PUBLISHER'S PREFACE

The *Crossword Puzzle Dictionary*, compiled by Andrew Swanfeldt, has been for many years the most comprehensive dictionary designed solely for crossword puzzle enthusiasts. Since the first edition appeared in 1940, the book has been the richest mine of entry and answer words to be found in any book that could conveniently be used in working puzzles. That advantage has been greatly increased in this third edition by the addition of more than 100,000 new answer words in 153 more pages. The number of entries has not been increased, however, so now there are more answers, but fewer places to look for them.

Moreover, the new edition introduces a feature unique among dictionaries—the Instant Finder System. For years crossword puzzle fans have wanted a dictionary in which the answer words in each entry were listed according to number of letters. Desirable as this arrangement was, it was not practical to produce such a book until the development of electronic computers made it possible to count the letters by mechanical means. The third edition of the *Crossword Puzzle Dictionary* has been printed entirely by computerized equipment. It is, in fact, one of the most complex reference books to be produced by this method, which holds numbering errors to a minimum.

The text of the new edition was prepared entirely by Andrew Swanfeldt, but, regrettably, he did not live to see the fruit of his years of research. For the demanding work of editorial preparation of the manuscript the publishers are indebted to an able staff which was headed, during most of the process, by Anne Vaughan.

CROSSWORD PUZZLE DICTIONARY

3rd Edition

ANDREW SWANFELDT

BARNES & NOBLE BOOKS
A DIVISION OF HARPER & ROW, PUBLISHERS
New York, Cambridge,
Philadelphia, San Francisco, London,
Mexico City, São Paulo, Sydney

ISBN: 0-06-463552-X
82 83 84 85 86 10 9 8 7 6 5 4 3

Abbreviations Used in This Book

abbr.	abbreviation	It.	Italian
Ar.	Arabic	L.	Latin
c.	capital	pert. to	pertaining to
comb. form	combining form	P.I.	Philippine Islands
D.	Dutch	pl.	plural
F.	French	Russ.	Russian
G.	German	Sc.	Scottish
Gr.	Greek	Sp.	Spanish
Ind.	Indian	W.	Welsh
Ir.	Irish	Yid.	Yiddish

CROSSWORD
PUZZLE
DICTIONARY

A

aa: 4 lava

aal, al: 8 mulberry

  dye: 8 morindin

aardvark: 8 anteater, edentate

Aaron: *associate:* Hur

  brother: 5 Moses

  burial place: Hor

  sister: 6 Miriam

Aaronic: 9 Levitical

abaca: 4 hemp 5 fiber, lupis 6 linaga

abacus: 4 slab 5 stone 10 calculator

Abadite, Ibidite: 6 Muslim

abaft: aft 4 back, baft 5 abaff 6 astern, behind 8 rearward

abalienate: 8 alienate

abalone: ear 5 awabi, ormer, shell 6 asseir, sea-ear 7 mollusk

abandon: ego 4 cast, drop, flee, junk, quit 5 allay, ditch, expel, leave, remit, scrap, waive, yield 6 abjure, banish, desert, devest, disuse, maroon, recant, reject, relent, resign, vacate 7 discard, forsake 8 abdicate, forswear, rashness, renounce 9 surrender 10 enthusiasm, exuberance, relinquish

abandoned: bad 4 left, lost 7 corrupt, forlorn 8 derelict, flagrant, forsaken 9 desolated, destitute, dissolute, shameless, unbridled 10 dissipated, profligate 12 unrestrained

abandonment instrument: 6 waiver

abase: 5 lower, shame 6 bemean, debase, defame, deject, demean, depose, humble, lessen, reduce 7 degrade, depress, mortify 8 disgrace, dishonor 9 denigrate, humiliate 10 depreciate

abash: awe, cow 4 dash 5 shame 6 humble 7 mortify 8 bewilder, browbeat, confound 9 discomfit, embarrass, humiliate 10 disconcert, intimidate

abashed: 7 ashamed 8 sheepish

abate: ebb, end 4 fall, omit, slow, void, wane 5 allay, annul, let up, lower, quash, relax, remit, slake 6 deduct, lessen, reduce, relent 7 abolish, assuage, nullify, slacken, subside 8 decrease, diminish, mitigate, moderate 9 alleviate

abatement: 6 rebate 8 decrease 9 allowance, deduction, reduction 10 diminution, relaxation, subsidence

abatis: 8 obstacle 9 barricade 13 fortification

abba: 5 title 6 father

abbe: 4 monk 6 cleric, curate, priest 12 ecclesiastic

abbess: 4 amma 9 prelatess

abbey: 6 priory 7 convent, nunnery 8 cloister 9 monastery, sanctuary

abbot: 5 coarb, abbas

  assistant: 5 prior

abbreviate: cut 4 clip, dock 5 prune 6 digest 7 abridge, curtail, shorten 8 contract, condense, truncate 9 epitomize

abdicate: 4 cede, quit 5 demit, expel, leave, remit 6 depose, disown, forego, resign, retire, vacate 7 abandon 8 disclaim, renounce 9 surrender 10 disinherit, relinquish

abdomen: 5 belly, pleon, tharm 6 paunch

abduct: 4 lure, take 5 steal 6 kidnap 7 capture

abecedarian: 4 tyro 6 novice 7 learner 8 beginner 12 alphabetical

abecederium: 4 book 6 primer

abed: 4 sick 7 resting, retired 8 sleeping

Abel: *brother:* 4 Cain, Seth

  parent: Eve 4 Adam

Abelard's beloved: 7 Heloise

aberrant: 4 wild 7 deviant 8 abnormal, straying 9 wandering

aberration: 4 slip 5 error, fault, lapse, mania 8 delirium, delusion, insanity 9 deviation 12 eccentricity 13 hallucination

abet: aid, egg 4 back, help 5 boost, coach 6 assist, foment, incite, second, succor, uphold 7 connive, espouse, forward, further, support, sustain 8 advocate, befriend 9 encourage, instigate, subsidize 11 countenance

abettor: 6 fautor 8 advocate, promoter 9 accessory, auxiliary 10 accomplice 11 confederate, conspirator

abeyance: 9 cessation 10 expectancy, suspension 11 suppression

abhor: 4 hate, shun 6 detest, loathe 7 despise, dislike 8 execrate 9 abominate

abhorrence: 5 odium 6 hatred 7 disgust 8 aversion 9 antipathy 10 repugnance 11 detestation

abide: be 4 bear, bide, last, live, stay 5 await, delay, dwell, exist, pause, tarry 6 endure, linger, remain, reside, submit 7 sojourn, sustain 8 continue, tolerate 9 acquiesce, withstand

abies: 4 firs 5 trees 10 evergreens

abigail: 4 maid

Abigail's husband: 5 David, Nabal

ability: can 5 force, power, skill 6 energy, talent 7 caliber, faculty, potency 8 aptitude, capacity, strength **9** dexterity, ingenuity **10** capability, competence, efficiency **11** proficiency

abject: low **4** base, mean, poor, sunk, vile **5** helot **6** paltry, sordid, supine **7** forlorn, ignoble, servile, slavish **8** beggarly, cringing, degraded, downcast, listless, wretched **9** groveling, miserable **10** despicable **12** contemptible

abjure: **4** deny **5** spurn **6** eschew, recall, recant, reject, resign, revoke **7** abandon, disavow, retract **8** abnegate, disclaim, forswear, renounce **9** repudiate

ablaze: **4** alow **5** afire, alowe **7** burning, glowing, radiant **8** gleaming, inflamed

able: apt, can, fit **5** adept, smart **6** clever, facile, strong **7** capable **8** dextrous, skillful, suitable, talented, vigorous **9** competent, effective, efficient, qualified, versatile **10** proficient

ablution: **4** bath **6** lotion **7** baptism, washing **9** cleansing
vessel: **5** basin **9** washbasin

abnegate: **4** deny **6** abjure, forego, refuse, reject **7** disavow **8** disclaim, forswear, renounce **10** relinquish

abnormal: **5** queer, utter **7** erratic, unusual **8** aberrant **9** anomalous, eccentric, irregular, unnatural **10** exorbitant **11** exceptional **13** extraordinary

aboard: on **4** onto **6** across **7** athwart

abode: cot, dar, hut **4** bode, cell, flat, home **5** bower, house, manor, suite **6** estate **7** cottage, habitat, lodging, mansion **8** domicile, dwelling, tenement **9** apartment, residence **10** habitation
animal: zoo **9** menagerie
of Dead: Dar **4** Aaru, Hell **5** Aralu, Hades, Orcus, Sheol **6** Heaven **9** Purgatory
of gods: **4** Meru **6** Asgard **7** Asgarth, Olympus **8** Asgardhr

abolish: end **4** kill **5** abate, annul, erase, quash **6** cancel, recall, repeal, revoke, vacate **7** destroy, nullify, rescind **8** abrogate **9** eradicate **10** invalidate, neutralize **11** countermand, discontinue, exterminate

aboma: boa, bom **5** snake **7** serpent

abominable: **4** vile **6** odious **9** atrocious, execrable, loathsome **10** unpleasant **12** disagreeable

abominate: **4** hate **5** abhor **6** detest, loathe **8** execrate

abomination: **4** evil **5** crime, curse **6** horror, plague **7** disgust **8** aversion **9** antipathy **10** abhorrence, odiousness, repugnance **11** detestation

aboriginal: **5** first, natal **7** primary **8** original **9** beginning, primitive **10** indigenous

aborigine: **6** Indian, native, savage **10** autochthon

abortion: **7** failure **8** feticide, misbirth **9** foeticide **11** miscarriage, monstrosity **13** misconception

abortive: **4** idle, vain **6** futile **9** fruitless **12** unsuccessful

abound: **4** flow, teem **5** fleet, swarm **8** overflow **9** exuberate

abounding: **4** rife **5** flush **7** replete, teeming **8** abundant **9** luxuriant, plenteous, plentiful
prefix: **4** poly

about: in, re **4** in re, near, some **5** anent, astir, circa **6** active, almost, around **8** circiter **10** concerning, throughout **11** surrounding **13** approximately
prefix: amb

above: on, up; oer **4** atop, over, past, upon **6** beyond, higher **8** overhead, superior **9** exceeding, foregoing **12** transcendent
comb. form: **5** super, supra, hyper

abrade: rub **4** bark, file, fret, gall, rasp, sand, wear **5** chafe, erase, grate, grind **6** scrape **8** irritate **9** excoriate

abrader: **4** file, rasp **5** emery **6** grater, sander **7** grinder, scraper **9** sandpaper **10** grindstone

Abraham: *birthplace:* Ur
brother: **5** Nahor
concubine: **5** Hagar
father: **5** Terah
grandfather: **5** Nahor
grandson: **4** Esau
nephew: Lot
son: **5** Isaac, Medan, Shuah **6** Midian, Zimran **7** Ishmael
wife: **4** Sara **5** Hagar, Sarah, Sarai **7** Keturah

abrasion: **4** gall, scar **9** attrition

abrasive: **4** sand **5** emery **6** pumice, quartz **7** erodent **8** corundum **9** sandpaper **11** rottenstone

abreast: **4** even **6** beside **9** alongside

abret: **5** bread, wafer

abridge: cut **4** dock **5** brief, limit, rasee, razee **6** reduce, shrink **7** curtail, deprive, shorten **8** abstract, compress, condense, contract, diminish, retrench **10** abbreviate

abridgement: **6** digest, precis, sketch **7** epitome, summary **8** synopsis **9** lessening **10** compendium, diminution

abrii: **4** shed **5** cover **6** cavity, dugout **7** shelter

abrini: **8** licorice

abroad: off **4** asea, away **5** astir, forth **6** afield, astray, widely **7** distant

abrogate: **5** annul, quash, remit **6** cancel, repeal, revoke **7** abolish, nullify, rescind **8** overrule

abrogation: **9** abolition, cassation **11** dissolution

abrupt: **4** bold, curt, fast, rude **5** bluff, blunt, brief, hasty, quick, rough, sharp, sheer, short, steep, terse **6** craggy, rugged, sudden **7** angular, brusque, violent **8** headlong, vertical **9** impetuous **10** unexpected **11** precipitate, precipitous **12** disconnected **13** perpendicular, unceremonious

Absalom: *captain:* 5 Amasa
father: 5 David
slayer: 4 Joab
abscess: 4 boil, moro, sore 5 ulcer 6 fester, lesion 9 gathering
abscond: fly, run 4 bolt, flee, hide, quit 5 elope, scram 6 decamp, depart, desert, eloine, escape, levant 8 withdraw
absence: 4 lack, void, want 5 blank, leave 6 vacuum 7 vacancy 8 furlough 10 deficiency, withdrawal 13 nonappearance, nonattendance
absent: off, out 4 away, AWOL, gone 7 lacking, missing 8 absorbed 10 abstracted
absent-minded: 6 musing 8 distrait, dreaming 9 engrossed 10 abstracted 11 inattentive, preoccupied
absolute: 4 dead, fine, free, mear, meer, mere, plat, pure, rank, real, true 5 plumb, sheer, stark, total, utter, whole 6 entire, simple 7 certain, perfect, plenary 8 complete, explicit, implicit, positive 9 arbitrary, downright 10 autocratic, disengaged, peremptory 11 categorical, terminative, unalienable 13 authoritative, unconditional
absolutely: yea, yes 4 amen 6 wholly 8 evendown 10 thoroughly 13 unequivocally
absolution: 6 pardon 8 shriving 9 acquittal, cleansing, remission 11 exculpation, forgiveness
payment: 7 sin rent
absolve: 4 free 5 clear, remit 6 acquit, excuse, exempt, finish, pardon, shrive, unbind 7 cleanse, forgive, release 8 dispense, liberate, overlook 9 discharge, exculpate, exonerate, vindicate
absorb: eat, sop 4 soak, take 5 amuse, drink, merge, unite 6 devour, engage, engulf, imbibe, occupy 7 combine, consume, engross, immerse, occlude, swallow 10 assimilate 11 incorporate
absorbed: 4 deep, lost, rapt, sunk 6 absent, buried, intent 7 plunged, riveted 8 immersed 9 engrossed 11 preoccupied
absorbent: 5 fomes
abstain: 4 deny, fast 5 avoid, cease, spurn, waive 6 desist, eschew, forego, refuse, reject 7 forbear, refrain 8 restrain teetotal, withhold
abstemious: 5 sober 7 ascetic 8 moderate 9 abstinent, temperate
absterge: 4 wipe 5 bathe, clean, purge, rinse
abstract: 4 cull, deed, draw, part, take 5 brief, ideal, steal 6 deduct, divert, precis, remove 7 abridge, excerpt, purloin, summary 8 abstruse, argument, separate, synopsis, withdraw 9 difficult, epitomize, recondite, summarize 10 compendium 11 abridgement, theoretical
being: ens 5 entia (pl.)
abstruse: 4 dark, deep 6 hidden, mystic,

remote, subtle 7 obscure 8 abstract, acroatic, esoteric, profound 9 concealed, recondite 10 acroamatic, mysterious 16 incomprehensible
absurd: 4 wild 5 droll, false, inane, inept, silly 6 stupid 7 asinine, foolish 8 fabulous 9 fantastic, ludicrous, senseless 10 irrational, ridiculous 11 incongruous, nonsensical 12 inconsistent, inharmonious, preposterous, unreasonable
abundance: 4 flow, mort 5 depth, store 6 foison, plenty, riches, wealth 8 fullness, opulence 9 affluence, amplitude, plenitude 10 exuberance
suffix: ose
abundant: 4 free, lush, much, rife 5 ample, flush 6 galore, hearty 7 copious, fertile, fulsome, profuse, replete, teeming 8 fruitful, generous, numerous 9 abounding, bountiful, plenteous, plentiful 10 sufficient 11 overflowing
abuse: mar, tax 4 flay, harm, hurt, maul, rail, ruin, slam 5 crime, curse, fault, scold, spoil 6 berate, defile, ill-use, injure, insult, malign, misuse, punish, ravish, revile, vilify, yatter 7 affront, bedevil, deceive, falsify, misbede, miscall, obloquy, outrage, pervert, slander, traduce, upbraid, violate 8 dishonor, maltreat, misapply, mistreat, reproach 9 blaspheme, contumely, desecrate, disparage, invective, objurgate 10 adulterate. opprobrium, scurrility 12 vituperation
abusive: 4 foul 7 corrupt 8 cheating, insolent, libelous 9 offensive, perverted 10 calumnious, fraudulent, scurrilous 11 blasphemous 12 catachrestic, vituperative
abut: 4 join, rest 5 touch 6 adjoin, border 7 project
abutment: 4 pier 6 alette 8 buttress
abysmal: 4 deep 6 dreary 8 profound, unending, wretched 10 bottomless
abyss: pit 4 deep, gulf, hell, void 5 abysm, chaos, chasm, depth, gorge 6 bottom, vorago 7 gehenna 8 downfall, interval
Abyssinia: See **Ethiopia.**
acacia: gum 4 tree 5 babul, siris 6 arabic, locust
academic: 5 rigid 6 formal 7 classic, erudite, learned 9 scholarly 10 collegiate, scholastic 11 quodlibetic, theoretical 12 conventional
academy: 4 USMA, USNA 6 lyceum, manege, school 7 college, society 8 seminary 9 Annapolis, institute, West Point 10 university
acantha: fin 5 spine, thorn 7 prickle
acarus: 4 mite, tick 6 insect
acaudal: 6 bobbed 7 anurous 8 ecaudate, tailless
accede: let 5 agree, allow, grant, yield 6 accord, assent, comply, concur 7 concede, conform, consent 9 acquiesce 11 acknowledge

accelerate: rev, run 4 race, urge 5 drive, hurry, speed 6 hasten 7 advance, forward, further, quicken 8 dispatch, expedite, increase 9 stimulate 11 precipitate

accelerator: 8 throttle

accent: 4 beat, burr, mark, tone 5 ictus, pitch, pulse, sound, throb 6 brogue, rhythm, stress 8 emphasis 9 emphasize, pronounce, underline 10 accentuate, inflection, intonation

accented: 7 marcato

accentuate: 6 accent 9 emphasize, intensify

accept: 4 fang, take 5 admit, adopt, agree, allow, honor, marry 6 assent 7 approve, believe, embrace, espouse, receive 9 acquiesce 10 understand 11 acknowledge

acceptable: 7 welcome 8 pleasant 9 palatable 11 comfortable 12 satisfactory

accepted: 7 popular 8 approved, credited, orthodox, standard 9 canonical, prevalent 12 conventional

access: way 4 adit, door, gate, path, road 5 entry, going, route 6 accost, avenue, entree, portal, street 7 advance 8 approach, entrance, paroxysm 9 admission 10 admittance, passageway 13 accessibility

accessible: 4 near, open 5 handy 6 at hand, patent 7 affable 8 familiar, pervious, sociable 9 available, reachable 10 attainable, convenient, obtainable, procurable 12 approachable

accession: 5 enter 8 addition, increase 9 agreement, inaugural, induction 11 acquisition, enlargement 13 reinforcement

accessorius: 5 nerve

accessory: 4 aide, ally, tool 5 extra, scarf 6 helper 7 abettor, adjunct 8 additive 9 adjective, appendage, assistant, auxiliary 10 accidental, accomplice, attachment, incidental, subsidiary 11 appurtenant, concomitant, confederate, contingency, subservient 12 accompanying, appurtenance, circumstance, contributary 13 accompaniment, supplementary

accident: hap 4 case, luck 5 event 6 chance, hazard, injury, mishap 7 fortune 8 calamity, casualty, disaster, fortuity, incident 9 mischance 10 misfortune 11 catastrophe, contingency, contretemps 12 misadventure

accidental: 6 casual, chance, random 9 dependent, extrinsic, haphazard, secondary 10 collateral, extraneous, incidental, undesigned, unexpected, unforeseen, unintended 11 conditional, subordinate 12 adscititious, adventitious, nonessential, unexpectedly 13 unintentional 14 unpremeditated

acclaim: cry 4 clap, laud, root 5 cheer, claim, eclat, extol, shout 6 praise 7 applaud, ovation, plaudit, welcome 8 applause 11 acclamation, approbation

acclimate: 5 inure 6 harden, season 8 accustom 9 habituate 10 naturalize 11 acclimatize

acclivity: 4 bank, brow, hill, rise 5 grade, pitch, slope, slant 6 ascent, height 7 incline 9 ascendant, ascendent 11 inclination

accolade: 4 Emmy, kiss, rite, sign 5 award, honor, medal, Oscar, token 6 symbol 7 embrace 8 ceremony 10 salutation

accommodate: aid, bow, fit 4 give, help, hold, lend, suit 5 adapt, board, defer, favor, house, lodge, serve, yield 6 adjust, comply, favour, oblige, settle 7 conform 8 attemper, suitable 9 reconcile

accompaniment: 7 descant 8 obligato 9 accessory

accompany: see 4 fare, join, lead 5 pilot 6 assist, attend, concur, convey, convoy, escort, follow, squire 7 coexist, conduct, consort 9 associate, companion

accomplice: pal 4 aide, ally, chum 5 buddy, crony 6 helper 7 abettor, partner 9 accessory, assistant, associate, colleague 10 cooperator 11 confederate 12 participator

accomplish: do; end, win 4 fill, work 5 enact, equip, forth 6 afford, attain, effect, finish, fulfil, manage 7 achieve, chevise, compass, execute, fulfill, furnish, operate, perfect, perform, realize, succeed 8 complete, contrive, dispatch, engineer 9 implement, negotiate 10 consummate, effectuate

accomplished: apt 4 able, done 5 adept, ended 6 expert 8 talented 10 proficient

accomplishment: art 4 deed, feat 5 craft, skill 7 earning 10 attainment 11 achievement, performance

accord: 4 give, jibe 5 agree, allow, atone, award, grant, tally, unity 6 accede, adjust, assent, bestow, beteem, comply, concur, settle, unison 7 comport, compose, concede, concert, concord, consent, consort, rapport, respond 9 harmonize, reconcile 10 compliance, conformity, correspond, permission 11 composition, concurrence

accordant: 4 even 7 attuned 8 agreeing, coherent, suitable 9 congruous, consonant 10 compatible, concentual, consistent, harmonious 11 concentuous, conformable 13 correspondent

accordingly: so 4 then, thus 5 hence 9 therefore, wherefore 12 consequently 15 correspondingly

accost: 4 hail, meet 5 board, greet, speak 6 halloo, salute 7 address, solicit 8 approach, greeting 9 encounter

account: tab, 4 bill, deem, item, rate, sake, tale 5 chalk, count, judge, score, story, value, worth 6 credit, detail, esteem, profit, reckon, record, relate, report, repute 7 compute, explain, narrate, recital

8 consider, estimate, 9 advantage, biography, chronicle, discourse, inventory, narrative, reckoning, rehearsal, statement 10 commentary, importance, recitation 11 calculation, computation, description, enumeration, explanation

accountable: 6 liable 10 answerable, explicable 11 responsible 12 attributable

accountant: CPA 5 clerk 7 auditor 8 reckoner 10 bookkeeper, calculator

accouter: arm, rig 4 gird 5 array, dress, equip 6 attire, clothe, outfit 7 furnish, provide

accredit: 5 allot, vouch 6 credit, depute 7 appoint, approve, ascribe, believe, certify, confirm, endorse, license 8 sanction 9 attribute, authorize 10 commission

accretion: 4 gain 6 growth 7 deposit, exudate 8 addition, adhesion, increase 9 coherence 11 enlargement

accrue: add 4 earn, gain, grow 5 arise, ensue, inure, issue 6 mature, result, spring 7 acquire, collect, redound 8 cumulate, increase

accumulate: 4 grow, heap, pile, save 5 amass, hoard, store, total 6 accrue, garner, gather, muster 7 collect 8 increase 9 aggregate

accumulation: 4 fund, heap, mass, pile 5 stack, store 6 budget 7 cumulus 8 dividend, interest 10 acervation, congestion, cumulation

accurate: 4 just, leal, nice, true 5 close, exact, right 6 strict 7 careful, correct, precise 8 faithful 9 veridical 10 particular

accursed: fey 6 cursed, damned, doomed 9 execrable, execrated 10 detestable 13 anathematized

accuse: tax 4 call, file, show, slur, wray 5 argue, blame 6 attack, charge, defame, indict 7 appeach, arraign, attaint, censure, impeach 8 chastise, denounce, reproach 9 challenge 10 calumniate 11 incriminate, recriminate

accuser: 7 charger, delator 8 libelant 9 plaintiff 10 prosecutor 11 complainant

accustom: use 4 haft, wont 5 adapt, enure, drill, inure, train 6 addict, season 7 consort, toughen 9 acclimate, habituate 10 naturalize 11 familiarize

ace: jot, one, pip 4 atom, card, hero, mark, tops, unit, a-one 5 adept, basto, flyer, point 6 expert 7 aviator 8 particle, quantity 10 topnotcher

acerb: 4 acid, sour, tart 5 acrid, harsh, sharp 6 bitter, severe 10 astringent

acerbate: 8 embitter, irritate 10 exasperate

acetaldehyde: 5 ethyl 7 ethanal

acetic: 4 sour 5 sharp

acetic acid: 7 vinegar
salt: 7 acetate

acetylene: gas 5 tolan 6 ethine, tolane

ache: 4 hurt, long, pain, pang, pine 5 smart, throe, throb 6 desire, stitch, twinge 7 anguish 8 soreness

achieve: do; end, get, win 4 earn, gain 5 reach 6 afford, attain, effect, finish, obtain 7 compass, fulfill, produce, realize, succeed, triumph 8 complete, conclude, contrive 9 terminate 10 accomplish, consummate

achievement: act 4 deed, feat 6 action, career, result 7 exploit 9 execution, fosterage 11 performance 14 accomplishment

Achilles: *father* 6 Peleus
friend: 9 Patroclus
horse: 7 Xanthus
mother: 6 Thetis
slayer: 5 Paris
soldier: 8 Myrmidon
victim: 6 Hector
vulnerable part: 4 heel

achiote: 4 tree 7 annatto, arnatta, arnatto

achira: 5 canna 8 acheiria, handless

acid: dry 4 keen, sour, tart 5 acrid, amino, eager, harsh, sharp, ulmic 6 biting, bitter, oleate 7 acetose, acetous, vinegar 9 corrosive 11 acrimonious
comb. form: oxy 4 acer
nitric: 10 aquafortis
pert. to: 7 oleatic
radical: 4 acyl 6 acetyl 7 malonyl, benzoyl

acidity: 4 acor 8 acerbity, verjuice
measure: 10 acidimeter

acknowledge: nod, own 4 aver, avow, sign 5 admit, allow, grant, thank, yield 6 accede, accept, answer, assent, avouch, reward 7 concede, confess, declare, observe, profess 8 disclose 9 recognize

acme: cap, top 4 apex, peak 5 crest 6 apogee, climax, crisis, height, heyday, summit, zenith 8 pinnacle 11 culmination

acolyte: boy 6 helper, novice 7 learner 9 satellite

acomia: 8 baldness

aconic acid: 4 salt 7 aconate

aconite: 4 bikh 6 remedy 9 monkshood

acorn: nut 4 mast 5 ovest
dried: 6 camata
edible: 7 ballote, bellote

acorn-shaped: 8 balanoid

acquaint: 4 know, tell 5 teach, verse 6 advise, inform, notify, school 7 apprise, apprize, possess 11 familiarize

acquaintance: 4 kith 6 friend 8 affinity, intimate 9 companion, knowledge 10 fellowship

acquainted: 7 versant 10 conversant

acquiesce: bow 5 abide, agree, chime, yield 6 accede, accept, assent, comply, concur, submit 7 concede, conform, consent

acquire: add, buy, get, win 4 earn, gain,

grab, reap **5** adopt, amass, learn, reach, steal **6** attain, effect, obtain, secure, snatch **7** collect, conquer, procure, receive **8** contract **9** cultivate

acquit: 4 free **5** clear **6** excuse, pardon **7** absolve, comport, conduct, release, requite **8** liberate, overlook **9** discharge, exculpate, exonerate, quitclaim, vindicate

acre: 4 land **5** field **6** arpent **7** measure **8** farmhold

one hundred: **7** hectare

quarter: rod **4** rood

acreage: 5 ranch **6** estate **8** farmland

acrid: 4 acid, keen **5** harsh, rough, sharp, surly **6** biting, bitter **7** caustic, pungent, reeking **8** unsavory, virulent **9** acidulous, corrosive **10** irritating

acrimonious: mad **4** acid, keen **5** acrid, angry, gruff, harsh, irate, sharp, surly **6** bitter **7** caustic **8** stinging **9** rancorous

acroamatic: 4 oral **6** arcane, secret **8** abstruse, esoteric, profound

acrobat: 4 zany **7** gymnast, tumbler **8** balancer **10** ropedancer **13** contortionist, schoenobatist

garment: **7** leotard

acropolis: 4 fort, hill **7** citadel

across: 4 over, span **6** aboard **7** athwart **8** opposite **9** crosswise **10** transverse

prefix: dia **5** trans

acrostic: 4 agla, game, poem **6** phrase, puzzle **9** crosswise **11** composition

act: do, go; ape, law **4** actu, bill, deed, feat, play, skit, turn, work **5** actus, drama, edict, emote, exert, feign, karma, model, scene, stunt **6** behave, bestir, decree **7** comport, execute, exploit, perform, portray, pretend, statute **8** function, pretense, simulate **9** ordinance, portrayal, represent **10** observance **11** impersonate, instruction, performance

by turns: **6** altern **9** alternate

suffix: ure

action: 4 case, deed, fray, push, step, work **5** doing, edict, fight **6** affair, battle **7** conduct, process **8** behavior, conflict, function **9** animation, behaviour **10** deportment, enterprise **11** performance, transaction

field of: **4** bowl **5** arena, stage **7** stadium

legal: res **4** suit **5** actus **8** replevin **9** gravamina

pert. to: **9** practical

put out of: K.O. **7** disable

to recover property: **6** trover **8** replevin

word: **4** verb

active: 4 busy, pert, spry **5** about, agile, alert, astir, brisk, quick, ready, smart **6** hearty, lively, moving, nimble, prompt **7** kinetic **8** animated, athletic, diligent, spirited, vigorous **9** assiduous, effective, energetic, sprightly, unpassive **10** productive **11** industrious, progressive

activity: ado, gog, vir **4** life, stir **5** rally **6** action, bustle **8** business, exercise, function, movement

actor: ham **4** doer, hero, lead, mime, star **5** agent, extra, heavy, mimic **6** artist, mummer, player, stager **7** artiste, stormer, trouper **8** aisteoir (Ir.), comedian, juvenile, stroller, thespian **9** performer, portrayer, tragedian **10** personator **11** entertainer, pantomimist, protagonist

cue: **4** hint, word **6** prompt

group of: **4** cast **6** troupe **7** company **8** troupers

lines: **4** role, side

part: **4** role

actress: 4 diva, star **7** ingenue **8** thespian **9** soubrette **10** comedienne **11** entertainer

actual: 4 real, true **5** posit **6** bodily **7** factual, genuine **8** concrete, existing, material, positive, tangible **9** effective, veritable **11** substantial

actuality: 4 fact **5** being **6** verity **7** reality **9** existence, substance

actuate: egg, run **4** draw, move, urge **5** enact, impel, rouse, start **6** arouse, compel, incite, induce **7** agitate, animate, enliven, inspire, pointed, sharpen **8** motivate, persuade **9** instigate

acumen: wit **7** insight **8** keenness, sagacity **9** acuteness, mentality, sharpness **10** perception, shrewdness **11** discernment **12** perspicacity **14** discrimination

acute: 4 fine, high, keen **5** quick, sharp, smart, snell **6** astute, shrewd, shrill, subtle, urgent **7** intense, pointed **8** critical, incisive, poignant **9** ingenious, sensitive **10** discerning, perceiving **11** intelligent, penetrating **13** perspicacious **14** discriminating

ad-lib: 9 improvise

adage: saw **4** dict **5** axiom, maxim, motto **6** homily, saying, truism **7** bromide, precept, proverb **8** aphorism, apothegm

Adam:

grandson: **4** Enos **5** Enoch

rib: Eve

son: **4** Abel, Cain, Seth

teacher: **6** Raisel

wife, first: **6** Lilith

adamant: 4 firm, hard **5** stony **8** obdurate **9** loadstone **10** inflexible, unyielding

adamantine: 4 firm **5** stone **9** immovable **10** unyielding

pert. to: **5** boric

Adam's flannel: 7 mullien

Adam's needle: 5 yucca

adapt: apt, fit **4** suit **5** agree, apply, inure **6** adjust, change, comply, temper **7** arrange, conform, convert, prepare, qualify **8** attemper, equalize, regulate **9** acclimate, calculate, harmonize **10** assimilate **11** accommodate

adaptable: 7 pliable 8 flexuous 9 tractable 10 adjustable 11 conformable

add: say, sum, tot 4 gain, give, join, plus, tote 5 affix, annex, total, unite 6 accrue, append, attach, figure, reckon 7 accrete, augment, combine, compile, compute, enlarge, subjoin 8 increase 9 aggregate 10 supplement

adda: 5 scink, skink 6 lizard

added: and, eke 4 plus

adder: 5 krait, snake, viper 7 machine, serpent 13 mathematician

addict: fan 4 buff, user 5 fiend, hound, slave 6 devote 7 deliver, devotee, hophead 8 accustom 9 habituate 10 enthusiast

addiction: 5 habit 9 surrender 10 attachment 11 disposition, enslavement, habituation

addition: and, ell 4 also, else, plus 5 rider 6 prefix 7 addenda (pl.), adjunct, advance, codicil, joining 8 addendum, additory, increase 9 accession, accretion, amendment, appendage, extension 10 ascription 11 enlargement 12 augmentation
prefix: 5 super

additional: new 4 else, more 5 extra, fresh, other 7 besides, further 9 auxiliary

addle: 4 earn, home, idle, mire 5 amaze, filth, ripen, spoil 6 muddle, thrive 7 agitate, confuse 8 befuddle, bewilder, confound 9 fruitless

addled: 4 asea 5 empty 7 unsound

address: aim, woo 4 call, hail, pray, tact, talk, turn 5 abode, apply, court, greet, poise, skill 6 accost, adjust, appeal, devote, direct, eulogy, manner, salute, speech 7 consign, entrust, lecture, oration 8 approach, delivery, dispatch, facility, harangue, petition 9 discourse, statement 10 allocution, deportment, management, peroration

adduce: 4 cite, give, name 5 allay, argue, infer, offer, quote 6 allege, assign 7 advance, mention, present

ade: 8 beverage

adeps: fat 4 lard

adept: ace, apt 4 able 5 handy 6 adroit, artist, expert, versed 7 capable, dabster 8 skillful 9 alchemist, dexterous, masterful 10 conversant, proficient

adequate: due, fit 4 full, meet 5 ample, equal 6 enough, proper 7 condign 8 suitable 9 competent, effective 10 answerable, sufficient 12 commensurate, satisfactory 13 proportionate

Adhem: 4 Abon

adhere: 4 cleg, glue, hold 5 affix, cling, stick, unite 6 attach, cleave, cohere 7 accrete, persist 9 persevere

adherence: 8 fidelity 9 constancy 10 attachment 11 concurrence

adherent: ist, ite 4 aide, ally 6 factor, votary 8 believer, disciple, follower, partisan, servitor, upholder 9 supporter
suffix: ist, ite

adhesive: gum, wax 4 bond, glue, tape 5 paste 6 cement, gluten, mastic, sticky 8 mucilage 9 tenacious

adhibit: use 5 admit, affix, apply 6 attach 10 administer

adieu: 5 adios 6 good-by 7 good-bye 8 farewell 11 valediction

adipose: fat 4 hard, suet 5 fatty, obese, pursy, squat 6 tallow

adit: 5 entry, stulm 6 access 7 passage 8 approach, entrance 9 admission 10 passageway

adjacent: 4 nigh 5 close, handy 6 beside 7 meeting 8 abutting, touching 9 adjoining, bordering 10 contiguous, juxtaposed 11 neighboring 12 conterminous

adjective: 7 epithet 8 modifier 9 accessory, dependent
demonstrative: 4 that, this 5 these, those
limiting: the
suffix: ed, ic, il; ent, ial, ian, ile, ine, ish, ive, ous 4 ical, ular
verbal: 9 gerundive

adjoin: add 4 abut, join 5 touch 6 append, attach, border 7 contact

adjourn: end 4 move, rise, stay 5 close, defer, delay 6 recess 7 suspend 8 dissolve, postpone, prorogue 11 discontinue 13 procrastinate

adjudge: try 4 deem, find, give, hold, rate 5 allot, award, grant, judge, order 6 assign, decide, decree, ordain, regard 7 condemn 8 sentence 9 determine, forejudge 10 adjudicate

adjudicate: act, try 4 hear, pass, rule 5 judge 6 decide, esteem, reckon, regard, settle 8 consider, sentence 9 determine

adjunct: aid 4 help, word 5 annex 6 device, phrase 7 pertain, teacher 8 addition, appanage 9 accessory, appendage, associate, auxiliary, colleague 10 complement 11 contingency 12 appurtenance

adjure: ask, beg, bid 4 bind, pray 5 crave, plead, swear 6 appeal, charge 7 beseech, command, conjure, contest, entreat, request

adjust: fit, fix, set 4 form, free, gear, line, pare, rate, size, suit, trim, true 5 adapt, admit, align, frame 6 accord, attune, settle, temper, wangle 7 address arrange, balance, conform, compose, dispose, justify, prepare, rectify 8 compound, regulate 9 harmonize 10 concinnate, coordinate, straighten 11 accommodate, systematize

adjutant: 4 aide, ally 6 helper 7 officer 9 assistant, auxiliary
bird: 5 crane, stork 6 argala 7 marabou

adjuvant: 4 aide 6 helper 7 helpful 9 assistant, auxiliary

admeasure: 4 mete 7 measure 9 ascertain, apportion, determine

Admetus' wife: 8 Alcestis

administer: run 4 deal, dose, give, rule 5 apply, treat 6 direct, govern, manage, settle, supply 7 adhibit, conduct, control, execute, furnish, husband 8 dispense 10 distribute 11 superintend

administration: 4 rule, sway 6 policy 7 regimen 10 regulation

administrator: 7 manager, trustee 8 director, executor 9 dispenser, executive, executrix

admirable: 4 high 7 amiable, capital, elegant, ripping 9 estimable, excellent, marvelous, wonderful

admire: 4 like, love 5 adore, extol, honor, prize, value 6 esteem, marvel, regard, revere, wonder 7 approve, delight, idolize, respect 8 venerate

admirer: fan 4 beau 5 beaux (pl.), lover, swain 7 devotee 10 dilettante

admission: fee 4 adit 6 access, charge, entree, ticket 7 consent, ingress 8 entrance 10 admittance, aggregation, concession, confession, disclosure 15 acknowledgement

receipts: 4 gate

admit: ken, own 4 avow, take 5 agree, allow, enter, grant 6 accept, accede, adjust, assent, avouch, enroll, induct, permit, suffer 7 adhibit, concede, confess, include, profess, receive 8 initiate 9 recognize 11 acknowledge, matriculate

admixture: 5 alloy, blend, shade, tinge 6 flavor 7 mixture, soupcon 8 compound, infusion 11 composition

admonish: 4 warn 5 chide, scold 6 advise, enjoin, exhort, notify, rebuke, remind 7 caution, counsel, monitor, reprove 9 reprehend, sermonize

admonisher: 7 monitor

ado: 4 fuss, stir, to-do, work 6 bother, bustle, effort, flurry, hubbub, pother, ruckus 7 trouble, turmoil 9 commotion 10 excitement, hullabaloo

adobe: mud 4 clay 5 brick, house 6 mudcap

adolescence: 5 teens, youth 6 nonage 7 puberty 8 minority

adolescent: lad 5 young, youth 8 immature, teenager

adopt: 4 take 6 accept, assume, borrow, choose, follow, foster 7 acquire, embrace, espouse, receive, welcome 8 advocate, maintain 9 affiliate 10 naturalize 11 appropriate

adorable: 6 lovely 7 lovable 8 charming 10 delightful

adoration: 6 homage 8 devotion

adore: 4 dote, laud, love 5 honor 6 admire, esteem, praise, revere 7 glorify, idolize, worship 8 venerate

adorn: dub 4 deck, gaud, gild, pink, trim 5 array, begem, dight, drape, dress, grace, primp, prink 6 attire, bedeck, blazon, clothe, emboss, enrich, suborn, tassel 7 apparel, bedight, bedizen, commend, dignify, furnish, garnish, glorify, implume 8 beautify, decorate, emblazon, ornament 9 bespangle, caparison, embellish

Adriatic: *city* 6 Venice

island: Bua, Eso 7 Lagosta, Lastovo

peninsula: 6 Istria

port: 4 Pola 5 Fiume 6 Rimini 7 Trieste

resort: 4 Lido

river into: Po 4 Reno 5 Adige, Bosna, Drini, Kerka, Piave

wind: 4 bora 10 tramontana, tramontane (pl.)

adrift: 4 asea, lost 5 awaft, loose 6 afloat 8 derelict, floating, unmoored 10 unanchored

adroit: 4 deft, neat 5 handy, ready, smart 6 artful, clever, expert, habile 7 cunning 8 dextrous, skillful 9 dexterous, ingenious

adroitness: 4 ease, tact 5 knack 7 address 8 facility 9 dexterity, ingenuity

adulate: 4 fawn, laud 5 gloss, gloze 6 praise 7 flatter 10 compliment, overpraise

adult: man 6 mature 7 grown-up 9 developed

adulterate mix 5 alloy, taint 6 debase, defile, dilute, weaken 7 corrupt, falsify 8 denature 11 contaminate

adulterated cut 6 impure 8 spurious 11 counterfeit

adumbrate 5 shade, vague 7 obscure 8 intimate 10 foreshadow, overshadow

aduncuous: 4 bent 6 hooked

adust: 5 burnt, fiery 6 gloomy, sallow 7 parched 8 scorched, sunburnt

advance: aid, pay 4 gain, help, laud, lend, lift, loan, move, near, nose, pass, push, rise 5 avant, boost, exalt, extol, favor, offer, raise, serve 6 adduce, allege, amount, assign, better, favour, hasten, stride, thrive 7 benefit, elevate, forward, further, improve, proceed, process, promote, propose, succeed 8 addition, heighten, progress 9 encourage, promotion 10 accelerate, aggrandize, appreciate

guard: van 8 vanguard

military: 8 anabasis, anabases (pl.),

slowly: 4 inch, worm 5 creep

advanced: far 5 ahead 11 enlightened, progressive

equally: 7 abreast

most: 8 foremost, headmost

advantage: use 4 boot, edge, gain, odds 5 avail, favor, start, stead 6 behalf, behoof, profit 7 account, benefit, exploit, further, utility 8 handicap, interest, leverage, overplus 9 emolument, privilege 11 opportunity, superiority

advantageous: 6 useful 9 expedient, favorable, strategic 10 auspicious, beneficial, commodious, favourable, profitable, propitious 11 encouraging

advent: 6 coming 7 arrival 8 approach 11 incarnation

adventitious: 6 casual 7 foreign 8 acquired, episodic 9 extrinsic 10 accidental, fortuitous, incidental 12 adscititious, nonessential

adventure: 4 gest, lark, risk 5 event, geste, peril, quest 6 chance, danger, hazard, 7 fortune, venture 8 escapade, jeopardy 9 mischance 10 enterprise, experience 11 undertaking

story: 4 gest, yarn 5 geste

adventurer: 10 filibuster 11 condottiere, condottieri (pl.), enterpriser

adventuress: 7 demirep 12 demimondaine

adventurous: 4 rash 6 daring, errant 8 reckless 9 audacious, foolhardy, hazardous 10 courageous

adverb ending: ly; ily

adversaria: 5 notes 10 miscellany 12 commentaries

adversary: foe 5 enemy, rival, Satan 6 foeman 8 opponent 10 antagonist, competitor

adverse: foe, ill 4 evil 5 loath 6 averse 7 awkward, counter, diverse, froward, opposed 8 contrary, opposing, opposite 9 diametric, reluctant, repugnant 10 afflictive, calamitous 11 conflicting, disinclined, unfavorable 12 antagonistic, inauspicious, unfavourable, unpropitious

adversity: woe 5 decay 6 misery, sorrow 7 illness, trouble 8 calamity, distress 9 suffering 10 affliction, misfortune 11 contrariety

advert: 4 heed 5 recur, refer 6 allude, attend, return, revert 7 observe 8 consider

advertise: 4 plug, warn 6 inform, notify, parade 7 declare, observe, publish 8 announce, proclaim 9 broadcast, publicize 10 promulgate

advertisement: ad 4 bill, sign 5 blurb 6 dodger, notice, poster, teaser 7 affiche, placard 8 handbill 10 commercial

advice: 4 lore, news 6 notice 7 caution, counsel, opinion, tidings 8 monition 10 admonition, suggestion 11 instruction 12 consultation, deliberation 14 recommendation

seek: 6 huddle 7 consult

advisable: 6 proper 7 prudent 9 befitting, desirable, expedient

advise: 4 read, rede, warn 5 aread, areed, coach, guide 6 confer, exhort, inform, reveal 7 apprise, apprize, counsel 8 acquaint, admonish 9 encourage, recommend

adviser, advisor: 4 aide, tout 5 coach, tutor 6 doctor, lawyer, nestor 7 monitor, teacher 8 attorney, preacher 9 counselor, physician 10 admonisher, counsellor, instructor

advisory: 6 urging 7 prudent 9 expedient, hortative, hortatory

body: 5 board 7 cabinet, council

advocate: pro 4 abet 5 adopt, favor, plead 6 assert, backer, defend, lawyer 7 abettor, apostle, endorse, espouse, scholar, support 8 attorney, champion, partisan 9 apologist, barrister, counselor, paraclete, proponent, recommend 11 intercessor

of new laws: 9 neonomian

adz, adze: ax; axe 7 hatchet

Aeacus:

father: 4 Zeus

son: 6 Peleus 7 Telamon

Aeetes' daughter: 5 Medea

Aegean Sea:

ancient peoples: 5 Psara, Psyra 6 Samian 7 Leleges, Samiote

gulf: 5 Saros

island: Ios 4 Nios, Rodi, Scio 5 Chios, Naxia, Naxos, Paros, Patmo, Psara, Samos, Thera 6 Ikaria, Ipsara, Kariot, Lemnos, Patmos, Rhodes, Skyros 7 Amorgos, Nikaria 8 Cyclades, Mytilene, Mytilini, Santorin, Sporades 10 Dodecanese, Samothrace, Samothrake 11 Castelrosso 12 Castellorizo

port: 4 Enos

river into: 6 Struma, Vardar 7 Marista

rock: Aex

Aegeon's wife: 7 Aemilia

Aegir's wife: Ran

aegis, egis: 6 shield 7 auspice, defence, defense 9 patronage 10 protection 11 sponsorship

Aegisthus' father: 8 Thyestes

Aegyptus:

brother: 6 Danaus

father: 5 Belus

Aello: 5 Harpy

Aeneas:

companion: 7 Achates

father: 8 Anchises

great-grandson: 4 Brut

mother: 9 Aphrodite

son: 5 Iulus 8 Ascanius

wife: 6 Creusa 7 Lavinia

Aeneid:

author: 6 Vergil, Virgil

first word: 4 arma

hero: 6 Aeneas

Aengus' mother: 5 Boann

Aeolus' daughter: 6 Canace 8 Halcyone

aeon, eon: age, era 5 cycle, Kalpa 6 period

aerate: 6 aerify, charge 7 inflate 9 oxygenate, ventilate

aerial: 4 aery, airy 5 aeric, lofty 6 unreal

7 antenna 8 antennae (pl.), ethereal 9 imaginary 13 unsubstantial

aerialist: 10 trapeze man 11 entertainer
garment: 7 leotard

aerie: 4 nest 5 brood 9 penthouse

aeriform: 6 unreal 7 gaseous

aerify: 6 aerate, infuse 8 vaporize

aerobe: 8 organism 9 bacterium

aerodrome: 7 airport 8 airfield

aerolite: 9 meteorite 10 brontolite

aeronaut: 5 pilot 8 operator, traveler

aeronautics: 7 science 8 aviation
pert. to: 4 aero

aerose: 6 brassy

aerostat: 7 airship, balloon 8 aircraft

aerugo: 4 rust 6 patina 9 verdigris

aery: 6 aerial 8 ethereal 9 visionary 11 incorporeal

Aesculapian: 6 doctor 7 medical 9 medicinal, physician

Aeson's son: 5 Jason

aesthetic, esthetic: 8 artistic, tasteful 9 beautiful

Aeta: Ita 8 Filipino 10 Philippino

Aether's father: 6 Erebus

afar: off 4 away, saho 6 remote 7 distant

affable: 4 open 5 civil, frank, suave 6 benign, facile, urbane 7 amiable, likable 8 charming, familiar, friendly, gracious, pleasant, sociable 9 courteous 10 accessible 11 complaisant

affair: 4 case, duel 5 event, fight, levee, party, thing 6 action, battle, matter 7 concern 8 business, endeavor, intrigue, occasion 9 endeavour, rickmatic 10 engagement, proceeding 11 transaction 12 circumstance

affect: hit 4 melt, move, stir 5 allot, alter, fancy, feign, haunt, impel, mince, touch 6 aspire, assign, assume, change, desire, soften, strike, thrill 7 attinge, concern, emotion, feeling, impress, operate, passion, pretend, profess 8 allocate, disposed, frequent, interest, simulate 9 cultivate, distemper, influence 11 counterfeit, disposition, hypothecate, inclination
each other: 8 interact

affectation: air 4 pose, sham 5 mince 7 display, foppery, grimace, pietism 8 fondness, pretense 9 arrogance, hypocrisy, mannerism

affected: 4 airy 5 ailed, apish, moved 6 formal, seized 7 minikin, smitten, stilted, touched 8 attacked, disposed, mannered 9 cherished, unnatural 10 artificial 11 pretentious

affection: 4 love 5 amour, heart 6 cherte, esteem, malady, regard 7 ailment, charity, emotion, feeling, symptom 8 fondness, tendency 10 attachment, friendship, propensity, tenderness 11 disposition, inclination
parental: 6 storge

affectionate: 4 fond, warm 6 ardent, doting, loving, tender 7 amorous, devoted,

earnest, zealous 8 attached, parental, sisterly 9 brotherly

afferent: 4 bear 6 esodic 7 sensory 9 ascending 11 centripetal

affiance: 5 faith, trust 6 assure, engage, ensure, fiance, pledge, plight 7 betroth, promise 8 contract, reliance 9 assurance, betrothal 10 confidence

affiant: 8 deponent 9 affidavit

affidavit: 4 oath 7 affiant 9 statement 10 deposition 11 declaration

affiliate: 4 ally, unit 5 adopt, merge, unite 6 attach, branch, relate 7 ascribe, chapter, connect 9 associate 10 fraternize, subsidiary 11 incorporate

affinity: 6 family, liking 7 kinship, rapport 8 alliance, relation 10 attraction, conformity, connection 11 propinquity, resemblance 12 acquaintance, friendliness, relationship 13 companionship, consanguinity

affirm: 4 affy, aver, avow 5 posit, state, swear, vouch 6 allege, assert, attest, avouch, depose, ratify, verify 7 confirm, declare, profess, testify 8 maintain 9 predicate, pronounce 10 asseverate

affirmation: vow, yes 4 amen, oath, word 9 affidavit, assertion, statement 10 deposition 11 declaration, proposition 12 asseveration, ratification
by negative understatement: 7 litotes

affirmative: ay; aye, nod, yah, yea, yep, yes 4 amen, yeah 8 dogmatic, positive 10 cataphatic 11 affirmatory, declarative, predicative 12 conformative

affix: add, fix, pin 4 clip, join, nail, seal, 5 annex, stamp, unite 6 anchor, append, attach, fasten, settle, staple 7 adhibit, connect, entitle, impress, subjoin

afflatus: 4 fury 5 furor 6 frenzy, vision 7 impulse 9 breathing 11 inspiration

afflict: ail, rue, try, vex 4 hurt, pain, rack 5 array, beset, gripe, grill, harry, wound 6 burden, grieve, harass, humble, infect, pester, remord 7 chasten, oppress, torment, trouble 8 distress 9 overthrow, persecute

afflicted: sad 5 sorry 6 ailing, woeful 7 grieved, smitten 8 impaired, troubled 9 depressed, lacerated

affliction: woe 4 evil, loss, pain, sore 5 cross, grief 6 duress, misery, pathos, plague, sorrow 7 ailment, disease, illness, scourge, trouble 8 calamity, distress, hardship, severity, sickness 9 adversity, grievance, martyrdom 10 misfortune 12 wretchedness

affluence: 4 ease 6 afflux, influx, plenty, riches, wealth 7 fortune 8 opulence 9 abundance, concourse, plenitude, profusion, substance 10 prosperity 11 sufficiency

affluent: fat 4 rich 5 flush, river 6 stream 7 copious, flowing, opulent, wealthy 8 abundant 9 plenteous, tributary

afford: 4 bear, give, lend 5 grant, incur, stand, yield 6 confer, manage, supply 7 achieve, forward, furnish, further, produce, provide 8 minister 10 accomplish

affray: 4 feud, fray, riot 5 alarm, brawl, broil, fight, melee, scare 6 attack, battle, fright, strife, terror, tumult 7 assault, contest, quarrel, scuffle, startle 8 frighten 9 encounter 11 disturbance

affright: cow 4 fear 5 alarm, daunt, dread, scare 6 agrise, appall, dismay 7 confuse, startle, terrify 8 frighten 10 intimidate

affront: cut 4 defy, slap 5 abuse, beard, peeve 6 harass, injure, insult, nettle, offend, slight 7 outrage, provoke 8 confront, disgrace, illtreat, irritate 9 encounter, indignity, sobriquet 10 soubriquet

affusion: 7 pouring 8 infusion

affy: 4 join 5 trust 6 affirm 7 betroth, confide, espouse 8 affiance

afghan: rug 7 blanket 8 coverlet

Afghan carpet: 5 Herat

Afghan fox: 6 corsac

Afghanistan:
city: 5 Cabul (c.), Herat, Kabul (c.) 6 Ghuzni 8 Kandahar
coin: pul 6 abbasi, anania 7 afghani
mountain: 8 Sulaiman 9 Himilayas, Hindu Kush
native: 7 Sistani
pony: 4 yabu 5 yaboo
prince: 4 amir, emir 5 ameer, emeer
river: 5 Cabul, Indus 7 Hari Rud, Helmund 9 Archandab
tribe: 4 Safi, Ulus

aficionado: fan 7 amateur, devotee 8 follower

afield: 6 abroad, astray

afire: 4 alow 5 alowe, eager 6 ablaze, ardent 7 burning, flaming

afloat: 4 asea 5 awaft, awash 6 adrift, buoyed, natant 7 flooded, unfixed 8 floating

afoot: 5 about, astir 6 abroad 7 walking 9 unmounted

aforesaid: 5 ditto, named, prior 8 previous 9 foregoing 10 antecedent

aforethought: 8 prepense 10 deliberate 11 forethought 12 premeditated

aforetime: ere 8 formerly

afraid: rad (Sc.), 5 timid 6 aghast, craven, scared 7 afeared, alarmed, anxious, fearful, gastful 8 cowardly, ghastful, timorous 9 shrinking, terrified 10 affrighted, frightened 12 fainthearted 13 pusillanimous

afreet: 4 jinn 5 afrit, demon, giant, jinni 6 afrite

afresh: 4 anew, anon, over 5 again, newly 6 denovo, encore 8 repeated

Africa:
animal: ayu 4 arui 5 civet, genet, okapi, potto, ratel, zebra, zoril 6 aoudad, ayeaye, quagga, serval 7 nandine 8 aardvark, pangolin, suricate

antelope: gnu, kob 4 bisa, guib, koba, kudu, oryx, tolo, topi, tora, zenu 5 addax, beisa, bongo, eland, nagor, oribi, peele 6 duiker, grimme, impala, koodoo, rhebok 7 blaubok, blesbok, boshbok, defassa, gemsbok, grysbok, reitbok, sassaby, stembok 8 blesbuck, bontebok, bosehbok, steenbok, steinbok 9 steenbock 10 duikerbuck, hartebeest
ash: 4 atar
ass: 6 quagga
baboon: 5 drill 8 mandrill
bass: iyo
bean: 7 calabar
beer: 5 pombe
bird: 4 lory, taha 6 weaver 7 touraco, xurakoo 8 umbretti 9 hammerkop
blaubok: 5 etaac 8 antelope
boss: 4 baas
bread: 5 kisra
buffalo: 5 niare
bustard: 4 kori 5 paauw
camp: 4 boma 5 lager 6 laager
canoe: 7 almadia, almadie
cape: ras 4 juby, vert, yubi
cataract: 8 Victoria
catfish: 4 shal 5 schal 6 docmac
cattle: 5 niata
cattle pen: 5 kraal 6 zareba 7 zareeba
charm: 4 juju 5 saffi, safie 6 grigri, saphie 8 greegree
chief: 4 kaid 8 caboceer
city: 4 Oran 5 Accra, Cairo, Dakar, Lagos, Rabat, Tunis 6 Bangui, Ibadan 7 Algiers, Tripoli, Yaoundi 8 Cape Town, Freetown, Khartoum, Monrovia, Pretoria 9 Timbuctoo 10 Addis Ababa, Alexandria, Casablanca 11 Brazzaville, Dar es Salaam 12 Johannesburg, Leopoldville 14 Elisabethville
civet: 7 nandine
cloak: 5 jelab 6 jellab
coin: 4 akey, pesa 5 rupie, toque
colonist: 4 Boer
colony: see *country* below
conference: 6 indaba
country: 4 Chad, Mali, Togo 5 Congo, Egypt, Gabon, Ghana, Kenya, Libya, Niger, Sudan, Volta 6 Angola, Gambia, Guinea, Malawi, Twanda, Sahara, Somali, Uganda 7 Algeria, Burundi, Dahomey, Liberia, Morocco, Nigeria, Senegal, Tunisia 8 Cameroon, Ethiopia, Malagasy 9 Swaziland 10 Basutoland, Mauritania, Mozambique, Tanganyika 11 Sierra Leone
deity: 6 nyambe, nzambi
desert: 5 Igidi 6 Libyan, Sahara 8 Kalahari
desert region: 4 erg
dialect: Twi 4 Akan, Geez, Saho, Taal 5 Bantu, Fanti 7 Swahili
dish: 8 couscous
district: 4 Rand, Tibu 5 Nubia 6 Ruanda
dried meat: 7 biltong

drink: 8 skokiaan
dunes: erg
eagle: 8 berghaan
enclosure: 5 bomar, kraal
farmyard: 4 werf
fetish: see *charm* above
finch: 7 senegal
fly: 5 kivus 6 tsetse
food: 6 paw-paw 7 cassava
fox: 4 asse 5 caama 6 fennec
fruit: 5 terfa 6 terfez
gangster: 7 tsotsis
garden: 6 shamba
garment: 4 haik, tobe 6 kaross
gazelle: 4 admi, cora, dama, kudu, nohr, oryx 5 ariel, mhorr 7 buffalo, dibatag 9 springbok
grass: 4 alfa 5 fundi 7 esparto
grassland: 5 veldt
greenhorn: 5 ikona
groundnut: 5 gobbe
guard: 5 askar
gulf: 5 Gabes, Sidra 6 Guinea
gully: 5 donga 6 nullah
gun: 4 roer
harp: 5 nanga
headland: kop, ras
headman: 8 caboceer
helmet: 4 topi 5 topee
hemp: ife
hill: kop
hornbill: 4 tock
horse: 4 barb
horse disease: 5 surra
Hottentot: 4 Nama
house: 5 tembe
hunt: 6 safari
hut: 5 kraal
instrument: 5 nanga, rebab, zanze 6 balafo
Islamic sect: 9 Almohades
island: 6 Azores, Djerba 7 Bourbon, Comoros, Madeira, Reunion, Socotra 8 Canaries, St. Helena 9 Ascension, Cape Verde, Mauritius 10 Fernando Po, Madagascar, Seychelles 12 Prince Edward
jackal: 5 diebs
king 5 negus 8 Selassie
lake: 4 Asal, Chad, Lifu, Tana 5 Abayo, chott, Moero, Mweru, Ngami, Nyasa, Rirwa, Shott, Tchad, Tsana, Tumba 6 Albert, Dembel, Dilolo, Nyanza, Nyassa, Rudolf, Shirwa 7 Leopold, Malumba 8 Victoria 9 Bangweulu, Stephanie 10 Tanganyika 12 Albert Edward
language: 5 Bantu, Hausa 6 Hamite 7 Swahili
legislature: 4 raad
lemur: 5 potto 6 maholi 8 kinkajou 10 angwantibo
livestock: fe
lynx: 7 caracal
mahogany: 9 cailcedra
measure: ton 4 doti, muid, rood, rope 5 curba, darah, mkono 6 morgen 7 schepel 8 Cape foot

monkey: 4 mona, mono, waag 5 patas 6 grivet, guenon 7 guereza 8 talapoin
mortar: 5 swish
mountain: 4 Pare 5 Atlas, Kenia, Natal 7 Cathkin, Kabylic 8 Cameroon 10 Drakenberg 11 Kilimanjaro
narcotic: 5 dagga
native (see also *people* below): Jur, Vai, Vei 4 Bari, Egbo 5 Bantu, Felup, Sotik 6 Fellup 7 Dahoman 8 Gabunese
nurse: aja 4 ayah
nut: 4 cola, kola
oak: 7 turtosa
old name: 5 Libya
ostrich: 4 rhea
palm: 6 raffia, raphia
palmyra: 6 ronier
pass: Nek
peasant: 4 kopi
people: Ga; Abo, Ewe, Ijo, Jur, Kru, Vai, Vei, Yao 4 Akim, Akka, Akra, Arab, Asha, Bari, Boni, Efik, Egbe, Ekoi, Golo, Habe, Hutu, Ibok, Leda, Lozi, Luri, Madi, Majo, Moor, Nama, Nuba, Riff, Suto, Tshi, Viti, Zulu 5 Afifi, Bantu, Batwa, Dinka, Hausa, Inkra, Kafir, Mandi, Masai, Mende, Pygmy, Sanye, Temne, Tutsi 6 Berber, Damara, Djerma, Dorobo, Fulani, Hamite, Kikuyu, Somali, Sousou, Tuareg, Ubangi 7 Ashanti, Bambute, Bapindi, Batonga, Dahoman, Kindiga, Malinke, Nilotic, Sandawe, Songhai, Voltaic
pigeon: 7 namaqua
pine: 6 ronier
plant: 4 ocra 5 argel, calla 6 arghel
plateau: 5 karoo
poison: 7 calabar
polecat: 5 zoril 6 musang
port: 5 Dakar 8 Freetown 10 Casablanca
pygmy: 4 Akka 5 Afifi
reedbuck: 5 bohor, nagor 7 reitbok
religious sect: 6 Coptic 7 Abelite
residence: 4 tato 5 kraal
rhinoceros: 6 umhofo
ridge: 4 rand
river: Job, Nun 4 Athi, Geba, Liba, Nile, Tana 5 Beira, Binue, Chobe, Congo, Kongo, Niger, Shari, Volta 6 Chinde, Gambia, Joliba, Rovuma, Sabaki, Ubangi 7 Atabara, Calabar, Limpopo, Semliki, Senegal, Zambesi 9 Crocodile
river bed: 5 donga
rosewood: 7 mulompi
scrub: 4 bito
seaport: Ibo 4 Oran 5 Dakar, Lagos, Tunis
secret society: Mau 6 Mau-Mau
servant: 4 volk
shallow lake: 5 chott, shott
sheep: 4 zenu
snake: boa 5 elaps, mamba 12 schaapsteker
soldier: 5 spahi 6 askari
sorcery: obe, obi 5 obeah
sorghum: 4 imfe 6 imphee
soup powder: 4 lalo

spear: **7** assagai, assegai
spiritual power: **4** ngai
squirrel: **5** xerus
stockade: **4** boma **6** zareba **7** zareeba
stork: **6** simbil **7** marabou
tableland: **5** karoo
tick: **6** tampan
title: **4** baas, sidi
tree: **4** akee, baku, bito, cola, etua, kola, moli, odum, olax, shea **5** abura, artar, bumbo, njave, odoom, sassy, siris, tenio **6** baobab, dukuma **7** assagai, assegai **8** gamdeboo **9** sassywood
tribe: Edo, Yao **4** Boni, Nuba, Sara **5** Wa-yao **6** Wabena **7** Bapindi, Batonga
valley: **4** daal, wadi, wady
village: **4** stad **5** kraal, stadt
wheat: **6** imphee
wild sheep: **4** arui **6** aoudad
wind: **9** harmattan
witchcraft bean: **7** calabar
wolf: **5** aard
wood: **4** teak **5** ebony
worker: **4** volk
worm: loa
Afrikaans: **4** Taal
aft: **4** back, rear **5** abaft, after **6** astern, behind **9** posterior
opposite of: **4** fore
after: eft **4** anon, next, past **5** infra, later, since, apres (F.) **6** behind, beyond, follow, hinder **9** afterward, following, hereafter **10** subsequent, succeeding
awhile: **4** anon **5** later
prefix: **4** meta, post
after-dinner: **12** postprandial
afterbreast: **10** metathorax
aftermath: **4** loss **5** issue, rowen **6** eddish, effect, profit, result, sequel, upshot **7** stubble **11** consequence
aftermost: **4** last **8** hindmost
afterpiece: **5** epode, exode **8** postlude
afterward: **4** then **5** later **9** afterhend **10** thereafter **12** subsequently
afterwrist: **10** metacarpus
aga: **4** lord **5** chief **9** commander
wife: **5** begum
agacella: **8** antelope
again: bis, eft **4** anew, anon, back, more, over **6** afresh, denovo, encore, iterum (L.) **7** further **8** moreover
prefix: re
against: vs (abbr.); con, non **4** anti **5** anent **6** anenst, versus **7** opposed **8** adversus
prefix: ob **4** anti, para **6** contra
against the law: **7** illegal **8** unlawful
agalloch: **5** garoo **8** calambac **9** aloeswood, calambour, eaglewood
agallochum: **5** aloes
agama: **6** iguana, lizard
Agamemnon: *avenger:* **7** Orestes
brother: **8** Menelaus
daughter: **7** Electra **9** Iphigenia
father: **6** Atreus
rival: **9** Aegisthus

son: **7** Orestes
wife: **12** Clytemnestra
agape: **4** love, open **5** feast **6** gaping **7** yawning **10** bewildered
agar, agar-agar: **4** moss **6** gelose
agaric: **6** fungus
agasp: **5** eager **7** gasping **9** astounded
agate: taw **4** ruby **6** achate, marble, pebble, quartz **9** burnisher, drawplate **10** chalcedony
agave: **4** aloe **5** amole, datil **6** maguey, mescal, pulque **9** amaryllis
fiber: **4** pita **5** istle, sisal
age: eld, eon, era **4** aeon, olam, time **5** cycle, epoch, ripen, years **6** mature, mellow, period, siecle, wither **7** century **8** duration, eternity, lifetime, majority, maturity **9** senectude **10** generation
geological: see **geology** *age*
modern: **6** atomic
pert. to: **4** eval **6** senile **9** geriatric
aged: old **5** anile, hoary, olden, passe **6** feeble, infirm, mature, senile, ogyian **7** ancient, elderly **9** nestorian, senescent, venerable **10** antiquated
agee: **4** awry **5** agley, askew
ageless: **7** eternal **8** timeless
agency: **4** dint, hand **5** force, lever, means, moyen, proxy **6** bureau, medium, office **9** influence, operation **10** management **14** intermediation **15** instrumentality
suffix: eer, fic, ier **4** ator, ific
agendum: **5** slate **6** record, ritual **7** liturgy, program **10** memorandum
Agenor:
daughter: **6** Europa
father: **7** Antenor
son: **6** Cadmus
agent: spy **4** doer, gene, g-man, T-man **5** actor, buyer, cause, envoy, means, organ, proxy **6** broker, commis, dealer, deputy, factor, peskar, seller **7** bailiff, channel, coucher, facient, proctor **8** aumildar, emissary, executor, operator, promoter, salesman **9** canvasser, consignee, go-between, protector **10** commissary, instrument **11** facilitator **12** intermediary **14** representative
appoint: **6** depute **8** deputize
suffix: see **agency** *suffix*
symbol: Agt
agger: **4** road, tide **5** mound **7** rampart **9** earthwork **10** prominence
agglomerate: **4** heap, lump, mass, pile, wind **6** gather **7** cluster, collect **10** collection **12** conglomerate
agglutination: **8** adhesion
aggrandize: **4** lift **5** boost, exalt, raise **7** advance, augment, dignify, elevate, enlarge, magnify, promote **8** increase
aggravate: irk, nag, vex **4** load, twit **5** anger, annoy, taunt, tease **6** burden, pester, worsen **7** enhance, enlarge, magnify, provoke **8** aggrieve, heighten, increase, irri-

tate **9** intensify **10** exacerbate, exaggerate, exasperate

aggregate: add, all, sum **4** bulk, mass **5** bunch, gross, total, unite, whole **6** amount, volume **7** collect **9** accretion, composite **10** accumulate, collection **11** combination, composition

aggregation: **4** herd **5** flock, group **7** cluster **9** congeries **10** assemblage, collection **11** association

aggression: war **4** raid **6** attack, injury **7** assault, offense **8** invasion **9** intrusion **11** provocation **12** encroachment

aggressive: **7** pushing **9** assertive **12** enterprising

aggressor: **9** assailant

aggrieve: try **4** harm, hurt, pain **5** harry, wrong **6** injure **7** afflict, oppress, trouble **8** distress **9** aggravate, persecute

aggrieved: **4** sore

aggroup: See **group.**

aggry, aggri: **4** bead **5** charm

agha: See **aga.**

aghast: **6** afraid **9** horrified, terrified

agile: **4** deft, fast, lish, spry, wiry **5** alert, brisk, lithe, quick, withy **6** active, lissom, lively, nimble, supple **7** lissome, salient, springy **8** dextrous **9** dexterous

agio: **5** batta **7** premium **8** discount, exchange **9** allowance, brokerage, deduction **10** percentage

agist: tax **4** feed, rate **5** graze **7** pasture

agitate: fan, irk, jar, vex, wey **4** fret, move, plot, rile, rock, seek, stir, teem **5** alarm, churn, drive, harry, rouse, shake **6** arouse, debate, devise, excite, foment, harass, incite, jumble, manage, rattle, ruffle, seethe **7** actuate, canvass, commove, concuss, discuss, disturb, perturb, revolve, trouble **8** activate, contrive, convulse, disquiet, distract, transact **10** administer, discompose

agitation: gog **4** fear, gust, heat **5** hurry, storm **6** bustle, energy, flight, flurry, jabble, quiver, tumult **7** emotion, ferment, flutter, rampage, tempest, turmoil **8** paroxysm, upheaval **9** carfuffle, commotion, confusion, estuation **10** combustion, ebullition, excitement, turbulence **11** trepidation **13** effervescence

prone to: **9** emotional

aglet, aiglet: tab, tag **4** lace, stud **5** plate **7** pendant, spangle **8** hawthorn, staylace

agley: **4** awry **5** aside, askew, wrong

agnate: **4** akin **6** allied **7** cognate, kindred

agnomen: **4** name **5** alias **7** epithet, surname **8** cognomen, nickname

agnomination: **7** echoing **10** repetition **12** alliteration

agnostic: **7** doubter, skeptic **8** nescient **10** unbeliever **11** freethinker

ago: by **4** erst, past, syne, yore **5** agone, since

agog: **4** avid, keen **5** astir, eager **6** lively **7** excited **8** vigilant **9** expectant, impatient

agon: **6** debate **7** contest **8** argument, struggle

agonize: **4** bear, rack **6** strain, writhe **10** excruciate

agony: **4** pain, pang **5** dolor, grief, panic, throe, trial **6** aching **7** anguish, anxiety, emotion, torment, torture, travail **8** distress, paroxysm **9** suffering **11** tribulation

agora: **8** assembly

agouti, agouty: **4** paca **5** color **6** animal, rodent

agra: **4** pain **7** seizure

agrafe, agraffe: **4** hook **5** clamp, clasp **6** eyelet

agrarian: **5** rural **8** pastoral **10** campestral **12** agricultural

agree: fit, gee, pan, yes **4** gibe, jibe, side, suit **5** admit, allow, atone, grant, hitch, match, tally, yield, unite **6** accede, accord, assent, comply, concur, condog, cotton, engage, settle, square, submit **7** arrange, comport, concede, conform, consent, promise **8** coincide, contract, covenant, quadrate **9** acquiesce, congruous, co-operate, harmonize, reconcile, stipulate **10** astipulate, correspond, homologate

agreeable: **4** easy, good, joli, lief, nice **5** amene, jolie, ready, suave, sweet **6** comely, dulcet, savory **7** adapted, amabile, amiable, couthie, greable, welcome, willing **8** amenable, charming, grateful, pleasant, pleasing, sociable, suitable **9** accordant, appealing, compliant, consonant, desirable **10** acceptable, compatible, convenient, harmonious **11** acquiescent, conformable **13** companionable

render: **7** dulcify

agreeing: **11** consentient

agreement: nod **4** bond, deal, mise, pact **5** lease, terms **6** action, assent, cartel, treaty, unison **7** bargain, closure, compact, concert, consent, entente, harmony, oneness, paction, rapport **8** contract, sympathy **9** accedence, accession, character, collusion, communion, concordat, condition, congruity, consensus, convenant, indenture, statement, unanimity **10** accordance, compliance, compromise, conformity, consonance, conspiracy, convention, obligation **11** arrangement, concordance, concurrence, resemblance, stipulation **12** capitulation **13** understanding

written: **6** cartel **8** contract

agremens, agrements: **6** graces **9** amenities, ornaments **14** embellishments

agrestic: **5** rural **6** rustic **7** bucolic **10** unpolished

agricultural: **8** geoponic

agriculture: **7** farming, tillage **8** agronomy **9** husbandry **10** agrotechny

establishment: **4** farm **5** grove, ranch **7** orchard

god: **4** Nabu, Nebo, Thor **6** Faunus, Tammuz **8** Amaethon *goddess:* Ops 5 Ceres 7 Demeter

machine: 4 disk, plow 5 baler, drill, mower 6 binder, harrow, header, reaper, seeder, tedder 7 combine, tractor 8 thrasher, thresher 9 separator 10 cultivator 11 caterpillar

overseer: 8 agronome 10 agronomist

pert. to: 7 georgic

science: 11 arviculture

worker: 4 okie 5 Arkie 6 cocker, farmer 8 farmhand

agriculturist: 6 farmer, grower 7 planter, rancher 10 agricolist, husbandman, orchardist

agrise: 5 abhor, dread 6 loathe 7 shudder, terrify, tremble 8 affright

aground: 6 ashore 7 beached 8 stranded

agrypnia: 8 insomnia 13 sleeplessness

agua: 4 toad 5 water

aguacate: 7 avocado

aguamas: 7 pinguin

ague: 5 chill, fever 7 malaria

ague tree: 9 sassafras

Ahasuerus: *minister:* 5 Haman

wife: 6 Vashti

Ahaziah's sister: 9 Jehosheba 11 Jehosobeath

ahead: on 4 fore 5 afore 6 before, onward 7 forward, leading 8 adelante, advanced, anterior 9 preceding

prefix: pre

Ahriman's angel: div 4 deev, deva

ahu: 4 heap 5 mound 7 gazelle

ahuehuete: 5 cedar 6 sabino 7 cypress

ai: 5 sloth 8 edentate

aid: key 4 abet, back, beet, help, pony 5 allay, boost, coach, favor, grant, serve, treat 6 assist, favour, relief, remedy, rescue, second, succor, uphold 7 advance, forward, further, relieve, subsidy, support 8 befriend 9 alleviate, auxiliary 10 assistance, facilitate 11 collaborate, countenance

Aida's lover: 8 Radames

aide: 6 deputy, second 7 officer, orderly 8 adjutant 9 assistant 11 subordinate 12 underofficer

aigrette: 5 egret, heron, plume, spray 8 feathers

ail: 4 fail, pain, pine 6 affect, bother, falter, suffer 7 afflict, decline, trouble 8 complain, distress 13 indisposition

ailment (see also **disease**): ail 6 malady 7 disease, illness 8 disorder, sickness, weakness 9 affection, complaint, infirmity 13 indisposition

aim: end, lay, try 4 bent, butt, goal, head, plan 5 essay, guess, level, point, sight, train 6 aspire, design, direct, esteem, intend, intent, object, scheme, strive 7 address, purpose 8 consider, endeavor, estimate 9 calculate, endeavour, intention, objective 10 aspiration, conjecture, estimation

aimless: 4 idle 5 blind 6 chance, random

8 drifting 9 desultory 10 undirected 11 purposeless

aimlessness: 8 flanerie

aine: 5 elder 6 senior

air: sky 4 aria, aura, lilt, mien, pose, song, tell, tune, vent 5 beach(Sc.), ether, ozone, voice 6 aerate, aether, allure, aspect, broach, cachet, manner, melody, ostent, regard, vanity, welkin 7 bearing, display, exhibit 8 attitude, behavior, carriage, sandbank (Sc.) 9 behaviour, semblance, ventilate 10 appearance, atmosphere, deportment 11 affectation, haughtiness 12 stratosphere

comb. form: aer, atm 4 aeri, aero, atmo

containing: 9 pneumatic

current: 4 wind 5 draft 6 breeze 7 draught

downward motion (pert. to): 9 katabatic

element: 5 argon, xenon 6 oxygen 8 nitrogen

in the: 5 aloft

measuring device: 9 aerometer, airometer

musical: see **melody**

overcast: 4 haze

air fleet arrangement: 7 echelon 8 squadron

air navigation officer: 8 avigator

air pressure: 5 baric

air propeller: fan

aircraft (see also **airplane**): 4 kite 5 blimp, plane 6 glider 7 balloon 8 aerostat, airplane 9 dirigible, orthopter 10 helicopter

carrier: 7 flattop

fleet formation: 7 echelon

manufacturer: 4 Vega 5 Astra 6 Bendix, Boeing, Curtis, Hughes, United, Vultee, Wright 7 Convair, Douglas, Grumman 8 Lockheed, American, Northrop, Republic

motorless: 6 glider

part: fin 4 keel, tail, wing 5 cabin 6 cabane 7 aileron, cockpit, nacelle 8 fusilage 9 empennage

route: 6 skyway

route marker: 5 pylon

shelter: 6 hangar

unit: 5 squad 10 escadrille

vapor: 8 contrail

airing: 4 walk 6 pasear 8 exposure

airplane (see also **aircraft**): mig 4 zero 5 avion (F.), gyro, liner 6 copter, glider, 7 biplane, clipper 9 monoplane

inventor: 6 Wright

maneuver: 9 chandelle

operator: 5 flier, flyer, pilot 7 aviator 8 aeronaut

airport: 5 drome 8 airdrome, airfield 9 aerodrome

airs: 6 vanity 10 mannerisms, pretension 11 affectation, haughtiness, preciseness

airship: See **aircraft, airplane.**

airt: See **direct.**

airtight: 6 sealed 8 hermetic 12 impenetrable

airy: gay **4** cool, rare, thin **5** empty, huffy, light, merry **6** aerial, breezy, jaunty, jocund, lively **7** airlike, haughty **8** affected, animated, debonair, delicate, ethereal, flippant, graceful, trifling, volatile **9** sprightly, visionary, vivacious **11** atmospheric **13** insubstantial, unsubstantial

aiseweed: **8** goutweed

aisle: way **4** lane, walk **5** alley **7** passage **8** corridor **10** ambulatory, passageway

ait: oat **4** eyot, holm, isle **5** islet

aitchbone: **9** natchbone

aith: **4** oath

aitu: god **5** demon **6** spirit

aizle: **5** ember, spark

ajar: **4** open **10** discordant

Ajax's father: **7** Telamon

ajonjoli: **6** sesame

akimbo: **6** angled

akin: sib **4** like, near, nigh **5** alike, close **6** agnate, allied **7** cognate, connate, germane, related, similar **10** correlated **11** appropriate **14** consanguineous

al, aal: **8** mulberry
  dye: **8** morindin

ala: **4** axil, drum, wing **6** axilla, recess **8** winglike

Alabama: *city:* **5** Selma **6** Mobile **8** Anniston **10** Birmingham (c.)
  county: Lee **4** Bibb, Clay, Dale, Hale, Pike **5** Coosa, Lamar **6** Etowah **7** Chilton
  river: **5** Coosa
  state flower: **9** goldenrod

alabaster: **6** gypsum

alack: **4** alas **9** alackaday

alacrity: **5** haste, speed **8** celerity, rapidity **9** briskness, eagerness, readiness **11** promptitude, willingness **13** sprightliness

Aladdin's spirit: **4** jinn (pl.) **5** genie, genii (pl.)

a la diable: **7** deviled **8** seasoned

alameda: **4** mall, walk **9** promenade

a la mode: **4** mood **7** stylish **11** fashionable

alan: dog **9** wolfhound

alantin: **6** inulin

alar: **6** pteric, winged **8** axillary, winglike **10** wing-shaped

alarm: din, SOS **4** bell, fear, gast **5** alert, broil, clock, larum, noise, panic, rouse, scare, siren, upset **6** affray, alarum, appall, arouse, attack, buzzer, dismay, excite, fright, outcry, signal, terror, tocsin **7** disturb, gloppen, startle, terrify, warning **8** frighten, surprise **9** commotion, diversion **11** disturbance, trepidation **13** consternation

alarmist: **9** pessimist, terrorist **11** scaremonger

alarum: See **alarm.**

alas: ay: ach, heu, och, woe **5** alack, oimee **6** ochone **8** welladay, wellaway **12** interjection

Alaska: *animal:* **4** bear **6** Kadiak, Kodiak
  auk: **5** arrie, murre
  bird: auk **5** arrie, murre
  boat: **5** kayak, umiak **6** oomiac **7** angeyok, bidarka **8** bidarkee
  city: **4** Nome **5** Sitka **6** Juneau (c.), Kodiak, Seward, Valdez **7** Cordova, Douglas, Klawock, Skagway **8** Latouche, Wrangell **9** Anchorage, Fairbanks, Ketchikan **10** Metlakatla, Petersburg
  fish: **5** wacha **6** salmon **7** inconnu
  garment: **5** parka
  glacier: **4** Muir
  highway: **5** Alcan
  island: **4** Adak, Atka, Attu **5** Riska **6** Tanaka **8** Pribilof **9** Andreanof
  island group: Fox, Rat **4** Near **8** Aleutian
  liquor: **9** hoochinoo
  mountain: Ada **4** Muir **5** Logan **8** McKinley **9** Blackburn **10** Saint Elias **11** Fairweather
  native: auk **5** Aleut **6** Ahtena, Eskimo **7** Tlingit **8** Aleutian
  river: **4** Atna **5** Yukon **6** Copper, Innoko, Noatak, Tanana **7** Koyukuk, Susitna **9** Kuskokwim, Matanuska, Porcupine **10** Whitehorse

alate: ant **5** aphid **6** insect, winged

alb, albe: **7** camisia **8** vestment

albacore: **4** tuna **5** tunny **6** germon

Albania: *city:* **5** Berat **6** Avlona, Durres, Tirana (c), Tirane (c.), Valona **7** Chimara, Coritza, Durazzo, Elbasan, Koritza, Prevesa, Scutari **8** Tepeleni
  coin: lek **5** franc **6** qintar
  king: Zog
  lake: **7** Ochrida, Scutria
  river: **4** Arta, Drin
  soldier: **7** palikar

albatross: **4** bird **5** nelly **6** fabric **9** mallemuck

album: **4** book **6** record **8** register **9** scrapbook **10** collection

albumen seed: **9** endosperm

albuminoid: **7** elastin, keratin, protein **8** collagen

alburnum: **7** sapwood

alcalde, alcade: **5** judge **10** magistrate **11** burgomaster

alcazar: **6** castle, palace **8** fortress

Alcestis' husband: **7** Admetus

alchemist: **5** adept **8** hermetic

alchemy: art **5** magic **11** thaumaturgy
  god: **6** Hermes
  iron: **4** Mars

Alcinous: *daughter:* **8** Nausicaa
  wife: **5** Arete

Alcmaeon: *father:* **10** Amphiaraus
  wife: **10** Callirrhoe

Alcmene's husband: **10** Amphitryon

alcohol: (See also **alcoholic drink**): **5** ethyl, vinyl **6** liquor, methyl **7** ethanol **8** methanol

crystalline: **6** guaiol, talite **7** talitol
desire for: **10** dipsomania
liquid: **8** farnesol
radical: **4** amyl
solid: **6** sterin, sterol **11** cholesterol
standard: **5** proof
suffix: ol
alcoholic: 9 spiritous **11** dipsomaniac **12**
intoxicating
alcoholic drink: ale, gin, rum **4** beer,
grog, wine **5** julep, lager, negus, vodka **6**
brandy, liquor, porter, whisky **7** liqueur,
whiskey **8** cocktail, highball
Alcoran: 5 Koran
alcove: bay **4** nook **5** bower, niche, oriel
6 recess **7** cubicle, dinette, tablina (L. pl.)
8 alhacena (Sp.), tablinum **11** compartment
alder: arn (Sc.) **4** tree **5** shrub
genus: **5** almus
alderman: 6 bailie, senior **7** headman **10**
magistrate
ale: mum **4** beer, bock, brew, flip **5** clink,
lager, nappy stout **6** alegar, liquor, porter, stingo, swanky **8** beverage, hugmatee
mixed with sweetener: **7** bragget
alee: 5 ahead **7** leeward
opposite of: **5** stoss **8** aweather
alegar: ale
alehouse: pub **6** tavern **7** barroom **9** hosthouse
alert: 4 gleg, warn, wary **5** agile, alarm,
alive, awake, brisk, eager, ready, sharp,
siren **6** active, alarum, bright, lively, nimble, prompt, tocsin **7** wakeful **8** vigilant,
watchful **9** observant, wide-awake **11**
circumspect
alette: 4 wing **8** abutment, door jamb
Aleut: 4 Atka **8** Unalaska
Aleutian Island: 4 Adak, Attu **5** Kiska,
Umnak **6** Akutan, Amukta, Kodiak,
Seguam **7** Agamil **8** Amchitka, Unalaska
alewife: 4 fish **6** allice **7** herring, pompano, walleye **9** gaspereau (F.)
Alexander: *birthplace:* **5** Pella
horse: **10** Bucephalus
kingdom: **9** Macedonia
Alexandria:
bishop: **10** Athanasius
patriarch: **4** papa
theologian: **5** Arius
alfa: 7 esparto
alfalfa: hay **6** fodder, lucern **7** lucerne
alforja: bag **5** pouch **6** wallet **9** saddlebag
alga: 4 nori **6** desmid, diatom, nostoc **7**
seaweed **8** rockweed
genus: **5** dasya **6** alaria, padina **10** gloeo-
capsa
study: **8** algology
algate, algates: yet **6** always, wholly **10**
completely, everywhere **15** notwithstanding
Algeria: 7 Algerie, Numidia

cavalryman: **5** spahi **6** spahee
city: **4** Bona, Oran **5** Blida, Media **7** Algiers (c.), Tlemcen **11** Constantine
department: **4** Oran **7** Algiers **11** Constantine
grass: **7** esparto
measure: pik **5** rebis, tarri **6** termin **9** pik
halebi
monastery: **5** ribat
mountain: **5** Atlas
people: **5** Arabs **7** Berbers, Kabyles
river: **6** Shelif
ruler: bey, dey
seaport: **4** Bona, Bone, Oran, Orel
ship: **5** xebec
weight: **4** rotl
algid: 4 cold, cool **6** chilly, clammy
Algiers', native quarters: 6 Casbah,
Kasbah
algodon: 6 cotton
algodoncillo: 7 majagua
Algonquin (see also **Indian**):
spirit: **7** Manitou
Alhambra site: 7 Granada
Ali: *descendant:* **7** fatimid **8** fatimite
wife: **6** Fatima
Ali Baba: *brother:* **6** Cassim
word: **6** sesame
alias: 4 else, name **5** other, title **7** assumed, epithet, pen name **9** pseudonym,
sobriquet
alibi: 4 plea **6** excuse **7** apology, pretext
Alice in Wonderland: *author:* **7** Carroll
character: cat **5** Queen **6** rabbit, Walrus **9**
Mad Hatter **11** Cheshire cat, White
Rabbit
alien: ger **5** fremd, metic **6** exotic, remote
7 foreign, invader, strange **8** stranger,
transfer **9** foreigner, immigrant, outlander, peregrine **10** irrelevant, tramontane
11 incongruous **12** inconsistent **13** unsympathetic
alienate: 4 part, wean **5** avert **6** convey,
devest **8** amortize, disunite, estrange,
separate, transfer, withdraw **10** abalienate
alienist: 12 psychiatrist
aliform: 8 winglike **10** wing-shaped
alight: 4 land, rest, stop **5** lodge, perch,
roost **6** arrive, settle **7** descend, lighted **8**
dismount **9** disembark
align, aline: 4 tram, true **5** array, range **6**
adjust **7** arrange, marshal **10** straighten
alike: 4 akin, like, same **5** equal, twins **7**
equally, similar, uniform **9** congruent, duplicate, identical
comb. form: iso
aliment: pap **4** food **5** broma, manna **6**
viands **7** alimony, pabulum, rations **9** allowance, nutriment, substance **10** sustenance **11** nourishment
alimentation: 7 support **9** nutrition **10**
sustenance **11** maintenance, nourishment

alimony: 7 aliment 9 allowance 11 maintenance

aline: See **align.**

alive: 4 busy, keen, spry, vive (F.) 5 agile, alert, astir, brisk, quick, vital 6 extant, living 7 animate, vibrant 8 animated, existent, sensible, swarming 9 breathing, sensitive, sprightly, unexpired 14 unextinguished

alkali: lye, reh 4 kali, soda, usar
volatile: 7 ammonia

alkaline: *remedy:* 7 antacid
salt: 5 borax

alkaloid: 6 aricin, codein, conine, eserin 7 arabine, aricine, caffein, cocaine, codeine 8 atropine, caffeine, morphine 10 strychnine 13 physostigmine

all: sum 5 gross, quite, total, totum (L.), whole 6 entire, solely, wholly 7 plenary 8 entirely, everyone, totality 9 aggregate, everybody 10 altogether, completely, everything, thoroughly 11 exclusively
comb. form: pan 4 omni

all-fired: 7 extreme 9 excessive 10 inordinate

all-knowing: 10 omniscient

all right: OK; yes 4 okay 6 agreed 9 hunky-dory

all there: 4 sane

allanite: 6 cerite 7 mineral

allay: aid 4 calm, cite, cool, ease, help, hush 5 abate, allay, charm, check, quell, quiet, slake, still 6 adduce, pacify, quench, reduce, soften, soothe, stanch, subdue, temper 7 appease, assuage, comfort, compose, lighten, mollify, relieve, repress, staunch 8 mitigate, palliate 9 alleviate

allee: See **alley.**

allege: 4 aver, avow, cite 5 offer, plead, quote, state, swear 6 adduce, affirm, assert, assign, charge, depose 7 advance, ascribe, declare, lighten, present, profess, propose 8 allegate, maintain 9 attribute 10 asseverate

allegiance: tie 4 duty 5 honor 6 fealty, homage 7 loyalty, tribute 8 devotion, fidelity 9 constancy, obedience 10 obligation
violation of: 7 treason 9 treachery

allegory: 4 myth, tale 5 fable, story 7 parable 8 apologue, metaphor

alleviate: aid 4 ease, help 5 abate, allay 6 allege, lenify, lessen, pacify, soften, solace, soothe 7 assuage, compose, console, correct, lighten, relieve 8 diminish, mitigate, moderate, palliate 9 extenuate 11 tranquilize

alley: way 4 lane, mall, path, walk 5 allee, byway, chare, tewer 6 vennel 7 passage 10 passageway 12 thoroughfare
back: 4 slum

alliance: 4 pact 5 union 6 accord, fusion, league, treaty 7 compact, entente, society 8 affinity, agnation, covenant 9 coalition

10 federation, fellowship 11 association, combination, confederacy, partnership 13 confederation

allice: 4 shad

allied: 4 akin 6 agnate, joined, linked, united 7 cognate, germane, kindred, related, similar 9 analogous

alligator: 5 niger 6 caiman, cayman, jacare, yacare 7 lagarto 9 crocodile

alligator pear: 7 avocado 8 aguacate

alliteration: 10 repetition 12 agnomination

allmouth: 6 angler

allocate: 4 deal, dole, mete, rate 5 allot, award, share 6 affect, assign 9 apportion 10 distribute

allonge: 4 pass 5 lunge, rider 6 thrust

allophanamide: 6 biuret 8 compound

allot: fix 4 cast, deal, dole, mete 5 award, grant, share 6 assign, bestow, depute, design, ordain, ration 7 appoint, destine, prorate, specify, tribute 8 allocate 9 apportion, attribute, authorize, prescribe 10 distribute

allow: let 4 bear, lend 5 admit, defer, grant, stand, thole, yield 6 accept, accord, assign, bestow, beteem, endure, permit, suffer 7 approve, concede, confess, suppose 8 consider, sanction, tolerate 9 authorize 11 acknowledge

allowance: fee 4 agio, edge, gift, hire, odds, size 5 leave, share 6 bounty, margin, salary 7 aliment, alimony, pension, portion, stipend 8 appenage, approval, discount, quantity, sanction, 9 admitting, allotment, conceding, deduction, reduction, tolerance 10 permission 11 appointment, approbation 13 authorization
short: 6 ration 9 scrimping
traveling: 7 mileage
weight: 4 tare, tret 7 scalage

allowing for that: if

alloy: mix 5 mokum 6 garble 7 mixture 9 admixture 10 adulterate, amalgamate
black copper: 6 niello
carbon and iron: 5 steel
Chinese: 7 paktong 8 packtong
copper and aluminum: 9 duralumin
copper, iron and zinc: 4 aich 7 paktong, rheotan 8 packtong
copper and tin: 6 bronze, oreide, oroide, pewter
copper and zinc: 5 brass 6 oreide, oroide 8 arsedine
costume jewelry: 6 oreide, oroide
fusible: 6 solder
gold and silver: 4 asem
gold-like: 6 oreide, oroide 8 doralium
lead and tin: 5 calin, terne 6 pewter
mercurial: 7 amalgam
nickel and silver: 8 alfenide
nickel and steel: 7 elinvar
silver with copper or tin: 6 billon
sulphuric: 6 niello

allspice tree: 7 pimento

allude: 4 hint 5 imply, point, refer 6 advert, relate 7 connote, mention, suggest 8 indicate, intimate 9 attribute, insinuate

allure (see also **lure**): air, woo 4 bait, draw, lead, lure, move, sway 5 angle, bribe, charm, court, decoy, snare, tempt 6 entice, entrap, induce, seduce 7 attract, beguile, ensnare 8 blandish, inveigle, persuade 9 captivate, fascinate, influence

allurement: 4 cord 6 glamor 7 gudgeon 9 incentive 10 enticement, temptation 11 fascination

allusion: 4 hint, twit 7 inkling, mention 8 innuendo, instance 9 quotation, reference 10 intimation

alluvial: *clay:* 5 adobe

  deposit: mud 4 sand, silt, wash 5 delta, drift, geest 6 gravel, placer

  fan: 5 delta

alluvion: 4 flow, wash 5 flood 10 inundation 11 overflowing

ally: pal 4 aide, join 5 union, unite 6 backer, friend, helper 7 connect, partner 8 adherent 9 affiliate, assistant, associate, auxiliary, colleague, supporter 10 accomplice 11 confederate

almanac: 4 ordo 8 calendar 9 ephemeris

almighty: 5 great 7 extreme 8 powerful, puissant 10 omnipotent 12 irresistible

Almighty: God 7 Creator

almond: nut 5 badam 6 kanari

  paste: 8 marzipan

almost: 4 nigh 5 anear, close 6 amaist, feckly (Sc.), nearly 13 approximately

  prefix: pen 4 pene

alms: 4 dole, gift 6 aumous (Sc.), bounty, relief 7 charity, handout 8 donation, gratuity, offering, pittance 11 benefaction 12 philanthropy

  box: 4 arca 7 poor box

  dispenser: 7 almoner, almsman 11 eleemosynar

almshouse: 9 poorhouse, workhouse

almuce: 4 hood 6 tippet 9 headdress

alodium, allodium: 6 estate 8 property

aloe: 4 pita 5 agave 6 maguey

  compound: 5 aloin

  extract: 5 orcin 7 orcinol

aloes: 5 tonic 8 agalloch 10 agallochum

aloft: up 4 high 5 above 6 upward 7 skyward 8 overhead

aloha: 4 love 8 farewell, greeting, kindness 9 affection 10 salutation

alone: one 4 bare, lorn, only, sole, solo 5 aloof, apart, solus 6 single, unique 8 desolate, detached, isolated, separate, solitary 9 exclusive, matchless, unmatched 11 exclusively 12 incomparable, unparalleled 13 companionless, unaccompanied

along: on; via 4 away, with 5 ahead 6 beside, onward 7 forward 8 parallel, together 10 lengthwise

alongside: at, by 5 close 6 aboard 7 abreast 8 parallel

  prefix: 4 para

Alonso's son: 9 Ferdinand

aloof: shy 4 cold, cool 5 aback, alone, apart, proud 6 abeigh, frosty, remote, silent 7 distant, removed 8 detached, reserved, secluded, windward 11 indifferent

alopecia: 8 baldness 11 phalacrosis

alopecoid: 7 foxlike, vulpine

aloud: 4 oral 5 vocal 7 audible

alp: 4 peak 5 demon, mount, witch 8 mountain 9 bullfinch, nightmare

alpaca: 4 paco 5 llama

alpenstock: 5 staff 9 bergstock

alphabet: 4 ABC's, order 6 primer, sarada 10 abcedarium

  character: 4 ogam, ogum, rune 5 ogham 6 letter

  pert. to: 11 abecedarian

  Runic: 7 Futharc, Futhork

alphabetize: 7 arrange

Alpine: hat 5 stick 9 alpestral

  dance: 5 gavot

  goat: 4 ibex 8 steinbok

  herdsman: 4 senn

  pass: col

  plant: 9 edelweiss

  wind: 4 bora 5 foehn

Alps: *Austrian:* 5 Tirol, Tyrol

  division of: 7 Bernese 8 Maritime 9 Lepontine

  Italian: 9 Dolomites

  mountain: 5 Blanc 8 Jungfrau 10 Matterhorn

  pass: 5 Cenis 7 Brenner, Simplon

  tunnel: 5 Cenis 7 Arlberg, Gothard, Simplon 11 Loetschberg

  Yugoslav: 6 Julian 7 Dinaric

already: een, now 6 before

also: and, eke, too, yet 4 erst, more, plus 5 ditto 7 besides, further 8 likewise, moreover 9 similarly

altar: ara 5 table 6 autere, shrine 7 chancel, chantry 9 sanctuary

  boy: 7 acolyte

  carpet: 6 pedale

  cloth: 6 coster 7 frontal

  curtain: 6 coster, riddel

  enclosure: 4 bema

  hanging: 6 dorsal, dossal, dossel

  ledge: 7 retable

  platform: 8 predella

  portable: 10 superaltar

  screen: 7 reredos

  top: 5 mensa

alter: 4 geld, move, turn, vary, veer 5 adapt, amend, break, emend, reset, shift 6 adjust, change, modify, mutate, revise, temper 7 convert 9 transform 11 interpolate

altercation: 4 spat, tiff 5 brawl, broil,

fight **6** bicker, jangle, strife **7** contest, dispute, quarrel, wrangle **10** contention **11** controversy

alternate: 4 else, sway, vary **5** other, recur, shift **6** change, rotate, seesaw **8** intermit **9** oscillate **10** substitute **11** interchange, reciprocate

alternative: or **6** choice, either, option **8** election **10** preference
word introducing: **7** whether

althaea: 6 mallow

althorn: sax **4** alto **7** saxhorn

although: een **4** even **5** while **6** albeit, though **7** despite **15** notwithstanding

altitude: 4 apex, peak **6** height **7** stature **9** elevation, loftiness
measuring device: **9** altimeter

alto: 4 part **6** singer **7** althorn, saxhorn **8** vocalist

altogether: all **5** quite **6** wholly **7** totally, utterly **10** completely, thoroughly **12** collectively

altruism: 10 generosity **11** benevolence **12** philanthropy **13** unselfishness

aludel: pot

alula: 4 lobe, wing

alum: 7 styptic **10** astringent
rock: **7** alunite

alumina: 5 argil

aluminum: *calcium silicate:* **7** epidote
discoverers: **4** Davy **6** Wohler
hydrousphosphate: **9** wavellite
oxide: **7** alumina
sulphate: **8** alum

alumnus: 4 grad **5** pupil **8** graduate

alure: 7 gallery, passage **10** ambulatory

alveary: 4 hive **7** beehive **9** alvearium

alveolar plasma: 11 trophoplasm

alveolate: 6 pitted **9** faveolate **11** honeycombed

always: ay; aye, een **4** ever **6** semper (L.), **7** algates, forever **8** evermore **9** eternally, uniformly **10** constantly, habitually, invariably **11** continually, perpetually, unceasingly **13** everlastingly

alyssum: 6 alison

am: See **be**.

ama: cup **5** amula, cruet, diver **6** vessel **7** chalice **9** candlenut

amabile: 6 gentle, tender **9** agreeable

amability: 11 lovableness

amadou: 4 punk **6** tinder **9** touchwood

amah: 5 nurse **7** servant

amain: 7 greatly **8** forcibly **9** violently **10** vigorously **11** exceedingly

Amalekite king: 4 Agag

amalgamate: mix **4** fuse, join **5** alloy, blend, merge, unite **6** mingle **7** combine **8** coalesce, compound **11** consolidate

amanuensis: 6 penman, scribe, typist **8** recorder **9** scrivener, secretary **11** transcriber **12** stenographer

amara: 6 beetle

amaryllis: 4 girl, lily **5** agave **10** sweetheart **11** shepherdess

amass: 4 heap, mass, pile, save **5** gross, hoard, stack, store **6** gather **7** collect, compile **8** assemble **10** accumulate

amate: 4 tree **5** daunt, match **6** subdue **10** dishearten

amateur: ham **4** tiro, tyro **6** novice, votary **7** admirer, dabbler, devotee, fancier **8** beginner **10** dilettante, aficionado **15** nonprofessional

amative: 4 fond **6** ardent, loving **7** amatory, amorous **10** passionate

amaze: awe **4** stun **5** alarm **6** astony **7** astound, confuse, perplex, stagger, stupefy **8** astonish, bewilder, confound, dumfound, surprise **9** dumbfound, overwhelm

amazement: 5 ferly **6** frenzy, wonder **7** madness **13** consternation

Amazon: 5 river, woman **7** warrior
cetacean: **4** inia
estuary: **4** Para
headstream: **7** Maranon
mat: **4** yapa
rain forest: **5** selva **6** silvas
tributary: **5** Napo

ambage: 4 path **7** circuit, quibble **9** ambiguity **14** circumlocution

ambari: da **4** hemp **5** fiber **7** cordage

ambassador: 5 agent, envoy **6** deputy, legate, nuncio **8** diplomat, minister **9** messenger **10** ambassiate **12** intermediary **14** representative **15** plenipotentiary
pert. to: **8** legatine

amber: 4 gris **5** resin **6** yellow **8** amberoid, electrum **9** ambergris

amber-colored: 8 resinous

ambiance, ambience: 6 milieu **11** environment **12** surroundings

ambiguity: 6 ambage **7** paradox **9** duplexity, obscurity **10** hesitation **12** doubtfulness

ambiguous: 4 dark **5** vague **6** double **7** cryptic, dubious **8** doubtful **9** bifarious, equivocal, uncertain, unsettled **10** indefinite, indistinct, mistakable **11** problematic **12** inexplicable, questionable **13** indeterminate

ambit: 5 limit, scope, space **6** bounds, extent, sphere **7** circuit, compass **8** boundary, precinct **13** circumference

ambition: 4 goal, hope, wish **5** glory **6** desire **7** purpose **9** intention **10** aspiration

ambitious: 4 avid, bold, keen **5** eager, showy **7** emulous **8** aspiring

amble: 4 gait **7** meander, saunter

ambo: 4 desk **6** pulpit

Amboina pine: 8 galagala

ambos: 5 incus

ambrosial: 6 divine **8** fragrant **9** delicious

ambry: 4 safe 5 chest, niche 6 closet, pantry, recess 7 almonry, armoire 8 armarium, cupboard 10 repository

ambulate: gad 4 hike, move, walk

ambush: 4 lurk, trap 5 await, blind, snare 6 waylay 7 forelay 9 ambuscade, ambuscado

ameer: See **emir.**

ameliorate: 4 ease, help, mend 5 amend 6 better, reform 7 improve, promote 9 meliorate

amen: yea 5 truly 6 assent, verily, so-be-it 8 approval, sanction 9 assuredly, certainly 11 termination 12 ratification

Amen-Ra's wife: Mut

amenable: 4 open 6 liable, pliant 7 subject 9 tractable 10 answerable, responsive 11 accountable, responsible

amend: end 4 beet, mend 5 alter, emend 6 better, change, reform, remedy, repair, repeal, revise 7 convert, correct, improve, recover, rectify, redress, restore 8 chastise

amends: 6 reward 7 apology, redress 9 atonement, expiation 10 recompense, reparation 12 compensation, satisfaction

amenities: 8 agremens, niceties 9 agrements, etiquette 11 formalities

amenity: joy 6 comity 7 feature, suavity 8 civility, courtesy, mildness 9 geniality 10 gentleness 12 complaisance, pleasantness 13 agreeableness

ament: 4 cjat 5 idiot, moron 6 catkin 7 cachrys, cattail, gosling 8 imbecile, nucament

amerce: 4 fine 5 mulct 6 affeer, punish, sconce 7 condemn, forfeit 8 penalize

America (see also **North America, South America,** and specific countries, e.g., **Brazil, Canada, United States**): 8 New World 9 continent 10 hemisphere

animal: 4 puma 5 bison, tapir, vison 6 argali, marten, martin, ocelot, wapiti 7 musquaw, opossum 9 assapanic, chickaree

apple: 7 Roxbury

ash: 5 rowan, rowen

balsam: 4 tolu

bear: 7 musquaw

bird: 4 rhea, sora 5 colin, urubu 6 condor 7 shrupsh, tanager 8 squealer

butterfly 7 viceroy

buzzard: 5 buteo 7 vulture

deer: 6 wapiti

discoverer of: 5 Cabot 7 Ericson 8 Columbus

elm: 5 ulmus

finch: 5 junco

fir: 5 abies

lion: 4 puma 6 cougar

monkey: 4 titi

moth: io

plains: 6 pampas 7 prairie

rodent: 4 paca 6 gopher 8 capybara

shrub: 4 majo 5 guava, majoe, wahoo 10 frangipane, frangipani

tiger: 6 jaguar

toad: 4 agua, bufo, rana

tree: fir, lin, oak 4 pine 5 maple, savin 6 tupelo, walnut 7 hickory, redwood, sequoia 8 oneberry, zapetero

tropical tree: 5 acapu, balsa, dalli, guama, guara 6 babeen, grigri, grugru, mammee, pawpaw, sapota 7 wacapou 8 amarillo, sweetsop 10 manchineel

American: 4 Yank 6 Gringo, Yankee, Yanqui

American Indian: See **Indian** *American.*

Amerind: 6 Eskimo, Indian, native 8 American

clan symbol: 5 totem

memorial post: xat

amethyst: gem 7 onegite

Amfortas' father: 7 Titurel

ami: 5 lover 6 friend

amiable: 4 kind, warm 5 sweet 6 loving, mellow, tender 7 affable, lovable, winsome 8 charming, engaging, friendly, pleasing 9 admirable, agreeable, courteous 11 kindhearted

amicable: 8 friendly 9 peaceable 10 harmonious, neighborly

amice: 4 cape, cowl, hood 5 ephod 6 almuce, tippet, vakass 8 vestment

amid: in 5 among 6 amidst, during 7 amongst, between 10 surrounded

amino compound: 7 diamide, diamine 8 triamine

amir: See **emir.**

amiss: ill 4 awry, bias 5 agley, askew, wrong 6 astray, faulty 7 mistake 8 improper 9 erroneous, incorrect 10 inaccurate

amit: 4 lose

amity: 5 peace 6 accord 7 concord, harmony 10 friendship 12 friendliness

amma: 6 abbess, mother

ammonia: 9 hartshorn 11 refrigerant

derivative: 4 amid, amin 5 amide, amine 6 anilid 7 anilide, diamine

ammunition: 4 ammo, ammu, arms, shot 5 bombs 6 powder, shells 7 bullets 8 grenades, material, ordnance, shrapnel 9 munitions

case: 9 bandolier

wagon: 7 caisson

amnesia: 5 lapse 13 forgetfulness

amnesty: 6 pardon 11 overlooking

amnion: sac 6 serosa 8 membrane

amok, amuck: mad 5 crazy 6 crazed 7 violent 8 frenzied

among: in; mid 4 amid, with 5 amang,

midst **6** amidst **7** between
prefix: epi
amor: 4 Eros, love **5** cupid **7** amoroso
amora: 5 rabbi
amoral: 7 neutral **8** nonmoral **9** objective
Amorc member: 11 Rosicrucian
amorous: 4 fond **6** ardent, erotic, loving, tender **7** amatory, fervent **10** passionate **12** affectionate
amorphous: 5 vague **8** formless, resinous **9** irregular, shapeless **14** uncrystallized
amort: 8 dejected, lifeless **9** inanimate **10** spiritless **11** discouraged
amortize: 7 destroy **8** alienate **9** liquidate **10** extinguish
amotion: 7 ousting, removal **11** deprivation
amount: gob, lot, sum **4** dose, feck, ream, rise, unit **5** chunk, price, reach, stack, store, total, whole **6** degree, dosage, extent, number **7** advance, scruple, signify, slather **8** increase, quantity **9** aggregate
fixed: **4** rate
indefinite: any **4** some
relative: **5** ratio **6** degree
small: bit, tot **4** dash, dite, flow, lick, wisp **5** pinch, shred, taste, trace **6** morsel, trifle **7** dribble, driblet, modicum **8** fragment, spoonful **10** pennyworth
smallest: jot **4** iota, whit **5** grain, least **7** minimum
ampere unit: 4 volt, watt
ampersand: and **4** also, plus **9** character
amphibian: eft, olm **4** frog, hyla, newt, rana, toad **5** anura **7** caudate, proteus **8** tree toad **10** salamander
extinct: **5** eryop
family: **7** Ranidae
order of: **5** anura **7** aglossa
young: **7** tadpole **8** polliwog
amphibole: 7 edenite, oralite, uralite **9** tremolite **10** hornblende
Amphion:
father: **4** Zeus **5** Iasus
mother: **7** Antiope
twin brother: **6** Zethus
wife: **5** Niobe
amphitheater: 4 bowl, oval **5** arena, cavea **6** circus **7** stadium **10** auditorium
Amphitrite: *father:* **6** Nereus
husband: **8** Poseidon
mother: **5** Doris
Amphitryon's wife: 7 Alcmena, Alcmene
amphora: jar, urn **4** cadi(pl.), vase **5** cadus **6** pelike
ample: 4 full, good, much, rich, wide **5** broad, great, large, roomy **6** enough, plenty **7** copious, liberal, opulent **8** abundant, adequate, generous, handsome, spacious **9** bounteous, bountiful, capacious, extensive, plenteous, plentiful, unstinted **10** munificent, sufficient

amplify: mu; pad **5** farse, swell, widen **6** dilate, expand, extend, stress **7** augment, enlarge **8** ampliate, increase, lengthen, multiply **10** exaggerate
amputate: cut, lop **5** prune, sever **7** curtail **12** exarticulate
ampyx: 4 band **5** plate **6** diadem, fillet **9** headdress
amuck: See **amok**.
amula: ama **6** vessel
amulet: gem **4** mojo **5** charm, saffi, safie, token **6** fetish, grigri, saphie, scroll **7** periapt **8** greegree, ornament, talisman **10** protection
amuse: 6 absorb, delude, divert, engage, please, tickle **7** beguile, disport, gratify **8** bewilder, distract **9** entertain **10** exhilarate
amusement: fad, fun **4** game, jest, play **5** mirth, sport **7** pastime **8** pleasure **9** avocation, diversion, merriment **10** recreation, relaxation **13** divertisement, entertainment
place (see also **entertainment:** *place):* **4** park **5** movie **6** casino, cinema, circus, midway **7** theater
amusing: 5 droll, funny **7** comical, risible **8** humorous, pleasant **9** laughable, ludicrous, quizzical **10** ridiculous
amyl: 6 pentyl
an: one **7** article
ana: 6 events **7** sayings **9** anecdotes, anthology **10** collection **11** memorabilia
anabatic: 9 ascending
anaconda: boa **5** snake
anadem: 5 crown **6** diadem, fillet, wreath **7** chaplet, coronet, garland
anagram: 4 game **5** rebus **6** puzzle **9** logogriph **13** transposition
analabos: 5 cloak
analogous: 4 akin, like **5** alike **6** allied **7** cognate, related, similar **8** parallel **9** comparable, equivalent **11** correlative **13** correspondent
analogy: 10 congruence, proportion, similarity, similitude **11** resemblance
analysis: 4 test **5** study **8** solution, synopses **9** reduction, titration **10** exposition **13** investigation
analyze: 5 assay, parse, study, weigh **6** reduce **7** dissect, examine, resolve **8** diagnose, separate **9** decompose, determine
Anam: See **Annam**.
Ananas: 5 anana **9** pineapple
Ananias: 4 liar
wife: **8** Sapphira
anarchist: 5 rebel **8** nihilist **10** antisocial
anarchy: 4 riot **5** chaos **6** revolt **7** license, misrule **8** disorder **9** confusion **11** lawlessness
anathema: ban **4** oath **5** curse **7** censure **9**

blasphemy 11 imprecation, malediction 12 denunciation

Anatolia: 7 Armenia
goddess: Ma 6 Cybele
rug: 5 Tuzla

anatomize: 7 analyze, dissect

anatomy: *microscopic:* 9 histology
quick: 11 vivisection

Anaximander's principle: 7 apeiron

ancestor: 4 Adam, sire 5 elder 6 author, beldam, parent 7 beldame 8 forebear, relative 9 grandsire, precursor 10 forefather, forerunner, progenitor 11 predecessor
having common: 14 consanguineous
law: 6 stipes, stirps
remote: 6 atavus
worship: 10 ancientism

ancestral: 4 aval 6 avital, lineal 10 hereditary 11 patrimonial

ancestry: 4 race 6 family 7 descent, lineage 8 pedigree 9 paternity 11 antecedents
relating to: 6 atavic 9 atavistic

Anchises' son: 6 Aeneas

anchor: fix 4 bind, hook, moor, rest, stop 5 affix, berth, bower, kedge, rivet 6 attach, drogue, fasten, hermit, secure 7 chaplet, connect, grapnel, killick, support 9 anchorite
bill: pee 4 peak
hoist: 7 capstan
lift: cat
part: arm 4 palm 5 fluke, shank, stock
position: 5 atrip
ring: 4 tore 6 toroid
shaped: 8 ankyroid
tackle: cat
timber: 7 grouser

anchor bed: 9 billboard

anchorage: 4 dock, rade(Sc.) 6 harbor, refuge 7 moorage 8 berthage, location 9 roadstead

anchored: 4 stay

anchorite: 4 monk 6 hermit 7 ascetic, eremite, recluse, stylite 8 anchoret 9 pillarist

anchovy: 6 spratt 7 herring
sauce: 4 alec

ancient: eld, old 4 aged, auld(Sc.) 5 early, elder, hoary, olden 6 bygone, ensign 7 antique, archaic, archean, classic, oxygian 8 historic, obsolete, primeval, pristine 9 grandeval, primitive, venerable 10 antiquated 11 patriarchal

ancilla: 6 helper 7 adjunct, servant 8 handmaid 9 accessory

ancillary: 9 auxiliary 10 subsidiary 11 subordinate

ancon: 5 elbow 6 corbel 7 console 9 olecranon

and: et(F., L.); ant, too 4 also, plus 7 besides, further 8 moreover 9 ampersand 10 connective 11 furthermore

and so forth: etc 4 more 6 others 8 etcetera

Andean: 5 grand, lofty 8 Peruvian

Andes: *animal:* 5 llama
bird: 6 condor
camel: 5 llama
deer: 4 pudu 6 vanada
grass: 4 ichu
tableland: 4 puna 6 paramo
tribe: 4 anti 5 campa

andiron: dog 7 cobiron, firedog, hessian

andradite: 6 aplome, garnet

android: 5 robot 9 automaton

ane: one 4 once

anecdote: 4 joke, tale, yarn 5 story 6 sketch 9 narrative
collection: ana

anele: 5 bless 6 anoint, shrive

anemia: 5 surra 6 surrah

anemic: low 4 pale, weak 6 watery 8 lifeless 9 bloodless 10 exsanguine

anemone: 9 buttercup 10 windflower

anent: on, re 5 about 6 anenst, beside, toward 7 against 8 opposite 9 regarding 10 concerning

aneroid: 9 barometer

anesthetic: gas 5 ether 6 acoine, obtuse, opiate 7 cocaine, dulling, menthol 8 sedative 9 novacaine 10 chloroform

anew: 4 over 5 again, newly 6 afresh, denovo, iterum(L.), 8 recently

anfractuous: 6 spiral 7 bending, sinuous, winding 8 tortuous

angel: 4 deva 5 daeva, seraf(Sp.), yaksa 6 backer, cherub, seraph, spirit, yaksha 7 sponsor 8 cherubim, guardian, seraphim 9 harbinger, messenger
apostate prince: 5 Eblis 7 Lucifer
biblical: 7 Gabriel, Raphael
bottomless pit: 7 Abaddon 8 Apollyon
of death: 6 Azrael 7 Sammael
Paradise Lost: 5 Uriel 6 Belial 7 Ariocha
worship: 5 dulia

angelfish: 9 chirivita, isabelita, isabelite

angelic: 7 saintly 8 cherubic, heavenly, seraphic 9 celestial 10 beneficent

angelica: 4 herb 7 jellica

angelico: 5 nondo

angelus: 4 bell 6 prayer 8 devotion

anger (see also **angry**): ire, irk 4 bile, fell, fury, gall, rage, rile, roil, teem 5 annoy, pique, wrath 6 choler, dander, enrage, excite, grieve, nettle, offend, rancor, spleen, temper 7 burning, dudgeon, emotion, incense, inflame, passion, provoke 8 acrimony, distress, irritate, vexation 9 displease 10 affliction, antagonism, antagonize, resentment 11 displeasure, indignation
express: 5 snort

Angevin: 11 Plantagenet
angle: ell, tee 4 cant, coin, fish, fork, knee, peak 5 arris, bevel, bight, coign, elbow, phase, point, slant 6 allure, aspect, canton, corner, scheme 7 bastion, perigon 8 decalage, fishhook, intrigue
acute: 6 akimbo
equal (pert. to): 8 isogonal, isogonic
geological: 4 hade
mathematical: 6 octant, radian 9 incidence
measuring device: 10 semicircle
of branch and leaf: 4 axil
of keel and bowsprit: 6 steeve
without: 6 agonic
angler: 5 thief 7 rodster 8 allmouth, piscator 9 fisherman, sportsman
angleworm: ess
Anglian kingdom: 5 Deira
Anglo Saxon:
armor: 7 hauberk
army: 4 fyrd
assembly: 4 moot, mote 6 mancus
coin: ora 5 sceat
council: 9 heptarchy
court: 4 leet 5 gemot 6 gemote
deity: Ing 4 Frey, Wyrd 5 Freyr
epic: 7 Beowulf
freeman: 5 thane, thegn
king: Ine 5 Edgar 6 Harold
king's council: 5 witan
letter: edh, eth, wyn 4 wynn 5 thorn
money: ora
nobleman: 4 earl 5 thane, thegn
poet: 4 scop
sheriff: 5 reeve 6 gerefa
slave: 4 esne
tax: 4 geld
village: ham
writer: 4 bede
Angola: *coin:* 6 macuta, macute 7 angolar
river: 6 Coanza, Kunene, Kwanza
town: 6 Luanda(c.) 8 Benguela 10 Mossamedes
angora: cat 4 goat, hair, wool, yarn 6 rabbit
angry (see also **anger**): mad 4 grim, sore, wraw 5 cross, grame, huffy, irate, vexed, wroth 6 crouse, fuming, ireful 7 fretful, furious, iracund, painful 8 choleric, inflamed, rigorous, vehement 9 indignant, irascible, resentful 11 exasperated
anguilla: eel
anguish: woe 4 ache, pain, pang, rack 5 agony, dolor, grief, throe 6 misery, regret 7 remorse, torment, torture 8 distress
angular: 4 bone, bony, slim, thin 5 gaunt, sharp 6 abrupt 7 pointed, scrawny 8 angulose, angulous, cornered, rawboned
ani: 6 cuckoo 9 blackbird
anil: dye 6 indigo
anile: old 5 silly 6 doting, feeble, infirm, senile, simple 7 flighty, foolish 9 doddering 11 old-womanish

animadversion: 5 blame 6 remark 7 censure, comment, reproof, warning 8 monition, reproach 9 aspersion, criticism 10 perception, punishment 11 observation 12 chastisement, condemnation
animal (see also **amphibian, bird, carnivore, fish, insect, invertebrate, mammal, reptile, vertebrate**): 5 beast, biped, brute, fauna, gross, lusty 6 carnal, fleshy, mammal, roden 7 sensual 8 creature, organism, physical 9 carnivore, marsupial, quadruped
arboreal: 7 tarsier
Biblical: 4 reem 8 behemoth
body: 4 soma
burrowing: 4 mole 6 badger, gopher, rabbit, wombat 8 squirrel 9 armadillo
class: 5 genus 6 genera(pl.)
coat: fur 4 hair, hide, pelt, skin, wool 6 pelage
collection: zoo 4 herd 5 drove 9 menagerie
crawling: 4 worm 5 snake
cross-bred: 4 mule 5 hinny 6 hybrid
doctor: vet 12 veterinarian
domestic: cat, cow, hog, pet, pig 4 mare, mule 5 horse, stock 6 cattle
draft: ox 4 mule, oxen(pl.) 5 horse 8 elephant
enclosure: pen, sty 4 cage, coop, cote, yard 5 hutch, kraal, stall 6 corral 7 pasture
equine: ass 5 horse, zebra
extinct: 8 dinosaur, mastodon
fat: 4 lard, suet 5 cetin 6 tallow 7 lanolin
feathered: bird, fowl
feline: cat 4 pard 5 tiger 6 jaguar 7 cheetah
footless: 4 apod 5 apoda
group: 4 herd 5 drove
hibernating: 4 bear
hunted: 4 game, prey
life: 4 bios 5 fauna
life (god of): 6 Faunus
lover: 8 zoophile 10 zoophilist
male: mas, tom 4 bull, jack, stag 5 steed, steer 8 stallion
many-footed: 6 insect 7 decapod, hexapod 8 multiped 9 centipede
marine: orc 4 brit, fish, inia, seal 5 coral, otter, polyp, salpa, whale 6 dugong, walrus 7 dolphin, manatee, rotifer 9 jellyfish 10 ctenophore, ctenophran
microscopic: 5 ameba, monad 6 acarid, amoeba 8 rhizopod 9 protozoan 10 animalcule
monkey-like: 5 lemur, loris
mythical: 4 faun 5 snark 6 acephal, bagwyn, bunyip, dragon, garuda 7 alborak, centaur, griffen, unicorn 8 dingmaul, minotaur 9 rosmarine
nocturnal: bat, owl 4 coon 5 lemur, ratel, tapir 6 possum, racoon 7 opossum
one-celled: 5 ameba, monad 6 amoeba 8 protozoa 9 protozoan
ovine: 5 sheep

pack: ass **4** mule **5** burro, camel, horse, llama **6** donkey

parasitic: **8** entozoon

pert. to: **7** leonine **8** zoologic

porcine: hog, pig **4** boar

rabbit-like: **4** pika **6** marmot

ruminant: cow **4** deer, goat **5** camel, sheep **8** antelope

science: **7** zoology

scrawny: **5** scrag

symbol: **5** totem

timid: **4** deer, hare **5** sheep

ursine: **4** bear

vulpine: fox

water: **4** fish, seal **5** coral, otter, whale **6** beaver, walrus

winged: bat **4** bird

young: cub, kid, pup **4** babe, calf, colt, fawn, foal, lamb **5** bruin, chick, filly, puppy, whelp **6** kitten, lionet **8** chipling

animalcule: fly **5** ameba **6** amoeba **7** rotifer **8** rotifera(pl.)

animate: pep **4** fire, move, perk, stir, urge **5** alive, brisk, cheer, drive, flush, imbue, impel, liven, rouse **6** arouse, bright, ensoul, excite, incite, induce, living, prompt, vivify **7** actuate, comfort, enliven, inspire, quicken **8** activate, energize, inspirit, vitalize **9** encourage, stimulate **10** exhilarate, invigorate

animated: gay **4** glad **5** brisk, vivid, vital **6** active, ardent, blithe, lively **7** buoyant, jocular, sthenic **8** spirited, vigorous **9** sprightly, vivacious **12** enthusiastic

anime: **5** copal, elemi, resin, rosin **7** animato **9** oleoresin

animism: **8** naturism

animosity: **4** hate, **6** animus, enmity, hatred, malice, rancor **7** dislike **9** hostility **10** antagonism, opposition, resentment **11** acharnement, malevolence

animus: **4** mind, will **6** effort, spirit, temper **8** attitude **9** intention **10** antagonism **11** disposition, inclination

anion: ion **8** particle

anise: **4** anet, dill **5** cumen **6** fennel

anisette: **7** cordial, liqueur

anisic acid salt: **7** anisate

ankle: **4** coot, cuit, hock, tali(pl.), **5** talus, tarsi(pl.) **6** tarsus

comb. form: tar **5** tarso

ornament: **6** anklet

anklebone: **5** talus **8** astragal **10** astragalus, hucklebone

anklet: **4** sock **6** fetter

ann: **7** stipend

anna: **4** coin **7** hoatzin **8** hoactzin

annal: **6** record **7** archive, history **8** register **9** chronicle **11** publication

annalist: **6** writer **8** recorder **9** historian **12** chronologist

Annam: *boat:* **6** gayyou **8** gaydiang

city: Hue(c.) **4** Haoi

division: **7** Tonquin **11** Cochin China

measure: ly; con, dam, gon, mao, ngu, quo, sao, tat, vai **4** chai, phan, that **5** shita, thouc **6** tac tao, troung

river: **6** Songka

tribe: Moi

weight: li; can, fan, hao, nen, yen **4** binh, dong

Annapolis student: **4** pleb **5** plebe **10** midshipman

annates: **6** bounty **8** benefice

annatto, annotto, arnatto: dye **4** tree **5** urucu **6** salmon **7** achiote

derivative: **7** orellin

anneal: **4** bake, fuse, heat **5** smelt **6** temper **7** inflame, toughen

annectent: **7** linking **10** connecting

annelid: **4** worm

fresh water: **4** naid

annex: add, ell **4** join **5** affix, seize, unite **6** adject, append, attach, fasten **7** acquire, fixture, subjoin **8** addition **11** appropriate **12** appurtenance

Annie Oakley: **4** pass **6** ticket

annihilate: end **4** kill, raze, slay **5** annul, erase, wreck **6** devour, quench, reduce **7** abolish, destroy, expunge **8** decimate **9** eradicate, extirpate **10** extinguish, obliterate **11** exterminate

anniversary: **4** fete **5** feast **6** annual **7** jubilee **8** birthday, festival **11** celebration

hundreth: **10** centennial

one hundred fiftieth: **16** sesquicentennial

tenth: **9** decennial

third: **9** triennial

thousandth: **10** millennial **11** millenniary

twentieth: **12** vigentennial

wedding: see **wedding:** *anniversary.*

annotate: **4** edit, note **5** gloss **6** remark **7** comment, explain **9** elucidate **10** illustrate

annotation: **7** scholia(pl.) **8** scholium

announce: bid, cry **4** bode, call, deem, tell **5** bruit **6** assert, blazon, herald, inform, report, reveal, steven **7** declare, divulge, publish **8** foretell, intimate, proclaim **9** advertise, broadcast, enunciate, pronounce **10** annunciate, promulgate

announcement: **4** hat **5** banns, blurb, edict **6** decree, dictum, notice **8** bulletin **9** manifesto **11** declaration **12** notification, proclamation

announcer: **4** page **5** crier, emcee **6** nuncio **7** gongman, spieler **8** nunciate **9** messenger

of coming events: **4** seer **6** herald **7** prophet **9** harbinger

annoy: dun, get, hox, ire, irk, nag, try, vex **4** bait, bore, fret, gall, grig, hale, harm, nark, pain, rile, roil **5** chafe, chase, devil, harry, peeve, pique, spite, tease, upset, weary, worry **6** badger, bother, caddle, harass, heckle, hector, injure, molest, needle, nettle, offend, pester, rattle **7** disturb, trouble **8** distress, irritate **9** aggravate, displease, embarrass, incommode, persecute 10 exasperate 13 inconvenience

annoyance: 4 pest 5 thorn 6 insect 8 nuisance 11 disturbance 13 inconvenience

annual: 4 book 5 plant 6 flower, yearly 7 etesian 8 periodic, yearbook 11 anniversary, publication

annuity: 5 censo 6 income 7 pension, tontine

annul: 4 cass, undo, void 5 blank, elide, erase, quash, remit 6 cancel, negate, recall, repeal, revoke 7 abolish, cassate, nullify, rescind 8 abrogate, derogate, overrule 9 disaffirm 10 annihilate, extinguish, invalidate, neutralize, obliterate 11 countermand

annular: 6 banded, cyclic, ringed 8 cingular, circular

annulet: 4 ring 5 ridge 6 fillet 7 molding

annunciate: 8 announce

anoa: ox 8 sapiutan

anode: 9 electrode

anode deposit: 5 anion

anodic: 9 ascending

anodyne: 4 balm 6 opiate, remedy 7 soother 8 narcotic, sedative 10 painkiller, palliative

anoesia: 5 anoia 6 idiocy

anoint: oil, rub 4 balm, beat, cere, nard 5 anele, anoil, cream, crown, prune, slave, smear 6 chrism, grease, spread, thrash 7 moisten 8 chastise 10 consecrate

anole: 6 lizard

anomalous: odd 7 strange, unusual 8 aberrant, abnormal, atypical, peculiar 9 eccentric, irregular 10 dissimilar 11 exceptional

anomy: 7 miracle

anon: 4 once, soon 5 again, later 6 afresh, bedeen, bedene, thence 7 shortly 9 afterward, forthwith, presently 11 immediately, straightway

anonymous: 7 unknown 8 nameless, unavowed, unsigned 9 incognito

another: new 5 alias 6 second 7 further 9 different 10 additional

ansa: 4 loop 6 handle

anserine: 4 dull 6 stolid, stupid 9 goose-like

answer: do 4 echo, plea, suit 5 atone, avail, react, reply, serve 6 result, retort, return, result, ripost 7 defense, fulfill, respond, satisfy 8 pleading, rebuttal, repartee, response, solution 9 rejoinder 11 acknowledge 16 counterstatement

answerable: 5 equal 6 liable 7 fitting 8 adequate, amenable 10 equivalent 11 accountable, responsible 12 commensurate 13 proportionate

ant: 4 anai, anay, mire 5 emmet 6 eciton, insect 7 termite 8 formicid, micraner 9 myramicid 10 formicidae(pl.), hymenop-

ter, myrmicidae(pl.), 11 hymenoptera (pl.), 12 hymenopteron

comb. form: 6 myrmec 7 myrmeco

male: 9 ergataner 15 ergatandromorph

nonworker: 5 drone

worker (comb. form): 6 ergate, ergato

ant cow: 5 aphid

ant shrike: 6 batara

anta: 4 pier 5 tapir 8 pedestal, pilaster

antagonism: 6 enmity 9 animosity, antipathy, hostility 10 opposition 11 contrariety

antagonist: foe 5 enemy, rival 7 battler, warrior 8 copemate, opponent, wrangler 9 adversary, combatant 10 competitor

antagonistic: 7 counter, hostile 8 contrary, inimical 9 dissonant

Antarctica: *bird:* 4 skua 7 penguin

sea: 4 Ross

seal: 4 Ross 9 sterrinck

ante: pay 5 stake 6 before

anteater: 5 tapir 6 animal 7 echidna, tamandu 8 aardvark, aardwolf, edentate, tamandua

scaly: 5 manis 8 pangolin

antecedent: 4 fore 5 cause, prior 6 former, reason 7 premise 8 anterior, previous 9 foregoing, foretaste, precedent, preceding

antechamber: See **anteroom**.

antedate: 7 precede, predate 10 anticipate

antediluvian: 10 antiquated

antelope (see also specific countries, e.g., **Africa:** *antelope)* gnu, sus 5 eland, peron, takin, yakin 6 dik-dik, impala, mammal 7 bloubok, gazelle, gemsbok, leather, stembok 8 ruminant, steenbok 9 pronghorn 10 hartebeest

brown: 5 nagor

female: doe

forest: 5 bongo

four-horned: 6 chouka 7 chikara 10 chousingha

gazelle-like: 5 beira 7 gerenuk

genus: 4 oryx

goat-like: 5 goral, serow 7 chamois

golden: 6 impala

harnessed: 6 guib

large: gnu 4 aste, kudu, oryx 5 addax, beisa, bongo, cland 6 impala, koodoo, nilgai, nilgau 7 bubalis, defassa, gemsbok, sassaby 10 hartebeest

male: 4 buck

mountain: 7 chamois

pied: 8 bontebok

pronghorn: 6 cabree, cabrie, cabret, cabrit

reddish: 7 grysbok

royal: 5 ipete 9 kleeneboc

sheep-like: 5 saiga

short-maned: gnu 6 nilgau

small: 6 duiker, grimme 7 grysbok 9 duikerbok

tiger-like: 8 agacella

young: kid

antelope-like: 5 bovid 6 bovine

Antelope State: 8 Nebraska

antenna: 4 horn, palp 6 aerial, feeler, lead-in

insect: 5 clava

anterior: 5 front, prior 6 atloid, before 7 ventral 8 atlantal, previous 9 foregoing, preceding 10 antecedent

anteroom: 4 hall 5 foyer, lobby 8 entrance 9 vestibule 11 antechamber

anthelion: 4 halo 6 nimbus 7 antisun, aureole 10 countersun

anthem: 4 hymn, song 5 motet, psalm 9 antiphony, offertory 10 responsory

anther: tip 6 pollen, stamen

anthesis: 5 bloom 7 blossom 13 efflorescence

anthill: 4 bank 5 mound 9 formicary

anthology: ana 4 book 6 corpus 7 garland 9 potpourri 10 collection 11 compilation

anthozoan: 5 coryl, polyp 7 anemone

anthropoid: ape, lar 5 orang 6 gibbon, simian 7 gorilla, primate, siamang 9 orangutan 10 chimpanzee, troglodyte

anthropophagite: 8 cannibal

anti: 6 contra 7 against, opposed

anti-aircraft: *fire:* 4 flak

gun: 5 archy 6 pom-pom

piece: 6 pompom

antic: 4 dido, fool, wild 5 caper, clown, comic, droll, prank, stunt 6 gambol 7 buffoon, caprice, gambado 9 grotesque, ludicrous 11 merry-andrew, monkeyshine

anticipate: 4 balk, hope 5 augur, await 6 divine, expect, thwart 7 devance, forerun, foresee, obviate, portend, prepare, prevene, prevent 8 antedate 9 apprehend, forestall, foretaste

anticipation: 5 odium 6 augury 9 intuition, prolepsis 11 forethought 12 presentiment 13 preoccupation

anticipator: 4 seer 6 omener 7 prophet, seeress 8 foreseer

antidote: 6 bezoar, remedy 10 preventive

Antilles: *god:* 4 Zeme

native: 5 Ineri

pearl: 4 Cuba

antimacassar: 4 tidy 5 doily

antimony: 4 kohl

Antioch proselyte: 7 Nicolas

antipasto: 6 relish 9 appetizer, foretaste 12 hors d'oeuvres

antipathy: 6 enmity, nausea, rancor 7 disgust, dislike 8 aversion, distaste, loathing 9 disrelish, hostility 10 abhorrence, antagonism, reluctance, repugnance 11 contrariety, detestation 14 disinclination 15 incompatibility

antiquated: old 4 aged 5 passe 6 fossil, voided 7 ancient, archaic 8 obsolete, outdated, outmoded 9 primitive 12 antediluvian 13 superannuated

antique: 5 relic, virtu 9 venerable 12 old-fashioned

antiquity: eld 4 hpar, yore 5 relic 8 ancience, anciency, monument 9 anciently

antiseptic: 5 amido, amine, eupad, eusol, salol 6 iodine, phenol 7 alcohol, aseptic, loretin, sterile 8 creosote, metaphen 9 germicide 12 disinfectant

powder: 6 formin

antisocial: 7 hostile 11 anarchistic 12 misanthropic

antisociability: 14 anthropophobia

antispasmodic: 9 asadulcis

antithesis: 8 contrast 9 antipodes 10 opposition

antitoxin: 4 sera(pl.) 5 serum

antler: 4 horn

bay: 9 bezantler

branch: bay, bey 4 beam, brow, snag, tine, tyne 5 crown, royal 7 speller 8 tresting

knob: 6 croche

main stem: 4 beam

unbranched: dag 4 horn 5 dague, spike 7 pricket 9 greenhorn

Antony and Cleopatra character: 4 Eros, Iras 5 Menas, Philo 6 Gallus, Taurus 7 Agrippa

antrum: 5 sinus 6 cavern, cavity

anuran: 4 toad 10 salientian

anurous: 8 tailless

Anu's consort: 4 Anat

anvil: 5 block 6 stithy 7 bickern 8 beakiron

bone: 4 amos 5 incus 7 incudes(pl.)

point: 4 horn, beak

tinsmith's: 5 teest

anxiety: 4 care, fear 5 alarm, anger, doubt, dread, panic, worry 7 caution, chagrin, concern, scruple, trouble 8 disquiet, suspense 9 misgiving 10 foreboding, perplexity, solicitude, uneasiness 12 apprehension

anxious: 4 agog 5 eager 6 uneasy 7 carking, unquiet 8 desirous, restless, watchful 9 disturbed, expectant, impatient

any: an; ary, oni 4 part, some 8 quantity 11 appreciable

anybody: one 7 someone

anything: 5 aught

Anzac 7 soldier 10 Australian 12 New Zealander

aorist: 4 past 5 tense

aoristic: 10 indefinite 12 undetermined 13 indeterminate

aorta: 5 trunk 6 artery

aoudad: 4 arui 5 sheep

apa: 7 wallaba

apace: 4 fast 5 quick 7 quickly, rapidly 8 speedily

Apache: 4 Yuma 6 Indian 10 Chiricahua

beverage: 6 tiswin

chief: 7 Cochese 8 Geronimo

jacket: 6 bietle

Apache State: 7 Arizona

apar: 9 armadillo

apart: by 4 away, lone 5 alone, aloof, aside, riven, solus, split 6 atwain, lonely 7 asunder, enisled, removed, severed 8 divorced, secluded, separate 10 abstracted 11 dissociated

prefix: se; dia, dis

apartment: 4 digs, flat 5 abode, rooms, suite 7 chamber 8 building, dwelling, tenement 11 compartment

upper: 5 solar 6 sollar

apathetic: 4 calm, cold, cool, dead, dull 5 inert, stoic 6 torpid, supine 7 passive, unmoved 8 listless, sluggish 9 impassive, incurious, unfeeling 10 insensible, phlegmatic 11 indifferent, unemotional 12 uninterested 13 dispassionate, sensationless

apathy: 6 acedia, phlegm, torpor 7 languor 8 doldrums 9 lassitude, unconcern 12 indifference

apatite: 7 ijolite

ape (see also **anthropoid**): 4 boor, copy, dupe, fool, maha, mime, mock 5 clown, magot, mimic 6 baboon, gelada, langur, monkey, parrot, simian 7 buffoon, copycat, emulate, imitate, portray, primate 8 imitator, simulate 10 anthropoid, quadrumane 11 impersonate

dog-headed: 4 aani 11 cynocephali(pl.) 12 cynocephalus

largest: 7 gorilla

like animal: 5 lemur

apeak: 8 vertical

apeman: 6 alalus

aper: 4 boar, mime, snob 5 clown 6 mocker 7 buffoon, copycat

apercu: 6 digest, glance, sketch 7 insight, outline 10 conspectus

aperitif: 5 drink 9 appetizer

apert: 4 bold, open 7 evident 9 outspoken 15 straightforward

aperture: gap, vue 4 hole, leak, pore, rima, slit, slot, vent 5 chasm, cleft, crack, mouth, stoma 6 window 7 fissure, opening, orifice, ostiole 8 loophole, spiracle 11 perforation

apex: tip, top 4 acme, cone, cusp, noon, peak 5 crest, point, spire 6 apogee, climax, crisis, summit, tittle, vertex, zenith 7 cacumen 8 fastigia(pl.), pinnacle 9 fastigium 11 culmination

covering: epi

ornament for: 6 finial

rounded: 6 retuse

Aphareus: *brother:* 7 Lynceus

son: 4 Idas

aphid: 5 aphis, louse

aphorism: saw 5 adage, axiom, dicta(pl.), gnome, maxim, motto, sutra, sutta 6 dictum, saying 7 epigram, precept, proverb 10 apophthegm

aphoristic: 6 gnomic 8 gnomical 10 proverbial

Aphrodite: 5 Venus 6 Urania 9 priestess

consort: 4 Ares

mother: 5 Dione

priestess: 4 Hero

son: 4 Eros 5 Eneas 6 Aeneas

temple site: 6 Paphos

apiary: 4 hive, skep 8 beehouse

apiece: per 4 each 8 seriatim 14 distributively

apina: 7 apoidea

apis: bee 8 honeybee

Apis' manifestation: 7 Serapis

apish: 5 silly 7 foppish 8 affected

apishamore: bed 7 blanket

aplomb: 4 tact 5 nerve, poise 6 surety 8 coolness 9 assurance, stability 10 confidence, resolution

apocopate: 5 elide 7 shorten

apocryphal: 4 sham 5 false 6 unreal 8 doubtful, fabulous, mythical, spurious 9 imitative 10 fictitious, unorthodox 11 counterfeit, uncanonical, unauthentic

apodal: 8 footless

apode: eel 5 moray

apogee: 4 acme, apex, peak 6 climax, zenith 11 culmination

apograph: 4 copy 6 ectype 7 replica 9 imitation 10 transcript

apoidea: bee 4 apis 5 apina 6 apidae

Apollo: 6 Delius 7 Phoebus

abode of: 7 Helicon

beloved of: 6 Cyrene, Daphne 8 Calliope

birthplace: 5 Delos

father: 4 Zeus 7 Jupiter

mother: 4 Leto 6 Latona

oracle site: 6 Delphi

sister: 5 Diana 7 Artemis

son: Ion

twin: 5 Diana

Apollyon: 5 Satan, devil 7 Abaddon 9 archfield, Beelzebub, destroyer

apologetic: 5 sorry 9 defensive 10 remorseful

apologue: 4 myth 5 fable, story 7 parable 8 allegory

pert. to: 7 fabular

apology: 4 plea 5 alibi 6 amends, excuse, regret 11 explanation, vindication 13 justification 14 acknowledgment 15 acknowledgement

apoplexy: 4 esca 5 plant 6 stroke 12 black measles

apostate: rat 7 heretic, pervert, seceder 8 deserter, disloyal, recreant, renegade, turncoat 9 faithless 10 recidivist

apostle: 4 John, Jude, Paul 5 James, Judas, Peter, Silas, Simon 6 Andrew, Philip, Thomas 7 Matthew, teacher 8 Barnabas, disciple, follower, preacher 9 messenger 10 apprentice 11 Bartholomew

of Indies: 6 Xavier

pert. to: 7 petrine

to Gauls: 5 Denis

apothecary: 8 druggist **10** pharmacist
weight: **4** dram **5** grain, pound **7** scruple
apothegm, apophthegm: saw **4** dict **5**
adage, axiom, dicta(pl.), gnome, maxim,
sutra **6** dictum, saying, suttah **7** proverb
8 aphorism
apotheosize: 5 deify, exalt **7** elevate, glorify **10** consecrate
appall, appal: 4 stun **5** daunt, shock **6**
dismay, reduce, revolt, weaken **7** astound, depress, disgust, dismiss, horrify,
terrify **8** affright, astonish, enfeeble,
frighten, overcome **10** discourage,
dishearten
appalling: 5 awful **7** awesome **8** terrible,
terrific **9** frightful, unearthly
appanage, apanage: 5 grant **7** adjunct **9**
allowance, privilege, territory **10** dependency, perquisite **11** prerogative **12** appurtenance
apparatus (see also **device, instrument):**
4 gear, tool **6** dingus, gadget, graith, outfit
7 machine, utensil **8** equipage **9** appliance, equipment, machinery, mechanism,
trappings **10** furnishing **11** contrivance
12 appurtenance
apparel (see also **dress, vestment): 4**
deck, fare, garb, gear, robe, wear **5** adorn,
array, equip, tunic **6** attire, clothe, graith,
outfit **7** costume, furnish, garment, prepare, raiment, vesture **8** clothing, wardrobe **9** embellish, equipment **11** habiliments
apparent: 4 open **5** clear, overt, plain
6 patent **7** certain, evident, glaring,
obvious, seeming, visible **8** distinct, manifest, palpable, probable **9** appearant **10**
ostensible **11** discernible, perceptible,
unconcealed **12** unmistakable
apparition: 4 hant **5** dream, ghost, haunt,
shade, spook **6** aspect, eidola(pl.), idolum, spirit, sprite, wraith **7** display, eidolon, fantasy, phantom, specter, spectre **8**
phantasm, revenant **9** hobgoblin, semblance **10** appearance, phenomenon **13**
demonstration
appay: 5 repay **6** please, reward **7** content, satisfy
appeach: 6 accuse **7** asperse, impeach
appeal: ask, beg **4** call, case, plea, seek,
suit **5** apply, refer **6** accuse, adjure,
avouch, invoke, prayer, summon **7** address, conjure, entreat, implore, request,
solicit **8** approach, petition **9** challenge,
importune **10** appelation, supplicate
appealing: 4 cute, nice **6** catchy, clever **8**
pleasant **9** agreeable **10** attractive
appear: 4 come, dawn, look, loom, seem **5**
arise, enter, issue, occur **6** arrive, beseem, emerge **7** compear(Sc.), develop
appearance: air, hue **4** form, idea, look,
mien, show, view **5** blush, front, guise,
sight **6** aspect, manner, ostent **7** arrival,
display **8** illusion, presence, pretense **9**

semblance **10** disclosure, likelihood,
phenomenon **11** countenance, probability
13 manifestation
first: **4** dawn **5** debut **8** premiere
appease: lay **4** calm, ease, hush **5** allay,
alone, mease(Sc.), quiet, slake **6** defray,
pacify, please, soften, soothe **7** assuage,
content, gratify, mollify, placate, satisfy **8**
mitigate **10** conciliate, propitiate **11**
tranquilize
appellation: nom (F.), **4** name, term **5**
style, title **6** appeal **7** calling, epithet,
surname **8** cognomen, nickname **9** sobriquet **11** description, designation **12** denomination, nomenclature
appellee: 9 defendant **10** respondent
appenage: See **appanage.**
append: add, pin, tag **4** clip, hang, join **5**
affix, annex **6** adjoin, attach, fasten **7**
augment, subjoin **8** appendix
appendage: arm, awn, tab, tag **4** aril,
barb, caud, flap, lobe, tail **5** ceras, rider **6**
adnexa(pl.), bracht, palpus, suffix **7** adjunct, eodicil **8** addition, pendicle **9** accessory, belonging **10** dependency **12**
appurtenance
appendix: 5 organ **6** append **7** addenda(pl.), **8** addendum **10** supplement
operation: **12** appendectomy
appertain: 5 refer **6** belong, relate **7** pertain
appetite: yen **4** lust, urge, zest **5** gusto,
taste **6** desire, hunger, liking, orexis, relish **7** craving, longing, passion, wanting **8**
cupidity, tendency **9** appetency **10** preference, propensity
excessive: **5** greed **8** gluttony, gulosity **10**
polyphagia
voracious: **7** edacity **8** rapacity
appetizer: 5 sauce **6** canape, relish, savory **8** aperitif **9** antipasto **11** hors
d'oeuvre
applaud: 4 clap, laud, root **5** cheer, extol
6 praise **7** acclaim, approve, commend,
endorse **10** compliment
applauders: 6 claque
applause: 4 clap, hand **5** bravo, cheer,
eclat, huzza, salvo **6** hurrah **7** acclaim,
ovation **8** clapping, plaudits **11** approbation
device: **8** claptrap
applause-seeking: 9 captation
apple: 4 crab, pome **6** Esopus, pippin,
russet **7** Baldwin, Fameuse, winesap,
wealthy **8** Ben Davis, Cortland, Greening,
Jonathan, McIntosh **9** Delicious, Oldenberg **10** Rome Beauty **11** Gravenstein,
Northern Spy, Spitzenburg **12** Yellow
Newton, York Imperial **17** Yellow Transparent
acid: **5** malic
cider-making: **8** coccagee
dried: **6** beefin, biffin
family: **8** Malaceae

immature: 6 codlin 7 codling
juice: 5 cider 9 applejack
juice (pert. to): 5 malic
old variety: 6 rennet
pastry: 7 strudel
pulp: 6 pomace
ribbed: 7 costard
seed: pip
seller: 6 coster 12 costermonger
shriveled: 9 crumpling
tree: 4 sorb 5 malus, papaw 6 pawpaw
wild: 4 crab 6 doucin
apple grunt: pie 8 dumpling
appliance (see also **tool**): 4 gear 6 device,
gadget 7 utensil 9 implement 10 instrument 11 application, contrivance 12 appurtenance
applicable: apt, fit 4 meet 6 proper, useful
7 fitting, pliable 8 apposite, relative, relevant, suitable 9 compliant, pertinent 11
appropriate
applicant: 8 prospect 9 candidate, dec-
larant
application: use 4 form 5 blank, topic 6
appeal, effort 7 address, request 8 petition, practice, sedulity 9 diligence 10
compliance 11 requisition
applique: 6 attach, design 8 ornament 10
decoration
apply: ask, put, rub, use 4 give, toil, work
5 adapt, grind, labor, liken, smear 6 appeal, appose, bestow, betake, comply, devote, direct, employ 7 adhibit, compare,
conform, overlay, pertain, request, solicit,
utilize 8 dedicate, petition 9 persevere
10 administer
appoggiatura: 8 ornament 9 grace note
appoint: arm, fix, set 4 call, deck, name 5
allot, array, award, crest, dight, elect,
enact, equip, place 6 assign, assize, attach, decree, detail, devise, direct, ordain,
outfit, settle, steven 7 arraign, confirm,
destine, dispose, furnish, resolve 8 delegate, indicate, ordinate, nominate 9 designate, determine, establish, prescribe
10 constitute
as agent: 6 depute 8 delegate, deputize
appointment: 4 date 5 berth, order, tryst
6 billet, office, steven 7 command, station
8 position 9 allowance, equipment, interview, ordaining, ordinance 10 assignment, engagement, nomination, perquisite, rendezvous 11 assignation,
designation 12 capitulation 13 establishment
apport: 4 port 5 rents 7 bearing, produce,
tribute 13 contributions
apportion: lot 4 deal, dole, mete 5 allot,
award, grant, paral, share 6 assess, assign, divide 7 arrange 8 allocate 10 distribute
appose: add, put 5 apply, place

apposite: apt, pat 6 timely 7 germane 8
relative, relevant, suitable 9 pertinent 11
appropriate
appraise(see also **apprise**): 4 gage, rate 5
assay, judge, price, value 6 assess, esteem, evalue, ponder 7 adjudge, analyze,
commend 8 estimate, evaluate 10 adjudicate, appreciate
appreciable: any 11 perceptible
appreciate: 4 feel, love 5 judge, prize,
raise, value 6 admire, esteem 7 advance,
apprize, approve, cherish, realize 8 increase, treasure
appreciation: 5 gusto 9 gratitude 11
recognition 12 gratefulness
apprehend: cop, nab, see 4 fear, know,
note, take, view 5 catch, dread, grasp,
gripe, intue, seize 6 arrest, detain, intuit
7 believe, capture, imagine, realize 8
conceive, discover, overtake, perceive 9
recognize 10 anticipate, appreciate, comprehend, understand
apprehensible: 6 noetic 7 sensate 12
intelligible
apprehension: 4 fear, fray 5 doubt,
dread, worry 6 arrest, dismay 7 anxiety,
concern 8 distrust, mistrust, suspense 9
awareness, misgiving, suspicion 10 cognizance, conception, diffidence, foreboding, perception, solicitude, uneasiness 11
premonition 12 anticipation, intellection,
presentiment 13 signification
apprehensive: apt 5 jumpy 6 morbid 7
nervous 9 cognizant, conscious 10 discerning
apprentice: 4 tyro 6 helper, jockey, novice 7 learner, trainee 8 beginner, servitor
9 draftsman
apres: 5 after 10 afterwards
apprise, apprize (see also **appraise**): 4
warn 5 learn, teach 6 advise, inform, notify, reveal 8 acquaint, disclose 9 ascertain 10 appreciate, certiorate
apprised: 5 aware 7 knowing
approach: try 4 adit, come, near, nere,
road 5 board, coast, essay, stalk, verge 6
access, accost, advent, appeal, broach,
impend 7 advance, seagate 9 introduce
11 approximate 13 appropinquate
approbation: 4 test 5 favor, proof, trial 6
assent, favour, praise, regard, repute 7
plaudit 8 applause, approval, sanction 9
allowance 10 admiration 11 attestation
12 commendation, confirmation
appropinquate: 8 approach
appropriate: add, apt, due, fit 4 akin,
grab, meet, suit, take 5 annex, happy,
right, steal, usurp 6 assign, assume, borrow, pilfer, pirate, proper, timely, worthy
7 apropos, cabbage, condign, convert,
fitting, germane, grabble, impound,
preempt, purloin, related 8 accroach, be-

coming, deserved, idoneous, relevant, suitable **9** attribute, pertinent **10** applicable, assimilate, confiscate, convenient, plagiarize **11** conformable, felicitious
approval: **4** amen **5** eclat **6** assent **7** approof, support **8** sanction **10** imprimatur **11** approbation
approve: ok; try **4** like, okay, pass, test, vote **5** allow, favor, value **6** accept, admire, concur, ratify **7** applaud, certify, commend, confirm, consent, endorse, exhibit, indorse **8** accredit, manifest, sanction **9** authorize, establish **10** appreciate, experience **11** countenance **12** adscititious, authenticate
approximate: **4** near **5** about, circa, close **8** approach, estimate **10** resembling **11** approaching
approximately: **4** nigh **5** about **6** almost, around, nearly **7** roughly
appurtenance: **4** gear **5** annex **7** adjunct **8** appanage, appenage **9** accessory, apparatus, appliance, belonging
apricot: ume **4** ansu, tree **5** color, fruit **8** Blenheim
confection: **5** mebos **6** meebos
cordial: **7** perisco **8** periscot
vine: **6** maypop
apron: bib **4** base, boot, brat, tier **5** cover **6** barvel, bishop, napron, runway, shield, tarmac, touser **7** gremial **8** lambskin, pinafore **9** barmcloth **10** coverslut, protection
leather: **4** dick **6** barvel **7** barvell **8** barmskin
apropos: apt, fit, pat **4** meet **6** timely **8** relevant, suitable **9** opportune, pertinent **11** appropriate
apse: **5** niche **6** recess **10** projection
apt: fit, pat **4** able, deft, keen **5** adept, alert, happy, prone, quick, ready **6** clever, docile, liable, likely, suited **7** apropos, capable, fitting, willing **8** apposite, dextrous, disposed, idoneous, inclined, prepared, skillful, suitable **9** competent, consonant, dexterous, pertinent, qualified **10** proficient **11** appropriate
apteral: **8** apterous, wingless
aptitude: art **4** bent, gift, turn **5** craft, flair, knack **6** genius, talent **7** ability, faculty, fitness, leaning **8** capacity, instinct, tendency **10** propensity **11** disposition **12** suitableness
aqua: **5** water
aquamarine: gem **4** blue **5** beryl, color
aquarium: **4** bowl, pool, pond, tank **5** globe
aquatic plant: **4** lily **5** coral, lotus **6** enalid, sugamo **7** elatine, seaweed **10** hydrophyte
aqueduct: **4** duct **5** canal **7** channel, conduit, passage **9** conductor

aquifer: bed **6** bearer **7** stratum
aquila: **5** eagle
aquiline: **6** curved, hooked **7** curving **9** prominent
aquosity: **7** wetness **8** moisture **10** wateriness
ara: **5** macaw
Arab: **4** Oman, sleb, waif **5** gamin, horse, nomad, Saudi, tatar **6** Semite, urchin **7** Arabian, bedouin, Saracen **8** wanderer, Yemenite **9** Himyarite
araba: cab **5** coach, wagon **6** monkey **7** vehicle
Arabia: *alphabet:* see **Arabic:** *alphabet*
ancient: **4** Saha **5** Sheba
antelope: **5** addax
author: **6** lokman
banquet: **5** diffa
bird: **7** phoenix
caliph: Ali **6** sharif, sherif **7** shareef, shereef
chief: **4** amir, emir **5** ameer, emeer
city: **4** Aden, Hail, Riad, Sana **5** Mecca, Mocha **6** Medina **7** Oneizah
cloak: aba
coffee: **5** mocha
coin: **4** lari **5** carat, dinar, kabik, riyal
cosmetic: **4** kohl
country: **4** Asir, Iran, Iraq, Oman **5** Egypt, Syria, Yemen **6** Arabia, Jordan **7** Lebanon
demon: **4** jinn **5** afrit, genie, jinni **6** afreet, jinnee
desert: Nyd **5** Ankaf, Dehna, Nefud **6** Syrian
division: **4** Oman, Suez **5** Mecca, Sinai **6** El Hasa, El Nejd, Mahara **7** El Yemen, Medinah **8** El Hedjaz, El Tehama **9** Hadramaut
drink: **4** bosa, boza **5** bozah **6** lebban
drum: **9** tara-booka
fabric: aba **4** haik
father: abu **4** abba, abou
garment: aba **4** haik **6** cabaan **7** burnous **8** burnoose
gazelle: **4** cora **5** ariel
goddess: **5** Allat
grammar: **7** ajrumya
gulf: **4** Aden, Oman
horse: **6** anezeh **8** kadischi, palomino
infantryman: **5** askar
jasmine: **4** bela **10** sampaquita
judge: **4** cadi
measure: den, saa **4** ferk, foot, kist **5** achir, barid, cabda, cafiz, covid, cuddy, makuk, mille, qasab, teman, woibe, zudda **6** artaba, assbaa, covido, feddan, gariba, ghalva **7** caphite, farsakh, farsang, kiladja, marhale, nusfiah
mountain: **4** Nebo **5** Horeb, Sinai
noble: **4** amir, emir **5** ameer, emeer
nomad: **7** Saracen

palm: 4 doom, doum
peasant: 6 fellah
peninsula: 5 Sinai
plant: kat 5 retem
prince (see also *ruler* below): 6 sherif 7 shereef
raiders: 8 fedayeen
river bed: 4 wadi, wady
romance: 5 antar 6 antara
ruler: 4 amir, emir 5 ameer, emeer
shrub: kat 5 alhaj, retem
tambourine: 4 taar 5 daira
tea shrub: kat
tent encampment: 5 douar
tribe: Aus 4 Asir, Irad, Tema 5 Kedar 7 Diendel, Shukria 9 Hagarenes
vessel: 4 dhow 6 boutre, sambuk
weight: 4 rotl 5 cheki, kella, nasch, nevat, ocque, oukia, ratel, toman, vakia 6 bokard, dirhem, miskal, tomand 8 farsalah
wind: 6 simoom, simoon

Arabian Nights:
bird: roc 4 aqib
character: Ali 4 Sidi 5 Amina 7 Zobeide
dervish: 4 Agib
merchant: 7 Sindbad
prince: 7 Alasnam
sorceress: 5 Amine
youth: 7 Aladdin

Arabic: *alphabet:* ba, ta, ha, ra, za, fa, ha, ya; tha, jim, kha, dal, zay, sin, sad, dad, ayn, qaf, kaf, lam, mim, nun, waw 4 alif, dhal, shin 5 ghayn
script: 5 neski

arabic acid salt: 7 arabate
arable: 7 fertile 8 plowable, tillable
land: 5 laine
aracanga: 5 macaw
aracari: 6 toucan
arachnid: 4 crab, mite, tick 6 acarus, spider 8 scorpion 9 tarantula
arachnoid: 4 thin 5 hairy 8 araneous, delicate 10 cobweblike
Aram: 5 Syria
city: 5 arpad 6 arphad
deity: 6 Rimmon
Aramaic: 6 Syriac 9 Samaritan
araneous: 4 thin 8 delicate 9 arachnoid 10 cobweblike
araphorostic: 7 unsewed 8 seamless
araponga: 8 bellbird
Arawakan: *Indian:* 4 Uran 5 Araua, Bares, Guana, Moxos, Piros 6 Campas 7 Atorais, Banivas, Jucunas, Lucayos, Tacanan, Ticunan 8 Lorenzan
language: 5 Taino
arbiter: 5 judge 6 critic, oddman, umpire 7 adviser, daysman, oddsman, overman, referee 10 arbitrator
arbitrary: 6 severe, thetic 7 willful 8 absolute, despotic, masterly 9 imperious 10 autocratic, capricious, highhanded, peremptory, tyrannical 11 determinate 13 irresponsible

arbitrate: 6 decide 7 mediate 9 determine, intercede
arbitrator: ref 5 judge 6 umpire 7 arbiter, munsiff, referee 8 mediator 11 conciliator
arbor, arbour: bar 4 axle, beam 5 abode, bower, shaft 6 garden 7 mandrel, orchard, pergola, retreat, spindle, trellis 8 platform 11 latticework
arbustum: 5 copse 7 orchard 10 plantation
arc: bow 4 arch, bend, halo 5 curve, orbit, spark 6 radian 7 rainbow 9 spotlight
chord of: 4 sine
horizon: 7 azimuth
arc lamp rod: 6 carbon
arca: box 5 chest, paten 9 reliquary
arcade: 6 avenue, loggia, street 7 gallery, portico 8 arcature 9 collonade 10 passageway
Arcadia: 4 Eden 6 Arcady 8 paradise
huntress: 8 Atalanta
princess: 4 Auge
town: 4 Alea
woodland spirit: Pan
arcadian: 5 ideal, rural 6 rustic, simple 7 bucolic 8 pastoral, shepherd
arcane: 6 hidden, secret 10 mysterious
arcanum: 6 elixir, remedy, secret 7 mystery
arch: arc, bow, coy, sly 4 bend, span 5 arcus, chief, curve, great, prime, saucy, vault 6 arcade, clever, fornix, impish 7 archway, cunning, eminent, roguish, support, waggish 9 principal 11 mischievous
inner curve of: 8 intrados
kind of: 4 flat 5 round, Tudor 6 lancet 7 rampant, trefoil 9 horseshoe, primitive, segmental 10 shouldered 11 equilateral 12 basket-handle, four-centered 13 three-cornered
memorial: 6 pailoo, pailou, pailow
molding: 9 accoclade
part: 8 keystone, springer, voussoir
pointed: 4 ogee 5 ogive
arch-enemy: 5 devil, Satan
archaic: old 7 ancient 8 historic, obsolete 9 venerable 10 antiquated 12 old-fashioned
archangel: 5 Satan, Uriel 7 Gabriel, Michael, Raphael
archbishop: 7 prelate, primate
archbishopric: see
archer: 4 Clim, Clym, Tell 5 cupid 6 bowman 9 Robin Hood 10 archerfish 11 Sagittarius
archery:
locker: 6 ascham
lover: 11 toxophilite
target center: 5 clout
archetype: 4 idea 5 model 6 figure, sample 7 example, paragon, pattern 8 exemplar, original 9 prototype 10 manuscript
architect: 5 maker 6 artist, author 7 art-

isan, builder, creator, planner **8** designer **9** contriver, draftsman
architectural: 8 tectonic
architecture: *convexity:* **7** entasis
 order: **5** Doric, Ionic **10** Corinthian
 ornament: ove **5** gutta **6** dentil, rosace **7** rosette
 style: **5** Doric, Greek, Ionic, Tudor **6** French, Gothic, Lancet, Modern, Norman **7** Baroque, Cape Cod, English, Italian, Moorish, Spanish **8** Academic, Colonial, Egyptian, Etruscan, Georgian **9** Byzantine, Palladian **10** Corinthian, Romanesque **11** Renaissance
archive: 5 annal **6** museum, record **7** library **8** document, register **9** chronicle
archon: 5 ruler **8** director, official **10** magistrate
arctic: icy **4** cold, cool, shoe **5** gelid, polar **6** boreal, chilly, frigid, galosh **8** northern, overshoe
Arctic: *base:* **4** Etah
 bird: auk
 current: **8** Labrador
 dog: **7** samoyed **8** samoyede
 explorer: Rae **4** Byrd, Eric, Kane, Ross **5** Davis, Peary **6** Baffin, Bering, Button, Greely, Hudson, Nansen **7** McClure, Wilkins, Wrangel **8** Amundsen **9** Frobisher, Stefanson **10** Willoughby
 falcon: **9** gyrfalcon
 gull (genus): **4** xema
 headland: **5** Odden
 inhabitant: **4** Lapp **5** Aleut **6** Eskimo **7** Alaskan **9** Laplander
 jacket: **6** anorak
 plain: **6** tundra
 plant: **5** ledum
 sea: **7** Barents
 sea animal: **6** narwal **8** narwhale
Arctic Sea gulf: Ob
Arcturus: 4 star
arcuate: **4** bent **5** bowed **6** arched, curved, hooked
ardent: hot **4** avid, fond, keen, warm **5** eager, fiery, rethe(Sc.) **6** ablaze, fervid, fierce **7** amorous, earnest, feeling, fervent, flaming, forward, intense, shining, zealous **8** desirous, vehement **9** impetuous, perfervid **11** inflammable **12** enthusiastic
ardor, ardour: 4 dash, elan, glow, heat, love, zest **5** gusto, verve **6** desire, fervor, mettle, spirit **7** ardency, passion **8** devotion, vivacity **9** animation, calenture, constancy **10** enthusiasm
arduous: 4 hard **5** lofty, steep **6** trying **7** onerous **8** exacting, tiresome, toilsome **9** difficult, laborious, strenuous **10** exhausting
are: 5 exist
area: 4 belt, size, zone **5** court, field, range, realm, scene, scope, space, tract **6** areola, extent, locale, region, sector,

sphere, volume **7** areaway, circuit, compass, environ, expanse, purlieu, surface **8** district, province **9** bailiwick, extension, territory **12** neighborhood
 measure: **6** parish
 pert. to: **7** spatial
aread, areed: 4 read, tell, warn **5** guess **6** advise, decree, direct, divine **7** adjudge, counsel, declare, explain **9** interpret
areca: 4 palm **5** betel
arena: 4 area, oval, ring, rink **5** court, field, scene, scope, space, stage **6** circus, region, sphere, stadia(pl.), **7** cockpit, stadium, theater **8** province **10** hippodrome **12** amphitheater
 sports: see **field** *athletic*
arenaceous: 5 sandy **6** gritty **8** sabulous
areola: pit **4** area, ring, spot **5** space **9** periphery **10** interstice
areometer: 10 hydrometer
Ares: 4 Mars
 father: **4** Zeus
 mother: **4** Enyo, Hera
 sister: **4** Eris
 son: **6** Cycnus
arete: 4 crag **5** crest, ridge, valor **6** virtue **8** fishbone **9** manliness **10** excellence
argala: 7 marabou **8** adjutant
argali: 5 sheep **6** aoudad
argent: 4 coin **5** money, white **6** silver **7** shining, silvery **9** whiteness
Argentina: *barge:* **7** chalana
 city: **4** Acha, Azul, Goya, Puan **5** Bahia, Jujuy, Lanus, Salta **6** Blanca, Burras, Parana **7** Cordoba, La Plata, La Rioja, Mendoza, Rosario, Santa Fe, Tucuman **11** Buenos Aires (c.)
 coin: **4** peso **7** centavo **9** argentino
 cowboy: **6** gaucho
 dance: **5** tango **6** cuando
 estuary: **5** Plata
 garment: **7** chiripa
 Indian: **4** Lule
 Indian village: **8** tolderia
 measure: **4** sino, vara **5** legua **6** cuadra, fanega **7** manzana
 mesquite: **6** calden **9** algarroba
 plain: **5** pampa
 port: **7** Rosario
 province: **5** Chaco, Jujuy, Pampa, Rioja, Salta **6** Estero **7** Cordova, Formosa, Mendoza, San Juan, San Luis, Santa Fe, Tacuman **8** Santiago **9** Catamarca, Entre Rios, Patagonia **10** Corrientes
 river: **5** Negro, Plata **6** Parana, Salado **7** Vermejo **8** Colorado, Paraguay, Picomayo **9** Rio Grande
 tree: **4** coco, tala **5** ambay, timbo
 weight: **4** last **5** grano **7** quintal **8** tonelada
argil: 4 clay **7** alumina
argillaceous: 5 slaty **6** clayey, cledgy, doughy, spongy
argol, argal: 6 tartar

Argonaut: 5 Jason 8 wanderer 10 adventurer

Argos: *king:* 4 Abas 6 Danaus 7 Lynceus 8 Acrisius, Adrastus

princess: 5 Danae

argosy: 4 boat, ship 5 craft, fleet 6 vessel 7 galleon

argot: 4 cant 5 flash, lingo, slang 6 jargon, patois 7 dialect

argue: 4 moot, spar 5 cavil, orate, plead, prove, treat 6 accuse, adduce, caffle, debate, reason 7 arraign, contend, contest, discuss, wrangle 8 indicate, maintain, persuade 9 discourse 11 argey-bargey, expostulate, ratiocinate, remonstrate

argument: row 4 agon, case, fuss, plea, spar, text 5 clash, proof, set to, theme 6 combat, debate, hassle 7 dispute, polemic, rhubarb, summary 8 abstract, evidence 9 argy-bargy, discourse 10 indication 11 altercation, argey-bargey, controversy, disputation

fallacious: 7 sophism

negative side: con

positive side: pro

starting point: 7 premise

argumentative: 7 eristic 8 forensic 10 rhetorical 11 presumptive 12 disputatious 13 controversial

argute: 5 acute, sharp 6 shrewd, shrill, subtle 9 sagacious

argy-bargy, argey-bargey: 5 argue 6 haggle 7 dispute, wrangle

arhat: 4 monk 5 lohan, saint

aria: air 4 solo, song, tune 6 melody 7 arietta, ariette, sortita

arid: dry 4 bald, bare, dull, lean 6 barren, desert, jejune, meager 7 parched, sterile 8 withered 9 unfertile, waterless 10 desiccated, siccaneous 12 moistureless 13 uninteresting

ariel: 7 gazelle

Aries: ram

mother: 4 Enyo

aril: pod 7 arillus, coating 8 covering 9 appendage 10 integument

false: 8 arillode

ariose: 7 melodic 8 songlike 9 melodious

aris: See **arris.**

arise: 4 flow, lift, rear, rise, soar, stem 5 awake, begin, exist, issue, mount, raise, stand, surge, tower, waken 6 accrue, amount, appear, ascend, attain, derive, emerge, happen, spring 7 develop, emanate, proceed 8 develope 9 originate

arista: awn 5 beard 9 appendage

aristocracy: 4 rule 5 class, elite 8 nobility 10 government, patriciate

aristocrat: 4 lord 5 noble 7 grandee, parvenu 9 patrician

aristocratic: 4 tony 7 high-hat

Aristotle: 5 Greek 11 philosopher

birthplace: 6 Thrace 7 Stagira

category: 4 time 5 place 6 action 7 quality 8 position, quantity, relation 9 passivity, substance 10 possession

father: 10 Nicomachus

teacher: 5 Plato

arithmetic: 4 sums 8 textbook 11 mathematics

rule: 10 alligation

Arius' follower: 5 Arian

Arizona: *city:* 4 Yuma 5 Tempe 6 Tucson 7 Nogales, Phoenix

flower: 7 saguaro

Indian: 4 Pima, Yuma 6 Navaho, Navajo

river: 4 Gila

town: see *city* above

Arizona gourd: 11 calabazilla

ark: bin, box 4 boat, ship 5 barge, chest, hutch 6 basket, coffer, refuge, wangan 7 retreat, shelter, wanigan 8 flatboat

builder: Noe 4 Noah

resting place: 6 Ararat

Arkansas: *county:* Lee 4 Clay, Drew, Pike, Poke, Polk, Yell 5 Scott

mountains: 5 Ozark

arkose: 9 sandstone

arm: fin 4 limb, wing 5 bough, equip, fiord, firth, force, inlet, might, power, rifle 6 branch, energy, member, outfit, sleeve, tappet, weapon 7 flipper, forearm, fortify, furnish, prepare, protect, provide, support 8 soupbone, strength 9 appendage 10 instrument, projection 12 ramification

bone: 4 ulna 5 radii(pl.), ulnae(pl.) 6 humeri(pl.), radius 7 humerus

hollow at bend: 8 chelidon

joint: 4 ares 5 elbow, wrist

muscle: 6 biceps 7 triceps

part: 4 ares 5 elbow, wrist

armada: 4 army, navy 5 fleet 8 flotilla, squadron, warships

armadillo: 4 peva 5 poyou 6 mulita 7 tatouay 8 pangolin 10 pichiciago

giant: 4 tatu 5 tatou 6 peludo

small: 4 peba 11 quirquincho

three banded: 4 apar 5 apara 6 mataco

armamentarium: 5 store 6 armory 7 arsenal 8 armament, magazine 9 equipment 10 collection

armariolum: 5 ambry 8 armarium

armarium: 5 ambry 10 armariolum

armband: 8 brassard

Armenia: 5 Minni 8 Anatolia

angel or devil worshiper: 6 Yezidi

cap: 6 calpac

city: 6 Erivan(c.) 7 Erzurum, Yerevan

cumin: 7 caraway

lake: Van 8 Urumiyah

mountain: 6 Ararat, Taurus

people: 5 Gomer

river: Kur 4 Aras 5 Cyrus, Halys 6 Araxes, Tigris 9 Euphrates 10 Kizil-Trmak

town: see *city* above

armet: 6 helmet

armful: 6 yaffle

armhole: 4 mail, scye 7 armscye

armistice: 4 lull 5 peace, truce 9 cessation 10 suspension

armoire (see also **ambry**): 8 cupboard, wardrobe 12 clothespress

armor: 4 arms, egis, mail, tace 5 amure, plate, tasse 6 armour, brinie, brunie, byrnie, cuisse, graith, shield, tasset, tuille 7 cuirass, defense 8 materiel, ordnance 10 protection

arm: 8 brassard, brassart 9 gardebras

bearer: 6 squire 7 armiger, custrel

body: 6 byrnie, lorica 7 cuirass

elbow guard: 9 cubitiere

face: 6 beaver 7 ventail 8 aventail

horse: 5 barde 7 peitrel, peytrel, poitrel 8 poitrail, testiere

knee: 11 genouillere

leg: 4 boot, jamb 5 cuish, jambe 6 cuisse, greave, tuille 7 jambeau 11 braconniere

neck: 6 gorget 8 aventail, gorgelet

part: 6 lorica(L.)

shoulder: 7 ailette 9 epauliere

skirt: 4 tace 5 tasse 6 taslet, tasset

throat: 6 gorget

armored: 6 mailed 8 equipped, ironclad, mailclad 9 panoplied 11 encuirassed

armpit: ala 5 oxter 6 axilla 7 axillae(pl.)

pert. to: 7 axillar

arms depository: 7 arsenal

army: 4 here, host 5 array, crowd, force, horde 6 cohort, legion, number, throng, troops 7 militia 8 soldiers, warriors 9 battalion, multitude

camp: 6 campoo(Ind.)

car: 4 jeep

commission: 6 brevet

enlisted man in ranks: 7 mustang

follower: 6 sutler

meal: 4 chow

officer: tab 4 aide 5 major 7 captain, general 8 sergeant 9 centurion 10 lieutenant

pert. to: 8 military

post: 4 base, camp, fort

postal abbreviation: APO

unit: 5 corps, squad, troop 7 brigade, company, platoon 8 division, regiment 10 detachment

wing: ala(L.)

arnotto: See **annatto.**

aroba: See **araba.**

aroid: 4 taro 5 apium, tania 6 tanier 8 araceous

aroint: 6 begone

aroma: 4 odor 5 nidor, savor, scent, smell, spice 6 flavor 7 bouquet, perfume 9 fragrance, redolence

aromatic: 5 balmy, spicy, sweet 7 odorous, piquant, pungent 8 fragrant, redolent

gum: 5 myrrh

herb: 4 mint, nard 5 anise, clary, nondo 8 lavender

seed: 5 anise, cumin 6 nutmeg 7 aniseed

spice: 4 mace 5 clove

tree: 6 balsam 8 huisache 9 sassafras

weed: 5 tansy

around: 4 near 5 about, circa 10 encircling, enveloping

prefix: 4 peri

arouse: 4 call, fire, move, spur, stir, wake, whet 5 alarm, awake, evoke, pique, raise, rally, rouse, roust, waken 6 awaken, excite, foment, incite, kindle, revive, summon, thrill 7 actuate, agitate, animate, enliven, incense, inflame 8 inspirit 9 stimulate

arpeggio: 5 sweep 7 roulade 8 division, flourish

arpent: 4 acre

arraign: try 4 cite 5 argue 6 accuse, charge, impute, indict, indite, summon 7 appoint, impeach 8 denounce 9 challenge, prosecute

arrange: fix, set 4 edit, file, form, plan, size, sort, tier 5 adapt, aline, align, array, drape, ettle, frame, grade, range, score, space 6 adjust, design, devise, fettle, settle 7 bespeak, catalog, compone, compose, dispose, gradate, marshal, permute, prepare, seriate 8 classify, conclude, organize, regulate, tabulate 9 catalogue, collocate, construct, determine, 10 distribute 11 alphabetize

mutually: 5 agree 7 concert

arranged alternately: 4 paly

arrangement: 4 deal 5 index, order, setup 6 scheme, system, treaty 8 contract 9 direction 10 allocation 11 composition, disposition, permutation 12 dispensation

arrant: bad 5 thief 6 outlaw, robber 7 vagrant 8 rascally 9 confirmed, downright, itinerant, notorious, shameless 11 unmitigated 13 thoroughgoing

arras: 7 drapery 8 tapestry

array: don, fig 4 army, busk, deck, doll, garb, host, pomp, robe 5 adorn, align, aline, dress, habit, order 6 attire, attrap, bedeck, clothe, finery, invest, plight, series 7 address, affaite, afflict, apparel, arrange, company, envelop, furnish, marshal 8 accouter, accoutre 10 assemblage 11 preparation

arrear: 4 debt 6 behind, unpaid 7 arriere 8 backward

arrect: 5 alert, erect 6 direct, raised 9 attentive

arrest: cop, fix, nab 4 balk, curb, grab, halt, hold, jail, keep, pull, sist, stay, stop 5 arret, catch, check, delay, pinch, seize, stunt 6 attach, collar, decree, detain, engage, hinder pledge, retard, thwart 7 capture, custody, suspend 8 imprison, obstruct, restrain 9 apprehend, intercept, interrupt 11 concentrate

arresting: 8 pleasing, striking 10 impressive

arret: 5 edict 6 arrest, decree 8 decision, judgment

arride: 5 laugh, smile 6 please 7 delight, gratify

arrie: 5 murre

arris, aris: 4 pien 5 angle, piend

arrival: 5 comer 6 advent

arrive: 4 come, flow, gain, land 5 occur, reach 6 appear, attain, happen 7 compass

arrogance: 5 pride 6 hubris, hybris 7 conceit, disdain, egotism, hauteur 9 insolence 10 effrontery 11 affectation

arrogant: 4 bold 5 lofty, proud 6 lordly, uppish 7 forward, haughty 8 affected, assuming, cavalier, fastuous, impudent 9 audacious, conceited, insulting, presuming 10 hoity-toity 11 dictatorial, domineering, impertinent, overbearing, overweening 12 contemptuous, contumelious, presumptuous, supercilious

arrogate: 4 grab, take 5 claim, seize, usurp 6 assume

arrondissement: 4 ward 8 division

arrow: pin, rod 4 bolt, dart, reed 5 shaft 6 sprite, weapon 7 missile, pointer 9 indicator

case: 6 quiver

feathered: 4 vire

maker: 6 bowyer 8 fletcher

part: 4 barb, butt, head, nock 5 shaft, stele 7 feather

pert. to: 8 sagittal

point: neb 4 barb

poison: 4 inee, upas 5 urali 6 antiar, curare, sumpit, wagogo 7 woorali

rotating: 4 vire

arrow-shaped: 6 beloid 8 sagittal 9 sagittate

arrowroot: pia 4 musa 5 araru, canna, tacca, tikor 6 ararao

family: 11 marantaceae

arrowstone: 9 belemnite

arroyo: 5 brook, creek, gulch, gully, hondo, zanja 6 ravine, stream 7 channel 11 watercourse

arsenal: 6 armory, supply 8 dockyard, magazine 10 storehouse 13 armamentarium

arsenate: *copper:* 7 erinite

hydrous zinc: 7 adamite

red manganese: 9 sarkinite

arsenic: 6 poison 8 chemical

comb. form: 6 arseno

sulfide: 7 realgar

trisulfide: 8 orpiment

arsenic acid salt: 8 arsenate

arsenillo: 9 atacamite

arsenopyrite: 7 danaite

arsis: 4 beat 5 ictus 6 accent, rhythm

opposed to: 6 thesis, theses (pl.)

arson: 4 fire 5 crime 7 burning 12 incendiarism

arsonist: 10 pyromaniac

art: ars(L.) 4 wile 5 craft, knack, magic, skill, trade 7 calling, cunning, faculty, finesse, science 8 artifice, business, learning 9 dexterity, duplicity, ingenuity 10 profession 11 contrivance, cultivation

black: 5 magic 7 alchemy 8 wizardry 9 diablerie 10 demonology, necromancy 11 conjuration

fancier of: 6 votary 7 esthete, devotee 8 aesthete 10 dilettante 11 connoisseur

gallery: 5 salon 6 museum

manual: 5 craft, sloid, slojd, sloyd

school of: 4 Dada

style: 4 Dada 5 genre 7 baroque

Artemis: 4 Upis 5 Delia, Diana 6 Phoebe

brother: 6 Apollo

mother: 4 Leto

artel: 5 union 11 association, cooperative

artery: way 4 path, road 5 route 6 course, street, vessel 7 anonyma, conduit, highway 9 maxillary

main: 5 aorta 6 aortae(pl.)

neck: 8 caratoid

pulsation: 5 ictus

artful: apt, sly 4 foxy, wily 5 agile, suave 6 adroit, clever, facile, shrewd, smooth, tricky 7 crooked, cunning, politic, vulpine 8 stealthy 9 deceitful, deceptive, designing, dexterous, imitative, practical

artfulness: 8 subtlety 9 diplomacy, duplicity, stratagem 10 refinement

arthritis: 4 gout

arthron: 5 joint 12 articulation

Arthur: See **King Arthur.**

artichoke: bur 6 Canada, Cynara 7 Chorogi 9 Jerusalem

leafstalk: 5 chard

article: an, ye; one, the 4 item, term 5 essay, paper, piece, plank, point, story, theme, thing 6 clause, detail, object, report 7 feature 8 causerie, doctrine 9 condition, paragraph, statement 10 particular 11 composition, stipulation

French: la, le, un; les, une

German: das, der, die, ein

Spanish: el, un; las, los, una

articulate: 4 join 5 clear, speak, unite, utter, vocal 6 fluent, verbal 7 express, jointed 8 distinct 9 enunciate, pronounce 10 formulated 13 particularize

articulation: 5 joint, voice 6 arthra(pl.), suture 7 arthron 9 arthrosis, utterance 10 connection

artifice: art 4 gaud, hoax, plan, plot, ruse, wile 5 blind, cheat, dodge, feint, fraud, guile, skill, trick 6 cautel, deceit, device, 7 cunning, evasion, finesse, sleight 8 intrigue, maneuver, pretense, strategy, trickery 9 deception, expedient, imposture, ingenuity, invention, stratagem 10 artfulness, subterfuge 11 contrivance, machination 13 ingeniousness

artificer: See **artisan.**

artificial: 4 sham 5 faked, false 6 ersatz, forced, forged, unreal 7 assumed, bastard, feigned **8** affected, falsetto, spurious **9** insincere, synthetic, unnatural **10** factitious, fictitious, theatrical **11** adulterated, counterfeit **12** supposititious

artillery: **4** arms, guns **6** cannon **8** ordnance
emplacement: **7** battery
fire: **5** salvo **6** rafale **7** barrage

artilleryman: **6** gunner, lascar **8** topechee **9** cannoneer **10** bombardier

artiodactyl: ox; pig **4** deer, goat **5** camel, sheep **6** artiad **7** giraffe **8** antelope **12** hippopotamus

artisan: **5** smith **6** artist **7** artifex, workman **8** opificer, mechanic **9** artificer, craftsman, operative **14** handicraftsman

artist: dab **5** actor, adept **6** dancer, etcher, expert, fictor, master, singer, wizard **7** artisan, artiste, operant, painter, schemer **8** magician, musician, sculptor, sketcher **9** craftsman, performer **12** professional, practitioner
equipment: **5** brush, easel **7** palette
medium: oil **7** tempera **10** watercolor
signature word: **5** fecit
workshop: **6** studio **7** atelier

artistic: **6** daedal, expert **8** esthetic **9** aesthetic

artless: **4** naif, open **5** frank, naive, plain **6** candid, rustic, simple **7** natural **8** innocent **9** guileless, ingenuous, untutored **10** unaffected **11** undesigning **15** unsophisticated

arts: *goddess:* **4** Muse **6** Athena
liberal: **5** logic **6** trivia(pl.) **7** grammar, trivium **8** rhetoric

arui: **5** sheep **6** aoudad

arum: **4** arad, taro **5** aroid, plant **10** cuckoopint
family: **7** araceae
water: **5** calla

arundinaceous: **5** reedy

Aryan: **4** Mede, Slav **9** Caucasian
god of fire: **4** Agni
language: **8** Sanskrit

as: for, qua **4** like, that, thus, when **5** equal, since, while **7** because, equally, similar **9** therefore
above: **5** ditto, ut sup **7** ut supra
far as: to
if: **5** quasi
she is: **4** dyce
stated: so **4** thus
usual: **6** solito
well as: and
written: sic, sta **4** stet

Asa: **6** healer **9** physician
father: **4** Abia
son: **11** Jehoshaphat

asafetida: **4** hing **5** laser **6** ferula

ascend: up **4** rise, soar **5** climb, mount, scale, tower **7** clamber **8** escalate, progress

ascendancy: **4** sway **5** power **7** control, mastery, success **8** dominion, prestige **9** authority, influence, supremacy **10** domination **11** sovereignty **13** preponderance

ascent: sty **4** hill, ramp, rise, rist **5** glory, grade, mount, scend, slope, steps **6** stairs **7** incline, upswing **8** eminence, gradient **9** acclivity, ascension **11** advancement

ascertain: get **4** find **5** count, learn, prove **6** assure, attain **7** apprise, apprize, measure, unearth **8** discover **9** determine

ascetic: nun **4** monk, yogi **5** fakir, friar, stoic, Yogin **6** Essene, strict **7** austere, bhikshu, devotee, eremite, recluse, stylite **8** anchoret **9** anchorite **10** abstemious

ascot: tie **5** scarf **6** cravat **7** necktie **9** racetrack

ascribe: lay **4** aret **5** blame, count, guess, infer, refer **6** accuse, allege, arette, assign, attach, charge, credit, impute, reckon **8** accredit, dedicate, inscribe **9** affiliate, attribute

ascription: **8** addition **11** declaration
of praise: **6** gloria
popular: **6** repute

ascus: bag, sac

asea: **4** lost **6** addled, adrift **7** puzzled, sailing **8** confused **9** befuddled, uncertain **10** bewildered

aseptic: **5** clean **6** barren **7** sterile

ash: ase(Sc.), ron **4** coke, sorb, tree **5** artar, ember, rowan **6** cinder, corpse **7** clinker, residue **8** fraxinus
receptacle: bin, box, urn
reduce to: **7** cremate
tobacco: **6** dottel, dottle

ash holder: urn

ashamed: **7** abashed, hangdog **10** humiliated

ashen: wan **4** gray, grey, pale **5** waxen **6** pallid **7** ghastly **8** blanched **9** cinereous **11** cineritious

Asher: *daughter:* **5** Serah **6** Beriah
father: **5** Jacob
son: **4** Usui **6** Jimnah

ashkoko: **4** cony **5** daman, hyrax

ashore: **7** aground, beached **8** stranded

ashweed: **8** goutweed

Asia (see also **Asia Minor, Southeast Asia**): **4** East **6** Orient
ancient region: **4** Aria **5** Akkad, Sumer **6** Canaan **7** Babylon
animal: **5** bison **8** pangolin **10** chevrotain
antelope: **5** goral, serow **6** dzeren, dzerin, dzeron
ass: **6** onager, koulan
bird: **4** mina, myna **5** mynah, pitta **7** minivet **8** dotterel **9** brambling
blizzard: **5** buran
carnivore: **5** panda
central: **6** Tatary
Christian: **5** Uniat

city: 4 Amoy, Sian 5 Dacca 6 Bagdad,
Bombay, Singan 7 Comilla 9 Singapore
comb. form: 4 Indo
conjurer: 6 shaman
country: 4 Elam, Irak, Iran, Iraq, Siam 5
Accad, Araby, Assam, Burma, China,
India, Japan, Korea, Nepal, Syria, Tibet
6 Arabia, Malaya, Persia, Russia, Turkey
7 Armenia, Chaldea, Siberia 8 Cambodia,
Thailand
crowfoot: 9 buttercup
deer: roe 4 axis
desert: 4 Gobi
disease: 4 yaws 7 cholera, malaria 9 tra-
choman
district: 7 Fartary
dog (wild): 5 dhole
drink: 5 airan
eskimo: 4 Yuit 6 Innuit
fiber: 4 hemp 5 ramie
fox: 6 corsac
gangster: 6 dacoit
gazelle: ahu 4 cora
goat: 4 tahr
goddess: 4 Anta
grass: 4 coix, munj
greeting: 6 salaam
herb: 4 hemp
horse: 6 tarpan
island: 4 Java 5 Japan, Luzon, Malay 6
Borneo, Ceylon 7 Celebes, Formosa,
Sumatra, Wrangel 8 Mindanao, Sakhalin
11 Philippines
isthmus: Kra
jay: 7 sirgang
lake: Tai 4 Tami 6 Baikal 8 Balkhash
language: 5 Malay, Pamir, Tamil
lemur: 5 loris 6 macaco
lynx: 7 caracal
mammal: 10 chevrotain
market: 6 bazaar
measure: mou 4 tael
millet: 4 dari
mink: 8 kolinsky
mongoose: 4 urva
monkey: 6 rhesus
mountain: 5 Altai, Sayan 7 Everest 9
Himalayas, Hindu-Kush 14 Kanchinin-
jinga
mystic: 5 fakir
oasis: 4 merv
oil plant: 4 odal
owl: 4 utum
ox: yak
partridge: 6 seesee
peninsula: 5 Corea, Korea, Malay 6 Arabia 9 Kamchatka
people: Meo, Tai 4 Huns, Miao, Shan, Yuit
5 Kurds, Medes, Seres, Tatar, Todas 6
tartar 10 Mongolians
pert to: 8 Chaldean
pheasant: 8 tragopan
plain: 4 chol
plant: tea 4 atis, odal, soya 5 akebi, betel
plant (fiber source): 5 ramie

region: 7 Tartary
religion: 5 Islam 8 Buddhism, Hinduism
river: Ob; Ili, Obi 4 Amur, Yalu 5 Amoor,
Eelee, Indus, Putra 6 Branma, Mekong,
Tigris 7 Granges, Hwang-Ho, Yang-Tse,
Yeinsei 8 Chao Phya, Irawaddy 9 Euphrates
rodent: 4 pika 6 gerbil, marmot 7 gerbile
sandstorm: 6 simoon, tebbad
seaport: 5 Macao 6 Bombay 9 Singapore
shrub: tea
sea: 4 Aral, Azof 7 Caspian
sheep: 5 argal 6 argali
shrub: tea 4 tche, thea
squirrel: 8 jelerang 10 polatouche
storm: 5 buran 6 tebbad 7 monsoon, typhoon
tree: 4 asak, asok, dita, rata 5 asoka, siris
6 banyan, medlar, wampee
warehouse: 6 godown
weapon: 5 adaga
weight: 4 tael
wolf: 6 chanco
Asia Minor (see also **Asia**): 8 Anatolia
animal: 5 daman
city: 4 Myra, Myus, Teos, Troy 5 Haran,
Perga, Ushak 6 Aintab, Sardis, Tarsus 7
Ephesus, Miletus
coast: 5 Ionia
island: 5 Samos
mountain: Ida
mountain range: 4 Alai
region: 4 Aria 5 Caria, Eolis, Ionia, Troad,
Troas 6 Pontus
river: 5 Halys 8 Monderez
sea: 6 Aegean
seaport: 5 Issus
aside: off 4 away, gone, near, past 5 agley,
aloof, apart 6 aslant, astray, beside, beyond, byhand 7 lateral, private, whisper 8
reserved, secretly, separate, sidewise 9
alongside 10 indirectly
asinego: ass 4 fool
asinine: 4 dull 5 crass, dense, inept, silly
6 absurd, obtuse, simple, stupid 7 doltish, fatuous, foolish, idiotic 9 gooselike,
senseless
ask: beg, sue 4 pray, quiz 5 claim, crave,
exact, frayn, plead, query, speer (Sc.), 6
adjure, demand, expect, frayne, invite 7
beseech, bespeak, consult, entreat, implore, inquire, request, require, solicit 8
petition, question 9 obsecrate 11 interrogate
askance: 4 awry 5 askew 6 askant, askile
7 crooked 8 sideways 9 obliquely, suspicion 13 distrustfully
askew: cam 4 agee, alop, awry 5 agley,
amiss, atilt 6 askant, aslant, atwist 7
asquint, crooked, oblique 9 distorted 10
catawampus
asleep: 4 dead, idle 6 latent, numbed 7
dormant, napping 10 motionless, slumbering 11 unconscious
asomatous: 10 immaterial 11 incorporeal

asp: 5 aspen, snake, viper 7 serpent 8 ophidian
representative headdress: 6 uraeus
asparagus: 5 sprue
aspect: air 4 face, look, mien, side, view 5 angle, facet, guise, phase, sight, stage 6 glance, manner, visage 7 bearing, feature, outlook 8 carriage, prospect 9 semblance 10 appearance 11 countenance 13 consideration
aspen: aps, asp 4 tree 6 poplar 7 quaking 9 quivering, trembling, tremulous
asper: 4 coin 5 harsh, rough, stern 6 bitter
asperse: 4 spot, slur 5 abuse, decry, libel, spray 6 defame defile, malign, revile, shower 7 appeach, blacken, detract, lampoon, slander, tarnish, traduce 8 besmirch, forspeak, sprinkle 9 bespatter, discredit, disparage 10 besprinkle, vituperate
aspersion: 7 baptism, calumny 8 innuendo
asperity: ire 5 rigor 8 acerbity, acrimony, hardship, severity, sourness, tartness 9 briskness, harshness, roughness 10 bitterness, difficulty, unevenness 11 crabbedness 16 disagreeableness
aspersorium: 4 font 5 basin, stoup 11 aspergillum
asphalt: 4 brea 7 bitumen 9 chapapote 10 wurtzilite 11 courtzilite
asphyxia: 5 apnea 6 apnoea 8 acrotism 11 suffocation
aspic: asp 5 jelly 7 gelatin 8 gelatine, lavender
aspirant: 9 candidate
aspiration: 4 goal 5 ideal 8 ambition
aspire: aim 4 hope, long, rise, seek, soar, wish 5 ettle, mount, tower, yearn 6 desire, ascend, attain
ass: 4 dolt, fool 5 burro, chump, cuddy, dunce, kiang, kulan 6 donkey, onager, koulan 8 imbecile 9 blockhead, simpleton 10 rattlepate
comb. form: ono
assai: 4 very 6 enough
assail: woo 4 pelt 5 assay, beset, stone, whack, whang 6 accuse, attack, bullet, hurtle, impugn, molest, invade, malign, rattle, scathe 7 assault, belabor, bombard 9 encounter 11 assassinate
assailant: 9 aggressor
Assam: *city:* 4 Ledo 10 Shillangle (c.)
silkworm: eri 4 eria
tribesman: Ao; Aka 4 Ahom, Garo, Naga
assassin: 4 thag, thug 5 bravo 6 cuttle, killer, slayer 7 ruffian 8 murderer 9 cutthroat
assation: 6 baking 8 roasting
assault: 4 beat, raid, slug 5 assay, brunt, onset, pound, smite, storm 6 affray, assail, attack, buffet, breach, charge, invade 7 attempt, bombard, violate 8 outburst 9 incursion, onslaught 10 aggression

assay: try 4 test 5 prove, trial 6 attack, effort 7 analyze, attempt, examine, tasting 8 analysis, appraise, endeavor, hardship 9 determine 10 affliction, experiment
assaying: 8 docimasy
cup: 5 cupel
assemblage: 4 army, body, camp, crew, herd, host, mass, pack 5 bunch, crowd, drove, flock, posse, salon, swarm 6 convoy, galaxy, hookup, leveee, throng 7 cluster 9 community 11 aggregation 13 constellation
assemble: fit 4 call, mass, meet 5 amass, piece, rally, unite 6 couple, gather, huddle, muster, summon 7 collect, convene, convoke, recruit 9 aggregate 10 congregate, foregather
assembly: hui 4 baud, bevy, diet, feis, moot, raad 5 forum, group, junta, party, press, setup, synod, troop 6 assize, gemote, powwow, senate 7 comitia, company, council, husting, meeting, session, society 8 audience, conclave, congress, tribunal 10 consistory, convention, parliament 11 convocation, legislature
ecclesiastical: 6 coetus 8 sederunt
full: 5 plena
people's: 7 folcmot, folkmot 8 folkmote, folkmout 9 folcgemot
place: 5 agora
room: 4 hall 10 auditorium
assent: aye, bow, nod, yea, yes 4 amen 5 admit, agree, yield 6 accede, accept, accord, chorus, comply, concur, submit 7 approve, concede, conform, consent 8 adhesion, sanction 9 acquiesce, subscribe 10 compliance, condescend 11 acknowledge
assert: say 4 aver, avow, cite 5 claim, plead, posit, state, swear, utter, vaunt, voice 6 affirm, allege, assure, avouch, defend, depone, depose, uphold 7 advance, betoken, contend, declare, protest, support 8 advocate, champion, maintain 9 attribute, predicate, vindicate 10 asseverate
assertive: 8 dogmatic, positive 9 defensive, pragmatic 10 aggressive 11 affirmatory
assess: tax 4 cess, levy, mise, rate, scot, toll 5 cense, price, value 6 assize, charge, impose 7 measure 8 appraise, estimate 9 apportion
assessment: fee, tax 4 duty, levy, scot, toll 5 price, ratal, tithe, worth 6 extent, impost, surtax, tariff 7 scutage 9 valuation
assessor: 5 judge, rater 8 adsessor 11 adjudicator
assets: 5 goods, means, money 6 credit, wealth 7 capital, effects 8 accounts, property, resource 9 valuables
asseverate: say, vow 4 aver, avow 5 state 6 affirm, allege, assert, assure 7 assever, declare, protest
asseveration: 4 oath

assiduous: 4 busy 6 active 7 devoted 8 diligent, frequent, sedulous, studious 9 attentive, laborious, unwearied 10 persistent 11 industrious, painstaking, persevering, unremitting 13 indefatigable 14 unintermittent

assign: fix, set 4 cede, deal, dole, give, mete, rate, show, sign, seal 5 allot, allow, award, endow, refer 6 adduce, affect, allege, charge, convey, delate, depute, detail, reckon, select, settle 7 adjudge, advance, appoint, ascribe, consign, dispose, specify, tribute 8 allocate, delegate, transfer 9 apportion, attribute, designate, determine 10 commission, distribute 11 appropriate

assignation: 4 date 5 tryst 7 meeting 11 appointment

assignment: 4 duty, task 5 stent, stint 6 lesson 11 assignation

assimilate: mix 4 fuse 5 adapt, alter, blend, learn, merge 6 absorb, digest, imbibe 7 compare, concoct 8 resemble 9 transform 10 metabolize, understand 11 appropriate, incorporate

assist: aid 4 abet, back, help, join 5 avail, boost, coach, favor, serve, nurse, speed 6 attend, escort, prompt, second, squire, succor 7 benefit, relieve, support, sustain 8 befriend 9 accompany 10 facilitate

assistance: aid 4 alms, gift, help 5 heeze 6 relief, remedy 8 easement 9 patronage 11 furtherance

assistant: 4 aide, ally, hand, maid, mate, zany 5 clerk, groom, usher, valet 6 aidant, deputy, second 7 abettor, partner 8 adjutant, adjuvant, servitor 9 associate, auxiliary, secretary 10 accomplice 11 confederate, subordinate

assistants: 4 crew 5 staff 7 retinue 9 entourage

assize: fix 4 oyer, rate 5 court, edict, trial 6 assess, decree 7 hearing, measure, session, sitting, statute 8 assembly, standard, tribunal 9 enactment, ordinance 10 regulation

associate: mix, pal 4 aide, ally, band, chum, join, link, mate, moop, moup, peer, yoke, wife 5 blend, buddy, crony 6 cohort, fellow, friend, helper, hobnob, mingle, relate, spouse 7 adjunct, comrade, connect, consort, husband, partner 8 copemate, federate, intimate 9 accompany, affiliate, assistant, attendant, coadjutor, colleague, companion, conrector, socialize 10 accomplice, fraternize 11 concomitant

association: 4 body, bond, club, gild 5 artel, guild, hansa, hanse, union 6 cartel, league, pledge 7 company, consort, society 8 alliance, converse, intimacy, sodality 9 syndicate 10 assemblage, fellowship, sisterhood 11 aggregation, brotherhood, combination, confederacy,

conjunction, partnership 12 conversation 13 confederation

literary: 6 lyceum 9 athenaeum

secret: 5 cabal, lodge

assoil: rid 5 atone, clear, solve 6 acquit, pardon, refute 7 absolve, deliver, expiate, forgive, release, resolve 9 discharge

assonance: pun 5 rhyme 8 paragram 11 resemblance

assortment: lot, set 4 olio 5 batch, group, suite 7 mixture 10 collection, miscellany

assuage: 4 calm, ease 5 abate, allay, delay, slake 6 lessen, modify, pacify, quench, reduce, soften, solace, soothe, temper 7 appease, comfort, mollify, relieve, satisfy 8 diminish, mitigate, moderate 9 alleviate 11 tranquilize

assuasive: 4 mild 7 lenient 8 lenitive, soothing 9 emollient

assume: don 4 dare, fang, mask, sham, take 5 adopt, cloak, elect, feign, indue, infer, raise, usurp 6 accept, affect, betake, clothe 7 believe, premise, pretend, receive, suppose, surmise 8 accroach, arrogate, simulate 9 undertake 11 appropriate, counterfeit

assumed: 5 alias 9 fictional, uncertain 10 artificial, fictitious, precarious 12 hypothetical, suppositious

assuming: 5 lofty 8 arrogant, superior 10 assumptive 11 pretentious 12 presumptuous

different form: 7 protean

assurance: 4 seal 5 brass, faith, nerve, trust 6 aplomb, belief, credit, safety 7 courage, promise 8 audacity, boldness, coolness, firmance, security 9 certainty, certitude, impudence 10 confidence, effrontery 12 cocksureness

assure: 4 aver 5 hight 6 assert, avouch, ensure, insure, pledge, secure 7 betroth, confirm, declare, hearten, promise, protest 8 affiance, convince, embolden, reassure 9 ascertain, encourage, guarantee, vouchsafe 10 asseverate, certiorate, underwrite

assuredly: 4 amen 6 surely, verily 10 intrepidly, truthfully 11 indubitably, undoubtedly

Assyria: 5 Ashur, Assur 6 Asshur

city: 4 Hara, Opis 5 Al Sur, Calah 6 Arbela, Asshur, Kalakh 7 Antioch(c.), Nineveh(c.) 9 Dur Sargon

god: El, Zu; Ira, Sin 4 Adad, Anet, Asur, Nebo 5 Ashir, Ashur, Hadad, Ninip 6 Asshur, Nergal, Shamas

goddess: 4 Nana, Nine 5 Istar 6 Allatu, Ishtar 9 Sarpanitu

king: Pul 5 Belus 6 Sargon 8 Asnapper, Osnappar 9 Asenappar

measure: 4 cane, foot 5 makuk, gasab 6 artaba, gariba, ghalva 7 mansion

queen: 9 Semiramis

river: Zab 6 Adhiam

astart: **8** suddenly

asteism: **5** irony **8** derision, raillery, ridicule

aster: *family:* **10** carduaceae, compositae
 herb: **5** alant **6** arnica **7** boneset **10** elecampane

asterisk: **4** mark, star

astern: aft **4** baft, hind, rear **5** abaft, apoop **6** behind **7** occiput **8** backward

asteroid: **4** Eros, Hebe, Iris, Juno **5** Ceres, Flora, Irene, Metis, Vesta **6** Astrea, Egeria, Europa, Hygeia, Pallas, planet, Psyche, Thetis **7** Eunomia, Fortuna, Lutetia **8** Massalia, starfish, starlike, Victoria **9** Melpomene, planetoid **10** Parthenope, star-shaped
 first: **5** Ceres
 nearest earth: **4** Eros

asthmatic: **5** pursy **6** wheezy **7** panting, puffing

astipulate: **5** agree **6** assent **11** exstipulate

astir: up **4** agog **5** about, afoot, alert, going **6** active, moving, roused **7** abroach, excited **8** stirring, vigilant

astonish: awe **4** daze, stam **5** amaze **7** astound, impress, startle **8** bewilder, confound, surprise **11** flabbergast

astonished: **5** agape

astonishing: **8** fabulous .

astonishment: **5** ferly **6** dismay, wonder **10** admiration **13** consternation

astound: **4** stun **5** amaze, appal, shock **6** appall **7** stagger, stupefy, terrify **8** astonish, confound **9** overwhelm

astragal: **5** talus **7** molding **9** anklebone

astral: **6** remote, starry **7** stellar **8** sidereal, starlike **9** visionary

astray: **4** awry, lost **5** agley, amiss, aside, wrong **6** abroad, afield, errant, erring, faulty **7** sinning **8** mistaken, straying **9** wandering

astride: **4** atop **7** acheval **8** spanning **9** astraddle **10** bestriding, straddling

astringent: **4** acid, alum, sour, tart **5** acerb, harsh, stern **6** severe, tannin **7** austere, binding, styptic **11** acrimonious, compressive, contracting **12** constrictive
 extract: **7** catechu
 gum: **4** kino

astrologer: **4** Josh **6** Merlin **9** stargazer **10** astronomer **11** Nostradamus

astronomer: **10** Hipparchus

astronomical: far **4** huge **5** great **6** uranic **7** distant, immense **8** colossal, infinite
 instrument: aba **9** telescope **10** equatorial
 measurement: **5** apsis **7** azimuth
 Muse: **4** Clio **6** Urania

astute: sly **4** foxy, keen, wily **5** acute, canny, quick, sharp, smart **6** clever, crafty, shrewd **7** cunning, skilled **9** astucious, sagacious **10** discerning **14** discriminating

asunder: **5** apart, split **6** atwain, sunder **7** divided **8** divorced **9** separated
 prefix: dis

asylum: ark **4** home, jail **5** altar, cover, grith, haven **6** bedlam, harbor, refuge **7** alsatia, hospice, retreat, shelter **9** sanctuary **11** institution

asymmetrical: **4** skew

asymmetry: **13** disproportion

at: al, au, by, to; als **5** atten, there **6** hereat
 all: any, ava, eer **4** ever **5** aught **6** anyway, soever
 hand: by **4** near, nigh **7** present
 home: in; tea **4** here **5** levee, party **9** reception
 last: **7** finally **10** ultimately
 odds: out
 once: now, PDQ **4** anon **5** amain **6** presto **9** instanter **11** immediately
 that: **4** then **7** thereat, whereat **9** thereupon, whereupon
 this: **6** hereon **8** hereupon

Ata, Aeta: Ita **7** Negrito

atabal, attabal: **4** drum **5** tabor **10** kettledrum

atacamite: **9** arsenillo

Atahaulpa: **4** Inca **6** Indian

ataman: **5** chief, judge **6** hetman **7** Cossack, headman

atap: **4** nipa, palm

atavism: **9** reversion

atavus: **8** ancestor **11** grandfather

atelier: **6** studio **7** bottega **8** botteghe(pl.), workshop

ates: **8** sweetsop

Athamas: *daughter:* **5** Helle
 son: **7** Phrixos, Phrixus **8** Learchus
 wife: Ino

athanor: **4** oven **7** furnace

Athapascan Indian: **4** Dene, Hupa **5** Hoopa

atheist: **7** doubter **8** agnostic **11** nonbeliever

Athena, Athene: **4** Alea, Auge, Nike **5** Alera, Areia **6** Ergane, Hippia, Hygeia, Itonia, Pallas, Polias **7** Minerva **8** Apaturia, Athenaia **9** Parthenos, Poliuchos, Promachos **10** Chalinitis **11** Chalcioecus, Tritogeneia

Athens (see also **Attica, Greece**):
 alien resident: **5** metic
 assembly: **4** pnyx **5** boule
 assembly platform: **4** bema
 clan: obe
 coin: **5** oboli **6** obolus **7** chalcus, chalkos
 family: **11** Alcmaeonids **12** Alcmaeonidae
 festival: **8** Apaturia, Athenaea **11** Scirophoria
 general: **6** Nicias **7** Phocion **8** Zenophon
 hill: **9** Acropolis **10** Lycabettus
 historian: **8** Xenophon
 king: **6** Codrus **7** Cecrops, Pandion
 lawgiver: **5** Draco, Solon
 magistrate: **5** draco **6** archon, dicast

mountain: **6** Parnes
orator: **9** Isocrates
pert. to: **5** Attic
philosopher: **5** Plato **8** Socrates
platform: **4** bema **6** bemata(pl.)
rival: **6** Sparta
ruler: **6** archon
seaport: **7** Piraeus
statesman: **8** Pericles **9** Aristides
Athens of: *America:* **6** Boston
Ireland: **7** Belfast
Switzerland: **6** Zurich
the North: **9** Edinburgh
the West: **7** Cordoba
athlete: pro **4** star **5** boxer **7** amateur, acrobat, gymnast, tumbler **8** wrestler **9** aerialist
athletic: **5** agile, burly, lusty, vital **6** brawny, robust, sinewy, strong **8** muscular, powerful, vigorous **9** acrobatic, energetic, strapping
contest: **4** agon, game, meet, race **8** Olympics
field: **4** oval, ring, rink **5** arena, court, green **6** course **7** diamond, stadium **8** gridiron
prize: cup **5** medal **6** ribbon
athletics: **5** games, sport **8** exercise
athwart: **6** aboard, across, aslant **7** oblique **8** sidewise, traverse **10** perversely
atlantal: **6** atloid **8** anterior, cephalic
Atlantic:
island: **4** Cuba **6** Azores, Canary **7** Iceland **9** Greenland
seaport: **5** Colon **6** Boston **7** New York, Norfolk **8** Savannah **9** Baltimore **12** Philadelphia
atlas: **4** bone, book, list, maps, tome **5** titan **8** mainstay
Atlas' daughters: **4** Maia **6** Merope **7** Alcyone, Calypso, Electra, Kelaine, Taygete **8** Asterope, Pleiades
atloid: **8** atlantal
atmosphere: air **4** aura, mood, tone **5** ether **6** frowst, miasma, nimbus, welkin **7** feeling, qualify **10** background **11** environment
disturbance: **5** storm **6** static
phenomenon: **6** aurora, meteor
prefix: **4** atmo **5** atmos
pressure: **10** barometric
atole: **4** meal **5** gruel **8** porridge
atom: ace, bit, jot **4** haet, iota, mite, mote, whit **5** atomy, monad, shade, speck, tinge **7** atomize **8** molecule, particle, quantity **9** corpuscle, scintilla
adsorbed: **6** adatom
component: **6** proton **7** neutron
electrically charged: ion
nucleus: **6** proton
atomic: **4** tiny **6** minute **7** nuclear **9** molecular **13** infinitesimal
theory originator: **6** Dalton
atomize: **5** grate, spray **6** reduce **8** nebulize **9** devastate, pulverize

atomy: **4** atom, mite, mote **5** pygmy **8** skeleton
atone: **5** agree, amend **6** accord, redeem, repent **7** appease, expiate, restore **9** harmonize, reconcile **10** conciliate, propitiate
atonement: **7** penance **10** reparation **12** satisfaction
atonic: **7** unheard **9** voiceless **10** unaccented
atrabilious: **4** glum **6** gloomy, morose, sullen **10** melancholy
Atreus: *brother:* **8** Thyestes
father: **6** Pelops
half brother: **10** Chrysippus
mother: **10** Hippodamia
slayer: **9** Aegisthus
son: **8** Menelaus **9** Agamemnon **11** Pleisthenes
wife: **6** Aerope
atrio: **6** atrium, valley **10** depression
atrip: **6** aweigh
atrium: **4** hall **5** atrio, court **6** cavity **7** auricle, chamber, passage **8** entrance
atrocha: **5** larva
atrocious: bad **4** dark, rank, vile **5** awful, black, cruel, gross **6** brutal, odious, savage, wicked **7** heinous, ungodly, violent **8** grievous, horrible, terrible **9** execrable, frightful, nefarious **10** abominable, villainous
atrophy: **4** rust **5** stunt, tabes **6** shrink, starve, wither **8** stultify **10** emaciation
Atropos: **4** Fate
attach: add, fix, tag, tie **4** bind, glue, join, link, take, vest, weld **5** affix, annex, hitch, paste, seize, unite **6** accuse, addict, adhere, adjoin, append, arrest, cement, fasten, indict **7** adhibit, appoint, ascribe, connect, subjoin **9** affiliate, associate, garnishee
attached (see also **attach**): **4** fond **6** doting
at base: **7** sessile
to the land: **7** predial **8** praedial
attachment: **4** love **8** devotion, fondness **9** accessory, addiction, adherence, affection **10** engagement, friendship **11** inclination
attack: fit **4** bout, fray, pang, raid, rush, wade **5** alarm, assay, begin, beset, blitz, drive, fight, foray, ictus, onset, sally, spasm, storm **6** accuse, action, affray, assail, battle, charge, charge, invade, onrush, pounce, sortie, strike, stroke, thrust **7** assault, beseige, censure, descent, offense, potshot, seizure **8** paroxysm **9** diversion, encounter, onslaught **10** aggression
false: **5** feint
suicidal: **8** kamikaze
attacker: **9** aggressor **10** iconoclast
attain: get, hit, win **4** earn, gain, rise **5** reach, touch **6** accede, amount, arrive, aspire, effect, obtain, secure, strike **7**

achieve, acquire, compass, procure, succeed 8 overtake 9 ascertain 10 accomplish, comprehend

attar: oil 4 atar 7 essence, perfume

attempt: try 4 dare, fist, mint, mird, osse, seek, shot, stab, wage 5 assay, begin, essay, frame, onset, start 6 attack, effort 7 venture 8 endeavor, exertion 9 undertake 10 enterprise, experiment

attend: go, ho; see 4 hear, heed, mind, tend, wait 5 await, guard, nurse, serve, treat, visit, watch 6 assist, convey, follow, harken, listen, shadow 7 consort 8 champion, minister 9 accompany

attendance: 4 gate 6 number, regard 8 presence 9 attention 11 application, expectation

attendant: 4 maid, page, zany 5 gilly, guide, usher, valet 6 escort, famuli(pl.), friend, minion, porter, squire, varlet, waiter 7 chobdar, courier, famulus, footboy, orderly, pageboy 8 chasseur, follower, henchboy, henchman 9 assistant, associate, attentive, companion 10 consequent, subsequent 11 chamberlain, concomitant 12 accompanying

attendants: 5 train, suite 7 cortege, retinue 9 entourage

attention: ear 4 care, heed, hist, note 5 study 6 notice, regard 7 achtung(G.), respect 9 diligence, obedience, vigilance 10 observance 11 observation 13 concentration, consideration

attentive: 4 wary 5 alert, awake, civil 6 intent, polite 7 careful, gallant, listful, mindful 8 studious, watchful 9 advertent, assiduous, courteous, listening 11 circumspect

attenuate: sap 4 thin 5 water 6 dilute, lessen, rarefy, reduce, weaken 7 slender 8 decrease, diminish, enfeeble, tapering 9 subtilize

attest: 4 seal 5 prove, swear, vouch 6 adjure, affirm, invoke 7 certify, confess, confirm, testify, witness 8 evidence, manifest 9 subscribe 12 authenticate

attic: 4 loft 6 garret 8 cockloft

Attic: 5 Greek 8 Athenian

Attica (see also **Athens, Greece**):
  alien: 5 metic
  festival: 5 Haloa 8 Diipolia 9 Diipoleia
  legendary king: 6 Ogyges, Ogygos
  township: 4 deme
  valley: 6 Icaria

Attila: Hun 5 Etzel

attire: See **dress.**

attitude: air, set 4 bias, mien, mood, pose 5 angle, phase, slant, stand 6 action, aspect, manner 7 bearing, feeling, posture 8 behavior, position 11 disposition

attorney: 4 doer 5 agent, proxy 6 deputy, factor, lawyer, legist, muktar 7 proctor 8 advocate 9 barrister, counselor, solicitor 10 counsellor

attract: 4 bait, draw, lure, pull 5 catch,

charm, court, fetch, tempt 6 allure, engage, entice, invite, seduce 8 interest 9 captivate, fascinate, influence, magnetize

attracting: 9 allicient, attrahent

attraction: 4 card 6 magnet 7 gravity 8 affinity, penchant, witchery

attractive: 4 chic, cute, fair 5 bonny 6 lovely, pretty, taking 7 winning, winsome 8 alluring, charming, fetching, graceful 9 beautiful

attribute: fix, owe 4 mark, sign, type 5 asign, badge, blame, place, power, refer 6 allege, allude, assert, bestow, charge, impute, symbol 7 ascribe, pertain, quality 8 accredit, property 10 reputation 11 peculiarity 14 characteristic

attribution: 6 theory 8 etiology

attrition: 4 wear 5 grief 6 regret, sorrow 7 anguish 8 abrasion, friction 10 contrition

attune: key 4 tune 5 adapt, agree 6 accord, adjust, temper 7 prepare 9 harmonize

atua: 5 being, demon 6 spirit

atwain: 7 asunder

auberge: inn 7 albergo

auction: 4 cant, roup, sale, sell, vend 5 trade 6 barter, bridge 8 disposal

audacious: 4 bold 5 brash, hardy, saucy 6 audace, brazen, cheeky, daring 7 forward 8 arrogant, fearless, impudent, insolent, intrepid, spirited 9 barefaced, bodacious, imprudent, shameless 10 courageous 11 adventurous, impertinent, venturesome 12 presumptuous

audacity: 5 nerve 7 courage 8 boldness, temerity 9 assurance, hardihood, impudence, insolence, sauciness 10 effrontery 12 impertinence

audible: 5 aloud, heard

audience: ear 4 fans 5 audit, court, house 6 public 7 gallery, hearing 8 assembly, auditory, tribunal 9 audiencia, interview, reception

audit: 4 scan 5 check, probe 6 reckon, verify 7 account, examine, inquire, inspect 8 estimate

auditor: CPA 6 censor, hearer 7 apposer, audient 8 disciple, listener 10 accountant, catechumen 11 comptroller

auditorium: 4 hall, room 5 cavea, odeum 7 theater 8 auditory

auditory: 4 oral, otic 5 aural 8 acoustic

auger: bit 4 bore, tool 5 grill 6 gimlet wimble

aught: 5 owned 6 cipher, naught, worthy 7 nothing, valiant 8 anything, property 9 possessed

augite: 8 pyroxene

augment: add, eke 4 grow 5 exalt, swell 6 append, dilate, expand, extend 7 amplify enhance, enlarge, improve, magnify 8 heighten, increase, multiply 9 increment 10 aggrandize

augur: 4 bode, omen, seer 6 auspex, divine 7 betoken, foresee, portend, predict, presage, prophet, promise, signify 8 forebode, foreshow, foretell, forewarn, indicate, prophesy 9 auspicate, 10 anticipate, conjecture, soothsayer 13 prognosticate

augury: 4 rite, sign 5 token 6 hansel, ritual 7 handsel 8 ceremony 10 foreboding, forerunner

august: 5 awful, grand, noble 6 solemn 7 exalted, stately 8 imposing, majestic 9 dignified, venerable 11 magisterial

auk: 4 loom 5 arrie, lemot, noddy 6 puffin, rotche 7 dovekey, dovekie, 9 guillemot
family: 7 alcidae
genus: 4 alca, alle
razorbill: 4 falk 5 murre

aula: 4 hall, room 5 court 6 emblic

aumildar: 5 agent 6 factor 7 manager 9 collector

auncel: 7 balance

aunt: tia(Sp.) 4 bawd 5 tante(F.) 6 gossip 8 relative

aura: air 4 halo, odor 5 aroma, savor 6 breeze 7 buzzard, feeling 9 emanation 10 atmosphere, exhalation

aural: 4 otic 7 audible 9 auricular
appendage: ear

aureate: 6 golden, ornate, rococo, yellow 8 aurelian

aureole: 4 halo 5 crown, glory, light 6 corona, nimbus 8 gloriole

auricle: ear 5 pinna 6 atrium, earlet 7 trumpet
part: 7 earlobe

auricular: 4 otic 7 hearsay 12 confidential

aurochs: tur 4 urus 5 bison 6 wisent

Aurora: Eos 4 dawn 7 morning

auroral: 4 eoan, rosy 7 eastern, radiant

aurum: 4 gold

auscultate: 6 listen

auspex: 5 augur

auspicate: 5 augur 7 portend, predict 8 initiate 10 inaugurate

auspice: 4 care, egis, omen, sign 5 aegis 6 augury 7 portent 8 guidance 9 patronage 10 indication, protection 11 observation, sponsorship

auspicious: 4 fair, good 6 dexter 9 favorable, fortunate, opportune 10 favourable, propitious, prosperous 12 advantageous

Aussie: 9 Australia 10 Australian

austere: 4 cold, hard, sour 5 budge, grave, gruff, harsh, rigid, rough, sharp, stern, stiff 6 bitter, formal, severe, simple, somber, strict 7 ascetic, earnest, serious 8 rigorous 9 unadorned, unsmiling 10 astringent, forbidding, relentless 13 unembellished

Australia: *animal:* 4 tait 5 coala, koala, panda 6 bunyip, cuscus, wombat 7 das-

qure, wallady 8 duckbill, kangaroo, platypus 9 bandicoot, phalanger
apple: 6 colane
badger: 6 wombat
bag: 5 dilli
bear: 5 coala, koala
beefwood: 5 belar
beverage: 4 kava
bird: emu 4 emeu, lory 5 arara, crake, grebe, stint 6 gannet, leipoa 7 bittern, boobook, bustard, figbird 8 berigora, dabchick, dotterel, lorikeet, lyrebird, morepork, whimbrel 9 bower-bird, cassowary, coachwhip, friarbird, stipiture, 10 paradalote, pratincole, sanderling
boomerang: 5 kiley, kilie
brushwood: 6 millee
bush: ake
bustard: 7 bebilya
cake: 6 damper 7 brownie
call: 5 cooee, cooey
cape: 4 Howe
cat: 7 dasyure
catfish: 6 tandan
cattle stealer: 6 duffer
cedar: 4 toon
channel: 5 cowal 9 anabranch, billabong
coin: 4 dump
countryman: 8 Billijim
crayfish: 5 yabby 6 yabbie
cycad: 5 banga
dog: 5 dingo 6 Kelpie
duckbill: 8 platypus
eucalyptus: 6 bimbil, mallee 7 carbeen
fern: 5 nardu 6 nardoo
fish: 4 dart, mado, mako 5 yabby 6 tandan, yabbie
fruit: 5 nonda
gum: 6 tewart, tooart, touart
herb: 8 piripiri
horse: 7 brumbee 8 yarraman
hut: 6 miamia
insect: 4 laap, lerp
island: 5 Timor 8 Tasmania
kangaroo: 4 joey 5 tungo 7 bettong
kiwi: roa
lake: 4 Eyre 5 Carey, Cowan, Frome, Moore, Woods 6 Austin, Barlee, Bulloo, Harris, Mackay 7 Amadeus, Blanche, Eyerard, Torrens 8 Carnegie, Gairdner 9 Macdonald 14 Disappointment
language: 6 yabber
lorikeet: 6 parrot, warrin
mahogany: 6 jarrah 7 gunning
measure: 4 saum
mile: 4 naut
moth: 6 bogong
mountain: Ise 5 Bruce 6 Cradle, Garnet, Magnet, Morgan 7 Bongong 8 Cuthbert, Mulligan 9 Kosciusko, Murchison
mountain range: 7 Darling 8 Flinders
native: 4 Mara 5 binge 6 digger 8 Billijim,

Warragal, Warrigal
no: **4** baal, bail, bale
ostrich: **4** emeu
owl: **7** boobook **8** morepoke, morepork
palm: **8** bangalow
parakeet: **6** budgie **7** corella **10** budgerigar
parrot: **4** lory **7** corella, lorilet **8** lorikeet **9** cockateel, cockatiel
pepper: **4** arva, kava, yava **6** ava-ava
petrel: **4** titi
phalanger: **5** ariel
plant: **5** lakea **6** correa **7** calomba, waratah **8** warratau
pine: **5** kauri, kaury
pond: **9** billabong
rat: **8** hapalote **9** hapalotis
ratite: **4** emeu
rifleman: **5** yager
river: Hay **4** Avon, Daly, Swan, Yule **5** Comet, Namoi, Paroo, Roper, Yarra **6** Barcoo, Barwon, Bulloo, Culgoa, Dawson, De Grey, Hunter, Isaacs, Murray, Nepean, Norman **7** Darling, Fitzroy, Georges, Gilbert, Lachlan, Staaten **8** Brisbane, Burdekin, Clarence, Drysdale, Flinders, Gascoyne, Georgina, Goulburn, Mitchell, Thompson, Victoria, Werribee, Wooramel **9** Ashburton, Fortescue, Macquarie, Murchison, Saltwater **10** Diamantina, Leichhardt **11** Murrumidgee
rustler: **6** duffer
shark: **4** mako
shield: **8** heelaman, heilaman, hielaman, yeelaman
snake: **6** elapid
soldier: **5** Anzac **6** digger, swaddy **7** Billjim
sorcerer: **5** boyla **6** boolya
spear: **7** womerah, wommala, woomera **8** wommerah, woomerah **9** woomerang
state: **8** Tasmania, Victoria **10** Queensland **13** New South Wales **14** South Australia **16** Western Australia **17** Northern Territory
thicket: **6** mallee
throwing stick: **5** kiley, kylie **7** womerah, wommala **8** hornerah, wommerah, woomerah **9** boomerang, woomerang
town: Ayr **4** Yass **5** Dubbo, Perth, Wagga **6** Albury, Casino, Darwin, Hobart, Mackay, Sydney **7** Geelong, Ipswich, Kogarah, Mildura, Warwick, Waverly **8** Adelaide, Brighton, Brisbane, Canberra (c.), Hamilton, Maylands, Richmond, Toowomba **9** Bankstown, Caulfield, Melbourne, Newcastle **10** Hurtsville, Townsville, Wollongong **11** Rockhampton
toy: **8** weet-weet
tree: **4** toon **5** belah, belar, boree, gidya, penda **6** gidgea, gidgee, gidyea, marara **7** alipata **8** beefwood, curajong, flindosa,

flindosy, ironbark **9** koorajong **10** bunya-bunya
tulip: **7** waratah **8** warratau
valley: **5** Grose **8** Jamieson, Kangaroo, Megalong **11** Burragorang
war club: **5** waddy
weapon: **5** hulla, waddy **6** hullah **7** liangle **8** leeangle **10** hullanulla
wombat: **5** koala
wood: emu
workman: **7** Billjim
Austria: *coin:* **5** ducat, krone **6** florin, heller, zehner **8** groschen **9** schilling
crownland: **8** Dalmatia
legislature: **10** Herrenhaus
measure: **4** fass, fuss, joch, mass, yoke **5** halbe, linie, meile, metze, pfiff, punkt **6** achtel, becher, seidel **7** klafter, viertel **8** dreiling **10** muthmassel **12** futtermassel
measure of weight: **4** marc, saum, unze **5** denat, karch, pfund, stein **7** centner, pfennig **8** vierling **9** quentchen
native: **7** Styrian **8** Tyrolese
nobility: **6** Ritter
province: **4** Gorz **5** Tirol, Tyrol **6** Istria, Styria, Triest **7** Bohemia, Galicia, Moravia, Selesia **8** Bukowina, Carniola, Dalmatia, Gradisca, Salzburg **9** Carinthia **10** Vorarlberg
river: Inn **4** Elbe, Enns, Isar **6** Danube, Moldau
town: **4** Graz, Linz, Wien **5** Gratz **6** Vienna (c.), **7** Noricum **8** Salzburg
austringer: **8** falconer
Austronesian language: **4** Niue **7** Tagalog
autarch: **6** despot **8** autocrat
authentic: **4** pure, real, sure, true **5** exact, right, valid **6** actual, proper **7** correct, genuine, sincere **8** bonafide, credible, official, original, reliable **9** veritable **10** authorized **11** trustworthy **13** authoritative
authenticate: **4** seal **5** prove **6** attest, verify **7** approve, confirm
author: **4** doer **5** maker, ruler **6** factor, parent, source, writer **7** creator, founder **8** ancestor, begetter, compiler, composer, inventor, producer **10** bookwright, instigator, originator
authoritative: **8** official, oracular, positive **9** canonical, effectual, imperious, masterful **10** conclusive, convincing, legitimate, peremptory **11** dictatorial, excathedral, magisterial
authority: **4** sway **5** adept, board, power, riche, right, title **6** artist, author, expert, regent, regime, weight **7** command, dynasty, scepter, sceptre, warrant **8** dominion, prestige, sanction **9** influence **10** ascendancy, ascendency, commission, competence **12** jurisdiction **13** authorization, justification

judicial: **4** banc
preponderant: **8** hegemony
symbol: **7** scepter
woman's: **7** distaff
authorize: let **4** vest **5** allow **6** clothe, permit, ratify **7** approve, empower, endorse, entitle, indorse, justify, license, warrant **8** accredit, delegate, legalize, sanction **10** commission, legitimize
authorless: **9** anonymous
auto: See **automobile.**
autobiography: **4** vita **6** memoir
autochthonous: **6** native **7** edaphic, endemic **10** aboriginal, indigenous
autocrat: **4** czar, tsar, tzar **5** mogul **6** Caesar, despot **7** autarch, monarch **8** dictator **9** sovereign
autocratic: **8** absolute **9** arbitrary **10** tyrannical
autograph: **4** name, sign **9** signature
automatic: **7** machine **9** automatous, mechanical, self-acting **11** instinctive, spontaneous
automaton: **5** golem, robot **7** android, machine
automobile: **4** heap, jeep **5** coupe, crate, racer, sedan **6** jalopy **7** flivver, machine, phaeton **8** roadster **11** convertible
army: **4** jeep
British: AC, MG **5** Alvis, Riley, Rover **6** Allard, Anglia, Austin, Consul, Humber, Jaguar, Jowett, Morgan, Morris, Rapier, Singer, Zephyr **7** Bentley, Daimler, Hillman, Sunbeam, Triumph **8** Berkeley, Vauxhall **10** Rolls-Royce **11** Austintin-Healy, Hillman-Minx, Morris-Minor **12** Metropolitan **13** Sunbeam-Talbot
Czech: **5** Skoda
early: EMF, Reo **4** Alco, Benz, Cord, Knox, Moon, Olds, Sear, Star **5** Brush, Regal, Stutz **6** Auburn, Dupont, Duryea, Graham, Haynes, Kissel, Lozier, Marmon, Mercer, Saxson, Thomas, Winton **7** Autocar, Bugatti, La Salle, Maxwell, Oakland, Premier, Rambler, Simplex, Stevens, Tourist **8** Apperson, Chalmers, Chandler, Franklin, Mercedes, National, Overland, Peerless **9** Hupmobile **10** Cunningham, Duesenberg, Jackrabbit, Locomobile **11** Graham-Paige, Pierce-Arrow **12** Crane-Simplex, Owen-Magnetic, Pope-Hartford, White-Streamer **13** Baker-Electric, Ofeldt-Steamer, Stevens-Duryea, Wills-St. Claire **14** Stanley-Steamer **16** Columbia-Electric **22** International Auto Buggy
Europe: BMW **4** Benz **5** Aston, Metro, Prinz, Skoda **6** Martin, Denzel, Isetta, Zodiac **7** Bugatti, Prefect **9** Facel-Vega
French: DB **5** Simca **7** Citroen, Panhard, Peugeot, Renault **8** Dauphine
German: DKW **4** Opel **6** Taunus **7** Goliath, Porsche, Weidner **8** Borgward, Rometsch, Wartburg **10** Golomobile, Lloyd-

Wagon, Volkswagen **12** Mercedes-Benz
Italian: **4** Fiat **6** Lancia **7** Ferrari **8** Maserati **9** Alfa-Romeo
Japanese: **6** Datsun **7** Toyopet **13** Pringe-Skylark
part: **4** hood **5** motor, trunk **6** engine **7** chassis, magneto, tonneau **8** ignition
Russian: Zim **6** Pobeda **9** Moskvitch
Swedish: **5** Volvo
United States: **4** Ford, Jeep, Nash **5** Buick, Dodge, Edsel **6** De Soto, Hudson, Willys **7** Lincoln, Mercury, Packard, Pontiac, Rambler **8** Cadillac, Chrysler, Corvette, Imperial, Plymouth **9** Chevrolet **10** Oldsmobile, Studebaker **11** Continental, Thunderbird
autonomous: **4** free **11** independent
antopsy: **8** necropsy **10** dissection **11** examination
autumn: **4** fall **6** season **8** maturity **11** harvest-time
auxiliary: aid, sub **4** aide, ally **6** branch, helper **7** abetter, abettor, adjunct, partner **8** adjutant **9** accessory, adminicle, ancillary, assistant, coadjutor, secondary, tributary **10** additional, foederatus, subsidiary, supporting **11** confederate, cooperating, subordinate, subservient
ava: **4** kava
avail: do; aid, dow, use **4** boot, help **5** serve, stead, value **6** moment, profit **7** benefit, bestead, succeed, suffice, utilize **9** advantage **10** assistance
available: fit **4** free, open **5** handy, ready **6** patent, usable **7** present **9** effectual, practical **10** accessible, attainable, convenient, obtainable **11** efficacious
aval: **8** acceptor, indorser **9** ancestral
avalanche: **5** slide **9** landslide
avale: **4** doff, flow, sink **5** abase, lower, yield **6** submit **7** descend **8** dismount
avania: tax **6** impost
avanious: **12** extortionate
avantgarde: **8** vanguard
avarice: **7** avidity **8** cupidity, rapacity
spirit of: **6** Mammon
avaricious: **5** close **6** greedy, hungry, stingy **7** gripple, miserly **8** covetous, grasping **9** niggardly, penurious **12** parsimonious
avast: **4** hold, stay, stop **5** cease
avatar: **8** epiphany **10** embodiment **11** incarnation
avaunt: **5** boast, vaunt **6** begone, depart **7** advance, forward **9** dismissal
ave: **4** bead, hail **6** prayer **8** farewell, greeting **10** salutation, veneration
avellane: nut **5** hazel **7** filbert
avelonge: **4** oval **6** oblong **8** slanting
avenaceous: **4** oaty **5** oaten
avenge: **5** repay, wrack **6** awreak, punish **7** requite, revenge **8** chastise **9** retaliate, vindicate
avenger: **7** nemesis **10** vindicator

avenue: rue(F.), way **4** gate, mall, pike, road **5** allee, alley, drive, entry **6** access, arcade, artery, street **7** opening **9** boulevard **10** passageway **12** thoroughfare

aveolate: **6** favose

aver: say **5** claim, prove, state, swear **6** affirm, allege, assert, assure, avouch, depose, verify **7** declare, justify, protest **9** predicate **10** asseverate **11** acknowledge

average: par, sum **4** duty, fair, mean, norm, rule, so-so **5** ratio, usual, value **6** charge, medial, median, medium, middle, normal, tariff **8** estimate, mediocre, moderate, ordinary, quantity, standard **10** proportion **13** approximation

averse: **4** loth **5** balky, loath **7** adverse, against, opposed **8** inimical, opposite **9** disliking, reluctant, unwilling **11** disinclined, unfavorable

aversion: **4** hate **5** odium **6** enmity, hatred, horror **7** disdain, disgust, dislike **8** distaste **9** antipathy **10** repugnance **11** abomination **12** estrangement **14** disinclination

avert: **4** bend, fend, move, shun, ward **5** avoid, deter, dodge, evade, parry, sheer, twist **6** defray, divert, retard, shield **7** deflect, expiate, prevent **8** alienate, estrange, forefend **9** forestall

aviary: **4** cage **5** house **6** volery **8** ornithon **9** birdhouse, enclosure

keeper: **8** aviarist

aviation: **6** flying **10** airplaning **11** aeronautics

maneuver: **8** Immelman

aviator: ace **5** flier, flyer, pilot **6** airman, flying, Icarus **8** operator

signal: out **4** over **5** roger

aviatrix: **13** Amelia Earhart

avid: **4** agog, keen, warm **5** eager **6** ardent, greedy, hungry, jejune **7** anxious, athirst, craving, longing **8** desirous, grasping **9** devouring

avidity: **7** avarice **8** cupidity **10** greediness

avifauna: **5** birds, ornis

avile: **5** abase **6** debase, vilify **10** depreciate

avital: **6** avitic **9** ancestral

avocado: **4** coyo, pear, tree **6** chinin **8** aguacate, alligato

avocation: **4** work **5** hobby, trade **7** calling **9** amusement, diversion **10** recreation

avoid: **4** balk, quit, shun **5** annul, avert, dodge, elude, evade, feign, hedge, parry, shirk, slack, spair(Sc.), **6** blench, escape, eschew, refute, remove, vacate **7** abstain, evitate, forbear, forsake, refrain **8** sidestep

avoidance: **6** outlet **10** dismissing, withdrawal

avoirdupois weight: ton **4** dram **5** ounce, pound **7** long ton **13** hundredweight **17** long hundredweight

avolate: fly **6** escape **9** evaporate

avow: own **4** bind **5** admit, state **6** affirm, avouch, depone, depose, devote **7** confess, declare, justify, profess **8** maintain **11** acknowledge

avowal: **4** oath, word **14** representation

awa: **4** kava **8** milkfish

awabi: **8** abalone

await: **4** bide, heed, pend, wait **5** abide, tarry, watch **6** attend, expect, impend, waylay

awake: daw **4** stir, wake **5** alert, alive, aware, rouse **6** active, arouse, awaken, excite **7** careful, heedful **8** open-eyed, vigilant **9** attentive, conscious

awakening: **7** revival **14** expergefacient, expergefaction

award: **4** give, meed, mete **5** allot, grant, medal, prize **6** accord, addeem, assign, bestow, bounty, confer, decide **7** adjudge, appoint, consign, custody, keeping **8** accolade, sentence **9** apportion, determine, judgement **10** adjudicate

academic: **7** diploma **11** scholarship

cinema: **5** Oscar

aware: hep **4** reck, sure, wary **5** alert, alive **6** beware **7** knowing, mindful **8** apprised, apprized, informed, sensible, vigilant, watchful **9** cognizant, conscious **11** intelligent

away: awa(Sc.), fro, off, out, via **4** gone **5** along, apart, aside, forth, hence **6** abroad, absent, begone, onward, thence **7** distant, froward **8** fromward **9** fromwards, herehence

prefix: aph, apo

awe: cow **5** amaze, daunt, scare **6** fright, regard, terror, wonder **7** buffalo, respect **8** astonish, bewilder, overcome **9** fascinate, overpower **10** intimidate

aweband: **4** band, rope **5** check **9** restraint

aweigh: **5** atrip

awesome: **4** eery **5** awful, eerie, weird **6** solemn **7** dreaded, ghostly **9** appalling, unearthly

awful: **4** dire, ugly **6** august, horrid **7** awesome, fearful **8** dreadful, shocking, terrible **9** appalling, frightful **10** tremendous

awk: odd **6** clumsy **7** adverse **8** perverse

awkward: **4** gaum **5** gawky, inapt, inept **6** clumsy, gauche, rustic, uneasy **7** adverse, boorish, froward, loutish, stilted, uncouth, unhandy **8** bungling, clownish, lubberly, perverse, ungainly, untoward, unwieldy **9** graceless, inelegant, lumbering, maladroit, ponderous **10** backhanded, blundering, ungraceful, unskillful **11** heavyhanded **12** inconvenient

awl: **4** brog **5** brode, elsen, elson(Sc.) **6** elshin, gimlet

awn: ear **4** barb **5** beard **7** aristae, bristle **9** appendage

awning: **5** velum **6** canopy, tienda **8**

velarium 9 shameeana, shamianah(Ind.)
fastening: 6 earing
awreak: 6 avenge 7 condemn
awry: 4 agee, bias 5 agley(Sc.), amiss,
askew, gleed, gleyd, wrong 6 cammed 7
askance, asquint, crooked, oblique 8 perverse 9 distorted 10 crisscross
ax: adz 4 adze 5 hache 6 twibil 7 besague,
boucher, cleaver, hatchet, twibill 8 tomahawk
blade: bit
butt: 4 poll
handle: 5 helve
axeman: 8 woodsman 9 lumberman 10
woodcutter 11 woodchopper
axial: 7 central
axilla: ala 6 armpit 8 shoulder
axiom: saw 5 adage, dicta(pl.), maxim,
motto 6 byword, dictum, saying, truism 7
precept, proverb 8 aphorism, apothegm,
sentence 9 principle 11 proposition
axis: 4 axle, deer 5 stalk 6 chitra 7 spindle

axle: bar, cod, pin 4 axis 5 arbor, shaft 6
axtree 7 mandrel, spindle
axletree pin: 8 linchpin
axoloti: 4 newt 10 salamander
axweed: 8 goutweed
ay: 9 champagne
ayah: 4 maid 5 nurse 9 nursemaid
aye, ay: pro, yea, yes 4 ever 6 always, assent 7 forever 11 affirmative, continually
Azerbaijan city: 4 Baku(c.) 11 Eliza-
vetpol 12 Yelisavetpol
Azores: *district:* 5 Horta
port: 5 Horta
Aztec: *god:* 4 Xipe 9 Xipetotic 11 Xiuhte-
cutli
language: 7 Nahuatl
myth: 4 Nana, Nata
stone: 9 temelactl 12 chalchihuitl
azure: 4 bice, blue 8 cerulean 9 cloudless,
unclouded
azygous: odd

B

baa: **5** bleat
baahling: **4** lamb
Baal: god **4** idol **5** deity
 consort: **6** Baltis
baba: **4** baby, cake, male **5** child
babacoote: **5** lemur
babblative: **9** garrulous, talkative **10** loquacious
babble: **4** chat, gash **5** haver, prate **6** cackle, gabble, glaver, gossip, murmur, palter, tumult **7** blabber, blather, bluster, brabble, chatter, chipper, clatter, prattle, smatter, twaddle **8** glaister **11** stultiloquy
babel: **5** tower **6** medley, tumult **9** confusion, charivari
baboon: ape **4** papa **5** drill **6** chaema **7** babuina **8** mandrill
babul: **6** acacia
babushka: **5** scarf **8** kerchief **11** grandmother
baby: **4** baba, babe, doll **5** bairn(Sc.), child, humor, spoil **6** coddle, fondle, infant, moppet, pamper, puppet, weanie (Sc.) **7** bambino(It.), papoose **9** youngster
 carriage: **4** pram **6** gocart **8** stroller **12** perambulator
 cry: mew **6** squall
 food: pap **4** milk **6** pablum
 outfit: **7** layette
 shoe: **6** bootee
babyish: **6** simple **7** puerile **8** childish
Babylonia:
 abode of the dead: **5** Aralu
 army officer: **11** samagarnebo
 city: **5** Akkad **6** Calneh, Cunaxa, Cuthah
 cycle of moon: sar **5** saros
 division: **4** Elam **5** Sumer, Sumir
 era: **5** sumer **10** Nabonassar
 foe: **7** Elamite
 god: Ea, Zu; Anu, Aya, Bel, Hea, Hes, Ira, Ler, Sin, Utu **4** Adad, Anat, Apsu, Baal, Gula, Irra, Nebo, Utug **5** Alala, Alalu, Dagan, Enlil, Etana, Ninib, Nusku, Siris, Urash **6** Ishtar, Nergal, Oannes, Tammuz **7** Ninurta, Shamash **8** Merodach **10** Adramelech **11** Adrammelech
 goddess: Ai; Aya **4** Erua, Nana, Nina **5** Belit **6** Belili, Beltis **7** Mylitta
 hero of myth: **5** Adapa, Etana
 king: **14** Nebuchadnezzar, Nebuchadrezzar
 language: **5** Accad, Akkad
 mountain: **6** Ararat

 people: **7** Elamite
 priest: En
 priestess: **5** Entum
 region: **5** Aralu, Sumer, Sumir
 river: **6** Tigris **9** Euphrates
 ruler: **8** Exilarch
 sea: **4** Nina
 sun god's attendant: **6** Bunene
 tower: **7** zikurat **8** ziggurat
 waters: **4** Apsu
 weight: **4** mina **5** maneh
Babylonian: **5** Accad **8** Sumerian
bacalao: **5** murre **7** codfish, grouper **9** guillemot
bacca: **5** berry
baccalaureate degree: B.A. **8** bachelor
 player: **6** punter
 term: **5** banco
 variety of: **11** chemin-de-fer
bacchanal: **7** devotee, reveler **8** carouser
Bacchanal's cry: **4** evoe **5** evohe
bacchante: **6** maenad **9** priestess
bachelor: **4** seal **6** garcon **8** benedict, celibate **11** holluschick **13** holluschickie(pl.),
bachelor button: **8** milkwort
bacillus: **4** germ **5** virus **7** microbe
back: aid, fro, tub, vat **4** abet, beck, hind, nape, nata, rear, tail **5** again, angel, chine, dorsa(pl.), notum, splat, spine, stern **6** assist, dorsum, second, trough, uphold, verify **7** cistern, endorse, finance, sponsor, support, sustain **8** backward **9** encourage, posterior, reinforce **10** strengthen
 at the: aft **5** abaff, abaft, arear **6** astern **7** postern
 comb. form: **5** notus
 lower part of: **4** loin
 pain: **8** notalgia
 pert. to: **6** dorsal, lumbar, tergal
 prefix: re **5** retro
 toward: aft **5** abaft **6** astern, dorsad **7** postern
back off: ebb **6** recede, retire **7** retreat, reverse **10** retrograde
back out: **4** funk **5** welsh **8** crawfish, withdraw
back talk: lip **4** sass **9** insolence
backbone: **4** grit, guts **5** chine, nerve, pluck, spina, spine **6** mettle, spinae, spirit **7** stamina **8** vertebra
backgammon: **6** fayles **10** tricktrack

background: 4 rear 6 offing 7 setting 8 distance, training 9 education

backing: aid 6 lining, refuse 7 support 9 financing 10 embankment 11 endorsement

backlog: 7 reserve, surplus 12 accumulation

backslide: 4 fall 5 lapse 6 desert, revert 7 relapse 11 deteriorate

backward: fro, lax 4 back, dull, loth 5 arear, inapt, loath, unapt 6 astern, averse, bygone, stupid 7 bashful, laggard, lagging, reverse 8 dilatory, perverse, rearward 9 recessive, reluctant, unwilling 10 behindhand, hesitating, regressive, retrograde 11 unfavorable 13 retrogressive, retrospective, unprogressive

backwater: ebb 5 bayou 7 retract, retreat

backwoodsman: 4 hick 9 hillbilly

backwort: 7 comfrey

bacon: pig 4 pork 5 prize 6 rustic
fat: 5 speck
side: 6 gammon
slice: 6 rasher, collop

bacteria, bacterium: 4 germ 6 aerobe 7 aerobia, microbe 10 aerobacter
chain: 6 torula 7 torulae(pl.)
dissolver: 5 lysin
free from harmful: 7 asepsis, aseptic
rod-shaped: 7 bacilli(pl.) 8 bacillus
vaccine: 8 bacterin

bacteriologist: *culture:* 4 agar
wire: 4 oese

bactrian: 5 camel

bad: big, ill, sad 4 evil, full, lewd, poor, qued, sick, vile 5 gammy, nasty, sorry, worst, wrong 6 arrant, faulty, nought, rotten, severe, sinful, wicked 7 baleful, baneful, corrupt, harmful, hurtful, immoral, inutile, naughty, noughty, spoiled, tainted, unlucky, unmoral, unsound, vicious 8 annoying, criminal, depraved, flagrant, inferior, unsuited 9 abandoned, atrocious, blemished, dangerous, defective, incorrect, injurious, offensive, perverted, worthless 10 aggravated, distressed, inadequate, iniquitous, pernicious, unsuitable 11 deleterious, displeasing, inopportune, unfavorable 12 disagreeable, inauspicious
comb. form: dys, mal 4 caco, kako
prefix: mal, mis

bad blood: 4 hate 5 anger 10 bitterness, resentment

badderlocks: 6 murlin 7 henware, seaweed 9 honeyware

badge: pin 4 mark, sign 5 token 6 emblem, ensign, symbol 8 insignia 10 cognizance
policeman: 4 star 6 busser, shield

badger: nag 4 bait, mele, pate 5 annoy, brock, brush, chevy, chivy, phani, rated, tease, worry 6 bauson, bother, chivvy, haggle, harass, hawker, heckle, pester,

teledu, wombat 7 torment 8 carcajou, huckster, irritate 9 bandicoot, mistonusk 10 badgerweed 12 pasqueflower

Badger State: 9 Wisconsin

badgerweed: 12 pasqueflower

badinage: 4 fool 5 joker 6 banter 8 raillery, trifling 9 badinerie

badly: ill 4 illy, sick 6 poorly, unwell 8 faultily, wickedly 9 viciously 11 imperfectly 12 disagreeable, unskillfully 13 unfortunately

baff: 4 bang, beat, blow thud 6 strike, stroke 9 worthless

baffle: get 4 balk, foil, pose 5 cheat, check, elude, evade, fling, stump 6 blench, boggle, defeat, delude, infamy, outwit, resist, thwart 7 confuse, deceive, quibble 8 bewilder, confound, disgrace, juggling 9 confusion, discomfit. frustrate 10 circumvent, disappoint, disconcert

baft: 5 abaft 6 astern

bag: cod, net, pod, pot, sac 4 grip, poke, sack, trap, womb 5 belly, bouge, bulse, catch, pouch, purse, scrip, seize, snare, steal 6 budget, cavity, entrap, pocket, sachet, wallet, valise 7 alforja, balloon, capture, gamebag, handbag, reticle, satchel 8 entrails, knapsack, reticule, suitcase 9 cartridge, container, gladstone, haversack 10 collection, pocketbook 11 portmanteau
botanic: sac 4 asci 5 ascus, spore
canvas: 7 musette
fishing net: 4 bunt, fyke
hop: 7 sarpler
muslin: 6 tillot
traveling: 9 telescope

bagatelle: 4 game 5 verse 6 trifle

baggage: 4 arms, gear, minx 5 huzzy, nasty, tents, trash, wench 6 harlot, refuse, trashy, trunks 7 clothes, effects, rubbish, valises 8 carriage, rubbishy, utensils 9 munitions, viaticals, worthless 10 prostitute 11 impedimenta

baggy: 5 loose 6 flabby, puffed

Baghdad: *capital:* 4 Irak
merchant: 6 Sinbad 7 Sindbad

bagnio: 4 bath 5 bagne 6 prison 7 brothel 8 hothouse

bagpipe: 5 drone 7 musette 8 zampogna 10 doodlesack, sordellina
mouthpiece: 4 muse
pipe: 6 drones 7 chanter
player: 5 piper 7 doodler
sound: 5 skirl
tune: 4 port

bah: foh, pah, rot 5 faugh, pshaw 8 nonsense

Bahama Islands: 5 Abaco 6 Andros, Bimini 9 Eleuthera
capital: 6 Nassau

bahia: bay

bail: dip 4 bond, hoop, lade, lave, ring, rynd, yoke 5 ladle, scoop, throw, vouch 6 bucket, handle, secure, surety **7** custody, deliver, release **8** bailsman, bulwarks, security **9** guarantee

bailiff: **4** hind **5** agent, reeve, staff **6** bailie, bailli, beadle, deputy, factor, grieve, porter, staves(pl.), varlet, office **7** sheriff, steward **8** huissier, overseer, tipstaff **9** constable **10** magistrate **12** understeward
farm: **4** hind

bailiwick: **4** area **6** domain, office **8** province **9** bailiffry, bailliage **12** jurisdiction

bain: **4** near **5** lithe, ready, short **6** direct, limber, supple **7** forward, willing

bairn: **5** child

bait: bad **4** bite, chum, feed, halt, lure **5** decoy, tempt, worry **6** allure, attack, badger, entice, harass, repast **7** fulcrum, gudgeon, provoke, torment **9** persecute **10** allurement, enticement, exasperate, inducement, temptation **11** refreshment
artificial: **6** hackle
bird enticing: **5** shrap **6** shrape
salmon fishing: **5** haker

baize: **6** fabric **7** drapery

bake: dry **4** cook, fire **5** batch, broil, grill, parch, roast **6** anneal, harden **7** biscuit **8** clambake

baker: **4** oven **6** baxter **7** furnace, roaster, utensil
sheet: pan
shovel: **4** pale, peel
tool: **4** pale, peel

baker's dozen: **8** thirteen

baking dish: **7** cocotte, ramekin

baking ingredient: **4** soda **5** flour, yeast

baking soda: **9** saleratus

Bakongo goddess: **6** Nyambe, Nzambi

balance: **4** even, rest **5** peise, poise, scale, weigh, weihe **6** adjust, equate, offset, sanity **7** residue **8** equality, equalize, serenity **9** composure, equipoise, remainder, stability **10** neutralize, steadiness **11** equilibrium **12** counterpoise
lose: **4** trip **7** stagger
weighing: **6** auncel

balancer: **7** acrobat, athlete, gymnast

balate: **7** trepang

balcony: **5** oriel, porch **6** piazza, sollar **7** balagan, gallery, mirador, pergola, terrace **8** brattice, verandah
church singer: **8** cantoria
projecting: **6** gazabo, gazebo

bald: **4** bare, base **5** crude, naked, plain **6** callow, paltry, pilled, simple **7** epilose, literal **8** glabrous, hairless **9** unadorned, uncovered **11** undisguised, unvarnished

Balder: *father:* **4** Odin
mother: **5** Frigg
slayer: **4** Hoth, Loke **5** Hothr
son: **7** Forsete, Forseti
wife: **5** Nanna

balderdash: rot **5** trash **6** drivel, jargon **8** nonsense **9** balductum, rigmarole **10** flumdiddle

baldmoney: **7** gentian **8** spicknel

baldness: **6** acomia **7** calvity **8** alopecia **10** calavities **11** phalacrosis

baldric, baldrick: **4** belt **6** girdle, zodiac **7** balteus, support **8** baltheus, necklace

bale: no; not, woe **4** evil, fire, harm, pyre **5** crate, death **6** ballot, bundle, sorrow **7** package **8** compress, disaster **9** influence, suffering
of wool: **7** sarpler

Balearic Island: **5** Iviza **7** Cabrera, Majorca, Minorca **10** Formentera
measure: **5** palmo **6** misura, quarta, quarte **7** quartin **8** barcella, quartera
weight: **5** artal, artel, cargo, corta, libra, mayor, ratel, rotel **8** quartano

baleen: **5** whale **9** whalebone

baleful: bad **4** evil **6** deadly, malign, **7** noxious, ruinous **8** sinister, wretched **10** calamitous, pernicious **11** destructive

Bali (see also **Indonesia**):
dance: **5** ardja, baris, kriss **6** barong, ketjak, monkey **7** djanger **9** sanghyang **14** barong-landoeng
musical instrument: **7** gamelan **8** gamelang
religion: **8** Hinduism
rice field: **6** sawaii

balk: hue, jib, shy **4** beam, bilk, foil, heap, lick, loft, miss, omit, shun, skip, slip, stop **5** avoid, block, check, hunch, mound, rebel, reest(Sc.), ridge, waver **6** baffle, defeat, falter, hinder, impede, outwit, rafter, refuse, thwart **7** blunder, isthmus, mistake **8** omitting, overlook, skipping **9** discomfit, frustrate **10** disappoint **14** disappointment

Balkan: **4** Serb, Slav **7** Serbian **8** Albanian, Rumanian, Yugoslav
bandit: **6** haiduk, heydue **7** heyduck, heyduke
coin: **6** novcic
country: **6** Serbia, Servia **7** Albania, Rumania **10** Yugoslavia
instrument: **5** gusla, gusle

balky: **6** mulish **8** stubborn **9** obstinate

ball: bal(F.), bob, orb, toy **4** bead, pill **5** dance, globe, glome **6** bullet, muddle, pellet, pompon, rundle, sphere **7** confuse, mandrel, ridotto **8** spheroid **11** glomeration
lofted: fly, lob
low: **5** liner
minced meat: **5** pinda **7** rissole
wooden: **4** knur

ball game: cat **5** rugby **6** pelota, soccer **7** cricket **8** baseball

ballad: lai(F.) **4** lilt, poem, song **5** derry **6** ballet, sonnet **7** ballant, canzone

ballast: **4** load, trim **5** poise, stone **6** burden, gravel, weight **7** balance **9** saburrate

ballerina: **4** pony **6** dancer **8** danseuse

ballet: **5** dance, drama **6** ballad, masque **9** pantomime **12** choreography

movement: 4 jete 5 brise 8 glissade
posture: 9 arabesque
balloon: bag 5 blimp 6 expand, gasbag 7
airship, distend, inflate 8 aerostat 9 dirigible
basket: car 7 gondola, nacelle
ballot: 4 bale, poll, vote 5 elect, voice 6
billet, choice, ticket
cast: 4 vote
balm: oil 4 bito, daub, case 5 salve 6 balsam, embalm, lotion, relief, soothe, solace
7 annoint, anoydne, besmear, comfort,
cure-all, heal-all, perfume, soother, unguent 8 mitigate, ointment 11 assuagement
horse: 10 citronella
of Gilead: 6 balsam
balmy: 4 mild, soft 5 bland, daffy, moony,
spicy, sunny, sweet 6 gentle, insane 7
healing, lenient 8 aromatic, dressing, fragrant, soothing 9 assuaging 10 refreshing
11 odoriferous
balneary: 9 bathhouse
balneation: 4 bath
balneum: 4 bath 8 bathroom
baloney: 4 bunk 5 hooey
balsa: 4 raft, tree, wood 5 float
balsam: 4 balm, riga, tree, tolu 6 storay 7
copaiba 8 bdellium, ointment
apple: 4 vine 7 creeper 8 amargosa,
amargoso, ampalaya
Balt: Yod 4 Esth, Lett 8 Estonian 10
Lithuanian
Baltic: *barge:* 5 praam
city: 6 Danzig
island: 4 Dago, Faro, Osel 5 Alsen, Oesel,
Oland
language: 6 Lettic
seaport: 4 Kiel, Riga 5 Memel, Reval 6
Talinn
Baltic Sea: *canal:* 4 kiel
river: 4 Oder, Odra 5 Dvina, Peene, Wilsa
Baluchistan: *native:* 4 Mari 5 Marri
6 Marree
province: Lus
balustrade: 6 barrer 7 parapet, railing 8
balconet, baluster, banister 10 balconette
Balzac character: 4 Nana 6 Goriot
bam: 4 hoax, sham 5 cheat, trick 7 wheedle
bambino: 4 baby 5 child 6 infant
bamboo: 4 cane, reed, tree
sacred: 6 nandin
sprouts: 5 achar
sugar: 9 tabasheer
woven: 6 sawali
bamboozle: 4 dupe 5 cheat, cozen, grill
6 cajole, humbug 7 buffalo, defraud, deceive, mystify, perplex 11 hornswoggle
ban: bar, woe 4 tabu, veto 5 banal, block,
curse, edict, order, taboo 6 banish, enjoin, forbid, hinder, invoke, notice,
outlaw 7 condemn, exclude 8 anath-

ema, denounce, execrate, prohibit 9
interdict, proscribe 10 inhibition 11 forbiddance, imprecation, malediction 12
anathematize, denunciation, interdiction,
proclamation 15 excommunication
Bana: *conqueror:* 7 Krishna
daughter: 4 Usha
banal: 4 flat 5 corny, inane, silly, stale,
trite, vapid 6 jejune 7 trivial 9 hackneyed
11 commonplace 13 platitudinous
phrase: 6 cliche
banana: 4 musa 6 ensete 7 platano(Sp.) 8
plantain
bunch: 4 hand, stem
family: 4 musa 6 pesang 8 musaceae
leaf: 5 frond
wild: fei
Bananaland: 10 Queensland
band: bar, tie 4 belt, bond, came, cord,
crew, fess, gang, girt, hoop, ring, zona,
zone 5 ampyx, bandy, corse, label, strap,
strip, tribe, unite, zonae(pl.), 6 armlet,
binder, bundle, cohort, collar, collet, copula, fascia, fetter, fillet, girdle, hyphen,
norsel, pledge, string, stripe, swathe,
tether 7 aweband, bandeau, binding, circlet, company, fasciae(pl.), garland, orphrey, promise, shackle 8 banderol, biliment, bracelet, cincture, cingulum,
faisceau, ligament, ligature, tressour,
tressure 9 associate, banderole, bandoleer, guarantee, orchestra 10 obligation
armed: 5 posse
armor: 6 tonlet
brain: 6 ligula 7 ligulae
decorative: 7 cornice
garment fastening: 5 patte
narrow: 4 tape 5 stria 6 striae(pl.),
small: 8 bandelet 10 bandelette
bandage: 4 bind, tape 5 blind, clout,
dress, sling, spica, truss 6 fettle, fillet,
ligate, swathe 8 cincture, ligature 9
blindfold
fastener: 7 ligator
nose: 9 accipiter
surgical: 5 spica 6 fascia, spicae(pl.) 7
fasciae
bandeau: 4 band 5 strip 6 fillet
bandicoot: 4 rat 6 badger
bandikai: 4 okra
bandit: 4 caco 5 bravo, thief 6 banish,
outlaw, robber 7 bandido, brigand, ladrone 8 marauder, picaroon 10 highwayman
bandleader: 6 master 7 choragi, maestro
8 choragus 9 conductor
bandy: 4 band, cart, swap 5 trade 6
league, strive 7 chaffer, contend, discuss
8 carriage, exchange 11 reciprocate
bane: woe 4 evil, harm, kill, pest, ruin 5
curse, death, venon 6 injury, murder,
poison, slayer 7 nemesis, scourge 8 mischief, murderer, nuisance

baneful: bad, ill **4** evil, vile **7** harmful, hurtful, noxious, ruinous **8** venomous **9** sinistral **10** pernicious

bang: rap **4** baff, beat, blow, dash, dock, drub, slam **5** blaff, clash, drive, excel, force, impel, pound, sound, thump, whack, whang **6** bounce, cudgel, energy, strike, thrash, thunge, thwack **7** sardine, surpass **8** forelock

bang-up: **5** crack **6** tiptop **9** first-rate

bangle: **4** flap, roam **5** droop, waste **7** circlet, fritter, trinket **8** bracelet, ornament

Bani's son: Uel **4** Amzi **5** Amram

banish: ban **5** eject, exile, expel, fleme **6** bandit, deport, dispel, forsay, outlaw **7** abandon, condemn, dismiss, exclude **8** displace, relegate **9** ostracize, proscribe, transport **10** expatriate, repatriate

banished: **8** fugitive

banister: **7** railing **8** baluster **10** balustrade

bank: bar, bay, cop, rim, row **4** bink, brae, brew, caja, dike, dune, dyke, edge, hill, mass, pile, ramp, rive, sand, seat, tier, weir **5** banco, bench, bluff, brink, fence, levee, marge, mound, ridge, stack, share, shelf, shoal, shore, slope, stage, trust **6** causey, degree, depend, margin, reckon, rivage, strand **7** anthill, deposit, pottery, shallow **8** barranca, barranco, platform **9** acclivity, **10** depository, elevation, embankment

clerk: **6** teller

requirement: **5** funds, money **6** assets **7** surplus **8** deposits

bankroll: wad **5** bills **8** currency

bankrupt: sap **4** bung **5** broke, drain, smash, strip **6** busted, devour, ruined, quisby **7** failure **8** beggarly, depleted **9** destitute, insolvent **12** impoverished

banner: **4** fane, flag, jack **5** color **6** ensign, fannon, pennon **7** leading, pennant, salient **8** banderol, foremost, gonfalon, standard, vexillum **9** banderole, exemplary, oriflamme **10** surpassing

banns: **4** bans **6** notice **12** proclamation

banquet: **4** fete, meal **5** feast **6** dinner, junket, regale, repast **8** carousal, festival

room: **8** cenacula(pl.) **9** cenaculum

banquette: way **4** seat **5** shelf **7** footway **8** platform, sidewalk **10** embankment

bant: **4** diet, fast **6** reduce

bantam: **4** cock **5** saucy **7** chicken **9** combative **10** diminutive

breed: **8** Sebright

banteng: ox **5** tsine

banter: kid, rag **4** fool, jest, joke, josh, mock, quiz, rail **5** borak, chaff, rally, roast, trick **6** delude, deride, haggle, satire **7** badiner, stashie **8** badinage, chaffing, raillery, ridicule **10** persiflage, pleasantry

bantering: **9** quizzical

bantling: **5** child **6** infant

Bantu: *dialect:* **6** Chwana **8** Sechuana

language: Ila **4** Suto **5** Ronga **6** Thonga **7** Nyanaja **8** Nyamwezi **10** Wanymawezi

people: **4** Guha, Hehe, Yaka, Zulu **5** Duala, Kafir **6** Banyai, Damara, Kaffir, Waguha, Yakala **7** Swahili, Wachaga **8** Bechuana

banyan: bur **4** burr **6** banian

baobab: **4** tree **7** tebeldi

baptism: **9** cleansing **11** christening

robe: **7** Chrisom

vessel: **4** font **6** fontal, spring **7** piscina

water: **5** laver

baptize: dip **4** full, name **5** heave **6** purify **7** cleanse **8** christen, sprinkle

bar: ban, dam, fid, gad, law, rod **4** axle, band, bank, beam, bolt, cake, gate, hide, joke, lock, oust, pole, rail, reef, save, shut, stop **5** arbor, bench, bilco, block, close, court, deter, estop, fence, hedge, lever, perch, shade, shaft, strap, strip **6** billet, brooch, except, fasten, grille, hinder, meagre, saloon, stripe **7** barrage, barrier, confine, counter, exclude, prevent **8** conclude, handicap, obstacle, obstruct, preclude, prohibit, restrain, restrict, surround, tribunal **9** barricade, fastening, gatehouse, hindrance, interpose, ostracize **10** crosspiece, difficulty, impediment, inhibition, portcullis **11** obstruction

acrobat: **7** trapeze

bullion: **5** ingot

legally: **5** estop

millstone: **4** rynd

resisting pressure: **5** strut

supporting: fid, rod **9** stanchion

tamping: **7** stemmer

window: **5** jemmy, jimmy **7** forcing

barb: awn, bur, jag, mow **4** burr, clip, file, flue, hair, herl, hook, jagg **5** beard, horse, point, ridge **6** pigeon **7** bristle **8** kingfish **9** appendage **10** projection

anchor: **4** flue

feather: **4** harl, herl **5** ramus **7** pinnula, pinnule **8** pinnulae

Barbados native: Bim

barbarian: Hun **4** boor, Goth, rude, wild **5** alien, brute **6** savage, vandal **7** ruffian **9** foreigner, untutored **10** Philistine, unlettered **11** uncivilized

barbarism: **4** cant **8** savagism, solecism **10** savageness

barbarity: **6** ferity **7** cruelty **8** ferocity, rudeness, savagery **9** brutality **10** inhumanity

barbarous: **4** fell, rude, wild **5** cruel **6** brutal **7** foreign, Hunnish, inhuman, slavish, uncivil **8** ignorant **9** ferocious, primitive **10** illiterate, outlandish, tramontane, unpolished **11** uncivilized **12** uncultivated

Barbary: *ape:* **5** magot **6** simian

states: **5** Tunis **7** Algiers, Morocco, Tripoli

barber: 6 Figaro, poller, shaver, tonsor 7 scraper, tonsure 11 chirotonsor

bard: 4 poet, scop 5 druid, runer, scald 6 singer 8 minstrel, musician

India: 4 bhat

Bard of Avon: 11 Shakespeare

bare: 4 bald, mere, nude 5 alone, crude, empty, naked, plain, stark, strip 6 barren, callow, denude, divert, divest, expose, histie, meager, meagre, paltry, pilled, reveal, simple 7 divulge, exposed, unarmed, uncover 8 desolate, disclose, stripped 9 unadorned, uncovered, worthless 10 threadbare 11 defenseless, unconcealed, unfurnished 13 unaccompanied

barefaced: 7 glaring 8 impudent 9 audacious, shameless 11 undisguised

barefooted: 6 unshod 9 discalced

barely: 4 only 5 faint 6 hardly, merely, poorly 8 scantily, scarcely, slightly 13 unqualifiedly 14 insufficiently

bargain: 4 deal, huck, mise, pact, pick, sale, sell 5 cheap, fight 6 barter, dicker, haggle, higglo, palter 7 chaffer, compact, contend, contest, traffic 8 contract, covenant, purchase, struggle 9 agreement, negotiate, situation, stipulate 10 engagement 11 transaction

barge: ark, box, boy, tow, tub 4 bark, boat, pram, raft, scow 5 foist, lunge, lurch, praam, scold, shrew, vixen 6 barque, berate, praham, rebuke, thrust, tender, vessel 7 gabbard, gabbart, gondola, lighter, omnibus 9 houseboat, interfere

charge: 10 lighterage

coal: 4 keel

bargeman: pug 6 bargee 7 huffler

barium sulphate: 6 barite

bark: bag, bay, rub, wap, yap, yip 4 boat, coat, howl, husk, peel, pelt, pill, rind, ross, ship, skin, yawp 5 balat, barca, barge, cough, shell, shout, strip 6 abrade, cortex, girdle, vessel 7 solicit, tanbark 8 cortices, covering

aromatic: 6 sintoc 7 canella 9 sassafras

cloth: 4 tapa 5 tappa 8 mulberry

covered with: 9 corticate 10 corticated

medicinal: 4 coto 5 casca, madar, nudar, niepa 7 quinine 8 cinchona 9 sassafras

outer: 8 periderm

remove: 4 ross 5 scale

resembling: 8 cortical

rough: 4 ross

tanning: 5 alder

barkeeper: 6 barman 7 tapster

barker: dog 6 jumper, pistol, tanner 7 spieler 9 solicitor

barking: 4 spud 7 latrant 9 latration

barking deer: 7 muntjac, muntjak

barley: 5 grain

ground: 6 tsamba

pert. to: 11 hordeaceous

steep: 4 malt

variety: big 4 bere, bigg

barman: 7 tapster 9 barkeeper, barrister 11 metalworker

barmy: 5 foamy, silly 6 frothy, yeasty 7 flighty, foolish, idiotic

barn: 4 byre 5 stall 6 stable 10 storehouse

storage area: bag, mow 4 loft 7 hayloft

barn dance official: 6 caller

barnacle: *genus:* 5 Lepas

plate: 5 terga(pl.), 6 tergum

barnstorm: 4 tour

barometric line: 6 isobar

baron: 4 peer 5 noble 7 freeman

baronet: sir 8 commoner

barony: han 4 rank 6 domain 7 dignity

baroque: 6 ornate, rococo 9 grotesque, irregular 11 extravagant

barrack: 4 camp 6 casern 7 cuartel(Sp.), 8 quarters

barraclade: 7 blanket

barracuda: 4 fish, spet 5 barry, pelon 6 becuna, picuda, sennet 10 guaguanche 12 guanchepelon

barrage: bar 6 attack, volley 7 barrier 9 cannonade 10 barricuade, obtruction

barranca, barranco: 4 bank 5 bluff 6 ravine

barras: 5 linen 7 galipot 8 gallipot

barrator: 5 bully, rowdy 7 fighter

barred: 6 ribbed 7 striped

barrel: fat, keg, tun, vat 4 butt, cade, cask, drum, knag 6 runlet, tierce, vessel 7 cistern, rundlet 8 cylinder, hogshead 9 container, kilderkin

herring: 4 cade

maker: 6 cooper

part: 4 side, hoop 5 stave

raising device: 9 parbuckle

stopper: 4 bung

support: 4 hoop 6 gantry 7 gauntry

barren: dry 4 arid, bare, dull, gast, geld 5 blunt, drape, empty, gaunt, stark, stern 6 desert, effete, fallow, histie, hungry, jejune, meager, stupid 7 sterile 8 impotent, treeless 9 exhausted, fruitless, infertile, penurious 10 unfruitful 12 unproductive, unprofitable

barren oak: 9 blackjack

barren privet: 7 alatern 9 houseleek

barrette: bar 8 ornament

barricade: bar 4 stop 5 block, close, fence 6 abatis, prison 7 barrage, defense, fortify 9 roadblock 11 obstruction 13 fortification

barrier: bar, dam 4 door, gate, line, wall, weir 5 bound, chain, fence, hedge, limit 6 hurdle, screen 7 barrage, parapet, railing 8 boundary, fortress, frontier, stockade 9 palisades, restraint 10 difficulty, partcullis, tournament 11 obstruction

movable: 4 bars, door 5 blind, shade 6 window 7 certain 8 shutters

barrister: 6 barman, lawyer 7 counsel 8 advocate, attorney

barroom: pub 4 cafe 6 saloon 7 cantina(Sp.), doggery 8 dramshop, exchange

barrow: hod, hog 4 bank, dune, hill, mote 5 grave, gurry, mound 6 tumuli 7 hillock, trolley, tumulus 8 mountain

bartender: 7 tapster

barter: 4 chap, chop, cope, coup, hawk, sell, swap, vend 5 corse, trade, troke, truck 6 dicker 7 bargain, cambium, permute, traffic 8 commerce, exchange 9 excambion 11 reciprocate

bas: low

bas-relief: 9 plaquette

basal: 5 basic 7 basilar 11 fundamental

basalt: 6 marble, navite 7 pottery

base: bed, low 4 clam, evil, foot, foul, lewd, mean, poor, root, stem, step, vile 5 basis, cheap, dirty, muddy, petty, snide 6 abject, bottom, common, ground, menial, paltry, podium, shabby, sordid, vulgar 7 bastard, caitiff, comical, debased, hangdog, hilding, housing, ignoble, servile, slavish, support 8 coistrel, coistril, degraded, infamous, inferior, pedestal, scullion, shameful, stepping, unworthy, wretched 9 absorbent, degrading, establish, worthless 10 despicable, foundation, villainous 11 ignominious 12 contemptible, dishonorable, disreputable 13 dishonourable

architectural: 5 socle 6 plinth

military: HDQ 4 camp 5 depot 12 headquarters

structural: 6 plinth

baseball:

field: 7 diamond

hit: 4 bunt

official: 5 coach 6 umpire 7 manager

team: 4 nine

term: bag, bat, box, fan, fly, hit, lob, low, out, peg, RBI, run, tap, top 4 ball, bean, beat, bunt, burn, deck, foul, high, hill, hole, home, hook, miss, pill, pole, sack, save, turn, walk, wild 5 alley, apple, bench, booth, clout, coach, count, curve, drive, error, field, first, force, frame, glove, homer, lined, mound, pitch, plate, popup, punch, score, slide, swing, third 6 assist, batter, bungle, bottom, charge, clutch, double, dugout, groove, hitter, inside, lifted, lumber, middle, popout, putout, rubber, runner, screen, second, series, single, sinker, stance, strike, string, target, triple, wind-up 7 arbited, arbiter, battery, blooper, bullpen, circuit, cleanup, diamond, fielder, floater, infield, man-

ager, nothing, outside, pitcher, side-arm, squeeze, stretch, thumbed 8 delivery, grounded, grounder, knuckler, outfield, pinch-hit, pitchout, powdered, soupbone, spitball 9 full-count, hot corner, sacrifice, smothered, strike-out, two-bagger 10 scratch-hit 11 three-bagger

baseless: 4 idle 9 unfounded 10 gratuitous, groundless

basement: 4 base 6 cellar

bash: bat, lam 4 beat, blow, dent, mash, swat, wham, whop 5 abash, smash 6 bruise, strike

bashful: shy 4 copy, helo 5 blate, heloe, timid 6 modest 7 daunted 8 backward, blushing, dismayed, retiring, sheepish, verecund 9 diffident, shrinking

basic: 5 basal, vital 7 central 9 elemental 11 fundamental 13 indispensable

basil: 4 herb 5 plant, royal 6 fetter

basin: pan 4 bowl, dish, dock, ewer, font, tank 5 laver, stoup 6 chafer, marina, valley, vessel 7 cuvette, piscina 8 lavatory, receptor, washbowl 9 reservoir 10 aspersoria, depression 11 aspersorium

basis: 4 base, fund, root, sill 5 axiom 6 bottom, ground 7 footing, premise, support 10 foundation, groundwork

bask: sun 4 beek, warm 5 acrid, bathe, enjoy, revel 6 bitter 7 rejoice 9 luxuriate

basket: ark, fan, ped 4 trug 5 cassy(Sc.), cesta, chest, crate, scull 6 cassie, coffin, dorsel, dorser, dosser, gabion, hamper, hoppet, panier 7 canasta, hanaper, pannier, scuttle 9 container 10 receptacle

coal mine: 4 corf

eel: 4 buck

fig: 4 caba 5 frail 6 tapnet

fire: 5 grate 7 cresset

fish: pot 4 caul, cawl, corf, hask, skip, weel 5 creel, crate, maund 6 courge, gabion, hamper 7 pannier

fruit: 6 pottle, funnet

material: 5 otate

twig: 6 wattle

water-tight: 7 wattape

wicker: cob 4 cobb, coop 5 willy 6 hamper 7 hanaper 8 bassinet

willow: 5 osier 7 prickle

work: 4 caba 5 cabas, slath 6 slarth

basket-ball team: 4 five 7 cagemen

Basque: 5 waist 6 scoter 7 Iberian

cap: 5 beret

dance: 7 auresca 8 aurrescu, zortzico

game: 6 pelota

language: 6 Uskara 7 Eskuara, Euskara, Euskera

people: 7 Euscara, Euscaro

petticoat: 8 basquine

bass: low 4 deep, fish 5 voice 6 singer 7 achigan, jewfish

bassinet: 6 basket, cradle

basswood: lin 6 linden
bast: 4 bark 5 fiber, ramie 6 phloem
basta: 4 stop 6 enough
bastard: 4 base 5 false 6 cannon, galley, hybrid, impure 7 byspell, lowbred, mongrel 8 bantling, spurious 10 artificial 11 adulterated 12 illegitimate
baste: sew 4 beat, cane, cook, drub, lard, tack 6 cudgel, punish, stitch, thrash
bastion:
defensive: 4 fort 13 fortification
shoulder: 6 epaule
bat: hit, wad 4 bate, beat, club, gait, lump, mass, swat, wink 5 brick, piece, spree, stick 6 aliped, backie(Sc.), baston, beetle, cudgel, racket, strike, stroke 7 flutter, noctule, vampire 8 bludgeon, serotine 9 reremouse 10 battledore, chiroptera, packsaddle 11 rattlemouse 12 chauvesouris, flittermouse
European: 9 barbastel 11 barbastelle
species: 9 pipistrel 11 pipistrelle
batch: lot 4 mass, mess, sort 5 group 6 baking 7 mixture 8 quantity 10 collection
bateau: 4 boat
bath: dip 4 bate, pert 5 therm 6 plunge, shower 7 balneum 8 ablution 10 natatorium
pert, to: 7 balneal
public: 7 piscine
bathe: bay, tub 4 bask, lave, stew, wash 5 embay 6 enwrap 7 immerse, pervade, suffuse 8 permeate
bathhouse: 6 cabana 8 balneary
bathos: 8 comedown 10 anticlimax
bathroom: W.C.(abbr.) 6 hammam 8 sudatory 10 sudatorium 11 water closet
Bathsheba's son: 7 Solomon
baton: rod 4 bend 5 staff, stick 6 baston, cudgel 7 bourdon, scepter, sceptre 9 truncheon
batsman: 6 batter, hitter 7 striker
batten: 6 enrich, fatten, thrive 9 fertilize
batter: ram 4 beat, dent, maim 5 clour, dinge, frush, paste, pound 6 bruise, hammer, hatter, hitter, pummel 7 batsman, bombard, cripple, destroy, shatter, striker 8 demolish
battery:
floating: 4 cell 5 praam 7 parapet 9 artillery 11 bombardment
plate: 4 grid
battle: war 4 duel, fray, meet, tilt 5 brush, fight, joust 6 action, affray, combat 7 contend, contest, hosting, warfare 8 conflict, skirmish, struggle 9 encounter 10 engagement, tournament 11 competition
area: 5 arena, front 6 sector 7 terrain
cry: 6 slogan 9 catchword
formation: 5 herse 6 deploy
line: 5 front
order: 7 regalia 8 battalia

royal: 5 melee 9 scrimmage
site: 6 Shiloh 7 Bull Run 8 Manassas 10 Armageddon, Gettysburg
battleship: 7 carrier 11 dreadnaught 16 superdreadnaught
battologize: 6 repeat 7 iterate
batty: 5 crazy, silly 7 batlike, foolish
bauble: bow, toy 4 bead, gaud 6 button, gewgaw, trifle 7 trinket 8 gimcrack 9 plaything 10 knickknack
bauxite derivative: 8 aluminum
Bavaria:
beer: 10 Wurzburger
city: Hof 6 Munich(c.), 8 Augsburg, Nurnberg, Ratisbon, Wurzburg 10 Regensburg
community: 6 Passau
division: 7 Neuburg 8 Fraconia, Schwaben 10 Palatinate, Regensburg 13 Aschaffenburg
lake: 4 Wurm 5 Ammer, Chiem 8 Starber
measure: 4 fass, fuss, rute 5 linie, metze, ruthe 6 massel, morgen 7 juchert, tagwerk 10 dreissiger
mountain: 6 Vosges 8 Watzmann 9 Zugspitze
river: Inn, Nab 4 Eger, Isar, Iser, Lech 5 Iller, Regen, Saale 7 Altmuhl, Wornitz
university site: 8 Erlangen
weight: 4 gran 9 quentchen
bawd: 4 aunt, hare 5 dirty 6 defile 7 commode 8 procurer 9 procuress 10 fruitwoman
bawdry: 5 mirth 6 filthy, finery, gaiety, gayety 9 obscenity
bawdy: 4 foul, lewd 5 dirty 7 obscene 8 unchaste
bawl: cry 4 howl 5 golly, shout 6 bellow, boohoo, outcry 8 glaister 10 vociferate
out: 5 scold 9 reprimand
bawling: 10 vociferous
bay: dam, ria, voe 4 bank, bark, cove, gulf, hole, hope, howl, loch(Sc.), roan, tree, yaup, yawp 5 bahia(Sp.), berry, bight, color, creek, fiord, fjord, fleet, haven, horse, oriel, sinus 6 laurel, recess, window 7 enclose, estuary, silanga, ululate 11 compartment, indentation
bird: 5 snipe 6 curlew, godwit, plover
camphor: 6 laurin
Bay State: 13 Massachusetts
bayard: 5 horse
bayardly: 5 blind 6 stupid
Baylor University site: 4 Waco
bayou: 5 brook, creek, inlet, river 6 outlet, stream 7 rivulet 9 backwater
Bayou State: 11 Mississippi
bazaar, bazar: 4 fair, fete, sale 5 agora, burse 6 market 7 canteen 8 emporium 9 bezesteen 10 exposition
bazoo: 4 talk 5 kazoo, mouth
be: are 4 live 5 abide, exist, occur 6 remain 7 breathe, subsist 8 continue

beach: 4 bank, moor, ripa, sand **5** coast, plage(F.), playa(Sp.), shore **6** ground, shilla, strand **7** hardway, seaside, shingle

beacon: 4 mark, sign **5** baken, fanal, guide, phare **6** ensign, pharos, signal **7** cresset, seamark, warning **8** signpost **10** lighthouse, watchtower

light: **7** cresset, lantern

bead: 4 drop, foam **5** sewan, sight **6** bauble, bubble, prayer, wampum **7** globule, molding, sparkle, trinket

string: **6** rosary **7** chaplet **8** necklace

beadel: 5 crier, macer, usher **6** bedell, bumble, herald **7** bailiff, officer **8** servitor, summoner **9** apparitor, messenger **10** mace-bearer

beadsman, bedesman: 6 beggar, hermit **10** petitioner

beady: 5 round, small **8** globular **10** glistening

beak: neb, nib **4** bill, nose, prow **5** lorum, snout **6** master, speron **7** molding, rostrum **8** mandible **10** magistrate **11** stipendiary

beaker: cup **4** tass **5** bocal, bouse, glass **6** bareca, bareka, vessel

beam: bar, ray **4** balk, emit, glow, I-bar, sile(Sc), stud, T-bar **5** arbor, caber, flash, gleam, gleed, joist, light, shine, smile **6** binder, girder, rafter, timber, walker **7** bumpkin, chevron, radiate, support, trimmer **10** architrave

beaming: gay **4** rosy **6** bright, lucent **7** radiant, shining

beamy: 5 broad **6** joyous, lucent **7** massive, radiant **8** mirthful

bean: urd **4** chap, gram, head, Lima, pole **5** brain, skull **6** caster, collar, fellow, kidney, lentil, nipple, noggin, strike, thrash, trifle **7** calabar, frijole(Sp.) **11** castigation

climbing: **4** lima, pole

cluster: **4** guar

eye: **4** hila **5** hilum

kind: goa, soy, wax **4** lima, navy **6** castor, kidney, string **7** calabar

lima: **4** haba **5** sieva

locust: **5** carob

lubricant: ben

poisonous: **4** loco **7** calabar

bear: cub, lug **4** gest, tote, ursa **5** abide, allow, beget, breed, bring, brook, brown, bruin, carry, drive, geste, koala, Polar, press, stand, yield **6** affort, behave, endure, kadiak, kodiak, pierce, render, suffer, thrust, uphold **7** comport, conduct, forbear, grizzly, produce, support, sustain, undergo **8** forebear, tolerate **9** carnivore, transport **13** constellation

genus: **5** ursus

bear bane: 9 wolfsbane

bear bush: 8 inkberry

bear cat: 4 paud **9** binturong

bear-shaped: 8 ursiform

Bear State: 8 Arkansas

beard: ane, awn **4** avel, barb, defy **6** arista, goatee **7** affront, aristae, Vandyke **8** whiskers

bearded: 5 hairy **6** barbed **7** barbate, hirsute **9** whiskered **11** barbigerous

grain: rye **5** awned, wheat **8** aristate

bearer: 5 macer **6** beadle, porter **7** carrier **8** escudero, portator **9** supporter **10** pallbearer **11** gonfalonier

bearing: aim, air **4** gest, mien, orle, port **5** birth, front, geste, habit, poise, trend **6** allure, apport, aspect, course, gerent, manner, orient, thrust **7** address, conduct, meaning, posture, purport, support **8** amenance, attitude, behavior, carriage, demeanor, pressure, relation, tendency, yielding **9** behaviour, demeanour, direction, gestation, influence, personage, producing **10** cognizance, deportment **11** comportment, countenance **12** significance

fine: **6** belair

heraldic: **4** ente, orle **5** pheon

beast: 4 bete(F.) **5** brute **6** animal **7** monster **8** blighter **9** quadriped

mythical: **4** ogre, Rahu **5** Apepi, giant, harpy, hydra, Rahab **6** dragon, ellops, Empusa, garuda, Geryon, gorgon, Kraken, scylla, sphinx, triton **7** centaur, chimera, echidna, figfaun, griffin, griffon **8** chimaera, minotaur **9** bucentaur **10** jabberwock **11** chichevache

pertaining to: **7** leonine

royal: **4** lion

beast fly: 6 gadfly

beast of burden: ox; ass, yak **5** burro, camel, horse, llama **6** donkey, onager

beastly: 5 gross **6** brutal **7** bestial, brutish, inhuman, swinish **9** offensive **10** abominable, disgusting

beat: KO; bat, cob, dad, fan, fib, tap, taw, tew **4** baff, bang, bash, bate, belt, best, blow, bolt, bray, cane, chap, club, daud, ding, dint, drub, dump, dunt, fell, flap, flax, flog, frat, haze, lash, lump, maul, mill, pant, pelt, poss, prat, rout, scat, slam, tack, tick, tund, whip, whop **5** baste, berry, churn, clink, douse, feeze, fight, filch, flail, knock, pound, pulse, round, scatt, scoop, skelp, strap, threp, throb, thump, trump, whang, worst **6** accent, batter, beetle, bensel, buffet, cotton, cudgel, defeat, dowsel, feague, fettle, hammer, hamper, larrup, outrun, pummel, raddle, rhythm, squash, strike, stroke, swinge, switch, thrash, threap, threip, threpe, thresh **7** assault, battuta, belabor, blister, cadence, canvass, conquer, contuse, exhaust, fatigue, pulsate, reeshie, shellac, surpass, trounce, vibrate **8** belabour, fatigued, lambaste, overcome, shellack, slaister, van-

quish **9** exhausted, pulsation, throbbing
10 assignment
back: **7** repulse
into plate: **8** malleate
beat it: 4 scat **5** scram **7** vamoose
beater: rab **4** maul, seal **5** caner, lacer **6**
dasher, mallet **8** thresher **9** scrutcher
beatify: 6 hallow **7** enchant, glorify **8**
sanctify
beatitude: joy **5** bliss **7** benison **9** happiness **11** blessedness
beau: 5 beaux(pl.), blade, dandy, flame,
lover, spark, swell **6** garcon, escort, fellow, steady, suitor **7** admirer, bravery,
courter, coxcomb, cupidon, gallant **8** follower
Beau Brummell: 5 dandy
beautician: 10 beautifier, cosmetiste(F.)
11 cosmetician
beautifier: 8 cosmetic
beautiful: 4 fair, fine, glad, mear, meer,
mere **5** belle, bonny **6** blithe, bonnie,
comely, decore, freely, lovely, poetic,
pretty **7** elegant **8** charming, delicate,
fairsome, gorgeous, graceful, handsome **9**
exquisite
beautify: 4 gild **5** adorn, grace, hight,
preen, primp, prune **6** bedeck **7** adonize,
garnish **8** decorate, fairhead **9** embellish
beauty: 5 belle, charm, grace **6** looker,
polish **10** comeliness, goodliness, loveliness **11** pulchritude
goddess: Sri **5** Freya, Venus **6** Freyja **7**
Lakshmi **9** Aphrodite
lover: **7** esthete **8** aesthete
beaver: hat **4** coin **6** castor, rodent
cloth: **6** kersey
eater: **9** wolverine
skin: **4** plew
Beaver State: 6 Oregon
because: as, so; for **4** that **5** since **8** inasmuch
because of that: 7 thereby **9** therefore
bechance: 6 befall, chance
beche-de-mer: 4 grub, worm **6** pidgin **7**
trepang **8** language
beck: vat **5** becon, brook
becken: 7 cymbals
beckon: bow, nod **4** wave **6** curtsy, summon **7** bidding, command, curtsey, gesture **10** salutation
becloud: 4 hide **5** bedim **6** darken **7**
mystify, obscure **8** befuddle, overcast
become: get, wax **4** grow, pass, suit **5**
adorn, befit, grace **6** accord, befall,
beseem, betide, change **7** behoove, flatter
becoming: 4 good **5** right **6** comely, gainly **7** decorum, farrand, farrant **8** decorous, handsome, suitable **10** convenient
11 appropriate
becscie: 9 merganser
becuna: 9 barracuda

bed: cot, pad **4** base, bunk, doss, lair, plot
5 berth, couch, layer **6** bottom,
couche(F.), litter, matrix, pallet, strata **7**
channel, lodging, stratum **8** matrices,
plancher **9** basegrave, stretcher **10** apishamore, foundation
feather: tye
small: cot **4** crib **6** cradle, pallet **7** hammock, truckle, trundle **8** bassinet
straw: **9** shakedown
bed stay: 4 slat
bedbug: 5 cimex **6** chinch **7** cimice(pl.)
8 conenose
bedding: 6 quilts, sheets **8** blankets **10**
bedclothes
bedeck: gem **4** lard **5** adorn, array, dight,
grace **8** ornament **9** embellish
bedevil: 5 abuse, annoy, worry **6** muddle.
pester **7** bewitch, confuse, torment
bedim: fog **4** mist **5** cloud **6** darken **7** becloud, obscure
bedizen: 4 daub **5** adorn, array, dizen **6**
bedaub **9** overdress
bedlam: 4 riot **5** noise, rudas(Sc.) **6**
asylum, madman, tumult, uproar **7** lunatic, madness **8** madhouse **9** confusion
Bedouin: 4 Arab, Moor **5** nomad
bedridden: ill **6** ailing
bedrock: 5 nadir **6** bottom
bedroll: 6 bindle
bedroom: 4 flat **5** berth, cabin **11** compartment
bee: dor, fly **4** apis, ring **5** party **6** dingar,
insect, notion, torque **7** stinger **9** gathering **11** hymenoptera **12** hymenopteron
colony of: **5** swarm, yeast
comb. form: api
family: **5** apina **6** apidae
female: **5** queen
genus: **4** apis
house: gum **4** butt, hive, scap, skep **6** apiary **7** alveary, bee-butt **9** alvearium
house covering: **6** hackle
male: **5** drone
nose: **4** lora(pl.) **5** lorum
pert. to: **8** apiarian
pollen brush: **5** scopa **6** scopae(pl.), **9**
sarothrum
beech: 4 buck, tree **6** myrtle
genus: **5** fagus
beechnut: 4 mast
beef: 4 meat **5** gripe **8** complain
cut: **4** loin, rump, side **5** baron, chine,
chuck, flank, roast, round, shank, steak **6**
cutlet, saddle **7** brisket, knuckle, quarter,
sirloin **8** short-rib, shoulder **9** aitchbone,
rattleran **11** porterhouse
dried: **5** bucan, jerky, vifda, vivda **6** buccan **7** charqui
pickled: **5** bully
salted: **4** junk
spiced: **8** pastroma, pastromi

beefy: 5 hefty, heavy 6 brawny, fleshy, stolid

Beehive State: 4 Utah

beekeeper: 8 apiarist, skeppist 12 apiculturist

been: be; see

beer: ale, mum 4 bock, brew, grog, scud(Sc.) 5 kvass, lager, stout 6 liquor, porter, stingo, swanky 8 beverage

barley: 5 chang

cask: 4 butt

maize: 5 chica 6 chicha

mug: see *vessel,* below

vessel: mug 4 Toby 5 stein 6 flagon, seidel, tanker 8 schooner 9 blackjack

beery: 7 maudlin, muddled

beeswax substitute: 7 ceresin

beet: 5 chard, sugar 6 mangel 8 beetrave 9 vegetable

Beethoven:

birthplace: 4 Bonn

symphony: 5 fifth, first, ninth, sixth,·third 6 eighth, Eroica, fourth, second 7 seventh 8 Pastoral

beetle: bat, bug, jut, ram 4 beat, goga, gogo, maul, stag 5 amara, drive, gogga, hispa, meloe 6 chafer, golach, goloch, jutout, mallet, pestle, scarab, weevil 7 prinoid, project 8 lowering, overhang 9 prioninae(pl.) 10 battledore, projecting

bark: 5 borer

bright: 7 ladybug

family: 10 elateridae 11 clavicornes, clavicornia

fire: 6 cucuyo

genus: 5 fidia

ground: 5 amara

mustard: 9 blackjack

sacred: 6 scarab

beetle-head: 6 plover 9 blockhead

befall: hap 4 come 5 occur 6 astart, become, betide, happen 7 pertain 8 bechance

befile: 4 soil 6 defile

befit: dow 4 suit 5 beset 6 become, behove, beseem, betide 7 behoove

beflum: 7 deceive

befog: 5 cloud 6 obsane 7 confuse, mystify

before: ere 4 said 5 ahead, afore, avant, coram(L.), first, forby, front, prior 6 forbye, former, rather, sooner 7 already, earlier, forward 8 anterior, hitherto 10 beforehand, heretofore, previously

prefix: pre, pro 4 ante, prae

before long: 4 anon, soon 9 presently

before now: ere 4 gone, over 6 erenow

befoul: 4 soil 5 dirty 6 bemire, defile 7 pollute 8 entangle 11 contaminate

befriend: aid 4 abet, help 5 favor 6 assist, favour, foster, succor 7 benefit, support, sustain 11 countenance

befuddle: 5 addle, besot 6 muddle 7 becloud, confuse, fluster, mystify, stupefy

beg: ask, bid, sue, woo 4 coax, pray, sorn(Sc.) 5 cadge, crave, mooch, plead 6 adjure 7 beseech, entreat, implore, request, solicit 8 petition 9 importune, panhandle 10 supplicate

beget: 4 bear, sire 5 breed, yield 6 create, father 7 acquire, engraff 8 engender, generate 9 germinate, procreate

begetter: 4 sire 6 author, father, mother, parent

beggar: 4 ruin 5 asker, randy, rogue 6 alsman, bacach, bidder, canter, devour, mumper, pariah, pauper, wretch 8 palliard, stroller 9 maunderer, mendicant, schnorrer, suppliant 10 impoverish, panhandler, petitioner, starveling 12 hallan-shaker

speech: 4 cant

beggarly: 4 mean, poor 5 cheap, petty, sorry 6 abject, paltry 8 bankrupt, indigent 10 despicable 12 contemptible

begin: 4 fang, lead, open, rise 5 arise, enter, start 6 attack, spring 8 commence, inchoate, initiate 9 institute, introduce, originate 10 inaugurate

begin again: 4 anew, over 5 renew 6 resume 7 restart

beginner: 4 boot, tiro, tyro 5 rooky 6 novice, rookie 7 amateur, entrant, noviate, recruit, trainee, student 8 freshman, neophyte 9 candidate, debutante, postulate, 10 apprentice

beginning: egg 4 dawn, edge, germ, rise, root, seed 5 alpha, birth, debut, start 6 source 7 genesis, geneses(pl.), initial, nascent 8 entrance, exordium, inchoate, rudiment 9 embryonic, inception, incipient 10 conception, foundation, incunabula(pl.), initiation 11 incunabulum 12 commencement

begone: off, out, out 4 away, scat, shoo 5 scoot, scram 6 aroint, avaunt, depart 7 vamoose

begrudging: 6 loathe, grudge 7 envious, grumble 9 reluctant

beguile: fox 4 coax, foil, gull, lure 5 amuse, charm, cheat, cozen, elude, evade, trick 6 brique, delude, divert, entrap 7 deceive, ensnare, flatter, mislead 9 entertain

behalf: 4 part, sake, side 5 stead 6 affair, matter, profit 7 benefit, defence, support 8 interest 9 advantage

behave: act 4 bear, work 5 carry, react, treat 6 acquit, demean, deport, handle 7 comport, conduct, gesture, manager 8 function, regulate, restrain

behavior, behaviour: air 4 port, mien 5 guise 6 action, manner 7 bearing, comport, decorum 8 amenance, breeding, carriage **9** demeanour **10** deportment, governance

behead: **9** decollate **10** decapitate, guillotine

behemoth: **4** huge **5** beast, giant, hippo **7** monster

behest: bid, law **4** hest, rule **5** order **6** demand **7** command, mandate **10** injunction

behind: aft **.4** past, rear, ward, rump **5** abaff, abaft, after, ahind(Sc.), arear, later, passe, tardy **6** arrear, astern **8** backward, dilatory **9** posterior **10** afterwards

behold: lo; eye, see, spy **4** ecce, espy, gaze, hold, keep, look, scan, stop, view, wait **5** sight, voila, watch **6** descry, regard, retain **7** discern, observe, witness **8** consider, maintain, perceive

beholden: **7** obliged **8** indebted

behoof: use **6** profit **7** benefit **8** interest **9** advantage

behoove: dow, fit **4** need, suit **5** befit, ought **6** belong, proper **7** require **8** suitable **9** incumbent

beige: tan **4** ecru **5** color, grege(F.) **10** unbleached

being: ens **4** self **5** entia, entre(F.), gnome, human, troll **6** animal, entity, extant, living, mortal, person **7** essence, present, reality **8** creature, ontology, standing **9** actuality, existence **11** subsistence **12** constitution

abstract: ens **5** entia

actual: **4** esse

in front: **6** anteal

science of: **8** ontology

suffix: ure

beken: **7** commend, deliver, entrust, intrust

beknow: **7** confess **9** recognize **11** acknowledge

Bela's son: Ard, Iri **4** Uzzi **5** Ezbon

Bel's wife: **5** Belit **6** Beltis

belabor, belabour: ply **4** beat, drub, lash, work **6** assail, cudgel, hammer, hamper, thrash, thwack

belair: **7** bearing **10** deportment

Belait: **6** Europe

belamour: **5** lover **6** flower **8** ladylove

belated: **5** lated, tardy **7** delayed, overdue

belay: **5** beset **6** invest, waylay **7** besiege **8** encircle

belch: **4** boke, bolk, galp, rasp **5** eruct **8** eructate **10** eructation

beldam, beldame: hag **4** fury **5** crone, jixen **6** alecto, erinys, virago **7** Jezebel **8** ancestor **9** Tisiphone **11** grandmother

beleaguer: **5** belay, beset **6** invest **7** assault, besiege **8** blockade, surround **9** encompass

belfry: **4** shed **5** tower **7** clocher **9** campanile

Belgian: **7** Fleming, Walloon

Belgian Congo:

animal: **5** okapi

river: **4** Uele

ruminant: **5** okapi

tribe: Rua **5** Bantu, Warua **7** Batetla

Belgium:

anthem: **11** Brabanconne

city: Ans, Spa **4** Gand, Mons **5** Alost, Ciney, Eupen, Ghent, Jumet, Liege, Namur, Ypres **6** Bruges, Deurne, Lierre, Merxem, Ostend, Turnai **7** Antwerp, Berchem, Herstal, Hoboken, Ixelles, Louvain, Mechlin, Roulers, Seraing **8** Brussels(c.), Courtrai, Mouscron, Turnhout, Verviers **9** Charleroi, Molenbeek **10** Anderlecht, Borgerhout, Schaerbeek

coin: **5** belga, franc **7** centime

commune: Ath, Ely, Hal, Mol, Spa **4** Aath, Boom, Geel, Genk, Lier, Zele **5** Aalst, Alost, Evere, Genck, Jette, Ronse, Uccle, Ukkel

endive: **7** witloof

Gaul tribe: **4** Remi **6** Nervii

marble: **5** rance

measure: vat **4** aune, last, pied **5** carat **6** perche **8** boisseau

province: Spa **5** Liege, Namur **7** Antwerp, Brabant, Hainaut, Limburg **8** Flanders **9** Luxemburg

river: Lys **4** Dyle, Leie, Maas, Yser **5** Meuse, Rupel **6** Dender, Ourthe, Sambre **7** Schelde, Scheldt

seaport: **6** Ostend

tribe: **9** Bellovaci

weight: **4** last **5** carat, livre, pound **6** charge **7** chariot **8** esterlin

Belgrade native: **4** Serb

Belial: **5** devil, satan

belie: **6** belong, defame **7** besiege, falsify, pertain, slander, traduce **8** disguise, strumpet, surround **9** encompass **10** calumniate, contradict **11** counterfeit **12** misrepresent

belief: fay, ism **4** mind, sect, view **5** credo, creed, dogma, faith, tenet, troth, trust **6** credit **7** opinion **8** credence, doctrine, reliance **9** assurance **10** confidence, conviction, persuasion

liable to: **7** credent **9** credulous

believe: wis **4** deem, trow, ween **5** judge, think, trust **6** accept, credit **7** suppose **8** accredit, consider, credence

believer: ist **8** adherent

in all religions: **6** omnist

in God: **5** deist **6** theist

in predestination: **13** particularist

Belili's brother: **6** Tammuz

belittle: **5** decry, dwarf, sneer **6** slight **7** detract **8** minimize **9** denigrate, discredit, disparage **10** depreciate

bell: **4** call, fair, gong, ring, roar **5** chime, cloak, codon, flare, knell, swell **6** bellow, bubble(Sc.), crotal, curfew, tocsin **7** blossom, campana, campane, corolla **9** beautiful **13** tintinnabulum

axle bearing: cod

clapper: **6** tongue

kind of: cow **4** door, gong, hand **5** ship's **6** church, jingle, school, **8** electric

part: **7** baldric **8** baldrick

ringer: **6** toller **12** carillonneur

room: **6** belfry

sound: **4** ding, dong, toll **5** knell **6** tinkle

tower: **6** belfry **9** campanile

bell ear: 6 cannon

bell-mouthed: 5 evase(F.)

bell-shaped: 11 campanulate

belladonna: 5 dwale, plant **6** remedy **7** manicon **8** narcotic **9** dwayberry **10** nightshade

extract: **7** atropin **8** atropine

bellbird: 6 shrike **8** arapunga

Bellerophon:

father: **7** Glaucus

spring: **7** Pelrene

belles-lettres: 10 literature

bellicose: mad **5** irate **7** hostile, warlike **8** militant **10** pugnacious **11** belligerent

belligerent: 7 hostile, warlike **8** choleric, fighting, jingoist **9** bellicose, combative, irascible, litigious, wrangling **10** pugnacious **11** contentious, quarrelsome **12** disputatious

Bellini:

opera: **5** Norma

sleepwalker: **5** Amina

bellow: cry, low, moo, yap **4** bawl, beal, bell, roar, rout, yaup, yawp **5** belve, blart, croon, roust(Sc.), shout **6** buller, clamor **7** bluster, clamour, ululate **10** vociferate

bellware: 4 kelp

bellweed: 8 knapweed

bellwether: 5 sheep **6** leader

belly: bag, cod, gie(Sc.), gut, pod **4** bouk, kyte(Sc.) **5** bingy, bulge, pleon **6** hunger paunch **7** abdomen, stomach **8** appetite

bellying: 7 bunting

belong: 4 bear **5** apply, belie **6** inhere, relate **7** pertain **9** appertain

belongings: 4 gear **5** goods, traps **6** assets, estate **7** effects **8** chattels, property **9** household **10** appendages **11** possessions **13** appurtenances

beloved: 4 dear, idol **5** cheri(F.) **6** adored, cherie(F.) **7** darling **8** precious **9** inamorata, valentine

below: 4 alow, down **5** ablow, infra, sotto(It.), under **7** beneath **8** downward, inferior **10** downstairs, underneath

belt: 4 area, band, beat, blow, cest, gird, mark, ring, sash, zone **5** girth, strap, strip, tract, whack, zonar **6** bodice, cestus, cingle, fettle, girdle, invest, region, strait, stripe, zonnar, zonule **7** circuit, passage **8** cincture, encircle, surround **9** bandoleer, encompass **10** cummerbund, kummerbund

conveyor: **5** apron

ecclesiastical: **7** balteus **8** baltheus

sword: **7** baldric **8** boldrick

belted: 6 zonate **7** girdled **9** cinctured

bench: 4 banc, seat **5** judge, stool **6** settee

church: pew, pue **6** sedile(L.)

bend: bow, nid, ply, sag **4** arch, flex, kink, turn **5** angle, baton, bulge, crimp, crook, curve, stoop, twist **6** buckle, cotice, cotise, crouch, direct, divert, fasten, inflex, submit **7** bendlet, incline, refract **9** genuflect

backward: **6** retort

in timber: sny

bender: leg **5** drunk, spree **7** whopper **8** guzzling, sixpence

bending: 5 lithe **6** pliant, supple **7** anfract, flexion **8** flection

beneath: 5 aneth(Sc.), below, lower, under **6** aneath **10** underneath **11** underground

benedict: 4 mild **6** benign, kindly **7** blessed **8** bachelor, gracious, salutary **9** benignant, favorable, wholesome **10** propitious

Benedictine: 4 monk **7** Cluniac, liqueur

title: dom

benediction: 4 amen **6** prayer **7** benison **8** blessing **10** invocation

benefaction: 4 alms, boon, gift **7** benefit, present **8** benefice, donation, gratuity **11** beneficence

benefactor: 5 agent, angel, donor **6** friend, helper, patron, savior **8** promoter **14** philanthropist

benefice: feu **4** fief **5** favor **6** curacy, favour, living **7** benefit, rectory **8** kindness, vicarage **10** beneficium **11** benefaction

first fruit: **5** annat **6** annate

beneficence: 4 boon, gift **5** grace **6** bounty **7** charity **8** goodness, kindness **11** benefaction

beneficial: 4 good **6** useful **7** helpful **8** salutary **9** available, benignant, desirable, enjoyable, healthful, lucrative, wholesome **10** beneficent, profitable, salubrious **11** serviceable **12** advantageous, remunerative

beneficiary: 4 heir, user **5** donee **6** vassal **7** legatee **9** feudatory

benefit: aid, use **4** boon, boot, gain, gift, help, prow, sake **5** avail, boost **6** assist, behalf, behoof, better, profit, usance **7** advance, bespeak, concert, deserve, improve, service, utility **8** benefice, befriend, interest **9** advantage, emolument **11** benefaction, performance

benevolent: 4 good, kind **6** benign, loving **7** amiable, liberal **8** generous **9** benignant **10** altruistic, charitable, munificent **13** philanthropic

Bengal:

boat: **5** batel **6** baulea **7** bauleah

capital: **5** Dacca

city: see *town* below

cotton: **5** adati, adaty

district: **5** Dacca, Nadia

gentlemen: **5** baboo

hemp: **4** sunn

measure: **5** cotta **6** cottah **8** chattack

native: Ebo, Kol **4** Eboe **6** Banian
quince: bel **4** bael, bhel
root: **10** cassumunar
singer: **4** baul
town: **5** Dacca(c.) **6** Madras **7** Barisal, Rangoon **8** Calcutta **9** Tittacarh
tree: **4** bola
benign: **4** boon, good, kind, mild **5** bland **6** genial, gentle **7** affable **8** benedict, gracious, salutary **9** benignant, favorable, wholesome **10** benevolent, favourable, propitious, salubrious
benison: **8** blessing **9** beatitude **10** invocation **11** benediction
Benjamin:
descendant: **4** Aher
grandson: Iri
son: Ehi **4** Gera, Rosh
benne: **6** sesame
bent: aim, bow, set **4** bias, gift, turn **5** bound, bowed, crank, crump, flair, knack, prone, taste, trend **6** akimbo, biased, braced, courbe, course, curved, energy, genius, hooked, swayed, talent **7** crooked, curvant, flexion, flexure, impetus, leaning, leveled, pronate, purpose, stooped, tension **8** aptitude, declined, flection, penchant, tendency **9** curvature, direction, prejudice **10** determined, proclivity, propensity **11** disposition, inclination **13** prepossession **14** predisposition
benthonic plant: **6** enalid
benumb: nip **4** daze, dunt, numb, stun **5** daver **6** cumber, deaden **7** fretish, fretize, stupefy
benzine derivative: **6** phenol
Beowulf: **4** epic, poem
bequeath: **4** give, will **5** endow, leave, offer **6** bestow, commit, demise, devise, legate, quethe **7** bequest, commend **8** transmit **9** testament
bequest: **4** gift, will **6** legacy **8** bequeath, heritage, pittance **9** endowment
berate: jaw, nag **4** lash, rail **5** abuse, chide, scold, score **6** revile **7** censure, reprove, upbraid **8** chastise **10** vituperate
bereave: rob **5** strip **6** divest, sadden **7** deprive, despoil **10** dispossess
bereft: orb **4** lorn, lost, poor **7** forlorn **9** destitute **12** dispossessed
beret: cap, hat, tam **7** biretta, chapeau **8** berretta, chapeaux(pl.), headgear
berg: ice **4** floe **6** barrow **8** eminence, mountain
bergamot: **4** bose, mint, pear **5** snuff **6** orange **7** Bergama, essence, perfume
bergstock: **10** alpenstock
beriberi: **5** kakke
Berlin park: **10** Tiergarten
berm, berme: **4** bank, edge, path **5** ledge, shelf **7** terrace
Bermuda:
arrowroot: **5** aruru **6** ararao

barracuda: **4** spet
berry: **9** soapberry
capital: **8** Hamilton
catfish: **6** coelho
ceremony: **6** gombay
grass: **4** doob
berry: bay, dew, haw **4** beat, cran, rasp **5** acini, bacca, black, fruit, mound, salal, savin **6** acinus, baccae, burrow, sabine, thresh **7** currant, burrow, hillock
medicinal: **5** cubeb
oil: **5** olive
berry-like: **7** baccate
berserk: mad **5** bravo **6** pirate **7** enraged, warrior **8** frenzied, maniacal
berth: bed, job **4** bunk, dock, slip **5** place **6** billet, office **7** lodging, mooring **8** position **9** anchorage, situation **11** appointment
beryl: gem **5** jewel **7** emerald **10** aquamarine
green: **11** davidsonite
yellow: **8** heliodor
beseech: ask, beg, sue **4** pray **5** crave, plead **6** adjure, appeal, obtest **7** entreat, implore, solicit **9** impetrate, obsecrate **10** supplicate
beseeching: **9** precative
beset: ply **4** sail, stud **5** allot, belay, harry, siege, spend **6** assail, attack, harass, infest **7** arrange, besiege, perplex **8** blockade, encumber, obstruct, surround **9** beleaguer
beside: by **4** hear **5** along, aside **7** abreast **8** adjacent
comb. form: **4** para **5** juxta
besides: by; and, but, too, yet **4** also, else, over, then **6** beside, beyond, except **8** moreover **10** additional **11** furthermore
besiege: **4** gird, girt **5** belay, belie, beset, siege, storm **6** attack, pester, plague **7** solicit **8** surround **9** beleaguer
besmear: ray **4** balm, daub, soil **5** apply, cover, muddy, smear, sully, taint **6** bedaub **7** beslime, smother **8** besmirch
besmirch: **4** soil **5** smear, sully **6** smirch **7** asperse, blacken **8** discolor
besom: map **4** drab(Sc), **5** broom, sweep **6** sloven(Sc.), **7** heather
besot: **4** dull **6** muddle, stupid **7** stupefy **8** befuddle **9** infatuate
bespangle: dot **4** stud, star **5** adorn **8** sprinkle
bespatter: **4** blot, dash, soil, spot **5** muddy, plash, stain, sully **6** sparge **7** asperse, scatter **8** reproach, sprinkle
bespeak: **4** cite, hint, show **5** argue, imply, order, speak **6** accost, attest, engage, steven **7** address, arrange, benefit, betoken, discuss, exclaim, reserve **8** foretell, indicate **9** stipulate
best: ace **4** a-one, beat, most, tops, wale **5**

elite, excel, worst **6** choice, defeat, finest, flower, outwit, utmost **7** conquer, largest, optimum **8** greatest, outmatch, outstrip, vanquish **9** excellent, overmatch **11** superlative

comb. form: **5** arist **6** aristo

bestial: low **4** vile, wild **5** brute, feral **6** brutal, filthy **7** beastly, brutish, inhuman, sensual **8** depraved **10** irrational

bestir: **5** rouse

bestow: add, put, use **4** deal, dote, give **5** allot, allow, apply, award, beset, grant, lodge, place **6** accord, beteem, confer, demise, devote, divide, donate, employ, entail, extend, impart, render **7** collate, dispose, instate, present, quarter, tribute **8** bequeath **11** communicate

bestraddle: **8** bestride

bestride: **6** stride **8** straddle **10** bestraddle

bet: lay **4** ante, gage, play, plot, risk, wage **5** hedge, stake, wager **6** gamble, pledge

faro: **7** sleeper

roulette: bas **4** noir **5** carre **6** milieu **7** dernier, encarre, enplein

betake: go; hie **4** move **5** apply, catch, grant **6** assume, commit, repair, remove, resort **7** commend, journey

bete: **5** beast, silly **6** stupid **7** foolish

betel-nut: **5** areca

leaf: **4** buyo, puan

pepper: **4** ikmo, itmo

seed: **7** catechu

bethel: **6** chapel

Bethesda: **4** pool **6** chapel

bethink: **5** think **6** devise, recall **7** reflect **8** consider, remember **9** recollect **10** deliberate

Bethuel's son: **5** Laban

betide: hap **5** befit, occur, trite **6** become, befall, chance, happen **7** betoken, presage

betimes: **4** anon, rath, soon **5** early, rathe **8** speedily **9** forthwith **10** seasonably **12** occasionally

betise: **5** folly **9** silliness, stupidity

betoken: **4** mark, note, show **5** augur **6** assert, betide, denote, evince, import **7** bespeak, express, forbode, oblique, portend, presage, signify **8** forebode, foreshow, indicate **9** symbolize **10** foreshadow **13** prognosticate

betray: **4** blab, blow, boil, gull, sell, sile, sing, tell, undo, wray **5** peach, spill **6** accuse, delude, descry, reveal, seduce, snitch, squeal **7** beguile, deceive, falsify, mislead **8** disclose, discover

betrayer: rat **5** Judas, skunk **7** seducer, traitor **8** derelict

betroth: **4** affy **6** assure, engage, ensure, pledge, plight **7** espouse, promise **8** affiance, contract, handfast

better: aid, top **4** mend **5** amend, emend, excel, safer, wiser **6** bigger, exceed, re-form **7** advance, choicer, correct, greater, improve, promote, rectify, relieve, support, surpass **8** increase, superior **9** meliorate **10** ameliorate, preferable

better half: **4** wife

betting:

adviser: **4** tout

figures: **4** odds

odds: **5** price

between: **4** amid **5** amell, among, entre(F.) **7** average, betwixt **12** intermediate

law: **5** mesne

prefix: dia **4** meta **5** inter

bevel: **4** blow(Sc.), cant, edge, push(Sc.) **5** angle, bezel, miter, mitre, slant, slope **6** aslant **7** chamfer, incline, oblique

corners: **5** splay

end of timber: **5** snape

out: **4** ream

beverage: ade, ale, nog, pop, tea **4** beer, grog, mead, milk, soda, wine **5** cider, cocoa, draft, drink, lager, leban, negus, morat, punch, treat, water **6** coffee, eggnog, liquid, liquor, nectar, posset **7** potable **8** cocktail, potation **9** metheglin **10** melicratum

alcoholic: see **alcoholic drink**

container: vat **6** kettle **7** charger **9** separator

extract: **4** kola

malted wheat: **6** zythem, zythum

mixed: **5** negus, punch, smash **6** bishop

mulberry and honey: **5** morat

Oriental: rak **4** sake **5** rakee **6** arrack

pepper: **4** kava

South American: **4** mate

bevy: **4** herd, pack **5** covey, drove, flock, group, swarm **6** flight, school **7** company **8** assembly **9** gathering, multitude **10** collection

bewail: cry, rue **4** keen, moan, sigh, wail, weep **5** mourn **6** bemoan, grieve, lament, plaint, sorrow **7** deplore **8** complain

beware: **4** cave, heed, shun **5** avoid, spend **6** eschew **7** warning

bewilder: fog **4** daze, foil, gaum **5** abash, addle, amaze, amuse, deave **6** baffle, bemist, bother, dazzle, muddle, puzzle **7** buffalo, confuse, mystify, perplex, stagger, stupefy **8** astonish, confound, distract, entangle, surprise **9** embarrass, obfuscate **10** spifficate **11** spifflicate

bewildered: **4** asea, lost, mang **5** agape, dazed **8** confused, helpless **9** perplexed

bewilderment: awe, fog **4** daze **9** amazement, confusion **10** perplexity **11** distraction **13** distration

bewitch: hex **5** charm, fasci, spell **6** enamor, entice, glamor, grigri, hoodoo, thrill **7** bedevil, delight, enchant, glamour **8** ensorcel, forspeak, greegree **9** captivate, ensorcell, fascinate

bewith: **9** makeshift **10** substitute

bewray: 4 show, tell 6 accuse, betray, expose, malign, reveal 7 divulge 8 disclose
bey: 6 beylic, beylik 8 governor
beyond: by 4 free, over 5 above, aside, forby, ultra 6 forbye, yonder 7 besides, further 8 superior 9 hereafter
prefix: sur 4 meta 5 ultra
the sea: 11 ultramarine
the threshold: 12 ultraliminal
bezel, basil: rim 4 edge, ouch, seal 5 bevil, bezil, crown, facet 6 chaton, flange 8 template
bezezteen: 5 bazar 6 bazaar
bezzle: 5 drink, revel, waste 7 consume, plunder 10 gluttonize
bhagavat: 7 blessed
bhakta: 7 devotee 9 bhagavata, worshiper
bhalu: 4 bear
bhandar: 5 store 7 library 10 storehouse
bhandari: 7 steward 9 treasurer
bhang, bang: 7 hashish 8 narcotic 10 intoxicant
bharal: tur 5 sheep 6 nahoor
bhat: 4 bard 8 minstrel
bhikku: 4 monk 5 friar 6 priest 9 mendicant
bhikshu: 5 friar 7 ascetic 9 mendicant
bhoosa: 5 chaff, husks, straw
b'hoy: 5 rowdy 8 gangster
bias: 4 awry, bent, sway 5 amiss, color, slant, slope 7 bigotry, incline, oblique 8 clinamen, diagonal, tendency 9 clinamina(pl.), prejudice, procedure 10 favoritism, partiality, prepossess, propensity 11 declination, disposition, favouritism, inclination 12 predetermine, predilection 13 prepossession
biased: 11 tendentious
bib: sip 4 brat, fish 5 apron, drink 6 tipple, tucker 7 bavette(F.), 9 neckpiece 10 protection
bibelot: 5 curio 7 trinket 8 ornament
Bible:
angel: 5 Micah 7 Raphael
animal: 4 reem 5 daman 6 hydrax 8 behemoth
apocrypha: 5 Tobit 6 Baruch, Esdras, Jeremy, Judith, Syriac, Wisdom 7 Vulgate 8 Manasses 9 Maccabees 10 Septuagint 14 Ecclesiasticus
battle scene: 10 Armageddon
book: Job 4 Acts, Amos, Ezra, Joel, John, Jude, Luke, Mark, Ruth 5 Hosea, James, Jonah, Kings, Micah, Peter, Titus 6 Daniel, Esther, Exodus, Haggai, Isaiah, Joshua, Psalms, Romans, Samuel 7 Ezekiel, Genesis, Hebrews, Matthew, Numbers, Obadiah, Timothy 8 Habakkuk, Jeremiah, Nehemiah, Philemon, Proverbs 9 Apocrypha, Ephesians, Galatians, Leviticus, Zechariah 10 Chronicles, Colossians, Revelation 11 Corinthians, Deuteronomy,

Philippians 12 Ecclesiastes, Lamentations 13 Song of Solomon, Thessalonians
character: see *name* below
city: Ain, Dan 4 Arad, Aven, Cana, Elim, Elon, Gath, Gaza, Geba, Maon, Rome, Tyre 5 Akkad, Arvad, Ashur, Assur, Joppa, Sidon, Sodom 6 Bethel, Biblos, Gadara, Jerico, Tarsus 7 Babylon, Nineveh 8 Gomorrah, Nazareth 9 Jerusalem
clan: 6 Shelah
country: Nod, Pul 4 Aram, Bela, Edam, Elam, Gath, Hali, Moab, Seba, Seir 5 Ammon 6 Canaan 7 Galilee, Samaria
giant: 4 Anak, Emim 7 Goliath
giant killer: 5 David
hunter: 6 Nimrod
judge: 4 Agog, Elon
king: Og, Asa, Iva 4 Agag, Ahab, Ahaz, Amon, Bera, Omri, Reba, Saul 5 David, Herod, Tidal 6 Birsha 7 Jehoram, Solomon
kingdom: 4 Elam, Moab 5 Judea, Judah 6 Israel 8 Chaldeae
land of plenty: 6 Goshen
liar: 7 Ananias
mountains: Hor 4 Ebal, Nebo, Peor, Sina, Sion, Zion 5 Heres, Horeb, Sinai 6 Ararat, Gilead, Moriah, Olivet, Pisgah
name: Ai, Ar, Ir: Ahi, Asa, Eri, Eve, Evi, Hor, Iri, Koa, Lot, Ner, Ono, Reu, Toi, Uel, Uri 4 Abel, Acan, Acub, Adam, Ader, Adna, Ador, Agee, Aher, Aman, Anak, Anam, Aner, Aram, Arem, Arie, Asan, Asom, Ater, Aven, Azal, Cain, Cana, Dura, Edar, Edec, Edes, Eker, Enan, Enos, Eran, Esau, Etam, Gera, Irad, Iram, Isac, Mary, Neri, Obal, Omar, Oreb, Oren, Paul, Reba, Sami, Sara, Seth, Suba, Ucal, Vale 5 Ahlab, Alian, Amasa, Aroer, Bedan, Besai, Caleb, Elias, Ephai, Esrom, Hadad, Hanes, Isaac, Mered, Nehum, Oseas, Peleg, Rahad, Tarah, Vania 6 Naaman, Pilate, Ramath 7 Abadias, Abigail, Antioch, Elmodam, Idithum, Sidrach, Tabitha
navigator: 4 Noah
ornament: 4 urim
patriarch: 6 Israel
people: 4 Seba 5 Ammon 7 Amorite, Dodanim, Moabite
plotter: 5 Haman
pool: 6 Siloam
priest: Eli 5 Aaron 6 Levite
pronoun: ye; thy 4 thee, thou 5 thine
prophet: 4 Amos, Ezra 5 Elias 6 Elijah 8 Jeremiah
psalmist: 5 David
queen: 5 Sheba 6 Esther, Vashti
region: 4 Enon 5 Ophir, Perea 6 Bashan
reproach: 4 raca
river: Zab 4 Nile 5 Abana, Arnon 6 Kishon, Jordan

scholar: **7** Biblist **9** Biblicist
sea: Red **4** Dead **7** Galilee **8** Tiberias **10** Gennesaret
shepherd: **4** Abel **5** David
spice: **5** myrrh **6** stacte **12** frankincense
spy: **5** Caleb
stone: **4** ezel **6** ligure
tower: **4** Edar **5** Babel
town: see *city* above
valley: **4** Baca, Elah **6** Shaveh, Siddim
version: Av, RV **4** Geez **5** Douay, Itala **6** Syriac **7** Vulgate **8** Bohairic **9** Apocrypha, King James **10** New English **15** Revised Standard
weed: **4** tare
witch's home: **5** Endor
Biblical: 10 scriptural
bicker: war **4** bowl, spar, tiff **5** argue, brawl, cavil, fight **6** assail, attack, battle **7** contend, dispute, quarrel, wrangle **8** pettifog, skirmish, squabble **10** contention
bicycle: 4 bike **5** wheel
for two: **6** tandem
rider: **7** cyclist
bid: beg **4** call, hist, pray **5** clepe, offer, order **6** adjure, charge, direct, enjoin, invite, reveal, tender **7** command, declare, entreat, proffer **8** announce, proclaim, proposal
biddable: 6 docile **8** obedient
biddy: hen **7** chicken
bide: 4 face, stay, wait **5** abide, await, dwell, tarry **6** endure, remain, suffer **7** sojourn **8** continue, tolerate **9** encounter, withstand
bield: den **4** cozy **5** dwell **7** comfort, courage, hearten, protect, shelter **8** boldness, embolden **9** sheltered **10** confidence, habitation
bien, bein: 4 fine, good, snug **6** genial **8** pleasant, thriving **10** prosperous **11** comfortable
bier: 4 pyre **5** frame, grave **6** coffin, hearse, litter **7** support **10** catafalque, handbarrow
bifarious: 7 twofold **9** ambiguous
biff: 4 blow
bifid: 6 forked
bifocal: 4 lens
bifold: 6 double **7** twofold
bifurcation: wye **4** fork **5** split **6** branch **8** division
big: 4 bold, huge, vast **5** bulky, chief, grand, great, gross, large **6** mighty **7** bumping, eminent, leading, massive, pompous, violent **8** boastful, bouncing, enormous, generous, gigantic, imposing, pregnant **9** notorious **10** tremendous **11** magnanimous, outstanding, pretentious, threatening
Big Bend State: 9 Tennessee
big shot: VIP

bighorn: 5 sheep **6** argali, aoudad **8** cimarron
bight: bay **4** bend, coil, gulf, loop **5** angle, curve, inlet, noose **6** corner, hollow
bignou, biniou: 7 bagpipe
bigot: 6 cafard, zealot **7** fanatic **9** hypocrite
bigoted: 6 biased, narrow **9** hidebound, illiberal, sectarian **10** intolerant, prejudiced **12** narrow-minded
bijou: 5 jewel **7** trinket
bilbie: 6 refuge **7** shelter
bile: 4 boil, gall, hump **5** venom **6** choler, growth
bilge: 4 scum **5** bouge, bulge
bilingual: diglot
bilk: do, gyp **4** balk, hoax **5** cheat, cozen, trick **6** delude, fleece **7** deceive, defraud, swindle **9** frustrate **10** disappoint
bill: act, dun, law, neb, nib, tab **4** beak, note, peck **5** libel, score **6** caress, charge, indict, pickax, poster, strike **7** invoice, lampoon, mattock, placard, statute **8** billhook, document, headland, petition **9** memoranda(pl.), statement **10** broadsword, memorandum, promontory **13** advertisement
anchor: pee
five dollar: fin, vee
one dollar: **4** buck **8** frogskin
ten dollar: **7** sawbuck
bill of fare: 4 card, menu **5** carte
billet: bar, gad, log **4** loop, note, pass, post **5** berth, enrol, house, lodge, order, stick, strap **6** ballot, enroll, harbor, letter, notice, ticket **7** bearing, epistle, harbour, missive, pollack **8** coalfish, document, firewood, ornament, position, quarters **11** appointment, requisiton
billfish: gar **8** sailfish **9** spearfish
billiard:
cue: **4** mace
shot: **5** carom, masse **7** bricole
rod: cue
billiards: 4 game, pool
billionaire: 6 nabob
billow: sea **4** wave **5** bulge, float, surge, swell **6** ripple, roller **7** breaker **8** undulate
billowing: 5 tidal **7** surging
billy: caw **4** chap, club, goat, mate **6** cudgel, fellow **7** brother, comrade **8** billikin, bludgeon **9** blackjack
bin: ark, box, cub **4** bing, cart, crib, vina **5** frame, hutch, pungi, stall, store, wagon **6** basket, bunker, hamper, manger, trough, within **9** container **10** receptacle
coal: **6** bunker
fish: **5** canch, kench
binate: 4 dual **6** double, paired **7** coupled, twofold
bind: jam, tie **4** gird, hold, tape **5** stick **7** confine

to secrecy: **4** tile, tyle
tightly: **4** frap
binder: **4** band, beam, bond, cord, rope **5** baler, cover, frame, lever **6** fillet, folder, girder, header **9** bondstone
binding: **4** band, cord, rope, tape **5** valid **6** edging, ribbon **7** galloon, mousing, webbing **9** stringent **10** astringent, obligatory **11** restraining, restrictive
limp: **4** yapp
binge: bow, hit **4** blow, soak **5** beano, party, spree **6** cringe **8** carousal **9** obeisance
bingo: **4** game, keno **5** lotto **6** brandy
biography: **4** life, vita(It.) **6** memoir **7** account, history, memoire(F.), recount
saint's: **11** hagiography
biological class: **5** genus **6** genera(pl.) **7** species
biological factor: id **4** gene **5** idant
biology: **7** ecology **8** genetics
biose: **11** disaccharid **12** disaccharide
biotite: **4** mica **7** anomite
biplane: **4** spad **8** airplane
birch: **4** cane, flog, tree, whip **5** canoe **6** betula **7** hickory
bird: ani, daw, nun, pie, tit **4** avis(L.), crow, kite, lark, ruff, tern, wren **5** brant, egret, finch, hobby, pewee, pewit, raven, robin, snipe, terek, vireo **6** bulbul, dunlin, falcon, hoopoe, linnet, marten, mocker, oriole, phoebe, plover, shrike, thrush **7** bluejay, bustard, buzzard, catbird, flicker, halcyon, irrisor, jackdaw, kinglet, ortolan, peacock, redwing, skylark, sparrow, swallow, tanager, warbler, waxwing **8** airplane, bluebird, boatbill, bobolink, bobwhite, chicadee, grosbeak, kingbird, pheasant, redstart, starling, thrasher **9** blackbird, blackcock, brambling, bullfinch, goldfinch, partridge, phalarope, sandpiper **10** bufflehead, meadowlark, tropicbird, woodpecker **11** butcherbird, hummingbird **12** yellowhammer
adjutant: **5** stork **6** argala **7** hurgila, marabou
African: **4** taha **8** umbrette
American: **4** sora **5** robin, vireo **6** darter, fulmar, turkey **7** grackle, tanager **8** cardinal **10** bufflehead
Antarctic: **4** skua **7** penguin
aquatic: **4** duck, gull, loon, swan, tern **5** goose, grebe, small, terne **7** penguin **8** dabshick, flamingo
aquiline: **5** eagle
Arabian Nights: roc
Arctic: auk **6** fulmar
Asiatic: **4** mine, myna **5** pitta **7** hilltit **8** dotterel **9** brambling, feng-huang, feng-hwang
Attic: **11** nightingale
Australian: emu, roa **4** emeu, lory **5** arara **6** leipoa **7** boobook, bustard **8** lorikeet, lyrebird, platypus **9** cassowary, coach-

whip, friarbird, pardalote
black: ani, ano, daw, pie **4** crow **5** merle, raven **6** oriole **7** jackdaw **8** starling
brilliant plumage: **4** tody **5** jalep **6** oriole, trogon **7** jacamar, tanager **8** pheasant
Central American: daw **4** crow, rave, rook **5** raven **6** magpie **7** corvine, jacamar **8** puffbird
crane-like: **5** wader **6** chunga
crow-family: daw, jay, pie **4** craw **5** raven **7** jackdaw
crying: **6** ramage **7** limpkin
dressing of feathers: **5** preen
emu-like: **11** cassowaries
European: ani, daw, emu, mew, qua **4** cirl, darr, emeu, gled, kite, mall, moro, osel, rook, stag, whim, yite **5** amsel, boonk, glede, mavis, merle, ousel, ouzel, sacer, saker, serin, tarin, terek, terin, whaup **6** avocet, avoset, cushat, gaylag, godwit, linnet, loriot, marten, merlin, missel, redcap, whewer, windle, winnel, wranny **7** bittern, bustard, haybird, kestrel, motacil, ortolan, sakeret, starnel, whiskey, winnard, witwall **8** bargoose, chepster, dotterel, garganey, redstart, wheybird, whimbrel, wrannock, yoldring **9** brambling, gallinule, goldfinch, goosander, peregrine, swinepipe, wheybeard **10** chiffchaff, lammegeyer, turtledove, whitterick **11** capercailie, lammergeier **12** capercailzie
extinct: moa, roc **4** dodo, kiwi, mamo, rukh **7** offbird
finch-like: **7** chewink, tanager
fish-catching: **6** osprey **9** cormorant
flightless: emu, moa **4** emeu, kiwi **7** apteryx, ostrich, penguin, ratitae **9** solitaire
fly-catching **8** redstart **9** solitaire
flying backwards: **7** swallow, humming
food: hen **5** capon **6** pullet, turkey **7** chicken, rooster
frigate: ioa, iwa **6** tropic
gallinaceous: **6** peahen **7** peacock, peafowl
game: **5** quail, snipe **6** grouse **8** pheasant
genus: **4** alca, crax, otis **7** certhia **9** apatornis
gull-like: **4** tern **6** jaeger
Hawaiian: io, oo; ava, ioa, iwa **4** iiwi, mamo, moho
heron family: **4** benu, ibis **7** bittern
humming: ava **5** carib **7** colibri
insectivorous: owl **5** vireo
jay: gae **6** magpie
large: emu **4** emeu, guan **5** eagle **6** curlew, willet **7** bustard, megapod, ostrich, pelican, seriema **8** curassow, shoebill
lark-like: **5** pipit
long-billed: **5** snipe **7** pelican
long-legged: io **4** sora **5** heron, snipe, stilt, wader **6** avocet, avoset, curlew **7** seriema
long-necked: **4** swan **5** agami, crane, goose, geese(pl.), stork **7** ostrich
male: tom **4** cock **6** gander **7** peacock, rooster

marsh: **4** sora **5** snipe, stilt
meadow: **8** bobolink
Mexican: **6** jacana, towhee **7** jacamar
New Zealand: kea, moa, **4** kaka, kiwi,
  kulu, ruru, titi, weka **6** kakapo **7** apterix,
  apteryx **8** morepork, notornis **10** blight-
  bird
Northern: auk **6** gannet, puffin
of Athena: owl
of Juno: **8** peacock
of paradise: **8** manucode
of prey: owl **4** hawk, kite **5** eagle, elant **6**
  eaglet, elanet, owelet **7** goshawk, vulture
  9 accipeter
of Zeus: **5** eagle
oldest known: **13** archaeopteryx
oscine: **4** chat **6** dronge, oriole **7** tanager
ostrich-like: emu, moa **4** emeu, rhea **10**
  cassowarie
parrot-like: **11** budgereegah, budggerygah
parson: poe, tue, tui
parts of body: neb, nib **4** bill, cere, knee,
  lora, mala **5** lores **6** pecten, pileum, pinion, rostra, syrinx **7** ambiens **8** pec-
  tines(pl.),
passerine: **5** finch **7** sparrow, starnel **9**
  chatterer, coachwhip
pert. to: **5** avian, avine **8** ornithic **9** volu-
  crine
pink: **8** flamingo
plover-like: **5** drome **7** lapwing
Poe's: **5** raven
predatory: owl **4** kite **5** yager **6** falcon,
  shrike **9** cormorant
rare: **8** rara avis
ratite: emu, moa **4** emeu **7** ostrich **9** cassowary
sacred: **4** ibis
sea: auk, ern **4** erne, gony, gull, smew, tern
  5 eider, solan **6** gannet, petrel, puffin **7**
  pelican **9** albatross **10** shearwater
shore: ree **4** rail, sora **5** snipe, stilt, wader
  6 avocet, avoset, curlew, plover, willet
Sindbad's: roc **4** rock, rukh
singing: **4** lark, wren **5** finch, mavis, robin,
  shama, veery, vireo **6** canary, linnet,
  mocker, oriole, oscine, thrush **7** mocking,
  robinet **8** bobolink, redstart **12** whip-
  poorwill
small: tit **4** tody, wren **5** dicky, pipit, viero
  6 dickey, linnet, siskin, todies(pl.), tomtit **7** creeper, humming, sparrow, titlark,
  wheater **8** starling **9** didappers
South American: **4** guan, mina, myna **5**
  chaja, mynah **6** barbet, becard **7** cariama,
  oilbird **8** bellbird, boatbill, caracara, guacharo, hoactzin, puffbird
swallow-like: **4** cran **5** swift
swimming: **4** loon **5** grebe
talking: **4** mina, mino, myna **5** mynah
tall: **6** avocet, avoset
tropical: ani **4** koae, tody **6** barbet, trogon
unfledged: gor **4** eyas **6** gorlin **8** bubbling,
  nestling

wading: **4** hern, ibis, rail, sora **5** crane,
  heron, snipe, stilt, stork **6** avocet, jacana
  8 flamingo **9** sandpiper
web-footed: **4** duck, swan **5** drake, goose **6**
  avocet, avoset, gander
West Indies: **4** tody
white-tailed: ern **4** erne **5** egret
woodcock: **5** pewee
young: eya **4** gull **5** piper **7** flapper, nestler **8** birdikin, nestling **9** fledgling
bird cage: **6** aviary **7** paddock
bird clapper: **9** scarecrow
bird crest: **4** tuft
bird eye: **12** cuckoo flower
birdcage: **6** pinjra, volery
birdman: **6** airman **7** aviator **13** ornithologist
birds: **4** aves
  collective: **4** fowl
  domesticated: **7** poultry
bird's-eye view: **6** apercu
birdwoman: **8** aviatrix **9** aviatress, aviatrice
biretta, berretta: cap **5** beret **8** skullcap
biri: **9** cigarette
birl: **4** spin, toss, whir **5** whirr **6** rattle,
  rotate **7** revolve
birma: **6** calaba
birn: **5** brand **6** burden
birr: bur **4** blow, burr, push, rush, wind **5**
  force, storm, vigor **6** energy, thrust, onrush **7** impetus
birse: **6** temper **7** bristle **8** bristles **10**
  irritation
birsle: **5** broil, toast **6** scorch **9** scorching
birsy: **7** bristly **9** irritable
birth: **4** bear **6** burden, origin **7** descent,
  genesis, lineage **8** delivery, geniture, nascency, nativity **9** beginning, naissance,
  parentage **10** extraction
  after: **9** postnatal
  by: nee
  goddess: **5** Parca
  help with: **8** accouche
  new: **10** renascence **11** Renaissance
  nobleness: **6** eugeny
  pert. to: **5** natal **13** primogenitive
birth flower:
  April: **5** daisy
  August: **9** gladiolus
  December: **9** poinsetta
  February: **8** primrose
  January: **9** carnation
  July: **8** sweet pea
  June: **4** rose
  March: **6** violet
  May: **15** lily of the valley
  November: **13** chrysanthemum
  October: **6** dahlia
  September: **5** aster
birth stone:
  April: **7** diamond **8** sapphire
  August: **9** carnelian
  December: **4** ruby

February: **8** amethyst
January: **6** garnet
July: **9** turquoise
June: **5** agate
March: **6** jasper **10** bloodstone
May: **7** emerald
November: **5** topaz
October: **5** beryl
September: **10** chrysolite
birthday: **11** anniversary, celebration
ode: **12** genethliacon
pert. to: **10** genethliac **12** genethliacal
birthmark: **4** mole **5** naeve, nevus **6** naevus **7** blemish, spiloma
pert. to: **7** naevoid
birthplace: **10** incunabula(pl.) **11** incunabulum
birthright: **8** heritage
bis: **5** again, twice **6** encore, repeat **7** replica **9** duplicate
biscuit: bun **4** bake(Sc.), roll, rush, snap **5** scone, wafer **6** cookie **7** cracker, pentile, pretzel **8** hardtack **9** porcelain **11** earthenware
bisect: **4** fork **5** cross, halve, split **6** cleave, divide **8** separate
bishop: **4** pope **5** angel **6** archer, bustle, priest **7** pontiff, prelate, primate **8** director, overseer **9** clergyman, inspector, **13** administrator **14** superintendent
apron: **7** gremial
assistant: **6** verger **9** coadjutor
buskin: **6** caliga **7** caligae(pl.),
cap: **4** hura **5** miter, mitre **7** biretta **8** berretta, mitrella
first year revenue: **5** annat **6** annate
jurisdiction: see **7** diocese
private room: **9** accubitus
robe: **6** chimar, chimer **7** chimere
staff: **7** crosier
stave: **6** baculi(pl.) **7** baculus
throne: **4** apse
title: **4** abba, anba **7** prelate. primate
vestment: alb **4** cope **6** chimer, rochet **7** gremial, tunicle **8** dalmatic **10** omophorion
bishopric: see **7** diocese **10** episcopacy, episcopate
bishop's weed: **4** ammi **6** ammeos **8** goutweed
bismar: **9** steelyard
bismer: **5** scorn, shame **8** reproach
bison: **6** bovine **7** aurochs, bonasus, buffalo
bisson: **5** blind **8** blinding, purblind
bit: ace, jot, ort, wee **4** atom, bite, curb, doit, food, iota, item, mite, mote, part, snap, tool, whit **5** blade, check, crumb, drill, pezzo, piece, scrap, shred, speck **6** bridle, cannon, eating, morsel, smidge, splice, tittle, trifle **7** morceau(F.), portion, scatche, smidgen, smidgin, smigeon,

snaffle **8** fraction, fragment, quantity, smitchin, victuals **9** restraint
horse's curb: **6** pelham
Irish: **7** traneen
bite: bit, cut, eat, nip **4** bait, cham, chew, food, gash, gnap, gnaw, hold, knap, meal, snap **5** chack, chamm, champ, cheat, pinch, seize, smart, snack, sting, trick **6** crunch, morsel, nibble, pierce **7** cheater, corrode, impress, partake, sharper, slander **8** lacerate, puncture, victuals **9** denticate
biting: **4** acid, hoar, keen **5** acrid, sharp, snell **6** bitter, rodent, severe **7** caustic, cutting, mordant, nipping, pungent **8** incisive, poignant, scathing, stinging **9** corrosive, sarcastic, trenchant, vitriolic
biting dragon: **8** tarragon
bito: **4** balm, tree **7** hajilij
oil: **6** zachun
bitt: **4** post **5** block
bitter: gal **4** acid, bask, keen, sore, sour, tart **5** acerb, acrid, amara, bleak, harsh, irate, sharp **6** biting, picric, severe **7** austere, caustic, crabbed, cutting, galling, painful, pungent, satiric **8** poignant, stinging, virulent **9** malicious **11** acrimonious, distressful
bitter apple: **9** colocynth
bitter bush: **9** snakeroot
bitter gentian: **9** baldmoney
bitter grass: **9** colicroot
bitter oak: **6** cerris
bitter spar: **8** dolomite
bitter wintergreen: **10** pipsissewa
bittern: **4** bump **5** boonk, heron **6** kakkak
bitterness: rue **4** acor, bile, fell, gall **5** atter **6** enmity, malice, rancor **7** amarity **8** acerbity, acrimony, severity **9** amaritude, hostility, poignancy, virulence **11** malevolence
bitters: **4** amer(F.) **5** tonic **6** liquor
pert. to: **9** amaroidal
bittersweet: **10** confection, nightshade
bitterweed: **7** ragweed **9** horseweed **10** sneezeweed
bitterwort: **7** felwort **9** dandelion
bitumen: tar **5** pitch **7** asphalt **8** alkitran **9** alchitran, elaterite
bivalve: **4** clam, spat **6** cockle, diatom, mussel, oyster **7** mollusk, Pandora, scallop **10** brachiopod
genus: **5** pinna **6** anomia **7** toheroa **12** gastrochaena
bivocal: **9** diphthong
bivouac: **4** camp **5** etape, watch **6** encamp **10** encampment
biwa: **6** loquat
bizarre: odd **5** antic, dedal, outre, queer **6** quaint **7** curious **8** fanciful **9** eccentric, fantastic, grotesque **10** ridiculous **11** extravagant

blab: 4 chat 5 blart, blate, clack 6 babble, betray, gossip, reveal, tattle 7 blabber, chatter 8 telltale

black: jet 4 calo, dark, ebon, foul, inky 5 dusky, murky, Negro, noire(F.), raven, sable, sooty 6 atrous, dismal, gloomy, pitchy, sullen 7 melanic, Negrito, swarthy, unclean 8 mournful 9 atrocious 10 blackamoor, calamitous, forbidding
and white: 11 chiaroscuro
comb. form: 4 atra, atro, mela 5 melan 6 melano

black and blue: 5 livid
spot: 6 bruise, shiner 10 ecchymosis
black art: 5 magic 7 alchemy 8 wizardry 10 necromancy 11 conjuration
black cod: 6 beshow
black diamond: oil 4 coal 8 hematite
black earth: 4 mold 9 chernozem
black elder: 9 hackberry
black grunt: 10 tripletail
black hole: 4 cell 7 dungeon 8 solitary
Black Sea:
city: 5 Batum 6 Odessa
peninsula: 6 Crimea
black widow: 6 spider 7 pokomoo
blackamoor: 5 bleck, negro 7 negress
blackball: 4 pill 6 ballot 7 exclude, heeball 9 ostracize
blackberry: 6 agawam 8 dewberry
blackbird: ani, daw, pie 4 crow 5 amsel, colly, merle, ousel, ouzel, raven 6 colley 7 jackdaw
blackcap: 4 gull 7 warbler 8 chicadee, titmouse 9 raspberry
blackdamp: 9 chokedamp
blacken: ink, tar 4 char, soot 5 bleck, cloud, japan, sully 6 darken, defame, malign, vilify 7 asperse, slander, traduce 8 besmirch 10 calumniate
blackface: 5 actor, comic, sheep 8 boldface, minstrel
blackfin: 4 fish 5 cisco, sesis
blackfish: 5 whale 6 tautog 10 nigrescent
school: 5 grind
blackguard: 4 shag 5 gamin, guard, snuff 7 vagrant 8 criminal, hanger-on, vagabond 9 scoundrel
blackjack: oak 4 club, duck, flag, game, jack 5 billy 6 beetle, jerkin, vessel, weapon
blackleg: 4 scab, snob 7 disease, gambler 8 apostate, swindler 13 strikebreaker
blackmail: 5 bribe 6 coerce, extort 7 payment, tribute
blackmailer: 5 ghoul 7 leecher
blackmailing: 8 chantage 9 extortion
Blackmore heroine: 10 Lorna Doone
blackout: 6 darken 8 darkness, scrounge 11 suppression
blacksmith: gow 5 shoer, smith 6 plover,

smithy, stithy 7 farrier, striker 10 horseshoer
shop: 5 anvil, stith 6 smithy, stithy 8 smithery
blacksnake: 4 whip 5 racer, quirt
blackthorn: haw 4 sloe
Blackwater State: 8 Nebraska
blackwort: 8 comfrey
bladder: sac 7 blister, inflate, vesicle
comb. form: 4 asco
blade: bit, fop, oar 4 blow, bone, edge, leaf 5 blood, dandy, fluke, grain, knife, spark, spear, spire, sword 6 cutter, lamina, scythe, sickle 7 gallant, laminae(pl.), scapula 9 propeller
blae: blo 4 blue, gray 5 bleak, livid 7 sunless 10 unbleached
blague: lie 4 hoax 6 humbug 8 claptrap, raillery
blain: 4 sore 5 bulla 7 blister, inflame, pustule 8 swelling
blake: wan 4 pale 6 yellow 9 colorless
Blake's symbol: 4 Zoas
blamable: 6 faulty 8 culpable 11 blameworthy 13 reprehensible
blame: 4 call, hurt, onus, twit 5 chide, fault, guilt, odium, shend 6 accuse, charge, dirdum, rebuke, revile, scance 7 ascribe, censure, condemn, obloquy, reproof, reprove, upbraid 8 reproach 9 challenge, criticism, inculpate 10 accussation 11 culpability, reprobation 12 reprehension 13 animadversion
deserving: 8 culpable
blameless: 7 perfect 8 innocent, spotless 9 faultless, righteous 14 irreproachable
blanch: 4 fade, pale 5 chalk, scald, white 6 argent, bleach, blench, whiten 8 etiolate 9 whitewash
bland: 4 kind, mild, oily, open, soft 5 suave 6 benign, genial, gentle, smooth, urbane 7 affable, amiable, lenient 8 gracious 9 benignant, courteous
blandish: 4 coax 5 charm 6 allure, blanch, cajole 7 flatter, wheedle 10 compliment
blank: 4 bare, flan, form, shot, void 5 annul, blind, break, clean, empty, range, space 6 vacant 7 nonplus, unmixed, vacuous 8 unfilled 9 colorless, downright, fruitless, frustrate
blanket: 4 brot, wrap 5 cotta, cover, layer, manta, quilt, sheet, throw 6 afghan, poncho, serape 8 coverlet 10 barraclade
cowboy: 5 sugan 6 soogan, sougan, sugann
goat's hair: 6 cumbly
horse: 5 manta
Indian: 6 stroud
blare: 4 peal 5 blast, noise 6 blazon 7 fanfare, tantara, trumpet 11 flamboyance

blarney: 5 stone 6 butter 7 flatter, wheedle 8 flattery

blase: 5 bored, sated, weary 8 satiated 9 surfeited 11 indifferent

blaspheme: 5 abuse, curse 6 revile 7 defame, profane 10 calumniate

blasphemy: 7 calumny, cursing, impiety 8 anathema, swearing 9 profanity, sacrilege 10 execration 11 imprecation, irreverence, malediction 12 vilification

blast: bub, nip, wap 4 bang, blow, gale, gust, ruin, wind 5 split, stunt 6 attack, blight, wither 7 bluster, explode, shatter, shrivel 8 dynamite, outburst, proclaim 9 discharge, explosion 10 detonation

blast furnace:
lower part: 4 bosh
nozzle: 6 tuyere

blatant: 4 glib, loud 5 gross, noisy, silly, vocal 6 coarse, vulgar 8 brawling 9 bellowing, clamorous, inelegant, obtrusive 10 vociferous

blate: 4 blab, dull, pale, slow 5 blunt, prate, timid 7 bashful, ghastly 8 sheepish 9 diffident 10 spiritless

blather: 4 stir 5 bleat 6 babble 7 blither, prattle 8 nonsense 9 commotion

blaubok: 5 etaac 8 antelope

blaw: 4 blow, brag 5 boast

blaze: 4 burn, fire, glow, mark, shot 5 flame, flare, flash, glare, gleam, glory, shine, torch 6 bleeze 7 bonfire, pioneer 8 splendor 9 firebrand 10 effulgence 11 coruscation 13 conflagration

blazer: 6 jacket

blazon: 4 deck, show 5 adorn, blare, boast 6 depict, shield 7 declare, display, exhibit, publish 8 emblazon, inscribe 9 delineate, embellish 11 description, publication 14 representation

bleach: sun 5 chalk 6 blanch, blench, chlore, purify, whiten 7 decolor, lighten 8 etiolate

bleak: dim, raw 4 blae, blay, cold, gray, pale 5 sprat 6 bitter, bleach, dismal, dreary, frigid, pallid 7 cutting 8 desolate 9 cheerless 10 depressing

blear: dim 4 blur, dull 6 darken 7 deceive, mislead 8 hoodwink, protrude

bleat: baa 4 blat, blea 5 blart 7 blather, bluster, whicker

bleb: 4 blob 5 bulla 6 bubble 7 blister, pustule, vesicle 8 swelling

bleeding heart: 8 dicentra

blemish: mar 4 blot, blur, dent, flaw, gall, lack, mark, rift, scar, slur, spot, vice, want 5 blame, breck, crack, fault, mulct, speck, sully, tache, taint 6 blotch, breach, defame, defect, impair, injure, macula, macule, smirch, stigma 7 default, failing, fissure, maculae(pl.) 9 birthmark, deformity, discredit, disfigure 10 defacement, deficiency 12 imperfection 13 disfigurement

wood: 4 mote
wound: 4 scar 8 cicatrix 9 cicatrice

blench: 4 foil, shun, wile 5 avoid, elude, evade, quail, shake, shirk, trick 6 baffle, blanch, bleach, flinch, recoil, shrink 7 deceive 9 stratagem 10 disconcert

blend: mix 4 blot, fuse, join, meng 5 blind, cream, merge, shade, spoil, stain, tinge, unite 6 commix, dazzle, mingle 7 combine, confuse, corrupt, deceive, mixture, pollute 8 coalesce, tincture 9 admixture, associate, commingle, harmonize 10 amalgamate 11 incorporate

blended: 5 fondu, mixed 6 merged 7 mingled 9 confluent

blesbok: 5 nunni 8 antelope, blesbuck

bless: 4 keep, sain, wave 5 adore, anele, bensh(Yid.), extol, favor, guard, thank, wound 6 favour, hallow, praise, thrash 7 approve, beatify, glorify, protect 8 macarize, preserve, sanctify 10 consecrate, felicitate

blessed: 4 holy 5 happy 6 divine, joyful, sacred 8 benedict, bhagavat, blissful, hallowed 9 beatified, benedight 11 consecrated

blessing: 4 boon, gift 5 bliss, grace 6 praise 7 benison, worship 8 felicity 9 beatitude 10 benedicite, beneficent 11 benediction

blether: See **blather.**

blight: nip 4 ruin, rust, smut 5 blast, frost 6 mildew, wither 7 destroy 9 frustrate

blimp: 7 airship, balloon, colonel

blind: bet, pot 4 ante, dark, dull, hood 5 blank, blend, dunch, shade, stake, wager 6 ambush, bisson, dazzle, screen, secret 7 aimless, bandage, benight, eclipse, execate, eyeless, obscure, pretext, shutter 8 abortive, artifice, bayardly, blinding, hoodwink, ignorant, involved, jalousie, outshine, purblind 9 benighted, concealed, deceitful, defective, insensate, intricate, senseless, sightless 10 incomplete, misleading, subterfuge
as a hawk: seel
part of: 4 slat
printing for: 7 braille

blind alley: 7 dead end, impasse 8 cul-de-sac

blind me: 5 blimy

blind staggers: gid

blind worm: 5 orvet

blinder: 4 flap 5 bluff 7 blinker 8 hoodwink 9 blindfold 11 obstruction

blindfold: 4 dark 5 blink, bluff 7 bandage, blinder, obscure 8 heedless, hoodwink, reckless 9 concealed

blindness: 6 bisson, cecity 7 ablepsy, anopsia 8 ablepsia 9 ignorance
color: 13 achromatopsia 14 monochromatism
day: 11 hemeralopia
partial: 7 meropia 10 cecutiency

snow: 14 chiona-blepsia

blink: 4 shun, wink 5 blush, cheat, flash, gleam, shine, trick 6 glance, ignore, obtuse 7 blinter, condone, glimmer, glimpse, neglect, nictate, sparkle, twinkle 9 blindfold

blinker: eye 5 bluff, light 6 signal 7 blinder, goggles 8 coquette, hoodwink, mackerel

blinking: 5 utter 8 blooming, complete

blintze: 7 pancake

bliss: joy 4 Eden, kaif, seil(Sc.) 5 glory 7 delight, ecstacy, gladden, rapture 8 felicity, gladness, paradise, pleasure 9 happiness 11 contentment

place of: 4 Eden 6 Utopia 7 Elysium 8 Paradise

blissful: 4 holy 6 blithe 7 blessed, Elysian, Utopian 9 beatified, glorified

blister: 4 beat, bleb, blob, lash 5 blain, bulge 6 bubble, scorch 7 vesicle 8 vesicate 10 vesicatory

blithe: gay 4 glad 5 bonny, happy, jolly, merry 6 bonnie, jovial, joyous, lively 7 gaysome, jocular, winsome 8 cheerful, gladsome 9 sprightly

blitzkrieg: 4 raid 5 blitz 6 attack 11 bombardment

blizzard: 4 blow, gale, wind 5 purga 6 retort 9 snowstorm, squelcher

Blizzard State: 11 South Dakota

bloat: 5 puffy, swell 6 expand, tumefy 7 distend, ferment, inflate 8 drunkard

bloated: 5 bloat, cured 6 sodden, turgid 7 pompous

blob: lip, wen 4 bleb, blot, boil, daub, drop, lump, mark, mass 6 bubble, pimple, splash 7 blemish, blister, blossom, globule, postule, splotch 8 globular

bloc: 4 ring 5 cabal, party, union 6 clique 7 faction 11 combination

block: ame, bar, cob, dam, hob, nog, row, vol 4 bloc, cake, clog, cube, foil, head, mass, stop 5 check, chump, deter, nudge, parry, shape, spike, stump 6 hamper, hinder, impede, oppose, outwit, square, street, stymie, taplet, thwart 7 buckler, inhibit, outline, prevent 8 blockade, obstacle, obstruct, stoppage 9 barricade, blockhead, frustrate, hindrance 11 obstruction

architectural: 6 dentil, mutule

electrically insulated 6 taplet

football: 4 clip

for shaping metal objects: ame

ice: 4 cube 5 serac

metal type: 4 quad, quod

nautical: 7 deadeye

perforated: nut

blockade: dam 5 beset, block, siege 6 whisky 7 embargo 8 obstruct 9 beleaguer 11 obstruction, restriction

blockhead: ass, oaf 4 bust, coof, dolt, fool, mome 5 block, chump, cuddy, idiot,

ninny 6 noodle 7 dizzard, half-wit, tomfool 8 beefhead, clodpate, gamphrel, hardhead 9 blockpate, grouthead, hoddy-peak, numbskull, screwball, simpleton 10 beetlehead, dunderhead, hoddy-doddy

bloke: man 4 chap, toff 6 fellow 9 personage

blonde: 4 fair 5 light 6 flaxen, golden, yellow

blood: kin, sap 4 gore, life, mood, race 5 blade, fluid, serum, stock 6 indred 7 gallant, kinship, kinsman, lineage, youstir(Sc.) 8 relation 9 lifeblood 14 consanguineous

comb. form: 4 hema, hemo 5 haemo

deficiency: 6 anemia 7 anaemia

disease: 8 leucemia, leukemia 9 leucaemia, leukaemia

fluid part: 5 serum 6 plasma 7 opsonin

particle in: 7 embolus

mixed: See **hybrid.**

of the gods: 4 icor 5 ichor

stagnation: 4 clot 5 cruor, grume 6 stasis, stases

strain: 4 race 5 stock 6 family

testing instrument: 13 hemabarometer 14 haemabarometer

blood and thunder: 6 uproar 8 violence 9 melodrama

blood fine: cro(Sc.) 4 eric 7 galanas, wergild 9 bloodwite

blood horse: 12 thoroughbred

blood money: cro

blood pudding: 7 sausage

blood relationship: 7 kinsman 8 relative 13 consanguinity

blood vessel: 4 vein 5 hemad 6 artery 9 capillary

comb. form: vas

bloodhound: 4 lyam, lyme

bloodless: 4 dead 6 anemic 7 anaemic, inhuman 8 lifeless 9 unfeeling 10 exsanguine

bloodshed: 5 death 7 carnage 8 violence 9 slaughter

bloodshot: red 8 inflamed

bloodsucker: 5 leech 7 sponger 11 extortioner

bloodthirsty: 6 bloody, carnal 9 ferocious, murderous 10 sanguinary

bloody: 4 gory 5 cruel 6 cruent 8 bleeding, hematose, infamous 9 cruentous, ferocious, haematose, merciless, murderous 10 sanguinary 12 bloodstained, bloodthirsty, contemptible

bloodybones: 7 specter 9 hobgoblin

bloom (see also **flower**): dew 4 blow 7 blossom, blowing 8 floreate, flourish 13 efflorescence

bloomer: 5 error 6 blower 7 blunder, failure

bloomery: 5 forge 6 hearth 7 furnace

blooming: 4 rosy 5 green 6 abloom, florid

7 blowing, roseate 8 blinking 10 prospering

blossom (see also **flower**): bud 4 blob 5 bloom 7 prosper 8 flourish 13 efflorescence

small: 8 floweret

blot: mar 4 blob, blue, daub, soil, spot 5 blend, erase, smear, speck, stain, sully 6 blotch, cancel, damage, efface, impair, macula, shadow, smirch, smudge, smutch, stigma 7 blemish, eclipse, expunge, maculae(pl.), obscure, tarnish 8 disgrace, reproach 9 bespatter 10 obliterate, stigmatize 12 obliteration 13 disfigurement

blotch: dab 4 blot, gout, spot 5 patch, smear, stain 6 macula, mottle, smirch, stigma 7 blemish, maculae(pl.), pustule, splotch 8 eruption, maculate

blouse: 5 shirt, smock, tunic 7 casaque 10 shirtwaist

bushman's: 5 bluey

blow: bob, cob, cop, dub, jab, pat, rap, tap, wap 4 ande, baff, bang, bash, beat, belt, biff, birr, blad, blaw, brag, buff, bump, chap, conk, crig, cuff, daud, dint, dird, drub, dunt, dush, fleg, gale, gowf, huff, jolt, knap, lash, mint, oner, pant, plug, puff, scud, slam, slap, slug, sock 5 binge, blade, blast, blizz, bloom, boast, brunt, burst, clink, clour, clout, clump, crump, curse, douse, dowse, filip, flack, flick, gowff, ictus, impel, knock, peise, shock, skite, slipe, sound, spend, storm, swipe, thump, whack, whang 6 bensel, bensil, betray, bounce, buffet, depart, dirdum, expand, fillip, flower, frolic, larrup, wallop 7 assault, attaint, bensail, bensall, bensell, blossom, blowout, bluster, boaster, destroy, inflate, publish, shatter, whample 8 boasting, calamity, confound, diaster, disclose 9 bastinado

mock: 5 feint

up: 5 scene 7 explode, inflate 8 dynamite, outburst

blower: fan 5 whale 6 puffer 7 bloomer 8 braggart 9 swellfish 11 sacheverell

blowfly: 10 bluebottle

blowgun: 10 peashooter

blowhard: 8 braggart

blown: 5 stale, tired 6 opened 7 blossom, swollen, tainted 8 betrayed, flyblown, inflated 9 distended, exhausted, worthless

blowout: 4 blow, feed, meal 6 valley 10 depression

blowze: 5 trull, wench, woman 6 hoyden 8 slattern

blowzy: 5 dowdy 6 frowzy 10 disheveled, slatternly

blub: 4 bulb 5 swell 6 puffed 7 blubber, swollen

blubber: cry, fat 4 blub, foam, wail, weep 5 swell, thick, whine 6 bubble, flitch, medusa, nettle, seethe 7 blobber, bluster, swollen, whimper 9 disfigure

remove: 6 flense

whale: 5 fenks, speck 6 muktuk

blubbery: fat 5 obese 7 swollen 9 quivering 10 gelatinous 11 protuberant

bludgeon: bat, hit 4 club, mace 5 billy, stick 6 coerce, weapon

blue: low, sad, sky 4 aqua, bice, glum 5 azure, livid, perse, small 6 cobalt, gloomy, indigo, severe 7 celeste, gentian, learned, lobelia 8 cerulean, cynanine, dejected, literary 9 turquoise 10 despondent, melancholy

asbestos: 11 crocidolite

gray: 5 merle, pearl, slate 7 cesious 8 caesious

green: 4 bice, teal 5 beryl 8 calamine

red: 5 smalt 6 mallow 8 gridelin, mazarine 9 gris-de-lin

sheep: 6 bharal

blue blood: 5 noble 10 aristocrat 12 bluestocking

blue boneset: 10 mistflower

blue catalpa: 9 paulownia

blue dandelion: 7 chicory

blue earth: 10 kimberlite

Blue Grotto site: 5 Capri, Italy

blue gum: 4 tree 10 eucalyptus

Blue Hen State: 8 Delaware

blue huckleberry: 11 tangleberry

blue jaundice: 8 cyanosis

blue Joe: 8 bluegill

blue John: 4 milk

Blue Law State: 11 Connecticut

blue-pencil: 4 edit 6 delete, redact

Bluebeard's wife: 6 Fatima

bluebonnet: cap 4 Scot 7 bluecap 8 Scotsman 10 cornflower

bluebottle: 5 bluet 7 barbeau, blowfly 8 hyacinth

bluecap: 4 Scot 10 bluebonnet

bluefish: 4 bass, tuna 5 saury 8 weakfish

bluegill: 7 sunfish

bluegrass: poa

Bluegrass State 8 Kentucky

bluejacket: tar 6 sailor

bluejoint: 6 redtop

bluenose: 4 snob 8 moralist 11 Nova Scotian

bluepoint: 6 oyster

blueprint: map 4 plan, plot 5 draft, trace 6 sketch 7 diagram 9 cyanotype

bluer: 4 anil

bluerocket: 9 monkshood

blues: 4 song 5 dumps 6 cafard 7 megrims 10 melancholy, mulligrubs 11 despondency

bluestocking: 5 woman 12 intellectual

bluet: 5 plant 10 bluebottle 11 farkleberry

bluethroat: 7 warbler

bluey: 6 bundle 7 blanket

bluff: 4 bank, brag, curt, fool, rude 5 blunt, burly, cliff, frank, gruff, short, surly 6 abrupt, crusty 7 blinder, blinker, brusque, deceive, uncivil 8 barranca, barranco, churlish, hoodwink, impolite 9

blindfold, outspoken, precipice **13** unceremonious
Bluff King Hal: 5 Henry
blunder: err, mix **4** balk, bull, flub, gaff,
roil, slip, stir **5** boner, botch, break, error,
fault, lapse, misdo **6** boggle, bumble,
bungle, gazabo, gazebo, mingle, muddle **7**
bloomer, confuse, derange, failure, faux-
pas, mistake, stumble **8** solecism **9** confusion, mismanage **11** disturbance
blunderbuss: gun **9** espingole
blunk: 6 bungle **9** mismanage
blunt: 4 bald, curt, damp, dull, flat **5** bluff,
brusk, inert, plain, plump, stunt **6**
clumsy, deaden, obtund, obtuse, stupid **7**
brusque **8** hebetate **9** depressed, downright **10** point-blank **11** insensitive **13**
unceremonious
mentally: **8** hebitate
blur: dim, hum **4** blob, blot, mist, soil, spot
5 blear, cloud, smear, stain, sully **6** mackle, macule, smudge, stigma **7** blemish,
obscure **9** disfigure
blurb: ad **4** puff, rove **5** brief **6** notice **12**
announcement, commendation **13** adver-
tisement
blush: 4 glow, look **5** blink, color, flush,
gleam, tinge **6** glance, mantle, redden **8**
likeness **10** appearance, rubescence
blushing: red **4** rosy **5** ruddy **7** roseate **8**
flushing **9** rosaceous **10** erubescent **11**
embarrassed
bluster: 4 blow, huff, rage, rant **5** blast,
bleat, boast, bully, noise, storm, swank **6**
babble, bellow, bounce, hector, huffle,
tumult **7** blubber, bravado, gauster, roister, swagger **8** boasting, bullying, threaten
9 confusion, gasconade **10** swaggering,
turbulence **11** fanfaronade, rodomontade
bo, boh: 5 chief **6** leader **7** captain
boa: 5 aboma, scarf, snake **8** anaconda **9**
neckpiece
boa constrictor: 5 snake **6** giboia
boar: hog, sus **4** aper **5** swine **6** barrow,
hogget **8** sanglier **9** hoggaster
head: **4** hure
wound: **4** gore **5** ganch
board: 4 deal, diet, eats, fare, keep, lath,
slat **5** enter, found, house, lodge, meals,
panel, plank, stage **6** accost, planch,
shield **7** cabinet, council, duoviri, en-
plane, entrain, planche **8** approach, tribunal **9** authority, shipboard **10** commission, management, provisions **11** switchboard **13** entertainment
boast: gab **4** blaw, blow, brag, crow, pomp,
rave **5** brave, extol, exult, glory, prate,
roose, scold, skite, vapor, vaunt **6** bounce,
clamor, extoll, flaunt, menace(Sc.), outcry,
splore **7** bluster, clamour, display, glorify,
swagger **8** flourish, threaten **9** gasconade
11 rodomontade
boaster: 5 skite **6** crower, gascon, pedant
7 bouncer, bravado, cracker, ruffler **8**
blowhard, braggart, cacofogo, fanfaron,

glorioso, jingoist, rodomont **9** cacafuego
11 braggadocio
boastful: big **6** parado **8** fanfaron **9** gasconade, kompology **11** rodomontade, thra-
sonical
boat: (see also **canoe, ship, vessel**): ark,
cat, cot, gig, tub **4** bark, brig, carv,
dory, junk, raft, scow, ship, skag, tack,
trow, yawl **5** aviso, barca, barge, bully,
canoe, coble, craft, dingy, ferry, ketch,
liner, shell, skiff, skift, smack, xebec, zebec **6** baidak, bateau, carvel, chebec,
cruise, cutter, dinghy, dugout, garvey,
packet, vessel, zebeck **7** bateaus, che-
beck, coracle, gondola, lighter, nacelle,
pinnace, scooter, steamer **8** pessoner,
schooner **9** submarine, transport **10** watercraft
coal cargo: **7** collier
comb. form: **5** scapo
deck: **4** poop **5** orlop
engine-driven: **6** sampan
fishing: **8** bracozzo
front: bow **4** prow
garbage: **6** hopper
ornamental: **9** navicella
part: bow **4** beam, deck, hold, keel, prow **5**
bilge, cabin, stern **6** bridge, gunnel, kel-
son, saloon, thwart **7** capstan, gunwale,
keelson, painter, scupper **12** companionway
pin: **5** thole
post: poy **4** biff **7** bollard, capstan **9** sternpost
power: tug
propellant: oar, row **4** pole **5** motor, scull
ride: row **4** sail **6** cruise
round: **4** gufa **5** goofa **6** goofah
sailing: **4** pram, proa **5** praam, prahu
undersea: sub **9** submarine **11** submersible
boatman: 6 barger, Charon **7** hobbler,
hoveler, huffler **8** hoveller **9** gondolier **10**
barcajuolo
boatswain: 5 bosun **6** serang
whistle: **4** pipe
Boaz:
son: **4** Obed
wife: **4** Ruth
bob: bow, cut, dab, jog, rap, tap **4** ball,
blow, buff, calf, clip, coin, cork, duck,
grub, jeer, jerk, jest, knob, mock, worm **5**
bunch, cheat, dance, filch, float, flout,
shake taunt, trick **6** bingle, buffet,
curtsy, delude, pommel, strike, weight **7**
bobsled, bobtail, cluster, curtesy, haircut,
pendant, refrain **8** shilling **9** bobsleigh
bobac: 6 marmot
bobber: 4 cork, duck **5** float **6** bobfly **7**
dropper **8** deadhead
bobbery: 6 hubbub, tumult **8** squabble
11 disturbance
bobbie, bobby: cop **4** bull **6** peeler **7** officer **9** policeman
bobbin: pin **4** cord, pirn, reel **5** braid,

quill, spool **7** ratchet, spindle **8** cylinder **10** cuckoopint
frame: **5** creel
pin: **7** spindle
bobble: dib **6** fumble
bobolink: **4** bird, reed **7** bunting, ortolan **10** butterbird
bobsled: bob **6** ripper
bobtail: bob, cur **4** dock **6** rabble, strunt(Sc.) **7** curtail **8** sheepdog **9** deficient **11** abbreviated
bobwhite: **4** bird **5** colin, quail
bocardo: **6** dokhma, prison **7** bokardo
bode: **4** omen, stop **5** augur, offer **6** herald **7** message, portend, presage **8** forebode, forecast, foreshow, foretell, indicate **9** messenger **10** inaugurate **13** foreshadowing, prognosticate
bodice: **4** jupe **5** choli, gilet, waist **6** basque, corset
bodiless: **9** trunkless **11** incorporeal
bodily: **5** solid **6** actual, carnal **7** fleshly, somatic **8** corporal, entirely, material, physical **9** corporeal **10** completely **11** corporeally, substantial
bodily motion: **5** shrug **7** gesture
boding: **7** ominous **10** foreboding, prediction, prognostic
bodkin: awl, pin **6** dagger, needle **7** hairpin, poniard **8** stiletto **9** eyeleteer
body: **4** bole, bouk, bulk, form, mass, nave, rupa, soma, stem **5** flesh, stiff, torso, trunk **6** corpse, corpus, extent, licham, person **7** cadaver, carcass, company **8** extensum, majority **9** curcurbit, substance **10** assemblage, foundation **11** association, corporation
away from center: **6** distal
heavenly: sun **4** luna, moon, star **5** comet **6** meteor, planet **8** asteroid, luminary
joint: hip **4** knee **5** elbow, wrist **8** shoulder
motion: **7** gesture
of men: **5** posse **10** authorized
of persons: **5** corps, posse
of water: bay, sea **4** gulf, lake, pond, pool **5** ocean **6** lagoon, sealet **9** reservoir
path: **5** orbit
pert. to: **5** somal **8** physical, systemic
wall: **6** paries, septum
body politic: **4** weal **9** community
bodyguard: **5** thane **6** escort **7** retinue, trabant **9** lifeguard
Boeotia:
capital: **6** Thebes
region: **5** Ionia
Boer:
dialect: **4** Taal
general: **5** Botha
bog: bug, car, fen, gog, hag **4** bold, carr, cess, mire, moor, moss, ooze, sink, slew, slue, syrt **5** marsh, saucy swamp **6** morass, muskeg, slough **7** forward **8** quagmire **9** conceited

bog down: **4** mire **5** stall **6** bemire
bogey: bug, cow, hag **5** bogie, bogle, devil, gnome **6** boggle, booger, goblin **7** boggard, boggart, bugaboo, bugbear, gnomide, specter, spectre **9** hobgoblin, scarecrow **10** bullbeggar
boggle: jib, shy **4** balk, foil, stop **5** alarm, botch, demur, scare, start **6** baffle, bungle, goblin, shrink **7** bauchle, blunder, perplex, scruple **8** frighten, hesitate **9** dissemble, embarrass **10** difficulty
boggy: wet **4** miry, soft **5** gouty, fenny, haggy, mossy **6** quaggy, swampy **7** boggish, queachy
bogus: **4** fake, sham **5** false, phony **8** spurious **10** fictitious **11** counterfeit
bogy: See **bogey.**
bohemian: **4** arty **5** gipsy, gypsy **6** Picard
boil: sty **4** bile, blob, buck, coct, cook, rage, sore, stew, stye, teem **5** botch, brede, steam **6** betray, bubble buller, burble, decoct, seethe, simmer **7** anthrax, estuate, inflame **8** aestuate, ebullate **10** ebbulliate, effervesce
almost: **5** scald
boiler: **4** reef **6** copper, kettle, retort **7** alembic, caldron, furnace **8** cauldron
plate: **4** sput
tube scaler: **6** sooter
boisterous: **4** gurl, loud, rude **5** burly, gurly, noisy, rough, windy **6** coarse, stormy, strong, unruly **7** furious, massive, roaring, violent **8** cumbrous, strident, vehement **9** clamorous, excessive, excitable **10** blustering, tumultuous, unyielding
bold: big, bog, yep **4** derf, pert, rash, rude, yepe **5** bardy, bield, brash, brave, brent, frack, freak, freck, gally, hardy, large, manly, nervy, peart, saucy, steep, stout **6** abrupt, audace, brassy, brazen, crouse, daring, fierce, heroic, strong **7** assured, dashing, defiant, forward, grivois, haughty, massive, valiant **8** arrogant, familiar, fearless, grivoise, immodest, impudent, intrepid, malapert, powerful, resolute **9** audacious, bodacious, confident, dauntless, imprudent, undaunted **10** courageous, forritsome **11** venturesome **12** enterprising, overassuming, presumptuous, stout-hearted **13** overconfident
boldness: **4** brow **5** bield, nerve, vigor **6** daring **7** bravery, courage **8** audacity, temerity **9** assurance, hardiesse, hardihood, hardiness **10** brazenness, confidence, effrontery **11** intrepidity, presumption **13** dauntlessness
bole: **4** clay, dose, stem **5** bolus, crypt, trunk **7** opening
bolero: **5** dance, waist **6** jacket
Bolivia:
animal: **6** vicuna
city: **5** La Paz(c.), Oruro, Sucre(c.) **6** Potosi **10** Chuquisaca, Cochabamba

coin: **5** tomin **7** bolivar, centavo **9** bolivi-
ano
district: **5** La Paz, Oruro **6** Elbeni, Potosi,
Tarija **7** Colinas, El Chaco **9** Santa Cruz
10 Chuquisaca, Cochabamba
dried mutton: **7** chalone
Indian: Uro, Uru **4** Iten, Moxo, Uran **6** Arawak, Aymara, Charca, Chicha, Tacana **7**
Aymaran, Puquina, Sirione **10** Chiriguano
lake: **8** Aullugas, Titacaca **11** Desaguad-
ero
measure: **6** league **7** celemin
mountain: **5** Andes, Cusco, Cuzco **6** Sa-
jama, Sorata **8** Illimani
plateau: **9** Altiplano
river: **4** Beni **5** Orton **6** Mamore **7** Gua-
pore **8** Paraguay **9** Pilcomayo, San Miguel **10** Cordillera **11** Madre de Dios
weight: **5** libra, macro
boll: pod **4** bulb, grow, knob **5** onion **6**
bubble **7** capsule, measure **8** pericarp **12**
protuberance
bolo: **5** knife **7** machete, sundang **8** paci-
fist **9** defeatist
Bolshevist: **7** Russian **9** socialist
leader: **5** Lenin
bolster: aid, pad **6** pillow **7** cushion, support **8** compress, maintain
bolt: bar, pen pin, rod, run **4** beat, dart,
flee, gulp, lock, pawl, sift **5** arrow, bilbo,
close, elope, flash, gorge, latch, rivet,
shaft **6** assort, decamp, desert, fasten,
flight, garble, pintle, purify, refine, secure,
strong, toggle, winnow **7** missile, shackle,
thunder **8** fastener, separate, stampede **9**
lightning
bolus: cud **4** bole, clop, lump, mass, pill,
rock
bomb: dud, egg **5** blare, shell **6** ashcan **7**
bombard, grenade, marmite **9** pineapple
10 projectile **11** blockbuster
guide: fin
hole: **6** crater
bombard: **4** bomb **5** crump, shell **6** batter, bottle, strafe, vessel
bombardier: **6** gunner **12** artilleryman
bombardment: **5** blitz, siege **6** attack,
rafale, strafe **9** cannonade
bombast: gas, pad **4** rage, rant, rave **5**
stuff **6** padded **7** bluster, stuffed, tympany **8** boasting **9** turgidity **11** rodomontade **14** grandiloquence
bombastic: **5** tumid, vocal **6** fluent, heroic,
turgid **7** bombast, flowery, fustian, orotund, pompous, ranting, stilted **8** inflated
9 expansive, flatulent, grandiose, plethoric
10 lexiphanic **12** magniloquent
Bombay:
arrowroot: **5** tikor
division: **4** Sind
fabric: **5** rumal
hemp: **4** sunn **6** ambary

native: **5** Parsi **6** Parsee
state: **4** Edar
town: **5** Miraj, Poona, Surat
vessel: **7** patamar
bombyx: eri **4** eria, moth **8** silkworm
bon ami: **5** lover **6** friend **10** sweetheart
bonafide: **7** genuine **9** authentic
Bonanza State: **7** Montana
bonbon: **5** candy, cream **6** dainty **7** caramel **8** confetto, confetti **9** sugarplum
bond: tie, vow **4** bail, band, duty, glue,
knot, link, note, yoke **5** bound, chain,
nexus **6** binder, cement, connex, engage,
escrow, fetter, league, pledge **7** husband,
manacle, shackle **8** adhesive, contract,
covenant, guaranty, ligament, ligature,
mortgage, security **9** agreement, composure, guarantee **10** constraint, husbandman, obligation **11** association, householder
bondage: **4** yoke **7** helotry, serfdom,
slavery **9** captivity, restraint, servitude,
thralldom
bondsman: **4** carl, esne, peon, serf **5**
churl, Helot, slave **6** stooge, surety, thrall,
vassal **7** chattel, peasant, servant, villein
bondstone: **6** binder
bone: os; rib **4** ossa(pl.) **5** blade **6** fillet,
radius **7** humerus
anvil: **5** incus **7** incudes(pl.)
arm: **4** ulna **6** radius **7** humerus
breast: **6** sterna(pl.) **7** sternum
cartilage: **6** ossein
change into: **6** ossify
comb. form: os **5** osteo
dorsal: **4** ilia(pl.) **5** ilium
formation: **7** ostosis **10** parostosis
girdle: **12** sphenethmoid
manipulator: **9** osteopath
pert. to: **6** osteal
prefix: **4** oste
scraper: **6** xyster
bonefish: **8** ladyfish
bonelet: **7** ossicle
boner: **5** error **7** blunder, mistake
bones: **4** dice, ossa **8** skeletoa
boneset: **7** comfrey **8** hempweek **12** thoroughwort
bonfire: **5** blaze
boniface: **8** landlord **9** innkeeper
bonito: aku, atu **4** fish, nice **5** cobia **6**
bonita, pretty, robalo **8** skipjack
bonne: **5** nurse **9** nursemaid **11** maidservant
bonnet: cap, hat **4** hood **5** cover, decoy,
toque **6** capote, slouch **7** chapeau, coronet **8** headgear **9** headdress **10** accomplice, chinquapin
brim: **4** poke
bonny, bonnie: gay **4** fine **5** merry, plump
6 blithe, pretty, strong **7** healthy **8**
budgeree, handsome **9** beautiful **11**
good-looking

bonton: 5 elite

bonus: tip 4 gift, meed 5 award, bribe, bunce, pilon, prize, spiff 6 reward 7 cumshaw, premium, subsidy 8 dividend, lagnappe 9 allowance, lagniappe 12 compensation

bony: 4 hard, lank, leaw, thin 5 stiff, tough 6 osteal, skinny 7 osseous 8 skeletal

boo: 4 hoot, jeer 5 decry

boob: ass 4 fool 5 dunce, goony, neddy 6 nitwit

boobook: owl 6 cuckoo

booby: 5 dunce, idiot, loser, prize 6 sleigh, stupid 8 goosecap 9 simpleton

booby hatch: 4 jail 6 asylum

boodle: 4 swag 5 crowd, graft 6 noodle 7 plunder 8 caboodle

boohoo: sob 4 hoot, weep 5 shout 8 sailfish

book: mo; log, mss. 4 opus, text, tome 5 Bible, canto, diary, divan, enter, folio, liber, libri(pl.) 6 manual, record, volume 7 blotter, catalog, writing 8 brochure, document, libretto, register 9 catalogue, potboiler

accounts: day 5 bilan, liber 6 ledger 7 journal
alphabet: 9 abecedary
Apocrypha: 5 Tobit
back: 5 spine
best selling: 5 Bible
binding material: 5 cloth, paper 6 canvas 7 buckram, leather
blank: 5 album, diary 6 tablet
church music: 6 hymnal
collector: 12 bibliomaniac
cover ornamentation: 7 tooling
covering: 6 jacket 7 binding
design: 6 format, lay-out
destroyer: 11 biblioclast
devotional: 5 Bible 6 gospel, missal 7 diurnal, psalter
division: 7 chapter
elementary reading: 6 primer
fiction: 5 novel
group: 7 trilogy
Islam: 5 kitab, Koran
jacket notice: 5 blurb
lover: 11 bibliophile
make-up: 6 format
manuscript: 5 codex, draft 7 codices(pl.)
map: 5 atlas
mass: 6 missal
navigator's: log 7 logbook 9 portolano
obscene: 11 pornography
of hours: 4 Hora 5 Horae(pl.)
of psalms: 7 psalter
page: 5 folio
palm: 4 tara 7 taliera
part: 4 leaf, page 5 cover 7 binding, chapter, section 9 signature
pert. to: 13 bibliographic
school: 6 primer, reader 7 grammar, speller 9 geography 10 arithmetic

size: 6 octavo, quarto 8 twelvemo 9 duodecimo
translation: 4 pony
words of opera: 8 libretto
yearbook: 7 almanac
Zoroastrian: 6 Avesta

book dealer: 10 bibliopole 11 bonguiniste

bookbinder: 12 bibliopegist

bookkeeper: 7 auditor 10 accountant

bookkeeping term: 4 post 5 debit, entry 6 credit 9 statement

bookman: 6 bookie, dealer 7 scholar 9 publisher 11 litterateur

bookplate: 8 exlibris

bookworm: 6 reader 7 scholar 11 bibliophile

boom: jib 4 bump, crib, pole, roar, spar 5 croon 7 bumpkin, resound, support 8 bowsprit, flourish 9 bombilate, bombinate 10 prosperity

boomerang: 5 kiley, kalie 6 recoil 7 rebound 8 backfire, ricochet

boon: gay 4 bene, gift, good, kind 5 favor, grant, merry, order 6 benign, bounty, favour, goodly, jovial, prayer 7 benefit, command, present 8 blessing, intimate, petition 9 congenial, convivial, favorable 10 concession, prosperous 11 benefaction

boor: cad, oaf 4 Boer, carl, lout, pill 5 chuff, churl, clown, slave 6 carlot, clunch, hoblob, lubber, lummox, rustic 7 cauboge, grobian, peasant, villain 8 bosthoon 9 barbarian, roughneck 10 clodhopper, countryman, husbandman, tramontane

boorish: 4 rude 5 gawky, rough, surly 6 clumsy, rustic, sullen, vulgar 7 awkward, crabbed, hoblike, loutish, roister, uncouth 8 churlish, cloddish, clownish, lubberly, ungainly 9 bourgeois 10 uncultured, unmannerly

boost: aid 4 abet, back, help, lift, plug, push 5 coach, exalt, hoist, raise 6 assist, rear up 7 advance, commend, elevate, endorse, indorse, promote 8 increase 9 encourage 10 assistance 12 commendation

boot: pac, use 4 cure, gain, help, kick, shoe, sock 5 avail, booty, eject, jemmy, kamik, spoil 6 bootee, buskin, casing, crakow, enrich, fumble, galosh, sheath 7 benefit, galoshe 8 chassure(F.), covering 9 advantage, discharge, dismissal
half: pac 4 pack 6 buskin, cocker 7 blucher, bottine 8 cothurni(pl.) 9 cothurnus
heavy: pac 5 stogy 6 Brogan 8 Balmoral
high-water: 5 wader
loose-topped: 10 wellington
riding: 5 jemmy 7 gambado
small: 7 bottine 8 bottekin

booted: 4 shod 7 ocreate

booth: 4 loge, shed, shop, sook 5 bothy, cabin, crame, house, stall, stand 6 tienda 7 balagan

bootleg: 7 illegal, illicit 11 clandestine 12 illegitimate 13 surreptitious

bootless: 7 useless 9 incurable 10 remediless, unavailing 12 unprofitable

bootlick: 4 fawn 5 toady 7 flatter

booty: 4 boot, gain, loot, pelf, prey, swag 5 cheat, graft, prize 6 spoils 7 despoil, pillage, plunder 10 chevisance

booze: 4 bout 5 budge, drink, spree 6 fuddle, liquor

boozer: pub 5 toper 6 bouser

boquet: See **bouquet.**

bora: 4 wind

borax: 6 tincal

Bordeaux wine: (see also **wine**): 5 Bourg, cosne, medoc 6 claret 7 Margauz

border: hem, rim 4 abut, brim, dado, eave, edge, line, nark, orle, rand, rund(Sc.), roon, side, trim 5 bound, braid, brink, coast, costa, flank, forel, frame, limit, march, marge, plait, skirt, strip, touch, verge 6 adjoin, costae, edging, forrel, fringe, impale, margin, purfle, stripe 7 bordure, confine, selvage 8 boundary, frontier, neighbor, tressour, tressure 9 extremity, periphery 10 sidepieces

wall: 4 dado, ogee 7 cornice

Border State (Civil War): 8 Arkansas, Delaware, Kentucky, Maryland, Missouri, Virginia 9 Tennessee 13 North Carolina

bordering: 6 edging 8 abutting, adjacent

bore: bit, irk, tap 4 drag, hole, pall, poke, push, ream, size, tide, tire, tool 5 annoy, augur, chink, drill, eagre, gauge, prick, punch, tewel, trick, weary 6 befool, gimlet, pierce, thrust, tunnel 7 caliber, calibre, carried, crevice, opening 8 aiguille, diameter 9 annoyance, penetrate, perforate, terebrate 11 perforation 12 buttonholder

boreas: 4 wind 7 norther

Boreas' son: 6 Calais

bored: 7 ennuyee(F.)

boredom: 5 ennui 6 tedium

borer: 6 insect 7 hagfish, termite 8 shipworm

boric acid salt: 6 borate

boring: dry 4 flat 6 broach, tiring 7 tedious 8 piercing, tiresome 9 wearisome 11 displeasing, penetrating 13 uninteresting

born: nee(F.) 6 innate 7 nascent, natural 9 delivered

dead: 9 stillborn

prematurely: 8 abortive

well: 4 free 5 noble 7 eugenic

borne (see also **bear**): 4 rode 6 narrow 7 carried, endured

by the wind: 6 eolian

Borneo (see also **Indonesia**):

ape: 5 orang 9 orangutan

city: 5 Bruni

measure: 5 ganta 7 gantang

mountain: 8 Kini-Balu

native: 4 Dyak, Iban 5 Dayak

pepper plant: ara

pirates: 5 bajau

river: 5 Bruni, Kajan

sea: 4 Sulu

seaport: 4 Miri 5 Balik, Papan

timbertree: 7 billian

tribe: 4 Dyak, Iban 6 Dusuns

weight: 4 para 6 chapah

boron: 5 borax, boric 7 ulexite

borough: 4 burg, town 5 brush, burgh 6 burgus, castle 7 citadel, village 8 fortress, township

borrow: 4 copy, loan, take 5 adopt, steal 6 pledge, surety 7 chevise, hostage, tithing 11 frankpledge

bosh: end, rot 4 joke, show, talk, tosh 5 trash 6 bushwa, figure, flaunt, humbug, trivia 8 nonsense 9 poppycock

bosky: 5 bushy, tipsy, woody 7 fuddled 11 intoxicated

Bosnian native: 4 Slav 5 Croat

bosom: 4 barm(Sc.) 5 close, sinus 6 breast, cavity, desire, recess 7 beloved, embrace, inclose 8 intimate 9 cherished 11 inclination, indentation 12 confidential

boss: bur, pad 4 baas, buhr, burr, knob, stud 5 bully, chief, empty, knosp, order, owner 6 brooch, button, direct, emboss, hollow, manage, master, shield 7 capataz, cushion, foreman, hassock, headman, manager, phalera 8 director, domineer, overseer 9 supervise 10 politician, supervisor 12 protuberance 14 superintendent

logging camp: 5 bully

political: 7 cacique

shield: 4 umbo

bossy: cow 4 calf 11 dictatorial, domineering

bot: 5 larva

botch: mar, mux 4 boil, mend, mess, sore 5 bitch, bodge, spoil 6 boggle, bumble, bungle, cobble, jumble, repair 8 swelling 10 hodge podge

botcher: 6 grilse, salmon 7 bungler, butcher, clouter, cobbler

both: bo; two 7 equally

handed: 12 ambidextrous

prefix: bi 4 ambi

bother: ado, ail, nag, vex 4 fuss 5 annoy, deave, tease, worry 6 badger, bustle, dither, flurry, gravel, harass, meddle, moider, molest, pester, pother, puzzle, tamper 7 confuse, disturb, perplex, trouble 8 bewilder, irritate, nuisance

bothy: cot, hut 5 booth, lodge 6 bothie 8 barracks

bottle: jug 4 vial 5 cruet, cruse, flask, glass, gourd, house, phial 6 bundle, carafe, carboy, fiasco, flagon, magnum, vessel 7 canteen, costrel 8 building, decanter, demijohn, jeroboam, preserve 9 aryballos, aryballus, container

sealer: 6 capper

small: **4** vial **5** ampul, cruet, phial **6** doruck, flacon **7** ampoule, costrel **8** decanter **11** vinaigrette

bottom: bed **4** base, dale, fund, holm, lees, root **5** abyss, basis, dregs, floor, nadir **6** ground **7** bedrock, grounds, lowland, support, surface **8** buttocks, sediment **10** foundation, groundwork

boudoir: **4** room **5** cabin **7** bedroom, cabinet

bouffant, bouffante: **4** full **6** puffed **7** bulging

bough: arm, leg **4** limb, twig **5** shoot, spray, sprig **6** branch, ramage **7** gallows **8** offshoot, shoulder

boulder: **4** rock **5** stone
monument: **8** megalith
transported by ice: **7** erratic

boulevard: **6** avenue, street **7** highway **12** thoroughfare

bounce: **4** bang, blow, brag, bump, fire, jump, leap, sack **5** boast, bound, bully, carom, chuck, eject, knock, scold, thump, verve **6** spirit, spring, strike **7** address, bluster, dismiss, rebound, swagger **8** proclaim, ricochet **9** discharge, explosion, expulsion **10** resilience

bouncing: big **5** buxom, lusty, stout **7** healthy **9** excessive

bound: dap, end, hop **4** bent, bind, bond, brow, butt, dart, girt, jump, leap, mere, ramp, scud, skip, stem **5** ambit, bourn, going, limit, ready, stend, sting, tiled, vault, verge **6** border, bounce, bourne, curvet, define, domain, finish, hurdle, oblige, prance, spring **7** barrier, certain, chained, closure, confine, costive, delimit, dressed, rebound, saltate, secured, trussed **8** boundary, confined, destined, enclosed, frontier, handfast, landmark, precinct, prepared, shackled **9** compelled, inhibited, obligated **10** borderland **11** constrained, termination **12** circumscribe **13** circumference
back: **5** carom **6** resile
by a vow: **6** votary

boundary: ahu, end, rim **4** dole, dool, edge, line, mear, meer, mere, meta, mete, term, wall **5** ambit, bourn, fence, hedge, limit, march, metae, mound, verge **6** border, bourne, define **7** barrier, bounder, termini(pl.) **8** frontier, precinct, terminus **9** demarcate, perimeter **11** termination **13** circumference
comb. form: ori

bounder: cab, cad, cub **4** snob, rake, roue **7** dogcart

boundless: **4** vast **6** untold **7** endless, eternal **8** infinite **9** limitless, unlimited **10** immoderate, unconfined, unmeasured **11** illimitable, measureless **12** immeasurable, interminable

bountiful: **4** good, lush, rich **5** ample **6** freely, lavish **7** liberal, profuse **8** abun-

dant, generous **9** bounteous, plenteous, plentiful **10** munificent

bounty: **4** boon, gift, meed **5** award, bonus, grant, valor, worth **6** reward, virtue **7** largess, premium, present, prowess, subsidy **8** goodness, gratuity, kindness **9** allowance **10** generosity, liberality, recompense **11** beneficence, munificence

bouquet, boquet: **4** aura, odor **5** aroma, cigar, posey, spray **7** corsage, nosegay **9** fragrance **10** compliment **11** boutonniere

bourgeois: **6** common, stupid **7** boorish, burgher **8** mediocre **9** hidebound **12** capitalistic, conservative

bourn, bourne: **4** goal **5** bound, brook, limit, realm **6** bourne, domain, stream **7** rivulet **8** boundary **11** destination

bouse: cup **4** haul, lift, pull, tope **5** booze, drink **6** beaker **7** carouse

bout: go; job **4** turn **5** booze, essay, fight, match, round, set-to, trial **6** attack, fracas **7** attempt, carouse, circuit, contest, debauch, outside, without **8** conflict **10** knobkerrie

boutonniere: **6** boquet **7** bouquet **10** buttonhole

bovine: ox; bos, cow **4** bull, calf, dull, neat, slow, zebu **5** bison, steer **6** oxlike **7** patient, taurine **8** longhorn, sluggish
hybrid: **4** mule **6** catalo
genus: bos

bow: arc, nod, tie **4** arch, beck, bend, bent, duck, fold, knot, prow, stem, turn, wend **5** binge, conge, crush, curve, defer, kneel, noued, stoop, yield **6** archer, assent, bauble, buckle, curtsy, fiddle, ribbon, salaam, submit, swerve, weapon **7** depress, incline, inflict, rainbow **8** crescent, greeting **9** obeisance, prostrate
facing sea: **4** atry
of ship: **4** beak, prow, stem
oriental: **5** salam **6** salaam
toward: **5** afore
wood for: yew

bow-shaped: **6** arcate

bowed: **4** bent **5** kneed **6** arcate, curved **7** bulging

bowels: gut **5** belly, colon **8** entrails **10** compassion **11** disembowels, eviscerates

bower: **4** jack, nook **5** abode, arbor, joker, knave **6** anchor **7** berceau, chamber, cottage, embower, enclose, pergola, retreat, shelter

bowfin: **4** amia **6** lawyer **7** grindle, mudfish

bowie: tub **4** bowl, cask, pail **5** knife

Bowie State: **8** Arkansas

bowl: cap, cup, pan **4** coup **5** arena, basin, bowie, depas, phial, rogan **6** beaker, crater, syphus, tureen, vessel **7** stadium, whiskin

bowler: hat **5** derby **6** kegler **8** trundler

bowling: **7** tenpins
division: **5** frame

pin: **7** ninepin, skittle
place: **5** alley
score: **5** spare **6** strike
bowman: **5** cupid **6** archer
box: bin, lug, pix, pyx **4** arca, cage, caja, case, cist, crib, cuff, cyst, loge, pack, scob, seat, slap, slug, spar, stow, till, tray **5** barge, boist, buist, buxus, caddy, chest, clout, crate, fight, hutch, punch, shrub, stall, trunk **6** arcana(pl.), buffet, bunker, carton, casket, coffin, hopper, shrine, strike **7** arcanum, cabinet, caisson, casquet, cassone, confine, enclose, fostell, hanaper, package, trummel **9** container, fisticuff **10** receptacle
alms: **4** arca
ammunition: **7** caisson **9** bandoleer, bandolier
document: **7** hanaper
box sleigh: **4** pung
boxer: dog, hat **5** champ **6** bantam **7** bruiser, fighter, sparrer **8** pugilist **11** heavyweight
hand covering: **5** cesti, glove **6** cestus
boxing contest: **4** bout **5** match
boy: bub, lad tad **4** chap, nino(Sp.), page, puer(L.) **5** buddy, chabo, child, gamin, knave, rogue, valet, youth **6** garcon, nipper, rascal, shaver, urchin **7** gossoon, servant **8** henchboy **9** stripling, youngster
boy friend: **4** beau **5** beaux(pl.) **6** steady **10** sweetheart
boycott: **4** shun **5** avoid, debar **9** blackball **10** ostracized
brace: leg, tie, two **4** bind, case, frap, gird, mark, pair, prop, stay **5** nerve, strut **6** clench, couple, crutch, fasten, fathom, splint **7** embrace, refresh, stiffen, support **8** buttress, encircle **9** reinforce, stimulate, suspender **10** strengthen **11** mantelpiece
bracelet: **4** band, ring **5** chain **6** armlet, bangle, grivna **7** armilla, circlet, manacle, poignet **8** handcuff **10** calombigas
bracer: **5** drink, tonic **6** breeze **9** stimulant
bracing: **5** crisp, quick, tonic **10** salubrious **11** stimulating **12** invigorating **13** strengthening
bracken: **4** fern **5** plaid
bracket: **5** brace, class, level, shelf, strut **6** corbel, couple, sconce **7** console, fixture, spotted **8** category, speckled **9** merganser
brackish: **5** foist, salty **6** bracky, saline **7** saltish **8** nauseous **11** distasteful
bract: **5** glume, palea, palet **6** spadix, spathe
brad: pin **4** nail **5** rivet, sprig
brae: **4** bank, brow, hill **5** cleve, slope **6** cleeve, valley **8** hillside
brag: **4** blaw, blow, crow, defy, huff, yelp **5** bluff, boast, flird, preen, strut, vaunt **6** bounce, splore **7** display, gauster, roister,

swagger **8** braggart, flourish, pretense, threaten **9** gasconade **11** rodomontade
braggadocio: **7** boaster **8** braggart, rodomont **9** swaggerer **10** pretension
braggart: **4** brag **5** boast **6** blower, crower, gascon, potgun **7** boaster, cracker, ruffler **8** bangster, blowhard, fanfaron, rodomont **9** renommist **10** burgullian **11** braggadocio, rodomontade
Brahma: **5** Hindu **7** creator
first woman created by: **6** Ahalya
Brahman: **4** zebu **5** Aryan, Hindu **6** priest, pundit **9** Bostonian
land grant: **5** sasan
precept: **5** sutra, sutta
title: aya
braid: cue **4** band, jerk, lace, plat, trim **5** brede, fancy, freak, jiffy, lacet, onset, plait, pleat, queue, start, tress, trick, twine, vomit, weave **6** bobbin, border, moment, plight, ribbon, sennet, snatch, string **7** caprice, entwine, upbraid **8** brandish, ornament, reproach, soutache, trimming **9** deceitful, interlace **10** interweave
gold and silver: **5** orris
hemp: **5** tagal
knotted: **5** lacet
brain: mad **4** bean, harn(Sc.), mind, utac, wits **5** skull **6** psyche **7** furious **8** cerebrum(L.), conceive **9** intellect
box: pan **5** skull **7** cranium
membrane: **4** tela **8** meninges
operate on: **6** trepan
orifice: **4** lura
part: **4** aula **8** cerebrum **10** encephalon **11** pericranium
passage: **4** iter
white matter: pia **4** alba, dura
brainless: **5** silly **6** stupid **7** foolish, witless **11** thoughtless
brake: **4** cage, curb, drag, fern, rack, slow, trap **5** block, check, copse, delay, deter, snare, vomit **6** bridle, harrow, hinder, retard **7** dilemma, thicket **9** brushwood
brakeman: **6** brakie **8** trainman
bramble: **5** brier, thorn **6** bumble **10** cloudberry
brambly: **5** spiny **6** thorny **7** prickly
bran: **5** treat **6** cereal, chisel
branch: arm, bow **4** brog, bush, chat, fork, limb, part, rame, rami, snag, spur, stem **5** bough, creek, ramus, shoot, spray, sprig, vimen, withe **6** divide, member, outlet, raddle, ramage, ramify, stolon, stream **7** diverge, tendril **8** district, offshoot **10** department **11** bifurcation **12** ramification
angle of: **4** axil
of nerves: **4** rami(pl.) **5** ramus
pert. to: **5** ramal **6** remeal
branch herring: **7** alewife
branch-like: **5** ramal **6** ramose, ramous
branched: **5** forky **6** forked, ramate, ramose **7** cladine, cladose

brand: 4 birn, blot, burn, flaw, kind, mark, sear, smit, sort 5 buist, stain, stamp, sword, taint, torch 6 stigma 8 flambeau 9 cauterize, character, trademark 10 stigmatize
on stolen cattle: 4 duff
sheep: 4 smit
brandish: 4 dart, wave 5 bless, braid, shake, swing, wield 6 flaunt, hurtle 7 flutter, glitter, swagger, vibrate 8 flourish 9 coruscate, irradiate
brandy: 4 marc 5 bingo 6 cognac 11 aguardiente(Sp.)
and soda: peg
mastic: 4 raki 5 rakee
plum: 9 slivovitz
brank: 5 caper, mumps, strut 6 bridle, prance 7 pillory
brant: 4 rout 5 erect, goose, proud, quink, sheer, steep 7 steeply 8 straight
brash: 4 bold, rash 5 hasty, saucy, storm 6 attack 7 brittle, forward 8 impudent, tactless 9 irascible
brass: 4 cash 5 alloy, money, nerve 6 brazen 7 officer 9 impudence, insolence
brass hat: (army slang): 7 general, officer
brassica: 4 cole, rape 6 turnip
brassy: 4 bold 6 aerose, brazen 8 impudent
brat: bib, imp 4 film, scum 5 apron, bairn, bilsh, child, cloak 6 infant, mantle, urchin 7 garment 8 clothing 9 offspring
bravado: 4 pomp 5 brave, pride, storm 6 bravor, hector 7 bluster, bombast, bravade, bravery, swagger 9 gasconade
brave: 4 bold, braw(Sc.), dare, defy, face, fine, game, good, prow 5 adorn, boast, bravo, bully, felon, hardy, manly, Roman, stout, vaunt 6 breast, daring, heroic, manful, plucky 7 bravado, gallant, soldier, swagger, valiant, venture, warrior 8 cavalier, defiance, embolden, fearless, intrepid, stalwart, superior, valorous, virtuous 9 challenge, dauntless, excellent, undaunted 10 courageous 11 venturesome 12 stouthearted
bravery: 4 grit 5 valor 6 spirit, valour 7 bravado, bravura, courage, heroism 8 boldness 9 fortitude, gallantry, gentleman, hardihood
bravo: ole(Sp.), rah 4 thug 5 brave, bully 6 bandit, Indian 7 bravado, villain 8 applause, assassin 9 cutthroat, desperado
brawl: din, row 4 clem, fray, riot 5 broil, fight, melee, revel, scold 6 affray, bicker, fracas, habble, revile, rumpus, shindy, strife, tumult, uproar 7 brabble, discord, dispute, quarrel, scuffle, wrangle 8 complain, squabble 10 contention 11 altercation, disturbance
brawling: 5 noisy 7 blatant 9 clamorous 10 clamourous, vociferous 11 quarrelsome
brawn: 4 boar 5 flesh 6 fatten, muscle 8 strength 10 headcheese

brawny: 5 beefy 6 fleshy, robust, sinewy, strong, sturdy 7 callous 8 muscular, powerful, stalwart
bray: cry, mix, rub 4 beat, rout, tool 5 grind, noise, pound 6 bruise, heehaw, outcry, pestle, thrash, whinny
brazen: 4 bold, pert 5 brass, harsh, sassy 6 brassy 7 callous, forward 8 immodest, impudent, insolent, metallic 9 shameless
Brazil:
ant: 9 tucandera
bird: ara, iva 4 soco 5 agami, macaw 6 arvara, darter, tiriba 7 maracan, seriema
city: Rio(c.) 4 Lapa, Para 5 Bahia, Ceara, Natal 6 Manaos, Santos 8 Campinas, Sao Paulo 10 Pernambuco 11 Porto Alegre 12 Rio de Janeiro(c.)
coffee plantation: 7 fazenda
coin: 4 reis 5 conto, dobra 7 milreis 8 cruzeiro
dance: 5 samba 6 maxixe
drink: 5 assai
duck: 7 muscovy
estuary: 4 Para
fiber: 4 imbe
forest: 5 matta
Indian: 4 Anta 5 Acroa, Arara, Arana, Bravo, Carib, Guana, Hauri 6 Arawak, Caraja 7 Tariana 8 Amiranha, Araquaju, Botocudo
mammal: 5 tapir
measure: pe 4 moio, pipa, sack, vara 5 braca, fanga, legoa, milha, palmo, passo, tonel 6 canada, covado, cuarta, league, quarto, tarefa 7 alquier, garrafa 8 alqueire 9 pollegada, quartilho
monkey: sai 6 miriki 9 belzebuth
mountain: 5 Organ 8 Maririme 10 Serra do Mar 14 Serra dos Orgaos
palm: 4 jara 5 assai, inaja, tucum 6 babaca, jupati 7 babassu 9 barriguda
paste: 7 guarana
plant: 4 imbe, para, yage, yaje 5 caroa 7 ayapana, seringa 9 jaborandi
promontory: 4 frio
river: Apa 4 Para, Paru 5 Jurua, Negro, Purus, Xingu 6 Amazon, Parana 7 Madeira, Orinoco, Tapajos 8 Paraguay 9 Tocantins 12 San Francisco
seaport: Rio 4 Para 5 Bahia, Belem, Natal 6 Santos 7 Pelotas
state: 4 Para 5 Bahia, Ceara, Goyas 6 Parana, Piauhy 7 Alagoas, Sergipe 8 Amazonas, Maranhao, Parahiba, Sao Paulo 10 Mato Grosso, Pernambuco 11 Minas Geraes 13 Espirito Santo 14 Rio Grande do Sul, Santa Catharina 16 Rio Grande do Norte
tree: apa, ule 4 anda, assu, uhle 5 araca, tingi 6 biriba, brauna, satine 7 araroba, becuiba, gomavel, paraiba, seringa, wallaba 8 bakupari 10 barbatimao, dal guarabu
weight: bag 4 onca 5 libra 6 arroba, oitava 7 arratel, quilate, quintal 8 tonelada

wood: **6** embuia **8** kingwood

breach: gap **4** chap, flaw, gool, rent, rift **5** brack, breck, chasm, cleft, crack, pause, split, wound **6** bruise, harbor, hernia, hiatus, inroad, schism **7** assault, blemish, dispute, fissure, opening, quarrel, rupture **8** breaking, fraction, fracture, interval, trespass **9** violation **10** disruption, infraction **12** infringement, interruption **14** nonfulfillment **16** misunderstanding

breach pin: **4** tige

bread: bun **4** diet, fare, food, loaf, pone, roll, rush **5** batch **7** aliment, bannock(Sc.) **10** livelihood, sustenance

boiled: **4** cush **6** panada

browned: **5** toast **6** sippet **7** crouton

communion: **4** azym **5** azyme

crust: **4** rind

leavened: **5** kisra **6** cocket

pert. to: **6** panary

unleavened: **4** azym **5** azyme **6** matzos **7** bannock, matzoth **8** afikomen

breadth: **4** span **5** brede, scope, width **6** extent **8** diameter, distance, latitude **9** amplitude, dimension

breadwinner: **6** earner, worker

break: gap **4** boon, bust, dash, hint, knap, pick, plow, rend, rent, rift, rive, ruin, rush, slip, snap, stop, tear **5** alter, blank, burst, cleft, crack, craze, frush, lapse, pluck, sever, smash, wound **6** bruise, change, cleave, defeat, hiatus, impair, lacuna, pierce **7** blunder, caesura, crackle, crevice, crumble, destroy, disable, dispart, disrupt, exhaust, fissure, lacunae(pl.), opening, respite, rupture, shatter **8** caesurae, fraction, fracture, interval, separate **9** interrupt, penetrate **10** invalidate **12** interruption **14** discontinuance

down: **7** debacle, failure **8** collapse **9** cataclasm **10** catabolism

in: **4** slip **5** stave **7** blunder **8** initiate **9** interrupt

of day: **4** dawn, morn **5** sunup **7** morning

out: **4** rash **5** erupt **6** escape

up: **5** split **7** disband, disrupt **8** disperse, dissolve, separate

breakable: **7** brittle, bruckle, friable **8** delicate

breaker: **4** surf, wave **6** billow, comber, roller

breakwater: cob, dam **4** cobb, dike, mole, pier, pile, quay **5** jetty **6** refuge **11** obstruction

bream: tai **4** fish, scup **5** broom **7** sunfish

sea: **4** shad **6** sargus

breast: **4** crop **5** bosom, brave, chest **6** thorax **9** encounter

ornament: **8** pectoral

breastbone: **6** sterna(pl.) **7** sternum, xiphoid **9** gladiolus

pert. to: **7** sternal

breastplate:

armor: **4** urim **6** gorget, lorica, shield

7 poitrel, thummin **8** poitrail

ecclesiastical: **4** urim

breastwork: **4** fort **5** redan **7** brattle, parapet, rampart **10** forecastle

breath: **4** ande, gasp, huff, life, pant, pech, puff, sigh, wind **5** pause, scent, smell, vapor, whiff **6** breeze, pneuma **7** halitus, instant, respite **10** exhalation

breathe: **4** ande, live, pant, pech, puff, sigh **5** exist, speak, utter **6** aspire, exhale, inhale, wheeze **7** afflate, emanate, respire, suspire

hard: **4** gasp, pant

breather: **4** rest **5** break, pause, truce **6** recess, repose **9** armistice

breathing: **5** alive **7** gasping **9** spiration **11** respiration

difficult: **7** dyspnea **8** dyspnoea

orifice: **4** nose, pore **5** mouth, nares **7** nostril **8** spiracle

smooth: **4** lene

sound: **4** rale **5** snore, snort **7** stridor

breathless: **4** dead **5** stale, tense **6** stuffy **10** motionless

bred well: **6** polite **7** genteel **9** pedigreed

breech: **4** bore, butt, doup **5** block **7** droddum **8** buttocks, derriere **9** posterior

breeches: **5** chaps, jeans, levis **8** jodhpurs, knickers, trousers **10** pantaloons

breed: ilk **4** bear, kind, race, rear, sort **5** beget, brood, caste, cause, class, hatch, raise, stock, train **6** create, strain **7** educate, nourish, produce, progeny, species, variety **8** engender, instruct, multiply **9** offspring, originate, propagate **10** generation

breeding: **6** origin **7** descent **8** behavior, training **9** education, gestation **10** deportment, extraction **11** development, instruction

science: **8** eugenics

breeze: air **4** aura, blow, flaw, gale, gust, pirr, stir, wind **5** blast, rumor **6** breath, report, zephyr **7** freshen, quarrel, whisper **11** disturbance

land: **6** terral

breezy: **4** airy **5** brisk, fresh, windy **6** airish **9** vivacious

breve: **4** bird, mark, note, writ **5** brief, minim, order **6** letter **7** compose, precept **8** syllable

brevet: **6** confer **9** promotion **10** commission

breviary: **4** ordo **6** digest, portas **7** coucher, epitome, summary **8** abstract **10** compendium **11** abridgement

brevity: **9** briefness, shortness, terseness **11** conciseness **12** succinctness

brew: ale, mix **4** beer, boil, make, plot, pour **5** hatch **6** devise, dilute, foment, gather, liquor, seethe **7** concoct, incline, prepare **8** beverage, contrive

briar: saw **4** pipe

bribe: fee, oil, rob, sop, tip **4** bait, gift hire, meed **5** bonus, cuddy, graft, offer, steal, sugar, tempt **6** extort, grease, payola, suborn **7** corrupt **8** gratuity **10** allurement

bric-a-brac: **5** curio **7** bibelot **11** knickknacks

brick: **4** pave, tile **5** block, quarl, stone **6** fellow, quarle
handler: **6** hacker
sun-baked: bat **5** adobe
tray: hod
vitrified: **7** clinker
wood: nog **4** dook **6** scutch

bridal: **7** nuptial

bride: bar, tie **4** loop, rein, rose **6** bridle, kallah

bridesmaid: **9** attendant

bridge: way **4** game, link, pons, pont, span **5** cross **6** ponton **7** auction, bascule, connect, pontoon, trestle, viaduct **8** contract, traverse **9** alcantara, gangplank
combination: **6** tenace
lever: **7** bascule
of musical instrument: **5** magas **10** ponticello
pontoon plank: **5** chess
score: leg
support: **4** pier **5** truss
term: bid, bye, leg, set **4** book, game, pass, ruff, slam, suit, void **5** raise, trick, trump **6** renege, revoke **7** finesse **9** part-score

bridle: bit **4** curb, rein, rule **5** brake, brank, bride, check, guard, guide, strut **6** direct, govern, halter, master, simper, subdue **7** blinder, control, repress, snaffle, swagger **8** restrain, suppress **9** restraint
noseband: **6** musrol **8** cavesson

brief: few **4** curt, list, rife, writ **5** blurb, breve, charm, pithy, quick, short, terse **6** abrupt, common, letter **7** abridge, compact, compose, concise, invoice, laconic, mandate, outline, precept, summary **8** breviate, condense, fleeting, succinct, syllabus **9** catalogue, condensed, ephemeral, memoranda(pl.), prevalent **10** compendium, memorandum, transitory **11** compendious

briefness: **7** brevity

brier, briar: **4** barb, pipe **5** thorn **6** similax

brig: **4** boat, jail **6** prison, vessel **10** guardhouse

brigand: **5** thief **6** bandit, pirate, robber **7** cateran, ladrone, soldier **8** picaroon **10** highwayman

bright: apt, gay **4** fine, glad, rosy **5** acute, aglow, alert, anime, beamy, clear, fresh, gemmy, light, lucid, nitid, quick, riant, sharp, smart, sunny, vivid, witty **6** cheery, clever, florid, garish, limpid, lively, lucent, orient **7** forward, fulgent, radiant, ringing, shining **8** animated, cheerful, flashing, gleaming, luminous, lustrous, splendid, splendor **9** brilliant, cloudless, effulgent, refulgent, sparkling **10** brightness, epiphanous, glistening, glittering **11** illus-

trious, intelligent, resplendent, transparent

brighten: **4** gild **5** cheer, clear, light, liven, shine **6** cantle, engild, polish **7** animate, burnish, enliven, furbish, lighten **8** illumine **9** irradiate

brightness: **5** eclat, flame, gleam, gloss, nitor, sheen **6** acumen, bright, fulgor, luster **7** clarity, fulgour, sparkle **8** splendor **9** clearness **10** brilliance, effulgence

brilliance: **4** fame **5** eclat, flame, glory **7** keeness **8** radiance, splendor **10** brightness, effulgence

brilliant: gay **4** good, keen, sage, wise **5** breme **6** bright, clever, signal **7** eminent, flaming, radiant, shining **8** dazzling, glorious, luminous **9** effective, prismatic, refulgent, sparkling **10** glittering **11** prismatical, resplendent **13** distinguished

brim: lip, rim, rut, sea **4** edge **5** bluff, brink, marge, ocean, verge, water **6** border, margin **8** copulate, strumpet **9** periphery

brimming: **4** full

brimstone: **6** virago **7** sulphur **8** spitfire

brindled: **5** tawny **7** flecked **8** streaked

brine: sea **4** main, salt **5** ocean, tears **6** pickle **8** marinade
preserve in: **4** corn, cure, salt

bring: **4** bear, take **5** carry, fetch **6** convey, deduce **7** conduce, procure, produce **9** transport
about: **5** cause **6** create **7** achieve **10** accomplish
back: **6** effect, recall, return, revive **7** produce, restore **8** occasion, retrieve, transact **9** instigate **10** consummate
forth: ean(Sc.) **4** bear **5** educe, hatch, incur **6** adduce, beteem **7** produce
in: **5** usher **6** import, report, return **9** introduce
near to: **6** appose
on: **6** induce
to: **11** resuscitate
to earth: **4** land
to light: **6** elicit, reveal **7** unearth **8** disclose, discover
to naught: **4** dash **6** negate **7** confute **9** frustrate
together: **4** join **5** unite **7** compile
up: **4** rear **5** nurse, raise, train **7** educate **11** regurgitate

brink: end, eve, lip, rim, sea **4** bank, brim, edge, foss **5** marge, shore, verge **6** border, margin

briny: **5** brack, salty **6** saline

brioche: **4** roll **6** stitch **7** cushion, pudding, savarin

brisk: gay **4** busy, fast, keen, pert, racy, spry, yern **5** agile, alert, alive, budge, crisp, fresh, frisk, peart, perky, quick, sharp, smart, yerne **6** active, breezy, cocket, crouse, lively, nimble, snappy **7**

allegro **8** animated, friskful, spirited **9** energetic, sprightly, vivacious **11** stimulating **12** effervescing

bristle: awn **4** barb, hair, seta, tela **5** birse, brush, parch, preen, setae, strut, toast **6** chaeta, palpus, ruffle, setula **7** chaetae, setulae, stubble
comb. form: **4** seti
surgical: **4** seta **5** seton

bristle-like: **5** setal **8** setiform

bristling: **5** rough **6** hispid, horrid, setose, thorny **7** horrent, scrubby

Britain: See **England**.

British Columbia:
Indian: **5** Haida **7** Shuswap
river: **6** Nicola

Briton: **4** Celt, Scot

Brittany:
canvas: **8** vandelas
king: Ban
native: **6** Breton
poetry: **6** soniou

brittle: **4** frow, weak **5** brash, candy, crisp, crump, eager, frail, frowy, frush, short **6** crispy, crumpy, feeble, fickle, frough, infirm, slight **7** brickle, bruckle, fragile, friable, froughy **8** delicate, snappish **9** breakable, crumbling, frangible, irritable **10** perishable

broach: air, awl, cut, pin, rod, tap **4** open, ouch, shed, spit, spur, stab, veer, vent **5** begin, dress, drift, prick, rimer, spool, voice **6** boring, brooch, launch, pierce, reamer **7** enlarge, publish, spindle, violate **8** approach, broacher, deflower, incision **9** introduce **11** perforation

broad: **4** deep, free, vast, wide **5** ample, beamy, large, plain, roomy, thick, woman **6** coarse **7** evident, general, grivois, liberal, obvious, platoid **8** grivoise, spacious, tolerant **9** capacious, expansive, extensive, outspoken **12** unrestrained **13** comprehensive

broad-footed: **8** platypod

broad-minded: **7** lenient, liberal **8** Catholic, tolerant

broadbill: **4** bird, gaya, raya **5** scaup **8** shoveler **9** swordfish

broadcast: sow **4** seed, send, **5** radio, strew **6** spread **7** publish, scatter **8** announce, televise, transmit **9** advertise

broadcloth: **6** cotton, fabric, woolen **7** suiting **8** material

broaden: **5** brede, widen **6** dilate, expand, extend, spread **7** ennoble **9** expatiate **10** generalize

broadsword: **4** bill, kris **6** glaive, spatha **7** cutlass, Ferrara **8** claymore, scimitar

brocade: **5** cloth **6** broche, kincab **8** baudekin **9** baldachin

brocard: **4** gibe, rule **5** maxim **6** speech **7** sarcasm **9** principle

brochure: **4** book **5** tract **8** pamphlet, treatise

brocket: **4** deer, pita, stag **5** brock **7** spitter

brogan: **4** shoe **5** stogy **6** brogue

brogue: **4** hose, shoe **5** fraud, trick **6** accent, brogan **7** dialect **8** trousers

broil: row **4** burn, char, feud, fray, heat **5** alarm, brawl, grill, melee, scrap **6** affray, birsle, braise, splore, tumult **7** brulyie(Sc.), contest, discord, dispute, embroil, garboil, quarrel **8** conflict, grillade **10** contention, dissension **11** altercation, disturbance

broiler: **4** bird **5** grill **7** chicken

broke: **8** bankrupt **9** insolvent, penniless

broken: **4** rent, torn **5** burst, gappy, rompu(F.), rough, tamed **6** hackly, ruined, shaken **7** crushed, fracted, reduced, subdued **8** outlawed, ruptured, weakened **9** cashiered, dispersed, fractured, shattered **10** incoherent, incomplete **11** fragmentary **12** disconnected, intermittent

broker: **5** agent **6** corser, dealer, factor, jobber **7** brogger, changer, courser, peddler, realtor, scalper **8** broacher, huckster, merchant **10** pawnbroker

brokerage: fee **4** agio **10** commission

bromide: **5** trite **8** compound, sedative **9** platitude

bronco: **5** horse **6** cayuse **7** broncho, mustang **9** estrapade(Sp.)

bronco buster: **6** cowboy, ginete

Bronx cheer: boo **9** raspberry

bronze: aes(L.), tan **4** bust **5** alloy, brown **6** statue
film: **6** patina
gilded: **6** ormolu
nickel: **11** cupronickel

brooch: bar, pin **4** boss, ouch **5** cameo, clasp **6** fibula, plaque, shield **8** ornament **9** brochette

brood: fry, nye, set, sit **4** mope, nest, nide, race, weep **5** aerie, breed, covey, flock, group, hatch, issue, sedge, worry, young **6** cletch, clutch, family, litter, ponder **7** progeny, species **8** cogitate, incubate, meditate **9** multitude, offspring **11** contemplate

brook: run **4** bear, beck, burn, ghyl, gill, rill, rush, sike **5** abide, bayou, bourn, creek, stand **6** arroyo(Sp.), bourne, canada, endure, gutter, rindle, rivose, runlet, stream, suffer **7** comport **8** quebrada, tolerate **11** watercourse

brooklet: **4** beck, rill **6** rillet, runnel **7** rillock, rivulet **9** arroyuelo(Sp.)

broom: mop **4** fray, swab **5** besom, bream, brush, spart, sweep, whisk **8** splinter

broom plant: **5** hirse, spart **7** cyticus, genista, heather **8** deerweed

broomcorn millet: **5** hirse

broth: **4** bree, broo, soup **5** stock **6** brewis, jussal, jussel **7** pottage **8** consomme, jusshell

brother: bub, fra, kin, pal, sib 4 mate, monk, peer 5 billy, buddy, cadet, frere(F.), friar 6 fellow, fraile, frater(L.) 7 comrade, sibling
pert. to: 9 fraternal

brotherhood: 4 gild 5 guild, lodge 6 friary 8 bratstro, sodality 10 fellowship, fraternity 11 association 13 brotherliness, companionship; confraternity

brotherly: 4 kind 6 tender 9 fraternal 12 affectionate

brougham: 8 carriage

brought up: 4 cade

brow: top 4 brae, bree, edge, mien, snab(Sc.) 5 bound, brink, crest, front, ridge, slope 8 boldness, forehead 9 acclivity, gangplank 10 effrontery 11 countenance

browbeat: 5 abash, bully 6 hector 7 depress 10 disconcert, intimidate

brown: dun, tan 4 coin, cook, dark, sear 5 dusky, penny, sedge, sepia, tawny, tenne, toast, umber 6 gloomy, russet, sennet, tanned 9 half-penny
cocoa: 6 sahara
dark: 6 bister, bistre
light: tan 4 ecru, fawn 5 beige, khaki, tenne
purple: 4 puce
red: bay 4 cuba, roan 5 henna, sepia 6 auburn, russet, sorrel 8 chestnut
rich: 5 sepia

brown Bess: 6 musket

brown Betty: 7 pudding 10 coneflower

browned: 7 rissole

brownie: elk, nis 4 cake 5 cooky, nisse, urisk 6 goblin, uruisg(Sc.) 9 sandpiper

browse: 4 brut, crop, feed 5 graze 6 forage, nibble 7 pasture

bruin: 4 bear

bruise: 4 bash, bray, dent, dunt, hurt, maim, maul 5 break, crush, curry, delve, dinge, pound 6 batter, breach, hatter, injury, mangle, shiner 7 contuse, dammish, disable 9 pulverize, triturate

bruised: 4 hurt 5 livid 6 humble 7 froisse

bruiser: 5 boxer 8 pugilist

bruit: din 4 fame, rale, tell 5 noise, rumor, sound 6 blazon, clamor, report 7 declare, hearsay

brume: fog 4 haze, mist, smog 5 vapor

brumous: 5 foggy, misty 6 hiemal, sleety 7 wintery

brunette: 4 dark 5 brown, brune, gipsy, gypsy 7 swarthy

brunt: jar 4 blow, jolt 5 clash, force, onset, shock 6 attack, effort, impact 7 assault 8 outburst

brush: 4 comb, fray, skim 5 broom, clean, copse, fight, graze, sweep 6 badger, battle, brosse(F.), stroke 7 thicket 8 skirmish 9 brushwood, encounter 11 undergrowth

brushwood: 4 rone 5 brake, brush, copse,

frith, scrog, scrub 6 rammel 7 coppice, thicket

brusque: 4 curt, rude 5 bluff, blunt, brusk, gruff, hasty, rough, short 6 abrupt 7 violent 8 cavalier, impolite 12 discourteous

brut: dry 6 browse

brutal: 5 cruel, feral, gross 6 carnal, coarse, savage 7 bestial, beastly, brutish, caddish, inhuman 8 ruthless 9 atrocious, barbarous, ferocious, insensate

brute: 5 beast, yahoo 6 animal, savage 7 ruffian 9 scoundrel

bryophyte: 4 moss 5 plant 9 liverwort

Brython: 5 Welsh 6 Celtic 7 Cornish
god: Dea, Ler 4 Bran 5 Dylan, Lludd 8 Amaethon
goddess: Don 8 Rhiannon 9 Arianrhod

bubble: air, bub 4 bead, bell(Sc.), bleb, blob, boil, boll, dupe, foam, glob, seed, suds 5 caper, cheat, empty 6 burble, delude, seethe, trifle 7 blister, blubber, deceive, globule 8 delusive 10 effervesce 11 speculation

bubbling: gay 8 effusive 9 sparkling

buccaneer: 6 pirate, rifler, robber, viking 7 corsair, mariner, spoiler 8 Picaroon 10 freebooter
standard: 5 roger

buck: fob, ram 4 boil, butt, deer, dude, male, prig, rear, soak, stag, toff, wash 5 dandy, steep 6 basket, dollar, oppose, resist 7 sawbuck 8 antelope, prickett, sawhorse 9 buckwheat
first year: 4 fawn
fourth year: 4 sore

bucket: tub 4 bail, bowk, cage, pail 5 cheat, scoop, skeel 6 bailer, drench, hoppet, situla(L.), vessel 7 swindle 8 cannikin
handle: 4 bail
molten glass: 7 cuvette

Buckeye State: 4 Ohio

buckle: bow 4 bend, curl, kink, tach, warp 5 clasp, marry, twist 6 fibula(L.) 7 contend, fermail, fibulae(L.pl.), grapple 8 fastener, struggle 10 distortion
part: 5 chape 6 tongue

buckler: 4 crab 5 block 6 shield 7 rotella, roundel, shutter

buckram: 6 fabric 7 precise 10 cuckoopint, stiffening

buckthorn: 5 rhamn 7 alatern, cascara 8 lotebush 9 alaternus, chaparral

buckwheat: 4 black 8 sarrazin

buckwheat tree: 4 titi 6 teetee

bucolic: 4 idyl 5 local, naive, rural 6 farmer, rustic, simple 7 cowherd, eclogue 8 agrestic, herdsman, pastoral

bud: eye, gem, imp, pip 4 bulb, cion, germ, girl, grow, knop 5 child, graft, scion, shoot, youth 6 button, flower, germin, sprout, 7 blossom, brother, gemmule 8 bourgeon 9 germinate

arrangement: 11 aestivation
social: deb 8 debutant 9 debutante
Buddha: Fo; Foh 7 Gautama 10 Shaky-
amuni
cause of infinite existence: 6 nidana
center: 5 Lassa, Lhasa
church: 4 Tera
column: lat
dryad: 6 Yaksha, Yakshi
evil spirit: 4 Mara
fate: 5 karma
fertility spirit: 6 Yaksha, Yakshi
festival: bon
final beatitude: 4 raga 7 nirvana
for justice: 6 dharna, dhurna
gateway: 5 toran, torii 6 torana
god: 4 deva
greater: 8 Hinayana
Japanese image: 8 Daibutsu
language: 4 Pali
lesser: 8 Mahayana
mendicant: 6 bhikku 7 bhikshu
monastery: 4 Tera 6 Vihara
monk: bo 4 lama 5 arhat, yahan 7 poongee
8 poonghee, poonghie, talapoin
monument: 5 stupa
mother: 4 Maya
novice: 5 goyim
passion: 4 raga
priest: 4 lama 7 mahatma
relic mound: 5 stupa
retribution: 5 karma
rock temple: 4 rath 5 ratha
sacred city: 5 Lassa, Lhasa
scripture: 5 sutra
sect: 7 Jodo-shu
shrine: 4 tope 5 stupa 6 dagoba 7 chorten
stupa site: 9 Amaravati
throne: 5 asana
title: 7 Mahatma
tree: 5 pipal 6 botree
will to live: 5 Tanha
buddy: bo; boy, pal 4 mate 7 brother, comrade 8 tentmate 9 companion
budge: fur 4 move, stir 5 booze, brisk,
stiff, thief 6 jocund, liquor, solemn 7
austere, pompous 8 movement 11 nervousness
budget: bag 4 boot, pack, plan, roll 5
batch, bunch, stock, store 6 bottle, bundle, parcel, socket, wallet 7 program 12
accumulation
buds: 8 burgeons, dehisces
pickled: 6 capers
buff: ox; bob, fan, tan 4 blow, coat, curt,
firm 5 shine 6 buffet, polish, sturdy 7
leather, stammer, stutter 8 nonsense, seladang 10 enthusiast
buffalo: ox 4 anoa, buff, stag 5 bison, bugle 6 buffle, hamper 7 cariboo, caribou,
gazelle, overawe, timarau, zamouse 8 bewilder 9 bamboozle
large: 4 arna, arni 5 arnee
meat: 7 biltong

wild: 4 arna, arni 5 arnee 8 seladang
buffalo gourd: 11 calabazilla
buffalo tree: 10 rabbitwood
buffer: dog, pad 6 bumper, fender, pistol 7
cushion
buffet: bar, bob, box 4 beat, blow, buff,
cuff, slap, toss 5 filip, smite, stool 6 abacus, batter, fillip, strike, strive, thrash 7
contend, counter, hassock 8 credence,
credenza, cupboard 9 footstool, sideboard
10 affliction
bufflehead: 4 duck, fool 5 clown 6 buffle
9 merrywing
buffleheaded: 4 dull 6 stupid
buffoon: dor, wag, wit 4 aper, fool, jape,
mime, mome 5 actor, antic, buffo, clown,
comic, drole, droll, mimer 6 harlot, jester,
mummer, stooge 7 playboy 8 balatron,
gracioso, humorist, merryman, ridicule 9
harlequin 10 harlequina, hobby-horse 11
merry-andrew, Punchinello
bug: bog, dor 4 flaw, germ, idea, mite 5
bogey, bulge, roach 6 beetle, chinch, elater, insect, scheme 7 bellied, bugbear,
forward, pompous 8 hemipter, hobbyist 9
conceited, hobgoblin, prominent 10 enthusiast, flashlight 11 hunchbacked
June: dor
lightning: 7 firefly
needle: 7 ranatra
bugaboo: 4 bogy, fear, goga, gogo, ogre 5
alarm, bogey, bogie, gogga 6 bodach,
goblin 7 bugbear, specter, spectre 8 wor-
ricow(Sc.) 9 hobgoblin, scarecrow, wor-
riecow(Sc.) 10 mumbo-jumbo
bugbane: 4 herb 9 hellebore 10 rattleroot
bugbear: See **bugaboo.**
bugger: 4 chap 6 fellow, person, rascal 7
heretic 8 sodomite 11 Albigensian
buggy: (see also **carriage**) 4 cart, shay,
trap 5 nutty 7 caboose, foolish, vehicle 8
demented, infested, stanhope 9 gladstone
bughouse: 5 crazy, nutty 6 asylum, insane
bugle: ox 4 bead, horn 5 black 7 buffalo,
bullock, clarion, trumpet
blare: 7 tantara
call: 4 taps 6 alerte(F.), sennet, tattoo 7
retreat 8 reveille
note: mot
bugleweed: 4 mint 6 indigo
build: big 4 bigg, form, make, rear 5 edify,
erect, found, frame, raise, set up, shape 6
create, graith 7 fashion 8 assemble 9
construct, establish, fabricate
up: 7 enhance 8 increase 9 publicity 10
strengthen
builder: 5 maker 7 erector 8 tectonic 9
carpenter 11 constructor
labyrinth: 8 Daedalus
of wooden horse: 5 Epeus 6 Epeius
building: 4 casa(Sp.), pile 5 aedes, hotel, house 6 biggin, bottle, fabric 7 edifice, factory 8 dwelling 9 apartment,
structure 10 storehouse 11 edification

addition to: ell **4** apse, wing **5** annex **6** lean-to

dilapidated: **7** rookery **8** firetrap, tenement

exhibition: **6** museum

farm: **4** barn, crib, shed, silo

gateway: **5** pylon

material: **4** iron, wood **5** brick, glass, steel **6** cement

medieval: **6** castle

part: ell **4** apse

projection: ell **4** apse, wing **5** annex **6** dormer, lean-to **7** cornice

public: **5** edile **6** aedile, casino, church, museum, temple **7** capitol, library, theater **10** auditorium

rib: **9** tierceron

round: **7** rotunda

sacred: **4** fane **6** church, mosque, temple **7** edicule **8** pantheon **9** cathedral

stately: **6** castle, palace **7** edifice, mansion

buirdly: **5**husky **6** strong **8** athletic

bulb: bud **4** blub, corm, knob, lamp, root **5** globe, swell, tuber **6** bulbus **9** expansion **12** protuberance

edible: yam **4** sego **5** onion **6** garlic, potato

bulbous: **7** round **7** swollen

bulbul: **4** bird, kala

Bulgar: **4** Slav **5** Tatar **6** Slavic **9** Bulgarian

assembly: **8** Sobranje, Sobranye

capital: **5** Sofia

coin: lev, lew, **8** stotinka

commune: **6** Sliven, Slivno **7** Sistova

measure: oka, oke **5** krine, lekha

river: **5** Mesta **6** Danube, Marica, Struma **7** Marista

ruler: **4** czar, tsar **5** Boris

town: **4** Ruse **5** Byclu, Sofia(c.), Stara, Varna **6** Bleven, Burgas, Plevna, Shumen, Shumla, Sliven, Slivno, Widdin, Zagora **7** Plovdiv, Sistova, Tirnova **8** Rustchuk **9** Silistria

weight: oka, oke **5** tovar

bulge: bag, bug, jut **4** bump, cask, hump, knob, lump **5** belly, bilge, bloat, bouge, flask, pouch, swell **6** billow, cockle, extend, pucker, wallet **7** blister **8** protrude **9** convexity, gibbosity **10** projection **11** indentation **12** protuberance

bulged: **5** bombe

bulging: **4** full **5** bombe, bowed, pudgy **6** convex **7** gibbous **8** bouffant

bulk: **4** body, heap, hold, hulk, hull, mass, pile, size **5** cargo, gross, might, power, stall, swell **6** expand, extent, figure, volume **7** bigness **8** majority, quantity **9** aggregate, dimension, largeness, magnitude **11** massiveness

bulkhead: **5** check **9** partition, structure

bulky: big **5** burly, gross, large, stout **6** clumsy, stodgy **7** hulking, massive, weighty **8** unwieldy **9** corpulent, policeman, ponderous

bull: cop **4** apis, jest, male, seal, slip,

toro(Sp.), zebu **5** bobby, boner, drink, edict, error **6** bovine, letter, peeler, taurus(L.) **8** cajolery, document, flattery **9** detective, policeman, quadruped **10** zapaterito(Sp.)

angry: **5** gorer

castrated: **4** stot **5** steer **7** bullock

half man: **8** minotaur

hornless: **5** doddy **6** doddie

young: **4** stot(Sc.) **5** stirk **7** bullock

bull-like: **7** taurine

Bull Run:

battle: **8** Manassas

hero: Lee

bulla: **4** bleb, case, seal **5** blain **7** vesicle

bullate: **8** puckered

bulldoze: cow, dig, ram **5** bully, force, scoop **6** coerce, pistol **8** browbeat, restrain

bulldozer: **5** bully **6** grader **7** machine

bullet: **4** ball, lead, shot, slug **6** pellet, sinker, tracer **7** missile

diameter: **7** caliber

fake: **6** pellet

bulletin: **4** memo **6** notice, poster, report **7** program **9** statement **11** publication **12** announcement

bullfighter: . **6** torero **7** matador, picador **8** capeador, matadore, toreador

foot: **6** torero

mounted: **8** toreador

bullfinch: alp, olp **4** monk, nope, olph, pope **5** hedge

bullheaded: **6** stupid **8** stubborn **9** obstinate **10** headstrong

bullion: bar **5** ingot, metal **6** billot

bullock: **4** stot **5** bugle, steer, stirk **6** bovine **9** quadruped

bull's eye: **6** target

bully: **4** boat, boss, fine, good, huff, mate **5** brave, bravo, great **6** bounce, harass, hector, jovial, tyrant **7** bluster, bouncer, bullock, darling, dashing, gallant, gauster, huffcap, roister, ruffian **8** bangster, barrater, barrator, browbeat, bulldoze, domineer, frampler **9** blusterer, bulldozer, companion, excellent, scrimmage **10** burgullian, intimidate, sweetheart

bulrush: **4** reed, rush, tule **5** sedge **6** bumble **7** cattail, papyrus, scirpus

bulwark: **4** bail, fort, wall **5** fence, mound **7** bastion, defence, defense, parapet, protect, rampart **10** breakwater **12** propugnacula(L.pl.) **13** propugnaculum(L.)

bum: beg, din **4** hobo **5** drink, drone, idler, mooch, tramp **6** frolic, guzzle, sponge **7** guzzler **8** vagabond

bumble: bee **4** veil **5** botch, drone, idler **6** beadle, bungle, jumble, muffle **7** bittern, blunder, bramble, bulrush, bungler

bumblebee: dor **6** bumbee, bumble, insect

bump: cry, hit **4** blow, boom, jolt, lump, whop **5** bulge, clout, knock, thump **6** bounce, nodule, strike **7** bittern, collide **8** swelling **10** projection **12** protuberance

bumper: 4 bowl, fine, good 5 facer, glass 6 buffer, fender, goblet 8 carangid

bumpkin: yap 4 beam, boom, clod, gawk, hick, lout, rube, swab 5 churl, clown, robin, yahoo, yokel 6 lummox 7 cauboge, hawbuck 9 chawbacon

bun: jag, wig 4 boat, bunt, roll, stem, tail 5 stalk 6 rabbit 7 biscuit, chervil, stubble 8 squirrel 11 drunkenness

bunch: bob, set 4 bale, club, herd, hump, kick, pack, tuft, wisp 5 clump, fagot, flock, knoll, pahil(Ir.), thump 6 budget, bundle, finial, hobble, 8 quantity, swelling 9 aggregate 10 collection

of grapes: bob

pert. to: 5 comal

bund: 4 band, quay 5 praya 6 league 7 society 10 embankment, federation 11 confederacy

bundle: lot, wad, wap 4 bale, band, bolt, garb, hank, pack, roll, swag 5 bunch, fadge, group, sheaf 6 bindle, fardel, fascis(L.), gather, number, packet, parcel 7 package 10 collection

maker: 5 baler

bundle of:

arrows: 5 sheaf

firewood: 5 bavin

grain: 5 sheaf

sticks: 5 fagot 6 faggot

straw: 4 bolt

bung: 4 cork, dead, maul, plug, stop 5 plumb, purse, spile 6 parcel 7 smashed, squared, stopper, stopple, tampeon, tampion, tampoon 8 bankrupt, bunghole, 9 falsehood 10 pickpocket

bungle: err 4 goof, mess, muff 5 blunk, botch, spoil 6 boggle, bumble, foozle, fumble 7 bauchle, blunder 9 mismanage

bungling: 6 clumsy 7 awkward 9 maladroit, unskilled 10 blundering

bunk: bed, car 4 case 5 abide, berth, bunko, frame, hokum, hooey, leave, lodge, sleep, truck 6 bunkum, timber 7 baloney, boloney, chicory, hemlock, twaddle 8 buncombe, nonsense 9 crossbeam, skedaddle 10 humbuggery

bunker: bin, box 5 chest 6 hazard 8 obstacle, sandhole 11 compartment 12 entanglement

bunko: 5 bunco, cheat 6 scheme 7 swindle

bunt: bun 4 butt, push, sift, smut, tail 5 shove, 6 kernel, strike

bunting: 4 bird, flag, pape 5 dumpy, finch, plump 6 cotton, stocky, towhee, untidy 7 cowbird, etamine, garment, ortolan, rounded 8 bellying, bobolink, slovenly

bunyip: 4 sham 6 humbug, poster 8 impostor

buoy: dan 5 baken, elate, float, raise 6 marker 7 sustain 8 deadhead, levitate

mooring: 7 dolphin

trawling marker: dan

buoyant: gay 5 happy, light 6 blithe, floaty, lively 7 elastic, hopeful, lilting, springy 8 animated, cheerful, sanguine, spirited, volatile 9 resilient, vivacious 12 lighthearted

bur: See **burr**.

burble: 4 boil 6 bubble, gurgle, jabber, muddle, pimple 7 confuse, prattle, trouble 8 disorder

burbot: cod 4 fish, ling, lota 7 eelpout

burd: 4 lady 5 woman 6 maiden

burden: tax, vex 4 birn(Sc.), care, cark, clag, clog, duty, load, onus, seam 5 birth, cargo 6 charge, cumber, fardel, hamper, impose, lading, weight 7 ballast, fraught, freight, oppress, refrain, trouble 8 capacity, carriage, encumber, handicap, quantity 9 aggravate, grievance 10 imposition 11 encumbrance 14 responsibility

of complaint: 8 gravamen

with care: 4 cark

burdensome: 5 heavy 7 irksome, onerous, weighty 8 cumbrous, grievous, grinding 10 chargeable, cumbersome, oppressive 11 importunate, troublesome

burdock: 5 clite, lappa, plant 7 cadillo, clotbur, harebur, hurr-bur 9 cocklebur

bureau: 4 desk 5 chest 6 agency, office 7 dresser 10 chiffonier, department, escritoire

burg, burgh: 4 city, town 6 burgus 7 borough 9 community

burgeon: bud 4 grow 5 shoot 6 sprout

burgess: 7 citizen, freeman 8 commoner 10 magistrate

burglar: 4 yegg 5 thief 6 gopher, robber 7 yeggman 8 peterman 10 burglarize

burglary: 5 theft 7 larceny, robbery 8 stealage

burgomaster: 4 gull 5 mayor 7 alcalde 10 magistrate

burgoo, burgout: 4 soup, stew 5 gruel 7 pudding 8 porridge

burial: 9 interment 10 deposition

case: box 6 casket, coffin

ceremony: 7 funeral

litter: 4 bier

mound: low 5 grave 6 barrow 7 tumulus

pile: 4 pyre

place: 4 tomb 5 grave 7 pyramid 8 catacomb, cemetery, golgotha 9 graveyard, mausoleum 10 necropolis

preparation for: 4 cere 11 pollincture

buried (see also **bury**): 6 hidden 8 absorbed, imbedded

burin: 4 tool 6 graver

burl: 4 knot, lump 6 pimple 7 pustule 11 excrescence

in mahogany: roe

burlap: 5 gunny 6 fabric 7 bagging 8 wrapping

fiber: 4 hemp, jute

burler: 6 spiler 9 inspector

burlesque: ape, odd 4 copy, jest, mime 5 droll, farce, revue 6 comedy, overdo, parody **7** jocular, mockery, overact **8** ridicule, travesty **9** imitation, laughable, ludicrous **10** caricature

serenade: **9** charivari

burly: fat **5** bluff, bulky, heavy, husky, large, lusty, noble, obese, stout, thick, tramp **7** stately **8** imposing **9** corpulent, excellent, policeman **10** boisterous

Burma:

canopy: **7** tazaung

city: Ava **4** Pegu **5** Akyah, Prome **6** Lashio **7** Rangoon(c.) **8** Mandalay

dagger: dah **4** dout

deer: **6** thamin **7** thameng

demon: nat

division: **4** Pegu **6** arakam

garment: **6** tamein

head hunter: **4** Naga

hill dweller: Lai

knife: dah, dow

measure: dha, lan, tha **4** byee, dain, seit, taim, teng **6** palgat

musical instrument: **4** turr

native: Vu, Wa; Lai, Mon **4** Shaw **5** Karen **6** Kachin, Pequan

river: **6** Salwin, Sutang **7** Salween **8** Chindwin, Irrawadi **9** Irrawaddy

robber: **6** dacoit

sash: **7** tubbeck

skirts: **5** engis

spirit: nat

town: **4** Paan **5** Akyab, Manle **7** Bassein **8** Moulmein

traveler's shed: **5** zayat

tree: **4** acle **7** yamanai

tribe: Ao; Tai **4** Chin, Kuki, Shan, Thai, Tsin **6** Kachin, Karens **8** Kakhyens

tribesman: Lai

weight: mat, moo, vis **4** kait, ruay, viss **5** candy, tical, ticul

burn: **4** brew, char, fire, plot, raze, rill, sear, sere **5** adust, blaze, broil, brook, cense, flame, parch, scald, singe, waste, water **6** scorch, stream **7** combure, combust, consume, cremate, flicker, oxidize, rivulet, smolder **8** squander **9** cauterize **10** incinerate

midnight oil: **6** stay up **9** lucubrate

surface: **5** singe **6** scorch

burn up the road: **5** speed

burner: **6** Bunsen, censer **8** thurible

burning: hot **4** fire **5** afire, angry, blaze, calid, eager, fiery, flame, gledy **6** ablaze, ardent, fervid, torrid **7** caustic, cautery, fervent, flaming, glaring, glowing, mordant, shining **8** ardurous, exciting, inustion **9** consuming, cremating, inflaming **10** combustion, phlogistic **13** conflagration

bush: **5** wahoo

malicious: **5** arson

mountain: **7** volcano

taste: **5** acrid

burnish: rub **5** glaze, gloss **6** polish **7** furbish

burnisher: **4** tool **5** agate **6** buffer **7** frottom **8** polisher

burnoose, burnous: **5** cloak **7** garment **8** albornoz

burnt work: **10** pyrography

burr: nut, pad, rib **4** barb, birr, boss, buzz, halo, knob, ring, whir **5** briar, whirr **6** banyan, circle, corona, tunnel, washer **7** sticker **8** parasite **9** whetstone **10** sweetbread

burro: ass **6** donkey **9** quadruped

burrow: den, dig **4** heap, hole, mine, mole, root, tube **5** berry, couch, mound **6** furrow, tunnel **7** passage, shelter **8** excavate

bursa: sac **4** hall, sack **5** pouch **6** cavity **9** residence

bursar: **6** purser, terrar **7** boucher, cashier, student **9** treasurer

bursary: **8** treasury **11** scholarship

burse: **4** case, shop **5** bazar, purse **6** bazaar, bourse, pocket **8** exchange, treasury **11** scholarship

burst: pop **4** blow, bust, loss, rend, scat **5** blast, break, erupt, flash, reave, salvo, scatt, split **6** broken, damage, injury, sprout **7** explode, rupture, shatter **8** outbreak, sundered **9** interrupt

forth: **5** erupt, sally **9** blasted

inward: **7** implode

burster: **4** gale **7** cracker **9** explosive

bursting: **8** erupting **10** dehiscence

comb. form: **6** rrhage **7** rrhagia

bury: **4** hide, mool, veil **5** cloak, cover, earth, grave, inter, inurn **6** entomb, hearse, inhume, shroud **7** bedelve, conceal, engross, immerse, repress, secrete **8** submerge **9** overwhelm

bus: **6** jitney **7** vehicle **9** charabanc

busby: cap, wig **8** bearskin **9** headdress

bush: tod **4** buss, butt **5** bosch, clump, grove, shrub **6** branch, tavern **7** boscage, cluster, thicket **11** advertising

bushel: foo(Sc.), gob, lot **4** full

quarter of: **4** peck

forty: wey

bushing: **5** drill **6** collet, lining **7** padding

machine: **6** sleeve

bushman: san(pl.) **4** gung, saan(pl.) **5** bushy **6** Abatoa, Abatua, Abatwa, rustic **8** woodsman

blanket: **5** bluey

bushmaster: **5** snake, viper

bushwa: **4** bosh, bull **5** hooey, trash **7** baloney **8** bodewash

bushwacker: **5** papaw **6** pawpaw, scythe **8** guerilla

bushy: **5** bosky **6** dumose, dumous **7** bushman, queachy

hair: **4** shag

heap: tod

business: ado, art, job **4** care, firm, fuss,

game, line, task, work 5 cause, trade 6
affair, custom, matter, metier, office 7
calling, concern, trading, traffic 8 activity,
commerce, industry, vocation 9 diligence,
following, patronage, rickmatic 10 employment, enterprise, occupation, solicitude 11 disturbance, importunity, intercourse, transaction 13 attentiveness,
establishment
custom: 9 patronage
place of: 4 mart, shop 5 store 6 market,
office, shoppe 8 emporium
businessman: 9 executive
powerful: 6 tycoon
busk: hie 4 seek, stir, tack 5 array, dress 6
corset, hasten 7 prepare, stiffen
buskin: 4 boot, shoe 7 bottine, tragedy 8
cothurni(L. pl.), half-boot, stocking 9
brodequin, cothurnus(L.)
buss: 4 boat, bush, calf, deck, kiss 5
dress, smack 6 vessel 9 transport
bussock: 6 donkey
bussu: 4 palm 7 troolie
bust: 4 fail, ruin, tame 5 bosom, break,
burst, chest, flunk, spree 6 bronze, demote, reduce, statue 7 degrade, dismiss,
failure 8 bankrupt 9 blockhead
sculptured part: 5 gaine 6 pillar
bust-up: 5 party, spree 7 failure 8 collapse, outbreak 11 dissolution
bustard: 4 bird, kori 5 paauw 7 bebilya,
houbara 8 gompaaum
genus: 4 otis 6 otidae
bustee: 4 slum 6 hamlet 7 village
buster: 4 crab, wind 5 blade, child, spree
6 fellow
bustle: ado 4 fray, fuss, stir, todo, whir 5
frisk, haste, whirr 6 bishop, energy, fissle,
fistle, flurry, fustle, huddle, hustle, pother,
racket, tumult, unrest, uproar 7 clatter,
contend, scuffle 8 activity, struggle, tournure 9 agitation, commotion, stirabout
woman's: 6 bishop
busy: 4 fell 5 brisk 6 active, eident, intent, lively, occupy 7 engaged, humming,
operose, trouble 8 diligent, employed, occupied, sedulous, tireless, untiring 9 assiduous, attentive, detective, laborious,
officious, unwearied 11 industrious,
painstaking, persevering, unremitting 13
indefatigable
busybody: 4 busy 5 snoop 7 marplot,
meddler, snooper 8 factotum, quidnunc
but: lo, ma(It.); sed(L.), yet 4 mere, only,
save 5 still 6 except, unless 7 besides,
howbeit, however 12 nevertheless
butcher: 4 kill, slay 5 spoil 6 bungle,
murder, vendor 7 botcher, britten 8 pig-
stick 9 slaughter 10 pigsticker 11 executioner, slaughterer
hook: 7 gambrel
rabbi: 8 shochtim
tool: saw 5 knife, steel 7 cleaver

butcher-bird: 6 shrike
butchery: 6 murder 7 carnage 8 massacre, shambles 9 martyrdom, slaughter 12
manslaughter 14 slaughterhouse
butler: 6 yeoman 7 servant, spencer,
steward 10 manservant
butt: jut, mot, pit, ram, run, tup 4 buck,
bunt, burt, bush, cart, cask, fool, goad,
goal, goat, jolt, poll, push, stub, tope 5
bound, hinge, joint, mound, stump 6
breech, target, thrust 7 beehive, buttock,
parapet, project 8 flatfish, flounder
cigar or cigarette: 5 snipe
one third: 5 terce 6 tierce
butte: 4 hill 7 picacho 8 mountain
butter: 4 shea 6 beurre(F.), cajole, spread
7 blarney, flatter
artificial: 4 oleo, suin 8 margarin 9 butterine, margarine 12 oleomargarin 13 oleomargarine
lump: pat
semifluid: ghi 4 ghee
shea: 5 galam 6 bambui, bambuk 7 bam-
bara
tree: 4 shea 5 fulwa 8 phulwara
tub: 6 firkin
butter-and-eggs: 6 clover 7 ransted 8
ramstead, ranstead, toadflax
butterbur: 5 eldin, plant
buttercup: 6 flower 7 anemone 8 reindeer 10 butter-rose
fruit: 6 achene
butterfly: io 4 kiho 5 satyr 6 idalia, mor-
pho, ursula 7 admiral, buckeye, monarch,
skipper, vanessa, viceroy 8 arthemis,
cecropia, grayling 9 aphrodite, underwing
10 fritillary, lepidopter
expert: 13 lepidopterist
fish: 6 blenny
genus: 8 melitaea 10 heliconius
larva: 11 caterpillar
lily: 4 sego 8 mariposa
peacock: io
buttermilk: 8 sourdook(Sc.)
buttery: 6 larder, pantry, spence 9 apartment, storeroom, wheedling 10 flattering
button: bud 4 boss, chin, hook, knob, knop
5 badge, catch, pearl 6 bauble, buckle 8
fastener
ornamental: 4 stud
part: 5 shank
three jewel: 6 troche
buttonhole: 4 loop, slit 6 detain, eyelet
11 boutonniere
buttress: 4 pier, pile, prop, stay 5 brace 7
support 8 abutment 11 counterfort
butty: 4 chum 6 worker 7 partner, workman 9 companion, middleman
buxom: 4 mild 5 jolly, plump, prone,
sonsy 6 blithe, florid, humble, pliant, sonsie 8 bouncing, flexible, obedient,
obliging, yielding 9 compliant, courteous,
tractable 10 submissive 11 complaisant

buy: 4 chap, coff(Sc.), coup, gain, shop 5 bribe, trade 6 market, ransom, redeem, secure 7 acquire 8 purchase
cheaply: 4 snup
to sell at a profit: 7 regrate
buyer: 4 chap 5 agent 6 emptor, patron 7 chapman, shopper 8 customer, prospect 9 purchaser
stolen property: 5 fence
buying and selling: 11 nundination
buzz: hum 4 burr, call, hiss, huss, huzz, ring, whir 5 fancy, fling, phone, rumor 6 notion 7 whisper 9 bombilate, telephone
buzzard: 4 aura, fool, hawk, pern 5 buteo 6 beetle, curlew, stupid 7 vulture 9 senseless
bald: 6 osprey
honey: 4 pern
buzzer: bee 4 bell 5 alarm, badge 6 signal 7 whizzer 10 pickpocket, talebearer
by: at; ago, per 4 abut, anon, near, past 5 apart, aside, close 6 beside, toward 7 besides, through 9 alongside 10 concerning
means of: per 4 from, with 7 through
mouth: 4 oral

by-pass: 4 shun 5 evade, shunt 6 detour 7 circuit
bygone: 4 past, yore 5 olden 6 former 7 ancient, elapsed 8 backward, departed
byname: 6 byword 7 surname 8 cognomen, nickname 9 sobriquet
bypath: 4 lane 5 byway
byre: 4 barn 6 stable
Byron character: 4 Inez, Lara 6 Haidee 7 Don Juan
byssoid: 7 cottony 9 fiberlike 10 byssaceous
byway: 4 lane, path 5 alley
byword: 5 axiom, motto 6 byname, phrase, saying 7 proverb 8 nickname 9 catchword
Byzantine:
coin: 6 bezant
empress: 5 Irene
mosaic: 4 icon
scepter: 6 ferula

C

Caaba: 6 shrine
caama: fox 4 asse 10 hartebeest
cab driver: 5 cabby 6 cabbie, cocher(F.)
7 cochero(Sp.)
cabal: 4 plot, ring 5 junta, party 6 brigue,
clique, scheme, secret 7 chatter, consult,
council, dispute, faction, talking 8 intrigue 9 occultism, tradition 10 conspiracy 11 combination
pert. to: 9 factional
cabalistic: 6 mystic 10 mysterious
caballero: 6 knight 8 cavalier, horseman
9 gentleman
caballo: 5 horse
cabana: 9 bathhouse
cabaret: 4 cafe 5 table 6 tavern 9 nightclub 10 restaurant
cabbage: cab 4 chou, crib, kale, wort 5
filch, steal 6 pilfer, tailor 7 bowkail, purloin 8 borecole, colewort 11 appropriate,
translation
daisy: 11 globeflower
family: 12 brassicaceae
salad: 4 slaw 8 coleslaw
seed: 5 colza
tree: 7 angelin
variety: 4 cale, kale 5 colza, savoy 8 colewort, kohlrabi
cabbagehead: 5 dunce 9 screwball
cabby: 6 cabbie, cabman 9 cabdriver
caber: 4 beam, pole, spar 6 rafter
cabin: cot, den, hut 4 cave, cell, shed 5
booth, coach, hovel, lodge, shack 6 litter,
saloon, shanty 7 bedroom, boudoir, cottage 9 stateroom
cabin boy: 7 grummet
cabin car: 7 caboose
cabinet: box 4 buhl, case 5 habut, board,
chest 6 bureau, closet 7 almirah, boudoir,
console, council, etagere, whatnot 8 cellaret, cupboard, ministry 10 chiffonier
cable: 4 boom, link, rope, wire 6 ganger 8
telegram
lifter: 7 wildcat
post: 4 bitt
cable car: 6 telfer 7 telpher
cabling: 7 molding 9 rudenture
cabochon: gem 5 stone 8 ornament
caboodle: kit, lot 10 collection
caboose: cab, car 5 buggy 6 galley
cabotin: 5 actor 9 charlatan
cacao: 4 bean 5 cocoa, broma 6 arriba 9
chocolate
shell extract: 6 martol

cache: 4 bury, hide 5 store 6 screen 7
conceal 8 treasure 10 storehouse
cachet: 4 seal 5 stamp, wafer
cachexia: 7 illness, wasting 9 morbidity
12 malnutrition
cackle: 4 cank 5 clack, laugh 6 babble,
gabble, giggle, gossip, keckle, titter 7
chackle, chatter, snicker, twaddle 8
laughter
cacography: 11 misspelling
cacophonous: 5 harsh 7 raucous 8 jangling, strident 9 dissonant 10 discordant
11 unmelodious
cactus: 4 bleo 5 dildo, nopal, plant 6 cereus, chaute, chende, cholla 7 airampo,
saguaro 8 chichope
cad: cur 4 boor, chum, heel 5 churl 6 rascal, rotter 7 bounder, dastard 9 scoundrel
cadaver: 4 body 5 stiff 6 corpse 7 carcass
8 skeleton
cadaverous: 4 pale 5 gaunt 7 ghastly,
haggard
caddis fly: 4 bait 5 cadew 6 cadbit 7 cad-
bait, cadbote
caddle: 4 fuss, mess 5 annoy, tease, worry
6 gossip 7 confuse, trouble 8 disarray 9
confusion 13 embarrassment
caddow: 5 quilt 7 jackdaw 8 coverlet
caddy: box, boy, can 5 chest
cade: keg, pet 4 cask, lamb 6 barrel, coddle 7 indulge, juniper
cadence: 4 beat, lilt, pace, tone 5 meter,
metre, sound, swing, throb 6 rhythm,
8 clausula 10 modulation
cadent: 7 falling 10 descending, rhyth-
mical
cadet: son 5 plebe, youth 6 embryo, junior
10 midshipman
cadew: 4 worm
cadge: beg, tie 4 bind, hawk 5 carry,
mooch 6 peddle, sponge 8 scrounge
cadger: 6 dealer, hawker 7 carrier, packman, sponger 8 huckster
cadgy: 6 wanton 7 lustful 8 cheerful,
mirthful
Cadmus:
daughter: Ino 5 Agave 6 Semele 7 Autonoe
father: 6 Agenor
sister: 8 Europa
wife: 9 Harmonia
cadre: 4 core 5 frame, group 6 scheme 9
framework
caduceus: 4 wand 5 staff 6 symbol 7
insigne, scepter, sceptre

caducity: 5 lapse 8 senility 10 feebleness 14 perishableness

Caen stone: 9 freestone, limestone

Caesar:
capital: 4 Roma
country conquered by: 4 Gaul
fatal day: 4 Ides
place of victory: 6 Actium
river crossed by: 7 Rubicon
sister: 4 Atia
wife: 8 Cornelia 9 Calpurnia

caesura: 4 rest, stop 5 break, pause 8 interval 12 interruption

cafard: 5 bigot, blues 6 apathy, humbug 9 hypocrite 10 depression

cafe: 7 barroom, cabaret 8 teahouse 10 restaurant 11 coffeehouse

caffeine: 5 thein 6 theine 8 alkaloid 9 stimulant

cage: box, car, pen 4 coop 5 brake 6 aviary, basket, bucket, chapel, prison 7 chantry, confine 8 imprison, scaffold, strainer 9 enclosure, inclosure

cage hawk: mew 5 meute

caged: 4 pent

cagey, cagy: sly 4 wary

cahoots: 6 league 9 collusion 11 partnership

caiman: 6 cayman, jacare 9 alligator

Cain:
brother: Pur 4 Abel, Seth
descendant: 6 Lamech
land: Nod
nephew: 4 Enos

cairn: 4 pike 5 mound 8 stoneman

caisson: box 4 pont 5 chest, wagon 6 ponton 7 chamber, pontoon

caitiff: 4 base, mean, vile 6 coward, wicked 7 captive 8 cowardly, prisoner, wretched 10 despicable

cajole: cog 4 coax, flam, palp 5 carny, cheat, curry, decoy, jolly, tease 6 carney, delude, entice, fraise, humbug, whilly 7 beguile, flatter, wheedle 8 blandish 9 bamboozle 10 honey-fogle

cajolery: 5 fraik 6 butter 8 flattery

cake: bar, bun, wig 4 bake, flae, fool, lump, mass, tart 5 batty, block, crust, scone, torte, wafer, wedge 6 barkle, cimbal, eclair, harden, nacket, pastry 7 bannock, oatcake, pancake 8 solidify 9 coagulate, simpleton 11 griddlecake
almond: 7 macaron 8 macaroon
boiled in honey: 8 teiglech
corn: 4 pone 7 fritter
custard: 9 eclair 9 creampuff
dough: 6 batter
filled: 4 flan
fried: 7 cruller 8 doughnut
griddle: 7 bannock(Sc.), crumpet, hotcake, pancake
plum: 4 baba
rich: 5 torte 8 madeline 9 madeleine

sacrificial: 6 hallah
seed: wig 4 wiff
small: bun 4 tart 5 batty 6 jumble 7 cupcake
tea: 5 scone
thin: 5 scone, wager 8 tortilla(Sp.)
unleavened: 5 matzo 6 damper 8 tortilla

calaba: 4 tree 5 birma

calabash: 5 gourd 6 curuba

calaboose: jug 4 brig, gool, jail 6 prison 8 bastille

caladium: 4 taro

calamanco: 5 manco 6 fabric 7 garment

calamitous: sad 4 dire, evil 5 black, fatal 6 bitter, dismal, tragic, woeful 7 adverse, baleful, direful, hapless, ruinous, unhappy, unlucky 8 grievous, tragical, wretched 9 miserable 10 afflictive, deplorable, disastrous 11 distressful, unfortunate

calamity: 4 blow, evil, ruin 5 storm, wrack 6 misery, sorrow 8 accident, disaster, distress, fatality 9 adversity, mischance 10 affliction, misfortune 11 catastrophe, unhappiness 12 misadventure, wretchedness

calamus: pen 4 cane, reed 9 sweetflag

calangay: 8 cockatoo

calash: 6 calesa

calcar: 4 oven, spur 7 furnace

calcareous: See **calcite**.

calcite:
animal: 8 skeleton
deposit: 4 spar, tufa 5 tatar 10 stalactite, stalagmite
soil with: 4 marl

calcium:
carbonate: 4 tufa
oxide: 9 quicklime
sulphate: 5 hepar 6 gypsum

calculate: aim 4 plan, rate, tell 5 count, frame, think 6 design, expect, figure, number, reckon 7 average, compute, prepare 8 consider, estimate, forecast 9 determine, enumerate

calculation: 4 care 5 share 7 account, caution 8 forecast, prudence 9 logistics, reckoning 10 adjustment, discretion 11 computation

calculator: 5 table 6 abacus 7 soroban 10 accountant

calcutta:
hemp: 4 jute
weight: 4 pank, raik 5 hubba, pally

caldron, cauldron: pot, red, vat 4 afet 6 boiler, kettle, vessel 8 go-ashore

Caleb's son: Hur, Iru

Caledonia: 8 Scotland

Caledonian: 4 Pict, Scot 8 Scotsman

calefy: 4 heat, warm

calendar: 5 diary 7 almanac, calends, journal, kalends 8 register, schedule 9 repertory, ephemeris *church:* 4 ordo

French revolution: 6 Nivose 7 Floreal, Ventose 8 Brumaire, Fervidor, Gernubak, Messidor, Pluviose, Prairial 9 Fructidor, Thermidor 11 Vendemiaire

calenture: 4 fire, glow 5 ardor, fever 7 passion 9 sunstroke

calf: bob, boy, leg 4 buss, dolt 5 bobby, bossy, dogie, moggy, youth 6 bovine, muscle 7 bulchin, fatling 9 quadruped

flesh: 4 veal, veau(F.)

jelly: 7 fisnoga

motherless: 4 dogy 5 dogie 8 maverick

muscle: 9 plantaris

pert. to: 5 sural

Caliban:

adversary of: 8 Prospero

witch mother: 7 Sycorax

caliber: 4 bore, rank 6 degree, talent 7 ability, breadth, compass, quality 8 capacity, diameter

calico: 4 girl 5 pinto, sallo, woman 6 salloo 7 spotted 8 goldfish 9 womankind 12 multicolored

horse: 5 pinto

mix colors for: 4 teer

pigment: 7 canarin 8 canarine

printing: 4 teer 5 fondu, lapis

calid: hot 4 warm 7 burning

Calif: 6 Caliph

California:

bulrush: 4 tule

condor: 8 gymnogyp

county: 4 Inyo, Kern, Lake, Napa, Yolo, Yuba 5 Butte, Costa, Glenn, Kings, Marin, Modoc 6 Alpine, Amador, Colusa, Contra, Fresno, Lassen, Madera, Merced, Nevada, Orange, Plumas, Obispo, Shasta, Sierra, Solano, Sonoma, Sutter, Tehama, Tulare 7 Alameda, San Luis, Trinity, Ventura 8 Del Norte, Eldorado, Humboldt, Imperial, Mariposa, Monterey, San Diego, Siskiyou, Toulumne 9 Calaveras, Mendocino, Riverside, San Benito, Santa Cruz, San Joquin 10 Los Angeles, Sacramento, Santa Clara, Stanislaus 12 San Francisco, Santa Barbara 13 San Bernardino

fan palm: 7 erythea

Indian: 4 Hupa, Pomo, Seri 5 Hoopa, Yurok 10 Weitspekan

island: 4 Goat, Mare 7 Anacapa 8 Alcatraz, Catalina, Coronado, Nicholas, Treasure 9 Farollone, San Miguel, Santa Cruz, Santa Rosa 11 San Clemente 12 Santa Barbara

lake: 5 Tahoe

laurel: 7 cajeput, cajuput

motto: 6 Eureka

oak: 5 roble 6 encina

observatory: 4 Lick 7 Palomar 8 Mt. Wilson

plant: 7 tarweed

river: Eel, Mad, Pit 4 Kern 5 Kings, Smith 6 Merced, Salmon 7 Feather, Klamath, Russian, Salinas, Trinity 10 Sacramento, San Jacinto, Stanislaus

rockfish: 4 rena 5 reina, viuva 6 rasher 8 bocaccio

shrub: 5 salal 7 chamise, chamiso, tarbush 9 chaparral, manzanita

town: 4 Asti, Napa 5 Tracy 6 Arcata, Eureka, Fresno, Salina 7 Alameda, Arcadia

tree: 6 torrey 7 redwood, sequoia 12 Wellingtonia

caliginous: dim 4 dark 5 misty 7 obscure

caliph, calif: Abu, Ali 4 Bekr, Imam, Omar 6 Othman 9 caliphate

descendant: 5 Alide 7 Fatamid 8 Fatamite

fourth: Ali

calix: cup 7 chalice

calk: nap 4 copy, stop 5 close 7 occlude, silence

calking: 5 oakum

call: bid, cry, dub 4 cite, hail, name, page, stop, term, yell 5 claim, clepe, clock, elect, phone, rouse, shout, style, utter, visit, waken, yodel, yodle 6 accuse, appeal, arouse, demand, invite, invoke, muster, quethe, summon 7 address, appoint, collect, command, convene, convoke, entitle, impeach 8 announce, assemble, nominate, proclaim, vocation 9 challenge, reprimand, telephone, terminate 10 denominate

distress: S.O.S.

down: 5 scold 6 berate, invoke, rebuke 7 censure, reprove 8 denounce, execrate 9 reprimand

for: 4 page 5 exact 6 demand 7 request, require

forth: 5 evoke 6 arouse, elicit, invoke, signal, summon 7 evocate

out: 5 ascry, evoke 6 muster

to: 4 hail 5 ascry 6 accost, halloo 7 address

to attention: hop 6 remind

to mind: 4 cite 6 recall 8 remember

together: 6 muster, summon 7 convoke

callan, callant: boy, lad 4 chap 6 fellow 8 customer

calligrapher: 6 penman, writer 7 copyist 9 engrosser

calling: art, job 4 rank 5 trade 6 career, metier, naming, outcry 7 pursuit, station, summons 8 business, function, position, shouting, vocation 9 condition, summoning, utterance 10 employment, invitation, occupation, profession 11 appellation, convocation, undertaking 13 circumstances

callous: 4 hard 5 horny, tough 6 brawny, obtuse, torpid 8 obdurate 9 indurated, unfeeling 11 hardhearted, indifferent 14 pachydermatous

callow: 4 bald, bare 5 crude, green 6

marshy **7** meadow **8** immature, un-formed, youthful **9** unfledged **13** inexperienced **15** unsophisticated

calm: lee **4** cool, dill, easy, fair, hush, lull, mees(Sc.), mild, rest **5** abate, allay, charm, mease, peace, quell, quiet, sober, still, stoic **6** docile, gentle, irenic, pacify, placid, sedate, serene, smooth, soothe, steady **7** appease, assuage, halcyon, mollify, pacific, patient, placate, restful, unmoved **8** composed, decorous, peaceful, restrain, tranquil **9** collected, impassive, temperate, unexcited, unruffled **10** halcyonian, phlegmatic, unconfused **11** complacence, tranquilize, undisturbed **13** dispassionate, imperturbable **15** undemonstrative

calmness: **5** poise **6** repose **8** ataraxia, serenity **9** composure, placidity, quietness, sang-froid, stillness **10** equanimity **11** self-control, tranquility **12** peacefulness **13** impassiveness

calorie, calory: **5** therm **6** therme

calumet: **5** pipe

calumniate: **4** slur **5** belie, libel **6** accuse, attack, defame, malign, revile, vilify **7** asperse, blacken, slander, traduce **9** blaspheme

calyx: **4** leaf **5** sepal
helmet-shaped: **5** galea
of flower: **8** perianth

cam: cog **4** awry, lobe **5** askew, catch, wiper **6** tappet **7** crooked, trippet **8** perverse

camalig: hut **5** cabin **10** storehouse

camara: house **7** chamber

camarilla: **4** cell, ring **5** cabal, junta **6** clique **7** chamber, company **11** combination

camas, cammas: **5** plain **7** lobelia, prairie

Camboria: **7** Camboja **8** Cambodge

Cambria: See **Wales.**

cambric: **5** linen **7** batiste

Cambridge:
boat races: **4** Lent
college official: **6** bedell
council: **5** caput
honor examination: **6** tripos
student: **5** sizar, spoon **6** optime

camel: **4** cont **6** mehari **7** tylopod **8** bactrian, ruminant **9** dromedary **10** camelopard
driver: **6** sarwan **8** cameleer
female: **4** naga
fermented milk: **5** kumys **6** koumis, kumiss **7** koumiss, koumyss
keeper: **4** obil
two-humped: **8** Bactrian

Camelot:
lord: **6** Arthur
magician: **6** Merlin

camel's hair: aba **5** cloth **6** camlet **8** cameline
garment: aba

cameo: gem **7** camaieu(F.), carving, relievo, rilievo, phalera **8** anaglyph **9** sculpture
cutting tool: **5** spade
stone: **4** onyx **8** sardonyx

camera: **7** chamber **10** department, instrument
part: **4** lens **6** finder **7** bellows, shutter

cameraman: **8** camerist, operator **12** photographer **13** projectionist

Cameroon:
inhabitant: **4** Sara
river: **5** Shari

camion: bus **4** dray **5** truck, wagon **7** motorbus

camlet: **6** Angora, fabric, mohair **9** camelteen, camletine

camouflage: **4** fake, hide **6** muffle, screen **7** conceal **8** disguise **9** deception

camp: **4** pest, tent **5** etape(F.), horde, siege, tabor **7** bivouac, shelter **8** quarters **10** settlement
follower: **5** bidar(Ind.) **6** gudget(Sc.)
provision seller: **6** sutler

campaign: **5** drive, plain **7** canvass, crusade, solicit **9** champaign, operation

campanero: **8** arapunga, bellbird

campanile: **5** tower **6** belfry **7** clocher, steeple

camphor: **7** menthol, asarone

campus: **4** quad **5** field **7** grounds

can: cup, jug, may, tin **4** able, fire, jail **5** caddy, could, eshin, skill **6** vessel **7** ability, capable, dismiss **8** conserve, preserve **9** competent, container, discharge, knowledge **10** cleverness, receptacle

Canada:
airport: **6** Gander
boat: **6** bateau **7** bateaux(pl.), batteau **8** batteaux(pl.)
city: **5** Banff, Levis, Sorel **6** Ottawa(c.), Regina **7** Calgary, Toronto **8** Edmonton, Montreal, Victoria, Winnipeg **9** Carstairs, Saskatoon, Vancouver
court decree: **5** arret
fur company employee: **8** voyageur
gannet: **6** margot
goose: **5** brant **8** honker
lake: **4** Cree, Gras, Seul **6** Louise, Teslin
land measure: **6** arpent, roture
lynx: **5** pishu
measure: ton **5** minot, perch, point **6** arpent **7** chainon
mountain: **4** Gold **5** Logan **7** Cascade, Rockies St. Elias **9** Notre Dame **10** Laurentian, Shickshock
peninsula: **5** Gaspe
poplar: **5** liard
porcupine: **5** urson **7** cawquaw
province: **5** Sorel, Yukon **6** Quebec **7** Alberta, Ontario **8** Manitoba **10** Nova Scotia **12** New Brunswick, Saskatchewan **15** British Columbia
river: **4** Back, Leaf, **5** Peace, Trent **6** Al-

bany, Fraser, Nelson, Ottawa, Skeena **8**
Gatineau, Saguenay, Stickeen **9** Athabasca, Churchill, Great Bear, Great Fish,
Mackenzie, Richelieu, St. Maurice **10**
Coppermine, Great Slave, Peace Slave,
St. Lawrence **12** Saskatchewan
Canadian: **6** Canuck
canadine: **8** alkaloid
canaille: mob **5** flour **6** rabble **7** rifraff
canal: cut **4** cano, duct, tube **5** ditch,
  drain, fossa(L.), graff, zanje **6** fossae(L.pl.),
  groove, strait, trench **7** acequia(Sp.),
  channel, conduit, raceway, towpath **8**
  aqueduct **10** waterspout **11** watercourse
dredging machine: **7** couloir
famous: Soo **4** Erie, Kiel, Suez **6** Morris,
  Panama **7** Welland
footpath: **7** towpath
canape: **6** relish **9** appetizer **11**
  hors d'oeuvre
canard: **4** hoax **9** grapewine **11** fabrication
canary: **4** bird **5** dance **6** singer **8** informer, squealer
forerunner of: **5** serin
canary broom: **7** genista
Canary Islands: **4** Roca **5** Ferro, Lobos,
  Palma, Clara **6** Gomero **7** Inferno **8**
  Graciosa, Rocca Sta., Tenerife **9** Lanza-
  rote, Teneriffe **10** Allegranza **11** Grand
  Hierro **13** Fuerteventura
city: **6** Laguna **9** Santa Cruz(c.)
commune: **4** Icod
measure: **8** fanegada
mountain: **6** La Cruz **8** El Cumbre, Tenerife **9** Teneriffe **11** Gran Canaria
canary yellow: **6** meline
canasta: **4** game **5** cards, crate **6** basket,
  hamper
play: **4** meld
cancel: **4** blot, dele, omit **5** annul, erase,
  quash, remit **6** delete, efface, recall, remove, revoke **7** abolish, destroy, expunge,
  nullify, rescind, retract, scratch **8** abrogate **10** obliterate **11** countermand
cancion: **4** song **5** lyric
candent: hot **7** fervent, glowing
candescent: **7** glowing **8** dazzling **11** lu-
  minescent **15** autoluminescent
Candia: **5** Crete
candid: **4** fair, just, open, pure **5** blunt,
  clear, frank, naive **6** honest **7** artless, sincere **8** splendid **9** guileless, honorable,
  impartial, ingenuous, outspoken **10** immaculate **11** illustrious **15** straightforward
candidate: **7** nominee **8** aspirant, prospect **9** applicant
list: **4** leet **5** slate **6** roster
religious: **9** postulant
winning: **7** electee
candle: dip, wax **5** light, taper **6** cierge(F.)
  9 chandelle
holder: **6** lampad, sconce, sconse **9** giran-

dole **10** candelabra **11** candlestick
kind of: **8** bayberry
place of keeping: **9** chandlery
wax: **5** taper **6** bougie
candlelight: **4** dusk **8** twilight **9** nightfall
candlelighter: **5** spill **7** acolyte
candlenut tree: ama **5** kukui **6** bankul
candlestick: **6** lampad, sconce **8** flambeau, standard **9** flambeaux(pl.)
bracket: **6** sconce, sconse
branched: **5** jesse **8** dicerion, dikerion **9**
  girandole, tricerion, trikerion **10** chandelier **11** candelabrum
candlewood: **4** tree **5** shrub **9** coachwhip
candor, candour: **6** purity **8** fairness,
  kindness **9** frankness, innocence, unreserve, whiteness **10** brightness, brilliance,
  kindliness **12** impartiality **13** outspokenness
candy: **5** fudge, gundy, lolly, sweet, taffy **6**
  bonbon, comfit, nougate **7** brittle, caramel, congeal, fondate, flatter, sweeten **8**
  lollipop **9** granulate, sweetmeat **10** confection **11** crystallize
base: **8** fondant
mixture: **6** fourre
nut: **7** praline
pulled sugar: **5** taffy **6** penide
sugar: **7** fondant **8** alphenic
candytuft: **5** plant **6** flower, iberis
cane: rod **4** beat, dart, flog, pipe, reed,
  stem, tube, whip **5** birch, lance, staff,
  stick **6** bamboo, punish, rattan **7** calamus, hickory, malacca, scourge **9** crabstick
dense growth: **9** canebrake
knife: **7** machete
part: **7** ferrule
sugar: **7** sucrose
Canfield: **8** Klondike **9** solitaire
cangle: **7** dispute, quarrel, wrangle
canine (see also **dog**): cur, dog, fox, pup
  4 fisc, wolf **5** canis(L.) **7** doglike
tooth: **7** laniary
caning: **6** rattan
canister: box **9** container
canker: **4** rust **6** infect **7** consume, corrode, corrupt, tarnish **9** verdigris
cannibal: **6** savage **15** anthropophagite
cannon: bit, gun **5** crack, thief **6** mortar **7**
  bastard **8** howitzer, ordnance **9** artillery
  10 pickpocket
fire: **7** barrage
handle: **4** anse
muzzle plug: **7** tampion
part: **4** bore **5** chase **6** breech, muzzle **7**
  chamber, rimbase **8** cascabel, trunnion
shot: **5** grape
support: **8** trunnion
cannonade: **7** barrage
cannoneer: **12** artilleryman
cannot: **6** unable
canny: sly **4** cozy, snug, wary, wily, wise **5**
  lucky, pawky, quiet **6** clever, frugal,

gentle, shrewd **7** careful, cunning, knowing, prudent, quietly, thrifty **8** cautious, skillful, watchful **9** carefully, dexterous, fortunate, sagacious **10** cautiously **11** comfortable, sharpwitted

canoe: **4** boat, kiak, pahi, proa, waka **5** birch, kayak, prahu, skiff, umiak, waapa **6** ballam, dugout, oomiak, pitpan **7** almadia, bidarka, coracle, currane, pirogue
bark: **7** cascara
dugout: **5** banca **6** baroto, corial **7** pirogue, piroque **12** pambanmanche
large: **5** bungo
sailing: **4** proa **5** prahu
skin-covered: **4** kiak **5** bidar, kayak **7** baidara
war: **4** proa

canon: law **4** code, hymn, laud, list, rule, song **5** axiom, gorge, gulch, model, table, tenet **6** decree **7** precept, statute **8** decision, standard **9** catalogue, clergyman, criterion **10** regulation **12** constitution
enigmatical: **4** nodi(pl.) **5** nodus
resident: **8** stagiary

canonical: **8** accepted, orthodox **13** authoritative
hour: **4** laud, none, sext **5** matin, prime **6** tierce **7** vespers **8** compline

canopy: sky **4** ceil, cope, dais, hood **5** shade, vault **6** awning, celure, finial, tester **7** marquee, shelter **8** covering **9** baldachin, baldaquin, pavillion **11** baldacchino
altar: **7** ciboria(pl.) **8** baldakin, ciborium **9** baldachin, baldaquin **10** baldachino **11** baldacchino
bed: **6** tester **7** sparver

canorous: **5** clear **7** musical **8** sonorous **9** melodious **10** euphonious

cant: tip **4** coax, heel, lean, list, nook, sing, tilt, turn **5** argot, bevel, chant, herald, hield, lingo, lusty, merry, niche, pitch, share, slang, slant, slope, whine **6** careen, corner, intone, jargon, lively, patois, snivel **7** auction, incline, portion, singing, wheedle **8** cheerful, pretense, vigorous **9** barbarism, hypocrisy, vulgarism **10** intonation **13** colloquialism **17** sanctimoniousness

cantabank: **6** singer **7** chanter

cantaloupe, cantaloup: **9** muskmelon

cantankerous: **6** ornery **8** perverse **9** irritable, malicious **10** brabagious **11** contentious **12** crossgrained

cantata: **4** mote, poem **8** serenata **11** composition

cantatrice: **6** singer **9** chanteuse

canteen: K.T., P.X., bar **5** bazar, flask **6** bazaar **7** cantina

canter: jog, run **4** gait, lope, pace, rack **5** rogue **6** beggar, whiner **8** vagabond

Canterbury:
archbishop: Odo **4** Lang **6** Anselm, Becket **7** Cranmer
gallop: **5** aubin

canticle: ode **4** hymn, laud, song **5** canto **6** anthem, cantic, hirmos **7** bravura
church: **6** Te Deum, venite **10** magnificat

cantilena: **6** legato, melody **8** graceful

cantillate: hum **5** chant **6** intone, recite

cantina: bag **5** pouch, store **6** pocket, pommel, saloon **7** canteen

canting: **5** atrip, pious **12** hypocritical

cantle: **4** join, nook, part **5** cheer, piece, raise, slice **6** corner **7** portion, segment **8** brighten, fragment **11** cornerpiece

canto: air, fit **4** book, pace, song **5** verse **6** melody, passus

canton: **4** part **5** angle **6** corner **7** portion, quarter, section **8** district, division

cantor: **6** leader, singer **7** chanter, soloist **9** precentor

cantoria: **7** balcony, gallery

cantrip: **5** charm, spell, trick

cantus: **4** song **5** chant

canty: **6** lively **8** cheerful **9** sprightly

Canuck: **8** Canadian

canvas: **4** duck, sail, tarp, tent, tewk **5** scrim **6** burlap **7** picture, poldavy **8** painting
waterproof: **9** tarpaulin

canvasback: **4** duck **6** cheval

canvass: **4** beat, hawk, poll, sift **5** randy, study **6** debate, peddle, search **7** agitate, discuss, examine, solicit, trounce **8** campaign, consider **11** electioneer, investigate

canvasser: **5** agent **6** poller, rodman **7** counter **8** salesman

canyon: **5** cajon, chasm, gorge, gulch **6** arroyo, ravine
mouth: **4** abra
small: **6** canada

caoba: **5** quira **8** mahogany, muskwood

caoutchouc: **6** rubber
source: ule **6** caucho

cap: fez, hat, lid, taj, tam, tip, top **4** acme, coif, cork, dome, eton, hood, hure, mate, topi **5** beret, chief, cover, crown, excel, match, outdo, seize, topee **6** arrest, beanie, bonnet, climax, cornet, helmet, puzzle, summit, turban **7** commode, ferrule, overlie, overtop, perplex, surpass **8** headgear, surprise, tarboosh **9** detonator, headpiece **11** mortarboard
child's: **5** mutch, toque **6** biggin, bonnet
close-fitting: **4** coif **5** toque **6** cloche **7** calotte
covering: **8** havelock
ecclesiastical: **5** beret **6** barret **7** biretta, galerum, galerus **8** barretta
hunter's: **7** montero
ignition: **4** fuse, fuze
military: **4** kepi **5** busby, shako
muslin: **5** mutch
part: **4** bill, peak **5** visor
Scotch: tam **8** balmoral **9** glengarry **11** tamoshanter
skull: **5** beame **6** callot, pileus **7** calotte, yamilke **8** yarmulka

capa: **5** cloak **6** mantle

capability: 6 stroil 7 ability 8 capacity 9 potential 10 competence, efficiency

capable: apt, can, fit 4 able 5 adept 6 expert 7 skilled 9 competent, effective, efficient, qualified 10 proficient 12 accomplished

of being cut: 7 sectile 8 scissile

of being defended: 7 tenable

of being heard: 7 audible

of being molded: 7 plastic

of being touched: 8 tangible

of endurance: 4 wiry 5 tough

of extension: 7 tensile

of flying: 6 volant

of suffering: 8 passible 9 sensitive

render: 6 enable

capacious: 4 full, wide 5 ample, broad, large, roomy 6 goodly 8 captious, spacious 9 extensive 10 commodious 12 considerable

capacitate: 8 qualify

capacity: 4 bent, gift, size, turn 5 knack, power, skill, space 6 burden, extent, spread, talent, volume 7 ability, caliber, calibre, content, faculty, fitness 8 aptitude, strength 9 continent, endowment, intellect 10 capability, competence

caparison: 4 deck, trap 8 covering 9 adornment 10 decoration

capatas: 4 boss 7 capataz(Sp.), foreman 8 overseer

capcase: bag 4 case 5 chest 10 receptacle

cape: ras 4 cope, gape, head, look, neck, ness, writ 5 amice, cappa, cloak, fanon, fichu, orale, point, sagum, stare, stole, talma 6 bertha, chapel, mantle, sontag, tabard, tippet 7 leather, manteel 8 headland, lambskin, mantilla 9 inverness, peninsula, sheepskin 10 projection, promontory

crocheted: 6 sontag

lace: 5 fichu 6 bertha 8 collaret

Cape anteater: 8 aardvark

Cape armadillo: 8 pangolin

Cape Dutch: 9 Afrikaans

Cape elk: 5 eland

Cape gooseberry: 4 poha 12 ground cherry

Cape lancewood: 7 assagai

cape merchant: 10 supercargo

Cape polecat: 5 zoril 8 muishond

Cape Province:

people: 4 Xosa 5 Pondo

Cape Ruby: 6 garnet, pyrope

Cape Verde:

island: Sal 4 Fago

native: 5 Brava, Serer

caper: hop 4 dido, jump, leap, romp, skip, skit 5 antic, brank, dance, flisk, frisk, prank, sauce, shrub 6 cavort, frisco, frolic, gambol, gamond, prance, spring, tittup, vagary 7 corsair, courant, friscal, gambado 8 capricci(pl.), capriole, marigold 9 capriccio, condiment, privateer

family: 13 capparidaceae

capercaillie: 4 cock 6 grouse

courtship: lak

capernoited: 7 crabbed, peevish 9 irritable 11 intoxicated 12 muddleheaded

capernoitie: 4 head 6 noddle

capful: 4 puff 8 quantity

capias: 4 writ 7 process

capillus: 4 hair

capilotade: 4 stew 5 sauce 6 ragout

capital: 4 cash, city, good, main, rare, seat 5 basic, chief, fatal, great, major, money, stock, vital 6 deadly, letter, mortal, primal, wealth 7 central, chattel, leading, radical, serious, weighty 9 copacetic, excellent, paramount, principal, prominent 10 pre-eminent 11 scrumptious

ancient: 4 Roma

impairment of: 7 deficit 9 depletion

provide: 4 back 5 angel 7 finance

capital punishment: 7 hanging 8 shooting 12 death penalty 13 electrocution

capitalist: 8 investor 9 plutocrat

capitano: 5 chief 7 captain, headman, soldier

capitate: 8 headline

capitulate: 4 fall 5 agree, title, yield 8 headline 9 enumerate, surrender

caporal: 7 foreman, tobacco 8 overseer

capote: 4 hood 5 cloak 6 bonnet, mantle, topper 8 overcoat

capric acid salt: 6 rutate

caprice: fad 4 kink, mood, whim 5 antic, braid, fancy, freak, humor, quirk 6 maggot, notion, temper, vagary, whimsy 7 boutade, conceit, crochet, impulse, whimsey 9 capriccio 12 inconsistent

capricious: 5 dizzy, doddy, fluky, moody 6 fickle 7 comical, erratic, flighty, wayward 8 fanciful, freakish, humorous, unsteady, volatile 9 arbitrary, crotchety, fantastic, humorsome, whimsical 10 changeable, inconstant

Capricorn: 4 Goat 6 beetle 13 Constellation

star within: 5 Deneb

capriole: 4 leap 5 caper 6 spring 9 headdress

capripede: 4 goat 5 satyr

caprylate: 4 acid, salt 5 ester 7 octoate

capsize: 4 coup, keel 5 upset 8 overturn

capstan: 4 drum 5 hoist, lever 8 cylinder, windlass

catch: 4 pawl

capsule: pod 4 boll, case, pill 5 shell, theco, wafer 6 ampule, sheath 7 ampoule 8 pericarp 9 cartridge, detonator 10 repository

captain: bo; boh 4 head 5 chief 6 leader, master 7 capitan, foreman, headman, manager, skipper 8 capitano, governor 9 centurion, commander, principal 14 superintendent

boat: gig

caption: 5 title 6 leader, legend 7 heading 8 headline, subtitle

captious: 5 testy 6 crafty, severe 7 carping, cynical, fretful, peevish 8 alluring, caviling, contrary, critical 9 capacious, insidious, irascible 10 capricious, censorious 12 faultfinding 13 hypercritical

captivate: win 4 take 5 catch, charm 6 allure, enamor, please, ravish, subdue 7 attract, bewitch, capture, enamour, enchant 8 enthrall, overtake 9 enrapture, fascinate, infatuate

captive: 5 slave 6 enamor 7 caitiff 8 prisoner

captivity: 4 bond 6 duress 7 bondage, serfdom, slavery 9 servitude, thralldom 10 subjection 11 confinement 12 imprisonment

captor: 5 taker 6 victor 7 catcher

capture: bag, cop, get, nab, net, win 4 fang, grab, hook, land, prey, take, trap, tree 5 catch, prize, raven, seize 6 arrest, collar, obtain 9 apprehend, captivate 10 circumvent 12 apprehension

capuche: 4 cowl, hood

Capuchin: 5 friar 6 monkey, pigeon

caput: top 4 head 7 chapter, council, section 8 division 9 paragraph

car: box, bus 4 auto, jeep, rath 5 coach, hutch, ratha, sedan, train, wrong 6 basket 7 awkward, chariot, trailer, trolley, vehicle 8 roadster, sinister 10 automobile, left-handed 11 convertible
aerial cable: 6 telfer 7 telpher
armored: 4 tank
railroad: box, oil 4 club, flat, mail, tank 5 chair, coach, diner 6 buffet, hopper, parlor 7 baggage, caboose, express, freight, gondola, pullman, sleeper, tourist 9 furniture, passenger 12 refrigerator

car barn: 5 depot

carabao: 7 buffalo

caracara: 4 hawk

caract: See **character**.

carafe: 6 bottle

caramel: 5 candy, sweet 6 bonbon 9 flavoring 10 confection

carapace: 5 crust, shell 6 lorica

carara: 9 coronopus

caravan: van 4 trek, trip 5 fleet 6 cafila, convoy, safari, travel 7 journey, vehicle
slave: 6 coffle

caravansary: inn 4 chan, khan 5 hotel, serai 6 hostel, imaret 8 choultry, hostelry 9 resthouse

carbine: gun 5 rifle 6 musket, weapon 7 escopet 9 escopette

carbohydrate: 5 sugar 6 starch 8 dextrose 9 cellulose

carbon: 4 coal, coke, copy, soot 6 crayon 7 replica 8 graphite
deposit: 4 soot
point: 6 crayon

carbonate: 4 burn, char, fizz 6 aerate 7 enliven 9 carbonize

carborundum: 5 emery 8 abrasive

carcajou: 4 lynx 6 badger, cougar 9 wolverine

carcanet: 5 chain 6 collar 8 headband, necklace

carcass: 4 body 6 corpse 7 carrion

carcel: 4 jail 6 prison

carcoon: 5 clerk 7 manager

card: map, pam, wag 4 comb, menu, plan 5 chart, fiche, joker, tease 6 cartel, ticket 7 program 8 schedule 9 character, eccentric 10 attraction, pasteboard
wool: tum 4 comb, rove, toom

card game: lu; gin, hoc, loo, pam 4 bank, faro, hock, keno, ruff, skat, slam, snap, solo, spin, vint 5 beast, chico, cinch, comet, crimp, decoy, gilet, gleek, monte, omber, ombre, pedro, pique, pitch, poker, rummy, stuss, trump, two-up, waist, whist 6 basset, boston, bridge, casino, commit, ecarte, euchre, fantan, flinch, hearts, masset, piquet, rounce, sledge, smudge 7 baccara, bezique, cayenne, Chicago, canasta, cooncan, sevenup 8 baccarat, commerce, conquian, contract, cribbage, handicap, Napoleon, patience, pinochle, tresillo, vederuff 9 Newmarket, panguinui, solitaire 10 blackstone 11 everlasting, speculation
bid: 4 slam 6 misere
holding: 6 tenace
old: hoc, loo, pam 4 brag, ruff 5 comet, gilet, omber, ombre, trump 7 primero, reversi 8 penneech, penneeck
player who cuts: 4 pone
playing card: ace, pam, ten 4 jack, king, trey 5 basto(Sp.), deuce, joker, knave, queen, taroc, tarot
term: bid, bye, cat, pic 4 book, card, deal, hand, meld, pair, pass, suit 5 flush, raise, trump 6 renege, tenace, tricon 8 aequence, straight 9 doubleton, singleton 10 Yarborough
wild: 5 joker

cardigan: 6 fabric, jacket, wampus 7 sweater

cardinal: 4 bird, main 5 basic, chief, cloak, color, vital 6 cleric 7 radical 9 principal 10 underlying
notification of elevation: 9 biglietto

cards (see also **card game**): 4 deck, pack, suit

care: 4 cark, cure, duty, fret, heed, mind, reck, soin(F.), tend, wish, yeme 5 grief, guard, nurse, pains, worry 6 burden, desire, grieve, lament, regard, sorrow 7 anxiety, auspice, caution, cherish, concern, keeping, scruple, thought, tuition 8 business 9 attention, diligence, direction, oversight 10 management, solicitude 11 calculation, heedfulness 12 watchfulness 14 responsibility
for: 4 like, mind, tend 5 guard, nurse,

treat **6** foster, relish
requiring: **7** fragile **8** ticklish
under another's: **4** ward **6** charge **7** protege **10** apprentice
careen: tip **4** cant, heel, keel, list, tilt, veer **5** lurch, slope **7** incline
career: run, way **4** life, road **5** trade **6** charge, course, gallop **7** calling, pursuit, running **8** business, vocation **10** occupation, profession, racecourse **11** achievement
carefree: **4** easy **5** frank, happy **10** insouciant **12** lighthearted
careful: wary **5** canny, chary, exact **6** eident, frugal **7** anxious, guarded, heedful, prudent, thrifty **8** accurate, cautious, diligent, discreet, dreadful, gingerly, mournful, troubled, vigilant, watchful **9** advertent, attentive, exquisite, observant, provident **10** economical, meticulous, respectful, respective, scrupulous, solicitous, thoughtful **11** circumspect, considerate, painstaking, punctilious
carefully: **7** charily **8** gingerly
careless: lax **4** cool, easy, lash, rash **5** slack **6** casual, overly, remiss, supine, untidy, unwary **7** languid **8** heedless, listless, reckless, slattern, slipshod, slovenly **9** forgetful, haphazard, negligent, unheeding, unmindful **10** neglectful, nonchalant, regardless **11** inadvertent, inattentive, indifferent, perfunctory, spontaneous, thoughtless, unconcerned
caress: coy, hug, pat, pet **4** bill, dant(Sc.), kiss, neck **6** coddle, cosset, fondle, pamper, stroke **7** cherish, embrace **10** endearment
caretaker: **6** keeper **7** janitor **9** custodian **11** housekeeper
careworn: **5** lined
carfuffle: **6** flurry, ruffle **8** disorder **9** agitation **10** disarrange
cargador: **6** porter **7** carrier **9** stevedore
cargo: **4** bulk, load **6** burden, lading **7** freight **8** property, shipment **10** freightage
discarded: **6** jetsam
loader: **9** stevedore
space in ship: **4** hold
stabilizer: **7** ballast
take on: **4** lade, load
wrecked ship: **7** flotsam
Caribbean: *bird:* **4** tody
gulf: **6** Darien
island: **4** Cuba **6** Nassau
caribou: **4** deer **8** reindeer
caricature: ape **4** copy, mock, skit **5** farce, libel, mimic, squib **6** overdo, parody, satire **7** cartoon **8** travesty **9** burlesque **12** exaggeration
caries: **5** decay **10** ulceration **11** saprodontia
carillon: **5** bells **6** chimes **12** glockenspiel

cark: vex **4** care, heed, load **5** cavil, pains, worry **6** burden, charge, harass **7** anxiety, perplex, trouble **8** distress
carl: lad **4** boor, hemp **5** churl, snarl **6** carlot, fellow, rustic **7** bondman, villein **10** husbandman, pinchpenny
carling: **6** rafter **7** support
Carmelite: **4** monk **5** friar
barefoot: **8** Teresian
carmen: **4** poem, song **11** incantation
carmine: red **7** crimson, scarlet **8** coloring
carnage: **6** murder, pogrom **8** butchery, massacre **9** bloodshed, slaughter
carnal: **4** crow, lewd **6** animal, bodily, sexual, worldly **7** brutish, earthly, fleshly, secular, sensual **8** material, temporal **9** corporeal **11** unspiritual **12** bloodthirsty, unregenerate
carnation: **4** pink **5** flake **6** flower **7** picotee **9** grenadine(F.)
carnelian: **4** sard **10** chalcedony
carnival: **4** fete **7** revelry **8** festival **11** merrymaking
carnivore: cat, dog, fox **4** bear, coat, coon, lion, lynx, mink, puma, seal, wolf **5** civet, genet, hyena, otter, panda, pekah, ratel, sable, stoat, tiger **6** cougar, ermine, feline, ferret, jackal, jaguar, marten, ocelot, possum, serval, weasel **7** dasyure, genette, glutton, leopard, opposum, polecat, raccoon, tigress **8** mongoose **9** ichneumon
carnose: **6** fleshy
carol: lay **4** noel, sing, song **5** ditty, yodel, yodle **6** alcove, warble **8** madrigal
Carolina island: Yap **4** Palu, Truk **5** Pelew **6** Ponape
carom: **4** shot **6** bounce, glance, strike **7** rebound **9** richochet
carousal: **4** lark, orgy, riot, romp, toot **5** binge, feast, randy, revel, spree **6** frolic, shindy, splore **7** banquet, carouse, wassail **8** festival, jamboree **9** bacchanal
carouse: **4** bout **5** birle(Sc.), bouse, drink, revel, quaff, spree, toast **7** wassail **8** carousal
carp: nag **4** fish, sing, snag, talk, yerk **5** cavil, prate, scold, speak **6** censor, nibble, recite **7** censure, chatter, quibble **8** complain, goldfish **9** criticize, discourse
carpel: **9** carpophyl **10** carpophyll
carpenter: ant **6** framer, joiner, wright **8** tectonic **9** artificer **10** woodworker **12** cabinetmaker
machine: **5** lathe **6** planer, shaper
ship: **5** chips
tool: adz, awl, saw **4** adze **5** level, plane **6** gimlet, hammer, square **7** hatchet
carpet: mat, rug **4** kali **5** scold, tapet, tapis **6** fabric **8** covering **9** reprimand
design: **9** madallion
variety: **4** Agra **6** velvet, Wilton **7** ingrain **8** Brussels, moquette, Venetian **9** Axminster, broadloom

carping: **8** captious, caviling, critical **10** censorious **12** faultfinding **13** hypercritical

carpus: **5** wrist

carr, car: bog, fen **4** pool **5** grove

carrack, carack: **4** boat **7** galleon

carriage: air **4** gait, garb, hack, load, mien, shay **5** bandy, brake, break, buggy, coach, front, midge, poise, wagon **6** burden, convoy, landau, manner, surrey **7** baggage, bearing, conduct, gesture, hackney, phaeton, vecture, vehicle **8** behavior, demeanor, dormeuse, equipage, portance **9** behaviour, execution **10** conveyance, deportment, management **14** administration

baby: **4** pram **6** gocart **8** stroller **12** perambulator

closed: cab **4** hack, taxi **6** calash **7** caleche **8** brougham, clarence

covered: **6** Berlin, landau **7** ricksha **8** carryall, dearborn, stanhope

four-wheeled: **5** coupe **6** surrey, whisky **7** phaeton, whiskey **8** barouche, clarence, rockaway, victoria **9** chariotee, gladstone

one-horse: fly, gig **4** ekka (Ind.), shay, trap **5** sulky **6** dennet **7** cariole, dogcart **8** carriole

open: **7** dogcart, dos-a-dos **8** sociable

portable: **5** sedan

three-horse: **6** troika

two-seated: **6** tandem

two-wheeled: gig **4** shay, trap **5** essed, sulky, tonga **6** chaise, cisium, esseda, hansom **7** carreta, chariot, tilbury **8** carretta **9** caretella, carromata **11** jinrickshaw

carried: **5** borne, giddy, toted **6** carted, lugged, wafted **8** drifting, ravished **10** abstracted **11** transported

carrier (see also **conveyance**)**:** hod **4** ship **5** hamal, macer, plane **6** bearer, cadger, hamaul, hammal, khamal, porter **7** drayman, flattop, hammaul, postman, remover **8** cargador, portator, railroad, teamster **9** messenger

carrion: **4** vile **6** corpse, refuse, rotten **7** carcass, corrupt **9** loathsome

Carroll character: **5** Alice **6** hatter, rabbit **7** duchess

carrot: **4** root **5** plant **6** daucus **10** enticement

deadly: **5** drias

family: **8** ammaicea

genus: **5** carum

top: **7** red-head

wild: **8** hilltrot **10** laceflower

carrousel: **4** ride **12** merry-go-round

carry: hug, jag, lug **4** bear, cart, gest, hold, lead, take, tote, tump **5** bring, cadge, geste, guide, poise **6** behave, convey, convoy, delate, derive, extend **7** conduct, contain, produce, support, sustain, undergo **8** continue, transfer, transmit **9** prosecute, transport **11** comportment

away: **4** kill, take **5** eloin, reave, steal **6** eloign, kidnap, remove **9** transport

on: **4** rant, rave, wage **6** manage **7** conduct, perform, proceed **8** continue, maintain, transact **9** misbehave, prosecute

out: **6** effect **7** execute, perform, sustain **8** complete

over: **4** tide **5** table **6** extend, shelve **8** contango, postpone, transfer

the day: win **7** prevail

carryall: bag, bus **4** case **8** carriage

carrying: **6** gerent **9** gestation

cart: **4** butt, char, dray, haul, tote, wain **5** araba, bandy, bogie, carry, sulky, tonga, wagon **6** charet, convey **7** chariot, hackery, trolley, trundle, tumbler, tumbrel, tumbril, vehicle **8** charette

farmer: **7** morfrey **8** morphrey

freight: **8** carreton

horse: **8** cartaver(Sc.)

license: **6** caroon **7** caroome, carroon

racing: **5** sulky

rope: **5** wanty(Sc.)

strong: **4** dray

two-wheeled: bin, gig **4** shay **5** dandy, sulky, tonga **6** reckla **7** tumbril **8** carretta(Sp.)

cartage: **7** drayage, haulage

carte: map **4** card, list, menu **5** chart **7** charter, diagram

cartel: **4** card, defy, pact, pool, ship **5** paper, trust **6** corner, letter, treaty **8** contract **9** agreement, challenge **10** convention

carter: **7** drayman, trucker **8** horseman, teamster

Carthage: *citadel:* **5** Bursa, Byrsa

foe: **4** Cato

founder: **4** Dido

general: **5** Hanno **8** Hannibal

goddess: **5** Tanit **6** Tanith

language: **5** Punic

magistrate: **7** suffete

pert. to: **5** Punic

queen: **4** Dido

victor at Zama: **6** Scipio

cartilage: **6** tissue **7** gristle

ossified: **4** bone

cartload: **6** fother

cartograph: map **4** plat **5** chart

carton: box **4** case **9** container **10** receptacle

cartoon: **10** caricature

cartoonist: **4** Arno, Capp, Ding, Nast **6** Disney

cartridge: bag **4** case **5** shell **7** capsule

holder: **4** clip

carving: *in stone:* **5** cameo **8** intaglio **10** engrailing

pert. to: **7** glyphic, glyptic

relief: **5** cameo

caryatid: **6** figure **9** priestess

male: cap **7** telamon

casa: 5 house 8 building, dwelling
casaba: 5 melon 9 muskmelon
Casanova: 4 rake, roue 5 lover
cascade: lin(Sc.) 4 fall, linn(Sc.) 5 force(Sc.) 8 cataract 9 waterfall
casco: 5 barge 7 lighter
case: bag, box, hap, pod 4 bunk, burr, deed, file, pack, pair, suit 5 brace, bulla, burse, casus, cover, crate, event, folio, state, theca, trial 6 action, affair, binder, carton, chance, coffin, couple, matter, quiver, sheath, survey 7 cabinet, capcase, capsule, enclose, envelop, example, holster, inclose, lawsuit, satchel 8 accident, argument, cupboard, envelope, instance, situated 9 cartridge, condition, container, happening 10 occurrence, receptacle, sabretache 11 contingency
  book holder: 5 forel 6 forrel
  cigar: 7 humidor
  cosmetic: 7 compact
  document: 7 hanaper
  explosive: 5 shell 6 petard 11 firecracker
  grammatical: 6 dative 8 ablative, genitive, vocative 9 objective 10 accusative, nominative
  small: tye 4 etui 5 bulla, etwee 6 trouse
  toiletries: 4 etui 5 etwee
casement: 6 window 8 covering
cash: 4 coin, cush, dump, dust, jack, jake 5 blunt, brass, clink, darby, dough, funds, money 6 specie 7 capital, hemlock 8 currency 10 spondulics
  keeper: 6 bursar, teller 7 cashier 9 treasurer
cashew: nut 4 tree 7 maranon
casing: 4 boot, shoe, tire 5 gaine 6 coffin, collet, lining, sheath 8 covering 9 framework
cask: keg, tub, tun, vat 4 butt, cade, cowl, knag, pipe 5 bowie, bulge, foist 6 bareca, bareka, barrel, cardel, casque, firkin, tierce 7 barrico, fostell 8 cassette, hogshead, puncheon 9 kilderkin
  bulge: 5 bilge
  oil: 4 rier
  orifice: 8 bunghole
  rim: 5 chimb, chime
  stave: lag
  wine: fat, tun 4 butt, fust, pipe 6 tierce
casket: box, pix, tye 4 case, cask, cist, till, tomb 5 chest 6 Accera, chasse, coffer, coffin 7 casquet, fostell 8 cassette 9 reliquary
Caspian Sea: 5 Tates
casque: hat 4 cask 5 armor 6 helmet 9 headdress
cassation: 8 quashing 9 annulling, canceling 10 abrogation
cassava: 4 aipi 5 aipim 6 casiri, manioc 7 tapioca
cassena: 6 yaupon
cassette: 6 casket, holder, sagger
cassia: 4 drug, herb, tree 5 senna, shrub

  bark: 8 cinnamon
cassie: 6 basket 8 huisache
cassock: 4 gown 5 gippo 6 priest 7 pelisse, soutane 9 clergyman
cassone: box 5 chest
cassowary: emu 4 bird 5 murup 6 moorup
cast: 4 hurl, mold, molt, shed, spew, tint, toss 5 eject, fling, found, heave, mould, pitch, shade, sling, throw, tinge 7 cashier, deposit, discard
  aside: see *away* below
  away: 4 jilt, junk, shed 5 scrap, wreck 6 maroon, reject 7 abandon, discard, dismiss 8 squander 9 shipwreck
  down: 5 abase 6 abattu, deject, sadden 7 abattue, depress, destroy 8 demolish, dispirit 10 discourage
  lots: 5 cavel
  off: 4 free 5 untie 6 disown, unmoor 7 discard 9 eliminate
  out: 5 eject, expel 6 banish
  up: add 5 total, vomit 6 reckon 7 compute, measure 8 reproach
castaway: 4 waif 5 tramp 6 reject 7 outcast 8 derelict, stranded 9 shipwreck
caste: 4 rank 5 breed, class, grade, order 6 degree, status
  group: 5 varna
  merchant: 6 banian, banyan
  priestly: 4 magi(pl.) 5 magus
caster: 4 vial 5 cruse, cruet, phial, wheel 6 castor, hurler, roller 7 pitcher, trundle
castigate: 5 emend, scare 6 berate, punish, revise, strafe, subdue 7 censure, chasten, correct, reprove 8 chastise, lambaste 9 criticize
Castile: *hero:* Cid
  province: 5 Avila, Soria
Castilian: 7 Spanish
casting: *mold:* die 6 matrix 7 matrice
  rough: pig
castle: 4 fort, rock, rook 5 abode, morro 7 bastile, chateau, citadel 8 bastille, castillo, fastness, fortress 10 stronghold 13 fortification
  in the air: 5 dream 6 vision 7 fantasy 8 daydream 9 imagining
  tower: 4 keep
  wall: 6 bailey
  warden: 6 disdar, dizdar 9 castellan
castor: hat 4 bean, star 6 beaver 7 leather
Castor: *and Pollux:* 5 twins 6 Gemini 8 Dioscuri
  brother: 6 Pollux
  horse: 8 Cyllaros
  mother: 4 Leda
  slayer: 4 Idas
castrate: gib 4 geld, spay, swig 5 alter, capon, prune 6 eunuch, neuter 7 evirate 8 caponize, mutilate 10 emasculate
casual: 5 stray 6 chance, random 7 cursory, natural, offhand 8 informal 9 haphazard, uncertain 10 accidental, contingent, fortuitous, incidental, nonchalant,

occasional **11** indifferent **14** unconventional, unpremeditated

casualty: **4** loss **5** death **6** chance, hazard, injury, mishap **8** accident, disaster **9** mischance **10** misfortune **11** contingency **12** misadventure

casus: **4** case **5** event **8** occasion

cat: **4** flog, lion, lynx, pard, puma, puss **5** civet, felid, gatol(Sp.), moggy, ounce, pussy, tiger **6** cougar, feline, jaguar, malkin, mawkin, ocelot, tibert **7** cheetah, leopard, panther, tigress, wildcat **8** baudrons(Sc.) **9** carnivore, grimalkin **11** caterpiller **12** catamountain

breed: **4** Manx **5** alley, tabby **6** Angora **7** Maltese, Persian, Siamese

comb. form: **5** aelur **6** aeluro

cry: mew **4** hiss, meow, miau, purr **5** miaou, miaow, miaul

female: **9** grimalkin

genus: **5** felis **7** felidae(pl.)

cat-o-nine-tails: **4** lash, whip **7** cattail

cataclysm: **5** flood **6** deluge **7** debacle **8** diaster, overflow, upheaval **11** catastrophe

catacomb: **4** tomb **5** crypt, vault **8** cemetery

catalepsy: **6** trance **7** seizure

catalog, catalogue: **4** book, list, roll, rota **5** brief, canon, index **6** record, roster **7** arrange **8** classify, register, schedule **9** enumerate, inventory, repertory **11** systematize

Catalonia:

dance: **7** sardana

marble: **8** brocatel **10** brocatelle

catamaran: **4** raft, trow **5** balsa, float **6** vessel **8** auntsary

catamount: **4** lynx, puma **6** cougar

catapult: **5** throw **6** launch, onager **7** bricole **8** ballista, crossbow **9** slingshot

cataract: lin **4** linn **5** falls, flood **6** deluge **7** cascade, Niagara **8** Victoria **9** waterfall

cataria: **6** catnip

catarrh: **4** cold **5** rheum

catastrophe (see also **cataclysm**)**:** **8** accident, calamity, disaster **10** denouement, misfortune

catbird: **7** mimidae

catch: bag, cop, get, nab, net **4** draw, hasp, haul, hawk, hold, hook, land, pawl, snap, stop, trap, tree **5** grasp, hitch, ketch, knack, seize, snare, trick **6** button, clutch, corner, detect, detent, engage, enmesh, entrap, snatch **7** attract, capture, ensnare, grapnel **8** entangle, overtake, surprise **9** intercept

sight of: **4** espy **6** descry

up with: **8** overtake

catchfly: **6** silene

catching: **6** catchy **8** alluring **10** contagious, entrapping, infectious **11** captivating

catchword: cue, tag **5** motto **6** byword, phrase, slogan

catchy: **9** appealing

cate: **4** food **6** viands **8** dainties **10** delicacies, provisions

catechism: **5** guide **6** manual **8** carritch **10** carritches(Sc.),

catechumen: **5** pupil **7** audient, auditor, convert **8** beginner, neophyte

categorical: **8** absolute, explicit **11** dictatorial, unequivocal, unqualified

category: **4** rank **5** class, genus, genre(pl.), order **6** family **7** species **8** division **12** denomination **14** classification

catena: **4** link **5** chain **6** series

catenate: **4** link **11** concatenate

cater: **4** feed **5** humor, serve, treat **6** pander, purvey, supply **7** provide

caterpillar: cat **4** muga **5** aweto, eruca, larva **6** canker, erucae(pl.), risper, woubit **7** tractor

caterwaul: cry **4** wail **5** miaul

catface: **4** scar

catfish: mud **4** cusk, elod, pout, raad, shal **5** bagre, raash **6** docmac, hassar, raasch, tandau **7** candiru **8** bullhead **9** sheatfish

genus: **13** saccobranchus

cathartic: **8** lapactic, laxative **9** cleansing, purgative

cathode: **9** electrode

catholic: **5** broad, papal **7** general, liberal **8** tolerant **9** universal **10** ecumenical

Catholic: See **Roman Catholic**.

catlike: **6** feline **8** stealthy **9** noiseless

catnap: **4** doze

catnip: nep **6** catnep **7** cataria, catwort

Catoism: **9** austerity, harshness

cat's-cradle: **7** ribwort

cat's-paw: **4** dupe, gull, tool **5** cully

cattail: **4** flag, musk, rush **5** ament, cloud, raupo, reree **6** catkin **7** bulrush, matreed

family: **9** typhaceae

cattle: **4** cows, dhan(Ind.), kine, neat, oxen **5** beefs, bulls, stock **6** beasts, beeves, steers **7** bovines

assemblage: **4** herd **5** drove

brand: **4** duff **5** buist

breed: **4** Nata, Zobo **5** Angus, Devon, Dutch, Niata(dwarf) **6** Durham, Belted, Jersey, Sussex **7** Brahman, Brangus, Kerries **8** Ayrshire, Bradford, Charbray, Guernsey, Hereford, Holstein, Longhorn **9** Red Polled, Shorthorn, Teeswater **10** Beefmaster, Brown Swiss **11** Charollaise, Dutch Belted **14** French Canadian, Santa Gertrudis

call: **4** sook

dealer: **6** drover, herder

dehorned: **5** muley **6** mulley

genus: bos

goddess: **6** Bubona

group: **4** herd **5** drove **7** creaght(Ir.)

plague: **10** rinderpest

shelter: **4** byre **5** barth
yard: **6** cancha
catwort: 6 catnip
Caucasia:
   goat: tur
   ibex: zac
   language: laz, udi **4** andi, avar, laze, lazi,
      udic **5** udish **7** semetic **9** itranican
   race: **5** Aryan, Osset **6** Ossete
   tribe: **4** imer, kurd, laze, lazi, svan **5**
      pshav **7** kubachi
caucho: ule **4** tree **6** rubber
caudal: 4 rear **9** posterior
   appendage: **4** tail
caudata: 4 newt **5** snake **10** salamander
cauk: 5 chalk **9** limestone
caul: web **4** cawl, trug, veil **7** network, omentum **8** membrane, tressour, tressure
cauldrife: **4** cold **6** chilly **8** chilling **9**
   cheerless
cauldron: See **caldron.**
cauliflower: 7 cabbage **8** broccoli **9** disfigure
caulk, calk: **6** chinse **7** chintze
cause: aim, gar(Sc.), key **4** case, chat,
   move, root, spur, suit **5** agent, basis,
   breed **6** create, effect, gossip, ground, induce, malady, motive, object, origin, reason, source, spring **7** concern, disease,
   lawsuit, produce, provoke **8** business,
   engender, movement, occasion **9** originate, wherefore **10** mainspring
causerie: 4 chat, plea, talk **6** debate **10**
   discussion **12** conversation
causes, science of: 7 etiology
causeway: way **4** dike, road **7** chausse(F.),
   highway
causey: dam, way **4** bank, pave, road **5**
   mound **6** street **7** highway **8** sidewalk
caustic: lye **4** tart **5** acrid, sharp **6** biting,
   bitter, severe **7** burning, cutting, erodent,
   mordant, pungent, satiric **8** alkaline, scathing, snappish, stinging **9** corrosive, sarcastic, satirical, vitriolic **10** malevolent
   11 acrimonious
   agent: **7** cautery, erodent
cauterize:
4 burn, char, fire, sear **5** brand, inust, singe
   9 sterilize
caution: 4 care, heed, warn **6** advice,
   cautel, caveat, exhort **7** anxiety, counsel,
   precept, proviso **8** admonish, forecast,
   monition, prudence, wariness **9** diligence,
   vigilance **10** admonition, precaution,
   providence **11** calculation, forethought,
   reservation **12** watchfulness
cautious: 4 wary **5** alert, canny, chary,
   siker **6** fabian, sicker **7** careful, guarded,
   prudent **8** discreet, vigilant **10** scrupulous **11** circumspect
cavalcade: 4 raid, ride **5** march **6** parade,
   safari **7** journey, pageant **10** procession
cavalier: gay **4** curt, easy, fine **5** brave,

frank, rider **6** escort, knight **7** brusque,
   gallant, haughty, offhand, soldier **8** Royalist **9** cabellero, chevalier **10** disdainful **12**
   high-spirited, supercilious
Cavalleria Rusticana character: 4 Lola
   5 Alfio **7** Turiddu
cavalry: 6 horses, troops **8** horsemen **10**
   knighthood
   horse: **6** lancer
   weapon: **5** lance, saber
cavalryman: 5 spahi **6** hussar, lancer,
   spahee **7** courier, dragoon, soldier, trooper **8** gendarme, horseman
cave: den, tip **4** cove, hole, lair, rear, sink,
   toss, weem **5** antre, cavea, crypt, speos,
   store, upset **6** beware, cavern, cavity,
   cellar, forgou, grotto, hollow, larder, luster, pantry, plunge **7** reserve, spelunk **8**
   collapse, overturn **9** storeroom
   dweller: **10** troglodyte
   researcher: **9** spelunker **12** speleologist
   science of researching: **10** speleology
cave in: 5 stove, yield **6** submit **8** collapse
cavea: den **4** cage, cave **10** auditorium
caveat: 6 beware **7** caution, warning
cavern: 4 cave, grot, hole, lair, weem **5**
   antra(pl.), croft **6** antrum, cavity, grotto,
   hollow **7** spelunk
cavetto: 7 molding
caviar, caviare: ova, roe **4** eggs, ikra **5**
   ikary **6** relish **8** delicacy
   source: **7** sterlet **8** sturgeon
cavie: 4 cage, coop **7** hencoop
cavil: 4 cark, carp, haft **6** haggle **7** quibble
   9 criticise, criticize, exception, objection
caviling: 8 captious, picayune
cavity: bag, pit, sac **4** abri, cave, dalk,
   dent, hole, mine, vein, void **5** antra(pl.),
   atria(pl.), fossa, geode, lumen, mouth,
   sinus **6** antrum, atrium, camera, cavern,
   fossae(pl.), grotto, hollow, vacuum **7**
   cistern, vesicle **8** cul-de-sac **10** depression, excavation
   anatomical: **5** antra(pl.), fossa **6** antrum,
      fossae(pl.)
   brain: **6** coelia
   gun: **4** bore
   heart: **7** auricle **9** ventricle
   lode: vug **4** voog, vugg, vugh
   sac-like: **5** bursa **6** bursae(pl.),
   skull: **4** aula **5** fossa, sinus
   stone: **5** geode
cavort: 4 play **5** bound, caper **6** curvet,
   gambol, prance
cavy: 4 paca, pony **6** agouti, aperea, cayuse, rodent **8** capybara **9** guinea pig
caw: cry **4** call, cawl **5** croak, quark,
   quawk
cawl: 4 trug **6** basket
cay: See **key.**
cayuse: 4 cavy, pony **6** bronco **7** broncho
cease: end **4** halt, liss, quit, rest, stop **5**
   avast, douse, dowse, lisse, pause, peter **6**

desist, devall, finish **7** abstain, refrain **8**
intermit **9** terminate **11** discontinue
ceaseless: 4 ever **7** endless **8** unending **9**
continual, incessant, unceasing
ceasing: **9** cessation
cecidium: **4** gall
cecity: **9** blindness
Cecrops' daughter: **5** Herse **8** Aglauros
cedar: **4** toon, tree **5** savin **6** deodar, sa-
bina, sabine, savine **7** waxwing
camphor: **6** cedrol
green: **5** cedre(F.), color
moss: **8** hornwort
cede: **4** cess, give **5** award, grant, leave,
waive, yield **6** assign, resign, submit **8**
renounce, transfer **9** surrender **10** relinquish
cedrat: **6** citron
cedula: **8** document, schedule **11** certificate
ceil: **4** line **7** overlay **8** wainscot
ceilidh: **4** call **5** visit **12** conversation **13**
entertainment
ceiling: **6** lining, screen, soffit **7** curtain,
testudo **8** covering, paneling **10** testu-
dines(pl.) **11** wainscoting
covering: **9** calcimine, kalsomine
division: **5** trave
mine: **5** astel
wooden: **8** plancher
Celebes:
bovine: ox **4** anoa
island: **4** Muna
people: **6** toraja **7** toradja
celebrate: **4** keep, sing **5** extol, honor,
revel **6** extoll, praise **7** glorify, observe **8**
emblazon, eulogize, proclaim **9** solemnize
11 commemorate
celebrated: **4** kept **5** famed, noted **6**
famous **7** eminent, feasted, renomme **8**
glorious, observed, renowned **9** distingue,
prominent **10** solemnized **11** conspicuous, illustrious **13** distinguished
celebration: **4** fete, rite **6** renown **9** celebrity, festivity
celebrious: **6** famous **7** festive **8** renowned, thronged **10** frequented
celebrity: VIP **4** fame, lion, name, star **5**
eclat **6** renown, repute **11** celebration
celerity: **5** haste, hurry, speed **8** dispatch,
rapidity, velocity **9** prestezza, quickness,
swiftness
celery:
family: **9** ammiaceae
wild: **8** smallage
celeste: **4** stop **5** pedal **7** sky-blue
celestial: **4** holy **6** divine, uranic **7** angelic, Chinese, ethered **8** empyreal, ethereal, heavenly
being: **5** angel **6** cherub, seraph **8** sera-
phim(pl.)
body: **4** star **5** comet **6** meteor, nebula,
planet
elevation of mind: **7** anagoge
matter: **6** nebula

celibacy: **8** chastity
celibate: **6** chaste, single **8** bachelor,
spinster **9** unmarried
cell: egg **4** cage, germ, jail **5** cabin, crypt,
group, vault **6** cytode, prison **7** cellule,
chamber, cubicle, dungeon **9** hermitage
10 ergastulum **11** compartment
bull: **5** toril **7** toriles(pl.)
coloring: **10** endochrome
colorless: **10** achroacyte, lymphocyte
connecting: **10** heterocyst
generative: **6** gamete
lens-shaped: **8** lenticel
migratory: **9** leucocyte
structural unit: **7** energid, nucleus **10**
protoplast
substance: **5** linin
cell-like: **6** cytoid
cella: **4** naos
cellar: **4** cave **8** basement **9** storeroom
cellulose:
acetate: **7** acetose
elastic: **5** rayon
celsitude: **6** height **8** altitude **10** exaltation
Celt: **4** Gael, Gaul, Manx **5** Irish, Welsh **6**
Breton, Briton, Eolith **7** Cornish
Celtic: **4** Erse **7** Scotch
abbot: **5** coarb
chariot: **5** essed
chieftain: **6** tanist
divinity: **7** Taranis
foot soldier: **4** kern
god: Ler **4** Leir, Llyr
harp: telyn **11** clairschach
language: **4** Erse, Manx **5** Irish, Welsh **6**
Celtic, Cymric, Gaelic **9** Brythonic
peasant: **4** kern
priest: **5** Druid
sword: sax **4** seax
cembalo: **8** dulcimer **11** harpsichord
cement: fix **4** glue, join, knit, lime, lute **5**
imbed, paste, putty, stick, unite **6** cohere,
fasten, gulgul(Ind.), mortar, solder **7** asphalt **8** adhesive, hadigeon(F.), solidify
11 agglutinate
hydraulic: **4** paar
infusible substance: **4** lute
plastic: **8** albolite, albolith
quick-drying: **6** mastic
substance: **6** celite
window glass: **5** putty
cemetery: **6** litten **7** charnel **8** catacomb,
Golgotha **9** graveyard **10** necropolis **11**
polyandrium
cenchrus: **5** grass **6** millet
cenobite: nun **4** monk **5** friar **6** essene **7**
recluse **8** monastic **9** anchorite
cense: **4** rank **6** assess, rating **7** perfume
8 estimate, position
censer: **8** thurible
censor: **6** critic **8** restrict, suppress **9** detractor
censorious: **6** severe **7** carping **8** blame-
ful, captious, critical **9** satirical

censurable: **8** blamable, culpable **13** reprehensible

censure: **4** carp, flay **5** blame, chide, decry, judge, slate **6** accuse, berate, charge, rebuff, rebuke, remord, targue(Scot.), tirade **7** chasten, condemn, impeach, inveigh, reprove **8** disallow reproach **9** challenge, criticize, reprimand **10** animadvert, exprobrate, vituperate **11** disapproval **12** reprehension **13** animadversion **15** discommendation

census: **4** list, poll **5** count **11** enumeration

centaur:
bull's head: **9** bucentaur
killed by Hercules: **6** Nessus
Centennial State: **8** Colorado

center, centre: cor, hub, mid **4** axis, core, foci(pl.), nave, seat **5** focus, heart, midst, pivot, spine **6** middle **7** lineman, nucleus **8** centrate **12** headquarters
toward: **4** orad **5** entad **10** centerward
centerpiece: **7** epergne
centigrade: **5** scale **11** thermometer
centipede: **4** veri **6** earwig, golach, goloch **8** chilopod, myriapod **9** geophilus
central: mid **5** axial, basic, chief, focal, prime **6** median, middle **7** capital, centric, leading, pivotal, primary **8** dominant **11** equidistant
Central America:
agave: **5** sisal
ant: **5** kelep
bird: **7** jacamar **8** puffbird
canoe: **6** pitpan
country: **6** Panama **8** Honduras, Salvador **9** Costa Rica, Guatemala, Nicaragua
fishing boat: **6** cayuco
gopher: **7** quachil
Indian: **4** Maya **5** Carib
measure: **7** cantaro, manzana
monkey: **4** mono
mullet: **4** bobo
rodent: **4** paca
snake: **10** bushmaster
stockade: **4** boma
tragon: **4** bird **6** quezal **7** quetzal
tree: ebo, ule **4** eboe **5** amate **9** sapodilla
village: **4** boma
weight: **4** libra
Central Asia: See **Asia.**
central cylinder: **5** stele
centric: **5** focal **6** middle, tarete **7** central **9** clustered **11** cylindrical **12** concentrated
centrifugal: **9** radiating
centripetal: **8** afferent
century: age **6** siecle(F.)
ten: **7** chiliad **10** millennium
century plant: **4** aloe **5** agave **6** maguey
fiber: **4** pita, pito
ceorl: **5** churl, thane **7** freeman, villein
cepa: **5** onion
cephalagia: **8** headache
cephalic: **8** atlantal, cerebral

cephalopod: **5** squid **6** cuttle **7** inkfish, octopus
secretion: ink
ceral: **4** waxy **7** waxlike
ceramics: **5** tiles **7** pottery **9** stoneware
oven: **4** kiln
sieve: **4** laun
cerate: wax **4** lard **5** salve **8** ointment
ceratose: **5** horny
cereal grass genus: **6** secale
Cerberus: dog **7** monster **8** guardian **9** custodian
cere: wax **4** sere, wrap **6** anoint, embalm
cereal: rye **4** bean, bran, corn, mush, oats, rice **5** grain, maize, spelt, wheat **6** barley, farina, hominy **7** oatmeal, soybean **8** porridge **9** buckwheat
coating: **4** bran
grass: oat, rye **4** ragi, rice **5** grain, wheat **6** barley, raggee
spike: ear
cerebral: **6** mental
cerebration: **7** thought
cerement: **6** shroud **9** cerecloth
ceremonious: **5** grand, lofty, stiff **6** formal, proper, solemn **7** precise, stately, studied **10** respectful **11** punctilious **12** conventional
ceremony: **4** fete, pomp, rite, show, sign **5** state **6** augury, parade, powwow, review, ritual **7** display, pageant, portent, prodigy **8** accolade, function, marriage, occasion **9** formality, solemnity **10** ceremonial, observance **11** celebration
cerer: **10** undertaker
Ceres: **7** Demeter
mother: Ops
cerise: red **6** cherry
cerite: **7** mineral **8** allanite
cernuous: **7** nodding **8** drooping **9** pendulous
cero: **4** fish **6** sierra **7** cavallo, pintado
certain: **4** firm, real, sure, true **5** bound, clear, exact, fixed, plain, siker(Sc.) **6** actual, sicker, stated **7** assured, precise, settled **8** absolute, apparent, constant, official, positive, reliable, resolved, unerring **9** confident, steadfast, undoubted **10** dependable, inevitable, infallible, undeniable **11** determinate, indubitable, trustworthy **12** indisputable **13** incontestable **14** unquestionable **16** incontrovertible
certainly: **4** amen, ywis **5** iwiss, truly **6** certes, indeed, verily **7** hardily **8** forsooth
certie, certy: **5** faith, troth
certificate: **4** bond **5** check, libel, scrip **6** attest, ticket, verify **7** diploma, voucher **9** statement, testimony **10** credential **11** attestation, declaration, testimonial **13** certification
cargo: **8** navicert
land: **6** amparo(Sp.)
medical, for ill student: **8** aegrotat
money owed: **9** debenture

certify: 4 avow, vise 5 swear 6 affirm, assure, depose, evince, verify 7 endorse, license, testify 9 determine, guarantee
under oath: 6 attest
certiorari: 4 writ 6 review
certiorate: 6 assure 7 apprise, certify
cerulean: 4 blue 5 azure 6 coelin 7 sky-blue
cervine: elk 4 deer, stag 5 moose 6 cervid 8 cervidae(pl.), reindeer
cervix: 4 neck
cess: bog, tax 4 cede, duty, levy, luck, rate, tyrf 5 slope, yield 6 impost 7 measure 9 surrender 10 assessment, estimation
cessation: end 4 halt, liss, lull, rest, stay, stop 5 letup, lisse, pause, truce 6 recess 7 ceasing, respite 8 interval, stoppage, surcease 9 armistice, remission 12 intermission, interruption 14 discontinuance
of being: 8 desition
cession: 8 yielding 9 surrender 10 compliance, concession
cesspool: 4 sump 7 cistern
cest: 4 belt 6 cestus, girdle
cesta: 6 basket
cetacean: orc 4 cete, orca 5 whale 6 beluga 7 dolphin, grampus 8 porpoise
blind: 4 susu
genus: 4 inia
cete: 5 whale 7 cetacea
Ceylon: *aborigine:* 4 Toda 5 Vedda 6 Veddah
boat: 4 done, doni 5 balsa, dhoni, doney 11 warkamoowee
city: 7 Colombo(c.)
coin: 4 cent
Dravidian: 5 Tamil
garment: 6 sarong
gooseberry: 10 ketembilla
governor: 6 disawa
hemp: 6 sina-wa
hill dweller: 4 Toda
language: 4 Pali 5 Tamil
monkey: 4 maha 5 toque 6 langur, rilawa, rillow 10 wanderoock
moss: 4 agar, alga 5 jaffa 7 gulaman
native: 5 Vedda 6 Veddah
oak: 5 kusam
palm: 7 talipat, talipot
rat: 9 bandicoot
resthouse: 6 abalam
rose: 8 cleander
seaport: 5 Galle
sedan: 6 tomjon, tonjon
snake: 7 adjiger
soldier: 4 peon
tea: 5 pekoe
tree: 4 doon, tala 7 talipot
chabouk, chabuk: 4 whip
chabutra: 4 dais 7 terrace 8 platform
chack: 4 bite, snap 5 clack, snack 8 wheatear
chackle: 6 cackle, rattle 7 chatter
chacra: 4 farm 5 milpa, ranch

chaeta: 4 seta 5 spine 7 bristle
chafe: irk, rub, vex 4 fret, frig, fume, gall, heat, josh, rage, warm, wear 5 anger, annoy, grind, scold 6 abrade, banter, excite, fridge, harass, injury, nettle 7 incense, inflame 8 friction, irritate, raillery
chaff: guy, hay, pug 4 bran, caff(Sc.), guff, josh, quiz 5 borak, chyak, dross, glume hulls, husks, straw, tease, trash 6 banter, bhoosa, chyack, refuse 7 tailing 8 raillery, ridicule
chaffer: 5 bandy, sieve, wares 6 buying, dicker, haggle, higgle, market 7 bargain, chatter, selling, traffic 8 exchange 9 negotiate 10 bargaining 11 merchandise
chaffinch: 7 robinet
chaffy: 5 scaly 7 acerose, acerous, paleate, trivial 9 bantering, worthless 10 paleaceous
chain: guy, row, set, tew, tie, tye 4 bind, bond, file, gyve, join, link 5 cable, leash, suite, train 6 catena, chigon, collar, fasten, fetter, hobble, secure, series, string, tether 7 bobstay, catenae(pl.), connect, embrace, enslave, manacle, network, shackle 8 bracelet, restrain 9 constrain 10 chatelaine 13 concatenation
collar: 4 tore 6 torque
key: 10 chatelaine
mountain: 5 range, Rocky 7 Sierras
of rocks: 4 reef
set with precious stones: 7 sautoir
chain cable: 4 boom
chain grab: 7 wildcat
chain-like: 8 catenate
chains: 7 bondage, serfdom
chair: 4 seat 5 sedan, stool 6 office, pulpit, rocker
back: 5 splat
bath: 11 vinaigrette
bishop's official: 8 cathedra
cover: 4 tidy 12 antimacassar
easy: 6 morris, rocker
folding: 9 faldstool
occupy: 7 preside
portable: 5 sedan
chairman: 4 head 5 emcee 8 director 9 moderator 10 supervisor
chaise: gig 4 shay 7 curicle 8 carriage
chaitya: 6 shrine 8 monument
chalcedony: 4 onyx, opal, sard 5 agate 6 jasper, quartz 7 opaline 9 carnelian 11 chrysoprase
Chaldea: *astronomical cycle:* 5 saros
city: Ur
measure: 4 cane, foot 5 makuk, qasab 6 artaba, gariba, ghalva 7 mansion
chalet: hut 5 cabin, house 7 cottage 8 lavatory
chalice: ama, cup 4 bowl 5 calix, grail 6 goblet 7 calices(pl.)
cover: 4 pall 8 animetta
chalk: 4 cauk, pale, scar, talc, tick 5 creta, score 6 blanch, bleach, crayon,

credit, rubble, whiten **7** account **9** limestone, reckoning
challenge: **4** call, dare, defy, gage **5**
blame, brave, claim, query, stump **6** accuse, appeal, cartel, charge, dacker,
daiker, demand, forbid, impugn, invite **7**
arraign, censure, impeach, provoke, reprove, summons **8** question, reproach **9**
exception, objection **10** controvert **11**
impeachment
judge: **6** recuse
challenger: **7** duelist **8** pugilist
chamber: oda **4** cell, flat, hall, kiva, room
5 atria(pl.), bower, solar, soler **6** atrium,
camara, camera, hollow, sollar **7** bedroom, caisson, cubicle, lochlus **9** apartment, camarilla, vestibule **11** compartment
annealing: **4** leer
bombproof: **8** casemate
council: **10** consistory
drying: **4** kiln, oven
judge's: **6** camera
private: **5** adyta(pl.) **6** adytum **7** sanctum
8 conclave
underwater construction: **7** caisson
chamberlain: **6** factor **7** officer, servant,
steward **9** attendant, chamberer, treasurer **10** camerlengo **14** superintendent
papal: **10** camerlengo, camerlingo
chameleon: **5** anole, anoli **6** lizard
cameleonic: **6** fickle **10** changeable, inconstant
chamfer: **5** bevel, flute **6** furrow, groove **7**
channel **11** countersink
chamois: **4** gems, skin **5** cloth, gemse **6**
chammy, shammy, shamoy **7** leather **8**
antelope
male: **7** gemsbok
champ: **4** bite, chaw, firm, hard, mash **5**
field, gnash **7** trample **11** battlefield
champagne: ay **4** wine
center: **6** Troyes
champerty: **7** contest, rivalry **10** conspiracy
champion: ace, aid **4** abet, back, defy,
hero **6** assert, attend, defend, squire, victor **7** espouse, fighter, protect **8** advocate,
defender **9** challenge, combatant, first-
rate **10** unexcelled
championship: **5** title **7** defense **8** advocacy **9** supremacy **10** leadership
champleve: **6** enamel, inlaid
chance: die, hap, lot **4** case, dint, fate, luck,
odds, risk, tide **5** ettle, stake **6** betide,
casual, gamble, happen, hazard, mishap,
random **7** aimless, fortune, stumble, venture **8** accident, casualty, fortuity **9** adventure, haphazard, happening, mischance **10** contingent **11** contingency,
opportunity, probability
by: **5** haply
even: **6** tossup
favorable: **4** odds

chancel: *part:* **4** bema **5** altar
seat: **6** sedile **7** sedilia(pl.)
chancery petitioner: **7** relator
chandelier: **6** pharos **7** fixture **11** candelabrum
chandelle: lob **4** turn, zoom **5** climb **6**
candle **7** support
chandler: **6** dealer **10** chandelier **11**
candlestick
chang: **4** beer **5** noise **6** uproar
change: mew **4** move, turn, vary, veer **5**
adapt, alter, amend, break, coins, shift **6**
modify, mutate, remove, revamp, revise,
switch **7** commute, convert, deviate **8** re-
vision, transfer **9** diversity, permutate,
rearrange, transform, transmute, transpose, variation **10** alteration, correction,
difference, transition **11** vicissitude **13**
metamorphosis **15** diversification
character of: **8** denature
color: dye **5** blush **6** redden
course: **4** tack, turn, veer **5** sheer
music: **4** muta
changeable: **5** eemis, giddy, immis **6**
fickle, fitful, mobile **7** bruckle, erratic,
mutable, protean, variant **8** amenable,
catching, unstable, volatile **9** alterable,
irregular, mercurial, uncertain, unsettled
10 capricious, inconstant, irresolute **11**
chameleonic
in form: **9** metabolic
changeling: oaf **4** dolt, fool **5** child, dunce,
idiot **7** waverer **8** imbecile, renegade,
turncoat **9** simpleton **10** substitute
changing: *color:* **11** allochroous
pattern and color: **13** kaleidoscopic
channel: gat, ree, rut **4** cano, cava, dike,
duct, dyke, gool, gote, gout, pipe, vein,
wadi, wady **5** canal, chase, ditch, drain,
drill, flume, flute, glyph, media(pl.), regal, rigol, river, sinus, stria **6** arroyo, artery, furrow, groove, gutter, medium, rabbet, rivose, sluice, strait, stream,
striae(pl.), trough **7** conduct, conduit,
passage, rivulet, silanga, tideway **8** aqueduct, guideway
artificial: gat **4** leat **5** canal, drain, flume **6**
sluice **7** drainer
formed by cutting: **5** scarf
longitudinal: **6** rabbet
marker: **4** buoy
narrow: **6** furrow, strait
near port: **5** deeps
river: bed **6** alveni(pl.) **7** alvenus
ship: gat
vertical: **5** glyph
vital: **6** artery
water: gat **4** gote, gurt, leat, pipe, race **5**
canal, drain, flume **6** sluice **7** conduit **8**
aqueduct, millrace, tailrace
Channel Island: **4** Sark **8** Guernsey
measure: **4** cade **5** cabot
seaweed: **5** vraic
channelbill: **8** rainfowl

chant: 4 cant, sing, song 5 carol, psalm 6 anthem, cantus, intone, warble 7 introit, worship 10 cantillate

chantage: 9 extortion 12 blackmailing

chanter: 6 cantor, singer 7 bagpipe 8 songster 9 chorister

chanteuse: 6 singer 10 cantatrice

chantey, chanty: 4 song

chanticleer: 4 cock 7 rooster

chanty, chantey: 4 song

chaos: pie 4 gulf, mess, void 5 abyss, babel, chasm 6 jumble 7 anarchy, mixture 8 disorder, shambles 9 confusion
primordial: 4 Apsu
utter: 6 tophet 7 topheth

Chaos: *daugher:* Nox, Nyx
son: 7 Erebus

chaotic: 5 snafu 7 muddled 8 confused, formless

chap: boy, buy, man, rap 4 bean, beat, blow, chip, chop, cove, duck, kibe, mash 5 billy, bloke, bully, buyer, chink, cleft, crack, knock, lover, split, trade, youth 6 barter, breach, bugger, callan, choose, fellow, shaver, strike, stroke 7 callant, chapman, chappie, fissure, husband, roughen 8 blighter, customer, division
odd: 6 galoot
old: 6 geezer
young: 6 gaffer

chaparral: 9 buckthorn

chapel: 4 cage, cape, cope, cowl, hood 5 cloak 6 bethel, church, shrine 7 chantry, service 8 bethesda 9 reliquary, sanctuary
private: 7 oratory

chaperon: 4 hood 6 attend, duenna(Sp.), escort, matron 7 protect 8 guardian, trapping 10 escutcheon 11 gouvernante(F.)

chaplain: 5 padre 9 clergyman

chaplet: 4 bead, orle 5 crown 6 anadem, anchor, circle, fillet, rosary, trophy, wreath 7 coronal, coronet, garland 8 moulding, necklace, ornament

chapman: 4 chap 5 buyer 6 dealer, hawker, trader 7 peddler 8 customer, merchant

chaps: 4 boys, jaws, lads 5 flews 8 breeches, overalls

chapter: 4 body, cell, post 5 caput, lodge 6 branch 7 correct, meeting, section 8 assembly 9 reprimand 10 contingent
member: 9 capitular

char: 4 burn, cart, sear 5 broil, chark, chore, singe, trout 6 scorch 7 blacken, chariot 8 sandbank 9 carbonize

charact: 6 emblem

character: 4 bent, card, kind, mark, mold, note, part, rune, sign, sort, tone 5 brand, fiber, stamp, tenor, token, trait, write 6 caract, emblem, figure, letter, mettle, nature, repute, stripe, symbol 7 edition, essence, engrave, impress, quality 8 in-

scribe 9 agreement, ampersand 10 reputation 11 disposition
assumed: 4 role
bad: 5 drole(F.)
chief: 4 hero, lead, star 7 heroine
group: 5 ethos
vein: 6 streak
word-representing: 8 logogram 9 logograph

characteristic: 4 cast, mark, mien 5 trait 6 nature 7 feature, impress, quality, typical 8 property, symbolic 9 attribute, lineament 11 distinctive, pathognomic, peculiarity
individual: 9 idiopathy

characterize: 4 mark 6 define, depict 7 engrave, entitle, imprint, portray 8 describe, indicate, inscribe 9 delineate, designate, represent 11 distinguish

charade: 6 enigma, puzzle, riddle 7 picture, tableau

charco: 4 pool 6 puddle, spring

charcoal: 5 carbo, chark 6 carbon, fusain, pencil 7 blacken, drawing
animal: 9 boneblack
reduce to: 4 char

chard: 4 beet 7 thistle 9 artichoke

chare, char: job 4 lane, task, turn 5 alley, chore 6 finish, street 7 perform

charge: fee 4 bill, cark, cost, duty, fill, lien, load, onus, rate, rush, toll, ward 5 debit, onset, order, price, refer 6 accuse, adjure, allege, assess, attack, burden, career, credit, defame, demand, enjoin, impute, indict, tariff, weight 7 arraign, ascribe, assault, average, censure, command, concern, custody, expense, impeach, keeping, mandate, mission 8 chastise, overload 9 challenge, oversight 10 commission, impetition, impregnate, injunction, management 11 arraignment, encumbrance, incriminate, instruction 14 responsibility
customary: 4 dues
grazing: 5 agist
with gas: 6 aerate

chargeable: 6 costly, liable 7 weighty 9 expensive, important, momentous 10 burdensome 11 responsible, troublesome

charged: 5 tense 9 emotional 10 purposeful
with electricity: 4 live

chargeman: 7 blaster, foreman 10 batteryman

charger: 4 dish 5 horse, mount, plate, steed 6 vessel 7 accuser, courser, platter

charges: *boat carrying:* 7 boatage
legal: 4 dues, fees 5 costs 9 retainers
repairs to barrister's quarters: 9 detriment

charily: 8 frugally, gingerly 9 carefully 10 cautiously

chariness: 7 caution 9 frugality, integrity 11 heedfulness, sparingness

chariot: car 4 cart, char, wain 5 buggy,

essed, wagon **6** charet, esseda, essede **7** vehicle **8** carriage, charette

for carrying image of god: **4** rath **5** ratha

Greek: **8** quadriga

Roman: **5** essed **6** esseda, essede

two-horse: **4** biga

chariotee: **8** carriage

charioteer: **5** pilot **6** auriga, driver **7** wagoner **9** charioter

charitable: **4** kind **6** benign, humane **7** lenient, liberal **8** generous **9** favorable, forgiving, indulgent **10** beneficent, benevolent **12** eleemosynary **13** compassionate, philanthropic

charity: **4** alms, dole, gift, love, pity, ruth **5** mercy **6** bounty **7** handout, largess **8** lenience **9** affection **10** almsgiving, generosity, liberality, tenderness **12** philanthropy

dispenser: **7** almoner

charivari: **5** babel **8** serenade, shivaree **10** callithump **11** celebration

chark: cup **4** burn, char, coal, coke **5** glass **6** cinder, noggin **8** charcoal

charlatan: **5** cheat, faker, fraud, quack **7** cabotin, empiric **8** imposter, magician **9** pretender **10** medicaster, mountebank

Charlemagne: *brother:* **8** Carloman

court hero: **6** Roland

father: **5** Pepin

knight: **4** Gano **7** Ganelon, Paladin

nephew: **7** Orlando

peer: **6** Oliver **7** Paladin

pert. to: **8** Caroline

charlock: **4** weed **5** kraut **7** mustard

charlotte: **7** custard, dessert

Charlotte Corday's victim: **5** Marat

charm: obi **4** calm, jynx, mojo, play, song **5** allay, freet, freit, grace, obeah, magic, saffi, safie, spell, weird **6** allure, amulet, beauty, caract, enamor, entice, fetich, fetish, glamor, grigri, melody, please, scarab, saphie, soothe, subdue, summon **7** assuage, attract, beguile, bewitch, cantrip, conjure, control, delight, enamour, enchant, enthral, flatter, glamour, periapt, singing, sorcery **8** breloque, enthrall, entrance, greegree, practice, talisman **9** agreeable, captivate, fascinate, seduction **10** attraction, demonifuge **11** incantation

protective: **6** amulet

charmer: **5** siren **8** exorcist, magician, sorcerer **9** sorceress **11** spellbinder

charming: **7** amiable, eyesome, winning, winsome **8** adorable, delicate **9** agreeable, beautiful, glamorous **10** attractive, glamourous

charnel: **7** ghastly **8** cemetery **10** sepulchral

house: **7** ossuary **8** mortuary

charqui: **4** beef, meat **5** jerky

chart: map **4** card, plat, plan, plot **5** carte, graph **6** record, scheme **7** diagram, explore, outline, project **8** document, platform **10** cartograph

chartaceous: **6** papery

charter: let **4** deed, hire, rent **5** carte, chart, grant, lease **6** charta, permit **9** privilege **10** commission, conveyance

chary: shy **4** dear, wary **5** chere, scant **6** frugal, prized, skimpy **7** careful, sparing **8** cautious, hesitant, precious, reserved, vigilant **9** diffident, reluctant, treasured **10** economical, fastidious, scrupulous **11** circumspect

Charybdis rock: **6** Scylla

chase: **4** hunt, shag, sick **5** annoy, catch, chevy, chivy, harry, score **6** chivvy, emboss, follow, frieze, furrow, gallop, groove, harass, hollow, indent, pursue, quarry, scorse, trench **7** channel, engrave, pursuit **8** ornament

away: **4** rout **5** drive

goddess: **5** Diana

chaser: ram **5** drink **8** airplane, engraver

chasm: gap, pit **4** gulf, rift **5** abyss, blank, canon, chaos, cleft, gorge **6** breach, canyon, hiatus **7** fissure **8** aperture, crevasse, interval

chasse: **4** step **5** glide **6** liquor, shrine **7** dismiss **9** reliquary

chasseur: **6** hunter **7** footman **8** huntsman **9** attendant

chassis: **5** frame

chaste: **4** pure **5** clean **6** decent, honest, modest, proper, severe, vestal **7** refined **8** celibate, innocent, virtuous **9** continent, undefiled **10** immaculate

chasten: **4** rate **5** abase, smite, smote, sober **6** humble, punish, refine, subdue, temper **7** afflict, censure, correct **8** chastise, moderate, restrain **9** castigate, reprimand **10** discipline

chastise: **4** beat, flog, lash, slap, trim, whip **5** amend, blame, scold, spank, strap, taunt **6** accuse, anoint, berate, charge, punish, purify, rebuke, refine, swinge, temper, thrash **7** chasten, correct, reprove, scourge, suspect **9** castigate

chastity: **6** purity, virtue **7** modesty **8** goodness

chasuble: **6** deacon **8** vestment

chat: mag **4** bird, chin, cone, coze, gist, talk, tove, twig **5** ament, cause, dally, point, prate, speak, spike **6** babble, branch, catkin, confab, gabble, gibber, gossip, jabber, potato, samara **7** chatter, prattle **8** causerie, converse, spikelet, strobile **9** dalliance **11** confabulate **12** conversation

chateau: **5** house **6** castle **7** mansion **8** fortress

chatelaine: pin **4** etui, hook **5** chain, clasp, etwee, purse **6** brooch **8** mistress

chaton: **5** basil, bezel, bezil **7** setting

chatta: 8 umbrella

chattels: 4 gear 5 goods, money, wares 6 slaves 7 capital 8 bondsmen, property 9 livestock, principal

distraint: 4 naam

tenant's: 6 farleu, farley

to recover: 7 detinue

chatter: gab, jaw, mag, yap 4 blab, carp, chat, hack, rick, talk, tear, yirr 5 cabal, clack, garre, haver, prate, shake 6 babble, gabble, gibber, gossip, jabber, palter, rattle, shiver, tattle, yammer, yatter 7 blabber, brabble, chackle, chaffer, chipper, chitter, clitter, nashgob, prabble, prattle, shatter 8 verbiage 11 goosecackle

conjurer's: 10 hanky-panky

chatterbox: jay, mag 4 piet 5 clack 6 gossip, magpie 10 chatterbag, chattermag 13 chatterbasket

chattering: 8 babbling 9 prattling, talkative 10 loquacious

Chaucer: *inn:* 6 Tabard

Knight's Tale character: 7 Palamon

pilgrim: 5 reeve

chauffeur: 5 drive 6 driver 8 operator

chaussee: 4 road 6 street 7 highway 8 causeway

chaussure: 4 boot, shoe 7 slipper 8 footgear

chauve-souris: bat

chauvinism: 8 jingoism 10 patriotism

chavel: 4 gnaw 6 mumble, nibble

chaw: jaw, vex 4 chew, envy, mull 5 champ, grind 6 ponder 7 portion 8 ruminate 9 chawbacon, masticate

chawbacon: 4 chaw 5 yokel 6 rustic 7 bumpkin

chawn: gap 4 gape 5 cleft 6 cleave

cheap: low 4 base, poor, vile 5 close, gaudy, kitch, price, tight, tinny, value 6 abject, common, plenty, shoddy, sordid, stingy, tawdry, trashy 7 bargain, dealing 8 inferior, purchase 9 innkeeper 10 despicable 11 depreciated, inexpensive 12 contemptible

cheap jack: 6 hawker, pedlar, pedler 7 peddler 8 huckster 9 Cheap-John

cheat: do: bam, bob, cog, con, fob, gip, gum, gyp, nip 4 bilk, bite, clip, dupe, fake, flam, geck, gull, hoax, jilt, jouk, liar, mump, rook, sell, sham, sile, skin 5 blink, booty, bunco, bunko, cozen, cully, dodge, faker, fling, foist, fraud, gleek, gouge, guile, knave, mulct, rogue, scamp, spoil, trick, welsh 6 baffle, blanch, bubble, bucket, chiaus, chisel, chouse, daddle, delude, deride, doodle, duffer, fiddle, fleece, grease, humbug, illude, jockey, outwit, raddle, renege, shaver 7 abusion, beguile, deceive, defraud, escheat, faitour, finesse, foister, gudgeon, juggler, mislead, plunder, quibble, sharper, skelder, swindle 8 artifice, delusion,

dry-shave, hoodwink, impostor 9 bamboozle, fainaigue, hypocrite, imposture, scoundrel, stratagem, victimize 10 mountebank 15 prestidigitator

cheater: 4 bite, gull 5 knave 6 bilker, topper 7 sharper 9 trickster

check: bit, dam, nab, nip, tab 4 balk, curb, damp, rein, snub, stay, stem, stop, stub, test, twit, were 5 abort, allay, block, brake, catch, chide, chink, choke, crack, daunt, delay, deter, draft, limit, quell, repel, stall, still, stunt, tally, taunt, token 6 arrest, attack, baffle, bridle, defeat, detain, detent, gravel, hinder, impede, oppose, outwit, quench, rabbet, rebate, rebuff, rebuke, scotch, stifle, ticket, verify 7 backset, command, control, inhibit, monitor, refrain, repress, reproof, reprove, repulse, setback 8 bulkhead, encumber, obstruct, restrain, withhold 9 constrain, frustrate, interrupt, overpower, reprimand, restraint, supervise 10 difficulty 11 certificate, counterfoil, examination

checker: 5 freak, freck 6 damper

checkerboard: 7 dambrod 8 damboard

marked like: 10 tessellate

checkered: 4 pied, vair 5 diced, plaid 6 motley 10 changeable, variegated 11 diversified

checkers: 4 game 6 damrod, drafts 8 draughts

move: 4 dyke, fife, huff 5 cross 7 bristol

opening: 6 souter

checkerwork: 7 tessera 8 tesserae(pl.)

inlay: 6 mosaic

checkmate: 4 gain, lick, stop, undo 6 baffle, corner, defeat, outwit, stymie, thwart 9 frustrate

cheechako, chee-chaco: 10 tenderfoot

cheek: 4 chap, gall, gena, jole, jowl, leer, sass 5 bucca, chyak, genae(pl.), nerve, sauce 6 chyack, haffet, haffit 8 audacity, temerity 9 impudence

bone: 5 malar 6 zygoma

muscle: 10 buccinator

pert. to: 5 genal, malar 6 buccal

cheep: pip, yap, yip 4 hint(Sc.), peep, pule 5 chirp, creak(Sc.), tweet 6 squeak, tattle

cheer: ole(Sp.), rah 4 fare, food, root, viva, yell 5 bravo, elate, feast, heart, huzza, mirth, shout, whoop 6 cantle, gaiety, hurrah, huzzah, solace, viands 7 acclaim, animate, applaud, cherish, comfort, console, enliven, gladden, hearten, jollity, refresh, rejoice 8 applause, brighten, inspirit, pheasant, vivacity 9 animation, encourage, merriment 10 exhilarate, invigorate 11 acclamation hospitality 13 entertainment, hospitability

burst: 5 salvo

cheerful: gay 4 cant, glad, gleg(Sc.), rosy 5 cadgy, canty, chirk, douce, happy, jolly, merry, peart, ready, sunny 6 blithe, bright, cheery, chirpy, crouse, genial, hearty, hilary, jocund, lively **7** buoyant, chipper **8** cheering, gladsome, homelike, sanguine **9** contented, lightsome, sprightly **10** enlivening **11** comfortable **12** lighthearted

cheerless: sad **4** cold, drab, glum, gray **5** bleak, drear **6** dismal, dreary, gloomy **7** forlorn, joyless **8** dejected **10** dispirited, melancholy **11** comfortless **12** disconsolate

cheese: **4** Brie, Edam, Jack **5** cream, Gouda, mysost, Swiss, Ziega **6** Barrie, Dunlop, Glarus, Zieger **7** Cheddar, cottage, Gruyere, Stilton **8** American, Parmesan **9** Camembert, Gammelost, Limburger, Roquefort **10** Gorgonzola, Neufchatel **11** Liederkranz
brown: **6** mysost
curdy: **4** trip
dish: **4** cake **6** fondue, omelet **7** rarebit, souffle
large: **7** kebbock, kebbuck
milk whey: **5** ziega **6** zieger
Normandy: **7** angelot
pert. to: **6** caseic **7** caseous
poached: **10** gnocchetti
white: **11** Neufchatel
cheesecake: **7** dessert **10** photograph
cheesy: **4** fine **5** cheap, smart **6** shabby, sleazy **7** caseous **9** excellent, worthless
cheetah: cat **5** youse, youze **7** guepard **8** gueparde
chef: **4** cook **9** cuisinier **10** cuisiniere
chela: **5** slave **7** servant **8** disciple
chelicera: **8** mandible **9** appendage
chelonian: **6** turtle **8** tortoise
chemical: **4** acid, salt **7** alkalai **10** alchemical **13** iatrochemical
agent: **8** catalyst
compound: **4** imin **5** amide, azine, ceria, ester, imine, purin **6** boride **7** inosite, leucine, metamer
element: see **element:** *chemical*
measure: **4** dram, gram **5** liter, titer
salt: sal
suffix: ac, ol; ane, ein, ene, ile, ine, ion, ite, ole, ose **4** idin, olic **5** ylene
chemise: **5** shift, shirt, smock **6** camisa **8** lingerie
chemisette: **4** sham **6** guimpe
chemist: **7** analyst **8** druggist **9** alchemist **10** apothecary
vessel: **4** vial **5** ampul, cupel, phial **6** aludel, ampule, beaker, retort **7** ampoule
workroom: lab **10** laboratory
chequeen: **6** basket, sequin, zequin **8** zecchino
cheri, cherie: **4** dear **7** beloved, darling **9** cherished **10** sweetheart
cherish: aid, hug, pet **4** dote, hope, like, love, save **5** adore, cheer, cling, enjoy, nurse, prize, value **6** caress, esteem, faddle, fondle, foster, harbor, nestle, pamper,

pettle, revere **7** comfort, embosom, embrace, indulge, nourish, nurture, protect, support, sustain **8** enshrine, inspirit, preserve, treasure **9** cultivate, encourage, entertain

cherry: **4** bing, duke, gean **5** morel **7** capulin, chapman, lambert, morello, oxheart **8** amarelle, napoleon **9** bigarreau
acid: **7** cerasin
color: red **6** cerise
sour: **8** amarelle
sweet: **4** bing **7** lambert, oxheart
wild: **4** gean **7** marasca, mazzard
cherry finch: **8** hawfinch
cherry holly: **5** islay
cherry laurel: **7** cerasus
cherry orange: **7** kumquat
cherub: **5** angel **6** seraph, spirit **8** seraphim(pl.)
chervil: bun **4** herb
chess: *draw game:* **9** stalemate
finish: **4** draw, mate **7** endgame **9** checkmate, stalemate
Japanese: **5** shogi
move: **5** debut **6** castle, fidate, gambit **10** fianchetto
opening: **5** debut **6** gambit **10** fianchetto
pert. to: **8** scacchic
piece: man **4** king, pawn, rook **5** horse, queen **6** bishop, castle, knight
chest: ark, box, kit **4** arca, bust, cist, cyst, fund, safe **5** ambry, bahut, front, hoard, hutch, trunk **6** basket, breast, bunker(Sc.), casket, coffer, coffin, hamper, locker, shrine, stripe, thorax **7** caisson, capcase, cassone(It.), commode, deposit, enclose **8** cupboard, treasury **9** container, strongbox **10** contention, receptacle, repository **11** controversy, gardeviance
alms: **6** almoin **7** almoign
meal: **6** girnal, girnel
pert. to: **8** thoracic
sacred: ark **4** arca, cist
stone: **4** cist, kist
supply: **6** wangan, wangun **7** wanigan **8** wannigan
chesterfield: **4** coat, sofa **5** divan **8** overcoat **9** davenport
chestnut: **4** joke, ling, rata, tree **5** brown, horse **6** marron(F.), sativa **7** crenata, dentata
and gray: **4** roan
dwarf: **9** chincapin **10** chinquapin
genus of: **8** castanea
water: **4** ling **5** trapa
chevalier: **5** noble **6** knight **7** gallant **8** cavalier, horseman **10** greenshank
cheverel, cheveril: **6** pliant **7** elastic, kidskin **8** flexible
chevet: **4** apse **11** termination
chevin: **4** chub
chevisance: **5** booty, issue, spoil **6** remedy, supply **8** chivalry, resource **9** ex-

pedient, substance **10** enterprise, provisions **11** achievement, transaction

chevron: **4** beam, mark **5** glove **6** rafter, stripe **7** molding **10** gravystain

chevrotain: **4** napu **7** deerlet, kanchil, tragule

chevy: See **chivy**.

chew: cud **4** bite, cham, chaw, gnaw, quid **5** chamm, grind, munch, rumen **6** mumble **8** meditate, ruminate **9** denticate, manducate, masticate

chewink: **4** bird **5** finch, joree **6** towhee

chiastolite: **5** macle

chiaus: **5** cheat **8** sergeant, swindler **9** messenger

Chibcha: **4** zipa **5** zaque **6** Indian, zacqua

chic: **4** pert, posh, trig, trim **5** natty, nifty, smart **6** dapper, modish **7** elegant, stylish

chicadee: **8** titmouse

Chicago district: **4** Loop

chicanery: **4** ruse, wile **5** feint, trick **8** artifice, intrigue, trickery **9** deception, duplicity, sophistry, stratagem

chick: **4** girl, tick **5** child, natty **6** screen, sequin, sprout **7** chicken

chick-pea: **4** gram, herb **5** chich, cicer **8** garbanzo, garvance, garvanzo **9** garavance

chicken: hen **4** cock, fowl **5** biddy, capon, chick, child, chuck, fryer, layer, manoc, poult **6** chicky, pullet **7** broiler, rooster **8** cockerel **11** chickabiddy

breed: **7** Leghorn **9** Wyandotte **11** Rhode Island

raising device: **7** brooder

chickenhearted: **5** timid **8** cowardly

chickweed genus: **6** alsine

chicle: gum **5** latex

chicory: **4** bunk, root **5** plant **6** endive **7** succory, witloof

family: **12** cichoriaceae

chide: **4** rail, rate **5** blame, check, flite, flyte, scold **6** berate, rebuff, rebuke, threap, threep, threpe **7** censure, reprove, upbraid, wrangle **8** admonish, reproach **9** objurgate, reprehend, reprimand

chief: bo; aga, big, boh, cap, cob, dux, mir **4** agha, arch, boss, duce, duke, head, high, khan, main, rais, raja, reis, tyee **5** alder, elder, first, great, major, prime, rajah, ruler, sachem, staple, thane, titan, vital **6** adalid, cabeza, leader, master, rector **7** capital, captain, central, eminent, foreman, overman, palmary, prelate, premier, supreme **8** dominant, especial, foremost, intimate, sagamore **9** chieftain, commander, paramount, principal, prominent **11** predominant

chiffonier: **6** bureau **7** cabinet, commode

chigger: **4** mite **6** chigoe, insect, jigger, red-bug

chignon: **4** knot **5** chain, twist **6** collar

chigoe: **4** flea **7** chigger

chilblain: **4** kibe, mule(F.) **5** blain **6** pernio

child: (see also **children**): ben(Heb.), boy, bud, imp, kid, son, tad, tot **4** baba, babe, baby, bata, brat, chit, girl, page, tike, tyke **5** bairn(Sc.), chick, chiel(Sc.), gamin, issue **6** cherub, enfant, filius(L.), infant, moppet, urchin **7** bambino(It.), progeny **8** bantling, chiseler(Ir.), daughter **9** firstling, offspring, youngster **10** descendant **11** chickabiddy

advancement: **9** precocity

chubby: **8** rolypoly **10** butterball

comb. form: ped **4** paed, pedo **5** paedo

dainty: elf **5** fairy

homeless: **4** waif

illegitimate: **6** by-blow **7** bastard

killer: **11** infanticide

parentless: **6** orphan

patron saint: **8** Nicholas

puckish: imp

roguish: **6** urchin

spoiled: **4** brat **5** mardy **7** cockney

street: **5** gamin

unmannerly: **7** smatche(Sc.)

childbirth: **5** labor **7** lying-in, travail **11** confinement, parturition

goddess: **4** Apet, Auge, Upis **5** Damia **6** Lucina **7** Auxesia

childish: **4** weak **5** naive, petty, silly **6** puling, simple, weanly(Sc.), young **7** asinine, babyish, foolish, kiddish, puerile, unmanly **8** bairnish, brattish, immature, juvenile **9** credulous, childlike, infantile, kittenish

childlike: **4** meek **6** docile, filial **7** babyish, dutiful **8** childish, innocent, trusting **9** confiding, frivolous **10** submissive

children: **7** progeny **9** offspring

dislike of: **9** misopedia **10** misopaedia

medical science: **10** pediatrics **11** paediatrics

room: **7** nursery

study: **8** pedology **9** paedology

tender of: **4** amah **6** sitter **9** nursemaid

Chile: *arborvitae:* **6** alerce, alerse

city: **6** Arauco, Cobija, Serena **7** Caldera, Copiapo **8** Coquimbo, Santiago(c.), Valdivia **10** Concepcion, Valparaiso

coastal wind: **5** sures

coin: **4** peso **5** libra **6** condor, escudo

desert: **7** Atacama

Indian: Ona

measure: **4** vara **5** legua, linea **6** cuadra, fanega

mountain: **5** Maipu, Pular

mountain range: **5** Andes

national police: **11** carabineros

province: **5** Arica, Aysen, Maule, Nuble, Talca **6** Bio-Bio, Cautin, Chiloe, Curico **7** Atacama **8** Coquimbo, Santiago, Tarapaca, Valdivia **9** Aconcagua Colchagua **10** Concepcion, Valparaiso **11** Antofagasta

river: Loa **5** Itata, Maipu, Maule **6** Bio-Bio, Chuapa, Lontue **7** Illapel **8** Valdivia

rodent: **10** chinchilla
seaport: **4** Lota, Tome **5** Arica **8** Coquimba
shrub: **5** lithi **6** pepino
tree: **4** brea, pelu, ulmo **5** coleu, rauli, roble **6** alerce, alerse, coigue, muermo
volcano: **6** Antuco, Lascar, Llaima **7** Calbuco
weight: **5** grano, libra **7** quintal
workman: **4** roto
chill: ice, raw **4** ague, cold, cool, dazy(Sc.) **5** algor, gelid, rigor, shake **6** frappe, freeze, frigid, frosty, shiver **7** depress, frisson, malaria **8** coldness **11** refrigerate
chilling: **4** eery **5** eerie
chilly: raw **4** cold, cool, lash **5** algid, bleak, hunch **6** arctic, frosty **9** cauldrife
chilver: **4** lamb
chimaera: **7** ratfish
chime: din, rim **4** bell, edge, peal, ring, suit, ting **5** agree, prate **6** accord, cymbal, jingle, melody **7** concord, harmony **8** singsong
chimera: **5** fancy **6** mirage **8** illusion
chimerical: **4** vain, wild **7** utopian **8** delusive, fanciful, romantic **9** fantastic, imaginary, unfounded, visionary
chimes: **5** bells **8** carillon
chimney: **4** flue, pipe, tube, vent **5** gully, stack, tewel **6** funnel **7** fissure, opening, orifice **10** smokestack
cover: **4** cowl **7** turncap
deposit: **4** soot
piece: **5** parel **6** mantel
post: **5** speer
chimney corner: **8** fireside **9** inglenook
chimpanzee: ape **5** pigmy **10** anthropoid, troglodyte
chin: jaw **4** chat **5** menta(pl.) **6** mentum
comb. form: **5** genio
double: **4** fold **7** buccula
china: **4** ware **6** dishes **7** ceramic, pottery **8** Cinchona, crockery **9** porcelain **11** earthenware
fine: **5** Spode **6** Sevres **7** Limoges **8** Wedgwood
China: *aborigine:* Yao **4** Mans, Miao **6** Mantzu, Yao-min **7** Miaotse, Miaotze
alloy: **7** paktong **8** packtong
bamboo: **7** whangee
banker: **6** shroff
bat: ia
bean: soy **6** cowpea
boat: **4** bark, junk **6** sampan
brigand: **9** hunghutze, hunghutzu
Buddha: Fo; Foh
Buddhist paradise: **7** Chingtu
cabbage: **7** pakchoi
canton: Fu **5** Hsein
city: Su; Nom, Ude **4** Amoy, Tsin, Wuhu **5** Jehol, Macao, Macau, Pekin **6** Canton, Fachan, Fuchau, Hankau, Hankow, Huchau, Kalgan, Nankin, Ningpo, Suchau, Swatow, Tsinan, Yunnan **7** Chengte,

Chengtu, Chingtu, Fatshan, Foochow, Hanyang, Kaifeng, Lanchau, Nanking, Paoting, Taiyuen, Tunkuan, Wenchau, Wuchang, Yenping **8** Changsha, Chaochau, Fancheng, Hangchau, Hangchow, Kiaochau, Nanchang, Shanghai, Shaohing, Siangtan, Tengchau, Tientsin, Tungchau, Tunghwan, Yanphing **9** Changchau, Chinkiang, Chungking, Lienkiang **10** Chingkiang, Kingtechen
city (walled): **6** Peking
civet: **5** rasse
clay: **6** kaolin
cloth: sha **4** moxa, pulo, silk **6** nankin **7** nankeen
cloth-stiffening gelatin: **7** haitsai
coin: le, pu; fan, neu, sen **4** cash, cent, mace, tael, tiao, yuan **5** liang, tsien **6** dollar, ticket **9** candareen **10** Kupingtael **11** Haikwantael
comb. form: **4** Sino **5** Sinic
cosmic order: tao
customs collector: **5** hoppo
decigram: li
deer: **8** elaphure
department: Fu **5** Hsien
dialect: Wu **4** Amoy **5** Hakka **6** Canton, Ningpo, Swaton **7** Foochow, Wenchow
dish: **4** rice **7** fooyung **8** fooyoung
division: **4** chow, Miao **5** Hsien **6** canton
dog: **4** chow, peke
dragon: **6** chilin
drink: **6** samshu
duck eggs: **5** pidan
dulcimer: **7** yang-kin
dynasty: Fo; Han, Sui, Wei, Yin **4** Chin, Chou, Hsia, Ming, Sung, Tang, Tsin, Yuan **5** Shang
factory: **4** hong
festival: **9** Ching Ming
feudal state: Wei
figurine: **5** magot
flute: che **4** tche
fruit: **6** lichee, litchi
ginger: **9** galingale
god: **4** Ghos, Joss, Shen **5** Kuant
gong: **6** tamtam
gooseberry: **9** carambola
grass: bon **5** ramie
grass linen: **8** barandos
gruel: **6** congee, conjee
herb: tea **7** ginseng
herb genus: **7** nandina
houseboat: **5** tanka
idol: **4** joss **6** pagoda
isinglass: **4** agar **8** agar-agar
island: **4** Amoy **5** Macao **6** Hainan **7** Formosa
jute: **7** chingma
laborer: **6** coolie
lake: **6** Po-yang **8** Tung-ting
language: Wu **4** Shan **8** Mandarin **9** Cantonese
lemon: **6** citron

magistrate: **8** mandarin

magnolia: **5** yulan

mandarin's residence: **6** oyamen

measure: ho, hu, ko, li, mu, pu, ta, to, tu, yu; cho, fen, tou, yan, yin **4** chih, fang, kish, quei, shih, teke, tsan, tsun **5** chang, ching, sheng, shing **6** kung ho, kung li, kung mu, tching, tchung **7** kung fen **8** kung chih, kung shih **9** kung ching, kung sheng

measure of weight: **4** chin **5** catty

mile: li

money(see also *coin* above): mo, pu **4** mace, tael, tiao **5** sycee, tsien

mongol: hu

mountain: Omi **4** Omei, Sung **5** Tsins **6** Inshan, Pu-ling **7** Alashan, Kuen-lun, Ku-liang **8** Ta-yu-ling **9** Funiu-shan, Tsing-Ling

musical instrument: kin **5** cheng, sheng **7** samisen

Nationalist Party: **11** Kuomintang

noodles: **4** mein

official: **4** kuan, kwan **5** amban

oil: **4** tung

old name: **6** Cathay

orange: **7** kumquat **8** mandarin

ounce: **4** tael

ox: **4** zebu

pagoda: ta; taa **4** taag

parasol tree: **6** aogiri

peony: **6** moutan

philosopher: **4** Moti **5** Motzu **6** Laotse, Laotzu **9** Confucius

plant: tea, udo **4** rice, tche **5** ramie **7** ginseng

poet: **4** Li Po **7** Li Tai-Po

pony: **7** griffin

porcelain: **7** Celadon, Nankeen

porcelain glaze: **7** eelskin

porgy: tai

pottery: **4** Kuan, Ming, Ting **5** Chien **7** boccaro, Tzuchou

prefecture: fu

province: **4** Amur (Heilungkiang) **5** Chili, Honan, Hunan, Hupeh, Kansu **6** Fokien, Fukien, Shansi, Shensi, Yunnan **7** Kiangsi, Kiangsu, Kwangsi, Nganhui **8** Che-Kiang, Kweichau, Shantung, Szechuen **9** Kwangtung, Manchuria

provincial chief: **6** taoyin

puzzle: **7** tangram

race: **4** Lolo **5** Sinic, Soyot **6** Mongol

religion: **6** Shinto, Taoism **12** Confucianism

river: Si; Ili, Min, Pei, Wei **4** Tung, Yuan, Yuen **5** Hwang. Peiho, Pieho, Tarim **7** Hoangho, Sikiang **12** Yangtsekiang

roller: **7** sirgang

salutation: bow **6** kowtow

sauce: soy

sea port: **4** Amoy, Wuhu **5** Aigun, Shasi **6** Antung, Canton, Chefoo, Dairen, Harbin, Ichang, Ningpo, Pakhoi, Swaton, Szemao, Wuchow, Yochow **7** Foochow, Hangkow, Hunchun, Lungkow, Mengtsz, Nanking, Nanning, Samshui, Santuao, Soochow, Wenchow **8** Changsha, Hangchow, Kiukiang, Kongmoon, Lungchow, Shanghai, Tengyueh, Tientsin, Tsingtao, Wanhsien **9** Chinkiang, Chungking, Kiungchow, Newchwang **10** Chiankiang **12** Chingwangtao **14** Lungchingstsun

secret society: hui **4** tong

sedge: **4** mati

shrub: tea **5** ramie

silk: sha **5** pekin, tasar **6** pongee, tussah **7** taysaam. tsatlee **8** shantung

silkworm: **4** sina **6** tussah, tusser **10** ailanthus

silver: **5** sycee

skiff: **6** sampan

sleeping platform: **4** kang

society: **4** Hoey, Huey, Hung, Tong **5** Triad

squash: **6** cushaw

state(anc.): **4** Tsao **6** Cathay

stocks: **6** cangue

street: **6** hutung

student: **9** sinologue

sugar cane: **5** sorgo

taa: **6** pagoda

Tartar tribe: **4** Toda

tax: **5** likin

tea: cha **4** Tsia **5** bohea, congo, congu, Emesa, hyson

Temple: taa **6** pagoda

toy: **7** tangram

tree: **5** nikko **6** kinkan, litchi **7** gingkgo, hagbush, kumquat **9** bandoline, soapberry

tribe: Hu **4** Shan, Toba

vegetable: udo

vine: **5** kudzu **7** yangtao

walking stick: **7** whangee

warehouse: **4** hong

wax: **4** cere, pela

weight: li; fen, hao, kin, ssu, tan, yin **4** chee, chin, mace, shih, tael **5** catty, chien, liang, picul, tsien **6** kung li **7** haikwan, kung fen, kung ssu, kung tun **8** king chin **9** candareen **10** kuping tael **11** haikwan tael

wind instrument: **5** cheng, sheng

wormwood: **4** moxa

China Sea: *gulf:* **4** Siam

island: **6** Hainan **7** Formosa

Chinaberry: **9** soapberry

chinch: **6** bedbug

chine: **4** back, grow **5** chink, crack, crest, ridge, spine **6** cleave, ravine, sprout **7** crevice, fissure **8** backbone

Chinese (see also **China**): **5** Cerai, Seres, Seric, Sinic **6** Mongol, Sinico **7** Asiatic, Cataian, Sangley **9** Celestial

pert. to: **5** Seric **6** Serian **7** Sinitic **8** Senesian

chink: gap **4** bore, cash, coin, kink, rent, rift, rime **5** boore, check, chine, cleft,

crack, grike, money **6** cranny, sprain **7**
chinkle, crevice, fissure **8** aperture **9**
chaffinch **10** interstice

chinky: **5** rifty **6** rimose

Chinook: **4** wind **6** indian **8** Flathead
chief: **4** Tyee
people: **7** tilikum **8** tillicum
powwow: **4** wawa
salmon: **7** quinnat
woman: **10** klootchman

Chinook State: **10** Washington

chinquapin: oak **6** bonnet **8** chestnut,
wankapin **9** rattlenut

chintz: **5** cloth **7** pintado

Chios: **4** Scio(It.) **5** Khios(Gr.) **6** island
10 Sakis-Adasi

chip: bit, cut, hew, nig **4** chap, clip, knap,
nick, pare **5** crack, flake, piece, scrap,
spale, spalt, waste **6** chisel **7** counter **8**
fragment, splinter
of stone: **5** spall **6** gallet

chipmunk: **6** chippy, hackee, rodent **8**
squirrel

chipper: gay **4** spry **5** chirp, perky **6** babble, cockey, lively **7** chatter, chirrup,
twitter **8** cheerful

chirk: **5** chirp **6** lively **7** chirrup **8** cheerful

chirm: din, hum **5** chirp, croon, noise **6**
clamor

chirognomy: **9** palmistry **10** chiromancy

chirography: **6** script **7** writing **10** engrossing **11** handwriting

chiromancy: **9** palmistry **10** chirognomy

chiroptera: bat

chirp: pip **4** peek, peep, pipe **5** cheep,
chelp, chirk, chirl, chirm, chirt, tweet **7**
chipper, chirrup, chitter, rejoice, twitter,
wheetle

chirrup: **5** chirk, chirp, tweet **7** chipper

chirurgeon: **7** surgeon

chisel: cut, gad **4** chip, form, pare, tool **5**
burin, carve, cheat, gouge, hardy **6** chesil,
gravel, haggle **7** bargain, engrave, quarrel, shingle
ancient stone: **4** celt
engraving: **7** scooper, scorper
mine: gad **6** peeker
sculpture: **7** gradine **9** ebauchoir
stonemason's: **5** drove
toothed: **6** jagger

chiseled: **6** cisele(F.)

chiseler: **5** cheat, crook **6** gouger **9** bargainer

chiselled: **8** clearcut

chiselly: **6** gritty **8** gravelly **10** unpleasant
12 disagreeable

chit: dab, IOU **4** bill, girl, mind, note, rice **5**
child, draft, shoot **6** infant, letter, sprout
7 voucher **9** offspring **10** memorandum

chitarra: **6** guitar

chitchat: **4** talk **6** banter, gossip **12** conversation

chitter: **5** chirp **6** shiver **7** chatter, twitter

chivalrous: **5** brave, civil, noble **6** gentle,
polite **7** gallant, genteel, valiant, warlike
8 knightly **9** courteous, honorable

chive: cut **4** stab **5** clout, clove, knive, onion **6** bulbet

chivy, chivvy: run, vex **4** hunt, race **5**
chase, tease **6** badger, flight, harass, pursue **7** pursuit, scamper, torment **8** maneuver **9** confusion

chloral: **8** sedative

chloride: **4** salt **5** ester **7** calomel **8** compound

chlorine remover: **9** antichlor

chloroform: **4** kill **10** anesthetic
discoverer: **6** Liebig **7** Guthrie **9** Soubeiran
ingredient: **7** acetone
liquid used: **7** acetone

chobdar: **5** usher **9** attendant

chock: **5** block, chuck, cleat, wedge

chocolate: **5** candy, cocoa **8** beverage
family: **13** sterculiaceae
machine: **6** conche
powder: **5** cocoa **6** pinola
seed: **5** cacao
tree: **4** cola **5** cacao

choice: **4** a-one, best, fine, pick, rare,
wale, weal, will **5** cream, elite, prime,
voice **6** chosen, dainty, flower, option,
picked, select **8** delicate, election, eximious, uncommon, volition **9** excellent,
exquisite, recherche **10** preferable, preference **11** alternative

choicy: **6** choosy **10** fastidious

choir: **5** quire **6** chorus
leader: **6** cantor **9** precentor
member: **4** alto, bass **5** basso **7** songman,
soprano **9** chorister

choke: dam, gag **4** clog, plug, quar **5**
check, close, grane **6** hinder, impede,
stifle **7** querken, repress, silence, smother
8 obstruct, stoppage, strangle, suppress,
throttle **9** constrict, neckcloth, suffocate
10 extinguish

choke coil: **7** reactor

chokedamp: **9** blackdamp

choler: ire **4** bile, fury, rage **5** anger, wrath
6 spleen, temper **9** distemper **10** resentment **11** biliousness **12** irascibility

choleric: mad **5** angry, cross, fiery, huffy,
testy **6** fumish, touchy **7** bilious, enraged,
iracund, peevish, peppery, waspish **8**
wrathful **9** impatient, irascible **10**
passionate **11** belligerent, quarrelsome
render: **6** enrage

choose: opt **4** chap, cull, pick, pick, vote,
wale, weal **5** adopt, chuse, elect **6** prefer,
select **7** embrace, espouse

choosy, choosey: **7** finical **9** selective **10**
fastidious

chop: cut, hew, jaw, lop **4** chap, dice, gash,
hack, hash, jowl, rive, slit **5** carve, cleft,
crack, knock, mince, slash, stamp, trade,
truck, whang **6** barter, change, cleave,
incise **8** exchange **9** cotolette

eye of: **8** noisette
off: lop **4** drib **5** prune **8** amputate
chop-chop: 7 quickly **8** promptly
chophouse: 10 restaurant
chopping block: 7 hacklog
choppy: 5 rough
choragus: 6 leader **10** bandleader
chord: **4** cord, tone **5** nerve, triad **6** string, tendon **7** harmony **8** filament **9** harmonize
arc: **4** sine
harplike: **8** arpeggio
musical: **5** major, minor
ninth: **4** none
seventh: **6** tetrad
succession: **7** cadence
Chorda filum: 7 sealace
chore: job **4** char, duty, task **5** chare, stint **6** errand **9** housework
chorister: 6 singer **7** chanter **8** choirboy
chorten: 5 stupa **6** shrine **8** monument **9** reliquary
chortle: 5 laugh, snort **7** chuckle
chorus: **4** song **5** choir **6** accord, assent, unison **7** refrain, singers **8** response
girl: **6** dancer, singer **7** chorine
leader: **7** choragi(pl.) **8** choragus **9** conductor
chose: 5 thing
chosen: 5 elect, elite **7** elected **8** selected
Chosen: 5 Corea, Korea
chosen people: 10 Israelites
chouse: **4** dupe, gull, sham **5** chase, cheat, trick **6** harass **7** defraud **8** swindler **10** imposition
chowk: 5 bazar **6** bazaar, market
Christ: 4 Lord **7** Messiah, Saviour
christen: 4 name **7** baptize **10** denominate
Christian: 7 Gentile **8** Nazarene
early: **8** Galilean
Eastern: **6** Uniate
Egyptian: **4** Copt
persecuted: **6** martyr
Christian Science founder: 4 Eddy
Christiania: 4 Oslo
Christianity: *heretical sect:* **7** Docetae
love feast: **5** agape
martyr: **7** Stephen
symbol: **5** cross, orant **7** lehthus
theologian: **4** Kuhn **7** Aquinas, Niebuhr, Tillich **8** Bultmann **9** Augustine, de Chardin **10** Bonhoeffer **11** Kierkegaard
writer: **6** Origen
Christ's thorn: **4** nabk, nubk **5** shrub **6** jujube
Christmas: 4 noel, yule **7** holiday **8** festival, nativity, yuletide
carol: **4** noel **5** nowel
crib: **6** creche
decoration: **5** holly **6** tinsel **9** mistletoe
midnight mass supper: **9** reveillon
Christmas Carol: *author:* **7** Dickens
character: Tim **7** Scrooge
Christmas rose: 9 hellebore

chromium: 7 element, mineral
group element: **7** uranium **8** tungsten **10** molybdenum
symbol: Cr
chromo: 7 picture **10** lithograph
chromolithograph: 7 picture
chronic: 5 fixed **6** severe **7** intense **8** constant **9** confirmed, continual, lingering, prolonged **10** continuous, inveterate **12** disagreeable
chronicle: 5 annal, diary **6** record **7** account, archive, history, recital **8** register **9** narrative
chronicler: 6 writer **8** compiler, recorder **9** historian **11** memorialist
chronology: 6 record **11** arrangement **14** classification
according to: **5** datal
error in: **9** prolepsis **11** anachronism
chronometer: 5 clock **9** metronome, timepiece **10** timekeeper
chrysalis: 4 pupa **5** pupae(pl.)
chrysolite: 7 olivine, peridot
chrysoprase: 10 chalcedony
chub: **4** dace, dolt, fool, lout **5** chopa **6** chevin, shiner **8** fallfish, mackerel **9** hornyhead, squawfish
chubby: 5 chuff, fubsy, plump **6** choaty, rotund **8** rolypoly
chuck: hen, log, pig **4** beef, food, fowl, grub, hurl, jerk, lump, toss **5** chock, cluck, pitch, throw **6** bounce, collet **7** chicken, discard **9** dismissal
chuckle: 5 cluck, exult, laugh **6** giggle, titter **7** chortle
chuff: fat **4** boor **5** brick, churl, cross, miser, proud, sound, sulky, surly **6** chubby, elated, rustic **7** swollen **9** conceited **11** ill-tempered
chug: 4 puff
chum: cad, pal **4** bait, mate, pard **5** buddy, butty, crony **6** cobber, copain, friend **8** roommate **9** associate, companion
chump: ass **4** dolt, head **5** block **8** endpiece **9** blockhead, schlemiel, schlemihl
chunk: dab, gob, pat, wad **4** junk, slug **5** claut, piece, throw, whang
chunky: **4** game **5** lumpy, plump, squat, stout, thick
church: **4** tera(Jap.) **7** edifice **9** sanctuary, structure
altar end: **4** apse
attendant: **8** altarboy, choirboy
bench: pew, pue **4** seat
body of: **4** nave
calendar: **4** ordo
chapel: **7** oratory
congregation: **7** synaxis
council: **5** synod **6** Nicene
dignitary: **4** dean, pope **5** abbot, canon **6** bishop **7** prelate, primate
dominion of: **11** sacerdotium
endowed: **8** benefice
entrance chapel: **7** galilee

government: **9** hierarchy
home: **5** manse **7** deanery **8** convento **9** parsonage
member: **11** communicant
church: *morning service:* **5** matin
officer: **5** elder, vicar **6** beadle, deacon, lector, sexton, warden **7** prelate, sacrist **8** reverend **9** clergyman, moderator, presbyter, sacristan **11** headborough
part of: **4** apse, bema, nave **5** altar, solea **7** chancel, narthex **8** cantoria, transept **10** clearstory, clerestory
prayer: **5** kyrie **12** kyrie eleison
property: **5** glebe
reader: **6** lector
Roman: **7** lateran **8** basilica
room: **6** vestry **7** galilee **8** sacristy
seat: pew, pue **5** bench **6** sedile **7** sedilia(pl.)
service: **4** mass, rite **5** matin **7** vespers, nocturn **8** evensong
stand: **4** ambo
stipend: **7** prebend
vault: **5** crypt
vessel: ama, pyx **4** font **5** amula **7** columba, piscina **9** colymbion **10** monstrance
vestry room: **8** sacristy
wall: **6** cashel
warden's aide: **7** hoggler
wing: **5** aisle
church council (previous to): **10** antenicene
churchly: **9** religious, spiritual
churchyard: **6** litten **8** cemetery **9** graveyard
churl: cad, man **4** boor, carl, gnof, hind, lout, serf **5** carle, ceorl, chuff, gnoff, knave, miser **6** bodach. carlot, lubber, rustic, vassal, yeoman **7** bondman, freeman, haskard, husband, niggard, peasant, villain, villein **10** countryman, curmudgeon
churlish: **4** mean **5** bluff, gruff, rough, surly **6** crabby, rustic, sordid, sulkly, sullen, vulgar **7** boorish, crabbed, uncivil, violent **9** illiberal **10** ungracious, unyielding **12** cross-grained
churn: **4** beat, kirn(Sc.), stir **5** drill, shake **7** agitate
part: **6** dasher
chute: **4** rush, tube **5** flume, hurry, rapid, shoot, slide **6** hopper, trough **7** decline, descent **8** downfall, stampede
cibarious: **6** edible
cibol: **5** onion **7** shallot
ciborium: pix, pyx **6** canopy, coffer, vessel
cicada: **6** cigala, cagale, locust
noise: **5** chirr
cicala: **6** locust **11** grasshopper
cicatrix: **4** mark, scab, scar, seam
cicerone: **5** guide, pilot **6** mentor, orator **7** courier **9** conductor
cid: Ruy **4** epic, hero, poem **5** Bivar, chief,

title **9** commander
sword of: **6** colada, tizona
cider: **5** perry **6** perkin, swanky **8** beverage
pulp: **6** pomace
cienega: **5** marsh, swamp
cigar: **4** toby **5** claro, smoke **6** boquet, Corona, maduro, stogie **7** bouquet, cheroot, culebra **8** perfecto **9** Belvedere
cigarette: fag **4** biri, pill **5** cubeb, smoke **6** gasper, reefer **9** cigarillo
cigarfish: **4** scad **8** quiaquia
cilium: **4** hair, lash **7** eyelash **8** barbicel
cima: See **cyma.**
cimarron: **5** slave **6** maroon **7** bighorn
cimbia: **4** band **6** fillet
cimex: **6** bedbug, insect
cimmerian: **4** inky **5** black **6** gloomy
cinch: **4** belt, gird, grip, pipe, snap **5** girth **6** fasten **8** sinecure **9** certainty
cinchona extract: **7** quinine
cinct: **4** girt **9** encircled
cincture: **4** band, belt, gird, halo, list, ring **5** girth **6** cestus, collar, fillet, girdle **7** baldric, compass **8** encircle **9** enclosure **11** environment, surrounding
cinder: ash **4** gray, slag **5** chark, dross, ember **6** scoria **7** clinker, lapilla, residue
cinders: **5** gleed, track
cinema (see also **motion picture**): **4** film, show **5** flick, movie **6** screen
cinerarium: urn **8** mortuary
cinerator: **6** ashery **9** crematory **11** incinerator
cinerous: **5** ashen
cingle: **4** belt **5** girth **6** girdle
cingulum: **4** band **5** ridge **6** girdle
cingular: **7** annular **8** circular
cinnabar: ore **7** mineral **9** vermilion
derivative: **11** quicksilver
cinnamic acid derivative: **7** sinapic
cinnamon: **4** tree **5** canel, spice **6** canela, canell, canelo, cassia **7** canella, canelle **8** barbasco
cinnamon apple: **8** sweetsop
cinnamon oak: **8** bluejack
cinnamon stone: **6** garnet **8** essonite
cion: bud **5** graft, scion, shoot, uvula **10** descendant
cipher: key, nil **4** code, null, zero **5** aught, ought **6** device, decode, figure, letter, naught, nought, number, symbol **9** nonentity **10** cryptogram
cipo: **4** vine **5** liana
cippus: **6** pillar **8** landmark **10** gravestone
circa: **5** about **6** around **13** approximation
Circassian: *dialect:* **6** Adighe **8** Cherkess **9** Abkhasian, Kabardian
king: **9** Sacripant
Circe: **5** siren **7** tempter **9** sorceress **11** enchantress
father: **6** Helios
island: **5** Aeaea
niece: **6** Medea

circle: lap, set 4 disk, gyre, halo, hoop, loop, maru(Jap.), orbe, ring, rink, turn 5 class, crown, cycle, frame, group, monde, realm, rhomb, rigol, round, swirl, twirl 6 bezant, cirque, clique, collet, cordon, corona, diadem, girdle, rotate, rundle, spiral, system 7 chukkar, chukker, circlet, circuit, company, compass, coronet, coterie, enclose, revolve, ringlet 8 encircle, surround 9 circulate, encompass 13 circumference

geographic: 6 tropic
great: 7 equator
longest chord: 8 diameter
luminous: 4 aura, halo 6 corona, nimbus
part: arc 6 degree 7 segment
part of: arc 5 chord 6 radius, secant, sector

circlet: 4 band, hoop, ring 6 bangle, cirque 7 circuit 8 bracelet, headband
of light: 7 aureola, aureole

circuit: lap 4 area, bout, iter, loop, tour, zone 5 ambit, cycle, orbit, round, route 6 ambage, circle, detour 7 compass, itinera(pl.) 8 district 10 revolution 13 circumference
auxiliary: 5 relay
court: 4 eyre

circuitous: 4 mazy 6 curved 7 crooked, devious, oblique, sinuous, twisted, vagrant, winding 8 circular, flexuous, indirect, rambling, tortuous 9 ambagious, ambiguous, deceitful, underhand, wandering 10 roundabout, serpentine 12 disingenuous, labyrinthine

circular: 4 bill 5 libel, orbed, round 6 ringed 7 annular, cycloid, discoid, perfect 8 cingular, complete, encyclic, globular, pamphlet 9 orbicular 10 circuitous, roundabout 11 publication
indicator: 4 dial

circulate: air, mix 4 move, turn 6 rotate, spread 7 diffuse, publish 9 propagate 10 promulgate 11 disseminate
publicly: 6 report 9 broadcast

circumference: arc 5 ambet, girth 6 border, bounds, limits 7 circuit 8 boundary, surround 9 dimension, perimeter, periphery

circumlocution: 6 ambage 7 winding 8 verbiage 10 periphrase, redundancy, roundabout

circumscribe: 5 bound, fence, limit 6 define 7 confine, enclose, environ 8 encircle, restrain, restrict, surround 9 encompass

circumspect: 4 wary, wise 5 alert, chary 7 careful, guarded, prudent 8 cautious discreet, watchful 9 attentive 10 deliberate

circumstance: fix 4 fact, item 5 event, phase, state 6 affair, detail, factor, pickle 7 element, episode 8 incident, position 9 condition, situation 10 occurrence, particular 11 environment, opportunity 12 surroundings

circumstantial: 5 exact 6 minute 7 precise 8 detailed 9 pertinent 10 incidental, particular 11 inferential 12 nonessential

circumstantiate: 7 support 8 evidence

circumvent: 4 balk, dupe, foil 5 cheat, check, cozen, evade, trick, 6 baffle, delude, entrap, outwit, thwart 7 capture, deceive, defraud, ensnare, prevent 8 surround 9 encompass, frustrate, overreach, underfong

circus: 4 ring 5 arena 6 circle, cirque 9 spectacle 10 hippodrome 12 amphitheater 13 entertainment
arena wall: 5 spina
column: 4 meta
gear: 4 tent 5 rings 7 trapeze
rider: 8 desultor

cirque: 5 basin 6 circle, circus, corrie, recess 7 circlet, erosion

cirrus: 5 cloud 7 tendril 8 filament

cisco: 8 blackfin, whitefin

cist: box 4 tomb 5 chest 6 casket 7 chamber 9 cistavaen

cistern: sac, tub, vat 4 tank, well 6 cavity 7 cuvette 8 cisterna 9 reservoir, impluvium

cit: 8 townsman 9 tradesman 10 shopkeeper

citadel: arx 4 fort, hall 5 alamo, tower 6 castle 7 borough 8 fastness, fortress 10 stronghold 13 fortification
of Carthage: 5 Bursa, Byrsa

citation: 6 notice 7 mention, summons 8 monition 9 quotation, reference 10 allegation 11 enumeration

cite: 4 call, tell 5 allay, quote, refer 6 accite, accuse, adduce, allege, arouse, avouch, excite, notify, repeat, summon 7 arraign, bespeak, excerpt, extract, mention 8 indicate

citizen: cit 5 voter 6 native 7 burgess, burgher, citoyen(F.), denizen, elector, freeman, oppidan 8 civilian, commoner, occupant, resident 9 citoyenne(F.) 10 inhabitant
suffix: ese, ian, ist, ite

citizenship: *admission to:* 14 naturalization 15 enfranchisement
pert. to: 5 civic

citrine: 5 color 7 rhubarb

citron: 4 lime 5 lemon 6 cedrat, yellow

citrullus: 7 pumpkin 10 watermelon

citrus: *drink:* ade
fruit: 4 lime 5 lemon 6 citron, orange 7 kumquat, tangelo 8 mandarin, shaddock 9 tangerine 10 grapefruit

city: 4 burg, dorp, town, urbs(L.) 5 ville 6 ciudad, staple 9 community 10 metropolis 12 municipality
eternal: 4 Roma, Rome
hanging gardens: 7 Babylon
holy: 5 Mecca 6 Medina 9 Jerusalem

leaning tower: **4** Pisa
official: **5** mayor **7** manager, marshal **8** alderman **10** councilman
oldest inhabited: **8** Damascus
pert. to: **5** civic, urban
wicked: **5** Sodom **8** Gomorrah
City: *of Bells:* **9** Strasburg **10** Strasbourg
of Bridges: **6** Bruges
of Brotherly Love: **12** Philadelphia
of Churches: **8** Brooklyn
of David: **9** Jerusalem
of God: **6** church, heaven **8** Paradise
of Hundred Towers: .**5** Pavia
of Lilies: **8** Florence
of Masts: **6** London
of Saints: **8** Montreal
of Seven Hills: **4** Rome
of the Violet Crown: **6** Athens
of Victory: **5** Cairo
civet: cat, cit **5** rasse, zibet **6** bondar, musang, zibeth **7** fossane, nandine
civet-like animal: **5** genet
civic: lay **5** civil, suave, urban **6** polite, urbane **7** secular
civil: **4** hend **5** hende, suave **6** polite, urbane **7** affable, courtly, elegant, politic, refined **8** discreet, gracious, obliging, polished, wellbred **9** civilized, courteous **10** cultivated, respectful **11** complaisant **13** condescending
civil rights (extinction of): **9** attainder
civilian: cit **5** civvy **7** citizen, teacher **12** noncombatant, practitioner
dress: **5** mufti
civility: **6** comity **7** amenity **8** courtesy **9** propriety **10** affability, compliance, politeness **11** complacence **12** complaisance
civilization: **6** kultur(G.) **7** culture **10** refinement **11** cultivation
civilize: **4** tame **5** teach, train **6** polish, refine **7** educate **8** humanize, urbanize **9** cultivate **11** domesticate
clabber: mud **4** mire **6** curdle, lopper **12** bonnyclabber
clack: **4** blab **5** chack, cluck, crack **6** cackle, gossip, rattle, tongue **7** chatter, clacket, clatter, prattle **10** chatterbox
clad: **5** drest, robed **6** beseen, decked **7** adorned, arrayed, attired, clothed, covered, dressed **8** sheathed
cladose: **6** ramose **8** branched
clag: mud **4** clog, clot, daub, mire **5** fault, stick **6** adhere, burden
claggum: **5** taffy **7** treacle **8** molasses **9** sweetmeat
claim: ask **4** aver, call, case, lien, mine, name **5** exact, right, shout, title **6** assert, demand, elicit **7** acclaim, derecho, pretend, profess, require **8** maintain, pretence, pretense, proclaim **9** challenge, homestead, postulate, vindicate **11** encumbrance
claimant: **7** usurper **9** pretender, arrogator

clairvoyance: **7** insight **8** sagacity **10** divination **11** discernment, penetration
clairvoyant: **4** seer **6** omener **7** prophet, seeress
clam: **4** base, clog, daub, glam, hush, mean **5** clamp, crash, glaum, grasp, grope, smear, stick **6** adhere, clutch, sticky **7** bivalve, clangor, mollusk, steamer **8** adhesive
genus of: mya
kinds of: **4** mega **5** blunt, chama, razor, solen **6** gweduc, quahog **7** geoduck, quahaug
clamant: **4** loud **6** crying, urgent **9** clamorous
clambake: **4** bake **5** movie, rally **6** defeat **7** failure **9** gathering **11** performance
clamber: **5** climb, scale **6** claver **7** rammack **8** scramble, struggle
clamjamfry: mob **5** crowd **6** rabble **7** rubbish -
clammy: **4** damp, dank, soft, wack **5** moist, sammy **6** sticky, waughy
clamor: cry, din **4** bere, bunk, roar, rout, wail **5** blare, boast, bruit, noise, shout **6** bellow, hubbub, outcry, racket, tumult, uproar **7** stashie **10** hullabaloo, vociferate
clamorous: **4** loud **5** noisy **7** blatant, clamant, yelling **8** brawling, decrying **9** clamatory, turbulent **10** boisterous **11** openmouthed
clamp: lug, nip, pin **4** bolt, glam, grip, nail, vise **5** block, clasp, glaum **6** fasten **8** fastener, holdfast **10** clothespin
clan: set, sib **4** cult, race, sect, sept, unit **5** class, group, horde, party, tribe **6** clique, family..**7** society **8** division **10** collection, fraternity
emblem: xat **5** totem
head of: **5** chief, elder, thane
pert. to: **6** tribal
clancular: **6** secret **11** clandestine
clandestine: bye, sly **4** foxy **5** privy **6** covert, hidden, secret **7** bootleg, furtive, illicit **8** phratria, stealthy **9** clancular, concealed **10** fraudulent **12** hugger-mugger **13** surreptitious
clang: din **4** ding, peal, ring **5** clank, clash, noise **6** jangle, timbre
clangor: din **4** clam, roar **5** clang **6** hubbub, uproar
clank: **4** ring **5** sound **6** rackle
clansman: **10** Highlander
clap: **4** bang, flap, peal, slap **5** cheer, clink, crack **6** poster, strike, stroke **7** applaud, chatter, plaudit **9** explosion **11** thunderpeal
clapper: **6** rattle, tongue **7** knacker, knocker
support: **7** baldric **8** baldrick
claptrap: **5** trash **6** blague, device **7** fustian **8** nonsense, trickery **10** pretension **11** insincerity
clarify: **5** clean, clear **6** purify, refine,

render, settle 7 cleanse, explain, glorify 8 depurate, eliquate, simplify 10 illuminate 11 transfigure

clarinet: 4 reed, wind 10 instrument
  mouthpiece: 4 birn
  snake charmer's: 4 been

clarion: 5 clear 7 trumpet

clarity: 5 glory 8 splendor 9 clearness 10 brightness, brilliance 11 pellucidity

claro: 4 mild 5 cigar

clart: 4 clot, daub 5 smear, trash 6 sloven

clarty: 4 foul 5 dirty, gooey, muddy 6 sticky

clash: jar 4 bang, bolt, dash, news, slam 5 brawl, brunt, crash, fight, occur, prate, shock 6 affray, differ, gossip, hurtle, impact, strife, strike, tattle 7 collide, discord, scandal 8 argument, conflict 9 collision, interfere

clasp: hug, pin 4 fold, grab, grip, hasp, hold, hook, hoop, ouch, tach 5 cling grasp, morse, preen, seize, tache 6 agrafe, brooch, buckle, clench, clutch, enfold, enwrap, fasten, fibula, gimmer, gimmor, infold 7 agraffe, amplect, embrace, entwine, fermail, tendril 8 barrette, fastener, surround 9 constrain, safety-pin 10 chatelaine

class: ilk 4 clan, kind, race, rank, sect, sort, type 5 breed, caste, genus, genre, grade, group, order, tribe 6 circle, family, gender, rating 7 seminar, species, variety 8 category, division 9 abteilung 11 description 12 denomination
  animal: 5 genus 6 genera
  biological: 5 genus 6 genera(pl.),
  member: 4 coed 6 junior, senior 8 freshman 9 sophomore
  pert. to: 7 generic

classic: 4 book 5 Attic, model 7 ancient 8 standard 9 venerable 11 composition, masterpiece

classical: 4 pure 5 Attic, Greek, Latin, Roman 6 chaste 8 academic, masterly 9 firstrate

classification: 4 file, rank, rate, sort 5 genre, genra(pl.), genus, grade, order, taxis 6 genera(pl.), rating, system 8 analysis, category, division, taxonomy 12 distribution

classify: 4 list, rank, rate, size, sort, type 5 grade, group, label, range 6 assort, codify, divide, ticket 7 arrange, catalog, dispose, marshal 8 register 9 catalogue, segregate 10 categorize, distribute

classy: 4 tony 5 nifty, slick, smart 7 stylish

clat: 4 clod, clot, mess 5 dirty, prate 6 bedaub, gossip 7 chatter

clatter: din, jar 5 clack, noise, rumor 6 babble, gabble, gossip, rackle, rattle, tattle 7 blatter, chatter, clutter, prattle, reeshie 9 commotion 11 disturbance

claudicant: 4 lame 7 limping

clause: 4 part 5 close, plank, rider 6 phrase 7 article, passage, proviso 8 sentence 9 condition, provision 10 conclusion 11 stipulation

claut: 4 hand, lump, rake, tear 5 chunk 6 clutch, scrape 7 handful, scratch

clavecin: 11 harpsichord

clavel: 6 lintel, mantel

claver: 5 prate 6 clover, gossip 7 chatter, clamber

clavicle: 4 bone 10 collarbone

clavus: 4 band, corn 5 strip 6 bunion 7 callous

claw: dig 4 clee, fawn, hand, hook, nail, pull, sere, tear, unce 5 chela, cloof, clufe, court, grasp, griff, seize, talon, uncus 6 clutch, nipper, scrape, ungula 7 crubeen, flatter, scratch, wheedle 8 lacerate

clawk: 4 claw 6 snatch 7 scratch

clay: cob, pug 4 bole, galt, loam, lute, marl, mire 5 argil, brick, cloam, earth, gault, loess, ochre, rabat, tasco 6 cledge, clunch, kaolin 8 lifeless 9 inanimate
  building: 5 adobe, tapia
  casting: 4 slip
  covered with: 6 lutose
  deposit: 4 marl
  layer: 4 lias 5 sloam
  lump: 4 clag, clod
  made of: 7 fictile
  pert. to: 5 bolar
  piece: 4 tile
  pottery: 6 kaolin 7 kaoline

claybrained: 4 dull 6 stupid

clayey: 5 bolar, heavy, malmy, marly 6 cledgy, lutose 9 argillous 12 argillaceous

clead: 6 attire, clothe

cleam: 4 daub 5 smear, stick 6 adhere 7 plaster

clean: fay, fey, hoe, mop 4 dust, fair, pure, smug, swab, trim, wash, wipe 5 bream, clear, curry, empty, feigh, grave, scour, scrub, smart 6 chaste, clever, kosher, purify 7 apinoid, cleanse, clearly, furbish, perfect 8 absterge, brightly, dextrous, entirely, renovate, spotless, unsoiled 9 destitute, dexterous, guiltless, speckless, undefiled 10 immaculate 11 butterworth, untarnished 13 unadulterated

cleaner: 4 soap 5 borax, purer 6 ramrod 8 cleanser 9 detergent 10 dentifrice

cleaning agent: 4 soap 5 borax 9 detergent

cleaning implement: mop 4 swab 5 broom 6 ramrod 7 sweeper

cleanly: 4 pure 6 adroit, artful, chaste 7 correct, elegant 8 innocent, skillful 9 dexterous

cleanse: 4 farm, heal, soap, wash 5 brush, clean, dight, purge, rinse, scour, scrub 6 purify, refine 7 baptize, clarify, deterge, sweeten 8 renovate

cleanser: lye 10 clarifiant

cleansing: 4 bath 7 abluent, clysmic, washing 8 ablution, lavation 9 acquittal, cathartic, detergent **10** emundation **12** purification

clear: net, rid **4** free, gain, open, over, pure, quit **5** atrip, breme, brent, clean, lucid, plain, prune, sharp, vivid **6** acquit, assoil, bright, candid, clever, exempt, fluted, limpid, lucent, patent, purify, settle, smooth **7** absolve, clarion, clarify, crystal, deliver, evident, glaring, graphic, lighten, obvious, release **8** apparent, brighten, definite, distinct, explicit, manifest, pellucid, revelant **9** cloudless, discharge, disengage, elucidate, enigmatic, exculpate, exonerate, extricate, vindicate **10** unconfused **11** disentangle, perspicuous, transparent **12** intelligible
away: fay, fey **5** feigh **6** dispel **9** expurgate
out: **6** decamp, desert

clear-cut: **5** lucid, sharp **7** concise **8** definite, distinct, incisive **9** chiselled, **10** unconfused

clear-sighted: **10** discerning **13** perspicacious

clear-up: **5** solve **6** settle

clearing: *in woods:* **5** glade, tract **8** slashing
of land: **4** sart **6** assart

cleat: **4** bitt **5** block, chock, kevel, wedge **6** batten **7** bollard, coxcomb, support **9** butterbur

cleavage: **7** fission, fissure **8** division **9** partition **10** separation

cleave: cut, rip **4** chop, hold, join, link, part, rely, rend, rift, rive, slit, tear **5** break, carve, chawn, chine, clave, cleft, cling, clove, crack, sever, shear, split, stick **6** adhere, bisect, cohere, divide, pierce, sunder **7** dispart, fissure **8** separate

cleche: **4** urde **5** urdee **11** cross-shaped

cleek: **4** club, hook, link **5** crook, pluck, seize **6** clutch, snatch **8** fishhook

clef: key **9** character
bass: eff
treble: gee

cleft: gap **4** chap, chop, fent, flaw, reft, rift, rima, rive **5** break, chasm, chawn, chink, clove, crack, crena, riven, split **6** breach, cleave, cloven, cranny, crotch, divide, recess **7** crevice, divided, fissure, opening **8** aperture, fracture

cleft-lip: **7** harelip

cleg: **4** gleg **6** gadfly **8** horsefly

clem: **4** riot **5** brawl, fight **6** clutch, starve, thirst

clemency: **4** pity **5** mercy **6** lenity **7** quarter **8** kindness, leniency, mildness **10** compassion, indulgence

clement: **4** mild, soft, warm **6** gentle **7** lenient **8** merciful **9** forgiving **13** compassionate

clench: **4** fist, grip, grit, hold **5** brace, clasp, clint, close, grasp **6** clinch, clutch **9** interlock **10** strengthen

Cleopatra: *attendant:* **4** Iras
lover: **10** Marc Antony
river: **4** Nile
sister: **7** Arsinoe

Cleopatra's Needle: **7** obelisk

clepe: bid, cry **4** call, name **5** shout **6** appeal, invite, invoke, summon **7** address, mention

clergy: **4** cloth **9** clergymen
body of: **6** pulpit **7** college

clergyman: **4** abba, abbe, dean, Papa **5** canon, clerk, padre, pilot, prior, rabbi, vicar **6** bishop, cleric, curate, deacon, divine, domine, parson, pastor, priest, rector **7** cassock, prelate **8** cardinal, chaplain, minister, preacher, reverend **9** blackcoat, dignitary, presbyter **12** ecclesiastic
office: **4** cure **6** curacy **8** ministry **9** pastorate, priorship, rectorate
residence: **5** manse **6** priory **8** vicarage **9** parsonage

clergywoman: nun **8** rectress **9** priestess **10** religieuse

cleric: See **clergyman.**

clerical clothing: alb **5** rabat, stole, amice, cloth, fanon, orale **6** collar **7** biretta

clerk: nun **4** monk **5** agent, write **6** cleric, commis, hermit, layman, priest, scribe, teller, yeoman **7** carcoon, compose, gomasta, scholar **8** employee, greffier(F.), recorder, salesman **9** assistant, clergyman, registrar **10** accountant **11** salesperson **12** ecclesiastic
court: **11** protonotary **12** prothonotary

clerkly: **7** learned, scribal **9** scholarly

cletch: **5** brood **6** clique, clutch, family **8** hatching

cleuch: **5** cleft **6** clough, ravine **7** descent

cleve, cleeve: **4** brae **5** cliff **8** hillside

clever: apt, sly **4** able, cute, deft, fine, gnib, hend, keen **5** agile, alert, clean, clear, handy, mende, lithe, quick, slick, smart, witty **6** active, adroit, artful, astute, bright, expert, habile, heppen, neatly, nimble, pretty, shrewd **7** amiable, cunning, parlous **8** dextrous, handsome, obliging, skillful, talented **9** dexterous, ingenious **10** well-shaped **11** clean-limbed, dexterously, intelligent

cleverness: can **4** tact **5** skill **6** esprit **9** dexterity, ingenuity **10** adroitness, astuteness

clevis: **4** hake **5** copse **6** muzzle **7** fitting **10** connection

clew, clue: **4** ball, hint **5** globe, glome, skein **6** hurdle, thread

click: **4** pawl, tick **5** agree, catch **6** detent **7** ratchet

click beetle: **6** elater

client: **5** ceile **6** patron **7** patient **8** customer, henchman, retainer **9** dependent

clientele: **9** following

cliff: hoe **4** crag, hill, rock, scar **5** bluff,

cleve, heuch, heugh, scarp, shore, slope **6**
cleeve, height **7** clogwyn **8** hillside, palisade **9** precipice

climate: **4** mood **6** region, temper **8** attitude **9** condition

climax: cap, top **4** acme, apex, near, peak,
shut **5** mount, scale, tight **6** apogee, ascend, finish, opogee, summit, zenith **9**
gradation **11** culmination

climb: gad **4** ramp, rise, shin **5** creep,
grimp, mount, scale, speed(Sc.), twine **6**
ascend, ascent, shinny **7** clamber

climber: **6** rigger, scaler **11** mountaineer
12 alpenstocker

clime: See **climate**.

clinamen: **4** bias, turn **5** twist

clinch: fix, get, hug **4** bind, grip, nail, seal
5 clamp, cling, clink, clint, grasp, rivet,
seize **6** clench, clutch, fasten, secure,
snatch **7** confirm, embrace, grapple,
scuffle **8** complete, conclude, holdfast **9**
establish

cling: hug **4** bank, hang, hold, rely **5** clasp,
stick, trust **6** adhere, cleave, clinch, cohere, depend, fasten, shrink, wither **7**
cherish, embrace, shrivel **8** contract **9**
persevere

clink: ale, jug, put, rap **4** beat, blow, brig,
cash, clap, coin, jail, move, ring, slap **5**
latch, money, rhyme, seize **6** clinch, jingle, lockup, moment, prison, strike, tinkle
7 instant **9** assonance **10** guardhouse

clinker: **4** slag **5** waste

clinquant: **5** clink, showy **6** tinsel **8** tinseled **10** glittering

clip: bob, cut, dod, hug, lip, lop, mow, nip **4**
barb, chip, coll, crop, dock, dodd, hold,
pace, pare, poll, snip, trim **5** clasp, force,
prune, shear **6** clutch, fasten, hinder,
holder **7** curtain, curtail, embrace, scissor, shorten **8** diminish, encircle **9** encompass **10** abbreviate

clipper: **4** boat, ship **6** vessel **7** shearer,
workman

clique: cot, mob, set **4** bloc, clan, club,
gang, ring **5** cabal, write, group, junto **6**
circle, cletch **7** coterie, faction **8** conclave,
sodality **9** camarilla **11** combination

clit: **5** caked, close, heavy **6** doughy,
sticky

clitter: **5** noise **6** rattle **7** chatter **10** stridulate

cloak: aba **4** brat, capa, cape, hide, mant,
mask, pall, rail, robe, veil, wrap **5** capot,
cover, guise, manta, manto, sagum **6** assume, bautta, capote, caster, chapel, dolman, mantle, mantua, pharos, screen,
serape, shield, shroud, tabard, visite **7**
bavaroy, chlamys, conceal, garment,
manteau, manteel, pelisse, pretext, shelter, zimarra **8** albornoz, burnoose, disguise, intrigue, mantilla, palliate **9** dissemble **10** roquelaure **11** portmanteau
African: **5** jelab **6** jellab

Arabian: **7** feridgi, ferigee, ferijee **8** feridjee
baptismal: **7** chrisom
bishop's: **10** mantelleta
ecclesiastical: **4** cope
Greek: **6** abolla **7** chlamys
hooded: **6** camail
Jewish: **6** kittel **9** gaberdine
large-sleeved: **10** witzchoura
loose: **5** palla
monk's: **8** analabos
Punjabi: **5** choga
Roman: **5** sagum **7** alicula, paenula
Roman military: **10** paludament **11** palu-
damenta(pl.) **12** paludamentum
sleeveless: **6** dolman **7** paenula
Spanish: **4** capa **5** manta **6** mantle
worn over armor: **6** tabard

cloam: **4** daub **8** crockery **11** earthenware

clobber: **4** beat **5** patch, pound, smear **6**
cobble, defeat, strike

clocher: **6** belfry **9** bell tower, campanile

clock: nef **4** bell, call, dial, gong, time **5**
cluck, hatch, hurry, meter, watch **6**
beetle, Big Ben, crouch **8** horologe, incubate, ornament, recorder **9** clepsydra,
hourglass, indicator, taximeter, timepiece
11 chronometer, speedometer
maker: **9** horologer **10** horologist
part of: **4** dial **5** bundy **6** detent, foliot **8**
pendulum, recorder
regulating body: **8** pendulum **10** escapement
ship-shaped: nef

clocker: **5** timer **8** railbird **11** embroid-
erer

clockmaker: **9** horologer

clockwise: **6** deasil, dessil **7** deiseal **8**
positive

clod: sod **4** clat, clot, dolt, dull, lout, lump,
turf **5** clout, clown, divot, earth, glebe,
gross, knoll, yokel **6** ground, stupid **7**
bumpkin **9** coagulate **10** clodhopper

cloddish: **5** gross **6** stupid **7** boorish

clodhopper: **4** boor, clod, shoe **6** rustic **7**
plowman

clodpate: **4** clot, dolt, fool **7** ramhead **8**
clodpole, clodpoll, imbecile **9** blockhead

clog: gum, jam, log **4** clag, clam, cloy, curb,
load, lump, shoe, skid, stop **5** block,
check, choke, dance, sabot **6** adhere,
burden, chopin, fetter, galosh, hamper,
hobble, impede, patten, remora, sandal,
secque, weight **7** galoshe, perplex, shackle, trammel **8** coalesce, encumber, obstruct, overshoe, restrain **9** embarrass,
hindrance, restraint **10** difficulty **11** encumbrance
with mud: **4** daub **6** daggle

cloggy: **5** heavy, lumpy **6** sticky

clogwyn: **5** cliff **9** precipice

cloister: **4** hall, stoa **5** abbey, aisle,
stoae(pl.) **6** arcade, friary, immure,
piazza, priory **7** closter, convent, nunnery
9 cloistral, enclosure, hermitage, monas-

tery, sanctuary **11** ambulatoria(pl.) **12** ambulatorium

pert. to: **9** claustral, cloistral

cloistered: **7** recluse **11** sequestered

cloof, clufe: **4** claw, hoof **6** cleave

clop: **4** limp **5** sound **6** hobble

close: by; cap, end, hot **4** clit, firm, hard, hide, near, nigh, quit, seal, shut, slam, snug, stop **5** anear, block, cease, cheap, dense, finis, garth, gross, muggy, thick, tight **6** clause, clench, effect, expiry, finale, finish, narrow, nearby, period, stingy, strait **7** adjourn, compact, context, extreme, miserly, occlude, similar **8** accurate, adjacent, complete, conclude, familiar, imminent, intimate **9** barricade, extremity, niggardly, terminate **10** avaricious, conclusion **11** termination **12** parsimonious

a hawk's eyes: **4** seel

comb. form: **4** sten **5** steno

firmly: bar **4** lock, seal **5** tight **6** batten, cement

closefisted: **4** near **6** stingy **7** miserly **8** handfast **9** niggardly

closely: **4** just **6** almost, barely, narrow, nearly **9** compactly

closeness: **7** secrecy **8** fidelity, intimacy **9** parsimony, proximity **10** stinginess, strictness **11** literalness **12** consciseness **14** oppressiveness

closest: **4** next **7** nearest **9** proximate

closet: **4** ewry, room, safe **5** ambry, cuddy **6** armary, locker, pantry, secret **7** cabinet, conceal, private **8** conclave, cupboard, gardevin, wardevin, wardevin **9** gardevine **12** confidential

closing device: **4** lock **6** zipper

closure: end, gag **5** bound, limit **7** cloture **8** clausure **9** agreement, enclosure **10** conclusion **11** confinement, containment **12** entrenchment

clot: dot, gel **4** clag, clat, clod, gout, jell, lump, mass **5** clart, grume **6** balter, cotter **7** clodder, embolus, thicken **8** clodplate, coagulum, concrete, solidify **9** blockhead, coagulate **12** crassamentum

cloth (see also **fabric,** and names of individual fabrics: **cotton, linen, silk,** etc.): rag **5** bluet, toile(F.), tweed, twill **6** canvas, clergy, drapet, fabric, livery, napkin **7** acetate, drapery, garment, raiment, textile, worsted **8** dwelling, material, sheeting **10** cassinette

camel's hair: aba **6** camlet

coarse: **4** duck **5** crash, gunny **6** burlap, linsey

crinkled: **5** crape, crepe **10** seersucker

dealer: **6** draper, mercer

decorative: see *ornamental* below

dye method: tie **5** batik

figured: see *patterned* below

fine-textured: **4** mull, pima, silk **7** percale

flaw in: **4** rase

flaxen: **5** linen

glazed: **5** tammy

hemp: **4** jute **5** gunny **6** baline, burlap, canamo

homespun: **4** kelt

instrument: **8** ringhead

knitted: **6** jersey, tricot

light: **6** tissue **7** challis, etamine

lining: **5** serge **8** sarcenet, sarsenet

mesh: net **5** super, tulle **11** cheesecloth

metallic: **4** acca, tash

narrow: **4** tape **5** braid **6** edging, ribbon

old kind: **4** acca, tuke **5** tewke **6** samite

ornamental: **4** gimp, lace **6** lampas, riband **8** tapestry

poplin: **7** tabinet **8** tabbinet

print: **6** calico **7** percale

printer: **7** candroy

raised design: **7** brocade

remnant: **4** fent

roll: **4** bolt

rug: mat **7** matting

satin: see **fabric:** *satin*

shop: **7** mercery

silk: see **fabric:** *silk*

soft: **5** panne, plush, surah **6** fleece **9** montagnac

stiff: **7** taffeta **9** crinoline

stretcher: **6** tenter

synthetic: **5** nylon, rayon **6** dacron **7** acetate

clothe: don, dub, rig, tog **4** deck, garb, gird, gown, robe, vest **5** adorn, array, clead, cleed, dress, endow, endue, frock **6** attire, enrobe, invest, swathe **7** address, apparel, vesture **8** accouter, accoutre **9** authorize, represent

clothes (see also **dress**)**:** **4** duds, garb, gear, suit, tack, wear **5** habit **6** attire **7** apparel, baggage, costume, raiment, regalia, toggery, vesture **8** clothing, frippery, garments **9** vestments **10** bedclothes **11** habiliments

civilian: **5** mufti

dealer: **6** ragman **7** fripper **9** fripperer

informal: **5** smock **6** halter, shorts, slacks, trunks

pert. to: **8** vestiary **10** habilatory

presser: **7** sadiron

clothesmoth: **5** tinea

clothespress: **5** chest **7** armoire **8** wardrobe

clothing: (see also **garment**)**:** **4** wear **6** attire **7** apparel

coarse: **4** brat **5** burel

protective: **5** armor

woman's: **6** fardel

cloud: fog, nue(F.) **4** blur, dust, haze, hide, mist **5** bedim, befog, gloom, nubia, stain, sully, swarm, taint, vapor **6** cirrus, damage, darken, deepen, defame, nebula, nimbus, screen, shadow, stigma **7** blacken, confuse, cumulus, eclipse, obscure, tarnish **8** overcast **9** obfuscate **10**

overspread **11** thunderhead
comb. form: **5** nepho
kinds of: nue **4** rack, scud **6** cirrus, nebule, nimbus **7** cumulus, stratus, tornado **9** mare's tail
morning: **4** velo
cloud-built: **4** airy **9** imaginary **13** unsubstantial
cloud-like: **7** nebular
cloudless: **5** azure, clear **6** bright
cloudy: dim **4** dark, dull, hazy **5** filmy, foggy, misty, murky, shady **6** gloomy, lowery, opaque **7** blurred, clouded, nebular, obscure **8** confused, nubilous, overcast, vaporous **9** cloudlike **10** indistinct, lackluster
clough: **5** cleft **6** cleuch, cleugh, ravine, valley
clour: **4** blow, bump, dint **5** thump **6** batter
clout: bat, box, hit **4** beat, blow, bump, clod, club, cuff, join, mend, nail, slap, slug, swat **5** patch, smite **6** strike, target, thrash, washer **7** bandage **8** bosthoon **12** handkerchief
clouter: **7** botcher, cobbler
clove: gap **4** tree **5** cleft, spice **6** cleave, ravine
cloven: **5** cleft, split **9** bisulcate
clover: red **5** lotus, medic, nardu **6** alsike, luxury, nardoo **7** alfalfa, comfort, lucerne, melilot, trefoil **10** prosperity
clown: hob, oaf **4** aper, boor, fool, goff, joey, lout, mime, mome, zany **5** churl, comic, mimer, punch, zanni(It.) **6** august, bodach, hobbil, jester, lubber, rustic, stooge **7** buffoon, bumpkin, peasant, playboy **8** merryman **9** harlequin, joculator **10** bufflehead, countryman, harlequina **11** merry-andrew, punchinello **13** pickle-herring
clown's allheal: **8** woudword **9** clownheal
clownish: raw **4** rude, zany **5** gawky, rough **6** clumsy, coarse, rustic **7** awkward, boorish, hoblike, ill-bred, loutish, uncivil **8** ungainly **9** untutored
cloy: **4** clog, glut, nail, pall, sate **5** gorge, prick **6** pierce **7** satiate, satisfy, surfeit
club: bat, hit, set **4** beat, cane, join, mace, maul, polt, team **5** billy, bunch, clout, kebby, lodge, order, staff, stick, unite, yokel **6** clique, cudgel, kebbie, menage, weapon **8** bludgeon, sorority, spontoon **9** blackjack, truncheon **10** fraternity, knobkerrie, shillelagh **11** association
famous: **5** Lambs **6** Friars **7** Garrick
kinds of: bat **4** arum, mere **5** billy, plant **6** nullah, tawkee, tawkin, taiaha **7** pantoon **8** spantoon, spontoon **9** blackjack, espantoon, truncheon **10** knobkerrie, pogamoggan **12** nullahnullah
social: **4** card **6** bridge, cercle **10** fraternity
woman's: **7** Sorosis **8** sorority
club-shaped: **7** clavate

clubfoot: **7** talipes
clubs: **4** suit **5** cards, basto
clubstart: **5** stoat
clubweed: **8** knapweed
cluck: hen **4** call, fuss **5** chuck, clack, click, clock, sound
clue: key, tip **4** ball, clew, hint, idea **5** guide, twine **6** thread **8** innuendo **10** indication, intimation, suggestion **11** fingerprint
clump: tod **4** blow, bush, heap, lump, mass, mott, tope, tuft **5** bunch, group, grove, patch, tread **6** clunch, dollop **7** cluster, thicket
clumsy: awk **4** numb, rude **5** blunt, bulky, gawky, hulky, inapt, inept, stiff **6** gauche **7** awkward, boorish, ill-made, unhandy **8** benumbed, bungling, clownish, footless, tactless, ungainly, unwieldy **9** lumbering, maladroit, misshapen **10** cumbersome **11** heavy-handed **13** inappropriate
clunch: **4** clay, lump **5** clump, lumpy **9** limestone
clung: **5** stiff **8** shrunken, starving **9** collapsed, shriveled, toughened
cluster: bog **4** bush, cyme, knot, lump, tuft **5** bunch, clump, group **7** bourock, cluther **8** fascicle **9** glomerule **10** collection **11** agglomerate, aggregation
fern spore: **4** sori(pl.) **5** sorus
flower: **4** cime, cyme **5** ament, umbel **6** raceme **7** panicle **8** anthemia
flower-like: **7** rosette
clustered: **6** tufted **8** racemose **9** aciniform, aggregate, glomerate **10** coacervate
clutch: nab **4** clam, claw, clem, clip, fist, glam, grab, grip, nest **5** brood, catch, clasp, claut, cleek, glaum, grasp, gripe, hatch, lever, power, seize, talon **6** cleach, clench, cletch, clinch, retain, snatch **7** control **8** coupling
clutter: **4** mess **6** bustle **7** clatter **8** disorder **9** confusion **10** disarrange
Clytemnestra: *half-sister:* **5** Helen
husband: **9** Agamemnon
mother: **4** Leda
paramour: **9** Aegisthus
son: **7** Orestes
cnemis: **4** shin **5** tibia **7** legging
coach: bus, car **4** hack, help **5** araba, cabin, prime, teach, train, tutor **6** advise, direct, fiacre(F.), saloon **7** adviser, prepare, tallyho **8** carriage, dormeuse **10** instructor, stagecoach
railway: **7** Pullman, sleeper
coachman: fly **4** fish, jehu, whip **5** pilot **6** coachy, driver **7** coachee, coacher **8** yemschik
assistant: **10** postillion
Russian: **7** yamshik **8** yemschik **9** yamstchik
coadjustor: **6** bishop **7** partner **8** coworker **9** assistant, associate
coagulant: **6** rennet **7** styptic **8** gelatine

coagulate: gel, set **4** cake, clod, clot, curd, jell **5** quail **6** cotter, curdle, posset **7** clabber, congeal, thicken **8** solidify

coagulation: 4 gout **7** clotter

coal: 4 bass, fuel **5** chark, ember, gleed, stoke **6** carbon, cinder

agent: **6** fitter

bed: **4** seam

block: jud

constituent: **4** goaf **6** carbon, ethene, phenol, pyrene **7** benzene **8** creosote **11** naphthalene

dust: **4** coom, culm, smut, soot, swad **5** coomb

kind of: jud **4** dant, hard, soft **6** cannel **7** lignite **9** tasmanite **10** anthracite, bituminous

lump: cob

miner: **7** collier

mining implement: **7** breaker

oil: **8** kerosene

refuse: **4** coke, dust, slag **6** cinder **7** backing, clinker

size: cob, ett, nut, pea **4** lump **5** slack, stove **6** broken **8** chestnut **9** buckwheat

wagon: **4** corb, carf, tram

worker: **7** collier, geordie **8** chaffman

coal car part: 6 hopper

coalbin: 6 bunker

coalesce: mix **4** fuse, join **5** blend, merge, unite **6** embody **7** combine **10** amalgamate

coalescence: 5 union **6** fusion, league **11** combination

coalfish: sey **4** parr **5** cuddy **6** beshow, billet, cudden, podler, sarthe **7** baddock, glashan, pollack

coalition: 5 trust, union **6** fusion, league, merger **8** alliance **11** combination, confederacy, conjunction **13** confederation

coarse: low, raw **4** dank, hard, hask, lewd, loud, rank, rude, vile **5** bawdy, broad, crass, crude, dirty, gross, harsh, heavy, loose, randy, routh, thick **6** brutal, callow, common, earthy, impure, ribald, rustic, vulgar **7** blatant, fulsome, goatish, obscene, raucous, sensual **8** clownish, homespun, immodest, indecent, unchaste **9** inelegant, offensive, unrefined **10** boisterous, indelicate, unpolished

coast: 4 bank, land, ripa **5** beach, blide, shore, slide **6** adjoin, border, rivage, strand **7** seaside **8** approach, seaboard, seashore

area: **7** seaside **8** seacoast **9** coastline, shoreline

dweller: **7** orarian

pert. to: **7** coastal, orarian **8** littoral, riparian

projection: **4** cape, ness **8** headland **9** peninsula

Coast Guard: *boat:* **6** cutter

service-woman: **4** Spar

coaster: mat **4** sled **5** trout **8** toboggan **9** container

coat (see also **cloak**): **4** bark, daub, husk, rind, zinc **5** cloth, cover, crust, glaze, habit, layer, paint, plate, shell, terve **6** enamel, jacket, mantle, parget, pelage, veneer **7** garment, incrust, overlay, plaster, vesture **8** membrane, tegument **9** petticoat **10** integument

animal: fur **4** hair, hide, wool **6** pelage

fastener: **4** frog **6** button

Irish: **9** coatamore

kind of: pea **4** cape, jupe, mail, robe, sack, toga **5** armor, simar, tails **6** coatie, duster, jerkin, kirtle, mantle, reefer, rocket, topper **7** cassock, cutaway, haubeck, paletot, pelisse, surcoat, curcote, surtout **8** benjamin, mackinaw, overcoat **9** gaberdine, newmarket, redingote **12** chesterfield

neck: **6** george

part: **4** cuff **5** lapel, skirt **6** collar, george, pocket, sleeve

seaman's: **5** grego

coat of arms: 5 crest

pert. to: **8** heraldic

coati: 5 nasua **6** animal, narica

coating: 4 aril, film **6** patina, veneer **8** mucilage

coax: beg, coy, pet **4** cant, dupe, fawn, lure, urge **5** tease **6** cajole, cuitle, entice **7** beguile, cuittle, flatter, implore, wheedle **8** blandish, collogue, inveigle, persuade **9** influence **10** manipulate

coaxial: 12 conterminous

cob: ear, mew **4** beat, blow, gull, loaf, lump, mole, mule, pier, pony, swan, toss **5** block, break, chief, excel, horse, outdo, piece, stump, throw, thump **6** basket, cobnut, leader, muffin, peapod, spider, strike **7** beating, seagull, surpass, threash **8** dumpling **10** breakwater

cobber: pal **4** chum, mate **6** friend **9** companion

cobble: 4 darn, make, mend, pave **5** botch, patch, stone **6** bungle, repair **7** clobber **11** cobblestone

cobbler: pie **4** snob **5** sheep, soler, sutor **6** souter **7** botcher, catfish, crispin, dessert, pompano, saddler **8** chuckler, scorpion **9** killifish, shoemaker

pitch: **4** code

cobbra: 4 head **5** skull

cobby: 5 stout **6** hearty, lively, stocky **10** headstrong

cobra: asp, nag **4** naga, naja **5** snake, viper **6** uraeus

tree: **5** mamba

cobweb: net **4** trap **5** snare, wevet **8** gossamer **9** intricacy

cocaine: 4 snow **8** alkaloid, narcotic **10** anesthetic

source: **4** coca

Cochin-China: See **Vietnam.**

cock: tap **4** bank, fowl, heap, kora, pile, rick **5** fugie, fight, gallo, shock, stack, strut, valve, yowle **6** faucet, leader **7**

chicken, contend, gorcock, rooster, swagger **8** gamecock, malemass **10** cockalorum **11** chanticleer
gun: nab

cock-a-hoop: **4** awry **6** elated, lively **8** boastful, cockeyed

cockade: **4** knot **5** badge **7** rosette

Cockade State: **8** Maryland

cockatoo: ara **5** arara, cocky, galah, macaw **6** abacay, cockie, parrot **8** calangay, ganggang
genus: **7** cacatua, kakatoe

cocker: dog, pet **4** shoe **6** coddle, fondle, pamper, quiver, reaper **7** fighter, indulge, legging, nurture, spaniel

cockerel: **4** cock **6** bantam

cocket: **4** join, pert, seal **5** bread, brisk, merry, saucy **6** lively **7** mortise **8** document

cockfight: **4** game, spar **5** match **7** contest

cockhorse: **5** lofty, proud **7** astride, upstart **8** exultant

cockle: **4** boat, gall, gith, kiln, oast **5** bulge, shell, stove **6** darnel, pucker, ripple, wabble **7** mollusk, wrinkle **9** whimsical

cockpit: pit **4** ring, rink, well **5** arena, cabin, field **7** gallera

cocktail: **5** Bronx, drink **7** apertif, martini, sidecar **8** daiquiri **9** appetizer, Manhattan

cocky: **4** pert **6** crouse, farmer, jaunty **8** arrogant **9** conceited

cocoa, coco: **4** head, palm, tary **5** broma **6** yuntia **9** chocolate

cocoanut: **7** coquito
dried meat: **5** copra
fiber: **4** coir, kyar

cocoon: pod **4** clew, clue **5** shell **11** incunabulum

cod: bag, cor, pod **4** axle, bank, cusk, fish, fool, hoax, husk, rock **5** belly, pouch, scrod, torsk **6** burbot, codger, cultus, fellow, pillow **7** bacaloa, cushion
family: **7** gadidae
young: **5** scrod, sprag **7** codling

cod-like: bib **4** hake, ling **5** gadus

coda: **4** part **5** rondo **6** finale **10** conclusion

coddle: pet **4** baby, cade, cook **5** humor, nurse, spoil **6** caress, cocker, cotton, fondle, pamper **7** parboil

code: law **4** flag **5** canon, codex **6** cipher, digest, secret, signal **7** precept
inventor: **5** Morse
message: **6** cipher **10** cryptogram

codex: **4** code **5** annal **9** formulary **10** manuscript

codfish: See cod.

codger: cod **5** churl, crank, miser **6** fellow **7** niggard

codify: **5** index **6** digest **8** classify **11** systematize

coelenterate: **5** polyp **8** cnidaria

coerce: cow **4** curb, make **5** bully, check,

drive, force **6** compel **7** concuss, enforce, repress **8** bludgeon, bulldoze, restrain, restrict **9** blackmail, constrain, terrorize **10** intimidate

coercion: **5** force **6** duress

coeval: **12** contemporary

coffee: *after dinner:* **9** demitasse
alkaloid: **7** caffein
bean: nib
beverage: Rio **4** Java, Kona **5** Milds, Mocha **6** Bogota, Brazil, Santos **7** Sumatra **8** Medellin **9** Maracaibo
maker: urn **5** silex
refuse: **6** triage

coffee house: inn **4** cafe

coffeeberry: **6** jojoba **7** cascara, soybean **8** peaberry **9** buckthorn, chaparral

coffer: ark, box, dam **5** chest, hutch, trunk **6** casket, forcer, trench **7** caisson **8** ciborium, standard

coffin: **4** bier, case, cist, mold **6** basket, casing, casket **11** sarcophagus
cloth: **4** pall **5** cloak
support: **4** bier

cog: cam, lie **4** gear, jest **5** catch, cheat, cozen, tenon, tooth, trick, wedge, wheel **6** cajole **7** deceive, produce, quibble, wheedle **8** cockboat **9** fabricate, falsehood

cogent: **5** valid **6** potent, strong **7** telling **8** forcible, powerful **9** trenchant **10** conclusive, convincing, legitimate, persuasive

cogitate: **4** mull, muse, plan **5** think **6** ponder **7** connate, reflect **8** consider, meditate

cognate: kin **4** akin **5** alike **6** allied **7** kindred, related, similar **8** bandhava, relative

cognizance: ken **4** heed, mark **5** badge, crest **6** emblem, notice **7** bearing, cockade **9** knowledge **11** observation, recognition **12** apprehension

cognizant: **4** onto, ware **5** awake, aware **8** sensible **9** conscious **10** conversant **11** intelligent **12** apprehensive

cognize: **4** know **8** perceive **9** recognize

cognomen (see also **name**): **4** name **5** byname **7** agnomen, surname **8** nickname, patronym **11** appellation

cohabit: **4** live **5** dwell **6** occupy **8** accustom **9** accompany

cohere: fit **4** glue, suit **5** agree, cling, stick, unite **6** adhere, cement, cleave **7** connect **8** coincide **9** glutinate

coherence: **5** union **8** cohesion **9** congruity **10** accordance, connection, continuity **11** consistency

cohort: **4** band **7** company

coif, coiffe: cap **4** hood **6** beggin, burlet, hairdo **7** arrange **8** skullcap **9** headdress

coiffure: **6** hairdo **9** headdress

coign: **5** wedge **6** corner **8** position **10** projection

coil: ado, wip **4** ansa, clew, curl, fuss, hank, loop, roll, wind **5** helix, querl, tense, twine, twist **6** rundle, spiral, tu-

mult, windup 7 haycock, ringlet, trouble
8 cofusion, encircle 9 encounter 10 difficulty 11 convolution
electric: 6 teaser
coilet: 7 sinuous, tortile
coin: die, ori 4 cash, dime, make, mint 5
angle, brown, chink, clink, metal, money,
quoin, shape, stamp, token, wedge 6
change, corner, create, invent, specie,
strike 7 convert 8 currency 9 fabricate,
originate 11 cornerstone
copper: 4 cent 5 penny, bodle, brown
counterfeit: 9 brummagem
difference: 5 value 11 seigniorage
edge corrugation: 7 reeding
front: 4 head 7 obverse
imperfectly minted: 8 brockage
kind of: lap, ora 4 dime, doit, mite, rial,
rosa 5 cuyne, daric, disme, ducat, eagle,
groat 6 bawbee, beaver, besant, bezant,
cunzie 7 bezzant, carolus, crocard, louleau 8 bezantee, crockard 10 castellano
reverse side: 4 tail 5 verso
roll: 7 rouleau
science: 11 numismatics
silver: 4 batz, dime, dump, pina, tara 5
bezzo 6 tester, teston
stamper: 4 mill
weight: 6 shekel
coinage: 7 fiction, mintage
collector: 11 numismatist
coincide: gee 4 jibe 5 agree, tally 6 concur 9 harmonize 10 correspond
coincidence: 9 concourse 11 concurrence 12 concomitance, simultaneity
coincident: 4 even 8 together 9 consonant 10 concurrent 11 concomitant 12
contemporary 15 contemporaneous
coiner of new words: 9 neologian, neologist
coistrel: 4 base 6 menial, varlet 7 servile,
soldier
coition: 7 meeting 10 attraction 11 conjunction
cojuror: 12 compurgator
coke: ask 4 coal, core, dope 5 chark 7 cocaine
cokes: 4 gull 9 simpleton
col: 4 pass 10 depression
colander: 5 sieve 7 utensil 8 strainer
colate: 6 filter, strain
Colchean: See Colchis.
Colchis:
king: 6 Aeetes
princess: 5 Medea
cold: flu 4 dead, dull 5 algid, bleak, frore,
gelid, rheum, virus 6 arctic, chilly, frigid,
frosty, wintry 7 catarrh, chilled, distant,
glacial 8 reserved, rhigosis, unheated
9 apathetic, cheerless 10 insensible,
spiritless 11 hyperborean, indifferent,
unemotional 12 unresponsive 13 dispassionate, marblehearted 15 undemonstrative
cold and damp: raw 4 dank 5 bleak

cold feet: 4 fear 5 doubt 9 cowardice 12
apprehension
colder: 4 husk 6 refuse 7 rubbish
coleopthera insect: 6 beetle, insect,
weevil
colewort: 4 cole, kale 7 cabbage
colic: 10 mulligrubs
coliseum: 4 hall 7 stadium, theater 8
building 12 amphitheater
coll: hug 4 clip, poll 5 prune 7 embrace
collaborate: aid 9 cooperate
collagen: 7 protein 10 albuminoid
collapse: 4 cave, fall, fold 5 crash, slump,
wreck 6 bust-up 7 crumple, debacle, deflate, failure, flummox, smashup 8 contract, downfall 9 breakdown, telescope
11 prostration
collar: nab 4 band, eton, gill, grab, ring,
ruff 5 chain, fichu, ruche, seize 6 bertha,
gorget, tackle, torque 7 capture, chignon,
circlet, shackle 8 cincture, neckband,
necklace 9 neckpiece
horse: 6 hounce
kind of: 4 ruff 5 fanon, orale, phano,
ruche, rabat 6 carcan, rabato, rebato,
cangue 7 panuelo, bargham 8 carcanet
10 chevesaile
collar cell: 10 choanocyte
collarbone: 8 clavicle
collared monad: 16 choanoflagellate
collate: 6 bestow, confer, verify 7 compare, emamine
collateral: 4 side 8 indirect, parallel, security 9 ancillary 10 subsidiary 11 accidential, concomitant, subordinate
collation: tea 4 meal 5 lunch 6 repast,
sermon 7 address, reading 8 dejeuner,
parallel, treatise 10 collection, comparison, conference 12 consultation, contribution
collator: 6 critic 7 machine
colleague: 4 aide, ally 5 unite 6 deputy 7
adjunct, consort, partner 8 confrere, conspire 9 assistant, associate
collect: tax 4 call, heap, levy, pile, pool,
save 5 amass, glean, group, hoard, raise 6
accoil, accrue, confer, garner, gather,
muster, prayer, sheave 7 compile, engross, impound 8 assemble, contract 9
aggregate 10 accumulate, congregate 11
agglomerate
collected: 4 calm, cool 5 sober 6 serene
8 composed 9 aggregate, clustered 10
coacervate 11 agglomerate 13 dispassionate
collection: ana 4 bevy, clan, olio 5 batch,
group, store, suite 6 bundle, conger, sorite 8 assembly, caboodle 9 aggregate, anthology, collation, repertory 10 assemblage, assortment, cancionero
literary: ana 7 library 8 analects
miscellaneous: 4 olio 6 fardel
poems: 5 divan, sylva 9 anthology 10
cancionero
wild animals: zoo 9 menagerie

collectorship: 5 staff 6 office 9 residence 12 jurisdiction

colleen: 4 girl, lass, miss 5 belle 6 damsel, lassie, maiden

college: 5 lycee 6 school 7 academy 8 seminary 10 assemblage, university 11 institution 12 organization

building: gym, lab

campus: 4 quad 10 quadrangle

course: 5 major, minor 7 seminar

court: 4 quad

degree: A.B., B.A., B.S., C.E., D.D., M.A., M.D., M.S.; B.L.S., B.Sc., LL.B., LL.D., M.Sc., S.C.B., Ph.D. 5 Litt.D.

girl: 4 coed

graduate: 6 alumna, doctor, master 7 alumnus 8 bachelor

kind of: 9 electoral

living quarters: 4 dorm, hall

official: 4 dean 5 prexy 6 beadle, bursar, regent 7 proctor 9 president, registrar

student group: 4 frat 8 sorority 10 fraternity

term: 8 semester

U.S. oldest: 7 Harvard

U.S. woman's oldest: 9 Mt. Holyoke

collet: 4 band, ring 5 chuck 6 casing, circle, collar, flange, socket 7 bushing, ferrule 8 neckband

collide: hit, ram 4 bump, dash, hurt 5 clash, crash, wreck 6 hurtle, strike

collier: fly 4 boat 5 miner 6 plover, vessel 7 geordie

boy: 6 hodder

lung disease: 11 anthracosis

colliery: 4 mine

collieshangie: row 5 brawl 6 uproar 7 quarrel 8 squabble 11 disturbance

colliquate: 4 melt 7 liquefy

collision: 5 clash, crash, shock 7 smashup 8 clashing 9 encounter 10 opposition, percussion 12 interference

collocate: set 5 place 7 arrange

collogue: 4 coax, talk 5 gloze 6 confer 7 collude, flatter, wheedle 8 conspire, intrigue 12 conversation

colloquial: 8 familiar, informal 9 unstudied 14 conversational

colloquy: 4 chat, talk 6 parley 8 dialogue 9 discourse 10 conference 12 conversation

colluctation: 8 struggle 10 contention

collude: 4 plot 6 scheme 7 connive 8 collogue, conspire

collusion: 6 deceit 7 cahoots, secrecy 9 agreement 10 connivance

law: 5 covin

collusive: 8 covinous 10 fraudulent

colly: 4 dust, smut, soot 5 black, grime, sooty 9 blackbird

coloboma: 6 defect 7 fissure

Colombia: *city:* 4 Cali 5 Neiva, Pasto, Tunja 6 Bogota(C.), Cucuta, Ibaque, Quibdo 7 Leticia, Popayan 8 Medellin 9 Cartagena, Manizales, San Andres 10 Santa Maria 11 Bucaramanga 12 Barranquilla 13 Villavicencio

coin: 4 peso, real 6 condor, peseta 7 centavo

gulf: 6 Darien

Indian: 5 Boros 6 Betoya, Chitas, Tahami, Yahuna 7 Tunebos 8 Guacicos, Morcotes, Pedrazas, Quimbaya, Sinsigas

mahogany: 7 albarco

measure: 4 vara 7 celemin

plant: 5 yocco

province: 5 Cauca, Choco, Huila, Valle 6 Boyaca, Caldas, Narina, Tolima, Vaupes 7 Bolivar 9 Antioquia, Atlantico, Magdalena, Santander 12 Cundinamarca

river: 4 Sinu, Tomo 6 Atrato, Atroto, Pattia, Yapura 7 Putumay 8 Guaviara 9 Magdalena

seaport: 6 Lorica 9 Cartagena 10 Santa Marta 12 Barranquilla

weight: bag 4 saco 5 carga, libra 7 quilate, quintal

colon: 4 coin 6 farmer 7 planter 8 colonist 10 husbandman

colonial teak: 8 flindosa

colonist: 5 colon 7 pioneer, settler 8 emigrant

colonize: 5 found 6 gather, settle 7 migrate 9 establish

colonizer: ant 6 oecist 7 settler

colonnade: row 6 stoa 7 pergola, portico, terrace 9 peristyle

colony: 5 swarm 9 community 10 dependency, settlement

colophony: 5 resin, rosin

color (see also next entry): dye, hue 4 blee, cast, flag, tint, tone 5 badge, blush, paint, shade, stain, tenne, tinge 6 banner, ensign, redden 7 distort, pennant, pigment 8 standard, tincture 10 complexion

achromatic: 4 gray 5 black, white

change: 8 iridesce, opalesce

dull: dun 4 drab 5 terne

full of: 9 chromatic

graduation: 5 shade

healthy: tan

light: 4 tint

line of: 6 streak

malachite: 4 bice

mat white: 9 alabaster

mulberry: 7 morello

neutral: 4 ecru, gray 5 beige, black, white

painter: 6 Titian

pale: 6 pastel

primary: red 4 blue 5 black, green, white 6 yellow

quality: 4 tone

secondary: 5 green 6 orange, purple

shade of difference: 6 nuance

unhealthy: 6 sallow

value: see *quality* above

varying: 10 iridescent, opalescent

color: For colors see their names: **red,**

green, purple, etc.; for shades see main color. EXAMPLES: "reddish brown": see **brown**; "grayish green": see **green**.
color blindness: 9 Daltonism **13** achromatopsia **14** monochromatism
color organ: 8 clavilux
color photography inventor: 4 Ives
Colorado:
army camp: **6** Carson
city: **5** Aspen, Delta, Lamar **6** Denver, Meekar, Pueblo **7** Alamosa, Boulder, Greeley, Manassa **8** Trinidad **10** Walsenburg
county: Ada **4** Baca, Bent, Mesa, Park, Weld, Yuma **5** Adams, Grand, Kiowa, Logan, Otero, Ouray **6** Custer, Denver, Elbert, Moffat **7** Conejos, Crowley, Dolores, Douglas, Jackson, Lincoln, Prowers **8** Arapahoe **9** Archuleta, Montezuma
fort: **5** Logan
Indian: Ute **8** Arapahoe
mountain: Oso **7** Massive
mountain pass: **6** Alpine **7** Fremont **8** Marshall **9** Argentine, Tennessee **10** Cottonwood
mountain range: Elk **4** Book, Park, Roan **5** Raton **7** Sawatch
park: **5** Estes **9** Mesa Verde
peak: Oso **4** Yale **5** Baldy, Ethel, Evans, Grays, James, Pikes **6** Castle, Elbert, Long's, Maroon **7** Audubon, Harvard, Rosalie, Torreys **8** Arapahoe, Snowmass **9** Princeton
resort: **5** Aspen **7** Manitou
river: **4** Bear **5** Grand, Green, White, Yampa **7** Dolores, Laramie **8** Arkansas, Colorado, Gunnison
river tributary: **4** Gila
state flower: **9** Columbine
valley: **5** Estes
colorant: dye **4** anil **7** pigment
coloratura: 6 singer **7** soprano **8** vocalist
colored: 6 biased **9** distorted, prismatic **14** misrepresented
partly: **4** pied **6** motley **7** piebald **10** variegated
colorful: gay **5** vivid **9** brilliant
colorimeter: 10 tintometer
coloring: *cell:* **10** endochrome
matter: dye **5** morin **7** pigment **8** clorofil **10** endochrome **11** chlorophyll
colorless: wan **4** drab, dull, pale **5** ashen, blake, blank, plain **6** pallid **7** hueless, neutral **8** blanched **9** impartial **10** achromatic **11** transparent **13** uninteresting
colors, set of: 7 palette
colossal (see also **huge**): big **4** huge, vast **5** great, large **7** immense **8** enormous, gigantic **9** monstrous
colosseum: See **coliseum**.
colossus: 5 giant, titan **6** statue **7** monster, prodigy
colporteur: 6 hawker **7** peddler **11** distributor

colt: gun **4** foal **5** filly **6** pistol **9** quadruped, youngster
coluber: 5 snake **7** serpent
colubrine: 6 crafty **7** cunning **9** snakelike
Columbia River rapids: 6 Dalles
Columbia University symbol: 4 lion
columbine: 4 bird, dodo **5** plant **6** flower **8** dovelike
Columbus: *birthplace:* **5** Genoa
companion: **5** Ojeda
embarkation port: **5** Palos
ship: **4** Nina **5** Pinta **10** Santa Maria
column: lat, row **4** file, line, post **5** shaft, stela, stele **6** pillar **7** support **8** cylinder, pilaster **9** formation
arrange in: **8** tabulate
part: **4** anta, fust **5** galbe, socle, scape, shank **6** plinth **7** entasis, capital **8** pilaster
shaped like human figure: **7** telamon **8** atlantes, caryatid
type of: **5** Doric, Ionic **10** Corinthian
columnar: 6 terete **7** stelene **8** vertical
columnist: 6 writer
columns: *series of:* **9** colonnade
set in: **7** tabular
without: **7** astylar
coma: 4 tuft **5** bunch, carus, sleep **6** stupor, torpor, trance **7** cluster **8** lethargy **13** insensibility
comate: 5 hairy **6** comose **9** companion
comatose: out **6** drowsy **9** lethargic **10** insensible
comb: 4 card, lash, rake **5** brush, clean, crest, curry, tease **6** smooth **11** disentangle
comb. form: **4** cten **5** cteno
flax: **5** hacle
comb jelly: 10 ctenophore
comb-like: 8 pectinal **9** pectinate
comb rat: 5 gundi
combat: war **4** bout, cope, duel, fray, meet, rush, tilt **5** clash, fight, joust, repel, set-to **6** action, battle, oppose, resist, strife **7** contend, contest, counter, scuffle **8** argument, conflict, struggle **9** encounter, withstand **10** antagonize, contention
combatant: 6 dueler **7** battler, fighter **8** champion **10** contestant
combative: 6 bantam **8** militant **9** agonistic **10** pugnacious **11** agonistical, belligerent
comber: 4 wave **7** breaker **11** beachcomber
combinate: 6 joined **8** combined **9** betrothed
combination: key **4** bloc, gang, pact, pool, ring **5** cabal, junto, party, trust, union **6** cartel, clique, corner, merger **7** combine, consort, coterie, faction **8** alliance, ensemble **9** aggregate, camarilla, coalition, composite, composure, synthesis **10** concoction, conspiracy **11** association, coalescence, composition, confederacy,

conjunction, corporation **12** undergarment **13** incorporation

combine: add, mix, wed **4** bloc, join, pool **5** blend, marry, merge, total, unite **6** absorb, concur, merger, mingle, splice **7** conjoin, conjure, machine **8** coalesce, compound, concrete, condense, contract, federate **9** construct, cooperate **10** amalgamate **11** combination, consolidate

comble: **4** acme, heap, load **6** summit

comboy: **6** sarong

combust: **4** burn **5** burnt **8** consumed **10** incinerate

combustible: **4** fuel, peat **5** fiery **9** irascible **10** accendible **11** inflammable

material: gas, oil **4** coal, coke, peat **6** tinder

combustion: **4** fire, heat **5** therm **6** tumult **7** burning **9** agitation, confusion, consuming, cremation, oxidation **12** inflammation **13** conflagration

residue: ash, gas **7** clinker

come: **4** grow **5** arise, issue, occur, reach **6** accrue, appear, arrive, befall, emerge, happen, spring **7** advance, develop, emanate **8** approach, practice **9** eventuate

across: **4** find, meet **9** encounter **10** contribute

before: **7** precede, prevene **8** antecede

by: get **4** gain **6** obtain **7** acquire, inherit

in: **5** crash, enter **6** arrive **7** intrude

into view: **4** loom **6** appear, emerge

out: **6** appear, emerge, emerse, extend **8** protrude

to terms: **4** join **5** agree **6** assent, settle **7** approve, consent **8** coincide **9** acquiesce

together: **4** bump, join, meet **5** clash **7** collide, convene **8** assemble, converge

comeback: **5** rally **6** answer, retort, return **7** rebound **8** recovery, repartee

comedian: wag, wit **4** card, **5** actor, antic, clown, comic **6** jester **7** buffoon

comedown: **4** land **6** alight, bathos **7** descend

comedy: **5** drama, farce, revue **8** comoedia(L.), travesty **9** burlesque, slapstick

character: **9** Pantaloon

muse: **6** Thalia

pert. to: **7** thalian

symbol: **4** sock

comeling: **8** newcomer **9** immigrant, sojourner

comely: **4** fair, hend, pert **5** bonny, hende **6** decent, goodly, liking, lovely, pretty, proper **7** farrant **8** becoming, decorous, graceful, handsome, pleasing, suitable **9** agreeable, beautiful **10** gratifying, personable

comer: one **6** person **7** arrival

comestible: **4** food **5** manna, viand **6** edible **7** eatable, victual **8** esculent

comet: **6** meteor

discoverer: **5** Haley **6** Donati

part: **4** coma

tail: **8** streamer

comeuppance: **6** rebuke **7** deserts **12** chastisement

comfit: **5** candy **7** confect, praline **8** conserve, preserve **9** sweetmeat **10** confection

comfort: aid **4** ease, rest **5** bield(Sc.), cheer **6** endure, relief, repose, solace, soothe, succor **7** animate, assuage, cherish, confirm, console, enliven, gladden, refresh, relieve, support, sustain **8** inspirit, nepenthe, pleasure, reassure **9** encourage, well-being **10** strengthen **11** consolation

comfortable: **4** bein, bien, cosh, cozy, easy, like, snug, trig **5** comfy, scarf **7** relaxed **8** cheerful, euphoric, wristlet **9** contented **10** acceptable, commodious, complacent, gratifying **11** consolatory, encouraging

comforter: **4** puff **5** cover, quilt, scarf **6** tippet **7** cheerer **8** pacifier

comfortless: **7** forlorn **8** desolate **9** cheerless **12** inconsolable

comfrey: **5** daisy **9** blackwort

comic: **5** droll, funny **8** comedian, farcical **9** burlesque

comical: low **4** base **5** droll, funny, queer, witty **7** amusing, jocular, risible, strange, trivial **8** humorous, ticklish **9** diverting, laughable, ludicrous, quizzical, whimsical **10** capricious

coming: due **4** next **6** advent, future **7** arrival, forward **8** deserved **9** impending **11** approaching

coming out: **5** debut **8** issuance

command: bid **4** beck, bode, boon, call, fiat, hest, rule, sway **5** beken, check, edict, exact, force, hight, order, power, ukase **6** adjure, behest, charge, compel, degree, demand, direct, enjoin, govern, impose, master, ordain **7** appoint, behight, bidding, control, dictate, mandate, officer, precept, require **8** domineer, restrain **9** authority, direction, influence, ordinance, prescribe **10** commission **11** appointment

supreme: **9** hegemony

to a horse: gee, haw, hup **4** whoa

commander: cid, cio **4** head **5** chief **6** leader, master, rammer **7** captain, drungar, emperor, general, officer **10** commandant **11** commendador(Sp.) **13** generalissimo

of a thousand men: **9** chiliarch

commanding: **8** dominant, imposing **9** imperious, masterful **10** imperative **13** authoritative

commandment: law **4** rule **5** order **7** precept

commando: **6** raider, ranger

commemoration: **5** award, medal **6** plaque **7** service **8** memorial **11** celebration **13** solemnization

commence: **4** fall, open **5** arise, begin,

found, start 6 incept, spring 8 initiate 9 institute, originate

commencer: 4 tyro 8 beginner

commencing: 7 initial, nascent 9 incipient

commend: pat 4 give, laud 5 adorn, boost, extol, grace, offer 6 bestow, betake, commit, praise, resign 7 applaud, approve, bespeak, deliver, entrust, intrust 8 bequeath 9 predicate, recommend 10 compliment, ingratiate

highly: 5 extol 8 eulogize 10 panegyrize

to favor: 10 ingratiate

commendable: 4 good 6 worthy 8 laudable 9 exemplary, honorable

commensurate: 4 even 5 equal 6 enough 8 adequate 10 answerable, convenient 11 appropriate 12 proportional 13 corresponding, proportionate

comment: 4 note, talk, word 5 aside, gloss, gloze 6 notate, postil, remark 7 descant, discuss, explain, expound 9 criticise, criticism, critize, discourse 10 animadvert, annotation, commentary 13 animadversion

commentaries: 10 adversaria

commentary: 5 gloss 6 memoir 7 account, comment 8 glossary, treatise

commentator: 6 critic, glozer 9 annotator, expositor, glossator, scholiast 10 glossarist 13 glossographer

commerce: 5 trade 6 barter 7 traffic 8 business, exchange 10 connection 11 interchange

vehicle: 5 truck

commercial: 9 mercature 10 mercantile 13 advertisement

commingle: mix 4 fuse, join 5 blend, merge, unite 6 mingle 7 combine, embroil 10 amalgamate

comminute: 4 mill 5 crush, grind 9 pulverize, triturate

commiseration: 4 pity 7 empathy 8 sympathy 10 compassion, condolence

commission: 4 send, task 5 board, trust 6 brevit, charge, demand, depute, errand, office, ordain, permit 7 command, consign, empower, mandate, mission, warrant 8 delegate, encharge 9 allowance, authority, authorize, brokerage, establish 10 constitute 11 instruction 12 compensation, dispensation, perpetration 13 authorization

commissioner: 5 envoy 7 officer 8 delegate

commit: do 4 give 5 allot, refer 6 assign, betake, remand 7 command, confide, consign, deposit, entrust, intrust 8 bequeath, delegate, imprison, relegate 9 recommend 10 perpetrate

committee: 4 body 5 board, group, junta 7 council 9 executors, guardians

commixture: 7 mixture 8 compound

commode: cap 5 chest 8 cupboard 10 chiffonier

commodious: fit 5 ample, roomy 6 proper, useful 8 spacious, suitable 9 capacious 10 beneficial, convenient 11 comfortable, serviceable 12 advantageous

commodity: 4 ware 5 goods 6 staple 7 article

common: low 4 base 5 banal, brief, cheap, joint, stale, trite, usual 6 coarse, mutual, ornery, vulgar 7 average, current, general, generic, natural, plebian, popular, regular, trivial, unnoble 8 familiar, frequent, habitual, mediocre, ordinary, pandemic, trifling 9 bourgeois, customary, defective, hackneyed, prevalent, universal, unrefined 10 second-rate 11 commonplace

common fund: pot 4 pool 5 purse

commoner: 5 ceorl, plebe 7 burgess, citizen, student 8 roturier 12 participator

commonly: *accepted:* 7 popular, vulgate *thought:* 7 reputed 8 putative

commonplace: 4 dull, fade, worn 5 banal, daily, plain, prose, stale, trite, usual 6 common, garden, truism 7 humdrum, prosaic, tedious, trivial 8 ordinary 9 hackneyed 11 unimportant

remark: 5 style 6 cliche, truism 9 platitude

commonwealth: 5 state 6 public 9 community 10 commonweal, res publica

Commonwealth country: 6 Canada 8 Rhodesia 9 Australia 10 New Zealand

commotion: ado, din 4 bree, fray, fuss, heat, riot, stir, to-do, whir 5 alarm, flare, hurry 6 bustle, cathro(Sc.), fracas, flurry, garray, mutiny, pother, tumult, unrest, welter 7 clatter, tempest, turmoil 8 disorder, upheaval, uprising 9 agitation, confusion 10 concussion, convulsion, ebullition, excitement, turbulence 11 disturbance 12 perturbation

commune: 4 area, talk 5 argue, realm, share, treat 6 advise, confer, debate, import, parley, reveal 7 consult, discuss, divulge 8 converse, district, township 11 communicate, intercourse, participate 12 conversation

communicable: 4 open 5 frank 8 catching, sociable 9 knowledge, talkative 10 diffusible, infectious 13 communicative

communicant: 6 member 8 adherent 9 informant

communicate(see also **commune**)**:** 4 tell 6 bestow, convey, impart, inform, reveal, signal 7 declare, dictate, divulge 8 converse

communication: 4 note 5 favor 6 favour, letter 7 message 8 telegram 9 communion 10 communique, connection

means: 4 drum, flag, note, post 5 phone, radio, smoke 6 letter, movies, speech, tomtom 9 telegraph, telephone 10 television

communion: 4 cult, host, mass, sect, talk 5 creed, faith, share, unity 6 church, homily 7 concord 8 antiphon, converse, viaticum 9 agreement, eucharist, sacrament 10 confession, fellowship 11 intercourse 12 conversation, denomination 13 communication, participation

case: 5 burse

cloth: 8 corporal 9 corporale

consecrated food: 5 hagia

plate: 5 paten

table: 5 altar

vessel: pyx

communique: 6 report 7 message 12 announcement 13 communication

communism: 8 Leninism 10 Bolshevism

communist: Red 6 Soviet

community: mir 4 body, burg, city 5 firca, state, thorp 6 œnoby, colony, hamlet, nation, polity, public 7 society, village 8 district, likeness, province, township 9 frequency 10 commonness 12 commonwealth, neighborhood

pert. to: 8 societal

commute: 5 alter 6 change, travel 7 convert 8 exchange 10 substitute 11 interchange

comose: 5 hairy 6 comous, tufted

compact: 4 bond, case, firm, hard, knit, pact, plot, snug, trim 5 brief, close, dense, gross, pithy, solid, terse, thick 6 vanity 7 bargain, concise, concord, serried 8 alliance, condense, contract, covenant, solidify, succinct 9 agreement, concordat 10 compaction, compressed, conspiracy, federation 11 compendious, concentrate, confederacy, consolidate, sententious 13 understanding

compadre: pal 5 buddy 6 friend 9 companion

companion: pal 4 chum, fere, mate, peer, twin, wife 5 buddy, bully, butty, crony, cully, matey 6 attend, comate, escort, fellow, friend, spouse 7 compeer, comrade, consort, husband, partner 8 compadre, helpmate 9 accompany, associate, attendant 11 concomitant 12 acquaintance

companionable: 6 social 7 cordial 8 gracious, sociable 9 agreeable

company: mob, set 4 band, bevy, body, core, crew, fare, fere, firm, gang, gest, ging, host, rout, team 5 coven, covey, crowd, flock, geste, group, guest, horde, party, squad, troop 6 actors, circle, clique, cohort, covine, curney(Sc.), throng, troupe 7 battery, college, consort, society, visitor 8 assembly 9 camarilla, cavalcade, concourse, gathering 10 fellowship 11 association, partnership 13 companionship

comparable: 4 like 7 similar 9 analogous

comparative: as 4 than 5 equal, rival 7 compeer 8 relative

suffix: er, or; ior

compare: vie 4 even 5 apply, liken, match, scale 6 confer, relate 7 collate, examine, senible 8 contrast, estimate 10 assimilate

comparison: 6 simile 7 analogy, parable 8 likeness, likening, metaphor 9 collation 10 conference, similitude 11 examination

compartment: bay, bin 4 cell, part 5 abode, stall 6 alcove, bunker, region 7 cellule, chamber, section 8 division 9 apartment 10 pigeonhole

granary: 8 grintern

compass: 4 area, gain, room, size 5 admit, field, gamut, range, reach, scope 6 arrive, attain, bounds, circle, degree, device, effect, extent, sphere 7 achieve, caliber, circuit, confine, divider, enclose, environ, horizon, pelorus, 8 boundary, cincture, circuity, surround 10 accomplish

beam: 7 trammel

card: 4 rose

housing: 8 binnacle

ink leg: pen

kind of: sun 4 gyro 5 solar

part: 6 needle

pocket: 6 diacle

point: 4 airt 5 airth, rhumb 7 azimuth

sight: 4 vane

suspender: 6 gimbal

compassion: rue 4 pity, ruth 5 heart, grace, mercy, sorry 6 lenity 7 remorse 8 clemency, sympathy 10 condolence 12 misericordia 13 commiseration

compatible: 8 suitable 9 accordant, agreeable, congenial, congruous, consonant 10 consistent, harmonious 16 non-contradictory

compatriot: 10 countryman

compeer: 4 mate, peer, rank 5 equal, match 7 comrade 9 colleague, companion 11 comparative

compel: gar(Sc.) 4 make, move, urge 5 cause, drive, exact, force, impel, press 6 coerce, enjoin, extort, incite, oblige 7 actuate, command, dragoon, enforce, require 9 constrain, influence, instigate, overpower 11 necessitate, subjudicate

compelled: has 4 must 5 bound

compelling: 6 cogent 7 telling 8 forceful 9 demanding 10 conclusive, convincing, persuasive

compendious: 5 brief, short 6 direct 7 compact, concise 8 succinct 9 condensed 11 expeditious 13 comprehensive

compendium: 4 list 5 brief 6 apercu, digest, precis, sketch 7 catalog, compend, epitome, medulla, outline, summary 8 abstract, breviary, syllabus, synopsis 10 abridgment 11 compilation, composition, contraction 12 abbreviation

compensate: pay 4 jibe 5 agree, atone, repay, tally 6 recoup, reward, square 7 correct, redress, requite, restore, satisfy 8 compense **9** indemnify **10** recompense, remunerate **11** countervail **12** counterpoise **14** counterbalance

compensation: fee, pay, utu **4** hire **5** bonus, wages **6** amends, angild, gersum, offset, reward, salary **7** damages, payment, redress, stipend **8** pittance, requital **9** emolument, indemnity **10** recompense **11** restitution **12** counterpoise, remuneration, satisfaction **15** indemnification

compete: pit, vie **4** cope, tend **5** match, rival **6** strive **7** contend, contest, emulate

competent: apt, can, fit **4** able, good, meet, sane **5** adept, capax, smart **6** worthy **7** capable, endowed, skilled **8** adequate, suitable **9** effective, efficient, qualified **10** proficient, sufficient

competition: **4** game, heat **5** match, trial **7** contest, rivalry **8** conflict **9** emulation **10** contention, free-for-all, opposition

competitor: foe **5** enemy, rival **6** player **7** entrant **8** opponent **9** adversary, candidate, combatant **10** antagonist, contestant

compilation: ana **4** book, code **5** cento **6** digest **9** accretion **10** collection, compendium, confection

compile: add **4** edit **5** amass **6** gather, select **7** arrange, collect, compose, prepare **11** anthologize

compiler: **6** author, editor

complacent: **4** calm, smug **7** fatuous **9** satisfied **11** comfortable **13** self-satisfied

complain: ail, yip **4** beef, carp, fret, fuss, kick, moan, rule, wail, yelp, yirn **5** brawl, croak, croon, gripe, whine **6** bewail, charge, cotter, grieve, grizze, grouse, murmur, repine, yammer **7** deplore, grumble, protest **9** bellyache **11** expostulate

complainant: **5** asker **7** accuser, querent, relator **9** plaintiff

complaining: **9** plaintive, querulous

complaint: **6** lament, malady, plaint **7** ailment, disease, illness, protest **8** disorder, gravamen, jeremiad **9** execration, grievance **10** accusation **11** lamentation

complaisant: **4** able, easy, kind **5** buxom, civil, suave **6** polite, smooth, urbane **7** affable, amiable, lenient **8** gracious, obliging, pleasing **9** compliant, courteous, favorable **10** favourable **12** ingratiating

complect: **5** plait **7** embrace **9** interwine **10** interweave

complement: **4** crew, gang **5** force **6** amount **7** adjunct, obverse **10** completion, supplement **11** counterpart

complete: do; all, end **4** dead, deep, fill, full **5** close, every, plumb, quite, ripen, total, utter, whole **6** effect, entire, finish, intact, mature **7** achieve, execute, fulfill, germane, perfect, plenary, realize **8** absolute, blinking, circular, conclude, implicit,

thorough **9** implement, surfeited, terminate **10** accomplish, consummate, effectuate **11** unqualified **12** wholehearted

completeness: **5** depth **9** entelechy

completion: end **6** finish **9** plenitude

complex: **4** hard, mazy **5** mixed **6** knotty **7** network, tangled, twisted **8** involved, manifold, syndrome **9** composite, difficult, entangled, intricate, perplexed **10** interlaced **11** complicated

complexion: hue **4** blee, look, rudd, tint **5** color, humor, state, tenor, tinge **6** aspect, temper **10** appearance

compliance: **7** harmony **8** civility **9** obedience **10** concession, submission **11** application **12** complaisance

compliant: **4** easy, oily **6** pliant, supple **7** ductile, dutiful, willing **9** indulgent **10** applicable, manageable, obsequious, sequacious **11** complaisant

complicate: **6** intort, puzzle, tangle **7** involve, perplex **8** bewilder

complicated: **4** hard **6** knotty, prolix **7** complex, gordian, snarled, tangled **8** involved **9** difficult, elaborate, embroiled, intricate, plexiform **10** disordered

complication: **4** node, plot **5** nodus, snarl **9** complexus, confusion, intricacy **10** difficulty, perplexity

compliment: **4** gift, laud **5** extol **6** boquet, eulogy, praise **7** adulate, applaud, bou.juet, commend, flatter, tribute **8** encomium, flummery, gratuity **9** adulation, panegyric **12** blandishment, commendation, congratulate

comply: **4** cede, obey **5** abide, adapt, agree, apply, yield **6** accede, accord, assent, enfold, submit **7** conform, embrace, observe **9** acquiesce **11** accommodate

component: **4** item, part, unit **6** factor, member **7** element **8** integral **10** compounder, ingredient **11** constituent

comport: act **4** bear, jibe, suit **5** agree, brook, carry, tally **6** accord, acquit, behave, demean, endure, square **7** conduct **9** behaviour, harmonize **10** correspond, deportment **11** comportance

comportable: **8** suitable **9** endurable, tolerable **10** consistent

comportment: **7** conduct, dealing **8** behavior, demeanor **9** behaviour, demeanour **10** deportment

compose: pen, set **4** calm, dite, form, lull, make **5** allay, brief, clerk, dight, order, write **6** accord, adjust, create, design, indite, settle, soothe **7** arrange, compone, concoct, conform, dispose, fashion, produce **8** compound, comprise, comprize, regulate **9** alleviate, construct, formulate **10** constitute **11** tranquilize

composed: **4** calm, cool **5** quiet, sober, wrote **6** demure, placid, sedate, serene **7** written **8** compound, decorous, tranquil **9**

collected, composite, unruffled 13 dispassionate

composer: 4 poet 5 odist 6 author, writer 7 elegist 8 monodist, musician 10 compositor, typesetter

composition (see also **musical composition**): ana 4 mass, opus, work 5 cento, ditty, drama, piece, poesy, theme 6 accord, lesson, make-up, thesis 7 article, compost, mixture, picture, writing 8 acrostic, compound, fantasia 9 admixture, aggregate, composure, congruity, formation, invention, structure, synthesis 10 adjustment, compendium, composture, confection, manuscript 11 arrangement, combination, compositure, conjunction 12 constitution, construction

art of: 8 rhetoric

for two: 6 duetto 7 duetino

literary: ms(abbr.) 5 cento, drama, essay, novel, theme 6 satire, thesis 7 tragedy 8 treatise

metrical: 4 poem, rime 5 poesy, rhyme

mournful: 5 dirge

compositor: 4 type 6 setter 7 caseman, printer

compost: 6 mingle 7 compote, mixture 8 compound 10 composture, fertilizer 11 composition

composure: 4 bond, mien 5 quiet, union 6 repose 7 balance, posture 8 calmness, serenity 10 composture, equanimity, sedateness 11 combination, composition, tranquility

compote, compot: 4 bowl 5 fruit 7 dessert

compound: 4 fill, join 5 alloy, blend, ester, unite 6 adjust, jumble, medley, settle 7 amalgam, combine, complex, compone, compose, compost 8 ceromide 9 admixture, aggregate, composite, enclosure 10 amalgamate, commixture, compromise, concoction, confection, constitute, hodge-podge, settlement

alkaline: 4 soda

amorphous: 7 phenose

chemical: 4 amid, amin, azin, imid, imin 5 amide, amine, azine, azola, borid, ceria, ester, imide, imine, osone 6 borids 7 inosite, metamer, leucine 8 chloride

containing double bonds: 6 triene

containing two hydroxyl groups: 4 diol

crystalline: 5 aloin, oscin 6 amarin, anisil, phenol 7 tropine

hypnotic: 7 trional

organic: 4 amin 5 amine, ester, ketol 6 ketole, ketone

comprehend: get, see 4 know 5 grasp, imply, savvy, seize, sense 6 attain, digest, embody, fatham, follow, uptake 7 contain, discern, embrace, enclose, imagine, include, involve, realize 8 comprise, comprize, conceive, conclude, perceive 9 apprehend 10 understand

comprehensible: 8 exoteric, included 9 comprised 11 conceivable 12 intelligible

comprehension: 5 grasp 6 noesis 7 epitome, knowing, summary 9 inclusion, intension 10 conception 11 connotation

comprehensive: big 4 full, wide 5 broad, grand, large 7 concise, generic 8 encyclic, spacious 9 expansive, extensive, panoramic 11 compendious

compress: nip, tie 4 bale, bind, firm, wrap 5 cling, cramp, crowd, crush, press 6 gather, shrink 7 abridge, bolster, compact, curtail, embrace, deflate, flatten, repress, squeeze 8 astringe, condense, contract, restrain 9 constrain, epitomize 11 consolidate

medical: 5 stupe 7 bandage, pledget

compressor: 4 pump 6 device 7 machine

comprise, comprize: 4 hold 5 cover, imply, seize 6 attach, confer, embody 7 compose, contain, embrace, enclose, include, involve 8 conceive, perceive 10 comprehend

comprised: 4 rapt 8 included 9 engrossed 14 comprehensible

compromise: 8 compound, endanger 9 surrender 10 concession

opposition to: 13 intransigence

compt: 4 neat 6 spruce 8 polished

comptroller: 7 auditor, officer 10 controller

compulsion: 4 need, urge 5 force 6 duress, stress 7 impulse 8 coaction, coercion 10 constraint

compulsory: 8 coercive, forcible 10 imperative, obligatory

compunction: 5 qualm 6 regret, sorrow 7 remorse, scruple 9 misgiving 10 conscience, contrition, repentance

compute: add, sum 4 cast, rate 5 count, tally 6 assess, figure, number, reckon 7 account 8 estimate 9 calculate, enumerate

comrade: pal 4 ally, chum, mate, peer 5 billy, buddy, crony 6 copain(F.), digger, fellow, frater, friend, hearty 7 brother 8 copemate 9 associate, companion

comte: 5 count

comtesse: 8 countess

con: rap 4 anti, know, lead, look, pore, read, scan 5 cheat, guide, knock, learn, steer, study 6 direct, peruse, regard, versus 7 against, deceive, examine, inspect, opposed, swindle 10 understand

conation: 4 will 7 conatus 8 tendency, volition 11 inclination

concatenate: 4 join, link 5 chain, unite 7 connect 8 catenate

concave: 4 void 6 arched, dished, hollow 7 vaulted 8 incurved 9 depressed

conceal: 4 bury, hide, mask, sile, veil 5 cache, cloak, couch, cover, feign 6 closet, emboss, pocket, screen, shroud 7 secrete 8 bescreen, disguise, ensconce, withhold 9 dissemble 10 camouflage

goods: 5 cache, eloin 6 eloign

concealed: 4 dern(sc.) 5 blind 6 covert, hidden, latent, occult, perdue, secret, veiled **7** covered, larvate **8** abstruse **9** blindfold, disguised, insidious, recondite, withdrawn **11** clandestine

concealing: 10 obvelation

concede: own **4** cede **5** admit, agree, allow, grant, waive, yette, yield **6** accord, assent **7** confess **9** surrender **10** condescend **11** acknowledge

conceit: ego **4** idea **5** fancy, pride **6** notion, vagary, vanity **7** caprice, egotism, tympany **9** arrogance, conundrum **10** conception

conceited: bug **4** fess, vain **5** chuff, cocky, flory, huggy, proud **6** clever **8** arrogant, dogmatic, priggish, snobbish **9** pragmatic, whimsical **11** coxcombical, egotistical, opinionated

conceive: 4 form, make, plan, ween **5** begin, brain, dream, fancy, frame, think **6** devise, ideate, ponder **7** imagine, realize, suppose, suspect **8** comprise, comprize, contrive **9** apprehend, formulate **10** comprehend, understand

concent: 9 harmonize **10** accordance **11** consistency

concentrate: aim, fix **4** mass, pile **5** coact, exalt, focus, unify **6** arrest, attend, center, gather **7** compact, essence, thicken **8** approach, assemble, condense, contract **9** intensify **10** centralize **11** consolidate **12** conglomerate

concept: 4 idea **5** fancy, image **7** opinion, thought **11** disposition

conception: ens **4** idea **5** fancy, fetus, image **6** belief, design, embryo **7** conceit, purpose **8** notation **9** beginning **10** cogitation, impression **12** apprehension **13** comprehension

concern: 4 bear, care, firm, reck, sake **5** apply, cause, event, grief, touch, worry **6** affair, affect, behold, charge, employ, matter, regard **7** anxiety, article, company, disturb, involve, pertain, respect, trouble **8** business, interest **9** implicate, rickmatic **10** solicitude **11** corporation, distinguish **12** apprehension

concerned: 6 intent **7** anxious, worried **8** bothered

concerning: by, of, on, re; for **4** in-re **5** about, anent **6** anenst **9** regarding

concert: 4 plan **5** unite **6** accord, devise **7** arrange, benefit, concent, concord, consort, consult, harmony, recital **9** agreement **11** performance **13** entertainment

concertina: 9 bandonion

concession: 4 boon **5** favor, grant, lease **6** assent, favour, gambit **7** cession **9** admission, privilege **10** compliance, compromise **12** acquiescence **13** condescension **15** acknowledgement

conch: 5 shell **6** cockle, mussel

conchie, conchy: 8 objector

concierge: 6 porter, warden **7** janitor **9** attendant **10** doorkeeper

conciliate: get **4** calm, ease **5** atone **6** adjust, pacify **7** acquire, appease, concile,

mollify, placate, satisfy **9** reconcile **10** propitiate

conciliatory: 4 mild **6** gentle, giving, irenic **7** lenient, pacific, winning **8** irenical, lenitive **9** forgiving **10** mollifying **12** propitiating

concilium: 7 council

concinnity: 7 harmony **8** elegance

concise: 4 curt, neat **5** brief, crisp, pithy, short, terse **7** compact, laconic, pointed, precise, serried **8** mutilate, pregnant, succinct **9** condensed **10** compedious, contracted **11** sententious **12** epigrammatic **13** comprehensive

concision: 6 schism **7** faction **8** division **10** mutilation

conclave: 6 closet **7** chamber, meeting **8** assembly

conclude: bar, end **4** rest **5** close, estop, infer, judge, limit **6** clinch, deduce, figure, finish, gather, reason, settle **7** achieve, arrange, confine, embrace, enclose, resolve, suppose **8** complete, dispatch, graduate, restrain **9** determine, speculate, terminate **10** comprehend

conclusion: end **4** amen, coda, last **5** finis **6** finale, finish, period, result, upshot **7** finding, outcome **8** epilogue, judgment **9** diagnosis, inference **10** conjecture, settlement **11** probability, termination

conclusive: 4 last **5** final, valid **6** cogent **7** certain, extreme, telling **8** decisive, definite, ultimate **10** convincing, peremptory **11** irrefutable **12** unanswerable **13** determinative

concoct: mix **4** brew, cook, plan, plot, vamp **5** frame, hatch **6** decoct, devise, digest, invent, refine, scheme **7** compose, perfect, prepare **8** compound, intrigue **9** fabricate **10** assimilate

concomitant: 9 accessory, associate, attendant, attending, companion, conjoined, cooperant **10** coincident, concurrent **11** synchronous **12** accompanying **13** accompaniment

concord: 4 part **5** agree, amity, peace, union, unity **6** treaty, unison **7** compact, concent, concert, harmony, oneness **8** covenant **9** agreement, communion, congruity **10** accordance, consonance

concordant: 8 unisonal **9** agreeable, congruous, consonant **10** harmonious **13** correspondent

concourse: 5 crowd, place, point **6** throng **7** company **8** assembly **9** affluence, frequency, gathering **10** assemblage, confluence **11** coincidence, concurrence, conjunction, cooperation

concredit: 6 commit **7** entrust, intrust

concrete: 4 clot, firm, hard. real **5** beton, solid, unite **6** actual **7** combine, congeal, special **8** coalesce, compound, tangible **9** concresce **10** particular

construction: **6** tremie **7** caisson

concretion: 4 clot, mess **5** pearl **6** nodule **8** calculus

concubine: 5 woman 7 adalisk 8 mistress 9 odalisque

concur: 4 jibe, join 5 agree, chime, unite 6 accede, accord, assent 7 approve, combine, consent 8 coincide, converge 9 acquiesce, cooperate 10 correspond

concurrence: 5 union 6 assent, bestow 7 consent, consort, meeting 8 adhesion 9 adherence, agreement, concourse 10 conspiracy 11 coincidence, conjunction

concurrent: 6 coeval, united 7 meeting 10 associated, coincident 11 concomitant, synchronous 12 accompanying

concuss: jar 4 jolt 5 clash, force, shake, shock 6 coerce 7 agitate

condemn: ban 4 damn, doom, file, fine 5 blame, decry, judge 6 amerce, attain, awreak, banish, detest 7 adjudge, censure, convict 8 denounce, reproach, sentence 10 confiscate, disapprove

condemnation: 4 doom 5 blame 7 censure, decrial 11 reprobation 13 animadversion 14 disapprobation

condense: cut 5 brief, unite 6 decoct, digest, harden, lessen, narrow, reduce, shrink 7 abridge, combine, compact, deflate, distill, shorten, thicken 8 compress, diminish, solidify 9 constrict, epitomize, evaporate, intensify 11 concentrate, consolidate

condensed: 4 curt 5 brief 7 compact, concise 8 absorbed 11 compendious

condenser: 4 cric 6 aludel

condescend: 5 deign, favor, grant, stoop 6 assent, oblige, submit 7 concede, descend 9 patronize, vouchsafe

condescension: 7 disdain 8 courtesy 10 affability, concession 12 compliasance

condign: due, fit 4 fair, just 6 severe, worthy 8 adequate, deserved, suitable 11 appropriate

condiment: rea 4 herb, kari, mace, sage, salt 5 caper, curry, sauce, spice, thyme 6 catsup, cloves, pepper, relish 7 chutney, cuminos, ketchup, mustard, paprika, vinegar 8 allspice, turmeric 9 appetizer, seasoning

condisciple: 7 student 12 schoolfellow

condite: 7 pickled 8 seasoned 9 preserved

condition: if 4 case, mode, rank, rote, term 5 angle, birth, cause, class, estre, facet, place, stage, state 6 estate, fettle, gentry, morale, plight, status 7 article, calling, premise, proviso, station 8 covenant, occasion, position 9 agreement, exception, provision, requisite, situation 10 limitation 11 predicament, stipulation 13 circumstances

critical: 9 emergency
favorable: 4 odds
suffix: ile

conditional: 9 qualified 10 accidental

conditioned: 6 finite 7 limited

condolence: 4 pity, ruth 7 empathy 8 sympathy 10 compassion 13 commiseration

condone: 5 blink, remit 6 acquit, excuse, forget, ignore, pardon 7 absolve, forgive 8 overlook

condor: 4 coin 6 tiffin 7 vulture 8 gymnogyp

conduce: aid 4 help, hire, lead, tend 5 bring, guide 6 confer, effect, engage 7 advance, conduct, further, redound 10 contribute

conduct: act, run 4 bear, deed, gest, lead, mien, rule, wage 5 carry, geste, guard, guide, usher 6 action, attend, behave, convey, convoy, demean, deport, direct, escort, govern, manage, squire 7 bearing, channel, comport, conduce, conduit, control, execute, officer, operate 8 behavior, carriage, chaplain, demeanor, guidance, regulate, transact 9 accompany, behaviour, demeanour, supervise 10 administer, deportment, governance, government, proceeding 11 comportment, countenance, superintend

scandalous: 9 esclandre(F.)

conductor: cad 4 gude 5 guard 6 convoy, copper, escort, leader 7 cathode, maestro 8 aqueduct, cicerone, conveyor, director, employee 10 bandleader, propagator 11 impressario

conduit: 4 duct, main, pipe, tube, wire 5 cable, canal, sewer 6 trough 7 channel, conduct, culvert, passage 8 aqueduct

cone: 4 chat 5 crack, solid, spire 6 bobbin, object 7 cluster, fissure, strobil 8 strobile 9 container

section: 8 parabola

cone-shaped: 5 conic 6 pineal 7 conical

conenose: 6 bedbug

confab: 4 chat, talk 6 powwow 7 prattle 10 conference 11 confabulate 12 conversation

confect: mix 4 form, make 6 pickle 7 prepare 8 preserve 9 construct

confection: 5 candy, dulce, sweet 6 bonbon, comfit, cimbal, dainty, nougat 7 caramel, confect, fondant, mixture, praline, succade 8 compound, delicacy, preserve, sherbert 9 confiture, marmalade, sweetmeat 10 concoction 11 bittersweet, compilation, composition, preparation

Confederacy: *general:* Lee 4 Brag 5 Price 6 Morgan

president: 5 Davis

vice-president: 8 Stephens

confederate: aid, pal, reb 4 ally 5 rebel, stall, unite 6 league 7 abetter, abettor, conjure, fedarie, federal, partner 8 conspire, federate 9 accessory, assistant, associate, auxiliary 10 accomplice

confederation: 4 body 5 union 6 league

7 compact, society 8 alliance, covenant 9 coalition 10 conspiracy, federation 11 association, confederacy

confer: dub 4 give, meet, talk 5 award, endow, grant, treat 6 advise, bestow, donate, impart, invest, parley 7 commune, compare, conduce, consult, counsel, discuss, instate, present 8 comprise, converge 10 contribute, deliberate

conference: 4 talk 5 snyod, trust 6 confab, huddle, parley, pow-wow 7 council, meeting, palaver 8 colloque, colloquy, congress 9 collation, comparing, discourse, interview 10 comparison, discussion 11 association 12 consultation, conversation

confess: own 4 avow, sing 5 admit, grant 6 attest, avouch, beknow, reveal, shrive 7 concede, divulge 8 disclose, discover, manifest 11 acknowledge

confession: 5 credo, creed 6 avowal, shrift, shrive 9 admission, communion, statement 10 profession

confetti: 4 tape 5 candy 7 bonbons 9 sweetmeat 10 confection

confidant: 8 intimate

confide: 4 affy, rely, tell 5 trust 6 commit, depend 7 believe, consign, entrust, intrust

confidence: 4 hope 5 bield, faith, trust 6 aplomb, belief, credit, mettle, morale, secret, spirit 7 courage 8 affiance, boldness, credence, reliance, sureness 9 assurance, certitude, hardihood, hardiness 10 effrontery 11 presumption 12 impertinence

game: 5 bunco, bunko 7 swindle

lack: 10 diffidence

confident: 4 bold, smug, sure 5 hardy, siker 6 crouse, secure, sicker 7 assured, certain, hopeful, reliant 8 constant, fearless, impudent, sanguine, trustful 9 dependent, undaunted 10 dogmatical 11 trustworthy 12 presumptuous

confidential: 5 bosom, privy 6 covert, secret 7 private, subrosa 8 esoteric, intimate 9 auricular 11 trustworthy

law: 9 fiduciary

configuration: 4 form 5 shape 6 figure 7 contour, outline 10 topography

confine: 4 bar, box, dam, hem, new, pen, pin, sty, tie 4 bind, cage, coop, hasp, jail, keep, lock, seal 5 bound, cramp, delay, impen, limit, pinch, stint 6 border, compas, corral, fetter, forbar, hamper, hurdle, immure, impale, intern, pinion, pocket, tether 7 astrict, impound 8 boundary, conclude, imprison, restrain, straiten 9 carcerate, constrain, restraint 11 incarcerate 12 circumscribe

confined: ill 4 pent 5 bound, caged 6 sealed 7 cramped, cribbed, limited 8 impended, interned 9 impounded 10 cloist-

ered 13 incommunicado

to select group: 8 esoteric

confinement: mew 8 clausure, firmance 9 captivity, restraint 10 childbirth, constraint, internment 11 contraction 12 accouchement, imprisonment

place of: mew, pen 4 brig, cage, coop, goal, jail, stir 5 limbo 6 asylum, corral, prison 7 dungeon 9 calaboose 12 penitentiary

confirm: fix, set 4 firm, seal 5 prove 6 affirm, assent, assure, attest, avouch, clinch, ratify, settle, verify 7 approve, comfort, endorse, fortify, sustain 8 accredit, convince, sanction, validate 9 approbate, establish 10 comprobate, strengthen 11 corroborate, countersign 12 adminiculate, authenticate, substantiate

confirmed: set 5 fixed 6 arrant, stable 7 chronic 8 habitual, ratified 9 fortified, initiated 10 encouraged, inveterate 11 established

confiscate: 4 grab 5 seize, usurp 7 condemn 9 sequester 11 appropriate

conflagration: 4 fire 5 blaze, fever 7 burning 10 combustion 12 inflammation

conflict: war 4 bout, duel, fray, rift 5 broil, brush, clash, fight, grips, mix-up 6 action, battle, combat, mutiny, oppose, strife 7 contend, contest, discord, warfare 8 disagree, militate, struggle 9 collision, encounter, rebellion 10 contention 11 competition

final: 10 Armageddon

conflicting: 7 adverse 10 contending 12 incompatible, inharmonious

confluence: 5 crowd 7 conflux, meeting 8 junction 9 concourse 12 assimilation

conform: go; fit 4 lean, obey, suit 5 adapt, agree, apply, yield 6 accede, adjust, assent, comply, settle, submit 7 compose 9 acquiesce, harmonize, reconcile 10 correspond 11 accommodate

conformity: 7 harmony 8 affinity, likeness, symmetry 9 agreement, congruity, obedience 10 accordance, compliance, similarity, submission 11 affirmative 12 complaisance 13 acquiescence

to law: 6 dharma 8 legality

confound: mix 4 blow, dash, maze, rout, stam, stun 5 abash, addle, amaze, spend, spoil, waste 6 baffle, dismay, muddle, rattle 7 astound, confuse, confute, corrupt, destroy, flummox, perplex, stupefy 8 astonish, bewilder, distract, surprise 9 discomfit, dumbfound, embarrass, frustrate, overthrow 10 disconcert 11 intermingle

confraternity: 4 body 5 union 7 society 11 brotherhood

confrere: 6 fellow 7 comrade 9 colleague

confront: 4 defy, face, meet 5 beard, brave 6 oppose, resist 7 affront, compare

8 envisage, threaten **9** challenge, encounter

confuse: mix **4** dash, daze, maze, muss, rout **5** abash, addle, amaze, befog, blend, cloud, snarl **6** baffle, bemuse, bother, burble, caddle, flurry, fuddle, jumble, muddle, puzzle, rattle **7** bedevil, blunder, derange, fluster, mystify, nonplus, perplex, stupefy **8** befuddle, bewilder, confound, distract **9** barbulyie, discomfit, dumbfound, obfuscate **10** demoralize, disarrange, discompose, disconcert

confused: **4** asea, lost **5** foggy, muddy, vague **6** doiled, doited **7** chaotic, obscure **8** deranged **9** chagrined **10** bewildered, hurly-burly, topsy-turvy, tumultuous **13** helter-skelter

confusion: din **4** coil, dust, fuss, harl, mess, moil, riot **5** babel, chaos, chevy, chivy, deray, mix-up, snafu, snarl, strow **6** babble, bedlam, caddle, chivvy, habble, hubbub, huddle, jabble, jumble, muddle, pother, rabble, rumpus, tophet, tumult, uproar, welter **7** farrage, blunder, bluster, clutter, farrage, flutter, garboil, topheth, turmoil, widdrim **8** disarray, disorder **9** agitation, commotion **10** hullabaloo, hurly-burly **11** disturbance, trepidation **12** hugger-mugger, perturbation **13** embarrassment

confute: **4** deny **5** rebut **6** expose, refute **7** silence **8** confound, convince, disprove, infringe, overcome **9** overwhelm

conge: bow **6** curtsy **7** license, molding **8** farewell, passport **9** clearance, dismissal **10** permission **11** leavetaking

congeal: gel, ice, set **4** geal, jell **5** candy **6** cotter, curdle, freeze, harden **7** stiffen, thicken **8** concrete, solidify **9** coagulate **11** crystallize

congealing agent: **6** pectin **8** gelatine

congee: **5** gruel **9** departure

congenial: **4** boon **5** natal **6** native **7** connate, kindred **10** compatible **11** sympathetic

conger: eel **8** cucumber

congestion: jam **4** heap **8** crowding, stoppage **9** gathering **12** accumulation

conglaciate: **6** freeze **7** congeal

conglomerate: **4** heap, mass, pile, rock **5** stack **9** clustered **10** assemblage **11** agglomerate **12** concentrated

Congo: *tribe:* **4** Susa **6** Wabuma **7** Bangala

tributary: **6** Ubangi **7** Aruwima

congratulate: **4** laud **5** greet **6** salute **8** macarize **10** compliment, felicitate

congregate: **4** herd, mass, meet, teem **5** group, swarm, troop **6** gather, muster **7** collect, convene **8** assemble

congregation: **4** body, fold, host, mass **5** flock, swarm **6** church, parish **7** meeting, synaxes **8** assembly, brethren **9** gathering **10** collection **11** convocation

congress: **4** dail, diet **5** synod **7** council,

meeting **8** assembly, conclave **10** conference, convention, parliament **11** convocation, legislature

Congress: *building:* **7** Capitol
upper house: **6** Senate

congressman: **14** representative

congruity: **6** accord **7** concord, fitness, harmony **8** symmetry **9** agreement, coherence **10** conformity, consonance **11** composition, consistency, correctness, suitability **13** compatability **14** correspondence

conical: **8** tapering

conifer: fir, yew **4** pine, tree **5** cedar, larch **6** spruce **7** pinacle, pinales

conjecture: aim **4** plot, shot, view **5** augur, ettle, fancy, guess, opine **6** belief, divine, theory **7** imagine, opinion, presume, suppose, surmise, suspect **9** inference, speculate, suspicion **10** conclusion, estimation **11** contrivance, supposition

conjoined: **6** joined, linked **8** conjunct, touching **11** concomitant

conjoint: **8** combined **9** conjoined **10** associated **11** correlative **12** simultaneous

conjugal: **9** connubial **11** matrimonial

conjugate: **5** yoked **6** joined, united **7** coupled

conjunction: as, et, if, or: and, but, nor, tie **4** than **5** joint, since, union **7** coition, consort, **9** coalition, concourse **10** connection **11** association, combination, composition, concurrence

conjuration: art **5** charm, magic, spell **6** voodoo **10** necromancy **11** incantation, legerdemain

conjure: **4** pray **5** charm, halse **6** adjure, invent, invoke **7** beseech, combine, entreat, imagine **8** conspire, contrive, exorcise, exorcize **10** supplicate **11** confederate

conjuror: **4** mage, sear **6** pellar, shaman, wizard **7** juggler, warlock **8** magician, sorcerer **9** coswearer, enchanter **15** prestidigatator

conk: **4** fail, head, nose **5** faint, knock, stall

Conlaech: *father:* **10** Cuchulainn
mother: **5** Aoife

connach: **5** spoil, waste

Connacht king: **6** Ailill

connate: **4** akin, born **5** fused **6** allied, inborn, innate **7** cognate **9** congenial **10** congenital

connect: tie **4** ally, bind, glue, join, knit, link **5** affix, chain, marry, unite **6** attach, bridge, cement, cohere, connex, couple, fasten, relate **7** combine **8** continue **9** affiliate, associate, correlate, interlock **11** communicate

Connecticut: *city:* **4** Avon **6** Bethel, Darien **7** Meriden **8** Hartford(c.)
river: **10** Housatonic

connection: tie **4** bond, link **5** nexus, union **6** family **7** contact, kinship **8** affinity, alliance, commerce, intimacy, junction, relative, syndetic **9** coherence, reference, relevance **10** continuity **11** association, conjunction, intercourse **12** articulation, relationship **13** communication

connective: **8** syndetic **11** conjunction

connive: **4** abet, plot, wink **5** blink, cabal **6** assent, foment, incite **7** collude **8** intrigue, overlook

connoisseur: **5** judge **6** critic, experl **7** epicure, gormand, gourmet **9** collector **11** cognoscente

connotation: **6** intent **7** meaning **10** denotation **13** comprehension, signification

connote: **5** imply **8** indicate

connubial: **7** marital **8** conjugal, domestic **11** matrimonial

conquer: get, win **4** beat, best, down, gain, lick, rout, tame **5** crush, daunt **6** defeat, evince, humble, master, reduce, subdue, victor **7** acquire, prevail, subject, triumph **8** overcome, surmount, vanquish **9** checkmate, discomfit, overpower, overthrow, overwhelm, subjugate

conqueror: **4** hero **6** victor, winner **12** conquistador

conquest: **7** mastery, triumph, victory **8** invasion

consanguineous: **4** akin **7** kindred, related

consanguinity: **5** blood, nasab **7** kinship **8** affinity **12** relationship

conscience: **5** sense **7** scruple, thought **9** casuistry **10** compunction

conscientious: **4** fair, just **5** exact, rigid **6** honest, strict **7** dutiful, upright **8** faithful **9** honorable **10** scrupulous **11** punctilious

conscious: **4** keen **5** alive, awake, aware **7** feeling, knowing **8** rational, sensible, sentient **9** attentive, cognizant, concerned **10** perceptive **12** apprehensive

consciousness: **9** awareness

conscript: **5** draft, enrol **6** enlist, muster **7** recruit

consecrate: vow **4** fain, seal **5** bless, deify, devot **6** anoint, hallow, ordain **8** sanctify, dedicate **10** inaugurate **11** apotheosize

consecrated: **5** blest **6** oblate, sacred, votive **8** hallowed

consent: **5** agree, allow, grant, yield **6** accede, accord, assent, beteem, comply, permit **7** approve **9** recognize **10** permission **11** concurrence **12** acquiescence

consequence: end **4** bore **5** event, fruit, issue, worth **6** effect, import, moment, repute, result, sequel, weight **7** concern, outcome **8** aftering, interest, occasion **9** aftermath, emanation, inference **10** importance **11** consecution **13** consideration

consequently: so **4** ergo, then, thus **5** hence, later **8** pursuant **9** therefore **11**
accordingly **12** subsequently **13** consecutively

conservative: **4** safe, Tory **5** staid **6** stable **7** diehard **8** burgeois, moderate **11** reactionary **12** preservative

conservatory: **6** school **7** academy **10** glasshouse, greenhouse

conserve: can, jam **4** save **5** guard, jelly **6** defend, secure, shield, uphold **7** husband, protect, sustain **8** maintain, preserve **9** sweetmeat

consider: see **4** deem, heed, mull, muse, rate **5** ettle, judge, study, think, weigh **6** behold, debate, expend, impute, ponder, reason, reckon, regard **7** account, believe, canvass, examine, inspect, reflect, suppose **8** cogitate, estimate, meditate, ruminate **9** calculate, entertain, speculate **10** adjudicate, deliberate **11** contemplate

considerable: **5** geyan(Sc.), large, smart, smert **7** notable, several **9** capacious, important **10** cognizable, noteworthy, remarkable **11** perceptible, significant

considerate: **4** kind, mild **6** gentle **7** careful, heedful, prudent, serious **8** delicate **9** observant, regardful **10** deliberate, reflective, respectful, thoughtful

consideration: **4** sake **5** price, topic **6** aspect, esteem, motive, notice, reason, regard **7** respect, thought **9** attention, deference, incentive, influence **10** importance, inducement, recompense, reputation **11** consequence

considering: if **5** since

consign: **4** doom, give, mail, send, ship **5** allot, award, dight, remit, shift, yield **6** assign, commit, devote, remand, resign **7** address, confide, deliver, deposit, entrust, intrust **8** delegate, relegate, transfer **9** recommend **10** commission

consignee: **5** agent **8** receiver

consist: lie **4** hold **5** exist, stand **6** inhere, reside **7** contain, embrace **8** comprise **9** harmonize

consistency: **4** body **5** union **6** degree **7** concord, harmony **8** firmness, solidity, symmetry **9** adherence, coherence, congruity **10** consonance, uniformity **11** composition, persistency **14** correspondence, substantiality

consistent: **4** firm **7** durable, logical, uniform **8** coherent, enduring, suitable **9** accordant, congruous, consonant **10** changeless, compatible, persisting

consociate: **9** associate **11** confederate

consolation: sop **4** fine **6** relief, solace **7** comfort **10** booby prize

console: **4** calm **5** allay, ancon, cheer, organ, table **6** solace, soothe **7** bracket, cabinet, comfort, relieve, support, sustain **9** alleviate, encourage

consolidate: mix **4** knit, mass, pool, weld **5** blend, merge, unify, unite **6** harden, mingle **7** combine, compact **8** coalesce,

compress, condense, organize, solidify
10 amalgamate, strengthen 11 concentrate

consomme: 4 soup

consonance: 6 accord 7 harmony 9 resonance

consonant: 5 linis 6 dental, fortis, letter, sonant 7 palatal, spirant, unified 8 harmonic, suitable 9 accordant, agreeable, congruous 10 coincident, compatible, concordant, consistent, harmonious
pert. to: 7 palatal 9 bricative
smooth: 4 lene 5 lenis
voiceless: 4 lene, surd 6 atonic 7 spirate

consort: cot 4 aide, ally, join, mate, wife 5 group, unite 6 accord, attend, escort, mingle, spouse 7 company, concert, husband, partner 8 accustom, assembly 9 accompany, associate, colleague, companion, forgather 10 foregather 11 association, combination, concurrence, conjunction

conspectus: 4 list 6 survey 7 outline 8 synopsis 11 abridgement

conspicuous: 5 clear, famed, plain 6 extant, famous, marked, patent, signal 7 eminent, glaring, notable, obvious, pointed, salient, visible 8 apparent, manifest, striking 9 prominent 10 celebrated, egregrious, noticeable 11 discernable, distinctive, illustrious, outstanding, perspicuous 13 distinguished

conspiracy: 4 coup, plan, plot, ring 5 cabal, junto 6 scheme 7 compace 8 intrigue 9 agreement, champerty 11 combination, concurrence, confederacy, machination

conspire: 4 abet, plot 5 unite 6 league, scheme 7 collude, complot, conjure 8 contrive 9 cooperate 11 confederate

constable: cop 4 bull 6 beadle, harman, keeper, warden 7 bailiff, officer 8 tipstaff 9 policeman

constancy: 4 zeal 5 ardor 6 fealty 7 loyalty 8 devotion, fidelity 9 adherence, diligence, eagerness, integrity, stability 10 allegiance, attachment 11 earnestness 13 perserverance

constant: set 4 even, firm, leal, true 5 fixed, loyal, solid, still, tried 6 stable, steady 7 certain, chronic, durable, forever, lasting, regular, staunch, uniform 8 enduring, faithful, positive, resolute 9 confident, continual, immovable, incessant, permanent, perpetual, steadfast, unvarying 10 invariable, persistent, unwavering

Constantine's birthplace: 4 Nish

Constantinople: *foreign quarter:* 4 Pera
patriarch: 9 Nestorius

constate: 6 assert 9 establish

constellation (see also **star**): 5 group 6 dipper 7 cluster, pattern 10 assemblage 13 configuration
archer: 11 Sagittarius
Argo division: 4 Vela
balance: 5 Libra

bear: 4 Ursa
bird of paradise: 5 Apus
bull: 6 Taurus
crane: 4 Grus
cross: 4 Cruz
dipper: 4 Ursa
dog: 5 Canis
dragon: 5 Draco
eagle: 6 Aquila
fish: 6 Pisces
goat: 9 Capricorn
herdsman: 6 Bootes
hunter: 5 Orion
lion: Leo
lyre: 4 Lyra
maiden: 5 Virgo
northern: Leo 4 Coma, Lynx, Lyra, Ursa 5 Aries, Canes, Draco 6 Aquila, Auriga, Bootes, Cancer, Cygnus, Gemini, Taurus 7 Cepheus, Lacerta, Pegasus, Sagitta 8 Hercules 9 Andromeda, Delphinus, Vulpecula 10 Cassiopeia
peacock: 4 Pavo
ram: 5 Aries
sails: 4 Vela
southern: Ara 4 Apus, Argo, Crux, Grus, Pavo, Vela 5 Canis, Cetus, Hydra, Indus, Lepus, Libra, Mensa, Musca, Norma, Virgo 6 Antlia, Carina, Corvus, Crater, Dorado, Fornax, Pictor, Piscis, Puppis, Tucana, Volans 7 Columba, Phoenix, Sextans 8 Aquarius, Circinus, Sculptor, Scorpius 9 Centaurus, Chameleon, Monoceros, Reticulum 10 Horologium 11 Capricornus, Sagittarius 12 Microscopium
swan: 6 Cygnus
twins: 6 Gemini
water bearer: 8 Aquarius
whale: 5 Cetus
winged horse: 7 Pegasus

consternation: 4 fear 5 alarm, panic 6 dismay, fright, horror, terror 9 amazement, trepidity 11 trepidation 12 befuddlement

constituent: 4 item, part 5 piece, voter 6 detail, factor, matter, member 7 elector, element 9 component 10 ingredient

constitute: fix, set 4 form, make 5 enact, forge, found, shape 6 depute, graith, ordain 7 appoint, compose, station 8 compound, comprise 9 determine, establish 10 commission

constitution: law 4 code 5 being, canon, humor, state 6 custom, health, nature, temper 7 charter 8 physique 9 enactment, ordinance, structure 11 composition, disposition 12 organization

Constitution State: 11 Connecticut

constitutional: 4 walk 6 innate 8 exercise 9 essential, organical 10 congenital

constrain: 4 bend, bind, curb, fain, urge 5 chain, check, clasp, cramp, deter, drive, force, impel, limit, press 6 coerce, compel, oblige, ravish, secure 7 astrict, confine, enforce, oppress, repress, violate 8 compress, distress, restrain **9** constrict **10** constringe **11** necessitate

constraint: **4** bond **5** force **6** duress, stress **7** reserve **8** coercion, distress, pressure **9** captivity, restraint, stiffness **10** compulsion, obligation **11** compression, confinement

constrict: tie **4** bind, curb, grip **5** choke, cramp, limit **6** hamper, shrink, strait **7** astrict, deflate, squeeze, tighten **8** astringe, compress, condense, contract, restrict **9** constrain **10** constipate, constringe

breath: **8** strangle

constringe: See **constrict**.

construct: **4** form, make, rear **5** build, dight, erect, frame, model **6** devise **7** arrange, combine, compose, confect, fashion **8** construe, engineer **9** fabricate, originate

construction: **7** synesis **8** building

constructive: **7** helpful **8** creative, implicit, inferred

construe: **5** infer, parse **6** render **7** analyze, dissect, explain, expound, resolve **9** construct, interpret, translate

consuetude: use **4** wont **5** habit, usage **6** custom **8** practice

consul's recognition: **9** exequatur

consultant: **6** expert **7** adviser

consultation: **6** advice **7** council, counsel **9** collation, interview **10** conference, discussion **12** deliberation

consume: eat, use **4** burn, fret, rust, wear **5** drink, raven, spend, waste **6** absorb, absume, bezzle, canker, devour, engage, expend, perish **7** corrode, destroy, dwindle, engross, exhaust, swallow **8** squander **9** dissipate **10** incinerate, monopolize

consumer: **4** usee, user

consummate: end **4** fine, full, ripe **5** ideal, sheer **6** arrant, effect, finish **7** achieve, consume, crowned, perfect, perform **8** absolute, complete **9** culminate, exquisite **10** accomplish

consumption: use **5** decay, waste **7** expense **8** phthisis **11** destruction, expenditure **12** tuberculosis

contact: **4** abut, join, meet **5** touch, union **6** arrive, impact, syzygy **7** meeting **8** junction, tangency, touching **10** connection, contiguity **11** contingency **13** juxtaposition

contagion: pox **5** taint, virus **6** miasma, poison **9** infection **13** contamination

contagious: **7** noxious **8** catching **9** pestilent, spreading **10** infectuous

contain: **4** have, hold, keep **5** carry, check, cover, house **6** embody, retain **7** embrace, enclose, include, subsume, sustain **8** comprise, restrain **10** comprehend

container: bag, bin, box, can, cup, jug, keg, pan, pod, pot, tin, tub, urn, vat **4** cage, case, cask, crib, ewer, sack, silo, tank, vase **5** crate, cruet, gourd, pouch **6** barrel, basket, bottle, carboy, carton, hamper, hatbox, holder, shaker **7** band-

box, capsule, hanaper **8** canister, decanter, demijohn, hogshead, puncheon **10** receptacle

containing: For all phrases beginning with this word, see under the main word or phrase. EXAMPLES: "containing gold": see **gold** *containing;* "containing air": see **air** *containing.*

contaminate: **4** foul, harm, slur, soil **5** stain, sully, taint **6** befoul, debase, defile, infect, injure, poison **7** corrupt, debauch, pollute, tarnish, vitiate **8** dishonor **9** desecrate **10** adulterate

conte: **4** tale **9** narrative, novelette

contemn: **5** flout, hate, scorn, spurn **6** reject, slight **7** despise, disdain **8** contempt

contemplate: **4** muse, plan, scan, view **5** deign, study, think, weigh **6** ponder, regard, survey **7** propose, reflect **8** consider, meditate **9** speculate

contemplation: **5** study **6** musing, prayer, regard, theory **7** request **8** petition **9** intention **10** meditation **13** consideration

contemporaneous: **6** coeval, living, modern **7** current **8** existing, up-to-date **10** coincident **12** contemporary, simultaneous

contempt: **5** scorn, shame, sneer **6** slight **7** contemn, disdain, mockery **8** derision, disgrace **9** contumacy, contumely **10** disrespect **11** indignation

contemptible: low **4** base, mean, vile **5** cheap, petty, sorry **6** abject, paltry, scurvy, shabby, sordid, yellow **7** pitiful, scorned **8** beggarly, infamous, inferior, sneaking, unworthy, wretched **9** groveling, worthless **10** despicable **11** ignominious **12** dishonorable **13** insignificant

contemptuous: **7** haughty **8** arrogant, flouting, insolent, scornful **9** hubristic, insulting **10** despicable, disdainful **12** contemptible, supercilious

contend: vie, war **4** cope, race, wage **5** argue, bandy, brawl, claim, fight **6** assert, battle, bicker, buffet, bustle, combat, debate, oppose, reason, strive **7** bargain, compete, contest, dispute, quarrel **8** conflict, contrive, maintain, militate, squabble, struggle

contender: **7** entrant **10** contestant **11** protagonist

content: **4** calm, ease, gist, paid **5** happy **6** amount, please **7** appease, gratify, replete, satiate, satisfy, suffice, willing **8** capacity **9** satisfied **12** satisfaction

contented: **4** cozy **5** sated **8** cheerful **9** satisfied

contention: war **4** bait, bate, feud, riot, tiff **5** broil **6** combat, debate, strife **7** contest, discord, dispute, opinion, quarrel, rivalry, wrangle **8** argument, conflict, squabble, struggle, variance **9** rebellion **10** dissension, litigation **11** altercation, competition, controversy **12** disagreement

contentious: 7 peevish 8 perverse 9 litigious, wrangling 10 pugnacious 11 belligerent, quarrelsome 12 cantankerous, disputatious

contentment: 4 ease 5 bliss 8 pleasure 9 happiness 11 complacence 12 satisfaction 13 gratification

conterminous: 4 next 8 adjacent, proximal 9 adjoining

contest: bee, sue, try, vie 4 agon, bout, cope, duel, feud, fray, game, pitt, race, spar, tiff, tilt 5 broil, clash, fight, setto, trial 6 action, adjure, affray, battle, combat, debate, defend, oppose, resist, strife, strive 7 bargain, brabble, compete, contend, dispute, protest, tourney, warfare 8 argument, conflict, skirmish, struggle 9 champerty, encounter 10 controvert, tournament 11 altercation

kind of: 6 tryout 7 lawsuit 10 litigation

contestant: 4 vier 5 rival 6 player 7 agonist, entrant 8 finalist, prospect 9 combatant, candidate, contender, defendant, plaintiff 10 competitor 12 participator

contiguous: 4 next, nigh 6 nearby 8 abutting, adjacent, touching 9 adjoining, immediate, proximate 10 contacting 11 neighboring

continent: 4 Asia, land, mass 5 sober 6 Africa, chaste, Europe 7 content 8 capacity, mainland, moderate 9 Greenland, temperate 10 Antarctica, receptacle, restrained 12 South America

lost: 8 Atlantis

contingency: 4 case 5 event 6 chance 7 adjunct, contact 8 fortuity, incident, prospect 9 accessory 11 possibility, uncertainty

contingent: 6 casual, chance 8 doubtful, touching 9 dependent 10 accidental, fortuitous 11 provisional

continual: 7 endless, lasting, regular, undying, uniform 8 constant, enduring, unbroken 9 ceaseless, connected, incessant, perennial, permanent, unceasing 10 continuous, invariable 11 everlasting, unremitting 12 imperishable 13 unintermitted, uninterrupted

continually: aye 4 ever 6 always, hourly, steady 7 endless, eternal, forever 9 perpetual 10 constantly 11 incessantly, unceasingly

continuance: 4 stay 5 delay 6 sequel 8 duration 9 endurance, procedure 10 continuity 11 adjournment 12 postponement 13 perserverance

continue: be 4 bide, dure, last, live, stay 5 abide, carry, exist, unite 6 beleve, endure, extend, remain, resume 7 beleave, connect, persist, proceed, prolong, sustain 8 protract 9 persevere

continued: 5 still 6 serial 7 chronic 8 constant 9 continual, extending 10 continuous, protracted

continuity: 6 script 8 cohesion, scenario 9 coherence 10 connection

contort: wry 4 bend, coil, turn, warp 5 gnarl, screw, twist, wrest 6 deform, writhe 7 distort, pervert 8 obvolute 9 convolute

contortionist: 7 acrobat

contour: 4 form, line 5 curve, graph, shape 6 figure 7 outline, profile 9 lineament 10 appearance, silhouette 13 configuration

outline: 13 configuration

contra: 6 offset 7 against, counter, opposed 11 contrasting 12 contrariwise

contraband: 5 goods 7 illegal, illicit 8 smuggled, unlawful

contract: get 4 bond, knit, pact 5 catch, cramp, incur, lease, limit 6 cartel, engage, lessen, narrow, pledge, pucker, reduce, shrink, treaty 7 abridge, bargain, compact, crumple, curtail, promise, shorten, shrivel, wrinkle 8 condense, covenant, restrict 9 agreement, betrothal, constrict, indenture 10 abbreviate, constringe, convention, obligation 11 arrangement, concentrate, stipulation

unlawful: 10 chevisance

contraction: tic 5 cramp, spasm 6 intake, twitch 7 elision, epitome 9 gathering, reduction, shrinkage, stricture 10 abridgment, compendium, limitation 11 conciseness, confinement 12 abbreviation

common: een, eer, o'er oft, tis 5 aren't shant

heart: 8 systolic

contractor: 7 builder, remover 8 supplier

contradict: 4 deny 5 belie, rebut 6 forbid, impugn, negate, oppose, recant, refute 7 counter, gainsay 8 disprove 9 disaffirm 10 contravene, controvert

contradiction: 6 denial 7 paradox 8 antilogy

contradictory: 6 oppose 9 dissonant 12 incompatible, inconsistent

contraption: rig 4 tool 6 device, gadget 7 machine 11 contrivance

contrary: 5 snivy 6 averse, contra, ornery, snivey 7 adverse, counter, hostile, opposed, reverse, wayward 8 captious, contrair, inimical, opposite, perverse, petulant 9 refactory, repugnant, unpopular, vexatious 10 discordant, discrepant 11 prejudicial, unfavorable 12 antagonistic, cantankerous

to law: 7 illegal 16 unconstitutional

contrast: 6 strife 7 compare, contend 8 opposite 9 diversity 10 difference

contravene: 4 defy, deny 6 hinder, oppose, thwart 7 dispute, violate 8 infringe, obstruct 9 disregard 10 contradict

contravention: sin 4 vice 5 crime 6 breach 7 offense 9 violation 13 contradiction, transgression

contretemps: 4 slip 5 boner, hitch 6

mishap, scrape **8** accident **9** mischance **10** occurrence

contribute: aid **4** ante, give, help, tend **5** cause, grout **6** assist, bestow, concur, confer, donate, supply, tender **7** conduce, further **9** cooperate, subscribe

contribution: sum, tax **4** alms, boon, gift **5** essay, share **6** impost **7** article, largers, payment, present, renewal, writing **8** donation, offering **9** collation **10** imposition

contrite: **4** worn **5** sorry **6** humble, rueful **8** penitent **9** repentant, sorrowful

contrivance: art, gin **4** gear, plan, tool **5** shift **6** deceit, design, device, gadget, scheme **7** fiction, machine, project **8** adaption, artifice, resource **9** apparatus, appliance, doohickey, invention **10** conjecture, instrument **11** contraption

contrive: **4** brew, make, plan, plot **5** frame, fudge, hatch, weave **6** afford, design, devise, divine, invent, manage, scheme, wangle **7** achieve, agitate, concoct, consult, contend, fashion, procure, project **8** conspire, engineer, intrigue **9** fabricate, machinate **10** accomplish

contriver: **8** Daedalus **9** architect **10** originator

control: law, run **4** curb, hold, rein, rule, sway **5** charm, check, grasp, gripe, guide, power, skill, steer **6** bridle, direct, empire, govern, handle, manage, regime, subdue **7** command, conduct, mastery, preside **8** attemper, dominate, dominion, hegemony, regulate, restrain **9** influence, ordinance, prescribe **10** ascendancy, manipulate, moderation, possession, regulation **11** predominate, superintend

controversial: **7** eristic **9** debatable, polemical **12** disputatious **13** argumentative

controversy: **4** spat, suit **5** chest **6** debate, strife **7** dispute, quarrel, wrangle **8** argument **10** contention, difference, difficulty, discussion, litigation **11** altercation **12** disagreement

controvert: **4** deny, face, moot **5** argue **6** debate, oppose, oppugn, refute **7** contest, dispute, gainsay **9** challenge **10** contradict

contumacious: **6** unruly **7** riotous **8** insolent, mutinous, perverse, stubborn **9** obstinate, seditious **10** disdainful, headstrong, rebellious, refractory, unyielding **11** disobedient, intractable **13** insubordinate

contumely: **5** abuse, scorn **6** contek, insult **7** conteck, disdain **8** contempt, rudeness **9** arrogance **10** opprobrium **11** humiliation

contuse: **4** beat **5** pound **6** bruise, injure **7** squeeze

conundrum: pun **4** whim **6** enigma, puzzle, riddle **7** conceit **8** crotchet

convalesce: **4** mend **7** recover **10** recuperate

convene: sit **4** call, meet **5** unite **6** gather, muster, summon **7** convoke **8** assemble, converge **10** congregate, foregather

convenient: fit **5** handy, ready **6** proper, useful **7** adapted, helpful **8** becoming, suitable **9** agreeable, available, congruous, favorable, opportune **10** accessible, commodious **11** appropriate **12** commensurate

convent: **5** abbey **6** priory **7** convent, meeting **8** cloister **9** community, monastery, sanctuary

head: **5** abbot **6** abbess **8** hegumene **10** hegumeness

member: nun **4** monk **8** cenobite

pert. to: **6** friary

reception room: **8** arlatory

room: **9** parlatory

superior: see *head* above

convention: **4** diet, feis, mise, rule **5** synod, usage **6** cartel, caucus, custom, treaty **7** decorum, meeting **8** assembly, congress, contract, covenant, practice **9** agreement, gathering, tradition **10** conference **11** convocation

conventional: **4** more **5** nomic, right, trite, usual **6** decent, formal, modish, proper **7** correct, regular **8** academic, accepted **9** customary, hidebound **10** ceremonial, stipulated **11** contractual

conventionalize: **7** conform, stylize

converge: **4** join, meet **5** focus **6** concur **8** approach

conversant: **5** adept **6** busied, expert, versed **7** skilled **8** familiar, occupied **9** concerned, practiced **10** acquainted, proficient

conversation: **4** chat, talk **6** confab, parley **7** conduct, palaver **8** behavior, chitchat, colloquy, dialogue, parlance **9** discourse **10** conference **11** association, interchange, intercourse **13** communication **15** interlocution

of three: **7** trialog **9** trialogue

private: **7** ceilidh(Sc.) **8** collogue **9** tete-a-tete

converse: **4** chat, chin, live, move, talk **5** dwell, speak **6** confer, homily, parley **7** commune, obverse, reverse **8** colloque, exchange, opposite **9** discourse **11** association, confabulate

convert: **4** turn **5** alter, amend, apply, renew **6** change, decode, direct, novice **7** restore, reverse **8** converse, neophyte, persuade **9** acetalize, proselyte, transform, translate, transmute, transpose **10** regenerate

convertible: **4** auto **7** soft-top **10** automobile, changeable, equivalent, reciprocal, synonymous **15** interchangeable

convex: **5** bowed **6** arched, camber, curved **7** bulging, gibbous, rounded **9** cymbiform **11** protuberant

convey: **4** bear, cart, cede, deed, lead,

mean, pass, send, take, tote, will **5** bring,
carry, grant, guide, hurry, steal **6** assign,
convoy, delate, demise, devise, eloign,
impart, import, remove **7** auction, conduct, deliver, dispone, dispose **8** alienate,
bequeath, transfer, transmit **9** accompany, transport **11** communicate

conveyance: bus, car, sak **4** auto, cart,
deed, sled, taxi, tram **5** grant, stage, theft,
train, wagon **6** demise **7** charter, conduct,
rattler, trailer, trolley, vecture, vehicle,
waftage **8** carriage, carrying, stealing,
transfer **9** transport **10** automobile **11**
transmittal

public: el; bus, cab, car **4** taxi, tram **5** train
6 subway **7** omnibus, ricksha, steamer **8**
airplane, elevated, railroad, rickshaw **10**
jinricksha, jinrikisha

convict: **4** find **5** argue, felon, lifer, prove
6 attain, termer, trusty **7** attaint, captive,
condemn, culprit **8** criminal, jailbird,
prisoner, sentence **10** malefactor

conviction: **5** creed, dogma, faith, tenet **6**
belief, credit **7** opinion **8** sentence

convinced: **4** sold, sure **6** assure, subdue
7 certain **8** overcome, positive **9** persuaded

convincing: **5** sound, valid **6** cogent, potent **7** telling **8** forcible **10** conclusive,
persuasive

convivial: gay **4** boon **6** festal, genial,
jovial, social **7** festive, jocular **8** reveling

convocation: **4** diet **5** synod **7** calling,
council, meeting **8** assembly, congress **9**
gathering **10** convention **12** congregation

consult: ask **5** cabal, refer **6** advise, confer, decree, devise **7** concert, counsel,
discuss, meeting **8** consider, contrive, decision **9** agreement, determine **10** deliberate

convoke: bid **4** call, cite, meet **6** gather,
muster, summon **7** convene **8** assemble

convolute: **4** coil, roll, wind **5** twist **6** tangle, writhe **7** contort **8** obvolute

convolution: **4** coil, curl, fold **5** gyrus,
whorl **9** sinuosity

convolve: **5** twist **6** enwrap, enfold, infold,
writhe

convoy: **4** lead **5** carry, guard, guide, pilot,
watch **6** attend, convey, escort, manage **7**
conduct **9** accompany, conductor, safeguard

convulse: **4** rock, stir **5** shake **6** excite **7**
agitate, disturb

convulsion: fit **5** shrug, spasm, throe **6**
attack, tumult, uproar **8** laughter, paroxysm **9** agitation, commotion **11** disturbance

cony: das **4** hare, pika **5** daman, dassy,
ganam, hutia, hyrox, lapen **6** burbot, das-
sie, gazabo, gazebo, rabbit **7** ashkoko
catcher: **5** cheat **7** sharper **8** swindler

coo: **4** curr(Sc.), woot **6** murmur

coof: **4** dolt, lout **9** blockhead

cook: fix, fry **4** bake, boil, chef, make, sear,
stew **5** broil, grill, poach, roast, shirr,
steam **6** braise, decoct, sautee, seethe,
simmer **7** prepare, process, servant **8**
cusinero, magirist **9** cuisinier
partially: **7** parboil

cooked: **4** done

cookery: **7** cuisine, science **8** magirics

cookie, cooky: **4** cake, snap **6** hermit **7**
brownie, oatcake **8** seedcake **10** confection, gingersnap

cooking: *device:* **4** etna **5** range, stove **7**
brazier, griddle **10** rotisserie

vessel: pan, pot **4** etna, olla **6** caster,
chafer, spider, tureen **7** broiler, griddle,
roaster, skillet, steamer **8** colander, flesh-
pot **9** autoclave

cool: air, fan, ice **4** calm, cold **5** algid, allay,
chill, fresh, gelid, nervy, sober, staid,
whole **6** chilly, placid, quench, sedate,
serene **7** unmoved **8** careless, cautious,
composed, mitigate, moderate, tranquil **9**
apathetic, collected, officious, temperate,
unruffled **10** deliberate, nonchalant, unfriendly **11** indifferent, refrigerate, unconcerned **12** unresponsive **13** dispassionate, imperturbable **15** undemonstrative

cooled: **6** frappe

cooler: **4** icer, jail, olla **5** drink **6** icebox,
lockup, prison **11** refrigerant **12** refrigerator

coolie: **7** changar

cooling device: fan **7** freezer **12** refrigerator **14** air-conditioner

coolness: **5** nerve **6** aplomb **8** serenity **9**
assurance

coom, coomb: **4** smut, soot **5** frame,
grime **6** grease, refuse

coony: sly **4** cute, foxy **6** clever, crafty

coop: cot, cub, mew, pen, pot **4** cage, cote,
jail **5** cramp, hutch **6** basket, corral **7**
confine **9** enclosure **11** cooperative

cooperate: **4** tend **5** agree, coact, unite **6**
concur **7** combine, conduce, connive **8**
coadjute, conspire **10** contribute **11**
collaborate

cooperation: **8** teamwork

cooperator: **9** auxiliary, colleague **10** accomplice

coordinate: **5** adapt, equal **6** adjust **7**
arrange, syntony **8** classify **9** harmonize
10 concurrent

coordination: **4** bond **7** harmony, liaison
12 relationship

coorie: **5** cower, stoop **6** crouch

cooser: **8** stallion

coot: **4** duck, fowl, rail **5** smyth **6** beltie,
person, scoter **7** henbill **13** phalacrocorax

cooter: **4** idle **6** loiter, turtle **8** tortoise

cootie: nit **4** bowl, game **5** louse **6** vessel **8**
grayback

cop: bag, nab, rob **4** bank, blow, bull, head,
heap, lift, pile, trap, tube **5** catch, crest,
filch, mount, quill, shock, snare, steal,

stock, swipe **6** peeler, spider, strike **7**
capture **9** patrolman, policeman
copacetic: **4** fine **5** dandy, prime **6**
snappy **7** capital **12** satisfactory
copaiba: **4** tree **6** balsam **9** oleoresin
copain: pal **4** chum **7** comrade
copal: **5** anime, resin
cope: vie, war **4** cape, duty, face **5** cappa,
cloak, cover, dress, equal, fight, match,
notch, rival, vault, wield **6** barter, canopy,
chapel, combat, mantel, muzzle, oppose,
strike, strive **7** contend, contest **8** complete, exchange, struggle, vestment **9** encounter
copemate: **7** comrade, partner **9** associate
10 antagonist
copious: **4** full, good, lush, rich **5** ample,
large **6** fluent, lavish **7** diffuse, flowing,
fulsome, profuse, replete, teeming, ub-
erous **8** abundant, affluent, numerous **9**
exuberant, plenteous, plentiful, redundant
11 overflowing
copper: cu; cop **4** bull, cent **5** bobby, metal,
penny **6** cuprum, peeler **9** butterfly,
policeman
alloy: **5** brass **6** oroide **7** rheotan
arsenic sulfide: **8** enargite
comb. form: **5** cupro **6** chalco
copper nickel: **9** niccolite
Copperfield's wife: **4** Dora **5** Agnes
coppice: **4** wood **5** copse, firth, grove **6**
forest, growth **7** thicket **9** brushwood, underwood
copse: cut, hag **4** hasp, trim **6** clevis **7**
coppice, shackle
Copt: **8** Egyptian **9** Christian **11** monophysite
copula: **4** band, link **5** union **7** coupler
copy: ape **4** echo, edit, mime **5** dummy,
image, mimic **6** ectype, effigy, follow, record **7** emulate, estreat, imitate, redraft,
replica, reprint, tracing **8** apograph, likeness **9** abundance, antigraph, duplicate,
imitation, reproduce **10** transcribe, trans-
script **11** counterpart **12** reproduction
kind of: **6** carbon, ectype **7** estreat, extract, pattern, replica **9** duplicate, facsimile
true: **7** estreat
copying: **7** mimicry **8** mimetism
copyist: **6** scribe **7** copycat **10** plagiarist
pert. to: **8** clerical
copyread: **4** edit
coque: bow **4** loop **8** trimming
coquette: toy **5** dally, flirt **6** trifle **9** philander **11** hummingbird
coquettish: coy
cora: **7** gazelle
coral: red **4** pink **5** polyp **6** palule **8** skeleton, zoophyte **9** madrepore, millepore **10**
stalactite
division: **7** aporosa
formation: **5** palus
island: key **4** reef **5** atoll

corbel: **5** ancon **6** timber **10** projection
cord: rib **4** band, bind, bond, cord, welt **5**
nerve, twine **6** bobbin, sennet, string,
tendon **7** amentum, measure **10** aiqui-
lette, cordeliere
drapery: **7** torsade
goat's hair: **4** agal
parachute: **7** ripcord
cordage: da **4** rope, coir, eruc, feru,
hemp, imbe, jute **5** fiber **6** sennit **7**
rigging
Corday's victim: **5** Marat
corded: **4** tied **6** repped, ribbed, welted **7**
stacked, twilled
Cordelia's father: **4** Lear
cordelle: tow **4** cord, rope **7** towline, towrope
cordial (see also **liqueur**): **4** real, warm **5**
shrub **6** ardent, elixir, genial, hearty **7**
liqueur, sincere, zealous **8** anisette,
friendly, gracious, vigorous **9** courteous,
unfeigned **10** hospitable
apricot: **8** periscot
flavoring: **7** aniseed
core: cob, hub, nut **4** coke, gist, nave, pith
5 focus, heart, nowse, spool **6** center,
centre, kernel, matrix, middle, nodule **7**
company, corncob, essence, nucleus **9**
substance
corf: tub **4** cage, corb, skip **5** creel **6** basket, dosser
corge: **5** score **6** twenty
Corinth's king: **7** Polybus
corium: **5** layer **6** dermis
cork: oak **4** plug **5** float, shive **6** bobber **7**
soberin, stopper, stopple
pert. to: **7** suberic
tissue: **5** suber
wax: **5** cerin
corkscrew: **6** defect, spiral
corkwood: **5** balsa **6** blolly
cormorant: **4** bird, shag **5** norie, scart **6**
gormaw, scarth **7** glutton **8** ravenous **13**
phalacrocorax
young: **7** shaglet
corn: **4** salt, samp **5** grain, maize, mealy **6**
clavis, heloma, kernel **7** callous **8** preserve **9** granulate
bread: **4** pone
dealer: **10** cornmonger
ear: cob **5** mealy **6** mealie, nubbin
food: **6** hominy
ground: **4** meal **5** grist
hulled: **4** samp **6** hominy
Corncracker State: **8** Kentucky
corndodger: **4** pone **5** bread **8** dumpling
cornel: **4** tree **6** cherry **7** dogwood
corner: in; get, wro **4** bend, cant, coin,
nook, pool, trap, tree **5** angle, bight,
catch, coign, elbow, herne, ingle, niche,
quoin, trust **6** cantle, canton, coigne,
cranny, recess **8** monopoly
cornerpiece: **6** cantle
cornerstone: **4** coin **5** basis, coign **6**

coigne **7** support **9** curbstone **10** foundation
cornet: **4** horn **8** woodwind **10** instrument
cornflower: **7** barbeau **10** bluebottle
cornhouse: **7** granary **8** corncrib
cornice: **4** band, drip, eave **5** crown **6** geison **7** molding **8** astragal
basket: **4** caul
diamond: **6** quartz
support: **5** ancon
wolframite: cal
cornmeal: **4** masa, samp **5** atole **7** hoecake **10** johnnycake
cornucopia: **4** horn
Cornwall: *mine:* bal **5** wheal
ore: **5** whits
Cornwallis' surrender site: **8** Yorktown
corny: **5** banal, stale, trite **11** sentimental
corolla: **4** bell **8** perianth
part: **5** galea, petal
corollary: **5** dogma **6** result, truism **7** adjunct, theorem **9** deduction, inference **11** consequence, proposition
geometric: **6** porism
corona: **5** cigar, crown, glory **6** fillet, rosary, wreath **7** aureole, circlet, garland, scyphus
coroner: **6** elisor **7** officer **8** examiner
coronet: **4** band, burr **5** crown, tiara **6** anadem, circle, diadem, timbre, wreath **7** chaplet
coronopus: **4** herb **6** carara
corporal: NCO **4** fano **5** fanon, fanum, phano **6** bodily
corporal punishment: **5** death **7** penalty **8** spanking, whipping
corporate: **6** united **8** combined **9** aggregate
corporation: **4** body, firm **5** trust **10** fellowship, foundation **11** association, combination
corporeal: **4** real **5** hylic, somal **6** actual, bodily, carnal **7** somatic **8** material, physical, tangible **11** substantial
corpse: DOA **4** body **5** mummy, relic, stiff **7** cadaver, carcass, carrion
corpulent: fat **5** bulky, burly, husky, obese, plump, stout **6** fleshy, portly, rotund **7** adipose, bellied, weighty **8** rolypoly
corpuscle: **4** cell **9** leucocyte
redblood: **7** hematid **8** haematid **11** polkilocyte, schistocyte
corral: pen, sty **4** coop **5** atajo, pound **7** confine, enclose **8** stockage, surround **9** enclosure, inclosure
correct: O.K.; due, fit, fix **4** edit, lean, nice, okay, smug, true **5** amend, check, emend, exact, right **6** adjust, better, change, inform, proper, punish, rebuke, reform, remedy, repair, revamp, revise, strict **7** chasten, improve, perfect, precise, rectify, redress, reprove **8** accurate, chastise, definite, emendate, regulate, rigorous, truthful **9** castigate, faultless **10** immaculate, particular, scrupulous **11**

punctilious **12** conventional
comb. form: **5** ortho
correctable: **10** corrigible
correlated: **4** akin **7** related
correlative: or; nor **4** then **5** equal, still **6** either, mutual **7** neither **8** analogue, conjoint **9** analogous **10** reciprocal **13** correspondent
correspond: fit, gee **4** jibe, suit **5** agree, match, tally, write **6** accord, concur, square **7** conport, respond **8** coincide, parallel, quadrate **9** analogous, harmonize **11** communicate
correspondence: **4** mail **7** analogy, letters, traffic **8** homology **9** assonance, congruity **10** similarity
correspondent: **8** quadrate, suitable **9** accordant, analogous, congruous **10** accomplice, concordant, equivalent **11** conformable, contributor, correlative
corrida: **9** bullfight
corridor: **4** hall **5** aisle, oriel **6** arcade **7** couloir, gallery **8** coulisse **10** passageway
corrie: **6** cirque, hollow
corrigible: **8** amenable **10** corrective, punishable **11** correctable
corroborant: **5** tonic **10** supporting **12** invigorating **13** strengthening
corroborate: **5** prove **7** confirm, support, sustain **9** establish **11** countersign **12** substantiate
corrode: eat **4** bite, burn, etch, gnaw, rust **5** decay, erode, waste **6** be-gnaw, canker, impair **7** consume
corrosive: **4** acid **6** ardent, biting **7** caustic, erosive, fretful, mordant **9** sarcastic **11** destructive **14** disintegrating
corrugate: **5** crimp **6** furrow, rumple **7** crinkle, crumple, wrinkle
corrugation: **4** fold **6** crease, pucker **7** wrinkle
corrupt: bad, low, rot **4** evil, vile **5** blend, bribe, spoil, stain, sully, taint, venal **6** augean, canker, debase, impure, poison, putrid, ravish, rotten **7** abusive, attaint, carrion, crooked, defiled, degrade, deprave, envenom, falsify, immoral, pervert, pollute, putrefy, violate, vitiate **8** confound, empoison **9** abandoned, dishonest **10** adulterate, demoralize, flagitious, profligate **11** contaminate, purchasable
corsage: **5** waist **6** bodice, boquet **7** bouquet, flowers
corsair: bug **6** pirate, robber **8** picaroon, rockfish **9** privateer **10** buccanneer
body: **5** armor, cover
corset: **4** belt, busk **6** girdle **7** support
covering: **8** camisole
strip: **4** bone, busk
corslet: **6** bodice **8** corselet **11** breastplate
cortege: **5** suite, train **6** parade **7** retinue **10** procession
cortex: **4** bark, peel, rind **8** peridium
corundum: **4** ruby, sand **5** emeru, emery **7** alumina **8** abrasive, sapphire

coruscate: **5** blaze, flash, gleam, shine **7** glisten, glitter, radiate, sparkle **8** brandish **11** scintillate

corviform: **4** corvine **8** crowlike

cos: **7** lettuce, romaine

cosh: **4** neat, snug, tidy **5** happy, quiet, still **6** attack, lively, strike, weapon **7** assault **8** familiar, friendly **11** comfortable

cosher: pet **4** chat **5** feast, visit **6** pamper, sponge

cosmetic: **5** cream, henna, liner, paint, rouge **6** enamel, pomade, powder **7** mascara **8** lipstick

medicated: **6** lotion

white lead: **6** ceruse

cosmic: **4** vast **7** orderly **8** catholic, infinite **9** universal **10** harmonious

cosmopolitan: **5** urban **8** ecumenic **10** ecumenical **13** sophisticated

cosmos: **5** earth, globe, order, realm, world **6** flower **7** harmony **8** universe

Cossack: **4** Turk **5** tatar **6** ataman, hetman, tartar **7** Russian **10** cavalryman

captain: **6** Sotnik

chief: **6** ataman, hetman

regiment: **4** polk, pulk

squadron: **6** sotnia, sotnya

village: **8** stanitza

whip: **5** knout

cosset: pet **4** lamb **6** caress, coddle, cuddle, fondle, pamper

cossette: **4** chip **5** slice, strip **9** schnitzel

cossid: **9** messenger

cost: **4** loss, pain **5** price, value **6** charge, outlay **7** expense **8** estimate **9** detriment, sacrifice, suffering **11** deprivation, expenditure **14** characteristic

costa: rib **4** side, vein **5** ridge **6** border, midrib

Costa Rica: *city:* **7** Heredia, San Jose(c.) **8** Alajuela

coin: **5** colon **7** centimo

measure: **6** fanega, tercia **7** cajuela, manzana **10** caballeria

mountain: **6** Blanco **8** Chirripo

people: **6** Guaymi **7** Guaymie

port: **10** Porto Limon **11** Punta Arenas

weight: bag **4** caja

costate: **6** ribbed

costermonger: **6** coster, hawker, nipper **7** peddler

costly: **4** dear, fine, high, rich **6** lavish **8** gorgeous, precious, prodigal, splendid **9** dearthful, expensive, priceless, sumptuous **11** extravagant

costmary: **4** herb **5** plant, tansy **7** alecost

costrel: keg **4** head **5** flask **6** bottle

costume (see also **dress, vestment**): rig **4** garb, robe, sari, suit **5** dress, getup, habit **6** attire **7** apparel, clothes, raiment, uniform **8** clothing, ensemble **10** habiliment

costus root: **4** herb **6** pachak, pochok

cot: bed, hut, mat, pen **4** boat, coop, cote, fold **5** abode, cabin, couch, cover, house, stall **6** pallet, sheath, tangle **7** charpai,

charpoy, cottage, shelter **8** bedstead, dwelling **9** sheepfold, stretcher **11** fingerstall

cote: cot, hut **4** coop, fold, shed, wine **5** house, quote **7** cottage, shelter **8** hillside, outstrip, vineyard **9** inclosure, sheepfold

coterie: set **4** ring **5** junto, monde **6** circle, clique, galaxy **7** platoon, society **9** camarilla

cothamore: **8** overcoat **9** greatcoat

cothurnus: **4** boot **6** buskin

cotta: **6** mantle **7** blanket **8** surplice, vestment

cottage: cot, hut **4** bari, cosh **5** bower, cabin, house, lodge, shack **6** bohawn, cabana, chalet **7** shelter **9** hosthouse **10** guesthouse

partition: **5** speer **6** hallan

cottage cheese: **9** smearcase

cotter, cottar: mat, pin, vex **4** clot **6** fasten, potter, pucker, shrink, toggle, wither **7** congeal, cottier, peasant, shrivel, villein **8** cottager, cotterel, entangle **9** coagulate

cotton: **4** beat, flog **5** agree, bayal, derry **6** coddle, dhurry, fabric, nankin **7** algodon, dhurrie, garment, succeed **8** perceive **9** harmonize **10** fraternize, understand

and linen: **7** fustian

cleaner: **5** willy **6** willow

cloth: **4** baft, jean, lawn, leno, susi **5** bafta, bluet, denim, doria, khaki, lisle, manta, surat, terry, vichy, wigan **6** baline, calico, cangan, hum-hum **7** camboye, cotonia, galatea, jaconet, nankeen, percale, silesia

Egyptian: sak **4** Pima **5** sakel

extraction: **5** bolly

fiber: **4** lint **6** stapel

flowered: **6** chintz

knot in: nep **4** slub

light: **7** etamine

printed: **6** calico

refuse: **8** grabbots

seed pod: **4** boll **5** bolly

sheeting: **5** manta **6** muslin **7** percale **8** drilling

striped: **5** bezan **7** express

strong: **4** duck **5** scrim **6** canvas

thread: **5** lisle

waste: **4** noil **6** linter

cotton gin inventor: **10** Eli Whitney

Cotton State: **7** Alabama

cottonseed kernel: **4** meat

couch: bed, cot, lie **4** hide, lair, lurk, sofa **5** divan, inlay, lodge, press, skulk, slink, sneak, squat, stoop, utter **6** burrow, litter, pallet, settee **7** conceal, express, overlay, recline **8** disguise **9** accubitus(L.), davenport, embroider

couch grass: **5** quack, quick **6** quitch, scutch

couchant: **4** abed **5** prone **6** supine **7** lurking **9** crouching, squatting

cougar: cat **4** puma **7** panther **9** catamount

cough: **4** bark, hack **5** hoast **6** tussis **9**

pertussis
pert. to: **7** tussive
cough drop: **6** pastil, troche **7** lozenge **8** pastille
coulee: **4** lava **5** gorge, gulch **6** ravine
council: **4** body, dael, diet, rede **5** board, boule, cabal, divan, junta, junto, synod **6** senate **7** cabinet, consult, meeting **8** assembly, conclave, congress, hustling, ministry **10** conference, consistory, federation **11** convocation **12** consultation
pert. to: **7** cameral
table cover: **5** tapis
councilman: **11** concionator
counsel: **4** lore, rede, rule, warn **5** chide **6** advice, advise, confer **7** caution **8** admonish, advocate, prudence **9** barrister, counselor, recommend **10** counsellor **11** exhortation, instruction **12** consultation, deliberation
counselor, counsellor: **4** sage **6** lawyer, mentor, nestor **7** adviser, advisor, counsel, proctor **8** attorney **9** barrister
counselor-at-law: **9** barrister
count: add, tot **4** bank, cast, earl, foot, graf, name, rely, tell, tote **5** comte(F.), judge, score, tally **6** census, depend, esteem, figure, impute, number, reckon **7** account, ascribe, compute **8** numerate, sanction **9** ascertain, calculate, enumerate
Count of Monte Cristo: **6** Dantes
countenance: aid, mug **4** abet, brow, face, mien, puss, show, vult **5** favor, front **6** aspect, favour, visage **7** approve, bearing, conduct, endorse, feature, proffer, support **8** befriend, demeanor, sanction **9** demeanour, encourage, semblance **10** appearance **11** physiognomy
counter: bar **4** chip, dump, eddy, pawn **5** shelf, stand, table **6** combat, marker, oppose **7** adverse, contend, current **8** contrary, opposite **10** contradict
counter-irritant: **4** moxa **5** seton, stupe **6** arnica, iodine, pepper **7** mustard **8** liniment
counteract: **5** check **6** oppose, resist, thwart **7** balance, destroy, nullify **8** antidote **9** frustrate **10** compensate, neutralize **11** countermand **12** counterpoise
counterfeit: **4** base, copy, coin, duff, fake, mock, sham **5** belie, bogus, dummy, false, feign, forge, fudge, phony, queer **6** affect, assume, forged, pseudo, tinsel **7** falsify, feigned, imitate **8** deformed, simulate, spurious **9** brummagem, disguised, dissemble **10** adulterate, artificial, fictitious, fraudulent
counterfoil: **4** stub **5** check
countermand: **4** stop **5** annul **6** cancel, forbid, recall, revoke **7** abolish, rescind, reverse **8** abrogate, prohibit **9** frustrate **10** counteract

counterpart: **4** copy, like, mate, twin **5** image, match **6** double **7** obverse **8** parallel **9** duplicate, facsimile **10** complement, equivalent, similitude
counterpoint: **4** foil **7** deecant **8** contrast **11** arrangement **13** juxtaposition
counterpoise: **6** offset **7** balance **8** equalize **10** compensate, counteract **13** counterweight **14** counterbalance
countersign: **4** mark, seal, sign **6** signal **7** confirm, endorse **8** consigne, password, sanction **9** signature, watchword **11** corroborate
countersink: **4** ream **5** bevel **7** chamfer
countertenor: **4** alto **8** falsetto
countless: **8** infinite **10** numberless **12** incalculable
country: **4** home, land **5** addle, realm, state, tract, weald **6** ground, nation, people, region, sticks **8** district **9** champaign, territory **12** commonwealth
ancient: **4** Aram, Elam, Elis **5** Sheba
man: **4** jake, rube **5** swain, yokel **6** farmer, rustic **7** bumpkin, hayseed, plowman **10** compatriot, inhabitant
mythical: Oz
open: **4** moot, wold **5** heath, weald
pert. to: **5** rural **6** rustic **7** predial **8** agrestic, pastoral, praedial
place: **4** farm, peat **5** ranch, villa
reside in: **9** rusticate
county: **4** seat **5** shire **6** domain, parish **7** borough **8** district
coup: buy **4** blow, plan, play **5** scoop, upset **6** attack, barter, strike, stroke **7** capsize, traffic **8** overturn **9** stratagem
coup-cart: **8** dumpcart
couple: duo, tie, two **4** bond, case, dyad, join, link, mate, pair, span, team, twin, yoke **5** brace, leash, marry, twain, unite **7** bracket, connect, coupler **8** assemble
coupled: **5** yoked **6** joined, wedded **7** gemalad **8** geminate **9** conjugate
coupler: **4** link, ring **7** drawbar, shackle, tirasse
coupon: **4** form, slip, stub **5** check, stamp **7** portion
courage: **4** grit, guts, prow, sand, soul **5** heart, nerve, pluck, spunk, valor **6** daring, mettle, spirit **7** bravery, heroism, prowess **8** audacity, boldness, firmness, tenacity **9** assurance, fortitude, gallantry, hardihood **10** resolution
courageous: **4** bold, game **5** brave, hardy, manly, stout **6** daring, heroic, manful, plucky **7** gallant, spartan, staunch, valiant **8** fearless, intrepid, valorous **9** undaunted **11** adventurous **12** enterprising
courant, courante: **4** romp **5** caper, dance, music **6** letter **7** current, gazette, running **9** messenger, newspaper
courier: **4** post **5** guide, scout **7** estafet, orderly, postboy, soilage **8** cicerone, dra-

goman, estafeet, horseman **9** attendant, messenger **10** cavalryman

course: lap, run, way **4** bent, flow, game, heat, line, mode, path, race, rill, rink, road, rote, went **5** cycle, drift, orbit, route, tenor, track, trail, trend **6** artery, career, cursus, gallop, manner, method, series, stream, street, system **7** beeline, conduct, highway, passage, pathway, process, routine, running, subject, traject **8** curricle, progress, sequence, tendency **9** direction **10** curriculur proceeding, racecourse, succession **11** watercourse
alter: **4** veer **6** detour
easy: **4** pipe, snap **5** cinch **8** sinecure
habitual: rut, way **4** rote **7** regimen, routine
of action: **6** career **8** demarche **9** procedure
of study: **7** seminar **8** syllabus **10** curriculum
roundabout: **6** detour **11** indirection
courser: **5** horse, racer, steed **7** charger
court: bar, bid, see, sue, woo **4** area, body, quad, rota, seek, yard **5** arena, curea, curry, favor, forum, judge, patio, space, spark, tempt, train **6** allure, atrium, gemote, homage, invite, palace **7** address, attract, retinue, solicit **8** hustling, serenade, tribunal **9** attention, enclosure **10** quadrangle
attendant: **5** staff **6** elisor, staves
call to: **4** oyes, oyez **7** summons **8** subpoena **11** arraignment
circuit: **4** eyre, iter
crier: **6** beadle
ecclesiastical: **10** consistory
exemption: **6** essoin
hearing: **4** oyer, suit **5** trial **6** action
inner: **5** patio
minutes: **4** acta
of equity: **8** chancery
official: **5** clerk, crier, macer(Sc.) **7** bailiff
old: **4** leet **5** gemot **6** gemote **8** woodmote
participant: **4** jury **5** crier, judge **6** elisor **7** pleader **8** advocate, talesman **9** defendant, plaintiff
pert. to: **5** aulic **10** fornaneous
session: set **4** oyer **6** assize **7** sitting **8** sederunt **11** downsitting
writ: **6** capias **7** summons **8** subpoena
court game: **6** tennis **9** badminton
court-martial: **8** drumhead
courteous: **4** fair **5** buxom, civil, suave **6** polite, urbane **7** affable, cordial, gallant, genteel, gentile, refined **8** debonair, gracious **9** attentive **10** complaisant, respectful **11** considerate, gentlemanly
courtier: **4** bean **5** beaux(pl.), wooer **7** courter **8** courtman **9** attendant, courtling, flatterer
courtly: **4** hend **5** aulic, civil, hende **6**

polite **7** elegant, refined, stately **8** polished **9** dignified
courtyard: **4** area **5** patio **7** cortile **9** curtilage **10** quadrangle
cousin: coz, kin **4** akin **6** allied **8** relative
couthie: **4** smug **6** kindly, smooth **8** friendly, pleasant **9** agreeable **11** comfortable
couturier, couturiere: **8** designer **10** dressmaker
cove: bay, den **4** cave, chap, gill, hole, nook, pass **5** basin, bight, creek, inlet **6** fellow, hollow, recess, valley **7** molding
covenant: **4** bind, bond, mise, pact **5** agree **6** accord, cartel, engage, pledge, treaty **7** bargain, compact, concord, promise **8** alliance, contract, document **9** agreement, concordat, condition, stipulate, testament, undertake **10** convention **11** confederacy, stipulation
cover: cap, lid **4** coat, hide, mask, pave, roof, span, veil **5** drape, hatch **6** mantle, screen, shield **7** obscure, overlay, shelter
a bet: **4** fade
with straw: **6** thatch
with strips of bacon: **4** lard
covered: **4** clad, shod **5** mossy **6** covert, hidden **7** encased **8** screened **9** cleithral, concealed, panoplied, sheltered
covering: fur, hap **4** aril, bark, boot, case, hood, hull, husk, mask, pall, roof, tarp, tile **5** apron, armor, crust, quilt, shell, testa **6** awning, canopy, drapet, facing, heling, helmet, jacket, pelage, screen, sheath, shroud **7** capsule, ceiling, healing, overlay, pericap, wrapper **8** casement, clothing, coverlet, umbrella **9** coverture, operculum **10** integument **11** smokescreen
defensive: **5** armor **6** helmut **10** camouflage **11** smokescreen
thin: **4** film **6** veneer
coverlet: **5** quilt, rezai, throw **6** afghan, caddow, spread **7** blanket **8** coverlid **9** comforter **11** counterpane
coverslut: **5** apron **7** garment
covert: den, lie, sly **4** lair **5** niche, privy **6** asylum, harbor, hidden, latent, masked, refuge, secret **7** covered, defense, harbour, private, shelter, subrosa, thicket **9** concealed, disguised, insidious, shrubbery **10** underbrush **12** confidential
covet: **4** ache, envy, pant, want, wish **5** crave, yearn **6** desire, grudge, hanker
covetous: **4** avid, gair, gare **5** eager **6** frugal, greedy, stingy **7** miserly **8** desirous, grasping **9** mercenary **10** avaricious **12** parsimonious
covey: **4** bevy **5** brood, flock, hatch **7** company
covin, covine: **4** band, crew **5** fraud **7** company **8** assembly, trickery
cow: awe **4** beef, bogy, cowl, cush, faze,

kine, vaca **5** abash, alarm, bossy, brock, bully, daunt, dompt, moggy, scare **6** bovine, goblin, heifer, subdue, vacha **7** bugbear, depress, övertop, squelch, terrify **8** browbeat, dispirit, frighten, threaten **9** quadruped **10** intimidate

barn: **4** byre **7** vaccary

barren: **5** drape

cud: **5** rumen

hornless: not **4** moil **5** doddy, muley **6** doddie, mulley **7** pollard

young: **4** calf **5** stirk **6** heifer

cow pilot: 4 fish **9** chirivita **10** damselfish

cowardly: shy **4** argh **5** timid **6** afraid, cowish, craven, yellow **7** caitiff **12** fainthearted **13** pusillanimous

cowbird· 7 bunting **9** blackbird

cowboy. 5 rider, roper, waddi **6** gaucho, herder **7** llanero, puncher, vaquero **8** buckaroo, buckayro, wrangler **10** cowpuncher **12** broncobuster

breeches: **5** chaps, levis **8** jodhpurs

contest: **5** rodeo

cowcatcher: 5 guard, pilot

cowed: 8 downcast **11** crestfallen

cower: 4 fawn **5** quail, stoop, toady, wince **6** coorie, cringe, crouch, hurkle, shrink

cowfish: 4 toro **7** manatee, sirenia

cowherd: 7 bucolic **8** herdsman, neatherd

cowl: cap, lid, tub **4** hood, monk **6** bonnet, vessel **7** capuche

cowle: 5 grant **7** amnesty **10** engagement **11** safe-conduct

cowled: 6 hooded **9** cucullate

cowpea: 5 sitao

cowpuncher: 6 cowboy **7** puncher

cowslip: 8 auricula, marigold, primrose

coxcomb: fop, nob **4** buck, dude, fool, toff **5** cleat, dandy, hinge **7** princox **8** popinjay

coy: pal, shy **4** arch, coax, nice **5** aloof, chary, decoy, quiet, still **6** allure, caress, demure, modest, proper **7** bashful, distant **8** reserved **9** diffident **10** coquettish, disdainful, hesitating

Coyote State: 11 South Dakota

coypu: 6 nutria, rodent

cozen, cosen: cog, con **4** bilk, gull **5** cheat, trick **6** chisel **7** beguile, deceive, defraud, swindle **8** hoodwink **9** bamboozle

cozy: 4 easy, safe, snug **5** bield **6** chatty, secure, toasty **8** covering, familiar, gemutlich, homelike, sociable **9** contented, talkative **11** comfortable

crab: gin **5** anger, maian, racer, winch **6** buster, cancer, grouse, heemit, peeler **7** buckler, fiddler, grumble **8** arachnid, irritate, windlass **9** horseshoe **10** crosspatch, crustacean, curmudgeon

claw: **5** chela **6** nipper

fiddler: uca

genus: uca **6** birgus **7** squilla

crabbed: 4 ugly **5** cabby, cross, testy **6** bitter, crusty, morose, rugged, sullen, trying **7** boorish, cramped, cornish, crooked, gnarled, knotted, obscure, peevish **8** churlish, contrary, petulant, vinegary **9** difficult, fractious, intricate, irregular **11** perplexing **11** intractable

crabstick: 4 cane **5** crank, stick **6** cudgel

crabwood: 8 andiroba

crack: gag, pop **5** a-one, bang, blow, chap, chip, chop, clap, cone, flaw, jest, jibe, joke, kibe, leak, quip, rend, rift, rime, snap, yerk **5** brack, break, check, chine, chink, clack, cleft, craze, split **6** cleave, cranny **7** blemish, crackle, crevice, crevise, fissure **8** fracture

crackbrain: 8 crackpot **9** screwball

crackbrained: 5 crazy, nutty **7** erratic **12** unreasonable

cracker: 4 bake, liar **5** wafer **7** biscuit, boaster, breaker, burster, redneck, snapper **8** braggart **11** firecracker

Cracker State: 7 Georgia

crackle: 4 snap **5** break, crack **7** brustle, crinkle, sparkle, sputter **9** crackling, crepitate

crackpot: 7 erratic, lunatic **9** screwball

cracksman: 4 yegg **7** burglar, peteman

cradle: bed, cot **4** rest, rock **5** cader, frame **6** creche **7** berceau, shelter **8** cunabula **9** framework **11** incunabulum

song: **7** lullaby **8** berceuse

wicker: **8** bassinet

craft (see also **boat**): art **4** boat **5** fraud, guile, skill, trade **6** deceit, metier, talent, vessel **7** ability **8** aptitude, artifice, vocation **9** dexterity **10** employment, occupation **12** skillfulness

craftsman: 4 hand **5** navvy **6** artist, writer **7** artisan, workman **8** mechanic **9** artificer

aid: cad

crafty: sly **4** arch, foxy, wily **5** adept **6** adroit, astute, callid, shrewd, subtle, tricky **7** cunning, vulpine **8** captious, fetching **9** cautelous, deceitful, ingenious **10** fallacious, fraudulent **13** Machiavellian **15** Mephistophelean

crag: tor **4** craw, neck, rock, scar, spur **5** arete, brack, cliff **6** throat **9** precipice

craggy: 5 rough **6** abrupt, knotty, rugged

crake: 4 bird, crow, rail, rook **5** raven **8** railbird

cram: wad **4** bone, fill, glut, pack, stow, urge **5** crowd, crush, drive, force, gorge, grind, learn, press, study, stuff, teach

crame: 4 tent **5** booth, stall

cramp: 4 coop, kink, pain **5** crick, crowd, pinch, stunt **6** hamper, hinder, knotty **7** confine **8** compress, contract, restrain, restrict **9** constrict, difficult **11** contraction

cranberry: 7 pembina **8** bilberry, fox-

berry **9** mossberry, sourberry
habitat: bog
crane: job **4** bird, grus **5** davit, heron,
jenny, raise, wader **6** sarsus **7** derrick **9**
cormoran
arm: gib, jib
charges: **7** cranage
pert. to: **6** gruine
traveling: **5** jenny, titan
ship: **5** davit
small: **10** demoiselle
cranial nerve root: **5** radix **7** radices(pl.)
cranium: pan **4** head **5** skull **8** brainpan
crank: wit **4** bent, sick, weak, whim, wind
5 brace, loose, rogue, shaky, winch **6** ailing, boldly, grouch, handle, infirm **7** awkward, bracket, fanatic, lustily **9** distorted,
eccentric, sprightly **10** monomaniac, vigorously
crankle: **4** bend, turn, twist **6** zigzag
cranky: **4** ugly **5** crazy, cross, lusty,
shaky, testy **6** ailing, infirm, sickly **7**
crooked, grouchy **8** tortuous **9** crotchety,
difficult, irritable
cranny: **4** hole, nook **5** chink, cleft, crack
6 corner **7** crevice, fissure
cranreuch: **4** rime **9** hoarfrost
crants: **6** wreath **7** garland
crap: **5** dregs, money **7** gallows, greaves,
rubbish **8** nonsense, sediment
crape: **4** band, curl, friz **5** crepe, crimp,
drape, gauze **6** shroud **8** mourning
crapulence: **7** surfeit **8** gluttony **11**
overfeeding **12** intemperance, intoxication
crash: **4** fail, fall **5** blast, burst, cloth,
crush, shock, smash, sound **6** fiasco **7**
failure, shatter **8** collapse, splinter **9**
collision
crass: raw **4** dull, rude **5** crude, dense,
gross, rough, thick **6** coarse, obtuse, stupid **9** unrefined
cratch: **4** crib, rack **6** manger **7** grating
crate: box, car **4** case, crib **5** plane, seron
6 basket, cradle, encase, hamper, hurdle
7 canasta, vehicle **9** container **10** receptacle
bar: **4** slat
crater: cup, pit **4** cone, hole **5** fovea **6**
hollow **7** caldera
edge: lip
cravat: tie **4** teck **5** ascot, scarf, stock **7**
bandage, necktie, overlay **8** crumpler **9**
neckcloth **10** fourinhand **11** neckerchief
crave: ask, beg **4** long, need, pray, seek **5**
covet, yearn **6** desire, hanker, hunger,
thirst **7** beseech, entreat, implore, request, require, solicit **10** supplicate
craven: **6** afraid, coward, scared **7** dastard
8 cowardly, defeated, overcome, poltroon,
recreant, sneaking **10** vanquished **12**
fainthearted
craw: maw **4** crop **7** stomach **9** ingluvies

crawl: lag **4** drag, fawn, inch, ramp, swim **5**
creep, kraal **6** cringe, grovel, scride **7**
slither
crayfish: **5** yabby **6** yabbie **7** crawdad,
lobster **8** cambarus, crawfish **9** ecrevisse
10 crustacean
crayon: **4** plan **5** chalk **6** pastel, pencil,
sketch **7** drawing
craze: fad **4** flaw, mode, rage **5** break,
crack, crush, furor, mania, vogue **6** defect, impair, madden, weaken, whimsy **7**
derange, destroy, fashion, shatter, whimsey **8** distract **9** bedlamize, infirmity
11 infatuation
crazed: mad, ree **4** amok, loco, wild, wood,
zany **5** balmy, batty, daffy, dotty, manic,
nutty, potty, wacky **6** coocoo, dottle, insane, looney **7** lunatic **8** deleerit, delieret,
demented, deranged **10** crackbrain, distraught
creak: gig **4** rasp, yirr **5** cheep(Sc.), croak,
grind, groan **6** squeak
cream: **4** beat, best **5** creme, elite, froth,
sauce **6** bonbon **8** emulsion, ointment
cream of tartar: **5** argol
creamery: **5** dairy
creamy: **4** rich **5** reamy **6** smooth **8** luscious
crease: **4** fold, lirk, ruck, ruga, seam **5**
crimp, pleat **7** crumple, wrinkle
create: **4** coin, form, make, plan **5** build,
cause, forge, shape, write **6** design, invent
7 compose, fashion, imagine, produce
8 generate **9** establish, originate
creation: **5** world **6** cosmos, effect **7** fashion, product **8** creature, universe **10** production **11** masterpiece
creative: **9** demiurgic, inventive **10** productive **12** constructive
creativity: **6** genius
creator: **5** maker **6** author **8** designer **9**
architect
creature (see also **animal**): man **4** tool **5**
beast, being, slave, thing **6** animal, minion, person, wretch **8** hellicat(Sc.) **9**
dependent **10** animalcule, individual
fabled: elf **5** gnome **6** dragon, merman **7**
centaur, mermaid
ogre: **5** pixie **6** wyvern
creche: **4** crib **6** manger **7** nursery
credence: **5** faith, trust **6** belief, buffet,
credit **8** credenza **10** acceptance, confidence **11** reliability **15** trustworthiness
credential: **7** voucher **8** credence **11**
certificate, testimonial
credenza: **5** niche, shelf, table **6** buffet **8**
credence, cupboard **9** sideboard
credible: **6** likely **7** credent **8** probable **9**
authentic, plausible, reputable **11** trustworthy
credit: **4** loan **5** asset, chalk, faith, honor,
merit, tenet, trust **6** belief, charge, esteem, impute, renown, repute, weight **7**

ascribe, believe **8** accredit, credence **10** estimation

credulous: **4** fond **8** credible, gullible

creed: ism **4** cult, sect **5** credo, dogma, faith, tenet **6** belief **7** trowing **8** doctrine **10** confession

Christian: **6** Nicene **8** Apostle's

creek: bay, ria, rio **4** burn(Sc.), cove, kill, pill, rill, slue **5** bayou, bight, bogue, brook, crick, fleet, inlet, zanja **6** arroyo, estero, Indian, slough, stream **7** estuary, rivulet **11** watercourse

creel: **4** caul, cawl, rack, trap **6** basket

creem: hug **4** mash **5** crush **6** shiver **7** shudder, squeeze

creep: **4** fawn, inch, ramp **5** crawl, prowl, skulk, slink, steal **6** cringe, grovel, scride **7** cramble

creeper: ivy **4** shoe, vine, worm **5** snake **6** ipecac, romper, tecoma

creeping: **4** slow **7** reptant, servile **9** reptilian **11** reptatorial

creese: **4** kris, stab **5** sword **6** dagger, weapon

cremate: **4** burn **9** incremate **10** incinerate

Cremona: **5** Amati **6** violin

crena: **5** cleft, notch **7** scallop **11** indentation

crenic acid salt: **7** crenate

creole: **6** patois **7** mestizo

Creole State: **9** Louisiana

crepe: **6** fabric **7** frizzed, pancake **8** crinkled, wrinkled

crepitate: **4** snap **6** rattle **7** crackle

crescent: **4** horn, lune, moon, rool **5** curve, lunar **6** lunule **7** lunette, menisci(pl.) **8** meniscus **10** semicircle

point: **4** cusp

crescent-shaped: **6** bicorn, lunate **7** lunular **9** semilunar

crescive: **7** growing **10** increasing

cresset: **5** torch **6** basket, beacon, signal **7** furnace **8** flambeau

crest: cop, tip, top **4** acme, apex, comb, edge, knap, peak, seal, tuft **5** chine, crown, plume, ridge **6** copple, crista, finial, height, helmet, summit **7** bearing **8** pinnacle, whitecap **10** cognizance

rugged: **6** arete

crested: **6** muffed **7** crisate, crowned **8** pileated **9** coronated

crestfallen: **5** cowed **8** dejected **10** dispirited

creta: **5** chalk

Crete: **6** Candia

city: Hag **5** Canea(c.), Khora **6** Kisamo, Malemi, Mallia, Meleme, Retimo **7** Kasteli **8** Nikolaes, Sphakion **9** Heraclion, Tympakion **11** Palaiokhora

flier: **6** Icarus

goddess: **8** Dictynna

king: **5** Minos **9** Idomeneus

language: **6** Minoan

monster: **8** minotaur

mountain: Ida **9** Psiloriti

princess: **7** Ariadne

seaport: **5** Canea **6** Candia, Khania

cretin: **5** idiot

cretism: **5** lying **9** falsehood

crevasse: **5** chasm, split **8** cleavage

crevice: **4** bore, leak, nook, seam, vein **5** break, chine, chink, cleft, crack, grike **6** cranny **7** fissure, opening **8** crevasse, peephole **10** interstice

crew: men, mob, set **4** band, gang, herd, oars, team **5** hands, party, squad, staff **6** seamen, throng **7** company, faculty, members, retinue **8** equipage, mariners **10** assemblage, complement

crewel: **6** caddis **7** caddice **10** crewelwork, embroidery

crib: bed, bin, box, cab, cot, cub, hut, key **4** boom, dive, pony, rack, raft **5** boose, boosy, cheat, crate, frame, hovel, stall, steal **6** bunker, cratch, creche, manger, pilfer **7** purloin **8** cribbage **9** enclosure **10** plagiarize, storehouse

cribbage score: nob, peg

crick: **5** creek, hitch, spasm, twist

cricket: **4** game, grig **6** insect

run: bye

side: ons

team: **6** eleven

term: off, ons, rot **4** over **5** smick **6** yorker

crier: **6** beadle, herald, wailer **7** muezzin

crime: act, sin **4** evil **5** abuse, arson, blame, wrong **6** felony, murder, piacle **7** misdeed, offense **8** iniquity **9** violation **10** wickedness **11** abomination, malefaction **13** transgression

goddess of: Ate

scene of: **5** venue

Crimea: **4** Krym

city: **5** Kerch, Yalta **10** Sevastopal

people: **5** Tauri

river: **4** Alma

sea: **4** Azof, Azov

criminal: bad **4** yegg **5** crook, felon **6** guilty, inmate, nocent, slayer, wicked **7** convict, culprit, illegal **8** culpable, gangster **9** desperado, wrongdoer **10** blackguard, deplorable, flagitious, malefactor, malfeasant **11** blameworthy, disgraceful **13** reprehensible

habitual: **8** repeater **10** recidivist

refuge: **7** Alsatia **11** Whitefriars

criminology branch: **8** penology

crimp: **4** bend, curl, fold, friz, pote, wave, weak **5** cramp, flute, frizz, pinch, plait **6** goffer, ruffle **7** crinkle, friable, gauffer, wrinkle **8** obstacle **9** corrugate **12** inconsistent

crimson: dye, lac, red **4** pink **6** bloody, maroon, modena **7** carmine, scarlet

crine: **4** hair, mane **6** shrink **7** shrivel

cringe: bow 4 bend, fawn, jouk 5 binge, cower, crawl, quail, sneak, stoop, wince, yield 6 crouch, grovel, shrink, submit 7 crinkle, distort, truckle

cringing: 6 abject 7 hangdog

crinite: 5 hairy 6 fossil

crinitory: 5 hairy 7 crinose

crinkle: 4 bend, curl, kink, turn, wind 6 pucker, ripple, rumple, rustle 7 crackle, wrinkle 9 corrugate 11 convolution

cripple: mar 4 harm, hurt, lame, main 6 bacach, impair, injure, weaken 7 crapple, crumpet, disable, lamiter(Sc.) 8 handicap, mutilate, paralyze 9 hamstring 12 incapacitate

crisis: 4 acme, crux, pass, turn 5 panic, peril, pinch, trial 6 strait 8 decision, juncture 9 criterion, emergency 11 conjunction

crisp: new 4 cold 5 brisk, clear, curly, fresh, nippy, pithy, sharp, short, stiff, terse 6 biting, bright, lively 7 bracing, brittle, concise, cutting, friable 9 crackling

crisscross: 4 awry 7 network 8 confused 9 intersect

cristate: 6 ridged, tufted 7 crested

criterion: law 4 norm, rule, test, type 5 axiom, canon, gauge, nodel, proof 6 metric 7 measure 8 standard 9 yardstick 10 indication, touchstone

critic: 5 booer, judge, momus 6 carper, censor, expert, slater 8 collator, reviewer 9 detractor, literator 11 connoisseur, criticaster, faultfinder

critical: 4 edge 5 acute, exact 6 urgent 7 carping, exigent 8 captious, decisive, exacting 10 censorious, fastidious 12 faultfinding 14 discriminating

criticism: 5 blame 6 review 7 comment 8 critique, diatribe, judgment 9 stricture 13 animadversion

criticize: hit, pan, rap, rip 4 carp, flay, slam, slur, yelp 5 blame, blast, cavil, judge, knock, roast 6 rebuke, review 7 censure, comment, examine 8 critique 9 castigate 10 animadvert

cro: 7 payment 12 satisfaction

croak: caw, die 4 gasp, kill 5 creak, quark, speak 7 forbode, grumble 8 complain

Croatian: 4 Serb, Slav, Sorb, Wend 5 Sclav 6 Hrvati 7 Hervati, Slovene 8 European

crochet: 4 hook, knit 5 braid, plait, weave 8 crotchet

crock: jar, pig, pot 4 smut, soil, soot 5 stool 6 critch, smudge 8 potsherd

crockery: 5 china, cloam 6 dishes, plates 11 earthenware

crocodile: goa 5 gator 6 cayman, gavial, jacare, mugger 7 reptile 9 alligator
   genus: 11 goniopholis

crocus: 7 saffron

croft: 4 farm 5 crypt, field, garth, vault 6 bleach, cavern

cromlech: 6 circle, dolmen 7 gorsedd 9 cyclolith

Cromwell: 4 Noll 6 Oliver
   son-in-law: 6 Ireton

crone: hag 4 cive 5 witch 6 beldam 7 beldame 9 cailleach, cailliach
   father: 6 Uranus
   mother: 4 Gaea
   wife: 4 Rhea

crony: pal 4 chum 9 associate, companion

crook: 4 bend, turn, warp 5 cheat, cleek, crump, curve, pedum, staff, thief, trick 7 crosier, crozier 8 artifice, swindler 10 camshachle(Sc.)

crooked: cam 4 agee, awry, bent 5 agley(Sc.), askew, false, gleed 6 akimbo, artful, aslant, crabby, crafty, curved, tricky, zigzag 7 askance, asquint, corrupt, crabbed, oblique, turning, twisted, winding 8 tortuous 9 dishonest, distorted, irregular 10 circuitous, fraudulent, misleading 12 dishonorable

croon: hum, low 4 boom, lull, sing, wail 5 chirm, whine 6 lament, murmur 8 complain

crop: cut, maw, top 4 clip, craw, knap, reap, trim, whip 5 fruit, quirt, shear 6 gather, gebbie, silage 7 curtail, harvest, tillage 8 gleaning, ingulies
   second growth: 5 rowen

croquet: 5 roque

croquette: 5 cecil

crosier, crozier: 5 crook, cross, staff

cross: go; mix 4 ford, rood, span 5 angry, testy, trial 6 bisect, crabby, cranky, crouch, emblem, gibbet, grumpy, outwit, signum, sullen, symbol, thwart, touchy 7 athwart, crabbed, fretful, froward, oblique, peevish, pettish, potence 8 crotched, crucifix, petulant, snappish, suastica, swastika, traverse, vexillum 9 frustrate, intersect, irritable, plaintive 10 affliction, ill-humored, transverse 12 disagreeable
   barred: 11 trabeculate
   fiery: 8 crantara 9 crostarie
   stroke: 5 serif 6 ceriph
   tau: 4 crux 5 ankih
   type: 5 Greek, Latin, Papal 6 Celtic 7 Maltese 8 Egyptian

cross-examine: 5 grill 8 question

cross-grained: 7 gnarled 8 churlish, perverse 9 irascible 12 cantankerous

cross-rib: 4 arch 6 lierne

crossbar: 4 axle, rung 5 round 10 horizontal

crossbeam: bar 5 trave 6 girder

crossbow: 6 weapon 8 arbalest

crossbreed: 5 husky 6 hybrid 9 hybridize

crossing: 7 passage 8 opposing

crosspatch: 4 bear, crab 6 grouch

crosspiece: bar **4** spar, yoke **5** grill **8** crossarm **10** doubletree

crossroads: 9 carrefour **12** intersection
goddess: **6** Hecate, Hekate, Trivia

crossruff: 6 seesaw **9** alternate

crosswise: 6 across **7** athwart **8** acrostic, diagonal

crotch: 4 fork, pole, post **5** cleft, notch, stake **9** stanchion

crotchet: fad **4** hook, whim **5** fancy **6** vagary **9** conundrum **11** peculiarity **12** eccentricity

crotchety: 6 cranky **10** capricious

crouch: 4 bend, fawn, ruck **5** cower, squat, stoop **6** cringe **7** scrooch

crouching: 8 couchant

crouse: 4 bold **5** brisk, cocky **6** lively **8** cheerful **9** confident

crow: aga, caw, cry, daw **4** bird, brag, rook **5** boast, exult, raven, vaunt **6** carnal, corvas **7** grapnel, jackdow, swagger **9** blackbird

crow-like: 7 corvine

crowbar: pry **5** jemmy, jimmy, lever **7** gablock **8** gavelock

crowd: jam, mob, set **4** bike, cram, herd, host, pack, push, rout, rock, stow, swad **5** bunch, cramp, crush, drove, flock, group, horde, posse, press, serry, shoal, swarm, three, wedge **6** boodle, clique, hubble, huddle, jostle, rabble, throng **7** bourk(Sc.) company, squeeze **9** multitude **10** assemblage, clamjamfry(Sc.), confluence

penetrate: **5** elbow **6** needle

crowded: 5 close, dense, thick **6** filled **7** bunched, compact, serried, stipate, stuffed, teeming **9** congested

crowder: 6 loader **7** fiddler **8** thatcher

crown: cap, top **4** coin, pate, peak, poll **5** adorn, basil, bezel, bezil, crest, miter, mitre, tiara **6** anadem, circle, climax, corona(L.), diadem, fillet, invest, laurel, potong, reward, summit, trophy, wreath **7** aureole, chaplet, coronet, garland, install **8** coronate, enthrone, pinnacle, surmount, headdress, sovereign

pert. to: **8** coronal

cru: 8 vineyard

crucial: 5 acute **6** severe, trying **7** pivotal, telling **8** critical, decisive

crucible: pot **4** dish, etna, test **6** cruset, retort **7** furnace

crucifix: pax **4** rood **5** cross

crucify: vex **4** hang, kill **5** harry **7** mortify, torment, torture **8** cruciate **9** persecute

crud: 4 curd **6** refuse **7** thicken

crude: raw **4** bald, bare, rude **5** crass, green, harsh, rough **6** callow, coarse, savage, unripe, vulgar **7** uncouth **8** immature, impolite **9** primitive, unglossed, unrefined, untrained **10** incomplete, unpolished **11** undeveloped **13** inexperienced

cruel: 4 fell, hard **5** harsh **6** bloody, brutal,

fierce, savage, severe, unjust, unkind **7** bestial, brutish, inhuman, neronic **8** barbaric, diabolic, fiendish, inhumane, pitiless, ruthless, sadistic, tyrannic **9** atrocious, draconian, ferocious, heartless, merciless, rapacious, unfeeling **10** diabolical, sanguinary, vindictive **11** hardhearted

lover of: **6** sadist

cruet: ama, jar, jug **4** vial **5** cruse **6** bottle, caster, guttus, vessel **7** ampulla, burette **9** container

cruise: 4 boat, sail, trip **9** excursion

cruiser: 4 ship **6** vessel **7** warship

cruising: 4 asea

cruller: 7 olycook, olykock **8** doughnut **9** friedcake

crumb: bit, ort **5** piece **6** little, morsel **7** remnant **8** fragment

crumb covered: 7 breaded

crumble: rot **5** break, crush, decay, slake, spoil **6** molder, perish **7** moulder **9** decompose, pulverize **12** disintegrate

crumbly: 7 friable

crumpet: 4 cake **6** muffin **7** pikelet

crumple: 4 fold, muss **5** crush **6** crease, furrow, raffle, rumple **7** crunkle, wrinkle **8** collapse, contract **9** corrugate

crunch: 4 bite, chew **5** chomp, crump, crush, gnash, grind, munch, press **6** cranch **7** craunch, scrunch

crus: 5 shank

crusade: war **5** jehad, jihad **8** campaign **10** expedition

crusader: 7 pilgrim, Templar **8** reformer
enemy: **7** Saladin, Saracen

crush: bow, jam **4** cram, dash, mash, mill, mull **5** brake, break, crash, craze, crowd, force, grind, press, quash, quell, smash, tread, unman **6** bruise, burden, crunch, squash, subdue, thwack **7** conquer, crumple, depress, destroy, oppress, overrun, repress, scrunch, scrunge, shatter, squeeze, squelch **8** compress, overcome, suppress **9** overpower, overwhelm, pulverize

crust: 4 cake, hull, rind **5** shell **6** eschar, harden **7** coating **8** pellicle

crustacean: 4 crab, flea, scud **5** louse, prawn **6** endite, isopod, shrimp **7** lobster, squilla **8** barnacle
appendage: **5** exite
group: **7** caridea
larva: **5** alima
small: **6** isopod **7** copepod **8** barnacle
ten-footed: **4** crab

crusty: 4 curt **5** bluff, blunt, testy **6** morose **7** crabbed, peevish, pettish **8** snappish **11** ill-tempered

crux: nub **4** ankh, gist, pith **5** cross, point **6** puzzle, riddle **7** problem **10** difficulty

cry (see also **exclamation**)**:** ho; boo, caw, cri(F.), fad, hue, ole, sob, yip **4** bawl, bump, call, evoe, hawk, hoot, howl, keen, mewl, pule, rage, scry, wail, weep,

yell, yelp **5** clepe, crede, greet, groan, rumor, shout, sound, utter, vogue, whewl, whine **6** bellow, boohoo, clamor, demand, lament, outcry, quethe, scream, shriek, slogan, snivel, squeal, squall, wimick, yammer **7** clamour, exclaim, fashion, screech **8** proclaim **11** acclamation, lamentation
court: **4** oyes, oyez
derisive: bah, boo **4** hiss, hoot **6** phooey **7** catcall
gang's signal: **4** whyo
of relief: **4** phew, whew
of sorrow: ay; woe **4** alas **5** alack
of triumph: aha **6** hurrah
out: **5** blame, crake, deery **7** censure, protest **8** complain, denounce
crying: **6** urgent **7** clamant, heinous **8** pressing, recreant **9** notorious **11** exclamatory
crying bird: **7** limpkin
crying hare: **4** pika
crying out: **10** childbirth **11** confinement
crypt: pit **5** croft, vault **6** cavern, grotto, recess **7** chamber **8** follicle **10** depression
cryptic: **4** dark **5** vague **6** hidden, occult, secret **7** obscure **9** enigmatic, recondite **10** mysterious **12** hieroglyphic
cryptogram: **4** code **6** cipher **11** cryptograph
crystal: ice **4** dial, hard **5** clear, glass, lucid **6** limpid, pebble **7** acicula, diamond **8** pellucid **11** crystalline, transparent
gazer: **4** seer **7** seeress
ice: **6** frazil
twin: **5** macle
crystalline: **4** pure **7** crystal **8** pellucid **11** transparent
compound: **5** alban **6** anisil, oscine **7** aconite, amarine **8** atropine
mineral: **4** mica, spar **6** quartz **7** apatite **8** boracite, elaterin
salt: **5** borax **8** analgene, racemate
crystallize: **5** candy, sugar **7** congeal **8** solidify **9** granulate
cub: fry, pen **4** bear, coop, shed **5** stall, whelp **6** lionet, novice **7** codling **8** reporter **9** youngster
Cuba: *asphalt:* **9** chapapote
beverage: **4** pina
carriage: **7** volante
cigar: **6** Havana
city: **6** Guines, Havana(c.) **7** Palmira **8** Camaguay, Matanzas, Santiago **9** Cienfuego **10** Santa Clara **14** Puerto Principe
coin: **4** peso **7** centavo **8** cuarenta
dance: **5** conga, rumba **6** danzon, rhumba
dollar: **6** gourde
fish: **6** diablo **7** viajaca
hutia: **6** pilori
measure: **4** vara **5** bocoy, tarea **6** cordel, fanega **10** caballeria
mountain: **6** Copper **11** Pinar del Rio **12** Guaniguanico **13** Pico Turquinos

province: **6** Havana **7** Oriente **8** Camaguey, Matanzas, **10** Santa Clara **11** Pinar del Rio
root: **7** malanga
rum: **7** Bacardi
tobacco: **4** capa **6** vuelta
tree: **4** cuya **5** culla
weapon: **7** machete
weight: **5** libra **6** tercio
cubage: **6** volume **7** content
cubbyhole: **4** nook
cube: cut, die **4** dice **5** block, solid **10** hexahedron
cube spar: **9** anhydrite
cubic: **5** solid **9** isometric
decimeter: **5** liter, litre
meter: **5** stere
shape: **6** cuboid
cubicle: bay **4** cell, noak, room **5** booth, niche **6** alcove
cubitus: **4** ulna **7** forearm
Cuchullin's wife: **4** Emer **5** Eimer
cuckoo: ami **4** bird, fool, gowk, koel **5** clock, crazy, silly **7** boobook **8** rainfowl
kind: **6** coucal, kobird **7** kowbird, wryneck **8** coccyzus
cuckoopint: **4** arum **5** aaron, plant **9** wake-robin
cucullate: **6** cowled, hooded **7** covered **10** hood-shaped
cucumber: **4** cuke, pepo **6** conger, pepino(Sp.) **7** gherkin **9** elaterium
cucurbit: **5** flask, gourd **6** vessel **7** alembic, matrass
cud: **4** chew, quid **5** bolus, rumen **6** cudgel
cuddle: hug, pet **6** caress, cosset, fondle, nestle **7** embrace, snuggle
cuddy: ass **4** lout **5** bribe, cabin **6** donkey, galley, pantry **7** blockhead
cudgel: bat **4** beat, cane, club, drub, rack **5** baste, drive, kebby, kevel, staff, stave, stick **6** alpeen, ballow, baston, kebbie, thrash, weapon **7** belabor, bourdon, **8** bludgeon, shillala **9** bastinado, crabstick, fustigate, truncheon **10** shillelagh
cue: nod, tip **4** hint, mast, tail, wink **5** braid, cluff, plait, queue, twist **6** prompt, signal **7** pigrail **9** catchword **10** intimation
cuff: box **4** bank, blow, gowf, slam, slap, slug, swat **5** clout, fight, gowff, miser, smite **6** buffet, codger, mitten, strike **7** scuffle **8** gauntlet, handcuff
cuisine: **4** food, menu **5** table **7** cookery
cuittle: **4** coax **6** tickle **7** wheedle
cul-de-sac: **6** pocket, strait **7** deadend, impasse **10** difficulty
culicid: **8** mosquito
cull: opt **4** dupe, gull, pick, sift, sort **5** elect, glean, pluck **6** assort, choose, gather, remove, select **8** separate
cully: **4** dupe, gull, mate **5** cheat, trick **7** deceive **9** companion
culm: **5** slack **6** refuse **7** deposit

culmen: top **4** acme **5** ridge
culmination: end **4** acme, apex, noon **5** crown **6** apogee, climax, summit, vertex, zenith **10** completion **12** consummation
culpa: **5** fault, guilt **10** negligence **12** carelessness
culpable: **6** faulty, guilty, laches **7** immoral **8** criminal **10** censurable **11** blameworthy **13** reprehensible
culprit: **5** felon **7** convict **8** criminal, offender **10** malefactor
cult: **4** clan, sect **5** creed **6** church, ritual, school **7** worship **12** denomination
cultivate: ear, hoe **4** disk, farm, grow, plow, rear, tend, till **5** nurse, raise, study, train **6** affect, foster, harrow, plough **7** acquire, cherish, educate, husband, improve, nourish, prepare **8** civilize **9** encourage
cultivated: **5** civil **6** polite **7** refined **8** cultured **12** domesticated
land: **4** farm **5** arada, tilth
cultivation: **7** culture, tillage **9** culturing, husbandry **10** refinement **12** civilization
art: **9** geoponics
cultivator: **6** farmer, harrow, tiller **7** grubber, husband **10** husbandman
culture: art **4** agar **5** taste **6** polish **7** tillage **9** knowledge **10** discipline, refinement **12** civilization
culver: **4** dove **6** pigeon
culvert: **5** drain **6** bridge **7** conduit
cumbersome: **5** heavy **6** clumsy **7** onerous, weighty **8** cumbrous, unwieldy **10** burdensome
cumbrous: **8** clogging, unwieldy **9** difficult, vexatious **10** burdensome, cumbersome
cumin: **5** anise, cumic
cummer, kimmer: **4** girl, lass **5** witch, woman **6** friend **7** midwife **9** companion, godmother
cummerbund: **4** band, belt, sash
cumshaw: tip **5** bonus **6** thanks **7** present **8** gratuity
cumulate: **4** heap **6** gather **7** combine **10** accumulate
cuneal: **7** cuneate **11** wedge-shaped
cuneiform: **4** bone **6** wedged **7** writing **8** sphenoid
cunner: **5** canoe **6** nipper, wrasse
cunning: sly, wit **4** arch, cute, foxy, keen, wily **5** downy; guile, sharp. smart **6** adroit, artful, astute, callid, clever, crafty, deadal, deceit, shrewd, subtle, tricky, wisdom **7** curious, finesse, politic, vulpine **8** dextrous, skillful, stealthy **9** chicanery, colubrine, designing, dexterity, ingenious, knowledge, sagacious **10** fraudulent, witchcraft **13** Machiavellian
cup: ama, dop, mug, tyg **4** tass **5** bouse, calix, cruse, glass, grail, phial, stein, tazza **6** beaker, crater, goblet, noggin, potion, vessel **7** chalice, stirrup

assay: **4** test **5** cupel **6** beaker
diamond cutting: dop
eared: **6** quaich, quaigh
fungus: **6** aecium
horn-shaped: **6** holmos
looped handles: **5** kylix **9** cantharus, kantharos
pastry: **7** dariole
resembling: **9** oalicular
small: **4** shot **5** chark, cruse **6** noggin **8** cannikin **9** demitassè
two-handled: tig, tyg **5** depas
cup-shaped: **10** cyathiform
cupbearer of the gods: **4** Hebe **8** Ganymede
cupboard: kas **4** case, safe **5** ambry, cuddy **6** buffet, closet, larder, pantry **7** armoire, cabinet, dresser **8** credenza **9** sideboard
Cupid: Dan **4** Amor, Eros, love **7** Amorino
beloved of: **6** Psyche
mother: **5** Venus
cupidity: **4** lust **5** greed **6** desire **7** avarice, avidity, longing **8** appetite **12** covetousness
cupidon: **5** cupid
cupola: **4** dome, kiln **5** vault **6** turret **7** furnace, lantern, lookout
cur: dog, yap **4** fice, mutt, tike, tyke **5** feist **6** canine, messan, messin **7** bobtail, mongrel **9** goldeneye
curacao: **7** liqueur
Curacao island: **5** Aruba
curare: **5** urare, urari **6** oorali, poison
curate: cur **4** abbe **5** agent **7** doimine **8** minister **9** assistant, clergyman
curative: **7** healing **8** remedial, salutary, sanative **9** medicinal **11** restorative
curator: **6** keeper **7** manager, steward **8** guardian, overseer **9** custodian **14** superintendent
curb: bit **4** foil, rein **5** brake, check, curve, guard, limit **6** arrest, bridle, govern, hamper, thwart **7** control, inhibit, repress, shackle **8** moderate, restrain, restrict, withhold **9** constrain, hindrance **10** hamshackle
curculio: **6** weevil
curd: **6** curdle **7** caseine, clabber, congeal **8** fleeting **9** coagulate
curdle: **4** earn(Sc.), leep, quar, sour, yern **5** quail, quarl, spoil **6** posset, quarle **7** clabber, congeal, thicken **8** condense **9** coagulate
agent causing: **6** rennet
cure: dry **4** boot, care, heal, heed, help, jerk, salt, save **5** reest, smoke **6** charge, curate, priest, remedy, season **7** restore, therapy **8** antidote, preserve
by salting: **4** corn
in sun: **6** rizzar
cure-all: **4** balm **5** avens **6** elixir, remedy **7** panacea **10** catholicon
curfew: **4** bell **6** signal

curio: **5** relic, virtu **7** bibelot **8** keepsake, souvenir **9** bric-a-brac, curiosity

curious: odd **4** nosy, rare **5** queer **6** prying, quaint **7** cunning, strange, unusual **8** freakish, meddling, peculiar, singular **9** intrusive, wondering **11** inquisitive

curl: **4** bend, coil, kink, lock, roll, wave, wind **5** acker, crisp, tress, twist **6** buckle, frowse, ripple, spiral, writhe **7** crimple, flexure, ringlet, tendril **11** convolution **12** heartbreaker

curled: **7** savoyed

curlicue: ess **5** caper, curve **6** paraph **8** flourish

curling mark: tee

curly: **4** wavy **5** crisp **7** rippled **8** crinkled

curmudgeon: **4** crab **5** churl, miser **6** grouch **7** niggard

curn: **4** corn **5** grain

currant: **5** berry **6** raisin, rizzar
genus: **5** ribes

currency: **4** cash, coin **5** bills, money, scrip **6** specie **10** greenbacks

current: now, way **4** eddy, flow, flux, ford, rife, tide **5** drift, going, rapid, tenor, trend, usual **6** coeval, common, course, living, motion, moving, recent, stream **7** counter, flowing, general, present, running, thermal, torrent **8** frequent **9** prevalent **10** prevailing **11** electricity **15** contemporaneous
generator: **12** electromotor
measuring device: **7** ammeter
pert. to: **7** voltaic

currish: **4** base **7** cynical, ignoble **8** snarling **12** mean-spirited

curry: **4** comb, drub **5** clean, dress, groom **6** bruise, cajole, powder **7** prepare **9** condiment, seasoning
favor: **4** fawn **6** cajole, smooge

curse: ban **4** bane, blow, damn, oath **5** spell, swear **6** malign **7** beshrew, malison **8** anathema **9** blaspheme, imprecate, maranatha **10** execration, vituperate **11** deprecation, malediction **12** anathematize **13** excommunicate

cursory: **4** fast **5** brief, hasty, quick, short **6** fitful, speedy **7** passing, shallow **8** careless, rambling **9** desultory, irregular, transient **10** discursive, evanescent **11** superficial

curt: **4** buff, rude, tart **5** bluff, blunt, brief, brusk, short, terse **6** abrupt **7** brusque, concise **8** cavalier, succinct **9** condensed

curtail: cut, lop **4** clip, crop, dock, pare, stop **5** abate, short, slash, stunt **6** lessen, reduce, teaser **7** abridge, bobtail, shorten **8** diminish, minorate, retrench **9** decurtate, epitomize **10** abbreviate

curtain: end **4** boom, drop, mask, veil, wall **5** blind, drape, shade **6** purdah, screen, shroud **7** ceiling, conceal, drapery **8** portiere

half: **4** bise, cafe **5** brise
raiser: **9** forepiece

curtsy, curtsey: bob, bow **4** beck **5** conge **9** obeisance

curvature (see also **curve**): arc **4** bool, curl **8** kyphosis, lordosis **9** arcuation, scoliosis
center locus: **7** evolute
convex: **6** camber
surface: **5** plane

curve: arc, bow, ess **4** arch, bend, curb, ogee, turn, veer **5** ambit, bight, crook, crump, swirl, twist **6** bought, spiral **7** circuit, concave, contour, curvity, ellipse, flexure, inflect, sinuate **8** parabola, sinusaid **9** convexity, curvature
cusp: **7** spinode
double point of: **6** acnode
kind: **9** parabolic **10** memniscate
mathematical plane: **5** polar
parallel to an ellipse: **6** toroid

curved: **5** round, wound **6** convex, hamate, turned **7** arcuate, arrondi, crooked, curvant **8** anchorai, aquiline, arciform
inward: **5** adunc **6** hooked **8** aduncous

curvet: hop **4** leap, lope, skip, turn **5** bound, caper, frisk, prank **6** cavort, frolic, gambol, prance **8** corvetta(F.) **9** courbette

Cush: *father:* Ham
son: **4** Seba **6** Nimrod

cushion: bag, cod, mat, pad **4** boss, seat **5** gaddi, squab **6** buffer, insole, jockey, pillow, sachet **7** bolster, hassock **9** upholster
stuffing: **4** baru, down **5** kapok **8** feathers

cusk: **4** fish, tusk **5** torsk **6** burbot

cusp: **4** apex, horn, peak **5** angle, point, tooth **6** corner **8** paracone **10** projection

custard: **4** flan **5** flawn **6** doucet, dowcet, dowset **8** flummery **9** charlotte

custard apple: **5** anona **6** annona, pawpaw **8** sweetsop

custodian: **5** guard **6** bailee, keeper, warden **7** curator, janitor **8** guardian **9** caretaker, protector

custody: **4** care **5** trust **6** charge **7** control, durance, keeping, tuition **11** safekeeping **12** guardianship

custom: fad, law, mos (L.), tax, use **4** duty, form, garb, mode, more, rite, rote, rule, toll, wont **5** habit, haunt, usage, vogue **6** dastur, impost **7** costume, fashion, tribute **8** business, practice, **9** costumbre, patronage **10** consuetude, convention, observance **12** constitution
of peoples: **5** mores

customary: **5** nomic, usual **6** common **7** general **8** familiar, habitual, orthodox **10** accustomed **11** traditional **12** conventional **14** consuetudinary

customer: **4** chap **5** buyer **6** client, patron **7** callant, patient, shopper **8** prospect **9** purchaser

customhouse: **6** aduana(Sp.), dogana(It.) **9** chophouse.
customs: tax **4** cess, duty, levy, rate, toll **5** mores **6** tariff **7** trewage
officer: **8** douanier
cut: bob, hew, mow, nip, rit **4** bite, chip, chop, clip, crop, dock, fell, gash, hack, knap, mode, nick, pare, raze, slit, snee, snip, snub, trim **5** carve, flick, knife, lance, mince, notch, prune, razee, scarp, sever, shear, shorn, slash, slice, slish, snick, split **6** ablate, bisect, broach, chisel, cleave, divide, excise, haggle, ignore, incise, lessen, mangle, reduce, scotch, slight, swinge **7** affront, curtail, whittle **8** lacerate, retrench **9** engraving, intersect
across: **5** slice **8** transect **9** intersect, transcend
down: **4** pare **5** clear, slash **9** economize
in: mix **9** interpose, interrupt, introduce
in half: **5** halve **6** bisect, secant **8** dimidate
in small pieces: **4** dice, hash **5** mince **6** sliver
off: lop, nig **4** clip, crop, drib, poll **5** elide, roach, shave **7** deprive, divorce, exscind **8** amputate, truncate **9** apocopate, intercept **10** disinherit
out: **6** exsect **7** exscind **9** eliminate
roughly: jag **4** hack, snag **7** butcher
short: bob **4** clip, crop, dock, poll **5** abort, check, clipt **6** arrest **7** curtail
slanting: **4** bias **5** bevel, miter, mitre
with die: **4** dink
wool: dod **4** dodd **5** shear
cutaneous: **6** dermal
cutaway: **4** coat
cute: coy **4** keen **5** coony, dinky, sharp **6** clever, pretty, shrewd **7** cunning **10** attractive
cuticle: **4** hide, skin **8** membrane, pellicle **9** epidermis **10** integument
ingredient: **5** cutin
cutlass: **5** sword **6** dusack, tesack **7** machete
cutout: **9** decoupage
cutpurse: **5** thief **10** pickpocket
cutter: **4** beef, boat, sled **5** bravo, sloop, smack **6** cotter, editor, sleigh, slicer **7** clipper, incisor, ruffian **9** cutthroat, foretooth
cutthroat: **5** bravo **7** ruffian
cutting: hag, raw **4** curt, keen, kerf, slip, tart, twig **5** acute, bleak, crisp, scion, scrap, scrow, sharp **6** biting, bitter, secant, severe **7** caustic, mordant, painful, satiric **8** chilling, incisive, piercing, poignant, wounding **9** sarcastic, trenchant **10** blustering **11** abridgement, curtailment **12** adulteration.
edge: **5** blade
implement: ax; axe, bit, hob, saw **4** adze **5** knife, lathe, mower, plane, razor **6** chisel,

reaper, scythe, shears **8** scissors
of last letter: **7** apocope
cuttle: **4** thug **5** bully, knife **7** ruffian **8** assassin **9** swaggerer
cuttlefish: **5** sepia, squid **7** octopus, scuttle
ink: **5** sepia
cuvette: pot, tub **4** tank **5** basin **6** bucket, trench **7** cistern
cyanogen compound: **7** cyanide
Cybele: **4** Rhea
sweetheart: **5** Attis
Cyclades Island: Ios, Zea **4** Keos, Milo, Nios, Sira, Syra **5** Delos, Melos, Naxia, Naxos, Paros, Syros, Tenos, Tinos **6** Andros **7** Amorgos
cycle: age, eon, era **4** aeon, bike **5** epoch, pedal, round, saros, wheel **6** circle; course, period **7** bicycle, circuit, vehicle **8** tricycle **10** revolution
cyclone: **4** gale, gust, wind **5** blast, storm **6** baguio **7** tornado, twister, typhoon **9** hurricane, windstorm
cyclopean: **4** huge, vast **6** strong **7** massive **8** colossal, gigantic **9** herculean
Cyclopes: **5** Arges **7** Brontes **8** Steropes
Cyclops: **5** giant **7** monster
feature: **6** one eye
Cycnus' father: **4** Ares
cygnet: pen **4** fowl, swan
cylinder: **4** beam, drum, pipe, prim, tube **6** barrel, bobbin, gabian, piston, platen, roller **7** sleever
cylindrical: **5** round **6** terete **7** centric, tubular **8** teretial
cyma: **4** gola, gula ogee **7** molding
cymar: **4** robe **5** shift, simar
cymbal: tal, zel **8** doughnut
cymbals: **6** becken, piatti
Cymbeline's daughter: **6** Imogen
Cymric: **5** Welsh
god of dead: **5** Pwyll
god of sky: **7** Gwydion
god of sun: **4** Lleu, Llew
god of underworld: **4** Gwyn
cynic: **5** Timon **7** doubter **9** pessimist **11** misanthrope
cynical: **6** sullen **7** currish, doglike **8** captious, snarling
cypress: **9** belvedere
cyprinoid: See **fish**.
Cyprus: *city:* **6** Paphos **7** Limasol, Nicosia(c.) **9** Famagusta
coin: **4** para **7** piaster
measure: oka, oke, pik **4** cass **5** donum, kouza **6** gomari, kartos **7** medimno
mountain: **7** Troodos
weight: oka, oke **5** moosa **6** kantar
cyrenaic: **7** hedonic
cyst: bag, sac, wen **5** pouch **6** ranula **7** vesicle
czar, csar: **4** Ivan, tsar, tzar **5** Peter **8** Nicholas
daughter: **8** czarevna, tsarevna

son: **10** czarevitch, tsarevitch
Czechoslavakia: *city:* As **4** Asch, Brno,
Eger **5** Opava, Praha, Tuzla **6** Aussig,
Pilsen, Prague **7** Budweis, Teplitz **9**
Pressburg **10** Bratislava **11** Reichenberg
coin: **5** ducat, haler **6** heller, koruna
dance: **5** polka **6** redowa **7** furiant
measure: lan, sah **4** mira **5** liket, stopa **6**
merice

mountain: **5** Tatra
province: **7** Bohemia, Moravia
reformer: **4** Huss
river: Vag, Vah **4** Eger, Elbe, Gran, Hron,
Isar, Iser, Labe, Oder, Ohre, Waag **5** Ni-
tra **6** Moldau
czigany: 5 gypsy

D

dab: dap, hit, pat **4** blow, chit, lump, peck, spot **5** clout, dight, smear **6** blotch, expert, strike **7** dabster, portion, splotch **8** flatfish, flounder

dabble: dib **4** mess **5** dally **6** dibble, meddle, paddle, potter, splash, tamper, trifle **7** moisten, spatter **8** sprinkle

dabbler: **7** amateur, dabster **10** dilettante

dabby: wet **4** damp **5** moist **8** adhesive

dabchick: **5** grebe

dabster: See **dab**.

dace: **4** chub

dacoit: **6** robber **8** criminal **9** plunderer

dactylogram: **11** fingerprint

dactylopodite: **6** pollex

dactyloscopy: **14** classification, identification

dad: **4** beat, blow, hunk, lump, papa **5** knock, thump **6** father, strike

daddle: **4** fist, hand **6** dawdle

dado: **6** groove **7** solidum

daedal: **4** rich **6** varied **7** bizarre **8** artistic, skillful **9** ingenious, intricate **10** variegated

Daedalus' victim: **5** Talos

daemon (see also **demon**): **8** eudaemon

daffing: fun **7** fooling

daffodil: **5** dilly

daffy: See **daft**.

daft: gay **4** luny, wild **5** balmy, crazy, giddy, potty, silly **6** insane **7** foolish, idiotic **8** imbecile

dag: jag **4** stab **5** slash **6** daggle, pierce **7** daglock

Dag's horse: **8** Hrimfaxi **9** Skinfaksi

Dagda's kin: **5** Boann **6** Aengus, Brigit

dagger: **4** dirk, itac(Pl), kris, snee, spud, stab **5** crise, katar(Ind.), skean(Ir.) **6** anlace, bodkin, coutel, creese, diesis, kreese, panade, stylet, weapon **7** baslard, corteau, dudgeon, lalarao, poniard **8** puncheon, stiletto **10** misericord **11** misericorde

Dahomey people: Fon **4** Fong

daily: **4** aday **7** diurnal **9** hodiernal, newspaper, quotidian

daintily: **8** gingerly

dainty: **4** cate, nice, rare **5** acate, denty **6** bonbon, choice, costly, friand, mignon, minion, picked, scarce **7** elegant, finical, finicky, minikin **8** delicacy, delicate, migniard **9** exquisite, finicking, squeamish **10** confection, fastidious

dairy: **7** vaccary **8** creamery

food: **6** yogurt **7** yoghurt, yohourt **8** yoghourt

tool: **9** separator

dairymaid: dey **8** deywoman, milkmaid

dairyman: **7** milkman

dais: **4** seat **5** bench, podia(pl.), stage, table **6** canopy, podium, settle **7** estrade, terrace **8** chabutra, platform

daisy: **5** gowan, oxeye **6** shasta **10** moonflower

dak: **4** post

Dakota Indian: **5** Sioux **7** Arikara **8** Arikaree

dale: **4** dell, dene, glen, vale **5** spout **6** bottom, dingle, trough, valley

dalles: **6** rapids

dalliance: toy **4** chat, play, talk **6** gossip, trifle, tousel, tousle

dally: toy **4** chat, fool, idle, jake, jauk, play, wait **5** delay, flirt, sport, tarry **6** dabble dawdle, linger, loiter, trifle

Dalmatia:

channel: **7** Narenta

seaport: **7** Spalato

dam: bar, bay **4** stay, stem, stop, weir **5** block, check, choke, garth, mound **6** anicut, causey, mother, parent **7** annicut, barrier **8** blockade, obstacle, obstruct, restrain

dama: **7** gazelle

damage: mar **4** blot, cost, harm, hurt, loss, ruin, teen **5** burst, cloud, spoil, wound **6** charge, deface, defect, impair, injure, injury, scathe **7** expense, scratch **8** accident, disserve, mischief, sabotage **9** detriment, disprofit, vandalism **10** impairment **11** deleterious, impeachment **12** disadvantage

pert. to: **5** noxal

daman: **5** hyrax

Damascus:

people: **6** Syrian

river: **5** Abana **6** Abanah, Barada **7** Pharpar

damask: **5** linen

dame: **4** lady **5** woman **6** matron

correlative: **4** sire

dammar: **5** resin, rosin

damn: **5** curse

damnable: **6** odious **8** infernal **9** execrable **10** detestable

damnation: **9** perdition

damned: **5** bally **6** bloody **8** accursed

damnum: **4** harm, loss **9** detriment

damourite: 4 mica 9 muscovite

damp: deg, fog, wet 4 dank, dewy, dull, mist, roky 5 dabby, humid, moist, muggy, musty, rafty, rainy, soggy 6 clammy, dampen, deaden, muffle, quench, stupor 7 bedewed, depress, moisten 8 dejected, dispirit, humidity, moisture 9 depressed, stupefied 10 discourage

damper: 5 bread 7 checker 8 register

damsel: 4 girl 6 maiden 8 donzella, princess 10 demoiselle

Danae's kin: 4 Zeus 7 Perseus 8 Acrisius

danaite: 12 arsenopyrite

dance: bal(F.), bob, hop 4 ball, frug, hoof, prom, shag 5 caper, flisk, frike, frisk, rumba, tango, tread, stomp, twist, waltz 6 balter, Boston, hormos, masque, minuet, monkey 7 foxtrot, saltate 8 cotillon, fandango 9 allemande(G.), cotillion, farandole 10 roundabout, tripudiate

ancient: see *old* below

ballroom: 5 polka, waltz 7 czardas, foxtrot, mazurka, twostep

basket-carrying: 11 calathiscus

ceremonial: 6 areito

chorus: 5 strut 6 cancan, cordax

country: hay, hey 7 argeers, auresca 8 aurrescu, haymaker 10 villanella

designer: 12 choreographer 13 choreographer

exhibition: tap 6 ballet

fast: see *lively* below

gypsy: 7 farruca 10 zingaresca

involuntary: 8 tricotee

Latin American: 5 conga, rumba, samba, tango 6 maxixe, rhumba 7 carioca, criolla

lively: jig 4 reel, trot 5 fling, galop, gavot, polka, rumba 6 bolero, branle, canary, rhumba 7 coranto 8 galliard, rigadoon 9 allemande, schottish, shakedown, tambourin 10 corybantic 11 schottische

masked: 7 ridotto

modern: toe 4 dump, frug, pony, shag 5 twist 6 chacha, monkey 7 twostep 10 Charleston 12 mashed potato

movement: pas 4 jete, step 5 brise, coule, coupe 6 chasse, coupee 7 chassed, fouette, gambado 8 glissade 9 entrechat, pirouette

Muse: 11 Terpsichore

music: 10 gymnopedie

nineteenth-century: 7 tempete

old: 5 galop, gavot, loure, pavan, paven, pavin, rondo, volta 6 bource, branle, canary, carole, cebell, corant, minuet, morris, pavane 7 boutade, chaccon, chacona, coranto, courant, furlana, gavotte, lavolta 8 chaconne, faradole, gilliard 9 allemande, farandola, horedance, sarabande 10 tarantella, tarantelle

pert. to: 6 gestic 13 terpsichorean

round: 5 carol, waltz 6 carole 10 Charleston

rustic: See *country* above

shoes: 4 taps 5 pumps 8 slippers, toe-shoes

slow: 5 waltz 6 adagio, minuet, valeta

square: 7 argeers, lancers 8 lanciers 9 quadrille

step: See *movement* above

sword: 8 matachin 11 Flamborough

voluptuous: 5 belly 8 habanera

dance of death: 7 macaber, macabre

dancer: 6 artist, hoofer, happer 7 danseur 11 terpsichore 13 terpsichorean

Biblical: 6 Salome

female: 7 artiste, chorine 8 bayadere, coryphee, danseuse, devadasi 9 ballerina 15 terpsichorienne

garment: 7 leotard

instrument: 8 castanet

rope: nat

sword: 8 matachin

dancing: 7 saltant 11 choregraphy 12 choreography

dancing girl: See **dancer** *female.*

dandelion: 7 chicory 10 bitterwort

dander: 5 anger, scurf 6 stroll, temper, wander 7 passion, saunter 8 dandruff

dandified: 6 spruce 8 adonized

dandiprat: 5 dwarf, pygmy 6 urchin

dandle: 6 diddle, fondle, pamper

dandruff: 5 scurf

dandy: fop 4 beau, buck, dand, dude, fine, jake, prig, toff, yawl 5 dildo, swell 7 capstan, coxcomb, foppish, jessamy 8 sailboat 9 exquisite 11 scrumptious

female: 10 dandisette, dandizette

Dane: See **Denmark**.

danger: 4 fear, risk 5 doubt, peril 6 hazard 7 pitfall, venture 8 distress, jeopardy 9 adventure

signal: 4 bell 5 alarm, siren 6 tocsin

dangerous: bad, rum 5 nasty 6 fickle 7 parlous 8 insecure 9 desperate 10 precarious

dangle: lop 4 hang, loll 5 droop, swing 7 shoggle, suspend

dank: wet 4 damp 5 humid, moist 6 clammy, coarse, dampen 7 drizzle, wetness 8 moisture

danseuse: 6 dancer 9 ballerina

danta: 5 tapir

Dante:

circle of hell: 5 Caina

illustrator: 4 Dore

verse form: 7 sestina

Danube: 5 Ister

people: 6 Dacian

town: Ulm

tributary: 4 Drau, Raab, Raba 5 Drava, Drave, Siret

Danzig:

coin: 6 gulden 7 pfennig

liqueur: 7 ratafia

dap: dab, dib, dip 4 skip 6 bounce, dibble 7 rebound

Daphne: 8 Mezereon

father: **5** Ladon

dapper: 4 neat, trim **5** natty **6** spruce **7** finical, foppish

dappled: 6 dotted **7** flecked, mottled, spotted **8** freckled **10** variegated

darbies: 8 manacles **9** handcuffs

Dardanelles: 10 Hellespont

dare: 4 dast, defy, face, osse, risk **5** brave **6** assume **7** attempt, venture **9** challenge, undertake

dare not: 5 dasn't **6** daurna

daredevil: 6 madcap **12** swashbuckler

daring: 4 bold, rash **5** brave, hardy, manly, nerve **6** heroic **7** courage **8** boldness, devilish, fearless **9** audacious **10** courageous, jeopardous **11** adventurous, venturesome

dark: 4 dim, mum, sad, wan **4** dern, ebon, mirk, murk **5** black, blind, brown, cloud, dingy, dusky, faint, mirky, murky, shady, sooty, swart, unlit, vague **6** closed, cloudy, dimpsy, dismal, gloomy, opaque, swarth, wicked **7** melanic, obscure, rayless, stygian, swarthy **8** abstruse, darkling, gloomful, ignorant, lowering, sinister **9** ambiguous, atrocious, blindfold, Cimmerian, infuscate, recondite, secretive, tenebrous, uncertain, unlighted, unrefined **10** caliginous, indistinct, mysterious

darken: dim **4** dull **5** bedim, cloud, gloam, shade, sully, umber **6** deepen, shadow **7** becloud, benight, blacken, eclipse, obscure, opacate, perplex, tarnish **8** overcast **9** obfuscate, overcloud **10** overshadow

darkness: 4 dark, dern, dusk, murk **5** gloom, night, shade **6** shadow **7** dimness, privacy, secrecy **8** gloaming, iniquity, twilight **9** blackness **10** wickedness

realm: Po **6** Erebus

darling: 'jo; joe(Sc.), pet **4** dear, duck **5** aroon(Ir.), aruin, bully, cheri, deary, lieve, sweet **6** cherie, dautie(Sc.), dawtie(Sc.), minion, moppet **7** acushla(Ir.), pigsney, querida **8** favorite **9** favourite

darn: 4 mend **5** patch **6** repair

darnel: 4 tare, weed **5** grass **6** cockle

darner: 6 needle

dart: 4 bolt, flit, jouk, leap, plan **5** arrow, bound, fling, flirt, lance, skite, spear, speed, start **6** dartle, elance, method, scheme, spring **7** javelin, missile **9** fléchette

throwing machine: **10** anisocycle

dart-like: 8 dartling, spicular

D'Artagnan: *companion:* **5** Athos **6** Aramis **7** Porthos

creator: **5** Dumas

Dartmouth College Location: 7 Hanover **12** New Hampshire

Darwinian: 12 evolutionist

Das Kapital author: 4 Marx

dash: pep **4** bang, ding, elan, gift, hurl, line, pelt, race, ruin, rush, show, slam **5** abash, ardor, break, clash, crash, crush, fling, knock, smash, speed, spice, style, swash, throw **6** energy, hurtle, hyphen, shiver, spirit, splash, sprint, stroke, thrust **7** bravura, collide, depress, display, shatter, spatter, splotch **8** confound, gratuity, splinter **9** animation, bespatter, frustrate, overthrow

dasheen: 4 taro

dasher: 6 beater **7** plunger

dashing: 4 bold **5** bully, showy **6** swanky, veloce **7** stylish, swagger **8** spirited **11** fashionable

dastard: cad, sot **5** sneak **6** coward, craven **7** dullard **8** poltroon

dastardly: 4 foul

data: 5 facts **8** material **11** information

datary: 7 dataria

date: age, day, era **5** epoch, fruit **6** reckon **10** engagement, rendezvous **11** anniversary, appointment

erroneous: **11** anachronism

dated: 5 passe **8** outmoded **12** old-fashioned **13** unfashionable

dateless: 8 timeless **10** immemorial

dating: 6 timing

datum: 4 fact, item **11** information

daub: 4 balm, blob, blot, clag, clam, clat, coat, gaum, soil **5** clart, cleam, cover, paint, slake, smear **6** bedaub, grease **7** besmear, plaster, splotch **8** slaister

daughter: 4 bint **5** fille, filly **6** alumna **7** cadette

pert. to: **6** filial

Daughter of Moon: 7 Nokomis

daunt: awe, cow, daw **4** daze, faze, stun, tame **5** abash, amate, break, check, deter, dompt **6** dismay, subdue **7** conquer, control, overawe, repress, stupefy, terrify **8** dispirit, overcome **10** disconcert, discourage, dishearten, intimidate

dauntless: 4 bold, good **5** brave **7** aweless **8** fearless, intrepid **9** undaunted **10** courageous

davenport: 4 desk, sofa **5** couch, divan **12** chesterfield

daver: 4 fade, stun **5** droop **6** benumb, wither **7** stupefy

David: *chief ruler:* Ira

employer: **5** Nabal

kin: **5** Jesse, Tamar **6** Michal **7** Abigail, Absalom, Solomon

man of: Ira **4** Igal **7** Shammah

musician: **5** Asaph

traitor to: **10** Ahithophel

valley of Goliath's death: **4** Elah

David Copperfield character: 4 Dora, Heep, Rosa **5** Agnes, James, Uriah **6** Dartle **8** Micawber **9** Wickfield **10** Steerforth

daviely: 10 listlessly **12** spiritlessly

Davy: 4 lamp

daw: 4 dawn, drab **5** color, daunt **6** magpie **7** jackdaw **8** slattern, sluggard **9** blackbird, simpleton

dawdle: lag **4** idle, poke **5** dally **6** daddle, daidle, diddle, linger, loiter, pickle, piddle, putter, trifle **7** finnick, quiddle

dawn: **4** morn **5** sunup **6** aurora **7** morning, sunrise **8** daybreak **9** beginning
comb. form: eo
goddess: Eos **5** Ushas **6** Aurora
toward the: **8** eastward

dawny: **4** puny **5** small

day: yom(Heb.) **4** date, time **5** epoch **6** period **8** lifetime
before: eve **9** yesterday
early: see **daybreak**
father of: **6** Erebus
god of: **5** Horus
hot: **8** scorcher
joyful: **8** festival
judgment: **8** doomsday
pert. to: **6** ferial

day blindness: **11** hemeralopia

daybreak: **4** dawn, morn **5** sunup

daydream: **4** muse **6** vision **7** reverie

days: *fateful:* **4** Ides
fifty: **13** quinquagesima
fourteen: **9** fortnight

daysman: **6** umpire **7** arbiter **8** mediator

daze: fog **4** stun **5** daunt **6** astony, bemuse, benumb, dazzle, muddle, trance **7** confuse, stupefy **8** bewilder, dumfound

dazed: **4** asea **6** doiled, rotten **7** spoiled **8** astonied, withered **10** doitrified

dazzle: **4** daze **5** blind, glaik, shine **6** fulgor **7** eclipse **8** bewilder, outshine, surprise

dazzling: **5** flare, flash **6** garish **7** fulgent, glaring, radiant **8** gorgeous **9** brilliant **10** candescent, foudroyant **11** pyrotechnic

deacon: **5** adept **6** cleric, doctor, layman, master **10** adulterate

dead: **4** bung, cold, dull, flat, gone, mort(F.), numb, tame **5** amort, inert, napoo, quiet, slain **6** asleep, lapsed, napooh, refuse **7** defunct, exactly, expired, extinct, insipid, sterile, tedious **8** absolute, complete, deceased, departed, inactive, lifeless, obsolete **9** apathetic, bloodless, inanimate, nerveless, unsalable **10** breathless, lusterless, monotonous, motionless, spiritless, unexciting **11** indifferent, ineffectual, inoperative **12** extinguished, unproductive, unprofitable
region of: Po **5** Hades **6** Erebus

dead duck: **5** goner

Dead Sea: *city:* **5** Sodom
mountain: **6** Pisgah
pass: **8** Akrabbin
plateau: **4** Seir
territory: **4** Moab

deaden: **4** damp, dull, kill, mute, numb, stun **5** blunt **6** benumb, dampen, muffle, obtund, opiate, retard, weaken **7** petrify, repress **8** amortize, enfeeble **10** devitalize

deadfall: **4** trap

deadhead: **6** bobber

deadhouse: **6** morgue **8** mortuary

deadlock: tie **8** stoppage **9** stalemate **10** standstill

deadly: **4** dire, fell, mort **5** fatal **6** lethal, mortal **7** capital, deathly, fateful, ruinous **8** venomous, virulent **9** pestilent **10** implacable, pernicious **11** destructive, internecine

deaf: **5** dunch **9** unheeding

deafness: **6** asonia **8** anacusia, anacusis, cophosis
cause: **4** stun **5** deave(Sc.)

deal: **4** dole, part, sale **5** allot, board, plank, sever, share, trade, wield **6** bestow, divide, handle, parcel **7** bargain, deliver, inflict, portion, scatter, wrestle **8** dispense, separate **9** apportion, negotiate **10** administer, distribute **11** transaction
in: **4** sell **5** trade **6** purvey
with: **4** cope **6** handle

dealbate: **5** white **8** whitened

dealer: **5** agent **6** badger, broker, cadger, jobber, monger, seller, trader **7** chapman **8** merchant, operator **9** middleman, tradesman **10** negotiator, trafficker **11** distributer, distributor
secondhand goods: **6** broker **10** pawnbroker

dealing: **7** trading, traffic **8** exchange **11** intercourse
shrewd: **6** deceit **9** chicanery

dean (see also **dene**): **5** doyen **6** senior, verger **8** official

dear: jo; gra, joe, pet **4** agra, cara(It.), cher(F.), fond, high, lief, near **5** chary, chere(F.), honey, loved **6** costly, dearly, scarce, severe, worthy **7** beloved, darling, lovable, pigsney, querida **8** esteemed, glorious, precious, valuable **9** cherished, expensive, heartfelt, honorable, important **10** sweetheart **12** affectionate

dearly: **6** deeply, keenly, richly **8** heartily **9** earnestly

dearness: **6** dearth

dearth: **4** lack, want **6** famine **7** paucity, poverty **8** dearness, scarcity **10** costliness, deficiency

death: end **4** bale, bane, doom, mors, mort(F.), obit **5** decay **6** demise, expiry, murder **7** decease, quietus **8** biolysis, rawbones **9** bloodshed, departure, forthfare **10** expiration, extinction, pestilence
after: **10** posthumous
angel of: **6** Azrael
aware of portending: fey
eternal: **9** perdition
goddess: Hel **4** Dana, Danu
meditation: **11** thanatopsis
mercy: **10** euthanasia
notice: **4** obit **5** orbit **8** obituary
personification: **4** Mors **5** Ankou **6** Charos, Charus
put to: gas **4** hang, kill, slay **5** choke **6** murder, noyade, starve, stifle **7** garrote **8** strangle **9** suffocate **11** assassinate, elec-

trocute
rate: **9** mortality
rattle: **4** rale
register: **9** necrology
symbol of: **5** orant
type of: **5** lynch **6** halter, noyode **10** lapidation
deathless: 7 eternal, undying **8** immortal **12** imperishable
deathlessness: 9 athanasia **11** immortality
deathlike: 7 deathly, ghastly, macaber, macaber **8** ghastful, moribund
deathly: 5 fatal **6** deadly, mortal **8** mortally **9** deathlike **11** destructive
deave: din **4** stun **6** bother, deafen **7** stupefy **8** bewilder
debacle: 4 rout **7** failure **8** collapse, stampede **9** breakdown, cataclysm
debar: 4 deny, tabu **5** estop, taboo **6** forbid, hinder, refuse **7** boycott, deprive, exclude, prevent, seclude, suspend **8** preclude, prohibit **9** foreclose, interdict **10** disqualify
debark: 4 land **9** disembark
debarrass: 7 relieve **12** disembarrass
debase: 5 abase, alloy, avile, lower, stoop **6** defile, demean, impair, reduce, revile, vilify **7** corrupt, degrade, deprave, traduce, vitiate **10** adulterate, degenerate, depreciate **11** deteriorate
debased: 4 base, vile **7** corrupt
debatable: 4 moot
debate: 4 agon, moot **5** argue, fight **6** reason, strife **7** agitate, canvass, contend, contest, discuss, dispute, examine, palaver, quarrel, wrangle **8** argument, consider, militate, question **9** dialectic, quodlibet **10** contention, controvert, deliberate **11** controversy **12** dissertation **13** argumentation
pert. to: **8** forensic
place of: **5** forum
stoppage of: **7** cloture
debater: 16 controversialist
debating: 11 contentious
association: **6** lyceum
debauch: 4 bout **5** spree, taint **6** defile, guzzle, seduce, splore, vilify **7** corrupt, deprave, mislead, pollute, violate **8** squander, strumpet **10** depreciate, hellbender **11** contaminate
debauched: 4 lewd **8** rakehell **9** dissolute
debauchee: rip **4** rake, roue **6** lecher **8** rakehell **9** libertine
debilitated: 4 weak **5** seedy **6** feeble, infirm, sapped **9** enervated
debility: 5 atony **7** languor **8** weakness **9** infirmity, lassitude **10** feebleness
debit: 4 loss **6** charge
debonair: 4 airy **6** jaunty, polite **8** graceful, gracious
debouche: 4 exit **6** emerge, outlet **7** passage **9** emergence

debris: 5 trash, waste **6** refuse, rubble **7** rubbish **8** detritus
debt: sin **5** debit, fault **7** arrears **8** trespass **9** arrearage, liability **10** obligation
acknowledgement: I.O.U. **4** bill, note
debtor: 6 dyvour
proceed against: **6** excuss
debut: 7 opening **8** entrance **9** beginning **12** introduction
debutant, debutante: bud, deb **5** debby
decadent: 6 effete **7** decayed **9** declining **10** retrograde **12** deteriorated **13** retrogressive
decamp: 4 bolt **5** elope, scoot, vamos **6** depart, levant, mizzle, vamose **7** abscond, vamoose **8** clear out
decant: 4 emit, pour **6** unload **8** transfer
decanter: 6 carafe
decapitate: 6 behead **10** guillotine
decay: ebb, rot **4** conk, dote, doze, fade, fail, ruin, wast **5** death, spoil **6** caries, mildew, wither **7** decline, failure **8** decrease **9** adversity, decadence, decompose **11** destruction, deteriorate, dissolution **12** dilapidation, disintegrate, putrefaction **13** decomposition, deterioration **14** disintegration
decaying: 4 doty
decease: die **5** death **6** demise **9** departure **11** dissolution
deceased: 4 dead **7** defunct **8** departed
deceit: See **deception**.
deceitful: 5 false, gaudy **6** fickle, hollow **7** sirenic **8** tortuous **9** faithless, insidious, insincere **10** circuitous, fallacious **11** disaffected **13** machiavellian
deceivable: 8 gullible
deceive: cog, con, lie **4** bilk, dupe, flam, fool, gaff, gull, hoax, jilt **5** abuse, blear, blend, blind, bluff, catch, cheat, cozen, cully, dodge, gleek, hocus, trick **6** baffle, beflum, befool, betray, bubble, delude, divert, humbug, illude **7** beguile, defraud, mislead **8** flimflam, hoodwink **9** bamboozle, frustrate **11** doublecross **12** misrepresent
deceiver: 6 trepan **7** juggler, sharper, warlock **8** magician
decelerate: 4 slow
decency: 7 decorum **9** propriety
decennium: 6 decade
decent: 4 fair **6** chaste, comely, honest, modest, proper, seemly **7** fitting, gradely, shapely **8** decorous **11** appropriate, respectable
deception: dor **4** dole, gaff, ruse, sham, wile **5** cheat, covin, craft, fraud, guile, magic, trick **6** cautel, deceit, humbug **7** blaflum, cunning, evasion, fallacy, fiction, knavery, pretext, slyness **8** artifice, falsedad(Sp.), intrigue, prestige, subtlety, trickery, trumpery, wiliness **9** chicanery, collusion, duplicity, falsehood, hypocrisy, imposture, mendacity, sophistry, treach-

ery **10** artfulness, camouflage, dishonesty, imposition, infidelity **11** contrivance, counterfeit, dissembling **13** deceitfulness, dissimulation

deceptive: **5** false **8** delusive, illusory **10** fallacious

decided: **4** firm, flat **6** formed **8** clear-cut, decisive **14** unquestionably

decima: **5** tenth, tithe

decimal base: ten

decimate: **7** destroy

decipher: **4** read **6** decode, detect, reveal **8** discover, indicate **9** translate

decision: end **4** doom, fiat, grit **5** arret, canon, pluck **6** crisis, decree, ruling **7** consult, verdict **8** finality, judgment, sentence **9** precedent **10** conclusion, resolution **12** adjudication **13** determination

maker: **5** judge **6** umpire **7** referee **9** executive

sudden: **4** whim **7** impulse

decisive: **5** final **6** crisic **7** crucial **8** critical **10** conclusive, peremptory

deck: tog **4** buss, dink, heap, pink, trig **5** adorn, array, cover, dizen, dress, equip, floor, prink, store **6** blazon, clothe, fettle **7** apparel, bedight, bedizen, feather **8** beautify, decorate, platform **9** embellish **10** overspread

kind: gun **4** boat, main, poop, spar **5** berth, orlop, upper **6** bridge **7** shelter **8** hurrican, platform, splinter **9** promenade **10** forecastle, protective

part: **7** scupper

decked: **4** clad **6** beseen

deckle-edged: **5** erose

declaim: **4** gale, rant, rave **5** orate, speak, spout **6** recite **7** elocute, inveigh **8** denounce, harangue, perorate **9** discourse

declaration: **4** word **5** fuero, libel **6** oracle, placet **7** promise **9** affidavit, assertion, statement **10** allegation, deposition, exposition, intimation **11** affirmation, certificate, description, enunciation **12** announcement, asseveration, proclamation **13** advertisement, pronouncement **14** interpretation **15** acknowledgement

declare: bid, say, vow **4** aver, avow, deny, make, read, show, trow **5** aread, areed, posit, state **6** affirm, allege, assert, assure, avouch, blazon, depone, herald, indict, notify, relate **7** behight, express, profess, protest, signify, testify **8** announce, denounce, describe, indicate, maintain, manifest, proclaim **9** advertise, enunciate, nuncupate, pronounce **10** announciate, asseverate, promulgate **11** acknowledge, communicate

declination: **4** bias **5** decay, slope **6** regret **7** decline, descent, refusal **8** swerving **10** declension **11** declinature, inclination **13** deterioration

decline: dip, ebb, set **4** bend, fade, fail, fall, flag, sink, turn, wane **5** chute, droop,

heald, hield, lower, repel, slope, slump, stoop, stray **6** debase, refuse, reject, renege, weaken **7** descend, descent, deviate, disavow, dwindle, failure, forbear **8** decrease, forebear, languish, withdraw **9** decadence, declivity, recadence, repudiate **10** declension, retrograde **11** declination, degradation **13** deterioration

declining: **5** awane **8** decadent **13** deteriorating

declivity: **4** hang **5** cliff, scarp, slope **6** calade **7** decline, descent, hanging **9** acclivity, precipice

declivous: **5** prone **7** sloping

decoct: **4** boil, cook **5** smelt **6** excite, kindle, refine **7** extract **8** condense, diminish

decorate: **4** bind, cite, deck, pink, trim **5** adorn, dress, inlay, panel **6** decore, emboss, parget **7** festoon, garnish, miniate **8** ornament, titivate **9** embellish

decorated: **6** ornate **7** damasse, wrought **9** sigillate

decoration: **4** bahl **5** medal **6** frieze, plaque, tinsel **7** epergne, garnish, regalis **8** flourish, ornament **9** furniture, sgraffito **10** chambranle, decorament, decorement, sgraffiato

decorative: **5** fancy **9** beautiful **10** ornamental

decore: **5** adorn **8** beautify, decorate

decorous: **4** calm, good, prim **5** grave, quiet, sober, staid **6** decent, demure, modest, polite, proper, sedate, seemly, serene, steady **7** fitting, orderly, regular, settled **8** becoming, composed, mannerly **9** befitting, dignified, unruffled **11** appropriate

decorticate: **4** flay, hull, husk, pare, peel, pill, skin **5** strip **6** denude **9** excoriate

decorum: **9** propriety **10** convention

decoy: **4** bait, lure, tole **5** drill, plant, shill, tempt **6** allure, entice, entrap, pigeon **8** inveigle **9** shillaber

decrease: ebb **4** drop, fall, loss, sink, wane **5** abate, decay, taper, waste **6** impair, lessen, shrink **7** decline, dwindle, slacken, subside **8** diminish, moderate, retrench **9** decession, decrement **10** diminution

decree: act, law **4** fiat, rede, rule, will **5** aread, areed, arret, canon, edict, enact, irade, order, tenet, ukase **6** arrest, assize, decern, dictum, firman, indict, ordain **7** adjudge, appoint, command, decreet, mandate, statute **8** decision, decretum, rescript, sentence **9** determine, enactment, ordinance, preordain **10** adjudicate, plebiscite **12** adjudication, announcement

decrement: **4** loss **5** waste **8** decrease **10** diminution

decrepit: **4** lame, weak **6** feeble, infirm, senile **7** failing, invalid **9** bedridden

decrown: **6** depose **8** unthrone

decry: boo **4** slur **5** lower **6** lessen **7** asperse, censure, condemn, debauch, degrade, detract **8** belittle, derogate **9** discredit, disparage, underrate **10** depreciate, undervalue

decuman: **4** huge **5** large

decuple: **7** tenfold

decussate: **9** intersect

dedal: See **daedal**.

dedicate: vow **6** devote, direct, hallow, oblate **7** ascribe **8** inscribe **9** nuncupate **10** consecrate

deduce: **4** draw, lead **5** bring, drive, infer, trace **6** derive, elicit, evolve, gather **7** extract **8** conclude

deduct: **4** bate, dock, take **5** abate, allow **6** defalk, remove **7** curtail **8** abstract, discount, separate, subtract

deduction: **4** agio **6** rebate **7** reprise **8** illation **9** corollary, induction

deed: act **4** case, fact, feat, fiat, gest **5** actum, actus, chart, doing, title **6** action, convey, escrow, pottah, remise **7** charter, exploit **8** transfer **10** instrument **11** achievement, performance **14** accomplishment
benevolent: **4** boon **5** favor **8** benefice
evil: sin **11** malefaction

deeds: **9** res gestae

deem: say **4** hope, reck, tell **5** judge, opine, think **6** esteem, expect, ordain, reckon, regard **7** account, adjudge, believe, surmise **8** announce, consider, judgment, proclaim **10** adjudicate

deep: low, sea **4** howe, rapt **5** abyss, grave, great, gruff, heavy, ocean **6** hollow, intent **7** abysmal, intense, serious, unmixed **8** absorbed, abstruse, complete, powerful, profound, thorough **9** entangled, insidious, recondite **11** far-reaching

deepen: **5** cloud **6** darken **7** enhance, thicken **9** intensify **10** strengthen

deer: red, roe **6** animal, cervid, fallow, mammal **7** barking
antler: dag
Asian: **4** axis, maha, napu, shou, sika **5** maral **6** chitra, hangul, sambar **10** barasingha
barking: **7** muntjac, muntjak
cry: **4** bell
female: doe **4** hind
genus of: **8** cervilla
large: elk **5** moose **6** wapiti **7** caribou
male: **4** buck, hart, spay, stag **7** roebuck
meat: **5** jerky **7** charqui, venison
North American: elk **5** moose **6** wapiti **7**
path: run **4** slot **5** trail
pert. to: **6** damine **7** cervine
small: roe **7** roebuck
South American: **4** pudu **6** guemal, guemul, vanada **7** brocket
young: **4** fawn, spay **7** spitter

deerlet: **4** napu **10** chevrotain

deface: mar **4** foul, ruin, scar **5** erase, shame, spoil **6** damage, defame, defoil, deform, defoul, efface, injure, injury **7** destroy, detract, distort, slander **8** disgrace, dishonor, mutilate, outshine **9** blemished, discredit, disfigure, disvisage, vandalize **10** disfeature

defame: **4** foul **5** abase, belie, cloud, libel, smear **6** accuse, charge, deface, infamy, injure, malign, vilify **7** asperse, blacken, blemish, debauch, detract, publish, scandal, slander, traduce **8** dishonor **9** blaspheme, denigrate **10** calumniate, defamation

default: **4** fail, flaw **5** error, fault **6** offend **7** blemish, failure, mistake, neglect, offense **8** omission **12** imperfection **13** nonappearance

defeasance: **6** defeat **7** undoing **9** overthrow

defeat: win **4** balk, beat, best, drub, foil, loss, rout, ruin, undo **5** break, check, facer, floor, skunk, worst, wrack **6** baffle, cumber, derout, master, thwack, weaken **7** conquer, deprive, destroy, preempt, reverse, shellac **8** overcome, vanquish, Waterloo **9** discomfit, disfigure, frustrate, overpower, overthrow, overwhelm **10** defeasance, defeatment, disappoint **12** discomfiture

defeated: **4** lost **5** kaput **6** craven

defeatist: **4** Bolo **8** fatalist **9** handupper, pessimist **10** handsupper

defect: **4** flaw, lack, vice, want **5** craze, fault, minus **6** damage, desert, injury **7** blemish, debauch, detract, publish, scandal, slander, traduce **8** dishonor **9** blasshortcoming **12** imperfection
without: **5** sound **7** perfect

defective: bad, ill **4** poor **6** faulty **7** halting **8** vitiated **9** deficient, imperfect, **10** inaccurate, incomplete

defend (see also **defense**): **4** fend, hold, save, wear **5** guard, watch **6** assert, forbid, screen, secure, shield, uphold **7** contest, espouse, justify, prevent, protect, shelter **8** advocate, champion, conserve, maintain, preserve, prohibit **9** exculpate, patronage, vindicate

defendant: **8** appellee
answer: **4** plea **14** nolo contendere

defender: **11** propugnator

defense, defence (see also **fortification**): **4** egis, fort **5** aegis, alibi, fence, grith **6** answer, behalf, covert, sconce **7** contest, shelter **8** apologia, boundary, security **9** coverture, safeguard **10** protection **11** maintenance
movement: **4** spar

defenseless: **4** bare **5** naked **7** unarmed **8** helpless **9** unguarded

defensible: **7** tenable **9** excusable

defensive: **9** shielding **10** apologetic

defer: boy 4 wait 5 delay, honor, yield 6 esteem, humble, retard, revere, submit 8 consider, postpone, prorogue, protract 13 procrastinate

deference: 6 homage, regard 9 obeisance

defiance: 6 defial

defiant: 4 bold 5 brave 6 daring 8 insolent 11 challenging

deficiency: 4 lack, want 5 fault, minus 6 dearth, defect 7 absence, blemish, deficit, failing, failure 8 scarcity, shortage 9 indigence 10 inadequacy 11 destitution, shortcoming 12 imperfection 13 insufficiency

deficient: 6 meager, meagre 7 bobtail

defile: gut 4 file, gate, gowl, hals, pass, soil 5 abuse, beray, dirty, gorge, smear, sully, taint 6 debase, infect, ravish 7 corrupt, deprave, distain, passage, pollute, tarnish, violate 8 dishonor, maculate 9 desecrate 10 adulterate 11 contaminate

defiled: 6 impure 7 unclean 8 maculate

definable: 6 finite

define: end, fix, set 4 mere, term 5 bound, limit 6 decide 7 clarify, delimit, explain, expound 8 describe, discover 9 demarcate, determine, interpret, prescribe 11 distinguish 12 characterize, circumscribe

definite: 4 sure 5 clear, final, fixed, sharp 7 certain, limited, precise 8 distinct, explicit, limiting 10 conclusive 11 determinate, determining, unequivocal 12 determinable, unmistakable

definitive: 5 final

deflect: 4 bend, warp 5 parry 6 divert, swerve 7 deviate, inflect, reflect, refract

deflower: 6 ravage, ravish 7 despoil, violate

deform: mar 6 deface 7 blemish, contort, distort 8 disguise, dishonor, misshape 9 disfigure 10 disarrange

deformed: 7 crooked, hideous 8 formless 9 amorphous, loathsome, monstrous, shapeless, unshapely 11 counterfeit

defraud: rob 4 bilk, fake, gull, rook, trim 5 cheat, cozen, gouge, mulct, trick 6 chouse 7 deceive, swindle 8 dry-shave

defray: pay 5 avert 6 expend, prepay 7 appease, requite, satisfy 8 disburse 9 discharge, reimburse

deft: 4 neat, trim 5 agile, handy, quick 6 adroit, expert, heppen, nimble, spruce 7 deliver 8 dextrous, skillful 9 dexterous

defunct: 4 dead 7 extinct 8 deceased, departed, finished

defy: 4 dare, face 5 beard, brave, stump, tempt 6 forbid, reject 7 affront, despise, disdain, outface 8 champion, defiance, renounce 9 challenge, repudiate 10 contravene

deg: 6 dampen 8 sprinkle

degenerate: rot 6 debase 7 degrade, deprave 11 deteriorate

degradation: 7 descent 8 ignominy

degrade: 4 bust 5 abase, decry, lower, shame, strip 6 debase, demean, demote, depose, humble, reduce, vilify 7 corrupt, decline, depress 8 disgrace, dishonor 9 disparage, humiliate 10 degenerate, depreciate 11 deteriorate

degraded: 4 base 5 seamy 6 abject, fallen 7 debased, grieced 10 degenerate, diminished

degrading: 4 base 6 menial 8 shameful

degree: 4 bank, heat, rank, rate, rung, step, term, tier 5 class, grade, grece, honor, order, pitch, point, stage, stair 6 extent, medium, soever 7 measure, station 8 quantity, standing 9 gradation 10 attainment

academic: A.B., B.A., B.S., C.E., D.D., M.A., M.D., M.S.; B.L.S., B.Sc., L.L.B., L.L.D., M.Sc., Ph.D. 4 D.Lit. 5 Litt.D.

conferral: 10 laureation

equal: as

highest: sum 6 summit, utmost 7 extreme 8 cum laude

slight: ace 4 hair, inch 5 shade 8 slightly 9 gradation

degust, degustate: 5 savor, taste 6 relish

dehisce: 4 gape

dehort: 4 urge 8 dissuade

dehydrate: dry 9 desiccate, evaporate

deific: 6 divine 7 godlike

deify: 10 consecrate 11 apotheosize

deign: 5 stoop 10 condescend

deigning: 11 patronizing

deity (see also **god** and next entry)**:** god 4 deva, idol, muse 6 genius 7 creator, demigod, godling, godhead, godship 8 Almighty, divinity, governor

half-fish: Ea 6 Oannes

half-goat: 4 faun

hawk-eyed: Ra 5 Horus 6 Sokari 7 Sokaris

jackal-headed: 6 Anubis

tutelary: 5 genie, lares, numen 7 Hershef, penates

deity: For definitions using this word, see *god* and *goddess* under appropriate country or function. EXAMPLES: "Roman deity" see **Rome** *god*; "war deity" see **war** *god*.

deject: 5 abase, lower 6 humble, lessen 7 flatten 8 dispirit 9 overthrow 10 discomfort, discourage, dishearten

dejected: low, sad 4 damp, glum, sunk 5 amort 6 abased, gloomy, pining 7 alamort, humbled, unhappy 8 repining, wretched 9 cheerless, depressed, prostrate, woebegone 10 despondent, spiritless 11 crestfallen, downhearted 12 disconsolate, disheartened, fainthearted

dejection: 6 dismay 10 melancholy

dejeuner: 5 lunch 9 breakfast, collation

dekko: 4 look, peep

delapse: 5 lapse 7 descend

delate: 5 carry 6 accuse, assign, convey, inform, report, submit, tender 7 publish 8 denounce

Delaware: *Indian:* 6 Lenape

town: 5 Dover, Lewes 7 Chester 10 Wilmington

delay: lag 4 bode, mora, stay, stop, wait 5 abide, abode, allay, check, dally, defer, demur, deter, dwell, frist, stall, tarry 6 arrest, belate, detain, dilate, dilute, dretch, hinder, impede, linger, loiter, quench, remora, retard, taigle, temper, weaken 7 adjourn, assuage, barrace, confine, prolong, respite 8 demurral, hesitate, macerate, mitigate, moration, obstruct, postpone, stoppage 9 detention, hindrance, lingering 10 cunctation, moratorium, suspension 13 procrastinate 15 procrastination

delayed: 4 late 5 tardy 7 belated, overdue

delaying: 8 dilatory

dele: 4 omit 5 erase 6 cancel, delete, efface, remove 7 expunge 9 eradicate, extirpate 10 obliterate

delectable: 5 tasty 8 pleasing 9 delicious, desirable, diverting, enjoyable 10 delightful 11 pleasurable

delegate: 4 name, send 6 assign, commit, depute, deputy, legate, nuncio 7 appoint, consign, empower, entrust 8 emissary, transfer 9 authorize, surrogate 10 commission 12 commissioner 14 representative

delegation: 7 mission 9 committee 10 deputation

delete: 4 dele, omit 5 erase, purge 6 cancel, remove 7 destroy, expunge 9 eliminate, eradicate 10 obliterate

deleterious: bad 7 harmful, hurtful, noxious 8 damaging 9 injurious, malignant 10 pernicious 11 destructive, detrimental, prejudicial

delf, delft: pit, sod 4 mine, pond 5 ditch, drain, grave 6 quarry

Delhi district: 5 Simla

Delian god: 6 Apollo

deliberate: 4 cool, pore 5 think 6 advise, confer, debate, ponder 7 bethink, consult, reflect, resolve, studies 8 consider, measured, meditate 9 determine, leisurely, speculate, voluntary 10 purposeful 11 circumspect, intentional 12 premeditated 13 dispassionate

deliberation: 7 counsel 10 reflection

without: 4 rash 8 headlong

Delibes ballet: 5 Naila

delible: 10 eradicable

delicacy: roe 4 cate, ease, nori, tact 5 acate, taste 6 caviar, dainty, delice, luxury, nicety 7 caviare, finesse 8 niceness, pleasure, subtlety 9 exactness, precision 10 daintiness, effeminity, femininity, refinement 13 gratification

lacking: 5 gross

delicate: 4 airy, fine, lacy, nice 5 frail, light, silky 6 dainty, minion, petite, puling, queasy, slight, tender 7 elegant, finical, fragile, minikin, refined, subtile, tenuous 8 araneose, araneous, charming, ethereal, graceful, luscious, migniard, pleasant 9 agreeable, beautiful, delicious, exquisite, palatable, sensitive 10 delightful, fastidious 11 comfortable, considerate

delicatessen: 11 charcuterie

delicious: 8 delicate 9 ambrosial, exquisite, luxurious, nectareal, nectarean 10 delectable, delightful, nectareous, voluptuous

delict: 7 offense 13 transgression

delight: joy 4 glee, love 5 bliss, charm, feast, mirth, revel 6 admire, divert, liking, please, ravish, regale 7 ecstasy, enchant, gladden, gratify, rapture, rejoice 8 entrance, gladness, pleasure, savoring 9 delectate, enjoyment, enrapture, happiness 11 delectation

in: 6 relish

delightful: 4 nice 6 savory 7 elysian 8 adorable, delicate, glorious 9 delicious 10 delectable 11 pleasureful

Delilah's paramour: 6 Samson 7 Sampson

delimit: See **define.**

delineate: map 4 draw, limn, line 5 trace 6 blazon, depict, design, sketch, survey 7 outline, picture, portray 8 describe 9 represent 12 characterize

delineation: 10 expression

delinquency: 5 fault 7 failure, misdeed, offense 8 omission 9 violation 10 misconduct 11 malfeasance, misdemeanor, misfeasance

deliquesce: 4 give, melt 7 liquify 8 dissolve

delirious: mad 4 frey, gyte 5 manic 6 insane, raving 7 frantic, lunatic 8 brainish, deleerit, delieret, deranged, frenetic, frenzied 9 phrenetic 11 lightheaded

delirium: 4 fury, maze 8 idleness 10 aberration 13 hallucination

deliver: rid 4 bail, deal, free 5 serve, speak, utter 6 assoil, commit, convey, redeem, render, rescue, resign, succor, unbind 7 beteach, consign, declaim, dictate, present, release, relieve 8 dispatch, exorcise, exorcize, liberate 9 enunciate, pronounce, surrender 10 emancipate

deliverer: 7 drayman 9 preserver

deliverly: 6 deftly, nimbly 8 actively

delivery: 6 rescue 7 address 8 shipment 9 rendition 11 deliverance, parturition 12 accouchement

dell: den 4 dale, dean, dene, drab, glen, vale 5 trull, wench 6 dingle, ravine, valley

delphinium: 8 larkspur

delta: 8 alluvium, triangle

delude: bob 4 bilk, dupe, fool 5 cheat,

elude, evade, trick **6** befool, bubble, illude **7** beguile, deceive, mislead **8** hoodwink **9** mislippen **10** circumvent

deluge: sea **4** flow **5** flood, swamp **8** inundate, overflow, submerge **9** cataclysm, overpower, overwhelm, rainstorm **10** overspread

delusion: 5 trick **6** mirage, vision **7** chimera, fallacy, fantasm **8** illusion, phantasm **9** deception **13** appersonation, hallucination

delusory: 8 delusive

delve: den, dig, dip, pit **4** cave, dint, mine **5** ditch, plumb **6** bruise, exhume, fathom, indent **7** impress **8** excavate, inscribe

demagogic: 8 factious

demagogue, demagog: 6 leader, orator, rouser **7** speaker

demand: ask, cry **4** call, need **5** claim, exact, order, query **6** charge, elicit, expect, summon **7** command, inquire, mandate, request, require **8** question **9** challenge **10** commission **11** requisition

demandable: due

demarcate: 6 demark **7** delimit **8** separate **12** discriminate

demean: 5 abase, lower **6** debase **7** degrade **8** demeanon, maltreat

demeanor: 4 mien, port **5** habit **6** action, havior **7** bearing, conduct **8** behavior, carriage, portance **9** treatment **10** deportment, management **11** comportment, countenance

demented: mad **4** luny **5** buggy, crazy, nutty **6** insane **7** fatuous

demerit: 4 mark **5** fault **6** desert

demesne: 5 manor, place, realm **6** domain, estate, region **8** district

Demeter: 5 Ceres
daughter: **4** Cora, Kore **8** Despoina **10** Persephone, Proserpina, Proserpine **11** Persephassa
headdress: **5** polos
mother: **4** Rhea

demigod: 4 hero **7** godling
pert. to: **7** satyric
sylvan: **5** satyr

demirep: 11 adventuress

demise: 4 will **5** death **6** convey **7** decease **8** bequeath

demiss: 6 humble

demit: 5 lower **6** humble, resign **8** abdicate **10** relinquish **11** resignation

demiurgic: 8 creative

demoded: 5 passe

demoiselle: 5 crane **7** kaikara

demolish: 4 rase, raze, ruin **5** level, waste, wreck **6** batter **7** destroy, ruinate **9** devastate, overthrow

demon: hag, imp, nat **4** aitu, atua, ogre **5** devil, fiend, genie, lamia, Satan, witch **6** Abigor, afreet **7** villain, warlock **9** cacodemon **10** cacodaemon
possessed by: **9** energumen

demoniac: 7 demonic, lunatic **8** devilish, diabolic, fiendish, infernal **10** diabolical

demonstrate: 4 show **5** prove **7** display, portray **8** manifest

demonstration: 4 show, sign **5** proof **9** manifesto, portrayal **10** apparition **12** illustration **13** manifestation

demonstrative: 4 that, this **5** these, those **8** effusive **9** ostensive **12** ostentatious

demoralize: 6 weaken **7** confuse, corrupt, deprave, pervert **9** undermine **10** discourage, dishearten **11** disorganize

demos: 4 deme **6** people **8** citizens, populace

Demosthenes: *follower:* **5** Bryan **6** orator
oration: **9** philippic

demote: 4 bust **6** reduce **7** degrade

demotic: 7 popular

demulcent: 8 soothing **9** softening **10** mollifying

demur: 4 stay **5** delay, doubt, pause **6** boggle, linger, object **7** scruple, suspend **8** hesitate, suspense **9** objection **12** irresolution

demure: coy, mim, shy **4** prim **5** grave, staid, suant **6** modest, sedate **8** composed, decorous

demurral: See **demur.**

den: mew **4** cave, cove, dell, dive, glen, hole, lair, nest, room **5** bield, cabin, couch, haunt, study **6** burrow, cavern, covert, grotto, hollow, ravine **7** retreat **8** hideaway, snuggery, workroom

denary: 7 tenfold

dendroid: 11 arborescent

dene, dean: 4 dell, vale **5** mound **6** valley

denial (see also **deny**): no; nay

denizen: 6 native **7** citizen **8** resident **9** indweller **10** inhabitant

Denmark: *city:* **6** Odense **7** Aalborg, Aarhuus, Horsens, Randers **8** Elsinore **9** Helsingor **10** Copenhagen(c.) **13** Frederiksberg
coin: ore **5** krone
comb. form: **4** Dano
composer: **4** Gade
country: Amt **4** Soro **7** Aalborg **8** Aabenraa
downs: **7** Klitten
embroidery: **6** hedebo
flag: **9** Dannebrog
inlet: Ise **5** fjord
island: Oe; Als **4** Aero **5** Faroe, Samso **7** Seeland
king: **4** Cnut, Knut **6** Canute **9** Christian
knighthood order: **9** Dannebrog
measure: ell, fod, mil, pot **4** alen, favn, rode **5** album, kande, linje, paegl, tomme **6** achtel, paegel, paegle, skeppe **7** landmil, oltonde, skieppe, viertel **8** fjerding **9** korntonde, ottingkar
musical instrument: **4** lure
possession: **5** Faroe **6** St. John **7** Iceland **8** St. Thomas **9** Greenland, Santa Cruz

prince: **5** Ogier
river: 'Asa **4** Holm, Stor **5** Guden **7** Lonborg
seaport: **6** Aarhus
settlers: **6** Ostmen
tribunal: **7** Rigsret
weight: es; lod, ort, vog **4** eser(pl.), last, mark, pund, unze **5** carat, kvint, pound, quint, tonde **6** toende **7** centner, lispund, quintin **8** lispound, skippund **9** ship pound, skibslast **10** bismerpund

denominate: 4 call, name **5** title **6** denote **8** christen, indicate, nominate **9** designate

denomination: 4 cult, sect **5** class, title **7** society **8** category **9** communion **11** appellation
religious: **7** Baptist **8** Lutheran **9** Methodist, Unitarian **12** Episcopalian, Presbyterian **14** Congregational

denotation: 4 sign **5** token

denote: 4 give, mark, mean, name, show **6** import **7** betoken, connote, express **8** indicate **9** designate, recommend, represent **10** denominate

denouement: 4 end **5** issue **7** outcome **8** solution **11** catastrophe

denounce: ban **6** accuse, delate, descry, menace, scathe **7** arraign, condemn, declare, upbraid **8** proclaim, threaten **9** fulminate **10** stigmatize

de novo: 4 anew **5** again, newly **6** afresh

dense: 4 firm **5** close, foggy, gross, heavy, murky, silly, solid, thick **6** obtuse, stupid **7** compact, crowded, serried **11** thick-headed **12** impenetrable

dent: 4 bash, dint, nick, **5** dinge, notch, tooth **6** batter, hallow, indent **7** blemish, depress **10** depression, impression **11** indentation

dental: See **dentistry, tooth**.

dentation: 5 serra **10** projection

denticulate: 7 serrate

denticulation: jag **5** tooth **8** denticle

dentil: 5 block

dentin: 5 ivory **6** enamel

dentistry: *appliance:* dam **4** burr
branch: **9** exodontia **11** orthodontia **12** orthodontics
tool: **6** scaler **7** forceps

denture: 5 teeth, plate

denude: 4 bare **5** scalp, strip **6** devest, divest **8** denudate **11** decorticate

denunciation (see also **denounce**): **6** threat **8** diatribe **9** philippic **11** malediction **12** proclamation

deny: nay **5** debar, repel **6** abjure, disown, forbid, impugn, negate, refuse, refute, reject, renege **7** confute, deprive, disavow, dispute, forsake, gainsay, protest **8** abnegate, disclaim, forswear, renounce, withhold **9** disaffirm **10** contradict, contravene, controvert

deodand: 7 forfeit

deodar: 5 cedar

depart: go; die, mog **4** blow, pass, quit, vary **5** found, leave, mosey, sever **6** begone, decamp, demise, desist, divide, perish, recede, retire, sunder **7** abscond, deviate, forsake, get away, retreat, vamoose **8** farewell, separate, withdraw

departed: 4 dead **6** bygone **7** defunct **8** deceased, decedent

department: 4 part **5** realm **6** branch, bureau, sphere **7** portion **8** division, province **11** subdivision

departure: 4 exit **5** death, exode **6** congee, egress **7** decease **9** decession **11** abandonment, forthfaring, leavetaking

depend: 4 bank, hang, lean, rely, rest, turn **5** count, hinge, trust **7** confide

dependable: 5 siker, solid **6** sicker **7** certain **8** reliable **11** trustworthy

dependency: 5 taluk **6** colony **7** apanage **8** appanage

dependent: 6 client, minion, sponge, vassal **7** sponger, subject **8** clinging, follower **9** adjective, corollary **10** accidental, contingent, sequacious **11** subordinate

depict: 4 draw, limn **5** paint **6** blazon **7** picture, portray **8** describe **9** delineate, represent **12** characterize

depilous: 8 hairless

deplete: 5 drain, empty **6** reduce, unload **7** exhaust **8** diminish **10** impoverish

deplorable: sad **8** wretched **10** calamitous

deplore: rue **4** moan, sigh, wail **5** mourn **6** bemoan, bewail, grieve, lament, regret **8** complain

deploy: 6 unfold **7** display

deplume: 5 pluck, strip

depone: 5 swear **6** depose **7** testify

deponent: 7 affiant **10** incomplete

depopulate: 6 ravage **9** devastate, dispeople

deport: 5 exile **6** banish, behave, demean **7** bearing, conduct **9** transport **10** deportment

deportment: air **4** gest, mien **5** geste habit **6** action, deport, manner **7** address, bearing, comfort, conduct **8** behavior, breeding, carriage, demeanor **9** behaviour, demeanour

depose: 4 aver **5** abase **6** affirm, assert, depone, divest, remove **7** degrade, deposit, testify **8** dethrone, displace **10** dispossess **11** disenthrone

deposit: lay, set **4** bank, cast, dump, fund, hock, pawn **5** chest, lodge, place, store **6** entomb, pledge, repose, settle **7** consign, deposit, entrust **10** deposition, depository
black: **4** soot
earthy: as; ore **4** asar(pl.), gobi, lode, marl, sand, silt **5** delta, eskar, esker, geest, loess, manto, trona **6** placer, sludge **7** alluvia, moraine **8** alluvium
ore: vug
roric: dew

deposition: 6 burial **7** deposit, opinion **8** sediment **9** affidavit, statement, testimony

10 allegation 11 declaration 12 displacement 13 precipitation

depository: 4 bank, safe 5 attic, vault 7 ossuary 10 repository

depot: 4 base, gore(F.) 6 aurang(Ind.), aurung 7 station 8 magazine, terminal, terminus 9 warehouse 10 storehouse

deprave: 5 taint 6 debase, defile, malign, revile 7 corrupt, pervert, vitiate 10 degenerate, depreciate

depraved: bad 4 evil, ugly, vile 6 rotten, wicked 7 bestial, immoral, vicious 9 abandoned, graceless 10 profligate 11 demoralized 12 incorrigible

depravity: 4 vice 8 villainy

deprecate: 4 pray 6 invoke 7 beseech 10 depreciate, disapprove, supplicate

deprecation: 8 petition 14 disapprobation

depreciate: 4 fall 5 abase, avile, decry, slump 6 debase, lessen, reduce, shrink 7 cheapen, debauch, degrade, deprave, depress, detract 8 belittle, derogate, disprize, disvalue, minimize 9 disparage, dispraise, extenuate 10 undervalue

depreciation: 4 agio 8 discount 9 misprison

depredate: rob 4 prey, raze 5 spoil 6 thieve 7 despoil, destroy, pillage, plunder

deprehend: 5 seize 6 detect 7 capture 8 discover 9 apprehend

depress: bow, cow 4 dash, dent, fall, sink 5 abase, appal, chill, crush, lower, slump 6 appall, dampen, dismay, humble, indent, lessen, sadden, weaken 7 degrade, flatten, oppress, repress 8 browbeat, diminish, dispirit, enfeeble 9 disparage, subjugate 10 depreciate, discourage, dishearten

depressed: 4 sick 6 gloomy, hipped, hollow, lonely, oblate, somber, triste 8 dejected, downcast 9 afflicted, debruised 10 spiritless 11 downhearted, melancholic

depressing: 5 bleak 6 dreary

depression: col, dip, gat, pit 4 delk, doke, fall, foss, howe 5 atrio, basin, cowal, crypt, dinge, fossa, fosse, nadir 6 cafard, cavity, crater, dismay, gulley, ravine, valley 7 alveola, blowout 8 doldrums 9 dejection 11 despondency 13 disparagement

deprivation: 4 cost, loss, want 7 amotion 9 privation, restraint 10 diminution 11 destitution

deprive: bar, rob 4 bate, deny 5 debar, spoil, strip 6 amerce, defeat, depose, devest, dismay, divest, hinder, remove 7 abridge, bereave, cashier, despoil, exhaust 8 denature, desolate, evacuate 9 dismantle, forestall 10 dispossess

deprived: 4 reft

depth: 5 abyss, midst 8 deepness, strength 9 abundance, intensity 10 profundity 12 abstruseness, completeness, profoundness

depth charge: 4 mine 10 projectile

depths: 5 heart

depurant: 8 purifier 11 purificator

deputation: 7 mission 10 delegation

depute: 4 send 5 allot 6 assign, devote 7 appoint 8 delegate 10 commission, constitute

deputy: 4 aide 5 agent, envoy, proxy, vicar 6 commis, legate 7 bailiff 8 delegate 9 assistant, surrogate, vigilante 10 substitute

deracinate: 9 eradicate, extirpate

derange: 5 upset 7 disturb, perturb 8 displace, unsettle 9 interrupt 10 disarrange, discompose

deranged: 5 crazy 6 crazed 7 frantic 10 distraught, unbalanced

derangement: 5 mania 6 lunacy 7 madness, rummage 8 delirium, disorder, insanity 9 confusion 11 distraction, disturbance 12 irregularity 15 disorganization

deray: 8 disorder 9 confusion 11 disturbance

derby: hat 4 race, town 5 shire 6 bowler

derelict: 7 failure 8 betrayer, castaway 9 abandoned 10 delinquent, neglectful, unfaithful

derf: 4 bold 6 daring

deride: 4 geck, gibe, hoot, jape, jeer, mock, twit 5 fleer, rally, scoff, scorn, taunt 6 illude 8 ridicule

derision: 8 contempt

derive: get 4 draw, stem 5 carry, infer, trace 6 deduce, evolve, gather, obtain 7 extract, proceed, receive 9 originate

derm: 4 skin 7 cuticle

derma: 5 layer 6 corium, dermis

dern: 4 dark, darn, dire, evil, hide 5 drear 6 crafty, hidden, secret, somber, sombre 7 conceal 9 concealed, underhand

dernier: 4 last 5 final

derogate: 5 annul, decry 6 lessen, repeal 7 detract, slander 8 restrict, withdraw 9 disparage 10 depreciate

derrick: jib, rig 4 lift, spar 5 crane, davit, hoist 6 tackle 7 gallows, hanging, hangman

derringer: 6 pistol, weapon

derry: 7 dislike 8 aversion

dervish: 5 fakir 6 fakeer
cap: taj

descant: 4 sing, song 6 melody, remark, warble 7 comment 9 discourse 11 observation 12 counterpoint, dissertation 13 accompaniment

descend: 4 fall, sink 5 avale, lower, stoop 6 alight, derive 7 decline, delapse 9 originate 10 condescend

descendant: son 4 cion, heir, seed 5 child, scion 9 offspring

descendants: 7 progeny 9 posterity 10 generation

descended from same mother: 5 enate 6 enatic

descent: 4 drop, fall 5 birth, chute, issue,

scarp, slope, stock **6** escarp, strain **7** assault, decline, extract, lineage **8** ancestry, breeding, downfall, pedigree **9** avalanche, declivity, onslaught **10** declension, extraction, generation **11** declination, degradation, inclination

describe: **4** tell **6** define, depict, relate, report **7** declare, explain, express, narrate, outline, picture, portray, recount **8** inscribe **9** delineate, designate, discourse, enumerate, represent **10** transcribe **12** characterize

descry: see, spy **4** espy **5** sight **6** behold, betray, detect, reveal **7** discern, display **8** denounce, disclose, discover, perceive **9** determine **11** distinguish

Desdemona: *husband:* **7** Othello

traducer: **4** Iago

desecrate: **5** abuse **6** defile **7** pollute, profane, violate **8** unhallow **11** contaminate

desert: due, erg, rat **4** areg, arid, bolt, fail, flee, sand **5** waive, waste **6** barren, defect, lonely, renege, reward **7** abandon, abscond, demerit, forsake, hornada **8** desolate, renounce **9** backslide, wasteland **10** excellence, punishment, relinquish, wilderness

beast: **5** camel

driver: **8** cameleer **9** camelteer

dweller: **4** Arab **5** nomad

group: **7** caravan

hallucination: **6** mirage

pert. to: **6** eremic

rat: **10** prospector

region: erg

science: **9** eremology

ship: **5** camel

shrub: **5** retem **6** alhagi, raetam

train: **7** caravan

wind: **6** simoom, simoon **7** sirocco

desert candle: **5** plant **8** ocotillo

desert-like: dry **4** arid, sere

deserted: **6** lonely **7** forlorn **8** desolate, forsaken **9** abandoned **11** uninhabited

deserter: rat **6** bolter **8** apostate, fugitive, recreant, renegade

desertion: **14** tergiversation

deserve: **4** earn **5** merit, repay **7** benefit

deserved: **6** worthy **7** condign **11** appropriate

desiccate: dry **4** arid, sere **5** drain **9** dehydrate

desideratum: **4** need **6** desire

design: aim, end, map **4** draw, goal, idea, mean, plan, plot **5** allot, decor, drift, ettle, model, motif, shape **6** device, intend, intent, invent, layout, object, sketch **7** destine, diagram, fashion, outline, pattern, project, propose, purpose **8** contrive **9** calculate, delineate, intention **10** conception **11** contemplate, contrivance

of scattered objects: **4** seme

perforated: **7** stencil

skin: **6** tattoo

designate: set **4** mark, mean, name, show **5** label, style, title **6** assign, denote, intend, settle **7** appoint, entitle, specify **8** describe, identify, indicate **9** appellate, nuncupate **10** denominate **11** distinguish **12** characterize

designed: **8** prepense **11** intentional

designer: **7** planner, plotter, schemer **8** engineer **9** architect, intriguer

designing: **6** artful **7** cunning **8** planning, plotting, scheming **10** foreseeing, fraudulent, intriguing

desinential: **8** terminal

desipient: **5** silly **7** foolish

desirable: **7** amiable, welcome **8** desirous, eligible, pleasing, salutary **9** advisable, agreeable **10** beneficial

desire: yen **4** care, hope, itch, lust, need, urge, want, will, wish **5** ardor, bosom, covet, crave, mania, yearn **6** affect, aspire, hanker, hunger, prefer, thirst, yammer **7** craving, fantasy, inkling, longing, passion **8** appetite, cupidity **9** appetency, cacoethes **10** benedicite, desiderium

desirous: **4** fain, fond **5** eager, frack, freck **6** ardent **7** willing, wishing **8** covetous, spirited **10** delectable, solicitous

desist: ho **4** ease, halt, quit, stop **5** cease **6** depart **7** forbear **11** discontinue

desk: pew **4** ambo **5** board, table **6** pulpit **7** lectern **8** prie-dieu **9** davenport, monocleid, secretary **10** escritoire, monocleide

desman: **4** mole **7** muskrat

Desmanthus: **5** Acuan

desmid: **4** alga **5** algae(pl.)

desolate: sad **4** bare, lorn, ruin, sack, sole **5** alone, bleak, drear, gaunt **6** desert, dreary, gloomy, gousty, lonely, ravage **7** destroy, forlorn, goustie, lacking **8** deprived, deserted, forsaken, solitary **9** abandoned, destitute, dissolute, woebegone **11** comfortless, uninhabited **12** disconsolate

desolation: woe **4** ruin **5** gloom, grief, havoc **6** ravage **7** sadness **10** gloominess, loneliness, melancholy **11** deprivation, destitution, destruction, devastation **12** solitariness

area of: **5** waste **6** desert

despair: **5** gloom **11** desperation, despondency **12** hopelessness

despect: **8** contempt

desperado: **6** bandit **7** ruffian **8** criminal **10** lawbreaker

desperate: mad **4** rash **7** extreme, frantic **8** headlong, hopeless, perilous, reckless **9** dangerous **10** despairing, despondent, infuriated, outrageous **11** precipitate **13** irretrievable

despicable: **4** base, vile **5** cheap, dirty **6** abject, paltry, shabby, sordid **7** caitiff, pitiful **8** unworthy, wretched **9** beggarly, miserable **11** ignominious **12** contemptible, contemptuous

despise: **4** defy, hate **5** scorn, scout, spurn

6 detest, loathe, slight **7** contemn, despite, disdain **8** disprize, misprize, vilipend **9** disregard

despite: vex **7** despise **15** notwithstanding

despiteful: **5** cruel **8** insolent **9** insulting, malicious **12** contemptuous, contumelious

despiteous: **5** cruel **8** pitiless **9** malicious, merciless **12** contemptuous

despoil: rob **4** poll, raid, ruin **5** booty, harry, reave, rifle, spoil, strip **6** divest, fleece, ravage, ravish, remove **7** bereave, deprive, disrobe, pillage, plunder **8** deflower, disarray, unclothe **9** depredate

Despoina: **4** Kore **10** Persephone

despondency: **6** misery **7** despair **10** depression, melancholy **11** desperation

despondent: sad **4** blue **8** dejected, downcast, hopeless **9** desperate, heartless **10** despairing **12** heavy-hearted

despot: **4** czar, tsar, tzar **6** satrap, tyrant **7** autarch, monarch **8** autocrat **10** autocratix

despotic: **6** lordly **8** absolute, dominant **9** arbitrary **10** tyrannical

dessert: ice, pie **4** cake **5** fruit, glace(Fr.) **6** eclair, mousse, pastry, sweets **7** banquet, pudding, sherbet, strudel **8** ice cream, Napoleon, sillabub **9** poundcake, sweetmeat **10** blanc-mange

destination: end **4** goal **5** bourn **6** bourne

destine: **4** doom, fate **5** allot **6** depute, design, devote, intend, ordain **7** appoint **9** designate, destinate **10** foreordain, predestine **12** predetermine

destiny: lot **4** dole, doom, fate **5** karma, stars **6** kismet **7** fortune **8** foredoom
goddess: **4** Fate, Norn **5** Moira **6** Ciotho, Laches **7** Atripos

destitute: **4** poor **5** clean, needy **6** bereft, devoid, wasted **7** forlorn, lacking, wanting **8** bankrupt, beggared, defeated, deprived, desolate, forsaken, helpless, indigent **9** abandoned, defaulted, driftless **10** devastated, frustrated **12** disappointed, impoverished

destroy: eat, end, gut **4** blow, full, rase, raze, ruin, rush, slay, undo **5** break, craze, elide, erase, erode, fordo, havoc, quell, shend, smash, smite, spoil, stroy, wrack, wreck **6** blight, cancel, cumber, deface, defeat, delete, efface, famish, foredo, ravage **7** abolish, consume, expunge, forfare, nullify, overrun, perempt, ruinate, unbuild, whittle **8** amortize, confound, decimate, demolish, desolate, dissolve, infringe, mutilate, overturn, sabotage **9** depredate, devastate, discreate, dismantle, eradicate, extirpate, liquidate, overthrow **10** annihilate, counteract, disappoint, discomfort, extinguish, neutralize **11** assassinate, exterminate

destroyed: **5** kaput

destroyer: hun **6** vandal **7** warship **8** saboteur

destruction: end **4** bane, doom, loss, ruin **5** decay, havoc, waste **7** Abaddon(Heb.) **8** downfall, excision, shambles **9** holocaust, perdition **10** extinction, subversion

god: **4** Siva
goddess: Ara

destructive: **4** fell **5** fatal **6** deadly, mortal **7** baleful, deathly, fateful, harmful, hurtful, noisome, noxious, ruinous **8** wasteful **9** poisonous, truculent **10** catawampus, pernicious **11** catawampous, deleterious, internecine

desuetude: **6** disuse **12** obsolescence **14** discontinuance

desultory: **4** idle **5** hasty, loose **6** roving **7** aimless, cursory **8** rambling, unsteady, wavering **9** irregular, unsettled **10** discursive, inconstant **12** disconnected

detach: **5** sever **7** disjoin, isolate **8** disunite, separate, unfasten, withdraw **9** disengage

detached: **4** free **5** alone, aloof **8** unbiased **9** unconcerned, unconnected

detail: **4** item **6** assign, nicety, relate **7** account, appoint, article, itemize, minutia, narrate, specify **8** rehearse, salience **9** enumerate, narrative **10** particular **11** stipulation **12** circumstance **14** accountability **15** circumstantiate

detailed: **6** prolix **8** tiresome **9** wearisome **10** protracted

detain: **4** hold, keep, stay, stop **5** check, delay **6** arrest, hinder, retard **8** imprison, restrain, withhold
in time of war: **6** intern

detainment: **6** arrest **9** detention

detect: see, spy **4** espy, nose, spot **5** catch **6** descry, divine, expose, reveal **7** develop, discern, uncover **8** decipher, discover, overtake **9** deprehend

detection device: **5** radar

detective: tec **4** bull, dick **6** sleuth, tracer **7** gumshoe, scenter, spotter **8** flatfoot, operator, Sam Spade, The Saint **9** James Bond, Nero Wolfe **10** Martin Kane, Miss Marple, Nick Carter, Perry Mason, Peter Salem, Philo Vance **11** Charlie Chan, Ellery Queen, Green Hornet **12** investigator, Simon Templar **13** Hercule Poirot, Michael Shayne **14** Sherlock Holmes
story writer: **10** Ian Fleming **11** Ellery Queen **14** Agatha Christie **16** Arthur Conan Doyle **19** Earle Stanley Gardner

detector: **7** reagent
defect: **14** troubleshooter
storm: **7** sferics

detent: dog **4** pall, pawl **5** catch, click **7** ratchet

detention: **5** delay **7** capture **9** hindrance, restraint **10** arrestment, detainment

deter: bar **5** block, check, delay **6** hinder, retard **7** prevent **8** dissuade, restrain **9** constrain **10** discourage, dishearten, intimidate

deterge: **5** purge **7** cleanse

detergent: 4 soap 7 purging, smectic, solvent 8 cleanser 9 cleansing

deteriorate: 4 fail, wear 5 decay 6 debase, impair 7 decline, pervert 9 backslide 10 degenerate

determinable: 5 fixed 8 definite 9 judicable 10 mensurable, terminable

determinate: 7 certain 8 definite, resolute, resolved, specific 9 arbitrary 10 invariable 11 established

determinative: 5 final 7 shaping 8 limiting 9 directing 10 conclusive 13 authoritative

determine: end, fix, get 4 test 5 assay, award 6 assess, assign, decide, decree, define, descry, settle 7 adjudge, analyse, analyze, appoint, arrange, dispose, resolve 8 conclude 9 admeasure, arbitrate, ascertain, calculate, terminate 10 adjudicate, constitute, deliberate, predestine

determined: set 4 bent, firm 6 dogged, intent, mulish, sturdy 7 decided, settled 8 foregone, perverse, resolute, resolved, stubborn 9 obstinate, pigheaded 10 persistent, unyielding 12 determinable

deterrent: 9 hindrance 14 discouragement

detest: 4 damn, hate 5 abhor, curse 6 loathe 7 condemn, despise, dislike 8 denounce, execrate 9 abominate

detestable: 4 foul 6 horrid, odious 8 infamous 9 nefarious 12 antipathetic

dethrone: 6 depose, divest

detonate: 4 fire 5 blast 7 explode 9 fulminate

detonator: cap 7 torpedo 9 explosive

detour: 6 bypass 7 circuit 9 deviation

detract: 5 decry 6 defame, divert, vilify 7 asperse, traduce 8 belittle, derogate, distract, minimize, protract, subtract, withdraw 9 disparage 10 depreciate

detraction: 7 calumny, scandal, slander

detriment: 4 cost, hurt, loss 5 damna(pl.), wound 6 damage, damnum, injury 8 mischief 9 disprofit 10 impediment 12 disadvantage

detrimental: 7 harmful, hurtful 9 injurious 10 pernicious 11 deleterious

deva: 5 angel, deity

deval: 4 stop 5 cease, pause 9 cessation

devance: 8 outstrip 9 forestall 10 anticipate

devastate: 5 exile, havoc, waste 6 ravage 7 destroy, pillage, plunder, scourge 8 demolish 10 depopulate

devel: 4 blow 6 strike

develop, develope: 4 form, grow 5 arise, ripen 6 appear, detect, evolve, expand, flower, mature, reveal, unfold, unfurl 7 educate, enlarge, expound, uncover 8 disclose, discover, engender, generate, manifest 9 elaborate, germinate

development: 6 growth 7 stature 8 breeding, increase 9 evolution, expansion, formation, unfolding 11 elaboration

arrested: 7 aplasia

full: 8 maturity, ripeness

going back: 13 retrogression

devest: 5 strip 6 denude, divest 7 abandon, deprive, undress 8 alienate

deviate: err, yaw 4 lean, miss, vary, veer 5 drift, lapse, sheer, stray 6 change, depart, detour, recede, squint, swerve, wander 7 decline, deflect, digress, diverge

from the vertical: 4 hade

deviation: 7 anomaly 11 declination

device: gin, mot 4 tool 5 drift, meter, motto, shift 6 design, emblem, gadget, scheme 7 compass, fiction, impresa, imprese, project, vehicle 8 artifice, fastener, gimcrack 9 apparatus, appliance, doohickey, expedient, invention, regulator, stratagem 10 concoction, instrument 11 contraption, contrivance

curve measuring: 9 rotameter

holding: 4 vise 5 clamp

devil: imp 4 bogy, Deil(Sc.), haze, mahu 5 annoy, bogey, bogie, demon, fiend, Satan, tease 6 Amamon, diablo(Sp.), diable(F.), pester 7 Amaimon, Apollyn, clootie, diaboli(pl.), dickens, gremlin, torment, warlock 8 diabolus, Mephisto 9 archfiend, Beelzebub, cacodemon, deevilick, diablotin 10 cacodaemon

Dante's: 8 Cagnazzo

printer's: 10 apprentice

ruler: 10 diabolarch

tree: 4 dita

worship: 8 satanism

deviled: 9 a la diable

devilfish: ray 5 manta

devilish: 6 daring, rakish, wicked 7 demonic, extreme, hellish, inhuman, satanic 8 demoniac, diabolic, fiendish, infernal 9 excessive 10 diabolical 15 Mephistophelian

devilkin: imp

devious: 6 errant, roving, shifty, tricky 7 vagrant, winding 8 indirect, rambling, tortuous 9 eccentric, irregular 10 circuitous, farfetched, roundabout

devise: 4 plan, plot, will 5 array, frame, fudge, weave 6 convey, decoct, divide, divine, invent, scheme 7 appoint, arrange, bethink, concoct, consult, prepare 8 bequeath, contrive 9 construct, fabricate 10 distribute 11 distinguish

devitalize: 6 deaden 10 eviscerate

devoid: 4 free, void 5 empty 6 barren, vacant 7 wanting 9 destitute

devoir: 4 duty, task 6 effort

devolve: 4 pass 8 overturn, transfer, transmit

Devonshire: *boat:* 9 mumblebee

river: 4 Exe

devote: vow 4 ally, avow, doom, give 5 apply 6 addict, attach, bestow, depute, resign 7 address, consign, destine 8

dedicate, venerate **10** consecrate **11** appropriate

devoted: 4 true **5** liege, loyal, pious **6** devout, doomed, fervid **7** adoring, arduous, zealous **8** attached, constant, faithful **9** assiduous, religious **10** obsequious, venerating **11** whole-souled **12** affectionate, wholehearted

devotee: fan, nun **4** monk **6** votary, zealot **7** admirer, amateur, fanatic **8** follower, partisan **10** enthusiast

devotion: 6 bhakti, novena **7** loyalty **8** fidelity

excessive: **13** ecclesiolatry

object of: **4** idol **5** totem **6** fetich, fetish

devour: eat **4** fret **5** raven, waste **6** engulf **7** consume, engorge **10** annihilate

devout: 4 good, holy, warm **5** godly, pious **6** hearty, solemn **7** cordial, devoted, godlike, saintly, sincere **8** reverent **9** religious, righteous, spiritual **13** sanctimonious

devow: 7 disavow **8** disclaim, renounce

dew: 4 rime **5** bloom **7** moisten, refresh **8** moisture

dewlap: 4 jowl **7** wattles

dewy: 4 damp **5** moist, roral, roric **6** gentle, roscid **9** sparkling **10** refreshing

dexter: 5 right **6** honest **9** fortunate **10** auspicious **15** straightforward

dexterity: art **5** craft, knack, skill **6** stroil **7** ability, address, agility, aptness, cunning, finesse, sleight **8** aptitude, deftness, facility **9** adeptness, diplomacy, quickness, readiness **10** adroitness, cleverness, expertness, nimbleness

dextral: 10 auspicious **11** right-handed

dey: 5 pasha, ruler **7** servant **9** dairymaid

dhan: 6 cattle, wealth **8** property

diablerie: 7 devilry, sorcery **8** demology, mischief

diabolical, diabolic: 5 cruel **6** wicked **7** demonic, hellish, inhuman, satanic, violent **8** demoniac, devilish, fiendish, infernal **9** demonical, fiendlike

diacritic: 4 mark **5** tilde **6** umlaut **11** distinctive

diadem: 5 crown, tiara **6** anadem, circle, emblem, fillet **7** coronet **8** headband **11** sovereignty

diagnose: 7 analyze **8** identify

diagonal: 4 bias

diagram: map **4** plan, tree **5** carte, chart, epure(F.), graph **6** design, schema **9** blueprint

dial: 7 crystal **8** horologe **9** horoscope, indicator, telephone, timepiece

dialect: 5 argot, idiom, lingo **6** brogue, debate, patois, patter, speech **8** language **10** vernacular **11** phraseology

dialogue, dialog: 6 epilog, patter **8** epilogue **12** conversation

having nature of: **13** interlocutory **14** conversational

diameter: pi **4** bore **5** width

half: **5** radii(pl.) **6** radius

diamond: gem, ice **4** bort, rock **5** bortz, field, jager, jewel **7** lozenge **8** corundum **9** briolette

crystal: **7** glassie

famous: See **stone:** *famous*

glazier's: **6** emeril

holding device: dop **4** dopp

imitation: **5** paste **9** schlenter

necklace: **5** riviere(F.)

surface: **7** facet

diamond-hard: 7 adamant

Diamond State: 8 Delaware

Diana: 7 Artemis

diana monkey: 7 roloway

diaper: 6 hippen, hippin, napkin

diaphanous: 5 sheer **11** transparent

diaphragm: 4 riff **7** midriff

pert. to: **7** phrenic

diary: log **6** record **7** journal **8** register **9** ephemeris

diaskeuast: 6 editor **7** reviser, revisor

diastase: 4 malt **6** enzyme

diatribe: 6 screed **8** harangue **9** criticism, invective, philippic **10** discussion **12** denunciation

Diaz de Bivar's title: Cid

dibble: dap, dib **6** dabble, trifle

dibs: 5 syrup

dice: 4 cube **5** bones **6** reject **7** checker

cheater: **6** topper

throw of six: **4** sice

trick: cog

dicer: 5 derby **7** gambler

dick: lad **4** dike, whip **5** agent, apron, ditch **6** fellow **8** flatfoot **9** detective

Dickens: *character:* Tim **4** Dora, Nell **5** Fagin **6** Cuttle **7** Dorritt, Podsnap **9** Bill Sikes, Uriah Heep

pen name: Boz

dicker: 4 swap **5** daker **6** barter, haggle **7** bargain, chaffer **8** exchange **9** agreement, negotiate

dickey, dicky: 4 weak **5** shaky **6** donkey, rumble **7** haddock **9** petticoat

diet: saw **5** adage, maxim **6** saying **8** apothegm **10** apophthegm

dictate: say **4** dite, tell **5** dicta(pl.), utter **6** dictum, enjoin, impose **7** command, deliver, require, suggest **9** prescribe **11** communicate

dictatorial: 6 lordly **7** pompous **8** arrogant, dogmatic, positive **9** imperious, masterful, pragmatic **10** autocratic, peremptory **11** categorical, domineering, magisterial, opinionated, overbearing **13** authoritative

diction: 5 style **6** phrase **8** language, parlance, verbiage **10** vocabulary **11** enunciation, phraseology

dictionary: 7 lexicon **8** wordbook **10** vocabulary **11** onomasticon

compiler: **13** lexicographer

geographical: gazetteer
poet's: **6** gradus
dictum: **5** adage, axiom, edict **6** decree, saying **7** dictate, opinion **8** apothegm principle, statement
did: See **do.**
didactic: dry **7** preachy **10** moralistic
didacticism: **6** homily **8** pedantry
diddle: **4** hoax **6** befool, dandle, dawdle, jiggle, toddle **7** swindle
dido: **5** antic, caper, trick
Dido: *sister:* **4** Anna
wooer: **6** Aeneas
die: dod **4** coin, fade, mold, seal, wane **5** croak, stamp **6** chance, depart, expire, finish, perish, vanish, wither **7** decease, succumb **8** languish, puncheon **9** plaything
loaded: **6** fulham, fullam
symbol: ace
die-hard: **4** Tory
diet: **4** fare, fast, food **5** board **6** reduce, viands **7** regimen **8** congress **10** convention **11** convocation, legislature
convalescent: **5** broth
rule of: **7** dietary
difference: **5** clash **6** change **7** discord, dispute **8** division **10** alteration, dissension, unlikeness **11** controversy, discrepancy **12** disagreement
different: **4** many **5** other **6** divers, sundry, unlike **7** diverse, several, unalike, unusual, variant, various **8** distinct, manifold, separate **9** disparate, divergent **10** dissimilar, variegated **11** diversified
differentiate: **8** contrast **11** distinguish **12** discriminate
difficult: **4** hard **5** cramp, crank, spiny **6** crabby, cranky, strait, uneasy, uneath **7** arduous, crabbed, diffuse, labored, obscure, painful, practic **8** abstract, puzzling, stubborn **9** difficile, intricate, laborious **11** complicated, troublesome
prefix: dys
difficulty: ado, bar, rub **4** clog, coil, node, nodi(pl.), snag **5** cheek, nodus **6** boggle, habble, hobble, plight, scrape, strait **7** barrier, pitfall, problem **8** asperity, obstacle, severity, struggle **9** hindrance **10** impediment **11** controversy, obstruction **12** complication, disagreement
lack of: **4** ease
diffidence: **5** doubt **7** modesty, reserve, shyness **8** distrust, humility, timidity **9** suspicion **10** hesitation **11** bashfulness **12** apprehension
diffuse: **4** full, shed **5** strew **6** derive, dilate, divide, expand, extend, prolix, spread **7** copious, perplex, pervade, publish, radiate, scatter, verbose **8** confused, disperse **9** circulate, difficult, dissipate, expatiate, garrulous, irradiate, propagate **10** widespread **11** disseminate
diffusion: **6** osmose **7** osmosis
dig: hoe **4** claw, grub, howk, mine, moot,

pion, poke, root **5** delve, dwell, graft, lodge, spade, start **6** burrow, exhume, plunge, thrust **7** unearth **8** excavate
dig out: **5** scoop, shove, spade **8** excavate
digest: **4** code **5** ripen **6** codify, mature **7** concoct, epitome, pandect, summary **8** condense **10** abridgment, assimilate, compendium, comprehend **11** abridgement
digestion: **7** eupepsy **8** eupepsia **9** dyspepsia
agent: **6** pepsin, rennin **7** maltase
digger: pal **4** plow **5** miner **6** bildar, drudge **7** comrade, plodder **10** Australian **12** New Zealander
digging, fitted for: **7** fodient
dight: dab, rub **4** deck, wipe **5** adorn, dress, equip, order, raise, treat **6** manage, repair, winnow **7** appoint, consign, perform, prepare **9** construct
digit: toe **4** unit **5** thumb **6** figure, finger, number **7** dewclaw
diglot: **9** bilingual
dignified: **5** grand, lofty, manly, noble, staid **6** august, sedate, solemn **7** courtly, exalted, togated **8** ennobled, majestic **11** magisterial
dignify: **5** adorn, exalt, grace, honor **7** elevate, ennoble, promote
dignitary: don **4** raja **5** rajah **6** priest **7** prelate **9** clergyman
dignity: **4** rank **5** honor, pride, state **6** barony, repose **7** bearing, decorum, fitness, gravity, majesty, station **8** nobility **9** nobleness **10** excellence
digraph: **8** ligature
digress: **4** veer **6** swerve, wander **7** deviate, diverge **8** divagate **10** transgress
digression: **7** episode **8** excursus **9** excursion
dike, dyke: **4** bank, dick, pond, pool **5** digue, ditch, levee **7** channel **8** causeway **10** embankment **11** watercourse
dilapidation: **4** ruin **5** decay **9** disrepair **10** raggedness **14** disintegration
dilatation: **7** ectasia, ectasis **8** dilation
dilate: **5** delay, plump, swell, widen **6** expand, extend, spread **7** amplify, broaden, diffuse, distend, enlarge, inflate, prolong, stretch **8** disperse, increase, lengthen, protract **9** expatiate
dilatory: **4** slow **5** slack, tardy **6** fabian, remiss **8** backward, delaying, inactive, sluggish **10** behindhand **15** procrastinating, procrastinative
dilemma: fix **4** node **5** brake **8** quandary **11** predicament **12** complication
dilettante, dilettant, **5** lover **7** admirer, amateur, dabbler, dabster, esthete **8** aesthete
diligence: **4** heed **6** effort **7** caution **8** industry **9** constancy **11** application, earnestness, heedfulness
diligent: **4** busy, hard **6** active, eident, steady **7** careful, earnest, heedful, op-

erose **8** cautious, constant, sedulous **9**
assiduous, attentive, laborious **11** industrious, painstaking

dill: 4 calm **5** anise **6** pickle, soothe
seed: **4** anet

dillydally: lag, toy **4** loaf **5** stall **6** loiter,
trifle **9** vacillate

dilute: dil(abbr.) **4** thin **5** delay, water **6**
rarefy, reduce, weaken **8** diminish **9** attenuate, distemper

dim: wan **4** blur, dark, dull, fade, gray,
hazy, mist, pale, veil **5** bleak, blear,
dusky, faint, foggy, misty **6** bemist,
cloudy, darken, dimpsy, gloomy, obtuse,
shadow **7** darkish, eclipse, obscure, shadowy, tarnish **8** overcast **9** obfuscate **10**
indistinct, mysterious **11** crepuscular

dime: 4 coin **5** disme

dimension: 4 bulk, size **5** scope **6** extent,
height, length **7** breadth **9** magnitude,
thickness **10** importance, proportion **11**
measurement **13** circumference

diminish: ebb **4** bate, ease, fade, fret,
melt, pare, sink, wane, wear **5** abate,
lower, peter, taper **6** decoct, dilute, lessen, rebate, reduce, vanish, wither **7**
abridge, assuage, curtail, deplete,
depress, dwindle, qualify, relieve **8** ad-
minish, condense, decrease, diminute,
minorate, moderate, retrench **9** alleviate,
epitomize, extenuate

diminution: 8 decrease **9** abasement,
abatement, decrement **11** abridgement,
attenuation, curtailment, degradation,
deprivation, extenuation

diminutive: wee **4** tiny **5** banty, dwarf,
petty, runty, small **6** bantam, little, petite
9 minuscule **11** disparaging
suffix: el, et, ie; cle, ole, ule **4** cula, ette **5**
culus

dimmet: 4 dusk **8** twilight

dimness: 5 gloom **8** darkness **9** obscurity

dimple: 4 doke **6** ripple **8** fossette

din: bum **4** riot **5** alarm, bruit, clang, noise
6 clamor, hubbub, racket, rattle, steven,
tumult, uproar **7** clamour, clangor, clatter, discord, turmoil **9** commotion, confusion **10** hullabaloo

dindle: 4 ring **6** quiver, thrill, tingle, tinkle, tremor **7** vibrate **9** vibration

dine: eat, sup **5** feast **6** regale

diner: 7 epicure

dinette: 6 alcove **10** kitchen set

ding: 4 beat, dash, push, ring **5** clang,
drive, excel, fling, knock, pound, thump **6**
stroke, thrash, thrust

dinge: 4 dent, dint **6** batter, bruise **10**
depression

dinghy, dingy: 4 boat **5** skiff **7** rowboat,
shallop

dingle: 4 dale, dell, glen, vale **6** valley

dingus: 6 gadget **9** doohickey, doohickus,
doohinkey, doohinkus

dingy: dun **4** dark **5** dirty, dusky, grimy,
ourie, smoky **6** dinghy **8** smirched

dining: *room:* **7** cenacle, dinette **9** refectory
science: **10** aristology

dink: 4 deck, neat, trim **7** elegant

dinkey: 10 locomotive

dinkum: 4 fair **5** truly **6** honest, square **7**
genuine **8** honestly, reliable

dinky: 4 cute, neat, poor **13** insignificant

dinner: 4 meal **5** feast **6** repast **7** banquet
9 beanfeast
course: **4** nuts, soup **5** fruit, salad **6** entree
7 dessert
pert. to: **8** cenatory

dinornis: moa

dinosaur: 11 morosaurian, stegosauria,
stegosaurus, triceratops, tyrannosaur **12**
brontosaurus **13** tyrannosaurus
genus of: **10** diplodocus **11** apatosaurus

dint: 4 beat, blow, dent, nick **5** clour,
delve, dinge, force, notch, onset, power,
press, shock **6** attack, chance, effort,
strike, stroke **7** imprint **8** efficacy, striking **10** impression **11** indentation

diocese: see **8** district **12** jurisdiction
division: **6** parish **8** parishen(Sc.)

Dionysus: *attendant:* **6** Maenad
festival: **7** Agrania **8** Agrionia
mother: **6** Semele

diopside: 7 alalite **8** pyroxene

diorite: 7 diabase

Dioscuri's sister: 5 Helen **12** Clytemnestra

diose: 14 glycolaldehyde

dip: sop **4** bail, drop, dunk, lade, sink, soak
5 delve, ladle, lower, slope **6** candle, hollow, plunge **7** decline, immerge, immerse,
incline, moisten **8** submerge **10** depression, pickpocket
in water: **5** douse, rinse, souse

diploma: 6 degree **7** charter **11**
certificate

diplomacy: 4 tact **9** dexterity **10** artfulness

diplomat: 4 dean **6** consul **7** attache **8**
minister **10** ambassador
corps head: **4** dean **5** doyen

dipper: 5 ladle, scoop **10** pickpocket

dippy: mad **7** foolish **9** screwball

dipsomania: 9 potomania **10** alcoholism

dipthong, diphthong: ae, oe **7** bivocal

dird: 4 blow **5** thump **9** buffeting

dirdum: 4 blow **5** blame **6** rebuke, tumult, uproar **8** scolding **10** punishment

dire: 4 dern, evil **5** awful, fatal **6** deadly,
dismal, funest, tragic, woeful **7** doleful,
drastic, fearful **8** dreadful, horrible, terrible, ultimate **10** calamitous, oppressive,
portentous **12** overpowering

direct: aim, bid, con **4** airt, bain, bend,
boss, edit, even, flat, head, helm, lead,
open, rein, sway, turn **5** apply, blank,
coach, frank, guide, order, point, refer,
steer, teach, train, utter, write **6** ensign,
govern, handle, honest, impart, lineal,
manage **7** address, appoint, command,

conduct, control, convert, execute, express, officer, preside **8** dedicate, instruct, marshall, regulate, straight **9** categoric, downright, immediate, **10** administer, forthright, point-blank **11** categorical, compendious, superintend, superscribe **15** straightforward

direction: way **4** airt, bent, care, duct, east, road, rule, west **5** north, order, route, south, trend **6** course **7** address, bearing, command, control, mandate, precept **8** guidance, tendency **9** ordinance **10** injunction, management, regulation **11** appointment, arrangement, inclination, information, instruction **13** determination **14** superscription **15** superintendence
Biblical: **5** selah
court: **5** order
line of: **5** range
musical: see **musical direction**
pole to pole: **5** axial
printer's: **4** stet

direction finder: **7** compass

directly: **4** soon **8** promptly **9** instantly, presently **11** immediately, straightway

director: **4** boss, head **5** coach, guide, pilot **6** archon, bishop, leader, rector **7** manager, prefect, trainer **8** governor, producer **9** conductor, intendant **13** administrator **14** superintendent

directors, board of: **10** management

directory: **9** phonebook **10** collection, directoire(F.),

dirge: **4** keen, song **5** elegy **6** hearse, lament **7** epicede **8** epicedia(pl.), threnody **9** epicedium

dirigible: **5** blimp **7** airship **8** Zeppelin **10** Hindenburg
part: fin **7** nacelle

dirk: **4** snee **5** skean, sword **6** dagger, weapon

dirl: **4** ring **6** pierce, thrill, tingle **7** vibrate

dirt: fen, mud **4** dust, gore, muck, nast, soil **5** earth, filth, grime, trash **6** gravel, ground, refuse **7** mullock **8** muckment **9** excrement

dirty: low **4** base, clat, foul, soil **5** bawdy, cabby, dingy, foggy, grimy, gusty, horry, muddy, nasty, sully **6** bemire, clarty, defile, filthy, greasy, grubby, impure, mussed, smutty, soiled, sordid, stormy **7** begrime, brookie, bruckle, clouded, muddied, squalid, sullied, tarnish, unclean **10** despicable

dis: **5** Pluto

disable: **4** lame, maim **5** break, gruel, wreck **6** bruise, dismay, weaken **7** cripple **9** hamstring **10** disqualify **12** incapacitate

disaccharide: **5** biose **7** lactose, maltose, sucrose **10** saccharose

disadvantage: **4** hurt, risk **6** damage, injury **7** penalty **8** handicap **9** detriment

disadvantageous: **7** hurtful **10** derogatory **11** detrimental, prejudicial, unfavorable

disaffected 5 false **6** untrue **8** disloyal, forsworn, perjured, recreant **9** estranged, faithless, insidious **10** perfidious, traitorous **11** treacherous

disaffection: **6** deceit **7** disease, disgust, dislike **8** disorder **9** distemper, hostility **10** disloyalty, alienation, discontent **13** indisposition **14** disinclination

disaffirm: **4** deny **5** annul **7** reverse **9** repudiate **10** contradict

disagree: **4** vary **6** differ **7** dissent, quarrel **8** conflict

disagreeable: bad **4** sour, vile **5** cross, harsh, nasty **7** chronic, hateful **8** terrible **9** invidious, irritable, offensive, repugnant **10** abominable, forbidding, unpleasant **11** displeasing, distasteful **13** uncomfortable

disagreement: **5** clash, fight **7** discord, dispute, dissent, wrangle **8** variance **9** diversity **10** contention, difference, difficulty, dissension, dissidence, divergence, unlikeness **11** contrariety, controversy, discrepancy, displeasure, incongruity **16** misunderstanding

disallow: **6** forbid, reject **7** censure **8** disclaim, disprove, prohibit **10** disapprove

disappear: fly **4** fade, flee **6** vanish **7** evanish **8** evanesce

disappoint: **4** balk, bilk, fail, fall, mock, undo **6** baffle, defeat, delude, outwit, thwart **7** deceive, destroy, nullify **9** frustrate, mislippen

disappointment: rue **7** letdown **11** frustration

disapprobation: **5** odium **11** deprecation, disapproval **12** condemnation

disapproval: **4** booh, hiss, veto **7** catcall, censure **9** disliking **14** disapprobation

disapprove: **6** reject, resent **7** condemn, protest **8** disallow, disprove **9** deprecate

disarm: **6** subdue

disarrange: **4** muss **6** deform, ruffle **7** clutter, confuse, derange, disturb, rummage **8** dishevel, disorder, unsettle **9** dislocate **10** discompose, disconcert **11** disorganize

disarray: **4** mess **5** strip **6** caddle **7** despoil **8** dishevel, disorder **9** confusion **10** dishabille

disassociate: **8** separate **10** dissociate

disaster: woe **4** bale, blow, evil, ruin **6** mishap, stroke **7** reverse **8** accident, calamity, casualty, fatality **9** cataclysm, extremity, mischance **10** misfortune **11** catastrophe **12** misadventure

disavow: **4** deny **5** devow **6** abjure, dis-

own, recant, refuse **7** decline, retract **8**
abnegate, disclaim, renounce **9** repudiate

disband: **7** breakup, dismiss, release,
scatter **8** dissolve **9** discharge **12** disintegrate

disbelieve: **5** doubt **6** reject **7** suspect **9** discredit

disbeliever: **7** atheist, heretic

disburden: rid **4** ease **7** relieve **9** exonerate **11** disencumber

disburse: **5** spend **6** defray, expend, outlay **10** distribute

disc: **4** dial **5** medal, paten, plate, quoit **6** record **7** platter

discalced: **6** unshod **10** barefooted

discard: **4** cast, jilt, junk, omit, oust, shed **5** chuck, ditch, scrap, shuck, sluff **6** disuse, divest, excuss, reject **7** abandon, cashier, dismiss, forsake **9** eliminate, repudiate

discern: ken, see, spy **4** espy, read **5** sight **6** behold, descry, detect, notice **8** discover, perceive **10** understand **11** distinguish

discernible: **7** evident, visible **8** apparent, manifest **11** conspicuous, perceptible **15** distinguishable

discernment: eye **4** tact **5** flair, taste **6** acumen **7** insight **8** sagacity **9** sharpness **10** divination, perception, shrewdness **11** penetration **12** clairvoyance, perspicacity **14** discrimination

discharge: can **4** boot, cass, dump, emit, fire, free, pour, sack **5** eject, empty, expel, exude, shoot, speed **6** acquit, assoil, bounce, defray, effect, exempt, unlade, unload **7** absolve, cashier, disband, dismiss, exhaust, release, relieve **8** disgorge, displace, evacuate, mittimus **9** acquittal, dismissal, exculpate, exonerate, exudation, liquidate **10** discompose, liberation **11** acquittance, exoneration, performance, transaction

dishonorable: **7** bobtail, cashier

discharged from active service: **8** emeritus

disciple: ite **4** John, Mark **5** Judas, Peter, teach, train **6** hearer, punish **7** apostle, auditor, Matthew, scholar, student **8** adherent, follower **10** discipline

disciplinarian: **7** trainer **8** martinet

discipline: **4** whip **5** inure, teach, train **6** ferule, govern, punish **7** chasten, culture, educate, scourge **8** doctrine, instruct, learning, regulate, restrain, teaching, training, tutoring **9** education **10** punishment **11** instruction **12** chastisement

disclaim: **4** deny **5** devow **6** abjure, disown, refuse **7** disavow **8** abdicate, abnegate, disallow, renounce **9** repudiate

disclose: ope **4** bare, blow, open, tell **5** utter **6** betray, bewray, descry, expose, impart, reveal, shrive, unseal, unveil **7** confess, develop, display, divulge, exhibit, unclose, uncover **8** discover, indicate, manifest

discolor: **4** fade, spot **5** stain, tinge **6** smirch, streak **7** distain, tarnish **8** besmirch

discomfit: **4** rout **5** abash, upset **6** baffle, defeat **7** confuse, conquer, disturb, scatter **8** confound **9** embarrass, frustrate, overthrow **10** disconcert

discomfort: **4** pain **6** dismay, grieve, sorrow, unease **7** disturb **8** distress **9** annoyance, embarrass **10** discourage, uneasiness **11** displeasure **13** inconvenience **14** discouragement

discommendation: **5** blame **7** censure **8** reproach **9** dispraise

discommode: **7** trouble **9** incommode **13** inconvenience

discompose: **4** fret **5** upset **6** flurry, ruffle **7** agitate, confuse, derange, disturb, fluster, perturb **8** disorder, displace, disquiet, unsettle **9** discharge **10** disarrange, disconcert

disconcert: **4** faze **5** abash, daunt, feeze, upset, worry **6** baffle, blench, rattle **7** confuse, disturb, nonplus, perturb, squelch **8** browbeat, disorder **9** discomfit, embarrass, frustrate **10** disarrange, discompose **14** discountenance

disconnect: **4** undo **5** sever **6** divide **7** disjoin **8** dissolve, disunite, separate, uncouple

disconnected: **6** abrupt, broken **7** cursory **8** rambling **9** desultory, scattered **10** abstracted, disjointed, incoherent

disconsolate: sad **6** gloomy, woeful **7** forlorn **8** dejected, desolate, hopeless **9** cheerless, miserable, sorrowful **10** dispirited, melancholy **12** inconsolable

discontent: **8** disquiet **9** displease **10** dissatisfy, malcontent, uneasiness **11** displeasure **12** disaffection **15** dissatisfaction

discontinue: end **4** drop, quit, stop **5** break, cease, letup **6** desist, disuse, sunder **7** disrupt **8** intermit

discord: din, jar **5** broil **6** strife **7** faction **8** conflict, variance **9** cacophony, diversity **10** contention, difference, dissension, dissonance **12** disagreement

goddess of: Ate **4** Eris

discordant: **4** ajar **5** harsh **6** hoarse **7** jarring **8** contrary, jangling **10** discrepant **11** incongruous, quarrelsome **12** antagonistic, inconsistent, inharmonious **14** irreconcilable

discount: **4** agio **5** batta **6** rebate, reduce **9** allowance, deduction, disregard, reduction **12** depreciation

discourage: **4** carp **5** daunt, deter **6** dampen, deject, dismay **7** depress **8** dispirit, dissuade 10 discomfort, dishearten

discourse: 4 carp, talk, tell 5 orate, paper, speak, tract 6 eulogy, homily, parley, preach, sermon 7 account, address, comment, declaim, discuss, dissert, lecture, narrate, oration, prelect 8 argument, colloquy, converse, parlance, treatise 9 expatiate, narration, narrative, panegyric, sermonize, soliloquy 10 conference 11 description 12 conversation, dissertation
long: 6 screed, tirade 7 descant 9 philippic

discourteous: 4 rude 6 scurvy 7 uncivil 8 impolite, ungentle 10 unmannerly 11 ill-mannered, uncivilized 13 disrespectful

discover: see, spy 4 espy, find 5 learn 6 define, descry, detect, expose, invent, locate, reveal 7 confess, discern, display, divulge, exhibit, explore, uncover, unearth 8 decipher, disclose, manifest 9 apprehend, ascertain, deprehend 11 reconnoiter

discoverer: spy 5 scout 8 explorer, inventor 10 originator

discovery: 5 trove 6 espial 10 disclosure, revelation
gold: 6 strike

discreate: 7 destroy 10 annihilate

discredit: 5 decry, doubt, refel 6 deface 7 asperse, blemish, impeach, scandal, suspect 8 belittle, disgrace, dishonor, distrust 9 disparage, disrepute 10 disbelieve

discreet: 4 wary 5 civil 6 polite, silent 7 careful, guarded, politic, prudent 8 cautious, reserved, reticent 11 circumspect

discrepant: 8 contrary 9 different 10 discordant 11 disagreeing 12 inconsistent

discrepate: 6 differ 11 distinguish 12 discriminate

discretion: 4 tact 6 wisdom 8 courtesy 9 restraint 13 secretiveness

discriminate: 6 secern 8 perceive 9 demarcate 10 discrepate 11 distinguish 13 differentiate

discriminating: 4 nice 5 acute 6 astute 7 choosey 8 critical 10 discerning 11 distinctive

discrimination: 5 taste 6 acumen 11 discernment, distinction, penetration

discursive: 6 roving 7 cursory 8 rambling 9 desultory 10 digressive

discuss: air 4 moot 5 argue, bandy, treat 6 confer, debate, excuss, parley 7 agitate, bespeak, canvass, consult, dispute, dissert, examine, narrate 9 discourse, exagitate, ventilate 11 expostulate

discussion: 5 forum 6 hassel 8 causerie, diatribe, entreaty 12 dissertation
medium of: 5 forum
open to: 4 moot

disdain: tut 5 pride, scorn, spurn 7 con-

temn, despise 8 contempt 9 arrogance 11 haughtiness, indignation

disease: 4 harm 5 pinta 6 malady, morbus 7 ailment, illness, malaria, trouble, yellows 8 beriberi, distress, sickness 9 complaint, distemper, infirmity 10 discomfort, pestilence, uneasiness 12 disaffection
agent of: 4 germ 9 bacterium, contagium
animal: coe, pip, rye 4 rout 5 braxy, coath, colic, farcy, hoose, hooze, mange, nenta 6 amoeba, garget, hammer 7 dartars, spavins, takosis 8 asthenia, glanders, sacbrood 9 distemper, tularemia 11 myxomatosis, psittacosis
blood: 8 leucemia, leukemia 9 leucaemia
brain: 8 paranoia 13 schizophrenia
comb. form: nos 4 noso
contagious: pox 5 mumps 7 measles
crippling: 9 arthritis, sclerosis 10 rheumatism 13 poliomyelitis
declining stage: 9 catabasis
deficiency: 6 scurvy 8 pellagra
eye: 8 glaucoma, trachoma 9 pterygium 14 conjunctivitis
favorable termination of: 5 lysis
hair: 5 plica 7 xerasia 8 psilosis
heart: 8 aneurism, aneurysm
liver: 9 cirrhosis, hepatitis
local: 7 endemic
lung: 8 phthisis 9 emphysema, pneumonia 11 consumption 12 tuberculosis
nervous: see **mental disorder.**
plant: fen 4 bunt, rust, scab, smut 5 ergot, speck 6 calico, coleur, mildew 7 erinose, viruela, walloon 8 brindled, melanose
prediction about: 9 prognosis
recognition of: 9 diagnosis
science of children's: 10 pediatrics 11 paediatrics
skin: 4 acne, pian, rash 5 favus, hives, psora, tinea 6 courap, dartre, eczema, herpes, lichen, tetter 7 scabies, serpigo 8 impetigo, ringworm 9 frambesia, psoriasis, xeroderma 10 framboesia 11 scleroderma
suffix: 4 itis
wasting: 8 phthisic

disembark: 4 land 6 alight, debark

disembodiment: 4 soul 6 spirit

disembowel: gut 4 hulk 6 paunch 8 gralloch 10 eviscerate

disembroil: 8 untangle 9 extricate

disencumber: rid 4 free 9 disburden, disengage

disengage: 4 free 5 clear, untie 6 detach, evolve, loosen 7 release, unravel 8 liberate 9 extricate 11 disencumber, disentangle 12 disembarrass

disentangle: 4 comb, free 5 clear, loose, ravel 6 evolve, sleave 7 unravel 8 untangle 9 disengage, extricate 12 disembarrass

disenthrone: 6 depose
disfavor, disfavour: 5 odium 7 umbrage 9 disesteem 11 displeasure
disfigure: mar 4 blur, scar 6 deface, defeat, deform, injure, mangle 7 blemish 8 mutilate 10 disfashion
disgorge: 4 spew, vent 5 eject, empty, vomit 9 discharge 10 relinquish
disgrace: 4 blot, slur, soil, spot 5 abase, crime, odium, shame, stain 6 infamy 7 affront, attaint, degrade, scandal, slander 8 contempt, dishonor, ignominy, reproach 9 discredit, disesteem, disfigure, humiliate 10 attainture, defamation, opprobrium 11 displeasure, humiliation 13 disparagement
disgruntled: 4 sore 7 peevish
disguise: 4 hide, mask, veil 5 belie, cloak, couch, feign, gloze, guise 6 covert, deform, masque 7 conceal, obscure, pretend 8 palliate 9 coverture, dissemble, incognito 10 camouflage, intoxicate, masquerade 11 dissimulate
disgust: 5 repel, shock 6 degout(F.), horror, nausea, offend, revolt, sicken 8 aversion, distaste, loathing, nauseate 9 antipathy 10 abhorrence, repugnance 11 abomination 12 disaffection
disgusting: 4 foul, vile 5 nasty 6 filthy 7 beastly, fulsome, hateful, noisome, obscene 8 shocking
dish (see also **food**): cap 4 caup 5 basin, comal, nappy, paten, plate 6 bassie, critch, panada, patera, recipe, saucer, tureen 7 charger, cresset, epergne, patella, plateau, platter, ramekin, scuttle 9 casserole, clackdish
gravy: 4 boat
side: 6 entree
dishabille: 8 disarray, disorder, negligee
dishearten: 5 amate, daunt 6 deject 7 depress, flatten, unnerve 8 dispirit 10 demoralize, discourage
disheartened: 6 gloomy 8 downcast
dishevel: 4 muss 6 ruffle, tousel, tousle, tumble 8 disarray, disorder 10 disarrange
dishonest: 4 foul, lewd 5 cronk, false 7 corrupt, crooked, knavish 8 indecent, shameful, unchaste 9 deceitful, repulsive 10 fraudulent, perfidious 12 dishonorable 13 untrustworthy
dishonor, dishonour: 5 abase, abuse, shame, stain 6 defame, defile, infamy 7 degrade, obloquy, violate 8 disgrace, ignominy, reproach 9 discredit, disparage, disrepute 10 defamation, disworship, opprobrium 11 contaminate, impeachment, irreverence 13 disparagement
dishonorable, dishonourable: 4 base, foul, mean 5 nasty 6 yellow 7 ignoble 11 disesteemed
disillusion: 10 disenchant
disinclination: 7 dislike 8 aversion, distaste 9 antipathy 10 reluctance, repugnance 12 disaffection
disinclined: 6 averse 9 reluctant, unwilling 10 indisposed
disinfect: 7 cleanse 9 sterilize
disinfectant: 5 iodin 6 iodine, phenol 9 germicide 10 antiseptic
disingenuous: 5 false 10 circuitous
disinherit: 7 deprive 10 exheredate
disintegrate: 4 melt 5 decay, erode 7 crumble, disband 8 dissolve, separate 9 decompose
disinter: 6 exhume, unbury
disinterested: 4 fair 9 apathetic, impartial 11 unconcerned
disjasked, disjaskit: 5 jaded 7 decayed
disjoin: 4 part, undo 5 sever 6 detach, sunder 8 dissolve, disunite, separate 10 disconnect, dissociate
disjune: 9 breakfast
disk: 4 dial 5 cakra, medal, paten, plate, sabot, wheel 6 bezant, chakra, harrow, record, washer 7 medalet, phalera 9 cultivate, faceplate, medallion, millstone
metal: 4 flan, gong 6 ghurry, sequin 8 zecchino
dislike: 4 loth, mind 5 loath 8 detest 8 aversion, distaste 9 antipathy, disesteem, disrelish 11 detestation, displacency, displeasure 12 disaffection 14 disinclination
object of: 8 anathema
dislocate: 5 splay 8 disjoint, displace 10 disarrange
dislodge: 5 expel 6 remove
disloyal: 5 false 6 untrue 9 faithless 10 inconstant, perfidious, unfaithful 11 disaffected, treacherous
dismal: sad, wan 4 dark, dire, dull, glum, gray 5 black, bleak, drear, sorry 6 dreary, gloomy, triste 7 doleful, ghastly, joyless, ominous, unhappy 8 dolorous, funereal, lonesome 9 cheerless, sorrowful 10 acherontic, calamitous, lugubrious, melancholy 11 unfortunate
dismantle: 4 rase, raze 5 strip 6 divest 7 deprive, destroy, uncloak 8 dismount
dismay: 4 fear, ruin 5 alarm, appal, daunt, dread 6 appall, fright, subdue, terror 7 depress, deprive, horrify, terrify 8 affright, confound 9 dejection 10 depression, discomfort, discourage 11 trepidation 12 apprehension 13 consternation 14 discouragement
dismember: 4 maim, part, rend 5 sever 6 mangle 7 dissect 8 disjoint, mutilate
dismiss: can 4 boot, bust, drop, oust 5 chuck, eject 6 banish, bounce, reject, remove 7 cashier, disband, discard 8 relegate 9 discharge, overthrow
dismissal: 5 conge 6 avaunt 8 mittimus
dismount: 5 avale 6 alight 9 dismantle
disobedient: 7 forward, froward, naughty,

ungodly, wayward **8** mutinous **10** rebellious, refractory **11** intractable **12** contumacious **13** insubordinate

disoblige: **6** offend **7** affront

disorder: pie **4** mess, muss, riot **5** chaos, deray, snafu, touse **6** burble, jumble, litter, malady, mucker, muddle, ruffle, tousle, tumult **7** ailment, clutter, confuse, derange, disturb, embroil, flutter, illness, misdeed, perturb, trouble **8** disarray, dishevel **9** commotion, complaint, confusion, distemper **10** disarrange, discompose, disconcert, misconduct **11** derangement, disorganize, disturbance, misdemeanor **12** disaffection, discomposure, irregularity **13** indisposition **14** disarrangement **15** disorganization

visual: **10** strabismus

disordered: **6** frouzy, frowsy, frowzy **10** topsy-turvy **11** lightheaded

disorderly: **5** randy **6** unruly **8** slipshod, slovenly **12** hugger-mugger, ungovernable, unmanageable

disorganize: **5** upset **7** confuse, derange, disband, disrupt **8** disorder, dissolve **10** disarrange

disour: **6** jester **11** storyteller

disown: **4** deny **6** reject **7** disavow, retract **8** abdicate, disclaim, renounce **9** reprobate, repudiate

disparage, desparage: **4** slur **5** abuse, decry, lower **6** slight **7** degrade, depress, detract, impeach **8** belittle, derogate, dishonor, disprize, minimize **9** discredit, dispraise, extenuate **10** depreciate

disparate: **7** unequal **8** separate **9** different **10** dissimilar **16** disproportionate

dispart: **4** open, rend, rive **5** break, sever, split **6** cleave, divide **8** separate

dispassionate: **4** calm, cool, fair **5** stoic **6** sedate, serene **8** composed, moderate, **9** collected, impartial, temperate, unruffled **10** deliberate, unimpaired **12** unprejudiced
deliver, depeche(F.), dispose **8** celerity, conclude, expedite **9** quickness **10** accomplish, promptness

dispatch: rid **4** free, kill, mail, note, post, send **5** haste, hurry, speed **6** hasten **7** celerate, accomplish, promptness

dispatch boat: **5** aviso **9** packet

dispatcher: **8** trainman **9** motor boss

dispel: **6** banish **7** scatter **8** disperse **9** dissipate

dispend: **5** spend **6** expend **8** dispense, squander

dispendious: **6** costly **9** expensive **11** extravagant

dispense: **4** deal, dole **6** effuse, excuse, exempt, forego, manage **7** absolve, arrange, dispend **9** exemption **10** administer, distribute **12** dispensation

dispenser: **7** manager, steward **10** pharmacist **13** administrator

information: **4** tout **7** tipster **11** stoolpigeon

dispeople: **10** depopulate

disperse: sow **4** fray, part, rout **5** strew **6** dilate, dispel, sparse, spread, vanish **7** diffuse, scatter **8** separate, squander **9** dissipate **10** dispergate, distribute **11** disseminate

dispirit: cow **4** damp **5** daunt **6** deject **7** depress, flatten **10** discourage, dishearten, intimidate

dispirited: **6** abattu **7** abattue **8** downcast **9** cheerless, woebegone **11** crestfallen **12** disconsolate

dispiteous: **5** cruel **8** pitiless, spiteful

displace: **6** banish, depose, mislay, remove **7** derange **8** dislodge, misplace, supplant **9** discharge, dislocate, supersede **10** discompose

display: air **4** brag, pomp, show, wear **5** boast, emote, scene, sight, sport, stage **6** blazon, deploy, descry, expose, extend, flaunt, ostent, parade, reveal, uncase **7** approve, etalage, exhibit, flutter, pageant, uncover **8** ceremony, disclose, discover, emblazon, exercise, flourish, indicate, manifest, splendor **9** spectacle **10** exhibition **11** affectation, demonstrate **13** demonstration, manifestation

displease: vex **4** miff **5** anger, annoy, pique **6** offend **7** provoke **8** irritate **10** discontent, dissatisfy

displeasing: bad, dry **7** irksome **9** offensive **10** unpleasant **11** distasteful **12** disagreeable

displeasure: ire **5** anger, mumps, pique **6** injury **7** dislike, offense, trouble, umbrage **8** disfavor, disgrace, distaste **10** discomfort, discontent, resentment, uneasiness **11** indignation

show: cry **4** pout **5** frown

dispone: **8** transfer **10** distribute

disport: **4** play **5** amuse, frisk **6** divert, frolic, gambol

disposal: **8** bestowal **11** arrangement, disposition

dispose: set **4** bend, give, mind **5** array, order, place **6** adjust, attire, bestow, settle **7** appoint, arrange, prepare **8** dispatch, regulate **9** determine **10** distribute

disposition: **4** bent, bias, mood, turn **5** tache **6** affect, animus, health, nature, temper **7** concept **8** aptitude, attitude, disposal, positure **9** affection, character, diathesis **10** adjustment, management, proclivity, propension, propensity **11** arrangement, inclination, temperament **12** constitution, distribution, organization **14** relinquishment

dispossess: **4** oust **5** eject, evict, expel, strip **6** depose, divest **7** bereave, deprive **8** disseize

dispraise: **5** blame **7** censure **9** disparage **10** depreciate, detraction **13** disparagement **15** discommendation

disprize: **10** undervalue **13** underestimate

disproof: 10 refutation 11 confutation

disproportion: 9 disparity 10 inequality

disproportionate: 14 incommensurate

disprove: 5 rebut, refel 6 negate, refute 7 confute, explode 8 disallow, redargue 10 disapprove

disputable: 5 vague 6 unsure 7 dubious, fallible 8 doubtful, insecure 9 uncertain 10 indefinite, precarious

disputation: 7 polemic 8 argument 9 dialectic 10 discussion 11 controversy 12 conversation

dispute: 4 deny, feud, fuss, moot, riot, spat 5 argue, brawl, broil, cabal, hurry 6 barney, bicker, cangle, dacker, daiker, debate, differ, fratch, haggle 7 brabble, contend, contest, discuss, dissert, faction, gainsay, quarrel, wrangle 8 argument, question, squabble 9 argy-bargy, encounter 10 contravene, controvert, litigation 11 altercation, controversy 12 disagreement

disqualify: 5 debar 6 outlaw 7 disable 9 indispose 12 incapacitate

disquiet: vex 4 fear, fret, pain 6 excite, unease, unrest 7 agitate, anxiety, disturb, inquiet, trouble, turmoil 9 incommode 10 discompose, discontent, uneasiness 12 inconvenience, restlessness

disquisition: 5 essay 10 discussion

disregard: 4 omit 5 waive 6 forget, ignore, slight 7 despise, neglect 8 discount, disvalue, overlook 9 pretermit 10 contravene 11 inattention

disrelish: 7 dislike 8 distaste 9 antipathy

disreputable: low 4 base, hard 5 seamy, shady 7 raffish 8 shameful 13 discreditable

disrepute: 7 disfame 8 dishonor, reproach 9 discredit, disesteem

disrespect: 8 rudeness 9 disesteem, insolence 10 incivility 11 discourtesy

disrespectful: 7 uncivil 8 impolite, impudent 10 irreverent 11 impertinent

disrobe: 5 strip 6 divest 7 despoil, undress

disrupt: 4 rend, tear 5 break 7 disrump 11 discontinue, disorganize

dissatisfaction: 8 distaste 9 annoyance 10 discontent 11 displeasure

dissect: 7 analyze 9 anatomize, dismember

disseize: 10 dispossess

dissemble: 4 hide, mask 5 cloak, feign 6 boggle 7 conceal 8 disguise, simulate 11 counterfeit, dissimulate

dissembler: 9 hypocrite

disseminate: sow 5 strew 6 effuse, spread 7 diffuse, publish, scatter 8 disperse 9 circulate, propagate 10 distribute

dissent: 4 vary 6 differ 7 contend, protest 8 disagree 9 exception 10 dissidence 12 disagreement, nonagreement 13 nonconformity 14 nonconcurrence

signal of: nay

dissenter: 7 heretic 8 recusant 9 meetinger, protestor 10 Protestant 13 nonconformist

dissentious: 8 factious 11 contentious

dissert: 7 discuss, dispute 9 discourse

dissertation: 5 essay, theme, tract 6 debate, thesis, theses(pl.) 7 descant, lecture 8 treatise 9 discourse 10 discussion

Dissertation on a Roast Pig (author): 11 Charles Lamb

disservice: 4 harm 6 damage, injury 8 mischief

dissever: 4 part 6 sunder 8 disunite

dissidence: 7 dissent 12 disagreement 13 nonconformity

dissimilar: 6 unlike 7 difform, diverse 9 anomalous, different, disparate 13 heterogeneous

dissimulate: 5 feign 7 deceive, pretend 8 disguise 9 dissemble

dissipate: 4 fray 5 spend, waste 6 dispel, expend 7 diffuse, scatter, shatter 8 disperse, dissolve, embezzle, evanesce, squander 9 evaporate

dissocial: 7 selfish 8 unsocial 10 unfriendly

dissociate: 5 sever 7 disjoin 8 disunite, separate

dissolute: lax 4 lewd, wild 5 loose, slack 6 rakish, wanton 7 immoral, lawless 8 desolate, rakehell, reckless, uncurbed 9 abandoned, debauched, libertine, unbridled 10 licentious, negligence 12 unrestrained

dissolution: 4 ruin 5 decay 6 bust-up 7 breakup, decease, divorce 10 abrogation 14 disintegration

dissolve: end 4 fade, fuse, melt, thaw 5 fleet, solve 6 relent, unbind 7 adjourn, destroy, disband, disjoin, divorce, liquefy 8 discandy, disunite, separate 9 decompose, dissipate 10 deliquesce, disconnect 11 disorganize 12 disintegrate

dissolved: 6 solute

dissolving: 7 diluent

dissonant: 5 harsh 7 grating, jarring 8 jangling 10 discordant 11 cacophonous, incongruous, unmelodious 12 inconsistent, inharmonious, unharmonious 13 contradictory

dissuade: 5 deter 6 dehort, divert 10 discourage, disincline

distain: 5 stain 6 defile 7 tarnish 8 discolor

distal: 6 remote 7 distant

opposite of: 8 proximal

distance: 4 step 5 depth, range, space 7 farness, mileage, reserve, yardage 8 interval, outstrip 10 background, remoteness

measuring device: 6 stadia 8 odograph, odometer, viameter 9 pedometer, telemeter

on earth's surface: 8 latitude 9 longitude

distant: coy, far, off 4 afar, away, cold,

yond **5** aloof **6** remote, yonder **7** faraway, foreign, removed **8** reserved **9** separated **10** discrepant
prefix: tel **4** tele

distaste: 6 degout **7** disgust, dislike **8** aversion **9** disrelish **11** displeasure **14** disinclination

distasteful: 7 hateful **8** brackish, nauseous, unsavory **9** loathsome, offensive, repugnant, repulsive **10** unpleasant **11** unpalatable **12** disagreeable

distemper: 4 soak **5** steep **6** choler, dilute, malady **7** ailment, disease, illness **8** disorder, sickness, unsettle **12** disaffection **13** indisposition

distend: 4 fill, grow **5** bloat, plump, swell, widen **6** dilate, expand, extend, spread **7** balloon, enlarge, inflate, stretch

distended: 4 wide **5** blown **8** patulous

distill, distil: 4 emit **6** infuse **7** trickle

distillation: 9 ascension
device: **6** retort **7** alembic
product: dew

distinct: 5 breme, clear, plain, vivid **7** diverse, legible, obvious, several, special **8** apparent, separate **9** different **10** articulate, individual **11** well-defined **13** distinguished

distinction: 4 note, rank **5** glory, honor **6** laurel, luster, lustre, renown **7** variation **10** prominence, reputation, separation **14** discrimination **15** differentiation

distinctive: 8 peculiar, talented **9** prominent **11** conspicuous **14** characteristic, discriminating

distingue: 7 eminent **8** affected **10** celebrated

distinguish: 6 decern, define, descry, secern **8** perceive, separate **9** designate, punctuate **10** discrepate **12** characterize, discriminate **13** differentiate

distinguished: 5 noted **6** famous, marked **7** eminent, notable, special **8** distinct, laureate, renowned **9** brilliant, prominent **10** celebrated **11** conspicuous, illustrious **13** extraordinary

distort: 5 screw, twist **6** cringe, deface, deform **7** contort, pervert **10** camshachle, disfeature

distorted: wry **4** awry **5** askew, crank **7** crooked, gnarled **9** misshapen **10** anamorphic **11** anamorphous

distract: mad **5** amuse, craze **6** bemuse, divert, harass, insane, madden, moider, puzzle, twitch **7** agitate, confuse, disturb, embroil, perplex **8** bewilder, confound **9** tosticate **10** distraught

distraught: mad **6** crazed **7** frantic **8** deranged, distract **9** perplexed

distress: ail **4** hurt, need, pain, teen **5** agony, anger, annoy, dolor, grief, gripe, worry, wound **6** danger, dolour, grieve, harass, harrow, misery, sorrow **7** afflict, anguish, anxiety, disease, misease, oppress, perplex, torture, trouble **8** ag-

grieve, calamity, straiten **9** adversity, constrain, martyrdom, necessity **10** affliction, constraint, discomfort **11** tribulation
call: S.O.S. **6** mayday

distressing: sad **4** hard, sore **7** carking, fearful, painful **9** sorrowful **11** troublesome

distribute: 4 deal, dole, mete, sort **5** allot, issue, share **6** assign, assort, divide, expend, impart, parcel **7** arrange, dispose, prorate **8** allocate, classify, dispense, disperse, separate **9** apportion, partition **10** administer **11** disseminate

distributively: 4 each **6** apiece **9** severally **10** separately **12** individually, respectively

distributor: 6 dealer **10** colporteur

district: 4 area, slum, ward **5** harsh, tract, vicus(L.) **6** canton, member, parish, region **7** circuit, country, demesne, diocese, quarter **8** distrito, precinct, province, rigorous **9** community, territory **12** neighborhood **13** neighbourhood
theater: **6** rialto

distrust: 4 fear **5** doubt **7** suspect **8** mistrust **9** suspicion **12** apprehension

distrustfully: 7 askance

disturb: vex **4** rile, roil **5** alarm, annoy, feeze, rouse, upset **6** harass, molest, ruffle, uncalm **7** agitate, commote, commove, derange, garboil, inquiet, perturb, trouble **8** convulse, disorder, disquiet, distract **9** discomfit, interfere, interrupt **10** disarrange, discomfort, discompose, disconcert

disturbance: 4 bree, dust, riot, rout **5** alarm, brawl, broil, deray, hurry, storm, strow, sturt, touse **6** affray, bother, breeze, cathro, fracas, hubbub, pother, rumpus, tumult, uproar **7** blunder, brulyie, brulzie, clatter, emotion, ferment, trouble, turmoil **8** business, disorder **9** agitation, annoyance, commotion, confusion, violation **10** convulsion, excitement **11** derangement, distraction, trepidation **12** discomposure, interruption, perturbation **13** collie-shangie(Sc.), inconvenience
emotional: **8** neurosis
ocean: **7** tsunami

disunite: rip **4** part **5** sever, untie **6** detach, divide, sunder **7** disband, disjoin, dissent, divorce, unravel **8** alienate, dissever, dissolve, estrange, separate **10** disconnect, dissociate

disuse: 6 misuse **7** abandon, discard **8** misapply **9** desuetude, disrepair **11** disaccustom, discontinue

disvalue: 9 disesteem, disregard **10** depreciate, undervalue

disyoke: 6 unteam

dit, ditt: 4 poem, said, song **5** adage, ditty **6** saying **7** reputed **8** obstruct, surnamed **9** appointed **10** expression

ditch: rut, sap **4** delf, dick, dike, dyke,

foss, gool, gout, ha-ha, holl, moat, sike **5**
canal, delft, delve, fence, fossa(L.),
fosse, graff, graft, grave, rhine, zanja **6**
fossae(pl.), gutter, trench, zanjon **7**
abandon, channel, grindle, gripple, zanjona

side: **5** scarp

dite: **4** mite, song **5** ditty **6** indict, indite **7**
compose, dictate, diction **11** composition

dither: **5** shake **6** bother, shiver **7** trouble
9 trembling

ditto: **4** same **6** repeat **8** likewise **9** duplicate

ditty: dit, lay **4** dite, poem, sing, song **5**
theme, verse **6** saying **7** dictate **9** utterance **11** composition

diuretic: **8** evacuant

diurnal: **5** daily **9** ephemeral

divagate: **6** wander **7** digress

divan: **4** book, hall, room, sofa **5** couch,
court **6** canape(F.), leewan, lounge, saloon,
senate, settee **7** council **9** davenport **12**
chesterfield

divaricate: **6** forked

dive: den **4** crib, duck, leap **5** haunt, swoop
6 header, plunge, resort **7** explore **8** submerge, tailspin **9** penetrate

kind of: **4** swan **6** gainer **8** jacknife

diver: **4** loon **7** pearler, plunger **9** submarine **10** pickpocket

disease: **5** bends

diverge: **6** branch, differ, divide, ramify,
spread **7** deviate, digress **8** disagree

divers: **4** evil, many **5** cruel **6** sundry **7**
several, various **8** perverse **9** different

diverse: **4** evil **6** motley, sundry, unlike,
varied **7** adverse, several, various **8** distinct, perverse, separate, varietal **9** different, multiform **10** dissimilar **13** heterogeneous

comb. form: **4** vari

diversify: **4** vary **5** freck **7** variate **9** variegate **13** differentiate

with colors: **6** begary **7** begarie **9** bespatter

diversion: jeu **4** game, play **5** alarm, feint,
hobby, sport **6** attack **7** pastime **9**
amusement, avocation, merriment **10** deflection, recreation, relaxation **11** delectation, distraction **13** divertisement, entertainment

diversity: **6** change **7** discord, variety **10**
difference, inequality **11** variegation **12**
disagreement

divert: **5** amuse, relax **7** beguile, deflect,
delight, detract, reflect **8** dissuade, distract, estrange, recreate **9** entertain

diverting: **5** droll **8** pleasant **9** laughable

divest: **4** bare, doff, reft **5** spoil, strip **6**
delawn, denude, depose, devest **7** be-
reave, deprive, despoil, disrobe, uncover
8 denature, dethrone, unclothe **9** dismantle **10** disfurnish, dispossess

of sham: **6** debunk

divide: cut, lot **4** deal, fork, mere, part, rift,

zone **5** cleft, divvy, sever, share, slice,
space, split **6** bisect, branch, cleave,
coteau, depart, devise, differ, parcel, ramify, sleave, sunder **7** aliquot, britten, diffuse, dispart, diverge, fissure, partake,
prorate **8** classify, crossect, disunite, graduate, separate **9** apportion, dismember,
intersect, multisect, partition, watershed
10 distribute

into parts: **4** paly **6** bisect, gobbet **7** quarter, trisect **9** bifurcate, septinate

divided: **4** ente, reft **7** fissate, partite **8**
aerolate, areolate, camerate **10** incom-
plete

comb. form: **6** schist

dividend: **5** bonus

divider: **7** compass

dividing wall: **5** septa(pl.) **6** septum **9**
partition

divination: **4** omen **6** augury **9** sortilege
11 discernment, rhabdomancy, sidero-
mancy **12** clairvoyance **13** machairo-
mancy

by monstrosities: **11** teratoscopy

divine: **4** holy **5** aread, areed, guess, pious
6 detect, devise, halsen, priest, sacred **7**
blessed, foresee, godlike, portend, predict, presage **8** ariolate, contrive, forebode, foreknow, foretell, heavenly, immortal, minister, perceive **9** ambrosial,
celestial, clergyman, religious **10** anticipate, conjecture, superhuman, theologian
12 supernatural

artificer: **8** tvashtar, tvashtri

being: **4** deva

messenger: **7** apostle

render: **5** deify

diviner: **4** seer **5** augur, sibyl **7** augurer,
prophet **8** haruspex **10** soothsayer **11**
clairvoyant **14** prognosticator

diving: **8** plunging **10** acrobatics, sub-
merging

hazard: **5** bends

divinity: See **god; goddess.**

divisible: **9** dividable, separable

division: **4** chap, clan, dole, neat, part, rift
5 group, realm, share **6** canton, schism,
sector **7** roulade, section **8** arpeggio, category, cleavage **9** Abteilung, allotment,
concision, departure, partition **10** department **11** bifurcation, compartment,
disjunction **13** apportionment, discon-
nection, dismemberment

between torrid and temperate zone: **6**
tropic

house: **5** estre

into hundred: **12** centuriation

plant: **15** archichlamydeae

play: act **5** scene

poem: **5** canto

political: **4** city, ward **5** state **6** county,
parish **7** borough **8** district

property: **9** gavelkind

religious: **6** schism

shield: **4** ente, paly

social: **5** caste, class, tribe **6** clique

time: day, eon **4** aeon, week, year **5** month **6** decade, minute, moment, second **7** weekend **9** fortnight

word: **8** syllable

divisional: **10** fractional, separative

divorce: **5** sever **6** sunder **7** asunder **8** dissolve, disunion, disunite, separate **10** separation **11** dissolution

Jewish law: get **4** gett

mill: **4** Reno

divot: **4** clod

divulge: **4** bare, show, tell **5** voice **6** beway, impart, reveal, spread, unfold **7** publish, uncover **8** disclose, discover, evulgate, proclaim **9** eliminate **11** communicate

divvy: **5** share **6** divide **7** portion

Dixie Land: **5** South

dizen: **7** bedizen **9** overdress

dizzard: **4** fool **6** jester **9** blockhead

dizziness: **6** megrim **7** vertigo **9** giddiness

with headache: **10** scotodinia

dizzy: **4** dunt **5** crazy, giddy **6** fickle, stupid **7** foolish **8** swimming, unsteady **10** capricious **11** lightheaded, vertiginous

djebel: **4** hill

do: act **4** bilk, dost, make, suit **5** avail, cheat, guise, serve, trick **6** answer, render **7** achieve, execute, perform, produce, satisfy, suffice **8** transact **10** accomplish, administer

musical: ut

poetic: **5** didst

do away with: rid **4** kill **7** abolish, destroy **9** liquidate **11** discontinue

do up: **4** wrap

do well: **7** prosper

dobbin: **4** mare

docent: **7** teacher **8** lecturer

docile: **4** calm, meek, tame **6** gentle **7** ductile, dutiful **8** biddable **9** tractable **10** manageable

dock: cut **4** bang, clip, moor, pier, quay **5** basin, wharf **6** marina, strunt **7** bobtail, curtail, shorten **8** canaigre **9** perforate

worker: **9** stevedore

yard: **7** arsenal

doctor: **4** dose **5** sugar, treat **6** deacon, healer, intern **7** teacher **9** internist, physician **11** aesculapian

aide: **5** nurse

animal: vet **10** veterinary **12** veterinarian

oath of: **11** hippocratic

specialist: **6** aurist, goofer, intern **7** interne, oculist, surgeon **9** hippiater, otologist **10** podiatrist **11** chiropodist, neurologist, optometrist, orthopedist **12** chiropractor, gynecologist, obstetrician, orthodontist, orthopaedist, psychiatrist, proctologist **13** cranioscopist, gynaecologist **15** ophthalmologist

doctrine: ism **4** doxy, lear, rule **5** credo, creed, dogma, maxim, tenet **6** belief, gos-

pel, theory **7** article, opinion, precept **8** position **9** principle **10** discipline

pert. to: **10** dogmatical **12** teleological

specific: **6** cabala, heresy, malism, Mishna **7** egotism, Mishnah **8** fatalism, hedonism **10** agathology, pragmatism **13** monarchianism

spreader: **12** propagandist

document: **4** bill, book, deed, writ **5** chart, lease, paper, teach **6** billet, patent, school **7** archive, missive, precept, writing **8** contract, covenant, instruct, mortgage **9** indenture **10** manuscript **11** instruction

addition: **5** rider **7** codicil **9** amendment

file: **7** dossier

original record: **8** protocol

provisional: **5** scrip

receptacle: **7** hanaper

signed by all parties: **8** syngraph

true copy: **7** estreat

dod, dodd: lop **4** clip, poll

Dodecanese Island: Coo, Cos **4** Caso, Lero, Simi, Syme **5** Leros, Lipso, Lisso, Patmo, Tilos **6** Calchi, Calino, Lipsos, Nisiro, Patmos **7** Nisyros, Piscopi **9** Karpathos, Scarpanto, Stampalia **10** Astropalia

dodder: **5** shake **6** totter **7** tremble

doddering: old **5** inane **6** infirm, senile **7** foolish

dodge: **4** duck, jink, jouk, ruse **5** avoid, cheat, elude, evade, shift, trick **6** escape **7** deceive, evasion **8** artifice, gilenyie **9** expedient **10** equivocate

dodger: **7** haggler **8** handbill **10** corndodger **13** advertisement

corn: **4** pone

doe: teg **4** faun, hind **6** female

doer: **5** actor, agent, maker **6** author, factor, feasor **7** facient, manager **8** attorney, executor **9** performer

suffix: er, or; ast, eer, ier, ist **4** ator, euse, ster

does: **4** doth

doff: off **4** daff, vail **5** avale, douse, dowse, strip **6** divest, remove **7** undress

dog: cur, mut, pug, pup, yap **4** mutt, pawl, tike, tyke **5** canis(L.), pooch, puppy, whelp **6** bowwow, buffer, canine, detent, yapper **7** mongrel, yapster **9** carnivore

African: **7** basenji

breed: pug **4** Dane **5** boxer, hound, Husky, pelon, sauki, spitz **6** Afghan, basset, beagle, borzoi, Briard, collie, Eskimo, gun dog, poodle, setter, Sussex **7** Basenji, bulldog, griffon, harrier, Maltese, mastiff, Mexican, owtchar, pincher, pointer, Scottie, sleughi, spaniel, starter, terrier, whippet **8** Airedale, Alsatian, Aleutant, chow chow, coach dog, Doberman, elkhound, Flanders, foxhound, labrador, landseer, Malemute, Malinois, papillon, Pekinese, Pyrenees, Samoyede, Sealy-

ham, shepherd, springer **9** boarhound, Brabancon, Chihuahua, dachshund, Dalmation, deerhound, Great Dane, greyhound, kerry blue, police dog, retriever, St. Bernard, schnauzer, shorthair, wolfhound, wolf spitz, Yorkshire **10** Bedlington, bloodhound, Boston bull, fox terrier, Manchester, otter hound, Pomeranian, Rottweiler, schipperke, toy terrier, weimaraner, wire-haired **11** bull terrier, Groenendael, ruby spaniel, Skye terrier **12** cairn terrier, field spaniel, gazelle hound, Gordon setter, gossett hound, Newfoundland, water spaniel, Welsh terrier **13** Boston terrier, Chesapeake Bay, cocker spaniel, Great Pyrenees, Prince Charles, yankee terrier **14** Chinese crested, clumber spaniel, highland collie, Tibetan spaniel **15** Brussels griffon, highland terrier, Riesenschnauzer **17** Bouvier de Flandres
close-haired: pug **5** boxer
Eskimo: **5** husky **7** samoyed **8** Malemute, samoyede
famous: **4** Asta, Fala, King, Tige, Toby **5** Devil **6** Feller, Lassie **8** Checkers **9** Rin-tin-tin **11** Strongheart
fox-like: **6** colpeo
German origin: **5** boxer **8** Doberman **9** Drahthaar **10** Weimaraner
hauling: **5** husky **7** samoyed **8** Malemute, samoyede **9** Dalmatian
house: **6** kennel
howling of: **9** ululation
hunting: **4** alan, rach **5** aland, alant, hound, rache, ratch, toler **6** basset, borzoi, beagle, saluki, setter, talbot **7** courser, harrier, pointer **8** Elkhound **9** retriever, wolfhound **10** bloodhound
iron: **7** firedog
large: **4** alan, Dane **5** boxer, bawty **6** briard, bawtie, collie, police **7** mastiff **12** Newfoundland
long-haired: **4** alco, chow **7** spaniel
multi-headed: **8** cerberus
pack: **8** canaglia, canaille
reward: **6** hallow
small: Pom, pug, pup **4** alco, fist, purp **5** ascob, feist **6** messan, messin **7** spaniel **8** Pekinese **9** chihuahua, Pekingese **10** Pomeranian
upper lip: **5** flews
wild: **5** adjag, dhole, dingo **6** jackal **7** agouara **8** cimarron
dog days: **8** canicule
dog-like: **13** cynocephalous
dog rose: **5** bucky **6** canker **9** eglantine
fruit: hip
dog salmon: **4** keta
dog star: **4** sept, sopt **6** sirius
dogboat: pig
dogcart: **6** tumtum **7** bounder **8** gadabout
dogfish: hoe **4** huss, tope **9** roussette
dogged: **6** sullen **7** doggish, doglike **9**

malicious, obstinate, tenacious **10** determined **12** pertinacious
doggerel: **6** trivia **9** burlesque
doggery: **7** barroom **8** grogshop
doggish: **5** sulky **7** currish, cynical, stylish **8** snapping
dogie: **5** stray
dogma: **5** creed, tenet **6** dictum **8** doctrine, document
pert. to: **9** levitical
dogmatic: **9** assertive, confident, pragmatic **10** intolerant, peremptory **11** affirmative, dictatorial, magisterial, opinionated, pragmatical
dogmatism: **10** positivism, pragmatism **11** intolerance **13** pontificality
dogwood: **5** osier, sumac **6** cornel, cornus
flowering: **7** boxwood
doily: mat **6** napkin
doing: act **4** deed, stir **5** event **6** action **8** function
doldrum: **5** dumps, ennui **6** tedium **7** dullard **8** confused, dullness **10** depression **12** listlessness
dole: lot **4** alms, deal, gift, goal, mete, part **5** allot, fraud, grief, guile, mourn, share **6** deceit, grieve, relief, sorrow **7** charity, dealing, destiny, handout, payment, portion **8** boundary, dispense, division, gratuity, landmark, pittance **9** allotment, apportion **10** distribute, misfortune **12** distribution
doleful: sad **5** drear, heavy **6** dismal, dreary, funest, rueful **7** flebile **8** dolesome, dolorous, mournful **9** sorrowful **10** lugubrious, melancholy
dolent: **9** sorrowful
dolente: **9** plaintive
dolesome: **6** dismal, gloomy **7** doleful **9** sorrowful
doll: toy **4** babe, baby **5** array, puppe(G.) **6** maumet, moppet, muneca(Sp.), poupee(F.), puppet **8** mistress **9** golliwogg **10** sweetheart
dollar: **4** bean, buck **5** berry, eagle **8** frogskin, simoleon
Doll's House heroine: **4** Nora
dolly: **4** drab **8** mistress, slattern **10** sweetheart
dolor, dolour: **5** calor, grief **6** sorrow **7** anguish, sadness **8** distress, mourning **11** lamentation
dolorous: sad **6** dismal **7** doleful **8** grievous **9** sorrowful
dolphin, delphin: **4** fish, inia **6** dorado **8** porpoise **9** goosebeak **10** bottlenose
river: **5** bouto
dolt: ass, oaf **4** asse, calf, chub, clod, coof, dult, fool, moke **5** chump, dummy, dunce, idiot **6** befool, cudden, doodle **7** bluntie(Sc.), dawcock, dullard, half-wit **8** bosthoon, clodpate, imbecile, mooncalf, numskull **9** blockhead, ignoramus, simpleton **10** dunderhead

doltish: 4 dull 6 stupid 7 foolish, sottish 8 blockish, doltlike 11 thickheaded

domain: 5 bound, bourn, realm, scope, state, world 6 barony, bourne, empery, empire, estate 7 demesne 8 dominion, province 9 bailiwick 12 commonwealth

Dombey and Sons: 6 Cuttle

dome: cap 4 cima 6 cupola 7 calotte, edifice

domed: 7 vaulted

domestic: 4 hind, maid 5 domal 6 hameil, hamelt, hamilt, homely, homish, housal, inland, inmate, native 7 servant 8 home-bred, homemade, intimate 9 enchorial, home-grown
establishment: 6 menage

domesticate: 4 tame 6 entame 7 amenage, reclaim 8 civilize 10 naturalize 11 domiciliate

domicile: 4 home 5 abode, house 6 menage 8 dwelling 9 residence 10 habitation
identification: 9 doorplate

dominant: 5 bossy, chief 6 ruling 7 central, regnant, supreme 8 superior 9 ascendant, imperious, paramount, prevalent, principal 10 commanding, pre-eminent, prevailing 11 outweighing, predominant 12 preponderant 13 overbalancing

dominate: 4 rule 5 reign 6 govern 7 control 8 domineer 11 predominate

domination: 7 control 8 dominion 9 supremacy 10 ascendancy, ascendency 11 sovereignty 12 predominance 14 possessiveness

domine: 4 Lord, rule 6 master 9 clergyman 11 predominate

domineer: 4 boss, lord, rule 5 bully, feast, revel, tower 7 command, swagger 8 dominate, overlord 11 predominate

domineering: 6 lordly 7 haughty 8 arrogant, masterly 9 imperious, masterful 10 tyrannical 11 dictatorial, magisterial, overbearing

Dominican: 9 predicant

dominie: 6 pastor 9 pedagogue 12 schoolmaster

dominion: 4 rule, sway 5 realm, reign 6 domain, empire 7 control, dynasty, poustie, regency 9 authority, hierarchy, ownership, supremacy 10 ascendancy, ascendency, domination 11 sovereignty 12 jurisdiction
church: 11 sacerdotium
joint: 11 condominium

domino: die 4 mask

dompt: cow 5 daunt 6 subdue

domus: 4 home 5 house

don: 4 wear 5 array, dress 6 assume, clothe, invest 8 nobleman 9 gentleman, professor 10 instructor

Don Juan's mother: 4 Inez

Don Quixote: *companion:* 11 Sancho Panza
steed: 9 Rosinante, Rozinante

donate: gie(Sc.) 4 give 6 bestow 7 present 10 contribute

donatio: 4 gift 8 donation

donation: 4 gift 5 grant 7 donatio, present 10 foundation 11 benefaction 12 contribution

done: 4 over 5 baked, ended 6 cooked 7 through 8 finished 9 completed, exhausted 12 accomplished

donee: 7 heritor 8 receiver 9 recipient 11 beneficiary

donkey: ass 4 moke 5 burro, cuddy, dicky, neddy 6 dickey, onager 7 bussock, fussock 9 quadruped

donkey engine: 6 yarder

donna: 4 lady, wife 5 madam, woman 8 mistress

donor: 4 give 5 giver 10 benefactor 11 contributor 14 philanthropist

donsie: 6 ailing 7 sickish 9 squeamish

doodle: 4 dolt, draw 5 cheat 7 cartoon, trifler

doodlesack: 7 bagpipe

doodling: 9 scrolling

doohickey: 6 device, gadget 11 contrivance

doolee: 6 litter

doom: law, lot 4 damn, fate, ruin 5 death 6 decree, devote, steven 7 condemn, destine, destiny, fortune, statute 8 decision, sentence 9 destinate, enactment, judgement, ordinance 10 adjudicate, predestine 11 destruction, discernment 12 condemnation 13 righteousness

doomed: fey 5 fatal 8 accursed 9 sentenced

door: 4 gate 5 hatch 6 portal 7 barrier, doorway, opening, passage, postern 11 entranceway
cross piece: 6 lintel
fastener: bar 4 bolt, hasp, lock 5 catch 8 fastener
frame: 4 jamb
part: 4 jamb, knob, risp 5 panel 6 alette, lintel
storm: 6 dingle
trap: 4 drop
way: 4 exit 8 entrance

doorkeeper: 5 tiler, usher 6 durwan, porter, warden 7 durwaun, janitor, ostiary 8 huissier, janitrix 9 concierge(F.), janitress, ostiarius

doorknocker: 6 hammer, rapper

doorlatch: 8 haggaday

doorpost: 4 durn, jamb 6 alette

doorway: 4 door, exit 6 portal 7 opening 11 entranceway

dope: hop 4 drug 5 opium, paste 6 heroin, opiate 7 predict, stupefy 8 narcotic 9 marijuana 13 nitroglycerin

doped: 10 narcotized, prophesied

dor, dorr: bee 4 joke, mock 5 joker, scoff, trick 6 beetle 7 buffoon, deceive, mockery 9 deception 11 drumbledore

dorbel: 6 pedant

dorian: 6 simple
Dorian festival: 6 Carnea 7 Carneia
doric: 6 rustic
Doric: *frieze bottom:* 6 taenia
frieze slab: 6 metope
dormancy: 6 torpor 8 abeyance 10 quiescence
dormant: 5 fixed 6 asleep, latent, torpid 7 resting, sleeper 8 dormient, inactive, sleeping 9 quiescent, unaroused 10 stationary
dormer: 6 window 7 lucarne
dormeuse: 4 seat 5 coach 8 carriage, nightcap
dormient: 7 dormant 8 sleeping
dormitory: 4 dorm 5 house 8 quarters
monastery: 6 dorter 7 dortour
dormouse: 4 loir 5 lerot
dornick: 5 linen
dorp: 4 city, town 5 thorp 6 hamlet, thorpe 7 village 8 township
dorsal: 5 notal 6 dorsel, dorser, dosser, tergal 7 hanging 9 posterior
dorsum: 4 back
dorty: 5 saucy, sulky 7 haughty
dose: 4 bole 5 draft, treat 6 doctor, drench, potion 7 draught 8 quantity
doss: 4 tuft
dot: 4 clot, lump, mote, peck 5 dowry, point, speck 6 period 7 speckle, stipple 8 particle, sprinkle 9 bespangle 10 besprinkle, distribute
over the letter i: 6 tittle
dotage: 4 dote 5 folly 6 drivel 8 senility 10 feebleness, imbecility
dotard: 5 silly 6 senile 8 imbecile
dote: rot 4 dove, doze, love 5 adore, decay, endow 6 bestow, dotage, dotard, drivel, stupor 8 imbecile
doting: 4 fond
dotish, doatish: 4 weak 7 foolish 8 imbecile
dotted: 7 spotted 8 speckled, stippled 9 scattered 11 distributed, diversified
dotterel: 4 dupe, gull, wind 6 plover 7 morinel
dottle: 4 fool, plug 5 silly 6 dotard
dotty: 5 crazy 6 feeble, spotty
doty: 10 discolored
Douay Bible: 4 Aree
double: ply 4 dual, fold, twin 5 duple, fetch 6 bifold, binary, binate, duplex 7 twofold 8 geminate 9 ambiguous, duplicate 11 counterpart
prefix: di
double dagger: 6 diesis
double dealing: 6 deceit
double-hue: 7 bicolor
doublecross: 5 cheat 6 betray 7 deceive, swindle 9 treachery
doublecrosser: rat
doubled: 5 gemel
doublet: 9 pourpoint
doubling: 4 loop
doubly: 5 twice

doubt: 4 fear 5 demur, dread, query, waver 7 dubiate, scruple, suspect 8 distrust, dubitate, hesitate, mistrust, question 9 discredit, misgiving, suspicion 10 diffidence, disbelieve, indecision 11 uncertainty 12 apprehension
doubter: 5 cynic 7 skeptic 10 unbeliever
doubtful: 7 dubious, fearful, perhaps 8 dreadful, perilous, wavering 9 ambiguous, dangerous, diffident, equivocal, uncertain, undecided 10 apocryphal, hesitating, irresolute, suspicious 11 distrustful, vacillating 12 apprehensive, questionable, undetermined 13 problematical
doubtfulness: 9 ambiguity
douce: 4 neat, tidy 5 sober, sweet 6 genial, modest, sedate 7 prudent 8 cheerful, pleasant 10 hospitable
douceur: 5 bonus 9 pourboire
dough: 4 cash, duff 5 money, paste 6 noodle, sponge 7 brioche
doughnut: 6 cymbal, sinker 7 cruller, olycook, olykoek, simball 9 freidcake
doughty: 4 fell 7 valiant 8 intrepid
dour: 4 glum, grim, hard, sour 5 rough, stern 6 gloomy, morose, severe, strong, sullen 7 ominous 9 obstinate 10 inflexible
douse, dowse: 4 beat, blow, doff, duck, quit, stow 5 cease, rinse, souse 6 drench, plunge, strike, stroke 7 immerse 8 downpour 9 drenching 10 extinguish
douzepers: 4 Ivon, Oton 5 Ivory, Gerin, Ogier, peers 6 Anseis, Gerier, nobles, Oliver, Roland, Samson, Turpin 7 knights 8 Engelier, paladins 9 Berengier 17 Gerard de Rousillon
dove: 4 doze 5 color 6 culver, cushat, pigeon 7 namaqua, slumber
home: 4 cote
pert. to: 9 columbine
sound: 4 curr
young: 8 doveling
dovecot, dovecote: 9 columbary 11 columbarium
dovekey, dovekie: auk 4 alle 5 rotch, rotge 6 rotche 8 dovelike 9 guillemot
dovelike: 4 pure 6 dovish, gentle 7 lovable 9 columbine
dover: 4 doze, stun 6 drowse
dovetail: 5 tenon
dovish: 8 dovelike, harmless, innocent
dow: 4 dull, fade 5 avail, befit, endow 6 thrive 7 behoove, prosper
dowd: 5 frump
dowdy: 4 poky 5 frump, pokey 6 blowzy, shabby, untidy 8 slovenly 10 slatternly
dowel: peg, pin 4 coak 6 pintle
dower: dos 5 dowry, endow 7 portion 9 endowment
down: 4 dowl, fell, flix, flue, fuzz, hill, lint 5 below, dowle, floor, fluff 6 bedown 7 hillock, plumage 9 overthrow
comb. form: bas(F.) 4 cata(Gr.)
poetic: 5 adown

prefix: de
down at the heel: 5 seamy, seedy
down in the mouth: 4 glum 7 unhappy 9 depressed 11 discouraged
down under: 8 Tasmania 9 antipodes, Australia 10 New Zealand
down wind: 7 leeward
down with: 4 a bas
downcast: sad 6 abject, gloomy 8 hopeless 9 depressed 10 despondent, dispirited, melancholy 11 discouraged 12 disheartened
downfall: pit 4 fate, ruin, trap 5 abyss 7 descent, undoing 8 collapse 9 precipice, ruination 11 destruction, ecroulement 12 degringolade
heavy: 7 torrent
downhearted: 8 dejected 9 depressed 10 melancholy
downpour: 4 pour, rain 5 douse, dowse, spill 7 torrent
downright: 4 flat, pure, rank 5 blank, blunt, plain, plumb, sheer, stark 6 arrant, direct 8 absolute, even-down, positive, thorough 10 completely, forthright, thoroughly 11 straightway 13 perpendicular, unceremonious 15 perpendicularly
downstairs: 5 below
downward: 5 below, lower 11 netherwards
poetic: 5 adown
slope: 9 declivity
downy: 4 soft 5 mossy, nappy, pilar, quiet 6 fluffy, placid 7 cunning, knowing 8 soothing
dowry: dos, dot 4 gift 5 dower 6 talent 7 portion 9 endowment
pert. to: 5 dotal
doxology: 13 glorification
doxy: ism 5 wench 6 harlot 7 opinion 8 doctrine
doyen: 4 dean
doze: nap, nod, rot 4 dote, dove 5 decay, dover, sleep, sloom 6 catnap, drowse, muddle, snooze 7 perplex, slumber, snoozle, stupefy
drab: box, daw 4 dell, drug, dull 5 besom, dolly, graze, wench, whore 6 malkin, poison 7 prosaic 9 colorless 10 monotonous, prostitute 13 uninteresting
drachma: 4 coin, dram
one-sixth: 4 obol
draconian: 5 cruel 6 severe
draff: 4 lees 5 dregs, drink 6 refuse 7 hogwash
draft: nip, sip 4 dose, dram, gust, levy, plan, swig, toot 5 drink, epure, swipe 6 drench, godown, minute, potion, redact, scroll, sketch, waucht, waught 7 drawing, outline, pattern, project 8 beverage, potation, protocol 9 conscript
draftsman, draughtsman: 6 drawer 7 tippler 9 architect
drag: lug, tow, tug 4 draw, hale, harl, haul, pull, snig, tear, tump 5 brake, drawl, ral-

ly, tease, trail, trawl 6 linger, school, taigle 7 grapnel
through mud: 7 bemire
dragnet: 5 trawl 7 trainel
dragon: 7 monster 8 basilisk
Biblical: 5 Rahab
biting: 8 tarragon
Vedic: Ahi
dragoon: 10 cavalry-man, carabineer, carabinier
drain: dry, gaw, sap 4 delf, gout, grip, gurt, lade, milk, sike, sink 5 bunny, canal, delft, dreen, empty, fleet, gully, rhine(dial.), sewer, siver 6 filter, furrow, guzzle, siphon, syphon, trench, zanjon 7 acequia, alberca, channel, deplete, exhaust, grindle, gripple, zanjona 8 thurrock 9 undermine 11 watercourse
arched: 7 culvert
blood: 12 exsanguinate
forces: 5 spend
drainage: 4 adit
area: 5 basin
drainpipe: 6 leader
dram: nip 4 mite, slug 5 draft, drink 6 drachm 7 snifter 8 potation, quantity 11 indifferent
drama: 4 mime, play 5 opera 6 comedy 7 atellan, history, theater, tragedy 8 operetta, pastoral 9 pantomime 11 composition
court: 5 trial
division: act 5 scene
for single actor: 8 monodram
main act: 8 epitasis
part: 4 role
short: 4 skit 7 saynete
spectacular: 12 extravaganza
third most important actor: 11 tritagonist
dramatic: 4 wild 5 vivid 6 scenic 10 theatrical 12 melodramatic
expression system: 8 delsarte
representation: 13 impersonation
dramatist: 5 actor 10 playwright
drank: See **drink.**
drape: 4 hang 5 adorn, cover, weave 7 curtain, hanging, valance
drapeau: 4 flag 8 standard
draper: 6 tailor
drapery: 5 baize, cloth 7 curtain, valance 8 mourning
drapet: 5 cloth 8 covering
drastic: 4 dire 5 harsh 7 extreme, radical 8 rigorous
drasty: 4 vile 9 worthless
draught: See **draft.**
Dravidian (see also **India**): 4 Gond, Kota, Toda, Tulu 5 Arava, Gondi, Khond, Malto, Oraon, Tamil 6 Andhra, Brahui, Kodagu, Kurukh, Telegu, Telugu 8 Kanarese 9 Malayalam
demon: 4 bhut
tribe: 6 Badaga 7 Colleri, Collery 9 Colleries
draw: lug, tie, tow, tug 4 drag, duct, hale,

haul, lade, limn, lure, pull **5** catch, educe, train **6** allure, deduce, depict, derive, design, elicit, entice, induce, inhale, select, sketch **7** attract, detract, extract, inspire, portray **8** inveigle **9** delineate, reproduce, statement

again: **5** remap **6** replat

away from: **6** shrink

back: **4** fawn **5** wince **6** cringe, rebate, recede, recoil, resile, retire, shrink **7** retract, retreat **9** deduction, hindrance

finely: **4** etch

near: hie **4** near **5** coast **8** approach

off: sap **5** drain **6** siphon, syphon **7** extract **8** abstract, withdraw

out: **4** lade, pump **5** educe **6** elicit, exhale **7** extract, tweezer **8** protract **9** exantlate **11** interrogate **12** cross examine

tight: **4** frap, furl, lace **5** brace, cinch **7** stretch

draw game: **9** stalemate

drawer: **4** till

drawers: **5** pants **7** panties **9** shintiyan

chest of: **7** commode

drawing: **5** draft, envol, epure **7** hauling, pulling **8** traction **9** attrahent **10** attracting, extracting **11** delineation, centripetal

absent-minded: **8** doodling

exaggerated: **7** cartoon **10** caricature

instrument: **9** eidograph **10** pantograph

drawing room: **5** salon **6** parlor, saloon

drawl: **5** drant, drunt **6** draunt, loiter

drawlatch: lag **6** dawdle **11** latchstring **12** eavesdropper

drawn: **7** haggard

drawstring: **5** latch

dray: **4** cart **5** wagon **6** camion **7** go-devil

drayage: **7** cartage, haulage

drayman: **6** carter **7** carrier, remover, wagoner

dread: awe **4** fear, fray **5** awful, doubt **6** adread, agrise, dismay, eschew, horror, terror **7** anxiety, dismiss **8** affright, dreddour, terrible **9** reverence **12** apprehension

object of: **4** bogy **5** bogey, bogie **7** bugaboo, bugbear

dread of: See **fear.**

dreaded: **7** awesome

dreadful: **4** dire **5** awful **6** grisly, horrid **7** careful, direful, fearful, ghastly, grimful, hideous **8** doubtful, ghastful, horrible, shocking, terrible, terrific **9** frightful **10** formidable

dreadnaught, dreadnought: **4** tank **7** warship **8** fearless **10** battleship

dream: **4** muse, reve(F.) **5** fancy **6** sweven, vision **7** fantasy, imagine, reverie, romance **8** phantasm **9** nightmare **10** apparition

god of: **8** Morpheus

interpretation: **13** oneirocritics **15** oneirocriticism

pert. to: **7** oneiric, somnial **9** oneirotic

dreamed: **7** fancied **8** visioned

dreamer: **4** poet **7** fantast **8** idealist **9** visionary **10** ideologist

dreaminess: **7** languor

dreamy: kef **4** soft **5** vague **6** poetic **7** faraway, languid, pensive **8** fanciful, soothing **9** visionary **11** imaginative

drear: **4** dern **5** gloom **6** dismal, gloomy **7** doleful, sadness **9** sorrowful **10** melancholy

dreary: sad **4** dire, dree, dull, flat **5** bleak, cruel, ourie **6** dismal, elenge, gloomy, gousty, lonely **7** doleful, goustie, howling, wilsome **8** grievous **9** cheerless, sorrowful **10** depressing, monotonous **11** distressful

dredge: mop **4** sift **5** scoop **6** deepen **8** excavate, sprinkle **9** sweetmeat

dredger: **6** duster **9** sprinkler

dree: `4 dull, slow **5** grief **6** dismal, dreary, endure, suffer **7** tedious **9** suffering **10** persistent

dregs: **4** crap, faex, lees **5** draff, dross, feces, grout, magma **6** bottom, dunder, faeces, refuse **7** grounds, grummel, residue **8** grummels, remnants, sediment, settling **9** excrement, feculence **10** subsidence **12** crassamentum

drench: **4** dose, hose, sind, sink, soak **5** douse, dowse, draft, drink, drouk, drown, souse, steep **6** bucket, douche, imbrue, potion **7** immerse **8** permeate, saturate, submerge

dress (see also **garment, gown, robe, vestment**): don, dub, fig, ray rig, tog **4** be-go, busk, buss, deck, garb, gear, gown, hone, knap, mill, rail, robe, suit, tire, trim, wear **5** adorn, array, curry, dight, equip, frock, guise, habit, magma, preen, primp, prink, prune **6** attire, broach, clothe, enrobe, fangle, fettle, graith, invest, outfit, revest, toilet **7** affaite, apparel, bandage, clothes, costume, garment, garnish, raiment, toggery, vesture **8** cleading, clothing, decorate, ornament, vestment **9** embellish, equipment, vestiture **10** garmenture, habiliment, habilitate, investment **12** accouterment, accoutrement

clerical: **5** cloth

cloth: **4** burl

court: **4** robe

flax: ted **5** dizen

gaudily: **5** primp, prink **6** dizene **7** bedizen

in full armor: **7** panoply

informal: **6** shorts, slacks **8** negligee **9** bluejeans

kind of: alb **4** huke **5** crape, crepe, ephod, get-up, mufti, tails, tenue, tunic, weeds **6** dirndl, finery, gaiter, kirtle, livery, tuxedo **7** regalia **8** lava-lava, negligee, peignoir **9** canonical, decollete, polonaise

mean: **4** rags

odd: rig **5** getup

ornament: **4** frog, lace **5** jabot, ruche **6**

sequin, zequin **7** ruching **8** chequeen, zecchino **10** embroidery

stone: nig **5** nidge, spall **7** scabble

surgically: **5** dight

dress up: tog **5** preen, primp, prink

dressed: **4** clad **5** bound **7** habited

well: **4** braw **5** smart **7** dallack, stylish **9** spruced-up

dresser: **5** rober **6** bureau **7** modiste **8** cupboard **9** appreteur **10** escritoire

leather: **7** currier **8** levanter

scrupulous: **4** dude **7** preener **11** Beau Brummel

dressing: **7** beating **8** scolding **11** castigation

kind of: **4** lint **5** salve **7** pledget **8** ointment, remolade

dressing room: **7** camarin

dressing stone: **9** scotching

dressmaker: **5** sewer **6** seamer **7** modiste **8** stitcher **9** couturier **10** couturiere, seamstress

model: **7** manikin **8** mannikin **9** mannequin

dretch: **5** delay **6** dawdle **7** trouble

drew (see also **draw**): **8** eelgrass

dribble: **4** drip, drop

driblet: **5** piece

dried: See **dry.**

dried out: **5** stale **6** effete

drift: sag **4** dene, dune, ford, herd, plot, tide, till **5** drove, fleet, float, flock, tenor, trend **6** broach, course, design, device, scheme, tunnel **7** impetus, impulse, pasture, purport **8** tendency **9** deviation **10** propulsion

along: **4** tide **5** float

sidewise: **4** crab **8** crescent

driftage: **7** flotsam **8** wreckage

drill: gad, sow, tap **4** bore, spud **5** auger, borer, churn, decoy, train, tutor, twirl, whirl **6** allure, entice, furrow, pierce, school, seeder, stoper **7** channel **8** exercise, instruct, practice **9** perforate

drilled: **9** practiced

drilling: **5** denim

drink (see also **beverage**): bib, bum, lap, peg, rum, sip, tea **4** dram, grog, horn, lush, mead, shot, slug, soak, swig, tiff, toot, tope **5** bever, booze, bouse, draft, julep, morat, punch, quaff, skink, sniff, snort, souse, toast, toddy, vodka **6** absorb, bezzle, bracer, chaser, coffee, drench, godown, guzzle, hooker, imbibe, potion, ptisan, swinge, tipple **7** diluent, draught, snifter, swallow **8** beverage, cocktail, highball, potation, refresco **9** decoction **10** intoxicant

alcoholic: ade, ale, gin, hum, rye **4** beer, beno, bosa, boza, chia, flip, mead, nipa, nogg, soma, swig **5** airah, bombo, bozah, bubud, bumbo, julep, lager, negus, posca, sling, vodka, zombi **6** brandy, casiri, caudle, fuddle, mescal, posset, rickey, zombie **7** cobbler, guarapo, sidecar **8** aperitif, rumbarge, sangaree, tequilla **9**

cointreau, ship belly **10** tangle-foot **13** whistle-belley

carbonated: fiz, pop **4** fizz, soda **9** gingerade, gingerale

farinaceous: **6** ptisan

frozen: **6** frappe

fruit: ade **5** assai, bland, julep, morat **6** rickey **7** ratafee, ratafia

hot: tod **5** cocoa, copus, negus, toddy **6** caudle

magic: **8** nepenthe

mixer of: **6** barman **9** barkeeper, bartender

molasses and vinegar: **6** swanky

money for: **8** bonamano **9** pourboire

much: **4** swig, tope **5** bouse, quaff, swill **6** waucht, waught **7** carouse

sassafras **6** saloop

small: hum, nip, peg, tot **4** bull, dram, pony, shot **5** sniff, snort, tabor **6** chaser **7** diluent, snifter

sweet: **6** nectar

drinkable: **7** potable

drinker: sot **5** toper **6** bender **7** imbiber, intaker, quaffer **8** drunkard **9** inebriate

drinking: **5** bever **6** guzzle **8** carousal **10** poculation

bout: **4** orgy **5** binge, spree **6** fuddle, shindy, splore **7** gaedown, wassail **8** carousal, potation **11** downsitting

salutation: **5** skoal **7** prosit

vessel: cup, mug **4** bowl, tass **5** glass, gourd, hanap, jorum, stein, stoop, stoup **6** beaker, cappie, dipper, goblet, noggin, patera, rumkin **7** bombard, canikin, hanaper, tankard **8** cannikin, schooner

drip: sie, sye **4** drop, leak, sile **5** eaves **7** dribble, dripple, trickle

frozen: **6** icicle

drive: cot **4** bang, bear, butt, cram, ding, goad, hunt, ride, send, spur, urge **5** chase, co-act, crowd, feeze, force, hurry, impel, infer, press, repel, roust, shove, sweep **6** attack, beetle, bensel, compel, cudgel, deduce, derive, hasten, plunge, propel **7** overtax **9** constrain

away: **5** chase, repel **6** banish, dispel **7** repulse

down: **4** tamp

frantic: **7** bedevil

out: **4** rout **5** exile, expel **9** eradicate

public: **9** esplanade

drive-in: **7** open-air **10** restaurant

drivel: **4** dote **5** drool **6** dotage, drudge, footle, menial, slaver **7** twaddle **8** nonsense

driveler: **4** fool **5** doter

driver: **4** jenu **5** drabi **6** cabman, caller, drover, jarvey, mallet **7** catcher, spanker, speeder **8** coachman, engineer, galloway, overseer, teamster **9** chauffeur, izvozchik, propeller **10** charioteer, taskmaster

of golden chariot: **6** Helios

drizzle: deg, mug **4** dank, haze, ling, rain, smur **5** misle, smurr **6** mizzle **8** sprinkle

drole: **7** buffoon

droll: odd **5** comic, drole, funny, merry,

queer 6 jester, jocose 7 amusing, buffoon, comical, jocular, strange, waggish 8 farcical, humorous 9 burlesque, diverting, laughable, ludicrous, whimsical 10 ridiculous

drollery: wit 4 jest 5 farce, humor 10 buffoonery

drome: 6 plover 7 airport

dromedary: 5 camel, delul 7 camelus, dromond

dromond: 7 warship

drone: bee, bum, hum 4 drum, slug 5 drant, idler, snail 6 bumble, draunt, lubber 7 bagpipe, humming, shirker, sleeper, speaker 8 loiterer, sluggard 9 bombilate

dronish: 4 slow 8 indolent, sluggish

drool: 6 drivel, slaver 7 slobber

droop: fag, lob, lop, sag 4 bend, drop, flag, hang, loll, pine, sink, wilt 5 daver, heald, hield 6 bangle, dangle, nutate, slouch 7 decline, flitter 8 languish

drooping: lop 4 limp 6 flaggy, nutant 7 nodding

of eyelid: 6 ptosis

on one side: 4 alop

drop: dap, sie, sye 4 bead, bede, blob, drib, drip, fall, gout, omit, shed, sile, sink, stop 5 droop, lower, minim, plump, plunk, slump 6 drappy, plunge 7 abandon, curtain, descent, dismiss, drappie, dribble, forsake, globule, guttula, guttule, plummet, release 8 decrease, quantity 10 relinquish 11 discontinue

lachrymal: 4 tear

syllable: 5 elide 7 elision

droplet: 7 globule

dropped: 6 fallen

dropper: 7 pipette

dropsical: 5 puffy 6 edemic 8 hydropic

dropsy: 5 edema

dross: 4 lees, scum, slag 5 chaff, dregs, sprue, waste 6 garble, refuse, scoria, scruff, sinter 7 cinders, leaving 9 recrement

drossel: 4 slut 5 hussy 6 drazel, drazil 9 dratchell

drought, drouth: 4 soka 6 thirst 7 aridity, dryness

drouk: 4 soak 6 drench 9 overwhelm

drove (see also **drive**): mob 4 sent 5 atajo, crowd, drift, flock 6 manada 7 disturb, trouble 8 driftway 10 assemblage

drover: 6 dealer, driver 8 herdsman

drovy, druvy: 5 muddy 6 filthy, turbid

drown: 6 drench 6 inundate

drowse: nod 4 doze 5 dover, sleep 6 snooze 7 slumber

drowsiness: 8 dullness 9 oscitance, oscitancy 10 sleepiness 12 sluggishness

drowsy: 4 dull, logy 5 noddy 6 sleepy, stupid, supine 7 lulling 8 comatose, oscitant, sluggish 9 somnolent, soporific 11 heavy-headed

drub: tap 4 bang, beat, blow, drum 5 array, curry, stamp, thump 6 cudgel, thrash 7 belabor, shellac 8 belabour, shellack

drubbing: 9 thrashing

drubly: 5 muddy 6 turbid 8 troubled

drudge: fag 4 grub, moil, plod, toil 5 grind, scrub, slave 6 digger, drivel, endure, slavey, suffer 7 hackney, plodder, slavery

literary: 4 hack 5 devil

drudgery: 4 moil, toil, work 5 labor, swink 7 faggery

piece of: fag

drug: 4 aloe, alum, dope, drab, dull, hemp, numb 5 hocus, japop, locus, opium, salol, senna, tonga, truck 6 heroin, ipecac, locust(pl.), opiate, peyote, peyotl 7 atebrin, stupefy, zedoary 8 medicine, nepenthe 9 asedulcis, marijuana 11 barbiturate, ipecacuanha 14 sulphapyridine

and ship: 8 shanghai

container: 7 capsule 8 gallipot

convulsion causing: 7 tetanic

crocus species: 7 saffron

for neuralgia: 5 tonga

Hippocratic: 5 mecon

of forgetfulness: 8 nepenthe

sleeping: 8 narcotic, sedative 12 somnifacient

drugget: mat, rug

druggist: 8 gallipot 10 apothecary, pharmacist 13 pharmaceutist

bible: USP

drugstore: 8 pharmacy

druid: 6 priest

lodge: 4 cove

symbol: 9 mistletoe

drum: 4 drub 5 drone, tabor 6 barrel, tambor, tympan 7 tambour, timbrel 8 cylinder, tympanum 9 reiterate

call to arms: 6 rappel

flourish: 7 roulade

kettle: 5 naker 6 atabal, nagara, timbal 7 attabal, timbale, timpano, timpani(pl.), tympani(pl.) 8 tympanum 9 tamburone

kind of: 4 base, gong, toph 5 gumbe, gumby, snare, tabor, tombe 6 kettle, tabour, tam-tam, timbre, tom-tom 7 capstan, taboret, timbrel 8 bamboula, darbukka, derbukka, tabouret 9 darabukka, tambouret, tambourin

roll: 4 dian 5 diana

string: 5 snare

tighten cords: 4 frap

drumbeat: dub 8 berloque, breloque

at hour for sleep: 6 tattoo

drummer: 7 roadman 8 salesman

drumstick: 6 tampon

drunk: See **drunken.**

drunkard: sot 4 soak 5 bloat, dipso, souce, souse, sowce, toper 7 fuddler, potshot, tippler, tosspot 8 borachio 9 alcoholic, inebriate 11 dipsomaniac

drunken: ree 4 gone 5 bousy, drown 6 blotto, fluffy 7 pickled, sottish 8 drenched, saturate, squiffed 9 drunkelew 10 inebriated 11 intoxicated

drunkenness: bun 7 potshot 9 inebriacy, inebriety 12 intoxication

bout of: 4 bust

drupelet: 5 acini(pl.), 6 acinus
dry: sec, ted 4 adry, arid, bake, brut, dull,
geld, hask, sere, wipe 5 drain, hasky,
parch, prosy, vapid, wizen 6 barren, boring, gizzen, jejune 7 brustle, insipid, sapless, sub-arid, sterile, thirsty, xerotic 8
tiresome 9 dehydrate, desiccate, drink-
less, exsiccate, exsuccous, fruitless, pointless, sarcastic, waterless 10 desicated,
evaporated, siccaneous, teetotaler 11
displeasing 12 moistureless, unprofitable
13 uninteresting
comb. form: ser, xer 4 xero
grass: hay
leather: sam
out: 5 steam, toast 6 rizzar 7 siccate
up: 4 sere 5 parch 9 dehydrate, desiccate, evaporate, exsiccate 10 dehumidify
dry shave: 5 cheat 7 defraud
dry spell: 7 drought
dryad: 5 nymph 6 yaksha, yakshi
dryness: 6 drouth 7 drought, siccity
abnormal: 7 xerosis 9 xerostoma 10
xerostomia
dryth: 6 thirst 7 drought, dryness
duad: 4 pair
dual: 4 twin 6 binary, double 7 twofold
dub: rub 4 blow, call, name, pool 5 adorn,
array, dress, style, thump 6 clothe, puddle, smooth, strike 7 entitle 8 beginner,
drumbeat, ornament 9 schlemiel, schlemihl
dubious: 8 doubtful, doubting 9 ambiguous, equivocal, uncertain, unsettled 10
disputable, precarious 12 questionable,
undetermined
ducal: 5 noble
duck: bob, bow, mig, pet 4 chap, dive, jouk
5 dilly, dodge, douse, dowse, mommy,
shirk, souse 6 fellow, person, plunge 7
darling, gadwall 9 sheldrake
black: 9 blackjack
bluebill: 5 scaup
brood: 4 team
dead: 5 goner
diving: 4 smew
eider: 4 colk, wamp
for cooking: 7 caneton
fresh-water: 4 teal
fresh-water genus: aix
genus of: 7 nettion
goldeneye: 7 gowdnie
heraldic: 6 cannet 8 cannette
hooked-bill: 9 merganser
kind of: 4 smee, smew, teal 5 eider, scaup
6 scoter 7 mallard, pintail, scooter 9
merganser 10 bufflehead, butterball
longtailed: 9 hareld
male: 5 drake
Muscovy: 4 pato
old squaw: 6 quandy
Old World: 7 pochard 9 sheldrake
pert. to: 7 anatine
pintail: 4 smee, smew 8 piketail 11
querquedule

rare: 5 merse
ring-necked: 5 bunty
river: 4 smee, teal 7 pintail 8 piketail,
shoveler 9 greenwing
ruddy: 6 bobber 9 blackjack
scaup: 9 blackjack
sea: 4 coot 5 eider, scaup 6 scoter 7
scooter 9 harlequin
tree: 7 yaguaza
wild: 4 teal 5 scaup 7 gadwall, mallard
wooden: 5 decoy
yellow-billed: 7 geelbec 8 geelbeck
young: 8 duckling
duck-on-the-rock player: 6 tenter
duckbill: 8 platypus 10 mallangong
duct: vas 4 main, pipe tube, vasa(pl.) 5
canal 7 conduit, ductule, leading, passage, trachea 8 aqueduct, guidance 9
direction
ductile: 4 soft 6 docile, facile, pliant 7
plastic, pliable, tensile 8 flexible, tractile
9 compliant, malleable, tractable 10 manageable, sequacious
dud: 7 failure
dude: fop 5 dandy 6 dudine 7 coxcomb
stage door: 7 Johnnie
dudeen: 4 pipe
dudgeon: ire 5 anger, pique 6 dagger 10
resentment
duds: 7 clothes 8 clothing, garments
due: owe 4 just, meed, owed, toll 5 endow,
endue, fated, owing 6 desert, extent, lawful, mature, proper, unpaid 7 exactly, fitting 8 adequate, directly, rightful, suitable 10 demandable, inevitable, sufficient
11 appropriate 12 attributable
duel: 4 tilt 5 fence, fight 6 affair, combat
7 contest 8 conflict
duelist: 7 fighter
aide: 6 second
duena: 8 landlady, mistress
duenna: 8 chaperon
dues: 5 tolls 6 droits 7 payment
duet: duo, two 7 twosome
upper part: 5 primo
duff: 5 alter, brand 7 pudding
duffer: 4 sham 5 cheat 6 hawker 7 peddler
dugong: 6 seacow
dugout: 4 abri, boat, cave 5 canoe, donga,
dunga 6 cayuca, cayuco 7 pirogue, shelter 10 excavation
duke: duc(F.) 4 peer 5 chief 6 leader
dukedom: 5 duchy 7 ducatus
dulcet: 5 sweet 8 soothing 9 agreeable,
melodious 10 harmonious
dulcimer: 6 citole, santir 7 cembalo,
yang-kin 9 pantaleon
dull: dim, dow, dry, lax, mat, sad 4 clod,
cold, dead, drab, dree, drug, dumb, flat,
gray, grey, logy, mope, poky, slow, tame 5
besot, blate, blear, blind, blunt, crass,
dingy, dunch, fishy, foggy, gross, heavy,
inert, matte, moron, noose, plump, pokey,
prose, prosy, shade, unapt, vapid 6 barren,

bovine, cloudy, dampen, darken, deaden, dismal, dreary, drowsy, glassy, hebete, leaden, muffle, obtund, obtuse, sleepy, somber, stodgy, stolid, stupid, torpid, triste **7** blunted, doltish, humdrum, irksome, lumpish, mumpish, prosaic, sottish, stupefy, tedious, vacuous **8** backward, blockish, boeotian, hebetate, lifeless, listless, overcast, sluggish, stagnant, tiresome **9** apathetic, colorless, heavisome, inanimate, lethargic, pointless, saturnine, tarnished, tasteless, unfeeling **10** insensible, lusterless, melancholy, monotonous, slow-witted **11** claybrained, displeasing, heavy-headed, thickheaded **12** buffleheaded **13** unimaginative
become: **4** pall **8** hebetate
noise: **4** klop

dullard: **4** dolt **5** dunce, idiot, moron **6** stupid **7** dastard, doldrum, pothead

dullness: **7** dimness, doldrum, duncery, fatuity, languor **8** hebetude, slowness, vapidity **9** bluntness, oscitancy, platitude, stupidity **10** drowsiness
of hearing: **9** baryecoia

duly: **5** fitly **8** properly **9** regularly **13** appropriately

Dumas: *character:* **5** Athos **6** Aramis
heroine: **7** Camille

dumb: **4** dull, mute **6** silent, stupid **9** senseless **10** speechless **11** meaningless **12** inarticulate, inexpressive

dumbbell: **9** screwball

dumfound, dumbfound: **4** daze, stun **5** amaze **7** confuse **8** confound, surprise **9** embarrass

dummy: **4** copy, dolt, mute, sham **6** silent **9** imitation **10** fictitious, figurehead **11** counterfeit

dump: sum **4** beat, cash, coin, fall, hole, jail, muse, nail **5** empty, house **6** grieve, plunge, unload **7** counter, deposit, reverie, sadness, storage **9** halfpenny **10** melancholy **11** despondency

dumping ground: **4** toom

dumpling: cob **7** gnoccho, gnocchi(pl.) **8** quenelle **10** appleberry

dumps: **8** doldrums

dumpy: **5** pudgy, squat

dun: tan **4** fort, urge **5** annoy, brown, crave, dingy, mound, sepia **6** pester, plague **7** swarthy **9** importune

dunce: ass **4** dolt, dult, gony **5** booby, idiot, ninny **6** hobbil, pedant **7** dullard, half-wit, sophist **8** numskull **9** ignoramus, simpleton **10** dunderhead

dunderhead: oaf **4** dolt **5** dunce **9** blockhead, numbskull

dune: bar **5** mound, towan **6** barkan **7** barchan, barkhan

dung: **4** gore, muck **5** filth, fumet **6** billet, manure, ordure **9** billeting, excrement, poppycock

dungeon: **4** cell, hell, hole **5** vault **6** donjon, prison **8** revolver **9** oubliette **10** er-

gastulum

dunghill: **5** mixen **7** mixhill **10** muckmidden

dunk: dip, sop **4** soak **5** steep **7** immerse, moisten

dunker: **7** tumbler

dunlin: **4** stib **9** sandpiper

dunt: **4** beat, blow **5** dizzy, knock, thump **6** benumb, bruise, strike, stupid **7** stupefy **10** heartthrob

duo: **4** duet, pair **6** couple

dupe: ape, fob, mug **4** coax, cull, fool, geck, gull, tool **5** cheat, cully, heald, mouth, trick **6** bubble, choose, delude, deride, plover, sucker, victim **7** catspaw, deceive, gudgeon, mislead, pidgeon, swindle **8** dotterel

dupery: **4** ramp

duple: **7** twofold

duplex: **6** double **7** twofold **8** dwelling

duplexity: **9** ambiguity

duplicate: bis **4** copy **5** alike, ditto, spare **6** double, repeat **7** estreat, mislead, replica, twofold **8** likeness **9** facsimile, reproduce **10** transcript **11** counterpart

duplicity: art **6** deceit **8** trickery **9** deception, falsehood **13** dissimulation

durable: **4** firm **6** stable, staple **7** lasting **8** constant, enduring **9** permanent **10** consistent, continuing, persistent **11** everlasting

durance: **6** duress **12** imprisonment

duration: age **4** span, term, time **5** space **6** period **7** durance **8** lifetime **9** extension **11** continuance
note: **4** time **5** clock
of ministerial charge: **9** pastorate
without beginning or end: **8** eternity

D'Urberville lass: **4** Tess

dure: **4** hard, last **5** rough **6** endure, severe, strong **7** sustain **8** continue

duress: **7** cruelty, durance **8** coercion, hardness, pressure **9** captivity, harshness **10** affliction, compulsion, constraint **12** imprisonment

durgah, dargah: **4** tomb **5** court **6** mosque, shrine

during: **4** time **5** while **6** whilst **7** pending **10** throughout

durst: **8** ventured

dusk: eve **5** gloom **6** dimmet, dimpsy **7** dimness **8** darkness, gloaming, twilight **11** crepusculum

dusky: **4** dim, sad, wan **4** dark **5** adusk, brown, dingy, tawny **6** gloomy, somber, sombre, swarth **7** swarthy **8** blackish **10** melancholy

dust: row **4** dirt, pilm, smut **5** clean, flour, pouce, stive **6** pollen, powder **7** eburine, remains, turmoil **9** commotion, confusion **10** kryokonite **11** disturbance
measuring device: **9** koniscope
speck: **4** mote

dust-like: **7** powdery

dusty: **5** adusk **6** poucey **9** pulverant

Dutch: See **Netherlands**.

Dutch East Indies: See **East Indies, Indonesia**.

Dutch Guiana: See **Surinam**.

Dutch South Africa: See **South Africa**.

Dutchware blue: 5 delft

duteous: 7 dutiful 8 obedient 10 respectful 11 subservient

dutiful: 6 docile 7 duteous 8 obedient, reverent 9 childlike, compliant 10 submissive 11 reverential 13 conscientious

duty: job, tax 4 care, onus, role, task, toll 5 chore, stint 6 burden, charge, devoir, excise, exitus, heriot, impose, impost, rivage, tariff 7 average, bailage, service, station, tribute 8 function, malikana 10 allegiance, obligation
on commodities: 6 excise
shirking: 7 truancy
spell of: 5 shift, trick, watch

dux: 5 chief 6 leader

dwarf: elf 4 grig, grub, runt 5 crile, crowl, elves(pl.), Galar, gnome, midge, pigmy, pygmy, scrub, stunt, troll 6 ablach, droich, durgan, durgen, midget 7 blastie, manikin, overtop, Pacolet 8 belittle, Cercopes, homuncio, homuncle, huckmuck, nanander 9 dandiprat, homuncule 10 diminutive, homunculus, overshadow

dwarfish: 5 pigmy, pygmy 6 grubby, nanoid 7 pigment, runtish, stunted

dwell: big, cot, dig 4 bide, bigg, haft, harp, live, stay 5 abide, bield, brood, delay, lodge, pause, tarry 6 linger, remain, reside 7 cohabit, inhabit 8 converse 9 expatiate 12 intermission, interruption

dweller: 6 tenant 8 habitant, occupant, resident 10 inhabitant
around city: 11 suburbanite
cave: 10 troglodyte
city: 8 urbanite
desert: 4 Arab 5 nomad 9 sourdough
earth: 9 tellurian
fellow: 6 inmate
formicary: ant
jungle: 5 beast 6 monkey
monastery: 8 cenobite
prairie: 9 plainsman
seacoast: 7 coaster 11 beachcomber
temporary: 6 lodger 7 boarder 9 transient
underground 4 mole 5 gnome

dwelling: dar, hut 4 casa(It.), flat, haft, home, nest, slum, tent 5 abode, cabin, hotel, house, hovel, motel 6 duplex, shanty, teepee 7 cottage, lodging, mansion, trailer, triplex 8 building, bungalow, domicile, tenement 9 apartment, habitance, residence 10 habitation

dwindle: 4 melt, pine, wane 5 peter, taper, waste 6 shrink 7 consume, decline 8 decrease, diminish, fordwine

Dyak Sea: 4 iban

dye: aal 4 anil, tint 5 color, eosin, fucus, imbue, stain, tinge 6 litmus, madder 7 aniline, toluene 8 colorant
blue: wad 4 anil, wade, woad
blue-red: 6 orchal, orchil
brown: 5 sumac 6 sumach
coal-tar: 6 magena
hair: 5 henna 6 rastik
indigo: al; aal 4 anil
morindin: al; aal
mulberry: al
quercitron bark: 6 flavin
red: 5 aurin, eosin 7 annatto, magenta 8 rhodamin 9 rhodamine 10 orseilline
red-brown: 5 henna
red-orange: 5 chica 7 fuchsin 8 morindin
violet: 6 archil
yellow: 4 weld, wold 5 arusa, woald, would
yellow-red: 6 anatta, anatto 7 annatto, annotto

dyeing apparatus: vat 4 ager
scrape: 6 harass

dyestuff: See **dye**.

dying: 8 moribund

dynamic: 6 potent 8 forceful 9 energetic

dynamite: 5 blast 9 explosive
kind of: 6 dualin 7 dualine 9 fulgurite 10 kieselguhr
inventor: 5 Nobel

dynamo: 9 generator
in distributing system: 7 booster
part: 5 rotor 7 brushes 8 armature 10 commutator

dynast: 5 ruler 6 prince 8 governor

dynasty: 4 race 5 realm, ruler 6 prince 7 monarch 8 dominion, governor, lordship 10 succession 11 sovereignty
Chinese: Fo; Han, Yin 4 Isin, Ming
French: 5 Capet

dysentery: 7 toxemia 8 diarrhea, epidemic
remedy: 14 sulfaguanidine

E

ea: 5 river 6 stream

Ea's daughter: 4 Nina

each: ea; all, ilk, uch 4 ilka, uche 5 every
8 everyone

eager: hot 4 acid, avid, gair, keen, sour,
warm, wave 5 afire, agasp, itchy, ready,
sharp 6 ardent, greedy, hetter, intent 7
anxious, athirst, brittle, burning, excited,
fervent, forward, provoke 8 desirous, irritate, spirited, vigorous, yearning 9 de-
sireful, impatient, impetuous, strenuous
12 enthusiastic, forereaching

eagerness: gog 4 elan, zeal 5 ardor 6 fervor 7 ardency, avidity 8 alacrity, cupidity,
fainness, fervency 9 alertness, constancy,
readiness 10 enthusiasm, impatience 13
impetuousness

eagle: ern 4 erne, gier, tern 6 aquila, ber-
gut, eaglet, formal, formel 8 allerion, ba-
taleur, berghaan 9 ossifrage

genus of: 10 haliaeetus

nest: 4 aery, eyry 5 aerie, eyrie

eaglestone: 7 aetites

eagre: 4 bore, wave

ear: lug(Sc.), 4 hear, heed, obey, plow, till 5
auris(L.), spike 6 listen 7 auricle, hearing 8 audience 9 attention, cultivate

absence of: 6 anotia

bone: 5 ambos, incus 6 stapes 7 malleus,
stirrup

cleaning device: 8 aurilave

combining form: oto

covering: 4 muff 6 earcap, earlap 7
earmuff

inflammation of: 6 otitis

middle: 4 drum 8 tympanum

near: 7 parotic

part of: 4 burr, lobe 5 helix, pinna 6 tra-
gus

pert. to: 7 entotic

science of: 7 otology

ear shell: 7 abalone

ear stone: 7 otolite, otolith

earbob: 7 earring

eardrop: 7 earring, pendant

eared seal: 5 otary

earl: 4 eorl, lord, peer 5 noble 8 nobleman

pert. to: 7 comital

earldom: 5 derby

earlet: 7 auricle

earlier: ere 4 erst, fore 5 elder 6 before,
former, sooner 8 previous

early: air, ere, old 4 rath 5 forme, rathe 6
timely 7 ancient, betimes 9 matutinal,
premature 10 forehanded

earmark: bit 14 identification

earn: get, win 4 fang, gain 5 addle, ettle,
merit 6 obtain 7 achieve, acquire, chevise, deserve

earner: 6 winner, worker 11 breadwinner

earnest: 4 hard 5 grave, sober, staid 6
ardent, hearty, intent, sedate, solemn 7
engaged, forward, serious, sincere, zealous 8 diligent, emphatic 9 heartfelt 10
expressive, thoughtful 12 affectionate,
wholehearted

earnest money: 5 arles 7 deposit, forfeit
8 security

earring: 4 grip 8 ornament 9 girandole

earshot: 7 hearing

earth: erd(Sc.), orb 4 bury, clay, dirt, grit,
land, loam, marl, mool, muck, rock, soil,
sory 5 glebe, globe, groot, inter, loess,
regur, terra(L.), trass, umber, world 6
coarse, ground 7 tierras, topsoil 8 mag-
nesia 10 terra firma

comb. form: geo

compound: 7 tierras

crust constituent: 6 silica

deposit: 4 marl, silt 5 loess 8 alluvium

dweller: 9 tellurian

god: Geg, Keb, Seb 5 Dagan

layer of: 5 sloam

lump of: 4 clod

metallic: ore

opposite side of: 9 Antipodes

pert. to: 4 geal 5 terra 8 telluric 9 planetary 11 terrigenous

prefix: geo

prepare for seeding: 4 plow 5 spade 6
harrow 9 cultivate

ridge of: 4 kame 6 rideau

satellite of: 4 moon

science: 7 geodesy, geology 9 geography

surface gravel: 6 eratum 8 erratice

earth bob: 4 grub 6 maggot

earth hog: 8 aardvark

earth lodge: 5 hogan

earthborn: 11 terrigenous 13 autochthonous

earthbred: low 6 vulgar

earthdrake: 6 dragon

earthenware: 4 delf 5 china, cloam,
crock, delft 7 biscuit, faience, pottery 8
crockery 9 porcelain, stoneware 10
terra-cotta

maker: 6 potter

peddler: 6 mugger

piece of: 5 shard

earthfall: 9 landslide

earthkin: 7 terella
earthly: 6 carnal 7 mundane, secular, terrene, worldly 8 temporal 11 terrestrial
earthnut: 5 arnot, chufa 6 peanut 7 truffle
earthquake: 5 quake, seism 7 temblor
measuring device: 10 seisometer
point directly above: 9 epicenter
science: 10 seismology
earthwork: 5 agger 7 rampart 10 breastwork 13 fortification
earthworm: ess 7 annelid, ipomoea
earwax: 7 cerumen
earwig: 6 golach, goloch
ease: 4 calm, rest 5 allay, knack, peace, quiet, relax 6 loosen, pacify, reduce, relief, repose, smooth, soften, soothe 7 appease, assuage, comfort, faculty, freedom, leisure, liberty, lighten, relieve, slacken 8 diminish, facility, mitigate, moderate, palliate, pleasure, security, unburden 9 alleviate, disburden, enjoyment 10 ameliorate, facilitate, relaxation, solicitude 11 contentment, naturalness, tranquility 12 satisfaction
at: 6 degage, otiose 7 relaxed
ease-off: 5 slack
easel: 5 frame 7 support
easily: 6 gently, glibly 7 readily 8 smoothly
east: 4 Asia 6 Levant, Orient 9 direction
East Africa: See **Africa**.
East Asia: *people:* 5 Seres
weight: 4 tras
East India:
agent: 8 gomashta, gomastah
animal: 7 tarsier
aroid: 4 apii
arrowroot: 2 tikor
bark: 4 lodh 5 niepa
bead tree: nim 4 neem 6 neemba
bird: 4 baya
boatswain: 6 serang
broadbill: 4 raya
bush: 4 sola
cattle: 4 dhan, gaur
cavalry troop: 7 ressala
cheroot: 6 lunkah
civet: 6 musang
dancing girl: 4 dasi
disease: 5 lanas
drink: 4 nipa
dye: aal
dye tree: 4 toon
food: 4 sago
freight boat: 5 oolak
fruit: 6 durian, durion 8 belleric, cardamom 9 myrobalan
gateway: 5 toran 6 torana
granary: 4 gola
grass: 4 kasa, ragi, usar 5 glaga, ragee, raggi, raggy 6 glagah, raggie
harbor master: 9 shabandar, shabunder
hawk: 5 bacha
hemp: 7 pangane

herb: pia, rea, til 4 chay, sola 6 sesame 7 roselle 8 eggplant
hog: 8 babirusa 9 babirussa 10 babiroussa
island: 4 Bali, Nias, Muna 5 Misal, Timor 6 Borneo 7 Celebes. Sumatra
juniper berry: 5 abhol
maid: 4 ayah
mammal: 7 tarsier
mangrove: 7 ceriops
market: 5 pasar
measure: kit, kos 4 bouw, depa, rood, rope 5 depoh, kilan, parah, takar 6 bamboo, coyang 7 gantang, tjenkal, toenbak
millet: 4 dura 5 durra 6 dhurra
money changer: 6 monkey, shroff 8 entellus
musical instrument: 4 bina, vina
muskmelon: 6 wungee
muslin: ban
nose flute: 6 upanga
nut: ben
palm: tal 4 nipa 7 jaggery, palmyra, tokopat
plant: da; rea 4 amil, jute, sola, sunn 5 benne 6 ambari, ambary, madder, sesame 7 ambaree
poison: 4 bikh
police chief: 7 darogah
post: dak 4 dawk
race: 4 swat
robber: 6 dacoit
rubber tree: saj
sailing vessel: 4 doni 5 dhoni
sardine: 4 lile
shrub: ak 4 odal, sola 5 mudar
snake: 7 bokadam
songbird: 5 shama
squirrel: 6 taguan
starch: 4 sago 5 tikor
sugar cane: 5 glaga 6 glagah 7 talthib
sword: 4 pata
tree: ach, bel, ber, bih, dar, eng, hur, mee, nim, saj, sal 4 alof, dhak, moli, neem, odal, poon, toon 5 dadap, fulwa, mahua, neeba, niepa, oodal, rohan, roman, salai, sapan, simal, siman, siris, sissu, tikur, uadal 6 banyan, chalta, chogak, deodar, illupi, sissoo, tikoor 7 champac, dhamnoo, gumihan, hollong, margosa 8 phulwbra 11 chaulmaugra, hursinghair
vehicle: 5 tonga
vessel: 7 patamar 8 gallivat
vine: 4 odal, soma
viper: 6 kupper
warrior: 5 singh
wood: eng
wood apple: bel
xylophone: 5 saron
East Indies: See **East India**.
Easter: 5 Pasch 6 Eostre, Pascha
Sunday before: 4 Palm
eastern: 6 ortive 7 auroral
Eastern Church: *choir platform:* 5 solea
convent head: 8 hegumene

festival day: **8** apodosis
prayer: **6** ectene, ektene
Eastland: 8 estriche
easy: 4 calm, cozy, eath, eith, glib, mild **5**
cushy, light, suave **6** facile, gentle, secure, simple **7** lenient, natural **8** carefree,
careless, cavalier, familiar, graceful,
homelike, moderate, tranquil, unforced **9**
compliant, indulgent, tractable, unhurried
10 manageable, unaffected **11** comfortable, complaisant, susceptible, unconcerned **13** unconstrained
easy mark: 5 chump **6** sucker
eat: sup **4** bite, dine, fare, feed, fret, gnaw,
grub, rust **5** erode, feast, munch, taste,
waste **6** absorb, begnaw, devour, ingest,
ravage **7** consume, corrode, destroy,
swallow **9** manducate
between meals: **5** bever
by regimen: **4** diet
fastidiously: **7** epicure **8** gourmand
grass: **5** graze **6** forage
greedily: **4** cram, wolf **5** gorge, raven **6**
gobble, goffle **8** gourmand **10** gormandize
pert. to: **7** dietary **8** dietetic, edacious
sparingly: **4** diet
sumptuously: **6** regale
eatable: 6 edible **8** esculent **10** comestible
eatage: 9 pasturage
eating-place: ınn **4** cafe **5** diner, grill, hotel **6** tavern **7** automat, tearoom **8** grubbery **9** cafeteria, chophouse
eave: 7 cornice
eavesdrop: 6 harken **7** hearken
eavesdropper: 9 drawlatch
ebb: 4 fail, sink, wane **5** abate, decay **6**
recede, reflux, retire **7** decline, subside **8**
decrease, diminish **9** backwater
ebb and flow: 5 estus **6** aestus
ebbing: 5 awane **8** refluent **9** refluxing
Eber's son: 6 Joktan
ebon: 4 dark **5** black, sable
ebony: 5 black
eboulement: 9 landslide
ebriate: 9 inebriate **11** intoxicated
ebrious: 5 tipsy
ebullate, ebulliate: 4 boil
ebullience: 8 overflow
ebullient: 7 boiling **12** effervescent
ebullition: 7 ferment **8** outburst **9** agitation, commotion **10** excitement **12** fermentation **13** effervescence
ecaudate: 8 tailless
ecce: lo **6** behold
eccentric: odd **4** card **5** crank, queer **6**
cranky **7** bizarre, devious, erratic, strange
8 abnormal, peculiar, singular **9** anomalous, erratical, irregular, quizzical, screwball, whimsical **15** idiosyncratical
eccentricity: 5 ferly **6** oddity **8** crotchet
9 queerness **10** aberration **11** peculiarity, strangeness **12** idiosyncrasy
ecclesiastic: 4 abbe **5** abbot, clerk **6**
priest **7** prelate **9** clergyman
belt: **7** balteus **8** baltheus

council: **5** synod
court: **4** rota
garment: alb **4** cope **5** amice, fanon, orale,
stole, cappa, rabat **6** callot **7** cassock,
biretta, calotte **8** berretta
head: **6** rector
land: **5** glebe
living: **8** benefice
ruler: **8** hierarch
service: **5** matin
unit: **6** parish
ecclesiastics: 11 gens d'eglise
eche: 4 grow **7** enlarge **8** increase
echelon: 8 maneuver **11** arrangement
echidna: *food:* **4** ants
three-toed: **6** nodiak
echinoderm, armed: 8 starfish
echo: eco **4** ring **6** repeat, second **7** imitate, iterate, resound, respond, revoice **8**
response **9** imitation **10** repetition **11**
reverberate **13** reverberation
eciton: ant
eclat: 5 glory **6** renown **7** acclaim, scandal
8 applause, facility, splendor **9** notoriety
10 brilliance, brilliancy **11** ostentation
eclectic: 7 liberal
eclipse: dim **4** bind, blot, hide **5** blind,
cloud, shade, sully **6** darken, dazzle, exceed **7** obscure, travail **8** outrival **10** extinguish, overshadow **11** obscuration, occultation
demon of: **4** Rahu
shadow: **8** penumbra **9** penumbrae
eclogue: 4 idyl, poem **5** idyll **7** bucolic
ecology, oecology: 9 bionomics
economical: 5 chary **6** frugal, saving **7**
careful, prudent, thrifty **9** provident
economics: *element:* **9** commodity
theoretical: **9** plutology
economize: 4 save **5** skimp, stint **6**
scrimp **7** husband, utilize **8** retrench **9**
housewife
economy: 6 saving, thrift **9** frugality,
husbandry **10** compendium, providence
bad: **11** cacoeconomy
practice: **7** scraped **8** scrimped
ecostate: 7 ribless
ecru: 5 beige, linen **10** unbleached
ecstasy: joy **5** bliss, swoon **6** trance **7** delight, emotion, madness, rapture **9** enrapture, happiness, transport
ecstatic: 4 rapt **8** glorious **9** entranced,
rapturous, rhapsodic **10** enraptured
ectad: 5 outer **7** outward **8** exterior
ectal: 5 outer **8** exterior
ectype: 9 imitation
ecu: 4 coin **6** shield
Ecuador: *animal:* **6** vicuna
city: **4** Loja, Suyo **5** Banos, Guano, Luisa,
Mocha, Piura, Quito, Zunga **6** Ambato,
Cuenca, Ibarra, Patate, Pujili, Tulcan **7**
Azogues, Cayambe, Guamote, Machala,
Pelileo, Pillaro, Salcedo, Salinas, Squisil
8 Babahoyo, Cevallos, Cujibies, Guar-
anda, Pansaleo, Riobamba **9** Guayaquil,

Latagunga **10** Esmeraldas **11** Puertoviejo
coin: **5** sucre **6** condor **7** centavo
Indian: **4** Cara **5** Palta **6** Canelo, Jibaro,
Jivaro
island: **9** Galapagos
measure: **5** libra **6** cuadra, fanega
mountain: **7** Cayambe **8** Antisana, Cotopaxi **9** Cotacachi, Pichincha **10** Chimborazo
province: **4** Loja **5** Azuay, Canar, El Oro **6**
Carchi, Guayas, Manabi **7** Bolivar, Los
Rios **8** Cotapaxi, Imbabura **9** Pichincha
10 Chimborazo, Esmeraldas, Tungurahua
river: **4** Napo **5** Tigre **6** Ambato **7** Pastaza
9 Guayaquil **10** Esmeraldas
town: See **Ecuador:** *city.*
tree: **5** balsa
ecumenic: **12** cosmopolitan
ecumenical: **7** liberal **8** catholic, tolerant
9 worldwide **12** cosmopolitan
eczema: **9** malanders
edacity: **8** appetite, voracity **12** raven-
ousness
edaphic: **5** local **13** autochthonous
Edda: **4** saga
Eddaic god: **4** Odin
eddish: **6** arrish **7** eegrass **9** aftermath
eddo: **4** taro
eddy: **4** gulf, purl, weel **5** acker, gurge,
shift, swirl, whirl **6** vortex **7** backset **9**
whirlpool **14** countercurrent
eddying: **4** wale
edema: **5** tumor **8** swelling
Eden: **6** heaven, utopia **7** arcadia, elysium
8 paradise
Edenic: **7** elysian, elysium **8** blissful **10**
paradisaic
Edenite: **9** amphibole
edental: **9** toothless
edentate: ai **5** sloth **7** ant bear **8** aardvark,
anteater, pangolin, tamandua **9** armadillo,
toothless
edge: hem, jag, lip, rim **4** bank, berm,
brim, brow, rand, side, trim, whet **5** arris,
berme, bevel, blade, brink, crest, frill,
knife, marge, ruler, sidle, splay, verge **6**
border, flange, impale, margin **7** margent,
sharpen, selvage **8** boundary, keenness,
selvedge **9** advantage, beginning, sharpness **10** escarpment
run along: **5** skirt
edged: **5** sharp, erose **7** crenate
edger: **7** whetter **9** sharpener
edging: hem **4** lace **5** frill, picot **6** border,
fringe **7** binding **8** rickrack **10** embroidery
loop: **5** picot
edgrew, edgrow: **5** rowen **9** aftermath
edgy: **5** sharp **7** angular **8** critical, snappish **9** irritable
edible: **7** eatable **8** esculent **9** cibarious,
vegetable **10** comestible
arum: **4** taro

fungus: **5** morel
gallingale: **5** chufa
mollusk: asi
parts of fruit: **4** pulp
rush: **5** chufa
seaweed: **4** agar **5** dulse, laver **6** delisk **8**
agaragar
seed: pea **4** bean
tuber root: oca, uva, yam **4** beet, eddo, taro
6 turnip **7** parsnip **8** rutabaga
edict: act, ban, law **4** bull, fiat **5** arret,
bando, bulla, irade, order, ukase **6** decree, dictum, notice **7** command, embargo, program, statute **9** ordinance, programma **12** announcement, proclamation
edification: **7** edifice **8** building **11** instruction **13** enlightenment
edifice: **4** dome **6** church **8** building **9**
structure **11** edification
kind: **6** palace, church, temple **7** capitol
10 tabernacle
edifier: **7** teacher
edify: **4** grow **5** build, teach **7** improve,
prosper **8** instruct, organize **9** construct,
establish
edile: **10** magistrate
Edina: **9** Edinburgh
edit: **5** emend **6** direct, redact, review,
revise **7** arrange, compile, correct, prepare, publish, rewrite **8** copyread **9** supervise
edition: **4** kind **5** issue, print, stamp **6**
source **7** version **9** character **10** extraction
kind of: **5** extra **7** revisal, reprint
editor: **8** redactor **9** emendator, publisher,
redacteur **10** diaskeuast, journalist
room: **7** sanctum
Edom: *district:* **5** Teman
king: **5** Hadad
mountain: Hor
Edomite's ancestor: **4** Esau
educate: **4** rear **5** breed, teach, train **6**
expand, inform, school **7** develop, nurture
8 develope, instruct **9** cultivate, enlighten
10 discipline, strengthen **12** indoctrinate
educated: **4** bred **6** taught **7** trained **8**
lettered, literate
education: **7** nurture **8** breeding, learning, training **9** erudition **10** background,
discipline **11** scholarship
institution: **6** school **7** college **8** seminary
10 university
organization: PTA **6** lyceum
educator: **7** teacher
educe: **5** evoke **6** elicit, evolve **7** extract **9**
eliminate
edulcorate: **7** sweeten
eegrass: **6** eddish **7** stubble
eel: ele **4** grig, ling, opah, snig **5** elver, moray, siren **6** conger, carapo, moreia, mu-
rene **7** eel pout, lamprey, muraena, sniggle, wriggle **8** Anguilla **9** snipefish

cut and cooked: **10** spitchcock
migration: **7** eelfare
trap: **6** eelpot
eel-shaped: 12 anguilliform
eelboat: 6 schuit
eeler: 9 fisherman
eelgrass: 9 grassweed
eellike: 10 anguilloid
eelpot: 4 trap
eelpout: 4 pout **6** burbot, guffer, yowler **10** muttonfish
eelworm: 4 nema
eely: 7 elusive, evasive, wriggly **8** slippery **9** wriggling
eemis, immis: 8 insecure **10** changeable
e'en: 4 even **7** evening
eerie, eery: 5 scary, timid, weird **6** dismal, gloomy, spooky **7** awesome, ghostly, macabre, strange, uncanny **8** eldritch, ghoulish **9** unearthly, unnatural, unworldly **10** frightened **11** phantomlike
efface: 4 blot, dele, rase, raze **5** erase **6** cancel, deface **7** destroy, dislimn, expunge **10** obliterate
effacement: 7 erasure
effect: 4 does, feck, prey **5** cause, close, eclat, enact, ettle **6** intent, result, sequel **7** achieve, acquire, compass, conduce, emotion, execute, fulfill, operate outcome, perform, produce, purport, realize **8** complete **9** execution, influence **10** accomplish, consummate, expression, impression **11** consequence, fulfillment, performance **13** manifestation **14** accomplishment
of past experience: **5** mneme
of wind on a shot: **7** windage
effective: 4 able, real **5** siker **6** active, actual, causal, potent, sicker **7** capable, telling **8** adequate, forceful, powerful, striking, vigorous **9** brilliant, competent, effectual, efficient **10** perficient **11** efficacious, influential
effectiveness: 10 efficiency
effects: 5 goods **7** baggage **8** movables **10** belongings
effectual: 8 adequate, powerful **9** available, effective, efficient **10** perficient, sufficient **13** authoritative
effectuate: 6 fulfil **7** fulfill **8** complete **10** accomplish
effeminancy: 10 muliebrity
effeminate: 5 milky **6** female, tender, weakly **7** citizen, epicene, womanly **8** feminate, feminine, oversoft **9** emolliate **10** voluptuous **12** overdelicate **13** overemotional
effervesce: 4 huff **6** bubble
effervescence: 10 ebullition
effervescing: 5 brisk **9** ebullient
effete: 4 sere **5** spent **6** barren **8** decadent, moribund **9** exhausted
efficacious: 5 valid **6** mighty, potent **8**

forcible, powerful, vigorous, virtuous **9** available, effective, officious, prevalent **10** legitimate **11** efficiently
efficaciousness: 10 efficiency
efficacy: 4 dint, feck **5** force, grace, might, power **6** virtue **7** potency **10** efficiency
efficiency: 5 power, skill **6** agency **7** ability **8** efficacy **10** capability, competence, competency **11** proficiency **13** effectiveness **15** efficaciousness
efficient: 4 able **6** potent **7** capable, feckful **8** powerful **9** competent, effective, effectual
efficiently: 13 efficaciously
effigy: 5 image **8** likeness **9** jackstraw
efflorescence: 5 bloom **7** blossom **8** anthesis
effluence: 5 issue **6** efflux **7** emanate **9** emanation
effluvium: 4 aura **9** emanation **10** exhalation
efflux: 7 outflow **8** effusion **9** effluence, emanation
effodient: 9 burrowing, fossorial
effort: try 4 dint, fist, toil **5** assay, brunt, drive, essay, labor, nisus, pains, power, trial **6** devoir, fizzle, fuffle, strain **7** attempt, trouble **8** endeavor, exertion, struggle **9** diligence **11** application
single: **4** solo **5** trice
violent: **4** adit **5** burst **8** struggle
effrontery: 4 brow, gall **5** front **8** audacity, boldness, temerity **9** hardihood, impudence, sauciness **10** confidence, incivility
effulgence: 5 blaze, glory **7** radiant **8** radiance, splendor **10** brightness, brilliance
effulgent: 6 bright **7** fulgent, radiant
effuse: 4 gush, shed **5** fling **7** emanate **8** dispense **11** disseminate
effusion: 6 efflux, foison
effusive: 5 gushy **7** gushing **8** bubbling **9** exuberant, rhapsodic **13** demonstrative
eft, evet: 4 newt **6** lizard, triton **10** salamander
egad: 4 ecod
egality: 8 equality **10** equanimity
egall: 5 equal
egeran: 11 vesuvianite
egeria: 7 adviser
egest: 4 void **7** excrete
egg: 4 abet, goad, ovum, prod, seed, spur, urge **5** ovule, spore **6** incite **7** actuate, coke-ney **9** instigate
case: **5** shell **6** ovisac **7** outheca
combining form: oo; ovi
fertilized: **4** zoon **7** oosperm
insect: nit
measuring device: **7** oometer
nest: **6** clutch
Philippine duck: **5** balut

prefix: oo
small: **5** ovule
tested: **7** candled
unfertilized: **8** oosphere
white of: **5** glair **7** albumen
egg case: 4 ovum **6** ovisac
egg on: 4 abet, goad, urge **6** incite
egg-shaped: 4 ooid, oval **5** ovate, ovoid **6** ooidal **7** obovoid, ovaloid, oviform
egg to anger: 7 provoke
egg yolk: 7 liaison **8** lecithin
egger: 4 moth
eggnog: nog **8** beverage
eggplant: 7 brinjal **8** brinjaul **9** berengena
eggs: roe **5** spawn **6** graine **7** ahuatle
eggs: *feeding on:* **9** ovivorous
poached in cream: **7** shirred
eggshell: 8 cascaron
egis: 5 aigis, armor **6** shield **7** defence, defense **10** protection
eglantine: 8 eglatere, woodbine **10** sweetbrier **11** honeysuckle
ego: 4 self **7** conceit **11** personality, selfishness
egoism: 5 pride **6** oneism, vanity
egoist: 8 believer
egotism: 5 pride **6** vanity **7** conceit
egotistic: 7 selfish **9** conceited
egotistical: 7 selfish **9** conceited
egregious: 4 fine **5** gross **7** eminent **8** flagrant, shocking **9** excellent, prominent **10** remarkable **13** distinguished
egress: 4 exit **5** issue **6** outlet **7** outgate, passage, regress **9** departure
egret: 5 heron, plume **6** gaulin **8** gaulding
egrimony: 6 sorrow
Egypt: UAR **18** United Arab Republic
animal: fox **4** adda, lynx **5** genet, hyena **6** jackal, jerboa **7** gazelle **9** ichneumon
antelope: **5** bubal
army chieftain: **6** sirdar
beer: **6** zythum
beetle: **6** scarab
bird: **6** sicsac
boat: **5** baris **8** dahabeah
body: Ka **4** Sahu
bottle: **6** doruck
bull: **4** apis
calendar: **4** Ahet, Apap, Tybi **5** Choik, Payni, Shemu, Thoth **6** Hathor, Mechir, Mesore, Paophi **7** Pachons **9** Phamenoth Pharmuthi
cap: fez
capital: **5** Cairo **10** Alexandria
Christian: **4** Copt
city: No **4** Sais **5** Cairo, Gizeh, Luxor, Tanis **6** Abydos, Armant, Thebes **10** Alexandria
civilization: **6** Tasian
clover: **7** berseem
cobra: **4** haje
coin: **5** girsh, pound **7** piaster **8** millieme
concubine: **5** Hagar
cotton: Sak **4** Pima

cross: **4** ankh
crown: **4** atef
dancers: **7** ghawazi **8** ghawazee
deity: Hor, Mut, Nut **4** Anta, Apet, Bast, Isis, Maat, Sati **5** Anaka **6** Hathor, Seshat, Tefnut **7** Nepthys **8** Nechebit
descendant: **4** copt **6** fellah
desert: **5** Scete, Skete
drink: **4** bosa, boza **5** bozah
drug: **8** nepenthe
elysium: **4** Aalu
emblem: **4** aten **5** lotus
gateway: **5** Pylon
governor: **5** Pasha
guard: **6** ghafir **7** ghaffir
gunde: **8** dragoman
herb: **5** anise
instrument: **7** arghool, arghoul, sistrum
isthmus: **4** Suez
king: So; Tut **4** Fuad, Mena **5** Menes **6** Ramses **7** Pharaoh, Ptolemy, Rameses **9** Amenhotep **11** Tutankhamen
laborer: **5** aperu
lake: **8** Menzaleh **13** Birket-el-Kurun
language: **6** Arabic, Coptic
lighthouse: **6** pharos
lily: **5** calla, lotos, lotus
lizard: **4** adda **5** scink, skink
lute: **5** nabla
measure: apt, dra, hen, rob **4** dira, draa, khet, ocha, roub, theb **5** abdat, ardab, ardeb, cubit, farde, keleh, sahme **6** artaba, aurure, baladi, kantar, kedlah, robhah, schene **7** choryos, daribah, malouah, roubouh, toumnah **8** kassabah, kharouba **10** dira baladi, dira mimari, kerat kamel, nief keddah **11** feddan nasri
monarch: **7** Pharaoh
monument: **7** obelisk
mountain: **5** Sinai
native: **4** Copt **5** Nilot
negro: **6** Nubian
oasis: **4** Siwa **6** Dakhel **7** Farafra, Khargeh **8** Bahriyeh **12** Wah-el-Khargeh
official: **5** mudir
paper: **6** papyri **7** papyrus
peasant: **6** fellah
peninsula: **5** Sinai
Pharaoh's headdress: **7** pschent
plant: **5** cumin **6** cummin, lentil
queen: **9** Cleopatra, Nofretete
relic: **5** mummy
river: **4** Bahr, Nile
rulers: **9** Ptolemeis
sacred bird: **4** ibis
sacred bull: **4** apis
sacred flower: **5** lotos, lotus
sanctuary: **5** secos, sekos
seal: **6** scarab
serpent: **5** apepi
shrub: kat
soul: Ba
stone: **7** rosetta
sun god: Ra; Tem, Tum **4** Atmu, Atum

symbol: uta **4** ankh **6** scarab
title: **4** atef **5** pasha **7** Pharaoh
tomb: **7** mastaba, pyramid
vase: **7** canopic
viper: **8** cerastes
waterway: **4** Nile
weight: ket, oka, oke **4** dera, heml, khar, okia, rotl **5** artal, artel, deben, kerat, okieh, ratel, uckia **6** hamlah, kantar **7** drachma, quintal
wind: **6** kamsin **7** chamsin, kamseen, khamsin **8** khamseen
Egyptian: **4** Arab, Copt **7** African, Ptolemy
eident: **4** busy **7** careful **8** diligent
eider duck: **4** colk
eidetic: **5** vivid
eidolon: **4** icon **5** ghost, image **7** phantom **10** apparition
eight: eta(G.), **6** ogdoad
combining form: **4** octo
group of: **5** octad, octet **6** octave **7** octette
set of: **5** octad **6** ogdoad
eight-sided: **9** octagonal
eighth:
circle: **6** octant
day after nones: **4** ides
order: **5** octic
eighty: pi(G.) **9** fourscore
Eire: **4** Erin
capital: **6** Tralee
legislature: **4** Dail
Eireannach: **8** Irishman
ejaculate: **5** blurt, eject **7** exclaim
ejaculation: **7** begorra **8** uttering **11** exclamation
eject: **4** boot, cast, emit, oust, spat, spew, spit, void **5** avoid, erupt, evict, expel, spout, spurt, vomit **6** banish, bounce **7** dismiss, exclude, extrude, obtrude **8** disgorge **9** discharge, ejaculate **10** disembogue, dispossess
ejection: **6** ouster **8** eviction **9** expulsion
eke: **4** also **7** augment, enlarge, husband, stretch **8** appendix, increase, lengthen, likewise **10** postscript, supplement
eking: **7** piecing **8** addition **12** augmentation
el: **4** bend
El Salvador: *coin:* **4** peso **5** colon **7** centavo
measure: **4** vara **6** fanega, tercia **7** botella, cajuela, manzana
weight: **4** caja
elaborate: **5** great **6** ornate, refine **7** develop, enlarge, labored, perfect **9** embellish, perfected **11** complicated, extravagant, painstaking
elaborated: **7** wrought **9** superfine
elaboration: **10** production **11** development
Elam: *capital:* **4** Susa
king: **12** Chedorlaomer
elan: **4** dash **5** ardor, gusto, verve **6** spirit,

warmth **7** potency **9** eagerness **10** enthusiasm
elanet: **4** kite
elapse: go; pass **4** slip **6** expire
elasmobranch fish: ray
elastic: **6** garter, spongy **7** buoyant, springy **8** cheverel, cheveril, flexible, stretchy **9** expansive, resilient **10** propulsive
fluid: gas
material from whales: **6** baleen
elasticity science: **9** elaterics
elastin: **10** albuminoid
elate: **4** buoy **5** cheer, exalt, exult, flush, lofty, raise **6** excite, please, thrill **7** elevate, gladden, inflate, success **8** elevated, heighten, inspirit **9** stimulate **10** exhilarate
elated: **5** chuff, happy, vogie **6** jovial **7** excited, exulted, jocular **8** exultant, inflated, jubilant **9** cock-a-hoop
elater: **6** beetle **8** skipjack
elaterite: **7** bitumen
elation: joy **4** glee **10** exaltation
Elbe tributary: **4** Eger, Iser
elbow: **4** bend **5** ancon, joint, nudge, shove **6** jostle
bone: **4** ulna **5** ulnae
elbowroom: **6** leeway
elcaja: **6** mafura
elchee, elchi: **5** envoy **10** ambassador
eld: **9** antiquity
elder: ain, iva **4** aine **5** prior **6** senior **7** ancient **8** ancestor, danewort **9** elderwort, presbyter **10** forefather
elderly: **4** aged, gray **6** senile
eldest: **5** eigne **6** oldest
eldritch: **4** eery **5** eerie, weird **7** uncanny **9** frightful
eleatic: **11** xenophanean
elect: **4** call, pick **6** assume, choose, chosen, decide, prefer, select **9** legislate
election: **6** choice **9** balloting **10** plebiscite **11** alternative
majority of votes: **9** plurality
electioneer: **5** stump
elective: **8** optional **9** voluntary
elector: **5** voter **6** elisor **7** chooser **11** constituent
Electra: *brother:* **7** Orestes
father: **9** Agamemnon
mother: **12** Klytemnestra
son: **8** Dardanus
electric: **4** elod **6** static **8** magnetic
carrier: **9** conductor
conductor: **6** ohmage
current: AC., DC.
current meter: **7** ammeter **9** voltmeter
current moderator: **5** coder **9** rheometer **10** attenuator
device: **8** divertor
generator: **6** dynamo
instrument: **6** dynamo **8** rheostat, rheotome **9** condenser, generator

light: arc 4 neon 12 incandescent
measuring unit: es; amp, ohm, rel 4 volt, watt 5 barad, farad, henry, joule 6 ampere, proton 7 coulomb 8 kilowatt
motion: 14 electrodynamic
motor part: 10 commutator
od: 4 elod
particle: ion
pole: 5 anode 7 cathode
power: 7 wattage
resistance: 6 ohmage
safety device: 4 fuse
strength: 8 amperage
transmission: 5 radio
wave meter: 9 ondometer
electrify: 7 startle
electrocute: 7 execute
electrode: 5 anode 7 cathode, kathode
controlling electron tube: 4 grid
negative: 7 cathode, kathode
electrum: 5 amber
eleemosynary: 4 free 7 almoner 9 dependent 10 charitable, gratuitous
elegance: 4 chic 5 grace, taste 6 finery, luxury, polish 8 courtesy, grandeur, splendor 9 propriety, recherche 10 concinnity, refinement 12 gracefulness
elegant: 4 chic, dink, fine, posh 5 civil 6 dainty, dressy, facete, minion, superb, urbane 7 cleanly, courtly, featish, featous, genteel, minikin, refined 8 delicate, graceful, handsome, polished, tasteful 9 admirable, beautiful, excellent, exquisite 10 concinnous, fastidious
elegantly: 8 gingerly
elegiac: 8 mournful 9 plaintive
elegiacal: 8 mournful
elegist: 4 Gray, poet 6 Milton 10 Propertius
elegit: 4 writ
elegy: 4 poem, song 5 dirge 6 lament 7 epicede 9 epicedium 11 lamentation
element: 5 metal, stuff 7 essence 8 rudiment 9 component 10 ingredient 11 constituent, environment
chemical: tin(Sn) 4 gold(Au), Iron(Fe), lead (Pb), neon(Ne), zinc(Zn) 5 argon(A), boron (B), radon(Rn), xenon(Xe) 6 barium(Ba), carbon(C), cerium(Ce), cesium(Cs), cobalt(Co), copper(Cu), erbium(Er), helium(He), indium(In), iodine(I), nickel(Ni), osmium(Os), oxygen(O), radium(Ra), silver(Ag), sodium(Na) 7 arsenic(As), bismuth(Bi), bromine(Br), cadmium(Cd), calcium(Ca), gallium(Ga), hafnium(Hf), holmium(Ho), iridium(Ir), krypton(Kr), lithium(Li), mercury(Hg), niobium(Cb), rhenium(Re), rhodium(Rh), silicon(Si), sulphur(S.), terbium(Tb), thorium(Th), thulium(Tm), uranium(U), yttrium(Y) 8 actinium(Ac), aluminum(Al), antimony(Sb), astatine(At), chlorine(Cl), chromium(Cr), Europium(Eu), fluorine(F), hydrogen(H), illinium(Il), lutecium(Lu), masurium(Ma), nitrogen(N), platinum(Pt), polonium(Po),

rubidium(Rb), samarium(Sm), scandium (Sc), selenium(Se), tantalum(Ta), thallium(Tl), titanium(Ti), tungsten(W), vanadium(V) 9 beryllium(Be), columbium (Cb), germanium(Ge), lanthanum(La), magnesium(Mg), manganese(Mn), neodymium(Nd), palladium(Pd), potassium(K), ruthenium(Ru), strontium(Sr), tellurium (Te), virginium(Vi), ytterbium(Yb), zirconium(Zr) 10 dysprosium(Dy), gadolinium(Gd), molybdenum(Mo) 11 phosphorous(P), 12 praseodymium(Pr) 13 protoactinium(Pa)
combining power: 7 valence
decomposed: 5 anion
different weight: 7 isotope
family: 7 halogen
minute: 5 monad
nonmetallic: 5 boron 6 bromin, iodine 7 bromine, silicon
poisonous: 7 arsenic
elemental: 4 pure 5 basic 6 primal, simple 7 primary 10 elementary 11 fundamental, rudimentary
elementary: 6 simple 7 initial 8 inchoate 9 elemental 10 rudimental, uncombined 11 fundamental, rudimentary
organism: 5 monad
reader: 6 primer
elemi: 5 anime, resin 9 oleoresin
pert. to: 7 elemine
elenge: 6 dreary, remote 7 tedious 9 miserable
elephant: cow 4 bull, calf 5 rogue, hathi 6 tusker, muckna 7 marmoth 8 oliphant, mastodon 9 pachyderm
call: 4 barr 7 trumpet
cry: 4 barr
dentin: 5 ivory
driver: 6 mahout
ear: 4 taro
goad: 5 ankus
keeper: 6 mahout
male: 4 bull
saddle: 6 howdah
seat: 6 howdah
tusk: 5 ivory 9 scrivello
trunk: 9 proboscis
elephantine: 4 huge 8 enormous, ungainly 9 ponderous
goddess: 4 Sati
elevate: 4 hain, lift, rear, rise 5 elate, erect, exalt, extol, heave, hoist, raise, setup, tower 6 uplift 7 advance, dignify, enhance, ennoble, glorify, promote 8 heighten, inspirit 10 exhilarate
elevated: el 4 high 5 great, lofty, noble, risen, steep 6 elated, raised, rising 7 exalted 8 majestic
elevation: 4 bank, hill, rise, toot 5 horst, mound, ridge 6 height, uplift 8 altitude, eminence, highness, swelling 10 exaltation
elevator: bin 4 cage, lift, silo 5 hoist 9 ascenseur

elf: fay, hob, imp, oaf, pug 4 fane, peri, pixy 5 dwarf, elfin, fairy, gnome, ouphe, pigmy, pixie 6 elfkin, goblin, sprite 7 brownie, incubus, succubi 8 succubus 10 changeling, leprechaun

elf dock: 10 elecampane

elfin: elf 5 child 6 urchin

elfish: 5 elfin 6 elvish, impish 7 elflike, tricksy 11 mischievous

elfland: 9 fairyland

elfwort: 10 elecampane

Elgin marbles: 10 sculptures

Eli: 4 Yale

Elian: 8 Eretrian

elicit: 4 draw, milk, pump 5 claim, educe, evoke, exact, wrest, wring 6 deduce, demand, entice, extort, induce 7 extract 9 elicitate

elide: 4 omit, skip 5 annul 6 ignore 7 destroy, nullify 8 demolish, suppress 9 apocopate

eligible: fit 6 worthy 8 suitable 9 desirable, qualified

eliminate: 5 educe, expel 6 delete, except, ignore, remove 7 divulge, exclude, excrete, release, silence 8 separate

elimination: 9 excursion

eliquate: 4 melt 5 smelt 6 strain 7 clarify, liquate, liquefy

elision mark: 10 apostrophe

elisor: 7 elector

Elissa's husband: 7 Acerbas

elite: 4 best 6 choice, flower, select 9 oligarchy 10 uppercrust 11 aristocracy 12 quintessence

    gathering: 6 galaxy

elixir: 6 spirit 7 arcanum, cordial, cure-all, panacea 12 quintessence

    of life: 6 amrita 7 amreeta

elk: 4 alce, deer 5 aland, eland, moose 6 sambar, wapiti 7 sambhur

    genus of: 5 alces

ell: 6 alnage 8 addition

ellipse: 4 oval

ellipsoidal: 4 oval

elliptical: 4 oval 5 ovate

elm: *family of:* 8 ulmaceae

    fruit of: 6 samara

    rock: 5 wahoo

elocute: 7 declaim

elocution: 7 oratory 9 eloquence

elocutionist: 6 reader 7 reciter

elodian: 8 tortoise

eloge: 6 eulogy 7 oration 8 encomium 9 panegyric

elogium: 7 oration 11 inscription

eloign: 6 convey, remove 7 conceal

eloine: 7 abscond

elongate: 6 remove 7 stretch 8 lengthen, protract

elongated: 4 lank, long 6 linear, oblong 7 prolate, slender 9 stretched

elope: 6 decamp 7 abscond, getaway

eloquence: 6 facund 7 fluency, oratory 9 elocution, facundity, loftiness

    teacher of: 6 rhetor

eloquent: 6 facund, fervid, fluent 7 renable 10 expressive, meaningful, oratorical, persuasive 11 impassioned, significant

else: or; ens 4 ense 5 other 7 besides, instead 9 otherwise 10 additional

elsewhere: 5 alibi

elt: 5 knead

elucidate: 5 clear, lucid 7 explain 8 simplify 9 interpret 10 illustrate

elude: 4 flee, foil, mock 5 avoid, dodge, evade 6 baffle, befool, delude, escape, illude 7 beguile, deceive 9 frustrate

elusive: 4 eely 6 subtle, tricky 7 elusory, evasive, subtile 8 baffling 9 lubricous 10 impalpable

elusory: 7 elusive, evasive

elver: eel

elves: See **elf.**

elvish: 11 mischievous

Elysian: 8 beatific, blissful 10 delightful

Elysium: 4 Eden 8 Paradise

emaciated: 4 lean 5 gaunt 6 peaked, skinny, wasted

emaciation: 5 niton, tabes 7 atrophy 8 marasmus 11 attenuation

emanant: 9 radiating

emanate: 4 flow 5 arise, issue 6 effuse 7 breathe, outcome, proceed, radiate 9 effluence, originate

emanation: 4 aura 5 aurae(pl.), niton 6 efflux 7 outcome 9 ectoplasm, effluence 10 exhalation 11 consequence

emanative: 7 issuant

emancipate: 4 free 7 manumit, release 8 liberate, unfetter 11 affranchise, enfranchise

emancipation: 7 freedom, release 10 liberation 11 deliverance, manumission 15 enfranchisement

emasculate: 4 geld 6 soften 8 castrate, enervate

embale: 4 pack

embalm: 4 balm, cere 5 mummy 6 balsam

embalmer: 5 cerer 10 undertaker

embankment: 4 bank, bund, dike, fill, quay 5 digue, levee, mound, revet 6 staith 7 backing 9 banquette

embar: 4 stop 6 hinder

embargo: 5 edict, order 8 blockade, stoppage 10 impediment, inhibition 11 prohibition, requisition

embark: 4 sail, ship 6 engage, enlist, invest

embarrass: 4 clog 5 abash, annoy, shame, upset 6 boggle, gravel, hamper, hinder, hobble, impede 7 confuse, flummox, nonplus 8 bewilder, confound, dumfound, encumber, entangle, handicap, obstruct, straiten 9 discomfit 10 complicate, disconcert

embarrassment: fix 5 shame 6 caddle, hobble 9 abashment, confusion 10 discomfort, impediment, perplexity 11 encumbrance, involvement 12 bewilderment, discomfiture, discomposure, entanglement 13 inconvenience

embassy: 7 ambassy 9 ambassade, embassage 10 ambassiate

embattle: 6 crenel 7 fortify

embattled: 7 crenele 8 crenelee, crenelle

embattlement: 7 parapet

embay: 5 bathe 7 shelter, suffuse 8 encircle, surround

embed: set 6 engage

embellish: 4 deck, gild, trim 5 adorn, dress, grace 6 bedeck, blazon, emboss, enrich, flower 7 apparel, bedrape, emblaze, garnish, varnish 8 beautify, decorate, flourish, ornament 9 elaborate, embroider

embellished: 6 florid, gested, ornate

embellishment: 7 agremen 8 agrement, mounting, ornament 9 fioritura, furniture, garniture 13 ornamentation

ember: ash 4 coal 5 aizle 6 cinder

embezzle: 5 steal 8 peculate, squander 9 dissipate

embezzlement: 5 theft

embitter: 4 sour 7 acidify, envenom 8 acerbate 9 acidulate 10 exacerbate, exasperate

emblaze: 5 adorn, honor 6 kindle 9 embellish

emblazon: 4 laud 5 adorn, extol 6 blazon 7 display, exhibit, glorify 9 celebrate

emblem: bar 4 aten, mace, orle, sign, star, type 5 badge, image, tiara, token 6 device, diadem, figure, sabcat, symbol 7 impresa, imprese, scepter, sceptre 8 allegory, colophon, insignia 9 character, laticlave, prototype 10 cognizance

emblematic: 5 typal 7 typical 8 symbolic 10 figurative

emblic: 4 aula 5 aulae(pl.)

embodiment: map 6 avatar 11 incarnation 15 personification

embody: 5 unite 7 contain 8 coalesce, organize 9 incarnate, personify 10 comprehend 11 incorporate

embolden: 5 bield, brave, nerve 6 assure 7 hearten 9 encourage, enhearten

embolus: 4 clot

embosom, imbosom: 6 foster 7 cherish, enclose, shelter 8 surround

emboss: 4 boss, hide, knob 5 adorn, chase 6 indent 7 conceal, enclose, exhaust, inflate 8 ornament 9 embellish, embroider, insheathe

embossing: 8 celature

embowed: 5 bowed

embower: 5 bower

embrace: hug 4 clip, coll, fold, love, neck, side 5 adopt, bosom, brace, chain, clasp, cling, enarm, grasp, halch, halse, inarm 6 abrazo, accept, caress, clinch, comply, cuddle, enfold, huddle, inclip, infold, plight 7 amplect, cherish, contain, enclose, espouse, include, involve 8 acco-

lade, complect, compress, comprise, comprize, conclude, encircle 9 encompass 10 comprehend 11 amplexation

embrangle: 7 confuse 8 entangle

embrocation: 6 arnica 8 liniment

embroider: tat 4 lace 5 couch, panel 6 emboss, frieze, stitch 8 ornament 9 embellish 10 exaggerate

embroidered: 5 brode 6 brodee 7 browden

embroidery: 4 lace 5 brede 6 bonnaz, edging, hedebo 7 orphrey 8 arrasene
frame: 7 taboret

embroil: 5 broil 6 jumble 7 perplex, trouble 8 disorder, distract, entangle 9 commingle, implicate 10 complicate

embrown: tan

embryo: 5 cadet, fetus, ovule 6 foetus 9 peritroch 10 conception

embusque: 7 shirker, slacker

eme: 5 uncle 6 friend, gossip 8 relative

emeer, emir: 5 pasha, ruler

emend: 4 edit, mend 5 alter, amend 6 better, reform, repeal, revise 7 correct, improve, rectify, redress

emendate: 7 correct, rectify

emendator: 6 editor

emerald: 5 beryl, color, green 7 smaragd

Emerald Isle: 4 Erin 7 Ireland

emerge: dip 4 loom, rise 5 issue 6 appear, plunge 10 disembogue

emergence: 4 need 8 debouche, exigence 9 occurence, outgrowth

emergency: 5 pinch 6 crisis, crises(pl.), strait 8 exigency, juncture 9 necessity

emergent: 6 rising

Emerson: *friend:* 7 Thoreau
philosophy: 17 transcendentalism

emery: 8 abrasive, corundum 11 carborundum

emetic: 8 evacuant

emetic holly: 6 yaupon

emeute: 6 tumult 8 outbreak

emigrant: 6 emigre 7 exodist, settler 8 colonist, stranger

emigrate: 4 move

emigre: 7 refugee

eminence: 4 berg, mote, note, rise, scar, toot 6 ascent, height, renown, rideau 9 elevation, loftiness 10 projection, prominence 12 protuberance 13 transcendency

eminent: big 4 arch, high 5 chief, great, lofty, noble, noted 6 famous, marked, signal 8 glorious, renowned, singular, towering 9 egregious 10 celebrated, noteworthy 11 conspicuous, illustrious, outstanding 13 distinguished

emir, emeer: 5 noble, ruler, title 6 leader, prince 8 governor 9 chieftain, commander
province: 7 emirate

emissary: spy 5 agent, scout 8 delegate

emission: 9 radiation

emissive: 8 exhalant

emit: 4 beam, cast, give, pour, send, shed,

vent **5** avoid, eject, exert, exude, fling, issue, utter **6** decant, evolve, exhale, expire **7** distill, exhaust, radiate **8** transmit **9** discharge, irradiate
heat: **4** glow
light: **4** glow **9** luminesce
offensive odors: **4** reek
emmet: ant **7** pismire **8** formicid
emolliate: **6** soften **10** effeminate
emollient: **7** lenient **8** lenitive
emolument: **4** fees **5** wages **6** income, profit, salary **7** benefit, stipend **9** advantage **12** compensation
emote: act **7** overact
emotion: ire **4** love **5** agony, anger, grief, heart **6** affect, effect, raptus, snivel **7** ecstasy, feeling, passion **8** gramercy, movement **9** affection, agitation, sentiment **11** disturbance **14** susceptibility
without: **9** apathetic
emotionable: **11** sensational
emotional: **7** emotive **9** rhapsodic **10** hysterical, passionate
emotionalism: **8** hysteria
emperor: **4** czar, king, tsar **5** Akbar, ruler **6** sultan **7** Baginda, monarch **9** commander, imperator, sovereign
empery: **6** empire **8** dominion **11** sovereignty
emphasis: **6** accent, stress **8** salience
emphasize: **6** accent, betone, stress **9** punctuate **10** accentuate
emphatic: **7** earnest, marcato **8** enfatico, forcible, positive **9** energetic
empire: **4** rule, sway **5** power, realm, reign, state **6** domain, empery **7** control, kingdom **8** dominion **11** sovereignty
empiric: **5** quack **8** impostor **9** charlatan **10** mountebank
emplacement: **7** battery **8** platform
employ: fee, use **4** busy, hire, wage **5** beset **6** bestow, engage, infold, occupy, supply **7** concern, enclose, involve, service, utilize **8** exercise
employed: **4** busy **6** unidle **7** engaged
employee: **5** clerk **11** salesperson
bank: **5** guard **6** teller **7** cashier **8** watchman **10** bookkeeper
minor: cog **6** helper **9** assistant
slaughterhouse: **5** sider
employees: men **4** help **5** hands
employer: **6** gaffer **7** manager **12** entrepreneur
employment: use **4** task, toil, work **5** craft, trade, usage **7** calling, purpose **8** business, vocation **10** engagement, occupation, profession
empoison: **5** taint **6** poison **7** corrupt, deprave, envenom
emporium: **4** mart, shop **5** bazar, store **6** bazaar, market, staple
empower: **6** enable **7** entitle **8** delegate, deputize **9** authorize **10** commission
empresa: **5** motto **6** device **7** tsarina
empress tree: **9** paulownia

empresse: **6** ardent **9** impetuous
emprise, emprize: **9** undertake **10** enterprise
empt: **5** empty
emptiness: **4** void **7** inanity, vacancy, vacuity **9** inanition
emptio: **6** buying **8** purchase
empty: rid **4** bare, boss, dump, empt, farm, free, howe, idle, leer, pour, toom, void **5** addle, avoid, blank, drain, equal, expel, inane **6** barren, bubble, devoid, hollow, jejune, unload, vacant, vacate **7** deplete, exhaust, untaken, vacuate, vacuous **8** disgorge, evacuate, evanesce, negation, unfilled **9** discharge, moonshine **10** unburdened, unoccupied **11** rodomontade
empty space: **4** void **5** blank **6** vacuum
emptying: **8** evacuant **9** avoidance
Empusa: **7** specter **9** hobgoblin
empyreal: **7** sublime **9** celestial
empyrean: **5** ether **7** heavens **9** firmament
emu: **4** rhea **6** ratite
emulate: ape, vie **4** copy **5** equal, excel, rival **7** compete, imitate
emulation: **6** strife **7** contest **10** contention **11** competition
emulator: **5** rival
emulsive: **9** softening
enable: **7** empower, entitle, qualify
enact: **4** pass **6** decree, effect, ordain **7** actuate, appoint, perform, portray **9** legislate, personate, represent **10** constitute
enactment: law **4** doom **6** assize, decree **7** statute **12** constitution **14** representation
enactor: **6** player **10** legislator
enamel: **5** glaze, gloss, paint **6** aumail **7** dentine, schmelz **8** cosmetic, schmelze
enamelled: **10** variegated
enamor, enamour: **4** love **5** charm **7** captive **9** captivate, fascinate
enamorata, inamorata: **5** lover **10** sweetheart
enamored, enamoured: **4** fond **5** epris **6** eprise **7** amorous, charmed, smitten **10** fascinated, infatuated
enarm: **4** lard **7** embrace, enhance
enarme: **5** strap
enate: **7** related
encamp: **4** tent **5** lodge, pitch **7** bivouac
encampment: **5** siege **7** bivouac, castrum(L.)
encase: **7** inclose
encave: **6** entomb
enchain: **6** fetter
enchant: **5** charm **6** delude, glamor **7** bewitch, delight, glamour **8** ensorcel **9** captivate, enrapture, ensorcell, fascinate, spellbind
enchanted: **4** rapt
enchanting: **10** bewitching
enchantment: hex **5** charm, magic, spell **7** chantry, gramary, sorcery **8** gramarye, witchery **9** chantment **10** necromancy, witchcraft **11** fascination, incantation

enchantress: 5 Circe, fairy, Medea 9 sorceress

encharge: 7 entrust 10 commission

enchase: 7 engrave

enchiridion: 6 manual 8 handbook

enchorial: 6 native 8 domestic

encina: oak

encipher: 4 code

encircle: orb 4 belt, clip, coil, gird, girt, hoop, pale, ring, rink, zone 5 belay, brace, embay, embow, girth, inorb 6 circle, emball, engirt, enlace, girdle, impale 7 betrend, embrace, enclose, environ, wreathe 8 cincture, ensphere, surround 9 encompass 12 circumscribe 13 circumference

encircling: 6 around 8 encyclic

encloak: 6 mantle

enclose: bay, box, hem, mew, orb, pin, rim 4 case, gird, pale, wall, yard 5 bound, bower, bught, chest, fence, hedge, house 6 bought, circle, corral, emboss, empark, employ, encase, encyst, enfold, enlock, impark, incase, picket, pocket 7 contain, embosom, embrace, envelop, harness, imbosom 8 comprise, comprize, conclude, encircle, imprison, palisade, surround 9 encompass 10 comprehend 12 circumscribe

enclosure: hag, haw, mew, pen, ree, sty 4 bawn, cage, coop, fold, sept, wall, yard 5 atajo, court, fence, kraal, pleck, pound, reeve 6 aviary, corral, cowpen, garden, hurdle, kennel, paling, prison 7 closure, paddock, puddock 8 cincture, clausure, cloister, sepiment

animal: pen, sty, par 4 yard, cage, cote, weir, yair, yare 5 booly, crawl, kench, gotra, kraal, atajo 6 booley, corral, runway, cancha, keddah 8 poundage 9 sheepcote

kind of: 4 bawn, boma, cage 5 bomar, carol, crawl 6 cruive 7 nacelle, paddock, stadium 8 delubrum, stockade 9 cofferdam

encomiast: 8 eulogist 10 panegyrist

encomium: 5 eloge 6 eulogy, praise 7 plaudit, tribute 9 panegyric 10 compliment

encompass: 4 be-go, belt, clip, gird, ring, wall 5 belie, beset 6 begird, circle, engird 7 embrace, enclose, environ, include 8 encircle, engirdle, surround 9 beleaguer, circulate 10 circumvent 12 circumscribe

encompassed: 5 bayed 6 begirt 10 surrounded

encompassing: 13 circumambient

encore: bis 5 again 6 recall, repeat 10 repitition

encorel: 5 again

encounter: 4 bide, coil, face, meet, rink 5 brush, fight, force, incur, onset 6 accost, affray, assail, attack, battle, breast, combat, oppose 7 address, affront, contest, counter, dispute, hosting 8 conflict, confront, skirmish 9 collision, interview 10 engagement, foregather, occurrence, tournament

courageously: 5 beard, brave 7 weather

encountered: 4 moot

encourage: 4 abet, back 5 boost, cheer, impel, nerve 6 advise, assure, exhort, foment, foster, incite, induce, second, uphold 7 advance, animate, cherish, comfort, confirm, console, enliven, forward, hearten, inspire, promote 8 embolden, inspirit, reassure 9 instigate, stimulate 10 strengthen 11 comfortable. countenance

encouragement: 5 flush 6 hurrah 7 fomento 9 incentive, patronage 11 fomentation

encouraging: 8 favoring 11 comfortable, inspiriting 12 advantageous

Encratite: 6 Tatian 9 Tatianist

encraty: 10 abstinence

encroach: 5 poach 6 invade, trench 7 impinge, intrude 8 entrench, infringe, intrench, trespass

encroachment: 6 inroad 10 aggression, infraction

encuirassed: 7 armored 8 loricate

encumber: 4 clog, load 5 beset, check 6 burden, hamper, hinder, impede, moider, retard, saddle, weight 7 involve, oppress 8 entangle, handicap, obstruct, overcome, overload 9 embarrass 10 overburden

encumbered: 5 heavy

encumbrance: 4 clog, lien, load 5 claim 6 burden, charge 7 trouble 8 mortgage 9 cumbrance 10 impediment, perplexity 11 impedimenta(pl.) 13 embarrassment

encyclic: 8 circular 10 encircling 13 comprehensive

encyclopedia: 4 tome

end: aim, tip 4 fate, goal, heel, stop, tail 5 amend, cease, close, death, ensue, finis, issue, limit, napoo, omega, raise, scrap, stash 6 define, design, expire, finale, finish, napooh, object, period, upshot, windup 7 abolish, achieve, closure, destroy, lineman, outgive, purpose, remnant 8 boundary, complete, conclude, dissolve, finality, surcease, terminal, terminus 9 cessation, determine, extremity, intention, objective, terminate 10 completion, conclusion, denouement, expiration 11 sequence, destruction, discontinue, termination 12 consummation 14 accomplishment

comb. form: 4 telo

remove: tip 4 clip

upper: tip 4 apex, head

End of World: 15 Gotterdammerung

endamage: 4 harm 6 injure

endanger: 6 hazard 7 imperil 10 compromise, jeopardize

endearing: 7 lovable 9 caressing

endearment: 6 caress
endeavor, endeavour: aim, try 4 best, mint, seek 5 assay, essay, ettle, exert, study, tempt, trial 6 affair, effort, strife, strive 7 afforce, attempt 8 exertion, struggle 9 undertake
ended: 4 done, over, past 8 finished
endemic: 5 local
ending: 6 finale 11 termination
adjective: ic
adverbial: ly
participial: ed
superlative: est
endive: 7 chicory 8 escarole
endless: 7 eternal, forever, undying 8 immortal, infinite, unending 9 boundless, ceaseless, continual, incessant, perpetual, unceasing 10 continuous 11 everlasting, measureless 12 interminable 13 uninterrupted
endlessly: 7 forever
endlong: 5 along 10 lengthwise 14 longitudinally
endmost: 8 farthest, remotest
endoderm: 8 entomere
endorse, indorse: 4 back, sign 5 boost 6 second 7 approve, certify, support 8 advocate, sanction 9 authorize, guarantee 11 countenance
endorsement: 4 fiat, visa 5 rider 7 backing 8 approval, sanction 9 signature
endow: dow, due 4 dote, vest 5 dower, endue, equip, found, indue 6 clothe, dotate, enrich, invest 7 furnish, instate 8 bequeath
with bodily form: 11 materialize
with power: 8 energize
endowment: 4 gift 5 dower, dowry 6 talent 7 apanage, chantry 8 appanage, dotation 9 mentality 10 foundation
endpiece: 5 chump
endue: due 5 endow, teach 6 clothe, invest 8 instruct
endurable: 7 livable 8 bearable 9 tolerable 10 sufferable 11 supportable
endurance: 5 pluck 7 durance, stamina 8 gameness, hardship, patience, strength 9 fortitude, suffering 10 sufferance 11 continuance, persistance, resignation 12 perseverance
endure: vie, 4 bear, bide, dree, dure, last, tide, wear 5 abear, abide, allow, brook, stand, thole 6 abrook, drudge, harden, remain, suffer 7 comfort, forbear, persist, sustain, toughen, undergo 8 continue, forebear, tolerate 9 exantlate, withstand 10 strengthen
endured: 5 borne
enduring: 4 fast 6 biding 7 durable, eternal, lasting, patient 8 immortal, remanent 9 continual, perennial, permanent 11 everlasting 12 imperishable
endwise: 7 erectly

enemy: fae, foe 4 Axis, feid 5 devil, fiend, Satan 6 foeman 7 hostile 8 opponent 9 adversary, ill-wisher 10 antagonist, backfriend
energetic: 4 fast, hard, live 5 brisk, dashy 6 active, hearty, hustle 7 arduous 8 emphatic, forceful, forcible, vigorous 9 dynamical, strenuous 10 expressive 12 enterprising
energize: 7 animate
energumen: 7 fanatic 8 demoniac 10 enthusiast
energy: go; pep, vim, zip 4 bang, bent, birr, life 5 force, nerve, power, steam, vigor 6 intake, output, spirit 7 potency 8 activity, strength 9 animation
lack: 5 atony 6 anergy 7 aneuria
measuring device: 9 ergometer
potential: 4 edar 5 ergal
unit: erg 5 ergon
enervate: sap 6 weaken 7 unnerve 8 enfeeble 9 enslumber 10 debilitate
enfeeble: 4 numb 5 shake 6 appall, deaden, impair, soften, weaken 7 depress 8 enervate 9 attenuate, undermine 10 debilitate
enfeebled: fey 4 numb 9 dissolute
enfilade: 4 rake
enfold: lap 4 wrap 5 clasp, cover, enrol 6 comply, enlace, enroll, enwrap, swathe 7 embrace, enclose, envelop
enforce: 5 exact 6 coerce, compel 7 execute, implant 9 constrain, prosecute
engage: 4 book, gage, hire, join, mesh, rent, sign 5 agree, catch, enter, lease, trade 6 absorb, arrest, embark, employ, enlist, induce, oblige, occupy, pledge 7 bespeak, betroth, conduce, consume, engross, involve, promise 8 contract, covenant, entangle, interest, persuade 9 interlock, undertake
engaged: 4 busy 5 hired 6 bonded, meshed 7 assured, earnest, entered, pledged, versant 8 embedded, employed, involved, occupied, promised 9 affianced, betrothed
engagement: 4 aval, date 5 cowle 6 affair, battle, escrow 7 bargain 9 betrothal, encounter 10 attachment, employment 11 appointment, involvement
engager: 6 surety
engaging: 5 sapid 6 taking 10 attractive 11 interesting
engastrimyth: 13 ventriloquist
engender: 5 beget, breed, cause 6 excite, gender 7 develop, produce 8 generate, occasion 9 procreate, propagate
engild: 8 brighten
engine: gas 5 motor, steam 7 turbine 8 gasoline 10 locomotive
covering: 4 cowl
kind of: ram 4 goat 5 dinky 6 diesel, helper, pusher 8 dollbeer

military: ram **4** tank **6** onager **7** robinet **8** ballista, helepole **9** espringal **11** ribaude-quin

engineer: **4** plan **6** driver, manage **7** planner, plotter **8** contrive, designer, inventor, maneuver **9** construct **10** accomplish **11** constructor, superintend

degree: C.E., E.E., M.E.

enginous: **6** crafty **9** ingenious

engirdle: **4** gird **9** encompass

engirt: **6** engird **7** envelop **8** encircle

England: **6** Albion **7** Britain **9** Britannia **12** Great Britain

admiral: **6** Nelson, Rodney, Vernon

admirer of: **10** anglophile

air force: R.A.F.

Antarctic explorer: **5** Scott

apartment: **4** flat

apple: **6** beefin, biffin, coling, rennet **7** beaufin, costard **8** coccagee **9** guarenden, guarender

apron: **8** barmskin

architect: **4** Wren

bailiff: **5** reeve

bed: **4** doss

boat: **7** coracle

cattle: **5** Devon

cattle tender: **7** byreman

Channel Island: **4** Sark

charity school scholar: **8** blue coat

cheese: **7** stilton, truckle

chinaware: **5** Spode **8** Wedgwood

church caretaker: **6** verger

church officer: **6** beadle

city: Ely **4** Bath, Hull, York **5** Derby, Erith, Leeds, Truro, Wigan **6** Bolton, Bootle, Exeter, Hanley, Jarrow, Leyton, London, Oldham, Rippon **7** Bristol, Burnley, Croydon, Grimsby, Halifax, Hornsey, Ipswich, Newport, Norwich, Preston, Reading, Salford, Seaford, Walsall, West Ham **8** Bradford, Brighton, Coventry, Dewsbury, Hastings, Plymouth, Rochdale, Wallasey, Wallsend **9** Birkenhead, Blackburn, Devonport, Gateshead, Leicester, Liverpool, Rotherham, Sheffield, Smethwick, Stockport, Tottenham, Willesden **10** Aston Manor, Birmingham, Manchester, Nottingham, Portsmouth, Sunderland, Warrington **11** Bournemouth, Northampton, Saint Helens, Southampton, Walthamstow **12** Huddersfield, Southshields, West Bromwich **13** Middlesbrough, South-end-on-sea, Wolverhampton **14** Stoke-upon-Trent, West Hartlepool **15** Barrow-in Furness **17** Newcastle-upon-Tyne

class: **4** form

clergyman: **4** Inge **5** Donne, Oates **6** Becket, Newman **7** Latimer

cloth: **5** tweed

coin: ora **4** rial, ryal **5** ackey, angel, crown, groat, pence, pound **6** bawbee, florin, guinea, seskin, teston **7** angelet, carolus **8**

farthing, shilling, sixpence, twopence **9** dandiprat, fourpence, halfcrown, half-penny, sovereign **10** threepence

composer: **4** Arne **5** Elgar, Neale **6** Delius, Handel **7** Britten, Stainer **8** Williams

conservative: **4** Tory

conveyance: **4** tram **6** waggon

county: **4** Kent **5** Devon, Essex, Hants, Shire **6** Dorset, Surrey, Sussex

court: **4** eyre, leet **5** gemot **6** gemote **8** hustling **9** Old Bailey

crown tax: **4** geld

dance: **6** morris

dandy: **4** toff

economist: **6** Keynes **7** Gresham, Ricardo

elevator: **4** lift

emblem: **4** Lion

entertainment: **4** busk **7** ridotto

estate: **4** este

explorer: **4** Cook, Ross **5** Cabot, Drake, Scott **6** Hudson

field: **5** croft

fish: **5** sewen **8** dragonet

flood: **5** spate

flower: **4** rose

food dealer: **12** costermonger

forest: **5** Arden

freeman: **5** ceorl

game: **5** darts, rugby **6** soccer **7** cricket

gun carrier: **4** bren

historian: **5** Acton, Grote **7** Toynbee **8** Macaulay

hog: **5** Essex

inspector: **9** exciseman

invader: **4** Dane **5** Engle, Roman, Saxon **6** Norman

island: Man **4** Holy **5** Farne, Lundy **6** Scilly, Thanet, Walney **7** Ireland, Sheppey **8** Anglesey, Holyhead, Shetland **11** Isle of Wight

jacket: **4** Eton

king: Hal, Lud **4** Bran, Brut, Cnut, Cole, Knut, Lear **5** Brunt, Henry, James, Sweyn **6** Alfred, Arthur, Bladud, Cnaute, Edward, Egbert, George **7** Artegal, Elidure, Richard, Stephen, William **8** Gorboduc

laborer: **5** navvy

lake: **7** Derwent **8** Coniston **9** Ullswater **10** Windermere

land: **5** laine

law: **4** soke **6** esnecy **7** danelaw **9** common law

lawyer: **7** bencher **9** barrister, solicitor

liberal: **4** Whig

lunch: **6** tiffin

magistrate: **4** beak

man: **6** Briton **9** Britisher, Sassenach

measure: ell, pin, rod, ton, tun, vat **4** acre, bind, boll, comb, cran, foot, gill, goad, hand, hide, inch, last, line, mile, once, palm, peek, pint, pipe, pole, pool, rood, sack, span, trug, wist, yard, yoke **5** bodge, carat, chain, coomb, cubit, digit, float, floor, fluid, hutch, mimim, perch, point, prime, quart, skein, stack, truss **6** barrel, bovate, bushel, cranne, fathom, firkin, gallon, hobbet, jugrum, league, manent, oxgang, pottle, runlet, strike, sulung, thread, tieree **7** furlong, hobbitt, quarter, quarten, rundlet, spindle, tertian, virgate **8** carucate, chaldron, hogshead, landyard, puncheon, quadrant, standard **9** kilderskin, shaftment, shaftmont **10** barleycorn, barn gallon, winchester **13** tablespoonful

molasses: **7** treacle

monk: **4** Beda, Bede **5** Baeda

mountain: **7** Pennine **8** Cumbrian, Scawfell

news agency: **7** Reuters

nobleman (see also *title* below)*:* **4** peer **6** milord

officer's civilian dress: **5** mufti

old kingdom: **6** Sussex

painter: **4** Opie **6** Turner **7** Hogarth, Millais, Poynter

Parliament proceedings: **7** Hansard

party member: **4** Tory, Whig **7** Liberal **8** Laborite **9** Labourite **12** Conservative

patron saint: **6** George

peasant: **5** churl

pert. to: **8** Anglican **10** Anglo-Saxon

philosopher: **4** Hume **5** Bacon, Locke **6** Hobbes **7** Russell, Spencer **9** Whitehead

pirate: **4** Kidd **5** Drake **6** Morgan **7** Hawkins

policeman: **5** bobby **6** copper, peeler

prairie: **4** moor **5** heath

prison: **4** gaol

public school: **4** Eton **5** Rugby **6** Harrow **9** Sandhurst

queen: **4** Anne, Mary **8** Victoria **9** Elizabeth

racing town: **5** Ascot **10** Epsom Downs

rebel: **5** Essex, Tyler **8** Cromwell **10** Washington

resort: **4** Bath **8** Brighton

rifle: **7** Enfield

river: Dee, Esk, Exe, Nen, Ure, Wye **4** Aire, Avon, Eden, Nene, Ouse, Tees, Tyne, Wash, Wear **5** Alton, Dudin, Trent **6** Humber, Mersey, Ribble, Severn, Thames **7** Caulder **8** Walbrook

royal house: **4** York **5** Tudor **6** Stuart **7** Hanover, Windsor **9** Lancaster **11** Plantagenet

royal household officer: **7** equerry

royal residence: **7** Windsor

seaman: **5** limey **6** rating

seaport: **4** Deal **5** Dover, Poole **8** Wallasey **9** Liverpool **11** Southampton

settler: **4** Jute, Pict **5** Angle, Saxon **6** Norman

sheep: **8** costwold **11** Wensleydale

shoemaker: **4** snob

sixpence: **5** sprat

soldier: **5** tommy **7** redcoat **8** fusileer, fusilier **10** carabineer, carabinier

stable: **4** mews

statesman: **4** Eden, Grey, Peel, Pitt **5** Bevin, Simon **6** Attlee **7** Asquith, Baldwin **8** Disraeli **9** Churchill, Gladstone, MacDonald, Macmillan **10** Walsingham **11** Chamberlain, Lloyd George

streetcar: **4** tram

tavern: pub

taxpayer: **9** ratepayer

tea muffin: **7** crumpet

thicket: **7** spinney

thrush: **5** mavis

title: **4** dame, duke, earl, king, lady, lord, peer **5** baron, noble, queen **6** knight, prince **7** baronet, duchess, marquis **8** baroness, countess, marquess, princess, viscount **11** marchioness, viscountess

tourist: **7** tripper

tribe: **5** Iceni

truck: **5** lorry

tutor: don

university: **6** London, Oxford **9** Cambridge

uplands: **5** downs

valley: **4** Eden, Tees, Tyne **5** coomb **6** coquet

weight: **5** stone

engorge: **4** glut **5** gorge **6** devour

engraft: **9** inoculate

engrave: cut **4** etch **5** carve, chase, grave, print, sculp **6** chisel, incise **7** enchase, impress, imprint, stipple **8** inscribe, ornament **9** character, sculpture

engraver: **6** chaser, etcher, graver **7** artisan **13** siderographer

tool of: **5** burin

engraving: *wax:* **8** intaglio **9** cerograph, xylograph **11** glyptograph

instrument: **6** stylet

pert. to: **7** glyphic, glyptic

engross: **4** bury **5** amass **6** absorb, engage, enroll, enwrap, occupy **7** collect, consume, immerse **9** fascinate, overwhelm, preoccupy

engrossed: **4** rapt **6** intent

engrosser: **12** calligrapher

engrossing: **11** chirography

engulf: **5** swamp, whelm **6** absorb, devour **7** swallow **8** submerge **9** overwhelm

enhance: **4** lift **5** enarm, exalt, raise **6** deepen **7** augment, elevate, enlarge, greaten, improve, sharpen **8** heighten, increase **9** aggravate, intensify **10** exaggerate

enhearten: **8** embolden

enigma: **5** griph, rebus **6** riddle, sphinx **7** griphus, mystery, problem **9** conundrum

enigmatic: **6** mystic **7** cryptic, obscure **8** mystical, puzzling **9** equivocal **12** inexplicable

enisle: **7** isolate

enjoin: bid **5** order **6** decree, forbid **7** command, dictate, require **8** admonish, prohibit

enjoyment: use **4** bask, ease, zest **5** gusto **6** liking, relish **7** delight **8** felicity, pleasure 9 happiness 11 delectation 12 satisfaction 13 gratification

enkindle: 7 incense, inflame 9 enlighten

enlace: tie 5 twine, twist, weave 6 enfold 7 entwine 8 encircle, entangle 10 interweave

enlarge: add, eke(Sc.), 4 grow, huff, ream 5 swell, widen 6 broach, dilate, expand, extend, fraise, spread 7 amplify, augment, distend, enhance, greaten, magnify, stretch 8 flourish, increase 9 elaborate, expatiate, intumesce 10 aggrandize, exaggerate

enlarged: 8 varicose

enlargement: 9 accession, accretion 10 ampliation 13 magnification

enlighten: 5 edify, teach 6 inform 7 educate 8 enkindle, instruct 9 irradiate 10 illuminate

enlightenment: 5 bodhi 6 wisdom

enlist: 4 join 5 enter 6 enbark, engage, enroll, induct 7 impress 8 register 9 volunteer

enlistment: 5 hitch 7 listing

enliven: 4 warm 5 cheer, rouse 6 revive 7 animate, comfort, inspire, refresh 8 brighten, inspirit 9 encourage, stimulate 10 exhilarate, invigorate

enlivening: 6 genial 9 sprightly

enlock: 7 enclose

enmesh: 4 trap 5 catch 7 ensnare 8 entangle

enmity: war 4 feud 5 spite 6 hatred, malice, rancor 8 aversion 9 animosity, antipathy, hostility 10 antagonism, repugnance, resentment 11 malevolence

ennead: 7 nine

ennoble: 5 exalt, honor, raise 6 uplift 7 dignify, elevate, glorify

ennui: 4 bore 6 tedium 7 boredom, doldrum

enorm: 8 abnormal, enormous 9 monstrous 10 outrageous 13 extraordinary

enormous: big, gob 4 huge, ream, vast 5 enorm, great, large 6 heroic, mighty 7 immense 8 abnormal, colossal, gigantic 9 excessive, monstrous 10 gargantuan, prodigious, stupendous 11 elephantine

Enos: *father:* 4 Seth
grandfather: 4 Adam
grandmother: Eve
uncle: 4 Abel, Cain

enough: 4 enow 5 ample, basta 6 plenty 7 suffice 8 adequate 10 sufficient 12 satisfactory

enounce: 5 state, utter 8 proclaim 9 enunciate, pronounce

enow: 9 presently

enrage: 4 anger 6 grieve, madden 7 incense, inflame 9 infuriate 10 exasperate

enraged: 5 irate 7 berserk 8 choleric, maddened

enrapture: 6 ravish 7 ecstasy, enchant 8 enravish, entrance 9 captivate, fascinate

enraptured: 4 rapt 11 imparadised

enravished: 4 rapt 10 enraptured

enrich: 4 boot, lard 5 adorn, endow 6 batten, fatten 7 furnish 8 ornament 9 embellish, fertilize

enrobe: 6 attire, clothe

enroll, enrol: 4 join, list 5 enter, write 6 billet, enfold, enlist, induct, record 7 ascribe, impanel 8 initiate, inscribe, register 11 matriculate 13 immatriculate

enroot: 7 implant

ens: 5 being 6 entity 9 existence

ensaint: 8 canonize

ensconce: 4 hide 5 cover 6 settle 7 conceal, shelter 9 establish

ensemble: 5 decor, whole 7 costume 11 combination

ensiform: 6 ensate 7 xiphoid

ensign: 4 flag, sign 5 badge 6 banner, signal, symbol 7 officer 8 gonfalon, standard 9 oriflamme

enslave: 5 chain 7 slavish 8 enthrall

ensnare: net, web 4 mesh, trap 5 benet, catch, noose, snarl 6 allure, attrap, enmesh, entoil, entrap, tangle, trepan 7 beguile, springe 8 overtake 10 circumvent, intertwine

ensorcell, ensorcel: 7 bewitch, enchant

ensoul, insoul: 7 animate

ensuing: 4 next 9 following, resulting 10 subsequent, succeeding

ensure: 6 assure, insure, secure 7 betroth, espouse, warrant 8 affiance 9 guarantee

entablature: 10 trabeation

entad: 6 inward
opposite of: 5 ectad

entail: 6 impose 7 involve, require 11 necessitate

ental: 5 inner
opposite of: 5 ectal

entame: 11 domesticate

entangle: 4 mat, web 4 foul, harl, knit, knot, mesh, mire 5 catch, ravel, snafu, snare, snarl, twist 6 befoul, cotter, engage, enlace, enmesh, entrap, hankle, inmesh, puzzle 7 confuse, embroil, ensnarl, involve, perplex 8 bewilder, encumber 9 embarrass, embrangle, imbroglio 10 intertwine, interweave

entangled: 4 deep 5 cotty 7 complex 10 interwoven

entanglement: 4 knot 6 bunker 8 obstacle 13 embarrassment

entellus: 6 monkey

entente: 6 treaty 8 alliance 9 agreement 13 understanding

enter: 4 join, post 5 admit, begin, share 6 accede, appear, engage, enlist, enroll, entrer(F.), hamper, incept, pierce, record 7 intrude 8 initiate, inscribe, register 9 introduce, penetrate 11 matriculate
militarily: 6 invade

enteric: 10 intestinal

enterprise: 5 essay 6 action, spirit 7 attempt, emprise, project, venture 8 business, gumption **9** adventure **10** initiative, management **11** undertaking

enterpriser: **12** entrepreneur

enterprising: **4** bold **9** energetic **10** aggressive, courageous **11** progressive

entertain: **4** fete, hold **5** amuse, treat **6** divert, regale **7** beguile, cherish **8** consider, interest

entertainer: **4** host **5** actor **6** amuser, dancer, singer **7** actress, hostess, regaler, speaker **8** comedian, magician, minstrel **9** soubrette(F.) **10** comedienne

entertainment: **4** fare, fete, glee, play **5** board, cheer, feast, opera, revue, sport **6** kermis, shivvo **7** banquet, ceilidh(Ir.), concert, festine, festino, kermess, pastime, ridotto **8** function, musicale **9** amusement, diversion, festivity, reception, wayzgoose **10** recreation

place: **4** gaff, park **5** movie **6** casino, cinema, circus, midway **7** cabaret, theater, theatre

enthrall, enthral: **5** charm **7** enslave **9** captivate

enthrone: **5** crown, exalt **6** throne

enthusiasm: **4** elan, fire, zeal, zest **5** ardor, flame, furor, mania, verve **6** fervor, spirit **7** ardency **9** animation, eagerness **10** ebullience, fanaticism

enthusiast: bug, fan, nut **5** bigot **6** rooter, zealot **7** devotee, fanatic **8** follower **9** energumen

enthusiastic: **4** keen, warm **5** rabid **6** ardent **10** forthgoing

entice: win **4** bait, coax, draw, lure, tole, wile **5** charm, decoy, tempt **6** allure, cajole, incite, induce, invite, seduce **7** attract, bewitch **8** inveigle, persuade

entire: all **4** full, mear, mere **5** clean, every, quite, sound, stark, total, utter, whole **7** perfect, plenary **8** absolute, allwhole, complete, unbroken **9** exclusive, integrate, undivided **10** unimpaired **11** unqualified **12** undiminished

entitle: dub **4** call, name, term **5** affix **6** enable **7** empower, qualify **8** nominate **9** authorize, designate **10** denominate, habilitate **12** characterize

entity: ens **4** unit **5** being, thing **7** essence, integer **9** existence

entoil: **5** snare **7** ensnare

entomb: **4** bury **5** inter, inurn **6** encave, hearse, inhume

entourage: **5** train **7** retinue **9** associate, attendant

entracte: **8** interval **9** interlude **12** intermission

entrail: bag, gut **5** bowel **6** giblet, mugget **7** viscera **8** gigerium

entrain: **5** board

entrance: **4** adit, boca(Sp.), door, gate, hall **5** charm, debut, entry, foyer, mouth, stulm, toran **6** access, atrium(L.), entree, portal, ravish, torana, zaguam **7** delight, gateway, hallway, ingoing, ingress, initial,

postern **9** admission, beginning, enrapture, fascinate, incursion, induction, overpower, threshold, vestibule **10** admittance **12** introduction

entranced: **4** rapt **8** ecstatic

entrant: **7** intrant, starter **8** beginner **11** participant

entrap: bag, net **5** catch, decoy, snare **6** allure, ambush, taigle(Sc.), tangle, trepan **7** beguile, ensnare **8** entangle, inveigle

entre(F.): **7** between

entreat: ask, beg, bid, sue **4** pray, seek **5** crave, plead **6** appeal, invoke **7** beseech, conjure, implore, prevail, request, solicit **8** persuade, petition **9** impetrate, importune **10** supplicate

entreaty: **4** plea, suit **8** petition **9** treatment **11** importunity, negotiation

entree: **5** entry **6** access **8** entrance **9** admission **10** permission

entrench, intrench: **6** invade **8** encroach, trespass

entrenchment: **7** closure

entrepreneur: **7** manager **8** employer **10** impresario **11** enterpriser

entresol: **9** mezzanine

entrust, intrust: **4** give **6** commit **7** address, commend confide, consign, deposit **8** delegate, encharge **9** concredit, recommend

entry: **4** adit, hall, item **5** debit **6** credit, entree, postea, record, ringer **7** ingress, passage **8** entrance, notandum, register **9** vestibule **10** adjustment, enlistment, enrollment

entwine: **4** lace **5** braid, twine, twist, weave **6** enlace **7** wreathe **9** interlace **10** intertwine

enucleate: **7** explain

enumerate: **4** tell **5** count **6** detail, number, recite, reckon, relate **7** compute, itemize, recount **8** estimate **9** calculate **13** particularize

enumeration: **4** list **6** census **7** account, catalog **9** catalogue

enunciate: **5** utter **7** declare, enounce **8** announce, proclaim **9** pronounce **10** articulate

enure: See **inure**.

envelop, envelope: **4** case, coma, husk **5** cover, round **6** bemist, enfold, engirt, enwrap, infold, invest, muffle, sheath, shroud, swathe **7** enclose, environ, wrapper **8** ensphere, surround **9** chevelure **10** integument

envenom: **7** corrupt, vitiate **8** embitter, empoison

envious: **7** jealous **8** enviable **9** invidious

environ: hem **4** gird **5** limit **6** girdle, suburb **7** envelop, inclose, involve, jealous, purlieu **8** district, encircle, surround **9** encompass, territory **12** circumscribe

environment: **6** medium, milieu **7** element, habitat, setting **8** ambiance, precinct

envisage: 4 face 8 confront 9 visualize
envision: 5 dream
envoy: 5 agent, envoi(F.) 6 deputy, legate 8 ablegate 9 messenger, missioner 10 ambassador 12 commissioner 14 representative 15 plenipotentiary
envy: 5 covet 6 grudge 8 begrudge, jealousy
enwrap: 4 roll 5 clasp 6 enfold, infold, kirtle 7 engross, envelop 8 convolve, envelope
enzyme: ase 6 cytase, lipase, olease, papain, pepsin, rennin, urease 7 adenase, amylase, casease, diatase, erepsin, ferment, guanase, inulase, maltase, pectase, pepsine, tannase 8 catalase, cytolist, eraptase, esterase, protease 9 biogenase, deamidase, deaminase, invertase, trehalase 10 amygdalase 11 gaultherase 14 acetaldehydase
eoan: 7 auroral
eolith: 4 celt
eon: age 8 eternity
epee: 5 blade, sword
epergne: 11 centerpiece
ephelis: 7 freckle
ephemeral: 5 brief, vague 7 passant, passing 9 temporary, transient 10 evanescent, short-lived, transitory 11 impermanent
ephemeris: 5 diary 7 almanac, journal 8 calendar, magazine 10 periodical 11 publication
Ephraim's descendant: 7 Resheph
epi: 5 spire 6 finial 8 pinnacle
epic: 4 Edda, epos, saga 5 grand, Iliad, noble 6 epopee, heroic 7 Beowulf 8 epyllion, Ramayana 9 narrative 11 Mahabharata
epicarp: 4 husk, rind
epicede, epicedium: ode 4 song 5 dirge, elegy
epicene: 7 sexless 10 effeminate
epichoric: 5 local
epicure: 6 friand 7 glutton, gourmet 8 gourmand 10 gastronome 11 connoisseur
epidemic: flu 6 plague 8 pandemic 9 influenza 10 pestilence
epiderm appendage: 4 horn
epidermis: 7 cuticle
epigram: 4 poem 6 englyn 11 inscription
epigramatic: 7 concise, piquant, pointed
epigraph: 7 imprint 11 inscription 14 superscription
epilogue, epilog: 8 appendix 10 conclusion
epinard: 7 spinach
Epiphany: 9 uphellyaa(Sc.)
episcopacy: 9 bishopric
Episcopal parish head: 6 rector
Episcopalian: 9 prelatist
episcopate: 9 bishopric

episode: 5 event, scene, story 8 incident 9 happening
episperm: 5 testa
epistaxis: 9 nosebleed
epistle: 6 letter 7 missive, writing
epitaph: 8 hicjacet 11 inscription
epithet: 4 name, term 5 title 6 phrase 7 agnomen 9 sobriquet 10 soubriquet 11 appellation
epitome: 6 digest, precis 8 abstract, synopsis 9 comprisal, statement 10 compendium 11 abridgement, contraction 13 comprehension
epitomize: 6 resume 7 curtail 8 compress, condense, diminish 9 summarize 10 abbreviate
epityphlitis: 12 appendicitis
epoch: age, era 4 date, time 5 event 6 period
epode: 7 refrain 9 aftersong
epopee: 4 epic, epos
epure: 5 draft 7 diagram, drawing, pattern
equability: 10 equanimity
equable: 4 even, just 5 equal, suant 6 smooth, steady 7 uniform 8 tranquil 9 equitable
equal: par, tie 4 cope, even, fere, isos(Gr.), just, like, meet, peer, same 5 alike, level, match, rival 6 equate 7 abreast, compeer, emulate, equable, identic, uniform 8 adequate, equalize, tranquil 9 equitable, identical, unruffled 10 answerable, equivalent, tantamount 11 comparative, countervail 12 commensurate, counterpoise 13 unfluctuating
combining form: iso 4 pari
prefix: iso 4 equi
equalire: 4 even
equality: 6 equity, parity 7 balance, egality 8 evenness, fairness 12 impartiality
legal: 7 isonomy
equally: as 4 both 5 alike 6 evenly, justly
equanimity: 5 poise 7 egality 8 calmness, evenness, serenity 9 composure 10 equability 11 tranquility
equate: 7 balance 8 equalize
equatorial: 8 tropical
equestrian: 5 rider 7 vaquero(Sp.) 8 horseman
equidistant: 7 central, halfway
equilibrium: 5 poise 7 balance 9 equipoise
being in: 7 astatic
science: 8 astatics
equine: 4 colt, foal, mare 5 filly, horse, zebra
equip: arm, rig 4 deck, gear, gird, heel, reek 5 array, dress, enarm, endow 6 attire, fit out, outfit, suborn 7 apparel, appoint, bedight, furnish, prepare, qualify 8 accouter, accoutre 10 accomplish, habilitate

equipage: 4 crew 5 suite, train 6 supply 7 retinue, turnout 8 carriage 9 apparatus, furniture 10 habiliment

equipment: 4 gear 6 attire, tackle 7 fitment, harness, panoply 8 armament, material, mounting 11 appointment 13 paraphernalia

equipoise: 5 poise 7 balance 11 equilibrium

equiponderate: 14 counterbalance

equitable: 4 even, fair, just 5 equal, right 6 honest 7 equable, upright 9 impartial, righteous 10 reasonable

equitation: 12 horsemanship

equity: law 7 honesty, justice 8 equality, fairness 9 rectitude 11 uprightness 13 righteousness

equivalent: 9 identical 10 synonymous, tantamount

equivocal: 7 dubious, obscure 8 doubtful, puzzling 9 ambiguous, enigmatic, uncertain 10 indefinite, mysterious, perplexing, suspicious 12 questionable, undetermined 13 indeterminate, problematical

equivocate: lie 5 dodge, evade, shift 6 escape, palter, trifle, weasel 7 quibble, shuffle 11 prevaricate

era: A.D., B.C.; age 4 aeon, date, time 5 epoch, stage 6 period

eradicate: 4 dele, weed 5 erase 6 delete, remove, uproot 7 abolish, destroy, outroot 9 extirpate 10 annihilate, deracinate 11 exterminate

erase: 4 blot, dele, rase, raze 5 annul 6 cancel, deface, delete, efface, excise, remove 7 destroy, expunge, scratch 9 eradicate 10 obliterate

erd: 4 land 5 earth 6 region

ere: 4 soon 5 early, prior 6 before 8 erewhile, formerly 9 aforetime 10 previously

Erebus: *parent of:* 5 Chaos
sister: Nox
son: 6 Charon

erect: big 4 bigg, rear, step 5 build, exalt, setup, stand 6 arrect, uplift 7 address, elevate, upright 8 straight, vertical 9 construct, establish, institute 10 upstanding 13 perpendicular

erelong: 4 anon, soon

eremite: 6 hermit 7 ascetic, recluse 8 anchoret 9 anchorite
hut: 4 cell

erewhile: ere 10 heretofore

ergastulum: 4 cell 7 dungeon

ergo: so 5 hence 9 therefore

erica: 5 heath 7 heather

Erin: 4 Eire 7 Ireland 8 Hibernia 9 Innisfail

Erinys: 4 Fury 6 Alecto 7 Megaera 9 Tisiphone

Eris' daughter: Ate

eristic: 12 disputatious 13 controversial

Eritrea: See **Ethiopia**.

ermine: fur 5 stoat, white 6 weasel 7 ermelin, miniver

erode: eat 4 gnaw, wear 7 corrode, destroy 9 undermine 12 disintegrate

Eros: 4 amor 5 Cupid

erose: 6 uneven 9 irregular

erotic: 6 loving 7 amatory, amorous

err: sin 4 miss, slip 5 lapse, misgo, stray 6 bungle, wander 7 blunder, deviate, misplay, mistake 8 misjudge 10 transgress 12 miscalculate, misinterpret

errand: 5 chore 7 journey, mission

errand boy: 4 page 7 courier 9 messenger

errant: 5 stray 6 astray, erring 9 deviating, itinerant, wandering 10 journeying 11 adventurous

erratic: 5 queer, wacky 6 whacky 7 strange, vagrant 8 vagabond 9 eccentric, irregular, wandering 10 capricious, changeable

erratum: 5 error 7 mistake

errhine: 7 sneezer

erring: 6 astray, errant

erroneous: 5 amiss, false, wrong 6 untrue 7 erratic 8 mistaken, straying, wrongful 9 incorrect, wandering

error: sin 4 bull, flub, muff, slip 5 bevue, boner, fault, fluff, lapse 6 fumble, miscue 7 bloomer, blunder, default, erratum, fallacy, falsity, misplay, misstep, mistake, offense, rhubarb 8 solecism 9 violation 10 inaccuracy 12 irregularity, malformation
measuring device: 11 aberrometer

ers: 5 vetch

ersatz: 10 artificial, substitute 11 replacement

Erse: 5 Irish 6 Celtic, Gaelic 8 Scottish

erst: 8 formerly

erstwhile: 6 former 8 formerly 10 heretofore

eruca: 11 caterpillar

erudition: 4 lore 7 letters 8 learning 9 education, knowledge 11 instruction, scholarship

erupt: 5 burst, eject

eruption: 4 rush 5 rupia, storm 6 blotch 8 outbreak, outburst 9 commotion

Esau: 4 Edom
brother: 5 Jacob
descendant: 7 Edomite
father: 5 Isaac
grandson: 6 Amalek
mother: 7 Rebekah

escapade: 5 prank, sally 7 runaway 9 adventure, excursion

escape: lam 4 flee, gate, jink(Sc.), miss, slip 5 avoid, dodge, elude, evade, issue, spill 6 eschew, outlet 7 getaway, leakage, mistake, outflow 9 evaporate

means: 8 loophole
escargot: 5 snail
escarole: 6 endive
escarp: 5 scarp, slope
eschalot: 5 onion
eschar: 4 scab 5 crust
escheat: 4 fall 5 lapse 6 revert 7 forfeit
eschew: 4 shun 5 avoid 6 escape 7 abstain
escolar: 8 mackerel
escort: see 4 beau, lead, show 5 guard, usher 6 attend, convoy, squire 7 conduct, consort, gallant 8 cavalier, chaperon 9 accompany, attendant, bodyguard, safeguard
escritoire: 4 desk 6 bureau 9 secretary
escrow: 4 bond, deed
esculent: 6 edible 7 eatable 10 comestible
escutcheon: 6 shield
band: 4 fess 5 fesse
cord: 10 cordeliere
eserine: 13 physostigmine
eshin: tub 4 pail
esker, eskar: as 4 kame
Eskimo: *Aleutian Islands:* 4 Atka 5 Aleut, Husky
Asiatic: 4 Yuit 6 Innuit
bird: 4 fute
boot: 5 kamik
canoe: 5 cayak, kayak, umiak 6 oomiac, oomiak 7 oomiack
coat: 5 parka 6 parkee, temiak
Diomede Islands: 11 Yikirgaulit
dog: 5 husky 8 Malamute, Malemute
dwelling: 4 iglu 5 igloo, topek, tupek, tupik 9 barrabora
goddess: 5 Sedna
Greenland: Ita
knife: ulu
medicine man: 7 angakok, angakut, angekok, angekut 8 angekkok
mountain: 7 nunatak
settlement: 4 Etah
sledge: 7 komatik
esne: 4 serf 7 bondman 8 hireling
esodic: 8 afferent
esophagus: 6 gullet
esoteric: 5 inner 6 mystic, secret 7 private 8 abstruse 9 recondite 10 acroamatic, mysterious 12 confidential
espadon: 9 swordfish
espalier: 7 lattice, railing, trellis
Espanol: 7 Spanish
espantoon: 4 club 8 spontoon
esparto: 4 alfa
especial: 5 chief 8 peculiar, uncommon 10 particular
esperance: 4 hope 11 expectation
espial: spy 5 scout 6 notice 9 discovery 11 observation
espiegle: 7 roguish 10 frolicsome
espionage: 4 espy 6 spying
agent: spy

esplanade: 4 walk 5 drive 6 maidan, marina 9 promenade
esplee: 6 profit 7 product
espousal: 8 ceremony
espouse: wed 4 affy, mate 5 adopt, marry 6 defend, spouse 7 betroth, embrace, husband, support 8 advocate, maintain
esprit: wit 6 spirit 10 cleverness 12 intelligence
esprit de corps: 8 devotion
espy: see 4 spot 5 sight, watch 6 behold, descry, detect, locate, notice 7 discern, observe 8 discover 9 espionage
esquire: 7 armiger
ess: 8 curlicue, curlycue
essay: try 4 seek 5 chria(L.), paper, theme, tract, trail 6 effort, satire, thesis 7 article, attempt, venture, writing 8 endeavor, exertion, treatise 10 enterprise, experiment 12 disquisition, dissertation
essayist: 4 Elia, Lamb
esse: 5 being 9 existence
essence: ens 4 atar, core, crux, gist, odor, otto, pith, soul 5 attar, basic, being, heart, ottar, ousia(G.) 6 nature 7 element, extract, medulla, perfume 9 existence, principle, substance 10 extraction
Essene: 7 ascetic
essential: 5 per se, vital 7 needful 8 inherent, material 9 intrinsic, necessary 11 fundamental 13 indispensable 14 constitutional
essonite: 6 garnet
establish: fix, set 4 base, rear, rest, seat 5 build, edify, erect, found, plant, prove, setup, state 6 avouch, clinch, create, ground, locate, ordain, ratify, settle, verify 7 appoint, approve, confirm, enstate, install, instate, preempt 8 colonize, constate, ensconce, identify, radicate, regulate, validate 9 determine, institute, originate 10 accomplish, constitute 11 corroborate
established: 4 fast, firm, sure 7 certain
establishment: 4 mill 5 plant 6 ecesis, menage 7 dounset(Sc.), factory 8 business, hacienda
estafette: 7 courier 9 messenger
estancia(Sp.): 4 farm 5 ranch
estate: 4 alod, fief, home, pomp, rank 5 acres, allod, finca, habit, manor, state, taluk 6 domain, ground 7 alodium, demesne, dignity, display, fortune 8 allodium, freehold, hacienda, position, property, standing 9 condition, situation 11 latifundium
fourth: 5 press 9 newspaper
owner: 9 hacendero
purchaser: 9 acquereur(F.)
rent deduction: 7 reprise
third: 9 tiers etat(F.)
to hold: 7 tenancy
esteem: 4 deem 5 adore, count, favor,

honor, pride, prize, value, worth **6** credit,
favour, regard, repute **7** account, opinion,
respect **8** appraise, venerate **9** deference,
reckoning, reverence **10** admiration, appreciate, estimation **13** consideration

ester: **6** oleate **7** acetate, tropate **8** compound, stearate

estero: **5** inlet **7** channel, estuary

esthesiometer: **10** tactometer

esthetic: See **aesthetic.**

estimable: **4** good **5** solid **6** worthy **9** admirable, honorable **11** respectable

estimate: set **4** rank, rate **5** cense, gauge,
guess, judge, prize, value **6** assess,
budget, esteem, reckon **7** average **8** appraise, consider **9** calculate **11** computation

low: **14** undervaluation

smallest: **7** minimum

too high: **8** overrate

estimation: aim **4** fame **5** honor **6** regard,
repute **7** opinion **9** judgement **10** conjecture

estoc: **5** sword

estocada: **6** thrust

Estonia: *city:* **5** Reval **7** Tallinn

coin: **4** sent **5** kroon **7** estmark

island: **4** Dago **5** Oesel, Saare

measure: tun **4** elle, liin, pang, sund, toll,
toop **5** faden, verst **6** sagene, versta,
verste **7** kulimet, verchoc, verchok **8**
tonnland **9** lofstelle

weight: **4** lood, nael, puud

estop: bar **4** fill, plug, stop **5** debar **6** hinder, impede **7** prevent **8** preclude, prohibit

estrade: **4** dais **8** platform

estrange: part, wean **6** divert **8** alienate,
disunite

estray: **6** wander

estreat: **4** copy, fine **5** exact **6** record **7**
extract **9** duplicate

estrepe: **5** spoil

estuary: **5** firth, frith, inlet **6** estero

estuate: **4** boil **5** heave, surge **7** agitate

esurient: **6** greedy, hungry **9** voracious

etaac: **7** blaubok **8** antelope

etagere: **7** whatnot

etalon: **14** interferometer

etat: **5** state

etch: **7** engrave **8** inscribe

eternal: **6** eterne **7** ageless, endless, lasting, unaging **8** enduring, immortal, timeless **9** boundless, continual, deathless,
immutable, perpetual, unceasing **10** perdurable **11** everlasting **12** imperishable,
unchangeable **13** uninterrupted

Eternal City: **4** Rome

eternally: ake, eer **4** ever **6** always **7** forever

eterne: **7** eternal

eternity: age, eon **4** aeon, olam

etesian: **6** annual **8** periodic

ethenol: **7** alcohol

ether: air, sky **5** ester **7** solvent **8** empyrean **10** anesthetic, atmosphere

ethereal, etherial: **4** aery, airy **6** aerial **7**
airlike, etheric, fragile, slender **8** delicate,
heavenly **9** celestial **10** spiritlike

ethical: **5** moral

ethics: *system of:* **8** hedonics

teacher of· **8** moralist

without: **6** amoral

Ethiopia: **4** Kafa **5** Kaffa **9** Abyssinia

animal: **4** kudu, lion, oryx **5** zebra **6** baboon, gelada, impala, jackal, monkey **7**
gazelle, giraffe, redbuck **12** hippopotamus

battleground: **5** Adowa

Catholic: **4** Cush, Geez **5** Uniat **6** Uniate

cattle: **5** sanga

city: **4** Axum, Gore **5** Adowa, Assab, Harar
6 Antalo, Asmara, Gondar, Harrar, Na-
pata **7** Ankober, Gambela, Magdala **10**
Addis Ababa(c.)

coin: **4** besa, harf **5** amole, girsh **6** kharaf,
talari **7** ashrafi, piaster, tallero

district: **4** Shoa **5** Harer, Tigre **6** Amhara

dollar: **6** Levant, talari **12** Maria Theresa

emperor: **5** Negus **6** Memnon **7** Menelik **8**
Selassie

fly: **4** zimb

garment: **6** chamma

governor: ras

lake: **4** Tana **5** Tanna, Tsana, Tzana,
6 Dembel **8** Stefanie

language: Ago **4** Afar, Geez, Saho **5** Galla,
Tigre **6** Harari **7** Amharic

lyre: **6** kissar

measure: tat **4** cubi, kuba **5** derah, messe
6 cabaho, sinjer, sinzer, tanica **7** entelam,
farsakh, farsang, ghebeta

mountain: **9** Ras Dashan

people: **4** Kala **5** Bejas, Negro **6** Ethiop,
Hamite, Harari **7** Somalis **10** Abyssinian

princess: **4** Aida **9** Andromeda

province: **4** Jima **5** Arusi, Gojam, Tigre,
Wallo **6** Harage, Sidamo, Walaga **8** Ba-
gemder, Gamagofa, Ilubabor

pygmy: **4** Doko

river: Omo **4** Baro, Gibe, Juba **5** Abbai,
Albai, Giubo, Rahad, Webbe **7** Tacazze

tableland: **4** amba

title: ras **5** abuna, negus

torah: **5** tetel

tribe: **4** Afar **5** Agows, Galas **6** Amhara,
Tigres **7** Donakus, Somalis

violin: **7** masinko

weight: pek **4** kasm, natr, oket, rotl **5**
alada, artal, mocha, neter, ratel, wakea **6**
wogiet **8** farasula **9** mutagalla

etiolate: **4** pale **6** bleach

etiquette: **4** form **6** manner **7** chanoyu,
decorum **9** propriety

breach of: **8** solecism

etna: **4** lamp

Etruria: *deity:* Lar, Uni **5** Tinia

pottery: **8** bucchero

Etruscan (see also **Etruria**): **8** Etrurian, Tursenoi, Tyrrheni

ettle: aim **4** plan **6** aspire, design, intend, intent, nettle **8** endeavor

etui, etwee: 4 case **8** reticule **10** needle-case

etymology: 6 origin

eucalyptus secretion: 4 laap, lerp **5** laarp

Eucharist: *box:* pix, pyx

bread plate: **5** paten

cup: **5** calix **7** chalice

wafer vessel: **8** ciborium

wine vessel: ama **5** amula

Euchite: 8 satanist

eugenic: 8 wellborn

eulogize: 4 laud **5** extol **7** glorify **9** celebrate

eulogy: 5 eloge **6** hesped(Heb.), praise **7** address, oration **8** encomium **9** panegyric **11** composition

eunuch: 7 gelding **8** castrate

pert. to: **8** spadonic

Euphrates tributary: 5 Habor **6** Tigris

euplexoptera: 6 earwig

eureka red: 4 puce

Europa's father: 6 Agenor

Europe: 9 continent

antelope: **7** chamois

ape: **6** baboon

ash: **4** sorb

badger: **5** brock

barracuda: **4** spet

bass: **6** brasse

bat: **8** serotine

bellflower: **7** rampion

bird: See **bird:** *Europe.*

bison: **7** aurochs

boar: sus(L.) **4** aper(L.)

boxing: **6** savate

broadcloth: **6** suclat

buckthorn: **7** alatern **9** alaternus

canal: **4** kiel

cavalryman: **4** Ulan **5** Uhlan **6** Hussar

cherry: **4** gean

city: Osb **4** Riga, Rome **5** Paris, Posen, Soest, Vichy **6** Berlin, Lisbon, Pilsen **9** Stockholm

clover: **6** alsike

coin: **5** ducat, taler **7** pistole

country: **5** Italy, Spain **6** France, Greece, Latvia, Norway, Poland **7** Austria, Belgium, Denmark, Finland, Germany, Holland, Hungary, Rumania **8** Bulgaria **9** Luxemburg **11** Switzerland

deer: roe **6** fallow

elder: **8** danewort

fish: id; gar, ide **4** blay, boce, dace, lote, rudd, tope **5** alose, barse, roach, ruffe, sprat, tench **6** barbel, besugo, braise, meagre, morgay, plaice, turbot **7** eperlan, homelyn, lavaret, osseter, picarel, topknot

8 John Dory, scirenga **9** John Doree

grape: **6** muscat

gulf: **4** Riga

herb: **4** dill, meum, woad **6** borage, lovage, yarrow **7** henbane **8** spicknel, tarragon

hundredweight: **7** zentner

industrial region: **4** Ruhr, Saar

invaders: **4** Huns **5** Alani, Alans, Arabs, Turks **7** Mongols

island: **4** Erin **5** Aland

juniper: **4** cade

kingdom: **5** Arles, Italy **6** Aragon, Norway, Sweden **7** Belgium, England, Holland, Navarre **11** Netherlands

language: **5** Ugric

larkspur: **10** stavesacre

lavender: **5** aspic

lime: **4** teil

measure: aam **5** liter, metre

mint: iva **6** hyssop **9** horehound

mountain: Alp

mountain ash: **4** sorb **5** rowan, rowen

mountainous region: **4** Alps **5** Tyrol

mouse: **4** loir, vole **5** lerot

nationality: **4** Dane, Finn, Goth, Lapp, Lett, Pole, Serb, Slav **5** Croat, Swede, Welsh

oak: **4** holm **7** durmast

ox: **4** urus

peninsula: **7** Iberian

plant: **4** ulex **7** azarole, eelware **8** lavender **9** elderwort, escobilla **10** sneezewort

polecat: **7** fitchet, fitchew

rabbit: **4** cony

republic: **4** Eire **5** Hesse **7** Andorra, Andorre

resort: spa **7** Riviera

river: Po; Bug **4** Drau, Eder, Eger, Elbe, Oder, Ruhr, Saar, Ural **5** Meuse, Rhine, Rhone **6** Danube **7** Narenta

rodent: erd **7** hamster

rustic: **7** peasant

sea: **4** Aral, Azov **5** North **6** Baltic

sedge: **5** chufa

squirrel: **5** sisel **10** polatouche

strait: **8** Bosporus

valley: **4** Ruhr

weasel: **5** stote **8** whitrack

wheat: **5** emmer **6** whizen **7** einkorn

worm: sao

Eurytus' daughter: 4 Iole

evacuant: 6 emetic **8** diuretic, emptying **9** cathartic, purgative

evacuate: 4 void **5** empty, expel **6** vacate **7** deprive, excrete, exhaust, nullify, vacuate **9** discharge

evade: 4 bilk, foil, jouk, shun **5** avert, avoid, dodge, elude, shirk **6** baffle, blench, escape, illude **7** beguile

evaluate: 6 ponder **8** appraise

evanesce: 4 fade **5** empty **6** vanish **9** disappear, dissipate

evanescent: 7 cursory, evasive 8 fleeting, fugitive 9 ephemeral, fugacious, transient vanishing 11 impermanent 13 infinitesimal

evangel: 6 gospel

Evangeline's home: 6 Acadia

evangelist: 6 Graham, Sunday 7 Edwards 9 McPherson

evaporate: dry 8 condense, vaporize 9 dehydrate

evasion: 4 jink 5 dodge, shift 6 escape 9 avoidance 10 subterfuge 12 equivocation

evasive: sly 4 eely 5 dodgy 6 shifty 7 elusive, elusory 9 deceitful 12 tergiversate

eve: 4 dusk 6 sunset 7 sundown 9 threshold

even: een, tie 4 fair, just 5 aline, equal, exact, flush, grade, level, match, plain, rival, suant 6 direct, placid, smooth, square, steady 7 abreast, balance, equable, flatten, regular, uniform 8 moderate, parallel 9 equitable, impartial 10 coincident 15 straightforward

even if: tho 8 although

even-tempered: 4 calm, mild 5 plane, still 9 impartial

evener: 7 leveler 9 equalizer 10 doubletree

evening: eve 5 abend 8 eventide

evening star: 5 Venus 6 Hesper, Vesper 8 Hesperus

evenness: 8 equality 10 equanimity, uniformity

event: hap 4 case, fact, fate, feat, tilt 5 casus(L.), doing, epoch 6 factum(L.), result 7 episode, miracle, tragedy 8 incident, occasion 9 adventure, happening, milestone 10 occurrence, phenomenon 11 catastrophe, consequence, termination 12 circumstance

first: 6 opener 8 premiere

happy: hit 5 birth 7 godsend 8 marriage

eventful: 7 notable 9 important, momentous

eventide: 6 vesper 7 evening

eventual: 4 last 5 final 8 ultimate

eventuate: 6 result

ever: ay; aye, eer 6 always 7 forever 10 constantly 11 continually, perpetually

Everglade State: 7 Florida

Everglades: 5 marsh, swamp

evergreen: fir, ivy 4 ilex 5 heath, holly, savin 6 laurel, savine 7 jasmine 9 mistletoe 12 rhododendron

genus of: 4 olax 9 cupressus 11 pittosporum

tree: fir, yew 4 pine 5 carob, cedar 6 balsam, calaba, larche

everlasting: 6 eterne 7 aeonial, aeonian, durable, endless, eternal, forever, lasting, tedious 8 enduring, immortal, infinite,

timeless 9 continual, incessant, perpetual, unceasing, wearisome 10 everduring, perdurable 12 imperishable 13 unintermitted, uninterrupted

everlasting flower: 6 orpine

everlastingly: 6 always 7 forever

evermore: 6 always

evert: 7 subvert 9 overthrow

every: all, ilk(Sc.) 4 each, ilka(Sc.) 6 entire 8 complete

everybody: all 8 everyone

everyday: 7 prosaic 8 ordinary

everything: all

evict: 4 oust 5 eject, expel 10 dispossess

evidence: 4 show 5 proof, scrip, token, trace 6 attest, reveal 7 exhibit, support 8 argument, manifest, muniment 9 testimony 10 indication 15 circumstantiate

piece of: 7 probate

evident: 5 apert, broad, clear, plain 6 patent 7 glaring, obvious, visible 8 apparent, manifest, palpable 10 noticeable 11 discernible, indubitable, transparent 12 demonstrable

evil: bad, ill, sin 4 bale, base, harm, poor, vice, vile 5 crime, malum(L.), wrong 6 menace, wicked 7 adverse, corrupt, disease, hurtful, immoral, misdeed, noxious, satanic, unsound 8 calamity, depraved, disaster, improper, iniquity, mischief, sinister 9 injurious, malicious, malignant, malignity, offensive, worthless 10 malevolent, misfortune, pernicious 11 malefaction, unwholesome 12 unpropitious 14 unsatisfactory

combining form: mal

incarnation of: 5 Satan

spirit: imp 5 demon, devil 6 daemon

evildoer: 10 malefactor

evince: 4 show 5 prove 6 subdue 7 conquer, display, exhibit 8 indicate, manifest

evirate: 8 castrate 10 emasculate

eviscerate: gut 10 devitalize, disembowel, exenterate

evoke: 5 educe 6 arouse, elicit, summon 7 evocate

evolute: 6 evolve, unfold

evolution: 7 biogeny 8 maneuver 11 development

evolutionist: 9 Darwinian

evolve: 4 emit 5 educe 6 derive, unfold, unroll 7 develop, evolute 9 disengage 11 disentangle

evulgate: 7 divulge, publish

ewe: teg 5 crone, sheep 6 theave

ewer: jug 5 basin, udder 7 pitcher 9 container

ewest: 4 next 7 nearest

ex: 6 former

exacerbate: 8 embitter, irritate

exact: ask 4 even, fine, levy, true 5 wreak, wrest 6 compel, demand, elicit, extort,

formal, minute, square, strict **7** careful, certain, command, correct, enforce, estreat, extract, literal, precise, regular, require **8** accurate, critical, explicit, rigorous, specific **9** religious **10** methodical, meticulous, scrupulous **11** punctilious **13** hypercritical **14** circumstantial

exacting: **6** severe **7** arduous, exigent **8** pressing

exactly: due **4** dead **5** spang, truly **6** evenly, nicely **9** precisely

exactness: **8** delicacy, identity, severity

exaggerate: **6** extend, overdo **7** amplify, enhance, enlarge, magnify, romance, stretch **8** increase **9** aggravate, embroider, overstate

exaggeration: **9** hyperbole **10** caricature

exagitate: **6** harass **7** agitate, censure, discuss

exalt: **5** arear, elate, erect, extol, heeze, honor, raise, set up, tower **6** ascend, refine **7** advance, augment, dignify, elevate, enhance, ennoble, glorify, greaten, inspire, magnify, promote **8** enthrone, heighten **9** intensify **10** aggrandize

exaltation: **7** elation, rapture **9** celsitude, elevation **10** apotheosis

exalted: **4** high **5** grand, noble **7** haughty, sublime **11** illustrious, magnanimous

examen: **7** inquiry **11** examination **13** investigation

examination: **4** quiz, test **5** assay, audit, check, trial **6** examen, review, survey, tripos **7** autopsy, inquest, inquiry **8** necropsy, research, scrutiny **10** comparison, inspection **11** exploration, inquisition **13** consideration, investigation **14** reconnaissance

examine: spy, try **4** feel, scan, sift, view **5** assay, probe, quest **6** candle, ponder **7** analyze, canvass, palpate, rummage **8** overhaul **10** introspect, scrutinize **11** expostulate, interrogate, reconnoiter, reconnoitre

examiner: **6** censor, conner **7** analyst, auditor, coroner **9** inspector **10** inquisitor

example: **4** case, norm, tipe(Sp.), type **5** model **6** praxis, sample **7** pattern **8** exemplar, exemplum(L.), foregoer, instance, paradigm, specimen **9** precedent **11** description **12** illustration **15** exemplification

exanimate: **8** lifeless **9** inanimate **10** spiritless

exasperate: ire, irk **4** bait, gall, heat **5** annoy **6** enrage, excite, nettle **7** inflame, provoke, roughen **8** irritate **9** aggravate

exasperated: **5** wroth **9** indignant

excavate: dig **4** mine, mole, pion **5** delve, scoop **6** burrow, dredge

excavation: cut, pit **4** hole, mine **5** grave, stope **6** cavity, groove, trench

into bank: **7** remblai

excavator: **6** bildar(Ind.), cleoid, digger **7** pioneer

exceed: top **4** best, pass **5** excel, outdo, outgo **6** better, outrun, outvie, overdo **7** eclipse, overtax, surpass **8** outrange, outstrip, overcome, overstep **9** overshoot, transcend **11** predominate

exceedingly: **4** tres(F.), very **5** amain **7** parlous **9** extremely

excel: cap, cob **4** best **5** outdo, outgo, shine **6** better, exceed **7** emulate, outpeer, surpass **8** outclass, outrival, outstrip **9** transcend

excellence: **5** arete(Gr.), merit **6** virtue **7** dignity **8** goodness **10** perfection

excellent: **4** best, braw(Sc.), fine, good **5** brave, bully, great, prime, super, wally(Sc.) **6** choice, famous, gentle, proper, select, spiffy, worthy **7** capital, corking, elegant, quality **8** eximious, generous, superior, valuable **9** admirable, first-rate **10** inimitable, preeminent **12** transcendent

except: but **4** bate, omit, only **6** exempt, unless **7** besides, exclude **9** eliminate

exception: **5** demur **7** dissent, offense **9** complaint, condition, objection

exceptional: **4** rare **7** unusual **8** abnormal, uncommon **9** anomalous **10** remarkable **11** outstanding **13** extraordinary

excerpt: **4** cite **5** quote, scrap **7** extract

excess: **4** over, plus, riot **5** flood **7** nimiety, overage, profuse, surplus **8** overmuch, overplus, plethora **10** exuberance, redundancy **11** excrescence, superfluity **12** intemperance **13** overabundance **14** superabundance

excessive: too **4** over **5** enorm(Sc.), undue **6** de trop(F.) **7** extreme, nimious **8** allfired, enormous, horrible, overmuch **9** exuberant **10** boisterous, exorbitant, immoderate, inordinate **11** extravagant, intemperate **12** extortionate, unreasonable

excessively: **11** parlous

exchange: set **4** cash, chop, cope, mart, sell, swap, swop **5** bandy, bolsa, corse, store, trade, truck **6** barter, bourse, dicker, excamb(Sc.), market, resale, rialto, scorse, shoppe **7** barroom, chaffer, commute, dealing, traffic **9** excambion(Sc.), transpose **10** substitute **11** interchange, reciprocate **12** headquarters

business: **5** bolsa

medium: **7** coinage

rate: **4** agio **5** batta

exchequer: **4** fisc(Sc.) **5** purse **7** finance **8** treasury

excise: tax **4** duty, toll **6** impost, resect **7** exscind **8** alcabala(Sp.) **9** extirpate **10** overcharge

officer: **8** revenuer

excision: cut **7** erasure **9** expulsion **11** destruction, extirpation **15** excommunication

excitability: 12 irritability

excitable: 9 spasmodic

excite: 4 fire, spur, stir, urge 5 alarm, amove, anger, chafe, elate, impel, pique, rouse 6 arouse, awaken, decoct, foment, incite, kindle 7 agitate, animate, inflame, provoke 8 disquiet 9 electrify, galvanize, instigate, stimulate, titillate 10 exasperate, intoxicate

excited: hot 4 agog 5 eager, ranty 6 heated 7 fevered, wakened 8 flurried, startled

excitement: ado 4 stir 5 fever, furor, larry 6 warmth 7 widdrim(Sc.) 9 commotion 10 irritation 11 disturbance

exciting: 6 hectic 8 stirring, terrific

exclaim: 6 clamor, outcry 9 ejaculate

exclamation: ah, ai, ay, bo, ha, hi, ho, la, lo, oh, ow, so; aha, aie, bah, boo, fie, foh, hep, hey, hic, huh, och, oho, pah, poh, suz, tut, ugh, wow, yah 4 ahem, alas, drat, egad, evoe, garn, hech, heck, hist, hola, phew, pish, pugh, rats, rivo, tush, wugg 5 alack, bravo, faugh, feigh, heigh, holla, humph, ohone(Ir.), pshaw 6 clamor, hurrah, indeed 7 hosanna 9 alackaday, expletive 12 interjection

exclude: bar 5 debar, eject, expel 6 banish, except, exempt, reject 7 foreign 9 blackball, eliminate, forestall, ostracize 13 excommunicate

exclusive: all 4 only, rare, sole 5 alone, whole 6 select 8 cliquish, entirely

excommunication: ban 8 excision

excoriate: 4 flay, gall 5 score, strip 6 abrade 11 decorticate

excrement: lee 4 dirt, dreg, dung, fece 5 faece 6 ordure, refuse

excrescence: 4 burl, lump, wart 6 excess, pimple 9 outgrowth, tubercule 11 superfluity

excrete: 5 egest 8 defecate 9 eliminate

excruciate: 4 rack 5 grind 7 agonize, torture

exculpate: 4 free 5 clear, remit 6 acquit, excuse, pardon 7 absolve, forgive, justify, release 8 palliate 9 discharge, exonerate, vindicate

excursion: row 4 ride, sail, tour, trip 5 jaunt, sally, tramp 6 cruise, junket, outing, ramble, voyage 7 journey 8 campaign, escapade 10 digression, expedition

excusable: 6 venial 9 allowable 10 defensible, pardonable 11 justifiable

excuse: 4 plea 5 alibi, remit 6 acquit, essoin, pardon 7 absolve, apology, condone, essoign, essoine, forgive, pretext 8 dispense, occasion, overlook 9 exculpate, exonerate, extenuate, vindicate

excuss: 7 discard, discuss

execrable: bad 8 accursed, damnable, wretched 9 nefarious 10 abominable, detestable, horrifying

execrate: ban 5 abhor, curse 9 imprecate, objurgate 12 anathematize

execute: do; act 4 hang, kill, obey, play, slay 5 lynch 6 direct, effect, finish, manage 7 conduct, enforce, perform 8 complete 10 accomplish, administer 11 electrocute

execution: 7 garrote, technic 8 garrotte 9 technique 10 fulfilment 11 achievement, fulfillment

executioner: 7 butcher, hangman, headman, lockman 9 deathsman, Jack Ketch

executive: 4 dean 5 mayor 7 cashier, manager, premier 8 governor, official 9 president 13 administrator

executor: 4 doer 5 agent 8 enforcer 9 performer 13 administrator

exegesis: 10 exposition 11 explanation 14 interpretation

exemplar: 5 model 7 example, pattern 9 archetype

exemplary: 8 laudable 11 commendable 12 praiseworthy

exemplification: 7 example 12 illustration

exemplify: 10 illustrate

exemplum: 7 example 12 illustration

exempt: 4 exon, free 6 fidate 7 exclude, release 8 excepted 9 discharge 11 exceptional

exemption: 7 freedom 8 immunity 12 dispensation

exenterate: 10 disembowel, eviscerate

exequy: 4 rite 7 obsequy 8 ceremony 10 procession

exercise: ply, ure, use 5 drill, etude, exert, longe 6 employ, lesson, parade, praxis, school 7 aufgabe, display, problem 8 activity, practice 9 athletics 10 exhibition, gymnastics, recitation 14 constitutional

exerciser: 5 groom

exert: 4 emit 5 spend 6 reveal, strain 8 endeavor, exercise

exertion: 5 essay, labor, trial 6 action, effort, strife 7 attempt 8 endeavor

exhalation: 5 steam 9 effluvium, emanation 10 expiration 11 evaporation

exhale: 4 cast, emit 6 expire 7 breathe, respire 9 transpire

exhaust: sap 4 emit, fail, jade 5 break, drain, empty, peter, waste, weary 6 abrade, overdo 7 deplete, deprive, fatigue 8 evacuate 9 discharge 10 impoverish

exhausted: 4 done, worn 5 blown, spent, tired 6 barren, beaten, effete 7 emptied, fordone 8 consumed, foredone, forspent 10 forwearied

exhausting: 7 arduous

exhaustion: 7 fatigue 9 depletion, inanition, lassitude 11 exinanition, prostration

exheredate: 10 disinherit

exhibit: air 4 fair, shew, show 5 stage 6 blazon, evince, expose, ostend, parade, reveal 7 approve, display, perform, produce 8 disclose, discover, emblazon, evidence, manifest 9 represent 11 demonstrate

exhibition: 4 fair, show 5 sight 6 salary 7 display, pageant, pension, present 8 exercise 9 allowance, cosmorama, spectacle 10 exposition, sustenance 11 maintenance 13 manifestation 14 representation

exhibitioner: 8 servitor

exhilarate: 5 cheer, elate 7 animate, enliven, gladden 10 invigorate

exhilarated: rad 9 ebullient

exhilaration: 6 gaiety 7 jollity 8 gladness, hilarity 9 merriment 10 joyousness

exhort: 4 urge, warn 6 advise, dehort, incite, preach 7 caution 8 admonish 9 encourage

exhortation: 6 advice 7 counsel 9 hortation

exhume: dig 5 delve 7 unearth 8 disinter, exhumate

exigency: 4 need, want 7 urgency 8 juncture

exigent: 5 vital 8 critical, exacting, pressing 13 indispensable

exiguity: 7 paucity

exile: 4 poor, ruin, thin 5 expel 6 deport, outlaw, scanty 7 outcast, refugee, slender 8 fugitive 9 devastate, foreigner, ostracize 10 banishment, expatriate 12 proscription

exility: 7 tenuity 8 fineness, subtlety, thinness 9 smallness 10 meagerness 11 slenderness

eximious: 6 choice, select 9 excellent

exinanition: 9 abasement 10 exhaustion 11 humiliation

exist: am, be, is; are 4 live
at same time: 15 contemporaneous
in name only: 7 nominal, titular
passively: 7 subsist 8 vegetate

existed: was 4 been, were, wert

existence: ens 4 esse, life, sein 5 being 6 entity, inesse 7 essence, reality 9 actuality
pert. to: 5 ontal, ontic

existent: 4 real 5 alive, being 6 extant 8 existing

exit: 4 door, gate 5 going, leave 6 egress, exitus, outlet 7 outgate, passage 8 debouche 9 departure

exitus: 4 exit 5 issue 6 exodus, outlet 7 outcome

exlex: 6 outlaw

exode: 9 departure 10 afterpiece

exodus: 5 exody 6 exitus 9 migration

exonerate: 4 free 5 clear 6 acquit, excuse, exoner, unload 7 absolve, relieve 9 disburden, discharge, exculpate, vindicate

exorbitant: 5 undue 8 abnormal 9 deviating, excessive, wandering 10 immoderate, outrageous 11 extravagant 12 extortionate, unreasonable

exordium: 7 preface 9 beginning 12 introduction

exotic: 5 alien 7 foreign, strange 9 glamorous, peregrine 10 extraneous, outlandish

expand: ope, wax 4 blow, bulk, flue, grow, open 5 splay, swell, widen 6 dilate, extend, spread, unfold, unfurl 7 amplify, balloon, broaden, develop, diffuse, display, distend, educate, enlarge, explain, inflate, stretch 8 dispread, increase, lengthen 9 disspread, expatiate, explicate, intumesce

expanded: 8 patulous

expanse: 4 area, room 5 reach, tract 6 extent, spread 7 stretch 8 separate
vast: 5 ocean 6 desert, empire

expansion: ala 6 growth 8 increase 9 extension 10 dilatation, distention 11 development, enlargement

expansive: 4 free 5 broad 6 genial 7 elastic, liberal 8 spacious 9 bombastic, diffusive, grandiose

expatiate: 5 dwell 6 dilate, expand, spread 7 broaden, descant, diffuse, enlarge

expatriation: 5 exile 10 banishment

expect: 4 deem, hope, stay, trow, wait, ween 5 await 6 attend, demand 7 require, suppose 9 calculate 10 anticipate

expectation: 9 esperance

expectorate: 4 spit

expedient: 4 wise 5 dodge, knack 6 device 7 politic, stopgap 9 advisable, makeshift 10 profitable 12 advantageous

expedite: hie 4 easy, free 5 hurry, speed 6 hasten 7 quicken 8 dispatch 9 expediate 10 accelerate, facilitate

expedition: 4 fare, trek 5 drave(Sc.), haste, hurry 6 safari, voyage 7 crusade, journey 8 progress 9 excursion

expeditious: 4 fast 5 hasty, quick, rapid, ready 6 prompt, speedy

expel: 4 oust 5 eject, evict, exile 6 banish, deport 7 exclude 8 dislodge, forjudge 9 discharge, eliminate, forejudge 10 dispossess, expatriate

expend: 5 spend, waste 6 occupy, ponder 7 dispend, overuse 9 dissipate 10 distribute

expenditure: 4 cost 5 outgo 6 outlay 10 lavishment 11 consumption 12 disbursement

expense: 4 cost, loss 5 batta, price 6 charge, gersum, outlay 8 overhead 11 consumption, expenditure 12 disbursement

expensive: 4 dear, high 6 costly, lavish 7 liberal 11 dispendious, extravagant

experience: see 4 feel, have, live, test 5 assay, skill, taste, trial 6 ordeal, suffer 7 calvary, feeling, undergo 9 adventure, knowledge

experienced: had, met 6 expert 7 veteran 9 practiced, underwent

experiment: try **4** test **5** assay, essay, trial **7** attempt

experimental: **9** empirical, tentative

expert: ace, dab **4** deft, good **5** adept **6** adroit. artist, au fait, clever. habile **7** artiste(F.), capable, skilled **9** authority **10** proficient **11** experienced **12** professional

expertness: **8** facility **9** dexterity, expertise

expiate: **5** atone, avert **6** assoil **10** propitiate

expiatory: **8** piacular

expiration: end **5** death **10** exhalation, extinction **11** termination

expire: die, end **4** emit **5** expel, lapse **6** elapse, exhale, perish

expiry: **5** close, death **10** extinction **11** termination

explain: **4** rede **5** aread areed, gloze, solve **6** define, expand, unfold **7** expound **8** describe, exegesis, manifest **9** elucidate, enucleate, explicate, interpret **10** understand

explanation: key **7** account, apology **10** exposition **11** description **13** clarification

expletive: gee **4** bosh, egad, gosh, oath **5** begad

explicate: **6** expand, unfold **7** account, explain **9** interpret

explicit: **4** open **5** clear, exact, fixed, plain **7** express, precise **8** absolute, definite, implicit, positive, specific **9** categoric, outspoken **11** categorical, unambiguous, unequivocal **13** unconditional **14** discriminating

explode: **4** fire **5** blast, burst **8** backfire, detonate **9** fulminate

exploit: act **4** deed, feat, gest, milk **5** geste, stunt **7** perform, success **9** advantage **11** achievement, performance

exploits: **9** res gestae(L.)

exploration: **5** probe **6** search **11** examination **13** investigation

explore: map **4** dive, feel **5** chart, range **8** discover

explorer: **4** Cook, Eric **5** Bruce, Cabot, Davis, diver, Drake **6** Baffin, Carter, Cortes, De Soto, Hearne, Hudson **7** pioneer, Pizarro, Raleigh **8** Amundsen, Columbus, Magellan, Vespucci **9** Frobisher **10** Chancellor, discoverer

explosion: pop **5** blast **6** blow-up, report **8** outburst **10** detonation

explosive: TNT **4** mine **6** amatol, powder, tonite **7** ammonal, lyddite, melnite **8** cheddite, dynamite, eruptive **9** fulminate, guncotton **10** detonative **13** nitroglycerin **15** trinitrotoluene

device: cap **6** petard **9** initiator

place of manufacture: **4** lydd

projectile: **5** shell **7** grenade **9** cartridge

exponent: **9** explainer, expounder **11** interpreter **14** representative

expose: **4** bare, open, risk **5** strip **6** bewray, detect, reveal, unmask **7** display, exhibit, expound, pillory, publish, uncover, unearth **8** disclose, discover, muckrake, ridicule, satirize, unclothe **10** exposition, jeopardize

exposed: **6** unsafe **11** unprotected

exposition: **4** fair **5** tract **6** expose **8** analysis, exegesis, exposure, treatise **10** exhibition, expounding **11** declaration, explanation **14** interpretation

expostulate: **5** argue **7** discuss, examine, protest **8** complain **11** remonstrate

expound: **5** gloze, treat **6** define, expose **7** develop, explain, exposit, express **8** construe **9** interpret

express: **4** vent **5** emote, opine, speak, state, utter, voice **6** denote, direct, phrase **7** declare, dictate, expound, testify **8** definite, describe, explicit, manifest **9** expatiate **10** articulate, particular, peremptory

expression: **4** form, pose, show, sign, term, word **5** idiom, token, voice **6** byword, oracle, phrase, symbol **8** laconism **9** euphemism, statement, utterance **10** holophrase **11** delineation, holophrasis **13** manifestation **14** representation

facial: **4** grin, **5** laugh, scowl, smile **7** grimace

hackneyed: **6** cliche

mathematical: **8** equation

metaphorical: **6** figure

of approval: **4** clap **5** smile **7** ovation **8** applause

of assent: **6** placet

of contempt: bah, fie **4** geck, hiss **5** pshaw, sneer

of gratitude: **12** thanksgiving

of incredulity: **6** indeed

of opinion: **4** vote

of sorrow: ay **4** alas **11** lamentation

of weariness: **4** sigh

expressionless: **5** stony **6** vacant **8** toneless

expressive: **6** poetic **8** eloquent, emphatic **10** indicative **11** significant

expressly: **6** namely

exprobrate: **7** censure, upbraid **8** reproach

expugn: **5** storm **6** attack **8** vanquish

expulsion: **5** exile **6** bounce **8** ejection **10** banishment

expunge: **4** blot, dele **5** erase **6** cancel, delete, efface, excise **7** destroy, scratch **10** annihilate, obliterate

expurgate: **4** gelt **5** purge

exquisite: fop **4** dude, nice **5** dandy, exact **6** choice, dainty **7** careful, elegant, refined **8** affected, delicate **9** beautiful, delicious, excellent, matchless, perfected, recherche **10** consummate, farfetched, fastidious **12** accomplished **14** discriminating

exsanguine: **6** anemic **9** bloodless

exscind: **6** excise **9** extirpate

exsert: 8 protrude
exsiccate: dry
exsuccous: dry 7 sapless
extant: 5 alive, being 6 living 7 visible 8 existing, manifest 10 protruding 11 protuberant
extempore: 7 affloof(Sc.), offhand 9 forthwith 11 immediately 14 extemporaneous, unpremeditated
extend: eke, lie, run 4 grow, rise, span 5 bulge, cover, reach, renew, seize, widen 6 amount, deepen, deploy, dilate, expand, spread, strain 7 amplify, broaden, diffuse, display, distend, enlarge, overlap, overrun, proffer, prolong, radiate, stretch 8 continue, increase, lengthen, protract, protrude 10 exaggerate, generalize
extended: 4 long, open 12 outstretched
extending widely: far
extension: 4 area 5 scope 8 addendum, addition, duration, increase 9 expansion 11 enlargement 12 augmentation 13 amplification
building: ell 4 wing 6 lean-to
of time: 4 stay 7 respite 8 reprieve
trench: sap
extensive: 4 vast, wide 5 ample, broad, large 7 immense 8 expanded 9 capacious 10 widespread 11 far-reaching 13 comprehensive
extent: due, tax 4 area, body, bulk, levy, writ 5 ambit, limit, range, reach, scope, space 6 amount, attack, degree, spread 7 acreage, assault, breadth, compass, expanse, seizure 8 increase, latitude, quantity 9 dimension, extension, magnitude, territory, valuation 10 assessment
extenuate: 4 thin 5 gloze 6 excuse, lessen, weaken 8 diminish, palliate 9 alleviate, attenuate, disparage, underrate 10 depreciate 13 underestimate
extenuation: 10 dimunition
exterior: 5 ectad, ectal, outer, shell 6 extern 7 outside, outward, surface 8 external
exterminate: 5 expel 6 uproot 7 abolish, destroy 9 eradicate, extirpate 10 annihilate
extern: 7 outward 8 exterior, external 9 extrinsic
external: out 5 outer 6 extern 7 outside, outward 8 exterior 9 extrinsic 10 peripheral 11 superficial
comb. form: 4 ecto
extinct: 4 dead 7 defunct 8 quenched 12 extinguished
extinction: 5 death 6 expiry 9 abolition 10 expiration 11 destruction 12 annihilation, obliteration
extinguish: 4 dout 5 annul, choke, douse, dowse, quell 6 quench, stanch, stifle 7 destroy, eclipse, obscure, staunch 8 suppress 9 suffocate 10 annihilate
extinguished: 4 dead 7 extinct

extirpate: 4 dele 5 erase, expel 6 excise, uproot 7 destroy, exscind 8 supplant 9 eradicate 10 annihilate, deracinate 11 exterminate
extirpation: 8 excision 11 destruction, eradication 12 annihilation
extol, extoll: 4 laud 5 bless, exalt 6 praise 7 applaud, commend, elevate, enhance, glorify 8 emblazon, eulogize 9 celebrate
extort: 5 exact, force, wrest, wring 6 compel, elicit, wrench 7 extract 9 blackmail
extortion 7 bribery 8 chantage, exaction, rapacity 10 oppression, overcharge
extortionate: 4 hard 9 excessive 10 exorbitant, oppressive
extortioner: 6 poller, shaver 11 blackmailer
extra: odd 4 more, orra(Sc.), over, plus 5 added, spare 7 special, surplus 8 superior 9 accessory, lagniappe 10 additional
extract: dig, pry 4 cite, draw, pull 5 educe, exact, quote, steep, wring 6 decoct, deduce, derive, elicit, evulse, extort, remove, render 7 descent, essence, estreat, excerpt, exhaust, summary 8 withdraw 9 decoction, quotation 11 preparation
extraction: 5 birth, stock 6 origin 7 descent, essence, extract 8 breeding, tincture 9 parentage
extraneous: 5 outer 6 exotic 7 foreign 9 extrinsic 10 accidental
extraordinary: odd 4 rare, unco(Sc.) 5 byous(Sc.), enorm 6 signal 7 notable, special, strange, unusual 8 abnormal, singular, uncommon 9 irregular, monstrous, wonderful 10 additional, phenomenal, remarkable, surprising, tremendous 11 exceptional 13 distinguished
extravagance: ela
extravagant: 4 wild 5 outre 6 costly, heroic, lavish 7 baroque, bizarre, fanatic, nimious, profuse, vagrant 8 prodigal, reckless, romantic, wanderer, wasteful 9 excessive, expensive, fantastic, luxurious 10 exorbitant, thriftless 11 dispendious 12 unreasonable, unrestrained
extreme: 4 last, rank, sore 5 close, final, great, limit, ultra, undue, utter 6 heroic, severe, utmost 7 drastic, forward, howling, intense, outward, radical, violent 8 devilish, farthest, greatest, terrible, terrific 9 desperate, excessive, outermost, stringent, uttermost 10 conclusive, immoderate
extremely: so 4 very 6 mighty 10 mortacious 11 exceedingly
extremist: 7 radical
extremity: end, tip 4 need, tail 5 close, limit, verge 6 border 8 disaster, terminal 9 bitter end
extricate: 4 free 5 clear, loose 6 rescue 8 liberate, untangle 9 disengage 10 disembroil 11 disentangle

extrinsic: 5 every **7** foreign, outward **8** external **10** accidental, extraneous, incidental **11** unessential **12** adventitious, nonessential

extrude: 4 spew **5** eject, expel **7** project **8** protrude

exuberance: 6 plenty **8** overflow **9** abundance, profusion **11** excrescence **14** superabundance

exuberant: 6 lavish **7** copious, fertile, rampart **8** effusive **9** abounding, excessive, luxuriant, plentiful

exudation: gum, lac, sap, tar **5** pitch, resin, rosin **9** discharge, secretion

exude: 4 emit, ooze **5** sweat **7** secrete **8** perspire **9** discharge, percolate

exult: 4 crow, leap **5** boast, gloat, glory **6** spring **7** rejoice

exultant: 6 elated

exultation: joy **7** rapture **10** jubilation

exulted: 6 prided **7** vaunted

exuviate: 4 molt **5** moult

eyas: 4 bird **8** nestling

eye: ee(Sc.); orb **4** disc, gaze, glim, lamp, loop, mien, ogle, scan, view **5** glare, watch **6** behold, goggle, oculus(L.), peeper, regard, vision **7** blinker, observe, witness **10** scrutinize **11** discernment

black: **5** mouse **6** shiner

covering: **6** eyelid **9** blindfold

defect: **4** cast **6** anopia, myopia **11** astigmatism

disease: **6** iritis **8** glaucoma, trachoma **14** conjunctivitis

hollow: **5** orbit **6** socket

instrument for examining: **8** otoscope **14** ophthalmoscope

part: **4** disc, iris, uvea **5** pupil **6** areola, cornea, retina

pert. to: **5** irian, optic **7** areolar, corneal, retinal **9** ocellated

science: **13** ophthalmology

simple: **6** ocelli(pl.) **7** ocellus

eye-like: 9 ocellated

eyebrow: 4 bree(Sc.) **6** eebree(Sc.)

eyeglasses: 5 specs **6** lenses **7** lorgnon, nippers **8** monocles, pince-nez **9** lorgnette

eyelash: 4 lash **5** cilia(pl.) **6** cilium

loss: **9** madarosis

eyelet: 6 agrafe, gromet, oillet **7** agraffe **8** peephole **10** buttonhole **11** perforation

eyeleteer: 6 bodkin **8** stiletto

eyelid: *drooping of:* **6** ptosis

pert. to: **9** blepharal

eyer: 8 beholder **9** spectator

eyeshot: 5 range, reach

eyesight: 4 view **5** sight **11** observation

eyesome: 11 good-looking

eyetooth: 6 cuspid

eyot: ait **5** islet

eyra: 7 wildcat

F

fabes: 10 gooseberry
fabian: 8 cautious
fabiform: 10 bean-shaped
fable: 4 myth, tale **5** feign, story **6** legend
7 fiction, parable, untruth **8** allegory,
apologue **9** falsehood, narrative **10** fabu-
losity
fabric: rep, web **4** felt, repp **5** baize, beige,
build, crepe, frame, lisle, rayon, serge,
terry, tulle **6** creton, etoile **7** texture **8**
cretonne, material **9** construct, cottonade
calico: **5** sallo **6** sallco
cotton: **4** susi **5** pique, wigan **6** burrah **7**
buckram, galatea, hickory **8** bourette
cotton knit: **10** balbriggan
cotton of light quality: **4** leno **7** jaconet,
organza **9** silka line
cotton mixture: **6** mashru **7** delaine, satinet, zanella **9** bombasine, grusaille
cotton print: **6** calico **7** percale **8** cretonne
cotton with silk embroidery: **8** agabanee
cotton twilled: **5** denim, sallo **6** sallco **7**
fustian, silesia
curtain material: **4** leno **5** scrim **6** moreen, velvet **7** silesia
finisher: **6** beetle
flag material: **7** buntine, bunting
linen: **4** crea(Sp.), ecru **5** carde, crash **6**
barras **7** buckram, drabbet, sinelon
linen and cotton: **9** huckaback
linen of light quality: **4** lawn **5** scrim
old: **9** ciclatoun
satin: **5** pekin **6** etoile
satin imitation: **6** sateen
silk: **4** alma, gimp, gros, ikat **5** caffa,
carde, crepe, ninon, rumal, satin, surah **6**
blatta, camaka, patola, samite **7** alamode,
chiffon, Xmantua, taffeta **8** barathea,
bourette, sarcenet, sarsenet **9** charmeuse,
levantine, matelasse **10** bombay-cine
silk (thin): **4** moff **5** tulle **6** pongee **7** hernani **8** eolienne
silk and cotton: **6** crepon, gloria **9** bombasine, bombazine
silk and linen: **8** brocatel **10** brocatelle
silk and wool: **6** crepon, gloria **7** challie,
challis **8** eolienne
silk imitation: **5** rayon **7** satinet
silk mixture: kin **4** acca **5** balda **6** mashru
7 grogram **9** baldachin, baldaquin, faran-
dine
silk-ribbed: rep **4** repp **6** faille **7** epingle **8**
marocain
silk yarn: **7** schappe

straw: mat **7** matting
striped: aba
suiting: **6** dacron **7** acrilan
surface: nap
synthetic: **5** nylon, orlon, rayon **7** plastic
textile: rep **5** moire **7** etamine
texture: **4** woof
thin: **5** gauze **8** gossamer, tarlatan **9**
grenadine
Turkish: **6** agaric **7** chekmak **8** cottonee
10 terry cloth
twilled: **4** alma **5** sallo, serge, surah **6** co-
burg, sallco **8** corduroy, shalloon, whipcord **9** bombasine, bombazine, gabardine,
levantine, messaline, tricotine **10** ker-
seymere
unbleached: **5** beige
upholstery: rep **4** repp **6** frieze **7** tabaret
velvet-like: **5** panne **6** velure **8** duvetine **9**
velveteen
waste material: **5** mungo
waterproof: **8** burberry
white: **8** coteline
wide: **6** cotele
wool: **5** baize, beige, casha, serge, tweed
6 burnet, frisca, moreen **7** bolivia, de-
beige, delaine, droguet, frisado, frizado,
hernani, worsted **8** cataloon, harateen,
rattinet, zibeline **9** catalowne, gabardine,
grenadine, harrateen, montagnac, zibelline
wool (coarse): **6** djersa, duffel, kersey,
witney **7** bocking
wool dress: **5** beige **7** delaine **8** wildbore **9**
grenadine
wool mixture: **7** delaine, zanella **9** gri-
saille
wool-ribbed: rep **4** repp **8** marocain
worsted: **7** etamine
woven: **4** lame **5** tweed, twill **6** tissue, tricot **7** blanket, damasse, textile
fabricate: 4 coin, form, make, mint **5**
build, frame **6** devise, invent **7** concoct,
fashion, produce **8** contrive **9** construct
11 manufacture
fabrication: lie **7** fiction, forgery, untruth
8 pretense **9** falsehood
fabricator: 4 liar **6** forger **12** manufacturer
fabricature: 9 structure **12** construction
fabula: 5 story
fabulist: 4 liar **5** Aesop
fabulous: 7 feigned **8** mythical, romantic
9 legendary **10** apocryphal, fictitious **11**
astonishing

facade: 4 face 5 front

face: map, mug, pan 4 dare, defy, dial, leer, line, meet, moue 5 cover, front, stand 6 facade, oppose, veneer, visage 7 feature, grimace, surface 8 confront, envisage 9 encounter, semblance 11 countenance, physiognomy
artery: 9 maxillary
bone: 5 malar 6 zygoma 7 maxilia 8 manduble
covering: 4 mask, veil
defect: 7 harelip
false: 4 mask
ornament: 4 veil 5 jewel, patch 9 cosmetics
paint: 4 fard 6 parget
part: eye, jaw, lid, lip 4 brow, chin, nose 5 cheek

face eastward: 9 orientate

face-to-face: 7 affront, vis-a-vis

face value: par

facer: 6 bumper 7 tankard

facet: 5 bezel, culet, phase

facete: 5 witty 9 facetious

facetious: 5 witty 6 facete, jocose 7 jocular 8 humorous, expertness 9 laughable

facia: 5 plate 6 tablet

facient: 4 doer 5 agent

facile: 4 able, easy 5 quick, ready 6 expert, fluent, gentle 7 affable, lenient

facilitate: aid 4 ease, help 5 speed 6 assist 8 expedite

facility: art 4 ease 5 eclat, knack, skill 7 address, freedom 9 dexterity, readiness 10 adroitness, expertness, pliability

facing: 5 front, panel 6 veneer 7 surface 8 covering, opposite
inward: 8 introrse
outward: 8 extrorse

facsimile: 4 copy 5 model 7 replica 9 duplicate imitation 10 similitude 11 counterpart

fact: 4 data(pl.), deed, fait(F.) 5 datum, event, truth 6 factum(L.) 7 keynote, lowdown, reality 9 actuality 12 circumstance
support: 15 circumstantiate

faction: 4 bloc, sect, side 5 cabal, junto, party 6 brigue, clique 7 dispute, quarrel 8 intrigue 9 concision 11 combination

factious: 9 seditious 11 dissentious

factitious: 4 sham 9 unnatural 10 artificial

factor: gen 4 doer, gene 5 agent, maker 6 author, detail 7 bailiff, factrix, steward 8 adherent, aumildar, gomashta, gomastah 11 chamberlain, constituent

factory: 4 mill, shop 5 plant 6 aurang, aurung 8 building, fabrique(F.), officina(Sp.), workshop 11 manufactory 13 establishment
book: 7 bindery

factual: 4 real, true 6 actual 7 literal

factum: 4 fact 5 event 8 memorial

faculty: wit 4 ease, gift 6 talent 7 ability 8 aptitude, capacity

fad: 4 rage, whim 5 craze, fancy, hobby 7 crochet, fashion 9 amusement

faddle: 6 trifle 8 nonsense

fade: 4 die, dim, dow, wan 4 flat, pale, vade, wilt 5 daver, decay, passe, peter 6 perish, vanish, wither 7 decline, insipid, lighten 8 diminish, discolor, dissolve, evanesce, languish 11 commonplace
camera device: 4 iris 9 diaphragm

fadge: fit 4 suit 6 bundle 7 succeed

faerie: See **fairy**.

Faerie Queen: *author:* 7 Spenser
character: Una 4 Alma 5 Guyon 6 Amoret 7 Artegal 8 Calidore, Gloriana 11 Britomartis

Faeroes: *district manager:* 4 foud
island: 6 Ostero
whirlwind: oe

Fafnir's slayer: 6 Sigurd 7 Sigurth 9 Siegfried

fag: 4 flag, tire, toil 5 droop, weary 6 drudge, menial 7 exhaust, fatigue, frazzle 9 cigarette

fagot, faggot: 5 fadge 6 bundle

faik: 6 lessen

fail: ebb 4 flag, fold, lose, sink, wane 5 flunk, peter 6 desert, falter 7 exhaust, flicker, founder 8 languish

failing: 5 fault 6 foible 7 blemish, frailty, weakness 9 infirmity 10 deficiency 11 delinquency, diminishing 12 imperfection

failure: dud 4 bust, flop, lack, loss, miss 5 bilge, decay, fault, lapse, lemon 6 fiasco, fizzle 7 bloomer, debacle, decline, default, neglect 8 abortion, collapse, omission 10 bankruptcy, deficiency 11 delinquency, miscarriage, shortcoming 13 deterioration 14 disappointment

fain: 4 fond, glad 5 eager 7 pleased, willing 8 desirous, inclined 11 constrained

fainaigue: 5 shirk 6 revoke, renege

faineant: 4 idle, lazy 5 idler 8 inactive, sluggard

fainness: 8 gladness 9 eagerness 11 willingness

faint: dim 4 dark, pale, pall, soft, weak 5 swoon, timid, waugh 6 evanid, feeble, sickly, 7 feigned, languid, obscure, syncope 8 cowardly, delicate, languish, listless, sluggish, timorous 9 simulated 10 indistinct

faintheart: 5 timid 6 afraid, craven 8 cowardly, timorous

faintness: 7 tenuity 8 weakness 9 dejection 10 feebleness 12 timorousness 16 faintheartedness

fair: 4 calm, even, just, mart 5 bazar, blond, clear, feria(L.), right 6 bazaar, blonde, decent, honest, kermis 7 exhibit, kermess 8 distinct, middling, unbiased 9 beautiful, equitable, impartial 10 auspicious, exhibition, reasonable 12 unprejudiced 13 disinterested, dispassionate

fair-haired: 5 blond 6 blonde

fairest: 6 flower

fairly: 4 well 7 plainly 8 properly, suitably 9 favorably, tolerably 10 handsomely 12 legitimately

fairness: 6 equity 7 honesty 8 equality 12 impartiality

fairy: elf, fay, hob, imp 4 perl, pixy, puck, shee, vila 5 pixie, sidhe 6 faerie, spirit, yaksha, yakshi 7 banshee, sylphid 8 folletto 10 leprechaun 11 enchantress

abode: 4 shee 5 sidhe

chief: 4 Puck

king: 6 Oberon

queen: Mab, Una 7 Titania

fairy-like: 5 elfin

fairyland: 7 elfland

fait: 4 deed, fact

faith: 5 certy(Sc.), creed, troth, trust 6 belief, certie(Sc.), credit 8 affiance, reliance 9 bona fides 10 confidence

article: 5 tenet 8 credenda 9 credendum

faithful: 4 fast, feal, firm, leal, true 5 liege, loyal, pious, tried 6 honest, steady, trusty 7 devoted, sincere 8 accurate, constant 9 steadfast, veracious 13 conscientious

faithfulness: 8 fidelity

faithless: 5 false, punic 6 fickle, hollow, unjust, untrue 7 atheist 8 apostate, delusive, disloyal, shifting, unstable 9 deceptive, mercurial 10 inconstant, perfidious 11 disaffected, incredulous, treacherous 12 unsatisfying

faithlessness: 7 falsity, perfidy, untruth 8 betrayal 10 infidelity

faitour: 5 cheat 8 imposter

fake: 4 hoax, sham 5 bogus, cheat, false, feign, fudge, phony 7 falsify, furbish, pretend, swindle 8 simulate, spurious 9 imitation 10 fictitious, fraudulent 11 counterfeit, manufacture

faker: 5 quack 6 humbug 7 peddler 9 charlatan, pretender

fakir: 7 dervish 9 mendicant

falbala: 7 flounce 8 furbelow, trimming

falcon: 4 hawk 5 hobby, saker 6 lanner, luggar, lugger, merlin, musket, tercel 7 kestrel 9 peregrine

falconer: 6 hawker 8 ostreger 10 austringer

summons: wo

fall: sag 4 drip, drop, flop, plop, ruin, ruse, sile, sink, slip 5 abate, cloit(Sc.), crash, hance, lapse, plump, rapid, shoot, slump 6 autumn, happen, perish, recede, season, topple, tumble 7 cascade, decline, degrade, depress, descend, devolve, dribble, escheat, plummet, retreat, stumble, subside 8 cataract, collapse, commence, decrease 9 backslide, prostrate, surrender 10 capitulate, depreciate, disappoint 11 precipitate

back: 6 recede 7 relapse, retreat

in: 4 cave 5 agree, lapse 6 concur 9 terminate

short: shy 4 fail, lack, miss

fallacious: sly 6 untrue 8 delusive, guileful, illusory 9 deceitful, deceptive, insidious 10 fraudulent, misleading 11 treacherous

fallacy: 5 error 6 idolum

fallfish: 4 chub

fallible: 7 errable

falling: 6 cadent 8 prolapse, windfall 10 subsidence

fallout: 9 radiation

fallow: 4 pale 6 barren 9 yellow-red, yellowish 12 uncultivated

fallow deer: 6 damine

false: 4 fake, sham 5 bogus, fause(Sc.), paste, phony, wrong 6 fickle, hollow, pseudo, untrue 7 bastard, crooked, feigned 8 disloyal, illusive, recreant, spurious 9 deceitful, deceptive, dishonest, erroneous, faithless, incorrect, insincere, irregular, pretended 10 apocryphal, artificial, calumnious, fictitious, groundless, mendacious, misleading, perfidious, traitorous, untruthful 11 counterfeit, disaffected, treacherous, unveracious 12 hypocritical

prefix: 6 pseudo

falsehood: cog fib, lie 4 flam, tale 5 fable 7 falsity, fiction, perfidy, romance, untruth 8 roorback 9 deception, duplicity, imposture, mendacity, treachery 10 pseudology 11 fabrication

falsify: lie 4 fake 5 belie, feint, forge 6 betray, doctor 7 violate 9 dissemble 10 adulterate 11 counterfeit

falsity: lie 5 error 7 untruth 9 falsehood, falseness, mendacity 13 deceitfulness, faithlessness 17 untrustworthiness

show: 5 belie 8 disprove

Falstaff's follower: Nym 6 Pistol

falter: 4 fail 5 pause, waver 6 boggle, flinch, totter 7 fribble, stumble, tremble 8 hesitate

faltering: 4 hink

Fama: 5 rumor

fame: 5 bruit, glory, honor, kudos, rumor 6 renown, report, repute 7 hearsay 9 celebrity 10 reputation

famed: 5 known, noted 7 eminent, renomee(F.) 11 illustrious, outstanding 13 distinguished

familiar: 4 bold, cozy, easy, free, tosh 5 usual 6 common, homely, versed 7 affable 8 frequent, habitual, intimate, sociable 9 customary, household, presuming, well-known 10 accustomed, conversant 12 acquaintance 13 unconstrained

familiarize: 4 haft 8 accustom 9 habituate 10 naturalize

family: lik, kin 4 clan 5 class, flesh, group, house 6 cletch 7 kindred, lineage, progeny **8** category **9** household **10** generation

head: **7** goodman, husband **9** patriarch **11** householder **13** pater familias(L.)

famine: **6** dearth, hunger **8** scarcity **10** starvation **11** destitution

famish: **4** kill **6** starve **7** destroy

famous: **5** grand, noted **6** namely **7** eminent, namable, notable **8** renowned **9** excellent, notorious **10** celebrated, celebrious **11** conspicuous, outstanding **13** distinguished

famulus: **7** servant **9** attendant

fan: **4** beat, cool **5** punka **6** basket, blower, colmar, punkah, rooter, shovel, spread, winnow **7** admirer, devotee **8** follower **9** flabellum, propeller **10** enthusiast

alluvial: **5** delta

fan-shaped: **10** flabellate

fanal: **5** light **6** beacon

fanatic: mad **5** bigot, crazy, rabid, ultra **6** zealot **7** devotee **8** frenetic **9** energumen, phrenetic **10** enthusiast, monomaniac **11** extravagant

fancied: **6** unreal **7** dreamed **9** imaginary **10** fictitious

fanciful: odd **5** ideal, queer **6** dreamy, quaint, unreal **7** bizarre, strange **8** romantic **9** conceited, fantasque, fantastic, grotesque, visionary, whimsical **10** capricious, chimerical, notionable **11** imaginative, unrealistic

fancy: fad **4** idea, love, maze, ween, whim **5** dream, freak, guess, humor **6** humour, ideate, liking, megrim, notion, ornate, vagary, vision, whimsy **7** caprice, chimera, conceit, crochet, fantasy, romance, suspect **8** chimaera, conceive, illusion, phantasm, phantasy **9** capriccio, fantaisie **10** conception, conjecture, decorative, impression, ornamental **11** imagination, inclination

fane: **4** flag **6** banner, church, temple **7** pennant **9** cathedral, sanctuary **11** weathercock

fanfare: **7** tantara **8** fanfaron, flourish **9** fanfarade **11** fanfaronade

fanfaron: **7** boaster, fanfare **8** braggart **9** swaggerer

fanfaronade: **7** bluster, fanfare **8** boasting **10** swaggering **11** ostentation

fanfoot: **5** gecko **6** lizard

fang: **4** earn, take, tusk, vang **5** begin, seize, snare, tooth **6** assume, obtain **7** capture, procure **9** undertake

fangle: **4** mode **5** dress **6** geegaw **7** fashion

fanion: **4** flag **6** guidon

fanon: **4** cape **5** orale **7** maniple

fantasque: **4** whim **5** fancy **7** fantasy **8** fanciful **9** fantastic

fantast: **7** dreamer **9** visionary

fantastic: odd **5** queer **6** absurd, unreal **7** bizarre **8** fanciful, freakish, romantic, singular **9** fantasque, grotesque, whimsical **10** capricious, chimerical **11** extravagant, imaginative **12** unbelievable

fantasy: **4** idea **5** dream, fancy **6** desire, vision **7** caprice, chimera, phantom, romance **8** chimaera, phantasm **9** fantasque **10** apparition **11** imagination, inclination **13** hallucination

fantom: See **phantom.**

far: **4** long **6** remote **7** distant

across: **4** wide

comb. form: tel **4** tele

down: **4** deep

far-reaching: **4** deep, vast **7** intense **8** profound

faraway: **6** dreamy, remote **7** distant **10** abstracted

farce: **4** mime **5** stuff **6** comedy **7** mockery **8** drollery **9** forcemeat

farceur: wag **5** joker

farcical: **5** comic, droll **7** Atellan **9** ludicrous **10** ridiculous

fardel: lot **4** furl, pack **6** bundle, burden **10** collection

fare: eat **4** diet, food, path, rate, wend **5** cheer, going, price, track, viand **6** happen, travel **7** journey, passage, proceed, prosper **8** progress **9** equipment, passenger, provision, sagaciate **10** expedition **11** nourishment **13** entertainment

farer: **8** traveler

farewell: ave(L.) **4** vale(L.) **5** adieu, adios, aloha, conge, final **7** goodbye, leaving, parting **9** bon voyage, departure **11** valedictory

farfetched: **6** forced **7** devious **8** strained **9** recherche **10** roundabout

farina: **4** meal **5** flour **6** starch

farinaceous food: oat, rye **4** meal **5** flour, grain, salep, spelt, wheat **6** barley, cereal **7** pudding **10** cornstarch

farm: **4** till **5** croft, empty, haras, ranch, range **6** barton, chacra, grange, rancho **7** cleanse, hennery, potrero **8** estancia, hatchery, hacienda **9** cultivate, farmstead

building: **4** barn, crib, shed, silo **7** farmery

laborer: **4** hand, hind

machine: See **agriculture** *machine;* **machine** *farm.*

steward: **7** granger

tenant: **6** cotter **7** cottier, cropper, metayer **12** sharecropper

farm out: let **4** hire

farmer: **4** tate **6** grower, tiller yeoman **7** granger, hayseed, planter, plowman, rancher **8** producer **9** hacendero(Sp.), ploughman **10** cultivator, husbandman **13** agriculturist

farmhouse: **6** grange **7** caserio(Sp.), onstead(Sc.)

farmland: **7** acreage

farmyard: **6** barton

farnesol: 7 alcohol
faro: 5 monte
 bet: 7 sleeper
 card: 4 soda
 card combination: 5 split 6 cathop
 player: 6 punter
farouche: shy 4 wild
farrago: 6 medley 7 mixture
farrier: 5 shoer, smith 10 blacksmith, horseshoer 12 veterinarian
farrow: pig, row 4 rake 6 litter
farseeing: 10 telescopic
farsighted: 6 shrewd 9 hyperopia, provident, sagacious 11 foresighted 13 hypermetropia
farther: 6 longer 7 remoter
farthest: 7 endmost, extreme, farmost, longest, outmost 8 remotest 11 farthermost
farthing: 4 coin 8 quadrans
fascia: 4 band, sash 6 fillet 7 molding
fascinate: 5 charm 6 allure, enamor 7 attract, bewitch, enchant, engross, philter, philtre 8 entrance, interest, intrigue 9 captivate, enrapture, spellbind
fascinating: 9 glamorous 10 attractive, glamourous
fascination: 5 charm, spell 11 enchantment
fashion: fad, ton(F.) 4 form, make, mode, mold, rage 5 craze, forge, frame, guise, model, mould, shape, style, vogue 6 create, custom, design, fangle, invent, manner, method 7 compose, portray 8 contrive 9 construct, fabricate
fashionable: 5 dashy, smart 6 modish 7 a la mode, dashing, stylish
fashioned: 6 carved 7 wrought
fast: 4 firm. Lent 5 agile, apace, brisk, fixed, fleet, hasty, quick, rapid, stuck, swift 6 lively, secure, speedy, stable, starve 7 abiding, settled 8 enduring, faithful 9 immovable, indelible, steadfast, unfadable, velocious 10 abstinence, stationary, unyielding 11 expeditious
fasten: bar, fix, pen, pin, tag, tie 4 bend, bind, bolt, clip, gird, girt, glue, knit, lace, lash, link, lock, moor, nail, rope, seal, snib, soud, weld, wire 5 affix, annex, belay, brace, chain, clamp, clasp, cling, latch, paste, rivet, seize, strap, truss 6 anchor, attach, batten, cement, clinch, picket, secure, solder, staple, tether 7 connect, padlock 8 transfix
fastener: bar, gib, nut, pin 4 agal, bolt, frog, hasp, lock, nail, snap 5 catch, clamp, clasp, latch, rivet, screw, strap, thong 6 buckle, button, hatpin, staple, zipper 7 latchet, padlock 8 staylace
fastidious: 4 fine, nice 5 chary, fussy, natty 6 choicy, choosy, dainty 7 choosey, elegant, finical, finicky, haughty, refined 8 critical, delicate, gingerly, overnice, scornful 9 exquisite, finicking, squeamish

10 meticulous, particular 14 overparticular
fastness: 4 fort 6 castle 7 citadel 8 fortress 10 stronghold
fastuous: 7 haughty 8 arrogant 12 ostentatious
fat: oil, tub 4 lard, lipa, rich, suet 5 adeps, brosy, cetin, chuff, ester, fleck, gross, lipid, lipin, obese, plump, podgy, pudgy, pursy, squab, stout, thick 6 fleshy, grease, lipide, portly, pubble, stocky, tallow 7 adipose, blubber, fertile, fulsome, lanolin, opulent, pinguid, stearin 8 extended, fruitful, lanoline, stearine, unctuous 9 corpulent 10 profitable 11 flourishing
 comb. form: 5 steat 6 steato
 liquid: 5 elain, olein 6 elaine, oleine
 pert. to: 6 adipic
 render: try 4 lard
 wool: 7 lanolin 8 lanoline
fatal: fey 4 dire 6 deadly, doomed, funest, lethal, mortal 7 capital, fateful, ominous, ruinous 8 destined 9 condemned, prophetic 10 calamitous, disastrous, pernicious, portentous 11 destructive
fatality: 5 wreck 8 calamity, disaster
fatbird: 8 guacharo
fate: end, lot 4 doom, ruin 5 event, karma 6 chance, kismet 7 destiny, fortune, outcome 8 downfall 14 predestination
 goddess: Ker 4 Norn 5 Tyche 8 Adrastea 9 Adrasteia
fated: 6 doomed 7 decreed 8 destined 10 inevitable
fateful: 5 fatal 6 deadly 7 ominous 9 momentous, prophetic 10 inevitable, portentous 11 destructive, predestined
Fates: *Greek:* 5 Moera, Moira 6 Clotho, Moerae 7 Atropos 8 Lachesis
 Roman: 4 Nona 5 Decum, Morta, Parca 6 Parcae
father: bu(Ar.), pa; abu(Ar.), ama, dad, pop 4 abba, abou(Ar.), baba(Ar.), bapu, papa, pere(F.), sire 5 adopt, babbo, beget, daddy, friar, padre(Sp.), pater(L.), vader(Dan.) 6 old man, parent, priest 7 tatinek(Czech.) 8 beaupere(F.), generate 9 confessor, paternity, procreate 11 acknowledge
 of geometry: 6 Euclid
 of gods and men: 4 Zeus
 of human race: 4 Adam
 of plenty: 8 Abiathar
Father of Waters: 11 Mississippi
fatherhood: 9 paternity
fathom: 5 brace, delve, solve 7 measure 9 penetrate
fathomless: 16 incomprehensible
fatidic: 9 prophetic
fatigue: fag 4 jade, tire 5 spend, weary 6 overdo, taigle(Sc.) 7 exhaust 8 fatigate
fatigued: 4 beat 8 tuckered 9 forjaskit, forjesket

fatiloquent: 9 fatidical, prophetic
Fatima: *husband:* Ali 9 Bluebeard
  descendant: 7 Fatimid 8 Fatimite
fatness: 10 pinguitude
fatten: 4 lard 6 batten, enrich, thrive
fatty: 5 suety 6 greasy 7 adipose, pinguid
  8 unctuous
fatuous: 5 inane, silly 6 stupid, unreal 7
  foolish, idiotic, witless 8 demented, illusory, imbecile 9 frivolous, insensate
faucet: tap 4 cock 5 valve 6 spigot 7 hydrant
faugh: bah
fault: sin 4 debt, flaw, flub, lack, slip, vice
  5 abuse, blame, culpa(L.), error, guilt,
  lapse, tache(Sc.) 6 defect, foible, vit-
  ium(L.) 7 blemish, blunder, default, demerit, failure, frailty, mistake, neglect,
  offense 10 peccadillo 11 culpability,
  delinquency, misdemeanor 12 imperfection 13 transgression
faultfinder: 5 momus 6 carper, critic 7
  caption, knocker, nagster
faultless: 4 pure 5 right 7 correct, perfect, precise 8 flawless 9 blameless 10
  impeccable 13 unimpeachable 14 irreproachable
faulty: bad, ill 5 amiss, unfit, wrong 9 incorrect 10 inaccurate
faun: 5 satyr
fauna and flora: 5 biota
Faust: *author:* 6 Goethe
  composer: 6 Gounod
fautor: 6 patron 7 abetter, abettor, favorer
  8 partisan 9 protector
faux pas: 4 slip 5 boner, error 7 misstep,
  mistake
faveolate: 6 favose 9 alveolate 11 honeycombed
favonian: 4 mild
favor, favour: aid, for, pro 4 boon, face,
  gree, help 5 bless, grace, leave, spare 6
  esteem, letter, uphold 7 advance, feature,
  forward, support 8 advocacy, befriend,
  goodwill, kindness, resemble 9 patronage,
  privilege, subscribe 10 assistance,
  concession, indulgence, permission 11
  accommodate, approbation, countenance
  13 communication
  pay: woo 5 court
favorable: 4 good, kind, rosy 5 clear 6
  benign 7 benefic, optimal, popular 8
  friendly, gracious, pleasing 9 approving,
  opportune 10 auspicious, charitable, convenient, propitious 12 advantageous
favored: 6 gifted 9 fortunate, preferred
favorer: 6 fautor 9 supporter
favorite: pet 6 minion 7 darling, popular
favoritism: 4 bias 8 nepotism 9 prejudice
favose: 8 aveolate 9 faveolate, honeycomb
fawn: 4 buck, deer, jouk 5 color, cower,
  crawl, kotow, toady, whelp 6 cringe, grovel, kowtow, shrink 7 adulate, flatter,

hangdog, servile, toadeat, truckle 9 parasitic, sycophant 10 ingratiate
  skin: 6 nebris
fay: elf, fit 4 join 5 fairy, unite 6 sprite
faze: 5 daunt, worry 10 disconcert
feal: 5 loyal 7 conceal 8 faithful
fealty: 6 homage 7 loyalty 8 fidelity 9
  constancy, obeisance 10 allegiance
fear: awe 5 alarm, doubt, dread, panic 6
  danger, dismay, fright, horror, phobia,
  terror 7 anxiety, suspect 8 affright, disquiet, distrust, venerate 9 agitation, reverence, revulsion 10 solicitude 12 apprehension 13 consternation
  of animals: 9 zoophobia
  of being alone: 24 monophobia
  of burial alive: 11 taphephobia
  of cats: 12 aelurophobia, ailurophobia
  of crowds: 11 ochlophobia
  of dirt: 10 mysophobia
  of enclosed places: 14 claustrophobia
  of fire: 10 pyrophobia
  of great heights: 10 acrophobia
  of open spaces: 11 agoraphobia
  of strangers: 10 xenophobia
  of thunder: 12 brontophobia 13 tonitro-
  phobia
  of water: 11 hydrophobia
fearful: 4 dire 5 awful, pavid, timid 6
  afraid 7 ghastly, nervous, panicky, worried 8 cautious, doubtful, dreadful, grewsome, gruesome, horrible, horrific, shocking, terrible, timorous 9 appalling,
  frightful, trembling 10 formidable, horrendous, meticulous 11 distressing 12
  apprehensive
  comb. form: 4 dino
fearless: 4 bold 5 brave 6 daring, heroic 8
  intrepid 9 audacious, confident, dauntless, undaunted 10 courageous
fearsome: 5 timid 8 timorous 9 frightful
feasible: 6 likely 8 possible, probable,
  suitable 9 practical 10 reasonable
feast: eat, foy(Sc.), sup 4 dine, fete, luau,
  meal 5 festa, treat 6 regale, repast 7
  banquet, delight, festino, gratify 8 festival, potlatch 10 burrakhana
  comb. form: mas
  Christian: 5 agape 9 eucharist
  funeral: 5 arval, arvel, dirgy(Sc.), 6 arthel,
  averil, dirgie(Sc.)
  of lights: 7 Hanukka 8 Chanukah, Ha-
  nukkah
  of lots: 5 Purim
  of nativity: 9 Christmas
  of tabernacles: 7 Succoth
  of weeks: 8 Shabuoth
  passover: 5 seder
feasting: 9 epulation
  companion: 7 convive
feat: act 4 deed, gest 5 geste, stunt, trick 7
  exploit, miracle 11 achievement, performance 14 accomplishment

feather: 4 deck, down, vane 5 adorn, penna, pinna(L.), pluma(L.), plume, quill, 6 clothe, fledge, fletch, hackle, pinion
barb: 4 harl, herl 7 pinnula
comb. form: 5 ptile
down: 4 dowl 5 dowle 7 plumule
mature: 10 teleoptile
quill: 5 remex 7 calamus
shaft: 5 scape
shank: 4 boot
shoulder: 4 cape
feather alum: 8 alunogen 12 halotrichite
feather-brained: 7 foolish 9 frivolous
feather-headed: 5 giddy 7 foolish
feather key: 6 spline
feather star: 8 comatula 9 comatulae(pl.), comatulid
feathered: 7 pennate, pinnate
feathers: *provide with:* 6 fletch
shed: 4 molt 5 moult
feathery: 6 fluffy
featly: 6 neatly, nimbly 8 graceful, properly
feature: 4 face 5 favor, motif, token, trait 6 aspect, favour 7 amenity, outline 8 salience 9 lineament 11 countenance 14 characteristic
natural: 9 geography
feaze: 4 fray 7 roughen, unravel, untwist
febris: 5 fever
feces, faeces: 4 dreg 5 drast, drest 6 ordure, refuse 8 sediment 9 excrement, feculence
feck: 5 value 6 amount 8 quantity
fecket: 9 waistcoat
feckful: 6 strong 8 powerful 9 efficient
feckless: 4 weak 9 shiftless, worthless
feckly: 6 almost, mostly
feculence: 5 dregs, feces 6 faeces 8 foulness 9 muddiness
fecund: 7 fertile 8 fruitful, prolific
fecundate: 9 fertilize, pollinate 10 impregnate
fed up: 5 bored 7 wearied 8 satiated 9 surfeited
fedarie: 10 accomplice 11 confederate
federacy: 8 alliance 11 confederacy
federation: 5 union 6 league, nation 8 alliance 11 association, confederacy
fedity: 8 impurity, vileness
fedora: hat
fee: 4 dues, feal, feul(Sc.), fier, hire, rate, wage 5 price 6 charge, dastur, employ, reward, salary 7 payment, stipend, storage, tribute 8 gratuity, malikana, retainer 9 allowance, bienvenne, emolument, pourboire 10 assessment, honorarium, perquisite, recompense 12 compensation
feeble: 4 flue, lame, mean, poor, puny, weak 5 faint 6 dotage, flabby, flimsy, foible, infirm, scanty, sickly, wankle, weanly 7 fragile, invalid, languid, queechy 8 decrepit, impotent, inferior, thewless(Sc.),

yielding 9 miserable 10 inadequate, indistinct 11 debilitated
feeble-minded: 5 anile, dotty 7 moronic 10 irresolute 11 vacillating
feed: eat, hay 4 bait, bran, fill, glut, grub, meal, oats, sate 5 agist, gorge, grass, graze, nurse 6 fodder, foster, repast, suckle, supply 7 blowout, furnish, gratify, herbage, indulge, nourish, nurture, satiate, satisfy, surfeit, sustain 9 replenish
to excess: 4 glut 6 agrote, pamper 7 surfeit 8 overfill 9 crapulate
feeder: 9 tributary
fire: 6 stoker
feel: 5 grope, sense, touch 6 handle 7 examine, explore, sensate 8 perceive 10 appreciate, experience
feeler: 4 palp 6 palpus 7 antenna, smeller 8 proposal, tentacle
feeling: 4 pity, tact, view 5 humor, touch 6 morale 7 emotion, opinion, passion 8 attitude, sentient 9 affection, sensation, sentiment 10 atmosphere, experience, perception 11 sensibility 13 consciousness 14 susceptibility
evocative of: 7 emotive
lack: 8 numbness 9 apathetic, insensate 10 anesthesia 11 anaesthesia 13 insensibility
feet (see also **foot**): 4 dogs
feeze: 4 rush 5 drive 6 impact 7 disturb
fegary: 4 whim 5 prank 6 finery, gewgaw
feign: act 4 fake, seem, sham 5 avoid, fable, shape, shirk 6 affect, assume, invent 7 conceal, fashion, imagine, pretend, romance 8 disguise, simulate 9 dissemble, personate 11 counterfeit, dissimulate, make-believe
ignorance: 7 connive
sickness: 8 malinger
feigned: 5 false 6 pseudo 7 fictive 9 insincere 10 artificial, fictitious
feil: 4 neat 11 comfortable
feint: 4 ruse 5 shift, trick 7 falsify, feigned 8 pretense 9 diversion
feirie: 6 active, nimble
feis: 8 assembly 10 convention
feldspar: 6 gneiss 7 syenite
felicitate: 12 congratulate
felicitous: 7 happy
felicity: joy 9 happiness, well-being
felid: cat
felidae: cat
feline: cat, sly, tom 4 lion, lynx, pard, puma 5 civet, tiger 6 jaguar 7 cheetah, leonine, leopard, wildcat 8 stealthy 9 grimalkin 11 treacherous
breathing: 4 purr
felis domestica: cat
fell: cut, fen, hew 4 down, hide, hill, moor, pelt, ruin, skin, very 5 cruel, eager, field, great, sharp 6 deadly, fierce, fleece, intent, mighty, savage, shrewd 7 brutish,

crashed, doughty, hideous, inhuman, tumbled **8** mountain, spirited, vigorous **9** barbarous, ferocious, marshland, momentous, prostrate **11** destructive

fellah: 7 peasant

fellow (see also **man; person**): bo; cod, guy, lad, man **4** bean, beau, bozo, carl, chal, chap, cove, dick, duck, hind, mate, peer **5** billy, bloke, chiel, match **6** bugger, callan, chield, codger, hombre(Sp.), person, sirrah **7** callant, chappie, comrade, cullies, partner, scroyle **8** neighbor **9** associate, companion **10** sweetheart **12** contemporary

awkward: oaf **4** club, gawk, lout, slam **5** booby, clown **6** galoot **7** bumpkin **9** dromedary **11** hobble-de-hoy

beggardly: **8** bezonian

conceited: **7** dalteen

craven: **6** coward

dissolute: **4** rake, roue **9** debaucher

dull: **4** drip, fogy **5** fogey **8** codshead

fat: **7** glutton

fine: **5** brick, bully **7** bawcock **8** bonhomme(F.),

foolish: sop **4** goff

funny: wag, wit **4** card **5** clown

honest: **6** trusty **9** truepenny

idle: **6** footer, stocah

ignorant: **6** gobbin

lazy: bum **9** drawlatch

little: bub **5** caddy **6** birkie, caddie, shaver **9** dandiprat

mean: cad **4** boor, carl, pleb **5** bucko, bully, catso, cavil, churl, yahoo **6** fouter, foutre **7** cullion **8** blighter, coistrel, coistril, smatchet(Sc.)

old: **6** geezer, gleyde

old-fashioned: **4** fogy

ragged: **10** ragamuffin **14** tatterdemalion

reckless: **4** buck **5** blade **9** daredevil, hell-raker

rowdy: **6** roarer **8** larrikin

shrewd: **6** gazabo, gazebo

silly: **8** dotterel

stupid: ass **4** clod, daff, dolt, gump, hash, simp **5** booby, dunce, moron **6** bayard, foozle **8** codshead **9** blockhead, heavyhead **10** bufflehead **11** blunderbuss, blunderhead

tricky: **5** knave, scamp **6** rascal

vain: fop

worthless: bum, cur **5** rogue, scamp **6** budzat **7** bobtail, brothel, budzart, vaurien(F.) **9** schlemiel(Yid.), schlemihl(Yid.), scoundrel

fellowship: 5 guild, union **7** company **8** alliance **9** communion **10** membership **11** association, brotherhood, camaraderie, comradeship, corporation, familiarity, intercourse, partnership **12** acquaintance, friendliness **13** companionship

felly: rim **6** keenly **7** cruelly **8** bitterly, fiercely, savagely, terribly **11** barbarously **13** destructively

felo-de-se: 7 suicide

felon: **4** wild **5** cruel **6** fetlow, fierce, wicked **7** convict, culprit, villain, whitlow **8** criminal **9** murderous **10** malefactor

felony: 5 arson, crime **7** offense

felt: hat **6** fabric, sensed

felwort: 7 gentian

female: 4 girl, gyne **5** woman **6** weakly **7** feminal, womanly **8** feminine, ladylike, womanish **9** womanlike **10** effeminate

animal: cow, doe, ewe, hen **4** mare, slut **5** bitch, filly, jenny **6** sheder **7** lioness, tigress

assistant: **8** adjutrix **9** adjutrice

figure: **5** orant **8** caryatid

monster: **6** gorgon

principle: **5** Sakti

saint: ste

sandpiper: **5** reeve

sheep: ewe

slave: **7** odalisk **9** odalisque

spirit: **7** banshee

warrior: **6** Amazon

feminine: **4** soft, weak **5** woman **6** female, tender **8** womanish **10** effeminate

femininity: 10 effeminacy, muliebrity **11** womanliness **12** womanishness

fere: **4** mate, peer **5** equal **9** companion

fen: bog **4** carr, fowl, moor **5** marsh, snipe, swamp **6** morass **8** quagmire

fence: bar **4** bank, duel, ha-ha, pale, rail, wall **5** guard, hedge **6** paling, picket, raddle, rasper **7** barrier, bulwark, defense **8** palisade, palisado **9** enclosure **12** circumscribe

fencer: 7 duelist, parrier **9** gladiator, swordsman

cry of: **6** touche **7** en garde

fencing: *attack:* **7** reprise

cry: **4** sasa

hit: **5** punto

movement: **4** volt

position: **5** carte, prime, sixte, terce **6** octave, quarte, quinte, tierce **7** seconde, septime

term: **4** bind **5** lunge **6** thrust, touche

thrust: **7** riposte

weapon: **4** epee, foil **5** saber, sabre, sword **6** rapier

fend: **4** ward **5** parry **6** defend, forbid, resist **7** support

fender: 5 guard **6** buffer, bumper, shield **11** splashboard

fennel: 4 hemp

fent: 4 slit **7** opening

feracious: 8 fruitful

feral: **4** wild **6** deadly, savage **7** bestial, untamed **8** funereal, unbroken **11** uncivilized **14** undomesticated

Ferdinand's wife: 8 Isabella

feria: 4 fair 6 fiesta 7 holiday

ferine: 4 rude, wild 6 savage 7 untamed 9 barbarous, ferocious 11 uncivilized

ferly: 6 marvel, wonder 9 amazement 12 astonishment

fermail: 5 clasp 6 buckle

ferment: 4 barm, heat, turn, work, zyme 5 fever, yeast 6 enzyme, foment, tumult, uproar 7 agitate 8 disorder 10 ebullition, exacerbate, excitement, turbulence

fermenting mixture: bub

fern: 4 tara 5 frond
genus: 7 onoclea, osmunda 8 psilotum
kind of: 4 nito 5 brake 6 pteris 7 bracken 8 polypody 10 maidenhair
scale: 7 ramenta(pl.) 8 ramentum

fern-like: 7 pteroid 13 pteridophytic

ferocious: 4 fell, grim, wild 5 cruel, feral 6 bloody, brutal, fierce, raging, savage 7 inhuman, ominous, violent 8 pitiless, ravenous, ruthless 9 barbarous, malignant, merciless, murderous, rapacious, truculent 10 implacable, malevolent, relentless, sanguinary 11 remorseless 12 bloodthirsty

ferret: hob 4 tape 6 weasel 7 polecat

ferrotype: 7 tintype

ferrule: cap 4 ring, virl(Sc.) 6 collet, pulley, verrel 7 bushing, verrell

ferry: 4 pont, scow 7 traject

ferryman: 6 Charon

fertile: fat 4 rank, rich 5 gleby 6 fecund, hearty 7 teeming 8 abundant, fruitful, generous, prolific 9 exuberant, feracious, inventive, luxuriant, plenteous, plentiful 10 productive, profitable
render: 6 enrich

fertility god: 4 Frey 5 Freyr

fertilize: 6 batten, enrich 8 fructify 9 fecundate 10 impregnate, inseminate

fertilizer: 4 marl 5 guano, humus 6 alinit, manure, pollen, potash 7 compote, nitrate 8 nitrogen 11 phosphorous 14 superphosphate

ferule: rod 5 ruler 6 fennel, ferula 10 discipline, punishment

fervency: See **fervor.**

fervent: hot 4 keen, warm 5 eager, fiery 6 ardent, bitter, fervid, fierce, raging, savage 7 boiling, burning, glowing, intense 8 vehement 9 religious 10 passionate 11 impassioned

fervid: hot 6 ardent, tropic 7 boiling, burning, fervent, zealous 8 vehement 9 impetuous 11 impassioned

fervor: 4 fire, heat, rage, zeal 5 ardor 7 passion 8 candency 9 eagerness, vehemence 10 enthusiasm 11 earnestness

fess: bar 4 band, pert 5 smart 6 lively 9 conceited

festa: 5 feast 7 holiday 8 festival

festal: gay 4 gala 5 gaudy 7 festive

fester: rot 4 scar 6 rankle 7 pustule, putrefy 9 cicatrice, cicatrize

festival: mas 4 fair, fete, gala, Holi 5 feast, feria, festa, gaudy, Haloa, Hooli, revel 6 fiesta, Hohlee 7 banquet, holiday 8 carnival, carousal 9 festivity
church: 4 Lent 6 Easter 9 Christmas
comb. form.: mas
epiphany: 7 uphelya

festive: gay 4 gala 6 festal, genial, joyous 7 holiday, jocular 8 mirthful, sportive 9 convivial 10 celebrious 11 merrymaking

festivity: 4 gala 5 mirth, randy, revel 6 gaiety, splore 7 jollity 8 festival, function 9 festivity 10 joyfulness 11 celebration, merrymaking 12 conviviality 13 entertainment, glorification
god: 5 Comus 7 Bacchus 8 Dionysus

festoon: 6 wreath 7 garland 8 decorate

fetch: fet 4 gasp, tack, take 5 bring, sweep, trick 6 double, wraith 7 achieve, attract 8 artifice, interest 9 stratagem

fetching: 6 crafty 8 alluring, pleasing, scheming 10 attractive 11 fascinating

fete: 4 fair, gala 5 bazar, feast 6 bazaar, fiesta, regale 7 banquet, holiday 8 ceremony, festival 9 entertain 11 celebration 13 entertainment

fetid: 4 olid, rank 6 rotten, virose 7 noisome 10 malodorous

fetish, fetich: obi 4 idol, obia 5 charm, huaca, obeah, obiah, totem 6 grigri, voodoo 7 sorcery 8 greegree, talisman 10 mumbo-jumbo

fetter: 4 band, bond, find, gyve, iron 5 basil, chain 6 anklet, garter, hamper, hobble, hopple, impede 7 confine, enchain, manacle, shackle, trammel 8 restrain 9 restraint

fettle: 4 beat, deck, fuss, mull, tidy 5 dress, groom 6 repair, strike 7 arrange, bandage, harness 9 condition

fetus, foetus: 5 birth, child, young 6 embryo 10 conception
human: 10 homunculus
limbless: 5 ameli(pl.) 6 amelus

feud: 4 fray 5 broil 6 affray, enmity, strife 7 contest, dispute, quarrel 8 vendetta 9 hostility 10 contention
blood: 8 vendetta

feudal: *estate:* 4 feod, fief
jurisdiction: soc 4 soke
lord: 7 vavasor 8 suzerain, vavasour
tenant: 6 vassal 7 homager

feudatory: 4 fief 11 beneficiary

fever: 4 ague, fire 6 febris 7 ferment 9 calenture 10 excitement 11 temperature 13 conflagration
kind of: 4 ague 5 octan 6 dengue, sextan, sodoku 7 feveret, helodes, malaria, quartan 10 calentural 11 brucellosis
without: 8 apyretic

feverish: 5 fiery 6 hectic 7 excited, febrile, frantic 8 restless 9 overeager 11 impassioned

few: 4 less, some 5 scant 7 limited 8 exiguous

fewness: 7 paucity

fey: 4 dead 5 fatal 7 unlucky 8 accursed 9 delirious, enfeebled, visionary

fez: cap 8 tarboosh

fiacre: 4 hack 5 coach

fiance: 5 trust 7 promise 8 affiance 10 confidence

fiasco: 5 crash, flask 6 bottle 7 failure

fiat: 5 edict, order 6 decree 7 command 8 decision, sanction 9 ordinance 12 announcement, proclamation

fib: lie, yed 4 beat, flaw, whid 6 pummel 9 falsehood 11 tarradiddle

fibber: 4 liar 12 prevaricator

fiber, fibre: 5 grain 6 strand, thread
  band: 6 fillet
  kind of: nap, nep, tal, tow 4 adad, aloe, bast, buri, coir, eruc, feru, flax, hemp, ixle, jute, kyar, lint, marl, noil, pita, silk, sola 5 abaca, civil, erizo, floss, istle, istli, ixtle, kapok, linen, mudar, nylon, oakum, orlon, ramee, ramie, rayon, sisal 6 amiray, cotton, dacron, manila, raffia, staple 7 acetate, acrilan, castuli, haurizo, sabutan 8 filament, fibrilla, keratose 9 gamelotte 10 anodendron, escobadura
  synthetic: 5 nylon, orlon, rayon 6 dacron 7 acetate, acrilan
  yarn: 6 strand

fibrin: 6 gluten

fibrose: 6 sinewy 7 stringy

fibula: 5 clasp 6 brooch, buckle 9 safety-pin

fickle: 4 gery 5 dizzy, false, giddy 6 mobile, puzzle, shifty, volage, wankle 7 casalty, caselty, cazelty, flatter, mutable 8 cassalty, casselty, gossamer, unstable, unsteady, variable, volatile, wavering 9 changeful, dangerous, deceitful, faithless, unsettled 10 capricious, changeable, inconstant, irresolute, highheaded 11 treacherous, vacillating

fiction: 4 tale 5 fable, false, novel 6 deceit, device, fabula, legend 7 coinage, fantasy, figment, forgery, romance 9 falsehood, invention 10 concoction, pretending 11 contrivance, dissembling, fabrication 14 counterfeiting

fictional: 7 assumed 11 make-believe

fictitious: 5 bogus, dummy, false, phony 7 assumed, feigned 8 fabulous, mythical, spurious 9 imaginary, imitative, pretended 10 aprocryphal, artificial 11 counterfeit

fiddle: bow 4 viol 5 cheat, gique 6 potter, trifle, violin 7 swindle

fiddler: 4 crab 7 crowder, scraper 8 sixpence, 9 violinist

fiddlesticks: 5 pshaw

fidelity: 5 troth, truth 6 fealty 7 honesty 8 adhesion, devotion, veracity 9 adherence,

closeness, constancy 10 allegiance 12 faithfulness

fidget: 4 fike, fuss, roil 5 hotch, worry 6 brevit, fissle, fistle, fridge, fusser 7 nervous 8 restless 9 impatient 10 uneasiness 12 restlessness

fidgety: 5 fussy 6 uneasy 7 restive 8 restless 9 impatient

fiducial: 4 firm 7 trusted 8 trustful 9 confident 11 trustworthy

fiduciary: 7 trustee

fief: fee, han 4 feud 8 benefice 9 feudatory

field: lea, lot 4 acre, ager(L.), area, fell, list, mead, rand, wong 5 campo, champ, croft, glebe, paddy, range, rowen, sawah 6 arrish, campus, champe, furrow, ground, machar, meadow, sphere 7 compass, garston, paddock, terrain 8 clearing 9 grassland 11 battlefield
  athletic: 4 oval, ring, rink 5 arena, court, green 6 course, stadia(pl.) 7 diamond, stadium 8 gridiron
  common share: 4 dale
  edge: 4 rand
  god: 4 Faun
  pert. to: 8 agrarian, agrestic

field mouse: 4 vole

field of blood: 4 ager 8 aceldama, akeldama 9 sanguinis

fieldwork: 5 lunet, redan 7 lunette 13 fortification

fiend: foe 5 demon, devil, enemy, Satan, trull 6 wizard

fiendish: 5 cruel 6 wicked 7 demonic 8 demoniac, devilish, diabolic 10 diabolical

fierce: 4 bold, fell, grim 5 breme, cruel felon, rethe 6 ardent, gothic, hetter, raging, savage 7 brutish, fervent, furious, grimful, scaddle, violent 9 felonious, ferocious, impetuous, truculent 10 catawampus, forbidding, passionate 11 catawampous 13 catawamptious

fiercely: 4 fell 5 felly

fiery: hot, red 5 adust 6 ardent, flashy, ignite 7 burning, fervent, flaming, furious, glowing, parched, peppery, violent 8 choleric, feverish, frampoid, inflamed, spirited, vehement 9 hotheaded, impetuous, irascible, irritable 10 mettlesome, passionate, phlogistic 11 combustible, inflammable

fiesta: 4 fete 5 feria, party 7 holiday 8 festival 9 festivity

fifty: nu(Gr.)

fig: rig 4 fico 5 array, breba, dress, eleme, elemi, pipal 6 trifle 7 furbish

fig basket: 5 cabas

fig-shaped: 8 ficiform

Figaro: 6 barber

fight: box, war 4 beat, bout, clem, cock, cope, cuff, duel, flog, fray, mell, tilt, wage 5 brawl, clash, hurry, melee, scrap 6 affair, affray, barney, battle, bicker, combat, debate, impugn, op-

pose, resist, rippit, strife, strike, strive
7 bargain, contend, contest, ruction
8 conflict, militate, struggle **9** encounter, pugnacity **10** free-for-all **11** altercation **12** disagreement **13** combativeness
against the gods: **9** theomachy
fighter: pug **4** vamp **5** boxer **6** cocker **7** battler, duelist, soldier, warrior **8** andabata, barrater, barrator, champion, pugilist, guerilla, scrapper **9** combatant, guerrilla
fighting: **7** warlike **8** militant **10** pugnacious **11** belligerent
figment: **7** fiction **9** invention **11** fabrication
figuration: **4** form **5** shape **7** outline
figurative: **6** florid **7** flowery, typical **9** allegoric **10** rhetorical **12** emblematical
use of words: **5** trope
figure: hue, vol **4** bosh, form, idea, star **5** digit, image, magot, shape **6** emblem, number, symbol, tattoo **7** chiffer, chiffre, compute, contour, numeral, outline **8** likeness **9** archetype, calculate **13** configuration
geometrical: **4** cone, cube, lune **5** prism, rhomb, solid **6** circle, gnomon, oblong, sector, square **7** ellipse, lozenge, pelcoid, rhombus **8** crescent, pelecoid, pentacle, triangle **9** ellipsoid, rectangle **16** parallelepipedon
human form: **4** nude **5** dummy, glyph, orant **7** telamon **8** Atlantes, caryatid
many-sided: **4** cube **6** isogon **7** decagon, hexagon, nonagon, octagon, polygon **8** pentagon, tetragon **10** hexahedron, octahedron **11** icosahedron **12** dodecahedron **13** quadrilateral
of speech: **5** trope **6** aporia, simile **7** imagery **8** metaphor, metonymy
praying: **5** orant
symbolic: **6** emblem
figure out: **4** dope **5** solve
Fiji Island: *capital:* **4** Suva
chestnut: **4** rata
drug: **5** tonga
filament: **4** dowl, hair, harl **5** fiber, fibre **6** mantle, strand, thread
lamp: **12** incandescent
filch: bob, nim, rob **4** beat, fake, prig **5** fetch, steal **6** pilfer, strike **7** purloin
file: row **4** line, list, rank, rasp, rate, risp, roll, tool **5** grail, index, track **6** accuse, carlet, befoul, defile, rascal **7** arrange, condemn, graille, quannet **10** procession
document: **7** dossier
filial: **9** childlike
filibuster: **5** orate **11** obstruction
filigree: **8** fanciful **13** unsubstantial
filing: **5** lemel **6** rasion **8** limation
Filipino: See **Philippines.**
filippic: See **philippic.**
fill: pad **4** cram, feed, glut, hold, pang, sate **5** estop, gorge **6** charge, fulfil, occupy **7**

distend, enlarge, execute, fraught, fulfill, inflate, perfect, perform, pervade, plenish, satiate, satisfy, suffuse **8** complete, compound, permeate **9** replenish **10** accomplish, embankment **11** sufficiency
cracks: **4** calk, shim **5** caulk
with zeal: **7** enthuse
fille: **4** girl **8** daughter
filled: SRO **5** sated, solid **6** loaded **7** implete, replete **9** saturated **11** preoccupied
fillet: **4** band, bone, orle, orlo, sole, tape **5** ampyx, crown, label, miter, snood, stria, tiara, vitta **6** anadem, binder, cimbia, diadem, fascia, norsel, quadra, ribbon, striae(pl.), taenia, turban **7** bandage, bandeau, fasciae(pl.), molding, taeniae (pl.), tresson **8** bandelet, cincture, tressour, tressure **9** sphendone **10** bandelette
architectural: **6** cimbia, lintel, listel, regula, taenia
filling: *dental:* **5** inlay
fabric: **4** weft, woof
fillip, filip: **4** blow, flip, snap, urge **5** flash, flirt, flisk **6** buffet, moment **7** project **8** stimulus **9** stimulate
filly: **4** colt, foal, girl, mare **9** youngster
film (see also **motion picture**): **4** brat, haze, mist, scum, skin, veil **5** flake, layer **6** mother, patina **8** beeswing, negative, pellicle **10** photograph
filmy: **4** hazy, miry, vile **5** dirty, drovy, gross, nasty **6** bawdry, impure, sordid **7** bestial, hoggish, obscene, squalid, unclean **8** sluttish **9** polluting **10** disgusting, licentious **11** disgraceful
fin: arm **4** hand, keel **5** pinna **7** acantha, flipper, ventral
fin-footed: **8** pinniped
finagle, fenagle: **5** cheat, trick **6** revoke **7** deceive
final: **4** last **6** latter **7** dernier, extreme, outmost **8** decisive, definite, eventual, farewell, ultimate **9** uttermost **10** concluding, conclusive, definitive **11** terminating **13** determinating
final outcome: **5** issue **6** upshot
finale: end **4** coda **5** close, finis, fugue, shank **6** ending **7** closing **9** uttermost **10** conclusion **11** termination
finalist: **10** contestant
finality: end **11** termination **12** decisiveness **14** conclusiveness

finance: tax **4** back **5** goods **7** revenue **8** taxation, treasure **10** underwrite

finances: **5** funds, purse **6** assets **9** exchequer

financial: **6** fiscal **7** solvent **8** monetary **9** pecuniary

financing: **7** backing

finch: **4** fink, moro, pape **5** serin, terin **6** burion, citril, linnet, siskin **7** chewink, redpoll, senegal, tanager **8** amadavat **9** snowflake

find: get **5** catch **6** locate **8** discover
by keen search: **5** probe **6** ferret

find fault: nag **4** carp, crab, fret **5** cavil, scold **8** complain **9** belly-ache, criticise, criticize

find guilty: **7** convict

find out: **5** learn **6** detect **8** discover **9** ascertain

fine: cro, rum, tax **4** bein, bien, braw, eric, good, jake, levy, nice, pure **5** bonny, brave, bully, dandy, frail, mulct, noble, sharp, sheer, wally **6** amerce, bonnie, bright, clever, crafty, finish, gersum, ornate, proper, slight, spiffy, tender **7** cunning, elegant, estreat, forfeit, fragile, penalty, perfect, refined, tenuous **8** absolute, bloodwit, delicate, handsome, penalize, pleasant, skillful, splendid, superior **9** beautiful, bloodwite, excellent, ingenious, sensitive **10** consummate, fastidious, pulverized, punishment, surpassing

fineness: **5** trick **6** finery, purity **7** exility **8** delicacy **9** clearness

finery: **4** gaud, waly **5** wally **6** bauble, bawdry, beauty, fegary **7** gaudary **8** elegance, fineness, ornament **9** fallalery **10** hufty-tufty, lavishness

finespun: **4** hair, thin

finesse: art **5** cheat, skill **6** purity, serene **7** cunning **8** artifice, delicacy, subtlety, thinness **9** clearness, dexterity, stratagem **10** artfulness, refinement

fingent: **7** molding **10** fashioning

finger: toy **5** digit, index, pinky **6** handle, meddle, pilfer, pinkie **7** annular, minimus, purloin
resembling: **8** digitate
snap with: **5** filip **6** fillip

finger board: **4** fret

fingerlike: **6** dactyl

fingerling: **4** parr **8** troutlet

fingernail moon: **6** lunule

fingerprint: **11** dactylogram
mark: **4** arch, loop **5** whorl **9** composite
science: **12** dactyloscopy

finial: epi, tee, top **4** knot **5** bunch, crest, final **8** ornament, pinnacle

finical: **4** nice **5** fussy **6** choosy, dainty, dapper, jaunty, prissy, spruce **7** choosey, finicky, foppish, mincing **8** delicate **9** squeamish **10** fastidious, meticulous **11** overprecise **14** overscrupulous

finis: end **4** goal **5** close **10** conclusion

finish: die, end **4** char, mill **5** bound, cease, chare, cheve, close, glaze, limit **6** fulfil, windup **7** achieve, execute, fulfill, perfect, surface **8** complete, conclude, terminal **9** erudition, terminate **10** accomplish, completion, conclusion, consummate, perfection
dull: mat **5** matte
glossy: **6** enamel

finished: did, oer, pau **4** done, fine, gone, over, ripe **5** ended, kaput **6** closed, ornate **7** refined, stopped **8** climaxed, lustered, polished **9** completed, concluded, perfected, performed **10** terminated **11** consummated **12** professional

finisher: **4** eyer **5** ender **7** beetler **8** enameler

finite: **7** limited **9** definable **10** restricted, terminable **11** conditioned

fink: **8** informer, squealer **13** strikebreaker

Finland: **5** Suomi
city: Aba, Abo **11** Helsingfors
coin: **5** penni **6** markka
composer: **8** Sibelius
division: **5** Ijore **9** Villipuri
forest god: **5** Tapio
island: **5** Aland **6** Aaland
isthmus: **7** Karelia
lake: **5** Enare
language: **4** Avar, Lapp **5** Ugric **6** Magyar, Ostyak, Tarast **7** Samoyed **8** Estonian
measure: **5** kannu, tunna, verst **6** fathom, sjomil **7** tunland **8** ottinger, skalpund, tunnland
parliament: **9** Eduskunta
tribe: **4** Veps **5** Vepse **6** Ugrian

fiord, fjord: ise **5** inlet

fippenny bit: fip

fir: **9** evergreen

Firbolg queen: **6** Tailte **7** Tailtiu

fire: can, feu(F.) **4** bale, burn, heat, zeal **5** ardor, arson, fever, gleed, light, shoot, stoke **6** arouse, excite, fervor, ignite, incite, kindle, spirit **7** animate, burning, dismiss, explode, fervour, glimmer, inflame, inspire **8** detonate, illumine, irritate, vivacity **9** calenture, cauterize, discharge, holocaust **10** combustion, enthusiasm, illuminate **12** inflammation **13** conflagration
comb. form.: **4** igni, pyro
containing: **7** igneous
fighter: **4** vamp
god: **4** Agni **6** Vulcan **10** Hephaestus
military: **4** flak **5** salvo **6** rafale **7** barrage
particle: arc **5** spark
pert. to: **7** igneous
set: **6** accend, ignite, kindle **7** inflame **8** enkindle, irritate
worshipper: **5** Parsi **6** Parsee **9** pyrolater **10** ignicolist

fire extinguisher: **6** pyrene **9** pyroleter

fire feeder: **6** fueler, stoker

firearm: gun **5** piece, rifle **6** musket, pistol **7** demihag **8** revolver

fireback: 7 reredos 8 pheasant

fireboat: 8 palander

firebrand: 5 blaze 6 bleery

firecracker: 5 squib 6 petard 7 cracker, snapper 9 skyrocket

fireman: 4 vamp 6 stoker, tizeur 9 fire-eater

fireplace: 5 focus, fogon, forge, foyer, ingle 6 hearth 8 cheminee

part: hob 6 mantel 9 ingleside 11 hearthstone

firer: 6 stoker 10 incendiary

fireside: 9 ingleside 11 hearthstone

firestone: 5 flint

firewood: 4 lena 5 fagot 6 billet, billot

fireworks: 4 gerb 5 gerbe 7 fizgigs, rockets 9 sparklers 10 girandoles 11 tourbillion 12 pyrotechnics

resembling: 11 pyrotechnic

firing: 4 fuel

firm: hui 4 buff, fast, hard, sure, trig 5 champ, dense, firma, fixed, hardy, house, loyal, rigid, solid, sound, stith, stout, tight 6 hearty, secure, settle, sinewy, stable, stanch, steady, stolid, strong 7 adamant, certain, compact, company, confirm, context, decided, durable, staunch, unmoved 8 constant, faithful, fiducial, obdurate, resolute, unshaken 9 backboned, establish, immovable, immutable, standfast, steadfast 10 consistent, determined, unslipping, unwavering, unyielding 11 established, partnership, substantial, substantive, well-founded

firmament: sky 7 heavens 8 empyrean

firmance: 9 assurance, stability 11 confinement

firmly fixed: 6 rooted, stable

firmness: 4 iron 7 courage 8 solidity, strength, tenacity 9 constancy, stability 10 immobility, steadiness 11 consistency 13 determination 15 indissolubility

first: 4 erst, head, high, main 5 alpha, chief, forme, nieve, prime 6 primal, primus 7 highest, initial, leading, primary 8 earliest, foremost, original 9 primitive, principal 10 aboriginal, primordial

comb. form: 5 proto

appearance: 5 debut 8 premiere

first-born: 5 eigne 11 protogenist

first class: 5 prime 9 excellent, topdrawer 10 first-cabin

first-rate: 4 good, jake 5 prime 6 tiptop 7 skookum 8 clipping, topnotch 9 admirable, excellent

firth: 4 kyle 5 frith, inlet 7 coppice, estuary

Firth of Clyde Island: 4 Bute

fisc: 9 exchequer

fiscal: 8 monetary 9 financial

fiscus: 8 treasury

fish: net 4 cast 5 angle, drail, seine, troll 7 poisson(F.)

Alaska: 6 iconnu

ascending river from sea: 7 anadrom

Atlantic Coast: 4 opah, pogy 6 bunker, salema 7 alewife, bugfish, bughead, fatback, oldwife 8 bonyfish, menhaden 9 greentail 10 mossbunker

Australian: 4 mado 6 groper 7 grouper

bait: 5 killy 9 killifish

barbed tail: 8 stinaree, stingray

California: 4 rena 5 reina 6 rasher 9 garibaldi

carangold: 4 scad 5 jurel

carp: id; ide, orf

catfish: 6 hassar 9 sheatfish

caviar-yielding: 7 sterlet 8 sturgeon

cod: bib 4 cusk, hake, ling 5 torsk 6 gadoid 7 bacalao, beardie

cyprinoid: id; ide 4 dace

devil: ray 5 manta

eel-like: 4 link, opah 6 conger, cuchia 7 eelpout, lamprey

electric: 4 raad 7 torpedo

elongated: eel, gar 6 saurel

European: id; ide, rud 4 boce, dace, rudd, spet 5 alose, bleak, bream 6 angler, barbel, braice, meagre, plaice 7 gudgeon, lavaret, picarel

female: 4 raun 7 henfish

flat: dab, ray 4 butt, dace, sole 5 bream, fluke, skate 6 plaice, turbot 7 halibut, sanddab, sunfish, torpedo 8 flounder

Florida: 5 crunt 6 atinga, salema 7 burfish, tomtate 8 burrfish

food: cod, eel, gar, iki, sey 4 bass, boga, carp, hake, scup, shad, sole, stew, tile, tuna 5 bolti, cisco, hilsa, jurel, siera, skate, smelt, trout 6 baleen, groupa, hilsah, mullet, pompon, salema, salmon, tautog, wahoon, weever, wrasse 7 alewife, escolar, garlopa, halibut, herring, pompano, pompoon, sardine, snapper 8 mackerel 9 barracuda 10 barracouta

fresh water: id; gar, ide, orf 4 bass, carp, chub, dace, orfe, pike, rudd 5 bream, loach, roach, tench 6 darter, redeye, sucker 7 crappie, mooneye

game: 4 bass, cero, tuna 5 trout 6 grilse, marlin, salmon, tarpon 8 grayling 9 swordfish

Hawaiian: aku 4 ulua 5 akule, lania

herring: 4 shad, brit 5 sprat, sprot 7 alewife 8 pilchard

Japanese: tai, ayu

kind of: id; cat, cod, dab, eel, gar, ide, orf 4 bass, carp, chub, dace, dorn, hake, hiku, jocu, lant, lija, ling, mado, masu, meat, mero, mola, opah, orfe, pega, peto, pike, pogy, pout, rena, roud, rudd, ruff, scad, scup, shad, sier, skil, sole, spot, spet, tope, ulua 5 bream, lance, midge, otter, perch, pogie, porgy, prane, roach, ruffe, scrod, seine, skate, smelt, trout, umbra, wahoo 6 barbel, caribe, launce, mullet, porgie, sauger, saurel, shiner, tomcod, turbot, wrasse 7 alewife, grunion, haddock, machete, pegador, pintado, piranha, poisson **8** gourhead, hardhead, pilchard sturgeon **9** teleostei **10** candlefish

large: **4** cusk, opah **5** chiro, sargo, shark **6** bichir, tarpon **7** escolar, gourami, sennett **8** arapaima, sturgeon **10** blanquillo, maskalonge, maskinonge **11** muskellunge

little: see *small* below.

long: eel, gar **7** lamprey

mackerel-like: **4** cero **5** tunny **6** coelho **7** escolar, pintado

Mediterranean: **5** porgy, sargo **6** chivey **9** menominee

New England: **4** hake

New Zealand: **4** hiku **5** hikus

newly-hatched: fry

Nile: **4** erse **5** saide

olive green: **7** lutfisk **8** ludefisk

one-horned: **9** monoceros

parasitic: **6** remora

pert. to: **7** piscine **8** ichthyic **9** piscatory

pike: gar **4** lude

pilot: **6** romero

ray-like: **5** skate

river: **8** arapaima **10** barramunda

rock: **4** rena **5** reina **8** buccacio

scaleless: **9** alepidote

serpentine: eel

shark-eating: som **4** pega **7** catfish

shell: **7** abalone

small: id; fry, ide, ihi **4** brit, dace, goby, spet **5** saury, sprat **6** blenny, cunner, limpet, minnow, riggle, sennet, shiner **7** sardine **8** halfbeak, seahorse, spearing

small bait: **5** killy **9** killifish

South American: **4** gogy, mapo **5** acara **6** acoupa, aimara, almara, caribe

sparoid: tai **5** porgy, sargo

spear-snouted: gar

star: **7** asteria

sucking: **6** remora

teleost: eel **6** iniomi

toad: **4** sapo **6** slimer

toothed: **7** piranha

total haul: **4** mess **5** catch

tropical: **8** coachman

tunny: **4** tuna

voracious: **4** pike **5** shark **6** caribe **9** barracuda

West Indies: **4** Boga, cero, sier **5** chopa **6** Blanco **7** guapena **12** walleyed pike

young: fry **6** alevin

fish basket: pot **4** caul **5** creel, slath

fish gig: **5** spear

fish handler: **4** icer

fish hawk: **6** osprey

fish hide: **7** eelskin

fish limb: fin

fish net: **4** bunt **5** seine, trawl **6** sagene

fish net line: **5** meter

fish net mender: **8** beatster

fish peddler: **6** ripier, ripper **7** rippier

fish pole: pew

fish preserve: **6** warren

fish relish: **7** botargo

fish roe: **6** caviar **7** caviare

fish sauce: **4** aléc **5** garum

fish spear: gig **7** trident

fish trap: **4** coop, fyke, weel, weir **5** willy **6** eelpot

fisher: **5** eeler, pecan **6** seiner, wejack **7** trawler, troller

fisherman: **5** eeler **6** angler, seiner **7** prawner, trawler **8** peterman, piscator **9** harpooner **11** Izaak Walton

fishery: **7** piscary **9** piscation

fishes: **5** raiae

fishhook: gig **5** angle, Kirby **6** Sproat **7** Kendall **8** Aberdeen, limerick, barbless, Carlisle

fishing duck: **9** merganser

fishing gear: lam, rod, tew **4** cork, flew, flue, gaff, gimp, hook, line, reel, trot **5** cadar, cader, float, sedge, seine, snell, shood **8** trotline

fishing ground: **4** haaf

fishing vessel: **5** smack **6** seiner **7** trawler

fishline: **5** snell **7** boulter

fishmonger: **8** pessoner

fishpond: **7** piscina

fishwife: **9** buttwoman

fishy: **4** dull **6** vacant **10** improbable, lusterless, suspicious, unreliable **11** extravagant

fissate: **7** divided **8** fissured

fissile rock: **5** shale

fission: **8** breaking, cleavage, cleaving **9** splitting **12** reproduction

fissle: **4** fuss, hiss **6** bustle, fidget, rustle **7** whistle **9** fidgeting

fissure: gap **4** chap, cone, flaw, gool, leak, lode, rent, rift, rima, rime, seam, vein, vent **5** chasm, chine, chink, cleft, crack **6** cleave, cranny, divide, lesion **7** blemish, crevice, opening **8** aperture, cleavage, coloboma, crevasse, quebrada

fissured: **6** rimate **7** fissate, rimosed

fist: job **4** nave, neif **5** grasp, nieve **6** clench, clutch, daddle, effort, strike **7** attempt **8** puffball, tightwad **11** handwriting

fistic: **10** pugilistic

fisticuff: box

fit: apt, fay, gee, pan, rig **4** able, ague, good, hard, meet, ripe, suit, well, whim **5** adapt, adept, besit, chink, fancy, ictus, ready, right, spasm **6** adjust, attack, become, behove, besort, habile, heppen, proper, seemly, stroke, strong, suited **7** adapted, behoove, capable, condign, conform, correct, healthy, prepare, qualify, tantrum **8** adequate, becoming, eligible, glooming, idoneous(L.), outbreak, paroxysm, passable, suitable, syncopes **9** befitting, competent, congruous, covenable, opportune, pertinent, qualified **10** applicable, commodious, correspond, convenient **11** accommodate, appropriate

out: **6** outfit **7** habille, prepare **9** equipment

together: fay **4** mesh, nest **5** panel **8** dovetail

fitful: **4** gery **7** cursory, flighty **8** restless, unstable, variable **9** impulsive, irregular, spasmodic, uncertain **10** capricious, convulsive **12** intermittent

fitly: pat **4** duly **6** gladly, meetly **7** happily **8** properly, suitably

fitness: **7** aptness, decency, decorum, dignity **8** aptitude, capacity, justness **9** rectitude **10** competence **11** suitability

fitout: **6** outfit **9** equipment

fitted: apt **4** able **6** suited **7** adapted **8** adjusted **9** qualified **10** convenient

for digging: **7** fodient, laniary

fitting: apt, due, pat **4** meet **5** happy **6** become, proper, seemly **8** decorous, graceful, suitable **9** befitting **10** adjustment, answerable, habiliment **11** appropriate

five: **4** cinq(F.), funf(G.) **6** cinque(It.) **7** epsilon(Gr.) quinque(L.)

comb. form: **4** pent **5** penta

group of: **6** pentad

five-dollar bill: "V"; fin, vee

Five Nations: **7** Cayugas, Mohawks, Oneidas, Senecas **9** Onondagas

founder: **8** Hiawatha

five-year period: **6** pentad **7** lustrum

fix: peg, pin, set **4** glue, mend, moor, nail, seal **5** affix, allot, found, imbed, limit, tryst **6** adjust, anchor, arrest, assign, assize, attach, cement, clinch, define, fasten, ficche, freeze, repair, revamp, settle, temper **7** appoint, arrange, confirm, delimit, dilemma, impress, imprint, prepare, station **8** renovate, transfix **9** determine, establish, stabilize **10** constitute **11** predicament **13** embarrassment

firmly: set **4** moor **5** brace, grave, imbed, stamp **6** anchor, cement, enroot **7** engraff

fixed: pat, set **4** fast, firm **5** siker, staid **6** frozen, intent, mended, sicker, stable **7** certain, dormant, settled, statary **8** arranged, attached, constant, definite, explicit, fastened, immobile, moveless, resolute, stubborn **9** immovable, indelible, inerratic, permanent **10** stationary **12** determinable, refrigerated

amount: **4** rate **6** ration **7** stipend **10** remittance

star: **4** Vega

fixer: **8** handyman

fixture: **5** annex **7** bracket, shelves **8** counters, shelving **10** furnishing

fizgig: **9** fireworks, whirligig

fizzle: **4** fuss **6** barney **7** failure, flivver, hissing **9** agitation

flabby: lax **4** fozy, lash, limp, weak **5** frush **6** feeble **7** flaccid

flabellate: **9** fan-shaped

flabent: **10** flickering

flaccid: **4** limp **6** flabby, flaggy **8** yielding

flack: **4** blow, flap **5** throb **6** stroke **7** flutter

flacker: **5** throb **7** flutter, tremble

flag: fag, sag, sod **4** fail, fane, pine, turf, waif, wilt **5** droop, woman **6** banner, colors, ensign, flower, pennon, signal **7** ancient, cattail, decline, drapeau, pennant **8** banderol, brattach, languish, standard, streamer, vexillum **9** banderole, flagstone, fourpence

kind of: **5** Roger **6** burgee, colors, danger, ensign, fanion, guidon, muleta **7** calamus, curtain, pennant **8** brattach, banderol, masthead, standard, streamer, vexillum **9** blackjack, banderole **10** Jolly Roger

flagellants: **4** albi

flagellate: **4** flog, whip **5** throw **6** thrash **7** flutter, scourge

flagellum: **4** whip **5** shoot **6** runner **7** scourge

flageolet: **4** pipe **6** zufolo **7** basaree, zuffolo

flagging: **4** weak **7** languid **10** spiritless

flaggy: **4** weak **7** flaccid, languid **8** drooping

flagitious: **6** wicked **7** corrupt, heinous **8** criminal, flagrant, grievous **10** scandalous, villainous

flagon: **5** stoup **6** bottle, vessel **7** flacket

flagrant: bad **4** rank **5** gross **6** odious, wanton, wicked **7** glaring, hateful, heinous, scarlet, violent **8** shameful **9** abandoned, atrocious, egregious, monstrous, nefarious, notorious **10** flagitious, outrageous, profligate, villainous

flagstone layer: **5** paver

flail: **4** beat, flog, whip **6** thrash, thresh

flair: ray **4** bent, odor **5** skate, smell, taste **6** talent **7** leaning **8** aptitude **11** discernment

flake: **4** chip, film, flaw, rack, snow **5** fleck, flock, scale, strip **6** hurdle, lamina, paling **7** flaught **8** fragment

flaky: **5** scaly **7** laminar **8** laminose

flam: **4** whim **5** cheat, false, freak, trick **6** cajole, humbug, untrue **7** deceive, pretext, rubbish **8** drumbeat, illusory, nonsense, pretense **9** deception, deceptive, falsehood

flambeau: **5** torch **6** kettle **11** candlestick

flamboyant: **6** florid, ornate **7** flaming **9** flamelike **11** resplendent

flame: **4** fire, glow **5** ardor, blaze, flare, flash, glare, gleed, light **7** burning **9** affection **10** brightness, brilliance, sweetheart

fire without: **4** punk

movement: **4** dart, lick

flaming: **5** afire, fiery, vivid **6** ardent **7** blazing, burning, flaring **9** brilliant, consuming, flamelike **10** flamboyant, passionate **12** illuminating

Flanders capital: 5 Ghent
flanerie: 6 stroll 7 loafing 8 idleness 9 aimlessly, strolling 10 pillowcase
flaneur: 6 loafer 7 trifler
flank: 4 leer, side 5 thigh 6 border
flannel: 4 lana 6 stamin
flap: rob, tab, tag, wap 4 clap, flip, loma, slam, waff 5 alarm, flack, flaff, flipe, lapel, skirt 6 bangle, faffle, lappet, strike, tongue 7 aileron, blinder, flounce, flutter, swindle 9 appendage, operculum 10 epiglottis
flapper: 7 snicket 9 backfisch 10 backfische
flare: 4 bell, flue 5 blaze, flame, flash, fleck, fusee, light, torch 6 signal, spread 7 flicker 8 outburst 10 illuminate 11 ostentàtion
flaring: 4 bell, flue 5 evase(F.), gaudy 7 flaming, glaring 8 dazzling
flash: 4 pool 5 blash, blaze, burst, flare, flame, fluff, glaik, gleam, glent, glint, marsh, spark 6 bottle, fillip, glance 7 fouldre, glimmer, glimpse, glisten, glitter, instant, shimmer, sparkle 11 coruscation, fulguration, scintillate
flashing: 6 bright, flashy 7 forward 8 meteoric, snapping 9 fulgurant, fulgurous
flashy: gay 4 flat, gaud, loud 5 fiery, gaudy, showy 6 frothy, slangy, sporty 7 insipid, tinhorn 8 dazzling, flashing, vehement 9 impetuous 10 spiritless
flask: 4 olpe 5 betty, bulge, girba 6 bottle, fiasco, flacon, guttus 7 ampulla, canteen, matrass 8 cucurbit 9 aryballos
flat: 4 dead, dull, fade, plat 5 abode, aflat, banal, blunt, level, plane, prone, molle, vapid 6 boring, dreary, flashy 7 decided, insipid, platoid, prosaic, uniform 8 directly, dwelling, lifeless, unbroken 9 apartment, downright, prostrate, tasteless 10 homaloidal, horizontal, monotonous, unanimated 12 unmistakable 13 uninteresting
flatboat: ark 4 scow 5 barge
flatfish: dab, ray 4 butt, dace, sole 5 bream, fluke 6 acedia, plaice, turbot 7 sanddab, sunfish, torpedo 8 flounder
flatten: 4 even 5 level 6 deject, smooth 7 depress 8 compress, dispirit 9 prostrate 10 complanate, discourage, dishearten
flattened: 6 oblate 7 planate
flatter: 4 bull, claw, coax, fage, fume, palp 5 charm, float, gloze, honey, smalm 6 become, cajole, fickle, fleech, fraise, glaver, soothe, smooge 7 adulate, beguile, blarney, flether, flutter, wheedle 8 blandish, bootlick, collogue 10 compliment, ingratiate
flatterer: 6 cogger, glozer 7 soother 8 courtier 9 sycophant 10 assentator, greasehorn
flattering: 7 buttery, candied 11 assentatory

flattery: 4 bull, bunk 5 fraik, gloze, salve, taffy 6 butter, fleech 7 blarney, fawning, flether, palaver 8 cajolery 9 adulation 10 compliment 14 obsequiousness
flatulent: 5 gassy, windy 6 turgid 7 pompous, ventose 8 inflated 9 bombastic
flaunt: 4 bosh, wave 5 boast, vaunt 6 parade, trapes 7 display, flutter, traipse 8 brandish
flavicant: 6 yellow
flavor, flavour: 4 gamy, odor, rasa, salt, tang, zest 5 aroma, devil, sapid, sapor, sauce, savor, scent, taste, tinge 6 asarum, relish, season 7 perfume 8 hautgout, piquancy 9 fragrance
flavorable: 5 sapid, sipid 6 savory 9 palatable
flavoring material: 4 mint, sage 6 orgeat 7 cumarin 8 coumarin, cumarone 9 coumarone
flavorless, flavourless: 5 stale, rapid 9 tasteless
flaw: fib, gap, lie, mar 4 gall, hole, rase, rift, spot, wind 5 brack, cleft, crack, craze, fault, flake 6 breach, defect 7 blemish, default, fissure, nullify, violate, whitlow 8 fracture, fragment, gendarme 10 intoxicate 12 imperfection
flawless: 5 sound 7 perfect 9 faultless
flax: pob, tow 4 card, harl, lint 5 hards, hurds, linen, linin, pouce 6 bobbin
holder: 7 distaff
prepare: ret
refuse: pob
remove seed: 6 ribble
tool: 7 hatchel, swingle
flaxen-haired: 4 bawn
flaxseed: 7 linseed
flay: 4 skin 5 strip 6 fleece 7 censure, pillage, reprove 9 excoriate 11 decorticate
flea: 10 sandhopper
genus: 5 pulex
flebile: 7 doleful, tearful
fleck: fat 4 flea, flit, spot, tuft 5 flake, flare 6 dapple, streak, stripe 7 flutter, speckle 8 particle 9 variegate
fledgling, fledgeling: 5 squab
flee: fly, lam, run 4 bolt, fleg, loup, shun 5 elude, speed 6 escape, vanish 7 abandon, abscond, forsake 8 liberate 9 disappear, skedaddle
fleece: abb, jib, teg 4 bilk, fell, flay, gaff, wool 5 cheat, fleck, pluck, shear 6 toison 7 despoil
fleecy: 5 wooly 6 linten, woolly
fleeing: 7 fugient 8 fugitive
fleer: 4 gibe, grin, jeer, leer, mock 5 flout, laugh, scoff, sneer, taunt 7 grimace 8 derision
fleet: bay 4 fast, flit, navy, sail, skim, swim 5 creek, drain, drift, evand, float, flote, hasty, inlet, quick, rapid, swift 6 abound, argosy, armada, hasten, nimble, speedy 7

estuary **8** flotilla **10** evanescent, transitory

fleeting: **5** brief **6** caduke, volage **7** flighty, passing **8** caducous, fugitive **9** ephemeral, fugacious, transient **10** evanescent, transitory **11** impermanent

fleetings: 5 curds **9** skimmings

fleg: fly **4** flee, kick **5** fling, scare **6** fright

Flemish: *geographer:* **8** Mercator

painter: **5** Bouts **6** Mabuse, Massys, Rubens **7** Gossart, Memling, Patinir, van Eyck **8** Breughel, Brueghel, Gossaert, van Cleve **12** van der Weyden

flesh: kin **4** body, meat, race **5** stock **6** family, muscle **7** kindred, mankind **8** humanity **9** mortality **10** sensuality

appendage: **5** palpi(pl.) **6** palpus

formation: **8** sarcosis

kind of: **5** brawn **6** chevon, chiver **7** carrion

resembling: **7** sarcoid

fleshbrush: 7 strigil

flesh-eating: 11 carnivorous

fleshy: fat **5** beefy, human, obese, plump, pulpy, stout **6** animal, bodily, brawny, carnal **9** corpulent

fruit: **4** pear, pome **5** berry, drupe, melon **6** tomato

fleur-de-lis: lis, lys **4** iris, liss, luce, lucy

flex: 4 bend

flexible: 4 limp, lush, soft **5** buxom, lithe, withy **6** limber, pliant, supple **7** ductile, elastic, flexile, lissome, pliable, willowy **8** cheverel, cheveril, yielding **9** tractable **10** manageable

shoot: **4** bine

tube: **4** hose

flexile: 6 pliant **7** plastic, pliable **8** flexible **9** tractable, versatile

flexuous: 6 zigzag **7** relaxed **8** softened, wavering **9** adaptable **10** circuitous, flickering

flexure: 4 bend, bent, curl, fold **5** curve **6** bought

flichter: 6 quiver **7** flicker, flutter, vibrate

flick (see also **motion picture**): cut, hit **4** blow, flip, flit, snap, toss, whip **5** flisk, throw **6** flitch, propel **7** flutter

flicker: 4 fail, flit **5** flare, flunk, waver **6** fitter, shiver, yucker **7** blinter, flimmer, flitter, flutter, tremble **8** flichter **9** flaughter, palpitate **10** woodpecker

flickering: 7 flabent, lambent **8** flexuous, unsteady

flier: ace **5** pilot **6** airman **7** aviator **8** operator

female: **8** aviatrix **9** aviatress, aviatrice

flight: hop **4** bolt, rout **5** chevy, chivy, flock, scrap, volee **6** chivvy, exodus, hegira, hejira **7** flaught, migrate, mission, scamper **8** stampede, swarming **9** agitation, migration **12** perturbation

of fancy: **5** sally

of steps: **6** perron

of wild fowl: **5** skein

pert. to: **5** volar

put to: **4** rout

flightiness: 9 lightness

flighty: 5 barmy, giddy, swift **6** fitful, nimshi, volage, whisky **7** foolish, giggish **8** fleeting, freakish **9** transient **10** capricious **11** harum-scarum **13** shuttlewitted

flimflam: fob **5** freak, trick **6** humbug, tricky, trifle **7** swindle **8** nonsense, trifling **9** deception, deceptive **11** nonsensical

flimmer: 7 flicker, glimmer

flimsy: 4 limp, vain, weak **5** frail, gaudy **6** feeble, paltry, sleazy, slight **7** shallow, tenuous **10** gossamered **11** superficial **13** insubstantial, unsubstantial

flinch: 4 funk, game **5** feign, start, wince **6** blench, falter, flense, recoil, shrink

fling: 4 buzz, cast, dart, dash, ding, emit, fleg, gibe, hurl, kick, toss **5** cheat, dance, flirt, pitch, sling, sneer, throw, whang **6** baffle, effuse, hurtle, plunge, rebuff, spirit **7** flounce, repulse, sarcasm, scatter, swindle **9** overthrow

flint: 5 chert, miser, silex **6** quartz **9** firestone, skinflint

flintlock: 6 musket

flip: tap **4** flap, snap, toss, trip **5** flick, flirt, slirt **6** fillip, limber, nimble, pliant, propel **7** journey **10** somersault

flipe: 4 flap, fold, peel

flippant: 4 airy, glib **6** fluent, limber, nimble **9** talkative

flipper: arm, fin, paw **4** hand

flirt: tap, toy **4** dart, fike, flip, gibe, jeer, jest, joke, mash, mock, play, toss **5** dally, flick, fling, throw **6** coquet, fillip, masher, spring, trifle **7** trifler **9** philander

flit: 4 dart, flow, scud **5** fleck, fleet, flick, float, flurr, hover, quick, scoot, swift **6** nimble **7** flicker, flutter, migrate

flite, flyte: 4 gibe, jeer **5** chide, scold **6** strife **7** contend, dispute, quarrel, wrangle

flitter: rag **5** droop, hover, piece, waver **6** tatter **7** flicker, flutter, shuffle **8** fragment

float: fly, sea **4** buoy, cork, flow, flux, hove, pont, raft, ride, sail, scow, soar, swim, waft, wave **5** balsa, drift, fleet, flood, hover, ladle **6** billow, bobber, bungey, ponton **7** flatter, flotter, pontoon **8** overflow **9** catamaran, podoscaph

aloft: **4** soar

floating: 4 free **5** awash, loose **6** adrift, afloat, flying, natant **7** movable **8** drifting, fluitant, shifting, variable **9** wandering

flocculent: 6 woolly

flock: mob **4** bevy, fold, herd, pack **5** brood, bunch, charm, covey, crowd, drift, drove, flake, fleck, group, sedge, shoal, swarm **6** flight, hirsel **7** company **9** multitude **10** assemblage **11** aggregation

kind of: nid, nye, pod **4** nide, sord **5** covey, sedge, tribe

pert. to: **6** gregal

flocks (god of): Pan

floe: 4 raft

flog: cat, tan **4** beat, cane, hide, lash, toco, toko, wale, whip **5** birch, excel, fight, flail, linge, quilt, skeeg **6** cotton, larrup, strike, switch, thrash **7** baleise, belabor, scourge, sjambok, surpass, trounce **8** slaister **10** flagellate

flood: sea **4** bore, flow, flux **5** eagre, float, spate **6** deluge, excess **7** debacle, freshet, torrent **8** alluvion, inundate, overflow **9** cataclysm **14** superabundance

flooded: 6 afloat **10** surrounded

floodgate: 5 hatch **6** sluice

floor covering: mat, rug **4** tile **6** carpet, planks **8** linoleum, oilcloth

floor plank: 5 chess

flop: 4 whop

flora: 6 plants **9** florilege **11** florilegium

flora and fauna: 5 biota

floreate: 5 bloom

Florence: *coin:* **6** florin **7** ruspone
 devotees: **4** neri
 family: **6** Medici
 iris: **5** ireos, orris

Florentine (see also **Florence**): **4** gold **6** finish

florid: 5 buxom, fresh, ruddy **6** ornate **7** flowery **8** blooming, rubicund, vigorous **10** figurative, flamboyant, rhetorical **11** embellished, full-blooded

Florida: *city:* **5** Miami, Ocala, Tampa **7** Orlando, Palatka, Pompano **8** Sarasota **9** Pensacola **11** Tallahassee(c.)
 fishing boat: **7** smackee
 islands: **6** Bahama
 palm: **5** royal
 plain: **7** savanna **8** savannah
 region: **10** Everglades

floss: 5 fluff, skein, waste **6** sleave, stream

flotage: 8 buoyancy

flotilla: 5 fleet

flotsam: 8 driftage

flounce: 4 flap, slam **5** fling, frill **6** ruffle **7** falbala, falbelo **8** flounder, furbelow, struggle

flounder: dab **4** butt, keel, roll, toss **5** bream, fluke, megin **6** grovel, muddle, plaice, turbot, wallow **7** flounce, plounce, stumble, sunfish, topknot, vaagmar, vaagmer **8** flatfish, struggle, vaagmaer

flour: *bleach:* **5** agene
 diabetic: **9** aleuronat
 maker: **6** miller
 sifter: **6** bolter
 testing device: **11** farinometer
 wheat: **4** atta

flourish: 4 boom, brag, grow, riot, rise, show, wave **5** adorn, bloom, boast, cheve, gloss, quirk, vaunt **6** parade, paraph, thrive **7** blossom, display, enlarge, fanfare, prosper, roulade **8** arpeggio, brandish, curlicue, curlycue, increase, ornament **9** embellish **10** decoration **11** ostentation

flourishing: fat **4** frim **5** green, palmy **7** florent **8** thriving **10** prosperous, successful

floury: 4 meal

flout: bob **4** gibe, jeer, mock **5** fleer, flite,

flyte, frump, scoff, scorn, scout, sneer, taunt **6** deride, insult **7** jeering, mockery **8** betongue

flow: ebb, jet, run **4** bore, flit, flux, fuse, gush, hale, lava, lave, melt, pour, roll, shed,. sile, teem, well **5** avale, drain, eagre, exude, fleam, float, flood, glide, issue, river, spill, spurt **6** abound, deluge, recede, stream **7** current, emanate, flutter, meander, spurtle **8** alluvion, inundate **9** streaming **10** menstruate, outpouring **12** menstruation

flower (see also **plant**): bud **4** best, blow, flag, iris, ixia, pink, posy, rose **5** aster, bloom, elite, lilac, pansy, tulip **6** azalia, crocus, dahlia, orchid, posies(pl.), unfold **7** blethia, blossom, develop, fairest, gentian **8** camellia, choicest, daffodil, freshest, gardenia, geranium, hyacinth, ornament **9** carnation, embellish, gladiolus **12** chrysantheum
 appendage: **5** bract
 artificial: **7** rosette **8** gloxinia
 band: **6** wreath
 bell-shaped: **4** lily **5** tulip
 blooming once a year: **6** annual
 blue: **6** lupine **8** harebell
 bud: **5** ament, caper **6** spadix
 cluster: **4** cime, cyme **5** ament, bract, umbel **6** corymb, racéme **7** panicle **9** glomerule
 of death: **8** asphodel
 desert: **6** cactus
 extract: **4** atar, otto **5** attar, ottar
 fall: **5** aster **6** cosmos
 of forgetfulness: **5** lotus
 garden: **4** iris, ixia, lily, pink, rose **5** aster, canna, daisy, lilac, pansy, peony, phlox, tulip **6** asalia, olivia, orchid, violet **7** camella, freesia, petunia, verbena **8** bletilla, daffodil, gloxinia, hyacinth, primrose **9** buttercup, carnation, gladiolus, narcissus **10** heliotrope, ranunculus **11** honeysuckle
 goddess: **5** Flora
 imaginary: **7** amarant **8** amaranth
 large: **5** canna, peony
 late-blooming: **5** aster
 mass: **8** anthemia
 meadow: **5** bluet
 modest: **6** violet
 obsolete: **5** pense
 part: **5** calyx, sepal **6** anther, pistil, stamen **7** nectary, petiole **8** peduncle, perianth, pericarp
 passion: **6** maypop
 pink: **4** rose **7** rhodora
 prickly: **4** burr
 purple: **5** lilac, pense
 receptacle: **4** vase **5** torus
 spring: **4** iris **5** lilac, peony, tulip **7** arbutus **8** hepatica
 stand: **7** epergne
 stylized: lis
 unfading: **7** amarant **8** amaranth
 unknown kind: **8** belamour

white: **5** gowan

wild: **4** sage **5** bluet, daisy **6** lupine **7** anemone, arbutus **8** bluebell, hepatica **9** buttercup, innocence

wind: **7** anemone

yellow: **5** daisy, gowan, pense **7** jonquil **8** daffodil, marigold **9** buttercup

Flower State: 7 Florida

flowering: 7 flowery **8** anthesis, blooming **11** florescence

flowering plant: rue **4** arum **5** avens, calla, canna, comos, orpin, phlox, yucca, zamia **6** alalea, bareta, oxalis, spirea, teasel **7** barreta, gentian, lobelia, pavonia, petunia, rhodora, spiraea, tamarix, torenia, waratah **8** acanthus, ageratum, damewort, geranium, gerardia, valerian **9** candytuft, coreopsis, gloxinias, goldenrod, hollyhock, monkshood **10** pulsatilla, snapdragon

flowerpot: 10 jardiniere

flowery: 6 florid **7** florent **9** flowering **10** figurative, flosculous

flowing: 4 flux **5** fluid, fluor, tidal **6** afflux, fluent **7** copious, current, cursive, emanent, fluxing **9** affluxion, emanation **10** transitive

together: **9** confluent

flu: 6 grippe

flub: 4 muff **5** error

fluctuate: 4 sway, vary, veer **5** waver **7** vibrate **8** undulate, unsteady **9** oscillate, vacillate **10** irresolute **12** undetermined

fluctuating: 8 unstable, unsteady

flue: net **4** barb, down, open, pipe, thin **5** flare, fluff, fluke **6** expand, feeble, funnel, sickly, tunnel **7** chimney, flaring, passage, shallow

fluency: 9 eloquence, profusion **10** smoothness

fluent: 4 glib **5** fluid, ready **6** facile, liquid, smooth, stream **7** copious, flowing, fluidic, renable, verbose, voluble **8** eloquent, flippant **9** talkative **13** talkativeness

fluff: nap **4** down, flue, lint, puff **5** flash, floss, whiff

fluffy: 4 soft **5** downy, drunk, fluey, fuzzy **6** linten **8** feathery, unsteady **12** undependable

fluid: ink **4** rasa **5** water **6** fluent, liquid, watery **7** flowing, fluible, fluxile, gaseous **8** floating, fluxible

kind of: gas, ink, oil, sap, tar **4** bile, icor, milk **5** blood, ether, grume, ichor, latex, nerol, plasm, serum **6** naptha **7** acetone, coaloil, tearlet **8** gasoline, kerosene

measure: rhe

without: **7** aneroid

fluke: 4 fish, flue **5** blade **8** flounder

fluky: 8 unsteady **9** uncertain **10** capricious

flume: 4 leat **5** chute, gorge, water **6** ravine, sluice, stream **7** channel

flunk: 4 bust, fail **7** flicker

flunky, flunkey: 4 snob **5** toady **6** cookee **7** footman, servant, steward

flurry: ado **4** gust, stir **5** haste, skirl **6** bother, bustle, scurry, squall **7** confuse, flusker, fluster, flutter, fooster **9** agitation, carfuffle **10** discompose

flush: 4 even, glow, pool, rose **5** blush, elate, rouge, vigor **6** aflush, excite, lavish, mantle, morass, redden, thrill **7** animate **8** abundant, affluent, prodigal, rosiness **9** abounding, encourage **10** prosperous

flushing: 8 blushing **9** rubescent

fluster: 5 shake **6** flurry, fuddle, muddle, pother, rattle **7** confuse, flusker, fooster **8** befuddle, flustrum **10** discompose

flute: nay **4** fife **5** crimp **6** flauto, goffer, zufolo **7** chamfer, channel, gauffer, magadis, piccolo, zuffolo **8** flautino

player: **5** piper **6** aulete **7** flutist, tootler **8** auletris, flautist

wood for: **5** kokra

fluting: 5 strix **7** gadroon, godroon, strigil **10** gadroonage, godroonage

flux: 4 flow, fuse, melt **5** float, flood, resin, rosin, smear, smelt **6** fusion, stream **7** euripus, flowing, outflow

fluxible: 5 fluid **7** pliable **8** changing **10** inconstant

fly: bee, hop **4** flee, fleg, flit, leap, melt, scud, soar, solo, whir, whiz, wing **5** agile, alert, float, midge, pilot, quick, sharp, whirr **6** aviate, insect, nimble, spring, vanish **7** avigate, avolate, knowing **8** coachman **9** disappear

enemy: **6** spider

fishing: bee **4** lure **5** nymph, sedge **6** Cahill **7** Babcock, grannom, huzzard **8** coachman, Ferguson, hare's ear **9** alexandra, **10** Barrington

genus: **5** dacus

kind of: bee, bot, fag, mau, plu **4** gnat, kivu, zimb **5** alder, cadew, horse, midge, whame **6** breeze, gadfly, seroot, tsetse **7** butcher, collier, tachina **8** housefly **9** shoemaker **10** bluebottle **11** caterpillar, trichoptera

two winged: **8** dipteron

flybane: 12 cinnamonroot

flycatcher: 5 pewee **6** phoebe, yetapa **7** fielder, grignet, grinder

flyer: ace **5** pilot **7** Pegasus **8** aeronaut, operator

flying: 5 awing **6** flight, volant, waving **8** aviation, floating **9** fugacious

pert. to: **7** aviatic

flying adder: 9 dragonfly

flying boat: 8 seaplane **9** amphibian

flying body: 6 meteor

flying device: 4 kite **6** glider

Flying Dutchman heroine: 5 Senta

flying expert: ace

flying machine: 5 plane **8** aerostat **9** gyroplane **10** helicopter

flying mammal: bat

flying ship: 5 blimp **7** aeronat, biplane **8**

airplane **9** amphibian, dirigible, monoplane **10** helicopter
Fo: 6 Buddha
foal: 4 colt **5** filly
foam: fob, sud **4** fume, head, scud, scum **5**
frost, froth, spume, yeast **6** bubble,
freath, lather **7** blubber
foaming: 6 yeasty **7** spumous
foamy: 5 barmy, spumy **6** frothy
fob: 4 buck, foam **5** cheat, froth, trick **6**
impose, pocket **8** flimflam, impostor, ornament, swindler
focal: 7 central, centric, nuclear, nucleus
13 concentrative
focus: 4 foci(pl.) **5** point, train **6** center,
hearth **8** converge **9** fireplace **11** concentrate
fodder: hay **4** feed, food, vert **5** mange **6**
forage, silage **9** provender
kind of: ers, oat, rye **4** corn, rape **5** batad,
maize, vetch, wheat **6** barley, clover,
millet **7** alfalfa **8** deerweed **11** bitter
vetch
storing place: **4** silo **5** bakie **6** haymow,
silage **8** ensilage
foe: 5 enemy, fiend, rival **7** adverse, hostile, opposer, saracen **8** opponent **9** adversary, ill-wisher **10** antagonist
foederatus: 4 ally
foeman: 5 enemy **9** adversary
fog: dag, rag **4** damp, daze, haar, haze,
mist, moke, moss, murk, prig, roke, smog
5 bedim, brume, cloud, grass, vapor **6**
nebula, salmon, stupor **7** obscure, pogonip **8** bewilder, moisture **10** aftergrass
12 bewilderment
foggy: dim **4** dull, hazy, moky, roky **5**
dense, dirty, misky, misty, murky, rooky
6 cloudy, marshy **7** brumous, muddled,
obscure **8** confused, nubilous **9** becloud-
ed
foghorn: 5 siren
fogy: 6 foozle
foible: 4 weak **5** fault, ferly **6** feeble **7**
frailty **8** weakness **9** infirmity **12** imperfection
foil: 4 balk, soil, tain **5** blade, blunt, elude,
evade, stain, stump, sword, track, trail **6**
baffle, blench, boggle, defeat, defile, outwit, stigma, stooge, thwart **7** beguile,
failure, pollute, repulse, trample **8** disgrace **9** frustrate, overthrow **11** frustration
foist: 4 cask **5** barge, cheat, fudge, fusty **6**
galley, suborn **7** swindle **8** brackish **9**
rascality **11** interpolate
fold: bow, lap, pen, ply, wap **4** bend, cote,
fail, flap, furl, loop, plie, ruga, tuck **5**
clasp, crimp, drape, flipe, flock, layer,
plait, pleat, plica, prank, sinus, yield **6**
bought, crease, double, hurdle, infold,
plight, pucker, rimple **7** crumple, embrace, flexure, placate, plicate **8** surround
9 enclosure, overthrow, plicature
kind of: **4** loop **5** bight, lapel, plica, quire

6 bought, dewlap, octavo **7** plicate **9**
replicate
folder: 5 cover, folio **6** binder **7** leaflet **8**
pamphlet
folderol, falderal: 8 nonsense
foliage: 6 leaves **7** leafage
folio: fo **4** case, leaf, page
folk: 6 daoine, people **7** friends **9** inti-
mates, relatives
folklore genie: 7 Sandman
folks: 6 people
folle: mad **8** reckless **11** extravagant
folletto: imp **5** fairy **6** goblin, spirit
follicle: 5 crypt
follow: 4 copy, hunt, next, seek, shag, tail
5 adopt, after, chase, ensue, snake, spoor,
trace, track, trail **6** attend, pursue, result,
shadow **7** imitate, observe, replace, succeed **8** practice, supplant **9** accompany,
alternate, supervene **10** comprehend, understand
follow behind: dog, lag, tag **4** heel, hunt,
nose, tail **5** hound, trace **6** shadow, trail
7 draggle **9** supervene
follower: fan, ist, ite, son **4** aper, beau,
zany **5** gilly **6** bildar, ensuer, gillie, gudget, sequel, sulter, votary **7** devotee,
grifter, pursuer, retinue, spaniel **8** adherent, disciple, henchman, partisan,
retainer, servitor **9** attendant, cauda-
tory, cuadrilla, dependent, satellite,
successor **10** aficionado, sweetheart **11**
cuadrillero
following: 4 next, sect **5** after, suant,
train **6** sequel **7** ensuing, sequent **8**
business, trailing, vocation **9** clientele **10**
posthumous, profession, sequential, subsequent, succeeding, successive
exact words: **7** literal
laws of arithmetical algebra: **6** scalor
folly: sin **6** betise, dotage, lunacy **7** daffery,
daffing, foolery, foppery, madness, mis-
take **8** fondness, idleness, lewdness,
morology, nonsense, rashness **9** silliness
10 imprudence, wantonness **11** foolishness **12** indiscretion
foment: 4 abet, brew, spur **5** rouse, stupe
6 arouse, excite, incite **7** agitate, ferment
9 encourage, instigate
fond: tid **4** dear, dote, fain, fool, fund,
weak **5** silly, stock, store **6** ardent, befool,
caress, dearly, doting, fondle, loving, simple, tender **7** amatory, amorous, beguile,
browden, foolish, insipid **8** desirous, enamored, sanguine, trifling, uxorious **9** credulous, enamoured, indulgent, savorless
10 curcuddoch, infatuated, passionate
12 affectionate
of dainties: **6** friand **9** friandise
of drink: **8** bibulous
of hunting: **7** venatic
fonda: inn **5** hotel **6** fonduk **7** fondouk,
funduck
fondle: pet **4** baby, coax, fond, neck, waly
5 daunt, wally **6** caress, cocker, coddle,

cosset, dandle, pamper, stroke **7** cherish **8** blandish, canoodle

fondling: pet **4** fool **5** ninny **9** caressing, dalliance, simpleton

fondly: **4** fond **6** dearly **7** foolish **8** tenderly **9** foolishly **14** affectionately

fondness: gra **4** love **5** folly, taste **8** dearness, weakness **9** affection **10** attachment, tenderness **11** affectation, foolishness **12** predilection **15** Philotherianism

fondu: **6** cheese **7** blended

fons: **6** source **8** fountain

font: **4** pila **5** basin **6** source, spring **7** piscina **8** delubrum, fountain **10** aspersoria(pl.) **11** aspersorium

fontal: **8** original **9** baptismal

food: bit, pap **4** bite, cate, chow, diet, eats, fare, farm, gear, grub, meat, peck, prog **5** bread, broma, cheer, foray, scaff, tripe **6** fodder, foster, morsel, viands, wraith **7** aliment, edibles, handout, pabulum **8** flummery, grubbery, victuals **9** nutriment, provender **10** provisions, sustenance **11** nourishment

comb. form: **4** sito **5** troph **6** tropho

container: jar **4** bowl, dish, olla **5** crock, plate **6** saucer

craving for: **4** pica **7** bulimia

devotee: **7** epicure, gourmet

dislike of: **6** asitia **9** sitomania **10** cibophobia

dressing: **5** sauce

element: **6** gluten **7** protein, vitamin

heavenly: **5** manna

kind of: pap. poi, sop **4** ants. chum, crum, mess, mush, sago **5** acate, balut, bread, broma, cates. gruel, jelly, manna, puree, salep, scaff, souse, tripe **6** cagmag, cereal, farina, forage, hominy, vivres **7** abalone, boscage, pemican, tapioca **8** ambrosia, aperient, beebread, pemmican **9** aperitive, rechauffe **10** rechauffee

list: **4** diet, menu **5** carte

of gods: **6** amrita **7** amreeta **8** ambrosia

pert. to: **8** cibarial **9** cibarious

protein: **4** fish, meat **6** cheese

provision of: **4** mess **6** ration **8** catering

seller: **6** grocer **7** viander

storage pit: **4** cist

southern: **4** okra, pone **5** gumbo **6** hominy **7** hoecake **11** chitterling

special dish: **4** hogo, olla, stew **5** bredi, pilaf, pilau, pilaw, pizza **6** haslet, hominy, majoon, omelet, panada, pilaff, ragout, salmis, scouse, sundae, zimmis **7** chowder, custard, rarebit, ravioli, souffle **8** cabeliau, hautgout, omelette, sillabub, sukiyaki **9** cabilliau, colcannon, galantine, sish-kebab, succotash **10** salmagundi

starchy: **8** macaroni **9** spaghetti **10** vermicelli

unclean: **4** tref

food and drink: **4** diet, fare **5** bouge, found **6** bouche **10** provisions

fool: ape, ass, cod, fop, fox, mug, nup, toy **4** butt, cake, chub, dolt, dupe, fond, gowk, gype, jape, jest, joke, mome, nizy, simp, toot, zany **5** bluff, clown, dally, goose, idiot, knave, moron, ninny, nizey, noddy, sammy, silly, snipe, spoof, trick **6** buffle, cudden, cuckoo, delude, dotard, dottle, jester, nidget, nimshi, nincom, nupson, tamper **7** asinego, buffoon, coxcomb, deceive, dizzard, foolish, fribble, gomeral, gomeril, haveral, haverel, mislead, omadawn, playboy, witling **8** badinage, driveler, fondling, hoodwink, omadhaun **9** blockhead, capocchia, driveller, fopdoodle, hoddy-peak, hoddy-poll, simpleton **10** bufflehead, hoddy-doddy, nincompoop

foolable: **8** gullible

foolhardy: **4** rash **11** adventurous **12** presumptuous

fooling: **6** banter **7** daffery, daffing **12** harlequinade

foolish: mad **4** bete, daft, fond, fool, rash, zany **5** barmy, batty, boggy, buggy, dizzy, gawky, goofy, goosy, inane, inept, noddy, silly **6** absurd, dotish, fondly, gotham, harish, mopish, simple, stupid, unwise **7** asinine, doatish, doltish, fangled, fatuous, flighty, foppish, gullish, idiotic, witless **8** fopperly, headless, heedless **9** brainless, childlike, desipient, doddering, imprudent, insensate, ludicrous, senseless **10** half-witted, hulver-head, indiscreet, irrational **12** preposterous **13** feather-headed **14** feather-brained

foolishness: **5** folly **6** barney, levity, rubble **8** fondness **9** absurdity **10** insipience

foot: paw, pes **4** base, hoof **6** gammon

animal: pad, paw **4** hoof **7** fetlock, pastern

comb. form: **4** pedi

deformity: **5** varus

metric: **4** iamb **5** arsis, paeon **6** dactyl, iambic, iambus **7** anapest, spondee, triseme **8** bacchius, epitrite, molossus, trochee

pain: **8** talalgia

part: toe **4** arch **6** instep, tarsus, thenar **10** metatarsus

pert. to: **5** pedal, podal

poetic: See *metric* above

worked by: **5** pedal **7** treadle

foot bone: **6** tarsus **10** metatarsus

foot doctor: **10** podiatrist **11** chiropodist

foot lever: **5** pedal **7** treadle

foot-like part: pes

foot-loose: **4** free **10** ambulatory **11** untrammeled

foot soldier: **8** infantry

football: **5** rugby **6** rugger, soccer **7** pigskin

coach: **5** Jones, Morre, Stagg, Wilce **6** Bezdek, Dorais, Harlow, Romney **7** Crisler, Heisman, Higgins, Rockney **8** Morrison **9** Cavanaugh

kick: **4** punt **6** spiral
play: **4** buck, pass, punt **7** spinner
score: **4** down, goal **6** safety **9** touchback, touchdown
term: **6** onside **7** offside
footboy: **4** page **9** attendant
footed: **6** pedate
multiple: **7** bipedal, octopod **8** multiped
large: **7** megapod
footer: **4** fall, idle, jump **6** plunge, potter, trifle, walker
footfall: **5** tread
footgear: See **footwear**.
foothold: **7** toehold
footing: par **5** basis, track **7** toehold **9** footprint
footle: **5** silly **6** drivel, potter, trifle **7** trivial, twaddle
footless: **4** apod **5** apoda, apode, inapt **6** apodal, clumsy, stupid **13** unsubstantial
footman: **6** flunky, lackey, varlet, walker **7** flunkey, footpad, servant **8** chasseur **10** pedestrian
footpad: pad **4** whyo **6** padder, robber **7** footman **10** highwayman
footpath: **4** lane **5** senda, trail **8** trottoir
footprint: **5** trace, track, tread
fossil: **9** ichnolite
rabbit: **5** prick
footrest: **4** rail **7** hassock **9** footstool
footrope: **5** horse **8** boltrope
footstalk: **7** pedicel, petiole **8** peduncle
footstep: **7** vestige
footstool: **4** mora **6** buffet **7** cricket, hassock, ottoman **8** footrest
footway: **4** path **9** banquette
footwear: pac **4** boot, clog, pack, shoe, sock **5** kamik, sabot **6** arctic, bootee, brogan, brogue, buskin, galosh, kamika(pl.), patten, rubber, sandal **7** galoshe, slipper **8** moccasin, overshoe, stocking
footy: **4** mean, poor **6** paltry
fooyoung, fooyung: **6** omelet **8** omelette
fop: **4** buck, dude, dupe, fool **5** dandy **7** coxcomb, jessamy **8** gimcrack, popinjay **9** exquisite
foppery: **9** absurdity
foppish: **5** apish, dandy, silly **6** dapper, spruce, stupid **7** fangled, finical, foolish **8** dandyish
foppishness: **13** dandification
for: **7** because **8** favoring **9** favouring **10** concerning
prefix: pro
for all voices: **5** tutti
for cash: **9** alcontado (Sp.)
for each: per
with full: **5** amain
for example: e.g.
for fear that: **4** lest
for nothing: **6** gratis, lanyap **8** gratuity **9** lagniappe
for shame: fie

for temporary use: **4** jury
for that reason: **4** ergo(L.) **9** therefore
for which reason: **6** whence
forage: ers, oat, rye **4** corn, mast, raid, rape **5** grass, maize, raven, spoil, wheat **6** barley, browse, clover, fodder, millet, ravage, russud **7** alfalfa **8** deerweed **9** pasturage **10** provisions **11** bitter vetch
foramen: **4** pore
forane: **6** remote **7** foreign
foray: **4** rade, raid **5** melee **6** ravage, sortie **7** chappow, hership, pillage **9** incursion
forbear, forebear: **4** bear, help, shun, sire **5** avoid, forgo, spare **6** desist, endure, forego, parent **7** abstain, decline, refrain **8** ancestor **10** ancestress, forefather, foreparent
forbearance: **5** mercy **6** lenity **8** mildness, patience **9** tolerance **10** abstinence, self-denial **13** self-restraint
forbearing: **7** patient **8** tolerant **9** desisting
forbid: ban **4** defy, deny, fend, tabu, veto **5** debar, taboo **6** defend, enjoin, impede, refuse **7** forfend, forwarn, gainsay, inhibit **8** disallow, forefend, forspeak, preclude, prohibit **9** challenge, interdict, proscribe **10** contradict **11** countermand
forbiddance: ban **4** veto **12** interdiction, proscription
forbidden: **4** tabu **5** taboo **6** banned, denied **8** verboten **10** prohibited
Jewish law: **4** tref
Forbidden City: **5** Lhasa
forbidding: **4** grim **5** black, gaunt, stern **6** fierce, odious, strict **9** offensive, repellent **10** unpleasant **11** displeasing, prohibiting **12** disagreeable, interdicting
forbode: See **forebode**.
force: gar, gut, vim, vis **4** bang, birr, clip, cram, dint, feck, make **5** co-act, drive, exert, farce, impel, might, peise, poach, power, press, repel, shear, stuff, wrest **6** coerce, compel, cudgel, energy, extort, oblige, ravish, stithy **7** ability, afforce, cascade, impetus, impulse, require, violate **8** coaction, coercion, efficacy, momentum, pressure, strength, validity, violence, virility **9** constrain, influence, puissance, restraint, waterfall **10** compulsion, constraint, constringe **11** necessitate
air upon: **4** blow
into smaller space: **8** compress
kinds of: od **4** army, birr, dyne, elod, soul, task **5** agent, cadre, dynam, enemy, fohat, nerve, posse, steam, tonal **6** nature **7** voltage **8** bionergy, battalia, sanction **13** reinforcement
onward: **4** urge **6** propel
out: **5** evict
producing rotation: **6** torque
to do without: **7** deprive

forced: 7 labored 8 spurious 9 reluctant 10 artificial, compulsory, farfetched 11 constrained, involuntary, spontaneous 12 artificially

contribution: tax 4 duty, levy, toll 6 demand, excise, impost 7 tribute 8 exaction 10 assessment

feeding: 6 gavage

forceful: 6 mighty, strong, virile 7 dynamic, violent 8 eloquent, enfatico, forcible, vigorous 9 effective, energetic

forceps: 7 pincers 8 dentagra

forces: 4 army 6 troops

forcible: 5 stout, valid 6 cogent, mighty, potent 7 violent, weighty 8 emphatic, forceful, powerful, puissant, vigorous 9 energetic, impetuous, necessary 10 compulsory, convincing, impressive, obligatory 11 efficacious, influential

forcibly: 5 amain 6 hardly 9 violently 10 vigorously

ford: 4 wade, wath 5 drift 6 stream 7 current 8 crossing 9 wathstead

fore: van, way 5 afore, ahead, front, prior, track 6 former 7 earlier, further, journey 8 advanced, formerly 10 antecedent, previously

forearm: arm

bone: 4 ulna

pert. to: 7 cubital

forebear: See **forbear**.

forebode, forbode: 4 bode, omen 5 augur, croak 6 divine 7 betoken, portend, predict, presage 8 foretell 13 prognosticate 15 prognostication

foreboding, forboding: 4 omen 5 black 6 augury, boding, gloomy 7 anxiety 8 bodement, sinister 10 prediction 11 pessimistic, presagement 12 apprehension, presentiment

forecast: 4 bode 6 scheme 7 caution, foresee, fortune, predict 8 foredeem, foretell, prophesy 9 calculate, foregleam, forepoint, forescent, foretoken, prognosis 10 foreordain, prediction, prognostic 11 calculation, foredestiny 12 predetermine 15 prognostication

forecaster: 4 seer 6 oracle 8 dopester 11 nostradamus 13 meteorologist

foreclose: 5 debar 6 hinder 7 prevent 8 preclude

foredoom: 7 destiny 10 predestine

forefather: 4 sire 5 elder 6 parent 7 forbear 8 ancestor 9 grandsire 10 forerunner, progenitor

forefinger: 5 index

forefoot: paw, pud

forefront: van 5 front

foregather: 4 meet 7 consort, convene 8 assemble 9 encounter 10 fraternize

forego, forgo: 5 waive 7 abstain, neglect, precede, refrain 8 dispense, renounce

foregoer: 7 example 8 ancestor 10 forerunner 11 predecessor

foregoing: 4 past 5 above 8 anterior, previous 10 antecedent

foregone: 4 past 8 previous

conclusion: 9 certainty

forehanded: 5 early 6 timely 7 prudent, thrifty

forehead: 4 brow 5 frons, front 7 frontes 8 sinciput

pert. to: 7 metopic

prominence: 8 glabella

foreign: 5 alien, fremd 6 exiled, exotic, forane, remote 7 distant, ecdemic, exclude, strange 8 barbaric, peregrin 9 barbarous, extrinsic, peregrine 10 extraneous, outlandish, tramontane 12 adventitious, exallotriote, exterraneous

comb. form: 4 xeno

geology: 7 epigene

foreign service: *official:* 6 consul 7 attache 8 diplomat 10 ambassador

residence: 9 consulate

foreign to: 6 dehors

foreigner: 5 alien, haole 6 gringo, pakeha 7 greener, pardesi 8 outsider, stranger 9 barbarian, estranger, outlander 10 tramontane 12 ultramontane

forejudge: 7 adjudge

foreknow: 6 divine 7 foresee 9 prescient 11 preconceive

foreknowledge: 10 prescience

forel: 4 case 6 border, sheath 7 selvage 8 slipcase

foreland: 8 headland 10 promontory

forelay: 6 ambush, hinder, waylay 8 obstruct

forelock: 4 bang 6 cotter 8 linchpin

foreman: 4 boss 5 chief 6 gaffer, ganger, leader 7 capataz, captain, headman, manager, steward 8 overseer 9 chargeman 10 supervisor

foremost: 4 head, high, main 5 chief, first, forme, front, grand 6 banner 7 leading, supreme 9 principal

forensic: 8 forensal 10 rhetorical 13 argumentative

foreordain: 7 destine, foresay, predoom 8 forecast 9 preordain 10 predestine 12 predestinate, predetermine

forepart: 5 front 9 stomacher

forerun: 6 herald, outrun 7 precede, prelude 8 announce 9 forestall, introduce, precourse, prefigure 10 anticipate, foreshadow

forerunner: 4 omen, sign 5 usher 6 augury, herald 8 ancestor, foregoer, fourrier 9 harbinger, messenger, precedent, precursor 10 forefather, foreganger, progenitor, prognostic 11 predecessor

foresaid: 9 aforesaid

foresee: 4 read 6 divine 8 forecast, foreknow 10 anticipate

foreseeing: 9 designing

foreshadow: 7 forerun 9 adumbrate, prefigure

foreshow: 4 bode 5 abode, augur 7 betoken 8 foretell, prophesy 9 auspicate, foretoken 13 prognosticate

foresight: 6 vision 8 prudence 9 prevision 10 prescience, prevoyance, providence 11 forethought 12 anticipation 14 farsightedness

foresighted: 9 prescient, provident 10 farsighted

forest: 4 gapo, wood 5 Arden, glade, gubat, sylva(L.), taiga, waste 6 jungle, timber 7 boscage 8 caatinga, woodland 10 wilderness

deity: 4 faun 5 satyr 7 Aegipan

glade: 5 camas 6 camass, cammas 7 quamash

god: Pan 5 Tapio

open place: 5 glade

pertaining to: 6 sylvan 7 nemoral 9 forestral

warden: 6 ranger

Forest City: 8 Portland, Savannah 9 Cleveland

forester: 7 montero, treeman, woodman 8 woodsman

foretaste: 4 gust 6 teaser 8 prospect 12 anticipation

foretell: 4 bode, erst, read, spae 5 augur, insee, weird 6 divine 7 bespeak, foresay, portend, predict, presage 8 forebode, forecast, foreshow, prophesy, soothsay 9 predicate, prefigure, prophetic 10 vaticinate 13 prognosticate

foretelling: 9 fatidical, prophetic

forethought: 7 caution 8 prepense, prudence 9 foresight, provident 12 aforethought, anticipation 13 premeditation

foretoken: 4 omen 7 promise 8 forecast, foreshow, foresign 9 auspicate 10 presignify 13 prognosticate

foretold: 10 annunciate

foretooth: 5 biter 6 cutter 7 incisor

forever: ay; ake, aye 4 ever 5 etern 6 always, eterne 7 endless 8 eternity 9 endlessly, eternally, perpetual 10 constantly, invariably 11 ceaselessly, continually, everlasting, incessantly, perpetually, unceasingly 12 interminably, unchangeably 13 everlastingly

forewarn: 5 augur

forewarning: 7 portent 11 premonition

foreword: 5 proem 7 preface 8 preamble 12 introduction

forfeit: 4 fine, lose 5 crime, dedit, forgo 6 forego 7 escheat, misdeed, penalty 8 forfault

law: 7 abandum

forfeiture: 4 fine 5 mulct 7 penalty 9 decheance 10 amercement

forfend, forefend: 5 avert 6 forbid, secure 7 prevent, protect 8 preserve, prohibit

forfex: 6 shears

forge: 4 mint 5 feign 6 smithy, swinge 7 falsify, fashion 8 bloomery 9 fabricate 11 counterfeit, fabrication, manufacture

nozzle: tew 5 tewel

on: 5 drive

forged: 10 artificial 11 counterfeit

forger: 5 smith 9 falsifier 10 coachsmith, fabricator

forgery: 4 sham 7 fiction 8 bloomery 11 counterfeit, fabrication 13 falsification

forget: 4 omit 7 neglect 8 overlook 9 disregard 11 disremember

one's lines: 5 fluff

forgetful: 8 careless, heedless 9 oblivious 10 neglectful 11 inattentive

forgetfulness: 7 amnesia, amnesty 8 oblivion

river of: 5 Lethe

forging: 11 fabrication

forgivable: 6 venial

forgive: 5 remit, spare 6 excuse, pardon 7 absolve, condone 8 overlook 9 exculpate

forgiveness: 6 pardon 9 remission 10 absolution 11 condonation

forgiving: 6 humane 7 clement 8 merciful, placable 9 remissive 10 charitable

forgo, forego: 4 quit 5 leave 7 abstain, forbear, forfeit, forsake, neglect, refrain 8 abnegate, forebear, overlook, renounce 10 relinquish

forgoing: 5 above

forjudge, forejudge: 4 oust 5 expel 7 adjudge, condemn

fork: 4 tine 5 prong 6 bisect, branch, crotch, divide 7 fourche 10 divaricate, fourchette

kinds of: 4 croc, evil 5 graip, pikle, glack 7 biprong 9 tormentor

forked: 5 bifid 6 furcal 7 divided, furcate 8 branched 9 furciform 10 bifurcated 11 forficulate

forleave: 7 abandon

forlorn: 4 lorn, lost, reft 5 stray 6 abject, bereft, ruined 7 forfare 8 deserted, desolate, forsaken, helpless, hopeless, pitiable, wretched 9 abandoned, cheerless, desperate, destitute, miserable 10 friendless 11 comfortless 12 disconsolate

form: ame 4 blee, body, make, mode, mold, plan, rite, thew 5 bench, build, frame, guise, image, model, shape 6 adjust, create, figure, invent, manner, ritual, schema, sponge 7 arrange, compose, confect, contour, develop, fashion, outline, pattern, portray, produce, profile 8 ceremony, conceive, likeness, organize, schemata(pl.) 9 construct, etiquette, fabricate, formation, structure 10 appearance, constitute, expression, figuration, observance, similitude 12 conformation 13 configuration, questionnaire

carved: 8 statuary

display: 4 rack 7 manikin 9 mannequin

geometrical: see **figure:** *geometrical*

into arc: 5 embow

into ball: **8** conglobe
into chain: **8** catenate
into fabric: **4** knit
into network: **10** reticulate
literary: ode **5** novel, poesy **6** satire, sonnet **7** romance
liturgical: **6** litany **7** service
lyrical: **6** rondel **7** sestina, sestine(pl.)
of greeting: bow **5** hello, salam **6** salaam, salute **7** curtsey
formal: set **4** prim **5** exact, stiff **6** solemn **7** orderly, precise, regular, solward, starchy, stilted **8** academic, affected, formular, starched **9** essential, officious **10** ceremonial, methodical **11** ceremonious, punctilious, superficial **12** conventional
formality: **8** ceremony **15** conventionality
format: **4** size **5** shape, style **7** pattern
formation: **4** form, rank **9** structure **10** procession **11** composition, development **12** construction
bone: **7** ostosis **10** parostosis
cell: **6** tissue
flesh: **8** sarcosis
geological: lia **4** ione **5** atoll, ledge **6** schist **7** tapeats, terrain, terrane
military: **4** line **5** herse **7** echelon
sand: **4** dene, dune
formative: **7** plastic
forme: **5** bench, early, first **6** former **8** foremost
formed: **5** built **7** decided, matured, settled, wrought **10** constitute
at foot of mountain: **8** piedmont
by law: **9** corporate
crudely: **9** roughhewn
from above: **8** catogene
ingeniously: **5** dedal **6** daedal
of clustered grains (bot.): **7** grumose
on earth's surface: **7** epigene
former: ex; die, old **4** erst, fore, late, once, past **5** forme, gauge, guide, maker, prior **6** whilom **7** ancient, creator, earlier, further, pattern, quondam, templet **8** previous, sometime **9** aforetime, erstwhile **10** antecedent
prefix: ex
formerly: ere, nee **4** erst, fore, once, then **5** grave **7** onetime, quondam **8** sometime **9** aforetime, anciently, erstwhile **10** heretofore
formicary: ant **7** anthill, dweller
formicid: ant
formidable: **7** fearful **8** alarming, dreadful, menacing, terrible **11** redoubtable, threatening
formless: **5** arupa **7** anidian, chaotic **8** deformed **9** amorphous, shapeless **13** indeterminate
Formosa city: **6** Taipei, Taiwan **7** Dai-Hoku
formula: law **4** rule **6** method, recipe, theory **7** receipt

formular: **5** model **6** formal, proper **7** regular **9** formulary
formulated: **6** stated **10** articulate
forsake: **4** deny, drop, flee, quit, shun **5** avoid, forgo, leave, waive **6** beleve, defect, depart, desert, forego, refuse, reject **7** abandon, beleave, discard **8** renounce, withdraw **9** surrender **10** relinquish
forsaken: **4** lorn **7** forlorn **8** deserted, desolate **9** abandoned, destitute
forset: bar **5** beset **6** invest, waylay **8** surround
forspeak: **4** help **5** avert, curse **6** forbid, hinder **7** asperse, bewitch, devance, exclude, forerun, obviate, prevent **8** renounce **9** intercept **10** anticipate
forswear: **4** deny **6** abjure, reject **7** abandon, perjure **8** abnegate, renounce
forsworn: **8** perjured **11** disaffected
fort: pa: dun, lis, pah **4** liss, shee **5** gotta, redan, sidhe **6** castle, strong **7** bastile, bastion, bulwark, citadel, fortify **8** bastille, castillo, fastness, fortress **10** blockhouse, protection, stronghold
forte: **8** strength **9** specialty
forth: out **4** away **6** abroad, manage, onward **7** forward **8** outdoors **10** accomplish
forthink: **6** regret, repent **10** reconsider
forthright: **7** frankly **9** downright **11** straightway **13** straightforth **15** straightforward
forthwith: now **6** bedene, believe, direct **7** betimes **8** directly **9** extempore, presently, therewith **11** immediately
fortification (see also **defense**)**:** **4** boma, moat, wall **5** redan, tower **6** abatis, castle, glacis, shield **7** bastion, bulwark, citadel, parapet, rampart, ravelin, redoubt **8** fortress **9** barricade **10** stronghold **12** machiolation
kind of: **4** fort **5** redan **6** abatis, sconce **7** lunette, ravelin, redoubt, parados, **8** ceinture, demilune, estacade **9** fortalice, bastionet
part: **5** redan **7** bastion, ravelin **8** barbette
fortify: arm, man **4** fort **5** spike **6** abatis, picket **7** bastile, confirm **8** bastille, embattle, fortress, palisade **9** barricade **10** invigorate, strengthen, stronghold
fortitude: **6** mettle **7** bravery, courage, heroism, stamina **8** strength **9** endurance **10** resolution **12** resoluteness **14** impregnability
fortress: **4** fort, keep **5** rocca **6** castle **7** alcazar, barrier, bastile, borough, castlet, castrum, chateau, citadel, fortify **8** alcalzar, alcazava, bastille, chateaux(pl.), fastness **10** stronghold **13** fortification, propugnaculum
fortuitous: **6** casual, chance, random **9** hazardous **10** accidental, contingent, incidental **12** adventitious

fortuity: 4 luck 6 chance 9 accidence

fortunate: edi, hap, sri 4 good, shri 5 faust, happy, lucky, shree 6 dexter 7 favored 8 gracious 10 auspicious, prosperous, successful

fortune: hap, lot 4 bahi, doom, fate, hail, luck 5 weird 6 chance, estate, mishap, riches, wealth 7 destiny, success 8 accident, hacienda 9 adventure 10 prosperity 13 circumstances
goddess: 5 Tyche

fortune teller: 4 seer 5 gypsy, sibyl, sybil 7 diviner, palmist

forty: 13 quadragesimal

forty-third asteroid: 4 Eros

43,560 square feet: 4 acre

forum: 5 court 8 tribunal

forward: on, to; aid, bog, bug 4 abet, bain, bold, free, help, pert, send, ship, step 5 ahead, along, brash, eager, favor, forth, frack, freck, front, hasty, ready, relay, remit, saucy, serve, spack, ultra 6 afford, ardent, avaunt, before, bright, coming, favour, forthy, hasten, onward, prompt 7 advance, earnest, extreme, further, promote, radical 8 adelante, arrogant, immodest, impudent, perverse, petulant, transmit 9 audacious, encourage, forthward, obtrusive, overready 10 accelerate, forritsome, precocious 11 disobedient, progressive

fosette: 5 ulcer 6 dimple, hollow

fossa: pit 4 foss, moat 5 canal, ditch, fosse, fovea, graff, grave 6 cavity, trench 10 depression

fosse: See fossa.

fossil: 6 dolite 7 antique, lituite 8 calamite, conodont
science: 12 paleontology

fossorial: 9 effodient

fostell: box 4 cask 6 casket

foster: 4 feed, food, help, rear 5 nurse 6 harbor 7 cherish, embosom, gratify, imbosom, indulge, nourish, nursing, nurture, promote, sustain 8 befriend, forester, nursling 9 cultivate, encourage, fosterage, offspring 11 nourishment

foster child: 5 nurry 7 stepson 12 stepdaughter

fosterage: 11 achievement

foudroyant: 8 dazzling, stunning 10 thundering

fougue: 5 ardor 11 impetuosity

foul: 4 base, hory, roil, vile 5 bawdy, black, dirty, grimy, horry, muddy, nasty, sully, weedy 6 clarty, defame, dirten, filthy, impure, malign, odious, putrid, rotten, soiled, unfair 7 abusive, defaced, fulsome, hateful, illegal, noisome, obscene, profane, smeared, squalid, unclean, vicious 8 entangle, indecent, stinking, wretched 9 dastardly, dishonest, loathsome, nastiness, obnoxious, offensive 10 detestable, disgusting, scurrilous 11 contaminate, unfavorable 12 dishonorable, inauspicious

foulmouthed: 7 abusive, obscene, profane 10 scurrilous 11 opprobrious

foulness: 9 feculence

found: fix, try 4 base, cast, rest 5 board, build, endow, erect 8 attach, depart 8 equipped, practice, provided, supplied 9 establish, institute, originate, supported 10 foundation

foundation: bed 4 base, body, fund, gist, sill 5 basis, bases(pl.), found, stock 6 bottom, legacy, reseau, riprap 7 bedding, bedrock, chantry, roadbed 8 donation, pedestal 9 beginning, endowment 11 corporation 12 substructure

founder: 4 fail 6 author, caster, dismay, dynast 7 stumble 8 miscarry 9 supporter, undermine 10 maintainer 11 dumbfounder, establisher
metal: 5 yeter 6 yetter

founding: 8 settling

foundling: oaf 4 waif 6 infant, orphan 8 nursling

fount: 4 fons 6 source 8 fountain 9 reservoir

fountain: 4 fond, head, syke, well 5 fount 6 phiale, pirene, source, spring 7 bubbler 8 aganippe 9 reservoir 12 fountainhead
nymph: 5 naiad

fountainhead: 6 origin, source

four: *comb. form:* 5 tetra
group of: 6 tetrad 7 quartet 8 quadriad 9 quartette

four-footed: 9 quadruped

four hundred: 5 creme, elect, elite 6 select

four-in-hand: 7 necktie

four-sided: 13 quadrilateral

fourchette: 4 fork 8 wishbone

fourflusher: 9 pretender

fourpence: 5 groat

fourrier: 9 harbinger 10 forerunner 13 quartermaster

fourscore: 6 eighty

fourth: 5 quart 6 fardel 7 quarter 8 quadrant

fourth estate: 5 press 10 newspapers

fowl: hen 4 bird, cock 5 chick, chuck, manoc 7 chicken, rooster 8 volaille
kinds of: 4 keel, coot 5 malay, banty, snipe, poult, brant 6 Houdan, bantam, Sussex, rumkin 7 minorca, galeeny

fox: tod 4 fool 5 trick 6 canine, outwit 7 beguile, stupefy, vulpine 10 intoxicate, perplexity
foot: pad
hunter's cry: 4 soho 5 yoick
kinds of: cub 4 asse, stag 5 vixen, zorro 6 fennec, corsac 7 Reynard, karagan
scent of: 4 drag

foxglove: 7 popdock

leaf: **9** digitalis
foxlike: 9 alopecoid
foxy: sly **4** wily **5** coony **6** shrewd **7** cunning, vulpine **10** fraudulent
foy: 4 gift **5** faith, feast
foyer: 5 lobby **6** hearth **8** anteroom, entrance **9** fireplace, greenroom
fra: 4 monk **5** friar **6** priest **7** brother
Fra Diavolo composer: 5 Auber
frab: nag **5** scold, worry **7** contend **8** struggle
fracas: 4 bout **5** brawl, melee, set-to **6** rumpus, uproar **7** quarrel **8** fraction **9** commotion **11** disturbance
fraction: bit **4** part **5** break, piece, scrap **6** breach, fracas, little **7** ruction, rupture **8** breaking, fracture, fragment
fractional: 7 partial
fractious: 4 ugly **5** cross **6** unruly **7** crabbed, peevish, waspish **8** perverse, snappish **9** irritable
fracture: 4 flaw, rend **5** break, cleft, crack **6** breach **7** rupture **8** fraction
fragile: 4 fine, frow, weak **5** frail, frowy, light **6** feeble, frough, infirm, slight **7** brickle, brittle, froughy, slender **8** delicate, ethereal **9** frangible
fragility: 8 delicacy **12** delicateness
fragment: bit, ort **4** blad, chip, flaw, grot, part, snip, wisp **5** broke, crumb, flake, groat, piece, relic, scrap, shard, sherd, shred, spall **6** gobbet, morsel, parcel, screed, sheard, sippet, sliver **7** cantlet, flinder, flitter, fritter, oddment, portion, remnant **8** fraction **10** smithereen
biographical: **8** anecdote
diamond: **4** bort
ice afloat: **5** brash
fragmentary: 5 hashy **6** broken
fragments: 5 frush **7** gubbins
literary: ana **7** analect
fragrance: 4 odor **5** aroma, scent, smell **6** flavor **7** flavour, incense, perfume **9** perfumery, redolence
fragrant: 5 balmy, olent, spicy **7** odorant, odorous, perfumy, scented **8** aromatic, redolent **9** ambrosial **11** odoriferous
fragrant ointment: 4 balm, nard
fragrant wood: 5 aloes, cedar
fraicheur: 5 chill **8** coolness **9** freshness
frail: 4 fine, puny, weak **5** crazy **6** basket, flimsy, infirm, sickly **7** brittle, bruckle, fragile **8** delicate **12** destructible **13** insubstantial
frailty: 5 fault **6** foible **7** failing **9** frailness, infirmity **10** peccadillo **12** imperfection
fraise: 4 fray, fuss, ream, ruff **6** cajole, defend, praise **7** defense, enlarge, flatter, pancake **8** cajolery **10** strawberry **11** disturbance
fraist: ask, try **4** seek **7** attempt **10** experience
fram: 5 spear

frambesia: 7 disease, sibbens, sivvens
frame (see also **framework**): go, bin **4** bunk, form, mold, plan, plot, sill **5** build, cadre, easel, panel, serve, shape, trave **6** abacus, adjust, binder, border, devise, fabric, invent, manage, profit, redact, resort, tenter **7** arrange, attempt, chassis, fashion, furnish, outline, portray, prepare, proceed, prosper **8** contrive, regulate **9** calculate, construct, fabricate, structure
kinds of: ame, mat **4** bier, calm, caum, gill, sash, sess, sime, sley, **5** airer, cadar, cader, dekle, easel, grate, herse, knape, trave, scray **6** abacus, deckel, deckle, tenter **7** drosser, hayrack, taboret,
frame-up: 4 plot **10** conspiracy
framework: 4 rack, sill **5** cadge, cadre, racke **6** replum, stroma **7** chassis, nacelle, trestle **8** skeleton
frampoid: 5 cross, fiery **7** peevish **8** spirited **9** vexatious **11** quarrelsome
franc: *piece of twenty:* **5** louis
twentieth part of: **7** centime
France: 4 Gaul **6** Gallia
airplane: **5** avion
and: et
appellation: nom
architect: **7** Lenotre **9** Corbusier
article: la, le, un; les, une
author: **4** Hugo, Loti **5** Dumas, Renan
bachelor: **6** garcon
bacteriologist: **7** Pasteur
ball: bal
ballad: lai **7** virelai
bay: **6** Biscay
beach: **5** plage
beast: **4** bete
billiards: **7** bouchon
bitters: **4** amer
boat: **8** chaloupe
bond: rente
boxing: **6** savate
boy: **6** garcon
brandy: **8** armagnac
brewery: **9** brasserie
brush: **6** brosse
butcher shop: **11** charcuterie
cafe: **9** estaminet
cape: **5** talma
capital: **5** Paris
card game: **6** ecarte **7** baccara **8** baccarat
care: **4** soin
cathedral city: **5** Reims, Rouen **6** Nantes, Rheims
champagne: Ay
chaperon: **11** gouvernante
cheese: **4** Brie **9** Roquefort
chemist: **5** Curie **7** Pasteur
chestnut: **6** marone, maroon
citizen: **7** citoyen
city: Ay; Aix, Pau **4** Caen, Metz, Nice, Riom, Sens, Vimy **5** Aries, Arles, Arras, Brest, Dijon, Harve, Lille, Lisle, Lyons, Nance, Nancy, Nerac, Nesle, Nimes,

Paris, Reims, Rouen, Sedan, Seine, Tours, Vichy **6** Amiens, Angers, Calais, Lemans, Nantes, Pantin, Perret, Rennes, Rheims, Senlis, Sevres, Tarare, Toulon **7** Bareges, Ferrand, Limoges, Orleans, Roubaix, Valence **8** Bordeaux, Clermont, Mulhouse, Rochelle, Toulouse **9** Levallois, Marseille, Tourcoing **10** Saint-Denis, Strasbourg, Strassburg **11** Montpellier **12** Saint-Etienne

cleric: **4** abbe
cloth: ras **5** toile **8** blancard
cloud: nue
coffee house: **9** estaminet
coin: ecu, sol, sou **4** gros **5** agnel, blanc, blank, franc, obole, livre **6** denier, dizain, teston **7** centime, dizaine, testoon **8** cavalier, Louis d'or, Napoleon
composer: **4** Lalo **5** Bizet, Ravel, Thome **6** Gounod, Halevy **7** Debussy
comrade: ami
concrete: **5** beton
conjunction: et
cordial: **8** anisette
cotton: **7** jasmine
cowboy: **6** baille **7** gardian
creamcake: **7** dariole
crown: ecu
curate: **4** abbe
custom: **9** Gallicism
daffodil: **10** polyanthus
daisy: **10** marguerite
dance: bal **5** gavot **6** branle, canary, cancan **7** bourree, boutade
dash: **4** élan
dead: **4** mort
dean: **5** doyen
dear: **4** cher
delicatessen: **11** charcuterie
department: Ain, Lot, Var **4** Aube, Aude, Cher, Eure, Gard, Gers, Jura, Nord, Oise, Orne, Tarn **5** Aisne, Corse, Doubs, Drome, Indre, Isere, Loire, Marne, Meuse, Rhone, Seine, Somme, Yonne **6** Allier, Ariege, Cantal, Creuse, Landes, Loiret, Lozere, Manche, Nievre, Sarthe, Savoie, Vendee, Vienne, Vosges **7** Ardeche, Aveyron, Correze, Dordgne, Gironde, Herault, Mayenne, Meurthe, Moselle **8** Ardennes, Calvados, Charente, Morbihan, Vaucluse **9** Finistere
designer: **4** Dior, Gres **5** Patou **6** Chanel **8** Givenchy **9** Courreges, St. Laurent **10** Balenciaga
diplomat: **5** Segur, Senet **7** Ronsard
directory: **10** directoire
division: **6** canton **7** commune **10** department **14** arrondissement
division, ancient: **5** Arles **6** Arelas **7** Arelate **9** Aquitaine
doorkeeper: **9** concierge
dramatist: **5** Piron **6** Halevy, Racine, Sardou **7** Moliere
dressmaker: **9** couturier **10** couturiere

duke: duc
dungeon: **6** cachot
dynasty: **5** Capet **6** Valois
ecclesiastic: **4** abbe
empress: **7** Eugenie
essayist: **4** Gide
F.B.I.: **15** Surete Nationale
farmhouse: mas
father: **4** pere
friar: **5** frere
friend: ami
gala: **4** fete
game: jeu **4** jeux(pl.)
good: bon
green: **4** vert
hairdresser: **7** friseur
hat: **5** beret **7** chapeau **8** chapeaux
health: **5** sante
heaven: **4** ciel
here: ici
high: **5** haute
horse stable: **6** ecurie
husband: **4** mari
income: **5** rente
island: ile **4** Elba
judgment: **5** arret
king: roi **5** Louis, Capet
lace: **10** colberteen, colbertine **12** Valenciennes
lake: **6** Annecy **7** Bourget
language: **7** Catalan **9** Provencal
laundry: **13** blanchisserie
lenten season: **6** Careme
liqueur: **5** creme **8** anisette **9** Cointreau
lord: **8** seigneur
lover: **5** amant
lyric: **6** rondel **7** descort, rondeau
magistrate: **7** echevin
maidservant: **5** bonne **7** lisette
mask: **5** loups
mathematician: **5** Borel
me: moi
measure: pot **4** aune, line, mile, mine, muid, pied, sack, velt **5** arpen, carat, lieue, ligne, minot, perch, pinte, point, pouce, toise, velte **6** arpent, hemine, league, perche, quarte, setier **7** chopine, heminee, poisson, septier **8** boisseau, quartaut, roquille **9** decillion, quarteron **12** tonneau de mer
money: See **coin** above
mountain: **4** Alps, Jura **6** Vosges **8** Auvergne, Cevennes, Cote d'Or, Pyrenees **9** Mont Blanc, Puy de Dome, Vignemale **10** Puy de Sancy
name: nom
national anthem: **12** Marseillaise
national flower: **4** lily
no: non
novelist: **4** Gide, Hugo, Loti, Zola **5** Camus, Dumas, Ohnet, Sagan, Verne **6** Halevy, Proust **7** Merimee **8** Flaubert
nursemaid: **5** bonne
of: de

officer: **7** prefect
one: une
opera: **5** Faust, Manon **6** Carmen, Mignon
painter: **4** Dore **5** Corot, Degas, Manet, Monet **6** Cormon, Legros, Renoir, Vernet **7** Chardin, Deveria, Lorrain, Poussin, Watteau **8** Steinlen **9** Deschamps
palace: **6** elysee
parish priest: **4** cure
Parliament chamber: **5** senat
party: bal
pastry shop: **10** patisserie
patron saint: **5** Denis, Denys **6** Martin
peer: duc **8** seigneur
philosopher: **4** Caro **5** Camus **6** Pascal, Sartre **8** Rousseau **9** Descartes
physicist: **5** Arago, Binet **6** Ampere
pocket: **5** poche
poem: dit, lai **7** rondeau
poet: **4** Labe **6** Racine **7** Rimbaud, Rostand **9** Deschamps, Desportes
police: **6** Surete **8** gendarme
porcelain: **7** Limoges
port: **4** Caen
preposition: de
president's residence: **6** elysee
priest: **4** abbe, cure, pere
pronoun: tu: moi **4** elle **6** tienne
queen: **5** reine
rabbit: **5** lapin
race course: **7** Auteuil
railroad: **10** tortillard
railroad station: **4** gare
rear: **7** arrière
Republic calendar: **6** Nivose **7** Floreal, Ventose **8** Brumaire, Fervidor, Frimaire, Germinal, Messidor, Pluviose, Prairial, **9** Fructidor, Thermidor **11** Vendemiaire
resort: Pau **4** Nice **5** Vichy **6** Cannes, Menton **7** Riviera
rest: **5** repos
restaurant: **6** bistro
Revolutionary hero: **6** Danton
Revolutionary leader: **5** Marat
Revolutionary radical: **7** Jacobin
river: Ain, Lot, Lys **4** Aire, Aude, Cher, Eure, Gard, Gers, Loir, Oise, Orne, Saar, Tarn, Yser **5** Adour, Aisne, Drome, Indre, Isere, Loire, Maine, Marne, Meuse, Rance, Rhone, Saone, Seine, Seyre, Somme, Veste, Yonne **6** Allier, Ariege, Escaut, Loiret, Nievre, Sambre, Scarpe, Vienne **7** Ardeche, Durance, Garonne, Gironde, Moselle, Scheldt **8** Charente, Dordogne, Nantaise
room: **5** salle
royal family: **5** Capet **6** Valois
saint: **5** Denis, Denys **6** Martin
savant: **7** Diderot
school: **5** ecole, lycee **8** Barbison, Barbizon
scientist: **5** Curie **7** Pasteur
sculptor: **5** Rodin
sea: mer

seaport: **4** Caen **5** Brest, Havre **6** Calais, Toulon **8** Bordeaux **9** Dunkerque
shield: ecu **5** targe
shoe: **9** chaussure
shopgirl: **9** midinette
slang: **5** argot
soldier: **5** assis, poilu **6** Zouave **8** chasseur
song: **5** caira **6** aubade **7** Madelon, virelai, virelay
soul: ame
stable: **6** ecurie
state: **4** etat
stock exchange: **6** bourse
store: **8** boutique
story: **5** conte
summer: ete
symbol: **4** lily **10** Fleur-de-lis
the: la, le; les(pl.)
theater: **5** odeon
then: **5** alors
ticket window: **7** guichet
title: duc **5** comte
tobacco: **5** tabac
town: **4** Agen, Aire, Caen, Sens, Sete **5** Douai, Ernee, Laval, Nerac, Ornes **6** Longwy, Sarlat, Tarbes, Troyes, Verdun **7** Castres **8** Le Perche, Rochelle, **9** esterling
Verdun battle: **4** Vaux
verse: **4** vers
verse form: lai **4** alba **6** rondel **7** ballade, virelay
very: **4** tres
vessel: **7** navette
vinegar: **8** vinaigre
vineyard: cru
waiter: **6** garcon
water: eau **4** eaux(pl.)
weight: **4** gros, marc, once **5** carat, livre, pound, tonne, uckia **7** tonneau **8** esterlin **9** esterling
who: qui
wicket: **7** guichet
wine: vin **4** Bois **8** sauterne **10** Roussillon
wine district: **5** Medoc **8** Burgundy **9** Champagne
wine shop: **6** bistro
woman: **5** femme
you: tu **4** vous
Franciscan: **8** Minorite, Capuchin **9** Cordelier
nun: **5** Clare
franchise: soc **5** grant **6** patent **7** license **8** freelage, suffrage **9** privilege
frangible: **7** brittle, fragile **9** breakable
frank: **4** free, open, rank **5** bluff, lusty, naive, plain **6** candid, direct, honest **7** artless, genuine, liberal, profuse, sincere, **8** carefree, cavalier, generous, vigorous **9** ingenuous, luxuriant, outspoken **10** licentious, unreserved **15** straightforward, unsophisticated
frankincense: **8** olibanum
Frankish hero: **6** Roland
Franklin's nickname: **11** Poor Richard

frankly: 6 freely, openly 7 plainly 8 candidly 9 artlessly, liberally, sincerely, willingly 10 forthright 11 ingenuously 12 unreservedly 13 undisguisedly

frankness: 6 candor 7 freedom 8 openness 9 telltruth, unreserve

frankpledge: 6 borrow

Franks: 7 Salians
hero: 6 Roland
king: 5 Pepin 6 Clovis
law of: 5 Salic

frantic: mad 5 rabid 6 insane 7 furious, lunatic, violent 8 deranged, feverish, frenetic, frenzied 9 delirious, desperate, phrenetic 10 distracted, distraught

frap: 4 beat 5 brace 6 strike 7 tighten 10 strengthen

frappe: ice 4 iced 5 chill 6 cooled, freeze, frozen 9 milkshake

frat: 11 brotherhood

fratch: 7 dispute, quarrel, wrangle

frater: 7 brother, comrade

fraternal: 9 brotherly

fraternity: 4 club 8 sorority 10 sisterhood 11 brotherhood

fraternize: 6 cotton 9 affiliate, associate, forgather 10 foregather

fraud: 4 dole, fake, gaff, gaud, gull, jape, ruse, sham, wile 5 cheat, craft, faker, guile, hocus, quack, trick 6 brogue, deceit, humbug 7 defraud, knavery, roguery, swindle 8 artifice, impostor, subtlety, trickery, trumpery 9 collusion, deception, imposture, stratagem 10 imposition 11 fraudulency 13 circumvention

fraudulent: 4 fake, wily 5 snide 6 crafty, quacky 7 abusive, crooked, cunning 8 cheating, covinous, guileful, spurious 9 deceitful, deceiving, deceptive, designing, dishonest, horsefair, insidious, underhand 10 fallacious, misleading 11 clandestine, counterfeit, treacherous

fraught: 4 fill, lade, load 5 cargo, equip, laden 6 burden, supply 7 freight 9 freighted, transport

fray: 4 feud, fret, riot 5 alarm, broil, broom, dread, feaze, fight, melee, panic, ravel 6 affray, assail, attack, battle, bustle, combat, fraise, fridge, fright, inroad, terror, tumult 7 contest, frazzle, ruction, terrify 8 disperse, frighten 9 commotion, dissipate 12 apprehension

frayed: 4 worn 7 raveled 10 threadbare

freak: 4 bold, flam, lune, mood, whim 5 braid, fancy, fleck, humor, prank, sport 6 frolic, greedy, humour, megrim, streak, vagary, whimsy 7 caprice, checker, crochet, monster, whimsey 8 capricci(pl.), flimflam 9 capriccio, variegate 11 monstrosity 12 whimsicality

freakish: odd 6 screwy 7 curious, flighty 9 fantastic, whimsical 10 capricious

fream: 4 roar

freath: 4 foam 5 froth 6 lather

freck, frack: 4 bold, hale 5 eager, lusty, ready, stout 6 dapple, strong 7 checker, forward 8 desirous 9 diversify

freckle: 4 spot 7 ephelis, frecken, lentigo

Frederick the Great: 6 Alaric

free: lax, rid 4 liss, open, quit, void 5 broad, clear, enode, frank, lisse, loose, ready, siker, slake, spare, untie 6 acquit, adjust, beyond, degage, devoid, exempt, gratis, immune, lavish, loosen, remove, rescue, sicker, unbind 7 absolve, deliver, forward, grivois, inexact, leisure, liberal, manumit, outside, release, relieve, unbound, willing 8 abundant, detached, dispatch, distinct, expedite, familiar, floating, generous, grivoise, indigent, innocent, liberate, overfree, separate, unfasten, unhamper 9 discharge, disengage, exculpate, exonerate, expansive, extricate, foot-loose, guiltless, ingenuous, outspoken, separated, unbridled, unchecked, unimpeded, unleashed 10 autonomous, emancipate, gratuitous, immoderate, licentious, openhanded, unattached, uncombined, unconfined, unfettered, unimpaired, unreserved 11 disencumber, disentangle, independent, magnanimous, spontaneous, untrammeled 12 uncontrolled, unencumbered, unrestrained, unrestricted 13 communicative, unconstrained
from bacteria: 7 aseptic, sterile
from blame: 5 clear 6 acquit 7 absolve, relieve 9 exonerate
from bondage: 7 manumit 10 emancipate 11 affranchise
from dirt: 7 apinoid
from moisture: dry 9 dehydrate
from suspicion: 5 clear, purge 6 acquit 7 absolve 9 exculpate, exonerate

free-for-all: 4 race 5 fight, melee 6 barney 11 competition

free of charge: 8 buckshee

free time: 4 rest 6 recess 7 leisure

freebooter: 5 rider 6 pirate 7 cateran, corsair 8 pillager 9 buccaneer, plunderer 10 filibuster

freed: 8 absolute 13 disencumbered

freedom: 4 ease 7 abandon, content, leisure, liberty, license, release 8 facility, freelage, immunity, latitude, openness 9 exemption, frankness, readiness 10 generosity, liberality, liberation 11 manumission, willingness 12 emancipation, independence 13 outspokenness 14 unreservedness
from activity: 4 rest 6 recess 7 respite
from fraud: 7 honesty 9 bonafides
from pain: 6 aponia
from strife: 5 peace
of access: 6 entree

freehold: 4 alod 5 allod 6 estate, tenure 7 alodium 8 allodium

freeholder: 6 yeoman

freeing: 8 acquital 11 manumission
freely: 4 lief 5 noble, nobly 6 gratis 7 frankly, largely, readily 8 heartily 9 beautiful, bounteous, bountiful, copiously, excellent, liberally, voluntary, willingly 10 abundantly, generously 11 beautifully, bounteously, bountifully, excellently, plenteously, plentifully, voluntarily 12 munificently 13 spontaneously 14 unobstructedly 15 unconditionally
freeman: 4 aire 5 ceorl, churl, thane, thegn 6 yeoman 7 burgess, burgher, citizen
Freestone State: 11 Connecticut
freethinker: 7 infidel, skeptic 8 agnostic 10 espritfort, unbeliever
freeze: ice 4 rime 5 chill 6 frappe, harden 7 chilled, congeal, impound 11 conglaciate, refrigerate
freezer: 4 icer
freezing: 4 cold 6 frigid, frosty
freight: 4 load 5 cargo, laden 6 lading 7 fraught 9 transport 10 freightage
freightage: 5 cargo 6 lading 7 freight
freighted: 5 laden 7 fraught
French: See **France.**
French-Belgian river: Lys 4 Yser
frenetic, phrenetic: mad 4 wild 5 crazy, fresh 6 insane, madman 7 fanatic, frantic, madness, violent, zealous 9 delirious 10 distracted, ornamental, passionate 12 absent-minded
frenzied: 4 amok, mang 5 amoke, amuck, rabid 6 ramage 7 berserk, frantic, furious 8 franetic, furibund, maddened 9 delirious
frenzy: mad 4 amok, fury, rage 5 amoke, amuck, furor, mania 7 frantic, madness, oestrus 8 delirium, insanity, maniacal 9 amazement 11 distraction
frequency: 5 crowd 6 throng 7 crebity 9 community, concourse 11 familiarity
  unit: 7 fresnel
frequent: 5 haunt, howff, often, usual 6 affect, common, effect, hourly, sundry 7 current, enhaunt, prevail 8 familiar, habitual 9 assiduous, crebrouse, habituate 10 persistent
frequented places: 5 dives 6 haunts 7 resorts
frequenter: 7 habitue
frequently: oft 5 often 6 hourly 8 ofttimes 10 repeatedly
fresco: 5 mural, shade 8 coolness
frese: 4 bend, furl 5 slack 6 unbend 7 untwine
fresh: new 4 cool, good, pure, racy 5 brisk, green, ruddy, saucy, sound, sweet, vivid 6 breezy, bright, caller, florid, lively, recent, strong, unused 7 unfaded, untired, untried 9 obtrusive, unspoiled 10 additional, meddlesome, refreshing, unimpaired 12 invigorating, presumptuous
  and lively: 4 racy
freshen: 5 renew 6 breeze, revive 7 refresh, sweeten

freshet: 5 spate 9 streamlet 10 inundation
freshly: 5 again
freshman: 5 bejan, frosh, plebe 6 bejant, novice
freshness: 4 verd 8 verdancy 9 fraicheur
  lose: dry 4 fade, wilt 6 wither
fret: nag, rub, vex 4 care, fray, gall, gnaw, pout, rage, stew 5 chafe, grate, pique, tease, worry 6 abrade, devour, harass, murmur, nettle, plague, rankle, ripple, ruffle, strait 7 agitate, consume, disturb, grizzle, roughen 8 diminish, disquiet, irritate, vexation
fretful: 5 angry, cross 6 repine, sullen 7 carking, frecket, gnawing, peevish, pettish 8 captious, corroded, fretsome, petulant, restless 9 corrosive, impatient, irascible, irritable, plaintive, querulous 10 ill-humored, ill-natured
Frey's sister: 5 Freya 6 Freyja
Freya's husband: 4 Oder
friable: 5 crimp, crisp, crump, loamy, mealy
friar: fra 4 fish, monk 5 frere 6 Bhikku, fraile, frater 7 Bhikshu, brother 8 monastic 9 Carmelite 10 Franciscan 11 Augustinian
friary: 8 cloister 9 monastery 11 brotherhood
fribble: 4 fool 6 falter, totter, trifle 7 stammer 8 trifling 9 frivolity, frivolous
fricassee: 6 potpie 10 blanquette 11 blanc-manger
friction: rub 5 chafe 9 attrition 10 dissension
  air: 7 windage
fridge: rub 4 fray 5 chafe 6 fidget 8 irritate
fried: 4 frit 7 sauteed
fried cake: 7 cruller 8 doughnut
friend: ami(F.), amy, eme, pal 4 ally, amie(F.), chum, kith 5 amigo(Sp.), amiga(Sp.), crony 6 bonami(F.), cummer, gimmer, kimmer 7 comrade, gremial, kinsman 8 cockmate, compadre, paramour, relative 9 associate, attendant, bonne amie(F.), broadbrim, companion, confidant 10 confidante 12 acquaintance
Friend: 6 Quaker
  church founder: 9 George Fox
friendless: 7 forlorn
friendliness: 5 amity 8 affinity, amicable, goodwill 10 fellowship 13 companionship
friendly: sib 4 cosh, good, kind 5 chief, howdy 6 blithe, genial, homely, howdie 7 affable, amiable, amicous, cordial 8 amicable, homelike, intimate, sociable 9 favorable 10 favourable, hospitable 11 warmhearted
friendship: 5 amity 6 amitie 8 relation 9 affection 10 attachment
frier: 6 pullet
frieze: 4 kelt(Sc) 5 adorn, chase 8 trimming 9 embroider 10 decoration
  band: 6 taenia

frigate (see also **boat, ship**): **5** zabra(Sp.)

Frigg's son: 5 Baldr **6** Balder

fright: awe, cow **4** fear, fray, funk, gast **5** alarm, gliff, panic, scare, shock **6** affray, dismay, horror, schrik, terror **7** startle **13** consternation

frighten: awe, cow **4** fray, funk, hare, haze, shoo **5** afear, alarm, appal, gliff, hazen, scare **6** affray, appall, ascare, boggle **7** frecken, startle, terrify **8** affright **10** intimidate

frightened: 4 awed, eery, gast **5** eerie, timid **6** afraid **8** skittish

frightful: 4 grim **5** awful, ferly **6** horrid, ugsome **7** affreux, fearful, gashful, ghastly, hideous **8** alarming, dreadful, fearsome, horrible, horrific, shocking, terrible, terrific **10** horrendous, tremendous

frightfulness: 13 atrociousness **15** schrecklichkeit(Ger.)

frigid: icy **4** cold **5** acold, bleak **6** arctic, frosty **8** freezing

frill: 4 purl **5** jabot, ruche **6** ruffle **7** flounce **8** furbelow **9** balayeuse **11** chitterling

fringe: 4 loma **6** border, edging, margin **8** ciliella, trimming

fringed: 9 laciniate **10** frimbriate

frisk: 4 leap, skip, whid **5** brisk, caper, dance, flisk **6** curvet, frisco, frolic, gambol, lively, search **7** disport, friscal **8** caracole **10** frolicsome

frisky: gay **4** pert **6** lively **7** playful **8** frisking, sportive **10** frolicsome

frisson: 5 chill **6** quiver, shiver, thrill **7** shudder

frith: 4 help **5** firth, hedge **6** hurdle, wattle **7** coppice, estuary, freedom **8** liberate, security **9** brushwood, copsewood, underwood **10** protection

fritter: 5 shred, spend, waste **6** bangle **7** pancake, scatter **8** fragment

frivol: 6 trifle **9** frivolous

frivolity: 6 levity **7** fribble, inanity **8** nonsense **9** lightness

frivolous: gay **5** giddy, inane, petty **6** frivol, futile **7** fatuous, fribble, shallow, trivial **8** gossamer **9** childlike, worthless **11** lightheaded **14** featherbrained

frizzed: 5 crepe **6** crispy

fro: 4 away, back, from **5** hence, since **8** backward

frock (see also **dress**): jam **4** gown, slip, wrap **5** tunic **6** cleric, jersey, mantle **7** workman **9** gaberdine

frog: 5 frosh, frosk, jakie **6** peeper **7** paddock, quilkin **8** ferreiro **9** amphibian

order of: see *zoological order* below.

rearing place: **7** ranaria(pl.) **8** ranarium

zoological order: **5** anura **6** anoura **9** salientia

frohlich: gay **5** happy **6** joyous

froise: 7 pancake

frolic: bum, gay **4** blow, game, gell, jink, lark, orgy, play, ramp, romp **5** caper, freak, frisk, merry, prank, randy, sport,

spree **6** curvet, gambol, plisky, prance, rollix, shindy, splore **7** disport, gammock, pliskie, scamper, stashie, wassail **8** carousal **9** gilravage **10** masquerade

frolicsome: gay **4** roid **5** gilpy **6** frisky, gilpey **7** jocular, waggish **8** espiegle, friskful, gamesome, sportive

from: fro

beginning to end: **4** over **7** through

head to foot: **7** capapie

here: **5** hence

that time: **6** thence

the egg: **5** ab ovo

the time that: **5** since

this time: **5** hence

front: bow, van **4** brow, face, fore, head, prow **5** afore **6** before, facade, facing, oppose, sector **7** forward, further, obverse **8** forehead, foremost, forepart **9** forefront **10** appearance, effrontery **11** countenance

toward the: **8** anterior

frontal: 6 sindon **7** metopic

frontier: 4 face **5** bound, march **6** border, oppose **7** barrier, defense **8** boundary

frontiersman: 4 Cody **5** Boone **6** Carson **7** settler

fronton: 7 jai-alai

frore: 4 cold **6** frosty, frozen

frost: ice, nip **4** foam, rime **7** failure

frosted: 4 iced **5** glace **6** frozen

frosting: ice, mat **5** icing

frosty: icy **4** cold, rimy **5** chill, frore, gelid, glary **6** frigid, froren **8** chilling, freezing

froth: fob **4** barm, foam, scum, suds **5** spume **6** freath, lather

frow: 4 frau, froe, wife **5** vrouw, woman

froward: 4 away **5** cross **7** adverse, awkward, peevish, wayward **8** contrary, perverse, petulant, untoward **9** obstinate **10** refractory, unyielding **11** disobedient, unfavorable **12** ungovernable

frown: 4 lour **5** gloom, glout, lower, scowl **6** glower, glunch **7** frounce

frowst, froust: 4 loll **5** stale **6** lounge, stuffy **10** atmosphere

frowsy, frowzy: 5 musty **6** blowzy **7** raffish, unkempt **8** slovenly **10** disordered

frozen: 4 hard **5** fixed, frore, gelid, glary **6** chilly, frappe, froren **7** chilled, frosted **8** hardened, immobile **9** congealed **10** unyielding **11** coldhearted **12** refrigerated **13** unsympathetic

fructify: 9 fertilize **10** impregnate

frugal: 4 mild **5** chary, roman, spare **6** saving **7** careful, sparing, thrifty **9** economize, provident **10** economical, unwasteful **12** parsimonious

frugality: 6 thrift **7** economy **9** chariness

fruit: fig **4** date, lime, pear, plum, pome **5** apple, berry, drupe, grape, lemon, melon, olive, peach **6** cherry, orange, result **7** apricot, azarole, product **8** dewberry **9** blueberry, nectarine, offspring, pineapple, tangerine **10** production

aggregate: **7** etaerio

apple-like: **4** pome **6** quince
astringent: **4** sloe
baccate: **5** berry
blackthorn: **4** sloe
buttercup: **5** akene **6** achene **7** achenia(pl.) **8** achenium
citrus: **4** lime **5** grape, lemon **6** orange **7** tangelo **9** tangerine
collective: **7** syncarp **10** syncarpium
cooked in syrup: **7** compote
desert region: **5** terfa **6** terfez
dried: **5** prune **6** orejon
dry: **5** regma **6** achene, samara,
early maturing: **8** rareripe
elm tree: **6** samara
fleshy: **4** pear, plum, pome **5** berry, drupe, melon **6** tomato
fleshy part: **9** sarcocarp
gourd family: **4** pepo
horseradish tree: ben
husk: **5** lemma
hybrid: **7** tangelo
imperfect: **6** nubbin
juicy: **4** lime, pear, plum **5** grape, lemon, peach **6** orange **7** apricot **9** pineapple **10** grapefruit
layer: **7** epicarp
lime & lemon: **6** citron
many-seeded: **11** pomegranate
maple: **6** samara
mild acid: **5** guava
multiple: **4** cone
of rose: **11** cynorrhodon
of strawberry: **7** etaerio
oily: **5** olive
one-seeded: **5** akene **6** achene, samara **7** achenis(pl.) **8** achenium
palm tree: **4** date
peach-like: **7** apricot **9** nectarine
pear-shaped: fig **7** avocado
plum-like: **4** sloe
pome: **4** pear **5** apple **7** azarole
preserving: **6** medlar
pulp: pap
pulpy: uva **4** pome **5** drupe, grape, berry
red: **4** plum **5** apple **6** cherry **9** raspberry **10** strawberry
rind: **7** epicarp
rose-bush: hip
seed: pip, pit
spore: **6** aecium
stalk: **8** peduncle
stone: **4** paip, plum **5** drupe, peach, prune **6** cherry **7** apricot **9** nectarine
strawberry-family: **7** etaerio
tropical: fig **4** date **5** guava, gourd, mango **6** banana, papaya, pawpaw **9** sapodilla
vine: **5** grape
winged: **6** samara
withered: **6** nubbin
yellowish: **5** papaw **6** quince
fruit basket: 6 pottel, pottle
fruit bats: 8 pteropid **10** pteropidae
fruit dealer: 9 frontsman, fruiterer **11** greengrocer
fruit of Jove: 9 persimmon

fruit of paradise: 6 pomelo **10** grapefruit
fruit stone: pit **4** paip **6** pyrene **7** putamen
fruitful: fat **6** fecund **7** fertile **8** abundant, prolific **9** feracious, plenteous, plentiful, procreant **10** productive
fruitgrower: 8 fruitist **10** orchardist **11** palmologist **14** horticulturist
fruition: 8 pleasure **9** enjoyment **11** realization
fruitless: dry **4** geld, vain **5** addle, blank **6** barren **7** sterile, useless **8** abortive **10** profitless **11** ineffectual **12** unprofitable, unsuccessful
frump: vex **4** mock, snub, sulk **5** dowdy, flout **6** gossip **7** provoke **8** irritate
frush: din, rub **4** rush **5** break, carve, crush, onset **6** batter, debris, flabby, polish **7** brittle, scratch **9** fragments
frustrate: 4 balk, bilk, dash, foil, null, vain, void **5** baulk, blank, block, check, cross, crush, elude **6** baffle, blight, defeat, delude, outwit, scotch, thwart **7** deceive, nullify, prevent, useless **8** confound, infringe, nugatory **9** checkmate, discomfit **10** circumvent, counteract, disappoint, disconcert, neutralize **11** countermand, ineffectual **12** unprofitable
frustration: 4 foil **6** fiasco **12** discomfiture **15** disillusionment
fry: 4 sile **5** brook, roast, saute, young **9** offspring
frying pan: 6 spider **7** griddle, skillet
fubsy: 5 fubby, plump, short **6** chubby, stuffy
fuddle: 5 booze, tiple **6** muddle **7** fluster
fuddled: fap, ree **5** bosky, tipsy **7** muddled
fudge: 4 fake **5** candy, foist, hunch **6** devise, humbug **8** contrive, nonsense **9** interlope, makeshift **10** substitute **11** counterfeit
fuel: gas, oil **4** coal, coke, peat, wood **5** argal, argol, argul, stoke **6** acetol, elding, firing, petrol **7** pabulum **8** charcoal, gasoline, kerosene **9** petroleum **11** combustible
fuff: 4 puff **5** whiff **8** splutter
fuffy: 5 huffy, light, puffy
fugacious: 6 flying **8** fleeting, volatile **10** evanescent
fuggy: 6 smelly, stuffy
fugient: 7 fleeing **8** retiring
fugitive: 5 exile, fleme **6** emigré, exiled, outlaw **7** fleeing, refugee, roaming, runaway **8** banished, deserter, fleeting, runagate, unstable, vagabond, volatile **9** fugacious, strolling, transient, uncertain **10** evanescent
fugue: 4 fuga **9** ricercare
exponent: **4** Bach **6** Handel
Fukien river: Min
fulcrum: 4 bait, prop **5** thole **7** support
fulfill: 4 fill, full, meet **6** effect, finish, occupy **7** achieve, execute, perform, satisfy **8** complete **9** implement **10** accomplish, effectuate
fulfillment, fulfilment: 6 effect **9** execu-

tion **10** completion **11** performance, realization **14** accomplishment

fulgent: 6 bright **7** shining **8** dazzling **9** effulgent

full: bad **4** good **5** ample, round, sated, solid, total **6** entire, fulfil, honest **7** baptize, copious, destroy, diffuse, fulfill, fulsome, orotund, perform, plenary, replete, teeming, trample **8** adequate, bouffant, brimming, complete, resonant **9** bouffante, capacious, plentiful **10** consecrate, exhaustive **13** comprehensive

suffix: ose **5** itous, ulent

full-blooded: 6 florid **8** rubicund **12** thoroughbred

full force: 5 brunt

full-grown: 6 mature **9** developed

full of: *cracks:* **6** rimose

glands: **7** adenose

hollows: **8** lacunose

minute openings: **6** porous

sand: **7** arenose

sap or juice: **7** succous **9** succulent

thorns: **6** briary

twists: **5** kinky **7** winding

wrinkles: **6** rugose

fuller: 7 creaser

fuller's grass: 8 soapwort

fullness, fulness: 5 fulth **6** plenty **7** satiety **8** pleonasm **9** abundance, amplitude, plumpness, repletion **10** fleshiness, perfection **12** completeness

fully: 5 amply **6** wholly **7** clearly, largely, utterly **8** entirely, maturely **9** perfectly **10** abundantly, completely, distinctly **11** plenteously, plentifully

fulminate: 7 explode, inveigh **8** detonate

fulsome: fat **4** foul, full **5** gross, plump, suave **6** coarse, wanton **7** copious, lustful, overfed **8** abundant, nauseous **9** offensive, overgrown, repulsive, satiating, sickening **10** disgusting, indelicate, nauseating

fumble: paw **4** boot **5** abase, error **6** bobble, bungle, faffle, haffle, huddle, mumble

fume: 4 foam, odor, rage, rant, reek **5** ewder, fumet, smoke, storm, vapor **6** exhale **7** flatter, fumette **8** fumigate, outburst **10** exhalation

fumid: 5 smoky **8** vaporous

fun: gag, gig **4** game, gell, hoax, jest, joke, play **5** mirth, sport **6** gaiety, gayety **9** amusement, horseplay, merriment **10** pleasantry

function: act, run, use **4** duty, role, work **5** doing **6** action, office **7** calling, operate, service **8** activity, ceremony, occasion **9** festivity, gathering, operating, operation **10** occupation, profession, providence **11** performance **13** entertainment

social: tea **4** ball **5** party **6** soiree **9** reception

trigonometrical: **4** sine **6** cosine, secant **7** tangent

fund: 4 fond, pool **5** basis, stock, store **6** bottom, ground, supply **7** deposit, reserve **10** foundation, groundwork **12** accumulation

fundamental: 5 basal, basic, vital **7** basilar, organic, primary, radical **8** original, rudiment **9** elemental, essential, important, principle **10** elementary

funds: 4 caja, cash **5** money **9** resources

funebre: sad **7** funeral **8** funereal

funeral: 6 burial, dismal, exequy **7** cortege, funebre **8** exequial, funereal **9** forthfare, obsequies **10** sepulchral

bell: **5** knell

oration: **5** eloge **6** eulogy **8** encomium **9** panegyric

pile: **4** pyre

song: **5** dirge, elegy, elogy, nenia **6** elegie **7** elogium, epicede **8** threnody **9** epicedium

structure: **10** catafalque

funereal: 5 feral **6** dismal, solemn **7** funebre, funeral **8** mournful **9** funebrial, funebrous **10** funebrious

funest: sad **4** dire **5** fatal **7** doleful

fungus: 4 bunt, cepe, mold, rust, smut **5** ergot, fungo, morel, moril, uredo, yeast **6** agaric, fungal, mildew, oidium, telium **7** agarics, amanita, blewits, fungoid, fungous, geaster, truffle **8** amanitin, mushroom, puffball **9** stinkhorn, toadstool **10** fungaceous

fungus-like: 6 agaric

funk: 4 kick, odor, rage **5** shirk, spark **6** coward, flinch, fright, recoil, shrink **8** frighten **9** cowardice, touchwood

funnel: 6 hopper

funny: odd **5** comic, droll, queer **7** comical, jocular, risible, strange **8** humorous **9** laughable, ludicrous

funnyman: wit **8** comedian

fur: 4 flix, pell, pelt **5** budge, stole **6** furrow, pelage

coat: **6** pelage

kind of: fox **4** mink, paen, scut, seal, vair, woom **5** budge, civit, coney, fitch, lapin, otter, sable **6** ermine, galyac, galyak, marten, martin, moutin, nutria **7** calabar, calaber, caracul, karakul, miniver, platina, sealine **8** karakule, ragondin **9** silver fox

piece: **5** stole

refuse: **4** kemp

fur-bearing animal: fox **4** mink, seal **5** genet, otter, sable **6** marten, martin

furbelow: 5 frill **6** ruffle **7** falbala, falbelo, flounce **8** trimming

furbish: fig, rub **4** fake, vamp **5** clean, scour **6** polish **7** burnish **8** renovate

Furies: 5 Dirae **7** Erinyes

individual: **6** Alecto, Erinys **7** Erinnys, Erinyes, Megaera **9** Tisiphone

furious: mad **5** angry, brain, irate, rabid **6** fierce, furied, insane, stormy **7** frantic, mankind, rushing, violent **8** frenzied, vehement, wrathful **9** impetuous, turbulent **10** boisterous, tumultuous, uproarious

furl: **4** fold, roll, wrap **5** frese **6** fardel, furdel, furdle

furlong: **5** stade **7** stadium **10** quarentene

furlough: **5** leave **6** permit **8** passport

furnace: **4** bosh, dome, kiln, oven **5** stove, tisar **6** calcar, cupola, heater **7** athanor, howells, rotator, smelter **8** bloomery, bruckner **9** scorifier **11** incinerator

furnish: arm **4** feed, give, lend **5** array, endow, equip, frame, indue **6** afford, graith, insure, render, supply **7** apparel, appoint, garnish, provide **8** minister, palisade **10** accomplish, administer
crew: man
with battlements: **9** crenelate
with meals: **5** board, cater

furnished: **5** boden, garni **8** equipped, provided, supplied **9** garnished

furnishing: **7** fitment **8** fixtures, muniment, ornament **9** adornment, apparatus, furniture **10** enrichment, habiliment

furniture: **6** graith, outfit **7** fitment, tallboy **8** equipage **9** equipment **10** decoration, encoignure, furnishing **13** embellishment
style: **6** Empire **8** Colonial, Sheraton **11** Chippendale, Hepplewhite, Renaissance

furor: **4** fury, rage **5** craze, mania **6** frenzy **7** madness

furrow: fur, rut **4** grip, plow, rout **5** chase, drain, drill, field, rigol, score, stria **6** groove, sulcus, trench **7** channel, crumple, windrow, wrinkle

furrowed: **6** rivose **7** sulcate, porcate **8** porcated **10** corrugated

furry: **5** hairy

furse: **4** whin **5** gorse

further: aid, and, yet **4** abet, also, fore, help, more **5** again, front, serve **6** afford, beyond, former **7** advance, earlier, forward, promote, remoter **8** moreover **9** advantage **10** accelerate, additional

furtherance: **6** assist **8** facility, progress **9** promotion **10** assistance **11** advancement

furthermore: and **7** besides **8** moreover

furthersome: **4** rash **7** helpful **11** venturesome **12** advantageous

furtive: sly **6** secret, sneaky **7** hangdog **8** mystical, sneaking, stealthy **10** creepmouse **11** clandestine

fury: ire **4** rage **5** anger, breth, furor, rigor, vixen, wrath **6** beldam, choler, frenzy **7** beldame, madness, oestrus **8** delirium, violence **9** furiosity, vehemence **10** fierceness, turbulence **11** indignation

fuse: **4** flux, frit, melt, weld **5** blend, smelt, unite **6** anneal, mingle, solder **7** liquefy **8** dissolve **10** amalgamate **11** incorporate

fusee: **5** flare, torch **6** signal

fusion: **4** flux **6** fusure, merger **8** alliance, blending **9** coalition **11** coalescence

fuss: ado, row, tew, vex **4** busk, fike, rout, spat, stir, todo **5** bearm, touse, whaup, worry **6** bother, bustle, caddle, fantad, fantod, fettle, fidget, fissle, fistle, fizzle, fraise, fuffle, fustle, pother, potter, tumult **7** dispute, friggle, fussock, quarrel, sputter, trouble **8** business **9** confusion **10** disconcert

fussy: **6** bustle, fidfad, spruce **7** fidgety, finical **8** overnice **10** fastidious, meticulous **14** overparticular

fustanella: **8** petticoat

fustian: **4** rant **5** tumid **7** bombast, pompous **8** claptrap, inflated **9** bombastic, worthless

futile: **4** idle, vain **6** otiose **7** useless **8** hopeless, trifling **9** frivolous, worthless **11** ineffectual

futility: **11** uselessness **13** frivolousness

future: **5** later **6** coming **9** hereafter

fuzz: nap **4** down, lint **5** fluff **8** puffball

fyke: net

G

gab: lie, yap **4** talk **5** boast, mouth, prate, scoff **6** gossip **7** chatter, deceive, prattle

gabardine: **5** cloth **6** fabric

gabbard, gabbart: **4** scow **5** barge **6** vessel **7** lighter

gabble: rai(Sc.), yap **4** cank, chat, talk **6** babble, cackle, gossip, habble, jabber, yabble **7** chatter, clatter, twaddle

gabbro: **4** rock **6** norite

gabelle: tax **4** duty **6** excise, impost

gaberdine: **4** coat, gown **5** frock, smock **6** mantle **7** garment **8** pinafore

gabi: **4** taro

gabirit: **4** mold **5** gauge, model

gable: **4** wall **6** dormer, pinion

gablock: See **gavelock**.

Gabriel's instrument: **4** horn **7** trumpet

gaby: **4** fool **5** dunce **9** simpleton

gad: bar, rod **4** band, goad, roam, rope, rove, whip **5** climb, ingot, prowl, spear, spike, staff, stick, stray **6** billet, chisel, ramble, switch, wander **7** traipse **9** gallivant

Gad: *chieftain:* Ahi
 father: **5** Jacob
 mother: **6** Zilpah
 son: Eri **5** Ezbon
 tribe of: **6** Erites

gadfly: **4** pest **6** botfly **7** annoyer, oestrid, tabanid **8** busybody **9** breezefly

gadget: **4** tool **5** gibbe(Sc.) **6** device, doodad, jigger **9** doohickey **11** contrivance

Gaelic (see also **Irish**): **4** Erse **8** Highland
 clan: **4** Sept
 John: Ian
 land distribution: **7** rundale
 poem: **4** Duan
 spirit: **5** kelpy **6** kelpie **7** banshee
 warrior: **5** Dagda **6** Fenian

gaff: **4** hoax, hook, pick, spar, spur, talk **5** fraud, laugh, spear, trick **6** clamor, deceit, fleece, gamble, outcry **7** prating **8** raillery

gag: **4** gegg, hoax, joke **5** choke, heave, retch **6** muffle, muzzle **7** prevent, silence **8** obstruct, throttle **9** imposture **13** interpolation

gage (see also **gauge**): bet **4** pawn, risk **5** stake, wager **6** pledge **8** appraise, defiance, security **9** challenge

gain: buy, get, net, win **4** boot, earn, good, pelf, reap **5** clear, lucre, reach **6** attain, effect, income, obtain, profit, secure **7** achieve, acquire, advance, benefit, conquer, prevail, procure, realize **8** increase **9** accretion, advantage, increment **12** appreciation

ill-gotten: **4** pelf **5** graft, lucre **6** payola **9** extortion

gainly: **7** shapely **8** becoming, gainsome, graceful, suitable

gainsay: **4** deny **6** forbid, impugn, oppose, refute, resist **7** dispute **10** contradict, controvert

gair: **4** keen **5** eager, piece **6** greedy, stingy **8** covetous **12** parsimonious

gait: bat, run, way **4** lope, pace, rack, step, trip, trot, volt, walk **5** amble, strut, tread **6** allure, canter, gallop **7** journey, shamble **8** distance

gaiter: **4** boot, spat **6** gaskin, puttee **7** cutikin(Sc.), legging **8** bootikin, gamashes **11** galligaskin

gala: gay **4** fete **5** merry **6** festal, fiesta **8** festival

galago: **5** lemur **6** monkey

Galahad: *father:* **8** Lancelot
 mother: **6** Elaine
 quest: **5** grail

Galatea: *lover:* **4** Acis
 suitor: **10** Polyphemus

galaxy: **6** nebula

gale: **4** blow, gust, wind **5** blast, storm **6** breeze, easter **7** declaim, tempest **8** outburst **9** hurricane, windstorm **11** northeaster, northwester, southeaster, southwester

galea: **6** helmet

Galen: **9** physician

Galician river: San **4** Styr

Galilean town: **4** Cana, Nain **8** Nazareth, Tiberias **9** Capernaum

Galileo's birthplace: **4** Pisa

galimatias: **6** jargon **8** nonsense **9** gibberish

galipot, gallipot: sap **5** rosin **6** barras

gall: vex **4** bile, fell, flaw, fret **5** annoy, chafe, cheek, spite **6** abrade, harass, injure, poison, rancor **7** blemish **8** acerbity, cecidium, irritate, temerity **9** excoriate, impudence **10** bitterness, effrontery, exasperate

gallant: gay **4** beau, prow **5** blade, brave, bully, lover, noble, showy, swain **6** escort, heroic, polite, suitor **7** amatory, amorist, amorous, conduct, stately, younker **8** cavalier, cicisbeo(It.), galliard, handsome, polished, splendid **9** attentive, chamberer, chevalier, courteous **10** chivalrous, courageous **11** fashionable **12** high-spirited

gallantry: 7 bravery, courage **11** intrepidity

galleon: 4 ship **6** carack, vessel **7** carrack

gallery: 5 alure, boyau(F.), porch, salon **6** arcade, dedans(F.), loggia, piazza **7** balcony, terrace, veranda **8** audience, brattice, cantoria, catacomb, corridor **9** promenade **10** ambulatory

galley: 4 aesc, tray **5** cuddy, foist **6** bireme, carvel, galiot, hearth **7** birling, birlinn, caravel, galliot, hexeris, kitchen, trireme, unireme **8** cookroom, crumster, galleass, hepteris, ramberge **9** caravelle **10** triaconter **13** tesseraconter

gallfly: 11 hymenoptera(pl.) **12** hymenopteron

galliard: 5 hardy **6** lively **7** gallant, valiant

Gallic: 6 French

gallimaufry: 4 hash **6** jumble, medley, ragout **7** mixture **10** hodgepodge

gallinae: 6 grouse, quails **7** rasores, turkeys **8** peafowls **9** curassows, pheasants

gallivant: gad **4** flit, roam **6** travel

gallop: run **4** gait, pelt **5** chase, speed **6** canter, career, course, hasten, pursue

galloping dominoes: 4 dice

gallows: 4 crap **5** bough **6** gibbet **7** potence

pert. to: **10** patibulary

galluses: 10 suspenders

gally: 5 worry **7** terrify **8** frighten

galoot: 6 fellow, marine, person **7** soldier **9** screwball

galore: 7 profuse **8** abundant **9** plentiful

galosh: 4 boot, clog, shoe **6** arctic, patten **8** overshoe

galvanize: 4 coat **6** excite **7** startle **9** stimulate

gam: leg **5** mouth, tooth, visit

gamb, gambe: leg **5** shank

gambado: 4 boot **5** antic, caper **6** spring **7** legging

gambit: 4 move **7** comment, opening **8** manouver **9** launching

gamble: bet **4** dice, gaff, game, risk, spec **5** stake, wager **6** chance, hazard, plunge **9** speculate **11** uncertainty

gambler: 5 dicer, shill **6** carrow(Ir.), player **7** playman, plunger, sharper **8** blackleg, gamester **10** speculator

gambling game: See **game** *gambling.*

gambling stake: pot **4** pool

gambol: hop **4** play **5** caper, frisk, prank **6** cavort, frolic

game: fun, jeu(F.) **4** lame, lark, plan, play, prey **5** brave, dodge, prank, sport, trick **6** course, frolic, gamble, gritty, plucky, quarry, racket, spunky **7** contest, foolery, pastime, project **8** enduring, resolute **9** amusement, diversion **10** courageous

ball: cat, tut **4** golf, polo, pool **5** fives,

rugby **6** hockey, pelota, soccer, squash, tennis, tipcat **7** cricket, croquet **8** baseball, football, handball **9** billiards

board: **4** keno **5** bingo, chess, halma, lotto, salta **6** squail **7** pachisi **8** checkers, cribbage, parchesi, parchisi, scrabble **9** crokinole, parcheesi **10** backgammon

card: gin, hoc, loo, lus, nap, pam **4** bank, brag, faro, hock, jass, ruff, skat, slam, snap, solo, spin, vint **5** beast, chico, cinch, comet, crimp, decoy, gilet, gleek, monte, omber, ombre, pedro, pique, pitch, poker, rummy, stuss, trump, two-up, waist, whist **6** basset, birkie, boston, bridge, commit, ecarte, flinch, hearts, loadum, masset, piquet, rounce, sledge, smudge **7** bezique, canasta, cassino, cayenne, Chicago, cooncan, hundred, old-maid, primero, reversi, seven-up **8** baccarat(F.), commerce, conquian, contract, cribbage, handicap, napoleon, patience, penneeck, tresillo, videruff **9** cinq-cents, grabouche, montebank, new market, solitaire, tredrille **10** heartsette **11** everlasting, speculation

carnival: **5** darts **6** hoopla

confidence: **5** bunco, bunko

court: **5** roque **6** pelota, squash, tennis **7** jai alai **8** handball **9** badminton **10** volleyball

dice: **4** ludo **5** craps **7** pachisi **8** dominoes, trey-trip

gambling: **4** beno, faro, keno, pico **5** beano, bingo, boule, craps, keeno, lotto, monte(Sp.), pique, pitch, poker, rondo, stuss **6** brelan(F.), fan-tan(Ch.), piquet, policy **7** baccara, barbudi, primero, rondeau(F.) **8** baccarat, crackloo, roulette **9** black-jack, crackaloo, montebank, twenty-one, vingt-et-un(F.) **10** panguingui(Phil. Is.)

goal: run **4** home **5** first, score, spare, tally **6** basket, strike **9** touchdown

kind of: **4** mora(It.) **6** merels, morris, quoits **7** diabolo, loggats, loggets, marbles **9** philopena **10** jackstraws, spillikins

official: **5** judge, timer **6** umpire **7** referee, starter **8** linesman **10** timekeeper

outdoor: **4** polo **6** tennis **7** cricket, croquet **9** badminton

parlor: **4** dibs **5** jacks **7** matador **8** charades **13** tiddledywinks

pin: **7** bowling, kegling, tenpins **8** ninepins, skittles

racket: **5** bandy **6** squash, tennis **8** lacrosse **9** badminton

small: **4** bird, fowl

stewed in wine: **5** salmi **6** ragout

war: **10** kriegspiel

word: **6** crambo **7** anagram **8** acrostic, scrabble

gamekeeper: 8 warrener

gamester: 5 dicer **6** player **7** gambler, playman

gamete: 6 zygote **8** oosphere

gamin: tad 6 urchin 7 hoodlum
  domain: 6 street
gaming cube: die
gammon: leg 4 bosh, dupe, foot, gull 5
  bacon, cozen, feign, thigh 6 delude, humbug 7 beguile, deceive, mislead, pretend
  10 backgammon
gammy: bad 4 lame, sore
gamp: 8 umbrella
gamut: 5 orbit, range, reach, scale 6 extent, series 7 compass
gamy: 5 spicy 7 lustful 8 spirited 10 malodorous 12 disreputable
ganch: 4 kill 6 impale 7 execute
gander: 5 goose 6 stroll, wander 9 simpleton
Gandhi: *name:* Bu; Aba, Abu 4 Abba,
  Abou, Bapu 7 Mahatma
  publication: 7 Harijan
ganef: 5 thief 6 rascal
gang: go; mob, set 4 band, crew, ging,
  pack, road, team, walk 5 group, horde,
  shift 6 clique, course, outfit, travel 7 company 9 pasturage 10 passageway 11
  combination
  member of: 4 b'hoy 5 rowdy, tough
Ganges River: *city:* 7 Benares
  dolphin: 4 susu
  goddess: 9 Gangadevi
ganglion: 5 tumor
gangplank: 4 brow 6 bridge 8 platform 9
  gangboard
gangrene: rot 7 mortify 8 necrosis 9
  sphacelus
gangster: 4 b'hoy, thug, whyo, yegg 5
  rough, thief 6 bandit 7 mobster, ruffian 8
  criminal, hireling
  female companion: 4 moll
gangway: 7 couloir 8 corridor 10 passageway
gannet: 4 bird, fowl 5 goose, solan
goal: 4 brig, jail 6 prison
gaoler: 5 guard 6 warden
gap: col 4 flaw, pass, rent 5 break, breck,
  chasm, chawn, cleft, clove, meuse, notch,
  space 6 breach, hiatus, lacuna, ravine 7
  fissure, lacunae(pl.), opening 8 aperture, interval, quebrada 10 interstice 12
  interruption 13 discontinuity
gape: ope 4 cape, gasp, gaum, gaup, gawp,
  gaze, pant, rent, yaup, yawn, yawp 5
  chawn, shout, stare 6 rictus, vacuum 7
  dehisce 8 oscitate
garage: 6 hangar, siding 8 building
garb (see also **dress**): 5 array, dress, habit,
  style 6 attire, bundle, clothe, custom,
  method 7 apparel, clothes, costume,
  fashion, raiment 8 carriage, clothing, ves-
  iture, vestment 10 appearance, habiliment
  kinds of: 4 toga 8 mourning 9 sackcloth
garbage: 5 offal, trash 6 bundle, faggot,
  refuse, scraps
garble: 4 bolt, cull, geld, sift, sort 5 alloy
  6 jumble, mangle, refine, refuse, select 7

distort, pervert, rubbish 8 disguise, mutilate
garboil: 9 confusion 10 turbulence
garcon: boy, lad 6 waiter 8 bachelor
garden: 4 Eden, hall. park, yard 5 arbor,
  patch, tract 6 arbour 8 outfield 9 cultivate, enclosure 11 commonplace
  implement: hoe 4 rake 5 mower 6 scythe,
  sickle, trowel, weeder
  kind of: 4 herb 5 oasis, truck 6 cactus,
  flower, formal 7 kitchen 8 chinampa,
  kailyard(Sc.), kaleyard(Sc.) 9 botanical,
  terrarium, vegetable 10 zoological
  protector: 7 Priapus
Garden City: 7 Chicago
garden plant: See **plant** *garden.*
gardener: 9 topiarist 14 horticulturist
garfish: 8 hornbeak, hornfish
gargantuan: 4 huge, vast 5 giant 7 titanic
  8 enormous, gigantic 9 monstrous
gargle: 9 mouthwash 11 collutorium
garish: 4 loud 5 cheap, gaudy, showy 6
  bright, tawdry 8 dazzling 9 offensive
garland: bay, lei 4 band 5 crown, glory 6
  anadem, corona. crants, diadem, laurel,
  rosary, wreath 7 chaplet, coronal, festoon
  9 anthology
garlic: 4 moly, ramp 5 chive, clove 6 ram-
  son
garment (see also **undergarment**): 4 brat,
  cape, coat, gear, gown, jupe, rail. robe,
  sari, vest 5 cloak, dress, habit 6 attire,
  kimono 7 apparel, leotard, raiment 8
  vestment 10 investment
  ancient: 4 toga 5 palla, stola 6 chiton 7
  chlamys 8 himation
  ecclesiastical: see **vestment**
  infant's: 6 woolly 7 bunting
  medieval: 5 simar 6 kirtle, rochet, tabard
  8 chausses
  men's: cap, hat, tie 4 belt, coat 5 pants,
  shirt, short, socks 6 jacket, slacks 7
  drawers 8 trousers 10 suspenders 11
  windbreaker
  mourning: 5 weeds
  outer: 4 coat, wrap 5 cloak, dress, pants,
  parka, shawl, skirt, stole 6 jacket, slacks
  7 sweater 9 coverslut, polonaise
  protective: 4 brat 5 apron, armor, chaps,
  smock 7 cuculla 8 overalls, pinafore 9
  coveralls, gaberdine
  sleeveless: aba 4 cape, vest 6 mantle 7
  sweater 8 slip-over
  upper: 4 coat, vest 5 jupon, shirt, tunic,
  waist 6 blouse, jersey, peplos, peplus 7
  sweater 8 guernsey, slip-over
garn: 4 yarn 7 worsted 11 exclamation
garner: 4 reap 5 store 6 gather 7 collect,
  granary 10 accumulate
garnet: 5 jewel, stone 7 garnate 8 essonite
  black: 8 melanite
  deep-red: 9 almandine, almandite
  green: 7 olivine
garnish: 4 trim 5 adorn, dress, equip 7

furnish **8** decorate, meringue, ornament **9** embellish

garret: **4** head **5** attic, solar, soler **6** gallet, soller, turret **7** mansard **8** cockloft **10** watchtower

garrote, garrotte: **4** kill **7** execute **8** strangle, throttle

garrulous: **5** talky, wordy **7** diffuse, voluble **8** fanfaron **9** talkative **10** long-winded, loquacious

garter: **6** garten **7** elastic **9** supporter

garth: dam **4** hoop, yard **5** close, girth **9** enclosure

garvey: **4** boat, scow

gas: **4** fuel, fume, reek, talk **5** radon, vapor **6** gossip, petrol **7** bombast **8** hydrogen **10** anesthetic, asphyxiate, illuminant

air: **4** neon **5** argon, ozone, xenon **6** oxygen **7** ammonia, krypton, sulfate **8** nitrogen

balloon: **6** helium

blue: **5** ozone

charcoal: **5** oxane

colorless: **5** keten, ozone **6** arsine, ethane **7** ammonia

comb. form: aer **4** aero

inert: **5** argon, xenon **6** helium **8** nitrogen

inflammable: **6** butane, ethane **7** methane

marsh: **7** methane

mustard: **7** yperite

oxygen: **5** ozone

poisonous: **6** arsine **7** mustard, stibine

gasbag: **7** balloon

gascon: **7** boaster **8** braggart **10** swaggering **12** swashbuckler

gasconade: **4** brag, crow **5** boast, vaunt **7** bluster, bravado **8** boasting

gaseous: **4** thin **5** fluid, light **7** tenuous **8** aeriform, gasiform, volatile **13** unsubstantial

gash: cut **4** bite, chop, slit, talk, trim, wise **5** sharp, slash, witty **6** babble, gossip, tattle **7** knowing **8** incision **9** talkative **11** well-dressed

gasket: **4** lute, ring, seal

gasoline: gas **6** petrol

gasp: **4** gape, pant **5** croak, fetch

gassy: **5** windy **8** inflated **9** flatulent

gast: **5** alarm, scare **8** frighten

gasthaus: inn **6** tavern

gastronome: **7** epicure **11** connoisseur

gastropod: **4** slug **5** harpa, oliva, snail **6** nerita, nerite, volute **7** mollusk **8** pteropod

ear-shaped: **7** abalone

marine: **5** cowry, murex **6** cowrie, limpet, tethys **7** aplysia

gat: gun **7** channel, passage **8** revolver

gata: **5** shark

gate: bar, dar, way **4** door, exit, hole, pass **5** hatch, valve **6** defile, escape, method, portal, wicket, zaguan **7** barrier, opening, postern **8** entrance **9** threshold, turnstile

flood: **6** sluice

gate money: fee **5** price **9** admission

Gates of Hercules: **9** Gibraltar

gatehouse: bar **5** lodge

gatekeeper: **6** porter, warden **8** guardian, watchman

gatepost: **4** durn

gateway: dar **5** pylon, toran, torii(Jap.) **6** portal, torana **8** entrance

gather: **4** bale, brew, cull, furl, herd, mass, meet, pick, rake, reap **5** amass, bunch, flock, glean, group, infer, pleat, pluck, raise, shirr **6** bundle, deduce, derive, garner, muster, scrape, summon **7** collect, compile, convene, convoke, harvest, recruit **8** assemble, colonize, compress, conclude, contract, increase **10** accumulate, congregate **11** agglomerate, concentrate **12** conglomerate

gatherer: **5** miser **7** gleaner **9** collector

gathering: bee, tea **4** bevy, fest, stag **5** crowd, party, troop **6** galaxy, plisse, shivoo, smoker **7** abscess, company, meeting, mooting **8** assembly, function, swelling **9** concourse **10** assemblage, collection, congestion, convention **11** contraction **12** accumulation, congregation

gauche: **4** skew **5** gawky **6** clumsy **7** awkward, twisted **8** tactless **10** left-handed

gaucho: **6** cowboy **8** herdsman

lariat: **5** bolas

gaud: **4** joke **5** adorn, fraud, paint, sport, trick **6** bauble, finery, flashy, gewgaw **7** trinket **8** artifice, ornament

gaudy: gay **4** loud **5** cheap, feast, showy **6** festal, flashy, flimsy, garish, tawdry, tinsel, tricky **7** brankie(Sc.), flaring, glaring, trinket **8** festival **9** brummagem, deceitful, flaunting, luxurious **11** pretentious **12** meretricious, ostentatious **13** entertainment

gaufre: **5** wafer **6** waffle

gauge, gage: **4** carp **5** judge **6** former **7** measure, scantle **8** estimate, udometer **9** indicator, manometer, manoscope **10** anemometer

Gaul: **6** France, Gallia(L.)

chariot: **5** esses **6** esseda, essede

god of thunder and rain: **7** Taranis

god of vegetation: **4** Esus

magistrate: **9** vergobret

people: **4** Remi

priest: **5** druid

river goddess: **8** Belisama

gaum: paw **4** daub, gape, heed, hold, mess **5** smear, stuff **8** perceive **9** attention **10** perception **13** understanding

gaunt: **4** bony, grim, lank, lean, slim, thin **5** spare **6** barren, hollow, meager, meagre **7** haggard, slender **8** desolate, rawboned **9** emaciated **10** attenuated, cadaverous, forbidding

gauntlet: **4** test **5** glove **6** ordeal

gauster: 4 brag 5 bully 6 gossip 7 bluster, swagger

gauze: 4 film, leno 5 crape, crepe, lisse 6 fabric, tissue 7 bandage

gavel: 4 mace, maul, rent 5 usury 6 hammer, mallet

gavelock: 4 gaff 5 lever, spear 7 crowbar, javelin

gaw: god 4 gape 5 drain 6 trench

Gawain's brother: 7 Gaheris

gawk: 4 gowk, left, lout 5 stare 6 gawney, lubber 7 bumpkin, rammack 9 simpleton 10 left-handed

gawky: 6 clumsy, gauche 7 awkward, foolish 8 clownish

gawn: tub 4 pail

gawney: 4 gawk 9 simpleton

gawp, gaup: 4 gape 5 stare 7 swallow 9 simpleton

gay: 4 airy, boon, daft, glad, gleg 5 bawdy, bonny, brisk, happy, jolly, loose, merry, riant, showy 6 blithe, bonnie, bright, flashy, frisky, garish, jocund, jovial, joyful, lively, wanton 7 festive, gleeful, jocular 8 cavalier, cheerful, colorful, mirthful, sportive 9 brillante, brilliant, convivial, sprightly, vivacious 10 frolicsome, licentious 12 lighthearted

gazabo: guy 6 fellow, person

gaze: eye, pry 4 gape, gouk, gowk, leer, look, moon, ogle, peer, pore, scan, toot 5 glare, gloat, sight, stare 6 behold, glower, regard

gazelle: ahu, goa 4 admi, cora, dama, kudu, mohr, oryx 5 ariel, mhorr 7 buffalo, chikara, corinne 8 antelope 9 springbok

gazelle hound: 6 saluki

gazette: 7 courant, journal 9 newspaper

gazetteer: 5 atlas 6 writer 10 dictionary

Ge's child: 5 Titan

geal: ice 5 jelly 7 congeal

gean: 6 cherry

gear: cam, cog, rig 4 food, tack 5 dress, equip, goods, stuff, tools 6 affair, aludel, doings, graith, liquor, matter, pinion, tackle, things, wealth 7 apparel, concern, harness, rigging, rubbish, trapeze 8 business, clothing, cogwheel, garments, material, ornament, property 9 equipment, mechanism, trappings, vestments 10 appliances, belongings, implements 12 appurtenance 13 accoutrements

geason: 4 rare 5 scant 6 scarce 12 unproductive

geaster: 9 earthstar

Geb's daughter: 8 Nephthys

gel: set 6 harden 7 congeal, thicken 8 solidify 9 coagulate

gelatin, gelatine: 6 collin 7 sericin 8 agar-agar

geld: dry 4 spay 5 alter, prune 6 barren, garble 8 castrate, mutilate 9 expurgate, fruitless 10 emasculate

gelid: icy 4 cold, iced 6 frozen

gell: fun 5 spree 6 frolic 8 carousal

gelt: 4 gold 5 money

gem: bud 4 keas, naif, onyx, opal, ruby, sard 5 agate, beryl, cameo, jewel, paste, pearl, stone, topaz 6 amulet, bedeck, garnet, muffin, scarab, spinel 7 diamond, emerald, paragon 8 intaglio, sapphire, tigereye 9 carnelian, germinate 10 aquamarine 11 masterpiece

blue: 8 sapphire 9 turquoise 10 aquamarine

face: 5 facet

green: 7 emerald, peridot 10 chrysolite

imperfect: 5 loupe

iridescent: 4 opal 5 pearl 7 cat's-eye 8 tigereye 9 moonstone

measure of weight: 5 carat

paste: 6 strass

purple: 8 amethyst

rectangular: 6 baguet 8 baguette

red: 4 ruby, sard 5 avena 6 garnet, pyrope 9 carnelian

relief-carved: 5 cameo

support: 7 setting

surface: 5 bezel, bezil, facet

Gem State: 5 Idaho

gemel: 4 twin 5 pairs, twins 6 hinged, paired 7 coupled, doubled

geminate: 6 binate, double 7 coupled

Gemini: 5 twins 6 Castor, Pollux

gemmule: bud 5 ovule

gemot, gemotte: 5 court 7 meeting 8 assembly

gemsbok: 4 oryx 8 antelope

gemutlich: 4 cozy 6 genial, kindly 8 cheerful 9 agreeable 11 comfortable, good-natured

gendarme: 7 soldier 9 policeman 10 cavalryman

gender: sex 4 kind, male, sort 5 class, genus 6 female, neuter 8 copulate, engender, generate

gene: 6 factor 10 determiner, uneasiness 13 embarrassment

genealogy: 4 tree 7 account, history, lineage, progeny 8 pedigree 9 offspring 10 generation

general: 5 broad, gross 6 common, leader 7 average, officer 8 catholic 9 commander, customary, prevalent, universal 10 prevailing, widespread

Civil War: Lee 5 Grant, Meade 7 Sherman

generalize: 5 widen 6 extend, spread 7 broaden

generate: 4 make 5 beget, breed, steam 6 create, gender 7 develop, produce 8 develope, engender 9 originate, procreate, propagate

generation: age, era 4 kind, race 5 breed, stock 6 family 7 descent, progeny 8 geniture 9 genealogy, offspring, posterity 11 abiogenesis, descendants, procreation

generative: 8 prolific 10 productive

generic: 12 encompassing 13 comprehensive

generosity: 7 largess 8 largesse

generous: big 4 free, good, kind, rich 5 ample, frank, noble 6 honest 7 fertile, liberal 8 abundant, gracious, handsome, highborn, spirited 9 bountiful, excellent, honorable, plenteous, unselfish, unstinted 10 benevolent, charitable, courageous, munificent, openhanded 11 magnanimous, stimulating, warmhearted

genesis: 5 birth 6 origin 9 beginning 11 origination

genet: 5 berbe, horse

genial: 4 bein, bien, warm 5 douce 6 benign, forthy, inborn, jovial, kindly, native 7 cordial, festive 8 cheerful, friendly, pleasant 9 benignant, expansive, gemutlich 10 enlivening, generative

genitor: 6 parent 7 creator 10 procreator

geniture: 5 birth 8 nativity 9 offspring 10 generation

genius: 5 genio 6 talent, wizard 8 aptitude 9 intellect 10 brilliance

Genoa: *coin:* 4 jane 8 genovino
magistrate: 4 doge

genre: 4 kind, sort, type 5 class, style 7 species 8 category 11 description 14 classification

gens: 4 clan 5 nomen 6 people

gent: 4 fine 5 noble 6 pretty 7 elegant 8 graceful

genteel: 4 nice 6 polite 7 stylish 8 graceful, lady-like, well-bred 11 fashionable

gentian: 6 flower 7 felwort 9 baldmoney

Gentile: 7 heathen 9 Christian

gentility: 8 breeding 10 refinement

gentle: moy 4 calm, deft, dewy, easy, fair, kind, meek, mild, soft, tame 5 bland, light, milky, quiet, sweet, tamed 6 benign, docile, facile, placid, polite, tender 7 amabile, bonaire, clement, gradual, lenient 8 amenable, dovelike, lenitive, maidenly, mansuete, moderate, peaceful, soothing, tranquil, well-born 9 courteous, excellent, honorable, tractable 10 chivalrous 11 considerate 13 compassionate

gentleman: don, rye, sir 5 sahib, senor 6 bayard, mister 7 younker 8 cavalier 9 caballero

gentlewoman: 4 lady

gentry: 4 rank 5 birth 6 people 8 gentrice 9 condition 10 gentlefolk

genty: 5 noble 7 genteel 8 graceful 9 courteous

genuflect: 5 kneel

genuine: 4 leal, pure, real, true, vrai(F.) 5 frank, plain, pucka, pukka 6 actual, dinkum, honest 7 germane, gradely, sincere 8 bonafide 9 authentic, heartfelt, intrinsic, true-penny, unalloyed, unfeigned, veridical, veritable 10 legitimate 13 unadulterated 15 unsophisticated

genus: 4 kind, sort 5 class, order 6 gender 8 category 14 classification

pert. to: 7 generic

geode: 5 druse 6 nodule

geology: 12 earth science
age: 7 Permian 8 Cambrian, cenezoic, Devonian, Jurassic, mesozoic, Silurian, Triassic 9 paleozoic 10 Cretaceous, cryptozoic, Ordovician 13 Mississippian, Pennsylvanian
division: age, era 4 lias, lyas 5 epoch. trias
period: 6 eocene 7 miocene 8 pliocene, tertiary 9 oligocene 10 quaternary 11 pleistocene
remains: 7 fossils
science: 12 paleontology 13 palaeontology

geometry: *angle:* 9 incidence
curve: 6 spiral 7 ellipse, evolute 8 parabola, sinusoid
father: 6 Euclid
figure: 4 cone, lune 5 prism, rhomb 6 circle, gnomon, oblong 7 ellipse, rhombus 8 triangle
proposition: 7 theorem
ratio: pi
solid: 4 cube 5 prism 7 pyramid
surface: 5 nappe, torus

geoponic: 5 rural 11 agriculture 12 agricultural

Georgia (Caucasus): *city:* 6 Iberia, Kutais, Tiflis
island: 6 Sapelo
people: 4 Svan 5 Svane
queen: 6 Tamara 7 Thamara

Georgia (U.S.): *city:* 5 Macon 6 Dalton 7 Cordele
county: Lee 4 Bibb, Clay, Cobb, Cook, Dade, Hall, Hart, Long, Pike, Polk, Tift, Ware 5 Bacon, Burke, Butts, Crisp, Early, Rabun, Troup

Geraint's wife: 4 Enid

germ: bud, bug 4 seed 5 spore, virus 6 embryo, germen, sprout 7 germule, microbe 8 rudiment 9 bacteriam, beginning 13 microorganism

germ cell: egg 4 ovum

German: 4 Goth 5 Boche, Saxon 6 Teuton

German measles: 7 rubello

germane: 4 akin, true 6 allied 7 genuine, related 8 relevant 9 pertinent 11 appropriate

Germany *ancient:* 6 Almain 7 Almaine
ancient tribesman: 4 Jute 6 Teuton 9 Ostrogoth
article: das, der, des, die
association: 6 verein 12 gesellschaft
cake: 5 torte 9 lebkuchen 11 pfeffernuss
canal: 4 Kiel
capital: 6 Berlin
castle: 7 schloss
Christmas: 11 Weihnachten
city: Aue, Ede, Ems, Ulm 4 Bonn, Jena, Kiel, Koln, Oder 5 Emden, Essen, Furth, Gotha, Hagen, Halle, Herne, Mainz, Pirna, Trier 6 Aachen, Altona, Barmen, Berlin, Bochum, Bremen, Cassel, Dessau, Erfurt, Kassel, Linden, Lubeck, Munich,

Plauen **7** Breslau, Cologne, Crefeld, Dresden, Gorlitz, Hamburg, Hanover, Harburg, Krefeld, Leipzig, Mayence, Munchen, Munster, Potsdam, Rostock, Spandau, Stettin, Zwickau **8** Augsburg, Chemnitz, Dortmund, Duisburg, Freiburg, Liegnitz, Nurnberg, Steglitz, Wurselen, Wurzburg **9** Bielefeld, Brunswick, Darmstadt, Elberfeld, Flensburg, Karlsruhe, Magdeburg, Nuremberg, Offenbach, Osnabruck, Pforzheim, Remscheid, Stuttgart, Wiesbaden **10** Braunsberg, Dusseldorf, Heidelberg, Konigsberg, Oberhausen, Schoneberg, Tuttlingen **11** Lichtenberg, Saarbrucken **12** Ludwigshafen **13** Gelsenkirchen **14** Charlottenburg, Mannheim-on-Ruhr **15** Frankfort-on-Main, Frankfort-on-Oder

coal region: **4** Ruhr, Saar **5** Sarre

code: **5** Salic

coin: **4** mark **6** kronen, thaler **7** pfennig **8** groschen

forest-keeper: **9** waldgrave

gnome: **6** kobold

hall: **4** aula, saal **5** diele

highway: **8** autobahn

home: **4** heim

iron region: **4** Saar **5** Sarre

knight: **6** ritter

lake: **9** Constance

language: **7** Deutsch

measure: aam, imi **4** last, sack, stab **5** carat, eimer, kanne, kette, maass **6** strich **7** klafter **8** scheffel, schoppen, stubchen **9** masskanne

mister: **4** herr

mountain: **4** Alps, Berg, Harz

nobleman: **4** graf **5** adlig **6** junker, ritter **7** younker

overture: **8** vorspiel

parliament: **9** Bundestag, Reichstag

port: **5** Emden **6** Bremen **7** Hamburg, Stettin

resort: Ems **5** Baden

river: Inn, Ulm **4** Alle, Eder, Elbe, Eser, Isar, Oder, Ruhr, Saar **5** Aller, Hunte, Rhine, Saale, Spree, Werra, Weser **9** Constance

school: **10** realschule, volkschule **14** oberrealschule

singing festival: **10** sangerfest **11** saengerfest

society: **4** bund **6** verein **10** turnverein **12** gesellschaft

song: **4** lied

teacher: **6** docent, dozent

vowel change: **6** umlaut

wine: **4** hock, wein **5** Rhine **7** Moselle

woman: **4** frau, frow **8** fraulein

germicide: 5 iodin **6** iodine **10** antiseptic **11** bactericide **12** disinfectant

germinate: bud, gem **5** beget, sprit **6** braird, evolve, sprout **7** develop **10** effloresce

geryon: 7 monster

gesso: 5 paste **7** plaster

gest, geste: 4 deed, feat, jest, tale **5** route, stage **7** bearing, company, conduct, gesture, lampoon, romance **9** adventure **10** deportment

gestation: 7 bearing **8** breeding, carrying **9** pregnancy

gesticulate: 6 motion **7** gesture

gesture: act, fig, nod **4** beck, bere, gest **5** geste, sneer **6** behave, motion, salute **7** posture **8** carriage **11** gesticulate **13** gesticulation

get: pen, win **4** earn, find, gain, take, trap **5** annoy, beget, catch, fetch, learn, reach, seize **6** appear, attain, baffle, become, corner, derive, induce, obtain, puzzle, secure, suffer **7** achieve, acquire, capture, conquer, possess, prepare, procure, realize, receive, recover **8** contract, irritate, overcome, persuade, retrieve, vanquish **9** ascertain, determine **10** comprehend, conciliate, understand

get along: 4 fare **5** hurry **7** advance, prosper, succeed **8** progress

get back: 6 redeem **7** recover

get on: 4 fare **5** board **6** embark

get out: 5 scram **6** elicit, escape, reveal **8** evacuate

get-together: bee **4** stag **6** social **7** meeting

get up: 5 arise, array, dress, style **6** invent **7** arrange, costume, prepare **9** construct

get well: 4 heal **10** recuperate

getaway: lam **4** scat **5** elope, leave, start **6** depart, escape

gewgaw: toy **4** gaud **6** bauble, fangle, fegary, trifle **7** trinket **8** gimcrack **10** knickknack

gey: 4 very **5** quite **6** pretty, rather **9** tolerable **12** considerable

ghastful, gastful: 6 afraid **7** alarmed, ghostly **8** dreadful **9** frightful **10** frightened

ghastly: wan **4** grim, pale **5** ghast, lurid **6** dismal, gashly, gousty, grisly, pallid **7** charnel, deathly, fearful, gashful, goustie, hideous, macaber, macabre **8** dreadful, grewsome, gruesome, horrible, shocking, terrible **9** deathlike, frightful, horrified, terrified **10** cadaverous

ghat: 4 pass **5** range **7** landing **8** mountain

gherkin: 6 pickle **8** cucumber

ghost: hag **4** bhut, hant **5** bugan, duppy, shade, spook, umbra **6** daemon, sprite **7** eidolon, haunter, lemures(pl.), phantom, specter, spectre **8** guytrash, phantasm, revenant **10** apparition, glimmering **11** poltergeist

ghostly: 4 eery **5** eerie, scary, weird **6** spooky **7** gastful **8** ghastful, spectral **9** spiritual

ghoulish: 4 eery **5** eerie

giant: 4 Bara, eten, huge, ogre, rahu, Ymir **5** Argus, Cacus, jumbo, titan, troll **6** afreet, nozzle, ogress **7** Antaeus, Cyclops, monster, warlock **8** behemoth, Bellerus, colossus **9** monstrous **10** gargantuan, prodigious, tremendous

gibber: **5** stone **6** pebble **7** boulder, chatter

gibberish: **6** jabber, jargon **9** rigmarole **10** galimatias

gibbet: **4** stob, tree **6** cudgel **7** gallows, potence

gibbon: ape, lar **6** monkey, wou-wou **7** hoolock, siamang **10** anthropoid

gibbous: **6** convex, humped **7** hunched, rounded **11** hunchbacked, protuberant

gibe, jibe: **4** gird, jape, jeer, mock, quib, quip, twit **5** agree, fleer, fling, flirt, flout, gleek, scoff, sneer, taunt **6** deride, heckle **7** prepare, sarcasm **8** ridicule

giddy: **4** daff, daft **5** dizzy **6** fickle, giglot, volage **7** carried, flighty, glaiket, glaikit **8** halucket, heedless **9** frivolous, hellicate **11** hairbrained **13** featherheaded

gift: sop **4** bent, boon, dash, dole **5** bonus, bribe, dower, dowry, favor, grant, knack, pilon, power, token **6** bounty, donary, gersum, hansel, legacy, talent **7** aptness, benefit, faculty, handsel, largess, present, subsidy **8** aptitude, bestowal, blessing, donation, gratuity, largesse, offering, pittance, potlatch **9** endowment, gratitude, lagniappe, readiness **10** compliment **11** benefaction, beneficence, serendipity **12** contribution

gifted: **8** talented **9** ingenious

gig: fun, top **4** boat, fool, goad, joke, spur, whim **5** rouse, spear, sport **6** kibble **7** provoke **8** carriage, hilarity

gigantic: big **4** huge, vast **5** giant, large **7** immense, mammoth, titanic **8** colossal, enormous **9** cyclopean, gigantean, monstrous **10** gargantuan, prodigious

giggle: **5** tehee **6** teehee, titter **7** snicker, snigger

gila: **5** trout **6** lizard **10** woodpecker

gild: **5** adorn, tinge **7** overlay **8** brighten, inaurate **9** embellish

Gilda's father: **9** Rigoletto

gilded: **5** aural **6** aurate **7** aureate **8** inaurate **11** embellished

gilet: **4** vest **6** bodice **9** waistcoat

gill, ghyl: ivy **4** cove, girl, lass **5** brook **6** collar, ravine, stream, tipple, valley, wattle **10** sweetheart

four: **4** pint

gilt: hog, sow **4** gold **5** money **6** gilded, golden

gimcrack: fop, toy **6** bauble, flimsy, gewgaw, trifle **7** trinket, trivial **8** ornament, trumpery **9** frivolous **10** knickknack **13** unsubstantial

gimp: jag, vim **4** trim **5** notch, orris **6** indent, spirit **7** cripple **8** trimming

gin: net **4** crab, grin, rack, sloe, trap **5** snare, trick **6** device, diddle, liquor,

scheme **7** springe **8** artifice, beverage, schnapps **10** intoxicant **11** contrivance

ging: **4** crew, gang **5** troop **7** company, retinue

ginger: pep, vim **5** spice, vigor **6** mettle, revive, spirit **8** piquancy, spirited

ginger cookie: **4** snap

ginger root: **4** race

gingerbread: **4** cake **5** money **6** wealth **8** trimming **13** pfefferkuchen(Ger.)

gingerbread tree: **4** doom

gingerly: **6** warily **7** charily **8** daintily **9** carefully, elegantly, finically, guardedly, mincingly **10** cautiously **12** fastidiously

gingham: **8** chambray

giraffe: **5** piano **6** animal, spinet **10** camelopard

girasol, girasole: **4** opal **5** thorn **9** artichoke

gird: **4** belt, bind, gibe, girt, hasp, hoop, jerk, mock, yerk **5** brace, equip, scoff, sneer **6** clothe, fasten, girdle, secure **7** besiege, enclose, prepare, provide **8** engirdle, surround **9** encompass

girder: **4** beam **6** binder

girdle: obi **4** band, bark, belt, bind, cest, gird, ring, sash, zona, zone **5** girth, sarpe **6** bodice, cestus, circle, circum, corset, moocha, zonule **7** baldric, balteus, environ, equator, griddle **8** baltheus, cincture, cingulum, encircle

girl: gal, sis **4** bint, chit, coed, gill, jill, lass, maid, minx **5** child, fille, filly, gilpy, quean, skirt, sylph, wench **6** amoret, calico, damsel, female, hoyden, kimmer, tomboy **7** camilla, colleen, flapper, ingenue **9** backfisch, debutante **10** jeune fille, sweetheart **11** maidservant

name: see **name** *female.*

girlish: **5** sissy **7** artless **8** immature

girt: **4** gird **6** belted, fasten **7** besiege **8** prepared **9** encircled **13** circumference

girth: **4** band, belt, gird, hoop **5** cinch, cinct, garth, strap, width **6** girdle **7** girding, measure **8** cincture, encircle **13** circumference

gist: **4** core, crux, pith **5** heart, point **7** essence **10** foundation

gitano, gitana: **5** gipsy, gypsy

give: gie(Sc.) **4** cede, dole, emit, hand, mete **5** apply, endow, grant, serve, yield **6** accord, afford, bestow, commit, confer, denote, devote, donate, impart, render, supply **7** consign, dispose, furnish, intrust, present, proffer, propose **8** bequeath **9** surrender, vouchsafe **10** administer, contribute, deliquesce

give away: **5** grant, yield **6** bestow, betray **7** present, succumb **8** disclose, telltale **9** sacrifice

give back: **4** echo **6** recede, remise, retire, return **7** replace, restore, retreat

give forth: **4** emit **8** eradiate

give in: 5 yield 6 relent 7 succumb 9 surrender

give off: 4 emit, quit 5 cease, exude, issue 7 publish

give out: 4 deal, emit, mete 5 exude, issue, peter, print 7 publish, release 9 circulate

give rise: 6 gender 7 produce 8 engender, occasion 9 originate

give up: 4 cede, emit, quit 5 demit, forgo, spare, waive, yield 6 betray, devote, forego, resign, reveal, vacate 7 abandon, deliver, despair, present 8 abdicate, renounce 9 sacrifice, surrender 10 relinquish

given: 5 fixed 6 stated 7 donated, granted 8 addicted, disposed, inclined 9 specified

givey: 4 soft

gizzen: dry 5 leaky 7 parched 10 shrivelled

glabrous: 4 bald 6 smooth 8 levigate

glace: ice 6 glazed 8 polished

glacier: 6 icecap 7 iceberg
deposit: as 4 asar(pl.) 5 eskar, esker 6 placer 7 moraine
direction: 5 stoss
fissure: 8 crevasse
fragment: 5 serac
hill: 7 drumlin
ridge: as, os 4 kame 5 eskar, esker
snow: 4 neve
snow field: 4 firn, neve

glacis: 5 slope 6 buffer 7 incline

glack: 6 ravine, valley

glad: gay 4 fain 5 eager, happy, merry, sunny 6 blithe, bright, joyous 7 pleased, shining, willing 8 animated cheerful, gladsome 9 beautiful, delighted, gratified, satisfied 11 exhilarated 12 lighthearted

gladden: 5 cheer, elate 6 please 7 gratify, rejoice

gladdy: 12 yellowhammer

glade: 4 vale 5 marsh 8 clearing
comb. form: 4 nemo

gladness: joy 5 bliss, mirth 6 blithe 8 fainness, pleasure 9 happiness 12 cheerfulness, exhilaration

glaiket, glaikit: 5 giddy 6 stupid 7 foolish 11 lightheaded, thoughtless

glamor, glamour: 5 charm, magic, spell 7 bewitch, enchant, mystery, romance 9 fascinate

glamorous, glamourous: 6 exotic 8 alluring, charming, romantic 11 fascinating

glance: 4 gleg, leer, ogle, peek, peep, scan, scry, skew 5 blink, blush, flash, glent, gliff, glime, glint, glisk, prink 6 aspect, scance 7 glimpse

gland: 5 liver, lymph 6 carnel, thymus 7 adrenal, parotid, thyroid 8 exocrine 9 endocrine 11 paranephros
comb. form: 4 aden 5 adeno
enlargement: 7 adenoma

secretion: 5 sebum 7 hormone
swelling: 4 bubo

glandular: 7 adenoid, adenose

glare: 4 gaze 5 blaze, flame, glaze, stare 7 glitter 8 radiance 9 showiness

glaring: 4 rank 5 clear, gaudy, glary, gross, plain, vivid 6 aglare 7 burning, evident, flaring, obvious, staring, visible 8 apparent, flagrant, manifest 9 barefaced 11 conspicuous

glary: 6 frosty, frozen 7 glaring, shining 8 slippery

glass: 4 frit, lens, pane 6 beaker, bottle, cloche, cullet, goblet, mirror 7 tumbler 9 barometer, telescope
alcohol: mug 4 pony 5 stein 6 rummer, seidel 8 schooner
colored: 5 smalt 7 opaline 10 aventurine
container: jar 6 bottle 7 matrass
design: 4 etch
molten: 5 metal 7 parison
pert. to: 6 vitric
remove bubbles: 5 plane

glassmaking *device:* 7 ironman
frame: 7 drosser
material: 4 frit 5 fritt
oven: 4 lehr

glassworker: 6 teaser

glasswort: 4 kali 5 plant 8 kelpwort

glassy: 4 hard 5 sharp 6 shrill 8 strident 9 apathetic 10 forbidding, lackluster, unwavering, unyielding

Glaucus: *father:* 8 Sisyphus
son: 11 Bellerophon

glaver: 7 flatter, wheedle

glaze: 4 coat, slip 5 cover, glare, sleet, stare 6 enamel, finish, polish, veneer, window 7 burnish, glidder, incrust, overlay, vitrify 8 couverte

glazier: 11 glassworker

gleam: ray 4 beam, glow 5 blink, blush, flash, glaik, glent, glint, glisk, sheen, shine 7 glimmer, glitter, shimmer, sparkle 8 radiance, splendor 9 coruscate 10 brightness 11 coruscation, scintillate

gleaming: 6 ablaze, bright

glean: 4 cull, reap 6 gather 7 collect

gleaning: 4 crop

glebe: sod 4 ciod, land, soil 5 earth, field

glebe house: 5 manse 9 parsonage

glee: joy 4 song 5 mirth, sport 6 gaiety 7 delight, elation 8 hilarity 9 merriment 10 minstrelsy 12 cheerfulness 13 entertainment

gleeful: gay 5 merry 6 joyous 7 jocular 8 gleesome

gleek: 4 gibe, jest, joke

gleeman: 8 minstrel, musician

gleg: gay 4 keen 5 alert, quick, sharp 6 bright, lively, nimble 8 cheerful

glen: den 4 dale, dell, vale 5 griff, heuch, heugh, kloof 6 dingle, valley 10 depression

glent: 4 slip 5 flash, gleam, glint, shine 6 glance 7 sparkle

glib: pat 4 easy, oily 5 slick 6 casual, fluent, smooth 7 offhand, shallow, voluble 8 flippant, unforced 9 impromptu, talkative, unstudied 10 nonchalant, unthinking 11 superficial

glibbery: 6 smooth 8 slippery 10 changeable, unreliable

glide: 4 flow, sail, sile, skim, slip, soar 5 coast, creep, merge, slide, steal 6 glance 7 slither 8 glissade

gliff: 4 look 5 scare, shock 6 fright, glance, moment 7 glimpse, instant 8 frighten

glim: bit, eye 5 light, watch 12 illumination

glimmer: 4 fire, glow 5 blink, flash, gleam 7 flimmer, glimpse, glitter, shimmer, sparkle

glimmering: 5 ghost

glimpse: 4 idea 5 blink, flash, glint, glisk, tinge, trace 6 glance, luster 7 glimmer, inkling

glint: 4 peep 5 flash, gleam, glent, shine 6 glance, luster 7 glimpse, sparkle 10 brightness

glisten: 5 flash, glisk, gliss, shine 7 glitter, sparkle 9 coruscate

glister: 5 shine 6 luster 7 sparkle

glitter: 5 flash, glare, gleam, glore, sheen, shine 6 scance 7 glimmer, glisten, glister, spangle, sparkle, twinkle 8 radiance 9 coruscate 10 brilliancy 11 coruscation, scintillate

glittering: 5 gaudy, gemmy 6 bright, fulgid 9 brilliant, clinquant, sparkling, twinkling

gloaming: eve 4 dusk 8 twilight

gloat: 4 gaze 5 exult

globe: orb 4 ball, clew 5 earth, monde, world 6 sphere 7 globule
half: 10 hemisphere
pert. to: 7 spheric

globular: 5 beady, round 6 beaded, globed 7 globose, spheric 9 globulous, orbicular, spherical 10 orbiculate

globule: 4 bead, blob, drop 6 bubble 7 droplet 8 particle, spherule

glockenspiel: 8 carillon

glom, glaum: 4 take 5 steal, swipe, watch 10 understand

gloom: 4 dusk, murk 5 cloud, drear, frown 7 despair, dimness, sadness 8 darkness 9 dejection, heaviness, obscurity 10 cloudiness, depression, desolation, melancholy

gloomy: dim, sad, wan 4 blue, dark, dour, eery, glum 5 adusk, adust, black, brown, drear, dusky, heavy, moody, murky, stern 6 cloudy, dismal, dreary, morose, somber, sullen 7 clouded, obscure, stygian 8 darkling, darksome, detected, desolate, dolesome, downcast, overcast 9 cheerless, darkening, depressed, saturnine, tene-

brous 10 depressing, despondent, foreboding, lusterless, melancholy, sepulchral, tenebrific 11 pessimistic 12 disconsolate, disheartened

glorify: 4 hery, laud 5 adore, adorn, bless, boast, exalt, extol, glory, honor, vaunt 6 praise 7 clarify, elevate, ennoble, magnify 8 emblazon, eulogize 9 celebrate 11 apotheosize

gloriole: 4 halo 7 aureole

glorious: 4 dear, mear, meer, mere 5 grand, noble 6 bright 7 eminent, haughty, radiant 8 boastful, ecstatic, gorgeous, renowned, splendid 9 hilarious, wonderful 10 celebrated, delightful 11 illustrious, intoxicated, magnificent, resplendent 12 praiseworthy, vainglorious

glory: 4 fame, halo 5 blaze, bliss, boast, eclat, exult, honor, kudos, pride 6 beauty, corona, heaven, praise, renown 7 aureole, clarity, garland, glorify 8 ambition, splendor 10 admiration, brilliancy, effulgence, reputation 11 distinction 12 magnificence, resplendence

gloss: 4 glow 5 dodge, gloze, sheen, shine 6 blanch, enamel, excuse, luster, polish, remark, veneer 7 burnish 8 annotate, flourish, palliate, pretense 9 semblance, sleekness 10 brightness, commentary 14 interpretation

glossal: 7 lingual

glossary: 6 clavis, claves(pl.)

glossy: 5 nitid, silky, sleek 6 bright, sheeny, smooth 7 shining 8 lustrous, polished, specious 9 plausible

glove: mit 4 cuff, mitt 6 mitten, sheath 7 chevron, dannock, gantlet 8 gauntlet
shape: 5 trank

glow: 4 beam, halo 5 ardor, blush, flame, flush, gleam, gloss, shine 6 warmth 7 glimmer 13 incandescence

glower: 4 gaze 5 frown, glore, scowl, stare

glowing: hot, red 5 aglow, fiery, vivid 6 ardent 7 burning, candent, fervent, radiant, shining 10 candescent

gloze: 4 fawn, glow, peer, pore 5 gleam, gloss, shine 6 speech 7 comment, deceive, explain, expound, flatter, wheedle 8 brighten, collogue, disguise, flattery, palliate, pretense 9 adulation, interpret

glucose: 5 sugar 6 starch 7 sucrose 8 dextrose

glue: fix 5 mount, paste, stick 6 adhere, attach, cement, fasten, gluten, sizing 7 sericin 8 adhesive, mucilage

glum: 4 dour, grum 5 moody, surly 6 dismal, gloomy, glummy, glumpy, morose, sullen 8 dejected, frowning, overcast 10 melancholy 11 threatening

glume: 4 leaf 5 bract

glut: 4 cloy, fill, gulp, sate 5 draft, gorge 6 englut, excess, pamper 7 engorge, satiate, surfeit, swallow 8 overfeed, overload, plethora, saturate

gluten: gum 4 glue 6 fibrin 8 adhesive

glutton: hog, pig 4 gulo 5 gulch 6 lecher, rascal, wretch 7 epicure 8 gourmand 9 scoundrel 11 gormandizer

gluttonous: 6 greedy 7 hoggish 9 voracious

gnar, gnarr: 5 growl, snarl

gnarl: 4 gnaw, knor, knot, nurl 5 growl, knurl, snarl, twist 6 nibble, tangle 7 contort, distort

gnarled: 6 knarry, knotty, rugged 7 crabbed, knarred, twisted 12 crossgrained

gnash: 5 champ, grind

gnaw: eat 4 bite, chew, fret 5 erode, gnarl, waste 6 be-gnaw, chavel, nibble 7 corrode

gnib: 5 ready, sharp 6 clever

gnome: elf, saw 5 adage, bogey, dwarf, elves(pl.), maxim, motto, pigmy, troll 6 goblin, kobold, sprite 8 aphorism, apothegm 10 apophthegm

gnomon: 4 nose 5 canon, style, tenet 9 indicator

gnostic: 4 wise 6 clever, shrewd 7 knowing 12 intellectual

gnu: 5 takin 6 mammal 8 antelope

go: be; act, bet, bid, die, gae, mog, run 4 fall, fare, gang, lead, mosy, move, pass, read, ride, turn, walk, wane, wend, work 5 break, elope, leave, occur, set-to, steal, visit 6 amount, attain, become, belong, betake, depart, elapse, follow, happen, intend, resort result, retire, travel 7 conduce, operate, proceed, succeed 8 diminish, traverse, withdraw 9 circulate, harmonize, undertake
aboard: 6 embark 7 entrain
ahead: 7 proceed 8 continue, progress
around: 6 detour 10 circumvent
ashore: 4 land 6 debark 9 disembark
astray: err 8 aberrate, miscarry
away: 4 exit, scat, shoo 5 imshi, leave, scram 6 begone, depart, retire 7 amscray
back: ebb 6 recede, return, revert 7 regress, retreat 10 retrogress
back on: 6 betray, recede 7 abandon, retrace
before: 4 lead 7 precede 8 antecede
between: 4 bhat 5 agent 7 arbiter, mediate 8 mediator 9 interpose 11 internuncio 12 intermediary
down: sag 4 fall, sink 5 lower 7 decline, descend, founder 8 decrease 11 deteriorate
forward: 4 fare 7 advance 8 progress
into: 5 audit, delve, enter, probe 7 examine
on: 5 enter 7 proceed 8 continue
over: 5 renew 7 retrace 9 backtrack
swiftly: run 5 scoot, speed
to and fro: 5 waver 6 totter, wig-wag 7 stagger 9 fluctuate, vacillate 11 shuttlecock
up: 4 rise 5 arise, raise 6 ascend

go-cart: 4 pram 5 wagon 12 perambulator

goa: 6 mugger 7 gazelle

goad: egg, gad, rod 4 brod, dice, edge, move, prod, spur, urge, yerk 5 ankus, decoy, impel, pique, prick, sting, thorn 6 incite 7 inflame, stimuli(pl.) 8 irritate, stimulus 9 incentive, instigate, stimulate 10 incitement

goal: aim, end 4 base, butt, dole, hail, mark, mete 5 bourn, finis, score, tally 6 object 7 purpose 8 ambition 9 intention, objective 10 aspiration 11 destination 12 consummation

goat: kid, ram, tur 4 ibex, tahr 5 beden, billy, goral 6 alpaca, chamal, pasang, victim 7 markhor 8 aegagrus, ruminant 9 bouquetin, stambecco, steinbock
disease: 7 takosis
flesh: 6 chevon
god of: Pan
pert. to: 6 capric 7 caprine, hircine

goatee: 5 beard

goatherd: 5 Damon

goatskin: 9 chevrette

gob: 4 hunk, lump, mass 5 chunk 6 sailor, seaman 7 mariner 8 quantity

gobbet: gob 4 lump, mass 5 piece 6 morsel 7 portion 8 fragment, mouthful

gobble: 4 gulp 6 gorble

Gobi Desert site: 4 Asia

goblet: cup 5 glass, hanap 6 vessel 7 chalice 8 standard

goblin: bog, cow, elf, hag, nis 4 bhut 5 bogey, bogle, bucca, gnome, nisse, ouphe, pooka 6 boggle, booger, churel, kobold, sprite 7 brownie, bugaboo, bugbear 8 barguest, bogey-man, folletto, folletti(pl.)

god (see also **deity** and next entry): As, Ea, Ra, Ve; Ada, Ani, Asa, Bel, Bes, Geb, Keb, Ler, Min, Pan, Ran, Seb, Tiu, Tyr, Ull, Van 4 aitu, Amen, Amón, Aten, Aton, Baal, deus(L.), deva, dieu(F.), Frey, Hler, idol, Kama, Loke, Loki, Nora, Odin, Orra, Ptah, Rama, Surt, Thor, Vali, Yama, Zeus 5 Aeger, Aegir, Asura, Baldr, Brage, Brama, Donar, Freyr, Hades, image, Othin, Pluto, Shiva, Surtr, Woden 6 Apollo, Brahma, Cronus, Elohim, Ganesa, Hermes, Hoenir, Kronus, Marduk, Njorth, Osiris, Saturn, Vulcan, Yahweh 7 Bacchus, creator, Forsete, godhead, Heimdal, Jehovah, Jupiter, Krishna, Mercury, Serapis, Vitharr 8 Almighty 9 Dionysius, Heindallr, Hlorrithi 10 Hephaestus 11 Ramachandra
false: 4 Baal 6 Mammon
love for: 5 piety 6 amadis, bhakti

god: For gods of specific localities, religions, or functions, see under the specific locality, religion, or function. EXAMPLES: "god of Thebes": see **Thebes** *god of;* "hindu god": see **Hinduism** *deity;* "god of war": *see* **war** *god.*

God be with you: 5 adieu, adios 7 goodbye

God blind me: 5 blimy

god-fearing: 5 pious 6 devout 9 religious

god-horse: 6 mantis

god-like: 5 pious 6 deific, devout, divine 8 immortal 9 religious

god of: For all definitions beginning with this phrase, see next important word. Ex-AMPLE: "god of flocks": see **flocks** *god of.*

goddess (see also **god**): Bau, Dis, Eir, Eos, Hel, Mut, Nut, Uma 4 Anta, Bast, Devi, Gaia, Hela, Hera, Isis, Juno, Kali, Nina, Norn, Saga, Urth, Wyrd 5 Belit, Ceres, Diana, Durga, Freya, Frigg, Gauri, Nanna, Venus 6 Athena, Aurora, Chandi, Freyja, Frigga, Hecate, Hestia, Shakti, Tiamat 7 Artemis, Asynjur, Demeter, Mylitta, Parvati 9 Aphrodite, Haimavati 10 Persephone, Proserpina

godfather: 7 sponsor

godforsaken: 8 desolate, wretched 9 neglected

godless: 6 wicked 7 impious, profane, ungodly 9 atheistic

godliness: 5 piety 13 righteousness

godling: 5 deity 6 godkin, godlet
woodland: 7 Selenus

godly: 5 pious 6 devout 8 gracious 9 religious, righteous

godmother: 6 cummer, kimmer 7 sponsor

gods' abode: 6 heaven 7 Olympus

God's body: 7 bodikin

Goethe drama: 5 Faust 6 Egmont

goety: 5 magic 10 necromancy

goffer, gauffer: 5 crimp, flute, plait

gog: bog 4 stir 8 activity, quagmire 9 agitation, eagerness

goggle: bug, eye 4 roll 5 stare 6 squint

goggler: 4 scad 5 akule

goggles: 8 blinkers

going: run, way 4 exit, fare, gait, gate, path, road 5 bound 6 access 8 behavior 9 departure 10 passageway

goiter: 6 struma 7 strumae(pl.)

gola: 4 cyma 7 granary 9 storeroom

gold: oro(Sp.) 4 gelt, gilt 5 aurum, metal 6 riches, wealth 7 bullion 9 clinquant
bar: 5 ingot
black: oil
fool's: 6 pyrite
heraldry: or
imitation: 6 ormolu, oroide
measure of weight: 5 carat
pert. to: 4 dore 6 aurous
uncoined: 7 bullion

gold-brick: 7 swindle

gold-plate: 4 gild, gilt

golden: 4 gilt, rich 5 auric, blest, blond, goldy 6 aureal, blonde, goldie, mellow, yellow 7 aureate, aureous, halcyon, shining 8 aurelian, precious 9 aureoline, Pactolian, yellowish 10 auriferous

golden age: 9 siecle d'or(F.)

golden apple giver: 5 Paris

golden chain: 8 laburnum

Golden Fleece: *keeper of:* 6 Aeetes
ship used: 4 Argo
seeker: 5 Jason 8 Argonaut

golden oriole: 5 pirol 6 loriot

goldeneye: cur 9 merrywing

goldenrod: 8 solidago

goldfinch: 8 graypate, greypate 12 yellowhammer

goldfish: 4 carp 6 calico 9 garibaldi, shubunkin

goldsmith: 7 artisan 9 artificer

golem: 5 robot 9 automaton, blockhead

golf: *assistant:* 5 caddy 6 caddie
club: 4 iron, wood 5 baffy, cleek, mashy, spoon 6 brassy, driver, jigger, mashie, putter 7 brassie, midiron, niblick
course: cup 4 link 5 green, links
cry: 4 fore
hazard: 4 trap 5 stymy 6 bunker, stymie
mound: tee
score: par 4 bogy 5 bogey, bogie, eagle 6 birdie, Nassau
stroke: 4 hook, loft, putt 5 drive, slice
target: cup 4 flag 5 green
term: lie, par, tee 4 baff, fore, hook 5 bogey, bogie, divot, dormy, eagle, green, slice, stimy 6 birdie, dormie, stymie, stroke 7 gallery

goliath: 5 giant

Goliath: *home:* 4 Gath
place of death: 4 Elah
slayer: 5 David

gollar, goller: 4 roar 5 growl, shout 6 gurgle

golly: 4 oath, yell

Gomer: *father:* 7 Japheth
husband: 5 Hosea

gondola: car 4 boat 5 barge, coach

gone: 4 left, lost 6 ruined 8 absorbed, advanced, finished, involved

gone by: ago, o'er 4 over, past 5 agone 6 bygone, passed

gonfalon: 4 flag 6 banner, ensign

goober: 6 peanut

good: bon(F.), fit 4 able, bein, bien(F.), boon, braw, fine, full, gain, kind, nice, prow 5 ample, brave, bueno, bully, moral, nifty, pious, sound, valid 6 benign, devout, expert, profit, proper 7 copious, gradely, helpful, liberal, trained, upright 8 becoming, budgeree, decorous, friendly, gracious, interest, orthodox, pleasant, pleasing, salutary, skillful, suitable, virtuous 9 agreeable, bountiful, competent, dauntless, enjoyable, estimable, excellent, favorable, fortunate, indulgent, reputable, righteous, well-being 10 auspicious, beneficial, benevolent, courageous, gratifying, profitable, sufficient 11 pleasurable, respectable, responsible, well-behaved 12 considerable, satisfactory, stouthearted, well-disposed

good-bye, good-by: 4 tata 5 addio, adieu(F.), adios(Sp.), ciaou(It.) 6 so-long 7 cheerio 8 farewell

good-for-nothing: 4 orra 7 useless 8 spalpeen(Ir.) 9 worthless 10 ne'er-do-well, 11 rapscallion

good health: 5 skoal 6 prosit 7 slainte

good-looking: 4 fair 5 bonny 6 comely, pretty 7 eyesome, winsome 9 beautiful 10 personable

good luck: 7 fortune
  image: 6 alraun

good-natured: 9 gemutlich

good spirit: 8 eudaemon

goodliness: 5 grace 6 beauty 8 goodness, kindness 10 comeliness, excellence

goodly: 4 kind 5 large 6 comely, portly 8 gracious, handsome 9 capacious, excellent 12 considerable

goodness: 6 bounty, purity, virtue 8 chastity, kindness 10 excellence, generosity, goodliness 11 beneficence, benevolence

goods: 4 fent, gear 5 stock, wares, wrack 7 chattel, finance 8 property 11 merchandise, possessions
  cast overboard: 5 lagan, ligan 6 jetsam, lagend
  in animal hides: 6 ceroon, seroon
  lost in shipwreck: 7 flotsam
  smuggled: 10 contraband

goodwill: 4 love 5 favor 9 readiness 10 heartiness 11 benevolence 12 friendliness

goody: 5 candy 9 sweetmeat

goof: 5 spoil 7 blunder

goofy: 5 silly 7 foolish 8 gullible

gool: 5 ditch 6 breach, sluice 7 channel, fissure

goon: sap 4 boob, dope, thug 6 bomber 7 slugger

goosander: 9 merganser

goose: 4 hiss 5 hansa, ninny, solan 6 cagmag, gander, goslet 7 gosling, widgeon 9 screwball, simpleton
  cry: 4 honk, yang 5 cronk
  mackerel: 9 phalarope
  pertaining to: 8 anserine 9 grossular
  resembling: 8 anserine
  snow: 4 chen 5 brant, wavey 9 whitehead
  tailor's: 8 flatiron

gooseberry: 4 fabe 6 groser 7 currant 8 feaberry, goosegog 9 honey-blob

gooseherd: 7 gozzard

gopher: 4 tuza 6 rodent 8 squirrel

Gopher State: 9 Minnesota

Gorboduc's son: 6 Porrex

Gordian: 9 intricate 11 complicated

gore: mud 4 burt, dirt 5 blood, cruor, filth, slime 6 gusset, insert, pierce 9 penetrate

gorge: 4 fill, gaum, glut, pass, sate 5 cajon, canon, chasm, flume, gulch, gully, kloof, strid 6 canyon, coulee, defile, englut, nullah, ravine, valley 7 couloir, overeat, pitcher, satiate 8 quebrada 10 gluttonize

gorgeous: 4 vain 5 grand, showy 6 costly 8 dazzling, glorious, splendid 9 beautiful,

luxurious 11 magnificent, resplendent

gorgon: 6 Medusa, Stheno 7 Euryale

gorilla: ape 10 anthropoid

gorse: 4 whin 5 furze 7 juniper

gory: 6 bloody 9 murderous 10 sanguinary 12 bloodstained

goshawk: gos 6 tercel
  keeper: 8 ostreger 10 austringer

gospel: 7 evangel, tidings 8 doctrine, teaching 9 veritable

gossamer: web 5 filmy 6 cobweb 8 raincoat

gossip: cat, gab, gup 4 aunt, chat, clat, gash 5 cause, clack, clash, clepe, clype, crony, rumor 6 babble, caddle, callet, claver, gabble, glaver, norate, tattle 7 chatter, chin-wag, clatter, comment, gauster, nashgob, scandal, sponsor, tattler 8 informer, quidnunc 9 chatterer 10 newsmonger, talebearer, tattletale 11 scuttlebutt

gossoon: boy, lad 5 youth

got: see **get.**

gotch: jug 7 pitcher

gote: 6 sluice, stream 7 channel

Goth: 8 Visigoth 9 barbarian, Ostrogoth
  hero: 5 Wudga

Gothamite: 9 New Yorker

Gothic: 4 rude 5 rough 6 fierce 8 barbaric, Teutonic

gouge: 4 tool 5 cheat, fraud 6 cavity, chisel, groove 7 defraud 9 extortion 10 overcharge

gourd: 4 hole, pepo 5 melon, pepos 6 bottle, vessel 7 anguria 8 calabash, cucurbit 9 colocynth 11 chilacayote

gourmand: 7 epicure, glutton, gourmet 11 connoisseur

gourmandise, gormandize: 6 guttle

gourmet: 7 epicure 8 gourmand 11 connoisseur

gousty: 6 dreary 7 ghastly 8 desolate 13 preternatural

gout: 4 clot, drop 5 ditch, drain, taste 6 blotch, sluice, splash 7 channel, podagra 9 arthritis 11 coagulation, discernment

goutweed: 8 aiseweed

govern: run 4 curb, rein, rule, sway 5 guide, regle, steer 6 bridle, direct, manage, police 7 command, conduct, control, preside, refrain 8 dominate, regulate, restrain 9 influence, supervise 10 administer, discipline

governance: 7 control 10 government, management

governante, gouvernante: 8 chaperon 9 governess 11 housekeeper

governess: 6 abbess 8 mistress 11 gouvernante

governing: 6 regent 7 leading 11 gubernative

government: 4 rule 5 power 6 empire, habits 7 conduct, regency, regimen 8 demeanor, monarchy, republic 9 autocracy, democracy, hierarchy, oligarchy 10 governance, management **11** aristocracy, gubernation

agent: **5** envoy **6** consul **8** diplomat, minister **10** ambassador

art of: **8** politics **13** statesmanship

by a few: **9** oligarchy

by church: **9** hierarchy **10** hierocracy

by three: **8** triarchy **11** triumvirate

derived from: **9** political

head: **4** czar, king, tzar **5** queen **7** emperor, empress, premier **8** dictator **9** president **10** presidente

official: **6** syndic **10** bureaucrat

opposition to: **10** antarchism

representative: **6** consul **10** ambassador

science: **8** politics

system: **6** regime

governor: bey **4** lord **5** deity, nabob, pilot, ruler **6** author, dynast, grieve, rector, regent **7** captain, control, dynasty, manager, viceroy **8** director **9** president, regulator **10** gubernator, magistrate

castle: **6** alcaid **7** alcaide **9** castellan

gowk: **4** fool, gawk **6** cuckoo **9** simpleton

gowl: **4** howl, yell **5** whine **6** throat

gown (see also **dress, garment**): **4** robe, toga **5** frock, habit, manto, toosh **6** clothe, invest, mantua **7** garment

dressing: **4** robe **6** kimono **8** peignoir

loose: **6** banian, camise, chimer **7** cassock, chemise, chimere

Moslem: **4** jama **5** jamah

goyle: **5** gully **6** hollow, ravine, valley

gozzard: **9** gooseherd

gra: **5** lover **6** liking **8** fondness **10** sweetheart

grab: nab, rap **4** boat **5** catch, clasp, grasp, seize **6** arrest, beclap, clutch, collar, snatch **7** capture, grapnel, grapple **11** appropriate

grabble: **4** grab **5** grope, seize **6** snatch, sprawl **7** grapple **11** appropriate

grace: **4** este **5** adorn, charm, favor, leave, mercy **6** beauty, become, bedeck, favour, polish, prayer, virtue **7** commend, dignify, gratify **8** beautify, easiness, efficacy, elegance, kindness **9** embellish, privilege **10** comeliness, goodliness, permission, refinement, seemliness **12** dispensation **14** attractiveness

Grace: **6** Aglaia, Charis, Thalia **10** Euphrosyne

mother of: **5** Aegle

graceful: **4** airy, easy, gent **5** genty **6** comely, gainly, mignon, seemly **7** elegant, fitting, genteel, tactful **8** charming, debonair, delicate **9** beautiful **11** appropriate

graceless: **4** ugly **5** cruel **7** awkward **8** depraved **9** abandoned, inelegant, merciless **10** ungracious **11** unfortunate

gracenote: **12** appoggiatura

graces: **8** agremens **9** agrements

gracile: **4** thin **6** slight **7** slender **8** graceful

gracious: **4** good, hend, kind, mild **5** civil,

godly, happy, lucky, suave **6** benign, goodly, kindly **7** affable **8** benedict, debonair, generous, handsome, merciful, pleasing **9** benignant, courteous, favorable, fortunate **10** beneficent, forthgoing, regenerate **11** complaisant

grackle: **4** myna

gradation: **4** rank, step **5** scale, stage **6** climax, degree, series **8** position **10** exaltation, succession

grade: peg **4** mark, rank, rate, size, sort **5** class, level, order, stage **6** ascent, assort, degree, rating, select **7** incline, inspect **8** classify, gradient, graduate **14** classification

grader: **9** bulldozer

gradient: **4** ramp **5** grade, slope

gradine, gradin: **5** shelf **7** retable

gradual: **4** easy, slow **6** gentle **9** leisurely

graduate: **5** grade **6** alumna **7** alumnus

Graeae, Graiae: **4** Enyo **5** Deino **8** Pephredo

graff: **5** canal, ditch, fosse **6** trench

graft: dig **4** cion, toil, work **5** ditch, gravy, labor, scion, trade **6** boodle, inarch, trench **7** engraff **10** occupation

grail: cup **7** chalice

grain: jot, rye **4** corn, curn, grit, meal, oats, rice, seed, wale **5** fiber, glebe, maize, scrap, spark, trace, wheat **6** barley, cereal, kernel, russud(Russ.) **7** granule, texture **8** particle **9** granulate

brewing: **4** malt

bundle: **5** sheaf

chaff: **4** bran, grit

coating: **4** bran

dried: **5** straw **6** groats, rissom, rizzom

ear of: **5** spike **6** ressum

foodstuff: **6** cereal

fungus: **5** ergot

funnel: **6** hopper

ground: **4** meal **5** flour, grist

line: **5** swath

measure: **6** thrave

mixture: **6** fodder **7** farrage **9** bullimong

outer membrane: **6** extine

parched: **7** graddan

price: **4** fiar(Sc.)

receptacle: bin **8** elevator

scoop: **5** shaul

spike: ear

stack: **4** rick

tool: **5** flail

warehouse: **8** elevator

graip: **5** gripe

graith: **4** gear **5** adorn, build, dress, stuff **6** wealth **7** apparel, compose, furnish, prepare **8** material **9** apparatus, furniture **11** possessions **12** acoutrements **13** accouterments

gram: *one-tenth:* **8** decigram

molecule: mol **4** mole

gramary: **5** magic **7** grammar **8** learning **10** necromancy **11** enchantment

gramercy: **6** thanks **7** emotion

grammar: 6 syntax 9 accidence 11 linguistics

case: nom 6 dative 8 ablative, genitive, vocative 9 objective 10 accusative, nominative

describe: 5 parse

direct address: 8 vocative

example: 8 paradigm

term: 6 phrase, simile 8 metaphor

grampus: orc 4 orca 5 whale 7 cetacea, dolphin 8 cetacean, scorpion

granada: 11 pomegranate

granary: bin 4 gola 6 garnel, garner, girnal, girnel, grange 8 cornloft 9 cornhouse 10 repository, storehouse

grand: 4 epic, main 5 chief, great, lofty, noble, showy 6 august, epical, famous, superb, swanky 7 exalted, immense, stately, sublime 8 foremost, glorious, gorgeous, majestic, splendid 9 dignified, grandiose, principal, sumptuous 10 impressive, preeminent 11 ceremonious, illustrious, magnificent 13 comprehensive

Grand Canyon state: 7 Arizona

Grand Duke of Hell: 6 Abogor

grand slam: 4 vole 5 homer 7 home run

grandchild: oe, oy; oye

great: 5 ieroe

grandee: 6 bashaw 7 magnate 8 nobleman 10 clarissimo(It.)

grandeur: 4 pomp 5 state 6 parade 7 majesty 8 elegance, splendor, vastness 9 greatness, immensity, loftiness, nobleness, sublimity 10 augustness 12 magnificence

grandeval: 7 ancient

grandfather: 6 atavus 8 grandfer, gudesire(Sc.)

grandiloquent: 6 heroic, turgid 7 pompous 9 bombastic 13 grandiloquous

grandiose: 4 epic 5 grand 6 turgid 7 pompous 8 imposing 9 bombastic, expansive, flaunting 10 impressive

grandmother: 6 beldam, granny, gudame(Sc.) 7 beldame, grandam, grannie 8 babushka(Russ.), grandame 9 eldmother

Devil's: 4 Baba

grange: 4 farm 7 granary 9 farmhouse

granger: 6 farmer

granite: 6 aplite 7 haplite, syenite 8 alaskite

granitic: 4 hard 7 austere 10 inflexible

grant: aid 4 boon, cede, gift, give, lend, loan, mise 5 admit, allot, allow, bonus, chart, cowle, spare, yette, yield 6 accede, accord, afford, assent, bestow, betake, beteem, bounty, confer, octroi, patent, permit, remise 7 adjudge, concede, consent, promise, subsidy, tribute 8 bestowal, donation, transfer 9 franchise, undertake 10 concession, permission, relinquish 11 acknowledge

granting: if 6 ceding, remise 7 lending 9 allowance, conceding

granular: 5 sandy 6 coarse, grainy 9 granulose

granulate: 5 grain 7 coarsen 11 crystallize

granule: 4 pill 5 grain 6 nodule, pellet 8 particle

grape: uva 5 Tokay 6 Agawam, Lalang, Malaga, Malage, Muscat 7 Catawba, Concord, Hamburg, Mission, Niagara 8 Delaware, Riesling, Thompson 9 muscadine 11 Scuppernong

acid: 7 racemic

cluster: 10 racemation

dried: 6 raisin

fermentation: 6 cuvage(Fr.)

gatherer: 8 vintager

genus of: 5 vitis

juice: 4 dibs, must, sapa, stum

refuse: 4 marc

residue: 4 marc, rape 6 pomace

seed: 6 acinus

grapefruit: 6 pomelo 8 shaddock

grapevine: 4 caro 5 rumor 6 canard, report

graph: 5 chart 7 contour 8 quantity

graphic: 5 vivid 11 picturesque

graphite: 6 carbon

grapnel: 4 drag, grab 5 catch, seize 6 anchor 7 grapple

grapple: 4 grab, hold 5 grasp, gripe 6 buckle, clinch, tackle 7 contend, grabble, grapnel, gripple, seizing, seizure, wrestle 8 struggle

grasp: nap, see 4 clam, fist, glam, grab, grip, hand, hent, hold, holt, take 5 catch, clasp, glaum, gripe, seize, snare 6 clench, clinch, clutch, grappe, snatch 7 control, embrace, grapple, gripple, seizure 8 handfast 9 apprehend 10 comprehend, understand 13 comprehension

grasping: 4 avid, hard 6 greedy, grippy 7 miserly 8 covetous 10 avaricious 12 apprehension, parsimonious

grass (see also **cereal**): 4 lawn, reed, turf 6 darnel 7 hassock, herbage, pasture 9 colieroot, vetiveria 10 greensward

blade of: 7 traneen

fiber: 4 flax 5 istle, ramee, ramie 6 bhabar

fodder: 4 dura, gama 6 millet

genus of: 5 stipa 6 clover, lygeum 7 setaria

kinds of: eel, fog, hay, poa 4 alfa, bent, cane, diss, leaf, reed 5 avena, grama, sedge, spart, spike, stipa 6 enalid, marram, quitch, redtop, sesame, sorrel 7 esparto, traneen 8 calfkill 9 bouteloua

grasschat: 8 whinchat

grasshopper: 4 grig 6 locust

grassland: lea 4 lawn, rakh(Ind.), vale 5 field, range, veldt 6 meadow 7 pasture, prairie

grassplot: 4 lawn 6 meadow

grassweed: 8 eelgrass

grate: jar 4 fret, grid, grit, rasp 5 grill, grind 6 abrade, basket, offend, prison,

scrape 7 grating 8 imprison, irritate
grateful: 8 thankful 9 agreeable 12 appreciative
gratification: 4 gust 6 reward 8 delicacy, gratuity, pleasure 9 enjoyment 10 recompense 11 contentment 12 satisfaction
gratified: 4 glad 5 proud 7 pleased 9 delighted
gratify: 4 feed, sate 5 adorn, amuse, feast, grace. humor, wreak 6 arride, foster, pamper, please 7 appease, content, delight, flatter, gladden, indulge, requite, satisfy, welcome 9 gratulate 10 remunerate
grating: 4 grid, heck, rasp 5 grate, gride, grill, harsh, raspy, rough 6 cratch, grille, hoarse 8 gridiron, grinding, strident 9 dissonant 11 latticework
gratis: 4 free 10 gratuitous
gratitude: 4 gift 5 favor 6 thanks 7 tribute 8 gratuity 12 thankfulness
gratuitous: 4 free 6 gratis, wanton 8 baseless, needless 10 groundless 11 superfluous, unwarranted
gratuity: fee, tip 4 dash, dole, gift, vail 5 bonus, bribe, pilon, spiff 6 bounty 7 cumshaw, pension, present 8 bakshish, bonamano, buckshee, lagnappe 9 baksheesh, buona-mano, gratitude, lagniappe, pourboire 10 compliment 11 benefaction 13 gratification
grave: dig, pit 4 bier, bury, deep, foss, slow, tomb 5 carve, ditch, fossa, fosse, heavy, inter, sober, staid, suant 6 burial, grieve, hearse, sedate, solemn, somber, sombre, trench 7 austere, earnest, engrave, serious, steward 8 decorous, overseer, sermonic 9 important, momentous, ponderous, sepulcher 11 influential 13 authoritative
comb. form: 5 serio
robber: 4 goul 5 ghoul
gravecloth: 6 sudary 8 cerement 9 cerecloth
gravedigger: 6 burier, fossor 7 fossore(pl.)
gravel: 4 dirt, grit, sand, stop 5 check 6 bother, chisel, eratum, sammel 7 perplex 8 alluvium, erratice 9 embarrass
graven: 6 etched 8 engraved 10 sculptured
graver: 5 burin 8 engraver, sculptor
gravestone: 5 blank, stela, stele 6 cippus, marker 8 monument 9 tombstone 11 sarcophagus
graveyard: 8 cemetery 10 churchyard
gravity: 7 dignity 8 enormity, sobriety 9 heaviness, influence, solemnity 10 importance 11 earnestness, seriousness, weightiness 12 significance 13 momentousness 17 authoritativeness
law discoverer: 6 Newton
gravy: jus(F.) 4 lear 5 graft, juice, sauce
gravy boat: 9 sauceboat

gray: dim 4 ashy, dull, gris, hoar 5 ashen, bleak, hoary, lyard, lyart, slate 6 dismal, leaden, mature 7 elderly, grisard, grizzly, hueless, neutral 9 cheerless 10 achromatic
bluish: 7 cesious
comb. form: 5 polio
dark: 5 taupe 6 Oxford 8 charcoal
light: 4 ashy 5 pearl
Quaker: 5 acier
gray whale: 7 ripsack
grayish: 7 grizzle 8 grizzled
grayling: 4 pink
graze: 4 drab, feed, rase, skim 5 agist, brush, shave 6 browse, ripple, scrape 7 pasture
grazing ground: 4 colp 5 range 6 collop, meadow 7 pasture
grease: fat, oil 4 daub, lard, mort, seak, soil 5 bleck, bribe, cheat, cozen, smear 6 creesh(Sc.) 7 lanolin 9 lubricate, overreach
greaser: 6 stoker
greasewood: 5 chico, orach, yolky 6 orache
greasy: fat 4 oily, rich 5 dirty, fatty, gross, porky, thick 7 smeared 8 indecent, unctuous 10 indelicate 11 threatening
great: big 4 deep, fell, huge, much, rial, unco, vast 5 ample, chief, grand, large, yeder 6 grande(F.), heroic, mickle 7 capital, eminent, extreme, howling, immense, intense, titanic, violent 8 almighty, elevated, enormous, favorite, horrible 9 elaborate, excellent, important, prolonged 10 delightful, omnipotent 11 magnificent
comb. form: 5 macro, megal
prefix: 4 arch
great albacore: 5 tunny 7 bluefin
great-aunt: 9 grandaunt
great blue heron: 5 crane
Great Britain: See **England**.
great deal: 4 gobs, lots
Great Divide: 7 Rockies
Great Lake: 4 Erie 5 Huron 7 Ontario 8 Michigan, Superior
great many: lac 4 lakh
Great Sea: 5 Black 13 Mediterranean
Great White Brother: 7 Mahatma
greatcoat: 5 grego, jemmy, jimmy 8 overcoat 9 cothamore
greaten: 5 exalt 7 enhance, enlarge, magnify 8 increase
greater: 6 better 8 majority, mightier
greatest: 4 arch, best, most 6 utmost 7 extreme, noblest, supreme
greatly: 4 fell, much 5 amain, nobly
greatness: 8 grandeur 9 magnitude 11 magnanimity
greave: 5 armor, grove 7 thicket
greaves: 9 crackling
Grecia: 6 Greece
Grecian: 5 Greek 9 Hellenist

gree: 5 favor, prize 7 mastery 8 gladness, pleasure 11 superiority 12 satisfaction
Greece (see also **Athens, Sparta**): 6 Hellas
 abode of gods: 7 Olympus
 administrator: 10 amphodarch
 alphabet: mu, nu, xi, pi; eta, rho, tau, phi, chi, psi 4 beta, zeta, iota 5 alpha, gamma, delta, theta, kappa, lamba, sigma, omega 7 epsilon, omicron, upsilon
 altar: 7 eschara
 ancient: 4 Elis 5 Doris 6 Achaea, Achaia, Attica, Epirus, Hellas, Sparta 7 Epeiros, Macedon 12 Peloponnesus
 Argolis valley: 5 Nemea
 army corps: 6 evzone
 basin: 6 louter
 beauty: 4 Lais
 cape: 5 Malea 7 Matapan
 chamber: 12 bouleuterion
 chariot: 4 biga
 citadel: 9 Acropolis
 city: 4 Elis 5 Barca, Chios, Drama, Eolis, Pella, Samos, Zante 6 Athens(c.), Edessa, Janina, Kozane, Larisa, Lesbos, Locris, Phocis, Phokis, Serrai, Serres, Sparta, Yanina 7 Corinth, Epeiros, Laconia, Larissa, Megaris, Rhodope 8 Ioannina, Komotine, Lassithi, Lessenia, Lessinia, Salonica, Salonika, Thessaly, Trikkala 9 Korinthos, Lasethion, Lasithion, Phthiotis, Rethymnon, Zakynthos 10 Negroponte 15 Alexandroupolis
 clan: 4 obes 5 genos
 cloak: 6 abolla 7 chlamys
 coin: 4 mine, obal 5 hecte, nomas 6 lepton, phenix, stater 7 diobolo, drachma
 column: 5 Doric, Ionic 10 Corinthian
 contest: 4 agon
 counselor: 6 Nestor
 cup: 5 depas
 dialect: 5 Doric, Elean, Eolic, Ionic 6 Aeolic
 dirge: 5 linos
 district: 4 Arta, deme 5 Canea, Chios, Corfu, Drama, Evros, Khios, Pella, Samos, Zante 6 Achaea. Attica, Epirus, Euboea, Khania, Kozane, Lesbos, Phocis, Serrai, Yanina 7 Achaiam, Aetolia, Arcadia, Argolis, Boeotia, Corinth, Florina, Kavalla, Laconia, Larissa, Rhodope 8 Cyclades, Ioannina, Messenia, Rethymne, Salonica, Thessaly, Trikkala 9 Acarnania, Korinthos, Lasithion, Macedonia, Phthiotis, Zakynthos 10 Cephalonia, Chalcidice, Khalkidike 11 Kephallenia
 doom: ker
 dramatist: 9 Aeschylus, Euripides, Sophocles 12 Aristophanes
 epic: 5 Iliad 7 Odyssey
 essence: 5 ousia
 fabulist: 5 Aesop
 Fate: 6 Clotho 7 Atropos 8 Lachesis
 festival: 5 delia, haloa 8 Apaturia

 flask: 4 olpe
 fleet commander: 7 navarch
 flute: 7 hemiope
 folk dance: 7 romaika
 foot soldier: 7 hoplite
 Fury: 6 Alecto, Erinys 7 Erinyes, Megaera 9 Tisiphone
 garment: 5 tunic 6 abolla, chiton, peplos, peplus 7 chlamys
 giant: 4 Otus 5 Mimas 7 Aloadae 9 Enceladus, Ephialtes
 god: Dis, Pan 4 Ares, Eros, Zeus 5 Hades, Momus, Pluto, satyr 6 Apollo, Cronus, Hermes, Kronos, Nereus, Triton 7 Bacchus 8 Dionysus, Poseidon
 goddess: Ge, Io; Ara, Ate, Eos, Not, Nyx, Ops 4 Alea, Dice, Dike, Enyo, Gaea, Gaia, Hebe, Hera, Leto, Nike 5 Horae, Irene, Metis, Moera, Niobe, Vesta 6 Athena, Eirene, Hecate, Hekate, Hestia, Selena, Selene, Semele 7 Ariadne, Artemis, Astarte, Demeter, Eunomia, Nemesis 9 Aphrodite
 gorgon: 4 Enyo 5 Deino 6 Graeae, Graiae, Medusa, Stheno 7 Euryale 8 Pephredo
 gymnasium: 4 xyst 9 palaestra
 hero: 4 Aias, Ajax, Idas 5 Jason 7 Cecrops, Theseus 8 Heracles
 historian: 7 Ctesias 8 Polybius, Xenophon 10 Thucydides
 hobgoblin: 6 Empusa
 hunter: 5 Orion
 instrument: 5 aulos 8 barbiton
 invader: 6 Dorian
 island: Ios, Nio 4 Keos, Milo, Paxi, Syra 5 Chios, Corfu, Crete, Delos, Khios, Krete, Melos, Milos, Naxos, Paros, Psara, Samos, Syros, Thera, Tinos, Zante 6 Andros, Candia, Cerigo, Ikaria, Ionian, Ithaka, Lemnos, Lesbos, Leukas, Patmus, Rhodes, Sifnos 7 Amorgos, Cythera, Kimolos, Kythera, Kythnos, Myconos, Mykonis, Serifus 8 Cyclades, Mytelene, Santorin 9 Antiparos, Santorini 10 Cephalonia, Samothrace 11 Anticythera
 jar: 7 amphora
 judge: 6 dikast 7 heliast
 jug: 5 ascos
 king: 6 Nestor
 lake: 6 Copais
 lawgiver: 5 Minos, Solon
 legislative council: 5 boule
 letter: see *alphabet* above.
 letter(primitive): san 5 koppa, sampi 7 digamma
 lover: 7 Rhoecus
 lyre player: 5 Arion
 man of brass: 5 Talos
 marker: 5 stela, stele
 market place: 5 agora
 mathematician: 6 Euclid 10 Archimedes
 measure: pik 4 bema, piki, pous 5 baril, cados, chous, cubit, diote, doron, pekhe, pygon, xylon 6 acaena, bachel, bacile,

barile, cotula, dichas, hemina, koilon, lichas, milion, orgyia, palame, pechys, schene, xestes **7** amphora, choemix, cyathos, diaulos, hekteus, metreta, stadion, stadium, stremma **8** condylos, daktylos, dekapode, dolichos, medimnys, palaiste, plethron, spithame, stathmos **9** hemiekton, oxybaphon

monster: **5** Hydra

mountain: Ida **4** Oeta, Ossa **5** Athos, Parus, Visti **6** Othrys, Pelion, Pindus **7** Helicon, Olympus **8** Hymettus, Taygetus **9** Cambunian, Cithaeron, Parnassus, Psiloriti **10** Lycabettus, Pentelucus

musical interval: **6** ditone, meseme

musical note: **4** mese, nete

musical system: **5** neume

mustard: **6** sinapi

nome: see *district* above

numeral: mu, nu, xi, pi; eta, san **4** beta, zeta, iota **5** alpha, gamma, delta, theta, kappa, koppa, sampi **6** lambda **7** epsilon, digamma, omicron

nymph: **5** Oread **8** Arethusa

old testament: **10** Septuagint

overseer: **5** ephor

paradise: **7** Elysium

patriarch: **5** Arius

patriot: **6** klepht

peninsula: **4** Alte **5** Morea

people: **5** demos **6** Argive, Cretan, Ionian **7** Hellene, Spartan **8** Athenian

pert. to: **6** Ionian **8** Hellenic **9** classical **11** Panhellenic

philosopher: **4** Zeno **5** Galen, Plato **6** Thales **8** Diogenes **9** Aristotle **10** Pythagoras

physician: **5** Galen

pitcher: **4** olla, olpe **8** oenochoe

platform: **4** bema **6** logeum

poem: **5** Iliad **7** Odyssey

poet: Ion **5** Arion, Homer **6** Pindar **9** Simonides, Sophocles

poetess: **5** Sapho **6** Sappho **7** Corinna

port: **4** Syra **5** Corfu **6** Patras **7** Piraeus

portico: **4** stoa, xyst

precinct: **7** temenos

priest: **4** papa

priestess: **4** Auge, Hero, Iole **8** Caryatid

province: **4** nome **5** nomos **7** eparchy

river: **4** Arta **5** Lerna **6** Peneus, Ruphia **7** Alpheus, Eurotas **8** Achelous, Arachtus **11** Aspropitamo **12** Basilipotamo

rose: **7** glaieul

sage: **6** Thales

sanctuary: **5** hiera

sculptor: **5** Myron **7** Phidias

seaport: **4** Enos, Volo **5** Pylos **8** Salonica, Salonika **9** Gallipoli

serpent: **4** seps

settler: **5** metic

shield: **5** pelta

ship: **4** saic **5** diota

shrine: **5** secos, sekos

skeptic: **5** Timon

slave: **5** helot **6** penest

slave woman: **5** Baubo, Iambe

soldier: **7** palikar

sorceress: **5** Circe, Medea, Siren

speech: **6** rhesis

statesman: **8** Pericles **9** Aristides **12** Themistocles

statue: **6** xoanon

temple: **4** naos **5** cella **7** Theseus

territory: see *district* above.

theater: **5** odeon, odeum

town: **4** Elea **5** Nemea **6** Actium **7** Eleusis **9** Pharsalus

township: **4** deme

valley: **5** Nemea

vase: **5** dinos

verse: **6** Alcaic

village: obe

weight: mna, oka, oke **4** mina **5** litra, maneh, minah, obole, pound **6** diobol, dramme, kantar, obolos, obolus, stater, talent **7** chalcon, chalque, drachma **8** diobolon, talanton **12** tetradrachma

greed: **7** avarice, avidity **8** cupidity, gulosity, voracity **11** miserliness

greedy: **4** avid **5** eager, gutty **6** stingy **7** miserly **8** covetous, esurient, grasping, ravenous **9** devouring, rapacious, voracious **10** avaricious, gluttonous, insatiable

Greek: See **Greece.**

green: new, raw **4** bice, live, verd, vert(Fr.) **5** cedre, crude, fresh, mossy, virid, young **6** callow, recent, unripe **7** untried, verdant **8** blooming, gullible, ignorant, immature, inexpert **9** malachite, undecayed, unskilled, untrained **11** flourishing **13** inexperienced **15** unsophisticated

blue: **4** cyan, saxe **7** sistine

gray: **5** olive

pale: **7** celadon

shade: **4** nile **5** apple, kelly **6** bottle **7** emerald

woodbine: **7** peridot

yellow: **7** opaline

Green Mountain Boy's leader: **10** Ethan Allen

Green Mountain state: **7** Vermont

green peak: **10** woodpecker

greenback: **8** frogskin

greenery: **7** verdure

greenhorn: yap **4** jake, tyro **5** ikona **6** novice **9** cheechaco, cheechako **10** tenderfoot

Greenland: *base:* **4** Etah

discoverer: **4** Eric

Eskimo: Ita

town: **4** Etah **8** Godthaab **11** Julianehaab **12** Angmagssalik

greenlet: **5** vireo

greenroom: **5** foyer

greens: **5** salad

greenstone: **4** jade **7** pounamu **8** nephrite **9** malachite

greensward: **4** turf **5** grass

greet: cry **4** hail **5** halse **6** accost, salute **7** address, receive, welcome

greeting: ave, bow **4** hail **5** aloha, hello, salut(Fr.) **6** accost, salute **7** address, slainte, welcome **8** saluting **9** reception **10** salutation **12** commendation

gregarious: 6 gregal, social **8** sociable **11** amadelphous

grego: 5 cloak **6** jacket **9** greatcoat

gremlin: imp **5** devil

grenade: 4 bomb **5** shell **11** pomegranate

grenadier: 4 fish **7** rattail, soldier

grenier: 5 attic

gres: 8 ceramics **9** stoneware

grey: See gray.

Greya's husband: 4 Oder

greyhound: 4 grew **9** grewhound

grid: 5 grate **6** buccan **7** grating **8** gridiron

griddle: 5 grill **8** gridiron

griddle-cake: 7 crumpet, pancake **8** chapatty

gridiron: 5 field, grill **7** brander, grating, griddle

grief: woe **4** care, dole, dool, dree, harm, hurt, pain, ruth, teen **5** agony, dolor, tears, trial, wrong **6** dolour, mishap, regret, sorrow **7** anguish, chagrin, emotion, failure, offense, sadness, trouble **8** disaster, distress, hardship **9** grievance, suffering **10** affliction, desolation, heartgrief **11** lamentation

grievance: 5 anger, grief **6** burden **8** gravamen, hardship **9** complaint, injustice **10** affliction, oppression **11** displeasure

grieve: rue **4** care, dole, pain, pine, sigh,**5** anger, grave, mourn, wound **6** bewail, enrage, lament, sadden, sorrow **7** afflict, bailiff, condole, manager, sheriff, steward, trouble **8** complain, distress, governor, overseer **10** discomfort

grieved: 4 sore **5** vexed **9** afflicted

grievous: sad **4** sore **5** heavy, sorry **6** bitter, dready, severe **7** heinous, intense **8** dolorous **9** atrocious **10** burdensome, calamitous, deplorable, flagitious, oppressive **11** gravaminous

griff: 4 glen **6** ravine

grig: eel **5** annoy, dwarf **7** cricket, heather **8** irritate **9** tantalize **11** grasshopper

grigri: 5 charm **6** amulet, fetish **8** talisman

grike: 5 chink **6** ravine **7** crevice

grill, grille: vex **4** reja(Sp.) **5** broil, grate, harsh **6** offend **7** grating, griddle, torment **8** distress, gridiron, grillade, irritate **12** cross-examine

grilse: 5 trout **6** salmon **7** botcher

grim: 4 dour, sour **5** angry, cruel, gaunt, harsh, stern **6** fierce, grisly, horrid, raging, savage, sullen **7** furious, ghastly, hideous, ominous **8** horrible, pitiless, ruthless, sinister **9** ferocious, frightful, merciless, repellent **10** forbidding, inexorable, relentless, unyielding

grimace: mop, mow, mug **4** face, mock, moue, mowe, mump, sham **5** fleer, smirk, sneer **8** pretense **11** affectation

grimalkin: cat **6** feline, she-cat

grime: 4 dirt, smut, soil, soot **5** colly, sully **7** begrime

grimly: 4 grim **5** stern **7** hideous

grimp: 5 climb

grimy: 4 foul **5** dingy, dirty **6** grubby, soiled **7** swarthy **8** begrimed

grin: gin **4** girn **5** fleer, smile

grind: vex **4** bray, chaw, chew, grit, joke, mill, mull, whet **5** chafe, crush, gnash, grate, study **6** abrade, crunch, drudge harass, pestle, polish, powder, satire **7** oppress, sharpen **8** satirize **9** blackfish, comminute, pulverize, triturate **12** steeplechase

grinder: 5 molar, tooth, tutor **9** announcer **10** flycatcher, goatsucker

grinding: 7 grating **10** burdensome **12** excruciating

grindle: 5 ditch, drain **6** bowfin

gringo: 8 American **9** foreigner **10** Englishman

grip: bag **4** holt, vice **5** cinch, clamp, clasp, cleat, ditch, drain, grasp, gripe, seize, spasm **6** clench, clinch, clutch, furrow, gutter, handle, trench, valise **7** earring, grapple, handbag, handful **8** gripsack, handfast, handgrip **9** constrict **12** sceneshifter

gripe: 4 grip **5** grasp, pinch **6** clench, clutch, grouse, handle, harass, snatch, timber **7** afflict, control, grapple, handful, mastery, vulture **8** complain, distress **9** apprehend **10** affliction, oppression

griph, griphus: 6 enigma, puzzle, riddle

grippe, grip: flu **9** influenza

gripper: 6 nipper

gripple: 5 grasp **7** grapple **9** tenacious **10** avaricious

gripsack: 4 grip **7** handbag

griskin: 4 chop, loin **5** steak

grisly: 4 grim **7** ghastly, hideous **8** dreadful, grewsome, gruesome, horrible, terrible

grison: 5 huron **6** weasel

grist: lot **8** quantity **9** provision

gristle: 9 cartilage

grit: 4 sand, soil **5** earth, grain, grate, grind, nerve, pluck **6** clench, gravel **7** bravery, courage **8** decision **12** perseverance

grith: 5 mercy, peace **6** asylum, refuge **7** defense, quarter **8** security **9** sanctuary **11** self-conduct

gritty: 4 game **5** sandy **6** plucky **7** arenose, arenous **8** resolute, sabulous **10** persistent

grivet: 6 monkey

grivois: 4 bold, free **5** broad **8** indecent

grizzle: 4 fret **7** grayish, whimper **8** complain

grizzly: 4 bear

Grizzly Bear State: 10 California

groan: 4 moan 5 creak, grank, grunt

grocer: 7 epicier(F.) 11 storekeeper

grog: rum 5 drink, rumbo 6 liquor 8 beverage

groggery: 7 shebeen(Ir.)

groggy: 5 shaky, tipsy 8 unsteady, wavering 9 tottering

groom: 4 mafu, syce, tidy 5 curry, dress, mafoo, strap 6 fettle 7 hostler, marshal, prepare, servant, shopboy 8 coistrel 9 assistant 10 bridegroom, manservant, palfrenier 11 horsekeeper

grooming: 8 toilette

groove: rut 4 dado, rake, slot 5 canal, chase, flute, glyph, regal, rigol, scarf, shaft, stria, sulci(pl.) 6 furrow, gutter, hollow, rabbet, raglet, scrobe, striae(pl.), sulcus 7 channel, striate 10 excavation

grope: 4 clam, feel, glam, test 5 glaum, probe, sound 6 handle 7 examine, grabble, gropple

grosbeak: 7 warbler 8 hawfinch

groser: 10 gooseberry

gross: big, fat, low, sum 4 bulk, clod, dull, mass, rank, rude 5 amass, broad, brute, bulky, burly, close, crass, dense, heavy, plain, rough, thick, total, whole 6 animal, brutal, coarse, earthy, entire, filthy, greasy, impure, vulgar 7 beastly, brutish, compact, fulsome, general, glaring, massive, obscene, obvious, sensual, swinish, witless 8 cloddish, flagrant, indecent 9 egregious, unlearned, unrefined 10 indefinite, indelicate, scurrilous

grot: 6 cavern, grotto

grotesque: 5 antic 7 baroque, bizarre 8 fanciful 9 fantastic, whimsical 11 incongruous 12 preposterous

grotto: den 4 cave, grot, hole 5 crypt, speos, vault 6 cavern, recess

grouch: 4 sulk 6 grouse 7 grumble

ground: 4 base, dirt, fund, land, root, soil 5 earth, field, train 6 bottom, estate, reason 7 country, premise, terrain 8 initiate 9 establish, territory 10 foundation, fundamenta(pl.) 11 fundamentum

kinds of: bog, lot 4 moor, acre, farm, plat, park 5 arada, glebe, tilth, range, marsh, swale, patch 6 meadow, calade, reseau, maidan 7 pasture, cripple, curragh

raised: 5 ridge 7 hillock, hummock

ground pine: iva

ground squirrel: 6 gopher 8 chipmunk

groundless: 4 idle 5 false 8 baseless 9 unfounded 10 gratuitous 11 unwarranted

grounds: 4 lees 5 basis, dregs, grout 6 bottom 8 sediment

college: 6 campus

military: 4 camp, fort 8 presidio 11 reservation

groundwork: 4 base, fund 5 basis, bases(pl.) 6 bottom, fundus

group: fry, mob, set 4 bevy, gang, herd, mass, ring, sect, team 5 batch, brood, cabal, class, clump, drove, firca, flock, genus, horde, party, squad, suite, tribe 6 bundle, clique, family, galaxy, gather, nation 7 arrange, cluster, collect, company, consort 8 assemble, assembly, classify, division 10 assemblage, assortment, collection, congregate 11 aggregation

animal: 4 herd 5 drove

pert. to: 7 generic

suffix: ery

grouse: 5 ganga, gripe 6 gorhen, grouch, repine 7 attagen, cheeper, gorcock, grumble 8 complain, squealer 9 gelinette, ptarmigan 10 whitebelly 12 capercaillie

grout: 4 lees, root 5 dregs, larry 7 grounds 8 porridge

grouty: 5 cross, sulky 6 sullen

grove: 4 bush, hewt, tope, wood 5 copse, hurst, lucus(L.) 6 aboret, bosket, greave, pinery 7 alameda, boscage, boskage, bosquet, coppice, thicket

pert. to: 7 nemoral

grovel: 4 fawn, roll 5 crawl, creep 6 cringe, tumble, wallow 7 grabble 8 flounder

groveling: 6 abject 7 hangdog 12 contemptible

grow: age, bud, get, wax 4 come, eche, rise 5 edify, raise, swell 6 accrue, batten, become, expand, extend, thrive 7 augment, develop, distend, enlarge, improve, nourish 8 develope, flourish, increase 9 cultivate 10 accumulate

grower: 6 farmer, raiser 7 rancher 10 orchardist 13 agriculturist 15 arboriculturist

growing: 6 rising 8 crescive

growl: 4 gurl, gurr, wirr, yirr 5 gnarl, snarl 6 gollar, goller, mutter, rumble 7 grumble, maunder 9 complaint

grown: 5 adult, risen 6 mature 7 matured 8 expanded

grownup: man 5 adult 7 matured

growth: 4 rise 5 swell 7 stature 8 increase, swelling 9 accretion, expansion, heterosis 11 development, enlargement 12 augmentation

in clusters: 8 racemose

on another: 8 parasite

on surface: 9 epigenous

organic: 9 accretion

promoting: 8 nutrient 9 nutriment

retarding: 9 paratonic

grub: bob, dig, eat 4 chow, feed, food, moot, plod, root 5 dwarf, larva, stump 6 drudge. larvae(pl.), maggot, search 7 plodder 8 victuals

grubby: 5 dirty, grimy, small 8 dwarfish, slovenly

grudge: 4 envy 5 covet, pique, spite 6 grutch 8 begrudge 10 resentment

grue: ice 4 snow 6 shiver 7 shudder 8 particle

gruel: 5 atole 6 burgoo, crowdy 8 porridge, wangrace

gruesome, grewsome: 4 ugly 6 grisly, horrid, sordid 7 fearful, ghastly, hideous, macabre 8 horrible

gruff: 4 deep, sour 5 bluff, harsh, rough, surly 6 hoarse, morose, severe, sullen 7 austere, brusque, quarrel

grumble: 4 crab, hone, kick 5 croak, growl, munge, snarl 6 grouch, grouse, mumble, murmur, mutter, repine, rumble, yammer 7 channer, gnatter, gruntle, maunder 8 begrudge, complain

grumpy: 5 cross, moody, surly 7 grumphy

grunt: 4 fish 5 groan, snork, snort 6 grumph 7 gruntle

grutch: 6 grudge, murmur 8 complain

guacharo: 7 fatbird, oilbird

guaiol: 7 alcohol

Guam: *breadfruit tree:* 6 nangca, nangka
capital: 5 Agana
native: 8 Chamorro

guanaco: 5 llama

guar: 4 bean

guarantee: 4 bail, band, bond, seal 6 assure, avouch, ensure, insure, surety 7 certify, endorse, hostage, warrant 8 guaranty, security, warranty 9 assurance, vouchsafe

guaranty: 4 bond, pawn, seal 6 pledge 7 warrant 8 security, warranty 9 guarantee

guard: 4 care, curb, herd, hold, keep, rail, tend, ward 5 bless, fence, hedge, watch 6 bantay, bridle, convey, custos, defend, dragon, escort, fender, gaoler, jailer, jailor, keeper, patrol, police, sentry, shield, warden 7 keeping, lineman, protect 8 conserve, preserve, restrain, security, sentinel, watchman 9 attention, custodian, protector, safeguard 10 cowcatcher, protection
foil: 6 button
line of: 6 cordon
on: 4 wary 5 alert, ready 8 vigilant, watchful 9 observant

guarded: 4 wary 6 manned 7 careful 8 cautious, defended, discreet, watchful 9 protected 11 circumspect

guardhouse: 4 brig 5 clink 6 prison 8 hoosegow

guardian: 4 herd 6 keeper, parent, pastor, patron, warden 7 curator, trustee, tutelar 8 defender, guardant 9 custodian, protector
heavenly: 5 angel
legal: 7 trustee
pert. to: 7 tutelar 8 tutelary

guardianship: 7 custody, keeping, tuition 8 custodia, tutelage 9 custodiae(pl.) 10 guardiancy

guasa: 7 grouper

Guatemala: *ant:* 5 kelep
city: 6 Salama 9 Guatemala 11 Ciudad Viega, Totonicapan 13 Quezaltenango
coin: 4 peso 7 centavo, quetzal
fruit: 4 anay
Indian: 4 Itxa, Ixil, Maya 5 Xinca
lake: 5 Dulce, Peten 7 Atitlan 10 Amatitland
measure: 4 vara 6 cuarta, fanega 7 cajuela, manzana 10 caballeria
port: 7 San Jose 10 Champerico, Livingston
river: 6 Chixoy, Pasion 8 San Pedro
volcano: 4 Agua 5 Fuego 7 Atitlan

Guaycuruan Indian: 4 Toba

gubbins: 6 refuse, scraps 9 fragments

gudame: 11 grandmother

gudesire: 11 grandfather

gudgeon: pin 4 bait, dupe, fish 5 cheat, pivot 7 journal 10 allurement

Gudrun's husband: 4 Atli

guerdon: 6 reward 8 requital 10 recompense

guess: aim 4 shot 5 areed, fancy, infer 6 divine 7 opinion, presume, surmise, suspect 8 estimate 9 speculate 10 conjecture

guest: 4 host 6 caller, inmate, lodger, patron, roomer 7 visitor 8 visitant

guesthouse: inn 5 hotel 11 caravansary

guff: 4 puff, talk 5 chaff, whiff 6 humbug

guffaw: 5 laugh 6 heehaw 8 laughter 10 horselaugh

Guiana: *cassava drink:* 7 paiwari
coin: bit
fowl: 4 keet
hut: 5 benab
river turtle: 8 matamata
tree: 4 dali, mora 5 dalli 6 camara

guidance: 4 duct, helm 7 auspice, conduct, guidage 8 steerage 9 direction 10 leadership, management 15 superintendence

guide: guy 4 airt, buoy, clue, lead, pole, rein, rule, show 5 airth, carry, longe, order, pilot, reign, steer, teach, treat, tutor, usher 6 bridle, convey, convoy, direct, former, govern, leader, manage 7 conduce, conduct, control, marshal, mercury 8 cicerone, director, instruct, polestar, regulate, textbook 9 catechism, conductor, guidebook, guidepost, itinerary, prescribe, regulator 11 superintend

guidebook: 8 baedeker, handbook 9 itinerary

guideway: 4 sley, slot 5 track 7 channel 8 slideway

guiding: 5 polar 7 leading

Guido: *fifth note:* sol
first note: ut
fourth note: fa
high note: la

second note: re
third note: mi
guild, gild: hui **6** gremio **7** society **10** fellowship **11** association, brotherhood
merchant: **5** hansa, hanse **6** cartel
guile: **4** dole, wile **5** cheat, craft, fraud **6** deceit, humbug **7** cunning **9** duplicity, treachery
guileful: **9** deceitful, insidious **10** fallacious, fraudulent **13** Machiavellian
guileless: **5** naive **6** candid, honest **7** artless **8** innocent **9** ingenuous
guillemot: auk **4** loom, quet **5** murre **7** dovekey, doveike
guillotine: **6** behead **10** decapitate
guilt: sin **5** culpa, fault **6** piacle **7** offense **8** iniquity **10** wickedness **11** criminality, culpability
guiltless: **4** free **8** innocent **9** righteous
guilty: **6** nocent, wicked **7** correal **8** culpable
Guinea: *measure:* **7** jacktan
seaport: **4** Bata
tree: **4** akee, dali, mora **5** dalli
weight: **4** akey, piso, uzan **5** benda, seron **6** quinto **8** aguirage
guinea fowl: **4** keet **7** galeeny, pintado
guinea pig: **4** cavy
Guinevere's husband: **6** Arthur
guise: hue **4** form, garb, mask, mien **5** cloak, cover, dress, habit, shape **6** aspect, attire, deceit, manner **7** arrange, fashion **8** behavior, disguise, likeness, practice **9** semblance **10** appearance, masquerade
guitar: uke **5** sitar, tiple **6** sancho **7** samisen, ukulele **8** chitarra **10** calascione
key: **5** dital
play: **5** strum
guitguit: **6** pitpit
gula: **4** ogee
gulch: **4** gulp **5** canon, gorge, gully **6** arroyo, canyon, coulee, ravine **7** glutton
gulf: **4** eddy **5** abyss, chaos, chasm **6** vorago **9** barathrum, whirlpool **10** separation
Gulf of Mexico islet: cay
Gulf States: **5** Texas **7** Alabama, Florida **9** Louisiana **11** Mississippi
gull: mew **4** dupe, fool, geck, sell, tern **5** cheat, cokes, cully, fraud, larid, trick **6** chouse, nilgai, teaser, victim, whilly **7** cheater, deceive, defraud, gosling, mislead **8** dotterel, impostor **9** kittiwake **10** mountebank
kinds of: cob **4** skua **5** allan, annet, pewit **6** larine, teaser, waggel **11** burgomaster
pert. to: **6** larine, laroid
gullet: maw **6** throat, weason **7** weasand **9** esophagus
gullible: **5** goofy, green, naive **9** credulous
gully: gut **4** sike **5** drain, gorge, goyal, goyle, gulch, knife, sword, zanja **6** arroyo, gutter, nullah, ravine, valley **7** couloir **11** watercourse

gulp: **4** glut, swig **5** gulch, quilt, swipe **6** glutch, gobble **7** swallow
gulp down: **4** bolt **6** englut
gum: **4** clog, hive, kino **5** cheat, nyssa, stick, trick **6** chicle, gluten, hashab, lumbug, impede, tissue, tupelo **7** bilsted, gingiva **8** mucilage **10** eucalyptus **11** masticatory
derivative: **8** bassorin **10** tragacanth, traganthin **12** tragacanthin
kinds of: **5** tuart **6** acacia, acacin, balata, touart **7** acacine, dextrin
resin: **5** elemi, gugal, myrrh **6** salban **9** sagapenum **12** frankincense
gum tree: **5** xylan
gumbo: **4** ocra, okra, soup **7** melange
gumma: **5** tumor
gummy: **6** mastic **7** viscous **8** adhesive
gumption: **10** enterprise, initiative, shrewdness
gums: ula **7** alveoli
gun: gat, rod **5** rifle, tommy **6** cannon, heater, pistol, weapon **7** carbine, shotgun **8** revolver **9** matchlock **11** blunderbuss
barrel cleaner: **6** ramrod
kinds of: **4** bore, bren, roer **5** baril **6** ack-ack, archie, barker **7** aerogun, bazooka **8** amusette
mount: **6** turret
part: **4** lock **5** stock **6** barrel, hammer, muzzle, rammer, safety **7** trigger
platform: **11** emplacement
gunfire: **4** rake **5** salvo **6** strafe **7** barrage **8** enfilade
gunlock: *catch:* **4** sear
hammer: **7** doghead
pawl: **4** sear
gunner: **7** shooter **9** cannoneer **10** bombardier **12** artilleryman
gunny: tat **4** jute **6** burlap
gunpowder: **5** nitro
gunroom: **8** quarters
gunshot: pop
Gunther's uncle: **5** Hagen
gunwale: **8** portoise
gurge: **4** eddy **5** surge, swirl
gurgle: **6** gargle, gollar, goller, guggle
Gurkha's sword: **5** kukri
gurl: **4** howl **5** growl, snarl
gurnard: **6** elleck, rochet **8** dragonet
guru: **5** guide **7** teacher
gush: **4** flow, pour, teem **5** issue, smarm, spate, spout, spurt **6** effuse, stream **10** outpouring
gushing: **5** agush **7** teeming **8** effusive, unctuous
gusset: **4** gore **8** piecette
gussie: pig **5** swine
gust: bub **4** flan, gale, puff, scud, waft, wind **5** blast, draft, gusto, storm, taste, whiff **6** flurry, liking, relish, squall **8** outburst **9** enjoyment, foretaste **11** inclination **13** gratification

gusto: **4** elan, gust, zest **5** taste **6** liking, relish **12** appreciation

gusty: **5** windy **6** savory, stormy **7** gustful, squally **8** agitated **11** tempestuous

gut: **5** belly, force, gully **6** bowels, defile, strait **7** courage, destroy, passage, plunder, stamina, stomach **8** entrails, gluttony **9** intestine **10** disembowel, eviscerate

gutta: **8** ornament

gutter: **4** grip, sink **5** brook, ditch, gully, siver(Sc.) **6** groove, guzzle, trench, trough, vennel **7** channel, scupper **11** watercourse

guttural: **5** burry, harsh, velar **7** rasping, throaty

guy: kid, rod **4** josh, rope, stay, twit **5** chain, guide, spoof, tease **6** decamp, fellow, gazabo, gazebo, person **8** ridicule

guy rope: **4** stay, vang

guzzle: **4** tope **5** drain, drink **6** gutter, throat

guzzler: bum **6** bender

gwyniad: **7** schelly

gymnast: **6** turner **7** acrobat, athlete, tumbler **8** balancer **10** gymnasiast

gymnastic: *stunt:* kip **9** handstand, headstand **10** handspring, headspring

  swing: **7** trapeze

gyp: **5** cheat, steal **7** sharper, swindle **8** swindler **10** overcharge

gypsum: **6** parget **8** selenite **9** alabaster *resembling:* **11** alabastrine

gypsy, gipsy: **4** calo **5** caird, nomad **6** Gitana, Gitano, roamer **7** czigany, tzigany, zincala, zincalo, zingana, zingano, zingara, zingaro **8** Bohemian, brunette, wanderer, zigeuner

  boy: **4** chal

  dance: **10** zingaresca

  devil: **4** beng

  dialect: **6** Romany **7** Rommany

  gentleman: rye

  horse: gri, gry

  husband: Rom

  non: **4** gajo

  Syrian: **5** Aptal

  village: gav

gyrate: **4** gyre, spin, turn **5** twirl, whirl **6** rotate **7** revolve

gyrator: top

gyre: **4** ring **6** gyrate, vortex **7** circuit **10** revolution

gyrfalcon: **6** jerkin

gyve: **4** iron **5** chain **6** fetter **7** shackle

H

H: 5 aitch 8 aspirate

haar: fog

haberdashery: hat 5 shirt 6 gloves 7 necktie 8 menswear

habile: fit 4 able 6 adroit, clever, expert 8 skillful, suitable

habiliment (see also **dress, gown**): 4 garb 5 habit 6 attire 7 apparel, clothes, costume, raiment 8 billiment, clothing, equipage, fittings, ornament, vestment 9 equipment, faculties 11 furnishings

habilitate: 5 dress, equip 6 clothe 7 entitle, qualify

habit (see also **dress**): rut, use 4 coat, garb, gown, suit, vice, wont 5 array, guise, haunt, thews, usage 6 attire, clothe, custom, estate, groove 7 bearing, clothes, costume, garment 8 demeanor, habitude, practice, tendency 9 cacoethes 10 consuetude, deportment, habiliment

habitant: 7 dweller

habitat: 4 home 5 abode, range 6 patria 7 station 8 locality 11 environment
combining form: eco 4 oeco, oiko

habitation: 4 home, tent 5 abode, house, hovel, igloo 6 harbor, warren 7 harbour, lodging 8 domicile, dwelling, tenement 9 chaumiere(F.), residence

habited: 6 garbed, gowned 7 arrayed, clothed, dressed 9 inhabited 10 accustomed

habitual: 5 usual 6 common, hectic 7 regular 8 familiar, frequent, ordinary 9 customary 10 accustomed, inveterate

habituate: use 5 enure, inure 6 addict, season 8 accustom, frequent 9 acclimate, 11 acclimatize, familiarize

habitude: 5 habit 11 familiarity

habitue: 10 frequenter

hacendero: 6 farmer

hacienda: 4 farm 5 ranch 6 estate 7 finance 10 plantation 13 establishment
proprietor: 9 hacendado

hack: cab, cut, hag, hew 4 chop, taxi 5 coach, cough 6 drudge, fiacre, hacker, hackle, haggle, mangle 7 butcher, chatter, hackney, stammer, stutter 8 carriage, mutilate 9 mercenary

hack writer: 7 penster

hackberry: 8 oneberry 10 sugarberry

hackee: 8 chipmunk

hackle: 4 bait, comb, hack 6 heckle 11 stickleback

hackly: 5 rough 6 broken, jagged

hackney: nag 4 hack, pony 5 horse, noddy 6 drudge 8 carriage, hireling

hackneyed: old 4 worn 5 banal, stale, trite 6 common 7 forworn 8 foreworn 10 habituated, threadbare 11 commonplace

had: See **have**.

Hades: dis, pit 4 hell 5 Orcus, Sheol 8 Tartarus 11 netherworld
god: 5 Pluto
mother: 4 Rhea
river: 4 Styx 5 Lethe 7 Acheron
wife: 10 Persephone

hadj, hajj: 10 pilgrimage

haet: bit 4 atom, whit

haff: 6 lagoon

haffet, haffit: 5 cheek 6 temple

haft: 5 dwell 6 handle, settle 8 accustom, dwelling 11 familiarize

hag: bog, cut 4 bogy, hack, wood 5 copse, crone, demon, ghost, marsh, notch, rudas(Sc.), witch 6 beldam, goblin, harass, spirit 7 beldame, fatigue, haggard, pasture, terrify 8 harridan, quagmire 9 cailleach, cailliach, enclosure, hobgoblin

Hagar's son: 7 Ishmael

hagdon: 7 seabird 10 shearwater

hagfish: 5 borer

haggard: 4 bony, lank, lean, pale, thin, wild 5 drawn, gaunt, spare 6 hagged, wanton 7 anxious, haglike, untamed 8 harrowed, unchaste 9 suffering, untrained 10 cadaverous 11 intractable

haggle: cut, hew 4 hack, prig 5 cavil 6 badger, banter, chisel, dicker, higgle, huckle, palter, scotch 7 bargain, chaffer, dispute, stickle, wrangle

haggler: 6 dodger 8 huckster

haggy: 5 boggy 6 uneven

hagioscope: 6 squint 7 opening

hagride: 4 ride 6 harass 7 torment

hail: ave 4 ahoy, call, goal 5 greet, sleet, sound, whole 6 accost, health, salute 7 address, fortune, graupel 8 greeting 10 salutation 13 precipitation

hain: 4 save 5 raise, spare 7 elevate

hair: fax, fur 4 barb, coma, mane, shag 5 crine, tress 6 crinet, nicety, trifle 7 bristle 8 capillus, filament, finespun 9 chevelure
accessory: 8 barrette
Angora goat: 6 mohair
braid: cue, pig 5 queue 7 pigtail
coarse: 4 kemp, seta, shag 7 bristle
disease: 8 dandruff, psilosis
false: rat, wig 6 peruke 7 periwig

fringe: **8** frisette, frizette
horse: **4** mane **5** seton **7** fetlock
intestinal: **6** villus
lock: **4** curl, feak, tate **5** flock, tress **6** berger **7** cowlick, elflock **8** lovelock **9** harigalds
loss: **8** alopecia, baldness
ornament: bow **4** comb **5** tiara **6** ribbon **7** coronet **8** barrette
pert. to: **6** crinal
plant: **6** villus
remover: **8** epilator **9** depilator, epilatory **10** depilatory
roll: **4** puff **5** twist **7** chignon **9** pompadour
short: **6** setula, setule
unruly: mop **6** tousle **7** cowlick
white: **4** snow
hairbrained: **5** giddy **8** heedless, volatile
hairbreadth: ace **6** margin
haircloth: aba **6** cilice
haircut: **7** tonsure
hairdo: bob **4** glib(Ir.) **5** braid **6** bubble, marcel **7** beehive, pageboy, pigtail, shingle **8** bouffant, ponytail **9** horsetail
hairdresser: **7** friseur **8** coiffeur **9** coiffeuse
hairless: **4** bald **8** depilous
hairnet: **5** snood
hairpin: **4** bend **6** bodkin **8** bobbypin
hairy: **5** pilar **6** comate, comous, pilary, piline, pilose, shaggy **7** crinose, hirsute
Haiti: *bandit:* **4** caco
city: **12** Port-au-Prince
coin: **6** gourde
island: **4** Mona **6** Gonave
magic: obi
spirit: **4** baka, bako
sweet potato: **6** batatas
hake: **4** idle **5** tramp **6** loiter, trudge
Halakoth collection: **6** mishna **7** mishnah
halberd: **4** bill **6** glaive, weapon **8** battle-ax
halcyon: **4** bird, calm **5** happy, quiet **6** golden **8** peaceful, tranquil **9** unruffled **10** kingfisher
Halcyone's husband: **4** Ceyx
hale: lug, tug, vex **4** draw, haul, heal, pull **5** annoy, frack, freck, sound **6** harass, hearty, robust, strong, summon, wholly **7** healthy **8** contract, vigorous
half: **4** demi, hemi, part, semi, term **6** moiety **7** partial, partner, portion **8** semester **11** imperfectly
half-ape: **5** lemur **7** tarsier
half breed: **5** metif, metis **6** mestee, metive, mustee **7** metisse, mestizo, mestiza, mulatto, mulatta **8** octoroon, quadroon
half brother: **7** half-sib **11** half-sibling
half circumference: **10** semicircle
half diameter: **6** radius
half-man: **4** faun **6** garuda **7** centaur **8** minotaur

half mask: **4** loup **6** domino
half-month: **9** fortnight
half-moon: **9** semilunar
half-turn: **8** caracole
half-wit: **4** dolt **5** dunce **6** nimshi **9** blockhead
half-witted: **5** dotty, silly **7** foolish **9** senseless
halfbeak: ihi **5** balao
halfpenny: mag **4** dump **5** brown **6** bawbee
halfway: mid **7** midship, partial **9** equivocal, partially **11** equidistant
halibut steak: **6** flitch
halidom, halidome: **8** holiness, sanctity **9** sanctuary
Halifax citizen: **10** Haligonian
hall: **4** aula, room, saal(G.) **5** entry, foyer, lobby, manor, odeon, odeum, salle **6** atrium, durbar, saloon **7** chamber, gallery, hallway, passage **8** anteroom, corridor **9** vestibule **10** auditorium, misericord, passageway **11** misericorde
music: **4** gaff **5** odeon, odeum
reception: **5** salon **6** parlor
student residence: **4** dorm **5** bursa **9** dormitory
hallanshaker: **5** scamp **6** beggar **8** vagabond
halloo: **5** shout **6** accost
hallow: **5** bless **8** dedicate **10** consecrate
hallowed: **4** holy
hallowed place: **4** fane **5** altar **6** bethel, chapel, church, shrine, temple **9** cathedral, synagogue
hallucination: d.t.'s **6** mirage **7** fantasy **8** delirium, delusion
halma: **4** game, jump
halo: arc **4** glow, nimb **5** glory **6** areola, areole, brough(Sc.), circle, corona, nimbus **7** areola, aureole **8** cincture, gloriole
halse, hals: col, hug **4** neck **5** greet **6** defile, salute, throat **7** conjure, embrace, entreat
halt: hop **4** bait, lame, limp, stem, stop **5** cease, hilch, hitch, pause, stand **6** arrest, desist, docked **7** limping **8** lameness, stoppage **9** cessation, mutilated, terminate
halter: **4** rope **5** leash, noose, strap, widdy **6** bridle, hamper **8** cavesson, restrain **9** hackamore
halting: **4** lame **7** limping **8** spavined **9** defective **10** hesitating **11** vacillating
halting place: **4** camp
halucket: **4** wild **5** crazy, giddy **10** halfwitted
ham: pig **4** pork **7** amateur
Ham: *brother:* **4** Shem
son: **4** Cush
son's land: **8** Ethiopia
hamadryad: **5** nymph **6** baboon
hamate: **6** curved, hooked **7** hamular **8** hamiform

hameil: 5 homey 8 domestic

Hamite: *father:* 4 Abel

language: 4 Afar, Agao, Beja 5 Belin, Galla 6 Berber, Kabyle, Shilha, Somali, Zenaga 8 Cushitic, Numidian, Tamashek 9 Ethiopian, Gaetulian 11 Mauretanian

people: 4 Beja, Bogo 5 Fulah 6 Berber, Gallas, Somali

hamlet: 4 dorp 5 aldea(Sp.), casal, hamel, moray, vicus(L.) 6 bustee, casale(It.), thorpe 7 clachan(Sc.), village 10 settlement

Hamlet: *character:* 7 Laertes, Ophelia 8 Gertrude, Polonius

country: 7 Denmark

friend: 7 Horatio

hammer: bit, tup 4 beat, claw, jack, maul, mell, reel, tack, tamp 5 gavel 6 batter, beetle, mallet, martel, pummel, sledge, strike, swinge 7 belabor 8 malleate 11 door-knocker

blacksmith's: 6 fuller, oliver

bricklayer's: 6 scutch

face: 4 trip

firearm: 4 cock 7 doghead

head: 4 peen, poll

medical: 6 plexor 7 plessor

stone: 5 kevel, spall

hammerhead: 5 shark

hammock: 7 machila

hamper: bin, ped 4 beat, clog, curb, load, slow 5 block, cramp, crate, rusky(Sc.), seron(Sp.) 6 basket, burden, fetter, halter, hinder, hopple, impede, panier 7 buffalo, confine, hanaper, manacle, pannier, perplex, shackle, trammel 8 encumber, entangle, obstruct, restrain, restrict 9 container, embarrass

hamstring: hox 4 hock, lame 5 hough 7 cripple, disable

hamulus: 4 hook

hanaper: 6 basket, hamper 10 receptacle

hance: 4 arch, fall 5 raise 6 lintel

hand: fin, paw, pud 4 claw, give, mano, mitt, neif, pass 5 claut(Sc.), grasp, nieve, power, share 6 clunch, daddle, famble, pledge, worker 7 ability, flipper, forepaw, laborer, proffer, workman 8 applause, bestowal, transmit 9 betrothal, craftsman, indicator, operative, signature 11 handwriting

back: 10 opisthenar

clenched: 4 fist

covering: 4 mitt, muff 5 glove 6 cestus(L.) 7 gantlet 8 gauntlet

deformity: 11 talipomanus

hollow: 6 gowpen, gowpin

palm: 6 thenar

part: 4 palm 5 thumb 7 fingers

pert. to: 6 manual

without: 7 amanous

hand-me-down: 5 cheap 9 ready-made 10 secondhand

hand mill: 5 quern

hand-picked: 5 elite 8 selected

handbag: bag 4 etui, grip 5 cabas, etwee, purse 6 valise 7 satchel 8 gripsack, pochette, reticule

handball: *game:* 6 pelota 7 jai alai

point: ace

handbarrow: 4 bier

handbill: 5 libel 6 dodger 13 advertisement

handbook: 6 manual 9 guidebook 11 enchiridion

handbreath: 4 span 6 spread

handcar: 6 gocart 7 go-devil

handcloth: 5 towel 6 napkin 12 handkerchief

handcuff: 4 cuff, iron 5 darby 6 nipper 7 manacle 8 bracelet, handbolt, handlock

Handel's oratorio: 7 Messiah

handfast: 4 bind, grip 5 bound, grasp 7 betroth, manacle 11 closefisted

handful: 4 grip, wisp 5 claut, gripe 6 gowpen, gowpin, yaffle 7 maniple 8 quantity

handicap: bar, law 4 lame, lisp 6 burden, hinder, impede 7 stammer, stutter 8 encumber 9 advantage, embarrass 12 disadvantage

handicraft goddess: 7 Minerva

handicraftsman: 7 artisan, workman 9 craftsman

handiwork: tat 7 sampler 12 embroidery

handkerchief: 5 clout, fogle 6 madras 7 bandana, belcher, sneezer 9 barcelona, handcloth, muckender, neckcloth 11 neckerchief

handle: ear, fan, lug, nob, paw, ply, use 4 ansa, bail, bool, deal, feel, gaum, grip, haft, hank, hilt, knob 5 gripe, grope, helve, lever, shaft, swipe, touch, treat, wield 6 behave, direct, finger, manage 7 control 8 handgrip 10 manipulate

bucket: 4 bail, bale

printing press: 6 rounce

pump: 5 brake

scythe: 5 snath, snead, thole 6 snathe

sword: 4 haft, hilt

whip: 4 crop

handled: 5 dealt 6 ansate

handling: use 7 control 9 treatment 10 management

handlock: 8 handcuff

handout: 4 alms, dole, food, meal, mete 5 snack 7 charity

handreading: 9 palmistry

handsel, hansel: 4 gift, luck, omen 5 money, token 6 augury

handsome: 4 braw(Sc.), fair, fine, pert 5 ample, belle, bonny, handy, ready 6 bonnie, clever, comely, goodly, heppen, limber 7 elegant, gallant, liberal 8 becoming, budgeree, generous, gracious, suitable 9 beautiful, dexterous 10 convenient, manageable 11 appropriate 12 considerable

handwriting: 4 fist, hand 5 ronde 6 script 10 griffonage, manuscript 11 chirography
on the wall: 4 mene 5 tekel 8 upharsin
study of: 10 graphology

handy: 4 deft, near 5 adept, ready 6 adroit, clever, heppen 8 adjacent, dextrous, handsome, skillful 9 available, dexterous, versatile 10 accessible, convenient

handyman: 5 fixer 8 repairer

hang: lop, sag 4 kilt, loll, pend, rest 5 drape, droop, hinge, knack, slope, swing 6 append, dangle, depend, gibbet, talter 7 crucify, execute, stretch, suspend 9 declivity 11 inclination
around: 4 loaf 6 loiter
back: 6 falter 8 hesitate
onto: 5 cling

hang fire: 4 pend 8 hesitate

hangar: 4 shed 6 garage, stable 7 shelter 9 penthouse

hangdog: 4 base 6 shifty 7 ashamed, fawning, furtive 8 cringing, sneaking 9 groveling

hanger-on: bur 5 toady 6 hangby, heeler 7 adjunct, dangler, slinger 8 bottomer, loiterer, onsetter, parasite 9 appendage, dependent, sycophant 10 blackguard

hanging: 5 arras, drape 6 celure, tippet 7 pendent, pensile, valance 8 inclined 9 declivity, execution, suspended 11 inclination

hangman: 6 hangie 9 Jack Ketch 11 executioner

hangnail: 6 agnail 10 backfriend

hangout: 5 joint 10 rendezvous

hangover: 8 residuum 11 aftereffect

hank: 4 coil, loop 5 skein 6 bundle, handle 7 control 9 influence

hanker: 4 long 5 crave, yearn 6 desire

hankle: 5 twist 6 fasten 8 entangle

Hannibal: *father:* 8 Hamilcar
place of victory: 6 Cannae

Hanse merchant: 7 hansard

hansom: cab

hap: lot 4 case, luck, wrap 5 check, seize 6 befall, chance, clothe, snatch 7 fortune, venture 8 covering 9 happening 10 occurrence, prosperity

haphazard: 6 casual, chance, random 8 careless 10 accidental

hapless: 4 poor 7 unlucky 11 unfortunate

happen: 4 come, fall, fare 5 evene, occur 6 arrive, befall, betide, chance, mayhap 7 perhaps, stumble 9 eventuate, transpire

happen again: 5 recur

happening: hap 4 case, fact 5 event 6 chance, faring 7 episode 8 incident, occasion 10 occurrence

happily: 5 fitly, haply 6 gladly 7 luckily 10 gracefully 11 contentedly, fortunately, opportunely, felicitously, peradventure, prosperously, successfully 13 appropria

happiness: joy 4 sele(Sc.), weal 5 bliss, mirth 6 felice 7 delight, ecstasy, felicia, rapture 8 felicity, gladness, hilarity 9 beatitude, enjoyment, eudaemony, transport, well-being 10 exaltation, prosperity 11 blessedness
god: 5 Ebisu
incapacity for: 9 anhedonia

happy: apt, gay 4 cosh, glad, gleg 5 blest, lucky, merry, ready, seely, sonsy, sunny 6 elated, sonsie 7 blessed, content, fitting, halcyon, radiant 8 carefree, frohlich, gracious, mirthful 9 contented, fortunate 10 felicitous, propitious, prosperous

happy-go-lucky: 9 easygoing

happy hunting ground: 6 heaven 8 paradise

harangue: nag 4 rave 5 orate, spiel 6 screed, sermon, speech, tirade 7 address, declaim, oration 8 diatribe, perorate 10 concionate

harass: fag, hag, nag, try, vex 4 bait, fret, gall, hake, hale, haze, jade, rack, raid, tire 5 annoy, beset, bully, chafe, chase, grind, gripe, harry, herry(Sc.), hurry, pique, tease, weary, worry 6 badger, bother, bucket, cumber, hatter, heckle, impede, molest, obsess, pester, plague, pother, scrape 7 afflict, affront, agitate, disturb, exhaust, fatigue, hagride, oppress, perplex, provoke, scourge, torment, trouble 8 distract, distress, irritate 9 exagitate, persecute, tantalize

harbinger: 4 camp, host 5 usher 6 herald 7 presage, shelter 8 fourrier, harbinge, harborer 9 messenger, precursor 10 forerunner
spring: 5 robin 6 crocus

harbor, harbour: inn 4 hold, port 5 haven 6 billet, breach, bunder, covert, foster, refuge 7 fairway, lodging, quarter, retreat, seaport, shelter 9 harborage
entrance: 4 boca

harborage, harbourage: 6 harbor 7 shelter

hard: fit 4 acid, cold, dear, dere, dure, firm, iron, mean, oaky, sour 5 champ, close, cruel, hardy, harsh, horny, rigid, rocky, rough, solid, stern, stiff, stony 6 coarse, frozen, knotty, marble, robust, severe, steely, strict, strong 7 adamant, arduous, austere, callous, compact, earnest, intense, onerous, scleral 8 diligent, granitic, grasping, hardened, obdurate, renitent, rigorous, scleroid, toilsome 9 difficult, energetic, fatiguing, inclement, intricate, laborious, petrified, repelling, reprobate, resistant, strenuous, stringent, unfeeling, wearisome 10 inflexible, oppressive, perplexing, persistent, relentless, ungraceful, unyielding 11 complicated, distressing, impregnable, persevering, unremitting 12 disreputable, extortionate, impenetrable, incorrigible,

unalleviated **13** unsympathetic
prefix: dys

hard corn: rye **5** wheat

hard drawn: **4** taut **5** tense

harden: gel, set **4** bake, cake, salt, sear **5** beath, enure, inure, steel **6** endure, freeze, ossify, temper **7** congeal, petrify, stiffen, thicken, toughen **8** concrete, condense, indurate, solidify **11** acclimatize

hardened: **4** hard **5** caked **6** frozen, gelled, inured **7** callous, steeled **8** obdurate **9** abandoned, reprobate **10** impenitent, impervious, inveterate, solidified **12** impenetrable

hardhead: **4** fish **5** whale **7** ribwort **8** knapweed, mackerel, menhaden **9** blockhead **10** niggerhead

hardheaded: **4** keen **6** shrewd **7** willful **8** stubborn **9** sagacious **10** longheaded **11** sharp-witted

hardhearted: **4** mean **5** cruel, stern **7** callous **8** obdurate, pitiless **9** unfeeling **13** marblehearted, unsympathetic

hardihood: **5** pluck, vigor **7** bravery, courage **8** audacity, boldness, temerity **9** hardiness, impudence, stoutness **10** confidence, effrontery, imprudence, resolution, robustness **11** intrepidity **13** audaciousness

hardly: **6** barely **7** faintly, hardily, harshly, roughly **8** forcibly, scarcely, severely, unfairly **11** unfavorably

hardness: **6** durity **8** severity, solidity **9** substance
measuring device: **9** durometer

hardpan: pan **7** bedrock **8** ortstein

hardship: **5** assay, rigor, trial **6** injury **7** penalty **8** asperity, hardness **9** endurance, grievance, injustice, privation **10** affliction

hardtack: **7** biscuit, galette(F.), pantile

hardwood: ash, oak **4** teak **5** maple **6** walnut **7** hickory **8** mahagony
genus: **7** quercus

hardy: **4** bold, firm, hard, rash, wiry **5** brave, lusty, manly, stout, tough **6** chisel, daring, robust, rugged, strong, sturdy **7** compact, spartan **8** galliard, intrepid, resolute, stubborn, vigorous **9** audacious, confident **10** courageous

hare: dol **4** bawd(Sc.) **4** pika **5** harry, lepus, tease, worry **6** malkin, rabbit **7** leporid, leveret **8** frighten, leporide
genus of: **5** lepus
pert. to: **8** leporine

harem: oda **4** odah **5** serai **6** serail, zenana **8** seraglio

haricot: **4** stew **6** ragout

harish: **7** foolish

hark: **4** hear, heed, hist **6** harken, listen **7** hearken, whisper

harl: **4** barb, drag, knot **5** leash, snarl **6** scrape, tangle **7** confuse, plaster, scraper **8** entangle **9** confusion

harlequin: **5** clown **7** buffoon **9** fantastic **11** masquerader

harlot: low, pug **4** base, doxy, lewd, slut **5** churl, knave, quean, rogue, whore **6** menial, rascal, wanton **7** buffoon, juggler **8** strumpet, vagabond **10** fricatrice, prostitute

harm: hob, ill **4** bale, bane, evil, hurt, pain, teen **5** abuse, annoy, grief, shend, wound, wrong **6** damage, damnum, injure, injury, scathe, sorrow **7** disease, impeach **8** disserve, endamage, nuisance **10** disservice, misfortune, wickedness **11** impeachment

harmful: bad **4** evil **5** nasty **6** nocent **7** baneful, hurtful, malefic, noisome, noxious **8** damaging, sinister **9** injurious **10** pernicious **11** contrarious, deleterious, detrimental, mischievous

harmonious: **6** cosmic, dulcet **7** cordial, musical, spheral, tuneful **8** amicable, peaceful **9** accordant, agreeable, congruous, consonant, harmonial, melodious, peaceable **10** compatible, concentive, concordant **11** harmoniacal, symmetrical **12** proportional

harmonize: go; gee, key **4** jibe, tone, tune **5** adapt, agree, blend, chime, hitch, rhyme **6** accord, adjust, attune, cotton **7** concent, concord, consist, consort **9** reconcile **10** correspond, sympathize

harmony: **4** tune **5** amity, music, peace **6** cosmos, melody **7** concert, concord, rapport **9** agreement **10** accordance, atmosphere, conformity, congruence, consonance **11** cooperation
bring into: **6** attune
lack: **7** discord

harness: **4** gear **5** heald **6** fettle, tackle **7** enclose, hitch-up **9** equipment, trappings
maker: **7** knacker, lorimer
part: bit, tug **4** hame, rein **5** blind, trace **6** billet, bridle, collar, saddle, terret **7** crouper **9** breeching, circingle, martingal, ridgeband, surcingle **10** breastband, crownpiece, martingale

harp: **4** arpa, koto, lyre **5** nanga **6** trigon **8** bedlamer **11** clairschach

harper: **4** coin **8** minstrel, musician

harpoon: **5** spear **7** javelin

harpsichord: **6** spinet **8** clavecin, virginal **12** clavicembalo

harpy: **5** Aello **7** Celaeno, Ocypete, Podarge **11** extortioner

harquebus: **6** hagbut **7** hackbut

harquebusier: **7** soldier **10** arcabucero

harridan: hag **5** crone, horse, vixen, woman **8** strumpet

harrier: dog **4** hawk

harrow: vex **4** disk, drag **5** brake, harry, wound **6** spader **7** oppress, torment **8** distress, lacerate **9** cultivate **10** cultivator

harrowed: **7** haggard

harry: rob, vex **4** sack **5** annoy, hound, hurry, spoil, steal, worry **6** harass, harrow, hector, plague, ravage **7** agitate, despoil, pillage, plunder, torment **9** persecute

harsh: raw **4** grim, hard, hask **5** acerb, acrid, asper, brute, crude, cruel, grill, gruff, raspy, rough, sharp, stern, stiff **6** bitter, brazen, coarse, severe, strict, sullen, unkind **7** austere, braying, drastic, grating, rasping, raucous **8** acerbate, catonian, clashing, croaking, district, guttural, jangling, rigorous, strident, ungentle **9** dissonant, inclement, insensate, repellent, squawking, truculent, unfeeling **10** astringent, discordant, oppressive, relentless **11** acrimonious, disagreeing **12** disagreeable

harshness: 5 rigor **6** duress **7** crudity, raucity **8** acerbity, acrimony, asperity, severity

hart: roe **4** deer, hert, stag **5** spade

hartebeest: 4 asse, tora **5** caama, kaama **6** lecama **8** antelope

hartshorn: 7 ammonia

harum-scarum: 4 rash, wild **7** flighty **8** reckless **11** thoughtless **13** irresponsible

Harun-Al-Rashid's wife: 7 Zobeide

haruspex: 7 diviner **10** soothsayer **14** prognosticator

harvest: 4 bind, crop, reap **6** foison, gather **8** ingather
god: **5** Ceres **6** Cronus
goddess: **5** Carpo

harvest home: 4 kern, kirn(Sc.)

harvester: 8 spalpeen

has: See **have.**

hash: 4 chop **5** mince **6** jumble **7** mixture **11** gallimaufry, olla podrida

hashish: 4 hemp **5** bhang **8** cannabis

hashmark: 6 stripe

hask: dry **4** cold **5** harsh **6** coarse

hasp: 4 gird **5** catch, clasp **7** confine **8** fastener

hassle: 4 talk **6** hustle **7** quarrel, wrestle **8** argument, squabble **9** commotion **10** discussion

hassock: 4 boss, pess **5** grass, sedge **6** buffet **7** cushion, tussock **8** footrest **9** footstool

haste: hie **4** rush **5** hurry, speed **6** bustle, flurry **7** urgency **8** dispatch, rapidity **9** quickness, swiftness **10** expedition, nimbleness **11** festination, impetuosity **12** precipitance **13** precipitation

hasten: hie, run **4** pell, race, rush, trot **5** crowd, drive, fleet, hurry, speed **6** expede, gallop, scurry **7** advance, scamper **8** dispatch, expedite **9** festinate **10** accelerate **11** precipitate

hastily: 6 nimbly **8** speedily **11** impatiently **13** precipitately

hasty: 4 fast, rash **5** brash, fleet, quick, swift **6** abrupt, daring, nimshi, speedy, sudden **7** cursory, forward, hurried **8** headlong, pell-mell, succinct **9** hotheaded, hurrisome, impatient, impetuous **10** indiscreet **11** expeditious, precipitate, precipitous

hasty pudding: 4 mush **6** supawn **9** stirabout

hat: cap, dip, fez, lid, nab, tam **4** baku, felt, topi **5** beany, benjy, benny, beret, boxer, cordy, derby, dicer, kelly, terai, topee, toque **6** Alpine, beaver, boater, bonnet, bowler, castor, claque, cloche, fedora, panama, shovel, turban **7** biretta, caubeen, chapeau, Homburg, petasus, salacot, shallow **8** capeline, copatain, headgear, sombrero **9** Dunstable, stovepipe, wide-awake **10** belltopper **11** mortarboard
covering: **8** havelock
crown: **4** poll
fiber: **4** felt, sola **5** straw
ladies: **5** caddy, cooie **6** Breton, caddie, slouch **7** leghorn **8** duckbill **9** harlequin **12** Gainsborough
medieval: **6** abacot **7** bycoket
military: **5** shako
opera: **5** crush, gibus **6** claque, topper
silk: lum(Sc.) **4** tile **5** opera **6** topper **7** catskin **8** gossamer
stovepipe: **8** caroline

hatch: 4 brew, door, gate, vent **5** breed, cleck, clock, cover **6** clutch, wicket **7** concoct **8** contrive, hatchway **9** floodgate
covering: **4** tarp

hatchel: 5 tease, worry **7** torment

hatchet: ax; adz, axe **4** adze, mogo **8** tomahawk

hatching: 6 cletch **8** breeding

hatchway: 7 scuttle

hate: 4 teen **5** abhor **6** detest, loathe, rancor, revile **7** contemn, despise **8** aversion **9** abominate, malignity **11** detestation

hateful: 4 foul **5** black **6** odious **7** heinous **8** flagrant **9** abhorrent, invidious, loathsome, malignant, obnoxious, offensive, revolting **10** abominable, detestable, disgusting, malevolent **11** distasteful **12** disagreeable

hatful: 4 lots, many, much **8** quantity

hatred: 5 odium **6** enmity, rancor **8** aversion **9** animosity, hostility, malignity **10** abhorrence, repugnance **11** abomination, detestation, malevolence
of argument: **8** misology
of children: **9** misopedia **10** misopaedia
of mankind: **11** misanthropy
of marriage: **8** misogamy
of strangers: **10** xenophobia

hatter: 5 worry **6** batter, bruise, harass **7** exhaust **8** milliner

haught: 4 high **5** noble **7** exalted, haughty

haughtiness: 4 airs **5** pride **6** morgue **7** hauteur **9** arrogance, insolence

haughty: 4 airy, bold, high **5** dorty, lofty, noble, proud **6** haught, snooty **7** exalted, fatuous, hontish, paughty, stately **8** arrogant, cavalier, glorious, scornful **9** imperious, masterful **10** disdainful, fastidious **11** domineering, magisterial, overbearing **12** contemptuous, presumptuous, supercilious

haul: lug, tow, tug **4** cart, drag, draw, hurl,

pull, tote **5** bouse, catch, heave, trice **8** cordelle **9** transport

haulage: **6** towage **7** cartage, drayage

hauler: **7** tractor

haunch: hip **4** huck **5** hance **12** hindquarters

haunt: den **4** dive, hawf, lair, nest **5** ghost, habit, hawff, skill **6** custom, infest, obsess, resort, spirit **7** terrify **8** frequent, practice **9** companion **10** fellowship

haunted: **6** filled, spooky **8** infested

haunty: **6** unruly **8** restless

hautboy, hautbois: **4** oboe **10** strawberry

hauteur: **5** pride **9** arrogance **11** haughtiness

Havana suburb: **5** Regia

have: hae(Sc.), own **4** hold **5** enjoy **6** retain **7** contain, possess **10** experience
on: **4** wear
to do with: **4** deal

haven: bay, lee **4** hope, port **5** hotel, inlet **6** asylum, harbor, recess, refuge **7** shelter **9** sanctuary

haver: oat **6** babble, holder **7** chatter, maunder, twaddle **8** nonsense **9** possessor

haversack: bag

havior, haviour: **8** behavior, demeanor

havoc: hob **4** ruin **5** waste **7** destroy **9** devastate **10** desolation **11** destruction, devastation

haw: gee **4** sloe, yard **5** fence, hedge **8** hawthorn **9** enclosure

Hawaii: *ballad:* **4** mele
basket: ie
beverage: **4** kava **8** kava-kava
bird: io, oo; ioa, iwa **4** iiwi, koae, mamo, omao, ooaa **6** palila **8** drepanis
bush: See *shrub* below
canoe: **5** waapa
channel: **4** Auau
chant: **4** mele
city: **4** Hilo **7** Wailuku **8** Honolulu(c.)
cloak: **4** mamo **6** ahuula
cloth: **4** kapa, tapa **5** tappa
cord: aea
crater: **7** Kilauea
dance: **4** hula
district: **4** Puna, Kona
farewell, hello: **5** aloha
feast: **4** luau **7** ahaaina
fern: **4** heii **5** ekaha, uluhi **6** iwaiwa **7** amaumau
fiber: **4** pulu
fish: ahi **4** ulua **5** akule
flower: **5** ilima
food: poi **4** kalo, taro
game: hei
garland: lei
garment: **6** holoku, muumuu **7** holomuu
god: **4** Kane **5** Wakea
goddess: **4** Pele
goose: **4** nene
grass: **6** emoloa

greeting: **5** aloha
hawk: io
herb: ape, pia **4** hola **5** awiwi **6** auhuhu
instrument: uke **7** ukalele, ukelele, ukulele
island: **4** Maui, Oahu **5** Kauai, Lanai **6** Hawaii, Niihau **7** Molokai **9** Kahoolawe
lava: aa **8** pahoehoe
loincloth: **4** malo, maro
lomilomi: rub **7** massage, shampoo
love: **5** aloha
massage: **8** lomilomi
morning glory: **5** koali
native: **6** Kanaka
octopus: hee
pantheon: **4** Kane
parrot fish: **5** lauia
partnership: hui
pepper: ava
pine: ie
pit for baking: imu
plant: pia **4** hala, taro **5** olona **8** pandanus
porch: **5** lanai
precipice: **4** pali
priest: **6** Kahuna
raven: **5** alala
root: **4** taro
root paste: poi
seaweed: **4** limu
shaman: **6** Kahuna
shrub: **4** akia **5** akala, olona **6** aupaka
song: **4** mele
staple: poi **4** taro
starch plant: pia
swordfish: au
temple: **5** heiau
thrush: **4** amao **6** olomao
tree: koa **4** aulu, ohia **5** aalii, alani **7** amaumau, walahee **8** mokihana
valley: **5** Manoa
vine: **5** kaiwi **9** awikiwiki
volcano: **7** Kilauea **8** Mauna Kea, Mauna Loa
white man: **5** haole
wind: **4** kona
woman: **5** haole
wreath: lei
yam: hoi

hawfinch: **8** grosbeak

hawk: io; cry, gos **4** eyas, kite, nyas, sell, vend **5** astur, cadge, catch, reach, retch **6** elanet, falcon, formal, formel, higgle, musket, osprey, peddle, rifler, tarcel, tarsel, tercel **7** buzzard, canvass, colport, harrier, kestrel, puttock, sparrow, vulture **8** brancher, caracara **9** accipiter **11** mortarboard
cage: mew
male: **6** tercel
leash: **4** jess, lune
nest: **5** aerie
pinion feather: **6** sarcel

hawk-headed deity: Ra

hawkbit: **9** dandelion

hawker: **6** badger, cadger, coster, duffer **7** chapman, mercury, packman, peddler **8**

falconer, huckster **9** colporter **10** colporteur **12** costermonger

Hawkeye State: 4 Iowa

hawklike: 11 accipitrine

hawser: 4 line, rope

block: **4** bitt

post: **4** bitt **7** bollard

hawthorn: haw, may **5** aglet **6** aiglet **8** cockspur, maybloom, quickset

hay: bed, net **4** park **5** chaff, fence, grass, hedge **9** provender

bundle: mow **4** bale, rick, wisp **5** gavel, stack, truss **7** hayrick

line: **5** swath **7** windrow

second cutting: **5** rowen

storage: mow **4** loft

haycock: 4 coil

hayfork: 4 evil **5** pikel

hayloft: mow **9** hay-tallat

hayseed: 5 yokel **6** farmer, rustic **10** countryman

hazard: die, lay, lot **4** risk **5** peril, stake **6** chance, danger, gamble **7** imperil, venture **8** accident, casualty, endanger, jeopardy **9** adventure **10** jeopardize

hazardous: 5 risky **6** chance, chancy, queasy, unsafe **8** insecure, perilous **9** dangerous, uncertain **10** fortuitous, jeopardous, precarious **11** adventurous

haze: fog **4** beat, film, mist **5** cloud, devil, scold, vapor **6** harass, vapour **7** drizzle **8** frighten

hazel: 8 noisette **11** avellaneous

hazelnut: nit **6** cobnut

hazy: dim **5** filmy, foggy, misty, smoky, thick, vague **7** nebular, obscure, unclear **8** nebulous **9** uncertain **10** indistinct

head: aim, cop, mir, nab, nob **4** bean, cape, coco, conk, crop, lead, pate, poll, tete(F.), turn **5** caput(L.), chief, chump, first, front, start, tibby **6** cabeza, cobbra, direct, garret, leader, manage, noggin, noodle, sconce, source, spring **7** captain, coconut, costrel, cranium, crumpet, leading, prelate **8** director, foremost, fountain, headland, initiate **9** intercept, president, principal **10** caper-nutie headmaster, promontory **11** caper-noitie

army camp: **10** commandant

back part: **7** occiput

bald: **9** pilgarlic

boar: **4** hure

bone: **8** parietal

crown: **6** cantle

muscle: **11** occipitalis

ornament: hat, wig **4** hair, veil **5** tiara **7** coronet

part: **4** pate **5** scalp **6** earlap, temple **7** cranium

pert. to: **8** cephalic

shaven: **7** tonsure

shrunken: **7** tsantsa

side of: **6** temple

top: **4** pate **5** scalp **6** coxcomb

head cook: 4 chef

head covering: (see also **cap, hat**): cap, fez, hat, tam, wig **4** barb, coif, hair, hood **5** beret, scalp, snood **6** bonnet, coiffe, peruke, toupee **7** biretta, chapeau, periwig **8** berretta, maharmah, sombrero **9** rigolette **10** fascinator

headache: 6 megrim **8** headwark, migraine **10** cephalagia

headband: 5 miter, mitre, vitta **6** diadem, fillet **7** circlet, coronet **9** sphendone

headdress: 4 caul, coif, pouf **5** ampyx, crown, cupee, miter, mitre, tiara, toque **6** almuce, bonnet, coiffe, faille, hennin, mobcap, pinner, turban **7** bandore, bycoket, coronet, topknot **8** biliment, binnogue, capriole, coiffure, stephane, tressure **9** rigolette

medieval: **6** abacot

military: **5** busby, shako **6** casque

sacred: **6** uraeus

headgear: See **headdress**.

headily: 6 rashly **9** violently

heading: 5 title, topic **7** caption **8** headline

topical: **5** trope

headland: ras **4** bill, cape, head, nase, naze, ness, peak **5** Morro, ridge, strip **8** foreland **10** promontory

headline: 7 caption, feature, heading

headliner: 4 star **11** personality

headlong: 4 rash **5** hasty, steep **6** abrupt, sudden **8** reckless **9** desperate, headfirst, impetuous, impulsive **11** precipitate, precipitous

headman: 4 boss **5** chief **6** ataman, cabeza, hetman **7** capitan, captain, foreman **8** alderman, caboceer, capitano **11** executioner

headmaster: 4 head **9** principal **11** gymnasiarch

headpiece: See **headdress**.

headquarters: 5 yamen **6** center **8** exchange, precinct

headstrong: 4 rash **5** cobby **6** unruly **7** hotspur, violent **8** stubborn **9** obstinate **10** bullheaded, forthright, hotspurred **11** intractable **12** contumacious, ungovernable

heady: 4 rash **7** huffcap, violent, willful **9** impetuous **11** precipitate **12** intoxicating

heal: 4 cure, hale, knit, mend, sain **5** amend **6** remedy, repair **7** restore **10** recuperate

heal-all: 4 balm **7** allheal, figwort, panacea

healer: asa **4** balm **6** doctor **9** naprapath **12** practitioner

healing: 5 balmy **8** covering, curative, sanative

agent: **6** balsam

pert. to: **7** medical **9** medicinal

science: **8** medicine **9** iatrology, latrology

health: 4 hale, hail **5** sante(F.), toast **7** slainte **8** eucrasia **11** disposition

goddess: **7** Minerva

poor: **4** sick **5** dawny
resort: spa
healthy: fit **4** hale, sane, well **5** bonny, hoddy **6** bonnie, hearty, robust **8** salutary, vigorous **9** wholesome **10** healthsome, salubrious
combining form: **4** sani
heap: ahu, cob, cop, mow **4** balk, bing, bulk, deck, dess(Sc.), hill, lump, mass, pile, pyre, raft, rick, ruck **5** amass, cairn, clump, crowd, spire, stack **6** burrow, hipple, jumble, plenty, throng **7** bourock, cumulus, hurrock **9** congeries, multitude **10** accumulate, collection, congestion, cumulation
hear: ear, see **4** feel, hark, heed, obey **6** attend, harken, listen **7** hearken **8** perceive **10** adjudicate
hear ye: **4** oyes, oyez
hearer: **7** audient, auditor **8** disciple, listener
hearing: ear **5** sound, trial **6** assize, report **7** earshot, lecture **8** audience, audition, scolding **9** attention, audiencia, interview, knowledge **10** attendance
court: **4** oyer
judicial: **5** trial **7** retrial
pert. to: **8** acoustic
hearken, harken: **4** hark, hear, heed, wait **6** attend, listen **7** inquire, whisper **9** eavesdrop
hearsay: **4** fame **5** rumor **6** report
hearse: **4** bier, bury, tomb **5** dirge, grave **6** coffin **8** monument, threnody
heart: ab; cor **4** core, gist, hati, love **5** cheer **6** center, centre. depths, middle, ticker **7** courage, emotion, essence, feeling **9** affection
cavity: **6** atrium
chamber: **7** auricle **9** ventricle
contraction: **7** systole
covering: **11** pericardium
expansion: **8** diastole
record: **17** electrocardiogram
stimulant: **8** thialdin **9** digitalis, thialdine **10** adrenaline, epinephrin **11** epinephrine
heart-shaped: **7** cordate
heartache: **4** pang **5** grief **6** sorrow
heartbeat: **5** pulse, throb **7** systole **9** pulsation
heartbreak: **5** grief **6** sorrow **7** tragedy
heartbroken: **12** inconsolable **13** brokenhearted, grief-stricken
heartburn: **4** envy **6** enmity **7** pyrosis **8** jealousy **10** cardialgia, discontent, heartscald, heartscaud
hearten: **5** cheer **6** spirit **7** refresh **8** embolden, inspirit, reassure **9** encourage
heartfelt: **4** dear, deep, real, true **7** earnest, genuine, sincere
hearth: **5** cupel, focus, fogon, foyer **8** bloomery, fireside
god: **6** Hestia

line: **6** fettle
heartily: **6** dearly, freely, warmly **8** actively, strongly **9** cordially, earnestly, profusely, sincerely, zealously, zestfully **10** abundantly, completely, vigorously **14** wholeheartedly
heartiness: **4** soul **8** goodwill, strength **9** soundness **10** cordiality
heartless: **5** cruel **8** hopeless, listless **9** merciless, unfeeling **10** despairing, despondent, spiritless **13** unsympathetic
heartsease, heartease: **5** pansy, peace **12** tranquillity
heartthrob: **4** dunt, love
heartwood: **4** dura **7** duramen
hearty: **4** firm, hale, real, rich, warm, well **5** cobby, heavy, sound **6** active, cheery, devout, robust, sailor, stanch **7** comrade, cordial, earnest, fertile, healthy, sincere, staunch **8** abundant, cheerful, heartful, vigorous **9** energetic, unfeigned, wholesome **10** nourishing **11** substantial, warmhearted
heat: ire **4** fire, mull, rage, warm **5** ardor, cauma, chafe, fever, roast, tepor **6** anneal, choler, degree, warmth **7** ferment, inflame, passion **8** fervency **9** agitation, animation, chauffage, commotion, vehemence **10** excitement **11** temperature **12** exasperation **14** passionateness
measure: **5** therm **6** calory, therme **7** calorie **10** centigrade, fahrenheit **11** calorimeter, pyronometer
pert. to: **7** thermic
quantity: **6** degree **11** temperature
white: **13** incandescence
heated: **7** excited **8** vehement **10** phlogistic
heater: **4** etna, oven **5** stove **6** boiler **7** choffer(Sc.), furnace **8** radiator
heath: **4** ling, moor **5** erica, plain
scrub: **9** chaparral
tree: **5** briar, brier
heathen: **5** pagan **6** ethnic, paynim **11** irreligious
deity: **4** idol
heather: **4** grig, ling **5** erica
family: **9** ericaceae
heatless: **8** athermic
heautarit: **7** mercury **11** quicksilver
heave: gag **4** cast, haul, heft, hurl, lift, pant, pull, push, quap, toss **5** hoist, pitch, raise, scend, throw **7** elevate, estuate **8** struggle
heaven: sky **5** dyaus, ether, glory **6** Himmel(G.) welkin, zodiac **7** Elysium, Nirvana, Valhall, Vahalla **8** devaloka, empyrean, paradise **9** firmament
combining form: **5** urano
pert. to: **6** uranic **9** celestial
queen: **7** Astarte
heavenly: **6** divine **7** angelic, olympic, sublime, uranian **8** ethereal, supernal **9** angelical, celestial, celestine

heavenly being: 5 angel 6 seraph
heavenly belt: way 6 galaxy, nebula, zodiac
heavenly body: sun 4 luna, moon, star 5 comet 6 planet 8 luminary
heavenly city: 4 Sion, Zion
heavenly twins: 6 Castor, Gemini, Pollux
heaviness: 5 gloom 6 weight 7 gravity, sadness 9 thickness 10 oppression 12 sluggishness
heavy: 4 clit, deep, dull, logy, loud 5 actor, beefy, burly, dense, grave, gross, hefty, hoggy, massy, thick 6 clayey, cloggy, coarse, gloomy, hearty, leaden, stodgy, strong, stupid 7 doleful, intense, massive, onerous, serious, villain, violent, weighty 8 burdened, grievous, inactive, lifeless, lowering, overcast, pregnant, profound, sluggish 9 heavisome, laborious, lethargic, ponderous, saturnine 10 afflictive, burdensome, cumbersome, encumbered, oppressive 13 consequential
heavy-headed: 4 dull 6 drowsy, stupid
heavy-hearted: sad 10 despondent, melancholy
hebdomad: 4 week 5 seven
hebetate: 4 dull 5 blunt
Hebrew (see also **Israel, Judaism**): Jew 6 Semite 7 Semitic 8 Hebraean 9 Israelite
acrostic: 4 agla
alphabet: He, Pe; Mem, Nun, Sin, Taf, Tet, Vav, Yod, Yud 4 Ayin, Beth, Caph, Koph, Resh, Shin 5 Aleph, Cheth, Gimel, Lamed, Tsade, Zayin 6 Daleth, Samekh
ancestor: 4 Eber
clean: 6 kosher
God: El 5 Eloah 6 Adonai, Elohim 7 Jehovah
greeting: 6 shalom
infinity: 6 adolam
Jehovah: 5 Jahve, Yahve, Yahwe 6 Jahvah, Jahveh, Yahveh, Yahweh 7 Jahaveh
juniper: 4 ezel
lawbreaking: 6 averah
lesson: 9 Haphtarah
man: rab 5 bahur, hakam
measure: cab, hin, kor 4 epha, omer, reed 5 cubit, ephah, homer
name for God: 6 Adonai, Elohim, Yahweh 7 Jehovah
parchment: 6 mezuza 7 mezuzah
school: 5 heder. schul
son: ben
teacher: 5 rabbi
thief: 5 ganef, ganof, gonof 6 gonoph
title: rab 4 abba
hecatomb: 9 sacrifice, slaughter
heckle: nag 4 gibe 5 tease 6 badger, hackle, harass, hector, needle
hectic: 8 exciting, feverish, habitual, restless 11 consumptive 13 constitutional
hector: nag 5 bully, harry, worry 6 harass, heckle, plague 7 bluster, torment 8

braggart, browbeat, irritate 9 roisterer, swagger 10 intimidate
Hector: *companion:* 8 Diomedes
father: 5 Priam
mother: 6 Hecuba
rescuer: 6 Agenor
slayer: 8 Achilles
wife: 10 Andromache
Hecuba: *daughter:* 9 Cassandra
son: 5 Paris 6 Hector 7 Helenus 9 Deiphobus
hedenbergite: 8 pyroxene
hedge: bar, haw, hem 4 boma 5 beard, fence, frith, guard, skulk 6 hinder, hurdle, privet 7 barrier, enclose, protect 8 boundary, obstruct, quickset, separate, sepiment, straddle, surround 14 counterbalance
hedgehog: 6 urchin 7 echinus 8 herisson, hurcheon 9 porcupine
hedonic: 8 cyrenaic
heed: ear 4 care, cark, cure, gaum, hark, hear, mind, note, obey, reck 5 await, watch 6 attend, beware, harken, listen, notice, regard, remark 7 caution, hearken, observe, respect 8 consider 9 attention, diligence 10 cognizance, solicitude 11 observation
heedful: 4 wary 5 chary 6 attent 7 careful, mindful 8 diligent, watchful 9 advertent, attendant, attentive, observant 10 respectful 11 considerate
heedless: 4 rash 5 giddy 6 remiss, unwary 7 languid, witless 8 careless, reckless 9 blindfold, forgetful, negligent 10 incautious, indiscreet, insouciant, regardless, unthinking 11 hairbrained, inadvertent, inattentive, indifferent, lightheaded, thoughtless, unobservant
heehaw: 4 bray 6 guffaw 10 horselaugh
heel: cad, end, tip 4 calx, cant, knob, tilt 5 talon 6 careen 7 incline 12 protuberance
heeze: 4 help 5 exalt, hoist, raise 6 assist
heft: 5 heave, raise 6 strain, weight 8 exertion 9 influence 13 ponderousness
hefty: 5 heavy, rough 6 rugged 7 massive, weighty 8 vehement vigorous
hegemonic: 6 ruling 7 leading 11 controlling, predominant
hegemony: 9 authority, influence 10 leadership
hegira, hejira: 6 exodus, flight 9 migration
heifer: 4 quey 5 stirk 10 colpindach(Sc.)
height: 4 acme, apex, mote 5 crest 6 summit 7 stature 8 altitude, eminence 9 celsitude, dimension, elevation, procerity, steepness 11 magnanimity
heighten: 4 lift 5 elate, exalt, raise 7 advance, augment, elevate, enhance 8 increase 9 aggravate, intensify
heinous: 6 crying, malign, odious, wicked 7 hateful 8 flagrant, grievous 9 atrocious,

malicious, nefarious 10 flagitious, outrageous

heir: son **5** heres, scion **7** heritor, legatee **9** firstborn, inheritor, successor **11** beneficiary

heiress: 5 begum **8** heretrix, heritrix

Hejaz city: 5 Mecca

held: See **hold.**

Helen of Troy: *abductor:* **5** Paris
brother-in-law: **9** Agamemnon
daughter: **8** Hermione
half-sister: **12** Clytemnestra **13** Clytaemnestra
husband: **8** Menelaus
mother: **4** Leda

heliacal: 5 solar

helical: 6 spiral

helicon: 4 tuba

Helios: *daughter* **5** Circe **8** Heliadae, Heliades
father: **8** Hyperion
son: **8** Phaethon

helix: 4 coil **6** spiral

hell: 5 limbo **6** prison **7** dungeon, inferno **9** barathrum

hell-bent: 8 reckless **10** determined

hellebore: 7 bugbane

Hellen: *father:* **9** Deucalion
son: **5** Dorus **6** Aeolus, Xuthus

Hellene: See **Greece.**

Hellenistic school: 9 Pergamene

Hellespont: 11 Dardanelles
swimmer: **7** Leander

hellgrammite: 6 dobson **8** sialidae

hellier: 5 tiler **8** slater **8** thatcher

hellish: 6 wicked **7** stygian **8** devilish, diabolic, infernal **9** malignant **10** detestable, diabolical

hello: 8 greeting **10** salutation

helm: 5 helve, steer, wheel **6** direct, tiller **8** guidance
position: **4** alee **5** aport

helmet: cap **4** sola, topi **5** armet, galea, topee **6** casque, heaume, morion, salade, sallet **7** basinet **8** schapska **9** casquetel, headpiece
part: **4** bell **5** crest **7** ventail **8** aventail

helmet-shaped: 7 galeate

helmsman: 5 pilot **9** steersman

Heloise's lover: 7 Abelard

helot: 4 serf **5** slave **6** vassal **7** bondman

help: aid, bot, S.O.S. **4** abet, boot, bote, cure, lift, mend, rede, tide **5** avail, boost, favor, frith, heeze, serve, speed, stead **6** assist, favour, relief, remedy, repair, succor **7** advance, benefit, forbear, forward, further, improve, promote, relieve, support, sustain **8** befriend, facility **9** adminicle, alleviate, forestall **10** assistance, contribute, facilitate, strengthen

helper: aid **4** ally **5** aider **7** abetter, abettor, striker **8** adjutant, adjutrix, helpmate **9** adjutrice, assistant, samaritan **10** apprentice, benefactor

helpful: 4 good **6** aidant, useful **8** adjuvant, helpsome, salutary **9** auxiliary **10** beneficial, profitable **11** furthersome

helpless: 4 numb, weak **6** unable **7** forlorn **8** unaiding **9** destitute, powerless **10** bewildered, unsupplied **11** defenseless, incompetent, unprotected **12** irremediable

helpmate: 4 wife **6** helper **8** helpmeet **9** companion

helpmeet: See **helpmate.**

helve: 4 haft **5** lever **6** handle

Helvetian: 5 Swiss **6** Suisse

hem: 4 edge, seam **5** hedge **6** border, edging, margin, stitch **7** confine, enclose, environ, inclose **8** surround **9** fimbriate

hem in: 5 beset, limit **6** impale **7** enclose, inclose **8** surround

hematite: 7 iron ore

hemeralopia: 6 defect **9** blindness

hemi: 4 half

hemlock: 4 bunk

hemmel: 4 shed **5** hovel **7** shelter **11** outbuilding

hemp: ife, pua, tow **4** bang, carl, flax, harl, jute, rine, sunn **5** abaca, bhang, istle, ramie, sisal, sizal **6** ambary, banana, cabuja, cabuya, fennel, hasish, manila

hen: pea **4** fowl, rail, wife **5** biddy, chuck, woman **6** gorhen, nester, pullet, towdie **7** chicken **9** gallinule

hen coop: 4 cavy(Sc.) **5** cavie

henbane: 10 nightshade

hence: so; fro **4** away, ergo(L.), thus **5** since **7** hereout, thither **9** therefore **11** accordingly

henceforth: 6 thence **12** henceforward

henchboy: boy **4** page **9** attendant

henchman: 4 page **6** gillie, squire **7** mobster **8** follower **9** attendant, supporter

Hengist: *brother:* **5** Horsa
daughter: **6** Rowena

henna: dye **6** alcana **7** alcanna

Henry VII's surname: 5 Tudor

Henry VIII: Hal
wife: **4** Anne

hent: get **5** catch, grasp, reach, seize **6** intent, obtain **11** opportunity

hepar: 5 liver

Hephaestus' wife: 6 Charis **8** Charites

heppen: fit **4** deft, neat **5** handy **6** clever **8** handsome **11** comfortable

heptad: seven **11** septivalent

Hera: 4 Juno
husband: **4** Zeus
mother: **4** Rhea
rival: Io
son: **4** Ares

herald: 4 bode **5** crier, usher **6** beadle, Hermes **7** declare, forerun **8** announce, blazoner, foretell, proclaim **9** harbinger, introduce, messenger, precursor **10** forerunner

heraldry: *band:* **4** fess **5** fesse

bell: **7** compane **10** campanella

chaplet: **4** orle

charge: vol **7** boterol, saltier, saltire **8** boteroll, tressour, tressure

cross: **4** paty **5** patee, patte **6** ermine, moline, pattee **7** erminee, patonce, saltier, saltire

device: **4** ente, orle **5** crest **6** altier

fleur-de-lis: lis, lys

gold: or

green: **4** vert

knot: **4** Lacy, Wake **5** Bowen, Dacre **7** Heneage **8** Stafford **9** Bourchier **10** Harrington

leg: **4** gamb, jamb **5** gambe, jambe

tincture: or **5** tenne

wreath: **4** orle **5** torse

herb: iva **4** anet, balm, dill, leek, mint, moly, sage, wort **5** anise, basil, chive, plant, sedge, thyme **6** annual, borage, catnip, clover, lovage, sesame, yarrow **7** carraway, oregano, parsley **8** marjoram tarragon

aromatic: **4** anet, dill, hemp, mint, nard, sage **5** anise, basil, clary, nondo, tansy, thyme **6** catnip, fennel, hyssop **7** chervil, mustard **8** wormseed **9** basilmint, spearmint

bitter: rue **4** aloe, woad **7** aletris, boneset **8** centaury **10** turtlehead

bog: **5** calla **9** steepweed, steepwort

climbing: **4** faba **5** vicia

coarse: **5** tansy **6** eringo, eryngo **7** leafcup **8** pokeweed

flowering: **7** anemone, dittane **8** stapelia **9** celandine

genus: iva **5** canna, cicer, cruca, galax, gavra, inula, lemna, loasa, rheum **6** aralia, asarum, cassia, dondia, isatis, mentha, nerine **7** anemone, cirsium, hedeoma, torenia **8** psoralea **9** grindelia

medicinal: rue **4** aloe **5** senna, sumac, tansy **6** arnica, lovage, tutsan **7** aconite, boneset

mythical: **4** moly

narcotic: **4** hemp

perennial: pia **4** balm, irid **5** sedum **6** fennel, madder, varrow **7** bugbane, lopweed **8** sainfoin, soapwort **9** digitalis

poisonous: **4** loco **6** conium **7** hemlock, henbane **9** hellebore

salad: **6** endive **7** chicory **10** watercress

shoot: udo

trinity: **8** hepatica

woody: rue

herbage: **5** grass **7** foliage, pasture

herbbane: **9** broomrape

herculean: **4** huge **10** superhuman

Hercules: *captive:* **4** Iole

companion: **5** Hylas

friend: **6** Iolaus

lion's home: **5** Nemea

mother: **7** Alcmene

stone: **9** loadstone

sweetheart: **4** Iole

victim: **5** Hydra

wife: **4** Hebe **8** Deianira

herd: mob **4** crew, ruck **5** bunch, crowd, drift, drove, flock, group, guard **6** hirsel, pastor, rabble **7** creaght, shelter **8** guardian **9** associate **10** assemblage, congregate **11** aggregation

herdsman: **5** booly **6** booley, cowboy, drover, gaucho, herder **7** bucolic, vaquero **8** garthman, ranchero(Sp.), wrangler

god: **5** Pales

here: ici(F.), **4** army, host **5** ready **6** hither **7** present

hereafter: **5** after, later **6** beyond, future

hereditary: **6** innate, lineal **8** heirship **9** ancestral, descended **11** inheritable, patrimonial

heredity: **4** line **10** inheritance

factor: **4** gene

heresy: **7** dissent **10** radicalism **11** unorthodoxy **13** nonconformism

heretic: **7** Patarin **8** Patarine **9** dissenter, miscreant, sectarian **10** schismatic, unbeliever **13** nonconformist

heretofore: **4** erst **6** before **8** erewhile, formerly, hitherto, previous **9** erstwhile

heritage: **9** heritance, patrimony **10** birthright **11** inheritance

heritor: **4** heir **5** donee **9** inheritor

heritrix, heretrix: **7** heiress

herl: fly **4** barb

hermaphrodite: **9** androgyne **10** androgynus

Hermes: **7** Mercury

birthplace: **7** Cyllene

cap: **7** petasos, petasus

father: **4** Zeus

mother: **4** Maia

son: **7** Evander **9** Autolycus

winged shoes: **7** talaria

hermetic: **8** airtight **9** alchemist

Hermione: *father:* **8** Menelaus

husband: **7** Orestes **11** Neoptolemus

mother: **5** Helen

hermit: **4** monk **5** clerk **6** anchor **7** ascetic, eremite, incluse, inclusa, recluse, stylite **8** anchoret, beadsman, bedesman, inclusus, marabout **9** anchorite

hut: **4** cell

hermit crab: **8** pagurian

hermitage: **7** ashrama **8** cloister **9** monastery, reclusery

hermitical: **8** eremitic

hernia: **6** breach **7** rupture

hero: ace **4** idol **5** darer **7** demigod **8** champion **9** conqueror **10** topnotcher **11** protagonist

deified: **7** demigod

legendary: **6** Amadis, Roland **7** Paladin

Hero's lover: **7** Leander

Herodias' daughter: **6** Salome

heroic: **4** bold, epic, huge **5** brave, great, large, noble **6** daring, epical **7** extreme,

gallant, spartan, valiant **8** enormous, fearless, intrepid, powerful **9** bombastic **10** courageous **11** extravagant, illustrious, magnanimous, outstanding, venturesome **13** grandiloquent
heroin: **4** drug **8** narcotic
heroine: **11** demigoddess
heroism: **5** valor **6** valour **7** bravery, courage **9** fortitude **13** unselfishness
heron: **4** hern, rail, soco **5** crane, egret, herne, quawk, wader **7** bittern, hernser, quabird **8** aigrette, gaulding, heronsew **9** cormorant, herneshaw, heronsewe, heronshaw
genus: **5** ardea
herring: **4** raun **7** alewife, anchovy **8** scud-dawn
barrel: **4** cade, cran
catch: **4** tack
fry: **4** sile
head: cob
lake: **5** cisco
young: **4** brit **5** sprat, sprot
hership: **4** loot, raid **5** foray
hery: **6** praise **7** glorify, worship
hesitancy: **10** hesitation, indecision, reluctance
hesitant: **4** loth **5** chary, loath **8** timorous **9** reluctant
hesitate: **4** wait **5** delay, demur, doubt, pause, stall, waver **6** boggle, falter, loiter, scotch **7** stammer
hesitating: coy **4** hink **7** halting **8** backward, doubtful **9** ambiguous **10** indecisive **11** vacillating
hesped: **6** eulogy **7** oration
Hesperides: **5** Aegle **6** Hestia **7** Hespera **8** Arethusa, Erytheia, Erytheis
hest: bid **6** behest, pledge **7** command, precept, promise **10** injunction
Hestia: *father:* **6** Cronus
mother: **4** Rhea
hetaera, hetaira: **8** mistress, paramour **9** companion
heterogeneous: **5** mixed **6** motley, unlike **7** diverse **10** dissimilar **13** miscellaneous **14** indiscriminate
Heteroousian: **5** Arian
hetman: **6** ataman **7** headman
heu: **6** alas
heugh, heuch: **4** bank, crag, glen **5** cliff, shaft **6** hollow
hew: cut **4** chip, chop, fell, hack **5** carve, wound **6** haggle, strike, stroke
hex: **4** jinx **7** bewitch
hexadecene: **6** cetene
hexoctahedron: **10** adamantoid
heyday: joy, May **4** acme **8** wildness **14** frolicsomeness
Hezekiah: *kingdom:* **5** Judah
mother: Abi
hi: **8** greeting **10** salutation
hiatus: gap **5** break, chasm **6** breach, lacuna **7** opening **8** interval **12** interruption
Hiawatha: *grandmother:* **7** Nokomis
mother: **7** Wenonah

Hibernia: **4** Erin **7** Ireland
hiccup, hiccough: **4** burp **5** spasm **9** singultus
hick: **4** jake, rube **6** hiccup, rustic **7** bumpkin
hickory: **5** pecan **9** bitternut, shellbark
hidage: tax
hidalgo: **8** nobleman
hidden: **4** lost **5** inner, overt, perdu **6** arcane, buried, cached, closed, innate, latent, masked, occult, secret, veiled **7** arcanum, covered, cryptic, obscure, recluse **8** screened, secluded, secreted **9** concealed, invisible, recondite **10** mysterious **11** clandestine, delitescent **12** subterranean
hide: bar, kip, lie **4** bury, coat, dern, fell, hill, hood, lurk, pelt, skin, stow, veil **5** cache, cloak, cloud, couch, cover, derne(Sc.), skulk **6** huddle, screen, shroud **7** abscond, conceal, eclipse, leather, secrete, shelter **8** carucate, disguise, ensconce, hoodwink, palliate, suppress, withhold **9** dissemble **10** camouflage
cleaning instrument: **6** slater
measured in: **8** hidation
worker: **6** tanner
hidebound: **6** narrow **7** bigoted, miserly **9** barkbound, bourgeois, illiberal, niggardly **10** restrained **12** conventional
hideous: **4** fell, grim, ugly **5** awful **6** grisly, horrid, odious, ogrish **7** ghastly, ogreish **8** deformed, dreadful, grewsome, gruesome, horrible, shocking, terrible **9** dismaying, frightful, revolting **10** detestable, discordant, terrifying
hideout: mew **4** lair **5** cache
hides: **4** furs **5** skins **6** peltry
hiding: **7** secrecy **8** flogging **9** coverture
hie: **5** haste, hurry, speed **6** betake, hasten, scurry, strive **8** expedite
hield: **4** heel, lean, tilt **5** droop, slope, yield **7** decline, incline
hiemal: **6** wintry
hierarchical: **9** episcopal
hieroglyphic: **7** cryptic **9** illegible
higgle: **6** haggle **7** bargain, chaffer
high: alt **4** dear, haut(F.), main, much, tall **5** acute, chief, first, lofty, sharp, steep **6** costly, shrill **7** eminent, exalted, haughty, violent **8** elevated, foremost, piercing, towering **9** admirable, expensive, important, principal, turbulent **10** tumultuous **11** mountainous
combining form: **4** alti
high-and-mighty: **8** arrogant **9** imperious **11** overbearing
high-brow: **7** egghead **14** intelligentsia
high-class: **6** classy **10** first-class
high-flying: **7** icarian **11** pretentious
high-handed: **6** lordly **8** arrogant, despotic **9** arbitrary **11** dictatorial, domineering, overbearing
high-hat: **4** snub **8** snobbish **12** aristocratic
high-pitched: **6** shrill **8** inclined

high-pressure: 8 forceful, pressing 9 insistent 10 aggressive
high-priced: 4 dear 6 costly 9 expensive
high priest: Eli
high sea: 4 main
high-sounding: 7 fustian, pompous 8 imposing 9 bombastic 10 altisonant
high-spirited: 5 fiery 6 lively 7 gallant 8 cavalier 10 mettlesome
high-strung: 5 tense 7 nervous 9 excitable
high-toned: 7 stylish 8 elevated 9 dignified 11 fashionable
highborn: 5 noble 8 generous 12 aristocratic
highbred: 7 genteel, refined
higher: 8 superior
highest: 6 upmost 8 bunemost, overmost
highest point: 4 acme 6 zenith
Highland war cry: 6 slogan
Highlander (see also **Scotland**): 4 Celt, Gael, Kelt, Scot 6 Tartan 8 clansman 9 Gluneamie
dance: 4 reel 5 fling
language: 4 Erse
pouch: 6 sporan 7 sporran
weapon: 8 claymore, skeandhu
highroad: 7 highway
highway: way 4 bahn(G.), iter(L.), path, pike, road 5 Alcan 6 Appian, artery, causey, course, rumpad, street 7 Lincoln 8 autobahn, causeway, chaussee(F.), highroad, turnpike 9 boulevard 12 thoroughfare
highwayman: pad 5 rider, thief 6 bandit, padder, robber 7 brigand, footpad, ladrone 8 hightoby 9 bandolero
Highwayman: *author:* 5 Noyes
hike: 4 jerk, toss, walk 5 march, raise, throw, tramp
hilarious: mad 5 funny, merry, noisy 6 jovial 7 jocular 8 mirthful 9 ludicrous
hilarity: gig, joy 4 glee 5 mirth 6 gaiety 7 jollity 9 happiness, joviality, merriment 10 joyousness 12 cheerfulness, exhilaration
hilch: 4 halt, limp
hill: ben, hoe, kop, pap, tor 4 bank, brae, bult, dagh, dune, fell, heap, hide, knap, knob, loma, mesa 5 bargh, butte, cerro(Sp.), cliff, cover, hurst, morro, mound, mount 6 ascent, barrow, copple, djebel 7 colline, picacho 9 acclivity, elevation, monadnock
glacial: 4 kame, paha 7 drumlin
Jerusalem: 6 Olivet
range: 5 ridge
hillock: 4 tump 5 croft, hurst, knoll, kopje, mound, toman(Sc.),
over grave: 7 tumulus
hillside: 4 brae, cote 5 cleve, cliff, slade, slope 5 cleve, falda(Sp.),
hilly: 5 steep
hilt: 6 handle 8 handgrip
hilum: 5 porta 7 nucleus
Himalaya: *animal, bear-like:* 5 panda

antelope: 5 goral, serow
bear: 5 bhalu
bearcat: 5 panda
cedar: 6 deodar
cypress: 6 bhutan
dweller: 8 Nepalese
goat: 4 kras, tahr, tair, thar
oxen: yak
peak: Api 7 Everest
sheep: 6 bharal, nahoor
swamp: 5 Terai
himene, himine: 4 hymn, song
himself: 4 ipse(L.)
Hinayana Buddhism: 5 shojo 6 lesser
hind: doe, lad, roe 4 back, chap, stag 6 fellow, rustic, worker 7 bailiff, peasant, servant, steward 8 cabrilla, domestic 9 posterior 11 hindquarter
hinddeck: 4 poop
hinder: bar, let 4 slow 5 after, block, cheat, check, choke, cramp, debar, delay, deter, embar, estop, hedge 6 arrest, detain, hamper, harass, impede, impend, injure, retard, scotch 7 deprive, forelay, impeach, inhibit, prevent 8 encumber, handicap, obstruct, preclude, prohibit 9 embarrass, foreclose, forestall, interrupt, posterior
hindmost: 4 last, rear 9 aftermost
hindrance: bar, rub 4 clog, curb, snag, stop 5 block, check, delay, hitch 6 arrest 7 barrier 8 obstacle 9 detention, deterrent, restraint 10 difficulty, impediment 11 impeachment, obstruction 12 interruption
Hindu: 4 Babu, Koli, Sikh 5 Tamil 6 Gentoo, Hindoo 8 Kolarian
unorthodox: 4 Jain 5 Jaina
Hinduism (see also **India**):
abode of gods: 4 Meru
adherent: Sik 4 Jain, Seik, Sikh 5 Jaina, Seikh
age of world: 4 yuga
alphabet: 6 Sarada
ancestral race: 5 Aryan
apartment: 5 mahal
Aryan race: 4 Swat
ascetic: 4 jogi, sadh, yati, yogi 5 sadhu
book: 4 Veda 6 Tantra 11 Yajna-valkya
calendar: Pus 4 Jeth, Asin, Kaur, Magh 5 Asarh, Sawan, Katik, Aghan, Chait 6 Bhadon, Kartik, Phagun 7 Baisakh, Sarawan, Phalgun
call to prayer: 4 azan
caste: Dom, Mal, Meo 4 Dasi, Gola, Koli, Kori, Mali, Pasi, Teli 5 Goala, Palli, Sudra 6 Babhan, Soodra 7 Brahman
caste member: Jat 4 Jain 6 Banian, Banyan, Rajput, Vaisya 7 Rajpoot 9 Kshatriya, Vakkaliga
charm: 6 mantra
chief: mir 6 sirdar
coin: ana, pai, pie 4 anna, pice 5 paisa, rupee
convert to Islam: 6 shaikh
cremation: 4 sati 6 suttee

dancer: 8 devadasi
deity: Dev 4 Deva, Dewa, Maya, Rama, Yama 6 Ganesa, Varuna, Vishnu 7 Ganesha, Krishna 9 Jagannath 10 Jagannatha, Juggernaut 11 Ramachandra
demon: 4 Bali, Bhut, Ketu, Rahu 5 Asura 6 Daitya
devotee: 4 yati
disciple: 4 sikh
divine being: dev 4 deva
doctrine: 5 Karma 6 dharma
drink: 4 soma
duty: 6 dharma
ejaculation: om, um
essence: 4 rata 5 atman 6 amrita
family: 5 gotra
female energy: 6 Sakati, Shakti
festival: 4 Holi, mela 6 Dewali, Hoolee 7 Dashara
flute: bin 5 pungi
garment: 4 sari 5 saree
gentleman: 4 babu 5 baboo, sahib
god (see also *deity* above)*:* 4 Agni, Deva, Kama, Siva, Yama 5 Asura, Shiva, Simia 6 Brahma, Ganesa, Skanda, Varuna 7 Ganesha
goddess: Sri, Uma, Vac 4 Devi, Kali, Shri, Vach 5 Durga, Gauri, Sakti, Shree, Ushas 6 Chandi, Shakti 7 Parvati 9 Haimavati
guitar: 5 sitar
headdress: 5 rumal
heaven: 5 dyaus
hermitage: 7 ashrama
hero: 4 Nala, Rama
holy book: 4 Veda 6 Sastra
holy sage: 5 rishi
hymn: 6 mantra
idol worship: 5 arati
incarnation: 6 avatar
Indra: 5 Sakka, Sakra
king: 4 Nala 5 Sesha 6 Shesha
lady: 4 devi, rani 5 ranee
language: 4 Pali, Urdu 5 Hindi, Tamil 8 Sanskrit 10 Hindustani
lawgiver: 4 Manu
leader: 5 Nehru 6 Gandhi, sirdar
life principle: 4 jiva 5 atman, prana
literature: 4 Veda 5 sruti 6 shruti
loincloth: 5 dhoti
magic: 4 jadu, maya 5 jadoo
magician: 5 fakir 6 fakeer
mantra: om, um
master: 5 sahib
mendicant: 4 naga 7 bairagi, vairagi 8 sannyasi
mental discipline: 4 yoga
monastery: 4 math
monkey god: 7 Hanuman
month: see *calendar* above
mother goddess: 6 matris
mystic: 4 yogi
noble: 5 rajah 8 maharaja
non-violence: 6 ahimsa
offering: 4 bali, lepa 5 pinda
paradise: 7 Nirvana
patriarch: 5 pitri

philosophy: 4 yoga 5 tamas
poem: 8 Ramayana 10 Mahabharta 12 Bhagavad-Gita
poet: 6 Tagore
policeman: 5 sepoy
prayer rug: 4 asan 5 asana
priest: 5 hotar
prince: 4 raja, rana 5 rajah 8 maharaja 9 maharajah
princess: 4 rani 5 ranee
queen: 4 rani 5 ranee 8 maharani 9 maharanee
religion: 5 Prana 7 Jainism, Sivaism 8 Shivaism
rite: 5 achar
ruler: 5 rajah
scripture: Li; rig 4 Veda 5 Sruti 6 Purana, Sastra, Smriti, Tantra 7 Shastra
sect: 4 Sikh, siva 6 Aghori
social division: 5 caste
soldier: 5 sepoy
soul: 4 atma 5 atman
spirit: 4 Jiva, Mara 5 Asura, Atman, Prana 7 Muktama
teacher: pir 4 guru
temple: 4 deul 6 vimana
title: aya, sri 4 mian, raja, shri, sidi 5 rajah, sahib, shree, swami 7 bahadur
tower: 5 stupa
triad god: 4 Siva
tunic: 4 jama 5 jamah
unknown god: Ka
Upanishad: 4 Isha, Veda 7 Vedanta
worship: 4 puja 5 pooja
Hindustan: Ind
language: 4 Urdu 5 Hindi
tribesman: 4 toda
hinge: har 4 butt, hang, turn 5 gemel, joint, pivot, stand 6 depend, gimmer, gimmor, hingle, lamina, pintle
Hinnom Valley: 7 Gehenna
hint: cue, tip 4 clew, clue, time, turn 5 cheep(Sc.), imply, trace 6 allude, moment 7 inkling, mention, suggest 8 allusion, innuendo, intimate, occasion 9 catchword, insinuate 10 indication, intimation, suggestion 11 insinuation
hip: hop 4 coxa, huck, limp, miss, skip 6 haunch, huckle
pert. to: 7 sciatic
hipbone: 5 ileum, ilium
hippodrome: 5 arena 6 circus 7 contest
hippopotamus: 6 seacow
hire: buy, fee, let, use 4 rent, sign, wage 5 bribe, lease, price, wages 6 employ, engage, retain, reward, salary 7 charter, conduce, stipend 9 allowance 12 compensation
hireling: 4 esne, serf 5 slave 8 gangster 9 mercenary
hirple: 4 limp 6 hobble
hirsel: 4 herd, land 5 flock
hirsute: 5 hairy, rough 6 coarse, shaggy
hispid: 7 bristly 8 strigose, strigous
hiss: 4 hish, sizz, whiz 5 whizz 6 fissle, fistle 8 goose cry 10 assibilate

hissing: 6 fizzle 8 sibilant 9 sibilance
hist: 4 hark, hush
historian: 8 annalist 10 chronicler
history: 4 tale 5 drama, story 6 annals, memoir, record 7 account 8 relation 9 biography, chronicle, genealogy, narrative
  muse: 4 Clio
histrion: 5 actor
histrionics: 6 acting 11 theatricals
hit: bat, lam, lob, ram, rap, tap 4 bump, bunt, cast, club, slog, slug, sock, swat, wham 5 clout, flick, knock, smack, smite, smote, throw, touch 6 attain, batted, bingle, strike 7 collide, success 8 bludgeon 10 production, succession
hit-or-miss: 6 casual, chance, habnab 8 careless 9 haphazard
hitch: hop, tie, tug 4 halt, hook, join, knot, limp, pull 5 agree, catch, crick, hotch, marry, unite 6 attach, enlist, hobble 8 obstacle, stoppage 9 harmonize, hindrance 10 enlistment, impediment 11 contretemps, obstruction
hitchhiker: 8 stowaway
hither: 4 here
hitherto: ago, yet 6 before
Hitler: *aerie:* 13 Berchtesgaden
  chosen race: 5 Aryan
  follower: 4 Nazi
hitter: 6 batter 7 batsman, slugger
Hittite storm god: 6 Teshub, Teshup
hives: 6 apiary 7 allergy
ho: 4 long, stop 5 yearn 6 attend, desist
hoar: 4 cold, gray, rime 5 hoary, musty, stale 6 biting 7 ancient 9 antiquity, venerable 13 venerableness
hoard: 4 save 5 amass, chest, hutch, stock, store 6 supply 7 husband 8 quantity, treasure, treasury 10 accumulate, collection
hoarder: 5 miser 6 storer 9 treasurer
hoarfrost: rag 4 rime 9 cranreuch(Sc.)
hoarse: 5 gruff, harsh, rocky, rough 7 grating, raucous 10 discordant
hoarseness: 4 frog 5 croup
hoary: old 4 aged, gray, hoar 5 moldy, mossy, musty 7 ancient, hoarish, whitish 9 canescent, venerable
hoax: bam, cod, fun, hex, kid 4 bilk, fake, gaff, gegg, gunk, joke, ruse, sell, sham 5 bluff, cheat, spoof, trick 6 canard, diddle, humbug, string 7 deceive 8 artifice 9 bamboozle, deception 11 hornswoggle
hob: elf, peg, pin, tap 4 game, mark, nail, nave 5 clown, fairy, ledge 6 ferret, rustic, sprite 7 mandrel 8 mischief 10 countryman, projection
hobbil: 4 dolt 5 clown, dunce, idiot
hobble: 4 clog, clop 5 bunch, cramp, hitch 6 fetter, hopple 7 cramble, perplex, shackle, spancel 9 embarrass 10 difficulty, perplexity 13 embarrassment
hobbledehoy: lad 5 youth
hobbler: 5 pilot 7 boatman, hoveler, laborer 8 retainer 12 longshoreman
hobbly: 5 rough 6 uneven

hobby: fad 5 horse 6 falcon 7 pastime 9 avocation, diversion
hobgoblin: bug, elf, hag, imp 4 bogy, Puck 5 bogey, bogie, bugan, poker, spook 6 boodie(Sc.) sprite 7 bugaboo 8 boggle-bo, worricow(Sc.) 9 coltpixie 10 apparition
hobo: bo; boe, bum 5 tramp 7 vagrant 8 vagabond
hock: ham, hox 4 pawn 5 ankle, hough, thigh 6 mallow, pledge 9 hamstring 10 houghsinew
hocket: 6 hiccup 8 obstacle 12 interruption
hockey: 5 bandy 6 shinny
  disk: 4 puck
hocus: 4 drug 5 cheat fraud 7 deceive 8 cheating, deceiver, trickery 10 adulterate
hocus-pocus: 5 cheat, trick 6 humbug 7 juggler 8 flimflam, quackery 9 trickster 12 charlatanism
hod: 4 soil 6 barrow 7 scuttle
hoddy-doddy: 4 fool 5 snail 7 cuckold 9 blockhead
hodgepodge: ana 4 mess, olio, stew 5 cento 6 medley 7 mixture 10 hotchpotch, miscellany 11 gallimaufry, ollapodrida 12 mingle-mangle
hoe: dig 4 brod, hill, till 5 clean, cliff, padle, worry 6 sarcle, scrape, dogfish 7 trouble 8 griffaun 9 cultivate 10 promontory
hog (see also **pig**): sow 4 bene, boar, dime, galt, gilt 5 shoat, shote, swine 6 barrow 7 hogling 8 shilling 9 boschvark 10 backfatter
  breed: 5 Essex 9 Hampshire
  genus: sus
hog peanut: 8 earthpea
hog plum: 4 amra
hog side: 6 flitch
hog thigh: ham
hogfish: 8 scorpene
hoggish: 5 hoggy 7 selfish, swinish 10 gluttonous
hogo: 5 taint 6 flavor, stench
hogshead: 4 cask 6 barrel, hogget, vessel
hogwash: 5 draff 7 pigwash
hoi polloi: mob 6 masses, rabble 8 populace
hoick: 4 lift, yank
hoist: cat, gin 4 jack, lift 5 boost, crane, davit, heave, heeze, horse, lewis, raise, setup, winch 7 derrick, elevate 8 elevator
hoist sail: 4 swig
hoistman: 8 bandsman 9 engineman
hoity-toity: 5 giddy, proud 6 snooty 7 flighty, haughty 8 arrogant 11 harumscarum, patronizing, thoughtless 13 irresponsible
hokum: 4 bunk 11 foolishness
hold: own 4 bind, bite, bulk, clip, fill, have, hook, keep, rely, seat, stow, tend 5 avast, carry, catch, grasp, guard, rivet 6 adhere, arrest, behold, cleave, clench, defend, detain, harbor, occupy, retain 7 adjudge,

contain, control **8** interest, maintain, thurrock **9** entertain **10** possession, stronghold

hold a brief for: **6** defend **8** advocate

hold back: dam **4** stem, stop **5** deter **6** detain, retard **7** inhibit, repress **8** restrain

hold fast: hug **5** cling, stick **6** cohere

hold forth: **5** offer **7** exhibit **8** continue, maintain, propound

hold in custody: **4** jail **6** detain, intern

hold on: **4** stop, wait **7** forbear **8** continue

hold out: **4** last **6** endure **7** exclude, pretend **8** continue

hold up: rob **4** halt, lift, rein **5** boost, check, raise **7** display, exhibit, robbery, support, sustain

hold water: **5** sound **10** consistent

holder: **5** haver **6** tenant **9** container **10** receptacle

holdfast: **5** clamp, miser **6** clinch **7** support **9** tenacious **10** persistent

holding: **5** asset **6** estate, tenure **8** property

adapted for: **10** prehensile

hole: bay, den, pit **4** bore, cave, cove, deep, dump, flaw, gate, gulf, leak, mine, nook, peck, rent, vent **5** abyss, chasm, shaft **6** burrow, cavern, cavity, cranny, crater, eyelet, grotto, hollow, pierce, prison, recess **7** dungeon, mortise, opening, orifice, ostiole **8** aperture, bunghole, peephole **10** excavation **11** perforation, predicament

instrument for making: awl **4** bore **5** drill **8** stiletto

wall: **4** muse **5** meuse, niche

Holi, Hoolee: **8** festival

holiday: **4** fete **5** feria, festa, merry **6** fiesta, jovial, outing **7** festive, playday **8** festival, vacation **9** convivial, Mardi Gras

holiness: **5** piety **7** halidom **8** halidome, sanctity **9** sanctuary **11** saintliness **13** righteousness

Holland: See **Netherlands**.

holler: **4** yell **6** shriek **7** protest

hollow: den, dip **4** boss, cave, cove, deep, dent, doke, glen, hole, holl, howe, huck, lean, thin, vain, void **5** bight, chase, cuppy, empty, false, gaunt, goyal, goyle, heugh, scoop, sinus, stria **6** cavern, cavity, cirque, groove, hungry, socket, sunken, vacant **7** concave, muffled, unsound **8** alveolus, fossette, specious **9** cavernous, deceitful, depressed, faithless, worthless **10** depression, sepulchral **11** treacherous **12** unsatisfying

hollow-eyed: **7** haggard

hollowed: **7** glenoid

hollowed out: **6** cavate

hollowness: **6** vanity **7** vacuity

holly: **4** assi, holm, ilex **5** yapon, yupon **6** hulver, yaupon, youpon

pert. to: **6** ilicic

holm: ait **5** holly, islet **7** bottoms, lowland

holm oak: **4** ilex **5** holly

holobaptist: **12** immersionist

holocaust: **9** sacrifice **11** destruction

holster: **4** case **7** housing **8** scabbard

holt: den **4** grip, hill, hold, lair, wood **5** copse, grasp **7** retreat

holy: **5** pious, sacre(F.), saint, santo **6** devout, divine, hallow, sacred **7** blessed, perfect, sainted, saintly **8** blissful, hallowed **9** inviolate, sanctuary, spiritual **10** sacrosanct **13** sanctimonious

combining form: **5** hagio

Holy City: **4** Kiev, Rome, Zion **5** Mecca, Lhasa, Medina, Moscow **7** Benares **9** Allahabad, Jerusalem

Holy Grail: **8** Sangraal, Sangreal

castle: **9** Monsalvat

knight: **7** Galahad

Holy Joe: **9** clergyman

Holy Land: **9** Palestine

pilgrim: **6** palmer

Holy One: God **6** Christ **7** Jehovah **12** Supreme Being

Holy Rood: **5** cross **8** crucifix

holy statue: **4** icon, ikon **5** ikono

holy water: *font:* **5** paten

receptacle: **5** stoup

sprinkler: **11** aspergillum

homage: **5** honor **6** eulogy, fealty, regard **7** loyalty, manrent, ovation, respect **9** adoration, deference, obeisance, reverence **10** allegiance

homager: **6** vassal

homard: **7** lobster

hombre: guy, man **6** fellow

Homburg: hat **4** felt

home: den **4** nest **5** abode, being, domus, house **6** asylum, estate, maison(F.) **7** habitat, hospice, village **8** domicile, dwelling **9** homestead, residence **10** habitation **11** hearthstone

at: **4** chez(F.)

wheeled: **7** trailer

home base: den **5** plate

homeborn: **6** native **10** indigenous

homefelt: **6** inward **7** private

homelike: **4** cozy **5** homey **6** homely, homish **8** cheerful, friendly, homesome **11** comfortable

homeliness: **9** plainness **10** simplicity **11** domesticity **17** unpretentiousness

homely: **4** rude, ugly **5** plain **6** hameil, hamelt, hamilt, kindly, simple **7** plainly **8** domestic, familiar, friendly, homelike, intimate **9** unsightly **10** intimately **12** unpretending **13** unpretentious

homemade: **5** plain **6** simple **8** domestic

Homer: *birthplace:* **5** Chios

character: **4** Ajax **6** Nestor **8** Achilles, Odysseus

poem: **5** Iliad **7** Odyssey

Homeric: **4** epic **6** epical

homesickness: **9** nostalgia

homespun: **4** kelt(Sc.), rude **5** plain **6** coarse

homestead: 4 toft, tref(W.) 7 onstead
homicide: 6 murder
homilist: 8 preacher
homily: 5 adage 6 sermon 8 assembly 9 communion, discourse 11 exhortation
hominy: 4 bran, samp
homo: man
Homo Americanus: 6 Indian
Homo sapiens: man
homogeneity: 8 equality, identity, sameness
homogeneous: 4 like 5 equal, solid 7 similar 10 comparable
homologous: 9 identical
homonym: 7 synonym 8 namesake
homunculus: 5 dwarf 7 manikin
Honduras:
city: 4 Yoro 6 Cedros, Iriona 7 Gracias 9 Juticalpa 11 Tegucigalpa(c.)
coin: 4 peso 7 centavo, lempira
Indian: 4 Ulua, Ulva 5 Lenca
measure: 4 vara 5 milla 6 mecate, tercia 7 cajuela, manzana 10 caballeria
mountain: 5 Ceiba, Colon
port: 8 Truxillo 10 San Lorenzo
river: 4 Ulua 5 Aguan, Negro 6 Patuca, Sulaco 9 Choluteca 10 Chamelicon
weight: 4 caja
hone: 4 long, pine 5 delay, dress, strop 6 lament 7 grumble, sharpen 8 oilstone 9 whetstone
honest: 4 fair, full, just, open 5 frank, roman 6 candid, chaste, decent, dexter, dinkum, proper, rustic, square 7 genuine, sincere, upright 8 bonafide, faithful, rightful, reliable, straight, suitable, truthful, virtuous 9 equitable, guileless, honorable, ingenuous, veracious 10 creditable 11 trustworthy 13 conscientious, incorruptible, unadulterated 15 straightforward
honestly: 5 truly 6 dinkum, justly 8 directly 9 telltruth
honesty: 5 honor 6 equity 7 decency, justice, probity 8 fairness, fidelity, veracity 9 constancy, integrity 10 generosity, liberality 11 uprightness 12 suitableness, truthfulness 15 honorableness 15 trustworthiness 19 straightforwardness
honey: mel 4 dear, niel(F.) 5 sweet 6 nectar 7 flatter 8 precious
combining form: 5 melli
honey badger: 5 ratel
honey buzzard: 4 hawk, pern
honey eater: iao 6 manuao
honeybee: 7 deseret 8 angelito
disease: 8 sacbrood
honeycomb cell: 7 alveola 8 alveolus
honeycombed: 6 favose, pitted 8 alveolar
honeydew: 5 melon 6 mildew, orange
honeyed: 5 sweet 6 sugary 7 candied 11 mellifluous
honeysuckle: 6 azalea, widbin
Hong Kong:

city: 8 Victoria
coin: 4 cent 6 dollar 13 British dollar 14 Hong Kong dollar
honor: 4 fame, fete, prow 5 adore, exalt, glory, grace, izzat 6 credit, decore, esteem, homage, laurel, praise, regard, repute, revere 7 dignify, dignity, emblaze, ennoble, glorify, honesty, respect, worship 9 celebrate, deference, reverence 10 estimation, reputation
pledge: 6 parole
honorable: 4 dear 5 moral, noble, white 6 gentle, honest 7 upright 8 generous, honorary 9 dearworth, estimable, reputable 10 creditable 11 commendable, illustrious, magnanimous, meritorious, respectable
honorarium: fee, tip 6 reward, salary 7 douceur, payment 8 gratuity
hood: cap 4 coif, cowl, hide 5 amice, blind 6 biggin, bonnet, burlet, camail, canopy, chapel, tippet 7 calotte, capuche, surtout 8 capsheaf, caputium, chaperon, covering
academic: 8 liripipe, liripoop
monk's: 4 atis, cowl 5 atees
saddle: 8 tapadera, tapadero
vehicle: 6 bonnet, capote
hooded: 9 cucullate 10 capistrate
hoodlum: yap 5 rowdy 6 goonda 8 hooligan
hoodoo: 4 jinx 5 Jonah 6 voodoo 7 bewitch, unlucky
hoodwink: 4 fool, hide, wile 5 blear, blind, bluff, cheat, cosen, cover, cozen 6 befool, delude 7 blinder, blinker, deceive, mislead 9 blindfold
hooey: 4 bunk 6 bunkum 7 baloney, boloney 8 buncombe, nonsense
hoof: 4 clee, foot, walk 5 cloof, cloot, cluif, dance, tramp 6 ungula
hoofer: 6 dancer, walker
hook: 4 barb, gaff, hake, hock, hold, huck 5 catch, cleek, hamus, hitch, larin, seize, steal 6 agrafe, anchor, larree, pilfer, tenter 7 agraffe, capture, grunter, hamulus, hitcher 8 crotchet 10 chatelaine
hook money: 5 larin 6 larree
hooka, hookah: 4 pipe 7 nargile 8 narghile 9 narghileh
hooked: 6 hamate 7 hamular, uncinal 8 ankyroid, aquiline, uncinate
hookey player: 6 truant
hooligan: 6 loafer 7 ruffian
hooly: 4 slow, soft, wary
hoop: 4 bail, band, ring, tire 5 clasp, garth, girth, shout 6 circle, frette 7 circlet, trundle 8 encircle, surround
hoopskirt: 9 crinoline
hoosegow: jug 4 jail 6 lockup, prison 10 guardhouse
hoosh: 4 lift, urge 5 boost, hoist
Hoosier State: 7 Indiana
hoot: boo 4 jeer, whoo 5 shout, whoop 6 boohoo 7 ululate

hop: fly, hip **4** dope, halt, jump, leap, limp, skip **5** bound, dance, hitch **6** flight, gambol, spring

hop back: vat

hop kiln: **4** oast

hop stem: **4** bine

hopbush: **6** akeake

hope: **4** deem, spes(L.), want, wish **5** haven, trust **6** aspire, desire, expect, morale **7** cherish, confide **8** prospect, reliance **9** esperance **10** aspiration **11** expectation **12** anticipation

lack: **7** despair

hopeful: **8** sanguine **9** confident, expectant **10** optimistic

hopeless: **4** gone, vain **6** futile **7** forlorn, useless **8** downcast **9** desperate, heartless, incurable **10** despairing, despondent, desponding, remediless **11** ineffectual **12** disconsolate, irremediable **13** irrecoverable, irretrievable

hophead: **6** addict

Hopi Indian: **4** Moki **5** Moqui

god: **7** Kachina, Katcina **8** Katchina

hoplite: **7** soldier

hopper: box **5** chute **6** dancer, leaper **10** receptacle

hoppet: **4** yard **6** basket, bucket

hopple: **6** fetter, hamper, hobble **8** entangle

hopscotch: **7** pallall

hopvine: **4** bine

horde: **4** army, camp, clan, pack **5** crowd, group, swarm **6** legion, throng **9** multitude

horehound: **6** henbit

Horite chief: **4** Seir

horizon: rim **4** edge, goal **8** prospect

horizontal: **4** flat **5** level

hormigo: **5** quira **7** ant tree

horn: **4** scur, tuba **5** brass, bugle, cornu, drone, siren **6** antler, cornet, rhyton **7** antenna, trumpet **8** oliphant **9** alpenhorn **10** cornucopia

blast: **4** mort, toot **7** fanfare, tantara **9** tantarara

combining form: **4** kera

crescent moon: **4** cusp

Hebrew: **6** shofar **7** shophar

player: **6** bugler **9** cornetist, trumpeter

without: **5** doddy **6** doddie, polled **7** acerous

hornbill: **4** bird, tock **6** homrai

genus of: **7** buceros

hornet: **4** wasp

hornswoggle: **4** hoax **9** bamboozle

horny: **4** hard **8** ceratoid **9** calloused **10** semiopaque

hornyhead: **4** chub

horologe: **4** dial **5** clock, watch **9** timepiece

horoscope: **4** dial **7** diagram

horrendous: **7** fearful **8** horrible **9** frightful

horrible: **4** dire, grim **5** great **6** grisly, horrid **7** fearful, ghastly, hideous, horrent **8** dreadful, gruesome, horrific, shocking, terrible **9** atrocious, excessive, frightful, horrified, nefarious **10** horrendous, tremendous

horrid: **4** grim, ugly **5** awful, rough **6** rugged **7** hideous **8** dreadful, grewsome, gruesome, horrible, shocking **9** bristling, frightful, obnoxious, offensive, revolting **10** detestable, terrifying **13** objectionable

horrific: **7** fearful **8** horrible **9** frightful **10** horrifying

horrified: **6** aghast **7** ghastly

horrify: **5** shock **6** appall, dismay

horrifying: **8** horrific **9** execrable

horror: **4** fear **5** dread **6** terror **8** aversion **10** abhorrence **11** abomination, detestation **13** consternation

hors d'ouevre: **6** canape, relish **7** zakuska **8** aperitif **9** antipasto, appetizer

horse: gee, nag, pad **4** barb, mare, plug, prad **5** brock, caple, capul, draft, filly, hobby, hoist, mount, pacer, raise, shier, steed, waler **6** cheval, equine, geegee, ladino, pelter, rouncy **7** caballo(Sp.), cavallo(Sp.), cavalry, charger, clipper, courser, hackney, mustang, saddler, sheltie, sleeper, stepper, trestle **8** bathorse, cartaver(Sc.), footrope, jackstay **10** breastband

Achilles': **7** Xanthus

ankle: **4** hock

breastplate: **7** peytrel, poitrel

breed: **4** Arab, Barb **5** Shire **6** hunter, Morgan **7** Belgian, harness, Suffolk, trotter **8** Galloway, Normandy, Shetland **9** Percheron **10** Clydesdale

brown: bay **6** sorrel **8** chestnut

buyer: **5** coper **6** trader **7** knacker

calico: **5** pinto

color: bay **4** pied, roan **5** pinto **6** calico, sorrel **8** chestnut, palomino, schimmel

combining form: **5** hippo

command: gee, haw, hup **4** whoa **6** giddap

covering: **9** caparison

cry: nie **5** neigh **6** whinny

dappled: **4** roan **5** pinto **7** piebald

dark: **4** zain

dealer: **7** chanter, scorser

disease: **5** surra **6** heaves, lampas **7** lampers, quittor, spavins **9** distemper

docked-tail: **6** curtal **8** cocktail

draft: **4** aver **5** aiver, hairy

driver: **6** jockey **7** sumpter **8** coachman

farm: **6** dobbin

feeding box: **6** manger

female: **4** mare, yaud **5** filly

foot: **4** frog, hoof **7** coronet, fetlock, pastern

forehead: **8** chanfrin

gait: run **4** lope, pace, rack, trot, vott, walk **6** canter, gallop

genus: **5** equus

goddess of: **5** Epona
golden: **8** palomino
gray: **8** schimmel
guide: **4** rein **5** longe
harness: **5** pacer **7** trotter
hired: **4** hack **7** hackney
horned: **7** unicorn **9** monoceros
leg: **6** instep **7** fetlock
lover: **10** hippophile
male: **4** stud **6** entire **7** gelding **8** stallion
measure: **4** hand
menage: **6** school **7** academy
pace: **4** lope, trot **5** amble **6** canter
pack: **5** bidet **7** sumpter
pair: **4** span, team
pert. to: **6** hippic
piebald: **5** pinto
prehistoric: **8** Eohippus
relay: **6** remuda
round-up: **5** rodeo
saddle: cob **5** mount **7** palfrey
small: cob, nag, tit **4** pony **5** bidet, genet **6** cayuse, jennet(Sp.) **8** galloway, Shetland
sorrel: **4** roan **8** chestnut
spirited: **4** Arab **5** steed **6** rearer **7** cour-ser
stable of: **6** string
talking: **5** Arion
track slope: **6** calade
trainer: **5** valet
trapping: **6** tackle **7** harness **9** caparison
trotting: **6** Morgan
turn: **7** passade
war: **5** steed **7** charger, courser **8** destrier
white-streaked face: **4** shim **5** blaze, reach
wild: **6** bronco, brumby, tarpan **7** mustang **8** warragal, warrigal
winged: **7** Pegasus
working: **4** aver **5** aiver **6** dobbin
worn-out: nag **4** hack, jade, moke, plug **5** crock, skate **6** garran, garron, gleyde **7** knacker **8** harridan **9** rosinante
horse-and-buggy: rig **12** old-fashioned
horse collar: **7** bargham(Sc.)
horse mackerel: **4** fish, scad **5** atule, tunny **6** bonita, saurel
horse opera: **7** western
horse tackle: **7** harness
horseback: *on:* **7** a cheval(F.)
horse tackle: **7** harness
horseback: *on:* **7** a cheval(F.)
horsefly: **4** cleg **5** clegg **6** botfly, gadfly
horsehair: **4** mane **9** haircloth
horsehide: **8** cordovan
horsekeeper: **5** groom **7** hostler
horselaugh: **5** snort **6** guffaw, heehaw
horseman: **5** rider **6** carter, cowboy centaur, courier, vaquero **8** buckaroo chevalier **10** cavalryman, equestrian **12** broncobuster, equestrienne
horseman goad: **4** spur
horsemanship: **6** manege **10** equitation
rearing: **6** pesade
sidewalk: **4** volt

turn: **8** caracole
horsemen: **7** cavalry **11** equestrians
horseradish tree: ben **5** behen
horseshoe:
point: **6** sponge
spur: **4** calk
rim: web
horseshoer: **7** farrier **10** blacksmith
horticulturist: **8** gardener
Horus: Ra, Re
brother: **6** Anubis
father: **6** Osiris
mother: **4** Isis
hory, horry: **4** foul **5** dirty **6** impure
hose: **4** sock, tube, vamp **5** water **6** drench **8** stocking
Hosea's wife: **5** Gomer
hospice: inn **5** house **6** asylum, imaret **9** hospitium
hospitable: **5** douce **6** cheery **7** cordial **8** friendly **9** receptive **10** hospitious
hospital: **6** creche, refuge, spital **9** infir-mary **10** sanatorium **11** xenodochium **12** ambulatorium
attendant: **5** nurse **7** orderly
mobile: **9** ambulance
host: inn **4** army, here **5** crowd, guest, swarm **6** housel, legion, myriad, throng **7** company, lodging **8** landlord **9** harbinger, multitude, sacrifice **10** assemblage **11** entertainer
hostage: inn **5** hotel **6** pledge **8** security **9** guarantee
hostel: inn **5** hotel, lodge **7** lodging **12** lodginghouse **13** entertainment
hostelry: inn **5** hotel **6** hostel, hostry, tav-ern **11** caravansary **12** lodginghouse
hostile: foe **5** black, enemy, fremd **7** ad-verse, opposed, warlike **8** contrary, inim-ical **9** resisting **10** malevolent, unfriendly **11** belligerent **12** antagonistic **13** unsym-pathetic
hostility: **4** feid, feud **6** animus, enmity, hatred, rancor **7** ill-will, warfare **9** ani-mosity, antipathy **10** antagonism, bitter-ness, opposition, resistance **12** disaffec-tion **14** unfriendliness, vindictiveness
hosting: **6** battle **9** encounter, gathering, incursion
hostler: **5** groom **6** ostler **9** innkeeper, stableman
hot: **5** acrid, calid, eager, fiery, spicy **6** ardent, biting, fervid, recent, strong, sul-try, torrid, urgent **7** burning, excited, fer-vent, flaming, glowing, intense, lustful, peppery, pungent, thermal **8** sizzling, vehement **9** impatient, impetuous **10** passionate
hot cakes: **7** kneepad, pancake **11** griddle cake
hot-tempered: **7** iracund **8** choleric **9** irascible
hot-water bottle: pad, pig
hotbed: **4** nest

hotchpotch: 4 stew 6 jumble 8 hotchpot 9 tripotage(F.) 10 hodgepodge

hotel: inn 5 fonda, haven, house 6 hostel, imaret, tavern 7 gasthof, hostage 8 building, dwelling, gasthaus 11 caravansary 12 caravanserai, lodginghouse
auto: 5 motel

hothead: 5 raver 7 inciter 11 reactionary

hotheaded: 5 fiery, hasty 8 reckless 9 impetuous

hothouse: 6 bagnio 10 greenhouse

hotspur: 4 rash 6 madcap 7 violent 8 reckless 9 impetuous 10 headstrong

Hottentot: *dialect:* 4 Gona, Kora, Nama
garment: 6 kaross
instrument: 4 gora 5 gorah, goura
tribe: 4 Gona, Kora, Nama 6 Damara, Griqua 7 Sandawe, Sandawi
war club: 10 knobkerrie

hound: dog 4 hunt 5 harry 6 addict, talbot 7 harrier 9 persecute
tail: 5 stern

hounds: 4 pack 8 avantlay

hour: *canonical:* 4 none, sext
class: 6 period
lights out: 4 taps 6 curfew

hourly: 5 brief, horal 6 horary, recent 7 quickly 8 frequent 9 continual 10 frequently 11 continually

hourglass: 5 clock 7 shapely

house: cot, hut 4 casa(It.), cote, dorm, dump, firm, flat, flet, haus(G.), home, nest 5 abode, bahay, booth, cabin, cover, dacha, domus(L.), hovel, lodge, manor, shack, villa 6 biggin, billet, bottle, camara, casino, duplex, family, grange, maison(F.), palace, shanty 7 cabildo, chateau, cottage, enclose, mansion, quarter, shelter, theater 8 ancestry, audience, building, domicile, dwelling, tenement 9 dormitory, playhouse, residence 10 habitation
cluster: 4 dorp 6 hamlet 7 village
combining form: eco
commercial: 4 firm 5 store 8 emporium
eating: inn 4 cafe 6 tavern 9 chophouse 10 restaurant
English royal: 5 Tudor 6 Stuart 7 Windsor
guest: inn 5 hotel 11 caravansary
Newfoundland: 4 tilt
Oriental: 5 serai
pert. to: 5 domal
public: inn 5 hotel 6 hostel, tavern 7 hospice 8 hostelry
religious: 4 kirk 6 chapel, church, priory, temple 9 cathedral, synagogue 10 tabernacle
summer: 6 gazebo 9 belvedere
Upper: 6 Senate

house servant: 4 maid 8 domestic

houseboat: 5 barge 6 wangan, wangun 7 wanigan 8 dahabeah, wannigan

household: 5 meiny 6 common, family, housal, menage 8 familiar 9 belonging

gods: 5 Lares 7 Penates

regulation: 6 thrift 7 economy 9 husbandry

housekeeper: 6 matron 7 janitor 8 janitrix 9 caretaker, janitress

houseleek: 8 sengreen

housemaid: 6 duster 7 servant

houseplant: ivy 5 aphis, calla 6 coleus 7 begonia, violets 11 asphidistra

housewarming: 6 infare

housewife: 8 hausfrau(G.) 9 economize

housework: 5 chore 8 drudgery

housing: pad 6 garage

hove: See heave.

hovel: hut, sty 4 crib, hulk, hull, shed 5 cabin, hutch, lodge 6 cruive, hemmel, shanty 7 shelter 10 tabernacle

hoveler: 7 boatman, hobbler

hover: 4 flit 5 float, pause 7 flitter, flutter

howdy, howdie: 7 midwife 10 salutation

howe: 4 deep 5 empty, lowly 6 hollow, humble, hungry 10 depression

however: but, tho, yet 5 still 6 though 8 although 10 howsomever 12 nevertheless 15 notwithstanding

howf, howff: 4 loaf 5 haunt, lodge 6 resort, tavern 7 shelter, sojourn 8 frequent

howitzer: 6 cannon

howl: bay, cry, wow(Sc.), 4 bawl, gowl, gurl, hurl, wail, wawl, yawl, yell, yowl, yowt 5 whewl 6 lament, steven 7 ululate

howling: 4 wild 5 great 6 baying, dreary, savage 7 extreme, ululant 10 pronounced

howsoever: 8 although

howsomever: 8 although 12 nevertheless

hox: 4 hock 5 annoy, worry 6 pester 7 trample 9 hamstring

hoyden, hoiden: 4 romp, rude 6 blowze, tomboy 7 ill-bred 10 roistering

Hreidmar's son: 5 Otter, Regin 6 Fafnir, Reginn

huaca: 4 holy, idol, tomb 6 fetish, sacred, shrine, temple

hub: 4 core, nave 6 center, centre

Hub: 6 Boston

hubble: 5 crowd 6 hubbub, uproar

hubble-show: 6 rabble 9 commotion, confusion

hubbub: ado, din 4 stir 5 noise 6 clamor, hubble, racket, rumpus, tumult, uproar 7 bobbery 8 hubbuboo 9 commotion, confusion 11 disturbance

hubby: 7 husband

hubristic: 4 vain 7 insolent 8 arrogant 12 contemptuous

huck: hip 4 husk 6 haunch, higgle 7 bargain

huckle: hip 6 haunch

huckleberry: 9 blueberry
family: 9 ericaceae

Huckleberry Finn:
author: 9 Mark Twain 13 Samuel Clemens
character: Jim

huckster: 5 adman, cheap 6 badger,

broker, cadger, cagier(Fr.), hawker 7 haggler, peddler 8 regrater, retailer 9 middleman

hud: 4 hull, husk 5 shell

huddle: hug 4 hide, raff 5 crowd, hurry 6 bustle, fumble, jumble, mingle 7 conceal, embrace, scrunch 8 assemble, disorder 9 confusion 10 conference 14 conglomeration

hue: 4 balk, blee, form, tint 5 color, guise, shade, shout, tinge 6 aspect, clamor, depict, figure, outcry 7 clamour 8 shouting 10 appearance, complexion

hueless: 4 gray 9 colorless

huff: dod, pet 4 blow, brag, puff 5 bully, peeve, swell 6 hector 7 bluster, enlarge 8 boasting, offended

huffcap: 5 bully, heady 6 strong 9 blusterer 10 blustering, swaggering

huffy: 4 airy 5 fuffy, puffy, windy 7 pettish 8 arrogant 9 conceited 10 swaggering

hug: lug 4 clip, coll 5 carry, clasp, cling, creem, halse, press 6 cuddle, huddle, huggle 7 cherish, embrace, squeeze

huge: big 4 stor(Sc.), vast 5 enorm, giant, great, jumbo, large 6 heroic 7 banging, bumping, immense, massive, monster 8 colossal, enormous, gigantic, titantic 9 monstrous, pyramidal 10 gargantuan, prodigious, tremendous, unmeasured 11 elephantine

hugger-mugger: sly 6 jumble, muddle, secret 7 secrecy 8 confused, secretly 9 confusion 10 disorderly 11 clandestine 13 clandestinely

hui: 4 firm 5 guild 7 society 8 assembly 11 partnership

huisache: 4 wabe, wabi 5 aromo, shrub 6 cassie 7 popinac

huitain: 6 octave, stanza

huke: 4 cape 5 cloak, dress

hulk: 4 bulk, hull, loom, ship 5 hovel 10 disembowel

hulking: 5 bulky, hulky, husky 7 loutish, massive 8 unwieldy

hull: hud, hut, pod 4 bulk, hulk, husk, shed 5 hovel, shell, strip 8 covering 11 decorticate
grain: 4 bran

hullabaloo: ado, din 5 noise 6 clamor, hubbub, racket, tumult, uproar 7 clamour 9 confusion

hulver: 5 holly

hum: 4 blur, buzz, huss, huzz, sing, whiz 5 croon, drink, drone, feign, whizz 6 murmur 9 bombinate 11 bombilation, bombination

human: 6 humane, mortal 7 hominid 9 enigmatic

human being: man 6 mortal, person 7 Adamite 8 creature

humane: 4 kind 5 kindly, tender 8 merciful 9 forgiving 11 sympathetic 13 compassionate, tenderhearted

humanitarian: 14 philanthropist

humanity: 5 flesh 6 lenity 8 kindness 9 mortality

humanize: 6 refine 8 civilize

humble: low 4 mean, meek, mild, poor 5 abase, abash, lower, lowly, plain, stoop 6 debase, deject, demean, demiss, modest, reduce, simple 7 afflict, conquer, degrade, depress, mortify 8 contrite, deferent, disgrace, reverent 9 humiliate 10 submissive

humbug: gum, kid, pah 4 bosh, flam, guff, hoax, sham 5 cheat, faker, fraud, fudge, guile, trick 6 barney, blague, bunkum, cafard, cajole, gammon 7 deceive, flummer, mislead 8 flimflam, flummery, huckmuck, pretense 9 bamboozle, deception, imposture, stratagem 10 flumdiddle 11 flumadiddle

humdrum: 4 dull 7 irksome, prosaic 10 monotonous 11 commonplace, indifferent 13 uninteresting

humect: wet 7 moisten

humerus: 4 bone

humid: wet 4 damp, dank 5 moist 6 sultry 8 humorous, vaporous

humidity: 8 dampness

humiliate: 5 abase, abash, shame 6 debase, humble 7 degrade, mortify 8 belittle, disgrace

humility: 7 modesty 8 meekness, mildness 9 lowliness 10 diffidence

humming: big 5 brool 6 strong 7 buzzing, droning 8 frothing, seething 13 extraordinary

humming bird: ava 5 carib 6 hummer 8 froufrou 9 sheartail
genus of: 6 sappho

hummock: 4 hump 5 knoll

humor, humour: pet, tid, wit 4 baby, mood, whim 5 fancy, freak, vapor 6 levity, megrim, please, temper 7 caprice, gratify, indulge 8 drollery, moisture 11 inclination, temperament

humorist: wag 5 joker

humorous, humourous: 5 comic, droll, funny, humid, moist 6 watery 7 amusive, comical, jocular, playful 8 pleasant 9 facetious, laughable, whimsical 10 capricious

hump: 4 bile, hunk, lump 5 bouge, bulge, bunch, crump, hunch, mound, ridge 6 gibber, gibbus, hummie 7 hummock 12 protuberance

humpback: 9 hunchback 10 huckleback

hun: 6 vandal 9 barbarian

hunch: 4 balk, bend, hump, hunk, lump, push 5 fudge, shove 6 chilly, frosty, thrust 9 intuition 12 protuberance

Hunchback of Notre Dame: 9 Quasimodo

hundred: 7 cantred, cantref
combining form: 5 centi, hecto

hundred-eyed being: 5 Argus

hundred percent: 6 entire 7 genuine,

perfect **9** unalloyed **13** thoroughgoing **14**
unquestionable

hundred years: **7** century **9** centenary

hundredfold: **8** centuple **12** centuplicate

hundredweight: cwt **6** cental **7** quintal

hung: See **hang**.

Hung Wu: **4** Ming

Hungary: *army:* **6** Honved **9** Honvedseg
cavalryman: **6** Hussar
city: **8** Budapest(cap.), Debrecen, Szeg-
edin **9** Budapesth, Debreczin, Kecskemet
16 Hodmezo-Vasarhely
coin: **4** gara **5** balas, pengo **6** filler, korona
commune: Mor
dance: **7** czardas
gypsy: **7** tzigane
lake: **7** Balaton **9** Blaten See **13** Neusied-
ler See
measure: ako **4** hold, joch, yoke **5** antal,
itcze, marok, metze **7** huvelyk, merfold
mountain range: **10** Carpathian
people: **6** Magyar
poet: **5** Arany
river: **4** Raab **5** Drave, Maros **6** Danube,
Poprad, Theiss **7** Vistula
Slav: **5** Croat **6** Croatian
weight: **7** vamfont **8** vammazsa
wine: **5** tokay

hunger: **4** long, want **5** belly **6** desire,
famine, starve **7** craving **8** appetite, voracity **9** esurience
abnormal: **7** bulimia **10** polyphagia

hungry: **4** avid, howe, poor **6** barren, hollow, jejune **7** uneaten **8** esurient, hun-
gered **10** avaricious

hunk: dad **4** daud, hump, lump **5** hunch,
piece

hunks: **5** miser

hunt: dig **4** drag, seek **5** chase, chevy,
chivy, delve, drive, hound, probe, quest,
stalk, track, trail **6** chivvy, ferret, follow,
forage, hunter, pursue, search, shikar **11**
inquisition
god of: **5** Ninip **6** Apollo

hunted: **4** game, prey

hunter: **4** hunt **5** jager, yager **6** chaser,
nimrod **7** stalker **8** chasseur, huntsman **9**
sportsman
attendant: **5** gilly(Scot.) **6** gillie
mythological: **5** Orion
Golden Fleece: **5** Jason
patron saint: **6** Hubert

hunting: *cry:* yoi **4** toho **5** chevy, chivy,
hoick **6** chivvy, hoicks, yoicks
game: **6** shikar, venery
horn note: **4** mort

huntsman: **5** jager **6** hunter **7** catcher,
venerer **8** chasseur
changed into stag: **7** Actaeon

Hur's son: Uri

hurdies: **4** hips, rump **8** buttocks

hurdle: pen **4** clew, fold, leap **5** bound
cover, crate, frith, hedge **6** raddle **7** barrier, confine **8** obstacle, surmount **9** enclosure

hurdy-gurdy: **4** lira, rota

hurkle: **5** squat **6** crouch

hurl: **4** cast, dash, haul, howl, hurl, pelt,
roar, send, toss, turn **5** fling, heave, pitch,
sling, smite, throw, twist, whang **6** elance
9 overthrow

hurlement: **6** tumult **9** confusion

hurly: **6** uproar **7** turmoil **9** confusion

hurly-burly: **4** hurl **5** storm **6** tumult,
uproar **8** confused **9** confusion **10**
tumultuous

huron: **6** grison

hurrah: joy **5** cheer, huzza, shout **7**
triumph **8** applause **13** encouragement

hurricane: **4** wind **5** storm **7** cyclone,
prester, tempest **8** chubasco **9** hurricano, windstorm

hurried: See **hurry**.

hurry: ado, hie, run **4** pass, pell, race, rese,
rush, scud, stir, trot, urge, whir **5** drive,
fight, haste, impel, slide, speed, worry **6**
convey, harass, hasten, hustle, scurry,
tumult **7** agitato(It.), dispute, quarrel,
quicken **8** dispatch, expedite **9** agitation,
commotion **10** expedition **11** disturbance,
festination, precipitate

hurst: **4** hill, wood **5** copse, grove **7** hillock **8** sandbank

hurt: **4** harm, maim, pain **5** abuse, blame,
grief, sorry, wound **6** damage, grieve, impair, injure, injury, mittle, scathe, strike **7**
afflict, collide, hurting **8** distress, mischief, nuisance **9** detriment **12** disadvantage

hurtful: bad **4** evil **6** nocent **7** baneful,
malefic, noisome, noxious **10** pernicious
11 deleterious, destructive, detrimental,
prejudicial

hurtle: **4** dash **5** clash, fling, whirl **6** assail, jostle **7** collide **8** brandish

husband: eke, man, rom **4** bond, buck,
chap, keep, mate, save **5** churl, hoard,
marry, store **6** manage, spouse, tiller **7**
consort, espouse, partner, plowman, steward **8** conserve **9** cultivate, economize **10**
cultivator, husbandman
more than one: **9** polyandry
property right: **7** curtesy

husbandman: **4** bond, boor, carl **5** colon
6 farmer, tiller **7** acre-man, husband **8**
agricole **10** cultivator

husbandry: **6** thrift **7** economy **8** managery **11** cultivation
god: **6** Faunus

hush: tut **4** calm, clam, hist, lull **5** allay,
quiet, still **6** soothe **7** appease, repress,
silence

husk: cod, hud **4** bark, bran, coat, hulk,
hull, leam, rind **5** lemma, scale, shack,
shell, shuck, straw, strip **6** colder **7** envelop, epicarp **8** covering, envelope **11**
decorticate

husks: **5** chaff **6** bhoosa

Husky: dog **6** Eskimo

huss: **7** dogfish

hussar: 7 soldier 10 cavalryman
headdress: 5 busby
uniform jacket: 6 dolman
hussy: 4 jade 5 besom(Sc.), gipsy, gypsy, madam, quean 7 drossel 9 housewife 11 housekeeper
hustle: 4 push 5 crowd, hurry, shove 6 bustle, jostle, thrust 7 pushing 8 activity
hustler: 6 peeler 8 go-getter
hut: cot 4 bari, cote, crib, hulk, shed 5 benab, bohio, bothy, cabin, choza, house, hovel, humpy, hutch, lodge, scale, shack, toldo, wurly 6 bohawn, canaba, chalet, gunyah, gunyeh, rancho, shanty 7 bala-gan, bourock, camalig, cottage, huddock, wickiup 8 barabara, chantier
fisherman's: 4 skeo
hermit's: 4 cell
mining: coe
shepherd's: 5 bothy
hutch: ark, bin, box, car, hut, pen 4 coop 5 chest, hoard, hotch, hovel 6 coffer, humped, shanty 7 hunched, shelter 9 in-closure
huzza: 5 cheer, shout 6 hurrah, huzzah 9 roisterer
huzzar: 6 hussar
huzzy: See **hussy.**
hyacinth: 7 greggle 8 bluebell, harebell
hyalite: 4 opal
hybrid: 5 blend 7 mongrel 9 composite
bovine: 7 cattalo
horse and ass: 4 mule 5 hinny
horse and zebra: 7 zebrula, zebrule 8 ze-brinny
zebra and donkey: 7 zebrass
hydrant: 4 plug 6 faucet
hydraulic engine: ram
hydrazoate: 4 azid 5 azide
hydrocarbon: 6 butane, carane, nonane, retene 7 benzene, olefine, pentane
gaseous: 6 ethane, ethene
liver oil: 8 pristane
tree: 7 terpene
hydrocyanic acid: 7 prussic
hydrogen: gas 5 arsin 6 arsine
hydromel: 4 mead 5 aloja 10 melicratum

hydrometer: 9 areometer
hydromica: 4 mica 9 muscovite
hydrophobia: 5 lyssa 6 rabies
hydrophyte: See **aquatic plant.**
hygienic: 8 sanitary
hymenopteron: ant, bee 4 wasp 6 sawfly 7 gallfly 9 ichneumon
hymn: ode 4 sing, song 5 psalm 6 himene, himine, hirmos, hirmus 7 introit 8 canti-cle 11 recessional 12 processional
following psalm: 9 sticheron
funeral: 5 dirge
praising: 4 pean 5 paean
ritual: 8 encomium
tune: 6 choral 7 chorale
victory: 9 epinicion, epinikion
hyoscyamus: 8 narcotic
hyperbole: 12 exaggeration 13 over-statement
Hyperborean sage: 6 Abaris
hypercritical: 7 carping 8 captious 12 overcritical, supercilious
hyphen: 4 band, dash
hypnotic: 6 opiate 8 narcotic 9 soporific 12 somnifacient
hypnotism: 5 sleep 8 hypnosis 9 mes-merism
hypnotist: 6 Mesmer 9 mesmerist
hypnum: 4 moss
hypochondria: hyp 6 megrim
hypocrisy: 4 cant 10 simulation
hypocrite: 6 Levite 7 Tartufe
hypocritical: 4 nice 5 exact, false 7 bi-goted, canting, carping 8 captious spe-cious 9 deceptive, insincere 11 dissem-bling, pharisaical 13 sanctimonious
hypostatic: 5 basic 9 elemental
hypotenuse: 5 slant
hypothesis: ism 6 system, theory 9 postu-late 10 assumption 11 supposition
hypothetical being: ens 6 entity
hypocrisy: 6 deceit
hyrax: 8 procavia
Hyrtacus' son: 5 Nisus
hyssop: 4 mint 11 aspergillum
hysteria: 6 nerves
hysterical: 9 emotional 12 uncontrolled

I

I do not wish to contend: 14 nolo contendere(L.)
I have found it: 6 eureka
I understand: 5 roger
Iago's wife: 6 Emelia
Iberian: 4 Pict
ibex: tur, zac
ibis: 5 guara, stork 9 gourdhead
Ibsen: *character:* Ase 4 Gynt, Nora
  play: 11 Rosmersholm
Icarus' daughter: 7 Erigone 8 Penelope
ice: 4 cool, geal, grue(Sc.), rime 5 chill,
  frost, glace(F.) 6 freeze 7 congeal, diamond, hauteur 10 confection 11 refrigerant, refrigerate
  crystals: 4 snow 5 frost
  floating: 4 berg, floe
  fragment: 5 brash
  glacier: 4 neve 5 serac
  mass: 4 berg, floe
  patch: 4 rone(Sc.)
  pendant: 6 icicle
  sea: 6 sludge
  sheet: 4 floe
ice cream dish: 4 soda 6 frappe, sundae
  7 parfait
ice river: 7 glacier
icebox: 6 cooler 12 refrigerator
icecap: 7 calotte
Iceland: *assembly:* 7 Althing
  bishopric: 5 Holar 8 Skalholt
  capital: 9 Reikjavik, Reykjavik
  coin: 5 aurar, eyrir, krona
  epic: 4 Edda
  giant: 4 Atli
  hero: 4 Bele
  measure: fet 4 alin, lina 5 almud, turma 6
  almenn, almude, ferfet, pottur 7 fathmur,
  feralin, fermila, oltunna, sjomila 9 korn-
  tunna 10 ferfathmur, kornskeppa, thum-
  lungur 11 angjateigur 12 tundagslatta 13
  ferthumlungur
  mountain: 5 Jokul 10 Orafajokul
  volcano: 4 Laki 5 Hekla
  weight: 4 pund 5 pound 11 tunna smjors
ichneumon: 8 mongoose 11 hymenop-
  tera(pl.) 12 hymenopteron
ichnography: map
ichnolite: 6 fossil 9 footprint
ichthyosis: 9 sauriosis
icicle: 7 shoggle
  limestone: 10 stalactite, stalagmite
icing: 7 topping 8 frosting

icon, ikon: 5 image 6 eidola(pl.), idolon,
  symbol 7 eidolon, picture 8 portrait 12
  illustration
iconolater: 9 worshiper
icterine: 9 yellowish
ictus: fit 4 blow 6 attack, stress, stroke
icy: 4 cold 5 gelid 6 arctic, frigid, frosty 8
  chilling
Idaho: *capital:* 5 Boise
  county: Ada 5 Butte, Katah, Lewis
  motto: 12 esto perpetua
  river: 7 Kutenai, Kutenay 8 Kootenai,
  Kootenay
  town: 5 Boise, Nampa 7 Preston 9 Poca-
  tello
ide: orf
idea: 4 idee(F.) 5 fancy, ideal, image 6
  design, figure, notion 7 conceit, concept,
  fantasy, inkling, opinion, project, thought
  8 gimcrack 9 archetype 10 appearance,
  cogitation, conception, impression,
  reflection
  comb. form: 4 ideo
  impracticable: 7 chimera 8 chimaera
  prompting action: 6 motive
ideal: 5 dream, model 6 mental 7 paragon, perfect, Utopian 8 abstract, fanciful,
  standard 9 imaginary, visionary 10 aspiration, conceptual, consummate 12 intellectual
ideate: 5 fancy 7 imagine 8 conceive 9
  prefigure 11 preconceive
identic: 4 same 5 equal
identical: one 4 same, self, very 5 alike,
  equal, samen(Sc.) 8 selfsame 10 equivalent, tantamount
identify: 4 mark, name 5 brand, prove 7
  earmark 9 designate, establish
identity: 4 name 5 unity 7 oneness 8
  sameness 9 exactness 11 homogeneity
  false: 5 alias
ideologist: 7 dreamer 8 theorist 9 visionary
idiasm: 11 peculiarity 12 idiosyncrasy
idiocy: 7 anoesia, fatuity
idiograph: 9 signature, trademark
idiom: 6 phrase 11 peculiarity
idiosyncrasy: way 6 idiasm, manner 11
  peculiarity 12 eccentricity
idiot: oaf 4 dolt, fool 5 booby, dunce 6
  cretin, hobbil, nidget 7 dullard, omadawn
  8 imbecile, omadhuan 9 blockhead, simpleton 10 changeling

idiotic: 4 daft, zany 5 barmy, inane 7 asinine, fatuous, foolish 9 senseless

idle: 4 lazy, loaf, sorn(Sc.), vain 5 dally, empty, shool 6 asleep, cooter, dawdle, futile, loiter, otiant, otiose, unused, vacant 7 aimless, loafing, sluther, useless 8 baseless, faineant, inactive, indolent, slothful, trifling 9 desultory, unfounded, worthless 10 groundless, unemployed, unoccupied 11 ineffectual

idleness: 5 folly 6 vanity 7 inertia 8 flanerie, inaction, laziness 9 silliness 10 inactivity 15 lightheadedness

idler: bum 4 hake 5 drone 6 bodaud, bumble, loafer, stocah 7 faitour 8 faineant, loiterer

idol: god 4 Baal, hero 5 afgod, image, satyr 6 fetish 7 phantom 8 impostor 9 pretender

idolater: 5 pagan 6 adorer 7 Baalite 9 worshiper

idolatrous: 5 pagan

idolize: 5 adore 6 admire, revere 7 worship 8 venerate

idolon: 5 image 6 eidola(pl.) 7 eidolon, phantom 10 apparition

idolum: 7 fallacy 8 phantasm

idoneous: apt, fit 8 suitable 11 appropriate

idyl, idyll: 4 poem 7 eclogue

idyllic: 7 bucolic 8 pastoral

if: si(F., It., L.) 8 granting, provided 9 supposing

i'faith: 5 truly 6 indeed

igneous rock: 4 trap 6 basalt, gabbro 7 granite, peridot

ignite: hot 4 fire 5 fiery, light 6 ardent, kindle

ignition cap: 4 fuse, fuze

ignoble: low 4 base, mean, vile 6 adject, sordid 8 shameful 11 disgraceful 12 dishonorable

ignominious: 4 base 6 odious 8 infamous, shameful 9 degrading 10 despicable, mortifying 11 disgraceful, humiliating 12 contemptible, dishonorable

ignoramus: 4 dolt 5 dunce 6 nitwit

ignorance: 6 agnosy

ignorant: 4 dark 5 green, young 6 stupid 7 artless, unaware, uncouth 8 nescient, untaught 9 unlearned, unskilled, untutored 10 illiterate, unlettered 11 unconscious

ignore: cut 4 omit, snub 5 blink, elide 6 slight 7 neglect 8 overlook 9 disregard, eliminate

Igorot, Igorrote: 6 Bontok 7 Nabaloi 8 Kankanai

   chief: Apo

iguana: 6 lizard 7 tuatara

Iguvine: 7 Umbrian 8 Eugubine

ihi: 4 fish 7 skipper 8 halfbeak 9 stichbird

Ihlat: 8 Sunnites

ijolite: 7 apatite, calcite 8 titanite

ikary: 6 caviar

ikbal: 7 arrival 8 prestige 10 prosperity

ikey: 5 proud

ikon: 5 image 6 symbol 7 picture 8 portrait 12 illustration

ikona: 9 greenhorn, simpleton

ikra: 6 caviar

ilex: 5 holly

Iliad: 4 epic, poem

   character: 4 Ajax 5 Priam 6 Hector 8 Achilles 9 Agamemnon, Cassandra

Ilium, Ilion: 4 Troy

ilk: 4 each, kind, same, sort 5 breed, class, every 6 family

ill: bad 4 evil, harm, poor, sick 5 amiss, badly, wrong 6 ailing, faulty, wicked 7 adverse, ailment, baneful, noxious, trouble, unlucky 8 improper 9 adversity, defective 10 indisposed, iniquitous, misfortune 11 unfortunate

   prefix: mal

ill at ease: 7 awkward

ill-boding: 4 dire 12 inauspicious

ill-bred: 6 hoiden, hoyden 7 plebian, uncivil 8 clownish, impolite, malapert 9 bourgeois 11 impertinent

ill-favored: 4 ugly 9 offensive 10 unpleasant 12 disagreeable

ill-humor: tid 5 anger 7 dudgeon

ill-humored: 5 cross 6 cranky, morose 7 fretful, peevish

ill-natured: 4 dour 5 nasty, surly 6 crabby 7 fretful

ill-tempered: 5 cross, moody 6 crusty 7 bilious

ill-treat: 5 abuse 8 maltreat

ill will: 5 spite 6 animus, malice, mauger 9 hostility

   showing: 7 hostile 8 choleric 9 bellicose, irascible, litigious, wrangling 10 pugnacious 11 belligerent, contentious, quarrelsome 12 disputatious

ill-wisher: foe 5 enemy

illation: 9 deduction 11 inferential

illegal: 4 foul 7 bootleg, illicit 8 unlawful 10 contraband

illegitimate: 7 bastard, bootleg, unusual 8 abnormal, improper, spurious, unlawful, wrongful 9 illogical

illiberal: 6 stingy 7 bigoted 8 churlish 9 hidebound 13 ungentlemanly

illicit: 7 bootleg, illegal 8 improper, unlawful 10 contraband

illimitable: 4 vast 8 infinite 9 boundless 11 measureless 12 immeasurable

Illinois: *county:* Lee 4 Cook, Ogle, Polk 6 Hardin

   town: 4 Pana 5 Alton, Elgin 6 Aurora, Breese, Joliet, Moline 7 Decatur, Wheaten 8 Streator 10 Springfield(c.)

illiterate: 6 unread 8 ignorant, untaught 9 barbarous, unlearned, untutored 10 unlettered

illness: 5 colic 6 malady, morbus 7 ail-

ment, cachexy, disease **8** cachexia, disorder, sickness **9** complaint, distemper **10** affliction, wickedness **13** indisposition
feign: **8** malinger
mental: See **mental disorder**.
illogical: **7** invalid **12** inconsequent
illude: **4** bilk, mock **5** cheat, elude, evade **6** delude, deride **7** deceive
illume: See **illuminate**.
illuminant: gas **9** petroleum
illuminate: **4** fire **5** adorn, flare, light **6** illume, kindle **7** clarify, emblaze, lighten **8** brighten, illumine **9** enlighten, irradiate **10** illustrate
illumination: *device:* **4** lamp **5** torch **7** lantern **10** flashlight
measure: **4** phot
illumine: See **illuminate**.
illusion: **5** fancy **6** mirage **7** chimera, fallacy, mockery, phantom **8** delusion **9** deception **10** appearance
illusive: **4** flam **5** false **6** unreal **7** fatuous **8** illusory **9** deceitful, deceptive, fantasmal **10** fallacious, phantasmal **16** phantasmagorical
illusory: See **illusive**.
illustrate: **5** adorn **7** picture **9** elucidate, exemplify, represent **10** illuminate
illustration: **4** icon, ikon **7** example, exempla(pl.) **8** exemplum, vignette **13** demonstration **15** exemplification
illustrator: **6** artist
illustrious: **5** famed, grand, noble, noted **6** bright, candid, heroic **7** eminent, exalted **8** glorious, renowned **9** honorable **10** celebrated **11** conspicuous **13** distinguished
ilvaite: **6** yenite
image: god **4** copy, form, icon, idol, ikon **5** eikon, image **6** effigy, eidola(pl.), emblem, figure, idolon, statue, symbol **7** eidolon, phantom, picture, portray **8** likeness **9** semblance, simulacre **10** conception, reflection, similitude, simulacrum
good luck: **6** alraun
maker: **10** iconoplast
mental: **4** idea **6** recept **7** concept **8** phantasm **10** conception
rainbowlike: **7** spectra(pl.) **8** spectrum
stone: **5** herma **6** hermae(pl.)
televised: **5** video
wooden: **4** tiki **6** xoanon
image-breaker: **10** iconoclast
image-like: **10** simulacral
image-worshiper: **8** idolator **9** conolater
imaginary: **5** ideal **6** unreal **7** fancied, feigned **8** mythical, notional **9** fantastic, visionary **10** artificial, chimerical, fictitious
imagination: **5** fancy **7** fantasy
imaginative: **6** dreamy, poetic **8** fanciful **9** fantastic
imagine: **4** ween **5** dream, fancy, feign,

think **6** vision **7** picture, suppose, surmise **8** conceive, envision **9** apprehend **10** comprehend, conjecture
imago: bee
imam: **5** calif **6** caliph
last: **5** Mahdi
imaret: **7** hospice **11** caravansary, caravaserai
imbecile: **4** dolt, dote **5** anile, daffy, idiot, moron **6** cranky, dotard, dotish **7** fatuous **9** driveling **10** changeling, half-witted
imbed: fix **5** embed, inset **6** cement
imbibe: sip **4** soak **5** drink, imbue, steep **6** absorb **7** swallow **8** saturate **10** assimilate
imbricate: **5** tiled **6** scaled
imbroglio: **12** disagreement **16** misunderstanding
imbrue: wet **4** soak **5** stain, steep **6** defile, drench **7** moisten **8** saturate
imbue: dye **4** soak **5** steep, tinge **6** imbibe, infuse, leaven **7** animate, ingrain, inspire, instill, pervade **8** permeate, saturate, tincture **9** inoculate **10** impregnate
imburse: pay **10** recompense
imidogen compound: **4** imid, imin **5** imide, imine
imitant: **9** imitation **11** counterfeit
imitate: ape **4** copy, echo, mime, mock **5** mimic **6** follow, repeat **7** copycat, emulate **8** resemble, simulate **9** dissemble **11** counterfeit
imitation: **4** copy, echo, fake, sham **5** dummy, paste **6** parody **7** imitant **9** emulation, facsimile, imitative, schlenter
derisive: **7** mimicry, mockery
fantastic: **8** travesty
imitator: **4** mima **5** mimae(pl.)
immaculate: **4** pure **5** clean **6** candid, chaste **7** correct, perfect **8** innocent, spotless, unsoiled **9** faultless, undefiled, unspotted, unstained, unsullied
immalleable: **10** unyielding
immane: **4** huge, vast **5** great **6** fierce **7** immense, inhuman **9** atrocious, monstrous
immanent: **8** inherent **9** intrinsic **10** indwelling
immaterial: **6** slight **8** trifling **9** asomatous, spiritual **10** impalpable, intangible **13** insignificant, unsubstantial
immatriculate: **6** enroll **11** matriculate
immature: **5** crude, green, young **6** callow, unripe **7** girlish, puerile, untried **8** youthful **9** premature **10** incomplete, unfinished **11** undeveloped
immeasurable: **7** immense **8** infinite **9** boundless, unlimited **10** indefinite **11** illimitable, measureless **12** immensurable
immediate: **4** next **6** direct **7** instant **8** imminent **9** proximate **10** contiguous, succeeding
immediately: now **4** anon **6** presto **8** directly **9** extempore, forthwith, presently

immemorial: 7 ageless, ancient 8 dateless 11 prehistoric, traditional

immense: 4 huge 5 grand, great, large 7 titanic 8 enormous, gigantic, infinite 9 extensive, monstrous 10 prodigious, unmeasured 12 immeasurable

immensurable: See **immeasurable**.

immerge: See **immerse**.

immerse: dip 4 bury, duck 5 bathe, douse, dowse, souse 6 absorb, drench, plunge 7 engross, ensteep, immerge

immigrant: 8 comeling

Israel: 6 halutz 7 chalutz

imminent: 9 impending

immitigable: 10 implacable

immobile: set 4 firm 5 fixed, inert 6 frozen, stable 8 moveless 9 immovable 10 motionless, stationary

immoderate: 4 free 5 undue 7 extreme 9 boundless, excessive, voracious 10 exorbitant, inordinate 11 intemperate 12 unreasonable

immodest: 4 bold 6 brazen, coarse 7 forward, obscene 8 indecent, unchaste 9 shameless 10 indecorous

immolation: 9 sacrifice

immoral: bad 4 evil 5 loose, wrong 7 corrupt, vicious 8 culpable, depraved, indecent 9 dissolute 10 licentious 11 unwholesome

immortal: 6 divine 7 endless, eternal, godlike 8 enduring 9 ceaseless, deathless 11 amaranthine, everlasting 12 imperishable 13 incorruptible

immortality: 8 athanasy 9 athanasia 13 deathlessness 15 everlastingness

immovable: pat, set 4 fast, firm 5 fixed rigid 7 adamant 8 constant, immobile, obdurate 9 steadfast 10 adamantine, stationary

immunity: 7 freedom 9 exemption 11 unrestraint

immunize: 7 vastate 9 inoculate 10 haffkinize

immure: 4 wall 7 confine 8 cloister, imprison 11 incarcerate

immutable: 4 firm 7 eternal 10 invariable, unchanging 11 unalterable 13 unadulterated

Imogen's mother: 9 Cymbeline

imp: bud, elf 4 brat, cion, slip 5 child, demon, devil, graft, rogue, scamp, scion 6 sprite, urchin 7 gremlin, implant, progeny 8 devilkin, folletto, folletti(pl.) 9 hobgoblin, offspring 13 mischiefmaker 15 flibbertigibbet

impact: 4 pack, slam 5 brunt, feeze, shock, wedge, whang 6 stroke 7 impulse

impair: mar 4 blot, harm, hurt, wear 5 break, spoil, waste 6 damage, debase, injure, lessen, reduce, sicken, weaken 7 blemish, impeach, vitiate 8 decrease, enfeeble

impaired: 9 afflicted

impala: 7 rooibok 8 rooyebok

impale: 4 edge, spit 5 spear, spike 6 border, pierce 7 confine 8 encircle, surround

impalpable: 7 elusive 10 immaterial, intangible

impar: odd 7 unequal

impark: 7 enclose

impart: 4 give, lend, tell 5 share, yield 6 bestow, confer, convey, direct, impute, reveal 7 divulge, inspire, instill 8 disclose, discover 10 distribute 11 communicate

impartial: 4 even, fair, just 6 candid 8 unbiased 9 colorless, equitable 12 irrespective 13 disinterested, dispassionate

impassable: 5 solid 10 impervious

impasse: 8 cul-de-sac(F.) 9 stalemate

impassible: 9 impassive, unfeeling 11 unendurable

impassioned: 6 fervid 7 fervent 8 eloquent, feverish

impassive: 4 calm 5 stoic 6 serene, stolid 7 passive 9 apathetic 10 impassible 13 imperturbable

impatient: hot 5 eager, hasty, testy 7 fidgety, fretful, peevish 8 choleric, petulant, restless 9 irascible, irritable

impavid: 8 fearless

impeach: 4 call, harm 6 accuse, charge, hinder, impair, impede, indict 7 appeach, arraign, censure, prevent 9 challenge, discredit, disparage

impeachment: 4 harm 6 damage, injury 8 dishonor, reproach 9 challenge, hindrance 10 accusation, impediment 11 obstruction

impeccable: 9 faultless

impecunious: 4 poor 9 penniless

impede: gum, let 4 clog 5 block, check, choke, delay, estop 6 fetter, forbid, hamper, harass, hinder, retard, stymie 7 impeach, prevent 8 encumber, handicap, obstruct, preclude 9 embarrass

impediment: bar, bur, rub 4 clog, snag 5 hitch 6 defect, malady, remora 7 embargo 8 obstacle 9 detriment, hindrance 10 difficulty 11 encumbrance, impeachment, obstruction 13 embarrassment

impedimenta: 7 baggage

impel: pat 4 blow, goad, move, send, spur, urge 5 drive, feeze, force, hurry 6 compel, excite, incite, induce 7 actuate 8 motivate 9 constrain, encourage, influence, instigate, stimulate

impending: 8 imminent, menacing 9 hindering 11 threatening

impenetrable: 4 hard 5 dense 8 airtight, hardened 10 impervious 11 inscrutable 12 unfathomable

impenitent: 8 hardened, obdurate 11 unrepentant

imperative: 8 pressing, verb form 9 imperious, mandatory 10 commanding, compulsory, peremptory

imperator: 6 leader 7 emperor, general
imperceptible: 10 insensible, intangible 13 inappreciable, indiscernible 17 indistinguishable
imperfect: 4 cull, poor 5 rough 6 faulty, second 9 defective 10 inadequate, incomplete, unfinished
prefix: mal 5 atelo
imperfection: 4 flaw, vice 5 fault 6 defect, foible 7 blemish, default, failing, frailty 8 weakness 10 deficiency 11 shortcoming
imperfectly: 4 half 5 badly
imperial: 5 regal, royal 6 kingly 8 majestic
cap: 5 crown
domain: 6 empery, empire 8 emperies(pl.)
imperil: 4 risk 6 expone, hazard 8 endanger 10 jeopardize
imperious: 6 lordly 7 haughty 8 arrogant, despotic, dominant, pressing 10 commanding, imperative, tyrannical 11 dictatorial, domineering, magisterial, overbearing 13 authoritative
imperish: 6 impair, injure
imperishable: 7 eternal, undying 8 enduring, immortal 9 continual, deathless 11 everlasting 14 indestructible
impermanent: 8 fleeting 9 ephemeral, temporary, tentative, transient 10 evanescent
impersonal: 4 cold 7 general
impersonate: act, ape 4 pose 6 typify 9 exemplify, personify
impersonator: 5 actor 7 actress
impertinence: 4 sass 8 audacity 9 insolence 10 confidence, incivility 11 impropriety, irrelevance
impertinent: 4 rude 5 sassy, saucy 7 ill-bred 8 arrogant, impudent 9 audacious, officious 10 inapposite 12 inconsequent 13 disrespectful
imperturbable: 4 cool 6 placid, serene 8 tranquil 9 impassive 10 phlegmatic
impervious: 5 tight 8 hardened 10 impassable 12 impenetrable
impetition: 6 charge 10 accusation
impetrate: 7 beseech, entreat, procure
impetuosity: 5 haste 6 fougue
impetuous: hot 4 ramp, rash 5 eager, fiery, hasty, heady, sharp 6 abrupt, ardent, fervid, fierce, flashy, sudden 7 furious, hotspur, violent 8 forcible, headlong, vehement 9 impulsive 10 hotspurred 11 precipitate
impetus: 4 bent, birr, fard 5 drift, faird force 6 swinge 7 impulse 8 momentum, stimulus 9 incentive
impi: 8 soldiers, warriors
impiety: 9 blasphemy 11 irreverence, ungodliness
impignorate: 6 pawned 7 pledged
impinge: 6 strike 8 encroach

impious: 6 unholy 7 godless, profane, ungodly 9 atheistic, nefandous, undutiful 10 irreverent 11 irreligious
impish: 6 elfish 7 warlock 11 mischievous
implacable: 6 deadly 9 ferocious 11 immitigable 12 unappeasable 14 irreconcilable
implant: sow 4 root 5 infix, inset 6 enrace, enroot, infuse 7 enforce, engraft, impress, inspire, instill 9 inculcate, inoculate, insinuate, introduce
implement: (see also **tool**): 4 gear 7 enforce, fulfill, utensil 8 complete, material 9 apparatus, appliance 10 accomplish, instrument
ancient: 4 celt 6 amgarn, eolith 9 paleolith
baker's: 4 peel
barbed: 7 harpoon
cleaning: mop 4 swab 5 broom, brush 6 vacuum 7 sweeper
cutting: 5 knife, mower, razor 6 reaper, scythe, shears 8 scissors 9 jackknife 11 pocketknife
enlarging: 6 reamer 7 dilator
furcate: 4 fork
garden: hoe 4 rake 5 mower 6 sickle, weeder
grasping: 5 tongs 6 pliers 8 tweezers
hide cleaning: 6 slater
kind of: 5 dolly 6 fraise, mortar, pestle, rabble 7 mattock, sadiron, scraper
kitchen: pot, pan 5 corer 6 kettle 7 skillet, spatula
lifting: pry 5 lever, tongs
logging: 4 tode 5 peavy, peevy 6 peavey, peevey
nap-raising: 5 tease 6 teasel, teasle, teazel, teazle
printer's: 5 biron, press
reaping: 5 mower 6 reaper, scythe, shears, sickle
shovel-like: 5 scoop, spoon 6 trowel
surgical: 7 scalpel 9 tenaculum
threshing: 5 flail
war: 6 armory, onager, petard
implete: 6 filled 7 replete
implicate: 7 concern, embroil, entwine, involve 10 interweave
implicit: 5 tacit 8 absolute, complete, explicit 12 constructive
implied: 5 tacit 6 hinted 11 inferential
implore: ask, beg 4 coax, pray 5 crave, plead 6 appeal 7 beseech, entreat, solicit 8 petition 10 supplicate
imply: 4 hint 5 infer 6 infold 7 connote, involve, premise, signify 8 comprise, intimate 9 insinuate, predicate 10 comprehend
impolite: 4 rude 5 bluff, crude, rough 7 ill-bred, uncivil 10 indecorous, ungracious, unmannerly, unpolished 12 discourteous 13 disrespectful

impolitic: 6 unwise 10 indiscreet 11 inexpedient, injudicious 12 undiplomatic

import: 5 sense, value 6 convey, denote 7 betoken, meaning, signify 8 indicate 9 substance

tax: 4 duty 6 tariff

importance: 4 bore 6 moment, weight 7 account, gravity 8 prestige 9 dimension 11 consequence 13 consideration

to be of: 6 matter

important: 4 dear, high 5 grave, great 6 urgent 7 pompous, serious 8 eventful, material 9 momentous, ponderous 10 chargeable 11 considerate, fundamental, influential, significant 12 considerable 13 consequential

importunate: 6 urgent 7 teasing 8 exigeant, pressing 9 exigeante 10 burdensome 11 inopportune, troublesome

importune: beg, dun, nag, ply, woo 4 urge 5 plead 6 appeal 7 entreat, solicit 10 supplicate

importunity: 8 business, entreaty

impose: fob 4 dupe, fool, levy, sorn 6 burden, charge, delude, entail 7 blaflum, command, dictate, inflict, obtrude

imposing: big 5 burly, proud 6 august 7 stately 9 grandiose, pyramidal 10 commanding, impressive, obligatory 11 outstanding

imposition: tax 4 duty, levy 5 fraud, gouge, trick 6 burden, chouse 7 penalty 8 artifice 9 deception, imposture

impossible: 13 impracticable

impost: tax 4 duty, levy, task, toll 6 annale, avania, custom, excise, surtax, tariff, weight 7 tribute 8 chaptrel

India: 5 abwab

salt: 7 gabelle

impostor: fob 4 gull, idol, sham 5 cheat, fraud, gouge, quack 6 bunyip 7 empiric, faitour 8 deceiver 9 charlatan, pretender 10 mountebank

imposture: gag 4 sham 5 cheat, fraud, trick 6 deceit, humbug 8 artifice, delusion 9 deception, falsehood 10 imposition

impotence: 7 acratia 8 weakness 10 feebleness

impotent: 6 barren, unable 7 sterile 9 powerless

impound: 5 seize, store 6 freeze 7 collect 11 appropriate

impouring: 6 influx

impoverish: 4 ruin 6 beggar, weaken 7 deplete, exhaust

impoverished: 4 poor 8 bankrupt

impracticable: 10 impossible

impractical: 9 visionary

imprecate: 4 pray 5 curse 6 invoke 8 execrate 10 supplicate

imprecation: ban 4 oath 5 curse 8 anathema 9 blasphemy 10 execration 11 deprecation, malediction

impregnability: 9 fortitude

impregnable: 4 hard 12 inexpugnable

impregnate: 4 soak 6 charge, infuse, leaven 8 fructify, permeate, saturate 9 fecundate, fertilize

impresa: 5 maxim, motto 6 device, emblem 7 proverb

impresario: 7 manager 9 conductor, projector 12 entrepreneur

impress: fix 4 bite, levy, mark, seal, tool 5 affix, brand, delve, infix, press, print, stamp 6 enlist 7 engrave, implant, impress, imprint 9 character, inculcate, influence 14 characteristic

impressed: 4 awed 8 affected

impression: 4 dent, dint, idea, mark 5 fancy, print, stamp 6 effect, signet 7 opinion 8 reaction 10 conception

printing: 6 macule

impressionable: 7 plastic 9 sensitive 10 responsive 11 susceptible

impressive: 5 grand 6 solemn 8 forcible, imposing 9 arresting, grandiose

imprevu: 10 unforeseen

imprimatur: 7 license 8 approval, sanction

imprint: fix 4 dint, mark 5 press, stamp 7 engrave, impress 12 characterize

imprison: 4 cage, jail, seal 5 grate, limit 6 arrest, commit, detain, immure 7 confine, enclose 8 restrain 9 carcerate 11 incarcerate

imprisonment: 6 arrest, duress 7 durance 8 coercion 9 captivity, restraint 11 confinement 13 incarceration

improbable: 5 fishy 8 unlikely

impromptu: 7 offhand 9 extempore 14 extemporaneous

improper: ill 4 evil 5 amiss, undue, unfit, wrong 6 unjust 7 illegal, illicit 8 indecent, shameful, unseemly 9 incorrect 10 inaccurate, indecorous, indelicate, unbecoming 12 illegitimate

improperly: 5 amiss

impropriety: 5 shame 8 solecism 12 impertinence

improve: 4 grow, help, mend 5 amend, edify, emend, moise 6 better, enrich 7 advance, augment, benefit, correct, enhance, perfect, promote, rectify, retouch 9 cultivate, intensify, meliorate 10 ameliorate

improvident: 8 prodigal, wasteful 9 negligent 10 thriftless 11 thoughtless

imprudent: 4 rash 6 unwary, unwise 7 foolish 8 reckless 10 incautious, indiscreet 11 injudicious 12 shortsighted

impudence: lip 4 gall 5 brass, cheek, folly 8 audacity 9 arrogance, assurance, hardihood, insolence 10 confidence, effrontery 11 presumption 13 shamelessness

impudent: 4 bold, pert, rude 5 brash, sassy, saucy 6 brazen 7 forward 8 insolent 9 barefaced, officious 11 impertinent 13 disrespectful

impugn: 4 deny 5 fight 6 assail, resist 7 gainsay 9 insinuate 10 contradict

impulse: 4 urge 5 drift, force 6 impact, motive 7 impetus 8 instinct 9 incentive 11 instigation

blind: ate

characterized by: 7 sensory

divine: 8 afflatus

traveling: 10 wanderlust

impulsive: 5 quick 6 fitful 8 headlong 9 impellent, impetuous

impure: 4 foul, hory, lewd, vile 5 dirty, gross, mixed 6 coarse, filthy, unholy 7 bastard, defiled, obscene, unclean, vicious 8 indecent, inferior, unchaste 10 unhallowed 11 adulterated, incongruous, unwholesome

impurity: 6 defect, fedity 8 solution 9 pollution 10 corruption

impute: 4 give 5 count 6 charge, credit, impart, reckon 7 arraign, ascribe 8 consider 9 attribute

impy: 11 mischievous

in: at 4 amid, into, nook 5 among 6 corner 7 arrived 9 incumbent

a chamber: 8 incamera

a flutter: 7 pitapat

a frenzied manner: 5 amuck

a row: 4 arow 6 alined, serial 7 aligned

a standing position: 7 statant

a vertical line: 5 apeak

accordance with: 8 pursuant

addition: too, yet 4 also, more, plus 5 aside 7 besides

advance: 5 ahead 6 before

another direction: 4 away

any case: 4 ever

as much: 5 since 7 because

capacity of: qua

case: 4 lest

common: 5 alike

company of: 4 with

concert: 8 together

contact: 9 attingent

equal degree: as

every way: 5 fully 6 wholly 7 totally 8 entirely 10 completely, thoroughly

excess: too 4 over

existence: 6 extant

fact: 5 truly 6 indeed 7 de facto(L.)

favor of: pro

few cases: 5 seldom

good season: 5 early 6 betime

great need: 7 straits

manner of: ala

place of: for 5 stead 7 instead

prefix: en, il

regard to: 5 anent

same place: 4 ibid

so far as it is: qua

spite of: 4 over 6 mauger, maugre 7 despite

store: 8 awaiting

that case: so 4 then

the case of: 4 in re(L.)

the center of: 4 amid

the know: hep

the main: 9 generally

the same period: 15 contemporaneous

the time of: 6 during

this: 6 herein

this way: 4 thus

truth: 6 certes, indeed, verily 8 forsooth

what way: how 7 quomodo

year of: 4 anno

inability: 9 impotence 10 incapacity 12 incompetence

to articulate: 7 anaudia

to chew: 8 amasesis

to comprehend: 11 acatalepsia

to name correctly: 9 paranomia

to read: 6 alexia

to speak: 6 anepia

to stand erect: 7 astasia

to swallow: 7 aphagia

to understand speech: 7 aphasia

inaccessible: 12 unattainable 14 inapproachable, unapproachable

inaccuracy: 5 error 7 mistake

inaccurate: 5 loose 6 faulty, unjust 7 inexact 8 improper 9 defective, imperfect 10 unfaithful

Inachus's daughter: Io

inaction: 8 idleness 9 inertness

temporary: 5 pause 6 recess 7 abeyant, respite

inactive: lax 4 dead, idle, slow 5 heavy, inert, prone, slack, still 6 latent, otiose, supine 7 dormant, passive 8 dilatory, faineant, indolent, sleeping, slothful, sluggish 9 quiescent, recumbent, sedentary 10 unemployed

inadequate: bad 4 lean 6 feeble 9 deficient, imperfect 12 insufficient

perilously: 7 Icarian

inadvertence: 10 negligence 12 carelessness, heedlessness 15 thoughtlessness

inadvisable: 4 rash 10 indiscreet

inalterable: 9 steadfast

inamorato: 7 amorado 8 amoretto

inane: 5 empty, silly, vapid 6 vacant 7 fatuous, foolish, idiotic, vacuous 8 trifling 9 doddering, frivolous, pointless, senseless, worthless 11 nonsensical 13 characterless

inanimate: 4 dead, dull, flat 5 brute, inert 6 stolid 8 lifeless 10 insensible 11 insensitive, unconscious

inanition: 7 fasting 9 emptiness

inanity: 7 vacuity 9 emptiness, frivolity, silliness 10 flimsiness, triviality 13 senselessness

inapposite: 10 irrelevant 11 impertinent 13 inappropriate

inappreciable: 10 invaluable 13 imperceptible

inappropriate: 5 inept, undue 6 clumsy 10 unsuitable

inapt: 5 inept 6 clumsy 7 awkward 8 backward 10 amateurish, unsuitable

inarch: 5 graft

inarm: 7 embrace

inarticulate: 4 dumb, mute

inartistic: 9 tasteless

inattention: 7 neglect 9 disregard 10 negligence

inattentive: lax 6 absent, remiss 8 careless, heedless 9 forgetful, negligent, unheeding, ummindful 10 abstracted, neglectful 11 inadvertent, thoughtless 13 inconsiderate

inaugurate: 4 open 5 augur, begin, start 6 induct 7 install 8 initiate 9 auspicate, introduce 10 consecrate

inauspicious: bad 4 foul 7 adverse, ominous 8 sinister 12 unpropitious

inauthentic: 5 false 6 mythic, unreal 8 doubtful, spurious 9 ambiguous, uncertain 10 apocryphal, fictitious

inborn: 6 inbred, innate, native 7 connate, natural 8 inherent 10 congenital

inbreak: 6 inroad 8 invasion 9 incursion

inbred: 6 inborn, innate 10 congenital

Inca: 9 Atahualpa

empire: 4 Peru

god: 5 Iraya

priests: 6 Amauta

ruler's sister-wife: 5 Ccoya

incalculable: 6 untold 9 boundless, countless, uncertain 11 illimitable 12 immeasurable

incandescence: 4 glow, heat

incantation: 5 chant, charm, dawut, magic, spell 6 carmen(L.) 7 sorcery 9 cantation 11 conjuration, enchantment

incapable: 6 unable 11 inefficient, unqualified 12 disqualified

incapacitate: 4 lame 7 cripple, disable 10 disqualify

incarcerate: 4 jail 6 immure 7 confine 8 imprison 9 carcerate

incarnate: 6 embody 8 embodied

incarnation: 6 advent, avatar, Christ 10 embodiment

of Vishnu: 4 Rama

incase: 5 cover 7 enclose 8 surround

incasement: 11 emboitement

incautious: 4 rash 6 unwary 8 careless, heedless, reckless 9 impolitic, imprudent, unguarded 10 indiscreet

incendiarism: 5 arson

incendiary: 4 goon 5 firer 9 seditious 12 inflammatory

incense: 5 anger 6 arouse, enrage, incite 7 provoke 8 enkindle, irritate 9 instigate

burner: 6 censer 8 thurible

spice: 6 balsam, stacte

vessel: 6 censer 7 navette(F.)

incentive: 4 goad, spur 5 spark 6 motive 7 impetus, impulse 8 stimulus 9 influence 10 incitement, inducement 11 provocation 13 consideration, encouragement

incept: 8 commence 9 undertake

inception: 6 origin 9 beginning, reception 10 initiation 12 commencement

incessant: 6 steady 7 endless, eternal 8 constant 9 ceaseless, continual 11 everlasting, unremitting

incessantly: 7 forever 11 continually, unceasingly

inch: 5 uncia

one-thousandth: mil

three-quarters of: 5 digit

inch along: 4 worm

inch forward: 4 edge 7 crowhop

inches: *forty-five:* ell

four: 4 hand

nine: 4 span

39.37: 5 meter

two and one-quarter: 4 nail

inchmeal: 9 gradually

inchoate: 5 begin 8 commence, initiate 9 incipient 10 incomplete

inchpin: 10 sweetbread

incident: 5 event 7 episode 8 accident, casualty, occasion 9 happening 11 contingency

incidental: 6 casual 8 episodic 9 accessory, extrinsic 10 accidental, contingent, fortuitous, occasional 12 adventitious 14 circumstantial

incidentally: 6 byhand, obiter

incinerate: 4 burn 7 combust, consume, cremate

incinerator: 7 furnace 9 crematory

incipient: 6 induct 7 initial 8 inchoate 10 commencing, inaugurate

incise: cut 4 chop, etch, rase 5 carve 7 engrave

narrowly: 9 laciniate

incision: cut 4 gash, slit 5 lance 6 broach, scotch 10 laceration

incisive: 5 acute, sharp 6 biting 7 cutting 9 sarcastic 11 penetrating

incisor: 6 cutter 9 foretooth

incite: egg, hie 4 abet, fire, goad, move, prod, sick, spur, urge 5 impel, sting 6 arouse, compel, entice, excite, exhort, foment, induce 7 actuate, agitate, animate, commove, provoke 8 motivate 9 encourage, instigate, stimulate

incitement: 6 motive 8 stimulus 9 incentive

incivility: 8 rudeness 9 surliness 10 disrespect, effrontery 11 discourtesy 12 churlishness, impertinence 14 unmannerliness

inclemency: 4 asperity

inclement: raw 4 hard, rude 5 harsh, rough 6 severe, stormy 8 rigorous 10 unmerciful

inclination: 4 bent, bias, broo, hang, love, urge, will 5 bevel, fancy, heald, hield, slant, taste, tenor, trend 6 affect, animus, ascent, device 7 conatus, descent, fantasy, hanging, inkling, leaning 8 penchant, tendency 9 acclivity, affection, direction, proneness 10 attachment, proclivity 11 declination, disposition 12 predilection 13 prepossession

incline: apt, bow, dip, tip 4 bend, brew, cant, heel, lean, list, ramp, tend, tilt 5 bevel, grade, heald, hield, humor, shape, slant, slide, slope, trend **6** careen, humour **7** upgrade

inclined: apt, dip **4** fain, wont **5** alist, atilt, prone **6** biased, leaned **7** hanging **8** addicted, affected **11** predisposed

inclip: **7** embrace, enclasp, inclasp

inclose: hem, pen **4** case **5** embar **6** encase, incase **7** environ

inclosed: **8** interior

inclosure: ree(Sc.) **8** sepiment **10** impalement

animal: pen, sty **4** cage, cote, fold **5** hutch, kraal **6** corral

include: **7** contain, embrace, involve **8** comprise, comprize **9** encompass **10** comprehend

incognito: **7** unknown **8** disguise

incoherent: **6** broken **9** illogical **11** incongruous **12** disconnected, inconsequent, inconsistent

income: **4** gain **5** rente(F.) **6** profit, return **7** produce, revenue **8** interest, proceeds, receipts **9** emolument

receiver: **7** rentier

incommensurate: **7** unequal **12** insufficient **16** disproportionate

incommode: vex **5** annoy **6** molest, plague **7** trouble **8** disquiet **9** disoblige **10** discommode **13** inconvenience

incomparable: **8** peerless **9** matchless, unequaled, unrivaled **10** surpassing **11** superlative **15** incommeasurable

incompatible: **9** repugnant **11** conflicting, incongruous **12** inharmonious **13** contradictory, unsympathetic **14** irreconcilable

incompetence: **9** inability, unfitness **10** disability

incompetent: **5** inept, unfit **6** unable **8** helpless **9** incapable, unskilled **10** untalented **11** inefficient, unqualified **12** insufficient

incomplete: **5** blind, crude, rough **6** broken, undone **7** divided, lacking **8** immature, inchoate **9** defective, imperfect, partially **10** unfinished

incomprehensible: **8** abstruse **9** graspless **10** fathomless, mysterious, unreadable **11** unthinkable **12** unimaginable **13** unconceivable **14** unintelligible

inconclusive: **10** indefinite **11** ineffective

incongruity: **9** inharmony **10** dissonance **11** incoherence **12** disagreement **13** inconsistency **14** unsuitableness

incongruous: **5** alien **6** absurd, impure **9** grotesque **10** discordant, unsuitable **12** disagreeable, inconsistent, inharmonious **13** inappropriate

inconsequent: **7** invalid **9** illogical **10** irrelevant **11** unimportant **12** inconsistent **13** inconsecutive

inconsiderable: **5** petty **7** trivial **8** careless, unworthy **10** negligible **13** inconsiderate

inconsiderate: **4** rash **6** unkind **8** careless **9** imprudent, negligent **10** incautious, indiscreet, neglectful **11** improvident, injudicious, thoughtless **14** inconsiderable

inconsistent: **5** crimp **6** absurd **9** dissonant **10** capricious, discordant, discrepant, incoherent, inconstant **13** contradictory **14** irreconcilable

inconsolable: **11** comfortless, heartbroken **12** disconsolate

inconstant: **6** fickle **7** bruckle **8** disloyal, fluxible, variable **9** desultory, faithless **10** capricious, changeable **12** inconsistent

incontestable: **4** sure **7** certain **10** undeniable **11** indubitable

incontrovertible: **7** certain **10** undeniable

inconvenience: **5** annoy **8** disquiet **9** annoyance, incommode **10** discomfort, discommode, uneasiness **11** awkwardness, disturbance **12** discomfiture **13** embarrassment

inconvenient: **7** awkward, unhandy **8** annoying **10** unsuitable **11** troublesome **12** unreasonable

incorporate: mix **4** fuse, join **5** blend, merge, unite **6** absorb, embody **10** assimilate

incorporation: **10** absorption **11** combination

incorporeal: **4** aery **8** bodiless **9** asomatous, spiritual, sprightly **13** unsubstantial

incorrect: bad **5** false, wrong **6** faulty **9** erroneous

incorrigible: **4** hard **9** abandoned

incorruptible: **4** just **6** honest **7** upright

incrassate: **7** stupefy, swollen, thicken **10** inspissate

increase: add, eke, wax **4** eche, gain, grow, rise, rist **5** boost, raise, swell **6** accrue, amount, better, dilate, expand, extend, gather, growth **7** amplify, augment, enhance, enlarge, greaten, inflate, magnify **8** addition, ampliate, flourish, heighten, multiply **9** accession, advantage, aggravate, expansion, extension, increment, intensify **10** accelerate, accumulate, aggrandize, appreciate **11** aggravation, development, enlargement **12** augmentation **13** amplification **15** intensification

in sound: **9** crescendo

possessions: **5** amass **6** enrich

salary: **5** raise

incredulous: **8** doubting **9** faithless, skeptical

incremate: **7** cremate

increment: **4** gain **6** growth, income **8** increase **12** augmentation

increscent: **6** waxing **7** growing **9** enlarging **10** increasing

incriminate: **6** accuse **7** impeach

incrust: **4** coat **5** glaze **6** barkle

incubate: **5** brood

incubator: **8** couveuse **11** eccaleobion

inculcate: **5** infix **6** infuse, instil **7** implant, impress, instill

inculpate: 5 blame 11 incriminate

incumbent: 9 impending 11 threatening

incunabulum: 6 cocoon, cradle, origin 7 infancy 9 beginning 10 birthplace

incur: 8 contract 9 encounter

incurable: 8 hopeless 10 remediless 11 irreparable 12 irremediable 13 irretrievable

incurious: 9 apathetic 11 unconcerned, uninquiring 12 uninterested

incursion: 4 rade(Sc.), raid 5 foray 6 inroad 7 assault, descent, hosting 8 invasion 10 dragonnade

incurved: 7 concave

incus: 5 ambos, anvil

indebted: 8 beholden 9 obligated

indecency: 8 impurity 9 immodesty, indecorum, obscenity 10 indelicacy

indecent: 4 foul 5 gross, nasty 6 coarse, greasy, impure 7 grivois, immoral, obscene 8 grivoise, immodest, improper, unseemly 9 dishonest 10 scurrilous

indecipherable: 9 illegible

indecision: 5 doubt 9 hesitancy 10 hesitation 11 uncertainty, vacillation 12 irresolution

indecorous: 4 rude 6 coarse 7 uncivil 8 immodest, impolite, improper, unseemly 10 unbecoming

indeed: aru, yea 4 awat(Sc.), iwis, ywis 5 truly 6 i'faith 8 forsooth

indefatigable: 4 busy 8 tireless, untiring 9 assiduous 10 persistent, unwearying 11 persevering

indefensible: 11 inexcusable 12 unpardonable 13 insupportable

indefinite: 5 loose, vague 7 inexact, neutral 8 aoristic 9 ambiguous, equivocal, uncertain, unlimited 10 inexplicit 12 inconclusive

pronoun: any, one 4 some

indehiscent fruit: uva

indelible: 4 fast 5 fixed 9 permanent 10 inerasable 12 ineffaceable, ineradicable, inexpungible

indelicate: raw 5 broad, gross 6 coarse, greasy 7 fulsome 8 impolite, improper, unseemly 9 offensive, unrefined 10 indecorous, unbecoming

indemnification: 10 reparation 11 restitution

indemnify: pay 6 recoup 9 reimburse 10 compensate, recompense

indemnity: 7 amnesty 9 exemption 10 protection 12 compensation

indent: jag 4 dent, gimp 5 chase, delve, inlay, notch, press, stamp, tooth 6 bruise, emboss 7 depress

indentation: bay 4 dent, dint, doke, nick 5 bulge, choil, crena, notch 6 crenae(pl.), dimple, recess 8 crenelet 10 impression

indented: 6 dented, jagged, milled 7 notched, sinuous 9 crenelate, impressed 10 undulating

indenture: 5 notch 8 contract 9 agreement

independence: 7 freedom 10 competency

independent: 4 free 5 proud 9 sovereign, uncoerced 11 self-centred 12 self-centered, uncontrolled, unrestricted

independently: 5 apart 10 absolutely

indestructible: 10 inviolable 12 imperishable

indeterminate: 5 vague 8 formless 9 uncertain, unlimited

indetermined: 9 ambiguous, equivocal

index: 4 file, list 5 table 7 catalog 9 catalogue, repertory

India: See also **Hinduism**.

acrobat: nat

agent: 4 amin 5 ameen 6 muktar 8 gomashta, gomastah

air conditioner: 5 tatty

ambassador: 5 vakil 6 vakeel

animal, ox-like: 4 zebu

antelope: 5 sasin 6 nilgai, nilgau 7 chikara, nilghai

apartment: 6 zenana

army officer: 4 naig, naik 6 naigue, naique 7 jemadar, jemidar

attorney: 6 muktar

awning: 9 shamianah

baby: 4 baba

bandit: 6 dacoit

bathing place: 4 ghat 5 ghaut

bazaar: 5 chawk, chowk

bean: urd

bear: 4 balu 5 baloo

bearer: 6 sirdar

bed: 7 charpai, charpoy

bed cover: 9 palampore

bedstead: 7 charpao, charpoy

bill of exchange: 5 hundi

bird: 5 shama 8 amadavat, amaduad 9 amaduvade

blight: 4 soka

boat: 7 almadia, almadie, masoola

body servant: 6 sirdar

boy: 6 chokra, Mowgli

bracelet: 6 sankha

bread: 8 chapatty, chupatty

breakfast: 5 hazri

brick: 6 soorki, soorky 7 soorkee

buck: 5 sasin

buffalo: 4 arna 5 arnee

butter: ghi 4 ghee

buzzard: 4 tesa

cabinet: 6 almura, almyra 7 almirah, almyrah

cannabis: 5 ganja

capital: 5 Delhi

carpet: 4 agra

carriage: 4 ekka 5 bandy, tonga 6 gharri, gharry

caste: Jat, Mal, Meo 4 Ahir, Gola, Mali 5 Dhoby, Sansi 6 Dacoit, Dhanuk, Dhobie, Lohana, Vaisya 7 Agarwal, Brahmin, Dhangar, Vaishya

cavalryman: 5 sowar 6 risala 7 ressala

cedar: 6 deodar

chamber: 4 Kiva 8 Tahkhana

charm: **6** mantra
chief: mir **4** raja, rana **5** rajah **6** sirdar
cigarette: **4** biri
city: See *town* below.
civet: **5** rasse, zibet **6** zibeth
clarinet: **4** been
class: **5** caste
clerk: **4** babu **5** baboo
cloth: **7** dhurrie
coast: **7** Malabar
coin: lac, pie **4** anna, fels, lakh, pice, tara
  5 abidi, crore, paisa, rupee
college: Tol
colonialist: **5** Clive
combining form: **4** Indo
cook: **8** bawarchi
corn: zea
coronation: **8** abhiseka
court official: **5** nazir
cowrie: **5** zimbi
crane: **5** sarus
crocodile: **6** gavial, muggar, mugger, mug-
  gur
crop: **4** rabi
cymbal: tal
dagger: **5** katar
dais: **8** chabutra
dance: **6** nautch **7** cantico
dancer: nat **8** bayadere
deer: **4** axis **5** kakar **6** chital, chitra, sambar, sambur **7** cheetal, cheetul
demon: **4** bhut **5** asura **6** daitya
deputy: **5** nabob, nawab
desert: **4** Thar
devil tree: **4** dita
dialect: **4** Urdu **5** Hindi, Tamil **7** Prakrit
dignitary: **5** rajah
dill: **4** soya
district: **4** Sibi **5** Nasik, Patna, Simla **6**
  Zillah **7** Malabar, Nellore **8** Mofussil
dog: **5** dhole **6** pariah
Dravidian: **5** Arava, Tamil
drink: **4** soma **6** arrack
dust storm: **7** shaitan, sheitan
earth: **5** regur
educated man: **4** babu **6** pundit
educated woman: **7** pundita
elephant: **5** hathi
elephant driver: **6** mahout
epic: **8** Ramayana **11** Mahabharata
fabric: **6** tanjib, zenana
falcon: **6** shahin **7** shaheen
fan: **5** punka **6** punkah
father: **4** babu
festival: **4** Holi, mela
fiber: **6** ambary
fig tree: **5** pipal **6** peepul
flower: **5** lotus
founder of Mogul dynasty: **5** Baber
fruit: bel
garment: **4** sari **5** burqa, saree
god: **4** Deva, Yama **5** Shiva
goddess: **4** Amma **5** Amman
gossip: gup

government: **6** sircar
governor: **5** nazim
grass: **4** kusa **5** kusha, roosa **6** bhabar,
  darbha, doorba
griddlecake: **8** chapatty
grinding stone: **4** mano **6** metate
grove: **5** Sarna
guard: **7** daloyet
guide: **7** shikari **8** shikaree
hall: **6** durbar
handkerchief: **7** malabar
harem: **6** zenana
heiress: **5** Begum
hemp: kef **4** bang, carl, kaif, keef **5** bhang,
  ramie **7** chirata
herb: pie **6** sesame **7** curcuma, tumeric,
  zeodary
hero: **4** Rama
holy: sri **4** shri **5** shree
house: **5** mahal **8** bungalow
instrument: **5** ruana, sarod **7** sarinda
intoxicant: **4** soma
jungle: **5** shola
justice: **7** adawlut
king: **4** Nala, raja **5** rajah
knife: dah
laborer: **4** toty **7** totyman
lady: **7** sahibah
lake: **4** jhil **5** jheel **6** Chilka, Kolair
language: **4** Urdu **5** Hindi, Tamil **6**
  Siouan, Telugu **8** Sanskrit
law opinion: **5** futwa
legal claim: hak **4** hakh
leopard, hunting: **7** cheetah
literature: **7** akhyana
loincloth: **5** dhoti
lord: **4** mian
mahogany: **4** toon **5** toona
mail: dak **4** dawk
mangrove: **5** goran
master: **5** saheb, sahib
meal: ata **4** atta
measure: ady, dha, gaz, gez, guz, jow, kos,
  lan, ser **4** byee, coss, dain, dhan, hath,
  jaob, koss, kunk, moot, para, rati, raik,
  seit, taun, teng, tola **5** bigha, cahar, covid,
  crosa, danda, denda, drona, garce, gireh,
  hasta, krosa, pally, parah, ratti, salay, yo-
  jan **6** adhaka, amunam, angula, covido,
  cudava, cumbha, geerah, lamany, moo-
  lum, mushti, palgat, parrah, ropani, ti-
  pree, unglee, yojana **7** adoulie, dhanush,
  gavyuti, khahoon, niranga, prastha, vitasti
  8 okthabah
merchant: **5** banya **6** banian **8** soudagur **9**
  brinjaree
money: see *coin* above
mountain: **4** Meru **5** Ghats **7** Siwalik,
  Vindhya **8** Suleiman **9** Himalayas,
  Hindu-kush, Nilghiris **12** Neilgherries
mulberry: al; aal, ach **6** alroot
musical instrument: **4** vina **5** ruana
muslin: **5** adati, dorea, doria **6** gurrah **9**
  charkhana

narcotic: **4** bang **5** bhang **7** hashish
native: **5** Hindu, Sepoy, Tamil **8** Assamese **10** Hindustani
nonviolence: **6** ahimsa
peasant: **4** ryot
people: **4** Bhil **5** Kotar **6** Hubshi, Badaga
pheasant: **5** monal **6** monaul, moonal
pipe: **6** hookah
poetic name: Ind
policeman: **4** peon **5** sepoy
priest: **5** mobed, mulla **6** mullah
prince: **4** bana, rana **5** rajah
princess: **4** rani **5** begum, ranee
property: **4** dhan
province: **5** Assam, Bihar **6** Bengal, Gujara, Kerala, Madras, Mysore, Orissa, Punjab **7** Kashmir, Manipur **9** Rajasthan **11** Utar Pradesh **13** Andhra Pradesh, Madhya Pradesh **14** Himachi Pradesh
Punjabi caste: **5** Sansi
Punjabi people: **4** Sikh
queen: **4** rani **5** begum, ranee **8** maharani
race: **5** Hindu **9** Dravidian
rainy season: **6** varsha **7** monsoon
region: **7** Malabar
religion: **5** Islam **8** Buddhism, Hinduism
rice: **4** boro
river: Ai; Dor **4** Kosi, Kusi, Sind **5** Bhimi, Indus, Rapti, Tapti **6** Chenab, Ganges, Kistna, Sutlej **7** Cauvery, Irawadi, Krishna **8** Godavari, Hydaspes, Nerbudda, Vindhyas **9** Irrawaddy **10** Bhagirathi **11** Brahmaputra
rubber: **10** caoutchouc
rule: raj
ruler: **4** rana **5** nawab, rajah
sacred grove: **5** Sarna
saffron: **7** tumeric, zedoary
sage: **6** pandit, pundit
seaport: **6** Bombay, Madras **8** Calcutta
servant: **4** maty **6** bearer **10** mussalchee
shirt: **6** banian
shrine: **6** dagaba, dagoba
silk: **4** muga **6** cabeca
silkworm: eri
snake: **5** krait
soldier: **4** peon **5** sepoy **6** gurkha
spinning wheel: **6** charka **7** charkha
supreme court: **6** Sudder
storm: **5** tufan **7** peesash
sun worshiper: **5** parsi **6** parsee
tapir: **8** saladang
tariff: **6** zabeta
tax: **10** chaukidari
teacher: **4** guru **5** akhun, mulla **6** akhund, mullah, pandit, pundit **7** akhoond
tenant: **4** ryot
title: sri **4** mian, raja **5** sahib, singh **6** sirdar **7** gaekwad, gaekwar, gaikwar, sahibah **8** guicowar **9** ahluwalia
town: **4** Agra, Gaya, Puna, Rewa **5** Adoni, Akola, Arcot, Bhera, Dacca, Daman, Delhi, Girot, Kalpi, Naida, Patan, Patna, Poona, Salem, Simla, Surat **6** Ajmere,

Ambala, Bareli, Baroda, Bhopal, Bombay, Dum-Dum, Howrah, Indore, Jaipur, Lahore, Madira, Madras, Madura, Meerut, Multan, Muttra, Musore, Nagpur, Rampur **7** Aligarh, Benares, Calicut, Cawnpur, Dinapir, Gwalior, Jodhpur, Karachi, Laswari, Lucknow, Rangoon, Rangpur **8** Amritsar, Bhatinda, Bhatpara, Calcutta, Cawnpore, Dinapore, Jabalpur, Kolhapur, Mandalay, Mirzapur, Peshawar, Sholapur, Srinagar **9** Ahmadabad, Allahabad, Berhampur, Berhampir, Bhagalpur, Bungalore, Cuddalore, Darjiling, Gorakhpir, Hyderabad, Kurrachee, Moradabad, Nagapatam, Srirangam **10** Darbhangah, Darjeeling, Haidarabad, Jubbulpore, Rawalpindi, Saharanpur **11** Barrackpore **12** Shahjahanpur, Trichioopoli
tree: bel, dar, lin, sal **4** dita, teak **5** anjan, pipal, salai **6** banyan, deodar **7** majagua
tribe: Ao; Gor **4** Bhil **6** Badaga **7** Sherani, Shirani
turban: **8** seerband
vessel: **4** doni **6** shibar
viceroy: **5** nabob, nawab
village: **5** abadi **6** mouzah
weight: moo, pai, ser, vis **4** dhan, drum, kona, myat, pala, pank, pice, raik, rati, ruay, seer, tank, tola, yava **5** adpao, bahar, candy, catty, hubba, masha, maund, pally, pouah, ratti, retti, tical, ticul, tikal **6** abucco, dhurra, karsha, ruttee **7** chittak, peiktha **8** chittack
wheat: **4** suji **5** sujee
wine: **5** shrab

Indian (see also **India**): red **5** indic **6** savage **9** aborigine
agricultural: **6** Pawnee
Alaska: **5** Aleut
Aleutian: **4** Attu
Algonquin: Sac **4** Cree, Sauk **5** Miami **6** Abnaki, Micmac, Ottawa, Sokoki **7** Arapaho, Mohican, Ojibway, Shawnee **8** Cheyenne, Delaware, Illinois **9** Blackfoot **10** Montagnais **11** Massachuset
American: Aht, Kaw, Oto, Red, Sac, Ute **4** Cree, Dene, Erie, Hopi, Ioni, Iowa, Otoe, Pima, Tana, Taos, Yuma, Zuni **5** Banak, Caddo, Coree, Creek Huron, Kania, Kansa, Keres, Miami, Omaha, Osage, Piute, Sioux, Tinne **6** Abnaki, Apache, Dakota, Kansas, Lenape, Mohave, Mojave, Navaho, Navajo, Nootka, Oneida, Ottawa, Paiute, Pawnee, Redman, Sambos, Seneca, Siwash **7** Abenaki, Amerind, Arapaho, Choctaw, Keresan, Redskin **8** Apalachi, Cherokee, Chippewa, Comanche, Hitchiti, Iroquois, Kickapoo, Onondaga, Pokonchi, Sagamore, Seminole, Shoshone **9** Algonquin, Apalachee, Chickasaw, Winnebago **10** Muskhogean **12** Narragansett
Arawakan: **5** Guana
Arizona: **4** Pima, Yuma **6** Navaho, Navajo

Athapascan: 4 Dene, Hupa 5 Hoopa, Tinne 6 Apache, Navaho, Navajo, Tinneh
blanket: 6 stroud 9 strouding
Bolivia: Uro 4 Iten, Moxo 6 Aymara 10 Chiriguano
Brazil: 5 Bravo 7 Tariana
British Columbia: 7 Gitksan
Caddoan: Ree 4 Adai, Ioni, Waco 6 Eyeish, Hainai 7 Andarko, Arikara 8 Arikaree 9 Nachitoch
Calgary: 5 Sarsi
California: 4 Pomo
Canadian: 4 Cree, Dene 5 Tinne 6 Tinneh 7 Sanetch 9 Athabasca 10 Athabascan
Cariban: 4 Yaos 5 Arara, Trios 6 Caribs, Oyanas 7 Akawais, Aparais, Chaymas, Macusis 8 Arecunas, Bakairis, Woyaways, Yauapery 9 Tamanacos 11 Cumanagotos 12 Maquiritares
ceremonial chamber: 4 kiva
chief: 6 sachem 8 sagamore
child: 7 papoose
Copehan: 6 Wintun
corn: zea 4 samp 5 maize
council: 6 powwow
craft: 5 canoe, kayak 6 dugout
Dakota: Ree
daughter of moon: 7 Nakomis, Nokomis
Delaware: 6 Lenape
female: 5 squaw 6 mahala, mahaly
festival: 8 potlatch
fighter: 5 Boone, Miles 6 Custer
flathead: 7 Chinook
Fuegian: Ona 4 Yahgan 8 Alikuluf
game: 6 canute
Great Lake: 4 Erie 5 Huron
guardian spirit: 5 totem
hatchet: 8 tomahawk
headdress: 7 topknot
Hopi: 4 Moki 5 Moqui
hut: 5 hogan, toldo 6 wikiup 7 wickiup
Iroquois: 4 Erie 6 Oneida, Seneca 7 Wyandot 9 Hochelaga
Keresan: Sia
liquor: 9 firewater
lodge: 5 tepee
man: 4 buck 5 brave, chief 6 sannup
Manitoba: 4 Cree
meal bread: 8 corncake
memorial post: xat 5 totem
Missouri: 5 Osage
moccasin: pac
money: 6 seawan, wampum 7 seawant
Muskhogean: 5 Creek 8 Hitchiti
Nebraska: 4 Otoe 5 Omaha
Nevada: 6 Digger
New Mexico: Sia 4 Tano, Taos 5 Keres
New York: 4 Erie 6 Oneida, Seneca 9 Tuscarora
North Carolina: 5 Coree 7 Buffalo
Northwest: 4 Cree
Oklahoma: 5 Creek, Kansa, Osage 6 Pawnee, Quapaw 7 Choctaw 8 Cherokee

Oregon: 5 Modoc
Orinoco Valley: 9 Guahiribo
Panama: 4 Cuna 6 Guaymi 7 Guaymie
Paraguay: 8 Guayaqui
Paru River: 8 Araquaju
Payaguas: 4 Agaz
Peban: 5 Yagua
peace pipe: 7 calumet
Peru: 4 Ande, Cana, Inca, Inka, Peba, Yutu 5 Boros, Campa, Carib, Panos 6 Aymara, Jibaro, Jiyaro, Kechua, Lamano 7 Quechau
pillar: lat, xat
Piman: 5 Opata
Platte River: 6 Pawnee
pony: 6 cayuse
porridge: 4 samp
potato: 4 yamp 9 breadroot
prayer stick: 4 paho
Pueblo: 4 Taos
Quapaw: 5 Ozark
Quechuan: 4 Inca
Rio Grande: Tao
Salishan: 7 Tulalip
Shoshone: Ute 4 Hopi, Otoe, Utah 5 Piute 6 Paiute 8 Comanche
Sioux: Kaw, Oto 4 Otoe 5 Omaha, Osage 6 Biloxi, Hidata, Saponi, Tutelo
snake dancer: 4 Hopi
sorcery: ob; obe, obi
South American: Ges, Ona 4 Inca 5 Aztec, Carib
spirit: 5 totem 7 Manitou
tent: 5 tepee 6 wigwam
Tierra del Fuego: Ona 4 Agni
token of victory: 5 scalp
Uchean: 5 Uchee, Yuchi
Utah: Ute 5 Piute 6 Paiute
Vancouver Island: Aht 5 Sooke 9 Ehatisaht
Venezuela: 5 Carib 6 Timote 7 Timotex 8 Guaruano
village: 6 pueblo
Wakashan: 6 Nootka
wampum: 4 peag 5 peage
warrior: 5 brave
weapon: 8 tomahawk
Western: Kaw 4 Seri
wigwam: 5 tepee
Wisconsin: Sac
woman: 5 squaw
Xingu River: 5 Aneto
Yucatan: 4 Maya
Yukian: 4 Yuki 5 Wappo 7 Huchnom
Zuni Land: 6 Cibola
Indiana: *and Ohio river:* 6 Maumee
city: 4 Peru 5 Floyd 6 Brazil, Fowler, Marion, Muncie 7 Bedford, Hammond, Laporte 8 Danville 10 Huntington 11 Bloomington 12 Indianapolis(c.), Kendallville 14 Jeffersonville
county: 8 Lagrange
native: 7 Hoosier
indicate: say 4 bode, cite, mark, read,

show **5** argue, augur, point **6** allude, denote, evince, import, reveal **7** bespeak, betoken, connote, declare, display, signify, specify **8** decipher, disclose, evidence, manifest, register **9** designate **10** denominate **12** characterize

indicated: 6 marked, signed **9** betokened

indicating: *chemical group:* azo
literal transcript: sic
succession: **7** ordinal

indication: 4 clew, clue, hint, mark, note, omen, sign **5** proof, token, trace **6** augury, signal **7** auspice, sympton **8** argument, evidence **10** denotation **11** designation **13** manifestation

indicative: 10 expressive **13** argumentative

indicator: 4 dial, hand, sign, vane **5** arrow, clock, gauge, index **6** gnomon, marker **7** indices(pl.), pointer **11** annunciator **15** telethermometer

indicium: 4 mark, sign **5** token **10** appearance, indication

indict: 4 bill, dite **6** accuse, attach, charge, decree **7** arraign, impeach **8** proclaim

indictive: 8 declared **9** appointed **10** proclaimed

indictment: 10 accusation

indifference: 6 apathy **8** coldness, froideur **9** aloofness **10** negligence **11** insouciance **12** carelessness, heedlessness, lukewarmness **13** insensibility, pococurantism

indifferent: ill **4** cold, cool, dead, dram, sick, soso **5** aloof, blase, blaze, shrug, stoic **6** casual, poorly, supine **7** neutral, uneager **8** careless, listless, mediocre **9** apathetic, Laodicean **10** nonchalant, regardless **11** adiaphorous, pocucurante **12** nonessential

indigence: 4 lack, need, want **6** penury **7** beggary, poverty **10** deficiency

indigene: 6 native

indigenous: 5 natal **6** inborn, innate, native **7** endemic, natural **8** homeborn, inherent **10** aboriginal **13** autochthonous

indigent: 4 free, poor, void **5** needy **7** lacking, wanting **8** beggarly **9** destitute, penniless **11** impecunious, necessitous

indigestion: 6 apepsy **7** apepsia

indign: 8 unworthy **10** undeserved **11** disgraceful, undeserving

indignant: 5 angry, irate, wroth **7** annoyed **8** incensed, wrathful **11** exasperated

indignation: ire **4** fury **5** anger, wrath **7** disdain **8** contempt **11** displeasure

indignity: cut **6** insult, slight **7** affront **13** disparagement

indigo: 4 anil, blue
artificial source: **6** isatin
natural source: **4** anil **7** indican

indirect: 4 side **7** devious, oblique **8** circular **9** dishonest **10** circuitous, collateral, misleading, roundabout
expense: **8** overhead

indirectly: 5 aside

indiscernible: 13 imperceptible **17** indistinguishable

indiscreet: 4 rash **5** hasty, silly **6** unwise **7** foolish, witless **8** careless, heedless **9** impolitic, imprudent, unadvised **10** incautious **11** injudicious **12** undiscerning **13** inconsiderate

indiscretion: 5 folly **8** fredaine **10** imprudence

indiscriminate: 5 mixed **7** mingled **9** wholesale **13** heterogeneous

indispensable: 5 basic, vital **7** exigent **9** essential, requisite **10** imperative

indisposed: ill **4** sick **6** ailing **8** unsuited **11** disinclined **12** disqualified

indisposition: ail **6** malady **7** ailment, illness, malaise **8** disorder, sickness **9** distemper **10** discomfort, reluctance **12** disaffection **13** unwillingness

indisputable: 4 sure **7** certain, evident **8** positive **10** undeniable **11** indubitable **12** irrefragable **13** incontestable **14** unquestionable **16** incontrovertible

indissolubility: 8 firmness

indistinct: dim **4** dark, hazy **5** faint, misty, vague **6** cloudy **7** blurred, obscure, shadowy **9** ambiguous, unrefined **10** indefinite **17** indistinguishable

indistinctly: 6 feeble

indite: pen **4** dite **5** write **7** compose **8** inscribe

individual (see also **person**): one **4** self, sole, unit **6** person, single **7** special **8** distinct, selfsame, solitary **9** identical **11** inseparable
combining form: **4** idio
physiological: **4** bion
selfish: **6** egoist
smug: **4** prig

individuality: 5 seity **7** oneness **14** indivisibility, inseparability
rare: **5** seity

individually: 9 severally **10** personally **14** distributively

individuate: 9 undivided **11** inseparable

Indo-Aryan deity: 5 Indra

Indo-China: *dialect:* ao
kingdom: **4** Anam **5** Annam
language: Ao, Hu, Wa; Aka, Lai, Lao, Sai, Tai, Yao **4** Bama, Mrus, Shan, Thai **7** Burmese
linguist stock: Tai
native: see *people* below
people: Mru, Tai **4** Naga
race: see *people* above
region: **4** Laos **5** Annam
river: Te
tree: eng, mee

Indo-European: 4 Slav **5** Aryan

Indo-Iranian: 5 Aryan

Indo-Portuguese: *Christian half-caste:* 5 Topas, Topaz 6 Topass
measure: 5 covid 6 covido
indoctrinate: 5 imbue, teach, tutor 7 educate 8 instruct
indolence: 5 scorn, sloth 7 inertia, languor
indolent: 4 idle, lazy 5 inert 6 otiose, supine 7 dronish 8 inactive, slothful, sluggish
indomitable: 10 invincible 11 intractable 13 unconquerable
Indonesia: *base:* Lae
capital: 7 Jakarta
Indian: Ata
island: 4 Bali, Java 5 Timor 6 Flores, Lombok 7 Madoera, Sumatra 8 Soembowa 9 New Guinea
Luzon: 6 Igorot
market: 5 pasar
measure: 4 depa 5 depoh
news agency: 5 Aneta
people: 6 Tapiro
race: 4 Dyak 6 Battak, Bontok, Ifugao, Igorot, Manobo 7 Lampong
sea gypsy: 6 selung
shop: 4 toko
tribe: Ata 4 Atta
weight: 6 soekoe
indorse: See **endorse**.
Indra: 5 Sakka, Sakra
elephant: 8 Airavata
heaven capital: 9 Amaravati
indubious: 7 certain
indubitable: 4 sure 7 assured, certain, evident 8 apparent 10 infallible, undeniable 12 irrefragable 13 incontestable 16 incontrovertible
induce: get 4 draw, lure, urge 5 infer, tempt 6 elicit, suborn 7 actuate 8 persuade 9 encourage, influence
induced: led 5 moved, urged 6 caused 7 allured, engaged, enticed, incited 8 impelled 9 motivated, persuaded 10 instigated
inducement: 4 bait 5 prize 6 motive, reason 9 incentive, influence 10 enticement 13 consideration
induct: 5 enrol 6 enlist, enroll 7 install 8 initiate 9 introduce 10 inaugurate
inductile: 10 inflexible, unyielding
induction: 8 entrance 9 accession, deduction 10 initiation 12 commencement, introduction
indue: 5 endow 6 assume, clothe, invest 7 furnish
indulge: pet 4 cade, feed, waly 5 favor, humor, wally 6 cocker, favour, foster, humour, pamper, please 7 cherish, gratify
in antics: 7 skylark
in fault finding: 5 cavil
in recreation: 4 play
in revelry: 5 roist

to excess: 6 pamper
indulgence: 5 favor, spree 6 favour 8 clemency, humoring 9 tolerance 13 gratification 17 self-gratification
indulgent: 4 easy, fond, good, kind, mild 7 lenient 8 tolerant 9 compliant 10 charitable
indurate: 5 inure 6 harden 9 calloused
indurated: 4 hard 5 inure 7 callous, scleral 8 hardened, obdurate, scleroid, stubborn 9 sclerotic
Indus tribesman: Gor
industrial magnate: 6 tycoon
industrious: 4 busy 6 active 7 zealous 8 diligent, sedulous 9 assiduous 11 painstaking 13 indefatigable
industry: 5 labor, skill 8 business 9 assiduity, diligence, ingenuity 10 occupation
indweller: 7 denizen 9 sojourner 10 inhabitant
indwelling: 8 immanent, inherent 9 immanence
inearth: 4 bury 5 inter
inebriacy: 11 drunkenness 12 intemperance
inebriate: sot 5 drunk 6 excite 7 ebriate 8 drunkard 9 stupefied 10 exhilerate, intoxicate 11 intoxicated
inebriated: 5 drunk
ineffable: 11 unspeakable, unutterable 13 indescribable, inexpressible 15 unpronounceable
ineffaceable: 9 indelible 12 ineradicable
ineffectively: 6 feebly
ineffectual: 4 dead, idle, vain, weak 6 futile 7 useless 8 hopeless, nugatory 9 fruitless, frustrate 10 unavailing 11 inefficient 13 inefficacious
inefficient: 4 poor 6 unable 7 useless 11 incompetent
inelastic: 4 limp 10 inflexible, unyielding
inelegant: 6 vulgar 7 awkward, blatant 9 graceless
inept: 4 dull, slow 5 unfit 6 absurd, clumsy 7 awkward, foolish 8 backward, unsuited 10 unbecoming, unsuitable 11 incompetent 13 inappropriate
inequal: 5 rough 6 uneven 7 unequal
inequality: 4 odds 9 disparity, diversity 10 unevenness 13 disproportion
inequity: 9 injustice 10 unfairness
ineradicable: 7 lasting 9 indelible, permanent 12 ineffaceable
inerrable: 8 unerring 10 infallible
inerrant: 8 unerring 10 infallible
inerratic: 5 fixed 7 settled 11 established
inert: 4 dead, dull, lazy, slow 5 still 6 stupid, supine, torpid 7 passive 8 immobile, inactive, indolent, lifeless, slothful, sluggish 9 apathetic, lethargic 10 motionless, phlegmatic
inertia: 5 sloth 8 idleness 9 indolence
inesculant: 8 inedible

inessential: 9 extrinsic 11 unimportant
inestimable: 9 priceless 10 invaluable 12 incalculable
inevitable: due 5 fated 7 certain, fateful 11 ineluctable, unavoidable
inexact: 4 free 5 rough 10 inaccurate
inexorable: 4 grim 5 stony 6 strict 7 ominous 8 rigorous 9 unbending 10 inflexible, relentless, unyielding 11 unrelenting
inexorability: 5 rigor
inexpedience: 6 unwise 9 imprudent 10 indiscreet 11 inadvisable 12 unprofitable 15 disadvantageous
inexpedient: 6 unwise 9 impolitic, imprudent 10 indiscreet 11 inadvisable, injudicious 12 unprofitable 15 disadvantageous
inexpensive: 5 cheap 6 frugal
inexperienced: raw 5 crude, green, naive, young 6 callow 7 untried 8 inexpert 10 amateurish
inexpert: 5 green 9 unskilled
inexplicable: 9 ambiguous, enigmatic 12 supernatural 13 preternatural
inexpressible: 8 nameless 9 ineffable 11 unutterable
inexpressive: 4 dull, dumb 13 unintelligent
infallible: 4 sure 7 certain 8 inerrant, unerring 9 inerrable, unfailing 11 indubitable
infamous: 4 base 6 bloody, odious 8 shameful 9 nefarious 10 detestable 11 ignominious 12 contemptible
infamy: 5 stain 6 baffle, defame 8 disgrace, dishonor, reproach 10 opprobrium
infancy: 10 incunabula(pl.) 11 incunabulum
infant: 4 babe, baby 5 child, minor 7 bambino, chrisom 8 bantling 9 foundling
murder: 11 infanticide
infantile paralysis: 13 poliomyelitis
infantryman: 6 doggie 7 dogface 8 fusilier 9 musketeer
infare: 12 housewarming
infatuate: 5 besot 6 befool 9 captivate
infatuated: mad 4 fond 6 engoue 7 engouee 8 enamored 9 enamoured
infatuatedness: 7 fatuity
infatuation: ate 4 rave 5 craze, folly 6 beguin 9 engoument 10 engouement
infect: 5 taint 6 canker, defile, poison 7 pollute 11 contaminate
infectious: 8 catching 9 vitiating 12 demoralizing, pestilential
infelicitous: 7 unhappy 11 unfortunate
infelicity: 6 misery 10 misfortune 11 unhappiness 12 wretchedness
infer: 4 hint 5 drive, educe, guess, imply 6 adduce, deduce, derive, gather 7 surmise 8 conclude, construe
inferal: 7 stygian
inference: 9 corollary, deduction 10 assumption, conclusion, derivation 11 consequence
inferential: 7 implied 8 illative 9 deductive
inferior: bad 4 base, cull, less, poor 5 baser, below, lower, minor, petit, petty, snide, worst 6 cagmag, common, feeble, impure, lesser, nether 7 cheaper, humbler, unequal 8 mediocre 9 underling 10 inadequate 11 subordinate 12 contemptible 13 insignificant
infernal: 7 avernal, hellish, satanic, stygian 8 all-fired, damnable, devilish, diabolic 9 tartarean 10 acherontic, demoniacal, diabolical
inferno: 4 fire, hell
infertile: 4 poor 6 barren 7 sterile
infest: vex 5 beset, haunt 6 plague 7 overrun, torment
infester: 8 nuisance
infidel: 5 deist, pagan 6 giaour, Kaffir, paynim 7 atheist, skeptic 8 agnostic 10 unbeliever 11 freethinker
infiltrate: 4 leak, seep
infinite: 6 Ananta 7 endless, immense 9 boundless, countless, limitless, unlimited 11 everlasting, illimitable, measureless 12 immeasurable, interminable
absorption into: 7 nirvana
infinitesimal: 4 tiny 5 small 6 atomic, minute 10 evanescent
infinity: 4 olam 8 eternity
infirm: old 4 lame, weak 5 anile, crank, crazy, frail 6 cranky, feeble, senile, sickly 7 brittle, casalty, caselty, cazelty, craichy, dowless, dwaible, dwaibly, fragile 8 cassalty, casselty, decrepit 9 doddering 10 irresolute 11 debilitated, vacillating
infirmary: 8 hospital
infirmity: 4 vice 7 ailment, disease, failing, frailty 8 debility, sickness, weakness 10 feebleness
infirmness: 8 weakness
infix: 5 inset 6 insert 7 engrave, implant, impress, ingrain, instill 9 inculcate
inflame: 4 boil, fire, goad, heat, stir 5 anger, blain, chafe 6 anneal, arouse, enrage, excite, kindle, madden, rankle, redden 7 inflame 8 enkindle, irritate 10 exasperate
with love: 6 enamor
with rage: 6 madden
inflamed: red 5 angry, fiery 6 ablaze
inflaming: 7 burning
inflammable: 5 fiery 6 ardent, tinder 7 bitumen, piceous 9 excitable, irascible, irritable 10 accendible 11 combustible
inflammation: 4 fire 10 combustion, phlegmasia 13 conflagration
kind of: 4 gout 5 felon 6 iritis, omitis, otitis 7 coxitis, gonitis, rickets 8 adenitis, cystitis, myositis, rachitis, sarcitis 9 arthritis, gastritis, phlebitis, rhachitis 12 encephalitis 13 poliomyelitis

inflate: 4 blow, fill 5 bloat, elate, swell 6 aerify, dilate, emboss, expand, tumefy 7 bombast, distend 8 increase

inflated: 4 blew 5 blown 6 elated, turgid 7 aerated, bellied, bloated, bombast, dilated, fustian, pompous, swollen 8 expanded 9 bombastic, distended, flatulent, plethoric

inflect: bow 4 bend 5 curve 7 deflect 8 modulate

inflection: 4 tone
of words: 8 paradigm

inflex: 4 bend 7 inflect

inflexibility: 8 acampsia

inflexible: 4 dour, hard 5 eager, rigid, stiff, stony 6 strict 7 adamant 8 granitic, obdurate, rigorous 9 immovable, inelastic, unbending 10 implacable, inexorable, relentless 14 uncompromising

inflict: 4 deal 5 wreak 6 impose
great pain: 7 torture
vengeance: 5 wreak

infliction: 7 scourge

inflorescence: 6 raceme

inflow: 6 influx, infuse

influence: win 4 bale, coax, egis, hank, heft, lead, move, pull, rule, sway 5 bribe, force, impel, lobby 6 affect, aspect, compel, effect, govern, induce, infuse, leaven, miasma, motive, sphere 7 attinge, attract, bearing, command, control, gravity, impress, inspire, mastery 8 hegemony, persuade, prestige, reaction 9 authority 10 ascendancy, ascendency, attraction, inducement 13 consideration
by fixed idea: 6 obsess
by reward: 5 bribe
region of: 5 orbit 6 sphere

influenced: 6 biased 8 affected
easily: 7 pliable

influential: 5 grave 6 potent 8 forcible 9 effective, important, momentous

influenza: flu 5 virus 10 coqueluche

influx: 4 tide 6 inflow 7 illapse 9 affluence, influence, inpouring

infold: lap 4 fold, wrap 5 clasp, twine 6 employ, enwrap 7 embrace, envelop 8 envelope

inform: 4 post, tell 5 train 6 advise, notify, preach 7 apprise, apprize, educate, lighten 8 acquaint, instruct 9 advertise 11 communicate

informal: 8 sociable 10 colloquial 13 unceremonious 14 unconventional
conversation: 4 chat

information: 4 data(pl.), dope, news, word 5 aviso, datum 6 notice 7 tidings 9 direction, knowledge 11 instruction
condensed: 6 digest
detailed: 7 dossier
giver: spy 4 fink 5 stool 7 stoolie 8 informer, squealer, telltale 10 tattletale 11 stoolpigeon
personal: 7 dossier

informed: up; hep, hip 4 wise 5 aware 6 posted 7 knowing 8 apprised 11 enlightened

informer: spy 4 fink, tout 5 stool 6 canary, gossip, pigeon, teller 7 delater, delator 8 observer, squealer, telltale 9 informant 10 discoverer, talebearer
military: spy 5 agent

infortune: 4 Mars 6 Saturn 7 Mercury 10 misfortune

infra: 5 after, below, under

infraction: 6 breach 8 trespass 10 intrustion 12 encroachment, infringement 13 transgression

infrequency: 6 rarity 8 rareness, solitude 9 isolation 12 uncommonness

infrequent: 4 rare 6 scarce, seldom, sparse 8 sporadic, uncommon, unwonted 10 occasional

infrequently: 6 rarely, seldom 12 occasionally

infringe: 6 defeat, refute 7 confute, destroy, intrude 8 encroach, trespass 9 frustrate
upon: 7 violate

infringement: 6 breach 8 trespass 9 violation 10 infraction 13 transgression 14 nonfulfillment

infuriate: vex 6 enrage, madden 7 enfelon

infuscate: 6 darken 7 obscure

infuse: 5 spoil, steep 6 aerify 7 engrain, implant, instill 9 inculcate, influence, insinuate, introduce

ingang: 5 porch 8 entrance 10 intestines

ingeminate: 6 repeat 8 redouble 9 reiterate

ingenious: 4 cute, fine 5 acute, dedal, sharp, smart, witty 6 adroit, clever, crafty, daedal, gifted, subtle 7 cunning 8 dedalian, enginous, skillful, talented 9 daedalian, deviceful, inventive 11 intelligent, resourceful

ingeniousness: 5 skill 8 artifice

ingenuity: art 7 address, cunning 8 artifice 10 adroitness, cleverness 11 originality 13 inventiveness

ingenuous: 4 free, naif 5 frank, naive, noble, plain 6 candid, honest, innate, simple 7 artless, sincere 8 freeborn, innocent 9 guileless 10 unaffected, unreserved 15 unsophisticated

ingenuousness: 7 naivete 9 innocence

ingest: eat 7 swallow

ingle: 4 fire 5 blaze, flame 9 fireplace

inglenook: 11 cornerstone

ingleside: 8 fireside

ingluvies: 4 craw, crop

ingoing: 8 entrance

ingot: *metal:* gad, pig
worker: 6 barman

ingrained: 6 imbued, innate, native 7 inhered 9 saturated 10 inveterate

ingratiate: 4 fawn 7 commend, flatter 9 insinuate, introduce

ingredient: 7 element 9 component 11 constituent
baking: 4 alum, soda 5 yeast
cough-syrup: 8 glycerin
facial: 5 cream, rouge 6 powder 7 lanolin 8 lanoline
incense: 6 stacte
ink: 6 tannin
varnish: lac 5 drier, resin, rosin
ingress: 4 adit 5 entry 8 entrance
ingrowing nail: 7 acronyx
inhabit: 5 dwell 6 occupy, people, settle 7 possess 9 establish
inhabitant: cit 6 inmate, native, people, tenant 7 citizen, denizen, dweller 8 habitant, resident
desert: 4 Arab 5 nomad
earliest known: 9 aborigine
foreign: 5 alien 10 alienicola
local: 6 native
moon: 8 selenite
northern: 11 septentrion
suffix: ese, ite
inhabited: 5 lived 7 dwelled, habited, peopled 9 populated
inhabiting: *caves:* 7 spelean 8 spelaean
grove: 7 nemoral
island: 7 nesiote
lake: 9 lacustral
sea: 7 pelagic
inhale: 4 draw 7 attract, breathe, respire 9 embreathe
inharmonious: 6 absurd, atonal 7 jarring 9 dissonant, unmusical 10 discordant 11 conflicting 12 antagonistic
inhere: 6 belong, innate 7 ingrain
inherent: 6 inborn, innate 7 infixed 8 immanent 9 essential, immanence, intrinsic 10 indwelling, subsistent 13 indispensable
inheritable: 10 hereditary
inheritance: 6 legacy 8 heirship, heredity, heritage 9 cleronomy, heritance
by first-born: 13 primogeniture
portion: 8 legitime
restricted: 10 entailment
Scotch law: 5 annat
seizer: 6 abator
inherited: 6 native
inheritor: 4 heir 7 heiress, heritor, legatee
inheritrix: 7 heiress
inhibit: 4 curb 5 check 6 forbid, hinder 8 prohibit, restrain 9 interdict
inhibition: ban, bar 7 embargo 9 restraint 11 prohibition 12 interdiction
inhuman: 4 fell 5 cruel 6 brutal, savage 7 beastly, bestial, brutish 8 devilish 9 barbarous, bloodless, ferocious 10 diabolical
inhumane: 5 cruel 6 brutal
inhumanity: 7 cruelty 9 barbarity
inhume: 4 bury 5 inter 6 entomb 7 deposit
inimical: 6 averse, frosty 7 hostile 8 con-

trary 9 repugnant 10 unfriendly 11 unfavorable
iniquitous: bad, ill 5 wrong 6 sinful, unjust, wicked 9 nefarious
iniquity: sin 4 evil, vice 5 crime, guilt 8 darkness 9 injustice 10 wickedness
initial: 5 first 6 letter 7 opening 8 entrance, monogram 9 beginning, incipient 10 commencing, elementary
design of: 8 monogram
initiate: 4 head, open 5 admit, begin, enrol, start 6 enroll, ground, induct 7 install, instate 8 commence, inchoate 9 introduce, originate 10 inaugurate
initiation: 9 admission, beginning, induction 10 admittance, introduced 12 commencement
initiative: 5 getup 6 energy 8 aptitude, gumption, petition
injection: 4 hypo 5 enema
injudicious: 6 unwise 9 impolitic, imprudent 10 indiscreet 11 inexpedient
injunction: 4 hest, writ 5 order 6 behest, charge 7 mandate, precept, process 9 direction
injured: 9 aggrieved
injury: ill, mar 4 bane, evil, harm, hurt, loss, risk, scar, tort 5 burst, chafe, wound, wrack, wrong 6 damage, deface, lesion, mayhem, scathe, trauma 7 hurting, scratch 8 crepance, hardship, nuisance, traumata(pl.) 9 contusion, detriment, injustice 10 aggression, disservice, impairment 11 displeasure, impeachment 12 disadvantage
pert. to: 5 noxal
injustice: 5 wrong 6 injury 8 hardship, inequity, iniquity 9 grievance 10 imposition, unfairness
ink: 7 blacken 8 millrynd
pert. to: 10 atramental
inkling: 4 hint, idea 5 rumor, scent 6 desire, report 7 glimpse 10 glimmering, intimation 11 inclination
inky: 5 black 9 cimmerian 11 atramentous
inlaid: 6 mosaic 9 champleve, decorated
inland: 8 domestic, interior
sea: 4 Aral 5 Black
inlay: 5 adorn, couch 6 insert 7 enchase 8 ornament 9 marquetry
work: 6 mosaic 9 certosina, certosino, champleve
inlet: oe; arm, bay, cay, geo, gio, ria 4 cove, hope, rias(pl.), slew, sloo, slue 5 admit, bayou, bight, creek, fiord, fjord, firth, fleet, haven, inlay, sound 6 estero, slough, strait 7 estuary, orifice 8 entrance
inmate: 5 guest, lifer 6 termer 8 domestic, occupant, prisoner 10 inhabitant
harem: oda
inmost: 8 intimate 9 innermost
inn: pub 4 host, khan 5 fonda, hotel, house, serai, tambo, venta 6 fonduk, har-

bor, hostel, hostry, imaret, public, tavern 7 albergo, auberge, boliche, fondaca, fondouk, fonduck, gasthof, harbour, hospice, hostage 8 choultry, gasthaus, hostelry, wayhouse 9 hosthouse 10 harbergage, herbergage 11 caravansary 12 caravanserai

innards: 4 guts 7 numbles 8 entrails

innate: 4 born 6 inborn, inbred, inhere, native 7 connate, natural 8 inherent 9 ingrained, intrinsic 10 congenital, hereditary 11 instinctive 14 constitutional

inner: ben 5 ental 6 inside, inward 8 esoteric, interior, internal

comb. form: ent 4 ento 5 ental

innermost: 6 inmost

innet: 7 ensnare

Innisfail: 4 Eire, Erin 7 Ireland

innkeeper: 4 host 5 cheap 7 hostler 8 boniface, caupones, traiteur 10 aubergiste

innocence: 6 purity 7 naivete 11 sinlessness 13 guiltlessness

innocent: 4 free, naif 5 bluet, naive 6 chaste, dovish, simple 7 artless, chrisom, cleanly, upright 9 blameless, childlike, guileless, guiltless, ingenuous, stainless 10 immaculate, unblamable 12 simpleminded 15 unsophisticated

Hebrew: 8 zaccheus 9 zacchaeus

innocuous: 8 harmless, innocent 9 innoxious 11 inoffensive, unoffending

innovation: 6 novity 7 novelty

innuendo: 4 clue, hint, slur 8 allusion 10 intimation 11 implication, insinuation

innumerable: 4 many 6 legion, myriad

Ino's grandfather: 6 Agenor

inoculate: 6 immune 7 engraft, implant

inodorous: 8 odorless 9 scentless

inoffensive: 8 harmless 9 innocuous

inoperative: 4 dead

inopinate: 10 unexpected

inopportune: bad 8 ill-timed, untimely 10 malapropos 11 importunate 12 unseasonable

inorb: 8 encircle

inordinate: 5 undue 8 all'fired 9 excessive 10 disorderly, immoderate 11 unregulated 12 unrestrained

inorganic: 7 mineral

inquest: 5 quest 6 search 7 inquiry 11 examination 13 investigation

official: 7 coroner

inquiet: 6 uneasy 7 disturb 8 disquiet, restless 9 disturbed

inquire: ask, esk(Sc.) 4 seek 5 frayn, price, query, spere 6 demand, frayne, harken 7 examine, hearken 8 question 11 interrogate, investigate

inquirer: 5 asker 6 seeker 7 zetetic 8 searcher

inquiring: 7 curious

inquiry: 5 query 6 examen 7 examine 8

question, research 11 examination 13 investigation

for lost goods: 6 tracer

inquisition: 4 hunt 6 search 11 examination 13 investigation

inquisitive: 4 nosy 5 nosey 6 prying 7 curious 8 meddling 10 meddlesome

inquisitiveness: 9 curiosity

inquisitor: 5 prier 6 tracer 8 examiner

inroad: 4 raid 5 foray 6 breach 8 invasion 9 incursion, irruption 12 encroachment

insane: mad 4 daft, luny 5 balmy, crazy, daffy, loony, manic 6 cranky, crazed 7 frantic, furious 8 bughouse, demented, deranged, distract, frenetic 9 delirious, phrenetic, psychotic

insanity: 5 folie, mania 6 frenzy, lunacy 7 madness, vesania 8 delirium, dementia 9 psychosis 10 aberration, alienation 11 derangement

temporary: 7 amentia

insatiable: 6 greedy 9 voracious

insatiate: 10 insatiable 11 unsatisfied

inscribe, enscribe: 4 etch 5 delve, enter, stamp, write 6 blazon, enroll, indite, scroll 7 ascribe, engrave 8 dedicate, describe 9 character 12 characterize

inscribed: 8 lettered 9 dedicated

on stone: 10 lapidarian

with Teutonic characters: 5 runed

inscription: 6 legend 7 epigram, writing 8 epigraph 11 description 14 superscription

appropriate: 5 motto

end of book: 8 colophon

explanatory: 6 tituli(pl.) 7 titulus

on coins: 5 sigla

tomb: 7 epitaph

inscrutable: 6 secret 10 mysterious 12 impenetrable, inexplorable, unfathomable 16 incomprehensible

insculpture: 7 carving 11 inscription

insect: ant, bee, bug, fly 4 flea, gnat, goga, gogo, lice, mite, moth, tick, wasp 5 emmet, gogga, roach 6 beetle, earwig, mantis, spider, weevil 7 cricket, katydid, termite 9 bumblebee, centipede

adult: 5 imago

destructive: 5 scale 7 termite 8 predator

genus of: 4 nepa

hymenopterous: ant, bee 4 wasp 6 sawfly 7 gallfly 10 ichneumons

immature: 4 pupa 5 larva 6 larvae(pl.) 9 chrysalis

kind of: dun, loa 5 aphid, aphis, bicho, borer 6 cicada, earwig, tremex, tsetse, vermin 7 attacus, Diptera, stinger 9 centipede, ephemeral

long-legged: 5 emesa

order: 7 diptera 17 palaeodictyoptera

organ: 8 plantula 9 plantulae(pl.)

parasitic: 4 lice 5 louse

part of: 4 nota 5 chirr, media, palps 7

antenna **8** pronotum, tentacle
pert. to: **11** entomologic
plate: **6** scutum
science: **10** entomology
secretion: lac
small: **4** flea, gnat, mite **5** aphid, aphis, micro, midge **6** garfly **8** bullhead
social: ant, bee **5** emmet
stage: **4** pupa **5** imago, larva **6** instar **9** chrysalis
stinging: ant, bee **4** wasp **6** hornet **7** sciniph **12** yellowjacket
trap: web
winged: bee **4** wasp **6** hornet **12** yellowjacket
wingless: **4** flea **6** aptera(pl.)

insecticide: **9** hellebore

insecure: **5** eemis, immis, loose, risky, shaky **6** infirm, unsafe, unsure **7** casalty, caselty, cazelty **8** cassalty, casselty, perilous, unstable **9** dangerous, hazardous **10** precarious

insecurity: **5** peril

insee: **8** foretell

inseminate: sow **7** implant, instill **9** fertilize **10** impregnate

insensate: **4** surd **5** blind, harsh **6** brutal, stupid **7** brutish, fatuous, foolish **9** senseless, unfeeling, untouched **10** insensible

insensibility: **4** coma, damp **6** trance

insensible: **4** dull **7** brutish **8** obdurate **9** inanimate, insensate, unfeeling **10** insentient **11** insensitive, meaningless, unconscious **13** imperceptible

insensitive: **5** blunt **9** inanimate, unfeeling **10** insensible, insentient **16** unimpressionable

insentient: **10** insensible **11** insensitive

insert: **5** foist, infix, inlay, inset **9** interpose **11** intercalate, interpolate
for growth: **5** graft **7** engraft
triangular: **4** gore **5** wedge

insertion: **5** inset
kinds of: **5** shinn **11** parenthesis **13** interpolation **15** intercalalation

inset: **4** gore **5** imbed, infix, panel **6** gusset, insert **7** appoint, engraft, implant **9** insertion

insheathe: **6** emboss

inside: **5** inner **6** lining, within **8** interior **9** partition
toward: **5** entad **6** inward

insidious: **4** deep **6** covert **7** cunning **8** guileful **9** concealed, deceitful **10** fallacious, fraudulent **11** disaffected, treacherous

insight: ken **11** discernment **12** clairvoyance

insignia: **4** mark **5** badge **6** emblem
kind of: tie **7** caducei(pl.), regalia **8** caduceus

insignificance: **10** effacement

insignificant: **4** puny **5** dinky, petit, petty **6** paltry **7** trivial **8** inferior, trifling **9** minuscule, senseless **10** immaterial **12** contemptible
part: bit **4** iota **5** tithe **8** molehill

insincere: **5** false **7** feigned **9** deceitful, deceptive **12** hypocritical

insinuate: **4** hint **5** imply **6** allude, infuse **7** implant, instill **9** introduce, penetrate **10** ingratiate, serpentine

insinuation: **4** hint **8** innuendo

insipid: dry **4** dead, fade, flat, fond, pale, pall, tame **5** bauch, prosy, stale, tepid, vapid, waugh **6** flashy, jejune **7** prosaic **8** lifeless **9** pointless, tasteless **10** monotonous, spiritless, unanimated **13** uninteresting

insipience: **9** stupidity **11** foolishness

insist: **6** demand **9** persevere

insistence: **7** urgency **11** persistence

insnare: web **4** trap **5** benet, noose **6** enmesh, trapan, trepan

insolence: **5** nerve **6** insult **8** audacity **9** arrogance, contumacy, contumely, impudence **11** haughtiness, presumption **12** impertinence

insolent: **4** pert, rude **5** bardy **6** brazen **7** abusive, defiant **8** arrogant, impudent **9** audacious, hubristic **11** overbearing **12** contemptuous, contumelious

insolvency: **7** failure **10** bankruptcy

insolvent: **5** broke **6** busted, ruined **8** bankrupt **9** destitute **12** impoverished

insomnia: **7** ahypnia **8** agrypnia

insouciant: **4** calm **8** carefree, heedless **10** unbothered **11** indifferent, unconcerned

inspect: pry, see **5** aview, grade, visit **6** peruse **7** examine **8** consider **9** supervise **10** scrutinize

inspection: **4** oyer **6** parade, review **8** scrutiny **11** examination

inspector: **6** bishop, conner, sealer **8** examiner, overseer

inspiration: **4** muse **6** breath **8** afflatus **9** afflation **10** aspiration
poetic: **7** pierian
pretender to: **6** eolist

inspire (see also **inspirit**): **4** draw, fire, move, stir **5** exalt, imbue **6** aspire, inhale **7** actuate, animate, enliven, implant **8** motivate **9** encourage, influence, stimulate

inspired: **5** vatic

inspirit (see also **inspire**): **4** stir **5** cheer, elate, rouse **7** cherish, comfort, hearten, quicken **10** invigorate

inspissate: **7** thicken **8** condense **10** incrassate

instability: **8** fluidity **11** flexibility **12** unsteadiness **13** changeability **14** disequilibrium

install: **4** seat, vest **6** induct, invest **7** instate **8** initiate **9** establish **10** inaugurate

installation: 9 vestiture

instance: 4 case, sign, urge 5 token 7 example, present, request, symptom 8 presence 9 importune 10 succession 11 demonstrate, instigation

instancy: 7 urgency 8 pressure 9 imminence 10 insistence 17 instantaneousness

instant: 4 urge 5 clink, flash, gliff, glisk, trice 6 breath, minute, moment, second, urgent 7 solicit 8 pressing 9 handwhile, immediate 11 importunate

instantly: now 4 just 8 directly

instate: set 5 endow 6 bestow, confer, invest 7 install 8 initiate 9 establish

instead: 4 else 6 in lieu 10 equivalent, substitute

of: for

instigate: egg 4 abet, goad, move, prod, sick, spur, urge 5 impel 6 compel, excite, foment, incite, prompt, suborn 7 provoke 8 motivate 9 encourage, stimulate

instigator: 6 author 10 ringleader

instill: 5 imbue, infix 6 impart, infuse 7 implant, pervade 9 inculcate, insinuate

instinct: 5 knack 7 impulse 8 aptitude 11 instigation

instinctive: 6 innate 7 natural 8 inherent, original 9 automatic, intuitive 11 involuntary, spontaneous

institute: 5 begin, erect, found 6 asylum, ordain 7 academy 8 academie, initiate, organize 9 establish, originate 10 inaugurate

institution: 6 clinic, school 7 academy, college 8 hospital, seminary 10 university 12 constitution

instruct: 4 lead, show 5 breed, coach, drill, edify, guide, teach, train, tutor 6 direct, inform, preach 7 counsel, educate 8 document 9 enlighten 10 discipline 12 indoctrinate

instruction: act 4 lore, news, tora 5 torah 6 advice, assize, charge, lesson 7 precept, tuition 8 practice 9 erudition, knowledge 10 commission 12 propaedeutic

period: 4 term, year 7 quarter, session 8 semester 9 trimester

place of: 13 conservatoire

instructive: 8 didactic, sermonic

instructor: don 5 coach, tutor 6 docent, mentor 7 acharya, teacher, trainer 9 preceptor, professor

instrument (see also **apparatus; device; tool**): 4 deed, writ 5 agent, means 6 medium 7 utensil, writing 9 appliance, implement 11 contrivance

board: 5 panel

calculating: 6 abacus 9 sliderule

cutting: 5 knife, razor 6 scythe, shears, sickle 8 scissors

percussion: 12 Glockenspiel

sacred: 4 urim

sealed: 4 deed 5 crypt, vault 6 escrow

sharp-edged: 5 knife, razor 6 scythe, shears, sickle 7 cutlery 8 scissors

instrumental: 5 organ 6 needed, useful 7 helpful, organic 11 ministerial

instrumentalist: 5 luter 6 harper 7 flutist, harpist, pianist 8 minstrel 9 cornetist 10 trombonist

instrumentality: 5 means 6 agency, medium

insubordinate: 5 rebel 6 unruly 7 riotous 8 mutinous, perverse 9 seditious 10 headstrong, refractory, unyielding 11 disobedient, intractable 12 contumacious

insubstantial: 4 airy, thin 5 frail 6 flimsy 10 intangible 12 apparitional

insufficient: 4 bare, poor 5 short 6 feeble, scanty, scarce 7 unequal, wanting 9 deficient 10 inadequate 14 incommensurate

insular: 8 islander, isolated 9 separated

insulate: 7 isolate 8 isolated 9 segregate 10 quarantine

insulated: 5 isled, taped

insulator: 4 tape 5 cleat

insult: cag 4 slap, slur 5 abuse, flout, frump 6 offend, revile 7 abusion, affront, offense, outrage 9 contumely, indignity, insolence

insulting: 4 rude 8 arrogant 9 offensive 10 despiteful, scurrilous 11 opprobrious 12 contumelious

insurance: 8 guaranty, warranty 9 assurance 10 protection

official: 7 actuary 8 adjuster

insure (see also **ensure**): 6 assure 7 furnish 10 underwrite

jointly: 8 coinsure

insurgent (see also **insubordinate**): 5 rebel 10 rebellious

insurmountable: 10 impassable, invincible 11 insuperable 13 unconquerable

insurrection: 6 mutiny, revolt, rising 9 rebellion

insusceptible: 6 immune 9 unfeeling

intact: 5 sound, whole 8 complete, unbroken 9 undefiled, undivided, uninjured, untouched 10 unimpaired

intaglio: cut, gem 9 represent

intake: net 4 gain, gate 6 profit 8 receipts 11 contraction

intangible: 5 vague 10 immaterial, impalpable 13 imperceptible, insubstantial

integer: one 5 whole 8 integral

integral: 5 whole 8 totality

integrate: mix 4 join 5 unite 6 entire

integrity: 7 honesty, probity 9 chariness, constancy

integument: 4 aril, coat 5 testa 7 cuticle, envelop 8 covering, envelope 10 investment

intellect: wit 4 mind, nous 5 brain 6

genius, reason **9** mentality **12** intelligence

limited in: **7** moronic

intellection: **6** notion **9** cognition, knowledge **12** apprehension **13** comprehension, understanding

intellectual: **5** ideal **6** brainy, mental, noetic, sophic **7** egghead **8** highbrow **9** epistemic

intelligence: **4** chit, mind, news, word **5** sense **6** esprit, notice, wisdom **8** learning **13** understanding

used alone: **6** noesis

without: **5** inane

intelligencer: spy **9** informant, messenger **10** newsmonger

intelligent: **5** acute, aware, smart **6** bright, mental **7** knowing **8** rational, sensible **9** cognizant **13** understanding

intelligentsia: **13** intellectuals

intelligible: **5** clear, plain **10** conceptual **11** perspicuous **12** apprehensive **13** apprehensible, intellectible, suprasensuous **14** comprehensible

intemperate: **4** pure **6** severe **7** extreme **9** excessive, inclement, inviolate, undefiled **10** immoderate, inordinate **12** ungovernable

intend: aim **4** mean, mint, plan **5** allot, ettle **6** design **7** destine, purpose

intended: **6** fiance **7** fiancee

intense: hot **4** deep, hard, keen **5** acute, great, heavy, vivid **6** ardent, severe, strong **7** chronic, earnest, extreme, fervent, violent, zealous **8** grievous, powerful, strained, vehement **9** assiduous, excessive, strenuous **11** far-reaching

intensify: **5** exalt **6** deepen **7** enhance **8** condense, heighten, increase **9** aggravate **10** accentuate **11** concentrate

intensity: **5** depth **6** chroma, timbre

intensive: **7** intense **8** vehement **9** ascensive

intent: aim **4** deep, dole(Sc.), fell, rapt **5** eager, ettle, fixed, tense **6** design, effect **7** earnest, meaning, purpose **8** absorbed, diligent, sedulous **9** attentive, engrossed, intention, steadfast **10** determined

intention: aim, end **4** goal, hent, will **6** animus, attent, design, intent, object **7** meaning, purpose **11** designation **13** contemplation

intentional: **8** designed **9** voluntary **10** deliberate

inter: **4** bury **5** earth, grave **6** entomb, inhume

interagent: **6** medium **12** intermediary

intercalary: **8** inserted **12** intercalated, interpolated

intercede: **7** mediate **9** arbitrate, interpose, intervene

intercept: **4** bury, head **5** catch **8** gaincope, retrench **9** forestall, interrupt

intercessor: **8** advocate, mediator

interchange: **4** vary **7** commute, permute **8** converse, exchange **9** alternate **10** transposal **11** reciprocate **12** conversation

interchangeable: **10** reversible **11** convertible

interconnection: **5** nexus

intercourse: **7** dealing **8** business, commerce, converse **9** communion **10** connection, fellowship **12** conversation **13** communication

interdict: ban **4** veto **5** debar, fence **6** forbid **7** inhibit **8** prohibit **9** proscribe

interdiction: **4** tabu **5** taboo

interest: **4** good **5** fetch **6** behalf, behoof, engage, profit **7** attract, concern **8** sympathy **9** advantage, anatocism, entertain, fascinate

exorbitant: **5** usury

lose: **4** tire

rate: **5** yield

without: **6** jejune **9** apathetic

interested: **4** rapt **6** caring

interfacing: **7** dineric

interfere: **5** barge, clash **6** meddle, tamper **7** collide, disturb, intrude **8** obstruct, sabotage **9** interpose, intervene

interference: **6** static

interferometer: **6** etalon

interim: **8** interval, meantime

interior: ben **5** ental, inner **6** inland, inside **8** midlands

interjection: aw, lo; boo, hic, rah **4** ahem, alas, amen, egad, ouch, well **6** aroint **7** criminy **11** exclamation

interlace: mat **5** braid, twine, weave **6** pleach, raddle **7** entwine **9** interfret, interlink **10** intertwine, interweave **11** interpolate

interlaced: **7** complex

interlock: **4** knit **5** unite **6** clench, engage **9** interlace **11** interrelate

interlocution: **12** conversation **13** communication

interlocutory: **12** intermediate

interlope: **6** insert **7** intrude, obtrude **8** trespass **11** intermeddle, interpolate

interlude: **5** truce **6** verset **8** entracte, ritornel **10** ritornelle

intermediary: **5** agent **6** medium **8** mediator **9** go-between **10** ambassador, interagent

interminable: **7** endless, eternal **8** infinite, timeless, unending **9** boundless, limitless, unlimited

interminably: **7** forever

intermingle: **8** intermix **10** infiltrate

intermission: **4** rest, stop **5** dwell, pause **6** devall, recess **7** respite **8** entracte, vacation **9** cessation **10** suspension **13** interposition **14** discontinuance

intermittent: **6** broken, fitful **8** periodic **9**

recurrent, spasmodic 11 alternating, interrupted 12 pretermitted

intermix: 6 mingle 10 interweave

intern: 6 doctor, inhume 7 confine, trainee

internal: 5 inner 6 inward, mental 8 enclosed 9 spiritual

combustion engine part: 5 timer

international: 9 world-wide

International: 4 song 9 Comintern

internecine: 6 deadly

interpellation: 7 summons 10 prevention 12 interception, intercession, interruption

interpolate: 5 alter 6 insert 9 introduce 11 intercalate

interpose: 6 thrust 7 intrude, mediate 9 intercede, interfere, intervene

interpret: 4 read, rede 5 aread, areed, gloze 6 decode, define, expose, render 7 explain, expound 8 construe 9 elucidate, explicate, translate 10 literalize, understand

interpretation: 5 gloss, sense 6 oracle 7 anagoge 8 exegesis 11 declaration

of science: 8 exegesis 12 hermeneutics

interpreter: 7 ulema 7 exegete 8 exponent 9 exegesist, hermeneut 11 oneirocritic

interrogate: ask 5 query 7 examine, inquire 8 question

interrogative: how, who, why 4 what, when 5 where 8 question

interrupt: 4 stop 5 break, burst, cease, check 6 arrest, hinder, thwart 7 derange, disturb, suspend 8 obstruct 9 intercept, pretermit 11 discontinue

interruption: gap 5 dwell, pause 6 breach, hiatus 7 caesura 9 cessation 12 intermission

intersect: cut 4 meet 5 cross 6 divide, pierce 9 decussate

intersection: 6 secant 7 chiasma

interstice: 4 mesh, pore, seam 5 chink, crack, space 6 areola, areole, cranny 7 crevice 8 interval

intertwine: 4 knit, lace 5 twist 6 tangle 7 ensnare, ensnarl, entwine 8 entangle 9 interlace 10 intertwist

intertwist: 10 intertwine

interval: gap 4 rest, span 5 break, space 6 breach, hiatus, recess 7 caesura, respite 8 entracte 9 cessation 12 intermission

at irregular: 12 sporadically

musical: 5 fifth, ninth, sixth, tenth, third 6 fourth, octave, second 7 seventh

intervene: 7 mediate 9 intercede, interpose

intervening: 5 mesne(law) 12 intermediate

interview: see 7 consult, hearing 8 audience, question 9 encounter 10 conference 12 consultation

interweave: mat 4 plat 5 braid, plait 6 enlace, raddle, splice, wattle 8 entangle, intermix 9 interlace

intestinal: 7 enteric

intestine: gut 5 inner 6 inward 7 viscera 8 domestic, internal

combined form: 6 entero

part: ile 5 ileum, ilium

intice: See **entice.**

intimacy: 8 affinity 10 connection

intimate: sib 4 boon, hint, homy, near 5 bosom, chief, close, homey, imply 6 allude, chummy, homely, inmost, secret 7 signify, suggest 8 announce, domestic, familiar, friendly, informal, personal 9 associate, confidant 11 contubernal 12 acquaintance, confidential

intimately: 4 inly

intimation: 4 clue, hint, wind 5 scent 6 notice 7 inkling 10 suggestion 11 declaration

intimidate: awe, cow 5 abash, bully, daunt, deter, scare 6 hector 7 overawe, terrify 8 browbeat, dispirit, frighten 9 blackmail, terrorize

into: *prefix:* en

that: 9 thereinto

intolerance: 9 misoneism

intolerant: 6 narrow 7 bigoted 8 dogmatic 9 illiberal, impatient 10 prejudiced

intonation: 4 sing 5 chant, sound 7 sonance

intonational: 7 tonetic

intone: 4 cant, sing 5 chant 8 modulate 10 cantillate

intoxicant (see also **alcoholic drink, liquor**): fox, gin, rum 4 wine 5 drink 6 excite, liquor 7 whiskey 9 inebriate, stimulate

intoxicated: 4 high, shot, tosy 5 bosky, drunk 6 boiled, soused, stewed 7 excited, screwed 8 besotted, glorious 9 crapulous 10 crapulated, inebriated, tosticated 11 capernoited

intoxicating: 5 heady

intractable: 6 unruly, wilful 7 haggard, restive 8 indocile, mutinous, obdurate, perverse, stubborn 9 obstinate 10 headstrong, refractory 11 disobedient, unteachable 12 contumacious, ungovernable 14 uncontrollable

intrada: 7 prelude 12 introduction

intranquillity: ado 12 restlessness

intransigent: 7 radical 14 irreconcilable, uncompromising

intrepid: 4 bold 5 brave, hardy, nervy 6 daring, heroic 7 assured, doughty, gallant, valiant 8 fearless, resolute, valorous 9 dauntless, dreadless, nerveless 10 courageous

intricate: 4 hard 5 dedal 6 daedal, knotty 7 complex, Gordian, sinuous 8 involved 9 Daedalian, difficult, involuted 10 perplexing 11 complicated 12 labyrinthine

intrigue: 4 plot 5 cabal, charm 6 brigue, deceit, design, scheme 7 faction 8 artifice, collogue 9 fascinate 10 concoction, conspiracy 11 machination

intrinsic: 4 real, true 6 inborn, inbred,

innate, native **7** genuine, natural **8** immanent, inherent, intimate **9** essential, necessary **11** inseparable **13** indispensable

intrinsically: 5 per se

introduce: 5 begin, enter, start, usher **6** broach, herald, infuse, insert **7** forerun, implant, precede, preface, present, sponsor **8** approach, initiate **9** insinuate **10** ingratiate

introduction: cue **5** debut, proem **7** intrada, introit, isagoge, preface, prelude **8** entrance, exordium, foreword, preamble, prologue, protasis **11** preparation

introductory: 8 exordial **9** prefatory, prelusive

introit: 8 entrance **12** introduction

intrude: 6 invade, meddle **7** obtrude **8** infringe, trespass **9** interfere, interlope, interpose

intruder: 8 outsider

intrusion: 10 aggression, infraction

intrusive: 7 curious

intrust: See **entrust**.

intuit: 4 feel **5** sense **8** perceive **9** apprehend

intuition: 5 hunch **8** instinct

inunction: 8 ointment **9** anointing

pert. to: **7** aliptic

inundate: 4 flow **5** drown, flood **6** deluge **8** overflow, submerge **9** overwhelm **10** overspread

inundation: 8 alluvion

inure, enure: 5 steel **6** harden, season **7** toughen **8** accustom **9** habituate **10** discipline **11** acclimatize

inurn: 4 bury **6** entomb

inustion: 7 burning **13** cauterization

inutile: bad **7** useless **8** unusable **9** worthless **12** unprofitable

inutterable: See **unutterable**.

invade: 4 raid **6** irrupt, offend **7** assault, intrude, overrun **8** encroach, entrench, intrench, trespass

invader: Hun **4** Pict **6** raider **8** intruder

invalid: 4 null **6** feeble, infirm, sickly **8** nugatory **11** ineffective **14** valetudinarian

invalidate: 4 undo **5** annul, break **7** abolish

invaluable: 8 precious **9** priceless **11** inestimable **13** inappreciable

invariable: 4 same **6** steady **7** uniform **8** constant **9** continual, immutable **10** unchanging **11** determinate **12** unchangeable

invariably: 6 always **7** forever

invasion (see also **invade**): **6** inroad **9** incursion **10** aggression

invective: 5 abuse, taunt **6** tirade **7** railing **8** diatribe, reproach **12** vituperation

inveigh: 9 fulminate

inveigle: 4 coax, lure **5** snare **6** allure, entice, entrap **8** persuade

invent: 4 coin, form, make, vamp **5** feign, forge, frame **6** create, design, devise, patent **7** concoct, fashion **8** contrive, dis-

cover, engineer **9** fabricate, improvise, originate **11** manufacture

invention: 7 fiction, figment

inventive: 6 adroit **7** fertile **9** ingenious

inventor: 6 author, coiner **7** creator **8** engineer **10** discoverer, originator

airplane: **6** Fokker, Wright

baseball: **9** Doubleday

cotton gin: **7** Whitney

dynamite: **5** Nobel

electric light: **6** Edison

electric motor: **9** Davenport

elevator: **4** Otis

gun: **4** Colt **9** Remington

internal combustion engine: **6** Lenoir **7** Daimler

logarithm: **6** Napier

phonograph: **6** Edison

photography: **6** Niepce, Talbot

power loom: **10** Cartwright

printing: **9** Gutenberg

printing press: Hoe

radio: **7** Marconi **8** de Forest

sewing machine: **4** Howe **6** Lester

steam locomotive: **10** Stephenson

steamboat: **5** Fitch **6** Fulton, Rumsey

telegraph: **5** Morse

telephone: **4** Bell

television: **6** Nipkow

wireless: **7** Marconi

inventory: 4 list **7** account, catalog, listing **8** register, schedule **9** catalogue

inveracity: fib, lie **9** falseness

inverse: 8 opposite

invert: 4 turn **7** reverse

invertebrate: 4 worm **5** polyp **6** insect, sponge **7** mollusk **8** arachnid **12** coelenterate

group: **7** radiata

invest: don **4** belt, gird, gown, robe, vest, wrap **5** array, crown, dress, endow, endue, imbue **6** clothe, confer, embark, ordain **7** envelop, install, instate **8** accredit, enthrone, surround

investigate: pry **4** nose **5** probe, study, trace **6** search **7** examine, explore, inquire **10** research **10** scrutinize

investigator: 6 prober, tracer **9** detective

body of: **4** jury **5** panel **9** committee

investiture: 7 clothes, vesture **8** clothing

investment: 7 garment **8** vestment

list: **9** portfolio

investor: 10 capitalist, shareowner **11** stockholder

inveterate: 6 rooted **7** chronic **8** habitual, hardened **9** confirmed, ingrained

invidious: 6 odious **7** envious, hateful **9** malignant **12** disagreeable

invigorate: pep **5** brace, cheer, nerve, renew **6** vivify **7** animate, enliven, fortify, refresh **9** stimulate **10** exhilarate, strengthen

invigorating: 5 tonic **11** corroborant

invincible: 10 unbeatable **11** indomitable

inviolate: 4 holy **6** sacred **9** undefiled,

unstained 10 inviolable, sacrosanct 13 incorruptible 14 indestructible

invisible: hid 6 unseen 10 indistinct, unapparent 13 undiscernible

invitation: bid 4 call 7 bidding 8 biddance, entreaty 9 challenge

invite: ask, bid 4 call 5 court 6 allure, entice 7 attract, provoke, request, solicit

invocation: 4 plea 6 prayer, sermon 7 benison 8 entreaty 11 benediction

invoice: 4 bill 5 brief 7 account 8 manifest 9 statement

invoke: 4 call, pray 6 appeal, attest 7 conjure, entreat, provoke, solicit 9 imprecate 10 supplicate

involuntary: 6 forced 9 reluctant, unwilling 11 instinctive, spontaneous

involve: 4 wrap 5 imply, snare 6 bemist, employ, engage, entail, tangle 7 concern, embrace, ensnare 8 comprise, comprize, encumber, entangle 9 implicate 10 complicate, comprehend

involved: 7 complex 12 labyrinthine

inward: 5 entad, inner 6 inside 8 homefelt, interior 10 internally

iodine: *combining form:* iod 4 iodo
  compound: 6 iodide
  salt: 6 iodate
  source: 4 kelp
  substitute: 7 aristal
  treat with: 6 iodate

Iolcus king: 6 Pelias

Ionia: *coin:* 4 obol 5 obolo
  gulf: 4 Arta
  island: 5 corfu, Zante 6 Cerigo, Ithaca 7 Kythera 10 Cephalonia
  monk: 5 Aidan

iota: bit, jot 4 atom, whit 6 tittle 8 particle

Iowa: *college:* Coe
  county: 5 Adair, Onawa 7 Wapello
  town: 4 Ames 5 Anita 7 Ottumwa 9 Davenport, Oskaloosa

ipecac: 4 evea
  substance: 7 emetine

Iphis' daughter: 6 Evadne

iracund: 8 choleric 9 irascible

irade: 5 edict 6 decree

Irak: See **Iraq.**

Iran: 6 Persia
  almond: 5 badam
  angel: Mah
  assembly: 6 Majlis, Mejlis,
  bed: 4 sofa 5 divan
  books: 5 Koran, Yasna 6 Avesta, Gathas, Yashts 8 Vendidad, Vispered
  capital: 7 Teheran
  caste: 4 magi
  chief: Mir
  city: 4 Amol 7 Teheran(c.)
  coin: pul 4 asar, cran, kran, lari, rial 5 bisti, daric, dinar, larin, shahi, toman 6 shahee, stater 7 ashrafi, kasbeke, pahlavi
  comedy: 7 temacha

country: 4 Elam 5 Media
demigod: 4 Yima
demon: 7 Apaosha, Ahriman
diadem: taj
dynasty: 6 Safavi, Seljuk 7 Safavid, Safawid 10 Sassanidae
fire-worshipper: 5 Parsi 6 Parsee
founder: 5 Cyrus
garment: 6 chedar
god: 6 Ormazd 7 Mithras
governor: 4 khan 6 satrap
grass: 6 millet
hat: fez 6 turban
hero: 4 Yima
javelin: 5 jerid 6 jeerid
king: 4 shah 6 Darius, Xerxes 7 Jamshid, Jamshyd 9 Giamschid 10 Artaxerxes
Koran student: 5 hafiz
lake: 5 Niriz, Urmia 6 Sahweh 8 Urumiyeh
language: 4 Zend 7 Pahlavi, Pehlevi
measure: guz, mou, zar, zer 4 cane, foot 5 gareh, jerib, kafiz, makuk, qasab 6 artaba, charac, chebel, gariba, ghalva, ouroub 7 capicha, chenica, farsakh, farsang, mansion, mishara 8 parasang, piamaneh, sabbitha, stathmos 9 collothun, colluthun
mountain: 4 Kush 5 Hindu 6 Ararat, Elburz 8 Demavend 11 Parapanisus
New Year's Day: 7 Nowroze
nomad: 4 Luri
oil center: 6 Abadan
Parliament: 6 Majlis, Mejlis
peasant: tai
people: Lur, tai 4 Kurd, Mede, sart 5 Kajar, Mukri, nomad, Perse, Tajik 6 Iranic, Tadjik 7 Hadjemi, Persian
poet: 4 Omar 5 Saadi
port: 7 Bushire 11 Bandar Abbas
religion founder: 9 Zoroaster 11 Zarathustra
religious doctrine: 6 babism 7 babiism
revenue officer: 9 tahsildar 10 tahseeldar
river: 4 Mand, Mund 5 Karun 6 Tigris 8 Safid Rud 9 Euphrates, Kizil Uzen
ruler: 4 shah 6 atabeg, atabek, satrap, sultan
saint: 6 Safavi 7 Safavid, Safawid
screen: 6 purdah
sect: 5 Shiah, Sunni 6 Shiite, Sunnee 7 Sunnite
tapestry: 7 susanee
tax collector: 9 tahsildar 10 tahseeldar
tent-maker: 4 Omar
throne room: 5 aiwan
tiara: 7 cidaris
title: mir 4 azam, shah 5 mirza
tobacco: 6 tumbak, tumbek 7 tumbaki, tumbeki
town: Fao, Kom 5 Niriz, Resht 6 Kasvin, Kerman, Meshed, Shiraz, Tabriz, Tauris 7 Hamadan, Ispahan, Tabreez, 9 Balfroosh
traders: 4 sart

trumpet: **6** kerana **7** kerrana
vessel: **6** aftaba
water-pipe: **5** hooka **6** calean, hookah **8** narghile **12** hubble-bubble
water wheel: **5** noria
weight: ser **4** dram, dung, rotl, sang, seer **5** abbas, artal, artel, maund, pinar, ratel **6** batman, dirhem, gandum, karwar, miscal, miskal, nakhod **7** abbassi **8** tcheirek **9** saddirham
Iraq: *capital:* **6** Bagdad **7** Baghdad
coin: **5** dinar
district: **5** Basra
town: **5** Amara, Basra
irascible: **5** brash, fiery, hasty, irate, techy, testy **6** snappy, touchy **7** fretful, peevish **8** captious, choleric, petulant, snappish **9** impatient, splenetic **10** passionate **11** bad-tempered, belligerent, combustible, hot-tempered **13** quick-tempered
irate: mad **5** angry, het up, wroth **6** bitter, wrathy **7** angered, enraged, furious **8** incensed, provoked, wrathful **9** indignant, irascible
ire: vex **4** fury, heat, rage **5** anger, annoy, wrath **6** choler, temper **8** asperity, vexation **9** vehemence **10** exasperate, resentment **11** displeasure **12** exasperation
Ireland: **4** Eire, Erin **5** Ierne, Irena **7** Ivernia **9** Innisfail
ancestor: Ir; Mil **6** Miledh **8** Milesius
assembly: **6** aenach, aonach
basket: **7** skeough
battle cry: abu
bay: **6** Galway
boat: **7** pookaun **8** pookhaun
cabstand: **6** hazard
cap: **6** barrad
capital: **4** Tara **6** Dublin
cattle: **5** Kerry
chamber of deputies: **4** Dail
chemist: **5** Boyle
chieftain: **6** Tanist
church steward: **7** erenach
clan: **4** sept **5** Cinel
club: **8** shillala **9** shillalah, shillelah **10** shillelagh
coin: rap **4** real
cordial: **10** usquebaugh
county: **4** Cork, Down, Mayo **5** Cavan, Clare, Kerry, Louth, Meath **6** Antrim, Armagh, Galway, Offaly, Tyrone, Ulster **7** Donegal, Kildare, Leitrim, Wexford, Wicklow **8** Fermangh, Kilkenny, Limerick, Longford, Monaghan **9** Tipperary, Westmeath **11** Londonderry
dagger: **5** skean
dance: **10** rinkafadda, rinncefada
dirge: **4** keen
dish: **4** stew
epic tales: **4** tain, tana(pl.)
exclamation: och **4** arra **5** arrah, ohone
fair: **6** aenach, aonach

fairy: **4** shee **5** sidhe **7** banshee, banshie **10** leprechaun
festival: **4** feis
fort: Lis **4** rath
freebooter: **8** rapparee
freeman: **4** aire
fuel: **4** peat
garment: **4** inar
goblin: **5** pooka
god's mother: Ana, Anu
god of love: **5** Dagda **6** Aengus, Oengus
god of sea: Ler
goddess: **4** Badb, Bodb, Dana
good-for-nothing: **8** spalpeen
groggery: **7** shebeen
harvester: **8** spalpeen
herring: **8** scud-dawn
holiday: **10** Whitmonday
infantryman: **4** kern
islands: **4** Aran
king: Ri; Rig **5** Ardri
king's home: **4** Tara
lamentation: **6** ochone
landholding system: **7** rundale
lawyer: **6** brehon
legislature: **4** Dail **10** Oireachtas
lord: **6** tanist
measure: **4** mile **6** bandle
melody: **7** planxty
moccasin: **9** pampootee, pampootie
monk: **6** culdee
monk's cell: kil **4** kill
mountain: **7** Wicklow **10** Carrantual **11** Lugnaquilla **13** Macgillicuddy
name: **4** Sean **5** Moira
national emblem: **8** shamrock
negative: **5** sorra
novelist: **4** Shaw
oath: **5** bedad
patriot: **5** Emmet **6** Oakboy
patron saint: **7** Patrick
peasant: **4** kern **5** kerne
peat: gor
people: **4** Celt, Erse, Gael **6** Celtic **9** Hibernian
person: **4** aire, kern, kern **5** kerne, paddy **7** shoneen **8** spalpeen **10** Eireannach
pert. to: **6** Celtic, Gaelic
pig: **5** bonav
playwright: **4** Shaw **5** Wilde
poem: **6** amhran
poet: **5** Moore, Wilde, Yeats
priest: **5** druid
princess: **6** Iseult
proprietor: **6** tanist
province(see also *country* above)*:* **6** Ulster **7** Munster **8** Leinster **9** Connaught
republicanism: **9** Fenianism
revolutionist: **6** Fenian
river: Lee **4** Bann, Deel, Erne, Suir **5** Boyne, Clare, Feale, Flesk, Foyle, Laune **6** Bandon, Barrow, Liffey, Martin **7** Munster, Shannon **10** Blackwater
robber: **8** woodkern

seaport: **4** Cobh **6** Tralee
servant: **5** biddy
society: **4** aire
soldier: **6** bonagh **8** rapparee
soldiers' quartering: **7** bonaght **8** bonaught
song: **4** rann
spirit: see *fairy* above
stock: **4** daer
straw load: **5** barth
surgeon: **6** Colles
sweetheart: gra
symbol: **4** harp **8** shamrock
tax: **7** bonaght **8** bonaught
tenant: **4** saer
tenure: **6** sorren **7** sorehon
term of endearment: **7** asthore
town: **4** Cork **5** Adare **6** Dublin, Lurgan **8** Limerick **9** Killarney, Tipperary **10** Abbey Feale **12** Castle Island
tribesman: see *person* above
trout: **7** gilaroo
verse: **4** rann
whiskey: **6** poteen **10** usquebaugh
womanhood: **4** emer
writing system: **4** ogam **5** ogham
irenic: **4** calm **5** irene **7** henotic, pacific **8** irenical, peaceful **12** conciliatory
iridescence: **9** irisation
iridescent: **6** irised **7** opaline **9** prismatic **10** opalescent
iridium: *pert. to:* **6** iridic
symbol: ir
iris: lis **5** orris, sedge **6** orrice **7** rainbow **10** Florentine **11** ambassadeur
combining form: **4** irid
family: **4** irid **8** tileroot
layer: **4** uvea
part: **4** uvea **6** argola **7** argolae(pl.),
pert. to: **5** irian
problem of: **6** iritis **8** aniridia
Irish (see also **Ireland** *people*): **6** Celtic, Gaelic **9** Hibernian
Irish bit: **7** traneen
Irish confetti: **6** bricks
Irish dividend: **10** assessment
Irish Free State: See **Ireland**.
Irish pennant: **6** thread **8** raveling
Irish Sweepstakes: **7** lottery
irk (see also **ire**): vex **4** bore **5** anger, annoy, chafe, peeve, tease, upset, weary **6** nettle **7** trouble **8** irritate **10** exasperate
irksome: **4** dull **6** tedium **7** humdrum, painful, tedious **8** tiresome **9** fatiguing, wearisome **10** burdensome, monotonous, unpleasant **11** displeasing
irne: **4** iron
iron: fer(F.) **4** gyve, hard, irne **5** goose, metal, power, press **6** fetter, trivet, robust, strong, yetlin **7** manacle, shackle, yetling **8** firmness, gridiron, handcuff, hematite, siderite **10** unyielding
comb. form: **6** sidero
compound: **5** steel
containing: **6** ferric

dross: **6** sinter
magnet: **8** armature
lump: pig
marking: **7** brander
meteoric: **8** siderite
pert. to: **6** ferric
sulphate: **7** ilesite
Iron City: **10** Pittsburgh
iron sand: **6** iserin
ironclad: **7** armored, monitor
ironer: **6** mangle **7** presser
ironic: **7** satiric **9** sarcastic
irons: **6** chains **7** garters **8** creepers, shackles
ironwork: **8** ferament
ironworker's tool: **6** lifter
irony: **6** satire **7** asteism, sarcasm **8** ridicule **13** dissimulation
Iroquois Indian: **4** Erie **5** Huron, Litre **6** Cayuga, Mohawk, Neuter, Oneida, Seneca **7** Wyandot **8** Cherokee, Nottoway, Onondaga **9** Conestoga, Tuscarora **10** Tionontati
irradiance: **11** irradiation
irradiate: ray **4** beam, emit **6** bright **7** diffuse, radiate **8** brighten **9** enlighten **10** illuminate **11** illuminated
irrational: **4** surd **5** brute **6** absurd, stupid **7** bestial, brutish, foolish **9** senseless **10** ridiculous **12** preposterous, unreasonable **13** unintelligent
irreclaimable: **4** lost **8** hopeless **9** abandoned **11** irrevocable
irreconcilable: **9** repugnant **10** discordant, implacable **12** incompatible, inconsistent, intransigent
irrecoverable: See **irreclaimable**.
irredeemable: See **irreclaimable**.
irrefutable: **10** conclusive
irregular: **4** wild **5** erose, false **6** ataxic, fitful, rugged, spotty, uneven, unlike **7** atactic, crabbed, crooked, cursory, devious, erratic, snatchy, unequal, wayward **8** abnormal, atypical, sporadic, unlawful, unstable, unsteady, variable **9** anomalous, desultory, eccentric, unsettled **10** changeable, disorderly, immoderate **11** intemperate **12** uncontrolled, unsystematic **13** extraordinary
irregularity: **5** error **7** anomaly **8** disorder **11** derangement **12** perturbation
irrelevant: **9** unrelated **10** inapposite **11** inessential, unessential **12** inconsequent
irreligious: **5** pagan **6** wicked **7** godless, heathen, impious, profane
irremediable: **8** helpless, hopeless **9** desperate, incurable **11** irreparable **13** irretrievable
irreproachable: **8** spotless **9** blameless, faultless
irresistible: **8** almighty **10** resistless **11** ineluctable **12** spellbinding
irresolute: **6** fickle, infirm, unsure **8** doubtful, unstable, wavering **9** uncertain,

undecided **10** changeable, inconstant **11** fluctuating **12** undertermined
irresponsible: 8 carefree **10** fly-by-night **11** harum-scarum **12** undependable **13** unaccountable
irretrievable: See **irremediable.**
irreverence: 7 impiety **8** dishonor **9** blasphemy, impudence, profanity
irrevocable: 4 firm **5** final **6** stable **9** immutable **11** unalterable
irrigate: wet **5** water **6** sluice **7** moisten
irritable: 4 edgy **5** birsy, cross, fiery, techy, testy **6** cranky, ornery, tetchy, touchy **7** fretful, iracund, peevish, pettish **8** snappish **9** excitable, fractious, impatient, querulent **11** capernoited **12** disagreeable
irritate: get, irk, nag, rub, vex **4** crab, fret, gall, goad, grig, rasp, rile, roil **5** anger, annoy, chafe, cross, frump, grate, peeve, pique, spite, sting, tease **6** abrade, badger, bother, enrage, excite, fridge, harass, hector, madden, needle, nettle, ruffle **7** affront, incense, provoke **8** acerbate **9** aggravate, displease, stimulate **10** exacerbate, exasperate
irritating: 5 acrid **8** rankling
irritation: 4 itch, sore **5** birse **6** temper
is: 6 exists **10** represents **11** personifies
is not: nis, nys
Isaac's kin: 4 Esau **5** Jacob **7** Abraham
isagoge: 12 introduction
Ishmael: 5 rover **6** pariah **7** outcast
  kin: **5** Hagar **7** Abraham **8** Nebaioth
Ishtar's lover: 6 Tammuz
isinglass: 4 mica
Isis: *kin:* **5** Horus **6** Osiris
  shrine: **5** Iseum **6** Iseium
Islam: *adherent:* **6** Moslem, Muslim
  festival: Eed
  founder: **7** Mahomet
  holy city: **5** Mecca **6** Medina
  judge: **4** cadi
  law: **5** sheri **6** sharia, sheria **8** sheriyat
  paradise: **5** jenna
  place of pilgrimage: **5** Caaba, Kaaba **6** Kaabeh
  priest: **4** imam
  scriptures: **5** Koran
  tambourine: **5** daira
island: ait, cay, ile(F.), key **4** calf, eyot, holm, ilot, inch(Sc.), isle **5** atoll, holme, islet, islot **8** insulate
  group: **5** Faroe, Samoa **8** Antilles, Caroline, Marshall **11** archipelago
  mythical: **4** Meru **6** Avalon, Bimini **8** Atlantis
  pert. to: **7** insular
  snake-free: **4** Erin
Island of Saints: 7 Ireland
isle: See **island.**
Isle of Man: *city:* **4** Peel **6** Ramsey **7** Douglas **10** Castletown
  judge: **8** deemster, dempster
  legislature: **7** tynwald

measure: **6** kishen, kishon
mountain: **8** Snaefell
part: **4** Ayre
pert. to: **4** Manx
watering place: **4** Ryde
islet: See **island.**
ism: 5 ology, tenet **6** belief **8** doctrine **10** hypothesis
isolate: 4 isle **6** detach, enisle, island **7** seclude **8** insulate, separate **9** segregate, sequester **10** quarantine
isolated: 4 sole **5** alone **6** lonely **7** insular **8** singular, solitary
Isolde's lover: 7 Tristan
Israel: (see also **Hebrew, Judaism**):
  anthem: **7** Hatikva **9** Hattikvah
  child: **5** sabra
  city: **5** Jaffa, Joppa **9** Jerusalem(c.)
  dust storm: **8** khamseen
  government body: **7** Knesset **9** Sanhedrin
  judge: **4** Elon **6** Samson **7** Sampson, Shamgar **8** Jephthah
  king: **4** Ahab, Jehu, Omri, Saul **5** David, Pekah **7** Jehoram, Solomon **8** Jehoahaz, Jeroboam, Pekahiah
  labor federation: **9** Histadrut
  labor party: **5** Mapai
  land of plenty: **6** Goshen
  lawgiver: **5** Moses
  measure: cab, cor, hin, kab, kor, log **4** bath, epha, ezba, omer, reed, seah **5** cubit, ephah, homer, kaneh, qaneh **11** handbreadth
  priest: Eli
  seaport: **5** Aqaba **7** Tel Aviv
  settlement: **6** moshav **7** kibbutz
  tribe: Dan **4** Aser, Levi **5** Asher **6** Reuben
issuance: 5 issue **6** sortie **7** issuing **9** emanation **12** distribution
issue: end, son **4** come, emit, fate, flow, gush, pour, send **5** arise, child, sally, spout, topic, utter **6** accrue, egress, emerge, escape, exitus, expede(Sc.), source, upshot **7** descent, edition, emanate, fortune, outcome, problem, proceed, progeny **9** effluence, offspring **10** denouement, distribute
issuing: 9 affluence, affluxion
ist: 7 devotee **8** adherent, believer, disciple, follower
Istanbul: 9 Byzantium **14** Constantinople
  part: **4** Pera **5** Fanar
isthmus: 4 neck **6** strait **9** peninsula
it may be: 5 haply
Ita: Ata **4** Aeta **7** Negrito
italicize: 9 emphasize, underline **10** underscore
Italy: *actress:* **4** Duse
  article: el, il
  artist: **7** Cellini
  astronomer: **6** Secchi **7** Galileo
  author: **5** Dante
  card game: **5** tarot
  carriage: **7** vettura

cathedral: **5** duomo
cereal: **5** arzun
cheese: **6** Romano **8** Parmesan
chest: **7** cassone
city: Bra, Ora **4** Alba, Asti, Bari, Este, Lodi, Nola, Pisa, Pola, Roma, Rome **5** Aosta, Fiume, Genoa, Lucca, Massa, Milan, Ostia, Padua, Parma, Pavia, Trent, Turin, Udine **6** Ancona, Foggia, Mantua, Modena, Naples, Spezia, Venice, Verona **7** Bologna, Catania, Ferrara, Leghorn, Livorno, Marsala, Messina, Palermo, Perugia, Pompeii, Ravenna, Taranto, Trieste **8** Brindisi, Cagliari, Florence, Sorrento **11** Alessandria
coin: **4** lira, sudo, tari **5** grano, paoli, soldo **6** ducato, sequin, teston, zequin **8** chequeen, zecchino **9** centisimo
commune: Bra **4** Dego, Este, Nola **5** Asola, Eboli **6** Rivoli
composer: **5** Verdi **7** Puccini **8** Mascagni **9** Scarlatti
condiment: **6** tamara
country: **7** Etruria
dance: **9** rigoletto **10** tarantella
deity: **4** faun
department: **4** Roma **5** Marca **6** Apulia, Emilia, Umbria **7** Liguria, Sicilia, Tuscana, Venetia **8** Calabria, Compania, Piemonte, Sardinia **9** Lombardia **10** Basilicata **13** Aruzzi e Molise
dictator: **9** Mussolini
engraver: **8** Raimondi
entertainment: **6** ridoto
estate: **11** latifundium
family: **4** Asti, Este **5** Amati, Cenci, **6** Medici
festival: **5** festa
food: **5** pizza **7** ravioli **10** zabaglione
gentleman: ser **6** signor
god: **5** Liber, Picus **6** Consus
goddess: Ops **4** Juno **5** Diana, Salus, Venus **6** Pomona **7** Feronia, Minerva
grape: **6** verdea
guessing game: **4** mora
gulf: **7** Salerno
hamlet: **5** casal **6** casale
hero: **7** Orlando
holiday: **5** festa
house: **4** casa **6** casino
immigrant: **6** guinea
infant cupids: **7** amorini
inlay work: **6** tarsia
inn: **7** locanda
innkeeper: **7** padrone
instrument: **10** colascione
island: Cos **4** Elba **5** Capri, Leros **6** Ischia, Lipari, Sicily **8** Sardinia
king: **4** Rene **5** Murat **6** Alonso
lady: **5** donna **7** signora
lake: **4** Como **5** Garda **6** Albano, Lugano **7** Bolsena **8** Maggiore **9** Trasimene
land: **7** maremma
landlord: **7** padrone

leader: **4** duce
limestone: **7** scaglia
lover: **7** amoroso
macaroni: **5** pasta
magistrate: **7** podesta
marble: **7** carrara
master: **7** padrone
mayor: **6** syndic
measure: pie **4** orna **5** canna, carat, palma, piede, punto, salma, staio, stero **6** barile, miglio, moggio, rubbio, tavola, tomolo **7** boccale, braccio, secchio **8** giornata, polonick, quadrato
medieval faction: **4** Neri
millet: **4** buda, moha **5** mohar, tenai
monk: **5** padre **6** abbate
mountain: **4** Alps **5** Amaro, Somma **8** Vesuvius **9** Apennines, Appennino
musician: **5** Guido
native: **5** Italo **6** Tirano **7** Sienese **9** Calabrian
needlework: **8** trapunto
noblewoman: **8** marchesa
omelet: **8** frittata
opera: **4** Aida **5** Norma, Tosca **9** Pagliacci
opera house: **5** Scala
organization: **7** Balilla
painter: **4** Reni, Tisi **5** Colle, Lippi, Lotto **6** Crespi, Guardi, Sacchi, Titian **7** Amigoni, di Credi, di Paolo, Raphael, Robusti, Strozzi, Tiepolo **8** Bronzino, Cagliari, Mainardi, Sassetta **9** Correggio, del Piombo, Giorgione, Veneziano **10** Botticelli, Caracciolo, Tintoretto
painting: **9** tenebrosi
patriot: **9** Garibaldi
peasant: **9** contadini, contadino
people: **5** Latin, Oscan, Roman **6** Sabine, Tuscan **8** Venetian
philosopher: **7** Rosmini
physicist: **5** Volta **7** Galvani
pie: **5** pizza
plays: **7** Vangeli
poet: **4** Redi **5** Dante, Tasso
poetic name: **7** Ausonia
police officer: **6** sbirri, sbirro
policeman: **11** carabiniere, carabinieri
porridge: **7** polenta
port: **6** Rimini
possession: **6** Dhalak **7** Eritrea, Tripoli **10** Somaliland
pottery: **8** majolica
prelate: **4** Rici
priest: fra
prince: **4** Asti, Este
printer: **6** Bodoni
procession: **5** corso **7** trionfi, trionfo
province: **4** Bari, Este, Pola **5** Aosta. Cuneo, Parma, Udine **6** Istria, Verona **7** Salerno
region: **5** Carso
resort: **4** Lido
river: Po **4** Adda, Arno, Liri **5** Adige, Melfa, Oglio, Piave, Tiber **6** Panora, Ra-

pido, Tevere, Ticino **7** Rubicon, Secchia, Trebbia **8** Volturno **10** Garigliano

rock: **7** scaglia

saint: **4** Neri

sausage: **6** salami

sculptor: **5** Leoni **6** Canova **7** Bernini **8** Canonica **9** Egenesean

sea: **8** Adriatic

seaport: Aci **4** Bari, Mola, Pola, Zara **5** Genoa, Ostia, Trani **7** Otranto, Trieste

secret society: **5** Mafia **7** Camorra **9** Carbonari

section: **7** maremma

soldier: **10** carabineer, carabinier **11** bersagliere, carabinieri

song: **10** villanella, villanelle

soprano: **5** Patti

soup: **8** minestra **10** minestrone

spice: **6** tamara

straits: **7** Messina

summer house: **6** casino

theme: **4** tema

theologian: **7** Peronne

town: Bra **4** Alba, Elea, Este, Meda, Pisa **5** Acqui, Aosta, Capua, Genoa, Milan, Parma, Teano **6** Naples, Napoli, Torino **7** Bologna, Caserta **9** Caporetto

university: **5** Padua

vessel: **9** trabacolo **10** trabascolo

violin maker: **5** Amati

violinist: **7** Corelli, Tartini

volcano: **4** Etna **5** Somma **8** Vesuvius **9** Stromboli

weight: **5** carat, libra, oncia, pound **6** denaro, libbra, ottava **11** chilogrammo

wine: **4** Asti **6** Barolo, Massic **9** Vernaccia

itch: **4** reef, yeuk(Sc.) **6** desire **9** cacoethes, hankering **10** irritation

ite: **8** adherent, disciple, follower

item (see also **object**): ad, bit **5** entry, scrap, thing, topic **6** detail **7** account, article, product **8** personal **9** paragraph **10** particular **12** circumstance

curious: ana

itemize: **9** enumerate

iterate: See **reiterate**.

Ithaca king: **8** Odysseus

Ithunn's husband: **5** Brage, Bragi

itinerant: **6** errant, roving **7** migrant, nomadic **8** traveler, wanderer **9** migratory, transient, traveling, unsettled, wandering **11** peripatetic

itinerary: **4** plan, tour **5** guide, route **6** record **8** roadbook **9** guidebook

itinerate: **6** travel **9** traveling

itineration: **4** eyre, tour **7** circuit, travels

Ivan the Terrible: **4** Tsar

wife: **9** Anastasia

Ivanhoe character: **4** Tuck **6** Rowena

ivory: **6** creamy, dentin **7** dentine, ivoride, ribzuba **8** ribazuba

carving: **9** toreutics

rasping: **5** scobs

ivy: tod **4** gill, hove **6** hedera, hibbin

crowned with: **9** hederated

pert. to: **7** hederic

poison: **5** sumac **6** sumach

izzat: **5** honor **6** credit **8** prestige **10** reputation

J

jab: hit, jag **4** poke, prod, stab **5** lunge, punch **6** thrust
Jabal's father: 6 Lamech
jabber: 4 chat **6** burble, gabble **7** chatter **9** gibberish
jabot: 5 frill
jacare: 6 caiman
jacent: 5 prone **9** recumbent
jack: nob **4** card, lift **5** knave, money **6** wenzel **8** zapetero
group of 4: **8** quatorze
jack-of-all-trades: 6 tinker
jackal: 5 diebs
jackdaw: coe, daw **6** caddow **7** dawcock **9** blackbird
jacket: 4 bajo, coat, Eton **5** acton, grego, wamus **6** anorak, banian(Ind.), bietle, blazer, bolero, dolman, reefer, sliver, wammus, wampus **7** cassock, doublet, ristori, spencer **8** camisole, chaqueta, hanselin **9** habergeon, peajacket **10** carmagnole(F.), roundabout **11** nightingale
knitted: **5** gansy **6** gansey, sontag **7** sweater **8** cardigan, penelope
jackknife: 6 barlow
jackrabbit: 4 hare
jackstay: 4 rope **5** horse, staff
jackstones: 4 dibs
Jacob: *brother:* **4** Edom, Esau
daughter: **5** Dinah
descendant: **6** Levite **9** Israelite
father-in-law: **5** Laban
new name: **6** Israel
parent: **5** Isaac **7** Rebekah
retreat: **5** Haran
son: Dan, Gad **4** Aser, Levi **5** Asher, Judah **6** Bononi, Joseph, Reuben, Simeon **7** Gershon, Zebulun **8** Benjamin, Issachar, Naphtali
wife: **4** Leah **6** Rachel
vision(scene): **6** Bethel
jade: fag, nag **4** hack, minx, plug, tire **5** hussy, weary **6** harass **7** exhaust, fatigue, hilding, pounamu **8** nephrite **10** greenstone
jaded: 9 forjaskit, forjesket
jag: dag, jab, rag **4** barb, hair, load, mess, stab **5** carry, notch, prick, scrap, shred, slash, souse, spree, tooth **6** indent, tatter **7** bristle, pendant, portion **8** quantity **13** denticulation
jager: 6 hunter **7** diamond **8** huntsman

jagged: 5 erose, rough, sharp **6** hackly, ragged **7** cutting
jaguar: 5 ounce
jai alai: 4 game **6** pelota
court: **7** fronton
jail: can, jug **4** brig, dump, gaol, keep, stir **5** clink **6** asylum, carcel, cooler, lockup, prison **7** hoosgow **8** hoosegaw, hoosegow, imprison **9** calaboose **11** incarcerate
jailer, jailor: 4 caid **5** guard **6** gaoler, keeper, warden **7** alcaide, turnkey
Jairite: Ira
jake: 4 fine, hick, rube **5** dandy **6** rustic **9** first-rate, greenhorn
jalousie: 5 blind **7** shutter
jam: 4 bind **5** crowd, crush **6** spread **7** squeeze **9** marmalade **10** congestion
Jamaica dogwood: 8 barbasco
ginger alcohol: **4** jake
James' father: 7 Zebedee
jangle: 4 ring **6** bicker **7** prattle, quarrel, wrangle **11** altercation
jangling: 5 harsh **9** dissonant **10** discordant **11** cacophonous
janitor: 6 porter **9** caretaker **10** doorkeeper **11** housekeeper
japan: 7 lacquer, varnish
Japan: 5 Nipon **6** Niphon, Nippon
abacus: **7** soroban
abalone: **5** awabi
alcoholic beverage: **4** sake, saki
alloy: **5** mokum
allspice: **12** chimonanthus
apricot: ume **4** ansu
art design: **5** notan
baron: **6** daimio, daimyo
battle cry: **6** banzai
bay: ise
biwa: **6** loquat
boxes: **4** inro
brake: **6** warabi
brazier: **7** hibachi
brocade: **7** nishiki
Buddha: **5** Amida, Amita
Buddhist festival: Bon
Buddhist sect: Zen **7** Jodo-shu, Shin-shu
bush clover: **4** hagi
button: **7** netsuke
calculator: **6** abacus **7** soroban
calisthenics: **4** judo
cape: **4** mino
cherry: **4** fuji
chess: **5** shogi

chevrotain: **4** napu
church: **4** tera
circle: **4** maru
city: Ome **4** Kobe, Kura, Nara, Ueda **5** Atami, Kioto, Kyoto, Nikko, Osaka, Otaru, Tokio(c.), Tokyo(c.), Ujina **6** Nagoya, Sasebo, Sendai **7** Fukuoka, Niigata, Okayama, Okazaki, Sapporo **8** Hako Date, Kamakura, Kanazawa, Kumamoto, Nagasaki, Wakatama, Yokahama, Yokosuka **9** Hiroshima, Kagoshima, Tokushima **11** Akamagaseki
clan: **7** Satsuma
class: eta, roi **6** heimin **7** kwazoku, samurai, shizoku
coin: bu; rin, sen, yen **4** oban **5** koban, obang, tempo **6** cobang, ichebu, ichibu, itzebu, itzibu, kobang **7** itzeboo, itziboo
combine: **8** zaibatsu
composition: **6** haikai
costume: **7** netsuke
court: **5** dairi
crepe: **8** chirimen
crest: mon **7** kikumon
deer: **4** sika
deity: **9** Amaterasu
dextrose: ame
dish: **7** tempura **8** sukiyaki
dog: **6** tanate
door: **6** fusuma
drama: no
drink: **4** mate, sake, saki
drum: **5** tarko
dye process: **5** yuzen
earthenware: **5** banko **8** rakuware
emperor: **6** Makado **8** Hirohito
emperor's title: **5** Tenno **6** Mikado
ethics: **7** Bushido
explosive: **7** shimose
fabric: **6** birodi **7** habutai, nishiki **8** chirimen, habutaye
family concern: **8** zaibatsu
fan: ogi
felicitation: **6** banzai
festival: Bon **7** Matsuri
fish: ayu, tai, tho **4** fugu, funa
flag: **7** sunflag
flower: **9** nelumbium
flute: **4** fuye
game: go **5** goban **6** gobang
garment: **5** haori **6** kimono, mompei
gateway: **5** torii
girdle: obi
girdle receptacle: **4** inro
girl: **6** geisha, mousme **7** mousmee
god: **5** Ebisu, Hotei **6** Benten **7** Daikoku, Jurojin **8** Bishamon **10** Fukurokuju
goddess: **9** Amaterasu
governor's title: **6** shogun, taikun, tycoon
harp: **4** koto
herb: udo
island: Iki **4** Oita **5** Bonin, Hondo, Kuril, Sikok **6** Honshu, Kiushu, Kiusiu, Kurile, Kyushu, Niphon, Riu-kiu **7** Cipango, Loo-

Choo, Shikoku **8** Hokkaido
kelp: **4** kome
lacquer: **6** urushi
lake: **4** Biwa
litter: see *palanquin* below
loquat: **4** biwa
lyric: **5** haiku, hokku
magnolia: **5** yulan
measure: bu, jo; boo, cho **4** hiro **5** tsubo **11** kujira-shaku
measure of land: se; tan
measure of weight: mo; fun, kin, kon, rin, shi **4** kati, kwan, niyo **5** carat, catty, momme, picul **6** kwamme **8** hiyak-kin **11** komma-ichida
medicine case: **4** etui, inro
metalwork: **5** zogan
Mikado: **5** dairi
monastery: **4** tera
money: mo, ro
money of account: mo; rin, yen
mountain: Usu **4** Fuji **5** Asama, Hondo, Yesso **6** Asosan, Kiusiu **7** Fujisan **8** Fujiyama
music and dancing: **7** san-gaku **8** sarugaku
musical instrument: **4** fuye, koto **5** tarko **8** samisen, truyume
nautical mile: **5** kairi
nobility: **7** kwazoku
ornament: **4** inro
outcaste: eta **5** ronin
overcoat: **4** mino
pagoda: taa
painting style: **4** kano **7** ukiyoye
palanquin: **4** kago **5** cango **7** norimon
paper mulberry: **4** kozo
paper screen: **5** shoji
people: **4** Aino, Ainu **6** Nippon **9** Nipponese
persimmon: **4** kaki **7** Hyakume
plant: udo **5** kudzu **6** sugamo
porcelain: **5** Hizen, Imari **6** Hirado **9** Nabeshima
port: **4** Kobe **5** Hiogo, Osaka, Otaru **7** Niigata **8** Hakodate, Nagasaki, Wakatama, Yokohama
porter: **5** akabo
potato: imo
prefecture: **5** ehime **9** Yamaguchi
province: Ise **5** Iwaki **6** Yamato **7** Satsuma
religion: **6** Shinto **8** Buddhism **9** Shintoism
rice cake: ame
rice flour: ame
rice paste: ame
river: **4** Yalu **8** Tonegawa
robe: **6** kimono
ruler: **6** shogun
salad plant: udo
samurai: **5** ronin
sash: obi
seaweed: **4** nori
self-defense: **4** judo **7** jujitsu, jujutsu

Shinto temple: Sha **5** Jinja **6** Jinsha **7** Yashiro
shoe: **4** geta, zori
silk: **7** habutai **8** chirimen, habutaye
silkworm: **7** yamamai
silkworm disease: uji
sock: **4** tabi
song: uta
sovereign: **5** tenno
storm: **7** tsunami
street: **5** Ginza
suicide: **7** seppuku **8** hara-kari, hara-kiri, hari-kari, kamikaze
suntree: **7** hinokis
sword: **5** catan **6** cattan **8** wacadash
sword guard: **5** tsuba
syllabic writing: **4** kana
tea ceremony: **7** chanoyu
tea girl: **6** mousme **7** mousmee
temple: **4** tera
throne: **6** shinza
title: **4** kami **6** shogun
tortoise shell: **5** bekko
tree: **4** kozo, sugi **5** akeki, kiaki, yeddo **6** urushi **7** camphor **8** akamatsu **10** shirakashi
vehicle: **7** ricksha **8** rickshaw **10** jinricksha, jinrikisha
velvet: **6** birodi
verse: **5** tanka
vine: **5** kudzu
volcano: Aso **5** Asama, Asame **6** Asosan **8** Fujiyama **9** Asamayama
wall: **5** shoji
windstorm: **5** taifu
winged being: **5** tengu
wrestling: **4** judo, Sumo **7** jujitsu, jujutsu **8** jiujitsu, jiututsu
writing: **4** kana
zitherharp: **4** koto
Japanese-American: **5** Issei, Kibei, Nesei, Nisei **6** Kibbei, Sansei
japaneer: **9** varnisher
jape: **4** fool, gibe, jeer, jest, jibe, jipe, joke, mock **5** fraud, trick **6** deride
japery: **10** buffoonery
Japeth: *father:* **4** Noah
  son: **5** Magog, Tubal **7** Meshech
jar: jug, ola, urn **4** jolt, olla, vase **5** banga, clash, cruse, shake, shock **6** croppa, hydria, krater, tinaja **7** agitate, amphora, clatter, concuss, discord **10** jardiniere
  rubber: **4** lute
  top: lid
jardiniere: jar, jug, urn **4** vase **5** stand **7** garnish **9** flowerpot
jargon: **4** cant **5** argot, idiom, lingo, slang **6** pidgin **9** baragouin, gibberish **10** balderdash **11** grimgribber
jarring: **5** rough **9** dissonant **10** discordant
Jason: *father:* **5** Aeson
  men: **9** Argonauts
  ship: **4** Argo

jauk: **5** dally **6** trifle
jaundice: **7** gulsach, icterus
jaunt: **4** ride, trip **5** sally, tramp **6** ramble **7** journey **9** excursion
jaunty: **4** airy **5** cocky, perky, showy, smart **7** finical, stylish **8** debonair **9** debonaire, sprightly
Java: *arrow poison:* **4** upas
  badger: **5** ratel **6** teledʾı
  berry: **5** cubeb
  carriage: **4** sado **5** sadoo
  city: **7** Batavia, Jakarta **8** Samarang, Surabaya **9** Surakarta **10** Jokjokarta
  civet: **5** rasse
  community: **5** Dessa
  cotton: **5** kapok
  dancers: **6** bedoyo
  drama: **6** topeng
  Dutchman: **6** blanda
  fabric: **4** ikat
  fig tree: **7** gondang
  grackle: beo
  island: **4** Bali
  lomboy: **4** plum
  measure: **4** paal **5** palen
  mountain: **4** Gede **5** Lawoe **6** Raoeng **7** Semeroe, Slameta **8** Soembing
  musical instrument: **5** saron **6** bonang, gender **7** gambang, gamelan **8** gamelang
  orchestra: **7** gamelan **8** gamelang
  ox: **7** bantens
  pepper: **5** cubeb
  plum: **5** duhal **6** jambul, lomboy **7** jambool
  port: **7** Batavia **8** Surabaya
  puppet show: **6** wajang, wayang
  rice field: **5** sawah
  speech: **5** krama, ngoko
  straw: **6** peanit
  sumac: **6** fuyang
  temple: **5** candi **6** chandi, tjandi
  tree: **4** upas **6** antiar **7** gondang
  village: **5** Dessa
  weight: **4** amat, pond, tali **5** pound
  wild dog: **5** adjag
Java almond: **7** talisay
Java cotton: **5** kapok
Javan squirrel: **8** jelerang
Javanese skunk: **6** teledu
javelin: **4** dart **5** lance, spear **7** assagai, assegai, harpoon
  cord: **7** amentum
jaw: maw **4** chaw, chop, talk **5** scold **6** jabber **7** chatter **8** scolding
  lumpy: **13** actinomycosis
  muscle: **8** masseter
  part: **4** chin
  pert. to: **5** malar **7** gnathic
jawab: **5** reply **6** answer **7** balance **8** building
jawbone: **7** maxilla
Jayhawker: **6** Kansan
jazz: hot **4** cool **5** funky, swing **6** modern **7** ragtime **11** barrelhouse, progressive

jealous: 6 yellow 7 envious 10 suspicious 11 mistrustful

jeer: bob, boo 4 gibe, hoot, jape, jibe, mock 5 fleer, flite, flout, scoff, scout, sneer, taunt 6 deride 8 ridicule

jeering: 6 glaiks 7 sarcasm

Jehiada's wife: 9 Jehosheba 12 Jehoshabeath

Jehoahaz's mother: 7 Hamutal

Jehoiachin's successor: 9 Salathiel

Jehoshaphat: *father:* Asa
son: 4 Jehu

jehu: 6 driver

Jehu's father: 11 Jehoshaphat

jejune: dry 4 arid, avid, dull, flat 5 empty, inane, prosy, trite, vapid 6 barren, hungry, meager 7 insipid, sterile 8 foodless, lifeless

jell: 9 coagulate 11 crystallize

jellify: gel 5 jelly

jelly: gel 4 geal, sapa 5 aspic, kisel 6 cullis, pectin, spread 7 fisnoga, gelatin 8 gelatine

jellyfish: 6 medusa 7 acaleph
group: 10 discophora
part: 10 exumbrella

jellylike: 10 gelatinous

jeofail: 7 mistake 9 oversight

jeopardize: 6 expose 7 imperil 8 endanger

jeopardous: 6 daring 11 venturesome

jeopardy: 4 risk 5 peril 6 danger, hazard, menace 9 adventure

jequirity: 8 licorice

Jerahmeel's son: 4 Oren 5 Achia

jeremiad: 6 lament, tirade 9 complaint

Jericho: *publican:* 8 Zaccheus 9 Zacchaeus
woman: 5 Rahab

jerk: bob, tic, tit 4 hike, lipe, shog, yank, yerk 5 chuck, hitch, pluck, tweak

jerkin: 4 coat 6 jacket, salmon 9 blackjack, waistcoat

jerky: 5 wagon 7 charqui 8 saccadic, staccato

jeroboam: 4 bowl 6 bottle, goblet

jersey: 6 gansey 7 sweater

Jersey tea: 11 wintergreen 12 checkerberry

Jerusalem: 4 Sion, Zion 5 Salem
captor: 4 Omar
garden: 10 Gethsemane
mosque: 4 Omar
mountain: 4 Sion, Zion 6 Moriah, Olivet
oak: 7 ambrose
pert. to: 14 Hierosolymitan
pool: 6 Siloam 8 Bethesda
priest: 5 Zadoc, Zadok
prophetess: 4 Anna, Anne
region: 5 Perea
spring: 5 Gihon 6 Siloam
temple treasury: 6 Corban
thorn: 6 retama
town: 14 Hierosolymitan

Jerusalem artichoke: 5 tuber 7 girasol 8 girasole 10 topinambou

Jerusalem corn: 5 durra

Jerusalem haddock: 4 opah

jess: 5 strap, thong 7 binding

jessamy: fop 5 dandy

jest: bob, cog, fun 4 bull, fool, gaud, jape, joke, mime, quip, skit 5 bourd, droll, flirt, gleek, sport 6 banter, japery, trifle 8 drollery 9 burlesque 10 jocularity

jester: 4 fool, mime 5 clown, droll 6 disour 7 buffoon, dizzard 8 merryman 9 joculator 11 merry-andrew

Jesuit: *founder:* 6 Loyola
motto: 4 A.M.D.G.

Jesuits' bark: 8 cinchona

jet: 4 ebon, gush 5 black, ladle, raven, spout, spurt 6 nozzle 8 fountain, spouting

Jethro's daughter: 8 Zipporah

jetty: 4 mole, pier 5 groin, wharf 6 groyne

jeu: 4 game, play 9 diversion

jeune fille: 4 girl, miss

Jew (see also **Judaism**): 6 Essene, Semite
ascetic: 6 essene
harp: 8 guimbard
horn: 6 shofar

jewel: gem 4 opal, ruby, sard 5 beryl, bijou(F.), regal 6 garnet 7 diamond 8 amethyst, ornament
box: 6 casket 7 casquet
case: tye
connoisseur: 10 lapidarist
set: 6 parure
weight: 4 tola

jeweler: 7 gemmary
glass: 5 loupe

jewelry: 10 bijouterie
alloy: 6 oreide, oroide
artificial: 5 paste 6 strass 7 costume
cutting device: dop
false: 5 paste 6 strass 7 costume
piece: 4 ring 6 brooch 8 bracelet, necklace
set: 6 parure 8 lavalier, necklace 9 lavaliere 10 lavalliere
setting: 4 pave

Jezebel's husband: 4 Ahab

jib: gib 4 balk, boom, sail

jibe: See **gibe.**

jiffy: 5 braid, flisk, hurry, trice 6 gliffy, moment, second 7 instant

jig: top 4 boat 5 dance, prank 6 fiddle 8 carriage, fishhook

jigger: cup 4 club 5 glass 6 bridge, gadget 7 support

jiggle: jar 5 dance, shake 6 diddle, teeter

jihad, jehad: war 6 strife 7 contest, crusade 8 campaign

jill: 4 girl 5 woman 10 sweetheart

jilt: mau 4 girl, gunk 5 cheat, woman 6 begunk, mitten, reject 7 abandon, deceive, discard

jimmy: bar, pry 4 neat, spot 5 dandy, jemmy 6 spruce 7 crowbar 9 greatcoat

Jimsonweed: 6 datura
jingle: 4 ring 5 clank, clink, rhyme, verse
6 tinkle 7 chinkle
jingoist: 10 chauvinist
jinni: 6 afreet, Alukah, Yaksha, Yakshi(fem.)
jinx: hex 5 jonah 6 hoodoo
jitters: 5 panic 6 dither 11 nervousness
jittery: 5 jumpy 7 fidgety, nervous
job: 4 char, duty, snap, task 5 chare,
chore 8 sinecure
Job: *friend:* 6 Zophar
home: Uz
jobber: 6 dealer 10 wholesaler
Jocasta: *daughter:* 6 Ismene 8 Antigone
husband: 7 Oedipus
son: 7 Oedipus 8 Eteocles 9 Polynices 10
Polyneices
jockey: 4 gull 5 rider, trick 6 fellow, laddie, outwit 8 maneuver 10 manipulate
jocular: gay 4 airy 5 droll, funny, jolly,
merry, silly, witty 6 blithe, elated, jocose,
jocund, jovial, joyous, lively, ribald 7
comical, festive, gleeful, jesting, playful,
waggish 8 animated, cheerful, gladsome,
humorous, mirthful, sportive 9 burlesque,
convivial, facetious, hilarious, vivacious
10 frolicsome
joculator: fod 4 mime 6 jester 7 juggler 8
conjurer, jongleur, minstrel 11 entertainer
jog: bob, mog 4 lope, poke, prod, shog, trot
5 dunch, nudge 6 canter 7 refresh 9
stimulate
joggle: 5 hotch 7 shoggle
John: Ian 4 Ivan, Juan, Sean
John the Baptist: *father:* 7 Zachary 9 Zachariah, Zacharias
mother: 9 Elizabeth
join: add, fay, mix, tie, wed 4 abut, affy,
ally, club, fuse, knit, knot, link, mate,
meet, seam, team, weld, yoke 5 annex,
atone, blend, chain, clout, enrol, enter,
graft, hitch, marry, merge, miter, nally,
piece, unite 6 adject, adjoin, assist, attach, cantle, cement, cocket, concur, couple, engage, enlist, enroll, mingle, solder,
splice, suture 7 combine, conjoin, connect, consort, mortise 8 accouple, coalesce, compound, copulate 9 associate
10 amalgamate, articulate, consociate 11
incorporate
joined: 8 conjugal
joiner: 7 splicer 9 carpenter 10 woodworker
joining: 6 syzygy 8 abutting, addition
joint: ell, hip, tee 4 ares, butt, coxa, knee,
node, seam 5 alula, ancle, ankle, cross,
elbow, hinge, scarf, tenon, wrist 6 arthra(pl.), mutual, rabbet, resort 7 arthron, calepin, hangout, knuckle, pastern
8 coupling 12 articulation
pert. to: 5 nodal 9 articular
put out of: 9 dislocate

turned outward: 6 valgus
without: 10 acondylose, acondylous
wooden: 5 tenon
joist: 4 beam 7 sleeper 8 studding
joke: dor, egg, fun, gag, gig, pun 4 fool,
gaud, gibe, hoax, jape, jest, jibe 5 flirt,
prank, rally, sport, tease 6 banter, humbug 7 bromide 8 chestnut
joker: out, wag, wit 4 card 5 catch 6 gagger, jester 7 farceur 9 mistigris
Joktan's son: 5 Ophir
joll: 5 lurch
jollity: fun 5 cheer, mirth, revel 6 gaiety,
gayety 7 revelry 8 hilarity 9 amusement,
festivity, joviality, merriment 11 merrymaking 12 cheerfulness, exhilaration 13
jollification
jolly: 5 buxom, rally 6 cajole, jovial, mellow 7 jocular 11 merrymaking
jolly boat: 4 yawl
jolt: jar 4 blow, bump, butt, shog 5 knock,
shake, shock 6 jostle, jounce
Jonah: 4 jinx
jongleur: See **joculator**.
Jordan: *region:* 5 Perea 6 Basham
joree: 7 chewink
Joseph: *brother:* Dan, Gad 4 Levi 5 Asher,
Judah 6 Reuben, Simeon 7 Zebulun 8
Benjamin, Issachar, Naphtali
buyer: 8 Potiphar
father: 5 Jacob
mother: 6 Rachel
son: 4 Igal 7 Ephraim
josh: guy, kid, rib 4 joke 5 chaff, spoof,
tease 6 banter, string
Joshua: *associate:* 5 Caleb
father: Nun
place of importance: 7 Aijalon
Joshua tree: 5 yucca
jostle: jar, jog 4 jolt, push, shog 5 crowd,
elbow, shove 6 hurtle, hustle
jot: ace, bit 4 atom, iota, whit 5 grain, minim, point 6 tittle 8 particle
jouk: 4 dart, duck, fawn, hide 5 cheat,
dodge, evade, skulk 6 cringe
jounce: 4 jolt 5 shake 6 bounce
journal: log 5 diary, paper 6 record 7
daybook, gazette, gudgeon, logbook 8
magazine 10 periodical
keeper: 7 diarist
journalist: 6 editor 8 reporter 9 columnist
journey: go; run 4 eyre, fare, iter(L.),
ride, sail, tour, trek, trip 5 jaunt, route 6
errand, travel, voyage 7 circuit, odyssey,
passage, travail 8 navigate 9 excursion
10 expedition, pilgrimage 13 peregrination
journeying: 6 errant
joust: 4 tilt 6 combat 7 tourney 10 tournament
field: 4 list
ready to: 5 atilt
jovial: gay 4 boon 5 bully, jolly, merry 6

elated, genial, jocose, jocund, joyous 7
jocular 9 convivial, hilarious
jowl: jaw 4 chop 5 cheek 6 dewlap, wattle
7 jawbone
joy: 4 gaud, glee 5 bliss, mirth, revel 6
gaiety, gayety 7 delight, ecstasy, elation,
rapture, revelry 8 felicity, gladness, hilarity, pleasure 9 beatitude, festivity,
happiness, rejoicing, transport 10 exultation, joyfulness, joyousness 12 cheerfulness, exhilaration
Muse: 4 Tara
joyless: 6 dismal 9 cheerless
joyous: gay 4 glad 5 merry 6 blithe, festal,
festus 7 blessed, gaudful, festive, gleeful,
jocular 8 cheerful, gleesome, mirthful 9
blitheful, delighted
Jubal's father: 6 Lamech
jubilant: 6 elated 8 exulting 9 rejoicing
10 triumphant
Judah (see also **Judea**):
daughter-in-law: 5 Tamar
descendant: 4 Anub 9 Jerahmeel
king: 4 Ahaz 6 Uzziah
sea: Er
son: Er
Judaism (see also **Hebrew, Israel**):
abode of the dead: 5 Sheol
ascetic: 6 essene
Bible: 4 Tora 5 Torah
Bible text: 5 miqra
Book of Psalms: 8 Tehillim
bread: 5 echem, matzo 6 hallah, matzos 7
matzoth 8 afikomen
butcher: 6 shohet 8 shochtim
cabalistic book: 5 Zohar
calendar: see *month* below
ceremony: 8 habdalah
community: 6 aljama 8 kehillah
confession of sins: 5 Alhet 7 Ashamnu
convert: ger
Day of Atonement: 9 Yom Kippur
devil: 6 Belial
dispersion: 5 golah 8 diaspora
doctor of law: 6 scribe
doctrine: 6 Mishna 7 Mishnah 8 Ko-
dashim
drum: 4 toph
festival: see *holiday* below
garment: 5 shawl, talis 7 tallith
harp: 5 nebel
healer: Asa
heretical doctrine: 7 Karaism
holiday: 5 Pesah, Purim 6 Pesach, Suc-
cos, Sukkos 7 Sukkoth 8 Hanukhah, Lag-
bomer, Shabouth 9 Tishahbab 11 Rosh
Hashana 12 Simhath Torah
horn: 6 shofar 7 shophar
immigrant: 4 oleh 6 halutz 7 chalutz
instrument: 4 asor 5 nebel
instrument player: 9 psalterer, psaltress
judge: 7 shophet
land: 4 Zion
law: 4 Chok, Tora 5 Torah 6 Chukah,

Talmud 7 Halacha, Halakah 8 Kashruth
lawgiver: 5 Moses
liturgy: 6 Maarib, Minhah 9 Shaharith
lyre: 4 asor
marriage broker: 8 shadchen
marriage custom: 8 levirate
meat inspection: 7 bedikah
miter: 7 petalon
month: Ab 4 Adar, Iyar, Elul 5 Tebet, Ni-
san, Sivan 6 Tishri, Kislev, Shebat, Bea-
dar, Tammuz 7 Heshvan
mourning period: 6 Shivah
New Year: 11 Rosh Hashana
Old Testament division: 11 Hagiographa
patriarch: 5 Isaac
patriot family: 8 Maccabee
pioneer: 6 halutz 7 chalutz
poems: 6 yigdal 8 Azharoth
prayer: 5 Alenu, Shema 7 Geullah
prayer book: 6 mahzor, siddur
priest: 4 Ezra 5 Aaron, Cohen 6 Levite
priestly caste: 7 Cohanim, Levites
prophet: 4 Amos, Ezra 5 Elias, Hosea,
Jonah, Micah, Nahum 6 Daniel, Elijah,
Elisha, Haggai 8 Habakkuk, Jeremiah 9
Zechariah
prophetess: 6 Huldah
proselyte: ger
psalm of praise: 6 hallel
redeemer: 4 goel
revelation: 5 Torah
ritual: see *ceremony* above
sabbath: 8 Saturday
sacred objects: 4 urim
sage: 4 Agur
scarf: 5 abnet 7 tallith
scroll: 11 Sepher Torah
sect member: 6 Essene, Hassid
skullcap: 6 kippah 7 yamilke 8 yarmulka
song: 8 hatikvah 9 hattikvah
spirit: 8 Asmodeus
synagogue: 5 schul
tassel: 6 zizith
teacher: 5 rabbi
temple precentor: 6 cantor
trumpet: 6 shofar 7 shophar
vestment: 5 ephod
women's organization: 8 Hadassah
Judas's place of suicide: 8 Aceldama,
Akeldama
Judea (see also **Judah**):
governor: 6 Pilate
king: Asa 4 Ahaz, Amon 5 Herod 7 Jehoram 8 Manesseh 10 Jehoiachin 11
Jehoshaphat
place: 5 Berea
judge: try 4 deem, gage 5 count, court,
gauge, opine, trier 6 critic, decide, dicast,
puisne, umpire 7 account, adjudge, arbiter, believe, referee, shamgar, suppose 8
consider, deemster, dempster, estimate,
sentence 9 criticise, criticize, determine
10 adjudicate, appreciate, arbitrator,
chancellor

bench: **4** banc **6** bancus
chamber: **6** camera
circuit: **4** iter
gavel: **4** mace
group: **5** bench
kind: **6** deputy **9** assistant
of the dead: **6** Osiris
judgment: **4** deem, doom **5** arret, award, sense, taste **6** steven **7** censure, opinion, verdict **9** criticism **10** astuteness, visitation **11** sensibility
left to one's: **13** discretionary
judicable: **12** determinable
judiciary: **5** bench
document: **4** writ **8** decision
judicious: **4** wise **9** sagacious **10** discerning
jug: jar **4** ewer, jail, olla, toby **5** ascos, askos, ascus, buire, cruse, gotch **6** gomlah, lockup, prison, tinaja, urceus **7** pitcher **8** cruisken **9** container, cruiskeen **10** bellarmine, jardiniere **13** schnabelkanne
juggle: **7** conjure, shuffle **10** manipulate
juggler: **5** cheat **6** harlot **8** conjurer, conjuror, deceiver, jongleur **14** legerdemainist
jugglery: **8** trickery **9** deception **10** escamotage(F.), hanky-panky **13** sleight-of-hand
Jugoslavia: See **Yugoslavia**.
juice: jus(F.), oil, sap **4** broo **6** cremor **8** gasoline **10** succulence **11** electricity
apple: **5** cider
fruit: rob **4** must, stum, wine **5** cider **6** casiri **7** vinegar
plant: sap **4** milk **5** latex **6** achete
juicy: **4** frim, racy **5** spicy **6** lively **7** piquant **9** succulent
juju: **5** charm **6** amulet, fetish
jujube: ber
julep: **5** drink **8** beverage
jumble: **4** hash, heap, mess, raff, stir **5** botch, shake **6** bumble, huddle, medley, muddle **7** agitate, confuse, embroil **8** disorder, riffraff **9** confusion **10** hodgepodge **12** hugger-mugger
jump: hop, lep **4** leap, loup, lowp **5** bound, caper, halma, scold, vault **6** prance, spring **7** saltate
stick for: **4** pogo, pole
jumpy: **7** jittery, nervous **12** apprehensive
junction: **4** axil, seam **5** joint, union **6** suture **7** contact, meeting **8** crossing, juncture **10** confluence, connection
juncture: **4** pass **5** union **6** choice, crisis, strait **7** quandry **8** exigency, junction **9** emergency **11** conjuncture, predicament
June bug: dor **4** dorr
June grass: poa
jungle: **5** shola
dweller: **5** beast, snake **6** savage
junior: son **6** puisne **7** younger **8** namesake

juniper: **4** cade, ezel **5** gorse, retem, savin **6** sabine, savine
junk: **4** boat, bunk, dope, drug, lump, rush **5** chunk, scrap, waste **6** heroin, refuse **7** discard, rubbish **8** nonsense **9** narcotics
junket: **4** trip **5** feast **6** picnic **9** excursion **13** entertainment
Juno: **4** Hera
special messenger: **4** Iris
junta: **7** council **8** tribunal **9** committee **10** government
junto: **5** cabal **6** clique **7** coterie, faction **11** combination
jupe: **4** coat **5** shirt, skirt, stays, tunic **6** bodice, jacket
Jupiter: **4** Jove, Zeus
angel: **7** Zadkiel
daughter: **4** Bura
epithet: **6** Stator
lover: Io
Roman temple: **7** Capitol
satellite: Io **6** Europa **8** Ganymede, Callisto
son: **6** Castor, Pollux
juridical: **5** legal **7** juridic
jurisdiction: law, see, soc **4** soke **5** venue **6** county, parish **7** diocese **8** dominion **9** authority, bailiwick, patronate **10** patriarchy **13** collectorship
jurisprudence: law
juror: **7** assizer, juryman **8** talesman
group: **4** jury **5** panel
jury: **5** panel
additions: **5** tales **8** talesmen
attempt to influence: **9** embracery
form: **7** impanel
person: **8** talesman
summons: **6** venire
just (see also **joust**): due, fit **4** even, fair, only, true **5** equal, exact, legal, valid **6** candid, honest, merely, normal, purely, simply **7** correct, equable, upright **8** accurate, unbiased **9** equitable, impartial **10** legitimate
justice: law **6** equity **7** honesty, nemesis
god: **7** Forsete, Forseti, Forsite
goddess: **4** Maat
pert. to: **9** juridical
seat: **4** banc **5** court **6** bancus **8** tribunal
justification: **6** excuse **7** apology **9** authority, rationale
justify: **4** avow **6** adjust, defend, excuse **7** support, warrant **8** maintain, sanction **9** authorize, exculpate, vindicate
jut: **4** butt **5** bulge **6** beetle **7** project **8** overhang, protrude **10** projection
jute: **4** desi **5** gunny **6** burlap **7** sacking
Jutlander: **4** Dane
jutting: **7** salient
juvenile: **5** actor, young **8** immature, youthful **11** undeveloped
juxtaposition: **7** contact **8** nearness **9** adjacence, adjacency, proximity **10** contiguity

K

kaama: 10 hartebeest
kae: 7 jackdaw
Kaffir, Kafir: 4 Xosa 5 Bantu, fondo, Tembu 8 Matabele
servant: 6 umfaan
warriors: 4 Impi
weapon: 4 keri 10 knobkerrie
kaka: 6 parrot
kakapo: 6 parrot
kaki: 4 bird 5 stilt 9 persimmon
kakkak: 7 bittern
kale: 4 cole 5 green 7 cabbage, collard 8 colewort
kalends: 7 calends
Kamchatka: *codfish:* 6 wachna 9 wachna-cod
salmon: 6 mykiss
kamias: 7 bilimbi
Kanaka: 8 Hawaiian 10 Melanesian, Polynesian 11 Micronesian
kangaroo: 5 bilbi, bilby 6 turatt 7 bettong, wallaby 8 bettonga, boongary, forester 11 macropodian
female: doe, gin, roo
male: 6 boomer
young: 4 joey
Kansas: *county:* 4 Reno
fort: 5 Riley
river: 5 Osage
town: 4 Iola 5 Dodge, Lyons, Paola, Sedan 6 Salina, Topeka(c.) 7 Abilene 8 Lawrence 11 Leavenworth
kaput: 6 broken, ruined 8 defeated 9 destroyed
Karakul: 5 sheep
karma: 4 fate 7 destiny
kasha: 4 mush 5 grain 6 cereal
Kashmir: *alphabet:* 6 sarada
capital: 8 Srinagar
deer: 6 hangul
official: 6 pundit
kava: ava, awa
bowl: 5 tanoa
kazoo: 5 gazoo
kebbie: 4 club 5 stick 6 cudgel
keek: spy 4 look, peep
keel: vat 4 ship 5 upset 6 careen, carina 7 capsize, carinae(pl.) 8 flounder, navigate
part: 4 skeg
right angle to: 5 abeam
without: 9 ecarinate
keel-shaped: 8 carinate
keelbill: ani
keeling: 7 codfish

keen: yap(Sc.) 4 avid, fell(Sc.), gleg(Sc.), nice, wide 5 acute, awake, eager, sharp 6 ardent, astute, bewail, biting, clever, hearty, lament, severe, shrewd 7 cunning, fervent, intense, parlous, pungent 9 trenchant 10 hardheaded 12 enthusiastic 13 perspicacious
keenly: 6 dearly
keenness: 4 edge 6 acumen, genius, talent
keep: 4 fend, hold 5 board, guard, lodge, place 6 arrest, behold, detain, stable 7 confine, contain, husband 8 fortress, maintain, preserve, restrain, withhold 9 celebrate 10 livelihood
going: 7 sustain
keep back: bar, dam, hap 6 detain 7 reserve
keep in: 6 retain
keep out: 4 save 5 debar 7 exclude, reserve 8 withhold
keeper: 5 guard 6 alcade, alcaid, custos, pastor, warden 7 alcaide, alcayde, curator 8 custodes(pl.), guardian 9 constable, custodian 10 maintainer
keeping: 4 care 5 award, guard, trust 6 charge 7 custody 10 caretaking, possession 11 maintenance 12 guardianship
keepsake: 5 token 7 memento 8 giftbook, souvenir
keeve: tub, vat 5 basin
kef: 7 languor, tobacco 8 euphoria 10 dreaminess 12 tranquillity
keg: cag 4 cade, cask 6 barrel 7 barrico
open: 6 unhead
kegler: 6 bowler
kelly: hat 5 color, derby, green
kelp: 5 varec 6 varech 7 seaweed 8 bellware(Sc.)
ken: 4 know(Sc.), view 5 admit, sight 7 discern, insight 9 knowledge, recognize 10 cognizance, understand 13 understanding
kench: bin
kennel: 5 drain, sewer 6 cannel, gutter, stable 9 enclosure
Kent: *freedman:* 4 laet
sheep: 6 romney
tribal law: 4 laes
kentledge: 5 metal 7 ballast
Kentucky: *college:* 5 Berea
county: 4 Owen 6 Harlan
town: 5 Benge, Berea 7 Paducah 10 Louisville

Kentucky bluegrass: Poa
Kentucky coffee tree: 6 bonduc, chicot
kerchief: 5 curch(Sc.) 7 panuelo 8 head-rail 12 handkerchief
kerchoo: 6 sneeze
  answer to: 10 gesundheit 11 God bless you
kerf: cut 4 slit 5 notch 6 groove 7 cutting
kermis, kermess: 4 fair 8 carnival 11 celebration
kernel: nut 4 bunt, core, meat, pith, seed 5 acini(pl) grain 6 acinus, nuclei(pl.) 7 nucleus
kestrel: 6 falcon, fanner 7 stannel 9 windhover
ketch: 4 boat, saic 8 sailboat
ketone: 7 acetone, camphor, shogaol 8 acridone, civetone, deguelin 9 heptanone 14 cyclopentanone
  oily: 5 irone 6 carone
kettle: pot, vat 4 cazo(Sp.) 5 lebes 6 hollow 7 caldron 8 cauldron, flambeau 9 teakettle 10 kettledrum
  nose: 5 spout
kettledrum: 5 naker, tabor 6 atabal, nagara(Ind.), timbal 7 attabal, timbale, timpano, timpani(pl.), tympani(pl.)
kevel: bar, bit, peg 4 bolt 5 cleat, staff 6 cudgel 7 bollard
key: cay, fin 4 clef, isle, quay, reef 5 dital, islet, pitch 6 claves(pl.), clavis, island, opener, spline, tapper 7 digital 8 clavecin, solution, tonality 11 explanation
  notch: 4 ward
  part: bit
  pert. to: 5 tonal, tonic
  skeleton: 4 gilt 5 screw 7 twirler
keyboard: 6 manual 7 clavier 8 pedalier 10 claviature
keyed up: 4 agog 5 eager 7 excited 10 stimulated
keynote: do 5 theme, tonic, topic 7 feature
keystone: 8 voussoir
Keystone State: 12 Pennsylvania
Khnemu's consort: 6 Anukit
Khyber Pass tribe: 6 Afridi
kiang: ass
kibble: 5 grind 6 bucket
kibe: 4 chap, sore 5 crack
kick: toe 4 boot, fleg, funk(Sc.), punt, yerk 5 bunch, fling 6 fitter(Sc.), object, recoil 7 grumble 8 complain 10 calcitrate, enthusiasm
kid: guy 4 hoax, joke 5 child, suede, tease 6 banter 7 fatling, leather 8 cheverel, cheveril 9 youngster
kidcote: 6 prison
kidnap: 6 abduct
kidney: 4 neer
  comb. form: 4 reni
  pert. to: 5 renal
Kilauea goddess: 4 Pele
kilderkin: 4 cask 6 barrel 7 measure
kill: 4 fake, hang, slay 5 croak, fordo,

stone 6 deaden, diddle, famish, foredo, murder 7 achieve, execute, poniard 8 deathify, dispatch, lapidate 9 slaughter 11 assassinate
killed: 4 slew 5 slain 9 immolated
killer: 6 gunman 7 soldier, torpedo 8 genocide, homicide, murderer 10 triggerman 11 infanticide
  of relative: 8 filicide 9 matricide, parricide, patricide 10 fratricide, sororicide
killer whale: orc 4 orca 7 grampus
killing: 6 murder 7 slaying 8 homicide 9 euthanasy, martyrdom, slaughter 10 euthanasia
kiln: 4 oast, oven 5 clamp, stove, tiler 6 cockle 7 furnace
kilt: 4 hang 5 pleat 6 fasten 7 filibag
kimmer: 4 girl 5 witch 6 cummer, friend
kin: (see also **kinship**): 4 clan, race, sept 5 flesh, tribe 6 family 7 kindred, kinfolk, related 8 affinity, cousinry, kinsfolk, relation, relative 12 relationship
kind: ilk, kin 4 boon, gest, good, kith, mild, soft, sort, type 5 breed, class, genre, genus, geste, order 6 benign, blithe, gender, genera(pl.), genial, gentle, goodly, humane, kindly, tender 7 amiable, clement, couthie, species, variety 8 amicable, benedict, friendly, generous, gracious, merciful 9 benignant, brotherly, favorable, indulgent, squeamish 10 benevolent, charitable, favourable, generation 11 considerate, description, kindhearted, sympathetic 13 compassionate
  comb. form: 4 geno
  same: 10 homogeneal
kindle: 4 beet, fire, move 5 beete, brood, light, young 6 alight, arouse, decoct, excite, ignite, illume, incite, litter 7 animate, emblaze, inflame, inspire, provoke
kindling: 5 fagot 6 faggot, sticks, tinder 7 akindle
kindness: 5 aloha 6 bounty 8 benefice 9 benignity 11 beneficence
kindred: kin, sib 5 blood, flesh 6 allied, family 7 cognate, kinsmen 8 affinity, kinsfolk 9 congenial 12 relationship
kinetic: 6 active
king: dam, rex(L.), rey(Sp.), roi(F.) 4 czar, tzar 5 ruler 7 cacique, regulus 9 sovereign
  chamber: 9 camarilla
  child: 6 prince 8 princess
  domestic officer: 8 palatine
  family: 7 dynasty
  legendary: Lud 4 Bran 5 Hogni, Lludd, Midas, Sesha 6 Oberon, Shesha 11 Prester John
  murderer: 8 regicide
  personnel: 5 thane 6 avener 7 avenuer, dapifer, viceroy
  symbol: 7 scepter, sceptre
  title: Sir 4 Sire 7 Majesty 8 Highness

King Arthur: *abode:* **6** Avalon
character: **6** Elaine, Merlin
court site: **7** Camelot **8** Caerleon
crowner: **6** Dubric
father: **5** Uther
fool: **7** Dagonet
lady: **4** Enid
nephew: **6** Gareth **7** Mordred
parent: **5** Uther **7** Igraine
queen: **8** Guinever **9** Guinevere
sister: **7** Morgain **11** Morgan le Fay
sword: **9** Excalibur

king of beasts: **4** lion
king's evil: **8** scrofula
king's yellow: **8** orpiment
kingdom: **5** realm, world **6** empire, region
kingfish: **4** barb, opah **6** bagara
kingfisher: **7** halcyon
kingly: **5** regal, royal **6** regnal **7** basilic, leonine **8** imperial, majestic
kink: **4** bend, curl, loop **5** bunch, chink, cramp, quirk, snarl, twist **6** buckle, tangle **7** caprice **11** peculiarity
kinkajou: **5** potto **6** mammal
kinship (see also **kin**): **5** blood, nasab **8** agnation, nearness **10** connection **11** propinquity **13** consanguinity
father's side: **5** agnat **6** agnate **8** agnation
mother's side: **5** enate **7** enation
kinsman (see also **kin, kindred**): **4** ally **6** friend **8** bandhava **9** rishtadar
kipe: **6** basket
kirtle: **4** coat, gown **5** cover, dress, skirt, tunic **6** enwrap **7** garment **9** petticoat
kismet: **4** fate **7** destiny
kiss: **4** bass, buss **5** smack **6** caress **8** osculate
kiss-me-quick: **6** bonnet
kiss of peace: pax
kist: box **4** cist **5** chest **6** locker
kit: bag, box, cat, lot, set **6** kitten, outfit **7** catling **8** caboodle **10** collection
kitchen: ben(Sc.) **4** chil(Ind.) **5** calan(P.I.) **6** chilla(Ind.) **7** cuisine **8** scullery
pert. to: **8** culinary
kith: **6** friend **10** associates **12** acquaintance
kittenish: coy **6** frisky **7** playful **8** childish
kittiwake: **4** gull **5** annet
kitty: **4** bowl, pool **6** stakes
kiwi: roa **7** Apteryx
Klondike: See **Alaska.**
kloof: **4** glen **5** gorge **6** ravine, valley
knack: art **5** ease, gift, hang **5** catch, skill, trick **8** facility **9** dexterity **10** adroitness
knap: cut, rap, top **4** bite, blow, chip, crop, hill, snap **5** break, crest, knoll **6** nibble, strike, summit **7** hilltop
knapsack: bag **6** wallet
knapweed: **5** bluet **7** harweed **8** bellweed, clubweed, hardhead, harshwee **10** harebottle
knarred: **6** knarry, knotty **7** gnarled
knave: boy, nob, pam **4** fool, jack **5** cheat,

churl, losel, rogue, scamp **6** harlot, rascal, varlet **7** villain **9** miscreant, scoundrel, trickster
knavery: **5** fraud **8** mischief **10** dishonesty **12** sportiveness
knead: elt(Sc.), mix **5** malax **7** massage **8** malaxate **9** masticate **10** manipulate **11** incorporate
knee: bow **5** joint **10** supplicate
armor: **11** genouillere
bend: **5** kneel
bone: **7** patella
knee breeches: **8** knickers **12** small-clothes
kneecap: **7** patella
kneel: **4** genu **9** genuflect
kneepan: **6** rotula **7** patella
knell: **4** bell, omen, ring, toll **6** stroke, summon **7** warning **8** proclaim
knickknack: toy **6** bauble, bawble, gewgaw, trifle **7** novelty, trinket **8** gimcrack
knife: cut **4** bolo, cane, corn, shiv, snee, stab **5** bowie, bread, chive, corer, gully, kurki, sword **6** barong, campit, colter, coutel, cuttle, dagger, trevet, worker **7** carving, machete, spattle, spatula, whittle, yatagan **8** belduque, serpette
case: **6** sheath
maker: **6** cutler
sharpener: **4** hone **5** steel, stone
surgical: **6** catlin **7** catling, scalpel
knight: sir **5** eques **6** equite, Ritter **8** banneret, cavalier **9** caballero, caveliere, chevalier
attendant: **6** squire
banner: **8** gonfanon
cloak: **6** tabard
famous: **7** Caradoc, Cradock, Galahad **9** Lohengrin
servant: **4** page **6** varlet
title: sir
wife: **4** lady
wreath: **4** orle
knight-errant: **7** paladin
knightly: **5** brave **9** courteous **10** chivalrous
knit: **4** bind, heal, join, mend, purl **5** plait, unite, woven **6** cement, fasten **7** conjoin, connect, crochet, wrinkle **8** contract, entangle **10** intertwine **11** compaginate, consolidate
knitter: **6** legger
knitting: **5** craft **9** handiwork
rod: **6** needle
term: **4** purl **7** castoff
knob: bob, bur, nub **4** boss, buhr, burr, club, heel, knot, lump, node, tore, umbo **5** bulge **6** button, croche, emboss, handle, pommel **12** protuberance
knobby: **5** gouty, hilly **6** knotty
knobkerrie: **4** club **5** stick
knock: con, dad, hit, rap, tap, wap **4** beat, blow, bolt, bump, chap, chop, dash, daud, ding, dunt, hill(Sc.), jolt, knap, polt, poss,

rout, slay **5** pound, thump **6** bounce **7** hillock(Sc.) **9** criticize **12** faultfinding
knock down: **4** fell **5** floor **9** prostrate
knockout: K.O. **4** kayo **5** facer
knoll: **4** knap, knob, lump **5** mound **7** hillock
knop: **5** knosp **6** button **8** ornament
knot: bow, nep, tie **4** bond, burl, burr, harl, knag, knar, knob, knur, loop, lump, node, snag **5** gnarl, hitch, knurl, nodus, snarl **6** finial, granny, nodule, puzzle, tangle **7** chignon, cockade, laniard, lanyard, rosette **8** entangle **12** entanglement, protuberance
running: **4** slip **5** noose
pert. to: **5** nodal
knotted: **5** noded **6** knotty **7** crabbed, nodated **9** intricate
knotty: **4** hard **5** gouty **6** craggy **7** complex **9** difficult, intricate **10** perplexing
know: can, con, ken(Sc.), wis, wot **4** wist **9** realize **8** perceive **9** recognize **10** comprehend, experience, understand
know-it-all: **6** smarty **8** wiseacre
know-nothing: **8** agnostic **9** ignoramus **11** scissorbill
knowing: **4** able, gash, wise **5** cagey, downy, leery, smart, witty **6** scient, shrewd **7** gnostic, sapient, stylish **8** informed **9** cognitive, conscious, gnostical, wide-awake **10** experience, perceptive **11** intelligent **13** comprehension
knowledge: ken **4** lore **6** wisdom **7** cunning, hearing, science **8** learning, sapience **9** cognition, erudition **10** cognizance, experience **11** information, instruction **12** acquaintance **13** enlightenment, understanding
instrument: **7** organon
lack of: **9** ignorance, nescience
object of: **7** cognita(pl.), scibile **8** cognitum
pert. to: **7** gnostic
seeker: **10** philonoist
slight: **7** inkling, smatter **8** sciolism **10** smattering
summary: **13** encyclopaedia
systematized: **7** science

universal: **9** pantology
known: **5** couth, famed **6** famous **7** notable **8** familiar, renowned **9** notorious
knucklebone: **4** tali(pl.) **5** dolos, talus **7** dolosse(pl.)
kobird: **6** cuckoo
kobold: nis **5** gnome **6** goblin **7** Hodeken(G.) **10** nissespire
kohl: **8** antimony
kokopu: **4** fish, para
kopecks (100): **5** ruble
kopje: **4** hill **5** mound **7** hillock
Koran: **7** Alcoran
compiler's son: Ali
division: **4** Sura
interpreter: **5** ulema **7** alfaqui **8** alfaquin
register: **5** sijil **6** sijill
Korea: **6** Chosen
money: won **4** hwan
peninsula: **6** Ongjin
river: Kum **4** Hans, Look, Yalu **5** Imjin **7** Naktong
town: **5** Fusan, Heijo(c.), Kanko, Keijo(c.), Kimpo, Moppo, Rigen, Seoul(c.) **6** Andong, Antung, Gunzan, Inchon, Jushin, Kaeson, Keishu, Pochon, Rashin, Reigui, Wonzan **7** Capyong, Kenjiho, Moonsan, Samchok, Seishin **8** Chunchon, Pingyang **9** Chinnampo, Chuminjun, Shingishu
kosher: **8** Kashruth
not: **4** tref
meat maker: **6** porger
kra: ape **7** macaque
kraal: **5** crawl **9** enclosure
Krishna: *grandson:* **9** Aniruddha
mother: **6** Devaki
paradise: **6** Goloka
kudo: **4** fame **5** glory **6** praise, renown **8** prestige **9** extolling
Kurd: **7** Persian
ancestors: **9** Gordyaean
Kurile island: **6** Iturup
Kurland Peninsula inhabitant: **4** Lett
kurrajong: **4** tree **5** shrub **6** calool
Kwantung seaport: **6** Dairen
Kyushu: See Japan.

L

La Boheme: *composer:* 7 Puccini
  heroine: 4 Mimi
laagte: 6 bottom, valley
Laban's daughter: 4 Leah 6 Rachel
label: tab, tag 4 band 5 brand 6 docket,
  lappet, tassel 8 classify 9 designate 10
  definition
labile: 8 unstable
labium: lip
labor: 4 moil, task, toil, work 5 sweat,
  yakka 6 effort, labour, stress, strive 7
  travail 8 business, drudgery, exertion,
  industry, struggle 11 lucubration
labor organization: AFL, CIO, UMW 5
  union, ILGWU
labored: 5 heavy 6 forced 8 strained 9
  difficult, elaborate
laborer: man 4 hand, hind, peon, prol 5
  cooly, plebe 6 coolie, toiler, worker 7
  bracero, dvornik, hobbler, wetback,
  workman 10 bluecollar
laborious: 4 hard 5 heavy 7 arduous, operose, tedious 8 diligent 9 assiduous, difficult 11 displeasing, painstaking
Labrador retriever: 12 Newfoundland
Labrador tea: 5 ledum 8 gowiddie 9 evergreen
labyrinth: 4 maze 7 circuit
labyrinthine: 8 involved, puzzling, tortuous 9 intricate 11 complicated
lac: 4 milk 5 resin 6 veneer
lace: gin, net, tat 4 band, beat, cord, lash,
  line 5 braid, noose, plait, snare, twine,
  unite 6 fasten, ribbon, string 7 ensnare,
  entwine, laniard, lanyard 8 biliment,
  openwork 9 embroider, interlace 10 embroidery, intertwine, shoestring
  edge: 5 picot
  frilled: 5 jabot, ruche
  gold and silver: 5 orris
  kind: 5 lisle, orris, tulle 7 alencon, allover,
  guipure, macrame, potlace 9 Alostlace
  10 colberteen, colbertine 12 Valenciennes
lacerate: cut, rip 4 bite, rend, rive, tear 6
  harrow, mangle
laceration: rip 4 tear 5 wound
lacework: See **lace.**
lachrymose: sad 5 teary, weepy
laciniate: 7 fringed
lacis: 4 lace 7 network
lack: 4 need, void, want 5 fault, minus 6
  dearth 7 absence, failure, paucity, pov-

erty 8 scarcity 9 indigence 10 deficiency
  11 destitution
lackadaisical: 4 blah 7 languid 8 listless
  10 spiritless 11 sentimental
lackaday: 4 alas
lackey: 5 toady, valet 7 footman, servant
lacking: shy 5 short 6 absent, barren 7
  wanting 8 desolate 9 deficient, destitute
lackluster: 4 dull 6 cloudy 8 dullness
Laconia: *capital:* 6 Sparta
  people: Obe
laconic: 5 brief, pithy, short, terse 7 concise, pointed, summary 8 succinct
lacquer: 7 shellac, varnish
lactate: 4 salt 5 actol, ester
lacteal: 5 milky
lacuna: gap 5 break
lacy: 7 weblike 8 delicate
lad: boy 4 carl, dick, hind 5 caddy, youth 6
  caddie, shaver 9 stripling 10 adolescent
  on call: 4 page 7 bellboy 9 messenger
  serving: 7 gossoon 8 coistrel, coistril
ladder: run, sty 4 stee 7 scalade
  on fortification: 8 escalade
  step: 7 ratline
ladderlike: 6 scalar
lade: dip 4 bail, draw, lave, load, ship 5
  drain, scoop 6 burden, charge, weight 7
  fraught, freight
laden: 4 lade 7 fraught 9 freighted, oppressed
ladies' man: 4 beau
lading: 4 load 5 cargo 6 burden 7 freight
  10 freightage
ladle: dip 4 bail 5 scoop, serve, spoon 6
  dipper
ladrone: 5 rouge, thief 6 bandit, robber 7
  brigand 10 highwayman
lady (see also **woman**): 4 burd, dame,
  dona(Sp.), rani(Ind.) 5 begum(Ind.),
  donna(It.), madam, ranee(Ind.) 6 dom-
  ina(L.), female, senora(Sp.) 7 signora(It.)
  11 gentlewoman
  noble: 5 queen 7 duchess 8 countess,
  princess
  young: 7 damozel 10 demoiselle, jeune
  fille(F.)
lady-killer: 4 wolf 5 sheik 7 Don Juan 8
  Casanova
Lady of the Lake: 5 Ellen
lady's maid: 5 woman 9 tirewoman
lady's thumb: 9 peachwort, persicary
ladybird genus: 9 epilachna

ladyfish: oio **6** wrasse

ladylike: **6** female, polite **7** genteel **8** feminine

ladylove: **5** amour, lover **8** mistress **10** sweetheart

laet: **8** freedman

lag: **4** flag, rift, tire **5** delay, stave, tarry, trail, weary **6** dawdle, linger, loiter **9** drawlatch **10** dillydally **11** retardation

lager: ale **4** beer **5** drink **8** beverage

laggard: **4** slow **6** remiss **8** backward, loiterer, sluggish **9** straggler

lagging: **5** tardy **8** backward

lagniappe: tip **4** gift **5** bonus, pilon **7** present **8** gratuity

lagoon: **4** cove, haff, pond, pool **5** liman **6** laguna(Sp.)

Lagoon Islands: **6** Ellice

laic: **6** layman **7** secular **15** nonprofessional

laid-down: **5** posed **6** thetic **8** academic **10** prescribed **11** traditional

lair: den, lie **4** holt, rest **5** haunt **6** cavern **7** hideout, retreat **8** quagmire

Lais: **7** Burmese

laissez-faire: **8** inactive, tolerant **9** donothing, unconcern **11** philosophic **12** indifference, mercantilism **15** individualistic, noninterference

laity: **6** laymen

Laius' son: **7** Oedipus

lake: red, sea **4** loch, mear, mere, pond, pool, shat, shot, tarn **5** chott, color, lough, shott **7** pigment
  deposit: **5** trona
  highest: **8** Titicaca
  Indian: **4** Erie
  marshy: **5** liman

Lake Chad: *people:* **4** Maba
  river: **5** Shari

lakelet: **4** pond

lakhs (100): **5** crore

lam: hit **4** bash, beat **6** thrash

Lamaism: *dignitary:* **8** hutukhtu
  priest: **6** Getsul
  stupa: **7** Chorten

lamasery: **9** monastery

lamb: ean **4** yean **5** agnus(L.) **6** agneau(F.), cosset **7** chilver, fatling, hogling
  hand-raised: hob
  leg of: **5** gigot
  pet: **4** cade **6** cosset

Lamb of God: **8** Agnus Dei

Lamb's penname: **4** Elia

lambskin: **4** case **5** suede **6** bagdad **7** baghdad

lambent: **7** glowing, radiant **8** wavering **9** brilliant **10** flickering

lame: **4** game, halt **5** gammy **6** feeble **7** cripple, halting **8** crippled, decrepit, disabled, handicap **9** defective, hamstring **12** incapacitate

Lamech's son: **5** Jabal, Jubal **9** Tubal-cain

lament: cry, rue **4** care, howl, keen, moan, pine, sigh, wail, weep **5** croon, dolor, dirge, elegy, greet, grief, mourn **6** bemoan, bewail, beweep, dolour, grieve, lament, ochone, outcry, plaint, regret, repent, repine, yammer **7** condole, deplore, elegize **8** jeremiad **9** complaint

lamentable: sad **8** wretched **11** distressing

lamia: **5** witch **7** vampire **9** sorceress

lamina: **5** blade, flake, hinge, layer

lamp: **4** davy, etna **5** light, torch **7** lantern **8** lanthorn **9** veilleuse

lampblack: **4** soot

lampoon: **5** squib **6** satire **8** ridicule, satirize **10** pasquinade

lamprey: eel **6** ramper
  migration: **7** eelfare

lanai: **5** porch **7** veranda

lanate: **5** wooly **6** woolly

Lancashire section: **6** Eccles

lance: cut **4** dart, hurl **5** joust, spear **6** faucre, lancet, launch, pierce, weapon **7** javelin
  head: **5** morne

Lancelot's lover: **6** Elaine

lancer: **4** ulan **5** uhlan **7** soldier, spearer **10** cavalryman

lancet: **5** fleam

lancinate: **4** stab **5** gouge **6** pierce **8** lacerate

land: erd **4** ager(L.), soil **5** catch, earth, glebe, realm, shore, terra(L.) **6** alight, arrive, debark, ground **7** acreage, capture, country, terrene **9** disembark, territory
  alluvial: **5** delta
  ancestral: **5** ethel
  arid: see **desert**
  barren: see **wasteland**
  body: **9** continent
  church: **5** glebe **8** abadengo
  cultivated: **4** farm **5** arada, arado, ranch, tilth **7** orchard, tillage
  dealer: **7** realtor
  depressed: **6** graben
  elevated: alp **4** hill, mesa **5** mound, ridge **7** plateau **8** mountain
  grazing: **5** field, plain, range **6** meadow **7** pasture
  heritable: **4** alod, fief, odal **5** allod **7** alodium **8** allodium
  hilly: **4** down
  householder's: **6** barton, casate **7** demesne
  in foreign territory: **7** enclave
  living on: **11** terrestrial
  low: **4** vale **5** carse(Sc.) **6** polder, valley **9** intervale
  measure: ar; are, rod **4** acre, mile, rood **5** meter, perch **6** decare
  mythical: **4** Eden **6** Utopia **7** Erewhon, Lemuria **9** Shangri-La
  narrow: **4** neck **6** strake **7** isthmus **9** peninsula
  open: **4** moor, vega, wold **5** heath, slash,

weald
owned: see *heritable* above
pasture: ham **5** grass **6** meadow
pert. to: **11** continental
piece: lot **4** acre, farm **5** laine, ranch, range, solum (law) spong **6** estate
plowed: **5** arada, arado, field **6** arable, fallow, furrow **7** thwaite
profit: **4** crop, rent **7** esplees
public: **4** parc, park
reclaimed: **6** polder **7** novalia(Sc.),
river drained: **5** basin
sandy: **4** dene
tilled: see *plowed* above
treeless: **5** llano **6** steppe **7** prairie, savanna **8** savannah
triangular: **4** gore
uncultivated: **5** heath, waste **6** desert, forest
uplifted: **5** horst
waste: see **wasteland**
waterlocked: ile(F.) **4** isle **6** island
watery: bog **4** flow, moor **5** marsh, swamp **6** morass **7** maremma(It.)
Land of Plenty: **6** Goshen
land's end guardian: **8** Bellerus
landed: See **estate; land.**
landholder: **5** laird **6** coscet, yeoman
landholding: **6** tenure
landing: **8** arrivage
kind: **5** crash **10** three-point
place: **4** dock, pier **5** wharf **7** airport **8** airplace, arrivage
landlady: **5** duena **7** hostess **8** mistress **9** concierge
landlord: **4** host **5** laird(Sc.) **6** lessor
landmark: **4** copa, dole, dool, mere **5** bound, cairn, senal(Sp.) **9** milestone
landscape: **4** plan **5** plant, scene **7** scenery, paysage, picture **8** decorate
landslide: **9** avalanche **10** eboulement
landsman: **6** lubber, sailor
lane: way **4** char, path, race **5** aisle, alley, byway, chare, chase, tewer **6** boreen, bypath, gullet, street, throat, vennel **7** pathway **8** footpath **10** passageway
language: **4** chib **5** argot, idiom, lingo, slang **6** jargon, speech, tongue **7** dialect, diction
ancient: **4** Pali **5** Aryan, Greek, Latin **6** Hebrew **7** Chinese **8** Sanskrit
change: **8** misquote **9** interpret, translate **10** paraphrase
classical: **5** Greek, Latin
common: **6** French, German **7** Chinese, English, Italian, Russian, Spanish
Cretan: **6** Minoan
figurative: **7** imagery
international: od, ro; ido **7** volapuk **9** esperanto
nonmetrical: **5** prose
pert. to: **8** semantic
pompous: **4** bull, wind **7** bombast, oratory **8** rhetoric

principles: **7** grammar
Romance: **5** Latin **6** French **7** Catalan, Italian, Spanish **8** Rumanian **10** Portuguese
sacred: **4** Pali
secret: **5** argot
Semitic: **6** Arabic, Hebrew
spoken: **7** diction **13** pronunciation
unintelligible: **9** gibberish
languid: **4** dull, slow, weak **6** dreamy, tender **8** indolent, listless, lovesick, sluggish **9** lethargic **11** indifferent
languish: die **4** fade, fail, flag, long, pine, wilt **5** droop, dwine, faint, swoon **6** linger, repine **7** decline
languor: kef **4** kaif, keef, kief **5** ennui **7** boredom **8** debility **9** lassitude **10** stagnation
langur: **6** monkey **8** wanderoo
lanky: **4** lean, slim, tall, thin **5** gaunt, rangy, spare **6** gangly, meager, meagre, skinny **7** haggard, slender **8** gangling, ungainly **9** elongated **12** loose-jointed
lanose: **5** wooly **6** woolly
lantern: **4** lamp **5** bowet **8** absconce
lanyard, laniard: **4** cord, knot, rope
Laodamia's father: **7** Acastus
Laodicean: **8** lukewarm **9** apathetic **10** uninvolved **11** indifferent
Laomedon's son: **8** Tithonus
lap: sip **4** fold, lick, wash **5** drink, slurp **6** circle, cuddle, enfold, infold **7** circuit
lap robe: rug **5** throw **6** afghan **7** blanket
lapactic: **8** laxative **9** cathartic
lapel: **5** rever **6** revers
lapidary: **7** jeweler **8** engraver **9** gem cutter
instrument: dop **4** dial
lapidate: **4** pelt **5** stone
lapin: **6** rabbit
lappet: **4** lobe **5** label **6** fabric
lapse: err **5** break, error, fault **6** expire **7** delapse, escheat, failure, relapse **8** caducity, slipping **9** backslide
lapsed: **4** dead, null, void
laputan: **6** absurd, dreamy **7** utopian **9** visionary **10** unfeasible **11** impractical
lapwing: **5** pewit **6** plover
lar: **6** gibbon
larboard: **4** left, port
larceny: **5** theft **7** looting, robbery **8** burglary, stealage
lard: fat, oil **4** mort **5** adeps(L.), baste, enarm, inarm **6** enrich, fatten, grease
larder: **4** cave **6** pantry, spence, spense **8** cupboard
large: big **4** bold, free, huge, main, vast, waly **5** ample, broad, bulky, burly, enorm, giant, great, hulky, massy, wally **6** goodly, heroic **7** copious, immense, liberal, massive, titanic, weighty **8** colossal, enormous, gigantic **9** capacious, extensive, plentiful **12** considerable **13** comprehensive

comb. form: **5** macro

largess, largesse: 4 gift **6** bounty **7** charity, present **10** generosity, liberality **11** beneficence

lariat: 4 rope **5** lasso, noose, reata(Sp.), riata(Sp.)
loop: **5** honda, hondo **6** hondoo, hondou

larix: 5 larch **7** larches

lark: 6 frolic **7** carouse **8** carousal

larkspur: 10 delphinium

larrigan: 8 moccasin

larrup: 4 beat, blow, flog, whip

larry: hoe **5** grout, noise **6** mortar **9** confusion **10** excitement

larva: bot, fly, loa **4** bott, grub **5** eruca **6** botfly, woubit **7** atrocha, oestrid **8** cercaria, horsefly **11** caterpillar
aquatic: **12** hellgrammite

larvate: 6 masked **7** covered **9** concealed

lascar: 6 sailor **12** artilleryman

lascivious: 6 wanton **7** blissom **9** lecherous, salacious, seductive **10** libidinous, licentious

lash: 4 beat, bind, blow, flog, lace, whip, yerk **5** slash **6** berate, fasten, strike, stroke, swinge **7** belabor, eyelash, scourge

lasket: 8 latching

lass: gal **4** gill, girl, maid, miss **5** trull, woman **6** cummer, kimmer, lassie, maiden **7** colleen **10** sweetheart **11** maidservant

lassitude: 5 ennui **7** languor **8** debility, lethargy **10** exhaustion

lasso: 4 rope **5** noose, reata(Sp.), riata(Sp.) **6** lariat

last: 4 dure, tail **5** abide, final, omega **6** endure, latest, utmost **7** dernier, extreme, tail-end **8** continue, eventual, hindmost, rearmost, ultimate **9** aftermost **10** concluding
but one: **6** penult
long: **7** outwear **9** perendure

Last of the Mohicans: 5 Uncas

Last Supper: *representation:* **4** cena
room: **7** cenacle

lasting (see also **last**)**: 6** stable **7** chronic, lasting, eternal **8** constant **9** perennial, permanent, steadfast **11** everlasting
briefly: **9** ephemeral, temporary

latch: 5 catch, sneck **6** fasten **8** fastener

latchet: tab **5** thong

late: new **4** sere **5** tardy **6** former, recent **7** belated, overdue **8** neoteric, serotine **10** behindhand
comb. form: neo

latent: 6 hidden **7** dormant **9** concealed, potential, quiescent, suspended **11** undeveloped

later: 4 anon, soon **5** after, newer **6** behind, future, puisne **7** elderly, neozoic **9** hereafter, posterior, presently **10** subsequent **12** subsequently

lateral: 4 side **8** indirect, sideward

latest: 4 last **6** newest

lath: 4 slat **5** spale, stave
attachment: **7** setover
operator: **6** turner
part: **7** mandrel

lather: 4 foam, soap, suds **5** froth **6** freath

Latin (see also **Rome**)**: 5** Roman **7** Italian, Romanic
bath: **7** balneum
barracks: **6** canaba
bowl: **6** patina
booth: **7** taberna
boxing glove: **6** cestus, ceston
bronze: aes
building: **5** aedes
cape: **5** sagum **6** byrrus
cistern: **9** impluvium
connective: et
contract: **5** nexum
couch: **9** accubitum
dish: **4** lanx **6** lances, pateral, patina
foot: pes
garland: **6** corona
ghosts: **7** lemures
grammar: **5** donat, donet
grammatical case: **6** dative **8** ablative, genitive, vocative **10** accusative, nominative
javelin: **4** pile **5** aclys, pilum
ornament: **5** bulla
post: **4** meta
pronoun: tu; ego, hic **4** ille, ipse, iste
ram: **5** aries
rite: **4** orgy **5** sacra
roof opening: **10** compluvium
seat: **5** sella
shelter: **7** taberna
towel: **5** mappa
trumpet: **4** tuba **6** buccin **7** buccina

Latinus' daughter: 7 Lavinia

latite: 4 lava

latitude: 5 scope, width **6** extent **7** breadth, freedom **8** distance
complement: **10** colatitude
measure: **6** degree **8** parallel
zero degrees: **7** equator

latrant: 7 barking **8** snarling **11** complaining

latrine: 5 privy **6** toilet

latter: 4 last **5** final **6** latest

Latter Day Saints: 7 Mormons

latterly: 4 anew **6** lately **8** recently

lattice: 6 pinjra(Ind.) **7** trellis **8** espalier

latticework: 5 arbor, grate **6** arbour **7** grating

Latvia: *city:* **4** Riga(c.) **5** Libau **6** Dvinsk, Libava **8** Dunaburg **10** Daugavpils
coin: lat **6** rublis **7** kapeika **8** santimas
measure: **4** stof **5** kanne, stoff, verst **6** kulmet, sagene, versta, verste **7** verchoc, verchok **8** krouchka, kroushka, pourvete **9** deciatine, lofstelle **10** tonnstelle
parliament: **6** Saeima
people: **5** Letts

river: Aa
university site: **4** Riga
weight: **9** liespfund
laud: **4** lute **5** extoll **6** extoll, praise **7** adulate, applaud, cittern, commend, glorify, magnify **8** emblazon, eulogize **9** panegyric **10** compliment
laudable: **9** allowable, exemplary **12** praiseworthy
laugh: **4** gaff, haha **5** fleer, snort **6** cackle, giggle, guffaw, hawhaw, nicker, titter **7** chortle, grizzle, snicker **9** cachinate
disposed to: **7** risible
incipient: **4** grin **5** smile
laughable: odd **5** comic, droll, funny, merry, queer, witty **7** amusing, comical, risible, strange, waggish **8** gelastic, humorous, sportive **9** burlesque, diverting, facetious, grotesque, ludicrous **10** ridiculous
laughing: **5** riant
laughing bird: **4** gull, loon **5** pewit **10** woodpecker
laughing owl: **5** wekau
laughter: **5** mirth, risus(L.)
pert. to: **7** risible
launder: tye **4** wash
laundry: **4** wash **10** laundromat **13** blanchisserie(F.)
laureate: **13** distinguished
laurel: bay **4** fame **5** honor **6** daphne, myrtle, tarata, trophy **7** garland, taratah **9** spoonwood **11** distinction
lava: aa, oo **4** slag **5** ashes **6** coulee, latite, scoria, verite **7** clinker **8** pahoehoe
lavabo: **5** basin **8** washbowl **9** cleansing
lavaliere, lavalier: **7** pendant
lavation: **4** bath **6** lavage **7** washing **9** cleansing
lavatory: **5** basin **8** washbowl, washroom
lave: **4** bail, lade, pour, wash **5** bathe, rinse
lavender: **6** pastel, purple, violet
laver: **5** basin **6** trough, vessel **7** cistern
Lavinia: *father:* **7** Latinus
husband: **6** Aeneas
mother: **5** Amata
lavish: **4** free, lash, rank, wild **5** flush, spend, waste **7** opulent, profuse **8** prodigal, reckless, splendid, squander **9** bountiful, expensive, exuberant, impetuous, luxuriant, sumptuous, unstinted **10** immoderate **11** extravagant, magnificent **12** unrestrained **13** superabundant
law: act, bar, ius(L.), jus(L.), lex(L.) **4** code, doom, rule, Tora **5** canon, edict, mesne, sutra, Torah **6** custom, decree, equity, noetic, sutrah, suttah **7** derecho, justice, precept, statute **8** handicap **9** enactment, ordinance, principle **11** commandment, legislation **12** constitution, jurisdiction **13** jurisprudence
action: res **4** suit **5** actus **8** replevin **9** gravamina

body of: **4** code
claim: **4** lien
contrary to: **7** illegal, illicit **8** unlawful **16** unconstitutional
degree: LLD
delay: **4** mora
document: **4** deed, writ **6** capias, elegit
expounder of: **6** jurist
goddess: **4** Maat
male succession: **5** Salic
man of: **5** judge **6** jurist, lawyer **7** counsel, justice **8** attorney **9** barrister
Manu: **5** sutra, sutta
offender: **8** criminal **9** desperado, wrongdoer
offense: **4** tort **5** crime, malum **6** delict
oral: **5** parol **11** nuncupative
order: **4** writ
permitted by: see **lawful**
pert. to: **5** legal **7** canonic **9** canonical, judiciary **11** legislative
philosophy of: **13** jurisprudence
warning: **6** caveat
lawful: due **5** legal, licit, valid **7** canonic, ennomic **10** legitimate
lawgiver: **5** Moses
lawless: **4** lewd **6** unruly **7** illegal **8** anarchic **9** dissolute **10** anarchical, disorderly, tumultuous
lawmaker: **5** solon **7** senator **10** legislator
lawn: **5** arbor, grass, sward **6** arbour **7** batiste **9** grassland, grassplot, grasswork
lawsuit: **4** case
one engaged in: **8** litigant
subject: res
lawyer: **6** avocat(F.) **8** attorney, commoner **9** barrister, counselor **10** counsellor
bad: **7** shyster **11** pettifogger
lax: **4** dull, free, limp, open, pave, slow **5** loose, slack, tardy **6** remiss **7** lenient **8** backward, careless, inactive **9** dissolute, negligent **10** unconfined **11** inattentive **12** unrestrained
lay: bet, put, set **4** bury, poem, rest, song **5** carol, ditty, place, quiet, stake, still, wager **6** ballad, entomb, hazard, impose, impute, melody **7** appease, ascribe, deposit **14** unprofessional **15** nonprofessional
lay aside: **5** table **6** shelve **7** abandon, discard, neglect
lay away: See **lay by.**
lay bare: **4** show **5** strip **6** denude, expose, reveal **7** uncover
lay by: **4** hive, save **5** amass, cache, hoard, store **7** deposit, husband, reposit **8** treasure **10** accumulate
lay down: set **5** posit **9** establish, surrender
lay hold of: **4** grab, grip **5** grasp, gripe, seize **9** apprehend
lay out: **4** plan **5** set up, spend **6** expend, extend, invest

lay up: See **lay by.**

lay waste: 6 harass, ravage **7** destroy **8** desolate **9** depredate, devastate

layer: bed, hen, ply **4** coat, film, fold, seam, tier, zona **5** paver **6** folium, lamina, veneer **7** bedding, provine, stratum **8** laminate **10** substratum

pert. to: **7** stratal

layered: 7 laminal, laminar **8** tunicate

layman: 4 laic

laymen: 4 laic **5** laity

layout: 4 plan **6** design, make-up **7** pattern

lazar: 5 leper

lazy: 4 idle, laze **5** inert **8** indolent, slothful, sluggard

lea: 6 meadow **7** pasture **9** grassland

leach: wet **7** moisten **9** lixiviate, percolate

lead: con, van, wad **4** head, lode, star, wadd **5** carry, first, guide, krems, metal, pilot, steer, usher **6** bullet, ceruse, convey, deduce, direct, escort, induce, manage **7** command, conduct, pioneer, precede **8** graphite, instruct, outstrip **9** influence

astray: **4** lure **6** allure, delude, entice, seduce **7** deceive, mislead, pervert **8** inveigle

color: **4** dull, gray **5** livid, olive

ore: **6** galena

paste: **6** strass

pig: **6** fother

sounding: **7** plummet

sulphide: **6** galena

leaden: 4 dull, gray **5** heavy **8** plumbean, sluggish **9** plumbeous

leader: bo; boh, cob, dux **4** cock, duce, duke, head, line, wire **5** chief, coach, pilot, sinew, snell **6** cantor, Fuhrer(G.), tendon **7** captain, demagog, foreman, Fuehrer(G.) **8** caudillo, choragus, headsman, preceder **9** chieftain, demagogue, drainpipe, principal **10** bellwether **11** condottiere, gymnasiarch

ecclesiastical: fra **4** pope **5** rabbi **6** bishop, father, priest **8** cardinal, minister, preacher **10** evangelist

leadership: 8 guidance, hegemony **9** authority

leading: big **4** duct, head, main **5** ahead, chief, first **6** banner **7** capital, central, guiding, premier, stellar **8** foremost **9** conducive, directing, governing, hegemonic, inductive, principal **11** controlling

leaf: ola, ole, pan **4** foil, olay, olla, page **5** blade, bract, folio, frond, palet, scale, sepal **6** areola, insert, spathe **7** tendril

aperture: **5** stoma

appendage: **6** ligula, stipel **7** stipule

aromatic: see **herb**

circle: **7** corolla

edge: **9** crenation

floating: pad

kind: **5** calxy, petal, sepal **7** corolla

part: pen **4** axil **5** costa, stoma **6** pagina **7** petiole, stomate

set: **5** calyx **7** corolla

vein: rib **5** costa

leafage: 7 foliage

leaflet: 5 pinna, tract **6** folder **7** booklet **8** pamphlet

leafstalk: 6 celery

leafy: 5 green, shady **6** foliar **7** sepaled

league: 4 bond **5** union **7** compact **8** alliance, covenant **9** coalition **10** federation **11** association, combination, confederacy **13** confederation

League of Nations city: 6 Geneva

Leah: *father:* **5** Laban

sister: **6** Rachel

son: **6** Simeon

leak: 4 drip, hole, loss, ooze, seep **5** crack **6** escape **7** channel, crevice, fissure

leaky: 6 gizzen

leal: 4 just, real, true **5** legal, loyal **6** lawful **7** correct, genuine **8** accurate, faithful

leam: 4 husk

lean: 4 bend, cant, lank, mean, poor, rely, slim, tend, thin, tilt **5** gaunt, lanky, scant, spare **6** depend, hollow, meager, meagre, skinny **7** conform, deviate, haggard, incline, recline, scrawny, slender **8** rawboned, scragged **9** deficient, emaciated **10** inadequate **12** unproductive

lean-to: hut **4** shed **5** shack

Leander's sweetheart: 4 Hera, Hero

leaning: 7 pronate **8** penchant **9** accumbent

leap: fly, hop **4** dart, dive, jump, loup, skip **5** bound, caper, exult, frisk, lunge, salto, vault **6** bounce, breach, cavort, curvet, gallop, gambol, hurdle, hurtle, spring **7** saltate **8** capriole **9** ballotade, entrechat

leaping: 7 salient, saltant **9** caprizant, saltation

lear: 4 lore **6** lesson **8** learning

Lear's daughter: 5 Regan **7** Goneril **8** Cordelia

learn: con, get **4** find, here, lere **6** master **7** acquire, apprise, apprize, realize **8** memorize **9** ascertain

learned: wot **4** blue, read, sage, wise **6** astute, doctus **7** clerkly, cunning, erudite **8** lettered, literary, literose **9** scholarly **10** omniscient

learner: 5 pupil **7** scholar, trainee **8** disciple, opsimath **10** apprentice

learning: art **4** lear, lore **6** wisdom **7** cunning **8** pedantry **9** education, erudition, knowledge **10** discipline, experience **11** scholarship

display of: **8** pedantry

love of: **9** philology

man of: **6** pundit, savant **7** scholar, teacher **9** philomath, professor **12** intellectual

lease: let **4** hire, rent **6** demise, engage, rental, tenure **7** charter **8** contract **10** concession

leash: **4** bind, cord, harl, jess, lune **5** strap **6** couple, tether

least: **6** fewest, little, lowest **7** minimal, minimum **8** shortest, smallest **9** slightest

leather: tan **4** napa, whip, yuft(Russ.) **5** balat, leder, strap **6** thrash

artificial: **7** keratol

drying: sam **4** samm **5** sammy

finish: **4** buff

inspector: **6** sealer

kind: elk, kid, kip **4** bock, buff, calf, doze, napa, roan, seal, vici **5** aluta, basil, mocha, suede, trank **6** castor, levant, oxhide, skiver **7** buffalo, canepin, chamois, morocco, saffian **8** cheverel, cheveril, Cordovan

pare: **5** skive

piece of: **4** rand, welt **5** clout, strap, thong **6** latigo

prepare: tan, taw

tool: **6** skiver

waste: **6** tanite

worker: **6** chamar, tanner **8** chuckler

leatherback: **6** turtle

leatherneck: **6** marine

leave: go; let **4** bunk, exit, quit **5** favor, forgo, grace, scram **6** beleve, decamp, depart, desert, entail, favour, forego, forlet, permit, retire, vacate **7** abandon, beleave, forsake, getaway, liberty, license **8** bequeath, emigrate, furlough, vacation **9** allowance **10** permission, relinquish

behind: **11** outdistance

in the lurch: **6** desert, maroon, strand

leave of absence: **5** exeat **8** furlough

leave off: **4** quit, stop **5** cease, elide **6** desist **10** abbreviate

leave out: **4** omit, skip **5** elide

leave-taking: **5** adieu, conge **6** congee **7** parting **8** farewell **9** departure

leaven: **5** imbue, yeast **7** lighten **10** impregnate

leaves (see also **leaf; leave**): **7** foliage

having: see **leafy**

medicinal: **5** senna

leavings: See **lees; rubbish**.

Lebanon: *castle:* **5** Saida, Sidon, Toron **8** Beaufort

city: **4** Arca, Tyre **5** Ehden, Saida **6** Beirut(c.) **7** Tripoli **8** Beyrouth **9** Broummana

dance: **6** dabkeh

fort: **6** Byblos

money: **5** livre **7** piastre

mountain: **4** Mzar **7** Sannine **8** Kadischa, Kenisseh

people: **4** Arab

river: **5** Lycos **6** Damour, Litani **8** Kasemieh

seaport: **4** Tyre **6** Beirut **8** Beyrouth

tree: **5** cedar

lech: **4** slab **8** capstone, monument

lecher: **7** glutton **8** gourmand, parasite **9** debauchee, libertine

lecherous: **4** lewd **7** boarish, goatish, lustful **9** salacious

lectern: **4** ambo, desk **10** escritoire

lecture: **5** scold **6** lesson, preach, sermon **7** address, hearing, lection, oration, prelect **9** discourse, sermonize **12** dissertation

lecturer: **6** docent, reader **9** prelector, professor

led: See **lead**.

Leda's son: **6** Castor, Pollux

ledge: **4** berm, sill **5** bench, berme, shelf **7** retable

ledger: **4** tome **6** record

lee: **5** haven **7** shelter **10** protection

leech: **8** parasite **9** blackmail **11** bloodsucker

leer: **4** face, lear, lehr, loin, look, lust, ogle, void **5** empty, flank, fleer, smirk **6** entice, unlade **7** grimace

leery, leary: **4** wary **7** knowing **10** suspicious **11** distrustful

lees: **5** draff, dregs, dross, grout **6** bottom, dunder, refuse, ullage **7** grounds **8** emptings, sediment, settling **9** excrement

leeward: **4** alee

drift: **4** crab

Leeward group island: **5** Nevis **7** Antigua, Barbuda, St. Kitts **8** Anguilla, Dominica, Windward **10** Montserrat

leeway: **4** room **5** space **9** elbowroom

left: **4** port **8** larboard

toward: haw **5** aport **9** sinistrad

left-handed: car **6** gauche **8** southpaw **9** portsided

left-over: See **lees; rubbish**.

leftist: red **7** radical **13** revolutionary

leftward: **5** aport

leg: **4** gam **4** gamb, hoof, limb, prop, walk **5** bough, brace, gambe, shank **6** bender, gammon **8** cabriole

bone: **4** shin **5** femur, ilium, tibia **6** fibula

muscle: **8** peroneus **9** peronaeus

ornament: **6** anklet

part: **4** calf, crus, knee, shin **5** ankle, thigh **11** anticnemion

pert. to: **6** crural

legacy: **4** gift **6** legate **7** bequest **8** windfall **10** foundation

inheritor: **4** heir **7** legatee

legal (see also **law**): **5** licit, valid **6** lawful **7** juridic **9** juridical **10** authorized, legitimate

legal matter: res

legal right, by: **6** ex jure

legalize: **9** authorize

legate: **5** envoy **6** deputy, legacy, nuncio **8** bequeath, delegate **9** messenger **10** ambassador **14** representative

legatee: **4** heir

joint: **6** coheir

legend: **4** edda, lore, myth, saga, tale **5** fable, story **6** record **7** fiction, proverb **9** tradition

legerdemain: 5 magic 6 deceit 8 trickery 9 conjuring

legging: 4 spat 5 chaps 6 cnemis, cocker, puttie 7 bottine, gambado 8 bootikin, chivarra, chivarro, gamashes 11 galligaskin, spatterdash 12 antigropelos

legible: 8 distinct, readable 14 understandable

legion: 4 army, host 9 multitude

legislate: act 5 elect, enact

legislation: act, law 7 statute

legislative: 12 nomothetical

legislative body: 4 diet, rada 5 house, junta 6 senate 7 althing 8 congress 9 Reichstag 10 parliament

legislator: 5 solon 7 enactor, senator 8 lawmaker 9 statesman

legislature: 4 Dail, diet 6 senate 8 assembly, congress

legitimate: 4 fair, just, real, true 5 legal, licit, valid 6 cogent, lawful 7 genuine 11 efficacious

legume: pea, pod, uva 4 bean, soya 5 pulse 6 lentil, loment 9 vegetable

lei: 6 wreath 7 flowers, garland

leisure: 4 case, free, idle, time 5 otium(L.), spare 6 otiose 7 freedom 10 relaxation, unemployed, unoccupied 11 convenience, opportunity 12 unproductive

leisurely: 4 slow 7 gradual 12 deliberately

leman: 5 lover 8 mistress, paramour 10 sweetheart

lemma: 5 bract 8 membrane

lemonade: 5 drink 6 cooler 8 beverage

lemur: 4 maki, vari 5 avahi, indri, loris, potto 6 aye-aye, colugo, galago, macaco, maholi 7 half-ape, semiape, tarsier 8 kinkajou 9 babacoote 10 angwantibo

lend: 4 loan 5 grant, prest 6 afford, impart, settle 7 advance, furnish 11 accommodate

lene: 6 smooth 9 consonant 11 unaspirated

length: 4 pace, term 7 yardage 9 dimension

measure: mil 4 foot, inch, yard

lengthen: eke 6 dilate, expand, extend 7 amplify, produce, prolong, stretch 8 elongate, increase, protract

lengthwise: 5 along 7 endlong, endways 14 longitudinally

lengthy: 4 long 8 extended 10 protracted

lenient: lax 4 easy, kind, mild 6 facile, gentle, humane 7 clement 8 lenitive, merciful, mitigant, relaxing, soothing, tolerant 9 assuasive, emollient, softening 10 charitable, forbearing, palliative

Leningrad: 9 Petrograd

lens: 4 unar 5 toric 7 bifocal 8 meniscus 10 anastigmat

Lent: 6 Careme(F.)

Lenten: 5 plain 6 meager, meagre, somber, sombre 8 meatless 14 unostentatious

lentigo: 7 freckle

lentil: 6 legume

Leo star: 7 Regulus

leonine: 8 lionlike, powerful

leopard: cat 4 pard 5 ounce 7 cheetah, panther

lepidopter: 4 moth 9 butterfly

leprechaun: elf 5 fairy

leprosy: 5 lepra

lerot: 8 dormouse

Les Miserables author: 4 Hugo

lesion: cut 4 sore 5 ulcer, wound 6 injury 7 fissure

less: 5 fewer, minus, under 7 smaller 8 inferior

lessee: 6 leaser, renter, tenant 7 hu-urder(D.)

lessen: 4 bate, ease, wane 5 abase, abate, decry, lower, peter 6 impair, reduce, soften, shrink, weaken 7 amenuse, assuage, curtail, depress, relieve 8 belittle, condense, contract, decrease, derogate, diminish, minimize, mitigate, palliate, retrench, truncate 9 alleviate, attenuate, disparage, extenuate 10 depreciate 11 deteriorate

lesser: 5 minor

lesson: 4 lear, task 5 moral, study 6 rebuke 7 example, lecture, precept, reading, reproof, warning 8 exercise 10 assignment 11 composition, instruction

lessor: 8 landlord

lest: 8 anaunter

let: 4 hire, rent 5 allow, lease, leave 6 hinder, impede, permit, suffer 7 prevent 8 obstacle 9 hindrance

fall: 4 drop, slip 5 lower, spill 7 mention

forth: 4 emit

in: 5 admit, enter 6 insert

let it stand: sta 4 stet

letdown: 5 slump 8 comedown, drawback 10 anticlimax, relaxation, slackening

lethal: 5 fatal 6 deadly, mortal, poison 9 poisonous 12 death-dealing

lethargic: 4 dull 5 heavy, inert 6 drowsy, sleepy, torpid 8 comatose, sluggish 9 apathetic

lethargy: 5 sopor 6 stupor, torpor

Lethe: 8 oblivion 13 forgetfulness

Lett: 4 Balt 7 Latvian

letter: 4 bull, chit, line, note 5 breve, brief, chain, favor, vowel 6 billet, cartel, charta, favour, screed, symbol 7 collins, courant, epistle, message, missile, missive 9 consonant, semivowel 13 communication, semiconsonant

Anglo-Saxon: edh, eth, wen, wyn 4 wynn

decorated: fac

sloping: 6 italic

letter carrier: 6 correo(Sp.) 7 mailman, postman 9 messenger

letter for letter: 9 literally, literatim
lettered: 7 learned, stamped 8 educated, literate 9 inscribed
lettuce: *kind of:* cos 4 head, leaf 6 butter 7 romaine, simpson
  sea: 4 alga 5 laver
letup: 7 respite 9 abatement, cessation
leucite: 5 lenad 9 amphigene
levant: 5 wager 6 decamp 7 abscond
Levant: 4 East 6 Orient 13 Mediterranean
  garment: 6 caftan
  river: 4 wadi, wady
  ship: 4 jerm, saic
  valley: 4 wady
levee: 4 bank, dike, dyke, pier, quay 6 durbar 9 reception 10 embankment
level: aim, par 4 even, flat, rase, raze, true 5 equal, grade, peavy, plane, point, scalp 6 evenly, peavey, peavie, smooth 7 flatten, uniform 8 demolish 10 horizontal 12 standardized
  comb. form: 5 plani
  social: 5 caste, class
  tool: 5 plane 6 gimbal
level-headed: 8 sensible
lever: bar, lam, pry 5 helve, jemmy, jimmy, peavy, pedal, prise, swipe 6 binder, garrot, peavey, peavie, tappet, tiller 7 crowbar, treadle 9 rockshaft
  part: 7 fulcrum
leveret: 4 hare 8 mistress
Levi: *descendant:* 6 Levite 7 Gershon
  father: 6 Jacob
levigate: 6 polish, smooth
levin: 9 lightning
levity: 5 humor 6 gaiety, humour 8 buoyancy 9 frivolity, lightness, silliness 11 foolishness
levy: tax 4 cess, fine, wage 5 exact, stent 6 assess, extent, impose, impost 7 collect 10 assessment, imposition
lewd: 4 base, rude 5 bawdy 6 carnal, coarse 7 lustful, obscene, rammish, sensual 8 unchaste 9 debauched, dissolute, lecherous, salacious 10 lascivious, libidinous, licentious 12 pornographic
lexicographer: 6 author 8 compiler 9 onomastic
lexicon: 7 calepin 10 dictionary 11 onomasticon
Leyte capital: 8 Tacloban
liability: 4 debt, loan 5 debit 6 burden 10 obligation
liable: apt 8 amenable 10 answerable 11 accountable, responsible
liaison: 4 bond 8 intimacy, intrigue
liana: 4 cipo 5 plant
liang: 4 tael
liar: 5 cheat 6 fibber 7 Ananias, cracker 8 deceiver, fabulist 10 fabricator 11 pseudologue 12 prevaricator, pseudologist 14 misrepresenter

lias: 4 rock 9 limestone
libation: 5 drink 8 potation
libel: 4 bill 6 defame, malign, vilify 7 calumny, lampoon, request, scandal, slander 8 circular, handbill, roorback 10 calumniate, defamation 11 certificate, declaration 12 supplication
libelant: 7 accuser
liberal: 4 free, good, open 5 ample, broad, frank, noble 6 honest 7 electic, profuse 8 eclectic, generous, handsome 9 benignant, bounteous, bountiful, expansive, expensive, plenteous, plentiful 10 benevolent, charitable, ecumenical, munificent
Liberal: 4 Whig
liberate: rid 4 flee, free 5 clear, loose, remit 6 acquit, redeem, rescue 7 deliver, manumit, release 8 unfetter 9 discharge, disengage, extricate 10 emancipate
Liberia: *boatman:* kru
  city: 8 Buchanan, Marshall, Monrovia(c.) 10 Greenville
  measure: 4 kuba
  people: Gi; Kru, Kwa, Vai, Vei 4 Kroo, Toma 5 Bassa, Gibbi, Greba 6 Krooby, Kruman 7 Krooboy, Krooman
  river: 5 Manna 8 San Pedro
libertine: 4 rake, roue 7 sceptic 9 debauchee, dissolute 11 freethinker
liberty: may 4 ease, play 5 leave, right 7 freedom, license 9 privilege 11 presumption
library: 7 bhandar 8 atheneum 9 athenaeum 11 bibliotheca
libretto: 4 book 5 words
Libya: *city:* 7 Tripoli
  measure: 5 bozze, donum, jabia, teman 6 barile 7 mattaro
  measure of weight: 4 kele 5 uckia 6 gorraf 7 termino 8 kharouba
  seaport: 5 Derna, Derrn 6 Tobruk 7 Bengazi 8 Benghazi
  wind: 7 sirocco
Libya's child: 5 Belus 6 Agenor
lice: See **louse**.
license: tax 5 exeat, leave 6 patent, permit 7 dismiss, freedom, liberty 8 escambio, passport, sanction 9 approbate, authority, authorize, franchise 10 permission 11 imprimateur, unrestraint
licentious: gay, lax 4 free, lewd 5 frank, loose 6 unruly 7 immoral, obscene 9 dissolute 10 lascivious, profligate 12 pornographic, uncontrolled, unrestrained
lichen: 4 moss
  genus: 5 usnea 7 evernia 10 pertusaria
lich-house: 8 mortuary
licit: 5 legal 6 lawful 9 permitted
lick: lap, win 4 flog 5 slake 6 thrash 7 conquer 8 overcome, vanquish
licorice: 5 abrin, anise 8 absinthe 9 jequirity
  pill: 6 cachou

seed: **9** jequirity
lid: cap, hat, top **5** cover **7** shutter **9** operculum
lie: cog, fib, gab **4** bask, cram, flaw, hide, loll, rest **5** exist **6** covert, extend, grovel, remain, repose **7** cracker, crammer, deceive, falsify, falsity, pronate, untruth **8** position, roorback **9** deception, fabricate, falsehood, mendacity, prostrate **10** equivocate, inveracity, taradiddle **11** fabrication, prevaricate, tarradiddle **13** prevarication
in ambush: **4** lurk **6** hugger **9** insidiate
Liebestraum composer: **5** Liszt
lief: **4** dear, fain **5** leave **6** freely, gladly **7** beloved, happily **8** pleasing, precious **9** willingly **10** permission
liege: **5** loyal **6** vassal **7** devoted, subject **8** faithful, overlord **9** sovereign
lien: **5** claim **6** charge **8** mortgage **9** trust deed **11** encumbrance, garnishment
lieu: **5** place, stead **7** instead
lieutenant: **4** zany
lieve: See **lief.**
life: vie **5** blood, hours **6** biosis, energy, spirit **8** vitality, vivacity **9** animation, biography, existence **11** anilopyrine
animal: **4** bios **5** biota, fauna
comb. form: bio
god of: **6** Faunus
pert. to: **5** vital **6** biotic, mortal **8** biotical
plant: **4** bios **5** biota, flora
principle: **5** atman, prana, tenet
professional: **6** career
science: **7** anatomy, biology, zoology **12** paleontology
sea: **5** coral **8** halibios, plankton
simple form: **5** ameba **6** amebic, amoeba **7** amoebic, amoebae(pl.)
staff of: **5** bread
without: **4** dead **5** azoic **9** inanimate
life insurance: **7** tontine
life jacket: **7** Mae West
life-like: **9** realistic
lifeless: **4** arid, dead, dull, flat **5** amort, heavy, inert, vapid **6** anemic, jejune, torpid **7** anaemic **8** inactive **9** bloodless, examinate, inanimate, powerless, tasteless **10** spiritless, unanimated
comb. form: **4** abio
lifer: **7** convict
lifetime: age, day, eon **4** aeon **5** being **8** duration
lift: pry **4** help, jack, perk, rear **5** boost, exalt, heave, hoick, hoist, hoosh, raise, scend **6** cleach, cleech **7** derrick, elevate, enhance **8** elevator, heighten
ligament: **4** band, bind, bond **6** artery **7** bandage
ligan, lagan: **6** debris
ligate: **4** bind **7** bandage
ligature: tie **4** band, bond **6** taenia **7** bandage
light: dey, gay **4** airy, deft, easy, fire, glim,

lamp, mild, moon, neon, soft **5** agile, blond, fanal, filmy, flaky, flame, flare, merry, torch **6** alight, beacon, bright, candle, floaty, gentle, ignite, kindle, lively, lumine, nimble, pastel, volant **7** buoyant, cresset, flyaway, fragile, trivial **8** brighten, cheerful, delicate, ethereal, gossamer, graceful, illumine, luminary, luminous, trifling **10** illuminate
circle: **4** halo **7** aureola, aureole
cloud: **6** nimbus
faint: **7** glimmer, shimmer **9** starlight **10** glimmering, shimmering
globe: **4** bulb
god: **5** Baldr **6** Balder
kind of: arc **4** lamp **5** klieg, torch **7** lantern **9** headlight **10** flashlight **12** incandescent
measure: lux, pyr, rad **5** lumen **6** Hefner
overpower with: **6** dazzle
portable: **4** lamp **5** flare, taper, torch **6** candle **7** lantern **10** flashlight
reflector: **4** lens **6** mirror
refractor: **5** prism
science: **6** optics
source: sun
lighten: **4** ease, fade **5** allay, clear **6** alight, allege, bleach, illume, leaven **7** gladden, relieve **8** brighten **9** alleviate **10** illuminate
lightening: **10** levitation
lighter (see also **light**): **4** scow **5** barge, spill **7** fidibus, gabbard, gabbart, pontoon **8** chopboat
lightheaded: **5** dizzy, giddy **6** fickle **7** flighty, glaiket, glaikit **8** flippant, heedless, unstable, unsteady **9** delirious, frivolous **10** disordered, inconstant **11** thoughtless
lighthearted: gay **4** glad **5** merry **7** buoyant **8** carefree, cheerful, gleesome, volatile **9** vivacious
lighthouse: **5** phare **6** beacon, pharos **7** seamark, warning
lightness: **6** levity
lightning: **4** bolt **5** levin
defier of: **4** Ajax
pert. to: **8** fulgural
protective device: **8** arrester
lightning bug: **7** firefly
lightning rod: **8** arrester
lightning stone: **9** fulgurite
lights: **5** lungs
lights out: **4** taps
ligneous: **5** woody
lignite: **4** coal
ligula: **4** band
ligulate: **11** strap-shaped
likable: **6** genial **7** winning **8** charming, pleasant **10** attractive
like: as **4** love, same **5** alike, enjoy, equal **6** admire, prefer, relish **7** similar **9** analogous, semblance **10** preference, synonymous **11** counterpart, homogeneous

suffix: ar, ic; ose

like a: For definitions beginning with these words, see following important words. EXAMPLES: "like a cat": see **catlike:** "like a house": see **house:** *pert. to.*

likelihood: **10** appearance **11** probability **14** verisimilitude

likely: apt **5** prone **6** liable **7** tending **8** credible, feasible, probable, suitable **9** promising **11** verisimilar

liken: **5** apply **7** compare **10** assimilate

likeness: **4** copy, form, twin **5** guise, image **6** effigy, figure, statue **7** analogy, parable, picture, replica **8** parallel, portrait **9** duplicate, facsimile, imitation, semblance, simulacre **10** comparison, photograph, similarity, similitude, simulacrum **11** counterfeit **12** reproduction **14** representation

likewise: and, nor, not, too **4** also **5** ditto **7** besides **8** moreover

liking: goo **4** gust, lust **5** fancy, gusto, taste **6** comely **7** delight **8** affinity, appetite, fondness, penchant, pleasing, pleasure **9** affection **10** sensuality **12** predilection

lilac: **5** mauve **7** syringa

Lilith's successor: Eve

lilliputian: **4** tiny **5** petty, small **6** midget **7** dwarfed

lilt: air **4** sing, song, tune **7** cadence

lily (see also **water lily**): ki, ti; **4** aloe, ixia, sego **5** calla, niobe, tiger, water, yucca **6** titree **8** mariposa

family: **9** liliaceae

genus: **7** bessera

lily iron: **7** harpoon

Lily Maid of Astolat: **6** Elaine

lily of France: **10** fleur-de-lis

lily of the valley: **6** mugget, mugwet **10** convallily

family: **15** convallariaceae

lily-of-the-valley tree: **8** sourwood **10** fetterbush, pepperbush

lily-shaped: **7** crinoid

lima: **4** bean

liman: bay **5** marsh **6** lagoon **7** estuary

limation: **6** filing **9** polishing

limb: arm, fin, leg **4** wing **5** bough **6** branch, member **7** flipper, pleopod, support

flexion: **9** anaclasis

limber: **4** bain, flip, limp **5** lithe **6** pliant, supple, swanky **8** flexible, flippant, handsome, yielding

limbo: **4** hell **9** purgatory

lime: **5** color, green **6** cement, citrus

pendent: **10** stalactite

phosphate: **7** apatite

lime tree: **4** teil **6** linden, tupelo

limen: **9** threshold

limestone: **4** calp, cauk, malm **5** chalk, ganil, poros(Gr.) **6** clunch, marble, oolite **7** hurlock **8** peastone, pisolite

limey: **6** sailor **7** soldier **10** Englishman

limit: end, fix **4** curb, mete **5** ambit, bound, bourn, check, fence, hedge, scant, stint, verge **6** border, bourne, curfew, define, extent, finish **7** astrict, barrier, closure, confine, environ, extreme **8** boundary, conclude, contract, deadline, restrain, restrict, terminal, terminus **9** condition, constrain, extremity **10** limitation **11** restriction, termination **12** circumscribe **13** determination, qualification

combining form: ori

limited: few **5** local, scant **6** finite, narrow, scanty, strait **8** reserved **9** parochial **10** restricted **11** topopolitan

limiting: **10** relational

limitless: **4** vast **8** infinite **9** boundless, unbounded, unlimited **11** measureless

limn: **4** draw **6** depict, sketch **7** portray **8** describe **9** delineate

limp: hop, lax **4** himp, soft, thin **5** hilch, hitch, loose **6** flabby, flimsy, hirple, hobble, limber, wilted **7** flaccid **8** drooping, flexible **9** inelastic **13** unsubstantial

limpid: **4** pure **5** clear, lucid **6** bright **7** crystal **8** pellucid **11** translucent, transparent

limping: **4** halt **10** claudicant

limy: **6** sticky **7** viscous

Lincoln: *friend:* **5** Speed

secretary of state: **6** Seward

secretary of war: **7** Stanton

son: Tad

linden: lin **4** lime, teil **8** basswood

genus of: **5** tilia

line: pad, ray, row, wad **4** axis, ceil, cord, dash, etch, face, file, mark, mere, race, rein, rope, rule, seam, wire **5** curve, front, leger, queue, route, serif, snell, steen, stich, stria, swath **6** border, ceriph, cordon, fettle, hawser, isobar, metier, nettle, streak, string, stripe, suture **7** barrier, carrier, contour, radiant, scratch **8** boundary, crossbar, isotherm, wainscot **9** delineate

comb. form: **4** lino

conceptual: **6** agonic, tropic **7** equator, isother **8** latitude, meridian **9** longitude

diagonal: **4** bias

geometrical: arc, ess **4** cant, sine **6** secant **7** tangent **8** parallel **9** asymptote

nautical: **6** earing, hawser, ratlin **7** marline, painter, ratline

pertaining to: **5** filar **6** linear

raised: **4** weal, welt **5** ridge

with boards: **8** wainscot

lineage: **4** race **5** birth, blood, caste, tribe **6** family, havage, stirps **7** descent, stirpes(pl.) **8** ancestry, heredity, pedigree **9** genealogy **10** progenitor

lineal: **6** direct, racial **9** ancestral **10** hereditary

lineament: **7** feature **14** characteristic

linear: **9** elongated

lineate: **7** striped **8** streaked

lined: 5 ruled 6 notate 7 striate 8 care-worn 9 lineolate

lineman: end 5 guard 6 center, tackle 7 wireman

linen: 4 brin, crea(Sp.), lawn 5 toile 6 barras, damask, dowlas, forfar 7 brabant, cambric, dornick 13 linsey-woolsey

fabric: 7 taffeta

household: 6 napery, sheets

source: 4 flax

yarn: lea

liner: 4 boat, ship 6 vessel 7 steamer 9 steamship

wrecked: 7 Titanic

lines: net 7 network, reticle

ling: 4 fish, hake 5 heath 6 burbot 7 heather 8 chestnut

linger: lag 4 drag, stay, wait 5 dally, delay, dwell, hover, tarry 6 dawdle, loiter, remain

lingerie: 9 underwear 11 underthings

lingering: 4 slow 7 chronic

lingo: 4 cant 5 argot 6 jargon, patter, tongue 7 dialect 8 language 10 vernacular

lingot: 4 mold 5 ingot

lingua: 6 glossa

lingual: 7 glossal 10 linguistic, tongue-like

linguist: 8 polyglot

linguistics: 7 grammar 9 philology

lingy: 5 agile 6 active, heathy, limber, nimble 8 heathery

linhay: 4 shed 8 outhouse

liniment: 11 embrocation

lining: 5 stean, steen 7 backing, ceiling 8 wainscot 12 wainscotting

link: tie 4 join, yoke 5 cleek, nexus, torch, unite 6 braced, catena, copula, couple, course, fasten 7 conjoin, connect 8 catenate 10 connection, golf course 11 concatenate

series: 5 chain 13 concatenation

linking: 9 annectant, annectent

linn, lin: 4 pool 6 linden, ravine 8 cataract 9 precipice, waterfall

linnet: 5 finch, twite 9 gorsebird

linseed: 8 flaxseed

lint: 5 fluff 7 charpie 8 raveling

lintel: 5 hance 6 clavel 7 transom

lion: 4 puma, star 5 simba 6 cougar, roarer 9 carnivore, celebrity

hair: 4 mane

winged, with woman's head: 6 sphinx

young: cub 6 lionet

Lion of God: Ali

lionlike: 7 leonine

lip: rim 4 brim, edge, kiss 5 brink, labia(pl.) 6 labium, margin 7 labella 8 labellum

ornament: 6 labret

part: 8 philtrum

pert. to: 6 labial 11 labiodental

lipa: fat

liparoid: 5 fatty

liparous: 5 obese

lipless: 8 achilary

lipped: 7 labiate

liquefy: 4 fuse, melt 6 fusile 7 liquate 8 dissolve, eliquate 10 colliquate, deliquesce

liqueur: 5 creme, noyau 6 genepi 7 cordial, ratafee 8 anisette, beverage 9 cointreau 11 benedictine

liquid: 5 fluid 6 fluent, watery 8 beverage

colorless: 5 water 7 alcohol

container: cup, jar, jug, mug, pan, pot 4 etna, ewer, vase, vial 5 cruse, glass, phial 6 boiler, bottle, bucket, goblet, kettle 7 creamer, pitcher 8 decanter, demijohn

gasified: 5 steam, vapor

inflammable: see *volatile* below

measure: 4 pint 5 ounce 6 gallon, tierce

oily: 6 cresol, octane 7 aniline, picamar

particle form: 4 mist 5 spray

sweet: 5 sirup, syrup 7 treacle 8 molasses

volatile: gas 5 ether 6 butane 7 alcohol, ligroin 8 gasolene, gasoline, ligroine

liquidate: 6 settle 8 amortize 9 discharge

liquor (see also **liqueur**): ale, bub, dew, gin, rum, rye 4 arak, bang, beer, beno, brew, grog, nipa, raki, sake, saki, soma 5 bhang, booze, budge, lager, pisco, stout 6 arrack, brandy, porter, pottle, scotch, stingo, strunt, tipple 7 bitters, whiskey 8 beverage 9 moonshine

bad: 5 smoke 6 rotgut 10 balderdash

cabinet: 8 cellaret

crude: 5 hooch 6 rotgut 9 hoochinoo, moonshine

drugged: 5 hocus 6 mickey 10 mickey-finn

manufacturer: 6 abkari 9 distiller

measure: 4 dram 5 rouse 7 snifter

mix with: 4 lace

mixture: 5 bogus 7 bragget

residue: 4 must 5 dregs 8 heeltaps

server: 6 barman 7 barmaid, skinker, tapster 9 barkeeper, bartender

shop: bar 6 saloon, tavern 7 shebeen

vessel: ama, keg 4 bowl 5 amula, flask 6 barrel, bottle, flagon 7 bombard, psykter, stamnos 8 cruisken, decanter 9 cruiskeen

lira (one-twentieth): 5 soldo

liripipe, liripoop: 4 hood, task 5 scarf 6 lesson, tippet

lirk: 6 crease 7 wrinkle

lish: 5 agile, quick 6 active, nimble

lisk: 4 loin 5 flank, groin

lisp: 7 prattle

lissome, lissom: 5 agile, lithe 6 limber, nimble, supple 8 flexible

list: tip 4 bill, cant, cast, file, item, keel, leet, memo, ordo, roll, rota, rote, tilt 5 brief, canon, index, panel, scrip, slate 6 careen, docket, roster 7 catalog, incline 8 manifest, register, schedule, tabulate 9 catalogue, inventory, portfolio, repertory 10 repertoire 11 enumeration

listen: ear **4** hark, hear, heed, note **5** audit **6** attend, harken **7** hearken **8** overhear **9** eavesdrop **10** auscultate

listener: **6** hearer **7** audient

lister: **8** assessor **9** appraiser **10** cataloguer

listful: **9** attentive

listing: **5** atilt **7** tilting, tipping **8** register **10** enlistment, enrollment

individual: **4** item **5** entry

listless: **4** dull **5** faint, inert **6** abject, drowsy, supine **7** languid **8** careless, heedless, sluggish **9** apathetic, heartless **10** spiritless **11** indifferent **13** uninteresting

listlessness: **8** doldrums

litany: **6** ectene, ektene, prayer **8** rogation **11** orapronobis

liter: kan(D.) **7** measure

literal: **4** bald, dull **5** exact **7** factual, precise, prosaic **8** verbatim **13** unimaginative

literate: **6** reader, writer **8** educated, lettered

literati: **14** intelligentsia

literator: **6** critic

literature: **7** letters

extracts: **9** anthology

form: **5** novel **6** poetry **7** fiction **9** technical **10** nonfiction, scientific **11** pornography

lithe: **4** bain, slim **6** clever, limber, lissom, pliant, supple, svelte **7** lissome, slender **8** flexible

lithograph: **6** chromo

Lithuania: *city:* **5** Kovno(c.), Memel, Vilna

coin: lit **5** litas, marka **6** centas, fennig **7** ostmark **8** auksinas, skatikas

dialect: **5** Zmudz

Lithuanian: **4** Balt, Lett **5** Zhmud **6** Litvak **7** Yatvyag

litigant: **4** suer **6** suitor **7** accuser

litigation: **4** moot, suit **7** contest, dispute, lawsuit **10** contention, discussion

one involved in: **8** barrater, barrator, litigant

litigious: **10** disputable **11** belligerent, contentious **14** controvertible

litten: **7** lighted **8** cemetery **10** churchyard

litter: bed, hay **4** bier, mess, raff **5** cabin, couch, dooly, mulch, straw, trash, young **6** doolie, refuse **7** cacolet, mullock, rubbish, rummage **8** brancard(F.), disorder **9** offspring, stretcher **10** untidiness

litterateur: **7** bookman

little: sma(Sc.), wee **4** poco(It.), puny, tiny **5** crumb, petit, small **6** petite **8** fraction **10** diminutive

comb. form: **5** steno

little finger: **7** minimus

little toe: **7** minimus

Little Women: Jo; Amy, Meg **4** Beth

author: **6** Alcott

surname: **5** March

littoral: **7** coastal

lituite: **6** fossil

liturate: **7** spotted

liturgy: **4** rite **6** ritual **7** service

livable: **8** bearable **9** endurable, tolerable

live: **4** fare, room **5** abide, alive, dwell, exist, green, vital, vivid **6** reside **7** animate, blazing, breathe, subsist **8** animated, continue, converse **9** energetic **10** experience

in: **7** inhabit

in the country: **9** rusticate

passively: **8** vegetate

permit to: **5** spare **8** reprieve

livelihood: **4** keep **5** being **6** living

liveliness: **6** spirit **8** vitality

lively: **4** gay, vif(F.) **4** airy, cant, fast, pert, racy, vive, yare **5** agile, alert, alive, brisk, canty, chirk, cobby, desto(It.), fresh, peart, peppy **6** active, blithe, bright, cheery, chirpy, cocket, crouse, dapper, frisky, nimble, snappy **7** allegro(It.), animate, animato(It.), buoyant, chipper **8** animated, galliard, spirited **9** energetic, sprightly, vivacious

liven: **5** cheer **7** animate **8** brighten

liver: **4** foie **5** hepar **8** tomalley

fluid: **4** bile

pert. to: **7** hepatic

liverwort: **4** moss **8** agrimony, hepatica **9** bryophyte

genus: **6** riccia

livery: **7** uniform **8** clothing

livestock: **6** cattle **7** chattel

livid: **4** blae, blue **5** bleak **10** discolored

living: **4** keep **5** alive, being, vivid **6** extant **7** animate **8** animated, benefice **10** livelihood, sustenance **11** subsistence,

again: **6** reborn **9** redivivus

correct: **7** regimen **11** orthobiosis

off others: **8** entozoic **9** parasitic, raptorial

together: **11** contubernal

Livonian river: Aa

lixiviate: **5** leach

lixivium: lye

lizard: dab, eft **4** adda, dabb, dhab, evet, gila, ibid, newt, seps, uran **5** agama, anoli, dhabb, gecko, gekko, goana, scink, skink, varan, waran **6** ameiva, anolis, dragon, goanna, iguana, lacert, moloch, worral, worrel **7** cheecha, geitjie, monitor, saurian, tuatera **8** basilisk **9** chameleon, galliwasp **10** chuckwalla **12** scheltopusik

comb. form: **5** sauro

family: **12** xenosauridae

genus: uta **5** agama **6** ameiva

mammal similar to: **10** salamander

lizard-like: **8** iguanoid

llama: **6** alpaca

habitat: **5** Andes

llanero: **6** cowboy **8** herdsman

llano: **5** plain **7** lowland, prairie

Llyr's son: **4** Bran **7** Branwen

lo: but **4** ecce(L.), look **6** behold **7** observe

load: jag **4** clog, jagg, lade, onus, pack,

tote, stow **5** cargo, weigh **6** burden, charge, hamper, lading, steeve, weight **7** fraught, freight, oppress **8** carriage, encumber **9** aggravate, exonerate **10** adulterate **11** encumbrance

small: jag **4** jagg **5** hurry

loader: **9** stevedore

loadstone: See **lodestone**.

loaf: **4** idle, laze **6** dawdle, loiter, lounge **10** dilly-dally

loafer: bum **4** hood **5** idler **7** flaneur, hoodlum, lounger **8** hooligan, larrikin **11** chairwarmer

loam: rab **4** silt **5** loess, regur(Ind.) **6** cledge

constituent: **4** clay, lime **5** chalk

deposit: **4** silt **5** loess

loan: **4** dhan(Ind.), lend **5** prest **6** borrow **7** advance **10** obligation, provisions **13** accommodation

loan shark: **6** usurer

loath, loth: **6** averse, odious **7** hateful **8** backward **9** reluctant, repulsive, unwilling

loathe: **4** hate **5** abhor **6** detest **7** adverse, condemn, despise, dislike **9** abominate

loathsome: **4** foul, ugly, vile **7** carrion, cloying, hateful **8** abhorent, deformed **9** offensive, repellent, repugnant **10** abominable, detestable, disgusting **11** distasteful

lob: hit **4** bowl, lots, lout, lump, step, till, toss, vein **5** droop, stair, throw **6** propel **7** pollack **9** chandelle

lobate: **8** lobelike

lobby: **4** hall, room **5** foyer **8** anteroom, coulisse **9** enclosure, vestibule

lobbyist: **8** promoter **12** propagandist

lobe: **5** alula **6** alular, earlap, lappet, lobule

lobelike: **6** lobate

loblolly: **4** mush **5** gruel **6** puddle **7** mudhole

lobo: **4** wolf

lobster: *claw:* **5** chela **6** nipper

part: **4** claw **6** pincer, telson, thorax

roe: **5** coral

trap: pot **5** creel **6** bownet

lobster pot: pot **4** corf **5** creel, trunk

local: **7** bucolic, endemic, limited, topical **8** regional, specific **10** restricted

locale: **4** loci(pl.), site **5** locus(L.), place, scene **6** region **9** situation

locality: **4** loci(pl.), seat, site, spot **5** locus, place, situs **6** region **7** habitat **8** district, position **12** neighborhood

localize: **7** situate **8** pinpoint

locate (see also **place**): sat **4** espy, find, seat, show, site, spot **5** stand, trace **6** settle **7** situate, station **8** discover **9** establish

located: **7** bestead

locatio: **7** leasing, letting

location: **4** area, seat, site, spot **5** place, scene, situs **6** ubiety **7** habitat **9** situation

loch: bay **4** lake, pond, pool **5** lough

loci: See **locus**.

lock: **4** bolt, curl, frib, hank, hasp **5** latch, sasse, tress **6** fasten **7** confine, cowlick **8** fastener

locker: **6** ascham

lockjaw: **7** tetanus, trismus **11** ankylostoma

remedy: **11** antitetanic, antitetanus

lockman: **11** executioner

lockup: jug **4** jail **5** clink **6** cooler **7** hoosgow **8** hoosegaw, hoosegow **9** calaboose

locomotive: **5** dolly, mogul **6** diesel, dinkey, engine, mallet **8** electric

part: cab **5** pilot

service car: **6** tender **7** coalcar

locus: **4** area, site **5** place **8** locality

locust: **5** bruke, cicad **6** cicada, cicala, cigala **11** grasshopper

locust bird: **7** grackle **8** starling

locust plant: **5** senna

locust tree: **5** carob **6** acacia

locustberry: **5** drupe, nance **9** glamberry

lode: **4** path, road, vein **5** canal, drain, ledge **6** course **7** deposit, fissure **8** waterway

cavity: vug **4** vugg, vugh

lodestone, loadstone: **6** magnet **7** adamant **8** terrella **9** magnetite

lodge: dig, lie **4** crib **5** board, couch, dwell, hogan **6** alight, bestow, encamp, hostel **7** deposit **8** harbinge **11** brotherhood

lodger: **5** guest **6** roomer, tenant

lodging: bed, hut, inn **4** camp, gite(F.), host, howf, nest, room, tent **5** abode, cabin, hotel, house, hovel, howff **6** billet, tavern, teepee, wigwam **7** mansion **8** barracks, dwelling, hostelry, quarters **9** dormitory, harborage, residence **10** habitation, harbourage

cost: **4** rent

loess: **4** loam, silt

loft: bin **4** balk **5** attic

lofty: **4** aery, epic, high, tall **5** aerie, elate, grand, noble, proud, steep **6** aerial, Andean, andine **7** Andesic, arduous, eminent, haughty, sublime **8** arrogant, assuming, elevated, eloquent, majestic **9** cockhorse, dignified, overproud **11** magisterial, mountainous

log: **4** clog, wood **5** diary **6** billet, loggat, logget, record, timber **7** journal

kind: **4** slab **5** spalt **8** puncheon

mass: **5** drive

revolve: **4** birl **7** logroll

log gin: **6** jammer

logarithm: *unit:* bel

inventor: **6** Napier

loge: box **4** room **5** booth, stall

logger: **6** sniper **9** lumberman **10** lumberjack, woodcutter **11** woodchopper

boot: pac **4** pack

loggerhead: **4** head **6** turtle **9** blockhead

loggerheads: **4** odds, outs

loggets, loggats: **4** game

loggia: **7** gallery

logging: *sled:* **4** tode **7** travois **8** travoise *tool:* 4 pevy 5 peavy, peevy 6 nigger, peavey

logic: 9 reasoning
 inductive: 7 epagoge
 specious: 7 sophism
 term: 5 ferio, lemma 7 ferison

logical: 4 sane 5 sound, valid 8 coherent, rational 10 consistent, reasonable

logion: 5 maxim, motto 6 saying 11 observation

logogriph: 5 rebus 6 puzzle, riddle 7 anagram

logroll: 4 birl

logy: 4 dull 5 heavy 6 drowsy 8 sluggish

lohan: 4 monk 5 Arhat

Lohengrin: *character:* 4 Elsa 8 Parsifal
 composer: 6 Wagner

loincloth: 5 pagne

loir: 8 dormouse

Loire: *river:* 5 Liger
 town: 6 Nantes

loiter: lag 4 idle, loaf 5 dally, delay, drawl, shool, tarry 6 cooter, dawdle, linger 7 saunter 8 hesitate

loiterer: 4 slug 5 drone, idler 7 laggard 8 sluggard

Loki: *child:* Hel 4 Hela, Naro
 mother: 9 Angrbodha
 wife: 5 Sigyn

loll: 4 hang 5 droop, tarry 6 dangle, froust, frowst, lounge, sprawl 7 recline

loma: 4 hill

lombard: 6 cannon

Lombardy lake: 4 Como

lomilomi: rub 7 massage, shampoo

lomita: 4 hill

London: *bus conductor:* 6 clippy
 coffee shop: 5 Wills
 district: 4 Soho 5 Acton 7 Adelphi, Alsatia, Mayfair
 monument: Gog 5 Magog 8 Cenotaph
 porter: 6 George 8 Georgina
 promenade: 4 Mall
 roisterer: mun
 society: 7 Mayfair
 square: 9 Leicester
 stables: 4 mews
 street: 4 Bond 6 Savile 7 Wardour 9 Cheapside, Haymarket
 suburb: Kew
 theater: 7 Adelphi
 timepiece: 6 Big Ben

Londoner: 7 Cockney

lone: 4 sole 5 alone, apart 6 single 7 retired 8 solitary 9 unmarried 12 unfrequented

Lone Star State: 5 Texas

loneliness: 8 solitude 9 dejection, isolation 10 depression, desolation 12 lonesomeness

lonely: 4 lorn, sole 5 alone, apart 6 dismal, dreary 7 deavely, forlorn 8 deserted, desolate, lonesome, secluded, solitary 11 sequestered 12 unfrequented

long: far 4 hone, hope, pine 5 yearn 6 aspire, hanker, hunger, prolix, thirst 7 lengthy, tedious 8 extended, tiresome 9 elongated, prolonged, wearisome 10 protracted
 and slender: 5 lathy, reedy 6 linear 9 elongated
 for: 4 miss, want, wish 5 covet, crave 6 desire

long ago: 4 yore

long dozen: 8 thirteen

long-suffering: 7 patient 8 patience 9 endurance 10 forbearing

long-winded: 6 prolix 9 garrulous

longe: 4 rein, rope 5 guide, strap, trout 8 exercise

Longfellow hero: 8 Hiawatha

longheaded: 4 wise 6 shrewd 10 hardheaded 11 foresighted

longing: yen 6 desire 7 athirst, craving, wistful 8 appetite, cupidity, yearning 9 nostalgia 10 desiderium

longitudinally: 7 endlong 10 lengthwise

longshoreman: 9 stevedore

loo: pam 8 napoleon

look: lo; con, pry, see 4 gaze, leer, ogle, peek, peep, peer, pore, scan, seem, skew 5 blush, dekko, fleer, glare, gliff, glime, gloat, gloom, glout, lower, sight, smile, snoop, stare 6 aspect, behold, gander, glance, glower, glunch, regard, search, squint, visage 7 observe 8 demeanor 10 appearance
 forward to: 5 await 6 expect 10 anticipate
 like: 8 resemble
 toward: 4 face

look after: 4 tend 6 attend

look at: eye, see 4 glom, view 6 behold, regard 7 examine, observe

look back: 6 recall, relive, review 7 rethink 8 remember 10 retrospect

look down on: 7 despise

look for: 4 seek 5 await 6 expect 10 anticipate

look into: 5 study 7 examine, inspect 11 investigate

look over: 6 ignore, survey 8 overlook 9 disregard 11 reconnoiter, reconnoitre

looker-on: 8 audience, beholder 9 bystander, spectator

lookout: 6 conner 7 atalaya(P.I.) 8 bantayan(P.I.), cockatoo 10 watchtower

looks (see also **look**): 4 face 8 features 10 attraction

loom: auk 4 hulk, loon, tool 5 dobby, weave 6 appear, emerge, gentle, puffin, vessel 7 machine 9 guillemot, implement 10 receptacle
 part: bar, lam 4 caam, leaf, reed, sley 5 easer, lathe 6 hanger, heddle 7 harness

loon: nut, sap 4 dolt, lout 5 diver, rogue, scamp, wabby 6 cobble, rascal

loop: eye, tab 4 ansa, coil, fold, hank, kink, knot, oese 5 bight, bride, coque, honda, hondo, noose, picot, terry 6 becket, billet, circle 7 circuit, curette, folding 8 doubling 11 aiguillette

loop-shaped: 9 fundiform

loophole: out 4 muse 5 meuse, oilet 6 escape, eyelet 7 opening 8 aperture, weakness

loose: gay, lax 4 floa, free, open 5 baggy, bulgy, crank, loose, relax, slack, vague 6 coarse, dangly, random, unlash, wobbly 7 immoral, movable, relaxed, unbound, unleash 8 insecure, unstable, withdraw 9 desultory, dissolute, unbridled, unchecked 10 indefinite, licentious, unattached, unconfined, unfastened 11 untrammeled 12 uncontrolled, unrestrained 14 unconventional

loose ends: 4 dags 5 bored 7 tagrags 8 restless

loose-jointed: 5 lanky, rangy 6 clumsy, wobbly 7 rickety 10 ramshackle

loosen: pry 4 ease, free, undo 5 relax, untie 7 slacken 8 liberate, unfasten 9 disengage, extricate 11 disentangle

loot: rob, sum 4 sack, swag 5 booty, strip 6 pilfer, ravage, spoils 7 pillage, plunder
receipt of: 9 theftbote

lop: bob, cut, dod 4 clip, flop, hang, sned(Sc.), snip, trim 5 droop, prune, slice 6 dangle 7 pendant, pendent 8 truncate

lope: jog 4 gait 6 canter 7 dogtrot

lopper: 4 clot 6 curdle 7 clabber 9 coagulate

lopsided: 4 alop 7 crooked 10 unbalanced

loquacious: 5 gabby 6 verbal 7 prating 8 cackling 9 garrulous, talkative 10 babblative, chattering

loquat: 4 biwa

lord: aga 4 agha, earl, peer, rule, tsar 5 liege, ruler 6 domine, master, prince 7 marquis, vavasor 8 domineer, governor, nobleman, seigneur, suzerain, vavasour, viscount 9 dominator
attendant: 5 thane

Lord have mercy upon us: 5 Kyrie 12 Kyrie eleison

Lord's Prayer: 11 Paternoster

lordly: 5 proud 6 uppish 8 arrogant, despotic 9 imperious, masterful 10 tyrannical 11 dictatorial, domineering, magisterial, overbearing

lordship: 7 dynasty 10 allegiance

lore: 4 lear 6 advice, wisdom 7 counsel 8 learning 9 erudition, knowledge, tradition 11 instruction

Lorelei: 5 siren

lorgnette: 8 eyeglass 10 opera glass

lorikeet: 6 parrot

loriot: 6 oriole

lorn: 6 bereft 7 forlorn 8 desolate, forsaken, lonesome 9 abandoned

Lorraine: *capital:* 4 Metz
river: 4 Saar

lose: 4 amit, fail, miss 5 waste 6 defeat, mislay 7 forfeit 9 dissipate

losel: bum 6 loafer 10 ne'er-do-well

loss: 4 cost, leak, ruin, toll 5 price, waste 6 damage, damnum, defeat, injury, ullage 7 expense, failure 8 amission, decrease 9 decrement, detriment, privation 10 affliction, bankruptcy 11 bereavement, deperdition, deprivation, destruction

lost: 4 gone, lorn 5 perdu(F.) 6 absent, hidden, ruined 7 forlorn, mislaid, strayed 8 absorbed, confused, defeated, estrayed, obscured, prodigal 9 abandoned, forfeited, perplexed, reprobate, subverted 10 abstracted, bewildered, dissipated, overthrown 11 preoccupied 13 irreclaimable

lot: hap 4 dole, doom, fate, land, luck, much, plat, plot 5 batch, field, grist, group, share, weird 6 amount, bundle, chance, divide, hazard, parcel 7 destiny, fortune, portion 8 caboodle, quantity 9 allotment, apportion 13 apportionment
appointment by: 9 sortition
miscellaneous: 6 fardel, joblot

Lot: *father:* 5 Haran
grandson: 7 Moabite
nephew: 7 Abraham
place of flight: 5 Sodom
sister: 6 Milcah
son: 4 Moab

lotion: 4 balm, wash 6 loture 8 ablution, linament

lots: 4 gobs 5 scads 6 plenty

lottery: 6 raffle 10 sweepstake

lotto: 5 bingo, keeno

lotus, lotos: 7 nelumbo 10 chinquapin

lotus bird: 6 jacana

lotus tree: 4 sadr 9 persimmon

loud: 5 gaudy, heavy, noisy, showy, vivid 6 coarse, flashy, vulgar 7 blatant, clamant, obvious, raucous 8 emphatic, strepent, vehement 9 clamorous, insistent, turbulent, unrefined 10 blustering, boisterous, stentorian, tumultuous, vociferous 11 thersitical 12 obstreperous

louder: 9 crescendo

lough: sea 4 lake, loch, pool 5 water

Louisiana: *county:* 6 parish
decree: 5 arret
dialect: 6 creole
native: 5 Cajun 6 creole
town: 4 Begg 6 Gretna 10 Shreveport
university: LSU 6 Tulane

lounge: 4 idle, loaf, loll, sofa 5 bange, couch, divan, relax 6 froust, frowst, loiter

loup: 4 flee, jump, leap

louse: nit 5 aphid, aphis 6 cootie, slater

lousy: 9 pedicular 10 pediculous

lout: bow, oaf 4 bend, boor, clod, coof, dolt, fool, gaum, gawk, hulk 5 clown, cuddy, stoop, yahoo, yokel 6 curtsy, lubber 7 bumpkin, grobian

loutish: 4 rude 5 crude 6 clumsy, gauche(F.), stupid 7 awkward

lovable, loveable: 4 dear 7 amative, amiable 8 adorable, dovelike 9 endearing

love: gra(Ir.), loe(Sc.), loo(Sc.) 4 dear, dote, like 5 adore, aloha, amore(It.), amour(F.), Cupid, fancy, liebe(G.), lover 6 enamor 7 charity, embrace, idolize 8 fondness, goodwill, idolatry 9 adoration, affection **10** attachment, sweetheart **11** inclination

god of: **4** Amor, Ares, Eros, Kama **5** Bhaga, Cupid

goddess of: **5** Athor, Freya, Venus **6** Freyja, Hathor, Ishtar **9** Aphrodite

science of: **9** erotology

token of: **6** amoret

love apple: **6** tomato

love feast: **5** agape **7** banquet **9** gathering

love knot: **6** amoret

love-potion: **5** charm **7** philter, philtre **11** aphrodisiac

love story: **7** romance

lovebird: **6** parrot

loveliness: **6** beauty **11** pulchritude

lovelock: **4** curl **5** tress **12** heartbreaker

lovely: **5** sweet **6** loving, tender **7** amiable, amorous, angelic **8** adorable, angelina, charming, graceful **9** beautiful **10** attractive

lover: ami(F.), gra(Ir.) **4** beau, chap **5** amant(F.), leman, Romeo **6** adorer, amadis, amante(F., fem.), bonami **7** admirer, amateur, amorist, amoroso, Don Juan, gallant **8** belamour, Lothario **9** bonne amie(fem.), enamorata, inamorata **10** dilettante, sweetheart **11** philanderer

meeting place: **5** tryst

patron saint: **9** Valentine

rustic: **7** Celadon

lovesick: **6** pining **7** longing **11** languishing

loving: **4** fond **6** erotic, lovely **7** adorant, amative, amatory, amorous **9** affecting **12** affectionate

comb. form: **4** phil **5** phile

low: bas(F.), moo **4** base, bass, blue, deep, hill, mean, neap **5** dirty, gross, snide **6** bellow, coarse, common, earthy, feeble, filthy, humble, humbly, slight, sordid, vulgar **7** bestial, ignoble, plebian, shallow, slavish **8** dejected **9** depressed, earthbred **10** melancholy **11** undignified, unfavorable **12** contemptible, disreputable

Low Country: **7** Belgium, Holland **9** Luxemburg **11** Netherlands

low-lived: **4** mean **10** despicable **12** contemptible

low-necked: **9** decollete

low tide: ebb **4** neap

lowbred: **5** crude **6** coarse, vulgar **11** ill-mannered

lower: dip **4** alow, bate, drop, sink, vail **5** abase, abate, baser, below, decry, demit, frown, glare, scowl, under **6** bemean, debase, deepen, demean, derate, glower, humble, lessen, meaner, nether, reduce **7** beneath, degrade, depress, descend, subside **8** diminish, downward **9** disparage **10** depreciate, nethermore

lowering: **4** dark **5** heavy **6** beetle, cloudy, gloomy, lowery, sullen **8** overcast **11** threatening

lowest: **5** least, nadir **6** bottom **7** bedrock **10** nethermost

lowing (see also **low**): **7** mugient **9** bellowing

lowland: **4** flat, holm, spit **5** terai(Ind.) **6** valley **7** bottoms

Lowlander (see also **Scotland**): **4** Scot **9** Sassenach

language: **6** Lallan **7** Lalland

lowly: **4** base, mean, meek **6** humble, modest **7** ignoble **12** unpretending **13** unpretentious

lox: **6** salmon

loy: **4** tool **5** spade

loyal: **4** feal, firm, leal, true **5** liege, pious **6** stanch **7** devoted, staunch **8** constant, faithful

loyalty: **6** homage **10** allegiance

Loyolite: **6** Jesuit

lozenge: **4** pill **5** candy **6** jujube, pastil, tablet, troche **7** diamond **8** pastille

lubber: **4** boor, gawk, lout **5** churl, drone **8** landsman

lubricate: oil **4** dope **6** grease **7** moisten

lubricous: **4** lewd **6** shifty, tricky, wanton **7** elusive **8** slippery, unstable **10** lascivious

luce: **4** pike

lucent: **5** clear, lucid **6** bright **7** shining **11** translucent, transparent

lucerne, lucern: **7** alfalfa

lucid: **4** sane **5** clear **6** bright, lucent **7** crystal, shining **8** luminous, pellucid **11** resplendent, translucent

Lucifer: **5** devil, Satan

luck: hap, lot, ure **4** cess, eure, fate **5** deuce **6** chance, hansel **7** ambsace, fortune, handsel, success **8** fortuity **9** mischance

bringer: **5** Jonah **6** clover, mascot **9** horseshoe **10** rabbit-foot

stroke of: **5** fluke

token for: **5** charm **6** amulet, mascot **7** periapt

lucky: **5** canny, happy, sonsy **6** sonsie **8** gracious **9** fortunate **10** propitious, prosperous, successful **12** providential

lucrative: **6** paying **7** gainful **10** beneficial, productive, profitable **12** remunerative

lucre: **4** gain, loot, pelf **5** booty, money **6** profit, riches, wealth

ludicrous: **4** antic, awful, comic, droll, funny **6** absurd **7** comical, foolish, risible **8** farcical **9** burlesque, laughable **10** ridiculous

luff: **4** sail

lug: box, ear **4** drag, draw, pull, tote, worm, haul **5** carry **10** projection

lugubrious: **4** sad **6** dismal **7** doleful **8** mournful

lukewarm: **5** tepid

lull: **4** calm, hush, rock **5** allay, quiet, still **6** pacify, soothe **7** compose **8** calmness, mitigate **9** cessation **11** tranquilize

lullaby: **5** baloo, balow

lumber: **4** raff, wood **6** refuse, timber

lumbering: **7** awkward

lumberman: 6 logger, sawyer, scorer 10 lumberjack
boot: pac
sled: 4 tode 7 travois 8 travoise
luminary: sun 4 star 5 light 12 illumination, intellectual
lumine: 5 light 8 illumine
luminous: 5 clear, lucid 6 bright 7 shining 9 brilliant 11 illuminated, transparent 14 phosphorescent
lummox: 4 boor, lout 5 yahoo 7 bumpkin, bungler
lump: bat, cob, dab, dad, dot, gob, nub, wad 4 beat, blob, burl, cake, clog, clot, daud, heap, hump, hunk, knob, knot, mass 5 bulge, claut, clump, clunk, hunch, wedge 6 dollop, gobbet, nodule, nugget 12 protuberance
lumpfish: 6 paddle
lumpish: 4 dull 5 heavy, inert 6 stodgy, stupid 8 sluggish 9 shapeless
lumpy: 5 rough 6 choppy
lunacy: 5 folly, mania 7 madness 8 delirium, insanity 9 craziness 11 derangement
lunar (see also **moon**): 6 lunate 8 crescent 9 satellite
lunatic: mad 6 insane, madman 7 frantic 8 demoniac 9 bedlamite 10 moonstruck
lune: 5 leash 8 crescent
lung: *disease:* 11 anthracosis
having: 9 pulmonate
sound: 4 rale
lunge: jab 4 foin, leap, stab 5 barge, longe, lurch, pitch 6 plunge, thrust
luny: 5 crazy 8 demented
lupine: 6 fierce 7 wolfish 8 ravenous, wolflike
lurch: rob 4 jolt, reel 5 barge, cheat, fraud, lunge, pitch, steal, trick 6 careen, career, swerve 7 stumble
lure: 4 bait, draw, trap 5 decoy, snare, tempt 6 allure, entice, seduce 7 attract, beguile, pitfall 8 inveigle 10 allurement, attraction, enticement
lurer: 4 bait 5 siren 7 trapper
lurid: wan 4 pale 5 gaudy, livid 6 dismal, gloomy 7 ghastly, hideous 8 gruesome, shocking, terrible
lurk: 4 hide 5 skulk, slink, sneak 6 ambush
luscious: 4 rich, ripe 5 sweet 6 creamy 7 cloying 8 delicate 9 delicious 10 voluptuous
lush: 4 soft 5 drunk 6 limber, mellow 9 alcoholic, luxuriant, succulent 11 intoxicated
lusory: 7 playful 8 sportive
lust: 6 desire, liking 7 passion 8 appetite, cupidity 11 inclination
luster, lustre: 4 cave, naif 5 sheen, shine, water 6 polish 8 glister 8 schiller, splendor 11 distinction, iridescence

lusterless: mat, wan 4 dead, dull 5 faded, fishy 6 gloomy 9 tarnished
lustful: hot 4 gamy, lewd 5 cadgy 7 fulsome, rammish 9 lecherous, salacious
lustrous: 5 nitid 6 glossy, orient 7 radiant 8 nitidous 9 brilliant 11 illustrious, transparent
lusty: 4 cant 5 crank, frack, frank, freck, hardy 6 cranky, gawsie, robust, strong, sturdy 8 bouncing, vigorous
lute: tar 4 clay, ring 6 cement 7 dyphone 10 instrument
luxe: 8 elegance, richness
Luxemburg: *measure:* 5 fuder
river: 7 Moselle
luxuriant: 4 lush, rank, rich 5 frank 6 lavish 7 fertile, opulent, profuse, teeming 8 prolific 9 exuberant 10 voluptuous
luxuriate: 4 bask, riot 5 revel
luxurious: 4 posh, rich 5 gaudy 6 costly 7 elegant, opulent 8 gorgeous, sensuous, 9 sumptuous 11 comfortable, extravagant
luxury: 8 delicacy
lover of: 8 Sybarite
Luzon: *city:* 5 Gapan 6 Ilagan 10 Cabanatuan
dialect: 6 Itaves
mountain: Iba
people: Ata, Ita 4 Aeta, Atta 5 Tagal 6 Aripas, Arupas, Igorot, Isinay, Itaneg 7 Igorote, Italone, Tagalog
seaport: 6 Aparri, Manila
volcano: 5 Mayon
lyam: 5 leash 10 bloodhound
lycee: 6 lyceum, school
Lycian city: 4 Myra 6 Sardis
Lydia: *king:* 5 Gyges 7 Croesus
river: 8 Pactolus
lye: 6 potash 7 caustic 8 lixivium
pert. to: 8 lixivial
lying: 4 flat 5 awald, awalt, prone 6 supine 8 couchant 9 dishonest, mendacity 10 pseudology
lying-in: 11 confinement 12 accouchement
lymph: sap 5 water 6 plasma, spring
lynch: 4 hang 6 murder 7 execute
lynx: cat 5 pishu 6 bobcat, lucern 7 caracal 8 carcajou
Lyra star: 4 Vega
lyrate: 9 spatulate
lyre: 4 asor, harp 6 kissar, trigon 7 cithara, kithara, testudo
lyre turtle: 11 leatherback
lyric: lai, lay, ode 4 alba, odic, poem 5 epode, gazel, melic 6 ghazel, poetic, rondel 7 cancion, canzone(It.), descort, rondeau 9 dithyramb
Muse: 5 Erato 8 Polymnia 10 Polyhymnia
lyrical: 6 epodic 7 sestina
lyrichord: 11 harpsichord
lyssa: 6 rabies 11 hydrophobia

M

macabre: 4 eery, grim 5 eerie 7 ghastly 8 grewsome, gruesome 9 deathlike

macaca: 5 lemur 6 monkey

macadam: tar 8 pavement

macaque: 4 bruh 6 monkey, rhesus

macaw: ara 4 arra, bird 5 arara 6 parrot 7 maracan 8 aracanga, ararauna

Macbeth: *character:* 5 Angus 6 Banquo
title: 5 Thane
victim: 6 Duncan

maccaboy: 5 snuff

mace: dod, rod 4 club, maul, rush 5 spice, staff 6 mallet 7 swindle
bearer: 6 beadle
royal: 7 scepter, sceptre

Macedonia: *mountain:* 7 Olympus 8 Olympiad
people: 6 Greeks 8 Serbians 9 Albanians 10 Bulgarians

macer: 6 beadle, bearer 8 swindler

macerate: ret 4 soak 5 steep

machete: 4 bolo, fish 5 blade, knife 6 guitar

Machiavellian: 4 wily 6 crafty 7 cunning 8 guileful 9 deceitful 11 treacherous

Machiavelli's book: 6 Prince

machila: 7 hammock

machin: 7 macaque

machination: 4 plan, plot 5 cabal 6 scheme 8 artifice, intrigue 10 conspiracy 11 contrivance

machine: car 4 auto 5 robot 6 device, engine 9 apparatus, appliance, automatic, automaton, mechanism 10 automobile 11 contrivance, machination 12 organization
hydraulic: 9 telemotor

machine gun: 4 Sten 5 Maxim 7 Gatling 9 Hotchkiss 10 chatterbox
place: 4 nest

mackerel: 4 scad 5 akule, atule, tunny 7 escolar, tassard 8 hardhead
genus: 7 scomber
net: 7 spiller
young: 5 spike 6 tinker 7 blinker

mackerel bird: 7 wryneck 9 kittiwake

mackle: See **macula**.

macle: 8 chrystal 11 chiastolite

macula: 4 blot, blur, spot 5 stain 6 blotch, mackle, macule 7 blemish

maculate: 6 defile, impure 7 speckle 8 besmirch

mad: 4 gite, gyte, hyte(Sc.) 5 angry, crazy, folle, irate, rabid, vexed 6 frenzy, insane 7 enraged, foolish, frantic, furious 8 demented, frenetic, incensed, maniacal 9 desperate, fanatical, hilarious, phrenetic, psychotic 10 distracted, distraught, infatuated, infuriated 11 fantastical 12 arreptitious, unreasonable

Madagascar: *animal:* 6 aye-aye, tanrec, tenrec 7 tendrac
city: 7 Mojanga 8 Tamatave 10 Tananarive, Tananarivo 12 Antananarivo(c.)
civet: 7 fossane
island group: 7 Aldabra
lemur: 5 avahi, indri 6 aye-aye 9 babacoote
measure: 7 gantang
native: 4 Hova 8 Sakalava
palm: 6 raffia
people: 4 Hova
tree: 11 antankarana
tribe: 4 Bara 5 Hovas 8 Betsileo, Malagasy, Sakalava 13 Betsimasaraka

madam, madame: Mme., Mrs. 4 bawd, lady 5 donna, hussy, title, wench 6 senora 8 mistress 9 courtesan

madcap: 4 wild 7 hotspur 8 reckless

madder: al; aal 7 munjeet 8 dyestuff
family: 9 rubiaceae

made: 10 artificial

Madeira wine: 4 bual 5 tinta, tinto 7 malmsey, sercial 8 verdelho

mademoiselle: 4 miss

madhouse: 5 chaos 6 asylum, bedlam 8 bughouse

madid: wet 5 moist

madman: 6 maniac 7 furioso, lunatic 8 frenetic 9 phrenetic, psychotic

madness: ire 4 fury 5 folly, furor, mania 6 bedlam, frenzy, lunacy, rabies 7 dewanee, ecstasy, widdrim 8 delirium, dementia, insanity 9 amazement, furiosity, nosomania, phrenetic 11 derangement

Madras: *district:* 7 Malabar, Nellore
hemp: 4 sunn
measure: 4 para 5 cawny, manei, parah 6 cawney, mercal, ollock, olluck, parrah, puddee
town: 5 Adoni, Arcot 7 Calicut
weight: ser 4 cash, powe, seer 5 fanam 6 pagoda, pollam 7 chinnam, varahan 8 mangelin

madrepore: 5 coral 6 fossil

madrigal: ode 4 glee, poem 5 lyric 6 verses

Maecenas: 6 patron
maelstrom: 4 eddy 5 swirl 7 current,
turmoil 9 whirlpool
maenad: 9 bacchante
maestro: 6 master 7 teacher 8 composer
9 conductor 10 bandleader 11 choirmaster 13 kapellmeister
di-cappella: 11 choirmaster 13 kapellmeister
maffle: 6 muddle, mumble 7 confuse, stammer 8 bewilder, squander
mag: 4 chat 6 magpie 7 chatter, magneto
8 titmouse 9 halfpenny 10 chatterbox
Magadha king: 9 Bimbisara 10 Ajatasa-
tru
magadis: 5 flute 9 monochord
magazine: 4 pulp 5 depot 7 almacen, arsenal, chamber, journal 9 ephemeris,
reservoir, warehouse 10 periodical, repository, storehouse 11 armamentary
mage: See **magician.**
magenta: dye 7 fuchsia
maggot: 4 grub, mawk, whim 5 larva,
mathe 6 gentle, notion 7 caprice
magi: 5 Sages 6 Gaspar 8 Melchior 9
Balthasar
magic: art 4 rune 5 fairy, obeah, spell,
turgy 6 glamor, voodoo 7 glamour, gramary, sorcery 8 brujeria(Sp.), gramarye
9 deception, diablerie 10 necromancy,
witchcraft 11 conjuration, enchantment,
legerdemain, thaumaturgy 12 invultuation
lantern: 11 epidiascope 12 stereopticon
perform: hex 6 sorcer 7 conjure
staff: 4 wand 7 rhabdos 8 caduceus
symbol: 5 charm 6 caract 8 pentacle
tree: 13 polemoniaceae
word: om, um 5 selah 6 presto, sesame,
shelah 10 abacadabra
magical: 5 goety 6 goetic, occult 8 charming 10 bewitching 11 necromantic
magician: 4 mage, magi 5 magus 6 goetic, Merlin, wabeno, wizard 7 juggler 8
conjurer, conjuror, mandrake, sorcerer 9
archimage, charlatan, enchanter 11 entertainer, necromancer, thaumaturge 13
thaumaturgist 15 prestidigitator
assistant: 6 famuli(pl.) 7 famulus
manual: 8 grimoire
motion: 4 pass
magirist: 4 cook
magisterial: 5 lofty, proud 6 august, lordly 7 haughty, stately 8 arrogant, dogmatic
9 dignified, imperious 11 dictatorial,
domineering, overbearing 13 authoritative
magistrate: 4 beak, doge 5 edile, judge 6
alcade, alcaid, archon, bailie, bailli, syndic 7 alcaide, alcalde, bailiff, burgess, po-
desta(It.) 8 alderman, governor, mittimus, official 11 burgomaster
orders: 4 acta(pl.) 5 actum
magma: 4 rock 5 dregs 8 sediment
basalt: 10 limburgite

magnanimous: big 4 free 5 lofty, noble 6
heroic 7 exalted, liberal 8 generous 9
honorable, unselfish, unstinted 10 high-
minded, high-souled 13 disinterested
magnate: 4 lord 5 mogul, noble 6 bashaw,
tycoon 7 grandee, richman 10 clarissimo
11 millionaire
magnesian limestone: 8 dolomite
magnesium: *silicate:* 4 talc
sulphate: 7 loweite
magnet: 7 terella 8 solenoid, terrella 9
loadstone, lodestone
end: 4 pole
pole: red
magnetic: 5 polar 10 electrical
unit: 5 weber
magnetize: 4 lure 7 attract 9 captivate
magnificent: 4 rial, rich 5 grand, great,
noble, regal 6 august, lavish 7 exalted,
stately, sublime 8 glorious, gorgeous, palatial, splendid, striking 9 beautiful,
sumptuous 10 munificent
magnificence: 4 pomp
magnify: 4 laud 5 exalt, extol 6 praise 7
enhance, enlarge, glorify, greaten 8 increase 9 aggravate, overstate 10 exaggerate
magniloquent: 6 turgid 9 bombastic 13
grandiloquent
magnitude: 4 bulk, mass, size 6 extent 7
bigness 9 dimension, greatness
magnolia: 5 yulan
magnum: 6 bottle
magnum opus: 4 work 11 achievement
magot: ape 6 figure
magpie: daw, mag, pie 4 pica, piet 5
madge, ninut, scold 9 chatterer, haggister
diver: 4 smew
shrike: 7 tanager
magsman: 8 swindler
maguari: 5 stork
magus: 4 magi 8 magician
Magyar: 9 Hungarian
maha: 4 deer
mahajan: 11 moneylender
mahala: 5 squaw
mahogany: 4 toon 6 acajou, totara 7 albarco, gunnung 8 bangalay 9 cailcedra
maholi: 5 lemur
Mahomet: See **Mohammed.**
Mahometan: See **Muslim.**
Mahound: 5 devil 8 Mohammed
mahout: 6 driver, keeper
mahu: 5 devil
Maia's son: 6 Hermes
maid: may 4 ayah, girl, help, lass 5 bonne,
woman 6 damsel, maiden, slavey, virgin 7
Abigail, ancilla, colleen, servant 8 domestic, suivante 9 attendant, cameriera,
tirewoman
changed to heifer: Io
changed to spider: 7 Arachne
mythical: 5 nymph
Maid of Astolat: 6 Elaine
maiden: deb 4 girl, jill, lass 5 nymph,

sylph 6 damsel 7 damosel, damozel 8 da-
mozell 9 damosella, damoysell, debutante
maiden duck: 8 shoveler
maiden name: nee
maidenhair: 4 fern 8 adiantum
tree: 6 ginkgo
maidenly: 6 gentle, modest, virgin
mail: bag 4 post, send, ship 6 wallet 8 dispatch
boat: 6 packet
coat: see **armor**
maim: 4 hurt 6 mangle 7 cripple, disable
8 mutilate 9 dismember
main: sea 4 duct, high, pipe 5 chief, first,
grand, ocean, prime 7 capital, conduct,
conduit, leading, purpose 8 foremost 9
principal
main gauche: 6 dagger
Maine: *bay:* 5 Casco 13 Passamaquoddy
city: 4 Bath, Milo, Saco 5 Hiram, Orono 6
Bangor 7 Augusta(c.) 9 Skowhegan
county: 5 Waldo
lake: 5 Moose 6 Sebago
motto: 6 dirigo
mountain: 5 Kineo 8 Katahdin
river: 4 Saco 8 Kennebec
university town: 5 Orono
mainferre: 5 armor 8 gauntlet
mainland: 8 fastland 9 continent
mainsheet: 4 rope
mainstay: key 7 support
maintain: 4 avow, bear, fend, hold, keep
5 argue, claim 6 affirm, allege, assert,
avouch, defend, retain, uphold 7 bolster,
contend, declare, espouse, justify, support, sustain 8 conserve, preserve 9 vindicate
again: 8 reassert
maintainable: 7 tenable
maintenance: 5 batta 6 upkeep 7 alimony, prebend 10 livelihood
maison: 5 house
de sante: 6 asylum 8 hospital 10 sanatorium
maize: 4 corn 5 grain 7 mealies
genus: Zea
majagua: hau 4 baru, bola 5 guana 8 bal-
ibago 12 algodoncillo
majestic: 5 grand, lofty, noble, regal, royal
6 august, kingly 7 leonine, stately, sublime 8 elevated, imperial, splendid 9
dignified, sovereign 11 magnificent
major: wig 5 chief 7 capital, greater, officer 8 superior 9 principal
music: dur
major-domo: 7 bailiff, steward 9 seneschal
majority: age 4 body, more, most 6 quorum 7 greater
make: do; cut, gar(Sc.) 4 coin, form 5
build, force, frame, shape 6 compel,
create, invent, render 7 compose, confect, fashion, prepare, produce 8 contrive,
generate 9 construct, fabricate 11 manufacture

suffix: fy; ify
make do: eke 9 improvise
make fun of: rib 5 scoff 8 ridicule
make known: 6 impart, reveal 7 divulge,
publish, uncover 8 disclose, discover,
proclaim 9 advertise, publicize
make over: 4 redo 6 revamp 9 refashion
make up: 8 complete, cosmetic
make up for: 5 atone 10 compensate
maker: 4 doer 6 author, factor 7 creator 8
declarer, inventor 9 architect 10 originator 12 manufacturer
makeshift: 4 rude 9 temporary
maki: 5 lemur
makluk: 4 seal
mal: bad 4 evil
de mer: 11 seasickness
du pays: 12 homesickness
Malabar: *bark:* 5 ochna
canoe: 5 tonee
palm: 7 talipot
malachite: 4 bice 7 azurite, mineral
maladive: ill 4 sick 6 sickly, unwell 9 unhealthy
maladroit: 6 clumsy 7 awkward, unhandy
8 bungling, inexpert
maladventure: 6 mishap 8 escapade
malady (see also **disease**): 7 ailment, illness 8 disorder, sickness 9 affection.
complaint, distemper 10 affliction 13 indisposition
malagma: 7 plaster 8 poultice
malanders: 6 eczema
malapert: 4 bold 5 saucy 7 ill-bred 8 impudent 9 unskilled
malapropism: 7 mistake
malapropos: 11 inopportune
malar: 6 zygoma 8 zygomata(pl.) 9 cheek-
bone
malaria: 4 agie, ague 5 chill, fever, miasm
6 miasma
antidote: 7 quinine
malaxate: 5 knead
Malaya: *archipelago:* see **island** below
ape: lar
boat: 4 proa 5 praam, prahu 6 praham 7
cougnar
buffalo: 7 carabao 8 seladang
Christian: 7 Ilokano
coin: tra 4 trah 7 tampang
condiment: 6 sambal, sambei 7 semball
crane: 5 sarus
disease: 4 amok, lata 5 amuck, latah
form of address: 4 tuan
garment: 6 sarong
island: Aru, Goa, Kei, Oma 4 Bali, Buru,
Gaga, Java, Sulu 5 Ambon, Arroe, Arrou,
Banca, Banda, Buton, Ceram, Misol,
Sangi, Sumba, Timor 6 Boefon, Boeroe,
Borneo, Flores, Jilolo, Lombik, Madura, Musool, Sangir, Soemba, Talaur,
Waigeu 7 Amboina, Amboyna, Celebes,
Morotai, Salwati, Sumatra, Sumbawa 8
Belitong, Billiton, Djailolo, Soembawa,
Tanimbar, Tenimber 9 Belitoeng, Halma-

hera, New Guinea, Singapore, Timorlaut
10 Sandalwood
isthmus: Kra
jacket: **4** baju
knife: **4** cris, kris **5** crise **6** crease, creese,
kreese, parang
language: **7** Tagalog
mammal: **10** chevrotain
measure: **4** tael, wang
mountain: **6** Gunong, Gunung
musical instrument: **7** anklong
ox: **5** tsine **7** banteng
palm: **4** ejoo, sago **5** areng **6** arenga, ge-
bang, gomuti, nibong, nibung **7** talipot
parrot: **4** lory **6** lories
people: Ata **5** Bajau, Tagal **6** Aripas, Sem-
ang **7** Bisayan, Tagalog, Visayan
pepper: **4** siri **5** sirih
rice field: sawah
state: **5** Kedah, Perak **6** Johore
town: **7** Malacca
tree(see also *palm* above): **4** upas **5** kapur,
niepa, terap **6** durian, durion
malconformation: **9** imperfect **16** disproportionate
malcontent: reb **5** rebel **6** uneasy **8** agitator, Frondeur **10** discontent, rebellious
12 discontented
male: man, mas **4** gent **5** manly **7** mankind, manlike, mannish **9** masculine
animal: tom **4** buck, bull, hart, jack, stag,
stud **8** stallion
malediction: ban **5** curse **7** malison, slander **8** anathema **9** blasphemy **11** imprecation **12** denunciation
malefactor: **5** felon **7** convict, culprit **8**
criminal, evildoer, offender **9** wrongdoer
malefic: **7** harmful, hurtful **11** mischievous
malevolence: **4** evil, hate **5** pique, spite **6**
enmity, hatred, malice, rancor **8** ferocity
9 animosity, hostility, malignity **10** bitterness
malevolent: **4** evil **7** hateful, hostile **9**
rancorous **11** ill-disposed
malfeasance: **5** crime, wrong **8** trespass
11 delinquency
malheur: **10** misfortune
malice: **5** pique **6** enmity **9** animosity **13**
maliciousness
malicious: **4** evil **5** catty, depit **6** bitter **7**
heinous **8** sinister, spiteful **9** felonious,
malignant, rancorous, resentful **10** calumnious, despiteful, despiteous, malevolent
11 ill-disposed **12** cantankerous, unpropitious
action: **5** arson **8** sabotage **9** vandalism
intention: **6** animus
malign: **4** evil, foul **5** abuse, curse, libel **6**
bewray, defame, revile, vilify **7** asperse,
baleful, blacken, deprave, hurtful, slander
8 virulent **10** calumniate, pernicious
malignant: **4** evil **6** wicked **7** hateful,
heinous, hellish, noxious, vicious **8** spite-

ful, venomous, virulent **9** cancerous, felonious, ferocious, invidious, malicious,
poisonous, rancorous **10** rebellious **11**
deleterious
malignity: **10** malignancy
malikana: fee **4** duty **7** payment
malison: **5** curse **11** malediction
malkin: cat, mop **4** drab, hare **6** sponge **8**
slattern **9** scarecrow
mall: **4** walk **5** allee, alley **6** mallet **7**
meeting **9** promenade
mallard: **4** duck
genus: **4** anas
malleable: **4** soft **7** ductile, pliable
mallemuck: **6** fulmar, petrel **9** albatross
mallet: tup **4** club, mace, mall, maul,
mell(Sc.) **5** gavel, madge **6** beater, beetle, driver, hammer
maline: net
mallow: maw **4** hock, weed **5** altea **6** escoba **7** althaea, gemauve
malm: **4** marl **9** limestone
malnutrition: **7** cachexy, wasting **8**
cachexia
malodorous: **4** rank **5** fetid **6** putrid,
smelly **7** noisome **9** odiferous
malt: **8** diastase
beverage: ale **4** beer, brew **5** lager, stout **6**
zythem
froth: **4** barm
ground: **5** grist
vinegar: **6** alegar
worm: **5** toper **7** tippler
Malta: *capital:* **7** Valetta
coin: **5** grain, grano
hamlet: **5** casal **6** casale
measure: **4** salm **5** canna, salma **7** caffiso
suburb: **7** Florian
weight: **4** rotl, salm **5** artal, artel, parto,
ratel, salma **6** kantar
maltose: **6** amylon
maltreat: **5** abuse, dight **6** defile, defoul,
demean, huspel, huspil, misuse, mohock
malty: **5** drunk
malum: **4** evil **5** wrong **7** offense
mammal (see also **animal**): cat **5** beast,
ovine, swine **6** bovine, equine, feline,
monkey, rodent **7** primate **8** edentate,
ruminant, ungulant **9** carnivore, marsupial
amphibious: **5** otter
antlered: elk **4** deer **5** moose **7** caribou **8**
reindeer
aquatic: **4** seal **5** otter, shark, whale **6**
desman, dugong, manati, rytina, walrus **7**
dolphin, manatee, sealion **8** sirenian **12**
hippopotamus
aquatic order: **4** cete **7** cetacea
arboreal: ai **5** lemur, sloth **6** fisher, monkey **7** glutton, opposum, raccoon **8**
banxring, kinkajou **9** orangutan
armored: **9** armadillo
badgerlike: **5** ratel **8** balisaur
bearlike: **5** panda
bovine: ox; bos, cow **4** bull, calf, zebu **5**

bison, steer **7** taurine **8** longhorn
burrowing: **4** mole **6** badger, gopher, wombat **8** squirrel **9** armadillo
camel-like: **7** guanaco
caprine: **4** goat
carnivorous: **9** carnivore
cetacean: see *aquatic* above
coat: fur **4** hide, skin **6** pelage
cud-chewing: **8** ruminant
deerlike: **10** chevrotain
desert: **5** camel
dolphinlike: **4** inia
domestic: cat, cow, dog **5** horse, sheep **6** cattle
edentate: **7** ant bear **8** anteater, pangolin, tamandua
equine: **4** colt, foal, mare **5** filly, horse, zebra **8** stallion
extinct: **6** rytina **8** mastodon
feline: cat
fish-eating: **5** otter
fleet: **4** deer, hare **8** antelope
flying: bat
fur-bearing: **4** coon, mink **5** coypu, otter, sheep, skunk **6** badger, ermine, marten, martin, nutria, rabbit **7** genette, raccoon **8** squirrel
giraffe-like: **5** okapi
gnawing: **6** rodent
hands different from feet: **6** bimana
hedgehog-like: **6** tenrec
herbivorous: **5** daman, tapir **6** bovine, dugong, equine **7** manatee **8** ruminant **9** orangutan **10** rhinoceros **12** hippopotamus
highest order: **7** primate
horned: ox; cow **4** gaur, goat, reem **5** bison **7** buffalo, unicorn **8** antelope, reindeer, seladang **10** rhinoceros
insectivorous: bat **6** tenrec **7** tendrac
large: **5** whale **7** mammoth **8** behemoth, elephant, mastodon **10** rhinoceros **12** hippopotamus
largest: **5** whale
lemurine: **5** potto
leopard-like: **4** lion, lynx, pard, puma **5** tiger **6** cougar, jaguar, ocelot **7** polecat, wildcat
llama-like: **6** vicuna
lowest order: **9** marsupial **11** marsupialia
marine: see *aquatic* above
meat-eating: **9** carnivore
mole-like: **6** desman
monkey-like: **5** lemur, loris
mouselike: **5** shrew
musteline: **5** otter, ratel
nocturnal: bat **5** hyena, lemur, ratel, tapir **6** macaco, racoon **7** raccoon, tarsier **8** kinkajou, platypus
omnivorous: hog, pig **5** swine
plantigrade: **6** racoon **7** raccoon
porcine: hog, pig **4** boar **5** swine **7** peccary
pouched: **9** marsupial
raccoon-like: **5** coati

retentive: **8** elephant
rhinoceros-like: **5** tapir **14** baluchitherium
ring-tailed: **4** coon **5** lemur
ruminant: ox; yak **4** deer, goat **5** bison, camel, llama, moose, okapi, sheep, steer **6** alpaca, cattle, chewer, vicuna **7** buffalo, giraffe **8** antelope
scaled: **8** pangolin
shelled: **9** armadillo
short-tailed: **7** bobtail
skunk-like: **5** zoril
slow-moving: **5** loris, sloth
smallest: **5** shrew
snake-eating: **8** mongoose
spiny: **6** tenrec **9** porcupine
thick-skinned: **8** elephant **9** pachyderm **10** rhinoceros
toothless: **8** edentate
tropical: **5** coati, rhino **7** peccary **9** coati-modi **10** coati-mundi, rhinoceros
tusked: **6** walrus **7** mammoth **8** elephant, mastodon
viverrine: **8** falanaka
vulpine: fox **4** wolf
web-footed: **5** otter
wing-footed: **6** aliped
winged: bat
zebra-like: **6** quagga
mammock: **4** tear **5** break, scrap **6** mangle
mammon: **6** riches, wealth
mammoth: **5** large **8** gigantic
man (see also **fellow, person**): bo; guy, vir(L.) **4** aner(Gr.), chal, chap, homo(L.), male, mann(G.), uomo(It.), work **5** bloke, chiel, guard, homme(F.), human, valet **6** andros(Gr.), chield, hombre(Sp.), mensch (Yid.) **7** counter, fortify, homines(L.pl.), husband, laborer, mankind, operate **8** creature **9** anthropos(Gr.)
aged: vet **4** cuff, sire **5** senex(L.), uncle **6** gaffer, stager **7** grandpa, starets(Russ.), **8** grandpop **9** grandsire, patriarch **10** Methuselah **11** grandfather **12** octogenarian
bad-tempered: **6** bodach **10** curmudgeon
bald: **9** pilgarlic **10** pillgarlic
big: cob
brass: **5** Talos
brave: **4** hero, lion
coarse: **5** churl, knave **7** ruffian
comb. form: **4** homo **5** andro **8** anthropo
conceited: **7** coxcomb
cruel: **4** ogre **7** monster, ruffian, villain
cunning: **5** rogue **7** shyster **9** trickster **10** mountebank
dissolute: **4** roue
eccentric: **6** codger
elderly: see *aged* above
enlisted: G.I. **6** rating, sailor **7** private, soldier **8** sargeant
fashionable: fop **4** dude **5** dandy **10** Corinthian **11** Beau Brummel **12** boulevardier

handsome: 6 Adonis
hard-pressed: Job
hardheaded: 5 boche
henpecked: 10 hoddy-doddy 11 milquetoast
impetuous: 7 hotspur
important: VIP 4 hero, name 5 nabob 7
grandee
ladies': 4 beau 5 beaux(pl.)
learned: PhD 4 bhat 6 doctor, pundit, savant 7 erudite, scholar, teacher 8 literati
9 literatus, professor 11 philologist
little: 6 mankin, shrimp, squirt 8 homuncio 10 homunculus
mechanical: 5 robot 9 automaton
medicine: 6 priest, shaman
money: 9 paymaster
mother of: Eve 6 Cybele
newspaper: 6 editor 8 reporter 9 columnist 10 journalist
of all work: 4 joey, mozo 8 factotum, handyman
of the world: 6 layman 10 secularist 11
cosmopolite 12 sophisticate
old: see *elderly* above
old-clothes: 4 poco
outdoor: 6 camper, hunter 7 athlete 9
fisherman
personifying: 15 anthropomorphic
pert. to: 5 human 6 humane, mortal
political: 7 senator 8 diplomat 9 statesman
10 ambassador 11 assemblyman 14
representative
poor: 6 pauper 7 peasant 8 beadsman,
bedesman
primitive: 6 savage 8 urmensch(Yid.)
resembling: 7 android 10 anthropoid
rich: 5 Midas, nabob 6 tycoon 7 Croesus,
magnate 9 plutocrat 10 capitalist 11
billionaire, millionaire
science: 9 ethnology 12 anthropology
self-important: 10 cockalorum
shadowless: 6 ascian
single: 4 stag 7 widower 8 bachelor, celibate
undercover: spy 5 agent 9 detective 12
investigator
unemployed: 6 batlan, batlon(Yid.),
unmarried: see *single* above
white: 6 buckra 7 cachila(P.I.) 8 pale-
face
wicked: 7 villain
wise: 4 sage, seer 5 solon 6 nestor 7 Solomon
young: boy 5 youth 6 varlet
man fungus: 9 earthstar
Man of Destiny: 17 Napoleon Bonaparte
Man of Galilee: 11 Jesus Christ
man of God: 5 rabbi, saint 6 pastor,
priest 7 ascetic, prelate 8 minister 12
ecclesiastic
man of war: 7 frigate, soldier, warrior
deck: 5 orlop

Man O'War: 5 horse 6 winner
manacle: 4 bond, cuff, iron 5 chain, darby
6 fetter, hamper 7 confine, shackle 8
handcuff 9 restraint
manada: 4 herd 5 drove, flock
manage: man, run 4 boss, head, lead, rule
5 dight, frame, guide, order, steer, wield
6 convoy, demean, direct, govern, handle
7 conduct, control, dispose, execute, husband, operate, oversee 8 contrive, dispense, engineer, maneuver 9 supervise
10 accomplish, administer, manipulate
frugally: 6 eke out 7 husband 9 economize
hard to: 6 ornery
manageable: 4 easy, tame, yare 6 docile,
wieldy 7 ductile, pliable 8 flexible, maniable, workable 9 compliant, tractable 10
governable
management: 4 care 6 agency, charge,
menage 7 address, economy, gestion 8
carriage, demeanor 9 demeanour, governail, ordinance 10 enterprise, governance
11 generalship
good: 6 eutaxy 7 eutaxie
poor: 11 cacoeconomy
manager: 4 doer 6 gerent, grieve 7 captain, curator, foreman, steward 8 aumildar 12 entrepreneur
managery: 7 cunning 8 artifice 9 frugality, husbandry 10 management 11
managership
manatee: 6 seacow 8 sirenian
Manchuria: *city:* 5 Hulan, Kirin 6 Harbin,
Mukden 9 Niuchwang
province: 5 Jehol
river: 4 Amur, Liao, Yalu
manciple: 5 slave 7 servant, steward 8
purveyor
mandarin: 6 orange 7 Chinese 9 tangerine
residence: 5 yamen
mandate: 4 writ 5 brief, order 6 behest,
charge, decree, demand, firman 7 bidding, command, precept 9 direction 10
commission, injunction, referendum
mandatory: 10 imperative, obligatory
mandible: jaw 4 beak 9 chelicera
part: 5 molar
mandrel: hob 4 axle, ball, pick 5 arbor 7
spindle
mandrill: 6 baboon
manducate: eat 4 chew 9 masticate
mane: 4 hair, juba 5 brush 6 grivna 8 en-
colure
maneuver: 4 ploy 6 deploy, jockey, tactic
7 echelon 8 artifice, contrive, engineer 9
evolution, stratagem 10 manipulate
aviation: 4 loop, spin 7 echelon, flathat 9
chandelle, Immelmann
military: 6 tactic
manful: See **manly.**
mang: 8 frenzied 10 bewildered

manga: 6 poncho

mange: eat 4 itch, meal, scab 6 fodder, scurvy

manger: bin, box 4 crib, meal 5 stall 6 trough 7 banquet

mangle: cut, mar 4 hack, maim 6 bruise, garble, ironer, smooth 8 calender, lacerate, mutilate 9 dismember

mango: *bird:* 6 oriole 11 hummingbird
fish: 9 threadfin
tree: 4 tope

mangy: 4 mean 5 seedy 6 ronion, ronyon, scurvy, shabby 7 squalid 12 contemptible

manhandle: 4 maul

mani: 6 peanut

mania: 5 craze, furor 6 frenzy, furore 7 madness, passion 8 delirium 9 cacoethes 11 derangement
buying: 9 oniomania
stealing: 11 kleptomania

maniable: See **manageable**.

maniac: 6 madman 7 lunatic

manic: 9 afflicted

manifest: 4 open, show 5 argue, clear, index, overt 6 attest, evince, extant, graith, patent, reveal 7 approve, confess, declare, develop, display, evident, exhibit, explain, express, glaring, invoice, obvious, signify, visible 8 apparent, develope, disclose, discover, evidence, indicate, palpable 11 conspicuous, demonstrate, discernible, indubitable, perspicuous 12 indisputable, unmistakable

manifestation: 4 sign 5 phase 6 effect, ostent

manifesto: 5 edict 7 placard 8 evidence 9 statement 11 declaration 13 demonstration

manifold: 4 many 7 various 8 multiple, numerous 9 different, multifold, multiplex, replicate 12 multifarious

manikin: 4 puny 5 dwarf, model, pygmy 7 phantom 8 homuncio, homuncle 9 homuncule, homunculi(pl.), mannequin 10 diminutive, homunculus

Manila: *creek:* 6 estero
hemp: 5 abaca, abaka 6 banana
nut: 6 peanut

manioc: 7 cassava, tapioca

manipulate: rig, use 4 work 5 treat, wield 6 handle, manage 7 control, operate

manis: 8 anteater, pangolin

mankind: man 4 Adam, male 5 flesh, world 6 humans, people 8 humanity
division: 4 race 5 tribe 6 people
hater: 11 misanthrope

manlike: 4 male 5 manly 7 android, mannish 9 masculine 10 anthropoid

manly: 4 bold, male 5 brave, hardy, noble 6 daring 7 manlike, mannish 8 resolute 9 dignified, masculine, undaunted 10 courageous

manna: 7 Godsend 10 gazangabin

mannequin: See **manikin**.

manner: air, way 4 cost, form, mien, mode, more, thew 5 guise, trick 6 aspect, course, method 7 address, bearing, fashion, quomodo 8 attitude, behavior 9 behaviour, technique 10 appearance, deportment
law: 4 modi(pl.) 5 modus

mannerism: 4 mode, pose 5 trait 7 bearing 11 affectation, peculiarity

mannerly: 4 nice 5 civil, moral 6 decent, polite, seemly 8 decorous

manners: 5 lates 8 courtesy 9 amenities, etiquette

Mannus' father: 6 Tuisto

mano: 4 hand 9 handstone

manoc: 4 fowl 7 chicken, rooster

manor: 4 hall 5 abode, house 6 estate 7 mansion
land: 6 barton 7 demesne

manred: 6 homage 9 vassalage

manse: 7 rectory

manservant: 4 help, mozo, syce 5 gilly(Sc.), groom, valey 6 Andrew, butter, garcon, gillie 8 factotum

manship: 5 honor 6 homage 7 courage, manhood 8 courtesy, humanity 9 manliness

mansion: 4 hall, home, stay 5 abode, house, manor, siege 7 chateau, lodging, sojourn 8 chateaux(pl.), dwelling 9 residence
papal: 7 Lateran

manslaughter: 6 murder 7 killing, slaying 8 butchery

mansuete: 4 kind, tame 6 gentle

manta: 4 wrap 5 cloak, cloth 7 blanket, bulwark, shelter 8 mantelet 9 devilfish

mantegar: ape

manteel: See **mantle**.

mantel: 4 arch, beam 5 brace(Sc.), ledge, shelf, stone 6 clavel, lintel 10 manteltree

mantelet: 4 cape 5 cloak 6 mantle, screen, shield 7 shelter 8 galapago

mantilla: 4 cape 5 cloak

mantis crab: 7 squilla

mantle (see also **cloak**): 4 brat, capa, cape, coat, cope, hood, mant, robe 5 blush, cover, manto 6 capote, kittel 7 encloak, manteau, manteel, whittle 8 envelope, mantelet, mantilla 10 witzchoura

manto: 4 gown 5 cloak 6 mantle, mantua

mantoid: 6 mantis

mantua: 4 gown 5 cloak, manto 9 overdress

manual: 4 book 7 clavier, didache 8 grimoire, handbook 9 catechism 11 enchiridion
art: 5 craft

manuduction: 5 guide 7 leading 8 guidance 9 direction 12 introduction

manufactory: 7 factory

manufacture: 4 fake, make 5 forge 6

invent **7** confect, produce **9** fabricate

manufactured: **4** made **10** artificial

manufacturer: **8** employer **9** fabricant, operative **10** fabricator **12** entrepreneur **13** industrialist

manumission: **7** freedom, freeing, release **10** liberation **11** deliverance **12** emancipation

manure: **4** dung **5** addle **7** compost **10** composture

manuscript: MS **4** copy **5** codex **7** papyrus, writing **8** document **9** archetype, minuscule **11** composition, handwriting

back: **5** dorso
space: **6** lacuna
copier: **6** scribe
mark: **5** obeli(pl.) **6** obelus

many: **4** fele, raff **6** divers **7** diverse, several, various **8** manifold, numerous **9** different, multifold, multitude **10** multiplied

prefix: **4** poly, vari **5** multi

many-footed: **8** multiped

many-sided: **9** versatile **12** multilateral

mao: **7** peacock

Maori: *bird:* poe, tue, tui
canoe: **4** waka
charm: **7** heitiki
chief: **5** ariki
club: **4** mere, patu, rata
compensation: utu
fort: pa; pah
hen: **4** weka
hero: **4** Maui
house: **5** whare **8** wharekai **9** wherekura **12** wharewananga
oven: umu
priest: **7** tuhunga
store: **6** pataka
tatooing: **4** moko
tree: **5** mapau **6** manuka **9** tanehakas
tribe: Ati **4** Hapu
village: pa; pah **4** kaik **5** kaika **6** kainga
weapon: **4** mere, patu, rata

map: **4** card, plan **5** carte, chard, chart, image **6** design, sketch, survey **7** diagram, epitome, explore, outline, picture **8** roadbook **9** delineate **10** cartograph, embodiment **14** representation

book: **5** atlas
copier: **10** pantograph
maker: **7** charter **8** Mercator **12** cartographer
townsite: **4** plat
weather line: **6** isobar

maple: **4** acer
cup: **5** mazer
derived from: **6** aceric
family: **9** aceraceae
sap: **5** humbo
scale: **10** pulvinaria
seed: **6** samara
spout: **5** spile

mar: **4** amar, blot, scar **5** botch, spoil **6** damage, deface, deform, impair, injure, mangle **7** blemish **8** obstruct **9** disfigure

marabou: **5** stork **6** argala **7** faleric **8** adjutant, marabout

maral: **4** deer

maranatha: **5** curse

maranon: **6** cashew

marasca: **6** cherry **10** maraschino

marasmus: **5** waste **10** emaciation **13** contabescence

maraud: **4** loot, raid, rove **7** pillage, plunder

marauder: **6** bandit, pirate **7** cateran(Sc.)

marble: **4** cold, hard **5** agate, rance, stone **6** basalt **7** cipolin **8** brocatel, dolomite **9** unfeeling **10** brocatelle

game: taw
mosaic: **7** tessera
playing: mib, pea, taw **4** doby **5** alley, dobie **6** glassy **7** shooter
slab: **5** dalle(F.)

marble flower: **5** poppy

marblehead: **6** fulmar

marbler: **6** carver **8** sculptor

marc: **6** refuse **7** residue

marcato: **6** marked **7** pointed **8** accented, emphatic

march: **4** hike, trek **5** route, troop **6** border, defile, parade **8** boundary, frontier, smallage **9** cavalcade **10** procession

day's: **5** etape
horsemen: **9** cavalcade
spirited: **9** quickstep

March (15th day): **4** ides

March King: **5** Sousa

marchland: **8** frontier **10** borderland

marcid: **4** weak **7** decayed, tabetic **8** withered **9** exhausted **10** emaciating

marcor: **5** decay **7** maramus

mare: yad **4** jade, yade, yaud(Sc.) **5** gilot, horse, meare **6** dobbin, equine, grasni
young: **5** filly

mare's tail: **5** cloud **6** cirrus

marge: See **margin**.

margin: hem, lip, ori, rim **4** bank, brim, edge, orae(L.), rand, side **5** brink, shore, verge **6** border, fringe, leeway **7** margent
narrow: **4** hair
note: **7** apostil **8** scholium **10** annotation
set in: **6** indent

Marianas: **4** Guam **6** Saipan

marigold: **5** boots, caper, gools **6** buddle **7** cowslip, elkslip, golland

marijuana: boo, hay, pot, tea **5** grass
cigarette: mu **6** greefa, griffo, moocah, mooter, muggle, reefer **7** mohasky **8** joy-smoke, loco weed, Mary Jane **9** Indian hay **10** bambalacha, Mary Warner, Mary Weaver **11** giggle-smoke
cigarette holder: **6** crutch
user: **7** pot head **10** muggle-head

marina: **4** dock **5** basin **9** esplanade, promenade

marinade: **5** brine **6** pickle **8** marinate

marinal: **6** marine, sailor, saline **7** mariner **8** nautical

marine: tar **5** jolly, naval, water **7** aquatic,

marinal, mariner, oceanic, pelagic **8** hali-
mous, maritime, nautical **9** aequoreal **11**
leatherneck
crustacean: **8** barnacle
instrument: aba **5** radar **7** pelorus, sextant
plant: **4** alga **5** algae **6** enalid **7** seaweed
science: **10** oceanology **12** oceanography
skeleton: **5** coral
slogan: **6** gungho
marine animal: orc **5** coral, polyp **9**
jellyfish
marine fish: **8** menhaden
mariner: gob, tar **5** Jacky **6** galoot, sailor,
seaman **7** buscarl **8** buscarle, seafarer,
waterman **9** aequoreal
card: **5** chart
compass card: **4** rose
compass points: **6** rhumbs
marinheiro: **6** acajou
marionette: **6** puppet **10** bufflehead
marital: **9** connubial **11** matrimonial
maritime: See **marine**.
marjoram: **4** herb, mint **6** origan
mark: dot, hob, tee **4** belt, goal, line, note,
rist, scar, wale **5** badge, brand, grade, label, score, stamp, track, watch **6** accent,
beacon, caract, denote, notice, target **7**
betoken, blemish, earmark, impress, imprint, insigne, observe **8** identify, insig-
nia(pl.), standard **9** character, designate
10 indication **11** distinguish **14** characteristic
bad: **7** demerit
diacritical: **5** breve, tilde **6** macron, umlaut **7** cedilla(F.),
down: **5** lower
out: **6** cancel, define **7** measure **10** obliterate
possessive: **10** apostrophe
printer's: **4** dele, fist, stet **5** caret, obeli **6**
dagger, diesis, obelus **7** obelisk
pronunciation: see *diacritical* above
punctuation: **4** dash **5** colon, comma **6**
period **8** dieresis **9** diaeresis, semicolon
11 parenthesis, parentheses(pl.),
question: **7** erotema, eroteme
reference: **4** star **6** dagger **8** asterisk
tiny: dot
white: **5** rache, ratch
with critical notes: **8** annotate
Mark Twain's name: **22** Samuel Lang-
horne Clemens
markaz: **8** district **11** subdivision
marked: **5** fated **7** eminent **10** empha-
sized **11** conspicuous, outstanding
with lines: **5** ruled **6** gyrose, linear, notate
marker: peg **5** arrow **6** scorer, signal **7**
brander, counter, monitor **8** bookmark,
marksman, recorder **9** milestone **10**
gravestone
air course: **5** pylon
floating: **4** buoy
market: **4** gunj(Ind.), mart, sale, sell, shop,
sook **5** agora(Gr.), bazar, gunge, halle,
pasar, plaza, store, tryst **6** bazaar, rialto,

shoppe **7** chaffer **8** cheaping, debouche
(F.), emporium
marketable: **8** vendible
markhor: **4** goat
marksman: **4** shot **6** sniper
marl: **4** clay, malm **6** manure **7** marlite **9**
greensand **10** fertilizer, overspread
marli: **4** lace **5** gauze, tulle
marlin: **6** curlew, godwit **9** spearfish
marlinespike: fid **4** skua **6** Jaeger
marlock: **4** ogle **5** prank, sport, trick **6**
frolic
marmalade: jam **6** sapote **8** preserve
quince: **8** co-diniac, quiddany
tree: **5** mamie
marmit: pot **6** kettle
marmoset: **4** mico **6** monkey, sagoin,
wistit **7** tamarin, wistiti
marmot: **5** bobac **6** rodent **8** burrower,
whistler **9** woodchuck
marmota: **8** arctomys **9** woodchuck
maroon: **6** enisle, strand **7** isolate, reddish **8** cimarron, purplish
marooner: **6** pirate **9** buccaneer
Marpessa's abductor: **4** Idas
marplot: **7** meddler, snooper **8** busybody
9 addle-plot
marquee: **4** tent **6** canopy
marquetry: **5** inlay
marquis: **4** peer
marriage: **5** match **6** splice **7** wedding,
wedlock **9** matrimony
absence of: **5** agamy
broker: **9** schatchen(Yid.)
forswearer: **8** celebate
fourth: **9** tetragamy
god: **5** Hymen
goddess: **4** Hera
more than one husband: **9** polyandry
more than one wife: **6** bigamy **8** polygamy
notice: **5** banns
of aged: **8** opsigamy
of gods: **8** theogamy
open to slaves: **12** contubernium
pert. to: **7** marital, spousal **8** hymeneal **9**
connubial, endogamic
portion: dot **5** dowry
secret: **9** elopement
to promise: **7** betroth **8** affiance
to two people: **6** bigamy
marriageable: **6** nubile
married: **5** wived **6** wedded **8** espoused **9**
connubial
married person: **4** wife **6** spouse **7** husband **8** benedict
marrow: **4** best, pith **5** reest(Sc.) **6** inmost, medula **7** essence, medulla
bones: **5** knees
marry: **4** join, mate, wive, yoke **5** cleek,
hitch, unite **6** buckle, couple **7** espouse,
husband
Mars: **4** Ares **6** planet, war god
inner moon: **6** Phobos
planet belt: **5** Libya

planet spot: **5** oasis, oases(pl.)
priests of: **5** Salii **6** Deimos
region (dark): **4** mare
twin sons: **5** Remus **7** Romulus
Marseillaise author: 13 Rouget de Lisle
marsh: bog, fen, hag **4** mire, moor, slew,
   sloo, slue **5** flash, liman, slash, swale,
   swamp **6** morass, palude, slough **7** cienaga, maremma(It.) **8** quagmire **9** everglade
bird: **4** sora **5** snipe, stilt
crocodile: goa
elder: iva
fever: **7** helodes
gas: **7** methane **8** firedamp
grass: **4** tule **5** sedge, spart
hawk: **7** harrier
marigold: **5** boots
pert. to: **8** paludine
salt: **6** salina **7** corcass
shrub: **8** moorwort
marsh plant genus: 6 caltha **7** elatine
marshal: **4** lead **5** align, aline, array,
   groom, guide, usher **6** direct, parade **7**
   arrange, farrier, officer **8** official
marshland: fen **4** fell
marshmallow: 5 altea
marshwort: 9 cranberry
genus: **4** sium
marshy: wet **5** fenny **6** callow **7** helodes,
   paludal, paludic **8** paludine **9** paludinal
lake: **5** liman
marsupial: **4** tait **5** coala, koala **6** possum, wombat **7** dasyure, opossum **9** bandicoot
Australian: **4** tait **6** cuscus **7** dasyure **8**
   kangaroo **9** phalanger
bearlike: **5** coala, koala **6** wombat
genus: **10** diprotodom
mart: **4** fair **5** bazar **6** bazaar, market,
   rialto **8** emporium
martel: 6 hammer
marten: fur **5** sable **6** animal, fisher, martin
beech: **4** foin
genus: **7** mustela
stone: **4** foin
martial: **7** warlike **8** military
Martian: 5 Arean
comb. form: **4** areo
martin: 7 swallow
martinet: 6 tyrant **14** disciplinarian
Martinique volcano: 5 Pelee
martyr: 5 saint **8** sufferer **10** sacrificer
first Christian: **7** Stephen
royal: **7** Charles
martyrdom: **7** killing, passion, torment,
   torture **8** butchery, distress **10** affliction
place of: **8** Golgotha
marvel: 5 ferly **6** admire, wonder **7** miracle, portent **8** astonish **9** horehound **12**
   astonishment
marvelous: **7** strange **8** wondrous **9** excellent **10** improbable, incredible
Maryland *city:* **9** Baltimore
race track: **5** Bowie

mas: **9** masculine
masa: **8** cornmeal
masculine: mas **4** male **5** manly **6** strong,
   virile **7** manlike, mannish
mash: **4** chap, mess, ogle **5** champ, cream,
   crush, flirt, smash **6** muddle **7** farrago,
   mixture, trouble
mashal: **7** parable, proverb
masher: **4** chap **5** flirt, ricer
mask: **4** hide, veil **5** cloak, cover, guise,
   visor **6** screen **7** conceal, curtain **8** defi-
   lade, disguise **9** dissemble
half: **4** loup(Fr.) **6** domino(Fr.)
top knot on: **5** onkos
masked: **6** covert **7** larvate, obscure **8**
   larvated
masker: **6** domino, mummer
maskery: 10 masquerade
maslin: **5** brass **7** mixture **9** potpourri
mason: **7** builder **11** stoneworker
mixing rod: rab
Masons: *doorkeeper:* **5** tiler
order: **8** Templars
masonry: **6** ashlar **7** blocage **9** stonework
masquerade: **5** guise **8** disguise
mass: bat, gob **4** blob, body, bulk, clot,
   heap, lump, size, swad **5** amass, batch,
   gross, group, store **6** gather, gobbet,
   prayer **7** phalanx, service **8** assemble **9**
   aggregate, magnitude **10** accumulate, assemblage, congregate **11** agglomerate,
   composition, compositure, concentrate,
   consolidate **12** congregation
book: **6** missal
cloudlike: **6** nebula **7** nebulae(pl.)
comb. form: mas
confused: cot **5** chaos **6** welter **9** imbroglio
   10 hotchpotch
for dead: **7** requiem
of particulars: **9** aggregate
pert. to: **5** molar
small: dab, pat, wad **4** floc
tangled: mop **4** shag
Massachusetts: *cape:* Ann
city: **4** Lynn **5** Acton, Salem **6** Boston(c.),
   Hadley, Lowell, Malden, Quincy, Wianno,
   Woburn **7** Chelsea, Metheun, Waltham
   8 Brockton, Plymouth **9** Braintree, Cambridge, Worcester **10** Framingham **11**
   Charlestown, Springfield, Summerville
island: **9** Nantucket **15** Martha's Vineyard
mountain: Tom
mountain ridge: **7** Taconic
oyster: **6** Cotuit
port: **5** Salem **6** Boston
school: **7** Andover
state flower: **7** arbutus
massacre: **6** pogrom **7** carnage **8** butchery
   9 slaughter
massage: rub **5** knead
massager: **7** masseur **8** masseuse
massed: **7** serried
Massenet's opera: **5** Manon, Thais
massive: big **4** bold, huge **5** beamy, bulky,

gross, heavy, large, massy **7** hulking, weighty **9** cyclopean, ponderous **10** boisterous

mast: cue **4** spar **5** stick **6** forage **8** beechnut
  against: **5** aback
  crosspiece: fid
  inclination from perpendicular: **4** rake
  middle: **8** mainmast
  wood for: ash **4** poon

mastaba: **4** tomb **8** platform

master: get, man, rab **4** baas, boss, lord, mian, rule, sire **5** chief, rabbi, sahib(Ind.), tutor **6** bridle, buckra, defeat, doctor, domine, govern, humble, subdue **7** captain, conquer, maestro, padrone(It.) **8** amaister, overcome, regulate, surmount, vanquish **9** commander, overpower, preceptor, subjugate **10** proprietor
  Eton: **4** beak
  fencing: **7** lanista
  harbor: **7** havener, havenor
  hard: **6** despot, Legree
  of house: **13** paterfamilias
  ship's: **7** captain, skipper

Master of Arts: A.M., M.A.

master of ceremonies: M.C. **5** emcee

master stroke: **4** coup

masterful: **6** lordly **7** haughty **8** arrogant, masterly **9** arbitrary, imperious **10** commanding **11** dictatorial, domineering, magisterial, overbearing **13** authoritative

mastermind: **4** plan **6** expert **8** wiseacre

mastery: **4** gree **5** gripe **7** control, victory **8** conquest, facility **9** influence

mastic: **5** gummy **8** adhesive

masticate: **4** chaw, chew **5** crush, gnash, grind **6** crunch **9** manducate

masticatory: gum **7** chewing

mastiff: dog **5** burly **7** massive

mastodon: **5** giant **7** mammoth

mat: cot, rug **4** felt **5** doily, platt, snarl **6** carpet, cotter, petate(Sp.), tangle **7** cushion, drugget, gardnap **8** entangle **10** interweave, lusterless

mat grass: **4** nard

matador: **11** bullfighter
  staff: **6** muleta
  sword: **7** estoque

matagasse: **11** butcherbird

match: go: **4** cap, pit, tir(F.) **4** bout, cope, even, mate, pair, peer, side, spar, suit, team, wife **5** amate, equal, fusee(F.), marry, rival, tally, torch, vesta **6** fellow, spouse **7** compare, compeer, contest, husband, lucifer(Eng.) **8** equalize, lampwick, marriage **9** allumette(F.) **10** candlewick, correspond **11** counterpart, countervail, parallelize

matchless: **5** alone **6** unlike **8** peerless **9** exquisite, unequaled **10** inimitable **12** incomparable

matchlock: gun

mate: cap, pal, wed **4** fear, fere, join, pair, peer, wife **5** billy, buddy, bully, cully,

feere, marry, match **6** bunkle, cobber, couple, fellow, spouse **7** brother, compeer, comrade, consort, espouse, husband, partner **9** associate, companion **10** yokefellow

matelot: **6** sailor

mater: ma; mom **4** mama **6** mother

material (see also **cloth, fabric, substance**)**:** **4** data, gear **5** goods, stuff **6** bodily, carnal, graith, matter **7** weighty **8** physical, tangible **9** corporeal, essential **12** nonspiritual
  discard: **4** junk, slag **5** scrap, trash, waste **6** refuse **7** rubbish
  glass-like: **5** plass
  raw: ore **6** staple

materialism: **8** hylonism

materialize: **5** reify

materiel: **8** supplies **9** apparatus, equipment

maternal: **8** motherly
  relation: **7** enation

matey: **9** companion **13** companionable

matezite: **7** pinitol **10** caoutchouc

matgrass: **4** nard **8** fogfruit

math: **6** mowing **9** monastery **10** arithmetic **11** mathematics

mathe: **4** grub **6** maggot

mathematician: **5** adder **7** figurer

mathematics: *abbreviation:* Q.E.D.
  branch: **7** algebra, geodesy **8** calculus, geometry **9** logarithm **10** arithmetic **12** trigonometry
  constant (arbitrary): **9** parameter
  deduction: **8** analysis
  diagram: **5** graph
  equation: **4** surd
  exercise: **7** problem
  factor: **10** quaternion
  instrument: **6** sector **7** compass **8** arbalest
  line: **6** vector
  number: **5** digit **12** multiplicand
  operation: **7** operand
  operator: **5** nabla **10** quaternion
  proposition: **7** theorem
  quantity: **6** scalar
  ration: pi **4** sine **8** derivate
  symbol: **7** faciend, operand **12** multiplicand
  term: **4** root, sine **6** cosine

mathemeg: **7** catfish

mathes: **7** mayweed

matie: **7** herring

matin: **4** call, song **6** prayer **9** matutinal
  song: **6** aubade

matinee: **5** party **6** soiree **8** negligee **9** reception **13** entertainment

matka: **4** seal

matranee: **7** servant, sweeper

matrass: **4** tube **5** flask **6** bottle **8** bolthead

matriculate: **5** adopt, enter **6** enroll **8** register **10** naturalize **13** immatriculate

matrimonial: **7** nuptial, spousal **8** conjugal, hymeneal **9** connubial

matrimony: 7 wedlock 8 marriage
matrix: bed, die, mat 4 form, mold, womb
 5 plasm 6 gangue 7 pattern
 plate: 6 stereo
matron: 4 dame, wife 5 widow 11 housekeeper
matte: 7 regulus
matter: pus 4 gear, malm, mass 5 solid,
 topic 6 affair, behalf 7 article, concern,
 problem, signify, trouble 8 business, material 11 constituent
 law: res
 particle: 4 atom
 property: 4 mass 7 inertia
 rarefied: fog, gas 4 mist 5 vapor 6 miasma
matter of fact: 7 literal, prosaic 9 pragmatic 11 utilitarian
matthiola: 5 stock
mattock: ax; axe 4 bill 5 tubal 6 twibil 7
 twibill
mattress: 6 pallet
 cover: 4 tick 7 ticking
mature: age, old 4 aged, form, gray, grow,
 ripe 5 adult, grown, ripen 6 accrue, autumn, decoct, digest, mellow, season 7
 develop 8 complete, develope
maturing: 8 rathripe 9 ratheripe
matutinal: 5 early, matin
maud: rug 5 plaid, shawl
maudlin: 5 beery, corny, tipsy 7 tearful,
 weeping 10 lachrymose 11 sentimental
mauger: 5 spite 7 ill-will 9 unwilling 15
 notwithstanding
maul: paw 4 beat, bung, club, mace, mall,
 mell, moth 5 abuse, gavel, staff 6 beater,
 beetle, bruise, hammer, mallet 9 manhandle
maumet: god, guy 4 doll, idol 5 image 6
 puppet
maund: beg 6 basket, hamper
maunder: 5 growl, haver 6 beggar 7
 grumble
Mauser: arm, gun 5 rifle 6 weapon 7
 firearm
mausoleum: 4 tomb 8 baradari(Ind.)
mauve: 5 lilac 6 purple, violet
mauvetaupe: 5 copra
maux: 8 slattern, slipshod 10 prostitute
mavis: 6 thrush
maw: 4 craw, crop 6 gullet, mallow 7
 stomach
mawk: 6 maggot
mawkish: 5 vapid 6 sickly 8 nauseous 9
 squeamish 10 disgusting 11 sentimental
maxim: saw 4 dict, rule, word 5 adage,
 axiom, gnome, logia(pl.), moral, motto 6
 logion, saying 7 brocard, precept, proverb
 8 aphorism, apothegm, doctrine, moral-
 ism 9 erudition, principle 10 apophthegm
maximum: 4 most, peak 5 limit 7 highest, largest 8 greatest
may: can 4 mote 5 might, shall 6 maiden 8
 possible
May: *festival:* 7 Beltane
 goddess: 4 Maia

May curlew: 8 whimbrel
May gowan: 5 daisy
Maya: *day:* 5 uayeb
 month: 6 uninal
 people: Mam 8 Pokonchi
 year: 4 haab
mayapple: 8 mandrake
maybe: 7 perhaps 11 possibility, uncertainty
maybird: 6 thrush
maycock: 5 melon 6 maypop, plover
mayfish: 9 killifish
mayflower: 7 arbutus 8 hawthorn, marigold 10 stitchwort 12 cuckooflower
Mayflower's sister ship: 9 Speedwell
mayfly: dun
mayfowl: 8 whimbrel
mayhap: 6 happen 7 perhaps 12 peradventure
mayor: 5 maire(F.) 7 alcalde(Sp.) 8 official 10 magistrate 12 burgomeister(G.)
maze: 4 daze 5 amaze, fancy 7 confuse,
 stupefy 8 bewilder, confound, delirium,
 delusion 9 amazement, deception, labyrinth 12 bewilderment
mazer: 4 bowl
mazy: 7 complex 9 intricate 10 circuitous,
 perplexing
mead: 5 drink 6 meadow 8 hydromel 9
 metheglin
meadow: ing, lea 4 mead, vega, wish, wong
 5 field, haugh 6 saeter 7 pasture 9
 grassland, grassplot
 piece of: 5 swale
meadow bell: 8 harebell
meadowlark: 6 medlar
meadowmouse: 4 vole 8 arvicole
meadowsweet: 7 spiraea
meager: bar 4 arid, bare, lank, lean, poor,
 slim, thin 5 gaunt, scant, spare 6 barren,
 jejune, lenten, meagre, narrow, pilled,
 scanty, scarce, sparse 7 scranny, starved,
 sterile, tenuous 9 emaciated 10 inadequate
meagerness: 7 exility
meal: tub 4 bite, dune, feed, menu 5 feast,
 flour, lunch, padar, salep, snack 6 bucket,
 dinner, morsel, nocake, repast, supper
 7 banquet, blowout, potluck 8 sandbank
 9 breakfast, collation, pulverize
 army: 4 chow, mess
 coarse: 5 grout 7 cribble 8 gurgeons
 last course: 7 dessert
 wheat: 4 atta(Ind.)
meals: 5 board
mealy: 4 pale 6 floury, spotty 7 friable,
 starchy 8 farinose 9 personate 11 farinaceous
mealy back: 6 cicada
mean: low 4 base, clam, hard, lean, norm,
 poor 5 argue, footy, nasty, petty, ratty,
 snide, snivy, sorry 6 abject, chetif,
 coarse, common, denote, design, dirten,
 feeble, humble, intend, medial, medium,
 middle, narrow, paltry, pilled, snivey,

sordid **7** average, caitiff, ignoble, pitiful, purport, purpose, signify **8** baseborn, beggarly, churlish, recreant, shameful **9** niggardly, penurious, truculent **11** disgraceful, hardhearted **12** contemptible, dishonorable, intermediate, parsimonious

mean line: 9 bisectrix

meander: 4 roam, turn, wind **5** amble **6** wander **8** straggle **9** labyrinth

meaning: 5 sense **6** import, intent, spirit **7** anagoge, bearing, purport, purpose **9** intending, intention, knowledge **10** definition **11** designation **12** apprehension, significance **13** signification, understanding

comb. form: **5** iatro, iatry

meanly: 6 humbly, poorly **8** beggarly, shabbily

means: 4 cost **5** agent **6** agency, method **7** quomodo **8** averages **10** instrument **11** wherewithal **12** intermediary

financial: **5** funds **7** capital **9** resources

of livelihood: **4** work **5** labor, trade **8** vocation **10** profession

support: **4** hold **6** income **7** aliment **11** maintenance

meantime: 7 interim **8** interval

meanwhile: 9 adinterim

mear: 8 boundary

measles: 7 rubeola

measly: 4 mean **6** skimpy, slight **9** worthless **12** contemptible

measure (see also **measuring instrument**): pe **4** bole, boll, cess, gage, mete, rule, span, tape, time **5** clock, gauge, girth, meter, ruler, scale **6** assize, degree, stadia **7** battuta, caliper **8** odometer, tapeline **9** admeasure, calculate, criterion, rotameter

astronomical: **7** azimuth

Biblical: cab, hin, kor, log **4** epha **5** cubit, aphah, homer

cable: **4** naut

capacity: **4** cask, gill, orna, peck, pint **5** liter, quart **6** barrel, bushel, gallon

cloth: ell **4** yard

cubic: **4** cord **5** stere **10** hectostere

degree of angle: arc

distance: see *length* below

dry: **4** bale, peck **6** bushel

established: **8** standard

fish: vog **4** cran(Sc.) **5** crane, crans

flexible: **4** tape **8** tapeline

heat: **5** therm **6** calory, therme **7** calorie **10** centigrade, fahrenheit

horse: **4** hand

land: ar; are, rod **4** acre, area, mile, rood **6** decare **7** hectare, kiliare

length: dra, ell, pik, rod **4** foot, inch, knot, mile, nail, pace, pole, yard **5** cubit, digit, meter, metre, perch, toise(F.) **6** league, micron, mikron **9** decimeter, kilometer **10** centimeter, hectometer, millimeter

liquid: aam, keg **4** gill, pint **5** lagen, liter, quart **6** barrel, gallon, magnum, minims,

runlet, tierce **7** rundlet **8** hogshead **9** hectolite, kiloliter

nautical: **4** knot **6** fathom

paper: **4** page, ream **5** quire, sheet

printer's: em, en **4** pica **5** agate, empen

short: **6** ullage

sound: bel

space: **6** parsec

time: day **4** hour, week, year **5** month **6** decade, minute, moment, second

water depth: **5** sound

weight: ton **4** bale **5** carat, liter, ounce, pound **9** kiloliter **10** hectoliter

wheat: **4** trug

wine: tun **4** butt, pipe

wire: mil **5** stone

work: erg **5** ergon

yarn: lea **4** heer, typp **6** denier **7** spindle

measured: 7 careful, guarded **10** deliberate

measureless: 4 vast **7** endless, immense **8** infinite **9** boundless, limitless, unbounded, unlimited **11** illimitable **12** immeasurable

measurement: 9 dimension **11** mensuration

pert. to: **6** metric **11** dimensional

measuring instrument: 4 gage, tape **5** chain, gauge, meter, ruler **7** alidade **8** measurer, tapeline **9** container, yardstick **13** saccharimeter

acidity: **10** acidimeter

heat: **11** calorimeter

lumber: **6** scaler

surveying: **11** stratameter

thickness: **7** caliper

measuring wheel: 8 odometer **12** perambulator

meat: 4 beef, food, gist, lamb, pork, veal **5** flesh **6** chevon, mutton **7** chilver, venison **9** nutriment

ball: **7** rissole **9** croquette, fricandel **11** fricandelle

bony: **5** scrag **9** spareribs

cured: ham **5** bacon **6** flitch, salame, salami **7** biltong, bultong, sausage **8** pastrami, pastroma **9** biltongue

cut: ham, rib **4** chop, loin **5** flank, roast, steak **6** cutlet, rasher **7** icebone, sirloin **9** aitchbone

dish: **5** pasty **6** potpie, ragout **7** goulash, haricot, ravioli **8** fricando **10** fricandeau

dish(with vegetables): **4** stew **8** mulligan **9** lobscouse **10** lobscourse

dried: **5** jerky **7** biltong, bultong, pemican **8** pemmican **9** biltongue

frozen: **5** frigo

ground: **7** rissole, sausage **9** hamburger

pin: **6** skewer

potted: **7** rillett **8** rillette

roasted: **5** brede, cabob, kabob

sauce: **4** A-one **5** caper, gravy **14** Worcestershire

slice: **6** collop

smoking place: **5** bucan

unwholesome: 6 cagmag
meated: fed 8 fattened
meatless: 6 lenten, maigre
meatman: 7 butcher
meatus: 4 burr, duct 5 canal 7 foramen, passage
meatworks: 8 abattoir 14 slaughterhouse
meaty: 5 pithy, solid 11 substantial
Mecca (see also **Muslim**):
deity: 5 Hobal, Hubal
mosque: 5 Caaba, Kaaba 6 Kaabeh
pilgrimage: 4 hadj
mechanic: erk(F.) 7 artisan, workman 8 operator 9 artificer, craftsman, operative
mechanical: 9 automatic 10 uninspired 11 automatical, involuntary, perfunctory, stereotyped
mechanical part: 5 rotor 6 stator, tappet
mechanics branch: 7 statics 8 dynamics
mechanism: 4 gear, tool 9 apparatus, machinery
driving: 9 propeller
eccentric: cam
self-moving: 8 automata(pl.) 9 automaton
meconin: 7 opianyl
medal: 4 disk 5 badge 6 plaque 7 medalet 10 decoration
medallion: 4 coin 8 ornament 11 contorniate, contorniato
Medb's consort: 6 Ailill
meddle: 4 nose 5 snoop 6 dabble, finger, monkey, potter, tamper 7 intrude 9 interfere
meddler: 7 marplot 8 busybody
meddlesome: 4 busy 5 fresh 7 curious 8 meddling 9 officious 10 handersome
Mede: 5 Aryan, Mesne 6 Median
caste: 4 magi
king: Evi
media: See **medium**.
medial: 6 middle 8 ordinary
median: 4 mean 6 medial, middle 7 average, central 12 intermediate
Median: See **Mede**.
mediate: 7 referee 8 ruminate 9 arbitrate, intercede, interpose
mediator: 7 daysman 9 go-between 10 amboceptor, interagent 12 intermediary
medic: 6 clover, doctor, intern, medico 7 luterne, student, surgeon 8 resident 9 physician
false: 10 medicaster
medical: 6 iatric 11 aesculapian
medical student: 6 extern, intern 7 externe, interne 8 resident
medicinal: 6 curing 7 healing 8 salutary 9 relieving 11 aesculapian
bark: 6 cartex
berry: 5 cubeb
compound: 4 pill, sera 5 hepar, iodin, serum 6 iodine 7 turpeth
nut: 4 cola
plant(see also *root* below): rue 4 aloe 5 ergot, senna, tansy 6 arnica, cohosh, ipe-

cac 7 chirata 8 valerian
remedy: 8 antidote
root(see also *plant* above): 5 artar, jalap, orris 6 seneca, senega 8 licorice
solution: 8 tincture
tablet: 4 pill 6 troche 7 lozenge
medicine: 4 drug 5 tonic 6 physic, remedy 7 placebo 10 abirritant, alterative
amount: 4 dose 6 dosage
institution: 6 clinic 8 hospital
instrument: see **surgery instrument**
mild: 6 tisane
noncuring: 6 ptisan
patent: 7 nostrum
vessel: 4 vial 5 ampul, phial 6 ampule 7 ampoule 8 gallipot
medicine dropper: 7 pipette
medicine man: 6 doctor, shaman 8 magician, sorcerer 9 physician
mediety: 6 moiety
Medina (see also **Muslim**): Aus
citizen: 5 Ansar
mediocre: 4 mean, soso 6 common, medium 7 average 8 middling, ordinary, passable 11 commonplace, indifferent
meditate: 4 chew, mull, muse, pore 5 brood, study, think, watch, weigh 6 ponder, reason 7 reflect, revolve 8 cogitate, consider, ruminate 10 deliberate 11 contemplate
meditation: 4 yoga 8 higgaion 14 omphaloskepsis
meditative: 7 pensive
mediterranean: 6 inland 7 midland 10 landlocked
Mediterranean: sea
boat: nef 4 saic 5 setee, xebec, zebec 6 galiot, mistic, settee, tartan, zebeck 7 felucca, mistico, polacre
coast: 7 Riviera
country: 5 Italy 6 France, Greece 7 Algeria
Eastern: 6 Levant
falcon: 6 lanner
fish: aco 6 remora
fruit: 5 olive 7 azarole
gulf: 5 Tunis
island: 4 Elba 5 Crete, Ibiza, Iviza, Malta 6 Candia, Cyprus, Ebusus, Lesbos, Lipari, Rhodes, Sicily 7 Majorca, Panaria 8 Sardinia 9 Stromboli
pert. to: 9 Levantine
port: 5 Tunis 7 Tunisia
shrub: 7 azarole
tree: 5 carob, 6 mastic 7 azarole,
wind: 6 otesan, solano 7 gregale, mistral, sirocco 8 levanter 10 euroclyden
medium: 4 mean 5 media(pl.), midst, organ 6 degree, medial 7 average, channel, psychic 8 mediator 10 instrument, interagent 11 environment 12 intermediary, intermediate
communication: 4 note 5 cable, phone, radio 6 letter 9 telegraph, telephone 10

television
culture: 4 agar
news: TV 5 radio 7 journal 8 magazine 9
newspaper 10 periodical, television
medley: 4 olio 6 jumble 7 farrago, melange,
mixture 8 mingling 9 bariolage(F.), potpourri 10 hodgepodge 11 gallimaufry 12
mingle-mangle
musical: 8 fantasia
medrick: 4 gull, tern
medulla: 4 pith 6 marrow 7 essence, summary 10 compendium
Medusa: 6 Gorgon 7 blubber 9 jellyfish
representation: 9 Gorgoneum
slayer: 7 Perseus
meed: due 4 gift 5 award, bribe, merit,
repay, worth 6 desert, reward 7 bribery
10 excellence, recompense
meek: 4 deft, kind, mild 5 lowly 6 docile,
gentle, humble 7 pacific, patient 8 moderate, sheepish, yielding 9 childlike,
spineless 10 spiritless, submissive
meerkat: 6 monkey 8 suricate
meerschaum: 7 seafoam 9 sepiolite
meet: fit, kep(Sc.), sit 4 duel, face, join,
tidy 5 equal, occur, touch, tryst 6 battle,
combat, confer, gather, proper 7 contact,
convene, fitting, fulfill 8 assemble, assembly, confront, moderate, suitable 9
encounter, forgather, gathering, intersect
10 congregate, experience, foregather
11 appropriate
athletic: 8 gymkhana 10 tournament
meeting: 4 mall, moot 5 gemot, rally, union 6 caucus, gemote, huddle, parley 7
coition, consult, session 8 adjacent, assembly, conclave, congress, junction 10
concurrent, conference, confluence, rendezvous 11 convocation
meetinger: 9 dissenter
meg: 6 guinea 9 halfpenny
megagamete: 11 macrogamete
megalithic chamber: 6 dolmen
megaphone: 8 vamphorn
Megara king: 5 Nisus
megrim: 4 whim 5 blues, fancy, freak,
humor, whiff 7 vertigo 8 flounder, headache 9 dizziness 12 hypochondria
tribe: Moi
Mekong River: *site:* 4 Asia 7 Vietnam
mel: 5 honey
melancholia: 6 athymy 7 athymia
melancholy: sad 4 blue, dram, dull, dump,
glum 5 dolar(L.), drear, dusky, gloom 7
dismal, somber, sombre, sorrow, yellow 7
chagrin, doleful, pensive, sadness, unhappy 8 atrabile, downcast, tristful 9
cheerless, dejection, plaintive 10 alli-
cholly, depression, desolation 11 despondency, downhearted 12 disconsolate,
heavy-hearted, hypochondria, mournful-
ness
Melanesia: *language:* 5 Santo
people: 4 Fiji

melange: 4 olio 6 medley 7 mixture
melanic: 5 black
meld: 4 play 5 unite
mele: 4 poem, song 5 chant, lyric 6 ballad
melee: row 4 fray, riot 5 brawl, fight, foray,
mix-up 6 affray, fracas, ruckus 7 ruction,
scuffle 8 dogfight, skirmish
melicocca: 5 genip
melicratum: 4 mead 8 beverage, hydromel
melilotus: 6 clover
meliorate: 6 better, soften 7 improve 10
ameliorate
melisma: 7 cadenza
mell: mix 4 maul 5 fight, honey 6 beetle,
hammer, mallet, meddle, mingle
mellifluous: 7 honeyed, sugared
mellow: age 4 aged, rich, ripe, soft 5 ripen
6 mature, tender 7 matured 8 patinate
melodeon: 9 seraphine
melodious: 6 ariose, arioso, dulcet 7 lyrical, melodic, musical, tunable, tuneful 8
canorous 10 harmonious
melodist: 6 singer 8 composer 9 harmon-
ist
melodramatic: 8 dramatic 9 emotional
10 theatrical 11 sensational
melody: air, lay 4 aria, lilt, note, raga(Ind.),
solo, song, tune 5 charm, music,
theme 6 strain 7 arietta, harmony, rosalia, sortita 9 cantilena 11 tunefulness
characterization: 6 ariose, arioso
counter: 7 descant
outline: 5 melos
pert. to: 6 plagal
unaccompanied: 4 solo 6 monody
melon: 4 musk, pepo 5 gourd, water 6
casaba, papaya 7 Persian 8 honeydew 10
cantaloupe, paddymelon
melon pear: 6 pepino
melongena: 8 eggplant
melos: 4 song 6 melody
melt: rin(Sc.), run 4 flow, flux, fuse, thaw
5 smelt, sweal 6 render, soften 7 dwindle, liquefy 8 discandy, dissolve, eliquate
10 colliquate, deliquesce 12 disintegrate
partly: 4 frit
member: 4 limb, part 5 organ 6 branch,
fellow 7 section 8 district 11 communicant
new: 6 novice 7 entrant 8 neophyte 10
apprentice
oldest: 4 dean
membership: 4 seat 10 fellowship
membrane: web 4 caul, coat, skin, tela 5
amnia(pl.), lemma, telae(pl.) 6 amnion,
amnios, retina 7 cuticle, eardrum, velamen 8 striffin
fold of: 5 plica
fringe: 4 loma
spore: 6 intine
memento: 5 relic, token 6 trophy 8 keepsake, reminder, souvenir
memo: 4 chit 8 reminder

memoir: 4 note 5 eloge 6 record, report 7 history 8 memorial 9 biography, narrative 10 commentary

memorabilia: ana

memorable: 7 namable, notable, special 9 reminding 10 remarkable 11 reminiscent 13 distinguished, extraordinary

memorandum: 4 bill, note, stub 5 brief 6 agenda(pl.) 7 agendum, memento, minutes, notanda(pl.), proctol 8 notandum, notation, reminder

book: 5 diary 6 agenda 7 tickler 8 calendar

legal: 5 jurat

memoria: 6 chapel, church, shrine, temple 9 reliquary

memorial: ahu 5 facta(pl.), relic 6 factum, memoir, record, trophy 8 mnemonic, monument 11 remembrance 12 recollection 13 commemorative

carved: 5 totem

stone: 5 cairn 6 statue 9 mausoleum

memorist: 8 prompter

memory: 4 mind, rote 8 memorial 9 retention 11 remembrance 12 recollection, reminiscence 13 retrospection

aid: 8 mnemonic, reminder 10 anamnestic

goddess: 9 Mnemosyne

loss: 5 blank, lethe 7 amnesia, aphasia 13 forgetfulness

pert. to: 6 mnesic 7 mnestic 8 mnemonic

vivid: 7 eidetic

memory book: 5 diary 9 scrapbook

Memphis (see also **Egypt**):

chief: Evi

god: Ra 4 Ptah

men: 4 crew 6 people

armed body: 4 army 5 posse

party: 4 stag 6 smoker

section of Greek church: 6 andron

wise: 4 Magi 6 Gaspar 8 Melchior 9 Balthasar, Balthazar

menace: 5 boast, peril 6 impend, threat 8 denounce, jeopardy, threaten 9 fulminate

menacing: 10 formidable

menaden's young: 7 sardine

menage: 4 club 7 society 8 domicile 9 household 10 management 12 housekeeping

menagerie: zoo 10 collection

menald: 8 speckled 10 variegated

menaspis: 5 shark

mend: fix, sew 4 beet, darn, heal, help, knit 5 amend, beete, botch, clout, emend, moise, patch 6 better, cobble, repair, solder 7 improve, restore 10 ameliorate, convalesce

mendacity: lie 5 lying 6 deceit 7 falsity, untruth 9 falsehood

mender: 6 tinker 7 cobbler 9 repairman

mendicant: 4 monk 5 fakir 6 beggar, begger, bhikku, fakeer, frater, gosain, gusain 7 ajivika, bhikshu

Menelaus: *brother:* 9 Agamemnon

daughter: 8 Hermione

wife: 5 Helen

meng: mix 5 blend 6 mingle

menial: fag 4 base 6 drivel, harlot, sordid, stocah, varlet 7 servant, servile, slavish 8 coistrel, coistril, servitor 9 degrading, underling

meniscus: 4 lens

mennom: 6 mennon, minnow

Menominee whitefish: 6 chivey

mensk: 5 adorn, favor, grace, honor 6 credit 8 ornament 9 reverence 12 graciousness

mensuration: 11 measurement 13 determination

mental: 5 ideal 7 phrenic 11 intelligent 12 intellectual

mental aberration: fog 4 daze, haze 5 lapse 6 stupor 7 doldrum, madness 8 insanity

mental deficient: 5 idiot, moron 8 imbecile

mental disorder: 6 ataxia 7 aphasia 8 neuritis, neurosis, paranoia 9 melomania, paranomia, psychosis 11 megalomania 12 hypochondria 13 schizophrenia

specialist: 12 psychiatrist

mental faculties: 4 mind, wits

mental image: 4 idea 5 dream, idola(pl.) 6 idolum 7 fantasy 8 phantasm 10 conception

mental state: 5 blues 6 morale 7 doldrum 8 euphoria

mentality: 4 mind 5 sense 6 acumen, reason 9 endowment, intellect 11 rationality 12 intelligence

mentiferous: 10 telepathic

mention: 4 cite, hint, mind, name 5 clepe, refer, speak, trace 6 allude, denote, notice, record 7 specify, vestige 8 allusion, citation 9 statement 10 indication

implied: 11 connotation

mentioned: 8 foresaid 9 aforesaid

mentor: 4 guru 7 monitor, teacher 9 counselor 10 counsellor, instructor

menu: 4 card, meal 5 carte 10 bill of fare

part of: 4 soup 5 salad 6 entree 7 dessert, special 9 appetizer

Mephistophelean: sly 4 evil 6 crafty

Mephistopheles: 5 devil, Satan

mephitis: 4 odor 5 smell 6 stench

mercantile: 7 trading 10 commercial

mercenary: 4 hack 5 venal 6 sordid 7 Hessian 8 covetous, hireling, vendible 10 galloglass(Sc.) 11 gallowglass 13 stipendiarian

merchandise: 4 ware 5 goods, wares 7 chaffer

cheap: 7 camelot

merchant: 4 Seth(Ind.) 6 dealer, seller, sutler, trader, vender, vendor 7 chapman, goladar, howadji, vintner 8 purveyor 9 tradesman 10 shopkeeper 11 storekeeper

group: **5** guild, hansa, **6** cartel
wholesale: **6** packer
merciful: 6 benign **7** sparing **9** benignant, forgiving **10** charitable
merciless: 4 grim **5** cruel **6** savage **8** pitiless **9** ferocious, graceless, heartless **10** despiteous, relentless
mercurial: 8 changing **9** faithless
mercury: 5 azoth, guide, thief **6** hawker **9** messenger, newspaper **11** quicksilver
derivative: **11** quicksilver
Mercury: 6 Hermes **9** newspaper
son: **5** Cupid
staff: **8** caduceus
winged cap: **7** petasos, petasus
winged shoes: **7** talaria
mercury subchloride: 7 calomel
mercy: law **4** pity, ruth **5** grace, grith **6** lenity **7** charity **8** clemency, humanity, kindness, lenience, leniency, mildness **9** tolerance **10** compassion, indulgence, tenderness **11** forbearance, forgiveness
show: **5** spare **6** pardon **7** forgive **8** reprieve
mercy-killing: 10 euthanasia
mere: but, sea **4** bare, club, lake, mear, pool, pond, pure, sole **5** bound, limit, plain, sheer, utter **6** divide, entire, famous, scarce, simple **7** unmixed **8** absolute, boundary, glorious, landmark, trifling **9** beautiful, undiluted **11** unqualified
merely: 4 also, just, only **5** quite **6** anerly
merganser: 4 smee, smew **5** harle, robin **7** becscie, bracket, garbill **9** goosander
merge: 4 fuse, join, meld **5** blend, unify, unite **6** absorb, mingle **7** combine, conjoin **8** coalesce **9** commingle **10** amalgamate **11** consolidate, incorporate
mericarp: 8 hemicarp
meridian: 4 noon **6** midday **11** culmination
meringue: 5 icing
Merino: 4 wool **5** sheep **6** fabric **7** Delaine
merit: 4 earn, meed **5** worth **6** desert, reward **7** deserve **10** condignity, excellence
merited: fit **7** fitting **8** adequate, suitable
meritorious: 8 valorous **9** honorable
merkin: mop
merlin: 6 falcon
Merlin: 8 magician **9** alchemist
Merlin's grass: 9 quillwort
mermaid: 5 nymph, siren **6** merrow
mero: 5 guasa **7** grouper
Merob's alphabet: 8 Armenian
meropia: 9 blindness
meropodite: 5 meros
merriment: fun **5** deray **9** amusement, diversion **11** galliardise
merrow: 7 mermaid
merry: gai(F.), gay **4** agog, airy, boon, cant, glad **5** bonny, droll, happy, jolly, sunny **6** blithe, bonnie, cocket, hilary, jocose, jocund, jovial, joyous, lively **7** gleeful, jocular **8** cheerful, chirping, game-

some, gleesome, mirthful, pleasant, sportive **9** hilarious, sprightly **10** blithesome, frolicsome **11** exhilarated **12** lighthearted
merry andrew: 4 zany **5** antic, clown, joker **6** jester **7** buffoon **8** merryman
merry-go-round: 8 carousel **9** carrousel
merrymaking: 5 jolly, revel **6** splore **7** festive, revelry, wassail **8** carnival **9** festivity, merriment **12** conviviality
merrythought: 8 wishbone
merrytrotter: 5 swing **6** seesaw
merrywing: 9 goldeneye **10** bufflehead
merse: dip **5** marsh **6** plunge **7** immerse
merycism: 10 rumination
mesa: 7 plateau **8** plateaux(pl.) **9** tableland
mescal: 5 cacti(pl.), drink **6** cactus, peyote, peyotl
mesel: 5 leper **7** leprosy
mesh: net **4** moke **5** snare **6** areola, engage, macula, tangle **7** areolae, ensnare, maculae(pl.), netting, network **8** entangle **10** reticulate
mesial: 6 median, middle
mesmerize: 9 hypnotize
mesne: 6 middle **11** intervening **12** intermediate
Mesopotamia: 4 Irak, Iraq
captives' place: **5** Halah
city: **5** Mosul **6** Bagdad(c.) **7** Edessan, Kerbela
people: **5** Iraki, Iraqi **7** Aramean
river: **6** Tigris **9** Euphrates
wind: **6** shamal
mesosperm: 9 secundine
mesotais: 4 base **10** groundmass
mespil: 6 medlar
mesquin: 4 mean **6** shabby, sordid
mesquite: 9 algarroba
mess: jag, row **4** clat, jagg, meal, mull, muss, soil **5** batch, botch, cauch, dirty, lelee **6** bungle, dabble, jumble, litter, muddle, rumple, tousle **7** crumple, mixture, wrinkle **8** disarray, dishevel, disorder, scramble, slaister, squabble **9** commotion, confusion **10** hodgepodge, picklement
message: 4 bode, line, memo, news, note, wire, word **5** cable **6** brevet, letter **7** bodword, depeche, mission, missive, tidings **9** memoranda **10** communique, memorandum **13** communication
good news: **7** evangel
messenger: 4 bode, page, sand, toty **5** angel, envoy, miler **6** beadle, chiaus, herald, legate, nuncio **7** apostle, carrier, courant, courier, hi-carra, mercury, prophet, totyman **8** hi-carrah, minister, nunciate, portator **9** harbinger **10** ambassador, evangelist, forerunner **11** internuncio
mounted: **6** cossid(Ind.) **7** courier, estafet **9** estafette
of the gods: **6** Hermes

Messiah: 6 Christ, Savior 7 prophet, Saviour
Messina Strait rock: 6 Scilla, Scylla
messy: 5 dirty 6 untidy
mestive: 8 mournful
met (see also **meet**): 7 measure, opposed 11 measurement
metad: rat
metagnomy: 10 divination
metagnostic: 10 unknowable
metal: ore, tin 4 gold, iron, lead, zinc 6 cobalt, copper, oroide, pewter, radium, silver, sodium, spirit 7 bullion, gallium, mercury 9 potassium, substance
bar: gad 5 ingot
base: 5 dross, sprue
cake: 4 slag
containing: 13 metalliferous
crude: 5 matte
decorate: 4 etch 6 emboss 9 damascene, damaskeen
decorative: 6 chrome, niello
deposit: 4 lode
disc: 5 paten 6 patten
fastener: pin 4 bolt, brad, nail 5 rivet, screw 6 cotter, solder
filings: 5 lemel
heavy: 6 osmium 7 uranium
impure mass: 7 regulus
layer: 4 seam 5 stope
lightest known: 7 lithium
lump: pig 4 slug 6 nugget
magnetized: 13 electromagnet
mixture: 5 alloy
nonexpanding: 5 invar
oblong piece: sow
patch: 6 solder
plate: gib
rare: 4 zinc 6 cerium, erbium 7 iridium, terbium, uranium, yttrium 8 lutecium, platinum
refuse: 4 slag 5 dross 6 scoria
scrap: 6 filing
shaper: 5 swage
sheet: 4 foil 5 lames, plate 6 lamina, latten, tagger
spike: gad
stannic: tin
strip: 6 spline
test: 5 assay
tin-like: 7 cadmium
unrefined: ore
waste: 4 slag 5 dross 6 scoria 9 recrement
worker: 5 smith 6 barman 7 riveter 8 tinsmith 9 goldsmith 11 coppersmith, silversmith
metallic: 6 brazen 13 metalliferous
content: ory
metamere: 6 somite 8 somatome
metamerism: 12 segmentation
metamorphose: 6 change 9 transform, transmute 16 transubstantiate

metaphor: 5 trope 6 simile 8 allegory 10 comparison 11 tralatition
metaphorical: 10 figurative
metastrophe: 11 interchange
mete: 4 dole, give, goal, post 5 allot, award, bound, limit, stake 7 measure 8 allocate 9 apportion 10 distribute
meteor: 5 bolis, Cetid, comet, Lyrid 6 Antlid, bolide, Lyraid 8 aerolite, fireball 9 Andromede 10 Andromedid
August: 8 Perseids
November: 6 Leonid
meteorite: 8 aerolite, aerolith, siderite 9 asiderite 10 siderolite
meteorological instrument: 6 bolide 9 barometer 11 thermometer
meteorologist: 10 forecaster
meter: 4 beat, time 5 metre, verse 6 rhythm 7 cadence, measure 8 measurer
cubic: 5 liter, litre, stere
one-hundredth: 10 centimeter
one-millionth: 6 micron
one-tenth: 9 decimeter
one-thousandth: 10 millimeter
square: 7 centare
unit: 4 mora 5 morae(pl.)
meterist: 10 verse-maker
meters: *10:* 9 decameter
100: 10 hectometer
100 square: ar; are
1,000: 9 kilometer
10,000: 10 myriameter
methane hydrocarbon: 8 paraffin 9 paraffine
metheglin: 4 mead 8 beverage
mether: cup
method: way 4 dart, form, garb, mode, rule 5 means, order, style, usage 6 course, manner, system 7 fashion, formula, process 9 procedure, technique 11 orderliness
customary: rut 5 habit 7 routine
methodical: 5 exact 6 severe 7 precise
methodize: 8 regulate
Methuselah's father: 5 Enoch
methyl: *cyanide:* 7 nitrile
ethyl ketone: 8 butanone
ketol: 6 acetol
meticulous: 4 neat, nice, prim 5 fussy, timid 7 careful, fearful, finical 10 fastidious, scrupulous
metier: 4 line 5 trade 7 calling 8 business 10 occupation, profession
metis: 8 octoroon 9 halfbreed
metric: 8 criteria(pl.) 9 criterion
measure: ar; are 5 carat, liter, litre, meter, stere, tonne 6 decare, hectar, micron, miglio 7 centare, deciare, dekiare, hectare, kiliare, manzana, myriare 8 centiare, dekagram, milliare 9 decaliter, decameter, decastere, deciliter, decimeter, decistere, dekaliter, dekameter, dekistere,

kiloliter, kilometer, kilostere, megameter **10** centiliter, centimeter, centistere, dekadrachm, hectoliter, hectometer, hectostere, microliter, milliliter, millimeter, millistere, myrialiter, myriameter **15** micromillimeter

metrical beat: **5** ictus

metrical foot: **4** iamb **6** iambic, iambus **7** anapest

accented syllable: **5** arsis

four syllables: **6** syzygy

three short syllables: **8** tribrach

two syllables: **7** spondee, trochee

two together: **6** dipody

metrist: **4** poet **9** metrician

metronome: **5** timer

metropolis: see **4** city, seat **6** center

metropolitan: cit **5** chief, urban **7** bishops, leading **9** principal

mettle: **4** fire **5** ardor, nerve, pluck, spunk **6** ginger, spirit **7** bravery, courage **9** fortitude

meuse: gap **4** hole, lurk **7** conceal, opening **8** loophole

mew: den **4** cage, cast, coop, gull, maas(Sc.), molt, shed **5** miaow, miaul **6** change **7** conceal, confine, enclose, garages, stables **8** spicknel **9** enclosure **11** concealment, confinement

mewl: cry, mew **6** squall **7** whimper

Mexico: *agave:* **5** datil **6** zapupe

alcoholic beverage: **6** mescal, pulque **7** tepache, tequila

American: **6** gringo

annuity: **5** censo

antelope: **9** pronghorn

bean: **6** frejol, frijol **7** frijole

bedbug: **8** conenose

beverage: **4** chia

bird: **6** jacana, towhee **7** jacamar, tinamon **8** zopilote

blanket: **6** serape

bread: **6** tamale

brigand: **7** ladrone

bull: **4** toro

cactus: **6** bavoso, chaute, chende, mescal **8** alicoche, chichipe **11** alfilerillo

candlewood: **8** ocotillo

cat: **6** margay

chaps(leather): **10** chaparajos, chaparejos

city: **4** Leon **5** Tepic **6** Colima, Jalapa, Juarez, Merida, Mexico(c.), Oaxaca, Puebla, Potosi **7** Durango, Orizaba, San Luis, Tampico **8** Culiacan, Mazatlan, Monterey, Saltillo, Vera Cruz, Victoria **9** Chihuahua, Luis Potos **10** Hermosillo **11** Guadalajara

cloak: **5** manta **6** serape

cockroach: **9** cucaracha

coin: **4** peso **5** adobe **6** azteca **7** centavo, piaster

conqueror: **6** Cortes, Cortez

cottonwood: **5** alamo

dish: **5** atole, tamal **6** tamale **9** enchilada

drug: **7** damiana

fiber: **4** pita **5** istle, sisal **6** catena

fish: **6** salema **7** totuava

garment: **5** manga **6** serape **7** chiripa

gopher: **4** tuza **7** quachil

grapefruit: **7** toronja

grass: **5** otate **7** sacaton, zacaton **8** hanequen, hanequin

guardian spirit: **6** nagual

hero: **4** Diaz **6** Juarez

hog: **7** peccary

house: **5** jacal

Indian: see *people* below

ivy: **6** cobaea

laborer: **4** peon **7** bracero, wetback

lake: **7** Chapala

land owner: **8** ranchero

masonry: **5** adobe

mat: **6** petate

measure: pie **4** alma, vara **5** almud, baril, jarra, labor, legua, linea, sitio **6** almude, fanega **7** pulgada **9** cuarteron, cuartillo **10** caballeria

measure of weight: bag **4** onza **5** carga, libra, marco **6** adarme, arroba, ochava, tercio **7** quintal

mountain: **7** Orizaba **12** Citlaltepetl, Ixtaccihuatl, Popocatepetl

musical instrument: **6** clarin, guiros **7** cabacas, maracas **11** chiapanecas

onyx: **6** tecali

orange: **7** choisya

pancake: **5** arepa

peasant: **4** peon

peninsula: **7** Yucatan

people: Mam **4** Cora, Maya, Seri, Xova **5** Aztec, Hauve, Lipan, Nahau, Opata, Otomi, Yaqui, Zoque **6** Indian, Mixtec, Otonia, Toltec **7** Haustec, Tepanec, Zacatec, Zapotec **8** Totonaco, Zacateco **9** Campesino **10** Cuitlateca, Cuitlateco

plant: **4** chia **5** agave, amole, datil, jalap, sotol **6** chaute, maguey, slavia **7** tequila **8** acapulco **9** sabadilla

porter: **5** tamen

ranch: **8** hacienda

river: **6** Panuco **7** Tabasco

rubber tree: ule

sandal: **8** gauracha, guarache, guaracho, huarache, huaracho

sauce: **7** tabasco

scarf: **6** rebozo, tapalo

shawl: **6** serape

shrub: **6** anagua, anaqua, colima **7** choisya

state: **6** Colima, Sonora **7** Durango, Hidalgo, Sinaloa, Tabasco, Yucatan **9** Michoacan

sugar: **7** panocha

tea: **6** basote **7** apasote **9** alpasotes

thong: **5** romal

tree: ule **4** sero **5** abeto, amapa, ebano, ocote **6** chacte, colima, mezcal, sabino **7**

capulin, colorin **8** chaparro, ulmaceae **9**
ahuehuete, canadulce **10** anacahuita
village: **6** ejidos, tecali
volcano: **6** Colima **7** Jorullo **9** Paricutin
12 Popocatepetl
yucca: **5** isote
mezereon: **5** shrub **6** daphne **8** camillia
mezzanine: **5** story **7** balcony **8** entresol
mias: **9** orangutan
miasma: **7** malaria
miaul: mew **4** meow, wraw **5** miaou,
miaow, miaul **9** caterwaul
mib: **6** marble
mica: **4** talc **5** glist **7** biotite **8** silicate **9**
damourite, hydromica, isinglass, muscov-
ite **10** lepidolite
micaceous: **7** talcose
miche: **4** lurk **5** skulk, sneak **6** pilfer **7**
conceal
micher: **5** cheat, thief **6** truant **8** panderer
Michigan: *city:* **4** Alma, Caro **5** Flint,
Ionia **7** Detroit, Lansing(c.) **8** Muske-
gon **9** Marquette
county: **4** Kent
motto: **6** Tuebor
river: **4** Cass **5** Huron
state flower: **5** apple
mickle: **4** much **5** great
mico: **8** marmoset
micraner: ant
micro: **4** moth
microbe: **4** germ **8** bacillus, organism
microcosm: **5** world **7** village **8** universe
9 community
microorganism: **4** germ **5** virus **6** aerobe
7 aerobia **8** aerobium **9** autoblast, spiril-
lum **10** spirochete **11** spirochaete
microscopic: **5** small **6** minute **9** engy-
scope
microspore: **6** pollen
microsporophyll: **6** stamen
mid: See **midst.**
mid-wifery: **10** obstetrics
midday: **4** noon **8** noontide
intermission: **5** lunch **7** nooning **8** noon
hour
nap: **6** siesta
middle: **4** mean **5** mesne, midst, waist **6**
center, centre, centry, median, mesial **7**
average, central, centric **11** intervening
12 intermediate **13** intermediator
combining form: mes **4** medi, meso
way: **6** midway **7** halfway **10** moderation
Middle East: **6** Levant
middleman: **5** agent, butty **6** dealer,
trader **8** huckster, retailer **9** go-between
12 interlocutor, intermediary
middling: **4** fair, soso **6** fairly, medium **8**
mediocre, moderate, ordinary, somewhat
10 moderately
midge: fly **4** fish, gnat **5** dwarf, stout **6** insect, midget, punkie **8** carriage
midget: **5** dwarf, small **9** miniature
midnoon: **4** noon **6** midday
midrib: **5** costa **6** costae(pl.)

midshipman: **5** cadet **6** reefer
midst: **4** amid, mean **5** among, depth **6**
amidst, center, centre, medium, middle,
mongst **7** between, halfway, setting **11**
surrounding
midwife: **4** baba, dhai(Ind.), gamp **5**
howdy **6** cummer, howdie, kimmer **7** he-
bamme **9** gracewife **11** accoucheuse, finger-smith
mien: air, eye **4** brow, vult **5** guise **6** aspect, manner, ostent **7** bearing, conduct **8**
attitude, behavior, carriage, demeanor **9**
behaviour, demeanour **10** appearance,
deportment **11** countenance
miffed: **5** sulky, vexed **8** offended **10** displeased
mig: **4** duck **6** marble
migale: **5** mouse, shrew
migeloid fish: **4** bobo
might: arm **4** mote **7** ability
mighty: big **4** bulk, fell, vast, very **5**
felon, great **6** potent, strong **7** violent **8**
enormous, forceful, forcible, powerful,
puissant, vigorous **9** extensive, extremely,
gigantean **10** omnipotent **11** efficacious
migniard: **6** dainty, minion **7** mincing **8**
delicate, mistress
mignon: **5** small **6** dainty, petite **8** delicate, graceful
mignonette: **6** reseda
vine: **7** Madeira, tarweed
migraine: **4** whim **8** headache **10** hemi-
crania
migrant: See **migratory.**
migrate: **4** flee, flit, move, pass, trek **8**
colonize, transfer
migration: **5** exode **6** exodus, flight
migratory: **6** roving **7** nomadic **9** peregrine, wandering
mihrab: **4** slab **5** niche **7** chamber
Mikado: **9** sovereign
court: **5** dairi
office: **9** mikadoate
mike: **10** microphone
milady: **4** dame **5** madam **10** noblewoman
11 gentlewoman
milarite: **8** silicate
mild: moy **4** calm, easy, kind, meek, soft,
tame **5** balmy, bland, claro **6** benign,
gentle, humble **7** clement, lenient **8** benedict, favonian, gracious, lenitive, merciful, moderate, soothing, tranquil **9** assuasive, forgiving, indulgent, temperate **10**
forbearing, mollifying **11** considerate
milder: **6** molder
mildew: **4** mold, rust **5** mould **6** blight,
fungus **8** honeydew
genus of: **7** erysibe **8** erysiphe
mildness: **6** comity
mile: *nautical:* **4** knot, naut
one-eighth: **7** furlong
mileage: **8** distance
milepost: **5** stela, stele **6** marker, stelae
miler: **6** runner
milestone: **8** milepost

milfoil: 6 yarrow 9 ahartalav
milieu: 11 environment 12 surroundings
militant: 7 martial, soldier, warlike 8
fighting 9 combating, combative 10 aggressive
military (see also **army, troop**): 7 martial
advance: 8 anabasis
adventurer: 10 filibuster
area: 6 sector
assistant: 4 aide 8 adjutant
base: 4 camp 5 depot, field 7 billets 8
barracks, quarters 10 encampment
call: 6 tattoo
chest: 5 funds
cloak: 5 sagum
commander: 7 marshal
commission: 6 brevet
force: 5 guard 6 legion, troops 7 reserve
front: 5 lines 6 sector
guard: 6 patrol
hat: 4 kepi 5 shako 6 helmet
hat covering: 8 havelock
horsemen: 7 cavalry, Hussars
informer: spy
inspection: 5 drill 6 parade, review
maneuver: 6 tactic
messenger: 7 estafet
obstruction: 6 abatis 7 abattis
officer: 5 major 7 captain, colonel, general
8 corporal, sergeant 9 brigadier, subaltern 10 lieutenant
operations: 8 campaign, strategy
order: 7 command
organization: 5 cadre
pit: 10 trou-de-loup
police: M.P. 9 gendarmes 12 constabulary
punishment: 9 strappado
quarters: 4 camp 7 billets 8 barracks
rank: 6 brevet 8 banneret
salute: 5 salvo
signal: 7 chamade
staff officer: 4 aide
storage place: 7 arsenal
supplies: 8 materiel, ordnance
survey: 11 reconnoiter
unit: van 4 rear 5 cadre, corps, squad,
troop 7 company, platoon, 8 division,
regiment
vehicle: 4 jeep, tank 6 camion 7 caisson
weapon: 4 croc 6 onager 7 robinet 8 ballista 9 catapult
work: 4 fort
militate: 5 fight 6 debate 7 contend 8
conflict
milk: lac 4 lait(F.) 5 drain, nurse 6 elicit,
suckle
coagulator: 6 rennet
combining form: 5 lacti, lacto
curdled: 6 yogurt 7 clabber, yoghurt, yogourt 8 yoghourt
curdler: 4 ruen 6 rennet
deodorizer: 7 aerator
derived from: 6 lactic
fermented: 5 kefir, kumys 6 koumis, koumys, kumiss 7 koumiss, matzoon

first after delivery: 9 beestings, biestings,
colostrum
food: 10 lacticinia
mouse: 6 spurge
pail: soa, soe 5 bowie
pert. to: 6 lactic 7 lactary, lacteal
preparation: 9 lactarene, lactarine
protein: 6 casein
sap: 5 latex
selling place: 5 dairy 9 lactarium
separator: 7 creamer
sour: 4 whig 6 blinky
sugar: 7 lactose
thickened part: 4 curd
watery: 8 blue John
watery part: 4 whey
with: 6 aulait(F.)
milk glass: 7 opaline
milkfish: awa 6 sabolo
milkman: 7 chalker 8 dairyman
milksop: 5 sissy 7 cockney 11 mollycoddle
milkweed: *down:* 4 silk
family: 14 asclepiadaceae
fluid: 5 latex
milkwood: 9 paperbark
milkwort family: 12 polygalaceae
milky: 4 meek, mild, tame 5 timid, white
6 chalky, gentle 7 lacteal, opaline 8 timorous 10 effeminate
Milky Way: 6 galaxy
black spaces in: 9 coalsacks
mill: box 4 beat, nurl 5 crush, dress, fight,
grind, knurl, shape, thief 6 finish, powder,
thrash 7 factory, machine 8 snuffbox,
vanquish 9 comminute, transform 12
housebreaker
beetle: 9 cockroach
bill: adz
end: 7 remnant
kind of: 5 quern 7 central 8 arrastra, arrastre, trapiche
race: 4 lade
run: 7 average 8 millrace, ordinary
sail: 7 vane
mill-wheel: *current:* 8 millrace
float: 5 ladle
millclapper: 10 chatterbox
millcourse: 8 millrace
millefleurs: 7 perfume
millenarian: 8 chiliast
millepede: 8 myriapod
millepore: 5 coral
miller: ray 4 moth 5 boxer 7 harrier 8
pugilist 10 flycatcher
miller's thumb: 4 bird 7 warbler 8 cottidae, titmouse 9 goldcrest
millerite: 8 sulphide
millesimal: 10 thousandth
millet: 4 buda, moha 5 bajra, bajri, chena,
cumbu, hirse, milly, mohar, proso, tenai 6
bajree, hureek 7 zaburro 8 cenchrus
millimeter: *one millionth:* 15 micromillimeter
one thousandth: 6 micron

milliner: 6 hatter
millions of millions: 9 trillions
millpond: dam
millrace: 4 lade(Sc.) 10 millcourse
 below wheel: 8 tailrace
millrind: 6 moline
millstone: *part:* 4 rynd
 support: 4 rind, rynd
millstream: 5 fleam
Mills bomb: 7 grenade
milo: 5 grain
milpa: 6 chacra
milt: 6 spleen
mim: shy 4 prim 5 quiet 6 demure, modest
mime: ape 4 aper, copy, jest 5 actor,
 clown, drama, farce, mimer, mimic 6 jester 7 buffoon, imitate 9 represent
 chief: 9 archi-mime
mimeograph: 7 stencil
mimer: 4 mime
mimesis: 7 mimicry
mimic (see also **mime**): 4 mima, mimo(G.),
 mock 6 parrot 7 copy-cat, copying, mi-
 metic 9 burlesque 11 counterfeit
mimic thrush: 11 mockingbird
mimidae: 7 catbird 8 thrasher 11 mockingbird
mimmock: 6 dainty 10 fastidious
mimsey: 4 prim 7 prudish
min: 5 ruler 6 memory, prince, remind 8
 remember 11 remembrance
mina: 5 money
minar: 4 myna 5 tower
minaret: 4 lamp 5 tower 10 lighthouse
minatory: 8 menacing 11 threatening
minaway: 7 minuet
mince: cut 4 chop, hash 6 affect 7 finnick
 9 subdivide 11 affectation
mincemeat: 5 gigot
minchery: 7 nunnery
minchiate: 5 tarot
mincing: 5 fussy 7 finical, minikin
mincingly: 8 gingerly
mind: min(Sc.) 4 care, chit, heed, obey,
 reck, tend, will 5 besee, brain, ma-
 nas(Ind.), watch 6 animus, burrow,
 memory, notice, psyche, regard 7 dislike,
 dispose 9 intellect, mentality 11 inclination, remembrance 12 intelligence, recollection
 keep in: 9 entertain
 origin and development: 13 psychogenesis
 pert. to: 6 mental, noetic 7 phrenic 13
 psychological
 split: 13 schizophrenic
 state of: 4 mood, tune
Mindanao: *island:* 5 Samal
 people: Ata 5 Lutao 6 Bagobo, Illano, Lu-
 tayo
 town: 4 Dapa
 volcano: Apo
mindful: 5 aware 7 heedful 9 attentive,
 observant, regardful

mine (see also **mining**): my; bal, dig,
 mio(Sp.), pit, sap 4 delf, hole meum(It.)
 5 bargh, delft, delve 6 cavity, gopher,
 threat 7 gallery, passage 8 colliery 10
 excavation
 basket: 4 corf
 ceiling: 5 astel
 coal: rob
 entrance: 4 adit 5 stulm
 excavation: 5 stope
 floor: 4 sill
 gold: 9 Homestead(S.D.)
 guardian: 5 gnome
 passage: 4 sill 5 stope
 platform: 6 sollar, soller
 prop: 5 sprag
 refuse: 4 dead 5 attle
 reservoir: 4 sump 8 standage
 rich: 4 lode 7 bonanza 8 golconda
 roof support: nog
 shaft: 4 sump
 surface: 6 placer
 sweeping device: 8 paravane
 tunnel: 4 adit 5 stulm
 vein: 4 lode
 wagon: 4 tram
 waste: gob 4 goaf 7 rubbish
 worker: 5 cager, miner 6 canary 7 cage-
 man, trapper 8 onsetter
mine run: 6 common 7 average 10 unas-
 sorted
mine-thrower: 6 minnie 11 minenwerfer
miner: 6 dammer(Sc.), digger, sapper 7
 collier
miner's anemia: 15 ancylostomiasis
miner's consumption: 8 phthisis
miner's worm: 8 hookworm
mineral (see also **ore, metal**): cal, tin 5
 irite 6 barite, iolite 7 alumite, ataxite, uralite 9 celestite, galactite, inorganic,
 uraninite 10 gadolinite, retinalite
 amorphous: 6 pinite
 black: jet 4 coal 5 irite 6 cerine, yenite 7
 knopite, niobite 8 graphite 10 minguetite
 blue-green: 5 beryl
 brittle: 7 euclase
 brown: 6 cerine, egeran, rutile 8 lederite
 9 elaterite
 calcium and magnesium: 8 diopside
 calcium carbonate: 7 calcite 8 calcspar
 combining form: 4 lite
 crystalline: 4 spar 6 yenite 7 apatite, felsite, felspar, knopite 8 boracite, elaterin,
 felspath
 deposit: 4 lode, nest, vein 6 placer
 deposit cavity: vug 4 voog, vugg, vugh
 earth like: 5 glebe
 fibrous: 8 asbestos, oakenite
 flaky: 4 mica
 gray-green: 7 edenite
 gray-white: 5 trona 14 chromiumptrona
 green: 7 alalite, apatite, epidote, erinite,
 prasine, uralian 9 demantoid

gunpowder: **5** niter
hard: **6** spinel **7** adamant **8** corundum, spinelle
lustrous: **4** spar **7** blendes **8** smaltine, smaltite
magnetic: **9** lodestone
mixture: **5** magma
native: ore
non-combustible: **8** asbestos
non-metallic: **4** spar **5** boron **6** gangue, iodine
plaster of paris: **6** gypsum
potash: **4** alum
potassium sulphate: **8** misenite
quartz-like: **5** opal
rare: **7** euclase, thorite
red: **5** balas **6** garnet, rutile
salt: **4** alum
seam: **4** vein
silicate: **4** mica
smelting: ore
soft: **4** talc **6** gypsum
spot: **5** macle
tallow: **11** hatchettine
tar: **4** brea **6** maltha
transparent: **4** mica **5** fluor
vitreous: **4** spar **7** apatite
wax-like: **9** ozocerite
white: **6** barite **8** smaltine, smaltite
yellow: **4** iron **5** topaz **6** pyrite
yellowish green: **7** epidote
mineral jelly: **8** vaseline
mineral oil: **5** colza
mineral spring: spa **4** well
mineral water: **6** selter **7** seltzer
ming: **6** remind **7** mention, recount **8** remember
minge: **5** midge
mingle: mix **4** amix, fuse, join, meng, mool **5** admix, blend, merge, unite **6** huddle **7** blunder, combine, compost **8** coalesce, compound, intermix **9** associate, commingle **10** amalgamate **11** consolidate
mingle-mangle: **6** medley **7** mixture **10** hodgepodge
mingwort: **8** wormwood
mingy: **4** mean **6** stingy
minhag: **6** custom, manner **7** conduct
miniate: **5** paint **8** decorate, luminate **9** rubricate
miniature: **4** copy, tiny **5** small, teeny **6** little, minute **8** painting, portrait **9** lineament, miniating **10** diminutive **11** rubrication **12** illumination **14** representation
minikin: **6** dainty **7** elegant, mincing **8** affected, delicate **10** diminutive
minim: jot **4** drop, fish **5** minnow, minute **7** tiniest **8** smallest **9** miniature **10** diminutive
minimize: **6** reduce **7** detract **8** belittle **9** disparage **10** depreciate
minimum: **5** least **6** lowest
minimuscular: wee **4** tiny **5** small

mining: **4** gwag
chisel: gad
deposit: **4** lode, nest, vein **6** placer
extraction: ore, tin **4** gold, lead **6** silver **8** diamonds **11** quicksilver
instrument: **4** dial
lamp: **4** davy
nozzle: **5** giant
partition: **8** brattice
place: **6** minery, mining
shack: coe
terms: hat **4** hade **6** clinic
tool: van
waste: **5** attle
minion: **4** idol, neat **5** lover **6** dainty, pretty **7** darling, elegant **8** creature, delicate, favorite, ladylove, mistress, paramour **9** underling
minister: **4** tend **5** angel, serve **6** afford, attend, cleric, curate, divine, pander, parson, pastor, supply **7** furnish, provide, servant **8** executor, preacher, reverend **9** attendant, clergyman, upstander **10** administer, ambassador
home: **5** manse **9** parsonage
minestrone: **4** soup
minitant: **11** threatening
Minnesota: *city:* Ely **6** Duluth, Winona **7** Bemidji, Mankato **8** Owatonna **9** Rochester **11** Minneapolis
iron range: **6** Cuyuna, Mesabi **9** Vermilion
lake: Red **7** Bemidji **10** Minnewaska **12** Winniboshish
minnow: **5** guppy **6** baggie
Mino: *children:* **7** Ariadne, Phaedra
lover: **6** Scylla
wife: **8** Pasiphae
minor: **4** less **5** petit, petty, youth **6** infant, lesser, slight **7** smaller **8** inferior **11** subordinate **15** inconsequential
minorate: **7** curtail **8** diminish
minority: **6** nonage **10** immaturity
Minotaur: *owner:* **5** Minos
slayer: **7** Theseus
minster: **6** church **9** cathedral, monastery
minstrel: **4** bard, bhat(Ind.), moke, poet **6** harper, jockey, singer **7** gleeman, goliard, Pierrot **8** jongleur, musician **9** blackface, troubador **10** gleemaiden, mountebank, troubadour **11** entertainer
accompanist: **7** harpist
minstrel show: *endman:* **5** bones
middleman: **12** interlocutor
part: **4** olio
minstrelsy: **4** glee
mint: aim, iva **4** blow, coin, sage **5** basil, feint, money, thyme **6** catnip, hyssop, intend, mentha, ramona **7** attempt, dittany, potherb, purpose, venture **8** bergamot, calamint, endeavor, lavender, marjoram **9** fabricate, horehound
charge: see *levy* below
family: **9** lamiaceae

genus of: **7** melissa **10** moluccella
geranium: **8** costmary
herb family: **4** balm **5** basil **6** hyssop
levy: **8** brassage **11** seigniorage
mintage: **5** stamp **7** coinage
minuend: **6** lessen **8** diminish
minuet: **5** dance
movement: **7** scherzo
minus: **4** lack, less **6** defect, devoid **7** lacking, without **8** negative, subtract **10** deficiency
minuscule: **4** tiny **5** petty, small **6** minute **10** diminutive, manuscript **13** insignificant
minute: jot, wee **4** mite, nice, note, time, tiny **5** draft, exact, petty, small **6** atomic, little, moment, record, slight, tittle **7** instant, minutia, precise **8** detailed, trifling **9** memoranda(pl.) **10** memorandum **13** imperceptible **14** circumstantial
glass: **9** hourglass
minutely: **7** exactly **9** continual, unceasing
minutes: **4** acta **5** actum **6** record
minutia: **6** minute **7** details **11** particulars
minx: dog **4** girl, jade **5** woman
Minyae king: **7** Athamas
minyan: **6** quorum
mir: **4** head **5** chief **9** community
mirabilia: **7** marvels, wonders **8** miracles
mirac: **6** mirach **7** abdomen
miracle: **4** feat **5** anomy **6** marvel, wonder **10** occurrence, phenomenon
scene of: **4** Cana
wheat: **7** Poulard
worker of: **8** magician **11** thaumaturge
miraculous: **9** unnatural **12** supernatural
mirador: **5** oriel **6** loggia, turret **7** balcony **10** watchtower
mirage: **5** serab **7** chimera **8** delusion, illusion **10** phenomenon, refraction
mirandous: **8** wondrous
mirate: **6** wonder
mird: toy **6** meddle **7** attempt
mire: bog, mud, wet **4** glar, moil, ooze, slew, slob, sloo, slud, slue **5** addle, embog, glaur(Sc.), marsh, sluig, slush, stall, swamp **6** defile, slough, sludge **7** clabber, sludder **8** entangle
mire duck: **7** mallard
mirific: **9** wonderful
mirky: See **murky**.
mirror: **5** glass **7** reflect **8** speculum **9** girandole
mirth: fun, joy **4** glee **5** cheer **6** bawdry, gaiety, levity, spleen **7** delight, jollity **8** gladness, hilarity, laughter **9** festivity, happiness, merriment **10** jocularity, joyousness **12** cheerfulness
god: **5** Comus
mirthful: **5** cadgy
miry: **5** boggy, muddy **6** claggy, clashy, filthy, lutose **7** guttery

mis: **5** amiss, wrong
misadventure: See **misfortune**.
misanthropic: **7** cynical **10** antisocial
misapplication: **5** abuse **6** disuse **10** perversion
misappropriate: **5** steal
misbear: **9** misbehave
misbede: **5** abuse, wrong **6** injure
misbegotten: **7** bastard **12** illegitimate
misbehave: **7** disobey, misbear, mislead
misbeliever: **7** heretic, infidel **9** miscreant
misbirth: **8** abortion
miscalculate: err **9** overshoot
miscall: **5** abuse **6** revile **7** slander
miscarriage: **5** lapse **6** mishap **7** failure, misdeed, mistake **8** abortion **9** mischance **11** misdemeanor **13** mismanagement
miscarry: err **5** misgo **7** founder
miscellaneous: **5** mixed **6** sundry, varied **8** assorted **13** heterogeneous **14** indiscriminate
miscellany: **4** olio **10** adversaria, hodgepodge
mischance: See **misfortune**.
mischief: ate, hob, ill **4** bane, evil, harm, hurt **5** prank, wrack **6** damage **7** cantrip **9** devilment, diablerie **10** disservice
god: **4** Loki
goddess: Ate **4** Eris
mischiefmaker: elf, imp, wag **5** knave, rogue
mischievous: sly **4** arch, impy **5** elfin, hempy **6** elfish, elvish, impish **7** harmful, knavish, malefic, mocking, naughty, parlous, roguish, teasing, waggish **8** prankish, sportive, venomous **9** injurious
miscible: **7** mixable
misconception: **8** abortion **16** misunderstanding
misconduct: **7** offense **8** disorder **9** mismanage **11** delinquency, malfeasance, misbehavior, misdemeanor
mark of: **7** demerit
miscreant: **5** knave **6** rascal, wretch **7** heretic, infidel, villain **8** criminal **9** heretical, scoundrel **10** unbeliever **11** misbeliever, unbelieving **12** unscrupulous
miscue: **4** miss, slip **5** error **7** mistake
misdeed: sin **5** crime, wrong **7** forfeit, offense **8** disorder **11** delinquency **13** transgression
misdemeanor: sin **5** crime, fault **6** delict **7** misdeed **8** disorder **11** delinquency **12** misdemeanant
misdirect: **7** pervert
mise: **4** levy, pact **5** grant **6** layout, treaty **8** immunity **9** agreement, privilege
misease: **7** poverty **8** distress **10** discomfort, uneasiness
misenunciation: **9** lallation
miser: **4** cuff **5** churl, flint, hayne, hunks, Nabal **6** codger, huddle, nipper, snudge, wretch **7** hoarder, niggard **8** holdfast **9** skinflint **10** curmudgeon

miserable: bad **4** dawy **6** abject, chetif, elenge, feeble **7** forlorn, pitiful **8** pitiable **10** despicable, discomfort, inadequate **12** disconsolate **13** commiserative

miserere: **4** boss **7** bracket

misericord: **4** hall, pity **5** mercy **6** dagger **9** refectory **10** compassion

miserly: **4** mean **5** close, gnede **6** greedy, grippy, stingy **8** covetous, grasping **9** penurious, scrimping **10** avaricious **12** parsimonious

misery: woe **4** ache, pain **5** agony **6** sorrow, **7** anguish, avarice, poverty, sadness, squalor **8** calamity, distress **9** adversity, privation, suffering **10** affliction, depression, misfortune **11** despondency, unhappiness **12** covetousness, wretchedness **13** niggardliness **14** unpleasantness

misfare: **6** mishap **8** miscarry **9** misbehave **10** misfortune

misfeasance: See **malfeasance**.

misfortune: woe **4** dole, evil, harm, slip **5** grief **6** misery, mishap, scathe **7** ill-luck, misfare, reverse, trouble **8** accident, calamity, casualty, disaster **9** adversity, holocaust, infortune, mischance **10** affliction, ill-fortune **11** catastrophe, contre-temps, miscarriage **12** misadventure

misgiving: **5** doubt, qualm **7** anxiety **12** apprehension

misgo: err **8** miscarry

misguess: err

misguide: **5** abuse **6** injure **7** mislead **8** maltreat **9** misbehave, misdirect, misgovern, mismanage

mishap: See **misfortune**.

mishmash: **4** olio **6** jumble **10** hodgepodge

misinterpret: err **4** warp

misjudge: err

misky: **5** foggy, misty

mislay: **4** lose

misle: **4** mist, rain **6** mizzle **7** drizzle

mislead: **4** dupe, fool **5** blear, cheat **6** betray, delude, humbug **7** beguile, debauch, deceive **8** hoodwink, misguide **9** duplicate, mismanage

misleading: **5** false **7** crooked **10** fallacious, fraudulent

mismanage: **5** blunk **6** bungle

misplace: **4** lose **6** mislay

misplay: err **5** error **6** renege

misprision: **5** scorn **6** slight **7** despite, mistake **8** contempt, misprise, misprize **10** misconduct **11** misdemeanor **12** depreciation **14** undervaluation **16** misunderstanding

mispronunciation: **8** cacology

misrepresent: lie **5** belie **6** garble **7** deceive

miss: err, fau, hip **4** balk, chit, fail, lack, lass, lose, muff, omit, skip, slip, snab,

want **5** lapse, title **6** escape, lassie, miscue **7** deviate, failure **8** mistress, overlook **10** desiderate, jeune fille, prostitute **12** mademoiselle

missay: **5** abuse **6** vilify **7** slander

missel: **9** mistletoe

misshapen: **4** ugly **6** clumsy **8** deformed **9** distorted, misformed, monstrous **11** counterfeit

missile (see also **guided missile**): **4** bola, bolt, dart, shot **5** arrow, shaft, spear **6** bullet, weapon **7** missive, outcast **8** brickbat **9** boomerang **10** projectile

    pert. to: **9** ballistic

missing: out **4** lost **6** absent

mission: **6** charge, errand **7** message **10** commission, delegation, deputation

missionary: **6** Marist **7** apostle

Mississippi: *county:* **5** Amite **8** Pontotoc

    mussel: **8** deerhorn

    nickname: **5** Bayou

    town: **6** Biloxi **7** Jackson, Memphis, Natchez **8** Gulfport, Tutwiler

Mississippian: **15** Eocarboniferous

missive: **4** note **6** billet, letter **7** epistle, message, missile **8** document

    love: **9** valentine

Missouri: *gourd:* **11** calabazilla

    skylark: **5** pipit

    town: **5** Edina **7** Clayton, Sedalia

misspelling: **10** cacography

misspend: **4** lose **8** squander

misstep: **4** slip, trip **5** error **7** faux pas

mist: dag, dim, fog, hag, rag, ure(Sc.) **4** blur, damp, drow(Scot.), film, haze, moke, scud, soup, smog, smur **5** bedim, brume, cloud, dabby, drisk, misle, smurr, vapor **6** mizzle, serein, shadow **7** mystery **9** obscurity **13** precipitation

mistake: err **4** balk, bull, slip **5** amiss, boner, error, fault, folly **6** astray, erring, escape, miscue, renege **7** blunder, default, erratum, rhubarb **10** inaccuracy **12** inadvertence **13** misconception **15** misapprehension

mistaken: **5** wrong

mistletoe: **7** allheal, gadbush

    family: **12** loranthaceae

mistonusk: **6** badger

mistreat: **5** abuse **7** violate

mistress: **4** amie, doll, dozy **5** amiga, dolly, donna, duena, leman **7** hetaera, hetaira, hostess **8** gudewife(Sc.), guidwife, ladylove **9** chamberer, concubine, courtesan, courtezan, governess **10** chatelaine, sweetheart

mistrust: **5** doubt **8** distrust **12** apprehension

misty: **4** roky **5** rouky, vague **10** indistinct **13** unilluminated **14** unintelligible

misunderstanding: **6** breach **7** quarrel **9** imbroglio **12** disagreement

misuse: **5** abuse **6** disuse **7** abusion, pervert **8** maltreat, mistreat **9** misemploy

mite: bit **4** atom, dite, dram, tick **5** acari(pl.), atomy, speck **6** acarid, acarus, minute, smidge **7** acarina, chigger, smidgen, smidgin **8** acaridan, arachnid, particle, smidgeon, smitchin

miter: **4** belt **5** frank, mitre, tiara **6** fillet, girdle, gusset, tavern **8** headband **9** headdress
flower: **8** cyclamen
Jewish part: **7** Petalon

mithridate: **8** antidote **9** electuary **12** alexipharmic

mitigate: **4** balm, bate, cool, ease, tone **5** abate, allay, delay, mease(Sc.), relax, remit, slake **6** lessen, pacify, soften, temper **7** appease, assuage, mollify, qualify, relieve, sweeten **8** diminish, lenitive, moderate, palliate **9** alleviate, meliorate

mitt: mit **5** glove **6** mitten

mitten: **4** cuff, jilt, mitt **5** glove, hands

mittimus: **4** writ **6** notice **7** quietus, warrant **9** discharge, dismissal **10** magistrate

mittle: **4** hurt **8** mutilate

mix: pug **4** amix, fuse, join, meng, stir **5** admix, alloy, blend, cross, knead, merge, unite **6** jumble, mingle, muddle, wuzzle **7** blunder, confect, confuse, shuffle **8** coalesce, compound, confound **9** associate, commingle **10** amalgamate **11** incorporate, intermingle

mix-up: **5** fight, melee **6** tangle **8** conflict **9** confusion

mixable: **8** miscible

mixed: **6** impure, motley **7** piebald **11** farraginous **13** heterogeneous **14** indiscriminate

mixed blood: See **hybrid**.
person of: **5** metis **6** Baluga, Ladino, mestee, mustee **7** mestizo, metisse, mulatta, mulatto

mixen: **7** mixhill **8** dunghill

mixer: **5** party, paver **9** bartender

mixhill: **5** mixen **8** dunghill

mixture: **4** hash, mash, olio **5** batch, blend **6** medley **7** amalgam, compost, farrage, farrago, melange **8** blendure **9** admixture, potpourri **10** concoction, hodgepodge **11** composition **12** minglemangle

mizar star: **5** alcor

mizmaze: **9** confusion **12** bewilderment

mizzle: **4** mist, rain **5** misle **6** decamp **7** confuse, drizzle, speckle **9** disappear, misinform

mizzy: bog **8** quagmire

mnemonic: **8** memorial

mo: **4** book **6** moment, volume

moa: **4** bird **6** ratite **8** dinornis **13** dinornithidae

moab: hat

Moab: *city:* Kir
descendants: **8** Moabites
god: **7** Chemosh

king: **5** Eglon, Mesha
mountain: **4** Nebo
people: **5** Emims

moan: cry **4** sigh, wail **5** groan **6** bemoan, bewail, grieve, lament **7** deplore, whimper **8** complain **9** complaint **11** lamentation
as the wind: **4** sugh **5** sough

moat: **4** foss, lake, pond **5** ditch, fosse, fossa **6** trench

mob: set **4** crew, gang, herd, rout **5** cohue, crowd, drove, flock, group, volge **6** clique, masses, rabble **7** undress **9** multitude **10** dishabille, prostitute
member: **6** rioter
worship: **9** mobolatry

mobbish: **7** lawless **10** disorderly

mobile: mob **6** fickle, vision **7** movable **8** populace **9** wandering **10** changeable

moble: **4** wrap **6** muffle **8** movables **9** furniture

mobsman: **10** pickpocket

mobster: **8** gangster

moccasin: pac **4** pack, shoe **5** snake, tegua **6** loafer, **7** slipper **8** larrigan **11** cottonmouth

moch: **4** moth

mocha: **6** coffee **7** leather
stone: **5** agate

mochy: **4** damp **5** misty, moist, muggy

mock: ape, bob, dor, gab **4** gibe, gird, jape, jeer, leer, sham **5** bourd, elude, false, fleer, flirt, flout, frump, hoker, mimic, scoff, sneer, taunt **6** banter, deride **7** deceive, grimace, imitate **8** ridicule **9** imitation **10** disappoint **11** counterfeit
brawn: **10** headcheese
cucumber: **5** apple
nightingale: **7** warbler **8** blackcap
orange: **7** seringa, syringa, syringe
ore: **10** sphalerite
plane: **8** sycamore

mocker: **4** bird **7** flauter **11** mockingbird
nut: **7** hickory

mockery: **5** bourd, farce, glaik, irony **6** satire **7** hething, sarcasm **8** futility, illusion, travesty **9** burlesque

mocking: **8** fleering

mode: cut, fad **4** form, thew **5** modus, order, state, style, vogue **6** course, custom, fangle, manner, method, regime, system **7** fashion **10** convention

model: act, sit **4** form, mold, norm, plan, plot, pose, type **5** canon, ideal, shape **6** design, sitter **7** example, fashion, manikin, paragon, pattern, templet **8** ensample, exemplar, formular, fugleman, mannikin, paradigm, specimen, standard, template **9** archetype, construct, exemplary, facsimile, flugelman, mannequin, miniature, precedent, prototype

moderate: **4** bate, calm, ease, easy, even, meek, mild **5** abate, lower, slake, sober **6** ease-up, frugal, gentle, lessen, soften, temper 7 average, control 8 attemper, decrease, diminish 9 abstinent, alleviate, temperate 10 abstemious, reasonable 12 conservative 13 dispassionate

moderating: 9 remissive

moderation: 7 control 9 restraint 10 abstinence, diminution, governance, limitation, mitigation 11 restriction 13 temperateness

moderator: 6 umpire 7 arbiter 8 mediator

modern: new 4 late 6 latter, recent 8 neoteric

modernize: 8 renovate

modest: coy, mim(Sc.), shy 4 deft, prim 5 douce, lowly 6 chaste, decent, demure, humble 7 bashful 8 decorous, maidenly, reserved, retiring, verecund, virtuous 9 diffident 10 unassuming 13 unpretentious

modicum: bit 6 amount 7 portion, soupcon

modify: 4 edit, tone, vary 5 alter, limit 6 change, master, temper 7 assuage, qualify 8 attemper, mitigate, moderate 9 influence

modish: 4 chic

modiste: 7 stylist 8 milliner 9 couturier 10 dressmaker

modulated: 5 toned 7 changed, intoned 8 softened, tempered 9 inflected, regulated

modulation: 9 inflexion 10 inflection

mog: jog 4 move, plod, walk 6 depart

moggan: leg 6 sleeve 8 stocking

moggy: cat, cow 4 calf 8 slattern 9 scarecrow

mogo: 7 hatchet

mogul: 5 tatar 6 tartar 7 magnate 8 autocrat 10 locomotive
capital: 4 Agra
emperor: 5 Akbar

moha: 6 millet

Mohammed: 7 Mahomet, Mahound 8 Muhammed
birthplace: 5 Mecca
daughter: 6 Fatima
descendant: Ali 5 Hasan 6 Hosein, Husain, She-rif 7 Ibrahim, She-reef
father: 8 Abdallah
flight from Mecca: 6 hegira, hejira
follower: 6 Wahabi 7 Wahabee, Wahabit, Wahhabi 8 Wahabite
horse: 7 Alborak
nephew: Ali
son-in-law: Ali
successor: 5 Calif 6 Caliph
title: 4 Iman
tomb: 6 Medina
uncle: 8 Abu-Talib
wife: 5 Aisha 6 Avesha, Ayesha 7 Khadija

Mohammedan: See **Muslim**.

Mohammedanism: 5 Islam

moho: 4 bird, rail 9 gallinule

mohock: 6 attack 8 maltreat

mohr: 7 gazelle

moider: 4 toil 5 worry 6 bother, wander 7 perplex, smother 8 distract, encumber

moieter: 6 roller

moiety: 4 half, part 5 share 7 portion

moil: bar 4 mire, soil, spot, tire, toil 5 labor, taint, weary 6 defile, drudge 7 torment, trouble, turmoil 8 drudgery, vexation 9 confusion 10 defilement

moire: 7 watered

moise: 4 mend 6 thrive 7 improve

moist: 4 dank 5 humid, rainy 6 clammy 8 humorous

moisten: dew, dip, ret, wet 4 moil 5 bedew, leach 6 anoint, dabble, dampen, humect, humify, imbrue, sparge 8 irrigate, sprinkle 9 humectate

moisture: fog 4 bree(Sc.), drip, drop 5 humor, vapor, water 6 humour, liquid 8 aquosity, humidity
excess: 5 edema
remove: dry, 4 wipe 5 wring 9 dehydrate

moisture-laden: 6 sodden

moistureless: dry 4 arid 6 burned 7 parched 8 scorched 10 desiccated

mojo: 4 Moxo 5 charm 6 amulet 7 majagua

mokaddam: 5 chief 7 headman

moke: fog, net 4 dolt, mesh, mist 5 horse 6 donkey 7 network 8 minstrel 9 performer

moki: 4 raft 9 trumpeter

moko: 9 tattooing

moko-moko: 6 lizard

mokum: 5 alloy

molar: 5 tooth 7 grinder 8 grinding

molarimeter: 11 thermometer

molasses: 5 syrup 7 claggum, treacle 8 theriaca 10 blackstrap

molave: 5 vitex

mold: die, fen 4 calm, cast, caum, core, form, mool, mull, must, soil 5 frame, humus, knead, model, mould, plasm, shape 6 coffin, matrix, mildew 7 fashion, matrice, moulage, pattern 9 ceroplast, character
opening: 6 ingate
part: 5 nowel, sprue
pert. to: 5 humic
pouring hole: 5 sprue

moldable: 7 fictile

Moldavia: *Rumania capital:* 4 Iasi
department: 4 Iasi 5 Jassy
measure: 4 faltche

molder: rot 5 decay 7 crumble

molding: ess 4 bead, beak, cima, cove, cyma, gula, ogee, reed, tore 5 angle, arris, conge, ogive, ovolo, splay, talon, thumb, torus 6 baguet, baston, fascia, fillet, listel, nebule, reglet, scotia 7 annulet, beading, cavetto, cornice, fingent, reeding, shaping 8 astragal, bageette, bezante 9 trochilus
case: 5 chape

combination: **9** ledgement
convex: **5** torus
ogee: **5** talon
pedestal: **7** surbase
rule for: **6** screed
moldy: **5** fusty, hoary, mucid, musty, stale **7** foughty **8** mildewed
mole: cob **4** cobb, pier, pile, quay **5** fault, jetty **6** anicut, burrow, rodent **7** annicut, barrier **8** excavate, starnose, tunneler **10** breakwater **12** imperfection
cricket: **9** churrworm
mole-like animal: **4** tape **6** desman
molecast: **8** molehill
molecule: *component:* **4** atom
gram: mol **4** mole
molehead: **8** pierhead
moleskin color: **5** taupe
molest: vex **5** annoy, tease **6** assail, bother, harass, pester **7** disturb, trouble **9** incommode, interfere **10** discommode
molge: **8** triturus
moliminous: **7** massive **9** laborious, momentous
moline: **8** millrind
molition: **6** device, effort **11** contrivance
molka: **10** cloudberry
moll: gal **5** wench **8** mistress **9** companion **10** prostitute
mollescent: **9** softening
mollhern: **5** heron
mollichop: **8** delicate
mollicrush: **4** beat, chop **9** pulverize
mollify: **4** bate, calm, ease **5** allay, relax, sleek **6** pacify, relent, soften, soothe, temper **7** amolish, appease, placate, sweeten **8** mitigate **9** attemper **10** conciliate
mollifying: **4** mild **9** demulcent
mollitious: **8** sensuous **9** softening, luxurious
molluscous: **6** flabby **9** spineless
mollusk: **5** snail, whelk **6** chiton, limpet **7** abalone **10** cuttlefish
bivalve: **4** leda, spat **5** chama **6** cockle, mussel, oyster **7** scallop
eight-armed: **7** octopus
fresh water: **7** etheria
gastropod: **4** slug **5** snail, whelk **7** abalone **12** taenioglossa
genus: **4** arca, leda(pl.) **5** eolis, ledum
group: **8** pteropod
larval: **7** veliger
marine: asi **4** welk **5** murex **7** abalone, scallop **8** nautilus
one shell: **5** snail **8** univalve
shell: **4** test **5** cowry, testa **6** cowrie, testae
shell concretion: **5** pearl
shell-less: **4** slug
teeth: **6** radula
ten-armed: **5** squid
used for bait: **5** squid **6** limpet
wrinkled shell: **6** cockle
young: **4** spat
molly: **4** moll **6** basket **7** milksop **9** malle-

muck **11** mollycoddle
mollycoddle: **6** coddle, pamper
moloch: **6** lizard
molt: mew **4** cast, mute, shed **5** moult **8** exuviate
moly: **4** herb **6** garlic
momble: **6** jumble, tangle
mome: **4** fool **5** clown **6** critic **7** buffoon **9** blockhead
moment: mo; sec **4** gird, hint, tick, tide, time **5** avail, braid, clink, filip, gliff, point, trice, value **6** fillip, minute, second, weight **7** instant **9** handwhile, twinkling **10** importance **11** consequence **13** signification
critical: **4** inch, nick **6** crisis, crises
particular: **4** then, when
momentary: **9** ephemeral, transient **10** transitory **13** instantaneous
momentous: **4** fell **5** grave **7** fateful, serious, weighty **8** eventful **9** important, ponderous **10** chargeable **11** influential
momentum: **5** force, power **7** impetus
momist: **5** momus
mommy: **4** duck **5** mammy **6** mother
momus: **6** critic, momist **8** ridicule **11** faultfinder
mon: **5** badge
monachist: **7** monkish
monad: **4** atom, unit **5** deity, henad **8** particle, zoospore
monarch: **4** csar, czar, tsar, tzar **5** ruler **6** despot, prince **7** dynasty, emperor **8** autocrat **9** butterfly, potentate, sovereign
monarchal: **5** regal, royal **8** imperial
monastery: **5** abbey, badia **6** friary, mandra, priory **7** convent, hospice, minster, nunnery **8** cloister, lamasery **9** sanctuary
Carthusian: **7** certosa
head: **5** abbot **7** hegumen
officer: **5** prior
room: **4** cell
superior: **5** prior
title: dom
monastic: **4** monk **5** friar **6** oblate **7** monkish **8** abbatial
monde: **5** globe, mound, world **6** circle **7** coterie, society
monetary: **9** financial, pecuniary
money: (see also **bill, coin**) oof, tin, wad **4** bill, cash, coin, cush, dubs, dump, gelt, gilt, grig, jack, jake, kale, loot, lour, mina, moss, pelf **5** blunt, brass, bread, bunce, chink, clink, dough, funds, livre, lucre, maneh, rhino **6** argent, boodle, change, flimsy, hansel, mazuma, siller(Sc.), spense, steven, wampum, wealth **7** chattel, handsel, lettuce, ooftish **8** currency **9** spondulix **10** spondulics
ancient: aes
blood: cro **7** breaghe
bag: **4** fels **6** follis, wealth **8** follicle
box: **4** arca, safe, till **5** chest **6** drawer **8** register
bribe: **6** boodle

broker: **7** changer
changer: **5** saraf, seraf **6** shroff
chest for: **7** brazier
coinage: **4** mint
coined: **6** specie
counterfeit: **5** queer **6** boodle
cowrie: **6** shells
dealer: **6** broker
depreciation: **4** agio **9** inflation
earnest: **5** arles(Sc.), arrha **6** hansel **7** deposit, handsel **8** handgeld
gambler's: **6** barato
gate: **9** admission
gift: **4** alms **7** bequest, charity **9** endowment
given to lord: **6** farleu, farley
found: **5** trove **8** treasure
hearth: **6** fumage
held: **6** escrow
hook: **4** lari **5** larin **6** larree
lender: **6** banker, usurer **7** shylock **9** loanshark **10** pawnbroker
lots of: pot **4** heap, mint, pile
maker: **4** mint **7** moneyer
manual of exchange values: **7** cambist
metal: **4** coin **6** change, specie **7** coinage
overdue: **7** arrears
oversupply: **9** inflation
paid down: **4** cash **7** deposit **11** downpayment
paper: **4** bill, kale **6** flimsy **7** lettuce
premium: **4** agio
ready: **4** cash **5** asset, darby **9** alcontado(Sp.),
roll of coin: **7** rouleau
sent: **10** remittance
small amount: **4** mite **7** peanuts **11** chickenfeed
standard bank: **5** banco
transactions: **7** banking, finance
unit: ora, yen **4** lira, mark, mina, peso, real, tael **5** frank, krona, krone, maneh, pound, ruble, rupee **6** dollar, piatre, talent **7** drachma, guilder, milreis, piaster **8** cruzeiro
without: **4** poor **5** broke **11** impecunious
money of account: ora
money plant: **9** moneywort
moneyed: **4** rich **6** heeled **7** wealthy **8** affluent
moneyer: **6** banker, coiner, minter **13** counterfeiter
weight: **4** mite **5** blank, droit, perit
mong: mix **5** crowd **6** barter, mingle **7** mixture, traffic **8** mingling **11** intercourse
monger: **6** dealer, trader
mongler: **9** sandpiper
Mongolia:
ass: **8** chigetai
caravan leader: **5** bashi
city: **4** Urga **5** Kobdo **14** Ulan Bator Khoto
coin: **5** mungo **6** tugrik
conjurer: **6** shaman
desert: **4** Gobi

measure: lan
monk: **4** lama
people: Hu; Lai, Rai **4** Garo, Lapp, Shan **5** Asian, Eleut, Tatar **6** Buriat, Tartar **7** Asiatic, Kalmuck, Khalkha **8** Annamese, Oriental **9** Mongoloid
priest: **6** shaman
province: **6** Chahar
religion: **9** Shamanism, Shintoism **12** Confucianism
river: Pei **4** Onon **5** Peiho
Mongoloid: See **Mongolia** *people.*
mongoose: **4** urva **5** lemur **9** ichneumon
Kipling's jungle book: **14** Rikki-Tikki-Tavi
mongrel: cur, dog, mut **4** mutt **6** hybrid **7** bastard, piebald **9** sandpiper
whitefish: **8** tullibee
monial: nun
moniker: **4** name **5** alias **8** nickname
monish: **8** admonish
monition: **5** order **6** advice, notice **7** caution, summons, warning **8** citation **10** admonition, indication, intimation **11** instruction **13** animadversion
monitor: **4** ibid **6** lizard, mentor, nozzle **7** inciter **8** ironclad, reminder **9** catamaran **10** instigator
bug: **8** conenose
lizard: **4** uran **5** varan
monk: dom, fra **4** saki **5** clerk, friar, padre(Sp.) **7** devotee **8** anchoret, cenobite, monastic **9** anchorite, baldicoot, bullfinch, hieronach
Buddhist: bo **4** lama **5** arhat, goyim, yahan **6** bhikku **7** bhikshu, poongee **8** poonghee, poonghie, talapoin
cap: **5** kulah **6** kullah
Eastern Church: **7** caloyer, starets
hair cut: **7** tonsure
hood: **4** cowl
Muslim: **7** dervish
Roman Catholic: **6** Culdee **8** Capuchin, Trappist
time in monastary: **9** monachate
monk's-head: **9** dandelion
monkey (see also **ape**)**:** lar **4** fool, sime **5** burro **6** meddle, nisnas, simian, tamper, trifle **7** colobin **9** catarhina, catarhine **10** catarrhina, catarrhine
African: **4** waag **5** potto **6** grivet, vervet
American: **4** saki **5** acari **6** grison, miriki **7** ouakari **8** marmoset, orabassu **9** beelzebub
Asiatic: **4** douc **5** toque **6** langur **7** macaque
bearded: **8** entellus
beautiful: **7** guereza
bonnet: **4** zati
Callicebus: **5** yapok **6** yapock
capuchin: sai **7** sapajou
cebine: sai
Diana: **7** roloway
entellus: **7** hanuman **10** hoonoo-maun
genus of: **5** cebus **8** alouatta
god: **7** Hanuman

grivet: **4** tota
handsome: **4** mona
howling: **4** mono **5** araba **7** gauriba, stentor **8** alouatta
large: **5** sajou
long-tailed: sai **4** maha **5** patas **6** guenon, langur **7** hanuman **8** entellus, telapoin, wanderoo
macaque: **6** rhesus
proboscis: **4** kaha **7** noseape
purple-faced: **8** wanderoo
rhesus: **6** bandar
saki: **6** couxia, couxio
small: **4** titi **6** apelet, teetee **7** apeling **8** marmoset
spider: **6** ateles, coaita **9** belzebuth
squirrel: **6** samiri
tailless: ape
monkey bear: **5** koala
monkey bread: **6** baobab
monkey flower: **7** mimulus **8** toadflax
monkey-nut: **6** peanut
monkey pot: **5** fruit
monkey wrench: **7** spanner
monkeyboard: **9** footboard
monkeyshines: **6** antics, pranks, tricks **7** aperies
monkshood: **4** atis **5** atees **7** aconite **8** napellus
monoceros: **7** sawfish, unicorn **9** swordfish
monochord: **7** harmony, magadis **9** agreement, sonometer
monocle: **8** eyeglass
monocleid: **4** desk **7** cabinet
monocracy: **9** autocracy
monodist: **6** singer, writer **8** composer
monody: ode **4** poem, song **5** dirge **7** oration
monogram: **6** cipher, sketch **7** outline **8** initials **9** character
monolith: **6** menhir, pillar, statue **8** monument
monologue: **9** soliloquy
monomachy: **4** duel **6** combat
monomaniac: **5** crank **12** single-minded
monophone: **9** homophone
Monophysite: **4** Copt **8** Jacobite
monoplane: **5** Taube
monopole: **8** emporium, monopoly **11** combination
monopolize: **7** engross
monopoly: **5** grant, right, trust **6** cartel, corner **7** appalto, charter, control **9** privilege, syndicate
monosaccharide: ose **5** sugar
monostele: **8** prostele
monotonous: **4** dead, drab, dull, flat, same **6** dreary **7** humdrum, tedious, uniform **8** unvaried **9** wearisome **10** repetitive
monotony: **9** treadmill
monoxylon: **4** boat **5** canoe
monster (see also **beast**): **4** huge, ogre **5** bilsh, freak, giant, teras **6** geryon, sphinx **7** centaur, chimera, warlock
combining form: **5** terat **6** terato
handless: **8** acheirus
headless: **9** acephalus
human: **5** teras **6** terata
medical: **5** Teras
nine-headed: **5** hydra
short-limbed: **9** nanomelus
two-bodied: **7** disomus
two-headed: **10** dicephalus
winged: **5** harpy
without hind limbs: api **4** apus
monster-like: **8** teratoid
monstrous: **4** huge, vast **5** enorm, large **7** hideous, immense, strange **8** colossal, deformed, enormous, flagrant, gigantic, horrible, shocking, titantic **9** atrocious, unnatural **10** outrageous, prodigious, stupendous, tremendous **12** overpowering, overwhelming **13** extraordinary
Montana: *river:* Sun **4** Milk **5** Teton **6** Willow **7** Madison, Shields **8** Missouri **11** Yellowstone
town: **4** Kipp **5** Butte, Havre, Libby **6** Circle, Helena, Laurel **8** Anaconda, Billings, Browning, Glendive, Lewiston, Missoula **9** Kalispell
montant: **6** rising **8** mounting
montanto: **5** sword **10** broadsword
monteith: **4** bowl **12** handkerchief
Montenegro coin: **4** para **6** florin **7** perpera
montero: cap **6** ranger **8** forester, huntsman, mountain
Montezuma cypress: **9** ahuehuete
month: *excess of calendar over lunar:* **5** epact
following: **7** proximo
half: **9** fortnight
preceding: **6** ultimo
monticule: **4** hill **5** mount **7** hillock **8** monticle, mountain
montilla: **6** sherry
Montmorency: **6** sherry
Montrachet: **8** Burgundy
monture: **5** horse, mount
monument: **4** tomb **5** cairn, relic, vault **6** bilith, effigy, hearse, menhir, record, statue **7** chaitya, chhatri, funeral **8** bilithon, cenotaph, cromlech, memorial, monolity **9** antiquity, sepulcher **10** gravestone
pillar-like: **5** stela, stele **6** stelae
moo: low **6** bellow
mooch: beg, bum **4** loaf **5** cadge, skulk, sneak, steal **6** loiter, pilfer, sponge **7** vagrant
moocha: **6** girdle
mood: tid(Sc.) **4** tune, vein, whim **5** freak, humor **6** humour, temper **7** caprice, feeling **10** atmosphere **11** disposition
assumed: **4** pose
recollection of past: **13** retrospection
moody: sad **4** glum **6** gloomy, grumpy, sullen **7** pensive **8** brooding **9** depressed

10 capricious **11** ill-tempered

mool: 4 bury, mold, soil **5** earth, grave **6** mingle **7** crumble

mools: 10 chilblains

moon: orb **4** Dian, Luna, lune(F.) **5** Diana, lunar **6** Phoebe **7** Cynthia, selenic **8** satelles, selenian **9** satellite

above: **10** superlunar

age at beginning of calendar year: **5** epact

areas on: **4** mare

aspect: **5** phase

combining form: **5** selen

crescent: **7** menisci **8** meniscus

crescent point: **4** cusp, horn **6** apogee **7** perigee

distance between apogee and perigee: **5** apsis

festival: **8** neomenia

first quarter: **8** crescent

geographer: **13** selenographer

god: Sin **6** Nannar

goddess: **4** Luna **5** Diana, Tanit **6** Hecate, Hekate, Salena, Selene, Tanith **7** Artemis, Astarte

inhabitant: **8** Selenite

instrument: **11** selenoscope

Jupiter's: Io

mock: **10** paraselene

new: **6** phasis

pert. to: **5** lunar **7** selenic

phase: **7** horning

picture: **11** selenograph

position: **6** octant

Uranus': **5** Ariel

moon fern: 8 moonwort

moon lily: 10 moonflower

moon-mad: 7 lunatic

moon-shaped: 6 lunate

half: **10** semilunate

moon valley: 5 rille

moonack: 9 woodchuck

moonbeam: ray

moonbill: 4 duck

mooncalf: 4 dolt, mole **7** monster **11** monstrosity

mooncreeper: 8 moonseed **10** moonflower

moondown: 7 moonset

mooned: 8 crescent

moonery: 7 madness

moonet: 9 satellite

moonfall: 7 moonset

moonfish: 4 opah **7** sunfish **9** spadefish

moonflower: 5 daisy, oxeye **6** achete

moonglow: 9 moonlight

moonish: 7 flighty **10** capricious

moonlighting: 4 raid **9** adventure **10** expedition **11** moonshining

moonman: 5 gipsy **6** robber

moonraking: 13 woolgathering

moonshine: 4 idle **5** empty, month, sauce **6** liquor **7** trivial, whiskey **8** nonsense **10** balsamweed

moonsick: 7 lunatic

moonstone: 10 hecatolite

moony: 5 round, silly **6** dreamy **8** listless

moor: bog, fen, fix **4** fell **5** heath, lande, marsh, swale, swamp **6** anchor, fasten, secure

Moor: 6 Berber, Moslem, Muslim **7** Bedouin, Othello, Saracen **8** Moroccan

moor blackbird: 5 ouzel

moor buzzard: 7 harrier

moor evil: 9 dysentery

moor game: 6 grouse **8** moorfowl

moor hawk: 7 harrier

moorage: 8 berthage **9** anchorage

moorbird: 6 grouse

moorburn: 7 quarrel **9** illtemper

moorcock: 6 grouse **9** blackcock

moorfowl: 6 grouse

moorhen: 4 coot **9** gallinule

Moorish: 8 Moresque

alcazar: **8** Alhambra

garment: **5** jupon **7** burnous **8** albornoz, burnoose

horse: **4** barb

judge: **4** cadi

kettledrum: **5** tabor **6** atabal

opiate: **4** kief

palace: **8** Alhambra

moorland: fen **5** moose

moose: elk **4** alce **5** eland

mooseberry: 10 hobblebush

moot: dig **4** grub, plea, root, tell **5** argue, plead, speak **6** debate **7** discuss, meeting **8** argument, assembly, complain, disputed **9** debatable, encounter, gathering, undecided **10** discussion, litigation

mooth: wet **4** damp **5** misty

mop: 4 pout, swab, wash, wipe **5** bunch, clean **6** merkin, moppet, scovel **7** cleanse, grimace

mope: 4 pout, sulk **5** brood

mopish: 6 gloomy **7** foolish **8** confused

moppet: tot **4** baby, doll, tike **5** child **7** darling, toddler **9** youngster

mopsy: son **6** moppet **8** slattern

moquette: 6 carpet **10** upholstery

mora: 5 delay, stool **7** default **9** footstool **12** postponement

mora tree: 6 fustic

moral: 4 good, pure **5** ethic **7** dutiful, epimyth, ethical, upright **8** priggish, virtuous **9** honorable, righteous

failure: sin

teaching: **5** maxim **7** precept **8** apologue **9** preaching **10** preachment **11** edification

morale: 4 hope, mood, zeal **6** spirit **8** morality **9** condition **10** confidence

morals: 6 ethics

description: **10** ethography

morass: bog, fen **4** flow **5** flush, marsh, swamp **8** quagmire

morass weed: 8 hornwort

moration: 5 delay

moray: eel **6** conger, hamlet **7** muraena

morbid: 4 sick **6** grisly **8** diseased, gruesome, horrible **9** debatable, unhealthy **11**

unwholesome 12 apprehensive, pathological
morbilli: 7 measles
morbus: 7 disease, illness
mordant: 4 keen 5 sharp 6 biting 7 burning, caustic, pungent 8 scathing 9 corrosive, sarcastic
more: piu 4 also, mair, plus 5 again, extra
6 custom, manner 7 folkway, further,
greater 10 additional, convention
or less: 4 some
than: 4 over 5 above
than enough: too 9 excessive
than one: few 4 many 6 couple, plural 7
several
than this: yea
morel: 8 mushroom 10 nightshade
morena: 8 brunette
moreover: and 4 also, then 5 again 7 besides, further 8 likewise 11 furthermore
morepork: 4 peho, ruru 7 boobook
morgay: 7 dogfish
morglay: 5 sword
morgue: 8 mortuary 9 deadhouse, sto-
lidity 11 haughtiness, impassivity
moribund: 5 dying 6 effete 8 decadent,
decaying 10 acherontic, terminated
morindin dye: al
morinel: 8 dotterel
moringa oil: ben
morion: 6 helmet, quartz 8 cabasset
mormo: 7 bugbear 10 shemonster
Mormon: 6 Danite 8 mandrill
brothers: 7 Danites
emblem: bee
officer: 5 elder
priesthood: 7 Aaronic 11 Melchizedek
prophet: 6 Moroni
Mormon State: 4 Utah
Mormonweed: 6 flower, mallow
morning: 4 dawn, morn 5 matin 6 aurora
7 sunrise
concert: 6 aubade
coat: 7 cutaway
performance: 7 matinee
pert. to: 5 matin, wight 7 matinal 9 matutinal
morning glory: nil 7 gaybine, ipomoea
family: 14 convolvulaceae
morning star: 4 Mars 5 Venus 6 Saturn
7 Daystar, Jupiter, Lucifer, Mercury
moro: 5 finch
Moro: *chief:* 4 Dato 5 Datto
dialect: 4 Sulu
island: 8 Mendanoa
knife: 6 barong
people: 4 Sulu 5 Lanao, Yakan
priest: 4 atli 5 sarip
morocco: 7 leather
imitation: 4 roan
Morocco: *cape:* Nun
city: (see also *port* below): Fez 4 Assa 5
Rabat 6 Rabbat 7 Morocco 9 Marrakech

coin: 4 okia, rial 5 okieh 8 mouzouna
district: Sus 4 Riff
emperor: 9 Miramolin 11 Miramomolin
government: 7 Maghzen, Makhzan, Mach-
zen
hat: fez
island: 7 Madeira
Jew's quarter: 8 El Millah
measure: 4 sahh 6 fanega, tomini
military expedition: 5 harka
mountain: Rif
people: 4 Moor 6 Berber, Kabyle, Moslem,
Muslim 7 Maghzen, Makhzan, Makhzen
port: 5 Ceuta, Rabat 6 Agadir, Rabbat,
Tetuan 7 Mogador, Tangier 8 El Araish,
Laraiche 10 Casablanca
ruler: 6 she-rif, sultan 7 she-reef
soldier: 5 askar
tree: 4 arar 5 argan 6 alerse 8 sandarac
weight: 4 rotl 5 artal, artel, gerbe, ratel 6
dirhem, kintar 7 quintal
morology: 5 folly 8 nonsense
moron: 4 dull, fool 5 ament 6 stupid 7
dullard 8 imbecile, sluggish
moronic: 4 dull 6 stupid 7 idiotic 8 sluggish
morose: 4 dour, glum, grum, sour 5 gruff,
moody, sulky, surly 6 crusty, gloomy,
sullen 7 crabbed, clumpse, clumpst,
crooked, unhappy 8 strounge 9 splenetic
10 embittered, ill-humored
moroseness: 8 asperity
morphia: 8 morphine
morphine derivative: 6 heroin
morro: 4 hill 5 bluff, point 6 castle 8
headland
Mors: 5 death
morse: 5 clasp 6 brooch, walrus
Morse code signal: dit, dah
morsel: bit, ort 4 bite, snap 5 crumb,
piece, scrap, snack 6 tidbit, titbit 7 mor-
ceau, rarebit 8 fragment
morsing: 7 priming
morsure: 4 bite 6 biting
mort: 4 dead, lard 5 death, fatal 6 deadly,
grease, salmon 9 abundance
mortacious: 4 very 9 extremely
mortal: 4 dire 5 being, fatal, human 6
deadly, lethal 7 capital, deathly, fleshly 8
grievous 9 extremely 10 implacable 11
destructive
mortar: 5 compo, putty 6 cannon, cement, holmos, petard 7 perrier
carrier: hod
mixer: rab
tray: hod
mortarboard: cap 4 hawk
mortgage: 4 bond, deed, lien 5 trust 6
pledge, wadset(Sc.) 11 encumbrance
giver: 6 lienee
receiver: 6 lienor
mortician: 10 undertaker
mortification: 5 shame 7 chagrin 8 gan-

grene, necrosis, vexation 11 humiliation 13 embarrassment

mortified: 10 sphacelate

mortify: 5 abase, abash, spite 6 ashame, humble, offend 7 crucify

mortifying: 11 ignominious

mortise: 6 cocket
complement of: 5 tenon
law: 8 amortize

mortuary: 4 gift 6 morgue 7 funeral 9 deadhouse, lich-house, sepulcher

morvin: 7 mallein

mosaic: 5 tiled, tiles
formed like a: 10 tesselated

mosaic gold: 6 ormolu
piece: 7 tessera

moschate: 5 musky

Moscow citadel: 7 Kremlin

Moses: 6 leader 8 lawgiver
brother: 5 Aaron
emissary: 5 Caleb
father-in-law: 6 Jethro
law: 4 tora 5 torah 10 pentateuch
mountain: 4 Nebo
sister: 6 Miriam
successor: 6 Joshua
wife: 8 Zipporah

mosey: 4 mosy 5 amble 6 depart, ramble, stroll, wander 7 shuffle

mosker: 5 decay 6 molder

Moslem (see also **Muslim**): 7 Islamic, Saracen 9 Moslemite, Mussulman 10 Mohammedan

mosque: 4 mosk 5 Caaba, Kaaba 6 church, dargah, durgah, Kaabeh, Kiblah, masjid, shrine, temple
official: 4 imam 5 imaum
tower: 7 manarat, minaret 8 minarete
warden: 5 nazir

mosquito: 5 aedes 7 culicid 11 gallinipper
genus of: 5 aedes, Culex 9 Anopheles
killer: 8 culicide
larvae: 8 wigglers

mosquito bee: 5 karbi 8 angelito

mosquito boat: P.T.

mosquito fish: 8 gambusia

mosquito hawk: 9 dragonfly, nighthawk

mosquito plant: 4 mint 10 pennyroyal

Mosquito State: 6 Jersey

moss: bog, fog, rag 5 swamp, usnea 6 lichen, morass 9 bryophyte, treebeard
animalcule: 8 bryozoan
club: 7 lycoped
edible: 4 agar 8 agaragar
like: 7 hepatic

moss cheeper: 5 pipit 7 bunting

moss coral: 8 bryozoan

moss corn: 10 silverweed

moss duck: 7 mallard

moss fruit: 11 sporogonium

moss-grown: 10 antiquated 12 old-fashioned

moss hammer: 7 bittern

moss polyp: 8 bryozoan

moss-trouper: 6 raider 8 marauder

mossback: 4 fogy 5 fogey

mossberry: 9 cranberry

mossbunker: 8 menhaden

mosshead: 9 merganser

mosswort: 9 bryophyte

mossy: 4 dull 5 boggy, downy, green, hoary 6 marshy, stupid 7 covered 9 abounding, overgrown

most: 4 best 5 chief 6 utmost 7 maximum 8 majority 9 principal

mostly: 6 feckly

mot: 4 butt, mark, moat, word 5 motto, piece 6 device 7 epigram, opinion

mote: dot, may 4 atom, hill, iota 5 atomy, match, might, speck, squib, stalk, straw 6 barrow, fescue, height, trifle 7 tumulus 8 eminence, particle

motel: inn 5 hotel

motet: 4 song 6 anthem 11 composition 12 contrapuntal

moth: io 5 tinea 6 bogong, lappet, mallet, miller, tineah, tinean, tineid 7 tineina 8 chloasma, forester 11 yellowshell
family: 7 arctiid, tineina 9 arctiidae
genus of: 5 sesia
larva: 11 caterpillar
spot: 8 chloasma, fenestra
suborder: 10 heterocera

moth-eaten: 4 worn 7 decayed 8 decrepit, out-dated
moth hawk: 10 goatsucker
moth hunter: 10 goatsucker

mother: dam 4 dame, womb 5 adopt, dregs, mater(L.), nurse 6 matron, patron 8 genetrix 10 ancestress
of gods: 4 Rhea 9 Brigantia
of graces: 5 aegle
of man: 6 Cybele
of states: 8 Virginia
of the months: 4 moon
spiritual: 4 amma
three deliveries: 7 Tripara

Mother Carey's goose: 6 fulmar

Mother Carey's hen: 6 petrel

mother gate: 4 bord 7 tramway

Mother Hubbard: 4 gown 5 dress

mother-in-law: 9 eldmother

mother of coal: 8 charcoal

mother of pearl: 5 nacre

mother superior: 6 abbess

mother's mark: 9 birthmark

mothered: 5 thick 6 viscid

motherland: 4 home 10 fatherland

motherly: 8 maternal

motion (see also **bodily motion**): 4 fard, idea, move 5 faird 6 unrest 7 gesture, impulse, propose, request, suggest 8 movement, petition, proposal 10 suggestion 11 application, inclination 13 gesticulation
circular: 4 gyre 10 revolution

convulsive: 11 vellication
due to: 7 kinetic
expressive: 7 gesture
impetuous: 6 bensel, bensil 7 bensail,
bensall, bensell
pert. to: 7 kinetic 9 kinematic 11 kine-
matical
quality: 8 momentum
rate: R.P.M. 4 time 5 speed, tempo 11
steerageway
science: 10 ballistics, kinematics
transmitter: cog 4 belt, gear
upward: 5 scend 8 upthrust
motion picture: 4 film, show 5 flick,
movie, talky 6 cinema 7 flicker 9 photoplay
arc lamp: 5 kleig, klieg
award: 5 Oscar
cowboy & Indian: 7 Western
machine: 9 projector 11 kinetoscope 12
animatograph, theatrograph 13 cinematograph 14 cinematographe
outline: 6 script 8 scenario
play: 5 movie 6 cinema 9 photoplay
prize: 5 Oscar
motionless: 4 dead 5 inert, rigid, still 6
asleep 8 becalmed, immobile, stagnant,
stagnate, stirless 9 quiescent, sedentary
10 breathless
motivate: 4 move 5 impel 6 incite, induce
7 inspire 9 influence, instigate, stimulate
motive: 4 sake, spur 5 cause 6 object,
reason 7 impulse, purpose 8 pressure,
stimulus 9 incentive, objective 13 consideration
ostensible: 7 pretext
motley: 4 fool 5 mixed 6 jester 7 diverse,
mottled, piebald 9 checkered 10 variegated 13 heterogeneous
man of: 4 fool 6 jester 7 Pierrot
motor: car 4 auto, ride 6 engine 7 kinetic,
machine 8 motorcar 10 automobile
electric: 6 dynamo
hand-powered: 9 baromotor
part: cam 6 piston
rotary: 7 turbine
motor-bike: 10 motorcycle
motor-boat: 8 palander
motor speed control: 8 rheocrat
motte: 5 grove
mottled: 4 pied, roed 5 pinto 6 motley 7
brocked, clouded, dappled, piebald, spotted 8 blotched 10 variegated 11 varicolored
motto: mot 4 word 5 adage, axiom, gnome,
maxim 6 device, saying 7 empresa, precept 8 aphorism 10 shibboleth
mouche: 5 patch
mouchoir: 12 handkerchief
moue: 4 face 7 grimace
moufflon: 5 sheep
mould: See mold.
moulrush: 7 pollack
moulting: 7 ecdysis

mound: ahu, cop, dam, dun, tee 4 balk,
bank, butt, dene, dher, doon, dune, heap,
hill, hump, pile, terp 5 agger, berry, cairn,
dheri, globe, huaca, knoll, stack, to-
man(Scot.) 6 barrow, bounds, burrow,
causey 7 bourock, bulwark, hornito, rampart, tumulus 8 boundary 9 elevation 10
embankment
pert. to: 7 tumular
mound bird: 8 megapode
Mound City: 7 St. Louis
mound of light: 8 kohinoor
mount: 4 glue, hill, pony, rise 5 arise,
climb, horse, paste, steed 6 ascend, aspire 8 escalate, increase, mountain 10
promontory 13 fortification
two-legged: 5 bipod
Mount Etna city: 7 Catania
Mount Everest peak: 6 Lhotse
Mount Helicon fountain: 8 Aganippe
mount horizontal bar: kip
Mount Ida nymph: 6 Oenone
Mount of Olives: 6 Olivet
Mount Parnassus fountain: 8 Castalia
mountain (see also **peak**): ben(Scot.),
kop 4 berg, dagh, fell, mont(F.) 5 onlay
6 barrow, bundoc 8 bundocks
base of: 8 piedmont
beyond: 10 tramontane 11 transalpine
Biblical: See **Bible:** *mountain.*
burning: 7 volcano
combining form: oro 4 oreo
depression: col
devil: 6 moloch
formation: 7 orogeny 9 orogenesy 10 oro-
genesis
gap: see *pass* below
highest: 7 Everest
low: 5 butte
mythical: Kaf, Qaf 4 Meru 5 candy, glass
7 Helicon 9 Parnassus
nymph: 5 dryad, oread
pass: col, gap 4 cove, gate, ghat 5 ghaut,
gorge, kotal 6 defile
pert. to: 10 orological
range: 4 Alps, Ghat, Ural 5 Andes, chain,
Coast, ridge, Rocky, Teton, White 6 Ala-
tau 7 Rockies, Sierras 8 Cascades, Cats-
kill, Pyrenees 9 Allegheny, Blue Ridge,
Himalayas 10 San Jacinto 11 Appa-
lachian, San Gorgonio
ridge: 4 aret, peak, spur 5 arete, crest 6
sierra, summit 7 sawbuck
rocky: 7 nunatak
science: 7 orology
sickness: 4 veta 7 soroche
snow: 5 jokul
study: 9 orography
mountain andromeda: 10 fetterbush
mountain ash: 5 rowan, rowen
mountain badger: 6 marmot
mountain balsam: fir
mountain banana: fei
mountain barometer: 8 orometer

mountain beaver: 8 sewellel
mountain bluet: 8 centaury
mountain cat: 4 lynx 6 bobcat, cougar 10 cacomistle
mountain cock: 12 capercaillie
mountain curassow: 10 oreophasis
mountain duck: 9 harlequin, sheldrake
mountain finch: 9 brambling
mountain flax: 8 centaury
mountain fringe: 8 fumitory, wormwood
mountain goat: 4 ibex
mountain ivy: 6 laurel
mountain leather: 12 palygorskite
mountain lion: 6 cougar
mountain magpie: 10 woodpecker 11 butcher-bird
mountain mint: 5 basil 8 calamint
mountain oak: 8 chestnut
mountain panther: 5 ounce 6 cougar 7 leopard
mountain parrot: kea
mountain partridge: 4 dove 5 quail
mountain pheasant: 6 grouse
mountain quail: 9 partridge
mountain raspberry: 10 cloudberry
mountain rose: 6 laurel
mountain snow: 4 neve
mountain spinach: 5 orach 6 orache
Mountain State: 7 Montana
Mountain States: 4 Utah 5 Idaho 6 Nevada 7 Arizona, Montana, Wyoming 8 Colorado 9 New Mexico
mountain tea: 11 wintergreen
mountaineer: 5 Aaron 7 climber, hillman 9 hillbilly
song: 5 yodel
mountainlike: 7 etiolin
mountainous: 4 high 6 rugged
mountaintop: 4 cone, peak 6 summit
mountebank: 4 gull 5 cheat, quack 7 empiric 8 impostor, minstrel 9 charlatan, pretender
aid: 4 zany
mounting: 7 setting 9 equipment 13 embellishment
mounting horizontal bar method: kip
moup: 6 nibble 9 associate
mourn: rue 4 dole, erme, long, sigh, wail, weep 6 bemoan, bewail, grieve, lament, murmur, sorrow 7 deplore 8 mourning
mournful: sad 5 black 6 repine 7 elegiac 8 funereal 9 elegiacal, plaintive, threnodic, woebegone 10 lugubrious, melancholy
mourning: 4 garb 5 dolor 6 dolour 7 drapery
bride: 5 plant 8 scabious
dress: 5 black, crape, weeds 6 sables
mouse: erd, pry 4 girl, hunt, knot 6 bruise, rodent 8 black-eye
field: 4 vole 7 harvest
leaping: 6 jerboa
like: shy 4 drab 5 mousy, quiet, timid 6 murine 8 retiring

male: 4 buck
meadow: 5 voles
milk: 6 spurge
mouse deer: 10 chevrotain
mouse-ear: 8 hawkweed 9 chickweed
mouse hare: 4 pika
mousebird: 4 coly 6 shrike
mouser: cat 9 detective
mouseweb: 6 cobweb 8 gossamer
mousing: 6 prying 7 binding 8 prowling 9 rapacious 11 inquisitive
mousle: 6 rumple
mousse: 7 dessert, messboy
mousy: 4 drab 5 quiet, timid
moutan: 5 peony, plant 6 flower
mouth: os; gab, gan, gob, mow, mug, mun, ora 4 boca(Sp.), dupe 5 front, stoma 6 cavity, gebbie(Sc.), mumble, rictus 7 flummer, opening, stomata 8 entrance 9 impudence
away from: 6 aborad, aboral
combining form: ori 5 stome
deformity: 7 harelip
disease: 4 noma 6 canker 10 stomatitis
muscle: 7 caninus
part: lip 5 uvula 6 palate 7 pharynx
pert. to: 4 oral 6 rictal 7 oscular, palatal 8 stomatic
projecting: 5 spout
roof: 6 palate
tissue: gum
toward: 4 orad
mouth organ: 9 harmonica
mouthful: lot, sup 4 bite, gulp 6 gobbet
mouthpiece: 5 bocal 6 lawyer 8 attorney
mouthwash: 9 collutory 11 collutorium
mouthy: 9 bombastic, talkative
mouton: fur, spy 4 wool 9 sheepskin
movable: 5 loose 6 fickle, mobile, motile 8 exorable, floating 10 changeable, inconstant 11 ephelcystic 12 figuratively
move (see also **go**): go; act, gee, mog 4 goad, pass, play, spur, stir 5 budge, cause, clink, impel, rouse, shift, start, sweep 6 affect, arouse, bestir, betake, excite, incite, induce, kindle, motion, prompt, quetch, remble, remove 7 actuate, advance, agitate, animate, inspire, migrate, propose, provoke, suggest 8 converse, emigrate, maneuver, motivate, transfer 9 influence, instigate, stimulate
along: mog 5 mosey, scram 7 maunder
away: shy 8 emigrate
back and forth: wag 4 flap, rock, tack 5 dodge, weave 6 falter, teeter, wabble, wiggle, wigwag, zigzag 7 shuttle 9 oscillate
false: 4 balk 5 feint 7 misstep
first: 10 initiative
forward: 4 edge 5 drive, forge, surge 7 advance 8 progress
heavily: lug 6 lumber, trudge
in water: 4 swim, wade
inwardly: 6 enmove

noiselessly: 4 slip 5 creep, glide, skulk, slink, sneak, steal 6 tiptoe 9 pussyfoot
noisily: 6 bustle 7 clatter, rollick
obliquely: 4 edge, joll, skew, slue 5 sidle
on wheels: 4 roll 7 trundle
quickly: fly 4 dart, dash, flit, jump, leap, race, scud, scur, whir 5 bound, hurry, scoot, skirr, spank, sweep, start 6 career, gallop, hurtle, scurry, spring
restlessly: 6 kelter, twitch
rhythmically: bob, jig, jog 5 dance, march
round and round: 4 eddy 5 swirl, twirl
sinuously: 5 snake 6 writhe
slowly: lag, mog 4 edge, inch, worm 5 crawl 6 trudge 7 crowhop
smoothly: 4 slip 5 glide, skate, slide
together: 5 unite 8 converge
moveless: See **immovable.**
movement: 5 tempo, trend 6 rhythm
music: 4 moto
surface: 6 seiche
movie: See **motion picture.**
moving: 7 current 8 ambulant, pathetic, poignant, touching 9 transient 10 ambulatory
about: 8 ambulent 10 ambulatory
moving picture: See **motion picture.**
moving staircase: 9 escalator
mow: bin, cut, lay, mew 4 barb, clip, goaf, heap, mass, math, pile, rick 5 mouth, stack 6 scythe, sickle 7 grimace 8 haystack 9 cornfield
mowana: 6 baobab
mowie: 9 stackyard
mowing: 7 mockery 8 derision 10 meadowland
mowland: 6 mowlot 10 meadowland
mowth: 6 mowing
moxie berry: 9 snowberry
moy: 4 mild 6 demure, gentle 8 affected
moyen: way 5 means 6 agency, course 8 property 9 influence, substance
mubarat: 7 divorce
mucago: 5 mucus 7 coating 8 mucilage
much: 4 fele, high, lots, many 5 great, heaps, scads 6 mickle 7 gaylies, geylies, greatly 8 abundant, uncommon 9 multitude
combining form: eri
music: 5 molto
mucid: 5 moldy, musty, slimy 6 mucous
mucilage: gum 5 paste 6 arabin, mucago 8 adhesive
mucilaginous: 5 gluey, slimy 6 sticky, viscid 8 adhesive
muck: 4 dirt, dung, mess 5 filth, money, slime, waste 6 manure, refuse, wealth
muckle: 4 fret 6 bother
mucoid: See **mucous.**
mucor: 9 hoariness, moldiness 10 filthiness
mucous: 5 moist, slimy 6 mucoid 7 viscous 8 blennoid, muculent

mud: fen 4 dirt, glar, gore, mire, ooze, slob, slud 5 glaur, gumbo, slime, slush, waise 6 sludge 7 clabber, sludder, sluther 12 offscourings
deposit: 4 silt
hole: pan 6 puddle, wallow 8 quagmire
like: 7 luteous
mud bath: 10 illutation
mud dab: 8 flounder
mud dabbler: 9 killifish
mud dauber: 4 wasp
mud devil: 10 hellbender
mud eel: 5 siren
mud lark: 5 gamin 6 magpie, urchin 8 shoveler 10 meadowlark
mud mark: 7 mudflow
mud peep: 9 sandpiper
mud puppy: 10 hellbender, salamander
mud snipe: 8 woodcock
mud sunfish: 4 bass 8 warmouth
mud volcano: 5 salse
Mudcat State: 11 Mississippi
muddle: mix 4 ball, daze, doze, mess 5 addle, besot, snafu 6 bemuse, burble, fuddle, jumble, pother 7 bedevil, blunder, confuse, fluster, mystify, perplex, stupefy 8 befuddle, bemuddle, bewilder, confound, disorder, flounder 9 confusion 10 intoxicate 12 hugger-mugger
muddled: ree 4 asea 5 beery, crazy, drunk, foggy, tipsy
muddy: 4 miry, roil 5 dirty, drovy, druvy, slaky, vague 6 claggy, clarty, clashy, cloudy, drubly, lutose, sludgy, slushy, turbid 7 clouded, guttery, obscure, sensual 8 confused, feculent 9 besmeared, spattered 11 bespattered
mudfish: 6 bowfin
mudhole: 4 slew, sloo, slue 6 slough
mudworm: ipo 9 earthworm
mudwort: 7 mudweed
muff: fur, vex 4 flub 5 crest, error 6 bungle, warmer 8 irritate
muffet: 5 mufty, muggy 11 whitethroat
muffetee: 7 muffler, wrister 8 wristlet
muffin: cob, gem 5 bread, scone 7 crumpet, popover
muffle: gag 4 damp, dull, mute, wrap 6 bumble, dampen, deaden, shroud 7 silence 8 envelope 10 camouflage
muffled: 6 hollow
muffler: 4 mute 5 scarf 6 tippet 8 silencer
mufflin: 8 titmouse
mufti: 4 alim 8 assessor, civilian, clothing, official 9 expounder
mufty: See **muffet.**
mug: cup 4 cram, dupe, face, fool, toby 5 mouth, mungo, pulse, sheep, stein, study 6 noggin, seidel 7 assault, canette, drizzle, goddard, grimace, tankard 8 schooner 10 photograph
muga: 11 caterpillar

mugger: goa **4** thug **6** tinker **7** peddler, puncher **9** crocodile
mugget: **6** mugwet **8** woodruff
muggins: **4** dupe, fool, game **9** simpleton
muggy (see also **muffet**): **4** damp, fozy **5** humid, moist, moldy
mughouse: **8** alehouse, pothouse
mugweed: **7** mugwort
mugwet: **8** woodruff
muir: **4** moor
mulberry bird: **8** starling
mulberry family: **8** Moraceae
mulberry fig: **8** sycamore
mulberry tree: **4** more
mulch: **5** cover, straw **6** litter **7** compost, sawdust
mulct: **4** balk, fine, scot **5** cheat **6** amerce, defect, fleece, punish **7** blemish, deceive, defraud, forfeit, penalty **8** penalize **10** amercement, forfeiture
mule: **4** mewl, mool, mute **5** coble, hinny **6** hybrid **7** bat-mule, slipper, tractor **9** chilblain **10** locomotive
   driver: See **muleteer.**
   leader in pack train: **8** cencerro
   male: **4** jack
   spinning: **7** ironman
   untrained: **9** shavetail
mule killer: **6** mantis
muleteer: **4** peon **6** driver **7** arriero(Sp.), skinner **9** almocrebe
mulga: **6** shield, wattle
mulish: **5** balky **6** hybrid, sullen **7** sterile **8** perverse, stubborn **9** obstinate, pig-headed **10** determined
mull: cow **4** crag, dust, heat, mess, mold, muse **5** cloth, crush, grind, snout, spice, think **6** fettle, muslin, muzzle, ponder, powder **7** crumble, failure, rubbish, squeeze, sweeten **8** cogitate, consider, ointment, snuffbox **9** pulverize **10** prom-ontory
mullein: **5** torch **6** agleaf **8** hagtaper **9** torchwort **10** hare's-beard
mullet: **4** bobo, liza **6** harder, puffin
mullet hawk: **6** osprey
mulligan: **4** stew
mulligatawny: **4** soup
mulligrubs: **5** blues, colic, sulks
mullock: **4** dirt **6** litter, refuse **7** rubbish
mulloway: **7** jewfish
mulmul: **6** muslin
multicolored: **4** pied **6** calico **7** dappled, spotted
multifarious: **7** diverse **8** manifold
multifold: **4** many **8** manifold, numerous
multiform: **7** diverse
multiple: **4** many **6** plural **8** numerous
multiplier: **7** facient
multiply: **5** breed **6** spread **7** amplify, augment, magnify **8** increase **9** reproduce
   by eight: **11** octuplicate
   by ten: **7** decuple

multitude: mob **4** army, heap, hive, host, many, mass, much, ruck **5** crowd, drove, flock, horde, shoal, swarm **6** legion, myriad, nation, throng
multitudinous: **8** manifold, numerous
mum: ale **4** beer, dark **5** still **6** mother, silent **7** silence **9** voiceless **10** speechless **13** chrysanthemum
mumble: **4** chew, mump **5** mouth **6** cha-vel, chavle, faffle, fumble, haffle, murmur, mutter, palter, patter **7** flummer, grumble
mumbo-jumbo: **4** idol **6** fetich, fetish **7** bugaboo
mummer: **4** mime **5** actor **6** guiser, player **7** buffoon **9** performer, puppeteer
mummy: **5** relic **6** corpse **7** cadaver, car-cass
mummy apple: **6** papaya
mump: **5** cheat, sulks **6** mumble, mutter **7** grimace **10** sullenness **11** displeasure
mumper: **6** beggar **8** impostor
mumps: **5** brank
mumruffin: **8** titmouse
mun: it; him, may **4** face, must, them **5** mouth, shall
munch: eat **4** chew **5** champ **6** growse, growze
mundane: **6** cosmic **7** earthly, prosaic, secular, terrene, worldly **8** temporal **10** terrestial
mungo: mug **8** mongoose
municipality: **4** city, town **7** cabildo
munificent: **4** free **5** ample **6** lavish **7** liberal **8** generous **9** bounteous, bountiful **10** benevolent
muniment: **6** record **7** defense **8** docu-ment, evidence, writings **9** valuables **11** furnishings **13** fortification
munitions: **7** baggage, weapons **10** am-munition
munity: **9** privilege
muntjac, muntjak: **4** deer **6** kidang
muraena: **5** moray
mural: **4** wall **8** painting
murchy: **8** mischief
murder: **4** bane, kill, slay **5** death **7** butcher, carnage, killing, murther **8** hom-icide **9** slaughter **11** assassinate **12** man-slaughter
   brother: **10** fratricide
   father: **9** patricide
   fine: **9** bloodfine
   king: **8** regicide
   mother: **9** matricide
   own child: **9** prolicide
   parent: **9** parricide
   prophet: **8** vaticide
   sister: **10** sororicide
   son or daughter: **8** filicide
   spouse: **10** mariticide
   wife: **9** uxoricide
   woman: **8** femicide
murderous: **4** gory **5** felon **6** bloody, bru-

tal **9** ferocious **10** sanguinary **12** bloodthirsty

mure: **4** meek, soft, wall **6** gentle, demure, immure, modest

murgeon: **7** grimace, grumble

muriatic: **12** hydrochloric

murid: rat **8** disciple

murky: dim **4** dark **5** black, dense, foggy, mirky, misty, thick **6** gloomy **7** obscure **12** impenetrable

murmur: coo, hum, pur **4** curr, fret, huzz, purl, purr, sugh **5** brool, grank, sough **6** babble, grutch, hummer, mumble, mutter, repine **7** grumble, whisper **8** complain **9** grumbling
nasal: hum

murphy: **6** potato

murrain: **6** plague **10** pestilence

murther: **6** murder

Musa: **6** banana

muscadine: **5** grape **11** scuppernong

muscle: **4** thew **5** brawn, flesh, sinew, teres **6** lacert **8** strength
affection: **5** crick **6** abasia, ataxia
column: **10** sarcostyle
contracting: **7** agonist
curve: **7** myogram
expansion: **7** dilator
lifting: **7** levator
limb-straightening: **8** extensor
round: **5** teres
segment: **8** myocomma
spasm: **5** tonus
straight: **6** rectus
stretching: **6** tensor
sugar: **7** inosite **8** inositol
trapezius: **10** cucullaris
triangular: **7** deltoid
turning: **7** evertor, rotator
two-headed: **6** biceps

muscovado: **5** sugar

Muscovite: Red **4** mica, Russ **7** Russian
mica: **4** talc
prince: **4** Ivan

muscular: **5** thewy **6** brawny, robust, sinewy, strong, torose, torous **8** athletic, vigorous

muse: **4** dump, mull **5** dream, think **6** loiter, ponder, trifle **7** reflect **8** cogitate, consider, meditate, ruminate **9** amusement **10** meditation **11** contemplate

museful: **6** silent **10** meditative, thoughtful

musery: **4** play **9** amusement

Muses: **4** Clio **5** Erato **6** Thalia, Urania **7** Euterpe **8** Calliope, Polymnia **9** Melpomene **10** Polyhymnia **11** Terpsichore
epithet: **7** Pierian
Fountain: **8** Aganippe
home: **5** Aonia **7** Helicon
mountain: **9** Parnassus
seat of worship: **6** Pieria

musette: air **4** oboe **7** bagpipe, gavotte

museum: **10** repository

custodian: **7** curator
director: **7** curator

mush: cut **5** atole, crush, gruel, march, notch, sepon **6** indent, sepawn, supawn, travel **7** confuse, journey, pudding, suppawn **8** flattery, porridge, sagamite, umbrella **14** sentimentality

mushroom: **4** grow **6** agaric, spread **7** parvenu, upstart
disease: **5** flock
edible: **5** morel **11** chanterelle
fairy-ring: **10** champignon
like: **7** fungous
part of: **4** gill **5** stipe, trama **6** pileus **7** annulus **8** basidium, hymenium, sterigma **12** basidiospore
poisoning: **8** mycetism
poisonous: **7** amanita **9** toadstool
stem: **5** stipe

mushy: **4** soft, weak **5** gushy, thick **8** effusive, yielding

music (see also **melody, song,** and entries under **musical**): air, art **4** tune **7** harmony
change to another key: **10** modulation **13** transposition
for eight: **5** octet
for five: **7** quintet
for four: **7** quartet
for nine: **5** nonet
for one: **4** soli, solo
for seven: **6** septet
for six: **6** sextet **7** sestole **8** sestolet
for three: **4** trio
for two: duo **4** duet
machine for: **5** radio **7** juke-box, pianola **8** musicbox **10** gramophone, phonograph
mania for: **9** melomania
Muse: **7** Euterpe
notation system: **5** neume
outdoor: **6** aubade **8** serenade
symbol: **4** clef, note, rest **5** staff
timing device: **9** metronome

music hall: **4** gaff, odea(pl.) **5** odeum, odeon

musical: **4** show **5** lyric, revue **7** lyrical, melodic **8** harmonic, rhythmic **9** melodious **10** harmonious

musical comedy: hit **4** flop, show **5** revue **6** review **7** musical

musical composition: **4** glee, opus **5** cento, fugue, opera, rondo **6** ballad, sonata **7** ballade, boutade, cantata, chanson, prelude, scherzo, virelai **8** berceuse, concerto, nocturne, operetta, oratorio, serenata, serenade, sonatina, symphony **9** cabaletta, interlude **10** intermezzo
aria-like: **6** arioso
dancer's: **10** gymnopedie
dawn: **6** aubade
declamatory: **10** recitative
ending: **4** coda **6** finale
exercise: **5** etude, study
feature: **5** motif, theme

interlude: **6** verset
jazz: rag **4** jive **5** bebop, blues, swing **7**
    ragtime **12** boogie-woogie
poetic: ode
prelude: **6** verset
religious: **4** mass **5** motet, psalm **6** an-
    them **7** cantata **8** oratorio
round: **5** canon, fugue, troll
suite: **7** partita
musical direction: *above:* **5** sopra
accented: **8** sforzato **9** sforzando
again: DC, DS; bis **6** da capo **8** dal segno
all: **5** tutti
always: **6** sempre
animated: **7** animato **9** spiritoso
ardent: **7** ardente **12** appassionato
as written: sta
bold: **6** audace
bowed: **4** arco
cold: **6** freddo
continue: va
devout: **6** divoto
disconnected: **8** staccato
dying away: **7** calando
emphatic: **7** marcato
evenly: **10** egualmente
everyone: **5** tutti
excited: **7** agitato **9** spiritoso
fast: **4** vivo **5** tosto **6** presto, veloce, vi-
    vace **10** tostamente
faster: **7** stretto
freely: **9** ad libitum
furious: **7** furioso
gay: **7** giocoso
gentle: **5** dolce
half: **5** mezzo
heavy: **7** pesante
held: **6** tenuto
hurried: **7** agitato
joyous: **7** giocoso
leap: **5** salto
less: **4** meno
little by little: **9** poco a poco
lively: **6** vivace **7** allegro, animato, giocoso
loud: **5** forte **10** fortissimo
louder: **9** crescendo
lovingly: **7** amabile, amoroso
lyric: **5** erato
majestic: **8** maestoso
marked: **7** marcato
moderate: **7** andante **8** moderato
more: piu
more rapid: **7** stretta, stretto
much: **5** molto
muted: **5** sorda
passionless: **6** freddo
plaintive: **7** dolente
playful: **7** giocoso **10** scherzando
plucked: **9** pizzicato
proceed: va
quick: **4** vite **5** tosto **6** presto **7** schnell
quick time: **9** alla breve
quickening: **11** affrettando
repeat: bis **6** ancoro **7** ripresa

sadly: **7** dolente **8** doloroso
sharp: **8** staccato **9** sforzando
silent: **5** tacet
singing: **9** cantabile
sliding: **9** glissando
slow: **5** grave, largo, lento, tardo **6** adagio
    7 andante **9** larghetto
slower: rit **6** ritard **10** ritardando
slowing: **11** rallentando
smooth: **6** legato
so much: **5** tanto
soft: **5** dulce, piano **10** pianissimo
softer: **10** diminuendo **11** decrescendo
solemn: **5** grave
somewhat: **4** poco
spirited: **7** animato **9** spiritoso
stately: **7** pomposo
strong: **5** forte **10** fortissimo
sustained: **6** tenuto **9** sostenuto, sustenuto
sweet: **5** dulce
tempo irregular: **6** rubato
thrice: ter
throughout: **6** sempre
together: **8** ensemble
tranquil: **7** calmato
turn: **9** gruppetto
very: tre **4** tres **5** assai, molto **7** dimolto
with: con
musical disc: **6** cymbal, record **9**
    recording
musical drama: **5** opera **8** operetta, ora-
    torio
musical instrument: **4** drum, fife, gong,
    harp, horn, lute, lyre, oboe, reed, tuba **5**
    banjo, flute, organ, piano, viola **6** cornet,
    guitar, spinet, violin **7** bassoon, ocarina,
    piccolo, saxhorn, trumpet, ukelele **8** cas-
    tanet, clarinet, dulcimer, mandolin, trom-
    bone **9** euphonium, flageolet, saxophone
    11 violoncello
ancient: **4** asor **5** rocta **6** rappel, sabeca **7**
    cithera, serpent **9** pantaleon
bass: **5** cello **11** violoncello
brass: **4** horn, tuba **5** bugle **6** tromba **7**
    althorn, helicon, saxhorn, trumpet **8** alto-
    horn, trombone **10** French horn
China: kin
East Indies: **4** bina
Egypt: **7** sistrum
helicon: **4** tuba
Java: **7** gamelon **8** gamelang
keyboard: **5** organ, piano **6** spinet **7** ce-
    lesta, clavier **8** melodeon **9** accordion **10**
    clavichord, concertina, pianoforte **11**
    harpsichord
lute-like: **7** angelot, bandore, cithern, cit-
    tern **9** bandurria **10** colascione
lyre-like: **4** asor **6** cither, zither **7** cithara,
    kithara
medieval: **5** rebab, rocta **7** chrotta
Mexico: **5** guiro **6** clarin **7** cabacas, mara-
    cas **11** chiapanecas
musical interval: **5** fifth, major, minor,
    sixth, third **6** ditone, fourth, octave, sec-

ond, unison **7** perfect, seventh, tritone **9**
augmented **10** diminished
mouthpiece: **4** reed **6** fipple
oboe-like: **5** shawm **7** musette
percussion: **4** drum, gong **5** bells, traps **6**
maraca **7** cymbals, marimba, timpani,
tympani **8** triangle **9** castanets, xylophone
10 tambourine **12** glockenspiel
piano-like: see *keyboard* above
reed: **4** oboe **7** bassoon **8** clarinet **9** saxophone **11** English horn
stringed: oud, uke **4** asor, bass, harp, lute,
lyre, viol, vina **5** banjo, cello, rebec, ruana, viola **6** citole, fiddle, guitar, rebeck,
violin, zither **7** bandore, cythara, gittern,
pandura, samisen, theorbo, ukelele **8** au-
toharp, dulcimer, mandolin **11** harpsichord, violoncello
supplementary: **7** ripieno
two-necked: **7** theorbo
viol-like: **5** rebec, ruana **6** rebeck **7** clav-
iol **8** claviole
wind: jug, sax **4** fife, horn, oboe, reed, tuba
5 brass, bugle, flute, organ **6** cornet **7**
althorn, bagpipe, bassoon, clarion, ocarina, panpipe, piccolo, saxhorn, serpent,
trumpet **8** altohorn, clarinet, recorder,
trombone, zampogna **9** flageolet, harmonica, saxophone **10** French horn **11** sar-
rusphone
xylophone-like: **7** marimba
musical medley: 4 olio **5** cento
musical note (see also **musical syllable**):
5 breve, minim, neume **6** quaver **9** semi-
breve
musical piece: See **musical composition; song.**
musical program: 5 opera **7** concert,
recital **8** musicale
musical rhythm: 4 beat, time **5** ictus,
meter, pulse, swing, tempo
measuring device: **9** metronome
musical scale (see also **musical syllable**):
5 gamut
musical sign: 5 segno
entrance: **5** presa
hold: **7** fermata, formata
key: **4** flat **5** sharp **7** natural
pitch level: **4** clef
silence: **4** rest
slur: **8** ligature
smooth: **4** slur
staff: bar
musical syllable: do, fa, la, mi, re, si, ti,
ut; sol
ancient: ce, ut; alt, are, ela **5** elami, neume
7 alamire
musical term: *arrangement:* **7** ridotto
ballad style: **8** a ballata
between acts: **8** entracte
cadence: **4** half **6** plagal **7** perfect **9** deceptive, imperfect
chapel-style: **9** a cappella
dance-style: **7** da ballo
embellishment: **8** ornament **9** fioritura **12**

appoggiatura
ending: **4** coda
florid: **7** bravura
flourish: **7** cadenza
half note: **5** minim
half tone: **8** semitone
major key: dur
melodic phrase: **5** motif **9** leitmotif, leitmotiv
melos: **4** song **6** melody
minor key: **4** moll
movement: **4** moto
note: **5** breve, neume
refrain: **5** epode **8** repetend
repeat: **5** rondo **7** reprise
run: **6** volata **9** glissando
shake: **5** trill **7** tremolo
soft pedal: VC **7** celeste
third: **6** tierce
thirty-second note: **14** demisemiquaver
three-note chord: **5** triad
time: see **musical rhythm**
tones: **5** chord
tremble: **5** trill **7** tremolo, vibrato
triplet: **6** tercet, triole
two notes: **5** duole
unaccompanied: **9** a cappella
upbeat: **5** arsis
vocal part: **5** canto
musical theme: 4 tema **5** motif **9** leitmotif, leitmotiv
musician: 4 bard **5** piper **6** singer **7**
drummer, flutist, gleeman, pianist **8**
bandsman, composer, flautist, minstrel,
organist **9** cornetist, performer, serenader, violinist **10** trombonist **11** clari-
netist, saxophonist
group: **4** band, duet, trio **5** choir, nonet **6**
chorus, septet, sextet **7** nonetto, quartet **8**
ensemble, septete, sextette **9** orchestra,
quartette
patron saint: **7** Cecelia
musing: 7 reverie **10** meditation, meditative **13** contemplation
musk: 4 deer **7** perfume
musk beaver: 7 muskrat
musk cat: 5 civet
musk cavy: 5 hutia
musk cucumber: 11 cassabanana
musk deer: 10 chevrotain
musk hog: 7 peccary
musk lorikeet: 8 parakeet
musk mallow: 8 abelmosk
musk shrew: 6 desman
muskeg: bog **5** marsh
muskellunge: 4 pike
musket: 4 hawk **5** fusil **6** falcon **7**
bundock, bundook, dragoon, firearm **8**
biscayen **9** flintlock
Musketeers: *Three:* see **Three Musketeers**
muskmelon: 6 atimon, casaba **10** cantaloupe
muskrat: 5 shrew **6** desman
Muslim, Moslem (see also **Islam, Mo-**

hammed): 4 Moro 6 Paynim 7 abadite, Islamic, Saracen 9 Mahometan, Mussulman 10 Mohammedan
angel: 6 Azrael 7 isrefel, israfil 8 israfeel
annual fast: 7 Ramadan
ascetic: 4 sufi 5 fakir 6 fakeer
bazaar: 4 sook
belt: 5 zonar 6 zonnar
Berber dynasty: 6 Hafsid 7 Hafsite
Bible: 5 Coran, Koran 7 Alcoran
bier: 5 tabut
calendar: 5 Rabia, Rajab, Safar 6 Jumada, Shaban 7 Ramadan, Shawwal 8 Zu'lhijah, Zu'lkadah 9 Mulharram
call to prayer: 4 adan, azan
cap: taj 5 kulah 6 kullah
caravansary: 6 imaret
caste: 5 mopla 6 moplah
chief: 4 rais, sidi 5 datto, sayid, sheik
city (sacred): 5 Mecca 6 Medina
coin: 5 dinar
council: 5 Ulema
creed: 5 Sunna
crusade: 5 jehad, jihad
decree: 5 irade
deity: 5 Allah, Eblis
demon: 5 afrit, eblis, jinni 6 jinnee
dervish: 6 Sadite, Santon
divorce: 5 ahsan, talak 7 mubarat
fast days: 7 Ramadan
festival: Eed 6 Bairam
freethinker: 7 Saracen 9 Aladinist
garment: 4 izar 6 jubbah
god: 5 Allah
guide (spiritual): pir
headdress: fez, taj 5 kulah 6 kullah, turban
hermit: 8 marabout
holy book: 5 Koran
holy city: 5 Mecca 6 Medina
holy war: 5 jehad, jihad
infidel: 5 kafir 6 kaffir
judge: 4 cadi, imam 5 hakim, imaum
lady: 5 begum
law: 5 halal 7 sheriat
lawyer: 5 mufti
leader: 4 amir, emir 5 ameer, emeer
men's quarters: 8 selamlik
minaret crier: 7 muezzin
minister of state: 6 vizier
monastery: 5 tekke
month: see *calendar* above
mosque: 6 masjid
mysticism: 6 Sufism
name: Ali
nymph: 5 houri
officer: aga
official: 5 hajib, mufti
orthodox: 7 hanif 7 Sunnite
people: Laz 4 Lazi, Moro, Sufi, Swat 5 Hanif, Isawa, Salar, Samal, Sunni, Swati 6 Dehgan, Senusi 7 Bazigar, Senousi, Senussi 8 Senusite 9 Senussian
physician: 5 hakim 6 hakeem
pilgrim: 4 haji 5 hadji, hajji
pilgrimage: 4 hadj

pilgrim's dress: 5 ihram
prayer: 5 namaz, salat
prayer call: 4 adan, azan
priest: 4 imam 5 imaum 6 wahabi
priests (body): 5 ulema
prince: 4 amir, emir, seid 5 ameer, emeer, nawab, sayid
princess: 4 tola 5 begum
religion: 5 Islam
ruler: aga 4 amir, emir 5 ameer, emeer, hakim, nawah 6 hakeem, sultan
saber: 7 yatagan 8 scimitar, scimiter, yataghan
sacred book: See *Bible* above.
saint: Pir 5 Abdal 6 Santon 8 Marabout
salutation: 5 salam 6 salaam
sect: 5 Isawa 6 Wahabi 7 Abadite, dervish, Sunnite 8 Ahmadiya, Sifatite
shrine: 5 Kaaba 6 Kaabeh
spirit: 4 jinn(pl.) 5 genie, jinni 7 jinnyeh
spiritual adviser: pir
student: 5 softa
supreme being: 5 Allah
teacher: 4 alim, imam 8 mujtahid
title: sid 4 said, sidi 5 nawab, sayid 6 sayyid
warrior: 7 Saracen
washing: 4 widu, wudu, wuzu
women's quarters: 5 harem

muslin: ban 4 mull 5 adati, dorea, doria, shela 6 cossas, gurrah, shelah 7 beteela, organdy 8 nainsook, seerhand, sheeting 9 charkhana, womanhood 10 femininity
muss: See **mess.**
mussel: 4 naid, unio 5 naiad 6 mucket, nerita 8 deerhorn
genus of: 8 modiolus
part: 6 byssus
mussitate: 6 mutter
Mussulman: See **Muslim.**
must: 4 bood, mold, musk, sapa, stum 5 juice, ought, shall 6 refuse 10 obligation
mustang: 5 pinto 6 bronco 7 broncho
mustard: 5 nigra, senvy 6 senapi 7 cadlock 8 charlock
chemical: 5 allyl
family: 12 brassicaceae
genus of: 7 sinapis
pod: 7 silicle
mustard plaster: 8 sinapism
muster: 4 call 5 erect 6 gather, roster, sample, summon 7 collect, marshal, pattern 8 assemble 10 accumulate, congregate
musty: 4 dull, sour 5 fusty, hoary, moldy, rafty, stale, trite 6 rancid 7 foughty, spoiled 10 antiquated
Mut: *child of:* 5 Chons
husband: 4 Amen, Amon
mutable: 6 fickle 8 variable 9 alterable 10 changeable, inconstant 11 vacillating
mutation: 6 change, revolt 9 posthouse 10 revolution, succession 11 vicissitude
mute: mum 4 dumb, lene, surd 6 deaden, muffle, silent 7 mourner, muffler 8

deadener, silencer **9** voiceless **10** speechless **12** inarticulate

mutilate: mar **4** hack, maim **6** deface, garble, injure, mangle, mittle(Sc.) **7** cripple, destroy **9** disfigure, dismember

mutinous: **6** unruly **9** seditious, turbulent **10** rebellious, refractory, tumultuous **11** disobedient, intractable **12** contumacious **13** insubordinate

mutiny: **6** revolt, strife **9** commotion **12** insurrection

mutt: cur, dog **7** mongrel **9** blockhead

mutter: **5** growl **6** mumble, murmur, patter **7** channer, grumble, maunder **9** mussitate

mutton: **4** meat **5** sheep **6** candle **10** prostitute

dried: **5** vifda, vivda

leg: **5** cabob, gigot **7** wabbler, wobbler

muttonbird: oii **6** petrel **10** shearwater

muttonchop: **7** whisker **8** burnside

muttonfish: **4** sama **5** pargo, porgy **7** eelpout, mojarra

muttonhead: **5** dunce **9** blockhead, screwball

mutual: **6** common **10** reciprocal, responsive

mutuality: **13** interrelation

mux: **4** mess **5** botch

muzhik: **7** peasant

muzz: **6** muddle

muzzle: gag **4** grub, nose, root **5** snout **6** clevis, muffle **7** sheathe **8** restrain **10** respirator

muzzy: **4** dull **5** fuzzy **7** blurred, muddled **8** confused **10** depressive

mycoid: **7** fungoid

mykiss: **6** salmon

myna: **7** grackle

myomorph: rat **5** mouse **6** rodent

myotic: **7** eserin **7** eserine

myriad: **9** countless **11** innumerable **13** multitudinous

myriapod: **9** centipede

myrmicid: ant

myrtle: **8** ramarama **10** periwinkle **11** candleberry

myself: **5** masel(Sc.)

mysterious: dim **4** dark **5** runic **6** arcane, mystic, occult, secret **7** cryptic, uncanny **8** abstruse **9** equivocal, recondite, sphinxine **12** inexplicable, unfathomable

mystery: **4** rune **5** craft, trade **6** cabala, enigma, puzzle, riddle, secret **7** arcanum, esotery **8** thriller, whodunit

mystic: **4** seer **5** epopt, runic **6** occult, orphic, secret **7** cryptic, epoptic, obscure **8** anagogic, esoteric, symbolic **9** enigmatic, recondite **10** cabalistic, mysterious

word: om, um **4** evoe **7** abraxas **11** abracadabra

mysticism: **6** cabala **8** cabalism

mystify: **5** befog **6** muddle, puzzle **7** becloud, confuse, perplex **8** befuddle, bewilder **9** bamboozle, obfuscate

myth: **4** saga, tale **5** fable, fancy, story **6** legend **7** parable **9** apocrypha

mythical: **9** imaginary **10** fictitious

N

nab: hat **4** grab, head **5** catch, seize **6** arrest, clutch, nibble, snatch **7** capture **9** apprehend

nabob: **5** nawab **6** deputy **7** viceroy **8** governor **9** plutocrat **10** viceregent **11** billionaire

nacelle: **7** shelter **11** compartment

nacket: boy **4** cake **5** lunch

nacre: **9** shellfish **10** conchiolin **13** mother-of-pearl

nag: tit **4** frab, fret, gnaw, jade, pony, twit **5** annoy, cobra, hobby, horse, scold, snake, tease **6** badger, berate, bother, harass, heckle, hector, padnag, pester, wanton **7** hackney **8** harangue, irritate **9** aggravate

naga, nag: **5** cobra, snake

nagor: **8** antelope, reedbuck

nahoor: sha, sna **5** sheep, urial **6** bharal, oorial

naiad: **5** nymph **6** mussel

naif: See **naive.**

nail: cut, fix, hob **4** brad, brag, brod, claw, cloy, dump, spad, stub, stud, tack, trap **5** affix, catch, clout, grope, spike, sprig **6** clinch, detain, fasten, hammer, secure, unguis, ungula **7** capture **8** fastener, sparable, spikelet **9** finishing, intercept

nais: **5** naiad, nymph

naissance: **5** birth

naive: **5** frank **6** simple **7** artless **8** childish, untaught **9** childlike, guileless, ingenuous, untutored, unworldly **10** unaffected **13** inexperienced, unphilosophic **15** unsophisticated

naked: **4** bare, nude, open **6** cuerpo **7** exposed **8** manifest **9** unadorned, unclothed, uncovered **11** defenseless, unprotected

namaycush: **5** lunge, togue, trout

namby-pamby: **7** insipid **10** wishy-washy **11** sentimental

name: dub, nom(F.) **4** call, term **5** claim, clepe, count, nemme, nemne, neven, nomen, style, title **6** adduce, appeal, monica, select **7** appoint, behight, enstyle, entitle, epithet, intitle, mention, moniker **8** christen, delegate, identify, identity, monicker, monniker, nominate **9** designate **10** denominate, denotation, reputation **11** appellation, designation **12** denomination, nomenclature

added: **6** agname **7** agnomen

assumed: **5** alias **6** anonym **9** incognito, pseudonym, sobriquet **10** nomdeplume, soubriquet

backwards: **6** ananym

based on location: **7** toponym

Biblical: See **Bible:** *name.*

derivation: **7** eponymy

family: **7** eponymy, sirname, surname **8** cognomen

female: Ada, Amy, Ann, Ava, Dot, Ena, Eva, Eve, Fay, Ida, Ina, Jen, Lil, Lou, Mae, May, Meg, Nan, Pam, Pat, Rae, Una, Zoe **4** Alma, Alta, Anna, Anta, Avis, Caro, Cora, Dian, Dona, Dora, Edla, Edna, Ella, Elsa, Enid, Erma, Etta, Eula, Fifi, Gail, Inez, Irma, Kate, Katy, Lena, Lida, Lila, Lois, Lola, Lona, Lora, Lula, Meta, Mina, Nena, Nina, Nita, Nora, Olga, Prue, Rena, Reta, Rita, Sara, Suke, Suky, Susy, Tess, Vera **5** Adele, Agnes, Aimee, Alice, Alida, Aline, Alsie, Anita, Annie, Aphra, Bella, Betsy, Betty, Celia, Clare, Delia, Della, Doris, Dulce, Edith, Eilen, Elain, Elena, Elise, Ellen, Elsie, Essie, Ester, Ethel, Ettie, Flora, Freda, Genie, Greta, Helen, Hilda, Irene, Janet, Karen, Laura, Lelia, Leona, Lucia, Lydia, Maida, Maria, Moira, Molly, Norah, Norma, Paula, Rhoda, Sally, Sarah, Sukey, Sukie, Susan, Susie, Tecla, Wilma, Zebina **6** Adelai, Alicia, Annice, Arline, Connie, Dagmar, Daphne, Dorcas, Elaine, Esther, Fedora, Flavia, Frieda, Gertie, Gloria, Gratia, Hedwig, Hermia, Honora, Isabel, Janice, Jennie, Lenora, Lenore, Louisa, Louise, Muriel, Pamela, Persis, Sallie, Sandra, Sheila **7** Abigale, Belinda, Cecilia, Celeste, Dolores, Eleanor, Emaline, Estelle, Eveline, Felicia, Heloise, Imogene, Juanita, Madelon, Mildred, Rosalia, Rosalie, Susanna, Waunita, Zulinde **8** Arabella, Drusilla, Hermiona, Hyacinth, Patricia **9** Anastasia

first: **9** praenomen

list: **11** onomasticon

masculine: Al, Ed, Si; Abe, Alf, Asa, Ben, Cal, Dan, Eli, Gil, Gus, Guy, Hal, Ian, Ike, Ira, Lem, Len, Lon, Moe, Nat, Ned, Ole, Pat, Ray, Rex, Roy, Sam, Sid, Ted, Tex, Tim, Ugo, Vic **4** Abel, Adam, Alan, Alex, Alva, Amos, Axel, Bart, Bert, Carl, Dian, Dick, Earl, Emil, Enos, Eric, Esme, Evan, Ezra, Gene, Hugh, Igor, Ivan, Joab, Joel,

Knut, Leon, Levi, Luke, Lynn, Marc, Mark, Neal, Neil, Noah, Noel, Olaf, Otto, Owen, Paul, Phil, Pius, Rene, Saul, Stan, Tony, Zeke **5** Aaron, Abiel, Abner, Abram, Agard, Allan, Alvan, Angus, Anton, Basil, Biron, Bryan, Bryon, Byron, Caleb, Cecil, Cliff, Clive, Denis, Edgar, Elias, Elihu, Elmer, Emery, Eneas, Enoch, Ernie Erwin, Ethan, Felix, Floyd, Giles, Hiram, Isaac, Jabez, Judah, Leigh, Leroy, Lloyd, Louis, Lysle, Moses, Nahum, Nigel, Orson, Peleg, Percy, Peter, Reuel, Roger, Rollo, Roman, Rufus, Silas, Titus, Urban, Uriah, Uriel, Zebee **6** Adolph, Adrian, Alaric, Albert, Alexis, Alfred, August, Austin, Caesar, Calvin, Caspar, Cedric, Daniel, Decius, Dexter, Donald, Dudley, Duncan, Dwight, Edmund, Egbert, Harvey, Hubert, Isaiah, Israel, Jairus, Jarvis, Joshua, Josiah, Jotham, Junius, Kasper, Lemuel, Lester, Lucius, Luther, Manuel, Marcus, Marion, Murray, Naaman, Nathan, Pierre, Reuben, Roland, Roscoe, Rupert, Samuel, Steven, Teague, Theron, Tobiah, Vergil, Victor, Vivian, Walter, Wilbur **7** Abraham, Anatole, Bertram, Chester, Clement, Dominic, Douglas, Eleazar, Elliott, Erasmus, Erastus, Eustace, Everard, Everett, Ezekiel, Flavius, Gabriel, Gifford, Gilbert, Godfrey, Isidore, Japheth, Lazarus, Leonard, Leopold, Lorenzo, Malachi, Maurice, Obadiah, Patrick, Phineas, Raphael, Raymond, Raymund, Rowland, Russell, Seymour, Stanley, Stephen, Ulysses, Zachary, Zebedee, Zebedei, Zebedia **8** Adelbert, Algernon, Alphonso, Benjamin, Claudius, Clifford, Ebenezer, Emmanuel, Fernando, Frederic, Gamaliel, Geoffrey, Gustavus, Hezekiah, Ignatius, Jeremiah, Laurence, Lawrence, Napoleon, Nehemiah, Octavius, Percival, Schuyler, Silvanus, Terrence, Thaddeus, Zebadiah **9** Anatasius, Archibald, Celestine, Cornelius, Demetrius, Ferdinand, Frederick, Lafayette, Launcelot, Llewellyn, Marcellus, Nathaniel, Rodolphus, Rudolphus, Siegfried, Sigismund, Silvester, Zachariah, Zacharias **10** Maximilian, Theophilus

objectionable: **7** caconym
tablet: **5** facia
nameable: **6** famous **7** notable **9** memorable
named: **6** yclept **7** ycleped
nameless: **7** bastard, obscure **9** anonymous, unnamable **12** illegitimate **13** indescribable, unmentionable
namely: viz **5** noted, towit **6** famous **8** scilicet **9** expressly, videlicit **10** especially **12** specifically
namesake: **6** junior
nandu: **4** rhea
nanism: **12** dwarfishness
nanny: **4** goat **5** nurse

nanny plum: **10** sheepberry
nanpie: **6** magpie
naos: **5** cella **6** shrine, temple
nap: nod **4** calk, doze, fuzz, lint, pile, shag, wink **5** fluff, grasp, seize, sleep, steal **6** siesta, snooze
nape: nod **5** nucha, nuque **6** scruff **7** niddick
napery: **5** linen
naphtha: **9** petroleum
napkin: **5** cloth, doily, towel **6** diaper **8** kerchief **9** handcloth, serviette **11** neckerchief **12** handkerchief
Naples biscuit: **10** ladyfinger
napless: **10** threadbare
Napoleon: *birthplace:* **7** Corsica
brother-in-law: **5** Murat
island of exile: **4** Elba
marshall: Ney
place of victory: **5** Ligny **10** Austerlitz
nappy: ale **4** dish **5** downy, heady, wooly **6** liquor, strong **7** foaming
napu: **7** deerlet **10** chevrotain
narcotic (see also **marijuana**): kat **4** bang, dope, junk **5** bhang, dagga, ether, opium **6** heroin, opiate **7** anodyne, cocaine, hashish **8** hasheesh, hypnotic, morphine, takrouri **9** soporific **10** belladonna, hyoscyamus, stramonium
dose: **5** locus
package: **4** deck **6** bindle
seller: **6** pusher **7** peddler
nard: **5** spice **6** anoint **7** rhizome **9** spikenard
nardoo: **6** clover
nargileh: **4** pipe **5** hooka **6** hookah **7** coconut
nark: spy, vex **5** annoy **8** informer, irritate **10** spoilsport **11** stool pigeon
narrate: **4** tell **5** state **6** detail, recite, relate, report **7** discuss, recount **8** describe, rehearse **9** chronicle, discourse
narrative: **4** epic, myth, saga, tale **5** conte, drama, fable, story **6** legend **7** account, episode, history, parable **8** allegory, anecdote **9** narration
narrator: **9** reconteur
narrow: **4** mean **5** close, scant, sound, taper **6** biased, linear, meager, meagre, strait, strict **7** bigoted, limited **8** condense, contract **9** constrict, hidebound, illiberal, niggardly **10** prejudiced, restricted, straighten, ungenerous **11** reactionary **12** parsimonious **13** circumscribed
combining form: **4** sten **5** steno
narsinga: **7** trumpet
narthex: **5** porch **7** portico **9** vestibule **10** antetemple
nasab: **7** kinship **13** consanguinity
nasal: **6** narine, rhinal, twangy
nascency: **5** birth **6** origin **7** genesis **9** beginning
naseberry: **9** sapodilla

nashgab: 6 gossip
nasi: 9 patriarch
nasicorn: 10 rhinoceros
nastika: 7 atheist
nasty: bad **4** foul, mean, ugly **5** dirty **6** filthy **7** harmful, obscene, squalid **8** indecent **9** dangerous, malicious, offensive **10** disgusting, ill-natured, nauseating, unpleasant **12** disagreeable, dishonorable **13** objectionable
nasutiform: 8 noselike
nat: 5 demon **6** spirit
natal: 6 native **7** gluteal **10** congenital
natant: 6 afloat **8** floating, swimming
natator: 7 swimmer
natatorium: 4 bath, pool
natchbone: 9 aitchbone
nation: 4 host, race **5** caste, class, state **6** people **7** country **9** community, multitude
national: 7 citizen, federal **11** gentilitian
National Guard member: 10 militiaman
native: 5 natal **6** genial, inborn, innate, normal **7** citizen, endemic, natural **8** domestic, inherent, original, resident **9** aborigine, congenial, ingrained, unbranded **10** congenital, indigenous, inhabitant
nativity: 5 birth **8** geniture **9** horoscope
natrium: NA **6** sodium
nattle: 4 gnaw **6** nibble
natty: 4 chic, neat, tidy, trig, trim **5** smart **6** spruce **10** fastidious
natural: 4 born, easy **5** usual **6** common, cretin, inborn, inbred, innate, native, normal **7** regular **8** inherent, ordinary, physical **9** primitive, unassumed, unfeigned **10** congenital **13** unenlightened
naturalize: 5 adopt **8** accustom **9** acclimate **11** acclimatize, domesticate, familiarize
nature: 4 kind, sort, type **7** essence **9** character **11** disposition, temperament
divinity: **5** nymph
god: Pan
goddess: **6** Cybele **7** Artemis
same: **10** homogeneal
naught: 4 evil, zero **5** aught, ought **6** cipher, nought, wicked **7** nothing, useless **9** worthless
naughty: bad **4** evil **5** wrong **6** wicked **7** obscene, wayward **8** improper **10** indelicate **11** disobedient, mischievous
nauntle: 4 fuss **5** raise, strut **6** potter
naupathia: 11 seasickness
nausea: 4 pall **7** disgust **8** loathing, sickness **10** queasiness
nauseating: 5 nasty, waugh **7** fulsome **8** brackish **9** loathsome, sickening **10** disgusting **11** distasteful
nautical (see also **navigation**)**: 5** naval **6** marine **7** oceanic **8** maritime
flag: **6** cornet, pennon
nautilus: 7 mollusk **9** argonauta
naval stores: tar **5** pitch **8** supplies **10** turpentine

nave: hob, hub, nef **4** apse, body, fist **5** aisle, nieve
navel: 9 umbilicus
navigate: 4 keel, sail **5** steer **6** direct, manage **7** journey, operate
navigation: 7 nautics **8** cabotage **10** seamanship
call: **4** ahoy **5** avast, belay
hazard: fog, sub **4** mine **9** submarine
instrument: aba **7** compass, pelorus, sextant
measure: ton **4** knot, seam **6** fathom **7** renning, sea mile **12** cable's length
signal: **4** bell, flag
term: **4** atry **5** abeam, atrip
navigator: 5 flyer, navvy, pilot **6** airman **7** aviator, copilot, laborer **8** aeronaut, seafarer, spaceman
navite: 6 basalt
navvy: 7 laborer **9** navigator
navy: 5 fleet
board: **9** admiralty
officer: **4** aide, mate **5** bosun **6** ensign **7** admiral, armorer, captain **8** armourer **9** commander, commodore **10** lieutenant
vessel: PT; sub **7** carrier, cruiser, flattop, gun boat **9** destroyer, submarine, transport **10** battleship
wireless operator: **6** sparks
nawab: 5 nabob, ruler **7** viceroy
nay: no; nai, not **4** deny, nyet(Russ.) **5** flute, never **6** denial, refuse **7** refusal **8** negative **11** prohibition
naysay: 6 denial **7** refusal
nayword: 6 byword **7** proverb **9** watchword
naze: 8 headland **10** promontory
Nazi: 9 Hitlerite
nazim: 7 viceroy **8** governor
neal: 6 anneal, temper
neanic: 8 immature, youthful
neap: 4 tide
near: by; gin, kin, nar(Sc.) **4** bain, dear, hend, nigh **5** anear, anent, aside, close, handy, hende **6** almost, around, beside, climax, narrow, stingy **7** advance, similar, thrifty, vicinal **8** adjacent, approach, intimate **9** niggardly, thriftily **10** contiguous, juxtaposed **11** approximate, closefisted **12** parsimonious **13** propinquitous
nearest: 4 next **5** ewest(Sc.) **7** closest **9** proximate
nearsighted: 6 myopic **12** shortsighted
neat: gim **4** cosh(Sc.), deft, dink, feil(Sc.), nice, prim, pure, snod(Sc.), snug, tidy, tosh, trig, trim **5** clean, compt, dinky, douce, natty **6** adroit, cattle, clever, dapper **7** concise, orderly, precise, refined, unmixed **8** skillful, tasteful **9** dexterous, shipshape, undiluted **10** concinnous, meticulous
neath: 5 below **7** beneath
neatherd: 7 cowherd **8** herdsman
neb: nib, tip **4** beak, bill, nose **5** snout

nebris: **8** fawnskin

nebula: sky **5** vapor **6** galaxy **10** atmosphere

nebulize: **7** atomize

nebulous: **4** hazy **5** foggy, misty, vague **6** cloudy **7** clouded, unclear **8** nebulose **10** indefinite, indistinct

necessarily: **8** perforce

necessary: **5** privy, vital **6** toilet **7** needful **8** forcible, integral **9** essential, mandatory, requisite **10** inevitable, undeniable **11** unavoidable, water-closet **13** indispensable

necessitate: **5** force, impel **6** compel, entail, oblige **7** require **9** constrain

necessity: **4** food, must, need, want **5** drink **7** ailment, poverty, urgency **8** distress **9** emergency **11** destitution

neck: pet **4** cape, crag, crop, hals, kiss **5** halse **6** caress, cervix, collum, fondle, strait **7** channel, embrace, isthmus
artery: **7** carotid
back of: **4** nape **5** nucha, nuque **6** scruff
muscle: **8** scalenus
part: **4** gula **7** withers
pert. to: **7** jugular **8** cervical
piece: bib, boa **5** amice, rabat, scarf, stole **6** collar **8** kerchief

neck and neck: tie **4** even **5** close

neckatee: **11** neckerchief

neckband: **6** collar, collet **10** collar-band

neckcloth: bib, boa **4** ruff **5** amice, choke, jabot, rabat, ruche, scarf, stole **6** choker, collar, cravat, dickey **7** bur-dash, pannelo **8** kerchief **9** barcelona **11** neckerchief

neckerchief: **4** gimp **7** belcher **8** kerchief, nectatee **12** handkerchief

necklace: **4** rope, torc **5** beads, chain, noose **6** collar, grivna, locket, torque **7** baldric, chaplet, haltern, necktie, riviere **8** baldrick, carcanet, lavalier **9** esclavage, lavaliere **10** lavalliere

necktie: bow, tie **4** band **5** ascot, scarf **6** cravat **10** four-in-hand

necktie party: **7** hanging **8** lynching

necrologue: **8** obituary

necromancy: art **5** goety, magic **7** gramary, sorcery **8** gramarye, wizardry **11** conjuration, enchantment

necropolis: **8** cemetery

necropsy: **7** autopsy

nectar: **5** honey **8** ambrosia

nectar bird: **7** sunbird

nedder: **5** adder

neddy: **6** donkey

nee: **4** born **8** formerly

need: **4** lack, want **5** crave **6** behove, demand, desire **7** behoove, poverty, require, urgency **8** distress, exigency **9** emergency, extremity, indigence, necessity, requisite **10** compulsion, dependence, obligation, retirement **11** destitution

needful: **5** vital **8** integral **9** essential **13** indispensable

needle: sew **4** acus(L.), darn **5** annoy **7** acicula, provoke, spicule **10** strengthen
combining form: acu
hole: eye
type: **4** sail **5** blunt, style **6** bodkin, stylus **7** darning, obelisk **8** knitting **10** hypodermic, phonograph, upholstery

needle bug: **7** ranatra

needle gun: **5** rifle **6** Dreyse

needlefish: gar **8** pipefish

needlelike: **6** acuate **7** acerate, acerose, acerous, aciform **8** acicular, belonoid

needleman: **6** tailor

needless: **10** gratuitous **11** superfluous, unnecessary

needlewoman: **10** seamstress

needlewood: **10** needlebush

needlework: **6** sewing **7** sampler, seaming, tatting **8** knitting **9** hemstitch **10** embroidery, crocheting

needy: **4** poor **9** penniless

neep: **6** turnip

ne'er-do-well: bum **5** losel, loser **9** schlemiel, worthless **11** incompetent

nef: **4** nave **5** clock

nefandous: **9** execrable

nefarious: **6** wicked **7** heinous, impious **8** flagrant, horrible, infamous **9** atrocious **10** detestable, iniquitous, villainous

nefast: **6** wicked

negation: not **5** empty **6** denial **7** refusal **9** annulment, blankness, nonentity **10** refutation **13** contradiction, nullification

negative: no, ne; nae(Sc.), nay, non(F.) nor, not **4** film, veto **5** minus, never **7** neutral
prefix: il, im, in, ir, un; dis, non

neglect: **4** fail, omit, slip **5** fault, forgo, shirk **6** forego, forget, ignore, slight **7** default, failure **8** omission **9** disregard, oversight, pretermit **10** negligence **11** inattention **12** inadvertence, indifference

neglectful: lax **6** remiss **8** careless, derelict, heedless **9** dissolute

negligee: **4** robe **7** undress **8** peignoir **9** nightgown **10** dishabille

negotiable: **12** transferable

negotiate: **4** deal **5** treat **6** dicker **7** bargain, chaffer, discuss **8** transact **10** accomplish

negotiation: **6** treaty **8** entreaty

negus: **8** beverage

neigh: **6** whinny

neighbor: **6** adjoin, border, fellow

neighborhood: **4** area **5** venue **6** locale, region **7** section **8** district, vicinage, vicinity **9** community, proximity, territory **11** propinquity

neighboring: **4** nigh **6** near-by **7** vicinal **8** adjacent **10** contiguous

neither: not

nema: **7** eelworm **9** roundworm

nemesis: 4 bane 7 avenger
nemoral: 6 sylvan
neophyte: 4 tyro 5 epopt 6 novice 7 amateur, convert 8 beginner 9 proselyte 10 catechumen
neoteric: new 4 late 6 modern, recent
nep: 6 catnep, catnip 7 catmint
Nepal: *city:* 5 Palan 8 Bhatgaon, Katmandu 9 Khatmandu
  cloth: 5 khadi 6 changa
  coin: 5 mohar
  mountain: 7 Everest 11 Dhawalagiri 12 Kinchinjinga
  people: Rai 4 Aoul 5 Bokra, Hindu, Limbu, Murmi, Newar, Tharu 6 Bhotia, Gurkha, Lepcha 7 Kiranti 8 Gorkhali
  river: 4 Kusi 6 Gandak 7 Karnali
  ruler: 4 Rana
  sheep: 6 bharal, nahoor, nayaur
  tree: sal 4 toon 5 sisoo
nepenthe: 7 anodyne
nephew: 6 nepote(Sc.)
nephrite: 4 jade 6 pounam 10 greenstone
nepote: 6 nephew
nepotism: 9 patronage 10 favoritism
Neptune: sea 5 ocean 6 seagod
  consort: 7 Salacia
  emblem: 7 trident
Nereides: *father:* 6 Nereus
  mother: 5 Doris
nerve: 4 grit 5 cheek, pluck, sinew, spunk, vigor 6 aplomb, daring, energy 7 courage 8 audacity, boldness, coolness, embolden, strength, temerity 9 encourage 10 brazenness, invigorate, resolution
  apparatus: 6 sensor
  cell: 5 cyton 6 cytone
  center: 8 ganglion
  combining form: 4 neur 5 neuro
  inflammation: 8 neuritis
  operation: 10 neurolysis
  pathway: 4 rete 5 hilum 8 ganglion
  pert. to: 5 neuro 6 neural
  root: 5 radix
  sensory: 8 afferent
  tissue: 7 cinerea
  tumor: 7 neuroma 9 neurinoma 11 neurocytoma 12 neuromatosis
nerve cell: 4 axon 6 neuron
  extension: 4 axon 7 neurite
  framework: 6 stroma
  process: 4 axon 5 axone 7 neurite
nerveless: 4 dead, weak 5 brave, inert 8 unnerved 9 foolhardy, powerless 10 courageous
nervous: 5 jumpy, timid 6 fidget, sinewy, touchy 7 fearful, fretful, jittery 8 neurotic, timorous 9 excitable, sensitive 10 highstrung 12 apprehensive
nervous disorder: See **mental disorder**.
nervous system: *center:* 5 brain
  description of: 11 neurography
  nomenclature: 9 neuronymy

  science: 9 neurology
nervy: 4 bold 6 brazen, sinewy, strong 7 jittery, nervous 8 impudent, vigorous 9 excitable
nescient: 7 infidel 8 agnostic, ignorant
ness: 4 cape 6 suffix 8 headland 10 promontory
nest: den, web 4 aery, bike, dray, drey, eyry, home 5 abode, aerie, eyrie, haunt, nidus, swarm 6 cuddle, hotbed 7 lodging, retreat 9 residence 10 nidificate
nester: 7 settler 8 squatter 11 homesteader
nestle: pet 4 nest 6 cuddle, pettle(Sc.) 7 cherish, shelter, snuggle
nestling: 4 baby, bird, eyas, nest 7 retreat 9 fledgling
nestor: 4 sage 7 adviser, advisor 9 counselor 10 counsellor
net: bag, gin, web 4 caul, flan, gain, lace, lawn, mesh, moke, neat, pure, rete, toil, trap, trim, weir 5 clean, clear, gauze, lacis, seize, snare, tulle, yield 6 bright, cobweb, entrap, maline, profit 7 dragnet, ensnare, network, protect, rinsing, shelter 8 meshwork 9 reticulum 10 reticulate 13 unadulterated
  fishing: lam 4 flew, flue, fyke 5 seine, trawl 6 sagene 7 trammel
  hair: 5 snood
  interstice: 4 hole, mesh
net-winged: 12 neuropteroid
nether: 5 lower, under 8 downward
Netherlands: 7 Holland
  bailiff: 6 schout
  cheese: 4 Edam 5 Gouda 7 cottage
  city: Ede 5 Asten, Breda, Hague 6 Aalten, Arnhem, Leiden 7 Commune, Haarlem, Utrecht 8 Aalsmeer 9 Amsterdam, Groningen, Rotterdam 10 Gravenhage
  coin: 4 cent, doit, raps 5 ryder 6 florin, gulden, stiver 7 ducaton, escalan, escalin, guilder, stooter 8 ducatoon 9 dubbeltje 12 rijksdaalder
  commune: Ede, Epe 5 Breda, Doorn, Hague 6 Dongen, Leyden 9 Amsterdam, Rotterdam 11 Doniawestal
  council: 7 heemrad 8 heemraad, heemraat
  fishing boat: 4 tode 6 hooker
  former colony: 4 Java 6 Borneo 7 Celebes, Sumatra 9 New Guinea
  gin: 8 schnapps
  inlet: 9 Zuider Zee
  island: 5 Texel 7 Ameland 8 Vlieland 9 Schelling
  island group: Aru 5 Arroe, Arrou
  lake: 7 Haarlem
  legislative assembly: 4 Raad
  measure: el; aam, ahm, aum, ell, kan, kop(pl.), mud, vat, zak 4 duim, lood, mijl, rood, rope, voet 5 anker, carat, roede, stoop, wisse 6 bunder, koppen,

legger, maatje, muddle, mutsje, streep **7**
leaguer, schepel **8** mimgelen, okshoofd,
steekkan **10** vingerhoed
native: **5** Dutch **8** Dutchman
painter: Lis **4** Hals, Kalf, Neer **5** Helst,
Steen **6** Leyden **7** De Houch, Hobbema,
Seghers, Vermeer **8** Kroninck, Mostaert,
Ter Borch **9** Rembrandt **10** Van de Velde
11 Van Ruisdael **19** Geertgen Tot Sint
Jans
people: **5** Dutch **7** Flemish, Frisian
possessions: **4** Saba **7** Curacao, Surinam
pottery: **4** delf **5** delft
11 Dutch Guiana, St. Eustacius
province: Epe **7** Brabant, Drenthe, Holland, Limburg, Utrecht, Zeeland **9** Friesland, Groningen **10** Gelderland, Overijssel
reclaimed land: **6** polder
river: Eem **4** Leck, Maas, Waal, Ysel **5**
Meuse, Rhine, Yssel **6** Ijssel, Kromme **7**
Scheldt
sheriff: **6** schout
town hall: **9** stadhouse
uncle: eme, oom
vessel: **4** koff **5** yanky **6** schuit, schuyt
weight: ons **4** last, lood, pond **5** bahar,
grein, pound **6** korrel **7** wichtje **8** esterlin,
9 esterling
woman: **4** frau, frow
netlike: **9** reticular
netop: **5** crony **6** friend **9** companion
netting: **4** lint, mesh **7** network
nettle: vex **4** fret, line **5** annoy, cnida, ettle, peeve, pique, sting **6** henbit, ruffle,
splice **7** affront, blubber, knittle, provoke
8 irritant, irritate **9** urticacea **10**
exasperate
nettle cell: **10** nematocyst
family: **10** Urticaceae
genus of: **10** parietaria
network (see also **net**): **6** plexus, reseau
neume: **6** pneuma
neural: **6** dorsal
neuralgia: **9** costalgia
neuter: **6** gender **7** neither, neutral, sexless **9** impartial
neutral: **4** gray **8** middling, negative **9**
colorless **10** achromatic, indefinite **11**
adiaphorous, indifferent **12** noncombatant
neutralize: **5** annul **7** abolish, balance,
destroy, nullify, vitiate **9** frustrate **10**
counteract **11** countervail **14** counterbalance
neutralizer: **6** alkali
Nevada: *lake:* **5** Tahoe
town: Ely **4** Elko, Reno **6** Carson, Fallon,
Minden, Sparks **7** Sulphur **8** Lovelock,
Mesquite **9** Henderson **10** Winnemucca
neve: **4** firn **6** nephew **7** glacier
never: nay, nie(G.), not **4** nary, ne'er
nevertheless: but, yet **5** still **7** how-be-it,
however **9** howsoever, natheless **10** howsomever

nevus: **4** mole **5** tumor **7** spiloma **9** birthmark
new: neu(G.) **4** late, nova(L.) **5** fresh,
green, novel **6** modern, recent, unused **7**
foreign, strange, untried **8** neoteric, original, untested **10** additional, promethean,
unfamiliar **11** fashionable, modernistic
12 unaccustomed **13** inexperienced
combining form: neo
prefix: neo
New Caledonia: *bird:* **4** kagu
seaport: **5** Numea
New England: *inhabitant:* **6** Yankee
of the West: **9** Minnesota
settler: **7** Pilgrim, Puritan
New Guinea: *bay:* Oro
city: Lae **4** Daru **5** Soron **6** Rabaul
export: **5** copra
gulf: **4** Huon **5** Papua
hog: **4** bene
island: Aru **5** Ceram
island group: **7** Solomon
mountain: **6** Albert **8** Victoria **9** Car-
stensz **10** Wilhelmina
parrot: **4** lory
people: **5** Karon **6** Papuan
port: Lae **4** Daru
river: Fly **5** Sepik **7** Amberno **10** Strick-
land **15** Kaiserin Augusta
section: **8** Bunagona
New Hampshire: *academy:* **6** Exeter
city: **5** Dover, Keene **6** Antrim, Exeter,
Nashua **7** Hanover, Laconia
county: **4** Coos
lake: **7** Sunapee
river: **4** Saco
state flower: **5** lilac
New Jersey: *city:* **6** Verona **7** Bayonne,
Raritan, Trenton
river: **6** Ramapo **7** Raritan
New Mexico: *county:* **4** Mora, Taos
resort: **4** Taos
river: **4** Gila **5** Pecos
state flower: **5** yucca
New Testament (see also **Bible**):
book: **4** Acts, John, Jude, Luke, Mark **5**
James, Peter, Titus **6** Romans **7** Hebrews, Matthew, Timothy **8** Philemon **9**
Ephesians, Galatians **10** Colossians,
Revelation **11** Corinthians, Philippians
13 Thessalonians
gospel: **4** John, Luke, Mark **7** Matthew
letter: **7** epistle
New York: *canal:* **4** Erie
city: Rye **4** Avon, Erie, Rome, Troy **5** Ilion, Nyack, Olean, Owego, Tioga, Utica **6**
Albany, Cohoes, Elmira, Esopus, Geneva,
Goshen, Gotham, Ithaca, Malone, Oneida,
Oswego **7** Buffalo, Endwell **8** Saratoga
11 Binghampton, Skaneateles **12** Niagara Falls
county: **4** Erie **5** Tioga, Wayne, Yates **6**
Cayuga, Monroe, Oneida, Oswego, Sen-
eca **7** Chemung, Genesee, Niagara, Ontario, Orleans, Steuben, Tompkin, Wyo-

ming **8** Allegany, Onondaga, Schuyler **9** Chatauqua, Courtland **10** Livingston **11** Cattaraugus

early land owner: **7** patroon

harbor entrance: **14** Ambrose channel

lake: **6** Cayuga, Croton, Oneida, Seneca **7** Saranac **8** Onondaga **11** Skaneateles

law: **6** Baumes

resort: **7** Saranac

river: **5** Tioga **6** Harlem, Hudson **7** Genesee, Niagara **8** Canisteo, Cohocton

state flower: **4** rose

university: **7** Colgate, Cornell **8** Columbia

New York City: **6** Gotham

island: **5** Ellis **6** Staten **7** Bedloes, Liberty, Welfare **9** Governors, Manhattan **10** Blackwells

prison: **5** Tombs

street: **4** Wall **6** Bowery

New Zealand: *anteater:* **7** echidna

bird: kea, moa, oii, poe, roa **4** kaka, kiwi, koko, kulu, ruru, titi, weka **6** kakapo **7** apteryx, wrybill **8** morepork, notornis

city: see *town* below

clay: **4** papa

fern: **4** weki **5** pitau, wheki

fish: ihi **5** hikus

flax: **8** harakeke

fort: pa; pah, pau

grass: **6** toetoe

gun: **6** tupara

heron: **6** kotuku

hut: **5** whare

island: **4** Otea **7** Stewart

kiwi: moa, roa **7** apteryx

lake: Ada **4** Gunn, Ohau, Rere **5** Hawea, Okaro, Taupo **6** Fergus, Pukaki, Rotoma. Sylvan, Teanau, Tekapo, Wanaka **7** Brunner, Diamond, Kanieri, Okareka, Rotoiti, Rotoroa, Rotorua **8** Okataina, Paradise, Rotoaira, Tarawera, Wakatipu **9** Manapouri, Rotokawau **10** Rotomahana **12** Rerewhakaitu, Waikaremoana

mahogany: **6** totara

mountain: **4** Cook **5** Ohope **6** Egmont **7** Aorangi, Pihanga, Raupehu, Ruapehu, Tauhara, Tauhera **8** Aspiring, Tarawera, Tauranga **9** Blackburn, Messenger, Ngauruhoe, Tongariro **10** Ngongotaha, Tapuaenuka

national bird: **4** kiwi

ostrich: moa

owl: **4** ruru

palm: **5** nikau

parrot: kea **4** kaka **6** kakapo

people: Ati **5** Arawa, Maori **7** Ringatu

pine: **4** rima **6** totara **9** kahikatea

port: Lae **7** Aukland, Dunedin **10** Wellington

reptile: **7** tuatara, tuatera

river: **7** Waikato **8** Wanganui **9** Taramakau, Tongariro, Whakapapa **10** Rangitikei **11** Waimakariri

settlement: pa; pah, pau

shark: **4** mako

song: **6** waiata

spa: **5** Aroha **7** Rotorua, Tearoha

storehouse: **5** whata

town: **5** Levin, Otaki, Taupo **6** Foxton, Napier, Nelson, Oamaru, Picton, Timaru **7** Dunedin, Raetihi, Rotorua **8** Auckland, Gisborne, Hamilton, Hastings, Tauranga, Wanganui **9** Ashburton, Greymouth, Masterton, Whangarei **10** Dannenirke, Palmerston, Queenstown, Wellington **12** Christchurch, Invercargill

tree: ake **4** mako, miro, pelu, puka, rata, rimu, tawa, toro, toru, whau **5** hinau, hinou, kauri, mahoe, maire, mapau, ngaio **6** ake-ake, karaka, kowhai, manuka, puriri, tarata, titoki **7** akepiro, taratah, wahahen **8** hiropito, makomako **9** kaiwhiria **10** pohutukawa

vine: aka

volcano: **6** Egmont **7** Ruapehu **9** Ngauruhoe

wages: utu

welcome: **8** haeremai

newcomer: **7** settler **8** comeling **9** immigrant

newel: **4** post

newfangled: **5** novel **6** modern

newly: **4** anew **5** again **6** afresh, lately **8** recently

news: **4** word **6** notice **7** tidings **11** information, instruction **12** intelligence

agency: AP, UP; DNB, INS, UPI **4** Tass(Russ.) **5** Domei **7** Reuters **13** International

gatherer: **8** reporter

media: TV **5** radio **7** journal **8** magazine **9** newspaper **10** periodical, television

statement: **8** bulletin

newsboy: **7** camelot

newsmonger: **6** gossip **7** tattler **8** reporter

newspaper: **4** News **5** daily, paper, sheet, Times **6** Herald **7** courant, Gazette, Mercury, tabloid, Tribune **9** newsprint **11** publication

article: **4** item

collectively: **5** press

employee: **6** editor **7** printer **8** pressman, reporter **9** columnist, linotyper **10** cartoonist, compositor, journalist **12** photographer **13** correspondent

file: **6** morgue

hoax: **6** canard

part of: ear **6** banner, sports **8** obituary **9** editorial

newsstand: **5** booth, kiosk, stall

newt: ask, eft **4** evet **6** lizard, triton **7** axolotl **10** salamander

next: **4** then **5** after, ewest(Sc.), neist(Sc.) **7** closest, ensuing, nearest **9** adjoining, following, immediate, proximate **10** contiguous, succeeding **12** conterminous

next to: **6** almost, beside, nearly **8** adjacent

nexus: tie **4** link **10** connection **15** interconnection

nib: pen **4** beak, bill **5** point, prong
nibble: eat, nab **4** bite, gnaw, knap **6** browse **7** chimble, gnabble, gnatter
Nicaragua: *city:* **4** Leon **6** Masaya **7** Granada, Managua **9** Choluteca **10** Chinandega
coin: **4** peso **7** centavo, cordoba
lake: **7** Managua
measure: **4** vara **5** cahiz, milla **6** suerte, tercia **7** cajuela, estadal, manzana **10** cabelleria
river: **4** Coco, Tuma **5** Wanks **7** San Juan
weight: bag **4** caja **8** tonelada
nice: **4** fine, good **5** exact **6** bonita, dainty, minute, peachy, queasy, subtle **7** elegant, finical, genteel, precise, prudish, refined **8** delicate, exacting, pleasant, pleasing **9** agreeable, appealing, exquisite, squeamish **10** appetizing, delightful, discerning, fastidious, particular, scrupulous **11** considerate, punctilious, scrumptious **13** hypercritical **14** discriminating
niche: **4** apse, nook **6** alcove, covert, recess **7** edicule, retreat **9** habitacle
nick: cut, nob **4** chip, slit **5** cheat, notch, tally, trick **6** arrest, record **7** defraud **9** indention
nickel alloy: **5** invar
nickel compound: **8** argenton
nickelodeon: **7** jukebox
nickname: **6** agname, byword **7** misname, moniker **8** cognomen, monicker **9** sobriquet **10** soubriquet
nicknaming: **12** prosonomasia
nictate: **4** wink **5** blink, twink **7** twinkle **9** nictitate
niddick: **4** nape
nide: **5** brood
nidge: **5** shake **6** quiver
nidget: **4** fool **5** idiot
nidification: **7** nesting
nidor: **5** aroma, savor, scent
nidus: **4** nest
nieve: **4** fist, hand, neif
niff-naff: **6** trifle
nifty: **4** good **5** smart **7** stylish
Nigeria: *people:* Aro, Ebo, Edo, Ibo, Ijo, Vai **4** Beni, Eboe, Efik, Ejam, Ekoi, Nupe **5** Benin
port: **5** Lagos **7** Calabar
province: Isa **4** Nupe, Ondo **5** Warri
river: Oli
town: Aba, Ede, Isa **4** Bidi, Offa **5** Lagos **6** Ibadan, Yakoba **9** Ogbomosho
tree: **5** afara
niggard: **8** scrimper **9** skinflint **10** curmudgeon
niggardly: **4** mean **5** close **6** narrow, scanty, stingy **7** miserly **8** churlish, wretched **10** avaricious **11** closefisted **12** parsimonious
niggle: **6** potter, putter, trifle
nigh: at **4** near **5** close **6** almost, nearly **8** adjacent **10** contiguous **11** neighboring
night: **4** nuit(F.) **8** darkness

goddess: Nox, Nyx
pert. to: **9** nocturnal
night bird: **10** shearwater **11** nightingale
night blindness: **10** nyctalopia
night-wandering: **11** noctivagant
nightcap: **6** biggin
nightchurr: **10** goatsucker
nightclub: **7** cabaret
nightfall: een, eve **4** dusk, even **8** twilight
nightingale: **8** philomel **9** philomela
nightjar: **5** potoo **9** nighthawk **10** goatsucker
nightmare: **5** dream, fiend **7** incubus **9** cauchemar(F.), ephialtes
nightshade: **5** morel **7** henbane, morelle **10** belladonna **11** bittersweet
nigrescent: **9** blackfish
nihil: **7** nothing
nihilist: **9** anarchist
nil: **4** zero **7** nothing
Nile: *bird:* **4** ibis **7** wryneck
boat: **5** baris **6** nuggar **8** dahabeah
captain: **4** rais, reis
dam: **5** Aswan
falls: **5** Ripon
fish: **5** saide **8** mormyrid **9** mormyroid
houseboat: **8** dahabeah
island: **4** Roda
people: **4** Madi **5** Nilot
plant: **4** sudd **5** lotus
reptile: **9** crocodile
river gauge: **9** nilometer
town: **5** Cairo, Rejaf **7** Rosetta
tributary: **6** Atbara, Kagera
nilgai: **8** antelope
nim tree: **4** neem **7** margosa
nimb: **4** halo
nimble: **4** deft, lish, spry **5** agile, alert, fleet, quick **6** active, adroit, clever, feirie, lissom, lively, prompt, volant **9** dexterous **11** quick-witted
nimbly: **6** featly **9** deliverly
nimbose: **6** cloudy, stormy
nimbus: **4** halo **5** cloud, vapor **6** gloria **7** aureole **10** atmosphere
nimiety: **6** excess **10** redundancy
nimmer: **5** thief
nimrod: **5** ruler **6** hunter, tyrant
nimshi: **4** fool **7** halfwit
nincompoop: **4** dolt, fool **5** moron, ninny **9** simpleton
nine: **6** ennead **8** ninefold
based on: **8** novenary
nine-eyes: **7** lamprey
nine-killer: **6** shrike
ninepin: **6** kayles **7** skittle **8** skittles
ninny: See **nincompoop**.
ninth: **5** nonus(L.)
ninut: **6** magpie
Niobe: *brother:* **6** Pelops
father: **8** Tantalus
husband: **7** Amphion
sister-in-law: **5** Aedon
nip: cut, sip **4** bite, clip, dram, tang **5** check, clamp, draft, drink, frost, pinch,

seize, sever, steal, sting **6** blight, catnip, snatch, tipple, twitch **7** squeeze **8** compress **10** pickpocket

nipa: 4 atap, palm **5** attap, drink **6** liquor

nipcheese: 5 miser **6** purser

nipper: boy, lad **4** claw, grab **5** biter **6** cunner, pliers, urchin **7** forceps, incisor, pincers **8** pincenez **9** handcuffs **10** eyeglasses

Nippon: See **Japan.**

nippy: 5 brisk, quick, sharp **6** active, biting, nimble **7** nipping **8** vigorous

nisse: 6 goblin, kobold, sprite **7** brownie

nisus: 6 effort **7** impulse **8** endeavor, striving

Nisus' daughter: 6 Scylla

nit: egg, nut **5** speck **6** insect **8** hazelnut

niter, nitre: 5 peter, petre **6** potash **9** saltpeter
  combining form: **5** nitro

nither: 5 blast **6** debase, shiver **7** tremble **9** humiliate

nithing: 6 coward **7** dastard

nitid: 6 bright, glossy **7** glowing, radiant **8** lustrous, nitidous

nitrate: 4 salt **5** ester
  sodium: **5** niter, nitre

nitrocotton: 9 guncotton

nitroform: 15 trinitromethane

nitrogen: 9 quinoline
  combining form: az; azo
  compound: **7** ammonia

niveau: 5 level

nivenite: 9 uraninite

niveous: 5 snowy **8** snowlike

nix: no **6** goblin, nobody, sprite **7** nothing

Njorth: *daughter:* **5** Freya **6** Freyja
  son: **4** Frey **5** Freyr
  wife: **6** Skathi

no: na(Sc.), ne; nae(Sc.), naw, nay, nea(Sc.), nit, nix, non(F.) **4** nein(G.), nyet(Russ.), play **5** drama **6** denial **7** refusal

no one: nix **6** nobody

Noah: *dove:* **7** Columba
  grandson: **4** Aram
  great-grandson: Uz; Hul
  place of debarkation: **6** Ararat
  raven: **6** Corvus
  son: Ham, Sem **4** Shem **7** Japheth
  wine cup: **6** Crater

nob: 4 head, jack

nobble: 5 bribe, cheat, steal **7** swindle **12** incapacitate

nobby: 4 chic **5** swell **7** stylish **9** excellent, first-rate **11** fashionable

noble: 4 epic, fine, free, gent, good, pure, rial **5** burly, ducal, grand, ideal, lofty, manly, proud **6** august, epical, famous, heroic **7** eminent, exalted, gallant, liberal, soulful, stately, sublime **8** elevated, generous, glorious, nobleman, precious, renowned, splendid **9** chevalier, dignified, excellent, honorable **10** idealistic, noblewoman **11** illustrious, magnanimous, magnificent

noble pine: 10 pipsissewa

nobleman: don **4** duke, earl, lord, peer **5** barin(Russ.), baron, count **6** knight, varlet **7** grandee(Sp.), hidalgo, marquis **8** marquess **10** aristocrat
  pert. to: **5** ducal **6** lordly

noblewoman: 4 lady **7** duchess, peeress **8** baroness, countess, marquise **10** marquiess **11** marchioness

nobody: 4 none **9** nonentity

nocent: 6 guilty **7** harmful, hurtful, noxious **8** criminal

noctambulism: 12 somnambulism

noctule: bat

nocturnal: 5 night **7** nightly **11** nightwalker

nocturne: 7 lullaby **8** serenade

nocuous: See **noxious, poisonous.**

nod: bow **4** beck, bend, doze, wink **5** droop **6** assent, beckon, drowse, nutate, salute **7** signify **8** nutation

nodding: 6 nutant **7** annuent **8** cernuous

noddy: auk **4** fool **5** ninny **6** fulmar, noodle **7** hackney **9** simpleton

node: bow **4** bump, knob, knot, lump **5** joint, nodus **6** nodule **7** dilemma, granule **8** swelling, tubercle **10** difficulty **12** complication, protuberance

nodule: 4 auge, node **5** geode **7** noblock **9** septarium

noel: 5 carol **9** Christmas

noetic: 12 intellectual

nog: ale, peg, pin **5** block **6** eggnog, noggin **8** beverage, treenail

noggin (see also **noodle**): cup, mug, nog **4** pate

noir: 5 black

noise (see also **sound**): air, din **5** bruit, rumor **6** gossip, norate, report

noiseless: 5 quiet, still, tacit **6** silent **7** catlike

noisemaker: 4 bell, horn **6** rattle

noisette: 5 hazel

noisome (see also **noxious**): **4** foul **5** fetid **7** harmful, hurtful **8** stinking **9** offensive **10** disgusting, malodorous, pernicious **11** destructive, unwholesome

noisy: 4 loud **6** clashy **7** blatant **8** brawling, clattery, strepent **9** clamorous, hilarious, turbulent **10** boisterous, tumultuous, vociferous **12** obstreperous

noll: See **noodle.**

nom: 4 name **10** nominative

nom de plume: 7 pen name **9** pseudonym

noma: 5 ulcer

nomad: 4 Arab, Luri, Moor **5** Alani, gypsy, rover **6** roamer, roving **7** Bedouin, Saracen, scenite **8** wanderer

nomadic: 9 itinerant

nomadism: 10 wanderlust

nome: 4 Elis **5** nomos **8** nomarchy, province **10** department

nomen: 4 gens, name

nomenclature: 4 list, name **8** glossary, register **9** catalogue, recounter **10** dictionary, vocabulary **11** appellation, designation

nomic: 8 ordinary **9** customary **12** conventional

nominal: 6 slight, unreal **7** titular, trivial **8** platonic **11** theoretical **13** unsubstantial

nominalist: 8 Occamist **9** terminist

nominate: 4 call, leet(Sc.), name **5** slate **7** appoint, entitle, propose, specify **10** denominate

nominee: 9 candidate

non-kosher: 4 tref

non-Mahometan: 5 Kafir

nomothetical: 11 legislative

nonage: 10 immaturity **12** youthfulness

nonaspirate: 4 lene

nonbeliever: 5 pagan **7** atheist **8** agnostic

nonce: 7 present **8** occasion

noncentric: 8 acentric

nonchalant: 4 cool **6** casual **8** careless **10** insouciant **11** indifferent **13** imperturbable

noncleric: 4 lay **4** laic

noncombatant: 8 chaplain, civilian, observer

noncompliance: 7 refusal **10** obstinance **13** recalcitrance

nonconcurrence: 7 dissent

nonconductor: 5 resin

nonconforming: 9 anomalous

nonconformity: 6 heresy **7** dissent **9** recusance, recusancy **10** dissidence **13** individualism

nondependent: 11 independent

nondescript: 13 indescribable **14** indeterminable

none: no; nae **4** nane(Sc.), neen

nonentity: 4 zero **6** cipher **7** nothing

nonessential: 9 extrinsic **10** adiaphoron **11** unnecessary **12** adventitious **14** circumstantial

nonesuch: 5 apple, model **7** paragon **8** paradigm **9** matchless, nonpariel, unequaled, unrivaled

nonexistent: 4 null **8** nonbeing

nonfestal: 6 ferial

nonfulfillment: 6 breach **12** infringement

nongrata: 9 unwelcome

nongypsy: 4 gajo

nonobjective: 8 abstract

nonobservance: 9 violation

nonpareil: 4 best **7** paragon, perfect, unequal **8** nonesuch, peerless **9** unrivaled

nonphysical: 7 psychic **9** psychical

nonplus: 5 blank, stump, trump **6** puzzle **7** perplex **9** embarrass

nonpositive: 8 negative **9** privative

nonproductive: 6 barren **7** sterile **10** unfruitful

nonprofessional: lay **4** laic **7** amateur

nonsense: bah, pah, rot **4** blah, bosh, buff, bunk, flam, tosh **5** blash, folly, fudge,

haver, hooey, stite(Sc) **6** bunkum, drivel, faddle, folder **7** blarney, blather, buncome, inanity, twaddle **8** blahblah, blathery, falderal, falderol, flimflam, trumpery **9** absurdity, fandangle, frivolity, moonshine, poppycock, silliness **10** balderdash, flapdoodle, flumdiddle, galimatias, triviality **11** flumadiddle, foolishness, monkeyshine **12** fiddle-dee-dee, flummadiddle, flummydiddle **16** preposterousness

nonsolid: 5 fluid **6** liquid

noodle: 4 bean, fool, head, nizy, noll, pate **5** ninny, nizey, noddy **6** boodle, noddle, noggin **9** blockhead, simpleton **10** caper-nutie **11** caper-noitie

nook: in; out, wro **4** cant, cove, glen, hole **5** angle, herne, niche **6** cantle, corner, cranny, recess **7** crevice, retreat

noon: 6 midday **8** meridian **11** culmination

noose: tie **4** bond, dull, grin, loop, trap **5** bight, grane, honda, snare, widdy **6** entrap, halter, lariat **7** ensnare, execute, laniard, lanyard, springe **8** slip-knot
armed with: **10** laquearian

nope: 9 bullfinch

nor: ner **7** neither **8** negative **10** connective

norate: 5 noise, rumor **6** gossip

nori: 4 alga **7** seaweed

noria: 5 wheel

norie: 9 cormorant

norite: 6 gabbro

norm: 4 rule, type **5** gauge, model, norma **7** average, pattern **8** standard, template

normal: 5 usual **7** natural, regular, typical

Normandy: *beach:* **5** Omaha
capital: **4** Caen **5** Rouen
conqueror: **5** Rollo **10** Eisenhower
department: **4** Eure, Orne **6** Manche **8** Calvados
duke: **5** Rollo

Norn: 4 fate, Urth, Wyrd **5** Skuld **9** Verthandi

Norse (see also **Scandinavia**)**: 4** mink **8** Teutonic **9** Icelandic, Norwegian **12** Scandinavian
alphabet: **5** runic
bard: **5** scald, skald **7** sagaman
chieftain: **4** jarl
demon: **4** Surt **5** Surtr
epic: **4** Edda
explorer: **4** Eric
fate: **4** Norn
first man: **4** Askr
giant: **4** Atli, Loke, Loki, Natt, Norn, Nott, Ymer, Ymir **5** Jotun, Mimer, Mimir, Thrym **6** Fafnir, Jotunn
god (see also *giant* above)**:** As, Ve; Asa, Ase, Ran, Tiu, Tyr, Ull **4** Frey, Hler, Loke, Loki, Odin, Surt, Thor, Vali **5** Aeger, Aegir, Aesir(pl.), Baldr, Brage, Bragi, Donar, Freyr, Gymir, Othin, Surtr,

Vanir(pl.), Woden **6** Balder, Hoenir, Njorth **7** Forsete, Forseti, Heimdal, Vitharr **9** Heimdallr, Hlorrithi
goddess: Dis, Eir, Hel **4** Hela, Nora, Saga, Urth, Wyrd **5** Freya, Frigg, Nanna **6** Freyja, Frigga **7** Asynjur
poem: **4** rune
saint: **4** Olaf **5** Olaus
sea serpent: **6** Kraken **7** Midgard
toast: **5** skoal
viking: **5** Rollo
watchdog: **4** Garm **5** Garmr
norsel: **4** band, line **6** fillet
North Africa: *antelope:* **5** addax **7** gazelle
country: **7** Algeria, Tunisia
fruit: fig **4** date
lyre: **6** kissar
measure: **4** rotl
oasis: **4** wadi, wady
people: **4** Moor **5** Nilot **6** Hamite
port: **4** Sfax
sheep: **6** aoudad
valley: **4** wadi, wady
North America: *bird:* **6** fulmar **7** grackle **8** cardinal, killdeer, kingrail **10** bufflehead
discoverer: **5** Cabot
herb: **4** sego
Indian: see **Indian**
marmoset: **7** tamarin
mountain: **5** Logan **8** McKinley
orchids: **9** arethusas
owl: **7** wapacut
people: **7** Mexican **8** American, Canadian
reindeer: **7** caribou
thrush: **5** robin
tree: lin **4** mabi, sorb, titi **5** balsa, papaw **6** balsam, pawpaw, redbud, tupelo **7** catalpa, hickory **8** basswood, oneberry, sweetsop **9** sassafras
North Atlantic: *island:* **7** Britain, Iceland, Ireland **9** Manhattan
seagull: **4** skua
North Britain: **8** Scotland **9** Caledonia
North Carolina: *cape:* **4** Fear **8** Hatteras
county: **4** Ashe **5** Anson, Avery **6** Lenoir
people: **7** Buffalo, Tarheel
river: Tar **5** Neuse **6** Pee Dee
town: **5** Boone **6** Durham, Lenoir, Oxford, Whynot **7** Edenton, Raleigh, Roxboro
North Dakota: *city:* **5** Fargo, Minot
county: **6** Traill
North Sea: *arm:* **9** Skagerrak, Skager-Rak
canal: **4** Kiel
river: **5** Weser
North Star: **7** polaris **8** loadstar, lodestar, polestar **10** tramontane
north wind: **6** boreas
northeaster: **4** blow, gale, wind **5** storm
northern: **6** boreal **13** septentrional
Northern Bear: **6** Russia
Northmen: See **Norse.**
Norway: *bird:* **4** rype
boat: **4** pram **5** praam **6** praham
capital: **4** Oslo

cart: **11** stolkjaerre
chieftain: **4** jarl
coin: ore **5** krone
counties: **5** amter
county: amt **5** fylke **6** fylker(pl.), Tromso **7** Finmark
dance: **7** halling
embroidery: **9** hardanger
goblin: **5** nisse **6** kobold
governor: **6** amtman
haddock: **8** rosefish
inlet: **5** fiord, fjord
language: **5** Norse
measure: fot, mal, pot **4** alen, maal **5** kande **6** fathom **7** skieppe **9** korntonde
mountain: **5** Sogne **6** Kjolen **7** Numedal **8** Telemark, Ustetind **9** Blodfjell, Harteigen, Ramnanosi **10** Galdhoepig, Glitretind, Hallingdal, Vibmesnosi **11** Myrdalfjell **14** Hallingskarvet, Hardangerjokul, Skagastolstind
parliament: **8** Storting **9** Storthing
plateau: **5** Dovre, fjeld **9** Hardanger
river: Oi; Ena **4** Tana **6** Lougen, Glomma
ruler: **6** hersir
saint: **4** Olaf **5** Olaus
town: Nes **4** Oslo(c.), Voss **5** Bjort, Skein, Skjak **6** Bergen, Horten, Larvik, Narvik **7** Alesund, Drammen **9** Stavanger, Trondhjem **10** Kristiania(c.) **11** Christiania(c.)
weight: lod **4** mark, pund **9** skaalpund **10** bismerpund
nose: neb, pry, spy **4** beak, conk, lora(pl.) **5** lorum, scent, smell, sniff, snoop, snout **6** detect, muffle, muzzle, nozzle, search, socket **7** advance, perfume **8** discover, informer, perceive **9** proboscis **11** investigate
cartilage: **6** septum
inflammation: **6** coryza **8** rhinitis
large: **6** nasute
medicine: **7** errhine
muscle: **7** nasalio
openings: **5** nares
partition: **5** vomer
pert. to: **5** nasal **6** narial, rhinal
snub: **6** simous
nosebleed: **9** epistaxis
nosegay: **4** odor, posy **5** scent **6** boquet **7** bouquet, perfume
nosegay tree: **10** frangipani
nosepiece: **5** nasal **6** nozzle **8** noseband
nosey: See **nosy.**
nosocomium: **8** hospital
nostalgia: **7** longing **10** melancholy **12** homesickness
nostic: **12** paragerontic
nostradamus: **4** seer **7** prophet **10** forecaster
nostril: **4** nare **5** nares(pl.), naris(pl.) **6** thrill
pert. to: **5** naric **6** narial, narine
nostril-shaped: **8** nariform

nosy: **6** prying **7** curious **8** fragrant **10** malodorous **11** inquisitive

not (see also **non**): na(Sc.); nae(Sc.), nay, nor **4** baal, bail, bale, nott **5** shorn **6** nought, polled, shaven **7** neither **8** hornless, negation, negative **11** nothingness

any: no; nul **4** nane(Sc.), nary, none

at all: **5** never **6** noways, nowise

either: **7** neither

final: **13** interlocutory

otherwise than: **6** merely

prefix: il, im, ir, un: non

the same: **5** other **7** another **9** different

notable: V.I.P. **6** fabled, famous **7** eminent, storied **8** eventful, historic **9** memorable, notorious **10** noteworthy, remarkable **12** considerable **13** distinguished, extraordinary

notal: **6** dorsal

notandum: **4** note **5** entry **9** memoranda(pl.) **10** memorandum

notar: **6** notary

notarize: **6** attest **7** certify

notary: **5** notar(Sc.), noter **7** graffer, notable **8** notebook, observer, official **9** notorious, scrivener

chief: **11** protonotary **12** prothonotary

notation: **4** memo, note **7** marking **10** annotation **14** representation

phonetic: **5** Romic

notator: **5** noter **8** recorder **9** annotator

notch: cut, dag, gap, hag, jag **4** cope, dent, dint, gimp, hila(pl.), nick, step **5** crena, grade, hilum, score, tally **6** crenae(pl.), crotch, defile, degree, indent, record, scotch **7** crenate, serrate **8** undercut **9** indenture **11** indentation

notched: **5** erose

note: I.O.U., jot, see **4** bill, chit, fame, heed, line, mark, memo, name, sign, sole, song, tone, tune **5** label, sound, token **6** billet, letter, minute, notice, record, regard, remark, renown, report **7** betoken, comment, message, missive, notanda(pl.), observe **8** annotate, breviate, dispatch, eminence, notandum, perceive **9** character **10** indication, memorandum, prominence, reputation **11** distinction, observation

accompanying: **8** overtone

bank: **6** finnip, flimsy **8** frogskin

bugle: mot

explanatory: **8** scholium **10** annotation

highest: ela

marginal: **6** postil **7** apostil **9** apostille

middle: **4** mese

prisoner's: **4** kite

promissory: bon

writer: **9** annotater

note well: N.B.(L.) **8** nota bene(L.)

notebook: log **5** diary **6** street **7** journal **10** adversaria

notecase: **10** pocketbook

noted: **9** distingue, well-known **10** celebrated **11** illustrious

notes: *literary:* ana

miscellaneous: **10** adversaria

noteworthy: **7** eminent, notable **10** remarkable **11** outstanding **12** considerable

nothing: nil **4** free, luke, nill, zero **5** aught, nihil **6** naught, nought, trifle **7** useless **10** triviality **12** nonexistence, unimportance **14** insignificance

nothing but: **4** mere, only

nothous: **8** spurious **12** illegitimate

notice: ad; ban, see **4** espy, heed, idea, mark, mind, news, note, sign **5** await, quote **6** advice, billet, espial, notion, regard, remark **7** affiche, article, discern, mention, observe, warning **8** apprisal, citation, civility **9** attention **10** cognizance, intimation **11** garnishment **12** announcement, intelligence, notification **13** consideration

book: **5** blurb

death: **4** obit **8** obituary

favorable: **4** rave

honorable: **8** citation

leave of: **8** mittimus

marriage: ban **4** bans **5** banns

official: **5** edict **8** bulletin **12** proclamation

paid: ad **13** advertisement

Patent Office: **6** caveat

refuse: **6** ignore

noticeable: **7** evident, notable, salient **8** striking **9** prominent **10** noteworthy, remarkable **11** conspicuous, outstanding, significant

notification: **6** notice

notify: bid **4** cite, page, tell, warn **6** inform **7** apprise, declare, frutify, publish **8** acquaint

notion: bee **4** buzz, idea, idee, view, whim **5** fancy, image **6** belief, desire, maggot, notice, theory, vagary **7** conceit, inkling, opinion, thought **9** intention **10** conception **11** inclination

notoriety: **5** eclat **9** publicity

notorious: big **5** known **6** arrant, crying, famous, notour **7** evident **8** apparent, flagrant, infamous, manifest **11** conspicuous

notum: **4** back

notus: **9** southwind

notwithstanding: yet **4** even **6** algate, mauger, maugre **7** algates, despite, however **8** although **12** nevertheless

nought: bad, nil **4** zero **5** wrong **7** nothing, useless **9** worthless **10** wickedness

noun: **4** name, word **11** substantive

indeclinable: **6** aptote

kind of: **6** common, proper

suffix: ac, et, ia, ic; ent, ery, ial, ier, ing, ion, ior, ist **4** ence **5** orium

verbal: **6** gerund

nourish: **4** feed, grow **5** breed, nurse **6**

foison, foster, suckle, supply **7** cherish, support, sustain, develop **9** cultivate, stimulate

nourishing: 4 alma **6** alible, hearty **8** nutrient **9** alimental, nutritive **10** alimentary

nourishment: 4 food, meat **5** manna **6** foison **7** aliment, pabulum **9** nutriment **10** sustenance **13** nutritiveness **14** nutritiousness

nous: 4 mind **6** reason **9** intellect

nova: new

Nova Scotia: 6 Acadia, Acadie
mountain ash: **8** dogberry
people: **8** Acadians **9** bluenoses

novel: new **4** book **5** fresh, story **6** recent **7** fiction, romance, strange, unusual **8** original, uncommon **10** newfangled
cut: **11** abridgment **12** condensation

novelette: 5 conte

novelty: fad **6** change **10** innovation

novice: dub **4** puny, tiro, tyro **5** rooky **6** rookie, tyrone **7** amateur, convert, learner **8** beginner, freshman, neophyte **9** greenhorn **10** apprentice **11** abecedarian

novitiate: 9 probation **14** apprenticeship

now: noo(Sc.) **4** here **5** today **7** present **9** forthwith **11** immediately

nowise: 5 navis

nowt: ox **4** lout, oxen **6** cattle **7** bullock **9** blockhead

noxious: ill **4** evil **6** nocent **7** baneful, harmful, hurtful, nocuous, noisome, vicious **8** virulent **9** injurious, miasmatic, poisonous **10** pernicious **11** deleterious, destructive, unwholesome **12** insalubrious

noy: 4 harm **5** annoy

nozzle: 4 nose, vent **5** snout

nuance: 5 shade

nub: 4 core, crux, gist, hang, knob, knot, knub, lump, neck, snag **12** protuberance

nubia: 4 wrap **5** cloud

nubile: 12 marriageable

nubilous: 5 foggy, misty, vague **6** cloudy **7** obscure **10** indefinite

nucament: 5 ament

nucha: 4 nape

nucleus: 4 core **5** focus, umbra **6** kernel
pert. to: **8** nucleate
starch: **4** hila(pl.) **5** hilum

nude: 4 bare **5** model, naked **6** statue **7** denuded, picture **8** painting, stripped **9** unclothed, uncovered, undressed

nudge: jog, nog **4** knub, lump, poke, push **5** block, elbow

nudist: 7 Adamite **12** gymnosophist

nugatory: 4 vain **7** invalid, trivial **8** trifling **9** frustrate, worthless **11** ineffectual

nugget: 4 hunk, lump, mass, slug

nuisance: 4 harm, hurt, pest **6** injury **9** annoyance **13** inconvenience

null: nil **7** nullify **11** nonexistent **13** insignificant

nullifidian: 7 skeptic

nullify: 4 flaw, null, undo, void **5** abate, annul, elide **6** cancel, negate, repeal **7** abolish, destroy **8** abrogate, evacuate **9** frustrate **10** counteract, disappoint, invalidate, neutralize

nullo: 4 game, task

numb: 6 asleep, benumb, deaden, stupid, torpid **7** stupefy **8** enfeeble, helpless **9** incapable **10** insensible

number: sum **4** curn(Sc.), data(pl.), many, mort, slew, herd, host **5** count, datum, digit, scads, score, total **6** bundle, encore, figure, myriad, reckon, hirsel **7** chiffer, chiffre, compute, decimal, several **8** numerate, quantity, fraction **9** aggregate, calculate, enumerate, multitude **10** collection, complement, percentage
cardinal: one, two **4** four **5** three
dice: **4** sise
indeterminate: **7** umpteen, zillion
irrational: **4** surd
ordinal: **5** first, third **6** second
prime: one, two **4** five **5** seven, three **6** eleven **8** thirteen
pure: **6** scalar
suffix: st, th; eth
third power: **4** cube
whole: **7** integer

numbles: 7 innards, nombles **8** entrails

numen: 5 deity **6** spirit **8** divinity

numerable: 11 enumerative

numeral: 4 word **6** figure, letter
style: **5** Roman **6** Arabic

numerate: 6 number

numerical group: duo **4** trio **5** octet **6** sextet **7** octette, quartet, twosome **8** foursome, sextette **9** threesome

numerous: 4 lots, many **7** copious, crowded **8** abundant, multiple, thronged **9** multifold, plentiful

Numidia: *bird:* **10** demoiselle
city: **5** Hippo

nun: 4 bird, snew **5** clerk **6** pigeon, sister, vestal **7** confine, devotee **8** titmouse, votaress **9** priestess **10** cloistress
chief: **6** abbess
Franciscan: **5** Clare
headdress: **6** wimple
Latin: **5** Vesta
order: **6** Marist **8** Trappist **9** Dominican, Lorettine
son: **6** Joshua

nun moth: 7 tussock

nunciate: 9 announcer, messenger

nuncio: 6 legate **8** delegate **9** messenger **14** representative

nuncupate: 7 declare **8** dedicate, inscribe, proclaim **9** designate

nuncupative: 4 oral **9** unwritten

nunnery: 5 abbey **7** convent **8** cloister
head: **6** abbess

nuphar: 12 nymphaeaceae

nupson: 4 fool

nuptial: 6 bridal, genial 7 marital, wedding 11 matrimonial

nur: 5 gnarl

nurse: 4 amah, ayah, baba, care, feed, rear, tend 5 bonne(F.), mammy, nanny 6 attend, cradle, foster, norice, suckle 7 cherish, nourice, nourish, nurture, promote

nursery: 6 creche

nursling: 4 baby 9 foundling

nurture: 4 diet, feed, food, rear 5 nurse, train 6 cocker, foster 7 cherish, educate 8 breeding, training 9 education, nutriment

nut: bur, guy, nit 4 burr, cola, core, head, kola, nute, pili, task 5 acorn, betel, crank, hazel, pecan 6 almond, Brazil, cashew, fellow, peanut, pyrene 7 filbert, hickory, problem 8 beechnut, chestnut 9 eccentric 11 undertaking

  collective: 4 mast 5 shack
  edible part: 6 kernel
  ivory: 4 anta
  kola: 5 bichy 9 gourou-nut
  medicinal: 4 cola, kola
  palm: 5 betel, lichi 8 cocoanut
  tropical: ben 4 cola, kola

Nut: *daughter:* 4 Isis 8 Nephythys
  son: Ra

nut-bearing: 10 nuciferous

nut-brown: 5 hazel 6 walnut 8 chestnut

nut coal: 10 anthracite

nut grass: 5 sedge

nutate: nod 5 droop

nutbreaker: 10 nutcracker

nutcake: 8 doughnut

nutcracker: 6 xenops 7 pillory 8 nuthatch 9 nutpecker 10 nutbreaker

nuthook: 6 beadle 9 constable

nutmeg: *covering:* 4 mace
  family: 13 myristicaceae

Nutmeg State: 11 Connecticut

nutpecker: 8 nuthatch

nutramin: 7 vitamin

nutrice: 5 nurse

nutrient: 10 nourishing

nutrify: 7 nourish

nutriment: 11 nourishment

nutrition: 11 nourishment 12 alimentation

nutritious: 10 nourishing

nutritive: 10 nourishing

nutty: 4 gaga 5 buggy, queer, spicy 7 amorous, piquant 8 demented, pleasant 10 unbalanced 12 crackbrained, enthusiastic

nuzzle: 5 nurse 6 foster, nestle 7 snuggle

nye: 4 eyas, nest, nide 5 brood

nylon: 5 crepe, ninon, tulle

nymph: 5 Aegle, naiad, siren, oread, slyph 6 nereid 7 Corycia 9 hamadryad
  Arcadian: 6 syrinx
  beloved of Narcissus: 4 Echo
  Cretan: 8 Cynosura
  hills: 5 Oread
  laurel tree: 6 Daphne
  Messina Strait: 6 Scylla
  Mount Ida: 6 Oenone
  mountain: 5 Oread
  Muslim: 5 houri
  ocean: 5 siren 6 Nereid 7 Galatea, Oceanid 10 Callirrhoe
  pursued by Apollo: 6 Daphne, Syrinx 8 Arethusa
  queen: Mab
  sea bird: 6 Scylla
  water: 4 Nais 5 Naiad 6 Egeria, Lurlei, Undine 7 Apsaras, Hydriad, Lorelei 8 Arethusa
  wood: 5 Dryad 6 Nereid 9 Hamadryad

nymphaea: 7 Castaly 8 Castalia, Castalie

nyssa: 6 tupelo

nystagmus: 4 tic

Nyx, Nox: *brother:* 6 Erebus
  daughter: Day 4 Eris 5 Light 10 Hesperides
  father: 5 Chaos
  husband: 5 Chaos 6 Erebus
  son: 6 Charon

O

O. Henry: 6 Porter

oaf (see also **fool**): 4 boor, dolt, lout 5 clown, idiot, yokel 9 blockhead, foundling, schlemiel, schlemihl, simpleton 10 changeling

oafish: 6 stupid

oak: 5 roble 6 barren, cerris, encina 7 ambrose, durmast, turtosa 8 chaparro 9 blackjack

bark: 4 crut

bitter: 6 cerris

black: 10 quercitron

blight: 5 louse

comb. form: 6 querci

evergreen: 4 holm

family: 8 fagaceae

fruit: 5 acorn 6 camata

fungus: 10 armillaria

gall: 8 oakapple

holm: 4 ilex 5 holly

immature fruit: 6 camata

seed: 5 acorn

tannin: 6 queric 9 quercinic

white: 5 roble

young: 8 flittern

oak beauty: 4 moth

oak fern: 8 polypody

oak web: 10 cockchafer

oaky: 4 hard

oam: 5 steam

oar: row 5 aloof, rower 6 paddle, propel 7 oarsman 9 propeller

blade: 4 palm, peel

collective: 6 oarage

fulcrum: 7 oarlock

part: 4 loom

short: 5 scull

steering: 5 swape, swipe

oarlock: 5 thole 7 rowlock

oarsman: 5 rower 6 stroke 7 sculler

oasis: ojo, spa 4 merv, wadi, wady

oat: ait(Sc.) 5 grain 6 angora 7 egilops 8 aegilops

oaten: 10 avenaceous 11 farinaceous

oath: vow 4 aith 5 aithe, curse, haith 6 appeal, pledge 7 serment 8 anathema 9 affidavit, expletive, profanity, swearword 10 adjuration, obligation 11 affirmation, imprecation

mild: 4 darn, drat, ecod, egad, gosh 5 golly 7 gee-wizz

take: 5 swear

oats: *paid as rent:* 7 avenage

unthreshed: 6 oathay

obclude: 4 hide

obduction: 7 autopsy

obdurate: 4 firm, hard 5 rough, stony 6 inured, rugged 7 adamant 8 hardened, stubborn 9 calloused, immovable, obstinate, unbending, unfeeling 10 impenitent, inflexible, insensible, persistent, unyielding 11 hardhearted, intractable, unrepenting 13 unsusceptible

obedience: 5 order 7 control 8 docility 10 compliance, conformity, submission 12 jurisdiction

obedient: 7 duteous, dutiful, heedful, mindful, obeying 8 biddable, yielding 9 attentive, observing, tractable

obedient plant: 10 dragonhead

obeisance: bow 5 binge, conge, salam 6 congee, curtsy, fealty, homage, saalam 7 curtsey 9 abaisance, deference, reference 10 submission 14 respectfulness

obelisk: 4 mark 5 pylon, shaft 6 dagger, guglia, guglio, needle, obelus, pillar 8 monument

Oberon: 4 king, poem 5 fairy, opera

wife: 7 Titania

obese: fat 5 plump, pudgy, pursy, stout 6 fleshy, pyknic, rotund 8 blubbery, liparous 9 corpulent

obey: ear 4 hear 7 execute

obfuscate: dim 6 darken 7 confuse, mystify, obscure, perplex, stupefy 8 bewilder 9 obfuscous

obi: 4 sash 5 charm, obeah 6 fetich, fetish, girdle

obit: 5 death 6 notice 8 obituary 9 obsequies 10 necrologue

obiter: 12 incidentally

object: aim, end 4 goal, item 5 argue, cavil, demur, thing 6 design, entity, motive, oppose, target 7 dislike, protest, purpose, quarrel 9 challenge, intention, interpose 10 disapprove 11 expostulate, remonstrate

rare: 5 curio 7 antique

sacred: 4 urim

object to: 4 mind

objection: but 6 cheson 7 chesoun 9 exception

legal: 5 demur

objectionable: 4 vile 6 horrid 9 obnoxious, offensive 11 exceptional 12 disagreeable

objective: aim, end 4 goal 6 motive, realty, target 7 purpose 8 detached 9 intention 10 impersonal

objet d'art: 4 vase 5 curio, virtu 7 bibelot 8 figurine

objurgate: 5 abuse, chide 6 berate, rebuke 7 reprove, upbraid 8 execrate

oblate: 4 monk 8 dedicate, monastic

oblation: 6 corban 7 charity 8 devotion, offering 9 sacrifice

obligate: 6 fasten, oblige

obligation: vow 4 band, bond, debt, duty, loan, must, oath, onus 6 pledge 7 promise 8 contract 9 agreement, liability 10 allegiance, compulsion 11 obstruction 12 indebtedness 14 responsibility

obligato: 13 accompaniment

obligatory: 7 binding, bounden 8 forcible, imposing 9 mandatory

oblige: 4 pawn 6 engage, please 7 gratify, require 8 mortgage, obligate 9 constrain 11 necessitate

obliged: 8 beholden

obliging: 4 kind 5 buxom, civil 6 clever 7 amiable 9 agreeable, courteous 11 complaisant 13 accommodating

oblique: 4 awry, bias, skew 5 askew, bevel, cross, slant 6 aslant, aswash 7 askance crooked, evasive, scalene 8 inclined, indirect, sidelong, sideways, sidewise, slanting 9 slantways, slantwise, underhand 10 circuitous 12 disingenuous

render: 5 splay

obliterate: 4 blot, dele, rase, raze 5 annul, erase 6 cancel, delete, efface, sponge 7 expunge 10 annihilate, extinguish

oblivion: 5 Lethe 6 pardon 7 amnesty 13 forgetfulness

oblong: 8 avelonge 9 elongated 11 rectangular

rounded: 7 ellipse

obloquy: 5 abuse, odium 6 infamy 7 calumny, censure 8 disgrace, dishonor 12 reprehension, vituperation

obnoxious: 4 foul, vile 6 horrid, odious, rancid 7 hateful 9 offensive, verminous 13 objectionable

oboe: 4 reed 5 shawn 6 surnai, surnay 7 hautboy, musette 8 szopelka

obrok: tax

obscene: 4 foul, lewd, nast 5 bawdy, gross, nasty 6 coarse, filthy, impure, vulgar 7 profane 8 immodest, indecent 9 loathsome, offensive, repulsive 10 disgusting, licentious 12 pornographic

obscure: dim 4 blot, blur, dark, hazy, hide 5 bedim, befog, blind, faint, foggy, inner, murky, vague 6 bemist, cloudy, darken, darkle, gloomy, mystic, remote 7 becloud, conceal, confuse, cryptic, eclipse, shadowy, unknown, unnoted 8 abstruse, darkling, disguise, mystical, nameless, obstruse, oversile 9 ambiguous, blindfold, difficult, enigmatic, equivocal, recondite,

undefined 10 caliginous, extinguish, indistinct, overshadow 14 uncomprehended

obsecrate: 4 pray 7 beseech, entreat 8 petition 10 supplicate

obsequious: 5 slick 7 devoted, dutiful, fawning, servile, slavish 8 obedient, toadying, toadyish 9 attentive, compliant 10 submissive 11 subservient

obsequy: 4 rite 6 exequy, ritual 7 funeral 8 ceremony

observance: act 4 form, rite, rule 6 custom, regard 8 ceremony, practice 9 attention, deference 11 observation 12 constitution

religious: 6 Novena 9 sacrament

observant: 5 alert 7 careful, mindful 8 watchful 10 perceptive 11 considerate

observation: 4 heed, note 6 remark 7 auspice, autopsy, descant

preliminary: 5 proem

observatory: 4 Lick 5 tower 7 lookout, Palomar 11 Mount Wilson

observe: lo; eye, see, spy 4 espy, heed, keep, look, nark, note, obey, tout, wait, yeme 5 study, watch 6 athold, behold, follow, notice, regard, remark 7 comment, discern, respect, witness 8 perceive, preserve 9 advertise, celebrate, solemnize 10 animadvert, scrutinize

observer: 8 audience, informer, onlooker 9 bystander, spectator 11 stool-pigeon

obsess: 5 beset, haunt 6 harass 9 preoccupy

obsidian: 5 lapis

obsignate: 4 seal 5 stamp 6 ratify

obsolescence: 9 desuetude

obsolete: old 4 dead 5 passe 7 ancient, archaic, outworn 8 out-dated, outmoded 9 discarded 10 antiquated 12 old-fashioned

obstacle: bar, dam, let 4 snag 5 block, hitch 6 bunker, hocket, hurdle 7 barrier 9 hindrance 10 difficulty, impediment 11 obstruction 12 entanglement

insurmountable: 7 impasse

obstetrician: 10 accoucheur

obstetrics: 9 maieutics

obstetrix: 7 midwife

obstinate: set 4 dour 5 balky, sulky, tough 6 assish, dogged, mulish, sullen, unruly 7 froward, willful 8 crotched, obdurate, perverse, stubborn 9 foreright, pigheaded 10 bullheaded, determined, headstrong, inflexible, persistent, refractory, selfwilled 11 intractable, opinionated 12 contumacious, pertinacious, recalcitrant

obstreperous: 5 noisy 6 unruly 9 clamorous 10 boisterous, vociferous

obstriction: 10 obligation

obstruct: bar, dam, dit, gag, mar 4 clog, ditt, stop 5 beset, block, check, choke, delay, hedge 6 arrest, cumber, forbar, hamper, hinder, impede, oppose, retard 7 barrier, forelay, occlude 8 blockade, encumber, incumber **9** barricade, embarrass, interfere, interrupt **10** filibuster **11** fillibuster

obstruction: **4** snag **5** gorce, hitch **7** barrace, barrage, barrier, blinder **8** embolism, obstacle **10** difficulty, impediment **11** impeachment

obtain: beg, bum, eke, get, win **4** earn, fang, gain, hent, reap **5** cadge, ettle, reach **6** attain, derive, secure, sponge **7** achieve, acquire, capture, chevise, prevail, procure, receive, succeed
by threat: **6** extort

obtainable: **9** available

obtent: **6** design **7** purpose

obtest: **7** beseech **10** supplicate

obtrude: **5** eject, expel **6** impose

obtruncate: lop

obtrusive: **5** fresh, pushy **7** blatant, forward, pushing **9** intrusive **10** aggressive **12** presumptuous

obtund: **4** dull **5** blunt, quell **6** deaden

obtuse: dim **4** dull **5** blink, blunt, crass, dense **6** stupid **8** boeotian, hebetate, purblind **11** insensitive

obvelation: **7** veiling **10** concealing

obverse: **4** face **5** front **8** converse **10** complement **11** counterpart

obviate: **7** prevent **8** preclude **9** forestall

obvious: **4** open **5** broad, clear, gross, overt, plain **6** patent **7** evident, glaring, visible **8** apparent, distinct, manifest, palpable **11** conspicuous

obvolute: **9** contorted, convolute **11** overlapping

oca: **5** tuber **6** oxalis, sorrel

occasion: **4** hint, sele, time **5** casus, cause, event, nonce, slant **6** excuse **7** pretext **8** ceremony, engender, exigency, function, incident **9** condition, happening
festive: **7** holiday

occasional: odd **4** orra **5** stray **6** daimen **8** sporadic **10** infrequent

occasionally: **7** betimes **9** sometimes

occasive: **7** setting **8** westward

Occidental: **4** West **6** ponent **7** Western **9** Hesperian, Westerner

occlude: **5** close **6** absorb **8** obstruct

occult: **5** magic **6** hidden, mystic, secret, voodoo **7** alchemy, cryptic **8** esoteric, mystical **9** concealed, recondite **10** mysterious, necromancy **11** supernormal **12** supernatural **13** imperceptible
science: **9** esoterics

occultation: **7** eclipse **13** disappearance

occultism: **6** cabala

occupant: **6** inmate, tenant **7** citizen, dweller **10** inhabitant

occupation: job **4** note, toil, work **5** graft, trade **6** career, metier, tenure **7** calling, pursuit **8** business, function, industry, vocation **10** employment, profession
transient: **5** hobby **9** avocation

occupied: **4** rapt

occupy: sit, use **4** busy, fill, hold, take **6** absorb, employ, engage, expend, fulfil, tenant **7** cohabit, engross, fulfill, oversit, pervade, possess **8** interest

occur: be **4** come, meet, pass **5** clash **6** appear, arrive, befall, betide, happen
again: **5** recur **6** repeat

occurrence: hap **4** case **5** event **7** episode **8** incident **9** encounter, happening **12** circumstance
supernatural: **7** miracle
unusual: **6** oddity

ocean (see also **sea**): **4** brim, deep, main **5** brine **6** Arctic, Indian **7** Pacific **8** Atlantic **9** Antarctic
approach: **7** seagate
floating matter: **5** algae **7** flotsam
mammal: **5** whale
periodic motion: **4** tide
phenomenon: **4** tide
swell: sea

Oceania: **6** Malaya **9** Australia, Melanesia, Polynesia **10** Micronesia, New Zealand **11** archipelago

Oceanid: **5** nymph

Oceanus: *daughter:* **5** Doris **7** Oceanid **8** Eurynome
sister: **6** Tethys
wife: **6** Tethys

ocellus: eye **6** stemma

ocelot: cat **7** leopard

ocher: rud, sil **5** tiver **6** abraum **7** almagra

ocrea: **6** sheath

octahedrite: **7** anatase

octapody: **9** octameter

octave: **4** utas **5** eight **6** eighth

octet: **7** huitain

octopean: **7** octopus

octopus: **5** polyp, poulp **6** poulpe **7** polypus **8** octopean **10** cephalopod
arm: **8** tentacle
ten arms: **7** decapod

octoroon: **5** metis **6** mestee, mustee **7** metisse

octose: **5** sugar

octroi: tax **5** grant **9** privilege **10** concession

octuple: **9** eightfold

ocuby: rum

ocular: **5** optic **6** visual

odd: awk **4** fell, left, lone, orra(Sc.), rare **5** droll, extra, funny, impar, outre(F.), queer, weird **6** quaint, uneven **7** azygous, bizarre, curious, strange, unusual **8** fanciful, freakish, peculiar, singular, unpaired **9** burlesque, eccentric, fantastic, grotesque, unmatched, whimsical **10** occasional **13** extraordinary

oddly: **6** featly

oddman: **6** umpire **7** arbiter, referee

oddment: ort **5** scrap **7** remnant **8** fragment

odds: **7** dispute, quarrel **8** variance **9** advantage **10** dissension **13** probabilities

ode: **4** hymn, poem **5** lyric, paean, psalm
7 epicede **8** canticle **9** epicedium
birthday: **12** genethliacon
kind of: **8** pindaric
part: **5** epode
victory: **9** epinicion, epinikion
odeon: **4** hall **5** odeum **7** gallery, theater
odeum: **5** odeon
odic: **5** lyric
odiferous: **11** odoriferous
Odin: **5** Wodan, Woden, Wotan
brother: Ve **4** Vili
descendant: **5** Scyld
father: Bor
hall: **7** Valhall **8** Valhalla
horse: **8** Sleipner
maiden: **8** Valkyrie
son: Tyr **4** Thor, Vali **5** Baldr **6** Balder
sword: **4** Gram
wife: **4** Fria, Rind **5** Frigg, Rindr **6** Frigga
wolf: **4** Gere, Geri **5** Freki
odious: **4** foul, loth, vile **5** loath **7** hatable,
hateful, heinous, hideous **8** damnable,
flagrant, infamous **9** abhorrent, invidious,
obnoxious, offensive, repugnant **10** abominable, detestable, disgusting, forbidding
11 ignominious, opprobrious
odium: **6** stigma **8** aversion, disfavor **9**
antipathy **14** disapprobation
odograph: **9** pedometer
odontalgia: **9** toothache
odor: **4** fume, funk, nose, olid, tang **5**
aroma, ewder, fetor, flair, fumet, nidor,
odour, scent, smell, stink **6** breath,
flavor, foetor, repute, stench **7** bouquet,
essence, flavour, fumette, perfume **9** fragrance, redolence **10** estimation, reputation
odoriferous: **5** balmy, olent **7** odorous **9**
odiferous
Odysseus: **7** Ulysses
magic plant: **5** moly
Odyssey: *author:* **5** Homer
sorceress: **5** Circe
oecist: **9** colonizer
oecodomic: **13** architectural
oeconomus: **7** manager, steward
Oedipus:
brother-in-law: **5** Creon
daughter: **6** Ismene **8** Antigone
father: **5** Laius
mother: **7** Jocasta
son: **8** Eteocles **9** Polynices **10** Polyneices
wife: **7** Jocasta
oeillade: **4** ogle **6** glance
Oenomaus daughter: **10** Hippodamia
oestrus: **4** fury **5** sting **6** desire, frenzy **7**
impulse **8** stimulus
of (see also next entry): de(F); van(D) **4**
from **5** about **10** concerning
of: For all definitions beginning with this
word, see under following main word or
phrase. EXAMPLES: "of the country":

see **country** *pert. to;* "of necessity": see
necessity *of.*
off: **4** away, doff, gone **5** aside, wrong **6**
absent, cuckoo, remote **7** distant, further,
removed
off-scouring: **5** filth **6** refuse **7** garbage,
rubbish
offal: **5** gurry, waste **6** refuse **7** carrion,
garbage, leaving, rubbish **8** gralloch
offend: cag, sin, vex **4** hurt, miff **5** abuse,
anger, annoy, grate, grill, pique, shock,
wrong **6** aguilt, attack, grieve, insult, revolt **7** affront, default, mortify, outrage,
violate **9** disoblige, displease **10** transgress
offended: **4** huff, sore **7** froisse
offender: **7** culprit
offense: **4** mala(pl.) **5** crime, error, fault,
guilt, malum **6** felony, pritch **7** misdeed,
umbrage **8** peccancy, trespass **9** indignity
10 aggression, peccadillo, resentment
11 delinquency, misdemeanor
civil: **11** stellionate
law: **5** delit **6** delict **8** delictum
moral: **4** evil
offensive: bad **4** foul **5** fetid **6** coarse,
horrid **7** beastly, fulsome, hateful,
noisome **8** invading **9** loathsome, obnoxious, repugnant **10** aggressive, disgusting,
forbidding, ill-favored, scurrilous, ungracious, unpleasant **11** distasteful **12**
disagreeable **13** objectionable
offer: bid **4** bode, tend **6** adduce, allege,
tender **7** advance, commend, present,
proffer, propine, propose, suggest **8**
avertment, bequeath, overture **9** volunteer
last: **9** ultimatum
solemn: **6** pledge
offering: **4** gift **6** corban **7** present **9** sacrifice
religious: **7** deodate **8** anathema, oblation
sacrificial: **5** hiera **7** sphagia(pl.) **8** spha-
gion
offering block: **4** aloe
offhand: **4** curt **6** casual **7** brusque **8**
cavalier, informal **9** impromptu **10** im-
provised **11** extemporary **14** extemporaneous, unpremeditated **15** autoschedias-
tic **16** extemporaneously
office: **4** post, wike **5** place, wiken **6** bureau **7** camarin, station **8** function, position **9** bailiwick, situation **10** commission
11 appointment **13** collectorship
chief: **7** manager
divine: **9** akolouthia
help: **5** clerk **6** typist **9** secretary **12**
stenographer
machine: **5** Xerox **9** stenotype **10** calculator, mimeograph, typewriter **11** comptometer
of third hour: **5** terce
paid without work: **8** sinecure
purchase or sale: **8** barratry

put in again: **7** re-elect **9** re-instate

officeholder: in **6** winner **8** official, placeman

officer: **4** aide **5** usher **6** direct, ensign, manage, tindal **7** command, conduct, general **8** adjutant

assistant: **4** aide

future: **5** cadet

law: cop **7** bailiff, marshal, sheriff **9** constable, detective, patrolman, policeman

naval: **4** mate **5** bosun **6** ensign, yeoman **7** admiral, captain, striper **9** boatswain, commander, commodore **10** lieutenant

presiding: **6** archon **7** speaker **8** chairman **9** moderator, president

warrant: **5** bosun **9** boatswain

officers: **5** staff

official: **6** formal **9** escribano(Sp.), executive, officious **10** authorized, bureaucrat, magistrate **11** ceremonious **13** authoritative

administrative: **5** reeve **6** gerefa **9** executive

assistant: **4** aide

city or town: **5** mayor **7** manager **8** alderman, marshall **10** councilman

civil: **5** judge, mayor **7** bailiff, marshal, sheriff **8** governor **9** constable, patrolman, policeman, president **10** magistrate

corrupt: **7** grafter

despotic: **6** satrap

excise: **8** revenuer **9** revenooer

former: aga

government: **6** syndic

judicial: **8** assessor, recorder **9** treasurer **11** comptroller

local: **6** bailie(Sc.), grieve **7** burgess

public: **6** notary

state: **8** minister **9** secretary

officiate: act **6** supply **7** perform **9** celebrate

officious: **4** busy, cool, pert **6** formal **8** arrogant, impudent, informal, official **10** impersonal, meddlesome **11** efficacious, impertinent, pragmatical **12** contemptuous **14** supererogatory **16** superserviceable

offing: **7** picture **10** background

offset: **6** contra **7** balance **10** compensate, complement **12** counterpoise

offshoot: rod **5** bough, scion **6** branch, sprout

offspring: fry, imp, kid, son **4** brat, chit, seed **5** brood, child, fruit, issue, scion **6** foster, result **7** outcome, produce, product, progeny **8** children, daughter, geniture **9** genealogy, youngster **10** descendant, generation

oficina: **5** works **6** office **7** factory **10** laboratory

oflete: **5** wafer **8** oblation, offering

often: **6** common **8** frequent, repeated **10** frequently **11** continually

ogdoad: **5** eight

ogee: See **molding**.

ogle: eye **4** gaze, leer **5** stare **7** examine

ogre: **5** demon, giant **6** tyrant, yaksha, yakshi **7** bugaboo, monster

ogtiern: son **4** lord **6** master

ogygian: **7** ancient **8** primeval

oh: ach(G.) **4** ouch

Ohio: *college:* **5** Hiram, State **7** Antioch **10** Wittenberg

county: **4** Erie, Ross

town: Ada **5** Akron, Berea, Cadiz, Niles, Xenia **6** Canton, Dayton, Girard, Lorain, Toledo **7** Bucyrus **8** Columbus, Sandusky **9** Cleveland **11** Chillicothe **13** Yellow Springs

oii: **10** muttonbird

oil: ben, fat, ile **4** balm, fuel **5** bribe, oleum **6** aceite, anoint, chrism, grease **7** lanolin **9** lubricate, petroleum

blasting: **14** nitroglycerine

bone: **6** olanin

butter: **4** ghee

cedar and juniper: **8** alkitran **9** alchitran

comb. form: **4** oleo

coal: **8** photogen

derived from: **5** elaic, oleic

linseed: **6** carron

liquid compound: **5** olein

mineral: **7** naphtha

orange-blossom: **6** neroli

prefix: ol

salt: **7** bittern

torch: **7** lucigen

vegetable: **8** macassar

vessel: **4** drum, olpe **5** cruet, cruse **6** tanker **7** cresset

whale: **5** sperm

oil beetle: **5** meloe

oil cask: **4** rier

oil lamp: **7** coal-oil **8** kerosene

oil plant: **6** sesame

oil rock: **5** shale **9** limestone

oil well: **6** gusher

oilbird: **8** guacharo

oilcan: **5** oiler

oilcloth: **8** linoleum

oiler: **6** oilcan, tanker

oillet: **6** eyelet

oilseed: til **4** teel **6** sesame **7** linseed **8** rapeseed **10** castorbean, cottonseed

oilstone: **4** hone **5** shale **9** whetstone

oily: fat **4** glib **5** bland, soapy, suave **6** greasy, oleose, supple **7** pinguid **8** slippery, unctuous **9** compliant, plausible **10** oleaginous **11** subservient

ointment: **4** balm, mull, nard **5** salve **6** balsam, cerate **7** unguent **9** spikenard

application: **11** embrocation

dry: **9** xeromyron, xeromyrum

hair: **6** pomade **7** pomatum

oil: **6** carron, cerate **7** oleamen

veterinary: **8** remolade **9** remoulade

wax: **6** cerate

oisivity: **8** laziness

ojo: 5 oasis
okay: ok 4 okeh 7 approve, correct
oket: 5 ounce
Okinawa capital: 4 Naha
Oklahoma: *county:* 6 Garvin
mountain: 5 Ozark
people: 5 Okies 7 Sooners
river: Red
state flower: 9 mistletoe
town: Ada 4 Alva, Enid, Hugo 5 Miami, Sayre, Tulsa 6 Beaver, Edmond, El Reno, Guymon, Idabel, Kansas, Lawton, Pawnee 7 Buffalo, Cordell, Cushing, Newkirk 8 Anadarko, Cheyenne, Coalgate, Eldorado 9 Drumright, Stillwell, Wilburton 10 Kingfisher 11 Pauls Valley
university: 6 Norman 10 Stillwater
okra: 5 bendy, gumbo 6 bendee 8 bandikai
olam: 8 eternity, infinity, universe
old: agy, ald, eld 4 aged, auld 5 anile, hoary, stale 6 former, infirm, mature, senile, shabby 7 ancient, antique, archaic 8 medieval, obsolete 9 doddering, hackneyed, senescent, venerable 10 antiquated 11 experienced 12 antediluvian
old age: 10 senescence 11 senectitude
Old Bailey: 4 gaol, jail 6 prison
Old Bay State: 13 Massachusetts
old boy: man 6 alumni(pl.) 7 alumnus
Old Dominion State: 8 Virginia
Old Faithful: 6 geyser
old-fashioned: 5 passe 6 fogram, fogrum, quaint 7 antique, archaic 8 obsolete 9 primitive 10 antiquated
Old Franklin State: 9 Tennessee
Old Gooseberry: 5 devil, satan
Old Hickory: 13 Andrew Jackson
Old Line State: 8 Maryland
old maid: 8 cardgame, spinster
Old Noll: 14 Oliver Cromwell
Old Rough and Ready: 6 Taylor
Old Sod: 4 Erin 7 Ireland
Old Testament: See **Bible.**
Old World: *ape:* 6 baboon 10 catarrhina, catarrhine
carnivore: 5 genet
dish: 5 tansy
falcon: 5 saker
olden: 6 bygone
older: 5 elder 6 senior 8 ancestor 11 forefathers 12 predecessors
oldest: 4 dean 6 eldest
olea: 5 olive
oleaginous: 4 oily
oleander: 11 rhododaphne 12 rhododendron
olecranon: 5 ancon
olefin: 6 alkene
olena: 8 turmeric
olent: 11 odoriferous
oleomargarine: 9 butterine, margarine
oleoresin: 5 anime, elemi, tolus 7 copaiba 10 turpentine
oleum: oil
olfact: 5 smell

olfaction: 7 osmesis 8 smelling
olid: 5 fetid
olinda bug: 6 weevil
olio: 4 stew 6 medley 7 melange, mixture 8 mishmash 9 potpourri 10 collection, hodgepodge, miscellany
oliphant: 4 horn 8 elephant
oliprance: 4 romp, show 7 jollity 11 merrymaking, ostentation
olitory: 6 garden 7 potherb
olive: 4 olea 9 appetizer
enzyme: 6 olease
overripe: 5 drupe
pert. to: 9 oleaceous
stuffed: 6 pimola
oliver: 6 hammer
olivet: 5 pearl
olivine: 10 chrysolite
olla: jar, jug, pot
ollapodrida: 4 hash, olio, olla 6 medley 10 assortment, hodgepodge, miscellany
olm: 10 salamander
ology: ism 7 science
oloroso: 6 sherry
olp: 4 olph 9 bullfinch
olpe: 5 flask 6 vessel 7 pitcher
olycook: 7 cruller, olykoek 8 doughnut
Olympus: *deity:* see **Greece:** *god*
pert. to: 7 exalted, godlike, Olympic 8 heavenly, majestic 9 celestial
omega: end 4 last
omelet: 5 amlet 8 fooyoung
omen: 4 bode, omen, sign 5 augur, boder, freet, freit, token 6 augury, handel, hansel 7 auspice, portent, presage, warning 8 bodement, forebode, foresign 9 foretoken 10 foreboding, forerunner, indication, prediction 11 premonition
omentum: 4 caul
ominous: 4 dour, grim 5 fatal 6 dismal 7 fateful 8 menacing, sinister 9 prophetic 10 inexorable, portentous 11 threatening
mark: 4 dele 5 caret 7 ellipse 10 apostrophe
pretended: 10 paralepsis, paralipsis
tacit: 7 silence
omit: cut 4 balk, drop, miss, skip, slip 5 abate, elide, spare 6 beleve, cancel, delete, except, forget, ignore 7 beleave, discard, neglect 8 overlook 9 disregard, pretermit
omneity: 7 allness
omnibus: bus 5 barge 10 shillibeer
omnicient: 4 wise 7 learned 8 powerful 10 all-knowing, allwitting 11 everpresent
omnipotent: God 4 able 5 deity, great 6 arrant, mighty 8 almighty, powerful 9 unequaled, unlimited 11 all-powerful
omnipresent: 10 ubiquitous 12 ubiquitarian
omnitude: 7 allness 8 totality 12 universality
omoplate: 7 scapula
omphalos: hub 4 boss, knob 5 navel 6 center
on: 4 atop, upon 5 about, above, ahead,

along, anent **6** anenst, within **7** forward **10** concerning

account of: for

all sides: **5** about **6** around

and on: **4** ever **7** forever, tedious

behalf: for

other side: **4** over **6** across

on the contrary: 6 rather

on the other hand: but **7** however **8** although **11** nonetheless **12** contrariwise, nevertheless

on time: 6 prompt

on what account: why

Ona: 7 Fuegian

onager: ass **8** catapult

once: ane(Sc.) **4** anes(Sc.), anis(Sc.), erst **5** aince(Sc.) **6** former **7** quondam **8** formerly, whenever

in a while: **9** sometimes **12** occasionally

more: **4** anew, echo **5** again **6** encore, repeat

upon a time: **8** formerly

oncorhynchus: 6 salmon

ondoyant: 4 wavy

one: ae(Sc.), an; ain(Sc.), ane(Sc.), ein(G.), tae(Sc.), una, une(F.), yae(Sc.) **4** same, sole, some, unal, unit **5** alone, unity **6** person, single, unique, united **7** numeral, pronoun **8** unbroken **9** singleton, undivided, unmarried **10** individual

after another: **8** serially, seriatim **11** consecutive **12** successively

by one: **6** apiece, singly **10** separately

comb. form: uni **4** mono

one-chambered: **10** unicameral

one-colored: **13** monochromatic

one-footed: **6** uniped

one-sided: **6** biased, uneven, unfair, unjust **7** bigoted, partial **10** prejudiced, unilateral

one tenth: 5 tithe

one thousand: mil

one twenty-fourth: 5 carat

oneberry: 9 hackberry

onefold: 6 simple, single **7** sincere **9** guileless

onegite: 8 amethyst

oneism: 6 egoism, monism

oneness: 7 concord **8** identity, sameness **9** agreement **11** singularity

onerous: 4 hard **5** heavy **7** arduous, onerose **8** exacting **9** laborious **10** burdensome, cumbersome, oppressive

onetime: 8 formerly

onfall: 5 onset **6** attack

onion: 4 boll, cepa, leek **5** cibol, pearl **7** Bermuda, onionet, shallot **8** eschalot, rareripe, scallion

onkos: 7 topknot

onlepy: 4 only, sole **8** solitary **9** unmarried

onlooker: 5 gazer **7** witness **8** audience, beholder **9** bystander, spectator **10** rubberneck

only: 4 just, lone, mere, sole **5** afald **6** anerly, barely, merely, simple, single, singly,

solely **9** allenarly, excepting **11** exclusively

onomasticon: 7 lexicon **10** dictionary

onomatopoeic: 6 echoic

onrush: 4 birr **6** attack

onset: 4 dash, dint, fard, rese, rush **5** braid, brunt, faird, frush, start **6** attack, charge **7** assault, attempt, brattle **9** beginning, encounter, onslaught **12** commencement

onslaught: 5 onset **6** attack **7** assault, descent

onstead: 9 farmhouse, homestead

Ontario: *capital:* **7** Toronto

town: **4** Galt **9** Kitchener

onto: 4 atop **6** aboard

onus: 4 duty, load **6** burden, charge **10** obligation

onward: 4 away **5** ahead, along, forth **7** forward

onyx: 10 chalcedony

oodles: 4 heap **5** scads **8** lashings **9** abundance

oolong: tea

oomiack, oomiak: 4 boat

oomph: 5 vigor **6** energy

oont: 5 camel

oopak: tea

oorali: 6 curare

oorial: sha **5** urial

ooze: bog, mud **4** drip, leak, mire, seep, slob **5** exude, gleet, marsh, slime, weeze **6** sludge **8** transude **9** percolate

opal: gem **5** noble, resin **7** girasol, hyalite **8** girasole **10** chalcedony

variety: **8** menilite **9** cacholong

opalescent: 7 opaline **8** irisated **10** iridescent

opaque: 4 dark, dull **6** obtuse, stupid **7** obscure **8** eyeshade **13** unilluminated **14** unintelligible

open: dup, ope **4** ajar, flue, free, undo **5** agape, apert, begin, clear, frank, lance, overt, naked, plain, start, untie **6** candid, direct, expand, expose, honest, patent, unbolt, unfold, unfurl, unlock, unseal, unstop **7** artless, dispart, obvious, sincere, unclose **8** apparent, commence, disclose, dispread, explicit, extended, initiate, manifest, patulous, unfasten **9** disspread, originate, uncovered **10** accessible, forthright, inaugurate, unreserved **11** unconcealed **13** undissembling **15** straightforward

bursting: **10** dehiscence

fully: **4** wide **5** agape **7** yawning **9** dehiscent, full-blown

partly: mid **4** ajar

open-eyed: 5 awake **8** vigilant, watchful **9** receptive **10** discerning

opener: key **4** knob **5** latch **6** seseame **8** aperient

openhanded: 4 free **7** liberal **8** generous **9** receptive **10** munificent

opening: os; gap, ora(pl.) **4** bore, door, fent, gate, hole, pass, rift, rima, slit, slot,

span, vent **5** brack, cleft, debut, mouth, start, width **6** avenue, breach, hiatus, lacuna, outlet, portal, spread **7** crevice, fissure, orifice **8** aperture, overture **11** opportunity
enlarge: **4** ream
escape: **4** muse **5** meuse
having: **10** fenestrate
mouth-like: **5** stoma .7 stomata(pl.),
small: **4** pore **5** chink **6** cranny, eyelet **7** foramen, pinhole **8** foramina(pl.),
openmouthed: **6** gaping, greedy **8** ravenous **9** clamorous **10** vociferous
openwork: **7** tracery
opera: **4** Aida **5** Faust **6** Boheme, Carmen, Otello **7** Fidelio **8** Falstaff, Parsifal, Traviata, Walkyrie **9** Lohengrin, Pagliacci, Rheingold, Rigoletto, Trovatore **10** Magic Flute, Tannhauser **11** Don Giovanni **16** Marriage of Figaro
comic: **5** buffa
division: **5** scena
horse: **7** Western
kind: **4** soap **5** horse **8** burletta
part: **4** aria
soap: **6** serial **9** melodrama
soprano: **4** Bori **5** Eames, Patti **6** Callas, Farrar
song: **4** aria **7** sortita **8** cavatina **9** cabaletta
star: **4** diva
opera glass: **9** lorgnette **10** binoculars
opera house: **7** theater
operant: **9** operative
operate: go; act, man, run **4** work **6** affect, effect, manage **7** conduct **10** accomplish
by hand: **10** manipulate
operation: **4** deed **6** agency **7** process **8** creation, function **9** actuation, influence, procedure **10** production **11** maintenance, transaction
operative: **4** hand **6** artist **7** artisan **8** mechanic **9** detective
beyond itself: **9** transeunt
for past: **11** retroactive
operator: **5** agent, quack **6** dealer **7** manager, operant, surgeon **9** conductor, operative **10** mountebank
operculum: lid **4** flap **8** covering
operose: **4** busy **8** diligent **9** laborious **11** industrious
ophidian: asp, eel **5** snake **6** conger **7** reptile, serpent
ophthalmic: **6** ocular
opiate: **4** dope, drug, hemp **5** dwale, opium **6** deaden **7** anodine, anodyne **8** hypnotic, narcotic **9** paregoric
opificer: **7** workman **9** artificer
opine: **4** deem **5** judge **6** ponder **7** suppose
opinion: **4** idea, view, ween **5** dicta(pl.), guess, tenet **6** advice, belief, dictum, esteem, notion, repute **7** concept, feeling, thought **8** decision, doctrine, estimate,

judgment **9** sentiment **10** conjecture, conviction, deposition, estimation, expression, evaluation, impression, persuasion **12** apprehension
erroneous: **13** misconception
expression: **4** vote
preconceived: **9** prejudice
united: **9** unanimous
unorthodox: **6** heresy
opinionated: **8** dogmatic **9** conceited, obstinate **11** dictatorial
opinions: *collected:* **9** anthology, symposium
professed: **5** credo
opium: **4** drug **10** intoxicant
alkaloid: **6** codein **7** codeine **8** morphine, narcotin **9** narcotine, papaverin **10** paraverine
camphorate tincture: **9** paregoric
concentrated form: **6** heroin
derivative: **7** meconic
Egyptian: **8** thebaine
poppy seed: maw
prepared: **6** chandu **7** chandoo
opossum: **9** marsupial
mouse: **7** marmosa, marmose **8** marmouse
water: **5** yapok **6** yapock
opponent: foe **5** enemy **7** opposer **9** adversary, assailant **10** antagonist
opportune: fit, pat **5** ready **6** timely **8** suitable **9** favorable, well-timed **10** auspicious, convenient, favourable, seasonable
opportunely: **7** apropos, happily
opportunity: **4** hent, sele **5** slant **6** chance **7** opening **8** occasion **9** advantage **12** circumstance
oppose: pit, vie **4** buck, cope, face, meet, stem, wear **5** argue, block, check, cross, fight, front, rebel, rebut, repel **6** breast, combat, object, oppugn, resist **7** contest, counter, gainsay **8** conflict, confront, contrast, frontier, obstruct **9** encounter, withstand **10** calcitrate, contradict, contravene, controvert
opposed: **4** anti **6** averse **7** adverse, against, hostile **8** contrary **11** contrariant
opposer: **8** opponent
opposite: **5** anent, polar **6** across, anenst, averse, facing **7** adverse, counter, inverse, reverse **8** contrary, contrast, converse **9** antipodal, repugnant **10** antipodean **12** antagonistic **13** contradictory
opposite to: **7** abreast, subtend
opposition: **5** atilt **9** animosity, collision, hostility, renitency **10** resistance **11** contrariety
oppress: **4** load, rape, thew **5** crush, grind, weigh, wrong **6** burden, defoil, defoul, extort, harass, harrow, ravish, subdue **7** afflict, depress, overlay, repress, trample **8** distress, encumber, pressure, suppress **9** constrain, overpower, overthrow, overwhelm **10** extinguish

oppressed: 5 laden 9 debruised 10 heavy-laden

oppression: 8 dullness 9 grievance, lassitude 11 obscuration

oppressive: 4 dire, hard 5 close, harsh, heavy 6 severe 7 onerous 8 rigorous 10 hardhanded 11 gravaminous, heavyhanded, overbearing 12 extortionate

oppressor: 4 csar, czar, Nero, tsar, tzar 6 tyrant

opprobrium: 5 abuse, odium, scorn 6 infamy, insult 7 calumny, offense, scandal 8 disgrace, dishonor, reproach 9 contumely 10 disrespect

oppugn: 6 oppose

oppugnacy: 9 hostility 10 antagonism

oppugnation: 6 attack 10 opposition

Ops: *associate:* 6 Consus
consort: 6 Saturn
daughter: 5 Ceres
festival: 6 opalia

opt: 4 cull, pick 5 elect 6 choose, decide, select

optic: eye 6 ocular, visual

optical: 6 ocular

optical: *instrument:* 4 lens 6 alidad 7 alidade 9 eriometer, optometer, periscope, telescope 10 microscope, teinoscope 11 stereoscope 15 ultramicroscope
organ: eye

optimistic: 4 rosy 6 joyous 7 hopeful, roseate 8 sanguine

option: 6 choice 7 refusal 9 privilege 11 alternative

optional: 8 elective 9 voluntary 10 permissive

opulent: fat 4 rich 5 ample 6 lavish 7 profuse, wealthy 8 abundant, affluent 9 luxuriant, plentiful

opus: 4 work 11 composition
overlabored: 11 lucubration

or: aut(L.), ere 6 either 11 alternative
heraldry: 4 gold 6 yellow

oracle: 4 seer 5 sibyl

oracular: 4 otic 5 vatic 7 vatical 9 prophetic 10 mysterious 11 dictatorial 13 authoritative

orage: 5 storm 7 tempest

oral: 5 aloud, parol, vocal 6 sonant, spoken, verbal 7 uttered 9 unwritten 10 acroamatic

orange: 4 mock 5 chino, color, hedge, Navel, Osage 6 bodock 7 Seville 8 bergamot, chinotti, mandarin, Valencia 9 tangerine
heraldry: 5 tenne
membrane: 4 zest
mock: 7 seringa, syringa, syringe
piece: 4 lith(Sc.) 7 segment
red: 7 saffron
seed: pip

orange-flower oil: 6 neroli

orange-shaped: 6 oblate

orangeat: 9 orangeade

orangeberry: 9 cranberry

orangebird: 7 tanager

orangeleaf: 6 karamu

orangewood: 5 Osage

orangutan: ape 4 mias 5 orang, pongo, satyr 7 primate 11 orangoutang

orate: 5 plead, speak, spiel, spout 7 address, declaim, lecture 8 harangue 9 discourse, speechify 10 filibuster 11 expostulate

oration: 6 sermon 7 concion 9 panegyric
funeral: 5 eloge 6 eulogy 7 elogium, encomia(pl.) 8 encomium

orator: 6 rhetor 7 demagog, speaker 8 cicerone, ciceroni(pl.) 9 demagogue, plaintiff 10 petitioner 11 rhetorician, spellbinder

oratorian: 6 priest

oratorical: 8 eloquent 10 rhetorical

oratory: 6 chapel 9 elocution, eloquence

orb: eye, sun 4 ball, moon, star 5 earth, globe 6 circle, planet, sphere 7 circuit, enclose 8 encircle, surround

orbed: 5 lunar, round

orbit: 4 path 5 track 6 socket 7 circuit, ellipse
point: 5 apsis, syzgy 6 apogee, epigee 7 apsides(pl.), perigee

orc: 4 orca 5 whale 7 grampus

orchard: 5 arbor 6 arbour, garden 8 arbustum 9 enclosure 10 plantation

orchestra: 4 band 5 group 8 ensemble
section: 4 wind, wood 5 brass 6 string 7 timpany

orchestra bells: 12 glockenspiel

orchestra circle: 7 parquet 8 parterre

orchestrate: 5 score 7 arrange, compose

orchid: 5 faham, petal, vanda 6 purple 7 aerides, calypso, lycaste, pogonia, vanilla 8 arethusa, labellum
appendage: 8 caudicle
genus of: 5 vanda 6 laelia 10 gymnadenia 14 gymnadeniopsis
leaves: 5 faham
meal: 5 salep
petal: 8 labellum
tuber: 5 salep 7 cullion

ordain: 4 deem 5 allot, enact, order 6 decree 7 adjudge, appoint, arrange, behight, command, destine, install, prepare 9 establish, prescribe 10 adjudicate, commission, constitute

ordeal: 4 gaff 5 trial 10 experience

order: ban, bid 4 boon, fiat, form, ordo, rank, rule, sect, will 5 align, array, class, dight, edict, genus, grade, guide 6 billet, charge, cosmos, decree, degree, demand, direct, enjoin, genera(pl.), graith, kilter, manage, method, ordain, police, series, system 7 adjudge, arrange, bespeak, bidding, command, compose, dispose, embargo, mandate, ordines(pl.), precept, process, society 8 decision, neatness, organize, regulate 9 direction, directive,

procedure **10** injunction, succession
11 appointment, instruction
back: **6** remand **8** recommit
connected: **8** seriatim
cosmic: tao **4** rita
good: **6** eutaxy **7** eutaxie
grammar: **5** taxis
lacking: **5** amiss, messy, mussy **7** chaotic,
unkempt **8** confused **10** disarrayed
law: **4** writ **7** summons **8** subpoena
Parliamentary: **9** procedure
writ: **7** precipe
orderly: **4** aide, tidy, trim **6** batman **7**
regular **8** decorous, obedient **9** peaceable,
regularly, shipshape **10** law-abiding **11**
well-behaved
ordinal: **4** book **6** number **7** orderly, regular
ordinance: law **4** doom, fiat, rite **5** bylaw,
edict **6** assize, decree **7** control, de-
creta(pl.), statute **8** decretum **9** direction, sacrament **10** management, regulation **11** appointment
ordinary: **4** lala, ruck, soso **5** nomic,
plain, prose, usual **6** common, normal **7**
average, natural, prosaic, trivial, vulgate
8 everyday, habitual, mediocre **9** customary **11** commonplace
ordinate: **7** appoint, orderly, regular **8**
moderate **9** temperate **10** methodical
ordnance: **4** guns **5** armor, orgue **6** petard **7** weapons **8** basilisk **9** artillery, tor-
pedoes **10** ammunition, serpentine
ordo: **5** order **7** almanac
ore (see also **mineral**): tin **4** gold, iron,
lead **5** favor, glory, grace, honor, mercy,
metal **6** copper **7** respect, seaweed **8**
clemency **9** reverence
crusher: **5** dolly
deposit: **4** lode **5** scrin **7** bonanza
fusing: **8** smelting
horizontal layer: **5** stope
impure: **6** speiss
iron: **5** ocher, ochre **8** hematite **9** magnetite
layer: **4** seam **5** stope
lead: **6** galena
loading platform: **4** plat
mercury: **8** cinnabar
refuse: **6** scoria **8** tailings
separator: **6** vanner
silver: **10** stephanite
sluice: **5** trunk
tin: **5** scove
tungsten: **4** cals
washing trough: **6** strake
worthless: **5** matte
oread: **5** nymph
Oregon: *capital:* **5** Salem
coin: **6** beaver
county: **4** Coos **5** Curry **7** Gilliam, Klamath, Malheur, Wallowa, Yamhill **8**
Umatilla **9** Deschutes, Multnomah, Tilla-
mook

crab apple: **7** powitch
mountain: **4** Hood **5** Coast **7** Cascade
river: **5** Rogue **7** Klamath **8** Columbia **9**
Deschutes **10** Willamette
town: **4** Bend **7** Medford **8** Portland
wind: **7** chinook
oreortyx: **5** quail
Orestes: *father:* **9** Agamemnon
friend: **7** Pylades
mother: **12** Clytemnestra
sister: **7** Electra
wife: **8** Hermione
orfevrerie: **7** jewelry
organ: **6** medium **9** equipment **10** instrument
auricular: ear
barrel: **8** autophon
bristle-like: **4** seta
cactus: **7** saguaro
desk: **7** console
elongated: **8** tentacle
fish: **8** drumfish
flutter device: **7** tremolo
footlike: pes
gallery: **4** loft
interlude: **6** verset
lymphoid: **6** tonsil
note: **9** tremolant
of living bodies: **8** organism
of motion: **6** muscle
of volition: **5** manas
olfactory: **4** nare, nose
opening: os; ora(pl.)
optical: eye
part: **4** reed, stop
piano: **9** melopiano
pipe: **4** reed **5** flute **7** mixture
portable: **5** regal
prelude: **6** verset
reed: **9** harmonium
respiratory: **4** lung
sawlike: **5** serra
secreting: **5** gland
sensory: ear, eye **4** nose
speech: lip **6** throat, tongue
tactile: **6** feeler
organ stop: **5** quint, viola **7** celesta, tertian **8** dulciana, gemshorn, register **9** di-
apaison, rohrflute **10** quindecima
adjust: **10** registrate
bell-like: **8** carillon
labial: **7** melodia
reed: **4** oboe **7** bassoon **8** possaune
storm-imitating: **5** orage
string: **5** gamba
two banks of pipes: **7** tertian
organic: **6** inborn **7** natural **8** inherent **9**
organlike **11** fundamental **12** instrumental **14** constitutional
organism: **5** plant **6** aerobe, animal
bacterial: **4** germ **7** microbe
body: **4** soma **6** somata(pl.)
elementary: **5** monad
minute: **5** ameba, monad, spore

pelagic: 6 nekton
process: 6 miosis 7 meiosis
vegetable: 4 tree 5 plant
organization: 5 setup 11 association, disposition 12 constitution
business: 4 firm 5 guild 11 cooperative, corporation, partnership 13 establishment
college: 4 frat 6 alumna, alumni(pl.) 7 alumnus 8 sorority 10 fraternity
political: 4 bloc 5 party
secret: K.C.; K.O.P., P.E.O., W.O.W. 4 B.P.O.E., Elks, frat 5 lodge, mafia, Moose 6 apache, maffia, Masons 8 sorority 9 Foresters, Maccabees 10 fraternity, Freemasons 11 underground
skeleton: 5 cadre
social: 4 club 5 forum
veterans: A.V.C., D.A.V., GAR, SAR, V.F.W. 5 Fidac 6 AMVETS 14 American Legion 21 Veterans of Foreign Wars
women's: D.A.R., W.A.F., W.R.C. 8 sorority
organize: 4 form 5 edify 6 embody 7 arrange 8 regiment
organized: 7 organic 10 systematic
organology: 10 phrenology 12 splanchnology
organophone: 9 harmonium
organoscopy: 10 phrenology
orgueil: 5 pride 11 haughtiness
orgy: 4 lark, romp 5 revel, spree 6 frolic, shindy 7 revelry, wassail 8 carousal, ceremony 10 observance 11 celebration, merrymaking
Oriana: *father:* 8 Lisuarte
lover: 6 Amadis
oribi: 8 antelope, bleekbok
oriel: bay 6 recess, window 7 balcony, gallery, portico 8 corridor
orient: 4 dawn 5 adapt, place 6 adjust, locate 7 sunrise 11 accommodate
Orient: 4 Asia, East 6 Levant
animal: 4 zebu
archangel: 5 Uriel
bearer: 5 hamal
beverage: 6 arrack
cap: 7 calpack
caravansary: 4 khan 5 serai 6 imaret
carriage: 10 jinricksha 11 jinrickshaw
cart: 5 araba
chief: 4 khan
Christian: 5 Uniat
coin: sen, yen 5 dinar
commander: ras 4 amir, emir, rais, reis 5 ameer, emeer
corn: 4 para
cosmetic: 4 kohl
council: 5 Divan
cymbal: zel
deity: Bel
destiny: 6 Kismet
disease: 8 beri-beri
drug: 6 heroin 7 hashish

drum: 7 anacara
dulcimer: 6 santir
dwelling: dar
emperor: 6 sultan
fan: ogi
food: 4 rice 5 salep
liquor: 4 sake, saki
litter: 5 dooli, dooly 6 dooley, doolie
lute: tar
manservant: 5 hamal
mansion: 5 yamen
market: 5 bazar 6 bazaar
measure: dra, mao
measure of weight: 4 kati, rotl, tael 5 abbas, bhaar, catty, picul 6 cantar, kantar, miskal
money of account: rin
monkey: 7 macaque
musical instrument: tar 5 sitar, surna, suray 6 santir 7 samisen
name: Ali
nomad: 5 Tatar 6 Tartar
nurse: 4 amah, ayah
oboe: 5 surna, suray
pagoda: tea
people: Tai, Tho 4 Sere 5 Asian, Tatar 6 Indian, Korean, Muslim, Tartar 7 Chinese, Eastern 8 Japanese 9 Easterner, Levantine 10 Mohammedan
pipe: 7 nargile 8 harghile, nargileh
plane-tree: 7 cheenar
porter: 5 hamal
rest house: 4 khan 5 serai
rice dish: 5 pilaf, pilau, pilaw
rice paste: ame
ruler: 4 amir, emir, khan, shah 5 ameer, calif, emeer 6 caliph, sultan
saber: 6 tulwar 7 tulwaur 8 scimitar
sailor: 6 lascar
salutation: 5 saheb, salam 6 kowtow, salaam
sash: obi
sauce: soy
sea captain: ras 4 rais, reis
shoe: 6 sandal
silkworm: 6 tussah, tusseh, tusser 7 tussore
slipper: 7 baboosh 8 babouche
smoking apparatus: 7 nargile 8 narghile, nargileh
tamarisk: 4 atle 5 atlee
tambourine: 5 daira
title: aga 4 amir, baba 5 pasha 6 huzoor
tower: 6 pagoda
tree: 4 atle 5 atlee
vessel: 4 dhow, saic
wagon: 5 araba
whip: 6 chabuk 7 chabouk
wind: 7 monsoon
worker: 5 cooly
oriental: 5 pearl 6 bright, ortive, rising 7 eastern, shining 8 lustrous, pellucid, precious 9 ascending, brilliant 11 resplendent

Oriental rug: 4 Baku, Kali 5 Herez, Mahal, Saruk, Senna, Sumak 6 Kashan, Kerman, Kirman, Meshed, Pamiri, Sarouk, Shiraz, Soumak, Tabriz 7 Bokhara, Bukhara, Chinese, Hamadan, Isfahan, Ispahan, Karajas, Meshhed 8 Lerestan, Sedjadeh 9 Kurdistan 10 Kermanshah
pattern: 7 ainaleh
orifice: 4 hole, vent 5 inlet, mouth 6 cavity, outlet 7 chimney, opening, ostiole 8 aperture
origin: nee 4 rise, root, seed 5 birth, cause, start 6 nature, parent, source 7 genesis, lineage 8 nascence, nascency 9 beginning, inception, naissance, parentage 10 extraction, incunabula(pl.) 11 incunabulum, provenience 12 commencement, fountainhead
foreign: 7 ecdemic
on earth: 7 epigene
original: new 5 first, novel 6 fontal, native, primal, primer 7 primary 8 pristine 9 authentic, inventive, primitive 10 aboriginal 11 fundamental, primigenial
originate: 4 coin, make, open, rise 5 arise, begin, breed, cause, found, start 6 create, derive, devise, invent 7 causate, emanate, produce 8 commence, contrive, discover, generate, initiate 9 construct, establish, institute
origination: 7 genesis 9 etymology
originator: 6 author
oriole: *family:* 9 icteridae
golden: 5 pirol 6 loriot
Orion: 5 Rigel 13 constellation
hound: 6 Aratus
slayer: 7 Artemis
orison: 6 prayer, speech 7 praying
oristic: 10 definitive 11 determinate
Orkney Island: *capital:* 8 Kirkwall
hut: 4 skio
land: 4 odal, udal 6 udaler 7 udalman 8 udalborn
largest: 6 Pomona
orle: 6 border, fillet, wreath 7 bearing, chaplet
orlean: 7 annatto
orlop: 4 deck
ormer: 7 abalone
ormolu: 4 gilt, gold 5 alloy 7 varnish
ornament (see also **decoration**): dub, fob, pin 4 etch, gaud, gear, tool, trim, waly 5 adorn, braid, chase, decor, gutta, inlay, wally 6 amulet, attire, bedaub, bedeck, billet, brooch, edging, emboss, enrich, finery, flower 7 agremen, engrave, garnish, spangle, trinket 8 agrement, applique, decorate, flourish, lavalier 9 arabesque, billiment, embellish, embroider, lavaliere 10 decorament, furnishing, habiliment, lavalliere 11 garnishment 13 embellishment
apex: 6 finial

bell-shaped: 9 clochette
Biblical: 4 Urim
boat-shaped: nef
claw-like: 6 griffe
crescent-shaped: 6 lunula 7 lunette, lunulae(pl.)
delicate: 7 tracery
diamond-shaped: 10 epigonatia(pl.) 11 epigonation
dress: 4 frog, lace 5 jabot 6 sequin, zequin 7 spangle 8 chequeen, zecchino 10 embroidery
flowerlike: 7 rosette
hanging: 6 bangle, fringe, tassel 7 pendant
magical: 6 amulet
mantel: 7 bibelot
neck: 5 chain 6 choker, gorget 8 necklace
pagoda: tee
pendant: 6 anadem, bangle, tassel 7 earring 8 lavalier 9 lavaliere 10 lavalliere
protuberant: 4 boss
scroll-like: 6 volute
silver: 6 tinsel
spiral: 5 helix 7 helices(pl.)
terminal: 6 finial
tufted: 6 pompon, tassel 7 pompoon, rosette
ornamental: 7 elegant 8 fanciful 10 decorative
ornamented: 6 ornate, tawdry 9 elaborate
ornate: gay 4 fine 5 fancy, showy 6 florid 7 aureate, flowery 9 elaborate, unnatural 10 flamboyant 11 overadorned
ornithologist: 7 Audubon, birdman
ornithon: 6 aviary
orotund: 4 full 5 clear, showy 6 mellow, strong 7 pompous 8 resonant 9 bombastic
orp: 4 fret, weep
orphan: 5 Annie 9 foundling
orpheum: 7 theater
Orpheus: *father:* 6 Apollo
mother: 8 Calliope
wife: 8 Eurydice
orphrey: 4 band 10 embroidery
orpiment: 7 arsenic
orpit: 7 fretful
orra: odd 10 occasional, unemployed 13 miscellaneous
orris: 4 gimp, lace 5 braid 7 galloon
ort: bit 5 crumb, scrap 6 morsel, refuse 7 leaving, remnant 8 fragment
orthodox: 4 good 6 proper 7 canonic, correct 8 accepted, standard 9 canonical, customary 12 conventional
orthographer: 7 speller
ortive: 7 Eastern
ortolan: 4 bird, rail 7 bunting 8 bobolink, wheatear
ortstein: 7 hardpan
oryx: 7 gazelle, gemsbok 8 antelope

os: 4 bone 5 eskar, esker, mouth 7 opening

oscillate: wag 4 rock, sway, vary 5 swing, waver, weave 7 vibrate 9 fluctuate, vacillate

oscillation: 11 trepidation

oscine: 9 scopoline

oscitant: 4 dull 6 drowsy, gaping, sleepy, stupid 7 yawning 8 careless, sluggish 9 apathetic

osculate: 4 buss, kiss

ose: 6 glucid 7 glucide 13 monosaccharid 14 monosaccharide

osier: rod 5 wand 6 basket, sallow, willow 7 dogwood, wilgers

Osiris: *brother:* Set 4 Seth
crown: 4 atef
enemy: Set 4 Seth 7 brother
father: Geb, Keb, Seb
mother: Nut
sister: 4 Isis
son: 5 Horus 6 Anubis
wife: 4 Isis

Osmanli: 4 Turk

osmesis: 8 smelling 9 olfaction

osprey: 4 bird, hawk, ossi

ossature: 8 skeleton

osse: 4 dare 7 attempt, presage, promise 8 prophesy 9 recommend, utterance

osseous: 4 bone, bony 6 osteal 10 ossiferous

ossianic: 7 flowery, pompous 9 bombastic

ossicle: 4 bone 5 incus 6 stapes 7 bonelet, malleus

ossifrage: 5 eagle 6 osprey 11 lammergeier

ossify: 6 harden

ossuary: urn 4 tomb 5 vault 10 depository, receptacle

ostend: 4 show 6 reveal 7 exhibit 8 manifest 11 demonstrate

ostensible: 7 seeming 8 apparent, specious 9 pretended, professed

ostensorium: pix, pyx 10 monstrance

ostent: air 4 mien 5 token 7 display, portent 10 appearance 13 manifestation

ostentation: 4 show 5 eclat, flare 6 parade 7 display, flutter, pageant, portent, presage 8 flourish, pretense 9 showiness, spectacle 10 exhibition 11 fanfaronade

ostentatious: 4 arty, loud 5 gaudy, showy 6 sporty 7 obvious, pompous 8 fastuous 9 elaborate, flaunting 11 pretentious

osteria: inn 6 tavern

ostiole: 4 pore 5 stoma 7 orifice, stomata(pl.) 8 aperture

ostler: 7 hostler 9 stableman

ostracize: bar 4 snub 5 exile 6 banish, reject 7 exclude 9 blackball, proscribe 10 expatriate

ostracon: 8 potsherd

ostreger: 8 falconer

ostrich: 4 rhea 5 nandu

extinct: mea
feather: boa, boo 5 plume

Otaheite: 6 Tahiti

otalgia: 7 earache

otary: 4 seal

Othello: 4 Moor
friend: 4 Iago
wife: 9 Desdemona

other: 4 else, more 5 ither(Sc.) 6 former 7 further 8 distinct 9 different 10 additional
combining form: 5 heter 6 hetero

other-worldly: fey 9 imaginary, spiritual

others: 4 rest

otherwise: or 4 else 5 alias 6 aliter 11 differently

otic: 5 aural 8 auditory, oracular 9 auricular

otiose: 4 idle, lazy, vain 6 futile, otiant 7 sterile, useless 8 inactive, indolent, reposing 10 unemployed 11 ineffective, superfluous

otium: 7 leisure

otologist: 6 aurist

ottavino: 7 piccolo

otter: fur 4 fish 6 tackle 7 annatto 8 paravane
sea: 5 kalan

ottoman: 4 pouf, seat 5 couch, divan, stool 6 fabric 9 footstool

Ottoman (see also **Turkey**): 4 Turk 5 Osman 6 Othman
court: 5 porte
governor: 5 pasha
imperial standard: 4 alem
leader of: 5 Osman
poetry couplet: 4 beyt
province: 7 Vilayet
subject: 4 Raia 5 Rayah

ouachitite: 4 dike

ouakari: 6 monkey

oubliette: 7 dungeon

ouch: oh 5 adorn, bezel, clasp 6 brooch, fibula 7 fibulae(pl.) 8 ornament 11 exclamation

ought: 4 bood, must, zero 6 cipher, naught, nought, should 7 behoove

ounce: ure 6 weight 7 measure
sixteenth of: 4 dram

oundy: 4 wavy 5 curly 6 waving

ouphe: elf 6 goblin

our: wir(Sc.) 5 notre(F.) 7 pronoun 10 possessive

ourie: 4 cold 5 dingy 6 dreary

ousia: 6 nature 7 essence 9 substance

oust: bar 5 eject, evict, expel 6 banish, remove 7 dismiss, 8 forjudge 9 forejudge 10 dispossess

out: 4 away 5 forth 6 absent, begone, issued 8 external 9 published 12 disadvantage
at elbows: 5 seedy
of: 4 from 6 dehors

of date: old **5** passe **10** antiquated

of kilter: **4** alop, awry **6** broken

of order: **5** amiss, kaput **6** faulty **9** deficient

of place: **5** inept **13** inappropriate

of play: **4** dead, foul

of, prefix for: ec, ex; ect, exo **4** ecto

of sorts: **5** cross **7** peevish

of the ordinary: odd **5** novel **6** unique **7** strange, unusual **8** peculiar, uncommon **9** different

of the way: **5** aside **6** afield, remote **10** farfetched

out-and-out: **5** sheer, utter **6** arrant, wholly **8** absolute, complete

outage: **4** vent **6** outlet **10** suspension **12** interruption

outas: **6** clamor, outcry

outbear: **4** bear, lead **7** sustain **8** outcarry

outbearing: **8** arrogant, demeanor **10** projection

outbraid: **4** draw **5** eject **7** upbraid

outbreak: fit **4** riot **5** burst **6** bust-up, emeute(F.), ruckus, tumult **7** boutade, outcrop, ruction **8** eruption **12** insurrection

new: **13** recrudescence

sudden: **5** spurt

outbreeding: **7** exogamy

outbuilding: **4** barn, shed **5** privy **6** barton, garage, hemmel **8** outhouse **9** backhouse

outburst: **4** fume, gale, gust, rage, tiff **5** blast, brunt, flare **6** blower, blow-up, tirade **7** outcrop, tantrum, torrent **8** eruption, outbreak **9** explosion **10** ebullition, outpouring

outcast: **5** exile, leper, ronin **6** outlet, pariah **7** missile **8** castaway, chandala, rejected, vagabond **10** expatriate

outclass: **5** excel **6** outwit **7** surpass **8** outcraft

outcome: **4** fate **5** issue **6** effect, exitus, outlet, result, sequel, upshot **7** emanate **9** aftermath, emanation **10** conclusion, denouement **11** consequence

outcraft: **8** outclass

outcrop: **5** ledge

outcry: ga; cry, hue, yip **4** bawl, bray, yell **5** alarm, boast, noise, shout **6** clamor, racket, shriek, steven **7** calling, clamour, exclaim, protest, screech, shil-loo **8** proclaim **9** objection **11** lamentation **12** vociferation

outdate: **7** outmode **9** antiquate

outdistance: **7** surpass **8** outstrip

outdo: cap, cow **5** excel **6** defeat, exceed **7** nonplus, surpass **8** overcome

outdoors: **5** forth **7** outside

outer: **5** alien, ectad, ectal, utter **7** foreign, outside **8** exterior, external **10** extraneous

outermost: **5** final, utter **6** utmost **7** extreme, outward **8** farthest, remotest **9** extremest, outermost, uttermost

outface: **4** defy **6** resist, subdue **8** overcome

outfield: **6** garden **7** pasture **8** moorland

outfit: kit, rig **4** gang, gear, suit, team, unit **5** equip **6** attire, fitout **7** furnish **8** equipage **9** equipment, furniture, grubstake **12** organization **13** paraphernalia

outflow: **4** flux **5** drain **6** efflux, escape

outgo: **4** exit **5** excel, issue, outdo **6** efflux, egress, exceed, outlay, outlet, outrun **7** outcome, outflow, product, surpass **11** expenditure, outdistance

outgrowth: **8** offshoot **9** emergence **11** excrescence

outhouse: **4** shed **5** privy **6** biggin **7** latrine

outing: **4** stay, trip **6** picnic **7** holiday **8** vacation **9** excursion

outknee: **6** bowleg

outlandish: **5** alien **6** exotic, remote **7** bizarre, foreign, strange, uncouth **8** peculiar **9** barbarous, fantastic, grotesque **10** tramontane

outlaw: ban **4** caco **5** exile, exlex, fleme, ronin **6** arrant, bandit, banish **8** fugitate, fugitive, prohibit **9** proscribe **10** disqualify, expatriate

outlawed: **7** illegal, illicit

outlay: **4** cost **7** expense **11** expenditure **12** disbursement

outlet: **4** exit, vent **5** issue **6** egress, escape, exitus **7** opening, outcast, outcome **9** avoidance

outline: map **4** form, plan **5** brief, chart, draft, frame, shape, trace **6** design, figure, sketch **7** contour, profile, summary **8** describe, skeleton, synopsis **9** delineate, perimeter **10** compendium, figuration, silhouette **11** delineation **13** configuration

outlive: **7** outlast, survive

outlook: **4** view **5** vista **6** aspect **7** purview **8** frontage, prospect **10** perception **11** expectation

medical: **9** prognosis

outmoded: **5** dated, passe **7** antique **8** obsolete, outdated

outpeer: **8** outclass

outpost: **7** station **8** forepost **10** settlement

outpour: **4** flow **7** outflow **8** outburst

output: cut **5** expel, power, yield **6** energy **10** production

outrage: **4** rape **5** abuse **6** insult, offend, ravish **7** abusion, affront, offense, violate

outrageous: **5** enorm **7** heinous, obscene, ungodly **8** flagrant, shocking **9** atrocious, desperate, execrable, monstrous **10** exorbitant

outre: **7** bizarre, strange **9** eccentric **11** exaggerated, extravagant

outreach: **5** cheat **6** exceed, extend, outwit, search **7** deceive, project, surpass **8** protrude **9** overreach

outright: 5 total, whole 6 direct, openly, wholly 8 complete, entirely 9 downright 15 straightforward

outrival: 5 excel 6 outvie 7 eclipse

outroot: 9 eradicate, extirpate

outrun: 4 beat, cote 6 exceed 7 forerun 9 forespeed

outset: 5 start 9 beginning

outshine: 5 blind, excel 6 dazzle, deface 7 distain, surpass

outside: 4 bout, free 8 exterior, external *comb. form:* ect 4 ecto

outsider: 5 alien 8 stranger 9 extra-nean(Sc.), foreigner

outspoken: 4 bold, free 5 bluff, blunt, broad, frank 6 candid, direct 7 artless 8 explicit 10 unreserved 12 unrestrained

outstanding: big 4 arch, rare 5 famed, noted 6 famous, heroic, marked, unpaid 7 eminent 9 principal, prominent, unsettled 10 noticeable, pre-eminent, projecting 11 conspicuous, exceptional, uncollected, unfulfilled 13 distinguished

outstretched: 5 stent(Sc.) 8 extended

outstrip: cap, top, win 4 best, cote, lead, pass 5 excel, out do 6 exceed 7 devance, surpass 8 distance 9 transcend

outvie: 8 outstrip

outward: 5 ectad, outer, overt 6 exodic, extern, formal 7 extreme, visible 8 apparent, exterior, external, obsolete 9 extrinsic 11 superficial

outweighing: 8 dominant 12 preponderant

outwit: fox 4 balk, best, foil 5 block, check, cross 6 baffle, jockey, thwart 9 checkmate, frustrate 10 circumvent, disappoint

ouzel: 4 piet 5 colly, ousel 6 thrush 8 whistler 9 blackbird

oval: 7 ellipse, stadium 8 avelonge 10 elliptical 11 ellipsoidal

ovary: 6 germen

ovate: 9 egg-shaped *inversely:* 7 obovate

ovation: 8 applause 10 exultation

oven: 4 kiln, oast 5 baker 6 calcar 7 furnace

oven mop: 6 scovel

over: oer, sur(F.), too 4 also, anew, done, upon 5 above, again, clear, ended, extra, vault 6 across, beyond, excess 7 surplus, through 8 finished 9 completed, excessive 10 terminated 11 consummated, superfluous *and above:* 7 besides 11 therewithal *combining form:* sur 5 hyper, super, supra *prefix:* sur 5 super, supra

overabundance: 6 excess 7 surplus 8 plethora

overact: 5 emote 9 burlesque 10 exaggerate

overage: 6 excess 7 surplus

overalls: 5 chaps 10 chaparajos, chapareras, chaparejos 11 chaparreras

overassuming: 4 bold

overbalance: 8 dominate

overbearing: 5 proud 6 lordly 7 haughty 8 arrogant, bullying, insolent, snobbish, subduing 9 imperious 10 disdainful, high-handed 11 dictatorial, domineering, magisterial 12 overpowering, supercilious

overburden: 8 encumber 9 surcharge

overbusy: 5 fussy

overcast: dim, sew 4 bind, dark, dull 5 cloud, heavy 6 cloudy, darken, gloomy, lowery 7 accloud, becloud, clouded

overcharge: gyp 6 excise 9 extortion

overcloud: dim 6 darken 7 obscure

overcoat: 5 benny 6 capote, raglan, slip-on(Sc.), ulster 7 paletot(F.), surtout, topcoat 9 balmacaan, greatcoat, inverness 12 chesterfield

overcome: awe, get, win 4 beat, best 5 charm, crush, daunt, fordo 6 appall, beaten, craven, defeat, exceed, foredo, master 7 confute, conquer 8 convince, encumber, outstrip, overbear, overturn, suppress, surmount, vanquish 9 overpower, overthrow, overwhelm, prostrate

overcrowded: 9 congested

overdo: 6 exceed 7 exhaust, fatigue 8 overcook, overwork 9 burlesque 10 caricature, exaggerate

overdue: 4 late 5 tardy 7 arrears, belated, delayed

overeager: 8 feverish

overeat: 5 gorge 7 satiate 8 gourmand 10 gluttonize

overfed: 7 fulsome

overflow: 4 slop, swim, teem, vent 5 float, flood, spate, spill 6 abound, debord, deluge, outlet 7 overrun 8 alluvion, inundate 9 abundance, cataclysm 10 ebullience, exuberance

overflowing: 5 awash 7 copious

overgrown: 7 fulsome

overhang: jut 6 beetle 7 project, suspend

overhaul: 7 examine 8 renovate 9 forereach

overhead: 5 above, aloft 7 expense

overissue: 9 inflation

overlapping: 8 obvolute 9 imbricate

overlay: cap, lap 4 ceil, coat 5 couch, cover, glaze, plate 6 cravat, spread, veneer 7 encrust, oppress, overlie 8 covering 10 overburden 11 superimpose

overload: 4 glut 6 charge 8 encumber

overloaded: 9 plethoric

overlook: 4 balk, miss, omit, skip 5 forgo 6 acquit, excuse, forego, forget, ignore, manage 7 absolve, condone, inspect, neglect 9 disregard

overlord: 5 liege 6 despot, satrap, tyrant 8 suzerain

overlying: 8 brochant

overman (see also **overseer**): 5 chief 6

leader 7 arbiter, foreman, referee 8 overseer 9 overpower

overmatch: 4 best 6 exceed 7 surpass 8 vanquish

overmodest: 4 prim 7 prudish

overmuch: too 6 excess 7 surplus 9 excessive

overnice: 5 fussy 7 precise 8 dentical 10 fastidious

overplus: 6 excess 7 surplus 9 advantage

overpower: awe 4 rout 5 crush, whelm 6 compel, defeat, deluge, master, subdue 7 conquer 8 convince, entrance, overbear, overcome, vanquish 9 enrapture, overthrow, overwhelm

overpowering: 4 dire 6 fierce 8 dazzling, stunning

overreach: do 5 cheat 6 grease, nobble, outwit 10 circumvent

overready: 7 forward

overrule: 4 veto 8 abrogate

overrun: 5 crush 6 infest, ravage, spread 7 destroy 9 overwhelm

overs: boots

oversee: 5 watch 6 survey 7 examine, inspect 9 supervise 11 superintend

overseer (see also **overman**): 4 boss 5 ephor(Gk.), grave, reeve 6 bishop, censor, driver, gaffer, grieve 7 bailiff, caporal, curator, foreman, manager 8 banksman, martinet 9 inspector 10 acequiador, supervisor 14 superintendent

agricultural: 8 agronome

spiritual: 6 pastor, priest

overshadow: dim 5 cover, dwarf 6 darken 7 eclipse, obscure 8 dominate 9 adumbrate

overshoe: gum 4 boot 6 arctic, galosh, golosh, patten, rubber 7 flapper

overshoot: 6 exceed

oversight: 4 care 5 error, lapse, watch 6 charge 7 blunder, control, mistake 8 omission 9 direction 10 inspection, negligence 11 supervision 12 surveillance 15 superintendence

overskirt: 6 peplum 7 pannier

oversleeve: 6 armlet

overspread: 4 deck, pall 5 brede, cloud, cover 6 deluge

overstate: 7 magnify 10 exaggerate

overstep: 6 exceed 10 transgress

overt: 4 open 6 patent, public 7 obvious 8 apparent, manifest

overtake: 5 catch 6 attain, detect 7 ensnare 9 apprehend, captivate

overtask: 5 drive

overtax: 6 exceed

overthrow: tip 4 dash, down, fell, foil, fold, hurl, raze, rout, ruin, rush 5 allay, evert, fling, upset, worst, wrack 6 defeat, unseat 7 afflict, conquer, destroy, dismiss, ruinate, unhorse 8 confound, demolish, overcome, overturn, reversal, supplant, vanquish 9 discomfit, overpower, over-

whelm, prostrate 10 defeasance 11 destruction 12 discomfiture

overtime: 8 extended

overtire: tax

overture: 5 offer, proem 7 opening, prelude 8 aperture, proposal 11 proposition

opera: 8 sinfonia

overturn: tip 4 cave, coup, tilt 5 throw, upset 6 topple 7 capsize, destroy, pervert, reverse, subvert 8 overcome 9 overthrow, overwhelm

overweening: 8 arrogant

overwhelm: 4 bury 5 amaze, cover, crush, drouk, swamp 6 defeat, deluge, engulf, quench 7 confute, conquer, engross, oppress 8 astonish, inundate, overturn, submerge 9 overpower, overthrow

ovine: 5 sheep 9 sheeplike

female: ewe

ovoid: 5 ovate 7 egg-like, obovoid, oviform

ovule: egg 4 seed 6 embryo 7 gemmule, seedlet

integument: 7 primine

ovum: *egg* 4 seed 5 spore

combining form: ova

owe: due, own 7 possess 9 attribute

ower: 6 debtor

owl: 4 lulu, momo 5 wekau 7 boobook, harfang, woolert 8 billy-wix, morepork 10 gillhooter, hob-houchin

call: 4 hoot

genus of: 5 ninox

like: 8 strigine

young: 4 utum 5 owlet

own: ain(Sc.), owe 4 avow, have, hold, nain(Sc.) 5 admit 7 concede, confess, possess 9 recognize 11 acknowledge

ownership: 5 title 7 tenancy 8 dominium 11 condominium 14 proprietorship

owse: 8 quagmire

ox: yak 4 anoa, aver, beef, buff, gaur, musk, reem, zebu 5 bison, bugle, gayal, steer, tsine 6 bovine 7 banteng, buffalo 8 seladang 9 quadruped

extinct: 4 urus

harness: 4 yoke

small: 4 runt

stall: 5 boose

wild: 4 gaur 8 seladang

oxen: 6 cattle

yoke: 4 span

oxeye: 4 boce 5 aster 6 dunlin

oxford: 4 shoe 5 cloth 7 college 10 saddleshoe, university

Oxford: *examination:* 5 great

officer: 5 bedel 6 beadle

scholarship: 6 Rhodes

oxhead: 4 dolt 9 blockhead

oxidation: 4 rust

oxide: *aluminum:* 7 alumina

barium: 6 baryta

calcium: 4 lime

hydrocarbon radical: 5 ether

iron: 4 rust

sodium: **4** soda
strontium: **8** strontia
oxidize: **4** rust **7** calcine
oxlike: **6** bovine **7** taurine
oxygen: gas
  acid: **7** chloric **9** sulphuric
  allotropic: **5** ozone
  binary: **5** oxide
oxygenate: **6** aerate
oyster: **6** huitre **7** bivalve, mollusk
  bed: **4** park, stew **5** layer **6** claire **9** oysterage

eggs: **5** spawn
fossil: **9** ostracite
gatherer: **7** tongman
kind of: **6** native **9** bluepoint
rake: **5** tongs
shell: **4** husk, test **5** shuck
spawn: **6** cultch
tree: **8** mangrove
young: **4** spat
oysterfish: **6** tautog **8** toadfish
Ozark State: **8** Missouri
ozone: air

P

pa, pah: dad, paw **4** fort, papa **5** daddy **6** father **7** village **8** stockade **10** settlement

pabulum: **4** food, fuel, prog **6** cereal **7** aliment, support **9** nutriment **10** sustenance

pac, pack: **4** boot **8** moccasin

paca: **4** cavy, lava **5** agout, labba **6** rodent

pace: way **4** clip, gait, lope, pass, rack, rate, step, trot, walk **5** amble, canto, speed, tempo, tread **6** canter, gallop, strait **7** channel, chapter, dogtrot, measure, passage **8** platform **10** passageway

pacer: **5** horse **9** pacemaker

pachisi: **4** game, ludo

pachyderm: **8** elephant **10** rhinoceros **12** hippopotamus

pacific: **4** calm, meek, mild **5** irene **6** irenic, placid, serene **8** irenical, peaceful, tranquil **9** appeasing, peaceable **12** conciliatory

Pacific coast state: **6** Oregon **10** California, Washington

Pacific Islands: *archipelago:* Aru **4** Sulu **5** Malay, Samoa **6** Tulagi

bird: **4** kagu

cloth: **4** tapa

collective name: **7** Oceania

grass: **4** neti

military base: **4** Guam

region: **9** Polynesia

tree: kou **4** ipil, taro **7** dasheen, madrona, madrono **8** eddyroot

Pacific Ocean: *archipelago:* **4** Sulu **5** Malay, Samoa

discoverer: **6** Balboa

island: Ie; Lae, Yap **4** Guam, Truk, Wake **5** Samoa **6** Tahiti **8** Tasmania **9** Carolines, Marquesas

shark: **4** mako

"stepping stones": **9** Aleutians

pacify: **4** calm, ease, lull **5** abate, allay, quiet, still **6** serene, soften, soothe **7** appease, assuage, mollify, placate **8** mitigate **9** alleviate, reconcile **10** conciliate, propitiate **11** tranquilize

pack: wad **4** bale, cram, gang, load, stow, tamp **5** crowd, flock, horde, steve, store, truss **6** barrel, bundle, duffle, embale, encase, fardel, impact, wallet **8** knapsack

pack animal: ass **4** mule **5** burro, camel, horse, llama **6** donkey

package: pad **4** bale **6** bundle, packet, parcel

packer: **5** baler, roper **6** canner

packet: **4** boat **6** bundle, parcel

packing: **4** rags **5** gauze, paper, straw, waste **7** stowage

material: **6** gasket, baline **9** excelsior

water-tight: **6** gasket

packing plant: **7** cannery

Pacolet: **5** dwarf, horse

pact: **6** cartel, treaty **7** bargain, compact **8** alliance, contract, covenant **9** agreement

Pactolian: **6** golden

pad: mat, wad, way **4** boss, path, road, walk **5** quilt, stuff, tramp **6** basket, buffer, jockey, pillow, tablet, trudge **7** bolster, bombast, cushion, footpad **8** footfall **10** highwayman

padcloth: **7** housing **11** saddlecloth

padding: **7** packing, robbery, wadding **8** stuffing

paddle: oar, row **4** spud, wade **5** aloof **6** dabble, toddle **8** lumpfish

paddlefish: **9** spadefish **10** shovel-fish

paddock: lot **4** frog, park **5** field **6** sledge **9** enclosure

paddockstone: **10** greenstone

paddockstool: **9** toadstool

Paddy: **8** Irishman

paddywhack: **4** beat, blow **9** thrashing

padlock: **4** lock **6** fasten **7** closing **8** fastener

padre: **4** monk **6** cleric, father, priest **8** chaplain

padrona: **8** landlady, mistress

padrone: **6** master, patron **8** landlord **9** innkeeper

paean, pean: ode **4** hymn, song **6** praise

pagan: **6** ethnic, paynim **7** heathen, infidel **8** idolator **10** idolatrous, unbeliever **11** nonbeliever

page: boy **4** call, leaf **5** child, folio, sheet **6** donzel, summon, varlet **7** footboy, servant **8** henchboy, henchman **9** attendant, messenger

beginning: **4** leaf **7** flyleaf

book: **5** folio **6** cahier

lady: **8** escudero

left-hand: vo **5** verso

number: **5** folio **10** pagination

paper: **5** sheet

reverse: **5** verso

right-hand: **5** recto

title: **5** unwan **6** rubric

pageant: **4** pomp, show **6** parade **7** tableau **8** aquacade **9** spectacle **10** exhibition, procession

pageantry: **8** splendor **11** ostentation
pagoda: taa **6** temple **10** kryailteyo **11** summerhouse
pah: pa **5** nasty **6** humbug **8** improper
paha: **4** hill **5** ridge
paideutics: **8** pedagogy
pail: can, cog(Sc.), pan, soa, soe **4** beat, bowk, gawn, meal, trug **5** bowie, cogue (Sc.), eshin, skeel **6** bucket, coggie(Sc.), harass, piggin, situla(L.), thrash, vessel **7** collock, situlae(pl.) **8** cannikin
pain: **4** ache, agra, care, cark, harm, hurt, pang **5** agony, cramp, grief, sting, thraw(Sc.), throe, wound **6** grieve, twinge **7** afflict, algesis, anguish, penalty, torture, travail, trouble **8** disquiet, distress **9** suffering **10** affliction, algophilia, discomfort, punishment
  darting: **6** twinge
  pert. to: **6** asonal **7** algetic
  relayer: **5** nerve
  sensitiveness to: **7** algesia
  suffix: **5** algia
painful: **4** sare, sore **5** angry **6** bitter **7** irksome **8** exacting **9** difficult, laborious **11** painstaking
painkiller: **6** opiate **7** anodyne, aspirin **8** reliever **9** analgesic, paregoric
painstaking: **4** busy **7** careful **8** diligent, exacting **9** assiduous, elaborate, laborious
paint: **4** coat, daub, gaud, limn **5** color, feign, fucus, rouge, stain **6** bedaub, depict, enamel **7** besmear, portray, pretend **8** decorate, disguise
  combining form: **5** picto
  glossy: **6** enamel
painted: **5** pinto **6** fucate **10** artificial, variegated
painter: **6** artist **7** artiste, panther, workman **9** decorator
painting: oil **5** mural **6** canvas **10** watercolor
  equipment: **5** brush, easel, paint **6** canvas, pallet **7** palette
  medium: oil **7** gouache, tempera **10** watercolor
  one-color: **8** monotint **10** monochrome
  plaster: **5** secco **6** fresco
  sacred: **5** pieta
  scenic: **5** scape **8** seascape **9** cityscape, landscape
  small: **9** miniature
  style: **5** genre
  three panels: **8** triptych
  wall: **5** mural, panel **6** fresco
pair: duo, two **4** case, diad, duad, dyad, mate, span, team, yoke **5** brace, match, unite **6** couple
paisano: **7** peasant **10** countryman
Paisley: **5** shawl **6** design, fabric **7** pattern
pal: **4** ally, chum, pard **5** buddy, crony **6** cobber, digger, friend **7** comrade, partner **9** associate, companion **10** accomplice **11** confederate

palace: **5** court, serai **6** castle, palais(F.) **7** alcazar, edifice, mansion **8** Alcalzar **9** pretorium **10** praetorium
  officer: **7** paladin **8** palatine
  papal: **7** Lateran
paladin: **4** hero, peer **6** knight **8** champion, douzeper
palamate: **9** web-footed
Palamon: *rival:* **6** Arcite
  wife: **6** Emelye
palanquin: **4** kago **5** dooli, dooly, palki, sedan **6** doolee, dooley, doolie, litter, palkee **10** conveyance
palatable: **5** sapid, tasty **6** savory **8** delicate, pleasing **9** agreeable, delicious **10** acceptable
  render: **4** salt **5** spice **6** season
palatal: **5** front, velar **8** gutteral **9** consonant
palate: **5** taste **6** relish **7** gourmet
  pert. to: **6** uranic
  soft: **4** cion, vela(pl.) **5** uvula, velum
palatial: **5** large **6** ornate **7** stately **11** magnificent
palatine: **4** cape **7** officer, paladin **8** palatial
palaver: **4** talk **6** debate, glaver, parley **7** chatter, flatter, wheedle **8** cajolery, flattery **10** conference **12** conversation
pale: dim, wan **4** ashy, fade, grey, gull, lily, pall, sick **5** ashen, blake, blate, bleak, faint, fence, livid, lurid, stake, stick, white **6** anemic, blanch, chalky, feeble, pallid, pastel, picket, region, sickly, whiten **7** anaemic, enclose, ghastly, haggard, insipid, obscure, whitish **8** encircle, etiolate **9** colorless
paleness: **6** pallor
Palestine: *coin:* mil **5** pound
  conquerors: **5** Turks
  country: **4** Edom **9** Philistia
  god: **4** Baal
  Jewish: **5** Erets, Eretz **7** Yisrael, Yisroel
  lake: **5** Merom **7** Galilee **8** Tiberias
  landmark: Dan
  language: **7** Aramaic
  mammal: **5** daman
  measure: **5** cubit, donum **6** sacred
  mountain: **4** Ebal, Nebo, Zion **6** Carmel, Gilead, Hermon, Moriah, Olives, Pisgah **7** Gerizim **8** Jebel Tur
  part: **4** Gaza **5** Haifa **6** Canaan, Ghazze
  people: **7** Amorite
  plain: **6** Sharon
  port: **4** Acre **5** Haifa, Jaffa
  province: **7** Galilee
  region: **5** Perea **6** Bashan
  river: **6** Jordan
  town: Tob **4** Bire, Cana, Gaza **5** Endor **6** Ghazze **7** Samaria **9** Jerusalem
palestra, palaestra: **6** school **9** gymnasium
paletot: **8** overcoat **9** greatcoat
palfrey: **5** horse

palimpsest: 6 tablet 9 parchment

paling: 4 pale 5 fence, flake, limit, stake 6 picket 7 fencing 9 enclosure

palinode: 10 retraction 11 recantation

palisade: 5 cliff, fence, stake 7 barrier, enclose, fortify, furnish 8 espalier, surround 9 implement

pall: 4 bore, cloy, pale, sate 5 cloak, cloth, faint, qualm, stale, weary 6 mantle, nausea 7 disgust, satiate 8 animetta, covering

pallbearer: 6 bearer

pallet: bed, cot, pad 5 couch, quilt 7 blanket 8 mattress, plancher 9 headpiece

palliard: 6 beggar, lecher, rascal 8 vagabond

palliate: 4 ease, hide 5 cloak, cover, gloss, gloze 6 lessen, soften 7 conceal, shelter 8 disguise, mitigate 9 alleviate, exculpate, extenuate

pallid: wan 4 ashy, pale, paly 5 bleak, white 7 ghastly 9 colorless

pallium: 4 band, pall 5 cloak 6 mantle 8 himation

palm: 4 hide 6 palmus(Lat.), thenar, trophy 7 conceal

betel nut: 5 areca, bonga

beverage: 5 assai

cabbage: 8 palmetto

climbing: 6 rattan

coconut: 4 coco

fan-leafed: 7 talipat, talipot, taliput 8 palmetto

feather: 5 howea 6 gomuti 7 urucuri, urucury

fiber: tal 4 buri 6 raffia

food: nut 4 sago 5 fruit

juice: 4 nipa, sura 5 taree, toddy

kind: ti 5 assai, royal, tucum 6 bacaba, tucuma 7 babassu, jaggery, tokopat 8 bangalow

leaf: ola, ole 4 olay, olla 5 frond

low: 5 bussu 6 trooly, trouie, ubussu

palmyra: ola, ole, tal 4 brab, olla 6 ronier

pert. to: 6 palmar 8 frondous 10 palmaceous

pith: 4 sago

reader: 7 palmist

sap: 5 toddy

seeds: 4 nipa

spiny: 6 grigri, grugru

starch: 4 sago

stem: 4 cane 5 ratan 6 rattan

stemless: 5 curua

thatch: 4 nipa 9 barriguda

wing-leaved: 6 cohune

palm off: 5 foist

palma: 5 yucca

palmary: 5 chief, palmy 6 palmar 8 superior 9 principal 10 pre-eminent, victorious

palmate: 4 flat 5 broad, lobed 6 palmed, webbed

palmed: 7 palmate

palmer: 5 louse 6 stroll, travel, votary, wander 7 pilgrim 15 prestidigitator

Palmetto State: 13 South Carolina

palmistry: 10 chirognomy, chiromancy

practicer: 11 chiromancer

palmodic: 5 jerky

palms down: 7 pronate

palmy: 7 palmary 10 prosperous, triumphant 11 flourishing

palp: 6 feeler, palpus 7 flatter 8 tentacle

palpable: 4 rank 5 plain 6 patent 7 audible, evident, obvious, tactile 8 apparent, distinct, manifest, tangible 10 noticeable, perceptive 12 recognizable

palpebra: 6 eyelid

palpebrate: 4 wink

palpitation: 4 beat, pant 7 flicker, flutter 9 pulsation, quivering, throbbing, trembling

palsied: 5 shaky 7 shaking 9 paralyzed, tottering, trembling

palter: fib, lie 6 babble, haggle, mumble, trifle 7 chatter, quibble 10 equivocate 11 prevaricate

paltock: 6 jacket 7 doublet

paltry: 4 bald, bare, base, mean, puny, vile 5 footy, petty, trash 6 chetif, flimsy, trashy 7 pitiful, rubbish, trivial 8 picayune, trifling 9 worthless 10 despicable 12 contemptible 13 insignificant

paludal: 6 marshy 8 paludine

pampas: 5 plain

pamper: pet 4 baby, cram, delt(Sc.), glut 5 spoil 6 caress, cocker, coddle, cosher, cosset, cuddle, dandle, fondle, posset 7 cherish, cockney, gratify, indulge, satiate, forwean

pamphagous: 10 omnivorous

pamphlet: 5 tract 6 folder 7 booklet, catalog, leaflet 8 brochure 9 catalogue

pan: fit, tab 4 part, wash 5 agree, basin, unite 6 frache(F.), lappet, vessel 7 cranium, hardpan, portion, subsoil 8 brainpan, ridicule 9 criticize 10 acetabulum

coal burner: 5 grill 7 brazier

frying: 6 spider 7 skillet

gold-washing: 4 tina 5 batea

Pan: 6 Faunus

instrument: 4 pipe, reed

place of worship: 7 Arcadia

son: 7 Silenus 8 Seilenos

panacea: 4 cure 6 elixir, remedy 7 allheal, cure-all, heal-all 8 nepenthe 10 catholicon 11 panchreston

panache: 5 plume

panachure: 8 mottling

panal: 7 biscuit

Panama: hat 6 Darien

city: 5 Colon 6 Panama 9 Aspinwall, Cristobal

coin: 6 balboa

gulf: 6 Darien

measure: 7 celemin

river: **5** Sambu, Tuira **7** Chagres
rubber: **8** Castilla
tree: **4** yaya **6** alfaje, cativo
Panama Canal: *dam and locks:* **5** Gatun **10** Miraflores
engineer: **9** de Lesseps
lake: **5** Gatun
port: **5** Colon **9** Cristobal
panatela: **5** cigar
panax: **4** herb
pancake: **5** arepa(Sp.), flawn **6** blintz, fraise, froise **7** blintze, fritter, hotcake **8** flapjack **11** griddlecake
delicate: **5** crepe
panda: wah **6** animal **7** bearcat
pandemonium: **5** noise **6** tumult, uproar **8** disorder **9** confusion
pander: **4** bawd, pimp **5** cater **7** whiskin **8** procurer **9** go-between, procuress
Pandora: *brother:* **10** Prometheus
husband: **10** Epimetheus
pane: **5** glass **7** section
panegyric: **5** eloge, elogy **6** eulogy, praise **7** encomia(pl.), oration, tribute, writing **8** encomium **9** discourse, laudation
panel: **4** jury **5** group **6** tympan **8** decorate
paneling: **4** wall **7** ceiling
panfish: **4** crab, king **9** horseshoe
pang: **4** ache, cram, fill, gird, pain, tang **5** agony, spasm, stuff, throe **6** twinge **7** anguish, travail **8** paroxysm **9** heartache
pangolin: **5** manis **8** anteater, edentate
order: **9** pholidota
panhandle: beg **5** cadge
Panhandle State: **12** West Virginia
panic: **4** fear, fray, funk **5** alarm, chaos, scare **6** fright, terror **8** stampede **13** consternation
pannier, panier: bag, ped **5** seron **6** basket, dorsel, dorser, dosser, pantry **9** overskirt
horse: **6** curagh **7** currach, currack, curragh, currock
panoply: **5** armor **8** armour
panorama: **4** view **5** scene, sweep, vista **7** picture, scenery **9** cyclorama
panpipe: **6** syrinx **8** zampogna
pansy: **9** heartease **10** heartsease
pant: **4** ache, beat, blow, gasp, puff **5** heave, throb, yearn **7** pulsate **9** palpitate **11** palpitation
Pantagruel: *companion:* **7** Panurge
father: **9** Gargantua
mother: **7** Badebec
pantalan: **5** wharf **8** platform
pantheon: **6** temple
panther: cat **4** pard, puma **6** cougar, jaguar **7** leopard, painter
pantile: **4** tile **7** biscuit **8** hardtack
panting: **8** anhelose, anhelous **10** anhelation
pantomimist: **4** mime **5** actor **7** Marceau
pantry: **4** cave **5** ambry **6** closet, larder **7** buttery, pannier, pantler **8** cupboard

pants: **5** jeans **7** drawers **8** trousers **10** pantaloons
leather: **5** chaps **10** chaparajos, chapareras, chaperejos, lederhosen(G.) **11** chaparreras
panuelo: **6** collar, ruffle **8** kerchief **9** neckcloth
pap: **4** teat **6** nipple **8** emulsion, mammilla
papa: pa; dad, paw, pop **6** baboon, father, potato, priest **7** vulture
papal (see also **Pope**): **9** apostolic **10** pontifical
papal court: see **5** curia
papaya: **5** papaw **6** pawpaw
paper: **5** essay, theme **6** cartel, report **7** journal, writing **8** document **9** monograph, newspaper, wallpaper **10** periodical **11** credentials, examination **12** dissertation **13** unsubstantial
absorbent: **7** blotter **9** towelling
case: **4** file **5** folio **6** binder
collection: **7** dossier
currency: **5** scrip
damaged: **5** broke, casse, salle **6** cassie
design: **9** watermark
detachable: tab **4** stub **6** coupon
fine: **5** linen **6** vellum
folded once: **5** folio
gummed: **5** label, stamp **6** paster **7** sticker
hard: **6** pelure
large-size: **5** atlas
legal: **4** writ
official: **5** targe **8** document
pad: **6** tablet
piece: **5** scrip, sheet
postage-stamp: **6** pelure
quantity: **4** page, ream **5** quire, sheet **6** bundle
size: cap **4** copy, demi, demy, pott **5** atlas, crown, folio, legal **7** bastard, emperor **8** foolscap, imperial **9** colombier
thin: **6** pelure, tissue **9** onionskin
writing-size: cap **8** foolscap
papist: **8** Catholic
papoose: **4** baby
pappy: pa; dad, paw **4** papa, soft **5** mushy **6** father
papule: **6** pimple
papyrus: **4** reed **6** biblos, biblus, scroll **7** bulrush
repository: **5** capsa
par: by **5** equal **6** normal **7** average **8** equality **9** enclosure **11** equivalence
par value: **4** face **7** nominal
parable: **4** myth, tale **5** fable, story **6** apolog, byword **7** byspell **8** allegory, apologue, forbysen **10** comparison, similitude
parabola: arc **5** curve
parachute material: **4** silk **5** nylon
paraclete: **6** helper **7** pleader **8** advocate, consoler **9** comforter **11** intercessor
parade: **4** pomp, show, walk **5** march, strut **6** flaunt, review, stroll **7** cortege,

display, exhibit, marshal **8** ceremony, flourish, grandeur, splendor **9** advertise, pageantry, promenade, strollers **10** callithump, pretension, procession **12** magnificence

paradigm: **5** model **7** example, pattern

Paradise: **4** Eden **5** bliss **6** Aidenn, heaven **7** Elysium

Buddhist: **4** Jodo

fool's: **5** limbo

Muslim: **5** Jenna

river: **5** Gihon

paraffin: **6** alkane

paragon: gem **4** type **5** ideal, model **7** pattern **9** nonpariel

paragram: pun

paragraph: **4** item, sign **5** caput **7** initial **8** material

Paraguay: *city:* Ita **8** Asuncion(c.) **9** Paraguari, Villa Rica

coin: **4** peso

measure: pie **4** line, lino, vara **5** legua, linea **6** cordel, cuadra, cuarta, fanega, league

money: **7** guarani

river: Apa **6** Parana **8** Paraguay **9** Tibiquare

tea: **4** mate **5** yerba

weight: **7** quintal

parakeet: **6** parrot, wellat **8** paraquet **10** budgerygah **11** budgereegah

parallel: **4** even **5** along, equal, match **8** analogue **10** collateral **11** counterpart

parallelism: **6** simile **10** similarity **11** resemblance **14** correspondence

parallelogram: **5** rhomb **6** oblong, square **9** rectangle

paralogist: **7** sophist

paralysis: **5** cramp, palsy **7** paresis **10** holoplexia **11** monoparesis

with: **7** paretic **9** paralytic

paralyzed: **4** numb **7** palsied **8** benumbed, crippled

paramount: **5** above, chief, ruler **7** capital, supreme **8** dominant, superior, suzerain **10** pre-eminent, proprietor

lord: **5** liege

paramour: **5** leman, lover, wooer **6** amoret, friend **10** sweetheart

female: **7** hetaera, hetaira **8** mistress

paranomasia: pun

paranymph: **10** bridesmaid

parapet: **4** butt, wall **5** redan **7** bulwark, railing, rampart **10** breastwork **12** embattlement **13** fortification

paraphernalia: **4** gear **9** apparatus, equipment, trappings **10** belongings **11** furnishings

paraphrase: **6** reword **7** version **9** translate **11** translation

parasite: bug, bur **4** burr, moss **5** leech, toady, virus **6** fungus, sponge **7** sponger **8** hanger-on **9** mistletoe, sycophant

animal: **8** entozoan

plant: **9** entophyte

trout: sug

parasol: **8** sunshade, umbrella **11** bumbershoot

paratrooper cry: **8** Geronimo

paravane: **5** otter

parcel: lot **4** deal, mete, pack, part **5** bulse, bunch, group, piece **6** bundle, divide, packet **7** package, portion **8** fragment **10** collection, distribute

parch: dry **4** burn, sear **5** roast, toast **6** scorch **7** bristle, brustle, graddan, shrivel

parched: **4** arid, sere **5** fiery **6** gizzen, torrid

parchment (see also **paper, scroll**): **6** charta

book cover: **5** forel **6** forrel

fine: vel **6** vellum

manuscript: **10** palimpsest

piece: **8** membrane

roll: **4** pell **6** scroll

pard: pal **4** chum **5** tiger **7** leopard, panther, partner **9** companion **10** camelopard

pardesi: **9** foreigner, outlander

pardo: **7** mulatto

pardon: **5** mercy, remit, spare **6** assoil, excuse **7** absolve, amnesty, condone, forgive **8** reprieve, tolerate **9** exculpate, remission **10** absolution, indulgence **11** forgiveness

general: **7** amnesty

stall: **12** confessional

pardonable: **6** venial **9** excusable

pare: cut **4** chip, peel, skin **5** shave **6** reduce, remove, resect **7** curtail, whittle **8** diminish **11** decorticate

paregoric: **7** anodyne

pareil: **4** mate **5** equal **8** equality

parel: **7** apparel **11** mantelpiece

parella, parelle: **6** lichen

parent: dad, dam **4** mama, papa, sire **5** daddy, mater(L.), pater **6** author, father, mother, origin **7** forbear, genitor **8** ancestor, begetter, forebear, guardian, producer **10** forefather, progenitor

parentage: **5** birth **6** family, origin **10** extraction, parenthood

parget: **4** coat **6** gypsum **7** plaster **8** decorate **9** whitewash

pariah: **7** Ishmael, outcast

parian: **6** marble, market **9** porcelain

Paris: *district:* **7** Auteuil

father: **5** Priam

mother: **6** Hecuba

palace: **6** Elysee, Louvre **9** Tuileries

river: **5** Seine

stock exchange: **6** bourse

suburb: **5** Passy

subway: **5** metro

thug: **6** apache

wife: **6** Oenone

parish: **12** congregation

head: **6** pastor, priest **8** minister

officer: **10** borsholder
official: **9** vestryman
paristhmion: **6** tonsil
parity: **7** analogy **8** equality **10** similarity **11** resemblance
park: hay **4** stop **7** commons, paddock **10** playground
parlance: **4** talk **7** diction **9** discourse **11** phraseology **12** conversation
parlay: **5** wager **6** paroli
parley: **5** speak, treat, utter **6** confer, paroli **7** discuss, palaver **9** discourse **10** conference, discussion **12** conversation
parliament: **4** diet **5** senat(F.) **7** council **8** congress, converse **9** parleying **10** conference
member: **4** lord
parlous: **4** keen **5** risky **6** clever, shrewd **7** cunning **8** perilous **9** dangerous **11** exceedingly, excessively, mischievous **13** disconcerting
parnassian: **4** poet
paroch: **9** clergyman
parody: **4** skit **6** satire **8** travesty **9** burlesque, imitation **10** caricature
paroemia: **7** proverb
parole: **6** pledge **7** promise
paronomasia: pun **12** agnomination
paroxysm: fit **4** pang **5** agony, spasm, throe **6** access, attack, orgasm **8** epitasis, outburst **9** agitation **10** convulsion **12** exacerbation
parrot: ara **4** copy, echo, lory **5** arara, mimic, polly **6** repeat, tiriba **7** corella **8** cockatoo, lorikeet, lovebird, parakeet **9** cockateel, cockatiel
disease: **11** psittacosis
gray: **4** jako
hawk: hia
like: **5** arine **11** psittaceous
long-tailed: **5** macaw
owl: **4** kaka **6** kakapo
sheep-killing: kea
small: **8** lovebird, parakeet
parrot fish: **4** scar **5** lania **6** scarus **9** labroidea
parry: **4** fend, ward **5** avoid, block, evade **6** thwart **7** deflect, evasion
parse: **7** analyse, analyze, diagram **8** construe
Parsee: See **Parsi.**
Parsi: **11** Zoroastrian
holy book: **6** Avesta
priest: **5** mobed **6** dastur **7** destour, dustoor
parsimonious: **4** mean, near **5** close, scant, spare **6** frugal, narrow, skimpy, sordid, stingy **7** miserly, sparing **8** covetous, grasping, wretched **9** illiberal, mercenary, niggardly, penurious **10** avaricious, economical, ungenerous **17** narrowheartedness
parsley: **5** cumin **6** eltrot
parsley camphor: **6** apiole

parson: **6** rector **8** minister, preacher **9** clergyman, guidepost
parson-in-the-pulpit: **10** cuckoopint
parsonage: **5** manse **7** rectory **9** pastorium
part (see also **parts**)**:** **4** deal, dole, half, role, rove, side, some, twin **5** piece, quota, sever, share **6** behalf, canton, cleave, depart, detail, divide, member, sunder **7** disjoin, element, portion, section, segment **8** alienate, disperse, dissever, disunite, division, estrange, fraction, fragment, separate **9** abteilung(G.), apportion, dismember **10** department **11** constituent
baglike: sac
basic: **4** core, pith **7** essence
central: **4** core **5** focus, solar **6** nuclei(pl.) **7** nucleus
choice: **5** cream, elite **6** marrow **7** essence
coarse: **5** dregs
distinct: **5** unit **7** article
essential: **4** core, gist, pith **6** factor
final: **5** shank
hardest: **5** brunt
highest: top **4** apex **5** crest **6** summit
inmost: **4** core **5** heart **6** center
main: **4** body **5** trunk
minor: bit, cog
moving: **5** rotor
narrow: **4** neck
revolving: **5** rotor **7** rotator
root-like: **7** radicle
small: bit, jot **4** atom, iota, mite **5** tithe **6** detail, moiety **7** snippet
suddenly: **4** rend, snap
uppermost: top **4** peak **6** upside **7** topside
part with: **4** give, lose, sell **5** leave **6** donate **7** abandon
partage: **4** part **5** share **7** portion **8** division
partake: **4** bite **5** share **6** divide **11** participate
of: use
partan: **4** crab
parted: **7** partite
parten: **6** impart **7** partake
partial: **4** half, part **6** biased, unfair **7** colored, halfway **8** coloured, inclined, one-sided, partisan **10** fractional, incomplete, prejudiced **11** predilected, predisposed
prefix: **4** semi, demi
participant: **5** party **8** partisan **10** accomplice **12** participator **13** participating
participate: **4** join, side **5** enter, share **7** compete, partake **9** cooperate
particle: ace, bit, dot, gru, jot **4** atom, grue, iota, mite, mote, whit **5** fleck, grain, shred, speck **6** smidge, tittle **7** smidgen, smidgin **8** smidgeon, smitchin
affirmative: yes
burnt: **6** cinder

co-ordinating: or
electrified: ion 5 anion 6 proton
incandescent: 5 spark
minute: jot, ort, ray 4 atom, iota, mite,
mote 5 grain, speck 7 granule, ram-
enta(pl.) 8 molecule, ramentum 9 scintilla
negative: nor, not
pluvial: 4 drop
small: see *minute* above
particular: 4 item, nice 5 fussy, thing 6
detail, minute 7 article, careful, correct,
precise, special, unusual 8 accurate, concrete, detailed, especial, exacting, item-
ized, specific 10 fastidious, noteworthy
11 scrumptious 12 circumstance 13 extraordinary 14 circumstantial
particularly: 9 expressly
parting: 5 death 8 farewell 11 leavetaking
partisan: 4 pike 5 staff 6 biased, fautor 7
devotee 8 adherent, follower, partizan 9
truncheon 10 factionary, factioneer, interested
unwavering: 6 zealot 8 stalwart
partite: 6 parted 7 divided 9 separated
partition: 4 wall 5 septa(pl.) 6 divide,
screen, septum 7 enclose, portion, scantle
8 cleavage, division 9 severance 10 distribute, enterclose, separation 11 compartment 13 apportionment
partitioned: 7 septate
partlet: hen 5 woman
partner: pal 4 ally, half, mate, wife 5 butty
6 fellow, sharer 7 comrade, consort, husband 8 camarada 9 associate, coadjutor,
colleague, companion 10 accomplice 11
confederate, participant
comedian's: 6 stooge
paid: 6 gigolo
partnership: hui 4 firm 7 cahoots, company 14 compagnieschap(D.)
partridge: 4 yutu 5 titar 6 chukar, chu-
kor, seesee 7 tinamou 9 francolin
flock: 5 covey
young: 7 cheeper 8 squealer
partridgeberry: 9 snowberry
parts (see also **part**):
innermost: 10 penetralia
together: 9 adhesions
totality: 5 unity
two: 6 binary
parturition: 7 travail 8 delivery 10
childbirth
party (see also **political party**): bal(F.) 4
clan, drum, sect, side 5 cabal, group 6
comite, fiesta, person 7 company, faction
9 gathering 10 detachment 11 association, combination 12 participator
afternoon: tea 9 reception
evening: 4 ball 6 soiree
guilty: 7 culprit
men's: 4 stag 6 smoker
reconnaissance: 6 patrol
seashore: 6 picnic 8 clambake

party man: 8 partisan
parure: 5 adorn 6 paring 7 apparel, peeling 8 ornament
parvenu: 4 snob 6 arrive 7 upstart 9 ar-
riviste 12 nouveauriche, nouvellerich
Pasch, Pascha: 6 Easter 8 Passover 10
Good Friday
paschal: 4 lamb 6 supper 8 Passover 11
celebration
pasear: 4 walk 6 airing 9 promenade
pasha: dey 4 emir
territory: 8 pachalic, pashalic, pashalik
Pasiphae: *children:* 7 Ariadne, Phaedra
husband: 5 Minos
pasqueflower: 6 badger 10 badgerweed
pasquinade: 5 squib 6 satire 7 lampoon,
pasquil
pass: go; col, end, gap 4 abra, beal(Sc.),
comp, cove, fare, ghat, hand, lane, pace,
step, wend 5 canto, enact, ghaut, gorge,
hurry, kotal, lapse, lunge, occur, relay,
smite, spend, utter, yodel 6 billet, convey,
defile, elapse, exceed, happen, passus,
permit, ticket, twofer 7 allonge, approve,
devolve, passage, undergo 8 beallach,
surmount 10 abjudicate, permission 11
Annie Oakley 13 complimentary
around: 5 skirt 6 detour
slowly: 4 drag
without touching: 5 clear
pass away: die 6 expire, perish, vanish 8
transfer 9 disappear, surrender
pass by: 4 cote, omit, skip 6 forego, ignore
8 overlook 9 disregard
pass off: con 5 foist
pass over: die 4 omit, skip 5 cross 6
elapse, expire, excuse, ignore 8 overlook,
transfer, traverse 9 disregard
lightly: 4 skim
quickly: 4 scan, scud
smoothly: 5 elide
pass through: 5 cross 6 pierce 7 pervade
8 permeate, traverse 9 penetrate
pass up: 6 reject 7 decline 9 disregard
passable: fit 4 fair, soso 7 genuine 8 adequate, mediocre, moderate, traveled 9
navigable, navigated, tolerable, traversed
10 admissable
passage: gat, gut, wro 4 adit, belt, door,
duct, exit, fare, flue, ford, gang, gate, hall,
iter, lane, pass, pawn, race, ramp, slip 5
aisle, allee, alley, alure, atria(pl.), entry,
going, gorge, meuse 6 access, arcade,
atrium, avenue, burrow, course, defile,
egress, strait, travel, tunnel, voyage 7
channel, couloir, estuary, gangway, itin-
era(pl.), journey, transit 8 aqueduct,
corridor, crossing 9 ventiduct 10 bottle-
neck 12 thoroughfare
air: 4 flue 9 ventiduct
literary: 4 text 7 excerpt 9 quotation
one outlet: 7 impasse 8 cul-de-sac
scripture: 4 text
subterranean: 4 mine 6 tunnel 8 cu-
niculi(pl.) 9 cuniculus

passageway: 5 aisle

passant: 4 past 7 current, cursory, passing, walking 9 ephemeral, excelling 10 proceeding, surpassing, transitory

passe: 4 aged, past, worn 5 faded 7 demoded 8 obsolete, outmoded 10 antiquated 12 old-fashioned 13 superannuated

passementerie: 8 trimming

passenger: 4 fare 8 ferryman, traveler, wayfarer

passerby: 9 saunterer

passing: 7 cursory 8 elapsing, fleeting 9 departing, ephemeral, exceeding 10 pre-eminent, transitory, surpassing

passion (see also **mania**): ire 4 fire, fury, heat, love, lust, raga, rage, zeal 5 anger, ardor 6 affect, choler, desire, fervor 7 emotion, feeling, fervour 8 appetite 9 calenture, martyrdom 10 affliction, enthusiasm

passion flower: 6 maypop
  family: 14 passifloraceae

passionate: 4 fond 6 fervid, fierce 7 amorous, flaming, peppery 8 frenetic 9 irascible, phrenetic 11 impassioned 12 affectionate

passionless: 4 cold 6 freddo(It.)

passive: 5 inert, stoic 6 stolid 7 patient 8 inactive, yielding 9 apathetic, impassive 10 submissive

passover: 5 phase

Passover: 5 Pesah 6 Pesach
  bread: 5 matzo 6 matzos 7 matzoth 8 afikomen
  festival: 5 Seder
  story: 7 haggada 8 haggadah

passport: 5 conge 6 dustuk 7 dustuck 8 furlough
  endorsement: 4 visa, vise

passus: 4 pace, part, step 5 canto 8 division

password: 11 countersign

past: by; ago 4 gone, yore 5 after, agone, aside, ended, since 6 behind, bygone 8 foregone 9 completed, foregoing 11 antecedents
  immediate: 9 yesterday
  pert. to: 8 historic
  tense: 11 preteritive

paste: hit, pap 4 beat, blow, duff, glue, pate 5 cream, dough, false, punch, stick 6 attach, batter, fasten, strass 7 filling 8 adhesive, mucilage 9 imitation
  aromatic: 6 pastil 7 pastile 8 pastille
  dried: 7 guarana

pasteboard: 4 card, sham 6 flimsy

pastel: 6 crayon 7 picture

pastern: 6 hobble, hopple, tether 7 shackle

pasticcio: 4 olio 6 jumble, medley 9 patchwork, potpourri 10 hodgepodge

pastime: 4 game 5 hobby, sport 9 amusement, diversion 10 yesteryear 13 entertainment

pastor: 4 herd 5 angel, rabbi 6 curate,

keeper, priest, rector 7 dominie 8 guardian, minister, shepherd 9 clergyman

pastoral: 4 poem 5 drama, rural 7 bucolic, idyllic, romance
  poem: 4 idyl 5 idyll 7 eclogue, georgic

pastry (see also **cake, pie**): pie 4 flan, huff, tart 6 eclair 7 carcake(Sc.), strudel 8 napoleon, turnover
  garnish: 5 cream, fruit 8 meringue
  shell: 7 dariole, timbale

pasturage: 4 gang 6 eatage, forage 7 herbage

pasture: hag, ham, ing, lea 4 heaf, hoga 5 agist, drift, grass, graze, veldt 6 meadow, saeter 7 grazing, vaccary 8 herdwick 9 grassland 10 agostadero
  god: Pan

pasturer: 7 grazier 8 herdsman

pasty: pie 6 doughy

pasty cement: 6 mastic

pat: apt, dab, tap 4 blow 5 fitly, fixed, impel, throw 6 caress, soothe, strike, stroke, timely 7 apropos, fitting, readily 8 suitable 9 immovable, opportune, pertinent 10 seasonable 12 commendation

Patagonia: *cavy:* 4 mara
  deity: 7 Setebos
  rodent: 4 cavy, mara
  tree: 6 alerce, alerse

patamar: 7 courier 9 messenger

patand: 4 base 6 plinth

patch: bit 4 mend, vamp 5 bodge, clout, clump, cover, piece, scrap 6 blotch, cobble, dollop, parcel, revamp, solder 7 clobber, remnant

patchwork: 5 cento 6 jumble, scraps 9 fragments 10 hodgepodge

pate: pie, top 4 head 5 crown, paste, pasty, patty 6 badger, noggin

patella: pan 4 dish, vase 7 kneecap, kneepan

paten: 4 arca, disc, dish, disk 5 plate 6 vessel

patent: 4 arca, open 5 berat(Orient), overt, plain 7 evident, license, obvious 8 apparent, archives, enduring, manifest 9 available, franchise 10 accessible, university 12 unobstructed
  notice: 6 caveat

pater: 6 father, priest

paterissa: 7 crosier

paternal: 8 fatherly

paternity: 6 father, origin 10 authorship, fatherhood 12 fatherliness

path: pad, rut, way 4 fare, lane, line, road, walk 5 alley, byway, going, piste, route, track, trail 6 camino, casaun, comino, course, groove 7 footway, highway, towpath
  hill: 4 berm 5 berme 6 roddin 7 borstal, rodding 8 borstall
  math.: 5 locus

pathetic: sad 5 teary 7 pitiful 8 stirring 9 affecting

pathic: 7 passive 8 catamite 9 suffering

pathological: 4 sick **6** morbid
pathway: run **4** lane, path **6** course, roddin **7** rodding
patience: 4 calm **8** stoicism **9** composure, endurance, fortitude **10** submission **11** forbearance, resignation **12** acquiescence
patient: 4 case, meek **6** bovine
patinize: 6 patine
patio: 5 court **9** courtyard
patois: 6 Creole **7** dialect
patriarch: 4 Enos, Levi, Nasi, Noah **5** elder **7** ancient **9** venerable
patrician: 5 noble **10** aristocrat **12** aristocratic
patrimony: 8 ancestry, heritage
patriot: 10 chauvinist, countryman **11** compatriate
song: **6** anthem **7** America
patrocinium: 9 patronage **10** protection
patrol: 5 guard, scout, watch **7** protect **10** detachment
patrolman: cop **5** guard **9** inspector, policeman
patron: 5 buyer, guest **6** client, fautor **7** sponsor **8** advocate, champion, customer, defender, guardian **9** protector, supporter **10** benefactor
stock exchange: **5** buyer **6** seller, trader
patron saint: See **saint.**
patronage: 5 aegis, favor **6** custom, favour **7** auspice, fomento **8** business **10** assistance **13** encouragement
patronize: 5 deign **10** condescend
patroon: 5 tract **6** patron **9** supporter **10** proprietor
patten: 4 base, clog, foot, shoe **5** skate, stand, stilt **6** sandal **7** support **8** overshoe, snowshoe
patter: 4 cant, talk **5** lingo **6** jargon **7** blatter, chatter
pattern: 4 form, norm, plan **5** bysen, draft, epure, guide, ideal, model, plaid **6** checks, design, format, former, sample, stripe **7** example, project, stencil, templet **8** exemplar, forbysen, paradigm, specimen, template **9** archetype, ensampler, precedent
patulous: 4 open **8** expanded **9** distended, spreading
paucity: 4 lack **6** dearth **7** fewness **8** exiguity, scarcity **13** insufficiency
paughty: 4 pert **5** saucy **7** haughty
Paul: *associate:* **5** Demas, Titus
companion: **5** Silas **7** Artemas **8** Barnabas
paunch: 5 belly, rumen **7** abdomen, stomach **8** potbelly **10** disembowel, eviscerate
pauper: 6 beggar **8** indigent
pause: 4 halt, lull, rest, stop, wait **5** abide, break, cease, delay, demur, dwell, hover, selah, tarry **6** breach, breath, falter, stance **7** caesura, respite **8** breather, caesurae(pl.), hesitate, intermit **9** cessa-

tion **10** hesitation **12** intermission, interruption
paut: paw **4** poke **5** stamp **6** finger
pavane: 5 dance
pave: lay **4** path, stud, tile **5** cover, floor **6** causey, cobble, smooth **7** overlay, prepare **10** facilitate, macadamize
pavid: 5 timid **6** afraid **7** fearful
pavilion: 4 flag, tent **5** kiosk **6** canopy, ensign, litter **8** covering **9** gloriette
paving: 4 flag, sett **5** block, brick, dalle, paver, stone **6** cobble, Tarmac **7** asphalt **9** flagstone
pavis: 5 cover **6** shield **7** protect
pavo: 7 peacock **13** constellation
paw: pud, toe **4** foot, gaum, hand, maul, paty **5** patte **6** fumble, handle, pattee **7** crubeen, flipper **8** forefoot
pawky: sly **4** arch, bold **5** canny, saucy **6** crafty, lively, shrewd **7** cunning, forward
pawl: cog, dog **4** bolt, sear, tent, trip **5** catch, click **6** detent, pallet, tongue **7** ratchet
pawn: 4 gage, hock, soak **6** lumber, pledge **7** counter, hostage, peacock **8** chessman, guaranty **11** impignorate
pawnbroker: 6 broker
pawnie: 7 peacock
pawpaw: 5 papaw **6** papaya **7** immoral, naughty **8** indecent **11** bushwhacker **15** euphemistically
pax: 5 board, peace **6** friend, tablet **10** friendship, osculatory
pay: fee, tip **4** ante, foot, meet, rent, wage **5** repay **6** defray, reward, salary **7** imburse, requite, satisfy, stipend, tribute **9** indemnify, reimburse **10** compensate, recompense, remunerate **11** retribution **12** compensation
back: **6** rebate, refund **9** reimburse, retaliate
extra: **5** batta, bonus **8** kickback
for: buy **4** rent **8** purchase
out: **5** spend **6** expend **8** disburse **10** distribute
up: **4** ante **6** settle **9** liquidate
paying: 10 profitable
paymaster: 6 bakshi, bukshi, purser **7** bukshee(Ind.) **8** buckshee **9** treasurer
payment: cro, fee, tax **4** bill, dole, dues, duty, feal, fine, gale, levy, toll **5** gavel, price **6** pledge, rebate, return, reward, tariff **7** alimony, annuity, customs, pension, stipend, trewage, tuition **8** defrayal, requital **9** acquittal, allowance, discharge, honoraria(pl.) **10** honorarium, recompense, remittance **12** compensation, contribution
demand: dun **4** bill
evade: **4** bilk **7** default
failure: **13** nonredemption
immediate: **4** cash **9** alcontado(Sp.),
on delivery: COD
press for: dun

without: **4** free **6** gratis

paynim: 5 pagan **7** heathen, infidel **10** Mohammedan

payoff: fix **5** bribe **6** climax **9** reckoning **10** settlement

payola: 5 bribe

payong: 8 umbrella

paysage: 7 picture **9** landscape

pea: dal **4** gram, seed **5** arhar, chick, cicer, pease **6** gandul, legume, pigeon **7** carmele, catjang **8** garvanro **12** peavetchling

dove: **7** zenaida

family: **8** fabaceae

finch: **9** chaffinch

flour: **9** Erbswurst

pod: **5** quash

sausage: **9** Erbswurst

seeds: **5** pulse

shaped: **8** pisiform

vine: **8** earthpea

peaberry: 11 coffeeberry

peabird: 6 oriole **7** wryneck

peace: pax(L.), paz(Sp.) **4** calm, ease, liss, rest **5** amity, grith, lisse, quiet **6** repose **7** concord, harmony **8** ataraxia, security, serenity **9** armistice, heartease **10** heartsease **11** tranquility

goddess: **5** Irene

pledge: **11** Frankpledge

symbol: **4** dove, toga **5** olive

peace pipe: 7 calumet

peaceable: 6 gentle **7** pacific, solomon **11** undisturbed

peaceful: 4 calm **5** still **6** irenic, placid **7** halcyon **8** irenical **11** undisturbed

peach: 4 blab **6** accuse, betray, indict, inform **7** impeach, whittle

family: **12** amygdalaceae

grafted on quince: **9** melocoton

kind: **6** Carman, Crosby, Salwey **7** Elberta **8** Crawford, quandang, quandong, quantong **9** freestone, nectarine **10** clingstone

origin: **5** China

stone: **7** putamen

peachwort: 9 persicary

peachy: 4 fine, nice **9** beautiful, excellent

peacock: mao **4** pavo, pawn

fan: **9** flabellum

feather fiber: **4** marl

female: **6** peahen

pert. to: **8** pavonine

tail spot: eye

peacock bittern: sun

peacock blue: 4 paon **7** pigment

peacock butterfly: io

peacock fish: 9 wrasse

peacock flower: 9 poinciana

peacock heron: 7 bittern

peacock ore: 7 bornite **12** chalcopyrite

peafowl: 6 peahen **7** peacock

peag, peage: tax **4** toll **5** beads **6** pedage, wampum

peak: Alp, ben, pic(F.), top, tor **4** acme,

apex, cima, cusp, dent, dolt, pico(Sp.) **5** crest, crown, point, slink, sneak, steal **6** shrink, summit **7** epitome, maximum **8** aiguille, headland, pinnacle **9** ascendant, ascendent, simpleton **10** promontory

ice: **5** serac

snow-capped: **7** calotte

peaked: wan **4** pale, thin **5** drawn **6** picked, sickly **9** emaciated

peal: 4 clap, ring, toll **5** chime **6** appeal, shovel **7** resound, summons, thunder **8** carillon

Peale Island: 4 Habe

pean, paean: ode **4** hymn, song

peanut: 4 mani **5** pinda **6** goober, pindal **7** beennut **8** earthnut, earthpea, grassnut, katchung

pear: 4 bosc **5** melon **6** beurre, burrel, warden, winter **7** kieffer, prickly **8** ambrette, Bartlett, bergamot **9** alligator **10** chaumontel

squash: **5** perry **7** chayote

pearl: gem **5** nacre, onion **6** bouton, orient **9** margarite

artificial: **6** olivet

seed: **7** aliofar

pearl blush: 7 rosetan

pearl moss: 9 carrageen

Pearl of Antilles: 4 Cuba

pearlbird: 6 barbet

pearl opal: 9 cacholong

pearlweed: 6 sagina **8** sealwort

pearlwort: 6 sagina

peart: 4 pert

peasant: 4 bond, boor, hind, kern(Ir.), kopi, peon, ryot, serf **5** churl, kerne(Ir.), knave, kulak, swain **6** cotman, cottar, cotter, farmer, fellah, rascal, rustic **7** bondman, laborer, paisano(Sp.) **9** chopstick, contadino(It.) **10** countryman

crop sharing: **7** metayer

pease: pea **5** quiet **6** pacify **7** appease **9** reconcile

pease brose: 7 pottage **8** porridge

pease crow: 4 tern

peashooter: 6 blower **7** blowgun **11** beanshooter

peat: gor(Ir.), pet **4** fuel, turf **6** lawyer, minion **7** darling **8** favorite **11** combustible

bog: **4** cess, moss

cutter: **5** piner(Sc.)

spade: **5** slane

peatwood: 11 loosestrife

peau d'ange: 6 fabric, finish **9** angelskin

peba: 9 armadillo

pebble: 5 scree, stone **6** gravel, quartz, sycite **7** chuckie, crystal **10** chuckstone

pebble-shaped: 9 calciform

peccadillo: 5 fault **7** offense **8** mischief

peccant: 6 morbid, sinner **7** corrupt, sinning **9** incorrect, unhealthy

peccary: 6 warree **7** tagassu, tayassu **8** javelina

pech: 4 pant, sigh 6 breath 7 breathe
pecht: 4 pict 5 fairy, gnome, pygmy
peck: dab, dot, nip 4 bill, carp, food, hole, jerk, kiss 5 pitch, prick, throw 6 nibble, stroke 7 chimble, measure
at: nag 4 twit 5 tease 6 attack, harass
four: bu. 6 bushel
pecker: 4 nose 5 eater 6 feeder 7 courage, spirits 10 resolution, woodpecker
pectase: 6 enzyme
peculate: 5 steal 6 misuse 8 embezzle 11 appropriate
peculiar: odd 5 queer 6 unique 7 curious, special, strange, unusual 8 especial, singular 9 eccentric, exclusive 10 particular 11 distinctive 14 characteristic
combining form: 4 idio
peculiarity: 4 kink 5 quirk, trait, twist 6 idiasm 9 attribute 12 idiosyncracy
of expression: 5 idiom 6 idioma, idiome
pecuniary: 9 financial
ped: 6 basket, hamper, panier 7 pannier
pedagogue: 5 tutor 6 pedant 7 dominie, teacher 12 schoolmaster
pedal: 5 lever 7 treadle
coupler: 7 tirasse
piano: 7 celeste
pedant: 4 prig 5 dunce, tutor 6 dorbel, purist, tassel 9 pedagogue 12 bluestocking, schoolmaster
pedantic: 7 bookish 8 teaching 10 didascalic, moralistic
peddle: 4 hawk, sell 5 cadge, trant 6 higgle, meddle, piddle, retail 7 colport
peddler: 5 faker 6 broker, coster, duffer, hawker, seller 7 camelot, chapman 8 huckster, pitchman 12 carpetbagger, costermonger
pedestal: 4 anta, base 6 pillar, podium 7 support 10 foundation
part: die 4 dado 5 socle 6 plinth, quadra
put on: 7 idolize 8 enshrine
pedestrian: ped 4 dull, slow 6 hoofer, walker 7 footman, prosaic 11 commonplace 13 unimaginative
pedicel: ray 4 stem 5 scape, stalk 8 peduncle 9 footstalk
umbel: ray
pedigree: 6 stemma 7 descent, lineage 8 ancestry, stemmata 9 genealogy
pedometer: 8 odograph 12 perambulator
pedum: 5 crook, staff
peduncle: 7 pedicel
peek: 4 peep
peekaboo: 4 game 6 bopeep, peep-bo 7 peepeye
peel: 4 bark, harl, hull, pare, rind, skin 5 flipe, slipe, stake, strip 6 shovel 7 undress 8 palisade, stockade 11 decorticate
peeler: 4 crab 5 bobby, corer 7 hustler 8 pillager 9 policeman
peeling: 4 rind, skin 6 paring
peep: pry, spy 4 peek, peer, pule, skeg 5

cheep, chirp, dekko, glint, snoop, tweet 6 glance, squeak
hawk: 7 kestrel
show: 5 raree
peeper: eye, Tom 4 frog
peepeye: 8 peekaboo
peephole: 4 hole 6 eyelet 7 crevice, eyehole
peeping: 4 nosy 5 nosey 11 inquisitive
peer: pry, vis. 4 duke, earl, fear, fere, gaze, look, lord, mate, peep 5 baron, equal, feere, gloze, match, noble, rival, stare, stime(Sc.), styme(Sc.), thane(Sc.) 6 appear, fellow 7 compeer, comrade, marquis 8 nobleman, superior, viscount 9 associate, companion 12 contemporary
residence: 6 barony
Peer Gynt: *author:* 5 Ibsen
character: 4 King 6 Anitra
composer: 5 Grieg
mother: Ase
peerage: 4 rank 7 dignity
peerdom: 8 equality
peerless: 9 matchless, nonpareil, unrivaled 11 superlative
peesoreh: 7 meminna
peesweep: 5 pewit 7 lapwing 10 greenfinch
peetweet: 9 sandpiper
peeve: irk 6 grudge, nettle 8 irritate 9 annoyance
peevish: 5 cross, techy, testy, wemod 6 crusty, hipped, snarly, sullen, touchy 7 crabbed, frecket, fretful, froward, pettish, spleeny, waspish 8 captious, choleric, crotched, frampoid, petulant, sawshach, snappish 9 fractious, impatient, irascible, irritable, plaintive, splenetic 10 ill-humored 11 caper-noited, contentious, disgruntled
peewee: 4 bird, lark 7 lapwing
peg: fix, hob, nob, nog, pin 4 plug, scob, step 5 cleat, dowel, drink, perch, piton, prong, spill, stake, throw, tooth 6 degree, dowell, marker, reason 7 pretext, support 8 fastener
pega, pagador: 6 remora
pegall: 6 basket
Pego: See **Burma**.
peho: 8 morepork
peignoir: 4 gown 5 dress 6 kimono 7 wrapper 8 negligee 9 housecoat 12 dressing-gown
peise: 4 blow 5 force, poise 6 impact, weight 7 balance, measure, oppress
pelage: fur 4 hair, pelt
pelagic: 6 marine 7 aquatic, oceanic
Peleus: *father:* 6 Aeacus
son: 7 Pelides 8 Achilles
wife: 6 Thetis
pelf: rob 4 gain 5 booty, lucre, money, spoil, trash 6 pilfer, refuse, riches, wealth 7 despoil, rubbish

pelham: bit
Pelican State: 9 Louisiana
pelike: jar 4 vase 7 amphora 8 amphorae
pell: 4 pelt
pellar: 6 wizard 8 conjurer
pellet: wad 4 ball, pill, shot 5 bolus, stone 6 bullet, pilule 7 granule
pellicle: 4 film, scum, skin 5 crust 7 cuticle
pellock: 8 porpoise
pellucid: 5 clear 6 bright, limpid 7 crystal 11 crystalline, translucent, transparent
pelmet: 7 valance
Peloponnesus: *city:* 6 Sparta
people: 7 Moreote
river god: 7 Alpheus
Pelops: *father:* 8 Tantalus
son: 6 Atreus 8 Thyestes
wife: 10 Hippodamia
pelota: 7 jai-alai
pelt: fur 4 beat, blow, cast, dash, fell, hide, hurl, pell, push, skin 5 fitch, flung, hurry, stone 6 gallop, hasten, pelage, refuse, strike, thrust 7 rawhide, rubbish 8 woolfell
dealer: 7 furrier
peltast: 7 soldier
peltmonger: 7 furrier
peludo: 9 armadillo
pelvis: *bone:* 4 ilia 5 ilium, pubes 7 ischium
pert. to: 5 iliac
pen: cot, cub, get, mew, pin, sty 4 bolt, cage, coop, fold, jail, yard 5 bught, crawl, hutch, kraal, quill, write 6 bought, corral, cruive, fasten, hurdle, indite, record, stylus, zareba 7 calamus, compose, confine, zareeba 9 enclosure 12 penitentiary
kind: ink 8 fountain 9 ball-point 12 stylographic
point: neb, nib 4 stub
seller: 9 stationer
pen-like: 7 styloid
pen name: 6 anonym 9 pseudonym 10 nom de plume
pen text: 5 ronde
penal: 8 punitive, punitory
penalize: 4 fine 5 mulct 6 punish
penalty: 4 fine, loss, pain 5 mulct 6 amende, amerce 7 forfeit 8 hardship 10 forfeiture, punishment 12 disadvantage
pay: aby 4 abye
penance: 6 sorrow 7 remorse 9 atonement, penitence, suffering 10 contrition, repentance
pencel: 4 flag 6 pennon 8 streamer 9 pennoncel
penchant: 4 bent 5 taste 6 liking 7 leaning 8 fondness 10 attraction 11 inclination
pencil: red, wad 4 blue, lead, wadd 8 charcoal 9 eversharp 10 mechanical
pert to: 6 desmic

worn-down: 4 stub
pendant, pendent: bob, jag 4 jagg, pend, tail 5 aglet 6 aiglet, tassel 7 pensile, support 8 gamaliel, lavalier 9 lavaliere, pendulous, suspended, undecided
pending: 6 during
pendulous: lop 7 hanging 8 swinging
Penelope: *father:* 7 Icarius
father-in-law: 7 Laertes
husband: 7 Ulysses 8 Odysseus
suitor: 7 Agelaus
penetralia: 6 secret 7 privacy
penetrate: 4 bore, dive, gore, stab 5 break, enter, imbue 6 fathom, ficche, pierce 7 discern, pervade 8 permeate 9 insinuate, perforate 10 understand
penetrating: 5 acute, sharp 6 astute, shrewd, shrill, subtle 7 knowing 8 incisive 9 sagacious 10 insightful 11 clairvoyant 14 discriminating
penetration: 6 acumen 13 understanding
penguin: auk 6 Johnny
home: 4 pole 7 rookery 10 penguinery
peninsula: 4 neck 6 penile 10 chersonese
penitence: rue 6 regret 7 remorse 10 contrition, repentance 11 compunction
penitent: 4 ruer 5 sorry 6 humble
penitentiary: jug, pen 4 jail, stir 5 tench 6 prison 8 big-house
penman: 6 author, scribe, writer 10 amanuenses, amanuensis 12 calligrapher
penmanship: 4 hand 6 script 7 writing
pennant: 4 fane, flag, whip 5 roger 6 cornet, banner, pennon, pinion 8 streamer 9 banderole
pennate: 9 penniform
penniless: 4 poor 5 broke, needy 8 bankrupt 9 insolvent 11 impecunious
pennon: 4 flag, wing 6 banner, pinion 7 feather, pennant
Pennsylvania: *borough:* 5 Avoca, Sayre 9 Homestead
county: 7 Venango
people: 5 Amish
port: 4 Erie
river: 6 Beaver, Lehigh 9 Allegheny, Conemaugh 10 Schuylkill 11 Monongahela, Susquehanna
town: Ono 4 Erie, York 5 Avoca 6 Easton, Sharon 7 Lebanon, Reading 8 Steelton
penny: 5 brown, pence 6 copper, saltee, stiver
penology: 11 criminology
pensile: 7 pendent
pension: 7 payment, stipend, subsidy, tribute 8 gratuity 9 allowance 10 exhibition
pensive: 5 sober 6 dreamy, musing 7 wistful 10 meditative, melancholy, reflective, thoughtful 13 contemplative
pent: 5 caged 8 confined, enclosed
pentacle: 4 star

pentastitch: 4 poem 6 stanza 7 strophe
Pentateuch: law 4 tora 5 Bible, torah
first book: 7 Genesis
pentene: 7 amylene
Pentheus: *grandfather:* 6 Cadmus
mother: 5 Agave
penthouse: 4 roof, shed 5 aerie 6 hangar
7 pentice 8 dwelling 9 apartment, tree-
house
pentyl: 4 amyl
penurious: 4 mean, poor 6 barren,
scanty, stingy 7 miserly, wanting 8 indigent 9 destitute 10 avaricious 12 parsimonious
penury: 7 beggary, poverty 9 privation
peon: 4 hand, pawn, serf 5 slave 6 thrall
7 footman, laborer, peasant, soldier 9 attendant, constable, messenger, policeman
state of: 7 peonage
peony: 4 piny 5 plant 6 flower, mouton
people (see also **person**): kin, men 4 folk,
gens, herd, pais(law) 5 demos, genté(Sp.),
laity, stock 6 daoine, gentry 7 tili-
kum(Ind.) 8 canaglia(It.), canaille(F.),
populate, tillicum(Ind.) 11 inhabitants
aggregation: 5 tribe
ancient: 4 Seba 5 Itali, Medes 6 Greeks,
Romans 7 Sabines 8 Grecians 9 Assyri-
ans, Egyptians, Etruscans
ape-shaped skull: 9 proghathi
body: 4 race 6 nation 7 society 8 assembly, populace 9 citizenry, community 10
public Rais
group: mob 4 army, band, team 5 corps,
crowd, posse 6 chorus, troupe, throng 7
company, coterie 8 assembly 9 orchestra
11 association
headless: 8 Acephali
mythical: 8 Acephali
pert. to: 6 ethnic 7 demotic
present: 5 class, crowd 10 assemblage,
attendance 12 congregation
well-bred: 9 gentility
pep: go; vim 4 dash 5 verve, vigor 6 energy, ginger 7 animate, quicken 9 animation, briskness, encourage, stimulate 10
initiative, invigorate, liveliness
peplos: 5 scarf, shawl
peplum: 5 shawl 8 kerchief 9 overskirt
pepo: 5 gourd, melon 6 squash 7 pumpkin
8 cucumber
pepper: ava, hot, red 4 kava, siri 5 betel,
green, sirih, sweet 7 paprica, paprika 8
capsicum, kavakava, pimiento
beverage: 4 kava 8 kavakava
grass: 5 cress
package: 6 robbin
pepper plant: ava 5 chile, chili 6 chilli
peppery: hot 5 fiery 7 piquant, pungent 8
choleric, spirited, stinging 9 irritable 10
passionate
per: by 4 each 7 through
per se: 6 itself 8 directly 11 essentially
13 intrinsically

peract: 7 perform
peradventure: hap 5 doubt, maybe 6
chance, mayhap 7 happily, perhaps 8
possibly 11 uncertainty
perambulate: 4 walk 6 ramble, stroll 8
traverse 9 promenade
perambulator: 5 buggy 12 baby-car-
riage, pushwainling
perceive: see 4 feel, hear, know, note 5
scent, sense, smell, taste, touch 6 behold,
descry, divine, notice 7 discern, observe,
realize, sensate 8 comprise, comprize 9
apprehend, recognize 10 articulate, comprehend, understand 11 distinguish 12
discriminate
perceivable: 11 perceptible
perceiving: 5 acute
percentage: 4 agio, part 5 share 6 profit
7 portion, rake-off 9 advantage
perceptible: 7 tactile, visible 8 palpable,
sensible, tangible 10 cognizable 11
appreciable, discernible, perceivable 12
intelligible
perception: 6 acumen 9 sensation 13
animadversion, consciousness
capable of: 8 sentient
perceptor: 5 tutor
perch: bar, peg, rod, sit 4 fish, mado,
okow, pike, pole, pope 5 barse, light,
roost, ruffe, staff 6 alight, sauger, settle,
weapon, zingel 9 trumpeter
perchance: 5 haply, maybe 7 perhaps 8
possibly
Percheron: 5 horse
perchers: 7 rooster 10 Incessores
percolate: 4 ooze, seep, sift, silt 5 exude,
leach 6 filter, strain
percolator: 6 biggin
percylite: 7 boleite
perdition: 4 hell, loss, ruin 9 damnation
11 destruction
perdrigon: 4 plum
perdue, perdu: 6 hidden 9 concealed
perdurable: 7 durable, eternal, lasting 8
enduring 9 permanent 11 everlasting
peregrinate: 6 travel, wander 7 journey,
sojourn 8 traverse
peregrine: 4 hawk 5 alien 6 exotic, falcon 7 foreign, pilgrim, strange
perempt: 5 quash 6 defeat 7 destroy
peremptory: 5 final, utter 7 express 8
absolute, decisive, dogmatic, positive 9
arbitrary, imperious 10 conclusive, imperative 11 dictatorial 13 authorititive
perennial: rue 4 tree 5 carex, liana, liane,
peony, plant, sedum 6 banana 8 enduring, geophyte, toadflax 9 continual, permanent, perpetual, unceasing 12 never-
failing
perfect: all 4 fill, fine, holy, pure 5 exact,
ideal, right, ripen, sheer, sound, utter,
whole 6 entire, finish 7 concoct, correct,
improve, plenary, precise, sinless, spheral
8 absolute, accurate, circular, complete,

finished, flawless, thorough **9** blameless, elaborate, exquisite, faultless, righteous **10** accomplish, consummate, immaculate, satisfying

combining form: **5** teleo

perfection: **4** acme, pink **5** ideal **7** fulness, paragon **8** fullness, maturity **10** excellence

realm of: **6** Utopia

perfectly: **5** quite **10** altogether

perfecto: **5** cigar

perfervid: **6** ardent

perficient: **6** actual **10** proficient

perfidious: **5** false, snaky **8** disloyal, spiteful **9** dishonest, faithless, felonious **10** traitorous **11** disaffected, treacherous

perfidy: **9** defection **10** infidelity

perforate: eat **4** dock **5** drill, punch **6** pierce, pounce, riddle **9** penetrate, torebrate **10** foraminate

perforation: **4** bore, hole **6** broach, eyelet, tresis **7** stencil **8** aperture

perform: do; act **4** char, fill, full, play **5** chare, dight, enact, exert **6** effect, fulfil, render **7** achieve, execute, exhibit, exploit, fulfill, furnish, gesture **8** transact **10** accomplish, perpetrate

again: **7** re-enact

inadequately: **6** bungle

while moving about: **11** peripatetic

with ceremony: **9** solemnise, solemnize

performance: act **4** deed, feat, show, test, work **5** stunt **6** acting, action, effect **7** benefit, concert, exploit, matinee **8** feasance, function **9** discharge, execution, rendition **10** completion, fulfilment **11** fulfillment **12** consummation **14** accomplishment

daytime: **7** matinee

first: **8** premiere

individual: **4** soli, solo

standard: **5** bogey

performer: **4** doer, moke **5** actor, shine **6** artist, worker **7** artiste **8** executor, thespian

company: **6** troupe

diligent: **5** plier **6** drudge **7** plugger

low-grade: **9** hamfatter

supplementary: **7** ripieno

top-notch: ace **4** star

perfume: **4** atar, nose, otto **5** aroma, attar, cense, irone, myrrh, ottar, scent, smell **6** chypre, flavor **7** essence, flavour, incense, odorize, sweeten **8** bergamot, fumigate **9** fragrance

base: **4** musk **5** civet **6** neroli **9** ambergris

container: **4** vial **5** phial **6** censer

medicated: **6** pastil **7** pastile **8** pastille

pad: **6** sachet

shrub source: **8** abelmosk

perfumed cherry: **7** mahaleb

perfunctory: **8** careless **10** mechanical **11** indifferent, superficial

pergola: **5** arbor, bower **6** arbour **7** bal-

cony, trellis **9** colonnade

perhaps: **4** haps **5** maybe **6** ablins, belike, happen, mayhap **7** ablings **8** doubtful, possibly, probably **9** perchance

peri: elf **5** fairy, houri **6** sprite

periapt: **5** charm **6** amulet

pericarp: pod **4** boll **5** berry

pericranium: **4** head **5** brain

periculum: **4** risk **5** peril **6** danger

peril: **4** risk **6** crises, crisis, danger, hazard, menace **7** apperil, imperil **8** jeopardy **9** adventure **10** insecurity

perilous: **8** doubtful **9** desperate

perimeter: rim **7** outline **8** boundary **9** periphery **13** circumference

period: age, dot, end, eon, era **4** aeon, span, stop, term, time **5** avail, close, cycle, epact, epoch, spell, stage **6** season **8** duration, semester **10** conclusion **11** termination

critical: **6** crises, crisis

festive: **7** holiday **8** vacation

holding: **6** tenure

infinite: **8** eternity

penitential: **4** Lent

playing: **4** half, hand **5** frame, round **6** inning **7** chukkar, chukker, quarter

sleep: **6** godown **11** hibernation

tertiary: **6** eocene **7** neocene

time: day **4** hour, week, year **5** month **6** decade, minute, second **7** century **9** fortnight

periodic: **4** eral **6** annual **7** etesian, regular **8** seasonal **12** intermittent

periodical: **5** daily, paper **6** annual, review, Tatler **7** etesian, journal, tabloid **8** bulletin, magazine **9** ephemeris, newspaper, Spectator

peripatetic: **8** rambling **9** itinerant, wandering

peripheral: **5** outer **6** distal **7** distant **8** confined, external

periphery: lip, rim **4** brim, edge **5** ambit, limit **6** areola, areole, border **7** areolae, outside **8** environs **9** perimeter **13** circumference

periphrastic: **14** circumlocutory

perique: **7** tobacco

perish: die **4** fade, fall, ruin **6** depart, expire **7** consume, crumble, forfare, succumb

perishable: **6** caduke **7** brittle

peristyle: **9** colonnade **10** peripteral

perite: **7** skilled

peritomy: **12** circumcision

peritroch: **5** larva **6** embryo

periwig: wig **6** peruke, toupee **10** periwinkle

periwinkle: **5** color, snail **6** mussel, myrtle

perjink: **4** neat, nice **7** precise

perjure: **8** forswear **9** aperjurer

perk: **5** preen, prink **7** smarten **8** animated **9** percolate **10** perquisite

perkin: 5 cider
permanent: 5 fixed 6 stable 7 abiding, durable, lasting 8 constant, enduring 9 continual, headdress, perennial 10 continuing
permeable: 6 porous
permeate: 4 fill 5 bathe, imbue 6 drench 7 pervade 8 saturate 9 penetrate
permirific: 8 wondrous
permit: let 4 leve, pass 5 admit, allow, conge, favor, grace, grant, leave 6 accord, beteem, dustuk, entree, favour, suffer 7 consent, dustuck, license, pompano, warrant 8 furlough, tolerate 9 authorize 10 permission
permutation: 6 change 10 alteration 11 interchange 13 rearrangement
pern: 7 buzzard
pernicious: bad 4 evil 5 fatal 6 deadly, malign, wicked 7 baleful, baneful, harmful, hurtful, noisome, noxious, ruinous 10 villainous 11 deleterious, destructive, detrimental
pernio: 9 chilblain
peronate: 5 mealy, wooly
perorate: 7 address, declaim 8 harangue
perpendicular: 4 sine 5 erect, plumb, sheer 6 abrupt 7 apothem, upright 8 binormal, vertical 9 downright
perpetrate: do 6 commit, effect 7 perform
perpetual: 5 etern 7 endless, eternal 8 constant, unending 9 continual, incessant, perennial, permanent, unceasing 10 continuous 11 everlasting 14 unintermittent
perpetually: 4 ever 6 always 7 forever
perpetuate: 8 continue, eternize, maintain, preserve
perplex: cap 4 clog, doze 5 amaze, beset 6 baffle, boggle, bother, cumber, darken, gravel, hamper, harass, hobble, muddle, pother, puzzle, twitch 7 bedevil, confuse, diffuse, embroil, mystify, nonplus 8 babulyie, bewilder, confound, distract, distress, entangle 9 bamboozle, obfuscate 10 complicate
perplexed: 10 distraught
perplexing: 4 hard 6 crabby 7 carking, complex, crabbed 9 equivocal 11 complicated
perplexity: fog 4 knot 6 tangle 7 anxiety, trouble 9 intricacy 11 encumbrance 13 embarrassment
perquisite: fee, tip 6 income 7 adjunct, apanage 8 appanage, appenage, gratuity 9 accessory 11 appointment, prerogative 12 appurtenance 13 accompaniment
presidential: 4 veto
perquod: 7 whereby
perse: 4 blue
persecute: 4 bait 5 annoy, harry, hound, wrack, wrong 6 harass 7 afflict, oppress, torment, torture

persecuted: 7 refugee
Persephone: 4 Kore 8 Despoina
daughter: 4 Cora, Kore
father: 4 Zeus
husband: 5 Hades, Pluto
mother: 7 Demeter
Perseus: *father:* 4 Zeus
grandfather: 8 Acrisius
mother: 5 Danae
star of: 4 Atik 5 Algol
victim: 8 Acrisius
wife: 9 Andromeda
perseverance: 4 grit 8 patience, tenacity 9 assiduity, constancy, diligence, endurance 10 insistence, steadiness 11 continuance, persistence, pertinacity 12 continuation 13 indefatigable, steadfastness
persevere: 4 tore
persevering: 4 busy 11 unremitting
Persia: See **Iran.**
Persian: *apple:* 6 citron
assembly: 6 majlis, meklis
bug: 5 miana
cat: 6 Angora
chief officer: 5 dewan, diwan
deer: 5 maral 6 fallow
gate: bab
gazelle: 4 cora
goddess: 7 Anahita
measure: gaz, guz
lynx: 7 caracal
nightingale: 6 bulbul
rug: 4 Kali 5 Saruk, Senna 6 Sarouk 7 Isfahan, Ispahan, Teheran 8 Serabend
tick: 8 miana bug
wheel: 5 noria 7 tympana 8 tympanum
Persian Gulf: *kingdom:* 7 Chaldea
port: 7 Bushire
province: 4 Fars
wind: 6 shamal, sharki 7 shurgee
persiennes: 6 blinds
persiflage: 6 banter 8 raillery
persimmon: 7 chapote
family: 5 ebony 9 ebenaceae
persist: 4 last 6 endure, insist, remain 8 continue 9 persevere
persistent: 4 dree, hard 6 gritty 7 durable 8 constant, enduring, frequent, holdfast, obdurate, resolute, stubborn 9 assiduous, continued, tenacious 10 consistent, continuing, determined, relentless 11 persevering 13 indefatigable
person (see also **people**): guy, man, one, urf 4 body, chap, self, soul 5 being, child, human, wight, woman 6 entity, fellow 10 individual
amusing: 8 comedian, comedien 10 comedienne
bad-luck carrier: 4 jinx 5 jonah
baptized: 10 illuminato 11 illuminatus
base: 7 caitiff, hangdog
beatified: 6 beatus

betrothed: **6** fiance **7** fiancee

blamed for others: **4** butt, goat **9** scapegoat

brilliant: **6** genius **10** mastermind

callow: **6** gorlin, smarty **7** gosling

canonized: **5** saint

careless: **6** tassel **11** pococurante

charitable: **9** samaritan

cheery: **8** optimist

contemptible: cad, yap **4** heel, toad **7** bauchle

cunning: **8** slyboots

deranged: nut **7** lunatic **10** monomaniac, psychopath

despicable: **5** hound **6** rotter **10** blackguard

detested: **8** anathema

disgruntled: **8** sorehead

dull: **5** dunce, moron **8** imbecile **9** blockhead, defective

eighty-year old: **12** octogenarian

enterprising: **8** go-getter

fearless: **10** fearnaught, fearnought **11** dreadnaught, dreadnought

fifty-year-old: **15** quinquagenarian

foolish: sop **4** zany **5** clown **6** dotard **7** half-wit **9** simpleton

forty-year-old: **14** quadragenarian

good-luck carrier: **6** mascot

gray-headed: **7** grisard

guilty: **7** culprit

half-grown: **6** haflin **8** halfling **9** stripling

held as pledge: **7** hostage

holy: ste.(F.) **5** saint

horned: **7** cornute

ill: **7** invalid, patient

indefinite: one **6** anyone **7** anybody, so and so, someone **8** somebody

indifferent to pleasure or pain: **5** stoic

injured: **6** victim **8** casualty

learned: **6** pundit, savant **7** scholar **9** professor **12** intellectual

left-handed: **9** portsider

married: **4** wife **6** spouse **7** husband

middle-class: **9** bourgeois **11** bourgeoisie

mischievous: imp **4** pest

named after another: **8** namesake

ninety-year-old: **12** nonagenarian

non-Jewish: **7** gentile

of mixed blood: **7** mestizo, mulatto **8** octoroon **9** half-breed

one-hundred-year-old: **11** centenarian

perfidious: **5** snake **7** serpent, traitor

proposed for office: **7** nominee

rapacious: **4** wolf **5** harpy, shark

representing another: **5** mimic, proxy **9** alternate

rude: **4** boor **7** caveman

scolding: **9** catamaran

second: you **4** thou

seventy-year-old: **14** septuagenarian

shiftless: bum **7** drifter

sick: **5** ailer **7** invalid, patient **9** aegrotant

sixty-year-old: **12** sexagenarian

skilled: **5** adept **6** artist, master, talent **7** artisan **8** mechanic

sponsored by another: **7** protege

studious: **5** grind, porer

stupid: ass **4** boob, clod, coot, dolt, fool, gump, moke **5** bucca, clout, moron, stirk, stock, stupe, sumph **6** boodle, duffer, gander **7** dullard **8** bonehead, dumbbell, gamphrel **9** boeoetian, simpleton

timid: **11** milquetoast

trustworthy: **7** standby

unmarried: **6** maiden **8** bachelor, celibate, spinster

wealthy: **5** nabob **9** plutocrat **10** capitalist **11** millionaire **12** millionnaire

white: fay **4** ofay **5** haole **6** albino **7** abiculi, redneck

young: **8** chipling **9** stripling **14** whippersnapper

personable: **6** comely **7** shapely **8** handsome **10** attractive **11** good-looking, well-favored

personage: **6** shogun, tycoon **7** magnate

personal: own **7** private **8** intimate
comb. form: **4** idio

personality: ego **4** self **8** selfhood **11** disposition **13** individuality
split: **13** schizophrenia

personate: See **impersonate.**

personification: **10** embodiment **11** incarnation **14** representation

personify: **6** embody **9** represent **11** impersonate

personnel: **5** staff **9** employees

perspicacious: **4** keen **5** acute **6** shrewd **10** discerning, perceptive **11** penetrating

perspicacity: **6** acumen

perspicuous: **5** clear, lucid, plain **8** manifest **11** conspicuous, translucent, transparent **12** intelligible

perspiration: **5** sudor, sweat **8** hidrosis, sweating **9** exudation **10** ephidrosis
pert. to: **7** sudoric
sheep: **5** suint

persuade: get, win **4** coax, gain, sway, urge **5** argue, suade **6** allure, assure, engage, entice, induce **7** entreat **8** convince, inveigle **9** influence

persuaded: **7** pliable **8** gullible **9** credulous

persuasion: **6** belief

persuasive: **6** cogent **8** eloquent **9** impelling

pert: **4** bold **5** alert, alive, bardy, brisk, cocky, quick, sassy, saucy, smart **6** active, clever, cocket, comely, dapper, frisky, lively **7** forward, paughty **8** handsome, impudent, insolent, petulant **9** exquisite, officious, sprightly **11** flourishing

pertain: **5** belie **6** befall, belong, relate **7** concern **9** accessory, appertain

pertaining to: For all definitions beginning

with this phrase, see under following main word or phrase. EXAMPLES: "pertaining to gold": see **gold** *pert. to;* "pertaining to the sun": see **sun** *pert. to.*

suffix: ac, ar, ic; ese, ile

pertinacious: 4 firm 6 dogged 8 adhering, stubborn 9 obstinate, tenacious 10 determined, inflexible, persistent, unyielding

pertinent: apt, fit, pat 6 proper, timely 7 adapted, apropos, germane, telling 8 apposite, relative, relevant 10 applicable, felicitous 11 appropriate 12 appurtenance

pertinentia: 6 things 8 fixtures

perturb: 5 upset, worry 7 agitate, confuse, derange, disturb, trouble 8 disorder 10 discompose, disconcert

perturbation: 6 flight, pother 7 turmoil 9 commotion 10 uneasiness 12 irregularity

pertuse: 7 pierced, punched 10 perforated

pertussis: 5 cough 13 whooping cough

Peru: *animal:* 5 llama 6 alpaca
city: Ica 4 Lima(c.) 5 Cuzco, Paita 6 Callao 7 Iquitos 8 Arequipa
coin: sol 5 libra 6 dinero 7 centavo
cormorant: 6 Guanay
dance: 5 cueca
department: Ica, Yca 4 Lima 5 Cusco, Cuzco, Piura, Tacna, Tagna
emblem of nobility: 6 llautu
empire: 4 Inca, Ynca
goddess: 4 Mama
king: 7 cacique
lake: 8 Titicaca
liquor: 5 pisco
llama: 4 paco 6 alpaca
measure: 4 topo, vara 5 galon 7 celemin 8 fanegada
people: 4 Ande, Cana, Inca, Inka, Peba, Yutu 5 Boros, Campa, Carib, Panos 6 Aymara, Jibaro, Jiyaro, Kechua, Lamano 7 Quechau
plant: oca 6 ulluco 7 rhatany
river: 5 Rimac, Santa 7 Maranon, Ucayale 8 Apurimac, Huallaga, Urubamba 11 Paucartambo
rodent: 10 chinchilla
ruler: 4 Inca, Inka
shrub: 6 shansa
tableland: 4 puna
tavern: 5 tambo
tinamou: 4 yutu
tree: 6 bucare 8 cinchona
tuber: oca
volcano: 5 Misti
weight: 5 libra 7 quintal

peruke: wig 6 toupee 7 periwig

perukier: 8 wigmaker

perula: 6 mentum

peruse: con 4 read, scan 5 study 6 handle, survey 7 examine, inspect 9 supervise

pervade: 4 fill 5 bathe, imbue 6 occupy 8 permeate, traverse 9 penetrate

pervading: 9 prevalant, universal 10 widespread

perverse: awk 4 awry, wogh, wraw 6 divers, wicked, wilful 7 awkward, distort, diverse, forward, froward, wayward 8 backward, camshach, contrary, crotched, petulant 9 camsteary, camsteery, difficult, fractious 10 determined 11 contentious, contrarious, disobedient, intractable 12 cantankerous, contumacious

perversely: 7 athwart

pervert: 4 ruin, skew 5 abuse, twist, upset 6 debase, divert, garble, invert, misuse, poison 7 contort, corrupt, deprave, distort, vitiate 8 apostate, misapply, overturn, renegade 9 misdirect 10 demoralize 12 misinterpret

perverted: bad 6 wicked 7 vicious

pervious: 9 permeable 10 accessible

pervulgate: 7 publish

peshkar: 5 agent 7 steward 8 minister 10 accountant

peshkash: tax 7 present, tribute 8 offering

pesky: 6 plaguy 8 annoying 9 pestering, vexatious 11 troublesome 12 disagreeable

pess: 7 hassock

pessimistic: 6 gloomy 7 alarmed, cynical

pessoner: 4 boat, ship 10 fishmonger

pest: 4 bane, weed 5 mouse 6 insect, plague, vermin 8 epidemic, nuisance 10 pestilence

pester: dun, nag, rib 5 annoy, devil, tease, worry 6 badger, bother, harass, molest 7 torment, trouble 9 aggravate

pestiferous: 4 evil 11 mischievous

pestilence: 4 pest 5 death 6 plague 7 disease 8 epidemic

pestilent: 6 deadly 7 noxious 9 poisonous 10 contagious, infectious

pestle: 4 bray 5 grind 6 beetle, bettle, muller

pet: cat, dog 4 coax, daut(Sc.), dawt(Sc.), dear, duck, huff, neck, sulk, tiff 5 drunt, humor, quiet, spoil 6 caress, coddle, cosher, cuddle, dautie(Sc.), dawtie(Sc.), faddle, fantad, fantod, fondle, pamper, stroke 7 cherish, darling, indulge, tantrum 8 favorite, fondling 9 cherished, favourite

petal: ala 4 alae

petal-bearing: 8 petalous

petals: 7 corolla
without: 9 apetalous

petard: 11 firecracker

peteman: 9 cracksman 10 safeblower

peter: 4 fade, fail, wane 5 cease 7 dwindle, exhaust 8 diminish

peterman: 5 thief 7 burglar 9 fisherman

petiole: 4 stem 5 stalk 8 peduncle 9 leafstalk 10 mesopodium

petit: 4 mean 5 minor, small 6 little 13 insignificant

petite: 4 trim 6 demure 10 diminutive

petition: ask, beg, sue 4 bill, boon, plea, pray, suit, wish 5 apply, orate, plead 6 appeal, prayer, steven 7 address, entreat, implore, oration, request, solicit 8 entreaty 10 supplicate 11 application, deprecation 12 supplication 13 contemplation

petitioner: 5 asker 6 beggar, seeker 8 appealer, beadsman, bedesman 9 applicant

chancery: 7 relator

petitor: 10 petitioner

peto: 5 wahoo

petrean: 5 rocky

petrel: 4 titi 5 mitty 7 assilag 8 allamoth 9 allamonti, allamotti, mallemuck

petrifying: 7 numbing 9 deadening, hardening 10 petrescent, terrifying 11 fossilizing

petrol: gas 8 gasoline

petroleum: oil 10 illuminant

by-product: 6 butane, deisel 7 propane 9 propylene

product: wax 4 coke 5 ethyl 6 petrol 7 alcohol, asphalt, canadol, naphtha 8 gasoline, kerosene, paraffin 9 righolene

petrosal: 4 hard 5 stony 7 petrous

petticoat: 4 kilt, slip 5 jupon, pagne 6 kirtle 7 whittle 8 basquine, halfslip, vasquine 9 undercoat, waistcoat 10 fustanella, underskirt 11 farthingale

tails: 7 teacake 9 shortcake

pettifogger: 6 lawyer 7 shyster 8 attorney

pettish: 8 petulant

pettle: 6 cuddle, nestle, potter 7 cherish, indulge

petty: 4 base, mean, orra, puny 5 minor, small 6 paltry, puisne 7 trivial 8 childish, inferior, nugatory, trifling 9 frivolous, minuscule 10 diminutive 11 subordinate, unimportant 12 contemptible 13 insignificant 14 inconsiderable

matter: 6 fidfad

morel: 9 spikenard 10 nightshade

whin: 10 restharrow

petulant: 4 pert 5 cross, huffy, saucy, short, testy 6 petted, sullen, wanton, wilful 7 forward, fretful, peevish, wayward 8 contrary, immodest, insolent, perverse 9 impatient, irascible, irritable, plaintive, querulous 10 ill-humored

pew: 4 desk, seat, slip 5 bench, bught, stall 6 bought

pewee: 10 flycatcher

pewter: tra 5 bidri, bidry 6 bidery, bidree 7 biddery

Phaedra: *father:* 5 Minos

husband: 7 Theseus

phaeton: 8 carriage

phalacrocorax: 4 coot 9 cormorant

phalacrosis: 8 alopecia, baldness

phalanger: 5 tapoa

phalera: 4 boss, disk 5 cameo

phantasm: 5 dream, fancy, vapor 7 phantom 8 delusion

phantasmal: 6 unreal 10 transitory

phantasy: 5 fancy

phantom: 4 idol 5 bogle, ghost, idola, image, shade, umbra 6 eidola(pl.), idolon, idolum, spirit 7 eidolon, fantasy, specter, spectre 8 illusion, phantasm 10 apparition

Pharaoh: 7 Rameses

ancester: Ra

Pharaoh's chicken: 7 vulture

Pharaoh's fig: 8 sycamore

Pharaoh's mouse: 9 ichneumon

phare: 6 pharos

pharisaical: 12 hypocritical

pharmaceutical: dia 7 mellite

pharmacist: 8 druggist 9 dispenser 13 pharmaceutist

pharmacy weight: 5 obole 6 obolus

pharos: 5 cloak 6 beacon 7 lantern 10 chandelier, lighthouse

phase: 4 side 5 angle, facet, stage 6 aspect 8 passover 13 manifestation

phasm: 6 meteor 7 phantom 10 appearance

pheasant: 5 cheer, monal 6 monaul, moonal, pukras 7 kallege 8 fireback, tragopan

breeding-place: 4 stew

brood: nid, nye 4 nide

pheasant cuckoo: 6 coucal

pheasant duck: 7 pintail 9 merganser

pheasant finch: 7 waxbill

phenate: 9 phenolate

Phenicia: See **Phoenicia.**

phenol: 6 orcine, thymol 9 germicide

derivative: 4 anol

phenolate: 7 phenate

phenomenal: 7 unusual 13 extraordinary

phenyl salicylate: 5 salol

pheon: 7 bearing

phial: cup 4 bowl, vial 6 bottle, vessel

philabeg: 4 kilt

philander: 5 flirt 10 flirtation

philanthropic: 6 humane 10 altruistic, benevolent, charitable 12 humanitarian

philanthropist: 5 donor 10 benefactor

philanthropy: 4 alms 10 almsgiving

universal: 15 omnibenevolence

philippic: 6 screed, tirade 8 diatribe

Philippines: *ant:* 4 anai, anay

archipelago: 4 Sulu

banana: 7 saguing

boat: 5 balsa, banca 8 balangay, barangay

breadfruit: 4 rima 8 casmansi

buffalo: 7 carabao, timarau, timerau

capital: 8 cabecera

carriage: 9 carretela, carromata

chief: **4** dato **5** datto, Iloco **7** Ilocano, Ilokano
Christianized tribe: **5** Bicol, Bikol, Tagal,
Vicol **7** Bisayan, Tagalog, Visayan
city: **4** Agoa, Cebu **5** Albay, Davao **6**
Aparri, Baguio, Cavite, Ilagan, Manila(c.)
7 Dagupan
coin: **4** peso **7** centavo
cyclone: **6** baguio
dagger: **4** itac **7** balarao
deity: **5** Dagon
discoverer: **8** Magellan
drink: **4** beno, vino **5** bubud **7** pangasi
farmer: lao, tao
fern: **4** nito
fetish: **5** anito
fiber: **4** eruc **6** buntal **9** pineapple
fish: **8** langaray
food: **4** baha, taro
fort: **4** Gota **10** Corregidor
garment: **4** saya
hardwood: **4** ipil **5** narra
hat: **7** salacot
hemp: **5** abaca **6** manila
house: **5** bahay
idol: **5** anito
island: **4** Cebu **5** Batan, Bohol, Leyte,
Luzon, Panay, Samar **6** Negros **7** Mas-
bate, Mindora, Palawan, Paragua **8**
Mindanao
kitchen: **5** calan
knife: **4** bolo, itac **7** balarao, machete
language: **4** Moro **5** Bicol, Tagal **6** Ibanag
7 Ilocano, Tagalog, Visayan
litter: **7** talabon
mammal: **7** tarsier
mango: **5** bauno **7** pahutan
market-day: **7** tiangue
measure: **4** loan **5** braza, caban, cavan,
chupa, ganta **6** apatan, balita, quinon
measure of weight: **5** catty, fardo, picul,
punto **6** lachsa **7** quilate **8** chinanta
mother: ina
mountain: Apo, Iba **5** Mayon
mountaineer: **8** mentesco
mudfish: **5** dalag
muskmelon: **6** atimon
Muslim: **4** Moro
native: see *people* below
parrot: **5** cagit
people: Ata, Ati, Ita, Tao **4** Aeta, Atta,
Etas, Moro, Sulu **5** Bicol, Bikol, Tagal,
Vicol **6** Igorot, Timaua, Timawa **7** Bisayan, Tagalog, Visayan **8** Filipino, Igorrote **10** Philippino
plant: aga **4** alem **5** abaca, baroi, batad **6**
agamid
plum: **6** sapote
priest: **7** pandita
province: **4** Abra **5** Albay **6** Iloilo
raft: **5** balsa
reptile: **6** python
rice: **4** paga **5** barit, bigas, macan
river: **4** Abra, Agno **5** Pasig **7** Cagayan **8**
Mindanao, Pampanga

road: **4** daan
sea: **4** Sulu
servant: **4** bata **5** alila
shirt: **4** baro
shrub: **4** alem, nabo **6** anilao
silk: **10** alcaiceria
slave: **6** alipin
slipper: **7** chinela
stream: **4** ilog
termite: **4** anai, anay
textile: **4** pina, saba **7** sina-may
timber: **5** cahuy
tree: dao, iba, tua, tui **4** acle, anam, ates,
bogo, dita, ipil **5** almon, amaga, anabo,
balao, balau, bayok, betis, bulak, guijo,
ligas, tabog, yacal **6** alagao, alagau, alupag,
amuyon, anagap, aranga, bancal, banuyo,
bataan, batino, botong, dungon, lanete,
marang, molave **7** amuguis, amuyong,
anabong,. apitong, banilad, binukau,
hapiton, mambong, tindalo **8** almaciga,
bitanhol, macaasim, malapaho, tanguile **9**
alintatad, batikulin, batitinan **10** batikuling **11** alibangbang, balinghasay
tree bark: aga **6** agamid
vine: iyo
volcano: Apo **4** Mayo
watchtower: **7** atalaya **8** bantayan
water buffalo: **7** carabao
water-jar: **5** bango
weapon: **4** bolo
Philistine: **9** barbarian, hypocrite
city: **4** Gath
god: **4** Baal **5** Dagan, Dagon
foe: **6** Samson
Philomela: **11** nightingale
father: **7** Pandion
sister: **6** Procne
philosopher: **4** Kant, sage **5** Plato, Renan, Solon **6** Nestor, Seneca **7** Emerson
8 Socrates, Voltaire **9** Epictetus
disciples: **4** sect **6** school
of Syracuse: **4** Dion
philosophical: **4** wise **8** rational **9** temperate, unruffled
philosophy: **4** yoga **7** dualism **8** stoicism
9 esoterics **10** empiricism, esthetics,
pragmatism **17** transcendentalism
philter, philtre: **5** charm **6** potion **7**
amatory **9** fascinate
phlebotomize: **5** bleed **8** venesect
phlegm: **5** gleet **10** equanimity
phlegmasia: **12** inflammation
phlegmatic: **4** calm, cool, dull, slow **5** inert
6 watery **7** viscous **8** composed, sluggish
9 apathetic, impassive **13** imperturbable
phloem: **4** bast
phlogistic: **5** fiery **6** heated **7** burning,
flaming **11** impassioned **12** inflammatory
phoca: **4** seal
Phoebad: **7** seeress **9** priestess **10** prophetess
phoebe: **4** bird **5** pewee, pewit **6** peewee
10 flycatcher
Phoebe: **5** Diane **6** Selene **7** Artemis

Phoebus: Sol, sun 6 Apollo
Phoenicia: *city:* 4 Tyre 5 Sidon
  colony: 8 Carthage
  god: 4 Baal
  goddess: 5 Tanit 6 Baltis, Tanith 7 Astarte
  king: 6 Agenor
  seaport: 5 Sidon
phonetic: 4 oral 5 vocal
  notation system: 5 romic
phonograph record: 4 disk 7 platter
phony: 4 fake, sham 5 bogus, false 8 impostor, spurious 9 charlatan 10 fictitious
  11 counterfeit
phosphate: 6 ehlite 7 apatite 9 wavellite
photoengraving: 15 heliotypography
photograph: mug 4 film, snap, X-ray 7
  picture, tintype 8 likeness, portrait, snapshot 9 ferrotype, pictorial 10 cheesecake, heliograph 13 daguerreotype
  bath: 5 fixer, toner 7 reducer 9 developer
  chemical: 5 metal, toner
  color tool: 5 blimp
  developer: 5 ortol 6 amidol 9 revelator
  fixing agent: 4 hypo
  instrument: 8 enlarger
  inventor: 6 Niepce(F.), Talbot
  kind: 5 panel, still 6 motion 7 boudoir,
  cabinet, diamond 8 imperial, passport,
  portrait 9 pictorial 10 commercial, scientific 12 composograph 13 carte de visite
  negative: 4 film
  printing: 7 ozotype
photographer: 9 cameraman
photology: 6 optics 7 photics
photometric unit: pyr, rad
phrase: mot 4 term, word 5 idiom, state 6
  clause, cliche, saving, slogan 7 adjunct,
  diction, epigram, epithet, thought 8
  acrostic 9 catchword, leitmotif 10 expression
phraseology: 7 dialect, diction, wording 8
  parlance
phratry: 4 clan
phrenetic: 8 frenetic
phrenic: 6 mental
Phrixos: *father:* 7 Athamus
  mother: 7 Nephele
  sister: 5 Helle
Phrygia: *enthusiast:* 9 Montanist
  god: 8 Sabazios
  god: 4 Atys 5 Attis
  king: 5 Midas
phyletic: 6 racial 12 phylogenetic
phyma: 5 tumor 6 nodule
physic: 5 purge 9 cathartic
physical: 6 bodily 7 natural, somatic 8
  material 9 corporeal, somatical
physician: asa, doc 5 curer, medic, quack
  6 doctor, intern, healer, medico 7 interne
  8 restorer 10 consultant, medicaster 11
  aesculapian, philospher 12 practitioner
  association: AMA
  combining form: 5 iatro
  group: AMA 5 panel, staff
  symbol: 8 caduceus

physicist: 10 naturalist
physiognomy: mug 4 face 8 portrait 11
  countenance
physique: 4 body 6 figure 8 strength 10
  appearance 12 constitution
physostigmine: 5 esere 6 eserin 7 eserine
piacle: sin 5 crime, guilt 7 offense 8 pi-
  aculum
pian: 4 yaws 9 frambesia 10 framboesia
piano: 5 grand 6 softly, spinet 7 clavial,
  quietly, upright 8 pianette 10 anemo-
  chord, pianoforte
  dumb keyboard: 9 digitoria 10 digitorium
  11 finger board
  key: 7 digital
  keyboard: 7 clavier
  pedal: 7 celeste
  pedal keyboard: 8 pedalier
piatti: 7 cymbals
piazza: 5 porch 7 gallery, portico, veranda
pic: 4 peak 8 picayune
picacho: 4 hill 5 butte
picador: wit 6 jester 7 debater 11
  bullfighter
picadura: 7 tobacco
picaro: 5 knave, rogue, tramp 7 sharper 8
  vagabond
picaroon: 5 rogue, thief 6 bandit, pirate,
  rascal 7 brigand, corsair 9 hooka-roon 10
  adventurer
pichiciago: 9 armadillo
pick: 4 gaff, pike, wale 5 adorn, beele,
  cavil, elect, elite, pluck 6 choice, gather,
  pickax, twitch 7 bargain, diamond 8
  plectrum
  on: 5 abuse, annoy, tease 9 criticize
  out: 4 cull, sort 5 glean 6 assort, choose,
  select
pickax: 4 bill, pick 6 tubber, twibil 7
  mattock, twibill
picked: 4 trim 5 spiny 6 dainty, peaked,
  spruce 7 pointed 8 stripped 10 fastidious
picket: peg 4 pale, post 5 fence, stake 6
  fasten, paling, tether 7 enclose, fortify
pickle: 4 alec, dill, mess, peck 5 achar,
  brine 6 capers, dawdle(Sc.), muddle,
  nibble, piddle, pilfer(Sc.), trifle(Sc.) 7
  chutney, condite, confect, gherkin, vitriol
  8 marinate 11 predicament
  mixed: 7 higdon
pickled: 5 drunk, soust 6 soused 11 intoxicated
pickpocket: dip 4 bung, hook, wire 5
  diver, filer, thief 6 buzzer, cannon, dipper, figboy, hooker, ratero(Sp.), robber 7
  foister, mobsman, stealer 8 clyfaker 11
  finger-smith
  helper: 4 duke 5 shill, stall 6 bulker
pickup: 5 truck 6 bracer, chippy 8 recovery 9 stimulant 10 hitchhiker 11 improvement, stimulation 12 acquaintance
  again: 6 resume
picnic: 5 gipsy, gypsy 6 junket, outing
picot: 4 loop

picotee: **9** carnation
pictograph: **5** glyph
picture (see also **motion picture**): oil **4**
copy, icon, idea, ikon **5** ikono, image,
photo, print, scene, vinet **6** chromo,
crayon, depict, marine, pastel **7** diorama,
etching, explain, imagine, paysage(F.),
portray, porture, reflect, tableau **8** describe, likeness, makimono, painting,
panorama, portrait, seascape, triptych,
vignette **9** delineate, landscape, miniature
10 illustrate, impression, photograph,
watercolor **16** chromolithograph
border: mat **5** frame
drawn with heated instrument: **11**
pyrogravure
section: **7** gravure
small: **5** cameo **9** miniature **15** micro-
photograph
stand: **5** easel
viewer: **9** projecter **11** alethoscope, stereoscope
picture puzzle: **5** rebus **6** jigsaw
pictured: **11** counterfeit
picturesque: **5** vivid **6** quaint, scenic **7**
graphic **8** informal, scenical, striking
picuda: **9** barracuda
piddle: toy **4** pick, play **6** dawdle, putter,
trifle
piddling: **6** paltry **7** trivial, useless **13**
insignificant
pie: **4** mess, tart **5** chaos, flawn, graft,
patty, pasty **6** jumble, magpie, pastry,
tourte **7** cobbler, dessert, mixture **8** crus-
tade, turnover **9** blackbird, confusion
with ice cream: **7** a la mode
piebald: **4** pied, piet **5** mixed, motly, pinto
6 bauson **7** mongrel, mottled **10** variegated **12** multicolored **13** heterogeneous
piece: bat, bit, cob, eke **4** chip, gare, hunk,
join, mend, part, slab, slat, snip, stub,
tate(Sc.) **5** crumb, flake, patch, pezzo(It.),
scrap, sheet, shred, slice, strip **6** cantle,
gobbet. morsel, parcel, sliver **7** cantlet,
driblet, flinder, flitter, morceau(F.), oddment, portion, section, segment, snippet **8**
assemble, dribblet, fraction
tapering: **4** gore, shim **6** gusset
piece of eight: **4** peso(Sp.) **6** escudo(Sp.)
pied: **7** piebald
pied antelope: **8** bontebok
pieplant: **7** rhubarb
pier: cob **4** cobb, dock. mole, pile, quay **5**
groin, stilt, wharf **6** bunder **7** landing,
support **8** buttress, pilaster **10** breakwater
architectural: **4** anta
base: **5** socle
pierce: dag, rit **4** bear, bite, bore, brod,
cloy, dirl, gore, hole, stab, tang **5** break,
drill, enter, gride, lance, probe, smite,
spear, spike, stick, sting **6** broach, cleave,
empale, ficche, impale, riddle **7** discern,

poniard **8** puncture **9** intersect, lancinate,
penetrate, perforate **10** comprehend
pierced: **5** ajour
piercer: awl
piercing: **4** fell, high, keen, tart **5** clear,
sharp **6** shrill **7** cutting, pungent **8** poignant **9** searching **10** foraminate
piet: **5** ouzel **6** magpie **10** chatterbox,
chattering
piety: **4** pity **7** loyalty **8** devotion, holiness,
religion **9** godliness, reverence **10** compassion, devoutness
pig (see also **hog**): far, ham, hog, sow **4**
boar, pork **5** bacon, chuck, crock(Sc.),
ingot, shoat, shote, swine **6** farrow, gussie, porker **7** casting, dogboat, glutton,
grumphy(Sc.) **8** grumphie(Sc.), pressman, sixpence
lead: **6** fother
litter: far **6** farrow
pert. to: **7** porcine
tender: **9** swineherd
yoke: **7** sextant **8** quadrant
young: elt **4** gilt, runt **5** grice(Sc.), piggy,
shoat, shote, snork **6** bonham, farrow,
piggie, piglet **7** teatman **9** gruntling
pig bed: sty **4** sand
pig deer: **8** babirusa **9** babirussa **10** babiroussa
pig hickory: **6** pignut
pig iron ballast: **9** kentledge
pig potato: **7** cowbane
pig rat: **9** bandicoot
pigboat: sub **9** submarine
pigs and whistles: **4** ruin **8** fragment,
wreckage
pigeon: **4** barb, bird, dodo, dove, dupe,
gull **5** decoy, pluck, squab, wonga **6** coward, culver, cushat, dodlet, fleece, isabel, pouter, turbit **7** cropper, fantail,
jacobin, namaqua, pintado, swallow, tumbler **8** squealer **9** frillback, harlequin
10 sweetheart, turbitteen, turtledove,
wonga-wonga
call: coo
carrier: **5** homer **6** homing **8** horseman
10 scandaroon
domestic: nun **4** barb, ruff, runt, spot **9**
satinette, trumpeter
feed: **7** saltcat
genus of: **7** columba
hawk: **6** falcon, merlin
pert. to: **9** columboid **12** peristeronic
young: **5** piper **8** squealer
pigeon blood: red **6** garnet
pigeon grass: **7** foxtail **9** crabgrass **12**
bristlegrass
pigeon house: **7** dovecot **9** columbary
pigeon-livered: **4** meek, mild **6** gentle
pigeon pea: dal, tur **4** herb, seed **5** arhar
6 gandul **7** catjang, cajanus
pigeon woodpecker: **7** flicker
pigeonberry: **8** pokeweed **9** Juneberry

11 coffeeberry
pigeonhearted: 5 timid 8 cowardly 14 chickenhearted
pigeonhole: 6 shelve 7 arrange, cubicle 8 classify
pigeonry: 7 dovecot 8 dovecote
piggery: 4 pigs 6 pigsty 8 crockery(Sc.)
piggish: 4 mean 6 filthy, greedy 7 selfish 8 stubborn 10 gluttonous
pigheaded: 7 willful 8 perverse, stubborn 9 obstinate 10 determined
pigment: 4 lake 5 color, paint 8 colorant
absence of: 8 alphosis
applied to canvas: 7 impasto
black: tar 5 sepia 7 melanin
blue: 4 bice 5 smalt 7 veriter
blue-gray: 4 bice
blue-white: 4 zinc
brown: 5 sepia, umber 6 bister, bistre, sienna 7 melanin
green: 4 bice 7 veriter
kind: 7 aniline, rubiate 8 alizarin, massicot 9 alizarine
red: 7 amatito, realgar, turacin
yellow: 5 ocher, ochre 7 etiolin 8 orpiment
pigmy: See **pgymy.**
pignus: 4 pawn 6 pledge
pigpen: 6 sty
pigsconce: 7 pighead
pigskin: 5 glove 6 saddle 8 football
pigsney: 4 dear 7 darling 10 sweetheart
pigsticker: 4 sled 5 sword 7 butcher 11 pocketknife
pigtail: 5 braid, queue
pigwash: 5 swill 7 hogwash
pika: 6 rodent
pike: ged(Sc.) 4 dore, fish, gedd(Sc.), luce, pick, road 5 cairn, point, spike, tower 6 beacon, pickax, summit 7 highway 8 poulaine 9 spearhead 11 muskallonge, muskallunge, muskellunge
pike perch: 4 dory 6 sauger
pikel, pikle: 7 hayfork 9 pitchfork
pikelet: 7 crumpet
piker: 5 thief, tramp 6 coward 7 gambler, quitter, shirker, vagrant 8 pilferer, tightwad 10 speculator
pilar: 5 downy, hairy
pilaster: 4 anta 5 antae 6 column
pilchard: 7 sardine
smoked: 6 fumado
pile: cop, mow, nap 4 bank, bing, cock, dass(Sc.), dess(Sc.), heap, mass, mole, pier, rick, sess, shag 5 amass, crowd, spile, stack, stake 6 pillar 7 fortune 8 buttress 10 accumulate, breakwater, coacervate
funeral: 4 pyre 5 mound
rubbish: 4 dump
pile-driver: *weight:* tup
pilewort: 6 ficary
pilfer: rob 4 hook, loot, pelf, take 5 filch,

sneak, steal, swipe 6 finger, snitch 7 purloin 8 scrounge
pilgrim: 5 ihram 6 palmer 8 crusader, traveler, wanderer, wayfarer 9 sojourner 12 peregrinator
bottle: 7 ampulla, costrel
ship: 9 Mayflower, Speedwell
pilgrimage: 4 hadj, trip 7 journey
pill: 4 ball, goli, pare, peel, pool 5 bolus, creek, strip 6 pellet, pilule 7 capsule, granule, pitcher, placebo 11 decorticate
pill bug: 5 louse 6 slater
pillage: 4 flay, loot, prey, sack 5 booty, foray, harry, rifle, spoil, strip 6 maraud, rapine, ravage 7 despoil, plunder 8 expilate, spoliate 9 depredate, devastate
pillager: 6 peeler 10 freebooter
of Rome: 6 Alaric
pillaging: 9 predatory
pillar: lat 4 pile, post 5 cippi(pl.), pylon, shaft, stela, stele 6 cippus, column, stelae(pl.), steles 7 obelisk, osiride, support 8 pilaster, pillaret 9 totem pole
capital: 7 chapter
pert. to: 6 stelar
resembling: 6 stelar
series of: 9 colonnade
without: 7 astylar
pillar-like: 6 stelar
pillar saint: 7 stylite
pillar-stone: 8 monument 11 cornerstone
pillarist: 7 stylite
Pillars of Hercules: 5 Abila, Calpe 9 Gibraltar
pillbox: cap, hat 7 shelter 8 brougham 11 emplacement 13 fortification
pilled: 4 bald, bare 6 barked, peeled, shaven 8 tonsured 12 decorticated
pillion: 6 saddle 7 cushion
pillory: 4 thew 5 stock, trone
pillow: cod, pad 5 block 7 bolster, cushion, support
stuffing: 5 eider, kapok 6 dacron
pillowcase: 4 sham, slip 5 cover, linen 8 flanerie
pilm: 4 dust
pilon: 4 gift 5 bonus 7 present 8 gratuity, lagnappe 9 lagniappe
pilose: 5 hairy
pilot: ace, fly 4 lead 5 flyer, guide, steer 6 leader 7 aviator, conduct, hobbler 8 chaplain, coxswain, director, governor, helmsman, preacher 9 clergyman, cockswain, steersman 10 cowcatcher
pilot bird: 6 plover
pilot fish: 6 remora, romero 9 whitefish
pilot snake: 4 bull 10 copperhead
pilot whale: 9 blackfish
pilotweed: 7 compass 9 rosinweed
pilum: 6 pestle 7 javelin
pimento: 7 paprika 8 allspice
pimple: 4 blob, burl, flaw 6 burble, papule 7 bubukle

pin: fed, fix, hob, nog, peg, pen, tit **4** axle, bolt, coak, dart, join, lill, scob **5** affix, arrow, badge, dowel, preen, rivet, spile, stake, style **6** bobbin, broach, brooch, cotter, fasten, pintle, secure, skewer **7** confine, enclose, eyebolt, gudgeon, jewelry, skittle, spindle, trenail **8** fastener, kingbolt, linchpin, ornament, spilikin, transfix **9** spillikin **10** chatelaine

pin grass: **9** alfilaria
pin plant: **5** tacca
pin-wing: **6** pinion
pinpoint: dot **5** point
pinafore: **4** slip **5** apron, dress, smock **6** daidly(Sc.) **8** sundress **9** gaberdine
Pinales: **5** trees **6** shrubs **11** Coniferales
pinbone: **7** hipbone
pince-nez: **5** specs **7** glasses, lorgnon **10** eyeglasses, spectacles
pincers: tew **5** chela **6** pliers, tenail **7** forceps **8** tenaille
pinch: nip, rob, wry **4** bite, raid **5** cramp, gripe, hinch, steal, stint, tweak **6** arrest, crisis, extort, snatch, snitch, twince **7** confine, squeeze **8** contract, straiten **9** emergency, vellicate
pinch bar: pry **5** lever
pinchbeck: **4** sham **5** alloy, cheap **8** spurious **11** counterfeit
pinchpenny: **4** carl **5** miser, stint **9** niggardly
Pindaric: ode
pine: ara, fir, iva, lim **4** ache, flag, hone, tree **5** cedar, droop, dwine, kauri, kaury, larch, pinon, vacoa, waste, white, yearn **6** balsam, grieve, lament, pandan, repine, spruce, totara, vacona, vacoua, wither **7** dwindle **8** galagala, languish, Northern **9** evergreen, Norwegian
acid: **5** pinic
exudation: **5** resin, rosin
fruit: **4** cone
leaf: **6** needle
mahogany: **6** totara
product: tar **5** resin **10** turpentine
pine bark aphid: **10** phylloxera
pine family: **8** pinaceae
pine gum: **8** sandarac
pine knot: **7** dovekie
pine siskin: **5** finch
pine tar: **6** retene
Pine Tree State: **5** Maine
pine tulip: **10** pipsissewa
pineapple: **4** bomb, pina(Sp.) **5** anana(It.) **7** grenade **8** ornament **10** decoration
family: **12** bromeliaceae
genus of: **6** ananas
segment: pip
pineapple weed: **8** marigold
pinecone: **4** clog **8** strobile
ping: **4** push, urge **5** prick
pinguid: fat **5** fatty
pinguin: **7** aguamas

pinguitude: **7** fatness, obesity **8** oiliness **10** greasiness
pinion: pin, tie **4** bind, gear, wing **5** quill **7** confine, disable, feather, pennant, shackle, trundle **8** cogwheel, restrain
pink: cut **4** deck, rose, rosy, stab, tint **5** adorn, color, coral, prick **6** flower, minnow, pastel, pierce, salmon **7** blossom, radical **8** decorate, grayling **9** carnation, embellish
family: **15** caryophyllaceae
genus of: **6** silene
pink needle: **9** alfilaria
pink pill: **7** cure-all
pinkeen: **6** minnow
pinkeye: **14** conjunctivitis
pinnace: **4** boat, ship **5** woman **6** tender **9** procuress **10** prostitute
pinnacle: epi, tee, top, tor **4** acme, apex, peak **5** crest, crown, serac **6** finial, needle, summit **8** gendarme
pinnate: **9** feathered **11** featherlike
pinnula: **4** barb
pinochle score: **4** meld
pintado: **4** cero, fish, sier **6** chintz, pigeon, sierra **7** siering
pintail: **4** duck, smee
pintle: **4** bolt **5** hinge, dowel
pinto: **4** pied, pony **5** horse **6** calico **7** mottled, painted, piebald
pinxter flower: **6** azalea **11** honeysuckle
pion: dig **8** excavate
pioneer: **5** miner **6** digger **7** settler **8** colonist, explorer **9** excavator
pious: **4** good, holy **5** froom, godly, loyal **6** devout, divine, pietic **7** canting, goddard, godlike, piteous **8** faithful **9** religious **11** reverential **13** sanctimonious
pip: **4** paip, peep, seed, spot **5** cheep, chirp, speck
pipe: oat **4** cask, duct, flue, lead, main, reed, tube **5** briar, canal, drain, spout, stack **6** dudeen, leader, outlet, tubule **7** calumet, conduit, fistula, larigot **8** mirliton(Fr.)
bend: el **5** elbow
clay: TD **4** tile **5** straw **12** churchwarden
connection: ell, tee **5** cross, elbow
end: **4** taft **6** nozzle
joint: "T", "Y"; ell, tee, wye **5** cross, elbow **7** calepin **8** coupling
Oriental: **5** hooka **6** hookah **7** nargile **8** narghile, nargileh **12** hubble-bubble
part: **4** bowl, stem
pastoral: oat **4** reed
player: **5** fifer **8** shepherd
smoke: **5** tewel
steam: **5** riser
pipe wrench: **8** Stillson
piperly: **7** trivial **9** worthless
pipette: **6** taster **7** dropper
measuring: **11** stactometer
piping: **6** edging, tubing
pipistrel, pipistrelle: bat

pipit: 6 wekeen 7 titlark
pippin: 5 apple
piquancy: 4 salt 6 flavor, ginger 7 flavour
piquant: 4 racy, tart 5 salty, sharp, spicy, tasty, zesty 6 biting, bitter 7 peppery, pungent 8 poignant, stinging 11 provocative, stimulating
pique: 4 fret, goad 5 annoy, pride, spite, sting 6 excite, grudge, harass, malice, nettle, offend, pritch, strunt 7 dudgeon, offense, provoke, umbrage 8 irritate, vexation 9 annoyance, displease 10 irritation, resentment 11 displeasure
piqued: 5 pouty
piquet: *score:* pic
tricks: 5 capot
pirate: 4 Kidd 5 rover 6 robber 7 brigand, corsair, omnibus 8 algerine, marauder, picaroon, predator 9 buccaneer, privateer 10 freebooter, plagiarize
flag: 5 Roger
piripiri: 4 weed 5 birch, mapau
pirl: 4 spin 5 twine, twist
pirn: 4 reel 5 spool 6 bobbin
pirogue: 5 canoe
pirol: 6 oriole
piscation: 7 fishery, fishing
piscator: 6 angler 9 fisherman 11 piscatorian
piscina: 4 tank 5 basin 8 fishpond 9 reservoir
piscine appendage: fin
pishogue, pishoge: 5 spell 7 sorcery 10 witchcraft
pismire: ant 5 emmet
piste: 4 path 5 spoor, track, trail
pistil: 6 carpel
pistle: 4 tale 5 story 7 epistle
pistol: dag, gat, gun, rod 6 barker, buffer 7 dungeon 8 bulldoze 9 automatic, derringer
case: 7 holster
lock: 5 rowet
piston: 7 plunger
pit: 4 butt, delf, foss, hell, hole, mine, pool, seed, sump, trap, weem, well 5 abyss, chasm, delft, delve, fossa, fosse, fovea, grave, shaft, snare, stone 6 cavern, cavity, fossae, hollow, oppose 7 abaddon, cockpit 8 downfall 9 barathron, barathrum, waterhole 10 depression, excavation 11 indentation
small: 7 alveola, foveola 8 alveolus, foveolae
pitch: dip, key, tar 4 cant, cast, hurl, line, roll, send, tone, toss 5 fling, heave, lunge, lurch, resin, rosin, throw 6 accent, encamp, patter, plunge, totter 7 asphalt, bitumen 8 alkitran 9 alchitran
above: 5 sharp
apple: 5 copei, cupay
below: 4 flat
high in: alt
pipe: 9 epitonion

pitch-color: 7 piceous
pitchblende: 6 radium 7 uranium
pitcher: jar 4 ewer, olla, olpe, toby 5 buire, gorge, gotch, ollae, olpae 6 carafe, heaver, hurler, tosser, urceus 7 canette, creamer 8 cruisken, oenochoe 9 container, cruiskeen 10 ballplayer
motions: 6 windup
place: 5 mound
pitcher plant: 8 nepenthe 10 cephalotus, sarracenia 12 chrysamphora, darlingtonia
pitcher-shaped: 9 urceolate 10 ascidiform
pitchfork: 4 evil 5 pikel, pikle 8 sheppeck, sheppick
pitchhole: 5 cahot
piteous: 5 pious 6 devout, moving, tender 7 pitiful, pitying 8 pitiable, touching 13 compassionate
pitfall: 4 lure, trap 5 snare 6 danger 10 difficulty
pith: jet, nub 4 core, crux, gist, meat, pulp 5 force, vigor 6 kernel, marrow 7 essence, medulla, nucleus 8 strength
pith helmet: 5 topee
pith tree: 7 ambatch
pithy: 5 crisp, meaty, terse 7 compact, concise, laconic 11 sententious 12 apothegmatic
pitiful: sad 4 mean 6 rueful, woeful 7 forlorn, piteous 8 pathetic, pitiable 9 miserable, sorrowful 10 despicable, lamentable 12 contemptible
pitiless: 4 grim 5 cruel, stony 6 savage 8 ruthless 9 ferocious, merciless 10 despiteous, dispiteous, relentless 11 hardhearted
pitpit: 8 guitguit
pittance: bit 4 alms, dole, gift, mite, song 6 trifle 7 bequest
pitted: 7 foveate, opposed, scarred 9 alveolate 10 pockmarked 11 honeycombed
pity: 4 ruth 5 mercy, piety 6 pathos 8 clemency, sympathy 10 compassion, condolence, tenderness 11 commiserate 13 commiseration
Pius: 4 Pope
pivot: toe 4 slew, slue, turn 5 hinge, swing 6 evener, swivel 7 gudgeon
pivot pin: 6 pintle 8 kingbolt
pivotal: 5 polar 7 central, crucial 8 cardinal
pixie, pixy: elf 5 fairy 6 sprite
pixilated: 5 dotty
placable: 4 calm 8 peaceful 9 agreeable, forgiving, peaceable
placard: 4 bill, post, sign 6 poster 7 affiche 9 manifesto 12 proclamation 13 advertisement
placate: 4 calm 5 quiet, sooth 6 pacify, please, soothe 7 appease 10 conciliate
place: lay, put, set 4 area, calm, city, lieu, loci, post, room, seat, site, spot, town 5 being, court, estre, locus, plant, posit,

siege, situs, space, stead **6** bestow, locale,
locate, region, repose, square **7** allodge,
bestead, demesne, deposit, dispose, situate, village **8** dwelling, location, locality,
position **9** collocate, residence, situation
again: **6** reseat **7** replace
before: **6** appose, prefix
beneath: **9** infrapose
between: **6** insert **9** interpose
by itself: **7** isolate
combining form: gea **4** gaea
end for end: **7** reverse
holy: **6** shrine
little hiding: **5** niche
one inside another: **4** nest
side by side: **9** collocate, juxtapose
placebo: **8** medicine **11** preparation
placed: **7** bestead
placid: **4** calm, even, mild **5** downy, quiet,
suant **6** gentle, serene **8** peaceful, tranquil **9** unruffled **11** undisturbed **13** imperturbable
placket: **4** slit **6** pocket **7** opening
pladaroma: **5** tumor
plage: **4** zone **5** beach **6** region **7** country
8 transept
plagiarize: rob **4** crib **5** steal **6** borrow,
pirate, thieve **7** purloin
plague: dun, pox, vex **4** fret, pest, twit **5**
annoy, harry, tease, worry **6** harass, hector, pester, wanion **7** scourge, torment,
trouble **8** calamity, epidemic, irritate,
nuisance **9** annoyance **10** affliction,
pestilence **11** infestation
carrier: rat
pert. to: **6** loimic
plaguy: **6** vexing **9** vexatious **12** disagreeable
plaice: **8** flounder
plaid: **4** maud **5** cloth **6** design, tartan **7**
bracken, garment, pattern **9** checkered
11 crossbarred
plain: lea **4** bald, bare, chol, down, even,
fair, mead, mere, mesa, moor, open, vega,
wold **5** blair, blunt, broad, camas, campo,
clear, corah, frank, gross, heath, homey,
llano, veldt **6** camass, cammas, coarse,
cuesta, graith, homely, humble, lenten,
meadow, pampas, simple, steppe, tundra,
undyed **7** artless, certain, evident, genuine, glaring, legible, obvious, prairie,
quamash, savanna **8** apparent, cam-
pagna(It.), campaign, distinct, explicit,
flatland, homemade, homespun, ordinary,
savannah, tailored **9** champaign, downright, outspoken, primitive, unadorned,
unfigured, untwilled **10** unaffected **11**
perspicuous, transparent, undisguised **12**
altiplanicie **13** unembellished **15**
straightforward
depression: **5** swale
salt-covered: **5** flats **6** salada
treeless: **7** savanna **8** savannah

plainstone: **6** paving **9** flagstone
plaint: **6** lament **9** complaint **11** lamentation
plaintiff: **4** suer **7** accuser **9** recoverer **11**
complainant
plaintive: sad **5** cross **7** elegiac, fretful,
peevish, pettish **8** dolorous, mournful,
petulant, repining **9** lamenting, sorrowful
10 melancholy **11** complaining **12** discontented
plait: cue **4** fold, knit **5** braid, brede,
crimp, pleat, weave **6** border, gather,
goffer, pleach, plight, wimple **7** gauffer **8**
complect **9** gathering **10** interweave
plaited: **7** browden
plan: aim, map **4** card, dart, form, game,
idea, plat, plot **5** draft, epure, ettle, frame
6 budget, decoct, design, devise, intend,
layout, method, policy, scheme, sketch,
system **7** arrange, concert, diagram,
draught, drawing, outline, program, project, purpose **8** conspire, contrive, engineer, platform, prepense, schedule **9** calculate, machinate, stratagem **10**
concoction **11** arrangement, contemplate,
contrivance, preconceive, precontrive,
premeditate
planate: **5** plane **9** flattened
plancher: bed **4** slab **5** board, floor, plank
6 pallet **7** ceiling **8** planking, platform
plancier: **6** soffit
plane (see also **airplane**): **4** even, flat,
soar **5** glide, level **6** aequor, chinar,
smooth **7** surface **8** sycamore
block: **5** stock
handle: **4** toat, tote
inclined: **5** chute, shute
kind of: **4** iron, jack **5** block **6** router **8**
grooving, tounging
on same: **8** coplanar
plane figure: *boundary:* **9** perimeter
four angles: **8** tetragon
nine-sided: **7** nonagon
plane iron: bit **5** blade
plane-tree: **8** sycamore
planer: **6** shaper **8** surfacer
planet: orb **4** Mars, moon, star **5** Earth,
Pluto, Venus **6** Saturn, sphere, Uranus **7**
Jupiter, Mercury, Neptune **8** asteroid,
terrella, wanderer **9** satellite
cone: **8** strobile
course: **5** orbit
orbit: **7** ellipse
orbit point: **5** apsis, nadir **6** apogee, zenith
8 parigree
path: **5** orbit
period: **9** alfridary
relation to another: **5** trine **7** sextile **10**
opposition **11** conjunction
ruling: **9** dominator
shadow: **9** umbra
planeta: **5** cloak
planetarian: **10** astrologer

planetarium: 6 orrery
planetary: 7 erratic 9 wandering, world-
  wide 10 astrologer 11 terrestrial
planeticose: 9 wandering
planetoid: 8 asteroid
plangor: 4 wail 11 lamentation
plank: 4 deal, slab 5 board, slate, stone 6
  lumber, timber 8 plancher 10 gravestone
  breadth: 6 strake
  increasing bearing surface: 5 shole
  lengthwise: 8 stringer
plank down: pay 7 advance, deposit
planking: 8 flooring
planner: 9 architect
plant: fix, set, sow, spy 4 arum, bush, fern,
  herb, hide, rape, root, seed, slip, trap,
  tree, weed, wort 5 berry, clote, decoy,
  found, fruit, grain, place, shoot, shrub,
  sotol, spice, trick, works 6 annual, clover,
  flower, legume, scheme, settle, teasel 7
  alyssum, aquatic, creeper, cutting, factory,
  furnish, pungent, sapling 8 aromatic,
  building, business, geophyte, narcotic,
  radicate 9 detective, establish, perennial,
  seasoning, succulent, swindling, vegetable
  13 establishment
  acid-juice: 5 ribes 6 nettle 8 knotweed 9
  smartweed
  arboreal: 4 tree
  aconite: 4 bikh
  amaryllis family: 5 agave
  ambrosia genus: 7 ragweed
  ammoniac: 5 oshac
  apiaceous: 4 ache
  appendage: 7 stipule
  aquatic: see **aquatic plant**
  aromatic: see **aromatic**
  arrowroot-yielding: 7 curcuma
  arum family: 4 arad, taro 5 aroid, calla
  aster family: 5 oxeye, tansy 8 fleabane
  asteraceous: 5 daisy
  bean family: 6 lupine 8 licorice 9 liquorice
  benthonic: 6 enalid
  bitter: ers, rue 9 colicroot
  blue-blossomed: 6 lupine 8 ageratum
  body: 6 cormus
  branched: 4 bush, tree 5 shrub
  breathing organ: 5 stoma 7 stomata(pl.)
  bulbous: 5 camas 6 camass, cammas,
  nerine 7 quamash
  cabbage family: 4 rape
  cactus family: 5 dildo 6 cereus, mescal
  cactus-like: 8 stapelia 9 xerophyte
  capsule: pod
  carrot-like: 7 parsnip
  cassia genus: 5 senna
  catnip family: nep 6 nepeta
  celery family: 5 anise
  celery-like: udo
  chlorophyll-rich: 4 alga 5 algae(pl.)
  class: 4 alga 5 algae(pl.)
  climbing: ive, ivy 4 bine, vine 5 liana,

liane, vetch 6 byrony, smilax 7 creeper
  clover-like: 5 medic 7 calomba
  coloring matter: 8 clorofil 10 endochrome
  11 chlorophyll
  crocus family: 4 irid
  crossbred: 6 hybrid
  crowfoot family: 5 peony 8 clematis
  cruciferous: 5 cress 7 alyssum
  cryptogamous: 4 moss
  cuticle: 5 cutin
  cyperaceous: 5 sedge
  decorative: ivy 4 bush, fern 6 flower
  dipsacus genus: 6 teasel
  disease: 4 scab, smut 5 ergot 7 blister
  division: 15 archichlamydeae
  dock-like: 6 sorrel
  dry-climate: 5 xerad 9 xerophyte 10
  ombrophobe
  dwarf: 5 cumin
  dye: 4 anil, weld, woad, wold 5 henna,
  woald, would 6 kamala, madder, wurras,
  wurrus 7 alhenna, orselle
  ebony family: 6 ebenad
  embryo: 8 plantule
  environmentally modified: 4 ecad
  erica genus: 5 heath 7 heather
  Euphorbia genus: 6 spurge
  exudation: gum, sap 4 milk 5 latex, resin.
  rosin
  fabaceous: pea
  family: 7 araceae
  fernlike: 8 filicoid
  fiber: see **fiber**
  flag-family: 4 irid
  floating: 7 frogbit
  flowering: see **flowering plant**
  forgetfulness-causing: 5 lotus
  fragrant: 5 orris 8 angelica
  garden: 4 geum, iris, ixia, rose 5 aster,
  calla, canna, daisy, pansy, phlox, poppy,
  stock, viola 6 bellis, bletia, celery, clivia,
  cosmos, crocus, lupine, oxalis, zinnia 7
  agathea, alyssum, anchusa, anemone, begonia, celosia, clarkia, gazania, gerbera,
  godetia, lettuce, lobelia, muscari, petunia,
  primula, statice, verbena 8 ageratum,
  arctotis, cyclamen, daffodil, dianthus,
  herebell, hyacinth, larkspur, marigold,
  myosotis, scabiosa, sparaxis, sweet pea,
  tithonia, watsonia 9 amaryllis, calendula,
  campanula, candytuft, carnation, cen-
  taurea, cinararia, coreopsis, digitalis,
  gladiolus, hollyhock, linararia, narcissus,
  nicotiana, penstemon, portulaca 10 delphinium, gaillardia, gypsophila, marguerite, ranunculus, snapdragon, sweet basil,
  wallflower 11 dusty miller, forget-me-not,
  helichrysum, hunnemannia, Madonna
  Lily, shasta daisy 12 nierembergia,
  rhodendron, salpiglossis, sweet William
  13 chrysanthemum, dimorphotheca,
  glory of the sun 14 canterbury bell 15
  Star of Bethlehem 16 spring snowflakes

genus: **4** dion
geography: **14** phytogeography
gourd family: **5** melon
grass cloth: **5** ramee, ramie
grass-like: **5** sedge
grassland: **6** baccar **7** bacchar
growing from inside: **7** endogen **9** endo-
   genae(pl.)
growing from outside: **6** exogen
growth layer: **7** cambium
growth on: **4** gall
habitat: **4** ecad
head: bud, bur **4** burr **5** fruit **6** flower
heather family: **4** ling **5** erica
herbaceous: see **herb**
honey-secreting organ: **7** nectary
house: see **houseplant**
interior chaff: **5** palea, palet
iridaceae: **4** irid
iris family: **4** irid, ixia **7** freesia
joint: **4** node
juice: see *exudation* above
leguminous: see **legume**
liliaceous: **4** aloe, leek **5** onion **9** birthroot
lily family: **4** aloe, sego **5** lotos, lotus,
   yucca **6** camass
linen-producing: **4** flax
main axis: **4** stem **5** stalk, trunk
male: mas **16** androgametophore
mallow family: **5** altea **6** escoba
manufacturing: **4** mill
marine: see **aquatic plant**
marsh: **4** fern, reed **7** bulrush, cattail
masculine: see *male* above
medicinal: hop, oak **4** aloe, dill, flax, herb,
   lime, sage **5** buchu, elder, erica, guaco,
   jalap, peony, poppy, senna, tansy **6** arnica, carrot, catnep, catnip, fennel, garlic,
   ipecac, kousso, laurel, nettle **7** aconite,
   boneset, calamus, camphor, caraway, catechu, copaiba, ephedra, gentian, hemlock, henbane, juniper, lobelia, mullein,
   mustard, parsley, rhubarb, saffron **8** barberry, camomile, crowfoot, foxglove,
   licorice, plantain, rosemary, valerian,
   wormwood **9** asparagus, bearberry, buckthorn, chamomile, colchicum, coltsfoot,
   dandelion, liquorice, monkshead **10** as-
   safetida, pennyroyal, peppermint, stavesacre **11** assafoetida, bittersweet
microscopic: **5** spore
moss-like: **6** orpine **7** hepatic
mottled leaf: **8** ratsbane
mushroom-type: **6** fungus
mustard family: **4** woad **5** cress **6** radish
   7 alyssum
native: **8** indigene
nettle family: **4** hemp
nightshade family: **6** tomato
oil-yielding: **4** odal **6** sesame
old-world: **5** lotus
one-seeded fruit: **9** olacaceae
onion family: **4** leek
onion-like: **5** chive **7** shallot

opening: **5** stoma **7** stomata(pl.)
packing: **7** cannery
painful to touch: **5** briar, thorn **6** nettle **8**
   knotweed **9** smartweed
parsley family: **4** dill **5** anise
part: **6** stamen, stipel **7** tendril
pert. to: **6** agamic **7** botanic, vegetal **9**
   botanical **10** vegetative
pigment-lacking: **6** albino
poaceae: **5** grass
poisonous: **4** atis **6** datura **7** amanita **8**
   oleander
poisonous to cattle: **4** loco **8** calfkill, lo-
   coweed
poisonous to fowls: **7** henbane
poppy family: **9** celandine
pore: **8** lenticel
potato-like: oca
preserving: **4** dill **7** cannery
prickly: **5** briar, brier, cacti(pl.), thorn **6**
   cactus, nettle, teasel **7** thistle **9** tear-
   thumb
reproductive organ: **5** spore
rope: **4** hemp
rose family: **5** avens
round-leaved: **9** pennywort
salad: **5** cress **6** celery, endive, greens **7**
   lettuce, romaine **8** purslane **10** watercress
science: **6** botany
sedge family: **5** carex
seedless: **4** fern
seller: **7** florist
silk: **5** floss
soap: **5** amole
solanaceous: **7** tobacco
sour-juice: **6** sorrel
starch: pia **4** arum, taro **7** cassava
tapioca-yielding: **6** casava, casave, casavi
   7 cassava
tequila-yielding: **5** agave
thistle family: **5** aster
thorny: see *prickly* above
three-leaved: **9** trifolium
tropical: **4** arum, palm, taro **5** agave, altea, canna, liana, liane, yucca, zamia **6**
   pepino **7** dasheen, hamelia **8** mangrove,
   redwithe
tufted: **4** moss
twining: see *climbing* above
type: **6** exogen
urticaceous: **6** nettle
valerian genus: **4** nard
verbenaceous: **7** lantana
vetch family: ers
wall: ivy
water-side: **5** sedge
woody: **4** bush, tree, vine **5** shrub
woody-vine genus: **5** vitis
xyloid: **4** tree
young: **4** cion **5** scion, shoot **6** sprout **7**
   vinelet **8** seedling
yucca-like: **5** sotol
plant life: **5** flora **10** vegetation

plant louse: 5 aphid
secretion: 4 laap, lerp 5 laarp
plant raising: *pert. to:* 13 floricultural
Plantagenets: 7 Angevin
plantain: 4 weed 6 banana, wabron 8 balisier
family: 14 plantaginaceae
plantain eater: 7 touraco
plantation: 4 farm 6 estate 8 hacienda
cacti: 7 nopalry
coffee: 5 finca 7 cafetal, fazenda
coniferous tree: 7 pinetum
oak tree: 9 quercetum
sugar: 8 trapiche
trees: 6 forest 7 orchard
willow: 4 holt 6 osiery
planter: 5 sower 6 farmer, grower, seeder 7 pioneer, settler 8 colonist 13 agriculturist
government by: 11 plantocracy
planting stick: 6 dibble
plantling: 8 plantlet
plaque: pin 5 medal 6 broach, brooch
plash: 4 pool 5 blash, hedge 6 pleach, puddle, splash 9 bespatter
plashy: wet 6 marshy
plasm: 4 mold 6 matrix
plasma: 5 lymph 11 trophoplasm
plaster: 4 daub, harl, teer, tere 5 cleam, cover, gatch, gesso, grout, salve, smalm, smear 6 mortar, parget
of Paris: 6 gypsum
stone: 6 gypsum
tool: 7 spatula
plastered: 5 drunk 11 intoxicated
plasterer: 5 mason
plastic: 4 soft 5 gesso 7 ductile, fictile, flexile, pliable 8 flexible 9 formative 14 impressionable
cotton-sizing: 7 viscose
dentist's: 6 cement
plastosome: 12 chondriosome
plastron: 7 calipee 8 trimming 11 breastplate
plat: lot, map 4 boat, flat, plan, slap 5 braid, chart, level, plain, plait 6 buffet 7 flatten, plateau 8 straight 9 tableland 10 interweave 15 straightforward
platanist: 4 susu
platano: 6 banana
plate: cut, gib 4 coat, disc, dish, disk, lame, tile 5 aglet, armor, facia, scute, stove 6 aiglet, discus, lamina, platen, tagger, veneer 7 lamella, laminae, overlay 8 assiette, lamellae, laminate 9 silverize
communion: 5 paten 6 patina
cooking: 4 grid
from matrix: 6 stereo 10 stereotype
horny: 5 scute
perforated: dog 4 grid 7 stencil
pitcher's: 4 slab
ship-shaped: nef
stereotype: 6 cliche
plate bone: 7 scapula

plate mark: 8 hallmark
plateholder: 8 cassette
plateau: 4 dish, mesa, seir 5 fjeld 6 hamada, plaque, salver 7 hammada, uplands 9 altiplano, tableland 12 altiplanicie
platen: 6 roller
platform: map 4 bank, bema, dais, deck, plan 5 bench, chart, floor, stage 6 bemata(pl.), podium, pulpit 7 estrade, program, rostrum, tribune 8 chabutra, plancher 9 banquette, gangplank, vestibule
church: 5 solea
reloading: 6 staith
salt-manufacturing: 6 hurdle
ship: 7 foretop, maintop 9 gangplank
sleeping: 4 kang
temple: 5 dukan
theater: 7 logeion
wheeled: 5 float
platic: 9 imperfect
platinum:
combining form: 6 platin 7 platino
crude: 7 platina
wire: 4 oese
platitude: 6 cliche, truism 7 bromide 8 dullness, flatness 9 staleness, triteness 10 triviality 11 commonplace 15 commonplaceness
platoid: 4 flat 5 broad
platonic: 9 spiritual, visionary 10 idealistic 11 impractical, theoretical
body: 4 cube 10 hexahedron, octahedron 11 icosahedron, tetrahedron 12 dodecahedron
philosophy follower: 9 academist
platoon: set 4 team, unit 5 squad 6 volley 7 coterie 8 division 9 formation
Platoon School: 4 Gary
platter: 4 dish, lanx(L.) 5 ashet(Sc.), grail, plate 7 charger
platter-shaped: 10 scutellate
platyfish: 8 moonfish
platypus: 8 duckbill
plaudit: 4 clap 6 praise 8 applause, approval, encomium 11 acclamation, approbation
plausible: 4 oily 6 glossy 7 colored 8 coloured, credible, specious 10 applausive, ostensible, plauditory
play: act, fun, jeu(F.), hit, toy 4 game, jeux(F.), move, romp 5 charm, dally, drama, enact, flirt, sport 6 cavort, frolic, gambol, rollix 7 disport, execute, perform 9 amusement, dalliance, diversion, pantomime 10 recreation 13 entertainment
badly: err 4 miff 6 bobble
festival: 9 festspiel
kind: 4 auto 5 farce 6 comedy, one-act 7 musical, tragedy 8 burletta 9 melodrama, pantomime 13 curtain-raiser
musical: 5 opera 8 burletta, operetta
on words: pun

outline: 8 scenario
part: act, bit 4 acte(F.), role 5 exode,
scene 7 prelude 8 epilogue, epitasis, prologue
put on: 5 stage 7 produce
playa: 4 lake 5 basin, beach
playboy: 4 fool 5 clown, idler 6 madcap 7
buffoon
playday: 7 holiday
played out: 5 tired 8 finished 9 exhausted
player: man 4 cast, star 5 actor 6 leader 7
enactor, gambler 8 gamester, thespian 10
competitor, contestant
card: 4 pone 6 dealer, eldest
leading: 4 star
poor: dub, dud, sub 12 second-string
strolling: 9 serenader, troubador 10 troubadour 11 barnstormer
player piano: 7 pianola
playful: 5 merry 6 frisky, joking, lusory,
wanton 7 jocular 8 gamesome, humorous,
playsome, sportive 10 frolicsome
playground: 4 park, yard
playhouse: 5 house, movie 6 cinema 7
theater
playing cards: 4 deck 6 tarots
hand: cat 4 deal
playlet: 4 skit
playman: 7 gambler 8 gamester
playock: 9 plaything
playsome: 7 playful
playtime: 6 recess
plaything: die, toy 4 hoop 6 bauble, trifle
playwright: 6 author 9 dramatist
plea: sue 4 suit 6 abater, answer, appeal,
excuse, prayer 7 apology, pretext, request, solicit 8 argument, entreaty, petition, pretense 12 supplication 14 nolo
contendere
pleach: 5 plait, plash 9 interlace
plead: beg, sue 5 orate 6 allege, assert 7
beseech, entreat, implore, solicit 8 advocate, appealed, petition 9 importune, intercede 10 supplicate
pleading: 4 oyer 6 answer 8 demurrer 9
suppliant 10 litigation 12 supplication
pleasant: gay 4 bien(F.), fine, good, hend,
joli, nice, waly 5 bigly, cushy, douce(F.),
hende, hoddy, jolie, lepid, merry, sweet,
wally 6 genial 7 amiable, amusing,
farrand, farrant, jesting, jocular, lee-
some(Sc.), playful, winsome 8 delicate,
gracious, humorous, pleasing, sportive 9
agreeable, appealing, diverting, enjoyable,
laughable, sprightly 10 acceptable, delightful, gratifying
pleasantness: 7 amenity
pleasantry: fun 4 jest, joke 6 banter 7
jesting 10 jocularity 11 gauloiserie 13
facetiousness
please: 4 suit 5 agree, amuse, elate, humor 6 arride, humour 7 aggrate, appease,
content, delight, gladden, gratify, indulge,
placate, satisfy

pleased: 4 fain 5 apaid, happy 8 gladsome
pleaseship: 10 litigation
pleasing: 4 glad, lief 5 amene, sooth 6
comely, eesome(Sc.), liking 7 roseate 8
fetching, pleasant 9 desirable, favorable,
palatable 10 attractive, delectable, favourable 11 pleasureful
pleasurable: 7 hedonic 8 pleasant
pleasure: fun, joy 4 ease, este, gree, will 5
bliss, mirth, sport, treat 6 gaiety 7 delight, jollity 8 delicacy, fruition, gladness,
hilarity 9 amusement, diversion, enjoyment, happiness, merriment 10 benepla-
cit 11 beneplacity, contentment, delectation 12 cheerfulness 13 gratification
god: Bes
insensitiveness to: 9 anhedonia
ground: 4 park 9 pleasance
pert. to: 7 hedonic
philosophy of: 8 hedonism
seeker: 5 sport 7 epicure, playboy 8 he-
donist
pleat: 4 fold, kilt, shir 5 braid, prank 7
plicate
pleater: 8 plicator
plebe: 5 toast 8 commoner, freshman
plebeian: 4 snob 6 coarse, common, vulgar 7 illbred, lowborn 8 baseborn, ordinary
plebiscite: 4 vote 6 decree 7 mandate 10
referendum
pleck: 4 spot 5 speck, stain 9 enclosure
plectrum: 4 pick 5 uvula 6 fescue,
tongue 7 malleus
pledge: bet, vas(L.), vow 4 adhi, band,
bond, gage, hand, hest, hock, oath, pawn,
seal, wage, word 5 siker, skoal, toast,
troth 6 arrest, assure, borrow, commit,
engage, lumber, parole, plight, sicker 7
betroth, earnest, espouse, hostage, promise 8 affiance, contract, guaranty, mortgage 9 assurance, certainty, sacrament
11 association, impignorate
security for: 5 gager
pledget: 4 swab 8 compress
Pleiad of Alexandria: 5 Homer 6 Aratus
8 Nicander 9 Lycophron 10 Apollonius,
Theocritus 11 Callimachus
Pleiades: 4 Maia 6 Merope 7 Alcyone,
Celaeno, Electra, Sterope, Taygeta 8 Asterope
plenary: 4 full 6 entire 7 perfect 8 absolute, complete 11 unqualified
plenipotentiary: 5 envoy 8 minister 10
ambassador
plenitude: 6 plenty
plenteous: 9 plentiful
plenteously: 6 freely
plentiful: 4 full, rich, rife 5 ample, sonsy
6 galore, plenty, sonsie 7 copious, fertile,
liberal, opulent, profuse 8 abundant, affluent, fruitful, generous, prolific 9
abounding, bounteous, bountiful, exuberant, plenteous 10 productive

plenty: 4 enow, heap, raff 5 ample, cheap, fouth 6 enough, foison, scouth 7 copious(L.) 8 fullness, opulence 9 abundance, affluence, plenitude, plenteous 10 exuberance, luxuriance, perfection, sufficient 11 copiousness, sufficiency 12 completeness

goddess: Ops

pleon: 6 telson 7 abdomen

pleonasm: 8 fullness 10 redundancy

plethora: 4 glut 6 excess 8 fullness 9 repletion 13 overabundance 14 superabundance

plethoric: 6 turgid 8 inflated, overfull 9 bombastic 10 overloaded

pleurapophysis: rib

pleurocarpous: 11 cladanthous, cladogenous

plexiform: 4 rete 5 retia 7 complex 9 intricate 11 complicated

plexus: 4 rete 5 retia 6 tangle 7 network

pliable: 4 easy, limp, soft, waxy 5 lithe 6 limber, pliant, supple 7 bending, ductile, flaccid, flexile, plastic, tensile 8 flexible, fluxible, informal, tractile, workable, yielding 9 adaptable, compliant, malleable, tractable 10 applicable 13 unconstrained

pliant: 4 flip 7 willowy 8 cheverel, cheveril 10 sequacious

plicate: 4 fold 5 pleat

plight: 4 fold, risk 5 array, braid, plait, state 6 engage, pledge, status 7 betroth, embrace, promise 8 position 9 betrothal, condition 10 difficulty 11 predicament

plinth: 4 base, orlo 5 block, couch, stone, table 6 course 8 skirting 9 baseboard

plod: dig, mog, peg 4 grub, slog, toil, tore, vamp, work 6 drudge, trudge

plop: 5 plump

plot: map 4 land, plan, plat 5 cabal, chart, draft, story 6 design, devise, scheme, secret 7 compact, connive, diagram, outline 8 conspire, contrive, engineer, intrigue, scenario 9 insidiate, machinate 10 conspiracy 11 machination

garden: bed 8 parterre

ground: lot 5 grave 7 terrain

inventor: 8 schemist

play: 4 node

plouk, plook: 4 knob 6 pimple

plounce: 6 plunge 8 flounder

plout: 4 dash 5 plash 6 splash

plover: 4 bied, crab, dupe 5 drome, sandy 6 kildee, piping 7 collier, killdee, lapwing 8 dotterel, killdeer, Wilson's 9 courtesan, turnstone 10 beetle-head, blacksmith

plow, plough: dig, ear 4 farm, mole, rove, till 5 break 6 digger, furrow 9 cultivate

kind of: 4 snow 5 sulky 6 gopher, lister, rotary, shovel 7 breaker 8 stirring, turnplow 9 moldboard 14 prairiebreaker

knife: 6 colter 7 coulter

part: 4 hale 5 sheth, slade, stilt 6 sheath

9 plowshare, sharebeam

plow spade: 9 plowstaff

plowgang: 4 area, land 6 bovate(Sc.), oxgang

plowhead: 4 beam 5 frame 6 clevis

plowing: 7 aration

plowland: 4 area 7 measure 8 carucate

plowman: 6 farmer, rustic, tiller 7 acreman, husband 10 clodhopper, countryman

command: gee, haw

plowman's-spikenard: 4 herb 8 aromatic 12 cinnamonroot

plowshare, ploughshare: 6 colter 7 coulter

bone: 5 vomer

ploy: 4 bend, joke 5 sport, trick 6 frolic, tactic 7 pastime 8 escapade 11 merrymaking

pluck: rob, tug 4 grit, jerk, pick, pull, sand, tear 5 cheek, nerve, spunk, strip, twang 6 daring, finger, fleece, gather, snatch, spirit, twitch 7 bravery, courage, deplume, plunder 8 decision, gameness 9 endurance, fortitude, hardihood 10 resolution

plug: peg, tap, tit 4 blow, bung, calk, cork, slog 5 boost, caulk, estop, knock, punch, shoot, spile, spill 6 dottle, tampon 7 bouchon, pledget, stopper, stopple, tampeon, tampion, tampoon 9 advertise

clay: bod 4 bott

medical: 4 clot 7 embolus

water: 7 hydrant

plug bib: 6 spigot

plug cock: 6 spigot

plug hat: 4 tile 5 gibus 6 topper

plug-ugly: 4 thug 5 rowdy, tough 7 ruffian 8 gangster

plugboard: 11 switchboard

plum: hog 4 amra, coco, gage, sloe 5 drupe, duhat, icaco, prune 6 damson, jambul, sapote 7 bullace, jambool 9 greengage 10 amatungula

family: 12 amygdalaceae

plum-colored: 4 puce

plum curculio: 6 weevil

plum duff: 7 pudding

plum weevil: 8 curculio

plumage: 4 down 5 dress 6 hackle 7 floccus 8 feathers 9 adornment

plumb: 4 bung 5 delve, probe, solve 6 chunky, fathom, plunge 7 explore, plummet 8 absolute, complete, entirely, vertical 9 downright 10 absolutely, straighten, understand 13 perpendicular

plumbago: ore 4 lead 5 plant 8 graphite, leadwort

plumbeous: 4 dull 6 leaden

plume: 4 tuft 5 crest, egret, preen, pride, prize, prune 6 aigret, plumet 7 feather, panache 8 aigrette, plumelet 9 plumicorn

plummet: 4 drop, fall, lead 5 plumb 6 weight

plump: fat **4** back, drop, fall, plop, sink, tidy **5** bonny, buxom, obese, plunk, stout **6** bonnie, chubby, dilate, flatly, fleshy, portly, rotund **7** bluntly, distend, fulsome, support **9** downright

plunder: gut, rob **4** boot, loot, pelf, prey, raid, sack, swag **5** booty, cheat, harry, pluck, poach, raven, reave, rifle, spoil, steal, strip **6** bezzle, boodle, creach(Sc.), creagh(Sc.), dacoit, maraud, pilfer, pirate, rapine, ravage, ravish, spoils **7** despoil, pillage, ransack **8** predator, spoliate **9** depredate, devastate

plunderer: **5** thief **6** bandit, vandal **8** marauder, predator **10** freebooter

plunge: bet, dig, dip **4** cave, dive, duck, dump, pool, sink **5** douse, dowse, drive, fling, lunge, merse, plumb, souse **6** absorb, emerge, footer, gamble, thrust **7** immerge, immerse **8** submerge

plunger: ram **6** risker **10** speculator

plunk: **4** drop, flop, pull, push, sink, toss **5** drive, pluck, plump, sound, throw **6** dollar, strike

plunther: **4** plod **8** flounder

plurality: **8** majority **9** multitude

plus: add **4** more, over **5** extra **6** excess **8** addition, positive

Pluto: Dis **5** Hades
kingdom: **5** Hades
wife: **10** Proserpina

plutocrat: **5** nabob

Plutus: *father:* **6** Iasion
mother: **7** Demeter

ply: web **4** bend, fold, mold, sail, urge, work **5** beset, layer, plait, wield **6** double, handle, travel **7** belabor, shuttle **8** belabour, exercise **9** importune, thickness
with drink: **5** birle

pneuma: **4** soul **5** neume **6** breath, spirit **9** breathing

pneumonia: **5** lobar, viral **9** bronchial

Po tributary: **4** Adda **9** Cispadane

poach: ram **4** boil, cook, poke, push, stab, stir **5** drive, force, shirr, spear, steal, steam **6** pierce, thrust **7** trample **8** encroach, trespass

poacher: **7** lurcher, stalker, widgeon

pochard: **4** duck, fowl, smee **6** dunker

pochette: **6** violin **7** handbag **8** envelope

pock: pit **4** scar **6** pimple **7** pustule

pocket: bin, cly, fob **4** poke, prat, sack **7** cantina, conceal, confine, enclose
ore: **4** lode **7** bonanza
water: **6** tinaja **7** alberca

pocketbook: bag, fob, lil **4** poke **5** hurse, pouch, purse **6** wallet **8** billfold **12** portemonnaie

pococurante: **9** apathetic **10** nonchalant **11** indifferent

pocosin, pocoson, pocosen: **5** marsh, swamp

pod: bag, bur, cod, kid, sac **4** aril, boll, hull, swad **5** belly, carob, pouch, shell, shuck **6** legume, loment **7** silicle

podesta: **5** judge, mayor **8** executor, governor, official **10** magistrate

podgy: fat **5** pudgy, squat

podium: **4** base, dais, wall **8** pedestal, platform **12** substructure

Poe: *bird:* **5** raven
poem: **5** Raven **6** Lenore **7** Ulalume

poem: ode **4** duan, epic, raff, rann(Ir.), rime, song, vers(F.) **5** canto, ditty, elegy, ionic, lyric, poesy, raffe, stave, verse **6** ballad, carmen, epopee, eulogy, iambic, jingle, poetry, screed, sonnet, tercet **7** ballade, dimeter, sestina, triolet, virelay **8** acrostic, doggerel, hexapody, senarius, trimeter **9** hexameter, hexastich, monometer, octameter, soliloquy **10** tetrameter **11** acatalectic
break in rhythm: **6** cesura **7** caesura
bucolic: **8** pastoral
division of: fit **5** canto
eight-line: **7** triolet
foot: **4** iamb **6** iambus **7** anapest, spondee
four-line: **8** quatrain
fourteen-line: **6** sonnet
heroic: **4** epic
line: **8** trimeter **9** hexameter **12** decasyllabic
love: **6** erotic
lyric: **4** alba
medieval: lai **4** alba
melodic: **5** lyric
moral: dit
mournful: **5** elegy
narrative: **4** epos
node: **4** plot
part: **4** feet, foot, line **5** canto, epode, stich, verse **6** epilog, stanza **7** refrain **8** epilogue
pert. to: **4** odic
religious: **4** hymn **5** psalm
satirical: dit(F.) **6** iambic, parody
seven-line: **10** heptastich
short: dit(F.) **5** ditty **6** sonnet **7** epigram **8** rondelet
six-line: **9** hexastich
six-stanza: **7** sestina
ten-line: **6** dizain **7** dizaine **9** decastich

poems: **5** poesy, verse **6** poetry
collection: **5** sylva

poesy: **4** poem **5** motto, verse **7** nosegay

poet: **4** bard, fili, scop **5** odist, rishi **6** lyrist **7** dreamer, imagist, metrist **8** idyllist, minstrel **9** bucoliast **13** cinque-centist
inferior: **5** rimer **6** rhymer **8** rimester **9** poetaster, poeticule, rhymester, versifier

poetic: **4** odic **5** lyric **6** dreamy **8** romantic **9** beautiful **11** imaginative

poetical: **8** sonnetic

poetry: *accented foot:* **5** arsis
god: **5** Bragi
inspiring to: **7** helicon
muse: **5** Erato **6** Thalia **8** Calliope

pogonip: fog

pogrom: **6** attack **8** massacre **9** slaughter

pogy: **8** menhaden

poietic: **8** creative

poignant: **4** keen, tart **5** acute, sharp **6** biting, bitter, moving **7** cutting, piquant, pointed, pungent **8** piercing, pricking

poind: **4** sell **5** seize **7** impound

point: aim, dot, jag, jet, jot, neb, nib, res, tip, wit **4** apex, barb, cape, crux, cusp, foci, gist, horn, peak, pith, pole, show, spit, spot **5** angle, focus, issue, level, prong, refer, sense, taper **6** allude, apices, cruces(pl.), degree, direct, tittle **7** apicula(L.), apiculi(L.), article, feature, meaning **8** apiculae(L.), apiculus(L.), emphasis, indicate, salience **10** promontory

cardinal: **4** east, west **5** north, south

compass: E., N., S., W.; N.E., N.W., S.E., S.W.; E.N.E., E.S.E., N.N.E., N.N.W., S.S.E., S.S.W., W.N.W., W.S.W. **4** airt **5** airth

final: end

finishing: **4** tape

highest: sum **4** acme, apex, noon, peak **6** apices, apogee, maxima, summit, zenith **7** maximum **8** meridian, pinnacle

law: res

lowest: **4** zero **5** nadir **6** bottom, pergee

pert. to: **6** apical

scoring: ace, run **5** punto **6** sponge

strong: **5** forte

supporting: **5** pivot **7** fulcrum

to the: **8** relevant **9** pertinent

turning: **4** tide **6** crisis, crises

utmost: **7** extreme

vibration: **4** node

weak: **4** flaw **5** fault **6** foible

point-blank: **7** blankly, bluntly, exactly **8** directly **9** perfectly, precisely **10** completely **13** unqualifiedly

point of view: eye **5** angle, sight, slant

pointed: **5** acute, tangy, terse **6** acuate, marked, picked **7** actuate, capapie, concise **8** aculeate, piercing, poignant, spicated, stinging **9** acuminate, apiculate, fastigate **11** conspicuous

pointer: arm, dog, tip **4** clue, hand, hint **5** index **6** fescue, gnomon **7** indices **9** indicator

pointless: **4** dull **5** blunt, inane, silly, vapid **6** stupid **7** insipid

points: *three:* **11** tricuspidal

twelve: **4** pica

pointsman: **7** flanker **9** switchman

poise: tee **5** carry, weigh **6** aplomb **7** balance, ballast, bearing, support, suspend **8** calmness, carriage, liberate, maintain **9** equipoise, stability **10** equanimity **11** equilibrium **12** counterpoise **14** counterbalance

poison: fig **4** bane, drab, gall **5** atter, taint, venin, venom, virus **6** amarin, infect, miasma **7** amarine, arsenic, corrupt, pervert, vitiate **8** empoison, ptomaine **11** contaminate

ant: **10** formmicide **11** formicicide

arrow: **4** haya, inee, upas **5** urali, urare,

urari **6** curare, curari

hexapod: **11** insecticide

kind: **4** bikh **5** abrin, nabee, ricin **6** antiar **7** arsenic, tanghin

pert. to: **9** arsenious

tree: **4** upas

poison ash: **5** sumac **6** sumach **9** torchwood

poison dogwood: **5** sumac **6** sumach

poison fish: **4** fugu **6** weever **8** scorpion, toadfish

poison flag: **4** iris

poison flower: **11** bittersweet

poison ivy: **5** sumac **6** laurel

poison tobacco: **7** henbane

poisoned: **6** sepsis

poisonous: **5** toxic **6** virose **7** noxious **8** virulent **9** malignant **11** destructive

herb: **8** aconitum

poisonwood: **5** sumac **10** manchineel

poisson bleu: **7** blue cat, catfish **8** grayling

poitrel: **5** armor, plate **6** armour **9** stomacher **11** breastplate

poke: bag, dig, hat, jab, jog **4** blow, bore, brod, prod, root, sack **5** nudge, probe, punch, purse **6** bonnet, dawdle, loiter, meddle, pocket, potter, putter, sleeve, thrust, wallet **7** dawdler, intrude, tobacco **8** slowpoke **10** pocketbook

poker: rod **4** dart, game

drawing by: **10** pyrography

forerunner: **7** primero

form: **4** draw, stud

stake: pot **4** ante **5** chips

pokeweed: **5** pocan **6** garget **8** inkberry

family: **14** phytolaccaceae

pokey, poky: **4** dull, mean, slow **5** dowdy **6** narrow, shabby, stuffy **7** tedious **8** trifling

Poland: **7** Polonia **8** Sarmatia

cake: **4** baba

carriage: **7** britska

city: **4** Lodz **5** Brest, Posen, Vilna **6** Cracow, Gdynia, Grodno, Krakow, Lublin, Tarnow, Warsaw **7** Beuthen, Lemberg, Litovsk **8** Gleiwitz, Tarnopol **9** Bialystok, Bielostok, Byelostok

coin: **5** ducat, grosz, marka, zloty **6** fennig, halerz, korona

dance: **7** mazurka **9** krakowiak, polonaise **11** cracovienne

dollar: **5** dalar

dynasty: **5** Piast

measure: cal **4** mila, morg, pret **5** linja, morga, sazen, stopa, vloka, wloka **6** cwierc, korzec, kwarta, lokiec **7** garniec **9** kwarterka

parliament: **4** Seim, Sejm, Seym **5** Senat

people: **4** Slav **5** Marur **8** Silesian

river: San **4** Styr **5** Dwina, Seret **6** Niemen, Pripet, Strypa **7** Vistula **8** Dniester, South Bug

szlachta: **6** gentry **8** nobility **9** landowner

title of address: **4** Pani

weight: lut **4** funt **5** uncya **6** kamian **7** centner, skrupul

polar: 6 Arctic **7** pivotal **8** opposite

polar plant: 9 rosinweed

pole: bar, pew, poy, rod, xat **4** axis, boom, brog, mast, palo(Sp.), pike, prop, spar, wand **5** caber, guide, nader, perch, sprit, staff, stake, stick, stool, sweep, totem **6** crotch **7** barling

circle: **11** circumpolar

electric: **5** anode **7** cathode, kathode **9** electrode

pert. to: **5** polar

vehicle: **4** cope, neap **5** thill

pole fluke: 8 flounder

pole horse: 7 wheeler

pole strip: 8 template

polecat: 5 skunk, zoril **6** ferret, musang **7** fitchet, fitchew, foumart

polehead: 7 tadpole

polemic: 8 argument **9** disputant **10** discussion **11** disputation **12** disputatious **13** argumentative, controversial

polenta: 4 mush **8** porridge

polestar: 5 guide **8** lodestar **10** tramontane

police: 5 guard, watch **6** govern, patrol **7** protect, rurales **8** officers **11** carabinieri(It.) **12** constabulary

headquarters: **4** tana **7** station **8** bargello, barracks **9** marshalcy

line: **6** cordon

officer: **6** kotwal **8** bargello

policeman: cop **4** bull **5** bobby, bulky, burly, rural, sepoy **6** bobbie, copper, peeler **7** crusher, gumshoe, officer, trooper **8** flatfoot, gendarme(F.) **9** burkundaz, constable, patrolman **11** burkundauze, carabiniere(It.)

badge: **6** buzzer, shield

club: **5** billy **9** espantoon, truncheon **10** nightstick

policy: wit **4** plan **6** wisdom **8** contract, prudence, sagacity **9** diplomacy, principle **10** artfulness, management, shrewdness **14** administration

polish: rub **4** buff **5** frush, glaze, gloss, grind, rabat, scour, sheen, shine, slick **6** finish, luster, lustre, rabbat, refine, smooth **7** burnish, culture, furbish **8** brighten, civilize, elegance, lapidate, levigate, urbanity **10** refinement

polished: 4 fine **5** compt, suave **6** polite **7** gallant

polisher: 5 rabat(F.) **8** abrasive

polishing: 8 frottage, limation

polite: 5 civil, suave **6** gentle, smooth, urbane **7** correct, courtly, cunning, gallant, genteel, refined **8** cultured, debonair, decorous, discreet, polished **9** courteous, debonaire **10** cultivated, debonnaire **11** complaisant

politesse: 10 politeness **11** cleanliness, courtliness **12** decorousness

politic: 4 wary, wise **5** suave **6** artful,

crafty, shrewd **7** prudent **8** discreet **9** expedient, politique, provident, sagacious **10** diplomatic **12** unscrupulous

political: *gathering:* **5** rally **6** caucus

group: **4** bloc, ring **5** cadre, party **6** caucus **7** faction, machine

hanger-on: **6** heeler

incumbents: ins

influence: **5** lobby

political party: G.O.P. **4** Tory, Whig **5** labor **9** Communist, Socialist **10** Democratic, Republican **12** Conservative

principles: **8** platform

program article: **5** plank

unit: **4** city, East, ward, West **5** state **6** county, parish **7** borough, hundred, kingdom **8** district **9** sultanate

politician: 7 schemer, senator, statist **9** intriguer, president, statesman **16** congressionalist

politico: 9 statesman **10** politician

polka dot: 4 spot **6** circle

poll: cow **4** clip, coll, head, list, trim **5** count, shave, shear **6** fleece, survey **7** canvass, despoil, listing **8** counting, register **9** enumerate

pollack: 4 fish, pool **6** billet **7** baddock(Sc.) **8** coalfish

pollan: 9 whitefish

pollard: cow **4** bran, deer, goat, stag, tree **5** sheep

polled: 8 hornless

pollen: 4 dust, meal **5** flour

pollen brush: 5 scopa **6** scopae

pollen grain: *mass:* **8** pollinia **9** pollinium

pollenization: 5 xenia

poller: 6 barber **9** plunderer **11** extortioner, taxgatherer

pollex: 4 inch **5** digit, thumb **7** phlange

pollicitation: 7 promise **8** proposal

pollinate: 9 fecundate

pollinosis: 8 hay fever

polliwog: 7 tadpole

pollute: 4 foul, soil **5** dirty, smear, stain, sully, taint **6** befoul, defile, ravish **7** corrupt, debauch, profane, violate, vitiate **9** desecrate **11** contaminate

pollution: 5 filth **8** impurity **11** uncleanness

Pollux: *brother:* **6** Castor

mother: **4** Leda

polo: *division:* **7** chucker, chukker

mount: **4** pony **5** horse

stick: **6** mallet

team: **4** four

Polonius: *daughter:* **7** Ophelia

son: **7** Laertes

Polony: 6 Polish **7** sausage **9** polonaise

polt: 4 blow, club **5** knock, thump

poltergeist: 5 ghost **6** spirit

poltfoot: 8 clubfoot

poltroon: cad **4** idle, lazy **6** coward, craven **7** dastard **8** cowardly, sluggard **9** dastardly

polverine: 6 potash **8** pearlash

polyandrium: 8 cemetery
polychromatic: 10 variegated **12** multi-colored
polygamy: 6 bigamy
polygon: 4 ngon **6** square **7** decagon, hexagon, nonagon, octagon **8** pentagon, triangle
Polynesia: *apple:* **4** hevi
chestnut: **4** rata
cloth: **4** tapa
dragon: ati
fern: **4** tara
garment: **5** pareu
god: Oro **4** Tane, Tiki
goddess: **4** Pele
herb: pia
homeland: **7** Havaiki
island: **4** Fiji **5** Samoa **7** Phoenix, Tokelau
language: **7** Tagalog
memorial: ahu
oven: umu
people: Ati **5** Malay, Maori **6** Kanaka, Samoan, Tongan **8** Hawaiian, Tahitian **9** Marquesan
pepper plant: **4** avas
pine: ara **4** hala
plant: **4** taro
ruler: **7** faipule
sling: ma
spirit: **4** Atua
statue: **4** Tiki
tree: ti **4** ahia, rata
wages: utu
yam: ube, ubi, uve, uvi
polyp: 5 hydra, tumor **6** seapen **7** anemone, hydroid
skeleton: **5** coral
polytrophic: 9 versatile
pomade: 5 salve **7** pomatum, unguent **8** cosmetic, ointment
pome: 4 ball, pear **5** apple, fruit, globe **6** quince, sphere
pomegranate: 6 granet **7** granate, grenade
sirup: **9** grenadine
pomelo: 8 shaddock **10** grapefruit
Pomerania: *capital:* **7** Stettin
city: **6** Anklam
island: **5** Rugen **6** Usedom
river: **4** Oder
Pomeranian: dog
pomme de terre: 6 potato
pommel: bat **4** beat, knob **6** handle **12** protuberance
pomp: 4 fare **5** boast, pride, state **6** estate, parade **7** cortege, display, pageant **8** ceremony, grandeur, splendor **9** pageantry, spectacle **10** ceremonial **11** ostentation **12** magnificence
pompano: 4 fish **7** alewife **9** poppy fish
pom-pom: gun **6** cannon
pompon: 4 ball, tuft **8** ornament **13** chrysanthemum
pompous: big **7** bloated, fustian, orotund, stately, stilted **9** bombastic, flatulent,

grandiose **10** altisonant, pontifical **11** altiloquent, dictatorial, magnificent, pretentious, stateliness **12** ostentatious **13** grandiloquent, self-important
pond: dam **4** delf, dike, dyke, lake, mere, pool, tarn **5** delft **6** lagoon **7** lakelet
fish: **7** aquaria, pisoina **8** aquarium
frog: **7** ranaria **8** ranarium
oyster: **6** claire
pond dogwood: 10 buttonbush
pond duck: 7 mallard
pond hen: 4 coot
ponder: 4 chaw, mull, muse, pore **5** brood, opine, weigh **6** reason **7** reflect, revolve **8** appraise, cogitate, consider, evaluate, meditate, ruminate **10** deliberate **11** contemplate
ponderous: 5 bulky, grave, heavy, hefty, massy **7** awkward, massive, weighty **8** unwieldy **9** important, momentous **11** elephantine
pondfish: 7 sunfish
pondokkie: hut **5** hovel
pone: 4 lump, turf **8** swelling **10** johnnycake
pongee: 4 silk **5** cloth **6** fabric **8** shantung
pongy: 4 monk **6** priest **8** Buddhist
poniard: 4 kill, stab **6** bodkin, dagger, pierce, stylet **8** stiletto
pont: 5 ferry, float **6** bridge **7** caisson, pontoon **9** ferryboat
pontiff: 4 pope **6** bishop
pert. to: **5** papal **7** sistine
pontifical: 5 papal **7** pompous **8** dogmatic
pontoon: 4 boat **5** barge, float **6** bridge, vessel **7** caisson
plank: **5** chess
pony: cab, cob, nag **4** crib **5** glass, horse **6** garran, liquor **7** hackney, measure
kind: **5** pinto, tatoo **6** cayuse, Exmoor **8** Shetland
pooch: dog **6** barbet **7** mongrel
pooh-pooh: 8 ridicule **9** denigrate
pook: 4 heap, pile, pull **5** pluck, stack
pooka: 6 goblin **7** specter
pool: car, dib(Sc.), dub(Sc.), lin, pit, pot **4** carr, dike, dyke, game, linn, loch, mear, meer, mere, pond, tank, tarn **5** flash, flush, funds, kitty, lough, plash, stake, trunk, trust **6** cartel, charco, flodge, lagoon, plunge, puddle, salina **7** alberca, carline, combine, jackpot, plashet **8** monopoly **9** billabong, billiards, reservoir, resources **10** natatorium **11** combination
ball: cue **4** spot **6** ringer
poon tree: 4 dilo **5** domba, keena **8** mastwood
poonghie: See **pongy.**
poop: 4 deck, fool, gulp, seat **5** cheat, cozen, stern **8** hinddeck **10** nincompoop **11** information
poor: bad, ill **4** bare, base, lean, mean **5** cheap, dinky, naked, needy, seedy **6** abject, barren, feeble, humble, hungry, paltry, pilled, scanty, shabby **7** hapless,

sterile, unlucky **8** indigent, inferior **9** defective, destitute, emaciated, imperfect, infertile, penurious **10** inadequate, ungenerous **11** impecunious, inefficient, unfortunate **12** contemptible, insufficient **13** improverished, insignificant **14** unsatisfactory

poor joe: 5 heron

poor John: cod **4** food, hake

poor man's pepper: 9 stonecrop **11** peppergrass

poor man's soap: 8 hardhack

poor man's weatherglass: 9 pimpernel

poor soldier: 9 friarbird

poor-spirited: 4 base **8** cowardly

poorer: 5 worse **8** inferior

poorhouse: 9 almshouse, workhouse

poorly: 13 disparagingly

pop: 4 dart **8** beverage **9** explosion

popadam: 4 cake **5** wafer **6** cookie

popdock: 8 foxglove

pope: 4 ruff **6** bishop, priest, puffin, shrike **7** pontiff **9** bullfinch, patriarch
cape: **5** fanon **7** mozetta **8** mozzetta
collar: **5** orale
court: **5** Curia
court office: **6** datary **7** dataria
court officer: **6** datary
crown: **5** tiara **9** triregnum
envoy: **6** legate **7** nuntius **8** ablegate
epistle: **8** decretal
headdress: **5** miter, mitre
letter: **4** bull
line: **6** papacy
name: Leo **4** John, Pius **5** Peter, Ratti, Urban **6** Adrian **7** Gregory, Zachary **8** Benedict
palace: **7** Lateran, Vatican
seal: **5** bulla
veil: **5** orale **6** fannel

popinac: 8 huisache

popinjay: 6 parrot **8** parakeet **10** woodpecker

poplar: 4 liar **5** abele, alamo, aspen, bahan, bolle, garab **7** populus **9** tacamahac **10** cottonwood

poppy: 5 plant **6** blaver, canker, flower **7** coprose, papaver, ponceau **8** foxglove **10** coquelicot
herb family: **9** celandine
seed: maw

poppycock: rot **4** bosh, dung **8** nonsense

populace: mob **4** mass **5** demos, plebs **6** people

popular: lay, pop **6** common, simple **7** demotic, favored **8** accepted, favorite **9** prevalent, well-liked **11** proletarian **12** nontechnical

popularity: 5 vogue

population: 9 habitancy **11** inhabitants
count: **6** census
study: **10** larithmics

porbeagle: 5 shark

porcelain: 4 frit **5** china **7** biscuit
clay: **6** kaolin **7** kaoline

furnace: **5** hovel
kind of: **6** Sevres **7** Celadon, Dresden, Limoges **8** Haviland **9** Wedgewood

porch: 4 door, stoa **5** lanai, plaza, stoae(pl.), stoop **6** harbor, loggia, piazza **7** balcony, galilee, gallery, portico, terrace, veranda **8** entrance **9** colonnade
sun: **7** solaria(pl.) **8** solarium

porcine: 7 piglike

porcupine: 5 urson **7** cawquaw **8** hedgehog
disease: **10** ichthyosis
genus of: **7** hystrix

porcupine anteater: 7 echidna

porcupine grass: 5 stipa
quill: pen

pore: con **4** gaze **5** gloze, stare, stoma, study **6** ponder **7** foramen, opening, orifice, ostiole, stomata(pl.) **8** lenticel, meditate

porgy: tai(Jap.) **4** fish, scup **6** besugo, pagrus **7** margate, pinfish **8** menhaden **9** spadefish

pork: ham, pig **5** bacon, money, swine **6** hamhog **7** griskin, sausage **8** position

porker: hog, pig **5** swine

porkfish: 4 sisi

porky: fat, pig **6** greasy **9** porcupine

pornographic: 4 lewd **7** obscene **10** licentious

porphyry: 4 rock

porpoise: 4 inia **6** seahog **7** dolphin, pellock(Sc.) **8** gairfish

porrect: 6 extend, tender **7** present

porret: 4 leek **5** onion **6** garlic **8** scallion

porridge: 4 samp **5** atole, brose(Sc.), grout, gruel **6** burgoo **7** brochan, burgout, oatmeal, polenta, pottage **9** stirabout **11** skilligalee
container: **6** bicker

port: 4 gate, toal, left, wine **5** carry, haven **6** apport, harbor, market, portal, refuge **7** bearing, harbour, meaning, purport, shelter **8** carriage, demeanor, larboard **9** demeanour, transport **10** deportment **11** destination

portable: 6 mobile **7** movable **8** bearable

portal: 4 arch, door, gate **7** gateway **8** entrance

portance: 7 bearing, conduct **8** carriage, demeanor

portcullis: bar **4** door, gate, shut **5** grate, herse **7** grating, lattice

porte-monnaie: 5 purse **10** pocketbook

portefeuille: 9 portfolio

portend: 4 bode **5** augur **6** divine **7** betoken, forbode, predict, presage **8** forebode, foretell, prophesy **10** foreshadow

portent: 4 omen, sign **5** event **6** marvel, ostent, wonder **7** meaning, prodigy **8** ceremony **10** prognostic **11** forewarning

portentous: 4 dire **5** fatal, grave **6** solemn **7** fateful, ominous **10** impressive **11** significant

porter: ale **5** carry, hamal, stout **6** bearer,

durwan, hamaul, hammal, khamal. redcap, suisse 7 bailiff, carrier, durwaun,
dvornik(Russ.), gateman, hummaul, janitor 8 beverage, cargador, janitrix 9 attendant, concierge, janitress, transport
10 doorkeeper

porteress: See **portress.**

Portia: *alias:* 9 Balthazar
  lover: 8 Bassanio
  maid: 7 Nerissa

portia tree: 5 bendy

portico: 4 stoa(Gr.), xyst 5 porch, stoae
(Gr., pl.) 6 atrium, piazza, xystus 7
narthex, pteroma, terrace, veranda 9 colonnade, pteromata(pl.) 10 ambulatory,
antetemple

portiere: 5 drape 7 curtain

portion: bit, cut, dab, dot, jag, lot, nip 4
chaw, deal, dole, dunt, fate, jagg, part,
some 5 allot, allow, divvy, dower, dowry,
endow, piece, quota, ratio, share 6 canton, divide, dowery, gobbet, moiety, parcel, rasher, ration 7 destiny, helping,
scruple, section, segment, serving 8 legitime, quantity 9 allotment, allowance,
apportion 10 distribute 13 apportionment

portly: fat 5 obese, stout 6 goodly 7 stately
8 imposing, majestic 9 corpulent,
dignified

portmanteau: bag 4 case 6 valise 8 suitcase 9 carpetbag, gladstone

Porto Rico: See **Puerto Rico.**

portoise: 7 gunwale 8 portlast

portrait: 4 copy, icon, ikon 5 image 7
picture 8 likeness 10 similitude
  sitting: 6 seance

portray: act 4 draw, form, limn, mime,
show 5 enact, frame, graph, image, paint
6 depict 7 fashion, picture 8 describe 9
delineate, pantomime, represent 11 demonstrate

portrayal: 8 portrait

portreeve: 5 mayor 7 bailiff, officer

portress, porteress: 6 porter 9 charwom-
an 10 doorkeeper

Portugal: *brandy:* 11 aguardiente
  city: 4 Ovar 5 Braga, Evora 6 Guarda,
Lisbon, Oporto 7 Coimbra 8 Braganca
  coin: rei 4 peca, real 5 conto, coroa, dobra,
indio 6 dobrao, escudo, macuta, macute,
pataca, pataco, testao, tostao, vintem 7
centavo, crusado, moidore, patacao 8
equipaga
  colony: Diu, Goa 5 Damao, Macao, Timor
6 Angola, Guinea 8 Principe, Sao Thome
10 Mozambique 11 Cape de Verde
  district: 4 Tete 5 Evora
  guitar: 7 machete
  harbor: 4 Faro, Ovar 5 Macao 6 Aveiro,
Lisbon, Oporto, Vianna 7 Setubal 8
Figueira
  island: 6 Angola, Azores 7 Madeira 8 Principe, Sao Thome
  legislature: 6 cortes
  liquid measure: 6 canada
  measure: pe; 4 alma, bota, meio, moio,
pipa, vara 5 almud, braca, fanga, geira,
legoa, linha, milha, palmo 6 almude,
covado, quarto 7 alquier, estadio, ferrado,
selamin 8 alqueire, tonelada 9 pollegada,
quartilho
  money: rei 4 peca 5 dobra 8 johannes
  mountain: 15 Serra d'Estrella
  noble: see *title* below
  people: 7 Iberian
  province: 4 Ovar 5 Beira, Minho 6 Azores
7 Algarve, Madeira 8 Alemtejo 11 Estre-
madura 12 Traz-os-Montes
  river: 4 Sado 5 Douro, Duero, Minho, Tagus 7 Mondego 8 Guadiana
  saint: Sao
  song: 4 fado
  title: dom 4 dona 6 senhor 7 fidalgo, sen-
hora 9 senhorita
  vessel: 7 caravel
  weight: 4 grao, onca, once 5 libra, marco
6 arroba, oitava 7 arratel, quintal 9 es-
cropulo

porwigle: 7 tadpole

posada: inn 5 hotel

posaune: 8 trombone

pose: set, sit 4 airs 5 model, place 6 baffle,
puzzle, stance 7 nonplus, posture 8 attitude, position, propound 9 mannerism 10
disconcert, expression 11 affectation, impersonate 12 attitudinize

Poseidon: 7 Neptune(L.)
  father: 6 Cronus
  mother: 4 Rhea
  servant: 7 Proteus
  son: 6 Albion, Triton 7 Alebion, Antaeus,
Antaios
  wife: 10 Amphitrite

poser: 5 facer 6 puzzle 7 problem 8
question

posh: 5 smart 6 spruce, swanky 7 elegant
9 luxurious

posit: 6 affirm, assert, assume 9 postulate

position (see also **place**): job, lie, set 4
loci(pl.), pose, post, rank, site 5 cense,
coign, locus, place, situs, stand 6 billet,
coigne, estate, locale, office, plight,
stance, status 7 calling, posture 8 attitude, doctrine, location, sinecure,
statuses(pl.) 9 condition, gradation, situation 11 affirmation, appointment, disposition 12 circumstance
  change: 4 move
  correct: 8 oriented
  relative: 5 grade 8 standing

positional: 6 situal

positive: set 4 plus, sure 6 actual, thetic 7
assured, certain 8 absolute, complete,
constant, dogmatic, emphatic, explicit 9
assertive, confident, downright, empirical,
practical 10 peremptory 11 affirmative,
dictatorial, opinionated, unqualified 13
authoritative, overconfident

positivism: 7 Comtism 11 materialism

positure: 7 posture 11 arrangement, disposition 13 configuration

poss: 4 beat, dash, push 5 drive, knock, pound, stamp 6 thrust

posse: 4 band

possess: get, owe, own 4 have 5 reach 6 occupy 7 inhabit 8 dominate, maintain

possessed: mad 8 demoniac

possession: 4 aver, hold 5 aught 6 havior, seisin, wealth 7 control, dewanee, haviour, mastery 8 property 9 ownership
family: 8 heirloom
of goods by finding: 6 trover
take: 5 seise
time: 5 lease

possessions: 5 goods 6 graith

possessor: 10 proprietor

posset: 4 turn 6 curdle, pamper 8 beverage 9 balductum, coagulate

possibility: 11 eventuality

possible: may 6 likely 8 feasible, probable 9 potential 10 contingent 11 practicable

possibly: may 5 maybe 7 perhaps

post: set 4 dole, dool, fort, mail, pole, ride, send 5 cippi(pl.), newel, place, stake, stock 6 assign, cippus, column, inform, office, pillar, travel 7 courier, placard, station 8 announce, dispatch, garrison, position 9 advertise, situation, sternpost 11 publication
easy: 4 pipe, snap 8 sinecure
middle: 8 kingpost

post chaise: 4 jack 5 coach 8 carriage

post office: 6 correo(Sp.)
letter box: 8 apartado(Sp.)

postage: 5 stamp
stamp design: 6 burele 8 burelage, spandred

postbox: 7 mailbox

postboy: 7 courier, yamshik(Russ.) 8 yemschik 9 postilion, yamstchik(Russ.)

postdate: 9 afterdate

postea: 5 entry 6 record

poster: 4 bill, clap, sign 7 affiche, courier, placard, sticker 10 billposter 13 advertisement

posterior: 4 back, hind, rear 6 behind, caudal, dorsal, hinder 10 subsequent

posterity: 6 sequel 10 generation 11 descendants

postern: 4 door, exit, gate 7 private 8 entrance 10 undercover

postfix: 6 append 7 suffix

postiche: wig 6 switch, toupee 8 pretense 9 imitation 14 counterfeiting

postil: 6 homily 7 comment 10 commentary

postilion: 7 postboy

postpone: 4 stay, wait 5 defer, delay, remit, table 6 remand, retard, shelve 7 adjourn, prolong 10 pigeonhole 11 subordinate 13 procrastinate

postponement: 4 mora 5 morae(pl.) 7 respite 8 reprieve 10 ampliation

postprandial: 11 after-dinner

postulant: 9 applicant, candidate 10 petitioner

postulate: 5 claim, posit 6 assume, demand 7 premise, require 10 hypotheses(pl.), hypothesis 11 proposition 12 prerequisite

posture: 4 pose 6 stance 7 bearing, gesture 8 attitude, carriage, position 9 composure
erect: 11 orthostatic

posy: 5 motto, verse 6 flower, legend 7 bouquet, nosegay 9 sentiment 11 composition

pot: bag, pan, win 4 dixy, pool 5 abyss, crewe, dixie, drink, kitty, shoot 6 aludel, basket, cruset, posnet, secure, vessel 7 caldron, capture, cuvette 8 cauldron, crucible, potation 11 deteriorate
arch: 4 kiln
earthen: 4 olla 5 crock, cruse 6 chytra
hat: 5 derby 6 bowler
lead: 8 graphite
wheel: 5 noria

pot-rustler: 4 cook

potable: 5 drink 8 beverage 9 drinkable

potage: 4 soup 5 broth

potash: 4 kali 5 niter, nitre, salin 6 alkali, saline 8 pearlash

potassium: *compound:* 4 alum 6 chrome, potash
sulphate: 4 alum

potation: 4 bout, dram 5 draft, drink 6 liquid, liquor 7 spirits 8 beverage, drinking

potato: ima, oca, yam 4 chat, papa, spud 5 rural, tuber 6 murphy 7 manroot
beetle: 8 hardback
bud: eye
disease: pox 4 curl
dish: 8 au gratin 9 lyonnaise, scalloped
family: 10 solanaceae *
planting ridge: 4 ruck
seed part: eye
starch: 6 farina
sweet: 6 batata, comote, patata 7 batatas, ocarina

Potato State: 5 Idaho, Maine

potbank: 7 pottery

potboiler: 4 book 8 painting 9 potwaller

potboy: 8 Ganymede 9 cupbearer

pote: 4 kick, poke, push 6 thrust

poteen, potheen: 6 whisky

potence: 5 cross 6 gibbet 7 gallows

potency: vis 5 force, might, power, vigor 6 energy 8 efficacy, strength, vitality 9 fertility

potent: 4 able 6 cogent, mighty 7 dynamic 8 powerful, puissant, virulent 9 effective, efficient 10 convincing 11 influential

potentate: 4 amir, emir 5 ameer, emeer, mogul, ruler 6 moghul, prince 7 monarch 9 sovereign

potential: 6 latent, mighty 8 possible 10 unrealized 11 influential, possibility, undeveloped

potentiality: 5 power

potgun: 6 pistol, popgun 8 braggart

pothead: 9 blackfish

pother: ado, row, vex 4 fuss, stir 5 worry 6 bother, bustle, harass, muddle, uproar 7 fluster, perplex, trouble 9 commotion, confusion 11 disturbance 12 perturbation

potherb: 4 kale, mint, wort 5 chard 6 greens 7 mustard, spinach

pert. to: 7 olitory

pothole: 6 tinaja

pothook: rod 4 hake, nine 5 crook 6 collar, scrawl

pothouse: 6 tavern 8 alehouse

potiche: jar 4 vase

potion: 4 brew, dose, drug 5 draft, drink 6 drench 7 draught, philter, philtre 8 nepenthe

sleeping: 5 dwale 6 opiate 8 narcotic 9 soporific 10 belladonna

potlatch: 4 gift 5 feast

potomania: 10 dipsomania

potpie: 4 stew 9 fricassee

potpourri: jar 4 olio, stew 6 medley 7 mixture 9 anthology 10 miscellany 11 salamagundi

potrero: 6 meadow 7 pasture

potsherd: bit 4 chip 5 shard 8 fragment

potshot: 5 shoot 6 assail, attack

pottage: 4 soup 6 brewis 8 porridge

pottah: 4 deed 5 lease 11 certificate

potted: 5 drunk 11 intoxicated

potter: fad, pry 4 fuss, mess, poke, push 6 cotter, dabble, dacker, daiker, dawdle, dodder, fiddle, footer, footle, loiter, meddle, putter, tamper, tinker, trifle 7 cloamer, fossick, saunter 8 ceramist 10 ceramicist

potter's clay: 5 argil

potter's wheel: 4 disk 5 lathe, palet, throw 6 jigger, pallet

pottery: 4 bank, ware 5 china, delft 7 Keramos(F.) 8 ceramics 9 delftware, Keramikos(Gr.), stoneware 11 earthenware

decorating paste: 9 barbotine

firing box: 6 saggar, sagger 7 saggard

fragment: 5 shard, sherd

kind: uda(Ind.) 4 delf 5 delft 6 basalt 7 aretine, bocraro 8 bucchero, Majolica, vitreous 9 delftware, sigillate 12 buccheronero

maker: 6 potter 8 ceramist

mineral: 8 feldspar

pottle: pot 6 basket, liquor 7 tankard

potty: pot 5 crazy, dotty, petty 7 foolish, haughty, trivial 9 eccentric 12 supercilious

pouch: bag, cod, pod, sac 4 cyst, sack 5 bulge, bursa, purse 6 budget, gipser, pocket, sporan 7 alforja, gipsire, mailbag, saccule, silicle, sporran 9 spleuchan 10 pocketbook

pouch bone: 9 marsupial

pouched: 9 sacculate

dog: 4 wolf

marmot: 8 squirrel 11 spermophile

pouf: 4 bang, puff 7 ottoman 9 hairdress

poulp, poulpe: 7 octopus

poultry: 4 fowl 5 ducks, geese 7 pigeons, turkeys 8 chickens 9 pheasants 10 guinea fowl

breed: 6 Ancona 7 Dorking, Leghorn 12 Plymouth Rock 14 Rhode-Island Red

dealer: 6 eggler

disease: pip 4 roup

dish: 9 galantine

yard: 6 barton

pounamu: 4 jade 8 nephrite 10 greenstone

pounce: nab 4 leap, pink, poke, stab 5 pound, prick, punch, stamp, swoop, talon 6 emboss, spring, thrust 8 ornament 9 comminute, perforate

pound: lb. 4 beat, bray, ding, maul, pond, tamp, unit 5 knock, thump 6 bruise, hammer, powder, weight 7 contuse 9 enclosure, pulverize

poundage: 6 charge, weight 8 distrain 9 constrain, enclosure 11 confinement

pounder: 6 pestle

pour: 4 emit, flow, gush, hale, lave, pass, rain, teem, tide, toom(Sc.), vent, well 5 birle, drain, empty, heald, hield, issue, spout, utter 6 affuse, decant, effuse, libate, stream 8 downpour 9 discharge

pourboire: fee, tip 7 douceur 8 gratuity 9 buona-mani(pl.), buona-mano

pout: bib, mop 4 moue, sulk 5 boody, pique 7 catfish, eelpout 8 bullhead 9 sulkiness

poverty: 4 lack, need, want 6 dearth, penury 7 paucity, tenuity 9 indigence 10 inadequacy, scantiness 11 destitution, inferiority

powder: 4 abir(Ind.), dust, kish, mull, talc 5 boral, boron, flour, grind 6 empasm, pollen, pounce, yttria 7 araroba, aristol, malarin, saponin, tripoli 8 cosmetic, sprinkle, tannigen 9 pulverize 10 epiplastic

case: 9 bandolier

container: 4 horn 7 arsenal 8 magazine

make: 4 bray 5 grind 7 calcine 9 pulverize

smokeless: 6 filite, poudre 7 cordite 8 amberite

powdered: 4 seme 5 semee 6 floury

power: arm, art, vis 4 bulk, dint, gift, hand, iron, rial, sway, thew 5 force, might, state, steam, vigor, vires(pl.), wield 6 agency, effort, empire, energy, foison, throne 7 ability, command, control, potence, potency, stamina 8 capacity, efficacy, momentum, strength, virility **9** authority, dominator, influence, intensity, puissance **10** domination, efficiency **12** jurisdiction, potentiality

deprive of: **4** maim **7** impeach **8** dethrone **12** deparliament

intellectual: wit **5** brain **6** genius

lack: **5** atony

natural: od **4** odyl **5** odyle

partnership: **9** champerty

provide with: **5** endue, endow

superior: **10** prepotency **12** predominance

symbol: **5** sword **7** scepter, sceptre

third: **4** cube

unit of: HP; RPM **4** watt

unlimited: **11** omnipotence

power of attorney: **5** agent **10** procurator

powerboat: **5** yacht **9** motorboat

powerful: **4** able, bold, deep **5** stout **6** brawny, cogent, heroic **7** feckful, leonine **9** effective, effectual **10** dominating **11** efficacious

powerless: **4** weak **6** feeble, unable **8** helpless, impotent, lifeless

Powhatan: *daughter:* **10** Pocahontas

pownie: **4** pony

powwow: **6** confer, priest **7** meeting **8** assembly, ceremony, congress, conjurer **10** conference

poyou: **6** peludo **9** armadillo

praam: **4** pram

prabble: **7** quarrel **8** squabble

prabhu: **4** lord **5** chief **6** writer

practic: **6** artful, shrewd **7** cunning **8** decision(Sc.) **9** practical, practiced

practical: **5** utile **6** actual, beaten, usable, useful **7** practic, working **8** feasible, possible, workable **9** available, practiced, pragmatic **11** pragmatical, utilitarian

joke: **4** hoax **5** prank, trick

practically: **6** almost, nearly **9** virtually **13** substantially

practice: do; ply, rut, try, use **4** plot, rote **5** apply, canon, cause, drill, habit, trade, train, usage **6** custom, follow, praxic **7** perform **8** exercise, intrigue, rehearse **9** construct, negotiate **10** experience

pert. to: **9** pragmatic

sharp: **4** game **5** dodge, fraud, usury **6** deceit **9** chicanery

practiced: **7** practic, skilled, veteran **10** conversant

practico: **5** guide **7** skilled **11** experienced

practitioner: **5** agent **6** artist, healer, novice **7** learner, plotter, schemer **8** civilian **9** assistant

prad: **5** horse

praenomen: **4** name **5** Caius, Gaius, Titus **9** first-name

pragmatic: **7** skilled **8** dogmatic, meddling **9** conceited, empirical, officious, practical **10** meddlesome, systematic **11** dictatorial, opinionated, pragmatical

prairie: bay **5** camas, llano, plain **6** camass, cammas, steppe **7** quamash **9** grassland **10** prairillon

prairie anemone: **12** pasqueflower

prairie antelope: **9** pronghorn

prairie apple: **9** breadroot

prairie berry: **9** trompillo

prairie breaker: **4** plow

prairie chicken: **6** grouse

prairie crocus: **12** pasqueflower

prairie dog: **6** marmot **11** wishton-wish

prairie dog weed: **8** marigold

prairie pigeon: **6** plover **9** sandpiper

prairie potato: **9** breadroot

prairie schooner: ark **5** wagon

Prairie State: **8** Illinois

prairie wolf: **6** coyote

prairieweed: **10** cinquefoil

praise: **4** hery, laud, tout **5** adore, allow, alose, bless, extol, glory, honor, kudos, roosa, roose **6** eulogy, extoll, kudize **7** acclaim, adulate, applaud, commend, encomia(pl.), glorify, hosanna, magnify, plaudit, tribute **8** applause, appraise, blessing, encomium, eulogize, macarism **9** adulation, celebrate, panegyric **10** compliment, panegyrize **11** approbation **12** commendation **13** glorification

praiseworthy: **9** exemplary **13** complimentary

praising: **9** laudative

Prakrit: **7** Bahlika **8** language **11** Dakshinatya

pram, praam: **4** boat, cart **5** barge **8** carriage, stroller **12** perambulator

prana: **9** principle

prance: **5** brank, caper, dance, strut **6** cavort, frolic **7** swagger

prancer: **5** horse, rider

prank: jig **4** dido, fold, lark, prat **5** adorn, antic, caper, freak, pleat, shine, trick **6** curvet, fegary, frolic, gambol **8** capricci(pl.), escapade, mischief **9** capriccio **11** monkeyshine

prat: **4** push **5** nudge, prank, trick

prate: gab **4** blab, buck, bukh, carp, chat, talk **5** blate, boast, clack, clash **6** babble, claver, tattle, tongue **7** blatter, chatter, deblate, prattle, twaddle **8** harangue **11** deblaterate

prattle: **4** gaff, lisp **5** prate **6** cackle **7** blather, blether, clatter **9** bavardage **11** confabulate

prawn: **10** crustacean

praxis: **6** action, custom **8** practice

pray: ask, beg, bid, sue **5** daven(Heb.) **6** appeal, invite, invoke **7** beseech, conjure, entreat, implore, request **8** petition **10** supplicate

praya: **4** road **5** beach **6** strand **9** esplanade **10** waterfront

prayer: ave **4** bead, bede, bene, boon, plea, suit **5** grace, matin **6** appeal, ectene, ektene, errand, orison **7** Angelus, bidding, collect, complin, gayatri, oration, request,

savitri **8** compline, entreaty, petition **9** competory, precation **10** paratheses(pl.), parathesis, requiescat **11** benediction, paternoster **12** intercession, supplication
call: **4** adan, azan, bell **5** chime **6** oremus
chancery: **7** relator
form of: **5** chant **6** litany
group: **12** comprecation
set: **9** akoluthia
prayer bead: 6 rosary
prayer book: 6 missal, portas, ritual **7** brevary, portass **9** porthouse
prayer desk: 8 prie-dieu
prayer shawl: 5 orale **7** tallith
prayer tower: 7 minaret
preach: 4 sugh **5** sough, teach **6** exhort, inform **8** advocate, homilize, instruct, moralize, proclaim **9** discourse, predicate, sermonize **10** concionate
preacher: 6 parson, rector **8** minister **9** clergyman, predicant, pulpiteer
preachy: 8 didactic **10** moralistic
preamble: 7 preface
preannounced: 10 annunciate
prebend: 4 land **7** stipend **9** allowance
precarious: 5 risky **7** assumed, dubious **8** insecure, perilous, unstable **9** dangerous, hazardous, uncertain, unsettled **11** unwarranted
precative: 10 beseeching **12** supplicating
precaution: 4 care **6** cautel **7** caution
precede: 4 lead **5** usher **6** forego **7** forerun, predate, preface **8** antecede, antedate **9** introduce
precedence: pas **8** priority
right: pas
precedent: 5 model, usage **7** example **8** decision, standard
preceding: 5 first **8** anterior
precentor: 6 cantor
precept: law **4** hest, rule, tora, writ **5** adage, axiom, breve, brief, maxim, order, sutra, torah **6** lesson **7** caution, command, mandate **8** doctrine, document, teaching **9** direction, principle **10** injunction **11** commandment, instruction
preceptive: 8 didactic **9** mandatory **11** instructive
preceptor: 5 tutor
precinct: 5 ambit, bound **6** hieron **7** temenos **8** boundary, district, environs **9** enclosure
precious: 4 dear, rare, very **5** chere(F.), loved **6** costly, valued **7** beloved **8** affected, esteemed, valuable **9** extremely **10** fastidious **11** overrefined
precious stone: See **gem.**
precipice: lin **4** crag, drop, linn, pali, scar **5** bluff, brink, cliff, steep **7** clogwyn **8** downfall **9** declivity
precipitate: 4 fall, floc, hurl, rash **5** hasty, heady, hurry, speed, throw **6** abrupt, hasten, sudden, tumble, unwary **8** headlong, settling, slapdash **9** desperate, impetuous, impulsive **11** precipitous

precipitation: dew **4** hail, mist, rain, snow **5** haste, sleet **8** downpour **9** hastening **10** deposition **11** impetuosity **12** acceleration
precipitous: 5 sheer, steep **6** steepy **7** prerupt **11** precipitate
precis: 7 epitome, summary **8** abstract **11** abridgement
precise: 4 even, nice, prim **5** exact, stiff **6** formal, minute, strict **7** buckram, certain, correct, finicky, literal, starchy **8** accurate, definite, delicate, explicit, overnice, priggish **9** faultless, veracious **10** ceremonial, fastidious, particular, scrupulous **11** ceremonious, painstaking, punctilious **14** circumstantial
preclude: bar **4** stop **5** avert, close, debar, estop **6** forbid, hinder, impede **7** obviate, prevent **9** foreclose
precocious: 6 unripe **7** forward **9** premature
preconceive: 5 dream **6** ideate, scheme **8** foreknow
precursor: 6 herald **8** ancestor, foregoer **9** harbinger, messenger **10** forefather, forerunner **11** predecessor
precursory: 11 preliminary, premonitory **12** introductory
predatory: 7 robbing **9** pillaging, piratical, rapacious, raptorial **10** plundering, predacious
predestine: 4 doom, fate **6** decree, ordain **7** destine, predoom **8** foredoom **9** determine, forepoint, preordain **10** foreordain **11** foredestine **12** predetermine
predetermine: 4 bias **6** decree **7** destine, predict **8** forecast **9** prejudice **10** prepossess
predicament: fix **4** hole, stew **5** state **6** pickle, plight, scrape **7** dilemma **8** quandary **9** condition, situation
predicant: 5 friar **8** preacher **9** dominican
predicate: cry **4** aver **5** imply **6** affirm, assert, preach **7** commend, declare, foresee, involve, predict **8** foretell, proclaim
predict: 4 bode, dope, omen **5** augur, weird **6** divine, halsen **7** forbode, presage **8** forebode, forecast, prophesy, soothsay **9** auspicate, predicate **13** prognosticate
prediction: 5 weird **7** bodword **12** forespeaking, vaticination
predictor: 4 seer
predilection: 4 bent, bias **8** fondness, tendency **9** prejudice **10** partiality, preference, propensity **11** inclination **14** predisposition, susceptibility
predisposition: 12 predilection
predominant: 6 ruling **8** dominant, reigning, superior **9** ascendant, ascendent, hegemonic, prevalent **10** dominating, noticeable, prevailing **11** controlling, outstanding **12** preponderant
predominate: 6 domine, exceed **8** domineer

pree: try 5 taste 6 sample

preeminent: big 4 star 5 grand 7 capital, palmary, ranking, supreme 8 dominant, superior 9 excellent, prominent 10 surpassing 11 outstanding

preempt: 5 usurp 9 establish 10 monopolize 11 appropriate

preen: pin, sew 4 perk, trim 5 adorn, clasp, dress, plume, press, primp, prink, prune 6 bodkin, brooch, smooth, spruce, stitch

preface: 5 front, proem 6 herald 7 forerun, precede, prelude 8 exordium, foreword, preamble, prologue 9 introduce 11 preliminary 12 forespeaking, introduction, introductory

prefect, praefect: 4 dean 7 monitor, officer 8 director, minister, official 9 president 10 magistrate

prefecture: 7 eparchy(Gr.) 8 district

prefer: opt 4 like 5 elect, favor 6 desire, favour, rather, select

preferable: 6 better

preference: 6 choice 8 appetite, priority 11 alternative 12 predilection

prefigure: 4 type 6 ideate, typify 7 forerun 8 foretell 10 foreshadow

pregnable: 10 assailable, expugnable, vulnerable 11 conquerable

pregnancy: 6 cyesis

pregnant: big 5 heavy 6 gravid 7 fertile, teeming, weighty 8 enceinte, fruitful, prolific 9 abounding, gestating, potential 10 germinable

prehend: 5 seize

prehistoric: 10 immemorial

preindicate: 7 presage 8 prophesy

prejudice: 4 bent, bias, harm, hurt 6 damage, hatred, impair 7 bigotry 9 suspicion 10 partiality, prepossess 11 inclination, intolerance 12 disadvantage, predetermine, predilection, prejudgement 13 prejudication

prejudicial: 8 contrary 9 injurious 11 contrarious, detrimental

prelate: 4 head 5 chief 6 abbess, bishop, priest 7 primate 8 superior 9 dignitary 10 archbishop 12 ecclesiastic

prelector: 6 reader 8 lecturer 9 professor 10 discourser, praelector

preliminary: 5 prior 7 preface 8 entrance, previous, proemial 9 prefatory, threshold 10 antecedent 11 preparatory

prelude: 6 verset 7 descant, intrada, opening, preface 8 overture, ritornel 10 ritornelle 12 introduction

premature: 6 unripe 8 immature, untimely 10 precocious 12 unseasonable

premeditate: See **meditate.**

premeditation: 11 forethought 12 aforethought

premier: 5 chief 7 leading 8 earliest, foremost 9 principal

premise: 6 ground 9 postulate 10 assumption 11 proposition

premium: 4 agio 5 bonus, prize, spiff 6 bounty, deport, reward 8 lagnappe 9 lagniappe 10 recompense

premonition: 4 omen 5 hunch 6 notice 7 bodword, warning 9 forescent 10 foreboding 11 forewarning, information 12 apprehension, presentiment

preoccupied: 4 lost, rapt 6 absent, filled 8 absorbed 9 engrossed

preordain: 10 predestine

preparation: 5 array 7 extract, product 8 cosmetic 9 condiment, decoction 10 confection 11 arrangement 12 introduction

place of: 10 laboratory, paratorium

without: 5 ad lib 8 careless 9 impromptu

prepare: arm, fit, fix, get, set 4 bush, busk, gibe, gird, pave, make, suit, tibe 5 adapt, alert, coach, curry, dight, equip, ettle, frame, groom, prime, ready, train 6 adjust, devise, graith 7 address, affaite(F.), apparel, arrange, concoct, confect, dispose, furnish, provide, qualify 8 accustom, compound, instruct, rehearse 9 calculate, condition, construct 10 concinnate

prepared: apt 4 yare

prepense: 8 designed 11 forethought 12 aforethought, premeditated

preponderance: 6 weight 9 dominance 10 ascendancy, ascendency, prevalence 12 predominance

preponderate: 4 sink 7 incline, surpass

prepose: 6 prefix 7 preface

preposition: at, by, in, on, to, up; but, for, off, out, tae(Sc.) 4 from, into, onto, over, unto, upon, with 5 about

prepossess: 12 predetermine

prepossessing: 10 attractive

prepossession: 4 bent, bias 9 prejudice 10 absorption 11 inclination 12 predilection 14 predisposition

preposterous: 6 absurd, screwy 7 foolish 9 grotesque, senseless 10 irrational, ridiculous 11 nonsensical

prerequisite: 9 postulate

prerogative: 5 right 7 apanage 8 appanage, appenage, priority 9 privilege 10 precedence

eldest son's: 6 esnecy

prerupt: 11 precipitous

presage: 4 bode, omen, osse, sign 5 augur, token 6 augury, betide, divine, import 7 betoken, forbode, meaning, portend, portent, predict, warning 8 forebode, foretell, prophecy, prophesy 9 foretoken, harbinger 10 foreboding, prediction, prognostic 11 foreknowing, preindicate 12 apprehension, presentiment 13 prognosticate

presbyter: 5 elder 6 priest 7 prester 8 minister 9 clergyman

presbytery: 5 court 7 council, rectory 9 residence

prescience: 9 foresight 11 omniscience 13 foreknowledge

prescind: 6 detach 7 isolate 8 abstract, separate

prescribe: set 5 allot, guide, limit, order 6 define, direct, ordain, outlaw 7 appoint, command, control, dictate 9 prescript 10 invalidate

prescribed: 6 thetic

prescript: 9 prescribe

prescription: rx 6 recipe

presence: 4 mien 5 being 6 spirit 7 bearing, company, dignity, spectre 8 assembly 9 influence 10 apparition, attendance, deportment

prefix: oxy

present: now 4 boon, gift, give, here 5 adsum(L.), being, bonus, cuddy, grant, nonce, offer, ready, today 6 adduce, allege, bestow, bounty, confer, donate, render, tender 7 cumshaw, display, exhibit, largess, perform 8 donation, gratuity, lagnappe 9 collected, introduce, lagniappe, personate 10 exhibition 11 benefaction, efficacious

again: 5 rerun

pert. to: 6 modern 7 current 12 contemporary

to guest or stranger: 6 xenium

with another: 8 collocal

present-day: 7 current 12 contemporary

presentiment: 10 foreboding 11 premonition 12 apprehension

presently: 4 anon, enow, soon 7 shortly 8 directly 9 forthwith 11 immediately

preservation: 11 safekeeping

preservative: 4 salt 5 spice 7 alcohol, vinegar 8 creosote 12 conservative

preserve: can, dry, jam, tin 4 corn, cure, keep, salt, save 5 bless, guard, jelly, spare, store, uvate 6 athold, comfit, defend, govern, retain, secure, shield, uphold 7 compote, condite, confect, forfend, protect, succade, sustain 8 conserve, forefend, maintain 9 confiture, safeguard

preside: 6 direct 7 control 8 moderate, regulate

president: mir 4 head 5 ruler 8 governor 9 sovereign

successor: 9 designado(Mex.)

President (U.S.): (1, 1789-97) George Washington; (2, 1797-1801) John Adams; (3, 1801-09) Thomas Jefferson; (4, 1809-17) James Madison; (5, 1817-25) James Monroe; (6, 1825-29) John Quincy Adams; (7, 1829-37) Andrew Jackson; (8, 1837-41) Martin Van Buren; (9, 1841) William Henry Harrison; (10, 1841-45) John Tyler; (11, 1845-49) James K. Polk; (12, 1849-50) Zachary Taylor; (13, 1850-53) Millard Fillmore; (14, 1853-57) Franklin Pierce; (15, 1857-61) James Buchanan; (16, 1861-65) Abraham Lincoln; (17, 1865-69) Andrew Johnson; (18, 1869-77) Ulysses S. Grant; (19, 1877-81) Rutherford B. Hayes; (20, 1881) James A. Garfield; (21, 1881-85) Chester A. Arthur; (22, 1885-89) Grover Cleveland; (23, 1889-93) Benjamin Harrison; (24, 1893-97) Grover Cleveland; (25, 1897-1901) William McKinley; (26, 1901-09) Theodore Roosevelt; (27, 1909-13) William H. Taft; (28, 1913-21) Woodrow Wilson; (29, 1921-23) Warren G. Harding; (30, 1923-29) Calvin Coolidge; (31, 1929-33) Herbert Hoover; (32, 1933-1945) Franklin D. Roosevelt; (33, 1945-1953) Harry S. Truman; (34, 1953-1961) Dwight D. Eisenhower; (35, 1961-1963) John F. Kennedy; (36, 1963-1969) Lyndon B. Johnson; (37, 1969-) Richard M. Nixon

nickname: Abe, Cal, Ike 5 Teddy

presignify: 7 presage 8 intimate 9 foretoken

press: hug 4 bale, bear, bind, cram, dint, iron, mash, spur, thew, urge 5 brize, brizz, chest, chirt, crowd, crush, drive, force, knead, preen, serry, wring 6 compel, crunch, impact, roller, smooth, throng 7 armoire, embrace, entreat, flatten, impress, imprint, scrunge, smasher, squeeze 8 calender, compress, straiten, wardrobe 9 constrain, embarrass, emphasize, importune 10 constipate, newspapers

corrector: 11 proofreader

critic: 6 censor

pressed: 5 dense 7 compact, serried

presser: 5 baler 6 ironer, mangle

pressing: 6 urgent 7 exigent 8 exacting 9 imperious 10 imperative 11 importunate

pressman: 7 printer

pressure: 4 heat, push 5 force 6 duress, stress 7 bearing, squeeze 8 exigency, instancy 10 affliction, constraint, impression, oppression 11 compression

equal: 8 isobaric

gauge: 9 manometer, manoscope

unit: 4 atmo, dyne 5 barad 7 mesobar

pressure group: 5 lobby

pressure measuring instrument: 10 piezometer

prest: 4 duty, loan 7 advance, pressed

prester: 4 vein 5 snake 6 priest 7 serpent 9 hurricane, presbyter, whirlwind

prestidigitator: 6 palmer 7 juggler 8 conjurer, magician

prestige: 6 renown 7 sorcery 8 illusion 9 deception, influence 10 importance, prominence

presto: 7 passing, quickly 8 suddenly 11 immediately 13 instantaneous

presumably: 8 probably 10 ostensibly, supposedly

presume: 5 guess 6 impose 7 daresay, suppose, venture 8 arrogate 9 postulate 10 conjecture, presuppose

presumptuous: 4 bold 5 fresh 7 forward, haughty, icarian 8 arrogant, assuming, familiar, impudent, insolent 9 audacious, confident, foolhardy 11 adventurous, venturesome

presuppose: 6 assume

pretend: act 4 pose, seem, sham 5 claim,

feign 6 affect, allege, assume, gammon 7 profess 8 disguise, simulate 11 dissimulate, make-believe

pretended: 4 fake 5 false 7 colored, reputed 8 coloured, intended, proposed 10 fictitious, ostensible

pretender: fop 4 fake, idol, snob 5 cowan(Sc.), faker, quack 6 poseur, seemer 8 aspirant, claimant, deceiver, impostor 9 charlatan 10 mountebank 11 fourflusher 12 dissimulator

pretense, pretence: act, peg 4 brag, cant, flam, plea, ruse, sham, show 5 claim, cloak, cover, feint, gloze, study, trick 6 excuse, humbug, tinsel 7 fiction, grimace, potiche, pretext 8 artifice, occasion 9 deception, moonshine, semblance 10 appearance, assumption, subterfuge 11 affectation, fabrication, make-believe, ostentation 13 stalking-horse

pretentious: big 4 arty 5 gaudy, showy 7 pompous 8 affected, assuming 11 highfaluten, highfalutin 12 highfaluting, ostentatious

pretermit: 4 omit 6 ignore 7 neglect, suspend 8 intermit 9 disregard, interrupt

preternatural: 6 gousty 7 goustie 8 abnormal, uncommon 9 irregular 12 supernatural

pretext: 8 pretense

pretty: gay, toy 4 cute, deft, fair, gent, joli 5 bonny, jolie, lindo(Sp.) 6 bonita, bonito, bonnie, clever, comely 7 dollish 8 betcheri, budgeree 9 beautiful, ingenious 10 attractive, knickknack, moderately

prevail: win 5 reign 6 induce, obtain 7 persist, succeed, triumph 8 dominate 11 predominate

prevail: *upon:* 4 urge 6 allure, induce 7 entreat 8 persuade

prevalent: 4 rife 6 common, potent 7 current, general 8 dominant, powerful 9 extensive 10 prevailing, successful, victorious, widespread 11 efficacious, influential

prevaricate: fib, lie 5 evade 7 quibble, shuffle 10 equivocate

prevarication: 10 subterfuge

prevene: 7 prevent

prevent: bar, gag, let 4 balk, bind, save, stop, warn 5 avert, debar, deter, estop 6 defend, forlet, hinder, impede, resist, thwart 7 forfend, impeach, obviate, prevent 8 antevert, forefend, preclude, prohibit, restrain 9 foreclose, forestall, frustrate 10 anticipate, circumvent

preventive: 12 prophylactic 13 precautionary

previous: ere 4 erst, fore, past 5 prior, supra 6 before, bygone, former 7 earlier 8 anterior, foregone, untimely 9 foregoing, preceding, premature 10 antecedent, beforehand, heretofore 11 unwarranted

prevision: 8 forecast 9 foresight 10 pre-

cience, prevoyance 13 foreknowledge 15 prognostication

prewar: 10 antebellum

prey: 4 feed 5 booty, raven, ravin, seize, spoil 6 quarry, ravage, ravine, victim 7 capture, plunder 9 victimize

living on: 9 predatory

Priam: *daughter:* 6 Creusa 8 Polyxena 9 Cassandra

servant: 7 Agelaus

son: 5 Paris 6 Hector 7 Helenus, Troilus 9 Deiphobus, Polydorus

wife: 6 Hecuba

price: fee 4 cost, fare, fiar(Sc.), fier(Sc.), hire, rate 5 cheap, value, worth 6 charge, ransom, reward 7 expense 8 appraise, evaluate 10 estimation, excellence 12 preciousness 13 consideration

maintain: peg

reduced: 4 sale 7 bargain

rising: 4 boom 9 inflation

priceless: 4 rare 6 absurd, costly, unique 7 amusing 8 valuable 10 invaluable 11 inestimable

prick: dot, jag 4 brod, brog, cloy, drob, goad, jagg, ping, pink, prod, stab, tang 5 briar, point, smart, spine, sting, thorn 6 broach, cactus, incite, nettle, pierce, skewer, tingle 7 bramble, pricker, prickle 8 puncture

pricking: 8 poignant

prickle: 4 seta 5 setae(pl.), sieve 6 basket 7 acantha, aculeus, spicula(pl.) 8 spiculum

prickly: 5 burry 8 echinate

prickly pear: 4 tuna 5 nopal 7 opuntia

pride: 5 glory, pique, plume, valor 6 egoism, esteem, spirit, vanity 7 conceit, disdain, egotism, elation, hauteur, respect 8 nobility, splendor, valiancy 9 arrogance, insolence, loftiness 10 lordliness, self-esteem 11 haughtiness, self-conceit, self-respect 12 independence 15 self-approbation 16 superciliousness

prier, pryer: 10 inquisitor

priest: en; fra 4 abbe, club, cura, cure(F.), imam, lama, papa(It.), pere(F.) 5 clerk, druid, hotar(Ind.), imaum, mulla, padre(Sp.), rabbi, sarip, vicar 6 bhikku, bishop, cleric, dastur, divine, father, gallah(Heb.), mullah, oblate, rector, vestal, wahabi 7 cassock, destour, dustoor, prester, tuhunga, wahabee, wahhabi 8 minister 9 clergyman, dignitary, oratorian, priesteen 10 hierophant, priestling 12 ecclesiastic

assistant: 7 acolyte

cap: 7 biretta

garment: alb 4 cope, robe 5 ephod, habit 8 scapular 9 vestments

habit ornament: 4 urim

headdress: 9 saghavart

neckpiece: 5 amice, stole

pert. to: 10 sacerdotal

scarf: **5** rabat **7** maniple
server: **7** acolyte
voodoo: **5** mambu **6** hungan **7** gangang
priesthood: 9 sacerdocy **11** sacerdotage
priestly: 10 sacerdotal
prig: beg, fop, pan **4** buck **5** dandy, filch, plead, prink, prude, steal, thief **6** haggle, pilfer, purist, tinker **7** bargain, entreat, pitcher **8** pilferer **9** precision **10** pickpocket
prigger: 5 thief
priggish: 4 prim, smug **8** thievish **11** overprecise
prill: 4 rill **6** button, nugget, pellet, stream
prim: mim, set **4** neat, nice **5** stiff **6** demure, formal, proper **7** correct, precise, prudish **8** accurate, decorous **10** ceremonial
prima donna: 4 diva, lead, star **6** singer **7** actress
famous: **4** Lind **5** Patti **7** Russell **13** Schumann-Heink
primary: 4 main **5** chief, first, prime **6** primal **7** capital, central, initial **8** earliest, original, primeval, pristine **9** elemental, primitive, principal **10** elementary, preeminent, primordial **11** fundamental
primate: ape, man **5** lemur, orang **6** bishop, monkey **8** marmoset **9** orangutan **10** anthropoid, archbishop **11** orangoutang
prime: 4 size **5** coach **7** prepare, primary **9** copacetic, excellent, undercoat
prime minister: 7 premier
primer: 8 hornbook, textbook **11** abecedarium
primeveal: 6 primal **7** ancient, ogygian **8** original, pristine **9** primitive
primitive: 5 basic, crude, first, rough **6** simple **7** ancient, archaic, primary, priscan, radical **8** barbaric, original, pristine **9** underived **10** aboriginal, antiquated **11** uncivilized **12** old-fashioned
primogenial: 6 primal **7** primary **8** original **9** primitive
primordial: 5 first **7** primary **9** elemental **11** fundamental
primp: 5 adorn, dress, preen, prink
primrose: 5 oxlip, spink(Sc.) **7** cowslip, primula **8** auricula
family: **11** primulaceae
primus: 5 first, stove
prince: bey, ras **4** amir, emir, rial **5** alder, ameer, emeer, ruler **6** despot, dynast, satrap **7** dynasty, monarch **8** archduke **9** potentate, princekin, princelet, sovereign **10** princeling
allowance: **8** appenage
pine: **10** pipsissewa
title: **6** serene
Prince of: *Apostles:* **8** St. Peter
Darkness: **5** devil, Satan **7** Ahriman **9** Beelzebub

Destruction: **6** Timour **9** Tamerlane
Evil Spirits: **7** Sammael
Liars: **5** Pinto
Peace: **7** Messiah
the Ode: **7** Ronsard
the Sonnet: **15** Joachim de Bellay
princedom: 4 rank **11** sovereignty **12** jurisdiction
princely: 5 noble, regal, royal **6** kingly **10** munificent **11** magnificent
princeps: 4 head **5** first, pagus **7** headman
princess: 5 begum(Muslim), ranee (Muslim)
loved by Cupid: **6** Psyche
loved by Zeus: **6** Europa
mythological: **8** Atalanta
Princeton symbol: 5 tiger
principal: top **4** arch, head, high, main, star **5** chief, first, grand, major, prime **6** leader, staple **7** capital, captain, chattel, leading, palmary, primary, stellar **8** cardinal, dominant, foremost **9** important, preceptor **10** headmaster **11** outstanding
principle: law **4** rule **5** axiom, canon, dicta(pl.), maxim, prana, tenet **6** dictum **7** brocard, essence, precept, theorum **8** doctrine **9** integrity **11** fundamental, uprightness
first: **4** base, seed **5** basis **8** rudiment **10** fundamenta(pl.) **11** fundamentum
general: **9** generalia **12** generalities
statement: **5** credo, creed, motto
vital: **4** soul **5** anima
principles: 5 creed
princox: fop **7** coxcomb
prink: 4 deck, perk, wink **5** adorn, dress, preen, primp, prune **6** bedeck, glance
print: 4 copy, film **5** issue, stamp **6** fabric **7** edition, engrave, impress, publish **8** negative **9** engraving, newspaper **10** impression
printer: 4 typo **8** letterer, pressman **11** typographer **12** lithographer
cross stroke: **5** serif **6** ceriph
direction: cut, tr. **6** delete
printing:
block: **4** wood **7** edition **8** linoleum
blurred appearance: **5** macul
color: **17** chromolithography
error: pi; pie **6** errata(pl.) **7** erratum
form: cut, die, mat **5** frame **6** matrix **7** matrice
implement: **5** biron **6** brayer, dabber, dauber
ink spreader: **6** brayer
mark: **4** dash, dele, list, stet **5** caret, obeli, tilde **6** dagger, diesis, obelus **7** obelisk **8** ellipses
measure: em, en **4** pica **5** agate, empen
metal block: **4** quad
plate: **6** stereo **10** stereotype
press part: **6** platen, roller, rounce **7** frisket

process: **6** offset **7** braille, typeset **8** cerotype **10** photolitho **11** lithography **14** photoengraving

second: **7** reissue

space block: **4** quad

type for spacing: **4** quad, slug

printer's aid: 5 devil

prion: 6 petrel

prionid: 6 beetle

prior: ex; ere **4** fore, past **5** elder **6** before, former **7** earlier **8** anterior, previous **10** antecedent **11** retroactive

priority: 8 position **9** privilege **10** precedence, preference **11** superiority

priory: 5 abbey **7** nunnery **8** cloister **9** monastery, sanctuary

priscan: 7 ancient **9** primitive

prism device: 8 iriscope

prismatic: 9 brilliant **10** iridescent **12** orthorhombic

prison: gib, jug **4** brig, cell, gaol, hell, hole, jail, keep, quod, rock, stir **5** bagne, clink, grate **6** bagnio, carcel, carcer, cooler, lock-up **7** Atlanta, Bocardo, college, dungeon, Gehenna, hoosgow, kidcote, Newgate **8** Alcatraz, Bastille, hoosegow, hoosegow, Sing Sing **9** Bridewell, calaboose, enclosure **10** guardhouse, panopticon **11** Leavenworth **12** penitentiary

guard: **5** screw

keeper: **5** guard **6** gaoler, jailer, jailor, keeper, warden **7** turnkey

room: **4** cell, hole, tank **7** dungeon **8** solitary

sentence: rap

spy: **6** mouton

prisoner: con **5** lifer **6** detenu(F.), inmate **7** caitiff, captive, convict, detenue(F.), parolee **9** collegian **10** emancipist **11** probationer

exchange agreement: **6** cartel

Prisoner of the Vatican: 4 Pope

prisoner of war: PW: P.O.W. **7** kriegie

prissy: 4 prim **5** fussy **7** finicky, precise, prudish **9** sissified **11** over-refined

pristav, pristaw: 8 official, overseer **12** commissioner

pristine: new **4** pure **5** early, fresh **7** ancient, primary **8** original **9** primitive, unspoiled, untouched **11** uncorrupted

pritch: 5 prick, spike, staff **6** pierce

privacy: 7 privity, retreat, secrecy **8** darkness, solitude **9** seclusion **10** penetralia **12** hugger-mugger

privado: 6 friend **8** intimate **9** confidant

private: 6 closet, covert, secret **7** soldier **8** esoteric, homefelt, personal, secluded, solitary **10** unofficial **12** confidential, unpublicized

private eye: 6 tailer **9** detective, operative **12** investigator

privateer: 4 Kidd **5** caper **6** pirate **7** corsair, drumler **8** drumbler

privately: 5 aside

privation: 4 loss, want **6** misery **8** hardship **11** deprivation, destitution

privet: 5 hedge, ibota, shrub **7** alatern, ibolium **9** houseleek

privilege: law, soc, use **4** soke **5** favor, grace, grant, right **6** favour, patent **7** charter, liberty **8** easement, immunity **9** advantage, exemption, franchise **10** concession **11** prerogative

privy: wc **4** gong **6** cloaca, hidden, secret, toilet **7** cloacae(pl.), furtive, private **8** familiar, intimate, out-house **9** backhouse, confidant, necessary **11** clandestine, water-closet **12** confidential **13** surreptitious

prix: 5 prize

prize: cup, pry **4** gree(Sc.), prix(F.), tern **5** award, bacon, booty, lever, medal, plate, purse, stake, value **6** esteem, glaive, reward, trophy **7** capture, premium, seizure **8** estimate, leverage, purchase, treasure **10** appreciate

prizefight: go **4** bout **5** match **7** contest

customer demand: K.O.

ring: **5** arena

prized: 4 dear **5** chary

pro: for **8** advocate, favoring **9** favouring **12** professional

probability: 4 odds **6** chance **10** appearance, likelihood, likeliness **11** credibility

probable: 6 likely **8** credible, feasible

probably: 6 belike, likely

probation: 4 test **5** trial **6** parole **9** novitiate **11** examination

probe: 4 acus, tent, test **5** grope, sound **6** pierce, search, seeker, stylet, tracer **7** examine, explore **9** penetrate **10** ankylomele, instrument, scrutinize **11** exploration, investigate **13** investigation

probity: 7 honesty **9** integrity, rectitude **11** uprightness

problem: nut, sum **4** crux, knot **5** hydra, poser **6** enigma, riddle **8** question **9** situation

problematical: 8 doubtful **9** ambiguous, equivocal, uncertain, unsettled **12** questionable

proboscis: 4 nose **5** snout, trunk

procacious: 4 pert **8** impudent, insolent, petulant

procavia: 5 hyrax **10** hyracoidea

procedure: 6 tactic **7** process, program, routine

proceed: go **4** fand, fare, move, pass, wend **5** arise, frame, issue **7** derive **7** advance, emanate, forthgo **8** continue, progress **9** originate

laboriously: mog **4** plod, plow, slog, wade **6** trudge

rapidly: run **5** speed **6** gallop

proceeding: 4 acta(pl.), step **5** actum, doing **6** affair, afflux, course **7** conduct, measure **9** affluxion, procedure **11** transaction

proceeds: 4 loot **5** booty **6** income, profit, return **8** stealage

procerity: 6 height 8 tallness

process: 4 cook, writ 5 lapse, order 6 capias, course, manner, method, notice, system 7 advance, mandate, summons 8 progress 9 operation, procedure, sterilize 10 injunction

procession: 4 file 5 march 6 course, exequy, litany, parade 7 cortege, pageant 9 cavalcade, formation, recession

proclaim: bid, cry 4 call, deem, toot, tout 5 blare, blast, blaze, claim, grede, knell, voice 6 blazon, bounce, defame, herald, indict, outcry, preach 7 declare, divulge, enounce, publish 8 announce, denounce, forspeak 9 advertise, celebrate, enunciate, forespeak 10 promulgate

proclamation: ban 4 bans, fiat 5 bando (Sp.), banns, blaze, edict, ukase 6 notice 7 bidding, placard 9 manifesto 11 publication 12 announcement, annunciation, denunciation, notification, promulgation

proclivity: 4 bent 6 talent 7 leaning 10 propensity 11 disposition, inclination

Procne: *husband:* 6 Tereus
sister: 9 Philomela

procrastination: 5 delay, stall 9 deferment 10 cunctation, inactivity 12 dilatoriness, postponement

procreant: 8 fruitful 9 producing 10 generating

procreate: 4 sire 5 beget 7 produce 8 engender, generate

procreation: 8 virility 9 offspring 10 generation, production

proctor: 5 agent, proxy 6 patron 7 steward 8 advocate, attorney

procurable: 10 accessible

procure: get 4 fang, find, gain 5 bring 6 effect, obtain, secure, suborn 7 acquire, chevise, receive 8 contrive 9 impetrate

procurer: 4 bawd, pimp

procuress: 4 bawd, hack 7 commode

prod: egg, jab 4 brog, goad, poke, urge 6 incite, thrust

prodigal: 5 flush 6 lavish 7 liberal, profuse, spender, wastrel 8 abundant, generous, wasteful 10 profligate, squanderer 11 extravagant, spendthrift, squandering

prodigious: 4 huge 5 giant 7 amazing, immense 8 enormous, gigantic 9 marvelous, monstrous, wonderful 10 portentous, tremendous 11 astonishing 13 extraordinary

prodigy: 4 omen, sign 6 marvel, ostent, wonder 7 miracle, portent 8 ceremony

prodition: 7 treason 8 betrayal 15 treacherousness

produce: do 4 bear, form, make, show 5 breed, carry, cause, shape, stage, yield 6 create, effect, fruits 7 exhibit 8 engender, generate 9 fabricate, offspring 10 production, vegetables 11 manufacture
new: 6 create, invent 9 originate

producer: 6 author, farmer, grower, parent 7 creator 8 director 12 manufacturer

product: 4 item 5 fruit 6 number, result 9 offspring, outgrowth

production: 4 work 5 fruit 6 output 11 performance

productive: 4 rich 6 active, parous 7 fertile 8 creative, fruitful, sonorous 10 generative 11 originative

proem: 7 preface, prelude 8 foreword, overture, preamble 12 introduction

profanation: 9 sacrilege

profane: hoa 4 foul 5 abuse 6 debase, defile, defoil, defoul, unholy, vulgar, wicked 7 godless, impious, obscene, secular, ungodly, violate, worldly 8 temporal 9 desecrate, vulgarize 10 irreverent, unhallowed 11 blasphemous 12 unsanctified

profanity: 4 oath 5 curse 9 blasphemy

profess: own 4 avow 5 admit, claim 6 affect, affirm, allege 7 confess, declare, protest 8 proclaim 11 acknowledge

professed: 9 pretended 10 ostensible

profession: art 5 craft, faith, forte, trade 6 avowal, career, metier(F.) 7 calling 8 function, vocation 9 following 10 employment, occupation

professional: pro 4 paid 5 hired 6 expert 7 artiste, skilled, trained 8 finished

professor: don, fly 7 teacher

proffer: bid 4 give, hand 5 offer 6 extend, tender 11 countenance

proficiency: 5 skill 7 ability, aptness 9 adeptness 10 capability, competence, efficiency, expertness 14 accomplishment

proficient: 6 actual, versed 9 effective, effectual 10 conversant

profile: 4 form 6 figure 7 contour, drawing, outline 10 silhouette 14 representation

profit: net, pay, use 4 boot, gain, good, help, mend, nett 5 avail, frame, lucre, melon 6 behoof, return 7 account, benefit, bestead, revenue, utility 8 increase, interest 9 advantage, emolument 12 remuneration
receiver of: 6 pernor

profitable: fat 8 repaying 9 expedient

profitless: 9 fruitless 12 unprofitable

profligate: 6 rioter 7 corrupt, riotous, spender, vicious, wastrel 8 depraved, flagrant, prodigal, rakehell, wasteful 9 abandoned, dissolute, reprobate 10 licentious 11 extravagant

profound: low 4 deep, sage, wise 5 heavy 7 abysmal, intense 8 abstruse, unbroken 9 recondite, sagacious 10 acroamatic, exhaustive 11 far-reaching 12 unfathomable

profuse: 4 lush 5 frank 6 galore, hearty, lavish 7 copious, liberal 8 abundant, generous, prodigal, wasteful 9 bountiful, exuberant, luxuriant, plentiful 10 munificent 11 extravagant, overflowing

profusion: 6 galore 8 opulence 9 affluence 11 prodigality

prog: 4 food 5 prick, prowl, tramp 6 forage 7 vagrant 8 supplies 9 provender

progenitor: 4 sire 6 parent 8 ancestor 10 forefather, foreparent, forerunner

progeny: imp, son 4 race, seed 5 breed, brood, brook, child, issue, scion, shoot 6 family, strain 8 children, daughter 9 genealogy, offspring 10 generation 11 descendants

prognostic: 4 omen, sign 5 token

prognosticate: 4 bode 5 augur 6 divine 7 betoken, forbode, forerun, portend, predict, presage 8 forebode, forecast, foreshow, foretell, prophesy 9 foretoken, hariolate

prognosticator: 4 seer 5 augur 6 divine 7 augurer, diviner, prophet 9 predictor 10 soothsayer

program: 4 card, list, show 5 draft, edict 6 agenda, notice 7 agendum, catalog, outline 8 bulletin, playbill, schedule, syllabus 9 broadcast 10 prospectus 12 proclamation

programma: 5 edict 6 decree 7 preface 12 prolegomenon

progress: 4 fare, flow, grow, tour, wend 5 march 6 course, growth, motion 7 advance, circuit, develop, headway, improve, journey, proceed 10 betterment, expedition 11 development, furtherance, improvement

planned: 7 telesia, telesis

progression: 5 stage 8 sequence 10 succession

progressive: 6 active, onward 7 forward, liberal 9 advancing, ascensive 12 enterprising

prohibit: ban, bar, bid 4 stop, veto 5 debar, estop, fence 6 defend, enjoin, forbid, hinder, outlaw 7 forfend, forwarn, prevent 8 disallow, forefend 9 interdict, proscribe 11 countermand

prohibited: 4 tabu 5 taboo 7 illegal, illicit 8 unlawful, verboten(G.).

prohibition: ban, nay 4 veto 7 embargo 8 estoppel 12 interdiction

prohibitionist: dry

project: jet, jut, lap 4 abut, apse, barb, butt, game, idea, plan, send, task 5 filip, shoot 6 beetle, design, device, fillip, scheme 7 extrude, imagine, pattern, problem 8 contrive, proposal, protrude 9 intention 10 enterprise 11 contrivance, proposition, undertaking

projectile: 4 bomb, dart, rock, shot 5 arrow, shell 6 bullet, rocket 7 missile, torpedo 8 shrapnel 9 cartridge

curve: 8 parabola

pert. to: 9 ballistic

projecting: 6 beetle 7 salient

projection: arm, cam, ell, hob, hub, jag, lee, lug, toe 4 apse, barb, croc, fang, lobe 5 bulge, crena, redan, socle, tenon, tooth 6 corbel, crenae(pl.), dormer, lobule,

tappet 7 cornice, empathy 8 abutment, ejection, eminence 9 crenation 10 protrusion 12 protuberance

projector: 8 bioscope 13 cinematograph, kinematograph

projet: 4 plan 5 draft

prolapse: 7 falling

prolate: 9 elongated

proletarian: 4 mean, rude 6 coarse, vulgar 7 laborer, working

prolific: 6 birthy, fecund 7 fertile, teeming 8 fruitful 9 abounding, plentiful 10 generative 11 propagative 12 reproductive

prolix: 5 wordy 7 diffuse, prosaic, tedious, verbose 8 tiresome 9 prolonged, wearisome 10 longwinded, protracted 11 displeasing 13 uninteresting

prolocutor: 6 orator 7 speaker 8 advocate, chairman 9 spokesman 10 mouthpiece

prolong: 5 defer 6 extend 8 continue, lengthen

prolonged: 5 great 6 prolix 7 chronic, delayed, dilated 8 extended 9 continued, postponed, sostenuto, sustained 10 lengthened, protracted

prom: 4 ball 5 dance

promenade: 4 deck, hall, mall, walk 5 prado(Sp.) 6 avenue, marina, parade, pasear(Sp.) 7 alameda, gallery 9 boardwalk, esplanade

Prometheus: *father:* 7 Iapetus

mother: 7 Clymene

prominence: 4 cusp 5 agger 8 eminence, prestige, salience 10 colliculus, promontory 11 distinction

prominent: 5 chief 6 marked, signal 7 capital, eminent, notable, obvious, salient 8 aquiline, manifest 9 egregious 10 celebrated, noticeable, projecting 11 conspicuous, distinctive 13 distinguished

promise: vow 4 band, hest, hote, oath, osse, sure, word 5 agree, grant, hight 6 assure, behest, engage, parole, pledge, plight 7 behight, betroth, fianced 8 affiance, contract, covenant 9 assurance, betrothal, foretoken 10 convenable, engagement, obligation 11 declaration

oral stipulation: 6 cautio 9 cautiones(pl.)

promissory note: I.O.U. 5 check 6 pledge

promontory: hoe 4 bill, cape, head, mull, nase, naze, ness, peak, scaw, skaw, spit 5 mount, point 8 headland 10 projection, prominence

promote: aid 4 help 5 boost, exalt, nurse, raise, speed 6 better, foster, prefer 7 advance, dignify, elevate, forward, further 9 advantage, encourage, patronize 10 aggrandize

promoter: 5 agent 7 abetter, abettor, booster, hustler 8 broacher, lobbyist

promotion: 6 brevet 7 advance 10 graduation, preferment 11 advancement, furtherance

prompt: apt, cue 4 move, yare(Sc.) 5 alert, quick, ready, yeder 6 active, assist, excite, nimble, remind 7 animate, forward 8 punctual 11 expeditious

prompter: aid 4 cuer 7 readier

promptly: 4 soon, tite(Sc.) 8 directly

promptness: 8 alacrity, dispatch

promulgate: 7 declare, publish 8 announce, proclaim 9 advertise

prone: apt 4 bent, flat 5 buxom 6 agroof, agrufe, agruif, supine 7 passive 8 addicted, disposed, inclined, pronated 9 declivous, groveling, prostrate, recumbent 10 decubitous

prong: nib, peg 4 fang, fork, horn, tine 5 point, tooth 6 branch

prongbuck: 9 pronghorn, springbok

prong key: 7 spanner

pronghorn: 4 deer 6 cabree, cabret, cabrie, cabrit 8 berrendo

pronoun: he, it, me, my, we, ye; any, her, him, his, its, one, our, she, thy, you 4 mine, ours, that, thee, them, they, this, thou, your 5 their, these, thine, those 6 itself, myself 7 herself, himself, oneself, ourself 8 yourself 9 ourselves 10 themselves, yourselves

interrogative: who 4 whom 5 whose

substantive: who 7 whoever 9 whosoever

pronounce: 4 pass 5 speak, utter 6 affirm 7 behight, declare, deliver, enounce 8 announce 9 enunciate 10 articulate

pronounced: 6 marked 7 decided, howling 12 unmistakable

pronouncement: 5 dicta(pl.) 6 dictum 9 manifesto, statement 11 declaration 12 announcement

pronto: 5 quick 7 quickly 8 promptly 11 immediately

pronunciation: 4 burr, lisp, slur 5 drawl, twang

correct: 8 orthoepy 9 phonology

incorrect: 7 cacoepy 8 psellism 9 psellisum

pronunciation mark: 5 tilde 8 dieresis 9 diacritic

proof: 4 test 5 trial 6 result 7 approof, probate, exhibit, outcome 8 argument, evidence 9 testimony 10 indication 11 approbation 12 confirmation, impenetrable, verification 13 certification, demonstration

proofreader mark: lc, tr; cap 4 dele, stet 5 caret, space

prop: leg, nog 4 stay 5 appui, brace, shore, sprag, staff, stell(Sc.); stilt 6 scotch, shorer 7 fulcrum, support, sustain 8 buttress 10 strengthen

propaganda: 4 plan 5 ideas 6 scheme, system 8 doctrine 12 brainwashing

propagation: 12 continuation

propagate: 5 breed 7 diffuse 8 engender,

generate, increase, multiply 9 circulate 11 disseminate

propel: gun, row 4 flip, move, pole, push, send, urge 5 drive, flick, force, impel, shove 7 project

propeller: fan, fin, oar 4 vane 5 screw 6 driver, paddle

arm: 4 vane

propensity: yen 4 bent, bias 6 liking 7 aptness, avidity 8 appetite, tendency 9 affection, proneness 10 proclivity, propension 11 disposition, inclination 12 predilection

proper: due, fit 4 fair, fine, good, meet, prim 5 right, stiff 6 behove, chaste, comely, decent, honest, modest, sedate, seemly, strict 7 behoove, correct, fitting, seeming 8 accurate, decorous, formular, suitable 9 advisable, allowable, befitting, beseeming, excellent 10 commodious, convenient, scrupulous 11 appropriate, respectable

properly: 6 featly, gladly 7 gradely

property: lot, res 4 acre, alod, aver, bona, dhan(Ind.), gear 5 addle, allod, asset, aught, glebe, goods, manor 6 domain, estate, havier, realty, wealth 7 acquest, alodium, chattel, haviour, holding 8 allodium 9 acensuada, attribute, homestead 11 appropriate, possessions 14 characteristic

act to regain: 8 replevin

bride's gift to husband: dos 5 dowry

charge against: 4 lien

conveyor of: 7 alienor, grantor

deceased wife's gift to husband: 8 courtesy

destruction of: 8 sabotage

found on the thief: 6 mainor

personal: 7 chattel

receiver: 7 alienee

settle: 6 entail

settlement: dos

stolen: 4 loot, pelf 5 booty, lucre, spoil

suit for: 6 trover

transferring party: 7 alienor

property right: 4 lien 8 easement

prophecy: 5 weird 6 oracle 8 bodement 9 utterance 10 prediction 11 declaration, foretelling 12 vaticination

pert. to: 9 vaticinal

prophesy: 4 dope, osse, spae 5 aread, areed, augur 6 divine 7 predict, presage 8 ariolate, forecast, foreshow, foretell 10 vaticinate 11 preindicate 13 prognosticate

prophet: 4 Amos, John, seer 5 augur, Elias, fatal, Hosea, Syrus 6 divine, Elijah, Elisha, leader, mantis, oracle 7 augurer, diviner, Malachi, teacher 8 Mohammed, Muhammed, presager 9 John Smith 10 soothsayer 11 vaticinator

prophetess: 5 Sibyl 7 Pythian, seeress 9 Cassandra

prophetic: 5 vatic 6 mantic 7 fateful, fatidic, vatical **8** foretell, oracular **9** prescient **10** divinatory, predictive, presageful, signifying **11** fatiloquent, foretelling, nostradamic **12** vaticinatory **14** interpretative

propine: **5** offer **6** pledge **7** present, propose

propinquity: **7** kinship **8** affinity, nearness, vicinity **9** proximity **12** neighborhood, relationship **13** appropinquity, neighbourhood

propitiate: **5** atone **6** pacify **7** appease, expiate, satisfy **9** reconcile **10** conciliate

propitious: **4** rosy **5** happy, lucky **6** benign **8** benedict **9** benignant, favorable, opportune, promising **10** auspicious, benevolent, favourable, prosperous **12** advantageous

proponent: **6** backer **8** advocate

proportion: **4** part, rate **5** quota, ratio, share **7** analogy, portion, prorate **8** relation **9** dimension

proportionate: **5** equal **7** ratable **8** adequate **10** answerable, equivalent **11** symmetrical **12** commensurate, proportional

proportionately: **6** fairly **7** prorata **10** adequately

proposal: bid **4** plan **5** offer **6** design, feeler, motion, scheme **7** project **8** overture **10** nomination, suggestion **11** proposition

propose: **4** give, moot, move **5** state **6** allege, design **8** propound **11** contemplate

proposition: **5** axiom, offer, point **6** affair, porism **7** premise, project, theorem **8** offering, overture, proposal, question **9** corollary, postulate, situation, statement **11** affirmation, undertaking

antecedent: **6** premise **7** premiss

preliminary: **5** lemma **7** lemmata(pl.)

propound: **4** pose **5** posit, state **7** propose

proprietor: **5** owner **6** master, tanist **7** lairdie

propriety: See also **proper 4** code, rule **7** customs, manners, quality **8** behavior, elegance, standard **9** attribute, etiquette **13** possessorship

propugnator: **8** defender **10** vindicator

propulsion: jet **5** drift **8** ejection **9** expulsion

prorate: **5** allot **6** assess, divide **9** apportion **10** distribute, proportion

prorogue: **5** defer **6** extend **7** adjourn, prolong **8** postpone, protract

prosaic: **4** drab, dull, flat **5** prosy **6** prolix, stolid, stupid **7** humdrum, insipid, tedious **8** tiresome, unpoetic **10** unexciting **11** commonplace **12** matter-of-fact **13** unimaginative, uninteresting

proscenium: **5** stage

front area: **5** apron

proscribe: ban **4** tabu **5** exile, taboo **6** banish, forbid, outlaw **8** prohibit **9** interdict, ostracize

prose form: **5** novel, story, tract **7** fiction, romance **8** treatise **10** nonfiction

prosecute: sue **4** urge **5** carry, chase, hound **6** accuse, charge, follow, indict, pursue **7** enforce **8** continue

prosecutor: D.A. **7** accuser, relator

proselyte: **5** alien **7** convert **8** neophyte, newcomer

proseuche: **7** oratory **9** synagogue

prosit: **5** toast **10** salutation

prosody: **5** meter

prospect: **4** hope, mine, view **5** buyer, scene, vista **6** aspect **7** outlook **8** customer, exposure **9** applicant, candidate, foretaste **10** contestant

prospective: **5** lofty **6** future, likely **7** eminent **8** expected, prospect **9** provident **11** anticipated, perspective

prospector: **9** sourdough

prosper: dow, hie, wax **4** fare **5** cheve, edify, frame, speed **6** thrive **7** blossom **8** flourish

prosperity: up; hap, ups **4** boom, weal **5** ikbal **6** thrift, wealth **7** fortune, success, welfare **9** happiness, well-being

god: **4** Frey

Prospero:

daughter: **7** Miranda

servant: **5** Ariel

prosperous: up **4** bein, bien, boon **5** flush, happy, lucky, palmy, sonsy **6** sonsie **7** well-off **8** thriving **9** favorable, fortunate **10** auspicious, propitious, successful **11** flourishing

prostitute: bat, cat **4** aunt, drab, hack, trug **5** broad, venal, whore **6** callet, debase, harlot **7** baggage, brothel, corrupt, Cyprian, hackney **8** berdache, commoner, customer, infamous, occupant **9** courtesan, courtezan **10** crosha-bell, hobbyhorse, licentious **12** streetwalker **13** commercialize

reformed: **8** Magdalen

prostitution house of: **6** bordel **7** brothel **8** bordello

prostrate: bow **4** fell, flat **5** prone **6** fallen, supine **7** exhaust **8** dejected, helpless, overcome **9** collapsed, flattened, overthrow, recumbent **10** subjugated, submissive

prosy: dry **4** dull **6** jejune **7** humdrum, prosaic, tedious **11** commonplace, displeasing **13** unimaginative

protagonist: foe **4** hero **5** actor, agent, enemy **6** leader **7** heroine **8** advocate, champion, defender **9** contender, principal, spokesman

protasis: **11** conditional, proposition **12** introduction

protean: **10** changeable

protect: arm **4** bind, hill, save, wear **5** bield, bless, guard, hedge, shade **6** assert, defend, insure, patent, police, screen, shield **7** bulwark, cherish, forfend, shelter, tuition **8** champion, conserve, forefend, preserve **9** copyright

protecting: **7** tutelar **8** tutelary

protection: bib, lee **4** egis, fort, moat, pass **5** aegis, apron, armor, frith, guard, shell, smock **6** amulet, armour, patent, safety **7** auspice, defence, defense, parapet, shelter, tuition, umbrage **8** passport, security **12** preservation

protector: **5** guard **6** fautor, patron, shield **8** defender, guardian **9** custodian

protectorate: **11** condominium

protege: **4** ward

proteid: **6** alexin **7** albumin **9** legumelin

Proteida family: olm **7** proteus **8** necturus **11** salamanders, typhlomolge

protein: **6** avidin, casein, fibrin **7** albumin, edestin, mucedin **8** aleurone, creatine, prolamin

group: **8** globulin

poison: **5** abrin, ricin **6** ricine

protest: **4** aver, beef, deny, kick **5** demur **6** affirm, assert, assure, holler, object, plaint **7** contest, declare, dissent, testify **8** complain **9** complaint, objection, stipulate **10** asseverate **11** expostulate, remonstrate

Protestant: **9** dissenter

sect: **9** orangeist

Proteus: olm **6** amoeba

Proteus:

friend: **9** Valentine

love: **6** Silvia

wife: **5** Julia

protograph: **7** writing **9** holograph **12** illustration

protoplasm: **5** ameba, spore **6** amoeba **7** sarcade

outer layer: **9** ectoplasm

substance: gel

protoplasmic: **10** archetypal, primordial

prototype: **5** model **6** emblem **7** pattern **8** antetype, original **9** archetype

protozoan:

genus of: **7** arcella

order: **6** lobosa

parasitic: **5** ameba **6** amoeba **8** amoebida

protract: **4** spin **5** defer, delay **6** dilate, extend **7** detract, prolong **8** continue, elongate, lengthen, protrude

protrude: jut **5** blear, bulge **7** extrude, project **9** interfere

protruded: **6** extant

protuberance: nub, wen **4** boll, boss, bulb, bump, heel, hump, knob, knot, lobe, lump, node, snag, umbo **5** bulge, bunch, caput, hunch, torus **8** eminence, swelling **9** gibbosity **10** projection, prominence, protrusion

protuberant: **6** convex, extant **7** bottled, gibbous **8** blubbery

proud (See also **pride**): **4** ikey **5** brant,

chuff **7** haughty, stately, valiant **8** imposing **9** cockhorse **10** impressive **11** magisterial, overbearing **12** presumptuous, supercilious

prove: try **4** aver, fand, pree, test **5** argue, essay, nurse, prive(Sc.) **6** argify, argufy, evince, verify **7** confirm, justify, probate **8** identify, manifest **9** ascertain, establish **11** corroborate, demonstrate

provenance: **6** origin, source **10** derivation **11** provenience

provender: hay **4** corn, feed, food, oats, prog **5** grain, straw **6** fodder **7** prebend **10** provisions

provenience: **10** provenance

proverb: saw **4** word **5** adage, axiom, maxim, motto **6** ballad, byword, enigma, saying **7** byspell, parable **8** allegory, aphorism, forbysen

proverbial: **11** sententious

provide: **5** cater, equip, stock, store, yield **6** afford, foison, purvey, ration, render, supply **7** chevise, furnish **8** accouter, accoutre **9** stipulate **10** contribute

provided: if; but **5** boden, found **6** sobeit **8** afforded, supplied **9** furnished **13** conditionally

provided that: if, so

providence: **8** function, guidance

provident: **4** wise **6** frugal, saving **7** careful, prudent, thrifty **8** cautious, discreet **9** farseeing **10** economical, farsighted **11** foresighted

providential: **5** lucky **9** fortunate

province: **4** area, nome **5** arena, range, realm, shire, tract **6** colony, domain, eparch, region, sphere **7** country, emirate **8** district, division **9** bailiwick, territory **10** department, palatinate **12** jurisdiction

pert. to: **5** nomic

provincial: **4** rude **5** crude, local **6** narrow, rustic **7** insular, limited **9** parochial **10** uncultured **11** countrified **15** unsophisticated

provision: **4** fare, food **5** board, cater, grist, stock, store **6** clause, supply, wraith **7** proviso **9** condition

seller: **6** sutler

provisional: **4** iffy **7** aeolian **9** provisory, temporary, tentative **10** contingent **11** conditional

provisions: **4** cate, chow, fare, food **5** board, bouge, terms **6** forage, stocks, stores, viands **7** rations **9** provender **10** chevisance

search for: **6** forage

stock of: **6** larder **8** magazine

proviso: **5** salvo **6** clause **7** article, caution **9** condition **11** stipulation

provisory: **11** provisional

provocative: **7** agacant **8** agacante **9** provoking **10** aggressive **11** stimulating

provoke: ire, vex **4** bait, move, spur, stir **5** anger, annoy, cause, eager, evoke, frump, pique, start, tease **6** arouse, excite, harass, incite, invite, invoke, nettle, summon **7** affront, incense, quicken **8** irritate **9** aggravate, challenge, displease, forthcall, stimulate **10** exasperate

provost: **4** head **5** chief **6** jailer, keeper **7** prefect **8** director, official **10** magistrate **13** administrator **14** superintendent

prow: bow **4** beak, nose, stem **5** brave, prore **6** steven **7** gallant, rostrum, valiant **9** honorable **10** courageous

prowess: **5** skill, valor **6** valour **7** bravery, courage **9** ingenuity **10** excellence

prowl: **4** lurk, roam **6** brevit, ramble, wander

proximal: **4** next **7** nearest **9** proximate **12** conterminous

proximate: **4** next **6** direct **8** proximal **9** immediate

proximity: **8** nearness, nighness, vicinage, vicinity **9** adjacence, closeness **10** contiguity **11** propinquity **13** approximation, juxtaposition

proxy: **5** agent, power, vicar **6** agency, deputy **7** proctor **8** function **9** authority **10** procurator, substitute

prudence: **10** management **11** calculation

prudent: **4** sage, wary, wise **5** canny, chary, douce, siker **6** frugal, sicker **7** careful **8** cautious, discreet, sensible **9** advisable, cautelous, provident, sagacious **10** economical, forehanded **11** circumspect, considerate, foresighted **14** forethoughtful

prudish: **4** nice, prim **8** priggish **10** overmodest

prune: cow, cut, lop **4** clip, coll, frog, geld, plum, sned(Sc.), trim **5** dress, fruit, plume, preen, purge, rasee, razee, shave **6** anoint **7** tonsure **8** castrate **9** simpleton

pruning knive: **8** serpette

prurient: **4** lewd **7** itching, longing, lustful **10** lascivious

Prussia:

bay: **4** Kiel **6** Danzig **10** Pomeranian

city: **4** Kiel **5** Essen **6** Aachen, Altena, Berlin, Tilsit **7** Breslau, Hanover, Munster, Stettin **9** Frankfort, Magdeburg **10** Dusseldorf, Konigsberg **14** Charlottenburg

district: **7** Stettin

island: **5** Rugen **6** Usedom, Wollin **7** Frisian

lagoon: **4** haff **7** Frische **8** Kurische **11** Pommerische

lancer: **4** Ulan **5** Uhlan

land-holding aristocracy: **6** Junker

legislature upper house: **10** Herrenhaus

measure: **4** fuss, rute, zoll **5** fuder, meile **6** morgen, oxhoft **8** scheffel

mountain: **4** Harz **7** Sudeten **11** Schneekoppe **13** Riesengebirge

province: **5** Posen **6** Berlin, Saxony **7**

Hanover, Prussia, Silesia **9** Pomerania, Rhineland **10** Westphalia **11** Brandenburg, East-Prussia, Hesse-Nassau, West-Prussia **12** Hohenzollern **17** Schleswig-Holstein

river: Ems **4** Alle, Eder, Elbe, Oder, Saar **5** Memel **6** Niemen, Pregel **7** Vistula **8** Passarge, Weichsel

seaport: **4** Kiel **5** Emden

spa: Ems

university town: **5** Halle

weight: **4** mark **9** quentchen

prussiate: **4** salt **7** cyanide **12** ferricyanide, ferrocyanide

pry: spy **4** gaze, lift, move, nose, peek, peep, peer **5** jemmy, jimmy, lever, mouse, prize, raise, snoop **6** potter **7** crowbar **8** leverage, scrounge **10** scrutinize

prying: **4** nosy **5** nosey **7** curious **11** inquisitive

psalm: ode **4** hymn, poem, song **11** composition

collection: **6** hallel **7** psalter

kind: **4** laud **6** hallel, Venite **7** Cantate, introit **8** Miserere

opening communion: **7** introit

sign: **5** selah

word of punctuation: **5** selah

psalmist: **5** David **6** cantor, writer **8** composer **9** precentor

psalterium: **4** lyra **6** omasum **7** stomach **9** manyplies

psammite: **9** sandstone

pseudo: **4** fake, mock, sham **5** bogus, false **7** feigned **8** spurious **9** pretended, simulated **11** counterfeit

pseudologist: **4** liar

pseudonym: **5** alias **6** anonym **7** anonyme

psittaceous: **10** parrotlike

psyche: **4** mind, soul **6** spirit

psychic: **9** animastic

psychotic: mad **5** crazy **6** insane **10** disordered **12** unreasonable

Ptah's wife: **6** Sekhet

ptarmica: **10** sneezewort

ptarmigan: **4** bird, ripa **6** grouse

pteric: **4** alar **8** winglike

pteroid: **8** fernlike, winglike

ptisan: tea **5** drink **6** tisane **9** decoction

Ptolemy: *astronomy work:* **8** almagest

wife: **12** Philadelphia

ptomaine: **6** poison

pub: bar, inn **5** hotel **6** boozer, tavern

pubble: fat **5** plump

public: inn **4** open **5** overt, state **9** community

discussion: **5** forum

record office: **7** archion **8** archives

service: **7** railway, utility **9** telegraph, telephone **10** waterworks

way: **4** road **5** alley **6** bridge, tunnel **7** highway **8** turnpike **9** boulevard

publican: **6** farmer, keeper **9** catchpole, catchpoll, collector

publication: 4 book 5 paper 6 annals, blazon, digest 7 booklet 8 pamphlet 9 ephemeris 10 periodical 12 notification, proclamation, promulgation
examiner: 6 censor
make-up: 6 format
permit: 7 release
preliminary: 9 prodromus
prepare for: 4 edit
regular: 10 periodical
publicist: 5 agent, solon 6 writer 10 journalist
publicity: air 7 buildup 9 promotion 11 advertising, information
publish: air 4 blow, edit, vent 5 issue, print 6 blazon, defame, delate, expose 7 diffuse, divulge, release 8 announce, evulgate, forspeak, proclaim, promulge 9 advertise, forespeak 10 promulgate 11 disseminate
without authority: 6 pirate 10 plagiarize
publisher: 6 editor, issuer 7 printer 8 broacher 10 journalist
copy: 5 blurb 8 colophon 12 announcement
Puccini: *heroine:* 4 Mimi
opera: 7 La Tosca
puck: elf 4 disk 5 fairy 6 roller, sprite, strike 9 hobgoblin 10 goatsucker
pucker: 4 fold 5 bulge, purse, reeve, smock 6 cockle, cotter, lucken 7 wrinkle 8 contract
puckered: 7 bullate
puckfist: 8 braggart, puffball
puckish: 8 annoying, pucklike 10 mysterious 11 mischievous
pud: paw 4 hand 7 pudding 8 forefoot
pudding: 4 duff, mush 6 burgoo, hackin, haggis(Sc.), panada 7 burgout, custard, dessert, hacking, sausage, tapioca 8 roly-poly 9 stir-about
puddle: dub 4 plud, pond, pool 5 plash, swamp 6 charco, flodge 7 plashet 8 quagmire
puddock: 7 paddock
pudency: 7 modesty 11 bashfulness, prudishness 13 embarrassment 14 shamefacedness
pudgy: fat 5 dumpy, plump, squat 7 bulging 8 roly-poly
pueblo: 4 town 7 village
Pueblo: 4 Hopi
assembly hall: 6 estufa
ceremonial chamber: 4 kiva
village: 4 taos
puerile: 4 weak 5 silly, young 7 babyish, foolish, trivial 8 childish, immature, juvenile, unworthy, youthful 10 unthinking
Puerto Principe: 8 Camaguey
Puerto Rico: *bark:* 4 mabi
beverage: 4 mabi
bird: 4 rola 7 yeguita
city: 5 Ponce 6 Dorado 7 Arecibo, San Juan(c.) 8 Mayaguez

conqueror of: 5 Miles
fish: 4 sama, sisi
island: 4 Mona
measure: 6 cuerda 10 caballeria
person of mixed blood: 6 gibaro
tree: 4 mora 5 yagua, yaray 8 guayroto 9 guaraguao
puff: 4 blow, chug, flam(Sc.), flan, fuff, gust, pant, pegh(Sc.), pouf, waff, waft 5 fluff, whiff
puff up: 5 bloat, swell 6 tumefy 7 distend, inflate
puffball: 4 fist, fuzz 8 fuzzball
puffbird: 6 barbet 8 barbacou
genus: 6 monasa
puffed up: 5 large 6 astrut 7 souffle 8 bouffant, imposing, inflated 9 bombastic, bouffante 11 pretentious
puffer: 6 blower 8 blowfish
puffy: 4 soft 5 pursy 6 flabby
pug: dog, elf 4 clay, plug, poke, puck 5 boxer, chaff, churn, dwarf, knead, track 6 harlot, refuse, sprite, thrust 7 trample 8 mistress, pugilist 9 footprint, hobgoblin
pug-nosed: 5 camus
puggy: 6 monkey(Sc.) 10 sweetheart
pugilist: lug 5 boxer 7 battler, bruiser, fighter
assistant: 6 second 7 handler
pugilistic: 6 fistic
pugnacious: 7 warlike 8 fighting 9 bellicose, combative 10 aggressive 11 belligerent, contentious, quarrelsome
puisne: 4 puny 5 judge, later, petty 6 feeble, junior 10 subsequent 11 subordinate 13 insignificant
puissance: 4 army, host 5 force, might, power, vigor 8 potency 8 strength 12 forcefulness
puke: 4 wool 5 vomit
pukka, pucka: 4 good, real 7 genuine 8 complete 9 authentic 11 substantial 13 thoroughgoing
pulchritude: 5 grace 6 beauty 10 comeliness, excellence, loveliness
pule: cry 4 peep 5 cheep, whine 6 repine, snivel 7 whimper 8 complain
puling: 4 puly 6 sickly 7 babyish 8 childish, delicate
pull: lug, tew, tit, tow, tug, wap 4 claw, drag, draw, duct, hale, haul, jerk, yank, yerk 5 bouse(naut.), heave(naut.), hitch, pluck, tweak 6 arrest, twitch 7 attract, revulse, stretch 9 influence
apart: rip 4 rend, tear 8 separate
away: 5 wrest 6 remove 8 withdraw
down: 4 raze 7 destroy 8 demolish
off: pug 6 avulse, manage 7 succeed
one's freight: 5 leave 6 depart
one's leg: 4 hoax 7 deceive 8 hoodwink
out: 7 extract 9 extirpate 10 deracinate
up: 5 elate, trice
pullet: hen 4 fowl 5 frier 6 earock(Sc.) 7 pollard 8 poullard

pulley: 4 ring 5 fusee, fuzee, wheel 6 sheave

part: 4 arse, drum 6 rigger

Pullman: car 5 coach 7 sleeper

pullulate: bud 4 teem 5 swarm 9 germinate

pulp: pap 4 marc, mash, mass, pith 5 chyme, magma 6 pomace 7 bagasse

machine: 9 macerater

pulpit: 4 ambo, bema, desk 5 chair, stage 7 lectern, rostrum 8 platform, scaffold

pulpy: 6 fleshy

pulsate: 4 beat, move, pant 5 throb 6 quiver, strike, thrill 7 vibrate

pulsation: 5 ictus

pulsatory: 8 rhythmic, 9 pulsatile, pulsative, systaltic, throbbing

pulse: mug 7 battuta 8 sphygmus

pulverize: 4 bray, meal, mull 5 crush, grind 6 bruise 7 atomize 8 demolish, levigate 9 comminute, triturate 12 contriturate

pulverized: 4 fine

pulverizer: 13 disintegrator

pulverulent: 5 dusty 7 crumbly, powdery 8 powdered

puly: 6 puling

puma: cat 6 cougar 7 panther 9 carnivore

pumice: 8 abrasive

pummel: fib 4 beat, maul 5 thump 6 batter, hammer

pump: gin, ram 4 jack 6 racker 7 stirrup, syringe 10 pulsometer

handle: 5 sweep, swipe

pumpernickel: 5 bread

pumpkin: 4 pepo 6 citrul, squash

head: 4 dolt 7 Puritan 9 blockhead

pumpkinseed: 7 sunfish 8 bluegill 10 butterfish

pun: mot 4 beat, joke 5 knock, pound 7 quibble 8 paragram 9 calembour, conundrum 11 paronomasia

punch: ade, jab 4 glog, poke, prod 5 douse, dowse, drink, negus, paste 6 pierce, strike 7 mattoir 8 beverage, puncture 9 perforate

Punch: 5 clown 7 buffoon, journal 8 magazine 10 periodical

first editor of: 5 Lemon

puncheon: die 4 cask, post, stud, tool 5 punch, stamp 6 timber

puncher: 6 cowboy 7 cowpoke 10 cowpuncher, perforator

Punchinello: 5 clown 7 buffoon

punctilious: 4 nice 5 exact 6 formal, proper 7 careful, correct, precise 8 exacting 10 ceremonial, scrupulous 11 ceremonious 13 conscientious

punctual: 6 prompt

punctuate: 4 mark 9 emphasize 11 distinguish

punctuation mark: dot 4 dash 5 colon, comma, quote 6 hyphen, period 8 ellipsis 9 semicolon 10 apostrophe 11 parenthesis

puncture: 4 bite, hole, stab, vent 5 prick, wound 6 pierce 9 perforate 11 perforation

pundit: 4 sage 5 swami 6 nestor 7 Brahman, scholar, teacher

pung: 4 sled 6 sleigh

pungent: hot 4 fell, keen, racy, tart 5 acrid, acute, cress, minty, salty, sharp, smart, spicy, tangy 6 biting, bitter, pepper 7 caustic, peppery, piquant 8 aromatic, piercing, poignant, stinging 10 expressive, irritating 11 acrimonious, stimulating

pungi: bin 4 pipe 5 flute

pungled: 8 shrunken 9 shriveled

Punic: 7 dialect 9 faithless 11 treacherous 12 Carthaginian

punish: 4 beat, fine, whip 5 abuse, mulct, scold, slate, smite, spank, strap, wreak 6 amerce, strike 7 chasten, correct, corrige, revenge, scourge 8 chastise, penalize 9 castigate 10 discipline 13 excommunicate

punishing: 8 grueling 9 gruelling

punishment: 4 loss, pain 5 peine(law), wrack 6 desert, dirdum, ferule 9 suffering 13 animadversion

device: rod 6 stocks

freedom from: 8 impunity

spare: 6 acquit 7 absolve 9 exculpate, exonerate

punitive: 5 penal 8 punitory 9 punishing 10 vindictive

Punjab: See India.

punk: bad 4 fuel, poor 5 conch, tramp 6 amadou, tinder 8 beginner, elephant, inferior, strumpet 9 beginning, miserable, touchwood, worthless 10 prostitute

punkah: fan

punt: 4 boat, kick 6 gamble

punter: 5 poler 6 bettor 7 scalper

puny: 4 weak 5 dawny, frail, petty, small 6 feeble, puisne, sickly, slight 8 droghlin, inferior 9 unskilled 13 inexperienced, insignificant

pupa: 9 chrysalis

case: 5 theca

pupil: 4 tyro 5 cadet, eleve(F.), minor, plebe, youth 6 junior, senior 7 ecolier(F.), learner, scholar, student 8 disciple, neophyte, freshman 9 sophomore

puppet: 4 baby, doll, tool 5 image 8 drollery 9 neuropast 10 marionette

show: 6 wajang, wayang

puppy: fop 5 whelp

pur: 4 purr

purblind: 5 blind 6 bisson, obtuse

purchasable: 5 venal 7 corrupt, salable 9 available 10 marketable

purchase: buy 5 acate, cheap, yield 6 emptio, income, obtain, return 7 acquire,

bargain, emption **11** acquisition
back: **6** redeem, regain
purchaser: **5** buyer **6** emptor, patron, vendee **8** co-emptor, customer **9** acquereur **13** adjudicataire
purdah: **6** screen **7** curtain **9** seclusion
pure: **4** fine, good, mear, meer, mere, neat, nice, pute, true **5** clean, clear, fresh, moral, sheer, utter **6** candid, chaste, simple, vestal, virgin **7** cleanly, genuine, perfect, refined, sincere, sinless, unmixed **8** absolute, complete, dovelike, filtered, innocent, virtuous, zaccheus(Heb.) **9** authentic, blameless, downright, elemental, faultless, guiltless, stainless, unalloyed, undefiled, unsullied **10** immaculate **11** crystalline, unblemished, uncorrupted, unqualified **13** unadulterated **15** unsophisticated
puree: **4** mush, soup **8** porridge
purely: **6** solely, wholly
purfle: hem **6** border **7** outline **8** decorate, ornament, trimming
purgative: **5** jalap **6** physic **8** evacuant **9** cathartic **10** alviducous
purgatory: **5** limbo
purge: rid **5** clear **6** physic, purify, remove, seethe **7** cleanse, deterge **8** absterge **9** exculpate, expurgate
purification: **9** catharsis
purify: **5** clean, clear, purge **6** bleach, filter, refine **7** baptize, clarify, cleanse, distill, epurate **8** depurate, lustrate, renovate **9** elutriate
Puritan: **9** Roundhead
puritanic: **6** strict **7** denying **8** rigorous
purl: rib **4** eddy, knit **5** frill, swirl **6** murmur, purfle, stitch
purlieu: **5** haunt **7** environ **12** neighborhood
purloin: **4** crib **5** filch, steal, swipe **6** finger, pilfer, pirate **7** cabbage **8** abstract **10** plagiarize
purple: **4** plum **5** grape, lilac, mauve, royal **6** blatta, emblem, maroon, ornate, tyrian, violet **7** cassius **8** amaranth, imperial, lavender **9** cathedral, elaborate
dye: **7** cassius
land of: **4** Tyre
seller of: **5** Lydia
purple coneflower: **9** echinacea
purple copper ore: **7** bornite
purple ragwort: **4** herb **6** jacoby
purport: **4** feck, gist, mean **5** drift, sense, tenor **6** effect, import, intent, object **7** bearing, meaning **9** intention, substance
purpose: aim, end, use **4** bent, goal, main, mean, plan, sake **5** avail **6** design, intend, intent, motive **7** mission **9** intention, objective, predesign **10** cogitation, conception, employment, resolution **13** determination

alleged: **7** pretext
lackin: **9** driftless
purposive: **5** telic **12** teleological
purpure: **6** purple
purr: hum **5** noise, sound **6** murmur
purse: bag, cly **4** bung, poke **5** bulse, burse, money, pouch **6** pucker, wallet **7** almoner, handbag **8** coco-wort, finances, treasury **9** exchequer **10** pocketbook **12** portemonnaie
purse crab: **5** ayuyu
purser: **6** bursar **7** boucher, cashier **9** paymaster, treasurer
pursue: run **4** hunt, seek **5** chase, chevy, chivy, hound, stalk **6** chivey, chivvy, follow, gallop **7** proceed **8** continue **9** prosecute
pursuer: **6** hunter **8** huntress
pursuit: **5** scent **7** calling **10** occupation
means: **7** dragnet
pursy: fat **5** obese, puffy **7** swollen, wealthy **9** asthmatic
purulent: **4** foul **5** pussy
purvey: tax **5** cater **6** supply **7** furnish, procure, provide **10** assessment
purveyor: **6** seller, sutler **7** caterer **9** victualer
push: go; pop, por **4** birr, bore, bunt, butt, ding, dush, pelt, ping, pole, porr, poss, prod, urge **5** bevel(Sc.), boost, crowd, drive, elbow, force, heave, hunch, impel, nudge, press, shove **6** clique, effort, energy, expand, extend, hustle, jostle, potter, propel, thrust **7** advance, promote **10** enterprise **14** aggressiveness
down: **7** detrude
in: **5** stove
pushy: **5** bossy **7** forward **9** officious
pusillanimous: **4** tame **5** timid **6** afraid **8** cowardly **10** irresolute **12** fainthearted
puss: cat **4** face, girl, hare **5** mouth, woman **8** baudrons(Sc.)
pustule: **4** blob, burl **5** achor, blain **6** blotch, pimple **7** blister **8** eruption, swelling
put (see also **place**): lay, set **4** cast, push, urge **5** clink, drive, fixed, force, impel, place, state, throw **6** appose, attach, bestow, incite, thrust **7** deposit, express **9** attribute, constrain
away: **4** kill **5** store **6** murder **7** consume
back: **6** demote **7** replace, restore
before: **7** apposed, present
by: **4** save **5** store **6** reject
down: **6** humble, record **7** degrade, depress **8** suppress **9** deposited
forth: **4** show **5** exert, offer **7** extrude, propose, publish **9** circulate
forward: **7** prepose, propone
in: **4** ante **5** defer, delay, elude **6** baffle, divert, insert **7** discard, enclose **8** postpone **9** frustrate
off: fob **4** doff, haft **5** defer, delay, evade

table **6** divert, shelve **7** discard **8** deferred, postpone
on: act, don **5** apply, endue, indue **7** assumed, feigned, pretend **10** exaggerate
out: irk, vex **4** oust **5** anger, annoy, eject, evict, exile, expel **6** banish, deport, retire **7** publish **8** displace, distress **9** ostracize **10** discompose, disconcert, expatriate, extinguish **14** discountenance
over: **4** bilk, hoax **5** cheat, trick **7** deceive
together: add **5** piece, unite **6** gather, muster **7** collect **8** assemble **9** construct **10** congregate
up: can **4** post **5** build, erect
up with: **4** bear, take **5** brook, stand **6** endure **7** stomach **8** tolerate
putrefy: rot **5** decay **6** fester **7** corrupt **9** decompose **12** disintegrate
putrid: **4** foul **7** friable, noisome, vicious **8** depraved **10** putrescent **11** displeasing **12** disagreeable
puttee: **4** spat **6** gaiter **7** legging
putty: **6** cement
puxy: **6** swampy **8** quagmire
puzzle: cap, get **5** glaik, griph, pinon, poser, rebus, stick **6** baffle, enigma, fickle, riddle **7** anagram, charade, confuse, foitter, griphus, mystery, mystify, nonplus, paradox, perplex **8** acrostic, bewilder, distract, entangle, intrigue **9** conundrum **10** difficulty, disconcert, palindrome
puzzled: **4** asea
puzzling: **9** equivocal
pygarg: **5** addax **6** osprey
Pygmalion:
brother: **4** Dido
sister's husband: **8** Sichaeus
statue: **7** Galatea

victim of: **8** Sichaeus
pygmy, pigmy: elf **4** pixy, runt **5** atomy, dwarf, gnome, minim, short **8** dwarfish **9** dandiprat **10** chimpanzee
pygmy musk deer: **10** chevrotain
pygostyle: **4** bone **5** vomer
pyknic: **5** solid, squat **6** stocky, sturdy **8** muscular **9** endomorph, squatness **11** endomorphic
pylon: **4** post **5** tower **6** marker **7** gateway **8** monument
pyramid:
inhabitant: **5** Khufu **6** Cheops
site: **4** Giza **7** Cholula
pyramidal: **4** huge **8** enormous, imposing
pyre: **4** bale, bier **6** suttee
Pyrenees: **7** bandit: **8** Miquelet
chamois: **5** izard
mountain peak: **5** Aneto
republic: **7** Andorra
resort: Pau
pyriform: **10** pear-shaped
pyromaniac: **7** firebug **8** arsonist
pyrotechnics: **9** fireworks
pyrotechnical device: **8** pinwheel
pyroxene: **6** augite **8** diopside **11** schefferite **12** hedenbergite
Pythagoras:
birthplace: **5** Samos
friend: **5** Damon
python: **5** snake **7** serpent
slayer: **6** Apollo
pythonic: **4** huge **8** inspired, oracular **9** monstrous
pyx, pix: box **4** case, test, vase **5** assay, capsa, carry, chest **6** casket, coffer, vessel **8** binnacle, ciborium, preserve **10** tabernacle

Q

Q: cue **5** queue

q.e.d.: 21 quod erat demonstrandum

qua *see also* **guaw:** as **4** bird **5** heron **7** quabird

quabird: 5 heron

quack: cry **5** couch, faker, fraud **6** crocus **8** impostor **9** charlatan, pretender **10** mountebank

quad: 4 quod **5** block **6** campus, person **7** sibling, quadrat **10** quadrangle

quadra: 6 fillet, listel, plinth

quadragesimal: 5 forty **6** Lenten

quadrangle: 5 court **8** tetragon

quadrant: 4 gill **6** fourth **8** farthing **9** antimeter **10** instrument

quadrate: 4 suit **5** agree, ideal **6** square **7** perfect, squared **8** balanced **9** rectangle **10** correspond **13** correspondent

quadriga: 4 cart **6** horses **7** chariot

quadrumane: ape **6** monkey **7** gorilla **10** chimpanzee

quadruped: 6 mammal **10** fourlegged

quaere: 5 query **7** inquiry **8** question

quaff: sip **5** draft, drink **6** waught

quag: 5 quake **6** quiver **8** quagmire

quaggy: 4 miry, soft **5** boggy **6** flabby, spongy **7** queachy **8** yielding

quagmire: bog, gog, hag **5** marsh, swamp **6** morass

quahog: 4 clam

quail: cow **4** bird **5** colin, cower, quake, shake **6** blench, cringe, curdle, flinch, recoil, shrink, tremor, turnix **7** massena, tremble **8** bobwhite **9** coagulate, courtesan, partridge

flock of: **4** bevy **5** covey

young: **7** cheeper **8** squealer

quail snipe: 9 dowitcher

quaint: odd **4** nice **6** crafty **7** antique, curious, strange, unusual **8** fanciful, graceful, peculiar, singular **9** whimsical

quake: 4 quag, rese **5** shake, waver **6** quiver, shiver, tremor **7** shudder, tremble, vibrate **10** earthquake

Quaker: Fox **4** Penn **6** Friend **9** broadbrim

Quaker City: 12 Philadelphia

Quaker gray: 5 acier

Quaker-ladies: 5 bluet **11** meadowsweet

Quaker State: 12 Pennsylvania

Quaker's founder: 9 George Fox

quaking: 5 aspen, quaky **6** trepid **9** trepidity

qualification: 7 ability **8** aptitude **9** condition, endowment, knowledge, requisite

10 adaptation, capability, competence, experience **11** acquirement, designation, restriction **12** capacitation, modification

qualified: 8 eligible

qualify: fit **5** abate, adapt, equip, limit **6** enable, modify, soften, temper **7** assuage, entitle, prepare **8** diminish, mitigate, moderate, restrain, restrict **10** habilitate

quality: 4 cost, kind, rank, rate, sort, thew, tone **5** class, grade, power, quale, taste, trait **6** nature, status, strain, virtue **7** caliber, calibre, element **8** capacity, nobility, property **9** attribute, character **10** excellence **11** superiority **14** accomplishment, characteristic

qualm: 4 drow, pall **5** spasm **6** attack, nausea, regret, twinge **7** scruple **8** sickness **9** faintness, misgiving **11** compunction **16** faintheartedness

quamash: 5 camas **6** camass, cammas **7** prairie

quandary: fix **4** pass **6** pickle **7** dilemma, nonplus **11** predicament **12** bewilderment

quant: 4 pole

quantity (See also **amount**): ace, any, bit, jag, jot, lot, sea, sum **4** atom, bulk, dash, dose, dram, drop, feck, iota, lick, lots, mass, mort, much, raff, raft, slew, unit **5** batch, bunch, grist, hoard, scads, stack, store **6** amount, capful, degree, extent, hirsel, morsel, number, weight **7** average, handful, modicum, portion, slather **8** dribblet **9** allowance **10** pennyworth

fixed: **8** constant

full: **10** complement

irrational: **4** surd

per unit: **4** rate

prescribed: **4** dose **6** dosage

without direction: **6** scalar

quantum: 4 unit **6** amount **7** portion **8** quantity

quarantine: ban **7** exclude, isolate **8** restrain **9** interdict

quaranty: 5 court

quarentene: 4 rood **7** furlong

quark: caw **5** croak, quawk

quarl, quarle: 4 tile **5** brick

quarrel: row **4** feud, fuss, spat, tiff **5** brawl, broil, cavil, flite, flyte, scene, scrap **6** affray, barney, bicker, breach, breeze, cangle, chisel, debate, fracas, fratch, hassle, jangle, quarry, strife **7** contend, dispute, faction, rhubarb, wrangle **8** argument, disagree, squabble **9** upscuddle **10** contention **11** altercation, controversy **13** collie-shangie **16** misunderstanding

quarrelsome: **7** fratchy, hostile **8** brawling, choleric, frampoid, petulant **9** bellicose, irascible, irritable, litigious **10** discordant, pugnacious **11** belligerent, contentious **12** disputatious **13** argumentative

quarry: **4** delf, game, prey **5** chase, delft **6** latomy, object, ravine **7** latomia, quarrel

quart: **6** fourth **7** measure
four: **6** gallon
metric: **5** liter, litre
one-eighth: **4** gill
two: **6** flagon

quartan: **5** fever **7** malaria

quarter: **4** coin, span **5** allot, grith, house, lodge, tract **6** assign, bestow, canton, charge, fourth, harbor, supply **7** bearing, furnish, harbour, shelter **8** clemency, contrada, contrade(pl.), district, division **9** apportion, dismember **11** forbearance

quarters: **4** camp, room **7** billets, lodging, shelter **8** barracks **9** dormitory
nautical: **6** fo'c'sle **7** gunroom **8** steerage, wardroom **10** forecastle
winter: **10** hibernacle
women's: **5** harem

quarter note: **8** crotchet

quartz: **4** onyx, sand, sard **5** agate, flint, prase, silex, topaz **6** jasper, silica **7** citrine, crystal, rubasse, sinople **8** amethyst **9** carnelian **10** calchedony

quartzite: **9** itabarite, sandstone

quash: **4** cass, drop, void **5** abate, annul, crush, quell, shake **6** cancel **7** abolish, cassare, destroy, pumpkin, shatter **8** abrogate, suppress **9** overthrow

quat: **4** boil, glut, quit(Sc.) **5** squat **6** pimple, squash **7** blister, pustule, satiate

quaver: **5** shake, trill **6** quiver **7** tremble, tremolo, vibrate **9** vibration

quaw: **8** quagmire

quawk: caw **5** heron **7** screech

quay: key **4** bund, dock, mole, pier, wall **5** levee, quell, wharf **6** bunder, subdue **7** landing **10** embankment

queach: fen **7** thicket

queachy: **5** boggy, bushy **6** marshy, quaggy, swampy

queasy: **5** timid **8** delicate, qualmish, ticklish, troubled **9** hazardous, nauseated, squeamish, uncertain, unsettled **10** fastidious **11** embarrassed **13** uncomfortable

Quebec:
cape: **5** Gaspe
county: **5** Laval
peninsula: **5** Gaspe
town: **5** Sorel
vehicle: **7** caleche

quebrada: gap **5** brook, creek, gorge **6** ravine, stream **7** fissure **8** brooklet

queechy: **4** puny, weak **5** small **6** feeble, sickly

queen: **4** fers, rani(Ind.) **5** ranee(Ind.), reine(F.) **6** regina **7** monarch **9** sovereign

queen of fairies: Mab, Pam, Una **7** Titania **8** Gloriand
gods: **4** Hera, Juno, Sati
Hearts: **9** Elizabeth
Heaven: **4** Hera, Mary, moon **7** Astarte
spades: **5** basta
underworld: Hel **4** Hela

Queen Anne's lace: **6** carrot

Queen City: **10** Cincinnati

Queen of the Adriatic: **6** Venice

Queen of the Antilles: **4** Cuba

Queen of the East: **7** Zenobia

Queen of Isles: **6** Albion

Queen of Palmyra: **7** Zenobia

Queen of Sheba: **6** Balkis

queen's arm: **6** musket

queen's-delight: oil **4** herb **9** perennial, queenroot

queen's-flower: **6** myrtle **9** bloodwood

Queensland:
river: **8** Brisbane
seaport: **8** Brisbane

queer: odd, rum **4** sham **5** comic, droll, drunk, faint, funny, giddy, rally, spoil **6** banter, insane **7** comical, erratic, strange, unusual **8** abnormal, doubtful, fanciful, humorous, peculiar, qualmish, ridicule, singular, spurious **9** dishonest, eccentric, fantastic **10** homosexual, suspicious **11** counterfeit, intoxicated **12** questionable

queest: **8** ringdove

queet: **4** coot

quell: **4** calm, cool, damp, dash, kill, quay **5** allay, check, crush, quash, quiet, still **6** obtund, pacify, reduce, soothe, spring, stanch, stifle, subdue **7** assuage, destroy, repress, satisfy **8** fountain, suppress **9** overpower, overwhelm **10** extinguish

queme: fit **4** neat, snug, tidy **5** handy, quiet **6** comely **7** fitting, satisfy **8** pleasant, suitable **9** agreeable

quench: **5** delay, slake

quenelle: **8** meatball **9** forcemeat

querent: **8** inquirer **9** plaintiff **11** complainant

querida: **5** lover **10** sweetheart

querist: **8** inquirer **10** questioner

querken: **5** choke **6** stifle

querl: **4** coil **5** twirl, twist

quern: **4** mill **7** grinder

quernstone: **9** millstone

querulous: **7** fretful, peevish, whining **9** complaint, plaintive, quizzical **11** complaining **12** querimonious

query: ask **5** doubt **6** demand, quaere **7** inquire, inquiry **8** question **9** challenge **11** interrogate

quest: ask **4** hunt, seek **6** search **7** examine, inquest, journey, pursuit, seeking **9** adventure **10** enterprise, expedition

question: ask **4** crux, quiz **5** doubt, grill, poser, query, scout, targe(Sc.) **6** appose, cruces(pl.), debate, demand, quaere, riddle, shrive **7** dispute, inquire, inquiry, problem, scruple, stumper **9** catechise, catechize, challenge, interview **10** discussion **11** examination, interrogate, proposition **12** interpellate **13** interrogation, interrogative, investigation
denoting: **15** interrogational
rhetorical: **10** eperotesis

questionable: **4** moot **7** dubious, suspect **9** ambiguous, equivocal, uncertain

questionnaire: **4** form, poll

quetch: **4** stir **6** twitch

quetzal: **6** trogon

queue: cue **4** line **5** braid **7** pigtail

quey: **6** heifer

quiaquia: **4** scad **9** cigarfish

quibble: cog, pun **4** carp, quib **5** cavil, cheat, evade **6** ambage, baffle, haffle **7** brabble, evasion, shuffle **9** previcate **10** equivocate **12** equivocation

quica: **7** opossum, sarigue

quick: apt, yap **4** deft, fast, flit, lish, live, spry, yare **5** acute, agile, alert, alive, apace, brisk, fiery, fleet, hasty, rapid, ready, sharp, swift, tosto(It.), yeder **6** abrupt, active, lively, moving, nimble prompt, speedy, sudden, volant **7** intense **8** animated, dextrous, shifting, vigorous **9** dexterous, impatient, sensitive, sprightly **10** celeritous, perceptive **11** expeditious **12** invigorating

quick bread: **7** muffins **8** biscuits **9** cornbread

quicken: **4** whet **5** hurry, speed **6** arouse, excite, hasten, incite, revive, vivify **7** animate, enliven, provoke, refresh, sharpen **8** expedite, inspirit **9** reanimate, stimulate **10** accelerate **11** resuscitate **12** reinvigorate

quicker than: ere

quicklime: **5** rusma

quickly: **4** fast, rath, soon, vite(F.) **5** alive, apace **6** belive, hourly, presto, pronto **7** rapidly **8** promptly, speedily, vigorous

quickness: **6** acumen **7** acidity **8** dispatch, progress, pungency, sagacity **9** acuteness **10** expedition

quicksand: **4** flow, syrt, trap **6** danger, syrtis

quickset: **5** hedge **7** thicket **8** hawthorn

quicksilver: **7** mercury **9** heautarit

quid: cud, fid **4** chaw, chew **5** pound, trade **6** barter, return **8** exchange, quiddity **9** sovereign

quiddany: **5** jelly, sirup

quiddit: **7** quibble **8** subtlety

quiddle: **6** dawdle, trifle

quidnunc: **5** frump **6** gossip, tatler **8** busybody

quiescent: **5** quiet, still **6** latent, static **7** dormant, resting **8** inactive, sleeping **10** motionless

quiet: sh; coy, pet **4** calm, cosh, dead, ease, fair, hush, lull, mild, rest, tame **5** allay, downy, inert, peace, privy, sober, still **6** gentle, hushed, merely, modest, placid, repose, secret, sedate, serene, settle, silent, smooth, soothe, static, stilly **7** appease, compose, halcyon, restful, retired, silence **8** composed, decorous, peaceful, secluded, tranquil **9** alleviate, contented, noiseless, peaceable, placidity, quiescent, reposeful, unruffled **10** motionless, silentness, unmolested **11** clandestine, tranquilize, undisturbed

quietus: **5** death **6** repose **8** mittimus **11** acquittance

quiff: **4** girl, puff **5** whiff **8** forelock

quill: cop, pen **5** remex, spina **6** bobbin, pinion **7** remiges(pl.), spindle

quillet: **4** tube **5** tract **7** quibble

quilt: pad, sew **4** gulp **5** eider **6** caddow, pallet, stitch **7** blanket, comfort, swallow **8** coverlet **9** comforter **11** counterpane

quink: **5** brant

quinoa: **5** seeds **7** pigweed

quinoline derivative: **7** analgen

quip: mot, pun **4** gibe, jest, joke **5** sally, taunt **6** saying **7** quibble

quire: **4** fold **5** choir, paper

quirk: **4** kink, quip, turn **5** clock, knack, sally, trait, twist **6** groove, strike **7** caprice, evasion **8** flourish **9** deviation **10** subterfuge **11** peculiarity **12** equivocation

quirquincho: **5** pichi **6** peludo **9** armadillo

quirt: **4** whip **5** romal

quis: **8** woodcock

quit: rid **4** free, stop **5** avoid, cease, clear, forgo, leave, repay **6** acquit, depart, desist, forego, resign, vacate **7** abandon, forsake, release, relieve **8** abdicate, absolved, liberate, renounce **9** surrender **10** relinquish **11** discontinue

quitclaim: **6** acquit **7** release **14** relinquishment

quite: all **4** very **5** stark, truly **6** really, wholly **7** totally, utterly **8** entirely **10** altogether, completely, positively **12** considerably

quite so: **7** exactly **9** precisely

quittance: **5** repay **6** return **7** requite **8** reprisal, requital **9** departure, discharge, repayment **10** recompense **11** acquittance

quitter: **4** seal, slag **5** piker **6** coward **7** shirker

quiver: **4** case, quag, tirl(Sc.) **5** bever, quake, quick, shake, thirl(Sc.), trill **6** active, arrows, bicker, cocker, dindle, lively, nimble, quaver, sheath, shiver, tremor **7** frisson, tremble, vibrate **8** flichter **9** palpitate, vibration

quivering: 5 aspen **6** ashake, didder **7** aquiver **8** blubbery

quiverleaf: 5 aspen

quixotic: 7 utopian **9** visionary **10** chivalrous, idealistic **11** impractical **13** impracticable

quiz: ask **4** exam, hiss, hoax, jest, joke, mock, test, whiz **5** chaff, probe **7** examine **8** instruct, question, ridicule **11** examination, questioning

quizzical: odd **7** amusing, comical, teasing **9** bantering, eccentric, perplexed

quizzing glass: 7 monocle **8** eyeglass

quod: jug **4** jail **5** court **6** prison

quodlibet: 6 debate, medley **8** fantasia, subtlety

quoin: 4 coin **5** angle, wedge **6** corner **8** keystone, voussoir

quoit: 4 disc, ring **5** throw **6** discus **8** cromlech
pin: hob

quomodo: 5 means **6** manner

quondam: 6 former **7** onetime **8** sometime

quop: 5 throb

quorum: 5 group **7** council **8** majority

quota: 4 part **5** share **6** divide, rating **8** dividend **10** contingent, proportion

quotation: 5 price, quote

quotation mark: 9 guillemet(F.)

quote: 4 cite, cote, name, note **5** motto, refer **6** adduce, allege, allude, notice, repeat, select **7** excerpt, extract, passage **9** quotation, reference, selection **10** memorandum

quoth: 4 said **5** spoke

quotha: 6 indeed **8** forsooth

quotidian: 5 daily **7** trivial **8** everyday, ordinary **9** recurring **11** commonplace

R

R: ar; rho **6** letter

Ra: Re; Shu, Tem, Tum **4** Aten **5** Horus **7** Chepera, Khepera, Sokaris **9** Harmachis
bull form: **5** Bacis
child: Mu; Mat, Shu **4** Maat **5** Athor
parent: Geb, Keb, Nut, Seb **5** Neith
wife: **4** Mout

raad: **7** catfish

rab: **6** beater

rabat: **5** rabbi **8** polisher

rabato, rebato: **4** ruff **6** collar

rabban: **6** master **7** teacher

rabbet: **5** check **6** groove, recess **7** channel

rabbi: **4** lord **5** amora **6** master, rabbin **7** amoraim, tannaim, teacher **8** sabaraim, saboraim **9** clergyman
assistant: **6** cantor
school: **7** yeshiva **8** yeshibah, yeshivah **9** yeshiboth(pl.)

rabbit: bun, doe **4** buck, cony, hare, tyro **5** bunny, capon, coney, lapin(F.) **6** coward, novice, rodent, tapeti
fur: **4** rack, scut
shelter: **5** hutch **6** burrow, warren **7** clapper
tail: fud(Sc.) **4** scut
young: **4** rack **6** gazabo, gazebo **7** starter

rabbit-ear: **6** cactus **8** toadflax

rabbit fever: **9** tularemia

rabbit flower: **8** foxglove, toadflax

rabbit-foot: **5** charm **8** talisman

rabbit-meat: **9** archangel

rabbit tobacco: **10** balsamweed

rabbit vine: **9** groundnut

rabbitfish: **8** chimaera

rabbitmouth: **10** harelipped

rabbitry: **5** hutch **6** warren

rabbit's-mouth: **10** snapdragon

rabbit's-root: **12** sarsaparilla

rabble: mob **4** herd, raff, rout **5** crowd **6** ragtag **7** bobtail **8** canaglia, canaille, riffraff **9** confusion **10** clamjamfry, hubbleshoo, hubble-show **11** commonality

rabble-rouser: **6** ragtag **8** agitator **9** demagogue

rabid: mad **6** raging **7** frantic, furious, violent, zealous **8** frenzied, virulent **9** fanatical **12** enthusiastic

rabies: **5** lyssa, lytta **7** madness **11** hydrophobia

race: cut, ilk, run **4** dash, gest, herd, kind, lane, line, root, rush, slit, sort, stem, stud **5** blood, breed, brood, caste, chevy, chivy, class, corso, flesh, geste, hurry, relay, speed, stock, track, tribe **6** arroyo, bicker, broose, chivvy, course, family, groove, hasten, hurdle, nation, people, slalom, sprint, stirps, strain **7** bombast, channel, contend, contest, dynasty, lineage, regatta, running, scamper, scratch **8** marathon **9** holethnos **10** freeforall, generation, passageway **11** competition, descendants, watercourse
combined form: **4** gend, geno
division: **7** Negroid **9** Caucasian, Mongolian
human: man **7** mankind **9** mortality
mixed: see **person:** *of mixed blood*
murder: **8** genocide
series: **7** regatta
science: **9** athletics, ethnology
starting line: **7** scratch

race board: **9** gangplank

race ginger: **10** gingerroot

raceabout: **5** sloop **8** roadster

racecourse: **4** heat, oval **6** career, circus, course **7** raceway
marker: **4** meta **6** pylon

racehorse: **6** maiden, mantis, plater

racer: **4** crab **5** miler, snake **6** runner **7** courser, serpent **8** sprinter **9** turntable **10** blacksnake

raceway: **5** canal **7** channel, fishway **8** millrace

Rachel: *children:* **6** Joseph **8** Benjamin
father: **5** Laban
husband: **5** Jacob
sister: **4** Leah

rachis: **4** stem **5** spine **8** backbone

rachitis: **7** rickets

rack: bar, fly, gin, jib **4** bink, crib, gait, pace, path, scud, skin, tree **5** airer, brake, creel, flake, horse, stand, touse, trace, track, vapor **6** course, cratch, gantry, harass, strain, wrench **7** agonize, grating, oppress, pathway, stretch, torment, torture, vestige **9** framework **10** excruciate, foresaddle

racket: bat, din **4** shoe **5** bandy, dodge, noise, trick **6** bustle, clamor, crosse, hubbub, outcry, scheme, strike **7** clangor, clatter, pattern, revelry **8** snowshoe **10** battledore, turbulence **11** merrymaking

rackle: **5** clank **6** rattle **7** clatter **8** reckless **9** impetuous **10** headstrong

raconteur: **8** narrator **11** storyteller

racy: **5** brisk, fresh, smart, spicy, swift **6**

lively, risque **7** piquant, pungent, zestful **8** indecent, spirited, stirring, vigorous **10** suggestive **12** exhilarating

rad: **5** eager, quick, ready **6** afraid, elated **11** exhilarated

raddle: rod **4** beat **5** color, ocher, twist **6** branch, cudgel, thrash **10** interweave

radial: ray **8** quadrant

radian: arc **7** auroral

radiance: **4** beam, glow **5** glare, gleam, glory, nitor, sheen, shine **6** luster **7** glitter, glowing, shining **8** lambency, splendor **9** brilliant **10** brightness, brilliancy, effulgence, refulgence

radiant: **7** auroral **11** resplendent

radiate: **4** beam, emit **5** shine **6** spread **7** diffuse, emanate **9** coruscate, irradiate **10** illuminate

radiating: **6** radial **8** stellate **11** centrifugal

radiation detector: **6** geiger

radiator: **6** heater

radical: red **4** root, surd **5** basal, basic, rebel, ultra **7** capital, drastic, extreme, forward, leftist, organic, support **8** cardinal, complete **9** extremist **10** foundation, iconoclast **11** fundamental **12** intransigent **13** revolutionary

chemical: ion **4** amyl, aryl **6** acetyl, adenyl, adipyl **7** tartryl **8** aluminyl

radicate: **9** establish

radicle: **7** rootlet

radio: set **8** portable, wireless **9** broadcast, radiogram **10** transistor **12** walkie-talkie

frequency: **5** audio

operator: ham **6** sparks **11** broadcaster

part: **5** diode **8** detector, selector

signal check: **7** monitor

radish: **5** radis(F.) **7** cadlock

radium:

discoverer: **5** Curie

emanation: **5** niton, radon

source: **7** uranite

radix: **4** root **6** etymon **7** radical

raff: **4** heap, raft, rake **5** trash **6** huddle, jumble, litter, lumber, rabble, timber **7** rubbish **8** leavings, riffraff

raffish: low **5** cheap **6** flashy, frowsy, tawdry **7** unkempt **9** worthless **11** disgraceful **12** disreputable

raffle: **4** raff **6** jumble, rabble, refuse, tangle **7** drawing, lottery, rubbish, serrate **8** entangle, riffraff

raft: cow **4** crib, floe, heap, moki, raff, spar **5** balsa, barge, float **6** rafter **9** catamaran, transport **10** collection

part: **5** brail

raft-breasted: **6** ratite

raft duck: **5** scaup **7** redhead **8** bluebill

rafter: **4** balk, beam, firm, raft, viga **7** carline, chevron

rafty: **4** damp **5** musty, stale **6** rancid

rag: jag **4** mock, rail, rate, tune **5** annoy, dance, scold, scrap, shred, tease **6** ban-

ter, harass, rumpus, tatter, uproar **7** quarrel, ragtime, remnant, wrangle

ragamuffin: **14** tatterdemalion

rage: fad, ire **4** beef, fret, fume, funk, fury, heat, rant, rave, tear **5** anger, chafe, craze, furor, mania, storm, wrath **6** choler, fervor, frenzy, furore, temper **7** amentia, bluster, bombast, emotion, fashion, fervour, passion, thunder **8** insanity, violence **9** vehemence **10** enthusiasm

ragged: **5** harsh, rough **6** jagged, shaggy, uneven **7** shreddy, unkempt **8** strident, tattered **9** defective, dissonant, imperfect, irregular **10** straggling, unfinished **11** dilapidated

ragged jacket: **4** seal

ragged lady: **5** guara **11** love-in-a-mist

ragged sailor: **10** bluebottle, cornflower

raggle: cut **6** groove

raggy: **6** ragged

raging: **4** grim **5** rabid **6** fierce **7** fervent, rageous **8** furibund **9** ferocious

raglan: **6** sleeve **8** overcoat

ragout: **4** hash, stew **5** salmi **6** salmis **7** goulash, haricot **8** salpicon **10** capilotade **11** gallimaufry

ragpicker: **6** bunter **10** chiffonier(F.) **11** chiffonnier(F.)

ragshag: **11** masquerader

rah: **5** cheer **6** hurrah

raid: **4** tala **5** foray **6** attack, creach(Sc.), creagh(Sc.), forage, harass, inroad, invade, maraud, piracy **7** chappow, despoil, hership **8** invasion **9** chevachie, incursion, roadstead, cavalcade

rail: bar, jaw **4** coot, flow, gush, jest, rant, rate, slat, sora **5** abuse, array, chide, cloak, crake, dress, guard, heron, plank, scoff, scold, soree, track **6** banter, berate, callet, revile, septum **7** arrange, bidcock, bilcock, clocker, footrest, garment, inveigh **8** decorate, Rallidae(pl.), reproach **9** spectator

genus of: **4** sora **6** rallus

railing: bar **5** fence **7** barrier, parapet **8** balconet, banister, espalier, rabulous **9** guardrail **10** balconette, balustrade **12** vituperation

raillery: **4** gaff **5** chaff, sport **6** banter, blague **8** badinage, ridicule **10** persiflage

railly: **4** jest, mock **5** rally **8** ridicule

railroad: **4** herd, line, push, rush **5** hurry, track **8** ceinture, monorail **9** transport

branch: **4** stub **6** feeder

car: **4** diner **6** parlor **7** caboose, coal-car, parlour, Pullman, sleeper

center: **7** station **8** terminal, terminus **10** roundhouse

signal: **5** fusee **9** semaphore

switch: **4** frog

worker: **6** boomer, porter **7** fireman **8** engineer, strapper **9** conductor

railway: **5** train **6** subway **8** elevated, jackstay, monorail **9** funicular

raiment: See **dress.**

rain: dag, fog **4** mist, pour **5** blizz, blout, misle, plash, spate, storm **6** deluge, mizzle, serein, shower **7** drizzle **8** downpour, sprinkle **10** cloudburst **13** precipitation
check: **4** stub **12** postponement
god: **8** Parjanya
icy: **4** hail, snow **5** sleet
unit of measure: **4** inch

rain cloud: **5** nimbi(pl.) **6** nimbus

rain gage: **8** udometer **10** hyetometer **11** pluviograph, pluviometer **15** hyetometrograph

rain glass: **9** barometer

rain leader: **9** downspout

rain-loving: **12** ombrophilous

rain tree: **5** saman, zaman **6** zamang **8** genisaro

rainbow: arc, bow **4** iris
measuring device: **12** spectrometer

rainbow chaser: **9** visionary **11** doctrinaire

rainbow-like: **6** iridal **10** iridescent

raincoat: **4** mino **6** poncho, ulster **7** slicker **10** mackintosh, trenchcoat

rainfall: *pert. to:* **6** hyetal

rainfowl: **6** cuckoo **10** woodpecker **11** channelbill

rainspout: **4** rone(Sc.) **10** waterspout

rainworm: **8** nematode **9** earthworm

rainy: wet **4** damp **5** moist **7** flooded **8** cluttery
season: **7** monsoon

rais, reis: **4** head **5** chief, ruler **7** captain

raise: up; end **4** buoy, grow, hain, heft, hike, levy, lift, rear, rise, stir **5** arear, boost, breed, crane, dight, elate, exalt, hance, heave, heeze, hoist, horse, rouse, set-up, start, trice **6** arouse, ascend, assume, awaken, cantle, create, emboss, excite, gather, incite, leaven, muster, obtain, remove, uplift **7** address, advance, chevise, collect, elevate, enhance, ennoble, lighten, present, procure, produce, promote **8** heighten, increase **9** cultivate, establish, institute, intensify, originate, propagate **10** aggrandize, appreciate, invigorate

raised: **4** hove **6** arrect, enleve(F.)

raisin: **5** lexia, zibeb **7** currant

raj: **4** rule **5** reign **11** sovereignty

rajah: **4** king **5** chief **6** prince **9** dignitary
wife: **4** rani **5** ranee

Rajmahal creeper: **4** jiti, vine

rake: gad, rue, rut **4** path, raff, roue, rove, trip **5** claut, glean, track **6** gather, groove **7** collect, gleaner, scratch **8** enfilade, rakehell **9** debauchee **11** inclination

rakehell: **4** rake **7** immoral **9** debauched, debauchee, dissolute **10** profligate

rake-off: **4** take **6** profit, rebate **10** commission, percentage

rakish: **4** lewd, pert **7** roguish **9** dissolute

rale: **6** rattle

rallidae: **5** coots, rails, wekas **6** crakes **10** gallinules

rally: **4** drag, mock **5** chaff, noise, rouse **6** arouse, attack, banter, deride, revive **7** recover, reunite **8** assemble, raillery, ridicule **10** recuperate, strengthen **11** concentrate

rallying cry: **6** slogan

ram: hit, pun, tup, wad **4** buck, butt, tamp, teap **5** Aries, crash, sheep, stuff **6** batter, beetle, chaser, rancid, strike, wether **7** collide, plunger **8** bulldoze

ram cat: tom **4** male

Rama's bride: **4** Sita

ramage: **4** wild **5** bough, rough **6** unruly **7** untamed **8** branches, frenzied, wildness

ramage hawk: **8** brancher

ramass: **6** gather **7** collect

ramate: **8** branched

ramble: gad **4** roam, rove, walk **5** jaunt, prowl, range **6** stroll, travel, wander **7** saunter **8** straggle **9** excursion

rambling: **7** cursory, devious **9** desultory, wandering **10** circuitous, discursive **11** peripatetic **12** disconnected

rambunctious: **4** wild **6** unruly **10** boisterous, disorderly, rampageous **12** obstreperous **14** uncontrollable

ramentum: **5** palea, palet **6** paleae(pl.), scales **7** shaving **8** particle

ramhead: arm **4** hook **5** lever **8** clodpate

ramie, ramee: **4** hemp, rhea **5** fiber

ramification: arm **4** rami(pl.) **5** ramus **6** branch, spread **8** division, offshoot **9** branching **10** divergence **12** embranchment

rammack: **4** rush

rammel: **5** trash **9** brushwood **11** undergrowth

rammish: **4** rank **5** rammy

ramose: **7** cladose **8** branched **9** branching

ramp: rob **4** bank, rage, walk **5** crawl, creep, slope, storm **6** dupery, unruly **7** incline, rampage, swindle **8** gradient, platform **9** helicline **10** cuckoopint

rampageous: **4** wild **6** unruly **9** rampaging **10** boisterous

rampant: **4** rife **6** fierce **7** violent **9** unchecked **10** rampageous, widespread **11** extravagant, flourishing, threatening **12** unrestrained **14** uncontrollable

rampart: **4** wall **5** agger, mound, redan **6** vallum **7** barrier, bulwark, parapet, ravelin **10** embankment **13** fortification
part: **4** spur

ramper: **7** lamprey

rampire: dam **7** fortify, rampart **10** embankment, strengthen

ramshackle: **5** loose, shaky **7** rickety **10** disorderly, dissipated, tumble-down

ramstam: **7** headlong, reckless **10** headstrong **11** thoughtless

ramus: **6** branch **10** branchlike

rancel: 6 search 7 ransack

ranch: 4 casa, farm, tear 5 finca, pluck 7 acreage, scratch 8 estancia, hacienda 9 estantion

worker: 4 hand 5 owner 6 cowboy, farmer 7 cowpoke, rancher 8 herdsman, ranchero(Sp.), ranchman

rancho: 5 ranch

rancid: 4 rank, sour 5 musty, stale 6 frowsy 7 spoiled 8 stinking 9 obnoxious, offensive 10 unpleasant

rancor, rancour: ire 4 gall, hate 5 spite 6 enmity, hatred, malice 8 rankling 9 animosity, antipathy, hostility 10 bitterness

rand: 4 edge 5 ridge, strip 6 border, margin

randan: row 4 boat 5 spree 7 rampage

random: 5 loose, stray 6 casual, chance 7 aimless 9 desultory, haphazard 10 accidental, fortuitous 11 purposeless

randy: 5 crude, revel, shrew 6 beggar, coarse, frolic, virago, vulgar 7 canvass 8 carousal 9 festivity 10 disorderly 12 unmanageable

range: ken, row 4 ally, area, farm, line, rank, roam, rove 5 align, aline, blank, class, field, gamut, order, reach, ridge, scope, space, stove, stray 6 extent, ramble, series, sphere, stroll, tether, wander 7 arrange, compass, explore, habitat, saunter 8 classify, distance 9 cookstove, grassland 11 systematize

range-finder: 6 stadia 9 mekometer, telemeter 10 trekometer

ranger: 4 seal 5 rover, sieve 6 keeper, warden 8 commando, rangeman, wanderer

rangy: 8 spacious

rank: row 4 army, file, foul, line, rate, sort, tier 5 array, caste, cense, class, frank, genus, grade, gross, order, proud, range, space 6 barony, coarse, degree, estate, fertid, gentry, mighty, rancid, rating, series, status, strong 7 caliber, calibre, calling, compeer, copious, corrupt, dignity, extreme, fertile, froward, glaring, haughty, noisome, overfed, peerage, quality, rammish, station, stratum, swollen, violent 8 absolute, abundant, classify, division, eminence, estimate, flagrant, gentrice, headlong, indecent, palpable, position, powerful, vigorous 9 condition, downright, excessive, exuberant, formation, gradation, hierarchy, luxuriant, offensive, overgrown, plentiful 10 coordinate 11 arrangement, distinction 14 classification

deprive of: 4 bust 5 break 6 depose 7 cashier

mark of: 6 stripe

military: PFC 5 major 7 captain, colonel, general, private 8 banneret, corporal, sergeant 10 lieutenant

rankle: 4 fret, gall 6 fester, rancor 7 inflame 8 irritate, ulcerate

rann: 5 verse 6 stanza, strain

ransack: 4 loot, rake, sack 5 rifle, steal 6 search 7 pillage, rummage

ransom: buy, fee 5 atone, price 6 redeem, rescue 7 deliver, expiate, release 9 redeeming 13 consideration

money: 10 redemptory

rant: 4 fume, rage, rail, rand, rave, riot, song, tune 5 dance, revel, scold, spout 6 frolic, speech, steven 7 bluster, bombast, carouse, declaim, fustian 9 discourse 11 merrymaking, rodomontade 13 jollification

rantipole: 4 wild 6 rakish, unruly 9 termagant

ranty: 4 wild 7 excited

ranula: 4 cyst 8 swelling

rap: bob, box, con, hit, tap 4 blow, chap, grab, knap, tirl 5 blame, clink, clout, knock, seize, smite, steal, utter 6 snatch, strike, thwack 7 deliver 8 sentence 9 criticize, criticism, enrapture, transport 10 punishment

rapacious: 6 greedy 8 covetous, grasping, ravening, ravenous 9 ferocious, voracious 10 avaricious, predacious

rapacity: 5 ravin 7 edacity 8 appetite 9 extortion

rape: 4 file, rasp 5 abuse, haste, hasty, hurry, quick, seize 6 defile, pomace, ravish, turnip 7 dispoil, hastily, pillage, plunder, robbery, scratch, violate 9 violation 10 plundering, spoliation

rapid: 4 fast 5 chute, fleet, quick, steep, swift 6 abrupt, moving, speedy 10 fastmoving 11 expeditions

rapidity: 5 haste 8 celerity, velocity

rapidly: 5 apace

rapier: 5 bilbo, sword 6 verdun 7 ricasso

rapine: 4 rape

rapparee: 6 robber 8 vagabond 9 plunderer 10 freebooter

rappee: 5 snuff

rapport: 6 accord 7 harmony 8 affinity, relation 9 agreement 12 relationship

rapscallion: 5 rogue 6 rascal, wretch 8 rascally 11 ne'er-do-well 14 good-fornothing

rapt: 4 deep 5 tense 6 intent 8 absorbed, ecstatic 9 comprised, enchanted, engrossed, entranced, transport 10 enraptured 11 preoccupied, transported

raptorial: 11 accipitrine

rapture: 5 bliss 6 trance 7 delight, ecstasy 8 rhapsody 9 enrapture, happiness, transport 10 exultation

rare: odd, raw 4 fine, good, nice, thin 6 choice, dainty, geason, scarce, seldom, unique 7 antique, capital, curious, extreme, special, tenuous, unusual 8 precious, uncommon, unwonted 9 beautiful, excellent, exclusive, exquisite, scattered, underdone 10 infrequent 11 distinctive, exceptional 13 distinguished, extraordinary

rarefied: **4** thin **7** diluted, ethered, gaseous, refined **8** aethered **10** attenuated

rarity: **5** curio, relic **6** geason **7** antique **8** rareness

ras: **4** cape **6** prince **8** headland **9** commander

rascal: boy, cad, imp **4** file, loon **5** foist, gipsy, gypsy, knave, rogue, scamp **6** ablach, budzat, coquin, harlot **7** budzart, glutton **8** hosebird, scalawag, sealpeen, widdifow **9** miscreant, reprobate, scallawag, scoundrel, trickster **11** rapscallion

rascally: **4** base, mean **6** arrant **9** dishonest, worthless **11** furciferous, mischievous

rase: **4** raze

rash: cut, mad **4** bold **5** brash, erase, hardy, hasty, heady, hives, scamp, shave, slash, uredo **6** daring, eczema, scrape, unwary **7** foolish, hotspur, icarian, scratch **8** careless, eruption, headlong, heedless, reckless, temerous **9** desperate, exanthema, foolhardy, foreright, impetuous, imprudent, overhasty, urticaria, venturous **10** headstrong, hotspurred, incautious, indiscreet, unthinking **11** adventurous, furthersome, harum-scarum, precipitate, precipitous, temerarious, thoughtless, venturesome, **13** adventuresome, efflorescence

rasher: **5** slice **7** portion **8** rockfish

rashness: **4** rese **5** folly **6** acrisy **8** temerity

Rasores: **8** Columbae, Gallinae

rasp: rub **4** file **5** belch, eruct, grate **6** scrape **8** bogberry, irritate **9** raspberry

rasping: **5** harsh, raspy, rough **6** hoarse, rasion **7** raspish, raucous **8** guttural **9** offensive

rasse: **5** civet

rasure: cut **6** filing **7** erasing, erasure, rasping, scratch, shaving **8** scraping **12** obliteration

rat: pad **4** scab **6** rodent, vermin **8** betrayer, deserter, informer, renegade, squealer **9** councilor, counselor **11** stool-pigeon **13** doublecrosser

kind: **5** metad, zemmi, zemni **6** tosher

poison: **8** ratsbane

rat hare: **4** pika

ratafia: **5** noyau **7** biscuit, cordial, liqueur

ratch: bar **4** rend **7** ratchet, stretch **8** distance

ratchet: **4** pawl **5** click **6** bobbin, detent

rate: fee, tax **4** fare, file, pace, rank **5** abuse, blame, chide, grade, price, scold, score, tempo, value **6** assess, assize, charge, reckon, regard, tariff **7** account, censure, chasten, despise, quality, reprove **8** appraise, classify, consider, estimate, evaluate **10** proportion **14** classification

ratel: **6** badger

ratfish: **8** chimaera

rathe, rath: **4** soon **5** eager, early, quick

6 prompt, speedy **7** betimes **8** promptly, speedily

rather: ere **4** erer **5** prior **6** before, choice, liever, sooner **7** earlier, quickly **8** somewhat **10** preferably, preference **11** immediately

rather than: ere

ratify: **4** amen, pass, seal **6** affirm, enseal, verify **7** approve, confirm **8** roborate, sanction **9** authorize, establish

ratihabition: **8** sanction **12** ratification

rating: **4** rank **5** cense, class, grade **6** rebuke **8** estimate, scolding, standing **9** reprimand **10** evaluation **14** classification

ratio: pi; cos **4** rate, sine **5** quota, share **6** cosine, degree, ration **7** average, portion **8** relation **10** percentage, proportion **11** capacitance

ratiocination: **5** logic **7** thought **8** argument **9** reasoning

ration: **4** dole, food, mete **5** allot, ratio, share **6** divide **7** portion **8** relation **9** allotment, allowance **10** distribute **11** calculation

rational: **4** sane **5** sober **7** logical **8** sensible **10** reasonable **11** intelligent **13** philosophical

rations: **8** buckshee **10** provisions

ratite: emu, moa **4** bird, emeu **7** ostrich **9** cassowary

genus: **7** apteryx **8** dinornis

ratoon: **5** shoot, stalk **6** spring, sprout

rattan: **4** cane, lash, palm, sega, whip **5** noose, thong **6** punish, switch, wicker

rattle: din **4** birl, rale, rick, stun, tirl **5** addle, annoy, clack, rouse, scold, upset **6** assail, racket, uproar **7** agitate, chatter, clapper, clatter, clitter, confuse, fluster, gnatter, maracas **9** crepitate, embarrass **10** disconcert

rattlebrained: **5** giddy **9** frivolous **11** empty-headed, harebrained

rattlemouse: bat

rattlepate: ass **4** dolt **9** chatterer **11** rattlebrain

rattleroot: **7** bugbane

rattlesnake: **8** cascavel, crotalus **9** sistrurus **10** crotalidae(pl.) **11** massasaugas

rattlesnake-bite: rue

rattlesnake fern: **9** sporangia

rattlesnake herb: **9** baneberry

rattlesnake pilot: **10** copperhead

rattle-top: **7** bugbane

rattletrap: **5** ratty **7** gewgaws, rickety **10** ramshackle **11** knickknacks

ratton: rat

ratty: **4** mean **6** shabby **10** rattletrap **11** dilapitated

ratwa: **7** muntjac

raucous: dry **4** loud **5** harsh, noisy, rough **6** coarse, hoarse **7** braying, rasping **8** strident **11** cacophonous

raun: roe **5** spawn

raupo: **7** cattail

ravage: eat **4** loot, prey, ruin, sack **5** foray,

harry, havoc, spoil, waste **6** forage **7** despoil, destroy, overrun, pillage, plunder, violate **8** deflower, desolate **9** devastate **10** depopulate, desolation **11** despoilment, devastation

rave: 4 rage, rant **5** blurb, crush, storm **7** bluster, bombast, declaim **8** harangue **11** infatuation **12** commendation

ravel: run **4** comb, fray, rail **5** snarl **6** runner, sleave, tangle, unwind **7** crumble, involve, railing, unravel, untwist, unweave **8** entangle, separate **11** disentangle

ravelin: 8 demilune **13** fortification

raveling: 4 lint **6** thread

raven (See also **ravin**): **4** crow **5** black **9** blackbird

ravenous: 6 greedy, hungry, lupine, toothy **8** edacious **9** cormorant, ferocious, rapacious, voracious **10** catawampus, gluttonous **12** catawampious **13** catawamptious

ravine: den, gap, lin **4** dell, ghyl, gill, linn, sike, wadi, wady **5** canon, chine, clove, ditch, flume, glack, gorge, goyal, goyle, griff, grike, gulch, gully, kloof, strid **6** arroyo, canyon, cleuch, clough, coulee, gulley, hollow, nullah **8** barranca, barranco, quebrado **10** depression

raving: 6 raging **8** frenzied **9** delirious **10** incoherent, irrational **12** arreptitious

ravish: rob **4** rape **5** abuse, charm, force, harry, seize **6** defile, snatch **7** afforce, corrupt, delight, despoil, enchant, plunder, violate **8** deflower, entrance **9** captivate, constrain, enrapture

ravishment: 7 ecstasy, rapture

raw: 4 cold, damp, dazy(Sc.), lash, nude, rare **5** bawdy, bleak, chill, crude, green, harsh, naked **6** abrade, chilly, unfair **7** cutting, natural, obscene **8** immature, indecent, uncooked **9** inclement, unexposed, unrefined, unskilled, untrained **10** indelicate, unfinished, unprepared, unseasoned **11** uncivilized, unpracticed, unprocessed **12** uncultivated **13** inexperienced

rawboned: 4 lean **5** gaunt **7** angular, scrawny

rawhide: 4 pelt, whip **5** knout, quirt, thong

ray: 4 beam, beta, dorn, soil **5** array, dress, flair, gleam, gleed, light, manta, order, shine, sight, skate **6** defile, glance, obispo, radial, streak, stripe, vision **7** besmear, homelyn, radiate, raiment **9** irradiate, selachian **10** perception, vertebrate **11** arrangement, irradiation

rayon: 5 moire, ninon, tulle **6** faille, pongee **7** taffeta

yarn size: **6** denier

raze, rase: cut, rub **4** rage, ruin, tear **5** erase, graze, growl, level, shave **6** efface, incise, scrape **7** destroy, scratch, subvert **8** demolish, dismantle **9** depredate, overthrow, prostrate **10** obliterate

razee: cut **5** prune **6** reduce **7** abridge

razor:
kind: **7** rattler **8** electric
sharpen: **4** hone **5** strop
razorback: hog **5** ridge **10** roustabout
razorbill: auk **7** skimmer
razor stone: 10 novaculite
razz: 5 chaff, tease **6** banter, deride, heckle **8** ridicule
razzia: 4 raid **5** foray **9** incursion
razzle-dazzle: 5 spree **6** dazzle **7** confuse **8** hilarity **9** confusion
Re: See **Ra.**
re: 5 anent **9** regarding **10** concerning
reach: toe **4** come, gain, hawk, hent, ryke(Sc.), seek, span, spit **5** grasp, retch, scope, vomit **6** advene, affect, amount, arrive, attain, extend, extent, strive **7** achieve, expanse, possess, stretch **9** culminate, penetrate **10** accomplish
under: **7** subtend
reachable: 10 accessible
reaching: 6 effort **8** profound
reaction: 4 kick **5** start **6** answer **7** tropism **8** response **9** influence **10** impression, opposition
read: con **4** pore, scan, skim, tell **5** aread, areed, drone, guess, solve, study **6** advise, browse, peruse, relate **7** counsel, declare, discern, foresee, learned **8** decipher, describe, foretell, indicate **9** interpret, supervise
ability to: **8** literacy
inability to: **6** alexia
readable: 7 legible
reader: 6 lector, lister, primer **7** reciter **8** lectrice, lecturer **9** assistant **10** instructor **11** proofreader **12** elocutionist
readiness: art **4** ease, gift **6** graith **7** address, freedom **8** alacrity, facility, goodwill, volition **9** dexterity, eagerness, quickness **10** promptness **12** preparedness
reading: 6 lesson **7** lection, lecture, perusal, recital, version **9** collation **10** prelection
ready: apt, fit **4** free, glib, here, pret(F.), ripe **5** alert, apert, bound, eager, handy, happy, point, quick **6** active, adroit, facile, fluent, prompt **7** forward, willing **8** cheerful, dextrous, handsome, prepared, skillful **9** agreeable, available, dexterous **10** convenient **11** expeditious **12** unhesitating
real: 4 very, true, vrai(F.) **5** being, loyal **6** actual, hearty **7** certain, cordial, factual, genuine, gradely, literal, sincere **8** existent, faithful, tangible **9** authentic, effective, heartfelt, intrinsic, unfeigned, veritable **10** unaffected
real estate: 4 alod **5** allod, lands **6** realty **8** freehold, premises, property, tenement **13** hereditaments
claim: tax **8** mortgage **9** trust deed **11** encumbrance
pert. to: **7** predial

realistic: 5 vivid 8 lifelike

realization: 8 fruition

realize: get 4 gain, know 5 sense 6 effect, obtain 7 achieve, acquire, convert, fulfill 8 complete, conceive 9 apprehend 10 accomplish, appreciate, understand

really: ara 5 quite, sooth 6 indeed 8 actually

realm: 4 land 5 bourn, clime 6 bourne, circle, domain, empire, region, sphere 7 country, demesne, dynasty, kingdom, terrene 8 division, dominion, province 9 territory 10 department 11 sovereignty 12 jurisdiction

realty: 7 honesty, loyalty, royalty 8 fidelity, property 10 possession

ream: 4 bore, draw, foam, scum 5 bevel, cream, froth, widen 7 enlarge, stretch 11 countersink

reamer: 5 drift 6 broach

reanimate: 5 rally, renew 6 revive 11 resuscitate 12 reinvigorate

reap: cut 4 crop, rake 5 glean 6 garner, gather 7 acquire, collect, harvest

rear: aft, end, fix 4 back, buck, cave, grow, last, lift, rere, tail 5 abaft, breed, build, erect, nurse, raise, stern, train 6 astern, behind, foster, nursle 7 arriere(F.), educate, elevate, nurture 9 construct, establish, posterior 10 background, forthbring

rearhorse: 6 insect, mantis

rearward: 8 backward 10 retrograde

reason: peg 4 mind, nous 5 argue, brain, cause, logic, sense, think 6 debate, ground, motive, ponder, sanity 7 meaning 8 argument, converse 9 discourse, intellect, rationale, wherefore 10 moderation, understand 11 expostulate, ratiocinate, rationality, rationalize 12 plausibility 13 consideration, understanding

alleged: 7 pretext

deprived of: 8 demented

pert. to: 6 noetic

want of: 5 folie 7 amentia, madness 8 insanity

reasonable: 4 fair, just 8 feasible 9 equitable 11 inexpensive

reasoning: 5 logic 8 argument 10 conclusion 13 argumentation

basis of: 7 premise

reassure: 6 assure 7 comfort, hearten 8 reinsure 9 encourage

reata, riata: 4 rope 5 lasso 6 lariat

reave: rob 4 tear 5 burst, seize, split 7 bereave, pillage, plunder

reb: 5 rebel

rebate: 5 check 6 lessen, reduce, refund, weaken 8 diminish, discount 9 abatement, deduction, reduction, remission

Rebekah:

husband: 5 Isaac

sister: 5 Laban

son: 4 Esau 5 Jacob

rebel: 4 rise 6 oppose, revolt 8 renegade 9 insurgent

rebellion: 6 mutiny, putsch, revolt 8 defiance, sedition, uprising 10 resistance, revolution 12 disobedience, insurrection, renunciation 15 insubordination

rebellious: 10 refractory 12 contumacious, recalcitrant

rebirth: 7 revival 10 conversion, renascence 11 renaissance 13 reincarnation

reboant: 7 echoing 13 reverberating

rebound: dap 4 echo, stot 5 bound, carom 6 bounce, carrom, recoil, re-echo, resile, return, spring 7 reflect, resound 8 ricochet 9 boomerang 11 reverberate

rebuff: cow 4 scat, slap, snub 5 check, chide, fling, repel, scold, spurn 6 lesson 7 censure, refusal, reprove, repulse 9 rejection, reprimand

rebuke: nip, tsk, tut 4 beat, snub, tush 5 barge, blame, check, chide, scold 6 berate, dirdum, lesson, rating 7 downset, lecture, repress, reproof, reprove 8 admonish, chastise, reproach, restrain 9 criticism, criticize, reprehend, reprimand 10 correction 11 comeuppance, reprobation

rebus: 6 enigma, puzzle, riddle

rebut: 5 reply 6 oppose, rebuff, refute, revile 7 repulse 8 disprove 10 contradict

recalcitrant: 5 rebel 6 unruly 7 defiant 9 obstinate 10 calcitrant, rebellious, refractory

recall: 5 annul 6 cancel, encore, remind, repeal, revoke 7 abolish, bethink, rescind, retrace, retract, summons 8 remember, withdraw 9 recollect, reminisce 11 countermand

recant: 6 abjure, revoke 7 abandon, disavow, retract 8 renounce, withdraw 9 repudiate 10 contradict

recapitulate: sum 5 essay 6 repeat, review 7 restate 8 argument 9 enumerate, reiterate, summarize

recapture: 6 recall, regain, retake 7 recover 9 reacquire

recede: ebb 6 depart, retire 7 deviate, regress, retreat 8 withdraw 10 retrograde

receipt: 4 stub, take 6 acquit, apocha, binder, recipe 7 formula 11 acquittance 15 acknowledgement

receive: get 4 take 5 admit, adopt, greet, reset 6 accept, assume, derive, obtain 7 acquire, procure 9 affiliate

receiver: 4 host 5 donee, fence 6 pernor, porter 7 breaker, catcher, hostess, rentier 8 cymaphen, receptor 9 collector, condenser, treasurer 12 receptionist

recense: 6 review, revise

recension: 6 review 8 revising 9 reviewing 11 enumeration, examination

recent: new 4 late 5 fresh 6 modern 7 current 8 neoteric

recently: 4 anew 8 latterly

receptacle: bin, box, can, cup, fat, pan, pot, tub, urn, vat 4 case, cell, cist, crib, etus, font, inro, pail, tray, vase, well, tank 5

basin, chest, etwee, torus 6 basket, bottle, bucket, carton, holder, hopper, trough
7 capcase, cistern, hanaper, humidor,
pitcher 8 canister, receiver 9 cannister,
container, continent, reservoir 11 chalkotheke

reception: tea 5 levee, party 6 accoil,
durbar, soiree 7 accueil, ovation, receipt,
welcome 8 greeting 9 admission, collation
10 admittance 13 entertainment

place: 4 hall 5 atria(pl.), foyer, salon 6
atrium, parlor 7 parlour 9 vestibule

receptive: 9 acceptant, recipient 10 hospitable

receptor: 5 basin 8 receiver 10 dispositor

recess: ala, bay 4 apse, cave, cove, grot,
hole, nook 5 ambry, cleft, crypt, niche,
sinus 6 alcove, closet, grotto, rabbet, retire 7 adjourn, conceal, retreat, seclude 8
interval, vacation 9 cessation, embrasure,
recession, remission, seclusion 1 retirement, suspension 11 withdrawing 12 intermission

recessive: 8 backward, receding

recherche: 4 rare 6 choice 8 uncommon
9 exquisite 10 farfetched

recidivation: 7 relapse 8 apostasy 11
backsliding

recipe: 7 formula, pattern, receipt 12
prescription

recipient: 4 heir 5 donee 7 alienee, dev-
isee, legatee 8 receiver 9 receiving, receptive

reciprocal: 6 mutual 9 alternate 11 convertible, correlative

reciprocate: 5 bandy, repay 6 return 8
exchange 9 alternate 10 recompense 11
countervail, interchange

recital: 4 saga, tale 5 story 6 report 7 account, concert, program 8 relation 9 narration, narrative, rehearsal, statement 10
recitation, repetition 11 declamation, description, enumeration

recitation: 7 reading, recital

recitative: 5 scena 9 narrative

recite: say 4 carp, scan, tell 5 chant, spout
6 intone 7 recount 9 enumerate 10
cantillate 12 recapitulate

reciter: 6 anteri, diseur(F.) 7 diseuse(F.)
8 narrator 12 elocutionist

reck: 4 care, deem, heed, mind 7 concern
8 estimate

reckless: 4 bold, rash 5 blind, folle, perdu
6 madcap, perdue 7 hotspur 8 careless,
headlong, heedless 9 blindfold, bodacious, daredevil, desperate, dissolute,
hotheaded, imprudent 10 neglectful, regardless 11 adventurous, extravagant,
harum-scarum, indifferent, thoughtless
13 inconsiderate, irresponsible

reckon: 4 aret, date, deem, rate, rely, tell
5 audit, count, think 6 arette, impute,
number, regard, repute 7 account, ascribe, compute, include, suppose 8 con-

sider, estimate, numerate 9 calculate,
enumerate 10 adjudicate 11 connum-
erate

reckoner: 5 abaci, brain 6 abacus 9 tabulator 10 calculator 11 comptometer

reckoning: 4 rate, scot, shot 5 chalk,
score 6 compot, esteem

machine: I.B.M. 5 adder, brain 6 abacus
9 tabulator 10 calculator

reclaim: 4 save, tame 5 train 6 ransom,
recall, redeem, reform, repair, rescue,
revoke 7 recover, restore, salvage 8 civilize, empolder 10 regenerate 11 domesticate

recline: lay, lie, sit 4 lean, loll, rest 6 repose 7 incline

reclining: 5 lying 6 supine 7 leaning,
lolling, passive, resting 8 reposing 9 accumbent, recumbent

recluse: nun 4 monk 6 hermit, hidden,
secret 7 eremite 8 anchoret, secluded,
solitary 9 anchoress, anchorite, cloistral
10 cloistered 11 sequestered

recognizance: 4 rank 5 badge, token 6
avowal, pledge, symbol 10 cognizance,
obligation, profession 11 recognition

recognize: ken, own, see 4 avow, know,
note, spot 5 admit, greet 6 accept, ack-
now, agnize, beknow, recall, review, revise, salute 7 consent, correct, recover 8
identify, perceive 9 apprehend 10 appreciate 11 acknowledge, distinguish

recoil: shy 4 kick 5 quail, wince 6 flinch,
shrink 7 rebound, retreat, reverse 8 withdraw 12 repercussion

recollect: 6 recall 7 bethink 8 remember

recollection: 4 mind 6 memory 8 memorial 9 anamnesis 11 remembrance 12
reminiscence

recommence: 6 resume

recommend: 4 tout 5 refer 6 advise,
commit, denote 7 commend, consign,
counsel, entrust 8 advocate

recompense: fee, pay 5 repay 6 amends,
bounty, reward, salary 7 premium, requite 8 requital 9 gratulate, indemnify,
reimburse, repayment 10 compensate,
remunerate 11 reciprocate, restitution,
retribution 12 compensation, remuneration 13 consideration, gratification

without: 4 free 6 gratis

reconcile: 4 wean 5 agree, atone 6 accord, adjust, pacify, regain, settle, shrive,
square 7 absolve, conform, expiate, explain, restore, reunite, satisfy 9 harmonize 10 conciliate, propitiate

recondite: 4 dark, deep 6 hidden, mystic,
occult 7 cryptic, obscure 8 abstract, abstruse, esoteric, profound 9 concealed

reconnoiter: spy 5 scout 6 survey 7 examine, explore, inquire 8 discover

record: log, tab 4 acta(pl.), book, dope,
file, memo, note, past, roll 5 actum, annal,
chart, diary, enrol, enter, entry, graph,

score 6 agenda, enroll, legend, memoir, postea, report **7** account, archive, blotter, calends, catalog, dossier, estreat, history, journal, kalends, rotulet **8** calendar, memorial, register **9** catalogue, chronicle, itinerary, narration **10** background, chronology, memorandum, transcribe, transcript
holder: **4** file **6** binder **7** cabinet
keeper: **8** recorder **9** registrar
official: **4** acta(pl.) **5** actum

recorder: 5 flute, judge **8** greffier, register **9** cartulary, registrar **10** chartulary

recount: 4 deem, tell **5** count **6** recite, reckon, relate, repeat, retail **7** account, include, narrate **8** describe, rehearse **9** enumerate

recoup: 7 recover **9** indemnify, reimburse **10** compensate, recuperate

recover: get **5** amend, rally, upset **6** obtain, recoup, reform, regain, rescue, resume, retake **7** reclaim, recruit, restore, salvage **8** overcome, retrieve **9** repossess **10** convalesce, recuperate

recovery: 13 convalescence

recreant: 5 false **6** coward, craven, crying, wretch, yellow **7** traitor **8** apostate, betrayer, cowardly, deserter, disloyal, yielding **10** traitorous, unfaithful **11** disaffected **12** mean-spirited

recreation: 4 meal, play **5** dance, hobby, sport **6** picnic **7** renewal **9** amusement, avocation, diversion **10** relaxation **11** delassement, refreshment **12** regeneration **13** divertisement, entertainment
time: **6** recess **7** holiday **8** vacation

recruit: 4 bleu(F.), boot **5** raise, rooky **6** gather, muster, revive, rookie, supply **7** draftee, private, recover, refresh, restore, soldier **8** assemble, bezonian, inductee **9** reinforce, replenish **10** recuperate, strengthen

rectangle: 6 oblong, square

rectify: 5 amend, emend, right **6** adjust, better, purify, refine, reform, remedy **7** correct, distill **8** emendate, regulate **10** straighten

rectitude 6 equity, virtue **7** fitness, honesty **10** straitness **11** uprightness **12** straightness

rector: 4 head **5** chief, ruler **6** leader, priest **7** proctor **8** director, governor, minister **9** clergyman, corrector **10** headmaster, proproctor

rectory: 5 manse **8** benefice **9** parsonage

recumbent: 4 idle **5** lying **7** leaning, resting **8** inactive, reposing **9** reclining

recuperate: 4 heal, rest **5** rally **6** recoup, regain **7** recover **9** reimburse **10** convalesce

recur: 6 advert, repeat, return **7** rearise, reoccur **8** reappear

recurrent: 9 recurring, returning **11** reappearing **12** intermittent

recusant: 9 dissenter **11** dissentient **12** nonconformer

red: 4 lake, puce, rosy, ruby **5** canna, color, coral, fiery, gules, peony, roset, ruddy **6** cerise, cherry, claret, garnet, maroon, rubric, sienna, titian **7** carmine, crimson, glowing, leftist, magenta, nacarat, radical, roseate, Russian, scarlet **8** amaranth, blushing, inflamed, rubicund **9** anarchist, bloodshot, Bolshevik, communist, Muscovite, vermilion **10** erubescent **12** bloodstained
antique: **5** canna
brown: **5** sepia **6** russet, sorrel
dye: aal, lac **4** chay, choy **5** aurin, eosin **6** aurine **8** morindin
marked with: **6** rubric
purplish: **4** lake **6** claret
yellow: **4** lama **5** aloma, brass, ochre, tenne **6** alesan, orange **7** saffron **9** alabaster, peachblow

red ape: 9 orangutan

red arsenic: 7 realgar

red-backed sandpiper: 6 dunlin

red bell: 9 columbine

red-bellied snipe: 9 dowitcher

red benjamin: 9 birthroot

red blotch: 10 adustiosis

red box: 8 official **12** bureaucratic

red bug: 7 chigger

red cedar: 5 savin **6** sabine, savine **7** juniper **8** flindosa

red cell: 11 erythrocyte

red chalk: 6 ruddle

red cobalt: 9 erythrite

red copper ore: 7 cuprite

red corpuscle deficiency: 6 anemia

red deer: roe **4** hart, hind, spay, stag

red-faced: 7 blushed, flushed **8** blushing

red fever: 10 erysipelas

red fir: 4 pine **6** spruce **7** Douglas

red gum: 10 eucalyptus, strophulus

red honeysuckle: 5 sulla

red lead ore: 8 corcoite

red man: 6 Indian

red pepper: 5 chile, chili **6** chilli

red perch: 8 rosefish

Red Planet: 4 Mars

Red Sea: 9 Erythrean
gulf: **4** Suez **5** Aqaba
peninsula: **5** Sinai
port: **9** Leningrad

red viper: 10 copperhead

red willow: 5 osier **6** cornel

redact: 4 edit **5** draft, frame **6** reduce, revise

redan: 7 rampart **8** fortress **10** breastwork **13** fortification

redargue: 6 accuse, refute **7** confute, convict, reprove **8** disprove, reproach

redbelly: 4 char **7** grouper **8** terrapin

redbird: 7 tanager **8** cardinal **9** bullfinch

redbird cactus: 7 jewbush

redbreast: 5 robin

redcap: 6 porter 7 carrier, specter, spectre 8 tarboosh 9 goldfinch, policeman

redden: 5 blush, flush, rouge

rede: saw 4 plan, tale, tell 5 story 6 advice, advise, relate, scheme 7 counsel, explain, narrate, predict, proverb 9 interpret, narration 10 prediction 11 explanation 14 interpretation

redeem: buy 4 save 6 ransom, regain, rescue 7 deliver, fulfill, reclaim, recover, release, restore 8 liberate 10 repurchase

redeye: 4 rudd 5 vireo 6 whisky 7 sunfish 10 copperhead

redhead: 5 finch 7 pochard 10 woodpecker

redolence: 4 balm, odor 5 aroma, odour, scent, smell 7 perfume 9 fragrance, sweetness

redouble: 6 reecho, repeat 7 reprise, retrace 10 ingeminate

redoubt: 6 schanz 10 breastwork 13 fortification

redoubtable: 5 dread 8 fearsome 10 formidable

redound: 5 react 6 accrue, recoil, return 7 conduce, resound 11 reverberate

redress: 5 amend, emend 6 adjust, relief, remedy 7 correct, relieve 10 compensate, reparation 12 compensation, satisfaction

redshirt: 9 anarchist 11 Garibaldian 13 revolutionist

reduce: cut 4 bant, bate, bust, diet, ease, pare, raze, thin 5 abase, abate, annul, break, level, lower, scale, slash, smelt 6 appall, change, debase, demote, depose, derate, dilute, equate, humble, impair, lessen, rebate, refine, subdue, weaken 7 abridge, assuage, commute, conquer, curtail, degrade, deplete, whittle 8 attemper, condense, contract, decrease, diminish, discount, emaciate, minimize, retrench 9 subjugate 10 annihilate, bantingize, depreciate

reduced: 6 broken 7 dwarfed 9 vestigial

reduction: cut 5 slice 6 rebate 7 cutting, meiosis 8 analysis, discount 11 contraction, degradation 12 annihilation

redundancy: 7 nimiety 8 pleonasm, verbiage 8 plethora 9 verbosity 11 periphrasis

redundant: 5 wordy 6 lavish, prolix 7 copious, diffuse, verbose 9 excessive, exuberant 10 pleonastic 11 overflowing, superfluous 12 overabundant, tautological 13 superabundant 17 circumlocutionary

redwing: 6 thrush 9 blackbird, francolin

redwood: 7 Sequoia

re-echo: 7 redoubt, resound 8 resonate 11 reverberate

reed: sag 4 dart, junk, pipe, sley, stem 5 arrow, grass, spear, stalk 7 bulrush, calamus, fistula

reed organ: 9 harmonium

reedbird: 7 warbler 8 bobolink

reedbuck: kob 4 koba 5 bohor, nagor 7 reitbok 8 antelope 9 waterbuck

reeder: 8 thatcher

reedy: 4 thin 11 arundineous

reef: bar, cay, key 4 cayo, itch, lode, vein 5 atoll, mange, shoal 6 boiler 7 shorten 8 eruption

reefer: 4 coat, eton 5 miner 6 jacket, oyster 9 cigarette 10 midshipman

reek: rig 4 emit, fume, heap, pile, vent 5 equip, exude, smell, smoke, steam, vapor 6 exhale, stench 7 seaweed 8 mountain 10 exhalation

reel: 4 drum, pirn(Sc.), roll, spin, sway, swim, wind 5 dance, lurch, spool, swift, swing, waver, whirl, wince 6 bobbin, hammer, teeter, totter, wintle 7 stagger 8 titubate, windlass

reelrall: 9 confusion 10 topsy-turvy 11 disturbance

reem: 4 uris 7 unicorn

reese: 6 scorch

reeve: pen 4 pass, wind 5 twist 6 pucker, thread 7 bailiff, wrinkle 9 enclosure, sheepfold

refection: 4 food 5 drink, lunch 6 repast 11 refreshment

refel: 6 refute, reject 7 deceive, repulse 8 disprove 9 discredit

refer: 4 cite, harp, send 5 recur 6 advert, allude, appeal, assign, charge, commit, direct, impute, regard, relate, return 7 ascribe, consult, mention, specify 8 identify 9 affiliate, appertain, attribute

referee: 5 judge 6 decide, umpire 7 arbiter 8 mediator 10 arbitrator

decision: nod

reference: 5 quote 6 aspect 7 respect 9 relevance 10 connection, pertinence 12 relationship 13 recommendance 14 recommendation

reference book: 5 atlas 7 almanac 8 handbook, syllabus 10 dictionary 12 encyclopedia

referendum: 4 vote 7 mandate 10 plebiscite

refine: 5 exalt, smelt 6 decoct, filter, finish, polish, purify 7 clarify, cleanse, concoct, elevate, improve, perfect 8 chastise, separate 9 cultivate, elaborate, subtilize 12 spiritualize

refined: 4 nice 5 civil 6 artful, chaste, polite, urbane 7 courtly, elegant, genteel 8 delicate, graceful, highbred 9 courteous, exquisite 10 fastidious

refinement: 7 finesse

refining cup: 5 cupel

reflect: 4 echo, muse, pore 5 think 6 divert, mirror, ponder 7 bethink, deflect 8 cogitate, consider, meditate, ruminate 9 reproduce 10 deliberate 11 contemplate, reverberate

reflected: 8 specular

reflection: 4 idea 5 image 6 musing 7 thought 8 likeness 10 cogitation, meditation, rumination 12 deliberation 13 consideration, contemplation
measuring device: 11 albedograph
reflective: 7 pensive
reflex: 4 bend, fold, turn 7 reflect 11 involuntary
reflux: ebb 6 ebbing, euripi(pl.), reflow 7 euripus 9 refluence, returning
refont: 6 recast
reform: 4 mend, trim 5 amend, emend, prune, renew 6 better, direct, punish, remass, repair, revise 7 censure, correct, improve, rebuild, reclaim, rectify, redress, reprove, reshape, restore 8 instruct 10 regenerate 11 reformation
refract: 6 dimish, impair 7 deflect, reflect
refraction:
device: 4 lens 5 prism 9 telescope
pert. to: 10 anaclastic
refractory: 6 immune, unruly 7 froward, restive 8 contrary, perverse, stubborn 9 camsteary, camsteery, obstinate 10 rebellious, unyielding 11 contrarious, disobedient, intractable 12 contumacious, ungovernable, unmanageable, unresponsive 13 insusceptible
refrain: bob 4 curb, shun 5 avoid, cease, check, epode, forgo 6 chorus, forego, govern 7 abstain, forbear 8 forebear, response, restrain, withhold
refresco: 5 drink 11 refreshment
refresh: 4 rest 5 bathe, cheer, renew, slake 6 caudle, revise, revive 7 comfort, enliven, freshen, hearten, quicken, restore 8 recreate, renovate 9 reanimate, replenish 10 invigorate, strengthen 12 reinvigorate
refreshing: 4 dewy 5 balmy, tonic 11 refectorial, refrigerant
refreshment: 8 refresco
refrigerant: ice 6 cooler 7 ammonia, coolant, cooling
refrigerate: ice 4 cool 5 chill 6 freeze
reft: 5 cleft 7 divided, forlorn 8 bereaved, divested
refuge: ark 4 home, port, rock 5 haven 6 asylum, bilbie, covert, harbor, resort 7 crannog(Sc.), harbour, retreat, shelter 8 crannoge(Sc.), hospital 9 sanctuary 10 protection, rendezvous, subterfuge
refugee: d.p. 5 exile 6 emigre 8 fugitive
refulgent: 6 bright 7 glowing, radiant, shining 8 splendid 9 brilliant 11 resplendent
refund: 5 repay 6 rebate 9 reimburse, repayment
refurbish: 5 renew 6 polish, revamp 7 freshen 8 brighten, renovate
refusal: no; nay, vee
refuse: nay, ort 4 balk, coom, culm, deny, dirt, dreg, junk, marc, nite, pelf, pelt, veto 5 chaff, coomb, crawm, debar, drast,

drest, dross, grith, offal, renig, repel, scrap, trash, waste, wrack 6 debris, forbid, garble, litter, lumber, reject, renege 7 backing, baggage, decline, disavow, forsake, garbage, gubbins, leaving, mullock, rubbish, repulse 8 disclaim, renounce, withhold 9 excrement, repudiate
refute: 4 deny, meet 5 avoid, rebut, refel 6 assoil 7 confute 8 disprove, infringe, redargue 9 overthrow 10 contradict
serving to: 8 elenctic 10 elenctical
regain: 6 recoup 7 recover 8 retrieve
regal: 5 jewel, royal 6 groove, kingly 7 channel, stately 8 imperial, majestic, splendid
regale: 4 dine, fete 5 feast, treat 7 delight, gratify 9 entertain
regalia: 5 crown, dress 6 finery 7 emblems, ensigns, scepter, symbols 8 costumes, insignia 11 decorations 13 paraphernalia
regality: 5 right 7 country, kingdom, royalty 8 kingship 9 privilege, territory 11 sovereignty 12 jurisdiction
regalo: 4 gift 6 dainty 7 banquet, present 8 delicacy
regard: air, awe, con, eye 4 care, deem, gaze, heed, hold, look, mind, note, rate, sake, view, yeme 5 honor, think, treat, watch 6 admire, aspect, attend, behold, esteem, glance, homage, notice, remark, repute, revere 7 adjudge, concern, observe, respect 8 consider, estimate, interest, relation 9 adoration, affection, attention, deference, reference 10 admiration, appearance, attendance, estimation, veneration 11 contemplate 13 consideration, contemplation
regarding: 5 about, anent 6 anenst
regardless: 9 negligent 10 neglectful
regatta: 4 race
regency: 4 rule 8 dominion 10 government
regenerate: 5 renew 6 reborn, redeem, reform, revive 7 convert, newborn, reclaim, restore 8 gracious, recreate, renovate
regent: 5 ruler 6 ruling 7 regnant, teacher 8 governor 9 governing
regimen: 4 diet, rule 6 system 7 control, hygiene 10 government, regulation 14 administration
regiment: 4 alai 5 cadre, order 11 systematize
member: 9 grenadier
nucleus: 5 cadre
officer: 5 boots 7 colonel
regina: 5 queen
region: des, erd, gay 4 area, belt, zone 5 clime, place, realm, space, tract 6 locale, sphere 7 climate, country, demesne, kingdom 8 district, division, latitude, province, vicinity 9 territory 12 neighborhood 13 neighbourhood

comb. form: **5** nesia

infernal: **5** Hades **7** Avernus **8** Tartarus **10** underworld

pert. to: **5** areal

surrounded by alien power: **7** enclave

upper: **5** ether

warm: **7** tropics

woodless: **4** wold **5** llano, plain, weald **6** desert, meadow, steppe **7** pasture, savanna **8** savannah

regional: 5 local **9** sectional **10** provincial

register: lid **4** book, list, roll, rota **5** album, annal, diary, enrol, enter, entry, slate **6** agenda, docket, enlist, enroll, record, roster **7** ascribe, calends, catalog, certify, coucher, kalends, license, stopper **8** archives, bookmark, calendar, recorder, registry, schedule **9** catalogue, chronical, inventory, registrar **10** enrollment **11** certificate, matriculate **12** authenticate, registration

cash: **6** damper

registrar: 8 greffier, recorder, register

regius: 4 king **5** royal **13** professorship

regle: 4 rule **6** govern **10** regulation

reglet: 5 strip **7** molding

regnal: 5 royal **6** kingly

regnant: 6 regent, ruling **8** dominant, reigning **9** prevalent **10** widespread **11** predominant

regress: 6 egress, return **10** retrograde, withdrawal **13** retrogression **14** retrogradation

regressive: 8 backward

regret: rew, rue **4** miss, ruth **5** grief, mourn, sorry, spurn **6** lament, repent, repine, sorrow **7** bethink, deplore, dislike, remorse **8** aversion, distress, forthink **9** penitence **10** misgivings, repentance **11** compunction, lamentation **14** disappointment

regular: 4 even **5** exact, sober, usual **6** formal, normal, proper, serial, stated, steady **7** amiable, correct, ordered, orderly, typical, uniform **8** complete, constant, decorous, formular, habitual, ordinary, ′ordinate, periodic, pleasant, rhythmic, rotative, standard, thorough **9** continual, customary, isometric **10** consistant, dependable, methodical, systematic **11** symmetrical

regulate: set **4** pace, rule, time **5** frame, guide, order **6** adjust, behave, direct, govern, settle **7** arrange, compose, conduct, control, correct, dispose, rectify **8** attemper, modulate **9** establish **10** discipline **11** standardize

regulating box: 8 rheostat

regulation: law **5** bylaw, canon, regle **6** assize, normal **7** precept, regimen, repulse, statute **8** ordinary **9** ordinance **14** administration

regulator: 5 valve

electricity: **9** rheometer

regulus: 4 king, star **5** matte, ruler

rehash: 7 restate **9** rechauffe

rehearse: say **4** cite, tell **5** drill, quote, speak, train **6** detail, recite, relate, repeat **7** mention, narrate, recount **8** describe, instruct **9** enumerate **12** recapitulate

rehoboam: hat **4** bowl **6** flagon **8** jeroboam

reif: 7 plunder, robbery

reign: raj **4** rule, sway **5** guide, power, realm **6** empire, govern **7** kingdom, prevail **8** dominate, dominion **9** authority, dominance **10** prevalence **11** predominate, sovereignty

reimburse: pay **5** repay **6** defray, recoup, refund **7** replace **9** indemnify **10** compensate, recompense, remunerate

reimkennar: 8 sorcerer **9** sorceress

Reims: 4 Loin, Remi

rein: 4 curb, slow, stop, turn **5** check, guide, leash, strap **6** bridle, direct, govern, haunch, kidney **7** control, repress **8** restrain **9** hindrance

reindeer: 6 tarand **7** caribou

genus: **8** rangifer

Santa's: See **Santa Claus** *reindeer.*

reinforce: 4 back **5** brace, reman **6** second **7** afforce, support **10** strengthen

reinforcement: 4 sput **9** accession

reinvigorate: 7 quicken, refresh

reit: 5 sedge **7** seaweed

reiterate: 4 drum, harp **6** repeat, resume **8** rehearse **10** ingeminate **12** recapitulate

reject: 4 defy, deny, scud **5** eject, repel, scorn, scout, spurn, vomit **6** abjure, disown, rebuff, recuse, refuse **7** cashier, decline, discard, dismiss, disobey, forsake **8** abnegate, castaway, disallow, forswear, relegate, renounce **9** blackball, ostracize, reprobate, repudiate **10** disapprove, disbelieve **13** excommunicate

rejoice: 5 cheer, elate, exult **6** please **7** delight, gladden **8** jubilate **10** exhilarate, tripudiate

rejoin: 5 reply **6** answer **7** respond, reunite

rekindle: 6 revive **7** relight

relache: 10 relaxation **12** intermission

relapse: 4 fall, sink, slip **5** lapse **7** setback, subside **9** backslide **10** recurrence **11** backsliding **12** recidivation

relate: 4 ally, tell **5** apply, refer, state **6** allude, detail, recite, report **7** connect, declare, narrate, pertain, recount, restore **8** describe, rehearse **9** appertain, associate, correlate, enumerate

related: kin **4** akin **7** cognate, germane, kindred **9** affiliate, connected **10** becousined **11** appropriate

on father's side: **6** agnate

on mother's side: **5** enate **6** enatic **7** cognate

relation: sib **5** blood, ratio **6** degree, family, status **7** account, bearing, history, kinship **8** affinity, relative, standing **10** connection, friendship **12** relationship **13** consanguinity

local: **6** ubiety

mutual: **11** correlation

second term of: **7** relatum

relative: pa: eme, kin **4** aunt, mama, papa **5** aunty, niece, uncle **6** auntie, cousin, father, friend, mother, nephew, sister **7** brother, kindred, kinsman, sibling **8** ancestor, apposite, relation, relevant **9** connected, kinswoman, pertinent **10** pertaining **11** comparative **13** corresponding, proportionate

female line: **6** bandju

material: **5** enate

relatives: **7** kinfolk **8** cousinry, kinsfolk

favoritism to: **8** nepotism

relax: **4** ease, open, rest **5** abate, loose, remit **6** divert, lessen, loosen, reduce, soften, unbend **7** mollify, release, relieve, slacken **8** mitigate

relaxation: **6** repose **7** detente(F.), relache **9** amusement **10** recreation **11** delassement

relaxed: **4** lash **7** lenient **8** flexuous

relay: **4** post, race **5** spell **6** remuda(Sp.), supply **7** forward, relieve, station **8** avantlay, transmit

release: **4** bail, drop, free, liss, trip, undo, vent **5** lisse, relax, remit, slake, untie **6** acquit, assoil, demise, exempt, loosen, parole, remise, rescue, spring **7** absolve, deliver, disband, freedom, manumit, publish, relieve, unleash, unloose **8** liberate, mitigate, unfasten **9** acquittal, discharge, disengage, eliminate, exculpate, extricate **10** emancipate, liberation, relinquish **11** acquittance, deliverance **12** emancipation

relegate: **5** exile **6** banish, commit, deport, remove **7** consign, dismiss

relent: **4** melt **5** abate, yield **6** soften **7** abandon, liquefy, mollify, slacken **8** dissolve **10** deliquesce

relentless: **4** grim, hard **5** harsh, stern, stony **6** strict **8** pitiless, rigorous **9** ferocious, immovable, merciless **10** inexorable, inflexible, persistent **11** unremitting

relevant: apt **6** timely **7** apropos, germain, germane **8** apposite **9** connected, pertinent **10** applicable **11** appropriate, referential

relevate: **5** raise **7** relieve, restore

reliable: **4** true **5** tried **6** dinkum, honest, steady, trusty **7** certain **9** authentic **10** dependable **11** trustworthy

reliance: **4** hope **5** trust **6** belief **8** affiance **10** confidence, dependence

relic: **5** curio, mummy **6** corpse, hallow, remain **7** antique, leaving, memento, remnant, residue **8** memorial, souvenir

pert. to: **9** reliquary

relic cabinet: **6** etager **7** etagere, whatnot

relict: **5** widow **7** widower **8** survivor

relief: bot **4** alms, boot, bote, dole **15** indemnification

relieve: aid **4** beet, ease, free, help, liss **5** abate, allay, beete, erase, lisse, raise, relay, slake, spare, spell **6** assist, lessen, remedy, remove, succor **7** assuage, comfort, console, deliver, lighten, redress, release, support, sustain, unloose **8** diminish, mitigate **9** alleviate, debarrass, disburden, discharge, exonerate

religieuse: nun **6** sister

religieux: **4** monk **5** pious **9** religious

religion (see also next entry)**:** **4** cult, sect **5** piety **6** voodoo **7** service, worship **8** devotion, fidelity **9** adoration, voodooism **10** conformity, observance, profession **17** conscientiousness

sect: **5** alogi

study of: **8** theology

system of: **5** faith

religion: See also under specific religions. EXAMPLES: "Jewish god," see **Judaism:**; *god of:* "Islamic priest," see **Islam:** *priest.*

religious: **4** holy **5** exact, godly, pious **6** devout, divine **7** fervent, godlike, zealous **8** devouted, faithful, monastic **9** pietistic, spiritual **10** devotional, scrupulous **13** conscientious

formally: **5** rigid **6** strict **8** orthodox **9** pharasaic

relinquish: **4** cede, drop, quit **5** demit, forgo, grant, leave, waive, yield **6** desert, forego, remise, resign **7** abandon, dispose, forsake **8** abdicate, abnegate, disgorge, renounce **9** surrender

reliquary: box **4** apse, arca **5** apsis, arcae(pl.), chest **6** casket, chasse, shrine **7** chorten

reliquiae: **6** relics **7** remains

relish: **4** dash, gust, like, tang, zest **5** achar, enjoy, gusto, sauce, savor, taste **6** canape, degust, flavor, palate, savour **7** delight, flavour **8** appetite, hautgout **9** appetizer, degustate, enjoyment, seasoning **11** inclination

kind: **5** achar, curry **6** catsup, caviar **7** botargo, chutney, mustard

relucent: **6** bright **7** radiant, shining **9** refulgent

reluct: **5** fight **6** revolt **8** struggle

reluctance: **6** revolt **8** aversion **9** aversion, hesitancy **10** opposition, repugnance, resistance **13** indisposition, unwillingness **14** disinclination

reluctant: **4** loth **5** loath **6** averse, forced **7** adverse **8** backward, grudging, hesitant, opposing **9** resisting, unwilling **11** disinclined

reluctate: **5** repel **6** oppose **9** repudiate

rely: **4** bank, base, hold, hope, lean, rest **5** count, rally, trust **6** belong, cleave, depend, expect, lippen, reckon, repose **7** believe, confide

remain: be; lie **4** bide, last, rest, stay, wait **5** abide, dwell, hover, stand, tarry, thole **6** endure, linger, reside **7** persist **8** continue

remainder: **4** rest, stub **5** stump **7** balance, remanet, remnant, residue, surplus **8** leavings, residual, residuum **9** leftovers

remains: **4** dust **5** ashes, relic, ruins, trace **6** corpse, fossil **7** vestige **9** remainder

remand: **6** commit **7** consign **8** recommit

remanent: **7** further, lasting, remains **8** enduring **9** permanent, remainder **10** additional **13** supplementary

remark: say **4** barb, heed, note, word **5** aside, gloss, state, write **6** notice, regard **7** comment, descant, express, observe **8** indicate, perceive **9** aspersion, platitude **10** animadvert, annotation, commentary, expression **11** distinguish, observation

embarrassing: **5** boner, break **7** blooper, faux pas

witty: gag, mot **4** quip **5** sally **7** sarcasm **9** witticism

remarkable: **7** notable, strange, unusual **8** uncommon **9** egregious, wonderful **11** exceptional **12** considerable **13** extraordinary

remble: **4** move, stir **6** remove

remedy: aid, bot **4** balm, boot, bote, cure, drug, gain, hale, heal, help **5** amend, salve, topic **6** arcana(pl.), relief, repair **7** arcanum, correct, cure-all, nostrum, panacea, placebo, rectify, redress, relieve **8** antidote, curative, medicine **9** treatment **10** assistance, catholicon, chevisance, corrective, reparation **13** counteractive

remember: **6** ideate, recall, record, remind, reward **7** bethink, mention **9** recollect, reminisce **11** commemorate

remembrance: **4** gift, mind **5** token **6** memory, minnie, notice, trophy **7** memento, mention **8** allusion, keepsake, memorial, souvenir **9** discourse, reference **10** impression **11** inscription **12** recollecting

remind: **6** recall

reminder: cue **4** hint, memo, note, prod, twit **7** memento, monitor **10** admonition

reminiscence: act **4** fact **5** power **6** memory **9** recalling **10** experience **11** memorabilia, remembering, remembrance **12** recollection

remise: **4** deed **5** remit **6** giving, return **7** release, replace, respite **8** granting **9** remission, surrender **10** remittance

remiss: lax **4** lazy, mild, pale **5** slack, tardy **6** gentle **7** diluted, languid, lenient, relaxed **8** careless, derelict, dilatory, heed-

less, moderate **9** dissolved, liquefied, negligent **10** neglectful **11** inattentive, thoughtless **13** irresponsible

remission: **4** liss **5** lisse **6** rebate **9** abolition, cessation, lessening **10** diminution

remit: pay **4** bate, send **5** abate, defer, enter, refer, relax **6** cancel, excuse, insert, pardon, resign, return, submit **7** abandon, absolve, forgive, forward, readmit, release, restore, slacken, suspend **8** abrogate, liberate, mitigate, moderate, postpone, recommit, transmit **9** exculpate, surrender

remittance: **9** allowance

remnant: bit, end, ort, rag **4** dreg, fent, left, part, rest, stub **5** crumb, piece, relic, scrap, trace, wrack **7** leaving, portion, remains, residue **8** fragment **9** remainder **10** suggestion

remodel: **6** change, recast **7** rebuild **11** reconstruct

remolade: **5** sauce **8** dressing, ointment

remonstrance: **10** benedicite **13** expostulation

remonstrate: **5** argue **6** object **7** declare, profess, protest **8** complain **11** demonstrate, expostulate

remora: **4** clog, drag, fish, pega **5** delay **7** pegador **9** hindrance **10** impediment

remord: **5** taint **6** excite, ponder, rebuke **7** afflict, censure, remorse **8** remember

remorse: rue **4** pity, ruth **5** grief, qualm **6** regret, sorrow **7** penance **8** distress **9** penitence, repentent **10** compassion, contrition **11** compunction

remote: far, off **4** afar, cool **5** alien, aloof, faint, vague **6** forane, slight **7** distant, faraway, foreign, removed **8** secluded, separate **10** abstracted, impersonal, unfriendly **12** inaccessible

more: **7** endmost, further **8** ulterior

most: **6** ultima **9** diametric

remove: rid **4** bate, dele, doff, fire, free, kill, move, oust, pare, raze, rend, sack, void, weed **5** amove, apart, avoid, elide, eloin, erase, evict, expel, strip **6** betake, cancel, change, convey, deduct, delete, depose, disbar, distal, eloign, recall, remble, retire, uproot **7** deprive, despoil, dismiss, extract, uncover, whittle **8** abstract, disclose, discover, dislodge, displace, relegate, separate, supplant, transfer **9** eliminate, eradicate, translate **10** disconnect **11** assassinate

removed: off **4** away, move **5** aloof, apart **6** remote **7** distant **10** abstracted

remover: **6** porter **7** carrier, drayman, solvent **9** scavenger **10** contractor

remuneration: pay **5** wages **6** reward **7** payment, stipend **8** requital **9** emolument, repayment **10** recompense **12** compensation, satisfaction **13** consideration, gratification, reimbursement

remunerative: **10** beneficial, profitable

Remus: *brother:* 7 Romulus
slayer: 7 Romulus

renable: 4 glib 5 ready 6 fluent 8 eloquent

renaissance: 7 rebirth, revival 10 renascence

rencounter: 4 duel, meet 5 clash, fight 6 action, battle, combat, debate 7 collide, contest, meeting 8 conflict 9 collision, encounter

rend: cut, rip 4 pull, rent, rive, slit, tear 5 break, burst, sever, split, wrest 6 breach, cleave, divide, enrive, pierce, remove, screed, sunder 7 abscind, dispart, disrupt, rupture 8 fracture, lacerate, separate 9 dismember 12 disintegrate

render: do; pay, put, try 4 emit, give, make, melt 5 treat, yield 6 depict, recite, repeat, return, submit 7 clarify, deliver, exhibit, extract, furnish, inflict, payment, perform, present, requite, restore 8 transmit 9 interpret, represent, surrender, translate 10 contribute

rendezvous: 4 date, meet 5 place, tryst 6 refuge 7 hangout, meeting, retreat 8 assemble, mobilize 9 agreement, gathering 11 appointment

rendition: 8 delivery 9 surrender 11 deliverance, performance, translation 14 interpretation

renegade: rat 5 rebel 6 bolter 7 traitor 8 apostate, deserter, fugitive, renegado, turncoat 10 changeling

renege, renig: 4 deny 5 welsh 6 desert, refuse, revoke 7 decline 8 renounce

renew: 4 beet 5 beete 6 extend, refill, repair, repeat, resume, revamp, revive 7 freshen, rebuild, refresh, replace, restore 8 reassume, re-create, renovate 9 replenish 10 invigorate, recommence, regenerate, rejuvenate 11 re-establish, resuscitate 12 redintegrate

renitent: 7 opposed 8 opposing 9 obstinate, resistant 12 recalcitrant

rennet: lab 5 apple 6 curdle, keslop 7 earning(Sc.) 8 cheeslep, cheeslip, earnings(Sc.), membrane 9 coagulate
ferment: 6 enzyme, rennin

renomme: 8 renowned 10 celebrated

renounce: 4 cede, defy, deny 5 cease, forgo, renay, renig, waive 6 abjure, desert, disown, forego, forlet, forsay, recant, reject, renege, repeal, resign 7 abandon, disavow, forsake, retract 8 abdicate, abnegate, disclaim, forspeak, forswear, renounce 9 repudiate, surrender 10 abrenounce, relinquish 12 abrenunciate

renovate: 4 redo 5 alter, clean, renew 6 purify, repair, resume, revive 7 cleanse, furbish, refresh, replace, restore 10 invigorate, regenerate

renown: rap 4 fame, note 5 eclat, glory, kudos, rumor 6 report 7 acclaim 8 eminence 9 celebrity 10 reputation 11 celebration, distinction

renowned: 5 known 11 illustrious

rent (see also **rend**): let, pay 4 gape, hire, hole, rime, toll 5 censo, chink, cleft, crack, cuddy, gavel, gorge, lease, share, split, yield 6 breach, engage, income, profit, return, reward, schism 7 fissure, opening, revenue, rupture, tribute
high: 8 rackrent
paid: tac
transfer: 6 attorn

rental: 4 cost, list 5 house 8 schedule 9 apartment

rente: 6 income 7 annuity, revenue

renter: 6 lessee, tenant 8 occupant

renverse: 7 reverse 8 overturn 9 overthrow

reopen: 6 resume 10 reeommence

repair: fix 4 darn, heal, help, mend 5 amend, patch, piece, refit, renew 6 remedy, return, revamp, revive 7 correct, rebuild 8 renovate

reparation: 4 bote 6 amende, amends, reward 7 damages, redress 8 requital 9 amendment, atonement, indemnity, repairing 10 recompense 11 restitution 12 compensation, distribution, partitioning 14 redistribution

repartee: wit 5 reply 6 retort 7 riposte

repast: tea 4 bait, feed, food, meal 5 bever, feast, snack, treat 6 dinner 7 banquet 8 mealtime 9 collation, refection 11 refreshment
pert. to: 8 prandial

repatriation: 6 return 11 restoration

repay: pay 4 meed 5 appay 6 avenge, profit, punish, refund, return, reward 7 deserve, requite, restore 9 gratulate, reimburse, retaliate 10 compensate, recompense, remunerate 11 reciprocate

repeal: 5 amend, annul, emend 6 appeal, cancel, recall, revoke 7 abolish, rescind, retract, reverse 8 abrogate, derogate, renounce, withdraw

repeat: bis(It.), din 4 cite, echo, rame 5 ditto, quote, recap, recur 6 encore, parrot, resume, retell 7 iterate, recount, reprise, restate 8 redouble 9 duplicate, reiterate 10 ingeminate, repetition 11 battologize 12 recapitulate

repeatedly: oft 5 often 10 frequently 11 continually 12 continuously

repeater: gun 5 rifle, watch 6 pistol 7 firearm 10 recidivist

repel: 4 beat, stop 5 check, debar, force 6 combat, defend, oppose, rebuff, refuse, reject, remove, resist 7 decline, disgust, repulse 8 vanquish 10 extinguish

repellent: 4 grim 5 harsh 9 repugnant 10 forbidding

repent: rue 5 atone 6 grieve, lament, regret 7 reptant 8 crawling, creeping, forthink, penitent

repentance: 4 pity, ruth 5 shame 7 penance, remorse **9** attrition, penitence **10** contrition **11** compunction

repentant: 11 penitential

repercussion: 4 blow **6** impact, recoil **7** rebound **8** reaction **10** reflection **11** reiteration **12** ballottement **13** reverberation

repertory: 4 list **5** index **7** theater, theatre **8** calendar, magazine, treasury **9** catalogue **10** collection, storehouse

repetition: bis **4** copy, echo, rote **5** rondo **6** dilogy, encore **7** replica, tremolo **9** iteration, rehearsal **10** redundancy **12** reproduction

of others: **7** echolia, mimicry **9** echolalia

repine: 4 fail, fret, pine, wane **5** mourn **6** grouse, lament, regret **7** grumble, whimper **8** complain, languish

replace: 4 stet **5** reset, stead **6** follow **7** relieve, restore, succeed **8** supplant **9** reimburse, supersede **10** substitute

replacement: 6 ersatz **9** successor **10** substitute

replenish: 4 feed, fill **5** renew, store

replete: fat **4** full, rife **5** sated, stout **6** filled, gorged **7** bloated, implete, stocked, stuffed **8** complete **9** abounding, surfeited

replica: 5 image **6** carbon, ectype **8** likeness **9** facsimile **10** repetition **12** reproduction

replicate: 4 bend, fold **5** reply **6** repeat **8** manifold, repeated **9** duplicate, multifold

reply: 4 echo, fold, sass **5** rebut **6** answer, oracle, re-echo, rejoin, repeat, retort, return **7** respond, retract, riposte **8** repartee, response **9** rejoinder **11** replication

report: pop **4** fame, tell, word **5** bruit, noise, rumor, state, story **6** breeze, cahier(F.), delate, digest, recite, relate, repeat, return, rumour **7** account, crackle, hansard, hearing, hearsay, inkling, narrate, recital, summary **8** announce, describe **9** circulate, grapevine, narration, narrative

false: fib, lie **6** canard **7** slander **8** tall-tale **12** misstatement

reporter: cub **6** writer **7** newsman **9** columnist **10** journalist

symbol: **6** thirty

repose: lay, lie, set, sit **4** calm, ease, rely, rest, seat **5** peace, place, quiet, sleep **6** relief **7** compose, confide, deposit, dignity, recline, replace, restore, support **8** calmness, serenity **9** composure, quietness **10** relaxation, repository **11** downsitting **12** requiescence, tranquillity

repository: ark, box **4** bank, file, safe, shop **5** ambry, capsa, chest, vault **6** closet, museum **7** arsenal, capsule, granary, storage **8** magazine, treasury **9** confidant, reliquary, sepulcher, warehouse **10** depository, storehouse

reposoir: 5 altar

repossess: 6 regain **7** recover

reprehend: 4 warn **5** blame, chide **6** rebuke **7** censure, reprove **8** admonish, disprove **9** reprimand

reprehensible: 8 criminal, culpable

represent: act **4** show **5** enact **6** clothe, denote, depict, typify **7** exhibit, express, picture, portray, produce, profess **8** describe, simulate **9** delineate, designate, exemplify, reproduce, symbolize **10** substitute **11** impersonate **12** characterize

representation: map **4** icon, idol, ikon **5** chart, graph, image, model **6** avowal, blazon, sample **7** account, diagram **8** likeness, notation **9** portrayal, statement **10** similitude **11** histrionics, performance, portraiture

favorable: **14** recommendation

representative: 4 heir **5** agent, envoy **6** consul, deputy, legate **7** tribune **8** delegate, executor, exponent, salesman **10** ambassador **12** illustrating, illustrative **13** administrator

repress: 4 bury, curb, hush, rein, stop **5** check, choke, crush, daunt, press, quell **6** bridle, deaden, reduce, stifle, subdue **7** depress **8** compress, restrain, suppress, withhold **9** constrain, overpower

reprieve: 5 defer, delay **6** escape **7** respite, suspend **8** postpone **12** postponement

reprimand: 4 call **5** check, chide, slate **6** rebuff, rebuke **7** censure, chapter, chasten, repress, reproof, reprove **9** reprehend **12** reprehension

reprint: 4 copy

reprisal: 7 revenue **8** requital

reprise: 8 reassume **10** compensate, recommence, repetition **12** reprehension

reproach: 4 blot, slur, twit **5** abuse, blame, braid, chide, shame, shend, sully, taunt **6** accuse, infamy, rebuke, revile, stigma, vilify **7** censure, condemn, reprove, traduce, upbraid **8** besmirch, disgrace, dishonor **9** bespatter, challenge, contumely, discredit, disrepute, invective **10** correction, exprobrate, opprobrium, scurrility **11** impeachment **12** vilification **13** animadversion **15** discommendation

reprobate: 4 hard **5** Satan, scamp **6** disown, rascal, reject **7** abandon, condemn, corrupt, vicious **8** castaway, denounce, hardened **9** blameable, reprehend, scoundrel **10** censurable, condemned, disallowed **11** blameworthy, disapproved **12** unprincipled **13** reprehensible

reproduce: 4 copy, draw **6** repeat **7** imitate **8** multiply **9** duplicate, propagate, represent **11** reconstruct

reproduction: 6 ectype **7** fission, replica **8** likeness **9** photostat **11** counterpart **13** proliferation

reproductive: 8 prolific

reprove: 4 flay, rate, slam **5** blame, check, chide, roast, scold, shame **6** be-

rate, rebuff, rebuke, refute, reject **7** censure, confute, correct, lecture, upbraid **8** admonish, carritch, chastise, disgrace, disprove, redargue, reproach **9** castigate, challenge, objurgate, reprehend, reprimand, reprobate **10** administer, animadvert, carritches **11** expostulate

reptant: 8 crawling, creeping

reptile: 4 croc, worm **5** snake **6** turtle **8** dinosaur, tortoise **9** alligator, crocodile, pterosaur **10** dinosauria(pl.), predentate **11** pterodactyl, pterosauria(pl.)

scale: **5** scute

reptiles: *age of:* **8** Mesozoic

group: **6** sauria

reptilian: low **4** mean **5** snaky **6** lizard, sneaky **7** reptant, saurian, serpent **8** crawling, creeping, ophidian **9** groveling, malignant **10** despicable

republic: 5 state **9** democracy **10** commonweal, government **12** commonwealth

imaginary: **7** Oceania

repudiate: 4 defy, deny **6** abjure, disown, recant, refuse, reject **7** decline, disavow, discard, divorce, retract **8** abrogate, disclaim, renounce **9** disaffirm

repugn: 6 oppose, resist

repugnance: 5 odium **6** enmity, hatred **7** disgust, dislike **8** aversion, distaste, loathing **9** antipathy, hostility, repulsion **10** abhorrence, antagonism, opposition, reluctance **11** abomination, contrariety, incongruity **13** inconsistency **14** disinclination **15** incompatibility **16** disagreeableness **17** contradictoriness

repugnant: 8 inimical **9** offensive, repellent **10** refractory **12** disagreeable **14** irreconcilable

repulse: 4 deny, foil, rout **5** check, fling, rebut, refel, repel **6** defeat, denial, rebuff, refuse, reject **7** exclude, refusal **9** rejection

repulsion: ug(Sc.) **7** dislike **8** aversion, distaste **10** repugnance

repulsive: 4 dain, evil, loth, ugly, vile **5** loath, toady **6** odious **7** fulsome, hateful, loathly **9** offensive, repellent, repugnant **10** disgusting, forbidding **11** distasteful, gorgonesque

repurchase: 6 redeem

reputable: 4 good **8** credible **10** creditable **11** responsible

reputation: 4 fame, lose, name, note, odor **5** glory, honor, izzat, odour, stamp **6** credit, honour, renown, repute **7** respect **9** attribute, character **11** distinction **13** consideration

loss of: **7** scandal

repute: 4 fame **5** honor, worth **6** credit, esteem, regard, revere **7** account, respect, suppose **9** character **10** ascription, estimation

reputed: dit **8** putative

request: ask, beg, sue **4** plea, pray, suit,

wish **5** apply, crave, order **6** appeal, b‹ hest, demand, invite **7** entreat, prithe‹ solicit **8** entreaty, petition, rogation **1** application **12** solicitation, supplicatio‹

requiem: 4 hymn, mass, rest, song **5** chant, dirge, peace, quiet **7** service

requiescat: 4 wish **6** prayer

requiescence: 6 repose

requin: 5 shark **8** man-eater

require: ask **4** lack, need **5** claim, crave, exact, force **6** behove, compel, demand, enjoin, entail, expect, oblige **7** behoove **9** postulate **11** necessitate

requirement: 4 duty **9** formality, requisite

requisite: 4 need **7** needful **9** condition, essential **11** requirement **13** indispensable

requisition: 5 order **6** billet, demand **9** embargo, request **11** application, requirement

requital: 7 guerdon **8** reprisal **9** vengeance **11** antapodosis, retribution

requite: pay **5** atone, repay **6** acquit, avenge, defray, return, reward **7** deserve, gratify, revenge **9** retaliate **10** compensate, recompense

reredos: 4 wall **6** screen **7** drapery **9** backplate, partition

reree: 7 cattail

reremouse: bat

res: 5 point, thing **6** matter

resale: 8 exchange

resay: 6 repeat **7** iterate

rescind: 4 void **5** annul **6** cancel, repeal, revoke **7** abolish, retract **8** abrogate **11** countermand

rescissible: 9 revokable **11** rescindable

rescript: 5 order **6** answer, decree **9** rewriting **11** counterpart

rescue: 4 free, save **6** ransom, redeem, succor **7** deliver, reclaim, recover, release, salvage **8** delivery, liberate **9** extricate **11** deliverance

rese: 4 rage, rush **5** hurry, onset, quake, shake **7** impulse, tremble **8** rashness

research: 7 inquiry **11** examination **13** investigation **15** experimentation

reseau: net **6** ground **7** network **10** foundation

resect: 6 excise

resemblance: 5 image **6** simile, symbol **7** analogy **8** affinity, likeness, vicinity **9** agreement, imitation, semblance **10** comparison, similarity, similitude **12** assimilation **14** representation

resembling: 4 like **5** alike **11** approximate

resentment: ire **4** gall **5** anger, depit, pique, spite **6** animus, choler, enmity, grudge, hatred, malice, rancor, spleen **7** dudgeon, umbrage **8** acrimony **9** animos ity, annoyance hostility, malignity **10** i‹ ritation **11** displeasure, indignation

reserve: 4 cash, cave, fund, keep, save 5 spare, stock, store 6 assets, retain, supply 7 backlog, bespeak, caution, modesty, shyness, silence, surplus 8 coldness, distance, forprise, preserve, withhold 9 exception, reservoir, restraint, retention, reticence 10 constraint, diffidence, discretion, limitation, substitute 11 reservation, taciturnity

reserved: coy 4 cold 5 aloof, staid, taken 6 sedate 8 backward, cautious 15 incommunicative, uncommunicative

reservoir: vat 4 font, pond, pool, sump, tank 5 basin, fount, stope, store 6 cenote, supply 7 cistern, favissa, forebay, piscina, reserve 8 favissae(pl.). fountain

re-set: 4 help 5 abode, alter 6 harbor, refuge, resort, succor 7 receipt, receive, replace, secrete, shelter 9 receiving 10 receptacle

resiance: 5 abode 9 residence

reside: big, lie 4 bigg, live, room, stay 5 abide, dwell, habit, lodge 6 remain, settle 7 inhabit, sojourn, subside 8 habitate

residence: 4 home, seat, shed 5 abode, house, villa 6 biding, castle, palace 7 habitat, mansion 8 domicile, residuum, sediment 9 apartment 10 habitation, villanette 13 collectorship

resident: cit 6 lessee, tenant 7 burgess, citizen 8 inherent, occupant

residue: ash 4 dreg, lees, marc, orts, rest, silt, slag 5 ashes, dregs 6 cinder, excess, relics, sludge, sordes 7 balance, remains, remnant 8 leavings, remanent, residuum, sediment 9 remainder

residuum: 8 hangover 9 remainder

resign: 4 cede, quit 5 demit, remit, yield 6 devote, submit 7 abandon, consign, deliver 8 abdicate, renounce 9 surrender 10 relinquish

resignation: 8 patience 9 endurance 12 acquiescence

resile: 6 recede, return 7 rebound, retract, retreat 8 withdraw

resilient: 5 toned 7 buoyant, elastic, springy 8 bouncing, stretchy 9 recoiling, returning 10 rebounding

resin, rosin: alk, gum, lac, tar 4 aloe, balm, folu 5 amber, anime, animi, copal, damar, elemi, gugal, gugul, loban, myrrh, pitch 6 balsam, charas, dammar, derrid, elemin, googul, salban, storax 7 acouchi, ambrite, aroiera, copaiba, copaiva, derride, exudate, fluavil, galipot, hartite, ladanum, retinol 8 alkitran, bdellium, fluavile, gedanite, glessite, guaiacum, labdanum, retinite, sandarac 9 alchitran, colophony, elaterite 11 colophonium 12 frankincense

purified: 7 shellac

resist: 4 buck, fend 5 rebel, repel 6 baffle, combat, defeat, defend, impugn, oppose, wither 7 contest, prevent 9 frustrate, gainstand, withstand

resistance: 6 rebuff 7 defence, defense 9 hostility, renitence 10 antagonism, oppugnance 13 recalcitrance

resistance box: 8 rheostat

resistant: 4 hard 8 obdurate, renitent

resolute: 4 bold 5 fixed 7 animose, animous 8 positive, resolved, stalwart, unshaken 9 unbending 10 unwavering

resolution: vow 4 grit, thew 5 heart, nerve 7 purpose, resolve, verdict 8 analysis, backbone, decision, firmness, proposal, strength 9 assurance, certainty, constancy, fortitude, hardihood, statement, sternness, stoutness 10 conviction, separation, steadiness 11 intrepidity, persevering 12 deliberation, faithfulness, perseverance, resoluteness 13 determination, inflexibility, steadfastness 14 simplification 15 disentanglement

resolve: 4 free, melt 5 relax, untie 6 answer, assoil, dispel, inform, loosen, reduce, remove, settle 7 appoint, dispose, explain, liquefy, scatter, unravel 8 conclude, dissolve, enfeeble, persuade, separate

resonant: 7 ringing, vibrant 8 sonorous, sounding 10 resounding 11 reverberant

resort: go; spa 4 howf 5 crowd, haunt, howff, joint, place, visit 6 betake, casino, refuge, return, revert, throng 7 company 8 frequent, habitual, recourse 10 assemblage, honkeytonk

health: spa 9 sanatoria(pl.) 10 sanatorium, sanitarium

place of: 5 haunt 7 purlieu

resound: 4 echo, peal, ring 5 clang 6 re-echo 11 reverberate

resourceful: apt 5 sharp 7 fertile

resources: 5 funds, means, money 6 assets, stocks, stores 7 resorts 8 reserves, supplies, supports 10 expedients 12 contrivances

guardian: 15 conservationist

respect: awe 4 heed 5 defer, honor, value 6 admire, esteem, homage, regard, revere 7 concern, neglect, observe, respite, tribute, worship 8 postpone, venerate 9 attention, deference, reference, reverence 10 admiration

pay: 5 greet 6 salute

respectable: 4 good 6 decent, honest, proper 7 fausant 9 estimable, honorable, reputable 10 creditable 11 presentable

respectful: 5 civil 7 careful, duteous 11 ceremonious

respective: 4 each 6 sundry 7 partial 9 regardful 10 individual, particular

respiration: 6 breath 7 eupnoea 9 breathing

difficulty: 4 rale 5 cough 7 dyspnea 8 dyspnoea

respire: 4 live, sigh 6 exhale, inhale 7 breathe

respite: 4 lull, rest 5 delay, pause 6 recess 7 leisure 8 interval, reprieve, sur-

cease **9** cessation **10** suspension **12** intermission, postponement

resplendent: 6 bright **7** aureate, blazing, radiant, shining **8** dazzling, glorious, gorgeous, lustrous, splendid **9** brilliant, refulgent **10** epiphanous, flamboyant

respond: 4 echo, feel **5** react, reply, write **6** accord, answer, pillar, rejoin, retort, return **8** response **10** correspond

response: 4 word **5** verse **6** anthem, chorus, phrase **7** refrain **8** sentence

responsible: 8 amenable **9** accordant, reputable **10** answerable, dependable, sufficient **13** correspondent

responsibility: 4 care, onus **6** burden, charge **9** liability **10** obligation **11** reliability **14** accountability **15** trustworthiness

responsive: 6 mutual **8** amenable **9** sensitive **11** sympathetic

res publica: 5 state **8** republic **10** commonweal **12** commonwealth

rest: lay, lie, set, sit **4** calm, ease, hang, lair, lean, liss, prop, rely, seat, slip, stay, stop **5** abide, ceast, found, lisse, pause, peace, quiet, relax, renew, repos(F.), sleep, stand **6** alight, cesura, depend, desist, remain, repose, settle **7** balance, caesura, comfort, leisure, refresh, remains, remnant, reposal, residue, respite, shelter, support, surplus **8** breather, interval, lodgment, vacation **9** cessation, establish, quietness, remainder, stillness **10** immobility, inactivity, relaxation **11** refreshment **12** intermission, peacefulness, tranquillity

noonday: nap **6** siesta

rest house: inn **4** chan, khan **5** hotel, serai **6** abalam, hostel, tavern **7** chhatri

restate: 6 reword **8** reassert

restaurant: inn **4** cafe **5** diner, hotel **6** bistro, tavern **7** automat, beanery, cabaret, tearoom **9** cafeteria, chophouse, hashhouse **10** rotisserie, steakhouse **11** rathskeller(G.)

restitution: 6 amends, return **8** recovery **10** recompense, reparation **11** restoration **12** compensation **13** reimbursement

restive: 5 balky **6** uneasy, unruly **7** fidgety, nervous **8** restless, stubborn **9** impatient **10** refractory **12** unmanageable

restless: 6 fidget, fitful, haunty, hectic, roving, uneasy **7** agitato(It.), fidgety, fretful, inquiet, restive, unquiet **8** agitated, feverish, stirring **9** disturbed, impatient, sleepless, unsettled, wandering **10** disquieted, reposeless **12** discontented

restoration: 10 reparation **11** restitution

restorative: 7 anodyne **8** salutary

restore: 4 cure, heal, mend **5** amend, atone, renew, repay, right **6** redeem, refund, repair, return, revive **7** convert, rebuild, recover, replace **8** renovate **9** reinstate, resurrect **10** regenerate **11** reconstruct, re-establish, resuscitate **12** redintegrate, rehabilitate

printer's mark: **4** stet

restrain: bar, dam **4** bate, bind, calm, clog, curb, hold, rein, rule, stay, stop **5** chain, check, cramp, deter, guard, limit, still, stint **6** arrest, behave, bridle, coerce, detain, fetter, forbid, govern, halter, hamper, hinder, pinion, tether **7** abridge, abstain, chasten, command, confine, contain, control, deprive, forbear, inhibit, prevent, repress, shackle, trammel **8** attemper, compesce, compress, conclude, imprison, prohibit, restrict, suppress, withhold **9** constrain, detention **12** circumscribe

restrained: 6 severe **8** reserved **9** hidebound **11** disciplined

restraint: bit **5** force **7** barrier, durance, reserve **9** avoidance, reticence **10** internment

restrict: bar **4** curb **5** bound, cramp, limit, scant, stint **6** censor, coerce, hamper, modify, ration **7** astrict, confine, repress, tighten **8** contract, derogate, prohibit, restrain, straiten **9** constrict **12** circumscribe

restricted: 5 local **6** finite, narrow, strait **9** parochial **10** provincial

restriction: 10 regulation **11** reservation **13** qualification

restrictive: 7 binding **8** limiting **9** stringent

resty: 5 quiet **6** rancid **7** restive **8** sluggish

result: go; end, sum **4** leap, rise **5** ensue, event, fruit, issue, score, total **6** accr◌, effect, follow, sequel, spring, upsho◌ outcome, proceed, redound **8** afte◌ decision **9** aftermath, eventuate, ◌ nate **10** conclusion **11** achieveme◌ ◌ sequence, termination

result in: 5 cause

resume: 5 renew **6** reopen, ◌ review **7** summary **8** continue, r◌ ◌y **9** epitomize, reiterate, summarize **10** recommence **12** recapitulate **14** recapitulation

resurrection: 7 rebirth, revival **11** restoration

resuscitate: 6 revive **7** quicken, restore **8** revivify

retailer: 6 dealer **8** huckster, merchant

retain: 4 hire, hold, keep, save **6** adhere, athold, behold, employ **7** contain, prevent, reserve **8** maintain, preserve, remember, restrain **9** entertain, recollect

retainer: fee **4** cage, hewe **5** frame **6** menial, minion, vassal **7** hobbler **8** follower **9** burkundaz **11** burkundauze

retaining: 9 retentive

retaliate: 5 repay **6** avenge, punish, retort **7** requite, revenge

retaliation: 6 talion **8** reprisal, requital **11** retribution

retard: 4 slow **5** brake, catch, defer, delay, deter, trash **6** belate, deaden, detain, hinder, impede **8** encumber, obstruct, postpone, restrain **10** decelerate

retardant: 8 obstacle

retardation: lag

retch: gag 4 hawk, spit 5 reach, vomit 6 expand, extend, strain 7 stretch

retention: 6 memory 7 holding, keeping 8 learning 10 retainment 11 maintenance, remembering

rethe: 5 cruel 6 ardent, fierce, severe

retiarius: 9 gladiator

reticent: 4 dark 6 silent 7 sparing 8 discreet, reserved, retiring, taciturn 9 secretive 10 mysterious 15 uncommunicative

reticule: bag 4 etui 5 cabas, etwee 6 pocket, sachet 7 handbag, reticle, workbag

reticulum: net 7 network, stomach 8 meshwork

retinaculum: 6 frenum

retinue: 4 band, crew, ging, rout, suit, tail 5 harem, meiny, suite, train 6 attend, escort 7 cortege, service 8 equipage 9 entourage, retainers 10 attendance, attendants

retire: go; ebb 5 leave 6 depart, recede, recess, remove, vanish 7 pension, retreat 8 withdraw 9 disappear, sequester

retired: 4 abed, lone 5 quiet 6 secret 7 private, recluse 8 abstruse, emeritus, reserved, secluded, solitary 9 recondite

retiring: shy 5 timid 6 modest 7 bashful, fugient 8 reserved 9 diffident 11 unobtrusive

retort: mot 4 quip, turn 5 facer, repay, reply, sally 6 answer, recoil, return, ripost 7 alembic, cornute, respond, riposte 8 blizzard, repartee 9 retaliate

retortion, retorsion: 7 bending 8 reprisal, twisting 10 reflection

retract: 4 bend 6 abjure, cancel, disown, recall, recant, remove, repeal, retire, revoke 7 disavow, prevent, rescind, retreat 8 restrain, withdraw 9 repudiate

retraction: 8 palinode

retral: 8 backward 9 posterior 10 retrograde

retreat: den 4 abri, cave, holt, lair, nest, nook, rout 5 arbor, bower 6 arbour, asylum, harbor, recede, recess, refuge, retire 7 harbour, privacy, retiral, shelter 8 solitude, withdraw 9 departure. hibernate, sanctuary, seclusion 10 rendezvous, retirement, sanitarium, withdrawal

retrench: cut 4 bate, omit, pare 6 delete, excise, lessen, reduce, remove 7 abridge, curtail, repress 8 decrease, diminish 9 economize, intercept

retrenchment: 5 ditch 7 parapet, rampart 8 traverse 10 breastwork 12 entrenchment

retribution: pay 6 return, reward 7 nemesis, revenge, tribute 8 requital 9 vengeance 10 punishment, recompense
    goddess of: Ate

retrieve: 6 recall, regain, revive 7 recover, restore 8 discover 10 recuperate

retrograde: 4 slow 6 recede, retral 7 decline, inverse, opposed, regress 8 backward, contrary, decadent, inverted, rearward, withdraw 9 catabolic, reversely 10 degenerate, retrogress 11 deteriorate

retrogression: 7 regress 8 fallback 9 decadence 12 degeneration 14 retrogradation

retrogressive: 8 backward

retrospective: 6 review 8 backward 11 retroactive 13 contemplative

retund: 4 dull 5 blunt 6 refute, subdue 9 attenuate

return: lob 4 bend, turn 5 recur, remit, repay, yield 6 advert, answer, profit, render, report, retort, revert 7 regress, replace, reprise, requite, respond, restore, revenue, reverse 8 requital, response 9 repayment, retaliate, reversion 10 recompense, recurrence 11 reciprocate, replacement, restoration 12 reappearance 13 reciprocation

reunite: 6 rejoin 9 reconcile

reus: 9 defendant

revamp: 5 renew

reveal: bid 4 bare, blab, jamb, open, show, tell, wray 5 exert 6 betray, bewray, descry, detect, expose, impart; unveil 7 confide, develop, display, divulge, exhibit, uncover 8 announce, decipher, develope, disclose, discover, evidence, manifest, revelate 11 communicate

reveille: 4 call, dian 5 diana, levet 6 signal

revel: joy 4 orgy, riot, wake 5 feast, randy, spree, watch 6 bezzle, gavall, high-go 7 carouse, delight, revelry, roister 8 carnival, carousal, domineer, festival 9 celebrate, festivity 11 celebration, merrymaking 12 conviviality

revelant: 9 pertinent

revelation: 4 tora 5 torah 9 discovery 10 disclosure 13 manifestation

reveler, reveller: 8 bacchant 9 bacchanal, roisterer 10 merrymaker
    cry: 4 evoe

revenant: 5 ghost 7 specter 9 recurring 10 apparition

revendicate: 7 reclaim, recover

revenge: 6 avenge 7 requite 8 requital 9 retaliate 11 retribution

revenue: 4 rent 5 yield 6 income, profit, rental, return 7 finance 8 interest

reverberate: 4 echo, ring 6 re-echo, return 7 reflect, resound

reverberating: 7 reboant 8 resonant 12 repercussive 13 reverberatory

revere: 4 love 5 adore, honor 6 admire, esteem, regard, repute 7 respect, worship 8 venerate

reverence: awe 4 fear 5 dread, piety 6 homage 8 devotion 9 deference, obeisance, solemnity
    gesture of: 8 kneeling 11 genuflexion 12 genuflection

reverend: sri **4** holy **5** abbot **6** clergy, sacred **9** clergyman, monsignor

reverent: **6** humble **7** dutiful

reverie: **5** dream **6** musing, vision **7** fantasy **8** daydream

reverse: **5** annul, upset **6** defeat, invert, regard, repeal, revoke **7** abolish, backset, convert, subvert **8** backward, contrary, converse, disaster, opposite, overturn **9** disaffirm, overthrow, transpose **10** misfortune **11** countermand

reversional: **9** atavistic

revert: **5** react **6** advert, return, revive **7** escheat, recover, reverse **9** backslide **11** antistrophe

revest: **4** robe **5** dress **6** attire, clothe **8** reinvest **9** reinstate

review: **4** edit **5** recap **6** parade, resume, survey **7** account **8** ceremony, critique **9** criticise, criticism, criticize, re-examine **10** certiorari, inspection, periodical, reconsider, retrospect **11** examination

revile: **4** hate, rail **5** abuse, blame, brawl, scold **6** debase, malign, vilify **7** deprave **8** reproach **9** blaspheme **10** calumniate

revince: **6** refute

revise: **4** edit **5** alter, amend, emend **6** change, redact **7** correct, improve, recense **8** readjust **9** castigate, reexamine, supervise

reviser, revisor: **10** diaskeuast

revival: **6** recall **7** rebirth **11** renaissance **12** reproduction **13** recrudescence

revive: daw **4** wake **5** rally, renew, rouse **6** return **7** enliven, freshen, quicken, recover, refresh, restore **8** reawaken, recreate, rekindle, revivify **9** reanimate, refreshen, resurrect **10** regenerate, rejuvenate **11** resuscitate **12** reinvigorate

revoice: **4** echo **5** refit **7** restore

revoke: **5** adeem, annul, check, renig **6** cancel, recall, recant, renege, repeal **7** abolish, fenagle, finagle, prevent, repress, rescind, retract, reverse **8** abrogate, restrain, withdraw **9** fainaigue **11** countermand

revolt: **5** rebel, repel **6** mutiny, offend **7** retreat **8** renounce, sedition, uprising **9** rebellion **12** insurrection, renunciation

revolting: **4** ugly **6** horrid **7** hateful, hideous **8** shocking **9** loathsome, offensive, repellent, repulsive **10** disgusting, nauseating

revolution: **4** gyre, turn **5** cycle **7** circuit **8** disorder, rotation, uprising **9** overthrow, rebellion **12** renunciation

revolutions per minute: RPM **4** revs

revolve: con **4** birl, roll, spin, turn, whir **5** recur, swing, trend, twirl, wheel, whirl, whirr **6** circle, gyrate, ponder, rotate **7** agitate, reflect, trundle **8** consider, meditate **10** deliberate

revolver: gat **6** pistol **7** firearm

revolving: **4** orby **6** rotary

part: **5** rotor **7** rotator

revue: **4** show **9** burlesque **13** entertainment

revulsion: **4** fear **6** change **8** reaction **9** reversion **10** withdrawal

reward: fee, pay, utu **4** heed, hire, meed, rent **5** ameed, award, bonus, check, crown, merit, medal, prize, repay, wages, yield **6** bounty, gersum, notice, profit, regard, return, salary, trophy **7** guerdon, premium, success **8** requital **9** honoraria(pl.) **10** compensate, honorarium, recompense, remunerate **11** retribution **12** compensation, remuneration **13** gratification

rewarding: **7** helpful **10** beneficial

rewrite: **4** edit **6** revise

rezai: **8** coverlet

rhamn: **9** buckthorn

rhapontic: **7** rhubarb **8** pieplant **9** knapweeds

rhapsodic: **8** ecstatic, effusive **9** emotional

rhea: emu **4** emeu **5** nandu **8** avestruz(Sp.)

Rhea: *child:* **4** Hera, Zeus **5** Hades **6** Hestia **7** Demeter **8** Poseidon
father: **6** Uranus
husband: **6** Cronus

rhema: **4** term, verb, word

rheoscope: **12** galvanoscope

rheotome: **11** interrupter

rhesus: **6** monkey **7** macaque

rhetor: **6** master, orator **7** teacher

rhetorical: **6** florid **8** forensic **10** figurative, oratorical

rhetorician: **6** master, orator, writer **7** speaker, teacher

rhetorics: *digression:* **6** ecbole
diminution: **7** litotes
figure of speech: **6** aporia, simile **7** epandos **8** metaphor **10** apostrophe **12** alliteration, onomatopoeia **15** personification

rheum: **4** cold **7** catarrh **8** rhinitis

rheumatism remedy: **5** salol **9** salacetol

rheumatism weed: **10** pipsissewa

rhexis: **7** rupture

rhine: **5** ditch, drain **6** runnel

Rhine: *city:* **8** Mannheim
magic hoard: **9** Rheingold, Rhinegold
nymph: **7** Lorelei
pert. to: **7** Rhenish
wine: **7** Moselle

rhino: **4** cash **5** money **10** rhinoceros

rhinoceros: **5** abada, topan **6** borele, umhofo **7** keitloa, upeygan

rhinoceros beetle: **4** uang

rhinoceros bird: **9** beefeater

rhipidion: **8** flabella(pl.) **9** flabellum

rhizoid: **8** rootcell

rhoda: **4** rose

Rhode Island founder: **13** Roger Williams

Rhodes festival: **10** Chelidonia

Rhodesia: *language:* Ila
people: **10** Balokwakwa
rhododaphne: 8 oleander
rhoeadales: 5 poppy
rhomboid: 13 parallelogram
rhonchus: 4 rale **7** snoring **8** croaking **9** whistling
Rhone: *town:* **5** Arles
tributary: **5** Isere, Saone
rhubarb: 5 error **6** hassle **7** mistake, yawweed **8** argument, pieplant **9** butterbur, rhapontic **10** discussion
derived from: **5** rheic
rhus tree: 5 sumac **6** sumach
rhyme: 5 verse **9** harmonize
rhymester: 4 poet **6** rhymer **8** rimester **9** poetaster
rhyptic: 9 detergent
rhythm: 4 beat, lilt, time **5** clink, meter, pulse, swing, tempo **7** cadence, measure
break in: **7** caesura **8** caesurae(pl.)
instrument: **4** drum **7** cymbals **8** triangle **9** tamborine
monotonous: **8** singsong
rhythmic: 6 poetic **8** metrical **9** recurrent
ria: bay **5** creek, inlet
rial: 4 king **5** great, noble, power, royal **6** prince **8** splendid **9** excellent **11** magnificent
rialto: 4 mart **6** bridge, market **8** exchange
rialty: 4 pomp **5** power, state **6** estate **8** grandeur **10** ceremonial
riant: gay **6** bright **8** cheerful, laughing, smiling
riata: 4 rope **5** lasso, reata **6** lariat
rib: 4 bone, hair, purl, stay, wale **5** costa, ridge, tease **6** costae(pl.), lierne **7** bristle, support **9** cotelette, tierceron
pert. to: **6** costal **7** costate
ribald: low **6** coarse, rascal, vulgar **7** obscene **9** offensive **10** irreverent, scurrilous **11** blasphemous
riband: 6 ribbon
ribband: bar **4** spar **5** plank, strip **6** bridge, timber **9** scantling
ribbed: 6 barred, corded **7** costate
ribbet: 5 rybat **6** rabbet, rebate
ribble row: 6 string **9** rigmarole
ribbon: bow **4** tape **5** braid, corse, padou, reins, shred, snood, strip, taste **6** cordon, fillet, riband, sliver, taenia, tatter **7** binding, taeniae(pl.) **8** banderol, decorate, tressour, tressure **9** banderole
ribbon-fish: 4 fish **7** cutlass, oarfish **8** bandfish, dealfish
ribbon gum: 8 eucalypt
ribbon-like: 8 taeniate, taenioid
ribbon worm: 9 nemertine
ribless: 8 ecostate **9** decostate
ribwort: 8 hardhead, plantain
rice: 4 boro, chit, paga, twig **5** arroz(Sp.), bigas, canin, macan, pilaf, pilau, stick **6** branch **7** risotto **9** brushwood

drink: **5** bubud
field: **4** padi **5** paddy
husk: **4** shud **5** shood
milk: **5** gruel **7** pudding **8** porridge
paste: ame
rice rail: 4 sora
ricebird: 7 bunting, sparrow **8** bobolink **9** gallinule
riceroot grass: 9 broomroot
rich: fat **4** dear, oofy **5** ample, opime **6** absurd, costly, creamy, daedal, fruity, greasy, hearty, mellow, mighty, oofier, potent **7** copious, fertile, moneyed, opulent, orotund, pinguid, wealthy **8** abundant, affluent, generous, luscious, powerful, valuable, well-to-do **9** abounding, bountiful, elaborate, laughable, luxuriant, plentiful, sumptuous **10** productive **12** concentrated, preposterous
richard: 9 plutocrat
richdom: 6 wealth **8** richness
riche: 4 rule **5** realm, reign **9** authority
riches: 4 gold, pelf, weal **5** lucre, worth **7** fortune **8** treasure
demon of: **6** Mammon
region of: **8** Eldorado
rick: 4 goaf, heap, pile **5** noise, scold, stack, twist **6** jingle, rattle, sprain, wrench **7** chatter
rickety: 4 weak **5** crazy, shaky **6** feeble, senile **7** unsound **8** unstable **9** tottering **10** ramshackle
rickmatic: 6 affair **7** concern **8** business
rickshaw: 6 samlor
ricochet: 4 skip **5** carom **6** bounce, glance **7** rebound
rictus: 4 gape, mask
rid: 4 free **5** clear, empty **6** assoil, remove, rescue **7** deliver, relieve **8** dispatch, liberate **9** eradicate **11** disencumber
ridder: 4 sift **5** sieve
riddle: ree **4** crux, sift **5** aread, areed, griph, rebus, sieve **6** enigma, pierce, puzzle **7** griphus, mystery, perplex **8** disprove, separate **9** conundrum, criticize, perforate
riddler: 8 screener
ride: 4 dosa **5** drive, float, motor, tease **6** harass **7** hagride, journey, torment **8** ridicule **9** carrousel, cavalcade, excursion **12** merry-go-round
to hounds: **4** hunt
without power: **5** coast, glide
rideau: 5 mound, ridge
rident: 5 riant **7** smiling **8** grinning, laughing
rider: 6 clause, cowboy, jockey, knight **7** allonge **8** addition, bucaayro, buckaroo, cavalier, desultor, horseman **9** amendment, performer, straddler **10** equestrian, freebooter, highwayman, horsewoman **11** endorsement, mosstrooper **12** broncobuster, equestrienne(fem.)
ridge: as, os; aas, rib, top **4** aret, asar,

back, balk, bank, barb, bult, dene, dune, gold, kame, lira, loma, osar(pl.), rand, reef, ring, ruck, ruga, seam, spur, wale, wave, weal, welt **5** arete, arris, bargh, chine, costa, crest, eskar, esker, hause, oesar(pl.), rugae(pl.), serac, spine, stria, varix, wheal, whelk **6** costae(pl.), crista, rideau, striae(pl.) **7** annulet, costula, cristae(pl.), hogback, porcate, varices(pl.), wrinkle, yardang **8** costulae(pl.), headland, sastrugi, zastrugi **9** elevation, razorback

ridge oak: 9 blackjack

ridicule: guy, pan **4** gibe, jeer, mock, quiz, razz, twit **5** borak, chaff, irony, roast, scout, sneer, taunt **6** banter, deride, expose, satire **7** asteism, buffoon, lampoon, mockery, pillory, sarcasm **8** derision, raillery, satirize **9** burlesque

deity: **5** Momus

object of: **13** laughingstock

ridiculous: 5 droll **6** absurd **7** amusing **8** farcical **9** laughable, ludicrous **10** irrational, outrageous **12** preposterous

riding: 9 chevachie **10** equitation

costume: **5** habit

pants: **8** jodhpurs

shoe: **8** solleret

riding school: 6 manege

riding whip: 4 crop **5** quirt

ridotto: 6 resort **7** redoubt, retreat **8** festival **9** gathering **10** masquerade **11** abridgement, arrangement **13** entertainment

riem: 5 strap, strip, thong

rier: 4 cask

rife: 5 brief **7** current, replete **8** abundant, numerous **9** abounding, plentiful, prevalent **10** prevailing, widespread

riff: 6 riffle, ripple **7** midriff **9** diaphragm

riffle: 4 plow, reef **5** rapid, shoal **6** rattle **7** shallow, shuffle **11** obstruction

riffraff: mob **4** raff, scum **5** trash **6** rabble, refuse **7** rubbish **9** sweepings

rifle: arm, gun, rob **4** tige **5** reeve, steal **6** furrow, groove, weapon **7** bundock, carbine, despoil, escopet, firearm, pillage, plunder, ransack **8** bandhook **9** chassepot, escopette

accessory: **6** ramrod

ball: **5** minie

instrument: **7** bayonet

kind of: **6** Garand, Mauser **7** Enfield **9** Remington **10** Winchester **11** Springfield

magazine: **6** Mauser

pin: **4** tige

rifleman: 5 jager, yager

rift: lag **4** flaw, rive **5** belch, break, chasm, cleft, crack, rapid, split **6** breach, cleave, divide **7** blemish, fissure, opening, shallow **8** division

rig: fig, fit, fix **4** fool, gear, hoax, wind **5** dress, equip, rifle, storm, trick **6** lateen, outfit, square, tackle **7** arrange, costume,

derrick, ransack, swindle, turnout **8** accouter, accoutre, carriage, equipage **9** apparatus, equipment **10** manipulate **11** contraption

part of: **4** spar

riga: 6 balsam

Riga Gulf island: 5 Oesel

rigadoon: 5 dance

rigescence: 8 numbness **9** stiffness

right: fit, gee, hak **4** fair, good, hakh, real, sane, soke, true **5** droit, sound **6** angary, dexter, equity, lawful, normal, patent, proper **7** correct, derecho, fitting, genuine, liberty, rectify, redress, upright **8** becoming, courtesy, easement, interest, straight, suitable, usufruct, virtuous **9** authority, equitable, faultless, franchise, privilege **11** appropriate, certificate, prerogative

exclusive: ex **7** patents **10** concession

proprietary: **8** interest

royal: **7** regalia

right-angled: 10 orthogonal, rectangled **11** rectangular

right down: 4 very **8** complete, thorough **10** positively, thoroughly

right-handed: 7 dextral **8** dextrous **9** dexterous

righteous: 4 good, holy, just **5** godly, moral, pious, zadoc, zadok **6** devout, worthy **7** perfect, sinless, upright **8** virtuous **9** blameless, equitable, guiltless

righteousness: 9 rectitude

rightful: due **4** fair, just, true **5** legal **6** honest, lawful, proper **7** fitting, upright **9** righteous **11** appropriate

rigid: set **4** firm, hard, taut **5** fixed, stark, stern, stiff, stony, tense **6** marbly, severe, strait, strict **7** austere **8** rigorous **9** immovable, stringent, unbending **10** inflexible, motionless, unyielding

rigmaree: 4 coin **6** trifle

rigmarole: 8 nonsense **10** balderdash

rignum: 9 horsemint

rigol: 4 ring **6** circle, furrow, groove **7** channel

rigor, rigour: 4 fury **7** cruelty **8** asperity, hardship, rigidity, severity, violence **9** austerity, harshness, rigidness, sharpness, stiffness **10** difficulty, exactitude, puritanism, strictness **13** inflexibility

rigorous: 5 angry, rigid, stern **6** severe, strait, strict **7** correct, drastic, precise **8** accurate **9** inclement **10** inexorable, oppressive, relentless

rikk: 10 tambourine

rile: vex **4** roil **5** anger, annoy, upset **7** agitate, disturb **8** irritate **9** turbidity

rill: 5 brook, creek, crick, ditch **6** course, furrow, groove, runnel, trench **7** rillock, rivulet **8** brooklet **9** arroyuelo(Sp.), streamlet

rim: lip **4** bank, brim, edge, orle, ring, tire **5** basil, bezel, bezil, brink, somma, verge

6 border, flange, margin, shield **7** enclose, horizon **8** boundary **9** perimeter

rima: **5** cleft **7** fissure **8** aperture **10** breadfruit

rimash: **9** hackberry

rimate: **8** fissured

rime: ice **4** hoar, poem, rent, rung, step **5** chink, crack, frost, rhyme, verse **6** freeze **7** fissure, versify **8** aperture **9** cranreuch(Sc.), hoarfrost

rimple: **4** fold **6** crease, ripple, rumple **7** wrinkle

rimption: lot **9** abundance

rind: **4** bark, husk, melt, peel, skin **5** crust, waste **6** cortex **7** clarify, epicarp, peeling **8** cortices(pl.)

rindle: **5** brook **6** runnel **7** rivulet

ring: bee, cut, rim, set **4** bail, band, cric, ding, dirl, echo, gyre, halo, hank, hoop, link, lute, peal, toll, tore **5** anlet, arena, bague, bezel, chime, clang, group, knell, longe, ridge, rigol **6** arenae, border, brough(Sc.), chaton, circle, circus, clique, collar, collet, corona, dindle, dingle, famble, gasket, girdle, terret, tingle, tinkle, toroid **7** annulet, annulus, circlet, coterie, curette, ferrule, grommet, resound, ringlet, tanbark, vibrate **8** bracelet, cincture, encircle, surround **9** archivolt, enclosure, encompass **10** racecourse **11** reverberate **14** tintinnabulate

carrier: **9** go-between

comb. form: **4** gyro

pert. to: **7** annular

ring finger: **5** third

ring ouzel: **6** thrush

ring plover: **5** sandy

ring-shaped: **7** annular **8** annulate **9** annulated

ring-tailed cat: **8** cacomixl **9** cacomixle **10** cacomistle

ring-worm: **5** tinea **7** serpigo **8** milleped **9** millepede

ringdove: **4** dove **6** cushat, pigeon **10** turtledove

ringed: **6** wedded **7** engaged, married **8** annulate, circular **9** annulated, decorated, encircled **10** surrounded

ringed worm: **7** annelid

ringent: **6** gaping

ringing: **4** clam **6** bright **7** orotund **8** resonant

ringle-eye: **7** walleye

ringleader: **10** instigator

ringlet: **4** curl, lock, ring **5** tress

rings: *interlocking:* **6** gimmal

series: **4** coil

rink: man **4** hero, race, ring **9** encounter

rinner: **6** runner

rinse: **4** lave, sind(Sc.), wash **5** douse **6** douche, gargle, sluice **7** cleanse

rinthereout: **5** tramp **7** vagrant **8** vagabond

rio: **5** river **6** coffee, stream

riot: din **4** clem **5** brawl, feast, melee, revel **6** affray, bedlam, clamor, excess, pogrom(Russ.), tumult, uproar **7** dispute, quarrel, revelry **8** carousal, debauche, disorder, outburst, sedition, uprising **9** commotion, confusion, luxuriate **10** donnybrook **11** dissolution, disturbance

riotous: **4** loud, wild **5** loose **6** wanton **10** boisterous, profligate **11** saturnalian **12** contumacious, unrestrained

rip: hag, rit **4** rend, rent, rive, tear **6** sunder **8** disunite, harridan, lacerate **9** debauchee **10** laceration

rip-roaring: **5** noisy **6** lively **8** exciting **9** hilarious **10** boisterous, uproarious

ripe: fit, rob **4** aged, bank **5** adult, ready, rifle **6** addled, august, mature, mellow **7** plunder **8** complete, finished, seashore **9** developed, full-grown, perfected, riverbank **10** consummate, seasonable **11** intoxicated

early: **8** rareripe

riposte, ripost: **5** reply **6** retort, return, thrust **8** repartee

ripper: **7** bobsled **9** bobsleigh

rippet: **4** romp **6** uproar **7** quarrel

ripping: **4** fine **8** splendid **9** admirable, excellent **10** remarkable

ripping iron: **8** ravehook

rippit: **5** fight

ripple: cut, lap **4** curl, fret, purl, riff, tear, wave **5** acker, graze **6** cockle, dimple, rimple **7** crinkle, scratch, wavelet, wrinkle **8** undulate

ripple grass: **7** ribwort

rise: **4** flow, grow, hulk, loom, rare, rear, soar, stem, well **5** arise, begin, climb, issue, mount, reach, rebel, stand, start, surge, swell, tower **6** amount, appear, ascend, ascent, aspire, assume, attain, derive, emerge, growth, mature, revolt, spring, thrive **7** adjourn, advance, elevate, emanate, prosper, succeed **8** eminence, flourish, increase, levitate **9** ascension, beginning, elevation, originate

again: **7** resurge **9** resurrect

and fall: **4** tide **5** heave **6** welter

risible: **5** funny **7** amusing **9** laughable, ludicrous

rising: **5** arist **6** orient, ortive **7** montant, nearing **8** gradient, uprising **9** ascendant, ascendent, ascension **11** approaching **12** extumescence, insurrection

risk: **4** dare, gage, wage **5** peril, stake **6** chance, danger, expose, gamble, hazard, injury, plight, plunge **7** imperil, venture **8** exposure, jeopardy **9** adventure **12** disadvantage

risky: **7** parlous

risley: **7** acrobat

risp: bar, rub **4** file, rasp, stem, tirl, wisp **5** grass, stalk **7** bulrush, scratch

risper: **11** caterpillar

risque: **4** racy **5** risky **6** daring **9** audacious, hazardous **10** suggestive

rissle: **4** pole **5** staff, stick

rist: 4 mark 5 wound 6 ascent 7 engrave, scratch 8 increase 12 insurrection, resurrection

risus: 5 laugh 8 laughter

rit: cut, rip 4 slit, tear 5 split 6 pierce 7 scratch

ritardando: 9 retarding 11 rallentando

rite: 4 cult, form, orgy 5 sacra 6 augury, exequy, novena, prayer, ritual 7 liturgy, obsequy 8 accolade, accolate, ceremony 9 ordinance, procedure, sacrament, solemnity 10 ceremonial, initiation, observance

Ritter: 6 knight

ritual: 4 cult, form, rite 7 liturgy, obsequy 8 ceremony 9 obsequies(pl.) 10 ceremonial

ritus: 5 usage 6 custom

ritzy: 6 modish 7 elegant 9 expensive, luxurious 11 fashionable

rivage: 4 bank, duty 5 coast, shore

rival: vie 4 even, peer 5 equal, match 7 compete, emulate, feuding 8 corrival, emulator, opponent 9 adversary, competing 10 antagonist, competitor, contending 11 comparative

rivalry: 11 competition

rive: rip, rob 4 bank, plow, pull, rend, rent, rift, tear 5 break, cleft, shore, split, steal 6 arrive, cleave, pierce, sunder, thieve, thrust 7 dispart 8 lacerate 9 disembark

rivel: 6 shrink 7 shrivel, wrinkle

river: ea; ree, ria(Sp.), rio(Sp.), run 4 wadi, wady 5 bayou, waddy 6 stream 7 channel 8 effluent 9 abundance 11 watercourse

arm: 7 estuary 9 tributary

channel: bed 6 alveus

comb. form: 6 potamo

current: 4 eddy 6 rapids

dam: 4 weir

god: 7 Alpheus, Inachus 8 Achelous

ice: 7 glacier

island: 4 holm

land: 5 carse(Sc.), flats

living in: 9 amphibian, rheophile

log run: 9 sluiceway

mouth: 4 beal(Sc.), lade 5 delta 7 estuary

mythical: 4 Styx

nymph: 4 nais 5 naiad

obstruction: 4 snag 5 gorce

of oblivion: 5 Lethe

passage: 4 ford 7 estuary

pert. to: 5 amnic 6 rivery 7 fluvial, potamic 8 riverine 9 fluminose, fluminous

sacred: 5 Ganga 6 Ganges

siren: 7 Lorelei

small: 5 brook, creek, tchai 6 stream 7 rivulet 8 riverlet 9 streamlet

thief: 6 ackman

winding part: ess

river dog: 10 hellbender

river duck: 4 teal

river horse: 5 hippo 12 hippopotamus

river mussel: 4 unio

River of Forgetfulness: 5 Lethe

River of Sorrows: 7 Acheron

riverbank: 4 ripa, ripe 5 levee

riverbed: 4 wadi, wady 5 waddy

riverboat: ark 5 barge 7 rowboat, towboat 8 flatboat

riverside: 4 bank 5 shore

riverweed family: 13 podostemaceae

rivet: fix 4 bolt, brad 6 clinch, fasten 8 fastener

riviere: 8 necklace

rivose: 5 brook 6 gutter 7 channel

rivulet: 4 burn, rill 5 bache, bayou, bourn, brook, creek 6 bourne, rindle(Sc.), runlet, runnel, stream 7 channel 9 streamlet

rix: 4 reed, rush

rixatrix: 5 scold 6 virago

rixy: 4 tern

rizzar: dry 4 cure 6 drying 7 currant

rizzom: ear 5 stalk, straw 8 particle

roach: bug, cut 4 fish, hill, rock, roll, soil, spot 6 braise 7 sunfish 9 cockroach

road: way 4 fare, gang, iter, path, raid, ride 5 agger, bargh, going, itero(pl.), route 6 avenue, camino, career, causey, chemin, course, street 7 calzada(Sp.), estrada, gangway, highway, itinera(pl.), journey, passage, railway 8 beallach, causeway, chaussee(F.), cul-de-sac, pavement, railroad 9 direction, incursion, roadstead 10 expedition

bend: 7 hairpin

edge: 4 berm 8 shoulder

machine: 4 harl 5 paver 6 grader 9 bulldozer

surface: tar 6 bricks, gravel, stones 7 macadam 8 concrete, pavement

road book: map 9 gazetteer, itinerary

road goose: 6 brant

road runner: 6 cuckoo 7 paisano(Sp.)

roadhouse: inn 6 tavern

roadman: 7 drummer, peddler 8 salesman 9 canvasser

roadster: 5 horse 7 bicycle 8 runabout

roadtrack: 9 roadstead

roadweed: 8 plantain

roam: err, gad 4 roil, rove 5 prowl, range, stray 6 bangle, ramble, stroll, travel, wander 7 meander 8 straggle 9 gallivant

roamer: 5 gipsy, gypsy, nomad 8 fugitive 12 peregrinator

roan: bay 9 sheepskin

Roanoke bell: 7 cowslip

roar: cry, din 4 beal, bell, bere, boom, bray, clap, hurl, rote, rout, yell 5 blart, brool, fream, laugh 6 bellow, buller, outcry, steven 7 thunder 8 shouting

roaring: 4 loud 5 aroar, brisk, noisy 7 riotous 10 boisterous, disorderly, stentorian

roaring game: 7 curling

roaring Meg: 6 cannon

roast: fry 4 bake, cook, razz, roti(F.) 5 asado(Sp.), brede, grill, parch 6 assate,

banter 7 torrefy, torrify **8** ridicule **9** criticize
prepare: **5** truss

roasting stick: 4 spit **6** skewer

rob: cop **4** fake, flap, loot, pelf, take **5** bribe, filch, harry, pilch, pinch, pluck, raven, reave, rifle, spoil, steal, strip, touch **6** burgle, pilfer, pirate, ravish, shrive, snatch, snitch, thieve **7** bereave, defraud, deprive, despoil, pillage, plunder **10** plagiarize

Rob Roy: 5 canoe

robber: 4 goul, yegg **5** ghoul **6** arrant, bandit, dacoit, pirate **7** brigand, corsair, footpad, ladrone, yeggman **8** marauder **9** bandolero, buccaneer, privateer **10** depredator, highwayman

robe (see also **dress, gown**): aba **4** skin, vest, wrap **5** array, camis, camus, cloak, cover, cymar, simar, talar, tunic **6** caftan, chimer, clothe, dolman, invest, kimono, mantle, revest **7** chimere, costume, garment, vesture **8** clothing, covering, vestment **10** sticharion

robin: 4 lout, tody **6** oriole, thrush **7** bumpkin, chewink **8** trimming **10** cuckoopint, toxalbumin

Robin Goodfellow: 4 Puck **5** fairy **6** sprite **9** hobgoblin

Robin Hood: *chaplain:* **9** Friar Tuck
follower: **4** John **9** Friar Tuck
sweetheart: **6** Marian

robin sandpiper: 9 dowitcher

robinet: 6 cannon **9** chaffinch

Robinson Crusoe: *author:* **5** Defoe
companion: **6** Friday

roborant: 5 tonic **13** strengthening

roborate: 6 ratify **10** strengthen **11** corroborate

roborean: 5 oaken, stout **6** strong

robot: 5 golem **7** android **9** androides, automaton

robust: 4 hale, hard, iron, rude **5** hardy, lusty, rough, sound, stout, wally **6** brawny, coarse, hearty, rugged, sinewy, strong, sturdy **7** healthy **8** athletic, muscular, vigorous **10** boisterous

roc: 4 bird **6** simurg **7** simurgh, soldier

rocca: 4 hold, keep **6** donjon **8** fortress

rochet: 5 cloak, frock **7** camisia, garment, gurnard **8** vestment

rock: dag, ore, tor **4** clay, crag, lull, peak, reef, reel, roll, scar, shog, spar, sway, trap, tufa, tuff, wash **5** agate, brack, candy, chert, cliff, earth, flint, geest, lytta, prase, scree, shake, shale, shaul, slate, stane(Sc.), stone, wacke **6** aplite, basalt, dacite, egeran, gneiss, gravel, issite, oolite, pebble, refuge, rognon, schist, silica, sinter, teeter, totter **7** adinole, akerite, alunite, defense, diamond, gondite, granite, greisen, support, tremble, vibrate **8** andesite, banakite, dolomite, laterite, obsidian, porphyry, psephite, rhyolite **9** ep-

idosite, flagstone, oscillate, phanerite **10** greenstone, promontory **11** petrography
boring tool: **6** trepan
debris: **5** talus **8** detritus
decomposed: **6** gossan
discarded: **5** attle
finely broken: **4** sand
fold: **8** syncline **9** anticline
fragments: see *debris* above
glacier deposit: **7** moraine
glacier-transported: **7** erratic
igneous: **4** boss, sial, sima, trap, tufa **5** trass **6** basalt, domite, latite **7** diabase, diorite, felsite, ijolite, peridot **8** extaxite, ijussite, porphyry **11** agglomerate
liquid: aa **4** lava
mythical: **6** Scylla
nodule: **5** geode
pert. to: **6** petric **7** petrean
point: **4** crag, peak
science: **9** petrology
strata: see *fold* above
suffix: ite, yte

rock badger: 4 cony

rock bass: 6 red-eye

rock bottom: 6 lowest **8** cheapest

rock dove: 9 guillemot **10** rockpigeon

rock eel: 6 gunnel

rock falcon: 6 merlin

rock geranium: 8 alumroot

rock goat: 4 ibex

rock grouse: 9 ptarmigan

rock hind: 7 grouper

rock hopper: 7 penquin

rock kangaroo: 7 wallaby

rock oak: 8 chestnut **10** California, chinquapin

rock oil: 9 petroleum

rock plant: 4 moss **6** lichen

rock rabbit: 5 hyrax

rock snake: 5 krait **6** phthon

rock starling: 5 ouzel

rock tar: 9 petroleum

rock tripe: 6 lichen

rockaway: 8 carriage

rockbell: 9 columbine

rockbird: 5 murre **9** sandpiper

rocket: 4 weld, wold **5** slate, woald, would **9** satellite **11** firecracker

rockfish: 4 bass **5** perch **7** grouper **9** killifish **10** priestfish

rockling: 4 fish, gade

rockrose: 6 cistus

rocky: 4 hard, weak **5** dizzy, shaky, stony **6** cliffy **7** petrean **8** obdurate, unsteady **9** unfeeling

Rocky Mountain: *goat:* **8** antelope
park: **5** Estes
range: **5** Teton **7** Wasatch
sheep: **7** bighorn

rococo: 4 arty **9** fantastic

rod: bar, gad, guy, rab, rib **4** axle, bolt, came, cane, crop, goad, I-bar, lath, pole, prod, race, scob, spit, wand, wire **5** arrow, baton, board, lytta, osier, perch, power, scion, spoke, staff, stick, stock, strip, tribe **6** baculi(pl.), batten, broach, carbon, etalon, eyebar, ferule, needle, pistol, piston, pontil, raddle, skewer, switch, toggle **7** baculus, caliper, crowbar, distaff, measure, scepter, sceptre, spindle, stemmer, support, tringle, tyranny **8** arrester, offshoot, revolver **9** authority **10** oppression **12** chastisement

bundle: **6** fasces

square: **5** perch

rod-like: **6** rhabdo **7** virgate

rodd: **8** crossbow

rodent: jap, rat **4** cavy, cony, cypu, degu, hare, mole, paca, pica, pika, utia, vole **5** aguti, hutia, jutia, lerot, mouse, ratel, zokor **6** agouti, agouty, beaver, biting, cururo, gerbil, gopher, gundie, jerboa, marmot, murine, rabbit, weasel **7** chincha, hamster, leveret, muskrat **8** capibara, capybrara, dormouse, gerbille, leporide, sewellel, squirrel, viscacha, vizcacha **9** porcupine **10** chinchilla

pert. to: **8** rosorial

rodeo: **7** roundup **9** enclosure **10** exhibition

rodge: **7** gadwall

rodman: **4** thug **10** highwayman

rodney: **5** idler **7** shirker **8** vagabond

rodomontade: **4** brag, rant **5** boast, empty **7** bluster, bombast **8** boastful, boasting, braggart

rodster: **6** angler **9** fisherman

roe: ra; ova, pea **4** deer, eggs, hart, hind **5** coral, spawn **6** caviar **7** caviare

roebuck: **4** girl **9** chevreuil

roestone: **6** oolite

rog: **4** pull, stir **5** shake **6** jumble

rogan: **4** bowl **10** receptacle

rogation: law **6** decree, litany, prayer **7** inquiry, request **8** petition **12** supplication

rogue: boy, gue, imp, wag **4** hemp, kite **5** catso, cheat, crank, decry, gipsy, gypsy, hempy, knave, scamp, shark, tramp **6** beggar, canter, coquin, harlot, pirate, rascal, wander **7** corsair, erratic, hellion, sharper, vagrant, villain, waggish **8** picaroon, swindler, vagabond **9** scoundrel, trickster **10** frolicsome, stigmatize **11** rapscallion

roguery: **5** fraud **8** mischief, trickery **15** mischievousness

roguish: sly **4** arch **5** pawky **6** wanton **7** playful, puckish **8** espiegle, sportive **9** dishonest, fun-loving **12** unscrupulous

roid: **5** rough **6** severe **7** riotous, roguish **10** frolicsome **12** unmanageable

roil: vex **4** foul, roam, romp, rust, stir **5** anger, annoy, muddy, rouse **6** cloudy, fidget, ruffle, wander **7** blunder, disturb **8** irritate **9** displease, unsettled

roily: **6** turbid

roister: **4** brag, rude **5** bully, revel, spree **7** bluster, boorish, reveler, swagger, violent **9** gilravage

roistering: **6** hoiden, hoyden

rojo: **6** Indian **7** redskin

roke: fog **4** mist, stir **5** smoke, steam, vapor **8** moisture

roker: ray **8** rockling **9** thornback

roky: **4** damp **5** foggy, misty, smoky **6** hoarse

Roland: *friend:* **6** Oliver

sword: **8** durendal

role: bit **4** cast, duty, part **6** office **8** business, function **7** character **13** impersonation **16** characterization

leading: **4** star

roll: bun, gad, rob **4** bolt, coil, file, flow, furl, list, pell, roam, rota, seel, sway, turn, wind, wrap **5** cadre, frisk, lurch, shift, surge, swing, trill, troll, wheel **6** bundle, enroll, enwrap, goggle, grovel, roster, rotate, scroll, spiral, tumble, wallow, wander, welter, whelve, wintle **7** biscuit, revolve, rissole, stagger, swagger, trundle **8** cylinder, flounder, register, undulate

roller: **4** band, wave **5** finer, inker, swath **6** canary, caster, fascia, fillet, pigeon, platen, rowlet, sponge **7** bandage, breaker, presser, sirgang, tumbler **8** cylinder **9** surcingle

rolleyway: **4** road **5** track **7** gangway, tramway

rollick: **4** romp **5** sport **6** frolic

rollicking: gay **6** jovial, lively **8** careless **9** hilarious

rolling stock: **4** cars **7** coaches, engines **8** cabooses, Pullmans, sleepers **11** locomotives

rolling weed: **10** tumbleweed

rollix: **7** rollick

roly-poly: **5** dumpy, pudgy, round **6** portly, rotund **7** pudding

rom: **4** buzz **5** gipsy, gypsy

romaine: cos **5** plant **7** lettuce

romal: **5** thong

Roman: **5** brave, Latin **6** frugal, honest, simple **7** Italian

Roman Catholic: *cassock:* **7** soutane, zimarra

church: **7** lateran

ecclesiastic: **7** Rosmini

priest: **4** abbe(F.) **6** father **8** sacerdos **9** monsignor

skullcap: **9** zucchetto

society: **7** Jesuits

romance: woo **4** gest, tale **5** court, dream, fable, fancy, feign, geste, novel, story **6** affair **7** chimera, fantasy, fiction, romanza **9** falsehood, sentiment **10** exaggerate **12** exaggeration

Romance language: **6** French **7** Catalan, Italian, Spanish **8** Rumanian **9** Provencal **10** Portuguese

Romanese: **7** gypsies **9** Walachian

romantic: **6** poetic, unreal **8** quixotic **9**

imaginary, visionary **10** idealistic **11** extravagant

Romany, Rommany: **5** gipsy, gypsy

tongue: **7** Romanes

romanza: **7** fiction, romance

Rome (see also **Latin**): **4** Roma

abode of gods: **7** Olympus

adviser to king: **6** Egeria

amphitheater: **9** colosseum

apostle: **4** Neri, Paul

army unit: **6** cohort

army wing: ala

assembly: **5** forum **6** senate **7** comitia

attendant: **7** aliptes **8** aleiptes

augur: **6** auspex

author (see also *biographer, historian, poet,* below): **5** Pliny, Varro

authority symbol: **6** fasces

basilica: **7** lateran

barracks: **6** canaba

battle array: **5** acies

biographer: **5** Nepos **9** Suetonius

boy: **4** puer **8** camillus

brothers: **5** Remus **7** Romulus

building: **5** aedes

Caesar's title: **9** imperator

captain: **9** centurion

carriage: **5** essed

citadel: arx

clans: **4** gens

coin: as; aes **5** asses(pl.), aurei(pl.), semis **6** aureus, dinder, solidu, triens **7** denarii(pl.), siliqua **8** decussis, denarius, sesterce, sesteria(pl.) **9** sesterium **10** sestertius, victoriate **11** victoriatus

comedy: **5** exode

comedy writer: **6** Cicero **7** Plautus, Terence

concert hall: **5** odeum

conqueror: **6** Alaric

conspirator: **8** Catiline

contract: **5** nexum

couch: **9** accubitum

court: **5** atria(pl.) **6** atrium

custodian: **10** neocorates

district: **5** Pagus **7** Pontine **8** Pomptine

diviner: **5** augur **6** auspex

division: **5** curia

earthwork: **5** agger

emperor: **4** Nero, Otho, Otto **5** Galba, Nerva, Titus **6** Caesar, Julian, Trajan **7** Hadrian **8** Augustus, Claudius, Domitian, Tiberius **9** Vespasian **10** Elagabalus **11** Constantine

empress: **7** Eudocia

encampment: **7** castrum

entrance hall: **5** atria(pl.) **6** atrium

family: **7** familia

farmer: **7** colonus **8** agricola

Fate: **4** Nona **5** Morta, Parca **6** Decuma, Parcae(pl.)

fighter: **9** gladiator

fortress: **7** castrum

founder: **5** Remus **7** Romulus

galley: **6** bireme **7** trireme

garment: **4** toga **5** palla, sagum, stola, stole, togae(pl.), tunic

general: **5** Sulla, Titus **6** Antony, Marius, Scipio **8** Agricola

god: Dis, Lar, Sol **4** Amor, Jove, Mars **5** Comus, Cupid, Fauns, Janus, Lares, manes, Orcus, Pluto **6** Faunus, Vulcan **7** Jupiter, lemures, Neptune, penates, Phoebus, Vatican **8** Dispater, Morpheus, Quirinus **11** Aesculapius

goddess: dea(L.) Lua, Nox, Ops, Pax **4** Caca, Juno, Luna, Maia, Paca **5** Ceres, Diana, Epona, Terra, Venus, Vesta **6** Aestas, Annona, Aurora, Lucina, Rumina, Tellus, Vacuna **7** Bellona, Fortuna, Minerva **8** Libitina **9** Abudantia, Discordia, Felicitas

greeting: ave

guard: **6** lictor

helmet: **5** galea **6** galeae(pl.),

highway: via **4** iter **5** itero(pl.) **6** Appian, **7** itinera(pl.)

holiday: **4** ides **5** feria **6** feriae(pl.)

hill: **7** Caelian, Viminal **8** Aventine, Palatine, Quirinal **9** Esquiline **10** Capitoline

historian: **4** Livy **5** Nepos

javelin: **4** pile **5** aclys, pilum

judge: **5** edile **6** aedile

jurist: **5** Gaius

king: **7** Romulus, Servius, Tullius **12** Ancus Martius **13** Numa Pompilius **15** Tullus Hostilius **18** Tarquinius Superbus

lake: **4** Nemi

language: **5** Latin

law: fas, lex **4** cern

magistrate: **5** edile **6** aedile, censor, pretor **7** praetor, tribune

measure: pes, urn **4** mile, pace, urna **5** actus, clima, cubit, juger **6** culeus, dolium, gradus, hemina, modius, palmus, passus, saltus, versus **7** amphora, congius, cyathus, digitus, stadion, stadium **8** centuria, hereduim, quadrant **9** decempeda, millarium, sextarius **10** acetabulum, quartarius

measure of weight: as; bes **4** pood **5** asses(pl.), libra, uncia **6** duella **7** dodrans, sextula, solidus **8** sicilium **9** scrupulus, scrupulum

military formation: ala **6** alares(pl.) **7** phalanx

military machine: **7** terebra

military unit: **6** cohort, legion **7** maniple

military vessel: **6** bireme **7** trireme

naturalist: **5** Pliny

nymph: **6** Egeria

official: **5** augur, edile **6** aedile, lictor **7** prefect, tribune **8** irenarch **9** nestorian

palace: **5** chigi **7** lateran

palace troops: **9** palatines

peace: **5** Irene

people: **5** Laeti **7** Sabines **8** plebians **10** patricians

pert. to: **9** classical

philosopher: **4** Cato **6** Seneca

physician: 9 archiater 11 Aesculapius

poet: 4 Ovid 5 Cinna, Lucan 6 Horace, Vergil, Virgil 7 Juvenal, Terence 8 Catullus, Tibullus 10 Propertius

port: 5 Ostia

praenomen: 5 Aulus, Caius, Gaius, Titus 6 Appius 7 Quintus, Spurius 8 Tiberius

priest: 5 epulo 6 flamen 7 luperci

priestess: 6 vestal

procurator: 5 Felix 6 Pilate

province: 5 Dacia 7 Cilicia

regulator: 6 censor

religious law: fas

river: Po 5 Tiber

room: ala 5 atria(pl.) 6 atrium 7 tablina(pl.) 8 fumarium, tablinum

shield: 5 scuta(pl.) 6 ancile, scutum 7 ancilia(pl.), clypeus

saint: 4 Neri

section: 5 Ostia

senate division: 5 curia

senate emblem: 9 laticlave

standard: 7 labarum, vexilla(pl.)   8 vexillum

standard-bearer: 9 vexillary

statesman: 4 Cato 5 Pliny 6 Caesar, Cicero, Seneca 7 Agrippa 8 Maecenas

tax gatherer: 8 publican

temple: 4 naos 5 cella 8 pantheon

treasurer: 8 quaestor

veteran: 7 emeriti(pl.) 8 emeritus

writing tablet: 7 diptych

Romeo: *father:* 8 Montague

rival: 5 Paris

rommack: 4 play, romp 7 rummage

romp: 4 hoit, play, roil 6 frolic, hoiden, hoyden 7 carouse, courant, gammock 8 carousal, courante

Romulus: *brother:* 5 Remus

father: 4 Mars

rond: 4 rand 5 shred 6 border

rondure: 5 round 6 circle, sphere 9 plumpness, roundness

rone: 5 brake 7 thicket 9 brushwood

rood: 5 cross 7 measure 8 crucifix

roodebok: 6 impala

roof: 5 cover 7 palate, shelter 8 covering

border: 4 eave

comb. form: 5 stego

style: hip 4 dome, flat, nave, sark 5 gable, spire 6 cupola 7 cricket, gambrel, mansard 8 penthouse, pyramidal 10 jerkinhead

timber: 6 rafter

roofing material: tar, tin 4 tile 5 paper, slate, straw, terne 6 copper, gravel, shakes, thatch 7 pantile 8 shingles

rook: 4 bird, crow 5 cheat, raven, steal 6 castle 7 defraud, sharper, swindle 8 swindler

rookery: 8 building

rookie, rooky: 4 tyro 6 novice 7 recruit, trainee 8 beginner

rooky: 4 roky 5 foggy 6 rookie, untidy 8 rascally 9 swindling 10 disheveled

room: ala, ben, den 4 aula, cell, hall, loge, sala(Sp.), seat 5 atria(pl.), aulae(pl.), cubby, divan, kiosk, lodge, place, salle(F.), salon, scope, space 6 atrium, casino, leeway, reside, saloon, scouth 7 boudoir, cabinet, chamber, cubicle, expanse, gallery, lodging, rotunda, theater 9 apartment, garderobe 10 auditorium

conversation: 6 exedra 7 exedrae(pl.) 11 drawing room

eating: 4 nook 7 cenacle, kitchen 8 cenacula(pl.) 9 cenaculum, refectory

private: 7 boudoir

provision: 4 ewry 5 ewery 6 larder 7 pantry 8 cupboard

reading: den 5 study 7 library

sleeping: 5 lodge 6 dormer 7 barrack, bedroom 8 roomette 9 dormitory

storage: 4 loft, shed 5 attic 6 cellar 9 storeroom

roomer: 5 guest 6 lodger, tenant 7 boarder

rooms: 4 flat 5 suite 9 apartment

roomy: 5 ample, broad, spacy 8 spacious 9 capacious 10 commodious

roorback, roorbach: lie 4 hoax 6 canard 7 fiction 9 falsehood

roose: 5 boast, extol, vaunt 6 praise

roost: sit 4 nest, pole, rest 5 abode, perch, sleep 6 alight, garret 7 lodging, support

rooster: 4 cock 5 gallo(Sp.) 11 chanticleer

root: dig 4 base, bulb, core, grub, moot, rout, stem 5 basis, cheer, grout, plant, radix, shout, tuber 6 bottom, etymon, ground, origin, settle 7 radical, radices(pl.), rootlet, support 9 beginning, establish 10 foundation

dyeing: 6 madder

edible: oca, roi, rue, uva, yam 4 beet, eddo, taro 5 orris, tania 6 carrot, ginger, orrice, radish, turnip 7 parsnip 8 rutabaga 9 sassafras

fragrant: 5 orris

outer layer: 7 exoderm

pert. to: 7 radical

principal: 7 taproot

pungent: 11 crinkleroot

root out: 4 stub 6 evulse 9 eradicate, extirpate 10 deracinate

rooted: 10 inveterate

rooter: fan 10 enthusiast

rootlet: 7 radicle, rhizoid

rope: gad, guy, tie, tow 4 bind, cord, hemp, line, stay 5 cable, longe, sheet, widdy 6 binder, fasten, halter, hawser 7 aweband, binding, bobstay, bollard, cordage, halyard, marline, painter 8 inveigle, prolonge

fiber: 4 coir, flax, jute 5 istle, sisal 6 cotton, Manila

holder: 6 becket

loop: 5 bight, noose 6 becket, parral, parrel

restraining: 6 tether

ship's: tye 4 colt, rode, stay, vang 5 sheet 6 hawser, inhaul, parral, parrel, ratlin,

shroud **7** halyard, lanyard, painter, ratline
throwing: **5** lasso, reata, riata **6** lariat
ropedancer: 7 acrobat **9** funambulo **11** funambulist
roper: 6 cowboy, packer
ropery: 6 banter **7** roguery
roque: 7 croquet
roric: 4 dewy, rory **5** roral **6** roscid
rosaceous: 4 rosy **5** rosal **8** blushing
rosary: 4 bede **5** beads **7** chaplet, garland **8** beadroll
rose (see also **rise**): ris **5** delta, flush **6** flower, nozzle **7** rambler, rosette **9** hellebore
family: **8** rosaceae
kind of: dog **4** moss, musk
oil: **4** atar, otto **5** attar, ottar
part: **5** petal
Rose City: 8 Pasadena, Portland
rose parakeet: 7 rosella
rose pogonia: 10 snakemouth
rosemary: 9 rosmarine
rosette: 7 cockade **8** ornament
rosilla: 10 sneezeweed
rosin: See **resin**.
rosiness: 5 blush, flush
ross: 4 bark, peel **5** waste **8** exterior
roster: 4 list, roll, rota **5** slate
rostrum: 4 beak, dais **5** snout, stage **6** pulpit **7** lectern, tribune **8** platform **9** proboscis
rosy: red **4** pink **5** ruddy **6** bright, florid **7** auroral, flushed, roseate **8** blooming, blushing, cheerful, rubicund **9** favorable, promising, rosaceous **10** favourable, optimistic
rot: ret **4** bosh, dote, doze, joke **5** chaff, decay, spoil, tease, trash **6** banter, fester, perish **7** corrupt, putrefy, rubbish, twaddle **8** nonsense **9** decompose, poppycock **10** degenerate **13** decomposition
rot grass: 9 flukewort **10** butterwort
rota: 4 list, roll **5** court, round **6** course, roster **8** register
rotate: 4 pass, roll, spin, turn **5** twirl, wheel, whirl **6** gyrate **7** perform, revolve, trundle **8** rotiform **9** alternate
rotation: 4 eddy **6** torque, vortex **9** pirouette
part: cam **4** axle **5** rotor, wheel
rote: 4 list **5** learn **6** course, custom, memory, repeat, system **7** routine **8** practice **9** automatic, condition **10** memorizing, repetition
rotiform: 6 rotate
rotor: 7 spinner **8** impeller
rotten: bad **4** evil, foul **5** fetid, nasty **6** putrid **7** carrion, corrupt, decayed, spoiled, tainted, unsound **8** depraved, unstable **9** offensive, putrefied **10** abominable, decomposed, putrescent, undermined **12** disagreeable **13** disintegrated **14** unsatisfactory
comb. form: **4** sapr **5** sapro

rotter: cad **7** shirker, slacker **10** blackguard
rotula: 6 troche **7** kneepan, lozenge, patella
rotund: 5 obese, plump, round, stout **6** chubby, portly **7** rounded **8** rolypoly, sonorous **9** spherical
roturier: 7 freeman **8** commoner
roue: rip **4** rake **9** debauchee, libertine
rouge: red **5** blush, color, flush, paint, score **6** redden, ruddle **8** cosmetic
rough: 4 hard, rude **5** acrid, brute, crude, hairy, harsh, husky, lumpy, raggy, rowdy, seamy, stern, surly, uncut **6** abrupt, broken, choppy, coarse, crabby, craggy, hoarse, jagged, rugged, severe, shaggy, uneven **7** austere, boorish, bristly, brusque, grating, hirsute, inexact, jarring, raucous, ruffian, ruffled, uncivil **8** churlish, clownish, gangster, impolite, obdurate, unplaned **9** imperfect, inclement, turbulent, unrefined **10** boisterous, discordant, incomplete, tumultuous, unpleasant, unpolished **11** approximate, tempestuous
roughen: 4 chap, fret, shag **5** feaze **7** engrail **10** exasperate
roughneck: 4 boor **5** rowdy, tough **7** sweater
roughness: 7 crudity **8** acrimony, asperity
rouky: 4 roky **5** foggy, misty
roulade: run **8** arpeggio, division, flourish
roulette: 10 epicycloid **11** epitrochoid **12** hypotrochoid
bet: bas **4** noir **5** carre, rouge **6** milieu **7** dernier, encarre, enplein
rounceval: 5 giant, large **6** virago **9** termagant
round: 4 beat, bout, full, rung **5** group, large, orbed, plump **6** circle, curved, period, rotund **7** bulbous, circuit, liberal **8** circular, complete, globular, rolypoly **9** spherical **11** cylindrical
round clam: 6 quahog
round dance: hay, ray **5** polka, waltz **7** roundel **9** roundelay, schottish **11** schottische
round robin: 6 letter **7** contest **8** document, petition **9** cigarfish **10** tournament
Round Table knight: Kay **6** Gawain **7** Caradoc, Cradock, Gaheris, Galahad **8** Lancelot, Tristram **9** Percivale
roundabout: 5 about, dance **6** detour **7** devious **8** circular, indirect, tortuous **10** circuitous, farfetched **13** approximately **14** circumlocution, circumlocutory
rounded: 4 oval **5** bombe, ovate **6** convex, rotund **7** arrondi, bunting, gibbous **8** circular **10** labialized
roundel: 4 guze
rounder: 4 roue **5** sport **8** criminal, drunkard, preacher **11** spendthrift
roundhead: 5 Swede **7** Puritan
roundup: 5 rodeo **9** gathering

roundworm: 4 nema 7 ascaris

roup: 4 sale 6 clamor 7 auction 8 shouting

rouse: daw, hie 4 call, move, stir, wake, whet 5 alarm, amove, awake, raise, rally, start, toast, upset, waken 6 arouse, awaken, bestir, bumper, excite, foment, frolic, revive 7 actuate, agitate, animate, disturb, enliven, startle 8 carousal, festival, inspirit 9 stimulate

roussette: 5 shark 7 dogfish

roust: 4 roar, stir, tide 5 rouse 6 bellow, tumult 7 current, roaring 9 bellowing

rout: ado, low, mob 4 band, beat, bray, dart, fuss, roar, root 5 crowd, knock, noise, scoop, shout, snore, snort, troop 6 bellow, clamor, defeat, furrow, rabble, search, strike, throng, tumult, uproar 7 company, confuse, debacle, repulse, retinue, retreat, rummage, slumber, trouble 8 assemble, assembly, confound, disperse, shouting, stampede, vanquish 9 bellowing, discomfit, hurricane, overpower, overthrow, overwhelm 11 disturbance 12 discomfiture

route: way 4 gest, lane, line, path, road 5 geste, march, trail 6 course, skyway 7 circuit, journey 9 direction, itinerary
circuitous: 6 detour
straight: 7 beeline

routh: 6 plenty 8 abundant 9 abundance, plentiful

routine: rut 4 rote 5 grind, habit, round, troll 6 course, groove, system 8 habitual 9 treadmill

rove: go; gad 4 move, part, pass, plow, roam, turn 5 prowl, range, stray 6 maraud, pierce, ramble, stroll, wander 8 straggle

rover: 5 nomad 6 pirate 7 corsair, Ishmael, migrant, vagrant 8 gadabout 9 itinerant

roving: 6 errant 7 cursory, devious 9 desultory 10 discursive

row: air, oar 4 bank, dust, file, fuss, line, list, rank, spat, tier 5 align, aline, brawl, broil, garry, noise, scull, swath 6 barney, clamor, paddle, pother, propel, rumpus, swathe 7 dispute, quarrel, ruction 8 argument, squabble 9 catalogue, commotion, excursion 11 disturbance 13 collieshangie

rowboat: cog, gig 4 dory, skif 5 canoe, cobil, coble, scull, skiff, skift 6 caique, galley, randan, wherry
stern: 7 transom

rowdy: 4 b'hoy, rude 5 rough, tough 6 roarer, tricky 7 hoodlum, vicious 8 larrikin 9 obstinate 10 boisterous

rowel: 4 spur 5 wheel 6 circle

rowen: 5 field 9 aftermath

rower: oar 6 punter 7 oarsman

rowing: 6 randan 8 sculling

royal: 4 real, rial, stag, true 5 basil, regal 6 august, kingly 7 stately 8 imperial, majestic, princely, splendid 9 excellent, sovereign 11 magnificent, monarchical

royal agaric: 8 mushroom

Royal Canadian Mounted Police: 7 Mountie

royal rock snake: 6 python

royal standard: 4 flag 6 banner, emblem

royalist: 4 Tory 8 Cavalier

royalty: 5 share 6 emblem 7 kingdom 8 kingship, nobility 10 kingliness, percentage 11 sovereignty
denoting: 5 crown 6 ermine, purple 7 scepter
symbol: 6 ermine

royet: 4 wild 6 unruly 7 romping 11 mischievous

rub: 4 bark, bray, buff, fret, rasp, wear, wipe 5 chafe, dight, feeze, grind, scour, smear 6 abrade, anoint, fridge, polish, scrape, smooth, stroke 7 burnish, massage 8 friction, irritate, obstacle 9 hindrance, triturate 10 difficulty, impediment

rub down: 4 comb 5 curry 7 massage

rub elbows: 9 associate 10 fraternize

rub out: 4 kill 5 elide, erase 6 cancel, efface, murder 7 expunge 10 obliterate

rubber: 4 band 5 brick 6 caucho, cutter, eraser 7 ebonite, masseur 8 masseuse, overshoe, polisher 9 vulcanite 10 caoutchouc
juice: 6 achete
source: 5 latex
substitute: 7 factice
synthetic: 4 buna
tree: 7 seringa

Rubber City: 5 Akron

rubber tree: ule 4 para 6 caucho 7 seringa 10 caoutchouc

rubbish: ket(Sc.), 4 flam, gear, junk, mull, pelf, pelt, raff, ross 5 crawm, dross, offal, trash, waste, wrack 6 colder, debris, garble, litter, refuse, rubble, trashy 7 baggage, beggary, mullock, rummage 8 nonsense, trumpery 9 worthless 10 clamjamfry 11 foolishness

rube: 4 hick, jake 6 rustic 7 bumpkin, hayseed 10 countryman

rubedity: 7 redness 9 ruddiness

rubellite: 10 tourmaline

rubeola: 7 measles, rubella

rubescent: red 4 pink 8 blushing, flushing 9 reddening 10 erubescent

rubicund: red 4 rosy, ruby 5 ruddy 6 florid 7 flushed, reddish, redness 11 full-blooded

rubor: 9 hyperemia

rubric: red 5 title 6 redden
book: 4 ordo 7 ordines(pl.)

ruby: gem, red 5 balas, jewel, stone 6 spinel 7 rubasse

ruck: rut, sit 4 fold, heap, mass, pile, rake, rick 5 cower, crowd, squat, stack 6 crease, crouch, furrow, pucker **7** crumple, wrinkle **9** multitude

ruckus: ado, row **6** rumpus, uproar **7** ruc't' **9** confusion **11** disturbance

ruction: **4** fray **5** fight, melee **6** uproar **7** quarrel **8** fraction, outbreak **11** disturbance

rudder: *control:* **4** helm **6** tiller
edge: **8** bearding
part: **4** yoke

ruddle: **5** rouge **6** redden

ruddy: red **4** rosy **5** fresh **6** florid, tanned **7** reddish **8** blushing

rude: **4** bold, curt, lewd **5** bluff, crude, harsh, rough, rowdy **6** bloody, borrel, brutal, clumsy, coarse, fierce, rugged, rustic, savage, severe, vulgar **7** artless, boorish, brutish, country, jarring, loutish, uncivil, uncouth, violent **8** churlish, clownish, homespun, ignorant, impolite, impudent, insolent, ungentle, untaught **9** barbarian, barbarous, ferocious, impetuous, inclement, inelegant, insulting, makeshift, truculent, turbulent, unskilled, untrained **10** boisterous, discordant, tumultuous, uncultured, ungracious, unmannerly, unpolished **11** acrimonious, impertinent, uncivilized **12** contumelious, discourteous

rudeness: **6** ferity

rudiment: **4** germ

rudimentary: **7** initial **9** elemental, vestigial **10** elementary **11** abecedarian, fundamental

rue: rew **4** pity, rake **5** dolor, grief, mourn **6** bewail, grieve, lament, regret, repent, sorrow, street, suffer **7** afflict, deplore, remorse **8** penitent **10** bitterness, compassion, repentance **14** disappointment

ruff: ree **4** bird, fish **5** perch, plait, reeve, stamp, trump **6** collar, fraise, hackle, pigeon, rabato, rebato, ruffle, tippet **7** applaud, sunfish **8** disorder, drumbeat **9** sandpiper

ruffian: **4** pimp, rage, thug **5** bully, cruel, rowdy **6** brutal, cutter, cuttle, pander, roarer, stormy **7** lawless, lustful, violent **8** assassin, gangster, hooligan, paramour **9** cutthroat, desperado, murderous **10** boisterous, licentious

ruffle: vex **4** beat, fret, roil, rool **5** annoy, brawl, crimp, frill, jabot, shake **6** nettle, riffle, ripple, tousel, tousle, tumult **7** agitate, derange, disturb, flounce, flutter, panuelo, roughen, swagger, wrinkle **8** brandish, dishevel, disorder, drumbeat, furbelow, irritate **9** balayeuse, carfuffle, commotion, confusion **10** disarrange, discompose **12** irregularity

ruffler: **5** bully, tramp **6** beggar **7** boaster, ruffian **8** braggart **10** attachment

rug: dog, mat, tug **4** Agra, cozy, haul, pull, snug, tear, wrap **5** Herat **6** afghan, carpet, frieze, kaross, liquor, runner, wrench **7** bargain, blanket, drugget, laprobe **8** Akhissar, Amritsar, covering, portiere **9** Samarkind **11** comfortable
Persian: see **Oriental rug**

ruga: **4** fold **6** crease **7** wrinkle **8** membrane

rugby: *formation:* **5** scrum
score: try

rugged: **4** hard, rude, sour **5** asper, hardy, harsh, rough, stern, surly **6** craggy, fierce, horrid, robust, seamed, severe, shaggy, stormy, strong, sturdy, uneven **7** austere, crabbed, gnarled, uncivil, unkempt **8** obdurate, vigorous, wrinkled **9** irregular, turbulent **10** ungracious, unpolished **11** tempestuous

rugose: **6** ridged **8** wrinkled **10** corrugated

Ruhr river: **4** Eder

ruin: gin **4** bane, bust, dash, doom, fall, fate, fell, harm, loss, undo **5** blast, break, decay, exile, fordo, havoc, spoil, wrack, wreck **6** beggar, blight, damage, deface, defeat, diddle, dismay, foredo, impair, injure, perish, ravage **7** decayed, despoil, destroy, pervert, ruinate, subvert **8** bankrupt, calamity, demolish, desolate, disaster, downfall **9** overthrow, perdition, ruination **10** bankruptcy, desolation, subversion **11** destruction, devastation, dissolution, ecroulement **12** delapidation

ruined: **4** dead **5** kaput **6** shabby **7** forlorn **10** tumbledown **11** dilapidated

ruinous: **10** pernicious

ruins: **5** ashes **6** debris **7** remains

rule: law **4** lord, norm, sway **5** by-law, canon, guide, maxim, order, regle, reign **6** course, decide, decree, direct, domine, empire, govern, manage, method, regime, screed **7** alidade, brocard, command, conduct, control, counsel, formula, precept, prevail, regency, regimen, theorem **8** behavior, decision, doctrine, domineer, dominion, persuade, practice, regulate, standard **9** authority, criterion, direction, enactment, influence, principle **10** convention, government, regulation **11** aristocracy, predominate **12** prescription **14** administration
pert. to: **5** rutic

rule out: bar **5** debar **6** forbid, refuse **7** prevent, scratch **8** preclude, prohibit

rule over: **6** manage **7** oversee **8** dominate **11** superintend

ruler: dey, min **4** amir, czar, emir, king, lord, tsar, tzar **5** alder, ameer, emeer, prior **6** archon, author, despot, dynast, ferule, gerent, prince, regent, satrap, sultan, tyrant **7** emperor, monarch, regulus, viceroy **8** autocrat, dictator, governor, hierarch, interrex **9** dominator, governail, imperator, matriarch, potentate, sovereign, yardstick **10** interreges(pl.) **12** straightedge *family:* **7** dynasty

former: Nhu **4** czar, Diem, tsar, tzar **5** Lenin **6** Fuhrer, Hitler, Stalin **7** Batista, Fuehrer, Leopold **8** Napoleon, Nicholas **9** Alexander, Mussolini

one of three: **7** triarch **8** triumvir

one of two: **6** duarch

wife: **4** rani **5** queen, ranee **7** czarina, empress, tzarina

rules: 4 code

infraction: **4** foul **8** cheating

ruling: law **7** average, current, inkling, regnant, statute **8** decision, dominant **9** ascendant, ascendent, hegemonic, prevalent **10** prevailing **11** predominant **13** predominating

rum: bad, odd **4** good, grog, poor **5** queer, tafia **6** liquor **7** Bacardi, cachaca, strange **8** beverage, peculiar **9** excellent

rumal: 8 kerchief

Rumania: *capital:* **8** Bucurest **9** Bucharest, Bukharest

coin: ban, leu, ley, lei **4** bani(pl.)

conservative: **5** boyar

king: **5** Carol **7** Michael

queen: **5** Marie

river: Alt, Jiu **5** Aluta, Arges, Schyl, Siret **6** Sereth

river port: **6** Galati, Galatz

town: **4** Arad, Iasi **5** Bacau, Jassy, Neamt, Turnu **6** Braila, Brasov, Galati, Galatz **7** Craiova, Focsani, Ploesti, Severin **8** Cernauti, Irongate, Kishenef, Kolsovar, Temesvar **9** Constanta, Cronstadt, Kronstadt, Nagyvarad, Timisoara **10** Czernovitz, Czernowitz **11** Klausenburg **12** Grosswardein

rumble: 4 seat **5** growl, rumor **6** murmur, polish, ramble, report, ripple, uproar **7** grumble **9** complaint **11** disturbance

rumbo: 4 grog

rumen: 6 paunch **7** stomach

ruminant: ox; yak **4** deer, goat **5** bison, camel, llama, moose, okapi, sheep, steer **6** alpaca, cattle, vicuna **7** buffalo, chewing, giraffe **8** antelope **10** meditative

female: cow, doe, ewe **5** nanny

genus: bos **5** capra

male: ram **4** buck, bull

stomach: **4** read, reed **5** rumen **6** omasum **8** abomasum, abomasus, roddikin **9** reticulum

ruminate: 4 chaw, chew, mull, muse **5** think, weigh **6** ponder **7** reflect **8** cogitate, consider, meditate

rummage: 4 rout, stow **6** gather, litter, search **7** collect, confuse, derange, examine, fossick, ransack, rubbish, stowage, turmoil **8** upheaval **9** confusion, searching **10** disarrange **11** derangement

rummer: cup **5** glass **6** better

rummy: rum **4** chap, game **5** drunk **8** drunkard

rumor: 4 buzz, sugh, talk, tell, word **5** bruit, noise, sough, story, voice **6** clamor, furphy, gossip, murmur, norate, report, spread, uproar **7** hearsay, message, tidings, whisper **9** grapevine, statement **10** reputation **11** scuttlebutt

personification: **4** Fama

repeat: **5** noise

rump: 4 dock **6** behind, insult **7** hurdies, plunder, remnant **8** bankrupt, buttocks **11** legislature

rump bone: 6 sacrum **8** edgebone **9** aitchbone

rumple: 4 fold, muss, rool, rump, tail **5** plait, touse **6** crease, frowse, tousle **7** crinkle, crumple, wrinkle

rumpus: row **5** brawl **6** barney, fracas, hubbub, uproar **9** confusion **11** disturbance

rumshop: bar **6** saloon, tavern **7** barroom, taproom

run: go; fly, gad, ply, rin(Sc.), sew **4** butt, cast, dart, dash, emit, flow, fuse, gait, grow, hare, hunt, melt, mold, move, pass, pour, race, roam, rove, sail, scud, tear, tend, trip, trot, turn, work **5** blend, brook, carry, climb, cover, creep, drive, enter, going, hurry, range, ravel, reach, recur, river, route, scoot, score, scour, speed, stand, trace, treat **6** ascend, bicker, career, charge, course, elapse, extend, gallop, govern, hasten, manage, output, pursue, refine, rotate, scurry, spread, spring, sprint, stream, thrust **7** conduct, contend, descend, develop, diffuse, journey, liquefy, migrate, operate, proceed, process, roulade, scamper, scutter, scuttle, smuggle, stretch, trickle **8** continue, dissolve, function, sequence, stampede, traverse **9** discharge, suppurate, transport **11** watercourse

across: **10** transverse

aground: **7** founder

run away: 4 bolt, flee **5** elope **6** decamp, desert, escape

run down: hit **4** kill, sink, stop **5** crush, decry **6** pursue **7** capture, decline, traduce **8** overbear **9** disparage, exhausted, overthrow **11** dilapidated

run-in: 4 tiff **5** fight **7** quarrel **11** altercation

run-of-the-mill: 6 common **7** average **8** ordinary

run off: 5 print, waste **7** impress

run out: 4 flow **5** expel, lapse, peter, spill, spilt, waste **6** elapse, expire, spread **8** squander

run over: 6 exceed, strike **8** overflow, rehearse

run through: 4 stab **6** pierce **7** examine, inspect, pervade **8** transfix

run up: 4 grow, rise **5** erect **7** enlarge **8** increase **9** construct **10** accumulate

runagate: 7 runaway **8** deserter, fugitive, renegade, vagabond, wanderer

runaway: 7 escapee 8 fugitive, runagate

rundle (see also **runnel**): 4 ball, drum, rung, step 5 round 6 circle, sphere

rundlet: tun 4 cask 6 barrel

rune: wen 5 magic 6 secret 7 mystery

rung: rod 4 spar, step 5 round, spoke, staff, stair, stake, stave, tread 6 cudgel, degree, rundle 7 girdled

runlet: 4 rush 5 brook 6 barrel, runnel 7 rivulet 9 streamlet

runnel: 4 rill 5 brook, creek, rhine 6 runlet, stream 7 channel, rivulet 9 streamlet 11 watercourse

runner: rug, ski 4 skee 5 agent, miler, racer, ravel, scarf 6 cursor, stolon 8 operator, smuggler, sprinter 9 collector, detective, messenger, solicitor

running: 4 care, trip 6 attack 7 contest, current, cursive, journey 8 skirmish 10 management, successive

running birch: 9 snowberry

running board: 9 footboard

running knot: 5 noose

running toad: 10 natterjack

runt: 4 chit, wrig 5 dwarf, pigmy, pygmy 6 durgan, durgen, titman

runty: 4 puny 5 small 7 stunted 8 dwarfish 10 diminutive, undersized 12 contemptible

runway: 4 file, path, ramp, road 5 chute, strip, track, trail 6 bridge, groove, trough 7 channel 8 platform 10 passageway

rupee, rupia: re., rs.(pl.)

rupia: 8 eruption

rupture: 4 part, rend, rent 5 break, burst, split 6 breach, hernia, rhexis 7 ruction, ruption 8 fraction, fracture 10 disruption, separating

rural: 6 rustic 7 bucolic, country 8 agrestic, Arcadian, geoponic, pastoral 11 countrified

life: 7 bucolic, georgic 8 pastoral

rurales: 9 policemen 12 constabulary

ruse: 4 fall, hoax, slip, wile 5 dodge, feint, fraud, shift, trick 6 deceit 8 artifice 9 stratagem 10 subterfuge

rush: sag 4 birr, dart, dash, junk, race, rout, scud, tear 5 break, brook, chute, feeze, haste, hurry, onset, press, sally, scoot, spate, sprat, sprot, straw, surge 6 attack, bustle, charge, combat, defeat, fescue, hasten, hurtle, hustle, runlet, sortie, trifle 7 assault, bulrush, cattail, destroy, rampage, repulse, tantivy 8 eruption, stampede 9 overthrow 11 undergrowth 13 precipitation

family: 9 juncaceae

load: 5 barth, gavel

rush hour: 4 peak

rush nut: 5 chufa

rush toad: 10 natterjack

rusk: 4 cake 5 bread, crisp, toast 7 biscuit

Russ: 7 Russian

Russia (see also **Soviet**): 4 USSR 7 Muscovy

alcoholic beverage: 5 kvass, quass, vodka 9 slivovitz

antelope: 5 saiga

apple: 9 astrachan

aristocrat: 5 Boyar 6 Boyard

automobile: Zis.

bondman: 4 serf

braid: 8 soutache

cabinet member: 9 commissar

cactus: 7 thistle

calendar: 6 Julian

cap: 4 aska

carriage: 6 drosky, troika 8 tarantas

cathedral: 5 sobor

caviar: 4 ikra 5 ikary

citadel: 7 Kremlin

city: 4 Kiev, Omsk, Orel, Perm 5 Gomel, Kasan, Kazan, Minsk, Pensa, Pskov 6 Kertch. Moscow(c.), Moskva, Nizhni, Odessa, Rostov, Samara, Sartov 7 Bataisk, Ivanovo, Kalinin, Rybinsk 8 Kostroma, Orenburg, Smolensk, Taganrog, Tashkent, Vladimir, Voronezh, Yaroslaf 9 Archangel, Astrakhan, Kuibishev, Petrograd 10 Michurinsk, Sebastopol, Sevastopol, Voznesensk 11 Cheliabinsk, Vladivostok 12 Ekaterinburg 13 Yekaterinburg 14 Nizhni Novgorod 15 Saint Petersburg

coal area: 6 Donets

coin: 5 altin, copec, kopek, ruble 6 copeck, grivna, kopeck 9 altininck, poltinnik 10 chervonets

collective farm: 6 kolhoz 7 kolkhos

commune: 6 kolhoz 7 kolkhos, kolkhoz

composer: Cui 9 Prokofiev 10 Stravinsky 12 Tschaikovsky 13 Shostakovitch 14 Rimsky-Korsakov

cossack: 6 Tartar

country house: 5 dacha

dance: 7 ziganka

decree: 5 ukase

delicacy: 6 caviar 7 caviare

devil: 5 chort

diplomat: 5 Malik, Zorin 6 Stalin 7 Gromyko, Molotov, Sobolev 8 Malenkov 9 Kuznetzov, Tsarapkin, Vishinsky 11 Shcherbakov

district: 7 Karelia

dog: 4 alan 6 borzoi 7 owtchah 9 wolfhound

dress: 7 sarafan

emperor: 4 czar, Ivan, tsar, tzar 5 Peter

empress: 7 czarina, tsarina, tzarina 8 tsaritza, tzaritza

exclamation: 7 nichevo 8 nitchevo

farmer: 5 kulak

fish: 6 beluga

flax: 6 bobbin

folk song: 6 bylina

forest: 6 tundra

fox: **6** corsac **7** karagan

gambling game: **6** coocoo

general: **10** Timoshenko **14** Tukhash-chevski

government group: **4** duma, rada, tsik **6** soviet **7** zemstvo **9** Politburo, Presidium **10** Praesidium **11** Politbureau

grandmother: **8** babushka

gulf: **4** Azov

hood: **7** bashlik, bashlyk

horse: **6** tarpan

house: **4** isba **5** dacha

image: **4** icon, ikon **5** ikono

imperial order: **5** ukase

kerchief: **6** analav

labor association: **5** artel

lagoon: **5** liman

lake: **4** Aral, Neva, Sego **5** Elton, Ilmen, Onega

language: **4** Russ

leader: **5** Lenin **6** Stalin **7** Molotov **8** Brezhnev **10** Khrushchev

measure: fut, lof **4** duim, fass, loof, stof **5** duime, foute, korec, ligne, osmin, pajak, stoff, vedro, verst **6** arshin, charka, liniya, osmina, paletz, sagene, tchast, versta, verste **7** arsheen, botchka, chkalik, garnetz, verchoc, verchok **8** boutylka, chetvert, krouchka, kroushka **9** chetverik **10** dessiatine **11** polugarnetz

mile: **5** verst

money: **5** ruble

monk: **7** starets **8** Rasputin

mountain range: **4** Alai, Ural

musical instrument: **5** gudok, gusla, gusle **9** balalaika

name: **4** Igor, Ivan, Olga **5** Peter, Sonya

naval academy: **6** Frunze

news agency: **4** Tass

newspaper: **6** Pravda **8** Izvestia

novelist: **5** Gorki **7** Chekhov, Tolstoi, Tolstoy **10** Dostoevsky

peasant: **5** kulak **6** muzhik, muzjik

peninsula: **4** Kola **6** Crimea **7** Karelia

people: Red **4** Lett, Russ, Slav **5** Ersar **7** Cossack, Russine **9** Muscovite **12** Byelorussian

poet: **6** Jehuda **7** Pushkin **9** Aleksandr, Pasternak, Sholokhov **11** Sergyeevich, Voznesensky, Yevtushenko

port: **4** Eisk **5** Anapa **6** Odessa **9** Archangel **10** Sevastapol **11** Vladivostok

prince **4** knez **5** knais, knyaz

revolutionist: **5** Lenin, Rykov **6** Stalin, Tomsky **7** Trotsky

river: Ik, Ob; Don, Ili, Ner, Oka, Ros, Ufa **4** Amur, Kara, Lena, Neva, Orel, Sura, Svir, Ural **5** Dnepr, Onega, Terek, Tobol, Volga **6** Donets, Irtish, Irtysh **7** Dnieper

saint: **4** Olga

satellite: **7** sputnik

sea: **4** Aral, Azof, Azov **6** Baikal

soup: **5** shchi **6** borsch **7** borscht

spa: Ems

stockade: **5** etape

tavern: **6** caback

urn: **7** samovar

villa: **5** dacha

village: mir

violinist: **5** Elman

worker: **7** dvornik **12** Stakhanovite

youth organizaton: **8** Comsomol, Komsomol

russud: **5** grain **6** forage

rust: eat **5** erode **6** aecium, aerugo, blight, canker, patina **7** corrode, erosion, oxidize **9** corrosion, oxidation, verdigris

rustic: hob **4** boor, carl, dull, hick, hind, jake, rube, rude **5** bacon, carle, chuff, churl, clown, doric, hodge, plain, rough, rural, swain, yokel **6** coarse, gaffer, honest, simple, sturdy, sylvan **7** artless, awkward, boorish, bucolic, bumpkin, bushman, Corydon, country, hayseed, peasant, plowboy, plowman, uncouth **8** agrestic, churlish, clownish, pastoral **9** agrestian, campesino, chawbacon, unadorned **10** clodhopper, countryman, unaffected, unpolished

rustle: **5** steal **6** fissle, fistle, scroop **7** crinkle

Rustum: *father:* Zal

son: **6** Sohrab

rut: rat, rit **4** brim **5** ditch, track **6** furrow, groove, strake **7** routine, wrinkle

rutabaga: **6** turnip

ruth: woe **4** pity **5** grief, mercy **6** regret, sorrow **7** remorse, sadness **10** compassion, repentance, tenderness **17** compassionateness

Ruth: *husband:* **4** Boaz

mother-in-law: **5** Naomi

son: **4** Obed

ruthless: **4** grim **5** cruel **6** savage **9** ferocious

rutter: **4** plow **5** guide **7** trooper **8** horseman

ruttle: **6** gurgle, rattle

rye: ree, rie **5** grain, grass **6** whisky **9** gentleman

disease: **5** ergot

ryke: **5** reach(Sc.)

ryot, raiyat: **6** farmer, tenant **7** peasant **10** cultivator

rytina: **12** hydrodamalis

Ryukyu: *island:* **7** Okinawa

S

S-shaped: 4 ogee **7** sigmate, sigmoid
sabana: See **savanna**.
sabbat: 8 assembly
saber, sabre: 8 scimitar, scimiter, yataghan
Sabine: *goddess:* **6** Vacuna
  people: **7** Vestini
sable: sad **4** dark, ebon **5** black, brush, saber **6** dismal, gloomy, marten, pellet **8** antelope, darkened **10** mysterious **11** threatening
  genus of: **7** mustela
  pert. to: **8** zibeline **9** zibelline
sablefish: cod **6** beshow **10** candlefish
sabot: 4 shoe
sabotage: 7 destroy **9** undermine **11** destruction
sabre: See **saber**.
sabutan: 5 fiber, straw
sac: bag, pod **4** cyst, sack **5** ascus, bursa, pouch, theca **6** cavity, saccus **7** cistern, utricle, vesicle **8** sacculus
saccadic: 5 jerky **9** twitching
saccharin: 7 gluside
saccharine: 5 sweet **10** sweetening
saccos: See **sakkos**.
sacculate: 7 pouched
sacerdotal: 8 clerical, priestly
sachet: bag, pad **4** oris **5** pouch, scent **8** reticule
sack (see also **sac**): bag, bed **4** base, fire, loot, poke, ruin **5** bursa, gunny, harry, pouch, purse, waste **6** budget, burlap, jacket, ravage, wallet **7** boucher, dismiss, musette, pillage, plunder **8** desolate **9** container, discharge, dismissal
sackless: 4 weak **7** bashful **8** harmless, innocent **9** guiltless, peaceable **10** dispirited, unmolested
sacrament: 4 sign **5** token **6** pledge, symbol **7** baptism, penance, promise, unction **8** ceremony, covenant **9** communion, Eucharist, matrimony **12** confirmation
sacrarium: 5 ambry **6** chapel, shrine **7** oratory **9** sanctuary **10** tabernacle
sacred: 4 holy **5** huaca, santo **6** divine **7** blessed **8** hallowed, reverend **9** geistlich, inviolate, venerated **10** inviolable, sacrosanct **11** consecrated **13** sanctimonious
  combining form: **5** hagio, hiero
  make: **8** enshrine
  most: **10** sacrosanct
sacred bean: 5 lotus
sacred beetle: 10 scarabaeus

sacred bo tree: 5 pipal
sacred fig: 5 pipal
sacred weed: 7 vervain
sacrifice: 4 host, loss **6** corban, homage, korban, victim **8** hecatomb, immolate, oblation, offering **9** holocaust, martyrdom, privation, surrender **10** immolation **11** destruction
sacrilege: 9 blasphemy **11** desecration, profanation
sacrosanct: 6 sacred
sad: bad **4** blue, dark, dram, dull **5** dusky, grave, sober, sorry, trist **6** dismal, dreary, gloomy, solemn, somber, sombre. triste(F.), wicked, woeful **7** doleful, dolente(It.), pensive, serious, unhappy **8** dejected, desolate, dolorous, downcast, grievous, mournful, pathetic, pitiable **9** afflicted, cheerless. depressed, plaintive, sorrowful **10** calamitous, deplorable, despondent, lugubrious **11** distressing, melancholic **12** disconsolate, heavyhearted
  combining form: **6** tragic
sadden: 7 attrist
saddle: 4 load **5** ridge **6** howdah **7** aparejo, pillion **8** encumber
  maker: **7** knacker
  pad: **5** panel **7** housing
  part: **4** horn, tore **5** arson, cinch, croup, girth, panel, pilch, skirt **6** cantle, corona, crutch, latigo, pommel **7** stirrup **8** sudadero **9** saddlebow
saddle horse: 4 pony **5** mount
saddle rock: 6 oyster
saddleback: 4 hill **5** ridge
saddlebag: jag(Sc.) **4** jagg(Sc.) **7** alforja, pannier
saddlecloth: 5 panel **7** housing **8** shabrack **9** shabraque
saddler: 4 seal **5** horse **7** cobbler, knacker, lorimer, loriner **9** shoemaker **11** saddlemaker
sadness: 5 blues, dumps
saeter: 6 meadow **7** pasture
safari: 4 hunt, trek **7** caravan, journey **9** excursion **10** expedition
safe: box **4** sure **5** chest, siker, sound, vault **6** armory, closet, coffer, holder, secure, sicker, unhurt **8** cupboard, unharmed **9** strongbox, untouched **10** depository **11** gardeviance, trustworthy
safe-conduct: 4 pass **5** cowle, guard **6** convoy **10** permission, protection

safecracker: 4 yegg 7 peteman

safeguard: 4 pass 5 guard 6 convoy, escort, safety 7 defense, protect 10 protection

safekeeping: 4 care 7 custody, storage 10 protection

safety: 6 surete(F.) 9 assurance

place of: ark 4 port 5 haven 6 asylum, refuge 7 retreat, sanctum

zone: 6 island

safety pin: 5 clasp 6 fibula

safety rail: 9 guardrail

saffron: 6 crocus, yellow 9 safflower

sag: 4 bend, flag, reed, rush, sink, wilt 5 drift, droop, sedge, slump 6 settle, weaken

saga: 4 edda, epic, myth, tale 5 story 6 legend 7 history, recital 9 narrative

narrator: 7 sagaman

sagaciate: 4 fare 6 thrive

sagacious: 4 sage, wise 5 acute, quick 6 argute, astute, shrewd 7 knowing, politic, prudent, sapient 9 judicious 10 discerning, farsighted, hardheaded 11 clairvoyant, penetrating 13 perspicacious

sagacity: 6 acumen 8 sapience

sagamore: 5 chief 6 sachem

sage: 4 herb, mint, seer, wise 5 clary, grave, rishi(Ind.), solon, spice 6 pundit, salvia, shrewd, solemn 7 learned, prudent, sapient 8 sagebush 9 counselor, judicious, venerable 10 counsellor, discerning, perceptive 11 philosopher

Sage:

of Chelsea: 13 Thomas Carlyle

of Concord: 17 Ralph Waldo Emerson

of Ferney: 8 Voltaire

of Monticello: 15 Thomas Jefferson

of Pylon: 6 Nestor

sage cheese: 7 cheddar

sage cock: 6 grouse

sage hen: 6 grouse 7 Nevadan

Sagebrush State: 6 Nevada

saginate: 6 fatten

Sagittarius: 6 archer, bowman

sago: 6 starch

sago palm: 7 coontie

sagoin: 8 marmoset

saguaro: 6 cactus

sagum: 5 cloak

Sahara: *people:* 4 Arab 5 nomad 6 Tuareg

plateau: 6 hamada 7 hammada

saic: 4 boat 5 ketch

said (see also **say**): dit(F.) 5 quoth 6 spoken, stated 7 reputed, uttered 8 supposed

Saida: 5 Sidon

saiga: 4 coin 8 antelope

sail: awe, awn, fly, rig, van 4 dart, duck, haul, keel, luff, move, scud, skim, soar, swim, trip 5 fleet, float, glide, sheet 6 canvas, depart, embark, voyage 7 journey 8 navigate 9 excursion

kind of: jib 5 royal 6 lateen, mizzen,

    square 7 balloon, lugsail, skysail, spanker, topsail, trysail 8 foresail, mainsail, staysail, studding 9 crossjack, foreroyal, spinnaker 10 topgallant 12 forestaysail

part: 4 bunt, clew, yard 5 leach, leech, sheet 6 earing 7 earring, yardarm

pert. to: 5 velic

prepare to: 4 trim

sail yard: rae(Sc.) 4 spar

sailboat: 4 bark, yawl 5 skiff, sloop, yacht 7 caravel 9 caravelle

sailcloth: 4 duck 6 canvas

sailfish: 8 billfish

sailing: 4 asea

sailing ship: cog 4 bark, brig, saic, yawl 5 sloop 6 barque, cutter, galley, sampan, vessel 7 frigate, galleon 8 schooner 10 barkentine, brigantine 11 barquentine

scoop: 5 skeet

sailor: gob, hat, tar, tot 4 salt 5 Jacky 6 hearty, lascar, ratiny 7 mariner, seafman 8 coxswain, seafarer, waterman 10 bluejacket, lobscouser

assent: aye

associate: 8 messmate

chapel: 6 bethel

group: 4 crew 5 hands

mess tub: kid

patron saint: 4 Elmo

song: 6 chanty 7 chantey 9 barcarole

saint: St.; Sao(Port.), Ste. 4 holy 5 santa(Sp.), santo 6 hallow 7 beatify 8 canonize, enshrine

England: 6 George

image: 5 santo

invocation of: 10 hagiolatry

Ireland: 7 Patrick

musician: 7 Cecilia

Scotland: 6 Andrew

worship: 10 hagiolatry, hierolatry

Saint Andrew's cross: 7 saltier, saltire

Saint Barnabas' prayer: 8 Ave Maria

Saint Elmo's fire: 5 flame 6 furole 9 corposant

Saint John's-bread: 5 carob

Saint Martin's: *bird:* 7 harrier

feast: 9 Martinmas

Saint Paul's companion: 4 Luke

Saint Peter: 5 Simon

Saint Veronica's handkerchief: 8 sudarium

saintly: 4 holy 5 pious 6 devout 7 angelic 9 angelical 13 sanctimonious

sake: end 5 cause, drink 6 behalf, motive, regard 7 account, benefit, concern, purpose 8 beverage 13 consideration

saker: 6 falcon

saki: 5 drink, yarke 6 monkey, yarkee 8 beverage

sakkos, saccos: 8 vestment

sal: 4 salt

sala: 4 hall

salaam, salam: bow 4 bend 6 salute 8

greeting **9** obeisance **10** compliment, salutation
salacious: 4 lewd **7** lustful, obscene **8**
scabrous **9** lecherous **12** pornographic
salad ingredient: 5 cress **6** celery, endive, greens **7** lettuce, romaine **8** scallion
10 watercress
salad tree: 6 redbud
salamander: eft, olm **4** evet, newt **6** triton
7 axoloti, axolotl, caudata, urodela, uro-
dele **10** hellbender
salami: 7 sausage
salary: fee, pay **4** hire **5** wages **6** reward **7**
stipend **8** pittance **9** allowance, emolu-
ment **10** exhibition, honorarium, recompense **12** compensation, remuneration
13 consideration
sale: net **4** deal, hall, vend **5** bower **6** market, palace, vendue, willow **7** auction,
bargain, chamber, rummage **8** contract,
transfer **9** utterance, vendition **10** conveyance **11** transaction
salesman: 5 agent, clerk **6** hawker, pedlar, seller, sutler, vendor **7** drummer,
hustler, peddler **8** pitchman, ven-
deuse(fem.) **9** solicitor **14** representative
salience: 5 point **7** agility **8** emphasis **9**
highlight **10** prominence
salient: 4 line **5** cabre, redan **6** trench **7**
jumping, leaping **8** bounding, extended,
striking **10** noticeable **11** conspicuous
salient angle: 5 arris
salient point: 5 heart **6** detail, source **7**
feature
salientia: 5 anura, frogs, toads **7** aglossa,
costata **8** Amphibia, linguata
salina: 4 lake, pond **5** marsh **6** salada **9**
saltworks
saline: 4 tear **5** brine, briny, salty **8**
brackish **10** saliferous
Salisbury steak: 9 hamburger
saliva: 4 spit **7** spittle
salix: 5 genus **6** osiers **7** sallows, willows
salle: 4 room
sallet, salade: 6 helmet
sallow: wan **4** pale, twig **5** muddy, osier,
shoot **6** pallid, willow **9** yellowish
sally: 4 leap, quip, rush, trip **5** dance, issue, jaunt, start **6** attack, escape, retort,
sortie, spring **7** darting, rushing **8** escapade, outbreak, outburst **9** excursion,
witticism **10** liveliness
salmagundi: 4 hash, olio **5** salad **6** medley **7** mixture **9** potpourri
salmon: gib, lax **4** chum, coho, kelt, keta,
mort, pike, pink, raun, slat **5** color,
haddo, holia, nerka, smolt, tecon **6** baggit,
kipper, laurel, sauqui, taimen **7** gilling,
saumont, shedder **8** schoodic, springer,
weakfish **9** ceratodus **10** barramunda
enclosure: 4 weir, yair, yare
smoked: lox
trap: 4 slap
salmon trout: 5 sewen

salmonoid: 4 ahyu **5** nelma, powan
Salome: *father:* 8 Herodias
grandfather: 5 Herod
salon: 4 hall, room **7** gallery **9** apartment,
reception **10** assemblage, exhibition
saloon: bar **4** hall, room **5** cabin, coach,
cuddy, divan, sedan **6** tavern **7** can-
tina(Sp.) **8** alehouse, groggery **9** apartment, barroom, brasserie(F.)
saloop: 5 drink, salep **9** sassafras
salpa, salp: 8 tunicate
salse: 7 volcano
salt: sal, tar, wit **4** alum, corn, cure **5** brine,
briny, ester, salic, sharp, witty **6** alkali,
flavor, halite, harden, lively, sailor, saline,
seaman, season **7** bromate, piquant, pungent, seadust **8** brackish, halinous **9** seasoning
combining form: 4 sali
deposit: 6 saline
oleic acid: 6 oleate
resembling: 5 halid **6** halide, haloid
rock: pig
working: 7 halurgy
salt-like: 6 haloid
salt marsh: 6 salina
salt pit: vat
salt tree: 4 atle **8** tamarisk
salt water: 5 brine
saltate: 4 jump, leap **5** bound, dance
saltcellar: 5 saler
salted: 4 alat **5** cured **6** corned
saltpeter, saltpetre: 5 niter, nitre
saltworks: 7 saltern, saltery
salty: See **salt.**
salubrious: 8 salutary **9** benignant,
healthful, wholesome **10** beneficial
salutary: 4 good **6** benign **7** healthy, helpful **8** curative **9** desirable, healthful,
medicinal, wholesome **10** beneficial **11**
restorative
salutation: hi; ave, bow **4** beck, hail **5**
aloha, hello, howdy, salam, skoal **6**
curtsy, kowtow, Mizpah, Mizpeh, prosit,
salaam, salute **7** address, welcome,
slainte **8** accolade, chin-chin, farewell,
greeting
salute: nod **4** hail **5** greet, halse, salvo **6**
accost **7** address **10** salutation
salvage : 4 save **6** rescue **7** reclaim **12**
compensation
salvager: 6 salvor
salvation: 6 rescue **10** redemption **12**
preservation
pert. to: 8 soterial **9** soterical
salve: 4 balm **6** anoint, cerate, soothe **7**
assuage, unguent **8** flattery, ointment,
palliate
salver: 4 tray **6** waiter
salvo: 6 excuse, salute **7** pretext, proviso,
quibble **9** exception **11** reservation
samadh: 4 tomb **6** shrine
samaj: 6 church **7** society **12** congregation

Samaritan: *alphabet:* i; ba, in, it; jud, mim, nun, phi, sen, tav, tit **4** alaf, bith, goph, kaph, rish, sadi, shan **5** dalat, gaman, labad **6** simcat
god: **6** Tartak
people: **8** Assyrian **9** Israelite
sambar, sambur: elk **4** deer, maha, rusa
same: id; ilk, one **4** ibid, idem, like, meme(F.), self **5** alike, ditto, equal **7** identic **9** identical, unchanged **10** invariable
sameness: **8** monotony **10** similarity **11** resemblance **14** correspondence
Samhain Eve: **9** Halloween
Samian philosopher: **10** Pythagoras
samlet: **4** parr **6** salmon **10** fingerling
sammy: **5** ninny **6** clammy, sodden, watery **9** simpleton
Samoa (see also **Polynesia**): *capital:* **4** Apia
fish: **6** ataata, sesele
hostess: **5** taupo **6** taupou
island: **5** Upolu **6** Savaii
mollusk: asi
mudworm: ipo
owl: **4** lulu
warrior: toa
samp: **4** meal, mush, soup **6** cereal, hominy **8** porridge
sampaloc: **8** tamarind
sampan: **4** boat **5** skiff
sample: **4** test **5** taste **6** swatch **7** example, pattern **8** specimen **12** illustration
sampleman: **6** taster **12** demonstrator
sampler: **5** model **6** taster **7** example, hanging, pattern **8** original, specimen **9** archetype
Samson's betrayer: **7** Delilah
Samuel: *home:* **5** Ramah
mentor: Eli
son: **5** Abiah
victim: **4** Agag, Agog
sanative: **6** curing **7** healing **8** curative, sanatory **9** healthful
sanatorium: spa **8** hospital
sanatory: **8** sanative
Sancho Panza: *island:* **9** Barataria
mule: **6** Dapple
sanctify: **8** dedicate **10** consecrate
sanctimonious: **4** holy **5** pious **6** devout, sacred **7** saintly **10** sanctified
sanctimoniousness: **4** cant
sanction: **4** amen, fiat **5** allow **6** assent, avouch, permit, placet, ratify **7** approve, confirm, endorse, indorse, support **8** accredit, approval **9** allowance, approbate, authority, authorize, encourage, subscribe **10** imprimatur **11** approbation, countenance, countersign, endorsement **12** ratification **13** authorization, encouragement
sanctity: **5** rites **6** purity **7** halidom **8** halidome, holiness, recesses **9** godliness, solemnity **10** sacredness **11** obligations, saintliness **13** inviolability

place of: **4** fane **5** altar, hiera **6** chapel, church, hieron, shrine, temple **7** chaitya **9** synagogue
sanctuary: ark **4** bema, fane, holy, naos **5** abbey, adyta(pl.), bamah, grith, haven **6** adytum, asylum, bemata, chapel, church, haikal, priory, refuge, shrine, temple **7** alsatia, chancel, convent, halidom, retreat, sanctum, shelter **8** cloister, halidome, holiness **9** monastery **10** protection, tabernacle **11** reservation
sanctum: den **5** study **6** adytum, office **9** sanctuary
sand: **4** grit **5** nerve **6** abrade, desert, gravel, smooth **7** courage **8** alluvium, asbestic
and clay: **4** loam
resembling: **7** arenoid
sand cock: **8** redshank
sand dune: **5** towan
sand eel: **4** grig **5** lance **6** launce
sand flounder: **5** fluke **10** windowpane
sand hill: **4** dene, dune
sand lob: **7** lugworm
sand widgeon: **7** gadwall
sandal (see also **moccasin**): **4** clog, shoe **6** buskin, caliga, charuk **7** rullion, slipper, talaria **9** alpargata **10** espadrille
sandarac: **7** realgar
wood: **6** alerce, alerse
sandbank: **4** dune, meal
sandbar: **4** dene, dune
sandia: **10** watermelon
sandpiper: ree **4** bird, knot, ruff **5** reeve, terek **6** dunlin, teeter, tiltup **7** brownie, chorook, fiddler, haybird **8** triddler, redshank **10** canderling
sandstone: **4** grit **5** hazel **6** arkose **8** ganister **9** gritstone
block: **6** sarsen
pert. to: **10** arenilitic
sandy: **6** gritty, plucky **7** arenose, arenous **8** shifting, unstable **9** arenulous **10** arenaceous **13** uninteresting
pert. to: **6** eremic
Sandy: **8** Scotsman
sane: **4** wise **5** lucid, sober, sound **6** normal **7** healthy, sapient **8** rational, sensible **10** reasonable
sang (see also **sing**): **5** blood
sangfroid: **8** calmness, coolness **9** composure **16** imperturbability
sanglier: **4** boar
sanguinaria: **6** yarrow **9** bloodroot
sanguine: red **4** fond, gory, warm **5** cruel, ruddy **6** ardent, bloody, crayon, savage, yarrow **7** buoyant, hopeful **8** cheerful, hematite **9** confident, ferocious, murderous **10** bloodstone, ensanguine, optimistic, sanguinary **12** bloodthirsty
sanitary: **8** hygienic
sanity: **6** reason **7** balance **8** lucidity, saneness **9** soundness **13** wholesomeness
sans: **7** without

Sanskrit: *dialect:* 4 Pali
  dictionary: 10 amara-kosha
  division of literature: 5 Sruti 6 Shruti
  epic: 8 Ramayana
  epic character: 4 Sita
  school: tol
  soul: 5 atman
Santa Barbara island: 8 Catalina
Santa Claus's reindeer: 5 Comet, Cupid,
  Vixen 6 Dancer, Dasher, Donder, Donner
  7 Blitzen, Prancer
santo: 5 image, saint
santon: 4 monk 5 image, saint 6 hermit 7
  dervish
sap: lac 4 dupe, fool, milk, mine, seve(F.),
  upas 5 drain, juice, latex, lymph, vigor 6
  energy, trench, weaken 7 exhaust, saphead 8 enervate, vitality, weakling 9 exudation, schlemiel, schlemihl, screwball,
  undermine 10 debilitate, devitalize
  dried: gum
  lose: 5 bleed
  spout: 5 spile
sapanwood, sappanwood: 4 tree 10
  brazilwood
saphead: See **sap.**
saphie, saffi: 5 charm 6 amulet 8 talisman
sapid: 5 tasty 6 savory 7 savoury 8 engaging 9 palatable 10 flavorable
sapient: 4 sage, sane, wise 6 shrewd 7
  knowing 9 sagacious 10 discerning
sapiutan: 4 anoa
sapless: dry 7 insipid 8 withered 9 exsuccous 11 devitalized
sapling: 5 plant, youth
sapo: 4 soap 8 toadfish
sapodilla, sapotilha, sapotilla: 5 chico
  6 sapota, sapote, zapote 7 nispero 9
  naseberry
saponaceous: 5 soapy 7 elusive 8 slippery
sapor: 5 gusto, savor, taste 6 flavor, relish
  7 flavour
sapper: 5 miner 6 digger
sappy: 5 juicy, moist, pithy, plump, silly 6
  sodden 7 fatuous, foolish 8 vigorous 9
  energetic, succulent 11 sentimental
sapsago: 6 cheese
sapsucker: 10 woodpecker
sapwood: 8 alburnum
Saracen: 4 Arab 5 nomad 6 Moslem
  Knight: 6 Rogero 8 Ruggiero
Sarah: *husband:* 7 Abraham
  slave: 5 Hagar
  son: 5 Isaac
sarcasm: 4 gibe, jeer 5 fling, irony, taunt
  6 attack, rebuke, satire 7 mockery 8
  acridity, reproach, ridicule 9 criticism
  pert. to: 8 ironical
sarcastic: dry 6 biting 7 cutting, mordant
  8 incisive, sardonic
sarcenet, sarsenet: 4 silk, soft 6 smooth
  8 tempered

sarcina: 8 bacteria 9 bacterium
sarcophagus: 4 tomb 6 coffin, cooler
sard: 7 sardine, sardius 9 carnelian 10
  chalcedony
sardine: 4 bang 8 pilchard
sardonic: 8 derisive 9 sarcastic
Sargon capital: 5 Accad
sarkinite: 8 arsenate
sarment: 4 cion 6 runner 7 cutting
sarong: 6 comboy
sarpler: 4 bale 6 weight 7 wrapper 8
  covering
sarrazin: 9 buckwheat
sarsen: 5 block 8 monument 9 sandstone
sartor: 6 tailor
sash: obi 4 band, belt, benn(Sc.) 5 scarf 6
  fascia, girdle 8 casement 9 waistband 10
  cummerbund
sasin: 4 buck 8 antelope
Saskatchewan capital: 6 Regina
sassaby: 8 antelope
sassafras tea: 6 saloop
Satan: 4 Nick 5 demon, devil, eblis, fiend
  6 Belial 7 Lucifer, tempter 8 diabolus 9
  archenemy, archfiend 14 Mephistopheles
  associate: 9 Beelzebub
  son: Imp
satanic: 4 evil 6 wicked 8 devilish, diabolic, infernal 10 diabolical
satchel: bag 4 case, grip 5 cabas 6 valise
satellite: Io 4 luna, moon, Rhea, vein 5
  Ariel, Dione, Mimas, Titan 6 Europa,
  planet, Tethys 7 Japetus 8 Callisto, follower, Ganymede, Hyperion 9 attendant,
  dependent, Enceladus
  man-made: 4 Oso 4 Anna, Echo, Mars 5 Ariel, Faith, Lunik, Midas, Relay, Samos,
  Tiros 6 Cosmos, Flight, Ranger, Syncom,
  Vostok 7 Courier, Mariner, Pioneer,
  Sputnik, Telstar, Transit 8 Alouette, Explorer, Telestar, Vanguard 9 Vela-Hotel
  10 Discoverer 12 Mercury-Atlas, Proj-
  ect-Score
satiat: 7 replete
satiate: 4 cloy, fill, glut, pall, sate 5 gorge.
  slake 6 pamper 7 content, gratify, overeat, satisfy
satiating: 4 rich 6 stodgy 7 fulsome
satiety: 7 surfeit
satin imitation: 6 sateen 7 satinet 9 satinette
satin pod: 7 honesty
satiny: 6 glossy 8 lustrous
satire: 5 grind, irony 6 banter, parody,
  satura 7 lampoon, mockery, sarcasm 8
  ridicule, travesty
satiric: dry 6 bitter, ironic 7 abusive, atellan, caustic, cutting 8 ironical, poignant
  10 censorious 11 reproachful
satirize: 4 lash 5 grind 6 attack, expose 8
  denounce 9 criticize
satisfaction: 4 ease, gree 6 amends 7
  content, payment 8 pleasure 9 atonement, enjoyment 10 bloodmoney, recom-

pense, reparation, settlement 11 complacence, contentment 12 compensation,
propitiation, remuneration 13 gratification 15 indemnification

satisfactory: pat 4 good 6 enough 8 adequate 9 allowable, expiatory 10 acceptable, satisfying

satisfied: fed 4 paid, smug 5 proud 9 contented, gratified 10 complacent

satisfy: do; pay 4 cloy, feed, fill, free, meet,
sate, suit 5 appay, atone, repay, serve,
slake 6 defray, please, supply 7 appease,
assuage, content, expiate, fulfill, gratify,
require, satiate, suffice, surfeit 8 convince, reparate 9 discharge 10 compensate, remunerate

satrap: 5 ruler 6 prince, tyrant 8 governor, official, overlord

sattva: 5 truth 6 purity, wisdom 8 goodness 12 tranquillity

saturate: ret, sog, sop, wet 4 fill, glut, soak
5 imbue, souse, steep 6 dampen, drench,
imbibe, imbrue, seethe 7 ingrain, satiate,
satisfy 8 permeate 9 penetrate 10 impregnate

saturated: 6 sodden

Saturday: 7 Sabbath
  pert. to: 9 sabbatine

Saturn: *ring part:* 5 ansae
  satellite: 4 Rhea 5 Dione, Mimas, Titan 6
  Tethys 7 Japetus 8 Hyperion 9 Enceladus
  temple treasury: 8 aerarium

saturnine: 4 dull 5 grave, heavy 6
gloomy, morose, sullen 8 sluggish, taciturn

satyr: 4 faun, idol 5 deity 7 demigod 9
butterfly

sauce: dip 5 gravy 6 flavor, relish 8 dressing, matelote 9 condiment
  kind: soy 4 alec, lear 5 garum 6 catsup 7
  catchup, gascony, ketchup, mustard 8
  chawdron, remolade 9 genevoise, remoulade 10 Bordelaise, mayonnaise 11 Hol-
  landaise

sauciness: 10 effrontery

saucy: 4 bold, coxy, pert, rude 5 brash,
fresh 6 bantam, cocket 7 forward 8 impudent, malapert 9 audacious, sprightly
11 impertinent

Saul: *concubine:* 6 Rizpah
  daughter: 6 Michal
  herdsman: 4 Doeg
  uncle: Ner
  wife: 7 Ahinoam

Saul of Tarsus: 4 Paul

Sault Sainte Marie: Soo

saumont: 6 salmon

sauna: 4 bath 9 bathhouse

saunter: lag 4 idle, roam, rove, walk 5
range, shool, stray 6 dander, dawdle, loiter, lounge, potter, ramble, stroll, wander
8 ruminate

saunterer: 8 passerby

saurel: 4 fish, scad 5 xurel

saurian: 6 lizard 8 dinosaur

saury: 4 fish

sausage: 5 gigot 6 salame, salami, wiener
7 balloon, balogna, baloney, saveloy 8
cervelat, drisheen, rollejee, rolliche 9 an-
douille, bratwurst, rollichie 11 wiener-
wurst 12 andouillette
  casing: 4 bung
  poisoning: 11 allantiasis

sausage-shaped: 9 allantoid 11 allantoi-
dal

savage: 4 fell, grim, rude, wild 5 brute,
crude, cruel, feral 6 brutal, ferine, fierce
7 brutish, furious, howling, inhuman, untamed 8 pitiless, ruthless 9 aborigine,
atrocious, barbarian, barbarous, ferocious, merciless, primitive, truculent 10
unpolished 11 uncivilized 12 uncultivated, unrestrained

Savage Island people: 5 Niuan

savanna, savannah: 5 plain 9 grassland

savant: 4 sage 5 Solon 6 pedant 7 scholar
9 scientist

savarin: 7 brioche 10 coffeecake

save: bar, but 4 hain, keep 5 amass, catch,
guard, hoard, salve, spare, store 6 defend,
except, redeem, rescue, retain, scrimp,
unless 7 deliver, husband, protect, reclaim, reserve, salvage 8 conserve, preserve 9 economize, excepting 10 accumulate

savin, savine: 7 juniper

saving: 6 frugal, thrift 7 thrifty 9 frugality

savings: 7 account, addlins 8 addlings

savoir faire: 4 tact 10 adroitness 11
worldliness 14 sophistication

savor, savour: 4 odor, zest 5 sapor, scent,
smack, smell, taste, tinge 6 degust, flavor,
relish, season 9 degustate

savory: 5 gusty, salty, sapid, tasty 7 piquant 8 pleasing 9 agreeable, palatable
10 appetizing, delightful

saw (see also **see**): cut 4 talk, word 5
adage, axiom, maxim, motto, rumor 6
cliche, saying 7 proverb 8 aphorism, apothegm 9 platitude 10 apophthegm
  combining form: 5 serri
  kind: 5 briar, edger, serra 6 stadda, trapan, trepan 8 trephine
  part: 4 tine 5 redan, tooth

saw-like: 8 serrated

sawbelly: 7 alewife

sawbones: 7 surgeon

sawder: 7 flatter

sawhorse: 4 buck 7 sawbuck

sawyer: 6 beetle, logman 9 lumberman 10
woodcutter

saxhorn: 4 alto, tuba

saxifrage: 6 seseli

Saxon: 9 Sassenach
  chief: 5 Horsa
  city: Ave
  king: Ine 6 Harold

lady: **6** Godiva, Rowena
serf: **4** esne
swineherd: **5** Gurth
warrior: **5** Thane
Saxony city: 7 Dresden
say: 4 aver, deem, silk, tell, wool **5** speak,
state, utter **6** advise, allege, answer, assert, bucket, direct, fabric, recite, relate,
remark, repeat, report **7** declare, dictate,
express, iterate, testify **8** announce, indicate **9** pronounce **10** asseverate
again: **6** repeat **9** reiterate
further: add
saying: mot, saw **4** quip, word **5** adage,
axiom, logia, maxim, motto **6** byword,
phrase **7** epigram, proverb **8** aphorism,
apothegm **9** statement **11** declaration
apt: **6** bon mot
collection: ana **9** gnomology
distinguishing: **10** shibboleth
scab: 5 crust, mange **6** eschar, ratter **8**
blackleg **9** scoundrel **13** strike-breaker
scabbard: 4 case **6** sheath, tsubas **7** holster
put in: **7** sheathe
tip: **7** crampit
scabby: low **4** base, mean **5** mangy **6**
scurvy, shabby, stingy **12** contemptible
scaddle: 4 wild **6** fierce **7** nervous **8** skittish **11** mischievous
scaffie: 9 scavenger
scaffold: 4 cage, loft **5** easel, stage **7** gallery **8** platform
scalage: 8 estimate **9** allowance **10** percentage
scalar: 10 ladderlike
scalawag, scallawag: 4 pony, runt **5**
scamp **6** rascal **10** scapegrace
scald: vex **4** burn **5** worry **6** blanch, excite,
scorch **7** inflame, torment
scale: cup, hut **4** bowl, film, husk, peel,
rate, rule, scut, shed, size **5** climb, flake,
gamut, lepis, palea, scute, shive, weigh **6**
ascend, lamina, rament, spread, vessel,
weight **7** balance, clamber, coating, compare, lamella, measure, scatter, vernier **8**
covering, disperse, separate **9** gradation,
steelyard **13** incrustation
note: do, fa, la, mi, re, ti; sol **8** dominant
10 supertonic
scale-like: 6 scurfy **7** leprose
scaling device: 6 ladder
scallion: 4 leek **5** onion **7** shallot
scallop: 4 quin **5** crena, notch **7** crenate,
mollusk
scalp: rob **4** skin **5** cheat **6** defeat, denude,
profit, trophy
scalper: 6 punter, trader **10** speculator
scaly: low **4** mean **6** stingy **8** squamous **10**
despicable
scamble: 6 sprawl **7** collect, shamble,
trample **9** scramble
scamp: imp **5** cheat, knave, rogue **6** rascal
8 scalawag, spalpeen, widdifow **9** scallawag, scoundrel **10** highwayman

scamper: run **4** race **5** speed **6** frolic, hasten, scurry **7** brattle, skitter **9** skedaddle
scan: eye **5** study, watch **6** behold, peruse,
survey **7** examine, observe **10** scrutinize
11 contemplate
scandal: 5 eclat, odium, shame **6** gossip **7**
calumny, outrage, slander **8** disgrace, ignominy **9** discredit **10** backbiting, defamation, detraction, opprobrium
scandalous: 6 unholy **8** libelous, shocking
9 offensive **10** flagitious **11** furciferous
scandent: 8 climbing
Scandinavia (see also **Norse; Teuton): 4**
Dane, Lapp **5** Norse, Swede **8** Norseman,
Suiogoth **9** Icelandic, Norwegian
alphabetical character: **4** rune
bard: **5** scald **7** sagaman
division: amt
explorer: **4** Eric
hero's place: **8** Valhalla
king: **4** Atli
land: **4** odal
legend: **4** edda, saga
legendary creature: nis **5** nisse, troll **6**
Kraken
measure: ass, lod, ort, vog **4** last, mark,
pund, sten, untz **5** carat **6** nylast **7** centner, lispund **8** lispound, skalpund, skeppund, skippund **9** shippound, skaalpund,
skibslast **10** bismerpund
minstrel: see *bard* above
money: **5** krone
nobleman: **4** jarl
pert. to: **5** Norse
plateau: **5** fjeld
rulers: Ros **10** Varangians
ship: **4** aesc
small bay: **5** fjord
trumpet: **4** lure
scant: few **4** lean **5** chary, stint **6** geason,
meager, meagre, narrow, scrimp, slight,
sparse **7** limited, sparing, wanting **12**
parsimonious
scanty: 4 bare **5** close, small, spare **6**
meager, meagre, scarce, sparse **7** limited,
niggard, scrimpy, sparing **8** exiguous **9**
niggardly **12** insufficient, parsimonious
scape: 4 slip, stem **5** fault, shaft **8** escapade, peduncle
scapegrace: 5 rogue, scamp **6** madcap,
rascal **8** scalawag **9** reprobate, scallawag
10 profligate
scar: arr, mar, shy **4** mark, rock, seam, slit,
wild **5** chink, cliff, crack, wound **6** cinder,
deface, scared **7** blemish, catface, clinker
8 cicatrix, mountain, pockmark **9** disfigure **13** disfigurement
scarab: 5 charm **6** beetle
scarce: 4 dear, rare **5** scant, short **6** geason, meager, meagre, scanty, sparse **8**
uncommon **9** deficient **10** infrequent **12**
insufficient
scarcely: 6 barely, hardly, merely
scarcity: 4 lack, need, want **6** dearth, famine, penury, rarity **7** paucity, poverty **8**

rareness **9** parsimony **10** deficiency, scarceness **11** infrequency, sparingness **12** uncommonness **13** insufficiency, niggardliness

scare: awe, shy **4** fleg **5** alarm, dread, gliff, gloff, panic **6** fright **7** scarify, startle, terrify **8** affright, frighten

scarecrow: **5** bogle

scared: **6** afraid

scarf: boa, tie **4** band, sash, wrap **5** adorn, ascot, barbe, cloud, cover, orale, shawl, stole, unite **6** cravat, groove, rebozo, runner, tapalo, tippet **7** dopatta(Ind.), muffler, necktie **8** liripipe, liripoop **9** comforter, cormorant **10** fascinator **11** comfortable, neckerchief

scarfskin: **7** cuticle **9** epidermis

scarify: See **scare**.

scarlet: red **4** lewd **5** bawdy **8** flagrant

Scarlett O'Hara: *home:* **4** Tara

 husband: **5** Rhett

scarp: cut **5** cliff, slope **6** escarp **7** descent **8** fragment **9** declivity

scart: **4** mark **6** scrape **7** scratch **9** cormorant

scarves: See **scarf**.

scary: **4** eery **5** eerie, timid, weird **6** spooky **7** ghostly, uncanny **8** alarming

scat: bop, tax **4** beat, riff, shoo **5** smash **6** begone, rebuff, shower **7** getaway, scatter, tribute, vamoose

scathe: **4** harm, hurt, sear **5** blast **6** assail, damage, injure, injury, scorch, wither **8** denounce **10** misfortune

scathing: **6** biting, severe **7** mordant **8** blasting, injuring, wounding **9** scorching, truculent, withering

scatter: sow, ted **4** deal, rout **5** fling, spray, strew, waste **6** dispel, shower, splash, spread **7** bestrew, confuse, diffuse, disband, fritter, radiate **8** dishevel, disperse, distract, separate, sprinkle, squander **9** bespatter, circulate, discomfit, dissipate **10** disconnect, distribute **11** disseminate

scatter-gun: **7** shotgun

scatterbrained: **5** giddy **7** flighty **9** frivolous

scattered: **6** sparse **7** erratic, strawed **8** rambling, sporadic **9** irregular **10** straggling

scatterer: **6** tedder

scatterling: **7** vagrant, wastrel

scatula: box

scavage: tax **4** duty, toll

scavenger: rat **7** vulture

scaw: **8** headland **10** promontory

scena: **10** recitative

scenario: **4** plot **6** script **10** continuity

scend: **4** lift **5** heave

scene: act **4** site, view **5** sight, vista **6** blow-up, locale **7** diorama, display, episode, picture, quarrel, tableau **8** prospect **9** landscape, spectacle

 last: **6** finale

scenery: **4** view **7** picture **9** landscape **14** representation

sceneshifter: **4** grip

scenic: **8** dramatic **9** panoramic **10** theatrical **11** picturesque

scenite: **5** nomad

scent: **4** nose, odor **5** aroma, odour, savor, smell, sniff, spoor, track **6** breath, flavor **7** bouquet, essence, flavour, inkling, perfume **8** effluvia **9** emanation, fragrance

scented: **5** olent

scepter, sceptre: rod **4** mace **5** baton, staff **6** emblem **7** trident **8** caduceus **9** authority **11** sovereignty

scerne: **7** discern

schedule: **4** card, list, plan, time **5** slate, table **6** tariff **7** catalog, routine, writing **8** calendar, document, register, tabulate **9** catalogue, inventory, timetable

schefferite: **8** pyroxene

schelm: **5** rogue **6** rascal

schema: **4** plan **6** figure, scheme **7** diagram, outline

scheme: aim, gin, web **4** dart, list, plan, plot **5** angle, cabal, cadre, draft, drift, table **6** design, device, devise, figure, racket **7** complot, concoct, diagram, epitome, outline, program, project, purpose **8** conspire, contrive, forecast, gimcrack, intrigue **9** statement **10** concoction, conspiracy **11** contrivance, machination, proposition

schemer: **6** artist

scheming: **6** artful, crafty, tricky **8** fetching **9** designing **10** intriguing

schism: **4** rent **5** split **6** breach **8** division **10** separation

schist: **5** slate

schlemiel: dub, oaf **4** clod, goof **5** chump **7** saphead

scholar: **5** clerk, pupil **6** pedant, savant **7** bookman, learner, student **8** disciple **11** academician, philologist

 servant: **7** famulus

scholarly: **7** erudite, learned **8** studious **10** scholastic

scholarship: **7** bursary **8** learning **9** allowance, education, erudition, knowledge **10** fellowship **11** instruction

scholiast: **9** annotator **10** glossarist **11** commentator **13** glossographer

school: gam, pod **4** cult, sect **5** drill, ecole(F.), flock, group, lycee(F.), shoal, teach, train **6** manege **7** academy, college, company, convent, educate, seminar **8** atheneum, document, exercise, instruct, seminary **9** athenaeum, cultivate **10** realschule(G.), university **11** institution, schoolhouse

 kind: **4** high, prep **5** grade **7** primary **8** military **9** finishing, secondary **10** elementary, vocational **11** preparatory

 official: **9** principal, scholarch **10** headmaster **14** superintendent

 task: **6** lesson **7** problem **10** assignment

11 composition
term: 7 quarter 8 semester 9 trimester
schoolbook: 4 text 5 atlas 6 primer, reader 7 speller 9 geography
schoolfellow: 11 condisciple
schoolmaster: 4 caji, head 7 dominie, manager, pedagog 9 pedagogue
schooner: 4 boat, brig, tern 5 glass 6 vessel 7 measure
builder: 14 Andrew Robinson
schout: 7 bailiff, sheriff
schrik: 5 panic 6 fright
science: art, sci 5 ology 9 knowledge 10 technology
principle: 5 logic
scient: 4 able 7 knowing 8 skillful 9 knowledge
scientific: 8 skillful 9 technical
scilicet: 6 namely 9 videlicet
scimitar, scimiter: 4 snee 5 saber, sword
scintilla: 4 atom, iota 5 spark, trace 8 particle
scintillate: 5 flash, gleam, spark 7 glitter, sparkle, twinkle 9 coruscate
scion, cion: bud, son 4 heir, twig 5 shoot, sprig 6 sprout 8 offshoot 9 offspring 10 descendant
scissor: cut 4 clip, trim 5 shear
scissors: 6 shears
scleroid: 4 hard 8 hardened 9 indurated
scoff: 4 food, gibe, gird, jeer, leer, meal, mock, rail 5 fleer, flout, gleek, scout, sneer, steal, taunt 6 deride 7 mockery, plunder 8 ridicule
scoffer: 5 clown 6 jester 10 unbeliever
scoke: 8 pokeweed
scold: nag, yap 4 haze, jump, rail, rant, rate 5 abuse, barge, boast, brawl, chide, score, shrew, slate 6 berate, bounce, rebuff, rebuke, revile 7 reprove, upbraid 8 chastise 9 objurgate 10 vituperate
scolding: 6 dirdum, rating, rebuke 7 combing, hearing, reproof 8 dressing
sconce: 4 fine, fort, head 5 cover, skull 7 bracket, bulwark, lantern, shelter 8 entrench 10 protection 11 candlestick
scone: 4 farl 5 farle 7 biscuit
scoop: dig 4 bail, beat, lade 5 didle, empty, gouge, ladle, skeet, spoon 6 bucket, chisel, dipper, dredge, gather, hollow, shovel, vessel 7 curette 8 excavate
scoot: 4 dart, dray, scud 5 shoot, slide 6 begone, decamp, scurry 9 skedaddle
scooter: toy 4 boat, plow 6 glider
scop: 4 bard, poet
scope: 4 area, goal, room 5 range, reach, theme, tract 6 domain, extent, import, intent, length, object, sphere, target 7 liberty 8 distance, latitude 9 dimension, extension, intention
having: 13 comprehensive
large: 7 general
scopic: 6 visual
scoptical: 7 jeering, jesting 8 scoffing

scorch: cut 4 burn, char, flay, sear, skin 5 adust, parch, score, singe, slash, sting, toast 6 birsle, scathe, wither 7 blister, scratch, shrivel
scorched: 4 sere 5 adust
score: cut, run, tab, taw 4 goal, line, mark, rate 5 chalk, chase, corge, count, judge, notch, scold, slash, tally 6 abrade, barter, berate, furrow, grudge, number, reason, record, scotch, twenty, weight 7 account, arrange, scratch, upbraid 8 incision 9 criticize, grievance, reckoning 10 obligation 11 enumeration, orchestrate 12 indebtedness
scoria: aa 4 lava, slag 5 dross 6 refuse
scorify: 5 smelt
scoring point: ace, hit, run 4 down, goal 5 tally 6 basket
scorn: 4 geck, jeer, mock 5 scoff 6 deride, reject, slight 7 condemn, despise, disdain 8 contempt, derision 9 contumely
scornful: 5 aloof 7 haughty, stuckup 8 arrogant, insolent 10 disdainful, fastidious
scorpion: 4 nepa 6 onager, weapon 7 scourge 8 arachnid, catapult 10 vinegaroon
Scorpion's Heart: 7 Antares
scorse: 5 trade 6 barter 8 exchange
scot: tax 4 levy 6 assess 7 payment 9 reckoning 10 assessment
Scot: 4 Gael, Pict 10 Caledonian, Highlander
scotch (see also **Scotland**): cut 4 stop 5 check, chock, notch, score, wedge 6 hinder, stingy, whisky 7 scratch, scruple 8 hesitate 9 frustrate
Scotchman: Mac 4 Gael, Scot 7 bluecap, Scottie 10 Highlander
Scotland: *accent:* 4 birr, burr
bird: gae 4 hern 6 grouse, snabby 7 snabbie 8 throstle 9 swinepipe
blessing: 6 rebuke 8 scolding
blood money: cro
bluebell: 8 harebell
boat: 4 zulu 6 scaffy, sexern 7 coracle, skaffie
bonfire: 6 tandle
bread: 5 briar 6 tammie 7 bannock
bread dish: 4 saps
briar: 4 rose
brook: 4 sike
broth: 4 soup
bull: 4 stot
bushel: fou
cake: 5 scone
camp follower: 6 gudget
cap: tam 6 bonnet, tassel, toorie 8 Balmoral 9 Glengarry 11 Tam O' Shanter
cap tassel: 6 toorie
cascade: lin 4 linn 5 force
cattle: 8 Ayrshire
celebration: 4 kirn
chafing dish: 7 choffer

chair: **5** regal
child: **4** dalt **5** bairn **6** scuddy **8** smatchet
church: **4** kirk
city: Ayr **5** Alloa, Leith, Perth, Troon **6** Dundee **7** Glasgow, Grunock, Paisley **8** Aberdeen, Stirling **9** Edinburgh, Inverness, St. Andrews **10** Kilmarnock
cloth: **4** kelt **6** tartan
coin: **4** demy **5** bodle, groat **6** baubee, bawbee
colt: **4** stag
congress: Mod
county: Ayr **4** Bute, Fife, Ross **5** Angus, Banff, Moray, Nairn, Perth **6** Argyll, Lanark, Orkney **7** Berwick, Kinross, Peebles, Renfrew, Selkirk, Wigtown **8** Aberdeen, Ayrshire, Dumfries, Roxburgh, Shetland, Stirling **9** Caithness, Dumbarton, Inverness **10** Kincardine, Midlothian, Sutherland **11** Clackmannan, West Lothian **13** Kirkcudbright
court officer: **5** macer
cross: **8** crantara **9** crostarie
cuddy: **6** draper **7** peddler
cup: **4** tass
curlies: **4** kale
dance: bob **4** reel **7** walloch **9** ecossaise **10** strathspey **13** Highland-fling
devil: **4** deil
district: Ayr **5** Rinns **6** Atholl **7** Lothian **8** Galloway **9** Tweeddale **11** Breadalbane
drapery: **4** pand
drinking bout: **6** screed
drinking vessel: **4** tass **6** quaich, quaigh
duck: **10** bufflehead
elm: **4** wych
excuse: **6** sunyie
fairy: **4** fane
farmer: **6** cottar, cotter **7** crofter
fashion: **7** Scotice
festival: Mod **7** Uphelya
fiddle: **4** itch
fingering: **4** wool, yarn
firth: Tay **4** Loch, Lorn **5** Clyde, Forth, Moray **6** Linnhe **8** Cromarty
fish: **4** sile **7** sillock **8** spalding
fish trap: **4** yare **5** yaire
fishing expedition: **5** drave
fog: **4** haar
fort: **4** dune **10** roundabout
garment: tam **4** kilt, maud **5** toosh **6** fecket, tartan **7** arisard **8** Balmoral **11** Tam o' Shanter
garter: **8** wooer-bab
ghost: **6** taisch
girl: **4** lass **5** quean **6** lassie, towdie **7** winklot
grandchild: oe, oy; oye
grandfather: **8** gudesire
granite: **5** gowan
gutter: **5** siver
hands: **8** paddling
hazelnut: nit
heater: **7** choffer

heath: **7** heather
hill: **6** strone
hillside: **4** brae
hoppers: **9** Hopscotch
icicle: **7** shoggle
inlet: gio
island: **4** Iona **5** Arran **6** Orkney **8** Hebrides, Shetland
kale: **8** borecole
king: **6** Robert
kiss: **8** smoorich
lake: dee **4** loch
lament: **6** ochone
land: **6** carses
land tax: **4** cess
landholder: **5** laird, thane
language: **4** Erse **6** Lallan **7** Lalland
liquor: **5** scour **6** athole **8** whittier
maurauder: **7** cateran
measure: cop **4** cran, fall, mile, peck, pint, rood, rope **5** crane, crans, lippy **6** firlot, lippie **7** auchlet, chalder, choppin **8** mutchkin, stimpart, stimpert **9** particate, shaftment, shaftmont
mist: ure
money: **6** siller
monk: **6** culdee
mountain: **8** Ben Nevis **9** Grampians
music festival: Mod
musical instrument: **5** pipes **7** bagpipe
musician: **5** piper
negative: **nae**
pastry: **5** scone **7** carcake
patron saint: **6** Andrew
peasant: **6** cottar, cotter
peninsula: **5** Rinns
people: **8** Damnonii **9** Dammonian
person: **4** Gael, Pict, Scot **7** Scottie **9** Lowlander, Scotchman **10** Highlander
plaid: **4** maud
pole: **5** caber
porridge: **5** brose
proprietor: **5** laird
pouch: **6** sporan **7** sporran
pudding: **6** haggis
queen: **4** Mary
ridge: run
river: Ayr, Dee, Don, Esk, Tay **4** Doon, Find, Norn, Nith, Spey **5** Afton, Annan, Clyde, North, Tweed **6** Teviot **7** Deveron
sausage: **9** whitehass **10** whitehawse
schoolmaster: dux
scurvy grass: **8** seabells
seaport: **4** Leth **5** Alloa **6** Dundee
sect: **9** Buchanite
servant: **5** gilly **6** gillie
sheepfold: ree
snow: **4** snaw
soldier: **7** cateran
song: **6** strowd
student: **5** bejan **6** nejant
tenure: **6** sorren **7** sorehon
tinker: **5** caird
tithe: **5** teind

title: **5** laird
to: tae
toad: ted **4** taed
tobacco: **5** elder
toe: tae
topaz: **6** tassel **9** cairngorm
tourist resort: **4** Oban
tower: **7** toorock
town hall: **8** tolbooth **9** tollbooth
tree: arm
uncle: eme
unit: ane
water spirit: **5** kelpy **6** kelpie
waterfall: lin **4** linn **5** force
weakling: **4** ribe **5** shilp **7** shilpit
weapon: **5** skean **8** claymore, skeandhu
weight: **4** boll, drop **5** trone **6** bushel
whirlpool: **7** swilkie **8** swelchie
whisky: **6** athole **9** Glenlivat, Glenlivit **10** Usquebaugh
whitefish: **7** vendace
window: **7** winnock
woodcock: **4** eggs
youth: **5** chiel **7** callant
Scott's character: 5 Norna **7** Ivanhoe **9** Lochinvar
Scottish: See **Scotland**.
scoundrel: cad **4** scab **5** cheat, filth, knave, scamp **6** rascal, varlet **7** glutton, villain, warlock **8** bezonian **9** miscreant, reprobate **10** blackguard
scoup: run **4** leap, skip **7** scamper
scour: rub, run **4** beat, rake, rush, wash **5** clean, purge, scrub **6** decamp, polish, punish, remove **7** cleanse, roister **8** brighten, traverse
scourge: **4** bane, flay, flog, lash, whip **5** harry, shoot, slash **6** plague, punish, swinge, switch **7** afflict, torment **8** chastise **9** devastate **10** affliction, discipline, flagellate, infliction, punishment
scout: guy, spy **4** chap, jeer, look **5** scoff, watch **6** fellow, search **7** despise, explore, lookout, observe **8** emissary, informer, ridicule, watchman **11** reconnoiter, reconnoitre
scouth: **4** room **5** range, scope **6** plenty
scovy: **7** blotchy, smeared, streaky
scow: **4** acon(F.), boat **5** barge, float **6** garvey **7** gabbard, gabbart, lighter
scowl: **5** frown, glare, glout, lower **6** glower
scrab: **7** scratch
scraffle: **7** wrangle **8** scramble, struggle
scraggly: **5** rough **6** jagged, ragged **7** unkempt **9** irregular **10** splintered
scraggy: **4** bony, lean, thin **5** rough, weedy **6** meager, rugged, skinny **7** knotted, scrawny
scram: **4** shoo **6** benumb **7** vamoose **8** paralyze, withered
scramble: mix **4** push **5** climb, crowd, crush **6** jostle, sprawl, spread, strive **7** clamber, pushing, scatter **8** struggle

scran: **4** grub **6** morsel, refuse **9** leftovers **10** provisions
scrannel: dry **4** lean, poor, thin, weak **5** harsh **6** slight **7** scrawny **11** unmelodious
scrap: bit, end, jag, ort, rag **4** chip, item, junk **5** fight, grain, piece, shred, waste **6** cullet, morsel, refuse **7** cutting, discard, extract, oddment, quarrel, remnant **8** fraction, fragment
scrape: bow, hoe, row, rub, saw **4** claw, grit, harl, rake, rasp, scud, trap **5** claut, erase, grate, graze, gride, hoard, order, shave **6** abrade, dredge, fiddle, gather, harass, refine, remove, sclaff **7** collect, corrode, scratch **9** situation **10** difficulty **11** predicament
scraper: **6** barber, rasper, xyster **7** fiddler, strigil **8** grattoir
scraping: **6** rasion, rasure
scrapper: **5** boxer **7** fighter **8** pugilist
scraps: **5** scran
literary: ana
scratch: dig, mar, rat, rit, rub, wig **4** claw, draw, feed, heap, line, mark, race, rake, rist, tear **5** break, claut, clawk, erase, expel, fluke, frush, score, wound **6** cancel, furrow, gather, injury, rasure, scotch, scrape, scrawl **7** expunge, roughen, scarify, scorify **8** incision, scribble, scrobble, withdraw **12** scratchbrush
scratcher: **6** forger **13** counterfeiter
scratching: **8** rasorial
scratchy: **6** uneven **10** straggling
scrawk: **6** squeak, squawk **7** scratch, screech
scrawl: **4** teem **5** crawl **7** scratch, writing **8** scribble
scrawm: **5** climb **7** clamber **8** scramble
scrawny: **4** lean, poor, thin **7** scraggy, scranny, scrubby **8** rawboned
screak: **4** rasp **5** creak, grate **7** screech
scream: cry **4** wail, yarm, yaup, yawl, yell, yowt **6** shriek, squall, yammer **7** screech
screamer: **5** chaja
scree: **5** stone, talus **6** pebble
screech: cry **4** yell **5** quawk **6** outcry, scream, shriek **7** ululate
screed: say **4** land, rend, rent, tear **5** board, shred, strip **6** scrape, smooth, tirade **7** leveler **8** diatribe, fragment, harangue **9** discourse
screen: **4** cage, hide, mask, mesh, reja, sept, sift, veil **5** arras, blind, chick(Ind.), , cloak, cover, grill, purda, scarf, shade, sieve, speer, spier **6** defend, filter, grille, purdah, settle, shield **7** conceal, curtain, protect, reredos, shelter **8** bescreen, covering, separate **9** breakwind, partition **10** protection
architectural: **5** spier
screw: key, pay **4** turn, wind, worm **5** cheat, guard, horse, miser, twist **6** gimlet, keeper, salary, spiral **7** contort, distort, robbery, squeeze, tighten, turnkey **9** bar-

gainer, propeller, skinflint **10** contortion, crustacean, instructor

screw-like: 6 spiral, spirod **7** helical

screw pine: 5 vacoa **6** vacona, vacoua **8** pandanus

screw-pine family: 11 pandanaceae

screwball: nut, sap **5** crank, crazy, dippy, goose **7** fanatic, galloot, saphead **8** crackpot, dumbbell **9** blockhead, eccentric **10** crackbrain, muttonhead

screwed: 5 drunk **11** intoxicated

screwy: 5 crazy, wacky **6** absurd, whacky **7** winding **8** freakish, peculiar **9** eccentric, fantastic **10** irrational, misleading, unbalanced **11** impractical **12** crackbrained, preposterous

scribal: 7 clerkly

scribble: 5 write **6** scrawl **7** scratch **8** scrabble

scribe: 5 clerk, write **6** author, copier, doctor, notary, penman, scrive, writer **7** copyist, graffer, teacher **8** inscribe **9** draftsman, scenarist, scrivener, secretary **10** amanuensis, journalist **11** transcriber **13** bibliographer

scriggle: 5 twist **6** squirm, wiggle **7** wriggle **8** curlicue

scrimmage: 4 play **6** battle, splore, tussle **8** football, practice

scrimp: 4 save **5** stint **6** meager, scanty **9** economize

scrimping: 7 miserly, sparing **9** niggardly

scringe: net **4** flog **5** glean, seine **6** cringe, flinch, search

scrip: bag **4** list **6** wallet **7** satchel, writing **8** schedule **11** certificate

script: 5 ronde **8** scenario **10** penmanship **11** chirography, handwriting

Arabic: **5** neski

Syriac: **5** serta

scriptor: See **scribe.**

scriptural: 8 Biblical

scripture: 4 text, word, writ **5** Bible, motto **7** passage, writing **10** manuscript, penmanship **11** composition, handwriting, inscription

interpreter: **7** exegete

Moslem: **7** Alcoran

part: **6** lesson

version: Vul **4** Vulg **5** Douay, Itala **7** Vulgate

scrive: cut **5** score, write **6** scribe **7** carving, scratch, writing **8** inscribe **11** handwriting

scrivener: See **scribe.**

scrofulous: 7 corrupt **10** degenerate **12** contaminated

scroll: 4 list, roll **5** draft **6** escrol, record, scrawl, spiral, volute **7** escroll, outline, writing **8** enscribe, inscribe, schedule, streamer

Hebrew: **6** mezuza **7** mezuzah

writing: **8** makimono

scrooch: 6 crouch, huddle

scroop: 5 creak, grate **6** scrape, squeak

scrouge: 5 crowd, press **7** squeeze

scrounge: 5 cadge, steal **6** pilfer, search, sponge

scroyle: 6 fellow, wretch **9** scoundrel

scrub: mop, rub **4** mean, poor, runt, wash **5** clean, dwarf, scour, small **6** drudge, paltry, shabby **7** cleanse **8** inferior **10** undersized **14** undernourished

scrub turkey: 6 leipoa **8** megapode

scruff: 4 film, nape, scum **5** crust, dross **6** refuse **7** coating **8** covering, dandruff

scrump: 6 shrink **7** shrivel, squeeze

scrumptious: 4 fine, nice **5** dandy **7** capital, elegant **8** splendid **9** delicious

scrunch: 5 crush **6** crunch, huddle **7** squeeze

scruple: 4 part **5** demur, doubt, qualm **6** amount, boggle **7** anxiety, portion **8** question **9** disbelief, misgiving **10** uneasiness

scrupulous: 4 nice **5** chary, exact **6** honest, proper, strict **7** careful, correct, precise, upright **8** accurate, cautious **9** reluctant **11** punctilious **13** conscientious

to excess: **7** finical, finicky, prudish **9** finicking **10** fastidious

scrutinize: eye, pry **4** scan, sift **5** probe **7** examine, inspect, observe

scrutiny: 4 gaze, look

scrutoire: 10 escritoire

scruze: 5 crush **7** squeeze

scry: cry **4** gaze, look **5** shout **6** descry, outcry

scud: ale, fly, run **4** beer, blow, foam, gust, mist, move, scum, skim, slap **5** hurry, spank, spray **6** scrape, shower **7** rushing **10** crustacean

scuff: 4 blow, cuff, drag, gust, toss, wipe **5** brush, evade, graze, rowdy, slare, touch, tread **6** buffet, rabble, scruff, shower, slight **7** scatter, shuffle, slipper **9** roughened, scratched

scuffle: 4 cuff **5** amble, fight, melee, scuff, shool **6** affray, bustle, clinch, combat, sclaff, strive, tussle **7** contend, shamble, shuffle **8** struggle

scug: 5 shade **6** shadow **7** protect, shelter **8** pretense, squirrel **9** schoolboy

sculch: 6 cultch, refuse

scull: oar **4** boat **6** basket, propel, wherry **7** rowboat **8** scullion

scullery: 5 ewery

scullion: 4 base **5** gippo, onion **6** menial, wretch **7** servant **8** scallion **10** blackguard

sculp: 4 pelt, skin **5** break, carve, scalp **6** sculpt **7** engrave **9** engraving, sculpture

sculptor: 6 artist, graver, imager

tool: **6** graver

sculpture: 4 bust, head **5** carve, grave, torso **6** emboss, relief, statue **7** engrave, relievo

pert. to: **7** glyphic, glyptic **9** glyptical

slab: **6** metope

scum: **4** brat, foam, scud, silt, skim **5** dross, froth, range, scour, spume, sweep **6** bubble, rabble, refuse, scoria **10** impurities **12** offscourings

scumfish: **5** choke **9** discomfit, overpower, suffocate

scuppernong: **4** wine **5** grape **9** muscadine

scurrilous: low **4** foul, vile **5** gross **6** ribald, vulgar **7** abusive **8** indecent, scurrile **9** insulting, offensive **11** foulmouthed, opprobrious

scurry: hie, run **4** race **5** harry, scoot, scour, skirr **6** flurry, hasten **7** scamper, scuttle, skelter **9** skedaddle

scurvy: low **4** mean **6** shabby **7** disease **8** scorbute **12** contemptible, discourteous

preventative: **6** citrus **13** antiscorbutic

scuttle: hod, run **4** dish, sink, veto **5** scoot **6** basket, bucket, scotch, scurry, shovel **7** octopus, platter **8** hatchway **10** cuttlefish

scuttlebutt: **5** rumor **6** gossip

Scylla: *father:* **5** Nisus

lover: **5** Minos

scythe: sy(Sc.); lea **6** sickle

handle: **5** snath, thole **6** snathe

sweep: **5** swath

sea: mer(F.) **4** meer(G.)

anemone: **5** polyp **7** actinia

approach: **7** seagate

arm: bay **4** gulf **5** bayou, firth, fjord, frith, inlet, lough **7** estuary

at: **4** asea

bottom: bed

combining form: mer

current: **4** tide **8** undertow

deity: Ler, Ran **5** Aegir, Doris **6** Nereus, Triton **7** Neptune, Phorcus, Phorcyn, Phorcys, Phorkys, Proteus **8** Palaemon, Poseidon

delicacy: roe **4** nori

description: **11** haliography

goddess: Ran **4** Nina **8** Eurynome **9** Leucothea **10** Amphitrite

king: Ler **5** chief **6** pirate, viking

land in: **6** island

life of: **8** halibios

little: **6** sealet

mammal: **4** seal **5** whale

open: **6** midsea

periodic motion: **4** tide

pert. to: **4** vast **5** naval **6** marine **7** oceanic, pelagic **8** maritime, nautical **9** aequoreal, thalassic

plant: **6** enalid

roughness: **5** swell, waves **6** lipper

route: **4** lane

spray: **9** spindrift **10** spoondrift

swell: **4** surf

term: **4** ahoy **5** avast, belay, trice

sea biscuit: **7** galette(F.) **8** hardtack

sea cow: **6** dugong, rytina, walrus **7** manatee **8** sirenian **12** hippopotamus

sea cucumber: **6** pedata **7** trepang **11** holothurian

sea dog: tar **4** seal **6** pirate, sailor **7** breaker, dogfish **9** privateer

sea duck: **5** eider **6** scoter **7** scooter

sea eagle: ern **4** erne, tern **6** osprey

sea-ear: **7** abalone

sea eel: **6** conger **7** lamprey

sea-foam: **5** froth **9** sepiolite **10** meerschaum

sea gate: **5** beach **7** channel

sea goose: **7** dolphin **9** phalarope

sea gull: cob, mew **4** cobb, gore

sea hog: **8** porpoise

sea horse: **6** walrus **8** whitecap **11** hippocampus

sea kale: **4** cole

sea lettuce: **5** laver **7** seaweed

sea nettle: **6** medusa **9** jellyfish

sea nymph: **5** siren **6** Nereid **7** Galatea, Oceanid

sea raven: **7** sculpin **9** cormorant **10** squaretail

sea robber: **6** jaeger, pirate **7** corsair **9** buccaneer, privateer

sea slug: **6** trepan **8** cucumber **10** nudibranch

sea soldier: **6** marine

sea squirt: **5** salpa **8** ascidian, tunicate

sea swallow: **4** tern **6** petrel

sea unicorn: **7** narwhal

sea urchin: **6** repkie **7** echinid, echinus **8** echinoid **10** echinoderm

rock hole: **5** geode

sea wolf: **4** seal **6** pirate **7** wolfish **9** privateer, submarine

sea worm: sao **7** annelid

seabird: auk, ern **4** duck, erne, gull, smew, tern **5** solan, yager **6** gannet, petrel **7** pelican **9** albatross **10** shearwater

seaboard: **5** coast **9** coastland, tidewater

seadog: **6** fogbow, fogdog **8** fogeater

seafarer: gob, tar **4** salt **6** sailor, seaman **7** mariner **9** navigator

seagoing: **5** naval **7** capable **9** seafaring **13** weatherbeaten

seal: cap, fix, hem, set, wax **4** bind, bull, cere, lute, rope, seel, shut, sign **5** bulla, chain, close, sigil, stamp, swile, token, wafer **6** attest, cachet, clinch, fasten, pledge, ranger, ratify, scarab, secure, signet **7** closure, confine, confirm, leather **8** breloque, document, guaranty, imprison, sealskin, validate **9** assurance, carnivore, guarantee, sigillate **10** obligation **12** authenticate **14** authentication

eared genus: **8** zalophus

limb: **7** flipper

pelt: **5** sculp

place: LS **7** rookery

polar: **5** otary, phoca, Ross's, ursal, ursuk **6** makluk **8** bedlamer, Ross seal, seecatch **9** sterrinck

school: pod

young: pup **6** beater, hopper **7** quitter, saddler **11** flipperling, holluschick

seal skin: 5 sculp

seam: sew 4 fash, fold, join, line, load, mark, scar 5 cleft, joint, layer, raphe, ridge, strip, unite 6 groove, streak, suture 7 crevice, fissure, stratum, wrinkle 8 cicatrix 10 packsaddle
pert. to: 7 suturic

seaman: See **sailor, seafarer.**

seamark: 6 beacon 8 landmark 10 lighthouse

seamer: 5 sewer 6 seamer 8 stitcher 10 dressmaker, seamstress

seamless: 5 whole 7 unsewed 12 araphorostic

seamy: 5 rough 8 degraded, wrinkled 12 disreputable

seance: 7 meeting, session, sitting
holder: 6 medium

seaport: 4 port 6 harbor

sear (See also **sere**): 4 burn, mark, scar 5 brand, brown, catch, parch, singe 6 braise, deaden, scorch, wither 9 cauterize

search: 4 comb, grub, hunt, look, nose, rout, seek 5 delve, frisk, probe, quest 6 brevit, ferret, forage, pierce, sphere, survey 7 canvass, examine, explore, inquire, inquiry, inspect, ransack, rummage 8 research, scrounge, scrutiny 9 penetrate 10 scrutinize 11 exploration, investigate

searching: 4 keen 5 acute, sharp 10 discerning

searing: 7 cautery

seashell: 4 clam 5 conch, snail 7 scallop

seashore: 5 beach, coast, shore 7 seaside 8 seabeach, seacoast
pert. to: 8 littoral

season: age, dry, tid, ver 4 beek, fall, salt, sele, tide, time 5 devil, imbue, inure, ripen, savor, spice, taste, tinge 6 autumn, embalm, flavor, mature, period, soften, spring, storm, summer, temper, winter 7 condite, flavour, Maytide, weather 8 accustom, marinate, occasion 9 habituate 10 impregnate 11 acclimatize, opportunity
religious: 4 Lent 6 careme

seasonable: pat 4 ripe 6 timely 7 apropos 8 suitable 9 opportune 11 appropriate

seasonably: 7 betimes

seasonal: 8 periodic

seasoned: 7 veteran 8 finished

seasoning: 4 herb, mace, sage, salt 5 cumin, onion, spice, thyme 6 celery, cloves, cummin, garlic, nutmeg, pepper, relish 7 caraway, cuminos, mustard, oregano, paprika, vinegar 8 allspice, cardamon, marjoram, rosemary, turmeric 9 condiment, coriander

seasons: 5 Horae
goddess: 4 Dike 5 Horae 6 Eirene, Eunomi

seat: fix, pew, see 4 apse, bank, form, hold, home, loge, room, site 5 asana, bench, chair, floor, place, sella(L.), siege, stool, usher 6 exedra, grange, howdah, locate, sedile, settee, settle, throne 7 capital, install, ottoman, situate, station, taboret, tendoor, tendour 8 bleacher, locality, location, tabouret 9 banquette, establish, residence, situation

seat bone: 7 ischium

seat worm: 7 pinworm

seaweed: ore 4 agar, alga, kelp, nori 5 algae, dulse, laver, varec, vraic, wrack 6 delisk, desmid, fucoid, varech 7 oreweek 8 agar-agar, hempweed, sargasso 9 desmidian
extract: 4 agar
genus of: 6 alaria
study: 8 algology

seaweedy: 6 algous

sebaceous: 5 fatty

sec: dry

secant: 7 cutting 12 intersecting

secede: 8 withdraw

seceder: 8 apostate

secern: 7 secrete 8 separate 11 distinguish 12 discriminate

seclude: bar 4 deny, hide 5 debar, expel 6 recess, remove, retire, screen 7 exclude, isolate, protect, retreat 8 prohibit, separate, withdraw 9 segregate, sequester

secluded: 5 aloof, apart 6 remote, secret 7 private 8 excepted, solitary

second: aid 4 abet, back, echo, time 5 other 6 assist, attend, backer, handle, moment 7 another, confirm, endorse, forward, further, instant, succeed, support, sustain 8 inferior 9 assistant, encourage, imperfect, prototype, reinforce, secondary, viscosity 10 additional 11 corroborate, subordinate 13 supplementary

second childhood: 6 dotage 8 senility

second-rate: 6 shabby 8 inferior, mediocre

second-sighted: fey 7 psychic 9 intuitive, visionary 11 clairvoyant 12 precognitive

second team: 6 scrubs 9 yannigans 11 substitutes

secondary: bye 5 minor 6 deputy 8 delegate, inferior 9 auxiliary, satellite 10 accidental 11 subordinate
color: 5 green 6 orange, purple

secondary school: 4 high, prep 5 lycee(F.) 7 academy 10 realschule(G.), vocational

secondhand: 4 used, worn 6 resold 7 derived 8 borrowed 10 unoriginal

secret: 4 dark, dern, hide, rune 5 blind, cabal, close, inner, privy 6 arcane, arcana, closet, covert, hidden, occult, remote, stolen 7 arcanum, cryptic, furtive, mystery, privacy, private, privity, retired, unknown 8 discrete, esoteric, intimate, mystical, reticent, secluded, stealthy 9 clancular, concealed, recondite, seclusion, secretive, underhand 10 confidence 11 clandestine, concealment 12 confidential, hugger-mugger 13 surreptitious

secret agent: spy 8 emissary, saboteur 10 counterspy

secretaire: 9 secretary 10 escritoire

secretary: 4 desk 5 clerk 9 confidant 10 amanuensis

secrete: 4 bury, hide, ooze, stow 5 exude 7 conceal

secretly: 4 inly 5 aside 13 clandestinely

sect: 4 clan, cult, part 5 class, group, order, party 6 school 7 faction, section 9 following 10 philosophy 12 denomination
distinguishing word: 10 shibboleth

sectarian: 7 bigoted, heretic, sectary 8 apostate 9 dissenter 12 narrow-minded 17 denominationalist

sectary: 4 sect 6 votary 8 adherent, disciple, follower, partisan 9 dissenter, sectarian 11 independent 13 non-conformist

section: 4 pane, part 5 piece, slice 6 canton 7 portion, segment 8 division 9 signature 11 subdivision
concluding: 8 epilogue

section hand: 6 worker 7 crewman, laborer

sector: 4 area 8 division

secular: lay 4 laic 5 civil 6 carnal, vulgar 7 earthly, profane, worldly 8 temporal 9 temporary 17 nonecclesiastical

secure: buy, get, pot, tie 4 bail, bind, bolt, easy, fast, firm, gird, moor, nail, safe, sure, tape 5 chain, guard, siker, spike, trice, truss 6 anchor, assure, clinch, defend, ensure, fasten, obtain, sicker, stable, strong 7 acquire, assured, certain, forfend, procure, protect 8 conserve, forefend 9 confident, constrain, guarantee 10 dependable 11 trustworthy, undisturbed 13 overconfident

security: 4 bail, bond, ease, gage 5 frith, grith, guard 6 pledge, safety, surety 7 defense, hostage, shelter 8 guaranty, warranty 9 assurance, certainty, guarantee, insurance 10 confidence, protection

sedan: car 4 auto 5 chair 10 automobile

sedate: 4 calm, cool, dope, drug 5 douce, grave, quiet, sober, staid 6 demure, proper, serene 7 earnest, serious, settled 8 composed, decorous 9 dignified, unruffled 12 tranquillize 13 contemplative, dispassionate

sedative: 6 remedy 7 aconite, bromide, chloral, nervine 8 barbital, lenitive, soothing 9 paregoric 10 palliative 13 tranquillizer

sedent: 6 seated 7 sitting

sedentary: 7 settled, sitting 8 inactive, slothful, tranquil 10 deliberate, motionless, stationary

sederunt: 7 session, sitting 8 assembly

sedge: sag 5 brood, flock 7 bulrush, hassock
genus of: 5 carex 7 scirpus

sediment: lee 4 crap, silt 5 dregs, magma, waste 6 bottom, refuse 7 deposit, grounds 8 settling

sedition: 6 revolt, strife, tumult 7 treason 9 commotion, rebellion 10 dissention, turbulence 12 insurrection

seditionary: 7 inciter 8 promoter 9 seditious 10 factitious, treasonist 12 contumacious

seduce: 4 lure 5 charm, decoy, tempt 6 allure, betray, entice 7 corrupt, debauch, mislead 8 inveigle

seducer: 8 Lothario

sedulous: 4 busy 8 diligent, untiring 9 assiduous, laborious, unwearied 10 persistent 11 industrious, persevering, unremitting

see: spy 4 espy, hear, ibid, look, meet, rank, scry, seat, view 5 besee, chair, power 6 attend, behold, descry, detect, escort, notice, office, throne 7 diocese, discern, examine, inspect, observe, undergo, witness 8 cathedra, consider, discover, perceive 9 accompany, apprehend, authority, bisphoric, encounter, interview, visualize 10 comprehend, experience, scrutinize, understand
above: vs(L.) 5 supra
below: vi(L.) 5 infra

seeing: 6 ocular 13 introspective

seed: ben, egg, pea, pip, pit, sow 4 germ, milt, tare 5 acorn, drupe, grain, ovule, plant, spore, stock 6 acinus, bubble, kernel, origin, samara, source 7 capsule, progeny, seedlet 8 ancestry 9 beginning, inoculate, offspring, posterity 10 descendant
apple: pip
aromatic: 5 anise 6 nutmeg 7 aniseed 9 anise-seed
case: pod 4 burr
cell: 4 cyst
coat: 4 aril, bran 5 testa
container: bur, pod 6 carpel, legume, loment
edible: pea 4 bean 6 lentil
expansion: ala
organ: 6 pistil
part: pod 4 aril 5 testa 6 tegman, tunica 9 endosperm
part with: 4 core
remove: gin, pit 5 picul
vessel: pod 6 carpel, legume

seed leaf: 9 cotyledon

seedy: 4 worn 5 tacky 6 shabby 7 scruffy 11 debilitated

seek: beg, sue, try, woo 4 busk, fand, hunt, sick 5 court, crave, essay, probe, quest, scout, trace 6 aspire, follow, fraist, pursue, search 7 attempt, beseech, entreat, examine, explore, inquire, request, solicit 8 endeavor 9 importune 11 investigate

seeker: 6 prober, tracer 7 pursuer, zetetic 9 applicant 10 petitioner

seel: 5 blind 8 hoodwink

seem: 4 look 5 feign 6 appear, beseem 7 pretend 8 manifest

seeming: 6 proper 9 befitting

seemingly: 5 quasi

seemliness: 5 grace 7 decorum

seemly: fit 6 comely, decent, proper,

rather, suited **7** fitting **8** decently, decorous, graceful, handsome, passably, suitable, suitably **10** becomingly **13** appropriately

seen (see also **see**): **7** visible

seep: run **4** leak, ooze **5** exude **8** transude **9** percolate **10** infiltrate

seer: **4** sage **5** augur, sybil **6** mystic, oracle, scryer **7** augurer, diviner, prophet **9** predictor **10** forecaster, foreteller, soothsayer **11** clairvoyant, Nostradamus **14** prognosticator

seesaw: **6** teeter, tilter, totter **9** alternate, crossruff, vacillate **10** reciprocal

seethe: hum **4** boil, soak, stew, teem **5** steep **6** bubble, buller, decoct **7** blubber **8** saturate

segment: arc **4** part **5** piece, tmema **6** cantle, divide, somite **7** isomere, portion, section **8** division, fragment, metamere, separate

segment-shaped: **5** toric

segregate: **4** part **5** sever **6** divide, select **7** isolate, seclude **8** classify, separate

seise: See **seize.**

seism: **10** earthquake

seity: **8** selfhood **13** individuality

seize: bag, cap, cly, cop, hap, nab, net **4** bind, bite, claw, fang, grab, grip, hent, hook, prey, take, trap **5** annex, catch, clink, grasp, reave, ravin, usurp, wrest **6** affect, arrest, attach, attack, betake, clinch, clutch, collar, fasten, ravene, snatch, strike **7** afflict, çapture, grabble, grapnel, possess, prehend **8** arrogate **9** apprehend, deprehend, raptorize **10** comprehend, confiscate, understand

seizure: fit **6** stroke **10** androlepsy **11** androlepsia, manucapture

Sekhet's husband: **4** Ptah

selachian: ray **5** shark **7** dogfish

seladang: **4** gaur **6** animal **7** buffalo

selcouth: **7** strange, unusual **9** marvelous, wonderful

seldom: **4** rare **6** rarely **10** infrequent **12** infrequently

select: opt **4** cull, draw, name, pick, wale **5** allot, elect, elite **6** assign, choice, choose, chosen, exempt, picked, prefer **8** eximious **9** excellent, exclusive, segregate **10** fastidious **11** outstanding

selection: **5** piece **7** analect, passage **10** collection

selective: **6** choosy **7** choosey **8** electric **9** demanding

selenium: *compound:* **7** selenid **8** selenide
soft acid: **8** selenate

self: ego, own, sel(Sc.), soi(F.) **4** same, very **5** being **6** myself **7** himself **8** personal **9** identical **10** particular **11** personality
combining form: **4** auto
pert. to: **8** personal

self-acting: **9** automatic

self-centered: **6** stable **7** selfish **10** egocentric, stationary **11** independent

self-confidence: **5** poise **6** aplomb **8** presence **9** composure

self-contained: **4** calm, cool **8** composed, reserved **9** collected **15** uncommunicative

self-control: **4** will **8** calmness **11** forbearance

self-defense: **6** boxing **7** fencing, j(i)ujitsu, j(i)ujutsu **8** fighting

self-denial: **10** abstinence, asceticism, puritanism **11** forbearance

self-evident: **5** clear **7** obvious **8** truistic **9** axiomatic **11** postulation

self-examination: **13** introspection

self-generated: **11** spontaneous

self-government: **8** autonomy **12** independence

self-important: **7** pompous

self-love: **6** egoism **7** egotism

self-possessed: **4** calm, cool **6** cooler **8** composed **11** undisturbed

self-reproach: rue **6** regret **7** remorse **9** penitence **10** contrition

self-respect: **5** pride

self-righteous: **11** pharisaical

self-satisfied: **4** smug **6** jaunty **10** complacent

self-subsistence: **12** independence

self-worship: **9** autolatry

selfish: **6** stingy **7** hoggish **9** dissocial, egotistic **10** egocentric **11** egotistical **12** self-centered

selfishness: **12** ego-centricity

selfsameness: **8** identity

sell: **4** bilk, cant, deal, dump, dupe, give, gull, hand, hawk, hoax, vend **5** cheat, trade, trick, yield **6** barter, betray, impose, market, peddle, retail **7** auction, bargain, deceive, deliver, dispose **8** convince, persuade, transfer **9** negotiate, wholesale

seller: **6** dealer, seller, sutler, trader, vender, vendor **7** peddler **8** salesman **9** tradesman **10** saleswoman, saltcellar

selling place: See **market.**

selvage: **4** edge, list **5** gouge **6** border, margin **8** sticking

semblable: **7** seeming **8** suitable **10** ostensible

semblance: air **4** copy, face, form, look **5** guise, image **6** aspect, figure **7** pretext **8** likeness, pretense **10** apparition, appearance, conformity, likelihood, similarity, similitude, simulacrum **11** countenance, presumption, resemblance **14** representation

Semele: *father:* **6** Cadmus
husband: **4** Zeus
son: **7** Bacchus **8** Dionysos **9** Dionysius

semester: **4** half, term **6** course, period

semi: **4** half

semiape: **5** lemur

semidiameter: **6** radius

seminar: 6 course, school 7 meeting
seminary: 6 school 7 academy, college 11 institution
semiopaque: 5 horny 11 translucent
Semiramis' husband: 5 Ninus
Semite: Jew 4 Arab 6 Hebrew 7 Moabite 8 Aramaean, Assyrian 9 Caucasian 10 Babylonian, Phoenician
god: 4 Baal 5 Anath, Hadad 6 Moloch 7 Shamash
language: 4 Geez 6 Arabic, Hebrew, Syrian 7 Hebraic, Maltese
people: 6 Shagia 7 Shaigia 9 Shaikiyeh
senate: 5 boule, divan 7 council 8 assembly 11 legislature
senator: 5 solon 8 lawmaker 10 legislator
senatorship: 4 toga
send: 4 hurl, mail, ship 5 drive, grant, impel, issue, relay, speed 6 bestow, commit, convey, depute, ordain, propel 7 address, consign, deliver, dismiss, forward, inflict, project 8 delegate, dispatch, transmit 9 discharge, vouchsafe 10 commission
back: 5 remit 6 remand, return
down: 5 demit
forth: 4 emit 6 effuse
out: 4 emit 5 exile 6 deport, export
to obscurity: 8 relegate
Senegal: *capital:* 5 Dakar
gazelle: 5 korin
timber: 9 cailcedra
senile: old 4 aged, weak 5 aging 6 daffle, dotard, infirm 7 ancient, elderly, rickety 8 decrepit 9 doddering 13 deteriorating
senility: 6 dotage 8 caducity
senior: 4 aine, dean 5 elder, older 7 ancient, student 8 alderman, superior 13 undergraduate
seniority: age 5 state 6 status 7 quality 8 priority 10 precedence
by birth: 13 primogeniture
Sennacherib: *father:* 6 Sargon
son: 8 Sharezer
sensation: 5 sense 7 emotion, feeling 8 interest 10 appearance, experience, perception 11 sensibility
lacking: 4 numb
sensational: 5 lurid 6 yellow 8 exciting 9 emotional, startling, thrilling 12 melodramatic
sense: 4 feel, mind 5 touch 6 import, intuit, reason, sanity, wisdom 7 feeling, meaning 8 judgment, perceive, prudence 9 apprehend, awareness, sensation, sentience, soundness 10 appreciate, cognizance, comprehend, perception 11 sensibility 12 intelligence 13 consciousness, sensitiveness, understanding 14 susceptibility
sense organ: ear, eye 4 nose, skin 5 nerve 6 tongue 8 receptor
senseless: mad 4 dumb 5 blind, inane 6 stupid, unwise 7 foolish, idiotic 9 insensate, unfeeling 10 half-witted, insensible, irrational 11 meaningless, nonsensical, purposeless, unconscious 12 unreasonable 13 unintelligent
senselessness: 5 folly
sensible: 5 privy 7 prudent 8 rational 10 responsive
sensitive: raw 4 nice, sore 5 acute, alive 6 tender, touchy 8 delicate 9 receptive 10 compatible, responsive 11 susceptible 14 impressionable
plant: 6 mimosa
sensual: 4 lewd 5 alive, gross 6 carnal, coarse, fleshy 7 bestial, brutish, fleshly, lustful, worldly 9 seductive 10 licentious, voluptuous
sent: See **send.**
sentence: rap 4 doom 5 award, axiom, maxim, motto 6 decide, decree, saying 7 adjudge, condemn, opinion, passage, proverb 8 aphorism, decision, judgment 9 destinate, statement 12 adjudication 13 determination
describe: 5 parse
part: 6 clause, phrase, object 7 subject 9 predicate
same backwards and forwards: 10 palindrome
sententious: 5 pithy, short, terse 7 compact, concise, laconic 10 moralistic, proverbial
sentient: 5 alive 6 animal, living 7 feeling 8 sensible 9 conscious
sentiment: 5 maxim, toast 6 lyrics, saying 7 emotion, feeling, meaning, opinion 9 sensation, substance 10 perception 11 sensibility 14 sentimentality, susceptibility
sentimental: 5 gushy 7 maudlin, mawkish, schmalz 8 romantic, schmaltz 9 fantastic 10 idealistic 11 susceptible 13 lackadaisical
sentinel: 5 guard, vedet(Sp.), videt(Sp.), watch 6 bantay(P.I.), sentry, warder 7 soldier 8 watchman 10 factionary, watchtower
sepal: 4 leaf
separate: 4 bolt, cull, deal, free, part, rend, rift, shed, sift, slay, sley, sort 5 alone, aloof, apart, aside, break, hedge, ravel, sever, space, strip 6 assort, breach, cleave, decide, deduct, depart, detach, divide, refine, remove, secede, secern, sejoin, single, sleave, sleeve, sunder, winnow 7 analyse, analyze, disjoin, dispart, diverse, divorce, expanse, isolate, segment, sejunct 8 abstract, alienate, detached, discrete, disperse, dissolve, distinct, disunite, prescind, secluded, solitary, withdraw 9 demarcate, different, disengage, dismember, disparate, eliminate, segregate, withdrawn 10 disconnect, dispossess, dissociate, distribute, individual, sejunctive 11 disembodied, distinctive, distinguish, fractionate, inde-

pendent, precipitate, unconnected 12 disassociate, disconnected, disintegrate

separation: 4 gulf 6 schism, tmesis 7 diacope 8 distance 9 cessation, partition 14 discontinuance
prefix: di; dis

separatists: 8 Pilgrims, Zoarites 9 Bimmelers

sepia: dun 7 pigment 10 cuttlebone, cuttlefish

sepiment: 5 hedge 7 defense 9 enclosure

sepoy: 9 policeman

seps: 5 snake 6 lizard 7 serpent

sept: 4 clan 5 seven, tribe

septum: 4 wall 9 partition

sepulcher: 4 bury, tomb 5 grave, inter, vault 6 entomb 8 monument 10 repository

sepulchral: 6 gloomy, hollow 7 charnel 8 funereal

sequacious: 6 pliant 7 ductile, servile 9 attendant, compliant, dependent, following, malleable

sequel (see also **sequence**): 4 next 5 issue 6 effect, result, upshot 7 outcome 8 follower, sequitur 9 aftermath, following, inference 10 conclusion 11 consequence, continuance 12 continuation

sequence (see also **sequel**): run, set 5 gamut, order, suite 6 course, series, tenace 8 straight 10 succession 11 progression

sequent: 8 follower 9 attendant, following 10 succeeding

sequential: 9 following 10 continuous, processive, succeeding 11 consecutive

sequestered: 5 alone 6 lonely, seized 7 private, recluse, removed, retired 8 isolated, secluded, solitary, withdrew 9 renounced, separated, withdrawn 10 cloistered, disclaimed, segregated 11 confiscated 12 appropriated

sequin: 4 disk 7 spangle

serac: 5 block 8 pinnacle

seraglio: 5 harem, serai 6 zenana 8 lodgings 9 enclosure, warehouse

serai: 5 harem 8 lodgings, seraglio 11 caravansary 12 caravanserai

serape: 5 cloak, shawl 7 blanket

seraphic: 4 pure 7 angelic, refined, sublime 8 cherubic 9 unworldly

seraphim: 5 angel 6 cherub

seraphine: 8 melodeon 10 instrument

Serb: 4 Slav

Serbia: *coin:* 5 dinar
combining form: 5 Serbo
measure: 4 ralo
prince: 4 Cral

sere, sear: dry, wax 4 worn 5 dried, talon 6 yellow 7 parched, several, various 8 scorched, separate, withered 10 desiccated, threadbare

serein: dew 4 mist, rain

serenade: 6 aubade 8 nocturne, serenata
burlesque: 8 shivaree 9 charivari 10 callithump

serenata: 6 serena 7 cantata 8 serenade

serene: 4 calm, cool, damp 5 clear, light, quiet 6 bright, pacify, placid, sedate, serein, steady 7 pacific 8 composed, decorous, peaceful, tranquil 9 collected, impassive, unruffled 10 unobscured 11 tranquilize, undisturbed 13 dispassionate, imperturbable

serenity: 6 repose 7 balance 10 equanimity

serf: 4 esne, peon 5 churl, helot, slave 6 servus, thrall, vassal 7 bondman, peasant, villein 8 bondsman, hireling

serge: 7 worsted

sergeant: 6 chiaus, tenant 7 esquire, servant, surgeon 9 attendant

seriation (see also **series**): 8 position 9 formation 11 arrangement

series: set 4 list 5 chain, gamut, suite, train 6 catena, course 8 beadroll, category, sequence, seriatim 9 gradation 10 succession
arranged in: 6 serial 7 seriate 11 installment

serious: 4 deep, grim, keen 5 grave, heavy, sober, staid 6 demure, sedate, severe, solemn 7 austere, capital, earnest, weighty 9 important, momentous 10 thoughtful 11 considerate

sermon: 4 talk 5 psalm, speak 6 homily 7 address, lecture 8 harangue 9 collation, discourse, preaching 10 admonition
subject: 4 text

sermonic: 5 grave

seroon: 4 bale 7 package

serous: 4 thin 6 watery

serpent: (see also **snake**): 7 entwine, reptile
elapine: 4 naia, naja
mythological: Ahi 5 Apepi, Dahak, Hydra 6 ellops, dragon 8 basilisk 11 Amphisbaena
pert. to: 7 anguine
victim: 7 Laocoon

serpentine: 4 file, wily, worm 5 snaky 7 sinuous, turning, winding 8 tempting 10 circuitous, meandering
variety: 10 antigorite

serrate: 5 notch, tooth 11 denticulate

serried: 4 dense 6 massed, packed 7 compact, crowded

serum: 4 whey 5 fluid 9 antitoxin

serum-like: 6 serous

servable: 6 usable 10 functional

servant: dey, gyp 4 amah, bata, cook, dasi, esne, girl, help, hewe, hind, maid, maty, mozo, syce 5 alila, biddy, boots, chela, gilly, groom, hamal, nurse, scout, slave, usher, valet 6 abigal, batman, bearer, bildar, butler, chakar, ewerer, flunky, garcon, gillie, hamaul, hammal, harlot, helper, khamal, menial, tenant, varlet, vassal **7** bondman, famulus, flunkey, footman, hummaul **8** chasseur, domestic, sergeant, servitor **9** atriensis **11** chamberlain

garment: **5** apron **6** livery **7** uniform

of God: **4** monk, pope **5** friar, rabbi **6** bishop, priest **8** chaplain, minister, preacher **10** Holy Father, missionary

pert. to: **8** famulary

retired: **8** emeritus

serve: do; act, aid **4** abet, give, help, mess, pass, suit, tend, wait **5** avail, cater, frame, ladle **6** answer, assist, attend, succor **7** advance, benefit, bestead, deliver, forward, further **8** function, minister **9** officiate **10** distribute

server: urn **4** tray **6** salver, waiter **7** caterer **9** assistant, lazy-Susan

Servia: See **Serbia**.

service: use **4** mass, rite **5** avera, favor, wages **6** employ, fealty, homage, repair, supply **7** chakari, retinue, slavery, utility **8** kindness, ministry **9** servitude **10** recompense **11** maintenance **12** installation, ministration

military: **4** duty **5** hitch **7** stretch **10** enlistment **12** conscription

public: **7** utility

service tree: **4** sorb

serviceable: **4** kind **6** useful **7** durable, helpful, lasting **8** obliging **9** available **10** beneficial, commodious

serviette: **6** napkin

servile: **4** base, bond, mean **6** abject, menial, sordid **7** fawning, slavish **8** cringing, enslaved **9** dependent, parasitic, truckling **10** obsequious, sequacious, submissive **11** subservient, sycophantic

servitor: **6** beadle, menial, squire **7** servant, soldier **8** adherent, follower **9** assistant, attendant **10** apprentice **12** exhibitioner

servitude: **4** yoke **7** bondage, peonage, serfdom, service, slavery **8** sentence **9** captivity, vassalage

sesame: til **4** herb, teel **5** benne **7** passkey **8** ajonjoli, password

seed: **7** gingili, tilseed

session: **4** term **7** meeting, sitting **8** sederunt **10** assemblage

Set: See **Seth**.

set: fix, gel, lay, put, sit **4** bent, clan, club, cock, crew, gang, laid, park, port, pose, prim, ring, seat, stud, suit **5** align, aline, brood, elect, elite, embed, fixed, group, imbed, place, plant, posit, range, ready, rigid, staid, stake, stand, suite **6** adjust, assign, cement, circle, clique, define, formal, harden, impose, impost, ordain, series, settle **7** appoint, arrange, company, confirm, congeal, coterie, decline, deposit, dispose, instate, platoon, station, stiffen **8** attitude, decorate, exchange, immobile, moveless, regulate, solidify **9** coagulate,

collocate, designate, determine, establish, immovable, obstinate, prescribe, stabilize **10** assortment, collection, constitute, stationary

about: **5** begin, start

afloat: **6** launch

apart: **5** elect **6** exempt **7** isolate, reserve, seclude **8** allocate, dedicate, separate **9** segregate, sequester

aside: **4** void **5** annul, table **6** except, reject **7** discard, dismiss, earmark, exclude, reserve **8** overrule, separate

at naught: **4** defy **7** despise **9** disregard

back: **4** loss **5** check **6** hinder **7** backset, relapse, reverse, setback

down: fix **4** seat **5** abase, enter, place, write **6** depose, encamp, ordain, reckon, record, regard, relate **7** appoint, descend, resolve, slacken **8** consider, estimate, register **9** attribute, determine, establish, humiliate, prescribe

forth: **5** adorn, offer, state **6** expone, expose **7** arrange, commend, display, enounce, exhibit, explain, expound, present, promote, propone, publish **8** announce, decorate, manifest **9** interpret, translate **10** promulgate

free: See **liberate**.

fresh: **5** relay

in operation: **4** jump, move, skip **5** slide, start **6** launch, plunge, spring

on end: **5** upend **10** topsyturvy

out: **4** plan **5** adorn, allot, equip, extol, issue, limit, start **6** embark, escort, outfit, recite **7** publish, started **8** describe, proclaim **9** embellish **10** promulgate

right: **4** file **5** align, aline, order **6** adjust **7** arrange, correct, ordered **11** systematize

to: go **4** bout **5** fight **6** fracas **7** contest **8** struggle

up: **4** post **5** build, erect, exalt, found, hoist, raise, treat **7** appoint, arrange, elevate **8** organize **9** establish

upon: **7** browden

seta: **6** chaeta **7** bristle

setaceous: **7** bristly

setal: **7** bristly

seth: **6** banker **8** merchant

Seth:

brother: **4** Abel, Cain

descendant: **4** Enos **7** Sethite

father: **4** Adam

son: **4** Enos

wife: **8** Nephthys

seton: **6** suture

setose: **7** bristly **9** setaceous

setout: **4** fuss **6** outfit **7** costume, display, exhibit **10** excitement **13** entertainment

settee: **4** seat, sofa **5** bench, divan

setter: dog **6** Gordon **10** compositor

setting: **4** eggs, trap, pave **5** decor, scene, snare, scena(It.) **6** locale **7** scenery **8** mounting **10** background **11** environment **12** surroundings

settle: fix, pay, sag, set **4** calm, dais, firm,

lend, nest, root, seat, sink, toit **5** affix,
agree, audit, bench, clear, couch, lodge,
order, perch, plant, quiet, serve, solve **6**
accord, adjust, alight, assign, decide, locate, purify, reduce, render, secure,
soothe **7** appoint, arrange, clarify, compone, compose, confirm, conform,
deposit, depress, dispose, provide, resolve, silence, subside **8** colonize, compound, conclude, ensconce, regulate **9**
conjobble, designate, determine, establish, habituate, liquidate, shrinkage **10**
accomodate, adjudicate, administer,
strengthen **11** tranquilize
strike: **7** mediate
settled: **4** alit, fast **5** fixed, staid **6** formed,
sedate **7** certain, decided, peopled, statary, testate **8** decorous **9** inerratic,
sedentary, steadfast **10** consistent, determined, unchanging **11** established
in advance: **13** predetermined
settlement: dos **4** camp, lees **5** abode,
dregs **6** colony, hamlet **7** payment, village
8 decision, disposal, fixation, sediment **9**
aldeament, community, residence **10** adjustment, conclusion, occupation, regulation **11** arrangement **12** colonization,
satisfaction **13** clarification, determination, establishment
arrange: **9** negotiate
settler: **6** sooner, vessel **7** planter, pioneer
8 colonist, emigrant **9** colonizer, immigrant **10** forehearth, receptacle
American: **7** Pilgrim, Puritan
seugh, seuch: rut **5** ditch, drain **6** furrow
seven: **4** zeta
combining form: **5** hepta
days and nights: **8** sennight
deadly sins: **4** envy, lust **5** anger, pride,
sloth **8** gluttony **12** covetousness
group of: **6** heptad, septet **8** hebdomad
Seven Churches: **6** Sardis, Smyrna **7**
Ephesos **8** Laodicea, Pergamos, Thyatira
12 Philadelphia
seven-faced: **11** heptahedral
seven-fold: **8** septuple
seven hills: See **Roman Hills**.
seven-sided: **10** heptagonal
sever: cut **4** deal, part, rend, slit **5** break **6**
breach, cleave, depart, detach, divide,
except, exempt, sunder **7** disjoin, dispart,
divorce, scatter **8** disunite, separate **9**
dismember segregate **10** disconnect,
dissociate **12** disassociate
from neck: **6** behead **9** decollate **10** decapitate
several: few **4** some **6** divers, single, sundry **7** diverse, various **8** distinct, peculiar
9 different **10** individual, respective
minimum: **5** three
severe: bad **4** dear, dere, dour, dure, hard,
keen, sore, tart **5** acute, breme, cruel,
grave, gruff, harsh, rethe, rigid, rough,
sharp, sober, stark, stern, stiff **6** biting,
bitter, chaste, coarse, hetter, sedate, sim

ple, solemn, strict, trying, unkind **7** ascetic, austere, caustic, chronic, condign,
crucial, cutting, drastic, extreme, intense,
serious, spartan, violent **8** captious, exacting, grievous, rigorous, scathing **9** difficult, draconian, inclement, strenuous,
stringent, unsparing **10** afflictive, astringent, censorious, forbidding, methodical,
oppressive, restrained **12** unornamented
severed: **5** apart
severity: **8** acerbity, acrimony, asperity
Seville cathedral tower: **7** Giralda
sew: hog, sow **4** bind, darn, join, mend,
seam **5** baste, broth, drain, sewer, shirr,
smock, unite **6** fasten, needle, stitch, suture **7** pottage
sewan: **5** beads, money **6** wampum
sewer: **5** drain **7** conduit, servant **10**
seamstress
opening: **7** manhole
sewing machine: *inventor:* **9** Elias Howe
part: **8** plicator **10** zipperfoot
sex: **6** gender
combining form: **4** geno
sexless: **6** neuter **7** epicene
sexton: **6** verger **7** sacrist **9** sacristan **12**
underofficer
sextuplet: **7** sestole **8** sestolet
sexy: **5** spicy **6** carnal, erotic **7** amatory,
earthly
sha: **5** sheep, urial **6** nahoor, oorial
shabby: old **4** base, mean, worn **5** dowdy,
faded, seedy **6** paltry, ragged, scurvy **7**
outworn, unkempt **8** shameful, tattered,
unworthy **9** beggardly **10** despicable,
threadbare **11** disgraceful **12** contemptible, deteriorated
shack (see also **shuck**): coe, hut **4** feed,
plug **5** cabin, catch, chase, hovel, tramp **6**
lean-to, refuse, shanty, wander **7** stubble
8 brakeman, retrieve, vagabond
shackle: tie **4** band, bind, bolt, bond, curb,
gird, idle, iron, loaf, ring **5** chain, gyves **6**
fetter, hamper, hinder, hobble, pinion,
secure **7** confine, manacle, trammel **8**
coupling, restrain **10** fetterlock
shad: **5** alose **6** allice **7** crappie, mojarra
shaddock: **5** fruit **6** pomelo **10** grapefruit
shade: bar, dim, hue **4** dark, dull, tint,
tone, veil **5** color, cover, ghost, hatch,
tinge, trace, umbra, vault **6** awning, canopy, darken, degree, nuance, screen,
shadow, spirit, sprite, shield **7** curtain,
eclipse, foliage, obscure, parasol, phantom, protect, shelter, spector, shutter, umbrage, vestige **8** clearing, darkness, ornament **9** adumbrate, variation **10**
apparition, difference, overshadow, protection, silhouette
light: **6** pastel
shaded: **10** umbrageous
shadetail: **8** squirrel
shadow (see also **shade**): dog **4** blot,
omen, tail **5** cleek, cloud **6** attend, follow,
shroud, symbol **7** remnant **8** penumbra **10**

indication, overspread 13 prefiguration
dispelling: 9 scialytic
figure: 10 silhouette
of death: 5 gloom, Sheol
outline: 10 silhouette
without: 6 ascian

shadowy: dim 5 faint, vague 6 opaque, shaded, umbral, unreal 7 obscure, retired 8 adumbral 10 impalpable, indistinct, overspread, transitory 12 inaccessible 13 unsubstantial

Shadrach: *companion:* 7 Meshach 8 Abednego
persecutor: 14 Nebuchadnezzar

shady: 7 shadowy, umbrous 11 underhanded 12 disreputable, questionable

shaffle: 4 limp 5 shirk 6 hobble, loiter 7 shuffle

shaft: bar, pit, ray, rod 4 axle, beam, bolt, cone, fust, hole, pole, stem, tige, tole 5 arbor, arrow, helve, heuch, heugh, irony, lance, scape, shank, spear, spire, stalk, stele, thill, trunk 6 arbour, column, groove, handle, pillar, tongue, upcast 7 chamber, chimney, Maypole, missile, obelisk, spindle 8 gatepost 9 flagstaff
part: 4 orlo
vehicle: 5 thill

shag: mat, nap 4 hair, mane, mass, pile, toss, wool 5 chase, fiber, shake 6 follow, rascal, refuse 7 garment, tobacco 9 cormorant 10 blackguard

shaggy: 5 bushy, furry, nappy, rough 7 hirsute, scrubby, unkempt, villous 8 straggly 10 unpolished

shagreen: 4 skin 7 leather, rawhide 8 galuchat

shaitan, sheitan: 5 devil, fiend

shake: go; bob, jar, jog, wag 4 free, jolt, move, pass, rese, rock, shog, stir, sway, toss, wave 5 churn, drink, eject, quake, shock, steal, swing, trill 6 depart, dither, dodder, goggle, hustle, joggle, quaver, quiver, rattle, shiver, totter, tremor, weaken 7 agitate, chatter, concuss, disturb, fluster, tremble, unnerve, vibrate 8 brandish, convulse, dislodge, enfeeble, flourish 9 agitation, dismissal 10 earthquake
down: bed, con 5 dance 6 extort, settle 9 blackmail
off: 4 shed 6 excuss 8 disagree

Shakespeare: *actor:* 4 Ward 6 Burton 7 Geilgud, Olivier, Sothern 8 Modjeska
alternate author: 5 Bacon
character: 4 Bone, Iago, Iras, Lear, Snug 5 Biron, Cleon, Henry, Regan, Romeo, Speed, Timon 6 Banquo, Juliet, Oberon, Portia, Simple 7 Antonio, Cassius, Othello, Salerio, Shylock, Silence, Slender, Titania 8 Falstaff
forest: 5 Arden
home: 4 Avon
play: 4 Lear 6 Caeser, Hamlet 7 Macbeth, Othello 9 Cymbeline

wife: Ann

shaking: 4 ague 9 tremulant, tremulous 10 concussion

shako: cap 9 headdress

shakti: 5 force, power

shaky: 4 weak 5 dicky 6 dickey, groggy, infirm, wabbly, wobbly 7 casalty, caselty, unsound 8 insecure 9 tottering, trembling, tremulous, uncertain 10 unreliable 12 questionable

shale: cod 4 husk, rock 5 metal, scale, shell, slate 7 shuffle 8 impurity

shall: may 4 must, will 5 would 7 obliged

shallop: 4 boat 6 dinghy, vessel

shallot: 4 tube 5 onion 8 eschalot

shallow: hat 4 cart, tray, weak 5 shoal 6 basket, flimsy, slight 7 cursory, trivial 9 depthless, frivolous 11 superficial

shalom: 5 peace

sham: 4 fake, hoax, mock 5 bogus, cheat, dummy, false, feign, fraud, trick 6 assume, bunyip, chouse, deceit, delude, device, duffer, humbug, shoddy 7 deceive, feigned, forgery, grimace, pretend 8 pretense, trickery 9 brummagem, deception, imitation, imposture, pretended, trickster 10 artificial, factitious, simulacrum, substitute 11 counterfeit, make-believe

shamal: 4 wind

shaman: 4 monk 6 beggar, priest 8 conjurer

shamash:
consort: Ai; Aya
worship center: 5 Larsa 6 Sippar

shamble: 5 bandy, bench, stall, stool, table 7 bauchle, butcher, counter, shuffle 9 footstool, malformed, slaughter

shambles: 8 abattoir

shame: 5 abase, abash 6 ashame, assume, bemean, bismer 7 degrade, mortify 8 contempt, disgrace, dishonor 9 embarrass, humiliate 10 repentance 11 degradation, shortcoming 12 illegitimacy 13 embarrassment, mortification

shamefaced: 6 humble, modest 7 bashful 9 diffident

shameful: 4 base, mean 5 gross 7 ignoble 8 flagrant, improper, indecent, infamous 9 degrading, dishonest 10 outrageous, scandalous, slanderous 11 disgraceful, ignominious, opprobrious 12 contumelious, dishonorable, disreputable, vituperative 13 dishonourable

shameless: 6 arrant, brazen 8 immodest, impudent 9 abandoned, audacious, barefaced 10 unblushing 11 brazenfaced

shammer: 4 aper 5 fraud 8 imposter

shammock: 4 loaf 6 dawdle, slouch

shamrock land: 4 Eire, Erin 5 Irena 7 Ireland

shandrydan: gig 6 chaise 7 vehicle

shandy: 4 wild 5 drink 9 visionary 11 unrealistic

Shang dynasty: Yin

shank: leg **4** gamb, shin, stem, tang **5** gambe, knife, ladle, ridge, shaft **8** leggings, stocking

shanny: shy **4** fish **5** giddy, silly **6** blenny

shanty: hut **5** cabin, hovel, hutch, shack **6** leanto **8** chantier, dwelling

shape: fit, hew **4** bend, cast, form, knap, make, mold, plan, tool, trim **5** block, boast, build, carve, feign, frame, guise, model, mould, state, torus **6** create, decree, design, devise, figure, format, happen, ordain **7** appoint, arrange, conform, contour, fashion, incline, phantom, posture, whittle **8** attitude, contrive **9** condition, determine, structure **10** apparition, appearance, figuration **11** arrangement **13** configuration

different: **8** variform

garden: **7** topiary

in: **4** trim

shapeless: **6** deform **8** deformed, formless **9** amorphous, contorted, distorted, misshapen, unshapely

shapely: fit **4** neat, trim **6** decent, gainly **8** suitable **11** symmetrical

shaping machine: **5** edger, lathe **6** shaper

shard: **5** scale, shell **8** fragment

share: cut, lot **4** cant, deal, dole, hand, part, rent **5** divvy, enter, quota, ratio, shear **6** cleave, divide, impart, moiety, ration **7** partake, portion **8** dividend, division **9** allotment, allowance, apportion, communion, plowshare **10** distribute **11** participate

widow's: **5** dower, dowry, terce, third **6** dowery

sharecropper: **7** metayer

Shari River: See **Cameroon.**

shark: **4** gata, haye, mako, tope **5** adept **6** expert, lawyer, usurer **7** dogfish, sharper, sponger **8** drunkard, maneater, parasite, swindler, thrasher, thresher **9** porbeagle, selachian, trickster **10** hammerhead

genus of: **11** carcharodon

pilot: **6** remora

young: **8** sharklet

sharp: **4** acid, cold, cute, edgy, fell, gash, gleg, gnib, high, keen, nice, sour, tart **5** acrid, acute, adept, alert, breme, brisk, crisp, eager, edged, fiery, harsh, salty, steep, tangy, witty **6** abrupt, active, acuate, astute, barbed, biting, bitter, clever, crafty, crispy, expert, peaked, severe, shrewd, shrill, snelly(Sc.) **7** angular, austere, caustic, cunning, cutting, gingery, grating, intense, lyncean, nipping, painful, piquant, pointed, pungent, rasping, sharper, violent, waspish **8** aculeate, distinct, handsome, incisive, piercing, poignant, vigilant, vigorous **9** attentive, beautiful, designing, impetuous, merciless, penetrant, sagacious, sarcastic, trenchant **10** discerning **11** acrimonious, intelligent, penetrating, underhanded

sharp-sighted: **6** astute

sharpen: nib, ted **4** edge, hone, whet **5** grind, point, reset, strop **6** acuate **7** enhance, quicken **9** intensify **10** cacuminate

sharper: gyp **4** bite **5** cheat, rogue **6** cogger, keener **7** cheater, gambler **8** deceiver, swindler **9** trickster

sharpness: **6** acumen

sharpshooter: **6** sniper **8** marksman

shastra class: **5** sruti **6** purana, smriti, tantra

shatter: **4** blow, dash **5** blast, break, burst, crash, smash, split, wreck **6** batter, damage, impair **7** clatter, derange, destroy, disable, scatter **8** disorder, disperse, splinter **9** dissipate

shattered: **6** broken **8** broozled, doddered

shave: ace, cut **4** pare, poll, trim **5** graze, skive **6** rasure, scrape **7** tonsure, whittle

shaveling: **4** monk **5** youth **6** priest **9** hypocrite, stripling

shaven: **4** bald **6** pilled **8** tonsured

shaver: boy, lad **4** chap **5** cheat **6** barber, fellow, tonsor **8** swindler **9** bargainer, youngster **11** extortioner

shavetail: **4** mule **10** lieutenant

shavie: **4** joke **5** prank, trick

shaving: **5** spale **8** ramentum

shaw: **4** wood **5** copse, grove **7** thicket

shawl (See also **vestment**)**:** **4** maud, wrap **5** manta, orale **6** serape(Mex.) **7** amlikar, paisley **8** epiblema

Shawnee Indian chief: **8** Tecumseh, Tecumtha

shay: **6** chaise **8** carriage

sheaf: **4** kern, kirn **5** bunch **6** bundle **7** cluster

group: **6** thrave

shear: cut **4** clip, gnaw, reap, rend, snip, trim **5** carve, force, mince, prune, sever, shave, strip **6** cleave, divest, fleece, nibble, pierce, remove **7** deprive, scissor, whittle **10** circumcise

shearing machine: **7** cropper

shears: **6** forfex **8** scissors, secateur

sheartail: **4** tern **11** hummingbird

shearwater: **4** crew **6** hagdon, haglet

sheatfish: **4** wels **7** catfish

sheath: cot **4** boot, case **5** dress, forel, ocrea, theca, stall **6** forrel, spathe **8** covering, envelope, scabbard

sheathe: **4** bury, case, ceil, dull **5** blunt, cover, glove **6** plunge **7** enclose, envelop

sheave: **5** wheel **6** pulley

sheaves: See **sheaf.**

Sheba: **4** Saba

shebang: **4** deal **6** affair, outfit **7** concern **8** business **11** contrivance **13** establishment

Shechem god: **10** Baalberith

shed: cut, hut **4** abri(F.), byre, cast, cote,

drop, emit, hull, lair, molt, nest, part, pour **5** booth, cabin, hovel, repel, scale, spill, tease **6** belfry, dingle, divide, effuse, hangar, hemmel, impart, lean-to, slough **7** cottage, diffuse, emanate, radiate, scatter, shelter, testudo **8** disperse, outhouse, separate, sprinkle, woodshed, workshop **9** irradiate, penthouse **11** intersperse, outbuilding

skin: **7** ecdysis

shedder: 4 crab **6** peeler, salmon **7** lobster

sheen: 4 fair **5** gleam, gloss, shine, shoes **6** bright, glossy, luster **7** exalted, glisten, glitter, radiant, shimmer, shining **8** brightly, lustrous, splendid, splendor **9** beautiful, shininess **10** brightness, glittering **11** beautifully, illustrious, resplendent

sheep: mug, sha **5** argal, dumba, ovine, urial **6** aoudad, argali, wether **7** bighorn, bleater, karakul, mouflon **8** karakule, moufflon, ruminant **9** blackface

breed: **4** Horn **6** Dorset, Exmoor, Merino, Romney **7** Cheviot, Delaine, Lincoln, Suffolk **8** Cotswold, Dartmoor **9** Leicester, Southdown, Teeswater **10** Corriedale, Oxford Down, Shropshire

coat: **6** fleece

cry: **5** bleat

dead: **5** braxy, traik

disease: coe, gid, rot

feed: **5** graze **7** pasture

female: ewe **6** gimmer, sheder

head: **5** jemmy

head broth: **9** powsowdy

kidney extract: **5** venes

male: ram, tup **5** heder **6** wether **10** bellwether

mark: **4** smit **5** brand

pathway: **6** roddin **7** rodding

pen: **5** bught(Sc.) **6** bought(Sc.)

second year: tag, teg

wild: sha **4** arui **5** argal, audad, urial **6** aoudad, argali, bharal, nahoor, nayaur **7** mouflon **8** moufflon

young: hog, teg **4** lamb, tegg **5** heder **6** bident, gimmer, hogget, sheder **7** twinter **8** hoggerel, shearhog **9** four-tooth, shearling

sheep dog: 6 collie **8** shepherd

sheep-like: 5 ovine

sheepfaced: See **sheepish.**

sheepfold: cot, pen, ree(Sc.) **4** cote, fold **7** sheppey **8** sheepcot **9** sheepcote, sheepfold **10** sheephouse

sheepheaded: 5 silly **6** stupid **12** simpleminded

sheepish: shy **4** meek **5** blate, silly, timid **7** abashed, awkward, bashful, daffish **11** embarrassed

sheepskin: 4 bond, cape **5** basil **7** diploma **9** parchment

leather: **4** roan

sheepwalk: run **5** range, slait **7** pasture

sheer: 4 fine, mere, pure, thin, turn **5** brant, clear, steep, utter **6** abrupt, bright, swerve **7** deviate, shining, unmixed, utterly **8** absolute, outright **9** deviation, downright, undiluted **10** diaphanous **11** transparent, unqualified **13** perpendicular

sheet: air **4** fine, page, rope, sail **5** chain, daily, linen, paper, plate **6** expand, lamina, shroud **7** tabloid **8** pamphlet **9** newspaper

shelf: 4 bank, berm, bink, reef, sill **5** altar, berme, ledge, shoal **6** gradin, mantel **7** bedrock, bracket, gradine, retable, sandbar, stratum **8** credence, credenza, sandbank **9** banquette **10** pigeonhole

shell: hud, pod **4** boat, bomb, coin, hull, husk, lyre, swad, test **5** balat, cameo, conch, cowry, crust, money, murex, scale, shuck, spoon, testa, troca **6** coffin, concha, cowrie, crusta, dolite, dugout, lamina, lorica, strafe **7** abalone, admiral, bombard, capsule, caracol, dariole, grenade **8** caracole, carapace, covering, exterior, frustule **9** cartridge **10** projectile, schoolroom

casing: **5** gaine

defective: dud

hole: **6** crater

measuring device: **11** conchometer

protected with: **8** loricate

unexploded: dud

shellac: lac **5** resin

shellacking: 6 defeat **7** beating **8** flogging, whipping

shellapple: 9 chaffinch, crossbill

shellfire: 6 strafe **7** barrage

shellfish: 5 nacre **6** limpet **7** mollusk **10** crustacean

shelter: cot, hut, lee **4** abri, barn, camp, cote, fold, gite(F.), herd, howf, port, roof, shed, skug, tent **5** benab, bield, boist, bower, cloak, cover, embay, haven, house, hovel, howff, hutch, shack **6** asylum, burrow, covert, defend, garage, hangar, harbor, hostel, refuge, sconce, sconse, screen, shield, trench **7** carport, cottage, defense, embosom, foxhole, harbour, hospice, imbosom, nacelle, pillbox, protect, retreat, trailer, umbrage **8** bescreen, ensconce, mantelet, quarters, security **9** coverture, harbinger, harborage, sanctuary **10** harbourage, protection

sheltered side: 7 leeward

on: **4** alee

shelve: tip **4** tilt **5** defer, ledge, shelf, table **6** mantel, retire **7** dismiss, project **8** overhang, platform **10** pigeonhole

shenanigan: 5 trick **7** evasion, foolery **8** mischief, nonsense, trickery

shend: mar **4** harm, lose, ruin **5** blame, shame, spoil, worst **6** damage, defeat, defend, injure, punish, revile, shield **7**

degrade, destroy, protect **8** confound, disgrace, dishonor, reproach **10** discomfort

Sheol: **4** hell **5** grave, Hades **10** underworld

shepherd: **4** herd, lead, tend **5** drive, guard, watch **6** attend, escort, feeder, gather, herder, leader, pastor, shadow **8** guardian, minister
band of: **10** pastoureau
clock: **7** salsify **9** pimpernel
dog: **6** Collie **8** Cebalrai
god: **5** Pales
pert. to: **8** pastoral
pipe: **4** reed **7** musette **11** flageolette
purse: **4** herb **9** blindweed

shepherdess: **7** bergere **9** Amarillis, Amaryllis

sherbet: ice

sherd: See **shard**.

sheriff: **6** grieve **7** bailiff, officer
aides: **5** posse
deputy: **6** elisor **7** bailiff
jurisdiction: **9** bailiwick

sherry: **4** wine **5** tokay **6** Solera **7** oloroso **11** amontillado

Shetland Island:
land: **4** odal, udal **6** udaler **7** udalman
measure: ure
musical instrument: gue
ounce: ure
tax: **4** scat

sheugh, sheuch: **5** ditch, gully **6** furrow, ravine, trench

sheyle: **6** squint **7** grimace

shibboleth: **4** test **8** password **9** criterion, watchword

shield: ecu(F.), rim **4** egis, hide, umbo **5** aegis, armor, avert, badge, board, cloak, cover, guard, shade, targe **6** blazon, brooch, canopy, defend, forbid, screen, target **7** buckler, conceal, defense, lirelle, prevent, protect, rotella, shelter, testudo **8** conserve, rondache **9** protector **10** escutcheon, protection
knob: **4** umbo
Minerva's: **4** egis **5** aegis
part of: **4** boss, ente, orle, umbo **6** pointe **7** bordure, impresa
rim: **4** orle

shield-bearer: **8** escudero

shield-shaped: **7** peltate, scutate **9** clypeolar

shieling: hut **7** cottage, pasture

shift: rid **4** deal, eddy, fend, jibe, move, quit, ruse, stir, tour, turn, veer **5** avoid, dodge, evade, feint, hours, order, shunt, slide **6** assign, bestir, change, device, divide, period **7** arrange, dispose, evasion, replace, shuffle **8** artifice, exchange, mutation, transfer **9** apportion, expedient **10** equivocate, subterfuge, transplant **11** contrivance **12** redistribute **13** transposition

shifting: **6** shifty **8** ambulant, drifting, floating

shiftless: **4** lazy **8** feckless **10** thriftless **11** inefficient

shifty: **4** haft **6** fickle, tricky **7** devious, hangdog **8** shifting **9** changeful, faithless **10** changeable

shikar: **4** hunt **5** sport **7** hunting

shikari, shikaree: **5** guide **6** hunter **9** sportsman

shillelagh: **4** club **6** cudgel

shillibeer: **6** hearse **7** omnibus

shilling: bob

shilpit: **4** flat, puny, thin, weak **6** feeble, sickly **7** insipid

shim: hoe **5** image, level, wedge **6** shadow, streak, washer **7** glimpse, shingle

Shimei's father: **4** Gera

Shimel's father: Ela

shimmer: **5** flash, light **7** glimmer, glisten

shimmy: **5** dance, shake **6** quiver **7** chemise, tremble, vibrate **10** shimmering

shin: run **4** kick, walk **5** climb, ridge, shank, tibia **6** cnemis, strike
pert. to: **7** cnemial

shindy: row **4** jump, lark, orgy, romp **5** brawl, dance, party, revel, spree **6** fracas, frolic, rumpus, uproar **7** shindig, wassail **8** carousal **9** commotion **11** disturbance, merrymaking

shine: ray **4** beam, beek(Sc.), glow, star **5** black, blaze, blink, excel, glaik, gleam, glent, glint, gloss, gloze, prank, sheen **6** liking, polish **7** glimpse, glisten, glister, glitter, radiate **8** eradiate, fondness, illumine **9** coruscate, irradiate, transluce

shiner: hat **4** chub **6** bruise **8** blackeye **9** bootblack

shingle: **4** sign, whip **7** haircut **9** signboard
splitting tool: **6** prower

shining: **4** glad, gold **5** aglow, glary, lucid, nitid, sleek **6** ardent, argent, bright, fulgid, glossy, lucent **7** beaming, eminent, fulgent, glowing, radiant **8** flashing, gleaming, luminous, lustrous, radiance, splendid **9** brilliant, effulgent, refulgent, sparkling, unclouded **10** glistening, glittering, remarkable **11** illustrious, irradiating, resplendent

shinplaster: **5** scrip

Shinto: *deity:* **8** Hachiman
temple: sha **5** Jinja **6** Jinsha **7** Yashiro

shiny: See **shining**.

ship: **4** boat, pink **5** setee **7** hagboat **8** balinger
abandoned: **8** derelict
ancient: **7** galleon
Arabian: **6** boutre
arctic: **6** sealer
Argonaut's: **4** Argo
armored: **7** carrack, cruiser **9** destroyer, ironsides, submarine
ascent: **5** scend

attendant: **7** steward
auxiliary: **6** tender
biscuit: **8** hardtack
boarding device: **6** ladder **9** gangplank
boat: **4** dory, life **5** barge, dingy **6** dingey, dinghy, tender **7** pinnace
body: **4** hull
breadth of: **4** beam
brutally disciplined: **8** hell ship
burden: **5** cargo
cabin: **6** saloon **9** stateroom
capacity: **7** tonnage
capacity unit: ton
cargo: **7** gaiassa
cargo invoice: **8** manifest
carpenter: **5** Chips
channel: gat **5** canal **6** narrow, strait
clean: **6** careen
clerk: **6** purser
coast guard: **6** cutter
coastal: hoy **4** dhow, grab **6** droger, trader **7** drogher
codfishing: **6** banker **8** walloper
commercial: **6** trader
company of: **4** crew **5** fleet, hands **6** armada
compass housing: **8** binnacle
cook: **6** slushy
course: **7** sealane
crane: **5** davit
curved planking: sny
deserter: rat
direction: **4** atry **5** abeam
enemy-watching: **7** vedette
employee: **5** oiler **6** purser, sailor **7** steward **8** deckhand, engineer, helmsman, steerman **9** navigator
fishing: **5** smack **6** hooker, lugger **7** trawler
flat-bottom: **4** keel **5** barge
fleet of: **6** armada
fuel: **5** barge, oiler **6** coaler, tanker **7** collier
group: **4** navy **5** fleet **6** armada
hoist: **4** boom **5** dairt **7** capstan
jail: **4** brig
lateral movement: **6** leeway
lifting device: **5** crane, davit **7** capstan
line: **7** marline, ratline
merchant: **6** argosy, galiot, holcad **7** galliot
middle: **9** amidships
movement: **6** leeway
oar: **6** bireme, galley, sampan **7** pinnace, rowboat, trireme
officer: **4** mate **5** bosun **6** purser **7** steward **9** boatswain
part: bow **4** beam, brig, deck, helm, hold, hull, keel, mast, prow **5** bilge, stern, waist, wheel **6** bridge, galley, rudder, steven **7** lazaret, scupper **8** binnacle **9** lazarette, lazaretto, sternpost
partition: **8** bulkhead
personnel: **4** crew **5** hands
pirate: **8** gallivat
planking: sny **6** strake

prison: **4** brig
privateer: **10** brigantine
prow: **5** prore
quarters: **6** fo'c'sle **8** steerage **10** forecastle
record: log
repair: **6** careen
repairing device: **7** drydock
rescue: ark
room: **4** brig **5** cabin, salon **6** galley **7** caboose **10** forecastle
rope: **4** line **6** hawser **7** halyard, lanyard, painter, ratline
sailing: **4** buss, dhow, proa, yawl **5** ketch, setee, sloop, smack, xebec **6** caique, chebec, hooker, lugger, mistic, saltie **7** galleon, Geordie, polacre
shovel: **5** skeet
side: **5** abeam
station: **5** berth
structure frame: **7** carcass
table frame: **6** fiddle
tender: **7** collier, pinnace
third-class: AE
tiller: **4** helm
timber: rib **4** bitt, keel, mast, spar **5** stick **7** bollard
twin-hulled: **9** catamaran
unseaworthy: **4** hulk **5** wreck **8** ballahoo, ballahou, derelict
upward movement: **5** scend
Venetian: **9** frigatoon
voyage record: log
war: (See also **warship**): sub **7** cruiser, flattop **8** corvette **9** destroyer, submarine **11** dreadnaught
windless: **7** capstan **8** becalmed
window: **4** port **8** porthole
wood for: **4** teak
worm: **5** borer **6** teredo
ship out: **6** enlist, export
shipboard: **5** board
shipment: **5** cargo **7** carload **8** delivery
shipping center: **7** seaport
shipshape: **4** neat, taut, tidy, trim **7** orderly
shipwright (launching slide marker): **6** wayman
shire: **5** derby, horse **6** county, region **8** district, province **11** subdivision
shirk: **4** duck, funk **5** avoid, dodge, evade, slack **6** desert **7** neglect **9** fainaigue
shirker: **6** loafer, truant **8** embusque
shirl: **4** slip **5** glide, slide
shirr: **6** gather
shirt: tee **4** jupe, polo, sark **5** dress, haire, kamis, parka, sport **6** camisa, camise, cilice, parkee
button: **4** stud
shirtfront: **5** dicky **6** dickey
shirtwaist: **6** blouse **9** garibaldi
shiver: **4** grue **5** chill, quake, shake **6** dither, quiver, tremor, twitch **7** flicker, frisson, shatter, shudder, tremble, vibrate **8** fragment, splinter
fit: **4** ague **6** chills **10** goosebumps

shivoo: 7 banquet, shindig 9 gathering 13 entertainment

shoal: bar 4 bank, mass, reef 5 barra, crowd, flock 6 school, throng 7 shallow 9 multitude

shock: jar, lot 4 blow, heap, jolt, pile, stun 5 appal, brunt, bushy, gliff, gloff, scare, shake 6 fright, impact, offend, parcel, shaggy, stroke, trauma 7 astound, collect, disgust, horrify, startle, terrify 8 paralyze 9 agitation, collision 10 assemblage, concussion

to reality: 5 sober

shock absorber: 7 snubber

shocking: 5 awful, lurid 6 horrid, unholy 7 fearful, ghastly, hideous 8 dreadful, horrible 9 egregious, revolting 10 disgusting

shod: 5 soled 6 booted 7 ensoled

shoddy: 4 poor 5 cheap 6 shabby 8 inferior

shoe: (see also **overshoe**): cue 4 boot, clog, flat, pump 5 gilly, sabot 6 brogan, brogue, buskin, caliga, crakow, gaiter, galosh, gillie, oxford, patten, sandal 7 blucher, flattie, slipper, sneaker 8 colonial, Congress, mocassin, moccasin, solleret 9 brodequin, pampootee 10 clodhopper, veldschoen

baby: 6 bootee

fix: 5 retap 6 polish, resole

form: 4 last, tree

grip: 5 cleat

part: box, cap, toe, top 4 heel, lift, pull, rand, vamp, welt 5 shank, strap 6 insole, tongue 7 counter, outsole 8 backstay, slipsole

paste: 7 clobber

piked: 6 cleats, crakow

repair: tap 5 retap 6 reheel, resole, stitch

rolling: 5 skate

rubber: 6 arctic, galosh 7 galoshe 8 overshoe

wooden: 5 sabot 6 patten

worker: 6 laster 7 cobbler

worn: 7 bauchle

shoelace: tie 5 lacet 7 latchet

tip: 5 aglet 6 aiglet

shoemaker: 4 snob 5 soler, sutor(L.) 7 cobbler, crispin, farrier 10 cordonnier(F.)

apprentice: 4 snob

patron saint: 7 Crispin

tool: 4 butt 5 elsin 6 elshin

shoes (see also **shoe**): 5 sheen, shoon

winged: 7 talaria

shoeshine: 9 bootblack

shog: jog 4 jerk, jolt, rock 5 shake 6 jostle

shoggie: 4 sway 5 swing

shoggle: 6 dangle, joggle

Shogun title: 6 tycoon

shole: 5 plank, plate

shoneen: 4 snob 5 toady

shoo: 4 away, scat

shook: See **shake.**

shool: 4 idle 6 loiter, scrape, shovel 7 saunter, scuffle, shamble, shuffle

shoot: bud, pot 4 bine, cast, chit, cion, dart, emit, film, fire, grow, move, plug, push, twig 5 bough, chute, drive, eject, plant, scion, snipe, spear, spout, spray, sprig, spurt, throw, tuber, utter, wound 6 branch, inject, propel, sprout, stolon, strike, thrust 7 burgeon, project 9 discharge 10 photograph 11 precipitate

objective: 6 target

shooting match: tir(F.) 5 skeet

shooting star: 5 comet 6 meteor 8 fireball

shop: 5 store 6 market, prison, tienda 7 bottega, factory 8 boutique, workshop

coffee: 4 cafe 6 bistro 9 estaminet

dairy: 8 cremerie

kind: 5 stith 6 smithy, stithy 7 mercery 8 saddlery, smithery 12 haberdashery

meat: 7 shamble 10 rotisserie 11 charcuterie

wine: 4 cafe 6 bistro

shopkeeper: cit 8 merchant, retailer 9 tradesman 11 businessman, storekeeper

shoplifter: 7 booster

shopper: 5 buyer 8 customer

shore: 4 bank, edge, land, prop 5 beach, brink, coast, drain, offer, scold, sewer 6 rivage, strand 7 seaside, support 8 threaten 9 foreshore

on: 8 littoral 9 amphibian

recess: bay 4 cove 5 bayou, inlet

shorebird: ree 4 ruff 5 snipe 6 curlew, plover 9 sandpiper

shorn: See **shear.**

short: 4 bain, curt, rude 5 bluff, brief, brusk, crisp, fubsy, harsh, scant, terse 6 abrupt, scanty, scarce 7 briefly, brusque, concise, crisply, curtail, friable, summary 8 abruptly, succinct 9 concisely, crumbling, deficient, shortstop 11 compendious 12 insufficient

and stout: 5 bunty, dumpy 6 stocky, stodgy, stubby 8 rolypoly, thickset

short-breathed: 5 pursy 6 winded 7 puffing

short-lived: 9 ephemeral

short-sighted: 6 myopic

short-spoken: 4 curt 5 gruff 7 laconic

shortage: 7 deficit 10 deficiency 13 insufficiency

shortcoming: 4 flaw 5 fault 6 defect 7 failure 10 deficiency, inadequacy 12 imperfection

shortcut: 5 alley 6 byroad 8 diagonal, gain cope

shorten: bob, cut, lop 4 clip, furl, reef 5 check 6 lessen, reduce 7 abridge, curtail, curtate, deprive 8 condense, contract, decrease, diminish 9 apocopate, decurtate 10 abbreviate 11 incapsulate

shorthand: 11 stenography 12 brachygraphy, speedwriting

system: 5 Gregg 6 Pitman

shortly (see also **short**): **4** soon **7** quickly **9** presently

shortness: 7 brevity

shortsighted: 4 dull **6** myopic, obtuse **11** nearsighted **13** opportunistic

Shoshone Indian: Ute **4** Hopi, Otoe, Utah **5** Piute **6** Paiute **8** Comanche

shot: (see also **shoot**): pop, try **5** blank, carom, drink, guess, masse, photo, range, reach, sally, tired, weary **6** bullet, pellet, stroke **7** attempt, missile **8** marksman, snapshot **9** exhausted, reckoning **10** conjecture, projectile **11** intoxicated

size: B; BB, FF, FT, TT; BBB **4** dust **8** air-rifle, buckshot

should: 5 ought

shoulder: 4 berm, edge **5** bough, raise **6** axilla

angle: **6** epaule

bone: **7** scapula

combining form: omo

muscle: **7** deltoid

ornament: tab **7** epaulet **9** epaulette

pain: **7** omalgia

pert. to: **4** alar **7** humeral **8** scapular

shoulder blade: 7 scapula

shout: boo, cry, hoy, hue **4** bark, bawl, call, crow, hoot, roar, root, roup, scry, yell, yelp **5** cheer, huzza, noise, whoop, yodel, yodle **6** clamor, gollar, goller, halloo, hurrah, outcry, yammer **7** acclaim **10** vociferate **11** acclamation

hunting: **5** hallo, holla **6** yoicks **7** tallyho **9** view-haloo

shove: 4 cast, push **5** drive, eject, elbow, hunch, shunt **6** hustle, jostle, propel, thrust

shovel: van **4** pale, peel **5** scoop, shool, skeet, spade **6** thrust **7** shuffle **8** strockle

shoveler: 9 broadbill

shovelfish: 9 spadefish **10** paddlefish

shovelhead: 5 shark **7** catfish **8** flathead, sturgeon

show: 4 bosh, dash, fair, lead, pomp **5** coach, farce, gloss, guide, movie, plead, prove, raree, revue, teach, train **6** accuse, afford, allege, assign, bestow, blazon, cinema, circus, confer, denote, detect, escort, evince, expose, flaunt, gaiety, gayety, inform, locate, parade, reveal, tinsel, unveil, veneer **7** bespeak, betoken, bravura, declare, display, divulge, exhibit, explain, perform, present, produce **8** ceremony, disclose, evidence, flourish, indicate, instruct, manifest **9** barnstorm, burlesque, designate, rareeshow, represent, semblance **10** appearance, exhibition, exposition, expression **11** countenance, demonstrate, performance **13** demonstration

false: **6** tinsel

forth: **7** publish **8** manifest, proclaim **9** publicize

stylized: **4** mime **6** parade **7** pageant **9** cavalcade, pantomime

way: **5** guide, usher **6** direct, escort **7** conduct

show up: 5 strip **6** appear, arrive, expose **7** display

showcase: 7 vitrine

shower: wet **4** bath, rain, sump, wash **5** bathe, party, spray, water **6** bestow, deluge **7** drizzle, scatter **8** revealer, sprinkle **9** exhibitor

showery: wet **4** damp **5** moist **7** tearful

showing: 4 sign **6** aspect **7** account **10** apocalypse, appearance

first: **8** premiere

showy: gay **4** arty, loud **5** dashy, gaudy, grand **6** flashy, garish, ornate, swanky **7** dashing, gallant, gaudful, pompous **8** gorgeous, splendid, striking **9** brillante, sumptuous **10** pretensive **11** pretentious **12** ostentatious

shrab: 5 drink **6** spirit **8** beverage

shrapnel: 10 projectile

shred: bit, cut, hew, jag, rag **4** fell, jagg, snip, tear, twig, wisp **5** blype, grate, piece, prune, scrap, sever, shard, strip **6** divide, screed, sliver, tailor, tatter **7** fritter, parings, vestige **8** fragment, particle

shrew: 5 curse, scold, vixen **6** mammal, tartar, virago **7** muskrat, villain **9** scoundrel, termagant

shrewd: bad, sly **4** cagy, cute, evil, foxy, hard, keen, sage, wily **5** acute, canny, harsh, sharp, smart, stern **6** argute, artful, astute, biting, clever, crafty, subtle, wicked **7** abusive, cunning, gnostic, hurtful, knowing, parlous, politic, sapient **8** depraved, grievous, piercing, shrewish **9** gnostical, ingenious, injurious, sagacious **10** discerning, farsighted, hardheaded **11** distressing, mischievous, penetrating, sharpwitted **13** perspicacious

shriek: cry, yip **4** yell **6** holler, outcry, scream **7** screech

shrift (see also **shrive**): **10** absolution, confession, disclosure **12** confessional **14** acknowledgment

shrill: 4 high, keen **5** acute, sharp **6** argute, biting, piping, shriek, squeak **7** screech **8** piercing, poignant, strident **11** highpitched, penetrating

shrimp: kid **5** dwarf **6** shaver **9** stripling **10** crustacean

shrine: box **4** case, naos, tomb **5** altar, caaba, chest, kaaba, huaca **6** abaton, adytum, chapel, chasse, dagaba(Ind.), dagoba(Ind.), entomb, hallow, temple **7** chaitya, enclose, memoria **8** canonize, enshrine **9** container, reliquary **10** receptacle

goddesses: **9** anaktoran

shrink: shy **4** fawn, funk, shun, wane **5** cling, cower, quail, rivel, shrug, wizen **6** blench, boggle, cutter, cringe, flinch, gizzen, huddle, humble, lessen, recoil, retire, wither **7** atrophy, dwindle, retract, shrivel

8 condense, contract, decrease, withdraw **9** constrict **10** depreciate

shrinking: shy **5** timid **6** afraid **9** diffident

shrive: rob **4** free **5** purge **6** pardon **7** absolve, confess **8** disclose **9** reconcile

shrivel: **5** blast, crine, parch, rivel, wizen **6** cotter, scrump, shrink, weazen, wither

shriveled: **4** wede

shroff: **6** banker, expert **7** changer, inspect **8** separate **12** moneychanger

shrogs: **9** brushwood

shroud: lop **4** hide, trim, veil **5** array, cloak, cover, crypt, dress, shade, sheet, vault **6** branch, clothe, screen, shadow **7** conceal, curtain, envelop, foliage, garment, plumage, protect, shelter **8** cerement, clothing, covering, envelope **9** cerecloth **10** protection

Shrove Tuesday: **10** Pancake Day

shrub: lop, tea, tod **4** bush, cade, coca, olea, sida, sola **5** elder, lilac, prune, punch, salal **6** cudgel, frutex **7** arboret, buckeye, chamise, chamiso, heather, scratch, tarbush **8** abelmosk, barberry, beverage, huisache **9** chaparral, manzanita

aromatic: tea **4** mint, sage **5** batis, thyme **8** rosemary

bean family: **4** ulex

collection: **10** fruticetum

desert: **5** retem **6** alhagi, raetam

evergreen: box **4** ilex, moss, titi **5** furze, heath, salal, savin **6** laurel, myrtle **7** jasmine, juniper **8** oleander **9** mistletoe

flowering: **5** lilac, tiara **6** azalea, laurel, myrtle, spirea **7** lantana, rhodora, spiraea, syringa **8** japonica, oleander, oleaster **9** mistletoe **10** mignonette

fruit: **5** salal

genus of: **5** erica, ledum **6** aralia

myrtle-like: **7** cajeput, cajuput

ornamental: **6** privet

parasitic: **9** mistletoe

pert. to: **9** fruticose, fruticous

poisonous: **5** sumac **6** sumach

prickly: **4** whin **5** briar, brier, gorse **7** bramble **8** allthorn, hawthorn

rubber: **7** guayule

tea-like: **7** kat **4** coca

tropical: **5** henna **6** olacad **7** lantana **10** frangipane, frangipani

yercum-yielding: **5** madar

shrubbery: **7** boscage, boskage

shruff: **5** dross **7** rubbish

shrug: don, tug **5** hitch **6** fidget, shiver, shrink **7** gesture, shudder **8** contract, hitching **9** handshake **10** convulsion

shrunken (see also **shrink**): **4** lank

Shu: *parent:* Ra **6** Hathor

sister: **6** Tefnut

wife: **6** Tefnut

shuck: pod **4** husk **5** shell, strip **6** recoil, remove **7** discard

shudder: **4** grue **5** quake, sha : **6** agrise, shiver **7** frisson, tremble

shuffle: mix **4** gait, plod **5** dance, scuff **6** huddle, juggle, jumble, mingle, remove, sclaff **7** evasion, quibble, scuffle, shamble **8** artifice **10** equivocate **11** prevaricate **12** equivocation

shuffling: **6** shifty **7** evasive **9** deceitful **13** opportunistic

shun: **4** balk, flee, hide **5** avert, avoid, evade, evite **6** eschew **7** forbear, forsake, refrain **8** forebear

shunt: **5** shift, shove **6** divert, remove, switch **9** conductor, rechannel, sidetrack

shut: bar, rid **4** free **5** close **6** climax, fasten, forbid **7** confine, exclude **8** prohibit **10** portcullis

in: hem, pen **4** cage, pent, wall **5** embar, embay, fence **6** bottle, hemmed **7** bottled, confine, enclose, impound **8** imprison **10** quarantine, surrounded

shut-in: **7** invalid, recluse **12** convalescent

shut out: bar **7** exclude **8** preclude

shut up: end, gag **7** seclude **8** conclude **9** terminate

shutter: **5** blind, cover **6** screen **7** buckler **8** jalousie

shuttle: **6** looper

shuttlecock: **4** bird **6** birdie

shy: coy, mim **4** jump, shun, wary **5** aloof, avoid, chary, scant, start, throw, timid **6** anerly, boggle, demure, modest, recoil, shrink **7** bashful, lacking **8** farouche, hesitant, reserved, retiring, secluded, sheepish, skittish **9** diffident, reluctant, shrinking **10** shamefaced, suspicious, unassuming **11** distrustful, unobtrusive **14** unostentatious

Shylock: *coin:* **5** ducat

friend: **5** Tubal

shyster: **11** pettifogger

si: yes

Siam: See **Thailand**.

Siamese twin: Eng **5** Chang

sib: kin **4** akin **6** allied, sister **7** brother, kindred, kinship, kinsman, related, sibling **8** friendly, relation, relative **9** congenial, kinswoman, relatives **12** well-disposed

Siberia: *antelope:* **5** saiga

carnivore: **5** sable

city: **4** Omsk **5** Chita, Tomsk **7** Barnaul, Irkutsk **11** Krasnoyarsk, Vladivostok **15** Blagovestchensk

dog: **7** Samoyed **8** Samoyede

forest: **5** Urman

fur: **7** calabar

gulf: Ob

hunters and fishers: **6** Giliak, Gilyak **7** Samoyed **8** Samoyede

hut: **8** barabara, barabora

mountains: **5** Altai

people: **5** Sagai, Tatar, Yakut **6** Kirgiz, Tartar, **7** Kirghis, Kirghiz, Yukagir **8** Yukaghir **9** Mongolian

plain: **6** steppe, tundra

region: **5** taiga

river: Ob, Om; Ili, Tom **4** Amur, Lena, Maya, Onon **5** Sobol, Tobol **6** Olenek
squirrel: **7** miniver
squirrel-skin: **7** calabar
storm: **5** buran
tanning plant: **5** badan
tent: **4** yurt **5** yurta
sibilant: s, z; ch, sh, zh; ess **7** hissing
sibling: (see also **sib**): **6** sister **7** brother
sibness: **7** kinship **10** connection **12** relationship
sibyl: **5** witch **6** Libyan, Samian, Trojan **7** Cumaean, seeress **8** Delphian, Phrygian **9** Cimmerian, Erythrean, sorceress, Tiburtine **10** prophetess **13** fortuneteller, Hellespontine
sibylline: **6** occult **7** cryptic **8** oracular **9** ambiguous, equivocal, prophetic **10** exorbitant, mysterious **11** prophetical
sic: so; set **4** seek, such, thus, urge **5** chase **6** attack, incite
sice: six **8** sixpence
Sicilian: **10** Trinacrian
Sicily: *cape:* **4** Boeo, Faro **7** Passaro
city: **4** Gela **5** Aetna, Bidis **6** Alcamo, Modica, Ragusa **7** Catania, Marsala, Messina, Palermo, Trapani **8** Girgenti **13** Caltanissetta
composer: **7** Bellini
crime society: **5** Mafia
god: **7** Adranus
harbor: **7** Palermo
island: **11** Pantelleria
king: **4** Eryx
measure: **5** salma **7** caffiso
mountain: **4** Etna
people: **5** Elymi, Sicel
river: **5** Salso **6** Belice, Simeto **7** Platani
seaport: Aci **7** Messina
volcano: **4** Etna
whirlpool: **9** Charybdis
youth: **4** Acis
sick: bad, ill, set, wan **4** abed, pale, seek, urge, weak **5** badly, chase, crank, cronk, fed-up, unfit, weary **6** ailing, attack, incite, unwell **7** unsound **8** impaired **9** crapulous, depressed, disgusted, instigate, nauseated, surfeited, unhealthy **10** indisposed **11** exasperated
deathly: **5** amort **7** alamort
sickbay: **6** clinic **8** hospital **9** infirmary **10** dispensary
sicken: **6** affect **8** languish
sickening: **7** fulsome **9** revolting **10** disgusting, nauseating
sicker (see also **sick**): **4** fast, firm, safe, sure **5** fixed **6** assure, pledge, safely, secure, stable **7** assured, certain **8** securely **9** assuredly, certainly, confident **10** dependable **11** established, trustworthy
sickish: **6** sickly **9** sickening
sickle: **6** scythe
sickly: ill, wan **4** flue, pale, puny, weak **5** cothy, faint, frail **6** ailing, cranky, feeble,

infirm, weakly **7** cothish, insipid, invalid, languid, mawkish, queechy **8** diseased **9** sickening, unhealthy
sickness: **6** malady, nausea **7** ailment, disease, disgust, illness **9** distemper, infirmity, weariness **12** qualmishness **13** indisposition
feign: **8** malinger
mental: See **mental disorder**.
side: far **4** edge, face, line, part, team, wall, wide **5** agree, ample, costa, facet, flank, latus, party, phase, place, proud, shore, slope, space, width **6** aspect, behalf, border, margin, region, severe **7** conceit, distant, faction, lateral, support, surface **8** district, position, spacious **9** declivity, direction, outskirts **10** collateral **15** pretentiousness
on the: **5** apart
pert. to: **7** lateral
piece: rib **5** stave
sheltered: lee **4** alee
side arm: **5** sword **6** pistol, weapon **7** bayonet **8** revolver
side by side: **8** parallel, together
side view: **7** profile
sideboard: **6** buffet **8** credence, credenza, cupboard, dressoir
sidekick: pal **4** chum **6** friend **7** partner **8** follower **9** assistant, companion, satellite **11** confederate
sideling, sidling: **5** askew, slope, steep **7** lateral, sloping **8** inclined, sidelong, sideways **9** inclining, laterally, obliquely
sidelong: **6** subtle **7** lateral, oblique, sloping **8** indirect, sideways, slanting **9** laterally, obliquely
sidepiece: rib **6** border
sidereal: **6** astral, starry **7** stellar **8** starlike
siderite: ore
siderolite: **9** meteorite
sideshow: **10** attraction
attraction: **5** freak
sideslip: **4** skid **5** slide **10** digression
sidestep: **4** duck **5** avoid, evade
sidetrack: **4** spur **5** shunt **6** divert, switch
sidewalk: **6** causey **9** banquette, boardwalk
part: **4** curb, kerb **5** crack **6** paving
sideway: **5** byway **6** bypath **7** postern **8** sidewalk, sideways
sideways: **5** aside **6** askant **7** askance, athwart, lateral **8** indirect, sidewise **9** laterally, obliquely
Sidi's wife: **5** Amine
sidle: **4** edge **6** loiter **7** saunter
sie: **4** drip, drop, sift **5** strain
siege: see **4** rank, seat **5** bench, beset, flock, place, privy **6** attack, throne **7** besiege, sitting, station **8** blockade **9** beleaguer **13** beleaguerment
Siegfried: *mother:* **8** Sieglind
slayer: **5** Hagen

wife: **9** Kriemhild
sierra: 5 range, ridge
Sierra Nevada: *fog:* **7** pogonip
  peak: **4** Dana **7** Whitney
siesta: nap **4** rest **5** sleep
sieve: 4 lawn, sift **5** tamis, temse **6** basket, bolter, filter, ranger, riddle, screen, sifter, strain **7** chaffer, cribble, measure **8** colander, separate, strainer
sievelike: 8 cribrate
sift: ree, sie, sye **4** bolt, cull, scry, seek **5** sieve, temse **6** dredge, filter, riddle, screen, search, strain, winnow **7** canvass, examine, inspect, scatter **8** separate **10** scrutinize
sigh: sob **4** moan, sugh, wail **5** mourn, sithe, sough, yearn **6** grieve, lament **7** suspire **11** respiration
sight: aim, ken, sum **4** bone, espy, gaze, look, show, vane, view **5** scene **6** aspect, behold, descry, glance, vision **7** discern, display, glimpse, insight, suspire **8** eyesight, quantity **9** spectacle **10** appearance, exhibition, inspection, perception **11** examination, observation, suspiration
  defect: **7** anopsia
  loss: **9** amaurosis
  obscurity: **6** caligo
  offending: **7** eyesore
  out of: **11** disappeared
  second: fey, ESP **7** psychic
sightless: 5 blind **6** unseen **9** invisible
sigil: 4 seal, sign, word **6** device, signet **9** signature
sigmoid: ess
sign (see also **signal**): ad; cue, nod **4** hire, mark, note, omen **5** badge, image, segno(It.), sigil, spoor, token, trace **6** banner, beacon, beckon, caract, effigy, emblem, engage, ensign, figure, motion, notice, poster, signet, symbol, wigwag **7** auspice, endorse, gesture, initial, insigne, message, picture, portent, prodigy, vestige, warning **8** password, pretense, standard **9** character, semaphore, semblance, subscribe, watchword **10** denotation, expression, forerunner, indication, prognostic, underwrite **11** countersign **13** advertisement, constellation, demonstration, foreshadowing
  astrological: **5** Aries **6** Gemini, Pisces, Taurus **8** Aquarius **9** Capricorn
  diacritical: **5** hamza, tilde **6** hamzah, tittle, umlaut **7** cedilla
  direction: **5** arrow
  illuminated: ad **4** neon **6** lights
  liturgical: **5** selah **6** shelah
  pert. to: **5** semic **8** semantic
  Zodiac: See **Zodiac** *sign.*
sign language: 11 dactylology
sign off: out **6** thirty
sign on: 4 hire, ship **6** engage, enlist, enroll **8** register
signal (see also **sign**): **4** flag **6** buzzer, en-

sign, notify, sennet **7** betoken, eminent, lantern, notable, presage, signify **9** memorable, prominent, semaphore, symbolize **10** remarkable **11** communicate, conspicuous **13** extraordinary
  distress: SOS **6** mayday.
  electric: **8** teleseme
  system: **4** code
  warning: **5** alarm, alert, flare, siren **6** alarum, beacon, tocsin **7** blinker
signature: 4 hand, mark, name, sign, visa, vise **5** sigil, stamp **9** allograph, autograph, birthmark, designate **10** directions, impression **11** countersign
signet: 4 mark, seal, sign **5** sigil, stamp **10** impression **12** authenticate
significance: 7 bearing, purport **13** signification
significant: 4 sign **5** grave, token **6** symbol **7** ominous, weighty **8** eloquent, sinister **9** important, momentous **10** expressive, indicative, meaningful, portentous, suggestive **13** consequential
signification: 4 sign **5** sense, token **7** meaning **10** importance, indication **11** consequence **12** apprehension, notification
signify: nod **4** mean, show, sign **5** augur, imply, spell, utter **6** amount, denote, import, inform, matter, signal **7** betoken, compare, declare **8** announce, foreshow, indicate, intimate, manifest **11** communicate
signor: man **4** lord **5** title **9** gentleman
signpost: 5 guide **6** beacon **9** guidepost
signum: 4 bell, mark, sign **9** signature
Sigurd: *horse:* Grani
  slayer: **5** Hogni
  wife: **6** Gudrun
sike: 4 rill **5** brook, ditch, drain, gully **6** ravine, stream, trench
siker: 4 safe **6** secure **7** assured **9** confident **10** dependable **11** trustworthy
Sikkim (see also **India**): *capital:* **7** Gangtok
  people: **4** Rong
silage: 4 feed **6** ensile, fodder **8** ensilage
sile: fry **4** beam, drop, fall, flow, pour, soil **5** glide, sieve, spawn **6** filter, rafter, strain **8** strainer
silence: gag **4** hush, mute, rest, stun **5** choke, floor, quiet, still, tacet **6** muffle **7** campion, confute, repress, secrecy **8** muteness, suppress **9** obscurity, reticence, stillness **10** silentness
  goddess: **8** Angerona
silencer: 4 mute **5** gavel **7** muffler
silene: 7 campion **8** catchfly
silent: mum **4** dumb, flat, mute **5** quiet, still, tacit **8** inactive, overcome, reserved, reticent, taciturn, unspoken **9** noiseless, secretive, unuttered **10** flavorless, speechless, unrecorded **11** unexpressed, unmentioned **15** uncommunicative
silex: 5 flint **6** quartz, silica

silica: 4 opal 5 silex 7 dioxide
silicate: 4 mica 6 cerite, iolite 7 epidote 8 calamine, severite, wellsite
silicon derivative: 5 monox
silk: 5 pekin, surah, tulle 7 foulard 8 florence, sarcenet, sarsenet
embroidery thread: 5 floss 8 arrasene
fabric: 4 gros 5 caffa, China, crepe, moire, ninon, pekin, satin, surah, tabby, tulle 6 cendal, faille, mantua, pongee, samite, sendal, tussah, tusser. tussur 7 alamode. marabou, sarsnet, taffeta, tsatlee, tussore 8 sarcenet, sarsenet
fishline: 4 gimp
hank: 4 hasp
Indian moth: 4 muga
refuse: 6 strass
substitute: 5 nylon, rayon
unspun: 6 sleave
waste: 4 noil 5 floss 6 frison
worker: 7 thrower 9 throwster
yarn: 4 tram 7 schappe
yarn size: 6 denier
silk-stocking: 4 ride 5 elite 7 elegant, wealthy 9 exclusive, luxurious 10 Federalist 12 aristocratic
silken: 4 fine, soft 5 quiet, silky, sleek, suave, sweet 6 gentle, glossy, smooth, tender 7 elegant 8 delicate, lustrous, silklike 9 luxurious, sericeous 10 effeminate 12 ingratiating
silkworm: eri 4 eria 6 tussah, tusser, tussur 7 tussore 8 bombycid
silkworm rot: 7 calcino
sill: 4 beam, seat, sile 5 bench, frame, ledge, shelf, stone 6 timber 9 threshold
silliness: 5 folly 6 betise(F.)
silly: mad 4 bete, daft, fond, fool, idle, simp, weak 5 anile, apish, barmy, dazed, dense, frail, goofy, goose, inane, plain 6 absurd, cranky, cuckoo, dotard, dottle(Sc.), feeble, footle, humble, infirm, paltry, rustic, sickly, simple, stupid, unwise 7 asinine, fatuous, foolish, foppish, shallow, witless 8 childish, fopperly, ignorant, imbecile, innocent 9 brainless, childlike, ludicrous, pointless, senseless, simpleton 10 half-witted, indiscreet 12 simple-minded 15 unsophisticated
silt: 4 scum 5 dregs 7 deposit, moraine, residue 8 sediment 9 percolate
silver: 4 pale 5 money, plate, sweet 6 argent, gentle 7 bullion, silvery 8 argentum, eloquent, lustrous, peaceful, precious, sterling 9 tableware 10 silverware 11 resplendent 13 argentiferous
containing: 5 lunar
pert. to: 9 argentine, argentous
reducing kettle: 4 cazo(Sp.)
symbol: Ag
silver and gold: *ornament:* 5 orris
silver fox: *fur:* 7 platina
silver oak: 11 flannelbush
silver plover: 4 knot(Sc.)

silver thaw: ice 4 rime 5 glaze
silver thistle: 8 acanthus
silver-tongued: 8 eloquent
silversmith: 9 artificer
silverware: 5 vases 6 dishes 8 platters 9 ornaments, tableware
ornament: 7 gadroon
silverweed: rue 5 tansy 9 jewelweed
silvery: 7 frosted 9 argentine 10 argenteous
simar: 4 robe 6 jacket 7 garment 12 undergarment
Simeon: *father:* 5 Jacob
mother: 4 Leah
simian: ape 6 monkey 7 apelike
similar: sib 4 akin, like, such 5 alike 6 evenly 7 uniform 8 analogic, parallel 9 semblance 10 analoguous, resembling 11 counterpart, homogeneous, resemblance 13 correspondent
comb. form: 4 homo 5 homeo 6 homoeo
simile: 10 comparison
similitude: 4 form 5 image 6 simile, symbol 7 analogy, parable 8 allegory, likeness 9 facsimile, semblance 10 similarity 11 counterpart, resemblance 14 representation
similize: 5 liken 7 compare
simmer: 4 boil, stew 6 braise
simmon: 9 persimmon
simnel: 5 bread 7 biscuit 8 cracknel 9 fruitcake
Simon: 5 Peter
Simon Legree: 6 driver 10 taskmaster
simon-pure: 4 real, true 7 genuine 9 authentic 11 unqualified
simony: 8 barratry
simper: 5 mince, smile, smirk 7 whimper
simple: 4 bald, bare, dull, easy, fond, mere, poor, pure, real, true, weak 5 folly, lowly, naive, naked, plain, Roman, silly 6 common, Dorian, homely, humble, oafish, rustic, severe, single, stupid 7 artless, austere, babyish, foolish, idyllic, natural, onefold, sincere, Spartan, unmixed 8 absolute, arcadian, childish, complete, gullible, homemade, ignorant, innocent, modestly, ordinary, tailored, trifling 9 childlike, elemental, ingenuous, primitive, unadorned 10 elementary, unaffected, uninvolved 11 homogeneous, undesigning, unimportant 12 inartificial, uncompounded, unpretending 13 insignificant, uncomplicated, unconstrained, unembellished 15 straightforward, undistinguished, unsophisticated
simple-minded: 6 simple, stupid 12 feeble-minded, unsuspecting 13 simple-hearted 15 unsophisticated
simpleton: ass, daw 4 boob, dolt, fool, gaby, gawk, gawp, gowk, lout, simp, tony, zany 5 dunce, goose, idiot, ninny, noddy, sammy 6 dawkin, gander, gawney, gulpin, nincom, nincum, nitwit, noodle 7 gomeral, gomerel, gomeril, muggins, widgeon

8 Abderite, fondling, numskull, omadhaun **10** changeling, nincompoop **11** ninnyhammer

simplify: **7** clarify, expound **9** elucidate, interpret

simulacrum: **4** sham **5** image **7** phantom **8** likeness, pretense, travesty **9** imposture, semblance **11** assemblance, counterfeit

simulate: act, ape **4** fake, mock, sham **5** feign, feiut **6** affect, assume **7** feigned, imitate, pretend **9** dissemble, personate, pretended **10** fictitious **11** counterfeit

simulation: **9** hypocrisy

simurgh, simurg: roc

sin: err **4** debt, envy, evil, lust, vice **5** anger, blame, crime, error, fault, folly, guilt, pride, sloth, wrong **6** acedia, felony **7** offense, violate **8** gluttony, iniquity, peccancy **9** deviation **10** immorality, peccadillo, transgress, wickedness, wrongdoing **11** misdemeanor, ungodliness, viciousness **12** covetousness **13** transgression

canonical: **6** heresy, murder **8** adultery, idolatry

Sinai mountain: **5** Horeb

sinapis: **7** mustard

since: as; ago, for, fro, now **4** ergo, gone, past, sith, syne(Sc.) **5** after, hence, later **7** already, because, whereas **8** inasmuch **9** afterward, therefore, thereupon **11** considering **12** continuously, subsequently .

sincere: **4** open, pure, real, true **5** frank, whole **6** candid, devout, hearty, honest **7** cordial, correct, earnest, genuine, unmixed, upright **8** faithful, truthful, virtuous **9** authentic, blameless, heartfelt, unfeigned, veracious **10** unaffected **11** unvarnished **12** wholehearted **13** unadulterated **15** straightforward

sinciput: **8** forehead

Sinclair Lewis character: **7** Babbitt

sind: **5** rinse **6** drench, quench

sinew: **5** snare **6** tendon

sinewy: **4** firm, wiry **5** thewy, tough **6** brawny, robust, strong **7** fibrose, nervous, stringy **8** forceful, muscular, powerful, vigorous **9** tendinous

sinful (see also **sin**): bad **4** evil **6** wicked **7** immoral, ungodly, vicious **10** iniquitous **11** unrighteous

sing: hum **4** cant, lilt, pipe, ring **5** carol, chant, chirl, croon, ditty, yodel, yodle **6** betray, intone, warble **7** chortle, confess, descant, rejoice, roulade, tweedle

singable: **7** lyrical, melodic, tuneful **9** cantabile

singe: **4** burn, char, sear **6** scorch

fiber: **6** genapp

singer: **4** alto, bard, bass, diva **5** basso, buffa, buffo, tenor **6** artist, cantor **7** artiste, chanter, crooner, soloist, songman, soprano **8** minstrel, vocalist **9** chanteuse,

chorister, contralto, descanter **10** cantatrice **11** entertainer

comic opera: **5** buffa

opera: **4** diva

singerie: **6** design **7** picture **10** decoration

singing: **4** cant **5** charm **9** cantation

group: **4** duet, trio **5** choir, octet **6** chorus, sextet **7** octette, quartet **8** chanters, sextette **9** quartette

pert. to: **6** choral **9** cantative

trio: **9** tricinium

single: one **4** lone, only, part, sole, unit **5** alone, unwed **6** unique **7** onefold, unusual **8** celibate, separate, singular, solitary, withdraw **9** sequester, unmarried **10** individual, particular **11** unsupported

combining form: uni

single out: **6** choose

singlet: **5** shirt **6** jersey **9** waistcoat **10** undershirt

singly: **4** once **5** alone **6** merely, solely **7** unaided **8** honestly **9** severally, sincerely **12** individually, particularly, singlehanded

singsong: **5** chime

singular: odd **4** each, rare, sole **5** queer **6** single, unique **7** eminent, private, strange, unusual **8** isolated, peculiar, separate, superior, uncommon **9** eccentric, fantastic, whimsical **10** individual, remarkable, unexampled, unparalled **11** exceptional **13** extraordinary, unprecedented

sinister: car(Sc.) **4** dark, evil, grim, left **5** wrong **7** adverse, baleful, corrupt, ominous **9** dishonest, injurious, malicious, underhand **10** disastrous, portentous **11** prejudicial, unfortunate **12** inauspicious

sink: bog, dip, ebb, sag **4** cave, drop, fail, fall, ruin, wane **5** avale, drain, droop, embog, heald, hield, lower, plump, sewer, slope **6** debase, dolina, doline, drench, extend, gutter, plunge, settle **7** decline, degrade, depress, descend, destroy, immerse, relapse, subside **8** decrease, diminish, submerge, suppress **9** penetrate

below horizon: set

ship: **7** scuttle

sinker: **6** weight **8** doughnut

Sinkiang: *capital:* **7** Urumchi

river: **5** Tarim

sinking: **10** depression

sinless: **7** perfect **8** innocent **9** righteous

sinner: **5** scamp **8** evildoer, offender, penitent **9** reprobate, wrongdoer **10** backslider, trespasser **12** transgressor

sinuous: **4** wavy **5** snaky **7** bending, crooked, curving, devious, sinuate, winding **9** deviating, intricate **10** circuitous, serpentine **11** anfractuous

sinus: bay **4** bend, fold **5** bosom, curve **6** cavity, hollow, recess **7** channel **10** depression *pert. to:* **5** sinal **7** sinusal

Sioux: Kaw, Oto **4** Crow, Iowa, Otoe **5** Brule, Omaha, Osage, Sioux **6** Dakota, Santee, Tutelo **8** Catawaba **9** Winnebago

division: **5** Teton

sip: bib, lap, sup **5** draft, drink, quaff, taste **8** toothful

sipe: **4** seep, soak **9** percolate

sir: **4** lord **5** title **6** knight, master **9** gentleman

sirdar: **5** chief, noble **6** bearer **7** officer, servant

sire: **4** lord **5** title **6** father, master, parent **8** ancestor, begetter **10** forefather, procreator, progenitor

siren: **5** lurer **7** charmer, foghorn, Lorelei, mermaid **9** Cleopatra **10** bewitching **11** fascinating

sirenian: **6** dugong **7** manatee

sirenic: **8** alluring **9** deceptive, melodious **11** fascinating

siriasis: **9** sunstroke

Sirius' master: **5** Orion

sirocco: **4** wind

sisal: **4** hemp **5** sizal

siskin: **5** finch, tarin

sissy: **7** girlish **11** mollycoddle

sister: nun, sis **4** girl **5** soror(L.) **7** sibling

murder: **10** sororicide

pert. to: **5** soral **8** sororate, sororial

younger: **7** cadette(F.)

Sister Superior: **6** abbess

sisterhood: **8** sorority

sistrusus: **11** rattlesnake

sit: lie, set **4** meet, pose, rest, seat **5** brood, dwell, model, perch, press, roost, squat **6** occupy, remain, repose **7** convene **8** incubate

carelessly: **4** loll **6** sprawl

sit in: **6** attend **7** protest **11** participate

sit on: **6** confer, rebuke **7** repress, squelch **8** suppress **9** reprimand **11** investigate

site: **4** ruin, seat, spot **5** locus(L.), place, scene, venue **6** locale, locate **8** location, position **9** situation

sitfast: **5** fixed, stone **9** immovable **10** stationary

sithe: **4** sigh

sitter: **5** model, rider

sitting: **4** seat **5** abode, place **6** clutch, posing, seance, sedent, sejaul **7** sejeant, session **8** sederunt

court: **6** assize **7** session

Sitting Bull's tribe: **5** Sioux

situated: **4** seat **5** basal **6** nether, placed, plight **7** located, station **8** marginal **13** circumstanced

between folds: **11** interplical

in the middle: **6** medial, median

on membrane enveloping the brain: **8** epidural

on right: **6** dexter

toward rear: **6** astern **7** postern **9** posterior

situation: job **4** case, need, post, seat, site **5** berth, place, siege, situs(L.), state **6** estate, locale, morass, plight, scrape, strait **7** bargain, dilemma, station, vantage **8** locality, location, position, quandary **9** condition, emergency, imbroglio **11** predicament, whereabouts **12** circumstance

situla: **4** pail, vase **6** bucket **10** receptacle

situs: **5** place **8** location, position **9** situation

Siva: *consort:* Uma **4** Devi

son: **6** Skanda

wife: **4** Sati

six: **6** senary, sestet **7** digamma, sestole **8** senarius

group: **5** hexad **6** hexade, senary, sextet **8** sextette

pert. to: **6** senary

prefix: **4** hexa, hexo

series of: **5** hexad **6** hexade

six-eyed: **9** senocular

six-footed: **7** hexaped **9** hexapodal, hexapodan

six-line stanza: **6** sestet

six on dice: **4** sice

six sheets: **7** sextern

sixfold: **8** sextuple

sixpence: **6** bender **7** cripple, fiddler

size: **4** area, bore, bulk, mass **5** cover, glaze, grade **6** adjust, amount, candle, extent, format, volume **7** arrange, stiffen **8** classify, standard **9** dimension, magnitude **11** measurement

book page: **9** duodecimo

hosiery: **4** pope

indefinite: nth

paper: cap **4** copy, demi, demy, pott **5** atlas, crown, felic, folio, legal **6** bagcap **7** bastard, emperor **8** foolscap, imperial **9** colombier

separation device: **6** grader

type: **4** pica, ruby **5** agate, canon, elite, pearl **6** minion, primer **7** brevier, diamond, English, paragon **9** bourgeois, columbian, nonpariel

yarn: lea **5** forty **6** denier

sizing: **4** glue **6** starch

sizy: **7** viscous **9** glutinous

sizz: **4** hiss

sizzle: fry **4** burn, sear, siss **7** shrivel

sizzling: hot **6** torrid

sjambok: **4** flog, whip

skag: **4** boat, skeg, tear **5** split, wound

skate: jag, ray **4** fish, plug, shoe, skid **5** flair, glide, horse

order: **4** raja **5** raiae **7** rajidae

skate blade: **6** runner

skating arena: **4** rink

skean: **4** dirk **5** sword **6** dagger

skedaddle: **4** bunk, flee **5** scoot **6** scurry **7** scamper

skeeg: **4** flog, lash, slap

skeel: tub **4** pail **6** bucket

skeesicks: 6 rascal 9 skinflint

skeet: 12 trapshooting

skegger: 4 parr

skeigh, skeich: shy 5 proud 10 mettle-some

skein: rap 4 hank, wind 5 flock 6 flight, hurdle, sleeve 7 spireme, thimble

skelder: 5 cheat 7 vagrant 9 panhandle

skelet: 5 mummy 8 skeleton

skeletal: 4 bony

skeleton: 4 past 5 atomy, bones, coral, ilium, mummy 6 sketch 7 outline, remains 9 framework

organization: 5 cadre

skell: 5 twist, upset 6 squint

skellum: 5 rogue, scamp 6 rascal

skelly: 4 chub 6 squint 9 chaffinch

skelp: say 4 beat, blow, kick, pare, push, rain, slap, walk 5 write 6 basket, colony, squall, stride, strike 7 beehive, measure, perform, quickly, scratch, scuttle 8 splinter, suddenly

skeppist: 8 apiarist 9 beekeeper

skeptic, sceptic: 7 doubter, infidel 10 pyrrhonist, unbeliever 11 disbeliever, freethinker, nullifidian

skeptical, sceptical: 8 doubting 9 faithless 11 questioning

skerrick: bit 5 scrap, trace 6 morsel

skerry: 4 isle, punt, reef, rock 6 potato

sketch: dot, jot, map 4 draw, limn, plan, play, skit 5 draft, paint, skate, story, trace 6 apercu, design, pastel 7 cartoon, croquis, drawing, outline, schizzo(It.) 8 describe 9 delineate, summarize 11 composition, delineation, description

sketchy: 5 rough, vague 10 inadequate, unfinished

skew: cup, cut, set 4 awry, fail, make, shun, slip, turn 5 askew, avoid, flunk, slant, stone, throw, twist 6 coping, escape, eschew, gauche, glance, offset, squint, swerve 7 blunder, distort, drizzle, oblique, pervert 8 slanting 9 deviating, distorted 12 misrepresent

skewer: pin, rod 5 prick, truss 6 fasten, pierce 7 hairpin 9 brochette

ski race: 6 slalom

skid: bar 4 clog, curb, drag, hook, rail, scud, shoe, slip, trig 5 brake, check, slide 6 fender, runner, timber, twitch 7 protect, skidpan, support 8 platform, sideslip

skiff: 4 boat, skif, skim 5 canoe, glide, graze, skift, touch 6 caique, flurry 7 currane, rowboat

skiing salutation: 4 heil

skill: art, can 5 craft, haunt, knack, virtu 7 ability, address, aptness, cunning, finesse, justice, mastery, science 8 artifice, capacity, deftness, facility, industry, judgment, rhetoric, training 9 adeptness, dexterity, knowledge, readiness 10 adroitness, artfulness, astuteness, capability, cleverness, competence, efficiency,

experience, expertness 11 discernment, information, proficiency 12 skillfulness 13 judiciousness, understanding

skilled: 5 adept 6 astute, expert, versed 7 capable 10 conversant, proficient

government: 9 statesman

skillful: apt 4 able, deft, fine, good, hend, just 5 adept, handy 6 adroit, artful, aufait, clever, crafty, daedal, expert, habile, proper 7 capable, cleanly, cunning 8 dextrous, tactical 9 daedalian, dexterous, ingenious, righteous 10 proficient, reasonable 11 intelligent 12 accomplished

skillfulness: 5 craft

skilligalee: 5 broth 8 porridge

skim: cut 4 film, flit, sail, scud, scum, skip 5 clear, cover, fleet, glide, graze, ready, study, throw 6 glance, refuse 7 examine

skim over: 5 skirr 6 passim

skimmings: 9 fleetings

skimp: 6 meager, scanty, scrimp 9 economize

skimpy: 5 chary, skimp, spare 6 scanty, stingy 9 niggardly 12 parsimonious

skin: 4 bark, derm, dole, fell, film, flay, hide, pare, peel, pell, pelt, rack, rind, scum 5 balat, cheat, cutis, derma, fraud, layer, plica, purse, scalp, shell, strip, sweep 6 callus, escape, fleece, scrape, spoils 7 callous, cuticle, defraud, plating, profits, sharper, surface, swindle 8 covering, membrane, pellicle, planking 9 epidermis, skinflint 10 integument, pocketbook 11 decorticate, outdistance

animal: fur 4 coat, hide, pelt, plew, rack, robe, vair 5 coney, sculp 6 hackle, peltry

burning sensation: 5 uredo

comb. form: 4 derm 5 derma 6 dermis

decoration: 6 tattoo

depression: 6 dimple

disease: 4 acne 5 hives, mange, psora, rupia, tinea 6 eczema, tetter

dressed: fur

excessive pigment: 8 melanism

fold: 5 plica 7 dewlaps

fruit: 7 epicarp

layer: 4 derm 5 cutis, derma

opening: 4 pore

pert. to: 5 deric 6 dermal 9 cuticular, epidermal

piece: 5 blype

prepare: taw

presser: 7 sammier

protuberance: 4 mole, wart

remover: 5 parer

resembling: 7 dermoid

sensitive layer: 5 cutis 7 enderon

tan: taw

unsheared pelt: 8 woolfell

worn by Dionysus: 6 nebris

skinflint: 5 flint, miser 6 huddle 7 niggard

skink: 4 adda, draw, hock, shin 5 drink, serve 6 liquor, lizard

skinker: 7 tapster

skinking: 4 thin 6 watery

skinkle: 5 strew 7 glitter, scatter, sparkle 8 sprinkle

skinned: *dark:* 7 melanic, swarthy
thick: 9 pachyderm 11 pachydermic

skinner: bet, gyp 5 cheat 6 driver 8 swindler

skinny: 4 bony, lean, thin 5 scant 6 meanly, stingy 9 emaciated, niggardly 10 membranous

skip: dap, hip, hop 4 balk, gait, jump, leap, miss, omit, skep, trip 5 bound, caper, elide, frisk, leave, salto, scout, vault 6 basket, bucket, escape, gambol, lackey, spring 7 abscond, captain, footman, servant 8 ricochet
along a surface: 7 skitter
school: tib

skip over: 5 elide
lightly: 4 skim
water: dap

skipjack: fop 4 fish 6 bonito, elater, jockey 7 upstart 8 sailboat 9 stripling 10 butterfish

skipper: ihi 5 saury 6 master 7 captain 9 butterfly
East Indian: 6 serang

skippet: box 4 boat 5 ladle, scoop, skiff 6 basket 8 envelope

skipping: 4 balk

skirl: fly 4 pipe, rain, snow 5 sweep, whirl 6 scream, shriek

skirling: 5 trout 6 salmon

skirmish: 5 brush, fence, fight, melee 6 action, battle, bicker, combat, effort 7 contest 8 conflict, flourish 9 encounter 10 velitation

skirp: 6 splash 7 spatter

skirr: fly, run 4 move, skim, tern 5 scour, whirr 6 scurry

skirt: lie, rim 4 edge, flap, girl 5 trend, woman 6 border, fringe 8 envelope, environs 9 outskirts, periphery, petticoat 10 underskirt
coat: 6 lappet
divided: 7 culotte
hoop: 6 peplum 9 crinoline, krinoline 11 farthingale
medieval armor: 4 tace 5 tasse 6 tasset
short: 4 kilt 6 kirtle
steel: 7 lamboys
velvet: 4 base

skit: act 4 gibe, girl, gust, hoax, jeer, jest, slap 5 caper, pound, revue, story, taunt, trick 6 parody, shower, sketch, splash 7 asperse, flounce 8 ridicule 9 enclosure 10 caricature, reflection

skite: 4 blow, dart, dash, fall, slip 5 boast, smite, trick 6 shower, squirt, strike 7 boaster 9 buffeting, squirting 12 yellowhammer

skitter: 4 pass, skim, skip 5 glide 7 scamper, scatter 8 sprinkle

skittish: coy, shy 5 jumpy 6 fickle, lively 7 nervous, playful, restive 8 spirited 9 ex-

citable, frivolous 10 capricious 12 undependable

skittle: 4 play 5 trash 7 ninepin 8 nonsense, squander 9 enjoyment

skive: 4 dart, pare, skim 5 shave, wheel

skiver: 6 impale, skewer 7 leather, scatter

skivvy: 9 underwear 10 undershirt

sklent: fib 5 slant 7 untruth 8 slanting

skoal: 5 toast 10 salutation 11 exclamation

skua: 4 gull 5 jager 6 jaeger

skulduggery: 8 trickery 10 craftiness, wickedness

skulk: 4 hide, lurk 5 dodge, evade, hedge, miche, shirk, slink, sneak 8 malinger

skull: 4 bean, head, mind 5 brain 6 cobra, crania(pl.) 7 cranium, harnpan
back part: 7 occiput
bone: 5 vomer 6 zygoma 7 frontal, maxilla 8 mandible, sphenoid
pert. to: 5 inial 7 cranial

skull cap: 5 calot 6 beanie 7 calotte 8 capeline, yarmulke, yarmelke(Yid.) 9 zucchetto
Arabian: 7 chechia
cardinal's: 10 berrettino
defensive: 4 coif 9 coiffette
ecclesiastical: 6 callot 7 calotte 9 zucchetto
felt: 6 pileus

skunk: 5 snipe 6 putois(F.) 7 polecat 8 betrayer

skunk-like: 5 civet 7 zorille

sky: 4 blue 5 azure, ether 6 welkin 7 heavens 9 firmament
god: Anu 4 Anat 5 Dyaus
goddess: 5 Frigg 6 Frigga
pert. to: 6 coelar

sky-blue: 5 azure 7 celeste 8 cerulean

sky pilot: 8 chaplain, preacher 9 clergyman 10 missionary

skylark: run 4 jump, lark, play, skip, yerk 6 frolic

skylight: 8 abatjour(F.)

slab: 4 tile 5 dalle, plate, slice, stela, stele 6 tablet

slab-like: 6 stelar 7 stelene

slack: lax 4 dull, idle, lull, slow, soft 5 chaff, evade, loose, relax, shirk, slake, tardy 6 abated, loosen, remiss 7 slacken 8 careless, dilatory, inactive, listless, sluggish, unsteady 9 dissolute, impudence, looseness, negligent 10 diminished, inadequate, neglectful 11 inattentive, indifferent

slacken: 4 ease, slow 5 abate, delay, relax 6 loosen, reduce, relent, retard 8 decrease, moderate

slackening: 7 detente(F.)

slacker: 4 spiv 7 coucher, shirker 8 embusque

slacks: 8 trousers

slade: den 4 cave, glen 5 glade, glide, slide 6 ravine, valley 7 peat bog 8 hillside

slag: 4 lava 5 dross, waste 6 cinder, debris, refuse, scoria **7** scoriae(pl.) **9** recrement **11** agglomerate

slain: **4** dead **6** fallen, killed **8** murdered **11** slaughtered **12** assassinated

slainte: **6** health **8** greeting **10** salutation

slaister: **4** idle, mess **5** smear **6** bedaub

slaistery: **4** dirt, miry **6** refuse, sloppy

slake: mud, wet **4** cool, daub, flag, free, lick, mire, sate **5** abate, algae, allay, gully, loose, slack, slime, smear, yield **6** aslake, deaden, lessen, quench, ravine, reduce **7** appease, assuage, crumble, refresh, relaxed, release, relieve, satisfy, slacken **8** decrease, mitigate, moderate **10** extinguish **12** disintegrate

slam: hit **4** bang, beat, blow, cuff, dash, push, shut, vole **5** abuse, clash, close, noise, throw **6** impact **7** flounce **9** criticize

slammock, slummock: **6** sloven **8** slattern, slipshod, ungainly

slander: **4** tale **5** belie, libel, shame **6** defame, malign, report, vilify **7** asperse, blacken, distort, scandal, traduce **8** derogate, disgrace, dishonor, reproach **10** defamation, depreciate, detraction, scandalize **12** misrepresent

slanderous: **8** libelous, shameful **11** disgraceful

slang: **4** cant **5** abuse, argot **6** jargon, rakish, vulgar **7** license, swindle

slant: tip **4** bend, bias, cant, skew, slab, tilt, turn, view **5** bevel, point, slope **6** biased, breeze, glance, sklent **7** incline, opinion **8** attitude, occasion **10** hypotenuse **11** inclination, opportunity

slanting: **4** bias, skew **5** askew, aside, atilt **6** askile, aslant, aslope **7** athwart, crooked

slap: box, hit, lap **4** beat, blow, clap, cuff, nick, pass, scud, snub, spat **5** click, clink, cluff, notch, plump, skelp, smack **6** break, buffet, insult, rebuff, slight, strike **7** attempt **8** suddenly

slapdash: **5** abuse, hasty **8** careless **9** impetuous, roughcast **10** abruptness **11** haphazardly **12** carelessness **13** precipitately

slape: **6** crafty, smooth **8** slippery **9** deceitful

slapjack: **7** pancake **11** griddlecake

slare: **4** slur **5** scuff, smear, sneer

slash: cut **4** dash, gash, lash, slit **5** crack, slosh, wound **6** attack, defeat, lessen, reduce, splash, strike, stripe **7** censure, scourge, slitter **9** criticize

slasher: **5** knife, sword **6** dagger **8** billhook **9** swordsman **12** swashbuckler

slashing: **4** huge **6** severe **7** dashing, driving, immense, violent **8** spirited **9** merciless **10** tremendous **11** criticizing

slat: bar, dab, rib **4** beat, blow, flap, hide, hurl, lath, slab, slap, toss **5** crack, split, throw **6** pummel, strike **8** fragment, splinter

slate: rag **4** list, rock, tile **5** board, color,

flesh, hound, plank, scold **6** berate, pummel, punish, pursue, record, roster, tablet, thrash **7** censure, roofing **8** nominate, register, schedule **9** criticize, reprimand, thrashing

break into slabs: **5** sculp

slater: **5** louse **6** critic **7** hellier

slath: **6** basket

slattern: daw **4** drab, frow, slut **5** dolly, idler, moggy, waste **6** blowze, faggot, sloppy **7** trifler, trollop **8** careless, slovenly

slatternly: **5** dirty, dowdy **6** blowzy, sordid, untidy **8** slovenly

slaty: **6** clayey **7** grayish **9** argillous **12** argillaceous

slaughter: **4** gash, kill, slay **6** battue, murder, pogrom, reduce **7** butcher, carnage, killing **8** butchery, hecatomb, massacre **9** bloodshed, reduction **10** butchering **11** destruction

slaughterhouse: **8** abattoir, butchery, matadero(Sp.)

Slav: **4** Pole, Serb, Sorb, Wend **5** Croat, Czech, Sider **6** Sclave, Slovak **7** Russian, Serbian, Servian **8** Bohemian, Croatian, Moravian, Silesian **9** Bulgarian **12** Czechoslovak

slave: **4** bond, esne, neif, peon, serf **5** chela, dasir, helot, thane **6** addict, cumhal, drudge, penest(Gr.), thrall, toiler, vassal, wretch **7** bondman, captive, chattel, enslave, odalisk, servant **9** gallerian, hierodule, odalisque

comedy: **5** Davus(L.)

dealer: **5** bichy

free: **10** emancipate

pen: **5** crawl

The Tempest: **7** Caliban

slave driver: **11** Simon Legree

Slave States: **5** Texas **7** Alabama, Florida, Georgia **8** Arkansas, Delaware, Kentucky, Maryland, Missouri, Virginia **9** Carolinas, Louisiana, Tennessee **11** Mississippi **13** North Carolina, South Carolina

slaver: **5** drool, smear **6** drivel, saliva **7** slabber, slobber

slavery: **7** bondage, service **8** drudgery **9** captivity, servitude, thralldom, vassalage **11** enslavement **12** enthrallment

release from: **8** liberate **10** emancipate **11** affranchise, enfranchise

Slavic: See **Slav.**

slavish: low **4** base, bond, vile **6** abject, menial **7** servile **8** despotic, enslaved **9** barbarous, dependent, imitative **10** oppressive, tyrannical

slaw: **8** coleslaw

slay: **4** kill **5** smite **6** murder, strike **7** butcher, destroy, execute **9** slaughter **10** annihilate **11** assassinate, exterminate

slayer: **4** bane **6** killer **8** criminal, genocide, murderer, regicide, vaticide **9** matricide, patricide, regicidal **10** fratricide, sororicide

sleave: 4 sley 6 cleave, divide, reduce, tangle 8 separate, untangle 11 disentangle

sleazy: 4 thin 6 flimsy

sled: 4 pung 6 jumper, sleigh 7 clipper, coaster, sledger, travois, vehicle 8 toboggan 10 conveyance

sledge: 4 dray, sled 5 break 6 hammer, hurdle, sleigh, strike

sleech: 4 ooze, silt 5 slime

sleek: nap 4 oily 5 gloss, preen, shiny, slick, smart, suave 6 finish, glossy, polish, smooth, soigne 7 flatter, mollify, soignee 8 polished, unctuous 10 flattering 11 insinuating

sleekit: 5 sleek 6 crafty, smooth 9 deceitful

sleep: nap 4 doss, doze 5 death, sopor 6 drowse, repose, snooze, stupor 7 slumber 8 lethargy 10 somnipathy 11 hibernation 15 unconsciousness
god: 4 Soma 8 Morpheus
inducer of: 6 opiate 7 sandman, sopient 8 sedative
pert. to: 7 somnial

sleeper: bet, tie 4 beam 5 horse, shark 6 rafter, rester, timber 7 dormant, earmark, Pullman, reposer 8 dormouse 9 dowitcher, slumberer 11 stringpiece

sleepiness: 10 drowsiness, somnolence

sleeping: 4 abed 6 latent 7 dormant 8 dormient, inactive 9 quiescent
place: bed 4 bunk, doss 5 berth, couch 6 pallet 7 cubicle 9 cubiculum, dormitory
sickness: 12 encephalitus

sleepless: 5 alert 7 unquiet, wakeful 8 restless, watchful 9 ceaseless

sleepy: 4 dull 5 tired 6 drowsy 8 sluggish, soporose, soporous 9 lethargic, somnolent 10 phlegmatic, slumberous

sleet: 5 glaze

sleeve: 5 gigot 6 armlet

sleigh: 4 pung, sled 6 cutter 7 cariole 8 carriole, toboggan

sleight: sly 5 craft, knack, skill, trick 6 crafty, wisdom 7 agility, conjure, cunning 8 artifice, deftness, prudence, trickery 9 dexterity, dexterous, quickness, stratagem 10 nimbleness

sleight-of-hand: 11 legerdemain
performer: 4 mage 8 conjurer, magician 15 prestidigitator

slender: 4 lean, slim, thin, weak 5 exile, gaunt, lanky, lithe, petit, reedy, small, sylph, wispy 6 feeble, lissom, meager, slight, svelte 7 gracile, tenuous, willowy 8 ethereal 9 attenuate, elongated 10 abstemious

slenderize: 4 slim

slenderness: 7 exility, tenuity

slent: 4 tear 5 slope, split 6 glance 9 declivity

sleuth: tec 6 tracer 7 tracker, trailer 9 detective, operative 12 investigator

slew: lot 4 slue, turn 5 twist 6 slough

sley: 4 part, reed 8 guideway

slice: cut, saw 4 jerk, part 5 carve, piece, share, shave, whang 6 cantle, divide, rasher, shiver, sliver 7 portion 8 separate, splinter

slick: 4 fine, neat, oily, tidy 5 alert, preen, sleek 6 adroit, chisel, clever, crafty, glossy, paddle, polish, smooth 7 smarten, thicket 8 slippery 9 enjoyable, excellent, ingenious 10 attractive, glistening 12 accomplished

slicker: 4 dude 5 cheat 7 gambler 8 raincoat 9 trickster

slide: 4 fall, skid, sled, slew, slip, slue 5 chute, coast, glide, hurry, scoot 6 sledge 7 incline, slither, sluther 8 glissade, ornament 9 avalanche, backslide, landslide
fastener: 6 zipper

slideway: 8 guideway

slight: cut 4 fine, slap, snub, thin 5 frail, leger(L.), light, minor, scant, scorn, sleek, small 6 flimsy, ignore, meager, scanty, simple, slight, smooth 7 distain, fragile, gracile, neglect, nominal, shallow, slender, trivial 8 careless, delicate 9 disesteem, disparage, disregard, indignity 10 immaterial 11 discourtesy, superficial, unimportant 12 contemptuous 13 disparagement, imperceptible, insignificant, unsubstantial
convexity: 6 camber
sound: 4 peep
variation: 6 nuance 7 shading

slightest: 5 least

slighting remark: 4 slur

slim: sly 4 lean, slur, thin 5 gaunt, small, spare 6 adroit, crafty, meager, meagre, scanty, slight, svelte 7 cunning, slender, tenuous 9 worthless 10 slenderize

slime: mud 4 gore, ooze 5 cover, gleet, smear 6 mucous

slimer: 8 toadfish

slimsy: 5 frail 6 flimsy

slimy: 4 vile 6 filthy, vulgar 7 viscous 9 glutinous, offensive, repulsive 10 disgusting

sling: 4 cast, hurl 5 drink, fling, throw 7 bandage 9 slingshot

slink: 4 lurk 5 crawl, sneak, steal

slip: err, imp 4 balk, clay, fall, omit, pier, shed, skid, slue 5 chute, elude, error, fault, frock, glide, lapse, leash, scion, shoot, slide 6 elapse, miscue 7 blunder, cutting, delapse, descend, faux pas, illapse, misstep, mistake, neglect, slither, sluther 8 pinafore 9 gaucherie 12 undergarment 13 transgression

slip-up: 5 error 6 miscue 9 oversight

slipe: 4 pare, peel, slip 5 glide, slice, sneak, split, strip 6 sledge, sleigh

slipknot: 5 noose

slipper: 4 mule, shoe 5 moyle, scuff 6 juliet, pliant, sandal 7 bauchle, scuffer, shuffle, willowy 8 babouche, slippery

slippery: 4 eely, glib 5 slick 6 crafty,

shifty, tricky, wanton **7** elusive, evasive, glidder **8** glibbery, unstable **9** deceitful, uncertain **10** unreliable **13** untrustworthy

slipshod: 8 careless, slommack, slovenly, slummock **10** disorderly

slipslop, slip-slop: 5 inane, slops **6** gabble **7** blunder, twaddle **10** wishy-washy **11** malapropism

slit: cut, rit **4** fent, gash, kerf, nick, race, rent, tear **5** sever, slash, split, unrip **6** cleave **7** fissure, opening **8** aperture, incision

slither: 4 slip **6** rubble **7** rubbish **8** slippery

slive: cut **4** slip **5** slice, slide, sneak, split **6** cleave, stroke

sliver: cut **5** shred, slice, slops, split **6** strand **7** slobber **8** fragment, splinter

slob: ice, mud **4** mire, ooze, snow **6** sloven, sludge

slobber: mud **4** gush, kiss, slob, slop **5** drool, slime, smarm **6** drivel, slaver, sloven **7** blubber, slabber

slobby: 5 boggy, muddy **8** slobbery

slock: bog **4** lure **5** drink **6** drench, entice, pilfer, quench **7** swallow

slocken: 5 slake **6** quench **8** saturate

sloe: haw **4** plum **10** blackthorn

slog: hit **4** blow, plod, plug, slam, slug, toil, work **5** drive **6** strike

slogan: cry **4** word **5** motto **6** phrase **9** catchword

sloop: 9 raceabout

slop: mud **4** gush, mash **5** slush, smock, spill, swill, waste **6** puddle, refuse, splash **7** cassock, clothes, garment, slobber **8** breeches, clothing, trousers

slope: dip, lie **4** bank, brae(Sc.), brow, cant, hang, ramp, rise, tilt **5** bevel, cliff, hield, scarp, slant, talus **6** ascent, aslant, aslope, bajada, depart, escarp, glacis **7** descent, incline, terrace, versant **8** gradient, hillside **9** acclivity, declivity, obliquely **10** declension **11** inclination
angle-measuring device: **10** clinometer
protective: **6** glacis

sloping: 6 aslant, aslope **7** oblique **8** inclined, slanting **9** declivous, inclining

sloppy: 5 messy **6** slushy **7** splashy **8** careless, slovenly **12** disagreeable

slosh: mud **5** slash, slush, spill, throw **6** wallow **8** flounder

slot: bar, cut **4** bolt, slat, stab **5** track, trail **6** groove, hollow, keyway, spline **7** keyhole, opening **8** aperture, guideway **10** depression

sloth: ai **4** idle, lazy, pack, slow, unau **5** delay **6** acedia, animal **7** accidie, inertia, neglect **8** edentate, idleness, laziness, slowness **9** indolence, tardiness **11** sleuthhound **12** sluggishness, wastefulness

slothful: 4 argh, idle, lazy **5** inert **8** inactive, indolent, sluggish **9** sedentary

slouch: hat **4** gait, lout, pipe **5** droop **6**

bonnet, loafer, lubber **7** posture **8** drooping, laziness **9** pendulous **13** shiftlessness

slough, slew, slue: bog, mud **4** fall, husk, mire, molt, ooze, plod, road, shed, skin, slew, slue **5** bayou, inlet, swamp **6** eschar, sheath, strike **7** channel, discard, mudhole **8** imprison

slounge: 4 idle, loaf **6** lounge

sloven: 4 slob **5** besom, clart **6** loafer **7** hallion **8** slovenly **9** scoundrel **11** undeveloped **12** uncultivated

slovenly: 4 lazy **5** dowdy, messy **6** blowzy, frouzy, frowsy, frowzy, grubby, sloppy, untidy **7** unkempt **8** careless, slattern, slipshod, sluttish **9** negligent **10** disorderly, slatternly

slow: lax **4** dull, late, poky **5** brosy, delay, grave, hooly, inert, pokey, slack, tardy **6** boring, hamper, hinder, retard, stolid, strike, stupid **7** dronish, gradual, laggard, slacken **8** boresome, dilatory, diminish, inactive, sluggard, sluggish **9** liesurely, lingering, slowgoing, unhurried **10** decelerate, deliberate, phlegmatic, retrograde **13** unprogressive

slow down: lap **4** idle **6** retard **7** decline **10** decelerate, deliberate

slow-witted: 4 dull **6** stupid

slowness: 6 lentor

slowpoke: 5 snail **7** dawdler

slubber: 4 daub, mire, slur **5** billy, botch, slime, smear, stain **6** darken **7** obscure, slabber

slud: mud **4** mire **5** slush **7** sludder

sludge: ice, mud **4** mire, ooze, slob **5** waste **7** deposit, mixture **8** sediment **9** settlings

slue, slew, slough: 4 turn, veer **5** pivot, swing, twist

sluff: 7 discard

slug: bat, hit **4** blow, dram, slow, snag, stud **5** delay, drink, limax, snail **6** bullet, hinder, loiter, nugget, strike **7** draught, mollusk, trepang **8** sluggard, sluggish **9** gastropod **11** caterpillar, obstruction
genus of: **4** doto **6** elysia

sluggard: daw **4** idle, lazy, slug **5** drone **8** faineant, sluggish

slugger: bat **4** goon **5** boxer **6** hitter, mauler **7** batsman **8** operator

sluggish: 4 dull, lazy, logy, slow **5** brosy, faint, heavy, inert **6** bovine, drowsy, leaden, supine, torpid **7** dronish, languor, lumpish **8** dilatory, inactive, indolent, slothful, sluggard, stagnant **10** tardigrade **15** procrastinating

sluice: 4 gash, gote, gout, pipe, race **5** flume, sasse, valve **6** breach, stream, trough **7** channel, launder, opening, passage **8** irrigate **9** floodgate

sluit: 5 ditch, gulch, gully

slum: 4 junk, room **5** alley

slumber: 4 coma, doze **5** sleep **6** drowse, repose

slumberous: 4 calm **5** quiet **6** drowsy,

sleepy **8** peaceful, tranquil **9** somnolent, soporific **10** slumbering

slump: sag **4** drop, fall, sink, slip **6** settle **7** decline **8** collapse **10** depreciate, depression

slur: **4** blot, blur, slip, soil **5** cheat, decry, elide, glide, slare, slide, smear, stain, sully, trick **6** insult, macule, slight, smirch, stigma **7** blemish, calumny, dimness, traduce **8** besmirch, disgrace, innuendo, reproach **9** aspersion, criticize, discredit, disparage, indignity **10** calumniate **11** contaminate **12** imperfection

slush: mud, wet **4** gush, mire, pulp, slud, wash **5** grout **6** drench, drivel, sloven, sluice, splash **7** mixture, sludder

slut: **4** jade **5** bitch, filth, quean **6** befoul, harlot **8** slattern **9** dratchell

sluther: **4** slip **5** slide **7** shuffle

sluttish: **4** lewd **5** gross **6** filthy, sordid **8** slovenly **10** disorderly

sly: **4** arch, cagy, foxy, ruse, slee, wily **5** coony, snaky **6** artful, clever, crafty, feline, secret, shrewd, slinky, sneaky, subtle, tricky **7** cunning, evasive, furtive, roguish **8** skillful, sneaking **9** cautelous, deceitful, secretive **10** fallacious **11** clandestine, dissembling, mischievous, underhanded **12** hugger-mugger

slyly spiteful: **5** catty

smack: bit, hit **4** blow, boat, buss, kiss, slap, tang **5** crack, savor, sloop, taste, touch, trace **6** cutter, flavor, strike, vessel **7** vestige **8** mouthful, sailboat **10** suggestion

smacking: **5** brisk, sharp **6** lively **8** spanking, vigorous

smaik: **6** rascal **9** scoundrel

small: dab, sma(Sc.), tot, wad, wee(Sc.) **4** cute, lite, mean, puny, thin, tiny, wisp, whit **5** dawny, minim, petty, scant **6** atomic, dapper, grubby, humble, little, mignon, minute, modest, petite(F.), slight **7** minimal, slender, trivial **8** atomical, picayune, trifling **9** miniature, minuscule, thumbnail **10** diminutive **13** insignificant
amount: mot **4** atom, chip, drop, iota, mote, tate **5** speck **6** detail, morsel **7** driblet, handful, modicum, morceau(F.), snippet **8** modecule
combining form: **5** lepto, micro
prefix: **5** micro

small-fry: **4** kids, tots **8** children **10** youngsters

small-minded: **4** mean **5** petty **6** narrow **7** selfish **10** prejudiced, ungenerous, vindictive

small talk: **6** babble **7** prattle **8** chitchat

smallage: **6** celery **7** parsley

smaller: **4** less **5** minor **6** lesser
combining form: mi; mio **4** meio

smallest: **5** least

smallness: **7** exility, paucity

smallpox: **7** variola

smalt: **4** flux

smaragd: **7** emerald

smarm: **4** gush **7** slobber

smart: **4** bite, braw, chic, neat, posh, smug, trig, wily, wise **5** acute, alert, brisk, clean, fresh, natty, nifty, quick, sharp, sting, witty **6** active, astute, bright, cheesy; clever, dressy, jaunty, lively, shrewd, spruce, suffer, swanky **7** capable, knowing, pungent, stylish **8** spirited, talented, vigorous **9** competent, dexterous **10** precocious **11** fashionable, intelligent

smarten: **6** spruce **7** improve **8** brighten, titivate

smash: hit **4** bash, blow, bung, dash, ruin **5** break, crash, crush, stave, wreck **7** destroy, shatter, smash-up, success **8** collapse, stramash(Sc.) **9** collision **10** bankruptcy

smashup: **4** ruin **5** wreck **6** defeat **7** failure **8** collapse **9** collision **10** bankruptcy

smatter: **4** smut, spot **5** break **6** babble, dabble, defile **7** chatter, clatter, crackle, shatter, spatter **9** fragments

smear: dab, rub **4** blot, blur, daub, gaum, soil, spot, stop **5** clart, cleam, slake, slare, stain, sully **6** anoint, bedaub, blotch, defame, defeat, defile, grease, malign, smirch, smudge, spread, thwart **7** besmear, plaster, pollute, slander, splatch **8** besmirch, ointment, slaister **9** overwhelm **10** overspread

smeared: **4** foul **6** greasy

smeary: **6** greasy, soiled, sticky **7** smeared

smectic: **9** detergent, purifying

smeddum: **4** dust **5** flour, vigor **6** powder, spirit

smeech: **4** dust **5** smell, smoke, stink, vapor

smeek: **4** reek **5** smoke

smell: **4** funk, fust, odor, olid, reek **5** aroma, fetor, flair, scent, sniff, trace **6** breath **7** hircine, noisome, perfume **9** fragrance **10** suggestiom **11** graveolence
loss of sense: **7** anosmia
pert. to: **9** olfactory

smell-feast: **7** sponger **8** parasite

smeller: **4** nose **6** feeler **7** antenna, bristle

smelling salts: **9** hartshorn

smelt: **4** fish, flux, fuse, melt, prim **6** iuanga(N.Z.), reduce, refine **7** scorify

smelting: *by-product:* **4** slag
cone: **4** pina

smew: **4** duck **9** merganser

smicker: **5** smile, smirk

smidge, smidgen: bit **4** mite

smile: **4** beam, grin **5** smirk, sneer **6** arride, simper

smirch: **4** blot **5** asoil, smear, stain, sully, taint **6** blotch, smudge, smutch **7** begrime, blacken, blemish, tarnish **8** besmirch, discolor, dishonor

smirched: **5** dingy

smirk: 4 leer, trim, yirn 5 quick, smart, smile 6 simper, spruce 7 grimace, smiling

smit: cut, hit 4 blow, smut, spot 5 brand, stain 6 infect, smirch, stroke, struck 7 tarnish 8 disgrace, punished

smite: hit 4 blow, clap, cuff, gird, hurl, kill, pass, slap, slay, swat 5 blast, knock, skite 6 attack, buffet, defeat, hammer, pierce, punish, strike 7 afflict, chasten, collide, destroy, disease, impress, inspire 8 distress

smith: 6 forger 7 farrier 10 blacksmith 11 metalworker

smithcraft: 6 smithy 8 smithery

smithereens: 4 bits 5 atoms 6 pieces 8 flinders 9 fragments

smithy: 6 forger 7 farrier 10 blacksmith

smitten: 8 affected, enamored, stricken 9 afflicted, enamoured

smock: 5 kamis, shift, tunic 6 camise 7 chemise 11 overgarment

smog: fog 4 mist

smoke: 4 floc, fume, funk, haze, mist, pipe, smog 5 cigar, cubeb, segar, smook(Sc.), vapor 6 smudge 7 cheroot, cigaret 9 cigarette

outlet: 7 chimney 8 fumeduct, fumiduct

wisp: 4 floc

smokejack: 6 funnel

smokeless powder: 6 poudre

smokestack: 4 pipe 6 funnel 7 chimney

smoking equipment: 7 nargile, tabagie

smoky: 4 hazy 5 dingy, fumid 6 fumish 9 fumacious

smolder, smoulder: 5 choke, smoke 6 smudge 7 smother 9 suffocate

smolt: 4 calm 5 clear 6 bright, salmon, smooth

smoodge, smooge: pat 6 pamper 7 wheedle

smooth: 4 clam, ease, easy, even, gleg, glib, iron, lene, mild, pave, sand 5 bland, brent, furry, glace, glary, gloze, level, plane, preen, press, quiet, silky, sleek, slick, soapy, suave 6 creamy, evenly, fluent, glassy, glossy, mangle, serene, sleeky 7 amiable, equable, erugate, flatten, plaster, sadiron 8 explicit, friendly, glabrous, levigate, palliate, pleasant, polished, soothing 9 courteous, unruffled 10 flattering 11 alabastrine 12 frictionless, ingratiating 13 mellifluently, uninterrupted

combining form: lio

phonetically: 4 lene

smoother: 7 abraser

smot: 4 mark 5 brand, stain

smote: hit 7 chasten

smother: 5 choke, smoor, smore 6 stifle, welter 7 overlie, smolder, turmoil 8 suppress 9 suffocate

smudge: 4 blot, blur, smug, smut, soil, soot 5 laugh, prink, smear, smile, stain 6 smutch 7 begrime, chuckle, smolder

smug: dig 4 neat, prig, tidy, trim 5 clean, grind, smart, steal, suave 6 pilfer, spruce 7 correct 9 confident 10 blacksmith, complacent 13 selfsatisfied

smuggler: 6 runner

smurr, smur: 4 mist 5 cloud 7 drizzle

smut: 4 bunt, coom, mark, soil, spot 5 coomb, grime, stain, sully, taint 6 blight, defile, smudge 8 colbrand 9 obscenity

smutch: 4 blot, dirt, smut, soot, spot 5 grime, stain, sully, taint, tinge, touch, trace 6 defile, smudge 7 blacken

smutty: 5 dirty, dusky, sooty 6 soiled, sordid 7 obscene, tainted 8 indecent

smytrie: 6 litter 10 collection

snack: bit, sip 4 ball, bite, jibe, part, snap 5 acute, alert, chack, lunch, quick, seize, share, smack, taste 6 adroit, morsel, repast, snatch 7 portion, quickly, sharply, teatime 8 grasping, snappish

snaffle: bit 4 loot 5 check, steal 6 pilfer 7 saunter, snuffle 8 restrain 9 restraint

snafu: 4 awry 6 muddle 8 disorder, entangle 9 confusion

snag: cut, hew, nag, nub 4 base, carp, knot, part, slug, tear, tine, tree, trim, unit 5 break, catch, point, snail, stump, tooth 6 branch, damage, hazard, tongue 8 obstacle 9 hindrance 10 difficulty, impediment 11 obstruction 12 protuberance

snagger: 8 billhook

snail: 4 slug, snag, wilk 5 drone, mitra 6 dodman, tritou, winkle 7 driller, mollusk, testudo 8 escargot, neritine, sluggard 9 gastropod 10 hoddy-doddy

genus of: 5 fusus 6 nerita 9 clausilia

snailflower: 7 caracol

snake: asp, boa, bom, esp, nag 4 bind, boma, curl, drag, draw, naga, skid, tail, turn, wind, worm 5 aboma, adder, arrow, braid, cobra, coral, crawl, cribo, filch, kriat, mamba, racer, sneak, steal, viper 6 katuka, python 7 bokadam, camoodi, elapine, hagworm, ingrate, meander, rattler, reptile, serpent 8 anaconda, bungarum, camoodie, moccasin, ophidian, ringhals 9 whipsnake 10 blacksnake, bushmaster, copperhead, massasauga, sidewinder 11 cottonmouth, rattlesnake 12 schaapsteker

expert: 13 herpetologist

genus of: boa 7 ophidia

horned: 8 cerastes

killer: 7 mongoos 8 mongoose

marine: 6 chital

mythological: See **serpent.**

resembling: 8 viperine

suborder: 6 asinea

snake dancers: 4 Hopi, Taos 5 Moqui

snake doctor: 9 dragonfly 12 hellgrammite

snake killer: 7 mongoos 8 mongoose

snake-shaped: 9 anguiform

snakeberry: 6 byrony 9 baneberry 11 bittersweet 14 partridge-berry

snakebird: 7 anhinga, wryneck

snakebite antidote: 5 guaco

snakeflower: 7 campion 8 blueweed 10 starflower, stitchwort

snakehead: 7 figwort 10 turtlehead

snakelike: 5 snaky 8 ophidian 9 colubrine 10 anguineous

snakemouth: 6 orchid

snakeroot: 6 seneca, senega 7 sangrel 9 birthwort 10 bitter-bush

snakeskin: 6 exuvia

snaky: sly 4 evil, wavy 5 angry 6 touchy 7 anguine, sinuous, winding, wriggly 8 spiteful, twisting, venomous 9 snakelike 10 perfidious, serpentine 11 exasperated, treacherous

snap: bit, rod 4 bark, bite, knap, lirp, pass, shut 5 break, catch, chack, cheat, cinch, close, crack, filip, flask, flick, ganch, grasp, hanch, quick, scrap, seize, sever, smart, snack, spell, stamp, steal, vigor, wafer 6 biting, cloyer, cookie, energy, fillip, morsel, report, retort, snatch 7 capture cozener, crackle, project, sharper, sparkle 8 interval, puncheon, sinecure, snapshot 9 crackling, crispness, fastening, handcuffs, interrupt, smartness, snatching 10 gingersnap 11 scintillate

snape: nip 4 snub 5 bevel, check, stint, taper 6 rebuke 7 snaping 8 beveling 10 disappoint

snapper: 4 bean, sesi 5 error 6 beetle, bonbon, turtle 7 cosoque, stumble, whopper 8 cachucho, fastener 9 castanets 10 stitchwort, woodpecker 11 firecracker, glassworker, phainopepla

snappish: 4 edgy, tart 5 crisp, cross, short, testy 7 brittle, cutting, peevish, uncivil 8 petulant 9 fractious, irascible, irritable 12 sharp-tongued

snappy: 4 frim 5 brisk, quick, sharp, smart 6 strong, sudden 7 stylish 8 pungency 9 briskness, copacetic, smartness

snapshot: 4 shot 5 photo 10 photograph

snare: bag, gin, net, pit, web 4 fang, grin, lure, mesh, toil, trap 5 benet, brake, catch, grasp, noose, steal 6 ambush, cobweb, entice, entoil, entrap, gilder, tangle, trapan, trepan 7 ensnare, involve, overnet, pitfall 8 entangle, inveigle 9 deception 12 entanglement

snarer: 6 spider 7 trapper

snarl: arr, gin 4 carl, girn, gnar, harl, hurr, knot, yarr, yirr 5 anvil, catch, ganch, gnarl, gnarr, growl, noose, scold, snare 6 tangle 7 confuse, ensnare, grizzle, grumble, involve, quarrel 8 complain, entangle 9 confusion 10 complicate 12 complication

snarly: 5 cross, surly 7 peevish, snarled, tangled 8 confused, snarling 10 ill-natured 11 bad-tempered

snash: 5 abuse 6 gibing 9 insolence

snatch: bit, get, hap, nab 4 grab, snap, take, trap, yerk 5 braid, catch, clawk, cleek, erept, grasp, gripe, pluck, seize, snare, spell, stint, swipe, wrest 6 clutch, kidnap, remove, twitch 7 excerpt, grabble 8 fragment

snatchy: 9 irregular, spasmodic 11 interrupted 12 disconnected

snath, snathe: lop 5 prune, shaft, snead 6 handle

sneak: 4 lurk 5 filch, miche, peach, skulk, slink, snoop, steal 6 coward, cringe, pilfer, snudge, tattle 9 fefnicute

sneaking: sly 4 mean, poor 6 craven, hidden, paltry, secret 7 furtive, hangdog 8 cowardly, stealthy 9 dastardly, niggardly, underhand 12 contemptible 13 surreptitious

sneap: spy 5 check, chide, snape, sneak

sneb: bar 4 bolt, snub 6 fasten, rebuke 9 reprimand

sneck: 5 catch, click, close, latch 6 fasten

sned: lop 5 prune

snee: cut 4 dirk 5 knife 6 dagger

sneer: 4 gibe, gird, grin, jeer, mock 5 fleer, fling, flird, flout, flurn, scoff, slare, snirl, snort 7 grimace, snicker 8 belittle, ridicule

sneesh: 5 snuff

sneeze: 5 neese(Sc.) 7 kerchoo 12 sternutation

sneezewort: 8 ptarmica, ptarmite 10 gesundheit

snell: 4 hard, keen 5 acute, eager, harsh, quick, sharp, smart, snood, swift 6 active, biting, clever, leader, severe 7 caustic, extreme, pungent, quickly, swiftly 8 piercing 10 vigorously

snib: bar 4 bolt, snub 5 catch, check, snuff 6 entrap, fasten, rebuff, rebuke 7 capture 8 restrain 9 fastening, reprimand

snick: cut, hit 4 blow, draw, kink, knot, move, nick, snip 5 click, notch, share, shoot, snack 6 pierce, strike 8 snicking

snicker: 5 knife, laugh, neigh, sneer, snirl 6 giggle, nicker, titter, whinny

snide: low, sly 4 base, mean 6 tricky 8 inferior, spurious 9 malicious

sniff: 4 nose 5 scent, smell, snuff 6 detect, inhale 7 sniffle 8 perceive 9 recognize

sniffy: 8 scornful 10 disdainful 12 contemptuous, supercilious

snifter: 4 blow, dram, good 5 drink, sniff, snort, storm 6 moment, snivel 7 dilemma, reverse 9 excellent

snig: eel, lop 4 chop, drag, jerk 5 snake, sneak 6 pilfer

snigger: 6 giggle 7 snicker

sniggle: 7 broggle

snip: bit, cut 4 clip, curb, snap 5 check, filch, notch, piece, shred, snack 6 snatch, stripe, stroke, tailor 8 fragment, incision, particle 9 disfigure

snipe: 4 bird, butt, fool 5 skunk 10 sharpshoot

snippy: 4 curt, mean, tart 5 brief, sharp 6 sniffy, stingy 8 snappish, snippety 11 closefisted, fragmentary 12 supercilious

snirl: 5 gnarl, snare, sneer, snort 6 tangle 7 snicker, wrinkle

snirt: 5 sneer, snort 7 snicker

snitch: 4 nose, tell 5 catch, peach, pinch, steal, thief 6 betray, inform, pilfer, smitch, snatch 8 informer, particle

snivel: cry 4 cant, fret 5 sniff, whine 6 pathos 7 emotion, snuffle 8 complain

snivy, snivey: 4 mean, ugly 8 contrary

snob: sob 4 aper, scab 5 toady 6 flunky 7 cobbler, cricket, flunkey, parvenu, plebian, shoneen, upstart 8 blackleg, bluenose, commoner, parvenue, townsman 9 pretender, shoemaker 10 fivestones

snobbish: 7 high-hat 11 overbearing

snod: 4 neat, snug, trim 6 smooth 7 cunning, trimmed 9 plausible

snood: bag, hat, tie 4 bind 5 braid 6 fasten, fillet, ribbon 7 hairnet

snook: pry 5 smell, sneak, sniff 6 follow, robalo, search 7 snuffle 9 barracuda

snool: cow 4 snub 6 craven, cringe

snoop: pry 4 look, nose, peek, peep 5 sneak 6 search 8 busybody

snooper: 7 marplot, meddler 8 busybody

snoot: 4 face, nose 7 grimace

snooty: 7 haughty 8 snobbish 10 hoitytoity 12 contemptuous, supercilious

snooze: nap 4 doze 5 sleep 6 drowse, siesta 7 snoozle

snoozle: 4 doze 5 sleep 6 cuddle, nuzzle, snooze 7 snuggle

snore: 4 rout 5 snork, snort

snoring: 5 stiff 7 roaring, stertor 10 stertorous

snork: pig 5 grunt, snore, snort

snort: 4 rout 5 drink, grunt, laugh, snirl, snore, snork

snotty: 5 dirty, nasty, slimy 6 offish, snooty 7 haughty, viscous 8 impudent, snotlike 9 offensive 12 contemptible, supercilious

snouch: 4 jibe, snub 5 taunt

snout: neb 4 mull, nose 5 groin, spout, trunk 6 nozzle 7 rostrum, tobacco

snout-nose: 4 gruntle 9 proboscis

snow: sna 4 grue, snaw(Sc.) 5 blizz, cover, opium 6 heroin 7 cocaine 8 obstruct 9 whiteness

glacial: 4 firn, neve
granular: 4 corn
half-melted: 5 slush
living in: 5 neval
mushy: 4 slob
resembling: 7 niveous
slide: 8 glissade 9 avalanche
wedding: 4 rice

snow and rain: 5 sleet

snow flurry: 5 skirl

snow mass: 9 avalanche

snow ridges: 8 sastrugi, zastrugi

snow runner: ski 4 skee

snowshoe: pac, ski 4 skee

snowstorm: 8 blizzard

snowy: 4 pure 5 nival, white 8 spotless, unsoiled

snub: cut, nip 4 chip, curb, slap, stop 5 check, frump, quell, scold, snool 6 ignore, rebuff, rebuke, remark, retort, slight, tauten 7 affront, neglect, repress, upbraid 8 restrain 9 interrupt, reprimand

snudge: 4 sulk 5 miser, sneak

snuff: 4 odor 5 pinch, pique, scent, smell, sniff, snort 6 detect, inhale 7 offense, umbrage 10 extinguish

kind of: 5 musty 6 rappee 8 bergamot, Maccaboy 10 blackguard, Copenhagen

snuff box: 4 mill, mull 9 tabatiere

snuffy: 5 sulky, vexed 6 horrid 7 annoyed 10 displeased 12 disagreeable, unattractive

snug: 4 bein, bien, cosh, cozy, neat, safe, tidy, trim, warm 5 close, quiet, tight 6 modest, secure, silent 7 compact, snuggle 8 reticent, secreted 9 concealed, seaworthy, secretive 10 prosperous 11 comfortable

snuggery: den

snuggle: 4 nest 6 cuddle, nestle

snugly: 6 cosily

sny: 4 bend 5 swarm 6 abound

so: sae, sic, sua 4 ergo, thus, very 5 hence 7 because 9 therefore 11 accordingly 12 consequently

so be it: 4 amen

so far: yet 4 thus

soak: dip, hit, ret, sog, sop, sot, wet 4 bate, blow, bowk, buck, hurl, ooze, pawn, sock 5 drink, drouk, imbue, punch, souse, spree, steep 6 drench, imbibe, imbrue, seethe 8 drunkard, macerate, permeate, saturate 9 distemper, percolate 10 impregnate, instructor, overcharge

soaked: wet 6 sodden

soaking: 4 slow 6 gentle 7 soakage

soap: 4 sape, sapo 5 money, savon 6 lather 7 cleanse, flatter 8 flattery 9 detergent

mottled: 7 castile 8 eschwege
plate: 4 sess
substitute: 5 amole, borax

soap plant: 5 amole 8 soapwort

soapmaking substance: lye

soapstone: 4 talc 8 steatite
full of: 7 talcose

soapweed: 5 yucca

soapy: 4 oily, soft 5 suave 6 smooth 7 saponic 8 lathered, unctuous 9 soapsuddy 10 latherable 11 saponaceous 12 ingratiating

soar: fly 4 lift, rise, sail 5 float, glide, hover, mount, plane 6 ascend, aspire 9 transcend

sob: cry, yex 4 sigh, soak, wail, weep 6
boohoo 7 whimper 8 frighten

sober: 4 calm, cool, poor, sane 5 douce,
grave, quiet, staid 6 ailing, feeble, gentle,
humble, sedate, severe, simple, solemn,
somber, steady, subdue, temper 7 chasten, earnest, regular, serious, subdued 8
composed, decorous, moderate, peaceful,
rational 9 abstinent, collected, temperate
10 abstemious 11 indifferent 13 unimpassioned, unpretentious

soberly: sad 5 grave 8 demurely

sobol: 5 sable 6 marten

soboles: 5 shoot 6 stolon, sucker

sobriety: 7 gravity 9 restraint, soberness,
solemnity, soundness 10 abstinence,
moderation, sedateness, temperance 11
seriousness 14 reasonableness

sobriquet, soubriquet: 4 name 5 alias,
chuck, title 6 byname 7 affront, epithet 8
nickname 11 appellation

soc: 12 jurisdiction

soccer player: 6 booter

sociability: 10 affability

sociable: 4 cozy, sofa 6 chummy, social 7
affable 8 carriage, familiar, friendly, informal, tricycle 9 aeroplane, agreeable,
reception 10 accessible, gregarious 13
communicative, companionable

social: tea 4 stag 5 party 6 smoker 9
agreeable, convivial, gathering 10 gregarious 13 companionable

affair: tea 4 ball 6 soiree 9 reception

career beginning: 5 debut

gathering: bee, tea 4 club, stag 5 party 6
smoker 7 reunion 9 reception

group: 4 clan, club 5 caste, class, lodge,
tribe 6 estate, family 7 coterie

insect: bee

outcast: 5 leper 6 pariah

person: 4 host 5 mixer 7 hostess

system: 6 feudal, modern, regime, tribal
11 traditional

worker: 7 analyst 8 do-gooder 9 clinician

socialism: 9 Communism 10 utopianism
13 Manchesterism

socialist: Red 9 Anarchist, communist 10
Bolshevist 11 nationalist 12 collectivist

socialize: 6 mingle

society (see also **organization**): 4 bund,
clan, gild 5 guild, order, union 6 menage
7 academy, company, hetaera, hetaira
8 academie, alliance 9 accademie, community 10 connection 11 association, cooperation, intercourse, partnership 12
denomination, relationship 13 companionship, confederation, confraternity, participation

low (member): 4 raff 8 riff-raff

kind of: 4 SPCA, frat, Tong 5 elite, order,
choir 7 societe 8 sorority 10 fraternity

secret: Hui 4 tong, egbo 5 mafia, lodge 6
maffia, ogboni 7 Camorra 9 Carbonari

symbol: 7 regalia

Society Island: 6 Tahiti

tree: 5 aitoa

sociology: 8 demotics

sock: hit, sew, udo 4 beat, blow, hurl, shoe,
sigh, vamp 5 drive 6 anklet, buskin, comedy, sandal, strike 7 slipper, socking 8
drainage, stocking 9 plowshare

sockdolager: 4 oner 8 finisher

socket: 5 lance, spear 6 budget, cavity,
collet, hollow 7 opening 9 plowshare

kind of: pan 4 birn 5 orbit 8 alveolus

Socrates: *biographer:* 5 Plato

dialogue: 4 Meno 6 Phaedo 8 Apologia

escape plotter: 5 Crito

love: 10 philosophy, Alcibiades

wife: 8 Xantippe 9 Xanthippe

sod: 4 delf, dove, flag, peat, soak, turf 5
delft, divot, glebe, soggy, sward 6 saddle,
sodden 7 stratum 9 fermented

pert. to: 8 alkaline

soda: sal 8 beverage 9 saleratus

sodality: 5 union, unity 6 chapel 10 fellowship, fraternity 11 association, brotherhood 13 companionship

sodden: 5 drunk, heavy, moist, sammy,
soggy 6 boiled, dulled, soaked, stewed,
stupid 7 bloated, drunken, steeped 8
spirited 9 saturated 11 intoxicated

sodium: 7 natrium

carbonate: 4 soda 5 borax, trona 6 natron
7 salsoda

chlorate: 5 NaClo

chloride: sal, tar 4 salt 7 saltcat

compound: 4 soda

nitrate: 5 niter

tetraborate: 5 borax

Sodom king: 4 Bera

sodomite: 6 bugger

sofa: 5 boist, couch, divan 6 lounge, settee
7 bergere, dosados 8 causeuse 9 davenport 12 chesterfield

soft: coy, low 4 feil, fine, limp, mild,
saft(Sc.), waxy, weak 5 bland, cushy,
downy, dolce, dulce, faint, givey, hooly,
mushy, piano, sooth 6 clammy, dreamy,
fluffy, gentle, gently, placid, silken,
smooth, tender 7 clement, ductile, lenient, lightly, quietly, squashy, subdued 8
delicate, feminine, flexible, tranquil 9
temperate, tractable, untrained 10 effeminate, peacefully 11 sympathetic 12
nonalcoholic 13 compassionate

and smooth: 5 furry, silky, soapy 6 mellow, supple 7 cottony

and sweet: 5 dolce 6 dulcet

and wet: 5 mushy 7 squashy

food: pap

mass: 4 pulp

music: 5 dulce, piano

palate: 4 cion 5 uvula, velum

soap: 4 gush 7 blarney, flatter, wheedle 8
flattery 9 wheedling

softa: 7 student 8 beginner

soften: 4 ease, melt 5 allay, malax, relax,

yield **6** affect, anneal, gentle, pacify, relent, soothe, subdue, temper, weaken **7** amolish, appease, assuage, mollify **8** attemper, enervate, enfeeble, lenitive, macerate, mitigate, modulate **9** alleviate, emolliate, meliorate **10** emasculate, intenerate **11** tranquilize

softening: **7** lenient **8** emulsive **9** demulcent **11** melioration
of brain: **8** dementia
of decayed fruit: **4** blet

soft-spoken: **4** mild **5** bland, suave **6** gentle, smooth **12** ingratiating

softhearted: **6** tender **13** tenderhearted

softheartedness: **4** pity

softly: low **4** soft **5** piano, sotto **6** fairly, gentle, gently **7** foolish, quietly **10** spiritless **13** unobtrusively

softness: **10** tenderness

sog: **4** soak **6** drowse **8** saturate

soggy: wet **4** damp **5** heavy **6** soaked, sodden, watery **9** saturated

soigne, soignee: **4** neat, tidy **5** sleek **11** well-groomed

soil: **4** blot, blur, daub, dirt, foil, grit, land, moil, mool, slur, spot **5** dirty, earth, filth, glebe, grime, smear, solum, stain, sully **6** assoil, bedaub, befile, befoul, bemire, defile, grease, ground, refuse, sewage, smirch, smudge **7** begrime, benasty, besmear, corrupt, pollute, tarnish **8** alluvium, besmirch, disgrace **9** bedraggle, bespatter, droppings, excrement **11** contaminate
goddess of: **7** Demeter
kind of: **4** clay, loam, marl, lair, malm, moss **5** adobe, loess, groot, humus
organic: **5** humus

soiled: **4** foul **5** dingy, grimy **6** smeary

soilure: **5** stain **6** smirch

sojourn: **4** bide, howf, rest, stay **5** abide, abode, delay, dwell, howff, lodge, tarry, visit **6** reside, travel **7** allodge, mansion **8** abidance **9** residence **11** peregrinate

sojourner: **7** boarder **8** comeling

sol: sun **4** gold **6** sun-god **7** Phoebus

solace: **5** allay, amuse, cheer **6** lessen, relief, soothe **7** assuage, comfort, console **9** alleviate, diversion, entertain **10** recreation, relaxation **11** alleviation, consolation

solacing: **6** dulcet

solar, soler, sollar: **4** room **5** floor, story **6** garret, heliac, tropic **7** chamber **8** heliacal **9** apartment
deity: Su; Shu
disk: **4** aten, aton

solar system: *member:* **6** planet
model: **6** orrery

sold (see also **sell**): **8** marketed

solder: **4** fuse, join, mend **5** braze, patch, unite **6** cement

soldering: *flux:* **5** resin, rosin
piece: lug

soldier: man, vet **4** swad, fogy **5** poilu, shirk, guffy, sammy, fogey **6** galoot, Zouave, marine, galoot **7** brigand, fighter, hobbler, palikar, private, trooper, veteran, warrior, regular, feedman, hotspur **8** buffcoat, cavalier, gendarme, malinger, servitor, tolpatch, shackman **9** grenadier, musketeer
detachment: **4** file
drinking flask: **7** canteen
female: **6** W.A.C.
foreign: **4** peon, kern **5** nezam, poilu, sepoy, kerne, spahi **6** sapper, lascar, askari **7** cateran, hoplite, Billjim **8** grognard, miquelet **10** base wallah, carmagnole, carabineer
group of: **4** band, file **5** corps, force, squad, troop **7** brigade, caterva, company, platoon **8** division **9** battalion
newly-trained: **5** cadet, plebe, rooky **6** rookie **7** chicken, recruit, trainee **8** bezonian **11** replacement
of fortune: **10** adventurer
overcoat: **6** capote
quarters: **7** billets **8** barracks
special functions: **6** lancer, sapper **7** velites, dragoon, trooper **8** fencible, fugleman **9** fantassin, targeteer, flugelman **10** cuirassier, velitation, carabineer, carabinier **12** antesignanus
trenching tool: **8** burgoyne
vacation: **4** pass **5** leave **8** furlough

soldierly: **5** brave **6** heroic **7** martial

sole: **4** dish, fish, foot, lone, mere, only, yoke **5** afald, alone, floor, plate, slade **6** bottom, entire, furrow, halter, hearth, lonely, single, unique, valley **7** outsole, subsoil **8** desolate, flatfish, isolated, solitary, unshared **9** exclusive, threshold, unmarried, unmatched **10** foundation, underframe, unsharable, windowsill
part: **5** shank
pert. to: **7** plantar

solecism: **9** barbarism, deviation **11** impropriety

solely: all **4** only **5** alone **6** merely, singly **8** entirely **9** allenarly **11** exclusively

solemn: sad **5** budge, grave, sober, usual **6** august, devout, formal, gloomy, ritual, sacred, severe, somber **7** earnest, serious, stately **8** funereal, splendid **9** customary, dignified, sumptuous **10** ceremonial, devotional, noteworthy **11** reverential **13** distinguished

solemnity: **7** gravity **8** ceremony

solemnization: **9** celebrity

solemnize: **5** exalt, marry **7** dignify, glorify, observe **9** celebrate **11** commemorate

soler: **7** cobbler **9** shoemaker

solert: **6** crafty **8** skillful

solicit: ask, beg, woo **4** bark, plea, seek, tout **5** court, crave, mooch, tempt **6** accost, entice, incite, invite, manage **7** beseech, canvass, entreat, forward, implore, request **8** campaign, disquiet, petition **9** importune, panhandle, prosecute **10** supplicate

solicitor: 4 tout **6** barker **8** attorney
chambers: **4** inns

solicitous: 5 eager **7** careful **8** desirous, troubled **9** attentive, concerned **10** thoughtful **12** apprehensive

solicitude: 4 care, coda, ease, fear, heed, yeme **7** anxiety, concern **8** business **11** carefulness **12** apprehension

solid: 4 cone, cube, firm, full, hard **5** cubic, dense, level, sound, stiff **6** bodily, sphere, stable, strong **7** bedrock, compact, uniform, weighty **8** constant, reliable, sterling, unbroken **9** estimable **10** consistent, dependable, inflexible **11** homogeneous, responsible, substantial, trustworthy
comb. form: **6** stereo
geometrical: **4** cone, cube **5** prism **7** pyramid **8** cylinder **11** heptahedron, pentahedron **12** dodecahedron

solidified: 8 hardened

solidify: gel, set **4** cake **6** cement, harden **7** compact **8** concrete, condense **9** coagulate **11** consolidate, crystallize

solidity: 8 firmness, hardness **9** solidness, soundness, stability **11** compactness, consistency **13** dependability

solidly: 10 completely

solidum: sum **4** dado

soliloquy: 4 poem **9** discourse, monologue, utterance

solitaire: 4 game **6** hermit, lonely **7** diamond, recluse **8** Canfield, patience, solitary **9** neckcloth

solitary: 4 hole, lone, monk, sole **5** alone **6** hermit, lonely, remote, simple, single **7** dungeon, eremite, recluse **8** desolate, lonesome, solitary **10** individual **12** unfrequented
combining form: **5** eremo

solitude: 6 dearth, desert **7** expanse, privacy, retreat **8** soleness **9** isolation, seclusion **10** loneliness, remoteness, retirement, uniqueness, wilderness **12** solitariness

solo: air **4** aria **5** alone, scena, radel **6** strain
accompaniment: **8** obligato **9** obbligato

soloist: 6 cantor, singer **7** aviator

Solomon: *father:* **5** David
mother: **9** Bathsheba
temple: **6** shamir

Solon: 4 sage **7** senator **8** lawmaker **9** publicist **10** legislator

soluble: 4 frim **6** solute

solus: 5 alone

solute: 4 free **5** loose, solve **7** arrange, soluble **8** dissolve, separate **9** dissolved **13** disintegrated

solution: key **6** answer **8** analysis **9** discharge, releasing **10** denouement, resolu-

tion **11** deliverance, explanation **14** disintegration **15** disentanglement
kinds of: lye **5** brine, eusol, iodin, titer, sirup, syrup **6** iodine, phenol
strength of: **5** titer

solve: 4 free, undo **5** break **6** assoil. fathom, unfold **7** explain, resolve, unravel **8** dissolve **9** interpret **11** disentangle

solvent: 8 solution **9** detergent

Somaliland: *city:* **7** Berbera **8** Mogdisho
coin: **4** besa
measure: top **4** caba **5** chela, darat, tabla **6** cubito
weight: **8** parsalah

Somalis division: 6 Hawiya

Somalis Proper: 4 Asha

somatic: 5 somal **6** bodily **8** parietal, physical **9** corporeal **13** somatopleuric

somber, sombre: sad **4** dark, dern, dull **5** dusky, gloom, grave, sober **6** dismal, gloomy, lenten, severe, solemn **7** austere **9** depressed **10** depressing, melancholy

sombrero: hat **8** headgear, sunshade

some: any, few, one **4** part **5** about **7** portion, several **13** approximately

somersault: 4 flip

something: 5 drink **6** liquor **7** aliquid **8** beverage, somewhat

sometime: 4 late, once **6** former **7** quondam **8** formerly **12** occasionally

somewhat: 6 rather **7** aliquid **9** something

Somme city: 6 Amiens

sommelier: 6 butler **9** cellarman

somnambulism: 12 noctambulism

somnolent: 6 drowsy, sleepy

somnus: 5 sleep

son: ben **4** fils **5** child, scion **6** filius, Jesuit, native **8** disciple, follower **9** offspring **10** descendant
as in Welsh names: ap
foster: **7** alumnus
pert. to: **6** filial
Scot.: Mac
youngest: **5** cadet

son-in-law: 5 gener **8** beau-fils

Son of God: 6 Savior **7** Saviour

sonance: 4 tune **5** sound

sonant: 4 oral **5** tonic, vocal **6** voiced **8** sounding **9** intonated

song: dit, lay, uta **4** aria, cant, dite, duan, fuss, glee, hymn, lied, lilt, noel, poem, tune **5** blues, canto, carol, chant, charm, ditty, lyric, melos, music, psalm, verse **6** ballad, cantic, cantus, canzon, carmen, chanty, clamor, himene, himine, melody, poetry, shanty, sonnet, strain, trifle **7** cancion, cantion, canzone, chantey, descant, shantey **8** canticle, pittance **9** cabaletta **11** composition
choral muse: **11** Terpsichore
college: **4** glee
collection: **9** anthology **10** cancionero
evening: **6** vesper **8** evensong, serenade
folk: **5** blues **6** ballad

funeral: **5** dirge, elegy, elogy **6** elegie, lament, threne **7** elogium, epicede **8** epicedia, threnody **9** epicedium
gay: **4** lilt
German: **4** lied **6** lieder(pl.)
gypsy: **10** zingaresca
love: **6** amoret, ballad, serena **8** serenade
mountaineer's: **5** yodel
mourning: see *funeral* above
obscure: **4** rune
part: **5** canon, round **8** madrigal
pert. to: **5** melic
sacred: **4** hymn **5** chant, motet, psalm **6** anthem **7** polymny
sailor's: **6** chanty, shanty **7** chantey, shantey **8** rumbelow **9** barcarole **10** barcarolle
wedding: **5** hymen
song-like: **6** ariose, arioso **7** lyrical
songbird: **4** lark, wren **5** mavie, mavis, robin, veery, vireo **6** canary, linnet, mocker, oriole, oscine, thrush **7** mocking, warbler **8** redstart
songman: **6** singer **7** gleeman **8** minstrel
songster: **4** poet **6** singer **7** chanter, warbler **8** songbird
songstress: **9** chantress
sonnet: **4** poem, song **5** octet, verse **6** sestet
conclusion: **6** sestet
sonority: **9** resonance
sonorous: **7** ringing **8** imposing, resonant **10** impressive
sons, sonse: **6** health **7** fortune **8** felicity **10** prosperity
sonsie, sonsy: **5** buxom, happy, lucky **6** comely **8** handsome, pleasing **9** plentiful **10** prosperous **11** comfortable
soodle: **6** stroll **7** saunter
soodly: **4** slow **9** leisurely
soogan: **4** rope **7** blanket
sook: **4** call **5** booth **6** market
soon: ere **4** anon, yern **5** early, later, quick, yerne **6** belive, rather, speedy **7** betimes, erelong, quickly, readily, shortly **8** directly, promptly, speedily **9** presently, willingly **10** beforetime **11** immediately
sooner: **4** erer, erst **6** before **9** Oklahoman
soot: **4** coom, smut, stup **5** colly, coomb, grime, sweet, smoke **6** carbon, gentle, smudge **7** blacken **9** melodious
pert. to: **10** fuliginous
sooth: **4** fact, real, soft, true **5** being, sweet, truly, truth **6** augury, smooth **7** comfort, genuine, present, proverb, reality **8** cajolery, pleasing, pleasure, soothing, truthful **10** delightful **11** soothsaying, trustworthy **12** blandishment
soothe: coy, pat, pet **4** balm, calm, dill, ease, lull **5** accoy, allay, charm, dulce, quiet **6** pacify, soften, solace, stroke **7** appease, assuage, comfort, compose, console, demulce, flatter, mollify, placate,

relieve **8** mitigate, palliate **9** alleviate, attemper **10** demulceate **11** tranquilize
soother: **4** balm **5** salve **9** emollient
soothing: **4** mild **5** balmy, downy, dulce **6** dreamy, dulcet, gentle **7** anodyne, calming **8** lenitive, sedative **9** appeasing, assuasive, demulcent **13** tranquilizing
soothsay: **4** omen **7** portent, predict, proverb **8** foretell
soothsayer: **4** seer **5** augur, weird, vates **6** ariole, mantis **7** augurer, diviner, prophet, seeress **8** haruspex, chaldean **10** hariolizer **14** prognosticator
sooty: **4** dark **5** black, colly, dusky **6** brokie **9** blackened **10** fuliginous
sop: **4** dunk, gift, heap, lump, mass, mess, soak, tuft **5** bribe, cloud, clump, steep **7** advance, milksop **8** saturate
sophism: **7** fallacy **8** argument
sophist: **7** casuist, teacher, thinker **10** paralogist **11** philosopher
sophistical: **8** captious **9** deceptive **11** adulterated
sophisticate: **5** alter, spoil **6** debase, garble **7** corrupt, falsify, mislead **10** adulterate
sophisticated: **4** wise **7** amended, refined, worldly **11** adulterated
sophistry: **6** deceit **7** fallacy, quibble, sophism **8** argument, trickery **9** deception
sophy: **4** sage **5** ruler, skill **6** wisdom **7** science **8** religion **9** personage **10** philosophy
sopie: **4** dram **5** drink
sopite: **5** draft, quash, quiet, sleep **6** drowsy **8** drooping
sopor: **5** sleep **6** stupor
soporific: **5** dwale **6** drowsy, opiate **8** hypnotic, narcotic **11** somniferous **12** somnifacient, somnivolency
soprano: **6** singer, treble
operatic: **4** Lind **5** Freni, Patti **6** Callas **7** Nilsson
sora: **4** rail
sorcerer: **4** mage, magi **5** boyla, brujo, Goeta **6** boolya, wizard **7** warlock **8** conjurer, magician **11** necromancer, thaumaturge **13** thaumaturgist
sorceress: **5** Circe, Lamia, sibyl, witch **6** Gorgon **11** enchantress
sorcery: art, obe, obi **5** magic, obeah, spell **6** fetich, fetish, voodoo **8** pishogue, prestige **9** diablerie, diabolism **10** necromancy, witchcraft **11** enchantment
sordellina: **7** bagpipe
sordid: low **4** base, mean, vile **5** dirty, gross **6** chetif, filthy, menial **7** ignoble, selfish, servile, squalid **8** churlish, covetous, grasping, grewsome, gruesome, sluttish, wretched **9** mercenary, niggardly **10** avaricious, despicable, slatternly **12** contemptible
sordo: low **4** deaf, dull **5** muted
sordor: **5** dregs **6** refuse **10** sordidness

sore: 4 boil, buck, evil, harm, kibe, pain, sair 5 angry, blain, botch, grief, ulcer, vexed, wound, wrong 6 bitter, bruise, fester, severe, sorrel, sorrow, tender, touchy 7 angered, annoyed, disease, extreme, grieved, painful, penance, trouble, violent 8 abrasion, grievous, inflamed, offended, sickness 9 detriment, irritated, sensitive, suffering, ulcerated, vexatious 10 affliction, afflictive, contrition, difficulty, distressed, unpleasant 11 disgruntled, distressing 13 temperamental, oversensitive

sorely: 7 greatly 8 severely, urgently 9 extremely, painfully, violently 10 grievously

soreness: 4 ache 8 severity, vexation, violence 11 painfulness 12 irritability

sorghum: 4 cush, dura, milo 5 batad, darso, durra, sorgo 6 shallu 8 feterita

sorite: 4 heap 10 collection

sorority: 4 club 7 society 10 fraternity, sisterhood

sorrow: rue, woe 4 bale, care, dole, harm, loss, sigh, teen, weal 5 devil, dolor, grief, mourn, rogue, scamp 6 grieve, lament, misery, plague, regret 7 sadness, trouble, waeness 8 calamity, distress, egrimony, mourning 9 adversity, penitence, suffering 10 affliction, compassion, contrition, discomfort, melancholy 11 lamentation, tribulation, unhappiness 12 wretchedness *over:* 6 bemoan, bewail, lament 7 deplore

sorrowful: sad 4 teen 5 drear, sadly 6 dismal, dolent, dreary, rueful 7 doleful, grieved, unhappy 8 contrite, dolesome, dolorous, grievous, mournful 9 afflicted, plaintive 10 lamentable, melancholy 11 distressing 12 disconsolate

sorrowing: 11 penitential 13 commiserating

sorry: bad 4 hurt, mean, poor 5 vexed 6 dismal, gloomy, regret, repent 7 chagrin, painful, pitiful 8 contrite, grievous, mournful, penitent, wretched 9 afflicted, chagrined, miserable, mortified, regretful, worthless 10 apologetic, melancholy 12 contemptible, disappointed

sort: ilk, ill, lot, set, wag 4 cull, gere, kind, race, part, race, rank, sift, suit, type 5 adapt, allot, batch, befit, breed, class, crowd, flock, genus, grade, group, order, swarm, vexed 6 adjust, assign, choose, garble, gender, manner, nature, punish, select 7 arrange, company, conform, fashion, quality, species, stripes, variety 8 classify, separate 9 character, disturbed 10 collection, distribute 11 accommodate, description

sorted: 6 chosen 8 assorted, selected 9 separated 10 classified

sortie: 4 knot 5 foray, sally 6 attack

sortilege: 7 sorcery 8 witchery 11 enchantment

sosh: jag 4 dash 5 drunk 11 intoxicated

soso: bad 4 poor 6 unwell 8 mediocre, middling, passable 9 tolerable 11 indifferent

soss: lap 4 mess, slop 5 plump, swill 6 muddle 7 heavily

sossle: 4 mess, slop 10 intoxicate

sot: 4 fool 5 child, fixed, toper, waste 6 befool, guzzle, tipple 7 dastard, foolish, sottish, stupefy, tippler, tosspot 8 drunkard, innocent, squander, stubborn 9 immovable, inebriate, obstinate, simpleton, swillbowl 10 winebibber

sotted: 5 bousy 8 besotted

sottish: 4 dull 6 stupid 7 doltish, drunken, foolish 9 senseless

sotto: 5 below, under

soubrette: 4 maid 7 actress 11 entertainer, maidservant

soucar: 6 banker 8 merchant, straight 9 honorable

soud: pay 4 join 5 unite 6 amount, enlist, fasten, solder 8 quantity 10 strengthen

soudagur: 8 merchant 10 shopkeeper

sough: die, sob 4 moan, sigh, whiz 5 chant, ditch, drain, rumor, whizz 6 murmur, report 7 breathe, moaning, whistle 8 singsong 9 murmuring

soul: ba; ame, God, ker 4 alma 5 atman, force, heart, saint 6 dibbuk, esprit, fervor, leader, pneuma, spirit 7 courage, essence 8 inspirer 10 embodiment, heartiness 11 anilopyrine 15 personification *loss:* 9 perdition

souled: 5 vital

soulless: 5 brute

sound: cry, din 4 birr, blow, bray, firm, good, hail, hale, rime, safe, sane, test, tone, true 5 alarm, blare, bruit(F.), chang, clang, fresh, grope, hoddy, inlet, legal, loyal, noise, plumb, probe, rhyme, solid, valid, whole 6 bedlam, bratte, clamor, entire, fathom, hearty, honest, hubbub, intact, measure, outcry, racket, report, robust, secure, stable, steven, strong, sturdy, tumult, uproar 7 bluster, clamour, clangor, clatter, clitter, clutter, examine, explore, healthy, hearing, measure, perfect, sonance, sputter 8 complete, flawless, orthodox, profound, reliable, shouting, splutter, thorough 9 honorable, undamaged 10 dependable, hullabaloo, scrutinize 11 trustworthy, undisturbed

amorous: coo
atonic: 4 surd
beating drum: 8 rataplan
bell-like: 4 ding 5 clang, knell 6 tinkle
breathing: 5 snore
buzzing: 4 whiz 5 whirr, whizz
contemptuous: 5 snort
contented: 4 purr
detection instrument: 10 hydrophone
discordant: 6 jangle 9 cacophony
distinctive: 6 timbre

dove's murmuring: **4** curr
drum: **4** roll
dry leaves: **6** rustle
engine: **4** chug, ping
explosive: pop **4** bang, boom, clap, roar **5** blast **6** report
guttural: **4** burr **5** grunt
harsh: **4** bray **5** creak, twang **9** cacophony
high-pitched: **4** ping, ting
hissing: zip **4** siss
hoarse: caw **4** bray
in doctrine: **8** orthodox
in mind: **4** sane
insect's: **5** chirr
jingling: **16** tintinnabulation
light: **5** swish **7** pitapat
loud: **4** boom, peal **5** blare, clang
magnifying device: **9** megaphone **11** loudspeaker
measurement of: bel
mentally: **4** sane **5** lucid **6** normal
metallic: **4** ping, ting **5** clang, clank **6** tinkle
monotonous: hum **4** moan **5** drone
mournful: sob
murmuring: **4** purr **5** groan
musical: **4** note
nasal: **5** snore, whine **7** stridor
of bell: **4** ding
of disapproval: boo, bah **4** hiss
of rising birds: **5** whirr
of surf: **4** rote
pert. to: **5** tonal **6** sonant **10** acoustical
pleasing in: **8** euphonic
respiratory: **4** rale
ringing: **5** clang **7** tinitus
shallow: **6** lagoon, laguna, lagune
shrill: **5** reedy, skirl
sibilant: **4** hiss, siss
small: **4** peep
solemn: **4** peal
speech: **5** vowel **8** phonetic
splashing: **5** swash
syllabic: **6** sonant
throat: **8** guttural
transposition: **10** spoonerism
trumpet: **5** blare **7** clarion
unvaried: **8** monotone
vibrant: **4** birr
vocal: **4** tone **6** hiccup **8** hiccough
warning: **5** alarm **6** alarum, tocsin
water: **4** klop, rote **5** plash, swish **6** splash
whispering: **8** susurrus
whizzing: **4** ping **5** swish
yelping: yip
sound out: **5** study **7** explore **11** investigate
sounded: **4** blew, rang, rung **5** oaten **6** tooted **7** clanged **8** syllabic
sounding: **6** sonant **8** plangent, resonant, sonorous, strident **9** bombastic **11** mellisonant **12** grandisonant, grandisonous
soundless: **5** quiet **9** noiseless **12** unfathomable

soundly: **6** deeply **7** healthy **8** securely **9** violently **10** completely, forcefully, profoundly, thoroughly
soundness: **5** truth **6** sanity **8** solidity, strength **9** integrity, rectitude **10** heartiness **11** healthiness
sounds: *having melody and rhythm:* **5** music
succession of: **4** peal
vocal symbols: **6** sonant
soup: **5** broth, puree, shchi, slash, stchi **6** borsch, borsht, oxtail **7** garbure, shtchee **8** consomme, gazpacho **12** mulligatawny
dish: **6** tureen
ingredient: **4** lalo, okra **7** noodles
thick: **4** bisk **5** hoosh, puree **6** bisque, burgoo **7** burgout, pottage **8** minestra **10** minestrone
thickener: **7** tapioca
soupcon: **5** taste, trace **7** modicum, portion **9** suspicion **10** suggestion
sour: wry **4** acid, dour, grim, hard, tart **5** acerb, acrid, cross, eager, gruff **6** acetic, bitter, cruety, morose, sullen **7** acetose, acetous, acidify, austere, crabbed, painful, peevish **8** acerbate, acescent, embitter **9** acidulate, acidulent, acidulous **10** afflictive, astringent, unpleasant **11** distasteful **12** disagreeable
source: **4** fons, font, germ, head, rise, root, seed **5** fount **6** ascent, origin, parent, spring **7** edition **8** fountain **9** beginning **10** wellspring **12** fountainhead
of caoutchouc: ule
of contrary action: **7** reagent
of gum arabic: **6** acacia
of income: **7** revenue
of indigo: **4** anil
of iodine: **4** kelp
of knowledge: **7** organon
of metal: ore
of phosphorus: **7** apatite
of vitamin "C": **6** orange
sourdook: **10** buttermilk
sourdough: **7** settler **10** prospector
sourness: **7** acidity **8** acerbity, acrimony, asperity **10** moroseness **16** disagreeableness
soursop: **9** guanabana
souse, souce, sowce, sowse: ear, jag **4** blow, cuff, duck, fall, prop, soak, wash **5** bathe, brine, douse, drink, swoop, thump **6** drench, pickle, plunge, pounce, strike, thwack **7** heavily, immerse, tippler **8** clumsily, drunkard, saturate, steeping, submerge **9** drenching
soused: **5** drunk **11** intoxicated
soutache: **5** braid **8** trimming
soutane: **5** cloak **7** cassock, zimarra
souter: **7** cobbler **9** shoemaker
South: **11** Confederacy
South Africa: *animal:* das **5** nenta **8** suricate
antelope: gnu **5** eland, leche, oribi, peele **6**

lechee, lechwe, rhebok **7** blaubok, blesbok, boshbok, grysbok, rheeboc, rheebok,
sassaby **8** blesbuck, bontebok, boschbok
armadillo: **4** para
ass: **6** quagga
assembly: **4** raad
aunt: **5** tanta
blaubok: **5** etaac
breastwork: **6** scherm
camp: **5** lager **6** laager
caterpillar: **6** risper
cattle enclosure: **5** kraal
cliff: **4** klip
coin: **4** cent, pond, rand **6** florin
colonist: **4** Boer
conference: **6** indaba
cony: das
corn: **5** mealy **6** mealie
council: **4** raad
criminal: **8** amalaita
dialect: **4** Taal
diamond: **5** jager **9** schlenter
Dutch: **4** Boer, Taal
Dutch speech: **9** Afrikaans
ferry: **4** pont
fox: **4** asse **5** caama
garment: **6** caross, kaross
goldfield: **4** rand
grass country: **4** veld **5** veldt
greenhorn: **5** ikona
gully: **5** donga
gun: **4** roer
hill: kop **8** spitzkop
hillock: **5** kopje
hippopotamus: **6** zeekoe
hog: **9** boschvark
hut: **8** rondavel, rondawel
legislative assembly: **4** raad
monkey: **6** vervet **8** talapoin
mountain: kop
pass: nek
pasture: **5** veldt
people: **4** Xosa **5** Bantu, Namas, Pondo **6**
Damara **7** Swahili **8** Bechuana **9** Hottentot
plain: **5** veldt
plant: **4** aloe
plot: erf
polecat: **6** musang
province: **9** Transvaal
race: see *people* above
region: **5** congo
river: **4** vaal
rodent: **5** ratel
settler: **4** Boer
shrub: **6** protea
simpleton: **5** ikona
snake: **5** elaps **8** eggeater
spirit: **8** tikolosh
starling: **5** sprew **7** spreeuw
stream: aar
sumac: **6** karree
thong: **4** riem **7** riempie
tick: **6** tampan

town: Aus **4** Stad **6** Durban **9** Germiston
12 Johannesburg
tract: **9** zuurveldt
trader: **7** Swahili
tree: **5** tenio **7** assagai **8** gamdeboo
tribe: see *people* above
village: **5** kraal
warrior: **4** impi
weaverbird: **4** taha
whip: **7** sjambok
South African: **4** Boer **10** Afrikander
South America: *aborigine:* **6** Arawak
animal: ai **4** paca **5** coati, coypu, llama,
sloth, tapir **6** alpaca, jaguar, nutria, vicuna **8** anteater **9** armadillo
ant: **5** sauba, sauva
anteater: **7** tamandu
arbor: **6** ramada
armadillo: **4** apar **7** tatouay **10** pichiciago
arrow poison: **6** curara, curare
balsam: **4** tolu
beast of burden: **5** llama
beef: **6** tasajo
beverage: **4** mate
bird: **4** aura, guan, mitu, myna, rara, taha
5 agami, arara, chaja, mynah **6** barber,
barbet **7** aracari, jacamar, oilbird, seriema, tinamou **8** bellbird, boatbill, curassow, guacharo, puffbird, screamer, terutero
blanket: **6** serape
boat: **6** cayuco
cactus: **7** airampo
catfish: **5** dorad
cattle ranch: **8** estancia **9** estantion
country: **4** Peru **5** Chile **6** Brazil **7** Bolivia, Ecuador **8** Colombia **9** Argentina,
Patagonia, Venezuela
cowboy: **6** gaucho **7** llanero, planero
cowboy's weapon: **5** bolas
dance: **5** mambo, samba **6** cha-cha
deer: **6** guemal, guemul
dove: **9** talpacoti
estuary: **4** Para **5** Plata
fish: **4** paru **6** aimara, caribe **7** scalare **8**
arapaima
fox: **4** asse
game: **6** pelota
garment: **6** serape
gold: oro
griddle cake: **5** arepa
hare: **6** tapeti
hawk: **8** caracara
herb: **9** romerillo
herdsman: **7** llanero
Indian: Ges, Ona **4** Auca, Inca, Tama, **5**
Carib, Tapas **6** Arawak, Jivaro **7** Caya-
pos, Goyanas, Guatoan, Pampero, Tapuyan **8** Camacans, Coroados, Timbiras
9 Caingangs, Chavantes **10** Patagonian
Indian hut: **5** toldo
Indian medicine man: **4** peai **6** shaman
Indian poison: **6** curara, curare, curari
island: **5** Aruba

knife: **7** machete **8** machette
language: Ona
lapwing: **8** terutero
liberator: **7** Bolivar
limestone: **5** tosca
liquor: **6** chicha
lizard: **4** teju **5** coati
mammal: ai **4** paca **5** coati, llama, tapir **6**
   alpaca, guanco **8** kinkajou, pacarana **10**
   coati-mondi, coati-mundi
marmoset: **7** tamarin
measure: **4** vara **7** manzana
mineral: **4** urso
monkey: sai **4** saki, titi **5** acari, araba **6**
   grison, teetee **7** ouakari, sapajou **8** marmoset, orabassu **9** barrigudo, beelzebub
mountains: **5** Andes
native: **5** Carib
opossum: **5** quica **7** sarigue
ostrich: **4** rhea
palm: **5** assai, bussu, datil, troly **6** tooroo,
   ubussu **7** troolie
parrot: **5** macaw
plain: **5** llano, pampa
plains dweller: **7** llanero
plant: **6** ipecac **8** crassula **10** tillandsia
porridge: **5** atole
rabbit: **6** tapeti
rancher: **10** estanciero
republic: **5** Chile **8** Colombia **9** Argentina,
   Venezuela
rodent: **4** degu, mara, paca **5** coypu **6**
   agouti, agouty **8** viscacha, vizcacha **10**
   chinchilla
root: oca
rubber tree: **4** para
ruminant: **5** llama **6** alpaca
scarf: **5** manta
serpent: **5** aboma
shrub: **4** coca
slaughterhouse: **11** frigorifico
snake: bom **4** lora **5** aboma **8** anaconda **10**
   bushmaster
sorrel: oca
stock: Ona
strait: **8** Magellan
tapir: **5** danta
tiger cat: **5** chati
toucan: **4** toco **7** aracari
tree: **4** fotu, lana, mora, para, vera **5**
   balsa, cacao, cebil, couma, pekea **6**
   chicha, simaba, yachan **7** bebeeru,
   quayabi **9** balaustre, couvatari **11**
   chichicaste
tribe: Ona
trumpeter: **5** agami
tuber: oca
ungulate: **5** tapir
vulture: **6** condor
walnut: **9** conacaste
weapon: **4** bola **5** bolas
wild cat: **4** eyra
wind: **7** pampero
South Australia: See **Australia**.

South Carolina: *fort:* **6** Sumter
   native: **6** weasel
   river: **6** Peedee, Saluda, Santee
South Dakota:
   capital: **6** Pierre
   Indian: **5** Brule
South India: See **India**.
South Pacific: *island:* **4** Fiji **5** Samoa,
   Tonga **7** Society **8** Pitcairn, Woodlark
   sea: **5** Coral, Timor **6** Tasman
South Pole bird: **4** skua **7** penguin
South Sea: *canoe:* **4** proa
   island: **4** Bali, Siam, Sulu
   island drink: ava
   island food: **5** taros
   island money: **6** wakiki
   islander: **5** Maori **6** Kanaka, Samoan
   plant: **4** taro
   product: **5** copra
   staple: **4** taro
South Western Indian: **4** Cree
south wind: **5** notus **6** auster
South Wind author: **7** Douglas
Southeast Asia (see also **Asia**): **4** Laos,
   Siam **5** Burma **6** Ceylon **7** Vietnam **8**
   Cambodia, Malaysia, Pakistan, Thailand
   9 Indonesia **11** Philippines
southeast wind: **5** eurus
southerly: **8** austrine
southern: **7** austral
Southern California: See **California**.
Southern dish: **4** okra **5** gumbo **7** hoecake
Southern France: **4** Midi
Southern tonic: **4** dope
southernwood: **9** abrotanum
Southwark inn: **6** Tabard
Southwest Pacific island: **5** Samoa
southwest wind: **4** afer
souvenir: **5** curio, relic **6** memory **7** memento **8** keepsake, reminder **12** recollection, remembrancer
sovereign: **4** king **5** chief, liege, royal,
   ruler **6** couter, Mikado, prince **7** emperor,
   highest, monarch, supreme **8** autocrat,
   greatest, princely, reigning, superior, suzerain **9** effectual, excellent, paramount,
   potentate **11** autocratrix, controlling, efficacious, independent
   female: **7** empress
   petty: **8** tetrarch
sovereign authority: **8** dominion
sovereign power: **6** throne
sovereign prerogative claim: **11** seigniorage
sovereignty: **4** rule, sway **5** realm **6** diadem, empery, empire, status **7** dynasty,
   majesty, scepter, sceptre **8** dominion **9**
   supremacy **10** ascendancy, ascendency,
   domination
   absolute: **8** autarchy
   joint: **11** condominium
Soviet (see also **Russia**):
   administrative committee: **9** presidium

government farm: **7** sovkhos, sovkhoz **8**
   sovkhose
hero: **5** Lenin **6** Stalin
news agency: **4** Tass
newspaper: **6** Pravda **8** Izvestia
police: **4** Ogpu
sow: hog, pig **4** heap, seed, shed **5** ditch,
   drain, drill, plant, stack, swine **6** runner, sluice, spread **7** channel, furnish,
   grumphy, implant, scatter **8** disperse,
   grumphie **9** broadcast, inoculate **10** salamander **11** disseminate
wild: **8** javelina
young: elt **4** gilt
sower: **7** seedman
of dragon's teeth: **6** Cadmus
soy: **4** silk
soy bean: **4** soja
soya: **4** dill **6** fennel **7** soybean
spa: **5** oasis, oases **6** resort, spring **8** Saratoga **10** sanatorium
space: gap **4** area, path, rank, roam, room,
   rove, void, walk **5** ambit, plena(pl.), range,
   track **6** course, divide, extent, plenum,
   region **7** areolae, arrange, expanse **8** capacity, distance, duration, interval, quantity **11** reservation **14** accommodations
architectural: **8** pediment
between eyes: **4** lore
between two intersecting lines: **5** angle
between two points: **8** distance
blank: **6** lacuna **7** lacunae(pl.)
breathing: **6** recess
cleared: **5** glade
coin: **7** exergue
empty: **4** void **5** blank, inane **6** vacuum
forest: **5** glade
hollowed: **7** mortice, mortise
included: **8** contents
limitless: **8** infinite
occupied: **6** volume
on surface: **4** area
partitioned: **4** room
pert. to: **5** areal
portion of: **5** place
safekeeping: **7** storage
small: **6** areola, areole **7** areolae
storage: **4** shed **5** attic **6** cellar **9** storeroom, warehouse
void: **5** chasm **7** inanity
wall: **5** niche
white: **6** margin
space for goods: **7** storage
space full of matter: **6** plenum
space of time: **8** interval
space theory: **7** plenism
spacer: bar
spacious: **4** vast **5** ample, broad, great,
   large, rangy, roomy **9** capacious, expansive, extensive **13** comprehensive
spack: **7** forward, knowing **11** intelligent
Spad: **7** biplane
spad: **4** nail
spadassin: **5** bravo **7** duelist **9** swordsman

spade: dig **5** graft **6** shovel
Irish: **5** slane
kind of: **6** scavel
narrow: loy
plasterer's: **6** server
sharp: **4** spud
triangular: **5** didle
turf: **5** slane
spadger: boy **7** sparrow
spae: **6** divine **8** foretell, prophecy
spahi, spahee: **7** cavalry
Spain: **6** Iberia
adventurer: **9** almogaver
article: el, la, un; las, los, una
author: **9** Cervantes
bayonet: **5** yucca
beach: **5** plays
belle: **4** maja
blanket: **6** serape
boat: **5** aviso
brandy: **11** aguardiente
bull: **4** toro
cape: **9** Trafalgar
cart: **7** carreta **8** carretta
cathedral city: **7** Seville
cedar: **6** acajou
champion: Cid
channel: **4** Cano
chaperone: **6** duenna
clerk: **11** escribiente
cloak: **4** capa **5** manta **6** mantle
coat: **7** zamarra, zamarro
coin: **5** dobla **6** cuarto, doblon, peseta **7**
   Alfonso, centimo, piaster **8** cuartino **9**
   cuartillo
conqueror: Cid **7** Pizarro **12** conquistador
contract: **7** asiento **8** assiento
council: **5** junta
count: **5** conde
dance: **4** jota **5** danza, tango **6** bolero, gitano **8** fandango, saraband **9** zapateado
   10 seguidilla
dish: **6** posole
district: **5** Xeres
dollar: **4** duro, peso, pezo **7** piaster,
   piastre
dumpling: **6** tamale
earth: **6** tierra
exclamation: **6** carajo **7** caramba
execution: **7** garotte, garrote **8** garrotte
explorer: **7** Mendoza **8** Coronado
fabric: **5** tiraz
fleet: **6** armada
friend: **5** amigo
frigate: **5** zabra
game: **5** omber **6** pelota **7** jai-alai
gentleman: don **5** senor **8** cavalier **9** caballero
goddess: **5** Diosa
gold: oro
governor: **10** idelantado
grass: **5** spart **7** esparto
griddlecake: **5** arepa
gunboat: **5** barca

gypsy: **7** zincalo
hall: **4** sala
head covering: **8** mantilla
herdsman: **8** ranchero
hill: **5** cerro, morro
holiday: **6** fiesta
horse: **7** caballo
hotel: **5** venta **6** posada
house: **4** casa
instrument: **8** castanet, zambomba
judge: **7** alcalde
kettle: **4** cazo
king: rey
kingdom: **4** Leon **6** Aragon **7** Castile
lady: **4** dona **6** senora
lagoon: **6** laguna
lariat: **5** reata, riata
leather: **8** cordovan
legislature: **6** cortes
letter carrier: **6** correo
linen cloth: **4** crea
lute: **7** vihuela
magic: **8** brujeria
man: don **6** hombre
mausoleum: **8** Escorial
mayor: **6** alcade **7** alcalde
measure: pie **4** codo, copa, dedo, moyo, paso, vara **5** aroba, braza, cafiz, cahiz, legua, linea, medio, milla, palmo, sesma **6** cordel, cuarta, estado, fanega, league, racion, yugada **7** azumbre, cantara, celemin, estadel, pulgada **8** aranzada, fanegada **9** cuarteron, cuartilla, cuartillo **10** caballeria
miss: **8** senorita
monk: **5** padre
mountain: **8** Asturian, Pyrenees **9** Mulahacem **10** Cantabrian, Guadarrama, Pic de Netou **11** La Maladetta **12** Sierra Morena **14** Sierra de Toledo
muleteer: **7** arriero
native: **7** Catalan, Iberian
nobleman: don **7** grandee, hidalgo
nun: **6** Teresa
officer: **8** alguacil, alguazil
operetta: **8** zarzuela
oyster: **5** pinna
painter: **4** Cano, Goya **6** Ribera **7** Zuloaga **9** Velasquez
palace: **8** Escorial
pancake: **5** arepa
parliament: **6** cortes
pear: **7** avocado
peasant: **7** paisano
peninsula: **6** Iberia
pepper: **5** chili **7** pimento
pickpocket: **6** ratero
plant: aji
porridge: **5** atole
port: **5** Palos
post office: **6** correo
priest: **4** cura **5** padre
promenade: **5** paseo
pronunciation mark: **5** tilde

raisin: **4** pasa
province: **4** Jaen, Leon, Lugo, Vigo **5** Alava, Avila, Cadiz, Soria **6** Burgos, Coruna, Cuenca, Gerona, Huelva, Huesca, Lerida, Madrid, Malaga, Murcia, Orense, Oviedo, Teruel, Toledo, Zamora **7** Almeria, Badajoz, Caceres, Cordova, Granada, Logrono, Navarra, Segovia, Seville, Vizcaya **8** Albacete, Alicante, Palencia, Valencia **9** Barcelona, Guipuscoa, Salamanca, Santander, Saragossa, Tarragona **10** Ciudad Real, Pontevedra, Valladolid **11** Guadalajara **15** Balearic Islands **18** Castellon de la Plana
rice: **5** arroz
rider: **8** herisson
river: ria, rio **4** Ebro **5** Douro, Tagus **8** Guadiana **12** Guadalquivir
road: **6** camino
room: **4** sala
seaport: **4** Adra **5** Palos
sentinel: **5** vedet, videt **7** vedette, vidette
shawl: **5** manta **6** serape
sherry: **5** Xeres **11** Amontillado
silk: **5** tiraz
sorcerer: **5** brujo
stanza: **10** seguidilla
street: **5** calle
sword: **5** bilbo
tax: **8** alcabala
title: don **5** senor **6** senora **7** hidalgo **8** senorita
tomorrow: **6** manana
town: **4** Irun, Leon, Olot **5** Cadiz, Gijon, Lorca, Ronda, Siero, Xeres **6** Bilbao, Madrid(c.), Malaga, Murcia, Toledo **7** Cordoba, Cordova, Granada, Seville **8** Valencia, Zaragoza **9** Barcelona, Cartagena, Salamanca, Santander, Saragossa **10** Carthagena, Valladolid **18** Jerez de la Frontiera
trail: **6** camino
trefoil: **7** alfalfa, lucerne
vehicle: **7** tartana
watchword: **6** alerta
watercourse: **6** arroyo
weight: **4** onza **5** frail, grano, libra, marco, tomin **6** adarme, arroba, dinero, dracma, ochava **7** arienzo, quilate, quintal **8** caracter, tonelada **9** escrupulo **10** castellano
wind: **6** solano
window: **7** ventana
witchcraft: **8** brujeria
woman: **6** senora
spal-peen: boy, fop, lad **5** scamp **6** rascal **7** laborer, workman **8** braggart **9** youngster
spald: **4** limb, open **5** joint, splay, split **8** shoulder, splinter
spale: bar **4** chip, fine, lath, rail **5** brace, spall **6** timber **7** shaving **8** splinter
spall: **4** chip, fall **5** break **6** reduce **7** breakup, crumble **8** fragment, shoulder
spalt: **4** chip, tear **5** crisp, split **7** brittle

span: **4** cock, pair, rope, swim, team, time **5** cover, grasp, reach, seize **6** attach, bridge, extend, fasten, fetter, hobble, inspan, spread **7** confine, matched, measure, stretch **8** distance, duration, encircle **9** encompass, perfectly **10** completely

spancel: tie **4** clog **6** fetter, hobble

spang: **4** bang, hurl, jump, kick, leap, yoke **5** clasp, crack **6** stride **7** spangle **8** abruptly, directly, ornament, straight

spangle: set **4** boss **5** adorn, aglet, gleam, plate **6** aiglet, sequin, zequin **7** glisten, glitter, sparkle **8** sprinkle, zecchino

spangly: **9** sparkling **10** glittering

Spaniard: **5** Latin **7** Espanol **9** Castilian *imaginary:* **9** Espriella

spaniel: **5** trasy **6** cocker **8** springer **9** sycophant

spank: **4** prat, whip **6** strike **8** chastise

spanking: **4** fine **5** brisk, fresh, large, stout **6** lively, strong **7** dashing **8** vigorous

spanner: **6** wrench

spar: bar, box, rod **4** beam, bolt, boom, gaff, mast, pole, raft, rung, shut, yard **5** close, fight, lunge, sprit, steve **6** barite, bicker, charge, fasten, rafter, strike, thrust, timber **7** contest, dispute, enclose, wrangle, yardarm **8** dolomite, lazulite

spare: **4** bear, free, gain, hain, lean, part, save, slim, slit, slow, stop, thin **5** avoid, chary, extra, favor, gaunt, grant, lanky, stint **6** desist, endure, favour, frugal, meager, scanty **7** deprive, forbear, forgive, haggard, leisure, opening, placket, refrain, relieve, reserve, sparing **8** dilatory, forebear, preserve, tolerate **9** duplicate, parsimony **11** replacement, superfluous **12** parsimonious

spare time: **7** leisure

sparge: **6** splash **8** sprinkle **9** bespatter

sparing: **5** chary, gnede, scant **6** frugal, meager, saving, scanty **7** careful, limited, thrifty **8** merciful, reticent, stinting **9** scrimping **12** parsimonious

spark: arc, woo **4** beau, funk, soil **5** aizle, belle, blade, court, flash, grain, lover **7** diamond, gallant, sparkle, spatter **8** sparklet **9** scintilla **10** sweetheart **11** scintillate
igniting property: **11** incendivity

sparked: **5** arced **7** courted, spotted **8** streaked **10** variegated

sparker: **5** lover **7** gallant **8** firework

sparkle: **5** blink, flash, gleam, glent, glint, shine, spark, strew, trace **7** diffuse, glisten, glitter, radiate, reflect, scatter, showing, spangle **8** disperse, sprinkle, vivacity **9** coruscate **10** effervesce, illuminate, liveliness **11** coruscation, scintillate **13** scintillation

sparkling: **4** dewy **5** crisp **6** bright, lively, starry **7** shining **8** animated, flashing, gleaming **9** brillante, brilliant, twinkling **10** glittering, reflecting **12** effervescent, effervescing

sparoid fish: **4** scup **5** porgy **10** sheepshead

sparple: **4** rout **7** scatter **8** disperse, sprinkle **11** disseminate

sparrer: **5** boxer **7** sparrow

sparrow: **7** chanter

sparse: **4** thin **5** scant **6** meager, meagre, scanty, thinly **7** scatter **8** disperse **9** scattered **10** distribute, infrequent

Sparta (see also **Attica, Greece**)*: army:* **4** mora
bondman: **5** helot
commander: **7** lochage
dog: **10** bloodhound
festival: **6** Carnea **7** Carneia
governor: **7** harmost
king: **8** Leonidas, Menelaus
king's wife: **4** Leda
magistrate: **5** ephor
method of cipher writing: **7** scytale
native: **8** Laconian
queen: **5** Helen
serf: **5** helot

spartan: **5** brave, hardy **6** frugal, heroic, severe **7** laconic **9** undaunted **10** courageous

sparver: **4** tent **6** canopy, tester

spasm: fit, tie **4** grip **5** crick **8** paroxysm **10** convulsion **11** contraction

spasmodic: **6** fitful, sudden **7** snatchy, violent **9** excitable **12** intermittent
disease: **7** tetanus

spat: row **4** blow, clap, fuss, slap, tiff **5** eject **6** gaiter, oyster, splash, strike **7** dispute, legging, quarrel

spate: **4** gush, rain **5** flood **7** freshet, outflow, torrent **9** overwhelm, rainstorm **10** waterspout

spatial: **5** areal **6** steric **8** sterical

spatter: jet **4** dash, drop, soil, spot **5** slart, spurt **6** dabble, defame, injure, splash, spread **7** scatter, spatule, sputter **8** splutter, sprinkle

spatulate: **6** lyrate

spawn: roe **4** eggs, germ, seed, spot **5** fungi **6** bulbis, source **7** cormels, deposit, produce **8** generate, mycelium

spay: **4** geld **8** castrate **9** sterilize

speak: say **4** carp, chat, hail, talk, tell **5** extol, honor, orate, utter **6** reveal **7** address, bespeak, declaim, declare, deliver, express, publish **8** converse, harangue, manifest, proclaim **9** celebrate, discourse, pronounce **10** articulate
affectedly: **4** mimp **5** mince
against: **6** oppose
curtly: **4** snap, birk
foolishly: **6** drivel
from memory: **6** recite
imperfectly: **4** lisp **7** stutter
in undertone: **6** mumble, murmur
of: **4** call **7** mention
offhand: **11** extemporize
oracularly: **11** pontificate
pert. to: **10** oratorical

profusely: **6** dilate **7** palaver

rapidly: **5** troll **6** patter **8** splutter

rhetorically: **5** orate **7** declaim

slightingly: **8** backbite **9** disparage

slowly: **5** drawl

softly: **7** whisper

thoughtlessly: **4** blat **8** splutter

through nose: **9** nasillate

to: **5** greet **6** accost **7** address

under breath: **6** mumble, mutter

speaker: **5** drone, sayer **6** lisper, orator, proser, ranter, talker **7** demagog, utterer **8** lecturer **9** demagogue **10** mouthpiece, prolocutor **11** entertainer, spellbinder

inspired: **7** prophet

of many languages: **8** linguist, polyglot

speaker's hammer: **5** gavel

speaking: *style:* **8** staccato, fluently

without preparation: **13** extemporizing

spean: **4** test, wean **5** prong **6** nipple

spear: **4** gad, rod **4** dart, fram, reed, shut, spar **5** apine, blade, lance, shoot, stalk **6** aprout, glaive, impale, pierce, strike **7** feather, harpoon, javelin, missile, trident **9** penetrate

kind of: **4** gaff **5** gidia, gidya **6** bident, fizgig, gidgea, gidgee, gidjee, gidyea **7** assagai, assegai, bourdon, harpoon, leister, trident

spear-shaped: **7** hastate

spearfish: **8** billfish

spearhead: **4** gaff

special: **4** dear, rare **5** chief, extra, local **6** unique **7** limited, unusual **8** concrete, detailed, favorite, intimate, paramour, peculiar, personal, specific, uncommon **9** specially **10** especially, individual, noteworthy, particular, restricted **11** distinctive, exceptional **12** particularly **13** distinguished, extraordinary

ability: **6** talent

edition: **5** extra

specialist: *atomic:* **9** physicist

city planning: **8** urbanist

ear: **6** aurist

eye: **7** oculist

medical (see also **doctor***):* **7** oculist, surgeon **9** otologist **11** orthopedist **12** obstetrician, orthopaedist, pediatrician **13** paediatrician

mineral: **12** mineralogist

money management: **9** economist

surgical: see **doctor**.

specialty: **5** forte, skill **8** aptitude **13** particularity

specie: **4** cash, coin **5** money

species: **4** kind, race, sort, type **5** breed, brood, class, genre, image **7** mankind, variety **8** category, humanity **9** spectacle **10** exhibition, reflection

spider: **5** acera

various: **5** genus **6** genera

specific: **5** exact **7** precise, special **8** concrete, definite, explicit, peculiar **10** par-

ticular, restricted, specifying **11** determinate

specifically: **6** namely **9** specially

specify: **4** name, tell **5** allot, state **6** assign, define, detail **7** mention **8** describe, nominate **9** designate, stipulate **10** articulate

in detail: **4** item **7** itemize

singly: **9** enumerate

specimen: **4** mark **5** model, relic, token **6** cotype, sample, swatch **7** example, pattern **11** examination

specious: gay **4** fair **5** showy **6** glossy, hollow **7** colored **8** coloured **9** colorable, plausible **10** ostensible **12** hypocritical

speck: bit, dot, nit **4** blot, iota, mark, mite, mote, spot, whit **5** glebe, stain **7** blemish, blubber **8** particle

speckle: dot **5** fleck **7** stipple

speckled: **6** menald **7** bracket

specs: **10** eyeglasses, spectacles

spectacle: **4** show **5** bysen, model, scene, sight **6** mirror **7** display, diorama, example, pageant, pattern **8** panorama, spyglass **9** cyclorama **10** exhibition **14** representation

structure for: **5** arena **7** stadium, theater, theatre **8** coliseum

spectacles: **7** glasses

part of: **6** bridge, temple

spectator: **4** eyer **6** espier **7** witness **8** beholder, kibitzer, looker-on, observer, onlooker

specter, spectre: **4** bogy **5** bogey, bogie, bogle, ghost, shade, spook **6** boggle, spirit, wraith **7** boggard, boggart, bugaboo, bugbear, phantom **8** boggle-bo, guytrash, phantasm, revenant **10** apparition

spectral: **6** ghosty, spooky **7** ghostly, phantom **12** apparitional **13** insubstantial

spectrum: **8** infrared

speculate: **5** guess, think **6** gamble, mirror, ponder, wonder **8** consider, meditate, ruminate, theorize **10** conjecture, deliberate, philosophy **11** contemplate

speculation: **6** bubble, vision **7** surmise **8** decision **9** guesswork, intuition **10** conclusion, conjecture

speculator: spy **4** lamb **7** lookout, scalper **8** explorer, observer, theorist **12** contemplator, investigator

sped: **4** hied **5** raced **6** darted, dashed **8** galloped, hastened **11** accelerated

speech: **4** talk **5** idiom, voice, slang **6** dilogy, epilog, orison, steven, tongue **7** address, dialect, oration, oratory, vinegar **8** colloquy, epilogue, harangue, language **9** utterance

abusive: **6** tirade

conclusion: **9** episcopal **10** peroration

defect: **4** lisp **6** alogia **7** stammer, stutter

denunciation: **5** frump **6** tirade **8** filippic **9** philippic

difficulty: **9** baryphony **10** baryphonia

element: **4** surd

expert: **9** phonetist

figure of: **5** irony, trope **6** aporia, simile **7** imagery **8** metaphor

goddess: Vac

hesitation: haw **7** stutter

impassioned: **6** tirade **9** dithyramb

insane: **9** bedlamism

loss: **6** alalia **7** aphasia **8** muteness

part: **4** noun, verb **6** adverb **9** adjective **11** conjunction, preposition **12** interjection

peculiar: **5** idiom

provincial: **6** patois **7** dialect

readiness: **9** facundity

religious: **6** sermon **9** preaching

representing: **8** phonetic

reserved: **8** reticent

summary: **5** notes

voiceless element: **4** surd **7** spirate

world language: **7** volapuk **9** esperanto

speechify: 5 orate **8** harangue

speechless: mum **4** dumb, mute **6** silent **9** voiceless

speed: go; hie, rip **4** fare, flee, help, race, rate **5** haste, hurry **6** assist, career, hasten, profit, succor **7** execute, prosper **8** celerity, dispatch, expedite, rapidity, velocity **9** advantage, discharge, quickness, swiftness **10** accelerate, expedition, facilitate **12** precipitance

full: **5** amain

great: **4** zoom **5** haste, spurt, amain **6** career **9** posthaste

measuring device: **11** speedometer, velocimeter

note: **4** time **5** clock

rate of: RPM **4** pace **5** tempo

speeder: 5 racer **11** accelerator

speedful: 5 rapid **6** expert, speedy **9** efficient, favorable **10** successful

speedily: 4 fast, soon **5** apace **6** presto **7** betimes, hastily, quickly, rapidly **8** promptly **13** expeditiously

speediness: 5 haste **8** dispatch, rapidity **9** quickness **10** promptness

speedometer: 5 clock **8** odometer **10** tachometer

speedy: 4 fast **5** fleet, hasty, quick, rapid, swift **6** active, prompt **7** helpful **12** advantageous

speel: 5 climb, mount **8** splinter

spell: bar, peg **4** chip, form, lath, mean, rung, save, tale, talk, tell, trap, turn, snap **5** brief. charm, curse, magic, relay, shift, spare, speak, spell, story, utter, weird **6** glamor, gospel, import, period, relate, relief, splint, trance **7** bewitch, cantrip, compose, glamour, relieve, shaving, signify, sorcery, drought, syncope **8** pishogue, splinter **9** discourse **10** constitute, demonifuge **11** conjuration, enchantment, fascination, abracadabra **12** entrancement **13** orthographize, prognosticate

in another alphabet: **13** transliterate

spellbind: 5 orate **7** enchant **9** fascinate

speller (according to pronunciation)**: 9** phonetist **11** phoneticist

poor: **11** cacographer

spelter: 4 zinc

spelunk: den **4** cave, lair **6** cavern

spence, spense: 6 larder, pantry **7** buttery **9** apartment

spencer: wig **4** coat **6** butler, jacket, pantry **7** buttery, steward, trysail

spend: run, use **4** blow, dash, flow, give, jump, pass, span **5** beset, exert. grasp, waste **6** attach, bestow, beware, devote, elapse, expend, fasten, lavish, manage, spread, spring, weaken **7** consume, dispend, exhaust, fatigue, perform **8** confound, disburse, squander **9** dissipate, sacrifice **10** distribute

spend the summer: 8 estivate **9** aestivate

spendful: 8 wasteful **11** extravagant

spendthrift: 6 waster **7** wastrel **8** prodigal, wasteful **10** dingthrift, profligate

Spenserian character: Una

spent: 4 beat, paid, used **5** weary **6** effete, wasted **8** lavished **9** exhausted **10** squandered

speos: 4 cave, tomb **6** grotto, temple

sperm: 4 seed **5** semen **12** spermatozoon

sperm whale: 8 cachalot

spet: 9 barracuda

spetch: 4 mend **5** patch **6** refuse **7** parings

spew, spue: bog **4** ooze, slip **5** eject, exude, strew, vomit **7** extrude, scatter **8** disgorge **10** afterswarm

sphacelate: 7 decayed, mortify **8** withered **9** mortified

sphenic: 11 wedge-shaped

spheral: 7 perfect **10** harmonious **11** symmetrical

sphere: orb, sky **4** ball, rank, star **5** ambit, arena, class, field, globe, orbit, order, range, scope **6** domain, orblet, planet **7** circuit, compass, heavens, stratum, station, theatre, terella **8** idiosome, position, province **9** idioblast **10** atmosphere, department **12** jurisdiction

perforated: **4** bead

spheric: 8 globular **11** globe-shaped

spherical: 5 orbic, round **6** rotund **7** globate, globose **8** globated, globular, obrotund **9** globulous, orbicular

sphericity: 9 rotundity, roundness

spheroid: 4 ball **5** earth

spherule: 7 globule

sphinx: *land of:* **5** Egypt

mother: **7** Echidna

site of: **4** Giza **5** Luxor

sphinxian: 10 mysterious **11** enigmatical, inscrutable

sphygmus: 5 pulse

spial: spy **5** scout, watch **6** espial

spica: 7 bandage

spice: 4 dash, kind, mace, mull, nard, odor, sort, vein 5 aroma, taste, touch 6 embalm, flavor, relish, season 7 modicum, perfume, portion, species, variety 8 quantity, specimen 9 admixture, condiment, seasoning 10 appearance
kind of: 4 mace, mull, sage 5 anise, cumin, curry, thyme 6 cloves, ginger, nutmeg, pepper, stacte, tamara 7 cayenne, mustard, oregano, paprika, pimento 8 allspice, cinnamon, marjoram, pimiento, turmeric
Spice Islands: 6 Indies 7 Molucca
spices: 9 aromatics
spicier: 4 racy 7 nuttier
spick: fat 5 split 6 grease 7 blubber 8 lavender, titmouse
spicknel: 9 baldmoney
spicule: rod 4 dart, nail, toxa 5 aster, spine 6 actine 7 prickle, rhabdus 8 sclerite, spikelet
spicy: hot 4 keen, racy 5 balmy, natty, showy, smart 6 active, risque 7 gingery, peppery, piquant, pungent 8 aromatic, fragrant, spirited
spider: cob, cop, hub, pan 5 arain 6 eresid, epeira, snarer, tripod, trivet 7 pokomoo, skillet, retiary 8 arachnid, attercop, telarian 9 tarantula 12 candleholder
family of: 7 attidae 9 drassidae 10 citigradae
genus of: 6 aranea, epeira
web-spinning organ: 9 spinneret
spider bug: 5 emesa
spider crab: 4 maia
spider monkey: 9 belzebuth
spider nest: web 5 nidus
spider species: 5 acera
spider web: 8 attercop
resembling: 9 arachnoid
spinner: 9 spinneret
spieler: 5 crier 6 barker, talker 7 sharper, speaker 8 lecturer 9 announcer 11 spellbinder
spiff: PM 5 bonus 7 premium 8 gratuity
spifflicate, spifflicate: 4 beat, kill 6 stifle 8 astonish, bewilder, confound
spigot: peg, pin, tap 4 cock, plug 5 spile, spout 6 dossil, faucet, pierce
spike: cut, cob, ear, gad 4 brob, chat, nail, tine, umbo 5 ament, block, prong 6 antler, cereal, earlet, fasten, finish, impale, pierce, secure, thwart 7 bayonet, disable, fortify, trenail 8 mackerel 9 frustrate, merganser 10 spadix-tine 13 inflorescence
spike hole: 5 spile
spike let: 4 chat, nail 7 spinule
spikenard: 4 nard 8 ointment
spile: pin, rod, tap 4 bung, heap, pile, plug, rule, tube 5 spill, spout, stake 6 spigot 8 forepole, splinter
spiler: 6 burler
spilikin: peg 7 pushpin 10 jackstraws

spill: die, mar, peg, pin, rod 4 disk, fail, fall, flow, kill, roll, ruin, shed, slip, slop 5 flosh, spile, spoil, spool, waste 6 injure, perish, punish, reveal, sheath, tumble, wasted 7 correct, destroy, divulge, scatter 8 chastise, downpour, gratuity, overflow, spillway, splinter, squander 11 deteriorate
spiloma: 5 nevus 9 birthmark
spin: 4 birl, burl, gyre, pirl, reel, turn 5 spurt, swirl, twirl, twist, whirl 6 gyrate, rotate 7 prolong, revolve 8 protract
spin a yarn: 7 narrate
spina: 4 wall 5 spine 8 backbone
spinach: 7 epinard, potherb
mountain: 5 orach, savoy 6 orache
spinal: 5 balas
column: 5 spine 8 backbone 9 vertebrae
cord: 4 alba 6 myelon
muscle: 5 psoas
spindle: pin, rod 4 axis, axle, hasp, stem 5 arbor, fusee, shaft, stalk, xeres 6 arbour, broach, fuseau, rachis 7 mandrel
spindling: 5 leggy 7 slender
spine: awn 4 back, turf 5 chine, ridge, sward, thorn 6 chaeta, needle, spirit 7 acantha, acicula, courage, prickle, spicule 8 backbone, spiculum 9 vertebrae
spine bone: 6 sacrum
spine-tingling: 4 eery 5 eerie 7 ghostly
spinel: gem 5 balas
spinet: 5 piano 7 giraffe 11 harpsichord
spinnaker: 4 sail
spinner: cap, top 5 spoon 6 spider, weaver 8 narrator 10 goatsucker
spinney: 5 copse, grove 7 thicket
spinning: 5 areel 6 rotary 8 whirling 9 revolving
device: 7 distaff
machine: 4 mule 5 jenny 8 throstle
rod: 7 distaff
spinning wheel: 6 charka 7 charkha
spinous: 5 spiny 7 spinose 9 acanthoid, spinelike
spinule: 8 backbone, spikelet
spiny: 6 picked, thorny 7 prickly 9 acanthoid, difficult
spiny-footed: 10 acanthopod 13 acanthopodous
spiracles: 4 hole 5 pores, vents 6 breath, spirit 8 blowhole, orifices 9 apertures
spiral: 4 coil, curl 5 curve, helix 7 coiling, curving, helical, winding 8 circling, helicoid 9 corkscrew 11 anfractuous
combining form: 5 helic, helix
spirate: 9 voiceless
spire: 4 coil, curl 5 blade, stalk, tower, twist, whorl 6 fleche, spiral, sprout 7 sapling, steeple
finial: epi 4 epis
ornament: 6 finial
spirit: hag, vim 4 aitu, alma, dash, dook, elan, fire, gimp, life, mood, soul, wind 5 angel, ardor, bugan, dhoul, ethos, fairy,

fling, ghost, haunt, metal, pluck, shade, spook, verve, vigor **6** ardour, asuang, breeze, elixir, energy, esprit, ginger, mettle, morale, pneuma, temper, yaksha (mas.), yakshi(fem.) **7** animate, bravery, courage, entrain, hearten, loyalty **8** folletto, phantasm, vivacity **9** animation, encourage **10** apparition, enterprise, enthusiasm **11** disposition, inspiration **12** cheerfulness, entrainement

animating: **6** animus

animation: pep **4** dash

avenging: Ate **6** alecto, erinys **7** megaera, nemesis **9** tisiphine

evil: Ate, imp, Ker **4** baka, beng, boko, drow, gyre **5** bugan, demon, devil **6** animus, asuang, daemon, daitya, dibbuk, Erynes, Lilith **9** cacodemon **10** cacodaemon

good: **5** genie, genus **7** eudemon **8** eudaemon

kinds of: Po; akh, imp, lar, nat **4** arac, gimp, Kuei, Kwei, soul **5** angel, Ariel, duffy, duppy, dusio, ethos, genie, jinni, manes, rakee, shade **6** animus, fulgja, jinnee, mammon, tangie, Undine **7** banshee

lose: **7** despond

spirit lamp: **4** etna

spirit-land: **9** fairyland

spirit-leaf: **8** manyroot

spirited: **4** fell, gamy **5** brisk, eager, fiery **6** active, audace, birkie, ginger, lively, spunky **7** animato, dashing **8** animated, desirous, frampoid, generous, vigorous **9** audacious, energetic, spiritoso, sprightly **10** mettlesome

spiritedness: **9** animation, animosity

spiritless: **4** cold, dead, meek **5** amort, blate, vapid **6** flashy **7** daviely, hilding **8** dejected, feckless, flagging, lifeless, listless, thewless **9** depressed, exanimate, heartless **10** dispirited

spiritlike: **8** ethereal

spiritous: **6** active, ardent **8** animated **9** vivacious

spirits: *dash of:* **5** lacer

dwelling place of: Po **5** Hades **7** Elysium

kinds of: **6** furies, uplift **7** elation, Sammael **9** firewater **13** aquacaelestis

lift: **5** elate **7** gladden

low: **5** blues, dumps, gloom **6** gloomy **8** doldrums

spirits and water: **4** grog

spirits of hartshorn: **7** ammonia

spiritual: **4** holy, pure, song **5** witty **6** clever, devout, divine, sacred **7** ghostly **8** churchly, internal, platonic, spirited **9** alcoholic, animastic, geistlich, unworldly **10** devotional, immaterial, spirituous **11** animastical, disembodied, incorporeal **14** ecclesiastical

apathy: **6** acedia

beings: **6** angels **7** seraphs

darkness: **4** Hell **5** tamas

spiritualistic meeting: **6** seance

spiritualize: **5** endow **6** purify, refine **7** animate **8** idealize **11** etherealize

spirituous: gay **4** airy, hard **5** vivid **6** active, ardent, lively **8** ethereal **9** alcoholic **10** immaterial **11** incorporeal

spiry: **4** tall **6** coiled, curled, spiral **7** slender **8** tapering, wreathed **10** serpentine

spit: dig, fix, rod **4** emit, hang, rain, reef, snow **5** eject, image, light, plant, reach, retch, shoal, spade, stick, sword, utter **6** broach, dagger, impale, saliva, skewer, sputum, thrust **7** spindle, spittle **8** broacher, likeness, sandbank, spadeful, sprinkle **9** brochette, secretion **11** counterpart, expectorate

spital: den **6** refuge, resort **7** shelter **8** hospital **9** lazaretto

spite: vex **4** hate, hurt, mood **5** annoy, depit, pique, shame, venom **6** enmity, grudge, hatred, injury, malice, mauger, maugre, rancor, thwart **7** chagrin, despite, dislike, ill-will, mortify **8** disgrace, dishonor **9** animosity, frustrate, humiliate **10** resentment **11** disposition, malevolence **12** spitefulness **13** mortification

spiteful: **4** mean **5** catty, snaky **6** sullen **7** waspish **8** annoying, venomous **9** malicious, malignant **10** dispiteous, irritating, vindictive **11** troublesome

spitfire: **9** brimstone

spitter: **4** deer **5** spade **7** brocket **8** spitball **12** expectorater

spitting: **6** saliva **10** exspuition

spittle: **4** spit **6** saliva

spittoon: **8** crachoir, cuspidor

spiv: **7** slacker

splash: lap **4** dash, daub, gout, lave, plop, pond, pool, spot **5** bathe, blash, plash, slart, slash, spray **6** blotch, dabble, flouse, floush, strike **7** display, scatter, spatter **8** splatter **9** dashingly **10** appearance, excitement **14** ostentatiously

splashboard: **4** gate, trap **5** board, plank **6** fender, screen **8** mudguard

splashy: wet **5** muddy, showy **6** blashy, slushy **8** striking **11** sensational, spectacular **12** ostentatious

splat: **4** open, plot, spot **5** patch **6** blotch **7** flatten

splatter: dab **4** dash, rush **6** hubbub, splash **7** cluster, spatter **9** splashing

splay: hem **4** awry, turn **5** adorn, bevel, carve, slant, slope **6** clumsy, expand, spread **7** awkward, display, sloping **8** ungainly **9** dislocate, expansion, obliquely, slopingly, spreading **10** slantingly **11** enlargement

spleen: fit **4** fire, milt, mood, whim **5** anger, ardor, freak, humor, mirth, organ, spite **6** malice, temper **7** caprice, dislike, impulse **8** laughter **9** lienculus, merriment **10** melancholy **11** impetuosity *pert. to:* **6** lienal

spleeny: 5 angry **7** fretful, peevish **9** irritable **10** melancholy

splendent: 6 glossy **7** beaming, shining **8** lustrous, splendid **9** brilliant **11** conspicuous, illustrious, magnificent, resplendent

splendid: gay **4** braw, fine, good, rial **5** grand, regal, showy, tinny **6** bright, candid, costly, superb **7** gallant, ripping, shining, sublime **8** glorious, gorgeous **9** brilliant, excellent, sumptuous **11** illustrious, magnificent, resplendent

splendor, splendour: 4 gite, pomp **5** blaze, eclat, gleam, glory, sheen **6** bright, fulgor, luster, parade **7** display, fulgour **8** elegance, grandeur, radiance, richness **9** pagaentry, showiness **10** brightness, brilliance, brilliancy, effulgence **12** gorgeousness, magnificence, resplendence **14** impressiveness

splenetic: 6 sullen **7** fretful, peevish, splenic **8** spiteful **9** depressed, irritable, malicious, spleenful **10** melancholy

spleuchan: 5 pouch

splice: 4 join **5** marry, unite **6** fasten **7** wedding **8** marriage **10** interweave

spliced: wed **6** joined, united **7** married

splint: 4 coal, lath, tace, scob **5** brace, plate, split, strip, tasse **6** fasten, shiver, tasset **7** confine **8** splinter

splinter: 4 chip, rend **5** break, broom, slice, smash, spale, split **6** fasten, shiver, sliver **7** confine, flinder, shatter **8** fragment

split: cut, rit **4** chap, rend, rent, rive, ruin, tear **5** break, burst, clave, cleft, crack, peach, reave, riven, share, wedge **6** betray, bisect, bottle, breach, broken, cleave, cloven, dilute, divide, rifted, schism, sliver, sunder **7** destroy, dispart, divided, fissure, portion, rupture, shatter **8** fragment, informer, separate, splinter **9** fractured, separated **10** separation

split pea: dal

splitfruit: 10 schizocarp

splitting: 5 funny **6** severe **7** comical, fission, rending **8** piercing

of mind: **13** schizophrenia

sploit: 5 spout **6** squirt

splore: 4 bout, brag, riot **5** boast, broil, revel **6** frolic **7** debauch, display **8** carousal, escapade **9** commotion, festivity, scrimmage **11** merrymaking

splotch: dab **4** blob, blot, dash, daub, spot **5** smear, stain **6** blotch, splash

splother: 6 splash **8** splutter

splurge: 6 effort **7** display **11** ostentation **13** demonstration

splutter: 4 fuff **5** hurry, noise, stuff **6** bustle, splash **7** dispute, glutter, quarrel, scatter, spatter, sputter, stammer **8** nonsense **9** confusion

spoil: mar, rob, rot **4** blad, boot, loot, pelf, prey, ruin, swag **5** bitch, blend, booty, carve, cheat, decay, harry, prize, seize, strip, taint, waste **6** coddle, damage, deface, divest, forage, impair, infuse, injure, pamper, perish, ravage **7** connach, corrump, corrupt, estrepe, deprive, despoil, destroy, indulge, pillage, plunder, violate, vitiate **8** confound, unclothe **10** chevisance, corruption, impairment

spoiled: bad **5** dazed, musty **6** addled, marred, molded, petted, preyed, rotted **7** botched, decayed, tainted **8** pampered, pillaged **9** plundered

spoiler: 6 robber **7** marplot **8** pillager **9** despoiler, plunderer **10** depredator

spoilsport: 10 wet-blanket

spoke: bar **4** clog, grip, rung, tale, talk **5** block, check, drone, round, spake, stake, stick **6** radius, speech **7** mention, uttered **8** handhold **10** impediment **11** enchantment

spoken: 4 oral, said **5** parol **7** uttered **9** declaimed

spoliate: rob **7** despoil, pillage, plunder

spoliation: 6 rapine **7** pillage, plunder, robbery **8** pillaged **13** despoiliation

spondulix: 5 funds, money

spondyl: 8 vertebra

sponge: bum, wet **4** form, swab, wipe **5** ascon, cadge, dough, erase, mooch **6** absorb, ascula, efface, rhagon **7** badiaga, cleanse, destroy, drinker, scrunge, zimocca **8** drunkard, parasite, scrounge

orifice: **6** oscula(pl.) **7** osculum

pen: **5** kraal

pert. to: **9** poriferal

spicule: **4** toxa

sponge tree: 8 huisache

sponger: 6 cadger **8** parasite

spongy: 4 fozy **5** rainy **6** porous, quaggy **9** absorbent

sponsor: 4 back **5** angel **6** backer, gossip, patron, surety **9** godfather, godmother, introduce

spontaneous: 4 free, wild **6** native **8** careless, untaught **9** automatic, impulsive **10** indigenous, self-acting **11** instinctive, involuntary

spontoon: 4 club, pike **7** halberd, pantoon **8** spantoon **9** espantoon, truncheon

spoof: guy **4** fool, hoax, joke **5** trick **7** deceive, swindle **8** nonsense **9** deception

spook: 5 ghost, haunt **6** spirit, wraith **7** specter **9** hobgoblin **10** apparition

spooky: 4 eery **5** eerie, weird **7** ghostly, haunted, uncanny **8** spectral

spool: 4 reel, wind **6** bobbin, broach **7** spindle **8** cylinder

spoon: 4 chip, neck **5** ladle, labis, lover, ninny **6** nestle, shovel, spoony **7** student **8** cochlear, simpleton

spoon-shaped: 8 cochlear

spoonbill: 5 ajaja **10** paddlefish

spoondrift: 5 spray **9** spindrift

spoor: 5 piste, scent, trace, track, trail
spore: 4 germ, seed
spore sac: 5 ascus
sport (see also **game** *official*): bet, fun, gig, toy 4 game, gaud, glee, jest, joke, mock, play, polo, romp 5 dally, freak, mirth, wager 6 frolic, gamble, racing, shikar 7 contest, gambler, jesting, mockery, pastime 8 derision, raillery 9 amusement, diversion, plaything 10 pleasantry, recreation 13 entertainment
summer: 6 diving, hiking, quoits, rowing, skiing 7 fishing, sailing 8 swimming
winter: 6 hockey, skiing 7 skating 8 sledding 11 tobogganing
sportive: gay 5 merry 6 frisky, lusory, wanton 7 amorous, festive, jocular, playful 8 frolicky, gamesome, playsome, pleasant 9 lecherous 10 frolicsome
sportiveness: 7 knavery
sports-minded: 8 athletic
sports official: 5 coach, judge 6 umpire 7 referee 8 linesman 10 timekeeper
sportsman: 6 hunter 7 shikari 8 shikaree
sportula: 4 gift 7 largess, present
sporty: 4 loud 5 showy 6 flashy
spot: bit, dab, dot 4 blot, blur, fish, flaw, mark, site 5 blaze, fault, fleck, nevus, patch, place, point, ready, speck, stain, sully, tache, taint 6 blotch, defect, detect, locate, macula, macule, naevus, remove 7 asperse, blemish, freckle, splotch 8 discolor, disgrace, handicap, locality, location, maculate, position, quantity, reproach 9 bespatter, recognize
kinds of: ace, dot, pip, tee 4 blet, fret, gall, rone, spil, wems 5 macle, oasis 6 alcove, bethel, mascle, mottle, mouche 7 freckle 8 bethesda, fenestra, fontanel
spotless: 5 clean, snowy 9 blameless, unspotted, unsullied 10 immaculate 11 unblemished, untarnished 14 irreproachable
spotlight: arc 4 beam
spotted: 6 bauson, calico, espied, marked, notate, sanded, ticked 7 bracket, dappled, guttate, mottled, noticed, stained, sullied 9 blemished, suspected, tarnished
spotter: 7 watcher 9 detective
spotty: 5 dotty 6 uneven 9 irregular
spousal: 7 wedlock 8 ceremony, marriage, nuptials
spouse: wed 4 give, join, mate, wife 5 annar, bride, marry, unite 6 fiance 7 consort, espouse, fiancee, husband, partner, promise, wedlock 8 affiance, espousal, marriage 9 companion 10 bridegroom
spout: jet, jut, lip 4 dale, flow, geat, gush, lift, pawn, pipe, rant 5 eject, issue, orate, shoot, speak, spile, spurt, utter 6 pledge, recite, spigot, spring, squirt, stream, trough 7 conduit, declaim 8 downpour,

gargoyle, pawnship 9 discharge, waterfall 10 waterspout
sprack: 4 deft 5 alert 6 active, lively, nimble, shrewd
sprag: 4 prop 6 billet
sprain: 5 chink 6 weaken 10 overstrain
sprang: 5 arose, spray 6 branch
sprangle: 5 spray 6 sprawl, spread 8 straggle, struggle
sprat: 5 bleak 6 garvie 7 herring 8 sixpence
sprattle: 6 sprawl 8 scramble, struggle
sprauchie: 6 sprawl 7 clamber 8 scramble
sprawl: 4 loll 7 grabble 8 struggle 9 sprauchie
spray: jet 4 chap, twig 5 bough, shoot, spree, sprig, water 6 boquet, branch, sparge, spread 7 atomize, bouquet, scatter 8 sprinkle 9 aspersion, discharge, spindrift
spread: fan, jam, ted 4 emit, meal, span, taft 5 cover, flare, jelly, reach, smear, splay, strew, widen 6 anoint, dilate, expand, extend, extent, ramify, unfold, unfurl 7 broaden, compass, diffuse, distend, diverge, divulge, enlarge, exhibit, expanse, overlay, overrun, prolong, protect, publish, radiate, scatter, slather, stretch 8 diffused, dispense, disperse, expanded, extended, increase, multiply, permeate, straddle 9 broadcast, circulate, dispersed, displayed, expansion, expatiate, propagate 10 distribute, generalize 11 disseminate
abroad: 5 bruit, noise, libel, rumor 6 delate, rumour, spring 7 delated, radiate 9 broadcast, publicize 11 disseminate
out: fan, lap, ted 4 bray, open, span 5 flare, widen 6 deploy, flange, sprawl, unfold
spreader: 6 tedder
spreading of light: 8 halation
spree: bat, jag 4 bout, bust, gell, lark, orgy, romp, toot, jagg 5 beano, binge, booze, revel 6 bender, buster, bust-up, frolic, high-go, shindy 7 carouse, debauch, wassail 8 carousal 10 indulgence
sprig: 4 brad, nail, trim, twig 5 bough, scion, shoot, smart, spray, youth 6 active, branch, spruce 7 tendril 9 stripling
sprightliness: 6 gaiety, gayety 8 airiness, alacrity, buoyancy 9 animation
sprightly: gay, tid 4 airy, pert 5 agile, alive, brisk, canty, crank, desto, elfin, peart 6 active, blithe, lively 7 briskly, buoyant, chipper, ghostly, quickly 8 animated, vigorous 10 enlivening, spiritedly, spiritlike 11 incorporeal
spring: ain, fly, hop, spa 4 bend, dart, font, head, jump, leap, lilt, rise, warp, well 5 arise, atart, bound, flirt, glent, issue, lymph, shoot, spurt, therm, tower, vault 6

accrue, bounce, emerge, therme, venero
7 diffuse, estuary, thermae 8 fountain 10
intoxicate
abruptly: 4 bolt
back: 6 recoil, resile 7 rebound
deposit: 5 trona
hot: 7 balneum, thermae, gipsies
kind of: ain, cee, spa, ver, hop, ojo 4 font 5
lymph 6 geyser, charco, source, saline 7
gambado 9 Castalian
pert. to: 6 vernal
up: 5 arise
spring-like: 6 vernal
springboard: 5 wagon 6 batule
springbok: 7 gazelle
springe: gin, set 4 trap 5 agile, catch,
noose, snare 6 supple 7 ensnare
springer: 7 grampus, spaniel 9 springbok
springing back: 7 elastic 9 renascent
springtime: May 8 germinal
springy: wet 6 spongy 7 elastic 8 flexible
9 resilient
sprinkle: deg, dot, wet 4 dart, rain, spot 5
color, flour, spray, strew, twist, water 6
affuse, bedrop, dabble, dredge, sparge 7
asperge, asperse, drizzle, scatter, spairge,
sparkle, spatter 8 disperse 9 bespangle,
bespatter 10 besprinkle, intoxicate
with flour: 6 dredge
with grains of mustard: 8 sinapize
with grit: 4 sand
with moisture: 5 bedew
with mud: 9 bespatter
with powder: 4 dust
with water: deg
sprinkler: 7 dredger 11 aspergillum
sprinkling: 4 seme 9 aspersion
sprint: run 4 dash, race 5 snare 6 bicker 7
springe
sprinter: 5 racer 6 runner 7 athlete
sprit: bud 4 dart, pole, rush, spar 5 shoot,
speck, sprat 6 sprint, sprout 8 bowsprit 9
germinate
sprite: elf, fay, hob, imp 4 elve, life, mind,
mood, peri, soul 5 Ariel, bucca, fairy, genie, ghost, gnome, nisse, pixie, shade, vital 6 goblin, person, spirit 7 essence 9
germinate, hobgoblin 10 apparition,
woodpecker 11 disposition, inspiration
kind of: nix 5 ariel, demon, Holda, naiad,
nixie 6 Kelpie 8 coltpixy 9 coltpixie 10
leprechaun, shoopiltie
sproil: 6 active, energy 7 agility 8 activity
9 energetic
sprout: bud, son, eye 4 cion, brod, chit,
chun, germ, malt 5 brode, chine, shoot,
spire, spout, sprig, spurt, achar 6 braird,
expand, germen, growth, ratoon 7 burgeon 8 offshoot 9 germinate
spruce: gim 4 deft, neat, posh, smug, trig,
trim 5 compt, fussy, natty, Picea, smart,
sprig 6 dapper, picked 7 dandify, finical,
smarten 8 overnice, titivate

sprue: 4 hole 5 dross 7 opening 8 psilosis
9 asparagus
sprunt: 4 hill, leap 5 brisk, steep 6 active,
spring, spruce 8 struggle
spry: 5 agile, brisk, quick, smart 6 active,
clever, nimble, spruce 7 knowing 8 vigorous 9 sprightly
spud: dig, man 4 hand 5 child, dough, drill,
knife, money, spade 6 dagger, paddle,
potato, reamer, remove, shovel 10 projection
spume: 4 foam, scum 5 froth
spumescent: 7 foaming 8 frothing
spumy: 5 foamy 6 frothy 7 spumous
spun: See **spin**.
spunk, sponk: 4 punk 5 anger, flame,
gleam, match, nerve, pluck, spark 6 kindle, mettle, spirit, sponge, tinder 7 courage, passion 9 touchwood
spunky: 4 game 5 quick 6 plucky, touchy
8 spirited 9 irritable 10 courageous,
mettlesome
spur: egg 4 calk, gaff, goad, move, prod,
prop, urge 5 arete, brace, drive, hurry,
impel, press, prick, range, ridge, rowel,
spine, spoor, strut, tower 6 arouse,
broach, calcar, digger, excite, foment,
griffe, hasten, incite, motive 7 gablock,
provoke, publish 8 buttress, stimulus 9
incentive, instigate, stimulate 10 blockhouse 11 publication
spur wheel: 5 rowel
spurge: 4 weed 5 purge 6 purify 8 milkweed 9 euphorbia
spurious: 4 fake 5 bogus, false, phony,
snide 6 forced 7 bastard 10 adulterate,
apocryphal, artificial, fictitious, fraudulent
11 counterfeit, superficial 12 illegitimate
14 supposititious
spurl: 6 sprawl 8 scramble
spurn: hit 4 blow, dash, kick, rush, spur 5
haste, scorn 6 affray, incite, pillar, rebuff,
refuse, reject, scrape, strike 7 contemn,
decline, despise, disdain, scratch, stumble 10 engagement
spurt: bud, jet, jut 4 dart, gush 5 expel,
shoot, spell, spout 6 sprout, squirt 8 increase, outbreak
sputter: ado 4 fuss, spit
spy: see 4 case, espy, keek, note, tout 5
scout, sneak, snoop, watch 6 behold,
descry, detect, espial, gaycat, mouton,
search 7 discern, examine, hi-carra, inspect, observe, snooper 8 discover, emissary, hi-carrah, informer, perceive 10
discoverer, scrutinize 13 intelligencer
spying: 9 espionage 16 counter-espionage
Spyri's heroine: 5 Heidi
squab: coy, fat, shy 4 drop, fall, flop, slop,
sofa 5 couch, crush, piper, plump, short,
thick 6 callow, pigeon, squash 7 cushion,
ottoman 8 nestling 9 fledgling, unfledged,
upholster

squabble: 5 brawl 6 bicker, jangle 7 bobbery, contend, dispute, quarrel, wrangle
13 collie-shangie
squabbling: 8 bangling
squadron: 6 armada 10 escadrille
squalid: 4 foul, mean, poor 5 dirty, nasty
6 filthy, sordid 7 unclean 8 wretched 9
miserable, repellant, repellent, repulsive
squall: cry, pet 4 dear, drow, gush, gust,
wawl 5 storm 6 flurry, scream, shower,
squawk, wretch 7 borasca, borasco, dispute, trouble 8 borasque 9 windstorm 11
disturbance
squalor: mud 4 dirt, mire 5 filth 9 roughness 10 filthiness 11 squalidness 12
wretchedness
squander: 4 burn, lash 5 spend, waste 6
befool, lavish, wander 7 consume, debauch, dispend, scatter 8 disperse, embezzle, misspend 9 dissipate
squanderer: 5 loser 7 wastrel
square: 4 even, parc, park, rule, true 5
agora, carre, clear, exact, hunky, plaza 6
dinkum, direct, honest, settle 7 commons,
pattern, quarrel, upright 8 justness, quadrate, standard 9 carre-four, criterion,
principle 11 unequivocal 13 parallelogram 15 straightforward
public: 5 plaza 6 common
squarehead: 4 dolt 5 Swede 6 German 8
numskull 9 screwball 12 Scandinavian
squares: 5 panes
squaring tool: 5 edger
squarish: 4 boxy
squark: 5 croak 6 squawk
squash: 4 beat, fall, ooze, pepo, stop 5
crush, press, quash 7 cymling, flatten,
pumpkin, squeeze, squelch 8 suppress 9
discomfit 10 disconcert
kind of: 6 banana, cushaw, simnel, summer, turban 7 cymling, Hubbard, Italian
8 cymbling, patty pan, zucchini 9 crook-
neck
squashy: wet 4 soft 5 boggy, muddy,
mushy 8 overripe
squat: sit 4 fall, sink, stub 5 cower, crush,
dumpy, pinch, pudgy, quash, quiet, stoop
6 bruise, crouch, fodgel, hurkle, settle,
splash, stubby 7 descend, silence,
squatty, squeeze 8 thickset
squatter: 4 flap 5 squat 6 crouch, nester,
plunge 7 confuse, flutter, nestler, scatter,
settler 8 bewilder, squander 9 sandpiper
Squatter State: 6 Kansas
squatting: 8 couchant
squatty: 5 dumpy, squat 8 thickset
squaw: 6 mahala, coween 10 klootchman
husband: 4 buck 6 sannup
squawfish: 4 chub 8 chappaul
squeak: cry, wee 4 peep 5 cheep, creak,
noise, speak 6 betray, escape, shrill 7
confess, disturb
squeal: yip 4 blab, sing 5 broil, frail, weary

6 betray, inform 7 dispute, protest, quarrel 8 complain
squealer: 4 duck, fink 5 quail, swift 6
grouse, pigeon, plover 7 traitor 8 informer
9 partridge
squeamish: shy 4 helo, nice, stir 5 dizzy,
heloe 6 bustle, dainty, dauncy, modest,
queasy 7 finical, prudish 8 overnice,
qualmish 9 dizziness, giddiness, reluctant, sensitive 10 fastidious, scrupulous
13 oversensitive
squeeze: eke, hug, jam 4 gain, mull, neck,
silk 5 chirt, creem, crowd, crush, force,
pinch, press, wring 6 corner, escape, extort, scrump, scruze, thrust, twitch 7 extract, oppress, procure, scrunch, scrunge
8 compress, condense, pressing, pressure, scrounge 9 constrict, influence 10
commission, constraint 11 compression
squeezer: 5 drier, noose 6 juicer, reamer
7 wringer 8 squeegee 9 extractor
squeezy: 7 cramped 8 confined
squelch: 4 blow, fall 5 crush, quash,
quell, stamp 6 rebuke, subdue 7 silence,
washrag 8 suppress 9 discomfit 10 disconcert
squelcher: 8 blizzard
squib: jet 4 ball, bomb, mote, pipe, skit,
tube 5 candy, match, throw, write 6
speech, squirt, writer 7 dispute, explode,
lampoon, pasquil, publish, torpedo, writing 9 bespatter 10 pasquinade 11
firecracker
squid: 6 loligo
pen: 5 quill
squiffer: 10 concertina
squiggle: 4 curl, line 5 shake, twist 6
squirm 7 wriggle 8 curlicue
squiggly: 4 wavy 8 twisting 9 wriggling
squinch: 4 arch 5 twist 6 lintel, quince,
squint, wrench 7 squeeze, squench 9
corbeling
squint: 4 bent, cast, glee, gleg, gley, skew
5 glent, trend 6 gledge, goggle 7 deviate
10 hagioscope, strabismus
squint-eyed: 5 gleed, gleyd
squire: 5 lover, title 6 donzel, escort 7
gallant 8 henchman, servitor 9 accompany, attendant, gentleman, landowner
squirrel: bun 5 sisel, xerus 6 chippy, gyrate 7 assapan 8 archilla, jelerang 9 assapanic, chickaree, shadetail
genus of: 7 sciurus
like: 8 sciuroid
nest: 4 dray, drey
shrew: 4 tana
skin: 4 vair
squirt: 5 chirt, skite, slirt, spout, spurt 14
whippersnapper
sri: 4 holy 7 Lakshmi 8 glorious, reverend
9 fortunate
stab: dag, jab, jag, try 4 gore, jagg, pink,
yerk 5 chive, drive, knife, knive, lunge,

prick, sound, stake, stick, stool, stump, wound **6** broach, dagger, pierce, strike, stroke, thrust **7** attempt, poniard, roughen **8** puncture **9** penetrate

stability: **5** poise **7** balance **8** firmance, firmness **9** constancy, fixedness **10** permanence, stableness, steadiness **12** immovability, immutability **13** steadfastness **15** indissolubility

stabilize: fix, set **5** poise **6** steady **8** regulate

stabilizer: **7** ballast

stable: **4** barn, fast, firm, shed, sure **5** fixed, set-up, solid, sound, stall **6** hangar, secure, steady, strong, sturdy **7** durable, equerry, lasting **8** constant, enduring, immobile **9** confirmed, establish, permanent, resistant, steadfast, unabashed, unvarying **10** stationary, unwavering **11** established, trustworthy **12** unchangeable
range: **4** mews
royal: **4** mews

stack: set **4** bike, heap, pile, rick, pike, stow, tier **5** group, hovel, mound, scroo, shock **7** chimney, conduit **9** fireplace

stack up: **4** tier **5** total

stackyard: **7** haggard **10** stackgarth

stad: **4** town **7** village

staddle: row **4** cane, tree **5** staff, stain, swath **6** crutch **7** sapling, support

stade: **7** furlong, stadium

stadium: **4** oval **5** arena, stade, stage **7** furlong **8** coliseum

staff: bar, gad, rod **4** cane, club, line, mace, maul, pole, prop, rung, wand **5** aides, baton, crook, lance, pedum, perch, spear, stave, stick, suite **6** baston, cudgel, stanza **7** attache, bailiff, caducei(pl.), scepter, sceptre, support **8** caduceus **9** constable, entourage, personnel **10** assistants, associates **12** quarter-staff
kinds of: **4** kent, wand **5** filch **6** croche, muleta **7** baculus, bourdon, cambuca, crosier, crozier, distaff, rhabdos **10** alpenstock
officers: **5** aides, cadre

stag: **4** colt, hart **7** pollard, shorten **8** informer
horn: **4** rial **9** bezantler

stage: era **4** dais, gest, step, tier **5** board, coach, floor, grade, level, phase, shelf, stair, story **6** degree, stadia **7** display, exhibit, produce, rostrum, stadium, theater **8** platform, scaffold **9** condition, gradation **10** proscenium, stagecoach **11** subdivision
extra: **4** supe **5** super
hanging: **7** scenery
on: **7** en scene
part: **4** role
pert. to: **6** scenic

stage direction: all **4** exit, sola **5** aside, enter, manet, omnes, solus **6** exeunt, sennet **8** loquitur

stagecoach: **9** diligence

stager: **5** actor **6** player

stagger: **4** reel, rock, stun, sway **5** lurch, shake, waver **6** hobble, totter, wintle(Sc.) **7** tremble, vibrate **8** hesitate, titubate, unsettle

stagnant: **4** dull, foul **5** inert, stale, still **8** sluggish, standing **10** motionless **13** unprogressive

stagnate : **4** dull **5** inert **10** motionless

stagnation: **6** stasis, stases, torpor

stagy: **8** affected **10** theatrical

staid: set **5** fixed, grave, sober **6** demure, sedate, steady **7** earnest, serious, settled **8** decorous **9** dignified, steadfast **10** cool-headed

stain: dye **4** blot, blur, soil, spot, tint **5** cloud, paint, smear, sully, tache, taint, tinge, trace **6** blotch, infamy, macula, smirch, smudge, stigma, vilify **7** blemish, corrupt, tarnish **8** discolor, disgrace, dishonor, maculate, tincture **9** bespatter, pollution **10** attainture **11** contaminate

stainless: **4** pure

stair: **4** step **5** stage, stile **6** degree
series of: **6** flight

staircase: **5** grece, grice **6** griece
moving: **9** escalator
on ship: **12** companionway
outdoor: **6** perron
part of: **4** rung **5** newel, riser, tread
portable: **6** ladder
spiral: **8** caracole

stake: bet, peg, pin, pot, set **4** ante, back, gage, pale, pile, pale, pole, pool, post, risk, spit, stob **5** anvil, prize, spile, stick, teest, wager **6** chance, gamble, hazard, picket **7** venture **9** grubstake
pert. to: **5** palar

stale: old **4** flat, hoar, lure, rung, worn **5** banal, blown, corny, decoy, frowy, moldy, musty, shaft, trite, vapid, waugh(Sc.) **7** insipid **9** hackneyed, tasteless **10** flavorless, prostitute **11** commonplace **13** uninteresting

stalemate: **4** draw **7** impasse **8** deadlock **10** standstill

stalk: bun **4** axis, halm, hunt, mote, risp, seta, stem **5** haulm, spear, stipe, straw **6** pursue, ratoon, stride **7** pedicel, petiole **8** peduncle
having: **9** petiolate
remove: **5** strig

stalker: **6** hunter

stalkless: **7** sessile

stall: bin, cot, pew **4** crib, loge, mire, seat, stop **5** boose, boosy, booth, check, crame, decoy, delay, stand **6** manger, stable **7** pretext, station **8** hesitate **9** enclosure **10** dilly-dally **11** compartment, confederate

stallion: **6** cooser(Sc.)

stalwart: **4** firm **5** brave, stout **6** brawny,

robust, strong, sturdy **7** valiant **8** partisan, resolute **10** unyielding
stamina: gut **4** grit **5** vigor **7** essence **8**
backbone, capacity, strength **9** endur-
ance, fortitude
stammer: **4** hack, stut **6** falter, hacker **7**
fribble, stumble, stutter **8** hesitate
stamp: die **4** beat, coin, form, kind, mark,
seal, tool, type **5** brand, class, crush,
drive, pound, press, print, stomp **6** signet,
strike, thresh **7** impress, imprint, postage,
sticker **8** inscribe **9** character **10**
impression **11** distinguish
collecting: **9** philately
fencing: **5** appel
madness for: **11** timbromania
paper: **6** pelure
space: **8** spandrel
stampede: **4** bolt, rout, rush **5** panic **6**
flight **7** debacle
stamping plate: die
stance: **4** pose **7** posture, station **8** position
stanch, staunch: **4** firm, stem, stop, true
5 allay, check, close, loyal, quell, sound **6**
hearty, quench, steady, strong, trusty **7**
zealous **8** constant, faithful, resolute **9**
steadfast **10** extinguish, unswerving, unwavering, watertight **11** substantial,
trustworthy
stanchion: bar **4** beam, post, prop **5** brace,
piton **7** confine, support, upright
stand: set **4** bear, dais, ease, halt, hold,
last, rack, stop **5** abide, arise, booth,
cease, erect, pause, table **6** afford, endure, podium, remain, resist, tripod, trivet
7 etagere, station, sustain, support, taboret, undergo **8** attitude, continue, hesitate, maintain, position, tabouret, tolerate
9 withstand
candles: **7** epergne **10** candelabra
for : **9** represent
on end: **5** upend
opposite: **4** face
ornamental: **7** atagere, etagere
still: ho **4** stop, whoa
stand-in: **10** substitute
standard: cup, par, set **4** fiar(Sc.), flag,
mark, norm, suit, type, unit **5** canon,
chest, grade, gauge, ideal, level, model **6**
assize, banner, beacon, coffer, ensign,
goblet, normal, sample, signal **7** classic,
example, labarum(L.), pattern, support,
upright **8** accepted, brattach(Sc.), gonfalon, orthodox, vexillum **9** criterion, oriflamme, yardstick **10** touchstone **11**
candlestick
bearer: **11** gonfalonier
golf: **5** bogey, bogie
of measurement: **6** metric
Turkish: **4** alem, toug
standardize: **9** calibrate
standing: **4** rank **5** being, erect, fixed **6**
estate, stable, stance, status **7** lasting,

settled, statant, station, upright **8** constant, duration, location, position, stagnant **9** permanent, situation **10** reputation, stationary
upright: **11** orthostatic
standing room only: S.R.O.
standstill: **4** halt, rest, stop **5** stand, state
8 deadlock **9** cessation, stalemate
stang: bar **4** ache, pang, pole **5** sting, throb
stanhope: **5** buggy
stank: **4** pond, pool **5** ditch
stanza: **5** envoi, stave, verse **7** strophe **8**
division **9** apartment
eight line: **6** huitan, octave **7** triolet
five line: **8** cinquain
four line: **8** quatrain
irregular: **13** alloeostropha
six line: **6** sestet
ten line: **6** dizain **7** dizaine
three line: **8** tristich
staple: **4** city, town **5** chief, fiber, shaft **7**
chaplet, support **8** fastener **9** principal
10 foundation
star (see also **constellation**): ace, orb,
sun **4** hero, lead **5** actor, badge, shine **6**
etoile **7** actress, estoile, heroine, ingenue,
stellar **8** asterisk, luminary, pentacle,
twinkler **9** bespangle, headliner, principal
10 preeminent, topnotcher
apple: **7** caimito
combining form: **5** astro **6** sidero
difference in direction: **7** paralax
divination: **9** astrology
evening: **5** Venus **6** Hesper, Vesper **7**
Evestar **8** Hesperus
evil: **7** sideral
exploding: **4** nova
group: **6** galaxy **13** constellation
in Aquila: **6** Altair
in Bootes: **8** Arcturus
in Canis Major: **6** Sirius
in Carina: **7** Canopus
in Cetus: **4** Mira
in Cynus: **5** Deneb **7** Albireo
in Draco: **6** Alsafi **7** Al Rakis, Eltanin
in Gemini: **5** Wasat **6** Alhena, Castor,
Pollux
in Leo: **7** Regulus
in Lyra: **4** Vega
in Orion: **5** Rigel, Saiph
in Perseus: **5** Algol
in Scorpius: **7** Antares
in Taurus: **8** Pleiades
in Ursa Major: **5** Alcor, Mizar **6** Alkaid
in Ursa Minor: **7** Polaris
in Virgo: **5** Spica
morning: **4** Mars **5** Venus **6** Saturn **7**
Daystar, Jupiter, Mercury
north: **7** polaris **8** loadstar, lodestar, polestar
pert to: **6** astral **7** astrean, stellar **8** sidereal, stellate
representation: **6** etoile
resembling: **8** stellate **9** stellated

shooting: 5 comet 6 Leonid, meteor
two: 9 bistellar
worshiper: 7 sabaist
star cluster: 6 nebula
star facet: 4 pane
star-like: 8 stellate
starch: vim 4 arum, sago 5 tikor, vigor 6 amylum, energy, farina, strong 7 cassava, precise, stiffen 8 activity, glycogen, strength 9 arrowroot, formality, stiffness 12 carbohydrate
combining form: 4 amyl
starchy: 5 rigid, stiff 6 formal 7 precise 9 unbending
stare: 4 gape, gaup, gawk, gawp, gaze, gouk, gowk, gype, look, ogle, peer 5 glare, glaze, glore 6 glower, goggle 7 bristle 8 starling
stargazer: 4 fish 10 astrologer, astronomer
staring: 6 astare, gazing 7 glaring 8 wide-eyed
stark: 4 bare, firm, hard, pure 5 bleak, harsh, quite, rigid, rough, sheer, stern, stiff, tense, utter 6 barren, severe, strong, wholly 7 violent 8 absolute, complete, desolate, entirely, obdurate, powerful, stalwart, stripped, vigorous 9 downright, unadorned 10 absolutely, unyielding 11 intractable
starling: 6 pastor
starry: 6 astral, bright 7 shining, stellar 8 sidereal, starlike, stellate 9 sparkling
Star-Spangled Banner author: 15 Francis Scott Key
start: fit, run, shy 4 dart, head, jerk, jump, lead, rush 5 alarm, begin, dodge, enter, flush, glent, lever, onset, rouse, sally, shock, wince 6 boggle, broach, flinch, fright, loosen, outset, spring, twitch 7 disturb, get away, impulse, provoke, retreat, startle 8 commence, displace, handicap, outburst 9 advantage, dislocate, introduce, originate
starter: 5 drill, punch 7 entrant 8 official 10 controller
startle: 5 alarm, rouse, scare, shock, start 6 excite 8 affright, frighten, surprise 9 electrify
startling: 7 rousing 8 alarming, restless, skittish 10 surprising
starvation: 6 famine
starve: 4 fast 6 famish, hunger
starveling: 4 lean 6 hungry, pining, wasted
starwort: 5 aster 9 chickweed, colicroot
stash: end 4 stop 5 store
stashie: 6 clamor
state: say 4 acme, aver, etat(F.), mode, pomp, rank, seat, tell, term, weal 5 chair, posit, style, utter 6 affirm, allege, assert, avouch, degree, empire, estate, height, nation, polity, recite, relate, report, status, throne 7 account, country, declare, dignity, enounce, express, narrate 8 cere-

mony, eminence, grandeur, position, property, propound, standing 9 community, condition, enunciate, pronounce, situation, territory 10 asseverate, possession 11 stateliness 12 circumstance, commonwealth
based on honor: 9 timocracy
bound by treaty: 4 ally
explicitly: 6 define 7 itemize, specify 13 particularize
ideal: 6 Utopia
member: 7 citizen
office of: 11 secretariat
pert. to: 7 federal
relating to: 6 statal
under foreign control: 12 protectorate
state police: 7 trooper
stated: 5 fixed 6 avowed 7 regular 8 declared 10 formulated 11 established
statehouse: 7 capitol
stately: 5 grand, lofty 6 august, formal, superb 7 courtly, gallant, haughty 8 imperial, imposing, majestic 9 dignified 10 deliberate 11 ceremonious, magisterial, magnificent
statement: 4 bill, word 5 audit, dicta 6 dictum, precis, remark, report, resume 7 account, address, article, bromide, epitome, invoice, recital, summary 8 abstract, averment(law), relation, sentence, schedule 9 affidavit, agreement, manifesto, narrative 10 allegation, deposition, expression 11 abridgement, affirmation, assertation, certificate, declaration 12 presentation 13 prevarication 14 circumspection
assumed true: 7 premise
defamatory: 5 libel
introductory: 5 proem 6 prolog 7 preface, prelude 8 foreword, prologue
mathematical: 7 theorem
of belief: 5 credo, creed
self-contradictory: 7 paradox
self-evident: 6 truism
statesman: 7 statist 10 politician
static: 7 resting 8 inactive 9 quiescent 10 stationary
station: fix, run, set 4 camp, halt, post, rank, seat, spot, stop 5 berth, depot, field, place, serai, siege 6 assign, church, degree, region, stance 7 appoint, calling, cuartel(Sp.), dignity, habitat, posture 8 attitude, location, position 9 condition, homestead, situation 10 constitute 11 equilibrium, institution
stationary: set 4 fast 5 fixed 6 stable, static 8 immobile, moveless 9 immovable, sedentary 10 unchanging
stationer: 9 publisher 10 bookseller
stationery: ink, pen 4 book 5 blank, paper 6 pencil 10 papeteries
statist: 9 statesman 10 politician
statistics collector: 7 statist 12 statistician

statue: 4 bust, icon, ikon, nude 5 image, orant ,6 bronze 7 Madonna 8 Colossus, figurine, likeness, monument
at Thebes: 6 Memnon
base: 6 plinth
in London Guildhall: Gog 5 Magog
that came to life: 7 Galatea
upper part of: 4 bust 5 torso
statuesque: 7 stately 8 graceful
statuette: 8 figurine
stature: 6 height
status: 4 rank 5 state 6 aspect, classe(F.) 8 position, relation, standing 9 condition
statute: act, law 4 rule 5 edict 6 assize, decree 9 enactment, ordinance 10 regulation
heading of: 5 title
volume of: 4 code 5 codex 7 codices
staunch: See **stanch.**
stave: bar 4 beat, rung, slat, stap(Sc.) 5 break, knock, lathi, staff, stick 6 baculi(pl.), cudgel 7 baculus 8 puncture
bundle of: 5 shook
staver: 6 totter 7 saunter
stay: dam, guy, lie, rib 4 bide, calm, halt, hold, live, prop, rely, rest, rope, stem, stop, tack, wait 5 abide, allay, avast, await, brace, cable, cease, check, delay, demur, dwell, pause, quell, stand, stare, tarry 6 arrest, depend, detain, endure, fasten, linger, pacify, remain, reside, resist, secure, shroud, status 7 appease, control, incline, refrain, satisfy, sojourn, support, sustain, triatic 8 continue, restrain 9 anchorage, cessation, hindrance, residence 10 impediment, permanence 12 postponement
stead: 4 farm, help, lieu, site, spot 5 avail, beset, place, trace, track 6 assist, behalf 7 benefit, bestead, impress, involve, replace, service, support 8 bedstead, locality, position 9 advantage, farmstead, situation, successor 10 substitute
steadfast, stedfast: 4 fast, firm, true 5 fixed, staid 6 stable, stanch, steady 7 certain, settled, staunch 8 constant, faithful, resolute 9 immovable 10 unchanging, unswerving 11 established, unalterable
steadiness: 5 nerve 7 balance 8 firmness 9 constancy
steading: 9 farmhouse, homestead
steady: 4 calm, even, firm 5 fixed, grave, sober, staid 6 direct, stable, sturdy 7 assured, equable, regular, uniform 8 constant, diligent, faithful, reliable, resolute 9 incessant, steadfast 10 continuous, controlled, invariable, sweetheart, unswerving 11 unfaltering, unmitigated 13 unfluctuating, uninterrupted
steak: 4 club 5 chuck, flank, round, shell, t-bone 7 griskin, New York, sirloin 9 entrecote 11 porterhouse
steal: bag, cly, cop, gyp, nim, rap 4 crib,

gain, glom, hook, lift, stem, take 5 bribe, creep, fetch, filch, harry, pinch, poach, shaft, stalk, swipe 6 abduct, burgle, convey, divert, extend, handle, kidnap, pilfer, pirate, rustle, snitch 7 purloin 8 embezzle, peculate 9 condiddle 10 plagiarize 11 appropriate 14 misappropriate
stealage: 5 theft 7 larceny 8 burglary
stealer: 5 thief 6 robber 7 burglar 10 plagiarist 11 biblioklept
cattle: 7 abactor, rustler
stealthy: sly 6 artful, secret 7 catlike, cunning, furtive 11 clandestine 13 surreptitious
walk: 5 stalk
steam: 4 boil, fume, reek 5 force, power, smoke, vapor 6 energy 8 vaporize, vexation 10 exhalation, irritation
jet: 8 soffione, soffioni
pipe: 5 riser
steamer: 4 boat, ship 5 liner 6 vessel 9 steamship
cabin: 5 texas
steaming: 5 aboil
steamship: 5 liner 7 steamer
route: 4 lane
stearic acid: 8 stearate
steatite: 4 talc 9 soapstone
stech: 4 cram 5 gorge 10 gormandize
steed: 4 Arab 5 horse 7 charger, courser
steek: 4 shut 5 close 6 fasten, stitch
steel: 4 rail 5 acier(F.), inure, press 6 damask, harden, smooth, toledo 8 Bessemer, Damascus 10 strengthen
process: 8 Bessemer 11 cementation
steelhead: 5 trout
steely: 10 unyielding
steelyard: 7 balance
steep: ret 4 bate, bath, bold, bowk, brew, buck, high, soak, stew, tall 5 bathe, brant, brent, heavy, hilly, imbue, lofty, proud, sharp, sheer 6 abrupt, bright, clifty, decoct, drench, imbibe, imbrue, infuse, seethe 7 arduous, extract, extreme, immerse 8 elevated, headlong, macerate, saturate, solution 9 difficult, distemper, excessive, precipice 10 exorbitant, impregnate 11 precipitous 13 perpendicular
steeper: vat 6 teapot, vessel 7 cistern
steeple: 5 spire, tower 6 cupola 8 pinnacle 9 campanile
steeply: 5 brant
steepness: 6 height
steer: ox; con, tip 4 conn, helm, lead, stot 5 guide, pilot 6 bovine, direct, govern, manage 7 bullock, control, oversee
close to wind: 4 luff
steerage: 8 guidance 9 direction 10 management, regulation
steering: aim 9 direction, mangement 10 government
apparatus: 4 helm 5 wheel 6 rudder, tiller
part: 10 rudderhead
superintend: con 4 conn

steery: 4 stir 6 tumult

steeve: 4 pack, stow 5 store, stuff

stein: mug 4 toby

steinbock: 8 antelope

steinkirk, steenkirk: 6 cravat 9 neckcloth

stela, stele: 4 slab 6 pillar 8 monument 10 gravestone

stelar: 10 columnlike

stellar: 5 chief 6 astral, starry 7 leading 8 starlike, stellate 9 principal

stellate: 8 starlike 10 star-shaped

Steller's sea cow: 6 rytina

stem: bow, bun, dam, ram 4 axis, base, body, bole, cane, culm, halt, hold, load, prow, race, reed, rise, risp, root, stop, tamp 5 check, haulm, shaft, stalk, steer, stipe, stock, trunk 6 branch, derive, oppose, stanch 7 lineage, pedicel, petiole, spindle 8 ancestry, contract, peduncle, restrain 9 originate, petiolule

bulblike: 4 corm 5 tuber 7 rhizome

climbing: 4 bine 7 tendril

joint: 4 node

part: 4 pith 5 stele

stemless: 11 acaulescent

stemma: 7 descent, lineage 8 ancestry, pedigree

stemmer: bar

stem-winder: 5 watch

stench: 4 fogo, odor, reek 5 fetor, smell, stink 6 foetor

stenographer: 5 steno

stenography: 9 shorthand 12 brachygraphy

stent: 5 tight 6 extend, extent 7 stretch 12 outstretched

stentor: 6 roarer

stentorian: 4 loud

step: sty, way 4 gait, pace, rank, rest, rung, walk 5 break, crush, dance, grade, ledge, level, plane, round, shelf, space, stage, stair, stalk, strut, trace, tread 6 action, degree, manner, squash, stride 7 advance, deprive, imprint, measure 8 distance, footfall, foothold, footrest, footstep, movement 9 footprint, gradation, procedure, promotion 10 proceeding, stepladder 11 translation

dance: pas 5 coule 6 chasse 8 glissade

introductory: 8 rudiment 10 initiative

measuring device: 10 passimeter

part: 5 riser, tread 8 nosing

recording device: 8 odograph

rope ladder: 7 ratline

series of raised: 6 gradin 7 gradine

step up: rev

step-by-step: 8 gradatim(L.)

step-in: 4 shoe 7 slipper

step-ins: 10 underpants

stepbrother: 9 beau-frere(F.) 11 beaux-freres

stepdame: 10 stepmother

steps: See **step, staircase**.

stepson: 8 beau-fils(F.) 9 beaux-fils

stere: 9 kiloliter

stereotype: 6 repeat 7 hackney

stereotyped: 5 trite

sterile: dry 4 arid, dead, geld 6 barren, meager, meagre, otiose 7 aseptic, useless 8 impotent 9 fruitless, infertile 10 unfruitful 11 ineffective 12 unproductive

sterility: 7 asepsis

sterilize: 9 disinfect

sterling: 5 penny 7 genuine 9 excellent

stern: 4 back, dour, firm, grim, hard, helm 5 harsh, rough, steer, stout 6 fierce, gloomy, mighty, rudder, savage, severe, strict, strong, sturdy, sullen, tiller, unkind 7 austere, massive 8 exacting, resolute, rigorous 9 unbending, unfeeling 10 astringent, forbidding, inexorable, inflexible, relentless, uninviting, unyielding 11 hardhearted 14 uncompromising

toward: aft 5 abaft 6 astern

sternforemost: 7 awkward 8 backward

sternness: 5 rigor 7 cruelty 8 hardness, severity 9 austerity, harshness, rigidness, stiffness 10 strictness 12 exactingness 13 inflexibility

sternutation: 6 sneeze 8 sneezing

sternward: aft 5 abaft 6 astern

sterol: 7 alcohol

stertor: 5 snore

stevedore: 6 loader, stower 8 cargador 12 longshoreman

steven: din 4 roar 5 noise, voice 6 outcry

Stevenson character: 4 Hyde

stew: 4 boil, cook, dive, fret, mess, olio 5 bathe, cloud, imbue, steep, study, sweat, worry 6 burgoo, ragout, seethe, simmer 7 brothel, haricot, swelter 8 hothouse 9 Brunswick, confusion 10 capilotade, excitement, hodgepodge, hotchpotch 11 predicament

steward: 4 hind 5 dewan, diwan, graff, grave 6 factor, grieve, waiter 7 bailiff, curator, foreman, granger, manager, officer, proctor 8 bhandari, employee 9 custodian, dispenser, seneschal 10 magistrate 11 chamberlain

monastery: 8 cellarer

ship: 6 flunky 7 flunkey

stewed: 5 drunk 10 inebriated 11 intoxicated

stey: 5 steep

sthenic: 6 active, strong

stib: 6 dunlin 9 sandpiper

stich: 4 line 5 verse

stick: bat, bow, cue, gad, gum, put, rod, set 4 bind, cane, clag, clam, club, fife, glue, kill, mast, poke, pole, push, shut, spit, stab, stem, stop, twig, wand 5 affix, baton, cheat, cleam, cling, close, delay, demur, flute, mount, paste, place, prick, shoot, shove, staff, stalk, stall, stave, trunk 6 adhere, attach, baffle, ballow, billet, branch, cement, cleave, cohere, cudgel, endure, fasten, ferule, fescue, impale, mallet, pierce, puzzle, rammer, strike, thrust **7** confine, defraud, drummer **8** bludgeon, clarinet, hesitate, puncture, revolver, tolerate **9** crabstick, drumstick

bamboo: **5** lathi **6** lathee

bundle of: **5** fagot **6** fasces **7** fascine

crooked: **5** caman **7** cammock, gambrel

measuring: **5** ruler **7** ellwand **8** yardwand **9** yardstick

mountain climbing: **10** alpenstock

stick out: **7** extrude

stick up: **6** hold up

sticker: bur **4** burr **5** knife, label, poser, thorn **6** paster, puzzle, weapon **7** bramble

sticking: **6** viscid **8** adhering, cohesive **12** stonewalling

stickit: **6** failed **7** botched **9** imperfect **12** unsuccessful

stickle: **5** demur, rapid, rough, steep **6** higgle, pacify **7** contend, current, scruple **8** separate **9** agitation, altercate, intervene **10** perplexity **11** participate **12** perturbation

stickleback: **6** bandie(Sc.)

stickler: **6** purist, second, umpire **7** arbiter, meddler **8** mediator

sticky: **4** clit **5** gluey, gooey, humid, messy **6** claggy, clammy, clarty, slushy, viscid, wooden **7** viscous **8** adhesive **9** difficult, glutinous **10** saccharine **13** uncomfortable

stife: **4** fume **5** smell

stiff: bum **4** deep, firm, hard, high, hobo, taut **5** brave, budge, clung, dense, fixed, grave, harsh, horse, money, rigid, steep, tense, thick, tramp, woody **6** clumsy, corpse, formal, loafer, proper, robust, severe, stanch, strong, sturdy **7** awkward, buckram, cadaver, precise, starchy **8** absorbed, exacting, resolute, rigorous, stalwart, starched, stubborn **9** difficult, laborious, obstinate, unbending **10** ceremonial, consistent, inflexible, unyielding **12** pertinacious **14** uncompromising

stiff-necked: **8** stubborn **9** obstinate **12** contumacious

stiffen: set **5** brace **6** benumb, harden, starch **10** inspissate

stiffness: **5** rigor **8** rigidity **10** constraint **11** starchiness

stifle: gag **4** stop **5** check, choke **6** muffle, quench **7** repress, smother **8** strangle, suppress, throttle **9** suffocate **10** extinguish

stigma: **4** blot, mark, scar, spot **5** brand, cloud, odium, stain, taint **6** defect **7** blemish **10** projection

stigmatize: **5** brand **8** denounce

stile: **4** step **5** style **6** gnomon **9** turnstile

stiletto: **4** kill, stab **6** bodkin, dagger, stylet **9** eyeleteer

still: but, een, low, mum, tho, yet **4** also, calm, cosh, drip, even, ever, hush, lull,

stop **5** allay, check, inert, quiet **6** always, distil, gentle, hushed, pacify, serene, soothe **7** appease, however, silence, subdued **8** habitual, inactive, restrain, suppress, tranquil **9** noiseless, uniformly **10** constantly, distillery, motionless, stationary, uneventful **11** continually **12** nevertheless

stillness: **5** peace, quiet **7** silence **8** calmness **9** quietness **11** taciturnity

stilly: **4** calm **5** quiet **7** quietly **8** silently

stilt: **4** limp, pile, pole, post **5** shaft **6** crutch

stilted: **6** formal **7** awkward, pompous **8** affected **9** bombastic, dignified **11** sententious

stimulant: kat **5** drink, tonic **6** bracer **8** beverage **9** sassafras

heart: **8** cardiant, thialdin **9** digitalis, thialdine **10** adrenaline, epinephrin **11** epinephrine

stimulate: fan, jog, pep **4** goad, move, spur, stir, urge, whet **5** brace, elate, filip, impel, rouse, sting **6** affect, arouse, excite, fillip, incite **7** animate, enliven, inspire, provoke, quicken **8** irritate, motivate **9** encourage, galvanize, instigate **10** exhilarate, invigorate

stimulating: **5** brisk **9** innerving **12** invigorating

stimulus: **4** goad, spur **5** filip, sting **6** fillip, motive **7** impetus **9** incentive

sting: **4** bite, dupe, goad, mast, pain, pike, pole, post, tang, urge **5** cheat, prick, shaft, smart, wound **6** impale, incite, nettle, pierce, tingle **7** stimuli **8** irritate, stimulus **9** stimulate **10** incitement

stinger: **4** blow **5** drink

stinginess: **9** closeness, frugality, parsimony **13** niggardliness

stinging: **6** biting, bitter **7** caustic, piquant, pungent **8** piercing **10** irritating **11** acrimonious

stingo: ale, vim, zip **4** beer, zest **6** energy

stingray: **6** obispo

stingy: **4** dree(Sc.), hard, mean **5** cheap, light, sharp, stint, tight **6** biting, greedy, meager, scanty **7** miserly, niggard, nipping, selfish **8** covetous **9** illiberal, penurious **10** avaricious **11** closefisted **12** parsimonious

stinking: **4** foul, rank **5** drunk, fetid **6** putrid, rancid **7** noisome **9** offensive **10** malodorous

stint, stent: **4** duty, stay, stop, task **5** bound, cease, check, chore, delay, limit, scant, serve, spare, stunt **6** assign, desist, divide, scrimp **7** confine **8** quantity, restrain, restrict, stoppage **9** cessation, economize, restraint **10** assignment, limitation, proportion **11** restriction

stinting: **7** sparing **8** scanting

stipe: **4** stem **5** stalk **6** caudex **7** petiole

stipend: ann, fee, pay **4** hire, wage **5** annal

6 income, salary **7** payment, prebend **9** allowance **12** compensation, remuneration

stipendiary: **4** beak **7** soldier, teacher **9** clergyman, mercenary **10** magistrate

stipple: dot **6** render **7** engrave, speckle

stipulate: **5** agree **7** bargain, specify **8** contract, covenant

stipulation: **4** bond, item **6** clause, detail **7** article, bargain, proviso **8** contract, covenant **9** agreement, prison, condition, situation **11** arrangement, undertaking

stipule of leaflet: **6** stipel

stir: ado, fan, gog, jog, mix, sir **4** busk, fuss, jail, move, plow, poke, roil, to-do **5** amove, budge, churn, doing, hurry, rally, rouse, shake, shift, shove, stoke, waken **6** arouse, awaken, bestir, bustle, excite, flurry, foment, hubbub, incite, motion, muddle, pother, prison, quetch, tumult **7** agitate, animate, blunder, disturb, flutter, inflame, provoke, trouble **8** activity, brandish, displace, movement **9** commotion, exagitate, stimulate **10** manipulate **12** penitentiary

together: **6** stodge

stirabout: **8** porridge

stirk: cow **4** bull **6** heifer **7** bullock

stirless: **10** motionless

stirps: **4** race **5** stock **6** branch

stirra: boy **6** sirrah **9** stripling

stirring: **5** astir **6** moving, tumult, uproar **7** rousing **8** activity, exciting, movement **9** agitation, animating, inspiring, thrilling **10** incitement **11** stimulating

stirrup: bar **4** ring, rope **5** clamp, strap **6** stapes **7** support **8** footrest

hood: **8** tapadera(Sp.)

stitch: bit, hem, sew **4** loop, pain, purl **5** baste, picot, ridge, unite **6** pierce, suture, tailor **8** distance **9** embroider

stitchbird: ihi

stitcher: **5** sewer **6** seamer **10** dressmaker

stitchwort: **9** chickweed

stithy: **5** anvil, forge **6** smithy **8** smithery

stive: **6** stifle **9** suffocate

stiver: **4** coin **5** money **7** bristle, stagger **8** struggle

stivy: **5** close **8** stifling

stoa: **7** portico **9** colonnade

stoat: **6** ermine, weasel **8** clubster **9** clubstart

stob: **4** post, stab **5** stake **6** pierce

stock: bar, cop, log **4** band, bond, butt, fund, hive, line, post, race, rail, stem **5** banal, block, blood, brace, breed, broth, estoc, flesh, frame, hoard, stake, stick, store, stump, swell, trite, trunk **6** assets, budget, common, cravat, handle, holder, pillar, strain, supply **7** cabbage, capital, catasta, descent, extract, lineage, provide, rhizome, support **8** ancestry, bitstock, colewort, material, ordinary, stoccado **9**

extirpate, hackneyed, livestock, provision, replenish, stockfish **10** foundation **11** commonplace, certificate **12** accumulation

framed on: **5** ramed

of food: **5** foray

of goods: **4** line

pair of: **5** cippi **6** cippus

preliminary: **5** scrip

racial: **8** pedigree

stockade: pen **5** etape, pound **6** corral, kennel **7** barrier, fortify, protect **8** poundage **9** enclosure

Africa: **4** boma **5** kraal **6** keddah, zareba **7** zareeba

stock exchange: **6** bourse(F.)

business: **9** arbitrage

patron: **5** buyer **6** seller, trader

stockfish: cod **4** hake, ling **5** torsk **7** haddock

stock-in-trade: **4** tool, ware **5** goods **7** capital **8** material **11** merchandise

stocked: **7** replete

stockholder: **8** investor, stockman

stocking: bas(F.) **4** hose **7** hosiery

bishop's: **6** buskin, caliga

cotton: **5** lisle

footless: **7** hushion

ornament: **5** clock

soleless: **7** traheen

worsted: **7** scogger

stockman: **6** herder **7** rancher **8** beastman

stocky: fat **4** cold, stub **5** cobby, stiff **6** chumpy, formal, stubby, sturdy **7** bunting, defiant **8** thickset **10** boisterous, headstrong

stodge: **6** trudge **7** satiate, satisfy

stodgy: **4** dull **5** bulky, heavy, thick **6** packed **7** crammed, lumpish, stuffed, tedious **8** thickset **9** satiating **10** uninspired **13** uninteresting

stogy: **4** boot, shoe **5** cigar **6** brogan, clumsy, coarse

stoic: **5** porch **7** ascetic, passive **9** impassive

Stoic School: **4** Stoa

founder: **4** Zeno

stoicism: **8** patience **11** impassivity **13** impassiveness

stoit: **5** lurch **7** stagger, stumble

stoke: **4** coal, fire, fuel, poke, stab, tend **5** stick **6** supply, thrust

stoker: **5** firer **7** fireman, greaser

glassworks: **6** teaser

stole: fur **5** scarf **7** garment, orarion **8** vestment **13** epitrachelion

stolen: **5** shoot **6** branch, runner **9** rootstock

stolid: **4** dull, firm, slow **5** beefy **6** stupid **7** brutish, clumpse, clumpst, passive **9** impassive, inanimate, unfeeling **10** impassable **12** unexciteable

stoma: **4** pore **5** mouth **7** opening, orifice

stomach: gut, maw **4** bear, craw, crop, kyte, vell **5** anger, belly, bingy, brook, pride, rumen **6** bingey, desire, endure, gebbie(Sc.), resent, spirit, temper **7** abdomen, gizzard, gizzern **8** appetite, tolerate **9** arrogance **10** resentment **11** inclination

acidity: **4** acor

pert. to: **7** gastric

ruminant's first: **5** rumen

ruminant's fourth: **4** read, rêed **8** abomasum, roddikin(Sc.)

ruminant's second: **6** bonnet **9** reticulum

ruminant's third: **6** omasum **9** manyplies **10** psalterium

used as food: **5** tripe

stomach ache: **5** colic **7** gullion

stomacher: **4** gimp **7** echelle **8** forepart

stomachy: **5** proud **8** paunched, spirited **9** irritable, obstinate, resentful **10** potbellied

stomp: See **stamp.**

stone (see also **rock**): gem, pit, rub **4** bone, pelt, rock **5** block, brick, lapis(L.), scour, scrub **6** chaton, cobble, domino, harden, marble, mirror **7** diamond, dornick, scruple, sharpen **8** gunflint, lapidate, memorial, monolith, testicle **9** hailstone, hemachate, milestone, millstone, whetstone **10** gravestone, grindstone

abrasive: **5** emery

and clay: **4** sere

architectural: **6** abacus

artificial: **8** albolite, albolith **9** granolith

base: **6** plinth

Biblical: **4** ezel

broken: **6** rubble

carved: **5** cameo

chip of: **5** spall **6** gallet

combining form: **5** litho

druid: **8** sarsen

drupe: **6** nutlet

eagle: **5** etite

famous: **4** Hope, Pitt **5** Green, Mogul, Sancy, Scone **6** Jonker, Nassak, Orloff, Regent, Vargas **7** Blarney, Dresden, Jubilee, Kohinur, Stewart, Tiffany **8** Braganza, Cullinan, Kohinoor **9** Excelsior, Polar Star **10** Florentine, Great Mogul **12** Plymouth Rock, Star of Africa **14** Star of the South

fruit: pit **4** paip **5** drupe **6** pyrene **7** putamen

gem cutting: **6** adamas

granitic: **6** gneiss

grave: **5** stela, stele **6** marker, stelae, steles **8** memorial, monument

grinding: **6** metate

hammering: **8** lapstone

hard: **9** chatoyant

heap: **5** cairn

hoist: **5** lewis

hollow: **5** druse, geode

hurling device: **9** trebucket

loose: **6** gibber

maize grinding: **4** mano

meteoric: **8** aerolite, aerolith

monumental: **4** lech **6** menhir

of arch: **8** keystone

paving: **4** flag, slab, slat

pert. to: **7** lithoid

precious: gem **4** keas, onyx, opal, ruby **5** beryl, pearl, topaz **6** garnet, jasper, lazuli, ligure **7** diamond, peridot **8** astroite, sapphire, tigereye **9** aromatite

pyramid-shape: **6** benben

shaped into pillars: **7** obelisk **9** monoliths

sharpening: oil **4** hone, whet

seam: dry

semiprecious: **4** jade, onyx, sard **5** agate, lapis **6** garnet, lazule, lazuli **7** olivine **8** murrhine **11** lapis lazuli

small: **6** pebble

squared: **6** ashlar

suffix: ith

uncut: **4** naif

upright: **5** bauta **6** menhir

used for cameos: **4** onyx

worker: **5** mason **6** slater

writing: **5** slate

Stone Age tool: **4** celt **6** eolith **7** neolith **10** palaeolith

stonecrop: **5** orpin **6** orpine

stonecutter: **6** jadder

disease: **9** silicosis

wooden receptacle of: **7** sebilla

stonelike: **7** lithoid

stoneman: **5** cairn **9** stonehand

stones: *fine:* **4** sand

heap of: **5** scree

loose: **6** eratum **8** erratice

mass of loose: **7** clitter

mound of: **4** carn, karn **5** cairn

pile of: **7** warlock

stonewall: **8** stubborn **9** obstinate **10** determined, filibuster

stonewalling: **8** sticking

stoneware: **4** gres **7** ceramic, pottery **11** earthenware

stonework: **7** masonry

stoneworker: **5** mason

stony: **4** cold, hard **5** fixed, rigid, still **7** adamant **8** obdurate, pitiless **9** petrified, unfeeling **10** inexorable, inflexible, petrifying, relentless, stupefying, unyielding **14** expressionless **15** uncompassionate

stood: **5** arose **7** endured

stooge: **4** foil

stook: **5** shock **6** pillar **12** handkerchief

stookie: **4** fool

stool: **4** base, mora, pole, seat, thew **5** bench, chair, decoy, morae, stand, stump **6** buffet, growth, throne, tiller, tripod **7** commode, creepie, taboret, trestle **8** kingship, platform, standard, tabouret **9** footstool **10** foundation **11** chieftaincy

stoolpigeon: spy **5** decoy, narks **7** peacher **8** betrayer, informer, observer

stoop: bow, lay **4** bend, bode, lean, post,

sink, tilt **5** deign, lower, porch, slant, souse, stake, stump, swoop, yield **6** alight, boggle, coorie, crouch, debase, gamble, huckle, humble, patron, pillar, pounce, submit **7** decline, degrade, descend, descent, subject, succumb, veranda **8** adherent, overcome, platform, stairway **9** prostrate, supporter **10** condescend **11** humiliation **13** condescension

stop: ho; bar, dam, end, inn, pug, wad **4** bait, bode, bung, call, calk, clog, drop, fill, halt, mend, pawl, plug, quit, stay, stem, stum, wear, weir, whoa **5** avast, basta, block, break, caulk, catch, cease, check, choke, close, delay, embar, estop, holla, hollo, parry, pause, point, repel, stall, stuff, tarry **6** alight, anchor, arrest, behold, boggle, defeat, desist, detain, finish, gravel, hinder, period, reside, scotch, stanch, stench **7** caesura, confine, counter, prevent, sojourn, station, staunch, stopper, suspend **8** caesurae(pl.), obstacle, obstruct, obturate, pinblock, preclude, prohibit, restrain, stoppage, suppress, withhold **9** barricade, cessation, hindrance, intercept, interrupt, punctuate **10** constipate **11** countermand, discontinue, obstruction **12** intermission, interruption, lodginghouse
organ: **5** orage, viola **7** posaune **8** dulciana, gemshorn **9** rohrflote
short: **5** delay, pause **7** respite **8** interval **9** cessation **12** intermission
stop watch: **5** timer
stope: **8** excavate **10** excavation
stoppage: **4** halt **5** block, choke, hitch **6** arrest, devall, strike **7** embargo, seizure **9** cessation, detention **10** arrestment, congestion **11** obstruction
debate: **7** cloture
temporary: **5** delay, pause **6** arrest, recess **10** arrestment **12** interception, intermission, interruption
stopper: wad **4** bung, cork, plug **6** fipple **7** bouchon
stopping: **4** halt **5** block, check **7** seizure **9** detention **11** obstruction
device: **5** brake
stopple: **4** bung, cork, plug **7** stopper
storage: **4** dump **11** safekeeping
battery plate: **4** grid
bin: mow **4** loft **7** granary **8** elevator
charge: **9** demurrage
place: bin **4** shed, silo **5** attic, depot **6** cellar, closet **7** arsenal, granary **8** cupboard, elevator **9** blood bank, reservoir, warehouse
prepare for: can
room: **6** closet, larder **7** lastage, lazaret **9** lazarette, lazaretto
storax: **5** resin **6** balsam
store: bin **4** cave, deck, deep, dose, fond, fund, hold, mass, save, shop, stow **5** amass, breed, cache, hoard, stock **6**

amount, budget, garner, repair, shoppe, supply **7** bhandar, collect, deposit, furnish, husband, provide, restore **8** emporium, reserves, supplies, treasure **9** abundance, chandlery, livestock, replenish, reservoir, resources, sweetshop, warehouse, **10** accumulate, collection, provisions, storehouse **12** accumulation
cargo: **5** steve
fodder: **6** ensile **8** ensilate
food: **6** market **9** sweetshop **12** delicatessen
fruit: **12** greengrocery
hidden: **5** cache
Hindu: **7** bhandar
in ground: **5** cache
in silo: **6** ensile
large: **4** raff, raft
lumber camp: van
milk: **5** dairy
slang: **5** stash
up: **4** hive **6** garner
storehouse: mow **4** barn, bike, crib, shed, silo **5** cache, depot, etape **7** arsenal, bhandar, camalig, camarin, granary **8** building, magazine, treasury **9** repertory, warehouse **10** commissary **11** chalkotheke
military: **5** depot **7** arsenal **10** commissary
public: **5** depot, etape
rural: mow **4** barn, crib, shed, silo **7** granary
wool: **6** lanary
storekeeper: **6** grocer **8** bhandari, merchant, storeman **9** shopkeeper **11** almacenista, stockkeeper
storeroom: **4** cave, gola, loft **6** bodega, cellar **7** buttery, genizah, granary **8** basement **10** repository
stork: **4** ibis **6** simbil **7** marabou **12** xenorhynchus
storken: **7** congeal, stiffen
storklike: **8** pelargic
storm: wap **4** birr, blow, bura, fume, gale, gust, hail, rage, rain, rand, rant, rave, snow, wind **5** blizz, brash, orage **6** attack, burran, expugn, shamal, shower, simoom, simoon, tumult, Wester **7** assault, bluster, borasca, borasco, bravado, cyclone, rampage, tempest, tornado, trouble **8** calamity, eruption, outburst, upheaval, violence **9** agitation, bourasque, commotion, hurricane **10** hurly-burly **11** disturbance
god: Zu **5** Rudra
revolving: **7** cyclone
sand: **6** tebbad
snow: **5** buran
stormcock: **6** petrel, thrush **9** fieldfare **10** woodpecker
stormy: **4** foul **5** dirty, gusty **6** raging **7** furious, riotous, violent **8** agitated, cluttery **9** inclement, turbulent **10** blustering, passionate, tumultuous **11** tempestuous

story: fib, lie **4** myth, plot, saga, tale, tier, yarn **5** etage, fable, floor, rumor, solar, soler **6** fabula, legend, record, report, sollar **7** account, article, episode, history, narrate, parable, recital **8** anecdote, intrigue **9** falsehood, happening, narration, narrative, statement, tradition **11** description

continued: **6** serial, sequel

exclusive: **4** beat **5** scoop

kind of: **4** epic, saga, tale, yarn **5** conte, fable **6** canard, legend, script **7** mystery, novella, parable, romance **8** allegory, scenario

upper: **5** attic **6** garret

storyteller: **4** liar **5** Aesop **6** disour, fibber **8** narrator **9** raconteur

stot: ox **4** bull **5** bound, horse, steer **6** bounce **7** rebound, stagger, stammer, stumble, stutter

stound: **4** ache, beat, blow, pain, pang, stun, time **5** grief, shock, sight, smart, swoon, throb **6** attack, benumb, bruise, moment, period, season, sorrow, thrill, twinge **7** assault, instant, stupefy **8** astonish, occasion **10** apparition **12** astonishment, stupefaction

stoup, stoop: cup **4** cask, pail **5** basin **6** bucket, flagon, vessel **7** measure, tankard **10** aspersoria **11** aspersorium

holy-water: **8** benitier **11** cantharus-ri(pl.) **12** kantharos-roi(pl.)

stour: fit, fog **4** dust, gale, gush, hard, huge, loud, move, pour, rise, rude, stir, vast **5** agony, chaff, drive, great, hardy, hurry, onset, rough, shock, spray, stern, stiff, storm, throe **6** breeze, coarse, combat, fierce, hoarse, robust, severe, strife, strong, tumult **7** assault, austere, conflict, meeting, quarrel, turmoil, violent **8** hardship, numerous, paroxysm **9** agitation, commotion, encounter **10** affliction, difficulty, excitement, inflexible, opposition

stourness: **7** bigness **9** greatness **10** sturdiness

stoush: **4** beat, blow **6** attack, strike, tirade **7** assault

stout: ale, fat **4** beer, bold, firm, gnat, hard **5** brave, bulky, burly, cobby, frack, freck, hardy, obese, plump, proud, shock, solid, tough **6** active, flagon, fleshy, liquor, porter, portly, robust, rotund, stable, stanch, stocky, stouty, strong, sturdy **7** defiant, haughty, violent **8** arrogant, bouncing, enduring, forceful, forcible, horsefly, insolent, powerful, resolute, stalwart, stubborn, thickset, vigorous **9** corpulent, energetic, obstinate, undaunted **10** courageous, determined, persistent **11** substantial **14** uncompromising

and rough: **5** burly

and short: **6** stocky **8** thickset

stout-hearted: **4** bold, good **5** brave **10** courageous

stoutly: **7** hardily

stoutness: **8** strength **9** hardihood

stove: **4** dent, etna, kiln **5** grate, plate, range, stave **6** cockle, heater **7** furnace **10** calefactor, glasshouse **12** conservatory

alcohol: **4** etna

charcoal: hod

grated: **8** chauffer

part: **4** oven **7** firebox, griddle

stow: box, cut **4** cram, crop, hide, hold, mass, pack, stop, trim **5** cease, crowd, douse, dowse, grant, lodge, place, shoot, slice, stack, store, stump **6** bestow, commit **7** arrange, contain, entrust, secrete **8** restrain

cargo: **5** steve(var.) **6** steeve

stowage: **6** charge **7** packing

stower: **9** stevedore

strabismus: **6** squint **8** cross-eye

straddle: **5** hedge **6** option, sprawl **7** astride, bracket **8** bestride **11** noncommital

straddler: **5** rider

strafe: **4** waif **5** shell, stray **6** punish **7** bombard **9** castigate

straggle: **4** rove **5** stray **6** ramble, wander **7** meander

straggler: **5** tramp **8** vagabond, wanderer

straight: **4** neat **5** brant, erect, euthy, frank, ortho, plain, recti, rigid, stern **6** aright, candid, direct, graith, honest, severe **7** rightly, sincere, stretch, through, unmixed, upright **8** accurate, directly, honestly, reliable, rigorous, sequence, unbroken, virtuous **9** correctly, honorably, undiluted **10** continuous, methodical, unmodified **11** immediately, straightway, undeviating, unqualified **12** continuously, unswervingly **13** unaccompanied, uninterrupted **15** straightforward

combining form: **5** euthy

straight course: **7** beeline

straight edge: **5** ruler

straight-haired: **12** leiotrichous **13** lissotrichous

straight-out: **6** direct **8** outright **11** unqualified **12** unrestrained **13** thoroughgoing

straight up and down: **15** perpendicularly

straighten: **5** align, aline, level, order, plumb **7** compose, rectify, unravel **11** disentangle

straightforward: **4** even, open **5** apert, frank **6** aright, candid, dexter, direct, honest **7** sincere **8** directly, outright, straight **9** foreright, outspoken **10** forthright **11** undeviating

straightforwardly: **8** directly

straightness: **9** rectitude

straightway: **4** anon **6** aright, bedene **8** directly **9** downright, forthwith **10** forthright **11** immediately

strain: air, hug, sie, sye, tax, try **4** balk, barb, bend, bind, curb, dash, gain, heft, kind, line, mood, note, ooze, race, sift, solo, sort, tone, tune, turn, urge, vein **5** begte, breed, clasp, class, exert, force, music, press, raise, shade, sieve, stock, style, tenor, touch, trace, track, trail, wield **6** burden, colate, effort, extend, extort, family, fasten, filter, injure, manner, melody, obtain, sprain, strand, stread, stress, strive, temper, thread, weaken, wrench **7** confine, descent, element, embrace, lineage, overtax, progeny, quality, squeeze, stretch, tension, trickle, variety **8** ancestry, brandish, compress, eliquate, exertion, restrain, tendency **9** begetting, character, constrain, constrict, percolate **10** distortion, generation **11** deformation, disposition
blood: **4** race **5** breed, stock **6** family **7** lineage
chief: **5** brunt
combining form: **4** tono
great: tax, tug **5** tense **6** stress **7** tension **8** exertion, overbear **11** tenterhooks
measuring device: **9** telemeter
strained: **4** taut **5** tense **6** forced **7** intense **8** weakened, wrenched **9** distorted **10** farfetched
strainer: **4** cage, sile **5** sieve, strum, tamis **6** filter, milsey, milsie, sifter **8** colander, colature, huckmuck **10** colatorium
strait: *between Labrador and Newfoundland:* **9** Belleisle
Strait of Gibraltar: 17 Pillars of Hercules
Straits Settlements:
city: **7** Malacca **9** Singapore **10** Georgetown
coin: **4** cent **6** dollar **13** Straits dollar
measure: pau, tun **4** para, pipe **5** parah **6** chupak, parrah **7** gantang
native state: **5** Perak **6** Johore, Pahang **8** Selangor **11** Sungei Ujong **13** Negri Sembilan
weight: **4** chee, hoon, saga **5** bedur, bhara, catty, koyan, picul, tahil
straiten: **5** limit **6** hamper **7** confine **8** contract, distress, restrict **9** embarrass
strait-jacket: **8** camisole
strait-laced: **5** stiff **6** severe, strict **8** stubborn **9** obstinate, puritanic **10** restricted **11** constrained **14** overscrupulous
strake: rut **4** band **5** crack **6** loiter, streak, stripe, stroll, trough, wander **7** stretch
stramineous: **6** chaffy, strawy **9** strawlike, valueless
strand: sea **4** bank, quay, wire **5** beach, fiber, shore, wharf **6** gutter, maroon, region, stream, thread **7** channel, current **8** filament
stranded: **6** ashore **7** aground, beached **8** castaway, marooned
strange: odd **4** fell, rare, unco **5** alien,

droll, eerie, fremd, novel, queer **6** exotic, quaint **7** curious, distant, erratic, foreign, uncanny, unknown, unusual **8** abnormal, estrange, fanciful, peculiar, reserved, singular, uncommon **9** couthless, different, eccentric, unnatural **10** outlandish, unfamiliar, unfriendly **12** unaccustomed, unacquainted **13** extraordinary, inexperienced, preternatural
combining form: xen **4** xeno
language: **4** cant **5** lingo **6** jargon **7** dialect
strangely: **5** oddly **6** featly
stranger: goy **5** alien, guest, odder **6** ganger, novice **7** comical, visitor **8** emigrant, estrange, intruder, newcomer, outsider **9** estranger, foreigner, outlander **10** tramontane **12** intermeddler
strangle: **4** kill, slay **5** choke, grane **6** stifle **7** garrote, repress **8** garrotte, suppress, throttle **9** suffocate
strangulate: **5** choke **8** compress, obstruct, strangle **9** constrict
strap: bar, fit, tie **4** band, beat, belt, bind, hang, rein, riem, whip **5** girth, groom, strip, strop, thong **6** billet, chaser, credit, enarme, fillet, halter, latigo, ligule, punish, secure **7** furnish, laniard, lanyard, sharpen **8** chastise
kind of: **4** jess, taws **5** guige, leash, strop, tawse, thong **6** chaser, enarme **8** bretelle **10** boondoggle
strap-shaped: **6** lorate **7** ligular **8** ligulate **9** ligulated
strapping: **6** robust, strong **7** beating **9** thrashing
strass: **5** glass, paste
strata (see also **stratum**): *geological:* **4** lias
later: **7** neozoic
social: **7** classes
stratagem: **4** coup, ruse, wile **5** cheat, fetch, fraud, trick **6** blench, device, humbug, scheme **7** finesse **8** artifice, maneuver **9** chicanery, deception, execution, slaughter **10** artfulness
smart: **8** liripipe, liripoop
strategic: **9** favorable **12** advantageous
strategy: **8** artifice, intrigue, maneuver
stratification: **7** bedding
stratum: bed **5** layer, level **6** couche **7** section **8** division
thin: **4** seam
stravagant: **7** vagrant **11** extravagant, irrelevance
stravage, stravaig: **6** stroll, wander **7** saunter
straw: hat, wap **4** gloy, mote, pipe, rush **5** chaff, strae, stree **6** fescue, litter, trifle **9** worthless, yellowish **11** meaningless **12** churchwarden
bundle of: **6** batten
color: **6** flaxen
colored: **11** stramineous
for hats: **6** sennit

half rotten: **5** mulch
load of: **5** barth
plaited: **6** sennit
threshing floor: **6** bhossa
used for hats: **7** sabutan
waxed: **6** strass
weaving: **5** rafia
strawberry: 6 fraise, runner **8** fragaria
strawlike: 11 stramineous
stray: err, gad **4** cavy, roam, rove, waif **5**
range **6** casual, course, errant, estray,
random, stroll, swerve, wander **7** decline,
deviate, digress, forlorn, habitat, saunter
8 detached, distract, isolated, straggle **9**
straggler, unrelated **10** incidental, occasional **12** unenumerated
straying: 6 astray **7** erratic **8** aberrant **9**
deviation, erroneous
streak: rub **4** line, rung, vein, wale **5** fleck,
freak, garle, hurry, layer, lined, round,
smear, spell, trace, trait **6** period, polish,
smooth, strain, strake, stripe, stroke **7**
stratum, striped **8** discolor
mottled: roe
narrow: **5** stria **6** striae
regular: **6** stripe
streaked: 4 liny **6** marked **7** alarmed,
brindle, striped, worried **8** brindled **10**
variegated
streaky: 4 liny **5** liney, mixed **6** uneven **8**
variable
stream: ea; run **4** burn, flow, flux, ford,
gote, gush, rill, rush **5** bache, bayou,
bourn, brook, creek, fleam, floss, flume,
fluor, force, issue, river, speed, trend **6**
amount, bourne, course, fluent, runnel **7**
channel, current, rivulet **8** affluent **9** anabranch **11** watercourse
diminutive: run **4** race **5** brook **6** rillet **7**
rivulet **9** streamlet
dry bed: **6** arroyo
living in: **9** amphibian, rheophile
ravine: **4** ghyl, gill
rushing: jet **7** torrent
small: run **4** rill, sike **5** brook, siket **6** rillet, runlet
underground: aar
upper part of: **6** source **9** headwater
streamer: jet **4** flag **5** strip **6** guidon, ribbon **7** feather, pendant, pennant **8** banderol, headline **9** banderole
streamlet: 4 rill **5** brook **6** rillet, runlet,
runnel **7** freshet, rivulet
streamline curve: 10 lissoneoid
streck: 6 direct **8** straight
streel: 7 saunter **8** slattern, straggle
street: rew(Sc.), way **4** char, lane, road **5**
calle, chare **6** avenue, causey, spread **7**
estreat, highway, roadway, strasse(G.) **8**
chaussee, contrada, contrade(pl.), notebook **9** boulevard **12** thoroughfare
Chinese: **6** hutung
degraded: **4** slum
India: **5** chawk, chowk
narrow: **5** alley, place

street roister: mun
street urchin: 4 arab **5** gamin
streetcar: 4 tram
strength: arm **4** beef, iron, thew **5** brawn,
force, might, power, vigor **6** energy, foison **7** ability, potency, stamina, sthenia **8**
capacity, firmness, puisance, solidity **9**
coherence, endurance, fortitude, intensity, lustiness, stoutness, toughness, vehemence **10** heartiness, robustness,
stronghold **14** impregnability
deprive of: **7** unnerve
diminish: **6** dilute
electric current: **8** amperage
loss: **8** asthenia
military: **8** armament
of character: **4** guts, sand **9** fortitude
poetic: **9** puissance
regain: **5** rally
solution: **5** titer, titre
source of: **5** asset
strengthen: 4 back, bind, frap, help, prop
5 brace, nerve, steel **6** clench, deepen,
endure **7** afforce, comfort, confirm, depth-
en, educate, fortify, toughen **8** roborate
9 encourage, reinforce **10** invigorate **11**
consolidate
with alcohol: **5** spike **7** fortify
strengthener: 6 gusset
strengthening: 7 bracing **8** roborant **10**
nourishing, supporting, sustaining **11**
corroborant
strenuous: 4 hard **5** eager **6** active, ardent, severe **7** arduous, zealous **8** vigorous **9** energetic
strepent: 4 loud **5** noisy
streperous: 4 loud **5** harsh, noisy **7** noisily **9** turbulent **10** boisterous
strepitant: 5 noisy **9** clamorous **10** strep-
itous
stress: 5 brunt, force, labor **6** accent, strain
7 afflict, amplify, overtax, tension, urgency
8 ampliate, distrain, distress, emphasis,
exertion, pressure **9** emphasize, intensity
10 constraint, importance, overstrain,
resistance **12** significance **13** inconvenience
mechanical: **8** erossure
metrical: **5** ictus
voice: **5** arsis **6** accent
stretch: eke **4** hang, span, walk **5** reach,
retch, space, toise, tract **6** course, dilate,
effort, expand, extend, period, spread,
strain **7** distend, enlarge, execute, expanse, tension **8** elongate, sentence **9** direction, extension **10** exaggerate
injuriously: **6** sprain
out: eke, lie, out
the neck: **5** crane
stretched: *out:* **6** craned **7** porrect **8** extended, prolated **9** elongated
tight: **4** taut **5** tense
while drying: **8** tentered
stretcher: 6 litter, racker **8** ringhead
neck: **6** craner

stretchy: 7 elastic, rubbery 9 resilient

strew: 6 litter, spread 7 diffuse, scatter 8 disperse, sprinkle 9 bespatter, broadcast 10 besprinkle 11 disseminate

strewing: 4 seme

stria: 4 band, line 5 ridge 6 fillet, furrow, groove, hollow, streak, stripe 7 channel 9 striation

striate: 5 lined 7 grooved 8 furrowed

stricken (see also **strike**): 7 smitten, wounded 13 incapacitated

strickle: 5 rifle 7 pattern 8 template

strict: 4 blue, hard 5 close, exact, harsh, rigid, stern, tense, tight 6 entire, narrow, severe 7 ascetic, austere, binding, correct, perfect, precise 8 absolute, accurate, intimate, limiting, rigorous, straight 9 confining, puritanic, stringent 10 compressed, forbidding, inexorable, inflexible, relentless, scrupulous 11 constricted, punctilious, puritanical, restricting, straitlaced, undeviating 14 uncompromising

disciplinarian: 8 martinet

discipline: 13 regimentation

striction: 12 constriction

strictly: 6 narrow 7 closely 9 precisely 10 positively, rigorously 11 stringently

strictness: 5 rigor 9 closeness

in law: 8 legalism

stricture: 4 sign 5 spark, touch, trace 7 binding, censure, closing 9 criticism 11 contraction 13 animadversion

strid: 5 gorge 6 ravine

stride: 4 step, walk 5 stalk 7 advance 8 bestride, progress, straddle 11 advancement

strident: 5 harsh 6 shrill 7 grating, raucous, yelling 11 cacophonous

stridulate: 7 clitter

strife: war 4 bait, bate, feud 5 fight, flite, flyte, noise, strow 6 combat, debate, estrif 7 contest, discord, hurling, quarrel 8 conflict, endeavor, exertion, struggle 9 emulation 10 contention 11 altercation, competition, controversy

about mere words: 9 logomachy

civil: 6 stasis

striffen: 4 skin 8 membrane

strigose, strigous: 6 hispid

strike: bat, bob, box, cob, cop, dab, dad, hew, hit, lam, pat, ram, rap, wap 4 baff, bang, bash, bean, beat, biff, bill, bump, bunt, chap, cope, coup, cuff, dash, daub, daud, dint, dunt, fist, flap, flog, frap, gird, gowf, hurl, hurt, knap, lash, pelt, rout, slap, slay, swat 5 clash, clink, clout, douse, dowse, dunch, fight, filch, gowff. impel, knock, punch, skelp, skite, slash. smear, smite, spank, swipe, touch, trend, whang 6 assail, attack, attain, bounce, buffet, fettle, hammer, hartal, punish. strike, stroke 7 afflict, cacanny, collide, impinge, impress 8 discover, struggle

a mean: 7 average

against: 4 bump 5 crash 7 collide

and rebound: 5 carom 6 carrom 9 carambole

down: 5 floor

dumb: 4 stun

heavily: lam, ram 4 bash, slog, slug

obliquely: 5 carom

on head: 4 bean

out: fan 4 dele 5 elide, erase 6 cancel, delete 9 eliminate

prepare to: 4 coil

producing musical sound: 5 chime

series of blows: 4 pelt

settler: 8 mediator

together: 7 collide

violently: ram 4 slam

with fist: 4 plug 5 punch, pound

with head: 4 butt

with wonder: awe 7 astound

striker: 4 scab, tern 6 batman, batter, helper, hitter, smiter 7 batsman, clapper, mobster 8 blackleg 9 assistant, harpooner

striking: 4 dint 7 salient 8 stunning 9 arresting, effective 10 noticeable, remarkable, surprising 11 conspicuous

effect: 5 eclat

strind: 4 cast, race 6 strain 7 kindred, progeny 9 offspring 10 generation 11 disposition

string: 4 band, cord, hoax, josh, line 5 bound, braid, chain, jolly, strip, twine 6 series, thread 10 conditions, succession 14 qualifications

course: 6 guidon

kinds of: 4 wire 5 lacet, snare 6 amenta, hypate, lachet 7 amentum, langate

of beads: 6 rosary 8 necklace

up: 4 hang, lace 5 lynch

string instrument: uke 4 harp, lute, lyre 5 banjo, cello, piano, viola 6 fiddle, guitar, spinet, violin, zither 7 ukalele, ukelele 8 mandolin 11 harpsichord

old: 4 lute, lyre 6 spinet 8 psaltery 11 harpsichord

stringency: 5 force, rigor 7 cogency 8 scarcity, severity 9 tightness 10 strictness

stringent: 4 hard, ropy 5 rigid, tense, tight 6 cogent, severe, strict 7 binding, extreme 10 convincing 11 restrictive

stringer: tie 4 rope, vein, wire 5 irons 6 string, timber 8 filament 9 handcuffs, libertine 11 stringpiece

stringy: 4 ropy 5 gluey 6 sinewy, viscid 7 fibrous, viscous 11 filamentous

strip: bar, rob, tab, tag, top 4 band, bare. bark, belt, doff, flay, hull, husk, peel, pull, skin, tear 5 clear, flake, fleck, pluck, shred, spoil, swath, unrig 6 border, denude, devest, divest, expose, flense, reduce, remove, runway, swathe 7 bandage, bandeau, bereave, degrade, deprive, despoil, disrobe, pillage, plunder, uncloak, uncover, undress, unleave 8 bandeaux(pl.), denudate, disarray, headland, outstrip, separate 9 dismantle, excoriate

10 disfurnish, dispossess **11** debenzolize, decorticate

kinds of: **4** came, cove, lead, rand, riem, tirr **5** cleat, ridge, stave **6** inwale, reglet **7** gunwale

leather: **4** welt **5** thong **6** latigo **7** belting

narrow: **4** slat, tape **5** reeve, strap **7** bandeau **8** bandeaux(pl.)

wooden: rib **4** lath, slat **5** stave **6** reglet

strip tease dancer: **9** ecdysiast

stripe: bar, roe **4** band, beat, belt, blow, kind, lash, line, mark, sort, type, wale, weal, welt, zone **5** chest, stria, strip **6** border, frenum, streak, strike, stroke, thrust **7** chevron, fraenum, lineate, pattern, rivulet **8** division **9** character

striped: bandy **6** banded, barred **7** lineate, vittate **8** bayadere, streaked

stripling: boy, lad **5** chiel, youth **6** chield

stripped: **4** bare, nude **6** picked

by trickery: **7** buncoed, bunkoed, fleeced

strive: aim, hie, tew, try, tug, vie **4** seek, toil **5** bandy, ensue, fight, labor, rival **6** battle, buffet, resist, strain **7** compete, contend, contest, emulate **8** contrast, endeavor, struggle

striving: **5** nisus

strobile: **4** chat, cone

strobilophyta: **4** cone

strockle: **6** shovel

stroil: **5** grass, power, weeds **9** dexterity **10** capability

stroke: bat, coy, fit, hew, hit, pat, pet, rub **4** baff, beat, blow, chap, coup, dash, ding, dint, flip, gowf, hurt, lash, mark, milk, oner, shot, walk, whet **5** chare, douse, dowse, flack, fluke, gowff, ictus, knock, power, pulse, rower, strut, throb, trait **6** attack, caress, effort, fondle, ictuse, impact, injury, soothe, stride **7** seizure, sharpen, whample **8** apoplexy, disaster **9** influence

kinds of: **5** eagle, cerif, serif, wedge **6** birdie **7** virgule

stroll: **4** mosy, roam, rove, walk **5** mosey, range, stray, tramp **6** dacker, daiker, dander, ramble, soodle, wander **7** saunter **8** flanerie

stroller: **4** cart, pram **5** actor, tramp **6** beggar, gocart, player, shuler **7** peddlar, peddler, shuiler, vagrant **8** bohemian, carriage, wanderer **9** saunterer

strolling: **7** roaming **8** flanerie, fugitive

stromming: **7** herring

strone: **4** hill **5** spout **6** stream

strong: fit, hot **4** able, bold, dure, elon, fere, firm, fort, hale, hard, rank, warm, wiry **5** bonny, clear, eager, frack, freck, fresh, great, gross, hardy, heavy, large, lusty, solid, sound, stout, tough, yauld **6** active, ardent, bonnie, brawny, buckra, cogent, feckle, mighty, potent, robust, rugged, sinewy, stable, stouty, strict, sturdy **7** buirdly, durable, fertile, greatly,

huffcap, humming, intense, sthenic, violent, zealous **8** athletic, distinct, flagrant, forceful, forcible, muscular, powerful, puissant, resonant, rigorous, severely, stalwart, strongly, vehement, vigorous **9** Atlantean, difficult, effective, fortright, impetuous, important, strapping, violently **10** boisterous, nourishing, outrageous, passionate, persuasive, productive, pronounced, remarkable **11** excessively **12** concentrated

upward movement: **5** surge

strong-arm: rob **4** beat, thug **5** force, power **7** assault, violent **8** violence

strong cloth: **5** scrim

strong man: *Biblical:* **6** Samson **7** Sampson

legendary: **5** Atlas

strong point: **5** forte

strongbox: **4** case, safe **5** chest, vault

stronghold: **4** fort, hold, keep **5** tower **6** castle **7** citadel, fortify **8** fasthold, fastness, fortress **13** fortification

strongly: **5** bigly **6** stably **8** heartily

strop: **4** hone, whet **7** sharpen

strophe: **6** stanza **10** heptastich

stroud: **5** harsh **6** morose **7** blanket

strow: **5** strew **6** strife **7** turmoil **9** confusion **11** disturbance

stroygood: **7** wastrel **11** spendthrift

strub: rob **5** strip **7** despoil

strubbly: **6** untidy **7** unkempt

struck: **4** smit **5** smote **7** smitten **8** punished

with amazement: **6** aghast

with small missiles: **6** pelted

with sudden fear: **7** alarmed

with terror: **6** aghast

with wonder: **6** aghast

struck out: **5** deled **6** elided, erased, fanned **7** deleted

struck smartly: **9** percussed

structural quality: **7** texture

structure: dam **4** form **5** frame **6** bridge, format, make-up **7** edifice, texture **8** building, bulkhead **9** formation **11** arrangement, composition, fabricature **12** constitution, construction

abnormal: **12** malformation

calcareous: **5** coral

conical: **7** pyramid

crown-like: **6** corona

curved: **4** arch

filamentous: **4** hair

floating: **4** raft

funeral: **10** catafalque

hallowed: **6** bethel, chapel, church, temple **8** basilica **9** cathedral, synagogue **10** tabernacle

high: **5** tower

human: **8** physique

keel-like: **6** carina

latticework: **7** trellis

looplike: **4** ansa

monumental: **5** pylon
on roof: **6** cupola, dormer **9** penthouse
Oriental: **6** pagoda
original: **6** isogen
osseous: **4** bone
over obstacles: **6** bridge
pergola-like: **6** ramada
projecting into water: **4** jiti **5** jetty **6** jettee
raised: **4** dais **5** altar, stage **8** platform
sacrificial: **5** altar
sheltering: cot **4** cote
supporting: **4** pier
tall: **5** tower **7** steeple **9** campanile
tent-like: **10** tabernacle
white: **6** albedo
strudel: **6** pastry
struggle: tug, vie **4** agon, cope, frab, wade
  5 fight, heave, labor **6** battle, buckle,
  bustle, combat, effort, Peniel, strife,
  strike, strive, throes, tussle, widdle **7**
  bargain, barrace, contend, contest,
  flounce, scuffle, warfare, wauchle, wrestle
  8 conflict, endeavor, exertion, flounder,
  scraffle, scramble **10** contention, difficulty
struggling: **12** colluctation
struma: **6** goiter, goitre
strummed: **8** thrummed
strumpet: **4** brim **5** belie, wench **6**
  blowen, harlot **7** cocotte, debauch, slander **8** harridan **10** prostitute
strung: **6** beaded
 highly: **5** tense **7** nervous
strunt: **4** dock **5** pique, strut, stump **6**
  liquor **7** stubble
strut: **4** brag, cock, gait, step, walk **5**
  brace, bulge, swell **6** parade, stride,
  strife, strunt, thrust **7** distend, peacock,
  provide, stiffen, stretch, support, swagger,
  wrangle **8** protrude **10** contention **11**
  protuberant
struthious: **4** emus **5** rheas **6** ratite **9** os-
  triches
stub: pen **4** beat, dolt **5** crush, drive, squat,
  stump **6** coupon, stocky **7** feather, remnant **8** thickset **9** blockhead, extirpate **11**
  counterfoil
stubble: bun **6** strunt **7** gratten, gratton **8**
  eelgrass
stubborn: set **4** rude **5** fixed, hardy, harsh,
  rough, tough **6** coarse, dogged, mulish,
  sturdy **7** restive **8** obdurate, perverse,
  resolute, starkish, vigorous **9** camsteary,
  camsteery, difficult, obstinate, pigheaded
  10 bullheaded, calcitrant, determined,
  hardheaded, headstrong, inflexible, refractory, unyielding **11** intractable **12**
  pertinacious
stubborness: **8** tenacity **9** contumacy,
  obstinacy **12** perverseness
stubby: **5** squat **6** stocky, stumpy **8** thickset
stuck: See stick.
stuck in the mud: **7** bemired
stuck-up: **4** vain **7** haughty **8** arrogant,

snobbish **9** conceited **12** supercilious **13**
  self-important
stud: dot, pin, rod **4** boss, knob, post, stem,
  stub **5** adorn, aglet, beset, brace, haras,
  study, stump **6** aiglet, button, pillar **7**
  chaplet, support **9** studhorse **10** besprinkle
 farm: **5** haras
 for shoe: **7** hobnail
 with jewels: **5** engem
 with radiating bodies: **6** enstar
student: **5** eleve(F.), pupil **6** bursar **7**
  educand, learner **8** disciple, observer
 according to grade: **6** termer
 agricultural college: **5** Aggie
 college: **4** soph **6** junior, senior **8** freshman **9** sophomore
 divinity: **9** theologue **10** theologian
 fellow: **9** classmate
 first year: **5** Fuchs(G.)
 girl: **4** coed
 group: **5** class
 hall: **5** burse **9** dormitory
 law: **8** stagiary
 medical: **6** intern **7** interne
 military: **5** cadet, plebe
 naval academy: **5** cadet **10** midshipman
 of birds: **13** ornithologist
 of crime: **10** penologist **13** criminologist
 of heavens: **13** uranographist
 of proverbs: **14** paroemiologist
 of punishment: **10** penologist
 of relics: **13** archaeologist
 of reptiles: **13** herpetologist
 of spiders: **13** arachnologist
 Oxford: **8** commoner
 residence: **5** house **6** hostel **9** dormitory
 room: **7** seminar
 stipend paid: **6** bursar
 West Point: **5** cadet, plebe
studied: **5** pored **6** intent **7** learned,
  planned **8** designed, inclined, reasoned **10**
  ceremonial, deliberate **12** premeditated
studies: *academic:* **4** arts **7** science **10**
  humanities
 advanced: **7** seminar **8** graduate
 chosen by students: **9** electives
 series of: **6** course
studio: **7** atelier, bottega **8** botteghe,
  workshop **11** ergasterion
studious: **5** booky **7** bookish, devoted,
  studied **8** diligent, sedulous **9** assiduous,
  scholarly **10** deliberate **13** contemplative
study: con, den, mug **4** bone, muse, muzz,
  pore, read, scan **5** grind **6** lesson, peruse,
  ponder **7** analyse, analyze, canvass, croquis, examine **8** consider, meditate **11**
  contemplate **13** consideration, contemplation
 animals: **9** zoography
 bees: **8** apiology
 closely: con **4** pore **7** examine
 course: **7** seminar
 fingerprints: **13** dactylography

fixed course: **4** rote
flowers: **12** anthoecology
handwriting: **10** graphology
hard: **4** bone
horses: **9** hippology
human generations: **15** anthropogenesis
insect's habits: **10** entomology
laborious: **11** lucubration
musical: **5** etude
optional: **8** elective
population: **10** larithmics
punishment: **8** penology
sacred edifices: **7** naology
sacred images: **9** iconology
wines: **7** enology
words: **9** etymology
stuff: pad, ram, wad **4** copy, cram, fill, gaum, junk, pang **5** crowd, farce, force, grain, pulse, steve **6** amount, fabric, graith, matter, refuse, stifle, supply **7** bombast, element, essence, filling, mixture, portion **8** material, medicine, nonsense, overload, stuffing **9** character, principle, substance, suffocate
full: **4** glut **5** gorge **6** stodge **7** satiate
harvested grain: **7** stubble
sticky: goo
worthless: **4** gear **7** hogwash
stuffed: **6** bourre, stodgy **7** bombast, replete **8** farctate
stuffing: **7** padding **8** dressing **9** forcemeat
prepare with: **8** marinate
stuffy: fat **4** dull, prim **5** angry, close, fubsy, fuggy, stout, sulky **6** froust, frowst, stodgy **8** resolute **9** obstinate **10** mettlesome, old-fogyish **11** strait-laced **12** conservative, old-fashioned
stuggy: **5** short **6** stodgy, sturdy **8** thickset
stulm: **4** adit **8** entrance
stultiloquy: **4** talk **6** babble
stumble: err **4** fall, slip, trip **5** lurch **6** boggle, chance, faffle, falter, happen, offend **7** blunder, failure, founder, perplex, scruple, stagger **8** confound, flounder
stumbling: **7** hurting
stump: cob, lop **4** butt, dare, foil, grub, snag, stab, stub **5** block, clump **6** baffle, corner, hobble, pillar, puzzle, strunt, thwart, travel **7** canvass, nonplus, perplex, rostrum, stumble **8** platform **9** challenge **11** electioneer
stumpy: **5** bunty **6** stubby **8** thickset
stun: **4** bowl, daze, tear **5** amaze, aston, daunt, daver, deave, dizzy, dover, shock **6** appall, astone, astony, benumb, bruise, crease, deaden, deafen **7** astound, dammish, scratch, stupefy **8** astonish, bewilder **9** dumbfound, overpower, overwhelm
stung (see also **sting**): **7** smarted
stunned: **10** astonished
stunning: **7** stylish **8** dazzling **9** beautiful **10** foudroyant
stunt: act **4** feat **5** angry, blast, blunt, check, cramp, crowl, dwarf, stamp, whale

6 abrupt, hinder **7** curtail, exploit **8** stubborn **10** undersized **11** performance
gymnastic: kip **4** kipp **10** handspring
stunted: **4** runt
stunty: **5** short **6** flashy, stocky **7** dwarfed
stupa: **5** mound, tower **6** shrine
lamaism: **7** chorten
stupe: **6** foment
stupefacient: **4** drug **8** narcotic **10** stupefying
stupefied: **8** benumbed **9** inebriate
stupefy: fox, sot **4** baze, daze, dope, doze, drug, dull, dunt, numb, stun **5** amaze, aston, besot, blunt, daunt, daver, deave, shock **6** astone, bedaze, bemuse, benumb, muddle **7** astound, confuse **8** astonish, bewilder, confound **10** incrassate
with drink: **6** fuddle
stupefying: **8** bemusing
stupend: **4** stun **7** astound, stupefy **10** stupendous
stupendous: **5** great **7** amazing, immense **8** enormous **9** monstrous, wonderful **10** astounding **11** astonishing **12** overpowering, overwhelming
stupent: **9** stupefied **11** dumbfounded
stupid: **4** bete, clod, dull, dumb, dunt, guam, lewd, slow **5** besot, blunt, booby, crass, dazed, dense, dizzy, goosy, heavy, inane, sumph **6** assish, barren, beetle, boring, bovine, dawkin, doiled, doited, drowsy, goosey, hebete, lurdan, oafish, obtuse, simple, stolid, torpid **7** asinine, brutish, buzzard, calvish, daffish, doldrum, doltish, duffing, dullard, fatuous, foolish, foppish, glaiket, glaikit, gomerel, goosish, gullish, lurdane, prosaic, stunned, vacuous, witless **8** anserine, anserous, backward, bayardly, blockish, boeotian, cloddish, deadened, footless, headless, retarded, sluggish **9** blocklike, bourgeois, brainless, codheaded, inanimate, insensate, insipient, plumbeous, pointless, senseless, stupefied **10** hardwitted, hulver-head, irrational, slow-witted **11** claybrained, heavy-headed **12** buffleheaded **13** unintelligent, uninteresting
render: **8** hebetate
stupidity: **6** betise, stupor **7** density, fatuity **8** dullness, hebetude, idiotism, numbness **9** crassness **12** astonishment, indifference, stupefaction **13** insensibility
stupidly: **10** bullheaded
stupor: fog **4** coma, damp, dote **5** sopor **6** trance **8** lethargy
pert. to: **7** carotic
stuprate: **6** ravish **7** debauch
sturdy: gid, set **4** buff, firm **5** felon, hardy, harsh, lusty, sound, stern, stiff, stout **6** brawny, robust, rugged, rustic, stable, steady, strong **7** violent **8** obdurate, resolute, stalwart, stubborn, vigorous **9** rigidness, obstinate **10** courageous, determined, unyielding **12** stupefaction
sturdy and stout: **5** burly

sturgeon: 6 beluga
small: 7 sterlet
white: 6 beluga
roe: 6 caviar
sturt: vex 4 stir 5 annoy 6 strife 7 startle, trouble 11 disturbance
sturtin, sturtan: 9 staggered 10 frightened
stutter: 7 stammer
stuttering: 8 psellism 9 psellisum
sty, stye: pen 4 boil, soar 5 climb, lodge, mount, stair, steps, stile 6 ascend, aspire, ladder 8 swelling 9 enclosure
stygian: 6 gloomy 7 hellish 8 infernal
style: air, dub, pen, pin, ton 4 call, garb, gere, kind, mode, name, sort, term, type 5 vogue 6 format, gnomon, graver, manner, method, needle, phrase, stylus 7 alamode, diction, entitle, fashion, variety 8 demeanor 9 designate, execution 10 denominate 12 characterize, construction
architecture: 5 Doric, Greek, Ionic, Roman, Saxon 6 Gothic, Norman 7 Italian 8 Colonial, Georgian, Monterey 9 Byzantine 10 Corinthian, Romanesque 11 Elizabethan, Renaissance 13 Mediterranean
art: 5 genre
artistic: 5 gusto
dress: 5 get-up
lofty: 4 epic
oratorical: 10 rhetorical
painting: 5 genre
penmanship: 4 hand
performance: 9 execution
stylet: pro 5 organ, probe 6 dagger 7 poniard 8 stiletto 9 appendage
surgical: 6 trocar
stylish: 4 chic, tony 5 dashy, nifty, smart, swell 6 classy, dressy, jaunty, modish, spiffy, swanky 7 alamode, dashing, doggish, genteel, knowing, swagger 11 fashionable
stylist: 7 modiste
stylites: 7 hermits 8 ascetics
styloid: 8 belonoid
stymie, stymy: 5 block 6 hinder, impede 8 obstruct
styptic: 4 alum 10 astringent
suant: 4 even 5 grave, quiet 6 demure, placid, smooth, steady 7 equable, regular 9 agreeable, following
suasion: 10 persuasion
suasive: 10 convincing, persuasive
suave: 4 easy, oily, smug 5 bland, civil, soapy, sweet 6 polite, smooth, urbane 7 fulsome 8 gracious, mannered, pleasant, polished, unctuous 9 agreeable 12 ingratiating
suavity: 6 comity 7 amenity 8 urbanity 10 politeness 12 complaisance
sub: 9 auxiliary, submarine
subdivide: 5 carve, mince 8 separate
subdivision: 6 sector, suburb 10 department
defensive position: 6 sector

lateral: 5 aisle
rocks: 5 range
subdue: cow 4 bend, quay, tame 5 accoy, allay, amate, atill, break, charm, crush, daunt, dompt, lower, quell, sober 6 adaunt, bridle, disarm, dismay, evince, master, mellow, reduce, soften, steady, subact 7 affaite, chasten, conquer, control, repress, squelch 8 convince, diminish, overcome, suppress, surmount, vanquish 9 captivate, castigate, overpower, subjugate
suber: 4 cork
subjacent: 10 underlying
subject: try 4 text 5 basis, cause, prone, theme, topic 6 liable, matter, motive, phrase, reason, submit, vassal 7 article, citizen, conquer, exposed, reality 8 disposed, incident, inferior, obedient 9 dependent, subjugate, substance 10 contingent, predispose, submissive, substratum 11 conditional, subordinate
of discourse: 5 theme, topic
of disease: 4 case 7 patient
of lawsuit: res
of verb: 4 noun
to abuse: 6 revile
to argument: 4 moot
to authority: 6 master
to be taught: 10 didascalic
to change: 7 mutable
to choice: 8 elective
to control: 7 rulable
to death: 6 mortal
to depression: 5 moody
to dislike: 8 aversion
to ill treatment: 6 misuse
to mistakes: 7 erratic
to taxation: 8 reteable
to whirling action: 11 centifugate
subjection: 8 thirling 9 captivity
subjoin: add 5 affix, annex 6 append, attack
subjugate: 6 compel, master, reduce, subdue 7 conquer, depress, overawe 8 overcome
sublate: 4 deny 6 cancel, negate, remove 9 eliminate
sublime: 5 exalt, grand, great, lofty, noble, proud 6 purify, refine 7 emotion, exalted, haughty, supreme 8 elevated, empyreal, heavenly, heighten, majestic, splendid, upraised 9 expletive
sublimity: 7 majesty 8 grandeur 12 magnificence
submarine: sub 4 boat 5 diver 9 periscope 11 submersible
detector: 5 sonar
projectile: 7 missile, Polaris, torpedo
submerge: dip 4 bury, dive, hide, sink 5 souse 6 deluge, drench, engulf, plunge 8 inundate, suppress
submiss: low 6 humble 7 subdued 10 obsequious, submissive
submission: 8 meekness 9 deference,

obedience, surrender **10** compliance, confession **11** resignation **13** nonresistance

to destiny: **8** fatalism

submissive: **4** meek **5** buxom **6** docile, humble **7** dutiful, passive, servile **8** obedient, resigned, yielding **9** childlike, compliant

to wife: **8** uxorious

submit: bow **4** bend, obey **5** abide, agree, avale, defer, heald, hield, lower, stoop, yield **6** assent, comply, delate, resign, soften, subdue, suffer, temper **7** exhibit, knuckle, propose, succumb, suggest **8** moderate **9** acquiesce, surrender **10** condescend

for consideration: **5** remit

proposal to: **4** move

to: **4** obey

subordinate: **5** minor, under **6** puisne, subdue **7** control **8** inferior, obedient, servient **9** ancillary, assistant, auxiliary, dependent, secondary, underling **10** accidental, collateral, incidental, submissive **11** subservient

activity: **8** parergon

adjunct: **9** appendage

officer: **4** exon

suborn: **5** adorn, bribe, equip, foist **6** father, incite, induce **7** furnish, procure, provide **9** instigate

subpoena: **4** writ

subreption: **6** secret, snatch, unfair **8** unlawful **9** deduction **11** underhanded

subscribe: **5** favor **6** assent, attest **7** ascribe, consent, support **8** sanction **10** acceptance, underwrite

subscriber of newspaper: **6** abonne

subscription to newspaper: **10** abonnement

subsequent: **5** after, later **6** puisne **7** ensuing **8** retainer **9** attendant, companion, following

to birth: **9** postnatal

subsequently: **5** later, since **10** afterwards, thereafter

subservient: **6** vassal **7** duteous, servile **9** accessory, ancillary, auxiliary, truckling **10** obsequious, submissive **11** subordinate

subside: ebb **4** bate, fall, lull, sink, wane **5** abate, cease, lower **6** settle **7** descend, flatten, relapse **8** decrease, withdraw

subsidence: **5** dregs

subsidiary: **7** reserve **9** accessory, assistant, auxiliary, tributary **10** collateral **13** supplementary

subsidy: aid **4** gift, help **5** bonus, grant **6** bounty **7** pension, reserve, support, tribute **10** assistance, subvention

subsist: be **4** feed, hold, live, stay **5** abide, exist, stand **6** obtain, remain **7** support, continue, maintain

subsistence: **6** living **9** allowance, inher-

ency, substance **10** livelihood, provisions **11** persistence

subsoil: bed, pan **4** sole **7** stratum

animal: **4** mole

substance: sum **4** body, core, gist, mass, meat **5** basis, metal, stuff **6** estate, ground, import, matter, realty, spirit, supply, wealth **7** aliment, essence, meaning, purport **8** hardness, majority, material, property, solidity **9** actuality, affluence, resources, solidness **11** consistency

amorphous: **5** resin, rosin **7** ferrite

animal: **7** gelatin

bitter: **4** acid **5** aloes, aloin, linin **6** ilicin **7** amarine, emetine **8** elaterin

dissolving: **9** resolvent

expansive: gas

reaction-inducing: **7** reagent

rubber-like: **5** gutta

simple: **7** element

sour: **4** acid **7** vinegar

starch-like: **6** inulin, olivil **8** alantine

sticky: goo, gum, tar **4** glue **5** paste

transparent: **9** celluloid

unctuous: oil **6** grease

vegetable: **4** peat **5** resin, rosin

white: **4** alba **6** inulin **7** alanine **8** elaterin

substantial: **4** firm, real, true **5** ample, large, meaty, solid, sound, stout **6** actual, bodily, hearty, stable, strong, sturdy **7** genuine, wealthy **8** tangible **9** corporeal, important **12** considerable

substantiality: See **substance**.

substantiate: **5** prove **6** assure, embody, verify **7** confirm **9** establish **11** corroborate

substantive: **4** noun **6** actual, entity **7** pronoun **9** essential **13** self-contained

substitute: **5** extra, fudge, proxy, vicar **6** deputy, ersatz(G.), ringer **7** commute, replace **8** exchange, nominate **9** alternate, makeshift, surrogate **10** viceregent **11** succedaneum **13** succenturiate

substructure: **4** base **6** podium **10** foundation

subsume: **6** assume, deduce **7** contain **8** classify **9** summarize

subterfuge: **4** plan, ruse **5** blind, trick **6** device, escape, refuge **7** evasion **8** artifice, pretense **9** deception **13** prevarication **14** tergiversation

use: **7** chicane **12** tergiversate

subterranean: **4** cave **6** cavern, hidden, secret

subtile: See **subtle**.

subtilize: **5** exalt **9** sublimate

subtle: sly **4** deft, keen, nice, wily **5** acute **6** artful, clever, crafty, expert, shrewd **7** cunning, elusive, refined, tenuous **8** abstruse, analytic, delicate, rarefied, skillful **9** beguiling, designing, ingenious, intricate **10** mysterious, perceptive **11** penetrating **14** discriminating

subtlety: **7** exility, finesse
subtract: **5** minus **6** deduct, remove **7** detract **8** withdraw, withhold
suburb: **8** environs **9** dissolute, outskirts, periphery
subvention: aid **4** help **5** grant **7** subsidy, support **9** endowment **10** assistance **13** appropriation
subvert: sap **4** ruin **5** evert, upset **6** uproot **7** corrupt, destroy, pervert **8** alienate, overturn **9** overthrow, undermine
subway: **4** tube **5** metro **6** tunnel **11** underground
entrance: **5** kiosk
succade: **8** preserve **10** confection
succedaneum: **6** remedy **8** medicine **10** substitute
succeed: win **4** fare **5** fadge, occur **6** attain, follow, happen, thrive **7** achieve, descend, inherit, prevail, prosper, replace **8** approach, flourish **10** accomplish
succeeding: **7** ensuing, sequent
success: go; hit, wow **4** luck **7** fortune **8** accolade **9** happiness **11** consequence
succession: row, run **6** course, series **7** dynasty **8** sequence **9** gradation
next in line: **4** heir
successive: **9** inherited **10** hereditary **11** consecutive
successor: **4** heir **5** heres **6** haeres, tanist **9** designado(Sp.)
succin: **5** amber
succinct: **4** curt **5** brief, short, terse **6** girded **7** compact, concise, laconic, summary **10** compressed
succor: aid **4** abet, cure, help **5** serve **6** assist, refuge, relief, rescue **7** comfort, deliver, provide, sustain **8** befriend, mitigate **9** alleviate **10** strengthen
succory: **7** chicory
succulent: **4** aloe, lush **5** fresh, juicy, pappy, tasty, vital **6** cactus, tender
succumb: die **5** yield **6** perish, submit
succursal: **6** branch **9** auxiliary **10** subsidiary
such: as, so; sic(L.) **4** kind, like, some **7** certain, similar
suck: rob, sip **4** draw, lick, swig **5** bleed, draft, drain, drink, nurse **6** absorb, adsorb, imbibe, inhale, suckle **7** consume, extract, suction **14** disappointment
sucker: **4** dupe **5** leech **6** victim **8** lollipop **9** simpleton
sucking fish: **6** remora **7** lamprey
suckle: **4** feed, rear, suck **5** nurse **6** foster **7** nourish **11** honeysuckle
sucrose: **5** sugar **10** saccharose
suction: **6** intake **7** drawing, lifting
sud: **4** foam **6** bubble
Sudan: *animal:* **4** dama **6** oterop
beer: **4** dolo
capital: **7** Khartum
language: Ga, Mo; Ewe, Ibo, Kru **4** Efik, Mole, Tshi **6** Yoruba **8** Mandingo

people: **4** Daza, Golo, Sere **5** Fulah, Hausa, Mossi
stockade: **6** zareba, zereba, zeriba **7** zareeba
stretcher: **7** angareb, angarep **8** angareeb
weapon: **8** trombash, trumbash
sudden: **4** rash, soon **5** brief, early, ferly, hasty, short, swift **6** abrupt, speedy **7** prerupt, violent **8** headlong, meteoric **9** alertness, impetuous, impromptu **10** unexpected, unforeseen, unprepared **11** precipitate, precipitous
suddenly: **6** presto
suddle: **4** soil **5** stain
suds: bog **4** beer, foam **5** dregs, filth, froth **6** lather, refuse **7** bubbles
sue: beg, woo **4** seek, urge **5** chase, court, ensue, plead **6** appeal, follow, guided, pursue **7** beseech, contest, entreat, proceed, request, solicit **8** continue, governed, petition, practice **9** prosecute
suer: **9** plaintiff
suet: fat **6** tallow
Suez Canal: *builder:* **9** de Lesseps
port: **4** Said
suffer: get, let **4** bear, bide, dree(Sc.) **5** admit, allow, groan, thole **6** endure, grieve, permit, submit **7** agonize, undergo **8** tolerate **10** experience
sufferance: **4** pain **6** misery **7** consent, respite **8** patience, sanction **9** passivity, suffering **11** forbearance **12** postponement
sufferer: **6** martyr, victim
suffering: ill **4** bale, dree(Sc.), loss, pain, **5** agony **6** ailing, injury **8** distress, sickness **9** adversity **10** affliction **11** tribulation
reliever of: **9** Samaritan
suffice: do **5** serve **6** answer **7** appease, content, satisfy
sufficiency: **4** fill **7** ability, conceit **8** adequacy, capacity **9** abundance **10** capability, competency
sufficient: due, fit **4** able, enow, good **5** ample, valid **6** enough, plenty **7** suffice **8** abundant, adequate **9** competent, effectual, efficient, qualified **11** responsible, substantial **12** satisfactory **13** well-qualified
sufflate: **7** inflate, inspire
suffocate: **4** kill **5** burke, choke **6** stifle **7** destroy, smother **8** compress, strangle, suppress, throttle **10** asphyxiate, extinguish
suffocation: **8** asphyxia
suffragan: **4** help **5** agent **6** bishop, deputy **9** assistant, auxiliary **11** subordinate
suffrage: aid **4** help, vote **5** right, voice **6** assent, ballot, prayer **7** witness **8** petition **9** franchise, testimony **10** assistance **12** intercession, supplication
suffuse: **4** fill, pour **5** embay **7** diffuse **10** overspread

sugar: gur, ose **4** cane **5** biose, candy, maple, money, oside **6** acrose, aldose, fucose, gulose, hexose, ketose, talose, triose **7** caramel, chitose, glucide, maltose, sucrose, sweeten, tetrose, threose **8** rhodeose **9** muscovado, raffinose, sweetness **10** digitoxose, piloncillo, saccharose **12** carbohydrate **13** dissaccharide **14** monosaccharide
boiling kettle: **8** flambeau
crystals: **5** candy
liquid: **5** sirup, syrup
measure: **13** saccharimeter
mixture: **5** syrup
preparation device: **10** granulator
raw: **9** cassonade
substitute: **5** honey **9** saccharin
syrup: **7** treacle **8** molasses
sugar apple: **6** biriba **8** sweetsop
sugar sand: **5** niter
sugarcane: *disease:* **5** sereh
pulp: **4** marc **6** megass **7** bagasse, megasse
refuse: **4** mare **6** begass **7** bagasse, begasse
stalk: **6** ratoon
sugarloaf: **4** hill **8** conoidal, mountain
sugarplum: **6** bonbon **9** sweetmeat
sugary: **5** sweet **7** honeyed **8** pleasant **10** flattering, saccharine **11** mellifluous
suggest: **4** hint, move **5** imply **6** allude, broach, prompt **7** connote, inspire, mention, propose **8** indicate, intimate **9** insinuate
suggestion: **4** idea **5** tinge, touch, trace **6** advice **7** inkling, remnant, soupcon **8** proposal **9** complaint **10** accusation, incitement, intimation, temptation **11** information
suidae: hog **5** swine
suing: **11** prosecution
suint: **5** sweat **6** grease **12** perspiration
suit: do **4** case(law), kind, plea, sort **5** adapt, agree, apply, cards, class, dress, fadge, group, habit, match, order, serve, tally **6** accord, adjust, answer, appeal, assort, attire, behove, outfit, please, prayer, series, trover, wooing **7** arrange, behoove, clothes, comport, conform, costume, request, satisfy, uniform **8** classify, courting, entreaty, petition, sequence **9** harmonize **10** correspond, litigation, succession **11** accommodate **12** solicitation
maker: **6** sartor, tailor
suitable: apt, due, fit, pat **4** able, fair, good, meet **5** right **6** comely, gainly, proper **7** a propos, seeming **8** adequate, apposite, becoming, coherent, eligible, feasible, idoneous, matching **9** competent, congruent, congruous, consonant, expedient **10** commodious, compatible, consistent, convenient, equivalent **11** appropriate **12** commensurate
render: **5** adapt **7** prepare

suitcase: bag **4** grip **6** valise **9** gladstone
suite: set **4** band **5** abode, group, staff, train **6** series **7** retinue **8** equipage **9** apartment, entourage **10** collection
member of: **7** attaché
musical: See **musical composition**.
suited: See **suitable**.
suiting: **4** wool **5** serge
suitor: **4** beau **5** wooer **7** gallant **8** follower **10** petitioner
sukey: **9** teakettle
sulcate: **6** fluted **7** grooved
sulfate: **5** treat **7** convert, sulphur **9** brimstone **10** impregnate
kind: **4** alum **5** hepar, matte **6** barite, blende **7** ilesite, loweite
sulfur: **9** brimstone
substance containing: **5** hepar
sulk: **4** dort(Sc.), mope, pout **5** grump **6** grouch
sulky: **4** cart, dull, weak **5** chuff, dorty, inert **6** gloomy, gocart, grouty, sullen **7** doggish, peevish **8** carriage, inactive **10** unyielding
sullage: mud **4** silt **5** filth **6** refuse, scoria, sewage **8** drainage **9** pollution **10** filthiness
sullen: sad **4** dour, dull, glum, grim, sour **5** alone, black, cross, felon, gruff, heavy, moody, pouty, stern, sulky, surly **6** crusty, dismal, dogged, gloomy, grouty, morose, silent, somber **7** baleful, boorish, crabbed, peevish, serious **8** churlish, lowering, petulant, solitary **9** obstinate, saturnine **10** depressing, ill-humored, ill-natured, refractory, unsociable **11** intractable, threatening **12** unpropitious
sully: **4** blot, blur, foul, soil **5** cloud, dirty, grime, smear, stain, taint **6** darken, defile, smirch **7** attaint, blacken, blemish, corrupt, pollute, tarnish **8** besmirch **9** bespatter **11** contaminate
sulphate: See **sulfate**.
sultan: **5** ruler **8** padishah **9** sovereign
decree: **5** irade
sultry: hot **5** close, fiery, humid, lurid **6** coarse, smutty, torrid **7** sensual **8** inflamed **10** oppressive, sweltering **13** uncomfortable
Sulu island: **6** Siassi
sum: add, end, tot **4** gist, host **5** count, gross, issue, total, whole **6** amount, degree, height, number, result, summit **7** integer, numeral, problem, summary **8** addition, assembly, entirety, perorate, quantity **9** aggregate, calculate, gathering, magnitude, substance, summarize, summation **11** epilogation **12** recapitulate
forfeited: **5** dedit
large: gob, pot
small: **4** drab **7** driblet **8** dribblet **11** chickenfeed
unexpended: **7** savings

sumac, sumach: 4 anam 7 dogwood 8
shoemake 11 balinghasay
genus of: 4 rhus
Sumatra: *animal:* 4 balu, tanu 5 orang
city: 5 Achin, Jambi, Medan 6 Padang 8
Bonkulin 9 Bencoolen, Indrapoor, Palem-
bang
deer: 4 napu
fiber: 6 caloee
language: 4 Nias
measure: 4 paal
raft: 5 rakit
river: 4 Musi 5 Jambi, Rokan 9 Indragiri
Sumer deity: Abu
summarize: sum 5 recap 6 digest 8 abstract 9 epitomize
summary: sum 4 gist 5 brief, recap, short
6 digest, precis, resume, summit 7 concise, epitome, extract, general, medulla 8
abstract, argument, breviate, succinct,
synopsis 9 condensed 10 compendium
11 abridgement 13 comprehension 14
recapitulation
summation: See **sum**.
summer: ete(F.) 8 estivate 9 aestivate
pass: 8 estivate
pert. to: 7 estival 8 aestival
summer teal: 8 garganey
summerhouse: 6 casino 9 belvedere
summery: 5 light 7 estival 8 delicate
summing up: See **sum**.
summit (see also **mountain, peak**)**:** bow,
cap, tip, top, van 4 acme, apex, knap,
roof 5 crest, crown, ridge 6 climax, comble, height, vertex, zenith 8 pinnacle 9
fastigium(L.) 11 culmination
pert. to: 6 apical
summon: ban, bid 4 call, page 5 charm,
evoke, rally, rouse 6 accite, appeal,
arouse, compel, demand, gather, muster
7 collect, command, convoke, provoke
summoner: 6 beadle 9 apparitor
summons: 4 writ 6 venire 7 command,
warning 8 citation 9 challenge 12
notification
sump: mud, pit 4 dirt, pool, pump, tank,
well 5 drain 6 puddle, shower 7 cistern,
depress 8 cesspool 9 reservoir 10
depression, excavation, receptacle
sumpter: 4 pack 6 burden
sumptuous: 5 grand 6 costly, lavish, superb 8 splendid 9 expensive, luxurious
11 magnificent
sun: orb, sol 4 bask, star 5 Titan 6 bleach
7 daystar, Phoebus 8 luminary 9 Harmachis
combining form: 5 helio
crossing equator: 7 equinox
god: Ra; Tem, Utu 4 Baal, Lleu, Llew,
Utug 6 Apollo, Helios 7 Chepera,
Khepara, Shamash, Sokaris 8 Hyperion
measuring device: 13 pyrheliometer

mock: 9 parhelion
near: 6 heliac
outer layer: 6 corona
part: 6 corona
path: 8 ecliptic
pert. to: 5 solar 6 heliac
protective devices: 7 parasol 8 blindage,
havelock
satellite: 6 planet
worshiper: 5 Parsi 6 Parsee 10 heliolater
sun-clock: 7 sundial
sun disk: 4 Aten
sun dog: 4 halo 7 rainbow 9 parhelion
sun room: 7 solaria 8 solarium
sun watch: 7 sundial 9 timepiece
sunburst: 6 brooch, ensign
Sunda Island: 4 Bali
Sunday: *pert. to:* 9 dominical
special: 4 Palm 6 Easter
sunder: rip 4 part, rend, rive 5 break, split
6 divide, severe 7 disjoin, disrupt, divorce 8 dissever, disunite, separate
sundial part: 6 gnomon
sundown: See **sunset**.
sundowner: 5 drink, tramp 7 captain 8
nightcap
sundry: 5 apart 6 divers 7 asunder, diverse, several, various 8 distinct, frequent, manifold, numerous, separate,
sundered 9 different, disunited 10 respective, separately 12 multifarious 13
miscellaneous
sunfall: See **sunset**.
sunfish: 5 bream 8 pondfish
genus of: 4 mola
sunflower: 8 marigold, rockrose 10 bal-
samroot, heliotrope
Sunflower State: 6 Kansas
sunk: (see also **sink**)**:** pad 4 bank, seat, turf,
5 couch 6 abject, hollow 8 absorbed,
overcome 9 depressed
sunket: 4 food 6 dainty 8 delicacy
sunless: 4 dark
sunny: gay 4 warm 5 clear, happy, merry
6 bright, golden, sunlit 8 cheerful 9
sparkling, vivacious
sunrise: 4 dawn
sunset: e'en, eve 4 dusk 7 evening, sundown, sunfall 8 twilight
pert. to: 9 acronical
reflection: 9 alpenglow
Sunset State: 6 Oregon 7 Arizona
sunshade: 5 visor 6 awning 7 parasol
sunshine: 5 cheer, light 6 warmth 8 sunburst 9 happiness, sunniness 11 fairweather 12 cheerfulness
Sunshine State: 9 New Mexico 11 South
Dakota
sunspot: 6 facula 7 freckle
sunstroke: 8 siriasis 9 calenture
sunwise: 6 deasil, dessil 7 deiseal 9
clockwise
sup: eat, sip 4 dine 5 drink, feast 6 absorb,

amount, liquor **7** consume, swallow **8** mouthful, quantity, spoonful

supawn: 4 mush **12** hasty pudding

super: 5 actor, watch **6** square **7** janitor **9** excellent, first-rate

superable: 12 surmountable

superabundance: 5 flood **6** excess **8** plethora **10** exuberance **11** superfluity

superabundant: 4 rank **6** lavish **9** redundant **11** overflowing

superannuate: 6 retire **7** outlast **8** obsolete **9** out-of-date **10** disqualify

superannuated: 5 passe **8** obsolete, outdated **10** antiquated **12** old-fashioned

superb: 4 fine, rich **5** grand, noble, proud **6** lordly **7** elegant, haughty, stately **8** enormous, majestic, splendid **9** excellent, luxurious, sumptuous **13** extraordinary

superbity: 9 arrogance **11** haughtiness

supercilious: 5 lofty, proud **6** uppish **7** haughty **8** arrogant, cavalier, snobbish **9** arbitrary **11** overbearing **12** contemptuous **13** hypercritical

superficial: 4 glib **5** hasty **6** casual, flimsy, slight **7** cursory, outward, shallow, surface **8** external

superfluity: 6 excess, luxury **9** abundance **11** prodigality

superfluous: 4 over **5** spare **6** de trop(F.) **7** surplus, useless **8** abnormal, needless, wasteful **9** excessive, redundant, worthless **10** gratuitous, inordinate **11** extravagant, unnecessary **12** nonessential **13** superabundant

superhuman: 6 divine **8** superman **9** herculean **12** supernatural **13** extraordinary

superhumeral: 5 amice

superimpose: 7 overlay

superintend: 4 boss **5** guide **6** direct, manage **7** conduct, control, inspect, oversee **8** engineer **9** supervise **10** administer

superintendence: 4 care **9** authority **14** responsibility

superintendent: 4 boss **6** bishop **7** captain, curator, manager **8** director, minister, overseer **9** inspector **10** supervisor **11** chamberlain

superior: 4 fine, head, lord, over, peer **5** above, eigne, extra, liege, upper **6** better, higher, senior **7** exalted, greater, haughty, palmary, prelate, ranking **8** alderman, arrogant, assuming, dominant, elevated, masterly **9** ascendant, ascendent, excellent, paramount, spiritual **10** preeminent, surpassing **11** predominant **12** supercilious, supernatural **13** comprehensive

superiority: 4 gree(Sc.) **8** priority **9** advantage, meliority, seniority **13** preponderance

position of: **10** domination

superlative: 4 acme, best, peak **6** utmost **7** supreme **8** peerless **9** excessive **11** exaggerated

suffix: est

supernal: 6 divine **8** ethereal, heavenly **9** celestial

supernatural: 5 magic **6** divine **9** marvelous **10** miraculous, superhuman **13** preternatural

superscribe: 5 write **6** direct **7** address, engrave

superscription: 5 title **9** direction **11** description, inscription

supersede, supercede: 7 replace, succeed **8** displace, override, supplant

supersensory: 12 extrasensory **13** supersensible

superstition: 5 freet, freit, magic **6** fetish, voodoo **8** idolatry

supervene: 5 ensue **6** follow, happen **9** supersede

supervise: 4 boss, edit, read, scan **5** check **6** direct, govern, manage, peruse, revise **7** conduct, correct, inspect, oversee **11** superintend

supervisor: 7 foreman **8** alytarch(G.) **9** spectator **10** roadmaster

supine: 5 inert, prone **6** abject, drowsy **7** leaning, passive, sloping, unalert **8** inactive, inclined, indolent, listless, sluggish **9** negligent **11** inattentive, indifferent

supper: tea 4 meal

supplant: 5 upset, usurp **6** follow, remove, uproot **7** replace, succeed **8** displace **9** extirpate, overthrow, supersede, undermine

supple: sly 4 bain, oily **5** agile, lithe **6** limber, lissom, nimble, pliant, swanky **7** cunning, elastic, fawning, lissome, pliable, servile **8** flexible, yielding **9** adaptable, compliant, resilient **10** obsequious, responsive **11** complaisant

supplement: add 8 addendum, addition, appendix **9** accessory **10** complement **13** reinforcement

supplemental: 12 adscititious **13** succenturiate

suppliant: 6 beggar **10** beseeching, entreating, petitioner

supplicate: beg, sue 4 knee, pray **5** crave, plead **6** appeal, invoke, obtest **7** beseech, conjure, entreat, implore, request, solicit **8** petition **9** importune, obsecrate

supplication: 6 litany **8** rogative

supply: aid, fit 4 feed, fill, fund, give, help, load **5** cache, cater, equip, hoard, relay, stock, store, yield **6** afford, employ, foison, purvey, relief, succor **7** fraught, furnish, granary, nourish, plenish, provide, replace, reserve, satisfy **8** minister, ordnance **9** profusion, reinforce, replenish, reservoir **10** administer, assistance, compensate, contribute

support: aid, arm, guy, leg, peg, rib 4 back, base, beam, bear, bibb, fend, help, keep, limb, pier, prop, stay **5** boost, brace, carry, cheer, cleat, easel, favor, found, hinge, shore, sling, staff, strut, truss **6** anchor, behalf, better, defend, endure, lintel, pillar, second, shield, splint, spring, suffer, tripod, trivet, uphold, verify **7** bolster, cherish, comfort, confirm, console, endorse, espouse, fulcrum, nourish, nurture, protect, provide, reserve, sustain, trestle **8** approval, baluster, befriend, evidence, maintain, pedestal, sanction, tolerate, underlie **9** adminicle, encourage, reinforce, stanchion, vindicate **10** assistance, foundation, strengthen **11** corroborate, countenance **12** alimentation, substantiate

supporter: **4** ally, knee **6** bearer, patron, rooter **7** abetter, abettor, booster, founder, support **8** adherent, advocate, assertor, follower, henchman, partisan **9** auxiliary

suppose: **4** deem, trow, ween **5** allow, imply, judge, opine, think **6** assume, expect, repute **7** believe, imagine, incline, opinion, presume, suspect **8** conceive, conclude, consider, obligate, supposal **9** apprehend, intention **10** conjecture, presuppose, substitute **11** expectation, supposition

supposed: See **supposititious.**

supposition: if **6** notion, theory **7** forgery, surmise **9** postulate **10** alteration, assumption, conjecture, estimation, hypothesis **11** expectation, proposition, uncertainty

supposititious: **7** feigned **8** fabulous, putative, spurious, supposed **9** imaginary, pretended **10** artificial **11** counterfeit **12** hypothetical, illegitimate

suppress: **4** hide, keep, kill, stop **5** check, choke, crush, elide, quash, quell **6** arrest, bridle, censor, harass, ravish, retard, stifle, subdue **7** abolish, conceal, destroy, exclude, oppress, prevent, refrain, repress, silence, smother, squelch **8** compress, prohibit, restrain, withhold **9** interdict, overpower, overthrow **10** dissolving, extinguish

suprarenal: **7** adrenal

supremacy: **4** sway **5** power **7** control, mastery **8** dominion **9** authority, autocracy, dominance, influence **10** ascendancy, ascendency, domination **11** sovereignty **12** predominance **13** preponderance

supreme: **4** last **5** chief, final **6** utmost **7** crucial, highest **8** foremost, greatest, loftiest, peerless, ultimate **9** paramount **10** preeminent

supreme being: **5** Allah, monad **7** creator

surcease: end **4** rest, stay, stop **5** defer, delay **6** desist, relief **7** refrain, respite, suspend **8** postpone **9** cessation

surcharge: tax **4** cost, fill, load **6** burden, impost **7** surfeit **8** overload, surprint **9** overcrowd, overprint, overstock **10** impregnate, overburden, overcharge

surcingle: **4** band, belt **6** girdle **8** cincture

surd: **7** radical **9** insensate, voiceless **10** irrational

sure: **4** fast, firm, safe, true **5** siker(Sc.) **6** indeed, secure, sicker(Sc.), stable, steady, strong **7** assured, certain **8** enduring, positive, reliable, unerring **9** authentic, betrothed, confident, convinced, steadfast, undoubted, unfailing **10** dependable, infallible **11** indubitable, trustworthy, unfaltering **12** indisputable **13** incontestable **14** unquestionable

surely: **6** atweel(Sc.), really

sureness: **9** certitude

surety: **4** bail **6** backer, pledge **7** engager, sponsor **8** bailsman, bondsman, security **9** assurance, certainty, guarantee, guarantor **10** confidence

post: **4** bond

surf: **4** foam, wave **5** spray, swell **7** breaker

sound of: **4** rote

surface: **4** area, face, pave, side, skin **5** facet, plane **6** facing, finish, patina **7** outside **8** boundary, exterior **11** superficial

flat: **4** area **5** plane, sheet **7** lateral

geometrical: **5** nappe **6** toroid

inclined: **4** cant, ramp

mellowed: **6** patina

pert. to: **6** facial

rounded: **9** concavity, convexity

toward: **5** ectad

surfacing: **6** gravel **7** asphalt, macadam

surfeit: **4** cloy, feed, glut, sate **6** excess, nausea, supply **7** disgust, replete, satiate, satiety, satisfy **8** disorder **9** satiation **10** discomfort **11** extravagant, overindulge, superfluity **13** overabundance **14** overindulgence

surfeited: **4** sick **5** blase, fed up **8** complete

surge: **4** rise, rush, tide, wave **5** gurge, swell **6** billow **7** estuate, rolling **8** sweeping, swelling

surgeon: **10** chirurgeon

surgeonfish: **4** tang

surgery: **9** operation, resection

instrument: **5** fleam, lance, probe, scala **6** bilabe, gorget, lancet, splint, stylet, trapan, trepan, trocar, vectis **7** forceps, levator, ligator, rongeur, scalpel, trilabe, trochar **8** bistoury, ecraseur, trephine, tweezers **9** goosebill, tenaculum, vulsellum **10** abaptiston, abaptistum, terebellum, tourniquet

perform: **7** operate

roller: **6** fascia **7** fasciae

stitch: **5** seton **6** suture

Surinam: *measure:* **7** ketting

toad: **4** pipa **5** pipal

surly: **4** glum, grum, rude **5** bluff, chuff, cross, gruff, gurly **6** abrupt, grumpy, morose, sullen **7** boorish, crabbed, haughty, uncivil **8** arrogant, churlish, growling **10** ill-natured **11** intractable

surmise: 4 deem 5 guess, infer, trace 6 charge 7 imagine, presume, suppose 9 suspicion 10 allegation, assumption, conclusion, conjecture 11 supposition

surmount: top 4 pass, rise, tide 5 climb, crown, excel, mount, total 6 ascend, exceed, hurdle, subdue 7 conquer, surpass 8 overcome 9 negotiate, transcend

surmountable: 9 superable

surmounting: 4 atop

surname: 6 byname 7 agnomen 8 cognomen 11 appellation

surpass: cap, cob, top 4 beat, flog 5 amend, excel, outdo 6 better, exceed, outvie 7 eclipse, outrank, outsoar 8 outclass, outreach, outstrip, surmount 9 transcend

surpassing: 4 fine 6 banner 9 excellent 10 inimitable, preeminent

surplice: 5 cotta, ephod

surplus: 4 over, rest 5 extra 6 excess 7 backlog, reserve 8 overplus 10 redundancy

surprise: awe, cap 5 alarm, amaze, catch, seize, shock 6 dazzle, detect, strike, wonder 7 astound, capture, gloppen, perplex, startle, uncover 8 astonish, bewilder, confound, dumfound, overcome 9 amazement, overwhelm 11 flabbergast

surprised: 5 agape

surprising: 10 unexpected 13 extraordinary

surrealist: 4 Dali

surrender: 4 cede, fall, give 5 remit, yield 6 remise, resign, tender, waiver 7 abandon, cession, concede, deliver, forsake 8 dedition, remittal 9 rendition 10 abdication, capitulate, compromise, relinquish 11 divestiture 12 cancellation

surreptitious: sly 6 secret 7 bootleg 8 sneaking, stealthy 9 underhand 11 clandestine

surrogate: 6 deputy 8 delegate 9 subrogate 10 substitute

surround: bar, hem 4 belt, fold, gird, ring 5 beset, embay, flood, hedge 6 circle, corral, encase, enring, invest 7 besiege, embosom, enclose, environ, imbosom 8 encircle, envelope, inundate, overflow 9 beleaguer, encompass 12 circumscribe 14 circumnavigate

with water: 4 isle 6 enisle

surrounded: in; mid 4 amid 5 among 6 amidst 7 bounded

surrounding: 5 about, midst 7 context, setting 8 ambiance 9 entourage 11 environment 12 circumjacent, circumstance

surtout: 4 coat, hood 7 garment 8 overcoat

survey: 4 poll, scan, view 5 study 6 regard, review, search 7 examine, history, inspect, oversee 8 consider, traverse 9 delineate, determine, treatment 10 exposition, scrutinize 11 description, recon-

noiter, superintend 13 triangulation 14 reconnaissance

surveyor: 6 gauger 9 arpenteur, inspector 14 superintendent

helper: 6 rodman 7 lineman, poleman 8 chainman

instrument: 11 stratameter

nail: 4 spad

tool: 6 alidad 7 alidade, transit 10 theodolite 12 perambulator

survival: 5 relic

survive: 7 outlast, outlive

susceptible: 4 easy, open 6 liable 7 exposed, subject 8 allergic, sensible 9 receptive, sensitive 10 responsive, vulnerable 11 softhearted, unresistant 13 tenderhearted 14 impressionable

susceptibility: 5 sense 7 emotion, feeling 11 sensibility 13 affectibility

suscitate: 5 rouse 6 excite 7 animate 9 stimulate

suslik: 5 sisel 8 squirrel 11 spermophile

suspect: 4 fear 5 doubt, guess 7 dubious, imagine, inkling, presume, suppose, surmise 8 conceive, distrust, mistrust 9 discredit 10 disbelieve, intimation, suspicious 12 apprehension

suspend: bar 4 hang, hold, oust, stop 5 cease, debar, defer, demur, expel 6 dangle, recess 7 adjourn, exclude 8 intermit, postpone, withhold 9 pretermit

suspended: 4 hung 6 latent 7 abeyant, pendent, pensile 8 inactive 11 inoperative

suspender: 5 brace 6 garter 7 galluse 9 supporter

suspense: 7 anxiety 8 cautious, hesitant, withheld 11 tenterhooks, uncertainty 12 apprehension 14 indecisiveness

in: 7 pending

suspension: 4 stop 5 delay 7 failure 8 abeyance, buoyancy, stoppage 9 remission 11 withholding 12 intermission, interruption

in air: 5 vapor

suspicion: 4 hint 5 doubt, touch, trace 7 askance, inkling 8 distrust, jealousy, mistrust 9 misgiving 10 diffidence, intimation, suggestion, uneasiness 11 expectation 12 apprehension

suspicious: 5 fishy, leery 8 doubtful 9 equivocal 11 mistrustful 12 questionable

suspire: 4 sigh 7 respire

sustain: 4 abet, back, bear, buoy, dure, feed, help, prop 5 abide, carry 6 assist, endure, foster, second, succor, suffer, supply, uphold 7 comfort, confirm, console, contain, nourish, prolong, provide, support, undergo 8 befriend, continue, maintain 9 encourage, withstand 10 strengthen 11 corroborate

sustenance: 4 food, meat 5 bread, viand 6 living, upkeep 7 aliment, support 9 nutrition, provision 10 exhibition 11 maintenance, nourishment, subsistence **12** alimentation

sustentation: **6** upkeep **7** support **10** sustenance **11** maintenance **12** preservation

sutler: **9** vivandier **10** vivandiere

suture: **4** line, seam **6** stitch **9** arthrosis **12** articulation

suzerain: **8** overlord **9** paramount, sovereign

svelte: **4** slim **5** lithe **6** lissom **7** lissome, slender **8** graceful

swab: mop **4** lout **5** brush, clean **7** epaulet, plunger **8** medicate

swack: **4** blow **5** whack **6** nimble, pliant, supple

swad: pod **4** mass **5** clown, crowd, shell **7** bumpkin, soldier

swaddle: **4** beat, bind, wrap **6** cudgel, swathe **7** bandage **8** restrict, surround

swag: pit, sag, tip **4** list, loot, sway **5** booty, lurch, spoil, swing, tramp **6** bundle, hollow **7** plunder, swagger **10** decoration

swage: **4** tool **5** shape **6** border, groove **7** assuage

swagger: **4** brag **5** bluff, boast, bully, lurch, strut, swell **6** cuttle, hector, prance **7** bluster, gauster, panache, quarrel, roister, ruffler, stagger, stylish **11** braggadocio, fanfaronade **16** ultrafashionable

swaggering: **6** gascon **7** huffcap

swagman: **9** sundowner

bundle: **5** bluey

swain: boy **5** lover, youth **6** rustic, suitor **7** admirer, gallant, peasant, servant **8** shepherd **9** attendant **10** countryman

swale: fen **4** moor, sway **5** marsh, shade, slash, sweal, swing, swirl **6** hollow, meadow, valley **8** coolness **10** depression

swallow: eat, sip, sup **4** bear, bolt, gaup, gawp, glut, gulp, tern **5** drink, merge, quilt, swift **6** absorb, accept, englut, engulf, go-down, gullet, imbibe, ingest, martin, recant, resorb, throat, vanish **7** believe, consume, engorge, retract **8** aperture, suppress, tolerate, withdraw **9** esophagus

swamp: bog, fen **4** mire, moor, muck, ruin, sink, slew, slue, thin, wham **5** clear, empty, flood, marsh **6** deluge, engulf, hollow, morass, slough **7** cienaga, pocosin, pocoson, slender **8** overcome, quagmire, submerge **9** overwhelm **10** Everglades

grass: **5** sedge

swan: cob, elk, pen **5** swear **6** cygnet **7** declare **8** surprise **9** trumpeter

Swan river: **4** Avon

swank: **6** active, lively **7** stylish, swagger

swanky: ale **4** beer **5** cider **6** active

swap: **4** bang, blow, move, slap **5** fling, smack, swoop, throw, trade **6** barter, dicker, pounce, strike, stroke **8** exchange

swape: bar, oar **4** pole

sward: sod **4** lawn, skin, turf **8** covering **10** greensward

swarm: fry, sny **4** bike(Sc.), byke(Sc.), host, move, shin, swim, teem **5** climb, cloud, crowd, flock, group, horde, mount **6** abound, throng **7** migrate **8** assemble **9** multitude **10** congregate

swarming: **6** aswarm **10** emigration

swart: **4** dark **6** dismal, gloomy **7** baneful, swarthy **8** blackish **9** malignant

swarthy: dun **4** dark **5** dusky **8** blackish

swash: bar **4** blow, move **5** noise, sound **6** strike **7** bluster, channel, dashing, swagger **9** splashing **12** swashbuckler

swashbuckler: **5** bravo **6** gascon **7** ruffian, slasher, soldier **9** daredevil, swaggerer

swashy: **4** weak **6** watery **7** insipid

swastika, svastika, swastica: **5** cross **6** fylfot **9** Gammadion

swat: bat, hit **4** blow **5** clout **6** strike

swatch: **5** swash **6** sample

swath, swathe: row **4** band, crop **5** strip, sweep **6** stroke **7** windrow

swathe: **4** band, bind, wrap **6** enfold **7** envelop, swaddle **8** surround

sway: **4** bend, bias, lean, move, reel, rock, rule, veer **5** force, grace, guide, lurch, power, shake, swing, waver, wield **6** direct, divert, govern, swerve, totter, waddle **7** command, control, deflect, shoggie **8** dominion, rotation **9** dominance, influence, oscillate, vacillate **10** ascendancy, ascendency **11** fluctuation, inclination **12** sovereignity **13** lithesomeness

swaying: **5** asway

sweal: **4** burn, melt **5** singe, waste **6** scorch

swear: vow **4** bind **5** curse, utter **6** adjure, affirm, assert, pledge, threat **7** declare, promise **8** execrate **9** blaspheme **10** administer, asseverate

to secrecy: **4** tile

false: **7** perjury

sweat: dry **4** emit, ooze, work **5** bleed, exude, hoist, labor, sudor(L.) **6** drudge, fleece **7** excrete, extract, ferment, putrefy, soldier **8** condense, overwork, perspire, transude

sweater: **5** shell **8** cardigan, pullover

Sweden: *artist:* **4** Zorn

bread: **10** knackebrod

city: **5** Boras, Edane, Falun, Gavle, Malmo, Ystad **6** Orebro, Upsala **7** Uppsala **8** Goteborg, Nykoping **9** Falkoping, Jonkoping, Stockholm **10** Eskilstuna, Gottenburg, Norrkoping **11** Halsingborg

clover: **6** alsike

coin: ore **5** krona

county: lan

dance: **6** polska

division: amt **4** Laen **5** Skane **8** Gotaland, Gothland, Norrland, Swealand

gulf: **7** Bothnia

island: **5** Oland **6** Oeland **8** Gotaland, Gothland

king: **4** Eric, Wasa **5** Oscar **10** Berradotte

lake: **5** Asnen, Malar, Wener **6** Siljan, Varern, Vatter, Wennen, Wetter **7** Hielmar, Malaren, Vattern

match: **12** taendstikker

measure: am; aln, fot, mil, ref, tum **4** famn, last, stop **5** carat, foder, kanna, kappe, linje, nymil, spann, stang, tunna **6** fathom, jumfru **7** kollast, oxhuvud, tunland **8** fjarding, kappland, koltunna, tunnland

money: **8** skilling

mountain: **6** Sarjek

parliament: **7** Riksdag

physicist: **5** Dalen

province: **6** Kalmar, Orebro, Upsala **7** Gotland, Halland **8** Blekinge, Elfsborg, Jemtland, Malmohus, Wermland **9** Gefleborg, Jonkoping, Kronoberg, Skaraborg, Stockholm **10** Kopparberg, Norrbotten **11** Westmanland **12** Oster Gotland, Sodermanland, Westerbotten **13** Christianstad **14** Westernorrland **18** Gottenborgoch Bohus

river: **4** Gota, Klar, Umea **5** Kalix, Lulea, Pitea, Ranea **6** Lainio, Ljusne, Tornea, Windel **7** Ljungan

soprano: **7** Nilsson **10** Jennie Lind

sour milk: **8** tatmjolk

state religion: **8** Lutheran

tribe: **6** Geatas

weight: ass, lod, ort **4** last, mark, pund, sten, untz **5** carat **6** nylast **7** centner, lispund **8** lispound, skalpund, skeppund **9** ship pound

writer: **6** Carlen **7** Bellman **8** Lagerlof

sweep: oar **4** line **5** besom, broom, brush, clean, clear, drive, range, scope, scour, strip, surge, swath **6** extend, remove **7** contour, stretch **8** traverse

sweeping: **8** complete **9** extensive **13** comprehensive, thoroughgoing

sweepings: **6** fulyie(Sc.), fulzie(Sc.)

sweer: **4** slow **5** loath **8** indolent **9** reluctant

sweet: **4** dear, fair **5** bonny, candy, dolce, douce(F.), fresh, soave **6** dulcet, gentle, lovely, pretty, sugary, syrupy **7** beloved, caramel, darling, honeyed, musical, winning **8** aromatic, fetching, fragrant, pleasant, pleasing, preserve **9** agreeable, ambrosial, melodious **10** attractive, confection, harmonious **11** mellisonant

sweet flag: **7** calamus

sweet potato: yam **6** batata **7** ocarina

sweetbread: **9** ris de veau

sweetbrier: **9** eglantine

sweeten: **4** mull **5** sugar **6** purify, refine, soften, solace **7** appease, cleanse, freshen, mollify, perfume, relieve **9** disinfect **10** edulcorate

sweetheart: jo(Sc.); gra **4** agra, beau, dear,

doll, doxy, gill, girl, jill, lass, love **5** bully, court, flame, leman **6** adorer, fellow, orpine **8** truelove

sweetly: **8** smoothly **10** pleasantly **11** comfortably **13** mellifluently

sweetmeat: **4** cake **5** candy, goody **6** comfit, dragee, pastry **7** caramel, dessert **8** confetti, conserve, hardbake, marzipan, preserve **9** marchpane, sugarplum **10** confection

sweetsop: **4** ates

swell: nob, sea **4** bell. bulb, bulk, grow, huff, rise, surf, toff, wave **5** bloat, bulge, grand, surge **6** billow, dilate, expand, extend, roller, tiptop, tumefy **7** augment, distend, enlarge, inflate, sea-gate, stylish **8** increase **9** elevation, excellent, firstrate, intumesce **10** prominence, thickening **11** fashionable **12** protuberance **16** ultrafashionable

swelled head: **6** egoist **7** conceit

swellfish: **6** puffer **8** puff-fish

swelling: sty **4** bleb, bubo, node **5** blain, botch, bouge, bunch, edema, tumor **6** aswell, gather, growth **7** gibbous, turgent **8** windgall **9** gibbosity

pert. to: **5** ensue **9** edematose, edematous

swelt: die **5** broil, faint, swoon **6** perish, scorch **9** suffocate

swelter: **4** fret, heat, rush **5** exude, faint, roast, sweat **6** wallow, welter **8** perspire

swerve: bow **4** skew, turn, veer **5** stray, yield **6** totter **7** deflect, deviate, digress

sweven: **5** dream, sleep **6** vision

swift: **4** cran(Sc.), fast, reel **5** alert, fleet, hasty, quick, rapid, ready **6** lizard, prompt, speedy, winged

swiftly: **4** fast **5** apace

swiftness: **5** haste **8** celerity

swig: **4** gulp, rock, sway **5** draft, drink, hoist, swash **6** tackle

swile: **4** seal

swill: **4** fill, wash **5** flood, rinse, swash, waste **6** basket, drench, guzzle, refuse **7** garbage, hogwash

swillbowl: sot **8** drunkard

swim: **4** reel **5** float, swoon **9** dizziness **13** forgetfulness **15** unconsciousness

pert. to: **8** natatory

swimmer: **7** natator

of the Hellespont: **7** Leander

of Tiber river: **7** Cloelia

swimming: **5** aswim **6** filled, naiant, natant **7** flooded, vertigo **9** dizziness

swimming pool: **4** tank **10** natatorium

swindle: con, gyp **4** bilk, dupe, fake, mace, rook **5** bunco, bunko, cheat, foist, fraud, spoof, trick **6** diddle, trepan **7** defraud **8** flimflam

swindler: fob **5** biter, cheat, crook, knave, rogue, shark **6** chiaus, chouse, shaver **7** sharper **8** blackleg

swine: hog, pig, sow **4** boar **7** peccary

breed of: **8** Cheshire, Tamworth **9** Berk-

shire, Hampshire, Yorkshire 11 Duroc-
Jersey, Poland China 12 Chester White
pert. to: 7 porcine
swinelike: 7 porcine
swing: 4 beat, bent, blow, hang, hurl, lilt,
slew, slue, sway, whip 5 fling, power,
shake, throw, trend, waver 6 dangle,
manage, rhythm, stroke, totter 7 flutter,
shoggie(Sc.), suspend, trapeze, vibrate 8
brandish, undulate 9 fluctuate, oscillate
swinge: 4 beat, lash, whip 5 whirl 6
thrash 7 impetus, revolve, scourge
swinish: 5 gross 6 coarse 7 beastly, boarish, piggish, sensual
swink: 4 toil 5 labor, slave 8 drudgery
swipe: cut, hit 4 blow, glom 5 draft, drink,
lever, steal, swape, sweep 6 pilfer,
snatch, strike
swirl: ess 4 curl, eddy 5 curve, gurge,
twist, whirl, whorl
swirly: 7 knotted, tangled, twisted
swish: 4 cane, flog, hiss, lash, whip 5
birch, smart, sound 6 rustle, strike
Swiss: See **Switzerland**.
switch: gad, rod 4 beat, flog, lash, turn,
twig, wand, whip 5 shift, shunt, swing 6
change, divert, strike 7 scourge 8 transfer 10 disconnect
switchboard: 5 panel
switchman: 7 shunter
Switzerland: 6 Suisse(F.) 7 Schweiz(G.)
8 Helvetia
ax: 6 piolet
bay: Uri
canton: Uri, Zug 4 Bern, Genf, Vaud 5 Basel, Basle, Waadt 6 Aargau, Geneva,
Geneve, Glaris, Glarus, Luzern, St. Gall,
Schwyz, Tessin, Ticino, Valais, Wallis,
Zurich 7 Grisons, Lucerne, Schwytz, So-
leure, Thurgau 8 Freiberg 9 Appenzell,
Neuchatel, Neuenberg, Solothurn 10
Graubunden 11 Sankt Gallen, Schaff-
house, Unterwalden 12 Schaffhausen
cheese: 7 Gruyere, sapsago 9 schweizer
10 Emmentaler 13 schweizer-kase
city: 4 Bale, Bern, Sion 5 Basel, Basle,
Berne 6 Geneva, Schwyz, Zurich 7 Fyza-
bad, Locarno, Lucerne 8 Faizabad, Lau-
sanne, Montreux, St. Gallen 9 Constance,
Neuchatel 10 Farukhabad, Winterthur
coin: 5 franc, rappe 6 rappen 7 angster,
centime, duplone 8 blaffert
commune: 5 Aarau
composer: 4 Raff
district: 6 canton
food: 12 bernerplatte
herdsman: 4 senn
hero: 11 Wilhelm Tell
lake: Uri 4 Thon 5 Leman 6 Bienne,
Brienz, Geneva, Lugano, Sarnen, Zurich 7
Lucerne, Lungern 8 Viervald 9 Constance, Neuchatel, Sarnersee, Thunersee
10 Stattersee 11 Brienzersee
language: 5 Ladin 6 French, German 7

Italian, Romansh 8 Romansch, Roumansh 14 Switzerduetsch
legislature: 8 grossrat 9 grosserat, gross-
rath
measure: imi, pot 4 aune, elle, fuss, immi,
muid, pied, saum, zoll 5 lieue, ligne, linie,
maass, moule, pouce, schuh, staab, toise
6 perche, setier, strich 7 juchart, klafter,
viertel 9 quarteron 11 holzklafter
mountain: 4 Alps, Jura, Rigi, Rosa 5
Blanc, Cenis, Genis 7 Pilatus 8 Jungfrau
9 St. Gothard 10 Matterhorn 11 Burgen-
stock
mountain pass: 5 Furka 7 Gothard, Grim-
sel, Simplon 8 Lotschen 13 Saint Gotthard
officer: 5 amman
people: 4 muff 6 French, German 7 Italian, Romansh 8 Rhaetian, Romansch,
Roumansh 9 Helvetian
pert. to: 5 Alpen
pine: 6 arolla
river: Aar, Inn 4 Aare 5 Doubs, Reuss,
Rhone
sled: 4 luge 5 luger
song: 5 yodel
tunnel: 5 Cenis 7 Gothard, Simplon 11
Loetschberg
weight: 5 pfund 7 centner, quintal 11
zugtierlast 12 zugthierlast
wind: 4 bise
wine: 7 Dezaley
valley: Aar
swivel: 4 turn
swollen: 4 blub 5 blown, pursy, tumid 6
turgid 7 blubber, bulbous, bulging, pompous 8 enlarged, inflated, varicose 9 distended, increased, tumescent
swoon: fit 4 dwam 5 dwalm(Sc.), faint,
sleep, spell 6 attack 7 ecstasy, syncope 8
languish
swoop: cut 5 seize, sweep 6 pounce 7 descend
sword: sax 4 dirk, epee, foil, pata 5 bilbo,
brand, estoc, glawe, gully, kukri, saber,
sabre 6 barong, creese, cutlas, Damask,
dusack, espada, floret, parang, rapier,
spatha, Toledo 7 ascalon, askelon, baslard, curtana, curtein, cutlass, espadon,
estoque, shabble, simitar 8 acinaces,
camplian, claymore, Damascus, falchion,
flamberg, scimitar, schlager, whinyard 9
achiavone, flamberge
blade of: 5 forte
cross guard: 7 quillon
handle: 4 haft, hilt
of the Cid: 6 Colada
sword lily: 9 gladiolus
swordfish: 6 espada 7 espadon 9 broadbill
swordlike: 5 xypho 6 ensate 8 ensiform,
gladiate
swordsman: 6 fencer 7 epeeist
swore: 5 curst 6 cursed

sworn: 7 devoted 8 affirmed, attested 9 confirmed 10 determined, inveterate

swot (see also **swat**)**:** 5 grind, labor, sweat

syagush: 7 caracal

sybarite: 7 epicure 10 voluptuary

Sybil: See **Sibyl**.

syce: 5 groom

sycophant: 5 toady 7 fawning, spaniel 8 informer, parasite 9 charlatan, flatterer 10 footlicker, talebearer

sycophantic: 7 servile, slavish

sye: sy; sie 4 fall, sink 7 descend

syllable: *added:* 6 prefix

deletion: 7 apocope

final: 6 ultima

lacking at end: 10 catalectic

musical: do, fa, la, mi, re, so, ti

next to last: 6 penult

second before last: 10 antepenult

short: 4 mora 5 breve

shortening: 7 apocope, elision, systole

unaccented: 6 atonic

syllabus: 7 outline, summary 8 headnote, synopsis 9 statement 10 compendium

sylloge: 10 collection, compendium

syllogism: 7 Sorites 8 argument 9 reasoning 10 epichirema 11 epicheirema

sylvan: 5 woody 6 rustic, wooded 8 woodsman 10 forestlike

sylvatic: 4 rude 11 uncivilized

symbol (see also **element**)**:** 4 icon, ikon, sign, type, word 5 badge, creed, crest, cross, image, token, totem 6 caract, emblem, ensign, figure, letter 7 diagram 9 character, hierogram, trademark 10 expression, similitude 12 abbreviation, contribution

put into: 6 notate

symbolical: 7 typical 8 mystical 11 allegorical, sacramental 14 representative

symbolize: 5 agree 6 concur, typify 7 betoken, combine, express, signify 9 harmonize, represent

symmetrical: 7 regular, spheral 13 commensurable

symmetry: 7 balance, harmony 9 congruity 10 conformity, consistency, proportion

sympathetic: 4 soft 6 humane, tender 7 pietoso, piteous 8 affected 9 condolent, congenial, expansive, sensitive 10 responsive 13 compassionate

sympathize: 6 bemoan 7 condole 11 commiserate

sympathy: 4 pity 6 accord, liking 7 harmony 8 interest 9 agreement 10 compassion, condolence, tenderness 13 commiseration, understanding

symphonious: 9 accordant 10 harmonious

symposium: 4 talk 7 banquet 8 dialogue 9 symposiac 10 conference, discussion 11 compotation

symptom: 4 mark, note, sign 5 token 10 indication

synagogue: 4 shul 5 group 8 assembly, building, religion 9 communion, community 12 congregation

platform: 7 almemar

Sephardic: 5 anoga

singer: 6 cantor, chazan 7 chazzan

synaxis: 7 meeting, service 12 congregation

synchronize: 7 arrange 8 regulate 12 contemporize

synchronous: 8 existing 10 concurrent 11 concomitant 12 contemporary, simultaneous 15 contemporaneous

syncope: 4 loss 5 faint, swoon 7 elision 9 cessation, haplology 10 suspension 11 contraction, hyphaeresis 15 unconsciousness

syndetic: 10 connective

syndic: 5 agent, judge, mayor 7 manager, officer, trustee 8 advocate, official 10 magistrate

syndicate: 4 sell 5 chain, group, trust, unite 6 cartel 7 censure, council 8 monopoly 9 committee 11 association 12 organization

synod: 4 body 5 court 7 council, meeting 8 assembly 10 convention 11 convocation

syne: ago 5 since

synonymous: 4 like 5 alike 10 equivalent

synopsis: 4 plan 7 summary 8 abstract 9 statement 10 compendium, conspectus 11 abridgment

syntax: 5 order 6 system 9 structure 11 arrangement

analyze: 5 parse

mistake: 8 solecism

synthesis: 5 summa 7 complex 11 combination, composition 13 incorporation

Syria: 4 Aram

animal: 5 addax, daman

bishop: 4 abba

church plan: 8 triconch

city: 4 Homs 5 Calno, Derra 6 Aleppo, Balbec, Beirut, Calneh 7 Antioch, Beirout, Beyrout 8 Damascus, Seleucia 12 Alexandretta

deity: El 4 Baal 5 Allat 6 Mammon 7 Resheph

district: 6 Aleppo, Hauran

goat: 6 angora

grass: 7 Johnson

gypsy: 5 Aptal

lake: 5 Merom 8 Tiberias

mallow: 4 okra

measure: 5 makuk 6 garava

money: 5 pound 6 talent 7 piaster

mountain: 6 Carmel 7 Libanus

peasant: 6 fellah

people: 5 Druse 7 Ansarie, Saracen

plant: 5 cumin

river: 6 Jordan 7 Orontes

script: **5** serta

tetrarchy: **7** abilene

weight: **4** cola, rotl **5** artal, artel, ratel **6** talent

wind: **6** simoon

syrt: bog **9** quicksand

syrup: **4** karo, sapa **6** orgeat **7** dhebbus, glucose, sarghum

system: ism **4** code **5** group **6** circle, method, regime, theory **7** regimen **8** religion, treatise, universe **9** procedure **10** assemblage, hypothesis, philosophy, regularity **11** aggregation, arrangement, orderliness

systematic: **4** neat **7** orderly, regular **9** organized **10** methodical

systematize: **6** adjust **7** arrange, catalog **8** organize, regiment **9** catalogue

T

t-shaped: tau
taa: 6 pagoda
Taal: 9 Afrikaans
tab: pan, tag 4 bill, drop, flap, loop 5 aglet, check, index, label, score, strap, strip 6 aiglet, eartab, record 7 account, latchet, officer 9 appendage, reckoning 10 accounting
tabac: 5 snuff 7 tobacco
tabard: inn 4 cape, coat 5 cloak 6 chimer, jacket, mantle 7 pendant
tabatiere: 8 snuffbox
tabby: cat, pad 4 gown, silk 5 dress 6 fabric, gossip, moreen 7 padding, taffeta 8 brindled
tabella: 6 tablet 7 lozenge
taberna: 4 shop, tent 5 booth 7 shelter
tabernacle: 4 tent 5 abode, dwell, hovel, niche 6 church, recess, reside, temple 7 deposit, shelter, support 8 enshrine 9 sanctuary, structure 10 habitation, receptacle
tabes: 7 atrophy 10 emaciation 11 consumption 12 tuberculosis
tabetless: 4 numb 7 foolish 9 senseless
table: hem 4 fare, feed, food, slab, wash 5 bench, board, canon, index, panel, plate, treat 6 indius, lamina, record, repast, tablet 7 console, surface 8 credence, feasting, postpone, schedule, synopsis, tabulate 10 collection 11 concentrate 12 stringcourse
  communion: 5 altar 8 credence, credenza
  cover: 5 baize, cloth, tapis
  dish: 6 tureen
  linen: 6 napery 7 napkins 11 tablecloths
  philosophers: 14 deipnosophists
  small: 5 stand, wagon 6 teapoy 7 cabaret, tendoor, tendour
  working: 5 bench
  writing: 10 escritoire
table-land: 4 mesa 5 karoo 6 karroo 7 plateau 8 balaghat, plateaux, plateaus 9 balaghaut 12 altiplanicie
tableau: 7 picture 8 register, schedule 14 representation
tablet: pad 4 bred, slab 5 facia, panel 6 troche 7 lozenge 10 receptacle
  medicine: 6 troche
  sculptured: 5 stela, stele 6 stelae, steles
  three-leaved: 8 triptych
  two-leaved: 7 diptych
  writing: pad 5 slate

tablinum: 4 room 6 alcove, recess
tabloid: 5 short 9 condensed 12 concentrated
taboo, tabu: ban 5 debar 6 forbid 8 prohibit 9 forbidden 12 interdiction
  opposed to: noa
tabor, tabour: 4 drum 6 atabal 7 attabal, eardrum, timbrel
taboret, tabouret: 4 drum, seat 5 stand, stool, tabor 6 tabour
tabu: See taboo.
tabulate: 4 list 7 arrange 8 schedule
tabulation: *grammatical:* 8 paradigm
  of the year: 8 calendar
taccaceous herb: pia
taccada: 9 fanflower
tache: pan, tie 4 spot 5 clasp, fault, habit, stain 6 attach, buckle 7 blemish, tarnish 11 disposition 14 characteristic
tacit: 6 silent 7 implied 8 implicit, unspoken, wordless 9 noiseless 10 understood
taciturn: 6 silent 8 reserved, reticent 9 saturnine 15 uncommunicative
tack: 4 beat, busk, clap, gear, haul, join, link, nail, rope, slap, trim 5 baste, catch, fetch, rider, spell, strip, tying, unite 6 attach, course, fasten, handle, method, secure, tackle 7 clothes, connect, payment 8 contract 9 agreement, endurance, fastening 10 stickiness, supplement 12 adhesiveness
  glazier: 4 brad
  nautical: 5 board
  to: 4 jibe
  to windward: 4 trip
  two-pointed: 6 staple
tackle: rig 4 arms, food, gear, tack 5 angle, drink, seize, stuff 6 attach, collar, secure 7 grapple, harness, rigging, weapons 8 mistress, windlass 9 apparatus, encounter, equipment, undertake
  fishing: tew
  single and double block: 6 burton
  strong: cat
tacky: 5 crude, dowdy, seedy 6 shabby, sticky, untidy 8 adhesive, slovenly
tact: 5 poise, touch 6 stroke 7 address, feeling 8 delicacy, graceful 9 appendage, diplomacy 10 adroitness, cleverness, discretion, perception 11 discernment 14 discrimination
tactfully: 7 happily
tactics: 6 method, system 9 procedure

tactless: 5 brash
tactlessness: 9 gaucherie
tad: 5 child 6 urchin
tadpole: 8 polliwog
taenia: 4 band 6 fillet 8 headband
Taffy: 8 Welshman
taffy: 5 gundy 7 glaggum 8 flattery
tag: dog, end, tab 4 flap, game, join, lock 5
aglet, label, shred, strip, touch 6 aiglet,
append, attach, eartab, fasten, follow,
rabble 7 refrain, taglock 9 appendage,
catchword 11 aiguillette
Tagalog (see also **Philippine Islands**): 8
Filipino
  child: 4 bata 5 Anacs
  deity: 6 Batala 7 Bathala
  gambling game: 10 panguingui
  learn: 4 aral
  mother: Ina
  peasant: Tao
  race: Ita
tagrag: rag, tag 6 rabble, tatter 8 vagabond
tagtail: 9 sycophant
Tahiti: *canoe:* 4 pahi
  capital: 7 Papeete
  centipede: 4 veri
  coronation robe: 4 maro
  food plant: 4 taro
  god: Oro 6 Taaroa
  mulberry: 4 aute
  old name: 8 Otaheite
  seaport: 7 Papeete
Tai, Thai: 7 Siamese
  race: Lao
taigle: 4 drag 5 catch, delay, trail 6 entrap, hinder, loiter 7 fatigue
tail: bun; cue, end 4 arse, back, bunt, last,
rear 5 cauda 6 follow, shadow, switch 7
limited, pendant, reduced 8 abridged,
buttocks, encumber, entailed 9 appendage, curtailed, extremity, fundament
  having a: 7 caudate
  kinds of: bob, bun, fud 4 bunt, scut 5
cauda, plume, stern, twist 6 strunt,
wreath 8 streamer 9 empennage
  pert. to: 6 caudal
tailed: 7 caudate
tailing: 5 chaff, waste 6 refuse
taille: fit, tax 4 form 5 build, shape, style,
waist 6 figure 10 imposition
tailless: 7 acaudal, anurous 8 acaudate,
ecaudate 9 excaudate
tailor: 4 snip 6 darzee, draper, sartor 7
cabbage 9 bushelman 11 bushelwoman
  goose: 8 flatiron
  iron: 5 goose
  lap board: 5 panel
  pert. to: 9 sartorial
tailzie: cut 5 agree, shape, slice, tally 6
entail 7 account, appoint, arrange 9
reckoning
taint: dip, dye, hit, hue 4 blow, evil, hogo,
spot, tint 5 cloud, color, imbue, prove,

spoil, stain, sully, tinge, touch, trace,
wound 6 accuse, defile, infect, poison,
stigma 7 attaint, blemish, convict, corrupt, debauch, deprave, pollute, vitiate 8
disgrace, empoison, hautgout, tincture 10
conviction, corruption, impregnate 11
contaminate
tainted: bad 5 blown
taipo: 5 demon, devil 10 theodolite
taisch: 5 ghost, voice
taissle: 6 puzzle, tangle 8 disorder
tait: 5 sport 6 lively 8 sportive 9 marsupial 12 cheerfulness
taivers, tavers: 6 babble, shreds 7 tatters
taj: cap 8 Taj Mahal
Taj Mahal site: 4 Agra
tajo: 6 trench
take: get, hit, win 4 doff, fang, glom, grip,
haul, lead, trap 5 adopt, atone, avail,
carry, catch, charm, cheat, check, fetch,
glaum, grasp, infer, seize, snare, spell,
steal, swear, touch, trick 6 absorb, accept, affirm, amount, arrest, assume, attach, attack, borrow, choose, convey, deduce, deduct, derive, employ, endure,
engage, number, obtain, profit, remove,
secure, select, strike, submit, tenure 7
capture, conduct, detract, extract, promise, receive, undergo 8 abstract, contract,
proceeds, quantity, receipts, subtract 9
apprehend, interrupt 11 appropriate
  aback: 5 check 8 astonish, confound
  account of: 6 notice, regard
  advice: 4 hear, heed, mind 6 listen
  aim: 5 level
  another's place: sub 9 alternate 10 substitute
  as actual: 5 posit
  as one's own: 5 adopt 6 borrow
  away: 5 adeem 6 adempt, deduct, devest,
recant, remove 7 deprive, detract, retract
8 subtract
  back: 6 recant 7 retract 8 withdraw
  beforehand: 7 pre-empt
  bold attitude: 5 brisk
  by craft: 6 entoil
  by force: 5 erept 8 ereption
  by stratagem: 4 trap
  care: 4 mind, reck 5 nurse, watch 6 beware, cuiado
  care of: 4 tend 5 nurse
  chair: sit
  cognizance of: 4 note 6 notice
  comb from beehive: 4 geld
  delight: 5 revel
  direction: 5 steer
  down: 5 abase, lower 6 escort, humble,
record, reduce 7 swallow 8 emaciate,
withdraw 10 distribute
  evening meal: sup 4 dine
  exception: 5 demur 6 object
  fire: 5 spunk

for granted: **6** assume **7** presume
forcibly: **5** seize
from: **5** wrest **6** deduct, divest **7** deprive, derived, detract **8** derogate, subtract
heed: **4** mind, reck, ware
hold: **5** grasp **6** obtain
in: **4** furl, open **5** admit, annex, brail, cheat, fence, trick, visit **6** attend, escort **7** deceive, embrace, enclose, explore, include, observe, receive **8** commence, comprise, contract **9** encompass **10** comprehend, understand
in hand: **5** seize **7** attempt **9** undertake
in sail: **4** reef
into custody: **6** arrest **9** apprehend
leave: **6** decamp, depart
legal possession of: **5** seise, seize
liberties: **7** presume
meals for pay: **5** board
no notice of: **9** disregard
notice: NB; see
off: **4** copy, doff, soar **5** abate, begin, deter, mimic, start **6** deduct, depart, lessen, remove **7** detract **8** discount, distract, subtract, withdraw **9** burlesque, calculate, determine, reproduce
off suspended list: **9** reinstate
offense of: **6** resent
on: **4** hire **6** assume, employ, engage, oppose, tackle **7** consort, receive **8** arrogate **9** associate, undertake
on cargo: **4** lade
one's way: **4** wend
out: **4** copy, dele, omit **5** elide **6** deduct, delete, efface, escort, except, remove **7** extract, unhitch **8** overall, separate
out by roots: **9** extirpate
out curves and bends: **10** straighten
out of pawn: **6** redeem
part: **4** join **5** share
part in contest: **7** compete
part of: **4** side
place: **5** occur
place again: **5** recur
place of: **4** else **8** supplant **9** supersede
pleasure in: **5** enjoy, fancy
positive opinion: **4** side
possession of: **5** enter, seise
rise: **7** emanate
service as seaman: **4** ship
shelter: **6** nestle
some of: **7** partake
stock: **5** count **6** survey **8** appraise, estimate **9** inventory
the stick: **5** steer
to court: sue
turns: **9** alternate
umbrage at: **6** resent
unawares: **5** seize **7** astound, capture, startle **8** astonish, confound, overcome, surprise **9** overwhelm
unlawfully: rob **5** steal, usurp **6** pilfer
up: buy **4** fill, lift **5** adopt, allow, check, enter, exact, mount, raise, seize **6** absorb,

accept, arrest, assume, borrow, employ, gather, occupy, remove, resume **7** collect, dissent, elevate, engross, receive **9** extirpate, reprimand **10** comprehend, understand
up again: **5** renew **6** resume
up weapons: arm **4** rise
with: **4** like **5** brook **6** accept **7** confess **11** acknowledge
without authority: **5** usurp
taken: **8** occupied
in all: **7** overall **9** inclusive
by twos: **5** duple
taker: **5** thief **6** captor **7** catcher **8** pilferer, purveyor **10** plagiarist
of court action: **4** suer
of income or profits: **6** pernor
taking: **4** take **5** catch, palsy **6** arrest, attack, blight, plight **7** capture, malefic, seizing, seizure **8** alluring, captious, catching, engaging, grasping, receipts **9** accepting, rapacious, receiving, reception **10** attachment, attractive, contagious, infectious **11** captivating **12** apprehension
different form: **7** protean **11** metamorphis
precedence: **7** ranking
unauthorized leave: **4** A.W.O.L.
takt: **4** beat **5** beats, pulse, tempo **7** measure
tala: **4** raid, ruin **11** destruction
talapoin: **4** monk **6** monkey **7** poongee **8** poonghee, poonghie
talc: **6** talcum **7** agalite **8** steatite **9** soapstone
tale: lie **4** gest, myth, saga, talk, tell, yarn **5** count, fable, geste, speak, story, tally, total **6** esteem, gossip, legend, reckon, report, speech **7** account, fiction, history, parable, recital **8** anecdote, category, consider, counting, relation **9** discourse, falsehood, narration, narrative, numbering, reckoning **11** declaration, enumeration, information **12** conversation
kind of: lai **4** gest, saga, yarn **5** bourd, geste, roman **6** legend **7** romance **8** allegory, jeremiad **9** storiette
talebearer: **6** buzzer, gossip **7** tattler **8** talepyet, telltale **10** newsmonger **13** scandalmonger
talent: **4** gift **5** anger, dowry, flair, gifts, knack, money, skill, talon **6** custom, desire, flavor, genius, powers, riches, wealth **7** ability, betters, faculty, feature, longing, passion **8** appetite, aptitude, capacity, gamblers, property **9** abilities, abundance, attribute **10** endowments **11** disposition, inclination **14** accomplishment
sale: **8** venality
special: **5** forte
talented: **4** able **5** smart **6** clever, gifted **8** addicted, disposed, inclined
talenter: **4** hawk
talents: **9** endowment

talesman: **5** juror **8** narrator
taletelling: **4** blab
taliation: **5** tally **10** adjustment
taliera: **4** tara
talion: **11** retaliation
talisman: **4** tara **5** charm, saffi, safie **6** amulet, fetich, fetish, grigri, saphie, scarab, telesm **8** greegree
talitol: **7** alcohol
talk: yap **4** buck, bukh, carp, chat, gaff, knap, talk, word **5** bazoo, lingo, parle, prate, rumor, speak, theme, utter **6** confer, debate, gabble, gossip, reason, report, speech, steven, tongue **7** address, chatter, consult, council, dialect, express, meeting, mention, palabra **8** causerie, chit-chat, collogue, colloquy, converse, parlance, verbiage **9** dalliance, discourse **10** conference, discussion **11** communicate **12** conversation
about: **6** gossip **7** discuss
abusive: **5** hoker
back: **4** sass **6** retort, ripost **7** riposte **8** repartee
big: **4** brag **5** boast
boastful: **4** gaff, rant
ceremonious: **8** chin-chin
common: **7** hearsay
complaining: **4** carp
confused: **10** galimatias
desultorily: **6** ramble
deliriously: **4** rave
effusively: **4** gush, rave
familiar: **6** confab
fast and idly: **7** gnatter
flattering: **7** palaver
fluent: **7** verbose, voluble
foolish: gab, gas **4** bosh, buff, bunk, gash **5** spiel **6** babble, bunkum, claver, fraise, patter **7** blabber, twaddle **8** buncombe, wishwash **9** poppycock, rigmarole **11** goose-cackle, stultiloquy
formal: **7** address, lecture
idly: gab, gas **5** prate **6** tattle **7** chatter, twaddle
imperfectly: **4** lisp **7** stutter
in sleep: **15** somniloquacious
indiscreetly: **4** blab
indistinctly: **7** sputter
irrationally: **4** rant, rave
persuasively: **6** reason
profuse: **4** chat **6** patter **7** palaver **10** persiflage
slowly: **5** drawl
small: gab **4** chat, chin **7** prattle **8** chitchat
table: ana **9** symposiac
tediously: **5** prose
to no purpose: **4** blat
together: **8** converse
turgid: **4** cant, rant
unintelligible: **6** drivel, jargon, patter **9** gibberish
wildly: **4** rave
with passion: **4** rave

talkative: **4** cozy, gash, glib **5** gabby **6** chatty, clashy, fluent **7** verbose, voluble **8** flippant **9** garrulous **10** babblative, loquacious
talkativeness: **9** garrulity, garrulous, loquacity
talker: **6** proser, ranter, rhetor **7** babbler, spieler **17** conversationalist
talkfest: **9** gathering **10** discussion
talking iron: gun **5** rifle
tall: **4** bold, deft, fine, high, lank, long **5** brave, grand, great, lanky, large, lofty, quick, rangy, ready, steep, tally **6** comely, docile, seemly **7** doughty, skyhigh, unusual **8** obedient, towering, yielding **9** excellent **10** courageous, incredible **11** exaggerated **13** grandiloquent
tallage: aid, due, fee, tax **4** toll **6** custom, impost, tarage
tallet: **5** attic **7** hayloft
talliar: **8** watchman
tallness: **9** procerity
tallote: **5** gourd **7** chayote **8** calabash
tallow: fat **4** suet **5** sevum, smear **6** fatten, grease
pert. to: **7** stearic
pot: **7** fireman
refuse: **9** crackling
sediment: **7** greaves
tallow-berry: **11** locustberry
tally: run, tab, tag **4** deal, goal, mark, mate, suit **5** agree, check, count, grade, label, match, notch, score **6** accord, reckon, record **7** account, compare, loftily **8** estimate **9** agreement, elegantly, reckoning **10** becomingly, correspond, resolutely **11** counterpart **14** correspondence
talma: **4** cape, coat
Talmud commentary: **6** Gemara
Talmudic academy: **7** Yeshiva **8** Yeshibah, Yeshivah **9** Yeshiboth
student: **5** bahur
talon: **4** claw, heel, sere **6** clutch, hallux **7** molding **11** certificate
talter: **4** hang
taluk: **5** tract **6** estate **10** dependency **11** subdivision **12** collectorate
talukdar: **9** collector, tahsildar **10** landholder, proprietor
talus: **5** ankle, scree, slope **6** debris **8** clubfoot **9** anklebone **11** knucklebone
tam: cap, hat **5** beret **8** headgear **11** tam-o-shanter
tamarack: **10** hackmatack
tamarind: **8** sampaloc
tamarisk: **4** atle **5** atlee
tamas: **7** inertia **8** dullness **9** ignorance
tamasha: **4** fuss, show **7** pageant **9** commotion, spectacle **10** excitement **13** entertainment
tambo: inn **6** corral, stable, tavern **7** station
tambour: cup **4** desk, drum **5** frame **7** drummer **8** buttress, ornament **9** em-

broider **10** embroidery, projection
tambourin: **4** drum **5** dance, tabor
tambourine: **4** dove, drum, taar **5** daira **7** timbrel, travale
tambreet: **8** duckbill
tame: cut **4** bust, dead, dull, mild **5** accoy, begin, break, daunt, prune **6** broach, docile, gentle, humble, soften, subdue **7** affaite, crushed, insipid, servile **8** cicurate, civilize, familiar, harmless **9** deficient, tractable **10** accustomed, cultivated, submissive **11** domesticate, ineffectual **12** domesticated **13** pusillanimous
  animal: pet **4** cade **6** cosset
  poison: **11** swallowwort
tamed: **6** broken, gentle
tameness: **10** mansuetude
Tamil: **9** Dravidian
  caste member: **7** Vellala
tamis: **5** sieve, tammy **8** strainer
Tammany Society officer: **8** Wiskinky **9** Wiskinkie
Tammuz: *love:* **6** Ishtar
  sister: **6** Belili
tamp: ram **5** drive
tamper: fix **4** fool, plot, tool **6** dabble, meddle, potter, scheme **7** machine **9** influence, interfere
Tampico fiber: **5** istle
tampion, tempeon, tampoon: **4** bung, plug **5** cover **7** stopper, turnpin
tampon: **4** plug **6** tympan **9** drumstick
  nasal: **9** rhinobyon
tan: dun, taw **4** beat, camp, ecru, flog, tent, whip **5** brown, color, toast **6** almond, bronze, switch, tannin, thrash **7** embrown, imbrown, sunburn, tanbark
  derived from: **5** tanic
tana: **8** banxring
tanager: **4** yeni
  genus of: **7** piranga
tanbark: **4** bark
tancel: **4** beat **5** abuse **6** thrash
tang: nip **4** butt, capt, fang, foil, odor, pang, pike, ring, root, spur, tine, zest **5** knife, prick, prong, shank, smack, sting, taste, tinge, trace, twang **6** branch, flavor, pierce, tangle, tongue **7** flavour, seatang, seaweed **8** rockweed **10** suggestion **11** surgeonfish
Tanganyika: *mountain:* **4** Meru
  people: **4** Goma **6** Wagogo, Wagoma **7** Wabunga
tangent: **8** touching
tangible: **4** real **6** actual **7** tactile **8** definite, palpable **9** objective, touchable **11** perceptible, substantial
Tangiers measure: **4** kula, mudd
tangle: bar, cot, mat **4** fank, harl, kink, knot, mesh, trap **5** frame, gnarl, ravel, snare, snarl **6** balter, entrap, icicle, medley, muddle, sleave **7** ensnare, involve, quandry **8** obstruct, scrobble **9** embarrass **10** intertwine, perplexity

  of thread: **5** snarl
tangle-foot: **5** aster, drink **6** whisky **8** deerweed
tangled: **11** complicated
tango: **5** bingo, dance
tania: **5** aroid
tank: hit, vat **4** bang, lake, pond, pool **5** basin, knock, trunk **7** cistern, cuvette, drinker, pachuca, piscina, stomach **9** container, reservoir
  part: **6** turret
tankard: **5** facer, hanap **6** pottle **7** goddard
tanker: **5** oiler
tanned: **5** brown, tawny **8** sixpence, sunburnt
tanner: **6** barker **8** sixpence
Tannhauser composer: **6** Wagner
tannic acid salt: **7** tannate
tannin: **10** astringent
tanning: *extract:* **5** cutch **7** amaltas
  material: **5** sumac **6** sumach
  method: **4** napa
  pert. to: **11** scytodepsic
  plant: **5** alder, sumac **6** sumach
tansy: **9** tanacetum
tanta: **4** aunt
tantadlin: **4** tart **6** dainty **8** dumpling
tantalize: **4** grig **5** taunt, tease **6** harass **7** torment
tantalus: toy **4** case **8** cellaret
Tantalus: *children:* **5** Niobe **6** Pelops
  father: **4** Zeus
tantamount: **5** equal **9** identical **10** equivalent
tantara, tantarara: **5** blare **7** fanfare
tantieme: **5** bonus, share **10** percentage
tantivy: cry **4** call, ride, rush, Tory **5** rapid, swift **6** gallop, speedy **7** swiftly **8** headlong, Royalist
tantrum: pet **4** rage
tantum: **5** stint **9** allowance
Tanzania: *people:* **7** Swahili
  title: **5** sayid
  weight: **8** farsalah
Taoism: Tao **12** cosmic reason
tap: bob, cut, hob, pat, rap, tit, vat **4** beat, blow, cock, flip, heat, hole, open, pipe, plug **5** break, fever, flirt, knock, leach, spile, touch, valve **6** broach, faucet, repair, signal, spigot, strike, tapnet **7** censure, connect, penance, reprove
  down: **4** tamp
tape: gin, tie **4** band, bind, mole **5** scale, strip **6** fillet, liquor, ribbon, secure **7** bandage, binding
  kind of: **4** lear, wick **5** inkle **6** ferret
taper: **4** ream, wick **5** light, point, snape **6** candle, cierge, lessen, narrow, trowel **7** conical, dwindle, trindle **8** decrease, diminish **9** acuminate **11** pyramidical
tapered: **7** conical
tapering: **5** conic **6** terete **7** conical **9** acuminate

blades: **6** spires
four-sided pillar: **7** obelisk
piece: **4** gore, shim **5** miter **6** gusset
solid: **4** cone
with circular cross section: **6** terete
tapestry: 5 arras, tapis **6** bayeux, dorser, dosser **7** dossier, gobelin **8** dossiere
tapeworm: 6 taenia **7** taeniae
embryonic form: **10** oncosphere
segments: **8** strobila **9** strobilae
hanging: **5** tapis
provide: **6** arrase
taphouse: bar, inn **6** saloon, tavern **7** taproom
tapioca-like food: 5 salep
tapir: 4 anta **5** danta **8** anteater, ungulate
tapirus Americanus: 4 anta
tapis: 4 band, hide, sash **6** carpet **7** hanging **8** tapestry **10** tablecloth
taplet: 5 block
tapnet: 5 frail **6** basket
tapper: 6 dancer **7** workman **9** decoherer, innkeeper **10** woodpecker
tappet: cam **5** lever **10** projection
tapster: 7 barmaid, skinker **9** barkeeper, bartender
Tapuyan: Ge; Ges **5** Gesan **6** Cayapo, Goyana, Timbra **7** Camacan, Coroado **8** Botocudo, Caingang, Chavante
tar: gob **4** brea, salt **5** black, pitch, tease **6** cresol, incite, sailor, seaman **7** blacken, mariner, provoke **8** alkitran, irritate, seafarer, telegram **9** alchitran **10** bluejacket
tar and feathers: 12 plumeopicean
tarantula: 6 spider
tarbet: 7 isthmus, portage
tarboosh: cap, fez
tarde: 4 late, slow **7** evening **9** afternoon
tardigrade: 8 sluggish
tardy: lag, lax **4** late, slow **5** delay, slack **6** remiss, retard **7** belated, lagging, overdue **8** dilatory **10** behindhand, unprepared **11** cunctatious
tare: 4 weed **5** vetch, weigh **6** darnel **7** leakage **9** allowance **13** counterweight
targe: 4 beat **5** paper, scold **6** harass, shield, targer, target **7** buckler, censure **8** document **9** reprimand **10** protection
targer: 5 scold, shrew
target: cut, tee **4** butt, coin, mark, vane **5** shred, sight, slice **6** cymbal, object, shield, tassel, tatter **7** buckler, pendant **8** bullseye, ornament, ridicule **9** indicator, objective, criticism
center: eye **5** clout
Tarheel State: 13 North Carolina
tariff: tax **4** duty, list, rate **5** scale **6** charge, scheme, system **7** average, tribute **8** schedule
favorer: **13** protectionist
tarn: 4 lake, pool
tarnish: dim **4** blot, dull, soil, spot **5** cloud, dirty, spoil, stain, sully, taint **6** canker,

darken, defile, smirch **7** asperse, blemish, destroy, distain, obscure **8** besmirch, diminish, discolor
taro: 4 coco, eddo, gabi **5** aroid, cocgo, eddoe, tania **7** dasheen **8** caladium
paste: poi
root: **4** eddo **6** eddoes
tarpaulin: hat, tar **4** coat, tarp **5** cover **6** sailor **7** sea-bred **10** sailorlike
tarpon: 9 savanilla **10** silverfish
tarriance: 5 delay **7** sojourn **8** awaiting, tarrying **9** hindrance
tarrock: 4 gull, tern
tarrow: 5 delay, tarry **6** linger **7** grumble
tarry: lag, vex **4** bide, loll, rest, stay, stop, wait **5** abide, await, black, dally, defer, delay, demur, dwell, lodge, pause, weary **6** arrest, bundle, hinder, linger, loiter, remain, retard, soiled, tarred, tarrow **7** fatigue, outstay, sojourn, unclean **8** irritate
tarrying: 6 arrest
tarsus: 5 ankle
fore: **4** pala
tart: pie **4** acid, flan, girl, keen, sour **5** acrid, acute, bowla, sharp **6** pastry, pielet, severe, tender, tourte **7** caustic, cutting, painful, piquant, pungent **8** piercing, poignant, turnover **9** acidulous, endearing, sensitive **10** astringent, prostitute
tartan: 4 sett, ship **5** plaid
tartar: 5 argol, shrew, valet **12** incrustation
Tartar: See **Tatar**.
tartarean: 8 infernal
Tartarus: 4 hell **5** Hades
Tartary prince: 4 Agib
tartness: 7 acidity **8** acerbity, acrimony, asperity, piquancy, sourness
tarve: 4 bend, turn
tarweed: 5 Madia
tash: 4 soil **5** stain **7** fatigue **8** disgrace
task: job, tax **4** busk, char, darg, duty, test, toil, work **5** chare, chore, labor, stent, stint, study **6** amount, burden, dargue, devoir, impost, lesson, strain **7** aufgabe, censure, oppress, overtax **8** quantity **10** accounting, assignment, employment **11** undertaking
easy: **4** pipe, snap **5** cinch **8** sinecure
taskmaster: 6 driver **8** overseer
Tasmania: *animal:* **6** wombat
lake: **12** Westmoreland
mountain: **4** Grey **5** Brown, Drome, Nevis **6** Barrow **8** Humboldt **9** Ben Lomond **10** Wellington
phalanger: **5** tapoa
river: **4** Huon **5** Tamar **6** Arthur, Jordan **7** Derwent
thylacine: **5** tiger
town: **6** Hobart **10** Launceston
wolf: **5** tiger
tass: cup, mow **4** bowl, heap **5** draft **6** goblet
tassel: 4 tuft **5** adorn, label **6** fringe, toor-

ie, zizith **7** pendant **8** ornament

taste: bit, eat, gab, goo, sip, try **4** bent, dash, gout, gust, heed, hint, rasa, tang, test **5** drink, flair, gusto, prove, sapor, savor, scent, shade, smack, smell, spice, touch, trace **6** degust, flavor, liking, little, palate, relish, relush, ribbon, sample, savour **7** flavour, soupcon, thought **8** appetite, delicacy, elegance, fondness **9** attention, degustate, judgement **10** experience, suggestion **11** discernment, inclination **14** discrimination

fundamental: **4** acid, salt **5** sweet **6** bitter
kind of: nip, sip **4** tang **5** prose, sapor, savor, smack **8** penchant
lacking in: **4** rude **8** ungentle **9** inelegant **10** unpolished **11** inaesthetic
pert. to: **7** palatal **9** gustative, gustatory
perversion: **7** malacia
refined: **7** elegant

tasted: **4** sipt
tasteful: **4** neat **5** tasty **6** savory **7** elegant
tasteless: **4** dull, flat **5** vapid **7** insipid **8** lifeless **9** savorless **10** inartistic
tasty: **5** sapid **6** savory **7** palatal **8** tasteful **9** flavorful, palatable, toothsome **10** delectable
tat: die, rag, tap **4** pony **5** touch **6** tangle **7** crochet **8** absolute **9** embroider

Tatar, Tartar: Hun **6** ataman, hetman **7** Cossack
militiaman: **4** Ulan **5** Uhlan
mounted band: **4** ulan **5** horde, uhlan **7** chambul
principality: **7** Khanate
republic capital: **5** Kazan
tribe: Hun **5** Alani, Alans **7** Shortzy

tatou, tatu: **9** armadillo
tatter: jag, rag **4** jagg, stir, tear **5** hurry, scold, scrap, shred, testy **6** bustle, gabble, ribbon, tattle **7** chatter, flitter, peevish **8** guenille **14** tatterdemalion
tatterdemalion: **6** ragged **8** tattered **10** ragamuffin
tattered: **4** torn **6** broken, jagged, ragged, shaggy **7** slashed **9** disrupted **10** disheveled **11** dilapidated
tattle: **4** blab, chat, gash, talk, tell **5** cheep, clash, clype, prate **6** gossip **7** chatter, clatter, prattle, stammer
tattler: **6** gossip **8** telltale **9** sandpiper **10** talebearer
tattletale: **6** gossip **7** tattler **8** telltale **10** talebearer
Taube: **9** monoplane
taught: See **teach.**
taunt: bob **4** dare, gibe, jeer, jibe, mock, quip, tall, twit **5** check, fleer, glaik, reply, slare, slart, sneer, tease, tempt **6** banter, deride, flaunt, rejoin **7** provoke, upbraid **8** reproach, ridicule **9** aggravate
taurine: **4** bull **6** bovine
taurocol: **4** glue
Taurus: **4** bull

taut: **4** firm, neat, snug, tidy, trim **5** rigid, stiff, tense, tight, tough **6** severe, strict **9** distended, shipshape
tauten: **5** tense **7** tighten
tautog: **9** blackfish
tautological: **9** redundant
tave: **4** rage, toss **5** hurry, labor **6** sprawl **8** struggle
tavern: bar, hut, inn, pub **4** bush, howf **5** booth, hotel, house, howff **6** saloon **7** cabaret, gasthof **8** alehouse, gasthaus, hostelry
tavert: **5** tired **6** stupid **8** confused
taw: tan, tew **4** beat, whip **5** agate **6** harass, marble **7** scourge, shooter, torment, toughen
tawdry: **5** cheap, gaudy, showy **6** sleazy, tinsel
tawny, tawney: tan **5** brown, dusky, olive, swart, tenne **6** Indian, tanned **7** fulvous, tigrine **8** brindled **9** bullfinch
tawse, taws: **4** whip **5** strap
tax: **4** cess, duty, feel, fine, levy, rate, scat, scot, task, toll **5** abuse, agist, exact, order, scatt, stent, stint, tithe, touch, value **6** accuse, assess, avania, burden, charge, demand, excise, extent, handle, hidage, impose, impost, settle, strain **7** censure, dispute, finance, gabelle, license, tailage, tallage, tollage, tribute **8** estimate, exaction, overtire, reproach **9** prescribe **10** assessment, imposition **12** contribution
assessment: **7** doomage
gatherer: **9** catchpole, catchpoll
kind of: cro, soc **4** cess, geld, scat **5** finta, tithe **6** abkari, excise, pavage, surtax, taille, vinage **7** boscage, chevage, patente, prisage, scewing, tailage **8** auxilium, carucage **9** surcharge **10** chaukidari
rate: **5** ratal **10** assessment
taxable: **10** assessable, censurable
taxation: tax **6** charge **7** finance, reproof, revenue **9** valuation **10** accusation, assessment
degree of: **5** ratal
taxi: cab **4** hack **5** jixie **6** litter **7** vehicle
taximeter: **5** clock
taxing: **10** accusation
taxpayer: **9** ratepayer
tchai: **5** brook, river **6** stream
tea: **5** party **6** repast, supper **8** beverage, function **9** collation, decoction, reception
cake: **5** scone
constituent: **8** caffeine
container: **8** canister
expert: **6** taster
family: **8** Theaceae
kind of: cha **4** chaa, chia, tsia **5** assam, black, bohea, congo, chias, Emesa, green, hyson, Ledum, oopak, pekoe, salop **6** congue, oolong, saloop **7** cambric **8** bouillon, go-widdie **9** gunpowder
plant: **4** thea
receptacle: **8** canister

room: **5** kiosk
table: **5** tepoy **6** teapoy
urn: **7** samovar
teach: **4** show **5** coach, edify, endue, guide, point, train, tutor **6** commit, direct, lesson, preach, school **7** apprise, apprize, beteach, conduct, educate **8** accustom, amaister, document, instruct **9** enlighten **10** discipline **11** demonstrate
teacher: **5** coach, guide, Plato, tutor **6** docent, doctor, mentor, pedant, pundit, reader, regent **7** adjunct, edifier, maestro, sophist, trainer **8** civilian, director, educator, gamaliel, moralist, preacher **9** pedagogue, preceptor **10** instructor
Alexandria: **6** Origen
association: NEA
Indian religion: **4** guru
Jewish: **5** rabbi
Mohammedan: pir **4** alim, imam **5** imaum, molla, mulla **6** mollah, mullah
of eloquence: **6** rhetor **7** sophist
of the deaf: **7** oralist
Russia: **7** starets
teaching: **5** moral **6** docent **7** precept **10** discipline **11** instruction
of a fable: **5** moral
of the Twelve: **7** Didache
pert. to: **9** pedagogic
teakettle: **4** suke, suky **5** sukey, sukie
teal: **5** crick **8** garganey
team: **4** crew, gang, join, pair, race, span, yoke **5** brood, chain, flock, group, wagon **6** convey, couple, number **7** lineage, progeny, vehicle **8** carriage **9** associate, stationed
kinds of: duo **4** crew **6** scrubs **7** varsity
supporter: fan **6** rooter
teamed with: **5** yoked **6** paired **7** matched
teamster: **6** carter, driver **7** carrier
tear: ram, rip, rit, run **4** claw, drag, fine, pull, rage, rend, rent, rive, rush, skag, snag, weep **5** break, claut, larme, reave, split, spree, touse, unrip, waste **6** cleave, dainty, damage, divide, flurry, lament, pierce, remove, screed, tatter, wrench **7** agitate, chatter, consume, destroy, disrupt, fritter, passion, shatter, torment **8** carousal, delicate, lacerate, lachryma, separate
apart: **4** rend
down: **4** rase, raze **11** disassemble
limb from limb: **9** dismember
to pieces: **6** tatter **10** dilacerate
up by the roots: **6** arache **9** eradicate, extirpate
tearcat: **7** ranting **9** blusterer **10** swaggering
teardrop design: **5** larme
tearful: sad **6** watery **7** flebile, snively, weeping **8** lacrimal
tearing: **4** rage **5** hasty, hurry **7** furious,

violent **8** splendid **9** furiously, harrowing, impetuous **10** impressive
tearpit: **7** larmier
tears: **5** grief
inducing: **9** rheumatic
pert. to: **8** lacrimal
poetic: **5** rheum
tease: beg, guy, irk, nag, rag, tew, vex **4** card, coax, comb, drag, fret, hare, razz, stir, tear, twit **5** annoy, chevy, chivy, devil, taunt, wrack **6** badger, bother, caddle, chivvy, harass, heckle, molest, pester, plague, teasel **7** disturb, hatchel, provoke, scratch, torment **8** irritate, separate **9** aggravate, importune, tantalize **11** disentangle
wool: tum **4** comb, toom
teasel: **4** comb
teaser: **4** gull **6** carder, curler, sniper, stoker, willow **7** curtain, fireman, problem **8** operator, pesterer, willower
teasing: **11** importunate
teaty: **5** cross **7** fretful, peevish
tebbad: **6** simoom **9** sandstorm
tebeldi: **6** baobab
technology of agriculture: **10** agrotechny
techy: **4** spot **5** habit **6** touchy, vexing **7** blemish, fretful, peevish, quality **9** irascible, irritable
teck: **6** cravat
tectonic: **7** builder, plastic **9** carpenter **10** structural **13** architectural
ted: **4** toad, turn **5** waste **6** spread **7** scatter
tedge: **6** ingate, runner
tedious: dry **4** dead, dree, dull, long, slow **5** bored, prosy **6** boring, borish, elenge, prolix **7** irksome, noxious, peevish, prosaic **8** dilatory, slowness, tiresome **9** exhausted, irritable, laborious, prolixity, wearisome **10** monotonous **11** displeasing, everlasting **13** uninteresting
tedium: **5** ennui **7** boredom, doldrum **11** irksomeness, tediousness **13** wearisomeness
tee: **5** mound
teem: go **4** bear, fill, gush, lead, pour, rain, swim **5** bring, drain, empty, fetch, swarm **6** abound, resort, seethe, summon **7** produce **8** abundant, conceive, generate, prolific
teeming: **4** full **5** agush **7** pouring, replete **8** crowding, prolific **9** abounding **11** overflowing **13** overabounding
teen: vex **4** harm, hate, keen, lose, pain, shut, tell, tind, tune **5** abuse, anger, grief, vexed **6** damage, injure, injury, sorrow **7** provoke, trouble **8** announce, distress, irritate, reproach, vexation **9** vexatious **10** affliction, calumniate
teeny: wee **4** tiny **5** small **7** fretful, peevish **9** malicious
teeny-weeny: **4** tiny **5** small **6** minute

teer: 4 daub 7 plaster
teeter: 4 rock 5 waver 6 jiggle, quiver, seesaw 7 rocking, rolling, tremble 9 sandpiper, vacillate
teeter board: 6 seesaw
teeth: 5 tines 7 canines
false: 5 plate 8 dentures
incrustation on: 6 tartar
large: 4 buck 5 snags
long: 5 fangs 6 tushes
outer covering of: 6 enamel
pert. to: 5 molar 6 dental
serpent: 5 fangs
sower of dragon's: 6 Cadmus
without: 10 edentulate, edentulous
teethy: 5 cross 6 biting 7 crabbed 9 irritable
teeting: 7 titlark
teetotal: 6 entire 7 abstain 8 complete
teetotaller: dry 7 nonuser 9 abstainer, rechabite, refrainer
teewhaap: 7 lapwing
teg: doe 5 sheep, woman 6 fleece
tegmen: 5 cover, plate 6 elytra 8 covering, fore-wing, tegument
tegua: 6 sandal
teguexin: 4 teju 6 lizard
tegula: 4 tile
tegument: 4 coat 5 cover, testa 6 testae 10 integument
tegurium: hut 5 cabin 6 shrine
tehee: 6 giggle, titter 7 snicker
Tehuantepec Gulf Indian: 5 Huave
teicher: 4 ooze 5 bleed
teiidae: 4 teju 7 lizards
teind: 5 tithe
teju: 6 lizard 8 teguexin
tekke: rug 6 carpet 7 convent 9 monastery
tela: web 6 tissue 7 bristle 8 membrane
telamon: 8 atlantes, caryatid
Telamon's son: 6 Teucer
teledu: 6 badger
telega: 4 cart 5 wagon
telegraph: 4 wire 5 cable
inventor: 5 Morse
key: 6 tapper
signal: dot 4 dash 9 semaphore
telegraphic communication: 10 lettergram
telephone: 4 buzz, call, dial 5 phone
inventor: 4 Bell
receiver: 8 cymaphen
Telephus' mother: 4 Auge
telescope: jam 5 glass 7 shorten 8 collapse, condense, simplify
object seen with: 11 debilissima
telescopic: 9 farseeing
telic: 9 purposive 10 purposeful 12 teleological
tell: say 4 chat, deem, hill, know, tale, talk, told 5 aread, areed, breve, count, mound, order, speak, state, utter, value 6 decide, direct, impart, inform, number, recite, reckon, regard, relate, repeat, report, reveal, tattle 7 account, command, dictate, discern, divulge, express, mention, narrate, publish, recount, request 8 acquaint, announce, disclose, rehearse 9 calculate, discourse, enumerate, recognize 11 communicate 12 discriminate
in advance: 4 warn
on: 4 sing 5 peach 6 snitch, squeal
revelatory facts: 6 debunk
secrets: 5 clype
thoughtlessly: 4 blab, blat
teller: 4 blow 5 shoot 6 remark, sprout 8 informer, narrator 9 describer 11 annunciator
telling: 5 valid 6 cogent 8 forceful, relation, striking 9 effective, pertinent 10 convincing
telltale: 4 blab, hint 7 tattler 8 betrayer, informer 9 betraying, indicator 10 indication, talebearer
telltruth: 7 honesty 9 frankness
telluride: 7 altaite
temblor: 10 earthquake
temerarious: 4 rash 6 chance 8 heedless, reckless 9 venturous 10 fortuitous, headstrong 11 venturesome
temerity: 4 gall 5 cheek, nerve 8 audacity, boldness, rashness 9 hardihood 10 effrontery 12 recklessness 13 foolhardiness 15 venturesomeness
temper: fit, ire, mix 4 bait, bate, coll, curb, cure, heal, mean, mood, neal, rage, tone 5 adapt, anger, birse, blend, delay, humor 6 adjust, animus, anneal, attune, church, dander, direct, govern, harden, manage, medium, mingle, modify, puddle, reduce, season, soften, soothe, steady 7 assuage, chasten, control, moisten, mollify, qualify, restore, toughen 8 attemper, chastise, compound, mitigate, moderate, modulate, regulate, restrain, 9 composure 10 equanimity, irritation 11 accommodate, disposition
even: 4 calm 5 staid 6 sedate
kind of: ire 4 huff, mood 6 choler, spleen
temperament: 4 mood 5 gemut, humor 6 crasis, crases(pl.), humour, nature, temper 7 caprice, climate, emotion 10 adjustment 11 disposition, temperature 12 constitution
temperance: 8 sobriety 10 abstinence, moderation
temperate: 4 calm, cool, mild 5 sober 6 soften, temper 8 moderate 9 continent 10 abstemious, restrained 13 dispassionate
temperature: 4 heat 5 fever, state 6 temper 7 mixture 8 compound, mildness 10 moderation, proportion 11 disposition, temperament 12 constitution
tempest: 4 gale, wind 5 orage, storm 6 tumult 7 agitate, borasca, borasco, turmoil 9 agitation, bourasque, commotion, hurricane 12 thunderstorm
Tempest characters: 5 Ariel 7 Caliban, Miranda 8 Prospero

tempestuous: 5 galey, gusty 6 stormy 7 violent 9 turbulent

template, templet: 4 beam, mold 5 basil, bezel, bezil, gauge 7 pattern

temple: 4 fane, naos, rath 5 candi, cella, edile, huaca, kovil, ratha, speos 6 aedile, chandi, church, haffet, haffit, hieron

basin: 5 laver

kind of: sha, taj 4 deul, Rath 5 jinja, Ratha 6 church, jinsha, pagoda 7 capitol 8 pantheon 9 Parthenon

part: 5 cella

sanctuary: 10 penetralia

tempo: 4 pace, rate, time 6 rhythm, timing

pert. to: 6 agogic

temporal: 4 laic 5 civil, scale 6 carnal, muscle 7 earthly, secular, worldly 9 ephemeral, political, temporary 10 transitory 11 impermanent 13 chronological

temporarily: 5 nonce

temporary: 6 acting, timely 7 interim, secular, topical 8 temporal 9 adinterim, ephemeral 10 transitory 11 provisional

contrivance: 9 makeshift

temporize: 5 delay, humor, yield 6 demand, parley, soothe 9 negotiate 13 procrastinate

tempt: try 4 defy, fand, lead, lure, test 5 decoy, probe, prove, taunt 6 allure, assail, entice, incite, induce, seduce 7 assault, attempt, attract, provoke 8 endeavor, persuade 9 endeavour, seduction 10 inducement

temptation: 4 bait 5 trial 7 testing 9 seduction 10 allurement, enticement, inducement

tempter: 5 devil, Satan 6 baiter

tempting: 8 alluring 9 seductive 10 attractive

temptress: 4 vamp 5 Circe, siren 7 Delilah, Lorelei, mermaid 10 Parthenope 11 enchantress

temse, tems: 4 sift 5 sieve

temulence: 12 intoxication

ten: 4 iota(Gk.) 5 decad 6 decade, denary

ares: 6 decare

dollars: 7 sawbuck

prefix: dec 4 deca

Ten Commandments: 7 Decalog 9 Decalogue

ten-footed: 7 decapod

ten-sided figure: 7 decagon

ten-stringed: 9 decachord

ten-year periods: 7 decades 9 decenniad, decennium

tenable: 10 defensible 12 maintainable

tenacious: 5 tough 6 cledgy, dogged, grippy, sticky 7 gripple, miserly, viscous 8 adhesive, cohesive, holdfast, sticking, stubborn 9 glutinous, niggardly, retentive 10 persistent 11 closefisted 12 pertinacious

tenaciously: 8 doggedly 10 persistent

tenacity: 8 firmness 9 toughness 11 miserliness, persistence, persistency 12 adhesiveness, cohesiveness, perseverance 13 glutinousness, retentiveness

tenancy: 6 estate, tenure 7 holding 9 occupancy 10 possession

tenant: 4 leud 5 ceile, dreng 6 bordar, drengh, geneat, holder, leaser, lessee, occupy, renter, vassal 7 chakdar, cottier, dweller 8 occupant 9 bordarius, collibert 10 inhabitant

tend: 4 burn, care, lead, move, wait, work 5 apply, await, guard, nurse, offer, reach, serve, swing, treat, watch 6 attend, direct, expect, extend, foster, intend, kindle, listen, manage, supply 7 conduce, hearken, incline, oversee, provide, purpose, stretch, tending 8 minister, tendency 9 accompany, attentive, co-operate, cultivate, gravitate

a fire: 5 stoke

to rise: 8 levitate

toward one point: 8 converge

tendency: set 4 bent, bias, tide 5 drift, drive, tenor, trend 6 course, effect, object, result 7 aptness, bearing, leaning 8 appetite, movement, relation 9 affection, direction, proneness, readiness 10 proclivity, propension, propensity 11 disposition, inclination

monistic: 11 unitariness

structural: 7 peloria

tender: bid, tid 4 boat, dear, fond, gift, keen, kind, mild, nice, soft, sore, thin, warm, weak 5 chary, frail, light, offer, young 6 delate, feeble, gentle, humane, loving, touchy, vessel, waiter 7 amabile, amatory, amorous, careful, fragile, pitiful, present, proffer, slender, sparing, steamer, subdued, tenuous, vehicle 8 delicate, feminine, immature, merciful, precious, proposal, ticklish 9 brotherly, sensitive, succulent 10 charitable, effeminate, scrupulous 11 considerate, softhearted, susceptible, sympathetic, warmhearted 12 affectionate 13 compassionate 14 impressionable

animals: 6 herder 10 husbandman

cattle: 6 cowboy, herder 7 byreman 8 neatherd 9 byrewoman

for cloth: 9 stenterer

horse: 5 groom 6 ostler 7 hostler, stabler

ship: gig 5 barge, dingy 6 dingey, dinghy 7 collier, pinnace

tenderfoot: 6 novice 7 greenie 8 beginner, neophyte, newcomer 9 cheechaco, cheechako, greenhorn

tenderhearted: 6 humane

tenderness: 4 love, pity 6 cherte 8 kindness, softness, sympathy, weakness 9 affection 10 compassion, gentleness 13 sensitiveness

tendon: 4 band, cord 5 chord, nerve, sinew 11 aponeurosis

comb. form: 4 teno

tendour, tendoor: 4 seat 5 table

tendril: 4 curl 5 clasp, sprig 6 branch, cirrus 7 ringlet, stipule
tendron: bud 5 shoot 6 sprout
tenebrous: 4 dark 5 dusky 6 gloomy 7 obscure 8 darkness
tenement: 5 abode 8 building, dwelling 9 apartment 10 habitation
tenet: ism 4 view 5 adoxy, canon, creed, dogma, maxim 6 belief, decree 7 opinion, paradox 8 doctrine 9 principle
tenfold: 6 denary 7 decuple
tengere: sky 7 heavens
teniente: 6 deputy 7 headman 10 lieutenant
tenmantale: tax 7 tithing 8 carucage
tenne: 5 brown, color
Tennessee: *first governor:* 6 Sevier
national park: 6 Shiloh
tennis: *between four persons:* 7 doubles
between two persons: 7 singles
game series: set
no score: 4 love
old form: 5 bandy
points: 4 aces
prize cup: 5 Davis
racket: bat
score: ace 4 love 5 deuce
shoe: 7 sneaker
stroke: cut, let, lob 4 chop 8 backhand
term: ace, cut, let, lob, set 4 love 5 deuce, fault, serve 6 volley 7 receive, service 9 advantage
trophy donor: 5 Davis
Tennyson: *character:* 4 Enid 5 Arden 6 Elaine
heroine: 4 Enid
"In Memoriam" subject: 6 Hallam
tenon: cog 4 coak 8 dovetail
tenor: 4 copy, feck, gist 5 drift, stamp, trend 6 course, intent, nature, singer 7 holding, purport, writing 8 tendency 9 character, condition, direction, discourse, procedure 10 transcript
falsetto: 8 tenorino
tens of thousands: 7 myriads
tense: 4 rapt, taut, time 5 rigid, stiff, tight 6 intent, tauten 7 intense 8 strained 9 stretched 10 breathless
past: 9 preterite
verb: 4 past 6 aorist, future 7 perfect, present 9 preterite 10 pluperfect 11 conditional
tensile: 6 pliant 7 ductile 8 tensible
tension: 4 bent 6 strain, stress 7 closure 8 pressure
tent: hut 4 camp, care, heed, show, stop, tend, test, wine 5 crame, frame, lodge, probe, teach, tempt 6 attend, beware, encamp, hinder, intent, pulpit, tender 7 observe, prevent, proffer, shelter 9 attention, attentive 10 habitation
dweller: 4 Arab 5 nomad 6 camper, Indian 7 scenite, tourist
kind: 4 pawl, yurt 5 darry, shool, tepee,

toldo, yurta 6 abbacy, wigwam, tienda 7 balagan, kibitka, marquee, sparver 8 pavilion 9 pretorium 10 praetorium
tentacle: 6 feeler 7 tendril 10 tentaculum
tentage: 5 camps
tentamen: 5 trial 7 attempt
tentative: 9 temporary 11 impermanent, provisional 12 experimental
tenter: 5 frame
tenterhooks: 6 strain 8 suspense
tenth: 5 tithe 6 decima 7 decimae 8 decimate
part: 5 tithe
tents: 4 camp 7 baggage 10 encampment
tenty: 7 careful 8 watchful 9 attentive, carefully 10 watchfully
tenuity: 6 rarity 7 exility, poverty 8 delicacy, fineness, rareness, thinness 9 faintness, indigence 10 meagerness, slightness 11 slenderness
tenuous: 4 fine, rare, slim, thin 6 flimsy, slight 7 gaseous, slender, subtile 8 delicate, ethereal 13 insignificant, unsubstantial
tenure: 4 term 5 lease 6 manner 8 courtesy 9 condition
tepee, teepee: 6 wigwam
tepid: 4 warm 8 lukewarm
tepidness: 5 tepor
tepor: 9 tepidness
tera: 6 church 9 monastery
Terah: *father:* 5 Nahor
son: 7 Abraham
teras: 7 monster
teratosis: 11 monstrosity
terceron: 7 mulatto
tere, teer: 4 daub 7 plaster
terebene: 10 antiseptic 12 disinfectant
terebra: 5 auger, drill
terebrate: 4 bore 9 perforate
teredo: 7 mollusk 8 shipworm
teres: 6 muscle
terete: 7 centric 8 columnar 11 cylindrical
Tereus: *son:* 4 Itys 6 Itylus
wife: 6 Procne
tergal: 6 dorsal
tergiversate: lie 5 shift 7 shuffle 10 apostatize, equivocate
tergiversation: 6 deceit 7 evasion 8 apostasy 10 subterfuge
tergum: 4 back
term: end 4 call, date, half, name, time, word 5 bound, limit, state 6 period, tenure 7 article, entitle, epithet, session 8 boundary, duration, semester 9 condition, extremity 10 definition, expression 11 appellation, termination
cricket: off, ons 6 yorker
fencing: hai, hay 4 bind 5 coupe 6 touche 8 tacautac
golf: lie, par, tee 4 baff, fore, hook 5 bogey, bogie, divot, eagle, green, slice, stimy 6 birdie, stroke, stymie 7 gallery

grammar: **6** phrase, simile, syntax
heraldry: **4** ente, urde
Hindu, of respect: sri
Jewish, of reproach: **4** raca
mathematics: **4** nome, root, sine **6** cosine
of address: sir **4** sire **6** milady, milord, sirrah
of endearment: **5** astor **8** ashstore
of office: **6** regime
printer: **4** dele, stet
rugby: try **5** scrum
school: **7** seminar **8** semester **9** trimester
science: azo, ame **4** beta **5** stoss
sea: **4** ahoy **5** avast, belay

termagant: **5** shrew **6** Amazon, tartar, virago **7** furious **8** scolding **9** turbulent **10** boisterous, tumultuous **11** quarrelsome

termed: **5** named **6** called, styled, yclept **7** ycleped

terminable: **6** finish, finite **9** limitable **12** determinable **13** discontinuing

terminal: end **5** anode, depot, final, limit **6** finish **7** cathode, closing, limital, station **8** desinent, terminus, ultimate **9** electrode, extremity **10** concluding **11** desinential, termination
negative: **7** cathode, kathode
positive: **5** anode

terminate: end **4** call, halt, stop **5** bound, cease, close, limit **6** define, direct, expire, finish, result **7** achieve, confine, destine, perfect **8** complete, conclude, restrict

terminating: **5** final **6** ending
distinct point: **9** apiculate
trefoil: **6** botone

termination: end **4** amen **5** bound, close, event, limit **6** ending, expiry, finale, finish, period, result, upshot **7** outcome, purpose **8** boundary, decision, finality, terminus **9** extremity **10** completion, concluding, conclusion, expiration **13** determination
malady: **5** lysis

terminative: **8** absolute, bounding, definite **10** concluding **11** determining, terminating

terminus: end **4** goal, post **5** depot, stone **6** marker **8** boundary, terminal **9** extremity **11** termination

termite: ant **4** anai, anay

termless: **8** infinite, nameless, unending **9** boundless, limitless **13** indescribable, inexpressible, unconditional, unconditioned

terms: **9** agreement **10** conditions, provisions **11** limitations **12** propositions **13** circumstances

tern: **4** darr, gull **9** wide-awake

ternary: **6** treble, triple **7** ternion, trinity **9** threefold

ternate: **12** trifoliolate

terne: **8** tinplate

terpsichore: **6** dancer **7** dancing

terra: **5** earth

terra firma: **5** earth **6** estate **8** mainland

terrace: **4** bank, dais, mesa, step **5** bench **7** balcony, gallery, portico **8** chabutra, platform **9** colonnade
wall: **6** podium

terrage: tax **4** toll **7** payment

terrain: **4** terr **5** tract **6** milieu, region **7** estrial, terrane, terrent **11** environment

terrapin: **4** emyd, emys **6** coodle, emydea, heifer, potter, slider, turtle **8** emydidae, emydinae

terrar: **6** bursar

terrene: **4** land **5** earth, realm **6** earthy **7** earthly, mundane, terrain, worldly **11** terrestrial

terrestrial: **6** earthy, layman, mortal **7** earthly, mundane, terrene, worldly **9** planetary

terret: **4** ring **7** cringle

terrible: **4** dire, gast **5** awful, lurid **6** severe, tragic **7** direful, extreme, fearful, ghastly, hideous, intense, painful **8** almighty, dreadful, horrible, terrific **9** appalling, atrocious, excessive, frightful **10** formidable, terrifying, tremendous, unpleasant **12** disagreeable

terribly: **4** very **5** felly **6** grisly **9** extremely **11** exceedingly

terrier: fox **4** Bull, Skye **5** Irish, Welsh **6** Boston **8** Scottish, Sealyham **10** Bedlington, Clydesdale

terrific: **7** extreme **8** dreadful, exciting, terrible **9** appalling, excessive, frightful **10** terrifying, tremendous

terrified: **4** awed **6** afraid, aghast **7** ghastly

terrifier: **5** haunt **7** haunter

terrify: awe, cow, hag **4** bree, fray **5** alarm, annoy, appal, daunt, deter, drive, haunt, impel, scare, shock, tease **6** affirm, afread, agrise, appall, bother, dismay, injure **7** torment **8** affright, frighten **9** importune

terrifying: **6** horrid **7** hideous **8** terrible

terrigenous: **9** earthborn **13** autochthonous

territorial division: amt **6** canton **7** commune **10** department **14** arrondissement

territory: **4** area, land **5** field, scope, state, tract **6** extent, ground, region, sphere **7** country, portion **8** district, environs, province **12** neighborhood
kind of: **5** banat **6** canton **7** banlieu, enclave **8** banlieue, Pashalic **10** palatinate
shut in: **7** enclave

terror: awe **4** fear, fray, pest **5** alarm, dread, panic **6** affray, dismay, fright, horror **8** dreddour **12** terribleness **13** consternation

terrorism: **11** subjugation **12** intimidation

terrorist: **5** rebel **8** alarmist **11** scaremonger

terrorize: awe **5** abash, appal, scare **6** appall, coerce **8** frighten **9** embarrass **10** intimidate

terry: 4 loop

terse: 4 curt, neat **5** brief, pithy **6** abrupt, claret, rubbed, smooth **7** compact, concise, laconic, pointed, refined **8** polished, succinct, unprolix **11** sententious, tight-lipped **12** accomplished

tertiary period: 7 neocene

tertulia: 4 club **5** party

tervee: 6 writhe **8** struggle

terzina: 6 tercet **7** triplet

terzo: 6 legion **7** brigade

tessel: 11 checkerwork

tessellated: 6 mosaic

tessera: 4 cube, tile **5** glass, label, token **6** billet, marble, pledge, tablet, ticket **7** voucher **8** password **9** rectangle **11** certificate

test: pot, try **4** exam, fand, feel, will **5** assay, check, cupel, grope, proof, prove, shell, taste, testa, trial, weave **6** ordeal, refine, sample **7** approof, approve, examine, witness **8** cupeling, evidence, potsherd, standard **9** construct, criterion, determine, testament, testimony **10** experience, experiment, touchstone **11** examination, performance **12** authenticate

in fineness and weight: pyx

ore: **5** assay

series: **7** gantlet

value: **5** assay

testa: 7 coating **8** covering, episperm, tegument **10** integument

testament: Job **4** will **8** covenant, landbook

testator: 7 legator, witness **9** testatrix

tester: 5 crown **6** canopy, conner, helmet, prover, teston **7** assayer, candler, sparver **9** chauffeur, headpiece

testicle: cob **6** testis, testes(pl.)

deer: **6** doucet, dowcet, dowset

testificate: 11 certificate, testimonial

testified under oath: 7 deponed

testifier: 7 witness **8** deponent

testify: 6 affirm, attest, depone, depose **7** declare, express, profess, protest **8** indicate, manifest, proclaim

testimonial: 4 sign **5** token **7** warrant, writing **8** evidence **9** testimony **10** credential **11** certificate

testimony: say **6** attest, avowal **7** witness **8** evidence **10** deposition, profession **11** affirmation, attestation, certificate, declaration **14** recommendation

testing: 5 assay **11** examination

testudo: 4 lyre, shed **5** cover, talpa, tumor, vault **6** screen **7** ceiling

testy: 6 touchy **7** crabbed, fretful, peevish, waspish **8** petulant, snappish **9** impatient, irascible, irritable, obstinate **10** headstrong

tetanus: 7 lockjaw

tetchy: 6 touchy **7** peevish **9** irritable, sensitive

tête-a-tête: 4 chat, seat, sofa **8** causeuse **12** conversation

tetel: 5 torah

tether: tie **4** band, rope **5** cable, chain, leash, limit, noose **6** fasten, picket **7** confine **8** restrain

tetragon: 6 square **7** rhombus **10** quadrangle

tetric: 5 harsh **6** gloomy **7** austere

Teuton: 4 Goth **6** German

Teutonic: 5 Dutch **6** German, Gothic **7** English **12** Scandinavian

alphabet character: **4** rune

deity: As, Er; Eir, Hel. Tiu, Tyr, Ull **4** Erda, Frea, Frig, Norn, Odin, Thor **5** Aesir, Baldr, Brage, Bragl, Donar, Othin, Tiwaz, Wodin, Wotan **6** Balder, Frigga, Saeter **7** Forseti **8** Heimdall

homicide: **5** morth

land: **4** odal

law: **5** Salic

race: **5** Danes, Goths, Jutes **6** Angles, Franks, Saxons **7** Germans, Vandals **8** Lombards **11** Burgundians, Norweigians **13** Scandinavians

water nymph: nis

tew: taw, tow, vex **4** beat, fuss, pull, work **5** knead, tease, tools **6** incite, strive, tackle, tuyere **7** fatigue **8** struggle

tewel: 4 bore, hole, pipe, tool, vent **6** funnel, tuyere **7** chimney, trumpet

tewer: 4 lane **5** alley

tewit: 7 lapwing

tewly: 6 sickly **8** delicate, qualmish

tewsome: 8 restless **11** troublesome

Texas: *broncho:* **7** mustang

citadel: **5** Alamo

city: **4** Waco **5** Cuero, Mexia, Paris **6** Austin, Dallas, El Paso, Laredo, Odessa **7** Abilene, Denison, Houston, Lubbock **8** Amarillo

cottonwood: **5** alamo

county: Bee **4** Leon, Polk, Rusk **5** Nolan, Starr, Tyler **6** Harris, Sutton, Walker **7** Houston, Madison, Navarro, Trinity **8** Anderson, Angelina, Cherokee **9** Freestone, Limestone **11** Nacogdoches

cowboy jacket: **8** chaqueta

fortress: **5** Alamo

founder: **6** Austin

itch: **5** mange **7** scabies

massacre site: **5** Alamo

mission: **5** Alamo

poplar: **5** Alamo

river: Red **5** Pecos **6** Neches, Nueces **9** Rio Grande

shrine: **5** Alamo

shrub: **6** anagua, anaqua

state police: **6** ranger

text: 4 copy **5** theme, topic **7** passage, subject **11** handwriting

operatic: **8** libretto

chunky, stocky, stodgy, stubby

thickskulled: 4 dull, slow 5 heavy 6 stupid 11 thickheaded

thicky: fat

thief (see also **stealer**): 4 chor, gilt 5 budge, scamp 6 ackman, arrant, bandit, cannon, cloyer, hooker, looter, nimmer, rascal, robber, sucker, waster 7 bramble, brigand, burglar, grifter, sneaker, stealer 8 cutpurse, gangster, larcener 9 larcenist, scoundrel 10 depredator, freebooter, highwayman, plagiarist

crucified beside Christ: 6 Desmas, Dismas, Dysmas

kind of: gun 5 ganef, ganof, gonof, snoop 6 ackman, angler, gonoph, pirate, swiper 7 gorilla, mercury, rustler 9 drawlatch 10 pickpocket

thieveless: 4 cold 5 bleak 6 frigid 7 aimless 8 bootless, listless 10 forbidding

thieves' Latin: 5 slang

thievish: sly 7 furtive, kleptic 8 stealthy 9 Hungarian

thig: ask, beg 6 borrow 7 beggary

thigh: ham 4 hock 5 carve, femur, flank, meros, merus 6 femora(pl.), gammon

bone: 5 femur, ilium

pert. to: 6 crural

thill: 5 plank, shaft 6 thwart 8 planking, wainscot

thimble: *conjurer:* 6 goblet

machine: 6 sleeve

thin: dim 4 bony, flue, lank, lean, pale, poor, rare, slim, weak 5 exile, faint, gaunt, lanky, lathy, scant, sheer, spare, washy, wizen 6 dilute, flimsy, hollow, meager, meagre, papery, rarefy, reduce, scanty, scarce, skinny, slight, slinky, sparse, watery, weaken, weazen 7 gracile, haggard, scrawny, slender, tenuous 8 araneous, gossamer, rarefied, scantily 9 attenuate, emaciated, extenuate, infertile, subtilize 10 inadequate 11 transparent 12 unbelievable, unconvincing 13 unsubstantial

and delicate: 8 araneous

and haggard: 5 gaunt

and slender: 4 lean 5 lanky

and vibrant: 5 reedy

and weak: 6 watery

and withered: 5 wizen 6 weezen

out: 5 peter

plate: 4 leaf, shim 5 wedge 6 lamina, tegmen

thine: 4 tuum

thing: act 4 deed, idea, item 5 cause, chose, court, event, point 6 affair, detail, matter, notion, object, reason, wealth 7 article, council 8 assembly, incident, property 9 happening 11 transaction 12 circumstance

accomplished: 4 acta, deed 5 actum, actus

added: ell 6 insert 7 addenda(pl.) 8 addendum, addition, appendix 9 insertion

10 additament, complement, supplement

admitted: 4 fact 5 datum 7 element 9 principle

aforesaid: 5 ditto

assumed: 7 premise, premiss 9 postulate 11 implication, stipulation 14 presupposition

brought into existence: 8 creation

capable of spontaneous motion: 8 automata 9 automaton

complete in itself: 5 unity

consecrated to a deity: 6 hieron, sacrum 8 anathema

cursed: 8 anathema

extra: 5 bonus 6 bounty, lanyap 7 premium 8 lagnappe 9 lagniappe

following: 6 sequel

forfeited to crown: 7 deodand

found: 5 trove

given as security: 4 gage 6 pledge

indefinite, unnamed: 7 so and so 11 nondescript

invariable: 8 constant

known by reasoning: 7 noumena 8 noumenon

known by senses: 9 phenomena 10 phenomenon

of no value: 4 bean 5 nihil 6 fillip, nought, stiver, trifle 7 bauchle, nothing, pinhead, trinket 8 picayune 9 nonentity, resnihili 10 resnullius

of remembrance: 5 token

personal property law: 5 chose

precious: 4 oner 5 curio, relic 6 pippin, rarity 8 treasure

small: dot, jot 4 atom, iota, whit 6 tittle 8 particle, scuddick

to be done: 5 chore 6 agenda 7 agendum

unusual: 5 freak 6 oddity 11 monstrosity 12 malformation

thingamajigs: 7 gadgets

things: res 4 gear 5 goods 7 clothes, effects 10 belongings 13 appurtenances

between extremes: 13 intermediates

done: 9 res gestae

for sale: 5 goods, wares 8 services 11 merchandise

gained by purchase: 10 acquirenda

hidden: 10 penetralia

holy: 5 hagia

jumble of: 4 mess, muss 14 conglomeration

linked in nature: 8 cognates

movable: 8 chattels 10 resmobiles

obtained from other things: 11 derivatives

prohibited: 7 vetanda

suitable for eating: 9 esculents

to see: 6 sights

worth remembering: 11 memorabilia

thingumbob: 9 doohickey, doohickus, doohinkey, doohinkus

think: wis 4 deem, feel, muse, seem, trow, ween 5 judge, opine 6 appear, esteem, expect, intend, reason, repute, **scheme** 7

believe, bethink, concoct, imagine, purpose, reflect, resolve, suppose, surmise **8** cogitate, conceive, consider, meditate, ruminate **9** calculate, determine, speculate **10** conjecture, deliberate, reconsider **11** contemplate
alike: **5** agree
for: **7** suppose, suspect
logically: **6** reason
out: **4** plan **5** solve **6** devise **7** develop, perfect **8** cogitate, contrive, discover **10** excogitate
over: **5** brood

thinker: 4 mind **5** brain **7** student **9** meditator **11** philosopher

thinking: 7 opinion **9** judgement **10** cogitation, reflection **13** ratiocination **17** intellectualizing
marked by exact: **13** ratiocinative

thinly: 6 airily **8** sparsely **14** insufficiently
metallic: **5** tinny
scattered: **6** sparse

thinner: 5 rarer **7** sheerer **10** turpentine

thinness: 6 rarity **7** exility, tenuity **11** attenuation

third: *combining form:* **4** trit
figure mood: **7** ferison
in number: **8** tertiary
music: **6** tierce
power of number: **4** cube

thirl: 4 hole, hurl, thin **5** drill, gaunt, whirl, wound **6** hungry, hurtle, pierce, sucken, thrill, tingle, window **7** enslave, nostril, opening, vibrate **8** enthrall, restrict, thirlage, traverse **9** penetrate, perforate, shriveled **11** perforation

thirlage: fee, pay **4** dues **5** right **7** multure, service **8** mortgage **9** servitude, thralldom

thirling: 7 bondage **10** subjection

thirst: 4 long **5** crave, dryth **6** desire **7** aridity, craving, longing
absence of: **7** adipsia
excessive: **9** anadipsia

thirsty: dry **4** adry, arid, avid **6** desire, drouth **7** athirst, craving, drought, longing, parched **8** droughty

thirty: 6 lambda(Gr.), trente(F.)

thirty nine and thirty seven hundredths inches: 5 meter

this: yis **4** esta(Sp.), haec(L.)

this way: 4 here

thistle: 4 weed **7** bedegar, caltrop **8** bedeguar **10** acanaceous
genus of: **5** layia

thistle-like plants: 7 carlina

thither: end, yon **5** hence, there **6** result, yonder **7** farther, thereat

thivel: 5 stick **7** spatula

thixle: ax: adz **7** hatchet

Thjazi: *daughter:* **6** Skathi
home: **9** Thrymheim

tho: 5 still

thole: peg, pin **4** bear **5** allow **6** endure, remain, suffer **7** undergo **8** tolerate

Thomas Hardy heroine: 4 Tess

Thomas Moore character: 5 Lalla

Thomas' opera: 6 Mignon

thong: 4 lace, lash, rein, riem **5** lasso, leash, romal, strap, strip, whang **6** twitch **7** amentum, laniard, lanyard, latchet **8** whiplash

thong-shaped: 6 lorate

Thor: *father:* **4** Odin
stepson: Ull
wife: Sif

thorn: 4 brod, goad **5** briar, brier, spine, worry **7** acantha **8** vexation **9** annoyance **10** irritation
apple: **5** metel **6** datura
combining form: **5** spini
Egyptian: **5** babul **6** gonake **7** gonakie
full of: **6** briery
small: **7** spinule

thorny: 5 sharp, spiny **6** spinal **7** brambly, bristly, prickly **8** spinated **9** acanthoid, difficult, vexatious **11** contentious

thorough: 4 deep, full **6** arrant **7** through **8** absolute, accurate, complete, finished **9** downright, intensive **10** exhaustive, throughout **11** painstaking **13** thoroughgoing

thorough-going: 6 arrant **7** radical

thoroughbred: 5 horse **7** trained **8** cultured, educated, well-bred **11** full-blooded

thoroughfare: 4 road **5** alley **6** avenue, street **7** highway, passage, transit **8** waterway **9** boulevard

thoroughly: all **4** inly **6** deeply **9** downright, intensive **10** absolutely, altogether

thoroughwort: 7 boneset

thorp, thorpe: 4 dorp **6** hamlet **7** village **9** community

thou: tha

though: 7 however **12** nevertheless

thought: 4 care, hope, idea, mind, view **5** trace **6** deemed, opined **7** anxiety, concept, judging, opinion **9** cogitated, reasoning **10** cogitation, conception, meditation, melancholy, reflection **11** cerebration, expectation, imagination **12** deliberation, recollection **13** concentration, consideration, ratiocination **16** intellectualized
continuous: **10** meditation
deep in: **10** cogitabund
form: **6** ideate
inability to express: **6** asemia
reader: **8** telepath
transference: **9** telepathy

thoughtful: 4 kind **5** moody **7** careful, earnest, heedful, mindful, pensive, prudent, serious **9** attentive, designing, regardful **10** cogitabund, meditative, melancholy, reflective, ruminative, solicitous **11** circumspect, considerate

thoughtfulness: 14 circumspection

thoughtless: 4 dull, rash **6** remiss, stupid **7** glaiket, glaikit **8** careless, heedless, reckless **9** brainless **10** unthinking **11** harum-scarum, inattentive, lightheaded **13** inconsiderate

thoughtlessness: 12 inadvertence

thousand: *combining form:* **4** kilo **5** mille
one: mil **5** grand **7** chiliad

Thrace: *goddess:* **6** Bendis
mountaineers: **5** Bessi
people: **6** Satrae **8** Bisaltae

thrall: 4 esne, serf **5** slave, theow **7** bondage, bondman, captive, enslave, slavery, subject **8** enslaved, enthrall **9** suffering **10** oppression, subjugated

thralldom: 7 bondage, slavery **9** captivity, servitude

thrangity: 6 bustle **8** business

thrash: lam, tan **4** bang, beat, bray, ding, drub, flax, flog, lash, rush, sail, whip, yerk **5** array, baste, bless, flail, pound, swing, threp, whang **6** anoint, defeat, fettle, raddle, strike, threap, threep, threip, threpe, thresh, thwack **7** trounce **8** belabour, blathery, vanquish **9** triturate **10** flagellate

thrashing: 4 bean **7** beating, milling **8** drubbing, flogging, whipping

thrast: 5 press **9** constrain

thrave: 4 bind **5** crowd **6** bundle, number, throng **8** quantity

thrawart: 7 adverse, crooked, peevish, twisted **8** backward, perverse, stubborn **9** reluctant **12** unpropitious

thrawn: 7 crooked **8** perverse **9** misshapen **10** unpleasant

thread: ray **4** line, vein, yarn **5** fiber, reeve, weave **6** strata, stream, string **7** quality, stratum **8** filament, fineness, raveling **9** ravelling **11** composition
a needle: **5** reeve
bits of: **4** lint **9** ravelings
cell: **5** cnida
combining form: nem
cone: cop
division of: **4** beer
in weaving shuttle: **4** weft
inserted beneath skin: **5** seton
kind of: **4** bast, bave, film, silk, yarn **5** floss, linen, lisle, rayon, seton, trame **6** cotton, lingel, lingle **8** arrasene
on spindle: cop
pert. to: **5** filar
raveled: **6** sleave
silk: bur **4** bave, burr **5** floss, trame **9** filoselle
skein of: **4** hasp
tape: **5** inkle
tester: **9** serimeter
used as core for tinsel: **4** poil
winding tube: cop

thread-like: 5 filar **6** filose

threadbare: 4 bare, sere, worn **5** stale, trite **6** frayed, pilled, shabby **9** hackneyed

threads: 4 beer, weft, woof **6** filler **8** clothing
combining form: **4** byss

**threap, threep, threip, threp, threpe:
4** beat, urge **5** chide, press, scold **6** affirm, assert, haggle, insist, thrash **7** dispute, quarrel, wrangle **8** complain, maintain

threat: vex **4** fail, lack, urge, want, warn **5** chide, crowd, peril, press, troop **6** compel, menace, misery, throng **7** oppress, portend, reprove, trouble, warning **8** maltreat, threaten **10** compulsion **12** denunciation

threaten: 4 brag **5** boast, lower, utter **6** charge, menace **7** portend, promise **8** denounce

threatening: big **6** greasy, lowery **8** lowering, menacing **9** impending **10** formidable

three: 5 crowd, gamma(Gr.), trias **7** Trinity
combining form: ter, tri
combination of: **7** triplet, ternary
consisting of: **7** ternate
group of: tre **4** trio **5** triad, trine **8** triumvir
months: **7** quarter **9** trimester
prefix: tri
ruling group: **8** triumvir
set of: **4** trio **5** triad **7** ternion

Three B's (in music): 4 Bach **6** Brahms **9** Beethoven

three-card monte: 9 montebank

three-cleft: 6 trifid

three-dimensional: 5 cubic **6** stereo **7** cubical

three-flowered: 9 trifloral

Three Graces; joy **5** bloom **6** Aglaia, Thalia **10** brilliance, Euphrosyne

three-headed goddess: 6 Hecate

three-hundredth anniversary: 13 tercentennial, tricentennial

three in one: 6 triune **7** trinity

Three Kingdoms: Wu: Shu, Wei

three L's: 4 lead **7** lookout **8** latitude

three-layered: 10 trilaminar

three-legged stand: 6 tripod, trivet

three-lined: 9 trilinear

three-masted vessel: 5 xebec **8** schooner

Three Musketeers: 5 Athos **6** Aramis **7** Porthos
author: **5** Dumas
friend: **9** D'Artagnan

three-piled: 4 best **6** costly **11** extravagant

three-pointed: 11 tricuspidal

three-score: 5 sixty

three-seeded: 11 trispermous

three-sided figure: 6 trigon **8** triangle

three-spot: 4 trey

three-square: 5 cross **9** irritable, threefold

three-styled: 10 trystylous

three-toed sloth: ai

Three Wise Men: 6 Gaspar **8** Melchior **9** Balthasar

threefold: 4 tern **5** trine **6** ternal, thrice, treble, trinal, triple, triply
combining form: ter

threesome: 4 trio

threne: 5 dirge 8 threnody 11 lamentation

threnody: 4 song 5 dirge 6 hearse

thresh (see also **thrash**): cob 4 beat, flog, lump, rush 5 berry, flail 6 thrash

threshed grain husks: 5 straw

thresher: 4 fail 6 beater 7 combine

threshing: *refuse:* 6 colder
  tool: 5 flail

threshold: eve 4 gate, sill 5 limen 6 outset 8 doorsill, entrance 9 beginning

threw: 4 cast, hove 5 flung, shied, slung 6 casted, heaved, hurled, pegged, pelted, tossed 7 chucked, elanced, pitched
  about: 7 sloshed 8 thrashed
  into confusion: 6 rioted 9 stampeded
  over: 6 jilted
  with force: 6 bunged

thribble: 6 triple 9 threefold

thrift: 4 work 5 labor 7 economy 9 frugality, husbandry 10 employment, occupation, prosperity, providence 14 forehandedness

thriftily: 4 near

thriftless: 6 lavish 8 prodigal, wasteful 11 extravagant, improvident

thrifty: 4 near 5 fendy, small 6 frugal, narrow, proper, saving, useful, worthy 7 careful, sparing 8 thriving 9 befitting, estimable, provident 10 economical, forehanded, prospering 11 flourishing, serviceable

thrill: 4 bore, cast, dirl, girl, hurl 5 drill, elate, flush, thirl, throw 6 dindle, pierce, quiver, tremor 7 frisson, tremble, vibrate 8 fremitus, transfix 9 penetrate, perforate, throbbing, vibration

thrilling: 9 throbbing, vibrating

thrilly: 8 stirring 11 sensational

thrimble: 6 fumble 7 squeeze, wrestle 8 hesitate

thrimp: 5 press 7 squeeze

thring: 4 cast 5 crowd, crush, press 6 batter, pierce, throng, thrust 7 squeeze

thrive: dow 4 gain, grow 5 addle, moise 6 batten, fatten 7 improve, prosper, succeed 8 flourish, increase

thriven: 4 wise 5 adult, grown 7 prudent 8 thriving 10 prosperous 11 experienced

thriving: 4 bein, bien 10 prosperous, successful 11 flourishing
  in shade: 11 sciophilous

thrivingly: 5 gaily, gayly

throat: maw 4 crag, crop, gowl, hals, lane, tube 5 halse 6 groove, gullet, guzzle, weason 7 channel, orifice, weasand 8 guttural
  combining form: 4 lemo
  covering: 4 barb
  infection: 5 croup 6 angina, quinsy 8 cynanche 9 squinancy 11 strep throat
  lozenge: 6 pastil, troche 7 pastile 8 pastille

part: 7 glottis
pert. to: 5 gular 7 jugular 8 guttural
sore: 6 housty
upper: 4 gula

throat skin: 6 dewlap

throaty: 6 hoarse 8 guttural 9 voracious

throb: 4 ache, beat, drum, pant 5 flack, pulse 7 flacker, pulsate, vibrate 9 palpitate, pulsation

throbbing: 4 beat

throdden: 4 grow 6 thrive

throddy: 5 plump 6 active 9 well-grown

throe: 4 pang 5 agony 6 effort 7 anguish 8 struggle

throne: see 4 apse, seat 5 asana, chair, exalt, gaddi, gadhi, power, siege 7 anguish, dignity 8 cathedra, enthrone 11 sovereignty
  remove from: 6 depose

throng: 4 busy, crew, heap, host, push, rout 5 close, crowd, horde, peril, press, swarm 6 busily, bustle, strain, stress 7 company, hurried 8 distress, familiar, hardship, intimate 9 confusion, frequency, multitude 10 affliction, constantly

thronged: 5 alive 7 peopled 10 celebrious

throttle: gun 5 check, choke 6 throat 7 garrote 8 compress, garrotte, strangle, suppress, windpipe 9 suffocate 11 accelerator
  open: gun

through, thru: by; per 4 over 5 athro, ended 6 across, coffin 7 perpend 8 athrough, finished 9 completed, tombstone 11 sarcophagus 12 thoroughfare, unobstructed
  the agency of: per
  the mouth: 7 peroral

throughgang: 5 labor 6 energy 11 overhauling 12 thoroughfare

throughgoing: 9 reprimand 11 examination, overhauling 12 thoroughfare

throughout: 5 about 6 bedene, during, sempre 7 perfect 8 thorough 10 completely, everywhere

throw: boa, cob, don, hit, lob, pat, peg, put, shy, wap 4 bail, bear, blow, cast, dash, fall, form, hike, hurl, rack, risk, shed, time, toss, turn, yerk 5 check, chuck, chunk, crank, drive, flick, fling, flirt, force, frame, heave, impel, pitch, place, scarf, sling, start, strip, trice, twist, whang, while, whirl 6 change, defeat, divest, elance, hinder, inject, retard, sprain, spread, spring, strike, stroke, thrust, thwart, wrench, writhe 7 advance, discard, fashion, present, produce, project, revolve, venture 8 catapult, coverlet, distance, obstruct 9 prostrate 10 flagellate
  a fit: 5 angry 7 excited 9 disturbed, irritated
  a scare into: 5 scare 7 terrify

about: **4** tack

at quoits: **6** leaner, ringer

away: **5** waste **6** refuse, reject **7** discard, leaflet **8** handbill, squander

back: **5** check, delay, repel **6** refuse, reject, retort, revert **8** reversal **9** reversion

double one at dice: **7** ambsace

down: **4** cast **5** fling **6** defeat, reject **7** refusal, subvert **9** overthrow, rejection **11** precipitate

down the gauntlet: **4** defy **9** challenge

dust in one's eyes: **7** deceive, mislead

from saddle: **7** unhorse

in: add **4** join **6** inject **10** contribute

in the towel: **4** cede, quit **5** yield **9** surrender

into confusion: **5** snafu **7** disturb **8** stampede **10** demoralize

into disorder: pif **4** pied **7** derange

into ecstasy: **6** enrapt

into shade: **7** eclipse

lazily: lob

light upon: **6** illume

lightly: **4** toss

off: **4** cast, emit, free, molt, shed **5** abate, expel, moult **6** reject **7** abandon, deflect, discard **10** disconnect

off the track: **6** derail

out: **4** emit, lade **5** egest, eject, evict, expel, utter **6** extend, reject **7** confuse, discard, excrete, project **8** distance **9** eliminate

out of order: **7** derange

over: **4** jilt **7** abandon

overboard: **8** jettison

six at dice: **4** sise **5** sises

underhand: lob

up: **4** rise **5** demit, vomit **10** relinquish

water upon: **5** douse

throwing rope: **5** lasso, reata, riata **6** lariat

throwing-stick: **6** atlatl **9** boomerang

thrown: **4** cast **6** hurled **7** twisted **8** unseated

thrum: bit **4** drum, lout, purr, tuft **5** strum, waste **6** fringe, recite, repeat, tangle, thatch **8** particle **10** threepence

thrush: dig **4** bear, birr, bore, butt, dash, ding **5** barge, mavie, mavis, ouzel, robin, veery **6** missel, oriole, shrike **7** bearing **8** bluebird, throstle **9** blackbird

European: **4** osel **5** mavis, ossel, ousel, ouzel **6** missel, shrite

migratory: **5** robin

thrust: dig, jab **4** bear, birr, bore, butt, dush, gird, jerk, pelt, poke, prop, push, stab **5** barge, clash, crowd, drive, force, hunch, impel, longe, lunge, onset, press, shove **6** attack, detude, extend, hustle, pierce, plunge, repost, ripost, spread, stress, throng **7** allonge, assault, collide, extrude, intrude, riposte **8** estocade, pressure, protrude **9** interject, interpose

against wall: **5** mured

thrutch: **4** push **5** crowd, press **6** throng, thrust

thrutchings: **4** whey

thud: **4** baff, blow, gust, move, push **5** press **6** strike **7** tempest **9** windstorm

thug: **5** rough **6** attack, cuttle, gunman **7** ruffian **8** assassin, gangster **9** cutthroat

thuggery: **6** murder **7** thuggee **10** ruffianism

thumb: **6** pollex, thenar **9** peachwort

part: **6** thenar

thump: cob, dad, dub, hit **4** bang, beat, blow, bump, daud, ding, dird, drub, dunt, polt, whip, yerk **5** blaff, bunch, clour, crump, knock, pound, throb **6** bounce, cudgel, hammer, strike, thrash, thunge

thumping: **5** large **6** tattoo **7** bumping **8** whopping

thunder: **4** peal, rage, roar **6** bronte **7** fouldre **9** Fulminate

god: **4** Thor, Zeus

witch: **4** baba

thunder and lightning: **8** ceraunic **9** fulminous

thunder-smitten goddess: **6** Semele

thunderbolt: **4** bolt **6** fulmen **7** fouldre **9** fulminant

thundering: **5** large **8** thumping, whopping **10** foudroyant

thunderpeal: **4** clap **11** thunderclap

thunderstorm: *Cuba:* **6** bayamo

West Indies: **7** houvari

thunge: **4** bang **5** sound, thump

thurible: **6** censer

Thursday: *god of:* **4** Thor

Holy: **5** Skire

thus: so; sae, sic **4** fiat **5** hence **9** therefore **12** consequently

thwack: rap **4** bang, blow, pack **5** crump, crush, drive, force, knock, whack **6** defeat, strike, thrash **7** belabor **8** belabour

thwart: **4** balk, foil, pert, seat **5** bench, block, brace, clash, cross, parry, saucy, spite, zygon **6** across, baffle, defeat, hinder, oppose, outwit, resist **7** athwart, oblique, prevent, quarrel **8** contrair, obstruct, perverse, stubborn, thwartly **9** frustrate, interpose **10** contravene, disappoint, opposition, transverse **11** intractable, obstruction

thy: tha

Thyestes: *brother:* **6** Atreus

father: **6** Pelops

son: **9** Aegisthus

thylacine: **4** wolf **5** tiger, yabbi

thyme: **8** hillwort

thymus: **5** gland

thyroid enlargement: **6** goiter

tiara: **5** crown **6** diadem, fillet **7** cidares, cidaris, coronet **8** frontlet **9** headdress

Tiber country: **7** Etruria

tibert: cat

Tibet: *animal:* **5** panda

antelope: goa, sus

ass: **5** kiang
banner: **5** tanka
beast of burden: yak
beer: **5** chang
capital: **5** Lassa, Lhasa
city: Noh **5** Lassa, Lhasa
coin: **5** tanga
deer: **4** shou
dialect: **9** Bhutanese
ecclesiastic: **4** lama **5** dalai
food: **6** tsamba
gazelle: goa
goat fleece: **5** pashm
kingdom: **5** Nepal
lama: **5** Dalai
language: **7** Bodskad
monk: **4** lama
ox: yak
people: **6** Bhotia **7** Bhotiya
pony: **6** tangum, tangun **7** tanghan
priest: **4** lama
religion: Bon
river: **5** Indus
ruminant: **5** takin
sheep: sha **6** bharal, nahoor, nayaur
wildcat: **5** manul
Tibetan: 6 Tangut
tibia: 5 flute **6** cnemis **8** shinbone
tiburon: 5 shark
Tiburon Island Indian: 4 Seri
tic: 9 twitching **11** vellication
tice: 6 entice, yorker **10** enticement
tichel: lot **5** troop **6** number
tick: dot, fag, ked, pat, tag, tap **4** beat,
case, dash, mark, mite, note, pest **5** acari,
chalk, click, count, cover, flirt, speck,
touch, trust **6** acarid, acarus, credit, fondle, insect, moment, record, second, tampon, talaje **7** acarina, instant, ticking **8**
acaridan, arachnid, garapata, indicate,
mattress, tickbean **10** pajahuello, paja-
roello
genus of: **5** argas
ticker: 5 clock, heart, watch
ticket: bid, tag **4** book, card, list, note, slip,
tick **5** check, ducat, fiche, label, score,
sight, slate, token **6** ballot, billet, notice,
permit, record **7** license, placard, voucher, warrant **8** document **9** cardboard, discharge, etiquette **10** memorandum **11**
certificate
complimentary: **4** comp, pass **11** Annie
Oakley
of leave: **6** parole
receiver of free: **8** deadhead
season: **6** abonne **10** abonnement
speculator: **7** scalper
tickey, tickie: 10 threepence
tickle: do **4** beat, nice, play, stir, take,
whip **5** amuse, annoy, frail, tease, touch **6**
arouse, cuitle, divert, excite, please, thrill,
tingle, touchy, wanton **7** capture, cuittle,
delight, gratify, operate, passage, portray,
provoke, tickler **8** chastise, delicate, in-

secure, tickling, ticklish, unstable, unsteady **9** difficult, squeamish, titillate,
vellicate **10** insecurely
tickled: 6 amused **7** pleased **9** gratified
tickler: pad, sip **4** book, cane, file **5** flask,
knife, prong, strap **6** pistol, puzzle,
record, weapon **7** problem
tickling: 7 craving **13** gratification
ticklish: 4 nice **5** risky **6** fickle, queasy,
touchy **7** comical **8** critical, delicate, unstable, unsteady **9** uncertain **10** changeable, precarious, unreliable **13** oversensitive
tid: 4 fond, mood **5** humor, silly **6** lively,
tender **8** childish, ill-humor **9** sprightly
tidal: *bore:* **5** eagre
creek: **6** estero
current: **8** tiderace
flow: **4** bore **5** eagre
wave: **5** aigre, eagre
tidbit, titbit: 5 goody **7** saynete **8** bea-
tille
tiddle: 4 rear **6** fidget, fondle, pamper,
potter, tickle
tiddley: 5 small **7** trivial
tiddy: 4 girl, tiny **5** child **7** babyish, trivial
8 childish
tide: sea **4** fair, flow, hour, pass, time **5**
carry, drift, drive, flood, point, space,
surge, tidal **6** befall, betide, endure, happen, moment, period, season, stream **7**
current, freshet, proceed **8** continue, fes
tival, occasion, surmount, tendency **11**
anniversary, opportunity
low: **4** neap
lowest of high: **4** neap
pert. to: **4** neap **7** cnemial
tidely: 5 fitly **7** smartly **8** cleverly, suitably **9** shipshape
tidewater: 8 seaboard
tiding: ebb **4** flow, news **5** event **6** advice,
gospel **7** account, message **9** happening
11 information **12** intelligence
tidy: 4 cosh, fair, good, meet(obs.), neat,
redd, smug, tosh, trig, trim **5** clean,
douce, great, groom, large, natty, plump **6**
comely, fettle, sleeky, tidily, timely, worthy **7** healthy, orderly, upright **8** diligent,
pinafore, skillful **9** shipshape **10** receptacle, seasonable **12** antimacassar, considerable, satisfactory
tie: ty: rod, sag **4** band, beam, beat, bind,
bond, cord, draw, duty, even, join, knot,
lace, link, post, rope, teck **5** angle, ascot,
brace, cadge, chain, equal, hitch, marry,
nexus, sheaf, trice, union, unite **6** attach,
cement, connex, couple, cravat, enlace,
fasten, pledge, string, tether, tiewig **7**
confine, connect, necktie, oxfords, sleeper
8 alligate, restrain, restrict, shoelace **9**
constrain, constrict, influence, stalemate
10 allegiance, obligation
down: **7** confine **8** restrain, restrict
fast: **5** belay

off: **4** snub **5** belay
ornament: pin **4** clip
securely: **4** lash **5** truss **7** shackle, trammel
up: **4** bind, moor, stop **5** truss **6** hinder, tether **8** obstruct
tied tightly: 5 bound **6** lashed
tienda: 4 shop, tent **5** booth **6** awning
tier: row **4** bank, rank **5** layer, place, stack, story **6** degree **7** antenna, arrange **8** pinafore
tierce: 4 cask **5** lunge, parry, third **7** measure **8** sequence
Tierra del Fuego Indian: Ona **4** Agni
tiff: fit, pet, sip **4** huff, mood, spat **5** draft, dress, drink, humor, lunch, order, scent, smell, sniff, spell, state, taste **6** liquor **7** quarrel **8** outburst **9** condition **11** altercation
tiffin: 5 lunch **6** eating **8** drinking
tiffle: 4 fray, idle **6** potter, trifle, tumble **7** unravel **8** entangle **10** disarrange
tift: 4 gust, pant, puff **5** hurry, sniff, whiff **6** flight **14** breathlessness
tig: pat, tag, tap **5** touch
tiger: cat, cub **4** howl, rake, yell **5** bully, groom **6** feline, jaguar **7** leopard **9** carnivore, swaggerer, thylacine **12** organization
tiger finch: 8 amadavat
tiger-hunting dog: 5 dhole
tigerish: 5 cruel **6** fierce, flashy **9** ferocious **10** swaggering **12** bloodthirsty
tigers-mouth: 8 foxglove, toadflax **10** snapdragon
tight: 4 fast, firm, hard, held, neat, snug, taut, tidy, trim **5** alert, bound, cheap, close, dense, drawn, drunk, fixed, ready, smart, solid, tense, tipsy **6** climax, comely, firmly, packed, severe, steady, stingy, strait, strict **7** capable, compact, concise, quickly, shapely, soundly, unmoved **8** constant, exacting, faithful **9** competent, condensed, energetic, mercenary, niggardly **10** impervious, vigorously **11** closefisted, intoxicated, restraining **12** parsimonious
making: **7** tensing
tight-fisted: 6 stingy **11** closefisted **12** parsimonious
tight-lipped: 5 terse **9** secretive
tighten: 5 tense **6** tauten **9** constrict
strings of drum: **4** frap
tightness: 9 closeness
tightwad: 4 fist **5** miser, piker
tigrine: 5 tawny
Tigris River city: 7 Nineveh
til: 6 sesame
tile: hat **5** brick, drain, plate, slate **6** tegula **7** carreau, quarrel
composed of: **7** tegular **9** tessellar
curved: **7** pantile
malting floor: **6** pament **7** pamment
mosaic: **7** tessera **8** abaculus

pert. to: **7** tegular
used in game: **6** domino
tile-like: 5 slaty
tiler: cat **4** kiln **5** field, thief **7** hellier **10** doorkeeper
tiles: 8 ceramics
till: at, by, of; box, far, for, get, hoe, sow **4** draw, earn, farm, gain, plow, tray **5** charm, dress, labor, train, while **6** casket, drawer, entice, strive, whilst **7** develop, prepare **9** cultivate **10** concerning
tillable: 6 arable **7** earable
tillage: 7 aration, culture **11** cultivation
tilled land: 5 arada
tiller: bar, bow **4** helm, hoer **5** lever, stalk, stick **6** farmer, handle, sprout **7** husband, rancher **10** cultivator, husbandman
tilt: tip **4** cant, duel, heel, lean, list, rush, tent **5** argue, fight, forge, heald, hield, joust, pitch, poise, slant, slope, speed, upend, upset **6** awning, canopy, careen, combat, hammer, oppose, seesaw, stroke, thrust, topple **7** contest, dispute, incline **8** covering, tiltyard **10** tournament **11** altercation
hammer: **6** oliver
skyward: **5** upend
tilter: 5 sword **6** avocet, seesaw **7** jouster **9** sandpiper
tilting: 5 alist **7** swaying **8** slanting
tilting match: 5 joust
timarau, timerau: 7 buffalo
timbal: 10 kettledrum
timber: log, rib **4** beam, fuel, gate, land, raff, stay, wood **5** build, cahuy, cover, fence, frame, gripe, spile, stile, trees **6** forest, lumber **7** support **8** building, contrive **9** construct, structure, underpier
bend: sny **6** camber, rafter
cut: **4** bunk **6** lumber **7** fallage **8** teakwood
decay: **4** conk, dote, doze
end: **5** tenon
estimator: **6** scaler **7** cruiser
parts of building: rib **4** sill **5** joist, spale **6** purlin, rafter **7** purline **8** stringer
partially decayed: **4** doty
peg: **4** coak
ship: bao, rib **4** bibb, bitt, keel, mast, spar, wale **5** snape, spale **7** stemson **8** sternson
sloping: **6** rafter
standing: **4** stud **5** spile **6** forest **8** puncheon, studding, stumpage
tree: ash, fir **4** pine **5** birch, cedar, maple **6** walnut **7** redwood **8** mahogany
wolf: **4** lobo
timber-jack: 10 lumberjack
timberman: 6 sawyer **7** cruiser **8** woodsman **9** carpenter, lumberman
timbre: 4 tone **5** crest, miter **7** coronet, quality, timbrel **9** character
timbrel: 4 drum **5** tabor **10** tambourine
time: age, day, eld, era, tid **4** date, fuss, hint, hour, sele, term, week, year **5** clock,

epoch, month, tempo, tense, watch **6**
during, indeed, minute, moment, period,
season, second, steven **8** duration, occasion, regulate, schedule, yuletide **9** fore-
sooth **13** demonstration
ahead of: **5** early **9** premature
allowed for payment: **6** usance
another: **5** again
at no: **5** never **9** nevermore
blossom: **9** blutezeit
break in: **6** hiatus
brief: **4** span **6** moment
Christmas: **8** yuletide
devoted to religion: **8** holytide
fast: **4** Lent
gone by: **4** yore **10** yesteryear
granted: **4** stay **5** delay, frist **8** reprieve
happy: **4** bust, lark **5** revel, spree **6** soiree
8 jamboree
intervening: **7** interim **8** meantime **9**
meanwhile
length: age, eon, era **6** moment, period
long ago: **4** yore
music: **6** presto
musical marker: **9** metronome
of great depression: **5** nadir
of highest strength: **6** heyday
olden: eld **4** syne(Sc.), yore
period of: age, day, eon, era **4** aeon, date,
hour, span, term, week, year **5** epoch,
month, spell, trice **6** decade, ghurry, minute, moment, recess, season, second **7**
century, instant **8** azoic age **9** fortnight
present: **5** nonce
right: tid(Sc.)
single: **4** once
to come: **5** tabor
waste: **4** idle, loaf **5** dally **6** dwadle, diddle, loiter **8** flanerie
wrong: **13** anachronistic
time being: **5** nonce
time clock: **8** recorder
Time Machine author: **5** Wells
timeless: **4** true **5** valid **6** eterne **7** ageless, eternal, undated **8** dateless, unend-
ing, untimely **9** co-eternal, premature **11**
everlasting **12** interminable
timeliness: **9** relevance
timely: apt, pat **4** soon **5** early **6** prompt **8**
temporal **9** opportune, pertinent **10** forehanded, seasonably **11** opportunity
timepiece: **4** dial **5** clock, watch **8** sun-
watch **9** horologue **11** chronometer **17**
chronothermometer
times: *many:* oft **5** often **10** frequently
olden: eld **9** yesterday **10** yesteryear
prosperous: ups **5** booms
timetable: **8** schedule
timid: shy **4** argh, eery **5** arghe, bauch,
blate, eerie, faint, mousy, pavid, scary **6**
afraid **7** bashful, fearful, gastful, nervous
8 cowardly, fearsome, ghastful, hesitant,
retiring, timorous **9** diffident, shrinking
12 fainthearted **13** pusillanimous **14**
chicken-hearted

timidity: **4** fear **7** shyness **9** funkiness **10**
diffidence **11** fearfulness
timish: **6** modish **11** fashionable
timon: **4** helm **5** cynic **6** rudder **11**
misanthropy
timor: **5** dread
Timor: *capital:* **4** Dili
coin: avo **6** pataca
island: **4** Leti
timorous: **5** faint, timid **6** afraid, cowish,
sheepy **7** fearful **8** fearsome, hesitant,
terrible **9** shrinking **12** fainthearted
timpani: **11** kettledrums
tin: box, can, pan **5** money, terne **6** latten **7**
stannic, stannum **8** preserve, prillion **9**
container
pert. to: **7** stannic, stranic
rubbish: **5** stent
tin and copper alloy: **6** pewter
Tin Can Island: **7** Niuafoo
tin dioxide: **8** tinstone
tin foil: **4** tain
tin-pot: **4** poor **6** paltry **8** inferior,
wretched
tinamou: **6** ynambu
tincal: **5** borax
tinct: dye **4** tint **5** color, imbue, tinge **6**
tinged, tinted **7** colored **8** coloured, tincture **10** impregnate
tincture: or **4** cast **5** color, gules, imbue,
myrrh, smack, stain, taint, tenne, tinge,
trace **6** elixir, imbrue **7** vestige **8** coloring
9 admixture, suspicion **10** extraction **12**
modification
for sprains: **6** arnica
of opium: **9** paregoric
tinder: *punk:* **6** amadou
vegetable: **6** amadou
tine: tub, vat **4** fine, fork, lose, pain, shut,
teen **5** grief, prong, spike, tooth **6** harrow,
perish, repair **7** destroy, enclose, forfeit,
trouble
tine branch: **4** snag
tinea: **8** ringworm
tinean: **4** moth
tineoidea: **5** moths
tinge: dye, hue **4** cast, odor, tint **5** color,
imbue, savor, shade, smack, stain, touch,
trace **6** affect, flavor **7** glimpse, quality **8**
coloring, discolor, tincture **9** influence **10**
suggestion
tinged with purple: **10** violaceous
tinglass: tin **7** bismuth
tingle: **4** dirl, girl, nail, ring, tack **5** alive,
patch, sting **6** dindle, tinkle **7** support,
tremble, vibrant **9** fastening, sensation,
stimulate
tinker: auk **4** fuss, mend, work **5** caird,
gypsy, murre, patch, rogue, skate, tramp
6 mender, mugger, potter, putter, rascal,
repair, wander **7** botcher, bungler, vagrant **8** mackerel **11** silversides
tinkle: **5** clink **6** dindle, dingle, tingle
tinner: **6** canner **8** tinsmith
tinny: **4** hard, rich, thin **5** cheap **6** bright

7 brittle, wealthy 8 metallic, tinsmith

tinplate: 5 terne

tinsel: 4 sham 5 gaudy, showy 6 tawdry 8 specious, splendor 9 clinquant 10 forfeiture, glittering

tinseled: 9 clinquant 10 glittering

tint: dye, hue 5 blush, color, stain, taste, tinge, trace 6 nuance 9 foretaste

cheeks: 5 rouge

tinter: 4 dyer

tintinnabulum: 4 bell 5 rhyme 7 rhythem 8 rhymster

tintype: 9 ferrotype

tiny: wee 5 child, small, teeny 6 atomic, infant, minute 9 miniature 10 diminutive 13 infinitesimal

tip: cap, cue, end, fee, neb, tap, toe, top 4 apex, barb, blow, cant, cave, clue, dump, fall, heel, hint, keel, lean, list, pile, tilt, vail 5 aglet, alist, chape, crown, drink, empty, point, slant, snick, spire, steer, touch, upset 6 aiglet, apices, arista, careen, corona, nozzle, summit, topple, unload 7 crampit, cumshaw, ferrule, incline 8 bakshish, bonamano, gratuity, overturn 9 baksheesh, buona-mano, buona-mani, extremity, overthrow, pourboire, protector 10 intoxicate

near to: 6 apical

tiple: 6 fuddle, guitar

tippet: boa, fur 4 barb, cape, hood, rope, ruff 5 amice, scarf, snell 6 almuce, sindon 7 hanging, muffler, patagia(pl.) 8 liripipe, liripoop, palatine, patagium 9 comforter, victorine

tipping: 5 alist 7 ripping, topping

up: 5 atilt

tipple: bib, nip, sip, tip 4 drip, gill, lose, suck, whet 5 drink, spend, upset 6 fuddle, liquor, sipple, tumble 8 overturn

tippled: 5 drank 6 beered

tippler: sot 5 souse, toper, winer 6 tipper, tipple, tumble 7 drinker, whetter 9 draftsman 11 draughtsman

tippy: 5 smart 6 tiptop 7 stylish 8 unsteady

tipstaff: 7 bailiff 9 attendant, constable

tipster: 4 tout 8 dopester 10 forecaster

tipsy: ree 4 awry 5 bosky, drunk, shaky, tippy 6 bungfu, groggy 7 crooked, ebriose, ebrious, foolish, fuddled, muddled, puddled, tipsify 8 unsteady 10 staggering 11 intoxicated

tiptoe: 5 alert, eager 6 roused, warily 7 eagerly, exalted, quietly 8 cautious, stealthy 10 cautiously 11 expectantly

tiptop: 4 best 9 first-rate 11 galumptious

tirade: 6 screed, speech 7 censure 8 harangue, jeremiad 9 philippic

tirailleur: 10 skirmisher 12 sharpshooter

tire: fag, lag, rim 4 band, bore, gnaw, hoop, jade, pall, prey, pull, shoe, tear, tier 5 dress, recap, seize, spare, weary 6 attire, casing, harass, satiate, tucker 7 apparel, exhaust, fatigue, frazzle, vesture 8 dec-

orate, enginery, overwork, pinafore 9 adornment, discharge, equipment, furniture, headdress, tiredness, weariness 12 accouterment

tired: 5 blown, spent, weary 6 aweary, fagged, sleepy 7 wearied 8 fatigued 9 exhausted

out: 5 jaded, spent

tireless: 4 busy 8 untiring 10 unwearying 13 indefatigable

tiresome: dry 4 dull, tame 6 boring, borish, dreary, prolix 7 irksome, prosaic, tedious 8 annoying, ennuyant 9 fatiguing, wearisome 10 irritating, monotonous 13 uninteresting

tirl: rap, tap 4 bout, turn 5 strip, twirl, twist, whirl 6 divest, rattle, thrill, unroof 7 uncover 9 vibration

tiro: See tyro.

tirr: 5 strip 6 unroof 7 uncover, undress

tirrivee: 7 tantrum 9 commotion

tirve: 5 strip 6 unroof 7 uncover

tissue: gum, web 4 tela 5 gauze, sheer, telae, weave 6 girdle, ribbon 7 network 8 meshwork 9 embroider, gauzelike 10 interweave

animal: fat, gum 4 bone, seur, suet 6 paxwax 7 keratin 8 gelatine

horny: 7 keratin

human: fat, gum 4 suet, tela 5 fiber 6 albedo, diploe, keloid, stroma, tendon 7 tonsils 8 ligament, stromata 10 aerenchyma

layer of: 6 strata 7 stratum

nerve: 8 ganglion

oily: fat

pert. to: 5 telar

resembling: 7 histoid

vegetable: 4 bast 5 xylem 6 lignin 7 endarch 8 meristem

wasting away of: 8 phthisis

tissue-like: 5 telar

tit: nag, pap, pin, tap, tee, tug 4 bird, blow, draw, girl, jade, jerk, plug, pull, teat, tite, twit 5 horse, woman 6 nipple, twitch 7 titlark 8 titmouse

Titan: Ge 4 Bana, Leto, Rhea 5 Coeus, Creus, Dione, giant, Theia 6 Cronus, Pallas, Phoebe, Tethys, Themis 7 Iapetus, Oceanus 8 gigantic, Hyperion 9 extensive, Mnemosyne

Titania's husband: 6 Oberon

titanic: 4 huge 5 great 7 immense 8 colossal, gigantic

titanite: 6 sphene 7 ijolite

tite: 4 soon 7 quickly 8 promptly 11 immediately

tithe: tax 5 teind, tiend, tenth 6 decima 7 decimae, decimal

pert. to: 7 decimal

tithing: 6 borrow, decime, denary 8 decenary 9 decennary

titi: 6 monkey

titillate: 6 excite, tickle 9 stimulate, vellicate

titlark: 5 pipit

title: Bey, sir **4** Czar, dame, deed, Duke, Earl, Emir, Khan, King, name, Raja, Shah **5** Baron, claim, Count, friar, Major, Mayor, Noble, right **6** assign, Ensign, Kaiser, Knight, legend, madame, Mikado, notice, Prince, record, squire, Sultan **7** Admiral, ascribe, Baronet, Captain, caption, Emperor, epithet, Esquire, General, heading, Justice, Khedive, Marquis, placard, Viceroy **8** Archduke, document, Governor, Viscount **9** Commander, Commodore, designate, President **10** appelation, capitulate, Lieutenant **11** designation **12** championship, denomination **13** Generalissimo

ecclesiastic: dom, fra **4** abba **8** reverend **10** excellency **11** monseigneur

feminine: **4** dame, lady **5** hanum, madam **6** hanoum, milady, missis, missus **8** mistress

foreign: aga, aya, Dan, don, mir, sha, sri **4** baba, Herr, lars, sidi, shri **5** basha, mirza, mpret, pasha, sayid, senor, shree, sieur **6** bashaw, shogun, squire **7** dominus, effendi **8** monsieur

of Athena: **4** Alea

pert. to: **7** titular

royal: hon., sir **4** sire **5** Grace **8** banneret **9** honorable

titmouse: mag, nun, tit **6** fuffit, puffer, titmal, tomtit, verdin **7** jacksaw, titmall, tomnoup **8** heckimal **9** chickadee, mumruffin

pert. to: **6** parine

titter: 5 laugh **6** giggle, rather, seesaw, sooner, totter, wobble **7** tremble

tittered: 7 giggled, teeheed **9** snickered

tittle: dot, jot **4** iota, sign, whit **5** point, tilde **6** accent, gossip, tattle **7** cedilla, whisper **8** particle

tittup: 5 caper, frisk

titubate: 4 reel **6** totter **7** stagger **8** unsteady **11** vacillating

titular: 7 nominal

tmema: 7 section, segment

TNT: 6 trotyl **8** dynamite **14** trinitrotoluol **15** trinitrotoluene

to (see also **next entries**): tae, till **4** unto **5** until **6** toward **7** forward

a conclusion: out

a place on: **4** onto

a point on: **4** onto

an end: out

be: **4** esse(L.), etre(F.), sein(G.) **5** einai(Gk.) **6** essere(It.)

be sure: **6** indeed

no extent: not

one side: **5** abeam

position into: **4** into

sheltered side: **4** alee

that time: **5** until

the left: haw **5** aport

the opposite side: **6** across

the rear: **5** arear **6** astern

this: **6** hereto

this place: **4** here **6** hither

the victor: **4** aboo

which: **7** whereto

wit: viz. **6** namely **8** scilicet **9** videlicet

your health: **5** skoal **6** prosit

to-deal, to-dele: 6 divide **8** separate **10** distribute **11** distinguish

to-do: ado **4** fuss, stir **6** bustle **9** commotion

to-draw: 4 pull, tear **7** detract **8** postpone, protract

toa: 7 warrior

toad: ted **4** agua, bufo, hyla, pipa, tade **6** anuran, peeper **7** crapaud, paddock, quilkin **9** amphibian, spadefoot

genus of: **4** bufo, hyla **6** alytes

order: **5** anura

toadeater: 5 toady **8** hanger-on, parasite **9** dependent, sycophant

toadfish: 4 sapo **6** angler, grubby, puffer, slimer **8** frogfish **10** midshipman

toadflax: 7 ransted **8** gallwort, ramstead, ranstead

toady: 4 fawn, snob, ugly, zany **6** flunky **7** flunkey, hideous, shoneen, truckle **8** bootlick, parasite, truckler **9** flatterer, repulsive, sycophant, toadeater

toast: dry, tan **4** soak, warm **5** brede, brown, drink, melba, parch, roast, skoal, worst **6** birsle, pledge, prosit **7** bristle, carouse, drinker, propose, swindle, tippler **8** cinnamon

toasted bread: 6 sippet

tobacco: *disease:* **6** calico **7** walloon

flavor mixture: **6** petune

holder: **4** pipe **7** humidor

hookah smoking: **7** goracco

ingredient: **8** nicotine

in pipe-bowl: **6** dottel, dottle

juice: **6** ambeer, ambier

kind of: **4** capa, shag **5** bogie, fogus, tabac **6** Burley, cowpen **7** caporal, henbane, Latakia, perique, Turkish **8** domestic, Virginia **9** salvadora

leaf moistener: **5** caser

paste: **7** goracco

pile: **4** bulk

receptacle: **4** pipe **7** humidor

roll: **5** cigar, segar **7** carotte

small portion: cud, fid, fig **4** quid **6** dottel, dottle **7** carotte

tobacco smoke hater: 11 misocapnist

toboggan: 4 sled **7** coaster, decline

toby: jug, mug, way **5** cigar, stein **6** street **7** highway, pitcher, robbery

toby-man: 10 highwayman

tocher: dot **5** dower **7** portion

toco: 6 toucan **8** flogging **9** thrashing

tocology, tokology: 9 midwifery **10** obstetrics

tocsin: 4 bell, sign **5** alarm **6** alarum, signal

tod: fox, mat **4** bush, load, pack **5** clump, shrub **6** bundle, weight

toddle: go **4** walk **5** dance **6** daddle, diddle, stroll **7** saunter

toddler: tot **4** trot **5** child

tode: **4** boat, haul, sled

toe: paw, tae, tai, tip **5** digit, pivot, reach, touch **7** journal **10** projection
little: **7** minimus
pert. to: **7** digital
without: **10** adactylous

toehold: **7** footing

toff: **5** bloke, dandy, swell

toffish: **5** smart **7** stylish

tog: **4** coat **5** dress **7** clothes, garment

toga: **4** gown, robe **5** tunic **7** garment

togated: **7** stately **9** dignified

together: mix **5** along, chain, union **6** bedene, fasten, unison **7** alongst, concert, contact, harmony **8** ensemble **9** cojointly, collision, courtship **11** association **12** cohabitation, coincidently **13** companionship, consecutively **14** simultaneously
prefix: co; com, con, syn

toggery: set **4** kind **5** dress **7** clothes, harness **9** trappings **12** haberdashery

toggle, toggel: pin, rod **4** bolt **6** cotter **10** crosspiece

togs: **7** clothes **8** clothing

togt: **5** draft, labor **7** drawing **10** enterprise **11** undertaking

togue: **9** namaycush

toil: fag, net, tug **4** drag, mesh, moil, plod, pull, rend, roll, task, trap, work **5** broil, cloth, graft, labor, slave, snare, weary **6** battle, canvas, drudge, effort, entrap, harass, strife, writhe **7** contend, ensnare, network, travail, turmoil **8** distress, drudgery, overwork, struggle, writhing **9** enclosure, wallowing **10** accomplish, contention, employment, occupation

toiler: **7** laborer, plodder, workman

toilet: **5** cloth, dress **6** attire **7** costume **8** bathroom, grooming, toilette **9** cleansing
case: **4** etui **5** etwee

toilsome: **4** hard **7** arduous **9** laborious, wearisome

toise: eye **4** look **6** extend **7** stretch

toit: **4** seat **6** dawdle, settle, totter **7** hassock, saunter

tokalon: **6** beauty **9** beautiful

token: **4** gift, mark, omen, sign **5** badge, check, medal, merit, proof **6** amulet, emblem, hansel, ostent, pledge, signal, symbol **7** betoken, betroth, feature, handsel, memento, portent, presage, signify **8** accolade, evidence, forbysen, keepsake, souvenir, tessella **9** character, symbolize **10** denotation, expression, indication, prognostic **14** characteristic
affection: **6** amoret, mascot **7** handsel **8** accolade
office: **5** badge

victory: **4** palm

toko: **4** shop **5** store **8** flogging

Tokyo: Edo **4** Yedo

tolbooth, tollbooth: **4** city, hall, jail, town **5** burgh **6** prison **9** tollhouse **11** customhouse

told: **4** tole **6** bidden **7** counted, related **8** narrated, reported
privately: **9** auricular
romances: **6** gested
stories: **6** yarned **7** tattled
without authority: **7** rumored

toldo: hut **4** tent

tole: **5** decoy **6** allure, entice

tolerable: gey **4** fair, so-so **8** bearable, passable **9** allowance, endurable **10** sufferable **11** comportable, supportable, translation **13** entertainment

tolerably: **5** geyah **6** fairly, pretty **7** gaylies, geylies **10** moderately

tolerance: **9** allowance, endurance, variation **10** indulgence **11** forbearance **13** understanding

tolerant: **5** broad **7** lenient, patient **8** enduring **9** indulgent **10** ecumenical **11** forebearing

tolerate: **4** bear, bide **5** abide, allow, broad, brook, stand **6** endure, permit, resist, suffer

toll: due, tax **4** chum, drag, draw, duty, lure, peal, pull, rent, ring **5** annul, decoy, knell, sound **6** allure, charge, custom, entice, excise, impost, invite, vacate **7** scatter, trewage **8** announce, exaction **10** assessment **12** compensation
gatherer: **8** customer, publican **9** collector **11** taxgatherer
kind of: **6** caphar **7** tronage **9** chiminage **10** ballastage
weight: **7** tronage

tolls: **4** dues

tolly: **4** cane **5** spire **6** candle

tolu: **6** balsam

toluic acid: **7** toluate

Tom Sawyer: *brother:* Sid
pal: **15** Huckleberry Finn

tomahawk: ax; axe, cut **4** kill **6** assail, attack, strike **7** hatchet **9** criticize

toman: **4** coin **5** mound **6** weight **7** hillock **8** division

tomato: **9** loveapple
relish: **6** catsup **7** ketchup
sauce: **6** catsup **7** ketchup

tomb: **4** bury **5** grave, house, huaca, speos, vault **6** burial, casket, cavity, entomb, hearse **7** chamber **8** catacomb, cenotaph, monument **9** sepulcher, tombstone
empty: **8** cenotaph
kind of: **4** cist **7** tritaph **8** cistvaen, kistvaen **9** mauseleum **11** sarcophagus

tombe: **4** drum

tomboy: meg **5** rowdy **6** harlot, hoiden, hoyden **8** strumpet

tombstone: 8 monument 9 headstone 10 gravestone

tomcat: gib

tome: 4 book 5 atlas 6 ledger, letter, volume 12 encyclopedia

tomfool: 4 fool 5 clown 6 stupid 7 buffoon, doltish, foolish, half-wit 8 rainbird 9 blockhead 10 flycatcher

tomfoolery: 8 nonsense 9 silliness

tommyrot: 8 nonsense 9 silliness

tomorrow: 6 domani(It.), manana(Sp.)

ton: 4 lots, mode 5 heaps, style, tunny, vogue 7 fashion

tonant: 7 blatant

tonca, tonka: 4 bean

wood: 6 camara

tone: 4 mood, note, tint 5 pitch, shade, sound, trend 6 accent, effect, intone, modify, temper, timbre 7 quality 8 coloring, mitigate, modulate 9 character, harmonize 10 atmosphere, inflection, intonation, modulation 12 modification

down: 6 soften

lacking: 5 atony 6 atonal, atonic

musical: 5 siren, syren 6 sirene

of cord: 8 concento

quality: 6 timbre

rapid: 7 tremolo

sharp: 4 tang

single: 8 monotone

singsong: 4 sugh 5 sough

succession: 5 melos

system of: 6 tonart

thin: 7 sfogato

third of diatonic scale: 7 mediant

vibrant: 5 twang

tone color: 6 timbre

toneless: 5 atony

tones: *combination of:* 5 chord

series of: 5 scale

Tonga island: Ono

tongs: 6 tenail 7 tueiron 8 tenaille

tongue: gab 4 bark, chib, fame, flap, howl, pole, sole, vote 5 chide, clack, lingo, prate, scold, speak, utter 6 report 7 beeweed, dialect, feather, lingula 8 language, lingulae, reproach, suffrage 9 pronounce

classical: 5 Greek, Latin 6 Hebrew

Jesus': 7 Aramaic

mother: 10 vernacular

oxcart: 4 cope

pert. to: 7 glossal, lingual

pivoted: 4 pawl

sacred: 4 Pali

seam: 5 raphe

serpent: 4 fang

tip of: 6 corona

wagon: 4 neap, pole

tongue-lash: 5 baste, scold

tongue-like: 7 lingual

tongued: 6 prated

tongueless: 4 dumb, mute 10 speechless

tonic: 5 aloes 6 bracer 7 bracing 8 medicine, roborant 9 sassafras, stimulant 10 refreshing 11 corroborant 12 invigorating

kind of: 4 dope 6 catnip 7 boneset, nervine

tonic leaf: 4 coca

toning down: 10 modulation

tonlet: 4 band

tonsil operation: 12 tonsilectomy

tonsorialist: 6 barber

tonsure: 5 shave 6 barber 7 haircut

tonsured: 4 bald 5 shorn 6 pilled, shaven 7 clipped

too: and, tae 4 also, over, very 6 overly 7 besides 8 likewise 9 extremely 11 exceedingly, excessively 13 superfluously

bad: 4 alas

late: 5 tardy 7 belated

small to matter: 13 inappreciable

soon: 9 premature

took: *away:* 4 reft

first: 9 preempted

ill: 8 resented

out: 5 deled 7 deleted 9 scratched 10 eliminated

part of: 5 sided 7 enacted

tool (see also **instrument**): ax; adz, axe, saw 4 adze, draw, dupe, file, form, ride 5 drive, plane, shape, sword 6 convey, device, finish, hammer, manage, puppet, weapon 7 cat's-paw, hatchet, utensil 8 ornament 9 appliance, implement 10 manipulate

abrading: 4 file

boring: awl, bit 5 auger, drill 6 gimlet, reamer 7 bradawl

bricklayer: 4 hock 5 float, level 6 hammer, trowel

butcher: saw 5 knife, steel 6 skewer, skiver 7 cleaver

carpenter: ax; bit, saw 4 rasp 5 auger, level, plane, punch 6 chisel, gimlet, hammer, pliers, square 7 handsaw, hatchet, scriber

chest: kit

chopping: 7 dolabra

cultivating: 4 plow 6 harrow, plough 7 leveler

cutting: ax; adz, axe, bit, hob, saw 4 adze 5 bezel, bezil, gouge, knife, plane, razor 6 chisel, graver, reamer, shears

edged: ax; axe 4 adze 5 knife, razor 6 chisel, reamer

excavating: 4 pick 6 pickax, shovel

garden: hoe 4 rake 5 edger, mower 6 sickle, trowel, weeder

gripping: 4 vise 5 clamp, tongs 7 pincers

kind of: awl, fid, fro, loy, tap, zax 4 celt, file, lute, sley 5 burin, edger, flail, lathe, loper, peavy, peevy, punch 6 chisel, cranny, eolith, flange, lifter, peavey, peevey, pommel, taster, trepan, trowel 7 setiron 8 burgoyne 12 straightedge

pointed: awl, fid, gad 4 barb, brod, brog, pick 6 gimlet, stylet

pounding: **6** pestle
prehistoric: **4** celt **6** eolith **9** paleolith **10** palaoelith
set: kit
slate-measuring: **7** scantle
smoothing: **4** file **5** plane **7** sleeker
temperer: **8** hardener
woodworking: adz **4** adze **7** edgeman, grainer, scauper, scriber **10** spokeshave
tool handle: *end:* **4** butt
fitted part: **4** tang
tools: tew **4** gear **7** gibbles(Sc.)
toom: **4** lank, lean, pour **5** empty **7** leisure
toomly: **4** idly **6** vainly **7** emptily **9** leisurely
toorie: **4** heap, knob **5** tower **6** tassel
toorock: **4** heap **5** tower
toosh: **4** gown, robe **9** nightgown
toot: pry, spy **4** blow, fool, gaze, peep **5** blast, draft, drink, shout, sound, spree **6** spread, sprout **7** carouse, trumpet, whistle **8** carousal, eminence, proclaim **9** elevation
tooter: spy **7** lookout **8** watchman **9** trumpeter
tooth: cog, jag **4** bite, dent, fang, jagg, snag, tine, tusk **5** molar, point, prong **6** cuspid, indent **7** consume, grinder, incisor, snaggle **10** projection
canine: **4** tush **6** cuspid, holder **7** laniary
combining form: **6** odonto
diminutive: **13** denticulation
double: **5** molar
drawer: **7** dentist
edge: **7** dentate
facing: **6** enamel
fore: **5** biter **6** cutter
gear wheel: cog **4** dent, tine
tooth covering: **6** enamel
tooth decay: **6** caries **8** cavities **11** saprodontia
"tooth for tooth": **6** talion
toothache: **4** worm(Sc.), **8** dentagra **10** odontalgia
toothed: *irregularly:* **5** erose
on edge: **8** serrated
toothful: sip **4** bite **5** drink **6** tipple **9** toothsome
toothless: **4** weak **6** futile **7** edental **8** decrepit, edentate **9** infantile **10** agomphious, edentulate
toothsome: **5** tasty **8** pleasing **9** agreeable, delicious, palatable
toozoo: **8** ringdove
top: ace, cap, fid, lid, tip, toy **4** acme, apex, crop, head, knap, lead, peak, pick, tent, tilt, tuft **5** caput, cream, crest, crown, drain, drink, equal, excel, outdo, prune, ridge, upset **6** apices(pl.), better, capote, culmen, exceed, finial, summit, swells, topple, tumble, upside, vertex, zenith **7** gyrator, highest, surpass, topmost **8** covering, dominate, forelock foremost, pinnacle, surmount, vertexes(pl.), ver-

tices(pl.) **9** uppermost **10** pre-eminent **11** aristocrats
altar: **5** mensa
head: **4** pate **5** scalp
wooden stand: **5** criss
top-hole: **6** tiptop **9** excellent **10** first-class
top kick: **8** sergeant
top-notch: **4** best **6** tiptop **7** highest **9** first-rate **11** unsurpassed
topaz humming bird: ani, ava **4** avas(pl.), aves(pl.)
topcoat: **6** reefer **8** overcoat
tope: **4** butt, wren **5** clump, drink, grove, shark, stupa **6** guzzle **7** dogfish, orchard
topechee: **12** artilleryman
topee, topi: cat, hat **6** helmet
toper: sot **5** shark **6** boozer, bouser **7** tippler, tosspot **8** drunkard
tophaceous: **5** rough, sandy, stony **6** gritty
tophet, topheth: **4** hell **5** chaos **8** darkness **9** confusion
topi: cap, hat **5** topee **8** antelope
topic: **4** item, text **5** issue, thema, theme **6** reason, remedy **7** heading, subject, themata **8** argument **11** application **13** consideration
topic of discourse: **5** theme
topical: **5** local **9** temporary
topknot: **4** hair, head, tuft **5** crest, onkos **7** commode **8** flounder **9** headdress
toplofty: **5** lofty **7** haughty **10** disdainful **12** contemptuous, supercilious
topmost: **6** apical **7** highest **9** uppermost
topnotcher: ace **4** hero, star
topper: hat **5** cover, float **6** stower **7** cheater, snuffer, topcoat **10** high-rigger **11** high-climber
toppiece: **4** head **6** toupee **11** masterpiece
topping: **4** bran, fine, good **5** icing, proud **6** refuse, tiptop **7** forlock, gallant, highest, topknot, topmost **8** arrogant, pleasant, superior **9** excellent, first-rate, skimmings **11** pretentious
topple: tip **4** fall, tilt **5** pitch, upset **6** totter, tumble **7** overset **8** overhang, overturn **9** overthrow **10** somersault **11** overbalance
toppy: **5** showy **7** stylish
topsman: **5** chief **6** drover **7** hangman, headman
topsy-turvy: **8** confused **10** disordered **11** widdershins, withershins
toque: hat **6** bonnet **9** headdress
tor: taw **4** crag, hill, peak **5** mound **8** pinnacle
tora, torah: law **5** tetel **7** precept **10** hartebeest, Pentateuch, revelation **11** instruction
torch: **4** lamp **5** blaze, brand, flare, fusee **7** lucigen **8** flambeau **9** flambeaux(pl.) **10** flashlight

frame: **7** cresset

tore: **4** knob, plod **5** grass **6** pommel **9** persevere

toreador: **11** bullfighter

torero: **11** bullfighter

torii: **7** gateway

torment: rib, vex **4** bait, pain, rack **5** agony, annoy, chevy, chivy, devil, force, grill, harry, tease, wrack **6** badger, chivvy, harass, harrow, hector, misery, pester, plague, strain **7** afflict, agitate, anguish, bedevil, crucify, distort, hagride, hatchel, tempest, torture, travail **8** distress, vexation **9** martyrdom, suffering, tantalize **10** cruciation **11** persecution

tormenting: **6** plaguy, vexing **9** harassing **11** troublesome

torn: **4** rent **5** riven **6** broken, ripped **9** lacerated

tornado: **4** wind **6** squall **7** cyclone, thunder, twister **9** hurricane, whirlwind, windstorm **12** thunderstorm

Tornado Junction: **8** Trinidad

toro: **4** bull, tree **7** cavalla, cowfish

torous, torose: **6** brawny **7** bulging, knobbed, swollen **8** muscular **11** protuberant

torpedinous: **9** benumbing **10** stupefying

torpedo: **4** mine, ruin **5** wreck **6** attack, benumb, damage, gunman **7** destroy, explode, shatter **8** firework, gangster, numbfish, paralyze **9** crampfish, detonator

torpid: **4** boat, dull, numb **5** inert **6** stupid **7** dormant, torpent **8** benumbed, inactive, lifeless, sluggish **9** apathetic, lethargic

torpor: **4** coma **5** sleep **6** acedia, apathy, stupor **7** accidie **8** dormancy, dullness, lethargy **10** inactivity, stagnation **12** sluggishness **13** insensibility

torque: bee **5** chain, sarpe, twist **6** collar

torrefy, torrify: dry **5** parch, roast **6** scorch

torrent: **4** flow, rush **5** flood, parch, roast, spate **6** stream **7** burning, channel, consume, current, roaring, rushing **8** downpour **9** impetuous

torrential: **10** outpouring **12** overwhelming

torrid: hot **4** arid **5** dried **6** ardent **7** burning, parched, zealous **8** inflamed, parching, scorched **9** scorching **10** oppressive, passionate

Torrid Zone boundary: **6** Tropic

tortoise: *marsh:* **6** gopher **7** elodian
order of: **8** chelonia
pert. to: **9** chelonian

tortuosity: **4** bend, turn **5** twist **7** flexure, winding **9** sinuosity **10** distortion **11** crookedness, deviousness

tortuous: **6** cranky, spiral **7** crooked, devious, immoral, sinuate, sinuous, winding, wriggly **8** wrongful **9** deceitful, injurious **10** circuitous, roundabout **11** anfractuous **12** labyrinthine

torture: **4** pain, rack **5** agony, twist, wheel **6** punish, wrench **7** agonize, anguish, crucify, distort, torment **8** distress, twisting **9** martyrdom **10** affliction, cruciation, distortion, excruciate, perversion, punishment
device: **4** rack

torus: **6** baston **7** molding **9** elevation **12** protuberance

torvity: **8** grimness, severity **9** sternness

torvous: **4** grim **5** stern **6** severe

tory: **6** bandit, outlaw, Papist **8** loyalist, marauder, Royalist **11** reactionary **12** conservative

tosh: **4** bath, bosh, neat, tidy **5** souse, trash **6** drench, neatly **7** bathtub **8** familiar, intimate, nonsense **10** intimately

toss: cob, cup, lob **4** cast, cave, flip, hike, hurl, rear, roll **5** chuck, flick, fling, flirt, heave, pitch, raise, serve, throw, wager **6** buffet, chance, fillip, harass, tossup, totter, uplift **7** agitate, disturb **8** disquiet **9** agitation, commotion **10** excitement
a coin: **4** flap, flip
about: **6** thrash, thresh
carelessly: **4** flip
head in derision: **4** geck
together confusedly: **8** scramble

tosspot: sot **5** toper **7** drinker **8** drunkard
bottle: **6** flagon

tosticate: **6** harass **8** distract **10** intoxicate

tosto: **4** fast **5** quick

tosy: **4** snug **10** comforting **11** intoxicated

tot: add, cup **4** item, note **5** child, count, drink, total, totum **6** amount, toddle, totter, tottum **7** jotting, toddler **8** exercise

tota: **6** grivet, monkey

total: add, all, sum, tot **4** full **5** gross, utter, whole **6** abrupt, amount, entire **7** concise, perfect, summary **8** absolute, complete, entirety **9** aggregate, undivided **10** accumulate

totality: all, sum **6** amount **7** allness **8** entirety **9** aggregate, wholeness **10** altogether

totally: **5** quite **6** wholly **8** entirely **10** altogether, completely

tote: all, lug, tot **4** bear, haul, lead, load **5** carry, count, total **6** handle, reckon **7** conduct **9** abstainer, transport

totem: **6** fetich, fetish

totem post: xat

toto: **4** baby

totter: **4** fall, hang, reel, rock, sway, toss **5** pitch, shake, swing, waver **6** dodder, falter, quiver, seesaw, staver(Sc.), toddle **7** fribble, stagger, tremble **8** titubate, unstable, unsteady **9** vacillate

tottering: **4** fall **5** shaky **6** groggy **7** adverse, rickety, shaking **8** collapse, unsteady, wavering **9** faltering **10** changeable **11** threatening, vacillating

tottery: **4** weak **5** shaky **8** unsteady **9** tottering

tottle: 4 boil, purl 5 count, total 6 reckon, simmer, toddle, topple, totter 9 reckoning
tottlish: 7 tottery 8 unsteady
tottum, totum: all, tot 5 child, whole
totty: 4 weak 5 child, dotty, shaky 7 tottery 8 unsteady 9 befuddled
toty: 7 laborer 9 messenger
toucan: 4 toco 7 aracari 8 hornbill 13 constellation
touch: dab, hit, rap, rob, tag, tap, tig, toe, use 4 abut, blow, feel, meet, rape 5 equal, reach, rival, steal, taste, trait 6 accuse, adjoin, affect, attain, border, borrow, extend, handle, molest, rebuke, strike, stroke 7 attinge, censure, contact, impinge, palpate, partake 8 perceive 9 mishandle
boundary line: 4 abut
closely: 8 osculate
combining form: tac
lightly: 5 brush 7 attinge, twiddle
measuring device: 10 haptometer
pert. to: 6 haptic 7 tactile, tactual
touching: 4 upon 6 moving 7 contact, meeting, tangent 8 adjacent, pathetic 9 affecting, attingent, conjoined 10 contacting, contiguous, contingent
a single point: 7 tangent
touchstone: 4 test 8 basanite, standard 9 criterion
touchwood: 4 funk, punk 5 sponk, spunk 6 amadou, tinder 8 punkwood
touchy: 4 sore 5 cross, risky, snaky, techy, testy 7 peevish 8 ticklish 9 irascible, irritable, sensitive 10 precarious 11 inflammable 13 over-sensitive
tough: 4 thug, wiry 5 hardy, rigid, rough, rowdy, stiff 6 brutal, robust, sinewy, sticky, strong 7 hickory, ruffian, violent, viscous 8 cohesive, enduring, hardened, leathery, rowdyish, stubborn, sturdily, toilsome, vigorous 9 difficult, glutinous, obstinate, ruffianly 10 aggressive, unyielding
and lean: 5 scrag 6 sinewy
tough-minded: 6 shrewd 7 willful 8 stubborn 9 practical, realistic 10 hardheaded 13 unsentimental
toughen: 5 inure 6 anneal, endure, temper
toughened: 5 clung 8 hardened, tempered
toupee: wig 6 peruke 7 periwig
tour: go 4 trip, turn 5 cover, drive, range, round, shift, spell, trick, watch 6 course, travel 7 circuit, compass, journey, proceed 9 barnstorm, excursion 10 appearance, revolution
tourbillion: 5 whirl 6 vortex 8 firework 9 whirlwind
tourelle: 5 tower 6 turret
tourist: 8 traveler
tourmaline: 6 schorl 9 rubellite
tournament: 4 tilt 5 joust, sport, trial 6 battle 7 contest, tourney 9 encounter

tourney: 10 tournament
tournure: pad 6 bustle
touse: 4 fuss, pull, rack, tear 5 worry 6 handle, rumple, tousel, tousle, tussle 7 turmoil 8 dishevel 11 disturbance
tousle, tousel: 4 drag, muss, pull, tear 5 touse 6 ruffle, rumple, tussle 7 rummage 8 dishevel, disorder
tousy: 5 rough 6 shaggy 7 tangled, tousled
tout: spy, vex 4 peep, peer, puff, toot 5 tease, thief, watch 6 praise 7 canvass, lookout, solicit, tipster, touting 8 informer, proclaim, smuggler 9 importune, recommend
tove: 4 emit 5 smoke
tow: tew, tug 4 drag, draw, flax, haul, lead, pull, rope 5 barge, chain 6 hawser 7 towboat, towrope, tugboat 8 cordelle
tow-row: 6 rumpus, uproar 9 racketing
toward: by; tae(Sc.) 4 near 5 anent 6 anenst, coming, future, onward 7 forward, willing 8 imminent, obliging 9 compliant, promising, tractable 11 approaching
prefix: ob, oc
towardly: 6 docile, gentle, kindly 7 affable 9 compliant, favorable, tractable 10 propitious
towel: dry, rub 5 cloth 6 napkin 8 vesperal 9 handcloth
tower: 4 rise, silo, soar 5 broch, exalt, mount, pylon, raise, reach, sikar, spire, stupa 6 ascend, belfry, castle, donjon, pagoda, prison, turret 7 bastile, bulwark, citadel, clocher, defense, elevate, mansion, minaret, mirador, overtop, shikara, steeple, surpass, zikurat 8 bastille, domineer, fortress, ziggurat, zikkurat 9 campanile 10 protection, stronghold
famous: 4 Pisa 5 Babel, Minar 6 Eiffel, London
glacier ice: 5 serac
towering: 4 high, tall 5 great, lofty, steep 7 eminent, intense, violent 11 overweening
towhee: 7 bunting, chewink
town: 4 burg, city, dorp, farm, stad, vill, yard 5 bourg, burgh, court, derby, house, manor, ville(F.), voter 6 ciudad(Sp.), garden, hamlet, parish, podunk, staple 7 borough, burgess, citizen, cluster, village 8 bourgade, township 9 enclosure, farmstead 10 electorate, metropolis 11 aggregation
Attic: 4 deme
official: 6 grieve
pert. to: 5 civic, urban 7 oppidon
plan: 4 plat
witch: 5 Salem
townsman: cit 7 citizen, oppidan 9 selectman 10 inhabitant
toxic: 9 poisonous
toxophilite: 6 archer
toy: pet, top 4 ball, daff, doll, fool, play,

whim **5** antic, dally, fancy, flirt, panda, sport **6** bauble, finger, gewgaw, hoople, rattle, trifle **7** caprice, conceit, pastime, trinket **8** aversion, flirting, gimcrack, interest, mistress, ornament, teetotum, weakling **9** bandalore, dalliance, headdress, plaything, rattlebox, teddybear **10** knickknack

toyish: 6 wanton **7** playful, trivial, useless **8** sportive, trifling **9** fantastic, frivolous, whimsical **13** unsubstantial

toze: 4 comb, pull **5** tease **11** disentangle

trabant: 9 attendant, bodyguard

trabeation: 6 beamed **11** entablature

trabuco: 5 cigar **11** blunderbuss

trace: 4 clew, clue, copy, draw, fall, file, hint, line, mark, nose, path, road, seek, sign, step, tang, walk **5** grain, march, probe, route, shade, tinge, track, trail, tread **6** amount, deduce, derive, detect, follow, locate, ramble, sketch, trudge **7** conduct, glimpse, impress, imprint, inquire, outline, remnant, soupcon, uncover, vestige **8** discover, evidence, quantity, traverse **9** ascertain, attribute, delineate, establish, footprint, scintilla **10** indication, procession **11** investigate

tracer: 5 horse **6** bullet, gilder, stylus **7** stainer **9** draftsman

trachea: 4 duct **8** windpipe

tracing: 4 copy **6** record **8** ergogram **10** cardiogram

track: 4 rut, way **4** drag, draw, hunt, line, mark, oval, path, rail, road, wake **5** march, route, scent, sight, spoor, trace, trail, tread **6** course, follow, infuse, pursue, teapot, travel **7** circuit, conduct, vestige **8** guideway, sequence, speedway, trackage, traverse **9** ascertain, footprint, spectacle **10** cinder path, succession

animal: run **4** slot **5** spoor

official: **5** judge, timer **7** referee, starter

race: **4** mile **5** relay **6** sprint

tracker: 5 guide, tower

tract (see also **land**): **4** area, mark, path, zone **5** campo, clime, essay, lapse, range, trace, track **6** course, estate, extent, region **7** country, expanse, leaflet, pteryla, quarter, stretch **8** brochure, district, duration, pamphlet, sequence, treatise **9** lineament, narrative, territory **10** exposition **11** subdivision **12** dissertation

tractable: 4 easy **6** docile, gentle, pliant **7** ductile, flexile **8** amenable, flexible, obedient, workable **9** adaptable, compliant, malleable **10** governable

tractate: 5 essay, tract **8** handling, treatise **9** treatment **10** discussion **12** dissertation

tractile: 6 pliant **7** ductile, tensile

traction: 5 power **7** drawing, utility **8** friction **9** influence **10** attraction

tractor: 9 agrimotor

trade: buy, way **4** chap, chop, deal, fuss, path, sell, swap, work **5** cheap, craft,

habit, track, trail, tread **6** action, barter, bother, course, employ, manner, method, metier, scorse **7** bargain, calling, dealing, pursuit, traffic **8** activity, business, commerce, exchange, practice, purchase **10** handicraft, occupation, profession **11** intercourse, nundination

association: NAM **5** hansa, hanse

combination: **4** gild **5** guild, hanse **6** cartel, merger

pert. to: **10** emporeutic

votes: **7** logroll

trademark: 5 brand

trader: 6 dealer, monger, seller, slaver, sutler **7** chapman **8** barterer, merchant **9** tradesman **10** shopkeeper

tradesman: 5 buyer **7** artisan, workman **8** merchant **9** craftsman **10** shopkeeper **11** storekeeper

supply: **4** line **5** stock **9** inventory

trading post: P.X. **7** station

tradition: 4 code, lore **6** belief, custom, legend **8** practice **9** surrender **10** convention

traduce: 4 slur **5** abuse, belie **6** debase, defame, malign, vilify **7** asperse, blacken, detract, pervert, slander **8** disgrace **10** calumniate

traffic: buy **4** coup, sell **5** trade **6** barter, market **7** chaffer, dealing **8** business, commerce, exchange **11** intercourse

in holy offices: **6** simony

trafficker: 6 dealer, trader **8** merchant

tragedy: 6 buskin, misery **8** calamity, disaster **10** misfortune

Muse: **9** Melpomene

tragic: sad **4** dire **5** fatal **7** doleful **8** mournful, pathetic, terrible

tragopan: 8 pheasant

tragule: 4 deer **10** chevrotain

trail: lag **4** drag, draw, hang, hunt, mark, path, slot, tail, wake **5** blaze, drail, piste, route, scent, spoor, trace, track, train, tramp, troll **6** camino(Sp.), course, follow, trapse **7** draggle, dwindle, traipse **8** footpath, straggle

blazer: **7** pioneer

marker: **5** cairn

trailer: **4** vine

truck: **4** semi

train: row **4** bait, drag, draw, file, form, gait, lead, line, lure, rack, rank, rear, tail, trap **5** breed, coach, decoy, drawl, drill, flier, guide, local, seine, snare, suite, teach, trace, trail **6** allure, coffle, convoy, cradle, direct, entice, ground, scheme, school, series, shaped **7** caravan, conduct, cortege, educate, prepare, retinue **8** accustom, artifice, equipage, instruct, protract, rehearse, sequence, trickery **9** condition, entourage, following, strategem, treachery **10** attendants, conveyance, discipline, procession **11** streamliner **13** accommodation

horses: **6** manege

men: 4 crew

trainer: 5 tamer 7 lanista 11 gymnasiarch

training: 4 diet 5 drill 8 breeding, exercise 9 education 10 background, discipline 11 supervision
lack of: 11 inappetence
manual: 5 sloid, sloyd

traipse, trapes: gad 4 walk 5 trail, tramp, tread 6 trudge, wander 8 gadabout, slattern

trait: 4 line, mark, note, thew 5 touch 6 streak, stroke 7 feature, quality 9 lineament, mannerism 11 peculiarity 14 characteristic

traitor: 5 Judas 8 betrayer, Iscariot, renegade
Norweigian: 8 Quisling

traitorous: 5 false 9 faithless, felonious 11 disaffected, treacherous, treasonable

traject: way 4 cast 5 ferry, route, throw 6 course 7 passage 8 transmit

trajet: way 5 route 6 course 7 passage, traject

tralatitious: 12 metaphorical

tram, trame: car, leg 4 beam, haul, limb 5 bench, shaft, wagon 6 thread 7 tramcar, trammel, tramway, trolley 9 streetcar 10 conveyance
tier: 4 deck

trammel: net, tie 4 clog, lock 5 check, gauge 6 braids, fasten, fetter, hamper, impede 7 compass, confine, pothook, prevent, shackle, tresses 8 restrain 9 intercept, plaitings 10 instrument

tramontane: 4 boor 5 alien 7 foreign 8 stranger 9 barbarous 10 outlandish 11 transalpine

tramp: bo; boe, bum, vag 4 hike, hobo, hoof, prog, step, tart, vamp, walk 5 caird, jaunt, tread 6 gaycat, trapes, travel, trudge, waffie, wander 7 traipse, vagrant 8 vagabond 9 excursion 10 prostitute

trample: 4 foil, hurt 5 crush, tread 6 injure 7 destroy, violate

trance: 4 coma, daze 5 spell, swoon 6 prance, raptus, stupor 7 ecstasy, enchant, passage 8 entrance 9 catalepsy, enrapture 10 passageway

traneen: bit 6 trifle

tranquil: 4 calm, cool, easy, even, mild 5 equal, quiet, still 6 gentle, placid, serene, steady 7 equable, pacific, restful 8 composed, peaceful 9 sedentary 10 motionless 11 undisturbed 13 imperturbable

tranquility, tranquillity: kef, kif 5 peace, quiet 8 serenity 10 equanimity 12 peacefulness

tranquilize: 4 lull 5 allay 6 settle, soften, soothe 7 appease, assuage 9 alleviate

transact: do 5 treat 7 conduct, perform 8 complete, transfer 9 negotiate

transaction: 4 deal, sale 6 action, affair 7 bargain 8 business 10 proceeding 11 proposition
unlawful: 10 chevisance

Transcaspian capital: 9 Ashkhabad

Transcaucasia: See **Armenia, Azerbaijan, Georgia.**

transcend: 5 climb, excel, mount, raise 6 ascend, exceed 7 elevate, surpass 8 outstrip, overstep, surmount

transcendent: 8 superior 13 extraordinary

transcendental: 5 ideal 8 ethereal 10 superhuman 12 metaphysical, supersensual, supranatural

transcribe: 4 copy 5 write 6 impute, record 7 ascribe, imitate 9 reproduce, translate 10 paraphrase

transcript: 6 record 8 apograph 9 duplicate 12 reproduction

transfer: 4 cede, deed, move, pass, sale, send 5 carry, grant, shift 6 assign, attorn, change, convey, decant, demise, depute, remove 7 dispose 8 alienate, delegate 9 translate, transport 10 abalienate 12 transmission 13 transposition

transference: 7 passage 10 conveyance

transfigure: 5 exalt 7 glorify 8 idealize 9 transform 12 metamorphose

transfix: fix, pin 5 spear, stick 6 fasten, impale, pierce 11 transpierce

transform: 4 turn 5 alter 6 change 7 convert 9 transmute 11 transfigure 12 metamorphose, transmogrify

transformation: 10 conversion 13 metamorphosis
into human form: 17 anthropomorphosis

transfuse: 5 imbue 6 infuse 7 instill 8 transfer, transmit

transgress: err, sin 5 break, cross 6 offend 7 disobey, violate 8 overstep

transgression: 5 crime, fault 7 misdeed 8 trespass 10 infraction 12 infringement 13 contravention

transient: 8 fleeting, fugitive 9 ephemeral, itinerant, migratory, momentary, temporary, transeunt 10 evanescent, shortlived, transitory 11 impermanent

transit: 6 change 7 passage 10 conveyance, transition 12 thoroughfare

transition: 5 phase, shift 9 metabasis 10 conversion

transitive: 7 flowing 12 transitional

transitory: 5 brief, fleet 8 caducous, temporal 9 ephemeral, temporary 10 evanescent

translate: 4 read, rede 6 change, decode, remove, render 7 convert 8 construe, decipher, entrance, transfer 9 enrapture, interpret 10 paraphrase

translation: 4 pony, trot 7 version 9 rendition 10 paraphrase 14 interpretation 15 transliteration

translucent: 6 limpid 9 alabaster 11 perspicuous, transparent

transmigration: 7 samsara

transmit: 4 emit, hand, send 5 carry, relay 6 convey, render 7 conduct, devolve, forward 8 bequeath 11 communicate

transmutation: 9 evolution
transmute: 6 change 7 convert 8 transfer 9 transform
transparent: 4 open 5 clear, frank, gauzy, lucid, sheer 6 candid, limpid, lucent 7 obvious, pelucid 8 luminous, lustrous 9 colorless 10 diaphanous 11 crystalline, perspicuous, translucent
transpierce: 6 pierce 8 transfix 9 penetrate
transpire: 6 happen
transport: dak 4 bear, boat, buss, haul, move, send, ship, tote 5 bring, carry, ferry, flute, truck 6 banish, convey, deport, ravish 7 convict, ecstasy, emotion, fraught, freight, passion, portage, rapture, smuggle 8 entrance, horsecar, overcome, palander, transfer 9 captivate, enrapture, happiness
transportation: *business:* 4 mail 7 air line, express 8 shipping 9 steamship 11 railroading
means: 7 rockets
system: 4 line
transpose: 5 shift 6 change, remove 7 convert, disturb, reverse 8 exchange, transfer 9 rearrange, transform, translate, transmute 11 interchange
transposition: 7 anagram 10 spoonerism 11 permutation
Transvaal: *capital:* 8 Pretoria
district: 4 Rand
policeman: 4 zarp
transverse: bar, way 4 bank, over, pass, rung, turn 5 argue, cross, pivot, route, shift, trace 6 across, denial, stripe, survey, swivel, thwart, travel 7 barrier, discuss, examine, impeach, oblique, pervade, quarrel 9 alternate, crossbeam 10 crosspiece 11 controversy
trap: bag, get, gin, net, pit 4 cage, lure, nail 5 brake, buggy, catch, goods, mouth, rocks, snare, steps, trick 6 ambush, corner, detect, enmesh 7 capture, cunning, ensnare, luggage, pitfall, springe 8 carriage, confound, covering, deadfall, separate, trapball 9 caparison, detective, policeman, stratagem 10 belongings, stepladder
animal: pot, web 4 weir 5 creel 6 bownet, eelpot
police: 7 dragnet 9 roadblock
trapdoor: 4 drop
trapes: See **traipse**.
trapeze: bar
trapping: 4 gear 5 cloth 7 harness 8 catching, covering, ornament 9 adornment, caparison, coverture 10 decoration 12 accouterment, accoutrement 13 embellishment, paraphernelia
theatrical: 4 prop 7 scenery 8 property
trapshooting: 5 skeet
trash: jog, lop 4 bosh, clog, crop, dirt, jade, pelf, plod, raff, tosh 5 leash, money,

tramp, waste, wrack 6 bushwa, debris, halter, hinder, rabble, refuse, retard, rubble, trudge 7 baggage, beggary, blather, rubbish 8 encumber, flummery, nonsense, restrain, riffraff, trumpery 10 balderdash 11 sleuthhound
trashy: 9 worthless
trauma: 5 shock, wound 6 injury
travail: 4 pain, pang, task, toil 5 agony, drive, labor 6 effort, travel 7 journey, torment, trouble 8 exertion 9 suffering 11 parturition
trave: 9 crossbeam
travel: go: run 4 fare, move, mush, post, ride, tour, trek, trip, walk, wend 5 coast 6 motion 7 commute, journey, migrate, passage, proceed, sojourn, torment, travail 8 traverse 9 gallivant, itinerate 10 locomotion 11 peregrinate
company: 7 caravan
pert. to: 6 viatic
traveler: 5 farer, tramp 6 viator 7 drummer, pilgrim, swagman, tourist, voyager 8 salesman, wanderer, wayfarer 9 itinerant 12 globe-trotter
travels: 7 odyssey
travesty: 6 parody, satire 8 disguise 9 burlesque, imitation 10 caricature
writer: 8 parodist
trawl: net 4 fish, line 7 boulter, dragnet
tray: hod 4 font 6 hurdle, salver, server 7 coaster
treacherous: 5 false, punic, snaky 6 fickle, hollow 8 disloyal, insecure, plotting, unstable 9 faithless, insidious 10 fraudulent, perfidious, traitorous, unreliable 11 disaffected 12 Machiavelian 13 Machiavellian, untrustworthy
treachery: 5 guile 6 deceit 7 perfidy, treason, untruth 8 betrayal
treacle: 4 cure 6 remedy 7 claggum 8 molasses
treaclewort: 4 herb 10 pennycress
tread: rut 4 gait, mark, pace, rung, step, volt, walk 5 clump, crush, labor, press, stair, stamp, trace, track, trail, tramp 6 balter, course, quench, subdue, trapes 7 conquer, repress, traipse, trample 8 copulate, footfall 9 footprint 10 employment, occupation
treadle: 5 pedal 7 chalaza
treason: 7 perfidy 8 betrayal 9 treachery
treasure: 4 roon 5 cache, hoard, pearl, prize, store, trove, value 6 gersum, riches, supply, wealth 7 cherish, finance 8 treasury 9 thesaurus(L.) 10 appreciate, collection 12 accumulation
Treasure State: 7 Montana
treasured: 5 chary
treasurer: 7 cashier, curator 8 bhandari, cofferer, deftedar, guardian, receiver 11 chamberlain
college: 6 bursar
treasury: 4 fisc, fund 5 chest, hoard 6

coffer **7** bursary, revenue **9** exchequer **10** repository, storehouse

Roman: **6** fiscus

treat: use **4** deal, dose, lead, urge **5** argue, besee, Dutch, feast, guide, touch **6** attend, confer, demean, doctor, govern, handle, parley, regale, regard, repast **7** address, bargain, control, discuss, entreat, expound **8** consider, transact, treatise **9** discourse, entertain, negotiate **10** manipulate

improperly: **4** snub **5** flout, scout, spite **6** ill-use, misuse **8** dishonor

tenderly: **5** spare **6** coddle, pamper

treatise: **5** essay, tract **6** thesis, treaty **7** account, grammar **8** brochure **9** discourse, narration, treatment **10** commentary **11** description **12** dissertation

treatment: **5** usage **8** demeanor, entreaty, handling **13** entertainment

harsh: **5** abuse **8** misusage, severity

compassionate: **5** mercy

treaty: **4** pact **7** article, concord, entente **8** contract, treatise **9** agreement, discourse **10** convention, discussion **11** arrangement, negotiation **13** understanding

treaty-bound: **6** allied

treble: **6** shrill, triple **7** soprano **9** threefold **11** high-pitched

treble clef: gee

tree (See also next entry): ach, ber, dal, dao, ebo, elm, fir, hur, iba, kou, lin, mee, oak **4** acle, alan, alof, anam, asak, asok, ates, ausu, bael, biti, bogo, bola, dali, dhak, dita, ipil, mabi, mora, odal, palm, pole, post, ship, toon, trap, wood, yaya **5** areca, asoka, betis, bongo, bulak, bumbo, cacao, carob, catch, cebil, couma, dadap, dalli, fulwa, genip, ligas, mahua, neeba, nepal, niepa, nitta, oodal, rohan, roman, salai, sassy, shaft, shift, siman, sissu, spade, staff, stake, stick, tikur, yacca **6** bahera, banyan, barbas, bariba, brauna, bucare, cativo, cedron, chalta, chogak, chupon, cocuyo, colima, corner, cudgel, design, gibbet, gomart, illupi, jarrah, locust, marane, marara, ramoon, sabino, simaba, sissoo, stemma, tikoor, timber **7** anubing, araraba, arboret, assagai, assegai, azarole, capture, champac, champak, cocullo, dhamnoo, diagram gallows, guaraba, gumihan, hautboy, hollong, madrona, madrono, malpaho, mambong **8** ahueuete, cockspur, gamdeboo, ironbark, magnolia, mangrove, mokihana, phulwara, seedling, tamarack **9** bandoline, betel-palm, bitanhole, canadulce, couratari, currajong, genealogy, sassywood **10** bunyabunya, chaulmugra **11** balinghasay, chaulmaugra, chaulmoogra, guachipilin, hursinghair

alder: arn **5** alnus, birch **12** ament-bearing

allspice: **7** pimento

aromatic: **9** sassafras

balsam: fir **9** torchwood

bark: **4** ross, tapa

basswood: **6** linden

bead: nim

bean: **5** sapan

bearing samara: ash

beefwood: **5** belah, belar

betel: **5** areca

bignoniacious: **7** catalpa

blinding sap: **7** alipata

boxwood: **5** seron

breadnut: **6** capomo

buckthorn: **7** cascara

buckwheat: **4** titi **6** teetee

Buddha's: **6** botree

bully: see *gum* below

burned, broken: **7** rampick, rampike

buttonball: **5** plane **8** sycamore

cabbage: **7** angelin

camphor: **5** kapur

candlenut: ama

caoutchouc: ule **6** rubber

caucho-yielding (see also *rubber* below): ule

cemetery: yew

chestnut: **10** chinqua pin

chocolate: **5** cacao

cinchona: **7** quinine **9** quinidine

cinnamon family: **6** cassia

clump: **4** tump **5** motte

coconut: **4** coco

coffee: **6** chicot

conebearing: fir, yew **4** pine **5** alder, cedar, larch **7** conifer **8** gnetales

coral: **6** gabgab

covering: **4** bark

cranberry: **7** pembina

derivative: **5** pinic

devil: **4** dita

drumstick: **11** canafistolo, canafistula, canafistulo

drupe bearing: **4** bito

dwarf: **5** scrub **7** abuscle **10** chinquapin

dwelling: **4** nest

dye yielding: tua, tui **4** mora **7** annatto **10** hursinghar

ebony: **9** diospyros

elder: **7** trammon

eucalyptus: **4** yati **6** mallee

evergreen: fir, yeu **4** pine, tawa **5** carob, cedar, holly, larch, ocote, olive **6** balsam, carobe, cazaba, coigue, tarata **7** bebeery, juniper, madrona, madrono, taratah

exudation: gum, lac, sap, tar **5** resin, rosin, xylan

fabacious: **5** agati

fiber: **5** bulak, simal, terap **7** bentang

fig family: **4** upas **5** pipal **7** gondang

flowering: **5** agati, elder, titis **6** mimosa, redbud **8** cleaster, oleaster

fodder: **5** mahoe **9** tagasaste

food: **4** akee

fruit: bel, fig, gab **4** gaub, lime **5** araca,

lemon, mahis, olive, papaw, topes **6** annona, banana, bearer, biriba, litchi, medlar, pawpaw, sapota **7** avocado, capulin, genipap, tangelo **8** bakupari, tamarind **9** tangerine **12** custard apple
gaucho: ule
group: **4** bosk **5** copse, grove, woods **6** forest **7** coppice, orchard
grower: **8** arborist
gum: **5** babul, balta **6** balata, sapota, sapote, tupelo, zapote **8** banildad **9** sapodilla, sapotilha, sapotilla **10** bansalague, eucalyptus
gum genus: **6** owenia
hardwood: **4** poon **5** aalii, gidia, gidya, mabee, maple, narra, ngaio **6** gidgea, gidgee, gidjee, gidyea, walnut **7** hickory, tindalo **8** macaasin, mahogany **9** quebracho
heartwood: **7** duramen
heath: **5** briar, brier
hickory: **5** pecan
holly: **4** ilex
honeberry: **5** genip
horseradish: **4** behn **5** behen
jobber: **10** woodpecker
juniper: **4** cade **5** cedar
kino: **4** bija
koranic: **6** zaggum
laurel: bay **7** tarairi
limb: **5** bough **6** branch
lime: lin **4** linn, teil **6** linden **9** tilicetum
linden: lin **4** lime, teil **8** basswood
locust: **6** acacia **9** courbaril
lotus: sad **4** lote
mafurra: **6** elcaja
magnolia: **5** yulan
mahogany: **4** toon
maple: **4** acer
margosa: **4** neem
marmalade: **5** mamey, mamie **6** mammee, sapote
medicinal: **5** sumac **6** sumach, wahahe
mimosaceous: **5** siris
monkeybread: **6** baobab
mountain ash: **4** sorb **5** rowan **7** service
mulberry: **4** more
nut: **4** cola **6** akhrot, chicha **9** almendron
oil: **5** mahua, mahwa **9** candlenut
oil-yielding: bel, ben **4** eboe, shea
olive: **4** olea
olive family: ash
orange-like: **5** osage
palm: ti; tal **4** coco **6** arengs
paradise: **8** aceituna
part: **4** bark, bole, knot, leaf, root, twig **5** shade, trunk **6** branch
pert. to: **8** arboreal
pine: see *evergreen* above
pipal: **6** botree
plane: **8** sycamore **10** buttonwood
plantain: **4** pala
pod-bearing: **7** catalpa
poisonous: **4** upas

poon: **4** dilo **5** keena
poplar: **5** abele, alamo, aspen, tulip **10** cottonwood
pottery: **7** caraipe, caraipi
rain: **5** saman, zaman **6** zamang **8** genisaro **9** algarroba
rare: **6** Joshua
resin: **4** arar
ribbon: **6** akaroa **7** houhere
rowan: see *mountain ash* below
rubber: ule **4** para **6** caucho **7** seringa **10** caoutchouc
rutaceous: **4** lime
salt: **4** atle **5** atlee
sandarac: **4** arar
sandbox: **6** assacu
science: **7** silvics
shade: ash, elm, lin, oak **5** maple **6** linden, poplar **7** catalpa **8** sycamore
smoke: **6** fustet **9** zante-wood
soft wood: lin **5** ambay, balsa, linde
sprout: **5** sprig **7** sapling
streaked wood: **6** baria
tallow: **4** cera
tamarisk: see *salt* above
tea: **6** manuka
teak: **4** teca
thorny: bel **4** bito, brea **7** colorin **9** barriguda **11** chichicaste
timber: ash, dar, eng, koa, saj, sal, yew **4** coco, cuya, ipil, pelu, pine, poon, rata, tala, teak, toon, ulmo **5** acana, almon, amate, balao, balau, bayok, beech, birch, cedar, culla, dalli, ebano, fotui, guijo, icica, kauri, kaury, maple, narra, pekea, penda, rauli, tenio, timbo, uadal, yacal, zorro **6** alerce, alerse, alfaje, ausubo, bacury, banaba, banaki, banago, bancal, banuyo, bataan, batinô, dagame, dungon, lanete, molave, satine, totara, walnut **7** batulin, becuiba, billian, camagon, capulin, cypress, gateado, gomavel, guacimo, hapiton, redwood **8** flindosa, flindosy, mahogany, zapetero **9** balaustre, guaraguao **10** batikuling
treatise: **5** silva
tropical genus: **8** bauhinia
tulip: **6** poplar
Turkey oak: **6** cerris
turpentine: **6** tarata **7** taratah **9** terebinth
walnut see *nut* above: **6** akhrot
wattle: **5** boree
willow: **5** osier
worship: **11** dendrolatry
yellow alder: **8** sagerose
tree: For trees of specific countries or regions, see under that country or region. EXAMPLES: "African tree", see under **Africa:** *tree;* "American tree," see under **America:** *tree.*
tree bear: **7** raccoon
tree runner: **8** nuthatch
treelike: **11** arborescent
treeless: **6** barren

plain: **5** llano, pampa **6** steppe **7** prairie, savanna **8** savannah

treen: 6 wooden

trefoil: 6 claver, clover

tregetour: 7 juggler **8** magician

treillage: 5 grill **7** trellis **8** espalier **11** latticework

trek: 4 draw, pull **5** march **6** travel **7** journey, migrate **10** expedition

trellis: 5 bower, cross **7** lattice, pergola **8** espalier **10** interweave **11** latticework

trematode worms: 8 cercaria **9** flatworms

tremble: 5 bever, quake, shake **6** didder, dither, dodder, falter, quaver, quiver, shiver, totter, tremor **7** flacker, flicker, shudder, vibrate **9** trepidate

trembling: 7 fearful, twitter **9** tremulous

tremendous: big **5** awful, giant, great, large **7** amazing **8** dreadful, enormous, horrible, powerful, terrific **9** frightful, momentous, monstrous **10** terrifying **13** extraordinary

tremolo: 6 quaver

tremor: 5 quake, shake **6** quiver, shiver, thrill **7** tremble **9** vibration

tremplin: 11 springboard

tremulous: 5 aspen, timid **7** fearful, nervous, palsied **8** timorous, unsteady, wavering **9** quavering, sensitive **11** palpitating

trench: cut, gaw **4** bury, gash, moat, sike **5** carve, ditch, drain, fosse, fossa(L.), graff, graft, slash, slice **6** furrow, groove, gutter **7** acequia **8** encroach, entrench, infringe **10** excavation

digger: **6** sapper

digging from within: sap

trenchant: 4 keen **5** acute, sharp **6** biting **7** cutting **8** clear-cut, distinct, forceful, incisive, vigorous **9** energetic **11** penetrating

trencher: 5 board, plate **7** platter **9** parasitic **11** sycophantic

trencherman: 7 sponger **8** hanger-on, parasite **11** gormandizer

trend: run **4** bend, bent, tone, turn, vein **5** drift, swing, tenor **6** extend, strike **7** incline **8** movement, tendency **9** direction **11** inclination

trendle: tub **6** trough

trepan: 4 lure, tool, trap **5** snare, trick **6** entrap **7** deceive, ensnare, swindle **9** perforate, stratagem

trepang: 10 beche-de-mer **22** holothurian-sea-cucumber

trepid: 7 quaking **8** timorous **9** trembling

trepidation: 4 fear **5** alarm, dread **6** dismay, tremor **7** quaking **9** agitation, confusion **11** disturbance **12** perturbation **13** consternation

trespass: sin **5** poach **6** breach, invade, offend **7** intrude **8** encroach, entrench, infringe **9** interlope **10** infraction, transgress **11** misfeasance

tress: 4 curl, hair, lock **5** braid, plait **7** ringlet

tressure: 4 band, caul **6** border, fillet, ribbon **9** headdress

trestle: leg **5** bench, horse, stand, stool **6** tripod, trivet **7** support, viaduct **9** framework

tret: 9 allowance

trew: 5 trust **7** believe

trews: 8 breeches, trousers **9** stockings

triad: 5 three, trine **6** triune **7** trinity **9** trivalent

trial: go; try **4** bout, case, pain, test **5** assay, cross, essay, grief, proof **6** assize, effort, ordeal, sample **7** approof, attempt, contest, hearing, inquiry **8** endeavor, evidence, hardship **10** experience, experiment, tournament **11** examination, tribulation **13** investigation

inconclusive: **8** mistrial

triangle: 5 delta **6** trigon **7** scalene, trigone **9** isosceles **11** equilateral

side: leg **11** hypothenuse

unequal sided: **7** scalene

triangular: 7 deltoid **13** three-cornered

piece: **4** gore **5** miter, mitre, wedge **6** gusset

triangular muscle: 7 deltoid

triarchy: 11 triumvirate

tribe: rod **4** band, clan, kind, race, sept **5** class, firca(Ind.), group **6** family **9** community

emblem: **5** totem

Germanic: **8** Alamanni, Alemanni

head: **5** chief **9** patriarch

New Zealand: ati

Roman: **5** Latin **6** Sabine **8** Etruscan

tribulation: 5 agony, trial **6** misery, sorrow **8** distress **9** suffering **10** affliction

tribunal: bar **4** banc, seat **5** bench, court, forum **7** tribune **8** assembly **10** consistory

tribune: 4 dais **6** throne **8** platform **10** magistrate

tributary: 5 ruler, state **6** feeder **7** subject **9** auxiliary, subsidary **11** subordinate **12** contributory

tribute: fee, tax **4** cain, dues, duty, gift, levy, rent, scat **5** grant **6** assign, eulogy, impost, praise, tariff **7** chevage, ovation, payment, respect **8** encomium **9** attribute, gratitude, laudation, panegyric **10** obligation **11** testimonial

tricar: 8 tricycle

trice: 4 bind, gird, haul, lash, pull **5** jiffy **6** moment, secure **7** instant **9** twinkling

trick: bob, boy, cog, dor, fob, fox, fub, gag, gum, toy **4** bilk, dupe, feat, flam, fool, gaff, gaud, girl, gull, hoax, jest, joke, prat, ruse, trap, turn, wile **5** catch, child, cully, dodge, feint, fraud, gleek, guile, knack, prank, shift, skite, spell, stunt **6** begunk, chouse, delude, humbug, palter, trepan, trifle **7** beguile, cantrip, deceive, defraud, finesse, gimmick, pretext, sleight, swindle **8** artifice, flimflam, illusion, maneuver **9** bamboozle, capriccio, chicanery, diablerie, imposture, mannerism, stratagem **10** subterfuge **11** hornswoggle, legerdemain

trickery: art **5** fraud, hocus **6** cautel, deceit, japery **7** knavery, roguery, slyness **8** cheating, trumpery **9** deception, duplicity **10** hanky-panky

trickle: **4** drip, flow, sipe(Sc.) **5** exude **6** distil **7** distill, dripple

trickster: **5** cheat **6** rascal **7** slicker

tricksy: **5** smart **6** spruce **7** evasive, playful, roguish **8** prankish, sportive **9** deceiving, deceptive, uncertain **11** embellished, mischievous

tricky: sly **5** dodgy **6** artful, catchy **7** devious **8** ticklish **9** deceitful, intricate

tricycle: **6** tricar

trident: **5** spear
bearer: **7** Neptune

tried: **6** ettled(Sc.), proved, select, tested **8** faithful, reliable **11** trustworthy

trier: **5** judge **7** refiner **8** examiner, renderer **12** experimenter, investigator

trifle: bit, fig, rap, toy **4** bean, doit, fike, jest, mock, mote, play **5** dally, flirt, straw, trick **6** bauble, coquet, dabble, dawdle, delude, dibble, doodle, fiddle, fidget, footer, footle, frivol, gewgaw, potter **7** deceive, dessert, fribble, nothing, traneen **8** flimflam, gimcrack, raillery **9** bagatelle **10** equivocate, knickknack, triviality

trifler: **7** flaneur

trifling: **4** airy, idle, mere **5** inane, petty **6** futile, little **7** shallow, wasting **8** badinage, frippery **9** dalliance **10** immaterial **13** insignificant

trifoliolate: **7** ternate **11** three-leaved

trifolium: **6** clover **8** shamrock

trig: run **4** chic, cram, deck, fill, firm, full, line, neat, prim, prop, stop, tidy, trim, trot **5** brisk, dandy, natty, smart, sound, stiff, stone, stuff, wedge **6** active, lively, spruce, steady, strong, trench **7** distend, foppish, precise, support **10** methodical

trigonometry function: **4** sine **6** cosine, secant **7** tangent

trill: **4** flow, move, turn **5** shake, twirl **6** gruppo, quaver, quiver, warble **7** mordent, trickle, vibrate, vibrato **8** grupetto **10** coloratura

trim: bob, cut, gay, lop **4** beat, chic, clip, crop, deft, dink, edge, fine, firm, neat, nice, snod(Sc.), snug, tidy, trig **5** adorn, braid, cheat, chide, dress, equip, fitty, natty, nifty, preen, prune, ready, shave, shear **6** adjust, dapper, defeat, modify, petite, punish, spruce, thrash **7** balance, compact, defraud, furnish, orderly **8**

chastise, decorate, ornament, pleasant, tailored **9** condition, embellish, excellent, shipshape **10** compromise **11** disposition

trimmer: **5** finer

trimming: **4** gimp, lace **5** braid, ruche **6** frieze, fringe, piping **7** falbala, ruching **8** furbelow, ornament, rick-rack **9** garniture **10** decoration **13** passementerie

trinal: **5** trial **9** threefold

trindle: **4** roll **5** wheel **7** trundle

trine: go **4** hang **5** march, triad **6** trigon. triple, triune **7** Trinity **9** favorable, threefold **10** auspicious

Trinidad music: **7** calypso

trinitrotoluene: TNT **6** trotyl **14** trinitrotoluol

trinity: **5** three, triad **6** triune **9** threeness **10** spiderwort

trinket: toy **4** bead, gaud, ring **5** bijou, jewel **6** bangle, bauble, gewgaw, trifle **7** bibelot **8** gimcrack, intrigue, ornament **10** knickknack

trinkle: **4** drip, flow **7** trickle

trio: **9** threesome

trip: run **4** gait, halt, hike, pawl, skip, slip, spin, tour **5** brood, caper, catch, danse, error, flock, jaunt, lapse, tread, wedge **6** cruise, falter, voyage **7** blunder, failure, journey, misstep, mistake, release, stumble **8** obstruct **9** excursion **10** expedition

trip-hammer: *operator:* **6** tilter

tripe: **5** trash **7** rubbish

triple: **5** trine **6** treble **9** threefold

triplet: **4** trin, trio

tripletail: **9** berrugate, spadefish

triplicate: **6** treble, triple **9** threefold

tripod: cat **5** easel, stand **6** trivet

Tripoli ruler: dey

trippet: cam

tripping: **5** quick **6** nimble **7** walking **8** trippant

triptych: *wing:* **5** volet

trismus: **7** lockjaw, tetanus

Tristan: *wife:* **5** Isolt **6** Iseult, Isolde
villain: **5** Melot

triste: sad **4** dull **6** dismal **9** sorrowful **10** depressing, melancholy

trite: **4** worn **5** banal, corny, stale, vapid **6** common, jejune **7** bromide, trivial **9** hackneyed **10** threadbare, unoriginal **11** commonplace, stereotyped **12** conventional **13** platitudinous

triton: eft **4** newt **7** demigod **10** salamander

triturate: rub **5** crush, grind **6** bruise **9** comminute, pulverize

triumph: win **4** gain **5** exult, glory **6** defeat, hurrah **7** conquer, prevail, rejoice, success, victory **8** flourish **11** achievement, celebration

triumvirate: *first:* **6** Caesar, Pompey **7** Crassus
second: **6** Antony **7** Lepidus **8** Octavius

trivet: **5** stand **6** tripod **7** support

trivial: **5** banal, fluff, inane, petty, small, trite **6** common, paltry, slight **7** nominal, piperly **8** doggerel, ordinary, trifling **9** frivolous **11** unimportant **13** insignificant **14** inconsiderable

trocar: **6** stylet **7** trochar

troche: **6** pastil, rotula, tablet **7** lozenge, pastile **8** pastille

trochilus: **7** warbler **9** goldcrest **11** hummingbird

trod: **4** path, walk **5** trace, track, tread **8** footpath, footstep

Trojan: **9** Dardanian

king: **5** Priam

prince: **5** Eneas, Paris **6** Aeneas, Hector

serpent victim: **7** Laocoon

soothsayer: **7** Helenus

War cause: **5** Helen

war hero: **5** Ajaix, Eneas **6** Aeneas, Agenor, Hector **9** Palamedes

Trojan horse: *builder:* **5** Epeus

troll: run, wag **4** bowl, fish, lure, reel, roll, sing, song, turn **5** angle, catch, chant, dwarf, giant, gnome, round, spoon **6** trolly **7** revolve, trolley, trollop **9** circulate

trolley: car **4** cart, tram **5** block **6** barrow, sledge **8** handcart **9** streetcar

trollop: **4** hang **5** slump **6** dangle, slouch **8** slattern **10** bedraggled, prostitute

trombone: **7** sackbut

tronk: **4** jail **6** lockup, prison

troop: lot **4** army, band, ging, line, rout, wave **5** crowd, group **6** number, troupe **7** battery, cavalry, company, echelon, militia, phalanx **8** quantity, soldiers **9** associate, gathering **10** congregate

Anglo-Indian: **6** risala **7** ressala, risalah

arrangement: **7** echelon

assembling: **6** muster

concealed: **6** ambush

German: **6** Panzer

raise: **4** levy **5** draft **9** conscript

sellers to: **6** sutler **10** vivandiere

trooper: **6** hussar **7** soldier **9** policeman, troopship **10** cavalryman

trope: **8** metaphor

trophy: cup **4** palm **5** prize **6** laurel, reward **7** memento **8** memorial, ornament

tropic: **5** limit **8** boundary

animal: **4** alco, eyra **5** agama, coati, potto **6** agouti, iguana **7** peccary

bird: ani **4** tody **5** jalap **7** jacamar

fish: **4** toro **6** salema **7** squetee

fruit: **4** date **5** guava, mango, papaw **6** banana, papaya **8** tamarind

genus of herb: **4** evea, sida **5** tacca, urena **8** laportea

plant: dal **4** aloe, arum, sida, taro **5** agave **6** alacad **7** cowhage, lantana **8** gardenia

plant genus: **5** rhoeo **6** cannas **7** bomarea, geonoma, hamelia

tree: ebo **4** coco, dali, eboe, etua, mabi, palm **5** acapu, amate, artar, assai, balsa, banak, bongo, cacao, dalli, guava, icica,

nepal, nitta, njave, papaw, seron, zorro **6** baboen, bacury, banana, barbas, cazaba, chupon, dagame, espave, mammee, pawpaw, sapota **7** anubing, gateado, guacimo **8** amarillo, mangrove, sweetsop, tamarind **9** huamuchli, quebracho, sapodilla, sapotilha, sapotilla **10** frangipane, frangipani, manchineel **11** guachipilin

trot: jog, run, tot **4** gait **5** child, hurry **6** hasten **7** toddler **11** translation

troth: **5** certy, faith **6** certie, pledge **8** fidelity **9** betrothal

trottoir: **8** footpath, pavement, sidewalk

trotty: **5** brisk **6** lively

trotyl: TNT **14** trinitrotoluol **15** trinitrotoluene

troubadour, troubador: **4** poet **6** singer **8** minstrel, musician

trouble: ado, ail, irk, vex, woe **4** busy, care, cark, fike, fuss, harm, pain, sore, stir **5** anger, annoy, grief, labor, tease, worry **6** bother, burble, caddle, cumber, dither, effort, harass, impair, matter, mishap, molest, pester, plague, pother, sorrow, unrest **7** afflict, agitate, anxiety, chagrin, concern, disease, disturb, embroil, illness, perturb, travail **8** aggrieve, calamity, disorder, disquiet, distress, exertion **9** adversity, incommode, interfere **10** difficulty, disarrange, discomfort, discommode, misfortune, perplexity, uneasiness **11** displeasure, encumbrance **13** inconvenience

troubled: **6** queasy **12** heart-scalded

troublemaker: **6** gossip **8** agitator

troublesome: **5** pesky **8** fashious **9** pestilent, turbulent, wearisome **10** burdensome, oppressive

troublous: **6** stormy, turbid **7** unquiet **8** restless **9** unsettled

trough: bin **4** boat, bosh, bowl, dale, tank, tomb **5** bakie, basin, canoe, chute **6** buddle, coffin, dugout, gutter, sluice **7** channel, conduit

trounce: sue **4** beat, flog **5** scold, tramp **6** cudgel, defeat, indict, punish, ramble, thrash **7** censure, journey

troupe: **4** band **5** group **7** company **9** cuadrilla(Sp.)

trouper: **5** actor

troupial: **6** oriole **7** cacique, cowbird **9** blackbird **10** meadowlark

trousers: **5** pants **6** skilts, slacks **8** breeches, culottes **9** pantalets, shintiyan **10** pantaloons

foreign: **7** shalwar **9** shaksheer, shulwaurs **10** calzoneras(Sp.)

trout: **4** char, peal **5** brook, sewen **6** finnac, grilse **7** gilaroo, rainbow **8** finnacle **9** steelhead **10** squeteague

lake: **9** namaycush

troutlet: **10** fingerling

trovatore: **10** troubadour

trove: **9** discovery

trow: 4 boat, hope 5 faith, fancy, smack, think, troll, trust 6 belief, expect 7 believe, imagine, suppose 9 catamaran

trowing: 5 creed 6 belief 7 opinion

Troy (see also **Trojan**): 5 Iliac, Ilian, Ilion, Ilium, Troas, Troad 8 Teucrian
defender: 6 Aeneas
founder: 4 Ilus, Tros
king: 5 Priam
mountain: Ida
pert. to: 5 Iliac 6 Trojan

troy weight: 5 grain, ounce, pound 11 pennyweight

truant: 4 idle 5 stray 6 beggar, errant 7 shirker, vagrant 8 vagabond, wanderer 9 shiftless
play: 5 miche

truce: 5 pause, treve(F.) 7 respite 9 armistice, cessation 12 intermission

truck: van 4 deal, dray 5 lorry, trade, trash 6 barrow, barter, camion, peddle, potter 7 bargain, rubbish, traffic, trundle 8 business, exchange, handcart 9 negotiate, transport, vegetable 10 handbarrow 11 association, intercourse

truckle: 4 fawn 5 toady, wheel 6 caster, cheese, cringe, submit 7 trundle

truckling: 7 servile

truculent: 4 mean, rude 5 cruel, harsh 6 fierce, savage 8 ruthless, scathing 9 barbarous, ferocious 11 destructive

trudge: pad 4 plod, walk 5 stoge, tramp 6 trapes 7 traipse

true: 4 just, leal(Sc.), pure, real, vera(L.), vrai(F.) 5 align, aline, exact, level, loyal, plumb, right, valid 6 actual, adjust, honest, lawful, proper, steady 7 certain, correct, devoted, factual, genuine, germane, precise, sincere, staunch, upright 8 accurate, bonafide, constant, faithful, reliable, unerring, virtuous 9 authentic, steadfast, truepenny, unfeigned, veracious, veritable 10 legitimate 11 unfaltering

truelove: 10 sweetheart

trueness: 7 reality 8 veracity 9 exactness 11 genuineness 12 faithfulness

truffle: 5 tuber 8 earthnut

trug: 4 caul, cawl, pail, tray 5 wench 6 basket, trough 7 measure 10 prostitute

truism: 5 axiom

trull: 4 dell, girl, lass 5 demon, fiend, giant, wench 6 blowze, callet 7 trollop 8 strumpet 10 prostitute

truly: 4 iwis 5 atweel, dinkum, indeed, verily 13 realistically

trump: cap, pam 4 beat, ruff 5 outdo, pedro 7 nonplus, surpass, trumpet 8 jew's-harp

trumpery: 5 fraud, showy, trash, weeds 6 deceit, paltry 7 rubbish 8 gimcrack, nonsense, trickery 9 worthless

trumpet: 4 horn 5 blare 6 bucina(Lat.), funnel, kerana, summon 7 begonia, clarion, publish 8 denounce, proclaim

blare: 6 sennet 7 fanfare, tantara
stage direction: 6 sennet

trumpet creeper: 5 plant 6 tecoma

trumpeter: 4 bird, swan 6 herald, pigeon, tooter 7 yakamik

truncate: cut, lop 6 lessen 7 shorten

truncheon: 4 club, stem 5 baton, staff 6 cudgel 8 fragment, splinter

trundle: bed 4 bowl, cart, hoop, roll 5 truck, twirl, wheel, whirl 6 barrow, caster, pinion, rotate 7 revolve, trindle 11 wheelbarrow

trundler: 6 bowler

trunk: box 4 body, bole, pipe, stem, tank, tube 5 chest, snout, stock, torso 6 caudex, coffer, corpse, thorax 7 baggage 9 proboscis

trunkless: 8 bodiless

truss: tie, wap 4 bind, furl, gird, hang, lade, pack 6 bundle, fasten 7 arrange, bracket, enclose, package, support, tighten 10 strengthen

trust: 4 affy, care, duty, hope, task 5 faith 6 belief, cartel, charge, credit, depend, merger 7 believe, confide, consign, custody, keeping, loyalty 8 affiance, commenda, credence, reliance, security 9 assurance, coalition, fiduciary, syndicate 10 commission, confidence 11 combination

trustee: 6 bailee 7 sindico 8 director, guardian 9 garnishee 13 administrator

trustful: 5 liege 7 devoted 9 confiding 13 unquestioning

trustless: 10 unreliable 11 distrustful, treacherous

trustworthy: 4 safe 5 siker, solid, tried 6 honest, sicker 7 certain 8 credible, fiducial, reliable 9 authentic, confiding 10 dependable 12 confidential

trusty: 8 faithful, trustful 9 confiding

truth: 4 fact 5 sooth, troth 6 certes, verity 7 honesty, loyalty 8 accuracy, fidelity, veracity 9 agreement, constancy, integrity, principle, sincerity 11 correctness, genuineness, uprightness 12 faithfulness 14 verisimilitude
goddess: 4 Maat
personification of: Una
seeming: 14 verisimilitude
self-evident: 5 axiom 6 truism

truthful: 6 honest 7 correct 9 veracious, veridical

try: do 4 cull, sift, test 5 annoy, assay, essay, ettle(Sc.), found, prove, trial 6 choose, effort, hansel, harass, purify, refine, render, sample, screen, select, strain, strive 7 adjudge, afflict, approve, attempt, contest, extract, handsel, subject, torment, venture 8 audition, endeavor, irritate, separate, struggle 9 ascertain, undertake 10 experience, experiment 11 demonstrate, investigate

trying: 6 severe 7 irksome, painful 8 annoying 12 exasperating

tryst: **4** fair **5** visit **6** market **7** bespeak, meeting **9** agreement, gathering **10** engagement, rendezvous **11** appointment, assignation

tsamba: **5** flour **6** barley

tsar: **4** czar, Ivan, tzar **5** Peter **6** despot **8** autocrat

tsine: **6** wild ox **7** banteng

tuatara, tuatera: **6** lizard **16** rhynchocephalian

tub (see also **barrel, cistern, vat, vessel**): box, kid, soe, vat **4** bath, boat, cask, cool, ship, tram **5** barge, bathe, bowie(Sc.), eshin, keeve, skeel **6** bucket, pulpit, vessel **7** bathtub, cistern, tubfish **9** container

wooden: soe

tuba: **7** helicon

tubal: **8** pipelike

Tubal's father: **7** Japheth

Tubalcain's father: **6** Lamech

tubbal: **7** mattock

tubber: **6** cooper, pickax

tube: **4** duct, hose, lull, pipe **5** chute, diode **6** cannon, siphon, tremie, triode, tunnel **7** cannula, conduit, fistula, pipette, tetrode **8** adjutage, bombilla(Sp.), cylinder **9** telescope

remove by: **6** siphon, syphon

system of: **6** pipage

tuber: oca, yam **4** beet, bulb, clog, eddo, root, taro **5** jalap, salep **6** potato **8** swelling **9** tubercule **10** tuberosity **12** protuberance

tubercle: **6** nodule **10** prominence

Tubuai island: **4** Rapa

tubular: **4** pipy **5** round **11** cylindrical

tuck: eat, jam, nip **4** cram, draw, fold, hang, poke **5** cramp, feast, pinch, press, scold, stuff, sword **6** energy, gather, hamper, rapier, upraid **7** consume, shorten, tighten **9** sweetmeat

tucked up: **7** cramped **8** hampered **9** exhausted

tucker: bib **4** food, meal, tire **5** board, weary **6** ration **7** fatigue **10** chemisette

Tudesque: **6** German

Tuesday: **5** mardi(F.)

god of: Tiu, Tyr

Shrove: **9** Mardi Gras

tufa: **5** trass

tufan: **5** storm

tuft: **4** beat, coma, disk **5** beard, bunch, clump, crest **6** button, comose, dollop, goatee, pompon, tassel **7** cluster, fetlock, scopula **8** imperial

pert. to: **5** comal

tuft-hunter: **4** snob

tug: lug, tit, tow **4** drag, draw, haul, maul, pull, rope, toil, yank **5** chain, exert, hitch, labor, strap, trace **6** drudge, effort, strain, strife, strive, tussle **7** contend, contest, tugboat, wrestle **8** struggle **11** counterpull

tuition: **4** care **5** watch **6** charge **7** cus-

tody **8** teaching **10** protection **11** instruction **12** guardianship

tule: **7** bulrush

tumble: **4** fall, leap, roll, trip, veer **5** pitch, slope, spill, whirl **6** rumple, spring, tousle **7** stumble **8** collapse, dishevel, disorder **9** confusion, overthrow **10** disarrange, handspring, somersault **11** precipitate

down: **10** dilapidate

tumbler: dog **4** cart, pupa **5** glass **6** dunker, pigeon, roller, vessel **7** acrobat, gymnast, tippler, tumbrel

tumbrel, tumbril: **4** cart **5** wagon **8** dumpcart

tumefy: **4** puff **5** swell **7** inflate

tumid: **6** turgid **7** bloated, bulging, fustian, pompous, swollen, teeming **8** bursting, enlarged, inflated **9** bombastic, distended, plethoric **11** protuberant

tumor: wen **4** beal, wart **5** edema, gumma **6** ambury, anbury, glioma, lipoma **7** bombast **8** blastoma, ganglion, hepatoma, neoplasm, papiloma, sarocele, swelling **10** distending **12** adamantinoma, protuberance

operation: **8** ancotomy

tumorous: **5** tumid **7** swollen **8** inflated **9** bombastic

tump: **4** heap **5** clump **7** hillock, tumulus

tumult: din, mob **4** fray, fuss, riot **5** babel, brawl, broil, noise **6** affray, babble, bedlam, bustle, dirdum(Sc.), émeute, hubbub, uproar **7** bluster, bobbery, ferment, tempest, turmoil **8** disorder, outbreak, outburst, uprising **9** agitation, commotion, confusion, distemper, hurlement **10** convulsion, excitement, turbulence **11** disturbance

tumultuous: **4** high, wild **5** rough **6** stormy **7** furious, violent **10** boisterous, hurly-burly

tumulus: **4** tump **5** mound **6** barrow **7** hillock

tun: cup, jar, tub, vat **4** cask **5** drink **6** guzzle, vessel **7** chimney

tune: air, key, pat **4** lilt, port, song, tone **5** dirge, drant, sound **6** choral, draunt, melody, string **7** chorale, concord, harmony, sonance **8** anglaise **9** agreement **10** adjustment

out: **6** detune

tuneful: **7** musical, tunable **9** melodious **10** concordant, euphonious, harmonious

tungsten ore: cal

tunic: **4** coat, jama, jupe, robe, toga **5** acton, frock, gippo, jamah **6** kirtle **8** colobium **10** cote-hardie, sticharion **11** houppelande

tunicate: **4** salp **5** salpa **12** marine animal

Tunisia: *cape:* bon

cities: **4** Sfax, Susa **5** Gabes, Gafsa, Tunis **6** Mateur, Nabeul **7** Bizerte **8** Tebourba, Zaghouan **9** Grombalia **10** Ferryville

gulf: **5** Gabes, Tunis **8** Hammamet

island: **6** Djerba

measure: saa, sah **4** saah **5** cafiz, whiba **6**
mettar **9** millerole

river: **8** Medjerda

ruler:. bey, dey

weight: saa **4** rotl **5** artal, artel, ratel, uckia
6 kantar

tunk: rap **5** thump

tunnel: net **4** adit, bore, flue, tube **6** burrow, funnel **10** smokestack

long: **5** Otira **6** Hoosac, Severn, Spiral **7**
Arlberg, Detroit, Gothard, Holland, Lin-
coln, Mont D'Or, St. Clair, Simplon **8**
Gunnison **9** Baltimore, Cascade Mt.,
Connaught, Gallitzin, Montcenis, Mt.
Roberts **10** Bitterroot, Cumberland,
Lotschberg, St. Gotthard, Wasserfluh **11**
Busk-Ivanhoe, Loetschberg, Trans-Andine

tunny: **4** tuna **8** albacore

tup: ram **5** cover, sheep **6** mallet **7** cuckold

tur: pea **4** goat

turb: **5** clump, crowd

turban: **6** fillet **9** headdress

turbid: **4** dark, dull **5** dense, gumly(Sc.),
muddy, roily, thick **6** cloudy, grumly(Sc.),
impure **7** muddled **8** confused, polluted **9**
perplexed

render: **4** roil

turbine wheel: **5** rotor

turbot: **5** brill **8** flatfish

turbulence: **4** fury **6** tumult, uproar **7**
bluster, ferment, rioting **8** disorder **9**
agitation, commotion **11** disturbance

turbulent: **4** wild **5** rough **6** stormy, unruly **7** furious, violent **9** clamorous **10**
boisterous, tumultuous **11** tempestuous

turf: sod **4** flag, peat, vell **5** divot, grass,
sward

turgid: **5** tumid **7** bloated, pompous,
swollen, turgent **8** inflated, swelling **9**
bombastic, distended, flatulent, grandiose
12 magniloquent **13** grandiloquent

Turk: aga **5** Tatar **7** Osmanli, Ottoman **9**
Kizilbash

turkey: tom **5** poult **7** bustard, failure,
gobbler

buzzard: **7** vulture

Turkey: *agent:* **6** Kehaya

army corps: **4** ordu **8** seraglio

army regiment: **4** alai

bath: **6** hamman

boat: **4** sail **6** mahone

cabinet: **5** divan

camp: **7** palanka

capital: **6** Ankara

carpet: **6** Smyrna

cavalryman: **5** spahi **6** spahee

chief (see also *ruler* below)*:* aga **6** kehaya
7 chambul

city: bir **4** Homs, Sert **5** Adana, Brusa,
Izmir, Konya, Siirt, Sivas **6** Aintab, An-
kara, Edessa, Edirne, Elaziz, Marash,
Samsun, Smyrna **7** Broussa, Erzurum,
Kayseri, Scutari, Skutari, Uskudar **8**
Istanbul, Stamboul **9** Eskisehir **10** Ad-

rianople, Diyarbekir **14** Afyonkarahisar,
Constantinople

commander: **4** amir, emir **5** ameer, emeer,
pacha, pasha **6** sirdar **9** seraskier

council: **5** divan, diwan

court: **5** porte

decree: **5** irade **11** hatti-sherif **12** hatti-
humaiun, hatti-humayum

deputy: **6** kahaya

dignitary: **5** pasha

district: **4** Pera **7** Beyoglu, Cilicia

division: **4** caza **5** adana **6** eyalet **7** vilayet **8** villayet

drink: **5** airan

dynasty: **6** seljuk

empire: **7** Ottoman

fig: **5** eleme, elemi

flag: **4** alem, toug **9** horsetail

general: **5** kamal

gulf: Cos

hat: fez **6** calpac

infidel: **6** giaour

inn: **6** imaret **7** cafenet

javelin: **5** jerid **6** jeered

judge: **4** cadi

liquor: **4** raki **5** rakee **6** mastic

man-of-war: **6** carvel **7** caravel **9** caravelle

measures: dra, oka, oke, pic, pik **4** alma,
draa, hatt, khat, kile, zira **5** almud, berri,
donum, kileh, zirai **6** almude, arshin,
chinik, djerib, fortin, halebi, parmak **7**
arsheen, arshine, nocktat, parmack **9**
pik halebi

military camp: **4** ordu

military rank: **6** chiaus **7** chaoush **8** bim-
bashi, binbashi

money: **4** lira, lire, para **5** akcha, attun,
asper, pound, rebia **6** akcheh, sequin, zequin **7** altilik, beshlik, chequin, chiquin,
pataque, piaster **8** medjidie, zecchino **9**
medjidieh

mosque: **4** jami

mountain: **6** Ararat

musical instrument: **5** canum, kanum **7**
kussier

musket: **8** tophaike

oak: **6** cerris

official: **4** amir, emir **5** ameer, emeer **6**
vizier **7** osmanli, subashi **8** subbassa

palace: **5** serai

policeman: **7** zaptiah, zaptieh

prayer rug: **5** kulah, melas, meles

province: **4** Sert **5** Siirt **6** Angora, Eyalet

religious war: **11** crescentade

reservist: **5** redif

river: **5** Mesta, Sarus **6** Seihun, Seyhan

ruler: bey, dey **4** khan **5** mudir **6** sultan **7**
chambul **9** president

saber: **6** obolus

sailor: **8** galionji **9** galiongee

seaport: **4** Enos

slave: **8** mameluke

soldier: **6** nizami **8** janizary **9** janissary
11 bashi-bazouk

statue: **8** tanzimat
storage place: **5** ambar
sultan: Ali **5** Ahmed, calif, Selim **6** caliph **7** Ilderim, Saladin
sword: **7** yatagan **8** yataghan
tambourine: **5** daira
tax: **5** vergi **6** caphar, avania
title: ali **4** amir, baba **5** ameer, basha **6** bashaw **7** effendi
tobacco: **7** chibouk, Latakia **9** chibouque
treasurer: **8** deftedar
veil: **7** yashmac, yashmak **8** maharmah
weight: oka, oke **4** dram, kile, rotl **5** artal, artel, cequi, cheke, kerat, kileh, maund, obolu, ratel **6** batman, dirhem, kantar, miskal **7** drachma, quintal, yusdrum
wheat: **6** bulgur
woman's clothing: **6** jelick **8** charshaf
turkey buzzard: **4** aura **9** gallinazo
Turkish: **7** Osmanli
Turkistan: *cities:* **6** Kokand **7** Andijan **9** Samarkand
highland: **6** Pamirs
land: **5** takyr
moslem: **5** salar
mountain: **4** Alai
peoples: **4** Sart **5** Tatar, Uigur, Usbeg, Usbek, Uzbeg, Yakut **6** Tartan
regiment: **4** alai
river: Ili
salt lake: **4** Shov
sea: **4** Aral
Turkmen: *capital:* **9** Ashkhabad
carpet: **5** Tekke, Yomud **6** Afghan **7** Bokhara
tribe: **5** Ersar **7** Viddhal
turmoil: ado, din **4** hurl, toil, toss **5** hurly, labor, touse, upset, worry **6** harass, tumult, unrest, uproar, welter **7** ferment, quarrel, tempest, trouble **8** disquiet, drudgery **9** agitation, commotion, confusion **10** turbulence **11** disturbance **12** perturbation
turn: bow, lap, rev **4** airt, bend, bent, bout, cant, char, head, plow, roll, slew, slue, spin, veer, vert **5** alter, avert, cramp, crook, curve, hinge, pivot, quirk, screw, tarve, wheel, whirl, whorl **6** bought, change, direct, divert, gyrate, invert, ponder, rotate, swerve, swivel, wimple(Sc.), zigzag **7** convert, derange, ferment, meander, rebound, reverse, revolve **8** exchange, nauseate, persuade **9** cinclamen, influence, pirouette, transform, translate **11** disposition **12** metamorphose
about: **9** alternate
inward: **9** introvert
left: haw **4** port, wynd, wyne
outward: **5** evert, splay **8** extrorse **9** extrovert
right: gee **9** starboard
sour: **5** blink **8** acescent
to one side: **4** awry, skew
turn away: shy **5** avert, avoid, deter,

evade, repel, shunt **6** depart, divert **7** decline, deflect, deviate, dismiss, diverge, swerve
turn back: **4** fold **5** repel **6** return, revert **7** evolute, retrace **9** inversion **10** retroverse
turn down: **4** fold, veto **6** invert, refuse, reject **7** decline
turn off: **4** hang **5** marry, shunt **6** detour, divert **7** con..ign, deflect, dismiss, putrefy **9** discharge
turn out: **4** oust, trig **5** array, evert, expel, prove **6** outfit, output, siding **7** abandon, dismiss, produce, reverse, striker **8** equipage **9** discharge, equipment, eventuate
turn over: **4** keel **5** spill, upset **6** invert, ponder, reform **7** evolute **8** delegate, overturn, transfer **10** relinquish
turn up: **6** appear, arrive
turncoat: **8** apostate, renegade **10** changeling
turned up: **9** retrousse
turner: **7** gymnast, tumbler
turning (see also **turn** above): **6** rotary **7** flexion, winding **8** flection, rotative, twisting **10** revolution **11** sinistrorse, vertiginous
turning point: **6** crisis **8** decision, landmark
turnip: **4** neep(Sc.) **5** watch **8** rutabaga **9** blockhead
turnkey: **5** screw **6** jailer, warder
turnover: **4** tart
turnpike: **7** highway **8** tollgate
gatekeeper: **7** pikeman
turnstile: **5** stile
turpentine: **4** thus **5** resin, rosin **9** oleoresin
residue: **5** resin, rosin
turpitude: **6** fedity **8** baseness, vileness **9** depravity
turquoise: **10** chalchuite
turret: **5** tower **8** gunhouse
turse: **4** load, pack **6** bundle
turtle: **5** arrau, caret, torup **6** cooter, emydea, jurara **7** snapper **8** chelonia, emydidae, matamata, shagtail, terrapin, tortoise **10** loggerhead, thalassian **11** leatherback
genus of: **4** emys **7** caretta, testudo **9** chelodina
part: **7** calipee
shell: **8** carapace
Tuscany: *city:* **4** Pisa
commune: **5** Greve
island: **4** Elba
river: **4** Arno
tusk: **4** fang **5** tooth **9** scrivello
tusker: **8** elephant
tussis: **5** cough
tussle: **5** fight **6** tousel, tousle **7** contend, contest, scuffle, wrestle **8** struggle **9** scrimmage
tussock: **4** tuft **5** bunch, clump **7** hassock

tut: 4 hush 6 rebuke

tutelage: 7 nurture 8 teaching 9 tutorship 11 instruction 12 guardianship

tutelar: 8 guardian

tutelary: 10 protecting
  gods: 5 Lares

tutor: 5 coach, mentor, school 7 grinder, peda-gog, teacher 8 guardian, instruct 9 peda-gogue, preceptor 10 discipline

tutta: all 5 whole

twaddle: rot 4 bunk 5 haver, prate 6 bab-ble, drivel, footle, gabble 8 nonsense

twangy: 5 nasal

tweak: 4 pull 5 pinch, twist 6 twitch

tweet: 4 peep 5 chirp 7 chirrup

tweezers: 7 pincers 9 merganser

twenty: 5 corge, kappa, score

twenty-faced: 11 icosahedral

twice: bis(L.) 6 doubly

twig: 4 beat, mode, pull 5 birch, bough, scion, shoot, spray, sprig, style, tweak, withe 6 branch, fescue, notice, sallow, switch, twitch, wattle 7 fashion, observe 8 perceive 10 comprehend, understand
  bundle: 5 fagot 6 barsom

twiggy: 4 thin 6 slight 7 slender 8 deli-cate

twilight: 4 dusk 5 gloam 6 dimmet 8 gloaming, glooming 9 cocklight 10 cre-puscule
  of the Gods: 8 Ragnarok 17 Goetterdaem-merung
  pert. to: 11 crepuscular

twill: rib 5 quill, weave

twin: two 4 dual, pair, part 5 gemel, sever, twain 6 couple, double, sunder 7 twofold 8 didymous 11 counterpart
  crystal: 5 macle
  one: 5 gemel
  stars: 6 Castor, gemini, Pollux

twinge: 4 ache, pain, pang 5 pinch, qualm, tweak 6 twitch

twine: ran 4 coil, turn, vine, warp, wind, wrap 5 braid, snarl, twist 6 encurl, en-fold, enlace, infold, string, tangle, thread 7 anamite, embrace, entwine, wreathe 8 encircle 9 interlace 10 intertwine, inter-weave 11 convolution, intermingle

twink: 4 wink 6 punish, thrash 7 twinkle 9 chaffinch

twinkle: 4 wink 5 blink, flash, gleam, shine 7 flicker, flutter, glimmer, glitter, sparkle 11 scintillate

twinkler: 4 star 8 sparkler

twinkling: 4 wink 5 flash, gleam, trice 6 moment 7 instant 13 scintillation

twire: 4 gaze, look, peer 5 gleam 6 glance 7 twinkle

twirl: 4 coil, curl, move, spin, turn 5 querl, twist, whirl 6 gyrate 7 revolve, twizzle 8 flourish, rotation 11 convolution

twist: 4 bend, coil, cord, curl, hang, hurl, silk, skew, slew, slue, spin, tirl(Sc.), turn,
wind, yarn 5 crink, crook, curve, gnarl, hinge, quirk, reeve, screw, snarl, swirl, tweak, twine, twirl, unite, wrest, wring 6 branch, enlace, hankle, rotate, spiral, squirm, thread, torque, wrench, writhe 7 confuse, contort, distort, entwine, flexure, meander, perplex, pervert, revolve, scat-ter, tendril, torment, torsion, torture, twizzle, wreathe 8 appetite, encircle, en-tangle, separate 9 constrain, deviation, insinuate 10 intertwine, interweave 11 convolution, peculiarity

twisted: cam, wry 6 warped 7 complex, tortile

twister: 4 roll, turn 7 cruller, cyclone, mallard, tornado 8 doughnut 10 somer-sault, waterspout

twistical: sly 7 evasive 11 underhanded

twistle: 5 twist 6 wrench

twisty (see also **twist** above): 6 tricky 7 bending, evasive, winding 9 dishonest

twit: guy 4 gibe 5 blame, chirp, taunt, tease 7 upbraid 8 reproach, ridicule

twitch: nip, tic, tie, tug 4 draw, jerk, pick, pull, skid, yank 5 pluck, start, thong, tweak 6 fasten, snatch 9 vellicate 11 contraction

twitter: 5 chirp, shake 6 giggle, titter 7 chatter, chitter, flutter, tremble 9 agita-tion

twizzle: 5 twirl

two: twa(Sc.) 4 beta(Gr.), both, duet, dyad, pair 5 twain, twins 6 couple 7 twosome
  chambered: 9 bicameral
  edged: 9 ancipital
  headed: 11 dicephalous
  metrical feet: 6 dipody
  months: 8 bi-mester
  parts: 6 bident 9 bifurcate 11 dichoto-mous
  pert. to: 4 dual 6 dyadic
  prefix: bi, di 5 dioxy
  winged: 7 bialate 8 dipteral 9 dipterous

two-bit: 5 cheap

two-faced: 5 false 9 deceitful 11 treach-erous 12 hypocritical
  god: 5 Janus

two-fisted: 6 virile 8 vigorous

two-foot: 5 biped 7 bipedal

two-pronged: 6 bident

two-sided: 9 bilateral 12 hypocritical

two-spot: 5 deuce

two-time: 5 cheat 7 deceive

two-tone: 7 bicolor

twofold: 4 dual 5 duple 6 bifold, binary, double, duplex 9 bifarious, duplicate

twopenny: ale 4 mean 5 cheap

tycoon: 7 magnate 9 financier 13 in-dustrialist

tyddyn: 4 farm 9 homestead

tydie: 4 bird, wren 8 titmouse

tye: 4 case, rope, wash 5 chain, close 6 common 7 pasture 9 enclosure

tyee: 5 chief

tyke, tike: cur, dog **5** child **6** shaver **7** bumpkin

tylopod: 5 camel

tympan: 4 drum **8** membrane

tympanum: 6 tympan **7** eardrum

tympany: 7 bombast, conceit **9** inflation **10** distention, turgidness

Tyndareus' wife: 4 Leda

typal: 8 symbolic

type: pi; gem **4** font, form, kern, kind, mark, norm, pica, sign, slug, sort **5** agate, class, doric, elite, genre, group, ideal, ionic, metal, model, order, pearl, roman, stamp, token **6** emblem, italic, minion, nature, symbol **7** brevier, English, example, impress, paragon, pattern, species **8** antetype, boldface, classify **9** archetype, bourgeois, character, condensed, nonpareil **11** Baskerville

block: **4** quad **7** quadrat

line: **4** slug

measure: em, en

mixed: pi

stroke: **5** serif

tray: **6** galley

typeset: 7 compose

typesetter: 8 linotype, monotype **10** compositor

typewriter part: key **6** platen, spacer **9** tabulator

typhoon: 4 wind **5** storm **7** cyclone

typical: 5 typal **6** normal **7** regular **9** schematic **10** emblematic, figurative **13** prefigurative **14** characteristic, representative

typify: 6 embody **9** prefigure, represent, symbolize

typographer: 7 printer

tyrannical: 5 cruel, harsh **6** lordly, unjust **7** slavish **8** despotic **9** arbitrary, imperious **10** oppressive **11** domineering

tyrannosaurus: 8 dinosaur

tyrannous: 5 cruel, harsh **6** severe, unjust **8** despotic **10** tyrannical

tyranny: 5 rigor **8** severity **9** despotism, harshness

tyrant: 4 czar, Ivan, Nero, tsar, tzar **6** despot **7** monarch, usurper **8** martinet **9** oppressor

murder: **11** tyrannicide

Tyre: *king:* **5** Belus, Hiram

noble: **7** Acerbas

prince: **8** Pericles

princess: **4** Dido

tyro: 4 tiro **5** pupil **6** novice **7** amateur **8** beginner, neophyte **9** commencer **10** apprentice **11** abecedarian

tzar, czar, tsar: 4 king **5** ruler **6** tyrant

tzigane: 5 gypsy

U

U-boat: sub **9** submarine
uang: **6** beetle
ubiety: **8** location, position, relation **9** whereness
ubiquitous: **10** everywhere **11** omnipresent
ubiquity: **12** omnipresence
Uganda: *capital:* **7** Entebbe
cattle: **6** ankoli
people: **7** Bunyoro
ughten: **4** dawn. dusk **7** evening, morning **8** twilight
ugly: bad **4** vile **5** awful, cross, snivy, toady **6** cranky, homely, snivey **7** crabbed, hideous, ominous **8** grewsome, gruesome, horrible, terrible, unlovely **9** dangerous, fractious, frightful, graceless, loathsome, offensive, repulsive, unsightly **10** ill-favored, ill-natured, unpleasant **11** ill-tempered, quarrelsome, threatening **12** cross-grained, disagreeable **13** objectionable
Ugrian: **4** Avar
ugsome: **6** horrid **9** abhorrent, frightful, loathsome
uhlan: **6** lancer **7** soldier **10** cavalryman
uitlander: **9** foreigner, outlander
ukase: **5** edict, order **6** decree **7** command **12** proclamation
Ukraine: *assembly:* **4** rada
coin: **6** grivna **7** schagiv
seaport: **6** Odessa
ulcer: **4** noma, sore **7** egilops **8** aegilops, fossette **9** cacoethes
ulceration: **8** helcosis
ule: **6** caucho
uliginous: wet **4** oozy **5** moist, muddy **6** swampy
ullage: **7** wantage **8** shortage **10** deficiency
ulna: **4** bone **7** cubitus
end of: **5** ancon
ulster: **4** coat **8** overcoat
ulterior: **5** later **6** future **7** further, remoter **10** subsequent, succeeding **11** undisclosed
ultimate: end **4** dire, last **5** final, telos(Gr.) **6** remote **7** extreme, maximum, primary **8** eventful, eventual, farthest **9** elemental **10** conclusive **11** fundamental
ultra: **6** beyond **7** extreme, forward, radical **9** excessive, extremist, fanatical **11** extravagant **14** uncompromising
ulu: **5** knife

ululate: bay **4** hoot, howl, wail, yelp **6** lament **7** screech
Ulysses: *antagonist:* **4** Irus
dog: **5** Argos
enchantress of: **5** Circe
enemy: **8** Poseidon
father: **7** Laertes
plant: **4** moly
son: **9** Telegonus **10** Telemachus
wife: **8** Penelope
umber: **5** brown, shade, visor **6** darken, shadow **7** protect, umbrere **8** grayling, umbrette
umbles: **7** numbles **8** entrails
umbra: **4** fish **5** ghost, shade **6** shadow **7** phantom, vestige
umbrage: **5** cloak, doubt, pique, shade, trace **6** offend, shadow **7** foliage, offense, pretext, shelter **8** disfavor, disgrace, disguise **9** disesteem, semblance, suspicion **10** overshadow, protection, resentment **11** displeasure
umbrageous: **5** shady **6** shaded
umbrella: **4** gamp **5** blind, guard, shade **6** brolly, chatta, payong, pileus, screen **7** parasol, protect, shelter **8** disguise **11** bumber-shoot
umbrette: **9** hammerkop
Umbrian river: **6** Tevere
umbrous: **5** shady
umiak: **4** boat
umpire: ump **5** judge **6** decide, oddman **7** arbiter, daysman, oddsman, referee **9** supervise **10** arbitrator
Una boat: **7** catboat
unable: **6** cannot **7** disable **8** helpless, impotent **9** incapable **11** incompetent, inefficient, unqualified **13** incapacitated
unaccented: **4** lene **6** atonic
unaccompanied: **4** bare, solo **5** alone
unaccountable: **7** strange **9** countless **10** mysterious **12** inexplicable, unfathomable **13** irresponsible
unaccustomed: new **7** strange **8** uncommon, unwonted **10** unfamiliar
unacquainted: **7** strange, unusual **10** unfamiliar **13** inexperienced
unadorned: **4** bald, bare **5** naked, plain, stark **6** rustic **7** austere
unadulterated: **4** pure **5** clean **6** honest **7** genuine, sincere, unmixed **9** immutable
unaffected: **4** easy, naif, real **5** naive, plain **6** rustic, simple **7** artless, genuine, natural, sincere, unmoved **8** unbiased **9**

ingenuous, unaltered, untouched **12** uninfluenced

unaging: 7 eternal

unalike: 9 different

unalleviated: 4 hard

unalloyed: 4 pure **7** genuine, unmixed **11** unqualified

unambiguous: 8 explicit

unanchored: 6 adrift

unanimous: 5 solid **6** united **8** agreeing **11** consentient

unanimously: 7 una voce

unanswerable: 5 final **10** conclusive

unappeasable: 10 implacable

unarmed: 4 bare **5** inerm **11** defenseless

unassailable: 12 invulnerable

unassuming: shy **6** modest **7** natural **8** retiring **9** diffident **14** unostentatious

unattached: 4 free **5** loose **6** single **9** unmarried **11** independent **13** noncollegiate

unattractive: 4 rude, ugly **10** ungracious

unau: 5 sloth

unavailing: 6 futile **8** bootless, gainless

unaware: 6 unwary **8** heedless, ignorant **11** thoughtless

unbalanced: 6 uneven **8** deranged, lop-sided, one-sided

unbecoming: 4 rude **5** inept **8** improper, unseemly, unworthy **10** indecorous, unsuitable **11** disgraceful **12** unattractive

unbefitting: 5 below **10** unsuitable

unbelief: 9 disbelief **10** skepticism **11** agnosticism, incredulity

unbelievable: 9 fantastic **10** incredible **13** inconceivable

unbeliever: 5 pagan **7** atheist, doubter, heretic, infidel, scoffer, skeptic **8** agnostic **11** freethinker

unbend: 4 rest, thaw **5** relax, untie, yield **6** loosen, uncock **7** slacken **8** unfasten

unbending: 5 rigid, stern, stiff **8** obdurate, resolute **10** inexorable, inflexible

unbiased: 4 fair, just **8** detached **9** impartial **12** unprejudiced

unbind: 4 free, undo **5** untie **6** detach, loosen **7** absolve, deliver, release **8** dissolve, unfasten

unbleached: 4 blae, ecru **5** beige **7** natural

unblemished: 4 pure **8** spotless

unblushing: 9 shameless

unbolt: 4 open **5** unbar, unpin **6** unlock **8** unfasten

unbound: 4 free **5** loose **10** unconfined

unbounded: 4 open **9** limitless, unchecked, unlimited **11** measureless **12** uncontrolled, unrestrained

unbrace: 4 free, undo **5** carve, relax **6** loosen, reveal, weaken **8** disjoint, enfeeble

unbridled: 4 free **5** loose **7** violent **9** dissolute, unchecked **10** licentious, ungoverned **12** uncontrolled, unrestrained

unbroken: one **4** flat **5** undug, whole **6** entire, intact **7** untamed **8** unplowed **9** continual, undivided, unsubdued **10** continuous **13** uninterrupted

unburden: 4 ease **5** empty, untax **6** unload **7** disload, relieve

uncanny: 4 eery **5** eerie, scary, weird **6** spooky **7** awkward, ghostly, strange **8** careless **9** dangerous, unnatural **10** mysterious

uncanonical: 10 apocryphal

unceasing: 6 eterne **7** endless, eternal **9** continual, incessant, perennial **11** everlasting **14** unintermittent

unceasingly: 7 forever **11** continually, incessantly

unceremonious: 4 curt **5** bluff, blunt **6** abrupt **8** familiar, informal **14** unconventional

uncertain: 4 asea, dark, hazy **5** fluky, vague **6** chancy, fitful, queasy **7** dubious **8** aleatory, doubtful, unsteady, variable **9** ambiguous, equivocal, hazardous, undecided **10** changeable, indefinite, precarious **12** questionable **13** indeterminate, problematical, untrustworthy

uncertainty: 4 were **6** gamble, wonder **7** dubiety **8** suspense **9** dubiosity **10** skepticism

unchanging: 7 eternal, forever, settled, uniform **9** immutable, steadfast, unvarying **10** invariable, stationary

unchaste: 4 lewd **5** bawdy **6** coarse, impure **7** haggard, obscene **8** immodest

unchecked: 4 free **5** loose **7** rampant **9** unbounded, unbridled

uncia: 4 coin, inch **5** ounce **7** twelfth

uncivil: 4 rude **5** bluff **7** ill-bred **8** clownish, impolite **9** barbarous **10** indecorous, ungracious, unsuitable **11** uncivilized **12** discourteous **13** disrespectful

uncivilized: 4 rude, wild **5** feral **6** brutal, ferine, savage **8** barbaric **9** barbarian, barbarous, primitive **10** unmannerly **13** unenlightened

uncle: eme. oom

unclean: 4 foul, tref, vile **5** black, dirty **6** common, filthy, impure **7** defiled, obscene **8** polluted, unchaste **11** unwholesome

unclose: ope **4** open **6** reveal **8** disclose **10** unreserved

unclothe: 5 spoil, strip **6** divest, expose **7** despoil, uncover, undress

unclothed: 4 bare, nude **5** naked

unclouded: 4 open **5** clear, sunny

unco: 5 great, weird **7** foreign, strange, uncanny, unknown **13** extraordinary

uncoil: 6 unwind

uncombined: 4 free **5** loose **10** elementary

uncomfortable: 6 uneasy

uncommon: odd **4** rare **5** novel **6** choice, scarce, unique **7** special, strange, unusual **8** especial, unwonted **10** infrequent, remarkable **11** exceptional **12** unaccustomed **13** extraordinary, preternatural

uncommunicative: 6 silent **8** reserved, reticent

uncompassionate: 5 stony

uncomplaining: 5 stoic **7** stoical

uncomplicated: 5 plain **6** simple

uncompromising: 4 firm **5** rigid, stern **6** strict **9** unbending **10** determined, inflexible, unyielding **12** intransigent

unconcealed: 4 bare, open **5** overt

unconcerned: 4 cool, easy **8** careless, detached **9** apathetic **10** insouciant **11** indifferent **12** uninterested

unconditional: 4 free **8** absolute, explicit

unconfined: lax **4** free **5** loose **9** boundless, limitless, unlimited

unconfused: 4 calm **5** clear **6** steady

unconnected: 5 gappy **6** abrupt **8** detached, rambling, separate **10** incoherent **12** disconnected

unconscious: out **6** asleep, torpid **7** stunned, unaware **8** comatose, ignorant, mindless **9** inanimate, lethargic **10** insensible

render: **4** stun

state: **5** swoon **8** apsychia

unconsciousness: 4 coma **5** faint **6** torpor

unconstrained: 4 easy, free **7** natural **8** familiar **11** spontaneous **12** unrestrained

uncontrollable: 4 wild **11** intractable

uncontrolled: 4 free, wild **5** loose **9** irregular, unbounded, unmanaged **10** hysterical, licentious, ungoverned **11** unregulated **12** unrestrained

unconventional: 5 loose, outre **6** casual **7** devious **8** Bohemian, informal **13** unceremonious

uncooked: raw **6** rawish

uncorrupted: 4 pure **8** pristine

uncouple: 5 loose **8** unfasten **10** disconnect

uncouth: odd **4** rare, rude **5** crude **6** clumsy, dismal, rugged **7** awkward, boorish, loutish, strange, uncanny, unknown **8** desolate, dreadful, ignorant, uncommon, ungainly **9** couthless, unknowing, unrefined, untrained **10** mysterious, outlandish, uncultured, unfamiliar, unpolished **11** comfortless **12** unacquainted, uncultivated

uncover: 4 bare, open, tirl(Sc.), tirr(Sc.) **6** denude, detect, divest, expose, remove, reveal, unveil **7** display, divulge, undrape, unearth **8** disclose, discover

uncovered: 4 bald, nude, open **5** naked **6** cuerpo **9** developed **10** bareheaded

uncrystallized: 9 amorphous

unctuous: fat **4** oily **5** bland, fatty, soapy, suave **6** fervid, greasy **7** gushing, pinguid, plastic **10** oleaginous

uncultivated: 4 arid, wild **5** feral **6** desert, fallow **7** deserty **9** barbarous

uncultured: 4 rude **7** artless, boorish **9** unrefined

uncurbed: 12 uncontrolled

undamaged: 5 whole **6** intact

undaunted: 4 bold **5** brave **7** spartan **8** fearless, intrepid, undashed **9** confident, dauntless, turbulent, unbridled, unchecked **10** courageous, undismayed **11** unconquered

undecayed: 5 fresh, green

undeceive: 8 disabuse **11** disillusion

undecided: 4 moot, pend **7** pending **8** doubtful, wavering **9** unsettled **10** inconstant, irresolute, unresolved **13** problematical

undefiled: 4 pure **6** chaste **8** innocent, virtuous **9** unlimited **10** immaculate

undemonstrative: 4 calm, cold, cool **8** reserved **10** restrained

undeniable: 4 true **7** certain **12** indisputable **13** incontestable

undependable: 7 erratic **13** irresponsible

under: 4 alow **5** below, neath, sotto(It.) **6** nether **7** beneath **10** underneath **11** subordinate

prefix: hyp, sub

the weather: **4** sick **5** drunk **6** ailing

under-set: 4 prop **6** sublet **7** provide, support **8** maintain, underlet **10** strengthen

underbrush 6 covert **7** abature

undercover: 6 secret **13** surreptitious

man: spy **5** agent **9** detective **10** counterspy

underdone: 4 rare

underestimate: 8 minimize **9** underrate **10** undervalue

undergarment: bra **4** slip **5** teddy **6** cilice, corset, flimsy; shorts, stepin **7** chemise **9** brassiere, chemilonn, nairshirt, petticoat, teddybear, underwear **10** foundation **11** camiknicker, combination

undergo: 4 bear, pass **5** carry **6** endure, suffer **7** sustain **10** experience

undergraduate: 4 coed **6** junior, senior **7** student **8** freshman **9** sophomore

underground: 5 train **6** hidden, secret, subway **7** beneath **10** undercover **15** surreptitiously

worker: **5** miner **6** mucker, pitman, sapper

undergrowth: 4 rush **5** brush **10** hypotrophy, underbrush

underhanded: sly **4** dern, mean **5** shady **6** byhand, secret, sneaky, unfair **8** sneaking, unfairly **9** deceitful **10** circuitous, fraudulent **11** clandestine, shorthanded, unobtrusive **13** unobtrusively **15** surreptitiously

underlie: 4 bear **7** support

underling: 6 menial, minion **8** inferior **11** subordinate

underlying: 5 basic **7** obscure **8** cardinal **11** fundamental

undermine: sap 4 cave 5 drain, erode 6 impair, weaken 7 founder, subvert 8 discover, enfeeble, excavate 10 demoralize

underneath: 5 below, under 6 secret 7 beneath 13 surreptitious

underpin: 7 justify, support 8 maintain 9 vindicate 12 substantiate

underprop: 4 prop 6 uphold 7 support 8 underpin

underrate: 5 decry 9 extenuate 10 undervalue 13 underestimate

underscore: 9 emphasize, italicize

undersea boat: sub 5 U-boat, wreck 9 submarine 11 submersible

eye: 9 periscope

undershirt: 4 vest 7 chemise

undershrub: 4 bush 7 heather

understand: con, dig, get, ken, see 4 know, sabe, twig 5 grasp, infer, sabby, savey, savvy, sense 6 follow, reason, savvey 7 discern, realize 8 conceive, perceive 9 apprehend, interpret, penetrate 10 comprehend

understandable: 5 clear, lucid

understanding: ken 4 feet, idea, news 5 amity, brain 6 humane, kindly, treaty 7 compact, concept, empathy, entente, knowing 8 attitude, contract, footwear, judgment, skillful, sympathy 9 agreement, diagnosis, knowledge tolerance 10 acceptance 11 intelligent, sympathetic 12 intelligence

understatement: 7 litotes

understeward: 7 bailiff

understood: 5 clear, lucid, tacit 8 implicit

undertake: try 4 dare, fand, fang 5 chide, grant, seize 6 accept, assume, engage, incept 7 attempt, emprise, emprize, execute, perform, promise, receive, reprove 8 contract, covenant, endeavor, overtake 9 guarantee, underfong

undertaker: 4 bant 5 cerer 6 surety 7 rebuker, sponsor 8 embalmer 9 mortician 12 entrepreneur

undertaking: 4 task 6 charge, pledge 7 calling, project, promise, venture 8 covenant 9 adventure, guarantee 10 enterprise 11 proposition

written: 6 cautio 9 cautiones

undertone: 5 aside

undervalue: 5 decry 8 disprize, disvalue 10 depreciate

underwater: *apparatus:* 6 tremie 7 caisson

chamber: 4 cave 7 caisson

underwear: 6 skivvy 7 dessous(F.), stepins 8 lingerie, skivvies 12 underclothes

underwood: 5 frith 7 boscage, coppice 10 underbrush 11 undergrowth

underworld: 4 hell 5 Hades, Orcus, Sheol 6 Erebus 7 xibalba 9 antipodes

deity: Dis 4 Bran 5 Hades, Pluto 6 Osiris 8 Dispater 9 Enmeshara 11 Ningishzida

goddess: 6 Allatu, Belili, Hecate, Trivia

underwrite: 6 insure 7 asssure, finance, sponsor 9 subscribe

undesigned: 6 chance 10 accidental

undesigning: 6 simple 7 artless, sincere

undetermined: 5 vague 7 dubious 8 aoristic, doubtful 9 equivocal

undeveloped: 5 crude 6 latent 8 immature

undeviating: 4 even 8 straight

undigested: 5 crude

undiluted: 4 mear, meer, mere, neat, pure 8 straight

undiminished: 6 entire

undirected: 6 misled 7 aimless 11 misdirected

undisciplined: 4 wild 6 unruly, wanton 9 untrained

undisclosed: 6 secret 8 ulterior

undisguised: 4 bald 5 frank, overt 9 barefaced

undisturbed: 4 calm 5 quiet 6 placid, secure, serene 9 unruffled

undivided: one 5 total, whole 6 entire, intact 8 complete, unbroken 10 continuous

undo: 4 open, ruin 5 annul, fordo, loose, solve 6 betray, cancel, defeat, diddle, foredo, unlash, unwrap 7 defease, destroy, disjoin, explain, nullify, release, uncover, unravel 8 unfasten 10 disappoint, disconnect, invalidate

undoing: 4 ruin 8 downfall 9 overthrow

undomesticated: 4 wild 5 feral 6 ferine

undone: raw 9 neglected 10 defeasible

undoubted: 4 sure 7 certain 8 accepted, admitted 11 indubitable

undress: 4 doff 5 strip 6 devest, divest 7 disrobe 8 unclothe 10 dishabille

undue: 7 extreme 8 improper 9 excessive 10 exorbitant, immoderate, inordinate, unsuitable 11 unwarranted 12 unreasonable 13 inappropriate

undulant: 7 aripple, sinuous 10 undulating, undulatory

undulate: 4 roll, wave 5 swing 6 billow 9 fluctuate

undulation: 5 crimp, swell 8 waviness

undutiful: 7 impious

undying: 6 eterne 7 ageless, endless, eternal 8 immortal, unending 9 continual, deathless 12 imperishable

unearth: dig 5 learn 6 exhume, expose 7 uncover 8 disclose, discover

unearthly: 4 eery 5 eerie, weird 7 awesome, uncanny, ungodly 8 terrific 9 appalling, fantastic 10 mysterious, outlandish 12 preposterous, supernatural 13 preternatural

uneasiness: 5 worry 6 unrest 7 anxiety, disease, trouble 8 disquiet 10 constraint, discomfort, discontent 11 displeasure, disturbance 12 apprehension 13 inconvenience 15 dissatisfaction

uneasy: 5 stiff 7 anxious, awkward, fidgety,

unquiet, restive **8** restless **9** difficult, perturbed, unsettled **13** uncomfortable

uneaten: 5 waste, whole **6** scraps

unemotional: 4 cold **5** stony, stoic **7** stoical **10** phlegmatic

unemployed: 4 idle **6** otiant, otiose **8** inactive, leisured

unenclosed: 4 open **9** fenceless

unencumbered: 4 free

unending: 7 endless, eternal, undying **8** timeless **9** ceaseless **12** interminable

unendurable: 10 impassible, unbearable **11** intolerable

unenthusiastic: 4 cool **9** apathetic **12** uninterested

unequal: 5 impar **6** uneven, unfair, unjust **8** variable **9** disparate, irregular **11** fluctuating **16** disproportionate

comb. form: **5** aniso

unequaled: 7 supreme **9** matchless, unmatched, unrivaled **10** surpassing **12** unparalleled

unequivocal: 5 clear, plain **7** sincere **8** definite, explicit **9** certainly **11** categorical **15** straightforward

unerring: 4 sure, true **5** exact **7** certain **8** inerrant **9** inerrancy, unfailing **10** infallible

unethical: 5 wrong **6** amoral

uneven: odd **5** erose, gobby, haggy, rough **6** hobbly, rugged, unfair, unjust, unlike **7** unequal, varying **9** irregular **10** illmatched **11** fluctuating, ill-assorted

unevenness: 8 asperity

unexamined: 8 apriori

unexcelled: 8 champion, superior

unexcitable: 6 stolid

unexcited: 4 calm **7** stoical

unexciting: 4 dead, tame **6** boring **7** prosaic **13** uninteresting

unexpected: 6 abrupt, sudden **9** inopinate, unguarded **10** accidental, unforeseen

unexpended: 6 saving **7** reserve, surplus

unexpired: 5 alive, valid **9** operative

unexpressed: 5 tacit

unextinguished: 5 alive

unface: 6 unmask

unfadable: 4 fast **9** memorable

unfaded: 5 fresh **6** bright

unfailing: 4 sure **7** certain **8** reliable, unerring **10** infallible, unflagging, unyielding **13** inexhaustible

unfair: 4 foul, hard **5** wrong **6** biased, uneven, unjust **8** unseemly, wrongful **9** dishonest, unethical **11** inequitable, underhanded, unfavorable **12** dishonorable

unfaithful: 7 infidel, traitor **8** derelict, disloyal, recreant, turncoat **9** dishonest, faithless **10** adulterous, inaccurate, traitorous **13** untrustworthy

unfaltering: 4 true **5** brave **6** steady

unfamiliar: new **7** strange, unknown **12** unaccustomed

unfashionable: 5 dated **9** distorted, unshapely

unfast: 6 unfirm, untrue **8** insecure

unfasten: 4 free, open, undo **5** loose, unbar, unfix, unpin, untie **6** detach, loosen, unlace, unlock **8** untether

unfathomable: 10 bottomless **12** impenetrable

unfavorable: bad, ill **4** foul **6** averse **7** adverse **8** contrary **15** disadvantageous

unfeeling: 4 dull, hard **5** cruel, harsh, stern, stony **6** brutal, marble, stolid · **7** callous **8** numbness, obdurate **9** apathetie, bloodless, heartless, insensate, senseless **10** impassible, insensible **11** hardhearted, insensitive **13** unsusceptible **16** unimpressionable

unfeigned: 4 real, true **6** hearty **7** genuine, natural, sincere

unfertile: 4 arid **6** barren

unfetter: 6 loosen

unfettered: 5 broad

unfilled: 5 blank, empty

unfinished: raw **5** crude, rough **7** sketchy **8** immature **9** imperfect **10** incomplete

unfit: bad **4** sick **5** inept, pasul(Heb.) **6** faulty **8** disabled, improper **10** unsuitable **11** handicapped, incompetent, unqualified **12** disqualified **13** incapacitated

unfix: 6 detach, loosen **8** dissolve, unfasten, unsettle

unfixed: 6 adrift, afloat **8** drifting, shifting

unfledged: 5 green **6** callow **8** immature **11** undeveloped, unfeathered

unflinching: 4 firm **6** stanch **8** resolute **9** steadfast **10** unwavering, unyielding

unfold: ope **4** open **6** deploy, evolve, expand, explat, flower, reveal, spread, unfurl, unwrap **7** develop, display, divulge, evolute, explain, explate, release **8** develope, disclose **9** explicate

unforced: 4 easy **7** natural, willing **9** voluntary

unforeseen: 6 casual **10** accidental

unformed: 6 callow **9** shapeless, uncreated **11** undeveloped

unfortunate: bad, ill **4** poor **5** worst **6** dismal, wretch **7** hapless, unhappy, unlucky **8** luckless, wretched **9** graceless **10** calamitous, prostitute, ungracious **12** inauspicious, infelicitous, unsuccessful

unfounded: 4 idle, vain **8** baseless **10** chimerical, groundless

unfriendly: 4 cool **6** remote **7** asocial, hostile **8** inimical, unsocial **9** dissocial

terms: **4** outs

unfruitful: 5 blunt **6** barren, wasted **7** sterile, useless **9** fruitless, infertile **12** unproductive, unprofitable

unfurl: 4 open **5** enrol **6** enroll, expand, spread, unfold, unroll **7** develop **8** develope

unfurnished: 4 bare **6** vacant

ungainly: 5 lanky **6** clumsy **7** awkward,

boorish, uncouth **8** clownish, slammock, slummock **11** elephantine

ungenerous: **4** mean **5** harsh, nasty **6** stingy

ungentlemanly: **7** ill-bred **9** illiberal

ungodly: **6** sinful, wicked **7** impious **8** dreadful **9** atheistic, atrocious, unearthly **11** unbelieving **12** hypocritical

ungovernable: **4** wild **6** unruly **7** froward **9** unbridled **10** disorderly, headstrong, licentious, rebellious **11** intractable **13** irrepressible **14** uncontrollable

ungraceful: **6** clumsy **7** angular, awkward **9** inelegant

ungracious: **4** hard, rude **6** wicked **8** churlish, disliked, impolite **9** graceless, offensive **10** unmannerly, unpleasant **11** unfortunate **12** discourteous, unattractive

ungrateful: **9** thankless

ungrounded: **8** baseless **9** unfounded **10** uninformed **12** uninstructed

ungrudging: **8** cheerful

ungual: **4** claw, hoof, nail **6** ungula

unguarded: **6** unwary **8** careless **9** imprudent **10** incautious **11** defenseless, thoughtless, unprotected

unguent: **4** balm **5** salve **6** cerate, ceroma, chrism **8** ointment **9** lubricant

unguinous: **4** oily **8** unctuous

ungula: **4** claw, hoof, nail **6** ungual

ungulate: hog, pig **4** deer **5** horse, tapir **6** hoofed **8** elephant **10** rhinoceros

unhallowed: **6** impure, unholy, wicked **7** impious, profane **10** desecrated

unhamper: **5** loose

unhandsome: **4** mean, rude **5** plain **6** homely, stingy **10** unbecoming

unhandy: **6** clumsy **7** awkward **12** inconvenient

unhap: **6** mishap **7** ill-luck

unhappy: sad **4** evil **6** dismal **7** unlucky **8** dejected, illfated, wretched **9** miserable, sorrowful, woebegone **10** calamitous **11** melancholic, mischievous, unfavorable, unfortunate **12** inauspicious, unsuccessful **13** inappropriate

unharmed: **4** safe **6** unhurt **8** harmless **10** scatheless

unharmonious: **9** dissonant

unharness: **6** disarm, divest, ungear **7** unhitch, unhorse

unhasp: **8** unfasten

unhealthy: ill **4** sick **6** sickly **11** unwholesome

unheard of: **7** strange, unknown **13** unprecedented

unheated: **4** cold

unheeding: **4** deaf **8** careless **12** disregarding

unhesitating: **5** ready

unhidden: **5** overt

unholy: **6** impure, wicked **7** impious, profane **8** dreadful, shocking **9** frightful **10** scandalous, unhallowed

unhonored: **12** dishonorable **13** dishonourable

unhorse: **5** throw **8** dislodge, dismount **9** overthrow, unharness

unhurried: **4** easy, slow **10** deliberate

unhurt: **4** safe **8** unharmed **9** uninjured

unicorn: **4** reem

unicorn fish: **7** narwhal **8** filefish

uniform: **4** even, flat, suit **5** equal, level **6** livery, outfit, steady **7** regular, similar **8** constant, equiform **9** continual, equitable, unvarying **10** consistent, equiformal, invariable, monotonous, unchanging **11** homogeneous

cord: **11** aiguillette

uniformly: **6** always

unify: **5** merge, unite **8** coalesce **9** correlate, integrate **11** consolidate

unimaginative: **4** dull **7** literal, prosaic

unimpaired: **4** free **5** fresh **6** entire, intact

unimpassioned: **6** steady

unimpeachable: **9** blameless, faultless **14** irreproachable, unquestionable **15** unexceptionable

unimpeded: **4** free

unimportant: **7** trivial

unimpressed: **6** unawed

uninformed: **8** ignorant

uninhabited: **5** empty **6** vacant **8** deserted, desolate

uninspired: **4** dull **6** stodgy

unintelligent: **4** dumb **5** brute **6** obtuse, stupid, unwise **7** foolish **8** ignorant **9** senseless **10** irrational

unintentional: **10** accidental **11** inadvertent

uninteresting: dry **4** arid, drab, dull, flat **5** stale **6** boring, jejune, prolix, stupid **7** humdrum, insipid, prosaic, tedious **8** tiresome **9** colorless **10** unexciting

uninterrupted: **7** endless, eternal **9** continual **10** continuous **11** everlasting

unio: **6** mussel

union: AFL, CIO, one, UAW **4** bloc **5** artel, ILGWU, unity **6** accord, copula, fusion, gremio(Sp.), league, merger, unicum **7** amalgam, concord, contact, entente, meeting, oneness, society **8** alliance, junction, knitting, marriage **9** coalition, coherence, composure **10** connection, copulation, federation, fellowship **11** association, coalescence, combination, concurrence, confederacy, conjunction, consistency

Union of Soviet Socialist Republics: **4** USSR **6** Russia, Soviet

unique: odd, one **4** rare, sole **5** alone, queer **6** single **7** notable, special, unequal, unusual **8** peculiar, singular **9** matchless **13** extraordinary

unison: **5** union **6** accord **7** concord, harmony **9** agreement, consonant, identical, unanimity, unisonant, unisonous 10 concordant, consonance, equivalent

unit: ace, one 4 item 5 digit, group, monad, whole 6 entity 10 individual
conductivity: mho
discord: 4 word
fluidity: rhe
flux density: 5 gauss
force: 4 dyne, volt 5 kinit, tonal
hypothetical: 6 pangen 7 pangene
illumination: 4 phot
inductance: 5 henry
light: lux, pyr 5 lumen
magnetic: 5 weber
measure: are, mil, rod 4 pint 5 meter, stere
measuring sound: 7 decibel
metrical: 4 dyne, mora 5 liter, morae
military: 4 army 5 corps, squad 7 brigade, company, platoon 8 division, regiment 9 battalion
physical: erg 7 atomerg
power: HP; bel 4 watt 5 dynam, horse
pressure: 5 barad, barye
reluctance: rel
resistance: ohm
social: 4 clan, sect 6 family
speed: 4 velo
stellar: 6 parsec
tale: 4 rees
telegraphic: 4 baud
thermal: 6 calory 7 calorie
time: day 4 bell, hour, week, year 5 month 6 minute, season, second
ultimate: 5 monad
velocity: kin 4 kine, velo
volume: oz, pd; cwt, ton 5 ounce, pound 13 hundredweight
weight: ton 4 dram, gram 5 carat, ounce, pound
work: erg 5 ergon, joule 6 kilerg

unite: add, fay, pan, sew, tie, wed 4 ally, band, bind, club, fuse, hasp, join, knit, link, meld, pair, seam, weld 5 affix, annex, blend, graft, hitch, marry, merge, piece, rally 6 adhere, adjoin, attach, cement, cohere, concur, couple, embody, mingle, pleach, solder, splice 7 combine, conjoin, connect, consort, convene 8 assemble, coalesce, compound, concrete, condense, conspire, continue, federate, regelate 9 affiliate, aggregate, associate, colleague 10 amalgamate, articulate, consociate, federalize 11 concentrate, compaginate, consolidate, incorporate 12 conglutinate

united: one 9 concerted, conjugate, corporate 10 corporated

United Nations Organization: UNO

United Provinces: 7 Holland, Utrecht, Zeeland 9 Friesland, Groningen 10 Gelderland, Overijssel

United States (see also **America**):
artist: 4 Pyle, Wood 5 Flagg, Homer, Ma-

rin, Moses, Peale, Ryder, Sloan, Wyeth 6 Benton, Eakins, Hopper, Stuart
author: Ade, Poe, Roe 4 Ames, Baum, Buck, Dana, Grey, Pyle, Ward, Wolf 5 Alger, Barth, Beach, Davis, Field, Harte, Hurst, Lewis, James, Quinn, Stowe, Tripp 6 Alcott, Bellow, Bryant, Cabell, Cooper, Ferber, Hersey, Holmes, Irving, London, Lowell, Jewett, Kantor, O Henry, O'Neill, Porter, Snyder 7 Barrett, Clemens, Dreiser, Emerson, Hayward, Malamud, Parkman, Saroyan, Stewart, Thoreau, Vaughan, Wallace, Whitman 8 Faulkner, Salinger, Sinclair, Whittier 9 Cenedella, Hawthorne, Hemingway 10 Longfellow, Tarkington
canal: 4 Erie 6 Panama
capital city: 5 Boise, Dover, Salem 6 Albany, Austin, Boston, Denver, Helena, Juneau, Pierre, St. Paul, Topeka 7 Atlanta, Augusta, Concord, Jackson, Lansing, Lincoln, Madison, Olympia, Phoenix, Raleigh, Santa Fe, Trenton 8 Bismarck, Cheyenne, Columbia, Columbus, Hartford, Honolulu, Richmond 9 Annapolis, Des Moines, Frankfort, Nashville 10 Baton Rouge, Carson City, Charleston, Harrisburg, Little Rock, Montgomery, Montpelier, Providence, Sacramento 11 Springfield, Tallahassee 12 Indianapolis, Oklahoma City, Salt Lake City 13 Jefferson City
coin: bit 4 cent, dime 5 eagle, penny 6 dollar, nickel 7 quarter
colonists: 5 Dutch 8 Pilgrims, Puritans
composer: 4 Foss, Kern 5 Foote, Nevin 6 Berlin, Foster, Grothe, Porter 7 Copland, Rodgers 8 Gershwin 9 Bernstein
dramatist: 4 Inge, Rice 5 Barry, Odets 6 Crouse, Miller, O'Neill 8 Crothers, Williams
editor: Bok 4 Dana, Ochs 5 White 7 Greeley
emblem: 5 eagle
essayist: Poe 5 Mabie 6 Lowell, Morley 7 Emerson, Thoreau
explorer: 4 Byrd, Long, Pike 5 Boone, Clark, Lewis, Logan, Perry
falls: 7 Niagara 8 Yosemite 9 Multnomah
flagmaker: 9 Betsy Ross
frontiersman: 4 Cody 5 Boone, Clark, Lewis 8 Crockett
humorist: Ade, Day, Nye 4 Cobb, Nash, Neal 5 Twain 6 Rogers 7 Lardner, Thurber
Indian: See under **Indian.**
inventor: Hoe 4 Bell, Howe 5 Fiske, Fitch, Morse 6 Edison, Fulton 7 Whitney
journalist: 4 Dana, Ochs, Pyle, Reid, Riis 5 Alsop, Block, Broun, White 6 Reston 7 Lorimer 8 Brisbane
measure: lea, mil, rod, ton, tub, vat 4 acre, bolt, cord, drum, foot, gill, hand, hank, heer, inch, iron, last, line, link, mile, nail,

pace, palm, peck, pint, pipe, pole, pool,
roll, sack, span, typp, vara, yard **5** block,
carat, chain, labor, minim, perch, point,
prime, quart, skein, stran **6** barrel, basket, bushel, fathom, gallon, league, pottle, square, strand, thread **7** quarter,
section, spindle **8** hogshead, quadrant,
standard, township **9** board foot, decillion, fluid dram **10** fluid ounce **11** tea-
spoonful **13** tablespoonful **16** Winchester
bushel

measure of weight: bag, keg, kip, ton **5**
carat, flask, grain, ounce, pound **6** denier
7 long ton, quarter, quintal **9** troy ounce,
troy pound **11** metric carat **13** hundredweight

mountain: **4** Hood **6** Cumbre, Elbert,
Helena, Shasta **7** Massive, Rainier,
Whitney **8** Katahdin, McKinley

naturalist: **4** Muir **5** Baird, Beebe, Seton
7 Thoreau

novelist: see *author* above

ornithologist: **7** Audubon

painter: see *artist* above

philanthropist: **4** Ford, Riis **5** Lenox **8**
Carnegie **11** Rockefeller

philosopher: **5** James **6** Edmans **7** Thoreau

physicist: **5** Tesla **6** Teller **7** Nichols

pioneer: see *frontiersman* above

pirate: **4** Kidd

poet: Poe **4** Nash **5** Benet, Field, Moore,
Reese, Riley, Stein, Towne, Wylie **6**
Bryant, Holmes, Kilmer, Lanier, Lowell,
Millay **7** Whitman **8** Whittier **10** Long-
fellow

polar explorer: **4** Byrd **5** Perry

vice-president: **4** Burr, King **5** Adams,
Dawes, Gerry, Nixon, Tyler **6** Arthur,
Colfax, Curtis, Dallas, Garner, Hamlin,
Hobart, Morton, Truman, Wilson **7** Bark-
ley, Calhoun, Clinton, Johnson, Sherman
Wallace, Wheeler **8** Coolidge, Fillmore,
Marshall, Tompkins, Van Buren **9** Fair-
banks, Hendricks, Jefferson, Roosevelt,
Stevenson **12** Breckinridge

units: *aggregate distance:* **7** mileage

biological: **6** idants

unity: one **5** union **6** accord **7** concord,
harmony, oneness **8** alliance, identity **9**
agreement, communion **10** singleness,
solidarity, uniformity **11** conjunction,
unification

universal: all **5** local, total, whole **6** common, cosmic, entire, public **7** general **8**
catholic, constant **9** continual, unlimited
12 allpervading

language: Ro; ido **9** Esperanto

military training: **5** draft

universe: **5** earth, monad, world **6** cosmos, nature, system **8** creation

controlling principle: **4** tien **5** logos

pert. to: **6** cosmic

science: **9** cosmology

university: **6** patent **7** academy, college **8**
academie **9** accademie

Ivy League: **4** Yale **5** Brown **7** Cornell,
Harvard **8** Columbia **9** Dartmouth,
Princeton **12** Pennsylvania

official: **4** dean **6** regent

rank: **6** docent **9** professor **10** instructor

univocal: **7** uniform **9** unanimous, unisonous **11** indubitable **12** unmistakable

unjust: **5** cruel **6** unfair **8** improper,
wrongful **9** dishonest, faithless **10** inaccurate, iniquitous, unfaithful

unked, unkid: odd **5** weird **6** lonely **7**
awkward, ghastly, strange, uncanny, uncouth, unknown **8** desolate **12** inconvenient **13** uncomfortable

unkeeled: **6** ratite

unkempt: **5** crude, messy, rough **6** frouzy,
frowsy, frowzy, shaggy, untidy **7** ruffled,
squalid, tousled **9** unrefined **10** disarrayed, disheveled, unpolished

unkind: bad, ill **4** vile **5** cruel, harsh,
rough, stern **6** severe, wicked **7** foreign,
strange **8** ungenial **9** inclement, undutiful, unnatural **10** degenerate, ungenerous, ungracious, ungrateful, unsuitable
11 unfavorable

unknit: **4** undo **5** ravel, relax, untie **6**
unknot **7** unravel **8** disperse, dissolve,
disunite

unknowable: **8** mystical, noumenon **9**
enigmatic

unknown: **4** unco **7** inconnu(F.), strange
9 anonymous, incognito **10** unfamiliar **12**
incalculable **13** inexpressible

unlace: **4** undo **5** loose **6** carver **7** undress, unravel **8** unfasten, untangle

unlawful: **7** bastard, illegal, illicit **8**
wrongful **9** irregular **10** contraband **12**
illegitimate

unlearned: **4** lewd **5** gross **6** borrel **7**
natural **8** ignorant, untaught **9** untutored
10 illiterate, uneducated **11** instinctive,
instinctual

unleashed: **4** free **5** loose **8** released

unless: **4** lest, nisi(L.), save **6** except **9**
excepting, provision **11** reservation

unlettered: **4** lewd **8** ignorant **9** barbarian
10 illiterate, uneducated

unlike: **6** uneven **7** difform, diverse **8** unlikely **9** different, irregular **10** dissimilar,
improbable **13** heterogeneous

unlikely: **5** unfit **10** improbable, unsuitable **11** unpromising **12** disagreeable,
unattractive **13** objectionable

unlikeness: **8** contrast **12** disagreement
13 dissimilarity

unlimited: **4** vast **9** boundless, limitless,
unbounded, undefined, universal **10**
indefinite, unconfined **11** illimitable, untrammeled **12** immeasurable, unrestricted
13 indeterminate

unlit: **4** dark

unload: 4 dump 5 empty, trash 6 decant, remove 7 deplete, discard, lighten, relieve 9 disburden, discharge, liquidate, sacrifice

unlucky: bad, fey, ill 7 hapless 8 illfated 9 illomened 11 unfortunate

unman: 5 crush 7 monster, unnerve

unmanageable: 5 randy 8 churlish 10 disorderly

unmanly: 8 childish

unmannerly: 4 rude 7 boorish, uncivil 8 impolite 10 ungracious 12 discourteous,

unmarried: one 4 lone 6 chaste, single

unmask: 6 expose, reveal, unface 7 uncloak 8 disclose 9 dismantle

unmatched: odd 5 alone 9 matchless

unmeasured: 4 huge, vast 7 immense 9 boundless 12 unrestrained

unmelodious: 9 dissonant 11 cacophonous

unmerciful: 5 cruel 8 pitiless, ruthless 9 inclement 10 relentless

unmethodical: 7 cursory, erratic 9 desultory

unmindful: 8 careless, heedless 9 forgetful, negligent 10 neglectful

unmistakable: 4 open 5 clear, plain 6 patent 7 evident, obvious 8 apparent, definite

unmitigated: 4 mere 5 sheer 6 arrant 8 absolute, clearcut 10 unmodified

unmixed: 4 deep, mear, mere, pure 5 blank, sheer, utter 7 sincere

unmoved: 4 calm, cool, firm 5 stony 6 serene 7 adamant 8 obdurate, stubborn, unshaken 9 apathetic,

unmoving: 5 inert

unnatural: 4 eery 5 eerie 7 strange, uncanny 8 abnormal, affected, farcical 9 irregular 10 artificial, factitious 11 counterfeit

unnecessary: 7 useless 8 needless 11 superfluous

unnerve: 5 unman 6 weaken 8 enervate 10 dishearten

unnoble: 7 ignoble

unobservant: 8 heedless

unobstructed: 4 free, open 9 panoramic

unobtrusive: 6 modest 8 retiring

unobtrusively: 9 underhand

unoccupied: 4 idle, void 5 empty 6 vacant 7 leisure 10 unemployed

unofficial: 7 private 8 informal

unoriginal: 4 copy 5 trite 10 secondhand

unorthodox: 9 heretical

unostentatious: 5 quiet 6 lenten, modest 10 restrained

unpaid: due 6 arrear 10 unrevenged

unpaired: odd

unpalatable: 10 unpleasant 11 distasteful

unparalleled: 5 alone 6 unique 7 unequal 8 peerless 9 matchless, unmatched 10 inimitable

unplaned: 5 rough

unpleasant: bad 7 irksome 9 offensive 10 abominable, forbidding, illfavored, ungracious 11 displeasing, distasteful 12 disagreeable
most: 5 worst

unpolished: 5 bruit, crude, rough 6 coarse, rugged 8 agrestic, impolite 9 barbarous 10 agrestical

unpopularity: 5 odium

unprecedented: new 5 novel 10 unexampled

unprejudiced: 4 fair 9 impartial 13 dispassionate

unpremeditated: 6 casual 9 extempore 10 accidental

unprepared: raw 5 unfit

unpretentious: 5 plain 6 homely, humble, modest, simple 10 unaffected

unprincipled: 4 lewd 9 abandoned 10 perfidious 12 unscrupulous

unprocessed: raw 5 crude

unproductive: 4 arid, dead, lean 6 barren, geason 7 sterile 10 unfruitful

unprofessional: lay 6 laical 7 amateur 9 unskilled 15 nonprofessional

unprofitable: dry 4 dead 6 barren 7 inutile, useless 8 bootless, gainless 9 fruitless, frustrate 10 unfruitful 12 frustraneous 15 disadvantageous

unpropitious: 4 evil 7 adverse, ominous, opposed 12 inauspicious

unprotected: 7 exposed 8 helpless 9 unguarded

unqualified: 4 bare, mear, meer, mere 5 sheer, unfit 6 entire, unable 7 plenary 8 absolute, complete, definite 9 categoric, downright, incapable 11 categorical, incompetent

unquestionable: 7 certain, decided, evident 8 implicit, positive 12 indisputable

unravel: 4 undo 5 feaze, ravel, solve 6 unfold, unlace 8 disorder, disunite, separate, untangle 9 disengage 11 disentangle

unready: 4 slow 5 unfit 6 clumsy 7 awkward 8 hesitant 9 undressed

unreal: 5 false, ideal 6 aerial 7 fancied fatuous, nominal 8 aeriform, fanciful, illusive, illusory, spurious 9 deceptive, fantastic, imaginary, pretended, visionary 10 apocryphal, artificial, barmecidal, fictitious, mandacious 11 counterfeit, imaginative 13 insubstantial, unsubstantial

unreality: 7 fantasy 9 fantastry

unreasonable: mad 6 absurd 9 excessive, senseless 10 exorbitant, immoderate, irrational 11 extravagant, impractical

unreasonableness: 5 alogy

unrecognized: 6 unsung 7 unknown 13 unappreciated

unrefined: raw 4 dark, loud, rude 5 broad, crass, crude, gross 6 coarse, common, earthy, vulgar 7 uncouth 12 uncultivated

unregenerate: **6** carnal, sinful **9** shameless **10** impenitent **11** unrepentent
unrelated: **5** fremd
unrelaxed: **4** taut **5** tense
unrelenting: **4** grim, hard, iron **5** cruel, stern **6** severe **8** rigorous **9** merciless **10** inexorable, inflexible, relentless, unyielding
unreliable: **5** fishy **6** fickle **7** casalty **10** capricious **12** undependable **13** irresponsible, untrustworthy
unremitting: **4** busy, hard **9** assiduous, continual, incessant **10** persistent **11** persevering
unrepentent: **10** impenitent **12** unregenerate
unreserved: **4** free **5** frank **6** candid **9** outspoken, unlimited
unresponsive: **4** cold, cool
unrest: **5** alarm **6** bustle, motion **8** disquiet **9** commotion **10** uneasiness **12** restlessness
unrestrained: lax **4** free, wild **5** broad, loose **6** wanton **7** riotous **9** abandoned, dissolute, expansive, unbounded, unbridled, unlimited **10** licentious, unmeasured **11** extravagant **12** uncontrolled
unrestraint: **7** license **8** immunity
unrevealed: **6** hidden, latent, masked **7** covered **9** concealed
unripe: **5** crude, green **6** callow **7** uncured, unready **8** immature **9** premature **10** precocious, unseasoned **12** unseasonable **13** inexperienced
unrobe: **7** disrobe, undress
unroll: **6** evolve, unfold **7** display **8** disclose
unruffled: **4** calm, cool **5** quiet **6** placid, poised, sedate, serene, smooth **8** decorous **11** undisturbed **13** dispassionate, philosophical
unruly: **6** haunty, ramage **7** lawless, restive **9** fractious, obstinate, turbulent **10** disorderly, headstrong, licentious, refractory **11** disobedient, intractable **12** recalcitrant, ungovernable, unmanageable
unsafe: **7** exposed **8** insecure, perilous **9** dangerous, hazardous **10** unreliable
unsatisfactory: **9** defective, imperfect **10** inadequate **11** inefficient
unsatisfied: **9** insatiate **15** dissatisfaction
unsatisfying: **6** hollow
unsavory: **7** insipid **9** offensive, tasteless **10** unpleasant **11** distasteful **12** disagreeable
unscrupulous: **8** rascally **9** dishonest, miscreant **12** unprincipled **13** untrustworthy
unseal: ope **4** open **8** disclose
unseasonable: **6** unripe **8** untimely **9** premature **11** inopportune
unseat: **6** remove **7** unhorse **9** overthrow
unseemly: **8** improper, indecent, unworthy **10** indecorous, unbecoming **13** inappropriate

unseen: **9** invisible, unnoticed **10** unobserved **11** unperceived **12** undiscovered
unselfish: **6** heroic **8** generous **10** altruistic, benevolent
unserviceable: **7** useless
unsettle: **5** upset **7** commove, derange, disturb **8** disorder, displace, disquiet **10** disarrange, discompose
unsettled: **4** moot **6** fickle, queasy **7** dubious **8** restless, unstable **9** ambiguous, desultory, itinerant, uncertain, unquieted **10** changeable, precarious, unoccupied **11** unpopulated **12** undetermined **13** problematical
unshaken: **4** firm **6** steady
unshapely: **8** deformed
unsightly: **4** ugly **5** messy **6** homely
unskilled: **4** rude **5** green **6** puisne **7** artless **8** ignorant, malapert
unskillful: **5** inept **6** bungly, clumsy **7** awkward **10** inexpertly **13** inexperienced
unskillfully: **5** badly
unsocial: **7** asocial **9** dissocial, nonsocial **10** antisocial
unsoiled: **5** clean **10** immaculate
unsophisticated: **4** naif, pure **5** frank, green, naive **6** callow, simple **7** artless, genuine **8** innocent **9** ingenuous, untutored
unsound: bad **4** evil, sick, weak **5** crazy, dotty, false, frail, risky, shaky **6** addled, fickle, flawed, hollow, rotten, weakly **7** decayed, wracked **8** diseased, impaired, insecure, weakened **9** defective, imperfect, tottering **10** illfounded
unspoiled: **4** racy **5** fresh
unspoken: **4** oral **5** tacit **6** silent **9** ineffable, unuttered
unspotted: **8** spotless **10** immaculate
unstable: **5** loose, sandy **6** fickle, fitful, flitty, labile **7** astatic, dwaible, dwaibly, erratic, flighty, plastic **8** insecure, ticklish, unhinged, unsteady, variable **9** eccentric, faithless, irregular, unsettled **10** changeable, inconstant, precarious, unreliable **11** fluctuating, vacillating
unstained: **8** spotless **10** immaculate
unsteady: **5** dizzy, fluky, shaky, tippy **6** fickle, flicky, fluffy, groggy, wabbly, wobbly **7** erratic, quavery, rickety, unsound, wayward **8** titubate, unstable, variable, wavering **9** desultory, irregular, uncertain **10** capricious, changeable, flickering, inconstant **11** fluctuating, lightheaded, vacillating
unstinted: **5** ample **8** generous
unstudied: **7** natural **8** careless, unforced, unversed **9** unlearned **10** colloquial, unaffected **11** spontaneous
unsubstantial: **4** airy, slim **5** filmy, light, paper **6** aerial, flimsy, papery, slight, unreal **7** folious, gaseous, nominal, shadowy **8** filigree, footless **9** visionary **10** immaterial

unsuccessful: 6 losing 7 failing, unlucky 8 abortive 9 fruitless 10 disastrous 11 ineffectual, unfortunate

unsuitable: bad 5 inapt, inept, undue, unfit 10 unbecoming 13 inappropriate

unsullied: 4 pure 8 spotless 10 immaculate

unsure: 4 weak 5 timid 6 infirm 8 doubtful 9 dangerous, hazardous 10 precarious 11 vacillating 13 untrustworthy

unsusceptible: 6 immune 8 obdurate

unsweetened: dry, sec 4 sour

unswerving: 4 firm, true 5 loyal 8 straight 9 steadfast

unsymmetrical: 8 lopsided 9 irregular 15 disproportional

unsympathetic: 4 hard 5 stony 6 frozen 7 hostile 9 heartless 11 hardhearted 12 unresponsive

untainted: 4 pure 9 unsullied

untalented: 8 mediocre 11 incompetent

untamed: 4 wild 5 feral 6 ferine, ramage, ramish, savage 9 unsubdued

untangle: 4 free 6 sleave 9 extricate 11 disentangle

untarnished: 5 clean 8 spotless

untaught: 5 naive 7 natural 8 ignorant 9 unlearned 10 illiterate, uneducated 11 spontaneous 12 uninstructed

untested: new 5 green 7 untried

unthinking: 4 rash 5 brute 6 casual 8 careless, heedless 9 impetuous 11 thoughtless 13 inconsiderate

unthrifty: 6 wanton 7 foolish, profuse 8 prodigal 10 profitless, profligate 11 extravagant

unthrone: 6 unseat 7 decrown 9 overthrow

untidy: 5 dowdy, messy 7 bunting 8 careless, littered, slovenly 10 disheveled, disordered, slatternly 11 disarranged

untie: 4 free, undo 5 loose 6 loosen, unbind, unlash 8 disunite, unfasten 9 disengage

until: to; til 4 till, unto

untimely: 8 immature 9 premature 11 inopportune 12 unseasonable

untiring: 4 busy 8 sedulous, tireless 13 indefatigable

unto: to 4 till 5 until

untold: 4 vast 9 boundless, unrelated 10 uninformed, unrevealed 12 immeasurable, incalculable

untouchable: 8 chandala 10 intangible

untouched: 6 intact 9 insensate

untoward: 6 unruly 7 awkward, froward, unlucky 8 improper, perverse, stubborn, unseemly 9 vexatious 10 indecorous, ungraceful 11 troublesome, unfavorable, unfortunate 12 inconvenient, unpropitious

untrained: raw 4 wild 5 green 7 awkward, untamed 8 undocile 9 unskilled 10 amateurish, unprepared

untrammeled: 4 free 5 loose 9 unlimited 10 unhampered

untransferable: 11 inalienable

untraversed: 6 untrod

untried: new 5 fresh, green 8 immature 13 inexperienced

untrue: 4 flam 5 false, wrong 8 disloyal 9 erroneous, faithless, incorrect 10 fallacious, unfaithful 11 disaffected

untrustworthy: 6 tricky 8 slippery 9 dishonest, uncertain 10 perfidious 12 undependable

untruth: lie 5 fable 7 falsity 9 falsehood, mendacity, treachery 11 fabrication, tarradiddle

untutored: 5 naive 6 simple 7 artless 8 clownish, ignorant, untaught 9 barbarian, unlearned 10 illiterate 15 unsophisticated

untwine: 5 frese, untie 6 unwind 11 disentangle

untwist: 4 free, open 5 ravel 7 unravel, untwine 8 separate 11 disentangle

unutterable, inutterable: 7 extreme 9 ineffable 11 unspeakable 13 inexpressible 15 unpronounceable

unused: new 4 idle 5 fresh 8 unwonted 12 unaccustomed

unusual: odd 4 rare 5 novel, queer, weird 6 quaint, unique 7 strange 8 abnormal, uncommon, unwonted 9 anomalous, different, eccentric 10 remarkable 11 exceptional 12 illegitimate 13 extraordinary

unvaried: 10 monotonous

unvarnished: 4 bald 5 plain 6 simple 8 unglazed 9 unadorned, unglossed 13 unembellished

unvarying: 7 uniform 8 constant

unveil: 6 reveal 7 uncover 8 disclose

unwarranted: 5 undue 11 unjustified

unwary: 4 rash 7 unaware 8 careless, heedless 9 unguarded 10 groundless 11 precipitate

unwavering: 4 firm 5 solid 6 stable 8 constant 9 steadfast

unwearied: 4 busy 8 tireless 9 assiduous 13 indefatigable

unweave: 4 undo 5 ravel 6 unfold

unwed: 6 single

unwelcome: 8 non grata, unwanted 9 intruding, intrusive

unwell: ill 4 evil, sick 5 badly 6 ailing, wicked

unwholesome: 4 evil 6 impure 7 corrupt, harmful, immoral, noisome, noxious, unclean 11 unhealthful

unwieldy: 5 bulky 6 clumsy 7 awkward, hulking 8 cumbrous, ungainly 9 ponderous 10 cumbersome 12 hippopotamic, unmanageable

unwilling: 4 loth 5 loath 6 averse, mauger, maugre 7 loathly 8 backward 9 eschewing, reluctant 11 disinclined

unwind: 5 ravel 6 uncoil 8 untangle 11 disentangle

unwise: **5** inane **6** simple **7** foolish, witless **9** brainless, impolitic, imprudent, senseless **10** irrational **11** injudicious **12** undiplomatic **13** unintelligent

unwonted: **4** rare **6** unused **7** unusual **8** uncommon **10** infrequent **12** unaccustomed

unworldly: **4** eery **5** eerie, naive, weird **9** spiritual, unearthly

unworthy: **4** base **7** beneath **8** shameful, unseemly **10** despicable, unbecoming **12** contemptible, dishonorable

unwrinkled: **5** brent(Sc.) **6** smooth

unwritten: **4** oral **5** blank, vocal **6** verbal

unwrought: **8** unworked

unyielding: set **4** fast, firm, grim, hard, iron **5** rigid, stern, stiff, stith, stony **6** frozen, steely **7** adamant **8** obdurate, stubborn **9** inelastic, obstinate, unbending **10** determined, immaleable, inexorable, relentless **12** contumacious, unsubmissive **14** uncompromising

unyoke: **4** free, part **5** loose **6** remove **7** disjoin, release **8** separate **10** disconnect

up: **4** busy, rise **5** aloft, astir, raise **6** active **7** success **9** according

up and down: **5** erect **6** direct, uneven **7** upright **8** vertical **9** downright, irregular **10** undulating **13** perpendicular

up to: **5** until

date: new **6** modern **7** stylish **11** fashionable

this time: **6** hereto **8** hitherto

upas tree gum: **6** antiar

upbraid: **4** draw, twit **5** abuse, blame, braid, chide, scold, score, taunt, twist **6** accuse, charge **7** censure, reprove **8** denounce, reproach **9** exprobate **10** denunciate

upbuilding: **8** increase **11** edification

upeygan: **6** borele **10** rhinoceros

upgrade: **5** raise, slope **6** ascent **7** incline

upheaval: **5** storm **6** revolt **7** rummage **9** agitation, cataclysm, commotion

upheave: **4** lift, rear, rise

uphill: **6** rising, tiring **9** ascending, difficult, laborious

uphold: aid **4** abet, back, bear, stay **5** favor, raise **6** assert, defend, favour, second **7** confirm, support, sustain **8** conserve, maintain **9** encourage **11** countenance

upholder: **6** dealer **8** adherent **9** tradesman **10** undertaker **11** upholsterer

upholstered: **9** cushioned

upholstering material: **6** damask, lampas, mohair **7** valance **8** tapestry

upkeep: **4** cost **6** repair **7** support **8** maintain **11** maintenance

upland: **4** wold **6** coteau **7** plateau

uplift: **4** head, lift, rock **5** erect, raise, tower **7** collect, improve **8** elevated, ennobled, upheaval **9** elevation

upon: on; oer, sur(law) **4** atop **5** about, above **8** touching **10** concerning

prefix: ep; epi

that: **7** thereat **9** thereupon

which: **7** whereat **9** whereupon

upper crust: **5** elite **7** segment

upper lips part: **5** flews

uppermost: **5** first **6** upmost, uptown **7** topmost **8** farthest, foremost **9** outermost **11** predominant

uppish: **5** proud **6** elated **7** haughty, peevish **8** arrogant, assuming, snobbish

upraised: **5** atilt **6** lifted, raised **7** erected **8** elevated, extolled, improved **10** encouraged

uprear: **5** erect, exalt, raise

upright: **4** good, just, true **5** erect, moral, piano, right, stela, stele, stile **6** honest, square **7** endwise, sincere **8** straight, vertical, virtuous **9** elevation, equitable, honorable, righteous **10** pianoforte, scrupulous **11** unambiguous **13** perpendicular

combining form: **5** ortho

uprightness: **9** rectitude

uprising: **4** riot **6** ascent, mutiny, putsch, revolt **7** ensuing **8** reaction **9** ascending, commotion, rebellion **10** increasing, insurgency, revolution **12** insurrection **17** counterrevolution

uproar: din **4** riot, rout **5** brawl, hurly, noise **6** bedlam, bustle, clamor, dirdum, fracas, habble, hubble, hubbub, rattle, tumult **7** clamour, ferment, turmoil **8** outbreak **9** commotion, confusion **10** convulsion, donnybrook, hurlyburly, rumbullion, tintamarre **11** disturbance, pandemonium

uproot: **8** supplant **9** eradicate, extirpate **11** exterminate

upscuddle: **7** quarrel

upset: irk **4** cave, coup, keel, rile **6** defeat, refund, topple **7** capsize, confuse, derange, disturb, outcome, pervert, quarrel, reverse, subvert **8** capsized, overturn **9** discomfit, embarrass, overthrow, perturbed **10** discompose, disconcert, disordered, distressed, overturned **11** disorganize

upshot: end **5** issue, limit **6** result, sequel **7** outcome **10** conclusion **11** termination **12** consummation

upside: top

upstage: shy **5** aloof **6** offish **8** backward, outshine, snobbish **9** conceited **12** supercilious

upstart: **4** snob **6** origin **7** dalteen, parvenu, saffron **8** parvenue **9** cockhorse

upstir: **6** incite **7** agitate **9** stimulate

upsurge: **4** boom **9** inflation

uptake: **4** flue, tube **5** shaft **6** upcast **10** collection, comprehend **13** comprehension, understanding

upward: **4** more, over **5** above, lofty **7** airward, skyward **8** airwards **9** ascending

combining form: ano

uraeus: asp 10 decoration
uralite: 9 amphibole
Urania's son: 5 Hymen
uranian: 6 uranic 8 heavenly 9 celestial 12 astronomical
uranium dioxide: 10 ianthinite
Uranus: *children:* 4 Rhea 5 Titan 7 Cyclops
 moon: 5 Ariel 6 Oberon 7 Titania, Umbriel
 mother: Ge 4 Gaea, Gaia
 satellite: 5 Ariel
urare: rat 6 curare
urbane: 5 bland, civil, suave 6 polite, smooth 7 affable, elegant, refined 8 polished 9 courteous 13 sophisticated
urbanity: 6 comity 12 complaisance
urchin: boy, elf, imp, tad 4 arab, brat 5 child, elfin, gamin 8 cylinder, hedgehog, hurcheon 9 dandiprat, hunchback, youngster
ure: use 4 haze, mist 6 custom 8 exercise, practice
urease: 6 enzyme
Urfa: 6 Edessa
urge: dun, egg, ert(Sc.), hie, ply, sue 4 brod, coax, goad, prod, push, spur 5 broad, drive, filip, force, hurry, impel, plead, press 6 allege, compel, demand, desire, excite, exhort, fillip, incite, induce, insist 7 animate, augment, commove, entreat, impulse, provoke, solicit 8 advocate, persuade 9 flagitate, importune, influence, prosecute, stimulate 10 exasperate
urgency: 4 need 5 haste, hurry 6 crisis, stress 8 exigency, pressure 10 insistence 11 importunity
urgent: hot 5 grave 7 clamant, exigent 8 critical, pressing 9 important 10 solicitous 11 importunate
urial, oorial: sha 5 sheep
urisk: 7 brownie
urn: jar, run 4 bury, ewer, urna, vase 5 grave, inurn, steen, theca 6 spring 7 capsule, cistern, pitcher, samovar, vaselet 8 fountain 9 container 10 jardiniere 11 watercourse
urn-shaped: 9 urceolate
urodela: 5 newts, order 7 Caudata 8 amphibia 10 salamander
Ursa: 4 Bear
ursine: 6 ursoid 8 bearlike
ursine baboon: 6 chacma
ursoid: 6 ursine 8 bearlike
urubu: 7 vulture
Uruguay: *city:* 4 Melo 5 Minas 6 Rivera 7 Durazno, Florida 8 Paysandu 9 Maldonado 10 Montevideo
 coin: 4 peso 9 centesimo
 estuary: 5 Plata
 lake: 5 Merin, Mirim
 measure: 4 vara 6 cuadra, suerte

 river: 4 Malo 5 Negro 6 Ulimar 7 Uruguay 9 Cebollary 10 Tacaurembo
 weight: 7 quintal
urus: ox; tur 7 aurochs
us: uns(Gr.) 4 nous(Fr.)
usable: fit 8 servable 9 available, practical 10 convenient, functional 11 serviceable, utilitarian
usage: use 4 wont 5 habit, haunt, idiom 6 custom, method 7 conduct, manners, utility 8 behavior, interest, practice 9 treatment 10 convention, employment, experience
usance: use 5 usage, usury 6 custom, income
use: try 4 boot, hire, vail, wont 5 apply, avail, guide, habit, right, spend, stead, treat, trope, usage, value, wield 6 behoof, custom, employ, expend, handle, hansel, occupy 7 benefit, consume, exhaust, exploit, utility, utilize 8 accustom, exercise, frequent, function, handling, practice 9 habituate, privilege, treatment 10 employment, manipulate 11 application, consumption, utilization
 refrain from: 7 boycott
 to be of: 5 avail
 up: eat 4 tire 5 spend 7 consume, deplete, exhaust, outwear
used: 10 secondhand 11 experienced
useful: 4 good 5 utile 7 helpful 9 practical 10 beneficial, commodious, profitable 11 serviceable 12 advantageous
usefulness: 5 avail, value 6 profit 7 utility
useless: 4 idle, null, vain 6 futile, otiose 7 inutile 8 bootless, hopeless 9 fruitless, worthless 11 ineffectual, inefficient, superfluous 12 unprofitable 13 unserviceable 14 goodfornothing
user: 4 lead, page 5 guide 6 beadle, escort, herald 7 chobdar, conduct, officer, precede, preface, servant, teacher 9 announcer, assistant, attendant, harbinger, introduce, precursor 10 doorkeeper, forerunner, inaugurate
usings: 8 property 10 belongings
usquebaugh: 6 whisky 7 cordial
U.S.S.R.: See **Union of Soviet Socialist Republics.**
ustion: 7 burning 13 cauterization
usual: 6 common, normal, wonted 7 average, general, regular, typical 8 familiar, frequent, habitual, ordinary, orthodox 9 customary 10 accustomed, prevailing 11 stereotyped 12 conventional
usurer: 5 shark 6 loaner 11 moneylender
usurp: 4 take 5 seize 6 assume 8 accroach, arrogate
usury: 7 gombeen
Utah: *lake:* 4 Salt, Swan, Utah 6 Sevier
 mountain range: 5 Uinta 7 Wasatch
 river: 5 Grand, Green, Weber 6 Jordan,

Sevier **8** Colorado
state flower: **4** sego
town: **4** Lehi **5** Delta, Heber, Kanab, Logan, Ogden, Provo **6** Beaver, Eureka, Payson, Tooele **7** Milford **9** Richfield

utensil: pan, pot **4** tool **5** sieve **6** grater, vessel **7** skillet **8** strainer **9** collander, implement **10** instrument
cleaning: mop **5** broom, brush **6** Hoover, ramrod, vacuum **7** Bissell, sweeper

utensils: 7 baggage

utile: 6 useful **9** practical **10** profitable **12** advantageous

utilitarian: 5 plain **6** useful **8** economic **9** practical **10** functional **12** matter-of-fact

utility: use **5** avail **6** profit **7** benefit, service

utilize: use **6** employ **9** economize

utmost: end **4** best, last **5** final **7** extreme **8** farthest, greatest **9** uttermost

Utopia: 4 Eden **9** Shangri La
Harrington's: **6** Oceana

Utopian: 5 ideal **8** idealist, Quixotic **9** visionary **10** chimerical

utricle: sac **7** vesicle

utter: add, say **4** blat, bray, emit, gasp, pipe, pray, rail, roar, tell, vent **5** blurt, clack, croak, drawl, final, issue, mince, sheer, speak, spill, spout, trill, stark, state, total, voice **6** assert, direct, entire, mumble, reveal, warble **7** bluster, deliver, divulge, enounce, express, extreme, iterate, publish **8** abnormal, absolute, complete, disclose **9** enunciate, pronounce **10** articulate, peremptory **11** unqualified **13** unconditional

utterance: gab **4** osse **5** aside, dicta, ditty **6** dictum, oracle, speech **7** calling **8** effusion, monotone, phonesis, rhapsody **9** phonation **10** expression, forthgoing **12** articulation
soft: **6** breath, murmur **7** whisper
voiced: **6** sonant
voiceless: **4** surd **7** spirate

uttered: 4 oral **5** spake

utterly: 5 fully, stark **6** merely **7** totally **8** entirely **10** absolutely, allutterly, completely **11** diametrally **17** straightforwardly

uttermost: 5 final **6** utmost **7** extreme, outmost

utu: 6 reward **12** compensation, satisfaction

uva: 5 fruit, grape

ux: 4 uxor(L.), wife

V

vacancy: gap **5** break, chasm, space **6** cavity, hollow **7** interim, vacuity **10** hollowness, interstice **11** vacuousness

vacant: **4** free, idle, open, void **5** blank, empty, fishy, inane, silly **6** barren, devoid, hollow, lonely **7** foolish, lacking, vacuous, wanting **8** unfilled **9** destitute **10** disengaged, unemployed, unoccupied, untenanted **12** unencumbered, unreflecting **14** expressionless

vacate: **4** quit, void **5** annul, avoid, empty, leave **7** abandon, abolish **8** abdicate, abrogate, evacuate

vacation: **4** rest **5** leave, spell **6** outing, recess **7** holiday, leisure, nonterm, respite **8** furlough **9** justitium **12** intermission

place: spa **4** city, lake, park **5** beach **6** forest, resort **7** seaside **9** mountains

vacationist: **6** camper **7** tourist

vaccinate: **9** inoculate

vaccination: *inventor:* **6** Jenner

vaccine: **4** sera **5** serum

discoverer of: **4** Salk **6** Jenner

vacillate: **4** sway **5** waver **6** dacker, daiker, seesaw, teeter, totter **7** flutter, stagger **8** hesitate, titubate **9** fluctuate, oscillate

vacillation: **5** doubt **7** halting, swaying **8** wavering **9** faltering, hesitancy, infirmity **10** fickleness, indecision, unsureness **11** uncertainty **12** irresolution **14** changeableness

vacuity: **7** inanity, vacancy

vacuous: **4** dull, idle **5** blank, empty **6** stupid **8** unfilled **9** evacuated, senseless **11** purposeless **13** unintelligent

vacuum: **4** void

vacuum pump: **10** pulsometer

vade mecum: **6** manual **8** handbook

vadimonium: **4** bond **6** pledge **8** contract, security

vagabond: vag **4** rove **5** scamp **6** beggar, canter, jockey, rascal **7** erratic, gadling, nomadic, vagrant, wayward **8** bohemian, brodyaga, drifting, fugitive, wanderer **9** shiftless, straggler, wandering, worthless **10** blackguard, ne'er-do-well **12** hallanshaker **14** good-for-nothing

vagarious: **7** erratic **13** unpredictable

vagary: **4** roam, whim **5** caper, fancy, freak, jaunt, prank, stray, trick, waver **6** action, breach, notion, oddity, ramble, totter, whimsy **7** caprice, conceit **8** flagarie, rambling **9** departure, excursion,

procedure, wandering **10** digression, divergence **13** manifestation

vagrant: bum, vag **4** hobo, prog **5** caird, rogue, tramp **6** arrant, roving, shuler, truant, vagrom **7** devious, drifter, nomadic, prowler, roaming, shuiler **8** brodyaga, vagabond **9** itinerant **10** capricious, circuitous, prostitute **11** extravagant

vague: dim **4** dark, hazy **5** loose, misty, stray **6** dreamy, vagary **7** obscure, shadowy, sketchy, unfixed, vagrant **8** confused, nebulous, vagabond, wanderer **9** ambiguous, uncertain, unsettled, wandering **10** ill-defined, indefinite, indistinct, intangible **13** indeterminate

vail: tip, use **4** doff, dole, veil **5** avail, bribe, lower, yield **6** humble, profit, return, submit **7** benefit, decline, descend, descent, subside **8** downflow, gratuity, proceeds **9** advantage **10** beneficial, profitable **12** advantageous

vain: **4** idle **5** empty, flory, petty, proud, silly **6** flimsy, futile, hollow, otiose, snooty **7** foolish, stuckup, trivial, useless **8** gorgeous, hopeless, ignorant, nugatory **9** conceited, emptiness, fruitless, frustrate, unfounded, worthless **10** chimerical, evanescent, unavailing, unrewarded **11** empty-headed, ineffectual, overweening, unimportant **12** unprofitable, vainglorious

vainglorious: **4** vain **8** boastful **9** selfproud

vair: fur

Vaishnavas: *deity:* **6** Vishnu

priest: **6** gosain, gusain

Vaisya caste: **6** Aroras

vakass: **5** amice

valance: **5** drape **6** pelmet **7** curtain, drapery, hanging

vale: **4** dale, dean, dell, dene, glen **5** bache, glade **6** dingle, valley **8** farewell

valediction: **5** adieu **7** address **8** farewell

valency: **5** power, value **10** importance

valerian: **4** drug **5** plant **7** allheal, panacea, setwall

valet: man **4** goad **5** stick **6** andrew, tartar **7** dresser **9** attendant, cameriere, chamberer **10** manservant

Vali's mother: **4** Rind **5** Rindr

valiant: **4** bold, prow **5** aught, brave, proud **6** heroic, robust, strong, sturdy **7** doughty **8** galliard, intrepid, powerful, stalwart, vigorous, virtuous **9** bounteous, excellent, steadfast **10** chivalrous, courageous **11** meritorious **12** stouthearted

valid: 4 good, just. true **5** legal. sound **6** cogent, lawful, robust, strong **7** binding, healthy, telling, weighty **8** forcible, powerful **9** authentic, effective, efficient **10** conclusive, convincing, sufficient **11** efficacious **12** well-grounded

validate: 7 confirm **9** establish

valise: bag **4** case, grip **7** baggage **8** suitcase

Valjean: *discover:* **6** Javert
friend: **6** Marius
protege: **7** Cosette

vallecula: 6 furrow, groove **7** channel **10** depression

Valletta people: 7 Maltese

valley: dip **4** brae, comb, coom, cove, dale, dean, dell, dene, ghyl, gill, glen, rill, vale, wadi, wady **5** atrio, basin, combe, coomb, dhoon, glack, gorge, goyal, goyle, gully, kloof, swale, waddy **6** bolson, canada, canyon, clough, coombe, coulee, dingle, gutter, hollow, ravine, rincon, strath, trough **7** blowout **10** depression

vallum: 4 wall **7** rampart

valor, valour: 5 arete, merit, value, worth **6** bounty, virtue **7** bravery, courage, heroism, prowess **8** position **9** valuation **10** importance **11** distinction **12** fearlessness **13** signification

valuable: 4 dear **5** asset **6** costly, prized, useful, worthy **8** precious **9** estimable, excellent, treasured **10** worthwhile **11** serviceable

value: use **4** cost, feck(Sc.), rate **5** avail, cheap, price, prize, worth **6** assess, assize, esteem, extend, moment **7** account, apprise, apprize, average, cherish, compute, opinion, respect, utility **8** appraise, estimate, evaluate, treasure **9** inventory, valuation **10** appreciate, estimation, importance
anything of little: **5** plack(Sc.) **6** trifle
equal: **6** parity
mathematical limit of: **8** derivate
mean: **7** average
net: **7** reserve
nominal: par
reduction: **12** depreciation

valued: 4 dear

valve: 4 cock, gate **6** piston

vamoose: lam **4** scat **5** leave, scram **6** decamp, depart

vamp: 4 hose, plod, sock **5** patch, tramp **6** invent, repair, seduce **7** beguile, concoct, fireman **9** fabricate, improvise

vampire: bat **5** lamia **6** alukah, corpse, usurer **7** seducer **11** blackmailer, bloodsucker, extortioner **12** extortionist

van: fan **4** fore, lead, wing **5** front, truck, wagon **6** shovel, summit, winnow **7** fourgon, vehicle **9** forefront

vandal: hun **9** plunderer

vandalize: mar **6** deface

Vandyke: 5 beard **6** artist **7** picture

vane: 7 feather **11** weathercock

vanguard: 10 avantgarde

vanilla substance: 8 coumarin

vanish: 4 fade, melt **8** disperse, evanesce **9** disappear

vanity (see also **vain**): **4** airs **5** pride **6** egoism **7** compact, conceit, egotism, falsity **8** futility, idleness **9** dizziness, emptiness **10** hollowness **11** fatuousness, foolishness, self-conceit

Vanity Fair character: 5 Becky **6** Amelia

vanquish: get, win **4** beat, best, rout **5** expel, floor **6** defeat, expugn, master, subdue **7** confute, conquer **8** confound, overcome, suppress, surmount **9** overthrow

vanquisher: 6 victor

vantage: fee **4** gain **6** chance, profit **9** advantage **10** perquisite **11** opportunity, superiority

vapid: dry **4** dull, flat, pall **5** inane, stale, trite **7** insipid, mawkish **8** lifeless **9** pointless, tasteless **10** flavorless, spiritless, unanimated, unexciting **13** uninteresting

vapor: fog, gas **4** fume, haze, idea, mist **5** boast, brume, cloud, ewder, fancy, humor, smoke, steam **6** breath, bubble, humour, nimbus, notion **7** halitus **8** contrail, humidity, phantasm **9** evaporate **10** blustering **11** braggadocio
frozen: **4** hail, rime, snow **5** frost, sleet

vaporizable: 8 volatile

vaporize: 5 steam **9** evaporate

vaporous: 8 fleeting **13** unsubstantial

vaquero: 6 cowboy **8** herdsman, horseman **10** equestrian

varec, varech: 4 kelp **7** seaweed

variable (see also **vary**): **6** fickle, fitful **7** protean, unequal, variant, varying **8** floating, unstable, unsteady **9** irregular, uncertain **10** capricious, inconstant

variance (see also **vary**): **7** discord, dispute **10** contention **11** discrepancy

variate: 4 vary **6** varied **8** variable

variation (see also **vary**): **7** variety **8** heterism, mutation **9** tolerance **10** aberration, deflection **11** distinction

varicolored: 6 varied **7** mottled **11** diversified

varicose: 7 dilated, swollen **8** enlarged

varied: 6 daedal **7** several, various **10** variegated

variegate: 9 diversify

variegated: 4 pied, shot **5** lyard(Sc.), lyart(Sc.) **6** daedal, menald, motley, varied **7** dappled, flecked, mottled, painted, piebald, tissued **8** speckled **9** different, enamelled **11** diversified

variety: 4 kind, sort **5** breed, class **7** species **9** diversity, variation **10** difference **16** multifariousness

variola: **6** cowpox **8** horsepox, smallpox

various: **4** many **6** divers, sundry **7** diverse, several **8** manifold, variable **9** different, uncertain, versatile **10** changeable, inconstant

varlet: boy **4** page **5** gippo, knave, noble, youth **6** menial, rabble, rascal, vassal **7** bailiff, footman, servant **8** coistrel, coistril **9** attendant, scoundrel

varmint, varment: **5** sharp **6** clever **7** amateur, cunning, dashing **8** sporting

varnish: **4** spar **5** japan **7** lacquer **8** brighten **9** embellish

ingredient: lac **5** copal, resin, rosin **6** dammar

vary: **5** alter, range, shift **6** change, depart, differ, modify, swerve **7** deviate, dispute, dissent, diverge, quarrel, variate **8** disagree **9** alternate, diversify, fluctuate, oscillate

vas: **4** duct **6** pledge, surety, vessel

vase: jar, urn **4** asci, vaso **5** ascus, askos, echea, tazza **6** crater, deinoi, deinos, krater **7** amphora **8** amphorae **10** cassolette, jardiniere

vassal: man **4** bond, esne, rule, serf **5** ceile, helot, liege, slave **6** varlet **7** bondman, feedman, feodary, geneate, homager, servant, servile, subject **8** dominate **9** dependent, feudatory **11** beneficiary, subordinate, subservient

pert. to: **6** feudal

vassalage: **5** valor **6** fealty, homage **7** courage, loyalty, prowess **8** dominion, services **9** authority, servitude

vast: **4** huge **5** broad, great, large, vasty **6** cosmic, lonely, mighty, untold **7** immense **8** colossal, enormous, gigantic, spacious **9** boundless, cyclopean, extensive **11** far-reaching, illimitable

vastness: **7** expanse **8** grandeur **9** magnitude

vat (see also **barrel, tub, vessel**): bac, fat, pit, tub, tun, wit **4** back, beck, cask, coom, gyle, keel, kier, tank **5** coomb, keeve, kieve, press **6** barrel, kettle, vessel **7** caldron, chessel, cistern **8** cauldron, chessart

vatic: **8** inspired, oracular **9** prophetic **11** prophetical

Vatican statuary group: **7** Laocoon

vaticanism: **9** curialism

vaticinate: **8** foretell

vaticinator: **4** seer **7** prophet

vaudeville: **5** revue

act: **4** skit, song, turn **5** dance

vaudevillist: **5** actor **6** dancer, hoofer, singer **7** acrobat, juggler **9** performer

vaudy: gay **5** gaudy, showy **6** elated, sturdy **8** cheerful

vault: box, pit **4** arch, bend, cave, cope, dome, jump, leap, over, roof, room, safe, tomb **5** bound, croft, crypt, curve, floor, groin, shade **6** cavern, cellar, crater, cupola, curvet, flaunt, grotto, hurdle, spring, welkin **7** ceiling, chamber, dungeon, glorify, testudo **8** flourish **9** concavity, staircase **10** depository, repository, testudines(pl.)

vaunt: van **4** brag, font **5** boast, roosa, roose **6** avaunt **11** ostentation

vaunty: **4** vain **5** brave, proud

veal: **4** calf, meat, veau(F.)

cutlet: **9** schnitzel

larded: **8** fricando **10** fricandeau

vedette: **5** vigil, watch **8** sentinel

Vedic: *artisans of gods:* **6** Ribhus

cosmic order: **4** Rita

fire god: **4** Agni

god: **6** Aditya

hymn: **6** mantra

language: **4** Pali **8** Sanskrit

sky serpent: ahi

sun god: **7** Savitar

text: **5** Sakha, Shaka

veer: yaw **4** slue, sway, turn **5** alter, shift **6** broach, careen, change, swerve **7** deviate, digress **9** fluctuate

veery: **6** thrush

vega: **5** tract **6** meadow

Vega's constellation: **4** Lyra

vegetable: pea, yam **4** bean, beet, corn, kale, leak, okra, soya **5** onion, pease, plant **6** carrot, celery, lentil, pepper, potato, radish, squash, tomato, turnip **7** brocoli, cabbage, lettuce, parsley, parsnip, peascod, rhubarb, spinach **8** broccoli, cucumber, eggplant, peasecod, rutabaga **9** artichoke **11** cauliflower **15** Brussels sprouts

carbonized: **7** lignite

dealer: **8** huckster **11** greengrocer **12** costermonger

decayed: **4** duff **5** humus

dish: **6** zimmis **10** chiffonade

esculent: **6** legume

exudation: lac, sap **5** resin

ferment: **5** yeast

green: **5** sabzi

oil: **8** macassar

pepsin: **6** caroid

poison: **5** abrin

salad: **4** leak **5** chard **6** endive **7** lettuce. romaine, shallot **8** scallion

stunted: **5** scrub

sugar-yielding: **4** beet

tinder: **6** amadou

vegetable caterpillar: **5** aweto

vegetable pear: **7** chayote

vegetant: **7** vegetal **9** animating **12** invigorating

vegetation: **6** growth **7** verdure

floating: **4** sadd, sudd

god: **4** Atys, Esus **5** Attis

vegete: **6** lively **7** healthy **11** flourishing

vehement: hot **5** angry, eager, fiery, hefty,

irked, yeder **6** ardent, fervid, flashy, heated, raging, urgent **7** animose, animous, fervent, furioso, furious, intense, violent **8** forceful, vigorous **9** impetuous **10** boisterous, passionate

vehemently: 5 amain

vehicle (see also **aircraft, ship**): ark, bus, car, van **4** auto, shay, wain **5** araba, brake, break, buggy, dilly, sedan, sulky, wagon **6** barrow, charet, device, hansom, landau, troika **7** chariot, kibitka(Russ.), tallyho **8** carriage, charette **9** buckboard, velociman **10** automobile, conveyance

army: **4** jeep, tank **9** ambulance

child's: **4** pram **5** buggy **6** walker **7** scooter **8** carriage, stroller, tricycle **10** velocipede

display: **5** float

hauling: van **4** dray, lory, sled **5** truck **7** tractor, trailer

passenger: bus, cab **4** hack, taxi, tram **5** train **6** hansom **7** minibus, omnibus, tramcar, trolley **9** charabanc

public: bus, cab, car **4** taxi, tram **5** train, **7** omnibus, ricksha **8** rickshaw **10** jinricksha, jinrikisha

two-wheeled: **4** cart **5** sulky, tonga **6** cisium **7** caleche **9** carromata(Fil.) **11** vinaigrette

wheelless: **4** ship, sled **6** cutter, sledge, sleigh

veil: dim **4** caul, film, hide, mask **5** cloak, cover, orale, velum, volet **6** bumble, fannel, masque, screen, shroud, soften **7** conceal, curtain, watcher **8** calyptra, disguise, headrail **11** amphithyron

veiling: 4 veil **5** tulle, voile **7** curtain **10** obvelation

vein: bed, rib **4** dash, hilo, lode, mood, seam, tang, vena, wave **5** costa, crack, scrin, shade, smack, spice, tinge, touch, trend, venae **6** cavity, costae, strain, streak **7** bonanza, channel, crevice, fissure, stratum **8** tendency **11** inclination, variegation

arrangement of: **9** neuration

fluid: **4** icor **5** ichor

inflammation: **9** phlebitis

pert. to: **6** veinal, venous

small: **6** venule **7** veinlet, veinule **8** veinulet

veinless: 7 avenous

veinstone: 6 gangue, matrix **9** lodestuff

velamen: 5 velum **8** membrane

velar: 7 palatal **8** guttural

velarium: 4 veil **6** awning **8** covering

veldt, veld: 6 meadow, plains **9** grassland

velitation: 7 contest, dispute **8** skirmish

velleity: 4 hope, wish **6** desire **8** volition **11** inclination

vellicate: 4 nip **4** pull **5** pinch, pluck **6** tickle, twitch **9** titillate

veloce: 7 dashing, rapidly **9** direction

velocious: 4 fast **6** speedy

velocipede: 4 ride **7** bicycle,` dicycle **8** tricycle **11** quadricycle

velocity: 4 pace **5** speed **8** celerity, rapidity **9** quickness, swiftness

instrument: **11** cinemograph

velum: 4 veil **6** awning, palate **8** membrane

velvet: 4 gain **5** drink **6** birodo(Jap.), profit **7** surplus **8** winnings

fabric like: **5** panne **6** velure

knife: **6** trevet

velvet dock: 6 mullen **7** mullein **10** elecampane

velvetbreast: 9 merganser

venal: 6 venous **7** corrupt, salable **8** saleable, vendible **9** mercenary

vend: 4 hawk, sell **5** utter **6** market, peddle **7** publish **8** transfer

vendetta: 4 feud

vendeuse: 9 salesgirl **10** saleswoman

vendible: 5 venal **7** salable **8** saleable **9** mercenary **10** marketable

vendition: 4 sale

vendor, vender,: 6 seller **7** alienor, butcher **8** merchant, salesman

vendue: 4 sale **7** auction

veneer: lac **4** coat, face, show **5** glaze, gloss, layer, plate **6** enamel, facing **7** overlay

venenate: 6 poison **8** poisoned **9** poisonous

venerable: old **4** aged, hoar, sage **5** hoary **6** august **7** ancient, antique, classic

veneration: awe **4** fear **6** esteem **7** respect, worship **8** devotion, idolatry **9** adoration, reverence

venerer: 6 hunter **8** huntsman

Venetian: See **Italy, Venice**.

Venezuela: *city:* **4** Aroa, Coro **6** Atures, Cumana **7** Barinas, Caracas(c.), Guanare, Maracay, Maturin, Ocumare, San Juan **8** Tacupita, Trujillo, Valencia **9** Barcelona, Los Teques, San Carlos, San Filepe **10** La Asuncion **11** San Fernando **12** Barquisimeto, San Cristobal

coin: **4** real **5** medio **6** fuerte **7** bolivar, centimo **8** morocota **10** venezolano

fiber: **5** erizo

Indian: **6** Timote

lake: **9** Maracaibo, Tacarigua

measure: **5** galon, milla **6** fanega **7** estadel

measure of weight: bag **5** libra

mountain: **5** Andes, Icutu **6** Concha, Cuneva, Parima **7** Imutaca, Roraima **9** Pacaraima **20** Sierra-Nevada-de-Merida

people: **5** Carib **6** Timote **7** Timotex **8** Guarauno

plain: **5** llano

port: **8** La Guayra **9** Maracaibo **13** Ciudad Bolivar, Puerto-Cabello

revolutionist: **7** Miranda

river: **5** Apure, Caura **6** Arausa, Caroni **7** Orinoco, Ventuar *snake:* **4** lora

state: **4** Lara **5** Apure, Sucre, Zulia **6** Aragua, Falcon, Merida, Zamora **7** Bolivar, Cojedes, Guarico, Monagas, Tachira, Yaracuy **8** Carabobo, Trujillo **10** Anzoategui, Portuguesa **12** Nueva Esparta

vengeance: **5** wrack **6** wanion **7** revenge **8** reprisal, requital **10** punishment **11** retaliation, retribution

god of: **6** Erinys **7** Alastor

goddess of: Ara, Ate **7** Nemesis

venial: **7** trivial **9** allowable, excusable, tolerable **10** pardonable **13** insignificant **15** unobjectionable

Venice: *beach:* **4** Lido

boat: **7** gondola **9** bucentaur

bridge: **6** Rialto

coin: **5** betso, bezzo, ducat **6** sequin **8** bagatino, gazzetta

court: **8** quaranty

island: **6** Rialto

magistrate: **4** doge

medal: **5** osela, osele **6** osella, oselle **7** oscella

painter: **6** Titian **7** Bellini **8** Veronese **9** Giorgione **10** Tintoretto

resort: **4** Lido

river: **6** Brenta

traveler and writer: **5** Conti **9** Marco Polo

wine measure: **6** anfora

Venice of the North: **9** Stockholm

venin: **6** poison

venison: **7** pemican **8** pemmican

vennel: **4** lane **5** alley, sewer **6** gutter

venomous: **5** snaky, toxic **6** attern, deadly **7** baneful, noxious **8** poisoned, spiteful, virulent **9** envenomed, malicious, malignant, poisonous, rancorous **11** mischievous

vent: **4** draw, emit, exit, hole, slit **5** brand, eject **6** cancel, outlet, report **7** fissure, opening, release **8** aperture, avacuate, disgorge, emission **9** discharge, embrasure **10** escapement

ventilate: air, fan **6** aerate, aerify, winnow **9** oxygenate

ventilation: **6** aerage **9** breathing

ventilator: **6** blinds, louver

ventral: **7** sternal

ventriloquist: **12** engastrimyth **13** gastriloquist

venture: hap, try **4** dare, luck, risk, wage **5** brave, essay, stake **6** chance, danger, feeler, hazard **7** attempt, courage, flutter, fortune, risking **8** trespass **9** adventure, speculate **10** enterprise **11** contingency, presumption, speculation, undertaking

ventured: **5** durst

venturesome: **4** bold, rash **5** hardy **6** heroic **8** fearless, heedless, reckless **9** audacious, dangerous, foolhardy, hazardous, venturous **11** adventurous, furthersome, temerarious

venturesomeness: **8** temerity

venturous: **11** venturesome

venue: hit **4** bout, site **5** lunge, match, onset **6** coming, ground, thrust **7** arrival, assault **9** encounter

Venus: **6** Hesper **8** Hesperus

son: **5** Cupid

sweetheart: **6** Adonis

venust: **6** comely **7** elegant **8** graceful **9** beautiful

veracious: **9** measuring, veridical **10** estimating

veracity: **5** truth **7** honesty **8** accuracy, trueness **9** judgement, precision, sincerity **11** correctness **12** faithfulness, truthfulness

veranda: **5** lania, porch, stoep **6** loggia, piazza **7** gallery, portico **8** verandah

verb: *auxiliary:* had, has, may, was **4** hast, will **5** might, shall, shalt, would

suffix: le; ire, ise

table: **8** paradigm

tense: **6** aorist

verbal: **4** oral **5** wordy **7** verbose **9** talkative **10** articulate

verbatim: **6** orally **7** literal **8** verbally

verbena: **7** aloysia

verberate: **4** beat **5** shake **6** quiver, strike **7** tremble

verbiage: **4** talk **7** chatter, diction, fustian, wording **9** verbosity, wordiness **10** redundancy

verbose: **5** windy, wordy **6** prolix **7** diffuse **9** redundant

verboten: **4** tabu **5** taboo **9** forbidden **10** prohibited

verdant: raw **5** fresh, green **8** immature, innocent **13** inexperienced **15** unsophisticated

Verdi's opera: **4** Aida **6** Ernani, Otello **7** Othello **8** Traviata **9** Rigoletto

verdict: **4** word **7** finding, opinion **8** decision, judgment

verdigris: **6** aerugo

Verdun river: **5** Meuse

verdure: **4** odor **5** scent, smell **6** flavor **7** acidity **8** greenery, strength, tapestry, tartness **9** freshness, greenness

Verein: **7** society **11** association **12** organization

verge: lip, rim, rod **4** edge, tend, twig, wand **5** bound, brink, limit, marge, range, scope, shaft, staff, stick, watch **6** border, margin **7** incline, virgate **8** approach, boundary, yardland **9** extremity, timepiece **13** circumference

verger: **4** dean **6** garden **7** justice, orchard **8** official **9** attendant

Vergil: See **Virgil.**

veridical: **7** genuine **8** accurate, truthful **9** veracious **12** truthtelling

verification: **8** averment **12** confirmation **14** authentication

verify: **4** aver, back, test **5** audit, check, prove **6** affirm, ratify, second **7** certify, collate, confirm, support **8** maintain **9** establish **11** certificate **12** authenticate, substantiate

verily: yea **4** amen **5** parde, pardi, pardy, truly **6** certes, indeed, pardie, really **9** certainly **11** confidently

verisimilitude: 5 truth **10** likelihood **11** probability

veritable: 4 real, true **6** actual, gospel, honest **7** genuine **9** authentic, veracious

verity: 12 faithfulness

verjuice: 5 juice **7** acidity **8** sourness, tartness

vermifuge: 12 anthelmintic

vermilion: red **8** cinnabar

vermin: 4 lice, mice, rats **5** filth, fleas, flies **7** bedbugs, rodents, weasels

verminous: 5 dirty **6** filthy **7** noxious **9** offensive

Vermont: *city:* **5** Barre **10** Montpelier(c.) *mountain range:* **7** Taconic

vernacular: 5 lingo **6** jargon, patois **7** dialect

vernal: 4 mild, warm **5** fresh, young **8** youthful **10** springlike

verneuk: 5 cheat **6** humbug **7** swindle

verrel: 7 ferrule

versate: 4 turn **7** revolve

versatile: 5 handy **6** fickle **7** flexile **8** unsteady, variable **10** changeable, inconstant, reversible

verse (see also **poem**): **4** turn **5** meter, stave, stich **6** stanza **7** revolve, stichos **8** consider **11** familiarize
Bible: **4** text
pert. to: **6** poetic
stress: **5** ictus

verse-maker: 8 meterist

versed: 5 adept **6** beseen **7** erudite, learned, skilled **8** familiar **9** practiced **10** acquainted, conversant, proficient

verset: 7 prelude **8** versicle **9** interlude

versification: 5 rhyme **6** poetry

versifier: 4 poet **5** rimer **6** verser **7** poetess **9** poetaster

versify: 6 berime **7** berhyme

version: 7 edition, turning **9** rendition **10** conversion, paraphrase **11** translation **14** transformation

verso: vo

versus: vs.; con **4** agin **7** against

vertebra: 4 axis **6** spondy **7** spondyl

vertebrae: 5 spine

vertebrate: ray **9** backboned
class: **4** aves
division: **6** somite
feathered: **4** bird
group: **9** amnionata

vertex: top **4** apex **6** summit **11** culmination

vertical: 4 acme **5** apeak, erect, plumb, sheer **6** abrupt, height, summit, vertex **7** upright **13** perpendicular

verticil: 5 whorl

vertiginate: 5 twirl, whirl

vertiginous: 5 dizzy, giddy **6** rotary **8** rotating, unstable, whirling **9** dizziness, giddiness, revolving **10** inconstant **11** vacillating

vertigo: 6 megrim **9** dizziness, giddiness

verve: pep **4** dash, elan **5** ardor, vigor **6** bounce, spirit, talent **7** ability **8** aptitude, vivacity **9** animation **10** enthusiasm

vervet: 6 monkey

very: so; too **4** fell, real, same, tres(F.), true, unco(Sc.) **5** assai(It.), molto(It.) truly, utter **6** actual, lawful, mighty, really **7** dimolto(It.), exactly, genuine **8** absolute, complete, especial, peculiar, rightful, truthful **9** extremely, identical, precisely, veracious, veritable **10** legitimate, mortacious **11** exceedingly
combining form: eri

vesica: 6 vessel **7** bladder

vesicate: 7 blister

vesicle: sac **4** bleb, cell, cyst **5** bulla **6** cavity, vessel **7** bladder, blister, utricle
air: **8** aerocyst

vesper: 7 evening **8** eventide

vespers: 6 prayer **7** service **8** ceremony, evensong

vessel: (see also **aircraft, boat, container, pail, ship**): can, cog, cup, jar, pan, tub, urn, vas **4** bell, cadi, drum, duct, ewer, olla, olpe, tank, tube, vase **5** bocal, cadus, canoe, cogue, craft, cruse, laver, liner, paten **6** aftaba, aludel, barrel, cootie, crater, firkin, funnel, goblet, goulah, holmos, krater, patera, situla, yetlin **7** aleyard, blickey, blickie, cistern, cresset, gabbard, gabbart, paterae, pinnace, pitcher, situlae, steamer, utensil, yetling **8** aiguiere, ciborium **9** alcarraza **10** receptacle
pert. to: **5** vasal
sacred: ama

vest: 4 robe **5** dress, endow, gilet **6** accrue, clothe, invest, jacket, jerkin, linder, weskit **7** furnish, garment **9** waistcoat **10** undershirt

vesta: 5 match

vestal: nun **4** pure **6** chaste, virgin

vestibule: 4 hall **5** entry, lobby, porch **7** chamber, narthex, passage **8** anteroom, entrance, vestible **10** antechapel

vestige: bit **4** mark, sign **5** relic, shred, smack, trace, track, umbra **8** footstep, tincture **9** vestigium

vestiture: 4 garb **5** dress **8** clothing

vestment (see also **dress**): **4** garb, gear, gown, hood, robe **5** cotta, dress, orale **6** chimer, chimre, gloves, rochet, tippet **7** cassock, garment, sandals **8** cincture, clothing, covering **10** habiliment
ecclesiastical: alb, cap **4** alba, cope **5** albae, amice, ephod, fanon, miter, orale, stole **6** lappet, palium, saccos **7** cassock, maniple, tunicle **8** chasuble, dalmatic, surplice

pert. to: **8** vestiary

vestry: 4 room **7** meeting **8** sacristy

vesture: 4 corn **5** cover, crops, grass **6** clothe, seizin **7** apparel, envelop, raiment, stubble, wrapper **8** garments, vestment **9** underwood **11** investiture

vesuvian: 5 fusee, match **8** volcanic

vet: 7 veteran **10** veterinary **12** veterinarian

vetch: ers **4** akra, tare, weed **5** fetch **7** arvejon

veteran: old **7** oldster **8** seasoned **9** practiced **11** experienced

veterinarian: 7 farrier

veto: 6 forbid **7** message **8** document, negative, overrule, prohibit **11** disapproval, forbiddance, prohibition **12** interdiction

vettura: 5 coach **8** carriage

veuve: 4 bird **6** whydah

vex: ire, irk, tew **4** cark, chaw, fret, fuss, gall, miff, rile, roil, toss **5** anger, annoy, chafe, harry, shake, spite, tease, worry, wrack **6** bother, cumber, madden, molest, nettle, offend, plague, pother, ruffle **7** afflict, agitate, discuss, dispute, disturb, harrass, perplex, provoke, torment, trouble **8** disquiet, irritate, vexation **9** annoyance, displease, infuriate **11** disturbance

vexation: 5 pique, thorn **7** fatigue **9** weariness **13** mortification

vexatious: 4 chaw, sore, vexy **5** pesky **8** annoying, cumbrous, frampoid, untoward **9** disturbed, pestilent **10** afflictive **11** contrarious, troublesome

vexed: 5 sorry **7** grieved

vexillum: web **4** flag, vane **6** banner **8** standard

via: way **4** road **5** right **7** passage, through

viaduct: 6 bridge **7** trestle

vial: 5 ampul, cruet, phial **6** bottle, caster, vessel **7** ampoule

viand: 4 fare, food **6** edible **7** aliment **8** victuals **10** provisions

choice: **4** cate

viaticum: 5 money **8** supplies **9** allowance **10** provisions

viator: 8 traveler, wayfarer

vibrant: 5 alive **8** sonorous, vigorous **9** vibrating

vibrate: jar, wag **4** beat, cast, dirl, rock, whir **5** pulse, quake, shake, swing, throb, throw, trill, waver, whirr **6** dindle, launch, quaver, quiver, shimmy, shiver, thrill **7** agitate, resound, tremble **8** brandish, flichter, resonate **9** fluctuate, oscillate, vacillate

vibration: 4 dirl(Sc.), tirl(Sc.) **5** thirl(Sc.) **6** dingle, quaver, quiver, thrill, tremor **7** flutter **8** stirring **11** oscillation, vacillation **14** changeableness

musical: **5** trill **7** sonance, tremolo, vibrato **8** overtone

point without: **4** node

vicar: 5 proxy **6** deputy, priest **8** minister **9** clergyman **10** substitute, vicegerent

assistant: **6** curate

vicarage: 4 dues **5** house **6** salary, tithes **8** benefice **9** household, pastorate, rectorate, residence

vice: sin **4** evil, grip, hold, turn **5** crime, fault, force, grasp, place, proxy, stead, taint **6** defect **7** blemish, failing, squeeze, stopper **8** iniquity, stairway **9** deformity, depravity **10** corruption, substitute, wickedness **11** harmfulness, viciousness **12** imperfection

viceroy: 5 nabob, nazim **6** exarch, satrap **8** governor **9** butterfly

vicinity: 6 region **8** nearness, vicinage **9** proximity **11** propinquity, resemblance **12** neighborhood **13** neighbourhood

vicious: bad, ill **4** evil, foul, lewd, mean, vile **6** faulty, wicked **7** corrupt, immoral, noxious **8** debasing, depraved, infamous, spiteful **9** dangerous, defective, dissolute, malicious, malignant, nefarious, perverted **10** corrupting, iniquitous, villainous

vicissitude: 6 change **8** mutation **10** difficulty, revolution, succession **11** alternation, interchange

victim: 4 dupe, goat, gull, prey **6** sucker

list: **4** toll

victor: 6 captor, winner **7** conquer **8** bangster, unbeaten **9** conqueror **10** vanquisher, victorious

victory: win **7** mastery, success, triumph **8** conquest **9** landslide, supremacy **11** superiority

celebrate: **9** epinician

goddess of: **4** Nike

ruinous: **7** pyrrhic

symbol: **4** palm

victrola: 9 turntable **10** phonograph **12** record player

victualler: 6 sutler **9** innkeeper

victuals: bit **4** bite, food, grub, meat **6** viands **7** vittles **11** nourishment

videlicet: viz **4** namely **8** scilicet

vie: bet, run **4** cope **5** bandy, rival, stake, wager **6** endure, hazard, oppose, strive **7** compete, contend, contest, emulate **8** panorama, prospect, struggle **9** challenge

Vienna: 4 Wien

palace: **10** Schonbrunn

park: **6** Prater

view: aim, eye, ken, see, vue(F.) **4** goal, look, scan **5** aview, scape, scene, sight, slant, tenet, vista, watch **6** admire, apercu(F.), aspect, behold, belief, object, regard, sketch, survey, vision **7** examine, inspect, opinion, picture, profile, summary, thought, witness **8** attitude, consider, panorama, prospect, synopsis **9** apprehend **10** appearance, inspection, perception, photograph, scrutinize, standpoint **11** contemplate, examination, expectation **13** contemplation

extended: **8** panorama
mentally: **8** envision
obstruct: **4** hide **7** conceal
open to: **4** bare **5** overt **6** expose
viewer: **9** spectator **11** stereoscope **14** superintendent
viewing instrument: **5** scope **9** telescope **10** binoculars
viewy: **5** showy **8** fanciful **9** visionary **11** spectacular, unpractical **12** ostentatious
vigil: eve **4** wake **5** guard **7** prayers, service **8** devotion, watchman
vigilant: **4** agog, wary **5** alert, awake, aware **7** careful, wakeful **8** cautious, watchful **9** attentive, observant, sleepless **11** circumspect
vigilantes: **5** posse
vigneron: **10** winegrower **13** viticulturist
vignettist: **6** artist, author, writer **7** painter **8** engraver **12** photographer
vigor, vigour: pep, vim, vir(Sc.), vis **4** birr, zeal **5** flush, force, nerve, power **6** energy, foison, growth, health **7** impetus, potency, stamina **8** activity, boldness, strength, virility, vitality **9** animation, fraicheur, hardihood, intensity, vehemence **10** invigorate
deprive of: sap **6** deaden **8** enervate
lose: fag, sag **4** fail, flag, pine **6** weaken **7** decline
period of: **6** heyday
vigoroso: **8** vigorous **9** direction, energetic
vigorous: yep **4** able, cant, fell, hale, spry, yepe **5** eager, frank, hardy, hefty, lusty **6** florid, hearty, lively, robust, rugged, sturdy **7** cordial **8** athletic, muscular **9** effective, energetic, strenuous **11** efficacious, energetical
vigorously: **5** amain
Viking: **4** Eric **5** rover **6** pirate **8** Norseman, Northman **12** Scandinavian
vilayet: **6** region **8** division
vile: bad, low **4** base, evil, foul, mean **5** cheap, lowly **6** abject, coarse, drasty, filthy, impure, odious, sinful, sordid, wicked **7** bestial, carrion, corrupt, debased, ignoble, unclean, vicious **8** baseborn, befouled, depraved **9** abandoned, degrading, loathsome, nefarious, obnoxious, offensive, repulsive, worthless **10** abominable, despicable, disgusting **12** contaminated
vileness: **6** fedity **9** turpitude
vilify: **5** abuse, avile, libel **6** bemean, debase, defame, malign, revile, slight **7** asperse, blacken, cheapen, debauch, degrade, despise, detract, slander, traduce **8** belittle, disgrace, dishonor, reproach, vilipend **9** blaspheme, disparage **10** calumniate, depreciate
vility: **8** vileness
vill: **4** town **7** village **8** division, township
villa: **5** aldea, dacha(Russ.), house **8** villakin **9** residence, villaette **10** villanette

village: gav, mir(Russ.), rew(Sc.) **4** dorp, home, stad(African), town, vici **5** aldea, bourg, kraal, thorp, vicus **6** bustee, castle, hamlet, pueblo, thorpe **7** borough, caserio(Sp.), endship **8** bourgade, villaget, villakin **9** aldeament **10** settlement **11** aggregation
villain: **4** boor, Iago, lout, serf **5** churl, demon, devil, heavy, knave, rogue **6** rascal **8** scelerat **9** miscreant, scoundrel **10** villainous
mythological: **4** ogre **5** giant **6** dragon
nemesis of: **4** hero
villainous: bad, low **4** base, evil, mean, vile **6** common, slight, vulgar, wicked **7** boorish **8** clownish, criminal, depraved, flagrant, wretched **9** dastardly, felonious **10** detestable, flagitious, iniquitous **12** disagreeable **13** objectionable
villainy: **5** crime **7** knavery **9** depravity
villatic: **5** rural **6** rustic
villein: **4** carl, serf **5** ceorl, churl **7** bondman, cottier
vim: zip **4** gimp **5** force, vigor **6** energy, ginger, spirit **8** strength
vina: **10** instrument
vinaigrette: box **6** bottle **7** vehicle **8** carriage
vincible: **11** conquerable **12** surmountable
vindicate: **4** free **5** clear **6** acquit, assert, avenge, defend, excuse, uphold **7** absolve, deliver, justify, propugn, revenge, support, sustain **8** advocate, maintain **9** exculpate, exonerate
vindication: **7** apology
vindicative: See **vindictive**.
vindictive: **7** hostile **8** punitive, spiteful, vengeful **10** revengeful **11** retaliatory, retributive, vindicative, vindicatory
vine: hop, ivy **4** akas, bine, gogo, odal, soma **5** betel, buaze, 'bwazi, guaco, liana, liane **6** maypop **7** creeper, cupseed, trailer **8** clematis **9** grapevine **10** chilicothe
vinegar: **4** acid **5** eisel **6** acetum, alegar, eisell **8** vinaigre(F.)
dregs: **6** mother
ester: **7** acetate
pert. to: **6** acetic
preserve in: **6** pickle
salt: **7** acetate
spice: **8** tarragon
vinegary: **4** sour **7** acetose, crabbed **9** unamiable **11** ill-tempered
vineyard: cru
protector: **7** Priapus
vinous: **4** winy **9** vinaceous
vintage: **4** crop, wine **5** cuvee, yield
vintner: **8** merchant
viol: **5** gigue, rebec **6** rebeck, vielle **7** quinton **9** violaalta
progenitor: **5** rebec
viola: **5** gamba **12** violapomposa

violate: 4 flaw, rape 5 abuse, break, force, harry, spoil, wrong 6 betray, broach, defile, defoil, defoul, injure, insult, invade, offend, ravage, ravish 7 corrupt, debauch, disturb, falsify, outrage, pollute, profane 8 deflower, dishonor, infringe, mistreat 9 constrain, desecrate, disregard 10 contravene, transgress

violation: 5 crime, error 6 breach 10 infraction 11 delinquency 13 nonobservance

violence: 4 fury 5 ardor 6 bensel, bensil, fervor, hubris, hybris 7 assault, bensal, bensall, bensell, outrage 8 ferocity 9 bloodshed 11 desecration, profanation 12 infringement

violent: 4 high, loud 5 acute, fiery, great, heady, heavy, hefty, rabid, rough, sharp, vivid 6 fierce, mighty, raging, savage, severe, stormy, strong 7 extreme, furious, hotspur, intense, rammish 8 flagrant, forceful, forcible, frenetic, vehement 9 atrocious, impetuous, phrenetic, turbulent 10 headstrong, hotspurred, immoderate, passionate, tumultuous 11 tempestuous

violently: 5 amain 8 slambang

violet: 5 mauve 6 blaver, flower, purple
perfume: 5 irone

violet root: 9 orrisroot

violet tip: 9 butterfly

violin: kit 4 alto, bass 5 Amati, cello, Rocta, Strad 6 fiddle 7 Cremona 8 Guarneri 10 Guadagnini, Guarnerius, Stradivari 11 violincello 12 Stradivarius
city: 7 Cremona
direction: 4 arco 9 pizzicato
forerunner: 5 rebab
part: peg 4 hole, neck 6 string 7 eclisse

violin-shaped: 7 waisted

violinist (first): 13 concertmaster 14 concertmeister

V.I.P.: 7 notable

viper: asp 5 adder, snake 8 cerastes 10 bushmaster, copperhead, fer-de-lance 11 rattlesnake.
genus of: 5 echis

viperish: 8 spiteful, venomous 9 malicious

vir: 5 green

virago: 5 randy, scold, vixen, woman 6 Amazon, beldam, callet 7 beldame 9 brimstone, termagant

vireo: 7 grasset 8 greenlet, songbird

Virgil: *birthplace:* 6 Mantua
character: 5 Amata, Damon 7 Corydon
friend: 8 Maecenas
hero: 5 Aneas, Eneas 6 Aeneis
language: 5 Latin
poem: 4 epic 5 Eneid 6 Aeneid

virgin: new 4 maid, pure 5 first, fresh 6 chaste, maiden, modest, vestal 7 initial 8 maidenly, spinster, virginal 9 unalloyed, undefiled, unsubdued, unsullied, untouched 10 uncaptured 11 undisturbed 12 uncultivated, unfertilized 13 unadulterated

Virgin Island coin: bit 5 daler, franc

Virgin Mary: *image:* 5 Pieta
mother: 4 Anna, Anne

virginal: 6 spinet, virgin 11 harpsichord

Virginia: *motto:* 17 Sic semper tyrannis
mountain: 5 Cedar
quail: 8 bobwhite
river: Dan 5 James 7 Potomac, Rapidan
town: 5 Luray 8 Danville 11 Falls Church

Virginia goat's rue: 6 catgut

Virginia snakeroot: 7 sangrel 9 birthwort 11 sangree-root

Virginia willow: iva 4 itea

Virginian: *author:* 6 Wister

virgularian: 6 searod

viridity: 5 youth 7 verdure 8 verdance 9 freshness, greenness 10 liveliness

virile: 4 male 5 manly 7 lustful 8 forceful, powerful, vigorous 9 masculine, masterful

virl: 7 ferrule

virose: 5 fetid 8 virulent 9 poisonous 10 malodorous

virtu: 5 curio 7 antique

virtually: 6 nearly 7 morally, totally 11 practically

virtue: 4 thew 5 arete, grace 6 bounty, purity 7 probity, quality 8 chastity, efficacy, goodness, morality 9 rectitude excellence 11 uprightness 13 righteousness
cardinal: 4 hope 5 faith 7 charity, justice 8 prudence 9 fortitude 10 temperance
paragon of: 5 saint

virtuoso: 6 expert, savant 7 scholar 8 aesthete, esthete 10 empiricist 11 connoisseur, philosopher

virtuous: 4 good, pure 5 brave, moral 6 chaste, honest, potent 7 goddard, thrifty, upright, valiant 8 valorous 9 righteous 11 efficacious, industrious

virulent: 5 acrid, rabid 6 bitter, deadly, potent 7 hostile, noxious 8 spiteful, venomous 9 festering, injurious, malignant, poisonous 10 infectious 12 antagonistic

virus: 5 venom 6 poison 8 acrimony

vis: 4 force, power, vigor, visit 6 visual 7 potency 8 strength

vis-a-vis: 4 seat, sofa 8 carriage, opposite

visage: 4 face, look, show 5 image 6 aspect 8 portrait 9 semblance 10 appearance 11 countenance

viscera: 4 guts 6 vitals 8 entrails 10 intestines

viscid: 7 viscous

viscount: 4 peer 6 deputy 7 sheriff 8 nobleman

viscous: 4 limy, ropy, sizy 5 gobby, gummy, tarry, thick 6 mucous, sirupy, sticky, viscid 7 stringy 8 adhering, sticking 9 glutinous, semisolid

vise: 5 clamp
part: jaw

Vishnu: *bearer:* 6 Garuda
consort: Sri 7 Lakshmi
epithet: 8 Bhagavat

incarnation: **4** Rama **6** avatar **7** Krishna **8** Balarama **11** Ramachandra

visible: **4** seen **6** extant **7** evident, glaring, obvious **8** apparent, manifest **9** available **11** conspicuous, discernible, perceivable, perceptible

Visigoth king: **6** Alaric

vision: eye **5** dream, fancy, image, sight **6** beauty, seeing **7** fantasy, imagine
combining form: **4** opto
defect: **6** anopia, myopia **14** metamorphopsae, metamorphopsia
illusory: **6** mirage
instrument of: **6** retina
lacking in: **8** purblind
measuring device: **9** optometer
pertaining to: **5** optic **6** ocular, visual

visionary: fey **4** aery, airy, wild **5** ideal **6** unreal **7** dreamer, fantast, laputan, utopian **8** delusive, idealist, quixotic, romantic **9** fantastic, imaginary **10** chimerical, ideologist **11** imaginative, impractical, speculative

visit: gam, see, vis **4** call, chat, hawk, slum, stay **5** apply, haunt **6** assail, attend, avenge **7** afflict, ceilidh(Sc.), inflict, sojourn **8** converse **10** inspection, visitation **12** conversation

visitant: **7** visitor

visitation: **8** disaster, visiting **9** migration **10** affliction

visitor: **5** guest **6** caller **7** company **8** visitant

visne: **4** jury, hood **5** venue **8** neighbor, vicinage

vison: **4** mink

vista: **4** view **5** scene **7** outlook **8** panorama, prospect

visual: **5** optic **6** ocular, scopic **7** optical, visible **11** perceptible

visualize: **6** ideate **7** imagine, picture **8** envisage **13** conceptualize

vital: **4** live **5** basic, chief, fatal **6** deadly, lively, living, souled, viable **7** animate, capital, exigent, supreme **8** vigorous **9** elemental, energetic, essential, important, necessary, requisite **10** imperative **11** fundamental **13** indispensable

vitality: sap, vim **6** biosis, foison

vitalize: **7** animate

vitals: **7** viscera

vitamin, vitamine: **6** biotin, citrin **7** choline **8** ascorbic, carotene, inositol, thiamine **10** calciferol, pyridoxine, riboflavin, tocopherol

vitiate: **5** pical, spoil, taint **6** debase, faulty, impair, impure, poison, weaken **7** corrupt, deprave, envenom, pervert, pollute **9** defective **10** adulterate, invalidate, neutralize **11** contaminate, ineffective

viticulturist: **8** vigneron **10** winegrower

vitiosity: **4** vice **5** fault **6** defect **9** depravity **11** viciousness **13** defectiveness

vitrella: **11** retinophore

vitrify: **5** glaze

vitriol: **4** sory

vitriolic: **5** sharp **6** biting, bitter **7** caustic **8** scathing, virulent **9** sarcastic

vituperate: **4** rail **5** abuse, curse, scold **6** berate, revile **7** censure

vituperative: **10** scurrilous **11** opprobrious

vivace: **9** direction, vivacious

vivacious: gay **4** airy **5** brisk, merry **6** active, breezy, lively, vivace(It.) **7** buoyant, zestful **8** animated, cheerful, spirited, sportive **9** long-lived, sprightly **12** lighthearted

vivacity: **4** fire, zeal **5** ardor, force, verve, vigor **6** gaiety, gayety **7** gayness **9** longevity **10** liveliness

vivandier: **6** sutler

vive: **5** brisk, vivid **6** lively, living **8** forcible, lifelike **9** perceived

vivers: **4** food **8** victuals

vivid: **4** keen, live, rich **5** clear, fresh, sharp **6** active, bright, lively, living, strong **7** eidetic, flaming, glaring, glowing, graphic, intense **8** animated, colorful, distinct, dramatic, spirited, striking, vigorous **9** brilliant

vivificate: **6** vivify

vivify: **5** endue **6** revive **7** animate, enliven, quicken **10** invigorate, vivificate

vivres: **9** foodstuff **10** provisions

vixen: fox, nag **4** fury **5** scold, shrew, woman **9** termagant

viz: **5** to-wit **6** namely **9** videlicet

vizard: **4** mask **5** guise, visor **8** disguise

vizcacha, viscacha: **6** rodent

vocabulary: **5** words **7** diction, lexicon **8** glossary, wordbook **10** dictionary

vocabulist: **13** lexicographer

vocal: **4** oral **5** vowel **9** unwritten

vocalist: **4** alto **5** basso, tenor **6** artist, singer **7** soprano **8** songster **9** performer **10** coloratura

vocalization: **11** melismatics

vocation: **4** call **5** trade **6** career **7** calling, summons **8** business **9** following **10** employment, occupation, profession

vociferate: cry **4** bawl, roar **5** shout, utter **6** assert, bellow, clamor **7** clamour

vociferation: **6** outcry

vociferous: **4** loud **5** noisy **7** blatant **8** brawling, strident **9** turbulent **10** boisterous **11** loud-mouthed, openmouthed **12** obstreperous

voe: bay **5** creek, inlet

vogie: **4** vain **5** merry, proud **6** elated

vogue: cut, ton(F.) **4** mode **5** style **6** custom **7** fashion **8** practice **10** popularity
in: **10** prevailing

voice: say, vox(L.) **4** emit, voce(It.), vote, wish **5** rumor, utter **6** choice, report, speech, steven, tongue **7** divulge, express, opinion **8** announce, falsetto, proclaim **9** utterance **10** expression **12** articulation
handicap: **4** lisp **7** stutter
loss of: **7** anaudia, aphonia

loud: **12** megalophonic **13** megalopho-
nous
male: **4** bass **5** basso, tenor **8** baritone,
barytone **12** countertenor
natural singing: **7** dipetto
part: **7** glottis
pert. to: **8** phonetic
principal: **6** cantus
quality: **6** timbre
quiet: **5** sotto
sound: **5** vowel **6** symbol
stop: **9** affricate
stress: **5** arsis
voice box: 6 larynx
voiced: 6 sonant
voiceless: mum **4** dumb, mute, surd **6**
atonic, flated, silent **7** aphonic, spirate **8**
aphonous **10** speechless
void: gap **4** free, idle, lack, null, vain, want
5 abyss, annul, blank, egest, eject, empty,
leave, space **6** devoid, hollow, remove,
vacant, vacate, vacuum **7** invalid, lacking,
leisure, nullify, opening, useless, vacuity,
wanting **8** evacuate **9** destitute, discharge, emptiness, frustrate **10** unemployed, unoccupied **11** ineffective,
ineffectual
voile: 5 ninon
voiture: 7 wagon **8** carriage
volage: 5 giddy **6** fickle **7** flighty **8** fleeting
volant: 5 agile, light, quick **6** flying, nimble **7** flounce **8** volitant
volary: 4 cage **6** aviary
volatile: 4 airy, bird **5** ether **6** fickle, fi-
gent, flying, lively, volage, volant **7** alcohol, ammonia, buoyant, essence, gaseous,
volatic **8** fleeting, fugitive, vaporous **9** fugacious, transient **10** capricious, changeable, transitory **11** hairbrained **12** lighthearted
volatilize: 9 evaporate
volcano: Apo **4** Etna **5** Askja, Pelee **6**
Ranier, Shasta **8** Cotopaxi, Krakatao,
Krakatau, Mauna Loa, Vesuvius **9** Stromboli **12** Popocatepetl
matter: aa, oo **4** lava, tufa **5** trass **6** pumice
mud from: **5** salse
opening: **5** mouth **6** crater **8** fumarole
rock: **5** trass **6** dacite **8** tephrite
scoria: **4** slag
vole: 6 craber, rodent
Volga: Rha
volition: 4 will **6** choice **13** determination
volley: 5 crowd, volee **6** flight **7** barrage,
company, platoon
voluble: 4 glib **5** wordy **6** fickle, fluent **8**
rotating, unstable **9** garrulous, revolving,
talkative **10** changeable, loquacious
volume: 4 book, bulk, coil, mass, roll,
tome, turn **6** amount, cubage, scroll **8** capacity, document, fullness, loudness,
quantity, strength **9** aggregate **10** crassi-
tude **11** convolution

measure: **11** stereometer
voluminous: 4 full **5** bulky, large
Volund's brother: 4 Egil **5** Egill
voluntary: 4 free **6** freely **7** willful, willing
8 elective **9** volunteer, willingly **10** deliberate, unimpelled **11** intentional, spontaneous **13** unconstrained
volunteer: 5 offer **6** enlist, worker **7**
proffer
Volunteer State: 9 Tennessee
voluptuous: 7 sensual **8** sensuous **9** luxurious **11** pleasurable
volute: 4 turn **5** whorl **6** cilery, scroll **7**
cillery
volution: 4 coil, turn **5** twist, whorl **7**
rolling **9** revolving **11** convolution
vomit: 4 boke, bolk, puke, spew **5** braid,
brake, reach, retch **6** emetic **8** disgorge
10 egurgitate **11** regurgitate
vomiting: 6 emesis **12** anacatharsis
voodoo: obe, obi **5** magic, obeah **6** fetish **8**
sorcerer
voracious: 5 eager **6** greedy, hungry **8**
esurient, ravening, revenous **9** cormorant,
rapacious **10** gargantuan, gluttonous, immoderate, insatiable
voracity: 7 edacity **10** greediness **12** rav-
enousness
vorago: 4 gulf **5** abyss
vortex: 4 apex, eddy, gyre **5** whirl **7** tornado **9** waterpool, whirlpool, whirlwind
10 waterspout
votary: 6 zealot **7** devoted, devotee **8** adherent, follower, promised **10** enthusiast
vote: aye, con, nay, pro, vow, yes **4** anti,
poll, wish **5** elect, grant **6** assign, ballot,
choice, confer, prayer **7** declare, opinion
8 dedicate, suffrage **10** plebiscite, referendum
group: **4** bloc
of assent: **6** placet
receptacle: **6** situla **7** situlae
voter: 6 poller **7** elector **8** balloter,
chooser **11** constituent
illegal: **8** repeater, underage **11** nonresi-
dent
voters (body of): 10 electorate
votive: 11 consecrated
vouch: vow **4** aver, back, bail, call, pray **6**
affirm, allege, assure, attest, second, summon **7** certify, confirm, declare, resolve,
support, warrant **8** accredit, maintain,
sanction **9** assertion, establish, guarantee
11 attestation **12** authenticate
voucher: 4 chit **7** receipt **9** debenture,
statement **10** credential
vouchsafe: 4 give **5** deign, yield **6** assure,
bestow, beteem **7** concede **9** guarantee
10 condescend
voussoir: 5 wedge **8** keystone
projection: ear
voust: 5 boast, vaunt
vow: vum **4** bind, hote, oath, wish **5** swear
6 behest, devote, pledge **7** behight, de-

clare, promise **8** dedicate **9** assertion **10** consecrate, obligation **12** asseveration, supplication

vowel: 5 vocal
contraction: **6** crasis, crases **9** diphthong

vowel: 5 vocal
contraction: **6** crasis, crases **8** dipthong
group: **6** digram
sound: **6** dental, labial **7** palatal
unaspirated: **4** lene

vox: 5 voice

voyage: 4 trip **6** cruise, travel **7** journey, passage, passing, project **8** proceeds **9** excursion **10** enterprise, expedition, pilgrimage **11** undertaking

voyageur: 7 boatman, trapper **8** traveler, woodsman

voyaging: 4 asea

vraic: 7 seaweed

vrouw: 4 frow **5** woman **8** mistress **9** housewife

vug, vugh: 6 cavity, hollow

Vulcan: *consort:* **4** Maia
epithet: **8** Mulciber
son: **5** Cacus **8** Caeculus

workshop: **4** Etna

vulcanite: 7 ebonite

vulcanize: 4 cure

vulgar: 4 lewd, rude **5** crude, gross **6** coarse, common, public, slangy **7** boorish, general, obscene, popular, profane **8** churlish, ordinary **9** customary, earthbred, inelegant, unrefined

vulgarian: 4 snob

vulgarism: 4 cant **9** vulgarity

vulnerable: 6 liable **7** exposed **9** pregnable, untenable **10** assailable **11** defenseless, susceptible
point: **12** Achilles heel

vulnerate: 4 hurt **5** wound

vulpine: fox **4** foxy **6** artful, clever, crafty, tricky **7** cunning **9** alopecoid

vult: 4 mien **6** aspect **10** expression **11** countenance

vulture: 4 papa **5** arend, grape, gripe, griph, urubu **6** condor, griphe **8** aasvogel, zopilote **9** gallinazo
genus of: **4** gyps

vum: vow

W

wabble: See **wobble**.

wabby: 4 loon

wabeno: 6 shaman

wacky, whacky: 5 crazy 6 screwy 7 erratic 9 eccentric 10 irrational

wad: bat, gag, pad, ram 4 cram, heap, lead, line, lump, mass, plug, roll, tuft 5 crowd, money, stuff, trace, track, would 6 bundle, insert, pledge, wealth 7 stopper 8 bankroll, compress, graphite

waddle: 5 tread 6 hoddle, toddle, widdle 7 trample

waddy: 4 beat, cane, club 5 stick 6 attack, cowboy

wade: go 4 ford, pass 6 paddle 7 proceed 8 struggle

wader: 4 boot, coot, hern, ibis, rail 5 crane, heron, snipe, stork 6 jacana 9 sandpiper

wadi, wady: 5 oasis, river 6 ravine, stream, valley 7 channel 11 watercourse

wadset: 4 pawn 6 pledge 8 mortgage

wady: See **wadi**.

wafer: 4 cake, disk, ring, seal, snap 5 close 6 fasten 7 biscuit, cracker

waff: wag 4 flap, gust, odor, puff, wave 5 ghost, whiff 6 paltry, wraith 7 flutter, lowborn 8 inferior 9 worthless 12 disreputable

waffie: 5 tramp 7 vagrant 8 vagabond

waft: 4 blow, buoy, flag, gust, odor, puff, turn, wave, weft 5 carry, drift, float, gleam, sound, taste, whiff 6 beckon, breath, direct, propel, signal, wraith 7 glimpse, pennant 9 transport

wag: wit 4 card, move, stir, sway 5 joker, leave, nudge, rogue, shake, swing 6 beckon, depart, signal 7 farceur, vibrate 8 brandish, flourish, humorist, jokester 9 oscillate

wagang: 5 death 9 departure 11 leavetaking

wage (see also **wager**): fee, pay, utu 4 hire, levy, pawn 5 bribe, fight, incur 6 employ, engage, reward, salary 7 attempt, conduct, contend, stipend 9 emolument 10 recompense 12 compensation

deduct: 4 dock

insurance: 7 chomage

wage earner: 6 worker 7 laborer 8 employee, mechanic 11 proletarian

wager: bet, bid, lay, vie 4 gage, risk 5 prize, sport, stake 6 gamble, hazard, parlay, pledge 7 venture

made in bad faith: 6 levant

waggery: 4 jest, joke 7 foolery 10 pleasantry 11 waggishness

waggish: 4 arch 5 droll, merry 7 jesting, jocular, parlous, playful, roguish 8 humorous, sportive 10 frolicsome 11 mischievous

waggle: wag 6 waddle, wobble

waggly: 8 unsteady

Wagner: *character:* Eva 4 Elsa, Erda 5 Hagen, Senta, Wotan 8 Parsifal

opera: 6 Rienzi 9 Lohengrin 15 Gotterdammerung

wife: 6 Cosima

wagon: bin, van 4 cart, dray, tram, wain 5 araba, aroba, dilly, gilly, lorry, lurry, tonga 6 camion, telega 7 caisson, chariot, fourgon, vehicle 8 carryall, schooner 12 perambulator

maker: 10 wainwright

part: 4 neap, pole, rave 5 thill 6 tongue

wagon-lit: 7 sleeper

wagonload: 6 fother 8 wagonful

wagonmaker: 10 wagonsmith, wainwright 11 wagonwright

wah: 5 panda

wahine: 4 wife 5 woman 8 mistress 10 sweetheart

wahoo: elm 4 fish, peto 8 nonsense, tommyrot 9 buckthorn, guarapucu

waif: 4 flag 5 stray 7 pennant, vagrant 8 castaway, homeless, wanderer 9 foundling

wail: cry, wow 4 howl, moan, weep, yarm 5 croon, mourn 6 bemoan, bewail, grieve, lament, plaint 7 deplore, ululate 9 complaint 11 lamentation

wain: 4 cart 5 fetch, wagon 6 convey 7 chariot, vehicle

wainscot: 4 line 6 lining 7 ceiling 8 paneling 9 partition

waist: 4 belt, wasp 5 shirt 6 basque, blouse, bodice, camisa, girdle 7 corsage 8 camisole 10 undershirt 12 undergarment

waistband: 4 sash

waistcoat: 4 vest 5 benjy, gilet 6 fecket, jacket, jerkin

wait: 4 bide, rest, stay, stop, tend 5 await, cater, court, dally, defer, delay, guard, serve, tarry, watch 6 ambush, attend, escort, expect, follow, harken, linger, remain 7 hautboy, hearken, observe 8 hesitate, inactive, postpone 9 accompany

10 stationary **11** expectation **12** watchfulness

waiter: spy **4** tray **6** garcon, salver, server, vessel **7** messboy, messman, servant, steward, watcher **8** servitor, watchman, waylayer **9** attendant

waive: put **4** cast, turn **5** cease, defer, forgo, leave, swing, yield **6** desert. forego, refuse, reject, vacate **7** abandon, forbear, forsake, neglect **8** postpone **9** disregard **10** relinquish

waka: **5** canoe

Wakashan: **6** Nootka

wake: **4** call, stir **5** guard, revel, rouse, track, trail, vigil, waken, watch **6** arouse, awaken, excite, revive **7** passage

wakeful: **5** alert **8** restless, vigilant **9** sleepless

wale: rib **4** best, flog, mark, pick, weal, welt **5** ridge, wheal **6** choice, choose, select, streak, stripe **7** timber **8** choicest

Wales (see also **Welsh**): **5** Cymru **7** Cambria

bard: **5** ovate

city: **6** Amlwch, Bangor **7** Cardiff, Rhondda, Swansea **8** Hereford, Holyhead, Pembroke **9** Carnarvon, Worcester **13** Kidderminster

cheese: **10** Caer-philly

deity: **4** Bran

emblem: **4** leek

fine: **6** saraad

language: **7** Cymraeg

law: **7** galanas

marriage fee: **6** amober

measure: **5** cover **7** cantred, cantref, lestrad, listred **8** crannock

musical instrument: **7** pibcorn

patron saint: **5** David

people: **5** Cymry, Kymry

person: **5** Taffy **8** Welshman

port: **7** Cardiff

river: Dee, Wye **4** Teme **5** Teifi **6** Severn

walk: mog, pad, wag **4** foot, gait, hike, hoof, limp, mall, pace, path, plod, ramp, reel, roam, roll, step, turn, wade **5** allee, amble, haunt, mince, scuff, stalk, stram, stray, strut, stump, trail, tramp, tread **6** arcade, hobble, loiter, lumber, pasear, prance, ramble, resort, stride, stroll, toddle, totter, trapes, trudge, wander **7** alameda, saunter, shuffle, traipse **8** ambulate, frescade, traverse **9** esplanade, promenade, tilicetum **11** perambulate, somnabulate **14** constitutional

a beat: **6** patrol

public: **4** mall **6** arcade **7** alameda **9** esplanade, promenade

walk-out: **6** strike

walk out on: **5** leave **6** desert **7** abandon

walker: **6** ganger **7** footman **8** stroller **10** pedestrian

walking: **7** passant (her.) **8** ambulant **10** ambulation **11** peripatetic

walking stick: **4** cane **5** kebby, staff, stilt, waddy **6** kebbie

wall: **4** dike, ha-ha **5** fence, levee, redan, scarp **6** bailey, cashel, escarp, haw-haw, paries, podium, septum **7** barrier, bastion, curtain, defense, enclose, parapet, rampart **9** barricade, enclosure, encompass, partition, revetment **13** fortification

bracket: **6** corbel

covering: **4** tile **5** cloth, paint, paper **8** paneling **9** calcimine, draperies, kalsomine, wallpaper

lining: **8** wainscot

masonry: **9** revetment

on: **5** mural

opening: **4** bole, door **6** window **7** scupper

ornament: **4** dado **6** mirror, plaque **7** hanging, molding, picture, placque **8** moulding, tapestry

part: **4** dado, pier **5** bahut, gable **6** coping, plinth **7** cornice

pert. to: **5** mural **8** parietal

up: **6** immure

wallaby: **8** kangaroo

wallah, walla: **5** agent, owner **6** fellow, master, person, worker **7** servant

wallet: bag, jag **4** jagg, pack, poke, sack **5** purse, scrip **6** budget **8** billfold, knapsack **10** pocketbook

wallop: **4** beat, blow, flog, lick, whip, whop **6** defeat, strike, thrash

walloping: **5** large **6** strong **8** enormous

wallow: pit **4** fade, mire **5** surge **6** billow, grovel, hollow, trough, welter, wither **7** founder **8** flounder, kommetje **10** depression

wallowish: **4** flat **7** insipid

wallpaper measure: **4** bolt

wally: **4** fine **6** robust, strong, sturdy **8** pleasant, pleasing, splendid **9** agreeable, excellent, first-rate

walnut: **6** bannut

walrus: **5** morse **6** seacat **9** rosmarine

flock: pod

limb: **7** flipper

walt: **8** unsteady

waltz: **5** dance, valse

kind of: **6** Boston, Vienna

wambly: **5** faint, shaky **8** unsteady **9** nauseated, squeamish

wame: **5** belly

wampish: **5** swing **9** fluctuate

wampum: **4** peag **5** beads, money **7** roanoke

wamus: **6** jacket **7** doublet **8** cardigan

wan: dim, one, sad **4** dark, fade, pale, sick **5** dusky, faint, livid **6** dismal, feeble, gloomy, pallid, pallor, peaked, sickly **7** ghastly, languid, wanness **8** paleness **9** colorless, sorrowful **10** lusterless

wand: rod **4** pole, twig **5** baton, shoot, staff, stick **6** switch **7** pointer, rhabdos, scepter, sceptre **8** caduceus **9** horsewhip

wand-shaped: **7** virgate

wander: err, gad **4** haik, hake, prog, rave, roam, roil, rove, wind **5** drift, prowl, range, shift, stray **6** cruise, dander, depart, ramble, stroll, trapes, travel **7** deviate, digress, meander, saunter, traipse **8** divagate, straggle, traverse **11** peregrinate

wanderer: vag **4** Arab, waif **5** gypsy, nomad **6** truant **7** migrant, pilgrim, vagrant **9** itinerant **11** extravagant

wandering: **5** vagus(anat.) **6** astray, errant **7** devious, erratic, journey, odyssey **8** aberrant **9** aberrance, planetary **10** circuitous, incoherent **11** noctivigant, perambulant

wanderlust: **8** nomadism **12** restlessness

wandle: **5** agile, lithe **6** supple

wane: go; ebb **4** fail, lack, sink, want **5** abate, decay, peter **6** absent, defect, repine **7** decline, dwindle, subside **8** decrease, diminish **10** defervesce

wang: **4** king **5** ruler **6** prince

wanga: **5** charm, spell **6** voodoo **7** philter, sorcery

wangle: **4** fake **5** shake **6** adjust, change, juggle, totter, wiggle **7** falsify, wriggle **8** contrive **9** extricate **10** manipulate

wanhap: **6** mishap **10** misfortune

wanion: **5** curse **6** plague **9** vengeance

wankle: **6** feeble, fickle, sickly **8** unstable, unsteady **10** irresolute

want: gap **4** hole, lack, lose, miss, mole, need, void, wish **5** crave, fault **6** besoin, dearth, desire, forget, hunger, penury **7** absence, beggary, blemish, craving, lacking, missing, poverty, require, straits, vacancy **8** exigency, scarcity, shortage **9** deficient, indigence, necessary, necessity, privation **10** deficiency, inadequacy **11** deprivation, destitution **12** difficulties

wanting: **4** less **5** minus **6** devoid **7** without, witless **12** feeble-minded

wanton: gay **4** lewd **5** cadgy, dally, frisk, merry, revel **6** frisky, frolic, giglet, harlot, lavish, trifle, unruly **7** fulsome, haggard, ill-bred, immoral, lustful, playful, sensual, wayward **8** arrogant, flagrant, inhumane, insolent, prodigal, spiteful, sportive, unchaste **9** dissolute, lecherous, luxuriant, luxurious, malicious, merciless **10** capricious, effeminate, frolicsome, gratuitous, lascivious, licentious, refractory, voluptuous **11** extravagant, mollycoddle **12** disregardful, unmanageable, unrestrained **13** undisciplined, unjustifiable

wantwit: **4** fool

wanty: tie **4** rope **5** girth **9** bellyband, surcingle

wap: **4** beat, bind, blow, whop, wrap **5** blast, fight, knock, storm, truss **6** bundle, strike **8** wrapping

wapiti: elk **4** deer, stag

war: *alarm:* **4** flap
  club: **4** mace **5** nulla **6** nullah

correspondent: **4** Pyle

fleet: **6** armada

god of: Ira, Tyr **4** Ares, Coel, Mars, Thor **6** Nergal

goddess: **4** Alea **5** Anath, Bella **6** Anunit, Ishtar **7** Bellona

instrument: **7** caltrap, caltrop **9** relocator

machine: ram **4** bomb, tank **6** rocket **7** missile **8** catapult

restriction: **8** blockade

vehicle: **4** jeep, tank

vessel: sub **6** corvet **7** cruiser **8** corvette **9** destroyer, submarine **11** dreadnaught

war hawk: **5** jingo

war-horse: **5** steed **6** leader **7** charger, standby **8** partisan **10** campaigner, politician

warbird: **7** aviator, tanager **8** airplane

warble: **4** sing **5** carol, chant, chirl, shake, trill, yodel **7** descant, twitter, vibrate

warbler: **4** wren **6** singer **8** blackcap, grosbeak, songbird, songster **9** beccafico **10** bluethroat **11** whitethroat

ward: **4** care, jail, rule, warn **5** watch **6** charge, defend, govern, prison, warden, warder **7** counsel, custody, defense, enclose, fortify, keeping, protect **8** district, garrison, guardian, watchman **9** safeguard, storeroom **10** protection **11** confinement **12** guardianship **14** arrondissement(F.)

pert. to: **9** pupillary

ward off: end **4** fend **5** avert, guard, parry, repel **7** forfend, prevent

warden: **4** caid **5** guard, nazir **6** disdar, dizdar, jailer, jailor, keeper, ranger, regent, sexton **7** alcaide, alcayde, turnkey, viceroy **8** director, governor, guardian, overseer, watchman **9** castellan, concierge, constable, custodian **10** doorkeeper, gatekeeper, supervisor

warder (see also **warden**): **5** staff **7** bulwark **8** sentinel **9** caretaker, truncheon **10** stronghold

wardrobe: **4** room **5** privy **6** closet **7** apparel, armoire, bedroom, cabinet, chamber, clothes **8** costumes **9** garderobe **12** clothespress

ware: **4** host, sage, shun, wary, wise **5** avoid, aware, china, goods, ready, spend, stuff, waste **6** people, shrewd **7** careful, chaffer, heedful, pottery, prudent, seaweed **8** cautious, products, squander, vigilant **9** cognizant, conscious, porcelain **11** commodities, earthenware, inhabitants, merchandise

warehouse: **4** silo **5** depot, etape, store **6** fonduk, godown **7** almacen, fondouk, funduck, storage **8** elevator, entrepot, magazine **10** storehouse

fee: **7** storage

warfare: See **war**.

warily: (see also **wary**): **8** gingerly

warkloom: **4** tool **7** utensil **9** implement

water sprite: See **water nymph**.

water thief: 6 pirate

watercourse (See also **water** *body*): run **4** dike, dyke, race, wadi, wady **5** brook, canal, chute, creek, drain, gully, river **6** arroyo(Sp.), course, gutter, nullah, ravine, sluice, stream **7** channel, trinket **8** barranca(Sp.)

watercraft: See **boat; ship**.

watercress: 9 brooklime

watered: 5 moire

waterfall: lin **4** linn **5** force **7** cascade, chignon, Niagara **8** cataract, Victoria, Yosemite

waterfowl: 4 coot, loon **5** diver

waterhead: 6 source **9** headwater **12** fountainhead **13** hydrocephalus

watering device: 4 hose, pump **5** spray **6** nozzle

watering place: spa **4** pool **5** oasis **6** aguada(Sp.), battis, resort, spring

waterless: dry **4** arid

watermelon: 6 citrul, sandia **7** anguria

waters: See **watering place**.

primeval: **4** Apsu

watershed: 5 ridge **6** divide

waterspout: 5 canal, spate **8** gargoyle **9** hurricano

waterwheel: 5 noria, sakia **6** sakieh **7** sakiyeh **8** tympanum

watery: wet **4** soft, thin, weak **5** fluid, sammy, soggy **6** blashy, serous, soaked, sweaty **7** aqueous, insipid, tearful, weeping **8** humorous **11** transparent

wattle: rod **4** beat, bind, flog, gill, twig, wand **5** cooba, fence, stick, twist, withe **6** acacia, coobah, dewlap, hurdle, lappet **9** boobyalla, framework, hackthorn **10** intertwine, interweave

waugh: 4 weak **5** faint, stale **7** insipid **8** nauseous

wave: ola(Sp.), sea, set, wag **4** bore, curl, flap, surf, sway, tide, vein **5** bless, crimp, curve, eager, eagre, float, flood, ridge, shake, surge, swell, swing, tilde, water, waver **6** beckon, billow, comber, fickle, flaunt, marcel, ripple, roller, signal **7** breaker, flutter, ripplet, seagate, tsunami, vibrate, wavelet **8** brandish, flourish, undulate, whitecap **9** fluctuate, permanent, vibration **10** undulation, unevenness

top: **5** crest

upward motion: **5** scend

waver: 4 reel, sway, twig **5** quake, swing **6** change, falter, teeter, totter, wiggle **7** flicker, flitter, flutter, sapling, stagger, tremble, vibrate **8** hesitate **9** fluctuate, oscillate, vacillate

wavering: 6 fickle **7** lambent **8** doubtful, flexuous, unsteady **9** desultory **10** irresolute

wavy: 4 ente(her.), onde(her.), unde(her.), undy(her.) **5** crisp, curly, snaky, undee (her.) **6** flying **7** billowy, sinuate, sinu-ous **8** undulant **9** undulated **10** undulating

wawl, waul: 4 howl, wail **6** squall

wax: 4 cere, grow, pela **5** putty **6** become **7** cerumen, suberin **8** adhesive, increase, paraffin **11** zietriskite

comb. form: cer

mixture: **6** cerate

pert. to: **5** ceral

preparation: **6** cerate

substance: **5** cerin

waxbill: 7 astrild

waxen: 4 soft, waxy **6** pallid, viscid **7** cerated, pliable **8** yielding **11** impressible **14** impressionable

waxy: 5 angry, vexed

way: via **4** cost, fore, gait, lane, mode, path, plan, road, room **5** alley, going, habit, milky, route, space, style, track **6** ambage, arcade, avenue, career, causey, chemin, course, detour, device, manner, method, scheme, street **7** advance, fashion, highway, opening, passage **8** causeway, contrada, progress **9** banquette, direction, procedure **12** idiosyncrasy

in: **7** contact **8** entrance

on: **7** en route

open: **7** pioneer

out: **4** exit **6** egress, escape

wayfarer: 6 viator **8** traveler

waygate: 4 path **9** departure **10** passageway

waylay: 5 await, belay, beset **6** ambush **7** forelay **8** surprise **9** ambuscade

waymark: ahu **5** arrow **9** milestone

wayward: 6 unruly **7** erratic, froward, naughty, willful **8** contrary, perverse, stubborn, unsteady, untoward **9** irregular **10** capricious, headstrong, refractory, self-willed **11** disobedient, fluctuating, intractable **13** unpredictable

waywiser: 8 odometer **9** pedometer **12** perambulator

we: nos(L.)

weak: 4 puny, soft, thin, worn **5** anile, bauch, chirp, crank, crimp, dicky, faint, frail, seely, washy, waugh, young **6** caduke, debile, dickey, dotish, faulty, feeble, flabby, flaggy, flimsy, foible, infirm, scream, sickly, squeak, tender, unwise, watery **7** brittle, doatish, dwaible, dwaibly, foolish, fragile, pliable **8** childish, decrepit, feckless, feminine, flagging, helpless, impotent **9** childlike, dissolute, enfeebled, nerveless, powerless **10** effeminate, inadequate **11** ineffective **12** unconvincing

weaken: go; sap **4** thin, tire **5** appal, break, craze, delay **6** appall, deaden, defeat, dilute, impair, lessen, rebate, reduce, soften **7** cripple, decline, depress, disable, exhaust, unnerve **8** enervate **9** attenuate, extenuate, undermine **10** debilitate, demoralize

weakness: 4 flaw 6 defect, foible 7 acratia, ailment, failing 8 debility, fondness 9 inability 11 attenuation 12 imperfection

weal: 4 line, mark, pomp, wale, welt 5 ridge, state, wheal 6 choice, choose, riches, stripe, wealth 7 welfare 9 happiness, wellbeing 10 commonweal, prosperity

wealth: 4 dhan, gear, gold, good, weal 5 money 6 assets, graith, mammon, riches 7 capital, fortune, welfare 8 opulence, property, treasure 9 abundance, affluence, wellbeing 10 prosperity 11 possessions

gained: 8 chevance 9 chievance

god of: 6 Plutus

wealthy: 4 full 5 ample, pursy

wean: 4 baby 5 child 6 detach, infant 8 alienate, estrange 9 reconcile

weanie: 4 baby

weanly: 6 feeble 8 childish

weapon: arm, dag, gun 4 beak, bola, bolo, celt, claw, dart, dirk, epee, foil, pike 5 arrow, bolas, glave, knife, lance, rifle, saber, sabre, shaft, sling, spear, sword, talon, vouge 6 bomber, dagger, eolith, glaive, mortar, pistol, poleax, rapier 7 bazooka, carbine, gisarme, halberd, halbert, machete, missile, poleaxe, trident 8 catapult, crossbow, fauchard, leeangle, revolver, stiletto, tomahawk 9 artillery, derringer 11 blunderbuss

lay down: 6 disarm 9 surrender

storage place: 7 arsenal

without: 7 unarmed

wear: don, rub 4 fray, tire 5 chafe, erode, grind, sport, weary 6 abrade, attire, endure, impair 7 apparel, clothes, consume, corrode, display, exhaust, exhibit, fatigue 8 diminish 11 deteriorate

away: 5 erode 6 abrade

wearable: 6 usable 7 garment 8 clothing

weariful: See **wearisome**.

weariness (see also **weary**): 5 ennui 6 tedium 7 fatigue 8 vexation 9 lassitude

wearish: 4 weak 5 faint 6 sickly 7 insipid 8 unsavory 9 squeamish

wearisome: 4 hard 6 boring, dismal, dreary, prolix, tiring 7 irksome, tedious 8 tiresome 9 fatiguing, laborious, vexatious 10 monotonous 11 displeasing, everlasting

weary: bad, fag, irk, sad 4 bore, jade, puny, tire, weak, worn 5 annoy, bored, curse, spent, timid, tired 6 harass, plague, sickly 7 exhaust, fatigue, irksome, tedious 8 fatigued, grievous, tiresome 9 forjaskit, forjesket, surfeited 10 defatigate, disastrous 11 unfortunate

Weary Willie: 5 tramp 7 shirker, vagrant 13 featherbedder

weasand: 6 gullet, throat 7 trachea 8 windpipe 9 esophagus

weasel: 4 cane, stot, vare 5 ratel, stoat 6 ermine, ferret 10 equivocate

family: 6 ermine, ferret, marten

weasel cat: 7 linsang

weasel-like: 9 musteline

weather: dry 4 hail, rain, snow, wind 5 erode, sleet 7 climate 8 discolor, windward 12 disintegrate

weather map line: 6 isobar

weathercock: 4 fane, vane

weathered: 5 faded 6 tanned 7 bronzed, stained 8 bleached, hardened 9 roughened, toughened

weatherman: 13 meteorologist

weave: 4 darn, knit, lace, spin 5 braid, drape, plait, unite 6 devise, enlace, wattle 7 canille, entwine, fashion 8 cannelle, contrive 9 fabricate, interlace, interwind 10 intertwine, intertwist

weaver's tool: 4 loom 5 sleys

weaverbird: 4 baya, taha

weaving:

cylinder: 4 beam

machine: 4 loom 6 carder 8 jacquard

weazen: See **wizen**.

web: mat, net, ply 4 caul, trap, veil, warp 5 snare 6 fabric, tissue 7 ensnare, network, texture, webbing 8 entangle, gossamer, membrane, vexillum 11 fabrication 12 entanglement

web-footed: 7 palmate 11 totipalmate

web-like: 4 lacy 7 spidery

half: 11 semi-palmate

webbing: 7 binding

wed: 4 join 5 elope, marry, mated, unite 6 joined, pawned 7 espouse, pledged, spliced 9 mortgaged

pert. to: 7 marital

wedding: 6 splice 8 ceremony, espousal, marriage, nuptials 11 anniversary

anniversary: tin 4 ruby 5 candy, china, coral, linen, paper, pearl, straw 6 floral, golden, silver, wooden 7 crystal, diamond, emerald, leather

proclamation: 5 banns

wedge: jam 4 club, heel, lump, shoe 5 cleat, crowd, ingot, piece, split 6 cleave, sector, wedgie 7 niblick 8 separate, triangle, voussoir 9 formation

wedge-shaped: 6 cuneal 7 cuneate 8 cuneated, cuniform 9 cuneiform

wedgie: 4 shoe

wedlock (see also **wedding**): 4 wife 9 matrimony

Wednesday (source of name): 5 Woden

wee: 4 tiny 5 bitty, small, teeny 6 little, minute 10 diminutive

weed: 4 band, garb, loco, milk, sida, tare 5 armor, cheat, dress, horse, vetch 6 darnel, datura, nettle, remove, sarcle, spurge 7 allseed, clothes, costume, garment, illness, mallows, purloin, ragweed, relapse, thistle, tobacco 8 clothing, plantain, purslane, sealwort, toadflax, trumpery 9 alfilaria, dandelion, eradicate 11 undergrowth

weed killer: 9 herbicide

weeds: 8 mourning

weedy: 4 foul, lean 5 lanky 7 scraggy 8 ungainly

week: 8 hebdomad

weekday: 5 feria

weekly: 5 aweek 10 hebdomadal, periodical 11 hebdomadary, publication

weeks (two): 9 fortnight

weel: 4 eddy, pool, trap 6 basket 9 whirlpool

weem: pit 4 cave 6 cavern

ween: 4 hope 5 fancy, think 6 expect 7 believe, imagine, suppose 8 conceive

weep: cry, sob 4 leak, tear, wail 5 exude, greet, mourn 6 bewail, beweep, boohoo, lament 7 blubber

Weeping Philosopher: 10 Heraclitus

weepy: 5 moist, seepy 6 oozing 7 tearful, weeping 8 mournful

weeshy, weeshie: wee 4 tiny 5 weeny

weet: wet, wit 4 know

weevil: 4 boll, lota 8 circulio

weeze: 4 ooze

weft: web 4 film, warp, woof, yarn 5 shoot, shute 7 filling

weigh: 4 bear, lift, tare, test 5 carry, hoist, poise 6 esteem, ponder, regard 7 balance, examine, measure, portion, support 8 consider, dispense, meditate 9 apportion 14 counterbalance

weigh down: sit 4 lade, load 7 depress, oppress

weigher: 5 trone 6 potdar, scaler 7 balance, trutine 8 computer 9 steelyard

weighing machine: 5 scale, trone 7 balance 9 steelyard

weight: bob, CWT, keg, lot, mol, tod, tom, ton, tup 4 beef, dram, gram, heft, lade, last, load, mina, onus, pari, rati, shot, tola 5 carat, clove, flask, grain, ounce, pfund, poise, pound, power, ratti, rider, scale, stein 6 barrel, burden, cental, charge, denier, fother, fotmal, gramme, grivna, import, moment 7 centner, drachma, gravity, oppress, plummet, quarter, quintal, scruple, tonnage 8 decagram, encumber, kilogram, micogram, pressure, vierling, vamfront, vammazsa 9 authority, centigram, hectogram, heaviness, influence, liespfund, milligram, myriagram, quentchen, zollpfund 12 significance 13 hundredweight, ponderability

allowance: 4 tare 7 scalage

comb. form: 4 baro

kind of: net 4 troy 5 gross 6 metric 8 jeweler's 10 apothecary 11 avoirdupois

inspector: 6 sealer

of container: 4 tare

official: 6 metage

pert. to: 5 baric 8 ponderal

system of: 4 troy 5 avoir 11 avoirdupois 12 apothecaries

weighted: 5 laden 6 loaded 8 burdened 9 evaluated, oppressed

weightiness: 4 pomp 7 dignity, gravity 9 solemnity

weighty: fat 5 bulky, heavy, hefty, large, massy, obese, solid 6 severe, solemn 7 capital, massive, onerous, serious, telling 8 forcible, grievous, powerful 9 corpulent, momentous, ponderous 10 burdensome, chargeable, cumbersome, impressive, oppressive

weir: dam 4 bank 5 fence, garth, levee 7 barrier, milldam 11 obstruction

weird: lot, odd 4 eery, fate, unco, wild 5 charm, eerie, queer, scary, spell 7 awesome, curious, destine, destiny, fortune, ghostly, macabre, predict, strange, uncanny, unusual 8 foretell, prophecy 9 unearthly 10 mysterious, prediction, soothsayer

weka: 4 rail

welcome: 4 hail 5 adopt, greet 7 acclaim, embrace 8 greeting 9 agreeable, bienvenue, desirable 10 acceptable, salutation

weld: 5 unite 11 consolidate

welding gas: 9 acetylene

welfare: 4 sele, weal 10 prosperity

goddess: 5 Salus

welkin: air, sky 10 atmosphere

well: fit, pit 4 bene(It., L.), bien(F.), fair, flow, gush, hole, sump 5 aweel(Sc.), fount 6 gusher, hearty, spring 7 cistern, gaylies, geylies, gradely, healthy 8 artesian, expertly, fountain 10 gratifying 11 excellently 12 satisfactory

comb. form: 4 bene

lining: 5 steen

pole: 5 sweep

prefix: eu

well-behaved: 4 good

well-being: 4 good, weal 6 health 7 comfort 8 eucrasia, felicity 9 eudaemony, happiness 10 prosperity

well-bred: 5 civil 6 polite 7 genteel, refined 8 cultured, wellborn 9 pedigreed 10 cultivated 11 gentlemanly 12 thoroughbred

well-defined: 8 distinct 11 distinctive

well-founded: 4 firm

well-groomed: 4 neat 5 clean, sleek 6 soigne 7 soignee

well-grounded: 4 firm 5 valid

well-heeled: 4 rich 7 moneyed 10 prosperous

well-known: 6 famous 7 eminent 8 familiar 9 notorious

well-liked: 7 popular

well-made: 9 affabrous

well-nigh: 6 almost, nearly

well-off: 5 lucky 8 thriving 10 prosperous

well-timed: 6 timely 9 opportune

well-versed: 7 erudite

wellborn: 4 rich 5 noble 7 eugenic

wellhead: 6 source, spring 8 fountain 12 fountainhead

Welsh, Welch (see also **Wales**): **6** Cymric **8** Cambrian

welsh drake: 7 gadwale, gadwall, gadwell

Welsh onion: 5 cibol

Welsh rabbit: 7 rarebit

welsh, welch: 5 cheat, evade, renig **6** renege **7** swindle

welt: 4 mark, turn, wale **5** ridge, upset **6** stripe, thrash **8** overturn

welter: 4 reel, roll, toss, wilt **5** upset **6** grovel, tumble, wallow, wither **7** stagger, turmoil **8** overturn **9** confusion

wem: 4 flaw, scar, spot **5** stain

wen: 4 cyst, rune **5** tumor **7** blemish **11** excrescence **12** imperfection, protuberance

wench: 4 dell, doxy, drab, gill, girl **5** child, gouge, trull, woman **6** blowen, blowze, damsel, maiden **7** consort, servant **8** strumpet **11** maidservant

wend: go; bow **4** fare, pass **5** alter, shift **6** depart, travel **7** circuit, journey, proceed **9** disappear

went (see also **go**): **4** lane, road **5** alley **7** passage **9** crossroad

wenzel: 4 jack **5** knave

were (see also **are**): **5** check, doubt, dread, guard **10** perplexity **11** uncertainty **12** apprehension

wergild: cro **4** eric

Wessex king: Ine, Ini

West: 8 frontier, Occident

West Indies:
bird: **4** arar, tody **6** mucaro
boat: **6** droger **7** drogher **9** catamaran
coin: **5** daler
fiber: **5** cajun
fish: **4** paru, pega, sesi **5** pelon **6** testar **7** pegador **8** scirenga **9** picudilla
fleas: **7** chigoes
fruit: **4** tuna **5** papaw **6** papaya, pawpaw **7** genipap
handkerchief: **7** malabar
herb: **4** ocra **6** vanglo **7** vangloe
island: **4** Cuba **5** Aruba, Haiti, Nevis **6** Bahama **7** Jamaica **8** Antilles, Barbados, Trinidad
king: **7** Cacique
liquor: **5** mobby, tafia **6** mobbie, taffia
lizard: **6** arbalo
mistletoe: **7** gadbush
people: Ebo **4** Eboe **5** Cuban **6** Creole
pert. to: **9** Antillean
region: **7** Malabar
republic: **5** Haiti
rodent: **5** hutia, jutia **6** agouti
shrub: **4** anil **7** joewood
snuff: **8** maccaboy, maccoboy
sorcery: ob; obe, obi **6** voodoo
sugar work: **5** usine
taro: **5** tania
tortoise: **7** hicatee **8** hiccatee
tree: **4** ausu, cera **5** acana, acapu, ebony, genip, papaw, yacca **6** aralie, ausubo, balata, cocuyo, gomart, pawpaw, ramoon **7** cocullo **8** aceituna, cockspur, drumwood **9** cocuswood, sapodilla
treewood: **5** galba
volcano: **5** Pelee

West Point:
island: **4** Iona
student: **4** pleb **5** cadet, plebe **8** yearling

West Virginia city: 5 Logan **10** Charleston(c.)

Westminster clock: Ben

Westphalian city: 7 Munster

wet: lax, off **4** damp, dank, dewy, lash, mire, rain, soak **5** bedew, bewet, dabby, foggy, humid, leach, misty, moist, mushy, rainy, soggy, soppy, sweat, wrong **6** clashy, dampen, drench, humect, imbrue, jarble, liquor, shower, soaked, sodden, watery **7** flotter, moisten, splashy, squashy **8** dampened, irrigate, moisture, sprinkle **9** misguided **11** intoxicated **18** anti-prohibitionist

wet blanket: 6 dampen **7** depress, killjoy **8** deadhead, dispirit **10** discourage, spoilsport

wet one's whistle: 5 drink

weta: 6 insect

wetbird: 9 chaffinch

wether: ram **4** wool **5** sheep **6** eunuch **7** dinmont

whack: hit, try **4** bang, beat, belt, blow **5** share, thump, trial, whang **6** chance, strike, stroke, thwack **7** attempt, portion **8** division **9** allowance, condition

whacking: 5 large **8** whopping **10** tremendous

whale: hit, orc **4** beat, cete, drub, lash, orca, wale, whip, whop **5** poggy, sperm, whack **6** baleen, beluga, blower, strike, thrash **7** Cetacea, grampus, ripsack **8** cachalot, hardhead **9** blackfish, mysticete, mysticeti, zeuglodon **10** bottlehead, zeuglodont **13** sulphur-bottom
blue: **9** sibbaldus
carcass: **5** kreng
cry: **4** fall
fat: **7** blubber
food: **4** brit
iron: **7** harpoon
order: **4** cete **7** Cetacea
pert. to: **5** cetic
school: gam, pod
secretion: **9** ambergris
skin: **6** muktuk
young: **4** calf **5** stunt **9** shorthead

whale oil: 10 spermaceti
cask: **4** rier

whaleback: 9 steamship **10** turtleback **12** grain-carrier

whalebird: 4 gull **6** petrel **9** phalarope, turnstone

whalebone: 5 stiff **6** baleen, severe **10** inflexible

whalehead: 8 shoebill

whaler: 4 ship 7 bushman, swagman, whopper 8 whaleman 9 sundowner, whaleboat
visit: gam

whaling:
cask: 4 rier 6 cardel
profit: lay

whample: 4 blow 6 stroke

whang: 4 bang, beat, blow, chop 5 chunk, slice, thong, throw, whack 6 assail, strike, thrash

wharf: 4 dock, pier, quai(F.), quay 7 landing
worker: 9 stevedore

wharf fish: 6 cunner

wharfmaster: 10 wharfinger

whatnot: 7 etagere

whaup: 4 fuss 6 curlew, outcry

wheal: 4 mark, mine, wale, weal 5 whelk 6 stripe 7 postule 9 suppurate

wheat: 5 durum, spelt, trigo 6 imphee 7 einkorn, semoule
chaff: 4 bran
head: ear
processed: 4 suji 5 grits 6 bulgur 9 middlings
state: 4 Ohio 5 Idaho 6 Dakota, Kansas 7 Indiana, Montana 8 Illinois, Missouri, Nebraska, Oklahoma 9 Minnesota 10 Washington 12 Pennsylvania
stubble: 6 arrish

wheat duck: 7 widgeon 8 baldpate

wheat louse: 5 aphid

wheat smut: 4 bunt 8 colbrand

wheatbird: 4 lark

wheatear: 8 chickell 10 gorsehatch

wheedle: cog 4 cant, coax 5 carny, tease, whine 6 banter, butter, cajole, carney, fleech, whilly 7 blarney, cuittle, flatter 8 persuade 9 influence

wheel (see also **gear**): cam, cog 4 bike, disk, helm, roll, turn 5 pivot, rotor, rowel, skeif, skive 6 caster, circle, roller, rotate, sheave 7 bicycle, chukkar, chukker, pedrail, revolve 10 revolution, waterwheel
part: cam, cog, rim 4 tire 5 felly, spoke, sprag 6 felloe 8 sprocket
pert. to: 5 rotal
potters: see **potter's wheel**
spinning: see **spinning wheel**
stopper: 5 brake
water-raising: see **waterwheel**

wheel-shaped: 6 rotate 8 circular, rotiform

wheelbarrow: hod 10 hurlbarrow

wheeler (see also **wheelman**): 7 cyclist, vulture 11 wheelwright

wheelman: 5 pilot 7 cyclist, steerer, wheeler 8 helmsman, pedalist 9 bicyclist

wheels (pair): 4 dish 6 camber 7 katydid

wheeze: gag 4 hint, joke 5 adage, dodge, hoose, hooze, trick 6 cliche, coghle(Sc.), device, saying 9 witticism

wheezy: 9 asthmatic

whelk: 4 acne 5 snail 6 papule, pimple, winkle 7 pustule

whelm (see also **overwhelm**): 5 cover, crush 9 drainpipe

whelp: cub, dog, pup 4 bear, fawn, lion, wale, welt, wolf 5 child, puppy, tiger, youth 7 leopard

whemmel, whemmle: 5 upset 6 tumble 8 overturn 9 confusion

when: as 5 until 7 whereas 8 although, whenever

where: 7 whither

whereas: as 5 since

wherefore: 5 cause 6 reason 9 therefore 11 accordingly

whereness: 6 ubiety

wherewithal: 5 means 9 resources

wherret: box, hit 4 slap

wherry: 4 boat 5 barge, carry, scull 7 lighter, rowboat, vehicle 9 transport

whet: 4 hone 5 grind, rouse, strop 6 excite 7 quicken, sharpen 9 stimulate

whether: if

whetstone: bur 4 buhr, burr, hone 5 stone 9 sharpener

whewl: cry 4 howl 5 whine

whey: 5 serum

which: who 4 that, whom

which was to be shown: QED

whicker: 5 neigh 6 whinny

whid: fib, lie 4 word 5 frisk

whiff: fan 4 flag, fuff, guff, gust, odor, puff, waft, wave 5 expel, fluff, jiffy, smell 6 breath, exhale, inhale, stench 7 instant 10 inhalation

whiffle: 4 blow, emit, idle, turn, veer, wave 5 expel, shake, shift 6 change, trifle 7 flicker, flutter, scatter 8 disperse 9 vacillate

whig: jog 4 whey 8 beverage 10 buttermilk

while: as; yet 5 until 6 whenas 7 whereas

whilly: 4 gull 6 cajole 7 wheedle

whilom: 4 erst, once, past 6 former 8 erewhile, formerly 9 erstwhile

whim: fad, fit, gig 4 idea, mood 5 fancy, humor, winch 6 megrim, notion, trifle, vagary, whimsy 7 boutade, caprice, capstan, whimsey 8 crotchet

whimper: cry, sob 4 mewl, moan, pule, weep 5 whine 6 murmur, yammer 7 grizzle, sniffle

whimsical: odd 5 droll, queer 6 cockle 7 bizzaro, comical 8 fanciful, freakish, notional 9 conceited, eccentric, fantastic, grotesque 10 capricious 11 fantastical

whimsy: See **whim**.

whin: 4 rock, whim 5 furze, gorse 9 whinstone

whinchat: 9 gorsechat, grasschat

whine: wow 4 cant, girn, moan, pule 5 croon, whewl 6 snivel, yammer 7 whimper 8 complain

whinnock: 7 whimper

whinny: 4 bray 5 hinny, neigh
whinyard: 5 sword
whip: cat, gad, tan 4 beat, cane, crop, flay,
  flog, jerk, lace, lash, urge, wind, wrap 5
  birch, flick, knout, outdo, quirt, spank,
  strap, swish 6 defeat, punish, stitch,
  strike, swinge, switch, thrash 7 belabor,
  chicote, conquer, overlay, scourge, sjambok 8 chawbuck, coachman, hunstman 9
  bullwhack, flagellum 10 discipline,
  flagellate
  mark: 4 wale, weal, welt
  part: 4 crop 5 snead 6 handle, socket
whir: bur, fly 4 birl, burr, move, whiz 5
  hurry, skirr, swirl, whizz 6 bustle, hurtle
  7 revolve, vibrate 9 commotion
whirl: 4 eddy, reel, spin, stir, tirl, turn 5
  drill, twirl 6 bustle, circle, gyrate, rotate,
  swinge, tumult, uproar, vortex 7 revolve 9
  commotion, pirouette
whirlbone: 7 kneepan, patella 10 hucklebone
whirlpool: 4 eddy 6 gurges, vortex
whirlwind: oe 7 cyclone, tornado 9 maelstrom
whirr: See **whir**.
whisht: 4 hush 7 silence
whisk: 4 tuft, whip, wisp 5 flisk
whiskers (see also **beard**): 6 growth 7
  stubble 9 sideburns, vibrissae 11 mut-
  tonchops
whiskey, whisky: rye 4 corn 6 poteen,
  redeye, rotgut, Scotch 8 blockade, bust-
  head 9 moonshine 10 usquebaugh
  maker: 9 distiller
  punch: 5 facer
whiskin: 4 bowl
whisper: 4 buzz 5 rumor 6 breeze, murmur
whisperer: 7 tattler 9 backbiter, slan-
  derer 10 talebearer
whist: 4 game, hush, mute 5 cards, quiet,
  still 6 silent 7 silence 8 silently
  hand: 6 tenace 10 Yarborough
whistle: 4 hiss, pipe, sugh, toot 5 siren,
  sough
whistle duck: 9 goldeneye
whistle-pig: 9 woodchuck
whistlewing: 9 goldeneye
whit: bit, jot 4 atom, doit, haet, hate, iota 5
  speck 8 particle
white: wan 4 ashy, bawn, hoar, pale, pure
  5 ashen, happy, hoary, ivory 6 argent,
  albino, blanch, chalky, grayed, honest,
  pallid, pearly 7 ivorine, silvery 8 harmless, innocent, spotless 9 colorless, fortunate, honorable 10 auspicious
  becoming: 9 canescent
white ant: 4 anai, anay 7 termite
white antimony: 11 valentinite
white cell: 9 leukocyte
white-collar: 5 clerk 6 typist 8 salesman
  9 bookeeper, secretary
white crow: 7 vulture

white elephant (land of): 4 Siam 5
  Burma, India 6 Ceylon 8 Thailand
white flag: 5 truce 9 surrender
white gentian: 9 feverroot
white grouse: 9 ptarmigan
white heat: 13 incandescence
white horse nettle: 9 trompillo
white Indian hemp: 8 milkweed
white iron pyrites: 9 marcasite
white jade: 9 alabaster
white lead: 6 ceruse
white lead ore: 9 cerussite
white-livered: 8 cowardly 13 pusillanimous
white merganser: 4 smew
white mica: 9 muscovite
White Monk: 10 Cistercian
White Mountain: 5 Adams
white mule: gin 6 liquor, whisky 7
  whiskey 9 moonshine
white mundic: 12 arsenopyrite
white nun: 4 smew
white partridge: 9 ptarmigan
white plague: 8 phthisis 11 consumption
  12 tuberculosis
white plantain: 9 pussytoes
white pudding: 7 sausage 9 whitehass
white pyrite: 9 marcasite
white sanicle: 9 snakeroot
white snipe: 6 avocet 10 sanderling
White Sunday: 10 Whitsunday
white walnut: 8 shagbark, sycamore 9
  butternut
white whale: 6 beluga
white widgeon: 4 smew
whitebelly: 6 grouse, pigeon
whiteboy: pet 8 favorite
whitecap: 4 wave 5 crest
whitefish: 5 cisco 6 beluga 8 menhaden
whiten: 4 pale 5 chalk 6 blanch, bleach 8
  etiolate
whiteside: 9 goldeneye
whitewash: 6 blanch, defeat, parget 7
  conceal
whiteweed: 5 daisy
whitewing: 4 sail 6. scoter 7 sweeper 9
  chaffinch
whither: 4 blow, hurl, rush, whiz 5 hurry,
  shake, throw, where 6 flurry, totter 7
  bluster, tremble 8 wherever
whiting: 4 fish 5 chalk
whitlow: 4 sore 5 felon 6 fetlow 12
  inflammation
whitster: 8 bleacher
whittaw: 7 saddler
whitten: 5 rowan
whitterick: 6 curlew
whittle: cut 4 pare, whet 5 knife, shape,
  shave, shawl 6 mantle, reduce, remove 7
  blanket 9 petticoat, whetstone
whiz: go; hum 4 buzz, hiss, pirr, whir 5
  hurry 6 corker, rotate 7 bargain
who: quo(L.), Wer(G.), wha(Sc.) 13 interrogative

whoa: 4 halt, stop

whole: all, sum 4 full, hail, hale, sole, unit 5 gross, total 6 entire, healed, intact, wholly 7 perfect 8 absolute, complete, ensemble, entirely, entirety, thorough, unbroken 9 unanimous, undamaged, un-divided 10 unimpaired

whole number: 7 integer

whole-souled: 7 devoted, sincere, zealous 8 generous 12 whole-hearted

wholehearted: 6 hearty 7 devoted, ear-nest, sincere 8 complete 10 unreserved 11 unmitigated

wholesale: 7 massive 9 extensive

wholesome: 5 sound 6 benign, hearty, robust 7 healthy 8 benedict, halesome, salutary, vigorous 9 favorable, healthful 10 beneficial, healthsome, propitious, salubrious

wholly: 5 quite 7 algates 10 altogether 11 exclusively

comb. form: 4 toto

whoop: 4 hoot, urge, yell 5 cheer, shout 6 halloo

whooping cough: 9 pertussis

whop: 4 beat, blow, bump, flop 5 knock, throw 6 strike, stroke

whopper: lie 5 story 6 bender, bumper 7 bouncer

whopping: 5 great, large 7 banging

whore: 4 drab 5 wench 6 harlot 8 strum-pet 9 courtesan 10 prostitute

whorl: 5 spire

why: 9 wherefore

whyo: 6 robber 7 footpad 8 gangster

wick: bay 4 bend, town 5 angle, creek, in-let 6 corner, hamlet, inwick 7 borough, village 9 farmstead

wicked: bad, ill 4 evil, vile 6 fierce, guilty, horrid, sinful, unjust 7 beastly, harmful, heinous, hellish, painful, profane, vicious 8 criminal, depraved, devilish, diabolic, felonous, fiendish, flagrant, indecent 9 atrocious, difficult, malicious, nefandous, nefarious, perverted 10 diabolical, flagi-tious, impassable, iniquitous, villainous 11 mischievous 12 inaccessible

wicket: 4 arch, door, gate, hoop 5 hatch 6 window 7 guichet, opening

wickiup: hut 7 shelter

widdershins, withershins: 10 contrarily, topsy-turvy 12 contrariwise

widdle: 7 wriggle 8 struggle

widdrim: 4 fury 7 madness 9 confusion 10 excitement

widdy: 4 rope 5 noose, widow, withy 6 halter 7 gallows

wide: 5 ample, broad, loose, roomy 6 opened 8 expanded, spacious 9 capa-cious, distended, expansive, extensive 12 farspreading 13 comprehensive

wide-awake: hat 4 keen, tern 5 alert 7 knowing 8 watchful 10 interested

widely: far 4 afar 6 abroad

widen: 4 ream 6 dilate, expand, extend, spread 7 amplify, broaden, enlarge 10 generalize

widespread: 4 rife 7 allover, diffuse, general 8 diffused, sweeping 9 extensive, pervasive, prevalent, universal 13 com-prehensive

widgeon: 4 duck 5 goose 8 baldpate 9 simpleton

genus: 6 mareca

widow: 5 widdy 6 relict 7 dowager 8 be-reaved

right: 5 dower 10 quarantine

suicide: 6 suttee

widow monkey: 4 titi

widowman: 7 widower

width: 5 girth 7 breadth 8 diameter, lati-tude, wideness

wield: ply 4 bear, cope, deal, rule 5 power, swing 6 direct, employ, handle, manage, ordain 7 control 8 brandish 9 determine 10 manipulate

wife: ux(L.); hen 4 frau, frow, mate, uxor(L.) 5 donna, mujer 6 gammer, spouse 7 consort 8 gudewife(Sc.), guid-wife(Sc.), helpmate, helpmeet

clergyman's: 8 curatess

lord's: 4 lady

pert. to: 7 uxorial

rajah's: 4 rani 5 ranee

slave's: 9 broadwife

wig: 4 gizz 5 busby, caxon, jasey, judge, scold 6 baguio, peruke, rebuke, toupee 7 censure, periwig, spencer 8 Chedreux 9 dignitary, Gregorian, reprimand

repair: 6 careen

wiggle: 5 shake 6 waggle, wobble 7 stag-ger, wriggle

wight: man 4 loud 5 brave, swift, witch 6 active, nimble, strong 7 swiftly, valiant 8 creature, powerful, strongly

wigwag: 6 signal

wigwam: 4 home 5 tepee 6 teepee

wild: mad, ree 4 daft, wowf(Sc.) 5 feral, rough, waste, weird 6 desert, ferine, ra-mage, savage, stormy, unruly 7 bestial, haggard, riotous, skeered(Sc.), untamed, wilsome 8 aberrant, agrestal, desolate, dramatic, farouche, frenetic, hellicat, reckless, untilled 9 agrestial, barbarian, barbarous, dissolute, disturbed, ferocious, hellicate, imprudent, primitive, turbulent, unbridled, visionary 10 chimerical, dis-sipated, irrational, licentious, tumultuous, wilderness 11 extravagant, harum-scarum, uncivilized, uninhabited 12 ob-streperous, uncontrolled, uncultivated 14 uncontrollable

wild alder: 8 goutweed

wild allspice: 9 spicebush

wild arum: 10 cuckoopint

wild banana: 5 papaw 6 pawpaw

wild carrot: 8 hilltrot

wild coffee: 9 feverroot

wild crocus: 12 pasqueflower
wild flower: See **flower**.
wild goose: 7 greylag 8 Jacobite
wild Irishman: 10 tumatakura
wild jalap: 8 mayapple
wild kale: 6 radish 8 charlock
wild masterwort: 8 goutweed
wild musk: 9 alfilaria
wild mustard: 8 charlock
wild passionflower: 6 maypop
wild pineapple: 7 pinguin
wild plum: 4 sloe
wild pumpkin: 11 calabazilla
wild sage: 5 clary
wild sago: 7 coontie
wild sheep: See **sheep**.
wild succory: 7 chicory
wild sweet potato: 7 manroot
wild turnip: 6 radish 8 rutabaga 9 breadroot
wildcat: cat 4 balu, eyra 6 ocelot, serval 7
panther 9 promotion
wildebeast: gnu
wilder (see also **wild**): 5 stray 6 wander 7
perplex 8 bewilder
wilderness: 5 waste 6 desert, forest
wildfowl: 4 duck 5 goose, quail 8 pheasant 9 partridge
flight: 5 skein
wildness: 6 ramage 8 ferocity 12 extravagance
wile: art 4 lure, ruse 5 fraud, guile, trick 6
allure, deceit, entice 7 beguile, cunning 8
artifice, trickery 9 stratagem
Wilkes Island: 4 Ashi
will: 4 lust, wish 6 animus, choose, decree,
desire, devise, prefer 7 command, longing
8 appetite, pleasure, volition 9 intention,
testament 11 disposition, inclination,
self-control 13 determination
appendix: 7 codicil
maker of: 8 testator
proof of: 7 probate
valid: 7 testacy
willful: mad 4 rash 5 heady 7 wayward 8
stubborn 9 camsteary, camsteery, impetuous, obstinate, voluntary 10 hardheaded 11 intentional
William II's residence: 5 Doorn
William Tell:
canton: Uri
hero: 4 Egil
William The Conqueror's burial place:
4 Caen
willing: apt 4 bain 5 prone, ready 6 minded
7 tending 8 desirous, disposed, unforced
9 agreeable 10 volitional
willingly: 4 fain, lief 5 lieve 6 freely,
gladly
willingness: 7 consent 8 alacrity
willow: iva 4 itea 5 osier, salix 6 teaser
willow wren: 10 chiffchaff
willowy: 5 lithe 6 pliant 7 slender 8 flexible, graceful

willpower: 7 purpose 10 resolution 12
resoluteness 13 determination
loss of: 6 abulia 7 aboulia
willy: 4 trap 6 basket, willow
Wilson's thrush: 5 veery
wilt: sag 4 fade, flag 5 droop, quail 6
wither 8 languish
wily: sly 4 foxy 5 canny, smart 6 artful,
astute, crafty, shrewd, subtle 7 cunning,
subtile 9 cautelous
wimble: awl 4 bore 5 auger, brace, scoop,
twist 6 active, gimlet, pierce 9 penetrate,
sprightly, whimsical
wimick: cry 7 whimper
wimple: 4 bend, fold, turn, veil, wind 5
curve 6 ripple 7 meander, wriggle 9
headdress
win: get, pot 4 earn, gain, take 5 charm 6
allure, attain, defeat, entice, obtain, secure 7 achieve, acquire, capture, conquer, prevail, succeed, triumph 8 vanquish 9 captivate, influence 10 accomplish, conciliate
all tricks: 4 slam
back: 7 recover 8 retrieve
over: 6 defeat 8 persuade 10 conciliate
wince: 4 crab, reel 5 start 6 cringe, flinch,
recoil, shrink 8 windlass
wind: oe; air 4 birr, bise, bora, coil, flaw,
gale, gust, kona, reel, wend, wrap 5 be-
lay(naut.), blast, buran, crank, curve,
foehn, noser, reeve, samum, siroc, storm,
trade, twine, twist, wield 6 boreas,
bought, breath, breeze, buster, gibleh,
simoom, simoon, solano, squall, writhe,
zephyr 7 chamsin, chinook, cyclone, entwine, entwist, etesian, gregale, khamsin,
meander, monsoon, pampero, revolve,
sirocco, tempest, tornado, typhoon,
wreathe, wriggle, wulliwa 8 blizzard,
khamseen, libeccio, williwaw, willywaw 9
harmattan, hurricane, libecchio, noreaster
10 euroclydon, tramontana, tramontane
combining form: 5 anemo
god of: 4 Adda, Adad, Vayu 5 Eolus 6
Aeolus, Eecatl
periodic: oe 7 etesian, monsoon
personification: 6 Caurus 7 Caecias 8
Favonius
pertaining to: 6 eolian 7 aeolian
wind gauge: 4 vane 10 anemometer 11
weathercock
wind instrument: sax 4 fife, horn, oboe,
tuba 5 flute, organ 6 cornet 7 hautboy 8
clarinet
wind up: end 4 coil 5 close 6 finish 8 conclude
windfall: 8 buckshee
windflower: 7 anemone
windhover: 7 kestrel
windiness: 7 conceit 9 puffiness 11 ver-
boseness 12 boastfulness
winding: 4 wily 6 screwy, spiral, tricky 7
coiling, crinkle, devious, pliable, sinuous,

twining, wriggly **8** flexible, rambling, tortuous, twisting **9** deceitful, intricate,
meandrous, sinuosity **10** anfracture, circuitous, meandering, serpentine **11**
amortisseur, anfractuous
device: **4** reel **7** capstan **8** windlass
windjammer: **4** ship **6** bugler, sailor,
talker **8** musician **9** trumpeter
windlass: **4** crab, reel **5** hoist, winch **7**
capstan
windle: **7** measure, redwing
windmill:
  blade: **4** vane
  pump: gin
  sail: awn, ban
window: bay **5** gable, glaze, oriel **6** dormer
  7 balcone, fenetre, lucarne, mirador, opening, winnock(Sc.) **8** aperture, casement
  arrangement: **12** fenestration
  frame: **4** sash
  leading: **4** came
  part: **4** came, sill
  pert. to: **9** fenestral
  recess: **6** exedra
  ship's: **4** port
  ticket: **6** wicket **7** guichet
  worker: **7** glazier
window glass (to supply): **7** impanel
windpipe: **6** artery, gullet, throat, weason
  7 trachea, weasand, weazand **9** esophagus
  pert. to: **8** trachean
windrow: **5** swath **6** furrow, swathe
windshake: **8** anemosis
windstorm (see also storm; wind): **4** gale
  7 cyclone, typhoon **9** hurricane
windward: **5** aloof **8** aweather
Windward Island: **7** Grenada
windy: **4** airy **5** empty, gusty, huffy, swift
  6 breezy, stormy **7** gustful, pompous,
verbose **8** boastful, skittish **9** aeolistic,
bombastic **10** boisterous, changeable,
intangible **11** harebrained, tempestuous
13 unsubstantial
Windy City: **7** Chicago
wine: vin(F.) **4** alac, Asti, Bual, cote, deal,
port, tent **5** Baden, Casel, drink, liane,
Medoc, merum(L.), Rhine, Tinta, tokay,
Yquem **6** Barolo, Barsac, Beaune, canary,
claret, Malaga, Massic, Muscat, Saumur,
sherry **7** Alicant, Banyals, Bastard, Cha-
blis, chacoli, Chateau, Chianti, Conthey,
Dezaley, Falerno, hollock, Madeira, Mar-
gaux, Marsala, Medeira, Moselle, Orvieto
8 Alicante, Ambonnay, beverage, Bordeaux, Bucellas, Burgundy, Florence,
Marsalla, muscadel, Muscatel, Rulander,
Riesling, Ruchelle, Rulander, sauterne **9**
Gladstone, hermitage, teneriffe, Zeltinger,
zinfandel **10** Beaujolais, Calon-Segur,
Hockheimer, Roussillon **11** Niersteiner,
scuppernong **12** Geisenheimer **15** schar-
lachberger
  apple: **5** cider

bag: **8** wineskin
bibber: sot **5** toper **7** tippler **8** drunkard
bottle: **6** fiasco, magnum **8** decanter, jeroboam
cask: tun **4** pipe
cask deposit: **6** tartar
cellar: **6** bodega
cruet: **7** burette
cup: ama **5** amula **6** goblet **7** chalice
deposit: **6** tartar
disorder: **5** casse
drink: **5** clary, mulse, negus, punch
film: **8** beeswing
god: **4** Soma **7** Bacchus **8** Dionysus
list: **4** card
lover: **11** oenophilist
maker: **6** abkari, abkary
measure: aam, aum **4** orna, orne
medicinal preparation: **5** mosto
merchant: **6** bistro(F.) **7** vintner **8** gourmand
new: **4** must
pitcher: **4** olpe **5** olpae **8** oenochoe
residue: **4** marc
scene of miracle: **4** Cana
shop: **6** bodega
spiced: **9** hippocras
stock: **6** cellar
study of: **7** enology
strength: **4** seve
sweet: **5** lunel
vessel: ama **5** amula **7** chalice
year: **7** vintage
wine and dine: **4** fete **6** regale
wineberry: **5** grape **7** currant **8** bilberry,
makomako **9** raspberry **10** gooseberry
winegrower: **8** vigneron **13** viticulturist
wineshop: bar **6** bistro, bodega
wing: ala, arm, ell, fin, fly, van **4** limb **5**
aisle, alula, pinna, shard, speed, volet,
wound **6** hasten, pennon, pinion **7** flutter
  arrangement: **7** alation
  pert. to: **4** alar **6** pteric
  under: **8** subalary
  vestigial: **5** alula
wing cover: **7** elytron
wing-footed: **5** swift **6** aliped **9** mercurial
wing-like: **4** alar **5** alary, alate **6** pteric **7**
aliform, pteroid
  part: ala **4** alae **7** aileron
winged: **4** aile, alar **5** alary, alate, lofty,
rapid, swift **6** alated **7** bialate, sublime,
wounded **9** aliferous, aligerous, feathered
Winged Horse: **7** Pegasus
wingless: **7** apteral **8** apterous
wings: *being with:* **5** angel **6** cherub, seraph
  7 Mercury
  conjoined: vol(her.)
wink: bat, nap, nod **4** hint **5** blink, flash,
gleam, prink, sleep **6** signal **7** flicker, instant, nictate, slumber, sparkle, twinkle **9**
nictation, nictitate, twinkling **10** periwinkle
winking: **13** blepharospasm

winks (forty): nap 6 catnap

winner: 6 earner, reaper, victor 7 face-man, sleeper 8 bangster 9 conqueror 11 breadwinner

winning (see also **win; winsome**): 5 shaft 6 profit 7 victory

winninish, winnonish: 6 salmon 10 ouananiche

winnock: 6 window

winnow: fan, van 4 beat, flap, sift 5 dight 6 assort, select 7 analyze, examine, scatter 8 brandish, disperse, separate 9 elimi-nate

winsome: gay 5 bonny, merry 6 blithe, bonnie 7 likable, winning 8 charming, cheerful, engaging, pleasant 9 agreeable 10 attractive 11 captivating 12 light-hearted

winter: 9 hibernate

pear: 6 seckel, warden

pert. to: 6 brumal, hiemal

winter quarters: 10 hibernacle 12 hi-bernaculum

winter teal: 9 greenwing

winterbloom: 6 azalea

wintergreen: 10 pipsissewa

wintle: 4 reel, roll 7 stagger, wriggle

wintry: icy 4 aged, cold 5 snowy, white 6 frigid, hiemal, stormy 8 chilling, hibernal, wintered 9 cheerless

winy: 6 vinous 7 drunken

wipe: dry, hit, mop, rub 4 beat, blow, draw, gibe, jeer, pass 5 brand, cheat, clean, dight, erase, stain, swipe, towel, trick 6 cancel, defeat, remove, sponge, strike, stroke 7 abolish, defraud, exhaust, sar-casm 8 disgrace 10 annihilate, obliterate 11 exterminate 12 handkerchief

wire: 4 coil 5 cable 6 fasten 8 telegram 9 cablegram, telegraph

bundle of: 5 cable

cutters: 6 pliers

measure: mil 5 stone

system: 7 network, reticle

wire cutter: 5 wirer 8 secateur

wiredraw: 5 wrest 7 distort, prolong 8 protract 9 attenuate 10 overrefine

wireless: 5 radio

wirework: 8 filigree

wiry: 4 lean 5 hardy, stiff, tough 6 sinewy, strong

wis: 4 deem, know 5 think 7 believe, im-agine, suppose

Wisconsin: *city:* 6 Beloit, Racine, Sparta 7 Kenosha, Madison(c.), Necedah, Oshkosh 10 Oconomowoc

native: 6 Badger

wisdom (see also **wise**): 4 lore 8 judgment

god of: 4 Nabu, Nebo 6 Ganesa 7 Ganesha

goddess of: 6 Athena 7 Minerva

wise: 4 mode, sage, sane, show, wary 5 aware, smart, sound, witty 6 advise, crafty, direct, inform, manner, shrewd, subtle, versed, witful 7 beguile, cunning, erudite, explain, fashion, heedful, know-ing, learned, politic, prudent, sapient, skilled 8 discreet, informed, instruct, persuade, profound, sensible, skillful 9 cognizant, dexterous, expedient, judi-cious, provident, sagacious 10 discerning, omniscient 11 calculating, circumspect, enlightened, intelligent, well-advised 13 sophisticated

infinitely: 10 omniscient

wise man: 4 sage 5 magus, solon 6 Cas-per, Gasper, Nestor, wizard 8 magician, Melchior 9 Balthasar, Balthazar, counci-lor

Wise Men: 4 Magi

wiseacre: 5 dunce 7 prophet 9 simpleton 10 mastermind 11 wisenheimer

wiselike: 6 decent 7 fitting 8 becoming, sensible 9 judicious 11 appropriate

wish: 4 hope, long, want 5 crave, yearn 6 behest, desire, invoke 7 longing, propose, request 8 petition, yearning 10 aspira-tion, invocation 11 imprecation

wishbone: 8 furculum 10 fourchette

wishful: 8 desirous 9 desirable 10 attrac-tive

wisht: 5 eerie 6 dismal, dreary 7 uncanny 8 wretched 10 melancholy

wishy-washy: 4 pale, sick, thin, weak 5 tepid 6 feeble, trashy, watery 7 insipid 13 unsubstantial

wisket: 6 basket

wisp: 4 band, ring, wase 5 broom, brush, bunch, clean, flock, shred, torch, whisk 6 bundle, parcel, rumple, wreath 7 crum-ple, handful 8 fragment

wispy: 5 filmy 6 slight 7 slender 8 gos-samer

wissel: 5 money 6 change 8 exchange 11 retribution

wist: 4 know

wistaria: 4 bush, fuji 6 purple, violet

wistful: 6 intent 7 longing, pensive 8 yearning 9 attentive, nostalgic

wistfulness: rue 6 regret

wit: wag 4 know 5 humor, irony, learn 6 acumen, esprit(F.), namely, reason, satire, wisdom 7 cunning, faculty, punster 8 co-median, drollery, funnyman, repartee 9 intellect 12 intelligence, perspicacity 13 understanding

witch: hag, hex 4 baba 5 charm, crone, lamia, woman 6 cummer, kimmer, wizard 7 bewitch 9 fascinate, sorceress

cat: 9 grimalkin

witchcraft: 5 charm, magic 7 cunning, hexerei, sorcery 8 brujeria(Sp.), pishogue, witchery, wizardry 9 sortilege 11 en-chantment, fascination 12 invultuation

goddess of: 5 Obeah 6 Hecate

practice: hex 7 bewitch

witchman: 6 shaman, wizard 8 sorcerer

wite: 4 fine 5 blame, fault 6 accuse 7 cen-sure 8 reproach 9 exemption 14 respon-sibility

with: wi(Sc.); con(It.), cum(L.), mit(G.) 4

avec(F.), near **5** along **9** alongside **12** accompanying

prefix: col, com, cyn, pro, syn

withdraw: go **4** void **5** avoid **6** absent, depart, detach, divert, recall, recant, recede, remove, retire, secede **7** abscond, decline, detract, extract, forbear, forsake, refrain, retract, retreat, subduce, subside **8** abstract, alienate, derogate, distract, evacuate, renounce, restrain, withhold **9** disengage, sequester **10** relinquish, retrograde

withdrawal (see also **withdraw**): **7** regress

withe: **4** band, bind, herb, rope, twig **5** osier, snare, withy **6** branch, fasten, halter, wattle, willow

wither: age, die, dry **4** fade, pine, sear, sere, wilt **5** blast, cling, daver, decay, wizen **6** blight, cotter, shrink, weaken **7** shrivel, wrinkle **8** languish

withered: **4** arid, sere **7** sapless **10** marcescent **11** sphacelated

withhold: **4** curb, deny, hide, keep **5** check **6** desist, detain, refuse, retain **7** abstain, forbear, prevent, refrain, repress, reserve **8** maintain, postpone, restrain

within: in, on; ben **4** inly, into **5** among **6** during, herein, inside **7** indoors **8** inwardly **10** underneath

comb. form: ent, eso **4** endo, ento

prefix: **5** intra

without: **4** bout, sans, sine(L.) **6** beyond **7** lacking, outside **9** outwardly **10** externally

prefix: se: ect, exo **4** ecto

without this: **7** sine hoc

withstand: **4** bear, bide, defy **5** abide **6** combat, endure, oppose, resist **7** gainsay **8** confront **9** gainstand **10** contradict, controvert

withy: **4** turn, twig, wind, wiry **5** agile, braid **6** branch, willow **8** flexible

witless: mad **5** crazy, gross **6** insane, stupid **7** foolish, unaware **8** heedless **9** brainless, pointless, unknowing **10** dullwitted, indiscreet

witness: eye, see, wit **4** know **5** teste **6** attest, beheld, behold, martyr **7** observe, sponsor, testify **8** beholder, evidence, observer, onlooker **9** spectator, subscribe, testifier, testimony **11** attestation **13** understanding

witter: tee **4** barb

witticism: mot, pun **4** gibe, jeer, jest, joke, quip **5** sally **11** gauloiserie

witting: **7** tidings **8** judgment **9** knowledge **10** deliberate **11** information, intentional **12** intelligence

wittol: **4** fool **7** cuckold **8** wheatear

witty: **4** gash, wise **5** comic **6** bright, clever, facete, jocose, jocund, versed **7** amusing, comical, jocular, knowing **8** humorous, informed **9** facetious **11** intelligent

wive: **5** marry

wizard: **4** mage, sage **5** fiend **6** genius, Merlin **7** magical, prodigy, warlock **8** charming, conjurer, magician, sorcerer **10** enchanting **11** necromancer, thaumaturge **12** thaumaturgus **13** thaumaturgist

wizardry: art **5** magic **7** sorcery **10** witchcraft

wizen, weazen: dry **6** wither **7** shrivel, wizened

woad: **8** dyestuff

wobble, wabble: **4** boil **5** shake, waver **6** quaver **7** tremble **9** vacillate

wobbly: **5** loose, shaky

woe: **4** bale, bane **5** grief **6** misery, sorrow **7** trouble **8** calamity, disaster **9** dejection **10** affliction, desolation, melancholy, misfortune

woeful: sad **4** dire **6** paltry **7** direful, pitiful, unhappy **8** mournful, wretched **9** miserable, sorrowful, woebegone **10** deplorable, dispirited **12** disconsolate

wold: lea **5** plain **6** meadow

wolf: **4** lobo **6** canine, chanco, coyote **9** thylacine **10** ladykiller **11** philanderer

cry: **4** howl

gait: **4** lope

wolf-like: **6** lupine **9** rapacious

wolfhound: **4** alan

wolfsbane: **7** aconite **9** monkshood

wolverine: **8** carcajou

genus of: **4** gulo

Wolverine State: **8** Michigan

woman (see also **girl; mother**): gin, hen, **4** bint, dame, dona, lady, maid, rani **5** begum, broad, chick, donna, femme, madam, mujer, ranee, skirt, squaw **6** calico, cummer, domina, female, heifer, kimmer, maness, senora **7** alewife, servant, signora **8** mistress, senorita **10** klootchman, sweetheart **11** gentlewoman

affected: **5** prude **7** cockney

attractice: **4** doll, peri **5** filly, pin-up, siren, sylph, Venus **6** beauty, looker **7** charmer, Zenobia **8** Musidora

brave: **7** hellcat, heroine

celibate: **7** agapeta

domain: **7** distaff

kept: **8** mistress **9** concubine **12** demimondaine

learned: **4** blue **7** basbleu(F.), seeress **12** bluestocking

little: **4** wife **7** ladykin

loose: tib **4** drab, flap, jilt, slut **5** hussy, quean, queen **6** chippy, giglet, giglot, harlot, wanton **7** cocotte, Jezebel, trollop **9** courtesan, courtezen, dratchell

married: **4** frau, frow, wife **5** vrouw **6** matron

mythical: **6** Gorgon

objectionable: hag **5** fagot, shrew, witch **6** faggot, gorgon, virago **8** harridan **9** grimalkin, termagant

old: gib, hag **4** baba, dame, trot **5** crone, frump **6** carlin, gammer, granny **7** car-

line, dowager, grandam **8** grandame,
spinster **9** cailleach, cailliach
organization: DAR, WAC, WSP **4** AMVS,
WAAC, WAVE, Wren **5** Ebell **6** circle **7**
sorosis **8** sorority **10** sisterhood
pert. to: **7** gynecic **8** gynaecic **9** muliebral
serving: See **servant.**
single (see also **maiden**): **6** virgin **8** mistress, spinster
staid: **4** lady **6** beldam, matron **7** beldame
state of: **10** muliebrity
strong: **6** Amazon, virago **8** titaness
talkative: cat, gad, hen **5** dolly, flirt, scold,
shrew, vixen **6** fizgig, virago **7** hellcat **9**
termagant
theater: **6** dancer **7** actress, chorine **9**
soubrette
unattractive: bag, dog **4** drab **5** crone,
dowdy, witch **8** slattern
young (see also **girl**): tib **4** burd, dell, drab,
lass **5** filly, trull, wench **6** lassie **7** damozel
10 demoiselle
woman chaser: **4** wolf **8** lothario **10**
sheepbiter **11** philanderer
woman hater: **10** misogynist
womanish: **5** anile **6** effete, female **8** feminine **10** effeminate
womb: bag **5** belly **6** uterus
wombat: **6** badger **9** marsupial
won (see also **win**): **4** live **5** abide, dwell **7**
inhabit
wonder: awe **4** evil, harm, sign **5** grief,
wrong **6** esteem, marvel **7** curious, miracle, prodigy **8** surprise **9** amazement,
speculate, uncertain **10** admiration, won-
derment **11** destruction **12** astonishment
performance: See **magic.**
worker of: See **wizard.**
Wonder State: 8 Arkansas
wonderful: **4** fine, good **5** super **6** lovely
7 amazing, amusing, corking, mirific,
strange **8** wondrous **9** admirable, excellent, marvelous **10** miraculous, surprising
11 astonishing, interesting **13** extraordinary
wong: **5** field **6** meadow
wonky: off **4** awry **5** shaky **6** feeble **7** tottery **8** unsteady **9** tottering
wont: use **5** dwell, habit, usage, usual **6**
custom, reside **8** inclined, practice **10**
accustomed
woo: beg, sue **4** coax, seek **5** court, spark **6**
assail, invite, splunt(Sc.) **7** address, beseech, entreat, solicit **9** importune
wood: hag, keg, mad **4** bois(F.), bosk, bowl,
cask, holt, wold **5** angry, cahuy, grove,
hurst, trees, xylem **6** forest, insane, lumber, timber **7** enraged, furious, violent **8**
woodland
ash: **6** potash
bundle of: **5** fagot
burned: ash **4** brae **8** charcoal
comb. form: **4** hylo, xylo **5** ligni
dealer: **10** xylopolist

derivative: tar **5** turps **6** balsam **10** turpentine
distillation from: tar **5** turps **10** turpentine
edge: **8** woodrime, woodside
fine-grained: yew **6** brauna
firing easily: **4** punk **5** sponk, spunk **6**
tinder **8** kindling, punkwood **9** touchwood
fragrant: **5** aloes, cedar
god: See **woodland:***deity.*
growth: **7** coppice
hard: ash, elm, eng, oak **4** lana, poon, rata,
teak **5** ebony, maple, zante **6** walnut **7**
hickory **8** mahogany
juice: sap
kind: See **tree.**
knot: nur **4** burl, knag, knar **5** gnarl
light: **4** cork **5** balsa
part: fid, nog, peg, rib **4** lath, shim, slat **5**
dowel, spile, sprag, stave, tenon **6** batten,
billet, reglet, splint **7** dingbat
pert. to: **5** treen
prefix: **4** xylo
steward: **9** woodreeve
striped: roe
supporting: **5** cleat
valuable: sal **4** teak
worker: **6** joiner, sawyer **7** paneler **9** carpenter
wood alcohol: **6** methyl **8** methanol
wood-ash salt: **6** potash
wood nymph: **4** moth **5** dryad **8** grayling
11 hummingbird
wood pigeon: **4** dove **6** cushat **8** ringdove
wood pussy: **5** skunk
wood sorrel: oca **6** oxalis **7** begonia **8**
haremeat
wood stork: **4** ibis
woodbine: **11** honeysuckle
woodchuck: **6** marmot **9** groundhog
woodcock: **4** dupe, fool **5** pewee **7** be-
casse(F.) **9** simpleton **10** woodpecker
woodcutter: **6** axeman, logger, sawyer **7**
chopper **8** woodsman **9** lumberman
wooded: **6** sylvan
wooden: dry **4** dull, wood **5** oaken, stiff,
treen **6** clumsy, stolid **7** awkward **8** lifeless **10** spiritless **11** insensitive **14** expressionless
wooden-headed: **4** dull **6** stupid **8** blockish
Wooden Horse: See **Trojan horse.**
woodkern: **6** outlaw, robber
woodland: **6** forest **7** woodlot **10** timber-
land
burnt over: **6** brulee
deity: Pan **4** faun **5** Diana, satyr, Silen **7**
Silenus **8** Seilenos
woodness: **4** fury, rage **7** madness **8** insanity
woodpecker: **4** chab **5** picus **6** picule,
yaffle, yockel, yuckle, yukkel **7** flicker,
piculet, whetile, wryneck, yaffler **8** hick-
wall, woodcock, woodhack **9** sapsucker,
woodchuck, woodspite **10** carpintero,

woodhacker, woodjobber **11** hickoryhead, woodknacker
pert. to: **6** picine
woods: 6 forest
love of: **9** nemophily
pert. to: **6** sylvan **7** nemoral
woodsman: 5 scout **6** hunter **7** bushman, trapper **8** forester **10** woodcutter **11** woodchopper
woodwind: 4 oboe **5** flute **7** bassoon, piccolo **8** clarinet **9** saxophone
woodworker: 6 joiner, turner **9** carpenter **12** cabinetmaker
machine: saw **5** edger, lathe **6** planer, router, shaper **7** sticker
tool: adz, saw **4** adze **5** plane **6** hammer
woody: 5 bosky **6** sylvan, xyloid **8** ligneous
woody fiber: 4 bast, hemp **5** xylem
wooer: 4 beau **6** suitor **8** courtier
woof: abb **5** cloth, weave **6** fabric **7** filling, texture **9** essential
wool: fur **4** hair, lamb **5** llama, sheep **6** fleece, mohair **8** barragan, barragon **9** cordillas
blemish: **4** mote
clean: **7** garnett
cloth: **5** baize, duroy, tweed **6** alpaca, angora, baline, duffel, frieze, hodden, kersey, melton, merino, mohair, vicuna **7** flannel, ratteen, stammel **8** cashmere, casimire **9** cassimere, haubergel **10** broadcloth, fearnaught, fearnought **11** dreadnaught, dreadnought
comb. form: **4** lani
fat: **5** suint **7** lanolin **8** lanoline
fibers: nep
implement: **6** carder, shears, teaser **7** distaff, spindle
kind: **4** noil, shag **8** mortling **9** downright, shearling
lock: **5** flock
mixed hues: tum
nap-raising plant: **5** tease
package: **5** fadge
piece: **4** frib, tate(Sc.) **7** cleamer
pulled: **5** slipe
rag: **5** mungo **6** shoddy
reclaimed: **5** mungo **6** shoddy
refuse: **7** backing
spun: **4** yarn
texture: nap
waste: fud
weight: tod **5** clove
worker: **8** shedhand
yarn: abb, eis **7** eiswool
wool-colored: 5 beige, camel
wool-dryer: 5 fugal
woolfell: 4 pelt
woolly: 6 fleecy, lanate, lanose **7** lanated **8** peronate
woozy: **5** drunk, shaky **7** muddled, strange, trembly **9** befuddled
word: 4 fame, news, talk, term **5** adage,

honor, maxim, motto, order, parol, voice **6** assent, avowal, phrase, pledge, remark, report, repute, saying, signal, speech **7** account, adjunct, command, comment, dispute, message, promise, proverb, tidings **8** acrostic, language, password **9** direction, discourse, statement, watchword **10** expression **11** affirmation, declaration, information **12** intelligence **13** communication
battle: **9** logomachy
colorful: **5** slang
complex of ideas: **10** holophrase **11** holophrasis
containing all vowels: **6** oiseau(F.) **7** eulogia, miaoued, sequoia **12** ambidextrous **14** undiscoverably **15** uncopyrightable
containing all vowels in reverse sequence: **10** duoliteral
containing all vowels in sequence: **8** caesious
containing four letters: **9** tetragram
containing no vowels: cwm, nth **5** crwth
containing uu: **6** mutuum, vacuum **7** duumvir, triduum **8** residuum **9** continuum, menstruum, perpetuum, zuurveldt **10** duumvirate
contraction: **9** haplology
corresponding: **8** analogue
derived from another: **7** paronym
figurative use: **5** trope **7** metonym
group: **6** clause, phrase **8** sentence
imitative: **9** onomatope
improper use: **8** solecism
inventor: **6** coiner **9** neologist
last sound omitted: **7** apocope
longest: **45** pneumonoultramicroscopicsilicovolcanokoniosis
meaning: **9** semantics
mystical: **7** anagoge
new: **9** neologism, neoterism
of action: **4** verb
of naming: **4** noun
of opposite meaning: **7** antonym
of same meaning: **7** synonym
pretentious: **10** lexiphanic
root: **6** etymon
sacred: om, um **5** selah **6** sesame, shelah
same backward and forward: **10** palindrome
same sound: **7** homonym **9** homophone
same spelling: **7** homonym **9** homograph
scrambled: **7** anagram
separation: **6** tmesis **7** diacope
square: **10** palindrome
substituted: **5** trope **7** metonym
transposition: **7** anagram
use of imitative: **12** onomatopoeia
use of new: **7** neology
use of unnecessary: **8** pleonasm
word blindness: 6 alexia
word for word: 7 exactly **8** verbatim **9** literally
word of honor: 6 parole **7** promise

word-sign: 8 ideogram, logogram 10 hieroglyph, pictograph

wordbook: 7 lexicon, speller 8 libretto 9 thesaurus 10 cyclopedia, dictionary, vocabulary

wordiness: 8 verbiage

wording: 8 phrasing 9 wrangling 10 expression

wordless: 5 tacit 6 silent

words: 4 text 6 lyrics 7 quarrel 8 libretto
depiction in: 8 vignette
excessive interest in: 10 verbomania
meaningless: 6 drivel 9 gibberish
misuse: 11 catachresis, heterophemy
put into: 5 state 6 phrase 7 express
written: 4 copy, text

wordy: 6 prolix 7 diffuse, verbose 9 garrulous, redundant

wore: See **wear**.

work: go; act, job, tew 4 beat, duty, feat, move, opus, plan, task, worm 5 chore, craft, draft, ergon, exert, graft, grind, knead, solve, stint, trade 6 arbeit(G.), design, effort, puddle, strive 7 belabor, ferment, operate, pattern, perform, travail 8 activity, belabour, business, drudgery, exertion, function, industry, struggle 10 accomplish, employment, manipulate, occupation, profession 11 achievement, performance, undertaking
agreement: 4 code, pact 8 contract
aversion to: 10 ergophobia
by day: 4 char 5 chare
defensive: See **fortification**.
divine: 7 theurgy
excess: 6 overdo 8 overwork
evade: 4 snib 9 goldbrick
for: 4 earn 5 serve
hard: peg, ply 4 char, moil, plod, plug, toil 5 chare, delve, drill, labor, sweat 6 drudge 7 travail 8 scrabble 9 lucubrate
incomplete: 7 ebauche
labored: 11 lucubration
lover of: 9 ergophile
musical: See **musical composition**.
period: day 4 hour, turn, week 5 month, shift, spell, trick, watch 8 schedule
slowly: 6 potter, putter 7 cacanny
together: 4 team 5 co-act 9 co-operate 11 collaborate
unit: erg 5 ergon, joule 7 calorie
women's: 7 distaff

work-a-day: 8 everyday, ordinary 11 commonplace

work-brittle: 11 industrious

work of art: 4 song 6 statue 7 classic, etching, picture 8 painting

work out: 5 erase, solve 6 efface 7 arrange, develop, exhaust 9 calculate, elaborate 10 accomplish

work over: 6 recast, rehash, revamp 8 persuade 9 brainwash, elaborate, influence

work up: irk 5 raise, rouse 6 arouse, excite, expend 7 advance, develop 9 elaborate 10 manipulate

workable: 4 ripe 6 mellow, pliant 8 feasible 9 practical 11 practicable

workbag: 8 reticule

worked: 7 wrought

worker: 4 arry, doer, hand, hind 5 navvy 6 earner, toiler 7 artisan, laborer 8 operator, opificer 9 artificer, craftsman, operative, performer 11 breadwinner
fellow: 5 buddy, butty 7 comrade 8 confrere
group: 4 crew, gang, team 5 corps, shift, staff 9 personnel
hard: 6 beaver, drudge, fagger
head: 4 boss 5 super 6 ganger 7 foreman 8 employer, overseer 14 superintendent
kind: 5 diver, mason, miner, smith, tuner 6 barman, cocker, hopper, joiner, laster, sapper, sawyer, slater, smithy, tanner, warper, wright 7 analyst, cobbler, collier, geordie, glazier, paneler, plumber, reedman, riveter, sandhog, spinner 8 chaffman, chuckler, enameler, mechanic, shedhand, strapper 9 carpenter, groundhog, machinist, stevedore
migrant: 4 hobo, Okie 5 Arkie 6 boomer 7 floater, wetback
objectionable: 4 scab 7 botcher, bungler 11 scissorbill 13 featherbedder
unskilled: 4 peon 6 coolie 7 laborer

workful: 8 diligent

workhorse: 7 trestle 8 sawhorse

workhouse: 6 prison 8 workshop 9 almshouse, poorhouse

working (see also **work**): 4 busy 5 alert 6 active, decree, effort 7 halurgy 8 employed, endeavor 9 ordinance, practical 10 contortion
not: off 4 idle 6 broken 10 unemployed

working-class: 7 laborer 11 proletariat

workman: See **worker**.

workman-like: 4 deft 5 adept 8 skillful 10 proficient

workroom: den, lab 4 mill, shop 5 plant, study 6 studio 7 atelier, bottega, factory, library 10 laboratory 11 ergasterion

works: 5 plant

worktable: 5 bench, siege

world: 5 globe, realm 6 cosmos, domain, people, public 7 kingdom, mankind 8 creation, humanity, universe
antedating creation of: 10 premundane
external: 6 nonego
lower: See **underworld**.
miniature: 9 microcosm
pert. to: 7 mundane, secular 11 terrestrial

worldly: 6 carnal, laical 7 earthen, earthly, mundane, secular, sensual, terrene 11 terrestrial 13 sophisticated

worldwide: 6 global 8 ecumenic, pandemic 9 planetary, universal 10 ecumenical 13 international

worm: bob, eel, eri, ess, ipo, loa, lug, pin 4 grub, nema 5 borer, larva, tinea 6 looper, maggot, palolo, teredo 7 annelid, ascarid, ipomoea, reptile, sagitta, serpent, tagtail 8 cercaria, helminth 9 angleworm, earthworm, nemertina, nemertine, nemertini, trematode 10 nemertinea, serpentine 13 platyhelminth

aquatic: sao 4 naid, nais, nema 5 cadew, leech 6 nereis 7 achaeta, annelid 8 annelida

genus of: 6 nereis 8 geoplana

parasitic: 8 trichina

worm-eaten: old 6 ragged, shabby 7 worn-out 8 decrepit 9 out-of-date, worthless

wormlike: 7 vermian 11 helminthoid

wormweed: 8 pinkroot

wormwood: 4 moxa

wormy: 6 rotten 8 diseased, crawling

worn: See **wear**.

worn down: 5 erose 6 eroded 7 abraded, attrite 8 attrited

worn-out: 4 sere, used 5 jaded, passe, seedy, spent, stale, trite 6 frayed, shabby 7 haggard 8 consumed, decrepit, impaired, weakened 9 enfeebled, exhausted, hackneyed 10 bedraggled, threadbare 11 commonplace

worricow: 5 devil 7 bugaboo 9 hobgoblin

worry: hox, nag, vex 4 bait, care, cark, faze, fear, fike, fret, fuss, hare, stew 5 annoy, brood, choke, gally, harry, hurry, touse 6 badger, bother, caddle, fidget, harass, hatter, hector, pester, plague, pother 7 anxiety, bedevil, chagrin, concern, disturb, perturb, torment, trouble 8 distress, strangle 9 worriment 10 disconcert, uneasiness

worse: 8 pejority

worsen: 10 retrogress 11 deteriorate

worship: 4 cult, fame, love 5 adore, dulia, honor, worth 6 credit, homage, latria, renown, repute, revere 7 dignity, idolism, idolize, liturgy, respect 8 blessing, devotion, hierurgy, idolatry, venerate 9 adoration, deference, monolatry, reverence, theolatry 10 admiration, allotheism, hagiolatry, hierolatry, hyperdulia, reputation, veneration, worthiness

form of: 4 rite 6 ritual

house of: dom 6 chapel, church, mosque, shrine, temple 9 cathedral, synagogue 10 tabernacle

nature: 11 physiolatry

object of: 4 icon, idol 5 totem 6 fetich, fetish

pert. to: 8 liturgic 10 liturgical

system of: 4 cult 6 cultus

worshiper: 6 adorer, bhakta, votary 7 devotee 8 disciple, idolater

worshipful: 7 notable 8 esteemed 9 honorable, respected 10 venerating 11 worshipping 13 distinguished

worst: bad 4 beat, best 6 defeat 9 discomfit, overthrow

worsted: 4 garn, yarn 5 serge 6 tamine 8 whipcord 9 gabardine

yarn: 6 caddis, crewel 7 caddice, genappe 9 fingering

wort: 4 herb 8 fleabane

worth: 5 merit, price, value 6 bounty, desert, esteem, riches, virtue, wealth 7 account, fitting 8 eminence 9 deserving, desirable 10 excellence, importance, possession, usefulness

sense of: 5 pride 7 dignity, respect

worthless: bad, rap 4 base, evil, idle, vain, vile 5 inane 6 cheesy, drossy, futile, hollow, paltry, putrid, rotten, trashy 7 fustian, inutile, useless 8 feckless, unworthy 9 frivolous, valueless 11 undeserving 12 contemptible 14 good-for-nothing

worthy: 4 dear, good 7 condign 8 deserved, eligible, meriting, valuable 9 competent, deserving, estimable, excellent, qualified 11 appropriate, meritorious

wound: cut 4 gore, harm, hurt, pain, stab, wing 5 break, ganch, sting 6 breach, damage, grieve, harrow, injury, trauma 7 afflict, attaint 8 distress, puncture

dressing: 7 bandage, pledget

mark: 4 scab, scar, welt 7 blister

sign: 4 scar 5 blood

woundwort: 7 allheal

wove: See **weave**.

woven (see also **weave**): 4 lacy 7 damasse

raised figures: 6 broche 7 brocade

wow: hit, mew 4 howl, rave, wail 5 whine 7 success

wowf: 4 wild 6 crazed

wrack: 4 kelp, rack, ruin 5 goods, trash, weeds, wreck 6 avenge, defeat, injury 7 destroy, seaweed, torment, unsound 8 calamity, mischief, wreckage 9 overthrow, shipwreck, vengeance 10 punishment 11 destruction, persecution

wraith: 5 ghost, spook 7 specter, spectre 10 apparition

wrangle (see also **quarrel**): 4 spar 5 argue, brawl, chide 6 bicker, debate, haggle 7 contend, dispute 11 altercation, controversy 12 disagreement

wrangler: 6 cowboy, hafter 7 student 8 herdsman, opponent 9 disputant 10 antagonist

wrangling: 11 belligerent, contentious

wrap: hap, rug, wap 4 cere, coil, fold, furl, hide, roll, wind 5 cloak, cover, nubia, twine 6 afghan, encowl, enfold, infold, invest, swathe 7 blanket, conceal, enclose, envelop, package 8 enshroud, enswathe, surround 9 encompass

wrapper: 4 gown 6 fardel 8 galabeah 9 undervest 10 undershirt

wrapping: wap 8 cerement

wrasse: 6 ballan

wrath: ire 4 fury, rage 5 anger 6 choler, felony 7 passion 8 violence 10 turbulence 11 indignation 12 exasperation

wrathful: 5 wroth 8 incensed 9 malignant

wreak: 5 exact 6 avenge, punish 7 gratify, indulge, inflict, revenge 9 vengeance

wreath, wreathe: lei 4 bank, coil, orle, roll, turn 5 crown, drift, torse(her.), twine, twist, whorl 6 anadem, corona, crants, crease, laurel, spirea, wrench 7 chaplet, contort, coronet, crownal, entwine, festoon, garland, spiraea, wrinkle 8 encircle, surround

wreck: 4 hulk, ruin 5 crash, ruins, smash, wrack 6 damage, defeat, thwart 7 destroy, disable, founder, shatter 8 demolish, derelict, sabotage 9 overthrow, shipwreck 11 destruction

wreckage: 7 flotsam 8 driftage

wrench (see also **wrest**): 4 jerk, pipe, pull, rack, tear, tool, turn 5 twist, wring 6 injury, monkey, sprain, strain, twinge 7 distort, spanner 8 Stillson 9 alligator, epitonion 10 distortion

wrest: 4 rend, ruse 5 exact, force, fraud, seize, trick, usurp, wring 6 elicit, extort, snatch 7 pervert, wrestle

wrestle: tug 6 squirm, strive, tussle, wraxle 7 contend, grapple, wriggle 8 struggle

wrestler: 6 mauler

wrestling: *place:* 4 ring 5 arena 8 palestra 9 palaestra

wretch: bum, dog 5 exile, loser 6 beggar, pauper 7 hilding, scroyle 8 derelict, recreant 9 miscreant 11 rapscallion

wretched: 4 base, foul, lewd, mean, poor 5 dawny 6 dismal, paltry, pilled, woeful 7 baleful, caitiff, forlorn, unhappy 8 dejected, grievous, inferior 9 afflicted, execrable, miserable, niggardly 10 calamitous, deplorable, depressing, despicable, distressed 11 unfortunate 12 contemptible, parsimonious 14 unsatisfactory

wriggle: 4 frig, turn, wind 5 dodge, evade, snake, twist 6 fitter, squirm, widdle, wiggle, wintle, writhe 7 meander 10 equivocate

wriggly: 8 tortuous

wring: 4 fret, rack 5 press, twist 6 elicit, extort, squirm, wrench 7 extract, squeeze, wrestle 8 compress, struggle

wrinkle: fad, rut 4 fold, idea, knit, lirk, ruck, ruga, seam 5 crimp, fancy, knack, reeve, ridge, rivel 6 cockle, crease, device, furrow, notion, pucker, rimple 7 crimple, crinkle, crumple, frumple, novelty, winding 8 contract 9 corrugate 10 prominence

wrinkled: 6 crepey, rugate, rugose, rugous 7 savoyed 8 rugulose

wrist:
bone: 4 ulna 6 carpus 9 capitatum
mark: 7 rasceta
ornament: 4 band 8 bracelet
pert. to: 6 carpal

wristlet: 4 band 5 strap 8 bracelet, handcuff 9 wristband 11 comfortable

writ: 5 breve, brief, tales 6 capias, elegit, extent, venire 7 exigent, process, writing 8 detainer, document, mittimus, replevin, subpoena 10 certiorari, distringas, injunction, instrument 11 fierifacias
of execution: 5 outre

write: pen 5 clerk, enrol 6 direct, enface, enroll, indite, record, scrawl, scribe 7 compose, engross, scratch 8 inscribe, scribble 9 character
letters: 10 correspond

write off: 4 drop 6 cancel, deduct, remove

writer: 4 hack, poet 5 clerk, odist 6 author, critic, glozer, lawyer, penman, scribe 7 copyist, glosser, hymnist, penster, realist, tropist 8 annalist, composer, gazeteer, literate, lyricist, novelist, parodist, prefacer, scriptor 9 annotater, columnist, craftsman, dramatist, glossator, scrivener, solicitor 10 amanuensis, chronicler, glossarist, journalist 12 calligrapher, epistolarian 13 glossographer
prose: 8 prosaist

writhe: 4 bend, bind, curl, turn 5 twist, wrest, wring 6 squirm 7 agonize, contort, distort, shrivel 8 encircle, enswathe 9 convolute, insinuate 10 contortion, intertwine

writhing: 4 eely 9 wriggling

writing: ms; ola 4 book, deed, olla, poem, writ 5 diary, essay, prose, verse 6 script 7 epistle, pothook 8 contract, covenant, document, makimono, pleading, spelling 9 allograph, cerograph, enrolment, esoterics 10 enrollment, instrument, literature, penmanship 11 chirography, composition, handwriting, inscription, orthography, pornography, publication
alternate: 13 boustrophedon
character: (see also **word-sign**): 4 sign 6 letter, symbol 9 cuneiform
excessive interest in: 11 graphomania
master: 7 stylist
material: pad 5 board, paper, slate 6 tablet 7 papyrus 9 parchment 10 stationery
pert. to: 7 scribal
sacred: 5 Bible, Koran 6 psalms, Talmud 9 hagiology, testament 10 scriptures
secret: 4 code 6 cipher 10 cryptogram 12 cryptography
tool: pen 5 chalk, stick 6 pencil, stylus 9 ballpoint

wrizzled: 8 wrinkled 9 shriveled

wrong: bad, car, ill, off, out, sin 4 awry, evil, harm, tort 5 abuse, agley, amiss, crime, error, false, grief, malum, unfit 6 astray, faulty, injure, injury, malign, seduce, sinful, unfair, unjust, wicked 7 crooked, defraud, immoral, misdeed, twisted, violate 8 dishonor, improper, iniquity, mistaken, tortuous, wrongful, wrongous 9 erroneous, incorrect, injurious, injustice, violation 10 dispossess, inaccurate, iniquitous, unsuitable 11 malfeasance, misfeasance **12** illegitimate **14** unsatisfactory

prefix: mis

wrongdoer: 6 sinner **8** criminal, violator **10** malefactor, tort-feasor, trespasser **12** transgressor

wroth: 5 angry, irate **7** violent **8** incensed, wrathful, wrothful **9** turbulent

wrought (see also **work**): **4** agog, made **5** eager **6** formed, shaped, worked **7** excited, operose **9** decorated, disturbed, fashioned, processed **10** elaborated, ornamented, stimulated **11** embroidered **12** manufactured

wrung: See **wring**.

wry: 4 awry, bend, bias, sour, tend, turn **5** avert, pinch, twist, wring **6** swerve, warped **7** contort, crooked, deflect, deviate, distort, incline **8** contrary, perverse

wryneck: 5 loxia **9** snakebird **10** woodpecker **11** torticollis

Wurttemberg:

city: Ulm **9** Esslingen, Heilbronn, Stuttgart

river: **6** Danube, Neckar

Wycliffe disciple: Hus **4** Huss **7** Lollard

wyliecoat: 9 petticoat, undervest **10** nightdress

wynd, wyne: haw **4** lane **5** alley, close, court

Wyoming:

mountain: **5** Moran, Teton

river: **5** Teton

town: **4** Cody **7** Laramie, Jackson, Rawlins **8** Cheyenne

X

xanthic: **6** yellow **9** yellowish
Xanthippe's husband: 8 Socrates
xebec: 4 boat, ship **6** vessel
xenagogue: 5 guide
xenagogy: 9 guidebook
xenium: 4 gift **7** present
xenodochy: 11 hospitality
xenogamy: 13 fertilization
xenon: Xe
Xenophanean: 7 eleatic
Xerus: 8 squirrel
Xerxes: *parent:* **6** Atossa, Darius
Xmas: 9 Christmas
X-ray: *inventor:* **8** Roentgen

measuring device: **11** quantimeter
science: **12** rontgenology **13** roentgenology
source: **6** target
type: **8** grenzray
xurel: 4 scad **6** saurel
xylograph: 5 print **9** engraving **10** impression
xyloid: 5 woody **8** ligneous
xylophone: 5 saron **6** gender **7** gambang, gamelan, marimba **8** gamelang, gigelira, sticcado
xyrid: 4 iris

Y

yabber: 4 talk 6 jabber 8 language 12 conversation

yabby, yabbie: 8 crayfish

yacht: 4 boat, race, sail, ship 5 craft 6 cruise, sonder

Yaff: yap 4 bark, yelp

yaffle: 4 yaff 6 armful 7 handful 10 woodpecker

yahoo: 4 lout 5 brute 6 savage 7 bumpkin

yak: ox 4 zobo 6 sarlak, sarlyk 7 buffalo
cross-bred: 6 yakalo 9 yakattalo

yakamik: 9 trumpeter

yakka: 4 work 5 labor

yaksha: god 4 jinn, ogre 5 angel, demon, dryad, fairy, gnome 6 spirit

Yakut river: 4 Lena

Yale: Eli 4 lock 10 University

yam: ube, ubi 5 tugui 6 buckra, igname, potato, uviyam 7 boniata 8 cush-cush 9 posthouse 11 sweetpotato

yamen: 6 office 7 mansion 9 residence 12 headquarters

yammadji: 6 native 11 blackfellow

yammer: cry 4 yell 5 crave, shout, whine, yearn 6 clamor, desire, lament, scream 7 chatter, grumble, stammer, whimper 8 complain

yang: cry 4 honk

yang-kin: 8 dulcimer

yank: 4 blow, jerk, pull 5 hoick 6 twitch

Yank, Yankee: 8 American 10 Northerner

yannigan: 5 scrub

yap: apt, cur, dog, gab 4 bark, keen, talk, yelp 5 cheep, eager, mouth, quick, ready, rowdy, scold 6 active, hungry, jabber 7 bumpkin, chatter, hoodlum 9 greenhorn

Yap Island money: fei 5 stone

yapock, yapok: 6 monkey 7 opossum

yapp: 7 binding

yard: rod 4 lawn, spar, wand 5 garth, staff, stick 7 confine 9 courtyard, curtilage, enclosure 10 correction, playground
sixteenth of: 4 nail

yards: *five and one-half:* rod
119.6 square: ar
600: 4 heer
two hundred twenty: 7 furlong

yardage: 6 length 8 distance

yardland: 7 virgate

yare: 4 well 5 brisk, eager, quick, ready 6 active, lively, prompt 8 entirely, prepared 10 manageable

yarm: 4 wail, yell 5 whine 6 scream

yarn: abb, eis, tow 4 garn, sley, tale 5 fiber, story 6 caddis, crewel 7 caddice, eiswool, genappe, schappe 9 fingering
croft: 8 ropeyard
holder: cop
quantity: cop, lea 4 clew, clue, hank, hasp 5 skein 7 spangle
size: 6 denier

yarr: 7 spurrey

yarrow: 7 allheal, milfoil

yashmak, yasmak: 4 veil

yataghan: 5 knife, saber

yatter: 7 chatter

yauld: 4 mare 5 alert, sharp 6 active, nimble, strong 7 healthy 8 vigorous 10 able-bodied

yaupon: 5 holly 7 cassena, cassina 9 evergreen

yaw: 4 turn, veer 5 steer 6 swerve 7 deviate

yawl: 4 boat, howl 6 scream, vessel

yawn: 4 galp, gant(Sc.), gape, yaup, yawp 5 chasm 7 opening 8 oscitate

yawp: bay, cry, yap 4 bawl, call, gape, yelp 6 bellow, scream 8 complain

yaws: 9 frambesia

yawweed: 7 rhubarb

yclept: 5 named 6 called

yea: ay; aye, yes 5 truly 6 assent, indeed, verily 11 affirmative

yean: ean 4 lamb

year: 5 annus(L.)
difference between lunar and solar: 5 epact
division: 5 raith(Sc.) 6 season
record: 5 annal 8 calendar

yearbook: 7 almanac

yearling: 4 colt 9 hornotine

yearly: 6 annual 7 etesian 8 annually

yearn: beg, vex, yen 4 ache, long, pine, sigh 5 crave 6 desire, grieve, hanker, yammer 7 request

yearning: 4 wish 5 eager 7 anxious

years: age, eon, era 4 time
eight: 9 octennial
fifteen: 9 indiction
five: 6 pentad 7 lustrum
hundred: 9 centenary
ninety: 12 nonagenarian
seventy: 12 septuagenary
ten: 6 decade 8 decenary 9 decennary, decenniad, decennium
thousand: 7 chiliad 10 millennium
two: 8 biennium

yeast: bee 4 barm, foam, rise 5 froth 6

leaven 7 ferment 9 agitation 14 tumultu-
ousness

yeasty: 5 light 8 restless 9 frivolous, unsettled 11 superficial

yegg: 5 thief 6 robber 7 burglar 8 criminal 11 safebreaker, safecracker

yell: cry 4 gowl, howl, roar, yarm, yowl 5
cheer, shout, whoop 6 outcry, scream,
shriek, yammer 7 yelloch

yelling: 8 strident 9 clamorous

yelloch: 4 yell

yellow: or(her.) 4 gull, mean, sere, turn,
yolk 5 amber, blake, color, favel, lemon,
ochre, tinge 6 butter, canary, fallow,
flavic, flavid, flaxen, golden, sallow 7 xanthic 8 cowardly, recreant 9 flavicant,
jaundiced, lutescent 10 flavescent, melancholy 11 sensational, treacherous 12
contemptible, dishonorable 13 dishonourable, untrustworthy

brown: dun 4 bran 5 aloma, amber, pablo,
straw 6 manila

dyestuff: 5 morin 6 orlean 7 annatto, annotto, arnatto

gray: 4 drab

green: 5 olive 6 privet 8 glaucous, tarragon 10 chartreuse, serpentine

orange: 9 grenadine

red: 4 lava, roan 5 sandy 6 orange 7 nacarat

yellow copper ore: 12 chalcopyrite

yellow copperas: 9 copiapite

yellow jacket: 4 wasp 8 eucalypt

yellow mustard: 8 charlock

yellow ocher: sil

yellow star: 10 sneezeweed

yellow starwort: 10 elecampane

yellowhammer: 4 bird, yite 5 ammer,
skite 6 gladdy 7 yeldrin 8 yeldrine,
yeldring, yeldrock, yeorling, yoldring 10
woodpecker

Yellowstone Park attraction: 4 deer 5
bears 6 geyser 11 Old Faithful

yelp: cry, yip 4 bark, brag 5 boast, cheep,
shout 6 greedy, outcry, shriek, squeal 7
ululate 8 complain 9 criticize

yeme: 4 care, heed 5 guard 6 govern, regard 7 observe 10 solicitude

Yemen: *people:* 4 Arab 7 Arabian
town: 4 Sana 5 Damar

yen: 4 urge 5 yearn 6 desire 7 longing 10
propensity

yeoman: 5 clerk 6 butler 8 retainer 9 assistant, attendant 10 freeholder, journey-
man, manservant 11 subordinate
of guard officer: 4 exon

yeomanly: 6 sturdy 8 faithful

yerk: 4 carp, cast, gird, goad, jerk, kick,
lash, pull, stab 5 crack, throw, thump 6
snatch, thrash, wrench 7 lashing

yes: da(Russ.), ja(G.), si(It., Sp.); aye, iss,
oui(F.), yeh, yep 4 yeah 5 agree 6 assent
9 assuredly 11 affirmation, affirmative

yesterday: 6 yester

yet: but 4 also 5 still 7 algates, besides,
further, however 10 eventually 11 nonetheless 12 nevertheless 15 notwithstanding

yew: ew

Yiddish: 6 Jewish

yield: bow, net, pay, sag 4 bear, bend,
cede, cess, elde, fold, give, obey, vail 5
addle, admit, agree, allow, avale, defer,
grant, heald, hield, repay, stoop, waive 6
accede, afford, comply, impart, profit, relent, render, return, reward, soften, submit, supply 7 abandon, concede, consent,
deliver, produce, revenue, succumb 9 acquiesce, surrender 10 capitulate, recompense, relinquish 11 acknowledge

yielding: 4 meek, soft, waxy 5 buxom 6
feeble, flabby, pliant, supple 7 flaccid 8
flexible, recreant 9 tractable 10 manageable

yill: ale

yin: one 8 feminine, negative

yip: 4 yelp

yird: 5 earth

yirr: 5 growl, snarl

Ymir, Ymer: 5 giant
slayer: Ve 4 Odin, Vili

yodel: 4 call, sing 5 carol, shout 6 warble
7 refrain

yogi: 4 yoga 5 fakir, yogin 6 fakeer 7 ascetic

yoke: tie 4 bail, bond, join, link, pair, span,
team 5 bangy, fight(Sc.), marry, seize(Sc.)
6 attack(Sc.), banghy, couple, inspan,
tackle(Sc.) 7 bondage, carrier, enslave,
harness, oppress, service, slavery 8 restrain 9 associate, servitude

yoked: 9 conjugate

yokefellow: 4 mate, wife 6 spouse 7 husband, partner 9 associate, companion

yokel: oaf 4 boor, clod, lout, rube 6 obtuse,
rustic 7 bumpkin, hayseed, plowboy 8
Abderite, gullible 10 countryman, slow-
witted

yoking: 4 bout 7 contest, mugging

yolk: 6 yellow 7 essence 8 vitellus

yon: 6 yonder

yond: 4 past 6 raging, yonder

yonder: yon 4 away 5 there 6 beyond 7
distant, farther, further, thither

yore: 4 past

Yorkshire: *river:* Ure
town: 5 Leeds

you: te, tu(F.), yi; sie(G.), yez

young: fry, raw 4 tyro, weak 5 brood, fetus, fresh, green 6 active, foetus, litter,
strong, tender 7 pliable 8 childish, ignorant, immature, juvenile, newcomer, vigorous, workable, youthful 9 offspring,
succulent 13 inexperienced

younger: 6 junior

youngling: 5 youth 6 novice 7 student 8
beginner, neophyte

youngster (see also **child**): boy, cub,

lad, tad, tot **4** baby, calf, colt, girl, lass, tike **5** filly, youth **6** moppet, shaver, urchin **9** stripling **10** midshipman

younker: 6 knight **7** gallant **8** nobleman **9** gentleman, youngster

your: thy

youth: bud **4** chap **5** chiel(Sc.), chabo **6** hoiden, hoyden **7** callant(Sc.), ephebos, ephebus, gossoon **9** youngster **10** adolescent **11** adolescence, hobbledehoy

goddess of: **4** Hebe

mythological: **5** Etana **6** Adonis, Apollo, Icarus

youthful: new **5** early, fresh, young **6** active **7** puerile **8** immature, juvenile, vigorous

yowl: cry **4** howl, wail, yell

yowt: 4 howl, yell, yelp **6** scream

yttrium: Yt

Yucatan: *people:* **4** Maya **5** Mayan

tree: **6** yaxche

yucca: 5 palma

Yugoslavia: *brandy:* **5** rakia **9** slivovitz

city: Nis **5** Agram **6** Morava, Mostar, Prilep, Skopje, Vardar, Zagrab, Zagreb **7** Cattaro **8** Belgrade, Monastir, Sarajevo, Subotica **9** Ljubljana, Subotitsa

coin: **4** para **5** dinar

commune: Pec **4** Stip **5** Veles

measure: rif **4** akov, ralo **5** donum, khvat, lanaz, stopa **6** motyka, palaze, ralico **9** dan oranja

monarch: **5** Peter

people: **4** Serb **5** Croat **7** Slovene

region: **5** Banat **6** Banate, Bosnia

river: **4** Sava **5** Drava, Drina **6** Danube, Morava, Vardar

weight: oka, oke **5** dramm, tovar, wagon **7** satlijk

yule: 9 Christmas **13** Christmastide

Z

Z: zed **6** izzard
Zacchaeus, Zaccheus: **4** pure **8** innocent
Zadok: **4** just **9** righteous
Zagreb: See **Yugolasvia**.
zaguan: **4** gate **8** entrance **11** entrance-way
Zambales (see also **Philippine Islands**):
  capital: Iba
  language: **4** Tino
Zamindar:
  chief: **6** mirdha **7** mirdaha
  overseer: **6** mirdha **7** mirdaha
zampogna: **7** bagpipe, panpipe
zanja: **5** canal, ditch, gully **6** arroyo
zanni: **5** clown
zany: **4** dolt, fool **5** clown, crazy, dotty, nutty, toady **7** acrobat, buffoon, idiotic **8** clownish, follower, imitator **9** assistant, attendant, simpleton **10** lieutenant **11** merry-andrew
Zanzibar: See **Tanzania**.
zeal: **4** fire **5** ardor, fervor **7** passion **8** devotion, interest **9** eagerness **10** enthusiasm, fanaticism
zealot: **5** bigot **6** votary **7** devotee, fanatic **8** partisan, votaress **10** enthusiast
zealous: **4** warm **5** rabid **6** ardent, fervid, hearty **7** devoted, earnest, fervent **8** frenetic, vigorous **9** phrenetic, strenuous **12** enthusiastic
Zebedee's son: **4** John **5** James
zebra: **4** dauw
zebrawood: **7** arariba **9** nakedwood **10** marblewood
Zulu:
  boy: **6** umfaan
zecchino: **6** sequin, zequin
zenana: **5** harem **8** seraglio
zenith: **4** acme, peak **6** summit **11** culmination
Zeno's follower: **5** stoic
zequin: **6** sequin **8** zecchino
zero: nil **6** cipher, naught, nought **7** nothing
zest: **4** tang **5** gusto, savor **6** flavor, relish **8** piquancy **9** enjoyment **10** enthusiasm
zestful: **4** racy **6** hearty **7** pungent
Zeus:
  beloved of: Io **6** Europa
  brother: **5** Hades **8** Poseidon
  daughter: Ate **4** Hebe, Kore **5** Irene **6** Athena, Athene **7** Artemis, Astraea **8** Despoina **9** Aphrodite **10** Persephone, Proserpina, Proserpine **11** Persephassa

  epithet: **5** soter **7** Alastor
  messenger: **4** Iris **6** Hermes
  nurse: **8** Cynosura
  oracle: **6** Dodona
  parent: **4** Rhea **6** Cronus, Kronos
  sister: **4** Hera
  son: Gad **4** Ares **5** Arcas, Argus **6** Aeacus, Apollo, Hermes, Tityus **7** Perseus **8** Dardanus, Dionysos, Dionysus, Heracles, Herakies, Hercules, Tantalus **10** Hephaestus
  victim: **4** Idas
  wife: **4** Hera **5** Danae, Metis **6** Semele
ziarat, ziara: **4** tomb **6** shrine
zigzag: **4** tack, turn **5** angle, crank, weave **8** flexuous
Zilpah's son: Gad **5** Asher
zimarra: **5** cloak **7** cassock, soutane
zimb: bug, fly **6** insect
zinc: Zn **7** adamine, adamite, spelter, tutenag **9** galvanize, tutenague
  ore: **6** blende
  sulphate: **7** ilesite
zing: pep, vim, zip **4** dash, snap **5** force, vigor **6** energy, stingo, spirit **10** enthusiasm
Zion: **4** hill
zip: **4** zing
zipper: **8** fastener
zippy: **5** brisk **6** snappy
zizith: **7** fringes, tassles
Zobeide's sister: **5** Amina
zodiac sign: Leo, Ram **4** Bull, Crab, Fish, Goat, Lion **5** Aries, decan, Libra, Scale, Twins, Virgo **6** Archer, Cancer, Fishes, Gemini, Pisces, Taurus, Virgin **7** Balance, Scorpio **8** Aquarius, Scorpion **9** Capricorn **11** Capricornus, Sagittarius, Waterbearer
zone: **4** area, band, belt, path **5** layer, tract **6** course, girdle, region, stripe **7** circuit **8** cincture, encircle, engirdle
  geological succession: **6** assise
  marked by: **6** zonate
zoom: **9** chandelle
zoo: **9** menagerie
zoophyte: **5** coral
zoril: **7** polecat
Zoroaster's works: **6** Avesta
Zorastrian: **5** Parsi **6** gheber, ghebre, Parsee
Zouave: **4** Zuzu
zounds: **4** egad
zufolo: **5** flute **9** flageolet

zuisin: 8 baldpate
Zulu: *regiment:* 4 impi
 spear: 7 assegai

zygote: 7 oosperm
zymogen activating substance: 6 kinase